Congressional Districts IN THE 1980s

CONGRESSIONAL QUARTERLY INC.
1414 22nd Street N.W.
Washington, D.C. 20037

Congressional Quarterly Inc.

Congressional Quarterly Inc., an editorial research service and publishing company, serves clients in the fields of news, education, business and government. It combines specific coverage of Congress, government and politics by Congressional Quarterly with the more general subject range of an affiliated service, Editorial Research Reports.

Congressional Quarterly publishes the *Congressional Quarterly Weekly Report* and a variety of books, including college political science textbooks under the CQ Press imprint and public affairs paperbacks designed as timely reports to keep journalists, scholars and the public abreast of developing issues and events. CQ also publishes information directories and reference books on the federal government, national elections and politics, including the *Guide to Congress*, the *Guide to the Supreme Court*, the *Guide to U.S. Elections* and *Politics in America*. The *CQ Almanac*, a compendium of legislation for one session of Congress, is published each year. *Congress and the Nation*, a record of government for a presidential term, is published every four years.

CQ publishes *The Congressional Monitor*, a daily report on current and future activities of congressional committees, and several newsletters including *Congressional Insight*, a weekly analysis of congressional action, and *Campaign Practices Reports*, a semimonthly update on campaign laws.

CQ conducts seminars and conferences on Congress, the legislative process, the federal budget, national elections and politics, and other current issues. CQ Direct Research is a consulting service that performs contract research and maintains a reference library and query desk for clients.

Library of Congress Cataloging in Publication Data

Main entry under title:

Congressional districts in the 1980s.

1. United States. Congress. House — Election districts. I. Congressional Quarterly, inc.
JK1341.C63   1983   328.73'07345   83-18988
ISBN 0-87187-264-1

Editor: Martha V. Gottron
Associate Editor: Wayne Walker
Assistant Editors: Mary Ames Booker, Esther D. Wyss
Major Contributors: Nancy A. Blanpied, Calvin Chin, Patricia M.
Russotto, Mark White
Contributors: Christopher Buchanan, Christopher Colford, Rhodes
Cook, Phil Duncan, Alan Ehrenhalt, Michael Glennon,
Diane Granat, Rob Gurwitt, Larry Light, Julia McCue,
Albert Menendez, Ann Pelham
Cover Design: Richard A. Pottern
Maps: Belle Burkhart, Patrick Murphy, Bob Redding
Dust Jacket Photos: George Kleiman, Frank Siteman, Joel Rogers/
UNIPHOTO

Congressional Quarterly Inc.

Eugene Patterson *Editor and President*
Wayne P. Kelley *Publisher*
Peter A. Harkness *Deputy Publisher and Executive Editor*
Robert E. Cuthriell *Director, Research and Development*
Robert C. Hur *General Manager*
I. D. Fuller *Production Manager*
Maceo Mayo *Assistant Production Manager*
Sydney E. Garriss *Computer Services Manager*

Book Department

David R. Tarr *Director*
Joanne D. Daniels *Director, CQ Press*
John L. Moore *Assistant Director*
Michael D. Wormser *Associate Editor*
Martha V. Gottron *Associate Editor*
Barbara R. de Boinville *Senior Editor, CQ Press*
Nancy Lammers *Senior Editor*
Margaret C. Thompson *Senior Writer*
Carolyn Goldinger *Project Editor*
Janet E. Hoffman *Project Editor*
Mary L. McNeil *Project Editor*
Patricia M. Russotto *Editorial Assistant*
Mary Ames Booker *Editorial Assistant*
Judith Aldock *Editorial Assistant*
Elizabeth H. Summers *Editorial Assistant*
Nancy A. Blanpied *Indexer*
Barbara March *Secretary*
Patricia Ann O'Connor *Contributing Editor*
Elder Witt *Contributing Editor*

Table of Contents

Redistricting for the 1980s

Republicans were supposed to do well in the elections of 1982. A popular Republican president sat in the White House, the nation seemed to be taking a rightward political turn and the reapportionment mandated by the 1980 Census shifted a large number of U.S. House seats from the Democratic North to the more conservative Sun Belt.

It didn't work out that way. With a substantial edge in the nation's state legislatures, particularly in those states that gained seats, Democrats were able to draw maps that helped them and hurt their opponents. After the 1982 elections, Democrats had won 26 additional seats in the House, including 10 of the seats created by redistricting.

But what might have a more lasting impact on the nation and its representative government was the new use to which the Supreme Court's edict of one person, one vote was put in the redistricting that followed the 1980 Census. In California, New Jersey and points between, Republicans and Democrats justified highly partisan remaps by demonstrating respect for the 1964 Supreme Court mandate that populations of congressional districts within states must be made as equal as possible. Other interests at stake in redistricting, such as the preservation of community boundaries and the grouping of constituencies with similar concerns, were brushed aside.

The Supreme Court itself seemed to approve this kind of partisan mapmaking. In June 1983 it overturned New Jersey's congressional district map on the ground that the population variations among the districts — the greatest of which was 0.69 percent — were too large and therefore unconstitutional. In its opinion the court ignored the fact that the map divided townships and cut up counties all across the state solely to give the Democrats a political advantage.

Other states had population variations as great or greater than New Jersey's. But it appeared unlikely that many of these plans would be challenged in court. What seemed more uncertain was how the Supreme Court's decision would affect the redistricting scheduled to follow the 1990 Census.

1980 Reapportionment

The reapportionment and redistricting process began on New Year's Eve 1980 when the Census Bureau sent state population totals to President Jimmy Carter, along with a calculation of the size of each state's congressional delegation, beginning with the 1982 elections. In February 1981 the bureau began to release more detailed data breaking down the nation's population, in some cases to the city-block level. The bureau's maps took up 31,715 sheets. Texas alone was spread across more than 2,000 census map sheets.

The census figures themselves were not immune to challenge. In 1980 Detroit officials claimed that minorities in the city had been undercounted and argued that this would cost the city federal funds and congressional representation. (Many federal welfare programs use census figures to determine how much assistance each locality is entitled to receive.) A Michigan district court ordered the bureau to revise its national population figures upward to include blacks, Hispanics and others allegedly overlooked in the 1980 Census.

But in June 1981 the 6th U.S. Circuit Court of Appeals reversed that decision, stating that the claim was "based on a state of affairs not yet in existence and ... so hypothetical in nature that it does not present a controversy capable of judicial resolution." The arguments used in the 1981 district court appeal dealt largely with the 1970 Census, in which the bureau's own research indicated census takers missed 2.5 percent of the population. More importantly, the bureau estimated it missed 7.7 percent of the nation's blacks, compared with only 1.9 percent of its whites. But the 1980 Census of these minority population counts unexpectedly turned out to be slightly higher than population estimates derived from demographic records, suggesting an apparent overcount rather than an undercount.

Nonetheless, the 1980 Census count confirmed that there was a dramatic decline in America's big city population during the 1970s. Most central city districts suffered severe shrinkage, and older suburban districts experienced slow growth, or none at all.

Meanwhile, there was substantial movement of the population from North to South and East to West. As a result, 17 House seats shifted from states in the Northeast and Midwest, the so-called Snow Belt, to those in the Sun Belt states of the South and West. Florida was the biggest gainer, receiving four new seats. Texas picked up three additional seats; California two; and Arizona, Colorado, Nevada, New Mexico, Oregon, Tennessee, Utah and Washington one each.

Status of Redistricting

(As of Oct. 1, 1983)

State	Redistricting Action
Alabama	Legislative plan enacted Aug. 18, 1981.
Arizona	Federal court approved legislative plan April 2, 1982.
Arkansas	Federal court plan enacted Feb. 25, 1982.
California	Voters rejected legislative plan, which was kept in place for 1982 elections. New plan not finalized as of Oct. 1, 1983.
Colorado	Federal court plan enacted Jan. 28, 1982.
Connecticut	Special commission plan enacted Oct. 28, 1981.
Florida	Legislative plan enacted May 23, 1982.
Georgia	First plan voided by Justice Department. Second legislative plan enacted Aug. 8, 1982.
Hawaii	Federal court approved special commission plan May 5, 1982.
Idaho	Legislative plan enacted July 30, 1981.
Illinois	Federal court plan enacted Nov. 23, 1981.
Indiana	Legislative plan enacted May 5, 1981.
Iowa	Legislative plan enacted Aug. 20, 1981.
Kansas	Federal court plan enacted June 2, 1982.
Kentucky	Legislative plan enacted March 10, 1982.
Louisiana	Legislative plan approved Nov. 12, 1981. Two New Orleans districts voided by federal court Sept. 24, 1983.
Maine	Special commission plan enacted March 30, 1983.
Maryland	Special commission plan enacted April 9, 1982.
Massachusetts	Legislative plan enacted Dec. 16, 1981.
Michigan	Federal court plan enacted May 17, 1982.
Minnesota	Federal court plan enacted March 11, 1982.
Mississippi	First plan voided by Justice Department. Federal court enacted temporary plan June 9, 1982; permanent plan not finalized as of Oct. 1, 1983.
Missouri	Federal court plan enacted Dec. 28, 1981.
Montana	Special commission plan enacted March 4, 1983.
Nebraska	Legislative plan enacted May 28, 1981.
Nevada	Legislative plan enacted June 3, 1981.
New Hampshire	Legislative plan enacted March 4, 1982.
New Jersey	Legislative plan, voided by federal court March 3, 1982, used for 1982 elections; Supreme Court upheld lower court ruling June 22, 1983; no new plan in place as of Oct. 1, 1983.
New Mexico	Legislative plan enacted Jan. 19, 1982.
New York	First plan voided by Justice Department. Second legislative plan enacted July 2, 1982.
North Carolina	First plan voided by Justice Department. Second legislative plan enacted Feb. 11, 1982.
Ohio	Legislative plan enacted March 25, 1982.
Oklahoma	Voters approved legislative plan Nov. 2, 1982.
Oregon	Legislative plan enacted Aug. 22, 1981.
Pennsylvania	Legislative plan enacted March 3, 1982.
Rhode Island	Legislative plan enacted April 9, 1982.
South Carolina	Federal court plan enacted March 8, 1982.
Tennessee	Legislative plan enacted June 17, 1981.
Texas	First plan voided by Justice Department Jan. 29, 1982. Federal court plan overturned by Supreme Court April 11, 1982. Second legislative plan enacted June 19, 1983.
Utah	Legislative plan enacted Nov. 11, 1981.
Virginia	Legislative plan enacted June 12, 1981.
Washington	Legislative plan voided in federal court Nov. 30, 1982. Special commission plan enacted March 29, 1983.
West Virginia	Legislative plan enacted Feb. 8, 1982.
Wisconsin	Legislative plan enacted March 25, 1982.

New York, which lost almost 700,000 people in the 1970s, according to the census, was hit with a five-seat loss, the biggest one-time drop-off in House representation since New York and Virginia lost six seats each in 1840. Illinois, Ohio and Pennsylvania each lost two seats, while Indiana, Massachusetts, Michigan, Missouri, New Jersey and South Dakota lost one each.

Drawing the Lines

Only 44 states go through the redistricting process. The other six — Alaska, Delaware, North Dakota, South Dakota, Vermont and Wyoming — each have only one representative elected at large.

Anticipating the apparent gains the population shifts would give the GOP — and anxious to capitalize on them — the Republicans undertook a nationwide campaign to win control of more state legislatures in preparation for the critical 1981 redistricting process. They had only scattered success in the November 1980 elections. Democrats still controlled 28 of the nation's state legislatures, while the Republicans held only 15. (The remaining legislatures were divided, except for Nebraska, which has a unicameral, nonpartisan legislature.).

Despite this nationwide disadvantage, Republicans in individual states were able to hold their own. In Florida, for example, the Democratic legislature drew only one new safe Democratic seat; the other three were expected to be competitive. In November 1982 the Democrats won two; the Republicans won the other two.

Partisan Maps

In several states where one or the other party was firmly in control, the redistricting process was overtly partisan. In Indiana the district map passed by the Republican-controlled Legislature April 30, 1981, was a textbook case of gerrymandering. Republicans drew the plan with the help of Market Opinion Research Corp.'s sophisticated computer system at a cost of more than $250,000. Its lines wove freely in and out of counties, concentrating Democratic voting strength into the districts of just three of the state's six Democratic incumbents and damaging the re-election prospects of the other three.

The state's Republicans made no apologies for their plan. As early as December 1980 they had made it clear they would take full advantage of their control of state government to secure a majority in Indiana's U. S. House delegation in the November 1982 election. As it turned out, their elaborate schemes went for nought, at least in 1982. The line-up after the election was 5-5.

Two partisan redistricting plans were the focus of GOP attacks. In California and Oklahoma, Republicans sought to nullify redistricting plans drawn by Democratic-controlled legislatures. California's plan, crafted by Democratic Rep. Phillip Burton, was designed to bring five more Democrats into the state's House delegation, which increased from 43 to 45 after the 1980 Census. Democrats in California held a 22-21 advantage in the 97th Congress. When Rep. William M. Thomas, R-Calif., called Burton's plan "an abomination," Burton countered that the Democrats had done only what Republicans had done in Indiana, and were attempting to do in Washington and Colorado. California Republicans filed sufficient signatures to hold a referendum on the redistricting plan, and in June 1982 the

state's voters rejected the map. However, six months earlier, the state supreme court had ruled that the Burton plan would stay in effect for the 1982 elections regardless of the outcome of the referendum. By October 1983 permanent district lines for the decade still had not been settled in California.

Court Plans

Sometimes, states cannot come up with a plan at all. This usually happens in states where control of the legislature is split between the parties, or where the governor's party does not control the state legislature. Philosophical or personal differences sometimes can interfere, even within parties. When deadlocks occur, the task of redistricting falls to the federal courts.

In Illinois, which lost two seats, no compromise could be reached between competing Democratic and Republican redistricting plans in 1981, and both parties filed suit in federal district court in Chicago. A three-judge panel, which included two judges with Republican backgrounds, heard the case and decided in favor of the Democratic plan. The Illinois Republicans' appeal to the U.S. Supreme Court was rejected.

A sharp drop in St. Louis' population cost Missouri one congressional seat. For most of 1981 it appeared that the problem might have to be solved by placing Democratic incumbents William Clay, a veteran black legislator, and Richard A. Gephardt, a "rising star," in the same district. The Democratic-dominated Legislature rejected this plan and failed to come up with another, leaving the decision up to a federal court panel. Much to the relief of the Democrats, the judicial plan penalized the Republicans, eliminating GOP Rep. Wendell Bailey's 8th District and forcing incumbent Republican Bill Emerson into a heavily Democratic district.

After Democratic Gov. Richard D. Lamm vetoed three redistricting maps passed by the Republican majority in Colorado's Legislature, a federal judge ordered Lamm and the legislative redistricting committee to negotiate. Talks in November 1981 failed to produce a compromise plan, so a federal court in Denver was given responsibility for drawing the district lines. The state gained one House seat, which Republicans easily won.

Minorities and Maps

Several states that managed to pass redistricting plans still had to clear another hurdle. Under the Voting Rights Act of 1965, the Justice Department has to approve redistricting plans in Alabama, Arizona, Georgia, Louisiana, Mississippi, South Carolina, Texas and Virginia, and parts of California, Colorado, Connecticut, Florida, Hawaii, Idaho, Maine, Massachusetts, Michigan, New Hampshire, New Mexico, New York, North Carolina and Oklahoma. The department could reject any redistricting plan in these states that diluted the voting strength or in any other way discriminated against blacks and other minorities.

This happened in several states in 1981. The North Carolina redistricting plan included a district that protected incumbent Democrat L. H. Fountain by curving around the heavily black community in Durham and the liberal university town of Chapel Hill. The Justice Department, in rejecting the plan, ruled on Dec. 8 that the "strangely irregular shape" of "Fountain's Fishhook" raised questions about the racial motivations of the state legislators. The legislators drew a second map, which put

Largest Districts

Listed below are the 25 congressional districts of the 98th Congress with the largest land areas, together with their population density.

Rank	District	Area in Square Miles*	Density/ Square Mile
1.	Nevada 2	105,860	3.8
2.	Montana 2	89,548	4.2
3.	Oregon 2	70,570	7.5
4.	Nebraska 3	59,836	8.8
5.	New Mexico 3	56,438	7.7
6.	Montana 1	55,841	7.3
7.	New Mexico 2	55,038	7.9
8.	Arizona 3	54,726	10.0
9.	Colorado 3	52,959	9.1
10.	Kansas 1	49,399	9.6
11.	Utah 1	46,994	10.4
12.	Texas 21	44,786	11.8
13.	Idaho 2	43,107	10.9
14.	Idaho 1	39,306	12.0
15.	Colorado 4	38,409	12.5
16.	Texas 13	34,619	15.2
17.	Utah 3	34,511	14.1
18.	Texas 17	31,592	16.7
19.	California 35	30,321	17.4
20.	Arizona 4	29,388	18.5
21.	California 14	27,376	19.2
22.	Maine 2	26,420	20.6
23.	Washington 4	25,778	19.9
24.	Oklahoma 6	25,638	19.6
25.	Minnesota 8	24,680	20.6

States with at-large seats were not included. If they had been, Alaska would be ranked first with 570,833 square miles (0.7 density), Wyoming third with 96,989 (4.8), South Dakota fifth with 75,952 (9.1) and North Dakota seventh with 69,300 (9.4).

Source: Bureau of the Census

Durham County in Fountain's district. That map was approved, Fountain decided to retire and a black came close to winning the Democratic nomination, winning 46 percent of the vote in a runoff.

In Georgia the Justice Department ruled that the Legislature improperly divided a "cohesive black community" in the Atlanta area between the 4th and 5th districts, reducing the chances that either would elect a black candidate to the House. Legislators then drew a plan that passed Justice Department review, but the elections for those two seats were postponed nearly a month to Nov. 30, 1982.

In Mississippi, Justice Department rejection of the legislative map resulted in creation of the state's first black-majority district since 1966. But the district was only 54 percent black, and civil rights leaders continued to pursue the matter in federal court. By October 1983 the Mississippi map still was pending in court.

In Louisiana, blacks demanded creation of a black-majority district in New Orleans, a concept endorsed by both the state House and state Senate. Republican Gov. David Treen opposed the black-majority district because the resulting boundaries would have endangered the seat of GOP U.S. Rep. Bob Livingston, who represented the New Orleans suburbs. The governor prevailed upon legislators to approve a remap protecting incumbents, and Justice approved that map. Blacks then went to court, which threw out the New Orleans district lines Sept. 24, 1983.

Hispanics were the beneficiaries of Justice Department review in Texas. In January 1982 the department ruled that the map improperly diluted the Hispanic vote in two south Texas districts by making one of them 80 percent Hispanic and the other 52 percent Hispanic. A federal court subsequently drew a map redistributing the voters in those two districts, and Hispanics won both seats in 1982.

Bipartisan Commission Plans

A number of citizens' groups have argued that partisan redistricting should be ended. One method, promoted by Common Cause, would establish a commission composed of an equal number of appointees from each party, which would be expected to choose a non-partisan chairman. The commission then would have full authority to redistrict the state according to the latest census. Only two states — Hawaii and Montana — redistricted by using such a system. Both had only two districts. However, other states used a variant of the commission system and some resorted to it after their legislatures were unable to reach agreement on redistricting maps.

One hybrid form of the Common Cause plan was adopted by Iowa in 1980. In spite of their total control of state government, GOP legislators agreed to let the non-partisan Legislative Service Bureau draw a plan, subject to the Legislature's approval. The bureau was instructed to follow objective criteria — population equality, compactness, contiguity, preservation of local boundaries — and to ignore partisan concerns or the wishes of incumbents.

The bureau's "non-partisan" plan, unveiled April 22, was a statistical beauty. The six districts were neat and compact, and they all followed county boundaries. None of the six varied in population from the state's ideal by more than 500 people.

But, to their surprise, two of the Republican incumbents found themselves living in the same district. The state Senate killed that plan. On its second try the bureau gave the two Republicans different districts but added a significant number of Democrats to one of them. Again the state Senate killed the plan. The third commission plan finally was approved even though the Republican legislators were not totally happy with it. They sensed, however, that the public was tiring of the time and expense being put into a supposedly non-partisan effort.

How Map Makers Fared in 1982

After all the votes were counted in November 1982, the anticipated Republican windfall had turned into a rout. Republicans lost 26 seats in the House; their numbers fell from 192 to 166.

The Sun Belt proved the Republicans' greatest disappointment. The GOP had hoped to take a dozen of the seats shifted to the Sun Belt and far West states. But Democratic legislative cartography and unfriendly federal court action got in the way, and in the end Democrats won 10 of the 17.

Democrats also managed to sidestep the brunt of district losses in the Northeast and Midwest. Legislative map makers eliminated Republican seats in Illinois and New Jersey, even though the population decline had been in urban Democratic areas. On Nov. 2 anti-Republican economic resentments took over, bringing victory to several Democrats in new districts that were nominally Democratic but had been voting conservatively in recent years. In all, in the 10 Northern states that lost districts, Republicans came out 18 seats short of where they stood before the election.

In most of the 11 states that gained seats, the GOP seemed the natural beneficiary of demographic changes. All 11 were carried by Ronald Reagan in the 1980 presidential race and eight went for Republican Gerald R. Ford in 1976.

Nonetheless, legislatures or courts in six of the states drew new districts favoring or leaning to Democrats. And, contrary to prediction, not one of these new constituencies nominated a conservative Democrat. As a result, liberals, including four Hispanics, made up a large portion of the Sun Belt's House contingent in the 98th Congress.

The Democrats' greatest boost came in California, where the remap masterminded by Rep. Phillip Burton dissolved three GOP-held seats and diluted a fourth enough to fatally weaken the incumbent. And although population gains entitled California to only two additional districts, Burton managed to give his party five new seats while strengthening its grip on most of the districts it already held. Three of the new California Democratic seats were in the Los Angeles area. A new district in San Diego and one around Fresno also sent liberal Democrats to the House.

Liberal Democrats also won new seats in New Mexico, Tennessee and Texas. Republicans expected to win at least one of the three new Texas seats but instead they were shut out. In the Republican-leaning 26th District between Dallas and Fort Worth, a conservative Democrat narrowly defeated the Republican candidate. Democrats easily won the other two.

Republicans' biggest gains came in Florida, where the party decisively won two of the state's four new seats. The GOP also picked up one seat each in Colorado, Nevada, Oregon, Utah and Washington.

In the Northeast and Midwest, Democrats used redistricting and the national Democratic tide to deny Republicans their apparent advantages of population shift. In Illinois and New Jersey, where population decline losses forced the removal of two seats and one seat respectively, Democratic legislatures dissolved existing GOP districts to bring delegation sizes down. They also left several Republican incumbents weaker. In New Jersey the GOP incumbent lost his seat in the 9th, which had gained several Democratic towns; in Illinois the GOP incumbent was evicted from a 20th District that had picked up three traditionally Democratic counties and lost Republican territory.

In Michigan Democratic legislators cut Republican territory out of the 6th District, which was held by a Republican freshman, and they gave the GOP incumbent staunchly Democratic Pontiac and its western Oakland County suburbs. In 1982 the GOP incumbent was unseated

Smallest Districts

Listed below are the 25 congressional districts of the 98th Congress smallest in land area together with their population density.

Rank	District	Area in Square Miles	Population Square Mile
1.	New York 15	7	73,772.7
2.	New York 16	8	64,550.6
3.	New York 12	11	46,998.5
4.	New York 18	13	39,854.3
5.	New York 17	13	39,710.7
6.	New York 11	15	34,544.3
7.	New York 13	17	30,523.9
8.	New York 9	21	24,578.2
9.	New York 7	22	23,588.7
10.	New York 10	23	22,310.4
11.	California 5	29	18,135.0
12.	Pennsylvania 2	29	17,835.0
13.	Illinois 1	32	16,220.2
14.	New York 19	32	15,993.8
15.	Illinois 8	33	15,728.3
16.	Pennsylvania 1	33	15,610.5
17.	New Jersey 14	34	15,493.5
18.	New York 8	36	14,233.3
19.	New Jersey 10	39	13,482.9
20.	Illinois 7	39	13,308.6
21.	New York 6	41	12,606.0
22.	Illinois 9	44	11,798.2
23.	California 28	47	11,184.7
24.	Maryland 7	49	10,767.1
25.	Pennsylvania 3	50	10,323.1

Source: Bureau of the Census

by the Democrat he had defeated just two years earlier. Although the Democrat trailed in the portion of the district that he held until 1980, he pulled in a 10,000-vote margin in the depression-plagued Pontiac area.

Only in Ohio did a change in a district prove fatal to a Democratic incumbent facing a challenger. In the 12th District the freshman Democrat saw his constituency lose Democratic portions of Columbus and gain rural and conservative territory; he was unseated by a New Right Republican.

Population and Politics

The important story about the 1980 reapportionment and redistricting process might not be which party won the most seats but rather how the "one-person, one-vote" prin-

Population Deviations in the Districts of the 98th Congress

State[1]	State Population	Number of Districts	Ideal District Size[2]	Largest District	Smallest District	Maximum Deviation[3]
Alabama	3,893,888	7	556,270	563,905	549,505	2.59%
Arizona	2,718,215	5 (+1)	543,643	544,870	542,918	0.36
Arkansas	2,286,435	4	571,609	573,551	569,116	0.78
California[4]	23,667,902	45 (+2)	525,953	528,091	524,346	0.71
Colorado	2,889,964	6 (+1)	481,661	481,854	481,512	0.07
Connecticut	3,107,576	6	517,929	518,700	516,232	0.48
Florida	9,746,324	19 (+4)	512,964	513,365	512,672	0.14
Georgia	5,463,105	10	546,311	550,268	540,865	1.72
Hawaii	964,691	2	482,346	482,347	482,344	—
Idaho	943,935	2	471,968	472,412	471,523	0.19
Illinois	11,426,518	22 (−2)	519,387	521,909	518,350	0.69
Indiana	5,490,224	10 (−1)	549,022	558,100	540,939	3.13
Iowa	2,913,808	6	485,635	485,961	485,480	0.10
Kansas	2,363,679	5	472,7366	473,180	472,139	0.22
Kentucky	3,660,777	7	522,968	526,284	519,009	1.39
Louisiana[4]	4,205,900	8	525,738	527,220	524,770	0.47
Maine[5]	1,124,660	2	562,330	581,185	543,475	6.71
Maryland	4,216,975	8	527,122	528,168	525,453	0.52
Massachusetts	5,737,037	11 (−1)	521,549	525,089	518,313	1.30
Michigan	9,262,078	18 (−1)	514,560	514,560	514,559	—
Minnesota	4,075,970	8	509,496	509,532	509,446	0.02
Mississippi[4]	2,520,638	5	504,128	504,714	503,617	0.22
Missouri	4,916,686	9 (−1)	546,298	546,882	545,921	0.18
Montana[5]	786,690	2	393,346	410,071	376,619	8.50
Nebraska	1,569,825	3	523,275	523,827	522,919	0.17
Nevada	800,493	2 (+1)	400,247	400,636	399,857	0.19
New Hampshire	920,610	2	460,305	460,863	459,747	0.24
New Jersey[4]	7,364,823	14 (−1)	526,059	527,472	523,798	0.70
New Mexico	1,302,894	3 (+1)	434,298	436,261	432,492	0.87
New York	17,558,072	34 (−5)	516,414	521,203	511,802	1.82
North Carolina	5,881,766	11	534,706	539,055	529,635	1.76
Ohio	10,797,630	21 (−2)	514,173	515,867	512,706	0.61
Oklahoma	3,025,290	6	504,215	505,869	502,974	0.57
Oregon	2,633,105	5 (+1)	526,621	526,968	526,120	0.16
Pennsylvania	11,863,895	23 (−2)	515,822	517,215	514,346	0.56
Rhode Island	947,154	2	473,577	474,429	472,725	0.36
South Carolina	3,121,820	6	520,303	522,688	519,273	0.66
Tennessee	4,591,120	9 (+1)	510,124	516,692	503,611	2.56
Texas[4]	14,229,191	27 (+3)	527,007	527,805	526,350	0.28
Utah	1,461,037	3 (+1)	487,012	487,833	485,729	0.43
Virginia	5,346,818	10	534,682	538,871	529,178	1.81
Washington[4]	4,132,156	8 (+1)	515,395	518,962	511,961	1.36
West Virginia	1,949,644	4	487,411	488,568	486,112	0.50
Wisconsin	4,705,767	9	522,863	523,225	522,477	0.14

[1] Alaska (401,851), Delaware (594,338), North Dakota (652,717), South Dakota (690,768), Vermont (511,456) and Wyoming (469,557) each elect only one U.S. Representative.

[2] Ideal district size is obtained by dividing the population of the state by the number of House seats assigned to that state.

[3] Maximum deviation is the percentage by which the difference between the most populated district and the least populated district varies from the ideal district size.

[4] Subsequent legislative or legal action was likely to change the population of the districts in these states.

[5] Maine and Montana did not redistrict until 1983.

ciple came into increasing use as a means to further partisan gerrymandering.

When the Supreme Court handed down its *Wesberry v. Sanders* ruling in 1964, congressional districts in many states were malapportioned to favor rural interests over urban dwellers or to make nearly impossible the election of a black candidate to the House. In Georgia one district had more than three times as many people as another, and the Legislature had not redrawn district lines in more than 30 years. *(Supreme Court on redistricting, p. 618)*

Responding to court pressure, 39 states realigned district boundaries between 1964 and 1970. But because legislators were working from outdated 1960 Census figures, significant population inequalities among districts persisted.

Meaningful implementation of the one-man, one-vote standard had to wait until publication of the 1970 Census figures. In 1972 voters elected representatives to the House from districts of nearly equal population for the first time in history.

At that time there still was lingering suspicion in many legislatures of the relatively new notion that one vote should have the same weight as another. Making district populations equal was seen by many legislators as a chore.

That has changed. Legislators who were uncomfortable with one-man, one-vote rule are now eager to use it to the advantage of their party. More than ever before, the dominant theme of redistricting has been partisanship.

In California, House candidates ran in 1982 in districts carefully crafted to meet the strictures of one-man, one-vote. In a state of nearly 24 million people, the average population variance among the 45 districts was only 67 people.

But while approaching mathematical precision in its population standards, the map blithely disregarded traditional community boundaries as it wound through the state throwing GOP incumbents together and creating territories where Democratic candidates should enjoy an edge. One of its districts joined together two disparate Democratic communities north of San Francisco whose only geographical link is a body of water. Californians rejected the plan in a June 1982 referendum, but candidates for Congress ran under it in 1982.

The three-judge federal panel in Missouri accepted the Democratic remap proposal over the Republican plan because it "achieves population equality better than any plan submitted to this court...." The Democratic plan achieved its population equality by dismantling a district in the south-central part of the state, where population was growing, and saving a district in inner-city St. Louis, where population declined markedly in the 1970s. The plan placed two Republican incumbents at a distinct disadvantage in 1982.

Michigan's districts were a tribute to the abilities of computerized line-drawing. Each district had either 514,559 or 514,560 people. But the lines for many districts cut through the hearts of many small cities and towns, placing their residents in two or three different districts.

So far most of the courts asked to review these highly partisan maps have relied solely on their population variations and not at all on claims that their partisan natures also constitute a violation of voting rights. In several instances challengers have not even raised that question, although the suits were brought solely to overturn the partisan maps.

In its 1983 New Jersey decision *(Karcher v. Daggett)*, the court appeared to make it even tougher to challenge maps on any grounds other than population deviation. The court majority said that minor variations might be justified by a "number of consistently applied legislative policies," including "making districts compact, respecting municipal boundaries, preserving the cores of prior districts, and avoiding contests between incumbent Representatives." The majority then cautioned that the state "must show with some specificity that a particular objective required the specific deviation in its plan, rather than simply relying on general assertions."

The court was divided 5-4 in the New Jersey case. Writing for the dissenters, Justice Byron R. White called the majority's ruling an "unreasonable insistence on an unattainable perfection...." He suggested that the quest for precisely equal populations within congressional districts could only move the country "closer to fulfilling [former] Justice [Abe] Fortas' prophecy that 'a legislature might have to ignore the boundaries of common sense, running the congressional district line down the middle of the corridor of an apartment house or even dividing the residents of a single-family house between two districts.'"

It was possible, however, that the court eventually might agree to hear a case based on the argument that a gerrymandered map had denied residents of a state equal protection of the laws as guaranteed by the 14th Amendment. Justice John Paul Stevens, who voted with the majority in *Karcher*, and Justice Lewis F. Powell Jr., who dissented, both indicated they would be willing to listen to such a challenge.

Sources and Explanations

Congressional Districts in the 1980s presents descriptive and statistical profiles of the 435 congressional districts based on the 1980 Census and subsequent reapportionment and redistricting. Information for each is provided as follows:

● First, for the 44 states that have two or more congressional districts, there is a narrative highlighting the congressional redistricting process for the state in 1981-83 — the politics, intended impact and actual results of redistricting as reflected in the 1982 congressional elections. For the six states that have a single representative in the U.S. House, the narrative describes the political character of the state itself.

● Second, a series of statistical tables including age of the population, income and occupation, school years completed, and housing and residential patterns.

● A map for each state showing its congressional district boundaries. Maps of cities divided between two or more congressional districts are also provided where appropriate. When the abbreviation (Pt.) appears on a map, it indicates that only part of the district is shown, the remaining portion being outside the city or county that is shown. The abbreviation (Pt.) appearing on a state map also may indicate a district or county with non-contiguous sections.

● Following this information are the profiles of each individual district in the state.

Age of Population

Source: Bureau of the Census, 1980 Summary Tape Files 1D and 3D, National Summaries.

For each district this table gives the population under 18 years of age, the voting age population, the population 65 years of age and older and the median age. Voting age population includes all persons 18 and over, that is, all potential voters, not just those who are registered. The percentage of the voting-age population that is 65 and older also is given.

The median age is the age that divides the population into two equal groups, one half of the persons being older than the median age, one half being younger.

Income and Occupation

Source: Bureau of the Census, 1980 Summary Tape Files 1D and 3D, National Summaries.

Median family income is the income level that divides families into two equal groups with half having incomes above the median and the other half having incomes below the median.

Percentages of white-collar, blue-collar, service and farm workers were calculated by Congressional Quarterly from figures provided by the Census Bureau. The Census Bureau divides employed persons into 12 major categories that Congressional Quarterly has regrouped into four categories as follows:

● White collar: managerial and professional specialty occupations including executive, administrative and managerial occupations and professional specialty occupations; and technical, sales and administrative support occupations including technicians and related support occupations, sales occupations and administrative support occupations including clerical.

● Blue collar: precision production, craft and repair occupations; and operators, fabricators, and laborers including machine operators, assemblers and inspectors; transportation and material-moving occupations; and handlers, equipment cleaners, helpers and laborers.

● Service workers: service occupations, including private household occupations and protective service occupations, and service occupations except protective and household occupations.

● Farm workers: farming, forestry and fishing occupations.

Education: School Years Completed

Source: Bureau of the Census, 1980 Summary Tape Files 1D and 3D, National Summaries.

Data on years of school completed refer to the adult population 25 years of age or over. Percentages were calculated by Congressional Quarterly.

The median number of school years divides adults 25 years or older into two groups, one having completed more, the other less, schooling than the median.

Black Districts

Listed below are the 25 congressional districts with the highest percentage of black residents. Districts are those in effect for the 98th Congress.

Rank	District	% of Blacks
1.	Illinois 1	92.1%
2.	New York 12	80.1
3.	Pennsylvania 2	80.0
4.	Maryland 7	73.3
5.	Michigan 13	71.1
6.	Michigan 1	70.7
7.	Illinois 2	70.3
8.	Illinois 7	66.9
9.	Georgia 5	65.0
10.	Ohio 21	62.3
11.	Tennessee 9	57.2
12.	New Jersey 10	54.8
13.	Mississippi 2	53.7
14.	Missouri 1	51.5
15.	New York 6	50.3
16.	New York 16	48.5
17.	New York 11	47.1
18.	California 29	46.6
19.	Mississippi 4	45.2
20.	Louisiana 2	44.5
21.	New York 18	43.7
22.	California 28	43.0
23.	South Carolina 6	40.9
24.	Texas 18	40.8
25.	North Carolina 2	40.1

Source: Bureau of the Census

Housing and Residential Patterns

Source: Bureau of the Census, 1980 Summary Tape Files 1D and 3D, National Summaries.

Housing units are broken down into owner-occupied and renter-occupied units. Housing units include both individual houses and individual apartments.

People classified as urban by the Census Bureau were those persons living in urbanized areas and in places of 2,500 or more outside urbanized areas. People classified as rural were all persons not classified as urban. The Census Bureau defines an urbanized area as one in which at least 50,000 people are concentrated, usually consisting of a central city and the surrounding, closely settled, contiguous territory generally referred to as suburbs.

District Profiles

Following the tabular material on all states is information for each individual congressional district. There are 13 categories under each district heading:

- An overview of the district — where its residents live and work and how redistricting affected the district and its politics.
- Presidential, gubernatorial, senatorial and U.S. House election returns within the area of the new district.
- The 1980 population of the district and the percentage change in size from the 1970 population.
- The area, in square miles, of the district and its population density.
- The counties or parts of counties in each district and their populations.
- The cities over 10,000 or parts of such cities in each district and their populations.
- The race and ancestry of the district's residents.
- The universities located in the district and their enrollments.
- The daily newspapers published in the district with their circulations.
- The commercial television stations within the district.
- The military facilities and/or activities in the district.
- The nuclear power plants in the district.
- The major industries in the district, their products and number of employees.

Every district does not necessarily include all 13 categories. If a district has nothing in a category, the category heading is omitted. For example, few districts have nuclear power plants; thus this category is omitted from most of the district profiles.

Election Returns

Source: Compiled by Scott J. Thomas and Mark Crain from official state election returns.

Returns for the 1976, 1978, 1980 and 1982 House races, the 1976 and 1980 presidential contests and any senatorial and gubernatorial elections between 1976 and 1982 are presented for the newly drawn districts and not as the districts existed at the time of each election. Thus, the figures reflect what the vote would have been in the district had the district lines for 1982 been in force in 1976, 1978 and 1980. In this way, it is possible to see the political history and trends within each current congressional district for the last four elections.

It should be noted that the House figures presented are strictly in terms of a party vote and are not necessarily comparable with the vote cast for a particular candidate, that is, the total may represent votes cast for more than one Democrat or Republican candidate where a district's boundary has been changed to include new areas. Votes also may appear for a party in a year in which there was no candidate of that party running for office. Such votes reflect the fact that the district gained territory during redistricting from other districts in which candidates of both parties ran for that office in that year.

Votes are for Democratic and Republican candidates only. Because minor party returns are not included percentages do not add to 100. When there was no major party opposition, a line is drawn in the space where the vote would have been recorded. In some instances, there were no official returns for candidates who had no opposition; these are indicated with a footnote.

Population, Land Area, Density

Source: Bureau of the Census, 1980 Summary Tape Files 1D and 3D, National Summaries.

The Census Bureau derived the population for each congressional district by adding together data from the 1980 Census for the various geographic components of each district. Where the smallest geographic unit was divided by a congressional district boundary, the bureau determined into which district the majority of the population fell and placed the entire area in that district.

Counties

Source: Bureau of the Census, 1980 Summary Tape Files 1D and 3D, National Summaries.

Most states are organized by counties. In Louisiana the equivalent divisions are known as parishes. Alaska has no counties. Virginia has a number of cities that are independent of any county and therefore are considered equivalent divisions. These are listed in the county section rather than the city section. Baltimore in Maryland, St. Louis in Missouri and Carson City in Nevada are also independent cities. The portion of Yellowstone National Park in Montana is considered equivalent to a county for census purposes.

In addition, two states have created new counties since the 1980 Census was taken. These are La Paz in Arizona, carved out of Yuma County, and Cibola in New Mexico, split away from Valencia County. The populations for these new counties are not reflected in the census figures.

Where one county is divided between two or more congressional districts, that is indicated by "(Pt.)" following the county name.

Cities

Source: Bureau of the Census, 1980 Summary Tape Files 1D and 3D, National Summaries.

The Census Bureau recognizes two kinds of places, those that are incorporated and those that are closely settled but that fall outside incorporated areas. Congressional Quarterly lists all those incorporated places whose total population exceeds 10,000.

In addition, widely recognized unincorporated places exceeding 10,000 in population are included for some districts and are followed by the abbreviation (CDP) — Census Designated Place. In some cases towns, townships and villages are also included.

Where a city is divided between two or more congressional districts, that is indicated by "(Pt.)" following the city name. A "0" means that the portion of the city or place in that district is unpopulated.

Race and Ancestry

Source: Bureau of the Census, 1980 Summary Tape Files 1D and 3D, National Summaries.

Hispanic Districts

Listed below are the 25 congressional districts with the highest percentage of residents of Spanish origin. Districts are those in effect for the 98th Congress.

Rank	District	Spanish Origin %
1.	Texas 15	71.7%
2.	California 25	63.6
3.	Texas 20	61.7
4.	Texas 27	61.5
5.	Texas 16	60.2
6.	California 30	54.2
7.	Texas 23	53.1
8.	New York 18	51.3
9.	Florida 18	50.7
10.	California 34	47.6
11.	New Mexico 3	39.0
12.	New York 11	38.0
13.	New York 16	37.9
14.	New Mexico 1	37.4
15.	Arizona 2	35.5
16.	New Mexico 2	33.6
17.	California 29	32.3
18.	Illinois 8	31.6
19.	Texas 18	31.2
20.	California 28	29.6
21.	California 17	28.3
22.	California 10	28.0
23.	California 15	26.8
24.	New Jersey 14	26.6
25.	California 24	26.4

Source: Bureau of the Census

The Census Bureau established five main racial categories: white; black; American Indian, Eskimo and Aleut; Asian and Pacific Islander; and other. All people responding to the 1980 Census were asked to identify which race they were. Census then grouped as white all those persons who responded "white" or who wrote in answers such as Canadian or Polish or Lebanese. It classified as black all those who said they were black or Negro or who reported such answers as Jamaican, Nigerian and black Puerto Rican.

Persons in the American Indian, Eskimo and Aleut category were those who said they were a member of one of those specific groups as well as those who reported a specific Indian tribe or said they were French American Indians or the like.

Census classified as Asian and Pacific Islander all those who responded they were Chinese, Filipino, Japa-

Wealthiest Districts

Listed below are the 25 congressional districts of the 98th Congress with the highest median family incomes. Median family income is the income level that divides families into two equal groups with half having incomes above the median and the other half having incomes below the median.

Rank	District*	Median Family Income
1.	Maryland 8	$33,404
2.	Michigan 18	33,080
3.	Illinois 10	31,471
4.	Texas 7	31,395
5.	Virginia 10	31,287
6.	New York 3	30,726
7.	Illinois 13	30,638
8.	New Jersey 12	30,287
9.	Virginia 8	29,850
10.	California 42	29,447
11.	Illinois 6	29,491
12.	Texas 3	29,302
13.	California 40	28,616
14.	California 21	28,479
15.	Minnesota 3	28,447
16.	New York 4	28,342
17.	California 12	28,237
18.	New Jersey 5	27,809
19.	Illinois 12	27,476
20.	New York 20	27,379
21.	California 23	27,256
22.	California 13	27,065
23.	Washington 8	27,016
24.	California 11	27,010
25.	Ohio 19	26,910

List does not include states with only one House member. If it did, Alaska would be 16th with a median family income of $28,395.

Source: Bureau of the Census

In some instances the sizable "other" category in the racial breakdown may be partially explained by the way in which the Census Bureau treated those persons of Spanish origin who listed their race as "other." Census reported that more people of Spanish origin marked the "other" category in 1980 than did in 1970. Moreover, in 1970 the Census Bureau reclassified as "white" those persons of Spanish origin who marked the "other" column, but who also gave themselves a Spanish designation such as Mexican or Venezuelan. In 1980 such persons were left in the "other" category.

Spanish Origin. Persons of Spanish origin or descent were asked to identify themselves by responding to a specific question in the 1980 Census. Persons of Spanish origin can be of any race. Census provided figures for persons of Spanish origin from both its full-count and sample-count data. Congressional Quarterly has listed percentages based on the full-count figures.

Ancestry. Persons responding to the 1980 Census sample questionnaire were asked to identify their ancestry, which Census defined as "a person's nationality group, lineage or the country in which the person or the person's parents or ancestors were born before their arrival in the United States." Census noted that the question reflected only a person's identification with an ethnic group and "not necessarily the degree of attachment or association the person had" with that particular group. Congressional Quarterly has included all such ancestry groups that make up at least 0.5 percent of each district's population.

Universities, Enrollment

Source: 1981-82 Accredited Institutions of Postsecondary Education, *published for the Council on Postsecondary Accreditation by the American Council on Education.*

Congressional Quarterly located by congressional district all colleges and universities that offered academic degrees or their equivalent, according to the Council on Postsecondary Accreditations. Junior and community colleges as well as technical, engineering and fine arts colleges are included. Most enrollment figures are as of the beginning of the 1980-81 school year. In a few instances where enrollment figures were not available, Congressional Quarterly contacted the school directly.

Newspapers, Circulation

Sources: Newspaper Rates and Data: Newspaper Circulation Analysis, September 1981, *published by Standard Rate and Data Service Inc.;* 1981 Editor & Publisher International Yearbook, *published by Editor and Publisher Co. Inc.*

Included under this heading are all daily newspapers (those that publish four days a week or more), and all daily foreign language newspapers.

The papers are listed in the congressional district in which the publishing company is located. The papers are listed alphabetically by name, together with the city of publication and circulation, as listed in the *1981 Editor and Publisher Yearbook.*

Times of publication are denoted as follows: m — morning; e — evening; S — Sunday; All Day — All Day. Sunday or weekend circulation figures are not used.

nese, Asian Indian, Korean, Vietnamese, Hawaiian, Samoan or Guamanian. In Census's full-count tabulations — that is, in the data in which every respondent was counted — persons who listed their race as Cambodian, Laotian, Pakistani and Fiji Islander were placed in the "other" category. In its sample-count data — that is, that data in which the total for a given category was extrapolated from a sample count — persons who listed these four races were classified as Asian and Pacific Islanders. Congressional Quarterly has listed the percentages based on the full-count figures for white; black; and American Indian, Eskimo and Aleut; and on the sample-count data for Asian and Pacific Islanders.

A newspaper's circulation often goes beyond the confines of a single congressional district. If a newspaper not published in a congressional district circulates in that district to the extent of at least 20,000 copies a day, it is noted. The Standard Rate and Data Service publication, *Newspaper Circulation Analysis*, lists newspaper circulation by county, from which Congressional Quarterly determined the extent of circulation by congressional district.

Commercial Television Stations, Affiliation

Source: Broadcasting/Cablecasting Yearbook 1982, *published by Broadcasting Publications Inc.*

Congressional Quarterly located all commercial television stations by congressional district. The stations are listed alphabetically by their call letters, with their location and network affiliation. When stations are not affiliated with one of the three national commercial networks, the word "None" is used. Spanish-language stations are so designated.

Congressional Quarterly also determined in which television Area of Dominant Influence (ADI) each congressional district is located. The ADI is a geographic market design that defines each TV market exclusive of another based on measurable viewing patterns. An ADI, as defined by Arbitron, is an area that consists of all counties in which the home market stations are viewed to any significant extent, including via cable. Each county in the United States, excluding Alaska and Hawaii, is allocated exclusively to only one ADI; there is no overlap. The Arbitron Co. is a television and radio marketing research firm based in New York City.

The wording used in this section is flexible because there are many variations in areas of TV coverage in congressional districts. A district may be entirely within one ADI or it may be divided among several ADIs. When the broadcasting city of an ADI is located in a state other than the congressional district under consideration, the state is identified.

Congressional Quarterly does not reproduce the exact boundaries of any ADIs nor any of the market data from Arbitron or the *Broadcasting/Cablecasting Yearbook*. Rather, Congressional Quarterly's purpose is to show what commercial television stations are received in each congressional district.

Military Installations

Source: Department of Defense

Congressional Quarterly lists by congressional district all military installations and facilities with full-time personnel in fiscal 1981. The listings in each district are alphabetical by name of the installation, together with the city nearest the installation and the total number of full-time military and civilian personnel.

Nuclear Power Plants

Sources: Nuclear Regulatory Commission, Atomic Industrial Forum Inc.

Congressional Quarterly located by congressional district the nation's nuclear power plants in operation or

Poorest Districts

Listed below are the 25 congressional districts in the 98th Congress with the lowest median family incomes. Median family income is the income level that divides families into two equal groups with half having incomes above the median and the other half having incomes below the median.

Rank	District	Median Family Income
1.	New York 18	$ 8,448
2.	New York 11	9,542
3.	New York 16	10,720
4.	Kentucky 5	11,578
5.	Mississippi 2	12,270
6.	Arkansas 1	12,580
7.	New York 12	12,690
8.	Michigan 13	12,825
9.	Pennsylvania 1	13,104
10.	Texas 15	13,313
11.	California 29	13,717
12.	Missouri 8	13,733
13.	Tennessee 4	13,733
14.	Pennsylvania 2	13,800
15.	Texas 20	13,809
16.	Illinois 1	14,017
17.	Oklahoma 3	14,125
18.	Florida 6	14,157
19.	North Carolina 3	14,188
20.	Kentucky 7	14,311
21.	Arkansas 3	14,337
22.	Mississippi 1	14,359
23.	Georgia 2	14,440
24.	Louisiana 5	14,576
25.	California 25	14,642

Source: Bureau of the Census

under construction as of March 1983. Each entry gives the name of the plant, the nearest city, the power supplier and contractor (in parentheses) and the date, if applicable, when the plant began commercial operation. Plants under construction are listed without a date. Shutdowns of already operating plants are noted.

Industries

Source: Dun & Bradstreet

Congressional Quarterly obtained from Dun & Bradstreet a list containing all plants and offices in the United States employing 500 people or more, the main products or line of business and employment for each location, a total of approximately 17,000 entries. The list was prepared in December 1981.

Congressional Quarterly eliminated from that list all those entries that were federal, state or local governing bodies, including school districts; public utilities; universities; hospitals that employed fewer than 1,000 people; retail establishments unless they were headquarters of a chain of stores, and many local service facilities, such as temporary employment agencies and delivery services.

Congressional Quarterly next determined the congressional district in which each remaining plant or office is located. Employment figures for hundreds of plants likely to have been affected by the recession of the early 1980s were determined by checking with the companies themselves. Much of the information was also checked with congressional offices, trade associations and local business associations

For each plant or office, Congressional Quarterly lists its name, its division name if applicable, whether it is a headquarters (HQ), its location, the main product or products made at that location and the number of employees. The plants are listed in descending order from the most employees to the fewest employees. In those instances where a company refused to give its employment figures, Congressional Quarterly assigned them a range, such as "more than 500."

With this information, the reader usually can discern the types of industry and business prevalent in a congressional district, what sort of products are made on a large scale in the district, and thus the types of employment that affect the economy of the district most.

In large cities, some distortion will result from the listing of many businesses in the downtown section. People who work there do not necessarily live there. In such cases the reader should examine the overall picture of the region by looking at the figures for all the congressional districts in the city and suburbs.

Congressional Districts IN THE 1980s

Alabama

District lines around Birmingham (Jefferson County) were the main issue as Alabama redrew its congressional map for the 1980s. Once legislators reached agreement on that subject, they finished their work quickly; three of the state's seven districts were left untouched.

Redistricting was not a dominant issue in the 1981 legislative year. The subject came up in a special session in August. State Rep. Rick Manley, co-chairman of a special redistricting committee, introduced a plan that would have excised from the 6th District the mostly-white, conservative areas that formed the basis of support for its freshman Republican incumbent. Manley's plan also would have given the district the Democratic industrial city of Bessemer.

Two Jefferson County legislators, Arthur Payne and Duane Lewis, objected strenuously to Manley's plan and drafted an alternative that won the support of the majority of Birmingham legislators. They said their plan was not designed to help or hurt the 6th District incumbent but was drawn to fit the wishes of their constituents.

Aware that any plan needed Jefferson County support to win, Manley agreed to go along with the Payne-Lewis boundaries, and they were adopted on a 52-11 vote in the House. The House then passed the entire bill Aug. 13, 1981, by a lopsided 93-9 vote. The Senate approved it the same day, 29-2. Democratic Gov. Fob James signed it Aug. 18, 1981.

The opposition to final passage came from black legislators who felt the plan was drawn to make the election of a black congressman nearly impossible. Although more than a fourth of the state population is black, the new redistricting plan followed the long-established pattern of dividing blacks nearly evenly among five districts. As a result no district was more than 34 percent black.

As it developed, the remap may have contributed to the defeat of the Republican incumbent in the 6th in 1982. He had narrowly won election to a first term in 1980; and the addition of some staunchly Democratic areas together with the industrial city's frustration with Reaganomics supplied the margin of victory for the Democratic challenger.

To preserve the existing boundaries of three of the seven districts, legislators were forced to accept a higher population variance than in the past. The largest district, the 1st, was 1.3 percent above the ideal district population

of 555,723. The smallest district, the 2nd, was 1.1 percent below the ideal, for a total deviation of 2.3 percent.

Age of Population

District	Population Under 18	Voting Age Population	Population 65 & Over (% of VAP)	Median Median Age
1	179,616	384,289	60,149 (15.7%)	28.3
2	166,355	383,150	64,624 (16.9%)	29.2
3	164,903	390,418	61,108 (15.7%)	28.2
4	165,012	397,076	71,872 (18.1%)	31.4
5	164,456	385,388	51,538 (13.4%)	29.3
6	149,374	404,782	67,231 (16.6%)	30.2
7	172,532	386,537	63,493 (16.4%)	28.4
State	1,162,248	2,731,640	440,015 (16.1%)	29.3

Income and Occupation

District	Median Family Income	White Collar Workers	Blue Collar Workers	Service Workers	Farm Workers
1	$ 16,622	47.3%	37.4%	12.5%	2.8%
2	15,295	48.3	35.1	12.6	4.0
3	15,489	41.5	44.3	11.8	2.5
4	14,798	35.9	50.3	9.8	4.0
5	17,787	48.5	38.0	11.1	2.5
6	18,668	58.4	28.7	12.3	0.6
7	16,316	46.5	38.0	12.8	2.6
State	$ 16,347	46.8%	38.7%	11.8%	2.7%

Education: School Years Completed

District	8 Years or Fewer	4 Years of High School	4 Years of College or More	Median School Years
1	22.3%	33.9%	11.4%	12.3
2	26.1	30.2	13.5	12.2
3	28.1	30.7	10.7	12.1
4	31.8	30.7	7.0	11.9
5	23.2	32.7	13.9	12.3
6	17.3	32.7	16.7	12.5
7	26.1	31.4	12.2	12.2
State	25.0%	31.8%	12.2%	12.2

ALABAMA

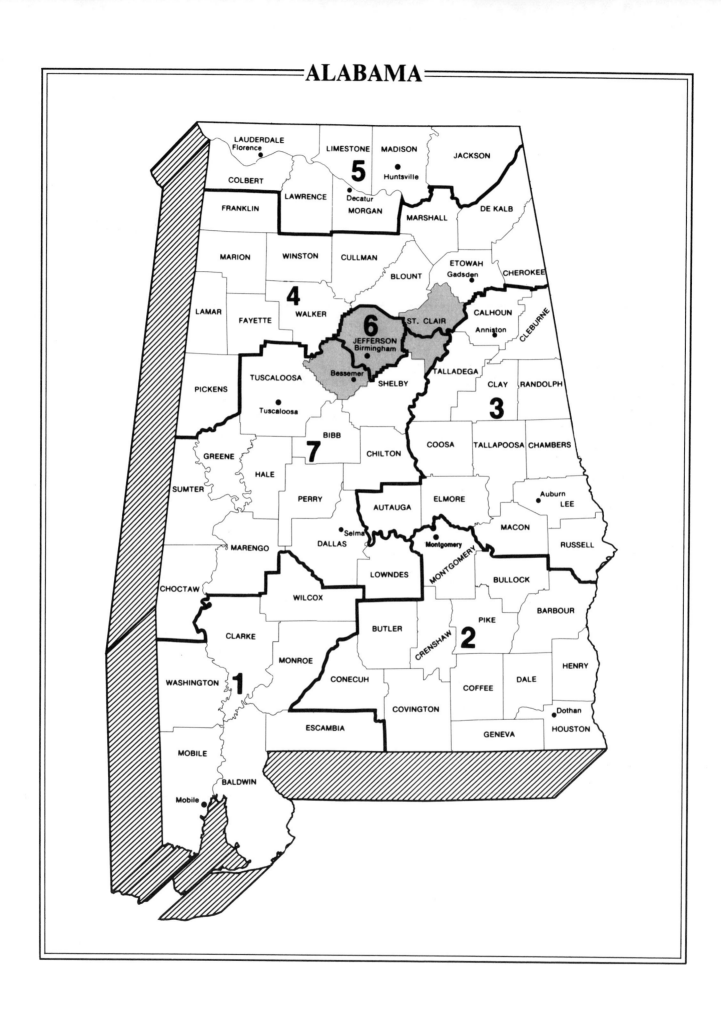

Housing and Residential Patterns

District	Owner Occupied	Renter Occupied	Urban	Rural
1	70.6%	29.4%	64.8%	35.2%
2	68.1	31.9	65.0	35.0
3	70.4	29.6	54.5	45.5
4	76.9	23.1	34.6	65.4
5	72.0	28.0	58.1	41.9
6	62.2	37.8	91.5	8.5
7	71.2	28.8	52.2	47.8
State	70.1%	29.9%	60.0%	40.0%

1st District

Southwest — Mobile

The 1st, covering seven counties in the southwest corner of the state, is dominated by the port city of Mobile. With a population of 200,452, Mobile is the state's second largest city, and the largest on the Gulf Coast between New Orleans and Tampa. Mobile is unique among Alabama's cities. Situated on the state's only coastline, it is isolated from the rest of Alabama, and its Spanish and French heritage and large Catholic population give the city a separate history. Because of the port, Mobile has always had a cosmopolitan, outward-looking air that distinguished it from more insular, inland Alabama.

Mobile County casts about two-thirds of the district vote. Like the neighboring Mississippi Gulf Coast, this area has been voting Republican in recent national elections, although in local elections Democrats still predominate, and Gov. George C. Wallace has always been popular here. The city of Mobile elected a female Republican to the state Senate in 1982; she is not only one of a handful of GOP members but the first woman elected to the Alabama Senate in the state's history.

The port is Mobile's largest employer. With the completion of the Tennessee-Tombigbee Waterway, which would connect Mobile Bay and the Tennessee River, the port of Mobile could compete with New Orleans in trade volume.

Shipbuilding is a major industry. In addition, the salt domes north of the city have given rise to a chemical industry, and several energy companies have been drilling offshore for oil and gas.

The other key industry in the 1st District is pulp and paper. International Paper and Scott Paper have large plants in Mobile County, and Mobile is now one of the more heavily unionized areas in Alabama.

The raw material for the paper industry comes from the forests that cover most of the district's rural counties. Cattle and pecans are raised in some, such as Washington, Clarke, Wilcox and Monroe.

The strong Republican vote in Mobile and coastal Baldwin County easily outweighs the Democratic strength found in the rural, heavily black counties in the northern part of the district and in the city of Prichard, a suburb of Mobile.

Wilcox County, more than two-thirds black, was one of just six Alabama counties to support Democratic Sen. George McGovern's presidential campaign in 1972. Blacks make up 31 percent of the district population. The dis-

trict's Republican representative was elected to a 10th consecutive term in 1982 with 62 percent of the vote.

Election Returns

1st District		Democrat		Republican	
1976	President	81,012	(48.4%)	83,622	(49.9%)
	House	58,906	(37.5%)	98,257	(62.5%)
1978	Governor	87,420	(76.4%)	24,789	(21.7%)
	Senate[1]	84,859	(94.0%)	—	
	Senate[2]	54,569	(50.2%)	51,686	(47.5%)
	House	40,450	(36.1%)	71,711	(63.9%)
1980	President	77,758	(40.7%)	107,679	(56.4%)
	Senate	69,641	(37.6%)	111,441	(60.2%)
	House	—		111,089	(94.8%)
1982	Governor	89,486	(58.0%)	60,275	(39.1%)
	House	54,315	(37.2%)	89,901	(61.6%)

[1] *Election for a full six-year term.*
[2] *Election for the remaining two years of the term of James B. Allen who died June 1, 1978.*

Demographics

Population: 563,905. **Percent Change from 1970:** 14.7%.

Land Area: 7,992 square miles. **Population per Square Mile:** 70.6.

Counties, 1980 Population: Baldwin — 78,556; Clarke — 27,702; Escambia — 38,440; Mobile — 364,980; Monroe — 22,651; Washington — 16,821; Wilcox 14,755.

Cities, 1980 Population: Mobile — 200,452; Prichard — 39,541.

Race and Ancestry: White — 67.9%; Black — 31.0%; American Indian, Eskimo and Aleut — 0.6%; Asian and Pacific Islander — 0.3%. Spanish Origin — 1.0%. English — 15.7%; French — 1.1%; German — 2.7%; Irish — 4.7%.

Universities, Enrollment: James H. Faulkner State Junior College, Bay Minette — 1,405; Jefferson Davis State Junior College, Brewton — 843; Mobile College, Mobile — 1,070; Patrick Henry State Junior College, Monroeville — 671; S. D. Bishop State Junior College, Mobile — 1,395; Spring Hill College, Mobile — 1,020; University of South Alabama, Mobile — 7,885.

Newspapers, Circulation: *Press* (eS), Mobile — 73,537; *Register* (mS), Mobile — 49,557.

Commercial Television Stations, Affiliation: WALA-TV, Mobile (NBC); WKRG-TV, Mobile (CBS); WPMI, Mobile (None). Most of district is located in Mobile-Pensacola (Fla.) ADI. Portion is in Montgomery ADI.

Industries:

Scott Paper Co. (Southern Operations); Mobile; paper mills — 4,000. **Alabama Dry Dock & Shipbuilding Co.;** Mobile; shipbuilding — 3,500. **V. F. Corp.** (Vanity Fair Mills); Monroeville; women's wear — 2,500. **Mobile Infirmary Assn. Inc.;** Mobile; hospital — 2,200. **International Paper Co. Inc.;** Mobile; paper bags — 1,700.

Ciba-Geigy Corp.; McIntosh; agricultural chemicals — 1,250. **MacMillian Bloedel Inc.** (Woodlands Div. - HQ); Pine Hill; lumber, plywood — 1,200. **Providence Hospital;** Mobile; hospital — 1,200. **Courtaulds North America Inc.** (HQ); Mobile; rayon, nylon fibers — 965. **Teledyne Industries Inc.** (Continental Motors Div.); Mobile; motor vehicle parts — 950. **Alabama State Docks Dept.** (HQ); Mobile; marine cargo handling — 863. **First Bancgroup-Alabama Inc.** (HQ); Mobile; bank holding company — 750.

Bender Shipbuilding & Repair Co.; Mobile; shipbuilding — 700. **Brown & Root Inc.;** Axis; highway construction — 700. **Allied Paper Inc.;** Jackson; pulp mills — 530. **International Systems Inc.;** Mobile; precast concrete products — 525. **Brewton Fashions Inc.;** Brewton; women's blouses — 500. **The Mitchell Co.;** Mobile; operative builders — 500. **Olin Corp.** (Olin Chemical Group); McIntosh; chemicals — 500.

2nd District

Southeast — Montgomery, Dothan

The unchanged 2nd District is growing steadily more Republican. Most of the 2nd, covering the southeast corner of the state, is rural. But half the population is concentrated in two urban centers found at opposite corners of the district.

At the northwestern edge is Montgomery County, with just under 200,000 people. The state capital, Montgomery, has long been a national Republican stronghold in Alabama, voting for GOP presidential candidates as far back as 1956. The city has a large white-collar government work force as well as a strong military influence from adjacent Maxwell and Gunter Air Force bases.

Montgomery was the first capital of the Confederacy, and to many the city represents the Fort Sumter of the civil rights movement. In Montgomery in 1955, a black woman refused to give up her seat to a white man; her arrest eventually resulted in the end of bus segregation.

At the southeastern corner of the district, near the Florida and Georgia borders, is the Houston County seat of Dothan, an old cotton and peanut market town that grew rapidly during the 1970s by attracting new industries. Although fiercely loyal to Gov. George C. Wallace, it voted for conservative Republican candidates in other contests with regularity during the 1970s.

Between these two population centers are the Piney Woods of Alabama and a portion of the state's Black Belt. Peanuts and cotton are still major crops. Overall, the new 2nd is 31 percent black.

Bullock and Barbour counties, Wallace's original home base, have large black populations and are loyally Democratic. As one moves south toward the Florida border, the black population drops sharply. The rural counties around Dothan are beginning to join the national trend toward supporting Republicans in statewide elections, although at the local level Democratic loyalties still prevail. In 1980, Ronald Reagan won seven of the district's 13 counties, taking 52 percent of the vote, his second highest mark in the state. As in the neighboring 1st, a Republican garnered a 10th consecutive House term in the 2nd in 1982, but by a majority of only 1,386 votes.

Election Returns

2nd District		Democrat		Republican	
1976	President	88,208	(53.1%)	75,528	(45.5%)
	House	66,288	(42.4%)	90,069	(57.6%)
1978	Governor	91,377	(81.6%)	19,308	(17.2%)
	Senate[1]	77,390	(92.8%)	—	
	Senate[2]	57,033	(54.2%)	46,342	(44.0%)
	House	49,341	(46.0%)	57,924	(54.0%)
1980	President	83,720	(44.2%)	99,283	(52.5%)
	Senate	86,870	(47.3%)	91,888	(50.0%)
	House	63,447	(36.7%)	104,796	(60.6%)
1982	Governor	102,579	(58.2%)	68,680	(38.9%)
	House	81,904	(49.6%)	83,290	(50.4%)

[1] *Election for a full six-year term.*
[2] *Election for the remaining two years of the term of James B. Allen who died June 1, 1978.*

Demographics

Population: 549,505. **Percent Change from 1970:** 11.7%.

Land Area: 9,209 square miles. **Population per Square Mile:** 59.7.

Counties, 1980 Population: Barbour — 24,756; Bullock — 10,596; Butler — 21,680; Coffee — 38,533; Conecuh — 15,884; Covington — 36,850; Crenshaw — 14,110; Dale — 47,821; Geneva — 24,253; Henry — 15,302; Houston — 74,632; Montgomery — 197,038; Pike — 28,050.

Cities, 1980 Population: Andalusia — 10,415; Dothan — 48,750; Enterprise — 18,033; Eufaula — 12,097; Montgomery — 177,857; Ozark — 13,188; Troy — 12,945.

Race and Ancestry: White — 68.5%; Black — 30.7%; American Indian, Eskimo and Aleut — 0.2%; Asian and Pacific Islander — 0.4%. Spanish Origin — 1.0%. English — 22.4%; French — 0.6%; German — 2.2%; Irish — 4.5%.

Universities, Enrollment: Alabama Christian College, Montgomery — 1,355; Alabama State University, Montgomery — 4,096; Auburn University at Montgomery, Montgomery — 4,810; Enterprise State Junior College, Enterprise — 1,918; George C. Wallace State Community College, Dothan — 1,928; Huntingdon College, Montgomery — 642; Lurleen B. Wallace State Junior College, Andalusia — 853; Troy State University, Troy — 6,687.

Newspapers, Circulation: *Alabama Journal* (e), Montgomery — 24,397; *Andalusia Star News* (eS), Andalusia — 5,204; *The Dothan Eagle* (eS), Dothan — 22,463; *The Enterprise Ledger* (eS), Enterprise — 8,013; *Montgomery Advertiser* (mS), Montgomery — 47,521; *The Troy Messenger* (eS), Troy — 4,630.

Commercial Television Stations, Affiliation: WCOV-TV, Montgomery (CBS); WDHN, Dothan (ABC); WKAB-TV, Montgomery (ABC); WMCF-TV, Montgomery (None); WSFA-TV, Montgomery, (NBC); WTUY, Dothan (CBS). Most of district is divided between Dothan ADI and Montgomery ADI. Portions are in Columbus (Ga.) ADI and Mobile-Pensacola (Fla.) ADI.

Military Installations: Dannelly Field (Air Force), Montgomery — 804; Fort Rucker, Daleville — 11,649; Gunter Air Force Station, Montgomery — 2,327; Hall Air National Guard Station, Dothan — 143; Maxwell Air Force Base, Montgomery — 4,724.

Nuclear Power Facilities: Farley 1, Dothan (Westinghouse, Bechtel), December 1977; Farley 2, Dothan (Westinghouse, Bechtel), July 1981.

Industries:

Daniel International Corp. (Daniel Construction Co. of Alabama); Dothan; heavy construction contracting — 2,400. **Northrop Corp.** (Northrop Worldwide); Fort Rucker; aircraft and airport services — 1,800. **Sony Magnetic Products Inc.;** Dothan; video, audio components — 1,700. **National Industries Inc.;** Montgomery; wiring harness — 1,350. **Alabama Farm Bureau Mutual Casualty Insurance Co. Inc.;** Montgomery; casualty insurance — 1,200.

The Baptist Medical Center; Montgomery; hospital — 1,200. **Houston County Hospital Board Inc.;** Dothan; hospital — 1,150. **Opp & Micolas Mills Inc.;** Opp; cotton sheeting — 1,150. **Alatex Inc.** (HQ); Andalusia; men's shirts — 1,100. **Brockway Glass Co. Inc.;** Montgomery; glass containers, cardboard boxes — 1,050. **Dorsey Trailers Inc.** (HQ); Elba; truck trailers — 875. **ConAgra Inc.;** Enterprise; poultry production — 820. **West Point-Pepperell Inc.;** Abbeville; sheets, pillowcases — 795. **Michelin Tire Corp.;** Dothan; tires — 700. **First Alabama Bank** (HQ); Montgomery; banking — 699. **Durr-Fillauer Medical Inc.** (Durr Drug Co.); Montgomery; surgical equipment — 685. **Akwell Industries Inc.** (HQ); Dothan; rubber products — 600. **Kleinerts Inc.;** Elba; women's wear — 600. **Covington Industries Inc.;** Opp; men's clothing — 550. **Hayes International Corp.;** Dothan; aircraft equipment — 550. **American Buildings Co.** (HQ); Eufaula; prefabricated metal buildings — 500. **Boss Mfg. Co.;** Greenville; gloves — 500. **Clinton Mills Inc.;** Geneva; broad-woven fabric — 500. **Blount Bros. Corp.** (HQ); Montgomery; building contractors — more than 500.

3rd District

East — Anniston, Auburn

Taking in the eastern side of the state from the outskirts of Montgomery to the hilly Piedmont Plateau, the 3rd is a conservative rural stronghold.

Although most of the voters throughout the district consider themselves Democrats, statewide Republican candidates are beginning to find favor, particularly in the more urbanized areas — Calhoun County (Anniston) in the north and Lee County (Auburn and Opelika) in the south. Ronald Reagan and Republican Senate candidate Jeremiah Denton carried both counties in 1980, although both trailed their Democratic opponents districtwide by slim margins.

The central part of the district has always been strong Wallace country and is still partisan toward Democratic candidates. Any national Democrat who stops short of outspoken liberalism can expect to win in these rural counties by a decent margin.

Textile mills are scattered around the 3rd District, reflecting the traditional prominence of cotton in the area's agricultural economy. There is a heavy concentration of industry in Opelika, located near the university town of Auburn and in Anniston. With slightly fewer than 30,000 people, Anniston is the district's largest city.

The only change in the district for the 1980s was the removal of predominently black Lowndes County, west of Montgomery. That leaves the 3rd with only one county — Macon — in which blacks are a majority. Blacks comprise 28 percent of the new 3rd.

Election Returns

3rd District		Democrat		Republican	
1976	President	90,034	(57.9%)	62,198	(40.0%)
	House	104,622	(98.9%)	—	
1978	Governor	83,617	(84.3%)	14,139	(14.3%)
	Senate[1]	72,593	(94.2%)	—	
	Senate[2]	59,959	(64.0%)	31,794	(33.9%)
	House	72,378	(100.0%)	—	
1980	President	86,753	(49.9%)	80,051	(46.1%)
	Senate	82,712	(50.1%)	76,906	(46.6%)
	House	104,511	(98.9%)	1,189	(1.1%)
1982	Governor	83,903	(59.1%)	52,910	(37.2%)
	House	100,864	(96.3%)	—	

[1] *Election for a full six-year term.*
[2] *Election for the remaining two years of the term of James B. Allen who died June 1, 1978.*

Demographics

Population: 555,321. **Percent Change from 1970:** 15.5%.

Land Area: 8,145 square miles. **Population per Square Mile:** 68.2.

Counties, 1980 Population: Autauga — 32,259; Calhoun — 119,761; Chambers — 39,191; Clay — 13,703; Cleburne — 12,595; Coosa — 11,377; Elmore — 43,390; Lee — 76,283; Macon — 26,829; Randolph — 20,075; Russell — 47,356; Talladega — 73,826; Tallapoosa — 38,846.

Cities, 1980 Population: Alexander City — 13,807; Anniston — 29,523; Auburn — 28,471; Opelika — 21,896; Phenix City — 26,928; Prattville — 18,647; Sylacauga — 12,708; Talladega — 19,128; Tuskegee — 13,327.

Race and Ancestry: White — 71.2%; Black — 28.2%; American Indian, Eskimo and Aleut — 0.1%; Asian and Pacific Islander — 0.3%. Spanish Origin — 0.9%. English — 23.3%; French — 0.5%; German — 2.2%; Irish — 5.7%.

Universities, Enrollment: Alexander City State Junior College, Alexander City — 1,229; Auburn University, Auburn — 18,603; Chattahoochee Valley State Community College, Phenix City — 1,434; Jacksonville State University, Jacksonville — 6,717; Opelika State Technical College, Opelika — 465; Southern Union State Junior College, Wadley — 1,591; Talladega College, Talladega — 784; Tuskegee Institute, Tuskegee Institute — 3,736.

Newspapers, Circulation: *Advance* (mS), Sylacauga — 3,105; *Alexander City Outlook* (eS), Alexander City — 4,505; *The Anniston Star* (eS), Anniston — 30,830; *Daily Home* (m), Talladega — 11,707; *Opelika-Auburn News* (eS), Opelika — 15,014; *Valley Times-News* (e), Lanett — 10,432.

Commercial Television Stations, Affiliation: WHMA-TV, Anniston (CBS); WSWS, Opelika (None). Most of district is divided among Birmingham ADI, Columbus (Ga.) ADI and Montgomery ADI. Portions are in Anniston ADI and Atlanta (Ga.) ADI.

Military Installations: Anniston Army Depot, Anniston — 4,782; Fort McClellan, Anniston — 7,446.

Industries:

Russell Corp. (HQ); Alexander City; knitted, woven fabrics — 8,000. **West Point-Pepperell Inc.** (Shawmut Apparel); Shawmut; broad-woven fabric — 3,000. **West Point-Pepperell Inc.** (Towel Services); Fairfax; towels — 2,000. **Kimberly-Clark Corp.;** Coosa Pines; newsprint pulp mills — 1,500. **Uniroyal Inc.** (Uniroyal Tire Co.); Opelika; tires, inner tubes — 1,420.

Ampex Corp.; Opelika; magnetic tape — 1,400. **Diversified Products Corp.** (HQ); Opelika; sporting goods — 1,200. **Northeast Alabama Regional Medical Center;** Anniston; hospital — 1,000. **Phelps Dodge Brass Co.** (Lee Fittings & Valves); Anniston; brass plumbing fixtures — 950. **Carisbrook Industries Inc.;** Blue Mountain; threads, twine — 900. **West Point-Pepperell Inc.** (Langdale Mill); Langdale; cotton fabrics — 845. **Avondale Mills Inc.** (Bevelle Plant); Alexander City; cotton fabrics — 750. **FMC Corp.** (Steel Products Div.); Anniston; steel forgings — 650. **Opelika Mfg. Corp.;** Opelika; cotton fabric — 650. **Allied Products Corp.** (Bush Hog/Continental Gin Co.); Prattville; textile machinery — 600.

Atlantic States Cast Iron Pipe (Union Foundry); Anniston; cast iron pipes — 600. **Dresser Industries;** Anniston; valves, pipe fittings — 600. **Southern Phenix Textile Inc.;** Phenix City; cotton fabric — 600. **Spring Valley Foods Inc.;** Ashland; poultry processors — 600. **Standard-Coosa-Thatcher;** Piedmont; yarn mills — 584. **Magic Chef Inc.** (Microwave Oven Div.); Anniston; cooking equipment — 580. **Palm Beach Co.;** Talladega; men's suits — 550. **Gurney Industries Inc.** (Manufacturing Div.); Prattville; yarn, knit fabrics — 500. **Neptune Water Meter Co.;** Tallassee; water meters — 500. **Wehadkee Yarn Mills Inc.;** Talladega; yarn spinning mills — 500. **West Point-Pepperell Inc.** (Bleachery & Dye Work Div.); Lanett; cotton fabrics — 500.

4th District

North Central — Gadsden

Stretching all the way across the northern part of the state, the 4th is rural, traditionally poor and overwhelmingly white. With just a 7 percent black population, it has a substantially different character from those districts further south.

The 4th has a long populist Democratic heritage. The "common man" rhetoric of Gov. George C. Wallace and former Gov. James E. Folsom Sr. always played well in this area. At the same time, with so few blacks, the area has been generally free of the extreme race-baiting found in other parts of the state.

Along with the 5th District directly to the north, the 4th has been the most predictably Democratic part of the state. But even here, the political complexion is changing. New residents are moving into this area at a faster pace than in any other district in the state, and many are voting Republican. The four counties with the fastest growth rates in the district during the 1970s — Blount and St. Clair near Birmingham, plus Winston and De Kalb — all voted for Ronald Reagan and GOP Senate candidate Jeremiah Denton in 1980. They were the only counties in the district to do so.

The western part of the district has a Republican bent that dates to the Civil War. Winston County seceded from Alabama when the state seceded from the Union. This part of the district contains coal mines that would be aided by completion of the Tennessee-Tombigbee waterway. The waterway would ease transportation from the mines to the port of Mobile.

Gadsden, an iron and steel center of 48,000 people, is the district's only city of substantial size. The remainder of the district is dominated largely by poultry, cotton and livestock farming operations.

Because of its 21 percent growth rate during the 1970s, the old 4th District was forced to give up population in redistricting. The Legislature shifted out about 9,000 people from the eastern side of Jefferson County, most of them Republicans, and 24,000 from the southern half of St. Clair County. The changes were too slight to have a major impact on politics in the district. If anything, these changes will strengthen the Democratic vote.

Election Returns

4th District		Democrat		Republican	
1976	President	121,138	(65.0%)	63,181	(33.9%)
	House	137,114	(80.2%)	33,840	(19.8%)
1978	Governor	73,143	(59.5%)	48,387	(39.3%)
	Senate[1]	80,414	(95.3%)	—	
	Senate[2]	64,758	(54.6%)	52,117	(44.0%)
	House	85,669	(100.0%)	—	
1980	President	104,802	(52.2%)	91.768	(45.7%)
	Senate	102,035	(52.2%)	90,283	(46.2%)
	House	125,419	(97.9%)	—	
1982	Governor	111,826	(62.0%)	63,886	(35.4%)
	House	x[3]		—[3]	

[1] Election for a full six-year term.
[2] Election for the remaining two years of the term of James B. Allen who died June 1, 1978.
[3] No votes tabulated where candidate was unopposed; x indicates winner.

Demographics

Population: 562,088. **Percent Change from 1970:** 19.7%.

Land Area: 9,186 square miles. **Population per Square Mile:** 61.2.

Counties, 1980 Population: Blount — 36,459; Cherokee — 18,760; Cullman — 61,642; De Kalb — 53,658; Etowah — 103,057; Fayette — 18,809; Franklin — 28,350; Lamar — 16,453; Marion — 30,041; Marshall — 65,622; Pickens — 21,481; St. Clair (Pt.) — 17,143; Walker — 68,660; Winston — 21,953.

Cities, 1980 Population: Albertville — 12,039; Cullman — 13,084; Fort Payne — 11,485; Gadsden — 47,565; Jasper — 11,894.

Race and Ancestry: White — 92.5%; Black — 7.2%; American Indian, Eskimo and Aleut — 0.1%; Asian and Pacific Islander — 0.1%. Spanish Origin — 0.6%. Dutch — 0.5%; English — 30.1%; French — 0.5%; German — 2.7%; Irish — 8.5%.

Universities, Enrollment: Brewer State Junior College, Fayette — 601; Gadsden State Junior College, Gadsden — 3,441; Northeast Alabama State Junior College, Rainsville — 998; Northwest Alabama State Junior College, Phil Campbell — 922; Snead State Junior College, Boaz — 1,032; Walker College, Jasper — 675.

Newspapers, Circulation: *The Cullman Times* (mS), Cullman — 7,975; *Daily Mountain Eagle* (e), Jasper — 11,875; *The Gadsden Times* (eS), Gadsden — 28,364; *Times Journal* (eS), Fort Payne — 6,395. *The Birmingham News* and *Birmingham Post-Herald* also circulate in the district.

Commercial Television Stations, Affiliation: WNAL, Gadsden (None). Most of district is located in Birmingham ADI. Portions are in Columbus (Miss.)-Tupelo (Miss.) ADI and Huntsville-Decatur-Florence ADI.

Military Installations: Martin Air National Guard Station, Gadsden — 168.

Industries:

Goodyear Tire & Rubber Co.; Gadsden; tires, inner tubes — 3,700. **Republic Steel Corp.;** Gadsden; steel production — 3,500. **Cooper Industries Inc.** (Nicholson File Div.); Cullman; machine tool accessories — 900. **H. D. Lee Co. Inc.;** Boaz; men's, boys' work wear — 800. **Haleyville Textile Mills Inc.;** Haleyville; women's wear — 750.

Health-Tex Inc.; Guin; children's wear — 750. **Health-Tex Inc.;** Gadsden; children's wear — 700. **Federal-Mogul Corp.;** Hamilton; ball and roller bearings — 689. **Blue Bell Inc.;** Oneonta; men's work wear — 625. **Spring Valley Foods Inc.;** Gadsden; poultry processing — 625. **Merico Inc.;** Fort Payne; cakes, bakery products — 575. **Gold Kist Inc.;** Boaz; poultry processing — 565.

Cluett Peabody & Co. Inc. (Arrow Co. Div.); Jasper; men's shirts — 550. **White Consolidated Industries;** Cullman; aluminum foundry — 550. **Cullman Product Corp.;** Cullman; metal panels — 500. **Grenoble Mills Inc.;** Fyffe; knit outerwear — 500. **Hyster Co.;** Sulligent; construction machinery — 500. **Republic Steel Corp.** (North River Energy); Berry; metal service centers — 500. **White Consolidated Industries** (Americold Compressor Div.); Cullman; metal stampings — 500.

5th District

North — Huntsville

The Tennessee River connects the seven counties of this district at the northern end of the state. Nearly half a century of natural resource development by the Tennessee Valley Authority (TVA) has contributed to the prosperity of this region, making it an atypical Alabama district.

The 5th has a relatively small black population (14 percent), several large federal installations in Huntsville and active labor unions in the metals, automobile and chemical plants along the Tennessee River. It is the state's most reliably Democratic territory in major statewide elections. In 1980 Jimmy Carter won 54 percent of the vote in this district, his best mark in the state of Alabama.

Huntsville (Madison County) was the only part of the 5th to side with Ronald Reagan in 1980, and only by a very slim margin. With 143,000 people, it is the state's fourth largest city and has a large white-collar work force. Boeing and IBM have high-technology plants in Huntsville, and the Army's Redstone Arsenal and the Marshall Space Flight Center have been economically important.

Located downstream along the Tennessee River are blue-collar towns such as Decatur and the Quad Cities of

Florence, Sheffield, Tuscumbia and Muscle Shoals. The Quad Cities are overwhelmingly Democratic. This was the only part of the state where white voters supported the Carter-Mondale ticket in 1980 by margins that approached those in the counties where blacks are the majority.

Because the population of the 5th District grew at about the same rate as the entire state in the 1970s, there was no need to alter the district lines. Except for the period 1962-64, when all of the state's representatives were elected at-large, the district has consisted of the same seven counties since the beginning of the century. Republicans ran for the seat in only 19 of the 42 elections during that period; only once — in 1970 — did a GOP candidate attain as much as 40 percent of the vote.

Election Returns

5th District		Democrat		Republican	
1976	President	106,191	(66.8%)	50,039	(31.5%)
	House	113,583	(100.0%)	—	
1978	Governor	63,033	(71.4%)	23,962	(27.1%)
	Senate[1]	65,069	(93.7%)	—	
	Senate[2]	49,189	(52.1%)	35,227	(40.9%)
	House	68,985	(96.8%)	—	
1980	President	96,169	(54.0%)	72,831	(40.9%)
	Senate	91,139	(52.3%)	78,226	(44.8%)
	House	117,626	(93.8%)	—	
1982	Governor	86,095	(59.2%)	54,473	(37.4%)
	House	108,807	(80.7%)	24,593	(18.2%)

[1] *Election for a full six-year term.*
[2] *Election for the remaining two years of the term of James B. Allen who died June 1, 1978.*

Demographics

Population: 549,844. **Percent Change from 1970:** 12.3%.

Land Area: 4,953 square miles. **Population per Square Mile:** 111.0.

Counties, 1980 Population: Colbert — 54,519; Jackson — 51,407; Lauderdale — 80,546; Lawrence — 30,170; Limestone — 46,005; Madison — 196,966; Morgan — 90,231.

Cities, 1980 Population: Athens — 14,558; Decatur — 42,002; Florence — 37,029; Huntsville — 142,513; Scottsboro — 14,758; Sheffield — 11,903.

Race and Ancestry: White — 84.9%; Black — 14.3%; American Indian, Eskimo and Aleut — 0.2%; Asian and Pacific Islander — 0.4%. Spanish Origin — 0.8%. English — 24.1%; French — 0.6%; German — 3.3%; Irish — 7.8%; Scottish — 0.5%.

Universities, Enrollment: Alabama Agricultural and Mechanical University, Normal — 4,245; Athens State College, Athens — 1,116; John C. Calhoun State Community College, Decatur — 5,264; Oakwood College, Huntsville — 1,263; University of Alabama in Huntsville, Huntsville — 5,009; University of North Alabama, Florence — 5,268.

Newspapers, Circulation: *Athens News Courier* (mS), Athens — 7,653; *The Decatur Daily* (eS), Decatur — 22,817; *Huntsville News* (m), Huntsville — 13,893; *The Huntsville Times* (eS), Huntsville — 52,506; *Sentinel* (eS), Scottsboro — 5,367; *The Times-Tri Cities Daily* (eS), Florence — 27,663.

Commercial Television Stations, Affiliation: WAAY-TV, Huntsville (ABC); WAFF, Huntsville (NBC); WHNT-TV, Huntsville (CBS); WOWL-TV, Florence (NBC). Most of district is located in Huntsville-Decatur-Florence ADI. Portion is in Chattanooga (Tenn.) ADI.

Military Installations: Redstone Arsenal (Army), Huntsville — 18,281.

Nuclear Power Plants: Bellefonte 1 and 2, Scottsboro (Babcock & Wilcox, Tennessee Valley Authority); Browns Ferry 1, Athens (General Electric, Tennessee Valley Authority), August 1974; Browns Ferry 2, Athens (General Electric, Tennessee Valley Authority), March 1975; Browns Ferry 3, Athens (General Electric, Tennessee Valley Authority), March 1977.

Industries:

Reynolds Metals Co. (Alloy Sheet & Plate); Sheffield; aluminum sheets — 2,855. **GTE Automatic Electric Co.;** Huntsville; telephone apparatus — 2,500. **Monsanto Co.;** Decatur; acrylic fibers — 2,400. **General Motors Corp.** (Saginaw Steering Gear Div.); Athens; auto parts — 1,750. **Chrysler Corp.;** Huntsville; electronic parts — 1,650.

Huntsville Hospital; Huntsville; hospital — 1,400. **Champion International Corp.** (Champion Papers Div.); Courtland; paper mills — 1,250. **M. Lowenstein Corp.** (Huntsville Mfg. Div.); Huntsville; cotton fabric mills — 1,250. **Eliza Coffee Memorial Hospital;** Florence; hospital — 1,150. **Ford Motor Co.;** Sheffield; auto parts — 1,100. **Dunlop Tire & Rubber Co.;** Huntsville; tires, inner tubes — 1,000. **Teledyne Inc.** (Teledyne Brown Engineering Co.); Huntsville; radio, TV transmitting equipment — 1,000. **Eltra Corp.** (Resto Lite Div.); Decatur; electrical equipment — 983. **Minnesota Mining and Mfg. Co.;** Decatur; plastics materials — 977. **SCI Systems Inc.** (HQ); Huntsville; electronic devices — 950.

UOP Inc. (Wolverine Tube Div.); Decatur; copper bars — 950. **Brown & Root Inc.;** Courtland; general building contracting — 800. **Central Bank of Alabama** (Commercial Billing Service - HQ); Decatur; banking — 800. **Intergraph Corp.** (HQ); Madison; commercial machine wholesaling — 800. **International Business Machines Corp.** (IBM Federal Systems Div.); Huntsville; business machines — 750. **Revere Copper & Brass Inc.** (Scottsboro Aluminum Sheet Div.); Scottsboro; aluminum foundry — 700. **Benham Corp.** (HQ); Scottsboro; men's, boys' wear — 650. **PPG Industries** (Aircraft Div.); Huntsville; glass aircraft products — 631. **Goodyear Tire & Rubber Co. Inc.;** Scottsboro; polyester yarns — 600. **The Boeing Co. Inc.** (Boeing Military Airplane Co.); Huntsville; automated test equipment —580. **Lawrence Corp.;** Moulton; women's wear — 550.

Sonoco Products Co. (Baker Div.); Hartselle; steel, wood, plastics products — 550. **Amoco Chemicals Corp.;** Decatur; petroleum refining — 520. **Thiokol Corp.;** Huntsville; ordnance and accessories — 520. **Candy Textile Co. Inc.** (Ballet Fabrics Inc.); Scottsboro; knitted stretch fabric — 500. **Chesebrough-Ponds Inc.;** Huntsville; cosmetics — 500. **ConAgra Inc.;** Decatur; poultry processing — 500. **Emhart Industries Inc.** (Mallory Co.); Huntsville; electrical industrial appliances — 500. **Martin Industries Inc.;** Huntsville; gas heaters — 500. **Onan Corp.;** Huntsville; motors — 500. **Reynolds Metals Co.** (Mill Products Div.); Sheffield; printed aluminum cans — 500. **United Space Boosters Inc.** (HQ); Huntsville; engineering services — 500.

6th District

Birmingham and Suburbs

The 6th is split almost evenly between Birmingham and its suburbs. The largest city in the state, Birmingham is often referred to as the Pittsburgh of the South because of its large steel plants. The city, which is 56 percent black, has an older, industrial flavor that the newer, white-collar Southern cities like Atlanta lack. It also has problems of urban decline more often associated with the North. It usually votes Democratic and has had a black mayor since 1979.

The suburbs of the 6th District are diverse. South of the Red Mountain, which forms the southern edge of the city, are Mountain Brook, Homewood and Hoover, all well-to-do areas that vote heavily Republican. The areas north and east of Birmingham in Jefferson County also tend to be Republican but are less densely populated. Redistricting added the Leeds area, in the extreme eastern corner of Jefferson County, previously in the 4th. Leeds showed its GOP bent in 1980 by supporting both Ronald Reagan and Republican Senate candidate Jeremiah Denton by large margins.

However, the Republican Leeds area has only a third the population of the other area the district gained, in what is called the Bessemer Cutoff. The new 6th District takes in only 1,000 residents of the labor-oriented steel town of Bessemer, but picks up six other blue-collar communities.

Brighton, Roosevelt City and Brownville are all largely black, Democratic areas. Fairfield, the largest added town, and Lipscomb are racially split but Democratic. Midfield, the remaining town, is nearly all white. Blacks make up about 34 percent of the new district.

Election Returns

6th District		Democrat		Republican	
1976	President	83,381	(45.5%)	96,737	(52.8%)
	House	83,154	(47.8%)	89,660	(51.5%)
1978	Governor	77,109	(63.5%)	41,891	(34.5%)
	Senate[1]	91,145	(94.1%)	—	
	Senate[2]	57,509	(48.7%)	59,144	(50.1%)
	House	50,100	(43.7%)	64,176	(56.0%)
1980	President	95,144	(43.6%)	111,373	(51.0%)
	Senate	90,060	(42.3%)	114,328	(53.6%)
	House	102,370	(50.9%)	93,547	(46.5%)
1982	Governor	77,239	(45.5%)	85,335	(50.3%)
	House	88,029	(53.2%)	76,726	(46.4%)

[1] *Election for a full six-year term.*
[2] *Election for the remaining two years of the term of James B. Allen who died June 1, 1978.*

Demographics

Population: 554,156. **Percent Change from 1970:** 3.3%.

Land Area: 617 square miles. **Population per Square Mile:** 898.1

Counties, 1980 Population: Jefferson (Pt.) — 554,156.

Cities, 1980 Population: Bessemer (Pt.) — 1,016; Birmingham (Pt.) — 280,261; Fairfield — 13,040; Homewood — 21,412; Hoover (Pt.) — 8,534; Mountain Brook — 19,718; Vestavia Hills (Pt.) — 14,138.

Race and Ancestry: White — 65.1%; Black — 34.4%; American Indian, Eskimo and Aleut — 0.1%; Asian and Pacific Islander — 0.3%. Spanish Origin — 0.7%. English — 17.6%; French — 0.6%; German — 2.5%; Irish — 4.5%; Italian — 1.2%; Scottish — 0.7%.

Universities, Enrollment: Birmingham-Southern College, Birmingham — 1,443; Jefferson State Junior College, Birmingham — 6,391; Lawson State Community College, Birmingham — 1,725; Miles College, Birmingham — 1,015; R.E.T.S. Electronic Institute, Birmingham — 475; Samford University, Birmingham — 3,980; Southeastern Bible College, Birmingham — 251; Southern Junior College of Business, Birmingham — 2,146; University of Alabama in Birmingham, Birmingham — 13,854.

Newspapers, Circulation: *The Birmingham News* (eS), Birmingham — 175,811; *Post-Herald* (m), Birmingham — 67,977.

Commercial Television Stations, Affiliation: WBMG, Birmingham (CBS); WBRC, Birmingham (ABC); WTTO, Birmingham (None); WVTM, Birmingham (NBC). Entire district is located in Birmingham ADI.

Military Installations: Birmingham Municipal Airport (Air Force), Birmingham — 1,294.

Industries:

University of Alabama Medical Center; Birmingham; hospital — 10,000. **American Cast Iron Pipe Co.** (HQ); Birmingham; ductile iron pipes — 2,800. **Hayes International Corp.** (HQ); Birmingham; aircraft parts — 2,440. **Stockham Valves & Fittings Inc.** (HQ); Birmingham; valves — 2,300. **Central Bank of Birmingham** (HQ); Birmingham; bank holding company — 2,165.

Carraway Methodist Medical Center Inc. (HQ); Birmingham; hospital, nursing care facility — 2,000. **Brookwood Health Services Inc.** (Brookwood Medical Center); Birmingham; hospital — 1,800. **First National Bank of Birmingham Inc.;** Birmingham; banking — 1,800. **Southern Co. Services Inc.** (HQ); Birmingham; management services — 1,680. **Ingalls Inc.;** Birmingham; fabricated structural metal — 1,600. **Veterans Administration;** Birmingham; veterans' hospital — 1,250. **Rust Engineering Co. Inc.** (HQ); Birmingham; general engineering contractors — 1,200. **St. Vincent's Hospital;** Birmingham; hospital — 1,180. **Blue Cross & Blue Shield** (HQ); Birmingham; health insurance — 1,140.

Liberty National Insurance Holding Co. (HQ); Birmingham; accident, health insurance — 1,040. **Birmingham Trust National Bank;** Birmingham; banking — 1,000. **Fontaine Truck Equipment Co.;** Birmingham; truck, bus bodies — 1,000. **Harbert International Inc.;** Birmingham; highway construction — 1,000. **Louisville & Nashville Railroad Co.;** Birmingham; railroad operations — 900. **Security Engineers Inc.** (HQ); Birmingham; security services — 900. **Alabama Cleaning Service & Supply Co.** (HQ); Birmingham; janitorial services — 850. **Birmingham News Co. Inc.** (HQ); Birmingham; newspaper publishing — 730. **Birmingham Coca-Cola Bottling Co.** (HQ); Birmingham; soft drink bottling — 650.

Connors Steel Co. (HQ); Birmingham; steel foundry — 650. **B. E. & K. Inc.;** Birmingham; general contracting — 649. **C. S. A. Satellite Communications of North America** (HQ); Birmingham; electronic communications apparatus — 640. **Chicago Bridge & Iron Co.;** Birmingham; iron plate fabricating — 600. **Southern Research Institute;** Birmingham; scientific research laboratory — 600. **Southern Natural Resources Inc.** (HQ); Birmingham; natural gas transmission — 550. **U. S. Industries Inc.** (United Chair Div.); Leeds; metal office furniture — 550. **Square D Co.** (Anderson Electric Co. Div.); Leeds; wiring devices — 530. **Southern Progressive Corp.** (HQ); Birmingham; book, periodical publishing — 500.

7th District

West Central — Tuscaloosa, Bessemer

The 7th has four separate but nearly equal parts. The new 7th still contains much of the intensely Democratic Black Belt of Alabama. While the term "Black Belt" is said not to refer to the racial composition but to the color of the rich, sticky cotton-growing soil, seven of the eight rural counties in this portion of the district have black majorities. One, Lowndes County, is newly added by redistricting. These eight Black Belt counties, which make up a quarter of the district's population, gave Jimmy Carter 60 percent of the vote in 1980. The black population in this area is 59 percent.

Republicans running in the district should be helped most in the booming area south of Birmingham. Shelby and Chilton counties have been voting increasingly Republican in recent years. Shelby, in particular, is experiencing a rapid population boom, as people continue to move out from Birmingham and Jefferson County.

The Jefferson County part of the 7th District has been leaning Republican in recent statewide contests. Any Republican candidate running in the district will still have to contend with a large black and Democratic vote in the city of Bessemer, which is part of Jefferson County, but Democrats lose strength with the transfer of six towns around Bessemer to the 6th District.

Tuscaloosa and Tuscaloosa County make up the remaining population bloc in the district. About one-quarter black, this county is a swing area; it went narrowly for Reagan in 1980 but comfortably for George C. Wallace for governor in 1982. With 75,000 people, Tuscaloosa is the largest city in the new 7th District. It has an industrial base centered around the manufacture of rubber, chemicals and fertilizer.

Election Returns

7th District		Democrat		Republican	
1976	President	88,502	(54.6%)	70,693	(43.6%)
	House	103,415	(97.0%)	3,144	(3.0%)
1978	Governor	76,187	(74.6%)	24,487	(24.0%)
	Senate[1]	75,584	(93.9%)	—	
	Senate[2]	58,022	(58.4%)	39,860	(40.1%)
	House	72,641	(92.1%)	3,365	(4.3%)
1980	President	92,384	(48.4%)	91,267	(47.8%)
	Senate	87,718	(48.7%)	87,290	(48.5%)
	House	114,760	(71.2%)	43,603	(27.0%)
1982	Governor	98,851	(62.6%)	53,384	(33.8%)
	House	124,070	(96.8%)	—	

[1] Election for a full six-year term.
[2] Election for the remaining two years of the term of James B. Allen who died June 1, 1978.

Demographics

Population: 559,069. **Percent Change from 1970:** 15.5%.

Land Area: 10,666 square miles. **Population per Square Mile:** 52.4.

Counties, 1980 Population: Bibb — 15,723; Chilton — 30,612; Choctaw — 16,839; Dallas — 53,981; Greene — 11,021; Hale — 15,604; Jefferson (Pt.) — 117,168; Lowndes — 13,253; Marengo — 25,047; Perry — 15,012; Shelby — 66,298; St. Clair (Pt.) — 24,062; Sumter — 16,908; Tuscaloosa — 137,541.

Cities, 1980 Population: Bessemer (Pt.) — 30,713; Birmingham (Pt.) — 4,152; Hoover (Pt.) — 11,258; Hueytown — 13,309; Northport — 14,291; Selma — 26,684; Tuscaloosa — 75,211; Vestavia Hills (Pt.) — 1,584.

Race and Ancestry: White — 66.3%; Black — 33.3%; American Indian, Eskimo and Aleut — 0.1%; Asian and Pacific Islander — 0.2%. Spanish Origin — 0.9%. English — 21.2%; French — 0.6%; German — 2.0%; Irish — 4.7%; Scottish — 0.5%.

Universities, Enrollment: George Corley Wallace State Community College, Selma — 1,554; Judson College, Marion — 346; Livingston University, Livingston — 1,100; Marion Military Institute, Marion — 256; Shelton State Community College, Tuscaloosa — 648; Stillman College, Tuscaloosa — 558; University of Alabama, University — 17,918; University of Montevallo, Montevallo — 2,593.

Newspapers, Circulation: *Selma Times-Journal* (eS), Selma — 10,214; *The Tuscaloosa News* (eS), Tuscaloosa — 29,223. *The Birmingham News* and *Birmingham Post-Herald* also circulate in the district.

Commercial Television Stations, Affiliation: WCFT-TV, Tuscaloosa (CBS); WSLA, Selma (CBS). Most of district is located in Birmingham ADI. Portions are in Montgomery ADI, Selma ADI, Tuscaloosa ADI and Meridian (Miss.) ADI.

Industries:

The B. F. Goodrich Co.; Tuscaloosa; tires, inner tubes — 2,000. **Druid City Hospital Inc.** (HQ); Tuscaloosa; hospital — 1,340. **Mead Corp.** (Mulga Coal Co.); Mulga; blast furnace — 700. **All Lock Co. Inc.**; Selma; hardware items — 500. **Avondale Mills;** Pell City; cotton blend fabrics — 500. **Bristol Steel & Iron Works Inc.** (Bessemer Galvanizing Co.); Bessemer; steel fabricating — 500. **McAbee Construction Inc.**; Tuscaloosa; industrial contracting — 500.

Alaska

The people of Alaska are spread over 570,833 square miles, but the vote is concentrated in a few centers of population. About half of it is cast in Anchorage, where the 1980 population of 174,431 marked a three-fold increase over what it had been in 1970.

The arrival of the U.S. military in World War II and the discovery of oil on the nearby Kenai Peninsula 15 years later turned Anchorage into a boom town. The continuing military presence, the fast-growth mentality of the oil industry and an influential conservative newspaper have combined to make Anchorage a GOP stronghold.

More than 300 miles north of Anchorage, at the end of the Alkan Highway, is Fairbanks, the traditional trading center for the hamlets of inland Alaska. In the 1970s, the city grew from 15,000 to 23,000, largely because of its role as supply center for the oil pipeline. Republicans usually do as well in Fairbanks as in Anchorage.

Southeast Alaska is separated from the rest of the state by two time zones, the St. Elias Mountains and the Gulf of Alaska. Juneau, the state capital, is inaccessible by land. Many of the state legislators say they feel "claustrophobic" amid the towering mountains and ever-present clouds that loom over the city.

In 1976 Alaska voters chose to move the capital to a site near Anchorage, but in 1982 a referendum to spend the $2.5 billion required to move the capital was soundly defeated. Losing the capital would devastate the Panhandle's economy, which apart from government, relies on lumber products and fishing. Government employees and a large native Indian population give Juneau and the other Panhandle towns, such as Sitka, Ketchikan, and Skagway a distinctly Democratic slant.

The great wilderness of Alaska is at least twice the size of Texas. With road building virtually prevented by harsh terrain and climate, the only access to the bush towns is by air.

Native Indians and Eskimos predominate in remote Alaska, which includes the Aleutian Islands. Poverty is endemic, even with the state oil boom. Most of the native residents back Democrats. The Republican voters are mainly whites who work in the oil fields north of Fairbanks.

Still, party label has little meaning in Alaska, which comes closer than any other state to having no organized parties at all. Independents outnumber both Democratic and GOP registrants.

Age of Population

District	Population Under 18	Voting Age Population	Population 65 & Over (% of VAP)	Median Age
AL	130,745	271,106	11,547 (4.3%)	26.1

Income and Occupation

District	Median Family Income	White Collar Workers	Blue Collar Workers	Service Workers	Farm Workers
AL	$ 28,395	59.9%	24.0%	13.6%	2.5%

Education: School Years Completed

District	8 Years or Fewer	4 Years of High School	4 Years of College or More	Median School Years
AL	9.0%	38.9%	21.1%	12.8

Housing and Residential Patterns

District	Owner Occupied	Renter Occupied	Urban	Rural
AL	58.3%	41.7%	64.3%	35.7%

Election Returns

At Large		Democrat		Republican	
1976	President	44,058	(35.7%)	71,555	(57.9%)
	House	34,194	(25.8%)	83,722	(70.8%)
1978	Governor	25,656	(20.2%)	49.580	(39.1%)
	Senate	29,574	(24.1%)	92,783	(75.6%)
	House	55,176	(44.4%)	68,811	(55.4%)
1980	President	41,842	(26.4%)	86,112	(54.3%)
	Senate	72,007	(45.9%)	84,159	(53.7%)
	House	39,922	(25.8%)	114,089	(73.8%)
1982	Governor	89,918	(46.1%)	72,291	(37.1%)
	House	52,011	(28.7%)	128,274	(70.8%)

ALASKA

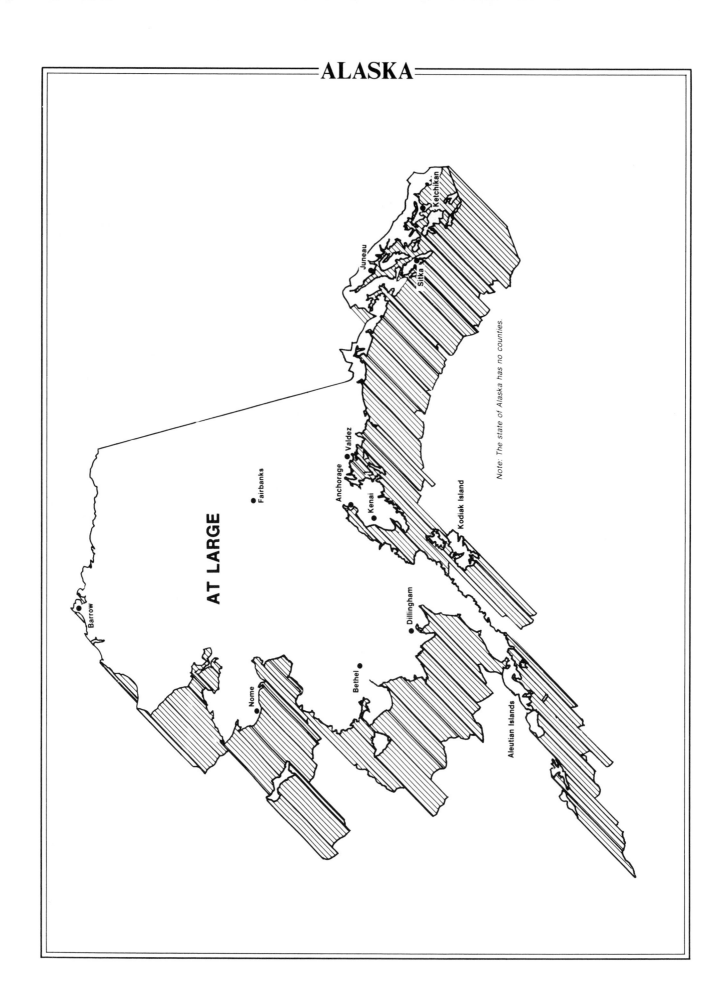

AT LARGE

Barrow

Fairbanks

Nome

Bethel

Anchorage
Valdez

Kenai

Dillingham

Kodiak Island

Juneau

Sitka

Ketchikan

Aleutian Islands

Note: The state of Alaska has no counties.

Demographics

Population: 401,851. **Percent Change from 1970:** 32.8%.

Land Area: 570,833 square miles. **Population per Square Mile:** 0.7.

Counties[1], 1980 Population: Aleutian Islands — 7,768; Anchorage — 174,431; Bethel — 10,999; Bristol Bay — 1,094; Dillingham — 4,616; Fairbanks North Star — 53,983; Haines — 1,680; Juneau — 19,528; Kenai Peninsula — 25,282; Ketchikan Gateway — 11,316; Kobuk — 4,831; Kodiak Island — 9,939; Matanuska-Susitna — 17,816; Nome — 6,537; North Slope — 4,199; Prince Of Wales-Outer Ketchikan — 3,822; Sitka — 7,803; Skagway-Yakutat-Angoon — 3,478; Southeast Fairbanks — 5,676; Valdez-Cordova — 8,348; Wade Hampton — 4,665; Wrangell-Petersburg — 6,167; Yukon-Koyukuk — 7,873.

[1] Alaska has no counties; the listing denotes census designated areas.

Cities, 1980 Population: Anchorage — 174,431; Fairbanks — 22,645; Juneau — 19,528.

Race and Ancestry: White — 77.1%; Black — 3.4%; American Indian, Eskimo and Aleut — 16.0%; Asian and Pacific Islander — 2.1%. Spanish Origin — 2.4%. Dutch — 0.8%; English — 8.9%; French — 1.5%; German — 8.1%; Irish — 4.1%; Italian — 1.0%; Norwegian — 1.7%; Polish — 0.8%; Scottish — 1.0%; Swedish — 1.1%.

Universities, Enrollment: Anchorage Community College, Anchorage — 7,142; Kenai Peninsula Community College, Soldotna — 967; Ketchikan Community College, Ketchikan — 396; Kodiak Community College, Kodiak — 487; Kuskokwim Community College, Bethel — 203; Matanuska-Susitna Community College, Palmer — 407; Sheldon Jackson College, Sitka — 198; University of Alaska, Anchorage — 2,826; University of Alaska, Fairbanks — 3,756.

Newspapers, Circulation: *Anchorage Daily News* (m), Anchorage — 26,071; *The Anchorage Times* (eS), Anchorage — 42,709; *Fairbanks Daily News-Miner* (e), Fairbanks — 15,647; *Juneau Empire* (e), Juneau — 6,120; *Ketchikan Daily News* (e), Ketchikan — 4,018; *Kodiak Daily Mirror* (e), Kodiak — 2,000; *The Peninsula Clarion* (m), Kenai — 2,381; *Sentinel* (e), Sitka — 2,645.

Commercial Television Stations, Affiliation: KIFW-TV, Sitka (CBS, ABC, NBC); KIMO, Anchorage (ABC); KINY-TV, Juneau (NBC, ABC); KJNP-TV, North Pole (None); KTTU-TV, Fairbanks (ABC, NBC); KTUU-TV, Anchorage (NBC); KTVA, Anchorage (CBS); KTVF, Fairbanks (CBS, ABC). Alaska has no ADIs.

Military Installations: Adak Naval Security Group, Adak — 561; Adak Naval Station, Adak — 1,241; Anchorage International Airport (Air Force), Anchorage — 214; Barter Island Distant Early Warning (DEW) Station (Air Force), Fairbanks — 104; Campion Air Force Station, Galena — 33; Cape Lisburne Air Force Station, Point Hope — 15; Cape Newenham Air Force Station, Platinum — 15; Cape Romanzof Air Force Station, Hooper Bay — 15; Clear Missile Early Warning Station (Air Force), Anderson — 527; Cold Bay Air Force Station, Cold Bay — 17.

Eielson Air Force Base, North Pole — 3,042; Elmendorf Air Force Base, Anchorage — 8,941; Fort Greely, Fairbanks — 1,104; Fort Richardson, Anchorage — 6,333; Fort Wainwright, Fairbanks — 3,636. Fort Yukon Air Force Station, Fort Yukon — 28; Galena Airport (Air Force), Galena — 319; Indian Mountain Air Force Station, Hughes — 28; King Salmon Airport (Air Force), Naknek — 379; Kotzebue Air Force Station, Kotzebue — 17; Kulis Air National Guard Base, Anchorage — 7.

Lonely DEW Station (Air Force), Fairbanks — 11; Murphy Dome Air Force Station, College — 67; Olitktok DEW Station (Air Force), Fairbanks — 11; Point Barrow DEW Station (Air Force), Fairbanks — 43; Point Lay DEW Station (Air Force), Fairbanks — 11; Shemya Air Force Base, Atka — 763; Sparrevohn Air Force Station, Iliamna — 28; Tatalina Air Force Station, McGrath — 28; Tin City Air Force Station, Wales — 15; Wainwright DEW Station (Air Force), Fairbanks — 11.

Industries:

Louisiana-Pacific Corp.; Ketchikan; pulp mills — 1,200. **Sohio Alaska Petroleum Co. Inc.;** Anchorage; oil production — 1,100. **Arctic Slope Regional Corp. (HQ);** Barrow; heavy construction — 800. **Wien Air Alaska Inc. (HQ);** Anchorage; airline — 730. **Sealaska Corp.;** Juneau; seafood packaging — 700. **Alaska Lumber & Pulp Co. Inc.;** Sitka; pulp mills — 500. **Alyeska Pipeline Service Co. (HQ);** Anchorage; crude oil pipeline — 500.

Arizona

Arizona earned its fifth House seat by growing 53.1 percent in the 1970s. The least populous of the new districts is the 2nd, which spreads south and west from Phoenix, with 543,187 people in the 1980 Census. The most populous, the new 3rd, stretching west and north from Phoenix to the California, Nevada and Utah borders, had a population of 544,870 — a difference of 1,683 people.

But the redistricting procedure was not without its problems. The first plan was passed Dec. 7, 1981, by the Republican Legislature over the governor's veto. The plan was challenged in court by Hispanics and other Democrats who claimed the remap hurt Mexican-Americans because it packed them into one district. According to the Democrats, this concentration diluted the strength of Hispanics in other sections of Arizona. Their suit also charged that the plan violated standards of compactness by linking widely separated areas of southwestern Arizona and that it divided the Tucson community of interest.

The resulting legal action forced a compromise in the Legislature that altered the lines but did not help the Democrats very much. After informal approval by party caucuses, the legislative leadership signed an agreement on the new boundaries March 22, 1982..A three-judge federal panel approved the plan and ordered it implemented April 2, 1982. The new plan received Justice Department review under the 1965 Voting Rights Act.

The compromise reshaped the 2nd to include Hispanic communities the previous plan had left out. The boundary was shifted to bring in parts of central Tucson placed initially in the new 5th District. The shift meant a transfer of many Hispanic neighborhoods and the University of Arizona from the 5th to the 2nd. One-third Hispanic, the redrawn 2nd now sprawls from Tucson northward to Phoenix and westward to Yuma on the California border.

The heavily Hispanic border town of Nogales also went to the 2nd from the 5th. Even with these changes the 2nd is largely a Phoenix-based district, with 45.8 percent of its population in that city and in other parts of Maricopa County.

In exchange for the Tucson-area additions to the 2nd, the Legislature moved eastern Pinal County from the 2nd to the 5th and switched an Anglo section of eastern Phoenix from the 2nd to the 1st. Minor changes made to the boundaries of the 3rd and 4th districts had little political impact.

Age of Population

District	Population Under 18	Voting Age Population	Population 65 & Over (% of VAP)	Median Age
1	144,049	399,698	62,119 (15.5%)	28.8
2	170,453	372,734	52,322 (14.0%)	26.5
3	155,720	389,150	79,881 (20.5%)	31.3
4	168,301	375,192	49,330 (13.1%)	29.6
5	152,964	389,954	63,710 (16.3%)	30.5
State	791,487	1,926,728	307,362 (16.0%)	29.2

Income and Occupation

District	Median Family Income	White Collar Workers	Blue Collar Workers	Service Workers	Farm Workers
1	$ 19,830	59.1%	25.8%	13.2%	1.9%
2	15,802	45.9	35.4	15.1	3.6
3	18,598	52.8	29.6	13.9	3.7
4	21,771	62.2	24.2	12.2	1.5
5	19,372	57.3	26.0	13.8	2.8
State	$ 19,017	55.7%	28.0%	13.6%	2.7%

Education: School Years Completed

District	8 Years or Fewer	4 Years of High School	4 Years of College or More	Median School Years
1	12.0%	34.5%	19.5%	12.8
2	24.8	32.3	10.9	12.3
3	13.8	37.0	15.5	12.6
4	12.3	33.7	20.6	12.8
5	12.9	33.9	20.0	12.7
State	15.0%	34.3%	17.4%	12.7

Housing and Residential Patterns

District	Owner Occupied	Renter Occupied	Urban	Rural
1	64.0%	36.0%	96.3%	3.7%
2	60.2	39.8	90.0	10.0

15

ARIZONA

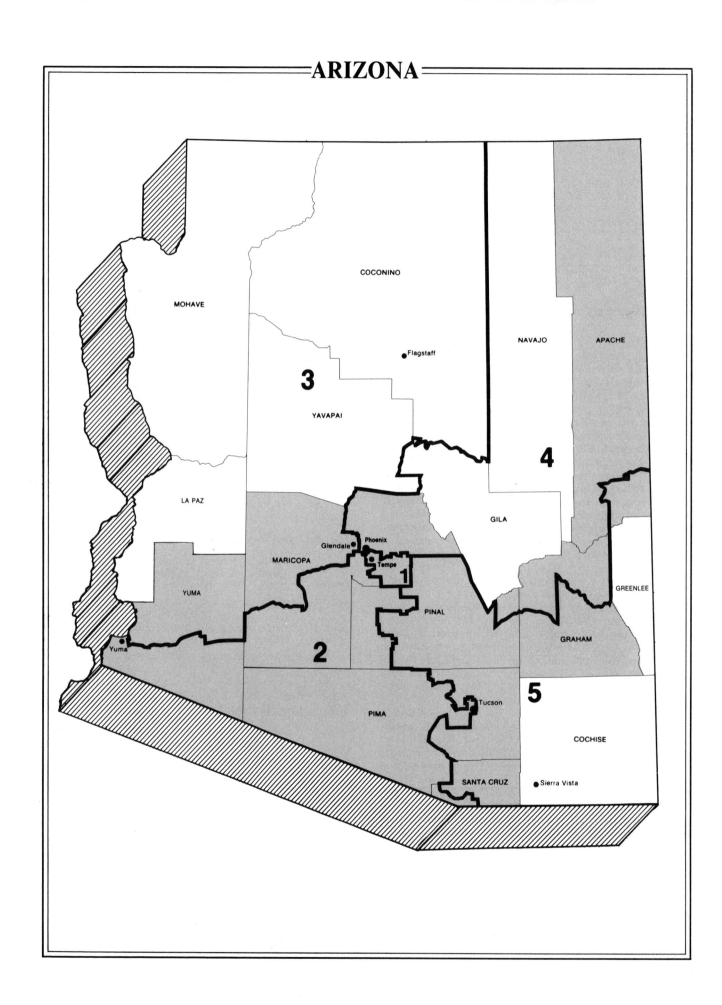

District	Owner Occupied	Renter Occupied	Urban	Rural
3	75.7	24.3	77.1	22.9
4	72.4	27.6	78.7	21.3
5	69.2	30.8	77.0	23.0
State	68.3%	31.7%	83.8%	16.2%

1st District

Eastern Phoenix, Tempe, Mesa

Republicans in Arizona's 1st District got a favorable constituency from the remap. Geographically, the 1st contracted by losing much of south Phoenix, whose Hispanic and black voters went to the new 2nd. While some minority areas remained, the Phoenix section of the district is mostly white, middle class and Republican.

The 1st District's balance of power is clearly in the Phoenix suburbs, where the bulk of the growth occurred during the 1970s. Mesa, for example, grew by almost 150 percent during the 1970s to 152,453. The large suburbs of Chandler and Tempe also remained in the 1st District, as did part of Scottsdale.

Throughout the district the Sun Belt technological boom is pronounced. Motorola and other electronics concerns are among the largest employers. Their managerial and technical personnel are reliable supporters of Republican candidates, joining the retirees who moved the area to the right a few years earlier. Aside from the Hispanic community in Phoenix, the best source of Democratic votes is Tempe, the home of Arizona State University.

Election Returns

1st District		Democrat		Republican	
1976	President	57,839	(36.7%)	93,155	(59.1%)
	Senate	81,662	(51.8%)	70,959	(45.0%)
	House	63,769	(40.7%)	89,595	(57.2%)
1978	Governor	54,557	(49.6%)	51,994	(47.3%)
	House	31,287	(29.0%)	76,485	(71.0%)
1980	President	44,473	(24.8%)	113,755	(63.4%)
	Senate	80,335	(44.3%)	96,967	(53.5%)
	House	32,634	(18.5%)	135,525	(76.7%)
1982	Governor	82,780	(59.0%)	49,959	(35.6%)
	Senate	71,264	(50.3%)	64,666	(46.2%)
	House	41,261	(30.5%)	89,116	(65.9%)

Demographics

Population: 543,747. **Percent Change from 1970:** 47.8%.

Land Area: 457 square miles. **Population per Square Mile:** 1,189.8.

Counties, 1980 Population: Maricopa (Pt.) — 543,747.

Cities, 1980 Population: Chandler — 29,673; Mesa — 152,453; Phoenix (Pt.) — 144,947; Scottsdale (Pt.) — 42,939; Tempe — 106,743.

Race and Ancestry: White — 87.3%; Black — 3.6%; American Indian, Eskimo and Aleut — 1.4%; Asian and Pacific Islander — 1.0%. Spanish Origin — 11.4%. Dutch — 0.6%; English — 11.3%; French — 1.0%; German — 8.0%; Irish — 3.9%; Italian — 1.9%; Norwegian — 0.7%; Polish — 1.1%; Scottish — 0.7%; Swedish — 0.9%.

Universities, Enrollment: Arizona State University, Tempe — 37,755; Mesa Community College, Mesa — 13,597.

Newspapers, Circulation: *The Chandler Arizonan* (e), Chandler — 6,429; *News* (mS), Tempe — 10,260; *Scottsdale Daily Progress* (e), Scottsdale — 18,694; *Tribune* (mS), Mesa — 31,983. Phoenix *Arizona Republic* and *The Phoenix Gazette* also circulate in the district.

Television Stations, Affiliation: KNXV-TV, Phoenix (None); KPAZ, Phoenix (None); KTVW-TV, Phoenix (None, Spanish). Entire district is located in Phoenix-Flagstaff ADI. *(For other Phoenix stations, see 2nd District.)*

Military Installations: Sky Harbor International Airport (Air Force), Phoenix — 943; Williams Air Force Base, Chandler — 3,770.

Industries:

Motorola Inc. (Semiconductor Group); Phoenix; semiconductors — 8,000. **The Garrett Pneumatic Systems Corp.** (Turbine Div.); Phoenix; aircraft parts — 6,000. **Motorola Inc.** (Semiconductor Group); Mesa; integrated circuits — 3,500. **Honeywell Inc.** (Process Management Systems Div.); Phoenix; data processing equipment — 3,000. **ITT Courier Terminal Systems** (HQ); Tempe; computers — 2,500.

The Garrett Corp. (Pneumatic Systems Div.); Phoenix; aircraft parts — 2,000. **The Greyhound Corp.** (HQ); Phoenix; meat, poultry packing; intercity busline, soap — 1,500. **St. Luke's Hospital & Medical Center;** Phoenix; hospital — 1,400. **Scottsdale Memorial Hospital;** Scottsdale; hospital — 1,350. **Samaritan Health Service;** Mesa; hospital — 1,180. **Mesa Lutheran Hospital;** Mesa; hospital — 1,100. **Medtronic Inc.** (Micro-Rel Div.); Tempe; electronic components — 815. **Ramada Inns Inc.** (HQ); Phoenix; hotel operations — 750. **Rogers Corp.** (Interconnection Products Group); Chandler; flexible cables — 700.

State Farm Fire & Casualty Co. (Sunland Regional Office); Tempe; life, casualty insurance company — 700. **Armour and Co.** (Armour Food Co.); (HQ); Phoenix; meat, poultry packing, cheese — 680. **Collins-Phoenix Corp.;** Tempe; engineering services — 596. **General Instrument Corp.;** Chandler; semiconductors — 500. **Midland Ross Corp.** (Capitol Castings Div.); Tempe; aluminum castings — 500.

2nd District

Southwest — Western Tucson, Southern Phoenix, Yuma

The 2nd District is the most Hispanic (35.4 percent) and Democratic district in the state. Subjected to the most changes in the second redistricting attempt, it stretches across southwestern Arizona, taking in parts of central Tucson and southwestern Phoenix, then moves across the state to Yuma, located on the California border. Its 14,169 square miles do not include a single whole county.

Because of its numbers, the city of Phoenix dominates the 2nd District politically. Maricopa County, in which Phoenix is located, casts a majority of the district vote, most of it in Hispanic areas. The parts of Tucson (Pima County) in the 2nd are also Democratic — the Hispanic neighborhoods in the city's western part, along with the University of Arizona community. Also favorable to Democrats are the copper mining town of Ajo and the Indian reservations of San Xavier and Papago.

The portion of Tucson within the 2nd District has a Hispanic population of 42.5 percent and a Democratic heritage that an influx of retirees and technical people had only begun to offset in the late 1970s. Change is certain to continue during the 1980s; a 1980 survey found that one in four of the residents of the areas in the 2nd District had

Phoenix Area

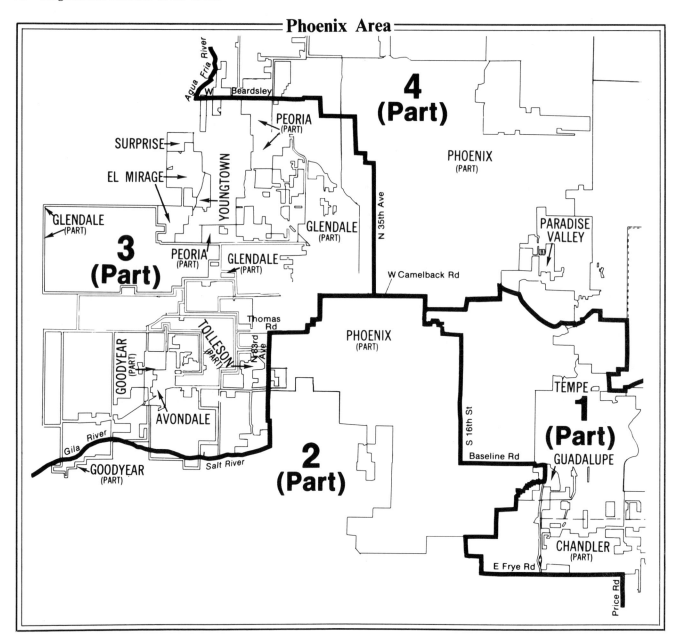

been there four years or less. However the 2nd likely will remain in the Democratic column in state and congressional contests.

The 2nd also takes in the southern tier of Yuma County, in which irrigated farm land grows citrus fruit and vegetables. The portion of Pinal County in the 2nd includes an important cotton belt.

Election Returns

2nd District		Democrat		Republican	
1976	President	38,769	(41.2%)	51,807	(55.0%)
	Senate	52,875	(56.3%)	38,670	(41.2%)
	House	46,851	(50.4%)	41,116	(44.2%)
1978	Governor	35,960	(53.5%)	29,674	(44.1%)
	House	38,545	(59.7%)	23,163	(35.9%)

2nd District		Democrat		Republican	
1980	President	46,830	(42.5%)	48,700	(44.2%)
	Senate	61,357	(58.2%)	40,765	(38.7%)
	House	71,453	(66.3%)	32,146	(29.8%)
1982	Governor	75,719	(72.2%)	23,883	(22.8%)
	Senate	72,637	(69.5%)	27,912	(26.7%)
	House	73,468	(70.9%)	28,407	(27.4%)

Demographics

Population: 543,187. **Percent Change from 1970:** 21.9%.

Land Area: 14,169 square miles. **Population per Square Mile:** 38.3.

Counties, 1980 Population: Maricopa (Pt.) — 248,449; Pima (Pt.) — 195,305; Pinal (Pt.) — 9,801; Santa Cruz (Pt.) — 16,393; Yuma (Pt.) — 73,239.

Cities, 1980 Population: Nogales — 15,683; Phoenix (Pt.) — 236,112; Tucson (Pt.) — 149,081; Yuma — 42,433.

Race and Ancestry: White — 69.4%; Black — 5.6%; American Indian, Eskimo and Aleut — 5.2%; Asian and Pacific Islander — 1.0%. Spanish Origin — 35.5%. English — 7.5%; French — 0.8%; German — 5.1%; Irish — 3.1%; Italian — 1.1%; Polish — 0.7%.

Universities, Enrollment: Arizona Western College, Yuma — 4,001; Lamson College, Phoenix — 1,778; Maricopa Technical Community College, Phoenix — 3,211; Phoenix College, Phoenix — 14,602; Pima County Community College, Tucson — 19,985; University of Arizona, Tucson — 30,960; University of Phoenix, Phoenix — 223.

Newspapers, Circulation: *The Arizona Daily Star* (mS), Tucson — 70,852; *The Arizona Republic* (mS), Phoenix — 247,999; *Herald* (e), Nogales — 3,317; *The Phoenix Gazette* (e), Phoenix — 106,220; *Tucson Citizen* (e), Tucson — 64,596; *The Yuma Daily Sun* (eS), Yuma — 18,667.

Commercial Television Stations, Affiliation: KGUN-TV, Tucson (ABC); KOLD-TV, Tucson (CBS); KOOL-TV, Phoenix (CBS); KPHO, Phoenix (None); KPNX, Phoenix (NBC); KTVK, Phoenix (ABC); KVOA-TV, Tucson (NBC); KYEL-TV, Yuma (NBC, ABC). District is divided among Phoenix-Flagstaff ADI, Tucson ADI and El Centro (Calif.)-Yuma ADI. *(For other Phoenix stations, see 1st District.)*

Military Installations: Gila Bend Auxiliary Airfield (Air Force), Gila Bend — 399; Yuma Marine Corps Air Station, Yuma — 4,463.

Industries:

St. Joseph's Hospital & Medical Center; Phoenix; hospital — 2,300. **Western Electric Co. Inc.;** Phoenix; steel wire drawing — 2,000. **Phoenix Newspapers Inc.** (HQ); Phoenix; newspaper publishing — 1,800. **Valley National Bank of Arizona** (HQ); Phoenix; banking — 1,500. **Southern Pacific Transportation Co.;** Tucson; railroad operations — 1,080.

Veterans Administration; Tucson; veterans' hospital — 1,030. **St. Mary's Hospital and Health Center;** Tucson; hospital — 1,000. **U-Haul International Inc.** (HQ); Phoenix; truck, trailer rental — 900. **Associated Grocers** (HQ); Phoenix; grocery wholesaling — 825. **Tucson Newspapers Inc.;** Tucson; newspaper publishing — 750.

Cyprus Pima Mining Co.; Tucson; copper, molybdenum mining — 710. **TEC Inc.** (HQ); Tucson; electronic computing equipment — 632. **First National Bank of Arizona Inc.;** Tucson; banking — 625. **First Interstate Bank of Arizona** (HQ); Phoenix; banking — 600. **Hyatt Corp.;** Phoenix; hotel — 600. **Revlon Inc.** (Princess Marcella Barghese Div.); Phoenix; perfume, cosmetics — 600. **Continental Security Guard** (HQ); Phoenix; security services — 550. **Pinkerton's Inc.;** Phoenix; security services — 550.

3rd District

North and West — Glendale, Flagstaff, Part of Phoenix

Once dominated almost entirely by "pinto Democrats" — ranchers and other conservative rural landowners — the 3rd District has become prime Republican turf over the years. With redistricting, it was made even more favorable to the GOP; the district lost much of Democratic Phoenix, keeping just a small portion on the west side.

More than 40 percent of the 3rd's population is in the Maricopa County suburbs west of the city. The most important towns are Glendale and Sun City, the latter a retirement community. Both towns produce mammoth Republican majorities. In Sun City the retirees have become very well-organized politically and boast turnouts of 90 percent or higher in congressional elections.

The 3rd lost the Hispanic areas of southern Yuma

County but kept the more conservative northern section, which has swung the county to Republican presidential candidates. Residents of this section moved to set up their own local government in June of 1982, passing a ballot initiative that transformed northern Yuma into brand new LaPaz County.

Mohave County, occupying the northwestern corner of the state, features three groups in constant political tension — Indians, pinto Democrats in Kingman and Republican retirees in Lake Havasu City. The county vote returns have been close between the two parties in statewide elections.

Perhaps the staunchest Republican stronghold in the 3rd District outside Maricopa County lies in Coconino County — the so-called "Arizona Strip" — a Mormon region located on the Utah border. The town of Sedona, at the southern end of the county, is filled with Republican retirees. Old-time Democratic loyalties persist in Flagstaff, the county's largest city and the commercial center of northern Arizona.

Election Returns

3rd District		Democrat		Republican	
1976	President	63,232	(38.5%)	95,078	(57.9%)
	Senate	84,534	(49.6%)	78,789	(48.0%)
	House	75,883	(47.6%)	68,345	(42.9%)
1978	Governor	59,664	(48.2%)	60,616	(48.9%)
	House	92,334	(82.4%)	3,325	(3.0%)
1980	President	48,133	(24.3%)	132,455	(67.0%)
	Senate	89,081	(44.9%)	105,621	(53.3%)
	House	117,859	(61.9%)	62,418	(32.8%)
1982	Governor	93,021	(56.9%)	61,422	(37.6%)
	Senate	83,790	(51.3%)	75,845	(46.4%)
	House	58,644	(36.7%)	101,198	(63.3%)

Demographics

Population: 544,870. **Percent Change from 1970:** 90.8%.

Land Area: 54,726 square miles. **Population per Square Mile:** 10.0.

Counties, 1980 Population: Coconino — 75,008; Maricopa (Pt.) — 328,537; Mohave — 55,865; Yavapai 68,145; Yuma (Pt.) — 17,315.

Cities, 1980 Population: Flagstaff — 34,743; Glendale (Pt.) — 96,982; Lake Havasu City — 15,909; Peoria (Pt.) — 12,251; Phoenix (Pt.) — 101,954; Prescott — 20,055; Sun City (CDP) — 40,505.

Race and Ancestry: White — 86.1%; Black — 1.5%; American Indian, Eskimo and Aleut — 5.1%; Asian and Pacific Islander — 0.7%. Spanish Origin — 11.8%. Dutch — 0.8%; English — 10.6%; French — 1.2%; German — 8.8%; Irish — 4.1%; Italian — 1.7%; Norwegian — 0.8%; Polish — 1.1%; Scottish — 0.8%; Swedish — 1.0%.

Universities, Enrollment: American Graduate School of International Management (Thunderbird campus), Glendale — 980; Glendale Community College, Glendale — 13,001; Mohave Community College, Kingman — 1,094; Northern Arizona University, Flagstaff — 12,094; Yavapai College, Prescott — 4,854.

Newspapers, Circulation: *The Arizona Daily Sun* (eS), Flagstaff — 9,660; *Courier* (eS), Prescott — 9,748; *Daily News-Sun* (e), Sun City — 13,690; *The Kingman Daily Miner* (e), Kingman — 6,556. Phoenix *Arizona Republic* and *The Phoenix Gazette* also circulate in the district.

Commercial Television Stations, Affiliation: KNAZ, Flagstaff (NBC); KUSK, Prescott (None). Most of district is located in Phoenix-Flagstaff ADI. Portion is in El Centro (Calif.)-Yuma ADI.

Military Installations: Luke Air Force Base, Litchfield Park — 7,446; Navajo Army Depot, Flagstaff — 379; Yuma Proving Ground (Army), Yuma — 1,449.

Nuclear Power Plants: Palo Verde 1, 2 and 3, Wintersburg (Combustion Engineering, Bechtel).

Industries:

Goodyear Aerospace Corp.; Litchfield Park; airborne radar systems — 1,458. **Walter O. Boswell Memorial Hospital;** Sun City; hospital — 1,200. **Del E. Webb Development Co.** (HQ); Sun City; real estate developer — 1,000. **Cyprus Mines Corp.** (Cyprus Bagdad Copper Co. Div.); Bagdad; copper mine — 840. **McCulloch Corp.;** Lake Havasu City; chain saws — 800. **Spring City Knitting Co.** (Western Div.); Glendale; knitted underwear — 700.

4th District

Northeast — Northern Phoenix, Scottsdale

The old 4th grew 55 percent during the 1970s, but its boundaries changed very little for the 1980s. It shed its excess population by giving small amounts of territory to the three other districts that come into Maricopa County. It lost most of Sun City, which it had previously shared with the 3rd.

The new lines do not affect the conservative complexion of the 4th. There are Democratic votes in the district's mining towns and on its Indian reservations, but the white-collar sections of northern Phoenix provide ample Republican majorities, as do adjoining suburbs such as Paradise Valley and wealthy Scottsdale. About 70 percent of the district's vote is cast in Maricopa County.

Much of the 4th's rural Democratic territory was transferred to the new 5th — parts of Pinal County, parts of Graham County, and all of tiny Greenlee County, the only county in the state that President Jimmy Carter carried in 1980. The only rural pinto county remaining in the district is copper-mining Gila. In Navajo and Apache counties, the Navajo and Hopi Indian tribes make up almost half the population. Of the two, the Navajos show greater Democratic fealty.

Election Returns

4th District		Democrat		Republican	
1976	President	58,837	(36.0%)	99,026	(60.5%)
	Senate	81,367	(49.8%)	77,293	(47.3%)
	House	74,737	(47.0%)	79,095	(49.7%)
1978	Governor	59,815	(50.7%)	56,968	(47.3%)
	House	40,137	(34.0%)	73,804	(62.5%)
1980	President	46,274	(23.7%)	130,172	(66.7%)
	Senate	87,135	(44.7%)	103,820	(53.3%)
	House	70,133	(37.0%)	119,126	(62.8%)
1982	Governor	87,815	(58.7%)	53,627	(35.8%)
	Senate	77,921	(52.3%)	67,128	(45.1%)
	House	44,182	(30.4%)	95,620	(65.7%)

Demographics

Population: 543,493. **Percent Change from 1970:** 65.9%.

Land Area: 29,388 square miles. **Population per Square Mile:** 18.5.

Counties, 1980 Population: Apache (Pt.) — 48,046; Gila — 37,080; Graham (Pt.) — 2,419; Maricopa (Pt.) — 388,319; Navajo — 67,629; Pinal (Pt.) — 0.

Cities, 1980 Population: Glendale (Pt.) — 190; Paradise Valley — 11,085; Peoria (Pt.) — 0; Phoenix (Pt.) — 306,691; Scottsdale (Pt.) — 45,473.

Race and Ancestry: White — 81.5%; Black — 0.6%; American Indian, Eskimo and Aleut — 15.4%; Asian and Pacific Islander — 0.7%. Spanish Origin — 5.3%. Dutch — 0.7%; English — 9.9%; French — 1.0%; German — 7.4%; Irish — 4.0%; Italian — 2.4%; Norwegian — 0.6%; Polish — 1.2%; Russian — 0.7%; Scottish — 0.7%; Swedish — 0.9%.

Universities, Enrollment: College of Ganado, Ganado — 132; DeVry Institute of Technology, Phoenix — 3,000; Grand Canyon College, Phoenix — 1,173; Navajo Community College, Tsaile — 1,609; Northland Pioneer College, Holbrook — 4,323; Scottsdale Community College, Scottsdale — 6,854; Southwestern Conservative Baptist Bible College, Phoenix — 215.

Newspapers, Circulation: Phoenix *Arizona Republic, The Phoenix Gazette* and *Scottsdale Daily Progress* circulate in the district.

Commercial Television Stations, Affiliation: Most of district is located in Phoenix-Flagstaff ADI. Portions are in Tucson ADI and Albuquerque (N.M.) ADI.

Industries:

Sperry Corp. (Sperry Flight Systems); Phoenix; electronic instruments — 4,422. **Honeywell Information Systems Inc.** (Large Computer Products Div.); Phoenix; data processing equipment — 3,928. **American Express Co.;** Phoenix; credit card operations — 2,000. **Honeywell Inc.** (Process Management Systems Div.); Phoenix; communications equipment — 1,500. **John C. Lincoln Hospital;** Phoenix; hospital — 1,000. **Phoenix Baptist Hospital & Medical Center;** Phoenix; hospital — 1,000.

Westin Hotel Co.; Phoenix; resort hotel — 850. **Atchison, Topeka & Santa Fe Railroad Co.;** Winslow; railroad operations — 800. **Sperry Corp.** (Avionics Div.); Phoenix; electronic instruments — 800. **Kennecott Copper Corp.** (Ray Mines Div.); Hayden; copper mining — 750. **GTE Automatic Electric Labs;** Phoenix; electronic components — 680. **Pointe Resorts Inc.;** Phoenix; resort — 600. **Best Western International Inc.** (HQ); Phoenix; motel operations — 550. **Asarco Inc.;** Hayden; copper smelting — 500. **Farmers Group Inc.;** Phoenix; life insurance — 500. **Southwest Forest Industries** (Snowflake Pulp & Paper Div.); Snowflake; paper mill — 500.

5th District

Southeast — Eastern Tucson

The 5th is 51 percent Democratic by registration, but since many of the Democrats are rural conservatives and often cross party lines, no Democrat can feel very secure. While the district takes in roughly 55 percent of Tucson, map makers placed most of the Hispanic neighborhoods in the 2nd, so the 5th cannot take advantage of the city's strongest Democratic vote.

Largely a college town and resort center in the 1950s, Tucson today is host to an impressive number of high-technology firms. A new International Business Machines plant on the southern outskirts of the city opened in 1977 and is already the largest employer in Pima County. White-collar professional communities with firm GOP loyalties dominate the city's burgeoning east side.

Well-to-do residents of the Santa Catalina foothills and retirees from Davis-Monthan Air Force Base add to the Republican vote. Green Valley, an outlying Pima

County town that rivals Sun City among the state's largest retirement communities, also has become a GOP force.

Democrats remain competitive in the Tucson portion of the district largely because of the University of Arizona community. While the university lies in the 2nd District, many of its students and faculty reside in the 5th. Outside the university, Democratic pickings are fairly meager, except in those Hispanic neighborhoods not transferred to the 2nd.

Outside the Pima County portion, the district is largely desert. In an area dominated by scrub oaks and cacti, the San Pedro River Valley provides the only relief, irrigating a fertile stretch of land cultivated for its grain and pecan crops. Greenlee County is burdened by a flagging copper industry.

The Old West county of Cochise anchors the southeastern corner of the state. Cochise is the home of Tombstone, "the town too tough to die." Notorious for its gold mines and its lawlessness in the early 1900s, Tombstone still mines some silver but relies mainly on tourism to boost the local economy.

Part of rural Democratic Graham County was given to the 5th from the old 4th District. Heavily Hispanic and Democratic Santa Cruz County on the Mexican border was transferred from the 2nd District.

Election Returns

5th District		Democrat		Republican	
1976	President	76,224	(47.2%)	79,013	(48.9%)
	Senate	102,051	(63.5%)	55,124	(34.3%)
	House	94,507	(58.7%)	62,327	(38.7%)
1978	Governor	72,283	(62.3%)	41,568	(35.8%)
	House	59,264	(50.9%)	53,796	(46.2%)
1980	President	60,700	(31.9%)	103,989	(54.6%)
	Senate	104,549	(54.1%)	84,665	(43.8%)
	House	102,196	(53.9%)	84,809	(44.8%)
1982	Governor	114,460	(68.2%)	46,986	(28.0%)
	Senate	106,358	(63.7%)	56,198	(33.6%)
	House	82,938	(49.7%)	80,531	(48.3%)

Demographics

Population: 542,918. **Percent Change from 1970:** 55.6%.

Land Area: 14,769 square miles. **Population per Square Mile:** 36.8.

Counties, 1980 Population: Apache (Pt.) — 4,062; Cochise — 85,686; Graham (Pt.) — 20,443; Greenlee — 11,406; Pima (Pt.) — 336,138; Pinal (Pt.) — 81,117; Santa Cruz (Pt.) — 4,066.

Cities, 1980 Population: Casa Grande — 14,971; Douglas — 13,058; Sierra Vista — 24,937; Tucson (Pt.) — 181,456.

Race and Ancestry: White — 88.0%; Black — 2.4%; American Indian, Eskimo and Aleut — 1.0%; Asian and Pacific Islander — 1.1%. Spanish Origin — 17.1%. Dutch — 0.7%; English — 10.8%; French — 1.0%; German — 7.7%; Irish — 3.9%; Italian — 1.7%; Norwegian — 0.5%; Polish — 1.0%; Russian — 0.5%; Scottish — 0.7%; Swedish — 0.8%.

Universities, Enrollment: Central Arizona College, Coolidge — 6,102; Chaparral Career College, Tucson — 298; Cochise College, Douglas — 4,069; Eastern Arizona College, Thatcher — 3,590.

Newspapers, Circulation: *Bisbee Daily Review* (eS), Sierra Vista — 1,838; *Casa Grande Dispatch* (e), Casa Grande — 5,904; *The Daily Dispatch* (e), Douglas — 2,989; *Daily Herald-Dispatch* (eS), Sierra Vista — 6,142. Tucson *Arizona Daily Star* and *Tucson Citizen* also circulate in the district.

Commercial Television Stations, Affiliation: KZAZ, Tucson (None). District is divided between Phoenix-Flagstaff ADI and Tucson ADI.

Military Installations: Air Force Plant 44, Tucson — 55; Davis-Monthan Air Force Base, Tucson — 6,740; Fort Huachuca, Sierra Vista — 10,332; Tucson International Airport (Air Force), Tucson — 971.

Industries:

International Business Machines Corp.; Tucson; electronic computing equipment — 4,000. **Magma Copper Co.;** San Manuel; copper mining, smelting — 3,726. **Hughes Aircraft Co.;** Tucson; military communications equipment — 3,500. **Tucson Medical Center;** Tucson; hospital — 2,460. **Gates Learjet Corp.;** Tucson; airplanes — 2,200.

Burr-Brown Research Corp. (HQ); Tucson; semiconductors — 1,480. **St. Joseph's Hospital of Tucson;** Tucson; hospital — 1,100. **Duval Corp.;** Sahuarita; copper mining — 800. **Mountain States Engineers Inc;** Tucson; engineering services — 600. **Anamax Mining Co.;** Sahuarita; copper, silver mining — 578.

Arkansas

The first state in the country to draw new congressional district lines for 1982, Arkansas was also the first to have its map thrown out in court. On Feb. 25, 1982, however, the three-judge federal panel that had voided the remap early in January handed down a plan only slightly different from the rejected version, leaving the state's four incumbent House members with little to worry about as they geared up for re-election campaigns.

After the first set of lines was enacted in June 1981, citizens from Garland and Grant counties, which had been placed in new districts, filed suit in Little Rock to have the map overturned. Although the real issue was the forced switch in their congressional representation, they based their case on a 1.87 percent variation between the populations of the smallest and largest of the redrawn districts, claiming that this violated the principle of one man, one vote. On Jan. 5, 1982, the court agreed. After Republican Gov. Frank D. White declined to call a special session of the Legislature to revise the map, the court took over the task of picking a redistricting plan itself.

The map the judges eventually chose was one that initially had served as the basis for the rejected plan. Drawn by state Rep. John Miller, D, it passed the Arkansas Senate in March 1981 but then underwent change in the state House. In the view of the federal panel, this original Senate-passed version, with only a .78 percent population variance, was more in line with the one-man, one-vote requirement.

Ironically, the court's decision did not leave the Garland County residents who brought the case any happier. They were moved out of the 3rd into the 4th District, just as they would have been under the first plan. Still, Garland County interests coincide with those of its new district. The heavily forested 4th long was a center of the timber industry, and Garland's economic base outside Hot Springs was mostly in lumber.

If Garland County residents gained nothing by their suits against the first redistricting plan, those from Grant County who joined in were more fortunate. The court chose to keep Grant in the 4th District, as its residents wanted. The county had been moved to the 2nd in the rejected version. Grant has been in the 4th since Arkansas lost two districts following the 1960 census. Heavily reliant on the lumber industry for jobs, it has been hard hit by the nationwide depression in housing and construction.

Age of Population

District	Population Under 18	Voting Age Population	Population 65 & Over (% of VAP)	Median Age
1	177,444	396,107	80,097 (20.2%)	30.4
2	168,012	401,104	60,593 (15.1%)	29.0
3	158,131	414,806	85,231 (20.5%)	32.0
4	167,787	403,044	86,556 (21.5%)	31.4
State	671,374	1,615,061	312,477 (19.3%)	30.6

Income and Occupation

District	Median Family Income	White Collar Workers	Blue Collar Workers	Service Workers	Farm Workers
1	$ 12,580	37.9%	40.0%	12.4%	9.8%
2	17,271	52.9	32.6	11.9	2.6
3	14,337	42.2	39.5	11.7	6.7
4	14,652	41.1	39.8	13.2	5.9
State	$ 14,641	43.9%	37.8%	12.3%	6.1%

Education: School Years Completed

District	8 Years or Fewer	4 Years of High School	4 Years of College or More	Median School Years
1	36.2%	29.0%	8.0%	11.9
2	18.8	35.6	15.0	12.4
3	25.5	34.5	10.8	12.2
4	26.7	33.6	9.7	12.1
State	26.8%	33.2%	10.8%	12.2

Housing and Residential Patterns

District	Owner Occupied	Renter Occupied	Urban	Rural
1	67.7%	32.3%	43.4%	56.6%
2	67.6	32.4	67.7	32.3
3	74.0	26.0	46.1	53.9
4	72.6	27.4	49.3	50.7
State	70.5%	29.5%	51.6%	48.4%

ARKANSAS

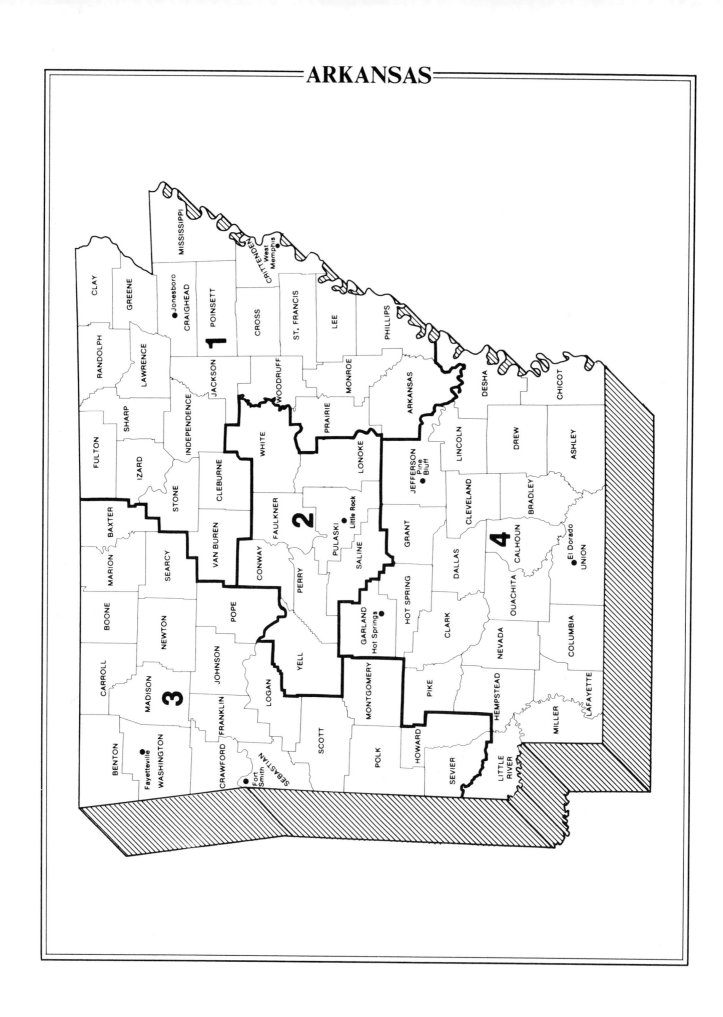

1st District

East — Jonesboro

Redistricting did little to change the Mississippi Delta character of this district. Covering most of the eastern third of the state and some hilly northern counties, the agricultural 1st is the part of the state with the strongest Deep South tradition. Although it is the poorest district in the state, its flat, fertile Mississippi delta traditionally has supported large plantations, some running into tens of thousands of acres. Tied to the cotton trade long before the Civil War, the area now is heavily reliant on rice and soybeans. Jonesboro, the home of Arkansas State University, and West Memphis, a suburb of Memphis, Tenn., are the district's only major cities. Despite the district's agricultural complexion, there is some industry, and Helena, West Memphis and Osceola, all on the Mississippi, are developing port cities.

The old district grew 9 percent in the 1970s, the slowest population increase in the state. So it was required to gain slightly more than 50,000 people. That was accomplished by adding three counties from the 2nd District. Two on the west side — Prairie and Arkansas — have sizable black populations (14 and 20 percent, respectively). Relatively poor farming counties, both are economically and politically similar to the other Delta counties on the eastern side of the district, many of which are nearly half black.

The third county added to the 1st is Cleburne, 55 miles north of Little Rock. Located at the eastern end of the Boston Mountains, it is nearly all white and has a strong recreational industry centered around the Greers Ferry Lake, near Heber Springs.

All three counties added to the 1st District usually support Democrats, with Prairie and Arkansas somewhat more Democratic. Cleburne narrowly went for Ronald Reagan for president in 1980.

Election Returns

1st District		Democrat		Republican	
1976	President	135,001	(70.0%)	57,776	(29.9%)
	Governor	158,241	(86.2%)	25,239	(13.7%)
	House	133,007	(70.9%)	54,646	(29.1%)
1978	Governor	97,662	(69.8%)	42,170	(30.2%)
	Senate	111,182	(79.8%)	17,056	(12.2%)
	House	7,471	(52.6%)	6,722	(47.4%)
1980	President	103,906	(52.2%)	88,732	(44.6%)
	Governor	99,855	(49.8%)	100,481	(50.2%)
	Senate	126,259	(65.1%)	67,603	(34.9%)
	House	4,115	(20.1%)	16,354	(79.9%)
1982	Governor	117,367	(60.6%)	76,412	(39.4%)
	House	124,208	(64.8%)	67,427	(35.2%)

Demographics

Population: 573,551. **Percent Change from 1970:** 9.5%.

Land Area: 15,911 square miles. **Population per Square Mile:** 36.0.

Counties, 1980 Population: Arkansas — 24,175; Clay — 20,616; Cleburne — 16,909; Craighead — 63,239; Crittenden — 49,499; Cross — 20,434; Fulton — 9,975; Greene — 30,744; Independence — 30,147; Izard — 10,768; Jackson — 21,646; Lawrence — 18,447; Lee — 15,539; Mississippi — 59,517; Monroe — 14,052; Phillips — 34,772; Poinsett — 27,032; Prairie — 10,140; Randolph — 16,834; Sharp — 14,607; St. Francis — 30,858; Stone — 9,022; Van Buren — 13,357; Woodruff — 11,222.

Cities, 1980 Population: Blytheville — 23,844; Forrest City — 13,803; Jonesboro — 31,530; Paragould — 15,248; Stuttgart — 10,941; West Helena — 11,367; West Memphis — 28,138.

Race and Ancestry: White — 80.6%; Black — 18.8%; American Indian, Eskimo and Aleut — 0.2%; Asian and Pacific Islander — 0.2%. Spanish Origin — 0.8%. Dutch — 0.5%; English — 19.7%; French — 0.6%; German — 3.8%; Irish — 6.6%.

Universities, Enrollment: Arkansas College, Batesville — 535; Arkansas State University (main campus), State University — 7,615; East Arkansas Community College, Forrest City — 851; Mississippi County Community College, Blytheville — 1,190; Phillips County Community College, Helena — 1,467; Southern Baptist College, Walnut Ridge — 379.

Newspapers, Circulation: *Batesville Guard* (e), Batesville — 8,628; *Courier News* (e), Blytheville — 12,145; *Evening Times* (e), West Memphis (e), 7,960; *Helena-West Helena World* (eS), Helena — 8,300; *The Jonesboro Sun* (eS), Jonesboro — 18,653; *Newport Daily Independent* (eS), Newport — 3,388; *The Paragould Daily Press* (e), Paragould — 8,080; *The Stuttgart Daily Leader* (e), Stuttgart — 4,831; *Times-Herald* (e), Forrest City — 3,932.

Commercial Television Stations, Affiliation: KAIT-TV, Jonesboro (ABC). District is divided among Jonesboro ADI, Little Rock ADI and Memphis (Tenn.) ADI. Small portion is in Springfield (Mo.) ADI.

Military Installations: Blytheville Air Force Base, Blytheville — 2,991.

Industries:

Sanyo Mfg. Corp.; Forrest City; radios, televisions — 2,000. **American Greetings Corp.;** Osceola; greeting cards — 1,500. **Wolverine World Wide Inc.** (Frolic Footwear Div.); Jonesboro; women's shoes — 1,500. **Emerson Electric Co.;** Paragould; electric motors — 1,250. **Halstead Industries Inc.** (Metal Products Div.); Wynne; copper tubing — 990.

Emerson Electric Co.; Batesville; automatic controls — 800. **General Electric Co.;** Jonesboro; electric motors — 700. **Monroe Auto Equipment Co.;** Paragould; auto parts, accessories — 700. **Monro & Co.** (Addison Shoe Div.); Wynne; men's shoes, boots — 660. **American Greetings Corp.;** Harrisburg; greeting cards — 600. **ConAgra Inc.** (Southerland Div.); Batesville; poultry, egg processing — 600. **Capital-Mercury Shirt Corp.** (Tri-County Shirt Co.); Salem; men's, boys' shirts — 600. **Poly-Products Inc.;** West Memphis; lubricants — 600. **Rainwater Enterprises;** Walnut Ridge; rice, soybeans, cotton — 600.

The Marmon Group Inc.; Paragould; store fixtures — 568. **Eaton Corp.;** Forrest City; hoists — 565. **Eastman Kodak Co.** (Arkansas Eastman Co. Div.); Batesville; organic chemicals — 550. **Universal Mfg. Corp.;** Blytheville; transformers — 550. **Borg-Warner Corp.** (Marvel-Schebler-Tillotson Div.); Blytheville; automotive parts — 500. **Brown-Jordan Co.** (American Lantern Co. Div.); Newport; metal furniture, light fixtures — 500. **General Industries Electric Co.;** Forrest City; electric motors — 500. **General Tire & Rubber Co.** (Industrial Products Div.); Batesville; hose, belting — 500. **Riceland Foods Inc.** (Jonesboro Grain Drying Co-op.); Jonesboro; grain warehousing, storage — 500. **Riceland Foods Inc.** (Soybean Div. - HQ); Stuttgart; soybean oil — 500.

2nd District

Central — Little Rock

The new 2nd District is centered around Little Rock, the state capital and largest city. The old district had grown by 24 percent during the 1970s, but redistricting trimmed its edges and reduced the total population by

31,000. That increased the impact of Little Rock's vote. Sixty percent of the new district's residents are concentrated in Pulaski County, and their political weight is usually enough to determine the outcome of the district's elections.

Three counties — Arkansas, Prairie and Cleburne — were moved from the 2nd District into the 1st. The 2nd gained about 17,026 residents with the addition of Yell County, west of Little Rock. Named after Arkansas' first U.S. House member, Archibald Yell, the county draws large numbers of tourists with its rivers and forests and the Holla Bend National Wildlife Refuge. The Arkansas River runs through Yell and a hydroelectric power plant at Dardanelle supplies wood mills and the poultry industry concentrated in the northern half of the county. Democrats outnumber Republicans in Yell County. The 2nd District also gained Perry, a lightly populated county largely devoted to the timber industry.

Southwest of Pulaski is Saline County, the nation's sole source of bauxite and home to a politically active union movement in the aluminum industry.

Election Returns

2nd District		Democrat		Republican	
1976	President	120,683	(67.5%)	57,936	(32.4%)
	Governor	146,790	(86.6%)	22,725	(13.4%)
	House	127,990	(86.1%)	20,738	(13.9%)
1978	Governor	79,600	(67.3%)	38,633	(32.6%)
	Senate	83,454	(75.3%)	19,026	(17.2%)
	House	56,621	(47.2%)	63,223	(52.8%)
1980	President	83,325	(47.1%)	90,488	(45.7%)
	Governor	105,830	(52.8%)	94,766	(47.2%)
	Senate	108,863	(63.7%)	61,668	(36.1%)
	House	38,163	(21.1%)	142,794	(78.8%)
1982	Governor	110,730	(57.3%)	82,514	(42.7%)
	House	82,913	(46.1%)	96,775	(53.9%)

Demographics

Population: 569,116. **Percent Change from 1970:** 24.5%.

Land Area: 6,000 square miles. **Population per Square Mile:** 94.9.

Counties, 1980 Population: Conway — 19,505; Faulkner — 46,192; Lonoke — 34,518; Perry — 7,266; Pulaski — 340,613; Saline — 53,161; White — 50,835; Yell — 17,026.

Cities, 1980 Population: Benton — 17,717; Conway — 20,375; Jacksonville — 27,589; Little Rock — 158,461; North Little Rock — 64,288; Searcy — 13,612; Sherwood — 10,586.

Race and Ancestry: White — 82.1%; Black — 16.8%; American Indian, Eskimo and Aleut — 0.3%; Asian and Pacific Islander — 0.4%. Spanish Origin — 0.8%. Dutch — 0.5%; English — 16.6%; French — 0.9%; German — 4.7%; Irish — 5.9%; Scottish — 0.5%.

Universities, Enrollment: Arkansas College of Technology, Little Rock — 484; Arkansas State University (Beebe campus), Beebe — 701; Capital City Junior College, Little Rock — 569; Central Baptist College, Conway — 235; Harding University, Searcy — 3,083; Hendrix College, Conway — 1,037; Philander Smith College, Little Rock — 596; University of Arkansas (Little Rock campus), Little Rock — 10,009; University of Central Arkansas, Conway — 5,739.

Newspapers, Circulation: *Arkansas Democrat* (mS), Little Rock — 61,315; *Arkansas Gazette* (mS), Little Rock — 128,141; *The Benton Courier* (e), Benton — 10,181; *The Daily Citizen* (eS), Searcy — 4,853; *Log Cabin Democrat* (eS), Conway — 9,332; *News* (eS), Jacksonville — 8,233.

Commercial Television Stations, Affiliation: KARK-TV, Little Rock (NBC); KATV, Little Rock (ABC); KTHV, Little Rock (CBS). Entire district is located in Little Rock ADI.

Military Installations: Little Rock Air Force Base, Jacksonville — 8,114.

Industries:

Timex Corp.; Little Rock; watches, clocks — 2,900. **Veterans Administration;** Little Rock; veterans' hospital — 2,870. **St. Vincent Infirmary;** Little Rock; hospital — 2,160. **Teletype Corp.;** Little Rock; teletype apparatus — 2,080. **Aluminum Co. of America;** Bauxite; aluminum production — 1,225.

Baptist Medical Center (HQ); Little Rock; hospital — 1,600. **Remington Arms Co. Inc.;** Lonoke; ammunition — 1,150. **Franklin Electric Co. Inc.;** Jacksonville; motors, generators — 1,040. **Maybelline Co.;** North Little Rock; cosmetics — 1,110. **Kellwood Co.** (Radcliffe Group Div.); Little Rock; women's blouses — 950. **Falcon Jet Corp.;** Little Rock; airport operations — 900. **Timex Corp.;** Little Rock; watch repairing — 850. **Arkansas Blue Cross-Blue Shield** (HQ); Little Rock; health insurance — 800. **Crompton Co. Inc.;** Morrilton; unfinished cotton fabric — 800. **Valmac Industries Inc.** (Foods Div.); Dardanelle; poultry processing — 800. **Virco Mfg. Corp.;** Conway; tables, school furniture — 800.

Westinghouse Electric Corp.; Little Rock; lamps — 700. **American Transportation Corp.;** Conway; bus bodies — 650. **Worthen Bank & Trust Co.** (HQ); Little Rock; banking — 610. **Pickens-Bond Construction Co.;** Little Rock; general contracting — 600. **Orbit Valve Co.** (HQ); Little Rock; valves, pipe fittings — 550. **A. O. Smith-Inland Inc.;** Little Rock; reinforced plastic — 525. **Arkansas Gazette Co.;** Little Rock; newspaper publishing — 500. **Burns International Security Services Inc.;** Little Rock; security services — 500. **Johnson & Johnson** (Chicopee Mfg. Div.); North Little Rock; non-woven felt goods — 500. **Sperry Corp.** Searcy; hydraulic valves — 500. **UMC Industries Inc.;** Conway; food storage equipment — 500.

3rd District

Northwest — Ozark Plateau, Fort Smith

The hilly 3rd District of northwestern Arkansas is the only strong Republican constituency in the state; Ronald Reagan won 58 percent of the vote here in 1980. It is overwhelmingly white, with a traditionally poor economy that has depended on relatively unproductive farm land. Vast pine forests have provided jobs in the saw mills scattered throughout the rural counties.

In the 1970s, however, the Ozark economy received a boost from a large influx of new residents. As older people from northern states began moving to the area in large numbers, the old 3rd grew by 33 percent. The Ozark region is best known for poultry, lumber and cattle. Tyson Foods Inc., one of the largest poultry-processing companies in the nation, has its headquarters in Springdale. In the Ouachita Mountains, timber is a chief source of income, and the large livestock business in the western portion of the district gives the area around Fort Smith a distinctly Western flavor.

The district's two major cities are Fort Smith, the state's second largest, and Fayetteville, home of the University of Arkansas. In the past both have supported Republicans even against popular Democrats. In 1980, when Democratic Gov. Bill Clinton and President Jimmy Carter were sharing the blame for housing Cuban refugees at Fort Chaffee near Fort Smith, Sebastian County (Fort Smith) expressed its opposition to the refugee camps by giving Clinton only 33 percent of the vote and Carter 27 percent.

Before redistricting, the 3rd District had another major city, Hot Springs, which was transferred to the 4th District. Many of the residents of Hot Springs argued vehemently against the change. The 3rd District also lost Yell and Perry counties to the 2nd and gained Sevier and Howard counties in the southwestern corner of the state. Sevier was marginally Democratic in the two close statewide contests won by Republican candidates in 1980.

Election Returns

3rd District		Democrat		Republican	
1976	President	111,118	(55.4%)	89,063	(44.4%)
	Governor	142,779	(74.2%)	49,524	(25.8%)
	House	—¹		x¹	
1978	Governor	87,100	(53.2%)	76,733	(46.8%)
	Senate	105,031	(70.2%)	35,083	(23.4%)
	House	29,418	(21.0%)	110,976	(79.0%)
1980	President	89,197	(38.5%)	134,908	(58.2%)
	Governor	91,710	(39.6%)	139,686	(60.4%)
	Senate	112,611	(47.1%)	126,325	(52.9%)
	House	—¹		x¹	
1982	Governor	88,968	(43.1%)	117,560	(56.9%)
	House	69,089	(34.0%)	133,909	(66.0%)

¹ No votes tabulated where candidate was unopposed; x indicates winner.

Demographics

Population: 572,937. **Percent Change from 1970: 33.3%.**

Land Area: 14,089 square miles. **Population per Square Mile:** 40.7.

Counties, 1980 Population: Baxter — 27,409; Benton — 78,115; Boone — 26,067; Carroll — 16,203; Crawford — 36,892; Franklin — 14,705; Howard — 13,459; Johnson — 17,423; Logan — 20,144; Madison — 11,373; Marion — 11,334; Montgomery — 7,771; Newton — 7,756; Polk — 17,007; Pope — 39,021; Scott — 9,685; Searcy — 8,847; Sebastian — 95,172; Sevier — 14,060; Washington — 100,494.

Cities, 1980 Population: Fayetteville — 36,608; Fort Smith 71,626; Rogers — 17,429; Russellville — 14,031; Springdale 23,458; Van Buren — 12,020.

Race and Ancestry: White — 96.3%; Black — 2.1%; American Indian, Eskimo and Aleut — 0.9%; Asian and Pacific Islander — 0.5%. Spanish Origin — 0.8%. Dutch — 0.6%; English — 18.3%; French — 0.8%; German — 5.8%; Irish — 6.2%.

Universities, Enrollment: American Junior College, Fort Smith — 302; Arkansas Tech University, Russellville — 3,171; College of the Ozarks, Clarksville — 720; John Brown University, Siloam Springs — 802; North Arkansas Community College, Harrison — 899; University of Arkansas (Fayetteville campus), Fayetteville — 18,280; Westark Community College, Fort Smith — 3,673.

Newspapers, Circulation: *Benton County Daily Democrat* (e), Bentonville — 4,604; *Daily Courier-Democrat* (eS), Russellville — 10,470; *De Queen Daily Citizen* (e), De Queen — 2,690; *Harrison Daily Times* (e), Harrison — 10,244; *Mena Evening Star* (e), Mena — 1,605; *Northwest Arkansas Morning News* (mS), Rogers — 13,970; *Northwest Arkansas Times* (eS), Fayetteville — 11,123; *Southwest Times Record* (all day, S), Fort Smith — 39,311; *The Springdale News* (eS), Springdale — 11,917.

Commercial Television Stations, Affiliation: KFPW-TV, Fort Smith (ABC, CBS); KFSM-TV, Fort Smith (CBS); KLMN, Fort Smith (NBC); KTVP-TV, Fayetteville (ABC). District is divided among Fort Smith ADI, Little Rock ADI and Springfield (Mo.) ADI. Portions are in Joplin (Mo.)-Pittsburg (Kan.) ADI and Shreveport (La.)-Texarkana (Texas) ADI.

Military Installations: Fort Chaffee, Fort Smith — 2,924; Fort Smith

Municipal Airport (Air Force), Fort Smith — 1,032.

Nuclear Power Plants: Arkansas 1, Russellville (Babcock & Wilcox, Bechtel), December 1974; Arkansas 2, Russellville (Combustion Engineering, Bechtel), March 1980.

Industries:

Whirlpool Corp.; Fort Smith; refrigeration equipment — 4,250. **Travenol Laboratories Inc.** (Baxter Laboratories Div.); Mountain Home; surgical instruments, pharmaceuticals — 2,000. **Sparks Regional Medical Center** (HQ); Fort Smith; hospital — 1,700. **Tyson Foods Inc.** (HQ); Springdale; frozen foods, meat processing — 1,500. **Rheem Mfg. Co. Inc.;** Fort Smith; heating, cooling equipment — 1,429.

Campbell Soup Co.; Fayetteville; frozen foods, meat processing — 1,300. **Emerson Electric Co.;** Rogers; motors, generators — 1,300. **Morton Frozen Foods Inc.;** Russellville; frozen dinners — 900. **Weyerhaeuser Co.;** Dierks; lumber — 850. **Tyson Foods Inc.;** Nashville; poultry processing — 800. **Victor United Inc.** (Daisy Mfg. Co. Div.); Rogers; games, toys, children's vehicles — 800. **Franklin Electric Co. Inc.;** Siloam Springs; electric motors — 750. **Emerson Electric Co. Inc.** (Weed Eater Div.); Nashville; power hand tools — 700. **Mountaire Poultry Inc.;** De Queen; poultry processing — 700. **Poultry Growers Inc.** (Cassady Broiler Div.); Nashville; poultry processing — 700. **Tyson Foods Inc.** (Ocoma Foods Div.); Berryville; poultry, egg processing — 700.

American Can Co. (Dixie Products Div.); Fort Smith; paper containers — 650. **The Moore Co. Inc.** (Arkansas Div.); Springdale; hand tools — 650. **TRW Inc.** (Carbide Tools Div.); Rogers; machine tool accessories — 650. **Mass Merchandisers Inc.** (HQ); Harrison; drug items wholesaling — 600. **Union Carbide Corp.** (Home & Automotive Products Div.); Rogers; plastic wrap — 600. **Shaw Willis Frozen Express Inc.** (HQ); Elm Springs; trucking — 595. **Levi Strauss Co.;** Harrison; men's, boys' clothing — 560. **North Arkansas Wholesale Co.** (Nadco Hobby & Craft Div. - HQ); Bentonville; craft supplies wholesaling — 550. **Crane Co.;** Rogers; valves and fittings — 525. **Simmons Industries Inc.** (Valley Farms Div. - HQ); Siloam Springs; poultry processing — 500. **Singer Co. Inc.** (Motor Products Div.); Clarksville; hand tools — 500. **Standard Brands Inc.** (Planters Peanut Div.); Fort Smith; peanut candies — 500.

4th District

South — Pine Bluff

Stretching across the southern third of the state from the Texas border to the Mississippi River, the 4th is so habitually Democratic that a contested general election is a rare event.

Adding Garland County (Hot Springs) from the 3rd District reduced the Democratic registration advantage somewhat. But the district's two other urban areas — Jefferson County (Pine Bluff) and Union County (El Dorado) — have twice as many people between them as Garland County. Pine Bluff is solidly Democratic. El Dorado voted Republican at the top of the ticket in 1980. The 4th lost Sevier and Howard counties to the 3rd District.

Sharing a 165-mile-long border with Louisiana, the 4th is in many ways a Deep South constituency like the 1st. In 1968, all but two counties within the boundaries of the new 4th District supported George C. Wallace for president. The two exceptions were Garland County, which voted Republican, and Chicot County, a largely black area along the Mississippi River, which voted Democratic.

Pine Bluff, the state's fourth largest city, is a railroad center with several pulp and paper mills. With a 49 percent black population, it casts the highest minority vote of any major Arkansas city. Altogether, the 4th is 27.8 percent black, more than any other district in the state.

Election Returns

4th District		Democrat		Republican	
1976	President	131,802	(67.6%)	63,128	(32.4%)
	Governor	157,287	(86.6%)	24,228	(13.3%)
	House	x[1]		—[1]	
1978	Governor	74,232	(66.1%)	38,014	(33.9%)
	Senate	98,784	(81.1%)	16,487	(13.5%)
	House	4,378	(23.2%)	14,453	(76.8%)
1980	President	111,613	(55.5%)	89,036	(42.7%)
	Governor	105,746	(51.2%)	100,751	(48.8%)
	Senate	123,609	(63.6%)	70,743	(36.4%)
	House	x[1]		—[1]	
1982	Governor	114,790	(58.6%)	81,010	(41.4%)
	House	121,256	(65.6%)	63,661	(34.4%)

[1] *No votes tabulated where candidate was unopposed; x indicates winner.*

Demographics

Population: 570,831. **Percent Change from 1970:** 11.4%.

Land Area: 16,079 square miles. **Population per Square Mile:** 35.5.

Counties, 1980 Population: Ashley — 26,538; Bradley — 13,803; Calhoun — 6,079; Chicot — 17,793; Clark — 23,326; Cleveland — 7,868; Columbia — 26,644; Dallas — 10,515; Desha — 19,760; Drew — 17,910; Garland — 70,531; Grant — 13,008; Hempstead — 23,635; Hot Spring — 26,819; Jefferson — 90,718; Lafayette — 10,213; Lincoln — 13,369; Little River — 13,952; Miller — 37,766; Nevada — 11,097; Ouachita — 30,541; Pike — 10,373; Union — 48,573.

Cities, 1980 Population: Arkadelphia — 10,005; Camden — 15,356; El Dorado — 25,270; Hope — 10,290; Hot Springs — 35,781; Magnolia — 11,909; Malvern — 10,163; Pine Bluff — 56,636; Texarkana — 21,459.

Race and Ancestry: White — 71.6%; Black — 27.8%; American Indian, Eskimo and Aleut — 0.2%; Asian and Pacific Islander — 0.2%. Spanish Origin — 0.8%. English — 18.6%; French — 0.8%; German — 2.8%; Irish — 6.4%.

Universities, Enrollment: Garland County Community College, Hot Springs — 1,486; Henderson State University, Arkadelphia — 2,941; Ouachita Baptist University, Arkadelphia — 1,671; Southern Arkansas University (main campus), Magnolia — 1,987; Southern Arkansas University (Technical campus), East Camden — 615; University of Arkansas (Monticello campus), Monticello — 2,031; University of Arkansas (Pine Bluff campus), Pine Bluff — 3,064.

Newspapers, Circulation: *Banner-News* (e), Magnolia — 4,244; *The Camden News* (e), Camden — 6,200; *El Dorado News-Times* (mS), El Dorado — 11,734; *Hope Star* (e), Hope — 4,824; *Malvern Daily Record* (e), Malvern — 5,443; *Pine Bluff Commercial* (eS), Pine Bluff — 23,302; *The Sentinel-Record* (mS), Hot Springs — 19,559; *Siftings Herald* (e), Arkadelphia — 4,223.

Commercial Television Stations, Affiliation: KTVE, El Dorado (ABC). Most of district is located in Little Rock ADI. Portions are in Monroe (La.)-El Dorado ADI and Shreveport (La.)-Texarkana (Texas) ADI.

Military Installations: Hot Springs Memorial Field (Air Force), Hot Springs — 138; Pine Bluff Arsenal (Army), Pine Bluff — 1,190.

Industries:

International Paper Co.; Pine Bluff; paper mill — 1,408. **Cooper Tire & Rubber Co.;** Texarkana; rubber hose, tires — 1,400. **St. Louis Southwestern Railway Cotton Belt Shops;** Pine Bluff; railroad operations — 1,350. **Country Pride Foods Ltd.** (El Dorado Poultry - HQ); El Dorado; poultry processing — 1,200. **Nekoosa Papers Inc.;** Ashdown; pulp, paper products — 1,200. **Potlatch Corp.;** Warren; lumber processing — 1,200.

Jefferson Hospital Assn. Inc.; Pine Bluff; hospital — 1,110. **Georgia-Pacific Corp.;** Crossett; plastics, synthetic resins — 1,000. **Feather-Lite Mfg. Co.** (HQ); Hot Springs National Park; aluminum storm doors and windows — 865. **Mastersons of Arkansas Inc.;** Camden; men's jackets — 700. **Central Moloney Inc.** (Components Operations - HQ); Pine Bluff; transformers — 650. **International Paper Co.;** Camden; paper mill — 650. **Weyerhaeuser Co.;** Mountain Pine; pine wood mill — 650.

Munro & Co. Inc. (Lake Catherine Footwear Co. - HQ); Hot Springs National Park; men's, women's footwear — 600. **General Dynamics Corp.** (Pomona Div.); Camden; electronic aircraft parts — 560. **Burlington Industries Inc.** (Area Rugs Plant); Monticello; tufted rugs — 550. **Champion Parts Rebuilders Inc.** (Standard Automotive Components); Hope; reconditioned auto engines — 500. **Great Lakes Chemical Corp.;** El Dorado; industrial inorganic chemicals — 500. **Reynolds Metals Co.;** Arkadelphia; aluminum production — 500. **Superior Surgical Mfg. Co. Inc.** (Eudora Garment Corp.); Eudora; clothing — 500.

California

In early September 1983 boundaries for California's 45 congressional districts were still not finally in place. The remap in effect for the 1982 elections had been superseded by a second plan that could be replaced by yet another plan. The effort to draw a congressional district map acceptable to both political parties and the state's voters involved a court decision and a statewide referendum in 1982, and other court decisions were anticipated before the final lines were settled.

The controversy, which also involved the lines for state Assembly and Senate seats, began after the 1980 census when U.S. Rep. Phillip Burton drew a congressional district map expressly for the purpose of strengthening Democratic control.

The state was guaranteed two additional House seats by its population growth during the 1970s. But while most of the 18 percent increase occurred in Republican-minded suburban areas, Burton carved the district lines so that the Democrats' 22-21 margin in the state's House delegation jumped to 28-17 after the 1982 elections.

The redrawn map resulted in the creation of two brand-new Democratic districts; three districts held by Republicans were carved up beyond recognition. In almost every case, the lines of the open districts were formed with particular Democrats in mind, usually friends from the California Legislature. Several of these districts were forced to take on unusual shapes to achieve their partisan objectives.

One of the two new Democratic districts was in the Central Valley around Fresno; the other was in inner-city San Diego. Both of the new districts were drawn to guarantee a Democratic registration advantage of more than 2-to-1.

The damage to the Republicans was concentrated in Los Angeles County. In the San Fernando Valley an open Democratic seat was created by placing two Republican incumbents in the same district. Burton created another Democratic seat in the western part of Los Angeles County by removing most of the Republican areas in the old 27th District. In the eastern part of Los Angeles County, Burton rearranged the districts to throw four Republican incumbents into two districts.

Providing only population figures of the 45 districts and a list of census tracts arranged by district, Burton convinced the Democratic majorities in both the state Senate and state Assembly to pass the new plan Sept. 15, 1981, without ever seeing a map. Democratic Gov. Edmund G. Brown Jr. signed the bill on Sept. 16, 1981.

Republicans were so outraged by the partisan nature of Burton's plan that they gathered enough signatures to qualify for a ballot referendum June 8, 1982. The Republican Party hoped to keep the new district map from taking effect in 1982. But in a 4-3 ruling handed down on Jan. 28, 1982, the state Supreme Court decided that the district lines as drawn by Burton would apply for the 1982 election regardless of the outcome of the referendum.

California voters rejected the Burton remap at the June 8, 1982, referendum. When Republican George Deukmejian was elected governor Nov. 2, outgoing Democratic Gov. Edmund G. Brown Jr. called a special session of the Democratic-controlled Legislature to redraw the map before Deukmejian took office Jan. 3, 1983. Working late, the newly elected Assembly passed a second Burton remap Dec. 28, 1982. State Senate passage followed Dec. 29, and Brown signed it into law Jan. 2.

The revised plan closely resembled the first Burton plan; most changes were only cosmetic. The remap changed radically only three of the most oddly-shaped districts. Fourteen other districts, generally in the southern California and San Francisco areas, were slightly altered and the remaining 28 districts were left largely untouched.

The political complexion of the state's districts was not significantly changed and most incumbents — Democrats and Republicans — were expected to be able to hold on to the seats they had just won.

Still dissatisfied with the second Burton remap, conservative Republican state Assemblyman Don Sebastiani early in 1983 drew new maps both for the state's congressional districts and its Legislature. Sebastiani's congressional district plan was drawn, its backers claim, along "good government" lines designed to create the largest possible number of politically competitive districts. Its effect, however, would be to dissolve the districts of several incumbents of both parties while ensuring Republicans significant gains in the U.S. House delegation and the state Legislature.

A petition campaign to put the Sebastiani proposal before the voters was successful, but the California Supreme Court Sept. 15 ruled it off the ballot; the vote had been scheduled for Dec. 13.

CALIFORNIA

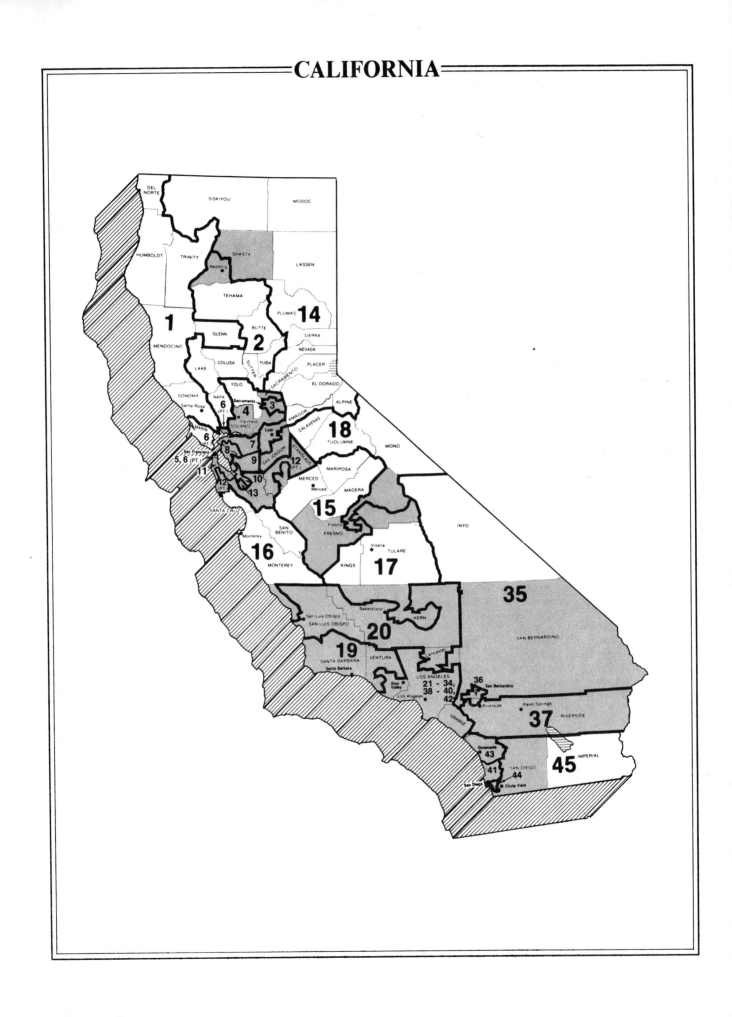

That left the second Burton plan in effect for the 1984 elections. However, Republicans were expected to challenge that map as an unconstitutional gerrymander and it was expected that the entire matter could end up before the Supreme Court of the United States.

The profiles that follow are for those congressional districts in place for the 1982 general elections.

Age of Population

District	Population Under 18	Voting Age Population	Population 65 & Over (% of VAP)	Median Age
1	139,471	386,887	65,953 (17.0%)	31.2
2	137,029	388,986	73,114 (18.8%)	31.8
3	135,426	390,358	52,459 (13.4%)	30.3
4	151,480	374,274	41,016 (11.0%)	28.0
5	90,201	435,713	83,685 (19.2%)	34.5
6	117,030	408,694	57,528 (14.1%)	32.6
7	146,492	378,842	49,302 (13.0%)	30.7
8	116,434	409,493	63,994 (15.6%)	32.1
9	137,262	387,387	52,594 (13.6%)	31.2
10	165,884	361,394	33,171 (9.2%)	27.0
11	120,973	404,129	54,831 (13.6%)	32.5
12	135,823	389,448	50,167 (12.9%)	32.1
13	146,228	380,351	35,559 (9.3%)	29.0
14	142,594	383,299	59,611 (15.6%)	31.9
15	166,574	359,314	51,657 (14.4%)	28.2
16	140,006	385,887	58,342 (15.1%)	29.1
17	169,713	355,077	49,408 (13.9%)	27.4
18	150,749	376,599	63,016 (16.7%)	29.3
19	142,028	384,040	56,547 (14.7%)	29.1
20	145,960	379,934	55,340 (14.6%)	29.3
21	157,465	367,512	35,439 (9.6%)	30.0
22	123,112	403,454	73,334 (18.2%)	34.4
23	99,671	426,336	66,676 (15.6%)	33.5
24	96,851	429,058	79,687 (18.6%)	33.3
25	167,522	357,889	48,642 (13.6%)	26.7
26	133,183	392,935	53,088 (13.5%)	31.2
27	109,403	416,355	50,216 (12.1%)	31.4
28	139,835	385,847	51,086 (13.2%)	28.7
29	179,131	346,664	47,886 (13.8%)	26.3
30	164,721	360,162	51,619 (14.3%)	27.4
31	172,300	353,829	36,364 (10.3%)	26.7
32	151,511	376,303	53,270 (14.2%)	29.2
33	155,652	370,644	42,136 (11.4%)	28.9
34	177,952	348,369	30,738 (8.8%)	26.2
35	153,861	372,537	55,801 (15.0%)	29.4
36	164,719	363,372	48,660 (13.4%)	27.4
37	141,651	383,312	86,429 (22.5%)	33.3
38	158,472	367,088	36,224 (9.9%)	27.2
39	145,099	380,905	37,185 (9.8%)	29.1
40	126,380	399,141	54,641 (13.7%)	31.3
41	128,890	397,122	45,909 (11.6%)	30.1
42	120,873	403,473	55,326 (13.7%)	33.4
43	140,574	387,512	64,623 (16.7%)	30.2
44	144,323	381,563	44,757 (11.7%)	25.8
45	138,450	387,456	57,220 (14.8%)	29.9
State	6,388,958	7,278,944	2,414,250 (14.0%)	29.9

Income and Occupation

District	Median Family Income	White Collar Workers	Blue Collar Workers	Service Workers	Farm Workers
1	$ 19,739	52.2%	27.5%	14.6%	5.7%
2	17,155	50.4	26.9	16.0	6.7
3	21,772	65.5	20.1	12.9	1.5
4	20,468	55.2	26.9	14.2	3.6
5	22,332	68.0	16.4	15.1	0.6
6	23,282	65.6	18.5	14.8	1.2
7	24,681	60.0	26.3	12.4	1.3
8	23,127	70.0	16.7	12.2	1.1
9	23,480	56.8	30.4	11.6	1.1
10	24,305	51.4	35.9	11.2	1.5
11	27,010	66.1	21.4	11.4	1.2
12	28,237	65.3	22.0	9.1	3.6
13	27,065	64.0	25.7	9.5	0.8
14	20,051	53.1	26.2	16.1	4.7
15	17,635	43.6	29.1	13.0	14.3
16	20,044	51.4	24.1	14.6	9.8
17	17,305	46.3	26.2	13.1	14.4
18	16,966	48.4	30.5	15.1	6.0
19	20,865	53.0	25.6	13.9	7.5
20	20,194	51.1	28.9	13.9	6.0
21	28,479	65.5	22.1	10.4	2.0
22	25,850	68.2	20.7	10.1	1.1
23	27,256	73.6	16.2	9.3	0.9
24	17,147	63.2	22.4	13.6	0.8
25	14,642	40.4	43.3	14.7	1.6
26	23,389	60.8	28.1	10.2	1.0
27	22,634	66.1	21.3	11.2	1.3
28	15,649	51.8	31.1	15.9	1.2
29	13,717	41.4	42.8	15.0	0.9
30	17,550	46.2	40.9	11.7	1.2
31	19,212	47.0	39.6	12.2	1.2
32	20,727	52.1	33.8	12.8	1.3
33	25,754	60.0	27.5	11.5	1.0
34	21,658	45.3	42.7	10.9	1.1
35	20,791	53.8	30.1	13.4	2.7
36	18,699	48.7	35.2	14.4	1.7
37	18,796	51.4	28.6	14.2	5.9
38	22,191	49.3	37.0	12.1	1.7
39	26,014	61.9	26.1	10.9	1.0
40	28,616	70.6	18.0	10.4	1.0
41	24,136	67.6	18.5	12.3	1.6
42	29,447	70.0	19.6	9.6	0.8
43	22,780	60.2	23.1	11.7	4.9
44	15,781	49.0	30.7	18.4	1.8
45	20,157	57.2	25.3	13.6	3.9
State	$ 21,537	57.7%	26.9%	12.6%	2.8%

Education: School Years Completed

District	8 Years or Fewer	4 Years of High School	4 Years of College or More	Median School Years
1	11.3%	35.3%	18.0%	12.7
2	13.9	35.6	14.2	12.6
3	9.9	32.5	22.2	12.9
4	12.0	36.6	16.3	12.7
5	14.3	25.6	29.8	13.0
6	11.7	27.1	27.7	13.0
7	9.8	34.6	20.6	12.8
8	10.7	23.0	35.6	13.3
9	12.2	36.7	15.5	12.7
10	16.0	32.7	16.1	12.6
11	8.5	30.9	26.9	13.0
12	10.6	26.3	30.8	13.2
13	7.7	31.9	24.1	13.0
14	10.8	37.1	16.0	12.7
15	25.7	30.1	11.2	12.3
16	16.3	29.0	20.7	12.8
17	25.6	28.7	12.8	12.3
18	21.9	31.3	11.5	12.4
19	15.1	31.0	19.8	12.8

District	8 Years or Fewer	4 Years of High School	4 Years of College or More	Median School Years
20	14.2	34.1	14.8	12.6
21	6.8	33.6	24.0	13.0
22	9.2	30.5	25.9	13.0
23	8.3	28.2	30.3	13.2
24	17.8	25.9	23.8	12.8
25	38.5	21.9	10.5	11.8
26	14.3	32.0	19.3	12.7
27	10.7	27.7	28.0	13.1
28	23.0	28.0	14.8	12.5
29	28.4	30.4	6.0	12.0
30	26.1	29.5	10.8	12.2
31	19.1	34.3	9.1	12.4
32	16.0	33.5	13.2	12.6
33	10.0	34.0	19.5	12.8
34	19.7	35.6	8.8	12.3
35	11.3	36.1	15.3	12.7
36	15.5	35.6	10.3	12.5
37	15.5	34.6	13.0	12.5
38	17.0	35.5	11.4	12.5
39	9.6	33.2	21.2	12.9
40	5.1	28.1	31.0	13.3
41	5.6	30.9	29.7	13.2
42	6.0	30.5	28.7	13.2
43	8.6	32.6	22.5	13.0
44	18.3	34.0	11.9	12.5
45	13.3	32.8	18.7	12.7
State	14.2%	31.4%	19.6%	12.7

Housing and Residential Patterns

District	Owner Occupied	Renter Occupied	Urban	Rural
1	63.4%	36.6%	56.5%	43.5%
2	64.5	35.5	64.6	35.4
3	58.8	41.2	98.2	1.8
4	61.5	38.5	89.4	10.6
5	38.9	61.1	100.0	0.0
6	45.8	54.2	97.2	2.8
7	65.7	34.3	96.6	3.4
8	48.9	51.1	99.7	0.3
9	59.4	40.6	98.4	1.6
10	62.4	37.6	99.0	1.0
11	57.6	42.4	99.0	1.0
12	62.1	37.9	85.5	14.5
13	60.7	39.3	99.9	0.1
14	68.9	31.1	46.8	53.2
15	61.3	38.7	64.3	35.7
16	56.0	44.0	77.5	22.5
17	62.0	38.0	73.9	26.1
18	58.4	41.6	78.7	21.3
19	54.7	45.3	92.9	7.1
20	62.9	37.1	78.1	21.9
21	74.4	25.6	94.2	5.8
22	57.4	42.6	95.8	4.2
23	45.4	54.6	100.0	0.0
24	23.4	76.6	100.0	0.0
25	38.0	62.0	100.0	0.0
26	55.0	45.0	100.0	0.0
27	36.8	63.2	97.3	2.7
28	32.7	67.3	100.0	0.0
29	42.5	57.5	100.0	0.0
30	46.6	53.4	100.0	0.0
31	53.3	46.7	100.0	0.0
32	50.5	49.5	100.0	0.0
33	71.1	28.9	97.4	2.6
34	70.6	29.4	100.0	0.0
35	70.6	29.4	80.1	19.9

District	Owner Occupied	Renter Occupied	Urban	Rural
36	63.4	36.6	99.6	0.4
37	71.0	29.0	77.8	22.2
38	56.9	43.1	100.0	0.0
39	59.2	40.8	100.0	0.0
40	61.1	38.9	99.2	0.8
41	59.4	40.6	94.5	5.5
42	58.8	41.2	100.0	0.0
43	65.8	34.2	88.8	11.2
44	46.3	53.7	100.0	0.0
45	53.2	46.8	87.3	12.7
State	55.9%	44.1%	91.3%	8.7%

1st District

Northern Coast — Santa Rosa, Eureka

Covering more than 300 miles of Pacific coastline stretching from Oregon to just north of San Francisco this district with its majestic stands of redwoods has a picturesque quality that masks the political tension growing within it.

For many years this area was the exclusive province of commercial fishermen and lumberjacks, some of whom made a few extra dollars every summer from the tourist trade. But since the early 1970s the northern coast has drawn a new class of immigrants — urban refugees from outside California who bring with them strongly held beliefs about protecting the environment at all costs. They are well organized politically, and their influence exceeds their actual numbers.

The 1982 remap gave this constituency a new number (it was the 2nd District in the 1970s) and removed from it Napa County, with its grape vineyards, wineries and Republican voters. Smaller Lake County was also taken out in exchange for Republican Glenn County. The net effect of redistricting combined with the changing demographics helped a Democratic challenger in 1982 defeat the Republican incumbent, a veteran of two decades in the House.

The three major coastal counties of the new 1st District — Humboldt, Mendocino and Sonoma — make up 90 percent of the district's population. This is primarily where the transplants have settled, enjoying a serene rural lifestyle epitomized by herbal teas and organic farming. Voting is on the liberal side, especially compared with the mountainous inland areas.

Voters in the three other, smaller counties — Del Norte on the coast and Trinity and Glenn inland — tend to be older and practice a more rigid conservative way of life that is reflected in their voting patterns. Glenn is the most staunchly Republican county in the district. In 1982, Republican Pete Wilson's 71 percent there was his highest mark in any county in his successful Senate bid against Gov. Edmund G. Brown Jr.

Sonoma County, at the southern end of the district, holds the key to winning in the 1st. With nearly 300,000 residents, it is the fastest-growing part of the district. Closer to the liberal San Francisco sphere of influence, Sonoma usually votes slightly more Democratic than either Humboldt or Mendocino. In 1980, when Democratic Sen. Alan Cranston won Sonoma with 61 percent, independent presidential candidate John B. Anderson scored a significant 11.2 percent, taking votes from both Ronald Reagan and Jimmy Carter.

Election Returns

1st District

1st District		Democrat		Republican	
1976	President	86,720	(51.3%)	79,280	(46.9%)
	Senate	81,792	(47.8%)	83,143	(48.6%)
	House	79,293	(44.4%)	93,840	(52.5%)
1978	Governor	93,523	(52.9%)	65,530	(37.1%)
	House	87,474	(47.4%)	92,187	(49.9%)
1980	President	79,246	(35.9%)	107,445	(48.7%)
	Senate	127,735	(59.3%)	69,587	(32.3%)
	House	92,884	(42.3%)	118,093	(53.8%)
1982	Governor	108,002	(49.4%)	101,922	(46.6%)
	Senate	89,476	(41.3%)	115,235	(53.2%)
	House	107,749	(49.8%)	102,043	(47.2%)

Demographics

Population: 526,358. **Percent Change from 1970:** 33.1%.

Land Area: 14,211 square miles. **Population per Square Mile:** 37.0.

Counties, 1980 Population: Del Norte — 18,217; Glenn — 21,350; Humboldt — 108,514; Mendocino — 66,738; Sonoma — 299,681; Trinity — 11,858.

Cities, 1980 Population: Arcata — 12,340; Eureka — 24,153; Petaluma — 33,834; Rohnert Park — 22,965; Santa Rosa — 83,320; Ukiah — 12,035.

Race and Ancestry: White — 92.2%; Black — 0.8%; American Indian, Eskimo and Aleut — 2.6%; Asian and Pacific Islander — 1.4%. Spanish Origin — 6.1%. Dutch — 0.8%; English — 9.9%; French — 1.4%; German — 7.4%; Irish — 5.2%; Italian — 3.7%; Norwegian — 1.0%; Polish — 0.5%; Portuguese — 1.4%; Russian — 0.5%; Scottish — 1.0%; Swedish — 1.3%.

Universities, Enrollment: College of the Redwoods, Eureka — 8,330; Humboldt State University, Arcata — 7,534; Mendocino College, Ukiah — 2,860; Santa Rosa Junior College, Santa Rosa — 21,352; Sonoma State University, Rohnert Park — 5,567.

Newspapers, Circulation: *Argus-Courier* (e), Petaluma — 8,522; *Orland Unit Register* (m), Orland — 1,298; *The Press Democrat* (eS), Santa Rosa — 64,673; *Times-Standard* (eS), Eureka — 21,507; *Ukiah Daily Journal* (eS), Ukiah — 8,836; *Willows Daily Journal* (e), Willows — 1,780. The San Francisco *Chronicle* and San Francisco *Examiner* also circulate in the district.

Commercial Television Stations, Affiliation: KFTY, Santa Rosa (None); KIEM-TV, Eureka (CBS, NBC); KVIQ, Eureka (ABC, NBC). District is divided among Eureka ADI, San Francisco ADI and Chico-Redding ADI.

Military Installations: Centerville Beach Naval Facility, Ferndale — 220; Klamath Air Force Station, Requa — 20; Point Arena Air Force Station, Anchor Bay — 45; Skaggs Island Naval Security Group Activity, Sonoma — 337.

Nuclear Power Plants: Humboldt Bay, Eureka (General Electric, Bechtel), August 1963.

Industries:

  Hewlett-Packard Co. Inc.; Santa Rosa; electronic instrumentation — 3,500. **Sonoma State Hospital;** Eldridge; hospital — 2,000. **Louisiana-Pacific Corp.;** (Regional headquarters); Samoa; plywood, sawmill — 1,600. **Simpson Timber Co.** (Simpson Redwood Co.); Arcata; forest products — 1,100. **The Pacific Lumber Co.;** Scotia; lumber mill — 1,000.

  Optical Coating Laboratory Inc. (HQ); Santa Rosa; optical film coated products — 900. **State Farm Fire & Casualty Co.;** Rohnert Park; casualty, life insurance — 900. **National Controls Inc.** (HQ); Santa Rosa; scales — 600. **Simpson Timber Co.;** Korbel; logging, sawmill — 550. **Masonite Corp.;** Ukiah; hardboard mill — 500.

2nd District

North Central — Napa, Redding

At first glance, 1982 redistricting changes looked unfavorable for the Republicans. The GOP incumbent lost his home base in the foothills east of Sacramento, along with most of the land area of the old district.

But there was little for Republicans to worry about. In political coloration, the new district is virtually identical to the old one. Most of the land it lost was in sparsely populated mountain counties; nearly two-thirds of the constituents remained.

The new 2nd District, which replaced the old 1st, is settled neatly in the Sacramento Valley north of the state capital. The area is almost exclusively devoted to ranching and farming.

The four new counties added to the district — Napa, Sutter, Lake and Colusa — are largely agricultural and Republican. The peach and tomato farmers of Sutter County are the most conservative of the new constituents. Sutter County gave Ronald Reagan 64 percent in 1980 and even backed Paul Gann, the inarticulate candidate put up by the GOP against Democratic Sen. Alan Cranston that year.

Across the low Vaca Mountains from Sutter and Colusa are the grape vineyards that cling to terraced hillsides in Napa and Lake counties. Napa County, the second most populous in the district, is known around the world for its wineries. Its politics has a Republican bouquet.

Barley and rice are the main crops of the Sacramento River basin. The 2nd District farmers who grow these crops tend to be conservative. At the northern end of the new 2nd District, near the headwaters of the Sacramento at Shasta Lake, the land is higher in elevation. This area, oriented toward ranching, often votes for Democrats.

Election Returns

2nd District		Democrat		Republican	
1976	President	83,928	(48.1%)	87,849	(50.3%)
	Senate	73,856	(42.1%)	95,886	(54.6%)
	House	104,245	(59.7%)	68,539	(39.3%)
1978	Governor	86,562	(51.3%)	68,523	(40.6%)
	House	85,647	(52.0%)	77,917	(47.3%)
1980	President	66,608	(32.1%)	117,948	(56.8%)
	Senate	105,780	(53.1%)	78,634	(39.5%)
	House	83,140	(40.3%)	112,679	(54.6%)
1982	Governor	81,130	(39.3%)	117,487	(57.0%)
	Senate	70,727	(34.6%)	123,276	(60.3%)
	House	81,314	(40.5%)	116,172	(57.9%)

Demographics

Population: 526,015. **Percent Change from 1970:** 32.5%.

Land Area: 9,857 square miles. **Population per Square Mile:** 53.4.

Counties, 1980 Population: Butte — 143,851; Colusa — 12,791; Lake — 36,366; Napa — 99,199; Shasta (Pt.) — 92,941; Sutter — 52,246; Tehama — 38,888; Yuba — 49,733.

Cities, 1980 Population: Chico — 26,603; Napa — 50,879; Paradise — 22,571; Redding — 41,995; Yuba City — 18,736.

Race and Ancestry: White — 91.3%; Black — 1.2%; American Indian, Eskimo and Aleut — 1.6%; Asian and Pacific Islander — 2.0%. Spanish Origin — 6.8%. Dutch — 0.8%; English — 12.3%; French — 1.5%; German — 7.8%; Irish — 5.1%; Italian — 2.0%; Norwegian — 0.8%; Portuguese — 0.9%; Scottish — 1.0%; Swedish — 1.1%.

Universities, Enrollment: Butte College, Oroville — 9,862; California State University at Chico, Chico — 13,826; Napa College, Napa — 5,963; Pacific Union College, Angwin — 2,053; Shasta College, Redding — 11,038; Yuba College, Marysville — 9,129.

Newspapers, Circulation: *Appeal-Democrat* (e), Marysville — 21,734; *Chico Enterprise-Record* (e), Chico — 25,453; *Colusa Sun-Herald* (e), Colusa — 3,032; *Corning Daily Observer* (e), Corning — 2,068; *Daily News* (e), Red Bluff — 7,992; *The Napa Register* (e), Napa — 20,019; *Oroville Mercury Register* (e), Oroville — 9,926; *Record Searchlight* (e), Redding — 33,632.

Commercial Television Stations, Affiliation: KHSL-TV, Chico (CBS, NBC); KRCR-TV, Redding (ABC, NBC). District is divided among Chico-Redding ADI, San Francisco ADI and Sacramento-Stockton ADI.

Military Installations: Beale Air Force Base, Marysville — 4,730.

Industries:
  Napa State Hospital; Napa; state psychiatric hospital — 1,700. **CHB Foods Inc.** (Harter Packing Co. Inc.); Yuba City; fruit canning — 1,000. **Louisiana-Pacific Corp.** (Sierra Div.); Red Bluff; lumber — 1,000. **Sunsweet Growers Inc.** (Sun-Diamond); Yuba City; dehydrated fruits, vegetables — 850. **Diamond International Corp.** (Fiber Products Div.); Red Bluff; building materials wholesaling — 800. **Simpson Paper Co.;** Anderson; paper products — 550. **Kaiser Steel Corp.** (Napa Fabrication Plant); Napa; steel pipe, plate work — 514.

3rd District

Most of Sacramento; Eastern Suburbs

With 275,741 inhabitants, Sacramento is the largest city in California's Central Valley. It is an agricultural center and major inland shipping port, but it draws its political identity from government — it is the capital of the nation's most populous state.

Close to 50,000 state employees live and work in Sacramento, providing the city with a strong pro-government, Democratic political base. The flagship newspaper of the McClatchy chain, the *Sacramento Bee*, takes a liberal editorial line that has been known to influence the outcome of elections in the area. Blacks and Hispanics — many of them state employees — make up more than a fourth of the city's population, which is another reason Democrats can usually count on carrying Sacramento.

The 3rd District includes all of the city except the primarily white, middle-to-upper-class area north of the American River. Also included in the 3rd are the suburban areas to the east, including Carmichael, which votes more Republican than the city. Because the old district was slightly overpopulated, the line was redrawn to exclude Folsom in the northeast corner of Sacramento County. The home of the large state prison, Folsom has the most conservative and Republican electorate in the county.

Since 1966, the 3rd District has been wholly contained within Sacramento County, and during that time it has never elected a Republican to the U.S. House. However Sacramento County's strong Democratic preference on the local and congressional levels is not always found in contests for statewide office. In 1982 the county went Republican in the Senate and gubernatorial elections.

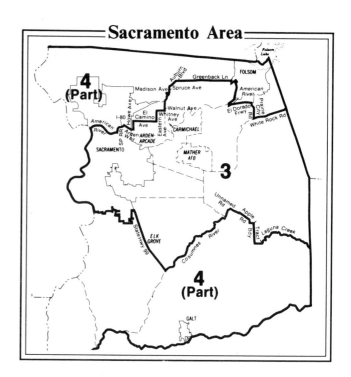

Sacramento Area

Election Returns

3rd District		Democrat		Republican	
1976	President	98,933	(52.5%)	87,248	(46.3%)
	Senate	85,624	(45.7%)	96,426	(51.4%)
	House	118,602	(72.8%)	44,308	(27.2%)
1978	Governor	96,249	(54.9%)	60,559	(34.6%)
	House	89,453	(53.3%)	78,302	(46.7%)
1980	President	86,632	(41.2%)	97,853	(46.5%)
	Senate	119,042	(58.1%)	69,620	(34.0%)
	House	144,451	(70.3%)	55,116	(26.8%)
1982	Governor	103,035	(44.9%)	119,824	(52.3%)
	Senate	107,494	(47.0%)	113,030	(49.4%)
	House	194,680	(89.6%)	—	

Demographics

Population: 525,784. **Percent Change from 1970:** 23.2%.

Land Area: 383 square miles. **Population per Square Mile:** 1,372.8.

Counties, 1980 Population: Sacramento (Pt.) — 525,784.

Cities, 1980 Population: Arden-Arcade (CDP) (Pt.) — 56,500; Carmichael (CDP) — 43,108; Folsom (Pt.) — 0; Rancho Cordova (CDP) — 42,881; Sacramento (Pt.) — 224,490.

Race and Ancestry: White — 78.6%; Black — 8.2%; American Indian, Eskimo and Aleut — 1.0%; Asian and Pacific Islander — 6.5%. Spanish Origin — 9.7%. English — 8.4%; French — 0.8%; German — 6.1%; Greek — 0.5%; Irish — 3.4%; Italian — 2.5%; Norwegian — 0.6%; Polish — 0.6%; Portuguese — 1.0%; Scottish — 0.6%; Swedish — 0.8%.

Universities, Enrollment: Bauder College, Sacramento — 487; California State University at Sacramento, Sacramento — 22,190; Cosumnes River College, Sacramento — 5,842; Sacramento City College, Sacramento — 15,340.

Newspapers, Circulation: *The Sacramento Bee* (mS), Sacramento — 194,484; *The Sacramento Union* (mS), Sacramento — 104,610.

Commercial Television Stations, Affiliation: KCRA-TV, Sacramento (NBC); KTXL, Sacramento (None); KXTV, Sacramento (CBS). Entire district is in Sacramento-Stockton ADI. *(For other Sacramento stations, see 4th district.)*

Military Installations: Mather Air Force Base, Rancho Cordova — 6,209; Sacramento Army Depot, Sacramento — 3,483.

Nuclear Power Plants: Rancho Seco 1, Clay Station (Babcock & Wilcox, Bechtel), April 1975.

Industries:
   Southern Pacific Transportation Co. Inc.; Sacramento; railroad operations — 2,000. **Kaiser Foundation Health Plan;** Sacramento; health insurance — 2,300. **Campbell Soup Co.;** Sacramento; canned food — 1,400. **McClatchy Newspapers Inc.** (HQ); Sacramento; newspaper publishing — 1,000. **Mercy San Juan Hospital;** Carmichael; hospital — 1,000. **California-Western States Life Insurance** (HQ); Sacramento; life insurance — 613. **Western Pacific Railroad Co.;** Sacramento; railroad operations — 500.

4th District

Suburban Sacramento to Bay Area

Looking like a large jaw about to clamp down upon the state capital, the 4th District surrounds Sacramento on three sides, taking in the northern part of the city as well. Nearly half the population of the new 4th lives in Sacramento County, although the outskirts of the district spread west through Yolo and Solano counties for more than 50 miles to San Pablo Bay.

The 1982 remap gave the 4th some additional areas around Sacramento, enhancing its suburban character. Most of this new territory, including the Folsom area and southern portions of Sacramento County, makes life more difficult for Democratic candidates. Partly suburban and partly agricultural, the southern section of the county is more Republican than the northern Sacramento suburbs that were already contained in the 4th District.

Outside the Sacramento area, the district has only four cities of any size. The largest is Fairfield, in Solano County, with 58,099 residents. Located adjacent to Travis Air Force Base, Fairfield usually votes Republican, as does Woodland, 35 miles to the north in Yolo County. Between the two are Vacaville and Davis. Davis is a liberal college community that gave John B. Anderson a full 20 percent of the vote in his 1980 independent presidential campaign. For Davis voters, the more liberal and anti-establishment a candidate is, the better. Although the turnout in Davis tends to be high, the town accounts for only about seven percent of the district vote.

In the old 4th, Democratic candidates could count on large pluralities in Vallejo, which was removed in redistricting. The loss of Vallejo's blue-collar voters, who work in the city's shipyards and warehouses, is a setback to any Democrat running in the district. Vallejo was the only city in Solano County that Jimmy Carter carried in the 1980 election.

To offset the impact of losing Vallejo, the Democratic map makers also took out two agricultural counties to the north — Colusa and Sutter. These two counties consistently voted more Republican than any other part of the district. Any Democratic candidate hoping to carry the 4th has to appeal to the middle-of-the-road Democrats in the northern Sacramento suburbs to overcome the GOP vote elsewhere in the district.

Election Returns

4th District		Democrat		Republican	
1976	President	81,686	(55.7%)	63,105	(43.1%)
	Senate	71,132	(48.6%)	70,914	(48.5%)
	House	84,378	(52.5%)	66,577	(41.4%)
1978	Governor	81,362	(56.9%)	47,656	(33.3%)
	House	89,752	(55.9%)	70,482	(43.9%)
1980	President	73,533	(40.6%)	89,728	(49.6%)
	Senate	104,754	(57.3%)	62,597	(34.2%)
	House	136,713	(65.6%)	61,839	(29.7%)
1982	Governor	86,629	(46.2%)	94,613	(50.5%)
	Senate	85,173	(45.6%)	92,836	(49.7%)
	House	118,476	(63.9%)	67,047	(36.1%)

Demographics

Population: 525,754. **Percent Change from 1970:** 32.2%.

Land Area: 2,398 square miles. **Population per Square Mile:** 219.2.

Counties, 1980 Population: Sacramento (Pt.) — 257,597; Solano (Pt.) — 154,783; Yolo — 113,374.

Cities, 1980 Population: Arden-Arcade (CDP) (Pt.) — 31,070; Benicia — 15,376; Davis — 36,640; Fairfield — 58,099; Folsom (Pt.) — 11,003; Sacramento (Pt.) — 51,251; Suisun City — 11,087; Vacaville — 43,367; Vallejo (Pt.) — 0; Woodland — 30,235.

Race and Ancestry: White — 82.8%; Black — 5.7%; American Indian, Eskimo and Aleut — 1.2%; Asian and Pacific Islander — 3.7%. Spanish Origin — 11.5%. Dutch — 0.6%; English — 9.2%; French — 0.9%; German — 6.4%; Irish — 3.5%; Italian — 1.8%; Norwegian — 0.6%; Polish — 0.5%; Portuguese — 1.0%; Scottish — 0.6%; Swedish — 0.7%.

Universities, Enrollment: American River College, Sacramento — 23,159; D-Q University-Lower Division, Davis — 167; Solano Community College, Suisun City — 9,860; University of California at Davis, Davis — 17,939.

Newspapers, Circulation: *The Daily Democrat* (e), Woodland — 12,613; *The Daily Republic* (e), Fairfield — 15,893; *The Davis Enterprise* (e), Davis — 7,371. *The Sacramento Bee, The Sacramento Union* and *Vallejo Times-Herald* also circulate in the district.

Commercial Television Stations, Affiliation: KRBK-TV, Sacramento (None). Most of district is in Sacramento-Stockton ADI. Portion is in San Francisco ADI. *(For other Sacramento stations, see 3rd district.)*

Military Installations: McClellan Air Force Base, Sacramento — 17,370; McClellan Storage Annex (Air Force), Folsom — 90; North Highlands Facility (Air Force), North Sacramento — 203; Travis Air Force Base, Fairfield — 15,035.

Industries:
   Aerojet-General Corp. Folsom; propulsion units — 3,200. **Basic Vegetable Products Inc.;** Vacaville; dehydrated vegetables — 600. **Environtech Corp.** (Wemco Div.); Sacramento; mining machinery — 584. **Anheuser-Busch Inc.;** Fairfield; brewery — 580.

5th District

Most of San Francisco

For 1983-84 the two San Francisco districts are divided along a line that roughly follows the Powell Street cable car. The 5th District portion occupies nearly all of the San Francisco peninsula west of the cable car line.

Contained completely within the city limits of San Francisco, the 5th (formerly numbered the 6th) occupies only 29 square miles but includes three-fourths of the city's population. The only parts of the city missing from the 5th are the eastern edge, which contains most of the city's business district, and the Haight-Ashbury and Hayes Valley sections.

The lines in San Francisco were drawn by Democratic Rep. Philip Burton to protect his brother, U. S. Rep. John L. Burton, who seemed vulnerable in the city's other district. Philip Burton tried to help John (who nevertheless chose to retire in 1982) by taking for himself the comfortable upper-income areas of Richmond and Pacific Heights and giving his brother the economically depressed and more Democratic Bayshore and Hunters Point sections in the southeast.

By all measures, San Francisco and the 5th District are liberal Democratic strongholds. The 5th has the highest percentage of registered Democrats — just under 60 percent — of any district in the state without a black or Hispanic majority. In 1982 when the rest of the state was drifting to the right, San Francisco stood alone by overwhelmingly supporting Gov. Edmund G. Brown Jr. in his losing Senate bid (67 percent), a handgun registration proposal (60 percent) and a nuclear freeze proposition (70 percent).

The district is an ethnic, racial and sexual pastiche. A fifth of its residents are Asian, mostly Japanese and Chinese, members of the largest Oriental community on this side of the Pacific Ocean. Mexican-Americans live in the Mission District. A large and expanding homosexual community is centered around Castro and Market streets.

There are white, middle-class neighborhoods of single-family homes on the western side of the city. And affluent professionals populate the neighborhoods around the Presidio, by the Golden Gate Bridge. These voters, while not as radical in their political outlook as other district residents, retain a socially conscious streak that manifests itself in a solid Democratic vote.

Election Returns

5th District		Democrat		Republican	
1976	President	97,347	(51.8%)	82,723	(44.0%)
	Senate	109,331	(58.7%)	73,040	(39.2%)
	House	104,741	(66.9%)	44,607	(28.5%)
1978	Governor	112,319	(68.3%)	39,517	(24.0%)
	House	103,890	(69.7%)	41,601	(27.9%)
1980	President	91,579	(50.7%)	59,018	(32.7%)
	Senate	133,384	(75.6%)	32,860	(18.6%)
	House	111,956	(65.5%)	51,233	(30.0%)
1982	Governor	114,838	(63.1%)	61,888	(34.0%)
	Senate	115,218	(63.9%)	59,745	(33.1%)
	House	103,268	(57.9%)	72,139	(40.5%)

Demographics

Population: 525,914. **Percent Change from 1970:** -3.1%.

Land Area: 29 square miles. **Population per Square Mile:** 18,135.0.

Counties, 1980 Population: San Francisco (Pt.) — 525,914.

Cities, 1980 Population: San Francisco (Pt.) — 525,914.

Race and Ancestry: White — 62.1%; Black — 8.0%; American Indian, Eskimo and Aleut — 0.4%; Asian and Pacific Islander — 22.5%. Spanish Origin — 13.2%. English — 5.0%; French — 1.1%; German — 4.1%; Greek — 0.7%; Irish — 5.0%; Italian — 4.4%; Polish — 0.8%; Russian — 2.1%; Scottish — 0.5%; Swedish — 0.6%.

Universities, Enrollment: Academy of Art College, San Francisco — 1,700; California Institute of Integral Studies, San Francisco — 173; City College of San Francisco, San Francisco — 25,386; New College of California, San Francisco — 379; San Francisco Art Institute, San Francisco — 726; San Francisco College of Mortuary Science, San Francisco — 72; San Francisco Conservatory of Music, San Francisco — 223; San Francisco State University, San Francisco — 24,131; Simpson College, San Francisco — 317; University of California at San Francisco, San Francisco — 3,812; University of San Francisco, San Francisco — 6,599.

Newspapers, Circulation: The San Francisco *Chronicle* and San Francisco *Examiner* circulate in the district. Foreign language newspapers: *Chinese Times* (Chinese), San Francisco — 11,000; *Nichi Bei Times* (Japanese), San Francisco — 7,115; *Russian Life* (Russian), San Francisco — 2,750.

Commercial Television Stations, Affiliation: KBHK-TV, San Francisco (None). Entire district is in San Francisco ADI. *(For other San Francisco stations, see 6th district.)*

Military Installations: Presidio of San Francisco (Army), San Francisco — 5,353.

Industries:

Mount Zion Hospital & Medical Center; San Francisco; hospital — 2,150. **Letterman General Hospital;** San Francisco; hospital — 1,850. **Schlage Lock Co.** (L N C Closer Div.); San Francisco; door locks — 1,600. **Veterans Administration;** San Francisco; veterans' hospital — 1,600. **Fireman's Fund Insurance Co.** (HQ); San Francisco; casualty, life, health insurance — 1,500. **Kaiser Foundation Hospital;** San Francisco; hospital — 1,500.

Children's Hospital of San Francisco; San Francisco; hospital — 1,350. **Pacific Medical Center Inc.** (HQ); San Francisco; hospital — 1,350. **National Surety Corp.** (HQ); San Francisco; surety company — 1,300. **St. Francis Hotel Corp.;** San Francisco; hotel — 1,100. **Hilton Hotels Corp.;** San Francisco; hotel — 984. **Fairmont Hotel** (HQ); San Francisco; hotel — 800. **Crown Building Maintenance Co.;** San Francisco; janitorial services — 675.

6th District

Eastern San Francisco; Marin County; Daly City

Of all the oddly shaped districts on the California map for the 1982 elections this one is the most bizarre. The 6th has four distinct and detached parts. Two are connected only by water, the other two by a narrow piece of land used for railroad yards.

The district was drawn this way so that John Burton might have enough Democratic constituents to win a fifth full term. Ironically, just three days before the filing deadline, Burton announced that he was retiring. Democrats retained the seat in 1982.

In land area and population, the largest of the four segments is Marin County, which accounts for 42 percent of the district's population but in 1982 cast 54 percent of the vote. Marin has been stereotyped in fiction and journalism as the home of "mellow" — a uniquely California lifestyle enjoyed by the rich and characterized by a social and cultural permissiveness that stops just short of intruding on another person's "space."

Politically, however, Marin County is not quite as liberal as its social image might suggest. It supported Ronald

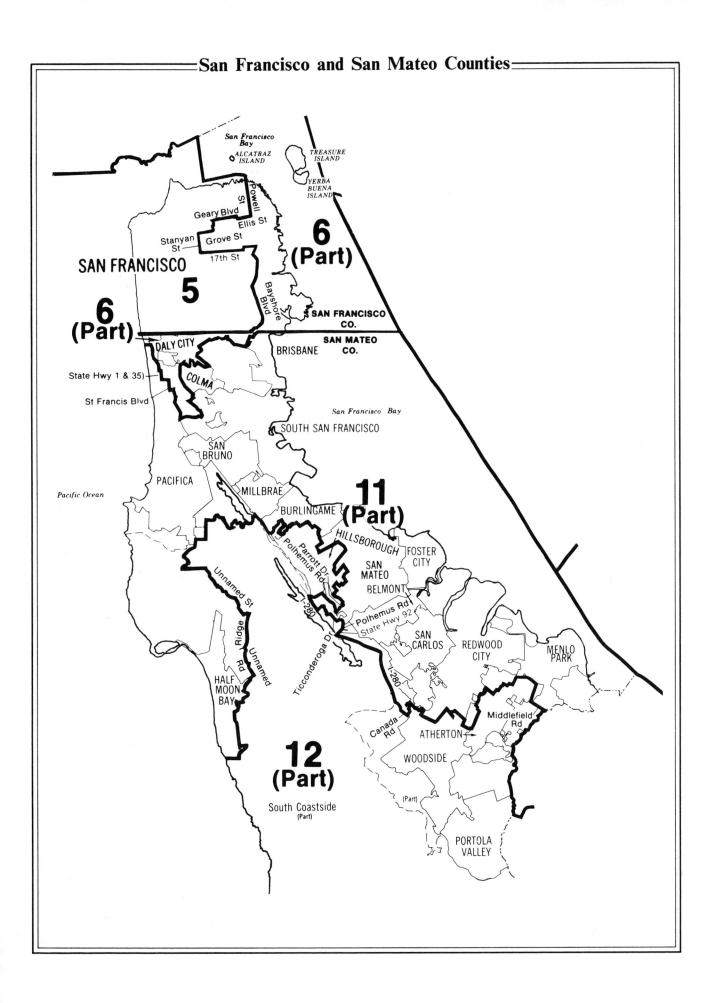

Reagan in 1980 and Gerald R. Ford in 1976. It favored tax-cutting Proposition 13 in the 1978 primary and the death penalty proposition in the 1978 general election. In 1980, John Burton lost Marin County to his GOP challenger.

About 30 percent of the residents of the 6th live in San Francisco, along the waterfront on the bay side and inland as far as Haight-Ashbury. Much of the city's large and politically active gay community is located in the 6th District, as well as many counterculture people busy reliving the 1960s. For the most part, the wealthier homes built in the hills are in the 5th District, as is most of Chinatown.

The two sections of the new district farthest from downtown San Francisco are Daly City to the southwest and Vallejo across the bay to the northeast. Vallejo, a city of 80,000, is socially, politically and geographically separate from the rest of the district. It is easier for Vallejo residents to get to Sacramento than to Haight-Ashbury. Formerly in the 4th District, Vallejo is a blue-collar, Democratic city that heavily relies on the defense industry for its economic support. Jimmy Carter carried Vallejo in 1980, although with less than a majority.

Daly City, slightly smaller than Vallejo, is an industrial suburb but it is not quite as heavily Democratic by registration as Vallejo.

Election Returns

6th District		Democrat		Republican	
1976	President	94,076	(53.3%)	77,024	(43.7%)
	Senate	95,390	(54.1%)	75,821	(43.0%)
	House	110,252	(59.4%)	71,788	(38.7%)
1978	Governor	106,096	(64.5%)	43,027	(26.2%)
	House	106,739	(63.0%)	60,943	(36.0%)
1980	President	89,964	(45.8%)	72,949	(37.2%)
	Senate	131,061	(68.9%)	43,535	(22.9%)
	House	111,621	(52.5%)	90,965	(42.8%)
1982	Governor	112,851	(60.3%)	67,263	(36.0%)
	Senate	105,766	(57.0%)	72,492	(39.1%)
	House	96,379	(52.4%)	82,128	(44.6%)

Demographics

Population: 525,724. **Percent Change from 1970:** 1.1%.

Land Area: 595 square miles. **Population per Square Mile:** 883.6.

Counties, 1980 Population: Marin — 222,568; San Francisco (Pt.) — 153,060; San Mateo (Pt.) — 69,676; Solano (Pt.) — 80,420.

Cities, 1980 Population: Daly City (Pt.) — 65,622; Larkspur — 11,064; Mill Valley — 12,967; Novato — 43,916; San Anselmo — 12,053; San Francisco (Pt.) — 153,060; San Rafael — 44,700; Vallejo (Pt.) — 80,303.

Race and Ancestry: White — 69.0%; Black — 13.7%; American Indian, Eskimo and Aleut — 0.6%; Asian and Pacific Islander — 12.7%. Spanish Origin — 8.4%. Dutch — 0.5%; English — 6.5%; French — 0.9%; German — 4.1%; Irish — 3.9%; Italian — 3.6%; Polish — 0.7%; Portuguese — 0.6%; Russian — 1.0%; Scottish — 0.6%; Swedish — 0.6%.

Universities, Enrollment: California College of Podiatric Medicine, San Francisco — 397; California Maritime Academy, Vallejo — 499; Cogswell College, San Francisco — 470; College of Marin, Kentfield — 7,032; Dominican College of San Rafael, San Rafael — 669; Golden Gate Baptist Theological Seminary, Mill Valley — 590; Golden Gate University, San Francisco — 9,567; Indian Valley Col-

leges, Novato — 1,552; Louise Salinger Academy of Fashion, San Francisco — 64; San Francisco Theological Seminary, San Anselmo — 956; University of California, Hastings College of Law, San Francisco — 1,470; World College West, San Rafael — 39.

Newspapers, Circulation: *Chronicle* (m), San Francisco — 508,016; *Examiner* (e), San Francisco — 157,206; *Independent-Journal* (e), San Rafael — 45,419; *Vallejo Times-Herald* (mS), Vallejo — 23,984. The San Mateo *Times and News Leader* and the *Peninsula Times-Tribune* also circulate in the district. Foreign language newspapers: *Chinese World* (Chinese), San Francisco — 3,311; *Young China Daily News* (Chinese), San Francisco — 7,300.

Commercial Television Stations, Affiliation: KDTV, San Francisco (None, Spanish); KGO-TV, San Francisco (ABC); KPIX, San Francisco (CBS); KRON-TV, San Francisco (NBC); KTSF, San Francisco (None); KTZO, San Francisco (None); KVOF-TV, San Francisco (None). Entire district is in San Francisco ADI. *(For other San Francisco stations, see 5th district.)*

Military Installations: Mare Island Naval Shipyard, Vallejo — 13,056; Mill Valley Air Force Station, Mill Valley — 30; Treasure Island Naval Station, San Francisco — 1,427.

Industries:

Bechtel Group Inc. (HQ); San Francisco; heavy construction, engineering services — 9,797. **Genstar Corp.**; San Francisco; building materials, land and real estate development, financial services — 8,500. **Wells Fargo & Co.** (HQ); San Francisco; bank holding company — 4,000. **Standard Oil Co. of California** (HQ); San Francisco; oil producing, refining; chemicals; fertilizers — 3,900. **BankAmerica Corp.** (HQ); San Francisco; bank holding company — 2,500.

San Francisco Newspaper Printing Co. (HQ); San Francisco; newspaper publishing — 2,110. **Crocker National Corp.** (HQ); San Francisco; bank holding company — 2,000. **Southern Pacific Co.** (HQ); San Francisco; railroad, trucking operations; title insurance; oil pipelines — 2,000. **St. Mary's Hospital & Medical Center**; San Francisco; hospital — 1,550. **Standard Oil Co. of California** (Chevron USA Inc. - HQ); San Francisco; oil producing, refining — 1,400. **International Business Machines Corp.**; San Francisco; machine wholesaling, data processing training — 1,400. **Blue Shield of California** (HQ); San Francisco; health insurance — 1,380. **Del Monte Corp.** (HQ); San Francisco; canned, frozen fruits, vegetables — 1,300. **Sohio Pipe Line Co.**; San Francisco; petroleum exploring — 1,300. **Metropolitan Life Insurance Co.**; San Francisco; life insurance — 1,250. **Chevron Transport Corp.**; San Francisco; deep sea transporting — 1,200. **Federal Reserve Bank of San Francisco** (HQ); San Francisco; banking — 1,200. **Mary's Help Hospital Inc.**; Daly City; hospital — 1,050. **American Building Maintenance Industries** (HQ); San Francisco; janitorial services — 1,000.

First Interstate Bank of California; San Francisco; banking — 1,000. **Fritzi of California Mfg. Corp.** (HQ); San Francisco; women's blouses — 1,000. **Prudential Building Maintenance Corp.**; San Francisco; janitorial, security services — 1,000. **Hyatt Corp.** (Hyatt Regency); San Francisco; hotel — 900. **Levi Strauss & Co.** (HQ); San Francisco; apparel — 900. **Industrial Indemnity Co.** (HQ); San Francisco; casualty insurance — 890. **Wells Fargo Investment Advisors**; San Francisco; investment advisers — 720.

Crown Zellerbach Corp. (HQ); San Francisco; paper products — 700. **Pillsbury, Madison & Sutro** (HQ); San Francisco; law firm — 668. **Foremost-McKesson Inc.** (HQ); San Francisco; drugs, liquor, chemical wholesaling — 650. **Pinkerton's Inc.**; San Francisco; security services — 650. **Atlantic Design Co. Inc.**; San Francisco; janitorial services — 600.

California Hyatt Corp.; San Francisco; hotel — 600. **Continental Insurance Co.**; San Francisco; health, accident insurance — 600. **Industrial Insurance Co.**; San Francisco; casualty insurance — 600. **United States Leasing International Inc.** (HQ); San Francisco; equipment leasing, financing — 600. **Dean Witter Reynolds Organization Inc.** (HQ); San Francisco; securities brokerage — 600. **Government Employees Insurance Co.**; San Francisco; auto insurance — 560. **International Engineering Co.** (HQ); San Francisco; design engineering services — 560.

The **Charles Schwab Corp.**; San Francisco; securities brokerage — 527. **American Patrol Service**; San Francisco; security services — 500. **The Bank of California** (HQ); San Francisco; banking — 500. **Bethlehem Steel Corp.** (Ship Building Div.); San Francisco; shipbuilding — 500. **Dinwiddie Construction Co.** (HQ); San Francisco; general contracting — 500. **Stauffer Chemical Co.**; San Francisco; administrative offices — 500. **Xerox Corp.**; San Francisco; commercial equipment wholesaling — 500.

7th District

Most of Contra Costa County; Concord; Richmond

The 7th and Contra Costa County are split almost evenly between the urbanized, industrial areas along the

east side of the San Pablo Bay and the new suburban tracts that have grown like crab grass behind the San Pablo mountain ridge. In forty years of largely unchecked expansion, the county's population has exploded from 100,000 to more than 650,000. Eighty percent of the county's population lives in the 7th District.

The Contra Costa shoreline looks more like northern New Jersey than Marin County, only five miles distant across the bay. The shoreline property from Richmond to Pittsburg is given over primarily to commerce, particularly shipping and oil and sugar refining. The blue-collar workers of Richmond and the crowded industrialized towns nearby are strongly Democratic. Richmond, 48 percent black, voted for Jimmy Carter in 1980 by an overwhelming margin.

The climate — both political and meteorological — is considerably different on the other side of the mountains

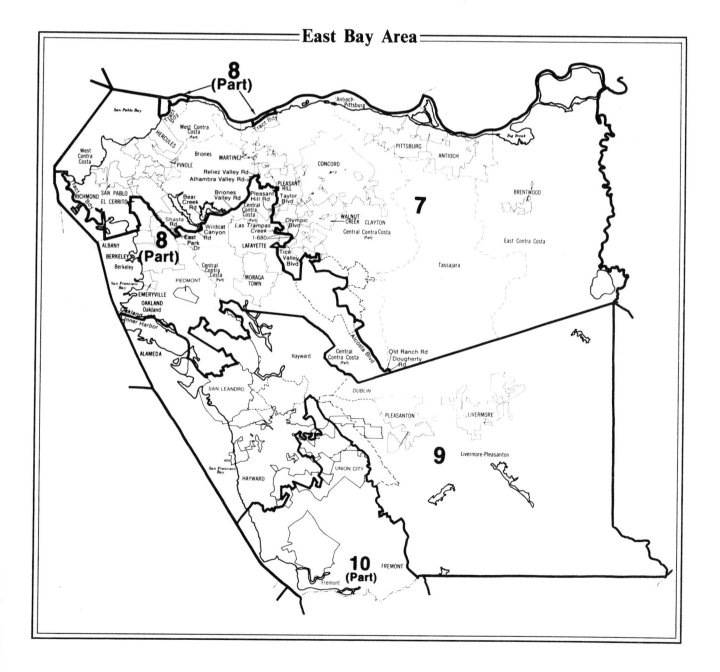

East Bay Area

that separate the coast from inland Contra Costa County. Once a fertile agricultural area, these inland areas are now largely occupied by housing developments.

Leaving the fog and the liberal politics on the other side of the hills, white-collar professionals have moved into communities such as Concord and Walnut Creek in massive numbers. The population of these two cities has increased by 242 percent since 1960, while Richmond has increased less than four percent. More of these commuters still register as Democrats than Republicans, but they tend to vote Republican. Thanks to a large Republican turnout on this inland side of mountains, Carter lost the new 7th District in 1980. Other statewide Democrats have been able to carry the district, but their margins are declining.

To reduce the district's population by about 30,000, the map makers removed part of the San Ramon Valley in the inland section. This gave portions of the Republican bedroom communities of San Ramon, Danville and Alamo to the new 8th District.

Election Returns

7th District		Democrat		Republican	
1976	President	94,291	(53.3%)	80,995	(45.8%)
	Senate	90,863	(50.9%)	84,033	(47.1%)
	House	134,858	(74.7%)	42,056	(23.3%)
1978	Governor	94,247	(57.8%)	53,299	(32.7%)
	House	100,573	(63.4%)	53,490	(33.7%)
1980	President	84,516	(41.0%)	96,765	(47.0%)
	Senate	127,509	(64.3%)	63,019	(31.8%)
	House	130,254	(63.3%)	64,629	(31.4%)
1982	Governor	94,997	(49.6%)	90,414	(47.2%)
	Senate	89,987	(47.3%)	92,659	(48.7%)
	House	126,952	(67.2%)	56,960	(30.2%)

Demographics

Population: 525,334. **Percent Change from 1970:** 15.2%.

Land Area: 627 square miles. **Population per Square Mile:** 837.9.

Counties, 1980 Population: Contra Costa (Pt.) — 525,334.

Cities, 1980 Population: Antioch — 42,683; Concord — 103,255; Martinez (Pt.) — 22,533; Pinole — 14,253; Pittsburg — 33,034; Pleasant Hill — 25,124; Richmond (Pt.) — 74,659; San Pablo 19,750; Walnut Creek (Pt.) — 53,642.

Race and Ancestry: White — 79.3%; Black — 10.8%; American Indian, Eskimo and Aleut — 0.7%; Asian and Pacific Islander — 4.6%. Spanish Origin — 9.7%. English — 7.9%; French — 0.8%; German — 5.1%; Irish — 3.5%; Italian — 3.5%; Norwegian — 0.6%; Polish — 0.5%; Portuguese — 1.3%; Scottish — 0.5%; Swedish — 0.7%.

Universities, Enrollment: Contra Costa College, San Pablo — 8,904; Diablo Valley College, Pleasant Hill — 18,850; Los Medanos College, Pittsburg — 4,464.

Newspapers, Circulation: *Contra Costa Independent* (eS), Richmond — 24,577; *Contra Costa Times* (mS), Walnut Creek — 50,363; *Daily Ledger* (eS), Antioch — 13,704; *Martinez News-Gazette* (m), Martinez — 3,000; *Pittsburg Post Dispatch* (eS), Pittsburg — 5,024. The *Oakland Tribune*, San Francisco *Chronicle* and San Francisco *Examiner* also circulate in the district.

Commercial Television Stations, Affiliation: District is divided between San Francisco ADI and Sacramento-Stockton ADI.

Military Installations: Concord Naval Weapons Station, Concord — 1,621.

Industries:

United States Steel Corp. Pittsburg; steel products — 2,000. **Chevron USA Inc.** (Accounting Center); Concord; accounting services — 1,700. **Safeway Stores Inc.;** Richmond; food processing, warehousing — 1,700. **Mt. Diablo Hospital District;** Concord; hospital — 1,340. **Shell Oil Co.;** Martinez; petroleum refining — 1,000.

Systron-Donner Corp. (HQ); Concord; precision sensing devices, electronic control systems — 900. **Tosco Corp.** (Avon Refinery); Martinez; petroleum refining — 760. **Chevron Chemical Co.** (Ortho Div.); Richmond; agricultural chemicals — 600. **Union Oil Company of California;** Rodeo; petroleum refining — 600. **East Bay Newspapers Inc.** (HQ); Walnut Creek; newspaper publishing — 535. **Dow Chemical Co.** (Western Div.); Pittsburg; industrial chemicals — 500. **United Grocers Ltd.** (United Distributing - HQ); Richmond; grocery wholesaling — 500. **Varian Associates** (Varian Instruments Group); Walnut Creek; analytical instruments — 500.

8th District

Northern Alameda County — Oakland; Berkeley

The Black Panther Party, the "free-speech movement" and the Symbionese Liberation Army all were born within this constituency, an intriguing mixture of poverty and intellectual ferment. Berkeley and most of Oakland account for about 60 percent of the district's voters and form its economic, philosophical and political base. To many of the left-wing activists who live and work in this area the term "liberal" has long been considered a pejorative.

The enormous University of California campus in Berkeley has provided an active political force in the area for decades, although in recent years it has been far less vocal than in the 1960s and early 1970s. It has been augmented by thousands of loyally Democratic black voters in Oakland, Berkeley's larger neighbor to the south and one of the poorest cities in the state. The portion of Oakland in the 8th District is 43 percent black; overall, the district is 26.5 percent black.

The 8th District in effect for the 1982 elections was expanded south to include some of the poorest black and Hispanic sections of Oakland, near the Alameda County Coliseum and the Oakland International Airport. The only part of the city not now included in the 8th District is an integrated middle-class area in the 9th.

The district also was pushed farther into the upper-class, conservative areas of Contra Costa County that adjoin Alameda County. The Lafayette-Moraga Town section of Contra Costa County has never given the district's black incumbent more than 40 percent of the vote; the portions of the San Ramon Valley communities newly added will not support him with any greater enthusiasm.

But Berkeley and Oakland make the district as a whole solidly Democratic. Even Jimmy Carter, who was swamped by Edward M. Kennedy in the 1980 presidential primary, was able to carry the new 8th in the fall. In fact, this was the only one of the redrawn East Bay districts he carried. Alameda County also was one of only five counties that former Gov. Edmund G. Brown Jr. carried in his unsuccessful 1982 bid for a Senate seat.

Third party candidates John B. Anderson and Barry Commoner took more than 15 percent of the vote in the district — the highest in the Bay Area outside of San Francisco. In Berkeley, Anderson and Commoner combined to outpoll Reagan by 2,500 votes.

Election Returns

8th District		Democrat		Republican	
1976	President	123,993	(58.7%)	84,206	(39.9%)
	Senate	126,323	(60.1%)	78,309	(37.2%)
	House	145,739	(63.5%)	76,976	(33.5%)
1978	Governor	122,389	(63.9%)	48,788	(25.5%)
	House	112,680	(58.2%)	79,857	(41.3%)
1980	President	116,652	(51.6%)	74,370	(32.9%)
	Senate	154,531	(70.8%)	50,382	(23.1%)
	House	129,149	(55.7%)	90,479	(39.0%)
1982	Governor	140,842	(63.6%)	74,050	(33.4%)
	Senate	134,526	(61.0%)	78,085	(35.4%)
	House	121,537	(55.9%)	95,694	(44.1%)

Demographics

Population: 525,927. **Percent Change from 1970:** 0.5%.

Land Area: 165 square miles. **Population per Square Mile:** 3,187.4.

Counties, 1980 Population: Alameda (Pt.) — 394,881; Contra Costa (Pt.) — 131,046.

Cities, 1980 Population: Albany — 15,130; Berkeley — 103,328; El Cerrito — 22,731; Lafayette — 20,879; Martinez (Pt.) — 49; Moraga Town — 15,014; Oakland (Pt.) — 262,201; Piedmont — 10,498; Richmond (Pt.) — 17; Walnut Creek (Pt.) — 1.

Race and Ancestry: White — 60.5%; Black — 26.5%; American Indian, Eskimo and Aleut — 0.5%; Asian and Pacific Islander — 8.6%. Spanish Origin — 6.5%. English — 6.9%; French — 0.7%; German — 3.9%; Irish — 2.8%; Italian — 2.3%; Norwegian — 0.6%; Polish — 0.7%; Portuguese — 0.7%; Russian — 1.3%; Scottish — 0.6%; Swedish — 0.7%.

Universities, Enrollment: American Baptist Seminary of the West, Berkeley — 171; Armstrong College, Berkeley — 452; California College of Arts and Crafts, Oakland — 1,150; California School of Professional Psychology at Berkeley, Berkeley — 292; Church Divinity School of the Pacific, Berkeley — 102; Dominican School of Philosophy and Theology, Berkeley — 85; Franciscan School of Theology, Berkeley — 120; Graduate Theological Union, Berkeley — 377; Holy Names College, Oakland — 666.

Jesuit School of Theology, Berkeley — 270; John F. Kennedy University, Orinda — 1,430; Laney College, Oakland — 9,733; Merritt College, Oakland — 9,365; Mills College, Oakland — 932; Pacific Lutheran Theological Seminary, Berkeley — 203; Pacific School of Religion, Berkeley — 189; Patten College, Oakland — 134; Saint Mary's College, Moraga Town — 2,451; Starr King School for the Ministry, Berkeley — 53; University of California at Berkeley, Berkeley — 30,462; Vista College, Berkeley — 8,441; Wright Institute, Berkeley — 187.

Newspapers, Circulation: *Berkeley Gazette* (eS), Berkeley — 7,338; *East Bay Today* (m), Oakland — 53,866; *Oakland Tribune* (eS), Oakland — 142,071. The *Contra Costa Times, Contra Costa Independent*, San Francisco *Chronicle* and San Francisco *Examiner* also circulate in the district.

Commercial Television Stations, Affiliation: KTVU, Oakland (None). Most of district is in San Francisco ADI. A portion is in Sacramento-Stockton ADI.

Industries:

Southern Pacific Co. Inc. (Southern Pacific Transportation Co.); Oakland; railroad operations — 2,000. **Blue Cross of Northern California** (HQ); Oakland; health insurance — 1,700. **Alta Bates Hospital;** Berkeley; hospital — 1,570. **Kaiser Foundation Hospital;** Oakland; hospital — 1,500. **Children's Hospital and Medical Center of Northern California;** Oakland; hospital — 1,400. **Kaiser Engineers Inc.** (HQ); Oakland; construction — 1,400.

Herrick Foundation Inc.; Berkeley; hospital — 1,300. **The Samuel**

Merritt Hospital; Oakland; hospital — 1,300. **American Protective Services** (HQ); Oakland; security services — 1,010. **Kaiser Aluminum & Chemical Corp.** (HQ); Oakland; aluminum — 1,000. **Oakland Tribune;** Oakland; newspaper publishing — 1,000. **Owens-Illinois Inc.;** Oakland; glass containers — 1,000. **Delaval Transamerica Inc.** (Delaval Engines & Compressors Div.); Oakland; generators — 850. **Brockway Glass Inc.;** Oakland; bottles, jars — 750. **Detective Intelligence Service** (HQ); Oakland; security services — 700.

The Clorox Co. (Food Service Products Div.); Oakland; specialty cleaning products — 650. **Oakland Scavenger Co. Inc.** (HQ); Oakland; refuse disposal — 635. **Grove Valve & Regulator Co.** (HQ); Emeryville; valves — 550. **American Brands Inc.** (Sunshine Biscuits); Oakland; biscuits, crackers — 500. **American Can Co.;** Oakland; metal cans — 500. **Central Banking System Inc.** (HQ); Oakland; bank holding company — 500. **Cutter Laboratories Inc.;** Berkeley; biological products — 500. **Dillingham Corp.;** Berkeley; general contracting — 500. **Sunset Designs Inc.;** San Ramon; craft kits — 500.

9th District

Suburban Alameda County — Hayward

The new 9th is Democratic but not nearly as liberal as the Democrat it sent to the House in every election between 1972 and 1982. The fastest-growing portions of this constituency have shown increasing willingness to vote Republican at the statewide level.

Like most of the East Bay districts, the 9th has two divergent parts. Working-class Democratic areas lie along the bay; a high-tech, suburban growth area is firmly established on the other side of the hills that form the eastern wall of the San Francisco basin.

The more densely populated bay-side area is dominated by warehouses and older factories. This area includes San Leandro, once largely a Portuguese enclave that still has a strong blue-collar voting bloc. San Leandro has voted for every recent Democratic presidential nominee except Jimmy Carter in 1980. Ronald Reagan's appeal to the economic interests of the voters here gave him a 48-41 margin.

To the north of San Leandro is Oakland. The transfer of black and Hispanic sections of the city to the 8th District left only a thin wedge of middle-class black and white communities in the 9th.

To the south, the 9th District in effect for the 1982 elections expanded to include most of Hayward, now the largest city in the district, with nearly 93,000 residents. The remaining 1,300 Hayward residents are in the 10th. Although the California State University Hayward campus is in the 10th, the 9th District contains much of the student population, which is a political benefit to the Democrats. Statewide Democratic candidates have consistently run several percentage points better in Hayward than in the rest of the district.

The area of greatest concern to Democrats in the 9th is on the eastern side of the San Leandro Hills, where high-tech research industries centered around Livermore have drawn thousands of affluent suburbanites.

Election Returns

9th District		Democrat		Republican	
1976	President	98,494	(55.5%)	77,158	(43.4%)
	Senate	93,624	(53.6%)	77,019	(44.1%)

9th District		Democrat		Republican	
1976	House	128,742	(71.1%)	48,108	(26.6%)
1978	Governor	89,588	(59.6%)	45,632	(30.3%)
	House	87,486	(65.3%)	42,128	(31.4%)
1980	President	75,939	(42.3%)	82,368	(45.8%)
	Senate	109,594	(62.2%)	56,242	(31.9%)
	House	102,359	(56.6%)	69,636	(38.5%)
1982	Governor	86,594	(49.3%)	82,918	(47.2%)
	Senate	88,908	(50.7%)	79,184	(45.2%)
	House	104,393	(60.7%)	67,702	(39.3%)

Demographics

Population: 524,649. **Percent Change from 1970:** 2.4%.

Land Area: 561 square miles. **Population per Square Mile:** 935.2.

Counties, 1980 Population: Alameda (Pt.) — 524,649.

Cities, 1980 Population: Alameda — 63,852; Castro Valley (CDP) — 44,011; Hayward (Pt.) — 92,846; Livermore — 48,349; Oakland (Pt.) — 77,136; Pleasanton — 35,160; San Leandro — 63,952; Union City (Pt.) — 19,270.

Race and Ancestry: White — 74.7%; Black — 11.6%; American Indian, Eskimo and Aleut — 0.7%; Asian and Pacific Islander — 6.6%. Spanish Origin — 13.5%. Dutch — 0.5%; English — 6.4%; French — 0.9%; German — 4.6%; Irish — 3.3%; Italian — 2.8%; Norwegian — 0.6%; Polish — 0.5%; Portuguese — 3.8%; Scottish — 0.6%; Swedish — 0.7%.

Universities, Enrollment: Chabot College, Hayward — 18,986; College of Alameda, Alameda — 6,900.

Newspapers, Circulation: *Alameda Times Star* (m), Alameda — 8,576; *The Daily Review* (eS), Hayward — 43,417; *Tri-Valley Herald* (mS), Livermore — 14,245; *Valley Times* (mS), Livermore — 6,160. The *Oakland Tribune*, San Francisco *Chronicle* and San Francisco *Examiner* also circulate in the district.

Commercial Television Stations, Affiliation: Entire district is in San Francisco ADI.

Military Installations: Alameda Naval Air Station, Alameda — 12,777; Camp Parks, Livermore — 425; Hayward Municipal Airport (Air Force), Hayward — 429; Oakland Naval Regional Medical Center, Oakland — 2,047; Oakland Naval Supply Center, Oakland — 5,259; San Francisco Naval Public Works Center, Oakland — 1,057.

Industries:

Western Electric Co. Inc.; San Leandro; warehousing — 1,200. **Sandia Laboratories;** Livermore; energy research — 1,050. **Transamerica Airlines Inc.** (HQ); Oakland; commercial airline — 1,000. **Hunt-Wesson Foods;** Hayward; canned fruits, vegetables — 1,000. **Mohawk Data Services Corp.** (Quantel Div.); Hayward; microcomputers — 1,000. **World Airways Inc.** (HQ); Oakland; commercial airline — 1,000.

Mack Trucks Inc. (Mack Western); Hayward; motor vehicles — 850. **Lucky Stores Inc.;** San Leandro; warehousing — 800. **Todd Shipyards Corp.;** Alameda; ship repairing — 600. **United Can Co.;** Hayward; metal cans — 600. **Intel Corp.;** Livermore; semiconductors — 500.

10th District

Southeast Bay Area — San Jose, Fremont

Sitting at the southeastern end of the San Francisco Bay area, the 10th is split between Alameda and Santa Clara counties. Of the four East Bay districts it is the most solidly blue-collar. Unlike the 7th and 9th it does not reach eastward into the hills, where Republican voting strength is growing.

As a result the new 10th is a few degrees more Democratic than the others. Its voters backed Ronald Reagan in 1980 by a slim margin, but they have shown few other signs of Republican flirtation.

The Alameda County part of the district is centered on Fremont, a city of 132,000 people. Fremont was once known as the Detroit of the West Coast. However, General Motors all but closed its assembly plant there in the early 1980s. Ford and Peterbilt trucks still are made in nearby Milpitas and Newark.

The Santa Clara portion is focused on San Jose, the fourth largest city in the state. Two-fifths of San Jose is included in the 10th. With a growing influx of Hispanic-Americans into San Jose, 28 percent of the new district's population is of Hispanic origin.

Although registered Democrats overwhelm Republicans in both the Alameda County and Santa Clara County portions of the district, there are differences in outlook. The Fremont voters are considerably more conservative than those living in San Jose. Reagan's slim victory in the district was a result of his 54-33 percent edge over Jimmy Carter in Fremont.

Carter's 1980 Fremont vote was a full 10 points below George McGovern's 1972 showing there, a marked demonstration of the shifting political values of the blue-collar voters of this area.

Apart from a minor adjustment in the district line through San Jose, the only other change moved most of Hayward into the 9th District.

Election Returns

10th District		Democrat		Republican	
1976	President	74,784	(59.0%)	50,300	(39.7%)
	Senate	69,278	(54.5%)	53,979	(42.5%)
	House	91,447	(71.2%)	32,874	(25.6%)
1978	Governor	70,021	(66.5%)	26,021	(24.7%)
	House	69,328	(65.7%)	35,573	(33.7%)
1980	President	57,207	(41.5%)	61,657	(44.8%)
	Senate	85,337	(63.8%)	39,082	(29.2%)
	House	84,727	(60.7%)	39,912	(28.6%)
1982	Governor	71,794	(56.8%)	49,970	(39.5%)
	Senate	67,275	(53.4%)	53,071	(42.1%)
	House	77,263	(62.7%)	41,506	(33.7%)

Demographics

Population: 527,278. **Percent Change from 1970:** 37.4%.

Land Area: 234 square miles. **Population per Square Mile:** 2,253.3.

Counties, 1980 Population: Alameda (Pt.) — 185,849; Santa Clara (Pt.) — 341,429.

Cities, 1980 Population: Fremont — 131,945; Hayward (Pt.) — 1,321; Milpitas — 37,820; Newark — 32,126; San Jose (Pt.) — 264,967; Union City (Pt.) — 20,136.

Race and Ancestry: White — 67.7%; Black — 5.6%; American Indian, Eskimo and Aleut — 0.9%; Asian and Pacific Islander — 10.1%. Spanish Origin — 28.0%. English — 5.1%; French — 0.6%; German

— 3.6%; Irish — 2.4%; Italian — 2.7%; Polish — 0.5%; Portuguese — 3.1%; Swedish — 0.5%.

Universities, Enrollment: California State University at Hayward, Hayward — 10,666; Holy Family College, Fremont — 116; Ohlone College, Fremont — 8,232; Queen of the Holy Rosary, Fremont — 228; San Jose Bible College, San Jose — 236; San Jose State University, San Jose — 25,821.

Newspapers, Circulation: *The Argus* (mS), Fremont — 18,705; *Mercury* (m), San Jose — 155,472; *News* (e), San Jose — 67,914. The *Oakland Tribune*, *Hayward Daily Review*, *Peninsula Times-Tribune*, San Francisco *Chronicle* and San Francisco *Examiner* also circulate in the district.

Commercial Television Stations, Affiliation: KICU-TV, San Jose (None); KNTV, San Jose (ABC); KSTS, San Jose (None). Entire district is in San Francisco ADI.

Industries:

FMC Corp. (Ordnance Div.); San Jose; weaponry — 5,900. **General Electric Co.** (Nuclear Energy Group); San Jose; engineering, research services — 5,000. **Ford Motor Co.**; Milpitas; auto, truck assembly — 2,480. **Tri-Valley Growers**; San Jose; fruit, vegetable canning — 2,000. **Northwest Publishing Inc.**; San Jose; newspaper publishing — 1,300.

San Jose Hospital & Health Center; San Jose; hospital — 1,200. **O'Connor Hospital Inc.**; San Jose; hospital — 1,050. **Kaiser Aerospace & Electronics Corp.** (Kaiser Electronics); San Jose; aircraft engines — 1,000. **L. S. Williams Co.**; Newark; vegetables — 1,000. **Qume Corp.** (HQ); San Jose; electronic computing equipment — 800. **Paccar Inc.** (Peterbilt Motors Co. Div.); Newark; trucks — 700. **Anderson-Jacobson Inc.** (HQ); San Jose; electronic computing — 550.

Fleming Companies Inc. (Fleming Foods); Fremont; grocery wholesaling — 500. **General Electric Co.** (Vertical Motor Products Div.); San Jose; vertical motors — 500. **Hewlett-Packard Co. Inc.**; San Jose; semiconductors — 500. **Magnuson Computer Systems Inc.** (HQ); San Jose; computers — 500. **Spectra-Physics Inc.**; San Jose; cromatographic instruments — 500. **Tymeshare Transactions Services** (HQ); Fremont; data processing services — 500.

11th District

Most of San Mateo County; Palo Alto

The 11th District put in place for the 1982 elections carefully skirts the most Republican areas of San Mateo County, drawing its population from the more Democratic territory between them.

Redistricting cost the 11th all but 13,000 residents of solidly Democratic blue-collar Daly City. But the district also shed Hillsborough, the most Republican part of the old district, and gained most of Palo Alto, a liberal bastion at the foot of the district's eastern leg.

The home of Stanford University, Palo Alto gave independent presidential candidate John B. Anderson more than a fifth of its vote in 1980 and still had enough Democratic strength for Jimmy Carter to eke out a plurality over Ronald Reagan.

Such Democratic presidential sentiment is not as evident elsewhere in the district. Both Reagan and Gerald R. Ford carried the area within the new 11th, even though registered Democrats outnumber Republicans by a 54-33 margin. But in contests for governor or U.S. senator, Democrats generally win by wide margins.

The district has two distinct legs that straddle the San Mateo Mountains. The western leg is primarily mist, fog and a smattering of small communities tucked into the mountains or perched on bluffs overlooking the sea.

The eastern segment, tied together by 30 miles of the Bayshore Freeway, has most of the voters living in a string of modest-sized suburbs ranging in population from Millbrae at 20,058 to San Mateo at 77,561. Two working-class enclaves, South San Francisco and San Bruno, occupy the northern end of this corridor. From Millbrae south to San Carlos are upper- and middle-class communities, all of which gave Reagan a majority in 1980.

Election Returns

11th District		Democrat		Republican	
1976	President	96,287	(49.2%)	97,407	(49.8%)
	Senate	98,673	(49.7%)	93,125	(46.9%)
	House	103,456	(52.9%)	85,658	(43.8%)
1978	Governor	104,662	(59.2%)	54,774	(31.0%)
	House	84,490	(50.4%)	76,001	(45.3%)
1980	President	79,707	(38.6%)	92,520	(44.8%)
	Senate	131,614	(66.6%)	47,554	(24.1%)
	House	78,998	(38.9%)	102,338	(50.4%)
1982	Governor	105,636	(53.5%)	85,342	(43.2%)
	Senate	96,136	(49.5%)	90,023	(46.4%)
	House	109,812	(57.1%)	76,462	(39.7%)

Demographics

Population: 525,102. **Percent Change from 1970:** 2.0%.

Land Area: 171 square miles. **Population per Square Mile:** 3,070.8.

Counties, 1980 Population: San Mateo (Pt.) — 459,152; Santa Clara (Pt.) — 65,950.

Cities, 1980 Population: Belmont — 24,505; Burlingame — 26,173; Daly City (Pt.) — 12,897; Foster City — 23,287; Menlo Park (Pt.) — 11,536; Millbrae — 20,058; Pacifica — 36,866; Palo Alto (Pt.) — 54,848; Redwood City — 54,951; San Bruno — 35,417; San Carlos — 24,710; San Mateo — 77,561; South San Francisco — 49,393; Stanford (CDP) — 11,045.

Race and Ancestry: White — 80.9%; Black — 5.8%; American Indian, Eskimo and Aleut — 0.4%; Asian and Pacific Islander — 8.0%. Spanish Origin — 11.4%. Dutch — 0.5%; English — 6.6%; French — 1.0%; German — 4.9%; Greek — 0.5%; Irish — 4.1%; Italian — 4.8%; Norwegian — 0.5%; Polish — 0.8%; Portuguese — 0.7%; Russian — 1.0%; Scottish — 0.6%; Swedish — 0.7%.

Universities, Enrollment: Canada College, Redwood City — 8,783; College of Notre Dame, Belmont — 1,444; College of San Mateo, San Mateo — 15,063; Saint Patrick's Seminary, Menlo Park — 83; Skyline College, San Bruno — 6,705; Stanford University, Stanford — 13,592.

Newspapers, Circulation: *The Peninsula Times-Tribune* (e), Palo Alto — 60,950; *Times and News Leader* (e), San Mateo — 48,769. The San Jose *Mercury*, San Jose *News*, San Francisco *Chronicle* and San Francisco *Examiner* also circulate in the district.

Commercial Television Stations, Affiliation: Entire district is in San Francisco ADI.

Industries:

United Air Lines Inc.; South San Francisco; commercial airline — 9,822. **Varian Associates** (HQ); Palo Alto; electronic systems, components — 5,000. **Ford Aerospace & Communications Corp.**; Palo Alto; electronic communications equipment — 3,500. **GTE Lenkurt Inc.** (HQ); San Carlos; telephone, telegraph apparatus — 3,000. **Raychem Corp.** (HQ); Menlo Park; wire cable — 3,000.

SRI International (HQ); Menlo Park; research services — 2,850. **Watkins-Johnson Co. Inc.** (HQ); Palo Alto; electronic communications equipment — 2,100. **The Folger Coffee Co.**; South San Francisco;

coffee — 2,000. **American Airlines Inc.;** South San Francisco; commercial airline — 1,700. **Ampex Corp.** (HQ); Redwood City; computer memory components — 1,640. **Veterans Administration;** Palo Alto; veterans' hospital — 1,500. **Peninsula Hospital District;** Burlingame; hospital — 1,250. **Sequoia Hospital District;** Redwood City; hospital — 1,200. **Mills Memorial Hospital;** San Mateo; hospital — 1,100. **Textron Inc.** (Dalmo Victor Operations); Belmont; radar systems — 1,100. **Western Air Lines Inc.;** South San Francisco; commercial airline — 1,000. **Lloyd W. Aubrey Engineering** (Calveyor); Burlingame; heavy construction — 900. **Consorcio Turimiquire;** South San Francisco; dam construction — 900. **Syntex U.S.A. Inc.;** Palo Alto; research, development — 900. **Teledyne Inc.** (Microwave Electronics Div.); Palo Alto; electronic communications equipment — 830.

Coherent Inc. (HQ); Palo Alto; lasers — 800. **Flying Tiger Line Inc.;** South San Francisco; air carrier — 800. **Hewlett-Packard Co. Inc.** (Laboratories Div.); Palo Alto; research — 775. **Lockheed Missiles & Space Co. Inc.;** Palo Alto; computer services — 750. **Litton Industries Inc.;** San Carlos; electron tubes — 710. **Siltec Corp.** (HQ); Menlo Park; silicon crystals, silicon processing equipment — 700. **Varian Associates** (EIMAC Div.); San Carlos; electron tubes — 675. **California Casualty Indemnity Exchange** (HQ); San Mateo; casualty insurance — 600. **Republic Airlines West Inc.** (HQ); San Mateo; commercial airline — 600. **Davy McKee Corp.;** San Mateo; engineering services — 550. **Alumax Fabricated Products Inc.;** San Mateo; aluminum sheet — 533. **Peabody Engineering Corp.** (Industrial Nuclear Co.); San Mateo; computer services — 510. **D H L Corp.;** Burlingame; air freight — 500. **Rocor International Inc.;** Palo Alto; trucking — 500.

12th District

Parts of San Mateo, Santa Clara and Stanislaus Counties

Used primarily by the Democratic cartographers as a "dumping ground" for GOP votes, the 12th District in effect for the 98th Congress takes in several areas with little in common except Republican inclinations.

The district is one of only two new districts in the state where Democrats do not have a majority in party registration. The 12th has a median housing value of nearly $140,000, the highest in California.

Starting just south of Millbrae and Burlingame and moving east, the district takes in the swank Hillsborough and Woodside sections of San Mateo County, where some of the residents commute to San Francisco by limousine. Some 65 percent of the Hillsborough voters are registered Republicans — the highest figure for any place in the Bay Area. In 1980, Jimmy Carter won only 13 percent in Hillsborough.

In Santa Clara County, the 12th includes Mountain View and Sunnyvale at the southern end of the electronics and computer corridor known as Silicon Valley. It has additional Republican turf taken from the 13th District — notably Saratoga and Cupertino.

Then the district takes in the southern tip of San Jose, turns east to cross the Diablo Mountains and enters Stanislaus County, in the heart of the agricultural Central Valley. It comes to an end in the shape of a large arrow pointing towards Yosemite National Park, 30 miles further east.

In Stanislaus County, the lines carefully skirt the wine-making capital of Modesto. By a quirk of cartography two residents of Modesto live in the 12th; the other 106,600 residents are part of the 15th. The 12th does take in smaller communities such as Turlock and Oakdale that often vote Republican. Several of the county's conservative

Democratic farming areas were added to the 12th, a move that does not threaten Republican control.

Election Returns

12th District		Democrat		Republican	
1976	President	74,075	(41.0%)	104,649	(57.9%)
	Senate	73,116	(40.2%)	104,546	(57.4%)
	House	92,080	(48.7%)	92,881	(49.1%)
1978	Governor	84,915	(52.8%)	61,369	(38.2%)
	House	61,213	(37.7%)	95,112	(58.4%)
1980	President	61,024	(30.1%)	109,355	(53.9%)
	Senate	109,842	(56.4%)	71,261	(36.6%)
	House	73,438	(36.1%)	115,402	(56.7%)
1982	Governor	86,038	(44.1%)	103,400	(53.0%)
	Senate	71,847	(37.4%)	112,640	(58.6%)
	House	61,372	(33.5%)	115,365	(63.0%)

Demographics

Population: 525,271 **Percent Change from 1970:** 18.1%.

Land Area: 2,642 square miles. **Population per Square Mile:** 198.8.

Counties, 1980 Population: San Mateo (Pt.) — 58,501; Santa Clara (Pt.) — 361,113; Stanislaus (Pt.) — 105,657.

Cities, 1980 Population: Cupertino — 34,015; Gilroy — 21,641; Hillsborough — 10,451; Los Altos — 25,769; Menlo Park (Pt.) — 14,833; Modesto (Pt.) — 2; Morgan Hill — 17,060; Mountain View — 58,655; Palo Alto (Pt.) — 377; San Jose (Pt.) — 12,297; Saratoga — 29,261; Sunnyvale (Pt.) — 106,618; Turlock — 26,287.

Race and Ancestry: White — 85.7%; Black — 1.4%; American Indian, Eskimo and Aleut — 0.6%; Asian and Pacific Islander — 5.9%. Spanish Origin — 12.1%. Dutch — 0.8%; English — 9.2%; French — 0.8%; German — 5.6%; Irish — 3.4%; Italian — 3.0%; Norwegian — 0.6%; Polish — 0.7%; Portuguese — 1.8%; Russian — 0.6%; Scottish — 0.7%; Swedish — 1.1%.

Universities, Enrollment: California State College at Stanislaus, Turlock — 3,910; De Anza College, Cupertino — 25,433; Foothill College, Los Altos Hills — 14,413; Gavilan College, Gilroy — 2,989; Menlo College, Menlo Park — 678; Saint Patrick's College, Mountain View — 63; West Valley College, Saratoga — 15,716.

Newspapers, Circulation: *The Dispatch* (e), Gilroy — 10,225; *Turlock Daily Journal* (e), Turlock — 8,842. *The Modesto Bee,* San Francisco *Chronicle,* San Francisco *Examiner, Peninsula Times-Tribune,* San Jose *Mercury,* San Jose *News* and San Mateo *Times and News Leader* also circulate in the district.

Commercial Television Stations, Affiliation: KCSO, Modesto (None, Spanish). District is divided between San Francisco ADI and Sacramento-Stockton ADI.

Military Installations: Moffett Field Naval Air Station, Mountain View — 6,664; Sunnyvale Air Force Station, Sunnyvale — 3,683; Riverbank Army Ammunitition Plant, Riverbank — 81.

Industries:

Lockheed Missiles & Space Co. Inc. (HQ); Sunnyvale; guided missiles, space vehicles, research — 21,000. **Hewlett-Packard Co. Inc.** (HQ); Palo Alto; electronic calculators, computers, instrumentation — 15,000. **Signetics Corp.** (HQ); Sunnyvale; integrated circuits — 3,600. **Fairchild Camera & Instrument Corp.** (HQ); Mountain View; semiconductor devices, photographic equipment — 3,500. **Amdahl Corp.** (HQ); Sunnyvale; electronic computing equipment — 3,000.

Shugart Associates (HQ); Sunnyvale; computer discs — 2,600. **Westinghouse Electric Corp.;** Sunnyvale; marine hardware — 2,500. **Intersil Inc.** (HQ); Cupertino; semiconductors — 2,200. **Four-Phase Systems Inc.** (HQ); Cupertino; electronic computing equipment —

2,100. **Atari Inc.** (HQ); Sunnyvale; coin operated amusement games — 2,000. **GTE Products Corp.;** Mountain View; cathode ray TV picture tubes — 2,000. **Western Electric Co. Inc.** (Pacific Regional Headquarters); Sunnyvale; administrative offices — 1,700. **El Camino Hospital District;** Mountain View; hospital — 1,600. **Hewlett-Packard Co. Inc.** (Data Systems Div.); Cupertino; mini-computers — 1,600. **Tandem Comput Inc.** (HQ); Cupertino; electronic computing equipment — 1,530. **Advanced Micro Devices Inc.** (HQ); Sunnyvale; integrated circuits — 1,500. **E S L Inc.** (HQ); Sunnyvale; electronic communications equipment — 1,500. **Hunt-Wesson Foods Inc.;** Oakdale; tomato canning — 1,500.

Hewlett-Packard Co. Inc. (Data Terminal Div.); Sunnyvale; computer terminals — 1,380. **United Technologies Corp.** (Chemical Systems Div.); Sunnyvale; aircraft engines — 1,200. **Itek Corp.** (Applied Technology Div.); Sunnyvale; electronic components — 1,050. **Printed Circuits International Inc.** (HQ); Sunnyvale; printed circuits — 1,000. **Verbatim Corp.** (HQ); Sunnyvale; magnetic data storage media — 1,000. **Raytheon Co. Inc.;** Mountain View; semiconductors — 950. **Acurex Corp.** (Aerotherm Div. - HQ); Mountain View; industrial controls — 850. **Tymshare Inc.** (HQ); Cupertino; data processing services — 850. **General Electric Co.** (Advanced Reactor Systems Dept.); Sunnyvale; transformers — 824. **Apple Computer Inc.** (HQ); Cupertino; electronic computing equipment — 800. **Measurex Corp.** (HQ); Cupertino; process control systems — 800. **Monolithic Memories Inc.** (HQ); Sunnyvale; semiconductor memories — 800. **Banquet Foods Corp.;** Turlock; frozen foods — 700.

Racal-Vadic Inc. (HQ); Sunnyvale; communications apparatus —

700. **Control Data Corp.** (Palo Alto Data Center); Sunnyvale; accounting services — 600. **Tri-Valley Growers;** Turlock; fruit, vegetable canning — 650. **Hershey Foods Corp.** (Hershey Chocolate Co.); Oakdale; chocolate — 600. **Universal Foods Corp.** (Rogers Foods); Turlock; dehydrated foods — 600. **Valchris Inc.;** Turlock; poultry processing — 600. **TRW Inc.** (Vidar Div.); Mountain View; semiconductor devices — 550. **Aertech Industries;** Sunnyvale; microwave ovens — 540. **Data General Corp.;** Sunnyvale; semiconductors — 500. **Informatics Inc.** (Programming Methods Div.); Mountain View; computer programming services — 500. **Syva Co.** (HQ); Palo Alto; reagents — 500. **Triad Systems Corp.** (HQ); Sunnyvale; mini-computers — 500.

13th District

Santa Clara County — Part of San Jose; Santa Clara

In three decades of post-World War II growth, suburbanization has crept down both sides of the San Francisco Bay and come together at San Jose in Santa Clara County, 50 miles south of San Francisco and 42 miles south of Oakland. The prune, cherry and apricot orchards that once made Santa Clara County a restful spot for Bay Area

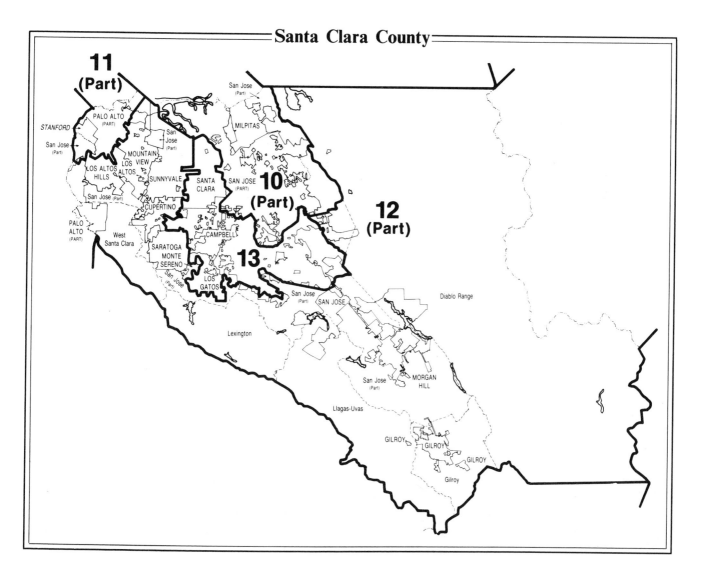
Santa Clara County

day-trippers have been replaced by electronics and aero-space plants and miles of tract homes occupied by young families.

The 13th is a relatively compact suburban district contained entirely within Santa Clara County. It includes about three-fifths of San Jose, although not the downtown area, and takes in the adjoining communities of Santa Clara, Campbell and Los Gatos. As the canneries and fruit-packing firms have given way to high-tech in this part of Silicon Valley, San Jose's white-collar population has grown accordingly. The part of San Jose included in the 13th is considerably more Anglo than the western side found in the 10th. Less than 15 percent of the population in the 13th is black or Hispanic, compared with 34 percent in the 10th.

Santa Clara, with 88,000 residents, is a new addition to the district and strengthens the 13th's already solid Democratic tendencies. The younger, more working-class residents of Santa Clara replace affluent Republicans in Saratoga, Cupertino and the eastern part of Santa Clara County, all transferred to the new 12th District. Santa Clara went for Ronald Reagan in 1980 — like the new district as a whole — but did not give the margins he collected in the areas that were removed.

Election Returns

13th District		Democrat		Republican	
1976	President	86,360	(47.7%)	92,787	(51.2%)
	Senate	79,270	(43.1%)	99,857	(54.3%)
	House	108,275	(58.9%)	71,373	(38.8%)
1978	Governor	95,795	(62.4%)	44,236	(28.8%)
	House	78,539	(50.3%)	72,360	(46.3%)
1980	President	66,607	(34.1%)	96,893	(49.6%)
	Senate	112,569	(59.4%)	64,368	(34.0%)
	House	100,742	(50.5%)	86,398	(43.3%)
1982	Governor	89,175	(52.0%)	77,327	(45.1%)
	Senate	76,249	(44.8%)	86,638	(50.9%)
	House	110,805	(65.9%)	52,806	(31.4%)

Demographics

Population: 526,579. **Percent Change from 1970:** 21.5%.

Land Area: 100 square miles. **Population per Square Mile:** 5,265.8.

Counties, 1980 Population: Santa Clara (Pt.) — 526,579.

Cities, 1980 Population: Campbell — 27,067; Los Gatos — 26,906; San Jose (Pt.) — 352,178; Santa Clara — 87,746; Sunnyvale (Pt.) — 0.

Race and Ancestry: White — 85.4%; Black — 2.3%; American Indian, Eskimo and Aleut — 0.6%; Asian and Pacific Islander — 6.4%. Spanish Origin — 11.6%. Dutch — 0.6%; English — 7.8%; French — 1.0%; German — 5.5%; Irish — 3.4%; Italian — 4.5%; Norwegian — 0.6%; Polish — 0.7%; Portuguese — 1.7%; Scottish — 0.6%; Swedish — 0.7%.

Universities, Enrollment: Bay-Valley Tech, Santa Clara — 323; Condie College of Business and Technology, San Jose — 325; Evergreen Valley College, San Jose — 6,814; Mission College, Santa Clara — 7,649; San Jose City College, San Jose — 14,135; University of Santa Clara, Santa Clara — 7,026.

Newspapers, Circulation: The San Francisco *Chronicle*, San Francisco *Examiner*, San Jose *Mercury*, San Jose *News* and *Peninsula Times-Tribune* circulate in the district.

Commercial Television Stations, Affiliation: Entire district is in San Francisco ADI.

Industries:

International Business Machines Corp.; San Jose; data processing equipment — 10,000. **National Semiconductor Corp.** (HQ); Santa Clara; semiconductors, computers — 9,000. **Intel Corp.** (HQ); Santa Clara; semiconductor devices, computing equipment — 5,500. **Memorex Corp.** (HQ); Santa Clara; peripheral computer equipment — 5,300. **Rolm Corp.** (HQ); Santa Clara; telephone apparatus — 2,740.

Hewlett-Packard Co. Inc.; Santa Clara; electronic counters — 2,000. **Santa Clara Valley Medical Center;** San Jose; hospital — 2,000. **Sperry Corp.** (ISS Div.); Santa Clara; peripheral computer equipment — 1,900. **Good Samaritan Hospital of Santa Clara Valley;** San Jose; hospital — 1,520. **Kaiser Foundation Hospital;** Santa Clara; hospital — 1,200. **Synertek;** Santa Clara; semiconductors — 1,200. **Siliconex Inc.** (HQ); Santa Clara; semiconductors — 1,100. **American Microsystems Inc.** (HQ); Santa Clara; integrated circuits — 1,050. **Dysan Corp.** (HQ); Santa Clara; computer memory equipment — 1,000. **Stanford Applied Engineering Inc.** (Circuits Div.); Santa Clara; electronic components — 1,000. **Avantek Inc.;** Santa Clara; electronic components — 900. **Owens-Corning Fiberglas Co.;** Santa Clara; fiberglass insulation — 900.

Versatec Inc. (HQ); Santa Clara; electronic computing equipment — 750. **Calma Co.** (HQ); Santa Clara; electronic computing equipment — 700. **Quadrex Corp.** (HQ); Campbell; engineering services — 700. **Northern Telecom Inc.** (Business Communications System); Santa Clara; communications apparatus — 657. **Precision Monolithics Inc.** (HQ); Santa Clara; integrated circuits — 650. **Stanford Applied Engineering Inc.** (Caltronics); Santa Clara; electronic components — 600. **Applied Materials Inc.** (HQ); Santa Clara; chemical vapor — 550. **Almaden Vineyards Inc.** (Almaden Wines); San Jose; winery — 500. **General Signal Mfg. Corp.** (Tempress Microelectric); Los Gatos; machine tools, special machinery — 500. **Intersil Inc.** (Mfg. Div.); Santa Clara; semiconductors — 500. **Stanford Applied Engineering Inc.** (HQ); Santa Clara; electronic components — 500.

14th District

Northeast; Part of San Joaquin County

The 14th took on a completely new look in 1982 as a result of redistricting. After years as an agricultural district focused on the canning town of Stockton, the district under the 1982 remap is an area of mountains, forests and lakes. It reaches north from Stockton to the Oregon border nearly 300 miles away and, geographically, is the second largest district in the state — slightly larger than West Virginia.

San Joaquin County, which includes Stockton, has a severely reduced role to play in district politics. In 1982 it cast less than a quarter of the vote in the 14th, and very little of that came from the city of Stockton. The city's 150,000 residents were nearly evenly split between the 14th and 18th districts.

In the new 14th agriculture is far less important than lumbering, ranching and recreation. The entire eastern flank of the long district is taken up by the Cascade and Sierra Nevada ranges, and much of the land is in the national forest system. Lake Tahoe and nearby Squaw Valley attract most of the tourist dollars.

Politically this is a marginal district. Although Democrats have a 51-38 percent registration edge, it means very little here. The district voters have an individualistic streak and resist party labels. Some of them refuse to state a party preference at all — for example, in Alpine County, 17 percent declare themselves independent, the highest such figure in the state.

In recent statewide elections, most voters have gone with the GOP. In 1980 Ronald Reagan carried all 12 counties in the district; the GOP Senate and gubernatorial candidates repeated the feat in 1982. Democratic Sen. Alan Cranston carried the district in 1980 but with only 48 percent, his poorest showing north of Los Angeles.

Election Returns

14th District		Democrat		Republican	
1976	President	77,369	(48.4%)	79,970	(50.0%)
	Senate	69,058	(42.8%)	87,026	(53.9%)
	House	110,617	(72.2%)	42,634	(27.8%)
1978	Governor	79,979	(47.7%)	70,922	(42.3%)
	House	82,303	(52.5%)	71,137	(45.4%)
1980	President	62,509	(30.8%)	117,495	(57.9%)
	Senate	94,495	(48.2%)	85,563	(43.6%)
	House	78,208	(39.3%)	109,126	(54.8%)
1982	Governor	79,979	(36.6%)	131,098	(60.0%)
	Senate	76,397	(35.3%)	128,919	(59.5%)
	House	77,400	(36.6%)	134,225	(63.4%)

Demographics

Population: 525,893. **Percent Change from 1970:** 57.5%.

Land Area: 27,376 square miles. **Population per Square Mile:** 19.2.

Counties, 1980 Population: Alpine — 1,097; Amador — 19,314; El Dorado — 85,812; Lassen — 21,661; Modoc — 8,610; Nevada — 51,645; Placer — 117,247; Plumas — 17,340; San Joaquin (Pt.) — 137,588; Shasta (Pt.) — 22,774; Sierra — 3,073; Siskiyou — 39,732.

Cities, 1980 Population: Lodi — 35,221; Roseville — 24,347; South Lake Tahoe — 20,681; Stockton (Pt.) — 67,563.

Race and Ancestry: White — 91.8%; Black — 1.1%; American Indian, Eskimo and Aleut — 1.4%; Asian and Pacific Islander — 2.5%. Spanish Origin — 6.8%. Dutch — 0.8%; English — 10.7%; French — 1.3%; German — 9.1%; Irish — 4.5%; Italian — 3.1%; Norwegian — 0.9%; Polish — 0.5%; Portuguese — 1.0%; Scottish — 0.9%; Swedish — 1.1%.

Universities, Enrollment: College of the Siskiyous, Weed — 1,312; Feather River College, Quincy — 1,108; Lake Tahoe Community College, South Lake Tahoe — 1,629; Lassen College, Susanville — 2,974; San Joaquin Delta College, Stockton — 16,460; Sierra Community College, Rocklin — 9,645; University of the Pacific, Stockton — 6,024.

Newspapers, Circulation: *The Auburn Journal* (m), Auburn — 12,868; *The Daily Tribune* (e), Roseville — 10,919; *Lodi News-Sentinel* (m), Lodi — 13,399; *Siskiyou News* (e), Yreka — 5,363; *Tahoe Daily Tribune* (e), South Lake Tahoe — 9,123; *The Union* (e), Grass Valley — 11,962. *The Sacramento Bee* and *Stockton Record* also circulate in the district.

Commercial Television Stations, Affiliation: District is divided among Chico-Redding ADI, Sacramento-Stockton ADI, Medford (Ore.) ADI and Reno (Nev.) ADI.

Military Installations: Sierra Army Depot, Herlong — 1,155; Stockton Naval Communication Station, Stockton — 511.

Industries:
The Grass Valley Group Inc.; Grass Valley; broadcasting equipment — 941. American Forest Products Co.; Martell; lumber, plywood, molding — 600. International Paper Co. (Western Region); Weed; sawmill, veneers — 600. Champion International Corp. (Champion Building Products); McCloud; sawmills — 560. General Mills Inc.; Lodi; cereal — 550. Formica Corp.; Lincoln; partitions; office, store fixtures — 500. Pacific Coast Producer; Lodi; fruit canning — 500. Shugart Associates; Roseville; computer discs — 500.

15th District

Mid-San Joaquin Valley — Modesto

State Highway 99 traverses nearly 100 miles of the level, fertile fields of the 15th District, connecting two major farm centers of the San Joaquin Valley — Modesto in the north and Fresno in the south.

In the 1970s, the district included the western half of the city of Fresno and was the most Democratic of the San Joaquin Valley districts. Having lost all but 27 residents of Fresno in the 1981 redistricting, the 15th is now only the second most Democratic.

The Democratic farmers of the Central Valley are not very loyal to their party these days, but given a choice and knowing little about either candidate, they will usually back the Democrat. That habit harks back to their political heritage in the Oklahoma dust bowl, brought with them to California more than a generation ago.

Although most of Fresno is outside the 15th, that city remains the major media center for the southern part of the district. The new 15th curves around the city from the south and takes in its outskirts on three sides. The district line around Modesto also has been altered, leaving the 15th with all but two residents of that city plus a long, thin corridor connecting Modesto to the rest of the district further south. Modesto most often is remembered for its restless teen-agers in the movie "American Graffiti" and for its large winery run by the Gallo Brothers.

Except for the population clusters at the northwest and southeast ends, the district is sparsely settled. Merced, with 36,499 people, is the only other major city. The rest of the population is scattered throughout the irrigated farm land. The eastern side of the district rises into the Sierra Nevadas, with Yosemite National Park providing some tourist-related employment.

Election Returns

15th District		Democrat		Republican	
1976	President	68,464	(51.4%)	63,101	(47.4%)
	Senate	60,030	(46.9%)	63,977	(50.0%)
	House	98,341	(71.3%)	39,517	(28.7%)
1978	Governor	65,724	(54.7%)	49,161	(40.9%)
	House	77,304	(57.9%)	55,984	(42.0%)
1980	President	62,240	(40.2%)	78,040	(50.3%)
	Senate	84,130	(57.8%)	49,601	(34.1%)
	House	103,684	(63.9%)	53,795	(33.2%)
1982	Governor	60,354	(42.2%)	78,562	(54.9%)
	Senate	55,149	(39.7%)	77,539	(55.8%)
	House	86,022	(63.7%)	45,948	(34.0%)

Demographics

Population: 525,888. **Percent Change from 1970:** 33.8%.

Land Area: 8,919 square miles. **Population per Square Mile:** 59.0.

Counties, 1980 Population: Fresno (Pt.) — 156,861; Madera — 63,116; Mariposa — 11,108; Merced — 134,560; Stanislaus (Pt.) — 160,243.

Cities, 1980 Population: Atwater — 17,530; Ceres — 13,281; Fresno (Pt.) — 27; Los Banos — 10,341; Madera — 21,732; Merced — 36,499; Modesto (Pt.) — 106,600; Reedley — 11,071; Selma — 10,942.

Race and Ancestry: White — 78.3%; Black — 2.6%; American Indian, Eskimo and Aleut — 1.1%; Asian and Pacific Islander — 2.4%. Spanish Origin — 26.8%. Dutch — 0.8%; English — 8.4%; French — 0.6%; German — 5.2%; Irish — 3.1%; Italian — 1.9%; Portuguese — 3.5%; Swedish — 0.7%.

Universities, Enrollment: Kings River Community College, Reedley — 3,346; Merced College, Merced — 7,950; Modesto Junior College, Modesto — 12,389; West Hills Community College, Coalinga — 2,420.

Newspapers, Circulation: *Madera Tribune* (e), Madera — 7,111; *Merced Sun-Star* (e), Merced — 22,075; *The Modesto Bee* (mS), Modesto — 64,001. *The Fresno Bee* also circulates in the district.

Commercial Television Stations, Affiliation: Most of the district is in Fresno ADI. A small portion is in Sacramento-Stockton ADI.

Military Installations: Castle Air Force Base, Merced — 5,824.

Industries:

Foster Poultry Farms (HQ); Livingston; poultry farming — 2,500. **E. & J. Gallo Winery Co.** (HQ); Modesto; wines, bottles — 1,800. **Doctors' Hospital of Modesto;** Modesto; hospital — 1,000. **Farmers Group Inc.;** Merced; life insurance — 1,000. **United Foods Inc.** (John Inglis Frozen Foods Div.); Modesto; frozen fruits, vegetables — 1,000.

Louis Rich Inc.; Modesto; poultry processing — 925. **Yosemite Park & Curry Co. Inc.;** Yosemite National Park; national park concessioning — 900. **J. R. Wood Inc.;** Atwater; frozen fruits, vegetables — 750. **Sun Maid Growers of California** (HQ); Kingsburg; raisins — 700. **Campbell Soup Co.** (Swanson Div.); Modesto; frozen foods — 600. **Foster Poultry Farms** (Fryer Production); Delhi; poultry processing — 600. **Fruehauf Corp.** (Liquid Bulk Tank Div.); Fresno; truck trailers — 600.

Sperry Corp. (New Holland Div.); Fowler; farm implements — 530. **Flintkote Co.** (Concrete Materials Div.); Modesto; ready-mix concrete — 500. **General Foods Corp.** (Food Products Div.); Modesto; vegetables — 500. **Keller Industries Inc.;** Merced; aluminum extrusions — 500. **Procter & Gamble Paper Products Co.;** Modesto; paper products — 500. **United Vintners Inc.;** Madera; winery — 500.

16th District

Central Coast — Salinas, Monterey

The new 16th hugs the California coast for 150 miles, living off agriculture and tourism and providing a secure political base for its Democratic incumbent.

The map in place for the 1982 elections made only one change — removal of the city of San Luis Obispo and some of the surrounding area on the south. By taking more than 67,000 residents of San Luis Obispo County out of the 16th District, the mapmakers centered the constituency even more on Monterey and Santa Cruz counties, which account for more than 90 percent of the population. Only the Morro Bay section of San Luis Obispo County remains in the new 16th District.

Although the House incumbent has gradually increased his majorities to 85 percent of the vote in 1982, the district is marginal in other contests. Ronald Reagan carried the area of the new 16th in 1980 with just under 49 percent of the vote; in 1976, Jimmy Carter drew just over 50 percent.

Monterey Bay at the northern end of the district, is one of Northern California's favorite playgrounds, with a wide variety of the state's lifestyles visible along its shores. A vibrant counterculture has emerged in Santa Cruz on the northern side of the bay. Young residents have been drawn to the area by the permissive atmosphere at the University

of California campus in Santa Cruz at the northern side of the bay.

Further south along the bay are Castroville, the artichoke capital of the world and Fort Ord, a major military installation that employs a large civilian work force.

Liberal Democrats and upper-income Republicans live just south of the bay on the luxuriant and exclusive Monterey Peninsula. A little further south is Big Sur, another gathering place for the mellow. And at the southern end of the district is San Simeon, the opulent mansion that newspaper magnate William Randolph Hearst built.

The areas contained in the 16th District are not all fun and games, as John Steinbeck and William Saroyan have illustrated in their novels and plays. The fishing industry, popularized in Steinbeck's *Cannery Row,* provides many of the jobs along the coast. Inland, agriculture is king, particularly around Salinas, which, with more than 80,000 inhabitants, is the largest city in the district. Although Democrats have the registration advantage in Salinas, the city favored Republican presidential candidates in 1980 and the three preceding elections.

Election Returns

16th District		Democrat		Republican	
1976	President	78,244	(50.2%)	75,211	(48.3%)
	Senate	69,365	(44.6%)	81,114	(52.1%)
	House	86,614	(53.5%)	75,248	(46.5%)
1978	Governor	77,936	(56.7%)	52,442	(38.1%)
	House	87,258	(62.6%)	52,051	(37.4%)
1980	President	64,704	(35.5%)	87,639	(48.7%)
	Senate	111,435	(63.7%)	50,696	(29.0%)
	House	130,472	(72.4%)	41,554	(23.1%)
1982	Governor	91,478	(52.4%)	76,112	(43.6%)
	Senate	77,053	(44.5%)	87,070	(50.3%)
	House	142,630	(85.4%)	24,448	(14.6%)

Demographics

Population: 525,893. **Percent Change from 1970:** 30.6%.

Land Area: 5,540 square miles. **Population per Square Mile:** 94.9.

Counties, 1980 Population: Monterey — 290,444; San Benito — 25,005; San Luis Obispo (Pt.) — 22,303; Santa Cruz — 188,141.

Cities, 1980 Population: Atascadero (Pt.) — 0; Hollister — 11,488; Marina — 20,647; Monterey — 27,558; Pacific Grove — 15,755; Salinas — 80,479; Santa Cruz — 41,483; Seaside — 36,567; Watsonville — 23,543.

Race and Ancestry: White — 76.6%; Black — 3.9%; American Indian, Eskimo and Aleut — 0.9%; Asian and Pacific Islander — 5.0%. Spanish Origin — 21.9%. English — 8.7%; French — 0.8%; German — 4.8%; Irish — 3.0%; Italian — 2.7%; Norwegian — 0.5%; Polish — 0.5%; Portuguese — 1.4%; Scottish — 0.6%; Swedish — 0.7%.

Universities, Enrollment: Bethany Bible College, Santa Cruz — 594; Cabrillo College, Aptos — 10,919; Hartnell College, Salinas — 7,375; Monterey Institute of International Studies, Monterey — 462; Monterey Peninsula College, Monterey — 6,617; Naval Postgraduate School, Monterey — 1,184; University of California at Santa Cruz, Santa Cruz — 6,472.

Newspapers, Circulation: *Evening Free Lance* (e), Hollister — 4,872; *Monterey Peninsula Herald* (eS), Monterey — 31,755; *Register-Pajaronian & Sun* (e), Watsonville — 12,479; *Salinas Californian* (e), Salinas — 24,911; *Santa Cruz Sentinel* (eS), Santa Cruz — 26,431.

The *San Luis Obispo County Telegram-Tribune* also circulates in the district.

Commercial Television Stations, Affiliation: KCBA, Salinas (None); KMST, Monterey (CBS); KSBW-TV, Salinas (NBC). Most of district is in Salinas-Monterey ADI. Portion is in Santa Barbara-Maria-San Luis Obispo ADI.

Military Installations: Fort Hunter Liggett, Jolon — 1,343; Fort Ord, Seaside — 19,317; Point Sur Naval Facility, Big Sur — 126; Presidio of Monterey (Army), Monterey — 3,852.

Industries:

Watsonville Canning & Frozen Foods Co. Inc.; Watsonville; frozen vegtables — 1,800. **D'Arrigo Bros. Co. of California** (HQ); Salinas; vegetable farming, packing, shipping — 800. **Amstar Corp.** (Spreckels Sugar Div.); Spreckels; beet sugar — 750. **Green Giant Co.;** Watsonville; frozen vegetables — 750. **Golden Gate Airlines USA Inc.;** Monterey; commercial airline — 730.

Texaco Inc.; San Ardo; oil production — 700. **McCormick Co. Inc.** (Grocery Products Div.); Salinas; spices — 600. **Plantronics Inc.;** Santa Cruz; telecommunications equipment — 585. **Growers Exchange Inc.;** Salinas; vegetable farming, packing — 550. **Pebble Beach Corp.;** Pacific Grove; resort hotel; golf course — 500.

17th District

Southern San Joaquin Valley

The 17th District is the food basket of the nation's most agriculturally productive state. Driving the length of the district from Fresno in the north to Bakersfield in the south, a traveler encounters virtually every kind of fruit and vegetable grown in the Temperate Zone.

Although parts of both Fresno and Bakersfield are in the new district, the majority of the population resides in smaller communities — dusty crossroads towns such as Pixley and Terra Bella, or small-scale farm centers such as Tulare and Visalia — all with fewer than 50,000 people.

The irrigated farm land stretches almost to the eastern border of the district, where the Sierra Nevada Mountains climb steeply into Sequoia National Park. The mountains attract some recreational dollars to the district, but in minuscule amounts compared with the valley's farm income.

The farmers and those whose livelihoods depend on the farm economy register as Democrats. More often than not, however, they vote Republican. Ronald Reagan and Gerald R. Ford both carried the area in the new 17th. The only major statewide Democrat to win this district in recent years was Edmund G. Brown Jr. when he was running for governor. As a Senate candidate in 1982, even Brown was demolished, winning less than 40 percent of the vote.

To wage an effective campaign in the district a candidate must have the financial resources to compete in two television markets and, above all, to attract support in the district's agribusiness community. The Republican House incumbent has been able to do that, making the huge Democratic registration advantage irrelevant, at least for the time being.

Overpopulated by nearly 80,000, the old 17th lost some densely settled parts of Fresno County (it retained the wealthier northeastern side of Fresno), and gained some lightly populated areas in Tulare County and the northern sector of Kern County, as far south as Bakersfield. More than a fourth of the new district's residents are of Spanish origin.

Election Returns

17th District		Democrat		Republican	
1976	President	59,227	(47.2%)	65,286	(52.0%)
	Senate	55,028	(44.8%)	64,373	(52.5%)
	House	74,577	(59.6%)	50,478	(40.4%)
1978	Governor	59,180	(50.8%)	50,970	(43.8%)
	House	52,115	(43.4%)	67,934	(56.6%)
1980	President	53,235	(37.1%)	80,523	(56.1%)
	Senate	81,424	(58.1%)	51,239	(36.5%)
	House	43,893	(29.7%)	103,789	(70.3%)
1982	Governor	64,952	(42.9%)	83,170	(54.9%)
	Senate	55,987	(37.2%)	88,737	(59.0%)
	House	68,364	(46.0%)	80,271	(54.0%)

Demographics

Population: 524,790. **Percent Change from 1970:** 39.4%.

Land Area: 10,051 square miles. **Population per Square Mile:** 52.2.

Counties, 1980 Population: Fresno (Pt.) — 103,381; Kern (Pt.) — 101,933; Kings — 73,738; Tulare — 245,738.

Cities, 1980 Population: Bakersfield (Pt.) — 30; Clovis — 33,021; Delano — 16,491; Fresno (Pt.) — 38,978; Hanford — 20,958; Porterville — 19,707; Tulare — 22,526; Visalia — 49,729.

Race and Ancestry: White — 73.4%; Black — 2.8%; American Indian, Eskimo and Aleut — 1.1%; Asian and Pacific Islander — 2.8%. Spanish Origin — 28.3%. Dutch — 0.7%; English — 9.5%; French — 0.7%; German — 4.8%; Irish — 2.9%; Italian — 1.2%; Portuguese — 2.5%; Swedish — 0.5%.

Universities, Enrollment: California State University at Fresno, Fresno — 16,227; College of the Sequoias, Visalia — 7,556; Porterville College, Porterville — 2,283; West Coast Christian College, Fresno — 207.

Newspapers, Circulation: *Advance-Register & Times* (e), Tulare — 8,810; *The Hanford Sentinel* (e), Hanford — 11,252; *Recorder* (e), Porterville — 12,295; *Visalia Times-Delta* (e), Visalia — 19,772. *The Bakersfield Californian* and *Fresno Bee* also circulate in the district.

Commercial Television Stations, Affiliation: KAIL, Clovis (None); KFTV, Hanford (None); KJEO, Fresno (ABC); KMPH, Visalia (None). Most of district is in Fresno ADI. Portion is located in Bakersfield ADI. *(For other Fresno stations, see 18th district.)*

Military Installations: Lemoore Naval Air Station, Lemoore — 5,811.

Industries:

Porterville State Hospital; Porterville; hospital — 1,900. **St. Agnes Hospital Inc.** (HQ); Fresno; hospital — 1,270. **Armstrong Rubber Co.** (Pacific Coast Div.); Hanford; tires — 800. **Giumarra Vineyards Corp.;** Edison; winery — 700. **Dixie Yarns Inc.** (Candlewick Yarns); Lemoore; yarn mills — 580. **Mike Yurosek & Son Inc.;** Lamont; vegetable farming — 550. **Beckman Instruments Inc.;** Porterville; electronic devices — 500.

18th District

Central Valley — Fresno

Like most of the districts drawn by Phillip Burton with particular candidates in mind, the new 18th has a very strange shape. If it were placed on its side, with the California-Nevada border as its base, it would look like a dragon.

The body of the dragon is found in three whole counties — Mono, Tuolumne and Calaveras. These counties often vote Republican but they have little impact on the political outcome of the district. Located high in the Sierra Nevadas, they have no population centers and account for less than one-eighth of the vote.

The political purpose of the dragon's body is to connect two Democratic farming centers. The larger of the two, Fresno, is found at the end of the dragon's long, thin southern neck. It is the home base of the Democrat that Burton's map helped propel into the U.S. House in 1982.

The other city, Stockton, is located in the dragon's tail. By joining these two distant sections of the Central Valley, Burton was able to come up with a wholly new Democratic district. The registration advantage is more than 2-to-1.

With a population of 218,000, Fresno is one of the most important agribusiness centers in the nation. While small portions of the city are in the 15th and 17th districts, nearly 180,000 Fresno residents are in the 18th. Although Fresno supported Ronald Reagan in 1980, it backs Democrats in most elections. Jimmy Carter defeated Gerald R. Ford there in 1976, and George McGovern carried it over Richard Nixon in 1972.

Stockton, in San Joaquin County, is split between the 18th and 14th districts, although the 18th has the larger portion. This city, too, is Democratic, but slightly less so than Fresno. In his two successful gubernatorial bids, Edmund G. Brown Jr. ran up healthy majorities in San Joaquin although his vote plummeted in his unsuccessful 1982 bid for the Senate. The major farm areas in the district are in the southern and eastern parts of San Joaquin County near Stockton.

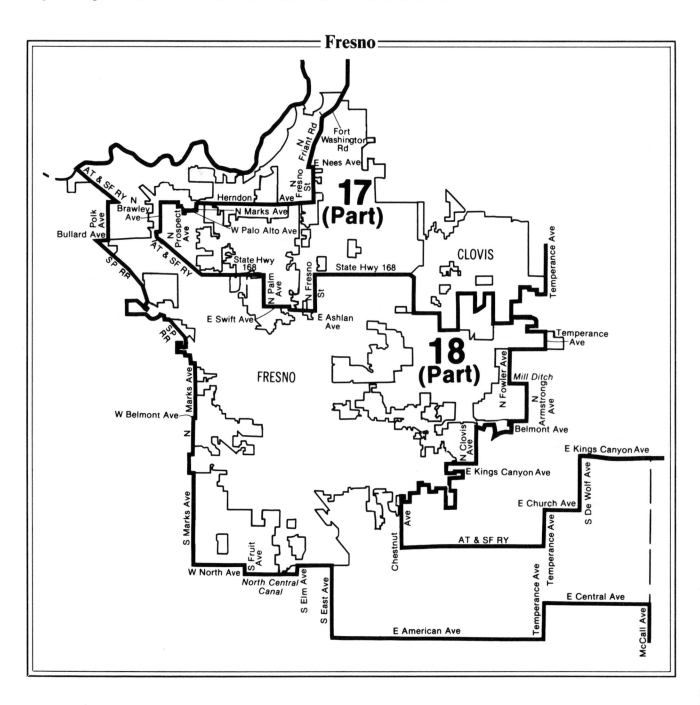

Fresno

Stockton and Fresno are 115 miles apart and are served by different media markets. Most of the land in between is in the 15th District, not the 18th. This is not an easy district to campaign in, but one issue — farm policy — unites the voters at both ends of the district.

Election Returns

18th District		Democrat		Republican	
1976	President	81,958	(55.2%)	65,043	(43.8%)
	Senate	73,037	(50.3%)	68,333	(47.0%)
	House	97,578	(71.8%)	38,340	(28.2%)
1978	Governor	79,019	(59.7%)	46,783	(35.3%)
	House	63,730	(47.3%)	67,894	(50.4%)
1980	President	68,985	(43.2%)	75,812	(47.5%)
	Senate	94,619	(61.2%)	50,261	(32.5%)
	House	61,775	(37.8%)	98,510	(60.2%)
1982	Governor	74,932	(45.9%)	82,822	(50.8%)
	Senate	76,304	(47.2%)	77,863	(48.2%)
	House	92,762	(59.5%)	59,664	(38.3%)

Demographics

Population: 527,348. **Percent Change from 1970:** 13.4%.

Land Area: 8,763 square miles. **Population per Square Mile:** 60.2.

Counties, 1980 Population: Calaveras — 20,710; Fresno (Pt.) — 254,379; Mono — 8,577; San Joaquin (Pt.) — 209,754; Tuolumne — 33,928.

Cities, 1980 Population: Fresno (Pt.) — 179,197; Manteca — 24,925; Sanger — 12,542; Stockton (Pt.) — 82,216; Tracy — 18,428.

Race and Ancestry: White — 73.4%; Black — 7.2%; American Indian, Eskimo and Aleut — 1.2%; Asian and Pacific Islander — 3.7%. Spanish Origin — 24.3%. Dutch — 0.9%; English — 8.0%; French — 0.8%; German — 5.7%; Irish — 3.1%; Italian — 2.6%; Portuguese — 1.4%; Scottish — 0.5%; Swedish — 0.7%.

Universities, Enrollment: California School of Professional Psychology at Fresno, Fresno — 158; Columbia College, Columbia — 3,057; Fresno City College, Fresno — 14,989; Fresno Pacific College, Fresno — 734; Humphreys College, Stockton — 255; Mennonite Brethren Biblical Seminary, Fresno — 141.

Newspapers, Circulation: *The Fresno Bee* (mS), Fresno — 127,076; *Manteca Bulletin* (mS), Manteca — 6,021; *Stockton Record* (eS), Stockton — 56,342; *The Union-Democrat* (e), Sonora — 8,498.

Commercial Television Stations, Affiliation: KFSN-TV, Fresno (CBS); KOVR, Stockton (ABC); KSEE, Fresno (NBC). District is divided between Fresno ADI and Sacramento-Stockton ADI. *(For other Fresno stations, see 17th district.)*

Military Installations: Sharpe Army Depot, Lathrop — 1,855; Tracy Defense Depot, Tracy — 1,571.

Industries:

Fresno Community Hospital & Medical Center (HQ); Fresno; hospital — 2,000. **Seabrook Foods Inc.** (Farms Div.); Sanger; vegetable farming — 2,000. **Valley Medical Center;** Fresno; hospital — 1,600. **Stockton State Hospital;** Stockton; state psychiatric hospital — 1,100. **Rich Products Corp.;** Escalon; strawberries — 1,000.

Libbey-Owens-Ford Co.; Lathrop; glass — 900. **E. Gottschalk & Co. Inc.** (HQ); Fresno; department store chain — 600. **McClatchy Newspapers;** Fresno; newspaper publishing — 600. **Owens-Illinois Inc.;** Tracy; glass containers — 600. **American Patrol Service Inc.** Stockton; security services — 550. **Troy Gold Industries Ltd.;** West Point; gold mining — 504. **American Forest Products Co.;** Stockton; sawmill — 500.

Atchison, Topeka and Santa Fe Railway Co.; Fresno; railroad operations — 500. **H. J. Heinz Co.;** Tracy; canned food — 500. **Louisiana-Pacific Corp.;** Standard; lumber, plywood — 500. **Occidental Petroleum Corp.** (Occidental Chemical Co.); Lathrop; agricultural chemicals — 500. **Ogden Food Products Corp.** (Tillie Lewis Div. - HQ); Stockton; fruit, vegetable canning — 500. **Riverbend Farms Inc.;** Sanger; citrus fruit — 500.

19th District

South Central Coast — Oxnard, Santa Barbara

Lying just beyond the northern fringe of metropolitan Los Angeles, the 19th has the potential to elect a Democrat to Congress. As long as the popular Republican incumbent, who won a fifth term in 1982, remains on the ballot, the district should stay firmly in the GOP column.

Democratic votes are found in the city of Santa Barbara, which has a large University of California campus, and in the Mexican-American community in Oxnard. Democrat Edmund G. Brown Jr. won the district in his 1978 gubernatorial campaign, and Democratic Sen. Alan Cranston carried it two years later. In 1982, however, it went Republican for U.S. Senate.

As drawn for the 1982 elections, the 19th District was contained in just two counties — Santa Barbara County, which accounted for slightly less than 60 percent of the vote, and the northern and western parts of Ventura County. The lightly populated southern portion of San Luis Obispo County, which had been in the district since 1974, was removed with little anticipated political impact. The district line cutting through Oxnard was altered slightly, but the differences there were likely to be inconsequential.

There are strong political, economic and social divisions within the 19th. The affluent Santa Barbara voters whose hillside homes overlook offshore oil rigs tend to place environmental issues at the top of their priority lists.

The oil workers of Oxnard, the ranchers in the foothills of the Coastal Range and the military families near Vandenberg Air Force Base are more interested in economic growth. A ballot proposition in 1980 authorizing the state of California to buy land around Lake Tahoe to preserve its scenic beauty was supported by 60 percent of the voters in Santa Barbara and rejected by 60 percent in Oxnard.

Election Returns

19th District		Democrat		Republican	
1976	President	84,000	(48.4%)	85,819	(49.4%)
	Senate	83,654	(48.3%)	84,980	(49.1%)
	House	62,657	(35.2%)	115,134	(64.8%)
1978	Governor	90,998	(58.1%)	55,600	(35.5%)
	House	39,649	(25.0%)	112,682	(71.1%)
1980	President	63,939	(33.8%)	100,387	(53.0%)
	Senate	107,095	(58.0%)	65,879	(35.7%)
	House	34,170	(17.7%)	149,858	(77.6%)
1982	Governor	92,038	(49.4%)	90,128	(48.3%)
	Senate	79,320	(42.9%)	98,936	(53.5%)
	House	66,042	(35.8%)	112,486	(61.1%)

Demographics

Population: 526,068. **Percent Change from 1970:** 17.3%.

Land Area: 3,997 square miles. **Population per Square Mile:** 131.6.

Counties, 1980 Population: Santa Barbara — 298,694; Ventura (Pt.) — 227,374.

Cities, 1980 Population: Carpinteria — 10,835; Lompoc — 26,267; Oxnard (Pt.) — 90,972; San Buenaventura (Ventura) — 74,393; Santa Barbara — 74,414; Santa Maria — 39,685; Santa Paula — 20,552.

Race and Ancestry: White — 77.1%; Black — 2.8%; American Indian, Eskimo and Aleut — 1.0%; Asian and Pacific Islander — 3.2%. Spanish Origin — 25.2%. Dutch — 0.6%; English — 8.5%; French — 0.9%; German — 5.1%; Irish — 3.1%; Italian — 1.6%; Norwegian — 0.6%; Polish — 0.6%; Scottish — 0.7%; Swedish — 0.7%.

Universities, Enrollment: Allan Hancock College, Santa Maria — 8,733; Brooks Institute, Santa Barbara — 792; Oxnard College, Oxnard — 5,772; Santa Barbara City College, Santa Barbara — 9,735; Thomas Aquinas College, Santa Paula — 120; University of California at Santa Barbara, Santa Barbara — 14,451; Ventura College, Ventura — 12,843; Westmont College, Santa Barbara — 1,077.

Newspapers, Circulation: *Daily Chronicle* (e), Santa Paula — 2,499; *Lompoc Record* (e), Lompoc — 9,371; *The Press-Courier* (eS), Oxnard — 20,312; *Santa Barbara News-Press* (eS), Santa Barbara — 46,014; *Star-Free Press* (eS), Ventura — 59,468; *Times* (e), Santa Maria — 18,309. The *Los Angeles Times, Los Angeles Herald Examiner* and Thousand Oaks *News Chronicle* also circulate in the district.

Commercial Television Stations, Affiliation: KCOY-TV, Santa Maria (CBS); KEYT, Santa Barbara (ABC). District is divided between Santa Barbara-Maria-San Luis Obispo ADI and Los Angeles ADI.

Military Installations: Vandenberg Air Force Base, Lompoc — 7,486.

Industries:

Santa Barbara Research Center; Goleta; applied electronic research — 2,000. **Santa Barbara Cottage Hospital;** Santa Barbara; hospital — 1,700. **Mission Industries** (HQ); Santa Barbara; industrial launderers — 1,650. **Raytheon Co.** (Electromagnetic Systems Div.); Goleta; electronic communications equipment — 1,570. **Federal Electric Corp.;** Lompoc; telephone communications services — 1,310.

Bud Antle Inc.; Oxnard; fruit farming, wholesaling — 1,000. **General Motors Corp.** (Delco Electronics); Goleta; electronic components — 980. **Vetco Inc.** (HQ); Ventura; oil field machinery, services — 900. **Saticoy Lemon Assn. Inc.;** Santa Paula; lemons — 850. **Vetco Inc.;** Ventura; oil field machinery — 800. **Applied Magnetics Corp.** (HQ); Goleta; electronic computing equipment — 700. **Burroughs Corp.;** Goleta; electronic computing equipment — 700. **Becton Dickinson & Co.** (Falcon Labware Div.); Oxnard; fabricated rubber products — 630.

Dalgety Foods Inc.; Santa Maria; frozen fruit, vegetables — 600. **Piper Aircraft Corp.;** Santa Maria; airport operations — 600. **Johns-Manville Sales Corp.;** Lompoc; non-metallic minerals — 595. **CBS Inc.;** Santa Maria; records — 500. **Gould Inc.** (Measuring Instruments); Oxnard; medical monitoring systems — 500. **Information Magnetics Corp.;** Goleta; magnetic disc equipment — 500. **Ventura Coastal Corp.** (Coastal Lemon Co. - HQ); Ventura; fresh, frozen lemons — 500.

20th District

Bakersfield, Lancaster, San Luis Obispo

Crossing the 20th District from east to west is like riding a roller coaster across half of Southern California. Beginning in the mountains at the southern end of the Sierra Nevada range, the district drawn for the 1982 elections dips down to Bakersfield in the central valley and then lifts up again across the Coastal Range before plunging to the Pacific Ocean around Pismo Beach in San Luis Obispo County.

Politically, however, there is not much variety in this area. It is uniformly conservative. Although registered Democrats outnumber Republicans by 48 percent to 41 percent, most of the district's voters, whether Republican or Democrat, share conservative views.

The new 20th is less agricultural than the district it replaced. It lost the Central Valley portion of Tulare County and much of the farm land in Kern County, including Delano, the one-time center of Cesar Chavez's United Farm Workers organization. In exchange, it picked up most of hilly San Luis Obispo County to the west, an area which has little in common with the Central Valley. Nonetheless, the real political power in the district still resides in the agribusiness community, outspoken in its conservative views, and the aerospace industry.

Bakersfield remains the political core of the district. All but 30 residents of this booming city of 106,000 were put in the 20th. Bakersfield has a Southern flavor, a legacy of the Texans and Oklahomans who moved there a generation ago to work in oil-related jobs.

The most conservative — and most Republican — section of the district is the remote northern end of Los Angeles County in the Antelope Valley. The communities of Lancaster and Palmdale are closer in spirit to Bakersfield than to the city of Los Angeles, and almost as close in miles. Separated from Los Angeles by the San Gabriel Mountains, the Antelope Valley relies economically on the aerospace industry that has developed around nearby Edwards Air Force Base.

Election Returns

20th District		Democrat		Republican	
1976	President	65,739	(42.9%)	85,383	(55.7%)
	Senate	60,507	(41.3%)	82,426	(56.2%)
	House	64,556	(40.0%)	96,889	(60.0%)
1978	Governor	68,479	(47.7%)	61,175	(42.6%)
	House	62,466	(42.4%)	84,606	(57.4%)
1980	President	51,337	(28.6%)	110,892	(61.8%)
	Senate	92,715	(52.7%)	70,583	(40.1%)
	House	67,466	(36.0%)	117,385	(62.6%)
1982	Governor	74,606	(39.7%)	109,269	(58.1%)
	Senate	60,329	(32.4%)	118,160	(63.4%)
	House	57,769	(31.9%)	123,312	(68.1%)

Demographics

Population: 525,894. **Percent Change from 1970:** 21.7%.

Land Area: 8,864 square miles. **Population per Square Mile:** 59.3.

Counties, 1980 Population: Kern (Pt.) — 301,156; Los Angeles (Pt.) — 91,606; San Luis Obispo (Pt.) — 133,132.

Cities, 1980 Population: Arroyo Grande — 11,290; Atascadero (Pt.) — 16,232; Bakersfield (Pt.) — 105,581; Lancaster — 48,027; Palmdale — 12,277; Ridgecrest — 15,929; San Luis Obispo — 34,252.

Race and Ancestry: White — 85.8%; Black — 4.0%; American Indian, Eskimo and Aleut — 1.4%; Asian and Pacific Islander — 1.8%. Spanish Origin — 11.9%. Dutch — 0.6%; English — 11.0%; French — 1.1%; German — 5.8%; Irish — 3.7%; Italian — 1.4%; Norwegian — 0.5%; Portuguese — 0.6%; Scottish — 0.6%; Swedish — 0.7%.

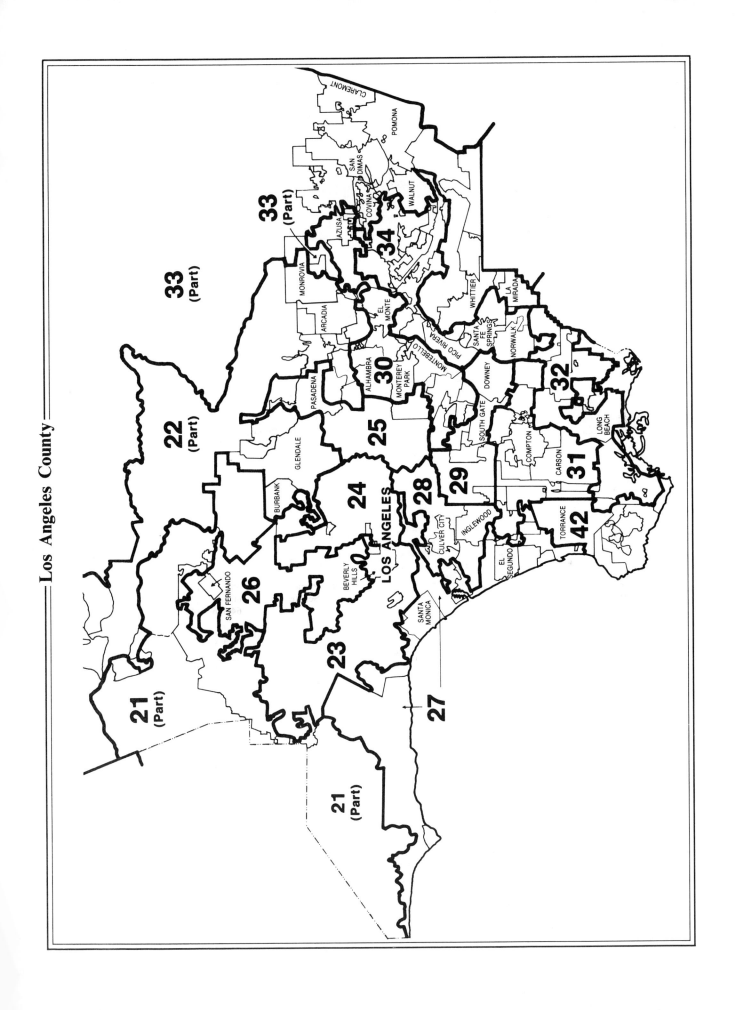

Los Angeles County

Universities, Enrollment: Antelope Valley College, Lancaster — 6,980; Bakersfield College, Bakersfield — 13,565; California Polytechnic State University at San Luis Obispo, San Luis Obispo — 16,048; California State College at Bakersfield, Bakersfield — 2,854; Cerro Coso Community College, Ridgecrest — 4,218; Cuesta College, San Luis Obispo — 5,848; Taft College, Taft — 1,192.

Newspapers, Circulation: *Antelope Valley Ledger-Gazette* (e), Lancaster — 8,693; *The Bakersfield Californian* (mS), Bakersfield — 70,048; *The Daily Independent* (e), Ridgecrest — 6,511; *Daily Midway Driller* (e), Taft — 4,091; *The Daily Press* (e), Paso Robles — 4,517; *San Luis Obispo County Telegram-Tribune* (e), San Luis Obispo — 24,914. The *Los Angeles Times* and *Los Angeles Herald Examiner* also circulate in the district.

Commercial Television Stations, Affiliation: KBAK-TV, Bakersfield (ABC); KERO-TV, Bakersfield (NBC); KPWR-TV, Bakersfield (CBS); KSBY-TV, San Luis Obispo (NBC). District is divided among Santa Barbara-Maria-San Luis Obispo ADI, Bakersfield ADI and Los Angeles ADI.

Military Installations: Camp Roberts, San Miguel — 1,435; Edwards Air Force Base, Rosamond — 6,119.

Nuclear Power Plants: Diablo Canyon 1 and 2, San Luis Obispo (Westinghouse, Pacific Gas & Electric).

Industries:

Rockwell International Corp. (North American Aircraft Operations); Palmdale; aircraft parts — 2,200. **Camarillo State Hospital;** Camarillo; hospital — 1,900. **United States Borax & Chemical Corp.;** Boron; sodium processing — 900. **Getty Oil Co.;** Bakersfield; oil and gas — 750. **Chevron USA Inc.;** Bakersfield; oil refining — 700. **Tenneco West Inc.** (HQ); Bakersfield; grape, date, nut farming — 600. **CTS Keene Inc.;** Paso Robles; electronic components — 500. **Occidental Peruana Inc.;** Bakersfield; oil exploration — 500.

21st District

Part of Ventura County; Western San Fernando Valley

No other part of the state embraced the 1978 property tax revolt — Proposition 13 — with as much fervor as the territory in the new 21st. Fully 82 percent of the voters in this collection of far-removed Los Angeles suburbs supported Howard Jarvis' plan to slash property taxes in half.

People in the Ventura County suburbs of Thousand Oaks and Simi Valley and the affluent Los Angeles County suburbs of Chatsworth and Hidden Valley were ripe for Jarvis' brand of government reform. For the most part they make a comfortable living, own well-landscaped homes and do not need the kinds of government services that have

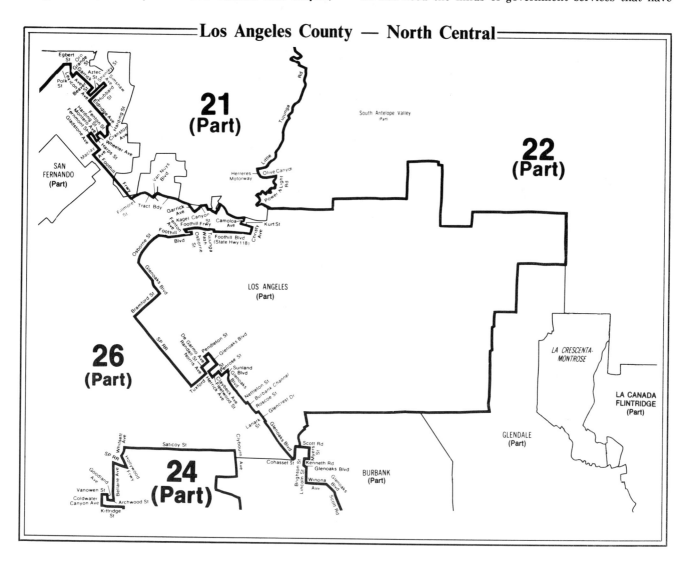

Los Angeles County — North Central

started to disappear as a result of the passage of Proposition 13.

The camel-shaped 21st District rides over the heart of the hot, flat San Fernando Valley, with the hump sitting in the foothills of the San Gabriel Mountains. The new 21st was drawn that way to incorporate staunch GOP areas at both ends of the valley while leaving out enough Democrats to populate two Democratic districts in between. The 21st District in place for the 1982 elections took in much of the old 20th District, including the entire Ventura County portion. Carried over from the old 21st were part of Van Nuys, Lakeview Terrace, Granada Hills and Selmar.

This is the kind of district where the Republican candidate with the strongest conservative credentials normally wins. In 1978, the area favored the bombastic law-and-order candidate, Ed Davis, over several more moderate contenders in the Republican gubernatorial primary.

Once nominated here, any Republican candidate is a likely winner. The area within the new 21st gave Jimmy Carter only 25 percent of the vote in 1980 and supported the weak GOP Senate candidate, Paul Gann. This is one of only six districts in the state where registered Republicans outnumber registered Democrats.

Election Returns

21st District		Democrat		Republican	
1976	President	65,665	(39.1%)	99,783	(59.4%)
	Senate	61,569	(38.9%)	93,474	(59.0%)
	House	58,911	(36.0%)	104,097	(63.6%)
1978	Governor	72,304	(46.4%)	71,211	(45.7%)
	House	52,032	(35.4%)	94,102	(63.9%)
1980	President	50,364	(25.1%)	129,662	(64.6%)
	Senate	90,348	(45.9%)	95,757	(48.6%)
	House	38,816	(20.1%)	146,298	(75.9%)
1982	Governor	75,755	(37.7%)	120,738	(60.2%)
	Senate	64,638	(32.5%)	128,181	(64.4%)
	House	46,412	(24.1%)	138,474	(71.8%)

Demographics

Population: 524,977. **Percent Change from 1970:** 37.4%.

Land Area: 906 square miles. **Population per Square Mile:** 579.4.

Counties, 1980 Population: Los Angeles (Pt.) — 223,177; Ventura (Pt.) — 301,800.

Cities, 1980 Population: Camarillo — 37,797; Los Angeles (Pt.) — 177,471; Oxnard (Pt.) — 17,223; Port Hueneme — 17,803; Simi Valley — 77,500; Thousand Oaks — 77,072.

Race and Ancestry: White — 89.6%; Black — 1.5%; American Indian, Eskimo and Aleut — 0.7%; Asian and Pacific Islander — 3.4%. Spanish Origin — 10.2%. Dutch — 0.7%; English — 8.9%; French — 1.0%; German — 6.2%; Hungarian — 0.5%; Irish — 3.6%; Italian — 3.0%; Norwegian — 0.7%; Polish — 1.2%; Russian — 1.6%; Scottish — 0.8%; Swedish — 0.8%.

Universities, Enrollment: California Institute of the Arts, Valencia — 797; California Lutheran College, Thousand Oaks — 2,636; College of the Canyons, Valencia — 3,673; Los Angeles Baptist College, Newhall — 349; Moorpark College, Moorpark — 9,361; Saint John's College, Camarillo — 190; Saint John's Seminary, Camarillo — 110.

Newspapers, Circulation: *The Camarillo Daily News* (mS), Camarillo — 9,183; *The Enterprise Sun & News* (eS), Simi Valley — 13,231; *News Chronicle* (eS), Thousand Oaks — 59,468. The *Los Angeles Times* and *Los Angeles Herald Examiner* also circulate in the district.

Commercial Television Stations, Affiliation: Entire district is in Los Angeles ADI.

Military Installations: Pacific Missile Test Center, Point Mugu — 8,588; Port Hueneme Naval Construction Battalion Center, Port Hueneme — 6,966.

Industries:

Hughes Aircraft Co. (Missile Systems Group); Canoga Park; research — 3,500. **Pertec Computer Corp.** (Peripheral Equipment Div.); Chatsworth; electronic computing equipment — 1,500. **Rockwell International Corp.** (Atomics International Div.); Canoga Park; research — 1,400. **State Farm Mutual Auto Insurance Companies;** Thousand Oaks; auto insurance — 1,380. **Olive View Medical Center;** Van Nuys; hospital — 1,200.

Bunker Ramo Corp. (Electronic Systems Div.); Thousand Oaks; electronic components — 1,000. **Burroughs Corp.;** Thousand Oaks; electronic computing equipment — 1,000. **Tandon Corp.** (HQ); Chatsworth; electronic components — 1,000. **Teledyne Industries Inc.** (Teledyne Systems); Northridge; electronic components — 1,000. **Abex Corp.** (Aerospace Div.); Oxnard; hydraulic pumps — 866. **Power-One Inc.;** Camarillo; electronic components — 850. **Minnesota Mining & Mfg. Co.;** Camarillo; data recording services — 800. **Northrop Corp.;** Newbury Park; target drones — 800. **Allegretti & Co.** (HQ); Chatsworth; electric yard equipment — 750. **Riker Laboratories Inc.** (HQ); Northridge; pharmaceuticals — 750.

Union Bank; Simi Valley; banking — 714. **C. E. Miller Corp.;** Port Hueneme; industrial machinery — 700. **Autologic Inc.** (HQ); Newbury Park; computerized photography equipment — 600. **Deluxe Check Printers Inc.;** Chatsworth; commercial printing — 600. **Viking Connectors;** Chatsworth; wiring devices — 600. **Litton Industries** (Aero Product Div.); Calabassas; aerospace systems — 580. **Scepter Mfg. Co.;** Simi Valley; plastic — 550. **Arco Solar Inc.;** Chatsworth; photovoltaic panels — 500. **Minnesota Mining & Mfg. Co.** (Mincom Div.); Camarillo; electronic computing equipment — 500. **Superscope Inc.** (HQ); Chatsworth; audio equipment — 500.

22nd District

Northern Los Angeles Suburbs; Glendale

By almost any standard of measurement, this is the most Republican district in California. It has the highest percentage of registered Republicans — 54 percent, compared to 38 percent registered Democrats. It is the only district that gave GOP gubernatorial candidate Evelle Younger a majority against Democratic Gov. Edmund G. Brown Jr. in 1978. Even the lackluster GOP Senate candidate Paul Gann picked up 54 percent of the vote here against Democratic incumbent Alan Cranston in 1980.

As redrawn by the state Legislature for 1982, the 22nd combined the old 22nd and 26th districts, both represented by conservative Republicans. The blue-collar communities at the far ends of each district were shaved off, leaving the most affluent parts in the 22nd. The result is a safe Republican district Democrats may as well ignore.

Burbank and Pasadena both were divided between two districts. The more Republican parts of both communities are in the 22nd. The middle-class black and Mexican-American areas of Pasadena have been pushed into the heavily Hispanic 25th; the infamous "beautiful downtown Burbank" is in the new 26th District.

The quiet bedroom community of Glendale is the largest town located entirely within the district. It overwhelmingly supports the Republican incumbent. The vote for Republicans is equally enthusiastic in San Marino, an exclusive community named for the tiny European republic whose main industry is postage stamps. Four out of five voters here are registered Republicans.

Arcadia and South Pasadena are only a rung or two down on the socio-economic ladder. Another step lower are Temple City, Sierra Madre and Monrovia — comfortable middle-to-upper-middle-class bedroom communities.

Election Returns

22nd District		Democrat		Republican	
1976	President	69,734	(31.6%)	146,518	(66.4%)
	Senate	60,044	(32.3%)	121,989	(65.6%)
	House	73,132	(36.4%)	127,813	(63.6%)
1978	Governor	75,764	(40.0%)	99,225	(52.4%)
	House	39,688	(25.4%)	116,856	(74.6%)
1980	President	50,520	(23.2%)	147,114	(67.5%)
	Senate	86,377	(40.8%)	114,619	(54.2%)
	House	57,620	(29.4%)	129,763	(66.2%)
1982	Governor	69,106	(33.0%)	136,139	(65.1%)
	Senate	60,779	(29.2%)	141,807	(68.1%)
	House	46,521	(23.5%)	145,831	(73.6%)

Demographics

Population: 526,566. **Percent Change from 1970:** 7.3%.

Land Area: 1,040 square miles. **Population per Square Mile:** 506.3.

Counties, 1980 Population: Los Angeles (Pt.) — 526,566.

Cities, 1980 Population: Arcadia — 45,994; Burbank (Pt.) — 37,979; Duarte (Pt.) — 0; Glendale — 139,060; La Canada Flintridge — 20,153; Monrovia — 30,531; Pasadena (Pt.) — 52,259; San Marino 13,307; Sierra Madre — 10,837; South Pasadena — 22,681; Temple City — 28,972;

Race and Ancestry: White — 87.9%; Black — 2.1%; American Indian, Eskimo and Aleut — 0.5%; Asian and Pacific Islander — 4.6%. Spanish Origin — 12.3%. Dutch — 0.7%; English — 9.6%; French — 0.9%; German — 5.9%; Hungarian — 0.5%; Irish — 3.5%; Italian — 3.6%; Norwegian — 0.7%; Polish — 0.8%; Russian — 0.6%; Scottish — 0.8%; Swedish — 0.9%.

Universities, Enrollment: California Institute of Technology, Pasadena — 1,709; Glendale Community College, Glendale — 10,011; Los Angeles College of Chiropractic, Glendale — 722.

Newspapers, Circulation: *Burbank Daily Review* (e), Glendale — 8,456; *Glendale News-Press* (e), Glendale — 13,656. The *Los Angeles Times* and *Los Angeles Herald Examiner* also circulate in the district.

Commercial Television Stations, Affiliation: Entire district is in Los Angeles ADI.

Industries:

The Burbank Studios; Burbank; motion picture production — 4,000. **Six Flags Corp.** (Magic Mountain); Saugus; amusement park — 3,000. **Pasadena Hospital Assn.;** Pasadena; hospital — 2,100. **Walt Disney Productions** (HQ); Burbank; motion picture production — 1,900. **Glendale Adventist Medical Center;** Glendale; hospital — 1,900.

Xerox Corp.; Pasadena; electronic components — 1,700. **Buena Vista Distribution Co.** (WED Enterprises Div.); Glendale; research, development lab — 1,600. **Unitek Corp.** (HQ); Monrovia; dental equipment — 1,600. **International Telephone & Telegraph Corp.** (General Controls Div.); Glendale; hydraulic controls — 1,500. **Warner Bros. Inc.** (HQ); Burbank; motion picture production — 1,500. **Coates Demonstrating Service Inc.** (Marketing Aid); Glendale; demonstration services — 1,400. **Textron Inc.;** Saugus; hydraulic aircraft engine parts —

1,400. **Bell & Howell Co.** (CEC Data Instrument); Pasadena; instrumentation equipment — 1,300. **Methodist Hospital of Southern California;** Arcadia; hospital — 1,100. **Kennedy Co.;** Monrovia; electronic computing equipment — 950.

The Singer Co. (Librascope Div.); Glendale; weapons control equipment — 900. **Dart Industries Inc.** (Thatcher Glass Mfg. Co.); Saugus; glass bottles — 850. **McDonnell Douglas Corp.;** Monrovia; electronic communications equipment — 750. **Burroughs Corp.;** Pasadena; electronic computing equipment — 735. **Zero Corp.** (HQ); Burbank; packing products, metal enclosures — 725. **Jacobs Engineering Group Inc.** (HQ); Pasadena; general contracting — 700. **Becton Dickinson & Co.** (The Digitran Co. Div.); Pasadena; digital testing equipment — 600. **Boskovitch Farms Inc.;** Saugus; vegetable farming — 600. **Travenol Laboratories Inc.** (Hyland Div.); Los Angeles; diagnostic equipment — 574. **American Hospital Supply Corp.** (American Pharmaseal Div.); Glendale; pharmaceuticals — 500. **TRE Corp.** (Advanced Structures Div.); Monrovia; aircraft parts — 500.

23rd District

Northwestern Los Angeles — Beverly Hills, Part of San Fernando Valley

The 23rd District is divided geographically and culturally by the Santa Monica Mountains.

On the southern slope of one of the world's few urban mountain ranges are the lush, well-tended neighborhoods of Bel Air and Westwood, the home of the sprawling U.C.L.A. campus. To the east, at the foot of the mountains is Beverly Hills, and to the south, Century City, Rancho Park and West Los Angeles. These are, for the most part, the provinces of wealthy, liberal families — many of them Jewish — that live in large single-family homes. They also vote Democratic.

On the other side of the Santa Monicas, where the ocean breezes seldom blow, is a different world. Here are the middle-class San Fernando Valley communities of Reseda, Tarzana, Canoga Park and Woodland Hills — flat, anonymous suburbs linked together by shopping centers and commercial strips. Although many of the voters in this area register as Democrats, most of them vote Republican.

To create a new, solidly Democratic district to the east — the 26th — the 23rd was pushed further west in the San Fernando Valley into territory that throughout the 1970s sent a conservative Republican to Congress. The redistricting changes in place for the 1982 elections pushed the Democratic registration down from 63 to 57 percent, and a majority of the voters now live on the valley side.

Election Returns

23rd District		Democrat		Republican	
1976	President	114,406	(49.7%)	111,766	(48.5%)
	Senate	114,759	(55.9%)	86,440	(42.1%)
	House	130,982	(55.6%)	104,177	(44.2%)
1978	Governor	112,113	(57.6%)	68,332	(35.1%)
	House	131,571	(65.5%)	68,872	(34.3%)
1980	President	83,686	(38.0%)	107,985	(49.1%)
	Senate	133,442	(62.3%)	70,357	(32.8%)
	House	121,471	(53.0%)	96,413	(42.0%)
1982	Governor	117,674	(55.2%)	91,586	(43.0%)
	Senate	110,252	(52.1%)	96,092	(45.5%)
	House	120,788	(59.6%)	82,031	(40.4%)

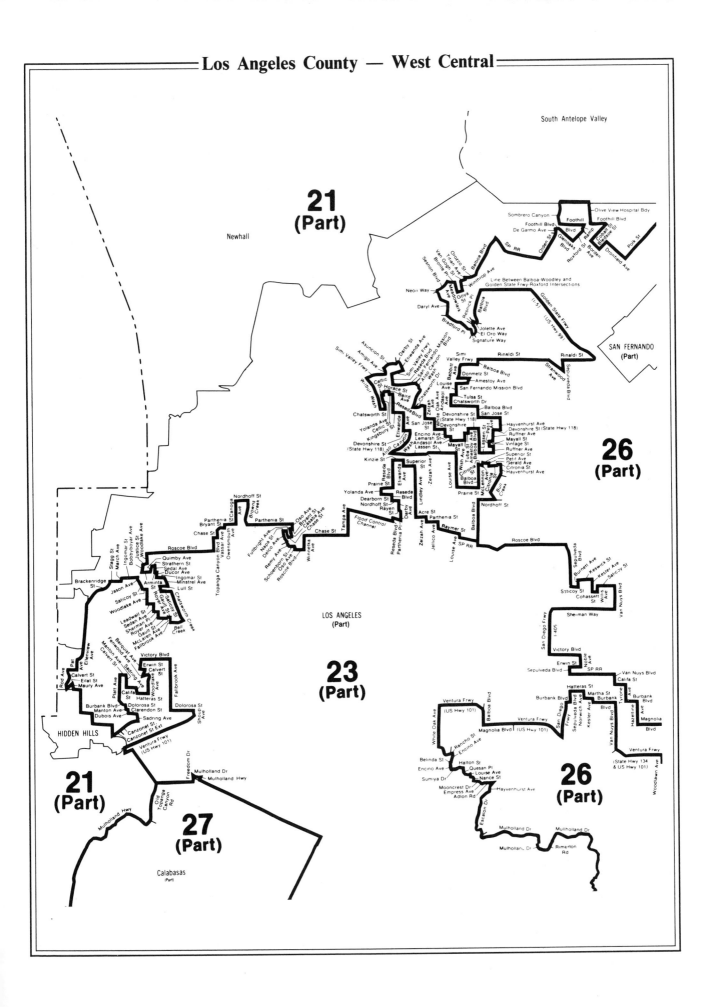

Demographics

Population: 526,007. **Percent Change from 1970:** 2.8%.

Land Area: 120 square miles. **Population per Square Mile:** 4,383.4.

Counties, 1980 Population: Los Angeles (Pt.) — 526,007.

Cities, 1980 Population: Beverly Hills — 32,367; Los Angeles (Pt.) — 468,598; West Hollywood (CDP) (Pt.) — 23,895.

Race and Ancestry: White — 88.7%; Black — 2.7%; American Indian, Eskimo and Aleut — 0.4%; Asian and Pacific Islander — 4.2%. Spanish Origin — 9.3%. Dutch — 0.5%; English — 7.1%; French — 1.0%; German — 5.0%; Hungarian — 1.4%; Irish — 3.0%; Italian — 2.8%; Norwegian — 0.5%; Polish — 2.9%; Russian — 6.2%; Scottish — 0.5%; Swedish — 0.7%.

Universities, Enrollment: California State University at Northridge, Northridge — 28,441; Los Angeles Pierce College, Woodland Hills — 22,954; Mount St. Mary's College, Los Angeles — 1,182; University of California at Los Angeles, Los Angeles — 34,031.

Newspapers, Circulation: *Los Angeles Times, Los Angeles Herald Examiner* and Los Angeles *Daily News* circulate in the district.

Commercial Television Stations, Affiliation: Entire district is in Los Angeles ADI.

Industries:

Cedars-Sinai Medical Center; Los Angeles; hospital — 5,000. **Rockwell International Corp.** (Rocketdyne Div.); Canoga Park; rocket engines — 5,000. **UCLA Hospital Center for Health Sciences;** Los Angeles; hospital — 4,500. **Litton Systems Inc.** (Litton Guidance & Control); Woodland Hills; aerospace guidance systems — 3,500. **Litton Systems Inc.** (Data Systems Div.); Van Nuys; military communications systems — 3,100.

Veterans Administration; Los Angeles; veterans' hospital — 2,750. **Blue Cross of Southern California** (HQ); Woodland Hills; health insurance — 2,050. **Northridge Hospital Foundation;** Northridge; hospital — 1,800. **International Telephone & Telegraph Corp.** (Gifillan Div.); Van Nuys; electronic components — 1,500. **Twentieth Century-Fox Film Corp.** (HQ); Los Angeles; motion picture production — 1,500. **Century Plaza Hotels Co.;** Los Angeles; hotel — 1,200. **Antenne II;** Los Angeles; motion picture production — 1,100. **HMO International;** Los Angeles; health maintenance organization — 1,100. **Marquardt Co. Inc.;** Van Nuys; aircraft engines — 1,000. **Nationwide Theatres Corp.;** Los Angeles; movie theater operations — 1,000.

Everest & Jennings Inc. (HQ); Los Angeles; wheel chairs — 968. **Dataproducts Corp.** (Lin Printer Div.); Woodland Hills; electronic computing equipment — 909. **Courtright Corp.** (Beverly Wilshire Hotel); Beverly Hills; hotel — 900. **Nordskog Industries Inc.** (HQ); Van Nuys; aircraft galleys — 900. **Anheuser-Busch Inc.;** Van Nuys; brewery — 700. **The Olga Co.** (HQ); Van Nuys; women's underwear — 650. **Teledyne Industries Inc.** (Controls Div.); Los Angeles; electronic control systems — 600. **20th Century Industries;** Woodland Hills; auto insurance — 540. **ITT Continental Baking Co.** (Wonder Bread Bakers Div.); Beverly Hills; bread — 518. **Petersen Publishing Co.** (HQ); Los Angeles; magazine publishing — 500.

24th District

North Central Los Angeles — Hollywood; Part of San Fernando Valley

More than any other district in the nation, the 24th depends on the entertainment industry for its economic well-being. It includes the symbolic center of the industry — the corner of Hollywood and Vine — as well as several movie studios and the West Coast headquarters of ABC and CBS.

Many of the heavily Jewish "bagel boroughs" of Los Angeles are also within the 24th District. Centered around the Wilshire Country Club, this area provides a solid core of votes for virtually any Democratic candidate. The new 24th was the only Los Angeles-area district without a large minority population that supported Jimmy Carter over Ronald Reagan in 1980.

Like the 23rd and 26th districts, this one straddles the Santa Monica Mountains. The district in place for the 1982 elections was pushed slightly further into the San Fernando Valley to include the Valley Plaza section. But this new territory, with its mostly middle-class, blue-collar residents, is not as conservative as the areas of the valley found farther to the west.

One of the few Republican-leaning communities in the 24th is Hancock Park, a favored home of Los Angeles "old money." During the years preceding World War II, its residents' exclusive attitudes forced the newly affluent — especially Jews — to look elsewhere for property. Beverly Hills thus became the address of choice for the arriving rich. Hancock Park now is the site of more modest neighborhoods, including a black community, but its select character still predominates.

The new 24th has the largest concentration of Asian-American voters in the state outside San Francisco. Many of them are Koreans, concentrated at the southern end of the district. There is a sizable homosexual community in Hollywood and West Hollywood.

Election Returns

24th District		Democrat		Republican	
1976	President	87,517	(54.3%)	69,667	(43.2%)
	Senate	77,810	(56.3%)	57,150	(41.3%)
	House	103,035	(67.8%)	47,929	(31.5%)
1978	Governor	87,116	(63.7%)	40,402	(29.5%)
	House	80,282	(62.5%)	42,332	(32.9%)
1980	President	67,571	(45.4%)	62,749	(42.4%)
	Senate	91,355	(63.2%)	43,952	(30.4%)
	House	87,423	(62.0%)	41,963	(29.7%)
1982	Governor	85,205	(60.1%)	53,139	(37.5%)
	Senate	85,950	(60.9%)	51,510	(36.5%)
	House	88,516	(65.0%)	42,133	(31.0%)

Demographics

Population: 525,909. **Percent Change from 1970:** 13.5%.

Land Area: 53 square miles. **Population per Square Mile:** 9,922.8.

Counties, 1980 Population: Los Angeles (Pt.) — 525,909.

Cities: 1980 Population: Los Angeles (Pt.) — 514,081; West Hollywood (CDP) (Pt.) — 11,808.

Race and Ancestry: White — 66.2%; Black — 6.3%; American Indian, Eskimo and Aleut — 0.5%; Asian and Pacific Islander — 12.4%. Spanish Origin — 26.4%. English — 5.3%; French — 0.8%; German — 3.1%; Hungarian — 1.0%; Irish — 2.3%; Italian — 2.0%; Polish — 1.9%; Russian — 3.3%.

Universities, Enrollment: California School of Professional Psychology at Los Angeles, Los Angeles — 319; College of the Center for Early Education, Los Angeles — 66; Columbia College, Los Angeles — 280; L.I.F.E. Bible College, Los Angeles — 466; Los Angeles City College, Los Angeles — 18,700; United College of Business, Los Angeles — 1,478; West Coast University, Los Angeles — 1,422.

Newspapers, Circulation: *Los Angeles Times, Los Angeles Herald Examiner* and Los Angeles *Daily News* circulate in the district.

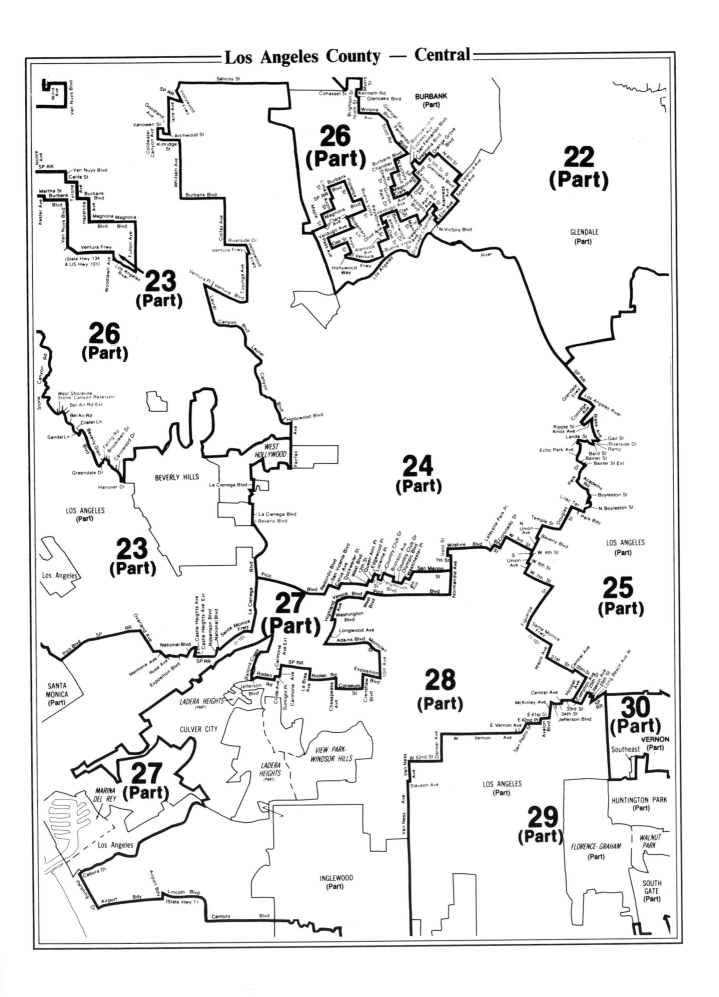

Commercial Television Stations, Affiliation: KABC-TV, Los Angeles (ABC); KCOP, Los Angeles (None); KHJ-TV, Los Angeles (None); KMEX-TV, Los Angeles (None, Spanish); KNBC, Los Angeles (NBC); KNXT, Los Angeles (CBS); KTLA, Los Angeles (None); KTTV, Los Angeles (None); KWHY-TV, Los Angeles (None, Chinese, Japanese and Korean). Entire district is in Los Angeles ADI.

Industries:

MCA Inc. (Universal Studios - HQ); North Hollywood; motion picture production — 8,000. **Kaiser Foundation Hospitals;** Los Angeles; hospital — 4,600. **Pedus Building Services Inc.** (HQ); Los Angeles; janitorial services — 3,500. **Children's Hospital of Los Angeles** (HQ); Los Angeles; hospital — 2,000. **Hewlett-Packard Co. Inc.** (Neely Sales Div.); North Hollywood; electrical supplies wholesaling — 2,000. **Prudential Insurance Co. of America;** Los Angeles; life, health insurance — 2,000.

Republic Corp. (Continental Graphics Div.); Los Angeles; printing & graphics — 1,300. **St. Vincent Medical Center Inc.;** Los Angeles; hospital — 1,300. **CBS Inc.** (CBS Studio Center); North Hollywood; motion picture production — 1,200. **American Broadcasting Companies;** Los Angeles; television broadcasting — 1,000. **California Federal Savings & Loan Assn.** (HQ); Los Angeles; savings & loan — 1,000. **CBS Inc.;** Los Angeles; television broadcasting — 1,000. **Equitable Life Assurance Society of the United States;** Los Angeles; life insurance — 1,000. **Hanna-Barbera Productions Inc.;** Los Angeles; motion picture, TV tapes production — 1,000. **Hollywood Presbyterian Hospital;** Los Angeles; hospital — 1,000.

Kaiser Foundation Health Plan; Los Angeles; health insurance — 1,000. **Fire Insurance Exchange;** Los Angeles; casualty insurance — 902. **Beneficial Standard Corp.** (HQ); Los Angeles; life, health, accident insurance — 900. **Interstate Brands Corp.** (Dolly Madison Cake); Los Angeles; cakes — 900. **Truck Insurance Exchange** (HQ); Los Angeles; casualty insurance — 900. **Farmers Insurance Exchange** (HQ); Los Angeles; casualty insurance — 836. **American Airlines Inc.;** Los Angeles; reservation office — 800. **California-World Financial Corp.;** North Hollywood; title insurance — 800. **Carnation Co.** (HQ); Los Angeles; dairy products, fruit and vegetable canning, pet foods — 800. **Chicago Title Insurance Co.;** Los Angeles; title insurance — 800. **Delta Air Lines Inc.;** Los Angeles; reservation office — 800. **Max Factor & Co.** (Moisturessence Cosmetics - HQ); Los Angeles; cosmetics, perfumes — 800.

Max Factor & Co.; Los Angeles; cosmetics, perfumes — 750. **Franciscan Ceramics Inc.;** Los Angeles; ceramic ware — 750. **Technicolor Inc.** (Professional Film Div.); North Hollywood; film processing — 750. **Van de Kamps Holland/Dutch Bakers;** Los Angeles bakery products wholesaling — 750. **Bendix Corp.** (Electrodynamics Div.); North Hollywood; electronics — 700. **Owens-Illinois Inc.;** Los Angeles; glass containers — 700. **Republic Corp.** (Consolidated Film Industries Div.); Los Angeles; film services — 650. **Fireman's Fund Insurance Co. Inc.;** Los Angeles; casualty insurance — 600. **Paramount Corp.;** Los Angeles; motion picture production — 600. **CNA Casualty Co. of California** (Marketing Div.); Los Angeles; casualty insurance — 500. **Home Savings & Loan Assn.** (HQ); Los Angeles; savings & loan, real estate — 500. **Kayser-Roth Corp.** (Cole of Calif. Div.); Los Angeles; women's wear — 500. **Quinn Martin Productions Inc.** (HQ); Los Angeles; TV motion pictures, tapes — 500.

25th District

Central and East Los Angeles

This is the most heavily Hispanic district in California. Nearly two-thirds of its residents identified themselves as being of Spanish ancestry in the 1980 census.

The district includes the shining glass-and-steel towers of downtown corporate Los Angeles. It has 10 expressways named for the places its professional people go home to each afternoon; for example, Pasadena, Pomona, Ventura, Glendale and Santa Ana.

But the real flavor of the 25th District is in the Hispanic barrios of Boyle Heights and East Los Angeles. It is there that poverty and unemployment run high and Democratic loyalty is strong.

Modest redistricting changes for the 1982 elections reduced the Hispanic population by about seven percentage points. The western side of the district, nearly all Hispanic, was sheared off and replaced by middle-class, racially mixed neighborhoods in western and northern Pasadena. Even with the changes, only a quarter of the population is Anglo and 10 percent is black.

But any group that votes in significant numbers can exert some influence here because voting participation in the district is the lowest in the state. The new 25th is the only constituency in California where fewer than 100,000 people voted for president in 1980 — less than half the statewide average. Among the 360,000 people in the district who were of eligible voting age, only 83,000 cast votes in the 1982 House election.

Election Returns

25th District		Democrat		Republican	
1976	President	59,537	(61.9%)	34,427	(35.8%)
	Senate	48,831	(60.5%)	29,636	(36.7%)
	House	61,029	(60.6%)	35,557	(35.3%)
1978	Governor	59,726	(71.2%)	19,684	(23.5%)
	House	48,340	(56.9%)	36,563	(43.1%)
1980	President	52,120	(57.0%)	30,850	(33.7%)
	Senate	60,537	(68.6%)	22,711	(25.7%)
	House	51,573	(54.3%)	38,481	(40.5%)
1982	Governor	59,994	(66.2%)	27,915	(30.8%)
	Senate	60,541	(67.3%)	27,058	(30.1%)
	House	71,106	(85.5%)	—	

Demographics

Population: 525,411. **Percent Change from 1970:** 6.6%.

Land Area: 64 square miles. **Population per Square Mile:** 8,209.5.

Counties, 1980 Population: Los Angeles (Pt.) — 525,411.

Cities, 1980 Population: East Los Angeles (CDP) (Pt.) — 89,124; Los Angeles (Pt.) — 345,682; Pasadena (Pt.) — 66,291.

Race and Ancestry: White — 50.4%; Black — 9.6%; American Indian, Eskimo and Aleut — 0.6%; Asian and Pacific Islander — 7.9%. Spanish Origin — 63.6%. English — 2.5%; German — 1.4%; Irish — 1.0%; Italian — 1.1%.

Universities, Enrollment: American Academy of Dramatic Arts West, Pasadena — 273; Art Center College of Design, Pasadena — 1,420; California State University at Los Angeles — 22,070; Fuller Theological Seminary, Pasadena — 1,286; Los Angeles Business College, Los Angeles — 655; Occidental College, Los Angeles — 1,701; Pacific Oaks College and Children's Programs, Pasadena — 274; Pasadena City College, Pasadena — 20,007; Sierra College of Business, Los Angeles — 1,843; Woodbury University, Los Angeles — 1,425.

Newspapers, Circulation: *Los Angeles Herald Examiner* (e), Los Angeles — 288,218; *Los Angeles Times* (mS), Los Angeles — 1,018,403; *Star News* (all day, S), Pasadena — 49,835. Los Angeles *Daily News* circulates in the district. Foreign language newspapers: *Kashu Mainichi* (Japanese), Los Angeles — 5,610; *La Opinion* (Spanish), Los Angeles — 36,965; *Rafu Shimpo* (Japanese), Los Angeles — 21,116.

Commercial Television Stations, Affiliation: Entire district is in Los Angeles ADI.

Industries:

University of Southern California Medical Center; Los Angeles; hospital — 9,000. Security Pacific National Bank Inc. (HQ); Los Angeles; banking — 5,000. Occidental Life Insurance Co. of California (HQ); Los Angeles; life, health insurance — 4,000. The Times Mirror Co. (HQ); Los Angeles; newspaper publishing — 4,000. John Portman & Associates Inc.; Los Angeles; hotel managing — 3,000. The Parsons Corp. (HD); Pasadena; heavy construction, engineering services — 3,000.

Bank of America National Trust & Savings Assn.; Los Angeles; data processing services — 2,700. Atlantic Richfield Co. (Solar Industries); Los Angeles; energy research — 2,500. Atlantic Richfield Co. (HQ); Los Angeles; petroleum producing, refining — 2,100. White Memorial Medical Center; Los Angeles; hospital — 1,550. Union Oil Co. of California (HQ); Los Angeles; petroleum producing, refining, marketing — 1,300. First Interstate Bank of California (HQ); Los Angeles; banking — 1,200. Golden State Transit Corp. (Los Angeles Yellow Cab); Los Angeles; taxi service — 1,120. Crocker National Bank Inc. (Crocker Commercial Services); Los Angeles; data processing services — 1,100. Lutheran Hospital Society of Southern California; Los Angeles; hospital — 1,100. National Railroad Passenger Corp. (Amtrak Purchasing); Los Angeles; railroad equipment wholesaling — 1,100. Six Flags Inc.; Los Angeles; holding company — 1,100.

Good Samaritan Hospital Corp.; Los Angeles; hospital — 1,030. Lawry's Food Inc.; Los Angeles; seasonings, salad dressing — 1,000. Times Mirror Press; Los Angeles; commercial printing — 975. The Hearst Corp.; Los Angeles; newspaper publishing — 900. Union Bank (HQ); Los Angeles; banking — 900. Crown Zellerbach Corp. (Zellerbach Paper Co. Div.); Los Angeles; paper wholesaling — 850. Arco Marine Inc.; Los Angeles; ship transportation — 800. Certified Grocers of California Ltd. (Food Service Div. - HQ); Los Angeles; grocery wholesaling — 800. Karen Corp. (Bekins Protection Services Co. - HQ); Los Angeles; security services — 800. Lloyds Bank of California (HQ); Los Angeles; banking — 800.

Biltmore Hotel; Los Angeles; hotel — 750. Arthur Andersen & Co.; Los Angeles; accounting services — 700. Wior Bros. Mfg. Co. Inc. (Gerry of California); Los Angeles; robes — 700. Phillippi of California Inc.; Los Angeles; women's handbags — 680. Ingersoll-Rand Co. (Proto Tool Div.); Los Angeles; tools — 650. Barth & Dreyfuss Co. of California (Royal Terry of California - HQ); Los Angeles; towels — 605. Hilton Hotels Corp. (Los Angeles Hilton); Los Angeles; hotel — 600. Northwestern Mutual Life Insurance Inc.; Los Angeles; life insurance — 600. Shield Security Inc.; Los Angeles; security services — 600. Southern Cal Davis Pleating (California Trimming); Los Angeles; pleating, decorative stitching — 600.

Trailways Inc.; Los Angeles; intercity bus transportation — 600. Transamerica Insurance Co. (HQ); Los Angeles; casualty, fire insurance — 600. Federal Reserve Bank of San Francisco; Los Angeles; banking — 560. Bendix Field Engineering Corp.; Pasadena; communication services — 500. New Otani America Inc.; Los Angeles; hotel — 500. O'Melveny & Myers (HQ); Los Angeles; law firm — 550. Coopers & Lybrand; Los Angeles; accounting services — 500. Peat, Marwick, Mitchell & Co.; Los Angeles; accounting services — 500. Southern Pacific Transportation Co.; Los Angeles; railroad operations — 500. Wells Fargo Bank Inc.; Los Angeles; banking — 500.

26th District

Santa Monica Mountains; Central San Fernando Valley

Phillip Burton took care to make sure the 26th was a safe Democratic district by including in it solid liberal territory that had been in the old 23rd.

Many of those voters reside in the fashionable Mulholland Drive area north of Beverly Hills. Further west the 26th District takes in Sherman Oaks and Studio City at the base of the mountains in the San Fernando Valley. This area normally supports liberal Democrats.

The less favorable part of the district for Democrats is in the heart of the San Fernando Valley — communities such as Panorama City, Sepulveda and part of Van Nuys. The ranch-style houses that line the endless straight streets here are home to some professionals and blue-collar workers, few wealthy and few poor. The aviation and electronics industries are still major employers.

Nearly all of the new 26th has been under Democratic representation for years in the state Legislature. But the 2-to-1 Democratic registration advantage belies its conservatism on many social and economic issues. The area warmly embraced tax-slashing Proposition 13 in 1978, and portions of it added from the old 21st District backed a conservative Republican House candidate in her 1980 victory there over a veteran Democrat.

The northernmost end of the district is the most industrialized part of the valley; it has attracted increasing numbers of blacks and Mexican-Americans. Thanks to migrations during the late 1970s to communities such as San Fernando City and Pacoima, in fact, the overall Hispanic population of the district is 25 percent. But because of low turnout, the Hispanic share of the vote is less than 10 percent.

Election Returns

26th District		Democrat		Republican	
1976	President	96,055	(50.4%)	90,592	(47.5%)
	Senate	86,737	(51.9%)	76,264	(45.6%)
	House	105,593	(58.3%)	70,470	(38.9%)
1978	Governor	89,315	(56.4%)	57,850	(36.5%)
	House	81,186	(54.3%)	63,933	(42.8%)
1980	President	70,376	(38.0%)	94,136	(50.9%)
	Senate	105,551	(58.5%)	65,515	(36.3%)
	House	80,056	(44.4%)	93,317	(51.7%)
1982	Governor	88,777	(52.1%)	78,266	(45.9%)
	Senate	85,786	(50.6%)	79,248	(46.7%)
	House	97,383	(59.6%)	66,072	(40.4%)

Demographics

Population: 526,118. Percent Change from 1970: 2.1%.

Land Area: 97 square miles. Population per Square Mile: 5,423.9.

Counties, 1980 Population: Los Angeles (Pt.) — 526,118.

Cities, 1980 Population: Burbank (Pt.) — 46,646; Los Angeles (Pt.) — 461,737; San Fernando — 17,731.

Race and Ancestry: White — 79.3%; Black — 4.4%; American Indian, Eskimo and Aleut — 0.7%; Asian and Pacific Islander — 3.7%. Spanish Origin — 25.3%. English — 6.1%; French — 0.8%; German — 4.4%; Hungarian — 0.8%; Irish — 2.7%; Italian — 3.0%; Polish — 1.6%; Russian — 3.3%; Swedish — 0.6%.

Universities, Enrollment: Los Angeles Mission College, San Fernando — 3,596; Los Angeles Valley College, Van Nuys — 25,474; University of Judaism, Los Angeles — 165.

Newspapers, Circulation: *Daily News* (mS), Los Angeles — 104,121. *Los Angeles Times, Los Angeles Herald Examiner* and *Burbank Daily Review* also circulate in the district.

Commercial Television Stations, Affiliation: Entire district is in Los Angeles ADI.

Industries:

General Motors Corp. (Assembly Div.); Van Nuys; auto assembly — 5,600. Hyatt Medical Enterprises Inc. (HQ); Encino; hospital managing, health services — 2,200. **Sisters of Providence in California** (Saint Joseph Medical Center - HQ); Burbank; hospital — 2,200. **Kaiser Foundation Hospital;** Van Nuys; hospital — 1,700. **Norris Industries Inc.** (Price Pfister Brass Mfg. Co. Div.); Pacoima; brass plumbing fixtures — 1,400.

Bendix Corp. (Electrodynamics Div.); San Fernando; aerospace electronics — 1,300. **Harman International Industries** (HQ); Northridge; stereo speakers — 1,300. **Valley Presbyterian Hospital;** Van Nuys; hospital — 1,300. **Walter Kidde Co. Inc.** (Weber Aircraft Co. Div.); Burbank; aircraft seats — 1,200. **Van Nuys Publishing Co.;** Van Nuys; newspaper publishing — 1,080. **Menasco Inc.** (HQ); Burbank; aircraft parts — 1,000. **SFE Technologies** (HQ); San Fernando; electronic components — 875. **Crane Co. Inc.** (Hydro Aire); Burbank; pumps, pumping equipment — 750. **Menasco Inc.** (California Div.); Burbank; aircraft parts — 700.

Whirlpool Corp. (Thomas International); Sepulveda; organs — 700. **R. G. Sloane Mfg. Co. Inc.** (HQ); Sun Valley; plastic pipe — 650. **CDI Corp.** (Sass-Widders Corp.); Encino; engineering service — 600. **Joseph Schlitz Brewing Co.;** Van Nuys; brewery — 650. **RCA Corp.** (Commercial Communications Systems Div.); Van Nuys; avionics — 600. **Bio-Science Enterprises** (Bio-Science Laboratories - HQ); Van Nuys; medical laboratory — 500. **Monarch Record Mfg. Co.** (Etan Products Co.); Sun Valley; phonograph records — 500. **Safeco Title Insurance Co.** (HQ); Van Nuys; title insurance — 500. **Sierracin Corp.** (HQ); San Fernando; aircraft ice protection systems — 500. **Stainless Steel Products Inc.;** Burbank; fuel gas ducting — 500.

27th District

Pacific Coast — Santa Monica

The old 27th, with its flamboyant conservative Republican House incumbent, was one of the prime targets for the Democratic map makers in 1981. The redrawn 27th retained most of the old district's Democratic parts, but the exclusive Palos Verdes Hills section at the southern end of the long coastal constituency was thrown into the new 42nd District.

With the exception of a long thin finger poking its way into the heart of Los Angeles, the new 27th is a coastal district. Santa Monica is its political and geographic hub. A city of 88,000 people, it is a mixture of elderly middle-class residents and young families that like being close to both the city and the ocean. Political activism runs high in Santa Monica, the home base for actress Jane Fonda and her husband, Tom Hayden, who was elected to the state Assembly in 1982.

Thanks in part to the activities of Hayden and Fonda, Santa Monica has received a reputation as a liberal community. But this image is not always reflected at the polls. Santa Monica has the second-highest Democratic registration of any community in the district, but it split its vote almost evenly between Ronald Reagan and Jimmy Carter in 1980.

Life is more "laid back" on either side of Santa Monica. The Pacific Palisades and Malibu Beach sections to the north provide the district's most interesting architecture and a strong upper-class voting element. The voters are polarized between the far left and the far right. To the south of Santa Monica is Venice, an artists' community that has been overrun by young beach-oriented people with roller skates, surfboards and blaring radios. The hot tub and Jaccuzi set is found a few blocks further south in the plush Marina Del Rey condominiums, and just beyond is the giant Los Angeles International Airport.

The communities south of the airport — upper-middle-class suburbs inhabited mostly by professional people — show little loyalty to either party. Manhattan Beach, Hermosa Beach and Redondo Beach have Democratic registration advantages, but all voted for Reagan in 1980 by margins of nearly 2-to-1 — about the same as El Segundo, the new GOP stronghold in the district.

Election Returns

27th District		Democrat		Republican	
1976	President	97,515	(50.0%)	92,507	(47.7%)
	Senate	87,895	(51.8%)	77,241	(45.5%)
	House	110,338	(54.2%)	93,286	(45.8%)
1978	Governor	97,033	(59.8%)	52,038	(32.1%)
	House	95,780	(57.6%)	70,601	(42.4%)
1980	President	80,577	(41.3%)	88,457	(45.3%)
	Senate	113,996	(60.2%)	63,702	(33.7%)
	House	108,936	(52.1%)	94,234	(45.1%)
1982	Governor	107,747	(56.3%)	79,317	(41.5%)
	Senate	101,216	(53.2%)	83,216	(43.8%)
	House	108,347	(59.5%)	67,479	(37.0%)

Demographics

Population: 525,758. **Percent Change from 1970:** 1.5%.

Land Area: 143 square miles. **Population per Square Mile:** 3,676.6

Counties, 1980 Population: Los Angeles (Pt.) — 525,758.

Cities, 1980 Population: El Segundo — 13,752; Hawthorne (Pt.) — 160; Hermosa Beach — 18,070; Inglewood (Pt.) — 396; Lawndale — 23,460; Long Beach (Pt.) — 3,189; Los Angeles (Pt.) — 218,794; Manhattan Beach — 31,542; Redondo Beach — 57,102; Santa Monica — 88,314.

Race and Ancestry: White — 74.5%; Black — 10.6%; American Indian, Eskimo and Aleut — 0.6%; Asian and Pacific Islander — 6.1%. Spanish Origin — 16.9%. Dutch — 0.5%; English — 7.5%; French — 1.0%; German — 4.7%; Hungarian — 0.5%; Irish — 3.4%; Italian — 1.9%; Norwegian — 0.5%; Polish — 1.2%; Russian — 1.9%; Scottish — 0.7%; Swedish — 0.7%.

Universities, Enrollment: The Fashion Institute of Design and Merchandising, Los Angeles — 2,115; Grantham College of Engineering, Los Angeles — 750; Pepperdine University, Malibu — 6,582; Rand Graduate Institute for Policy Studies, Santa Monica — 44; Santa Monica College, Santa Monica — 18,450; Southern California Institute of Architecture, Santa Monica — 300.

Newspapers, Circulation: *Evening Outlook* (e), Santa Monica — 33,349. *Los Angeles Times, Los Angeles Herald Examiner* and Los Angeles *Daily News* also circulate in the district.

Commercial Television Stations, Affiliation: Entire district is in Los Angeles ADI.

Military Installations: Los Angeles Air Force One Annex, Los Angeles — 75; Los Angeles Air Force Station, El Segundo — 3,162.

Industries:

TRW Inc. (Electronics & Defense Center); Redondo Beach; defense and space systems, microelectronics — 15,466. **Rockwell International Corp.** (North American Aircraft Operations); El Segundo; aircraft — 10,000. **Hughes Aircraft Co.** (Electro-Optical & Data Systems Group); El Segundo; electro-optics equipment — 9,900. **Hughes Aircraft Co. Inc.** (Radar Systems Group); El Segundo; electronic communications equipment — 9,800. **Hughes Aircraft Co.** (Space and Communications Group); El Segundo; electronic communications equipment — 7,700.

Los Angeles County — West Coastal

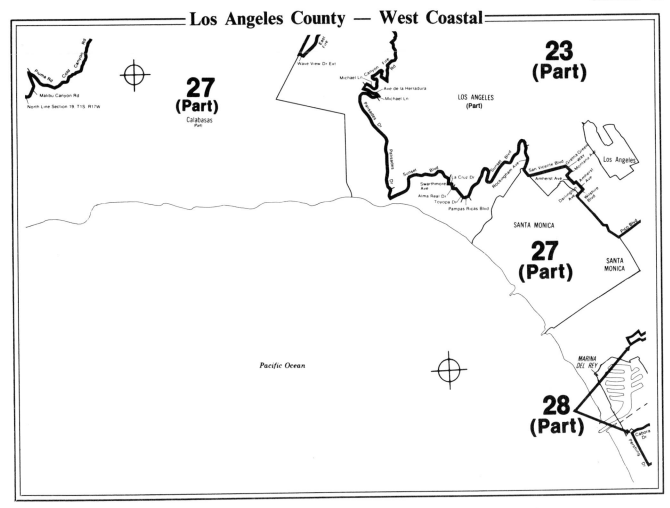

Western Air Lines Inc. (HQ); Los Angeles; commercial airline — 6,000. **Northrop Corp** (Aircraft Group); El Segundo; aircraft — 3,700. **Xerox Corp.** (Xerox Business Systems); El Segundo; electronic printing equipment — 3,500. **Trans World Airlines Inc.;** Los Angeles; commercial airline — 2,800. **The Flying Tiger Line Inc.** (HQ); Los Angeles; air cargo carrier — 2,000. **Volt Technical Corp.;** El Segundo; printing — 1,900. **System Development Corp.** (HQ); Santa Monica; computer programming, data processing services — 1,550. **Kaiser Permanente Medical Center;** Los Angeles; hospital — 1,500. **Lutheran Hospital Society of Southern California;** Santa Monica; hospital — 1,500. **Standard Oil Co. of California** (Chevron USA Inc.); El Segundo; refinery — 1,300.

American Protection Industries; Redondo Beach; security services — 1,200. **Xerox Corp.** (Computer Services Div.); Los Angeles; computer services — 1,200. **Borg-Warner Corp.** (Byron-Jackson Pump Div.); Los Angeles; centrifugal pumps — 1,000. **The Gillette Co.** (Santa Monica Mfg. Center); Santa Monica; writing instruments — 1,000. **Ernest W. Hahn Inc.** (HQ); El Segundo; general contracting — 1,000. **International Rectifier Corp.** (Semiconductor Div.); El Segundo; semiconductors — 1,000. **The Rand Corp.** (HQ); Santa Monica; research — 965. **Clougherty Packing Co.** (Farmer John Meat Co. - HQ); Los Angeles; meatpacking — 900. **Hughes Aircraft Co.** (HQ); El Segundo; electronic communications equipment — 900. **Teledyne Industries Inc.** (Teledyne Micro Electronics); Los Angeles; semiconductors — 900.

Ampex Corp. (Memory Products); El Segundo; electronic components — 800. **Oscar Mayer & Co. Inc.;** Los Angeles; meatpacking — 800. **Crocker National Bank;** El Segundo; data processing services — 700. **Hughes Helicopter Inc.;** Venice; administrative services — 700. **Pertec Computer Corp.** (HQ); Los Angeles; electronic computer equipment — 700. **Puritan-Bennett Corp. of California;** Los Angeles; medical instruments — 700. **Transaction Technology Inc.** (HQ); Santa Monica; computer programming, data processing services — 700. **G & H Technology Inc.;** Santa Monica; aircraft parts — 680. **Farr Co.** (HQ); El Segundo; filtration equipment — 675. **Computer Sciences Corp.** (HQ); El Segundo; computer services — 650. **Sperry Corp.** (Flight Systems Div.); Van Nuys; airborne communications systems — 625.

Collins Foods International; (HQ); Los Angeles; fast food restaurants — 600. **Transervice Lease Corp.;** Los Angeles; truck leasing — 600. **Vivitar Corp.** (HQ); Santa Monica; photographic supplies — 600. **Revell Inc.** (HQ); Venice; toys — 560. **Louverdrape Inc.** (HQ); Santa Monica; vertical blinds — 525. **Penncorp Financial Inc.** (HQ); Santa Monica; life, accident insurance — 525. **Fairchild Industries** (Fairchild Stratos Div.); Manhattan Beach; aircraft parts — 500. **Fun Striders Inc.** (Bare Traps); Los Angeles; shoes, sandals — 500. **Hughes Aircraft Co.** (Hughes Research Laboratories); Malibu; electronics research — 500. **IPM Technology Inc.** (HQ); Los Angeles; electronic components — 500. **Prudential Building Maintenance Corp.;** Los Angeles; janitorial service — 500. **Teledyne Inc.;** Los Angeles; electronic communications systems — 500.

28th District

Southern Los Angeles, Inglewood

Directly south of Beverly Hills and Hollywood and stretching to the edge of downtown Los Angeles, the new

28th is a racially mixed, middle-class Democratic stronghold.

Some 43 percent of its residents are black, giving it a black population second only to that of the poorer 29th District to the east. Since the district's creation in 1972 voters of both races have joined together to send black Democrats to the House.

During the 1960s and 1970s, middle-class blacks have been moving into the southern and western parts of the district in and around Inglewood. Except for the mostly black Coliseum area in the northeastern corner, the district is exceptionally well integrated with whites, blacks, Asians and Hispanics living next to each other in well-built single-family homes.

Three-fourths of the district's residents live in the city of Los Angeles or the unincorporated Windsor Hills area. The only noticeable change made to the district in 1981 was to remove the Mar Vista part of Los Angeles, near Santa Monica, and replace it with the more fashionable Playa Del Rey section just north of the Los Angeles International Airport.

Inglewood, a city of nearly 100,000, has seen a remarkable shift in its racial mix during the last generation. In 1960, it had a black population of less than 1 percent. By 1970, as the migration of blacks began, the percentage rose to 11 percent. The 1980 census revealed that 57 percent of Inglewood's residents were black; 19 percent, Hispanic.

This racial change has been reflected in Inglewood's politics as well. Richard Nixon carried the city in 1968 and 1972. But Jimmy Carter defeated Gerald R. Ford there by a 2-to-1 margin in 1976 and won it over Ronald Reagan in 1980 by nearly 3-to-1.

Culver City, the home of the MGM studios, is the only loyal Republican area left in the district. While the new 28th as a whole gave Carter his second highest percentage in the state in 1980 — 67.5 percent — Culver City went for Reagan. A growing Hispanic influence there, however, is also keeping the Republican vote lower than it once was.

Election Returns

28th District		Democrat		Republican	
1976	President	94,604	(67.6%)	43,058	(30.8%)
	Senate	80,275	(67.5%)	36,157	(30.4%)
	House	115,216	(74.2%)	39,378	(25.4%)
1978	Governor	86,907	(74.9%)	24,162	(20.8%)
	House	96,993	(85.1%)	16,101	(14.1%)
1980	President	91,477	(67.5%)	35,398	(26.1%)
	Senate	98,534	(75.9%)	26,042	(20.1%)
	House	108,265	(72.7%)	33,915	(22.8%)
1982	Governor	108,275	(76.9%)	30,718	(21.8%)
	Senate	105,044	(75.6%)	31,252	(22.5%)
	House	103,469	(78.9%)	24,473	(18.7%)

Demographics

Population: 525,682. **Percent Change from 1970:** 6.3%.

Land Area: 47 square miles. **Population per Square Mile:** 11,184.7.

Counties, 1980 Population: Los Angeles (Pt.) — 525,682.

Cities, 1980 Population: Culver City — 38,139; Hawthorne (Pt.) — 0; Inglewood (Pt.) — 93,849; Los Angeles (Pt.) — 374,922.

Race and Ancestry: White — 34.6%; Black — 43.0%; American Indian, Eskimo and Aleut — 0.5%; Asian and Pacific Islander — 5.8%. Spanish Origin — 29.6%. English — 2.9%; German — 1.6%; Irish — 1.2%; Italian — 0.8%; Russian — 0.5%.

Universities, Enrollment: Hebrew Union College-Jewish Institute of Religion, Los Angeles — 78; Los Angeles Trade-Technical College, Los Angeles — 17,229; Loyola Marymount University, Los Angeles — 6,051; National Technical Schools, Los Angeles — 1,059; Northrop University, Inglewood — 1,415; Otis Art Institute of Parsons School of Design, Los Angeles — 304; Southwestern University School of Law, Los Angeles — 1,653; West Los Angeles College, Culver City — 11,039.

Newspapers, Circulation: *Los Angeles Times, Los Angeles Herald Examiner* and Los Angeles *Daily News* circulate in the district.

Commercial Television Stations, Affiliation: Entire district is in Los Angeles ADI.

Industries:

Inter-Insurance Exchange Auto Club of Southern California; Los Angeles; auto insurance — 6,000. **Metro-Goldwyn-Mayer Film Co.** (HQ); Culver City; motion picture production — 2,000. **Brotman Medical Center;** Culver City; hospital — 1,500. **Centinela Hospital Assn.;** Inglewood; hospital — 1,500. **Burns International Security Services;** Culver City; security services — 1,400.

Thrifty Corp. (HQ); Los Angeles; drug store chain — 1,000. **Merle Norman Cosmetics Inc.** (HQ); Los Angeles; cosmetics — 830. **Knudsen Corp.** (HQ); Los Angeles; dairy products — 800. **Holland-America Insurance Co.** (HQ); Los Angeles; health insurance — 700. **Garrett Corp.** (AiResearch Industrial Div.); Los Angeles; fabricated plate work — 675. **Texaco Inc.;** Los Angeles; administrative offices — 600. **Sheraton Plaza La Reina Hotel;** Los Angeles; hotel — 550. **Transworld Services Inc.** (HQ); Los Angeles; engineering services — 550. **Fremont General Corp.** (HQ); Los Angeles; casualty insurance — 500. **Republic Corp.** (Continental Graphics); Culver City; miscellaneous publishing — 500. **Sobel, Bernstein & Green Co. Inc.** (HQ); Los Angeles; women's shoes — 500.

29th District

South-Central Los Angeles — Watts; Downey

Nearly four-fifths of the people who live in the 29th District are black or Hispanic. The 29th has the largest percentage of blacks in any California district. Nationally, the district ranks 18th in percentage of blacks, 17th in percentage of people of Spanish origin.

The riot-scarred Watts community makes up about 60 percent of the district with the Hispanics living in the adjacent suburbs of Huntington Park, Walnut Park and South Gate to the east. The poverty, high unemployment and housing shortages in Watts are about the same as they were during the 1965 riots, although the disturbances provoked an increased flow of state and federal funds to the community.

With their strong allegiance to the Democratic Party, black voters help place this district at the top of the Democratic list. It has the highest percentage of registered Democrats in the state — 78 percent — and Jimmy Carter's 69 percent showing here in 1980 was his highest mark anywhere in California.

The Hispanic communities do not always follow the Democratic voting patterns of the district's black voters. Huntington Park and South Gate both supported Ronald Reagan in 1980. In House elections the Hispanics have not faltered in their support for the black Democratic incumbent.

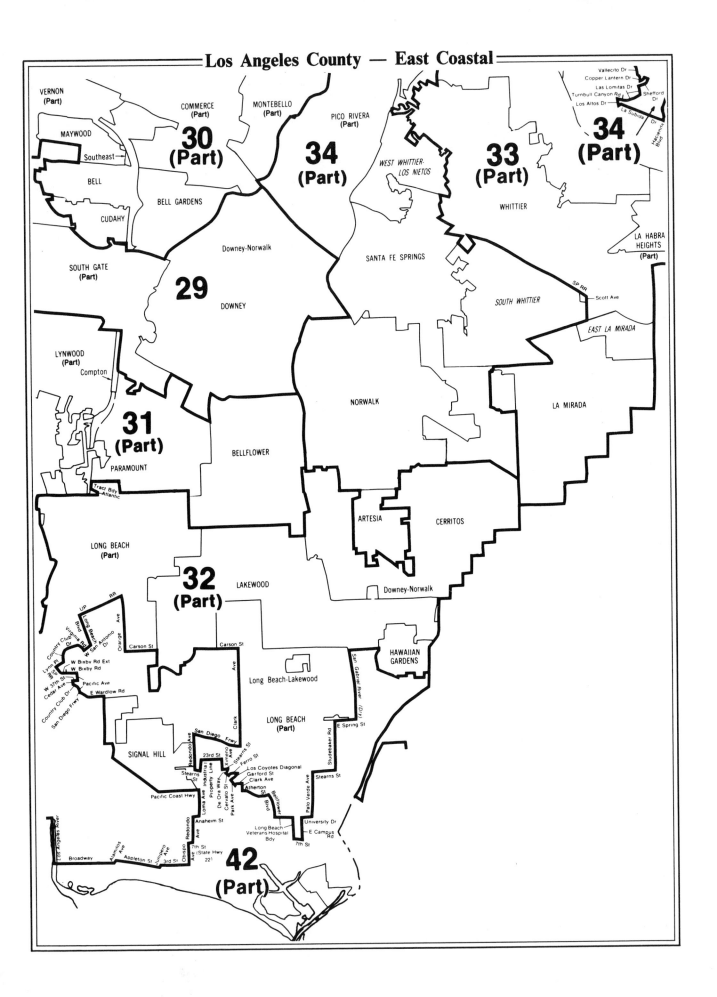

The 1981 redistricting changed the 29th somewhat by adding Downey, a mostly white, middle-class Republican suburb of 83,000 located east of the Hispanic part of the district. Downey gave Reagan 65 percent of the vote in 1980.

The change reduced the black population districtwide by 2.5 percentage points, to 46.6 percent. The Hispanic population dropped from 39 to 32 percent. The change, however, was not expected to have much effect on the district's ability to elect a minority Democrat to the House for the foreseeable future.

Election Returns

29th District		Democrat		Republican	
1976	President	91,966	(71.3%)	34,811	(27.0%)
	Senate	76,961	(71.4%)	28,664	(26.6%)
	House	88,371	(76.8%)	23,878	(20.7%)
1978	Governor	79,658	(75.1%)	22,752	(21.4%)
	House	69,765	(75.5%)	22,625	(24.5%)
1980	President	86,438	(68.5%)	34,792	(27.6%)
	Senate	88,780	(74.1%)	26,051	(21.7%)
	House	81,703	(72.6%)	28,479	(25.3%)
1982	Governor	99,204	(75.6%)	29,996	(22.9%)
	Senate	96,178	(74.8%)	29,879	(23.2%)
	House	97,028	(79.8%)	24,568	(20.2%)

Demographics

Population: 525,795. **Percent Change from 1970:** 2.1%.

Land Area: 51 square miles. **Population per Square Mile:** 10,309.7.

Counties, 1980 Population: Los Angeles (Pt.) — 525,795.

Cities, 1980 Population: Downey — 82,602; Huntington Park (Pt.) — 45,932; Los Angeles (Pt.) — 242,088; South Gate — 66,784.

Race and Ancestry: White — 38.1%; Black — 46.6%; American Indian, Eskimo and Aleut — 0.5%; Asian and Pacific Islander — 1.2%. Spanish Origin — 32.3%. English — 3.1%; German — 1.7%; Irish — 1.0%; Italian — 0.9%.

Newspapers, Circulation: *Daily Signal* (e), Downey — 11,271; *The Daily Southeast News & Downey Champion* (e), Downey — 5,785. *Los Angeles Times, Los Angeles Herald Examiner* and Los Angeles *Daily News* circulate in the district.

Commercial Television Stations, Affiliation: Entire district is in Los Angeles ADI.

Industries:

Rockwell International Corp. (Space Div.); Downey; spacecraft — 9,500. **Rancho Los Amigos Hospital;** Downey; hospital — 2,500. **American Building Maintenance Co.;** Los Angeles; janitorial services — 2,000. **Norris Industries Inc.** (Weiser Co. Div.); South Gate; cabinet hardware — 1,800. **Bechtel Power Corp.;** Downey; construction — 1,500.

ABMI Security Services Inc.; Los Angeles; security services — 1,000. **Dresser Industries Inc.** (Power Systems Group); Huntington Park; centrifugal pumps — 895. **Aerojet-General Corp.** (Ordnance & Mfg. Div.); Downey; ammunition — 800. **Leach Corp.** (Relay Div.); Los Angeles; electronic components — 800. **Modern Faucet Mfg. Co. Inc.;** Los Angeles; detergents — 740. **Latchford Glass Co. Inc.** (HQ); Huntington Park; bottles — 600. **Federal-Mogul Corp.** (National O-Rings); Downey; gaskets, sealing devices — 500. **General Motors Corp.** (Assembly Div.); South Gate; vehicle assembly — 500.

30th District

San Gabriel Valley — El Monte, Alhambra

As California's Hispanic population grew during the 1970s to 2 million, the Hispanic community moved beyond the inner-city barrios of Los Angeles to nearby suburbs such as the ones included in the new 30th District. Some 54 percent of the residents in the new 30th are of Spanish origin, a figure second only to that in the 25th District, just to the west.

The district cuts a diagonal swath across the San Gabriel Valley. The heaviest Hispanic concentration — as much as 85 percent in some places — is at the southwestern end, adjoining East Los Angeles. Suburbs such as Maywood, Cudahy and Montebello all have substantial Hispanic majorities. In the far eastern end of the district around Azusa there is a greater ethnic mix, although the neighborhoods are all blue-collar.

El Monte (population 79,494) links the eastern and western parts of the district. It is the largest of the 14 independent municipalities in the district. For years El Monte was a major hog-ranching center providing bacon for most of the Los Angeles area.

The only modestly Republican parts of the district are Alhambra and San Gabriel, once part of the old 26th. They helped Ronald Reagan carry the area in the new 30th in 1980.

Election Returns

30th District		Democrat		Republican	
1976	President	67,884	(52.8%)	57,892	(45.1%)
	Senate	54,012	(50.7%)	49,846	(46.8%)
	House	80,466	(58.4%)	57,018	(41.4%)
1978	Governor	64,224	(60.6%)	35,776	(33.7%)
	House	48,533	(46.5%)	55,931	(53.5%)
1980	President	50,316	(42.7%)	57,866	(49.1%)
	Senate	66,602	(58.2%)	41,241	(36.1%)
	House	68,310	(52.7%)	55,507	(42.9%)
1982	Governor	59,734	(51.9%)	52,191	(45.4%)
	Senate	61,144	(53.3%)	50,216	(43.8%)
	House	60,905	(53.9%)	52,177	(46.1%)

Demographics

Population: 524,883. **Percent Change from 1970:** 9.7%.

Land Area: 93 square miles. **Population per Square Mile:** 5,643.9.

Counties, 1980 Population: Los Angeles (Pt.) — 524,883.

Cities, 1980 Population: Alhambra — 64,615; Azusa — 29,380; Baldwin Park (Pt.) — 0; Bell — 25,450; Bell Gardens — 34,117; Commerce — 10,509; Cudahy — 17,984; East Los Angeles (CDP) (Pt.) — 20,893; El Monte — 79,494; Huntington Park (Pt.) — 291; Maywood — 21,810; Montebello — 52,929; Monterey Park — 54,338; Rosemead — 42,604; San Gabriel — 30,072.

Race and Ancestry: White — 67.3%; Black — 1.1%; American Indian, Eskimo and Aleut — 0.9%; Asian and Pacific Islander — 9.4%. Spanish Origin — 54.2%. English — 4.2%; French — 0.6%; German — 2.6%; Irish — 1.8%; Italian — 2.2%; Polish — 0.5%; Russian — 0.5%.

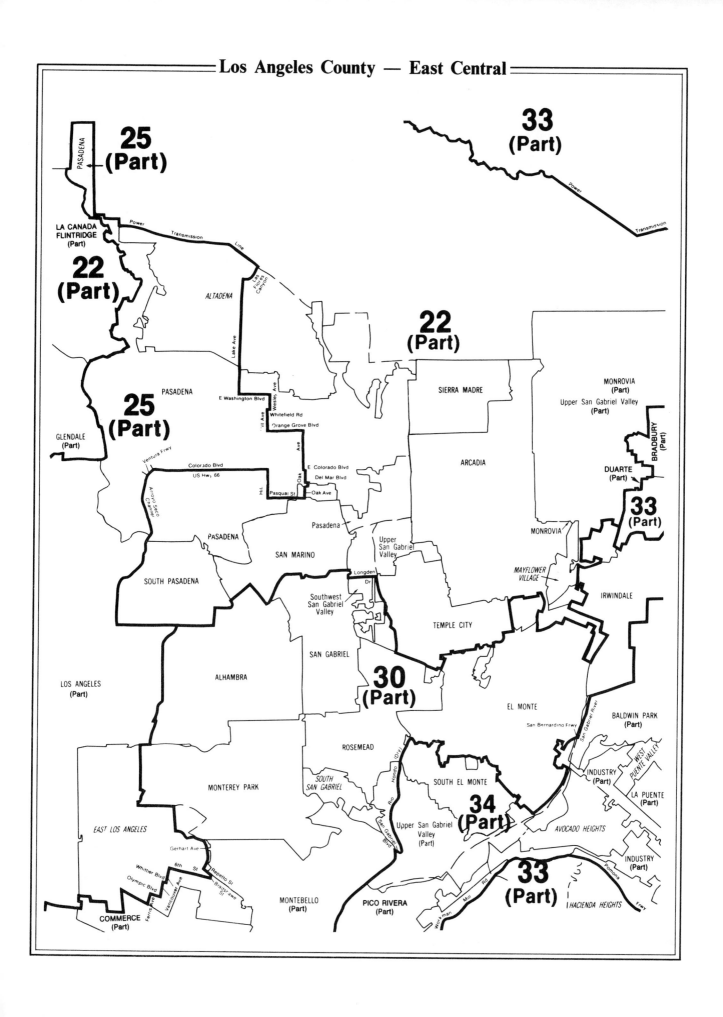

25
(Part)

33
(Part)

PASADENA

LA CANADA
FLINTRIDGE
(Part)

Power
Transmission
Line

Power
Transmission

22
(Part)

ALTADENA

Las Flores Canyon

22
(Part)

Lake Ave

SIERRA MADRE

MONROVIA
(Part)

Upper San Gabriel Valley
(Part)

BRADBURY
(Part)

PASADENA

Wesley Ave

E Washington Blvd

Hill Ave

Whitfield Rd
Orange Grove Blvd

Oak Ave

25
(Part)

GLENDALE
(Part)

ARCADIA

DUARTE
(Part)

Ventura Frwy

Colorado Blvd
US Hwy 66

Arroyo Seco Channel

Hill

E Colorado Blvd
Del Mar Blvd

Pasqual St
Oak Ave

33
(Part)

Pasadena

PASADENA

Upper
San Gabriel
Valley

MONROVIA

SAN MARINO

MAYFLOWER
VILLAGE

SOUTH PASADENA

Longden Dr

IRWINDALE

Southwest
San Gabriel
Valley

TEMPLE CITY

LOS ANGELES
(Part)

ALHAMBRA

SAN GABRIEL

30
(Part)

EL MONTE

BALDWIN PARK
(Part)

San Bernardino Frwy

San Gabriel River

ROSEMEAD

SOUTH EL MONTE

INDUSTRY
(Part)

WEST PUENTE VALLEY

MONTEREY PARK

SOUTH
SAN GABRIEL

Rio Hondo (D.V.)

LA PUENTE
(Part)

34
(Part)

Upper San Gabriel
Valley
(Part)

AVOCADO HEIGHTS

EAST LOS ANGELES

San Gabriel Blvd

INDUSTRY
(Part)

Gerhart Ave

6th St

Repetto St

Whittier Blvd

Bradshawe St

33
(Part)

Olympic Blvd

Ferris Blvd

Vancouver Ave

Pomona Frwy

MONTEBELLO
(Part)

PICO RIVERA
(Part)

Workman Mill Rd

HACIENDA HEIGHTS

COMMERCE
(Part)

Universities, Enrollment: Azusa Pacific College, Azusa — 2,102; Citrus College, Azusa — 9,395; Don Bosco Technical Institute, Rosemead — 315; East Los Angeles College, Monterey Park — 16,828.

Newspapers, Circulation: *Los Angeles Times* and *Los Angeles Herald Examiner* circulate in the district.

Commercial Television Stations, Affiliation: Entire district is in Los Angeles ADI.

Industries:

Santa Fe International Corp. (HQ); Alhambra; heavy construction — 3,200. **Union Pacific Railroad Co.;** Commerce; railroad operations — 1,600. **Aerojet-General Corp.** (Electro Systems Div.); Azusa; electrical industrial appliances — 1,350. **Bethlehem Steel Corp.** (Pacific Coast Div.); Vernon; steel alloy — 1,300. **Western Electric Co. Inc.;** East Los Angeles; telephone wholesaling — 1,300.

American Hospital Supply (Pharmaseal Lab Div.); Irwindale; disposable medical supplies — 1,250. **Aluminum Co. of America;** Vernon; aluminum tubing — 1,200. **Oroweat Foods Company Inc.** (Oroweat Baking Co.); Montebello; bakery products — 1,200. **Vons Grocery Co.** (HQ); El Monte; grocery chain — 1,200. **Miller Brewing Co. Inc.;** Irwindale; brewery — 1,180. **Norris Industries Inc.** (Thermador/Waste King Div.); Vernon; household appliances — 1,100. **Beverly Community Hospital;** Montebello; hospital — 1,000. **Filtrol Corp.;** Vernon; catalysts and absorbents; cement — 1,000. **Amfac Distribution Corp.** (Amfac Drug Supply Co.); Alhambra; drug supply wholesaling — 918. **Gould Inc.** (Navcom Systems Div.); El Monte; navigation communications equipment — 880.

Arcata Corp. (Pacific Press); Vernon; commercial printing — 850. **Lever Bros. Co.;** Commerce; soap, detergents — 800. **DuCommun Inc.** (Kierulff Electronics); Commerce; electron tubes — 780. **Flintkote Co.;** Vernon; roofing coating — 765. **Baker International Corp.** (Baker Packers); Commerce; oilfield, mining machinery — 750. **Glass Containers Corp.;** Vernon; glass — 700. **Kal-Kan Foods Inc.** (HQ); Vernon; pet food — 700. **Kayser-Roth Corp.** (Catalina Sportswear); Commerce; bathing suits, beachwear — 700. **Title Insurance & Trust Co.;** Rosemead; title insurance — 700. **Ball Corp.** (Ball Glass Container Group); El Monte; glass containers — 650.

Associated Beverage Co. (Seven Up Bottling Co. of Los Angeles - HQ); Vernon; soft drink bottling — 600. **Cal-Maine Foods Inc.** (Daisy Fresh Div.); Vernon; eggs — 600. **Crown City Plating Co.;** El Monte; commercial plating — 600.**Sargent Fletcher Co.;** El Monte; electrical industrial appliances — 538. **Atchison, Topeka & Santa Fe Railway Co.;** Commerce; railroad operations — 500. **Clayton Industries** (HQ); El Monte; industrial machinery — 500. **Federated Services Inc.** (HQ); Monterey Park; security, janitorial services — 500. **Indian Head Inc.** (Peerless Pump Div.); Montebello; pumps — 500. **Mand Carpet Mills;** Vernon; carpets — 500. **Pacific Tube Co.;** Commerce; steel tubing — 500.

31st District

Southern Los Angeles County — Compton, Carson

This is a working-class suburban district with more ethnic and racial diversity than can be found in almost any district in the state. More than a third of the residents are black, a quarter are of Spanish origin and nearly a tenth are Orientals. One thing most of them have in common is that they vote Democratic.

Only two other districts — the 28th and 29th, both with higher black populations — gave Jimmy Carter a higher percentage in 1980. The 31st is second only to the 29th in its Democratic registration percentage.

The 1981 remap added Bellflower at the eastern end of the district, bringing 38,000 more white voters to the district. But their impact was largely offset by the inclusion of Carson in the south, where blacks, Hispanics and Orientals

each number about 10,000 and nearly all are Democratic.

Bellflower and Paramount, with a combined population of 90,000 on the eastern side of the district, supported Ronald Reagan in 1980, as did Hawthorne, another mostly white suburb of about 56,000 people on the western end of the district. The four suburbs between the two ends — Carson, Compton, Gardena and Lynwood — all backed Jimmy Carter. Compton is poor and nearly all black. With 81,000 people — the same number as Carson — it gave Carter 19 votes for every one to Reagan.

The Asian vote in the district is located primarily in Gardena, a tidy suburb just off the Harbor Freeway, which bisects the district. Japanese-Americans have been a major part of Gardena's life and politics for several decades. On occasion the Japanese-American community supports Republicans.

Perhaps the district's most famous resident is the Goodyear blimp *Columbia*, whose permanent mooring is clearly visible from the intersection of the Harbor and San Diego freeways. Those two highways are important to the economy of the 31st District. Twice each day they are filled with commuters from the 31st going to their jobs in the defense or electronics industries. Throughout the rest of the day the highways are clogged with trucks hauling the goods the district produces: aircraft engines, semiconductors, Max Factor cosmetics and Mattel toys.

Election Returns

31st District		Democrat		Republican	
1976	President	83,912	(65.8%)	41,163	(32.3%)
	Senate	65,440	(62.2%)	37,170	(35.3%)
	House	97,315	(85.0%)	17,149	(15.0%)
1978	Governor	71,787	(70.5%)	25,291	(24.8%)
	House	70,865	(64.0%)	37,698	(34.1%)
1980	President	76,459	(59.0%)	45,544	(35.1%)
	Senate	87,810	(69.6%)	32,019	(25.4%)
	House	79,026	(59.8%)	51,506	(38.9%)
1982	Governor	84,855	(67.1%)	39,219	(31.0%)
	Senate	83,621	(66.7%)	38,554	(30.7%)
	House	86,718	(72.4%)	33,043	(27.6%)

Demographics

Population: 526,129. **Percent Change from 1970:** 2.1%.

Land Area: 81 square miles. **Population per Square Mile:** 6,495.4.

Counties, 1980 Population: Los Angeles (Pt.) — 526,129.

Cities, 1980 Population: Bellflower — 53,441; Carson — 81,221; Compton — 81,286; Gardena — 45,165; Hawthorne (Pt.) — 56,287; Los Angeles (Pt.) — 44,281; Lynwood — 48,548; Paramount — 36,407.

Race and Ancestry: White — 42.0%; Black — 33.7%; American Indian, Eskimo and Aleut — 0.6%; Asian and Pacific Islander — 8.4%; Spanish Origin — 25.1%. Dutch — 0.8%; English — 4.0%; French — 0.6%; German — 2.4%; Irish — 1.6%; Italian — 1.0%.

Universities, Enrollment: California State University at Dominguez Hills, Carson — 7,896; Compton Community College, Compton — 5,088; Los Angeles Southwest College, Los Angeles — 6,871.

Newspapers, Circulation: *Los Angeles Times*, *Los Angeles Herald Examiner* and Los Angeles *Daily News* circulate in the district.

Commercial Television Stations, Affiliation: Entire district is in Los Angeles ADI.

Military Installations: Compton Air National Guard Station, Compton — 140.

Industries:

Northrop Corp. (Aircraft Group); Hawthorne; aircraft — 10,700. **Martin Luther King Jr. General Hospital;** Los Angeles; hospital — 2,400. **Kaiser Foundation Hospital;** Bellflower; hospital — 2,100. **Mattel Inc.** (HQ); Hawthorne; games, toys, dolls — 1,700. **Robertshaw Controls Co. Inc.** (Grayson Controls Div.); Long Beach; thermostatic controls — 1,600.

St. Francis Medical Center; Lynwood; hospital — 1,500. **Martin Marietta Aluminum Inc.;** Los Angeles; aluminum — 1,350. **Northrop Corp.** (Electronic Div.); Hawthorne; inertial guidance systems — 1,300. **Atlantic Richfield Co.** (Watson Station Refinery); Carson; petroleum refinery — 1,100: **Max Factor & Co.;** Hawthorne; cosmetics, perfumes — 1,000. **Hiebert Inc.;** Carson; office furniture — 1,000. **Honeywell Inc.** (Residential Div.); Gardena; gas controls — 1,000. **Elixir Industries** (HQ); Gardena; metal stampings — 900. **Shell Oil Co.** (Wilmington Mfg. Complex); Carson; oil refinery — 850. **American Honda Motor Co. Inc.** (HQ); Gardena; auto, motorcycle wholesaling — 800. **Hitco** (Defense Products Div.); Gardena; specialized manufacturing — 800.

Western Gear Corp. (HQ); Lynwood; aircraft parts, industrial trucks, construction equipment — 800. **Paramount Energy Inc.;** Paramount; construction contracting — 730. **Northrop Corp.;** Hawthorne; data processing services — 699. **Alco Standard Corp.** (Rex Precision Products Div.); Gardena; foundry — 656. **California Strolee Inc.;** Compton; baby furniture — 650. **Macco Constructors Inc.** (HQ); Paramount; water, sewer, power lines constructing — 650. **Nissan Motor Corp. in U.S.A.** (HQ); Carson; auto wholesaling — 650. **Pacific Electricord Co.;** Gardena; electric cords — 650. **American Can Co.;** Carson; metal, fiber cans — 600. **Teledyne Industries Inc.** (Relays Div.); Hawthorne; relays — 600. **TRE Corp.** (Weslock Div.); Los Angeles; locks — 600.

Earle M. Jorgensen Co. (HQ); Lynwood; steel mill, forgings — 517. **Paul R. Briles Inc.** (PB Fasteners); Gardena; aircraft fasteners — 500. **Cherokee Shoe Co. Inc.** (Cherokee of California); Gardena; shoes — 500. **Lorber Industries of California;** Gardena; fabric printing — 500. **McDonnell Douglas Corp.** (Douglas Aircraft Div.); Compton; aircraft seats — 500. **Petroleum Maintenance Co.;** Lomita; oil field services — 500. **Plastiglide Mfg. Corp.** (HQ); Hawthorne; miscellaneous plastic, metal products — 500. **TRW Inc.** (Semiconductors Div.); Lawndale; semiconductors — 500. **Virco Mfg. Co.** (HQ); Los Angeles; metal school, office furniture — 500. **Western Indusrial Maintenance** (HQ); Paramount; janitorial services — 500.

32nd District

San Pedro, Long Beach

Driving along the freeways that crisscross the 32nd District, one can see fuel tanks, oil wells and, closer to the water, shipyards and loading docks. Behind this industrial landscape lie the older homes of Long Beach and San Pedro, where fishermen and sailors of many European nationalities provide a strong ethnic flavor not found in many places in the Los Angeles area.

Registered Democrats outnumber Republicans in the district by more than 2-to-1, but many split their tickets. Democrats usually prevail in statewide contests but not by the margins they enjoy in other districts where the registration advantage leans so heavily in their favor.

The 1981 redistricting preserved the nominal Democratic advantage, but it altered the 32nd significantly. The district picked up much unfamiliar territory to the east and saw some of its strongest Democratic areas removed. The heart of the district, however, remains the San Pedro-Long Beach area, which accounts for about two-thirds of the population.

Most of the new turf is on the eastern end of the old district around Lakewood and the comfortable Republican community of Cerritos, where Ronald Reagan won twice as many votes as Jimmy Carter in 1980. Lakewood is slightly more competitive than Cerritos. Combined, the two communities account for a quarter of the district's vote.

The Long Beach influence in the district was increased slightly by the addition of the eastern side of the city around the California State University branch campus. To the west and north, the district lost Carson with its strongly Democratic minority vote, and the poor neighborhoods of Torrance, which also voted Democratic.

The San Pedro Bay waterfront is no longer in the district, but maritime interests along that stretch of land remain vitally important. Thousands of constituents — old and new alike — are involved in the transportation and shipping industries.

Election Returns

32nd District		Democrat		Republican	
1976	President	84,321	(51.3%)	76,649	(46.6%)
	Senate	69,421	(49.4%)	67,242	(47.8%)
	House	103,086	(61.0%)	65,784	(38.9%)
1978	Governor	28,815	(58.1%)	48,653	(35.9%)
	House	78,588	(56.4%)	55,228	(39.7%)
1980	President	60,535	(38.3%)	82,728	(52.4%)
	Senate	86,246	(56.3%)	59,186	(38.6%)
	House	73,303	(44.8%)	84,784	(51.8%)
1982	Governor	67,913	(45.4%)	78,681	(52.5%)
	Senate	71,306	(48.0%)	72,727	(48.9%)
	House	84,663	(58.0%)	57,863	(39.6%)

Demographics

Population: 527,814. **Percent Change from 1970:** 8.3%.

Land Area: 72 square miles. **Population per Square Mile:** 7,330.8.

Counties, 1980 Population: Los Angeles (Pt.) — 527,814.

Cities, 1980 Population: Cerritos — 53,020; Hawaiian Gardens — 10,548; Lakewood — 74,654; Lomita — 18,807; Long Beach (Pt.) — 258,661; Los Angeles (Pt.) — 104,496.

Race and Ancestry: White — 70.5%; Black — 9.5%; American Indian, Eskimo and Aleut — 0.8%; Asian and Pacific Islander — 8.0%. Spanish Origin — 22.5%. Dutch — 0.8%; English — 6.7%; French — 0.9%; German — 4.2%; Irish — 2.9%; Italian — 2.1%; Norwegian — 0.6%; Polish — 0.5%; Swedish — 0.6%.

Universities, Enrollment: California State University at Long Beach, Long Beach — 31,246; Consortium of the California State University and Colleges, Long Beach — 409; Long Beach City College, Long Beach — 28,500; Los Angeles Harbor College, Wilmington — 12,825.

Newspapers, Circulation: *News-Pilot* (e), San Pedro — 14,071; *Press-Telegram* (all day, S), Long Beach — 71,483. *Los Angeles Times* and *Los Angeles Herald Examiner* also circulate in the district.

Commercial Television Stations, Affiliation: Entire district is in Los Angeles ADI.

Industries:

Todd Pacific Shipyards Corp.; San Pedro; shipbuilding, repairing — 5,200. **Memorial Hospital Medical Center;** Long Beach; hospital — 3,200. **Clopay Corp.** (Interior Door Div.); Artesia; metal doors —

1,600. **St. Mary Medical Center;** Long Beach; hospital — 1,500. **San Pedro Peninsula Hospital;** San Pedro; hospital — 1,300.

The Southland Corp. (Chief Auto Parts Div.); Artesia; auto parts wholesaling — 1,000. **Texaco Inc.;** Wilmington; petroleum production, refining — 800. **Marie Callender Pie Shops Inc.;** Long Beach; bakery products franchising — 750. **Twin Coast Newspapers Inc.;** Long Beach; newspaper publishing — 750. **Union Oil Co. of California;** Wilmington; petroleum refining — 600.

33rd District

Eastern Los Angeles — Pomona, Whittier

Most of the land in this sprawling outer suburban district is given over to largely uninhabitable mountains and hills. The northern end is dominated by the Angeles National Forest. In the southern end of the district, two modest-sized ranges divide the valley-dwelling population. A mountain named after cornflake king W. K. Kellogg separates working-class Covina from the white-collar communities of Pomona and Claremont, home of the several Claremont Colleges. And the La Puente Hills isolate Whittier and La Mirada from the rest of the district.

Slightly less than half the population of the new district belonged to the old 35th. This territory includes Pomona, with 92,000 residents, the largest city in the new constituency. Living more than 30 miles from downtown Los Angeles, Pomona residents are more likely to commute to San Bernardino and Riverside counties to the east or work in the Pomona-Claremont area than make the daily trip into Los Angeles.

The old 33rd was decimated by redistricting. The cities of Norwalk, Downey, Cerritos and Whittier made up more than half the old district's population. For the 1982 elections, the new 33rd retained only Richard Nixon's boyhood home of Whittier, which has fewer than 70,000 residents.

Merging the old 33rd and 35th districts combined two divergent elements of California's suburban culture. Voters south of the La Puente hills, in the old 33rd, tend to be middle-aged homeowners with grown children. Those to the north are more likely to be people who have come to California in the last 10 years.

Though far from unified geographically or culturally, the district is united in its Republican leanings. There are only a few more registered Democrats than Republicans, which in California means a Republican advantage in most elections. In the last several years most Republican statewide candidates have carried the district.

Election Returns

33rd District		Democrat		Republican	
1976	President	67,536	(39.5%)	99,999	(58.5%)
	Senate	57,626	(39.6%)	84,546	(58.1%)
	House	78,047	(45.8%)	92,351	(54.2%)
1978	Governor	70,243	(47.1%)	69,021	(46.2%)
	House	59,453	(42.9%)	79,255	(57.1%)
1980	President	49,694	(27.0%)	118,017	(64.1%)
	Senate	80,792	(45.1%)	88,944	(49.6%)
	House	61,763	(35.4%)	109,471	(62.7%)

35th District		Democrat		Republican	
1982	Governor	69,392	(38.6%)	106,892	(59.5%)
	Senate	61,906	(34.7%)	111,336	(62.4%)
	House	55,514	(32.2%)	112,362	(65.2%)

Demographics

Population: 526,296. **Percent Change from 1970:** 15.3%.

Land Area: 973 square miles. **Population per Square Mile:** 540.9.

Counties, 1980 Population: Los Angeles (Pt.) — 526,296.

Cities, 1980 Population: Claremont — 30,950; Covina — 33,751; Duarte (Pt.) — 16,766; Glendora — 38,654; La Mirada (Pt.) — 40,986; La Verne — 23,508; Pomona — 92,742; San Dimas — 24,014; Walnut — 12,478; Whittier (Pt.) — 69,717.

Race and Ancestry: White — 82.4%; Black — 5.2%; American Indian, Eskimo and Aleut — 0.7%; Asian and Pacific Islander — 4.2%. Spanish Origin — 19.0%. Dutch — 0.6%; English — 8.6%; French — 1.0%; German — 5.8%; Irish — 3.3%; Italian — 2.6%; Norwegian — 0.5%; Polish — 0.8%; Russian — 0.5%; Scottish — 0.6%; Swedish — 0.7%.

Universities, Enrollment: Biola University, La Mirada — 3,214; California State Polytechnic University at Pomona, Pomona — 15,448; Claremont Graduate School, Claremont — 1,690; Claremont Men's College, Claremont — 849; College of Osteopathic Medicine of the Pacific, Pomona — 161; Harvey Mudd College, Claremont — 497; Mt. San Antonio College, Walnut — 21,323; Pitzer College, Claremont — 787; Pomona College, Claremont — 1,354; Rio Hondo College, Whittier — 11,777; School of Theology at Claremont, Claremont — 373; Scripps College, Claremont — 579; University of La Verne, La Verne — 4,059; Whittier College, Whittier — 1,471.

Newspapers, Circulation: *The Daily News* (e), Whittier — 19,217; *Progress Bulletin* (meS), Pomona — 41,439; *San Gabriel Valley Daily Tribune* (meS), Covina — 64,903. *Los Angeles Times* and *Los Angeles Herald Examiner* also circulate in the district.

Commercial Television Stations, Affiliation: Entire district is in Los Angeles ADI.

Industries:

General Dynamics Corp.; Pomona; tactical weapons — 8,000. **Treasure Chest Advertising Co.;** Glendora; merchandising circulars — 2,200. **Denny's Inc.** (Denny's Restaurants - HQ); La Mirada; fast food restaurant chain — 1,900. **Lanterman State Hospital;** Pomona; state mental hospital — 1,700. **City of Hope Inc.;** Duarte; hospital — 1,500.

Presbyterian Intercommunity Hospital; Whittier; hospital — 1,450. **Pomona Valley Community Hospital;** Pomona; hospital — 1,100. **Honeywell Inc.** (Training Control Systems Operation); West Covina; combat radios — 1,000. **FMC Corp.** (Sweeper Div.); Pomona; street sweepers — 750. **Summit Companies Inc.;** La Mirada; trucking — 630. **Eastman Kodak Co.** (Pacific Southern Region); Whittier; photographic supply wholesaling — 600. **Potlatch Corp.** (Northwest & Paper Div.); Pomona; paper mill — 600. **Conrac Corp.;** Covina; TV monitors — 525. **Simpson Paper Co.;** Pomona; paper mill — 525. **The Perkin-Elmer Corp.** (Aerospace Div.); Pomona; fine optics — 500.

34th District

Los Angeles Suburbs — Norwalk, West Covina

This elongated slice of suburbia twists and slithers through parts of Los Angeles County tourists never see — unless they are racing by on one of four expressways that keep the area fragmented. The district more or less follows the San Gabriel River — a channelized concrete trough —

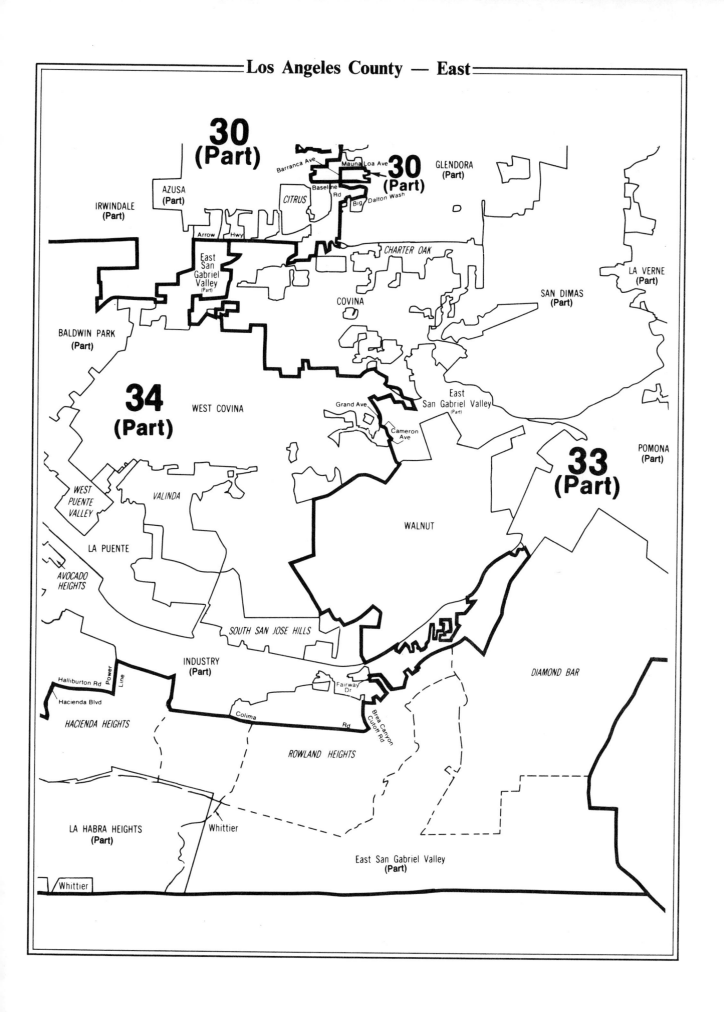

through blue-collar communities that have little interaction with each other.

At the two ends of the district are two very different cities of about 80,000 residents each. In the south is Norwalk, an older working-class suburb with a declining population but a growing Hispanic community — 40 percent in 1980. On the northern border is West Covina, a newer, still-growing and significantly more affluent town on the Los Angeles-San Bernardino axis.

In between are the district's most heavily Hispanic areas, around Pico Rivera and South El Monte. Three-fourths of the residents there are of Hispanic origin. Nearly every community in the district except West Covina has at least a one-third Hispanic population, making the new 34th 48 percent Hispanic altogether.

The district also contains the City of Industry. Although its population is only 664, it is home to dozens of businesses that bring thousands of workers into the area every day.

Thrown together from parts of five old congressional districts — the 26th, 30th, 33rd, 34th and 35th — this is an unpredictable area politically. Artesia and Norwalk in the south and Baldwin Park and West Covina in the north are most likely to vote Republican, as they all did in 1980 for Ronald Reagan. But the center of the district is solidly Democratic. The districtwide registration is 64-27 in favor of the Democrats.

If the Hispanic community is mobilized politically, it has the strength to elect one of its own, as it demonstrated in 1982 when a Hispanic challenger defeated the Democratic incumbent in the primary and went on to win the general election. Although Hispanic Democrats do not always turn out in large numbers, they can nearly always be decisive when a Hispanic candidate runs a well-organized campaign.

Election Returns

34th District		Democrat		Republican	
1976	President	75,721	(54.3%)	60,850	(43.6%)
	Senate	61,857	(52.3%)	53,231	(45.0%)
	House	80,361	(52.4%)	73,060	(47.6%)
1978	Governor	68,947	(60.6%)	38,266	(33.6%)
	House	59,867	(48.3%)	64,162	(51.7%)
1980	President	52,982	(39.8%)	69,299	(52.0%)
	Senate	73,086	(56.3%)	48,884	(37.7%)
	House	64,239	(42.4%)	83,637	(55.3%)
1982	Governor	63,916	(51.3%)	57,228	(46.0%)
	Senate	63,648	(51.3%)	56,310	(45.4%)
	House	68,316	(57.2%)	51,026	(42.8%)

Demographics

Population: 526,321. **Percent Change from 1970:** 3.9%.

Land Area: 100 square miles. **Population per Square Mile:** 5,263.2.

Counties, 1980 Population: Los Angeles (Pt.) — 526,321.

Cities, 1980 Population: Artesia — 14,301; Baldwin Park (Pt.) — 50,554; La Mirada (Pt.) — 0; La Puente — 30,882; Norwalk — 85,286; Pico Rivera — 53,459; Santa Fe Springs — 14,520; South El Monte — 16,623; West Covina — 80,291; Whittier (Pt.) — 0.

Race and Ancestry: White — 74.6%; Black — 2.3%; American Indian, Eskimo and Aleut — 0.8%; Asian and Pacific Islander — 4.3%.

Spanish Origin — 47.6%. Dutch — 0.7%; English — 5.0%; French — 0.7%; German — 3.3%; Irish — 2.1%; Italian — 1.5%; Polish — 0.5%; Portuguese — 0.5%.

Universities, Enrollment: Cerritos College, Norwalk — 22,225.

Newspapers, Circulation: *Los Angeles Times* and *Los Angeles Herald Examiner* circulate in the district.

Commercial Television Stations, Affiliation: Entire district is in Los Angeles ADI.

Industries:

Safeway Stores Inc. (Los Angeles Distributor Center); Santa Fe Springs; food warehousing — 9,710. **Bechtel Power Corp;** Norwalk; electrical engineering services — 3,200. **Queen of the Valley Hospital;** West Covina; hospital — 1,350. **Carrier Corp.** (Bryant-Day & Nite-Payne Div.); City of Industry; water heaters — 1,000. **Western Gear Corp.** (Applied Technology Div.); City of Industry; electrical machinery — 1,000.

International Telephone & Telegraph Corp. (Barton Instrument Div.); City of Industry; electricity testing devices — 800. **Utility Trailer Mfg. Co.** (HQ); City of Industry; truck trailers — 640. **Scovill Inc.** (Ajax-Nutone Div.); City of Industry; hardware — 630. **American Telecommunications Corp.** (Electronics Div.); City of Industry; telephone apparatus — 600. **Mattell Inc.;** City of Industry; toys, dolls — 600. **West Point-Pepperell Inc.** (Walter Carpet Mills); City of Industry; tufted carpets — 565. **Stoody Co.** (Wrap Div.); Whittier; castings — 530.

California Industrial Products; Santa Fe Springs; auto parts — 520. **Transcon Lines;** Santa Fe Springs; trucking — 520. **Challenge-Cook Bros. Inc.;** City of Industry; construction equipment — 516. **Magic Chef Inc.;** City of Industry; gas, electric ranges — 500. **Owens-Illinois Inc.** (Libby Products Group); City of Industry; glass tableware — 500. **Powerine Oil Co.** (HQ); Santa Fe Springs; petroleum refining, marketing — 500. **Spectrol Electronics;** City of Industry; electronics — 500.

35th District

San Bernardino and Inyo Counties

The newly drawn 35th covers a vast and sparsely populated desert area between Los Angeles and the Nevada border. Covering a fifth of the state's land area, it is the largest district in California.

The Mojave Desert, Death Valley and the nation's hottest town, Needles, are the best known parts of the district. But the voters who make this a reliably Republican constituency are elsewhere — squeezed into the southwestern corner of the district, surrounding the city of San Bernardino on three sides. For all intents and purposes, the 35th is a suburban district.

West of San Bernardino, near the border with Los Angeles County, are communities such as Chino and Upland that have been experiencing tremendous exurban growth in recent years. Most of the voters there side with the GOP, although Chino has a growing Hispanic population that tends to favor Democrats.

The cities of Redlands and Loma Linda, both university towns east of San Bernardino, are located in what was once a citrus-packing area at the edge of the nation's citrus belt. Today it primarily packs a huge suburban Republican vote, although orange groves still occupy a few small parcels of the region's red soil.

Despite the suburban majority, a successful candidate cannot ignore the concerns of voters living in desert towns such as Barstow, China Lake and Victorville. Water is the main political issue in those places.

San Bernardino - Riverside

Election Returns

35th District		Democrat		Republican	
1976	President	53,216	(42.9%)	69,275	(55.8%)
	Senate	50,523	(42.0%)	67,009	(55.7%)
	House	47,795	(33.3%)	93,583	(65.1%)
1978	Governor	61,764	(48.5%)	58,250	(45.7%)
	House	53,308	(39.5%)	78,743	(58.4%)
1980	President	46,323	(26.7%)	112,232	(64.7%)
	Senate	77,772	(46.0%)	81,984	(48.5%)
	House	50,667	(28.8%)	117,798	(66.9%)

35th District		Democrat		Republican	
1982	Governor	66,640	(38.6%)	101,594	(58.8%)
	Senate	56,829	(33.3%)	107,508	(63.0%)
	House	52,349	(31.7%)	112,786	(68.3%)

Demographics

Population: 526,398. **Percent Change from 1970:** 40.4%.

Land Area: 30,321 square miles. **Population per Square Mile:** 17.4.

Counties, 1980 Population: Inyo — 17,895; Los Angeles (Pt.) — 3,375; San Bernardino (Pt.) — 505,128.

Cities, 1980 Population: Barstow — 17,690; Chino — 40,165; Loma Linda — 10,694; Montclair — 22,628; Ontario (Pt.) — 0; Rancho Cucamonga — 55,250; Redlands (Pt.) — 43,619; San Bernardino (Pt.) — 0; Upland — 47,647; Victorville — 14,220.

Race and Ancestry: White — 87.1%; Black — 3.2%; American Indian, Eskimo and Aleut — 1.4%; Asian and Pacific Islander — 2.0%. Spanish Origin — 13.6%. Dutch — 1.2%; English — 9.9%; French — 1.1%; German — 6.8%; Irish — 3.4%; Italian — 1.9%; Norwegian — 0.5%; Polish — 0.8%; Portuguese — 0.5%; Scottish — 0.7%; Swedish — 0.9%.

Universities, Enrollment: Barstow College, Barstow — 1,800; Chaffey Community College, Alta Loma — 12,280; Crafton Hills College, Yucaipa — 3,865; Loma Linda University, Loma Linda — 5,351; University of Redlands, Redlands — 2,750; Victor Valley College, Victorville — 3,747.

Newspapers, Circulation: *Desert Dispatch* (e), Barstow — 7,135; *Redlands Daily Facts* (e), Redlands — 8,255; *Victor Valley Daily Press* (eS), Victorville — 14,609. The *Los Angeles Times*, San Bernardino *Sun* and Ontario *Daily Report* also circulate in the district.

Commercial Television Stations, Affiliation: Entire district is in Los Angeles ADI.

Military Installations: China Lake Naval Weapons Center, Ridgecrest — 5,214; Fort Irwin, Barstow — 2,854; George Air Force Base, Adelanto — 5,949; Marine Corps Air Ground Combat Center, Twentynine Palms — 7,805; Marine Corps Logistics Base, Barstow — 2,798.

Industries:

Kerr-McGee Chemical Corp.; Trona; potash, other mineral mining — 1,600. **San Antonio Community Hospital;** Upland; hospital — 1,020. **Atchison, Topeka & Santa Fe Railway;** Needles; railroad operations — 600. **Ameron Inc.** (Tamco); Rancho Cucamonga; steel products — 550.

36th District

San Bernardino, Riverside

Of the three districts covering the San Bernardino-Riverside metropolitan area, this is the only one a Democrat can win. The votes of the blue-collar residents of Riverside and San Bernardino and those of the growing Mexican-American population in San Bernardino have been enough to keep the Democratic incumbent in office since 1972.

To keep the district safe for the Democrats, the suburbs of Norco and Corona with their burgeoning Republican vote were removed from the 36th District, along with a large part of the city of Riverside. Only the Democratic north side of Riverside remains in the new 36th District.

The San Bernardino side of the district, which is usually more favorable to Democrats, was expanded. The district now extends westward to Ontario, once a shady residential town of a few thousand that has grown into a booming, industrial city of 88,000, supporting a major commercial airport and large Lockheed and General Electric plants. In recent years Ontario voters have turned increasingly toward Republican candidates, both statewide and congressional.

The new 36th takes in all of San Bernardino's 117,490 inhabitants. More than 50 miles from Los Angeles, the city once marked the eastern terminus for the big, red trolley cars of Los Angeles' Pacific Electric interurban rail system.

Today, San Bernardino residents have little contact with the Los Angeles area. A fruit-packing center in the 1930s, San Bernardino now forces its citrus industry to share space with the many electronics and aerospace firms in the area, as well as the Kaiser Steel Corporation's blast furnace in nearby Fontana. These industries, along with the large Atchinson, Topeka & Santa Fe railroad yards in San Bernardino, usually provide enough votes to put the city and nearby Rialto and Colton into the Democratic column.

Election Returns

36th District		Democrat		Republican	
1976	President	73,491	(57.3%)	53,212	(41.5%)
	Senate	74,311	(59.4%)	47,513	(38.0%)
	House	75,508	(60.1%)	45,108	(35.9%)
1978	Governor	72,301	(62.8%)	37,053	(32.2%)
	House	70,392	(63.5%)	40,096	(36.2%)
1980	President	58,253	(39.6%)	74,870	(50.8%)
	Senate	85,801	(59.5%)	49,175	(34.1%)
	House	74,379	(50.1%)	68,656	(46.2%)
1982	Governor	76,532	(52.6%)	65,121	(44.7%)
	Senate	71,553	(49.8%)	66,795	(46.5%)
	House	76,546	(54.3%)	64,361	(45.7%)

Demographics

Population: 528,091. **Percent Change from 1970:** 19.4%.

Land Area: 253 square miles. **Population per Square Mile:** 2,087.3.

Counties, 1980 Population: Riverside (Pt.) — 138,203; San Bernardino (Pt.) — 389,888.

Cities, 1980 Population: Colton — 21,310; Fontana — 37,111; Norco (Pt.) — 0; Ontario (Pt.) — 88,820; Redlands (Pt.) — 0; Rialto — 37,474; Riverside (Pt.) — 90,013; San Bernardino (Pt.) — 117,490.

Race and Ancestry: White — 76.5%; Black — 8.0%; American Indian, Eskimo and Aleut — 1.2%; Asian and Pacific Islander — 1.6%. Spanish Origin — 23.3%. Dutch — 0.7%; English — 8.0%; French — 1.0%; German — 5.3%; Irish — 3.1%; Italian — 1.7%; Polish — 0.7%; Swedish — 0.6%.

Universities, Enrollment: California State College at San Bernardino, San Bernardino — 4,231; Riverside City College, Riverside — 14,478; San Bernardino Valley College, San Bernardino — 15,004; Skadron College of Business, San Bernardino — 1,209; University of California at Riverside, Riverside — 4,707.

Newspapers, Circulation: *Herald-News* (e), Fontana — 4,268; *The Daily Report* (eS), Ontario — 33,236; *Press-Enterprise* (meS), Riverside — 105,538; *The Sun* (mS), San Bernardino — 81,870. *Los Angeles Times* also circulates in the district.

Commercial Television Stations, Affiliation: KTBN-TV, Fontana (None). Entire district is in Los Angeles ADI.

Military Installations: Norton Air Force Base, San Bernardino — 11,661; Ontario International Airport (Air Force), Ontario — 727.

Industries:

Kaiser Steel Corp.; Fontana; blast furnace — 8,300. **Rohr Industries Inc.;** Riverside; aircraft — 2,400. **Atchison, Topeka & Santa Fe Railway;** San Bernardino; railroad operations — 1,800. **Lockheed Aircraft Corp.** (Aircraft Service); Ontario; aircraft overhauling — 1,750. **Bourns Inc.** (HQ); Riverside; potentiometers — 1,200.

San Bernardino Community Hospital; San Bernardino; hospital — 1,150. **St. Bernardine's Hospital;** San Bernardino; hospital — 1,000. **Kasler Corp.** (HQ); San Bernardino; highway, pipeline construction — 990. **General Electric Co.** (Aviation Service Operation); Ontario; aircraft overhauling — 700. **The Toro Co.** (Irrigation Div.); Riverside; sprinkling systems — 625. **Kaiser Steel Corp.** (Fabricated Products

Div.); Fontana; fabricated structural metal — 600. **Sunkist Growers Inc.** (Orange Products Div.); Ontario; citrus packing — 600. **Owens-Illinois Inc.** (Libby Glass Div.); Mira Loma; glassware — 550. **The Harris Co.** (HQ); San Bernardino; department stores — 500. **Press Enterprise Co.**; Riverside; newspaper publishing — 698.

37th District

Riverside County

The suburban and desert areas of Riverside County in the 37th District are not very lucrative places for Democrats to look for votes. The district's population is dispersed over a huge expanse of Riverside County, but much of it is concentrated near Orange County in fast-growing Riverside suburbs such as Norco and Corona. This white-collar professional area supported Ronald Reagan by more than a 2-to-1 margin in 1980.

Further east in the desert are the oasis resorts of Rancho Mirage and Palm Springs, where the leisure economy pumps thousands of dollars into the hands of local businessmen. The returns from that area are every bit as Republican as the ones from the suburbs.

Agriculture also plays a major role in the district's economy and politics, as irrigation ditches from the Colorado River Aqueduct spread across the non-mountainous areas. Recently cotton and livestock growers have been voting for Republican House candidates.

During the 1960s and part of the 1970s, this district included all of the city of Riverside, which is more Democratic than the rest of the county. Riverside was removed completely from the 37th District in 1974. The 1982 remap placed some 81,000 Riverside residents back in the district, but they are in the southern half of the city, where the median housing values and the Republican vote are both about 20 points higher than elsewhere in Riverside.

Election Returns

37th District		Democrat		Republican	
1976	President	68,325	(47.5%)	74,296	(51.6%)
	Senate	71,339	(48.9%)	71,682	(49.2%)
	House	64,063	(40.9%)	87,263	(55.6%)
1978	Governor	74,709	(52.6%)	59,797	(42.1%)
	House	66,334	(45.7%)	75,565	(52.0%)
1980	President	56,492	(30.5%)	113,631	(61.4%)
	Senate	90,631	(49.7%)	80,920	(44.4%)
	House	65,299	(33.7%)	122,309	(63.1%)
1982	Governor	79,360	(42.8%)	102,608	(55.3%)
	Senate	69,281	(37.6%)	109,473	(59.4%)
	House	68,510	(38.5%)	105,065	(59.1%)

Demographics

Population: 524,963. **Percent Change from 1970:** 55.3%.

Land Area: 7,142 square miles. **Population per Square Mile:** 73.5.

Counties, 1980 Population: Riverside (Pt.) — 524,963.

Cities, 1980 Population: Banning — 14,020; Corona — 37,791; Hemet — 22,454; Indio — 21,611; Norco (Pt.) — 21,126; Palm Desert — 11,801; Palm Springs — 32,271; Riverside (Pt.) — 80,863.

Race and Ancestry: White — 83.5%; Black — 3.8%; American Indian, Eskimo and Aleut — 1.0%; Asian and Pacific Islander — 1.4%. Spanish Origin — 18.5%. Dutch — 0.8%; English — 9.9%; French — 1.0%; German — 6.1%; Irish — 3.4%; Italian — 1.7%; Norwegian — 0.6%; Polish — 0.8%; Russian — 0.5%; Scottish — 0.7%; Swedish — 0.8%.

Universities, Enrollment: California Baptist College, Riverside — 730; College of the Desert, Palm Desert — 5,214; Mt. San Jacinto College, San Jacinto — 2,723; Palo Verde College, Blythe — 590.

Newspapers, Circulation: *Daily Independent* (e), Corona — 6,497; *Daily News* (e), Indio — 8,079; *Desert Sun* (e), Palm Springs — 21,010; *The Hemet News* (e), Hemet — 14,818; *Record-Gazette* (e), Banning — 3,156. *Los Angeles Times* and Riverside *Press-Enterprise* also circulate in the district.

Commercial Television Stations, Affiliation: KBSC-TV, Corona (None); KESQ-TV, Palm Springs (ABC); KMIR-TV, Palm Springs (NBC). District is divided between Los Angeles ADI, Palm Springs ADI and Phoenix (Ariz.) ADI.

Military Installations: March Air Force Base, Sunnymead — 6,031.

Industries:

Deutsch Co. (Electronic Components Div. - HQ); Banning; relays, connectors — 1,000. **Kaiser Steel Corp.**; Eagle Mountain; iron ore mining — 1,000. **Bourns Inc.**; Riverside; electronic instruments — 500. **Fleetwood Enterprises Inc.** (HQ); Riverside; mobile homes — 500.

38th District

Northwestern Orange County — Santa Ana, Garden Grove

Situated between coastal Orange County and the Disneyland corridor, this district attracts no surfers and few tourists. It is an older suburban area that is home for young families and their children.

Although by no means a politically liberal district, the 38th is receptive to Democrats if they do not veer to the left of center; many of its residents came from Texas and Oklahoma, and there are some conservative Democratic sentiments remaining a generation later.

But Republicans are always competitive. Many Democrats here not only defected from the party's 1982 statewide slate but backed GOP assaults on a state Senate seat and one of the two Assembly seats Democrats held in the area.

About half of the district's residents live in Garden Grove and Santa Ana in the southern part of the district. They are for the most part working-class people, employed in Orange County's industrial and aerospace plants.

Santa Ana (population 203,713), the county seat, is 45 percent Hispanic. The city is split between two districts, but the territory in the the 38th includes three-fourths of the city's population and most of the Hispanic neighborhoods that are the foundation of the district's Democratic vote.

Garden Grove has a much smaller minority population. But the city's comfortable middle-American ethos, symbolized by the nationwide "positive-thinking" television ministry of Robert Schuller from his Crystal Cathedral, has been shaken in recent years by a heavy influx of Indochinese refugees. With an undercurrent of racial backlash running through the city, Garden Grove's blue-collar white voters have turned increasingly conservative.

The northern part of the 38th is equally mixed, with small working-class communities such as Stanton and

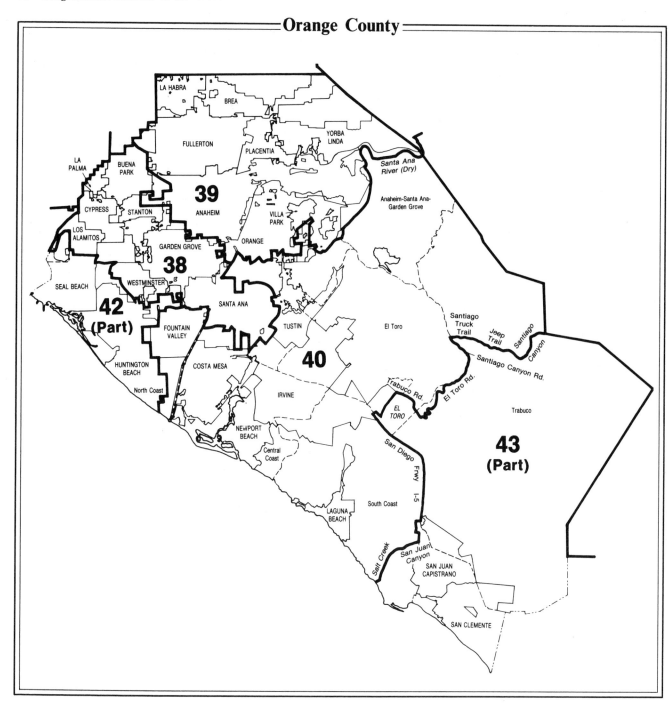

Orange County

Buena Park rubbing elbows with more prosperous Cypress, La Palma and Los Alamitos; these last three are marginally Republican.

Election Returns

38th District		Democrat		Republican	
1976	President	65,050	(44.6%)	79,018	(54.2%)
	Senate	70,834	(44.8%)	82,285	(52.1%)
	House	102,301	(62.0%)	62,651	(38.0%)
1978	Governor	73,021	(55.4%)	49,033	(37.2%)
	House	74,884	(56.8%)	56,875	(43.1%)

38th District		Democrat		Republican	
1980	President	45,316	(28.5%)	99,697	(62.6%)
	Senate	73,885	(47.2%)	72,165	(46.1%)
	House	89,584	(52.8%)	72,422	(42.7%)
1982	Governor	62,075	(42.5%)	80,277	(55.0%)
	Senate	55,033	(38.3%)	82,802	(57.6%)
	House	73,914	(52.4%)	61,279	(43.4%)

Demographics

Population: 525,560. **Percent Change from 1970:** 11.4%.

Land Area: 75 square miles. **Population per Square Mile:** 7,007.5.

Counties, 1980 Population: Orange (Pt.) — 525,560.

Cities, 1980 Population: Anaheim (Pt.) — 41,655; Buena Park (Pt.) — 54,664; Cypress — 40,391; Garden Grove (Pt.) — 123,307; La Palma — 15,399; Los Alamitos — 11,529; Santa Ana (Pt.) — 150,927; Stanton — 23,723; Tustin (Pt.) — 0; Westminster (Pt.) — 41,171.

Race and Ancestry: White — 77.6%; Black — 2.0%; American Indian, Eskimo and Aleut — 0.8%; Asian and Pacific Islander — 6.7%. Spanish Origin — 26.2%. Dutch — 0.7%; English — 7.4%; French — 1.0%; German — 5.0%; Irish — 3.0%; Italian — 1.9%; Norwegian — 0.5%; Polish — 0.7%; Scottish — 0.5%; Swedish — 0.5%.

Universities, Enrollment: Cypress College, Cypress — 12,958; Santa Ana College, Santa Ana — 18,772.

Newspapers, Circulation: *The Register* (all day, S), Santa Ana — 230,533. *Los Angeles Times* also circulates in the district.

Commercial Television Stations, Affiliation: Entire district is in Los Angeles ADI.

Military Installations: Los Alamitos Armed Forces Reserve Center, Los Alamitos — 2,583.

Industries:

International Telephone & Telegraph Corp. (Cannon Electric Div.); Santa Ana; wiring devices — 4,000. **Knotts Berry Farm (HQ);** Buena Park; amusement park — 2,580. **California Computer Products Inc. (HQ);** Anaheim; electronic computing equipment — 1,390. **Textron Inc.** (Townsend Co.); Santa Ana; aircraft parts — 1,100. **The Perkin-Elmer Corp.;** Garden Grove; analytical instruments — 900.

Ericsson Communications Co.; Garden Grove; electrical machinery — 800. **Butcher Boy Food Products Inc. (HQ);** Riverside; frozen meats — 700. **EECO Inc. (HQ);** Santa Ana; electronic components — 700. **Emerson Electric Co. Inc.;** Santa Ana; industrial controls — 670. **Cooper Industries Inc.** (Martin-Decker); Santa Ana; oil drilling equipment — 650. **Rockwell International Corp.** (Western Wheel Co.); La Palma; motor vehicle parts — 620. **Swedlow Inc. (HQ);** Garden Grove; plastic products — 570. **Beatrice Foods Co.** (Del Mar Window Coverings); Westminster; window blinds, shades — 550.

Lear Siegler Inc. (Energy Products Div.); Santa Ana; controlling devices — 550. **RCA Corp.** (Service Co. Div.); Santa Ana; business services — 530. **Zeno Table Co. Inc.;** Santa Ana; wooden furniture — 525. **Automatic Data Processing Inc.;** La Palma; data processing services — 517. **Federal-Mogul Corp.** (Arrowhead Products Div.); Los Alamitos; electronic components — 500. **General Telephone Directory Co.;** Los Alamitos; directory publishing — 500. **Stanford Applied Engineering;** Santa Ana; electronic connectors — 500.

39th District

Northeastern Orange County — Anaheim, Fullerton

The 1981 remap made few detectable changes in the 39th; it is so Republican that the map makers knew they were wasting Democratic votes by including them in it. A few neighborhoods around the edges — most notably those between Orange and Tustin — were removed to bring the district's population down some 65,000. But the net political effect was minimal. The new 39th, covering the heartland of Orange County, gave Ronald Reagan 69 percent of the vote, a margin he exceeded only in the new 43rd.

The 39th receives more visitors than most of the suburban Los Angeles districts, thanks to the presence of Disneyland and Anaheim Stadium, home of the California Angels. But it is the middle-to-upper-class families living around these sites in Anaheim and in the other Orange County suburbs that give the district its strong Republican flavor. These voters rarely even think about splitting their tickets. The new 39th was one of only two districts in the

state that gave a majority to Republican Senate candidate Paul Gann against Alan Cranston in 1980. In the 10 years between 1972 and 1982, the district supported a major statewide Democratic candidate only once — Gov. Edmund G. Brown Jr. carried it in his 1978 re-election.

The growth in the western part of the district — Anaheim and Fullerton — has slowed down somewhat in the last decade. The fast-growing communities now are ones such as Yorba Linda, Richard Nixon's birthplace, which more than doubled in size between 1970 and 1980. But Anaheim, Fullerton and Orange, the three major cities in the district, hold more than three-fourths of the electorate. In the three combined, Reagan received three votes in 1980 for every one of Jimmy Carter's.

Thirty years ago — before Disneyland and scores of electronics firms arrived in the area — Anaheim was a sleepy community in the middle of the orange groves that gave the county its name. Fewer than 15,000 people lived there. Today, with 219,311 residents, Anaheim is the eighth largest city in California. It would be the largest city in 19 other states.

Election Returns

39th District		Democrat		Republican	
1976	President	62,610	(36.0%)	109,704	(63.0%)
	Senate	65,030	(35.3%)	114,617	(62.3%)
	House	77,444	(41.9%)	107,330	(58.1%)
1978	Governor	79,551	(48.4%)	72,812	(44.3%)
	House	57,025	(36.8%)	98,127	(63.2%)
1980	President	44,258	(21.7%)	141,520	(69.4%)
	Senate	86,264	(43.0%)	102,260	(50.9%)
	House	49,334	(24.4%)	152,878	(75.5%)
1982	Governor	65,616	(35.0%)	118,242	(63.1%)
	Senate	54,287	(29.4%)	124,282	(67.3%)
	House	46,681	(26.0%)	129,539	(72.2%)

Demographics

Population: 526,004. **Percent Change from 1970:** 32.4%.

Land Area: 148 square miles. **Population per Square Mile:** 3,554.1.

Counties, 1980 Population: Orange (Pt.) — 526,004.

Cities, 1980 Population: Anaheim (Pt.) — 177,656; Brea — 27,913; Buena Park (Pt.) — 9,501; Fullerton — 102,034; La Habra — 45,232; Orange (Pt.) — 80,359; Placentia — 35,041; Santa Ana (Pt.) — 0; Yorba Linda — 28,254.

Race and Ancestry: White — 87.1%; Black — 1.1%; American Indian, Eskimo and Aleut — 0.7%; Asian and Pacific Islander — 3.9%. Spanish Origin — 15.5%. Dutch — 0.7%; English — 8.7%; French — 1.1%; German — 6.9%; Irish — 3.4%; Italian — 2.5%; Norwegian — 0.6%; Polish — 1.0%; Russian — 0.5%; Scottish — 0.7%; Swedish — 0.8%.

Universities, Enrollment: California State University at Fullerton, Fullerton — 23,125; Chapman College, Orange — 5,211; Control Data Institute, Anaheim — 436; Fullerton College, Fullerton — 19,062; Pacific Christian College, Fullerton — 655; Southern California College of Optometry, Fullerton — 396; Western State University College of Law of Orange County, Fullerton — 1,480.

Newspapers, Circulation: *Anaheim Bulletin* (e), Anaheim — 14,508; *Daily News Tribune* (e), Fullerton — 23,615; *Daily Star-Progress* (e), La Habra — 4,717. *Los Angeles Times* and Santa Ana *Register* also circulate in the district.

Commercial Television Stations, Affiliation: KDOC-TV, Anaheim (None). Entire district is in Los Angeles ADI.

Industries:

Hughes Aircraft Co. (Ground Systems Group); Fullerton; electronic defense systems — 13,000. **Walt Disney Productions** (Disneyland); Anaheim; amusement park — 8,076. **Beckman Instruments Inc.** (HQ); Fullerton; medical, surgical instruments — 4,500. **Rockwell International Corp.** (Autonetics Strategic Systems Div.); Anaheim; electronic communication equipment — 3,660. **Northrop Corp.** (Electro-Mechanical Div.); Anaheim; electronic communications equipment — 2,000. **St. Joseph Hospital;** Orange; hospital — 2,000.

Aerojet-General Corp. (General Valve Co.); Fullerton; aircraft parts — 1,500. **Alpha Beta Co. Inc.** (HQ); La Habra; grocery chain — 1,500. **Interstate Electronics Corp.** (Oceanics Div. - HQ); Anaheim; electronic communications equipment — 1,200. **St. Jude Hospital** (HQ); Fullerton; hospital — 1,100. **Anaheim Memorial Hospital Assn.** (HQ); Anaheim; hospital — 1,000. **Hunt-Wesson Foods Inc.** (HQ); Fullerton; canned tomatos, vegetable oils — 1,000. **Wrather Hotels Inc.;** Anaheim; hotel — 1,000. **Kirkhill Rubber Co.** (HQ); Brea; rubber speciality products — 940. **Century Data Systems** (HQ); Anaheim; magnetic tape — 920. **General Automation Inc.** (HQ); Anaheim; computers — 900. **CBS Inc.;** Fullerton; musical instruments — 850. **Environmentals Inc.** (Globe Laundry); Anaheim; linen rental — 845. **TRW Controls Corp.** (Information Services); Orange; administrative offices — 825. **Braegen Corp.;** Anaheim; business services — 800.

Kimberly-Clark Corp.; Fullerton; paper mill — 800. **Kraftco** (Kraft Foods Div.); Buena Park; margarine — 700. **Marriott Corp.;** Anaheim; hotel — 700. **Holmes & Narver Inc.** (HQ); Orange; engineering services — 625. **Santa Fe International Corp.** (Santa Fe Drilling Co.); Orange; oil well drilling — 600. **Western Plastering Inc.;** Orange; plastering, drywall work — 600. **CPM Research West Inc.;** Anaheim; marketing — 570. **Aerojet-General Corp.** (Aerojet Mfg. Co.); Fullerton; aerospace, nuclear products — 551. **Altec Corp.** (Sound Products Div. - HQ); Anaheim; sound equipment — 550. **Chevron Oil Field Research Co.;** La Habra; research — 550. **Pet Inc.;** Anaheim; food preparations — 550. **Albertson's Inc.** (Distribution & Mfg. Center); Brea; grocery warehousing — 500. **Varco International Inc.** (Varco Oil Tools - HQ); Orange; oil field tools — 500. **Wrather Inn Inc.;** Anaheim; hotel — 500.

40th District

Coastal Orange County

It is difficult for candidates to be too conservative for the voters in this region of Orange County. John G. Schmitz, who in 1982 was removed from the council of the John Birch Society for extremism, represented this area for a term in the House. The Republican registration of the new 40th District, 51.5 percent, is second only to the new 22nd.

Newport Beach, a wealthy enclave noted for its luxurious housing, remains the center of the district. A community of 62,556 people, Newport Beach regularly provides Republican candidates with tremendous margins at the polls. In 1980, Ronald Reagan topped Jimmy Carter by 74 to 16 percent there.

Many of the residents of the district either commute to jobs in Los Angeles or are employed by high-tech concerns that are scattered throughout the district. The University of California Irvine Campus is located in the district. But any liberal influence from this academic center is hardly noticed in the 40th District.

The only two incorporated areas in the district where registered Democrats outnumber Republicans are Costa Mesa and Laguna Beach, two quite different areas. Trendy Laguna Beach, which saw an influx of counterculture types in the 1960s and 1970s, today is home for many single adults and couples without children who live in comfortable condominium complexes along the ocean. Laguna Beach has been described in print as California's "grooviest beach resort."

Costa Mesa, whose airport is named after actor John Wayne, is not so groovy. Just north of Newport Beach, it is home for young families living in modest suburban homes built in the 1950s and 1960s. Although both communities supported Reagan by smaller margins than the rest of the district, they split on two policy questions in 1980. Costa Mesa voters joined those in Newport Beach in their opposition to requiring non-smoking areas in public places. They also objected to having the state purchase Lake Tahoe land to preserve it from development. Laguna Beach voters supported both ideas.

Election Returns

40th District		Democrat		Republican	
1976	President	55,991	(30.9%)	123,924	(68.3%)
	Senate	64,932	(33.3%)	125,883	(64.6%)
	House	70,946	(41.0%)	102,039	(59.0%)
1978	Governor	80,787	(45.5%)	83,822	(47.2%)
	House	52,798	(34.5%)	100,241	(65.5%)
1980	President	46,580	(20.7%)	155,576	(69.1%)
	Senate	96,050	(43.4%)	110,165	(49.8%)
	House	45,450	(22.1%)	146,136	(71.0%)
1982	Governor	75,234	(35.3%)	134,344	(63.1%)
	Senate	60,110	(28.6%)	144,258	(68.6%)
	House	52,546	(26.1%)	144,228	(71.5%)

Demographics

Population: 525,521. **Percent Change from 1970:** 50.6%.

Land Area: 326 square miles. **Population per Square Mile:** 1,612.0.

Counties, 1980 Population: Orange (Pt.) — 525,521.

Cities, 1980 Population: Costa Mesa — 82,562; Fountain Valley — 55,080; Huntington Beach (Pt.) — 34,351; Irvine — 62,134; Laguna Beach — 17,901; Newport Beach — 62,556; Orange (Pt.) — 11,429; Santa Ana (Pt.) — 52,786; Tustin (Pt.) — 32,317.

Race and Ancestry: White — 90.5%; Black — 1.3%; American Indian, Eskimo and Aleut — 0.5%; Asian and Pacific Islander — 4.5%. Spanish Origin — 7.8%. Dutch — 0.8%; English — 10.8%; French — 1.1%; German — 6.6%; Irish — 3.9%; Italian — 2.5%; Norwegian — 0.7%; Polish — 1.0%; Russian — 0.9%; Scottish — 0.9%; Swedish — 1.0%.

Universities, Enrollment: Christ College at Irvine, Irvine — 148; Coastline Community College, Fountain Valley — 23,536; Orange Coast College, Costa Mesa — 28,835; Southern California College, Costa Mesa — 740; University of California at Irvine, Irvine — 10,210.

Newspapers, Circulation: *Orange Coast Daily Pilot* (eS), Costa Mesa — 44,405. *Los Angeles Times* and Santa Ana *Register* also circulate in the district.

Commercial Television Stations, Affiliation: Entire district is in Los Angeles ADI.

Military Installations: El Toro Marine Corps Air Station, Irvine — 12,842; Tustin Marine Corps Air Station, Tustin — 2,908.

Industries:

Ford Aerospace & Communications Corp. (Aeronutronic Div.); Newport Beach; defense systems — 3,200. **American Hospital Supply**

Corp. (McGaw Respiration Therapy Div.); Irvine; orthopedic apparatus — 2,010. **Air Cal Investment Inc.;** Newport Beach; airline — 2,000. **Hoag Memorial Hospital;** Newport Beach; hospital — 1,850. **Smith International Inc.** (Smith Tool Co. Div.); Irvine; oil field machinery — 1,700. **Western Medical Center;** Santa Ana; hospital — 1,700.

American Hospital Supply Corp.; Newport Beach; pharmaceuticals — 1,500. **State Farm Fire & Casualty Co.;** Costa Mesa; casualty insurance — 1,500. **Parker-Hannifin Corp.** (Aerospace Group); Irvine; aircraft fluid, hydraulic power systems components — 1,400. **American Hospital Supply Group** (American Edwards Laboratories); Irvine; medical devices — 1,300. **Hughes Aircraft Co. Inc.** (Solid State Products Div.); Newport Beach; electronic office machines — 1,200. **Sperry Corp.** (Varian Data Machines); Irvine; electronic computing equipment — 1,200. **Burroughs Corp.** (Computer Systems Group); Mission Viejo; electronic computing equipment — 1,000. **Daniel International Corp.** (HQ); Irvine; general building contracting — 1,000. **Fountain Valley Community Hospital;** Fountain Valley; hospital — 1,000. **Microdata Corp.** (HQ); Irvine; computers — 1,000. **Pacific Mutual Life Insurance Co.** (HQ); Newport Beach; life, health insurance — 1,000. **Pertec Computer Corp.** (Business Systems Div.); Irvine; electronic computing equipment — 1,000.

Rockwell International Corp. (Collins Communications Systems Div.); Newport Beach; electronic components — 950. **Smithkline Corp.;** Irvine; pharmaceuticals — 950. **Steelcase Inc.;** Tustin; office furniture — 950. **Shiley Inc.** (HQ); Irvine; photographic equipment — 925. **Parker-Hannifin Corp.** (Aerospace Div. - Control Systems Div.); Irvine; aircraft components — 850. **Avco Financial Services Inc.** (HQ); Newport Beach; financing services — 840. **Printonix Inc.** (HQ); Irvine; computer line printers — 820. **Computer Automation Inc.** (HQ); Irvine; mini-computers — 800. **SPS Technologies;** Santa Ana; steel office furniture — 800. **Times-Mirror Co.;** Costa Mesa; newspaper publishing — 800. **Weyerhauser Co.** (Hines Wholesale Nurseries); Santa Ana; nursery wholesaling — 800.

Hughes Aircraft Co. (Connecting Devices Div.); Irvine; wiring devices — 764. **Bentley Laboratories Inc.** (HQ); Irvine; medical instruments — 750. **Hughes Aircraft Co.** (Microelectronic Systems Div.); Irvine; semiconductors — 700. **Management Assistance Inc.** (Basic/Four Information Systems Div.); Tustin; computer equipment — 700. **TRE Corp.;** Santa Ana; aircraft parts — 600. **MacGregor Yacht Corp.;** Costa Mesa; sailing yachts — 550. **Del Mar Avionics** (Avionics Biomedical Div - HQ); Irvine; surgical, medical instruments — 525. **Beckman Instruments Inc.;** Irvine; scientific instruments — 500. **Farmers Insurance Group** (Truck Underwriters Assn.); Santa Ana; casualty insurance — 500. **Fluor Engineers & Constructors Inc.** (HQ); Irvine; engineering services, heavy construction — 500. **International Telephone & Telegraph Corp.** (J. C. Carter Co.); Costa Mesa; special industrial machinery — 500. **MSI Data Corp.** (HQ); Costa Mesa; electronic computing equipment — 500. **Times-Mirror Cable TV Inc.** (HQ); Irvine; cable television — 500. **Western Digital Corp.** (HQ); Irvine; microcircuits — 500.

41st District

North San Diego and Suburbs

The 1981 remap made both the 41st and the nearby 45th more Republican in order to create a Democratic district in between the two — the 44th.

The redrawn 41st, essentially the northern half of San Diego, completely surrounds the huge Miramar Naval Air Station, which some would like to turn into the major commercial airport for San Diego. The presence of Miramar and other naval installations gives the district a large military constituency. Aerospace and electronics firms associated with the military are also in the area.

The further north one travels in San Diego County, toward the Orange County border, the more Republican the area becomes. The new 41st lost some of its southern

territory and was extended northward as far as Poway in the mountains and along the coast beyond Del Mar to Leucadia. All of the exclusive La Jolla section of San Diego is now in the district. The 41st also retained the Mission Bay and Pacific Beach sections, as well as the Republican suburb of La Mesa, on the eastern flank of the city. But most of the district's population — some 347,000 people — lives within the city limits of San Diego.

Voters here have shown a marked willingness to split their tickets. In 1980, Democratic Sen. Alan Cranston ran a full 30 points ahead of Jimmy Carter — the biggest difference between the two candidates in any district in the state. Ronald Reagan carried the district with 60 percent and Cranston was not far behind with 56 percent. But in recent House elections, the district has stayed firmly in the hands of Republicans.

Election Returns

41st District		Democrat		Republican	
1976	President	66,618	(40.3%)	97,306	(58.8%)
	Senate	63,718	(38.3%)	98,545	(59.2%)
	House	91,683	(41.0%)	131,998	(59.0%)
1978	Governor	106,070	(58.7%)	61,868	(34.2%)
	House	74,925	(39.9%)	113,036	(60.1%)
1980	President	60,346	(26.0%)	139,435	(60.0%)
	Senate	122,797	(56.1%)	82,837	(37.9%)
	House	91,391	(37.7%)	143,050	(59.0%)
1982	Governor	93,554	(44.3%)	112,585	(53.3%)
	Senate	78,686	(37.7%)	120,933	(57.9%)
	House	58,677	(28.8%)	140,130	(68.9%)

Demographics

Population: 526,012. **Percent Change from 1970:** 48.8%.

Land Area: 285 square miles. **Population per Square Mile:** 1,845.7.

Counties, 1980 Population: San Diego (Pt.) — 526,012.

Cities, 1980 Population: La Mesa — 50,308; Lemon Grove (Pt.) — 368; San Diego (Pt.) — 347,093.

Race and Ancestry: White — 90.1%; Black — 1.9%; American Indian, Eskimo and Aleut — 0.5%; Asian and Pacific Islander — 4.5%. Spanish Origin — 7.2%. Dutch — 0.6%; English — 10.1%; French — 1.3%; German — 6.8%; Irish — 4.1%; Italian — 2.6%; Norwegian — 0.7%; Polish — 1.2%; Russian — 1.0%; Scottish — 0.8%; Swedish — 0.9%.

Universities, Enrollment: California School of Professional Psychology at San Diego, San Diego — 266; Coleman College, San Diego — 323; National University, San Diego — 5,932; San Diego Mesa College, San Diego — 22,312; San Diego State University, San Diego — 33,117; United States International University, San Diego — 2,538; University of California at San Diego, La Jolla — 10,992; University of San Diego, San Diego — 4,428.

Newspapers, Circulation: *The San Diego Union* (mS), San Diego — 200,689. *Los Angeles Times* and San Diego *Evening Tribune* also circulate in the district.

Commercial Television Stations, Affiliation: KCST-TV, San Diego (NBC); KFMB-TV, San Diego (CBS); KUSI-TV, San Diego (None). Entire district is in San Diego ADI. *(For other San Diego stations, see 44th district.)*

Military Installations: Miramar Naval Air Station, San Diego — 10,329.

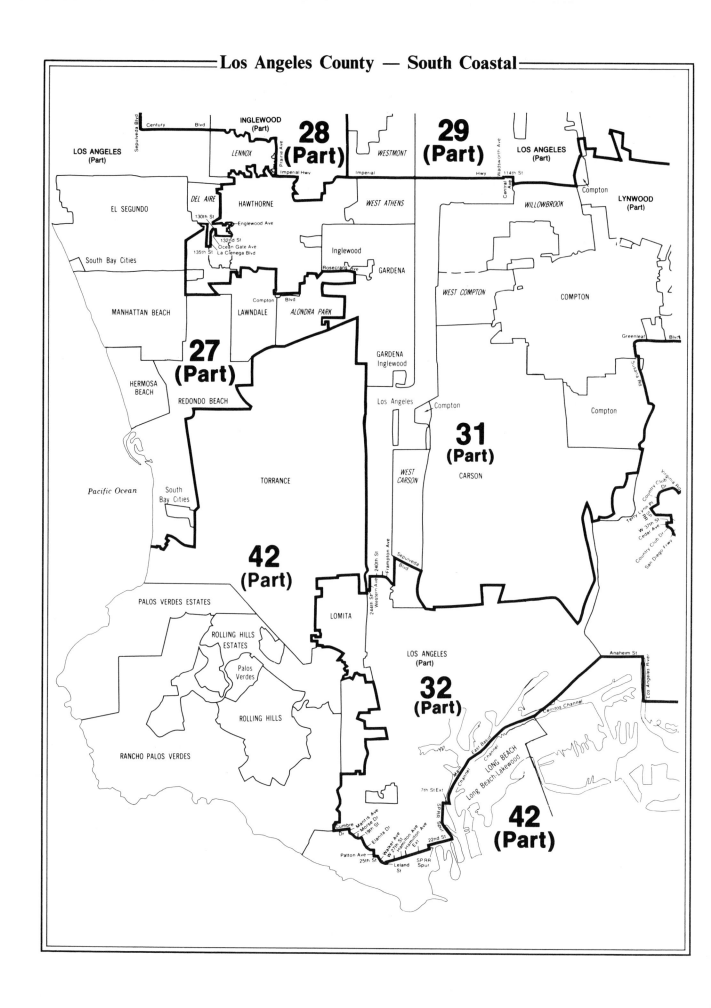

Industries:

General Dynamics Corp. (Convair Div.); San Diego; guided missiles — 7,970. **General Dynamics Corp.** (Electronics Div.); San Diego; electronic components — 3,200. **Scripps Clinic & Research Foundation** (HQ); La Jolla; hospital — 2,600. **General Atomic Co.** (HQ); San Diego; nuclear energy research, research reactors; 1,800. **Grossmont Hospital District**; La Mesa; hospital — 1,700.

Kaiser Foundation Hospital Inc. San Diego; hospital — 1,600. **Veterans Administration**; San Diego; veterans' hospital — 1,600. **Datagraphix Inc.** (HQ); San Diego; computer microfilm — 1,440. **Scripps Memorial Hospital** (HQ); La Jolla, hospital — 1,200. **Vanier Graphics Corp.**; Santee; business forms — 1,080. **Kyocera International Inc.** (HQ); San Diego; ceramic products — 1,000. **Soft Lenses Inc.** (Hydrocurve Soft Lenses); San Diego; contact lenses — 900. **Science Applications Inc.** (HQ); La Jolla; research — 700.

E. & E. Sanyo Corp.; San Diego; refrigerators — 630. **Merck & Co. Inc.** (Kelco); San Diego; medicinal chemicals — 600. **Scientific Atlanta Inc.**; San Diego; test equipment — 600. **Spectral Dynamics Corp.** (HQ); San Diego; electronic analyzing equipment — 520. **Cubic Corp.** (HQ); San Diego; electronic products — 500. **Imed Corp.** (Plastics Div. - HQ); San Diego; plastics products — 500. **University Mechanical Engineering Contractors** (HQ); San Diego; mechanical contracting — 500.

42nd District

Coastal Los Angeles and Orange Counties

The oddly shaped and heavily Republican 42nd District is another one of the side effects of the Democrats' efforts to create new Democratic seats in Los Angeles County.

The new 42nd is a combination of the most Republican portions of two old districts — the 27th and the 34th. A strip of land only a few hundred feet wide runs along the Los Angeles Harbor waterfront, joining the two segments. The Long Beach Naval Shipyard, the *Queen Mary* and Howard Hughes' "Spruce Goose" are all in this isthmus, but there are very few voters.

The northern and western end of the new 42nd, formerly in the 27th, includes the heavily Republican suburb of Torrance, with 129,881 people, and the lush, upper-income Palos Verdes Hills area. The Hills, forming a bluff overlooking the Pacific Ocean, include four exclusive communities — Palos Verdes Estates, Rancho Palos Verdes, Rolling Hills and Rolling Hills Estates. The voters who live there are overwhelmingly Republican and rarely split their tickets. Even Gov. Edmund G. Brown Jr., who in 1978 carried such Republican areas in the district as Torrance and Huntington Beach, was trounced in the Palos Verdes Hills.

The district's Orange County residents, carried over from the old 34th, account for just less than 40 percent of the new district's vote. This segment includes Seal Beach, Rossmoor, part of Westminster and all but the southeast side of Huntington Beach. Huntington Beach, with 170,000 people, is the district's southern anchor. Known as a haven for surfers who congregate around the city's pier, it is also a haven for Republican candidates, who can count on a large vote from the white-collar professionals who live in the area's cul-de-sacs.

A largely Democratic portion of the old 34th District, in Los Angeles County, was not included in the new 42nd. The communities of Lakewood, Bellflower, Artesia and

Hawaiian Gardens have been scattered among several other districts, along with the eastern part of Long Beach.

Election Returns

42nd District		Democrat		Republican	
1976	President	76,717	(35.3%)	137,552	(63.2%)
	Senate	74,714	(36.9%)	123,270	(60.9%)
	House	100,659	(51.7%)	94,186	(48.3%)
1978	Governor	91,202	(47.0%)	89,070	(45.9%)
	House	68,695	(44.3%)	82,725	(53.4%)
1980	President	57,371	(24.8%)	149,988	(64.9%)
	Senate	103,529	(45.8%)	110,714	(49.0%)
	House	71,781	(36.0%)	120,404	(60.3%)
1982	Governor	75,504	(34.7%)	137,756	(63.4%)
	Senate	69,919	(32.5%)	139,723	(64.9%)
	House	58,690	(28.3%)	142,845	(69.0%)

Demographics

Population: 524,346. **Percent Change from 1970:** 7.9%.

Land Area: 124 square miles. **Population per Square Mile:** 4,228.6.

Counties, 1980 Population: Los Angeles (Pt.) — 320,656; Orange (Pt.) — 203,690.

Cities, 1980 Population: Garden Grove (Pt.) — 0; Huntington Beach (Pt.) — 136,154; Long Beach (Pt.) — 99,484; Los Angeles (Pt.) — 14,700; Palos Verdes Estates — 14,376; Rancho Palos Verdes — 36,577; Seal Beach — 25,975; Torrance — 129,881; Westminster (Pt.) — 29,962.

Race and Ancestry: White — 88.7%; Black — 1.3%; American Indian, Eskimo and Aleut — 0.6%; Asian and Pacific Islander — 6.4%. Spanish Origin — 6.9%. Dutch — 0.7%; English — 9.8%; French — 1.0%; German — 6.5%; Greek — 0.5%; Irish — 3.8%; Italian — 2.7%; Norwegian — 0.8%; Polish — 1.1%; Russian — 0.9%; Scottish — 0.9%; Swedish — 0.9%.

Universities, Enrollment: Brooks College, Long Beach — 904; El Camino College, Torrance — 30,530; Golden West College, Huntington Beach — 21,636; Marymount Palos Verdes College, Palos Verdes — 387.

Newspapers, Circulation: *The Daily Breeze* (eS), Torrance — 86,954. *Los Angeles Times, Los Angeles Herald Examiner* and *Santa Ana Register* also circulate in the district.

Commercial Television Stations, Affiliation: Entire district is in Los Angeles ADI.

Military Installations: Fort MacArthur, San Pedro — 453; Long Beach Naval Regional Medical Center, Long Beach — 1,041; Long Beach Naval Shipyard, Long Beach — 7,518; Long Beach Naval Station, Long Beach — 4,511; Seal Beach Naval Weapons Station, Seal Beach — 2,546.

Industries:

The Garrett Corp. (AiResearch Mfg. Co.); Torrance; geoturbines, aircraft parts — 6,157. **McDonnell Douglas Corp.** (Astronautics Co.); Huntington Beach; space vehicles — 5,893. **Harbor General Hospital;** Torrance; hospital — 3,000. **Star-Kist Foods Inc.** (South Coast Fisheries Co. - HQ); San Pedro; fish canning — 3,000. **C H B Foods** (Pan Pacific Fishery Div.); San Pedro; tuna canning — 2,000.

Hughes Aircraft Co. (Electron Dynamics Div.); Torrance; electronic devices — 1,800. **Toyota Motor Sales USA Inc.;** (HQ); Torrance; auto wholesaling — 1,770. **Garrett Corp.** (Garrett Automotive Products Co.); Torrance; turbo chargers — 1,595. **First Interstate Services Co.;** Torrance; data processing services — 1,400. **Magnavox**

Government & Industrial Electronics Co. (Magnavox Advanced Products and Systems Co.); Torrance; computer software, hardware — 1,200. **Torrance Memorial Hospital Inc.;** Torrance; hospital — 1,100. **Long Beach Community Hospital Assn.;** Long Beach; hospital — 1,070. **Little Company of Mary Hospital;** Torrance; hospital — 1,020. **C H B Foods Inc.;** (HQ); San Pedro; pet foods — 1,000. **Armco Steel Corp.** (National Supply Co.); Torrance; oil field machinery — 950. **Wrather Corp.** (Wrather Port Properties Ltd.); Long Beach; recreational facilities — 900. **Norris Industries Inc.** (Weiser Lock Co.); Huntington Beach; door locks — 850. **Fiddlers Three Inc.** (Triple E Distributors); Long Beach; management service — 800. **Hi Shear Corp.** (HQ); Torrance; fasteners — 725.

Copley Press Inc.; Torrance; newspaper publishing — 700. **David Jones Inc.** (HQ); Long Beach; department store chain — 700. **Matrix Science Corp.;** Torrance; electrical connectors — 700. **Mark Controls Corp.** (Pacific Valves); Long Beach; valves — 650. **S. E. Rykoff & Co.** (Rogay Food Supply Co. - HQ); Los Angeles; grocery wholesaling — 650. **Teledyne Industries Inc.;** Torrance; aircraft power equipment — 600. **Tridair Industries** (HQ); Torrance; fasteners — 600. **United States Steel Corp.;** Torrance; steel products — 600. **The Garrett Corp.** (AiResearch Casting Div.); Torrance; steel foundry — 558. **Excellon Industries;** Torrance; circuit boards — 540. **Fala Corp.** (Western Security); Torrance; security services — 500. **Art Hale Inc.** (American Racing Equipment - HQ); Torrance; auto wheels — 500. **Reynolds Metals Co. Inc.;** Torrance; aluminum cans — 500. **Standard Brands Paint Co.** (HQ); Torrance; paint — 500.

43rd District

North San Diego County, South Orange County

The new 43rd District drawn is even more Republican than the old 43rd, where in 1980 GOP Rep. Clair Burgener received more votes than any other House candidate in U.S. history.

The district was made more compact by shedding the vast Imperial Valley and eastern San Diego County portions. The registration, which was split evenly between Democrats and Republicans in the old district, is now weighted toward the GOP by a 51-35 margin. Such a margin translates into enormous majorities for most GOP candidates. In the area of the new district, Ronald Reagan took 71 percent of the 1980 presidential vote to Jimmy Carter's 19 — Reagan's highest percentage in the state.

The new district runs along the Pacific coast from Carlsbad north to San Juan Capistrano, and inland about 30 miles into the mountains. About two-thirds of the voters live in the San Diego County portion of the district, which is similar in makeup to the smaller Orange County section. Both are upper-middle-class residential areas. There is little industry and the major incorporated cities, such as Oceanside and Escondido, are essentially aggregations of suburban housing developments. The huge Marine Corps base at Camp Pendleton is located just north of Oceanside.

The communities in the new 43rd were among the fastest-growing places in both Orange and San Diego counties in the 1970s. San Marcos, in the San Diego County hills near Escondido, grew by nearly 350 percent between 1970 and 1980. And the swallows of San Juan Capistrano find their community more crowded each March when they return to their historic mission. The population of that community quadrupled during the 1970s.

Because of its phenomenal growth, the 43rd District had to lose more people in redistricting than any other in

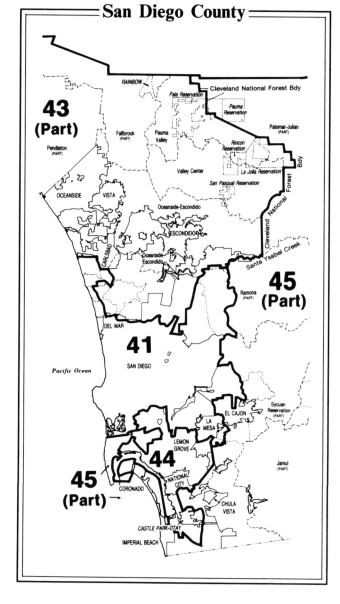

San Diego County

the state — more than 300,000. By removing the entire eastern end of the district, the booming western side of Riverside County, and the northern edge of the city of San Diego, the map makers took out enough population to allow them to add a heavily Republican slice of Orange County as well as Oceanside in San Diego County. With 76,000 people, Oceanside is the largest city in the district and the only one with more registered Democrats than Republicans. However, Reagan carried this residential, beach resort community in 1980 by nearly a 3-to-1 margin.

Election Returns

43rd District		Democrat		Republican	
1976	President	40,628	(32.7%)	82,189	(66.2%)
	Senate	40,378	(31.5%)	84,712	(66.1%)
	House	63,978	(37.3%)	107,610	(62.7%)
1978	Governor	68,887	(46.3%)	70,695	(47.5%)
	House	49,370	(32.0%)	104,955	(68.0%)

43rd District

		Democrat		Republican	
1980	President	38,525	(19.5%)	141,259	(71.4%)
	Senate	83,645	(44.4%)	92,665	(49.2%)
	House	37,649	(17.4%)	170,281	(78.6%)
1982	Governor	66,686	(34.8%)	120,885	(63.2%)
	Senate	52,493	(27.7%)	130,990	(69.2%)
	House	57,995	(32.1%)	56,297	(31.1%)

Demographics

Population: 528,086. **Percent Change from 1970:** 103.2%.

Land Area: 1,075 square miles. **Population per Square Mile:** 491.2.

Counties, 1980 Population: Orange (Pt.) — 151,934; San Diego (Pt.) — 376,152.

Cities, 1980 Population: Carlsbad — 35,490; Escondido — 64,355; Oceanside — 76,698; San Clemente — 27,325; San Diego (Pt.) — 21,229; San Juan Capistrano — 18,959; San Marcos — 17,479; Vista — 35,834.

Race and Ancestry: White — 87.2%; Black — 2.6%; American Indian, Eskimo and Aleut — 1.0%; Asian and Pacific Islander — 2.7%. Spanish Origin — 12.5%. Dutch — 0.7%; English — 10.4%; French — 1.2%; German — 6.9%; Irish — 3.8%; Italian — 2.3%; Norwegian — 0.8%; Polish — 0.9%; Russian — 0.5%; Scottish — 0.8%; Swedish — 0.9%.

Universities, Enrollment: Mira Costa College, Oceanside — 5,819; Palomar College, San Marcos — 16,583; Saddleback College, Mission Viejo — 24,841.

Newspapers, Circulation: *Blade-Tribune* (eS), Oceanside — 28,307; *Daily Sun-Post* (e), San Clemente — 7,034; *Times-Advocate* (e), Escondido — 31,678; *The Vista Press* (eS), Vista — 7,430. *Los Angeles Times*, Santa Ana *Register*, *San Diego Union* and *San Diego Evening Tribune* also circulate in the district.

Commercial Television Stations, Affiliation: District is divided between Los Angeles ADI and San Diego ADI.

Military Installations: Camp Pendleton Marine Corps Base, Oceanside — 28,824; Camp Pendleton Naval Regional Medical Center, Oceanside — 1,325.

Nuclear Power Plants: San Onofre 1, 2 and 3, San Clemente (Combustion Engineering, Bechtel).

Industries:

Oak Communications Inc.; San Diego; television broadcasting — 1,500. **Hewlett-Packard Co.;** San Diego; electrical equipment — 1,300. **Hughes Aircraft Co.** (Industrial Products Div.); Carlsbad; electron tubes — 1,100. **Tri-City Hospital District Inc.** (HQ); Oceanside; hospital — 1,010. **Sony Corp. of America;** San Diego; color televisions — 1,000.

Burroughs Corp. (Micro Components Div.); San Diego; electronic computing equipment — 810. **Oak Industries** (Oak Systems); Carlsbad; electronic components — 800. **Washington Patrol Service Inc.;** Escondido; security services — 800. **Armorlite Inc.** (HQ); San Marcos; ophthalmic goods — 700. **Gremlin Industries Inc.;** San Diego; electronics — 600. **Burroughs Corp.;** Carlsbad; electronic components — 550. **Endevco Corp.** (HQ); San Juan Capistrano; industrial measuring instruments — 550. **Emerson Electric Co.** (ACDC Electronics Div.); Oceanside; electronic components — 500.

44th District

Central San Diego

Although San Diego County has not voted for a Democratic presidential candidate in nearly four decades, the county has always contained enough Democrats for one safe Democratic district. For most of the 1970s that district was the old 42nd. But when the long-time Democratic incumbent was turned out of office by a Republican in 1980, it was clear some changes had to be made. Democrats solved the problem by drawing a new inner-city district comprising most of the old 42nd's area.

The new version, renumbered the 44th, is actually a better Democratic district than the old one. The party's registration advantage within the new lines is even better than the 2-to-1 margin the old district enjoyed, and the map was carefully drawn to exclude some heavily Republican precincts. By removing Coronado, sitting on a peninsula to the west of the San Diego Bay, map makers eliminated one of the most staunchly Republican areas in the old 42nd District.

The areas left are white, working-class residential neighborhoods near the center of the city and on toward the east; the blue-collar suburb of National City, further south; and all of San Diego's black and Mexican-American neighborhoods, including the San Ysidro ghetto, less than a mile from the Mexican border.

Many civilian government employees who are part of San Diego's vast naval operations live in the district. For local economic reasons, they tend to support a strong defense policy, which helps explain why Ronald Reagan carried the district by a 48-to-41-percent margin over Jimmy Carter in 1980. But in nearly every other contest for state and local office, Republican candidates find little support from the registered Democrats of the area.

Election Returns

44th District		Democrat		Republican	
1976	President	59,482	(54.7%)	47,944	(44.1%)
	Senate	56,776	(52.1%)	48,770	(44.8%)
	House	94,099	(61.1%)	59,924	(38.9%)
1978	Governor	76,967	(69.1%)	27,575	(24.8%)
	House	77,386	(58.7%)	54,440	(41.3%)
1980	President	54,114	(40.6%)	63,521	(47.7%)
	Senate	77,199	(63.9%)	35,554	(29.4%)
	House	67,433	(38.9%)	104,646	(60.3%)
1982	Governor	73,202	(58.7%)	47,751	(38.3%)
	Senate	68,668	(55.7%)	48,356	(39.2%)
	House	78,474	(65.0%)	38,447	(31.8%)

Demographics

Population: 525,886. **Percent Change from 1970:** 15.0%.

Land Area: 83 square miles. **Population per Square Mile:** 6,336.0.

Counties, 1980 Population: San Diego (Pt.) — 525,886.

Cities, 1980 Population: Chula Vista (Pt.) — 31,605; Lemon Grove (Pt.) — 20,412; National City (Pt.) — 48,772; San Diego (Pt.) — 394,481.

Race and Ancestry: White — 62.9%; Black — 14.2%; American Indian, Eskimo and Aleut — 0.7%; Asian and Pacific Islander — 9.0%. Spanish Origin — 26.1%. English — 6.0%; French — 0.9%; German — 4.4%; Irish — 2.8%; Italian — 1.5%; Polish — 0.6%.

Universities, Enrollment: California Western School of Law, San Diego — 715; San Diego City College, San Diego — 13,505.

Newspapers, Circulation: *San Diego Daily Transcript* (m), San Diego — 6,382. *San Diego Union* and *San Diego Evening Tribune* also circulate in the district.

San Diego

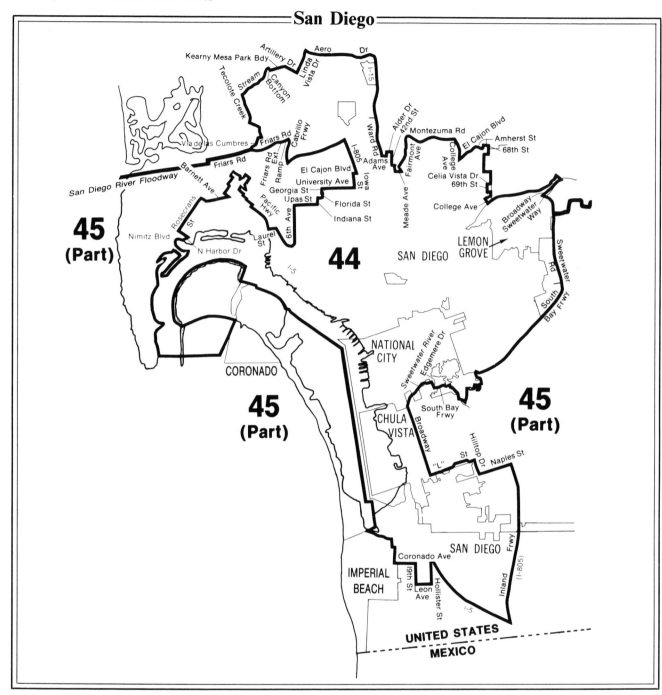

Military Installations: Pacific Fleet Anti-submarine Warfare Training Center, San Diego — 1,044; Pacific Fleet Combat Training Center, San Diego — 1,205; San Diego Marine Corps Recruit Depot, San Diego — 7,075; San Diego Naval Communications Station, San Diego — 226; San Diego Naval Public Works Center, San Diego — 1,807; San Diego Naval Regional Medical Center, San Diego — 3,603; San Diego Naval Station, San Diego — 43,904; San Diego Naval Supply Center, San Diego — 1,710; San Diego Naval Training Center, San Diego — 3,064.

Industries:

National Steel Shipbuilding Co. San Diego; shipbuilding — 6,000. **Rohr Industries Inc.** (HQ); Chula Vista; aircraft parts — 5,200. **Pacific Southwest Airlines** (HQ); San Diego; commercial airline — 3,500. **Sharp Memorial Hosp.;** San Diego; hospital — 1,580. **San Diego Financial Corp.;** San Diego; bank holding company — 1,300.

Armour Oil Co.; San Diego; petroleum marketing — 1,200. **Teledyne Industries Inc.** (Teledyne Ryan); San Diego; aircraft, aircraft parts — 1,200. **Children's Hospital & Health Center;** San Diego; hospital — 900. **Home Federal Savings & Loan Assn. of San Diego** (HQ); San Diego; savings & loan, real estate management — 800. **Ratner Corp.** (HQ); San Diego; men's suits — 800. **American Airlines**

Inc.; San Diego; commercial airline — 746. **Gamble-Skogmo Inc.** (HQ); San Diego; department store chain — 700. **Southwest Marine Inc.** (HQ); San Diego; ship repairing — 700. **Solar Turbines Inc.** (Solar Gear - HQ); San Diego; solar turbines — 500.

45th District

Imperial Valley and Part of San Diego

Crossing the entire southern border of the state from the Colorado River to San Diego's Sunset Cliffs, the new 45th is sparsely populated and overwhelmingly Republican.

The district was created to give the Republicans a safe seat and keep them from interfering with Democratic plans to regain the downtown San Diego district. Although the 45th is not the most Republican of the San Diego area's three GOP districts, it supported Ronald Reagan with 62 percent in 1980.

The 45th has two distinct parts. One is in the eastern suburbs of San Diego such as Chula Vista and El Cajon, as well as the spit of land — Coronado — that separates the Pacific Ocean from the San Diego Bay. Coronado is the home of many retired Navy officers who give the area a decidedly pro-military, Republican flavor.

The other segment of the district includes California's Imperial Valley. Below the level of both the Colorado River and the Pacific Ocean, the valley was relatively easy to irrigate at the turn of the century and has since become one of the most productive farm areas in the country.

As farmers and urban refugees move in with their house trailers, the valley is experiencing its first substantial population growth in several decades. Just under 100,000 people now live there. Although registered Democrats outnumber Republicans by 56 to 34 percent, the electorate here is conservative. In 1980, Reagan nearly reversed the registration figures and defeated Jimmy Carter, 56 to 37 percent. Imperial County has not voted for a Democratic presidential candidate since 1964.

Election Returns

45th District		Democrat		Republican	
1976	President	61,853	(42.2%)	82,830	(56.6%)
	Senate	59,025	(40.2%)	83,804	(57.0%)
	House	68,918	(46.6%)	78,954	(53.4%)
1978	Governor	83,393	(55.2%)	56,955	(37.7%)
	House	56,136	(43.0%)	74,524	(57.0%)
1980	President	50,729	(27.0%)	115,923	(61.7%)
	Senate	95,675	(53.8%)	70,764	(39.8%)
	House	39,947	(22.3%)	139,542	(77.7%)

45th District		Democrat		Republican	
1982	Governor	74,455	(42.0%)	97,819	(55.1%)
	Senate	65,491	(37.3%)	101,464	(57.8%)
	House	50,148	(29.2%)	117,771	(68.6%)

Demographics

Population: 525,906. **Percent Change from 1970:** 27.0%.

Land Area: 7,151 square miles. **Population per Square Mile:** 73.5.

Counties, 1980 Population: Imperial — 92,110; San Diego (Pt.) — 433,796.

Cities, 1980 Population: Brawley — 14,946; Calexico — 14,412; Chula Vista (Pt.) — 52,322; Coronado — 16,859; El Cajon — 73,892; El Centro — 23,996; Imperial Beach — 22,689; National City (Pt.) — 0; San Diego (Pt.) — 112,735.

Race and Ancestry: White — 84.1%; Black — 1.8%; American Indian, Eskimo and Aleut — 1.0%; Asian and Pacific Islander — 2.9%. Spanish Origin — 18.5%. Dutch — 0.5%; English — 9.3%; French — 1.1%; German — 6.2%; Irish — 3.6%; Italian — 2.1%; Norwegian — 0.6%; Polish — 0.8%; Portuguese — 0.8%; Scottish — 0.7%; Swedish — 0.7%.

Universities, Enrollment: Cuyamaca College, El Cajon — 2,033; Grossmont College, El Cajon — 14,629; Imperial Valley College, Imperial — 4,338; Point Loma College, San Diego — 1,803; Southwestern College, Chula Vista — 11,596; Western State University College of Law of San Diego, San Diego — 859.

Newspapers, Circulation: *The Brawley News* (e), Brawley — 15,311; *The Daily Californian* (e), El Cajon — 17,745; *The Evening Tribune* (e), San Diego — 124,349; *Imperial Valley Press* (e), El Centro — 15,311. *San Diego Union* also circulates in the district.

Commercial Television Stations, Affiliation: KECY-TV, El Centro (ABC). District is divided between San Diego ADI and El Centro (Calif.)-Yuma (Ariz) ADI.

Military Installations: Coronado Naval Amphibious Base, Coronado — 3,123; El Centro Naval Air Facility, El Centro — 676; Mt. Laguna Air Force Station, Mt. Laguna — 29; Naval Ocean Systems Center, Point Loma — 4,137; North Island Naval Air Station, San Diego — 35,816; San Diego Naval Submarine Base, San Diego — 8,850.

Industries:

Jim Enis; El Centro; vegetable farming — 3,000. **Trust Houses Forte Hotel Inc.;** El Cajon; hotel — 2,900. **Copley Press Inc.;** San Diego; newspaper publishing — 1,330. **Gourmet Farms;** El Centro; vegetable farming — 1,000. **Hotel Del Coronado Corp.;** Coronado; hotel — 1,000.

Abatti Bros.; El Centro; vegetable farming — 700. **Ametek Inc.** (Ametek Straza); El Cajon; machine tool accessories — 680. **American Towel Co.** (American Linen Supply); El Centro; linen supply service — 560. **Chem-Tronics Inc.;** El Cajon; jet engines — 560. **Computer Science Corp.** (Applied Technology Div.); San Diego; computer software services — 550. **Buck Knives Inc.** (Fine Blanking Div. - HQ); El Cajon; sport knives — 525. **The Fedmart Corp.** (HQ); San Diego; discount department store chain — 500.

Colorado

What Colorado politicians could not do in a year of arguing, federal judges did for them in a matter of weeks — revising substantially the congressional district lines within the state while preserving the basic partisan balance of power.

The congressional map approved by a three-judge federal panel in Denver Jan. 28, 1982, appeared to promote the re-election prospects of all five incumbents — three Democrats and two Republicans. It responded to the state's 31 percent population growth in the 1970s by creating a new, sixth seat in the Denver suburbs with an apparent Republican majority.

Democrats were pleased with the new map, but Republicans were left a bit disappointed. Before the court stepped in, Democratic Gov. Richard D. Lamm vetoed three plans passed by the Republican Legislature, all designed to give the GOP a congressional majority. Both parties sought to negotiate a compromise, but talks broke down in November 1981 in a dispute over the 3rd District which was represented by a Democrat. Acting on a suit filed by state Republican officials, a panel of three federal judges took over the redistricting process.

The judges' map eradicated the old district lines that had splintered the Denver and Colorado Springs vote and split western Colorado into northern and southern constituencies. Instead, the court followed the natural geography of the state to concentrate one district in the west and another in the eastern plains. Along the Front Range of the Rockies, where most of Colorado's population centers are located, district lines were drawn to keep virtually all the major cities and suburbs intact. The population division of the new map was nearly perfect. The variance in population between the largest and smallest districts was 12 people.

Age of Population

District	Population Under 18	Voting Age Population	Population 65 & Over (% of VAP)	Median Age
1	108,093	373,579	61,524 (16.5%)	30.3
2	142,000	339,617	25,890 (7.6%)	27.2
3	136,679	345,175	49,403 (14.3%)	28.9
4	138,767	342,745	49,097 (14.3%)	28.0
5	146,471	335,156	30,725 (9.2%)	27.7
6	136,803	344,879	30,686 (8.9%)	29.3
State	808,813	2,081,151	247,325 (11.9%)	28.6

Income and Occupation

District	Median Family Income	White Collar Workers	Blue Collar Workers	Service Workers	Farm Workers
1	$ 19,226	61.1%	23.3%	14.8%	0.7%
2	24,050	58.8	29.0	11.1	1.1
3	18,374	49.0	31.0	15.3	4.7
4	18,540	48.7	29.5	13.2	8.6
5	21,535	60.6	25.1	13.0	1.3
6	25,512	66.0	22.0	11.2	0.7
State	$ 21,279	57.7%	26.5%	13.0%	2.7%

Education: School Years Completed

District	8 Years or Fewer	4 Years of High School	4 Years of College or More	Median School Years
1	12.9%	29.8%	24.8%	12.8
2	6.7	36.7	24.8	12.9
3	14.8	35.1	17.9	12.6
4	16.4	35.1	18.4	12.6
5	6.8	36.1	24.7	12.9
6	5.6	35.3	27.0	13.0
State	10.6%	34.6%	23.0%	12.8

Housing and Residential Patterns

District	Owner Occupied	Renter Occupied	Urban	Rural
1	49.3%	50.7%	100.0%	0.0%
2	68.8	31.2	90.8	9.2
3	69.5	30.5	53.8	46.2
4	67.1	32.9	60.7	39.3
5	67.8	32.2	79.0	21.0
6	67.7	32.3	99.4	0.6
State	64.5%	35.5%	80.6%	19.4%

COLORADO

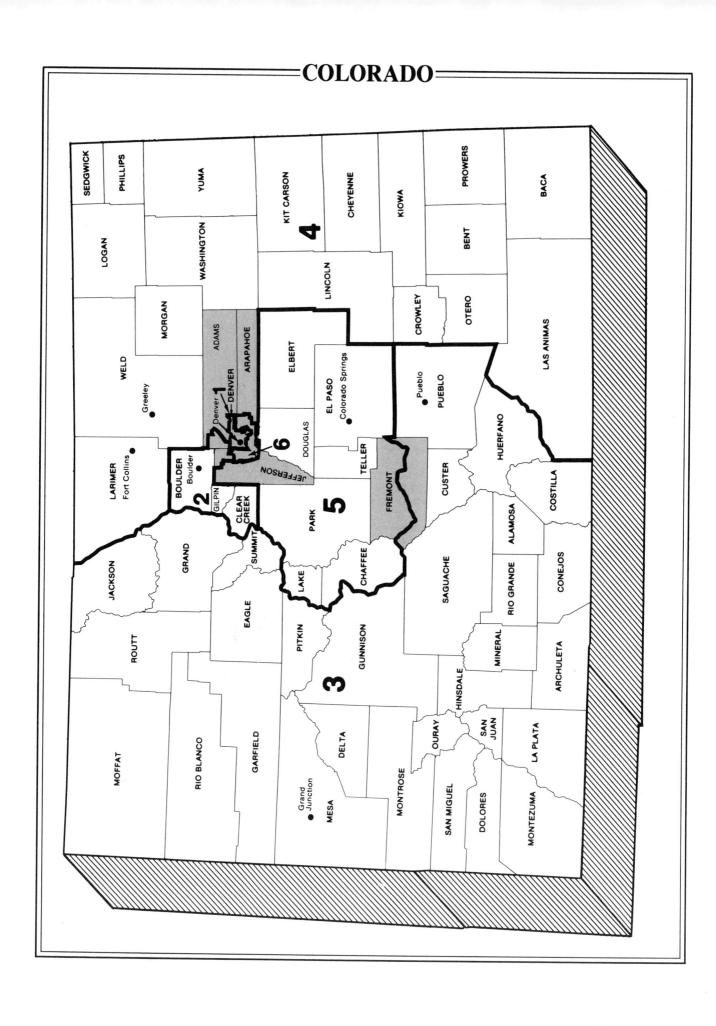

1st District

Denver

The new 1st includes virtually all of Denver, with its population of nearly a half-million, and is one of the few Democratic congressional strongholds in the Rocky Mountains region. Hispanics and blacks together comprise about one-third of the district population, and there is a strong liberal white-collar element.

Unlike its sprawling suburbs, Denver has ceased growing — it lost 4.5 percent of its population in the 1970s, partly because middle-class families sought to escape the impact of a federal court busing order that applied to the city. But Denver's national prominence increased as regional energy operations joined federal government establishments in making the city a focal point of commerce in the Rocky Mountains. Despite its scenic locale and casual, attractive lifestyle, Denver is bedeviled by racial tensions, serious air pollution and chronic water shortages.

Denver's highly mobile population and the historic absence of a political machine mean that party roots are not deep and Democratic majorities are not always large. The Democratic presidential candidate has not drawn more than 50.1 percent of the Denver vote since 1964. Ronald Reagan captured the city in 1980.

A heavy Democratic vote in Denver often bails out the party's statewide candidates. In 1980 Democratic Sen. Gary Hart won the city by 50,000 votes. He lost the rest of the state by more than 30,000.

Republican strength is concentrated in the middle- and upper-income neighborhoods of southeast Denver. Farther in that direction are newer subdivisions built in the hills along the Valley Highway (Interstate 25). Republicans also draw some votes downtown, where condominiums have mushroomed in the vicinity of Civil War-era Larimer Square.

Other parts of the city are reliably Democratic. Capitol Hills, perched on the eastern fringe of the downtown area, is home to a mixed population of students, young professionals and senior citizens. To the east and north are heavily black neighborhoods. Westward on the hills beyond the stockyards and the South Platte River live most of the city's Hispanics.

Redistricting returned to the 1st all of the Hispanic West Side and trimmed away about 16,500 residents in southwest Denver's Pinehurst section, an anti-busing stronghold. The new 1st also includes about 6,000 residents who live in Arapahoe County enclaves found within the Denver city limits. The major one is Glendale, a small community of shopping centers, office buildings and faddish bars and discos.

Election Returns

1st District		Democrat		Republican	
1976	President	101,957	(48.2%)	101,458	(48.0%)
	House	113,846	(54.6%)	93,585	(44.9%)
1978	Governor	100,475	(66.2%)	46,729	(30.8%)
	Senate	72,095	(49.2%)	71,946	(49.1%)
	House	90,816	(62.2%)	53,259	(36.5%)
1980	President	81,640	(41.6%)	81,196	(41.4%)

1st District		Democrat		Republican	
1980	Senate	118,585	(62.6%)	68,353	(36.1%)
	House	119,250	(61.6%)	69,450	(35.9%)
1982	Governor	115,434	(75.3%)	32,936	(21.5%)
	House	94,969	(60.3%)	59,009	(37.4%)

Demographics

Population: 481,672. **Percent Change from 1970:** -5.5%.

Land Area: 105 square miles. **Population per Square Mile:** 4,587.4.

Counties, 1980 Population: Adams (Pt.) — 0; Arapahoe (Pt.) — 5,803; Denver (Pt.) — 475,869.

Cities, 1980 Population: Denver (Pt.) — 475,869.

Race and Ancestry: White — 74.3%; Black — 12.3%; American Indian, Eskimo and Aleut — 0.8%; Asian and Pacific Islander — 1.8%. Spanish Origin — 18.9%. Dutch — 0.8%; English — 6.9%; French — 0.8%; German — 7.1%; Irish — 3.8%; Italian — 1.6%; Norwegian — 0.5%; Polish — 0.9%; Russian — 0.8%; Scottish — 0.6%; Swedish — 1.0%.

Universities, Enrollment: Bel-Rea Institute of Animal Technology, Denver — 100; Colorado Women's College, Denver — 509; Community College of Denver (Auraria campus), Denver — 3,373; Denver Conservative Baptist Seminary, Denver — 398; Iliff School of Theology, Denver — 359; Loretto Heights College, Denver — 929; Metropolitan State College, Denver — 14,464; Regis College, Denver — 1,169; St. Thomas Seminary, Denver — 146; University of Colorado at Denver, Denver — 8,744; University of Denver, Denver — 7,858.

Newspapers, Circulation: *The Denver Post* (eS), Denver — 266,408; *Rocky Mountain News* (mS), Denver — 272,297.

Commercial Television Stations, Affiliation: KBTV, Denver (ABC); KMGH, Denver (CBS); KOA-TV, Denver (NBC). Entire district is located in Denver ADI. *(For other Denver stations, see 6th district.)*

Military Installations: Lowry Air Force Base, Denver — 8,263.

Industries:

United Airlines Inc.; Denver; commercial airline — 4,814. **The Gates Rubber Co.;** (HQ); Denver; belting, hoses — 3,000. **Stearns-Roger Corp.;** (HQ); Glendale; engineering services, heavy construction — 3,000. **Continental Airlines Inc.;** Denver; commercial airline — 2,400. **United Banks of Colorado Inc.;** Denver; bank holding company — 2,270.

First National Bancorporation (HQ); Denver; banking — 2,000. **Frontier Airlines Inc.** (HQ); Denver; commercial airline — 2,000. **St. Joseph's Hospital Inc.;** Denver; hospital — 2,000. **Samsonite Corp.;** (HQ); Denver; luggage, furniture — 2,000.

First National Bank of Denver; Denver; banking — 1,700. **Brown Group Inc.** (Outdoor Sports Industries - HQ); Denver; camping gear, outerwear — 1,600. **The Denver Post Inc.** (HQ); Denver; newspaper publishing — 1,600. **Intra West Bank of Denver** (HQ); Denver; banking — 1,580. **St. Anthony Hospital;** Denver; hospital — 1,500. **Cobe Laboratories Inc.** (HQ); Denver; medical, surgical instruments — 1,450. **Porter Memorial Hospital;** Denver; hospital — 1,400. **United Bank of Denver;** Denver; banking — 1,350.

Rose Medical Center; Denver; hospital — 1,250. **Colorado National Bank;** Denver; banking — 1,200. **Mercy Medical Center;** Denver; hospital — 1,100. **Veterans Administration;** Denver; veterans' hospital — 1,050. **Rocky Mountain Hospital Medical Service** (HQ); Denver; medical insurance — 1,020. **Children's Hospital Assn.;** Denver; children's hospital — 1,000. **Exeter Drilling Northern Inc.;** Denver; oil, gas exploring — 1,000. **Keebler Co.;** Denver; cookies, crackers — 1,000. **Project Construction Co.;** Denver; general construction contracting — 1,000. **Amoco Production Co.;** Denver; oil production — 950. **Atlantic-Richfield Co.;** Denver; petroleum production, exploration — 850. **Chevron USA Inc.** (Chevron Oil Co.); Denver; petroleum products wholesaling — 800.

The Denver Publishing Co.; Denver; newspaper publishing — 790.

Norpac Exploration Services (HQ); Denver; oil, gas exploring — 700. **Prudential Building Maintenance Co. of Colorado;** Denver; janitorial services — 700. **Associated Grocers Co. Inc.** (HQ); Denver; grocery wholesaling — 675. **Central Bank of Denver;** Denver; banking — 650. **Blue Cross and Blue Shield of Colorado** (HQ); Denver; health insurance — 600. **Burlington Northern Inc.;** Denver; railroad operations — 600. **Burns International Security Service;** Denver; industrial security services — 600. **Conoco Inc.;** Denver; petroleum refining — 600. **Hilton Hotels Corp.;** Denver; hotel — 600. **Petro-Lewis Corp.** (HQ); Denver; oil, gas production — 600. **Union Pacific Railroad Co.;** Denver; railroad operations — 600.

Western Airlines Inc.; Denver; commercial airline — 600. **Nobel Inc.** (HQ); Denver; grocery wholesaling — 560. **Mobil Oil Corp.** (Denver Exploration & Producing Div.); Denver; oil, gas operations — 550. **Burroughs Corp.;** Denver; office supplies wholesaling — 520. **Fairmont Hotel Co.;** Denver; hotel — 520. **Burlington Northern Inc.;** Denver; railroad operations — 500. **Frankel Carbon & Ribbon** (HQ); Denver; typewriter ribbons, stencils, ink — 500. **Marriott Corp.;** Denver; hotel — 500. **Mastercraft Industries Corp.** (HQ); Denver; wooden kitchen furniture — 500. **Mobile-Premix Concrete Inc.** (HQ); Denver; readymix cement — 500. **Petroleum Information Corp.** (Energy Map Div. - HQ); Denver; publishing — 500. **Rio Grande Industries Inc.** (HQ); Denver; railroad operations — 500.

2nd District

Northern Denver Suburbs; Boulder

Redistricting changed the district's demographic mix, paring away the heavily Hispanic apartment houses of west Denver and removing 250,000 residents in the southern portion of Jefferson County, a suburban Republican bastion.

That shift moved the district north and east; Boulder County and the populous portion of Adams County added by the remap contain nearly three-quarter's of the district's residents.

The Colorado 2nd is rapidly becoming a Rocky Mountains version of California's Silicon Valley. Attracted by plenty of open space and a sizable white-collar work force, a half-dozen major high-technology firms have established operations in recent years in the Boulder area.

Broomfield, which sits on Boulder County's southern border, is bounded on one side by Western Electric and the other by Storage Technology, a major producer of computer components and the leading employer in the district with 7,500 workers. Fifteen miles due north is Longmont, twice as large as Broomfield with more than 40,000 residents. Historically, Longmont is a market for sugar beet farmers.

Boulder itself, is the centerpiece of the county. Its scenic location and relaxed lifestyle have made it a haven for the young. To control the city's expansion, Boulder officials have adopted a slow-growth policy that restricts the construction of new housing. The city grew by a relatively modest 15 percent in the 1970s — compared with 186 percent for Broomfield and 85 percent for Longmont.

Scientific firms such as Ball Corp. and IBM and government research outlets such as the National Oceanic and Atmospheric Administration provide major employment in Boulder. But there is also a variety of smaller, more esoteric businesses that fit in with prevailing cultural winds. For example, Boulder is home base for Celestial Seasonings, the herbal tea producer.

The large academic community at the University of Colorado and the young professional work force create a strong vote for liberal candidates, especially if they stress environmentalism and individual rights rather than traditional bread-and-butter issues. The Boulder vote gave independent presidential candidate John B. Anderson his healthy 16 percent countywide vote in 1980.

Southeast of Boulder is Adams County, whose suburbs literally have grown out of the grassy plains in the last quarter century. The breathtaking view of the nearby Rockies gives residents a sense of grandeur, if not community. The scores of new subdivisions that have sprouted on the rolling terrain are oriented to Denver, rather than Boulder, and follow Denver media.

Arvada, on the border between Adams and Jefferson counties, is the most affluent of the 2nd District suburbs. The others, such as Westminster, Thornton and Northglenn across the line in Adams County, are more blue collar and Democratic and have large Hispanic populations. Some of the Adams County suburbs have nearly as many mobile homes as houses. There is little heavy industry in Adams County, but the stockyards in north Denver and the myriad warehouses along Interstate 25 provide blue-collar jobs.

About half of the district's land area — but few of its voters — is in the mountains west of Boulder in Clear Creek and Gilpin counties, which were added for population balance. There, modern recreation areas are located near deserted mining towns. Central City in reliably Democratic Gilpin County and Georgetown in consistently Republican Clear Creek County were boom towns during the gold and silver strikes of the late 1800s.

Election Returns

2nd District		Democrat		Republican	
1976	President	76,702	(45.3%)	84,997	(50.2%)
	House	83,675	(50.8%)	77,758	(47.2%)

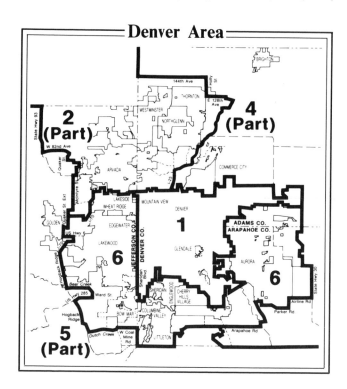

Denver Area

2nd District		Democrat		Republican	
1978	Governor	80,767	(63.2%)	41,750	(32.7%)
	Senate	56,404	(44.6%)	68,859	(54.5%)
	House	68,785	(54.7%)	56,200	(44.7%)
1980	President	60,570	(32.7%)	93,552	(50.4%)
	Senate	100,946	(54.3%)	83,306	(44.8%)
	House	108,686	(56.8%)	77,767	(40.6%)
1982	Governor	118,015	(71.1%)	43,673	(26.3%)
	House	101,194	(61.8%)	59,580	(36.4%)

Demographics

Population: 481,617. **Percent Change from 1970:** 50.4%.

Land Area: 1,442 square miles. **Population per Square Mile:** 334.0.

Counties, 1980 Population: Adams (Pt.) — 167,594; Boulder — 189,625; Clear Creek — 7,308; Gilpin — 2,441; Jefferson (Pt.) — 114,649.

Cities, 1980 Population: Arvada — 84,576; Boulder — 76,685; Broomfield — 20,730; Longmont — 42,942; Northglenn — 29,847; Sherrelwood (CDP) — 17,629; Thornton (Pt.) — 40,335; Westminster — 50,211.

Race and Ancestry: White — 93.4%; Black — 0.8%; American Indian, Eskimo and Aleut — 0.5%; Asian and Pacific Islander — 1.3%. Spanish Origin — 8.7%. Dutch — 0.6%; English — 8.4%; French — 0.9%; German — 11.1%; Irish — 3.3%; Italian — 2.2%; Norwegian — 0.8%; Polish — 0.7%; Scottish — 0.6%; Swedish — 1.1%.

Universities, Enrollment: Community College of Denver (North campus), Westminster — 4,756; Denver Institute of Technology, Sherrelwood — 561; Parks College, Sherrelwood — 617; University of Colorado at Boulder, Boulder — 23,241.

Newspapers, Circulation: *Daily Camera* (e), Boulder — 28,104; *Longmont Daily Times-Call* (e), Longmont — 16,994. *The Denver Post* and Denver *Rocky Mountain News* also circulate in the district.

Commercial Television Stations, Affiliation: Entire district is located in Denver ADI.

Industries:

Storage Technology Corp. (HQ); Louisville; computer tape discs — 7,590. **International Business Machines Corp.;** Boulder; copiers — 4,500. **Western Electric Co. Inc.;** Broomfield; aluminum foundries — 4,000. **Ball Corp.** (Aerospace Div.); Boulder; electronic communications equipment — 1,600. **Sundstrand Corp.** (Aviation Div.); Westminster; aircraft parts — 1,100. **A. C. Nielsen & Co. Inc.** (Neodata Services); Boulder; data processing services — 1,000. **Longmont Turkey Processors Inc.** (Longmont Foods Co.); Longmont; poultry dressing — 750. **Bell Telephone Labs Inc.;** Northglenn; commercial testing labs — 582.

3rd District

Western Slope, Pueblo, Grand Junction

After being divided for a decade between two congressional districts, Colorado's Western Slope has been reunited to form the heart of the revamped 3rd. The previous version of the district stretched across the southern half of Colorado; the new one covers roughly the western half of the state and two areas east of the Continental Divide — populous Pueblo County and the largely Hispanic San Luis Valley.

Pueblo was the center of the old 3rd, but it juts like a peninsula out of the southeastern corner of the new one. Still, it remains the district's population center, with one-quarter of the voters. Pueblo, population 101,000, is a steel-producing town and the hub of union activity in Colorado. It is a Democratic stronghold.

From the Pueblo County line the district boundary follows U.S. Route 50 west through Canon City to the Continental Divide. To the south is the San Luis Valley, an isolated lettuce- and potato-growing region that is the poorest part of the state. Two counties in the valley, Conejos and Costilla, have Hispanic majorities. Four others are at least 30 percent Hispanic. The valley, which makes up about 10 percent of the district vote, is a crucial source of Democratic votes.

Voters in the northern half of the new 3rd cast about 35 percent of the district vote. This area is Colorado's vacant sector; much of the land is federally owned forest. The largest city in the area, Grand Junction, located 25 miles east of the Utah border, has only 28,144 residents.

Although the oil shale boom in the northwestern part of the region is abating, the Western Slope is still one of the nation's leading suppliers of uranium and zinc. It is also the source of the Colorado and Gunnison rivers — which provide water for much of the Front Range and Southern California.

Politically the region has a slight Republican tilt. Democrats or independents have a registration advantage in half the 20 counties. But there are more Republicans in the three most populous ones — Mesa (Grand Junction), La Plata (Durango) and Montrose, which together comprise nearly 28 percent of the district population.

While voters on the Western Slope are essentially conservative, the region's resort communities such as Aspen are liberal outposts. Four Western Slope resort counties — Pitkin (Aspen), Summit (Dillon), San Juan (Silverton) and San Miguel (Telluride) — were among John B. Anderson's top 20 counties nationally in 1980. In statewide races these counties often vote Democratic.

Democrats also run well in the old mining towns in Colorado's southwestern corner. Many descendants of immigrants who came to work in the once-booming silver mines of Ouray and Silverton have remained, giving the Democrats a base in the area known as the "West End."

Beans and livestock are the key to the local agricultural economy, but there also is a heavy dependence on tourist dollars. Mesa Verde National Park and more than a half-dozen major ski areas attract a year-round stream of vacationers.

As one moves north out of the forested mountains into open ranching land, both the standard of living and the GOP vote increase. Rich oil shale reserves are found in Garfield and Rio Blanco counties in Colorado's northwest corner, and large coal deposits are located to the east.

Election Returns

3rd District		Democrat		Republican	
1976	President	74,039	(43.0%)	92,478	(53.8%)
	House	74,626	(43.6%)	87,376	(51.1%)
1978	Governor	80,205	(58.4%)	52,171	(38.0%)
	Senate	60,185	(43.4%)	77,143	(55.7%)
	House	64,766	(47.5%)	70,003	(51.3%)
1980	President	61,341	(32.6%)	106,846	(56.9%)
	Senate	91,330	(48.4%)	95,561	(50.7%)
	House	89,279	(46.9%)	98,081	(51.5%)
1982	Governor	103,999	(60.2%)	65,119	(37.7%)
	House	92,384	(53.4%)	77,409	(44.8%)

Demographics

Population: 481,854. **Percent Change from 1970:** 29.5%.

Land Area: 52,959 square miles. **Population per Square Mile:** 9.1.

Counties, 1980 Population: Alamosa — 11,799; Archuleta — 3,664; Conejos — 7,794; Costilla — 3,071; Custer — 1,528; Delta — 21,225; Dolores — 1,658; Eagle — 13,320; Fremont (Pt.) — 19,440; Garfield — 22,514; Grand — 7,475; Gunnison — 10,689; Hinsdale — 408; Huerfano — 6,440; Jackson — 1,863; La Plata — 27,424.

Mesa — 81,530; Mineral — 804; Moffat — 13,133; Montezuma — 16,510; Montrose — 24,352; Ouray — 1,925; Pitkin — 10,338; Pueblo — 125,972; Rio Blanco — 6,255; Rio Grande — 10,511; Routt — 13,404; Saguache — 3,935; San Juan — 833; San Miguel — 3,192; Summit — 8,848.

Cities, 1980 Population: Canon City (Pt.) — 7,278; Durango — 11,426; Grand Junction — 28,144; Pueblo — 101,686.

Race and Ancestry: White — 90.5%; Black — 0.7%; American Indian, Eskimo and Aleut — 1.1%; Asian and Pacific Islander — 0.4%. Spanish Origin — 17.1%. Dutch — 0.8%; English — 10.7%; French — 1.1%; German — 9.4%; Irish — 4.2%; Italian — 2.5%; Norwegian — 0.6%; Polish — 0.5%; Scottish — 1.0%; Swedish — 1.1%.

Universities, Enrollment: Adams State College, Alamosa — 1,837; Colorado Mountain College (West campus), Glenwood Springs — 741; Colorado Northwestern Community College, Rangely — 2,913; Fort Lewis College, Durango — 3,260; Mesa College, Grand Junction — 3,873; Pueblo Vocational Community College, Pueblo — 882; University of Southern Colorado, Pueblo — 4,682; Western State College of Colorado, Gunnison — 2,120.

Newspapers, Circulation: *Chieftain* (m), Pueblo — 38,737; *Canon City Daily Record* (e), Canon City — 7,890; *The Daily Sentinel* (eS), Grand Junction — 30,003; *Durango Herald* (e), Durango — 6,964; *The Glenwood Post* (e), Glenwood Springs — 4,857; *The Montrose Daily Press* (e), Montrose — 6,095; *Northwest Colorado Daily Press* (e), Craig — 3,048; *Star-Journal* (e), Pueblo — 14,419; *Valley Courier* (e), Alamosa — 5,905.

Commercial Television Stations, Affiliation: KJCT, Grand Junction (ABC); KREX-TV, Grand Junction (CBS, NBC); KREY-TV, Montrose (CBS, NBC); KREZ-TV, Durango (CBS, NBC). Most of district is located in Denver ADI. Portions are in Colorado Springs-Pueblo ADI, Grand Junction ADI and Albuquerque (N.M.) ADI.

Military Installations: Pueblo Army Depot Activity, Pueblo — 856.

Industries:

C F & I Steel Corp. (HQ); Pueblo; steel products — 5,700. **Colorado State Hospital;** Pueblo; state mental hospital — 1,400. **St. Mary's Corwin Hospital;** Pueblo; hospital — 1,200.

4th District

North and East — Fort Collins, Greeley

The 4th is Colorado's breadbasket, home of the state's agricultural heartland and its major farm markets. While the district is about as large as it was in the 1970s, the court remap made it far more homogeneous. The energy-rich desert landscape and ski resorts of the Western Slope have been removed, replaced by more of the rolling land of eastern Colorado.

Although the district gains nearly 150,000 new constituents, the 4th is as Republican as it was in the 1970s, if not more so. Most of the voters live near the northern flank of the Front Range in Larimer (Fort Collins) and Weld (Greeley) counties.

Both counties contain educational and trade centers for agricultural northern Colorado, an area that used to be one of the nation's top suppliers of sugar beets. As prices for beets dropped, many farmers switched to corn or beans.

Although Larimer and Weld counties regularly support GOP presidential and House candidates, both vote occasionally for Democrats in statewide races. Democratic Gov. Richard D. Lamm won Larimer and Weld easily in 1978; Democratic Sen. Gary Hart carried them both narrowly in 1980.

With nearly one-third of the district's population, Larimer County is larger, faster-growing and more economically diverse than Weld. Its growth rate of 66 percent in the 1970s far exceeded that of any other county in the district. Newcomers have been drawn by the spillover of high technology firms from the Boulder area to Fort Collins (pop. 65,092) and Loveland (pop. 30,244), the growing academic community at Colorado State University in Fort Collins, and the scenery.

In the southwest corner of the county is Estes Park, the eastern gateway to the Rocky Mountain National Park. The park's proximity ensures Larimer County a steady flow of tourist dollars.

Located to the east on the fringe of the Great Plains, Weld County is more dependent on agriculture. The county seat of Greeley (pop. 53,006) was an outgrowth of the Union Colony, an agricultural cooperative that was the brainchild of New York *Tribune* editor Horace Greeley. During its formative years in the late 19th and early 20th centuries, the Greeley area was an ethnic melting pot. The robust mixture of early German and Russian immigrants was the basis of James Michener's novel, "Centennial."

Ranching is also crucial to life in Weld County. For years Greeley has been the base of Monfort of Colorado, one of the largest feed lots and packing plants in the country. Smaller, family-run competitors dot the county.

The 4th used to extend into the blue-collar suburbs of Denver in western Adams County. But in redistricting, Democratic Northglenn and Westminster were exchanged for the rural, more Republican, eastern portion of Adams and Arapahoe counties. The 4th gained blue-collar Commerce City (pop. 16,234) on the outskirts of Denver and the neighboring Rocky Mountain Arsenal.

The territorial heart of the 4th is the eastern plains, a vast agricultural region that covers one-third of the state but holds barely 30 percent of the district residents. Of the 16 counties in the region, none has more than 25,000 residents.

The eastern counties are an extension of the Great Plains of the agricultural Midwest. Sparse rainfall and high winds made them part of the 1930s dust bowl. Now farmers graze livestock and grow wheat. Like neighboring Nebraska and Kansas, the area is conservative in outlook, but there are pockets of political ferment. The American Agricultural Movement was born in Springfield (Baca County) in the mid-1970s.

Election Returns

4th District		Democrat		Republican	
1976	President	76,026	(42.0%)	99,766	(55.1%)
	House	65,637	(37.1%)	95,929	(54.2%)
1978	Governor	79,112	(56.6%)	57,792	(41.4%)
	Senate	54,546	(38.9%)	84,509	(60.3%)
	House	52,779	(38.9%)	82,166	(60.5%)

4th District		Democrat		Republican	
1980	President	58,221	(29.2%)	115,469	(58.0%)
	Senate	101,461	(47.0%)	112,616	(52.2%)
	House	55,316	(28.2%)	137,091	(70.0%)
1982	Governor	96,488	(63.7%)	51,351	(33.9%)
	House	45,750	(30.2%)	105,550	(69.8%)

Demographics

Population: 481,512. **Percent Change from 1970:** 29.6%.

Land Area: 38,409 square miles. **Population per Square Mile:** 12.5.

Counties, 1980 Population: Adams (Pt.) — 48,969; Arapahoe (Pt.) — 13,577; Baca — 5,419; Bent — 5,945; Cheyenne — 2,153; Crowley — 2,988; Kiowa — 1,936; Kit Carson — 7,599; Larimer — 149,184; Las Animas — 14,897; Lincoln — 4,663; Logan — 19,800; Morgan — 22,513; Otero — 22,567; Phillips — 4,542; Prowers — 13,070; Sedgwick — 3,266; Washington — 5,304; Weld — 123,438; Yuma — 9,682.

Cities, 1980 Population: Brighton — 12,773; Commerce City — 16,234; Fort Collins — 65,092; Greeley — 53,006; Loveland — 30,244; Sterling — 11,385; Thornton (Pt.) — 8.

Race and Ancestry: White — 91.7%; Black — 0.5%; American Indian, Eskimo and Aleut — 0.4%; Asian and Pacific Islander — 0.8%. Spanish Origin — 13.7%. Dutch — 0.8%; English — 8.9%; French — 0.8%; German — 15.8%; Irish — 3.6%; Italian — 1.3%; Norwegian — 0.6%; Scottish — 0.6%; Swedish — 1.4%.

Universities, Enrollment: Aims Community College, Greeley — 3,558; Colorado State University, Fort Collins — 18,083; Lamar Community College, Lamar — 418; Morgan Community College, Fort Morgan — 531; Northeastern Junior College, Sterling — 1,701; Otero Junior College, La Junta — 880; Trinidad State Junior College, Trinidad — 1,865; University of Northern Colorado, Greeley — 10,830.

Newspapers, Circulation: *Chronicle-News* (e), Trinidad — 3,629; *Coloradoan* (eS), Fort Collins — 19,205; *Fort Morgan Times* (e), Fort Morgan — 6,151; *Greeley Daily Tribune* (eS), Greeley — 22,399; *The Lamar Tri-State Daily News* (e), Lamar — 3,225; *Loveland Daily Reporter-Herald* (e) Loveland — 14,458; *Rocky Ford Daily Gazette* (e), Rocky Ford — 3,032; *Sterling Journal-Advocate* (e), Sterling — 7,348; *Tribune-Democrat* (e), La Junta — 4,220. *The Denver Post* and Denver *Rocky Mountain News* also circulate in the district.

Commercial Television Stations, Affiliation: KTVS, Sterling (CBS, ABC). Most of district is divided between Colorado Springs-Pueblo ADI and Denver ADI. Portion is in Cheyenne (Wyo.) ADI.

Military Installations: La Junta Radar Bomb Score Site, La Junta — 107; Lamar Communications Facility Annex (Air Force), Lamar — 10; Rocky Mountain Arsenal, Commerce City — 405.

Nuclear Power Plants: Fort St. Vrain, Platteville (General Atomic Co., Ebasco Services Inc.), July 1979.

Industries:

Eastman Kodak Co. (Kodak Colorado Div.); Windsor; photographic supplies — 3,200. **Hewlett-Packard Co.;** Loveland; electronic devices — 2,811. **Hewlett-Packard Co.** (Calculator Products Div.); Fort Collins; computing equipment — 2,300. **Monfort of Colorado Inc.** (HQ); Greeley; cattle feeding; beef processing — 2,000. **Weld County General Hospital;** Greeley; hospital — 1,050. **Teledyne Industries Inc.** (Teledyne Water Pik); Fort Collins; dental supplies — 1,000. **State Farm Mutual Automobile Insurance Co.;** Greeley; surety company — 940. **Woodward Governor Co.;** Fort Collins; aircraft controls — 935.

5th District

South Central — Colorado Springs

Carefully designed after the 1970 census by a Republican-controlled state government, the 5th District was the leading GOP bastion in the state throughout that decade. The party's House candidates held the seat without difficulty, and in statewide elections the 5th was reliably Republican.

GOP margins may drop in the 1980s because redistricting pared away most of the conservative Arapahoe County suburbs. But their removal will be mitigated in part by the addition of new portions of Republican-oriented El Paso County (Colorado Springs), which has been reunited within the district.

During the 1970s about 70 percent of the El Paso County voters were in the 5th and 30 percent in the 3rd. Now El Paso County, with a population of 309,424, is the clear political center of the 5th District.

Both the county and the district revolve around Colorado Springs, the state's second-largest city and the southern anchor of the rapidly growing Front Range. It was originally a resort where sunny climate, nearby springs and Pikes Peak drew tourists from the East. So many English visitors established roots in the city that during the late 19th century the town gained the nickname "Little Lunnon."

Tourism remains a mainstay of the local economy. But after World War II, Colorado Springs became an important military center in the area. North of the city is the U.S. Air Force Academy; to the east is Peterson Air Force Base; to the south is Fort Carson; and deep in a mountain to the west is NORAD (the North American Air Defense Command), maintaining a round-the-clock alert for an enemy air attack on the continent.

The economy has diversified further, with electronics firms coming to the area. Among the major employers are Hewlett-Packard, TRW and Honeywell, which have made Colorado Springs a rival to Boulder as Colorado's center of high technology.

Yet while the economic base has changed, the politics of Colorado Springs has remained consistently conservative. Although there is a potentially decisive minority population — 8.5 percent Hispanic, 5.6 percent black and 2 percent Asian — the city strays into the Democratic column only during poor national Republican years.

Nearly two-thirds of the new district's population lives in El Paso County. Another 25 percent lives to the north in the Denver suburbs of southwest Jefferson, southwest Arapahoe and Douglas counties. All have Republican voting habits, although in the Jefferson County portion most of the registered voters are independents. In 1980 Ronald Reagan drew 64 percent of the El Paso County vote, his highest share in any major county along the Front Range.

The 5th contains about two-thirds of the land area of Jefferson County but less than one-fifth of its 371,753 residents. The major community within the district is Golden (pop. 12,237), the site of the Colorado School of Mines, the Adolph Coors brewery and Buffalo Bill's grave. Snuggled in the timbered mountains to the south are smaller suburban communities such as Conifer and Evergreen.

The 5th previously extended eastward from the Front Range to the Kansas border, but redistricting gave Cheyenne, Kit Carson and Lincoln counties to the 4th. The only plains county that remains in the 5th is Elbert, a cattle ranching area inhabited by rock-ribbed Republicans. Elbert is the lone county in Colorado that voted for both Alfred M. Landon in 1936 and Barry Goldwater in 1964. It gave Reagan 67.5 percent of the vote in 1980.

The remaining 9 percent of the district population

lives in sparsely populated mountain counties between Colorado Springs and the Continental Divide. Formerly a part of the 3rd District, this territory is not so reliably Republican.

Ranching, mining and tourism are mainstays of the mountain economy. Cattle roam throughout the northern half of Fremont County. Much of the land in Chaffee, Lake, Park and Teller counties is covered by national forests. Mining communities are the centers of Democratic strength in the mountain area. Lake and Chaffee are the only two counties in the district with a Democratic registration edge.

Election Returns

5th District		Democrat		Republican	
1976	President	64,460	(39.3%)	94,920	(57.9%)
	House	52,455	(39.8%)	78,804	(59.8%)
1978	Governor	65,121	(50.8%)	60,590	(47.2%)
	Senate	41,106	(32.2%)	85,545	(66.9%)
	House	38,693	(33.1%)	73,540	(62.9%)
1980	President	47,248	(24.7%)	121,490	(63.6%)
	Senate	72,733	(42.0%)	98,946	(57.1%)
	House	56,682	(31.9%)	117,131	(65.8%)
1982	Governor	81,405	(58.3%)	54,214	(38.8%)
	House	57,392	(40.5%)	84,479	(59.5%)

Demographics

Population: 481,627. **Percent Change from 1970:** 60.6%.

Land Area: 10,467 square miles. **Population per Square Mile:** 46.0.

Counties, 1980 Population: Arapahoe (Pt.) — 26,694; Chaffee — 13,227; Douglas — 25,153; El Paso — 309,424; Elbert — 6,850; Fremont (Pt.) — 9,236; Jefferson (Pt.) — 68,846; Lake — 8,830; Park — 5,333; Teller — 8,034.

Cities, 1980 Population: Canon City (Pt.) — 5,759; Colorado Springs — 215,150; Fort Carson (CDP) — 13,219; Golden — 12,237; Littleton (Pt.) — 128.

Race and Ancestry: White — 90.7%; Black — 4.1%; American Indian, Eskimo and Aleut — 0.5%; Asian and Pacific Islander — 1.3%. Spanish Origin — 6.8%. Dutch — 0.7%; English — 9.3%; French — 1.1%; German — 10.3%; Irish — 3.8%; Italian — 1.5%; Norwegian — 0.7%; Polish — 0.8%; Scottish — 0.7%; Swedish — 0.9%.

Universities, Enrollment: Blair Junior College, Colorado Springs — 277; Colorado College, Colorado Springs — 1,954; Colorado Mountain College (East campus), Leadville — 598; Colorado School of Mines, Golden — 2,907; Colorado Technical College, Colorado Springs — 585; Nazarene Bible College, Colorado Springs — 510; Pikes Peak Community College, Colorado Springs — 5,862; United States Air Force Academy, Colorado Springs — 4,485; University of Colorado at Colorado Springs, Colorado Springs — 4,787; Western Bible College, Morrison — 203.

Newspapers, Circulation: *Colorado Springs Gazette Telegraph* (meS), Colorado Springs — 77,057; *Colorado Springs Sun* (mS), Colorado Springs — 29,342; *Herald-Democrat* (e), Leadville — 2,050; *The Mountain Mail* (e), Salida — 2,403. *The Denver Post* and Denver *Rocky Mountain News* also circulate in the district.

Commercial Television Stations, Affiliation: KKTV, Colorado Springs (CBS); KOAA-TV, Colorado Springs (NBC); KRDO-TV, Colorado Springs (ABC). Most of district is located in Denver ADI. Portion is in Colorado Springs-Pueblo ADI.

Military Installations: Cheyenne Mountain Complex (NORAD), Colorado Springs — 1,952; Fort Carson, Colorado Springs — 23,463; Peterson Air Force Base, Colorado Springs — 2,197.

Industries:

Adolph Coors Co. (HQ); Golden; brewery, aluminum beer cans — 6,215. **Rockwell International Corp.;** Golden; electronic communications equipment — 5,360. **Hewlett-Packard Co.;** Colorado Springs; electronic measuring instruments — 2,400. **Coors Porcelain Co.** (Spectro Chemical Lab Div.); Golden; porcelain products — 2,000. **Ampex Corp.;** Colorado Springs; electronic components — 1,600. **Johns-Manville Corp.** (HQ); Lakewood; insulation, roofing materials — 1,600.

Digital Equipment Corp.; Colorado Springs; industrial measuring instruments — 1,598. **Penrose Hospital Inc.** (HQ); Colorado Springs; hospital — 1,550. **Broadmoor Hotel Inc.;** Colorado Springs; resort hotel — 1,400. **LooArt Press Inc.** (Current Inc.); Colorado Springs; greeting cards, stationery — 1,000. **TRW Colorado Electronics Inc.;** Colorado Springs; electronics communication equipment — 950. **Schlage Lock Co.;** Colorado Springs; locks — 762. **Kaman Sciences Corp.** (Digital Radiation Monitoring — HQ); Colorado Springs; nuclear research — 754. **Honeywell Inc.** (Solid State Product Center); Colorado Springs; electricity measuring instruments — 650. **Midwest Research Institute;** Golden; research — 650. **Western Forge Corp.** (HQ); Colorado Springs; hand tools — 625. **Inmos Corp.;** Colorado Springs; integrated circuits — 600. **Colorado Interstate Gas Co.** (HQ); Colorado Springs; natural gas extracting & distributing — 530.

6th District

Denver Suburbs — Aurora, Lakewood

Thanks to a statewide population increase of 680,368 in the 1970s, Colorado was entitled to a sixth congressional district for the 1980s, and the federal judges placed it in the Denver suburbs. It elected a Republican, as expected, in 1982.

The district forms a "U" around the east, south and west sides of the city, catching the homes of most white-collar commuters while missing the working-class suburbs to the north. Overwhelmingly white, the 6th has the lowest minority population of any district in the state.

Democrats see the large number of registered independents in the 6th — 41 percent — and the occasional success of a strong statewide democratic candidate such as Gov. Richard D. Lamm as hopeful signs. But as electronics and engineering firms have moved into the suburbs, the population has taken a big jump and Republicans have thrived. In 1980 Ronald Reagan ran about 5 percentage points better in the new 6th than he did statewide.

The district includes portions of four counties. More than half the population (51.4 percent) lives south and east of Denver in Arapahoe County. Another 39 percent lives west of the city in Jefferson County, with the rest divided between the southwest corner of Denver and a portion of Adams County northeast of the city near Stapleton Airport.

The largest community in the district is the city of Aurora (pop. 158,588), which straddles the Adams-Arapahoe county line. The smaller Adams County portion to the north is the only part of the district with a Democratic registration advantage. This area is one of the few minority enclaves in the 6th, with blacks, Hispanics and Asians comprising nearly one-quarter of the population. Large numbers of military retirees also have settled in the community.

The Arapahoe County portion of Aurora is a bit more affluent and Republican. It has been the center of the county's population boom. While Arapahoe County as a whole grew 81 percent in the 1970s — a faster pace than any of the other suburban counties — its Aurora portion grew by 170 percent as the city's inexpensive land and independent water supply lured suburban developers.

To the north and west is Jefferson County, which usually votes Republican but is less uniform in its conservatism. The county mixes business executives, government employees and factory workers.

The 6th District also includes about 16,500 residents in the southwestern part of Denver that juts out near the Arapahoe-Jefferson county line. During the 1970s it was a center of anti-busing sentiment in the city.

Election Returns

6th District		Democrat		Republican	
1976	President	60,365	(36.5%)	100,216	(60.6%)
	House	63,427	(38.7%)	100,321	(61.3%)
1978	Governor	72,189	(57.1%)	52,046	(41.2%)
	Senate	41,293	(32.5%)	84,706	(66.6%)
	House	51,896	(43.2%)	64,507	(53.7%)
1980	President	51,629	(26.1%)	117,916	(59.6%)
	Senate	93,757	(47.9%)	99,878	(51.1%)
	House	73,237	(37.8%)	116,688	(60.2%)
1982	Governor	104,370	(65.2%)	51,266	(32.0%)
	House	56,598	(35.6%)	98,909	(62.1%)

Demographics

Population: 481,682. **Percent Change from 1970:** 43.2%.

Land Area: 213 square miles. **Population per Square Mile:** 2,261.4

Counties, 1980 Population: Adams (Pt.) — 29,381; Arapahoe (Pt.) — 247,547; Denver (Pt.) — 16,496; Jefferson (Pt.) — 188,258.

Cities, 1980 Population: Aurora — 158,588; Denver (Pt.) — 16,496; Englewood — 30,021; Lakewood — 112,860; Littleton (Pt.) — 28,503; Wheat Ridge — 30,293.

Race and Ancestry: White — 93.1%; Black — 2.7%; American Indian, Es o and Aleut — 0.4%; Asian and Pacific Islander — 1.6%. Sp sh Origin — 5.3%. Dutch — 0.6%; English — 9.1%; French — 0.9%; German — 10.7%; Irish — 3.9%; Italian — 1.7%; Norwegian — 0.7%; Polish — 0.9%; Scottish — 0.6%; Swedish — 1.1%.

Universities, Enrollment: Arapahoe Community College, Littleton — 6,176; Community College of Denver (Red Rocks campus), Golden — 4,958; Engineering Drafting School, Denver — 170.

Newspapers, Circulation: *The Denver Post* and Denver *Rocky Mountain News* circulate in the district.

Commercial Television Stations, Affiliation: KWGN-TV, Denver (None). Entire district is located in Denver ADI. *(For other Denver stations, see 1st district.)*

Military Installations: Buckley Air National Guard Base, Aurora — 1,881; Fitzsimons Army Medical Center, Aurora — 3,505.

Industries:

Martin Marietta Corp. (Aerospace Div.); Littleton; aerospace data equipment — 8,700. **Swedish Medical Center Inc.;** Englewood; hospital — 1,600. **Western Electric Co. Inc.;** Aurora; telephone equipment — 1,600. **Lutheran Medical Center Inc.;** Wheatridge; hospital — 1,380. **MCA Financial Inc.** (Denver Tech Center Parkway); Englewood; savings and loan association — 900.

Indian Head Inc. (Information Handling Services); Englewood; microfilm indexing — 800. **C. A. Norgren Co.** (HQ); Littleton; pressure valves — 740. **Diners' Club Inc.;** Englewood; credit card operations — 700. **The Electron Corp.** (HQ); Littleton; gray iron foundries — 679. **Nekoosa Envelopes Inc.** (Rockmount Envelopes); Denver; envelopes, paper boxes, bags, stationery — 600. **Howard Electric & Mechanical Co. Inc.;** Lakewood; sheet metal work — 500. **Rocky Mountain Bank Note Co.** (HQ); Denver; commercial printing — 500. **Stone & Webster Engineering;** Englewood; engineering services — 500.

Connecticut

With a population that remained stable during the 1970s, Connecticut had to make only minor adjustments to its six congressional district boundaries. Not much was gained or lost politically in redistricting, but there was something to please both parties in the compromise that preceded the final ruling of the state's Reapportionment Commission.

The new district lines were expected to maintain the Democratic Party's modest statewide advantage in congressional districts. The Republican Party tightened its grip on the 4th District, already the GOP's most dependable territory.

The Democrats, controlling the governorship and solid majorities in both houses of the state Legislature, had the leverage to resist more ambitious GOP claims. The redistricting was to have been decided by an evenly balanced General Assembly committee, but the panel deadlocked over the parties' competing plans in midsummer 1981. That forced the appointment of a special commission, with four Republicans, four Democrats and one non-partisan member who would cast tie-breaking votes when necessary. The commission issued its new map on Oct. 28, 1981. Under rules established for the procedure, the commission's map was final.

The non-partisan ninth member of the commission was needed only to settle a dispute over the boundaries of the 6th District. Republicans had hoped to use the remapping of the 6th to improve their chances there in November 1982: Democrat Toby Moffett had given up his safe House seat to challenge Republican Sen. Lowell P. Weicker Jr. But when the Republicans tried to tailor the 6th District's lines to aid an expected GOP House candidate, a state senator, the Democrats balked at a "blatant, though limited, gerrymander."

The non-partisan commissioner endorsed a less controversial alternative that was expected to preserve the thin Democratic edge in the 6th without threatening the solid Democratic lead in the neighboring 1st District. However, the Republican candidate won in 1982 with 51.7 percent of the vote. The Democrats maintained their 4-2 advantage in the state's House delegation by defeating the Republican incumbent in the 3rd District.

The new congressional lines left the constituencies very closely balanced. No district deviated from the ideal population of 517,929 by more than 1,700 people.

Age of Population

District	Population Under 18	Voting Age Population	Population 65 & Over (% of VAP)	Median Age
1	132,673	383,559	65,558 (17.1%)	32.4
2	140,112	378,132	53,819 (14.2%)	29.5
3	130,937	387,740	64,393 (16.6%)	32.2
4	134,225	384,352	63,553 (16.5%)	33.8
5	146,698	372,002	57,224 (15.4%)	32.1
6	138,274	378,872	60,317 (15.9%)	32.3
State	822,919	2,284,657	364,864 (16.0%)	32.0

Income and Occupation

District	Median Family Income	White Collar Workers	Blue Collar Workers	Service Workers	Farm Workers
1	$ 23,026	62.4%	25.3%	11.5%	0.7%
2	21,176	51.5	33.7	13.0	1.8
3	22,267	58.4	29.4	11.6	0.6
4	25,879	63.2	25.2	10.9	0.8
5	23,927	55.8	32.9	10.5	0.7
6	23,548	54.5	33.7	10.7	1.1
State	$ 23,149	57.7%	30.0%	11.4%	1.0%

Education: School Years Completed

District	8 Years or Fewer	4 Years of High School	4 Years of College or More	Median School Years
1	16.7%	34.2%	20.8%	12.6
2	16.2	36.8	18.1	12.5
3	15.7	35.8	19.9	12.6
4	16.8	30.1	25.6	12.7
5	16.6	34.4	20.2	12.6
6	15.9	35.4	19.1	12.6
State	16.3%	34.4%	20.7%	12.6

Housing and Residential Patterns

District	Owner Occupied	Renter Occupied	Urban	Rural
1	57.8%	42.2%	88.4%	11.6%
2	64.8	35.2	54.8	45.2

CONNECTICUT

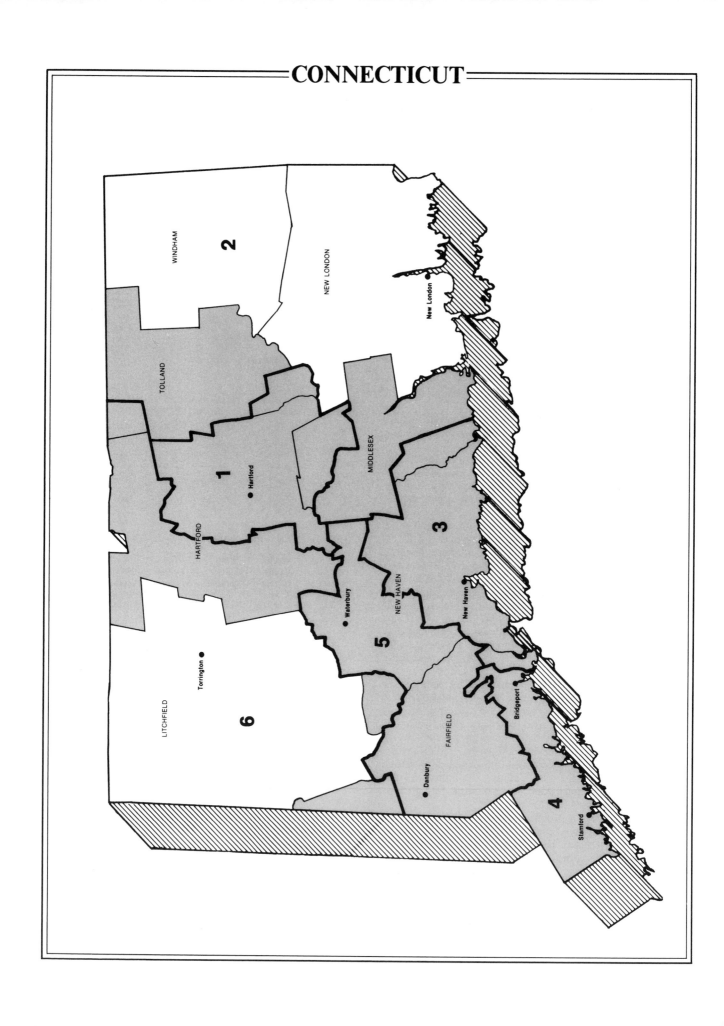

District	Owner Occupied	Renter Occupied	Urban	Rural
3	63.0	37.0	88.6	11.4
4	61.2	38.8	96.3	3.7
5	67.8	32.2	78.4	21.6
6	69.4	30.6	66.5	33.5
State	63.9%	36.1%	78.8%	21.2%

1st District

Central — Hartford

Centered around Hartford and its small-city neighbors, the 1st is primarily urban territory, and it has sent a Democrat to Congress in every election but one since 1948. Once the fiefdom of state party boss John Bailey, who died in 1975, the district in January 1982 elected his daughter, Barbara Bailey Kennelly, as its member of the U.S. House.

Following the statewide pattern, the small cities in the district gained population since the 1970 census at the expense of the inner city. Hartford lost 13.7 percent of its population, pacing the decline of Hartford County, the state's only county to lose population in the decade. Cities close to the capital also lost population, but several of the district's outlying towns grew, particularly in the Republican areas to the southeast.

The district has a two-to-one Democratic advantage in voter registration, although Hartford itself accounts for only one-sixth of the district vote. Fifty years earlier, Hartford had proportionally the third-largest Jewish population of any city in the nation; a variety of ethnic groups have traditionally shared power, and now the city has significant black and Hispanic communities.

As headquarters city for many of the nation's insurance firms, Hartford's economy still boasts a substantial white-collar sector. United Aircraft's Pratt & Whitney headquarters in East Hartford employs 18,000 people, and other aerospace and high-technology firms have attracted a skilled work force. Despite its population decline, Hartford entered the 1980s with more economic resources than some of the other Northeastern industrial cities.

The remap of the 1st added three new areas: East Windsor, north of the city, was shifted from the 6th. East Hampton and the remainder of Portland, to the south, were moved from the 2nd. All three towns usually vote Democratic. The 1st lost Bolton, which moved into the 2nd.

Election Returns

1st District		Democrat		Republican	
1976	President	125,895	(52.4%)	113,154	(47.1%)
	Senate	105,123	(44.1%)	131,493	(55.2%)
	House	134,878	(57.5%)	97,252	(41.5%)
1978	Governor	109,796	(60.2%)	72,652	(39.8%)
	House	108,426	(60.1%)	69,988	(38.8%)
1980	President	109,702	(45.6%)	93,750	(38.9%)
	Senate	153,323	(65.7%)	78,525	(33.6%)
	House	143,670	(62.9%)	84,730	(37.1%)
1982	Governor	107,332	(56.3%)	82,145	(43.1%)
	Senate	91,107	(47.9%)	92,919	(48.8%)
	House	126,798	(68.1%)	58,075	(31.2%)

Demographics

Population: 516,232. **Percent Change from 1970:** -1.7%.

Land Area: 455 square miles. **Population per Square Mile:** 1,134.6.

Counties, 1980 Population: Hartford (Pt.) — 483,559; Middlesex (Pt.) — 27,220; Tolland (Pt.) — 5,453.

Cities, 1980 Population: Berlin — 15,121; Bloomfield — 18,608; Cromwell — 10,265; East Hartford — 52,563; Hartford — 136,392; Glastonbury — 24,327; Manchester — 49,761; Newington — 28,841; Rocky Hill — 14,559; South Windsor — 17,198; West Hartford — 61,301; Wethersfield — 26,013; Windsor — 25,204.

Race and Ancestry: White — 83.2%; Black — 11.6%; American Indian, Eskimo and Aleut — 0.1%; Asian and Pacific Islander — 0.7%. Spanish Origin — 6.3%. English — 6.0%; French — 4.2%; German — 2.7%; Greek — 0.5%; Irish — 6.4%; Italian — 9.0%; Polish — 4.8%; Portuguese — 1.3%; Russian — 1.4%; Scottish — 0.5%; Swedish — 1.0%; Ukranian — 0.5%.

Universities, Enrollment: Greater Hartford Community College, Hartford — 2,875; Hartford College for Women, Hartford — 205; Hartford Graduate Center, Hartford — 1,316; Hartford Seminary Foundation, Hartford — 70; Hartford State Technical College, Hartford — 1,846; Holy Apostles College, Cromwell — 94; Manchester Community College, Manchester — 6,617; St. Joseph College, West Hartford — 792; Trinity College, Hartford — 1,781; University of Hartford, West Hartford — 9,836.

Newspapers, Circulation: *The Hartford Courant* (mS), Hartford — 213,101; *Journal Inquirer* (e), Manchester — 36,794; *Manchester Herald* (e), Manchester — 13,543. New Britain *Herald* also circulates in the district.

Commercial Television Stations, Affiliation: WFSB-TV, Hartford (CBS); WHCT-TV Hartford (None). Entire district is located in Hartford-New Haven ADI.

Industries:

United Technologies Corp. (Pratt & Whitney Aircraft Group - HQ); East Hartford; aircraft engines, parts — 18,000. **Aetna Life & Casualty Co.** (HQ); Hartford; casualty, life, health insurance — 11,000. **The Travelers Corp.** (HQ); Hartford; casualty, life, property insurance — 9,000. **CIGNA Insurance** (HQ); Bloomfield; life, casualty, health insurance — 4,700. **Combustion Engineering Inc.** (Steam Generation Systems); Windsor; steam turbines — 4,500. **Hartford Fire Insurance Co.** (HQ); Hartford; casualty, life insurance — 4,500.

Hartford Hospital Inc.; Hartford; hospital — 3,600. **Aetna Casualty & Surety Co.**; Hartford; casualty, surety insurance — 3,300. **St. Francis Hospital & Medical Center**; Hartford; hospital — 2,870. **Stanadyne Inc.** (HQ); Windsor; fuel pumps — 2,600. **Kaman Corp.** (HQ); Bloomfield; industrial supplies, musical instruments, aviation services — 2,098. **Colt Industries Operating Corp.** (Firearms Div.); Hartford; small arms — 2,000. **Mount Sinai Hospital Inc.**; Hartford; hospital — 1,500. **Emhart Industries** (Corbin Cabinet Lock); Berlin; locks — 1,467. **Connecticut Mutual Life Insurance Co.** (HQ); Hartford; life insurance — 1,450. **Hartford Accident & Indemnity Co.** (HQ); Hartford; health insurance — 1,200.

Manchester Memorial Hospital Inc.; Manchester; hospital — 1,150. **Pioneer Systems Inc.**; Manchester; parachutes — 1,150. **Chandler-Evans Inc.**; West Hartford; airborne systems — 1,100. **Aetna Insurance Co.** (HQ); Hartford; casualty insurance — 1,040. **American Airlines**; Hartford; commercial airline — 1,000. **Gerber Scientific Inc.** (HQ); South Windsor; drafting instruments — 1,000. **Hartford National Corp.** (HQ); Hartford; banking — 1,000. **The Institute of Living**; Hartford; psychiatric hospital — 1,000. **Phoenix Mutual Life Insurance Co.** (HQ); Hartford; life, accident insurance — 1,000. **Textron Inc.** (Fafnir Bearing Div.); Newington; ball bearings — 1,000. **United Technologies Corp.** (Power Systems Div.); South Windsor; fuel cells — 1,000. **Western Pacific Industries Inc.** (Veeder Root); Hartford; counting devices — 1,000.

Connecticut Bank & Trust Co.; East Hartford; banking — 998. **Building Maintenance Corp.**; Hartford; janitorial services — 900. **Connecticut Bank & Trust Co.** (HQ); Hartford; banking — 900. **Crouse-Hinds Co.** (Arrow Hart Div.); Hartford; electrical switchgear apparatus — 900. **Hartford National Bank & Trust Co.** (HQ); Hartford; banking — 870. **The Hartford Courant Co.** (HQ); Hartford; newspaper publishing — 850. **Atlantic Machine Tool Works;** Newington; aircraft parts — 800. **Sage-Allen & Co. Inc.** (HQ); Hartford; department stores — 760. **Emhart Industries;** Hartford; special industry machinery — 700. **Jacobs Mfg. Co.** (HQ); Bloomfield; machine tool accessories — 700. **Kaman Corp.** (Musical Instrument Div. - HQ); Bloomfield; musical instruments — 700. **The Wiremold Co.** (HQ); West Hartford; wiring devices, conduits — 700. **International Business Machines Corp.;** Hartford; data processing services — 600. **The Phoenix Insurance Co.** (HQ); Hartford; casualty insurance — 600. **Royal Business Machines Inc.** (Roytype Div. - HQ); Hartford; carbon ribbons, business forms — 600. **Terry Corp.** (Marine Div. - HQ); Windsor; steam turbines — 570. **Parker-Hannifin Corp.** (EIS Automotive Div.); Berlin; motor vehicle parts — 550. **Castle & Cooke Inc.** (East Windsor Mushroom Co.); Warehouse Point; mushrooms — 500. **Dunham-Bush Inc.** (HQ); West Hartford; heating, cooling equipment — 500.

2nd District

East — New London

Stretching from the shores of Long Island Sound to the state's upland hills, the 2nd District is the largest and least urbanized part of Connecticut, and its vote varies with its geography. Along the coast, dependably Democratic shipbuilding cities and fishing villages border wealthy WASPish towns that provide Republican votes. Inland, small manufacturing centers and bustling college towns deliver Democratic margins, while rural Yankee hill towns maintain their GOP tradition.

The fine balance among the areas helps give the 2nd District the state's most volatile congressional voting pattern, although Democratic trends now seem to predominate. When Democrats retained control of the seat in 1980 it was the first time in nearly 50 years that the district had changed hands without changing parties. Between 1934 and 1950, it switched parties every two years.

Historically a center for seafaring, the southern coast is the home of the General Dynamics shipbuilding installation, located in Groton. Home of the Trident nuclear submarine program, this is the district's largest industrial concern.

Like Connecticut as a whole, the coastal area's economy is heavily dependent on military spending. The Groton area's maritime complex also features the Naval Underseas Research and Development Center, a Navy submarine port and a submarine-training base.

Across the Thames River, in New London, is the U.S. Coast Guard Academy, which coexists peacefully with Connecticut College and several small plastics and hardware plants. To the east is Mystic Seaport, a tourist attraction commemorating the fishing life that once thrived here.

Further inland, college towns and mill towns are neighbors on the hilly landscape. In Willimantic, Eastern Connecticut State College adjoins needle-and-thread and wire-cable firms. The town of Storrs is dominated by the University of Connecticut campus, while Middletown is home to Wesleyan University.

The latest remap added to the 2nd District the small but fast-growing town of Bolton. The towns of Portland and East Hampton moved into the 1st, and all of Somers was put in the 6th District.

Election Returns

2nd District		Democrat		Republican	
1976	President	106,788	(50.0%)	105,737	(49.5%)
	Senate	93,963	(44.4%)	115,950	(54.8%)
	House	136,708	(65.1%)	71,528	(34.1%)
1978	Governor	98,828	(61.6%)	61,640	(38.4%)
	House	111,246	(69.8%)	48,014	(30.1%)
1980	President	85,537	(38.2%)	103,603	(46.3%)
	Senate	135,172	(62.0%)	81,073	(37.2%)
	House	114,369	(53.5%)	99,446	(46.5%)
1982	Governor	96,596	(56.2%)	73,851	(43.0%)
	Senate	79,129	(46.0%)	86,938	(50.6%)
	House	95,254	(55.8%)	74,294	(43.5%)

Demographics

Population: 518,244. **Percent Change from 1970:** 6.4%.

Land Area: 1,778 square miles. **Population per Square Mile:** 291.5.

Counties, 1980 Population: Middlesex (Pt.) — 86,626; New London — 238,409; Tolland (Pt.) — 100,897; Windham — 92,312.

Cities, 1980 Population: East Lyme — 13,870; Groton — 41,062; Killingly — 14,519; Ledyard — 13,735; Mansfield — 20,634; Middletown — 39,040; Montville — 16,455; New London — 28,842; Norwich — 38,074; Plainfield — 12,774; Stonington — 16,220; Storrs — 11,394; Vernon — 27,974; Waterford — 17,843; Willimantic — 14,652; Windham — 21,062.

Race and Ancestry: White — 95.3%; Black — 2.9%; American Indian, Eskimo and Aleut — 0.3%; Asian and Pacific Islander — 0.7%. Spanish Origin — 1.7%. English — 8.7%; French — 6.3%; German — 3.4%; Irish — 4.9%; Italian — 5.8%; Polish — 4.3%; Portuguese — 0.6%; Russian — 0.7%; Scottish — 0.7%; Swedish — 0.8%.

Universities, Enrollment: Connecticut College, New London — 1,974; Eastern Connecticut State College, Willimantic — 2,858; Middlesex Community College, Middletown — 2,774; Mitchell College, New London — 867; Mohegan Community College, Norwich — 2,368; Quinebaug Valley Community College, Danielson — 936; Thames Valley State Technical College, Norwich — 1,823; United States Coast Guard Academy, New London — 840; University of Connecticut, Storrs — 21,988; Wesleyan University, Middletown — 2,958.

Newspapers, Circulation: *The Chronicle* (e), Willimantic — 10,366; *The Day* (e), New London — 38,241; *The Middletown Press* (e), Middletown — 21,019; *Norwich Bulletin* (mS), Norwich — 35,310. *The Hartford Courant* also circulates in the district.

Commercial Television Stations, Affiliation: Most of district is located in Hartford-New Haven ADI. Portion is in Providence (R.I.)-New Bedford (Mass.) ADI.

Military Installations: New London Naval Submarine Base, Groton — 15,559.

Nuclear Power Plants: Haddam Neck, Haddam Neck (Westinghouse, Stone & Webster), January 1968; Millstone 1, Waterford (General Electric, Ebasco Services Inc.), March 1971; Millstone 2, Waterford (Combustion Engineering, Bechtel), December 1975; Millstone 3, Waterford (Westinghouse, Stone & Webster).

Industries:

General Dynamics Corp. (Electric Boat Div.); Groton; shipbuilding — 25,000. **Stone & Webster Engineering;** Waterford; engineering services — 4,700. **Pfizer Inc.** (Chemical Div.); Groton; medicinal chemicals — 3,000. **Lawrence & Memorial Hospital;** New London; hospital — 1,320. **Middlesex Memorial Hospital;** Middletown; hospital — 1,150.

United Nuclear Corp. (Naval Products Div.); Montville; fabricated plate work — 1,120. **King-Seeley Thermos Co.;** Norwich; insulated ware — 1,100. **Norwich Hospital;** Norwich; hospital — 1,100.

Connecticut Valley Hospital; Middletown; mental hospital — 1,060. **Glass Containers Corp.;** Dayville; glass containers — 1,000. **United Technologies Corp.** (Pratt & Whitney Aircraft Group); Middletown; aircraft parts — 1,000. **King-Seeley Thermos Co.;** Taftville; insulated ware — 950. **American Thread Co.;** Willimantic; thread — 900. **Brand-Rex Co.** (HQ); Willimantic; wire, cable, insulating materials — 820. **R. R. Donnelley & Sons Co.;** Old Saybrook; commercial printing — 500. **General Dynamics Corp.** (Eastern Data Systems); Norwich; data processing services — 500. **Kaman Corp.** (Aerospace Corp.) Moosup; special dies, tools — 500. **Monsanto Co.;** Deep River; plastics products — 500. **North American Philips Corp.** (Consumer Products Div.); Essex; electric housewares — 500. **Rogers Corp.** (HQ); Rogers; circuits, plastic products, insulating materials — 500. **Thames Valley Steel Corp.;** New London; fabricated structural metal — 500.

3rd District

South — New Haven

Although New Haven is the 3rd District's anchor and economic center, only one-fifth of the votes come from within that declining manufacturing city. The district's overall electorate is a mixture of blue-collar ethnics, who are the core of the city's shrinking population, and white-collar suburbanites, many of whom commute into the downtown business district from the fast-growing small- and medium-sized cities on the urban rim.

Once the state's largest city and a New England industrial powerhouse, New Haven was dominated in the 19th century by Yankee Republicans and for most of the 20th century divided its power among Italian, Polish and Irish communities. Today New Haven itself is almost one-third black, but the black population makes up only 10 percent districtwide.

Italian-Americans, 17 percent of the district's population, wield powerful political influence. Between 1952 and 1982, the area's congressional seat always was held by someone of Italian extraction — regardless of partisan label. The election of a non-Italian in 1982 broke that pattern, but Italians continue to dominate local politics.

Registered Republicans are outweighed two-to-one by Democrats in the 3rd, but independents outnumber both parties. In 1980 Ronald Reagan carried the district by 26,000 votes, but ticket-splitters gave Democrat Christopher J. Dodd a comfortable 24,000-vote margin in the U.S. Senate race. In 1982 GOP Sen. Lowell P. Weicker Jr. won the 3rd with just 49 percent of the vote.

Yale University is New Haven's best-known institution. The university does not take an active role in city politics, and the Yale student body — at least since the Black Panther trials that inflamed campus sentiment in the late 1960s — has been largely indifferent to the surrounding city's political affairs.

The town of Clinton, with a brisk 9 percent population growth since the 1970 census, was added to the 3rd in the 1981 remap. Clinton, which had been divided between the 2nd and 3rd districts, is usually Republican territory.

Election Returns

3rd District		Democrat		Republican	
1976	President	106,441	(46.1%)	122,995	(53.3%)
	Senate	92,865	(40.7%)	132,030	(57.8%)
	House	122,924	(54.7%)	97,622	(43.4%)

3rd District		Democrat		Republican	
1978	Governor	105,092	(61.6%)	65,522	(38.4%)
	House	102,370	(56.4%)	75,941	(41.9%)
1980	President	91,123	(38.7%)	118,469	(50.3%)
	Senate	124,337	(55.0%)	100,159	(44.3%)
	House	104,813	(46.4%)	118,429	(52.4%)
1982	Governor	97,514	(53.3%)	84,227	(46.0%)
	Senate	87,907	(48.0%)	89,702	(48.9%)
	House	90,638	(50.0%)	88,951	(49.0%)

Demographics

Population: 518,677. **Percent Change from 1970:** 1.6%.

Land Area: 394 square miles. **Population per Square Mile:** 1,316.4.

Counties, 1980 Population: Fairfield (Pt.) — 50,541; Middlesex (Pt.) — 15,171; New Haven (Pt.) — 452,965.

Cities, 1980 Population: Branford — 23,363; Clinton — 11,195; East Haven — 25,028; Guilford — 17,375; Hamden — 51,071; Madison — 14,031; Milford — 50,898; New Haven — 126,109; North Branford — 11,554; North Haven — 22,080; Orange — 13,237; Stratford — 50,541; Wallingford — 37,274; West Haven — 53,184.

Race and Ancestry: White — 87.3%; Black — 10.4%; American Indian, Eskimo and Aleut — 0.1%; Asian and Pacific Islander — 0.7%. Spanish Origin — 2.9%. English — 5.9%; French — 1.4%; German — 3.2%; Hungarian — 0.8%; Irish — 6.9%; Italian — 17.3%; Polish — 3.4%; Portuguese — 0.5%; Russian — 1.6%; Scottish — 0.6%; Swedish — 0.6%.

Universities, Enrollment: Albertus Magnus College, New Haven — 565; Quinnipiac College, Hamden — 3,903; Southern Connecticut State College, New Haven — 11,720; University of New Haven, West Haven — 7,531; Yale University, New Haven — 9,807.

Newspapers, Circulation: *Journal-Courier* (m), New Haven — 37,629; *Milford Citizen* (eS), Milford — 6,882; *The New Haven Register* (eS), New Haven — 100,252. Meriden *Record-Journal* also circulates in the district.

Commercial Television Stations, Affiliation: WTNH-TV, New Haven (ABC). Most of district is located in Hartford-New Haven ADI. Small portion is in New York (N.Y.) ADI.

Military Installations: Orange Air National Guard Communication Station, New Haven — 142; Stratford Army Engine Plant, Stratford — 5,110.

Industries:

United Technologies Corp. (Sikorsky Aircraft Div.); Stratford; helicopters — 7,800. **Olin Corp.** (Winchester-Western Div.); New Haven; sporting arms — 4,830. **Avco Corp.** (Lycoming Div.); Stratford; aircraft engines — 4,615. **United Technologies Corp.;** North Haven; aircraft engines — 4,000. **Yale-New Haven Hospital Inc.;** New Haven; hospital — 3,580.

Hospital of St. Raphael Inc.; New Haven; hospital — 2,300. **Raybestos-Manhattan Inc.** (Friction Materials); Stratford; asbestos products, gaskets — 1,600. **Northeast Bancorp Inc.;** New Haven; banking — 1,400. **U. S. Repeating Arms Co.** (Winchester - HQ); New Haven; sporting arms — 1,000. **Warner-Lambert Co.** (Consumer Products Group); Milford; razors, blades — 1,000. **Dresser Industries Inc.** (Industrial Valve & Instrument Div.); Stratford; environmental controls, valves — 950. **Walter Kidde & Co. Inc.** (Sargent & Co. Div.); New Haven; locks — 900. **The Jackson Newspapers Inc.;** New Haven; newspaper publishing — 890. **Bic Pen Corp.** (HQ); Milford; pens, cutlery — 850. **The Marlin Firearms Co.;** North Haven; firearms — 850. **Chesebrough-Pond's Inc.** (Prince Matchibelli Div.); Clinton; cosmetics — 800. **Blue Cross & Blue Shield of Connecticut** (HQ); North Haven; health insurance — 785. **Eyelet Specialty Co. Inc.** (HQ); Wallingford; cosmetic containers — 700.

American Cyanamid Co.; Wallingford; resin, plastic products — 675. **Automotive Controls Corp.** (HQ); Branford; auto electrical and fuel systems — 625. **The Armstrong Rubber Co.** (HQ); New Haven; tires, tubes — 600. **Dataproducts of New England** (HQ); Wallingford; telephone, telegraph apparatus — 600. **DeFrank & Sons Corp.** (HQ); New Haven; janitorial services — 600. **The Marmon Group Inc.** (Rockbestos Co.); New Haven; insulating wire, cable — 580. **Allegheny Ludlum Steel Corp.**; Wallingford; steel sheet, strip, bars — 570. **Circuit-Wise Inc.**; North Haven; printed circuits — 550. **Emerson Electric Co.** (U. S. Electric Motor Div.); Milford; electric motors — 500. **First Bancorp Inc.** (HQ); New Haven; banking — 500.

4th District

Southwest — Stamford, Bridgeport

Home to some of the wealthiest towns in the nation, the 4th is the best Republican territory in Connecticut. In 1980 Ronald Reagan won his biggest majority here, where towns such as Darien and Westport are symbols of upper-class New York City suburbia. Many of the voters are daily commuters to and from Wall Street and midtown Manhattan. Fairfield County is blanketed by newspapers and broadcasts that report the news of New York, not Connecticut. But the brand of Republicanism that usually holds sway in the area is liberal.

The suburbs here retained their high-income status in the 1970s, but they grew very little — in part because of restrictive zoning laws, and in part because children were growing up and moving away. The old district as a whole lost 5.4 percent of its population during the 1970s.

Despite the area's reputation as an enclave of white-collar Republican wealth, there remain several dependably Democratic areas, including Bridgeport, now the largest city in the state. Industrial Bridgeport actually lost 8.8 percent of its population between 1970 and 1980, but it surpassed Hartford in population because the decline in Hartford was far worse. Bridgeport's aging, heavy industries have been particularly sensitive to the economic downturns of the early 1980s.

While Stamford lost 5.8 percent of its residents in the decade, a more important trend may be the city's gradual change of character: what had once been a small-business center has become a haven for corporate headquarters fleeing New York's high tax rates. The largest single employer in the district in 1983 was Pitney Bowes' office equipment headquarters in Stamford. The 1981 redistricting returned the town of New Canaan to the 4th, where it had been until the 1970 remap. Also shifted into the 4th from the 5th District were part of Westport and most of Trumbull, both GOP areas.

Election Returns

4th District		Democrat		Republican	
1976	President	98,250	(42.3%)	139,270	(60.9%)
	Senate	86,530	(37.8%)	139,270	(60.9%)
	House	82,111	(36.0%)	141,581	(62.2%)
1978	Governor	93,725	(58.0%)	67,781	(42.0%)
	House	65,458	(41.2%)	93,268	(58.8%)
1980	President	82,004	(35.4%)	124,209	(53.6%)
	Senate	103,833	(47.0%)	115,432	(52.3%)
	House	82,168	(37.5%)	137,175	(62.5%)

4th District		Democrat		Republican	
1982	Governor	79,179	(47.2%)	87,530	(52.2%)
	Senate	68,439	(40.9%)	91,374	(54.6%)
	House	71,110	(42.9%)	93,660	(56.4%)

Demographics

Population: 518,577. **Percent Change from 1970:** -4.8%.

Land Area: 224 square miles. **Population per Square Mile:** 2,315.1.

Counties, 1980 Population: Fairfield (Pt.) — 518,577.

Cities, 1980 Population: Bridgeport — 142,546; Darien — 18,892; Fairfield — 54,849; Greenwich — 59,578; New Canaan — 17,931; Norwalk — 77,767; Stamford — 102,453; Trumbull (Pt.) — 19,271; Westport — 25,290.

Race and Ancestry: White — 84.3%; Black — 11.2%; American Indian, Eskimo and Aleut — 0.1%; Asian and Pacific Islander — 1.0%. Spanish Origin — 7.7%. English — 6.5%; French — 0.9%; German — 3.3%; Greek — 0.9%; Hungarian — 2.0%; Irish — 6.2%; Italian — 12.2%; Polish — 3.2%; Portuguese — 1.0%; Russian — 1.4%; Scottish — 0.7%; Swedish — 0.6%.

Universities, Enrollment: Bridgeport Engineering Institute, Bridgeport — 765; Fairfield University, Fairfield — 5,062; Housatonic Community College, Bridgeport — 2,600; Norwalk Community College, Norwalk — 2,980; Norwalk State Technical College, Norwalk — 909; Sacred Heart University, Bridgeport — 4,081; University of Bridgeport, Bridgeport — 6,805.

Newspapers, Circulation: *The Advocate* (e), Stamford — 30,144; *The Bridgeport Post* (eS), Bridgeport — 73,572; *The Greenwich Time* (e), Greenwich — 15,660; *The Hour* (e), Norwalk — 21,378; *The Telegram* (m), Bridgeport — 17,518. *New York Daily News* and *The New York Times* also circulate in the district.

Commercial Television Stations, Affiliation: Entire district is located in New York (N.Y.) ADI.

Industries:

Pitney Bowes Inc. (HQ); Stamford; mailing machinery — 5,800. **Bridgeport Hospital Inc.**; Bridgeport; hospital — 2,510. **General Electric Co. Inc.** (Housewares Div.); Bridgeport; electric appliance wholesaling — 2,450. **GTE Communications Network Systems**; Stamford; software, communications services — 2,000. **United Technologies Corp.** (Sikorsky Aircraft Div.); Bridgeport; helicopters — 1,940.

Bunker Ramo Corp. (Information Systems Div.); Trumbull; data processing equipment — 1,800. **Norwalk Hospital Assn.**; Norwalk; hospital — 1,700. **St. Vincent's Medical Center**; Bridgeport; hospital — 1,610. **American Can Co.** (HQ); Greenwich; metal, fiber cans — 1,500. **Clairol Inc.**; Stamford; hair preparations — 1,500. **White Consolidated Industries** (Bullard Div.); Bridgeport; machine tools — 1,350. **Continental Group Inc.** (HQ); Stamford; metal cans — 1,200. **GTE Service Corp.** (HQ); Stamford; business services — 1,200. **Remington Arms Co. Inc.** (HQ); Bridgeport; small arms, ammunition — 1,200. **Olin Corp.** (HQ); Stamford; chemicals, copper sheet, small arms, paper — 1,100. **The Stamford Hospital**; Stamford; hospital — 1,100.

Arnold Bakers Inc.; Greenwich; bakery products — 1,000. **Burndy Corp.** (HQ); Norwalk; electrical connectors — 1,000. **Carpenter Technology Corp.**; Bridgeport; electrometallurgical products — 1,000. **Connecticut National Bank Inc.** (HQ); Bridgeport; banking — 1,000. **Electrolux Corp.**; Old Greenwich; vacuum cleaners — 1,000. **General Electric Credit Corp.** (HQ); Stamford; credit operations — 1,000. **Norden Systems Inc.** (HQ); Norwalk; radar equipment — 1,000. **The Perkin-Elmer Corp.** (HQ); Norwalk; optical, scientific instruments — 1,000. **Textron Inc.** (Bridgeport Machines Div.); Bridgeport; milling machines — 1,000. **Stauffer Chemical Co.** (HQ); Westport; industrial chemicals — 850. **Harvey Hubbell Inc.**; Bridgeport; wiring devices — 800. **Machlett Laboratories Inc.** (HQ); Stamford; X-ray apparatus, electron tubes — 750.

Utica Tool Co. Inc.; Stamford; hand tools — 750. **Champion International Corp.** (HQ); Stamford; paper, plywood — 700. **Coldwater

Seafood Corp.; Rowayton; seafood processing — 700. **Westinghouse Electric Corp.** (Bryant Electric Co.); Bridgeport; steel sheet, strip, bars — 700. **American Cyanamid Co.** (Stamford Research Laboratory); Stamford; research — 690. **Jenkins Bros.**; Bridgeport; valves, pipe fittings — 680. **Dorr-Oliver Inc.** (HQ); Stamford; heavy industrial equipment — 650. **The Nash Engineering Co.** (HQ); Norwalk; pumps — 650. **Remington Products Inc.**; Bridgeport; electric housewares, cosmetics — 650. **Shamrock Maintenance Corp.**; Stamford; janitorial services — 620. **Condec Corp.** (HQ); Old Greenwich; valves, tire production machinery, semiconductors — 600. **General Electric Co.** (HQ); Fairfield; electric, electricity-related products — 600.

Pepperidge Farm Inc. (HQ); Norwalk; bread, rolls — 600. **Swank Inc.** (Crestline Div.); Norwalk; leather goods — 600. **Warnaco Inc.** (HQ); Bridgeport; men's, women's wear — 600. **Post Publishing Co. Inc.**; Bridgeport; newspaper publishing — 575. **Xerox Corp.** (HQ); Stamford; copiers, duplicators — 570. **Stewart-Warner Corp.** (Bassick & Co. Div.); Bridgeport; casters — 530. **Acme United Corp.** (HQ); Bridgeport; shears, scissors — 513. **American Hospital Supply Corp.** (Cystoscope Makers Div.); Stamford; medical instruments — 500. **General Electric Co.** (General Electric Supply Co.); Bridgeport; electric housewares — 500. **Glendinning Companies Inc.**; Westport; marketing, promotional services — 500. **Incom International Inc.** (Heim Div.); Fairfield; bearings — 500. **Moore Special Tool Co. Inc.**; Bridgeport; metal-cutting machine tools — 500. **State National Bank of Connecticut** (HQ); Bridgeport; banking — 500.

5th District

West — Waterbury, Danbury

Once a Democratic stronghold, the 5th has been slipping toward the Republican column in recent years. The last Democratic presidential candidate to carry the district was Hubert Humphrey in 1968, and his plurality was narrow. The zeal of the Democratic faithful in red-brick mill towns such as Waterbury — whose fervent election-eve campaign rally for John F. Kennedy in 1960 has become a political legend — has given way to split-ticket voting, with some GOP pockets. In 1980 Ronald Reagan rolled up a 44,000-vote majority here and won all but one community in the district.

Incorporating medium-sized manufacturing cities and bucolic villages, the 5th stretches through the central Connecticut hills from the New York line toward the well-populated New Haven-Hartford corridor. The economic core is the aging manufacturing area of the Naugatuck Valley, where the decline of small factories has made unemployment a chronic problem. But the district also includes several wealthy suburban towns, such as Wilton and Weston, within the orbit of New York City — staunchly Republican constituencies that help account for the recent GOP advances.

Democrats have depended on the 5th's urban areas to provide their winning margins, but the cities' recent growth has been uneven, despite the old district's overall population increase of 7.3 percent between 1970 and 1980. Waterbury, once a shirt-making center, lost 4.4 percent of its population during the 1970s as some of its oldest firms closed their doors or moved away. Danbury, whose hat makers once topped the nation, grew by 19.1 percent, paced by the arrival of corporate headquarters and sophisticated industries.

In the 1981 redistricting, the 5th District gained the town of Brookfield and the remainder of Newtown. Three solidly Republican areas — New Canaan, part of Westport and most of Trumbull — were shifted into the 4th District.

Election Returns

5th District		Democrat		Republican	
1976	President	99,444	(45.4%)	117,767	(53.8%)
	Senate	87,396	(39.2%)	132,851	(59.6%)
	House	75,186	(33.8%)	145,429	(65.4%)
1978	Governor	97,021	(54.2%)	82,026	(45.8%)
	House	89,822	(53.9%)	76,808	(46.1%)
1980	President	80,411	(34.6%)	123,976	(53.4%)
	Senate	112,906	(50.4%)	109,194	(48.8%)
	House	113,251	(51.4%)	107,104	(48.6%)
1982	Governor	92,426	(52.5%)	82,090	(46.7%)
	Senate	77,708	(44.2%)	91,361	(52.0%)
	House	101,362	(58.5%)	70,808	(40.8%)

Demographics

Population: 518,700. **Percent Change from 1970:** 8.2%.

Land Area: 595 square miles. **Population per Square Mile:** 871.8.

Counties, 1980 Population: Fairfield (Pt.) — 224,484; New Haven (Pt.) — 294,216.

Cities, 1980 Population: Ansonia — 19,039; Bethel — 16,004; Brookfield — 12,872; Cheshire — 21,788; Danbury — 60,470; Derby — 12,346; Meriden — 57,118; Monroe — 14,010; Naugatuck — 26,456; Newtown — 19,107; Ridgefield — 20,120; Seymour — 13,434; Shelton — 31,314; Trumbull (Pt.) — 13,718; Waterbury — 103,266; Wilton — 15,351; Wolcott — 13,008.

Race and Ancestry: White — 93.5%; Black — 4.2%; American Indian, Eskimo and Aleut — 0.2%; Asian and Pacific Islander — 0.5%. Spanish Origin — 3.3%. English — 5.7%; French — 2.5%; German — 3.7%; Hungarian — 0.7%; Irish — 6.6%; Italian — 13.3%; Polish — 4.1%; Portuguese — 1.7%; Russian — 1.0%; Scottish — 0.6%; Swedish — 0.6%.

Universities, Enrollment: Mattatuck Community College, Waterbury — 3,564; Post College, Waterbury — 1,136; Waterbury State Technical College, Waterbury — 1,715; Western Connecticut State College, Danbury — 5,656.

Newspapers, Circulation: *Naugatuck Daily News* (e), Naugatuck — 4,713; *The News-Times* (eS), Danbury — 39,500; *Record-Journal* (m), Meriden — 29,225; *Sentinel* (e), Ansonia — 18,519; *Waterbury American* (e), Waterbury — 35,815; *Waterbury Republican* (mS), Waterbury — 36,384. *The Bridgeport Post, New Haven Register, New York Daily News, The New York Times* and Stamford *Advocate* also circulate in the district.

Commercial Television Stations, Affiliation: WATR-TV, Waterbury (NBC). District is divided between Hartford-New Haven ADI and New York (N.Y.) ADI.

Industries:

Timex Corp. (HQ); Middlebury; watches, timing devices — 2,200. **Waterbury Hospital Corp.**; Waterbury; hospital — 2,100. **The Danbury Hospital Inc.**; Danbury; hospital — 1,800. **St. Mary's Hospital Corp.**; Waterbury; hospital — 1,650. **Century Brass Products Inc.** (HQ); Waterbury; metal tubing — 1,560.

The Perkin-Elmer Corp.; Danbury; optical instruments — 1,500. **Uniroyal Inc.** (Chemical Co.); Naugatuck; industrial inorganic chemicals — 1,500. **Emhart Corp.** (Farrel Connecticut Div.); Ansonia; heavy machinery — 1,260. **Fairfield Hills Hospital**; Newtown; state mental hospital — 1,100. **Meriden-Wallingford Hospital**; Meriden; hospital — 1,090. **The Griffin Hospital Inc.**; Derby; hospital — 1,010. **Union Carbide Corp.**; Danbury; administrative offices — 1,000. **General Datacomm Industries**; Danbury; data communications systems — 980. **Uniroyal Inc.** (HQ); Middlebury; tires, inner tubes — 980. **American Cyanamid Co.** (Davis-Geck Div.); Danbury; surgical supplies — 950. **Grolier Inc.** (HQ); Danbury; book publishing — 908

Bristol Babcock Inc. (HQ); Waterbury; industrial measuring controls — 881. **Colonial Bank** (HQ); Waterbury; banking — 875. **Textron Inc.** (Waterbury Farrel Div.); Cheshire; machine tools — 850. **The Barden Corp.** (HQ); Danbury; precision ball bearing mechanisms — 800. **Bunker Ramo Corp.** (RF Operations); Danbury; electronic components — 750. **Philips Medical Systems Inc.** (HQ); Shelton; X-ray equipment — 735. **Arco Metals American Brass** (Valley Mills Div.); Ansonia; brass mill products — 700. **National Semiconductors Corp.**; Danbury; semiconductors — 700. **North American Philips Corp.** (Airpax Div. - HQ); Cheshire; motors — 700. **Consolidated Controls Corp.** (HQ); Bethel; nuclear, aircraft control equipment — 600. **International Telephone & Telegraph Corp.** (Telecommunications Technology Center); Shelton; management services — 600.

Sperry Corp. (Gyroscope Div.); Waterbury; electronic products — 600. **Canberra Industries Inc.** (HQ); Meriden; nuclear control devices — 550. **The Napier Co.** (HQ); Meriden; jewelry — 525. **Automation Industries Inc.**; Danbury; automatic environmental controls — 520. **Anaconda Metal Hose**; Waterbury; industrial machinery — 500. **Buell Industries Inc.** (Anchor Fasteners Div. - HQ); Waterbury; metal fasteners — 500. **Burroughs Corp.** (Imaging Systems Div.); Danbury; communications equipment — 500. **Carabetta Enterprises Inc.**; Meriden; general building contracting — 500. **Harvey Hubbell Inc.**; Seymour; cordage, twine — 500. **International Silver Co.**; Meriden; stainless steel — 500. **Peter Paul Cadbury Inc.** (HQ); Naugatuck; candy — 500. **Pitney-Bowes Inc.** (Copier Div.); Danbury; copying equipment — 500. **Richardson-Vicks Inc.** (HQ); Wilton; pharmaceuticals, cosmetics, paints — 500.

6th District

Northwest — Bristol, Torrington

The 6th is diverse both geographically and politically. Any constituency that is home to both Ralph Nader and William F. Buckley Jr. is a challenging place in which to fashion a winning coalition. Extending from quiet villages in the pastoral Litchfield Hills to the Hartford-Springfield metropolitan area, the 6th is closely contested territory in most elections.

The "Nutmeggers" of rural Litchfield County, reflecting generations of small-town Yankee control, provide dependable Republican majorities. That pattern is offset by mill towns such as Torrington and Winsted, which usually deliver Democratic margins. To the east, the industrial cities of Bristol and New Britain are bedrock Democratic territory. New Britain lost 11.5 percent of its population between 1970 and 1980, while Bristol grew by 3.4 percent during the same period.

Extending through some upper-crust Hartford suburbs that vote Republican, the northern arm of the 6th reaches toward the industrial axis along the Connecticut River. The Democrats roll up their vote totals among the blue-collar, heavily Italian-American population of Windsor Locks and Enfield.

The district's largest employer, United Technologies' Hamilton-Standard aerospace division in Windsor Locks, provides 7,500 jobs. The headquarters of the Stanley Works hardware company has 4,000 employees in New Britain, while Textron's ball-bearing plant there employs 3,800 more.

The new map united the town of Somers, with a population that has grown 22.9 percent since the 1970 census, within the 6th District. East Windsor was shifted to the 1st District, and Brookfield and part of Newtown went to the 5th.

Election Returns

6th District		Democrat		Republican	
1976	President	111,077	(47.8%)	120,338	(51.7%)
	Senate	95,141	(41.2%)	134,089	(58.0%)
	House	129,923	(56.8%)	97,838	(42.8%)
1978	Governor	108,647	(59.9%)	72,695	(40.1%)
	House	115,074	(65.9%)	59,455	(34.1%)
1980	President	92,955	(38.5%)	113,203	(46.9%)
	Senate	134,398	(57.5%)	97,501	(41.7%)
	House	136,984	(59.2%)	93,293	(40.3%)
1982	Governor	105,217	(54.1%)	87,930	(45.2%)
	Senate	94,856	(48.7%)	93,693	(48.1%)
	House	92,178	(47.7%)	99,703	(51.7%)

Demographics

Population: 517,146. **Percent Change from 1970:** 6.4%.

Land Area: 1,426 square miles. **Population per Square Mile:** 362.7.

Counties, 1980 Population: Fairfield (Pt.) — 13,541; Hartford (Pt.) — 324,207; Litchfield — 156,769; New Haven (Pt.) — 14,156; Tolland (Pt.) — 8,473.

Cities, 1980 Population: Avon — 11,201; Bristol — 57,370; Enfield — 42,695; Farmington — 16,407; New Britain — 73,840; New Fairfield — 11,260; New Milford — 19,420; Plainville (Pt.) — 16,401; Plymouth — 10,732; Simsbury — 21,161; Southbury — 14,156; Southington — 36,879; Torrington — 30,987; Watertown — 19,489; Winchester — 10,841; Windsor Locks — 12,190.

Race and Ancestry: White — 96.9%; Black — 1.7%; American Indian, Eskimo and Aleut — 0.1%; Asian and Pacific Islander — 0.4%. Spanish Origin — 2.0%. English — 7.1%; French — 5.4%; German — 3.9%; Irish — 5.1%; Italian — 9.2%; Polish — 7.2%; Russian — 0.7%; Scottish — 0.6%; Swedish — 1.0%.

Universities, Enrollment: Asnuntuck Community College, Enfield — 1,739; Briarwood College, Southington — 496; Central Connecticut State College, New Britain — 12,250; Northwestern Connecticut Community College, Winsted — 2,468; St. Alphonsus College, Suffield — 68; Tunxis Community College, Farmington — 2,580.

Newspapers, Circulation: *The Bristol Press* (e), Bristol — 22,857; *The Herald* (e), New Britain — 40,025; *The Register* (e), Torrington — 12,351; *Winsted Evening Citizen* (e), Winsted — 5,029. *The Hartford Courant* also circulates in the district.

Commercial Television Stations, Affiliation: WVIT, New Britain (NBC). Most of district is located in Hartford-New Haven ADI. Small portion is in New York (N.Y.) ADI.

Military Installations: Bradley International Airport (Air Force), Windsor Locks — 722.

Industries:

United Technologies Corp. (Hamilton Standard Div.); Windsor Locks; aircraft engines, parts — 7,500. **The Stanley Works** (HQ); New Britain; hand tools — 4,000. **Textron Inc.** (Fafnir Bearing Div.); New Britain; ball bearings — 3,800. **United Technologies Corp.** (Pratt & Whitney Aircraft Div.); Southington; aircraft engine parts — 2,950. **Springfield Sugar & Products Co.** (New England Grocers Supply Co. Div.); Suffield; grocery wholesaling — 2,800.

General Electric Co. (Distribution Equipment Div.); Plainville; switchgear apparatus — 2,000. **General Motors Corp.** (New Departure-Hyatt Bearing Div.); Bristol; ball bearings — 1,900. **New Britain General Hospital**; New Britain; hospital — 1,600. **Sweet Life Foods Inc.** (HQ); Suffield; grocery wholesaling — 1,200. **Kimberly-Clark Corp.**; New Milford; paddings — 1,050. **Allstate Insurance Co. Inc.**; Farmington; health insurance — 1,000. **Litton Industrial Products Inc.**; New Britain; metal-cutting machine tools — 1,000. **Hi-G Co. Inc.**; Windsor Locks; switchgear apparatus — 900. **The Superior Electric Co.** (HQ); Bristol; transformers, motors, industrial controls — 900.

Torin Corp. (HQ); Torrington; fan blades — 900. **Choice Vend Inc.** (General Products Div.); Windsor Locks; vending machines — 760. **Connecticut Indemnity Co.** (Security Insurance Group - HQ); Farmington; casualty insurance — 750.

First National Stores Inc.; Windsor Locks; grocery warehousing — 750. **The Robert E. Morris Co.;** East Granby; machinery warehousing — 712. **C. E. Maguire Inc.;** New Britain; engineering services — 700. **T R W Inc.** (Bearings Div.); Plainville; ball bearings — 700. **Becton Dickinson & Co.;** Canaan; medical instruments — 600. **Litton Systems Inc.** (Winchester Electronics Div.); Oakville; electrical machinery, supplies — 600. **O Z-Gedney Co.** (HQ); Terryville; electric conduit fittings, iron castings — 600. **Connecticut Spring & Stamping;** Farmington; metal stampings — 575. **The Dexter Corp.** (HQ); Windsor Locks; filters, fabrics — 500. **Dynamics Corp. of America** (Waring Products Div.); New Hartford; metal stampings — 500. **Hallmark Cards Inc.;** Enfield; greeting card distributing operations — 500. **Tilcon Tomasso Inc.;** New Britain; paving contracting — 500. **U O P Inc.** (Aerospace Div.); Bantam; aircraft interiors — 500. **Wheeler Group Inc.** (Grayarc - HQ); New Hartford; office supplies wholesaling — 500.

Delaware

Delaware is divided by the Chesapeake and Delaware Canal. North of the canal, at the top of the Delmarva (Delaware-Maryland-Virginia) Peninsula, is Wilmington (New Castle County), the state's only real metropolitan area. Wilmington is dominated economically by E. I. du Pont de Nemours & Co., far and away its leading source of jobs.

Forty years ago, almost half of the state's people resided in Wilmington, but the city itself is down to a population of 70,195, less than 12 percent of the state's total population. Over half of Wilmington's population is black, but there are Italian, Irish and Polish neighborhoods as well. A Democratic candidate who hopes to win statewide must carry Wilmington by at least 10,000 votes. This means doing well among all segments of the city's electorate.

While the city has been shrinking, the suburban areas around Wilmington have been growing steadily, so about two-thirds of Delaware's vote is still cast within New Castle County. The Republican voting habits of suburban New Castle are frequently strong enough to overcome the solid Democratic margins turned in by Wilmington. In the 1980 presidential race, they were just strong enough — Ronald Reagan took the county over Jimmy Carter by one vote out of nearly 170,000 cast.

Below the Chesapeake and Delaware Canal, one notices a change in values, language and attitude similar to those of the border South. Kent and Sussex counties are mostly rural.

Dover, the state capital, has some light industry, but the largest industries in the two southern counties are poultry and tourism. Sussex is one of the largest poultry-producing counties in the United States. It also contains Rehoboth Beach, which attracts thousands of sunbathers every summer and whose year-round residents are firmly Republican.

If rural Kent and Sussex have similar cultures, they have slightly different voting habits. Sussex prefers conservative Republicans — it was the only one of the three counties to vote for the GOP House candidate in 1982. Kent, in pure partisan terms, is the most Democratic part of Delaware. But these Democrats are conservative — they joined Sussex voters in giving Reagan a comfortable majority in 1980. On the county level, Kent has the best Democratic organization in the state.

Age of Population

District	Population Under 18	Voting Age Population	Population 65 & Over (% of VAP)	Median Age
AL	166,595	427,743	59,179 (13.8%)	29.8

Income and Occupation

District	Median Family Income	White Collar Workers	Blue Collar Workers	Service Workers	Farm Workers
AL	$ 20,817	55.3%	29.1%	13.3%	2.3%

Education: School Years Completed

District	8 Years or Fewer	4 Years of High School	4 Years of College or More	Median School Years
AL	14.8%	36.2%	17.5%	12.5

Housing and Residential Patterns

District	Owner Occupied	Renter Occupied	Urban	Rural
AL	69.1%	30.9%	70.6%	29.4%

Election Returns

At-large		Democrat		Republican	
1976	President	122,596	(52.0%)	109,831	(46.6%)
	Governor	97,480	(42.5%)	130,531	(56.9%)
	Senate	98,055	(43.6%)	125,502	(55.8%)
	House	102,431	(47.7%)	110,677	(51.5%)
1978	Senate	93,930	(58.0%)	66,479	(41.0%)
	House	64,863	(41.2%)	91,689	(58.2%)
1980	President	105,754	(44.8%)	111,252	(47.2%)
	Governor	64,217	(28.5%)	159,004	(70.6%)
	House	81,227	(37.5%)	133,842	(61.8%)
1982	Senate	84,413	(44.2%)	105,357	(55.2%)
	House	98,533	(52.4%)	87,153	(46.3%)

DELAWARE

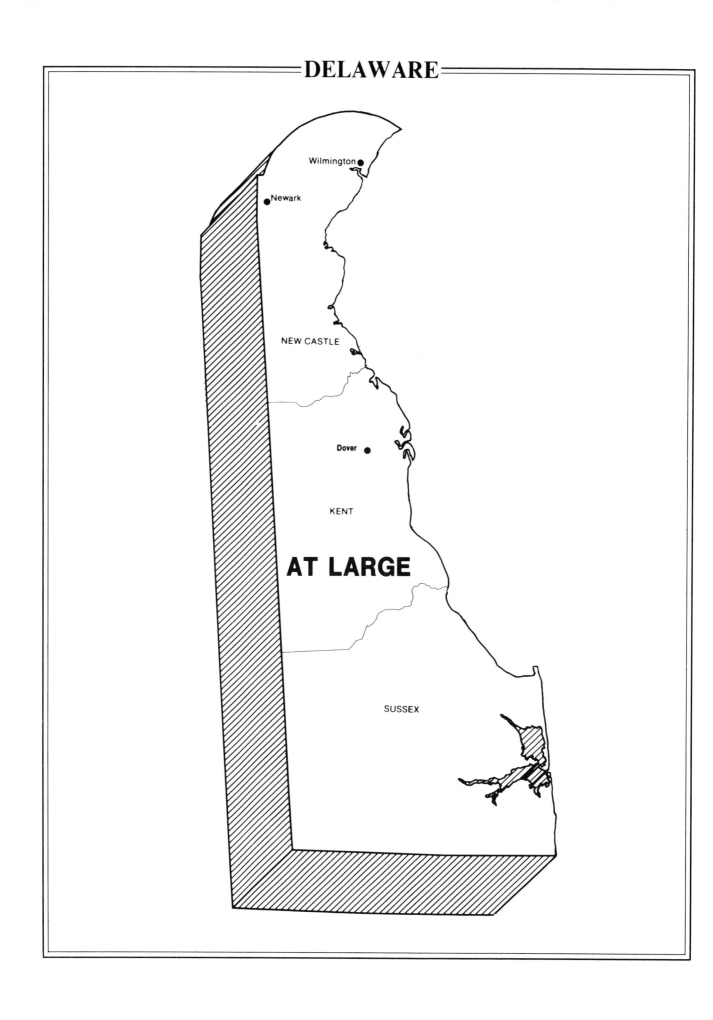

Wilmington

Newark

NEW CASTLE

Dover

KENT

AT LARGE

SUSSEX

Demographics

Population: 594,338. **Percent Change from 1970:** 8.4%.

Land Area: 1,933 square miles. **Population per Square Mile:** 307.5.

Counties, 1980 Population: Kent — 98,219; New Castle — 398,115; Sussex — 98,004.

Cities, 1980 Population: Dover — 23,512; Newark — 25,247; Wilmington — 70,195.

Race and Ancestry: White — 82.1%; Black — 16.1%; American Indian, Eskimo and Aleut — 0.2%; Asian and Pacific Islander — 0.8%. Spanish Origin — 1.6%. Dutch — 0.5%; English — 13.0%; French — 0.6%; German — 5.7%; Irish — 6.1%; Italian — 3.8%; Polish — 2.4%; Scottish — 0.5%.

Universities, Enrollment: Brandywine College, Wilmington — 862; Delaware Law School of Widener University, Wilmington — 764; Delaware State College, Dover — 2,083; Delaware Technical and Community College (Southern campus), Georgetown — 1,473; Delaware Technical and Community College (Terry campus), Dover — 1,194; Delaware Technical and Community College (Wilmington/Stanton campus), Wilmington — 3,838; Goldey Beacom College, Wilmington — 1,662; University of Delaware, Newark — 19,258; Wesley College, Dover — 1,316; Wilmington College, New Castle — 799.

Newspapers, Circulation: *Delaware State News* (eS), Dover — 25,696; *Evening Journal* (e), Wilmington — 80,062; *The Morning News* (m), Wilmington — 51,285. *The Philadelphia Inquirer* also circulates in the district.

Commercial Television Stations, Affiliation: Most of district is located in Philadelphia (Pa.) ADI. Small portion is in Salisbury (Md.) ADI.

Military Installations: Dover Air Force Base, Dover — 6,718; Greater Wilmington Airport (Air Force), Newport — 918.

Nuclear Power Plants: Hope Creek 1, Salem 1 and Salem 2. *See New Jersey Congressional District 2.*

Industries:

E. I. du Pont de Nemours & Co. (HQ); Wilmington; petroleum refining, synthetic fibers, plastics, pesticides, chemicals — 12,000. **General Motors Corp.** (GM Assembly Div.); Wilmington; automobiles — 4,300. **Chrysler Corp.;** Newark; auto assembly — 4,100. **E. I. du Pont de Nemours & Co.;** Seaford; nylon fibers — 3,000. **E. I. du Pont de Nemours & Co.** (Instrument Products Div.); Bear; scientific instruments — 2,000. **International Playtex Inc.;** Dover; latex, sanitary paper products — 2,000. **Rapid-American Corp.** (BVD Knitwear Div.); Dover; women's underwear — 2,000. **Wilmington Medical Center Inc.;** Wilmington; hospital — 2,000.

ICI Americas Inc. (HQ); Wilmington; chemicals — 1,900. **General Foods Corp.;** Dover; food processing, packaging — 1,500. **Hercules Inc.** (HQ); Wilmington; plastics, chemicals, explosives — 1,400. **XTRA Corp.;** Wilmington; truck manufacturing, rental — 1,300. **A B & F - Hosco Corp.;** Newark; janitorial services — 1,000. **NVF Co.** (HQ); Yorklyn; steel — 1,000. **St. Francis Hospital Inc.;** Wilmington; hospital — 1,000. **Getty Refining & Marketing Inc.;** Delaware City; petroleum refining — 800. **Anjou International Co.;** Wilmington; general industrial machinery — 730.

Atlantic Aviation Corp. (HQ); Wilmington; aircraft, auto leasing — 700. **ICI Americas Inc.** (Atlas Point Plant Site); New Castle; chemicals — 700. **Country Pride Foods Ltd.;** Milford; poultry processing — 600. **Gannett Co. Inc.;** Wilmington; newspaper publishing — 600. **Townsends Inc.** (HQ); Millsboro; soybean growers, wholesaling — 600. **Allied Chemical Corp.;** Claymont; industrial chemicals — 500. **Champlain Cable Corp.;** Wilmington; plastic products — 500. **Mountaire of Delmarva Inc.** (HQ); Selbyville; poultry processing — 500. **Sun Transport Inc.;** Wilmington; oil shipping — 500.

Florida

Florida's Legislature was charged with dispensing the spoils of phenomenal population growth — four new congressional districts. Population in Florida swelled by nearly three million during the 1970s, making the state paramount in House seats gained after the 1980 census.

But the legislators found more pain than pleasure in the remap process. Sporadic squabbling between the House and Senate persisted for months. Pressure from the congressional delegation, Democratic Gov. Robert Graham and federal judges finally induced completion of map drawing in a special session May 21, 1982.

Behind the delay was a continuing feud between the nominal leader of the Senate, moderate Democrat W. D. Childers, and a conservative coalition of Republicans and some Democrats that held the real power in the chamber. The struggle stalled proceedings, and the Legislature adjourned its regular session March 25, 1982, without producing bills on either legislative reapportionment or congressional redistricting.

On April 7, at the close of a special session establishing state legislative districts, there was an attempt to approve a map for U.S. House seats. But Senate and House proposals differed widely, and no consensus was reached.

The Senate plan would have split Orlando (Orange County) three ways to create an open north-central district friendly to Senate Majority Leader Pete Skinner, a Democrat who had his sights set on a place in Congress. The House refused to cannibalize Orlando. Gov. Graham concurred and said he would veto the Senate remap if it reached him.

Impatient to see a map approved before officially commencing his bid for Congress, Republican state Rep. Curtis Kiser of St. Petersburg filed suit in March asking federal judges to do the job. The Legislature's April 7 failure to reach a compromise prompted Kiser to offer the court a redistricting plan of his own design.

The court scheduled an initial hearing on Kiser's case for May 10, encouraging redoubled efforts to reach a legislative compromise. When Gov. Graham was persuaded that lawmakers could settle on a map, he called another special session.

The final plan produced by the Legislature closely resembled what the House had wanted all along: Orange County was divided into just two districts, the north Florida districts retained their old shapes and the newly added north-central district was a reasonably compact territory anchored in Gainesville.

The remap bill, which Graham signed May 23, left both parties more or less satisfied. None of the incumbents was seriously hurt by the redistricting although one had to shift his residence to remain with most of his constituents. Of the four newly created districts, the south Florida 16th is solidly Democratic, but elections in the 6th, 9th and 12th were expected to be competitive. In 1982 the Democratic candidate won the 6th with more than 60 percent of the vote. Republicans won the 9th with 51 percent and the 12th with 53 percent.

The 1982 elections gave the Republicans six seats in the Florida House delegation. Although the GOP gained no ground against the Democrats who also increased their numbers by two, it held the advances first made by the party in 1954 when Florida elected its first Republican to the House since 1875.

The massive influx of Republican retirees and upwardly mobile job-seekers has created regular two-party competition. Nonetheless, one constant remains: Democrats lose only when they become mired in internecine bickering.

Age of Population

District	Population Under 18	Voting Age Population	Population 65 & Over (% of VAP)	Median Age
1	150,330	362,491	43,293 (11.9%)	28.5
2	149,680	363,447	54,766 (15.1%)	28.6
3	150,420	362,272	49,479 (13.7%)	28.6
4	126,705	385,967	86,302 (22.4%)	34.6
5	139,018	373,987	61,889 (16.5%)	30.9
6	118,816	394,134	94,663 (24.0%)	34.3
7	136,427	376,478	62,422 (16.6%)	30.7
8	99,056	413,853	141,405 (34.2%)	45.2
9	108,830	404,361	123,085 (30.4%)	42.3
10	131,262	381,628	92,163 (24.1%)	34.5
11	132,680	380,011	59,741 (15.7%)	32.2
12	128,900	384,221	97,027 (25.3%)	35.8
13	99,571	413,477	136,938 (33.1%)	46.8
14	105,930	406,873	124,990 (30.7%)	41.6
15	101,368	411,582	116,583 (28.3%)	39.4
16	116,956	396,409	91,954 (23.2%)	37.0
17	127,849	385,199	80,913 (21.0%)	34.5
18	96,281	416,969	124,773 (29.9%)	44.3
19	139,557	373,329	45,187 (12.1%)	30.3
State	2,359,636	7,386,688	1,687,573 (22.8%)	34.7

FLORIDA

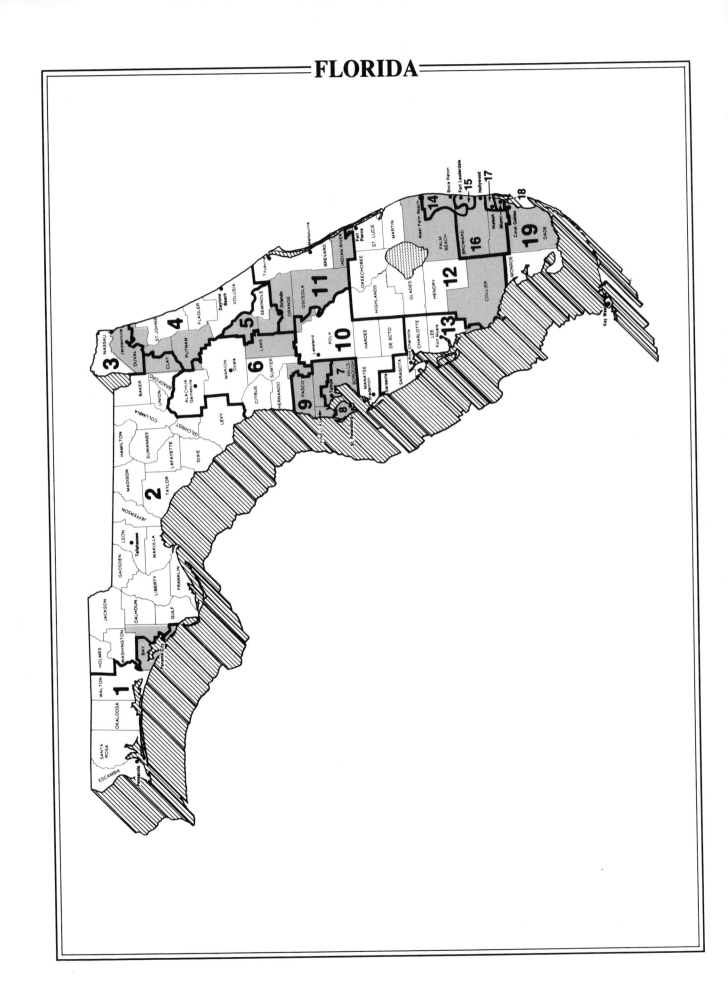

Income and Occupation

District	Median Family Income	White Collar Workers	Blue Collar Workers	Service Workers	Farm Workers
1	$ 16,256	53.2%	29.6%	15.3%	1.9%
2	14,802	52.2	27.4	14.7	5.7
3	16,918	54.1	30.4	14.2	1.3
4	16,783	56.8	24.8	15.2	3.2
5	18,228	56.2	25.2	14.6	4.0
6	14,157	52.8	26.7	14.8	5.7
7	17,346	56.0	28.9	13.2	2.0
8	16,206	56.7	25.7	15.9	1.7
9	16,309	55.2	28.4	13.6	2.8
10	16,170	46.8	32.2	14.0	7.1
11	18,650	56.8	26.2	14.4	2.5
12	17,114	48.7	28.1	14.5	8.7
13	17,299	55.3	26.3	15.2	3.2
14	20,071	58.8	24.5	14.4	2.3
15	18,622	55.4	26.0	16.7	1.9
16	20,947	60.9	25.3	12.5	1.3
17	17,740	53.6	30.3	14.9	1.2
18	14,703	50.9	31.5	16.5	1.2
19	22,368	65.1	18.9	12.9	3.0
State	$ 17,280	55.2%	27.1%	14.6%	3.1%

Education: School Years Completed

District	8 Years or Fewer	4 Years of High School	4 Years of College or More	Median School Years
1	16.1%	37.3%	14.4%	12.5
2	24.6	31.9	14.3	12.3
3	17.8	36.0	11.6	12.4
4	15.0	36.2	15.2	12.5
5	14.8	35.1	17.0	12.6
6	19.5	33.7	14.1	12.4
7	17.5	34.8	14.2	12.4
8	16.2	35.8	14.0	12.5
9	16.6	36.8	12.9	12.4
10	20.6	35.4	11.5	12.3
11	12.2	38.2	15.8	12.6
12	19.3	34.3	13.8	12.4
13	13.6	37.2	15.9	12.6
14	12.5	37.9	16.9	12.6
15	14.1	36.2	15.8	12.6
16	16.4	36.6	15.0	12.5
17	22.1	33.5	12.6	12.4
18	33.2	27.5	13.3	12.1
19	12.5	31.0	24.7	12.9
State	17.6%	35.0%	14.9%	12.5

Housing and Residential Patterns

District	Owner Occupied	Renter Occupied	Urban	Rural
1	68.5%	31.5%	78.8%	21.2%
2	71.0	29.0	39.9	60.1
3	63.4	36.6	94.0	6.0
4	71.3	28.7	73.1	26.9
5	66.1	33.9	88.9	11.1
6	73.0	27.0	46.0	54.0
7	64.9	35.1	94.0	6.0
8	71.3	28.7	100.0	0.0
9	77.8	22.2	80.1	19.9
10	72.1	27.9	72.3	27.7
11	69.2	30.8	87.5	12.5
12	69.7	30.3	71.7	28.3
13	76.7	23.3	86.2	13.8
14	78.0	22.0	96.8	3.2
15	66.8	33.2	100.0	0.0
16	74.2	25.8	98.3	1.7
17	61.7	38.3	100.0	0.0
18	35.3	64.7	100.0	0.0
19	66.7	33.3	93.6	6.4
State	68.3%	31.7%	84.3%	15.7%

1st District

Northwest — Pensacola, Panama City

The 1st is packed with military bases, among them Pensacola's Naval Air Station, Tyndall Air Force Base in Panama City and Eglin Air Force Base, which spans three counties. Their political influence is significant: The bases provide jobs for civilians, and many of the enlisted personnel remain in the area after they leave the service.

The 1st has found little to love in the recent policies of the national Democratic Party. Escambia County (Pensacola) has voted Republican in the last three presidential elections; Bay County (Panama City) gave Jimmy Carter a slight edge in 1976, but swung decisively back to the GOP in 1980.

But the district has remained faithful to the Democrats in other races. It has never given its three-term Democratic House member less than 59 percent of the vote, and in 1980 it supported the losing Democratic Senate candidate, giving him 50 percent of the vote.

In Pensacola, the district's largest city, the military's contribution to the economy is complemented by manufacturing of textiles and paper. Though Pensacola has a large natural harbor, its potential as a trading port is restricted because Mobile and New Orleans have a lock on much of the trade in the Gulf of Mexico.

The roughly 100-mile stretch of beach from Pensacola to Panama City, dubbed the "Miracle Strip" by civic boosters, also has been called the "Redneck Riviera" because it attracts a large number of visitors from nearby Georgia, Alabama and other Southeastern states.

Along that coastal strip, military retirees have settled in Fort Walton Beach and Destin (Okaloosa County), which are just a few miles from Eglin Air Force Base. Okaloosa County gave Ronald Reagan 70 percent in 1980.

Tourism, Panama City's leading industry, is at its peak from April through early September. As south Florida has become more crowded and expensive, however, the popularity of Panama City in the winter has increased. Canadians and New Englanders consider Panhandle winters tame, and they find the off-season rates attractive and the beach nearly deserted.

Inland, the sparsely settled rural areas of the 1st are occupied mostly by soybeans, corn, tomatoes, cantaloupes, cattle and pine trees.

Redistricting had little political impact. About 42,000 people living on farms and in small towns at the eastern end of the 1st were moved to the 2nd. Involved in the shift were western Holmes County, Washington and Gulf counties and the northern part of Bay County.

Election Returns

1st District		Democrat		Republican	
1976	President	79,481	(47.6%)	85,395	(51.1%)
	Senate	100,352	(64.8%)	54,536	(35.2%)
	House	x[1]		—[1]	
1978	Governor	63,849	(52.1%)	58,760	(47.9%)
	House	74,447	(61.0%)	47,606	(39.0%)
1980	President	67,301	(35.0%)	117,902	(61.4%)
	Senate	90,640	(50.3%)	89,583	(49.7%)
	House	106,149	(59.9%)	71,087	(40.1%)
1982	Governor	77,370	(70.1%)	32,942	(29.9%)
	Senate	67,225	(62.5%)	40,268	(37.5%)
	House	82,569	(74.4%)	28,373	(25.5%)

[1] *No votes tabulated where candidate was unopposed, x indicates winner.*

Demographics

Population: 512,821. **Percent Change from 1970:** 22.6%.

Land Area: 4,143 square miles. **Population per Square Mile:** 123.8.

Counties, 1980 Population: Bay (Pt.) — 91,819; Escambia — 233,794; Okaloosa — 109,920; Santa Rosa — 55,988; Walton — 21,300.

Cities, 1980 Population: Fort Walton Beach — 20,829; Panama City — 33,346; Pensacola — 57,619.

Race and Ancestry: White — 83.5%; Black — 14.0%; American Indian, Eskimo and Aleut — 0.6%; Asian and Pacific Islander — 1.4%. Spanish Origin — 1.7%. English — 15.4%; French — 1.0%; German — 4.7%; Irish — 5.3%; Italian — 1.0%; Polish — 0.5%; Scottish — 0.8%.

Universities, Enrollment: Gulf Coast Community College, Panama City — 4,017; Okaloosa-Walton Junior College, Niceville — 3,687; Pensacola Junior College, Pensacola — 8,200; University of West Florida, Pensacola — 5,485.

Newspapers, Circulation: *News-Herald* (mS), Panama City — 25,850; *Pensacola Journal* (mS), Pensacola — 56,944; *Pensacola News* (e), Pensacola — 13,113; *Playground Daily News* (mS), Fort Walton Beach — 20,905.

Commercial Television Stations, Affiliation: WEAR-TV, Pensacola (ABC); WJHG-TV, Panama City (ABC); WMBB, Panama City (NBC). District is divided between Panama City ADI and Mobile (Ala.)-Pensacola ADI.

Military Installations: Corry Station Naval Technical Training Center, Pensacola — 2,931; Eglin Air Force Base, Valpariso — 12,993; Eglin Auxiliary Air Field 3, Crestview — 1,369; Eglin 09/Hurlburt Auxiliary Air Field, Valpariso — 3,903; Ellyson Naval Education and Training Program Development Center, Pensacola — 763; Naval Coastal Systems Center, Panama City — 1,460; Pensacola Naval Air Station, Pensacola — 10,733; Pensacola Naval Medical Center, Pensacola — 955; Pensacola Naval Public Works Center, Pensacola — 799; Tyndall Air Force Base, Panama City — 5,566; Whiting Field Naval Air Station, Milton — 2,767.

Industries:
Monsanto Co. (Monsanto Textiles Co.); Pensacola; synthetic textiles — 4,600. **B. E. & K. Inc.;** Cantonment; general contracting — 1,650. **Baptist Regional Health Service;** Pensacola; hospital — 1,590. **St. Regis Paper Co.;** Cantonment; paper mill — 1,420. **Automation Industries Inc.** (Vitro Services Div.); Fort Walton Beach; engineering services, communications equipment — 1,200. **Hospital Corp. of America;** Pensacola; hospital — 1,200. **Sacred Heart Hospital of Pensacola;** Pensacola; hospital — 1,200.
Automation Industries Inc. (Vitro Services Div.); Pensacola; engineering services, communications equipment — 1,000. **American Fidelity Life Insurance Co.;** Pensacola; life insurance — 950. **S. W. F. Gulf Coast Co. Inc.;** Panama City; pressed wood — 800. **Southwest Forest**

Industries; Panama City; pulp, paper mills — 750. **American Cyanamid Co. Inc.** (Santa Rosa Plant); Milton; acrylic fibers — 600. **Armstrong World Industries Inc.;** Pensacola; acoustical tiles — 600. **Showell Farms Inc. of Florida;** DeFuniak Springs; poultry processing — 600. **Westinghouse Electric Corp.;** Pensacola; special industry machinery — 555. **Vanity Fair Mills Inc.;** Milton; women's underwear — 510. **Fairchild Industries Inc.** (Aircraft Service Div.); Crestview; aircraft, aircraft parts — 500. **Florida Drum Co. Inc.;** Pensacola; steel drums — 500.

2nd District

North — Tallahassee

This is the only Florida district where urban interests play a secondary role to rural concerns in politics. Nearly 30 percent of the district's people live in Leon County (Tallahassee), but the rest are scattered among 24 counties, none of which has a town with even 10,000 residents.

Alachua County (Gainesville), and Leon County cast more than half the vote in the old 2nd District. But in trying to draw districts of nearly equal population, map makers found that, at best, they could keep only part of Alachua in the 2nd. County residents objected to having their influence divided between two districts, so Alachua and Gainesville went into the newly created 6th District.

Many parts of the 2nd are unadulterated Dixie, little touched by the changes that have transformed much of the rest of the state. The "Big Bend" Gulf Coast from Gulf County to Levy County is mostly undeveloped, with just a few fishing villages. Pine trees cover seemingly endless acres, sustaining companies that make paper and pulp. Peanuts, soybeans and tobacco are among the important farm products.

With few outside pressures, Democratic loyalties forged a century ago are still strong. In 1980 unsuccessful Democratic Senate candidate Bill Gunter won virtually every county in the 2nd District, taking several by 2-to-1 margins.

Tallahassee, the capital of Florida, is economically dependent on state government and two large universities, Florida State and Florida A & M. These institutions are diversifying forces, but the city's elegant antebellum homes and flower gardens reveal a persistent Southern influence, and many south Floridians still view Tallahassee as a sleepy Southern city. Like the rural counties around it, Leon County votes solidly Democratic.

In addition to removing Alachua County, the remap also pulled the 2nd out of Marion County, south of Alachua. Joining the 2nd on the west were about 42,000 people who were in the old 1st; on the east, about 14,000 Clay County residents were brought in from the old 4th.

Election Returns

2nd District		Democrat		Republican	
1976	President	102,936	(60.2%)	63,809	(37.3%)
	Senate	105,451	(69.6%)	46,130	(30.4%)
	House	x[1]		—[1]	
1978	Governor	71,657	(69.0%)	32,244	(31.0%)
	House	82,860	(84.4%)	15,296	(15.6%)

2nd District		Democrat		Republican	
1980	President	96,530	(52.9%)	79,208	(43.4%)
	Senate	87,036	(64.6%)	47,678	(35.4%)
	House	95,390	(71.0%)	39,042	(29.0%)
1982	Governor	100,500	(76.2%)	31,410	(23.8%)
	Senate	95,508	(72.4%)	36,324	(27.6%)
	House	79,143	(61.7%)	49,101	(38.3%)

[1] *No votes tabulated where candidate was unopposed; x indicates winner.*

Demographics

Population: 513,127. **Percent Change from 1970:** 33.5%.

Land Area: 15,193 square miles. **Population per Square Mile:** 33.8.

Counties, 1980 Population: Baker — 15,289; Bay (Pt.) — 5,921; Bradford — 20,023; Calhoun — 9,294; Clay (Pt.) — 14,363; Columbia — 35,399; Dixie — 7,751; Franklin — 7,661; Gadsden — 41,565; Gilchrist — 5,767; Gulf — 10,658; Hamilton — 8,761; Holmes — 14,723; Jackson — 39,154; Jefferson — 10,703; Lafayette — 4,035; Leon — 148,655; Levy — 19,870; Liberty — 4,260; Madison — 14,894; Suwannee — 22,287; Taylor — 16,532; Union — 10,166; Wakulla — 10,887; Washington — 14,509.

Cities, 1980 Population: Tallahassee — 81,548.

Race and Ancestry: White — 74.8%; Black — 24.2%; American Indian, Eskimo and Aleut — 0.2%; Asian and Pacific Islander — 0.3%. Spanish Origin — 1.3%. English — 17.8%; French — 0.8%; German — 3.2%; Irish — 5.0%; Italian — 0.6%; Scottish — 0.7%.

Universities, Enrollment: Chipola Junior College, Marianna — 1,122; Florida Agricultural and Mechanical University, Tallahassee — 4,947; Florida State University, Tallahassee — 22,119; Lake City Community College, Lake City — 3,043; North Florida Junior College, Madison — 774; Tallahassee Community College, Tallahassee — 3,663.

Newspapers, Circulation: *Jackson County Floridan* (eS), Marianna — 4,813; *Lake City Reporter* (e), Lake City — 6,083; *Tallahassee Democrat* (mS), Tallahassee — 49,280.

Commercial Television Stations, Affiliation: WECA-TV, Tallahassee (ABC). District is divided among Gainesville ADI, Jacksonville ADI, Panama City ADI and Tallahassee ADI.

Industries:

Florida State Hospital; Chattahoochee; state psychiatric hospital — 2,500. **Hooker Chemical Corp.;** White Springs; phosphate mining — 2,000. **Tallahassee Memorial Regional Medical Center;** Tallahassee; hospital — 1,750. **Northeast Florida State Hospital;** MacClenny; state psychiatric hospital — 1,100. **Buckeye Cellulose Corp.;** Perry; pulp mills — 1,020.

St. Joe Paper Co.; Port St. Joe; pulp mill — 1,000. **E. M. Watkins & Co.;** Tallahassee; general contracting — 800. **Aero Corp.;** Lake City; aircraft — 750. **Ivaco Ltd.;** Quincy; paper mills — 720. **Gold Kist Inc.** (Gold Kist Poultry); Live Oak; poultry processing — 600.

3rd District

Northeast — Jacksonville

The 3rd was Florida's slowest growing district during the 1970s. Population increased by less than 4 percent in the old 3rd and by less than 5 percent in the new. This has not caused much alarm in Jacksonville, whose business and political leaders seem to prefer steady if unspectacular economic expansion based on the city's traditional economic foundations — shipping, insurance, banking and defense.

One sign that this strategy is working can be seen at the harbor, where hundreds of thousands of imported automobiles are unloaded and prepared for overland shipment. By touting its fine harbor and ready access to rail lines and roads that lead to dealers in the lucrative Southeastern market, Jacksonville has become the East Coast's leading port of entry for foreign vehicles.

When Japan bowed to U.S. pressure and agreed to curtail shipments of autos to the U.S., Jacksonville was not hurt; the Japanese decided to abandon other smaller ports and consolidate their business where most of it already was, in Jacksonville.

Workers handling cargo and building and repairing ships form a large segment of Jacksonville's blue-collar community. Prudential, Independent Insurance Group and Gulf Life are among the prominent white-collar employers in the city, which has headquarters or regional offices for two dozen insurance companies. Four of Florida's top 25 financial institutions are based in Jacksonville; only Miami has a larger share. The city's three naval air stations contribute more than $500 million annually to the local economy.

When Jacksonville was developing into a major Atlantic port and land transportation hub earlier this century, its jobs lured farm boys from south Georgia, South Carolina and the Florida Panhandle. People of Deep South origin are still dominant in the work force, giving Jacksonville an ambience quite different from that of Florida cities that have witnessed large-scale migrations of Northerners or Cubans.

The 3rd is a traditional Southern Democratic district. Jimmy Carter carried it in 1976 and 1980. The district encompasses most of Jacksonville, including large black communities in the north and northeast part of the city. Blacks account for 27.3 percent of the district's population, a larger proportion than in any other Florida district.

In the remap, the 3rd added about 43,000 people in southeast Jacksonville who previously were part of the 4th District. Southeast Jacksonville is a middle- and upper middle-income area prone to vote Republican in national elections.

Election Returns

3rd District		Democrat		Republican	
1976	President	80,412	(63.7%)	44,650	(35.4%)
	Senate	75,317	(67.2%)	36,762	(32.8%)
	House	x[1]		—[1]	
1978	Governor	52,089	(56.8%)	39,561	(43.2%)
	House	x[1]		—[1]	
1980	President	69,230	(52.7%)	58,864	(44.8%)
	Senate	70,186	(57.7%)	51,400	(42.3%)
	House	95,641	(77.0%)	28,521	(23.0%)
1982	Governor	76,287	(76.8%)	23,080	(23.2%)
	Senate	68,797	(71.2%)	27,619	(28.6%)
	House	73,802	(84.1%)	13,972	(15.9%)

[1] *No votes tabulated where candidate was unopposed; x indicates winner.*

Demographics

Population: 512,692. **Percent Change from 1970:** 4.7%.

Land Area: 1,276 square miles. **Population per Square Mile:** 401.8.

Counties, 1980 Population: Duval (Pt.) — 479,798; Nassau — 32,894.

Cities, 1980 Population: Jacksonville (Pt.) — 470,425.

Race and Ancestry: White — 71.0%; Black — 27.3%; American Indian, Eskimo and Aleut — 0.2%; Asian and Pacific Islander — 1.0%. Spanish Origin — 1.8%. English — 14.4%; French — 0.9%; German — 3.6%; Irish — 4.6%; Italian — 0.9%; Polish — 0.5%; Scottish — 0.6%.

Universities, Enrollment: Edward Waters College, Jacksonville — 836; Florida Junior College at Jacksonville, Jacksonville — 14,915; Jacksonville University, Jacksonville — 2,478; Jones College, Jacksonville — 1,197.

Newspapers, Circulation: *The Florida Times-Union* (mS), Jacksonville — 152,976; *Jacksonville Journal* (e), Jacksonville — 57,589.

Commercial Television Stations, Affiliation: WJXT-TV, Jacksonville (CBS); WTLV, Jacksonville (ABC); WXAO-TV, Jacksonville (None). Entire district is located in Jacksonville ADI. *(For other Jacksonville stations, see 4th district.)*

Military Installations: Cecil Field Naval Air Station, Jacksonville — 8,163; Jacksonville International Airport (Air Force), Callahan — 1,033; Jacksonville Naval Air Station, Jacksonville — 17,053; Jacksonville Naval Regional Medical Center, Jacksonville — 1,297; Mayport Naval Station, Mayport — 11,406.

Industries:

Family Line; Jacksonville; railroad operations — 3,000. **Prudential Insurance Co. of America;** Jacksonville; life, health insurance — 2,800. **Blue Cross/Blue Shield of Florida;** Jacksonville; health insurance — 2,410. **Independent Insurance Group Inc.;** (HQ); Jacksonville; life, health, casualty insurance — 1,800. **Southern Baptist Hospital of Florida;** Jacksonville; hospital — 1,800.

St. Vincent's Medical Center; Jacksonville; hospital — 1,740. **Jacksonville Shipyards Inc.** (Bellinger Shipyards Div.); Jacksonville; ship repairing — 1,700. **Pinkerton's of Florida Inc.;** Jacksonville; security services — 1,700. **Duval County Hospital Authority Inc.;** Jacksonville; hospital — 1,600. **Atlantic Bancorp.;** Jacksonville; bank holding company — 1,110. **Florida Publishing Co.** (HQ); Jacksonville; newspaper publishing — 1,020. **St. Luke's Hospital Assn.;** Jacksonville; hospital — 1,000. **Jacksonville Memorial Hospital;** Jacksonville; hospital — 1,000. **Anheuser-Busch Inc.;** Jacksonville; brewery — 850. **State Farm Mutual Automobile Insurance Co.;** Jacksonville; casualty insurance — 750. **Jon Swisher & Son Inc.** (HQ); Jacksonville; cigars, candy — 700. **Anchor Hocking Corp.;** Jacksonville; glass products — 600.

General Foods Corp. (Maxwell House Coffee Div.); Jacksonville; coffee — 600. **ITT Rayonier Inc.;** Fernandina Beach; pulp mill — 600. **B. B. McCormick & Sons;** Jacksonville; heavy construction — 600. **Florida National Bank of Jacksonville;** Jacksonville; banking — 585. **Gulf Life Insurance Co.** (HQ); Jacksonville; life, health insurance — 542. **Florida Machine & Foundry Co.** (Fleco Div.); Jacksonville; steel foundries — 500. **The Haskell Co. Inc.** (Capitol Prestress Div.); Jacksonville; building construction — 500. **Reynolds, Smith, Hills, Architects** (HQ); Jacksonville; engineering services — 500. **SCM Corp.** (Organic Chemical Div.); Jacksonville; industrial organic chemicals — 500. **Terminal Paper Bag Co.** (Trinity Bag & Paper Co. Div.); Yulee; kraft bags — 500.

4th District

Northeast — Daytona Beach

The old 4th had to be pared substantially by redistricting because its population had ballooned during the 1970s to 715,027, more than 200,000 above ideal district size. The legislators decided to move Marion County (Ocala) from the 4th and make it part of the newly created 6th. That left Daytona Beach (Volusia County) as the political focus of the new 4th.

Daytona's beach at low tide is as wide as a superhighway, and traffic clutter sometimes makes it resemble one. Ever since Florida's population began to boom in the 1950s, Daytona Beach has been the most popular resort on the state's east coast for vacationers who do not want to bother making a long trip down the peninsula.

Though the weather is sometimes cool, the city makes a special push to attract winter visitors from Canada, and the Daytona International Speedway schedules its Daytona 500 car race in February to lure tourists.

Parts of Daytona, however, look less than elegant. The boardwalk and some of the city's motels built in earlier boom days are reaching middle age, and competition from neighboring beaches has stepped up in recent years.

Volusia County, which has half the district's population, chooses Democratic candidates for statewide office, although it may prefer Republicans in presidential elections. Ronald Reagan carried Volusia with 52 percent in 1980.

Although Daytona's population increased by one-fifth in the 1970s, the rate of growth in Ormond Beach, just to the north, was more substantial. Flagler County, a few miles north, is receiving an influx of retirees that helped its population grow 40 percent between 1977 and 1981.

While the 4th gave up some of its southeast Jacksonville territory (Duval County) to the 3rd, it retained about 90,000 residents there, most of them from white-collar suburban communities. Besides the remap changes affecting Marion and Duval counties, redistricting also shifted parts of Clay, Putnam, Lake and Seminole counties to neighboring districts.

Election Returns

4th District		Democrat		Republican	
1976	President	101,649	(53.5%)	85,485	(45.0%)
	Senate	109,540	(62.9%)	64,504	(37.1%)
	House	x[1]		—[1]	
1978	Governor	77,700	(51.5%)	73,037	(48.5%)
	House	89,344	(73.0%)	33,119	(27.0%)
1980	President	90,665	(40.2%)	125,277	(55.6%)
	Senate	104,981	(49.9%)	105,593	(50.1%)
	House	123,553	(66.1%)	63,474	(33.9%)
1982	Governor	87,202	(66.1%)	44,674	(33.9%)
	Senate	74,584	(59.9%)	49,868	(40.1%)
	House	83,895	(66.9%)	41,457	(33.1%)

[1] *No votes tabulated where candidate was unopposed; x indicates winner.*

Demographics

Population: 512,672. **Percent Change from 1970:** 56.8%.

Land Area: 3,257 square miles. **Population per Square Mile:** 157.4.

Counties, 1980 Population: Clay (Pt.) — 52,689; Duval (Pt.) — 91,205; Flagler — 10,913; Putnam (Pt.) — 47,800; St. Johns — 51,303; Volusia — 258,762.

Cities, 1980 Population: Daytona Beach — 54,176; De Land — 15,354; Jacksonville (Pt.) — 70,495; Jacksonville Beach — 15,462; New Smyrna Beach — 13,557; Ormond Beach — 21,378; Palatka — 10,175; Port Orange — 18,756; South Daytona — 11,252; St. Augustine — 11,985.

Race and Ancestry: White — 88.0%; Black — 10.9%; American Indian, Eskimo and Aleut — 0.2%; Asian and Pacific Islander — 0.6%. Spanish Origin — 1.7%. Dutch — 0.6%; English — 14.7%; French —

1.5%; German — 6.6%; Irish — 5.5%; Italian — 2.4%; Polish — 1.1%; Scottish — 0.9%; Swedish — 0.5%.

Universities, Enrollment: Bethune-Cookman College, Daytona Beach — 1,747; Daytona Beach Community College, Daytona Beach — 8,133; Embry-Riddle Aeronautical University, Bunnell — 4,920; Flagler College, St. Augustine — 839; St. Johns River Community College, Palatka — 1,562; Stetson University, De Land — 2,977; University of North Florida, Jacksonville — 4,712.

Newspapers, Circulation: *Clay Today* (e), Orange Park — 5,533; *De Land Sun News* (eS), De Land — 8,758; *Journal* (mS), Daytona Beach — 51,347; *News* (eS), Daytona Beach — 29,719; *Palatka Daily News* (e), Palatka — 10,776; *The St. Augustine Record* (e), St. Augustine — 10,525. The Jacksonville *Florida Times Union* and *Jacksonville Journal* also circulate in the district.

Commercial Television Stations, Affiliation: WAWS, Jacksonville (None); WESH-TV, Daytona Beach (NBC); WJKS-TV, Jacksonville (NBC). District is divided between Jacksonville ADI and Orlando-Daytona Beach ADI. *(For other Jacksonville stations, see 3rd District.)*

Military Installations: Jacksonville Air Force Station, Orange Park — 5.

Industries:

Georgia-Pacific Corp; Palatka; paper, pulp mill — 1,700. **Halifax Hospital Medical Center;** Daytona Beach; hospital — 1,400. **General Electric Co.;** Daytona Beach; administrative offices — 1,300. **Florida Coca-Cola Bottling Co.;** Daytona Beach; soft drink bottling — 1,200. **Sherwood Medical Industries;** De Land; disposable medical instruments — 826.

Whittaker Corp. (Desco Marine); St. Augustine; shipbuilding, repairing — 700. **News Journal Corp.** (HQ); Daytona Beach; newspaper publishing — 600. **St. Augustine Trawlers Inc.** (St. Augustine Shipbuilding); St. Augustine; shrimp trawlers — 550. **Brunswick Corp.** (Technetics Div.); De Land; ammunition — 520.

5th District

North Central — Orlando, Northern Suburbs

The old 5th District grew 94 percent during the 1970s to a population exceeding 880,000. It was divided up to form the cores of three separate districts.

The new 5th contains all of downtown Orlando and the city's northern suburbs in Orange and southern Seminole counties. The tourism industry in this area boomed overnight with the 1971 opening of Disney World, 15 miles south of Orlando in the 11th District. Another boost came with the late 1982 opening of Disney's EPCOT Center, an area with futuristic pavilions that has been described as a permanent World's Fair.

Thousands of workers have been drawn to the area's numerous high-technology companies that got their start during the 1960s race to the moon; Orlando is the major city nearest the Kennedy Space Center in Titusville. Production of missiles, aircraft control systems, computer software, lasers and other sophisticated equipment provides a steady living for aerospace and defense contractors.

Growth has brought its share of problems to the district. Orlando sewage threatens the health of Lake Tohopekaliga to the south, and the capital improvements needed to control the problem are costly. Demand for water has increased dramatically; lowering of the water table was

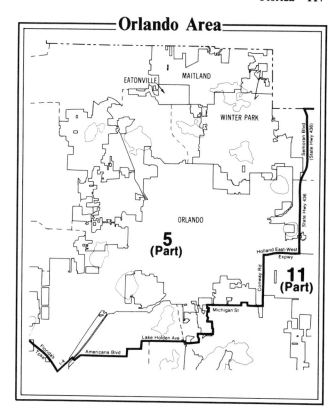

partly to blame for the massive sinkhole that opened up in Winter Park in 1981, swallowing buildings, cars and a swimming pool.

Affluent Orange County communities such as Winter Park and Maitland are home to Orlando's older, established elite, which provides strong support for Republican candidates. Many of the upper-level executives new to the area settle to the north in Seminole County, an area that gave two-thirds of its 1980 presidential vote to Ronald Reagan. Most of the district's Democratic voters come out of working-class areas within the city of Orlando.

Election Returns

5th District		Democrat		Republican	
1976	President	59,891	(45.9%)	68,991	(52.9%)
	Senate	72,041	(60.6%)	46,788	(39.4%)
	House	40,153	(33.8%)	78,696	(66.2%)
1978	Governor	53,991	(51.5%)	50,747	(48.5%)
	House	55,485	(53.7%)	47,803	(46.3%)
1980	President	51,295	(33.7%)	93,796	(61.5%)
	Senate	72,389	(46.2%)	84,435	(53.8%)
	House	75,979	(51.7%)	70,918	(48.3%)
1982	Governor	70,618	(60.3%)	46,433	(39.7%)
	Senate	61,463	(53.3%)	53,741	(46.6%)
	House	49,070	(41.2%)	69,993	(58.8%)

Demographics

Population: 513,005. **Percent Change from 1970:** 47.0%.

Land Area: 927 square miles. **Population per Square Mile:** 553.4.

Counties, 1980 Population: Lake (Pt.) — 22,078; Orange (Pt.) — 311,175; Seminole — 179,752.

Cities, 1980 Population: Altamonte Springs — 22,028; Casselberry — 15,247; Longwood — 10,029; Orlando (Pt.) — 108,393; Sanford — 23,176; Winter Park — 22,339; Winter Springs — 10,475.

Race and Ancestry: White — 81.9%; Black — 16.4%; American Indian, Eskimo and Aleut — 0.2%; Asian and Pacific Islander — 0.6%. Spanish Origin — 2.9%. Dutch — 0.5%; English — 13.8%; French — 1.3%; German — 6.3%; Irish — 4.5%; Italian — 2.0%; Polish — 1.0%; Scottish — 0.8%.

Universities, Enrollment: Jones College, Orlando — 1,519; Rollins College, Winter Park — 4,071; Seminole Community College, Sanford — 4,673; Valencia Community College, Orlando — 9,794.

Newspapers, Circulation: *Evening Herald* (eS), Sanford — 8,494; *Sentinel Star* (all day, S), Orlando — 195,448.

Commercial Television Stations, Affiliation: WCPX-TV, Orlando (CBS); WFTV, Orlando (ABC); WOFL, Orlando (None). Entire district is located in Orlando-Daytona Beach ADI.

Military Installations: Orlando Naval Training Center, Orlando — 17,263.

Industries:

Albertson's Inc.; (Southco Div.); Orlando; grocery chain — 10,000. **Adventist Health System** (HQ); Orlando; hospital — 3,000. **Orlando Regional Medical Center Inc.;** Orlando; hospital — 2,800. **Sentinel Star Co. Inc.** (HQ); Orlando; newspaper publishing — 1,500. **Stromberg-Carlson Corp.;** Sanford; communications equipment — 1,300.

Sun Bank Inc.; Orlando; banking — 1,160. **Sunland Training Center;** Orlando; state psychiatric hospital — 1,000. **Golden Gem Growers Inc.;** Umatilla; citrus growers, processors — 700. **Hubbard Construction Co.** (HQ); Orlando; highway, sewer, dam construction — 670. **American Bakeries** (Merita Bakery); Orlando; bakery — 600. **Piezo Technology Inc.;** Orlando; quartz crystal electronic components — 600. **NCR Corp.** (Scott Electronic Div.); Lake Mary; electronic components — 550. **The TRW Fujitsu Co.** (Financial Systems Div.); Orlando; electronic communications equipment — 550.

6th District

North Central — Gainesville, Ocala

This newly created district combines a fairly liberal university city with conservative rural areas and a coastal region rapidly filling with Republican retirees. When stirred together, these elements produce a district where Democrats have a slight edge.

The University of Florida, with more than 30,000 students and 2,500 faculty members, puts Gainesville and surrounding Alachua County clearly to the left of most of the Florida electorate.

In 1968, when surrounding north Florida counties were giving solid margins to George C. Wallace for president, Hubert H. Humphrey won a plurality in Alachua. The county was George McGovern's best in Florida in 1972, and John B. Anderson took 8 percent there in 1980. Thirty percent of the people in the 6th live in Alachua County.

From Alachua County, the district follows the southerly path of Interstate 75 to Ocala (Marion County). Motels, restaurants and gas stations strung along the highway service tourists drawn by the region's springs, rivers and lakes.

Some of central Florida's high-technology companies have been expanding operations northward in recent years; Martin Marietta and others moving into Ocala helped

boost that city's population by nearly 15,000 during the 1970s.

Outside Ocala, Marion County is mostly citrus groves and range land for horse and cattle farms. While the newcomers to Marion County tend to vote Republican, most of the rural people are traditional Southern Democrats. Those two groups were closely matched in 1976, when Jimmy Carter barely carried Marion County, but in 1980 Ronald Reagan won a solid majority there.

South of Marion, the district continues into Sumter and the western half of Lake counties. Watermelons, berries and other fruit are grown around Leesburg, the geographic center of Florida. Conservative retirees in Lake County's numerous trailer parks helped Reagan carry the county with 65 percent in 1980.

Finally, the 6th takes in the Gulf Coast counties of Citrus and Hernando, two of the four fastest-growing counties in Florida from 1977 to 1981. Retirees, who are responsible for much of the influx, generally help swing the vote to the right. Reagan in 1980 won 55 percent in Hernando and 58.5 percent in Citrus; in 1976 Carter carried both.

Election Returns

6th District		Democrat		Republican	
1976	President	81,083	(54.6%)	65,705	(44.3%)
	Senate	88,571	(65.1%)	47,508	(34.9%)
	House	29,768	(43.8%)	38,183	(56.2%)
1978	Governor	77,091	(51.1%)	73,699	(48.9%)
	House	91,766	(64.4%)	50,628	(35.6%)
1980	President	79,547	(41.6%)	101,489	(53.1%)
	Senate	111,108	(51.0%)	106,852	(49.0%)
	House	123,557	(60.1%)	82,005	(39.9%)
1982	Governor	90,692	(65.2%)	48,425	(34.8%)
	Senate	86,661	(61.4%)	54,512	(38.6%)
	House	85,825	(61.3%)	54,059	(38.6%)

Demographics

Population: 512,950. **Percent Change from 1970:** 70.9%.

Land Area: 5,012 square miles. **Population per Square Mile:** 102.3.

Counties, 1980 Population: Alachua — 151,348; Citrus — 54,703; Hernando — 44,469; Lake (Pt.) — 82,792; Marion — 122,488; Pasco (Pt.) — 30,129; Putnam (Pt.) — 2,749; Sumter — 24,272.

Cities, 1980 Population: Gainesville — 81,371; Leesburg — 13,191; Ocala — 37,170.

Race and Ancestry: White — 84.8%; Black — 13.9%; American Indian, Eskimo and Aleut — 0.2%; Asian and Pacific Islander — 0.5%. Spanish Origin — 2.3%. Dutch — 0.7%; English — 14.2%; French — 1.2%; German — 6.6%; Irish — 4.6%; Italian — 2.1%; Polish — 1.0%; Scottish — 0.8%; Swedish — 0.5%.

Universities, Enrollment: Central Florida Community College, Ocala — 2,512; Lake-Sumter Community College, Leesburg — 2,021; Santa Fe Community College, Gainesville — 7,355; University of Florida, Gainesville — 33,170.

Newspapers, Circulation: *The Daily Sun Journal* (e), Brooksville — 3,940; *Gainesville Sun* (mS), Gainesville — 38,519; *Leesburg Commercial* (eS), Leesburg — 10,409; *Ocala Star-Banner* (eS), Ocala — 30,675. Orlando *Sentinel Star* also circulates in the district.

Commercial Television Stations, Affiliation: WBSP, Ocala (None); WCJB, Gainesville (ABC); WIYE, Leesburg (None). District is divided among Gainesville ADI, Orlando-Daytona Beach ADI and Tampa-St. Petersburg ADI.

Nuclear Power Plants. Crystal River 3, Red Level (Babcock & Wilcox, J. A. Jones Construction), March 1977.

Industries:
General Electric Co.; Alachua; industrial machinery wholesaling — 1,300. **Veterans Administration;** Gainesville; veterans' hospital — 1,300. **General Electric Co.** (Battery Business Dept.); Gainesville; primary batteries — 1,200. **Alachua General Hospital Inc.;** Gainesville; hospital — 1,000. **Florida Farm Bureau Mutual Insurance Co.;** Gainesville; farm crop insurance — 725. **Martin Marietta Corp.;** Ocala; printed circuit boards — 725. **Certified Grocers of Florida;** Ocala; grocery wholesaling — 700. **Central Phosphates Inc.;** Zephyrhills; phosphatic fertilizers — 650.

7th District

West — Tampa

Ever since a Key West cigar factory moved to Tampa in 1886, this has been a city with a strong blue-collar orientation. Tampa still makes cigars, and other traditional industries are strong, among them brewing, commercial fishing and ship construction. The city is also a major port, giving it an interest in international markets.

Like industrial districts in Northern cities, the 7th votes Democratic in most elections, providing a sharp contrast to its neighbor across the bay, the Republican 8th District in St. Petersburg. But Tampa's traditional patterns were less noticeable in 1980 when there were not enough Democratic votes in the city to prevent Ronald Reagan from taking Hillsborough County on a tide of suburban GOP support.

Unlike many Northern industrial cities, Tampa has been able to diversify beyond its industrial base to compete for the lucrative tourist trade. Busch Gardens, which started as a simple brewery tour, has been expanded and transformed into a 300-acre amusement park featuring an African safari motif. It now is the second leading tourist attraction in Florida, trailing only Disney World in number of visitors per year.

The district is 11 percent Hispanic. The influence of the Cuban and Spanish culture is most pronounced in Ybor City, a long-established community in southeast Tampa named after the man who moved his cigar factory there from Key West.

Blacks, who account for 15 percent of the district's population, live mostly in inner-city Tampa. Several black political leaders believe they have more in common with predominantly black areas of downtown St. Petersburg than with the rest of the 7th District. Early in 1982, the Tampa and St. Petersburg NAACP chapters proposed a district that would unite the cities' blacks. Legislators gave the proposal no serious consideration.

In redistricting, the 7th lost northern Hillsborough County to the new 9th and took in some territory in southeastern Hillsborough that was part of the old 8th District. Those changes gave some Democratic votes to the 9th without damaging Democrats in the 7th.

Election Returns

7th District		Democrat		Republican	
1976	President	79,593	(53.8%)	66,684	(45.1%)
	Senate	99,498	(70.8%)	41,051	(29.2%)
1976	House	92,120	(65.8%)	47,784	(34.2%)
1978	Governor	66,084	(55.4%)	53,131	(44.6%)
	House	x[1]		—[1]	
1980	President	73,804	(43.2%)	87,705	(51.4%)
	Senate	87,064	(51.6%)	81,783	(48.4%)
	House	119,873	(72.4%)	45,750	(27.6%)
1982	Governor	84,862	(70.8%)	35,051	(29.2%)
	Senate	78,209	(67.8%)	37,094	(32.2%)
	House	85,331	(74.2%)	29,632	(25.8%)

[1] *No votes tabulated where candidate was unopposed; x indicates winner.*

Demographics

Population: 512,905. **Percent Change from 1970:** 25.3%.

Land Area: 638 square miles. **Population per Square Mile:** 803.9.

Counties, 1980 Population: Hillsborough (Pt.) — 512,905.

Cities, 1980 Population: Tampa — 271,523.

Race and Ancestry: White — 82.7%; Black — 14.9%; American Indian, Eskimo and Aleut — 0.2%; Asian and Pacific Islander — 0.6%. Spanish Origin — 11.3%. Dutch — 0.5%; English — 12.3%; French — 1.1%; German — 5.4%; Irish — 4.5%; Italian — 3.1%; Polish — 0.8%; Scottish — 0.6%.

Universities, Enrollment: Hillsborough Community College, Tampa — 10,824; Tampa College, Tampa — 1,412; United Electronics Institute, Tampa — 710; University of South Florida, Tampa — 25,054; University of Tampa, Tampa — 2,063.

Newspapers, Circulation: *The Tampa Times* (eS), Tampa — 24,942; *The Tampa Tribune* (mS), Tampa — 190,898.

Commercial Television Stations, Affiliation: WFLA-TV, Tampa (NBC); WFTS, Tampa (None); WTVT, Tampa (CBS). Entire district is located in Tampa-St. Petersburg ADI.

Military Installations: MacDill Air Force Base, Tampa — 7,034.

Industries:
Family Line; Tampa; railroad operations -- 2,500. **Hospital Authority of Hillsborough County;** Tampa; hospital — 2,200. **St. Joseph's Hospital Inc.;** Tampa; hospital — 2,000. **Busch Entertainment Corp.** (Busch Gardens); Tampa; amusement park — 1,600. **Veterans Administration;** Tampa; veterans' hospital — 1,500.

Honeywell Inc.; Tampa; semiconductors — 1,450. **Exchange Bancorp.;** Tampa; bank holding company — 1,290. **Maas Bros. Inc.** (HQ); Tampa; department store chain — 1,200. **Gardinier Inc.** (U. S. Phosphoric Products - HQ); Tampa; phosphate mining — 1,150. **University Community Hospital;** Tampa; hospital — 1,100. **Jim Walter Corp.** (HQ); Tampa; building materials — 1,000. **Singleton Packing Corp.** (HQ); Tampa; fresh, frozen fish, seafood — 980.
The Tribune Co. Inc. (HQ); Tampa; newspaper publishing — 800. **Treasure Isle Inc.** (HQ); Tampa; frozen shrimp — 760. **General Portland Inc.** (Florida Cement); Tampa; portland cement — 630. **G. T. E. Data Services Inc.** (HQ); Tampa; data processing services — 550. **Securex Inc.;** Tampa; security services — 550. **Burnup & Sims Inc.;** Tampa; utility construction — 500. **Tampa Ship Repair Drydock;** Tampa; ship repairing — 500.

8th District

West — St. Petersburg

In 1954 the influence of the conservative retirement community in St. Petersburg helped to elect Florida's first 20th-century Republican House member, William C.

Tampa - St. Petersburg Area

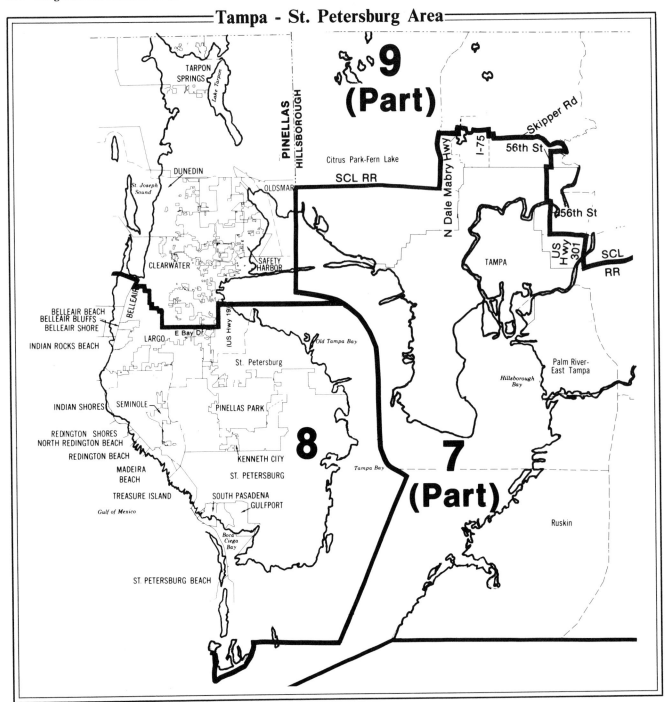

Cramer. In the years since then two-party competition in the 8th has just about ceased. The retirees who have settled in St. Pete — many are former storekeepers, office workers and civil servants from the small-town Midwest — clearly brought their political preferences to Florida with them. St. Petersburg has become more than just a haven for retirees in recent years, but the city is constant in its affection for the GOP.

Not too long ago, the St. Pete economy was mostly service oriented, geared to the needs of tourists and elderly residents. The morning rush hour saw many younger workers from St. Pete driving to jobs in Tampa, which offers employment in a variety of fields.

But during the 1970s, St. Petersburg sought to broaden its economic base by stressing that it offers a good climate for business. That promotional effort has been quite successful. Some existing manufacturers expanded, and new ones moved in. Firms such as E-Systems and Honeywell are busy with research, development, production and marketing of a broad range of computers, communications equipment and other high-technology items.

The median age of the Pinellas County population dropped during the 1970s because so many young people attracted to good-paying jobs moved into the area. The new arrivals have caused Republicans no political problems.

Redistricting changed the number of the district from

6 to 8, and it transferred into the new 9th District about 87,000 people in north Pinellas County.

Election Returns

8th District		Democrat		Republican	
1976	President	98,426	(48.9%)	100,586	(49.9%)
	Senate	109,266	(58.4%)	77,850	(41.6%)
	House	68,698	(34.8%)	128,665	(65.2%)
1978	Governor	76,698	(44.4%)	96,166	(55.6%)
	House	34,466	(21.2%)	128,090	(78.8%)
1980	President	97,234	(41.1%)	124,802	(52.7%)
	Senate	99,610	(46.9%)	112,567	(53.0%)
	House	—[1]		x[1]	
1982	Governor	107,846	(61.9%)	66,467	(38.1%)
	Senate	103,169	(59.3%)	70,830	(40.7%)
	House	—[1]		x[1]	

[1] *No votes tabulated where candidate was unopposed; x indicates winner.*

Demographics

Population: 512,909. **Percent Change from 1970:** 30.3%.

Land Area: 161 square miles. **Population per Square Mile:** 3,185.8.

Counties, 1980 Population: Pinellas (Pt.) — 512,909.

Cities, 1980 Population: Clearwater (Pt.) — 23; Gulfport — 11,180; Largo (Pt.) — 44,295; Pinellas Park — 32,811; St. Petersburg — 238,647.

Race and Ancestry: White — 90.3%; Black — 8.8%; American Indian, Eskimo and Aleut — 0.1%; Asian and Pacific Islander — 0.5%. Spanish Origin — 1.5%. Dutch — 0.8%; English — 12.7%; French — 1.8%; German — 9.5%; Hungarian — 0.5%; Irish — 5.2%; Italian — 3.2%; Polish — 1.8%; Russian — 0.5%; Scottish — 1.2%; Swedish — 0.9%.

Universities, Enrollment: Eckerd College, St. Petersburg — 1,122; St. Petersburg Junior College, St. Petersburg — 15,430.

Newspapers, Circulation: *Evening Independent* (e), St. Petersburg — 42,346; *St. Petersburg Times* (mS), St. Petersburg — 222,336.

Commercial Television Stations, Affiliation: WCLF, Largo (None); WTOG-TV, St. Petersburg (None); WTSP-TV, St. Petersburg (ABC). Entire district is located in Tampa-St. Petersburg ADI.

Industries:

Honeywell Inc. (Aerospace Div.); Largo; electronic communications equipment — 2,700. **Times Publishing Co.** (HQ); St. Petersburg; newspaper publishing — 1,925. **Paradyne Corp.** (HQ); Largo; electronic data equipment — 1,720. **E-Systems Inc.** (E C I Div.); St. Petersburg; electronic systems — 1,500. **Bayfront Medical Center Inc.**; St. Petersburg; hospital — 1,400.

General Electric Co. Inc. (Neutron Devices Dept.); St. Petersburg; semiconductors — 1,260. **National Medical Enterprises;** St. Petersburg; hospital — 1,100. **St. Anthony's Hospital Inc.;** St. Petersburg; hospital — 1,100. **Aircraft Porous Media Inc.** (HQ); Pinellas Park; aircraft parts — 625. **Suncoast Hospital Inc.;** Largo; hospital — 550. **Jack Eckerd Corp.** (Eckerd Drugs - HQ); Largo; drug store chain — 500. **Silor Optical Inc.;** St. Petersburg; glass, glassware — 500.

9th District

West — Clearwater, Parts of Pasco and Hillsborough Counties

Patching together pieces of three counties in the Tampa-St. Petersburg area, the 9th is a horseshoe-shaped district with a decided Republican bent. About 42 percent of the new district's residents come from Clearwater and nearby communities in Pinellas County, solidly Republican areas where a Democratic candidate is fortunate to win 45 percent of the vote. Clearwater, traditionally a beach resort, has benefited from the arrival of high-technology industry to the St. Petersburg metropolitan area.

Republicans also hold the upper hand in Pasco County, which accounts for about one-third of the district's population. But Democrats are more competitive there; many of the retirees who have settled in the county in recent years come from working-class backgrounds and cling to Democratic voting habits. The eastern part of Pasco County around Dade City also has rural Democratic voters among the farm lands and citrus groves.

Of the three counties placed in the new 9th, Hillsborough County, influenced by Tampa, is the friendliest to Democrats. But only about one-fourth of the district's people live in Hillsborough, and some in the mostly rural eastern part of the county are conservative and might switch to the GOP if they perceive the Democratic nominee as too liberal.

Because the Pinellas part of the district can be expected to go Republican, a Democratic candidate in the 9th has to carry Hillsborough solidly and neutralize the GOP advantage in Pasco to have much hope of winning.

Election Returns

9th District		Democrat		Republican	
1976	President	80,804	(50.8%)	76,330	(48.0%)
	Senate	87,895	(60.0%)	58,527	(40.0%)
	House	63,501	(42.6%)	85,409	(57.4%)
1978	Governor	66,094	(45.9%)	77,795	(54.1%)
	House	44,772	(40.1%)	66,988	(59.9%)
1980	President	82,783	(38.8%)	119,229	(55.9%)
	Senate	98,018	(47.3%)	109,396	(52.7%)
	House	77,205	(48.3%)	82,523	(51.6%)
1982	Governor	114,073	(61.6%)	70,985	(38.4%)
	Senate	105,887	(57.7%)	77,696	(42.3%)
	House	90,697	(48.8%)	95,009	(51.1%)

Demographics

Population: 513,191. **Percent Change from 1970:** 91.6%.

Land Area: 1,087 square miles. **Population per Square Mile:** 472.1.

Counties, 1980 Population: Hillsborough (Pt.) — 134,055; Pasco (Pt.) — 163,514; Pinellas (Pt.) — 215,622.

Cities, 1980 Population: Clearwater (Pt.) — 85,505; Dunedin — 30,203; Largo (Pt.) — 14,682; New Port Richey — 11,196; Plant City — 19,270; Tarpon Springs — 13,251; Temple Terrace — 11,097.

Race and Ancestry: White — 94.7%; Black — 4.2%; American Indian, Eskimo and Aleut — 0.2%; Asian and Pacific Islander — 0.3%. Spanish Origin — 2.5%. Dutch — 0.8%; English — 13.6%; French — 1.5%; German — 9.1%; Greek — 1.0%; Hungarian — 0.6%; Irish — 5.4%; Italian — 3.9%; Polish — 1.8%; Scottish — 1.0%; Swedish — 0.9%.

Universities, Enrollment: Florida College, Temple Terrace — 450; Pasco-Hernando Community College, Dade City — 3,268; Saint Leo College, St. Leo — 1,084.

Newspapers, Circulation: *Clearwater Sun* (mS), Clearwater — 41,523. *St. Petersburg Evening Independent, St. Petersburg Times, The Tampa Times,* and *The Tampa Tribune* also circulate in the district.

Commercial Television Stations, Affiliation: Entire district is located in Tampa-St. Petersburg ADI.

Industries:

Morton F. Plant Hospital Assn.; Clearwater; hospital — 2,300. **Mease Hospital Inc.**; Dunedin; hospital — 1,160. **Golf Hosts International Inc.** (HQ); Tarpon Springs; resort hotel — 1,000. **Sperry Corp.** (Sperry Gyroscope Div.); Clearwater; guidance, control systems — 1,000. **Sperry Corp.**; Oldsmar; industrial measuring devices — 900.

Lykes Bros. Inc.; Plant City; meatpacking — 750. **Lykes Pasco Packing Co.** (Dispenser Div.); Dade City; frozen, canned fruits — 700. **C F Industries Inc.**; Plant City; phosphatic fertilizers — 690. **Square D Co. Inc.** (Electromagnetic Industries Div.); Clearwater; electronic transformers — 600. **Amax Chemical Corp.** (Amax Phosphate); Plant City; phosphatic fertilizer, animal feed — 500. **Harsco Corp.**; Plant City; fabricated structural steel — 500.

10th District

Central — Lakeland, Winter Haven, Bradenton

All over Florida, land once devoted to agriculture is being eaten away by shopping centers, motels and condominiums. But in Polk County, centerpiece of the 10th District, citrus is still king.

Polk has 130,000 acres planted in citrus. Thousands of area jobs are connected with the growing, picking, packing, processing and loading of oranges, orange concentrate and grapefruit. Tropicana and Minute Maid have facilities within the district, and there are many lesser-known growers whose efforts combine to make Polk the nation's foremost citrus-producing county.

Occasional cold weather here is more than an inconvenience; if temperatures dip below freezing, millions of dollars of citrus may be lost.

Phosphate rock, the raw material of fertilizer, is another key element of the Polk County economy. Three-fourths of America's phosphate is strip-mined out of Polk, although the industry suffered in the early 1980s from slack demand. High interest rates were preventing domestic farmers from buying fertilizer at their typical pace, and a stronger dollar was pushing phosphate prices higher than foreign buyers prefer to pay.

Tourism also brings in substantial revenue to Polk County. The water ski shows at Winter Haven's Cypress Gardens have been running for 40 years, and they draw more than a million visitors annually.

Nearly 63 percent of the people in the 10th District live in Polk County, with the major concentration in the Lakeland-Winter Haven area.

The 10th has one Gulf Coast county, Manatee, which accounts for about 29 percent of the district's population. The city of Bradenton there grew 43 percent during the 1970s to a population exceeding 30,000. Like Pinellas County, Manatee is a popular retirement area for Republican voters from Central and Midwestern states. Registered Democrats once outnumbered registered Republicans in Manatee County by 3-to-1; that advantage has slipped to about 55-45.

The other two counties in the 10th are De Soto and Hardee. Predominantly agricultural, they have cattle ranches, citrus groves, a scattering of small towns and conservative Democratic voters. The remap transferred the part of heavily Republican Sarasota County formerly in the 10th to the new 13th District.

Election Returns

10th District		Democrat		Republican	
1976	President	77,872	(49.1%)	78,521	(49.5%)
	Senate	92,469	(61.0%)	59,178	(39.0%)
	House	86,813	(62.3%)	52,480	(37.7%)
1978	Governor	58,733	(46.4%)	67,737	(53.6%)
	House	x[1]		—[1]	
1980	President	71,059	(38.3%)	107,348	(57.9%)
	Senate	82,952	(46.8%)	94,228	(53.2%)
	House	116,932	(69.8%)	46,771	(27.9%)
1982	Governor	86,339	(64.6%)	47,244	(35.4%)
	Senate	81,492	(61.1%)	51,936	(38.9%)
	House	x[1]		—[1]	

[1] *No votes tabulated where candidate was unopposed. x indicates winner.*

Demographics

Population: 512,890. **Percent Change from 1970:** 44.3%.

Land Area: 3,966 square miles. **Population per Square Mile:** 129.3.

Counties, 1980 Population: De Soto — 19,039; Hardee — 19,379; Manatee — 148,442; Osceola (Pt.) — 4,378; Polk — 321,652.

Cities, 1980 Population: Bartow — 14,780; Bradenton — 30,170; Haines City — 10,799; Kissimmee (Pt.) — 3; Lakeland — 47,406; Winter Haven — 21,119.

Race and Ancestry: White — 84.9%; Black — 13.0%; American Indian, Eskimo and Aleut — 0.2%; Asian and Pacific Islander — 0.4%. Spanish Origin — 3.3%. Dutch — 0.8%; English — 14.6%; French — 1.0%; German — 6.1%; Irish — 5.0%; Italian — 1.2%; Polish — 0.7%; Scottish — 0.6%; Swedish — 0.5%.

Universities, Enrollment: Florida Southern College, Lakeland — 1,807; Lakeland College of Business and Fashion, Lakeland — 257; Manatee Junior College, Bradenton — 5,277; Polk Community College, Winter Haven — 4,624; Southeastern College of the Assemblies of God, Lakeland — 1,255; Warner Southern College, Lake Wales — 305; Webber College, Babson Park — 128.

Newspapers, Circulation: *The Bradenton Herald* (eS), Bradenton — 26,154; *Daily Highlander* (eS), Lake Wales — 5,900; *The Ledger* (mS), Lakeland — 46,646; *Winter Haven Daily News-Chief* (eS), Winter Haven — 15,945.

Commercial Television Stations, Affiliation: Most of district is located in Tampa-St. Petersburg ADI. Portion is in Orlando-Daytona Beach ADI.

Military Installations: Avon Park Weapons Range (Air Force), Avon Park — 265.

Industries:

Tropicana Products Inc. (HQ); Bradenton; citrus juices — 2,200. **International Minerals & Chemicals Corp.** (Noralyn Mine); Bartow; phosphate mining — 1,630. **Lakeland Regional Medical Center;** Lakeland; hospital — 1,600. **W. R. Grace & Co.**; Bartow; plastics, inorganic chemicals, phosphate mining — 1,400. **Winter Haven Hospital Inc.;** Winter Haven; hospital — 1,300.

Manatee Memorial Hospital; Bradenton; hospital — 1,250. **G. Pierce Wood Memorial Hospital**; Arcadia; hospital — 1,140. **International Minerals & Chemicals Corp.** (New Wales Chemical); Mulberry; phosphate mining — 1,100. **Irrigation South Inc.**; Haines City; farm equipment wholesaling — 1,040. **Piper Aircraft Corp.**; Lakeland; aircraft — 900. **Agrico Chemical Co. Inc.** (Agrico Mining Co.); Mulberry; phosphate mining — 905. **American Cyanamid Co. Inc.** (Brewster Phosphates); Mulberry; phosphate mining — 825. **Davy McKee Corp.**; Lakeland; engineering services — 800. **Pacific Packing Co.** (Lakeland Packing Co.); Highland City; citrus packing — 800.

Ringling Bros. Barnum & Bailey Circus (Circus World); Haines City; amusement park — 800. **United States Steel Corp.** (U.S.S. Agri

Chemicals Div.); Fort Meade; non-metallic minerals — 780. **Kraft Inc.;** Lakeland; citrus canning — 750. **The Coca-Cola Co. Inc.** (Minute Maid Div.); Auburndale; fruit juices — 700. **State Farm Fire & Casualty Co.;** Winter Haven; casualty insurance — 650. **Industrial Glass Co. Inc.;** Bradenton; glass containers — 600. **Mobil Oil Corp.** (Phosphorus Div.); Nichols; phosphate mining — 565. **Adams Packing Assn. Inc.** (HQ); Auburndale; frozen, canned fruits — 500. **Scotty's Inc.** (HQ); Winter Haven; lumber, building supplies — 500.

11th District

East — Melbourne, Titusville, Part of Orange County

The new 11th District is home to many of Florida's most popular tourist attractions. In addition to Disney World, and its new EPCOT Center, the 11th as redrawn contains Sea World, the Stars Hall of Fame and other diversions that offer many low-skill, minimum-wage jobs and rake in millions of visitors' dollars every year.

Also in the 11th is the National Aeronautics and Space Administration's Kennedy Space Center near Titusville in Brevard County. That area boomed during the era of space flights in the 1960s, then stalled in the 1970s when space exploration slipped from its status as a top-level national priority.

The high-technology industries that had been lured to the area were forced to trim jobs, but a core group of engineers and other skilled workers remained. The space shuttle program and President Reagan's plans to increase military spending have brought new opportunities for aerospace and defense-related work, and high-technology hiring in Brevard is again on the upswing.

Brevard contains slightly more than half of the people in the 11th District. Engineers and other professionals make up a significant share of the electorate; they are mostly conservative, partial to Republicans in presidential elections. Ronald Reagan won 60 percent in Brevard County in 1980.

The district also includes nearly all of Osceola and Indian River counties. Most of Osceola's people live in the northern half of the county, which lies on the outskirts of metropolitan Orlando. Southern Osceola is given over to cattle ranches and citrus groves.

Retirees who have settled in Vero Beach and other coastal towns in Indian River County tend to come from North-Central states — more Ohioans than New Yorkers. These older people are fairly affluent and accustomed to voting Republican.

Election Returns

11th District		Democrat		Republican	
1976	President	76,194	(47.4%)	82,160	(51.1%)
	Senate	94,620	(62.4%)	57,052	(37.6%)
	House	36,342	(24.5%)	111,766	(75.5%)
1978	Governor	69,486	(51.3%)	66,084	(48.7%)
	House	70,393	(63.7%)	40,067	(36.3%)
1980	President	65,216	(33.2%)	120,144	(61.2%)
	Senate	88,957	(46.9%)	100,664	(53.1%)
	House	119,592	(63.7%)	68,218	(36.3%)
1982	Governor	85,375	(59.9%)	57,147	(40.1%)

11th District		Democrat		Republican	
1982	Senate	77,573	(54.2%)	65,541	(45.8%)
	House	101,746	(70.6%)	42,422	(29.4%)

Demographics

Population: 512,691. **Percent Change from 1970:** 39.8%.

Land Area: 3,352 square miles. **Population per Square Mile:** 153.0.

Counties, 1980 Population: Brevard — 272,959; Indian River (Pt.) — 34,982; Orange (Pt.) — 159,841; Osceola (Pt.) — 44,909.

Cities, 1980 Population: Cocoa — 16,096; Cocoa Beach — 10,926; Kissimmee (Pt.) — 15,484; Melbourne — 46,536; Orlando (Pt.) — 19,898; Palm Bay — 18,560; Rockledge — 11,877; Titusville — 31,910; Vero Beach (Pt.) — 11,082.

Race and Ancestry: White — 90.0%; Black — 7.9%; American Indian, Eskimo and Aleut — 0.3%; Asian and Pacific Islander — 0.9%. Spanish Origin — 3.4%. Dutch — 0.6%; English — 13.4%; French — 1.5%; German — 7.6%; Irish — 5.2%; Italian — 2.5%; Polish — 1.1%; Scottish — 0.8%; Swedish — 0.5%.

Universities, Enrollment: Brevard Community College, Cocoa — 10,934; Florida Institute of Technology, Melbourne — 5,784; Morris Junior College of Business, Melbourne — 193; University of Central Florida, Orlando — 12,806.

Newspapers, Circulation: *Today* (mS), Cocoa — 65,738. Orlando *Sentinel Star* also circulates in the district.

Commercial Television Stations, Affiliation: WTGL-TV, Cocoa (None). Most of district is located in Orlando-Daytona Beach ADI. Portion is in West Palm Beach ADI.

Military Installations: Cape Canaveral Air Force Station, Port Canaveral — 4,037; Patrick Air Force Base, Cocoa Beach — 5,956.

Industries:

Walt Disney World Co. Inc.; Lake Buena Vista; amusement park — 16,000. **Martin Marietta Corp.;** Orlando; aerospace systems — 9,200. **Pan American World Airways** (Aerospace Services Div.); Cocoa Beach; aircraft parts — 2,000. **Rockwell International Corp.** (Space Systems Group); Kennedy Space Center; engineering services — 1,750. **Harris Corp.** (Government Aerospace Systems); Palm Bay; aerospace systems — 1,467.

Documation Inc.; Melbourne; data processing machinery — 1,400. **Harris Corp.** (Melbourne Division Support Operations); Palm Bay; administrative offices — 1,225. **Planning Research Corp.** (PRC Systems Services Co.); Cape Canaveral; engineering services — 1,150. **Computer Sciences Corp.;** Cocoa Beach; engineering services — 1,100. **James E. Holmes Regional Medical Center;** Melbourne; hospital — 1,100. **Piper Aircraft Corp.;** Vero Beach; airplanes — 1,100. **RCA Corp.** (International Services Div.); Cocoa Beach; commercial testing lab — 1,100. **Rockwell International Corp.** (Collins Avionics Div.); Melbourne; electronic communications equipment — 1,070. **Harris Corp.** (Government Information Systems); Palm Bay; information systems — 948. **Computer Services Corp.;** Kennedy Space Center; data processing services — 900. **Harris Corp.** (Semiconductor Div.); Palm Bay; semiconductors — 800. **Martin Marietta Corp.;** (Data Systems Div.); Orlando; data processing — 800.

Super Food Services Inc.; Orlando; grocery wholesaling — 750. **McDonnell Douglas Corp.** (Astronautics Div.); Titusville; aerospace systems — 700. **Harris Corp.** (Government Communications Systems); Palm Bay; communications systems — 628.

Hyatt Corp.; Orlando; hotel — 600. **Harris Corp.** (Controls Composition Div.) Melbourne; paper industries machinery — 580. **Harris Corp.** (Government Satellite Terminal Operations); Palm Bay; satellite communications equipment — 550. **Harris Corp.** (Satellite Communications); Melbourne; satellite communications equipment — 550. **Applied Devices Corp.** (Datatrol - HQ); Kissimmee; electronic computing equipment — 500. **Harris Corp.** (Semiconductor Custom Integrated Circuits); Palm Bay; integrated circuits — 500. **ITT Telecommunications Corp.;** Cape Canaveral; telephone apparatus — 500. **Valley Forge Life Insurance Co. Inc.;** Orlando; life insurance — 500.

12th District

South Central — Parts of Palm Beach and West Palm Beach; Fort Pierce

The huge new 12th encompasses much of inland south Florida and runs from the Gulf of Mexico to the Atlantic Ocean, but a candidate jealous of his time can spend most of it in just three east coast counties — Palm Beach, Martin and St. Lucie — where 70 percent of the people live.

In Palm Beach County, the district line divides Palm Beach and West Palm Beach, placing the northern part of each city in the 12th and the southern part of each in the 14th. In Palm Beach, where Rolls-Royce sedans carry their owners to Spanish-style seaside mansions, the spirit of noblesse oblige creates elaborate charity events but does not interfere with a monolithic conservative politics.

West Palm Beach, by contrast, is mostly middle class. Originally a railroad town and home to the Palm Beach servant community, it grew to dwarf the parent city. West Palm Beach today has some poor people and minorities in its population and usually votes Democratic. In addition to businesses that cater to the needs of the wealthy, West Palm has some high-technology employers, including Pratt & Whitney's engineering research and development facility for aircraft engines. Pratt & Whitney is the largest employer in Palm Beach County.

Just up the coast from West Palm Beach is Riviera Beach; that city's population is two-thirds black, and it is a reliable source of Democratic votes. Manufacturing of electronic components provides jobs there.

At one time Palm Beach was recognized as the northern limit of the densely populated "Gold Coast" region that begins south of Miami. But development is marching inexorably northward. In north Palm Beach County, the town of Jupiter tripled in size during the 1970s. Population in both Martin and St. Lucie counties jumped one-fourth from 1977 to 1981.

Some of the newcomers are retirees from the East and Midwest, but others are participants in a reverse migration — south Floridians fleeing the crime and crowding that is taking hold in areas where they originally settled.

Martin County is a GOP bastion, the only county on the east coast of Florida where there are as many registered Republicans as there are Democrats. Ronald Reagan won 68 percent there in 1980. St. Lucie County (Fort Pierce) is 2-to-1 Democratic by registration and has a noticeably liberal Democratic community. Even so, St. Lucie gave Reagan 61 percent in 1980.

At the other end of the state, on the Gulf Coast, the 12th includes about 39,000 residents of Collier County, a popular retirement area. Collier is one of the four Florida counties with more registered Republicans than Democrats.

Although the rural areas of the 12th are lightly populated, their agricultural output is an important component of the district's economy. Away from the developed coastal strip, much of Palm Beach County is planted in vegetables. The county harvests more acres of commercial vegetables than any other county in the state. The headquarters of the U.S. Sugar Corp. is located in Clewiston (Hendry County), and there are large cattle ranches in Hendry and Collier counties.

Lake Okeechobee, at the center of the district, sustains the agricutural areas and is the primary source of drinking water for south Florida. The pace of growth is taxing the capacity of the lake; during periods of drought mandatory limits on water use are imposed to keep the water table from dipping too low.

The bulk of the district's territory came from the old 10th District, which cartographers broke into several pieces because its population grew nearly 94 percent during the 1970s. It will take a strong Democratic U.S. House candidate to pull these voters away from their Republican habits.

Election Returns

12th District		Democrat		Republican	
1976	President	66,662	(47.9%)	70,289	(50.5%)
	Senate	68,791	(54.4%)	57,613	(45.6%)
	House	61,681	(51.4%)	56,508	(47.1%)
1978	Governor	62,575	(52.5%)	56,661	(47.5%)
	House	17,756	(55.3%)	14,345	(44.7%)
1980	President	62,153	(34.1%)	110,071	(60.5%)
	Senate	75,952	(42.6%)	102,403	(57.4%)
	House	57,971	(34.3%)	111,025	(65.7%)
1982	Governor	87,212	(57.8%)	63,617	(42.2%)
	Senate	86,814	(57.6%)	63,843	(42.4%)
	House	73,913	(47.4%)	81,893	(52.6%)

Demographics

Population: 513,121. **Percent Change from 1970:** 67.0%.

Land Area: 8,457 square miles. **Population per Square Mile:** 60.7.

Counties, 1980 Population: Collier (Pt.) — 38,900; Glades — 5,992; Hendry — 18,599; Highlands — 47,526; Indian River (Pt.) — 24,914; Martin — 64,014; Okeechobee — 20,264; Palm Beach (Pt.) — 205,730; St. Lucie — 87,182.

Cities, 1980 Population: Belle Glade — 16,535; Fort Pierce — 33,802; Naples (Pt.) — 5; North Palm Beach — 11,344; Palm Beach Gardens — 14,407; Port St. Lucie — 14,690; Riviera Beach — 26,489; Vero Beach (Pt.) — 5,094; West Palm Beach (Pt.) — 38,026.

Race and Ancestry: White — 77.4%; Black — 19.1%; American Indian, Eskimo and Aleut — 0.3%; Asian and Pacific Islander — 0.4%. Spanish Origin — 5.2%. Dutch — 0.5%; English — 11.5%; French — 1.2%; German — 6.1%; Hungarian — 0.5%; Irish — 4.5%; Italian — 2.6%; Polish — 1.3%; Russian — 0.9%; Scottish — 0.7%; Swedish — 0.6%.

Universities, Enrollment: Indian River Community College, Fort Pierce — 4,186; South Florida Junior College, Avon Park — 995.

Newspapers, Circulation: *Naples Daily News* (eS), Naples — 22,868; *The News Tribune* (mS), Fort Pierce — 13,781; *The Stuart News* (eS), Stuart — 14,638; *Vero Beach Press-Journal* (mS), Vero Beach — 13,837. Fort Lauderdale *Sun Sentinel*, *Fort Lauderdale News*, *The Miami Herald*, *The Miami News*, West Palm Beach *Post* and West Palm Beach *Evening Times* also circulate in the district.

Commercial Television Stations, Affiliation: WFLX, West Palm Beach (None); WPEC, West Palm Beach (ABC); WPTV, West Palm Beach (NBC); WTVX, Fort Pierce (CBS). Most of district is located in West Palm Beach ADI. Portions are in Fort Myers-Naples ADI and Tampa-St. Petersburg ADI.

Nuclear Power Plants: St. Lucie 1, Fort Pierce (Combustion Engineering, Ebasco Services Inc.), December 1976; St. Lucie 2, Fort Pierce (Combustion Engineering, Ebasco Services Inc.).

Industries:

United Technologies Corp. (Pratt & Whitney Aircraft Group

Div.); West Palm Beach; aircraft engines — 7,000. **U.S. Sugar Corp.** (HQ); Clewiston; raw sugar, molasses, livestock production — 2,500. **Ebasco Services Inc.;** Jensen Beach; engineering services, nuclear reactors — 2,000. **St. Mary's Hospital Inc.;** West Palm Beach; hospital — 1,200. **Grumman Aerospace Corp.;** Stuart; aircraft — 1,000.

Good Samaritan Hospital Assn.; West Palm Beach; hospital — 850. **Gulf & Western Properties Corp.** (Okeelanta Sugar Div.); South Bay; sugar cane processing — 700. **Northern Telecom Inc.** (Electronics Div.); West Palm Beach; electronics components — 680. **The Deltona Corp.;** Marco; general contracting — 625. **Flagler System Inc.** (HQ); Palm Beach; hotel — 600. **Marriott Corp.;** Marco; hotel — 600. **Sugar Cane Growers Co-op of Florida** (Glades Sugar House); Belle Glade; sugar cane processing — 600. **Mepco/Electra Inc.;** West Palm Beach; capacitors — 560. **Boran Craig Schreck Construction Co.;** Naples; general contracting — 500. **Dickerson Group Inc.;** Stuart; highway construction — 500.

13th District

Southwest — Sarasota, Fort Myers

A glimpse at the 1980 presidential vote from the four counties in the new 13th demonstrates just how prohibitive are the odds against a Democratic victory there. Ronald Reagan carried Lee, Sarasota and Charlotte counties, which are wholly included within the 13th, by 2-to-1 margins. And Collier County, more than half of whose residents are in the district, endorsed Reagan 3-to-1. The 13th seems likely to take a place next to St. Petersburg's 8th District as automatic Republican territory.

The political personality of the 13th is shaped by the thousands of residents who have chosen the sunshine of southwest Florida as their earthly reward for a lifetime of toil. Most who retire to this area come from the Central and Midwestern part of the country. These people changed their addresses but not their party registration, and they are a major contributor to the burgeoning strength of the Republican Party in Florida.

In some cases, the influx of people to the 13th is testing the limits of the infrastructure. Just getting around proves a trying task. Sections of Interstate 75 through the 13th District are open, but it may be years before completion of the entire north-south stretch that will link Naples with St. Petersburg. In the meantime, the unpleasant alternative is a plodding trip on traffic-cluttered U.S. 41.

Replacing outdated roads, inadequate sewers and overcrowded schools requires that governments raise revenue, and that is not an easy thing to do in southwest Florida. People who lived in high-tax states all their lives and are now on fixed incomes do not envision increased taxes as part of their Utopia.

Sarasota and Lee counties each have about 40 percent of the district's residents, with the remaining 20 percent divided roughly evenly between Charlotte County and the section of Collier in the 13th.

Sarasota cultivates a refined image with its art museums, theaters and symphony performances, and it draws a wealthier class of retirees than most other west coast communities. It is also the traditional winter home of the Ringling Brothers and Barnum & Bailey Circus, although much of the entourage now spends the winter months a few miles south, at Venice. In Lee County the city of Cape Coral, incorporated only in 1971, finished the decade with 32,103 people. But even that booming growth occupied

only a fraction of the land that was dredged, filled and marked off into residential lots when optimistic developers established the community.

Fort Myers, also in Lee County, is one of the southwest Florida communities having some difficulty meeting the demands of its growing population. There are occasional calls for the city to adopt a slow-growth policy, following the example of conservationists on the islands of Sanibel and Captiva located just offshore from Fort Myers. These islands enforce stringent restrictions on development to protect the islands' natural beauty and animal population.

The town of Naples (Collier County) advanced into the status of small city with a 46-percent population explosion during the 1970s, gaining exclusive high-rise condominiums to mark its maturity. Naples is the western terminus of the Alligator Alley highway, which crosses the Everglades to link Florida's west coast with Fort Lauderdale on the east.

Election Returns

13th District		Democrat		Republican	
1976	President	72,886	(40.9%)	102,769	(57.6%)
	Senate	86,646	(53.2%)	76,261	(46.8%)
	House	52,161	(31.5%)	113,426	(68.5%)
1978	Governor	68,748	(42.6%)	92,660	(57.4%)
	House	—[1]		x[1]	
1980	President	68,062	(27.5%)	165,630	(66.9%)
	Governor	88,715	(37.5%)	148,075	(62.5%)
	House	60,289	(26.0%)	170,304	(73.3%)
1982	Governor	101,421	(48.3%)	108,401	(51.7%)
	Senate	97,541	(46.7%)	111,468	(53.3%)
	House	71,239	(34.9%)	132,951	(65.1%)

[1] *No votes tabulated where candidate was unopposed; x indicates winner.*

Demographics

Population: 513,048. **Percent Change from 1970:** 86.5%.

Land Area: 2,170 square miles. **Population per Square Mile:** 236.4.

Counties, 1980 Population: Charlotte — 58,460; Collier (Pt.) — 47,071; Lee — 205,266; Sarasota — 202,251.

Cities, 1980 Population: Cape Coral — 32,103; Fort Myers — 36,638; Naples (Pt.) — 17,576; Sarasota — 48,868; Venice — 12,153.

Race and Ancestry: White — 92.9%; Black — 5.7%; American Indian, Eskimo and Aleut — 0.1%; Asian and Pacific Islander — 0.4%. Spanish Origin — 2.2%. Dutch — 0.8%; English — 13.0%; French — 1.4%; German — 9.6%; Hungarian — 0.6%; Irish — 4.7%; Italian — 3.0%; Polish — 1.5%; Scottish — 1.0%; Swedish — 0.8%.

Universities, Enrollment: Edison Community College, Fort Myers — 5,066; Ringling School of Art and Design, Sarasota — 497.

Newspapers, Circulation: *The Breeze* (e), Cape Coral — 5,613; *Daily Herald-News* (e), Punta Gorda — 9,518; *Fort Myers News-Press* (mS), Fort Myers — 66,192; *Herald-Tribune* (mS), Sarasota — 80,843; *Journal* (e), Sarasota — 5,946.

Commercial Television Stations, Affiliation: WBBH-TV, Fort Myers (NBC); WEVU, Naples (ABC); WINK-TV, Fort Myers (CBS); WXLT-TV, Sarasota (ABC). District is divided between Fort Myers-Naples ADI and Sarasota ADI.

Industries:

Sarasota Memorial Hospital Inc.; Sarasota; hospital — 1,700. **Lee Memorial Hospital;** Fort Myers; hospital — 1,400. **Schlumberger Ltd.**

Inc. (Sangamo-Weston Div.); Sarasota; electronic communications equipment — 1,200. **Fort Myers Community Hospital;** Fort Myers; hospital — 1,000. **General Development Corp.;** Punta Gorda; real estate development — 700. **Lehigh Corp.** (HQ); Lehigh Acres; real estate development — 600. **Yoder Bros. Inc.;** Fort Myers; nursery products — 535. **South Seas Plantation Co.;** Captiva; resort — 500.

14th District

Southeast — West Palm Beach; Boca Raton

The old district, which took in most of Palm Beach County and northeastern Broward County, was swamped by more than 390,000 newcomers during the 1970s. So the remap dramatically shrank its territory. A substantial Republican vote remained, but the remap enhanced Democratic strength in the district.

Included in the new 14th are the coastal strip of southeast Palm Beach County and a string of inland communities in northeast Broward. The Palm Beach County vote is dominant; seven in 10 residents of the new 14th live there.

The southern halves of Palm Beach and West Palm Beach are included in the 14th. The pleasant environment has lured the headquarters of several corporations to the area, bringing in a cadre of young, well-paid business executives and a few support personnel.

South of Palm Beach, retirees living in the condominium communities of Boynton Beach and Delray Beach are a potent political force. Some of the people in these complexes are Irish and Italian but most are Jewish, and nearly all come from a Democratic political background in the Northeast. The voter turnout rate among the condominium residents is very high.

Boca Raton, the next major city down the coast, is an upper middle-class area that generally votes Republican. It is also home to electronics manufacturer IBM, the largest employer in the district. Boca Raton's Florida Atlantic University recently opened a new engineering building; the school hopes to train a pool of skilled workers that can attract more high-technology employers to the area.

Boynton Beach, Delray Beach and Boca Raton each grew by more than 70 percent during the 1970s, but that seems trifling compared to the incredible population boom in the Broward County parts of the 14th.

In Broward County, the 14th includes Coral Springs, Margate, Tamarac, and parts of North Lauderdale, Lauderhill and Sunrise. Population in each of these communities grew by 300 percent or more during the 1970s; Coral Springs, for example, jumped from 1,489 residents in 1970 to 37,349 in 1980. These communities are moderate-to-liberal Democratic.

Election Returns

14th District		Democrat		Republican	
1976	President	85,922	(49.0%)	86,375	(49.3%)
	Senate	90,619	(56.5%)	69,821	(43.5%)
	House	130,988	(91.3%)	1,108	(0.8%)
1978	Governor	85,286	(58.4%)	60,706	(41.6%)
	House	81,287	(55.3%)	65,717	(44.7%)
1980	President	82,934	(36.5%)	128,344	(56.5%)
	Senate	92,769	(43.0%)	122,924	(57.0%)
	House	131,456	(58.8%)	91,982	(41.2%)

14th District		Democrat		Republican	
1982	Governor	120,947	(64.2%)	67,532	(35.8%)
	Senate	116,806	(62.9%)	68,792	(37.1%)
	House	128,646	(73.0%)	47,560	(27.0%)

Demographics

Population: 512,803. **Percent Change from 1970:** 126.3%.

Land Area: 419 square miles. **Population per Square Mile:** 1,223.9.

Counties, 1980 Population: Broward (Pt.) — 141,670; Palm Beach (Pt.) — 371,133.

Cities, 1980 Population: Boca Raton — 49,505; Boynton Beach — 35,624; Coral Springs — 37,349; Delray Beach — 34,325; Lake Worth — 27,048; Lauderhill (Pt.) — 8,229; Margate — 36,044; North Lauderdale (Pt.) — 18,479; Sunrise (Pt.) — 5,106; Tamarac (Pt.) — 25,406; West Palm Beach (Pt.) — 25,279.

Race and Ancestry: White — 94.4%; Black — 4.1%; American Indian, Eskimo and Aleut — 0.1%; Asian and Pacific Islander — 0.5%. Spanish Origin — 4.6%. Dutch — 0.7%; English — 8.9%; French — 1.4%; German — 7.2%; Hungarian — 1.0%; Irish — 5.2%; Italian — 6.0%; Polish — 2.8%; Russian — 3.9%; Scottish — 0.8%; Swedish — 0.7%.

Universities, Enrollment: The College of Boca Raton, Boca Raton — 528; Florida Atlantic University, Boca Raton — 7,550; Palm Beach Atlantic College, West Palm Beach — 641; Palm Beach Junior College, Lake Worth — 10,259; Seminary of Saint Vincent de Paul, Boynton Beach — 99.

Newspapers, Circulation: *Boca Raton News* (eS), Boca Raton — 12,555; *Evening Times* (eS), West Palm Beach — 29,796; *Palm Beach Daily News* (mS), Palm Beach — 4,511; *Post* (mS), West Palm Beach — 86,580. *Fort Lauderdale News,* Fort Lauderale *Sun Sentinel, Hollywood Sun Tattler, The Miami Herald* and *The Miami News* also circulate in the district.

Commercial Television Stations, Affiliation: District is divided between West Palm Beach ADI and Miami ADI.

Industries:

International Business Machines Corp.; Boca Raton; electronic computing equipment — 4,500. **Arvida Corp.;** Boca Raton; hotel — 1,500. **Arvida Corp.;** Boca Raton; real estate development — 1,200. **Modular Computer Systems Inc.** (HQ); Fort Lauderdale; computers — 900. **Palm Beach Newspapers Inc.;** West Palm Beach; newspaper publishing — 800.

Systems Engineering Labs (HQ); Fort Lauderdale; mini-computer equipment — 700. **National Enquirer Inc.** (HQ); Lake Worth; newspaper publishing — 600. **Cenvill Communities Inc.;** Boca Raton; operative builder — 500. **Siemens Corp.** (Telecommunications Div.); Boca Raton; research laboratory — 500.

15th District

Southeast — Fort Lauderdale

The new 15th was carved out of the old 12th District. Gone is the Democratic city of Hollywood in south Broward County; added are the oceanside communities of Pompano Beach and Deerfield Beach, north Broward County towns that buoyed Republican strength.

A Republican's biggest obstacle at election time in the new 15th is the well-organized Democratic political clubs based in the district's condominium communities. A Republican hoping to crack the condominium vote is pitted against the lifelong Democratic habits held by many of the northeasteners who have migrated here, attracted by advertising campaigns in the New York media.

Fort Lauderdale delivers solid Republican margins. Among the city's obvious signs of affluence are the private yachts that ply local waterways. Less obvious is the work of the investment managers who are kept busy overseeing the stock portfolios and trust funds held by wealthy residents of the city. But Fort Lauderdale has a substantial minority population; the blacks and Hispanics who walk its faded downtown streets live in a different world from the people who browse through the fashionable stores of Las Olas on the waterfront a short distance away. In recent years, some of Miami's drug traffic has migrated north to Fort Lauderdale, making some residents wealthy but creating an issue of political concern for most voters.

Fort Lauderdale's manufacturing sector concentrates on production of computer software, electronic circuitry and communications equipment. And the youth pilgrimage to its beaches every Easter serves to remind that tourism is an economic mainstay.

While the population of Fort Lauderdale increased nearly 10 percent during the 1970s, much more rapid growth in nearby Broward County towns defied planners' attempts to think ahead. What has grown up in Broward is a suburban metropolis with many people but not much personality, a sprawling accumulation of subdivisions, condominiums and shopping centers.

Broward County officials learned in 1981 that citizens are not much interested in paying to meet the burdens of growth. With demands for services stretching county government to the breaking point, the board agreed to increase county spending substantially and raise property taxes an average of 29 percent to pay the bills. Four thousand Broward Countians stormed the commission's meeting to protest the tax increase, and the board was later forced to endure a recall election, which it survived.

Election Returns

15th District		Democrat		Republican	
1976	President	82,690	(50.6%)	78,474	(48.1%)
	Senate	93,339	(63.1%)	54,611	(36.9%)
	House	85,065	(58.0%)	55,871	(38.1%)
1978	Governor	95,674	(63.5%)	54,991	(36.5%)
	House	77,527	(59.4%)	53,099	(40.6%)
1980	President	77,192	(35.8%)	123,753	(57.4%)
	Senate	94,745	(48.2%)	101,918	(51.8%)
	House	93,636	(51.2%)	89,401	(48.8%)
1982	Governor	92,697	(61.3%)	58,421	(38.7%)
	Senate	90,970	(60.0%)	60,076	(39.6%)
	House	67,083	(42.9%)	89,158	(57.1%)

Demographics

Population: 512,950. **Percent Change from 1970:** 34.0%.

Land Area: 169 square miles. **Population per Square Mile:** 3,035.2.

Counties, 1980 Population: Broward (Pt.) — 512,950.

Cities, 1980 Population: Dania (Pt.) — 1,360; Deerfield Beach — 39,193; Fort Lauderdale — 153,279; Hollywood (Pt.) — 1; Lauderdale Lakes — 25,426; Lauderhill (Pt.) — 29,042; Lighthouse Point — 11,488; North Lauderdale (Pt.) — 0; Oakland Park — 23,035; Plantation (Pt.) — 29,713; Pompano Beach — 52,618; Sunrise (Pt.) — 14,049; Tamarac (Pt.) — 3,970; Wilton Manors — 12,742.

Race and Ancestry: White — 81.0%; Black — 17.8%; American Indian, Eskimo and Aleut — 0.1%; Asian and Pacific Islander — 0.4%. Spanish Origin — 3.4%. Dutch — 0.5%; English — 8.6%; French — 1.4%; German — 7.0%; Hungarian — 0.8%; Irish — 4.8%; Italian — 5.4%; Polish — 2.4%; Russian — 2.9%; Scottish — 0.7%; Swedish — 0.6%.

Universities, Enrollment: Art Institute of Fort Lauderdale, Fort Lauderdale — 1,172; Broward Community College, Fort Lauderdale — 20,848; Fort Lauderdale College, Fort Lauderdale — 1,140.

Newspapers, Circulation: *Fort Lauderdale News* (eS), Fort Lauderdale — 99,453; *Sun-Sentinel* (m), Fort Lauderdale — 68,053. *Hollywood Sun-Tattler*, *The Miami Herald* and *The Miami News* also circulate in the district.

Commercial Television Stations, Affiliation: Entire district is located in Miami ADI.

Industries:

Motorola Inc. (Communications Div.); Fort Lauderdale; electronic communications equipment — 3,000. **Gould Inc.;** Plantation; computer services — 2,000. **Broward General Medical Center;** Fort Lauderdale; hospital — 1,800. **Bendix Corp.** (Avionics Div.); Fort Lauderdale; electronic communications equipment — 1,500. **Gore Newspapers Co.;** Fort Lauderdale; newspaper publishing — 1,500.

Holy Cross Hospital Inc.; Fort Lauderdale; hospital — 1,420. **Current Builders Inc.;** Fort Lauderdale; general contracting — 1,000. **Florida Medical Center Inc.;** Fort Lauderdale; hospital — 1,000. **Harris Corp.** (Computer Systems Div.); Fort Lauderdale; computers — 900. **F P A Corp.** (HQ); Pompano Beach; real estate development — 600. **Eastern Shores Food Corp.** (HQ); Fort Lauderdale; poultry processing — 550. **Sensormatic Electronics Corp.** (HQ); Deerfield Beach; shoplifting detection equipment — 540. **Peerless Electric Co. Inc.;** Pompano Beach; electrical contracting — 524. **Coral Ridge Properties Inc.** (HQ); Pompano Beach; land development — 500. **Gill Hotels Inc.;** Fort Lauderdale; hotel — 500. **Itek Corp.** (Ophthalmic Products Div.); Fort Lauderdale; ophthalmic goods — 500.

16th District

Southeast — Hollywood; Part of Dade County

The Legislature designed this seat to favor the Democratic Party. Anchored in Hollywood, it includes the towns of Pembroke Pines and Miramar and most of Dania and Hallandale, a collection that takes in many of the heavily Jewish, predominantly Democratic condominium areas of south Broward County.

The district reaches south into Dade County, incorporating the strongly Cuban Westchester and Sweetwater areas. These conservative communities may give the Dade segment of the district a Republican tilt, but since fewer than one-third of the residents in the new 16th live in Dade, Democrats should control the seat with solid margins in the Broward County part of the district.

After years in the shadow of larger Fort Lauderdale, Hollywood finally has a district it dominates. The city is different from the rest of Broward County; it does not have as much strip development, and it has more areas with single-family homes that offer a feeling of community. Rapid development of the city's southern beachfront in the 1960s and early 1970s packed it with condominiums. But a strain on roads and services induced a wave of anti-development sentiment that led local officials to restrict development of the city's northern beach.

This part of Broward County has a larger Jewish community than the part in the 15th District, which drew most of its population from among Midwestern Protestants and

Irish Catholics in the first big postwar migration. The voters who have come to the 16th are Eastern, urban oriented and generally liberal.

The district also has some traditional Deep South Democrats in communities such as Dania, an old tomato marketing town somewhat bewildered by all the growth around it. Voters in Dania contribute to the Democratic vote, even though they have little in common with the recent Democratic arrivals.

Election Returns

16th District		Democrat		Republican	
1976	President	90,882	(54.8%)	72.721	(43.8%)
	Senate	99,846	(66.4%)	50,508	(33.6%)
	House	87,383	(58.0%)	62,632	(41.6%)
1978	Governor	91,381	(65.3%)	48,593	(34.7%)
	House	70,241	(63.8%)	39,797	(36.2%)
1980	President	65,583	(34.6%)	107,954	(57.0%)
	Senate	84,631	(45.3%)	102,216	(54.7%)
	House	90,070	(52.8%)	80,636	(47.2%)
1982	Governor	91,999	(69.1%)	41,200	(30.9%)
	Senate	89,010	(68.7%)	40,289	(31.1%)
	House	91,888	(67.9%)	43,458	(32.0%)

Demographics

Population: 513,365. **Percent Change from 1970:** 74.6%.

Land Area: 1,507 square miles. **Population per Square Mile:** 340.7.

Counties, 1980 Population: Broward (Pt.) — 363,580; Dade (Pt.) — 149,785.

Cities, 1980 Population: Cooper City — 10,140; Dania (Pt.) — 10,451; Davie — 20,877; Hallandale (Pt.) — 36,460; Hollywood (Pt.) — 121,322; Miramar — 32,813; Pembroke Pines — 35,776; Plantation (Pt.) — 18,788; Sunrise (Pt.) — 20,526.

Race and Ancestry: White — 92.7%; Black — 5.0%; American Indian, Eskimo and Aleut — 0.2%; Asian and Pacific Islander — 0.5%. Spanish Origin — 21.0%. English — 5.9%; French — 1.3%; German — 4.9%; Hungarian — 1.0%; Irish — 3.7%; Italian — 6.9%; Polish — 2.4%; Russian — 3.5%; Scottish — 0.5%.

Universities, Enrollment: Florida International University, Sweetwater — 11,606; Nova University, Fort Lauderdale — 5,040; Prospect Hall College, Hollywood — 540; St. John Vianney College Seminary, Coral Way Village — 53.

Newspapers, Circulation: *Hollywood Sun-Tattler* (e), Hollywood — 40,373. *Fort Lauderdale News*, Fort Lauderdale *Sun Sentinel*, *The Miami Herald* and *The Miami News* also circulate in the district.

Commercial Television Stations, Affiliation: WHFT, Pembroke Park (None); WKID, Fort Lauderdale (None). Entire district is located in Miami ADI.

Industries:

American Express Co. Inc.; Fort Lauderdale; credit card operations — 2,700. **Racal-Milgo Inc.** (HQ); Sweetwater; data communications equipment — 2,400. **South Broward Hospital District;** Hollywood; hospital — 2,130. **South Florida State Hospital;** Hollywood; state psychiatric hospital — 1,550. **B. E. Hensley Forming Co. Inc.;** Hallandale; special trade contracting — 1,100.

Ryder Truck Rental Inc. (HQ); Sweetwater; truck rental — 969. **A N P Building Service Inc.;** Sweetwater; janitorial services — 600. **Intercontinental Hotels Corp.;** Fort Lauderdale; hotel — 600. **Nationwide Construction Inc.;** Sweetwater; heavy construction — 550. **Cordis Corp.** (HQ); Sweetwater; cardiac pacemakers — 500.

17th District

Southeast — North Miami, Part of Hialeah

The 17th is the strongest Democratic district in Dade County, thanks to the overwhelming turnouts among condominium residents who make this constituency the single most concentrated source of condominium votes in Florida.

All along the Dade County coast, from Golden Beach through North Miami Beach and North Miami down to Miami Shores, entire buildings seem to empty out as their people flock to the polls on election day. Some condominiums turn out so many people they become precincts in themselves, with the voting machines placed in their lobbies or recreation rooms.

Many of the condominium residents are middle-income retired people from the urban Northeast who maintain their lifelong Democratic voting habits. A sizable number — about one-quarter of the district's overall population — is Jewish.

About 80 percent of the condominium residents in the 17th vote a liberal Democratic line, and their combined tally can give a Democrat a lead of upwards of 30,000 votes in the district.

Also contributing to the Democratic majority in the 17th is the black population, which at 27 percent amounts to the second largest concentration of blacks in any of the Florida districts. About one-quarter of the electorate is Hispanic. In addition to the condominium-filled waterfront area, the district takes in the northern tip of Miami (down to N.W. 62nd Street) and suburban communities such as Opa-Locka and most of Hialeah.

Election Returns

17th District		Democrat		Republican	
1976	President	114,887	(65.6%)	57,720	(33.0%)
	Senate	107,396	(73.1%)	39,588	(26.9%)
	House	109,941	(77.8%)	31,373	(22.2%)
1978	Governor	98,369	(78.8%)	26,544	(21.2%)
	House	3,260	(63.1%)	1,904	(36.9%)
1980	President	82,646	(50.7%)	66,317	(40.7%)
	Senate	94,194	(62.0%)	57,770	(38.0%)
	House	113,280	(75.3%)	36,984	(24.6%)
1982	Governor	82,404	(78.0%)	23,196	(22.0%)
	Senate	81,526	(78.7%)	22,046	(21.3%)
	House	x[1]		—[1]	

[1] *No votes tabulated where candidate was unopposed; x indicates winner.*

Demographics

Population: 513,048. **Percent Change from 1970:** 25.6%.

Land Area: 106 square miles. **Population per Square Mile:** 4,840.1.

Counties, 1980 Population: Dade (Pt.) — 513,048.

Cities, 1980 Population: Hallandale (Pt.) — 57; Hialeah (Pt.) — 98,038; Miami (Pt.) — 34,081; North Miami — 42,566; North Miami Beach — 36,553; Opa-Locka — 14,460.

Race and Ancestry: White — 69.2%; Black — 26.7%; American Indian, Eskimo and Aleut — 0.1%; Asian and Pacific Islander — 0.7%. Spanish Origin — 24.7%. English — 4.6%; French — 0.9%; German

Miami Area

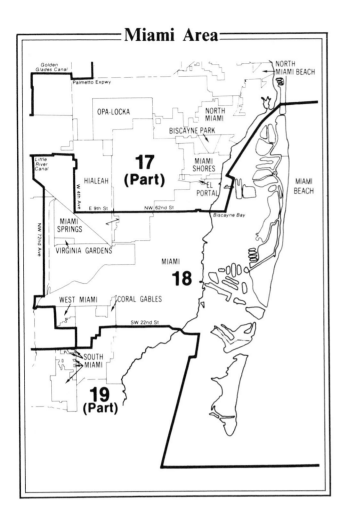

— 2.7%; Hungarian — 0.8%; Irish — 2.1%; Italian — 3.0%; Polish — 2.1%; Russian — 3.1%.

Universities, Enrollment: Barry College, Miami — 2,197; Biscayne College, Miami — 2,164; Florida Memorial College, Opa-Locka — 765; International Fine Arts College, Miami — 248; Miami Christian College, Miami — 263.

Newspapers, Circulation: *The Miami Herald* and *The Miami News* circulate in the district.

Commercial Television Stations, Affiliation: WCKT, Miami (NBC); WLTV, Miami (None, Spanish). Entire district is located in Miami ADI. *(For other Miami stations, see 18th district.)*

Industries:
Suave Shoe Corp. (HQ); Hialeah; footwear — 1,600. **Parkway General Hospital;** Miami; hospital — 1,380. **Palmetto General Hospital;** Hialeah; hospital — 1,200. **Injection Footwear Corp.** (HQ); Miami; rubber, plastic footwear — 1,190. **Northshore Medical Center Inc.;** Miami; hospital — 1,000.

Niki-Lu Industries Inc. (Miami Lakes Fashions - HQ); Hialeah; women's knitwear — 800. **First State Banking Corp.;** Miami; banking — 650. **Publix Supermarket Inc.;** Miami; warehouse — 600. **Western Electric Co. Inc.;** Miami; telephone equipment distributing — 600. **Solomon Corp.** (HQ); Miami; women's hosiery, footwear — 600. **Capeletti Bros. Inc.;** Hialeah; general contracting — 510. **A F A Consolidated Corp.** (Consumer & Closure Div. - HQ); Hialeah; hand sprayers — 500. **Alterman Transport Lines Inc.** (HQ); Opa-Locka; trucking — 500. **Jefferson Stores Inc.** (HQ); Miami; department store chain — 500. **Bennett M. Lifter Inc.;** Miami; hotel — 500. **Julius Resnick of Florida Inc.;** Opa-Locka; women's handbags — 500.

18th District

Southeast — Miami and Miami Beach

This is the core of the Cuban community in the Miami area, and it is a potentially important source of Republican votes. There are plenty of anti-Castro Cubans in Miami who have not trusted the Democratic Party since the Bay of Pigs invasion under President Kennedy in 1962. But Miami's conservative Cubans have not emerged with political influence proportional to their numbers. The 18th, which contains most of Miami and Miami Beach, has a number of different sides to its personality. Most noticeable is Little Havana, centered on Miami's S.W. 8th Street in the southern part of the district. English is a second language here and in many other parts of the district. In all, people of Hispanic origin account for more than half the population.

Many of the long-established Cubans in Miami came to this country in the early 1960s fleeing Fidel Castro's takeover. They were well-educated professionals and businessmen in their homeland, and they have achieved positions of status here. Cubans, Puerto Ricans and Haitians who have arrived recently tend to be unskilled workers, and integrating them into society is more difficult. There are tensions between the middle-class and underclass Cuban communities.

In the central part of the district is Liberty City, the black neighborhood that erupted in three days of rioting in May of 1980, leaving 18 dead. The violence began when a restive black community was infuriated by an all-white jury's decision to acquit four white Miami police officers in the beating death of a black insurance executive. The Chamber of Commerce has been pushing a program to create jobs for blacks and to promote black business ownership, but three years after the riots, the grim mood and appearance of Liberty City persists. About 16 percent of the people in the district are black.

Downtown Miami is going through a building boom, especially along Brickell Avenue, where a number of international financial institutions are establishing bases to take advantage of Miami's extensive commercial dealings with the Caribbean and with Central and South America. The city's emergence as a major center for trade in the Western Hemisphere has given its downtown area a vitality it lacked even five years ago.

Miami Beach is the part of the district that accounts for its high median age — 44 years. The Jewish community, which gives Miami Beach its New York flavor, usually prefers candidates who are moderately liberal on social issues, conservative on defense and strongly supportive of Israel.

Election Returns

18th District		Democrat		Republican	
1976	President	78,436	(55.0%)	62,204	(43.6%)
	Senate	77,398	(65.5%)	40,677	(34.4%)
	House	85,864	(72.4%)	32,792	(27.6%)
1978	Governor	75,712	(67.2%)	36,951	(32.8%)
	House	68,081	(65.2%)	36,407	(34.8%)
1980	President	58,549	(40.4%)	75,799	(52.3%)
	Senate	70,289	(51.5%)	66,113	(48.5%)
	House	100,851	(75.0%)	33,691	(25.0%)

18th District		Democrat		Republican	
1982	Governor	75,967	(72.7%)	28,640	(27.4%)
	Senate	73,122	(73.1%)	26,913	(26.9%)
	House	72,183	(71.2%)	29,196	(28.8%)

Demographics

Population: 513,250. **Percent Change from 1970:** 6.4%.

Land Area: 58 square miles. **Population per Square Mile:** 8,849.1.

Counties, 1980 Population: Dade (Pt.) — 513,250.

Cities, 1980 Population: Coral Gables (Pt.) — 17,022; Hialeah (Pt.) — 47,216; Miami (Pt.) — 277,335; Miami Beach — 96,298; Miami Springs — 12,350.

Race and Ancestry: White — 77.1%; Black — 15.8%; American Indian, Eskimo and Aleut — 0.1%; Asian and Pacific Islander — 0.6%. Spanish Origin — 50.7%. English — 3.1%; French — 0.7%; German — 1.9%; Hungarian — 0.8%; Irish — 1.1%; Italian — 1.3%; Polish — 2.1%; Russian — 3.7%.

Universities, Enrollment: Bauder Fashion College, Miami — 497; Florida Career Institute, Miami — 1,000.

Newspapers, Circulation: *The Miami Herald* (mS), Miami — 421,751; *The Miami News* (e), Miami — 58,989. Foreign language newspaper: *Diario Las Americas* (Spanish), Miami — 54,913.

Commercial Television Stations, Affiliation: WCIX-TV, Miami (None); WLRN-TV, Miami (None, Spanish); WLTV, Miami (None, Spanish); WPLG, Miami (ABC); WTVJ, Miami (CBS). Entire district is located in Miami ADI. *(For other Miami stations, see 17th district.)*

Industries:

Eastern Air Lines Inc. (HQ); Miami; commercial airline — 13,000. **G D V Inc.;** Miami; real estate holding company — 2,620. **Mount Sinai Hospital of Greater Miami;** Miami; hospital — 2,600. **Knight-Ridder Newspapers Inc.** (HQ); Miami; newspaper publishing — 2,500. **Veterans Administration;** Miami; veterans' hospital — 2,100.

Coulter Electronics Inc. (Coulter Diagnostics - HQ); Hialeah; scientific instruments — 1,800. **Southeast Banking Corp.** (HQ); Miami; bank holding company — 1,700. **Cedars of Lebanon Hospital;** Miami; hospital — 1,600. **Trusthouse Forte Inc.;** Miami; hotel — 1,500. **American Hospital Supply Corp.;** Miami; health care products — 1,200. **Miami Heart Institute;** Miami; hospital — 1,070. **Arco Metals Co.** (Extruded Products Div.); Miami; aluminum extruded products — 1,000. **Bobbie Brooks Inc.** (Miss Brooks); Hialeah; women's knitwear — 1,000. **Fontainebleau Hotel;** Miami Beach; hotel — 1,000. **Republic Airlines Inc.;** Miami; commercial airline — 1,000. **Whittaker Corp.** (Bertram Yacht Div.); Miami; shipbuilding — 1,000.

Deltona's Mackle-Built Construction; Miami; general contracting — 818. **The Sheraton Corp.** (Bal Harbour Hotel); Miami; hotel — 750. **Reynolds Metals Co.** (Can Reclamation Center); Miami; aluminum production — 715. **Gator Shoe Corp.** (HQ); Hialeah; rubber-soled tennis shoes — 700. **Doral Beach Hotel Corp.;** Miami Beach; hotel — 650. **Carillon Hotel;** Miami Beach; hotel — 600. **Joy Footwear Corp.** (Casino Casuals); Hialeah; footwear — 590. **American Bankers Life Assurance of Florida** (HQ); Miami; life insurance — 550. **Florida Building Services Inc.;** Coral Gables; janitorial services — 535. **Intercontinental Hotels;** Miami; hotel — 500. **Wometco Enterprises Inc.** (HQ); Miami; soft drink bottling — 500.

19th District

South — Coral Gables, Key West

Once the district for the whole Miami area, the 19th is now composed of the city's southern suburbs and rural country extending to the Florida Keys. There are still plenty of Democratic votes in the 19th but, with the liberal areas of Miami and Miami Beach gone, the remaining voters are more conservative and may be tempted to vote Republican.

Some of the conservative Democrats are preoccupied with south Florida's frustrating refugee problem. The symbol of that problem is located in the 19th — the Krome Avenue detention center, where about 400 Haitians were held until a federal judge in June 1982 ordered their release under the supervision of local relief agencies.

The state took in some 150,000 Cuban and Haitian refugees between 1980 and 1982, and many Floridians were enraged that, within days of their departure from Krome Avenue, some of the Haitians showed up at local welfare offices seeking assistance.

Much of the land in the 19th district is taken up by the Everglades National Park; the people live in eastern Dade County suburbs or farming areas or are scattered through the Florida Keys.

Coral Gables has liberal academics around the University of Miami, and there are poor and middle-class black neighborhoods as well as a large Cuban community. The Jewish vote in the Kendall area is sizable. Homestead and Florida City are markets for a vegetable and fruit-growing area and the domain of traditional rural Democratic voters.

In the Keys (Monroe County) there is a dispute over development policies. Some who have retired to the area want to discourage growth to preserve the islands in their current state. They are opposed by the Conchs, Keys' natives who see tourism and development as their livelihood and want to encourage growth.

Election Returns

19th District		Democrat		Republican	
1976	President	84,684	(53.6%)	70,567	(44.7%)
	Senate	91,812	(66.6%)	45,950	(33.4%)
	House	94,381	(70.4%)	39,618	(29.6%)
1978	Governor	77,345	(64.6%)	42,442	(35.4%)
	House	83,826	(73.5%)	30,239	(26.5%)
1980	President	56,728	(34.0%)	90,859	(54.5%)
	Senate	74,583	(46.6%)	85,501	(53.4%)
	House	105,105	(65.5%)	55,333	(34.5%)
1982	Governor	83,975	(68.1%)	39,407	(31.9%)
	Senate	80,165	(66.2%)	41,001	(33.8%)
	House	74,274	(58.8%)	51,969	(41.1%)

Demographics

Population: 512,886. **Percent Change from 1970:** 45.0%.

Land Area: 2,258 square miles. **Population per Square Mile:** 227.1.

Counties, 1980 Population: Dade (Pt.) — 449,698; Monroe — 63,188.

Cities, 1980 Population: Coral Gables (Pt.) — 26,219; Homestead — 20,668; Key West — 24,382; Miami (Pt.) — 35,449; South Miami — 10,944.

Race and Ancestry: White — 84.0%; Black — 12.0%; American Indian, Eskimo and Aleut — 0.1%; Asian and Pacific Islander — 1.4%. Spanish Origin — 21.8%. English — 8.1%; French — 1.0%; German — 4.6%; Hungarian — 0.5%; Irish — 3.4%; Italian — 2.3%; Polish — 1.2%; Russian — 1.8%; Scottish — 0.5%.

Universities, Enrollment: Florida Keys Community College, Key West — 1,918; Miami-Dade Community College, Miami — 35,536; University of Miami, Coral Gables — 15,970.

Newspapers, Circulation: *Key West Citizen* (eS), Key West — 7,089; *The South Dade News Leader* (e), Homestead — 13,821. *The Miami Herald* and *The Miami News* also circulate in the district.

Commercial Television Stations, Affiliation: WTKW, Key West (None). Entire district is located in Miami ADI.

Military Installations: Cudjoe Key Air Force Station, Perky — 14; Homestead Air Force Base, Homestead — 7,565; Homestead Naval Security Group, Homestead — 279; Key West Naval Air Station, Key West — 3,394.

Nuclear Power Plants: Turkey Point 3, Turkey Point (Westinghouse, Bechtel), December 1972; Turkey Point 4, Turkey Point (Westinghouse, Bechtel), September 1973.

Industries:

Mercy Hospital Inc.; Miami; hospital — 1,600. **South Miami Hospital Foundation;** Miami; hospital — 1,500. **Baptist Hospital of Miami Inc.;** Miami; hospital — 1,410. **Burger King Corp.** (HQ); Miami; fast food operation — 1,100. **The Wackenhut Corp.** (HQ); Miami; security services — 800. **Lennar Corp.** (HQ); Miami; real estate development — 516. **Ocean Reef Club Inc.;** Key Largo; resort, real estate development — 500.

Georgia

Controversy over creation of a black-majority district in Atlanta touched off a dispute that delayed House elections in the city's two congressional districts until Nov. 30, 1982, nearly a month after the regular general elections.

Georgia gained almost a million people in the 1970s, experiencing an overall 19.1 percent population growth, but it did not qualify for an 11th House seat, so black leaders tried to persuade the Legislature to carve a black-majority seat out of the existing ten. Nearly 27 percent of the state's population is black, but the one district that elected a black representative during the 1970s, the Atlanta-based 5th, was the most underpopulated constituency, falling 126,000 residents short of the ideal district size.

Blacks in the Legislature, led by state Sen. Julian Bond of Atlanta, sought to create a heavily black district in the Atlanta area to try to guarantee the election of a black to Congress. The state's House delegation has been all white since 1977, when Democrat Wyche Fowler won the 5th in a special election, replacing Andrew Young (D), who had joined President Carter's Cabinet.

Bond persuaded the state Senate to accept a plan that would have established a 69 percent black district in Atlanta and its southeast suburbs. But this map also would have thrown two incumbent Democratic representatives into the 4th District, which probably would not have included enough Democrats to elect either one of them. The two incumbents objected strenuously, and other critics accused Bond of trying to assure a safe district for himself in 1982 or later.

The Bond plan went nowhere in the Georgia House. A House reapportionment committee rejected it decisively and voted instead to make minor population adjustments throughout the state. In House-Senate conference, legislators finally settled on a map relatively close to what the House wanted. It gave the 5th District a 57 percent black majority, slightly greater than the 50 percent determined by previous district lines. The 4th District was left largely unchanged.

This plan cleared the Legislature on Sept. 17, 1981, and Democratic Governor George Busbee signed it into law five days later.

Bond appealed to the U.S. Department of Justice, which has jurisdiction over Georgia's redistricting as a result of the 1965 Voting Rights Act. He argued that the new map would deny blacks a fair chance of electing a U.S. representative by dividing their voting strength among two congressional districts. The appeal received some initial support from white Republicans, but was denounced by most liberal Democrats. The Atlanta *Constitution* accused Bond of trying to create a "ghetto" district and engaging in black racism.

In February 1982 the Justice Department disallowed the Georgia Legislature's plan. A three-judge federal panel concurred late in July. The state appealed this decision to the Supreme Court, which affirmed the lower court ruling Jan. 24, 1983.

Working under the federal panel's order to submit a new redistricting plan by Aug. 11, the Georgia Legislature Aug. 8 approved a remap of the 4th and 5th congressional districts in the Atlanta area. Under the new plan, the proportion of blacks in the 5th district was increased from 57 to 65 percent. The new plan was approved by the federal court and the Justice Department. Primaries in the eight unaffected districts — suspended at one point during the dispute — were rescheduled for Aug. 31.

Primaries in the 4th and 5th districts were conducted Nov. 2; ironically the white incumbent in the 5th received no primary challenge. Although two black independents did appear on the ballot in the Nov. 30 general election, the incumbent had little to worry about. He exceeded 75 percent of the vote even in some black precincts and coasted to victory with over 80 percent districtwide.

Age of Population

District	Population Under 18	Voting Age Population	Population 65 & Over (% of VAP)	Median Age
1	165,923	375,257	55,349 (14.7%)	27.7
2	180,371	369,606	60,160 (16.3%)	27.8
3	164,737	376,128	53,146 (14.1%)	27.8
4	142,665	399,703	44,801 (11.2%)	30.4
5	159,932	390,138	52,426 (13.4%)	28.3
6	173,750	375,209	44,363 (11.8%)	28.5
7	160,361	385,552	42,933 (11.1%)	29.7
8	168,996	372,727	62,836 (16.9%)	29.1
9	167,194	384,588	55,248 (14.4%)	29.9
10	162,201	388,067	45,469 (11.7%)	27.4
State	1,646,130	3,816,975	516,731 (13.5%)	28.7

GEORGIA

DADE
CA-TOO-SA
WHITFIELD
Dalton
MURRAY
FANNIN
UNION
TOWNS
RABUN

WALKER
7
CHATTOOGA
Dalton
GORDON
GILMER
PICKENS
LUMPKIN
DAWSON
WHITE
9
HALL
HABERSHAM
STEPHENS
BANKS
FRANKLIN
HART

FLOYD
Rome
BARTOW
CHEROKEE
FORSYTH
JACKSON
MADISON
ELBERT

POLK
PAULDING
Marietta
COBB
FULTON
GWINNETT
BARROW
CLARKE
Athens
OCONEE
OGLETHORPE
LINCOLN

HARALSON
6
DOUGLAS
5
DE KALB
4
WALTON
MORGAN
GREENE
10
WILKES
TALIA-FERRO
COLUMBIA

CARROLL
Atlanta
CLAYTON
FAY-ETTE
ROCK-DALE
NEWTON
McDUFFIE
WARREN
RICH-MOND
Augusta

HEARD
COWETA
HENRY
Griffin
SPALDING
BUTTS
JASPER
PUTNAM
HANCOCK
JEFFERSON
BURKE

TROUP
MERIWETHER
PIKE
LAMAR
MONROE
JONES
BALDWIN
WASHINGTON

UPSON
Macon
BIBB
WILKINSON
JOHNSON
EMANUEL
JENKINS
SCREVEN

HARRIS
TALBOT
CRAWFORD
PEACH
Warner Robins
TWIGGS
CANDLER
BULLOCH
EFFINGHAM

Columbus
MUS-COGEE
3
TAYLOR
MACON
HOUSTON
BLECKLEY
LAURENS
8
WHEELER
TREUTLEN
MONTGOMERY
TOOMBS
EVANS
1
BRYAN
Savannah
CHATHAM

CHATTA-HOOCHEE
MARION
SCHLEY
DOOLY
PULASKI
DODGE
TATTNALL
LIBERTY

STEWART
WEBSTER
SUMTER
CRISP
WILCOX
TELFAIR
JEFF DAVIS
APPLING
WAYNE
LONG
McINTOSH

QUIT-MAN
TERRELL
LEE
TURNER
BEN HILL
IRWIN
COFFEE
BACON
PIERCE
GLYNN

RANDOLPH
Albany
DOUGHERTY
2
WORTH
TIFT
BERRIEN
ATKINSON
WARE
BRANTLEY
CAMDEN

CLAY
CALHOUN
EARLY
BAKER
MITCHELL
COLQUITT
COOK
LANIER
CLINCH
CHARLTON

MILLER
SEMINOLE
DECATUR
GRADY
THOMAS
BROOKS
Valdosta
LOWNDES
ECHOLS

Income and Occupation

District	Median Family Income	White Collar Workers	Blue Collar Workers	Service Workers	Farm Workers
1	$ 15,112	45.5%	36.0%	14.1%	4.4%
2	14,440	41.9	37.2	12.6	8.3
3	16,069	45.0	38.1	13.4	3.5
4	24,538	70.1	19.9	9.3	0.6
5	15,431	55.2	26.5	17.7	0.7
6	19,410	48.6	39.4	10.9	1.1
7	20,296	55.0	34.0	10.0	1.0
8	15,075	42.9	39.0	13.0	5.2
9	16,943	41.4	45.5	9.6	3.5
10	17,935	52.1	33.6	12.3	2.0
State	$ 17,414	50.4%	34.6%	12.1%	2.9%

Education: School Years Completed

District	8 Years or Fewer	4 Years of High School	4 Years of College or More	Median School Years
1	25.3%	30.0%	11.4%	12.1
2	29.9	26.6	9.9	11.9
3	26.5	29.5	11.4	12.1
4	9.5	26.7	30.1	13.0
5	19.9	27.9	19.0	12.4
6	22.3	32.7	10.2	12.2
7	20.9	29.7	16.2	12.3
8	31.2	26.9	9.8	11.9
9	30.9	26.5	9.8	11.9
10	21.7	28.7	16.8	12.3
State	23.7%	28.5%	14.6%	12.2

Housing and Residential Patterns

District	Owner Occupied	Renter Occupied	Urban	Rural
1	64.0%	36.0%	59.1%	40.9%
2	64.9	35.1	50.2	49.8
3	64.4	35.6	64.2	35.8
4	60.8	39.2	87.2	12.8
5	46.5	53.5	97.6	2.4
6	70.1	29.9	57.9	42.1
7	69.8	30.2	70.7	29.3
8	68.1	31.9	48.2	51.8
9	76.8	23.2	22.2	77.8
10	65.9	34.1	67.0	33.0
State	65.0%	35.0%	62.4%	37.6%

1st District

Southeast — Savannah, Brunswick

The 1st District includes the city of Savannah, a significant Atlantic port as well as a tourist center, and the Golden Isles, Georgia's only seacoast. But the district also runs nearly 100 miles inland into the state's heavily-black rural counties.

Savannah, which celebrated its 250th anniversary in 1983, is one-half black and strongly unionized. Like other cities of the coastal South, it is a surprising ethnic melting pot, including Irish Catholics, French Huguenots and a substantial Jewish community. The mayor in 1983 was of Greek descent.

Republican candidates are beginning to do well in the Savannah area. Chatham County, which includes Savannah, went for Republican Mack Mattingly for the Senate in 1980 in his successful campaign against Democratic incumbent Herman E. Talmadge. The district's two fastest-growing counties in recent years have been Bryan and Liberty, narrow strips of land that contain Savannah suburbs but jut out from the coast into the cotton- and peanut-growing inland region.

The inland portion of the district, where blacks are a near majority in some counties, remains heavily Democratic. Talmadge carried some of these counties by 2-1 margins in 1980, allowing him to draw an overall 56 percent in the counties of the redrawn 1st District. The new 1st District is one-third black.

Under the new map, the 1st District gained Wayne and Brantley counties, but lost Johnson and Charlton counties, for a net population gain of about 13,000. No political changes are likely.

Election Returns

1st District		Democrat		Republican	
1976	President	92,126	(66.3%)	46,777	(33.7%)
	House	75,506	(98.0%)	1,442	(1.9%)
1978	Governor	43,476	(83.8%)	8,422	(16.2%)
	Senate	44,629	(83.6%)	8,731	(16.4%)
	House	37,566	(100.0%)	—	
1980	President	82,446	(55.3%)	63,003	(42.3%)
	Senate	81,506	(56.2%)	63,518	(43.8%)
	House	83,569	(98.5%)	1,262	(1.5 %)
1982	Governor	65,984	(59.2%)	45,410	(40.8%)
	House	65,625	(64.1%)	36,799	(35.9%)

Demographics

Population: 541,180. **Percent Change from 1970:** 15.9%.

Land Area: 9,604 square miles. **Population per Square Mile:** 56.3.

Counties, 1980 Population: Brantley — 8,701; Bryan — 10,175; Bulloch — 35,785; Burke — 19,349; Camden — 13,371; Candler — 7,518; Chatham — 202,226; Effingham — 18,327; Emanuel — 20,795; Evans — 8,428; Glynn — 54,981; Jenkins — 8,841; Liberty — 37,583; Long — 4,524; McIntosh — 8,046; Montgomery — 7,011; Screven — 14,043; Tattnall — 18,134; Toombs — 22,592; Wayne — 20,750.

Cities, 1980 Population: Brunswick — 17,605; Hinesville — 11,309; Savannah — 141,390; Statesboro — 14,866; Vidalia — 10,393.

Race and Ancestry: White — 65.7%; Black — 33.2%; American Indian, Eskimo and Aleut — 0.1%; Asian and Pacific Islander — 0.5%. Spanish Origin — 1.2%. English — 19.3%; French — 0.7%; German — 3.2%; Irish — 5.0%; Scottish — 0.5%.

Universities, Enrollment: Armstrong State College, Savannah — 2,882; Brewton-Parker College, Mount Vernon — 930; Brunswick Junior College, Brunswick — 1,134; Draughon's Junior College of Business, Savannah — 740; Emanuel County Junior College, Swainsboro — 450; Georgia Southern College, Statesboro — 6,626; Savannah State College, Savannah — 2,112.

Newspapers, Circulation: *The Brunswick News* (e), Brunswick — 14,846; *Savannah Evening Press* (e), Savannah — 20,938; *Savannah Morning News* (mS), Savannah — 56,092; *The Statesboro Herald* (mS), Statesboro — 6,629.

Commercial Television Stations, Affiliation: WJCL, Savannah (ABC); WSAV-TV, Savannah (NBC); WTOC, Savannah (CBS). Most of district is located in Savannah ADI. Portions are in Augusta ADI and Jacksonville (Fla.) ADI.

Military Installations: Fort Stewart, Hinesville — 20,661; Hunter Army Airfield, Savannah — 4,484; McKinnon Airport Communications Station (Air Force), St. Simons Island — 119; Naval Submarine Base, Kings Bay — 2,734; Savannah Air National Guard Communications Station, Savannah — 706; Savannah Municipal Airport (Air Force), Savannah — 416; Statesboro Bomb Scoring Site (Air Force), Statesboro — 45.

Nuclear Power Plants: Vogtle 1 and 2, Waynesboro (Westinghouse, Georgia Power Company).

Industries:

Union Camp Corp.; Savannah; paper, boxes — 3,500. **Gulfstream American Corp.** (Gulfstream American Aircenter); Savannah; aircraft — 2,711. **Seaboard Coastline Railroad Co.;** Savannah; railroad operations — 2,500. **Gilman Paper Co.** (St. Marys Kraft Div.); St. Marys; paper, paperboard — 1,600. **Chatham County Hospital Authority;** Savannah; hospital — 1,470.

ITT Rayonier Inc.; Jesup; pulp mills — 1,300. **Brunswick Pulp & Paper Co.** (HQ); Brunswick; pulp mills — 1,060. **St. Joseph's Hospital;** Savannah; hospital — 1,020. **Candler General Hospital Inc.;** Savannah; hospital — 1,000. **Hercules Inc.;** Brunswick; gum, wood chemicals — 923. **Great Dane Trailers Inc.** (HQ); Savannah; truck trailers — 900. **Sea Island Co.** (The Cloister - HQ); Sea Island; resort — 850. **Roper Corp.** (Roper Lawn Products); Savannah; lawn machinery — 800. **Oxford Industries Inc.;** Vidalia; men's shirts — 780. **Babcock & Wilcox Co. Inc.;** Brunswick; power generating systems equipment — 725. **Georgia Ports Authority;** Savannah; port — 689. **American Cyanamid Co.;** Savannah; pigments — 620. **Badische Co.** (Sylvania Spinning); Sylvania; carpet yarn — 600. **Claxton Mfg. Co. Inc.;** Claxton; women's underwear — 600. **Cooper Industries Inc.** (Cooper-Wiss); Statesboro; scissors, shears — 600. **ITT Grinnell Corp.;** Statesboro; foundry — 600. **Grumman Aerospace Corp.;** Savannah; aircraft — 575. **Emerson Electric Co. Inc.** (Brooks Instrument Div.); Statesboro; liquid meters — 535. **The Continental Group Inc.** (Continental Forest Industries); Port Wentworth; pulp mills — 500. **The Continental Group Inc.** (Mill Operations Div.); Port Wentworth; paperboard mills — 500. **Torrington Co. Inc.** (Sylvania Bearings Plant); Sylvania; bearings — 500.

2nd District

Southwest — Albany, Valdosta

The 2nd is rural South Georgia, with a black population of 36.5 percent and an economy primarily dependent on agriculture. Seven counties have black majorities. Peanuts, soybeans, cotton and vegetables are the major crops.

The only two urban areas of any significance are Albany and Valdosta (Dougherty and Lowndes counties). Both are turning Republican. Though Jimmy Carter easily carried the counties of the new 2nd District with nearly 57 percent of the vote in 1980, Ronald Reagan won in Lowndes and nearly carried Dougherty. Among white voters throughout the district there was a heavy decline in Carter's strength from 1976, when he won 70 percent of the vote in the areas now in the 2nd. As in other parts of Georgia, much of the Reagan strength came from the military population. The Valdosta area is home to Moody Air Force Base, and Albany has a Marine Corps supply center.

The old 2nd grew by 16 percent in the 1970s, slightly less than the statewide average. The small population imbalance was corrected by adding Echols, Irwin and Ben Hill counties, all of which had been in the 8th District. The new territory contains only 27,000 residents, all rural, and does little to interfere with the district's overall Democratic character.

Election Returns

2nd District		Democrat		Republican	
1976	President	93,296	(69.5%)	40,942	(30.5%)
	House	100,671	(98.4%)	1,426	(1.4%)
1978	Governor	45,756	(85.3%)	7,865	(14.7%)
	Senate	43,314	(83.6%)	8,487	(16.4%)
	House	44,815	(100.0%)	—	
1980	President	82,687	(56.9%)	60,378	(41.6%)
	Senate	90,125	(63.0%)	52,859	(37.0%)
	House	97,978	(74.1%)	34,259	(25.9%)
1982	Governor	81,026	(75.2%)	26,760	(24.8%)
	House	x[1]		—[1]	

[1] *No votes tabulated where candidate was unopposed; x indicates winner.*

Demographics

Population: 549,977. **Percent Change from 1970:** 13.7%.

Land Area: 11,104 square miles. **Population per Square Mile:** 49.5.

Counties, 1980 Population: Baker — 3,808; Ben Hill — 16,000; Berrien — 13,525; Brooks — 15,255; Calhoun — 5,717; Clay — 3,553; Colquitt — 35,376; Cook — 13,490; Crisp — 19,489; Decatur — 25,495; Dougherty — 100,718; Early — 13,158; Echols — 2,297; Grady — 19,845; Irwin — 8,988; Lanier — 5,654; Lee — 11,684; Lowndes — 67,972; Miller — 7,038; Mitchell — 21,114; Quitman — 2,357; Randolph — 9,599; Seminole — 9,057; Stewart — 5,896; Terrell — 12,017; Thomas — 38,008; Tift — 32,862; Turner — 9,510; Webster — 2,341; Worth — 18,064.

Cities, 1980 Population: Albany — 74,059; Bainbridge — 10,553; Cordele — 10,914; Fitzgerald — 10,187; Moultrie — 15,708; Thomasville — 18,463; Tifton — 13,749; Valdosta — 37,596.

Race and Ancestry: White — 63.0%; Black — 36.5%; American Indian, Eskimo and Aleut — 0.2%; Asian and Pacific Islander — 0.2%. Spanish Origin — 1.1%. English — 19.1%; German — 1.6%; Irish — 4.6%.

Universities, Enrollment: Abraham Baldwin Agricultural College, Tifton — 2,371; Albany Junior College, Albany — 1,999; Albany State College, Albany — 1,571; Andrew College, Cuthbert — 361; Valdosta State College, Valdosta — 4,901.

Newspapers, Circulation: *The Cordele Dispatch* (e), Cordele — 5,481; *Herald* (eS), Albany — 35,686; *The Moultrie Observer* (e), Moultrie — 7,912; *Thomasville Times-Enterprise* (eS), Thomasville — 10,705; *The Tifton Gazette* (e), Tifton — 10,169; *The Valdosta Daily Times* (eS), Valdosta — 17,954.

Commercial Television Stations, Affiliation: WALB-TV, Albany (NBC); WCTV, Thomasville (CBS); WTSG, Albany (None); WVGA, Valdosta (ABC). District is divided among Albany ADI, Columbus ADI, and Tallahassee (Fla.) ADI. Portion is in Dothan (Ala.) ADI.

Military Installations: Marine Corps Logistics Base, Albany — 3,621; Moody Air Force Base, Valdosta — 3,333.

Industries:

Sunnyland America Inc.; Thomasville; meat products — 1,740. **Great Northern Nekoosa Corp.** (Great Southern Paper Co.); Cedar Springs; liner board, plywood — 1,400. **Procter and Gamble Co.;** Albany; paper products — 1,300. **Coats & Clark Inc.;** Albany; thread — 1,200. **Miller Brewing Co.;** Albany; brewery — 1,200.

Amoco Fabrics Co. Inc.; Bainbridge; polypropylene — 1,150. **Amoco Fabrics Co. Inc.** (Nashville Mills Div.); Nashville; carpet backing — 1,100. **Phoebe Putney Memorial Hospital;** Albany; hospital — 1,000. **Levi Strauss & Co.;** Valdosta; men's jeans — 950. **Owens-Illinois Inc.** (Forest Products Div.); Valdosta; liner board — 900. **J. P. Stevens & Co. Inc.;** Tifton; wool fabric — 700. **Flint River Textiles Inc.** (HQ); Albany; cotton, wool fabrics — 578. **Riverside Mfg. Co.** (HQ); Moultrie; uniforms, work clothes — 575. **Wickes Corp.** (MacGregors Golf Co.); Albany; golf clubs, balls — 550. **Fitzgerald Underwear Corp.** (HQ); Tifton; women's, children's underwear — 500. **H. R. Kaminsky & Sons Inc.;** Fitzgerald; trousers, jeans — 500.

3rd District

West Central — Columbus

The 3rd District's most prominent citizen is former President Jimmy Carter, who resides in the southern end of it, in Sumter County. Carter held 60 percent of the 3rd District vote in 1980, a marked decrease from his 1976 showing, but still a comfortable victory.

The 3rd, like other Georgia districts, has a substantial black population — 34 percent — and is economically dependent on the military and the textile industry. The district is heavily agricultural, although its output lags behind textiles and the federal military payroll in its share of the district's annual gross product.

The dominant cities in the 3rd are Columbus (Muscogee County) and Warner Robins (Houston County), located at either end of the district. Situated on the Alabama border, Columbus (population 169,441) is the district's commercial center, with textiles the mainstay of the local economy.

Columbus' history as a manufacturing center dates back to the Civil War when it supplied uniforms, arms and food to the Confederate Army. These days the city's military ties are to Fort Benning, one of the Army's basic training centers. Warner Robins, on the district's eastern border, is home to Robins Air Force Base, a major air transport and Air Force supply center.

Ronald Reagan showed considerable strength within Columbus and Warner Robins in 1980. But he still lost both Houston and Muscogee counties to Carter.

The old 3rd grew by only 9 percent during the 1970s, less than any other Georgia district except the 5th. To add the necessary 40,000 voters, the Legislature gave the district Pulaski, Bleckley, Pike, Lamar and Butts counties, while removing Monroe County. All are rural and Democratic-leaning, and all went to Carter and Democratic Sen. Herman E. Talmadge easily in 1980.

Election Returns

3rd District		Democrat		Republican	
1976	President	92,186	(69.9%)	39,699	(30.1%)
	House	100,947	(86.3%)	15,994	(13.7%)
1978	Governor	62,205	(87.5%)	8,890	(12.5%)
	Senate	62,117	(89.0%)	7,674	(11.0%)
	House	58,091	(95.7%)	2,638	(4.3%)
1980	President	85,268	(60.4%)	52,307	(37.1%)
	Senate	75,742	(55.3%)	61,126	(44.7%)
	House	95,758	(93.9%)	6,240	(6.1%)
1982	Governor	80,892	(71.9%)	31,622	(28.1%)
	House	74,626	(71.0%)	30,537	(29.0%)

Demographics

Population: 540,865. **Percent Change from 1970:** 8.9%.

Land Area: 6,698 square miles. **Population per Square Mile:** 80.8.

Counties, 1980 Population: Bleckley — 10,767; Butts — 13,665; Chattahoochee — 21,732; Crawford — 7,684; Dooly — 10,826; Harris — 15,464; Houston — 77,605; Lamar — 12,215; Macon — 14,003; Marion — 5,297; Meriwether — 21,229; Muscogee — 170,108; Peach — 19,151; Pike — 8,937; Pulaski — 8,950; Schley — 3,433; Sumter — 29,360; Talbot — 6,536; Taylor — 7,902; Troup — 50,003; Upson — 25,998.

Cities, 1980 Population: Americus — 16,120; Columbus — 169,441; La Grange — 24,204; Warner Robins — 39,893.

Race and Ancestry: White — 64.2%; Black — 34.3%; American Indian, Eskimo and Aleut — 0.2%; Asian and Pacific Islander — 0.6%. Spanish Origin — 1.6%. English — 18.3%; French — 0.6%; German — 2.8%; Irish — 4.8%.

Universities, Enrollment: Columbus College, Columbus — 4,547; Fort Valley State College, Fort Valley — 1,814; Georgia Southwestern College, Americus — 2,147; Gordon Junior College, Barnesville — 1,160; La Grange College, La Grange — 947; Middle Georgia College, Cochran — 1,474; Phillips College, Columbus — 304.

Newspapers, Circulation: *The Columbus Enquirer* (mS), Columbus — 34,012; *The Columbus Ledger* (eS), Columbus — 30,827; *The Daily Sun* (eS), Warner Robins — 10,276; *La Grange Daily News* (e), La Grange — 13,917; *Times-Recorder* (e), Americus — 7,080.

Commercial Television Stations, Affiliation: WLTZ, Columbus (NBC); WRBL, Columbus (CBS); WTVM, Columbus (ABC). District is divided among Atlanta ADI, Columbus ADI and Macon ADI.

Military Installations: Fort Benning, Columbus — 21,719; Robins Air Force Base, Warner Robins — 22,213.

Industries:

Milliken & Co. Inc. (Industrial Div.); La Grange; house furnishings — 3,000. **The Bibb Co. Inc.;** Columbus; narrow fabrics — 2,250. **B. F. Goodrich Co.** (Tire-Group Textile Products); Thomaston; tire cord — 2,000. **Fieldcrest Mills Inc.;** Columbus; house furnishings — 1,830. **The Medical Center Hospital Authority;** Columbus; hospital — 1,420.

The William Carter Co. Inc.; Barnesville; children's underwear — 1,300. **Swift Textiles Inc.** (HQ); Columbus; cotton fabric — 1,240. **Columbus Foundries Inc.** (HQ); Columbus; ductile iron foundry — 1,200. **C P G Products Corp.** (Tom's Foods Div. - HQ); Columbus; snack food — 900. **Ex-Cell-O Corp.** (Davidson Rubber Div.); Americus; plastics products — 900. **Lummus Industries Inc.** (HQ); Columbus; textile machinery — 885. **American Family Corp.** (HQ); Columbus; life, health insurance — 860. **Milliken & Co.** (Hillside Plant); La Grange; tufted carpets — 800. **Seabrook Foods Inc.** (Southern Frozen Foods Div.); Montezuma; frozen fruits, vegetables — 767. **West Point-Pepperell Inc.;** Columbus; cotton, synthetic fabrics — 750. **Hog Slat Inc.;** Cobb; farm equipment — 710. **Hardaway Constructors Inc.;** Columbus; heavy construction — 700. **Garden Services Inc.** (Callaway Gardens - HQ); Pine Mountain; resort — 695. **Manhattan Industries Inc.** (Manhattan Shirt Co.); Americus; men's, women's shirts — 675. **Metalux Corp.** (Gibson Lighting - HQ); Americus; lighting fixtures — 673. **Blue Bird Body Co. Inc.** (Blue Bird Wanderlodge Div. - HQ); Fort Valley; bus bodies, trailers — 650. **Fieldcrest Mills Inc.** (Swift Spinning Mills); Columbus; yarn — 650. **Interstate Brands Corp.** (Dolly Madison Div.); Columbus; bakery products — 634. **Buckeye Cellulose Corp.;** Oglethorpe; pulp, paper — 625. **West Point-Pepperell Inc.** (Dixie Mill Div.); La Grange; cotton fabrics — 615. **W. C. Bradley Enterprises Inc.;** Columbus; cooking equipment, farm machinery — 600. **Blue Cross of Columbus, Ga.** (HQ); Columbus; health insurance — 555. **Sunshine Biscuits Inc.;** Columbus; cookies, crackers — 550. **Hanes Corp.** (Hanes Hosiery); La Grange; women's hosiery — 537. **Opelika Mfg. Corp.;** Hawkinsville; terry towel fabric — 525. **Daniel Construction Co.;** Oglethorpe; general contracting — 500. **Duracell International Inc.** (Mallory Battery Co.); La Grange; storage batteries — 500. **Pabst Brewing Co. Inc.;** Perry; brewery — 500.

4th District

Atlanta Suburbs — De Kalb County

The suburban 4th District contains some of the wealthiest communities in the South. De Kalb County, which makes up 73 percent of the district's population, often votes Republican. Portions of De Kalb regularly send Republicans to the state Legislature. Many of the voters prefer moderate Republican-style politics; De Kalb County chose Gerald R. Ford over Ronald Reagan in the 1976 Republican presidential primary. In some closely contested statewide elections, De Kalb voters have made the difference. The county gave GOP Senate candidate Mack Mattingly 70 percent of its vote in 1980; without that support, Mattingly would not even have come close against incumbent Sen. Herman E. Talmadge.

Democrats who win here do so largely because of the sizable black vote; the 4th District was 28 percent black as drawn during the 1970s, and Jimmy Carter carried it narrowly over Reagan in 1980.

The new map, however, reduced the district's black population to 13 percent and added some strongly Republican precincts in northern Fulton County, as well as in semi-rural Newton County.

The eastern portion of Fulton County remains in the 4th District, as does small Rockdale County, which is gradually moving out of its rural status and becoming a part of the Atlanta suburban sprawl. Rockdale has turned Republican as it has shed its rural character. Newton, by contrast, is dependably Democratic.

Election Returns

4th District		Democrat		Republican	
1976	President	116,288	(59.3%)	79,894	(40.7%)
	House	127,353	(68.7%)	58,082	(31.3%)

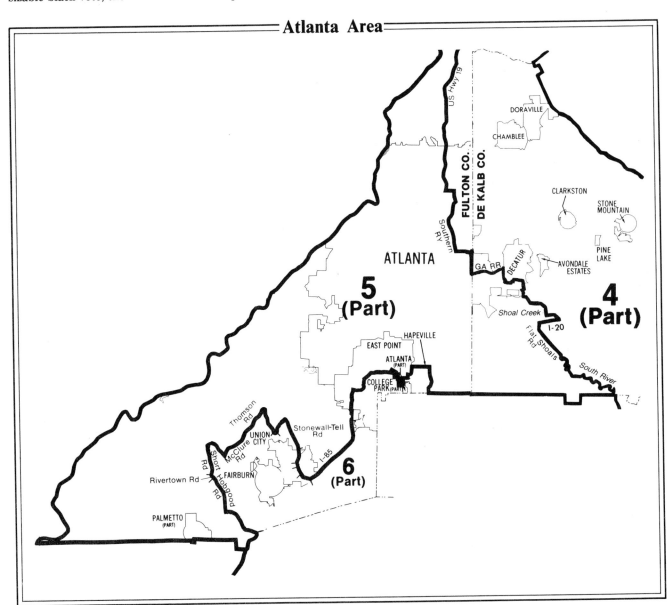

Atlanta Area

4th District		Democrat		Republican	
1978	Governor	68,561	(75.2%)	22,555	(24.8%)
	Senate	66,883	(77.6%)	19,339	(22.4%)
	House	67,146	(80.1%)	16,702	(19.9%)
1980	President	93,881	(51.2%)	79,568	(43.4%)
	Senate	71,798	(33.9%)	140,183	(66.1%)
	House	134,054	(69.1%)	59,814	(30.9%)
1982	Governor	55,201	(39.4%)	84,561	(60.5%)
	House	38,758	(65.5%)	20,418	(34.5%)

Demographics

Population: 542,368. **Percent Change from 1970:** 24.1%.

Land Area: 785 square miles. **Population per Square Mile:** 690.9.

Counties, 1980 Population: De Kalb (Pt.) — 397,728; Fulton (Pt.) — 73,404; Newton — 34,489; Rockdale — 36,747.

Cities, 1980 Population: Atlanta (Pt.) — 35,833; Covington — 10,586; Decatur — 18,404; Roswell (Pt.) — 6,215.

Race and Ancestry: White — 85.4%; Black — 12.9%; American Indian, Eskimo and Aleut — 0.2%; Asian and Pacific Islander — 1.0%. Spanish Origin — 1.6%. English — 20.1%; French — 0.8%; German — 4.3%; Irish — 5.0%; Italian — 0.9%; Polish — 0.6%; Russian — 0.8%; Scottish — 0.8%.

Universities, Enrollment: Agnes Scott College, Decatur — 541; Art Institute of Atlanta, Atlanta — 832; Bainbridge Junior College, Bainbridge — 565; Bauder Fashion College, Atlanta — 488; Columbia Theological Seminary, Decatur — 320; De Kalb Community College, Clarkston — 14,510; Emory University, Atlanta — 7,977; Mercer University in Atlanta, Atlanta — 1,628; Oglethorpe University, Atlanta — 1,153.

Newspapers, Circulation: *The Rockdale Citizen* (e), Conyers — 5,144. Atlanta *Constitution* and Atlanta *Journal* also circulate in the district.

Commercial Television Stations, Affiliation: WAGA-TV, Atlanta (CBS); WANX-TV, Atlanta (None); WVEU, Atlanta (None). Entire district is located in Atlanta ADI. *(For other Atlanta stations, see 5th district.)*

Industries:

General Motors Corp. (GM Assembly Div.); Doraville; autos — 5,500. **Western Electric Co. Inc.;** Atlanta; administrative offices — 2,500. **De Kalb County Hospital Authority;** Decatur; hospital — 1,700. **Hospital Authority of Fulton County** (Northside Hospital); Atlanta; hospital — 1,600. **National Service Industries** (Lithonia Lighting Div.); Conyers; electric lamps — 1,200.

Scientific-Atlanta Inc. (Telecommunication Group); Atlanta; telecommunications equipment — 1,050. **Watkins Associated Industries;** Atlanta; trucking, general contracting — 1,000. **Hercules Inc.;** Covington; polypropylene — 860. **Mobil Oil Corp.** (Mobil Chemical Co.); Covington; plastics products — 850. **Gold Kist Inc.** (Agricommodities Group - HQ); Atlanta; poultry processing, cottonseed oil, soybean oil — 800. **Kraft Inc.** (Kraft Foods); Decatur; cheese, salad dressings — 770. **Foote & Davies Inc.** (HQ); Atlanta; commercial printing — 750. **General Motors Corp.** (Parts Distribution Center); Doraville; automobile parts — 720. **Lanier Business Products Inc.** (HQ); Atlanta; dictating machines — 700.

Management Science of America; Atlanta; computer software services — 700. **Blue Cross/Blue Shield of Atlanta Inc.** (HQ); Atlanta; health insurance — 550. **Frito-Lay Inc.;** Atlanta; potato chips — 550. **Cotton States Insurance Co.** (HQ); Atlanta; insurance — 545. **Avon Products Inc.;** Atlanta; cosmetics wholesaling — 500. **Burnup & Sims Cablecom Inc.;** Lithonia; communication line construction — 500. **Minnesota Mining & Mfg. Co.** (Doraville); Atlanta; abrasive tapes wholesaling — 500. **National Data Corp.;** Atlanta; credit card operations — 500. **Rollins Inc.** (HQ); Atlanta; exterminating services, security services, cable TV, radio broadcasting — 500. **Simons-Eastern International** (HQ); Decatur; engineering services — 500.

5th District

Atlanta

The Democratic 5th combines Atlanta's glittering downtown area with its black inner city and some affluent suburban areas in northern Fulton County. Overall, blacks make up 65 percent of the 5th's population.

Capital of Georgia and symbolic capital of the New South, Atlanta is the commercial center for the Southeastern United States. Its banks and other white-collar industries attract a prosperous and sophisticated daytime population. Remaining behind at night, however, is a largely black and shrinking population.

The 5th includes 86 percent of Atlanta and surrounding Fulton County, and Fulton casts 84 percent of the district vote. The county as a whole is generally reliable Democratic territory, even with the suburbs included; Jimmy Carter took the county with 62 percent in 1980. But Republican Mack Mattingly garnered 57 percent of Fulton County's vote against incumbent Democrat Herman E. Talmadge in that year's Senate contest.

A pocket of GOP strength in Fulton County is Roswell, most of which is in the 5th. Roswell used to be a cotton milling center but is now a bedroom community. As white-collar, middle-level managers flocked to the Atlanta area in the 1970s, the population of Roswell mushroomed by 330 percent.

The 5th also contains the western half of Sandy Springs, another white bedroom community that is a step up the social ladder from Roswell. Carter drew 40 percent of its vote in 1980, twice as much as Sandy Springs gave Talmadge. South of Atlanta, the district takes in East Point, a lower-middle class community whose residents work in nearby manufacturing operations. Once a relatively stable city that delivered GOP votes, East Point lost population during the 1970s as white residents left. There is some residual GOP vote in East Point, but Democrats generally have an easier time there now.

Election Returns

5th District		Democrat		Republican	
1976	President	104,323	(67.5%)	50,151	(32.5%)
	House	99,452	(63.9%)	56,158	(36.1%)
1978	Governor	58,996	(78.0%)	16,602	(22.0%)
	Senate	61,042	(82.8%)	12,762	(17.3%)
	House	53,599	(69.8%)	23,186	(30.2%)
1980	President	111,457	(59.9%)	65,506	(35.2%)
	Senate	67,188	(43.0%)	89,022	(57.0%)
	House	102,003	(69.2%)	45,379	(30.8%)
1982	Governor	77,444	(67.1%)	37,927	(32.9%)
	House	53,264	(80.8%)	3,633	(5.5%)

Demographics

Population: 550,070. **Percent Change from 1970:** -6.4%.

Land Area: 367 square miles. **Population per Square Mile:** 1,498.8.

Counties, 1980 Population: De Kalb (Pt.) — 85,296; Fulton (Pt.) — 464,774.

Cities, 1980 Population: Atlanta (Pt.) — 389,189; College Park (Pt.) — 0; East Point — 37,486; Roswell (Pt.) — 17,122.

Race and Ancestry: White — 34.2%; Black — 65.0%; American Indian, Eskimo and Aleut — 0.1%; Asian and Pacific Islander — 0.4%. Spanish Origin — 1.1%. English — 9.7%; German — 1.5%; Irish — 2.2%.

Universities, Enrollment: Atlanta Christian College, East Point — 223, Atlanta College of Art, Atlanta — 268; Atlanta Junior College, Atlanta — 1,395; Atlanta University, Atlanta — 1,334; Clark College, Atlanta — 2,103; DeVry Institute of Technology, Atlanta — 2,000; Georgia Institute of Technology, Atlanta — 11,261; Georgia State University, Atlanta — 20,333; Interdenominational Theological Center, Atlanta — 273; Massey Business College, Atlanta — 768; Southern School of Pharmacy, Mercer University, Atlanta — 352; Morehouse College, Atlanta — 1,940; Morris Brown College, Atlanta — 1,611; Spelman College, Atlanta — 1,366.

Newspapers, Circulation: *Atlanta Daily World* (mS), Atlanta — 18,000; *Constitution* (mS), Atlanta — 215,130; *Journal* (eS), Atlanta — 204,424.

Commercial Television Stations, Affiliation: WATL-TV, Atlanta (ABC, CBS, NBC); WSB-TV, Atlanta (ABC); WTBS, Atlanta (None); WXIA-TV, Atlanta (NBC). Entire district is located in Atlanta ADI. *(For other Atlanta stations, see 4th district.)*

Military Installations: Fort McPherson, Atlanta — 3,694.

Industries:

The **Fulton De Kalb Hospital Authority;** Atlanta; hospital — 4,000. **Life Insurance Co. of Georgia;** Atlanta; life, health insurance — 3,590. **Trust Co. of Georgia;** Atlanta; bank holding company — 3,010. **Southern Railway Co.;** Atlanta; railroad operations — 3,000. **Cox Enterprises Inc.** (HQ); Atlanta; newspaper publishing — 2,500.

Seaboard Coastline Railroad; Atlanta; railroad operations — 2,200. **United States Steel Corp.** (USS Agri Chemical Div.); Atlanta; fertilizers — 2,100. **Georgia Baptist Hospital;** Atlanta; hospital — 1,800. **Atlantic Steel Co.** (HQ); Atlanta; steel products — 1,600. **The Coca-Cola Co. Inc.** (HQ); Atlanta; soft drinks, syrups — 1,400. **Bank South Corp.** (HQ); Atlanta; bank holding company — 1,300. **Hyprops;** Atlanta; hotel — 1,300. **Piedmont Hospital Inc.;** Atlanta; hospital — 1,300. **Tri-City Hospital Authority;** Atlanta; hospital — 1,300. **Westin Hotel Co.;** Atlanta; hotel — 1,300. **Allied Products Corp.** (Fabrics America Div.); Atlanta; fabrics, yarn — 1,050. **Owens-Illinois Inc.** Atlanta; glass containers — 1,020.

Atlanta News Agency Inc. (HQ); Atlanta; book wholesaling — 1,000. **Hyatt Hotels Corp.;** Atlanta; hotel — 1,000. **Nabisco Inc.;** Atlanta; cookies, crackers — 1,000. **Food Giant Inc.** (HQ); Atlanta; grocery store chain — 940. **Beers Construction Co. Inc.;** Atlanta; general contracting — 900. **Marriott Corp.;** Atlanta; hotel — 800. **Mead Corp.** (Mead Packaging Div.); Atlanta; administrative offices — 783. **Equifax Inc.** (HQ); Atlanta; business services — 750. **Federal Reserve Bank;** Atlanta; banking — 750. **Georgia Highway Express Inc.** (HQ); Atlanta; trucking — 750. **Hilton Hotels Corp.;** Atlanta; hotel — 720. **Roadway Express Inc.;** Atlanta; trucking — 700.

Atlanta Coca-Cola Bottling Co. (HQ); Atlanta; soft drinks — 682. **First Atlanta Corp.** (HQ); Atlanta; bank holding company — 600. **Allstate Insurance Co.;** Atlanta; auto insurance — 600. **Western Electric Co. Inc.;** Atlanta; repairing, warehousing — 600. **Simmons USA Corp.;** Atlanta; mattresses — 550. **Arco Metals** (Amarlite Div.); Atlanta; fabricated structural metal — 540. **Dittler Brothers Inc.** (HQ); Atlanta; commercial printing — 530. **Atlanta Janitorial Services;** Atlanta; janitorial services — 500. **Citizens and Southern National Bank;** Atlanta; banking — 500. **Shirley of Atlanta Inc.** (HQ); Atlanta; women's, children's outerwear — 500.

6th District

West Central — Atlanta Suburbs

The 6th is a mixture of suburban-Atlanta bedroom communities and rural piney-woods counties stretching west to the Alabama border. Growth has been rapid in recent years as suburbia has moved further from the city. Overall, the old 6th grew 37 percent during the 1970s, the second-highest rate among the state's districts. It had to lose about 80,000 residents in redistricting.

The changes made the district less suburban, removing areas of Fulton County south of Atlanta, along with tiny Pike, Lamar and Butts counties, and adding rural Polk and Paulding counties. The removal of southern Fulton reduced the black population from 23 percent to 15 percent, making the district less Democratic.

Several of the fast-growing counties closest to Atlanta have been moving in a Republican direction on their own. Clayton and Douglas, both of which grew more than 50 percent during the 1970s, switched from Jimmy Carter in 1976 to Ronald Reagan in 1980 and also backed successful GOP Senate candidate Mack Mattingly over Democratic incumbent Herman E. Talmadge. Fayette County, just south of Fulton, was Reagan's best county in the entire state, the only one which gave him more than 60 percent of the presidential vote. Four of the state's fifteen fastest growing counties (Fayette, Douglas, Clayton and Henry) are in this district.

There is no real population center in the 6th; Griffin, Carrollton, Forest Park, Newnan and the part of College Park in the district all have populations between 11,000 and 25,000. These towns are in the shadow of Atlanta and within commuting range of the city.

Outside the Atlanta orbit, the district's economy is largely dependent on textile mills, cattle, pecans and peaches. The western portions of the district are still loyally Democratic; all four of the district's counties along the Alabama border went for Carter easily in 1980.

Election Returns

6th District		Democrat		Republican	
1976	President	87,232	(67.9%)	41,333	(32.1%)
	House	63,107	(51.8%)	58,750	(48.2%)
1978	Governor	56,152	(78.4%)	15,513	(21.6%)
	Senate	57,361	(83.0%)	11,728	(17.0%)
	House	32,725	(47.4%)	36,277	(52.6%)
1980	President	75,853	(52.1%)	65,029	(44.7%)
	Senate	70,725	(47.5%)	78,282	(52.5%)
	House	60,670	(44.4%)	76,098	(55.6%)
1982	Governor	73,522	(62.0%)	45,148	(38.0%)
	House	50,459	(44.7%)	62,352	(55.3%)

Demographics

Population: 548,959. **Percent Change from 1970:** 41.4%.

Land Area: 3,276 square miles. **Population per Square Mile:** 167.6.

Counties, 1980 Population: Carroll — 56,346; Clayton — 150,357; Coweta — 39,268; Douglas — 54,573; Fayette — 29,043; Fulton (Pt.) — 51,726; Haralson — 18,422; Heard — 6,520; Henry — 36,309; Paulding — 26,110; Polk — 32,386; Spalding — 47,899.

Cities, 1980 Population: Atlanta (Pt.) — 0; Carrollton — 14,078; College Park (Pt.) — 24,632; Forest Park — 18,782; Griffin — 20,728; Newnan — 11,449.

Race and Ancestry: White — 84.3%; Black — 14.9%; American Indian, Eskimo and Aleut — 0.2%; Asian and Pacific Islander — 0.4%. Spanish Origin — 0.9%. English — 23.3%; French — 0.6%; German — 2.8%; Irish — 6.7%; Scottish — 0.5%.

Universities, Enrollment: Clayton Junior College, Morrow — 2,977; West Georgia College, Carrollton — 5,014.

Newspapers, Circulation: *Clayton News/Daily* (eS), Jonesboro — 6,082; *Griffin Daily News* (e), Griffin — 12,544; *Times-Georgian* (m), Carrollton — 12,001. Atlanta *Constitution* and Atlanta *Journal* also circulate in the district.

Commercial Television Stations, Affiliation: Entire district is located in Atlanta ADI.

Military Installations: Fort Gillem, Forest Park — 1,702.

Industries:

Eastern Air Lines Inc.; Atlanta; commercial airline — 7,500. **Southwire Co. Inc.** (HQ); Carrollton; wire — 2,900. **Ralston-Purina Co.;** Fairburn; pet food — 2,600. **Delta Air Lines Inc.** (HQ); Atlanta; commercial airline — 2,100. **Ford Motor Co.;** Hapeville; autos — 2,000.

Dundee Mills Inc. (Lowell Bleachery South - HQ); Griffin; cotton fabric — 1,800. **Reservco Inc.;** Atlanta; bridge, tunnel construction — 1,530. **Bremen-Bowdon Investment Co.;** Bowdon; men's suits — 1,200. **Dobbs Houses Inc.;** Atlanta; general warehousing — 1,200. **Clayton County Hospital Authority;** Riverdale; hospital — 1,140. **William L. Bonnell Co. Inc.** (HQ); Newnan; aluminum doors — 1,000. **Georgia Converters Inc.;** Bremen; trousers — 750. **Goodyear Tire & Rubber Co.** (Goodyear Aerospace Engineering Div.); Rockmart; engineered fabrics — 700.

La Mar Mfg. Co. (HQ); Bowdon; men's coats — 610. **Owens-Corning Fiberglas Corp.;** Fairburn; mineral wool — 600. **Douglas and Lomason Co. Inc.;** Carrollton; motor vehicle parts — 588. **NCR Corp.** (NCR Worldwide Service & Parts Center); Peachtree City; business machine wholesaling — 580. **Integrated Products Inc.;** Aragon; yarn — 550. **Custom Janitorial Service;** Forest Park; janitorial services — 500. **West Point-Pepperell Inc.** (Industrial Fabrics Div.); Newnan; synthetic yarn — 500.

7th District

Northwest — Rome, Marietta

The 7th District runs from the suburbs of Atlanta to those of Chattanooga, Tenn., more than 100 miles away. A majority of its population is in Cobb County, which borders Atlanta on the northwest and has 297,718 people. But there has been steady growth in many of the other counties as well, and the old 7th as a whole grew 32 percent during the 1970s.

Most of the district is heavily white, Baptist and conservative. The area within the new 7th gave Jimmy Carter 61 percent of its presidential vote in 1976 when most voters here saw Carter as an old-fashioned Southern Baptist. Four years later, perceived by many as a Northern-thinking liberal Democrat, Carter was able to win just 47 percent to Ronald Reagan's 49 percent. GOP Senate candidate Mack Mattingly was an easy winner here.

Redistricting added to the district Republican Catoosa County, on the Tennessee border, which went for Reagan and Mattingly. And it took away Gordon, Polk and Paulding counties, all Democratic.

Cobb County remains the core of the district. A collection of middle-income Atlanta suburbs, it went overwhelmingly for Reagan and Mattingly. Located in Cobb are Dobbins Air Force Base and a large Lockheed aircraft plant, both in Marietta, the county's largest city with 30,829 people.

The next largest concentration of voters, more than 100,000, are in the district's three northwestern counties — Dade, Catoosa and Walker — just south of Chattanooga.

Reagan and Mattingly carried all three in 1980. Between the two suburban ends of the district lie three rural counties dotted with small textile towns. Rome, a cotton and paper mill town in Floyd County, was once the largest city in the district. But its industrial base and population have been declining, and in 1980 it dropped below 30,000, placing it behind Marietta for the first time.

Election Returns

7th District		Democrat		Republican	
1976	President	85,939	(61.0%)	55,024	(39.0%)
	House	77,261	(55.5%)	62,115	(44.6%)
1978	Governor	49,901	(76.0%)	15,732	(24.0%)
	Senate	50,171	(78.9%)	13,433	(21.2%)
	House	42,443	(66.0%)	21,810	(33.9%)
1980	President	78,101	(47.1%)	81,442	(49.1%)
	Senate	63,396	(37.8%)	104,099	(62.2%)
	House	103,191	(65.8%)	53,389	(34.2%)
1982	Governor	65,885	(57.7%)	48,284	(42.3%)
	House	71,647	(61.1%)	45,569	(38.9%)

Demographics

Population: 545,913. **Percent Change from 1970:** 32.2%.

Land Area: 2,416 square miles. **Population per Square Mile:** 226.0.

Counties, 1980 Population: Bartow — 40,760; Catoosa — 36,991; Chattooga — 21,856; Cobb — 297,718; Dade — 12,318; Floyd — 79,800; Walker — 56,470.

Cities, 1980 Population: Marietta — 30,829; Rome — 29,654; Smyrna — 20,312.

Race and Ancestry: White — 93.3%; Black — 6.0%; American Indian, Eskimo and Aleut — 0.1%; Asian and Pacific Islander — 0.4%. Spanish Origin — 0.8%. English — 23.8%; French — 0.7%; German — 3.7%; Irish — 6.8%; Italian — 0.5%; Scottish — 0.6%.

Universities, Enrollment: Berry College, Mount Berry — 1,607; Covenant College, Lookout Mountain — 522; Floyd Junior College, Rome — 1,197; Kennesaw College, Marietta — 3,903; Shorter College, Rome — 809; Southern Technical Institute, Marietta — 2,583.

Newspapers, Circulation: *The Daily Tribune News* (e), Cartersville — 6,332; *Marietta Daily Journal* (eS), Marietta — 22,875; *Rome News-Tribune* (eS), Rome — 19,706. Atlanta *Constitution* and Atlanta *Journal* also circulate in the district.

Commercial Television Stations, Affiliation: District is divided between Atlanta ADI and Chattanooga (Tenn.) ADI.

Military Installations: Air Force Plant 6, Marietta — 133; Atlanta Naval Air Station, Marietta — 1,680; Dobbins Air Force Base, Marietta — 2,673; McCollum Air National Guard Station, Kennesaw — 316.

Industries:

Lockheed Corp. (Lockheed-Georgia Co.); Marietta; aircraft — 13,200. **Riegel Textile Corp.** (Apparel Fabrics Div.); Trion; wool fabrics — 2,850. **Salem Carpet Mills Inc.;** Ringgold; carpets — 2,000. **Curtis 1000 Inc.;** Smyrna; commercial printing — 1,620. **Burlington Industries Inc.** (Klopman Spun Woven Div.); Shannon; wool fabric — 1,550.

General Electric Co.; Rome; transformers — 1,400. **Cobb Kennestone Hospital;** Marietta; hospital — 1,300. **Bigelow-Sanford Inc.** (Georgia Rug Mills); Summerville; tufted carpet, rugs — 850. **Union Carbide Corp.;** Cartersville; plastic films — 800. **Tillotson Corp.** (Best Mfg. Div.); Menlo; work gloves — 775. **Spring City Knitting Co. Inc.** (E-Z Mills Div.); Cartersville; men's, boys' underwear — 700. **Bekaert**

Steel Wire Corp.; Rome; steel wire — 650. **Goodyear Tire and Rubber Co.**; Cartersville; tires, inner tubes — 650.

Stratton Industries Inc. (Celestial Carpet Mills - HQ); Cartersville; tufted carpets — 650. **Bigelow-Sanford Inc.** (Georgia Rug Mills); Lyerly; tufted carpet — 500. **Borg Textile Corp.**; Rossville; fur goods — 500. **Dixie Yarns Inc.** (Candlewick Yarns Div.); Ringgold; carpet, yarns — 500. **E & B Carpet Mills Inc.** (Trenton Spinning Mills Div.); Trenton; yarns — 500. **Roper Corp.** (Roper Appliance); LaFayette; household cooking equipment — 500. **Standard-Coosa-Thatcher Co.**; Rossville; cotton thread and yarn — 500.

8th District

South Central — Macon, Waycross

The oddly shaped 8th District twists all the way from the black-majority counties just south of Athens to the Okefenokee Swamp along the Florida border, a distance of some 250 miles. Throughout its length the district ranges from 10 to 100 miles wide. Covering 30 counties, it is one of the poorest areas of the state.

Its black population is 35 percent (up from 31 percent before redistricting). In both 1976 and 1980 this was Jimmy Carter's strongest district, and Democrat incumbent Herman E. Talmadge won it comfortably in his losing 1980 Senate campaign.

Most of this district is cotton, tobacco and peanut territory. The one large city is Macon (Bibb County), an old textile and railroad town which adjoins Robins Air Force Base in the 3rd District. Macon went for Carter by 2-1 in 1980. The city and surrounding Bibb county make up a little more than a quarter of the population of the redrawn district.

The old 8th grew by only 11 percent in the 1970s, well below the state average, and the Legislature gave it about 34,000 new residents in an unusual exchange of 18 counties. The counties added were Johnson, Charlton, Monroe, Jasper, Putnam, Greene, Taliaferro, Hancock, Washington, Glascock and Jefferson. Six of them have black majorities, and together they draw the constituency even further toward the Democratic side. Hancock, which is 78.2 percent black, gave Carter 78 percent of the vote in 1980, his best countywide showing in the state. The new counties make up 18 percent of the district population.

Wayne, Brantley, Echols, Irwin, Ben Hill, Pulaski and Bleckley counties left the 8th.

Election Returns

8th District		Democrat		Republican	
1976	President	117,623	(72.6%)	44,388	(27.4%)
	House	98,382	(73.3%)	35,790	(26.7%)
1978	Governor	45,091	(84.1%)	8,537	(15.9%)
	Senate	45,993	(88.0%)	6,297	(12.0%)
	House	39,731	(97.6%)	961	(2.4%)
1980	President	107,718	(64.6%)	55,844	(33.5%)
	Senate	101,111	(64.5%)	55,766	(35.5%)
	House	96,396	(76.5%)	29,682	(23.5%)
1982	Governor	83,487	(72.2%)	32,095	(27.8%)
	House	x[1]		—[1]	

[1] *No votes tabulated where candidate was unopposed; x indicates winner.*

Demographics

Population: 541,723. **Percent Change from 1970:** 10.6%.

Land Area: 13,123 square miles. **Population per Square Mile:** 41.3.

Counties, 1980 Population: Appling — 15,565; Atkinson — 6,141; Bacon — 9,379; Baldwin — 34,686; Bibb — 150,256; Charlton — 7,343; Clinch — 6,660; Coffee — 26,894; Dodge — 1,955; Glascock — 2,382; Greene — 11,391; Hancock — 9,466; Jasper — 7,553; Jeff Davis — 11,473; Jefferson — 18,403; Johnson — 8,660; Jones — 16,579; Laurens — 36,990; Monroe — 14,610; Pierce — 11,897; Putnam — 10,295; Taliaferro — 2,032; Telfair — 11,445; Treutlen — 6,087; Twiggs — 9,354; Ware — 37,180; Washington — 18,842; Wheeler — 5,155; Wilcox — 7,682; Wilkinson — 10,368.

Cities, 1980 Population: Douglas — 10,980; Dublin — 16,083; Macon — 116,896; Milledgeville — 12,176; Waycross — 19,371.

Race and Ancestry: White — 64.4%; Black — 35.3%; American Indian, Eskimo and Aleut — 0.1%; Asian and Pacific Islander — 0.2%. Spanish Origin — 0.9%. English — 22.9%; German — 1.5%; Irish — 4.8%.

Universities, Enrollment: Crandall College, Macon — 385; Georgia College, Milledgeville — 3,373; Georgia Military College, Milledgeville — 352; Macon Junior College, Macon — 2,335; Mercer University, Macon — 2,972; South Georgia College, Douglas — 1,152; Tift College, Forsyth — 791; Waycross Junior College, Waycross — 439; Wesleyan College, Macon — 422.

Newspapers, Circulation: *Dublin Courier-Herald* (e), Dublin — 10,489; *The Macon News* (eS), Macon — 21,479; *The Macon Telegraph* (mS), Macon — 52,195; *The Union-Recorder* (m), Milledgeville — 6,650; *Waycross Journal-Herald* (e), Waycross — 11,906.

Commercial Television Stations, Affiliation: WCWB-TV, Macon (NBC); WMAZ-TV, Macon (CBS, ABC); WWLG, Macon (ABC). District is divided among Albany ADI, Atlanta ADI, Augusta ADI, Macon ADI, Savannah ADI and Jacksonville (Fla.) ADI.

Military Installations: Lewis B. Wilson Airport, Macon — 153.

Nuclear Power Plants: Hatch 1, Baxley (General Electric, Georgia Power Company), December 1975; Hatch 2, Baxley (General Electric, Georgia Power Company), September 1979.

Industries:

Central State Hospital; Milledgeville; state psychiatric hospital — 4,300. **Macon-Bibb County Hospital Authority;** Macon; hospital — 1,650. **Amoco Fabrics Co.** (Patchogue Plymouth Div.); Hazlehurst; polypropylene — 1,500. **J. P. Stevens Co. Inc.** (Woolen and Worsted Div.); Dublin; woolen fabric — 1,450. **Brown & Williamson Tobacco Corp.**; Macon; tobacco wholesaling — 1,100.

B E & K Inc.; Dublin; general contracting — 1,020. **Armstrong World Industries Inc.**; Macon; ceiling tile — 1,000. **Phibro Corp.** (Edgar Operations); McIntyre; clay quarry — 1,000. **Levi Straus & Co.**; Macon; knit outerwear mill — 840. **American Hospital Supply Corp.** (American McGaw Labs Div.); Milledgeville; pharmaceuticals — 800. **Standard Container Co. Inc**; Homerville; metal cans — 800. **Keebler Co. Inc.**; Macon; cookies — 740. **Lancaster Colony Corp.** (Enterprise Aluminum Co. Div.); Macon; aluminum cookware — 700. **Rheem Mfg. Co.** (Rheem Air Conditioning Div.); Milledgeville; air conditioning systems — 700. **Thermo King Corp.**; Louisville; heating, cooling equipment — 660. **Campbell Soup Co.** (Joseph Campbell Co.); Douglas; poultry processing — 657.

Roydon Wear Inc.; McRae; boys', men's trousers — 650. **Lancaster Colony Corp.** (Enterprise Aluminim Co.); Eatonton; aluminum cookware — 600. **National Marketing Assn.**; Macon; electrical appliance wholesaling — 600. **J. P. Stevens Co. Inc.**; Milledgeville; wool dying — 600. **Yara Engineering Corp.** (Georgia Kaolin Corp.); Dry Branch; kaolin mining — 550. **Georgia Kraft Co.** (Mead Div.); Macon; paperboard — 540. **Cook and Co.**; Lumber City; steel tire cord — 500. **Grumman Aerospace Corp.**; Milledgeville; aircraft parts — 500. **Mohas Co. Industries Inc.** (Laurens Park Mill Div.); Dublin; tufted carpets — 500. **Oxford Industries Inc.**; Dublin; men's shirts — 500. **Swift & Co.**; Douglas; poultry processing — 500.

9th District

Northeast — Gainesville

It takes only a couple of hours to travel from the Atlanta suburbs at the southern end of the 9th to the mountains along its northern edge, but the trip is something of a cultural odyssey. The lives of Gwinnett County's white-collar suburbanites have little in common with the Bible-belt Baptism of Hall County's poultry farmers or the mountain-dwellers of Georgia's northeast corner.

About the only thing the two ends of the district share is an openness to Republicans not found in the rest of the 9th. It was on the strength of the GOP vote in metropolitan Atlanta and the mountain counties that Democratic Sen. Herman E. Talmadge was held to 51 percent in the 9th in 1980, a major reason he lost his re-election bid statewide.

Still, the district as a whole is undeniably Democratic. Rural people were as disenchanted here with Jimmy Carter in 1980 as they were elsewhere in the South, but he still won 57 percent districtwide.

The Democratic vote is strongest in the central portion of the district, which holds the bulk of its population. Although some of the residents of the area commute to Atlanta, most are employed locally. Textiles and tourism hold key places in the economy, but poultry is king. Chickens are raised and processed in Hall County and throughout the surrounding area. Gainesville, Hall's county seat and the second largest town in the district (population 15,280), calls itself the "broiler capital of the world." In the center of town stands the Georgia Poultry Federation's monument to the industry — an obelisk with a statue of a chicken mounted on top.

Development has begun to change the mountain region of northeast Georgia as urbanites and Floridians with their "Airstream" trailers flock to the unspoiled woods and streams. But the pace of change has been slow. Moonshiners still carry on their trade, and the backwoods folkways are alive enough for Rabun County high school students to chronicle them in the successful series of *Foxfire* books.

The counties in the northwestern corner of the 9th are more industrialized than the rest of the district. Dalton, the seat of Whitfield County and the district's largest city (population 20,939), is one of the country's chief carpet-making centers, with such companies as Coronet Industries and World Carpets anchoring the area's economy. The 9th lost Catoosa, Barrow and the southern part of Gwinnett in redistricting; it regained Gordon County.

Election Returns

9th District		Democrat		Republican	
1976	President	106,905	(73.5%)	38,570	(26.5%)
	House	96,499	(78.4%)	26,400	(21.5%)
1978	Governor	43,062	(79.4%)	11,171	(20.6%)
	Senate	43,349	(81.9%)	9,572	(18.1%)
	House	39,368	(77.7%)	11,295	(22.3%)
1980	President	92,811	(57.2%)	64,994	(40.0%)
	Senate	82,325	(50.9%)	79,408	(49.1%)
	House	101,490	(72.1%)	39,271	(27.9%)
1982	Governor	81,435	(67.7%)	38,846	(32.3%)
	House	86,514	(77.0%)	25,907	(23.0%)

Demographics

Population: 551,782. **Percent Change from 1970:** 35.1%.

Land Area: 6,467 square miles. **Population per Square Mile:** 85.3.

Counties, 1980 Population: Banks — 8,702; Cherokee — 51,699; Dawson — 4,774; Fannin — 14,748; Forsyth — 27,958; Franklin — 15,185; Gilmer — 11,110; Gordon — 30,070; Gwinnett (Pt.) — 77,674; Habersham — 25,020; Hall — 75,649; Hart — 18,585; Jackson — 25,343; Lumpkin — 10,762; Murray — 19,685; Pickens — 11,652; Rabun — 10,466; Stephens — 21,763; Towns — 5,638; Union — 9,390; White — 10,120; Whitfield — 65,789.

Cities, 1980 Population: Dalton — 20,939; Gainesville — 15,280.

Race and Ancestry: White — 94.3%; Black — 5.2%; American Indian, Eskimo and Aleut — 0.2%; Asian and Pacific Islander — 0.2%. Spanish Origin — 0.6%. English — 29.9%; French — 0.6%; German — 2.8%; Irish — 6.9%; Scottish — 0.5%.

Universities, Enrollment: Brenau College, Gainesville — 1,426; Dalton Junior College, Dalton — 1,428; Emmanuel College and School of Christian Ministry, Franklin Springs — 379; Gainesville Junior College, Gainesville — 1,569; North Georgia College, Dahlonega — 1,930; Piedmont College, Demorest — 390; Reinhardt College, Waleska — 509; Toccoa Falls College, Toccoa Falls — 619; Truett McConnell College, Cleveland — 754; Young Harris College, Young Harris — 528.

Newspapers, Circulation: *The Daily Citizen-News* (e), Dalton — 12,043; *Gwinnett Daily News* (eS), Lawrenceville — 18,505; *The Times* (eS), Gainesville — 20,647.

Commercial Television Stations, Affiliation: Most of district is located in Atlanta ADI. Portions are in Chattanooga (Tenn.) ADI and Greenville (S.C.)-Spartanburg (S.C.)-Asheville (N.C.) ADI.

Industries:

Coronet Industries Inc. (HQ); Dalton; tufted carpets — 2,500. **Scientific-Atlanta Inc.** (Optima Div. - HQ); Norcross; communications equipment — 1,826. **World Carpets Inc.** (HQ); Dalton; tufted carpets — 1,400. **Fieldale Corp.;** Baldwin; poultry processing — 1,300. **Coats & Clark Inc.;** Toccoa; finishing thread — 1,200. **West Point-Pepperell Inc.** (Carpet & Rug Div.); Dalton; carpets — 1,200.

Galaxy Carpet Mills Inc. (Galaxy Finishing Div.); Chatsworth; tufted carpets — 1,100. **Northeast Georgia Medical Center;** Gainesville; hospital — 1,070. **Johnson & Johnson;** Gainesville; baby powder, cotton swabs — 825. **Milliken & Co.;** Gainesville; industrial cotton fabric — 800. **Riegel Textile Corp.** (Apparel Fabrics Div.); Alto; synthetic fabrics, yarn — 750. **The Tappan Co.;** Dalton; vending machines — 750. **Burlington Industries Inc.;** Rabun Gap; tufted carpet — 700. **Westinghouse Air Brake Co.;** Toccoa; construction, mining equipment — 654. **Queen Carpet Corp.** (HQ); Dalton; tufted carpets — 650. **Sangamo Weston Inc.** (Sangamo Management Div.); Rabun Gap; transformers, switch gears — 650. **E & B Carpet Mills Inc.;** Dalton; carpets — 600. **Lawtex Industries Inc.** (HQ); Dalton; tufted rugs — 600. **The Lovable Co. Inc.;** Buford; corsets — 600. **Mar-Jac Inc.;** Gainesville; poultry processing — 600. **Monroe Auto Equiment Co.;** Hartwell; shock absorbers — 600.

Tyson Foods Inc.; Cumming; poultry processing — 580. **Peachtree Doors Inc.** (HQ); Norcross; metal doors — 550. **Sheller Globe Corp.** (Leece Neville Div.); Gainesville; electrical appliance wholesaling — 550. **Harmony Grove Mills Inc.;** Commerce; cotton fabrics — 540. **Levi Strauss & Co.;** Blue Ridge; work clothes — 510. **Burlington Industries Inc.** (Lees Div.); Dahlonega; yarn — 500. **Cagles Inc.;** Gainesville; poultry processing — 500. **Cables Inc.** (Plumbrook Farms Div.); Gainesville; poultry processing — 500. **Central Soya of Athens Inc.;** Canton; poultry processing — 500. **Country Pride Foods Ltd.;** Gainesville; animal feeds — 500. **Johnson & Johnson** (Chicopee Mfg. Co.); Royston; toiletries — 500. **Milliken & Co.;** New Holland; synthetic fabrics — 500. **Milliken & Co.** (Avalon Plant); Toccoa; yarn — 500. **O Jay Mills Inc.** (Heritage Spread Co.); Calhoun; house furnishings — 500. **The Pillsbury Co.** (Pillsbury Farms); Gainesville; hatchery, poultry processing — 500.

10th District

North Central — Athens, Augusta

The cities of Augusta and Athens anchor what is otherwise a rural district. Augusta, with a population just under 50,000, has a diverse array of industries. The city is a center for the surrounding agricultural areas in eastern Georgia and western South Carolina.

Augusta has a sizable population of retirees, mostly retired military people, who served at nearby Fort Gordon, the home of the Army Signal Corps. The retirees join other Augusta voters in favoring conservative Democrats.

Athens, with a population slightly below Augusta's, is the home of the University of Georgia. Largely a college town, it has attracted some light industry recently, including research firms associated with the university's schools of agricultural engineering and agricultural economics.

Cotton has been the major crop for generations in the district's rural areas, but it is declining in importance. In its place, farmers are raising soybeans, tobacco and corn.

Redistricting changed the political character of the 10th by giving it the suburban Atlanta areas of southern Gwinnett County while dropping eight heavily Democratic rural counties. Gwinnett grew by 131 percent in the 1970s, and much of this influx was made up of GOP-leaning corporate managers attracted by Atlanta's economic boom.

The counties that left the 10th District were Newton, Putnam, Greene, Taliaferro, Hancock, Washington, Glascock and Jefferson. In addition to southern Gwinnett County, the district also picked up Barrow County.

Election Returns

10th District		Democrat		Republican	
1976	President	83,491	(64.0%)	46,965	(36.0%)
	House	91,443	(94.0%)	5,733	(6.0%)
1978	Governor	61,372	(82.7%)	12,852	(17.3%)
	Senate	61,461	(85.1%)	10,785	(14.9%)
	House	56,726	(94.3%)	3,432	(5.7%)
1980	President	80,511	(53.2%)	66,097	(43.6%)
	Senate	72,227	(47.6%)	79,423	(52.4%)
	House	98,431	(73.3%)	35,780	(26.7%)
1982	Governor	69,214	(61.2%)	43,843	(38.8%)
	House	x[1]		—[1]	

[1] *No votes tabulated where candidate was unopposed; x indicates winner.*

Demographics

Population: 550,268. **Percent Change from 1970:** 32.1%.

Land Area: 4,218 square miles. **Population per Square Mile:** 130.5.

Counties, 1980 Population: Barrow — 21,354; Clarke — 74,498; Columbia — 40,118; Elbert — 18,758; Gwinnett (Pt.) — 89,229; Lincoln — 6,716; Madison — 17,747; McDuffie — 18,546; Morgan — 11,572; Oconee — 12,427; Oglethorpe — 8,929; Richmond — 181,629; Walton — 31,211; Warren — 6,583; Wilkes — 10,951.

Cities, 1980 Population: Athens — 42,549; Augusta — 47,532.

Race and Ancestry: White — 73.6%; Black — 25.0%; American Indian, Eskimo and Aleut — 0.1%; Asian and Pacific Islander — 0.8%. Spanish Origin — 1.4%. English — 20.8%; French — 0.7%; German — 3.7%; Irish — 4.9%; Italian — 0.5%; Scottish — 0.6%.

Universities, Enrollment: Augusta College, Augusta — 3,713; Medical College of Georgia, Augusta — 1,978; Paine College, Augusta — 748; Phillips College, Augusta — 460; University of Georgia, Athens — 23,470.

Newspapers, Circulation: *Athens Banner-Herald* (eS), Athens — 12,171; *Athens Daily News* (m), Athens — 7,881; *Chronicle* (mS), Augusta — 56,351; *Herald* (eS), Augusta — 18,687.

Commercial Television Stations, Affiliation: WAGT-TV, Augusta (NBC); WJBF, Augusta (ABC); WRDW-TV, Augusta (CBS). District is divided among Atlanta ADI, Augusta ADI and Greenville (S.C.)-Spartanburg (S.C.)-Asheville (N.C.) ADI.

Military Installations: Fort Gordon, Augusta — 13,153; Navy Supply Corps School, Athens — 579.

Industries:

University Hospital; Augusta; hospital — 2,600. **Western Electric Co. Inc.** (Atlanta Works); Norcross; cable wire — 2,600. **Veterans Administration;** Augusta; veterans' hospital — 2,220. **Gracewood State School & Hospital;** Gracewood; state psychiatric hospital — 1,890. **Uniroyal Inc.;** Thomson; rubber footwear — 1,300.

Babcock & Wilcox Co. Inc. (Insulating Products Div.); Augusta; cement refractory — 1,100. **Talley Industries Inc.** (Westclox Div.); Athens; clocks — 1,100. **Westinghouse Electric Corp.;** Athens; transformers — 1,100. **The Continental Group Inc.** (Continental Forest Industries); Augusta; fabricated wire products — 1,000. **Central Soya of Athens Inc.;** Athens; poultry processing — 950. **Spartan Mills** (John P. King Mfg. Div.); Augusta; cotton fabric — 925. **E. I. du Pont de Nemours & Co.** (Textile Fibers Div.); Athens; synthetic yarn — 840. **Portec Inc.** (Rail Car Div.); Winder; railroad equipment — 800. **Reliance Electric Co.;** Athens; motor vehicle parts — 800. **Columbia Nitrogen Corp.** (HQ); Augusta; nitrogen fertilizers — 752. **Nipro Inc.** (HQ); Augusta; caprolactam — 752. **Gold Kist Inc.** (Poultry Div.); Athens; farm supplies wholesaling — 725.

Beatrice Foods Co. (Murray Biscuit Div.); Augusta; cookies — 700. **Thomson Co.;** Thomson; men's clothing — 650. **Certain-Teed Corp.;** Athens; fiberglass — 600. **Graniteville Co.** (Sibley Div.); Augusta; cotton fabric — 600. **The Kendall Co. Inc.;** Augusta; cotton hospital supplies — 600. **Textron Inc.;** Augusta; children's vehicles, industrial trucks — 600. **Walton Mfg. Co.;** Loganville; suits, sport coats — 570. **Insurance Systems of America;** (HQ); Norcross; computer software services — 550. **TRW Inc.** (Drill & End Mill Div.); Evans; power hand tools — 502. **Johns-Manville Sales Corp.;** Winder; concrete products — 500. **Oxford Industries Inc.;** Monroe; men's slacks — 500.

Hawaii

A major alteration in redistricting procedures was of minor consequence for the Democratic incumbents of Hawaii's two congressional districts. A U.S. District Court in Honolulu struck down Hawaii's congressional and legislative redistricting plans in March 1982, ruling that the state's reapportionment commission had used an improper population base, counting only registered voters.

In May a three-judge federal panel accepted a new plan submitted by a group of five "special masters." While the revision expanded the 1st District westward in Honolulu, adding to it the Aiea area of the city, the change had little political impact. Both incumbents won re-election, one with 89 percent of the vote, the other with 90 percent. One of the six states Jimmy Carter carried in 1980, Hawaii is rivaled for its partisan consistency only by Rhode Island and Massachusetts.

From 1962 until 1970, Hawaii was represented by two at-large House members. The state switched to two districts for the 1970 election, following adoption of federal legislation providing that no state with more than one U.S. House seat could elect its representatives at large.

The state needed only modest adjustments to comply with the new census in 1981. Hawaii's 2nd District, covering the non-Honolulu portion of the state, had grown in population by approximately 40 percent during the 1970s and needed to transfer some 90,000 persons to the urban 1st District, where growth had been smaller.

The bipartisan state Reapportionment Commission accomplished that by extending the 1st District line northwest to bring in Pearl City and part of Waipahu, where dependably Democratic farm laborers and industrial workers live. The redistricting panel turned aside a Republican Party plan to expand the 1st toward Kailua, the home of upper middle-class voters who usually pull the Republican lever.

The commission approved the new map by a vote of 6 to 2 in September. Two of the four Republicans on the panel voted with the four Democrats in favor of it. State law allows challenges to a redistricting plan in state court within 45 days of the date of enactment, but that period ended in November 1981 with no challenges filed.

The federally mandated change in district lines came about due to a suit brought by the League of Women Voters and Hawaii Democrats. They challenged Hawaii's use of registered voters rather than pure population as the basis for reapportionment.

This latter procedure had been followed because of Hawaii's large number of transient military personnel and migrant laborers. But the suit successfully argued that the tabulation did not accurately reflect the makeup of the state.

Age of Population

District	Population Under 18	Voting Age Population	Population 65 & Over (% of VAP)	Median Age
1	119,554	362,790	42,985 (11.8%)	30.2
2	156,029	326,318	33,165 (10.2%)	26.5
State	275,583	689,108	76,150 (11.1%)	28.4

Income and Occupation

District	Median Family Income	White Collar Workers	Blue Collar Workers	Service Workers	Farm Workers
1	$ 24,714	60.4%	20.6%	17.7%	1.2%
2	21,227	49.5	26.5	18.0	6.0
State	$ 22,750	55.5%	23.3%	17.9%	3.4%

Education: School Years Completed

District	8 Years or Fewer	4 Years of High School	4 Years of College or More	Median School Years
1	15.4%	33.9%	23.1%	12.7
2	17.1	36.4	17.2	12.6
State	16.2%	35.1%	20.3%	12.7

Housing and Residential Patterns

District	Owner Occupied	Renter Occupied	Urban	Rural
1	47.7%	52.3%	99.9%	0.1%
2	56.1	43.9	73.1	26.9
State	51.7%	48.3%	86.5%	13.5%

HAWAII

Hilo

HAWAII

2
(PT.)

MAUI

KAHOOLAWE

2
(PT.)

MOLOKAI

LANAI

Kaneohe

Kailua

Honolulu

OAHU

1

2
(PT.)

KAUAI

2
(PT.)

NIIHAU

KAULA

1st District

Honolulu

Wholly contained on the island of Oahu, the 1st District is centered on Honolulu. A diverse and cosmopolitan city with Japanese, Chinese, Filipino, Caucasian and native Hawaiian populations, Honolulu is the site of numerous military installations as well as a world tourist center. The congressional redistricting in 1982 added to the military presence there; most of the Pearl Harbor naval base was moved from the 2nd District to the 1st District.

Compared with the rapid growth in the old 2nd, the old 1st District's 9 percent population increase during the 1970s was modest. The state redistricting commission's remedy, adding blue-collar suburbs such as Pearl City, deepened the Democratic sentiments of the 1st District. No Republican candidate has ever won its U.S. House seat.

Much of the GOP vote that does exist in the district comes from the military and managerial group involved with the major Honolulu corporations. It was military support that allowed Ronald Reagan to carry the 1st District narrowly over Jimmy Carter in November 1980. Independent John B. Anderson took 11 percent of the total vote.

Election Returns

1st District		Democrat		Republican	
1976	President	72,260	(49.3%)	72,302	(49.3%)
	Senate	82,763	(54.9%)	59,086	(39.2%)
	House	69,602	(46.6%)	55,460	(37.1%)
1978	Governor	75,785	(53.6%)	63,838	(45.2%)
	House	94,205	(53.6%)	25,547	(45.2%)
1980	President	64,149	(43.1%)	65,419	(44.0%)
	Senate	108,336	(77.0%)	27,394	(19.5%)
	House	110,046	(80.9%)	19,819	(14.6%)
1982	Governor	71,677	(46.1%)	40,764	(26.2%)
	Senate	123,801	(80.2%)	25,915	(16.8%)
	House	134,779	(89.9%)	—	

Demographics

Population: 482,344. **Percent Change from 1970:** 15.2%.

Land Area: 179 square miles. **Population per Square Mile:** 2,694.7.

Counties, 1980 Population: Honolulu (Pt.) — 482,344.

Cities, 1980 Population: Aiea — 32,879; Honolulu (Pt.) — 365,017; Pearl City — 42,575; Waipahu (Pt.) — 17,706.

Race and Ancestry: White — 29.4%; Black — 1.4%; American Indian, Eskimo and Aleut — 0.2%; Asian and Pacific Islander — 65.9%. Spanish Origin — 5.8%. English — 3.2%; German — 2.1%; Irish — 1.2%; Italian — 0.5%; Portuguese — 1.6%.

Universities, Enrollment: Chaminade University of Honolulu, Honolulu — 1,050; Hawaii Pacific College, Honolulu — 1,508; Honolulu Community College, Honolulu — 4,493; Kapiolani Community College, Honolulu — 5,009; Leeward Community College, Pearl City, Oahu — 5,535; University of Hawaii at Manoa, Honolulu — 20,311.

Newspapers, Circulation: *The Honolulu Advertiser* (mS), Honolulu — 83,479; *The Honolulu Star-Bulletin* (eS), Honolulu — 118,341. Foreign language newspapers: *Hawaii Hochi* (bilingual: English/Japanese), Honolulu — 9,558; *Hawaii Times* (bilingual: English/Japanese), Honolulu — 12,685; *New China Daily Press* (Chinese), Honolulu — 1,200; *United Chinese Press* (Chinese), Honolulu — 3,200.

Commercial Television Stations, Affiliation: KGMB-TV, Honolulu (CBS); KHON-TV, Honolulu (NBC); KIKU-TV, Honolulu, (None); KITV, Honolulu (ABC); KSHO, Honolulu (None). Hawaii has no ADIs.

Military Installations: Aliamanu Military Reservation (Army), Honolulu — 3; Camp H. M. Smith (Marine Corps), Honolulu — 974; Fort Derussy, Honolulu — 143; Fort Kamehameha, Honolulu — 34; Fort Ruger, Honolulu — 24; Fort Shafter, Honolulu — 2,728; Hickam Air Force Base, Honolulu — 9,493; Kapalama Military Reservation (Army), Honolulu — 233; Pearl Harbor Naval Public Works Center, Pearl Harbor — 1,520; Pearl Harbor Naval Shipyard, Pearl Harbor — 7,056; Pearl Harbor Naval Station, Honolulu — 12,610; Pearl Harbor Naval Submarine Base, Honolulu — 3,890; Pearl Harbor Naval Supply Center, Honolulu — 1,117; Tripler Army Medical Center — Honolulu — 2,448.

Industries:

The Queen's Medical Center; Honolulu; hospital — 1,800. **Sheraton Management Corp.** (Royal Hawaiian Hotel); Honolulu; hotel — 1,670. **Bank of Hawaii;** Honolulu; banking — 1,200. **Hilton Hawaiian Village;** Honolulu; hotel — 1,200. **St. Francis Hospital;** Honolulu; hospital — 1,200.

Kuakini Medical Center; Honolulu; hospital — 1,150. **Kaiser Foundation Hospital;** Honolulu; hospital — 1,020. **Pan American World Airways Inc.;** Honolulu; commercial airline — 1,000. **Straub Clinic & Hospital Inc.;** Honolulu; hospital — 1,000. **Hyatt Corp.;** Honolulu; hotel — 900. **Del Monte Corp.;** Honolulu; fruit canning — 851. **THI Hawaii Inc.** (Hawaiian Regent Hotel); Honolulu; hotel — 850. **Aloha Airlines Inc.** (HQ); Honolulu; commercial airline — 800. **Hawaiian Airlines Inc.** (HQ); Honolulu; commercial airline — 800. **First Hawaiian Bank** (HQ); Honolulu; banking — 709. **Ilikai Properties Inc.;** Honolulu; hotel — 700.

Western Airlines Inc.; Honolulu; commercial airline — 650. **Pacific Resources Inc.;** Honolulu; petroleum refining — 642. **Cal Lui & Associates Inc.** (HQ); Honolulu; travel agency — 600. **Castle & Cooke Inc.** (HQ); Honolulu; fruit, vegetable growing and processing — 600. **Hawaii Medical Service Assn.** (HQ); Honolulu; health insurance — 545. **WKH Corp.** (Kahala Hilton Hotel); Honolulu; hotel — 525. **Ala Moana Americana Hotel Co.;** Honolulu; hotel — 520. **C. Brewer and Co. Ltd.** (HQ); Honolulu; sugar growing, processing — 500. **Freeman Guards Inc.** (HQ); Honolulu; security services — 500. **Pacific Beach Corp.** (Pacific Beach Hotel); Honolulu; hotel — 500. **The Sheraton Corp.** (Princess Kaiulani Hotel); Honolulu; hotel — 500.

2nd District

Honolulu Suburbs and Outer Islands

The 2nd District encompasses virtually everything in the state but the city of Honolulu and some of its suburbs. The district includes all the islands outside of Oahu, where Honolulu is located, plus all but the southeastern portion of Oahu itself. Honolulu's fast-growing suburbs swelled the 2nd District's population during the 1970s and forced the map makers to transfer territory to the 1st District.

Since its creation for the 1970 elections, the 2nd District always has gone Democratic, usually by margins greater than those of the 1st. In 1976, it gave presidential candidate Jimmy Carter enough votes to allow him to lose the other district and still carry the state.

Although it lost much of the Pearl Harbor area in redistricting, the 2nd District retained many of Oahu's military installations, and these, along with wealthy residential neighborhoods located in and around Kailua, generate respectable Republican showings in national elections. In other contests, however, the Democratic strength elsewhere overwhelms Republican Party candidates. Pineapples and sugar cane are the major crops in the rural areas of Oahu, and the people who work in those industries have strong Democratic loyalties.

Oahu dominates the district politically. While the island of Hawaii is known as "the big island," comprising two-thirds of the state's entire land area, it has only one-eighth of Oahu's population. The island of Hawaii's main crop is sugar cane. Cattle, macadamia nuts, coffee beans and orchids also are key components of the island's agricultural economy.

The other islands of the Hawaiian chain contribute substantially to the state's agricultural wealth. The 2nd District's Maui County consists of the state's richest pineapple-growing land. Sugar cane and beef cattle are important commodities there as well as among the lightly populated islands in Kaui County.

Election Returns

2nd District		Democrat		Republican	
1976	President	75,115	(51.9%)	67,701	(46.8%)
	Senate	79,542	(52.6%)	63,638	(42.1%)
	House	114,564	(79.4%)	22,202	(15.4%)
1978	Governor	77,609	(55.3%)	60,772	(43.3%)
	House	108,619	(85.5%)	14,620	(11.5%)
1980	President	71,730	(46.4%)	64,693	(41.8%)
	Senate	116,149	(78.8%)	25,674	(17.4%)
	House	129,687	(89.8%)		
1982	Governor	69,366	(44.4%)	40,743	(26.1%)
	Senate	121,585	(80.0%)	26,156	(17.2%)
	House	132,072	(89.2%)	—	

Demographics

Population: 482,347. **Percent Change from 1970:** 37.4%.

Land Area: 6,247 square miles. **Population per Square Mile:** 77.2.

Counties, 1980 Population: Hawaii — 92,053; Honolulu (Pt.) — 280,221; Kalawao — 144; Kauai — 39,082; Maui — 70,847.

Cities, 1980 Population: Ewa Beach — 14,369; Hilo — 35,269; Honolulu (Pt.) — 31; Kahului — 12,978; Kailua — 35,812; Kaneohe —

29,919; Mililani Town — 21,365; Mokapu — 11,615; Schofield Barracks — 18,851; Wahiawa — 16,911; Wailuku — 10,260; Waipahu (Pt.) — 11,433.

Race and Ancestry: White — 36.7%; Black — 2.2%; American Indian, Eskimo and Aleut — 0.4%; Asian and Pacific Islander — 56.6%. Spanish Origin — 9.0%. English — 3.7%; French — 0.5%; German — 2.5%; Irish — 1.5%; Italian — 0.6%; Portuguese — 3.9%.

Universities, Enrollment: Brigham Young University (Hawaii campus), Laie, Oahu — 1,828; Hawaii Loa College, Kaneohe, Oahu — 297; Kauai Community College, Lihue, Kauai — 1,061; Maui Community College, Kahului, Maui — 1,869; University of Hawaii at Hilo, Hilo, Hawaii — 3,494; Windward Community College, Kaneohe, Oahu — 1,485.

Newspapers, Circulation: *Hawaii Tribune-Herald* (eS), Hilo, Hawaii — 17,825; *Maui News* (e), Wailuku, Maui — 15,150. *The Honolulu Advertiser* and *The Honolulu Star-Bulletin* circulate in the district.

Commercial Television Stations, Affiliation: KAII-TV, Wailuku, Maui (NBC); KGMD-TV, Hilo, Hawaii (CBS); KGMV, Wailuku, Maui (CBS); KHAW-TV, Hilo, Hawaii (NBC); KHVO, Hilo, Hawaii (ABC); KMAU, Wailuku, Maui (ABC). Hawaii has no ADIs.

Military Installations: Barbers Point Naval Air Station, Honolulu, Oahu — 4,267; Barking Sands Support Annex (Air Force), Kekaha, Kauai — 80; Bellows Air Force Station, Waimanalo, Oahu — 111; EPAC Naval Communications Area Master Station, Wahiawa, Oahu — 1,239; Helemano Radio Station (Army), Wahiawa, Oahu — 806; Kaala Air Force Station, Wahiawa, Oahu — 101; Kaena Point Facility (Air Force), Waialua, Oahu — 211; Kaena Point Military Reservation (Army), Waianae, Oahu — 87.

Kahuku Training Area (Army), Wahiawa, Oahu — 83; Kaneohe Bay Marine Corps Air Station, Kailua, Oahu — 10,731; Kekaha Naval Pacific Missile Range Facility, Kekaha, Kauai — 605; Kokee Air Force Station, Kekaha, Kauai — 293; Lualualei Naval Magazine, Waianae, Oahu — 422; Makua Military Reservation (Army), Waianae, Oahu — 2; Pohakuloa Training Area, Hilo, Hawaii — 89; Schofield Barracks Military Reservation (Army), Wahiawa, Oahu — 12,480; Wheeler Air Force Base, Wahiawa, Oahu — 1,136.

Industries:

Polynesian Cultural Center Inc.; Laie, Oahu; cultural park — 1,200. **Alexander & Baldwin Inc.;** Puunene, Maui; sugar processing — 1,150. **Oahu Sugar Co. Ltd.;** Waipahu, Oahu; sugar growing, processing — 950. **Kapalua Land Co. Ltd.;** Lahaina, Maui; resort developing — 681. **Westin Hotel Co.** (Mauna Kea Beach Hotel); Kamuela, Hawaii; hotel — 650.

Pioneer Mill Co. Ltd.; Lahaina, Maui; sugar growing, processing — 638. **Hyatt Corp.;** Kahuku, Oahu; hotel — 560. **McBryde Sugar Co. Ltd.** (HQ); Eleele, Kauai; sugar growing, processing — 550. **Hilo Coast Processing Co.** (HQ); Pepeekeo, Hilo; sugar processing — 500. **Intercontinental Hotels Corp.;** Kihei, Maui; hotel — 500. **Inter Island Resorts Ltd.;** Lihue, Kauai; resort — 500.

Idaho

Republicans, who dominated both chambers of the Idaho Legislature, passed a redistricting plan in 1981 that barely altered the state's congressional map.

The Democratic leader in the state Senate wanted to unite Ada County (Boise) in a single district, but the GOP rejected that concept because putting Republican Boise in one district might have improved Democrats' chances of winning Idaho's other district.

So the redistricting bill drafted by the GOP equalized population in the two districts simply by shifting 15 Boise precincts containing 20,633 people from the 1st District to the 2nd. That measure passed the Legislature July 16, 1981. Democratic Gov. John V. Evans, who had shown some interest in uniting Boise, finally signed the Republican remap into law July 30, 1981.

Democrats held a slight edge in most of the 15 shifted precincts, but the partisan balance in the precincts was so close that the political impact of their transfer was expected to be minimal. The population variance between the two new districts was 175.

During the 1970s Idaho sent militant conservative Republicans to the U.S. House. However, conservative dominance is a bit shaky. Since 1974, only one GOP House candidate in either district has won 60 percent of the vote. In 1982 neither GOP winner reached 55 percent.

Age of Population

District	Population Under 18	Voting Age Population	Population 65 & Over (% of VAP)	Median Age
1	147,903	324,509	49,720 (15.3%)	28.8
2	158,762	312,761	43,960 (14.1%)	26.3
State	306,665	637,270	93,680 (14.7%)	27.6

Income and Occupation

District	Median Family Income	White Collar Workers	Blue Collar Workers	Service Workers	Farm Workers
1	$ 17,708	49.6%	29.8%	13.5%	7.1%
2	17,308	49.5	27.7	12.1	10.7
State	$ 17,492	49.6%	28.8%	12.8%	8.9%

Education: School Years Completed

District	8 Years or Fewer	4 Years of High School	4 Years of College or More	Median School Years
1	13.4%	37.7%	14.9%	12.6
2	11.8	35.3	16.9	12.7
State	12.6%	36.5%	15.8%	12.6

Housing and Residential Patterns

District	Owner Occupied	Renter Occupied	Urban	Rural
1	73.3%	26.7%	51.6%	48.4%
2	70.7	29.3	56.4	43.6
State	72.0%	28.0%	54.0%	46.0%

1st District

North and West — Lewiston, Boise

Although the 1st is traditionally the more Democratic of Idaho's two districts, conservative Republicans are firmly in control. Democratic strength in the 1st stems from labor influence in the mountainous northern panhandle, where lumbermen and miners fought to organize unions early in this century. Adding to Democratic strength is a community of relatively liberal voters linked to the University of Idaho at Moscow in Latah County.

In the 1980 Senate contest, the nine northernmost counties in the state sided with Democrat Frank Church in his loss to Republican Steven D. Symms; several of those counties gave Jimmy Carter about 40 percent of the vote. Independent John B. Anderson's highest statewide tally (17 percent) and Ronald Reagan's lowest (47 percent) came in Latah County.

But the vote in the nine panhandle counties is more than offset by two heavily Republican urbanized areas at the southern end of the district — Canyon County and western Ada County — which have more than 40 percent of the district's residents.

The state capital of Boise is located in Ada County and

IDAHO

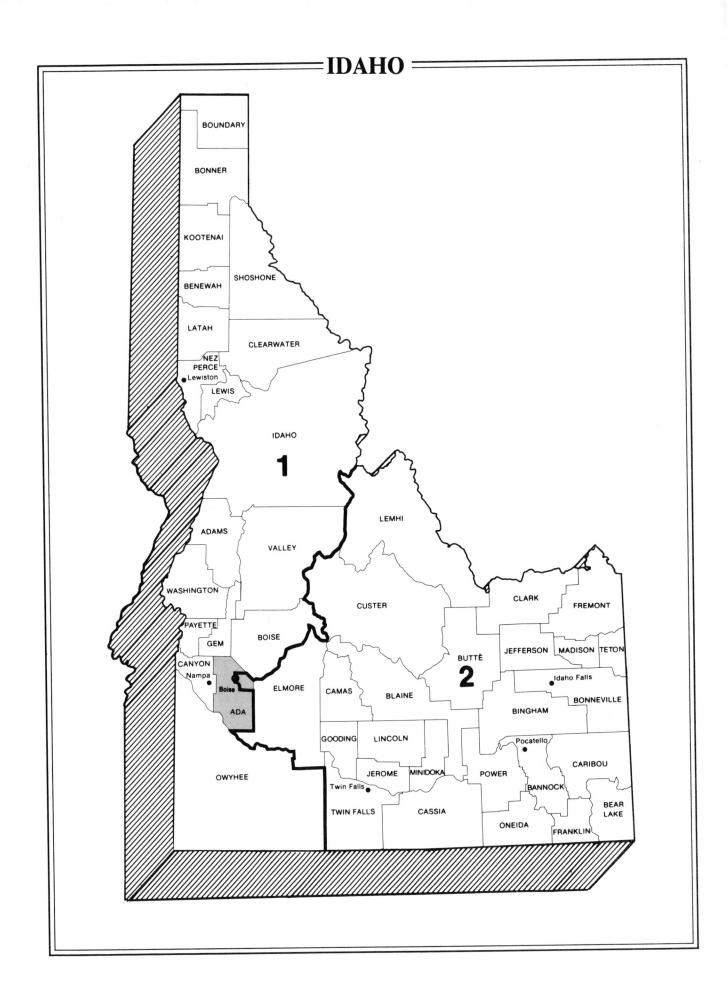

is almost evenly divided between the two congressional districts. It is Idaho's only city with more than 100,000 residents, and its Republican tendencies stem from the numerous lumber, paper, food processing and construction corporations that have their headquarters there. Canyon County contains the growing cities of Nampa and Caldwell — agricultural processing centers that usually vote a solidly Republican ticket.

In 1980, Canyon County and the 1st District portion of Ada County each gave 68 percent of their vote to Reagan. Demographic trends in Idaho's northern panhandle do not bode well for the Democratic Party. Shoshone and Clearwater counties were the only two counties in Idaho to lose population during the 1970s, and Nez Perce County (Lewiston) grew by less than 10 percent. Carter's highest 1980 percentages in Idaho came from those three counties.

Election Returns

1st District

		Democrat		Republican	
1976	President	65,243	(39.3%)	96,377	(58.1%)
	House	74,993	(45.1%)	91,443	(54.9%)
1978	Governor	89,452	(64.5%)	46,672	(33.6%)
	Senate	48,758	(35.3%)	89,212	(64.7%)
	House	54,783	(39.8%)	82,826	(60.2%)
1980	President	64,030	(28.8%)	134,454	(60.5%)
	Senate	112,476	(50.8%)	105,796	(47.8%)
	House	95,673	(46.0%)	112,282	(54.0%)
1982	Governor	85,856	(52.5%)	77,631	(47.5%)
	House	74,388	(46.3%)	86,277	(53.7%)

Demographics

Population: 472,412. **Percent Change from 1970:** 40.5%.

Land Area: 39,306 square miles. **Population per Square Mile:** 12.0.

Counties, 1980 Population: Ada (Pt.) — 121,951; Adams — 3,347; Benewah — 8,292; Boise — 2,999; Bonner — 24,163; Boundary — 7,289; Canyon — 83,756; Clearwater — 10,390; Gem — 11,972; Idaho — 14,769; Kootenai — 59,770; Latah — 28,749; Lewis — 4,118; Nez Perce — 33,220; Owyhee — 8,272; Payette — 15,722; Shoshone — 19,226; Valley — 5,604; Washington — 8,803.

Cities, 1980 Population: Boise City (Pt.) — 53,903; Caldwell — 17,699; Coeur d'Alene — 20,054; Lewiston — 27,986; Moscow — 16,513; Nampa — 25,112.

Race and Ancestry: White — 96.2%; Black — 0.2%; American Indian, Eskimo and Aleut — 1.1%; Asian and Pacific Islander — 0.7%. Spanish Origin — 3.4%. Dutch — 1.0%; English — 12.6%; French — 1.3%; German — 10.7%; Irish — 4.3%; Italian — 0.7%; Norwegian — 1.5%; Scottish — 1.1%; Swedish — 1.6%.

Universities, Enrollment: College of Idaho, Caldwell — 708; Lewis-Clark State College, Lewiston — 2,181; North Idaho College, Coeur d'Alene — 1,919; Northwest Nazarene College, Nampa — 1,320; University of Idaho, Moscow — 8,869.

Newspapers, Circulation: Bee (e), Sandpoint — 3,489; *Coeur d'Alene Press* (e), Coeur d'Alene -- 13,236; *Idahonian* (e), Moscow — 6,399; *The Idaho Free Press*, Nampa — 17,995; *The Idaho Statesman* (mS), Boise — 56,920; *The Kellogg Evening News* (e), Kellogg — 6,691; *North Idaho Press* (e), Wallace — 1,870; *The Tribune* (mS), Lewiston — 25,179.

Commercial Television Stations, Affiliation: KIVI, Nampa (ABC); KLEW-TV, Lewiston (CBS); KTRV, Nampa (None); KTVB, Boise (NBC). District is divided between Boise ADI and Spokane (Wash.) ADI.

Military Installations. Gowen Field Air Terminal (Air Force), Boise — 1,180; Wilder Radar Bomb Scoring Site (Air Force), Wilder — 56.

Industries:

Potlatch Corp.; (Wood Products Div.; Pulp Div; Consumers Products Div.); Lewiston; wood, pulp, paper products — 4,300. **Louisiana-Pacific Corp.** (Intermountain); Coeur d'Alene; lumber — 1,600. **J. R. Simplot Co. Inc.** (Food Div.); Caldwell; canned fruits, vegetables — 1,500. **Hewlett-Packard Co.;** Boise; electronic computing equipment — 1,350. **Boise Cascade Corp.** (Timber Wood Products Div.); Boise; sawmill — 650.

Diamond International Corp. (Northwest Lumber Div.); Coeur d'Alene; lumber — 650. **Asarco Inc.** (NW Mining Dept.); Wallace; lead, zinc, silver mining — 600. **Simplot Livestock Co.;** Grandview; cattle feed lot — 600. **Sunshine Mining Co.;** Kellogg; silver, antimony, copper mining — 600. **United Pacific Insurance Co.;** Boise; life insurance — 600. **Omark Industries Inc.;** Lewiston; small arms ammunition — 550.

2nd District

East — Pocatello, Idaho Falls

Mormons migrating north from Utah first settled southeastern Idaho in the mid-1800s, and today their influence is pervasive in the area. Almost two-thirds of the people in southeast Idaho are of the Mormon faith, and, like their religious brethren elsewhere, the Mormons here support conservative candidates and causes. In the 1978 gubernatorial election, a conservative Mormon Republican received majorities in many of the southeastern counties of the 2nd District while losing badly in the 1st District, where the Mormon influence is much less significant. Ronald Reagan's 77.6 percent in 1980 was the highest since Warren G. Harding's 70.5 percent in 1920 for any presidential candidate in Bonneville County (Idaho Falls).

The city of Idaho Falls processes potatoes grown in the surrounding upper Snake River Valley. It is located 30 miles from the nuclear plant test site that pioneered commercial nuclear power in the 1950s.

The other populous and reliably Republican county in southeast Idaho is Twin Falls. It is in the center of the Magic Valley farming area, so named because the sandy soil in this region, when irrigated with Snake River water, produces remarkable yields of potatoes, sugar beets and other cash crops. Twin Falls County gave Reagan 74 percent in 1980.

The most significant pocket of Democratic strength in the 2nd District is in Bannock County, which has 14 percent of the district's population and gave Democratic Sen. Frank Church nearly 59 percent of the vote in 1980. Located in Bannock County is southeast Idaho's largest city, Pocatello, a railroad and chemical center specializing in phosphate fertilizers. Democratic strength springs from a heavy labor vote and a sizable student vote from Idaho State University.

Two other centers of Democratic votes in the 2nd are in Blaine County, home of the Sun Valley resorts, and in the eastern section of Boise around Boise State University. Church won 69 percent of the Blaine County vote in 1980, his highest percentage in the state. The eastern section of Boise went Democratic in both the Senate and House elections in 1980, although Reagan won it comfortably.

The addition of 15 marginally Democratic Boise precincts to the 2nd District did not make much political difference. Despite the Democratic strength in Bannock and Blaine counties and in Boise, those areas together amount to less than a third of the total 2nd District vote. That is not nearly enough to offset overwhelming Republican majorities in Bonneville and Twin Falls counties and in the farm, ranch and wilderness region around them.

Election Returns

2nd District		Democrat		Republican	
1976	President	61,306	(35.0%)	107,774	(61.6%)
	House	86,906	(49.5%)	88,565	(50.5%)
1978	Governor	80,088	(53.5%)	67,477	(45.0%)
	Senate	40,877	(28.0%)	105,200	(72.0%)
	House	63,229	(42.8%)	84,445	(57.2%)
1980	President	46,162	(21.4%)	156,245	(72.6%)
	Senate	101,963	(46.7%)	112,905	(51.7%)
	House	86,388	(41.7%)	120,759	(58.3%)
1982	Governor	79,509	(48.8%)	83,526	(51.2%)
	House	76,608	(47.7%)	83,873	(52.3%)

Demographics

Population: 471,523. **Percent Change from 1970:** 25.1%.

Land Area: 43,107 square miles. **Population per Square Mile:** 10.9.

Counties, 1980 Population: Ada (Pt.) — 51,085; Bannock — 65,421; Bear Lake — 6,931; Bingham — 36,489; Blaine — 9,841; Bonneville — 65,980; Butte — 3,342; Camas — 818; Caribou — 8,695; Cassia — 19,427; Clark — 798; Custer — 3,385; Elmore — 21,565; Franklin — 8,895; Fremont — 10,813; Gooding — 11,874; Jefferson — 15,304; Jerome — 14,840; Lemhi — 7,460; Lincoln — 3,436; Madison — 19,480; Minidoka — 19,718; Oneida — 3,258; Power — 6,844; Teton — 2,897; Twin Falls — 52,927.

Cities, 1980 Population: Blackfoot — 10,065; Boise City (Pt.) — 48,548; Idaho Falls — 39,590; Pocatello — 46,340; Rexburg — 11,559; Twin Falls — 26,209.

Race and Ancestry: White — 94.9%; Black — 0.4%; American Indian, Eskimo and Aleut — 1.2%; Asian and Pacific Islander — 0.7%. Spanish Origin — 4.4%. Dutch — 0.8%; English — 23.7%; French — 1.1%; German — 8.4%; Irish — 2.8%; Italian — 0.7%; Norwegian — 0.8%; Scottish — 1.2%; Swedish — 2.0%.

Universities, Enrollment: Boise State University, Boise — 10,425; College of Southern Idaho, Twin Falls — 3,217; Idaho State University, Pocatello — 6,032; Ricks College, Rexburg — 6,342.

Newspapers, Circulation: *Idaho State Journal* (eS), Pocatello — 19,805; *The Morning News of Southern Idaho* (m), Blackfoot — 5,710; *The Post-Register* (meS), Idaho Falls — 25,696; *South Idaho Press* (eS), Burley — 6,752; *The Times-News* (mS), Twin Falls — 20,522. The *Idaho Statesman* also circulates in portions of district.

Commercial Television Stations, Affiliation: KBCI-TV, Boise (CBS); KID-TV, Idaho Falls (CBS); KIFI-TV, Idaho Falls (NBC); KMVT, Twin Falls (NBC, CBS, ABC); KPVI, Pocatello (ABC). Most of district is in Idaho Falls-Pocatello ADI. Portions are in Boise ADI, Twin Falls ADI, Missoula (Mont.)-Butte (Mont.) ADI and Salt Lake City (Utah) ADI.

Military Installations: Mountain Home Air Force Base, Mountain Home — 4,695.

Industries:

E G & G of Idaho Inc.; Idaho Falls; nuclear power research — 3,700. **Westinghouse Electric Corp.** (Atomic Div.); Idaho Falls; nuclear reactor parts — 2,500. **Morrison-Knudsen Co. Inc.** (HQ); Boise; heavy pipeline construction — 1,200. **Ore-Ida Foods Inc.**; Burley; frozen potatoes — 1,200. **St. Luke's Regional Medical Center**; Boise; hospital — 1,150.

Exxon Nuclear Idaho Co.; Idaho Falls; nuclear fuel processing — 1,000. **Bucyrus-Erie Co.**; Pocatello; mining machinery — 950. **Amfac Foods Inc.**; American Falls; frozen potatoes — 900. **Dart Industries Inc.** (Tupperware Co.); Jerome; plastic housewares — 725. **Boise Cascade Corp.** (HQ); Boise; paper products — 700. **Consolidated Foods Corp.** (Idaho Frozen Foods Div.); Twin Falls; frozen potatoes — 700. The **R. T. French Co.** (Potato Div.); Shelley; potato starch — 700.

The University of Chicago (Argonne National Laboratory); Idaho Falls; atomic research — 690. **Quality Inn**; Pocatello; motel — 635. **American Microsystems Inc.**; Pocatello; integrated circuits — 625. **FMC Corp.** (Industrial Chemical Group); Pocatello; inorganic chemicals — 600. **J. R. Simplot Co.**; Pocatello; fertilizer — 600. **Mitchell Construction Co. Inc.** (HQ); Pocatello; industrial contractors — 590. **Cal Ida Chemical Co.**; Boise; beef cattle feedlot — 500. **Gilbert Industrial Contracting Co.**; Challis; heavy construction — 500.

Illinois

The surprise ending of the Illinois redistricting saga was the approval of a partisan Democratic congressional map despite the presence of a Republican governor, a GOP-controlled state House and a three-judge federal panel with two Nixon appointees. The map eliminated two suburban Republican districts even though most of the state's population decline occurred in Chicago's inner city.

A major realignment was necessary because reapportionment cost Illinois two districts, forcing a reduction from 24 House seats to 22. Because control of the state Legislature was split between the parties, it was obvious early in 1981 that no compromise could be reached. As a result, the federal court took responsibility for selecting a redistricting plan.

Its ruling came Nov. 23, 1981, on a 2-1 vote that chose the redistricting map drawn up by Democrats in the Legislature over a Republican proposal. The decisive vote was cast by U.S. Appeals Court Judge Robert Sprecher, who had been named to the federal bench by President Richard Nixon. Sprecher sided with the one court appointee named by Jimmy Carter. The third judge, also a Nixon selection, said in his dissent that the map was a partisan effort to preserve urban Democratic constituencies in Chicago.

The Democratic victory was due in part to a computer program that made possible the creation of congressional districts having almost exactly equal population. The most populous district in the state had only 171 more residents than the least populous one. That accuracy seemed to impress the court, which did not express any concern over the fact that the redrawn district lines divided cities and carved up counties all over the state.

The court did commend the Democratic plan for preserving three black-majority districts in Chicago. Though the Republican plan also appeared to preserve the three districts, at least one would have been less than 65 percent black, and the court felt a 65 percent figure might be necessary to ensure continued black congressional representation. The Democratic plan kept all three districts at least 67 percent black.

Another explicit factor in the court decision was the overall strength of each party in the state. The court said Illinois appeared to be about evenly divided between Democrats and Republicans, based on recent election returns, and that the Democratic map would come closest to that split.

Democrats drew their map for the express purpose of protecting as many of their incumbents as possible. Led by Michael Madigan, the state House minority leader, they concentrated their cartographic ingenuity on the Chicago area.

The adjoining 1st, 5th and 7th districts in Chicago had suffered respective population losses of 20, 14.6 and 19.8 percent, making them obvious targets for consolidation. All but one of the other five city districts also had lost population. In contrast the surrounding suburban districts had gained population; the old 14th, for example, had grown by 34.8 percent. To retain the eight Democratic seats based in the city, Madigan extended them into the Republican suburbs, adding enough population to reach the ideal district size but leaving the city residents with the voting majority. Several districts reached outside the city limits for the first time. Only one district remained entirely within Chicago.

As a result of the new alignment, two sets of Republican incumbents were thrown into merged constituencies. On the northern edge of the city, the Democratic 9th District expanded into the heart of the old Republican, suburban 10th. The new 10th ended up with two Republican incumbents, forcing one to retire rather than face a primary battle.

In the southern and western suburbs, a GOP district was broken apart, placing two Republican incumbents in the new 4th District. The two faced each other in the primary, forcing the loss of another Republican seat.

After rearranging the Chicago districts, the cartographers focused their attention on the southern Illinois district, where the Democratic incumbent had barely held his seat in 1980. By borrowing about 40,000 Democratic voters from St. Clair County and shifting a few other counties, the map makers made the new 22nd a more firmly Democratic district.

Once these goals were accomplished, the Democrats worked a little mischief on downstate Republicans. They removed from the 20th District suburban Springfield, where Republicans had run well in the past, and added three Democratic counties and the industrial city of Decatur. The result was a 1982 Democratic victory over an 11-term Republican.

Elsewhere in the state, the computer cranked out population equality with little regard for county lines or other government jurisdictions. In Decatur, the district line

ILLINOIS

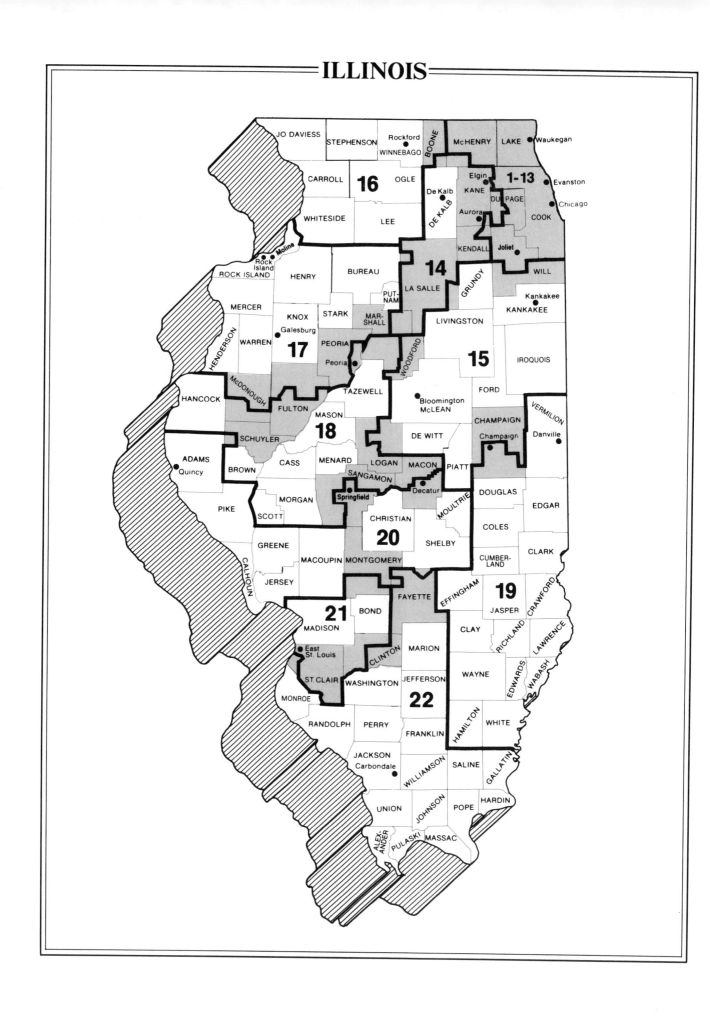

went through the middle of a Caterpillar Tractor plant, placing the plant manager in the 18th and the director of employee relations in the 20th. House Minority Leader Robert H. Michel got a district largely new to him, with his traditional home base of Peoria barely inside the line. The 15th District had to be given an artificial thumb to include the GOP incumbent's home.

The Democratic victory provided a form of revenge for the redistricting that took place a decade earlier, when a different federal panel accepted a Republican map that cost the Democratic Party two seats.

Age of Population

District	Population Under 18	Voting Age Population	Population 65 & Over (% of VAP)	Median Age
1	160,120	358,925	53,927 (15.0%)	28.4
2	178,104	340,827	35,955 (10.5%)	26.0
3	139,644	379,396	65,329 (17.2%)	32.0
4	162,525	356,524	43,743 (12.3%)	28.3
5	141,776	377,195	61,278 (16.2%)	30.2
6	151,099	367,916	38,548 (10.5%)	29.8
7	175,070	343,964	44,535 (12.9%)	26.2
8	143,848	375,186	64,532 (17.2%)	30.3
9	96,220	422,900	70,023 (16.6%)	32.4
10	151,049	368,611	40,566 (11.0%)	29.8
11	109,456	409,539	86,119 (21.0%)	37.4
12	162,242	356,939	35,082 (9.8%)	28.7
13	149,288	370,153	44,505 (12.0%)	31.0
14	154,468	367,441	49,852 (13.6%)	28.7
15	148,486	370,509	56,330 (15.2%)	28.5
16	154,211	364,824	58,988 (16.2%)	30.1
17	146,831	372,502	66,095 (17.7%)	30.3
18	150,367	368,659	62,341 (16.9%)	30.1
19	131,618	386,732	68,713 (17.8%)	29.3
20	143,251	375,764	75,365 (20.1%)	31.7
21	153,745	367,291	62,217 (16.9%)	30.0
22	139,619	381,684	77,842 (20.4%)	31.3
State	3,243,037	8,183,481	1,261,885 (15.4%)	29.9

Income and Occupation

District	Median Family Income	White Collar Workers	Blue Collar Workers	Service Workers	Farm Workers
1	$ 14,017	56.5%	25.6%	17.6%	0.2%
2	20,074	46.7	37.9	15.1	0.3
3	25,756	54.5	32.6	12.5	0.3
4	25,510	51.3	36.3	11.7	0.6
5	20,773	44.2	43.1	12.3	0.5
6	29,491	65.4	25.5	8.8	0.3
7	16,074	54.1	31.1	14.5	0.3
8	18,433	44.6	42.1	13.0	0.3
9	25,207	73.0	16.0	10.7	0.3
10	31,471	69.6	20.0	9.7	0.8
11	25,126	58.4	29.6	11.7	0.3
12	27,476	61.0	28.1	9.6	1.3
13	30,638	67.9	23.0	8.6	0.5
14	25,376	53.0	32.5	11.9	2.5
15	21,740	46.7	32.5	14.9	5.9
16	22,143	44.3	39.2	12.0	4.5
17	21,576	44.8	36.3	13.5	5.4
18	21,707	49.9	31.9	13.3	4.9
19	18,826	47.7	31.8	14.6	5.9
20	19,765	50.7	29.7	14.3	5.3
21	20,365	49.1	34.2	14.3	2.4
22	17,605	43.3	36.2	15.6	4.9
State	$ 22,746	54.2%	31.2%	12.5%	2.1%

Education: School Years Completed

District	8 Years or Fewer	4 Years of High School	4 Years of College or More	Median School Years
1	20.9%	26.8%	14.2%	12.3
2	21.0	33.8	6.8	12.2
3	16.2	40.2	12.1	12.4
4	15.0	38.9	14.6	12.5
5	32.1	31.0	6.4	11.9
6	8.9	36.4	23.8	12.8
7	22.7	27.0	16.1	12.3
8	33.7	27.4	8.5	11.9
9	13.0	23.5	35.4	13.2
10	8.9	29.0	33.3	13.1
11	20.2	33.7	15.2	12.4
12	9.4	37.9	21.4	12.8
13	8.4	34.4	27.7	12.9
14	13.9	38.1	18.5	12.6
15	17.5	41.1	13.7	12.4
16	17.6	41.5	11.7	12.4
17	17.0	42.9	11.4	12.4
18	17.3	40.9	13.8	12.5
19	21.7	36.9	14.9	12.4
20	19.8	40.4	12.4	12.4
21	22.9	36.7	11.3	12.3
22	29.8	34.4	9.6	12.2
State	18.5%	35.1%	16.2%	12.5

Housing and Residential Patterns

District	Owner Occupied	Renter Occupied	Urban	Rural
1	27.9%	72.1%	100.0%	0.0%
2	56.0	44.0	100.0	0.0
3	74.8	25.2	99.9	0.1
4	71.4	28.6	91.8	8.2
5	52.1	47.9	99.9	0.1
6	75.6	24.4	100.0	0.0
7	33.0	67.0	100.0	0.0
8	38.7	61.3	100.0	0.0
9	34.7	65.3	100.0	0.0
10	73.4	26.6	98.8	1.2
11	59.4	40.6	100.0	0.0
12	74.3	25.7	80.2	19.8
13	76.0	24.0	95.7	4.3
14	71.1	28.9	74.7	25.3
15	68.4	31.6	55.3	44.7
16	70.2	29.8	64.1	35.9
17	72.7	27.3	60.9	39.1
18	71.7	28.3	62.7	37.3
19	69.7	30.3	58.2	41.8
20	72.0	28.0	63.1	36.9
21	70.9	29.1	79.8	20.2
22	74.4	25.6	47.8	52.2
State	62.6%	37.4%	83.3%	16.7%

1st District

Chicago — South Side

The 1st contains the heart of Chicago's black South Side, an area that has been important in local politics since the 1920s — before most Northern cities even had substantial black populations. Although it is a very poor area, with the decaying buildings common to the inner city everywhere, it also has a stable black middle class. In the 1960s, when blacks on the more transient West Side rioted, this area was quiet.

Before World War II, most of the city's black population was concentrated here, just west of the wealthy residential areas on the shore of Lake Michigan. But in recent years, as color barriers have fallen in other parts of the city and its southern suburbs, people have been leaving the South Side in large numbers. During the 1970s, the 1st lost 20 percent of its population. To keep it in existence for the 1980s, map makers extended its boundaries in virtually every direction, bringing in voters from other urban districts, which in turn were stretched into the suburbs to gain back the population they gave up.

Like the old 1st, the new district is overwhelmingly Democratic. About 92 percent of its residents are black, the highest black percentage of any district in the U.S. Its small white population, centered around the University of Chicago in Hyde Park, is as Democratic as the black majority. Rep. Harold Washington, D, used his base in the district in 1983 to gain election as Chicago's first black mayor.

Some of the district's middle-class professionals live around the Michael Reese Hospital complex, newly added to the district on its northern border. Others live in Chatham, which has been a prosperous black residential neighborhood since the 1950s. Some blue-collar workers at the southern end of the district work in the steel mills of South Chicago.

Many of the district's poorer black residents live in public housing projects, buildings seen as enlightened urban renewal when built during the 1950s but now derided as "vertical ghettoes." One of them, the Robert Taylor Homes, is the largest such project in the country. It extends for 25 blocks and houses 75,000 people.

Election Returns

1st District		Democrat		Republican	
1976	President	188,194	(89.8%)	20,620	(9.8%)
	Governor	137,843	(69.0%)	61,714	(30.9%)
	House	168,176	(91.1%)	15,956	(8.6%)
1978	Governor	83,168	(67.6%)	38,223	(31.1%)
	Senate	74,329	(55.3%)	58,038	(43.2%)
	House	72,757	(66.2%)	36,564	(33.3%)
1980	President	177,491	(90.7%)	10,912	(5.6%)
	Senate	163,012	(91.2%)	11,620	(6.5%)
	House	160,075	(94.7%)	9,018	(5.3%)
1982	Governor	132,602	(73.0%)	47,313	(26.0%)
	House	172,641	(97.3%)	4,820	(2.7%)

Demographics

Population: 519,045. **Percent Change from 1970:** -18.9%.

Land Area: 32 square miles. **Population per Square Mile:** 16,220.2.

Counties, 1980 Population: Cook (Pt.) — 519,045.

Cities, 1980 Population: Chicago (Pt.) — 519,045.

Race and Ancestry: White — 6.4%; Black — 92.1%; American Indian, Eskimo and Aleut — 0.1%; Asian and Pacific Islander — 0.8%. Spanish Origin — 1.1%. English — 1.4%; German — 0.6%.

Universities, Enrollment: Catholic Theological Union, Chicago — 258; Chicago College of Osteopathic Medicine, Chicago — 395; Chicago State University, Chicago — 6,998; Chicago Theological Seminary, Chicago — 135; Illinois College of Optometry, Chicago — 598; Illinois Institute of Technology, Chicago — 7,254; Jesuit School of Theology in Chicago, Chicago — 96; Kennedy-King College, Chicago — 7,205; Lutheran School of Theology at Chicago, Chicago — 289; Meadville/Lombard Theological School, Chicago — 34; Olive-Harvey College, Chicago — 3,973; University of Chicago, Chicago — 9,048; VanderCook College of Music, Chicago — 121.

Newspapers, Circulation: Chicago *Sun-Times* and *Chicago Tribune* circulate in the district.

Commercial Television Stations, Affiliation: Entire district is located in Chicago ADI.

Industries:

Michael Reese Hospital & Medical Center; Chicago; hospital — 4,700. **Mercy Hospital & Medical Center;** Chicago; hospital — 2,000. **Chicago Osteopathic Medical Center;** Chicago; hospital — 1,550. **South Chicago Community Hospital;** Chicago; hospital — 1,280. **R. R. Donnelley and Sons Co.** (HQ); Chicago; commercial printing — 1,000.

Verson Allsteel Press Co. (HQ); Chicago; metal forming machine tools — 900. **IIT Research Institute** (HQ); Chicago; scientific research — 850. **McCormick Inn Corp.;** Chicago; hotel — 600. **Goodman Equipment Corp.;** Chicago; mining equipment — 570. **Cardwell Westinghouse Co.;** Chicago; railroad equipment — 520.

2nd District

Chicago — South Side; Harvey

For the first time, the 2nd District has crept beyond the city limits, into the southern suburbs formerly included in the 3rd. The politics of the district does not change dramatically, however.

The new lines of the 2nd were carefully drawn to take in communities with black majorities. As a result, blacks comprise 70 percent of the population, compared with 77 percent in the old city district. Harvey, an older industrial city, and Dixmoor, a suburb, are about two-thirds black. Phoenix, a village of about 3,000, has only 136 white residents. Phoenix has been nearly all-black for the past 60 years.

But the new 2nd also takes in some white suburban territory, including Riverdale, and parts of Dolton and Calumet City, all blue-collar in orientation and less than 10 percent black. Many of the people here moved out from the far South Side of the city in the 1960s and 1970s.

The district still includes the vast industrial area around the Calumet River, where the sky, trees and grass have long been blackened with soot, but where factory workers have been able to count on steady work and decent pay. By the early 1980s the grass was still gray, but the mills were in decline. Wisconsin Steelworks closed in 1980. Other steel mills were operating below capacity. Fewer freighters were using Chicago's ports, reducing the number of jobs available to dockworkers.

Election Returns

2nd District		Democrat		Republican	
1976	President	120,666	(72.5%)	45,713	(27.5%)
	Governor	95,455	(58.3%)	67,809	(41.4%)
	House	129,801	(79.0%)	34,270	(20.9%)
1978	Governor	62,665	(59.0%)	42,115	(39.7%)

2nd District		Democrat		Republican	
1978	Senate	62,302	(56.1%)	46,756	(42.1%)
	House	84,007	(80.7%)	18,414	(17.7%)
1980	President	151,227	(73.4%)	47,347	(23.0%)
	Senate	151,287	(85.0%)	23,955	(13.5%)
	House	133,773	(83.0%)	27,309	(16.9%)
1982	Governor	117,238	(70.1%)	48,372	(28.9%)
	House	140,827	(87.0%)	20,670	(12.8%)

Demographics

Population: 518,931. **Percent Change from 1970:** -1.9%.

Land Area: 68 square miles. **Population per Square Mile:** 7,631.3.

Counties, 1980 Population: Cook (Pt.) — 518,931.

Cities, 1980 Population: Blue Island (Pt.) — 6,296; Calumet City (Pt.) — 14,871; Chicago (Pt.) — 408,240; Dolton (Pt.) — 16,478; Harvey (Pt.) — 34,117; Markham (Pt.) — 5,480; Riverdale — 13,233; South Holland (Pt.) — 1,241.

Race and Ancestry: White — 25.3%; Black — 70.3%; American Indian, Eskimo and Aleut — 0.1%; Asian and Pacific Islander — 0.2%. Spanish Origin — 7.4%. English — 1.4%; German — 1.7%; Irish — 1.3%; Italian — 1.3%; Polish — 3.8%.

Universities, Enrollment: Thornton Community College, South Holland — 9,406.

Newspapers, Circulation: *The Daily Calumet* (e), Chicago — 8,648. Chicago *Sun Times* and Chicago *Tribune* also circulate in the district.

Commercial Television Stations, Affiliation: Entire district is located in Chicago ADI.

Industries:

Republic Steel Corp.; Chicago; steel mill — 4,500. **Ford Motor Co.** (Auto Div.); Chicago; auto assembly — 3,000. **The Sherwin-Williams Co.**; Chicago; paints — 2,200. **Ingalls Memorial Hospital;** Harvey; hospital — 1,900. **Interlake Inc.** (Iron & Steel Div.); Chicago; steel mill — 1,800.

M. W. Kellogg Co. (Pullman Standard Div.); Chicago; railroad equipment — 1,650. **Indiana Harbor Belt Railroad Co.;** Chicago; railroad operations — 1,600. **Wyman Gordon Co.** (Midwest Div.); Harvey; iron, steel forgings — 1,300. **United States Steel Corp.** (South Chicago Works Div.); Chicago; steel — 1,200. **Whiting Corp.** (Swenson Div. - HQ); Harvey; furnaces — 1,150. **Allis-Chalmers Corp.** (Engine Div.); Harvey; engines — 1,000. **Missouri Pacific Railroad Co.;** Dolton; railroad operations — 900. **Libby McNeill & Libby Inc.;** Chicago; canned meats — 800.

Allied Tube & Conduit Corp. (HQ); Harvey; conduit tubing — 700. **Ball Glass Containers Inc.;** Dolton; glass products — 700. **General Mills Inc.;** Chicago; cereals — 700. **Norfolk & Western Railway Co.;** Chicago; railroad services — 600. **Microdot Inc.** (Valley Mould & Iron Co. Div.); Chicago; steel mill — 550. **Bliss & Laughlin Industries** (Steel Co. Div.); Harvey; steel foundries — 500. **The Sherwin-Williams Co.;** Chicago; paints — 500. **Unarco Industries Inc.** (Leavitt Div.); Chicago; steel pipe, tubes — 500.

3rd District

Southwest Chicago and Suburbs

The line between the 2nd and 3rd districts is also the line between black and white Chicago. The 3rd District, concentrated on the west side of Western Avenue and in the suburbs just beyond the city, is less than 6 percent black.

About 40 percent of the population is new to the district. The new territory comes primarily from the old

4th District, a suburban constituency that Democratic map makers divided up and used to fill out underpopulated city-based districts. The 3rd lost some of its eastern portions to the 2nd.

The remaining city portions of the district are dominated by blue-collar ethnics, many of Polish and Lithuanian origin. Beverly, traditional home for Chicago's well-to-do Irish Catholics, is also included.

The suburbs in the 3rd include most of Blue Island, developed for Illinois Central railroad workers, and Oak Lawn, a 19th century suburb that now has a large Greek-American population. Midlothian and Oak Forest, built up in the 1960s, have drawn blue-collar workers from South Chicago. Most of the district's small black population is in Robbins, which has been majority-black for a generation, and Markham, which lost many of its white residents in the 1970s and is now about 70 percent black. South Holland has a significant Dutch population but has also attracted Italians, Poles and others from Chicago's South Side.

The area's voting patterns have been erratic. Many of the people here are ethnics who emerged into prosperity in the 1960s, left the city, and began to vote Republican in some contests. When the old 3rd was drawn in 1972, it was expected to send a Republican to the House. But it turned out the GOP incumbent for a Democrat in 1974 and returned him by comfortable margins for the rest of the decade. Many of these communities swing back and forth between the parties in state and national elections, choosing Republicans in better times and returning to the Democratic fold in years of recession.

Election Returns

3rd District		Democrat		Republican	
1976	President	79,792	(43.0%)	104,166	(56.1%)
	Governor	74,417	(40.4%)	109,470	(59.4%)
	House	96,815	(58.0%)	69,318	(41.5%)
1978	Governor	58,095	(42.3%)	78,508	(57.1%)
	Senate	68,972	(49.6%)	68,770	(49.5%)
	House	87,623	(65.8%)	45,636	(34.2%)
1980	President	95,274	(44.2%)	105,358	(48.8%)
	Senate	126,714	(60.7%)	79,743	(38.2%)
	House	112,360	(66.4%)	56,820	(33.6%)
1982	Governor	107,024	(55.6%)	82,950	(43.1%)
	House	137,391	(74.0%)	48,268	(26.0%)

Demographics

Population: 519,040. **Percent Change from 1970:** -2.0%.

Land Area: 105 square miles. **Population per Square Mile:** 4,943.2.

Counties, 1980 Population: Cook (Pt.) — 519,040.

Cities, 1980 Population: Alsip (Pt.) — 12,890; Blue Island (Pt.) — 15,559; Bridgeview (Pt.) — 2,644; Burbank — 28,462; Chicago (Pt.) — 206,990; Chicago Ridge — 13,473; Country Club Hills (Pt.) — 9,377; Crestwood (Pt.) — 6,250; Evergreen Park — 22,260; Glenwood (Pt.) — 969; Harvey (Pt.) — 1,693; Hazel Crest (Pt.) — 13,229; Homewood (Pt.) — 8,092; Markham (Pt.) — 9,692; Midlothian — 14,274; Oak Forest — 26,096; Oak Lawn — 60,590; Orland Park (Pt.) — 0; South Holland (Pt.) — 17,201; Tinley Park (Pt.) — 13,663; Worth (Pt.) — 2,872.

Race and Ancestry: White — 91.9%; Black — 5.7%; American Indian, Eskimo and Aleut — 0.1%; Asian and Pacific Islander — 0.7%.

Spanish Origin — 3.5%. Dutch — 1.7%; English — 2.0%; German — 6.7%; Greek — 1.0%; Irish — 11.2%; Italian — 4.2%; Polish — 9.1%; Swedish — 1.1%.

Universities, Enrollment: Richard J. Daley College, Chicago — 4,860; Saint Xavier College, Chicago — 2,203.

Newspapers, Circulation: The Chicago *Sun-Times* , *Chicago Tribune* and Chicago *Southtown Economist* circulate in the district. Foreign language newspaper: *Draugas* (Lithuanian), Chicago — 14,000.

Commercial Television Stations, Affiliation: Entire district is located in Chicago ADI.

Industries:

Nabisco Inc.; Chicago; cookies — 3,000. **Evangelical Hospital Assn.;** Oak Lawn; psychiatric hospital — 2,500. **Oak Forest Hospital;** Oak Forest; county hospital — 2,220. **Little Company of Mary Hospital;** Evergreen Park; hospital — 2,000. **Maryland Cup Corp.** (Sweetheart Cup Div.); Chicago; food containers — 1,800.

Holy Cross Hospital; Chicago; hospital — 1,600. **Rentar Industries;** Oak Lawn; trucking — 1,400. **Rheem Mfg. Co.** (Ruud Water Heating Div.); Chicago; metal shipping containers — 1,200. **Sisters of Mary Inc.;** Blue Island; hospital — 1,200. **Johnson & Johnson Products Inc.;** Chicago; fabricated rubber products — 1,100. **American Can Co.;** Chicago; metal cans — 1,035. **Tootsie Roll Industries Inc.** (HQ); Chicago; candy — 800. **General Foods Corp.** (Packaged Convenience Foods); Chicago; processed foods — 700. **C. W. Transport Inc.;** Oak Lawn; trucking — 650. **Douglas Furniture Corp.** (Advent Furniture Div.); Chicago; metal household furniture — 650. **Talman Home Federal Savings & Loan Assn.** (HQ); Chicago; savings & loan association — 650.

FCS Industries Inc.; Chicago; trucking — 600. **John Milton Co. Inc.** (Slumberon); Chicago; mattresses — 600. **Nalco Chemical Co.;** Bedford Park; medicinal chemicals — 600. **Federal Signal Corp.;** Blue Island; signaling equipment — 550. **Inland Steel Co.** (Container Co. Div.); Chicago; fabricated steel shipping containers — 525. **McLean Trucking Co.;** Oak Lawn; trucking — 511. **Borden Inc.** (Cracker Jack Div.); Chicago; candy — 500. **Ethicon Inc.;** Chicago; sutures — 500. **Illinois Central Gulf Railroad Co. Inc.;** Hazel Crest; railroad operations — 500. **Midas-International Corp.;** Chicago; motor vehicle parts — 500.

4th District

Southern Chicago Suburbs, Joliet, Aurora

The 4th is a new animal, built from remnants of the old 4th, 15th and 17th districts. It includes the southern end of Cook County, the section of Will County around the city of Joliet, and portions of Kane and Kendall counties around the city of Aurora. This conglomeration is firmly Republican, although it has pockets of Democratic voters in Aurora, Joliet and Chicago Heights.

The old 4th District, a suburban area that ran along the western edge of the city and then spread out to the southwest, was completely dismantled in the redistricting plan. Only Rich Township, an affluent suburban area, was left in the new 4th. The rest of the old district was a casualty of the geographic realignment designed to preserve the Democratic districts in Chicago.

Joliet, a largely blue-collar city of 78,000, has several oil refineries. Although once a major steel center, the city has lost most of its steel plants, including a U.S. Steel facility that shut down in late 1979. Joliet is also a center for barge traffic coming through the Chicago Sanitary and Ship Canal. It is essentially a Democratic city.

The old 17th District contributed Bloom Township to the 4th. Bloom includes the blue-collar communities around the industrial city of Chicago Heights, the site of the first steel-making facility in Chicago. The nearby bedroom community of Lansing was shifted from the 3rd District to the new 4th.

The town of Aurora, about 60 percent of which is in the new 4th, and a section of Kendall County around the small town of Oswego had been in the old 15th district. Aurora, a 19th century industrial city on the Fox River, still has a heavy equipment industry.

Election Returns

4th District		Democrat		Republican	
1976	President	111,214	(47.8%)	118,762	(51.0%)
	Governor	51,648	(28.5%)	129,234	(71.2%)
	House	78,979	(45.5%)	94,432	(54.4%)
1978	Governor	37,140	(30.9%)	82,111	(68.4%)
	Senate	48,773	(41.5%)	67,809	(57.6%)
	House	43,078	(36.2%)	75,864	(63.8%)
1980	President	71,355	(36.2%)	109,523	(55.5%)
	Senate	102,950	(52.9%)	89,370	(45.9%)
	House	71,578	(38.8%)	112,790	(61.2%)
1982	Governor	58,783	(41.0%)	82,497	(57.5%)
	House	66,323	(45.4%)	79,842	(54.6%)

Demographics

Population: 519,049. **Percent Change from 1970:** 13.9%.

Land Area: 204 square miles. **Population per Square Mile:** 2,544.4.

Counties, 1980 Population: Cook (Pt.) — 224,388; Kane (Pt.) — 68,203; Kendall (Pt.) — 3,866; Will (Pt.) — 222,592.

Cities, 1980 Population: Aurora (Pt.) — 54,757; Bolingbrook (Pt.) — 7,899; Calumet City (Pt.) — 24,826; Chicago Heights — 37,026; Country Club Hills (Pt.) — 5,299; Dolton (Pt.) — 8,288; Glenwood (Pt.) — 9,569; Hazel Crest (Pt.) — 744; Homewood (Pt.) — 11,632; Joliet (Pt.) — 77,938; Lansing — 29,039; Matteson — 10,223; Naperville (Pt.) — 628; Park Forest (Pt.) — 22,911; Romeoville — 15,519; Sauk Village — 10,906; South Holland (Pt.) — 6,535; Tinley Park (Pt.) — 29.

Race and Ancestry: White — 84.7%; Black — 11.2%; American Indian, Eskimo and Aleut — 0.2%; Asian and Pacific Islander — 0.8%. Spanish Origin — 6.9%. Dutch — 1.3%; English — 3.6%; German — 8.2%; Irish — 4.0%; Italian — 3.5%; Polish — 4.5%; Swedish — 1.0%.

Universities, Enrollment: College of St. Francis, Joliet — 3,251; Joliet Junior College, Joliet — 10,280; Lewis University, Romeoville — 2,813; Prairie State College, Chicago Heights — 5,721.

Newspapers, Circulation: *The Beacon-News* (eS), Aurora — 41,365; *Herald-News* (eS), Joliet — 50,196. Chicago *Sun Times* and *Chicago Tribune* also circulate in the district.

Commercial Television Stations, Affiliation: WFBN, Joliet (None). Entire district is located in Chicago ADI.

Military Installations: Joliet Army Ammunition Plant, Joliet — 338.

Industries:

Ford Motor Co. (Metal Stamping Div.); Chicago Heights; auto stampings — 2,500. **Caterpillar Tractor Co. Inc.;** Joliet; earth moving equipment — 2,400. **Franciscan Sisters Health Care;** Joliet; hospital — 1,890. **Barber-Greene Co.** (HQ); Aurora; asphalt machinery — 1,650. (Note: plant straddles 4th and 14th districts.) **Sisters of St. Francis Health Service;** Chicago Heights; hospital — 1,500.

Elgin, Joliet & Eastern Railway Co. (HQ); Joliet; railroad operations — 1,400. **Thrall Car Mfg. Co.** (HQ); Chicago Heights; railroad cars — 1,350. **Norlin Industries Inc.** (Lowery Electronics Div.); Lockport; musical instruments — 1,200. **Russ Togs Inc.** (R. & M. Kaufmann Div.); Aurora; women's dresses — 1,200. **Mercy Center Health Care Service;** Aurora; hospital — 1,100. **Silver Cross Hospital;** Joliet; hospital — 1,100. **Burlington Northern Inc.;** Aurora; rail terminal operations — 800. **Borg-Warner Corp.** (Sealmaster Bearing Div.); Aurora; ball, roller bearings — 700. **Union Oil Co.;** Romeoville; oil refinery — 687. **Allis-Chalmers Corp.** (Industrial Truck Div.); Matteson; industrial trucks — 640.

Stauffer Chemical Co.; Chicago Heights; inorganic chemicals — 635. **Armour-Dial Inc.;** Montgomery; soap products — 600. **GAF Corp.** (Industrial Products Div.); Joliet; felt roofing material — 600. **Material Service Corp.;** Lockport; concrete products — 600. **Olin Corp.;** Joliet; phosphates — 592. **Anchor Brush Co. Inc.** (Lakewood Metal Products Div. - HQ); Montgomery; brushes, sewing notions — 520. **Hobart Corp.;** Chicago Heights; commercial food machinery — 500. **Owens-Illinois Inc.;** Chicago Heights; glass, glassware — 500. **Pittway Corp.;** Aurora; fire detection devices — 500. **Roadway Express Inc.;** Chicago Heights; truck terminal — 500. **Thor Power Tool Co.;** Aurora; pneumatic power tools — 500.

5th District

South Central Chicago and Suburbs

Nearly twice the geographic size of the old 5th District, the new version begins about a mile from Lake Michigan and extends west to the split-levels of suburban Willow Springs, following the route of the Adlai Stevenson Expressway.

The 5th had to expand because it lost 15 percent of its population during the 1970s. But despite the realignment, it remains firmly Democratic territory; it keeps not only the home territory of the late Mayor Richard J. Daley, but also the political organization he dominated. The Daley machine has stayed intact in most of the city parts of the new 5th District, even though it has decayed elsewhere in Chicago.

Daley lived his entire life in Bridgeport, an almost exclusively Irish neighborhood, but Eastern Europeans, especially Poles, dominate the broader territory within the congressional district.

Some of the additions increase the district's Republican vote. The new 5th picked up the Czech and Bohemian enclaves of Cicero and Berwyn, which have been voting Republican in most contests, and the white-collar suburbs of Bridgeview and Hickory Hills, which lean to the GOP. But the inner suburban communities of McCook, Countryside, Hodgkins and Summit, all of which are industrial, echo the Democratic tendencies of the Chicago part of the district.

At the district's eastern end is the old Union Stockyards, a few blocks from the Daley home. Largely abandoned in the 1950s by the meatpacking industry, the huge stockyards area has in recent years become an industrial park, with two dozen new warehouses and light industrial operations.

Redistricting changed the racial makeup of the 5th dramatically. By 1980 the old 5th District had become 30 percent black, reflecting the movement of blacks into the southeastern part of the district, despite some white resistance. But the redistricting plan transferred these neighborhoods to the overwhelmingly black 1st District, and the suburbs brought into the 5th were virtually all white. Berwyn, a city of 47,000 for example, had only 13 blacks in the 1980 census. As a result, only 3 percent of the residents of the new 5th District are black.

The new 5th does retain a significant Hispanic population. About a quarter of its people are Hispanic, up from 17 percent in the old 5th.

Election Returns

5th District		Democrat		Republican	
1976	President	99,925	(53.2%)	87,259	(46.5%)
	Governor	99,925	(50.2%)	99,318	(49.8%)
	House	130,724	(70.5%)	54,791	(29.5%)
1978	Governor	108,833	(64.0%)	59,266	(34.9%)
	Senate	101,454	(58.7%)	69,245	(40.0%)
	House	100,633	(62.4%)	60,645	(37.6%)
1980	President	103,702	(51.8%)	83,448	(41.7%)
	Senate	121,296	(64.6%)	63,977	(34.1%)
	House	111,070	(56.8%)	84,585	(43.2%)
1982	Governor	89,381	(58.4%)	61,985	(40.5%)
	House	110,351	(75.4%)	35,970	(24.6%)

Demographics

Population: 518,971. **Percent Change from 1970:** -2.7%.

Land Area: 75 square miles. **Population per Square Mile:** 6,919.6.

Counties, 1980 Population: Cook (Pt.) — 518,971.

Cities, 1980 Population: Berwyn — 46,849; Bridgeview (Pt.) — 11,511; Brookfield (Pt.) — 8,248; Chicago (Pt.) — 309,662; Cicero — 61,232; Hickory Hills — 13,778; Justice — 10,552; La Grange (Pt.) — 2,590; Palos Hills (Pt.) — 6,557; Summit — 10,110.

Race and Ancestry: White — 79.6%; Black — 3.4%; American Indian, Eskimo and Aleut — 0.2%; Asian and Pacific Islander — 1.7%. Spanish Origin — 26.0%. English — 1.4%; German — 3.9%; Greek — 0.6%; Irish — 4.0%; Italian — 4.7%; Polish — 13.6%.

Universities, Enrollment: Morton College, Cicero — 3,482.

Newspapers, Circulation: *Southtown Economist* (eS), Chicago — 14,418. The Chicago *Sun-Times*, Chicago *Tribune* and Chicago *Daily Herald* also circulate in the district. Foreign language newspaper: *Denni Hlasatel* (Czech), Cicero — 6,769.

Commercial Television Stations, Affiliation: Entire district is located in Chicago ADI.

Industries:

General Motors Corp. (Electro-Motive Div.); La Grange; railroad equipment — 6,000. **Western Electric Co. Inc.** (Switching Equipment Div.); Chicago; telephone equipment — 4,400. **General Motors Corp.** (Fisher Body Div.); Willow Springs; auto assembly 2,800. **Burlington Northern Railroad;** Chicago; railroad terminal operation — 2,500. **Sweetheart Cup Corp.** (Northwest Cone Co. - HQ); Chicago; paper cups — 2,000.

Central Steel & Wire Co. (HQ); Chicago; metal service centers — 1,750. **Reynolds Metals Corp.** (Sheet & Plate Works); McCook; sheet metal works — 1,750. **CPC International Inc.** (Corn Products Div.); Argo; corn starch — 1,600. **General Electric Co.** (Major Appliance Business Group); Cicero; refrigerators, electric ranges, air conditioners, washers & dryers — 1,600. **MacNeal Memorial Hospital;** Berwyn; hospital — 1,540. **Campbell Soup Co.;** Chicago; soup — 1,400. **Maryland Cup Corp.;** Chicago; cookies, crackers — 1,400. **Minnesota Mining & Mfg. Co.;** Argo; paper coating, glazing — 1,000. **Rockwell Graphic Systems Inc.** (Miehle Commercial Products - HQ); Chicago; printing machinery — 1,000. **Pullman Inc.** (Trailmobile Div.); Chicago; motor vehicle wholesaling — 780. **Midland Ross Corp.;** Chicago; steel foundries — 750. **Federated Industries Inc.;** Chicago; wine, liquor wholesaling — 725. **The Bunker Ramo Corp.** (Amphenol North America Div.); Chicago; electronic connectors — 700.

Certified Grocers; La Grange; grocery wholesaling — 600. **Westinghouse Electric Corp.** (Control Center Div.); Chicago; motors, generators — 600. **Joslyn Mfg. & Supply Co. Inc.** (Hardware Div.); Chicago; iron, steel forgings — 560. **Pielet Bros. Scrap Iron & Metal** (Automotive Processing Div.); Argo; scrap materials wholesaling — 504. **Allied Products Corp.** (Phoell Mfg. Co.); Chicago; bolts, screws, rivets — 500. **Burlington Northern Inc.** (Bridge & Building Dept.); Chicago; railroad operations — 500. **Peter Eckrich & Sons Inc.;** Chicago; meatpacking — 500. **Schulze & Burch Biscuit Co.** (HQ); Chicago, cookies — 500. **Vulcan Materials Co. Inc.;** La Grange; concrete products — 500.

6th District

Far West Chicago Suburbs — Wheaton

Like the neighboring 4th, the old 6th was chopped up and grafted in pieces onto the western ends of inner-city Chicago districts that needed to gain population. Only a small area around Itasca and Wood Dale was carried over to the new 6th. The redrawn district takes in parts of Cook County, but Du Page County dominates, casting more than 60 percent of the vote.

Republicans are stronger in the new district. The old 6th had pockets of Democratic strength in Maywood and other moderate-income suburbs with significant black populations. There are no such enclaves apparent in the new district, whose suburban territory is nearly all white-collar and Republican.

The new 6th follows the route of two commuter railroad lines that drew Chicago residents westward as early as the 1930s. The suburbs of Elmhurst, Villa Park, Lombard, Glen Ellyn and Wheaton spread out from the city in the southern part of the district. Further north are Wood Dale, Itasca and Roselle, newer suburbs that still are expanding. Roselle has more than doubled in size since 1970. Schaumburg, which was rural in 1960, has tripled in size during the 1970s, with condominiums and apartment complexes cropping up around its enormous shopping center.

Less affluent is the area between the rail lines, including Glendale Heights and Addison, which have some light industry. A huge industrial park is located near Elk Grove Village, another fast-growing suburb to the north.

On its northeastern border, the new 6th District hooks into neighboring Cook County to take in most of the older, prosperous suburbs of Des Plaines and Park Ridge. Des Plaines adjoins O'Hare Airport and is the home of many airline employees.

Election Returns

6th District		Democrat		Republican	
1976	President	72,192	(33.0%)	142,229	(65.0%)
	Governor	44,825	(20.6%)	170,818	(78.6%)
	House	40,740	(16.2%)	210,697	(83.8%)
1978	Governor	10,884	(8.8%)	111,952	(90.4%)
	Senate	38,691	(31.1%)	84,063	(67.6%)
	House	36,805	(28.9%)	90,679	(71.1%)
1980	President	51,049	(25.4%)	126,318	(62.9%)
	Senate	88,306	(43.3%)	112,703	(55.3%)
	House	52,118	(25.2%)	154,722	(74.8%)

6th District		Democrat		Republican	
1982	Governor	40,179	(27.2%)	104,633	(70.9%)
	House	45,237	(31.6%)	97,918	(68.4%)

Demographics

Population: 519,015. **Percent Change from 1970:** 19.4%.

Land Area: 162 square miles. **Population per Square Mile:** 3,203.8.

Counties, 1980 Population: Cook (Pt.) — 193,311; Du Page (Pt.) — 325,704.

Cities, 1980 Population: Addison — 29,759; Bensenville (Pt.) — 16,121; Bloomingdale — 12,659; Carol Stream (Pt.) — 12,844; Chicago (Pt.) — 11; Des Plaines (Pt.) — 49,623; Downers Grove (Pt.) — 2,411; Elk Grove Village (Pt.) — 28,679; Elmhurst (Pt.) — 42,216; Glen Ellyn (Pt.) — 19,767; Glendale Heights — 23,163.

Hanover Park (Pt.) — 15,371; Hoffman Estates (Pt.) — 3,465; Lombard (Pt.) — 36,873; Mount Prospect (Pt.) — 9,383; Niles (Pt.) — 3,194; Park Ridge (Pt.) — 38,105; Roselle — 16,948; Schaumburg (Pt.) — 36,767; Villa Park (Pt.) — 21,507; Wheaton (Pt.) — 24,522; Wood Dale — 11,251.

Race and Ancestry: White — 95.2%; Black — 0.8%; American Indian, Eskimo and Aleut — 0.1%; Asian and Pacific Islander — 2.9%. Spanish Origin — 2.9%. Dutch — 0.5%; English — 3.3%; German — 10.8%; Greek — 1.1%; Irish — 4.7%; Italian — 6.2%; Norwegian — 0.7%; Polish — 6.1%; Swedish — 1.3%.

Universities, Enrollment: College of Du Page, Glen Ellyn — 21,530; Elmhurst College, Elmhurst — 3,311; Midwest College of Engineering, Lombard — 235; National College of Chiropractic, Lombard — 980; Northern Baptist Theological Seminary, Lombard — 192; Wheaton College, Wheaton — 2,496.

Newspapers, Circulation: *Chicago Tribune*, Chicago *Daily Herald*, and Chicago *Sun-Times* circulate in the district.

Commercial Television Stations, Affiliation: Entire district is located in Chicago ADI.

Industries:

Lutheran General Hospital Inc.; Park Ridge; hospital — 4,000. **UOP Inc.** (HQ); Des Plaines; inorganic chemicals, construction services, copper products, plastics — 3,500. **UAL Inc.** (HQ); Mount Prospect; air transportation, hotels, insurance claims adjusting — 3,320. **Power Systems Inc.;** Roselle; power systems construction — 2,500. **Memorial Hospital;** Elmhurst; hospital — 1,450.

Honeywell Inc. (Commercial Div.); Elk Grove Village; farm machinery, equipment — 1,230. **Alexian Brothers Medical Center;** Elk Grove Village; hospital — 1,200. **Union Oil Co. of California** (Union 76 Div.- Eastern Region); Roselle; petroleum refining — 1,200. **Bally Mfg. Corp.;** Bensenville; coin operated amusement machines — 1,000. **Littelfuse Inc.** (HQ); Des Plaines; circuit control devices — 930. **Household Merchandising Inc.** (Ben Franklin Div. - HQ); Des Plaines; general merchandise stores — 906. **Energy Cooperative;** Des Plaines; petroleum refining — 800. **Spraying Systems Co.;** Wheaton; spraying systems — 800. **Jovan Inc.** (Yardley of London); Bensenville; cosmetics — 750. **Brown & Root Inc.** (Chicago Engineering Div.); Lombard; engineering services — 700. **Zurich Insurance Co.** (HQ); Roselle; life insurance — 700. **International Telephone & Telegraph Corp.;** Des Plaines; telephone, telegraph equipment — 675. **Flick-Reedy Corp.** (HQ); Bensenville; hydraulic machinery — 660.

Desoto Inc. (HQ); Des Plaines; paints — 600. **Motorola Inc.** (Display Products); Wheaton; electronic communications equipment — 600. **General Telephone Directory Co.** (HQ); Des Plaines; telephone directories — 590. **The Meyercord Co. Inc.** (HQ); Wheaton; commercial printing — 575. **Ace Hardware Corp.** (HQ); Oak Brook; hardware — 550. **Federal Pacific Electric Co.** (Economy Fuse Div.); Des Plaines; electrical distribution & control equipment — 550. **AM International Inc.** (Services Div.); Roselle; welding repair services — 500. **Beeline Fashions Inc.** (HQ); Bensenville; women's apparel wholesaling — 500. **Container Corp. of America** (Folding Carton Div.); Wheaton; folding paper boxes — 500. **Field Container Corp.** (HQ); Elk Grove Village; folding cartons — 500. **McGraw-Edison Co.** (Halo Lighting Div.); Elk Grove Village; lighting — 500. **Motorola Communications** (Parts Dept.); Roselle; electronic parts wholesaling — 500.

7th District

Chicago — Downtown, West Side

The 7th District is home to much of Chicago's corporate life, which includes the headquarters of Sears, Roebuck & Co. and Marcor Inc., the holding company for Montgomery Ward & Co. Inc. But only a few blocks west of Chicago's lakefront, with its elegant high-rises and nearby shops, the rank poverty of the West Side begins, with burned-out buildings and abandoned factories that stretch for miles. The West Side has traditionally been a port of entry for migrants to the city: Jews and Italians early in this century, and blacks in the past generation. Roosevelt Road, running west from downtown out to the city limits, was the urban riot corridor in the 1960s.

The old 7th lost one-fifth of its population during the 1970s, but both parties wanted to preserve a black-majority district. So the 7th was redrawn to stretch twice its previous length, from Lake Michigan more than a dozen miles west to suburban Bellwood. Mixed in among the residential areas are industrial zones, with a major A & P warehouse and Sears trucking facilities. The campus of the University of Illinois at Chicago Circle is in the district, along with the West Side medical center complex.

Much of the new territory is made up of areas such as Austin along the city's western border, traditionally Eastern European in ethnic makeup but increasingly black during the 1970s. The new district lines increased the black population in the 7th from 50 percent to about 67 percent.

Further west, the 7th picked up some white-collar suburban territory, including Oak Park, one of the city's oldest suburbs, and Republican River Forest. Both communities feature several early Frank Lloyd Wright buildings. The suburbs of Maywood and Bellwood are predominantly black and vote Democratic.

Election Returns

7th District		Democrat		Republican	
1976	President	117,450	(68.2%)	53,344	(31.0%)
	Governor	98,721	(58.6%)	69,369	(41.2%)
	House	115,817	(85.1%)	20,263	(14.9%)
1978	Governor	65,397	(58.9%)	44,465	(40.0%)
	Senate	65,829	(57.5%)	47,080	(41.2%)
	House	76,601	(70.3%)	32,333	(29.7%)
1980	President	124,826	(70.1%)	40,421	(22.7%)
	Senate	136,335	(78.6%)	33,482	(19.3%)
	House	103,019	(68.9%)	46,424	(31.1%)
1982	Governor	109,858	(67.7%)	50,622	(31.2%)
	House	133,978	(86.5%)	20,994	(13.5%)

Demographics

Population: 519,034. **Percent Change from 1970:** -15.8%.

Land Area: 39 square miles. **Population per Square Mile:** 13,308.6.

Counties, 1980 Population: Cook (Pt.) — 519,034.

Cities, 1980 Population: Bellwood (Pt.) — 14,218; Chicago (Pt.) — 382,228; Forest Park (Pt.) — 4,919; Maywood — 27,998; Melrose Park (Pt.) — 15,286; Oak Park — 54,887; River Forest — 12,392.

Race and Ancestry: White — 29.0%; Black — 66.9%; American Indian, Eskimo and Aleut — 0.1%; Asian and Pacific Islander — 1.4%. Spanish Origin — 4.7%. English — 2.0%; German — 2.5%; Irish — 2.3%; Italian — 2.6%; Polish — 1.3%.

Universities, Enrollment: Alfred Adler Institute, Chicago — 120; American Academy of Art, Chicago — 980; American Conservatory of Music, Chicago — 369; Central Y.M.C.A. Community College, Chicago — 4,401; Chicago City-Wide College, Chicago — 4,880; Chicago College of Commerce, Chicago — 869; Chicago Conservatory College, Chicago — 58; College of Automation, Chicago — 625; Columbia College, Chicago — 3,827.

Concordia College, River Forest — 1,194; The Harrington Institute of Interior Design, Chicago — 460; Illinois College of Podiatric Medicine, Chicago — 642; Illinois Technical College, Chicago — 325; International Academy of Merchandising and Design, Chicago — 249; John Marshall Law School, Chicago — 1,606; Keller Graduate School of Management, Chicago — 1,131; Loop College, Chicago — 7,256; MacCormac Junior College, Chicago — 419; Malcom X College, Chicago — 4,179; Marion Adult Education and Career Training Center, Chicago — 389.

Moody Bible Institute, Chicago — 1,347; Ray-Vogue School of Design, Chicago — 386; Roosevelt University, Chicago — 7,046; Rosary College, River Forest — 1,590; Rush University, Chicago — 1,153; School of the Art Institute of Chicago, Chicago — 1,857; Sherwood Music School, Chicago — 40; Spertus College of Judaica, Chicago — 199; University of Illinois at Chicago Circle, Chicago — 21,001; University of Illinois at the Medical Center, Chicago — 4,912.

Newspapers, Circulation: *Chicago Defender* (m), Chicago — 16,789; *Chicago Tribune* (all day, S), Chicago — 784,925; *Sun-Times* (mS), Chicago — 667,200. Foreign language newspaper: *Abendpost* (German), Chicago — 10,000.

Commercial Television Stations, Affiliation: WBBM-TV, Chicago (CBS); WCFC-TV, Chicago (None); WCIU-TV, Chicago (None, Spanish); WFLD-TV, Chicago (None); WLS-TV, Chicago (ABC); WMAQ-TV, Chicago (NBC). Entire district is located in Chicago ADI. *(For other Chicago stations, see 8th and 9th districts.)*

Industries:

First National Bank of Chicago (HQ); Chicago; banking — 8,500. **Chicago, Milwaukee, St. Paul Pacific Railroad;** Chicago; railroad operations — 8,010. **Continental Illinois National Bank & Trust Co. of Chicago** (HQ); Chicago; banking — 7,000. **Sears, Roebuck & Co.** (HQ); Chicago; department stores — 7,000. **Young & Rubicam;** Chicago; advertising agency — 6,650.

Cook County Hospital; Chicago; hospital — 6,000. **Rush-Presbyterian St. Luke's Medical Center;** Chicago; hospital — 5,700. **Standard Oil Co. (Indiana)** (HQ); Chicago; oil production, refining — 5,300. **GTE Automatic Electric Inc.** (HQ); Melrose Park; telephone apparatus — 5,100. **Northwestern Memorial Hospital;** Chicago; hospital — 4,500. **Sargent & Lundy Engineers;** Chicago; engineering services — 4,500. **Chicago Tribune Co.** (HQ); Chicago; newspaper publishing — 4,100. **Montgomery Ward & Co. Inc.;** Chicago; administrative offices — 4,000. **American Home Products Corp.** (E. J. Brach & Sons); Chicago; candy — 3,830. **Loyola University Medical Center;** Maywood; hospital — 3,550. **Harris Trust & Savings Bank** (HQ); Chicago; banking — 3,500. **Marcor Inc.** (HQ); Chicago; holding company — 3,100. **Northern Trust Corp.** (HQ); Chicago; bank holding company — 3,030. **Veterans Administration;** Maywood; veterans' hospital — 3,000.

Aldens Inc. (HQ); Chicago; mail order house — 2,900. **Health Care Service Corp.** (HQ); Chicago; health insurance — 2,700. **Hospital Service Corp.** (HQ); Chicago; hospital insurance — 2,500. **National Kinney Corp.** (Maintenance Service Inc.); Chicago; janitorial services — 2,500. **University of Illinois Hospital;** Chicago; hospital — 2,500. **Federal Reserve Bank of Chicago;** Chicago; banking — 2,280. **General Electric Co. Inc.** (Hotpoint General Electric Co.); Chicago; household appliances — 2,200. **Sunbeam Corp.** (HQ); Chicago; electrical appliances — 2,200. **Skidmore Owings and Merrill;** Chicago; architects —

2,050. **Arthur Andersen & Co.** (HQ); Chicago; accounting services — 2,000. **Veterans Administration**; Chicago; veterans' hospital — 2,000. **Mount Sinai Hospital & Medical Center of Chicago**; Chicago; hospital — 1,940. **Bunker Ramo Corp.** (Amphenol Connector Div.); Maywood; electronic connectors — 1,800. **The Chicago Hotel Venture**; Chicago; hotel — 1,800.

Illinois Central Gulf Railroad Co. (HQ); Chicago; railroad operations — 1,800. **Time Inc.**; Chicago; periodicals publishing — 1,800. **Chicago & North Western Transportation Co.** (HQ); Chicago; railroad operations — 1,700. **Admiral Maintenance Service Co.**; Chicago; janitorial services — 1,500. **Joseph T. Ryerson & Son Inc.** (HQ); Chicago; steel wholesaling — 1,500. **Borg-Warner Corp.** (Spring-Brummer Div.); Bellwood; motor vehicle parts — 1,400. **Palmer House Co.**; Chicago; hotel — 1,400. **Leo Burnett Co. Inc.** (HQ); Chicago; advertising agency — 1,350. **American National Bank & Trust Co. of Chicago** (HQ); Chicago; banking — 1,300. **Pettibone Corp.** (Beardsley & Piper Div. - HQ); Chicago; construction machinery — 1,300. **Wieboldt Stores Inc.** (HQ); Chicago; department stores — 1,300. **Union Special Corp.** (HQ); Chicago; industrial sewing machines — 1,250. **Goldblatt Bros. Inc.** (HQ); Chicago; department stores — 1,200. **Hilton Hotels Corp.**; Chicago; hotel — 1,200.

The Quaker Oats Co. (HQ); Chicago; cereals — 1,200. **United States Gypsum Co.** (Wood Fiber Products Div.); Chicago; wood products — 1,190. **West Suburban Hospital Assn.**; Oak Park; hospital — 1,110. **Alexander Proudfoot Co.**; Chicago; management services — 1,100. **St. Anne's Hospital of Chicago Inc.**; Chicago; hospital — 1,100. **Chicago Title Insurance Co.** (HQ); Chicago; title insurance — 1,000. **Conticommodity Services Inc.** (Continfinancial Div.); Chicago; commodities brokers — 1,000. **Continental Casualty Co.** (HQ); Chicago; casualty, accident insurance — 1,000. **International Business Machines Corp.**; Chicago; business machine wholesaling — 1,000. **International Harvester Co.** (HQ); Chicago; trucks; farm, construction machinery — 1,000. **Joanna Western Mills Co.** (Standard Shade Roller Div. - HQ); Chicago; window shades — 1,000. **National Ben Franklin Insurance Co. of Illinois**; Chicago; fire, casualty insurance — 1,000. **Otis Elevator Co.**; Chicago; industrial elevators marketing — 1,000. **Pinkerton's Inc.**; Oak Park; security services — 1,000.

United States Gypsum Co. (HQ); Chicago; gypsum products — 1,000. **World Book-Childcraft International Inc.** (HQ); Chicago; book publishing — 1,000. **Allied Van Lines Inc.** (HQ); Maywood; trucking — 900. **Leaf Confectionery Inc.** (HQ); Chicago; candy, gum — 900. **Marriott Corp.** (Chicago Marriott Hotel); Chicago; hotel — 900. **The Baltimore & Ohio Railroad Co.** (Chessie System Railroads); Chicago; railroad terminal operations — 850. **Millard Maintenance Service Co. Inc.** (HQ); Chicago; janitorial services — 850. **A. G. Becker Inc.** (HQ); Chicago; securities dealers — 800. **Encyclopaedia Britannica Inc.** (F. E. Compton & Co. Div. - HQ); Chicago; book publishing — 800. **Walter E. Heller International** (HQ); Chicago; financing services — 800. **Chas. A. Stevens & Co.** (HQ); Chicago; women's clothing stores — 800. **Hyatt Corp.**; Chicago; business services — 780.

Peat Marwick Mitchell & Co.; Chicago; accounting services — 750. **Ritz Carlton of Chicago Inc.**; Chicago; hotel — 750. **Statistical Tabulating Corp.** (HQ); Chicago; computer programming, data processing services — 750. **Blue Cross Assn.** (HQ); Chicago; health insurance — 700. **Ernst & Whinney**; Chicago; accounting services — 700. **Harza Engineering Co.** (HQ); Chicago; engineering services — 700. **La Salle National Bank** (HQ); Chicago; banking — 700. **Ryan Insurance Group Inc.**; Chicago; life, health insurance — 700. **Travelers Insurance Co.**; Chicago; life, health insurance — 700. **Chicago Board Options Exchange** (HQ); Chicago; securities exchange — 680. **Henrotin Hospital**; Chicago; hospital — 650. **Inland Steel Co.** (HQ); Chicago; steel, iron ore mines — 650. **National Broadcasting Co.**; Chicago; radio, television broadcasting — 650. **Prudential Building Maintenance Corp.** (Chicago Floor Maintenance Corp.); Chicago; janitorial services — 650.

Radisson Hotel Corp.; Chicago; hotel — 650. **A. G. Becker-Warburg Paribas Becker Inc.** (HQ); Chicago; investment banking — 636. **Anadite Inc.** (Kropp Forge Div.); Chicago; forgings, foundries — 600. **Chicago Title & Trust Co.** (HQ); Chicago; title insurance — 600. **Fluor Power Services Inc.**; Chicago; engineering services — 600. **Follett Corp.** (Follett Library Book Co. Div. - HQ); Chicago; book publishing — 600. **Hyre Electric Co.**; Chicago; electrical contracting — 600. **Henry C. Lytton & Co.** (HQ); Chicago; family clothing stores — 600.

Morton-Norwich Products Inc. (HQ); Chicago; salt, household cleaning products — 600. **Natural Gas Pipeline Co.** (HQ); Chicago; natural gas transmission — 590. **The Hartford Fire Insurance Co.**; Chicago; fire, casualty insurance — 575. **CBS Inc.**; Chicago; television broadcasting — 550. **Chicago Executive House Inc.**; Chicago; hotel — 550. **The Exchange National Bank of Chicago** (HQ); Chicago; banking — 550.

Gulf & Western Mfg. Co. (Taylor Forge Div.); Chicago; valves, pipe fittings — 550. **Science Research Associates Inc.** (HQ); Chicago; book publishing — 550. **Swift & Co.** (HQ); Chicago; meatpacking — 550. **GATX Corp.** (HQ); Chicago; mining machinery, railroad equipment — 543. **United Insurance Co. of America** (HQ); Chicago; life, health insurance — 525. **Northwest Airlines Inc.**; Chicago; commercial airline — 510. **Amity Building Service Corp.**; Chicago; janitorial services — 500. **Beatrice Foods Co.** (The Stiffel Co.); Chicago; vehicular lighting equipment — 500. **Robert Bosch Corp.** (HQ); Maywood; fuel injection systems — 500. **Continental Illinois National Bank & Trust Co. of Chicago**; Chicago; data processing services — 500. **Dana Corp.** (Victor Products Div.); Chicago; gaskets, packing & sealing devices — 500. **Elkay Mfg. Co. Inc.**; Maywood; enameled iron sanitary ware — 500. **Evans Inc.** (HQ); Chicago; women's clothing stores — 500. **Fidelity & Casualty Co. of New York**; Chicago; accident, health insurance — 500.

FMC Corp. (HQ); Chicago; pesticides, industrial chemicals, mining equipment, industrial tractors — 500. **General Foods Corp.** (Breakfast Beverage Div.); Chicago; prepared foods — 500. **D. Gottlieb & Co. Inc.** (HQ); Melrose Park; amusement machines — 500. **Interstate Service Corp.** (HQ); Chicago; security services — 500. **Jenner & Block**; Chicago; law firm — 500. **Kirkland & Ellis** (HQ); Chicago; law firm — 500. **Litton Systems Inc.** (Jefferson Electric Div.); Bellwood; transformers — 500. **Mayer Brown & Platt** (HQ); Chicago; law firm — 500. **Needham Harper & Steers Advertising**; Chicago; advertising agency — 500. **Sidley & Austin** (HQ); Chicago; law firm — 500. **J. Walter Thompson Co. Inc.**; Chicago; advertising agency — 500. **Western Union Corp.**; Chicago; telegraph operations — 500.

8th District

Chicago — North and Northwest Sides

The 8th District expands northwest along Milwaukee Avenue, Chicago's traditional "Polish corridor," to take in such symbolic places as St. Hyacinth Parish, still a first-stop for Polish immigrants and a spot where a question asked in Polish will draw a ready response in the same language.

In the 1970s, the old 8th lost much of its ethnic Polish flavor as blacks and Hispanics moved into its southern and eastern portions, nearest to downtown Chicago.

The new 8th essentially follows its former residents in their movement northwest from the inner city. It is more than 70 percent white, thanks to the addition not only of Polish neighborhoods within the city but of suburbs to the west, including River Grove and Elmwood Park. The new suburban constituents have voted Republican in the past, but they are largely ethnic, recently transplanted from the city and could respond well to the Democrats.

Another important change was the shift of the southern arm of the old 8th to the new 7th. It was in this area, on Chicago's far West Side, that the black population of the old 8th had been concentrated. The new 8th is just 4 percent black.

There is, however, a substantial Hispanic population, increased to nearly 32 percent from the 27 percent in the old 8th. Lower Milwaukee Avenue, once the heart of the city's Polish community, is now overwhelmingly Hispanic.

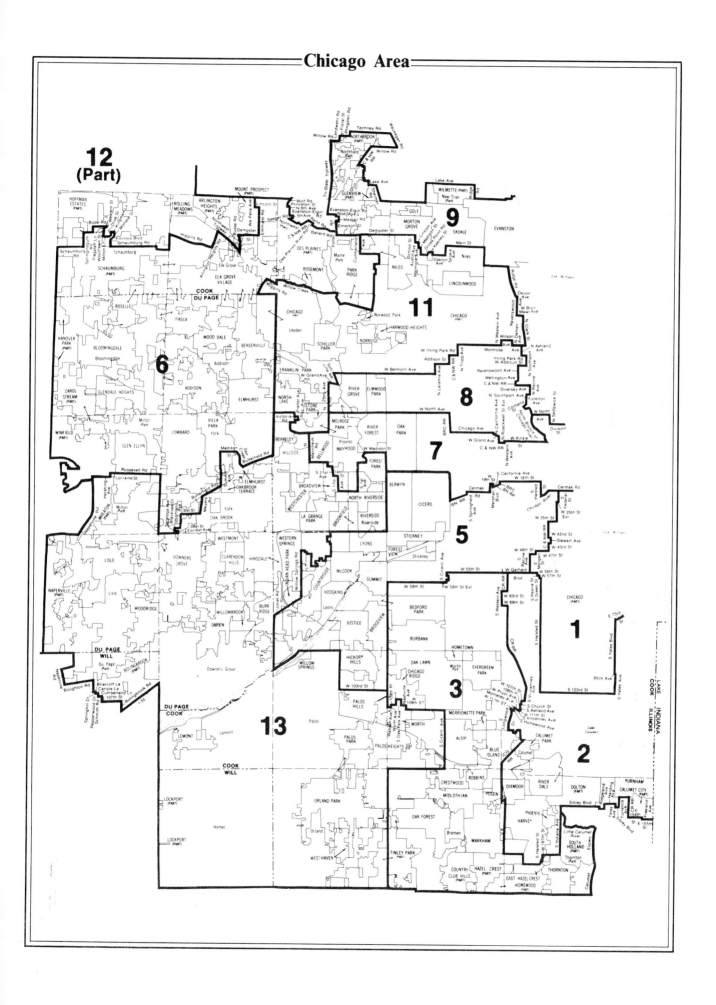

Election Returns

8th District		Democrat		Republican	
1976	President	122,652	(60.1%)	80,327	(39.3%)
	Governor	102,168	(50.9%)	98,108	(48.9%)
	House	134,016	(74.9%)	44,852	(25.1%)
1978	Governor	90,690	(60.1%)	58,976	(39.1%)
	Senate	96,521	(62.3%)	56,811	(36.7%)
	House	107,755	(77.4%)	31,489	(22.6%)
1980	President	111,965	(58.8%)	65,215	(34.3%)
	Senate	121,283	(69.9%)	49,087	(28.3%)
	House	123,040	(74.3%)	42,568	(25.7%)
1982	Governor	106,563	(69.6%)	44,942	(29.4%)
	House	124,318	(83.4%)	24,666	(16.6%)

Demographics

Population: 519,034. Percent Change from 1970: -9.3%.

Land Area: 33 square miles. **Population per Square Mile:** 15,728.3.

Counties, 1980 Population: Cook (Pt.) — 519,034.

Cities, 1980 Population: Chicago (Pt.) — 481,150; Elmwood Park — 24,016; Franklin Park (Pt.) — 1,541; Melrose Park (Pt.) — 1,955; River Grove — 10,368.

Race and Ancestry: White — 75.6%; Black — 4.3%; American Indian, Eskimo and Aleut — 0.3%; Asian and Pacific Islander — 2.4%. Spanish Origin — 31.6%. English — 1.5%; German — 5.8%; Greek — 0.9%; Irish — 3.4%; Italian — 6.7%; Norwegian — 0.5%; Polish — 13.2%; Swedish — 0.5%; Ukranian — 1.2%.

Universities, Enrollment: DeVry Institute of Technology, Chicago — 4,912; Northwestern Business College, Chicago — 272; Triton College, River Grove — 21,125.

Newspapers, Circulation: Foreign language newspaper: *Dziennik Zwiazkowy* (Polish), Chicago — 20,000. Chicago *Sun-Times* and *Chicago Tribune* also circulate in the district.

Commercial Television Stations, Affiliation: WGN-TV, Chicago (None). Entire district is located in Chicago ADI. *(For other Chicago stations, see 7th and 9th districts.)*

Industries:

Stewart-Warner Corp. (Alemite Div. - HQ); Chicago; meters, advertising displays, industrial machinery — 2,500. **St. Mary of Nazareth Hospital Center;** Chicago; hospital — 2,000. **Zenith Radio Corp.;** Chicago; radios — 1,800. **Schwinn Bicycle Co.** (HQ); Chicago; bicycles — 1,700. **Zenith Radio Corp.** (Plant #2); Chicago; radios — 1,600.

Alberto-Culver Co. (HQ); Melrose Park; hair care products — 1,550. **Ekco Products Inc.;** Chicago; food, service industry machinery — 1,500. **Motorola Inc.** (Systems Div.); Franklin Park; radios, televisions — 1,500. **Mars Inc.;** Chicago; chocolate candy — 1,400. **Zenith Radio Corp.** (Rauland Div.); Melrose Park; cathode ray, X-ray tubes — 1,219. **Williams Electronics Inc.** (HQ); Chicago; pinball games — 1,100. **Continental Group Inc.** (White Cap Div.); Chicago; food products machinery — 1,000. **Cotter & Co.** (HQ); Chicago; hardware, home furnishings wholesaling; paint — 1,000. **Helene Curtis Industries Inc.** (HQ); Chicago; hair care products — 1,000. **Chicago Rotoprint Co.;** Chicago; printing — 990. **Playskool Inc.** (HQ); Chicago; toys — 900. **Bodine Electric Co.** (HQ); Chicago; motors, generators, industrial controls — 850. **Brand-Rex Co.** (Pyle National Co.); Chicago; wiring devices — 850. **Danly Machine Corp.** (HQ); Chicago; machine tools, woodworking machinery — 812. **Advance Transformer Co.** (HQ); Chicago; transformers — 750. **Pepsi-Cola General Bottlers Inc.** (HQ); Chicago; soft drink bottling — 750. **Kimco Corp.;** Chicago; janitorial services — 700. **Stern Electronics Inc.** (HQ); Chicago; video machines — 700. **General Signal Corp.** (Lindberg Div.); Chicago; industrial furnaces — 650. **Wallace Murray Inc.** (Illinois Gear Div.); Chicago; gears — 600. **Wells-Gardner Electronics Corp.** (HQ); Chicago; televisions, electronic game monitors —

530. **Entenmanns Inc.;** Melrose Park; bakery goods — 500. **Illinois Tool Works Inc.** (Spiroid Div.); Chicago; special purpose machines — 500. **Pepsico Inc.** (Wilson Sporting Goods Co. Div.); River Grove; athletic goods — 500. **Procter & Gamble Co.;** Chicago; plastics products — 500. **Smoler Industries Inc.** (HQ); Chicago; dresses — 500. **Victor United Inc.** (HQ); Chicago; electronic calculators — 500. **WGN Continental Broadcasting Co.** (HQ); Chicago; radio, TV broadcasting — 500.

9th District

Chicago — North Side Lakefront, Northern Suburbs

The most striking characteristic of the new 9th is its shape. Narrow at its base along Lake Michigan, it widens and turns westward once it reaches the city's northern limits, ending in a hook around the suburbs of Glenview and Northbrook. The purpose of the elaborate cartography was to create a secure district for the Democratic incumbent by including liberal areas within the city and heavily Jewish suburban communities where he should run well.

The old 9th was confined to the city, but it lost nearly 10 percent of its population in the 1970s, forcing an expansion into the suburbs. The new 9th is still anchored on the North Side of Chicago, but it now runs north along the lake all the way to Evanston, and its western area takes in parts of Skokie and Wilmette, most of Morton Grove and a chunk of Northfield township. About 35 percent of the population is new to the district.

The city portion of the new 9th includes a mixture of neighborhoods, from the wealthy lakefront high-rises to the two- and three-story walkups just a few blocks to the west. These apartments house many of the prosperous singles and childless couples who work in professional jobs in downtown Chicago. There is also an urban restoration contingent living in older homes in the area. The city portion of the 9th contains some of Chicago's few remaining GOP wards.

The large Jewish population in the urban lakefront portion of the 9th is predominantly middle-aged, well-to-do and politically active. The 44th and 46th wards, west of the more prosperous neighborhoods, are mostly Hispanic; Hispanics comprise about 10 percent of the overall population of the district. The 9th is also about 10 percent black.

The parts of the district that lie beyond Chicago are not typically suburban in their political outlook. Evanston, once a bastion of conservative Republicanism, has a large liberal community around Northwestern University; it has also attracted young professional couples from Chicago in recent years, and they vote Democratic.

Aiding the Democrats in Evanston is the racial makeup: the city of 74,000 is 21 percent black. Morton Grove, west of Evanston, and neighboring Skokie both are heavily Jewish.

North and west of these communities, in Maine and Northfield townships, are newer suburban developments where voters generally preferred Ronald Reagan to Jimmy Carter in 1980. The part of Northfield in the 9th District was the only township the liberal Democratic incumbent failed to carry in 1982.

Republicans had thought they might have a chance at the seat if they ran an articulate candidate and a strong campaign. But their attempt in 1982 was fruitless; the incumbent won re-election with 67 percent of the vote.

Election Returns

9th District		Democrat		Republican	
1976	President	129,098	(51.2%)	121,293	(48.1%)
	Governor	87,336	(34.7%)	163,583	(65.1%)
	House	145,492	(62.9%)	85,961	(37.1%)
1978	Governor	64,609	(36.3%)	110,976	(62.3%)
	Senate	60,548	(33.5%)	117,697	(65.1%)
	House	115,378	(66.2%)	58,886	(33.8%)
1980	President	110,744	(48.5%)	83,961	(36.8%)
	Senate	145,139	(66.5%)	66,078	(30.3%)
	House	131,093	(59.6%)	88,727	(40.4%)
1982	Governor	110,545	(62.4%)	64,400	(36.4%)
	House	114,083	(66.5%)	54,851	(32.0%)

Demographics

Population: 519,120. **Percent Change from 1970:** -8.9%.

Land Area: 44 square miles. **Population per Square Mile:** 11,798.2.

Counties, 1980 Population: Cook (Pt.) — 519,120.

Cities, 1980 Population: Chicago (Pt.) — 318,899; Evanston — 73,706; Glenview (Pt.) — 17,315; Morton Grove (Pt.) — 20,940; Niles (Pt.) — 7,937; Northbrook (Pt.) — 4,391; Park Ridge (Pt.) — 599; Skokie (Pt.) — 37,670; Wilmette (Pt.) — 9,997.

Race and Ancestry: White — 78.5%; Black — 9.8%; American Indian, Eskimo and Aleut — 0.4%; Asian and Pacific Islander — 6.4%. Spanish Origin — 9.5%. English — 4.2%; French — 0.6%; German — 7.1%; Greek — 1.0%; Hungarian — 0.8%; Irish — 4.7%; Italian — 2.2%; Polish — 3.8%; Russian — 4.7%; Swedish — 1.2%.

Universities, Enrollment: DePaul University, Chicago — 12,857; Garrett-Evangelical Theological Seminary, Evanston — 324; Harry S Truman College, Chicago — 5,637; Kendall College, Evanston — 434; Loyola University of Chicago, Chicago — 15,782; McCormick Theological Seminary, Chicago — 618; Mundelein College, Chicago — 1,491; National College of Education, Evanston — 1,417; Northwestern University, Evanston — 15,539; Seabury-Western Theological Seminary, Evanston — 67.

Newspapers, Circulation: *Chicago Tribune* and Chicago *Sun-Times* circulate in the district. Foreign language newspaper: *Naujienos* (Lithuanian), Chicago — 30,540.

Commercial Television Stations, Affiliation: WSNS, Chicago (None). Entire district is located in Chicago ADI. *(For other Chicago stations, see 7th and 8th districts.)*

Military Installations: Naval Air Station, Glenview — 4,151.

Industries:

American Hospital Supply Corp.; Evanston; medical instruments — 2,000. **The Evanston Hospital Corp.;** Evanston; hospital — 1,900. **Children's Memorial Hospital;** Chicago; hospital — 1,800. **Illinois Masonic Medical Center;** Chicago; hospital — 1,800. **St. Joseph's Hospital;** Chicago; hospital — 1,800.

Edgewater Hospital Inc.; Chicago; hospital — 1,650. **Columbus-Cuneo-Cabrini Medical Center;** Chicago; hospital — 1,600. **The Kane Service** (HQ); Chicago; security services — 1,600. **Avon Products Inc.;** Morton Grove; cosmetics — 1,500. **Grant Hospital of Chicago;** Chicago; hospital — 1,500. **Sisters of St. Francis Health Service;** Evanston; hospital — 1,500. **Washington National Corp.** (HQ); Evanston; life, health insurance — 1,420. **Louis A. Weiss Memorial Hospital;** Chicago; hospital — 1,400. **Appleton Electric Co.** (HQ); Chicago; electric lighting fixtures — 1,300. **Oscar Mayer & Co. Inc.;** Chicago; processed meat products — 1,300.

S & C Electric Co. (HQ); Chicago; high voltage switchgears — 1,270. **Brunswick Corp.** (HQ); Skokie; bowling & billiards equipment; marine engines, aircraft parts — 1,000. **Combined Insurance Co. of America;** Chicago; accident, life insurance — 1,000. **Rand McNally & Co. Inc.** (HQ); Skokie; maps — 900. **American Hospital Supply Corp.** (HQ); Evanston; medical supplies, instruments, drugs — 790. **Anchor Corp.;** Evanston; management investment company — 600. **Aparacor Inc.** (HQ); Evanston; women's wear — 550. **A. Finkl & Sons Co. Inc.** (HQ); Chicago; iron, steel forgings — 540. **Andy Frain Security Services;** Chicago; security services — 500. **G. D. Searle & Co.** (HQ); Skokie; pharmaceuticals — 500.

10th District

North and Northwest Suburbs — Waukegan

The communities along Lake Michigan north of Chicago are the city's oldest suburbs and generally its most affluent. Fully developed long ago, they declined in population in the 1970s as the younger residents grew up and moved away. To erase the resulting population deficit, the map makers moved the district north to merge with portions of the old 12th and the old 13th, which was based in Waukegan. The new 10th extends north to the Wisconsin border, including the old lakefront towns, but sheds most of the newer suburban territory further west.

The hybrid district is firmly Republican. The only major Democratic enclave is the old port city of Waukegan, now a manufacturing center producing pharmaceuticals, hospital supplies and outboard motors. About 14 percent of Waukegan's population is Hispanic.

Much of the district's vote is cast in affluent Lake County towns such as Highland Park, Lake Forest and Deerfield, where most voters tend to prefer moderate Republicans but rarely cross over to the Democratic side. Many of the people who live here commute to professional jobs in downtown Chicago, but in recent years corporate outposts have sprung up among the bedroom communities.

In the 10th is the Great Lakes Naval Training Center, on the lake near North Chicago. The largest such operation in the country, it is the work place for more than 23,000 people.

Election Returns

10th District		Democrat		Republican	
1976	President	70,251	(32.9%)	139,680	(65.3%)
	Governor	38,637	(18.2%)	172,877	(81.4%)
	House	92,961	(42.3%)	125,664	(57.2%)
1978	Governor	31,996	(22.3%)	110,015	(76.8%)
	Senate	40,645	(27.2%)	107,077	(71.6%)
	House	43,625	(31.7%)	94,150	(68.3%)
1980	President	60,308	(27.7%)	129,386	(59.4%)
	Senate	102,986	(48.1%)	107,207	(50.1%)
	House	74,136	(32.8%)	151,994	(67.2%)
1982	Governor	53,072	(33.6%)	102,689	(65.0%)
	House	63,115	(41.0%)	90,750	(59.0%)

Demographics

Population: 519,660. **Percent Change from 1970:** 5.7%.

Land Area: 233 square miles. **Population per Square Mile:** 2,230.3.

Counties, 1980 Population: Cook (Pt.) — 234,696; Lake (Pt.) — 284,964.

Cities, 1980 Population: Arlington Heights (Pt.) — 54,926; Buffalo

Grove — 22,230; Deerfield — 17,430; Des Plaines (Pt.) — 3,945; Glenview (Pt.) — 14,745; Highland Park — 30,611; Lake Forest — 15,245; Libertyville (Pt.) — 16,519; Mount Prospect (Pt.) — 22,366; Mundelein (Pt.) — 9,069; North Chicago (Pt.) — 38,774; Northbrook (Pt.) — 26,387; Prospect Heights — 11,808; Rolling Meadows (Pt.) — 11; Waukegan (Pt.) — 66,342; Wheeling — 23,266; Wilmette (Pt.) — 18,232; Winnetka — 12,772; Zion — 17,861.

Race and Ancestry: White — 90.3%; Black — 5.6%; American Indian, Eskimo and Aleut — 0.1%; Asian and Pacific Islander — 1.9%. Spanish Origin — 4.3%. English — 5.3%; French — 0.5%; German — 9.4%; Greek — 0.8%; Irish — 4.3%; Italian — 3.2%; Norwegian — 0.7%; Polish — 3.6%; Russian — 2.3%; Scottish — 0.5%; Swedish — 1.4%.

Universities, Enrollment: Barat College, Lake Forest — 688; Lake Forest College, Lake Forest — 1,105; Lake Forest School of Management, Lake Forest — 354; Mallinckrodt College, Wilmette — 296; St. Mary of the Lake Seminary, Mundelein — 136; Trinity College, Deerfield — 687; Trinity Evangelical Divinity School, Deerfield — 833; University of Health Sciences-The Chicago Medical School, North Chicago — 688.

Newspapers, Circulation: *The News-Sun* (e), Waukegan — 44,126. *Chicago Tribune* also circulates in the district.

Commercial Television Stations, Affiliation: Entire district is located in Chicago ADI.

Military Installations: Fort Sheridan, Highland Park — 4,210; Great Lakes Naval Public Works Center, North Chicago — 688; Great Lakes Naval Regional Medical Center, North Chicago — 4,019; Great Lakes Naval Training Center, North Chicago — 23,088.

Nuclear Power Plants: Zion 1, Zion (Westinghouse, Commonwealth Edison), December 1973; Zion 2, Zion (Westinghouse, Commonwealth Edison), September 1974.

Industries:

Abbott Laboratories (Ross Laboratories Div. - HQ); North Chicago; pharmaceuticals, medical instruments — 8,000. **Allstate Insurance Co. Inc.** (HQ); Northbrook; auto, life insurance — 3,000. **Outboard Marine Corp.** (Stern Drive - HQ); Waukegan; outboard motors — 3,000. **Northrop Corp.** (Defense Systems Div.); Arlington Heights; electronic communications equipment — 2,200. **American Hospital Supply Corp.** (Scientific Products Div.); Waukegan; hospital supplies — 2,000. **Northwest Community Hospital;** Arlington Heights; hospital — 2,000.

Inventory Control Service Corp.; Buffalo Grove; business services — 1,800. **Kitchens of Sara Lee Inc.** (HQ); Deerfield; frozen bakery products — 1,530. **AM International Inc.** (Multigraphics Div.); Mount Prospect; office machines — 1,500. **Baxter Travenol Laboratories** (HQ); Deerfield; pharmaceuticals, medical instruments — 1,500. **Cherry Electrical Products** (HQ); Waukegan; switches, electronic keyboards — 1,400. **St. Therese Hospital Inc.;** Waukegan; hospital — 1,320. **Zenith Radio Corp.** (HQ); Glenview; radios, televisions — 1,260. **Combined International Corp.** (HQ); Northbrook; accident, life, health insurance — 1,130. **Underwriters Laboratories Inc.** (HQ); Northbrook; commercial testing lab — 1,100. **Household Finance Inc.** (HQ); Prospect Heights; consumer financing services — 1,050. **Holy Family Hospital;** Des Plaines; hospital — 1,040. **Victory Memorial Hospital;** Waukegan; hospital — 1,020.

Dresser Industries Inc. (International Hough); Libertyville; heavy construction equipment — 1,000. **Highland Park Hospital;** Highland Park; hospital — 1,000. **Walgreen Co.** (HQ); Deerfield; drugstores — 1,000. **Johns-Manville Sales Corp.** (Pipe & Industrial Products Plant); Waukegan; asbestos products — 955. **A. C. Nielsen Co.** (HQ); Northbrook; marketing research — 800. **Extel Corp.** (HQ); Northbrook; teleprinters — 800.

Kraft Inc. (HQ); Glenview; processed foods — 704. **Culligan International Co. Inc.** (HQ); Northbrook; water treating equipment — 670. **Fansteel Inc.** (Advanced Structures Div. - HQ); North Chicago; metal products, electrical contacts — 666. **American Home Products Corp.** (Ekco Products Inc.); Wheeling; housewares — 650. **International Minerals & Chemical Corp.;** Mundelein; fertilizer chemicals — 626. **SFN Companies Inc.** (HQ); Glenview; textbook publishing — 600. **General Binding Corp.** (HQ); Northbrook; binding; collating — 500.

11th District

Northwest Chicago and Suburbs

Concentrated entirely within Chicago during the 1970s, the 11th District takes on new Republican territory in the suburbs for the 1980s, following many of the old district's former residents in their flight to the suburbs.

The redrawn 11th stretches north to Niles and west to O'Hare Airport, taking in a collection of middle-class suburban developments built in the 1950s and early 1960s. Its residents are largely ethnic in background, but they have moved beyond their blue-collar roots; many of them voted for Republican candidates in statewide elections during the 1970s. Suburban Leyden and Norwood Park townships, both located almost entirely within the new 11th, voted for Ronald Reagan by comfortable margins in 1980.

The city part of the district was left intact except for a chunk in the southeast section shifted to the 8th district. Added to the eastern side of the 11th were some city neighborhoods from the 9th District. These should be reliably Democratic.

Like the old 11th, the new district is overwhelmingly white. About 6 percent of the population is Hispanic; less than 1 percent is black. The substantial Jewish community in Rogers Park, within the city limits, is joined by a large Jewish population in part of Skokie, which is split between the 11th and the 9th.

Election Returns

11th District		Democrat		Republican	
1976	President	123,612	(47.5%)	135,612	(52.2%)
	Governor	96,935	(37.6%)	160,883	(62.4%)
	House	150,310	(68.6%)	68,872	(31.4%)
1978	Governor	80,665	(41.6%)	111,181	(57.4%)
	Senate	88,857	(45.3%)	104,897	(53.4%)
	House	123,030	(66.9%)	60,734	(33.0%)
1980	President	111,641	(44.7%)	114,691	(45.9%)
	Senate	145,383	(62.4%)	84,273	(36.2%)
	House	127,419	(60.4%)	83,463	(39.6%)
1982	Governor	126,828	(65.6%)	64,458	(33.3%)
	House	134,755	(72.6%)	50,967	(27.4%)

Demographics

Population: 518,995. **Percent Change from 1970:** -7.8%.

Land Area: 71 square miles. **Population per Square Mile:** 7,309.8.

Counties, 1980 Population: Cook (Pt.) — 518,995.

Cities, 1980 Population: Bensenville (Pt.) — 3; Chicago (Pt.) — 378,847; Franklin Park (Pt.) — 15,966; Lincolnwood — 11,921; Melrose Park (Pt.) — 3,494; Morton Grove (Pt.) — 2,807; Niles (Pt.) — 19,232; Norridge — 16,483; Northlake (Pt.) — 10,269; Schiller Park — 11,458; Skokie (Pt.) — 22,608.

Race and Ancestry: White — 91.6%; Black — 0.4%; American Indian, Eskimo and Aleut — 0.2%; Asian and Pacific Islander — 4.9%. Spanish Origin — 6.1%. English — 1.8%; German — 9.4%; Greek — 2.9%; Hungarian — 0.7%; Irish — 5.5%; Italian — 8.3%; Norwegian — 0.6%; Polish — 11.8%; Russian — 2.8%; Swedish — 1.5%; Ukranian — 0.6%.

Universities, Enrollment: Felician College, Chicago — 280; Metropolitan School of Business, Chicago — 84; North Park College and Theological Seminary, Chicago — 1,242; Northeastern Illinois University, Chicago — 10,347; Oakton Community College, Des Plaines — 10,196; Wilbur Wright College, Chicago — 7,013.

Newspapers, Circulation: Chicago *Sun-Times*, Chicago *Daily Herald* and *Chicago Tribune* circulate in the district. Foreign language newspaper: *Polish Daily Zgoda* (Polish), Chicago — 17,473.

Commercial Television Stations, Affiliation: Entire district is located in Chicago ADI.

Military Installations: Chicago-O'Hare International Airport (Air Force), Chicago — 2,179.

Industries:

Bankers Life & Casualty Co. (HQ); Chicago; life, accident insurance — 3,600. **Bell & Howell Co.** (HQ); Chicago; photographic equipment, micro equipment, office machines — 3,300. **Teletype Corp.** (HQ); Skokie; telephone, telegraph apparatus — 3,300. **A. B. Dick Co. Inc.** (HQ); Chicago; copying machines — 2,500. **Houdaille Industries Inc.**; Morton Grove; general industrial machinery — 2,400.

Resurrection Health Care Corp.; Chicago; hospital — 1,500. **Trans World Airlines Inc.**; Chicago; commercial airline — 1,500. **Felt Products Mfg. Co. Inc.** (HQ); Skokie; gaskets — 1,440. **Midway Mfg. Co.**; Franklin Park; coin-operated amusement machines — 1,400. **Ravenswood Hospital & Medical Center**; Chicago; hospital — 1,400. **Standard Brands Inc.** (Curtiss Div.); Franklin Park; candy — 1,400. **Commerce Clearing House Inc.** (HQ); Chicago; legal publishing — 1,280. **International Harvester Co.**; Melrose Park; food products machinery — 1,200. **Duo-Fast Corp.** (HQ); Franklin Park; industrial staples — 1,100. **Northwest Hospital Inc.**; Chicago; hospital — 1,100. **Tempel Steel Co.**; Niles; metal products — 1,100. **Swedish Covenant Hospital**; Chicago; hospital — 1,050. **Chicago & North Western Transporation Co.**; Melrose Park; railroad operations — 1,000.

International Telephone & Telegraph Corp. (Bell & Gossett Div.); Morton Grove; bolts, screws, rivets — 1,000. **Wilson Jones Co.** (HQ); Chicago; blank books — 1,000. **Binks Mfg. Co.** (HQ); Franklin Park; spraying equipment — 950. **Switchcraft Inc.** (HQ); Chicago; electronic components — 950. **Gould Inc.** (Fluid Components); Niles; valves, pipe fittings — 900. **The Marmon Group Inc.** (Hammond Organ Div.); Chicago; musical instruments — 900. **Marriott Corp.**; Chicago; hotel — 900. **Republic Airlines Inc.**; Chicago; commercial airline — 900. **Sargent-Welch Scientific Co.** (HQ); Skokie; scientific instruments — 900. **Baxter Travenol Laboratories** (Dayton Flexible Products Div.); Morton Grove; pharmaceuticals, medical equipment — 875. **Bell & Howell Co. Inc.** (Business Equipment Group); Chicago; business machine wholesaling — 800. **Coca-Cola Bottling Co. of Chicago**; Chicago; soft drinks — 800. **Hyatt Corp.**; Rosemont; hotel management — 800.

Vapor Corp. (HQ); Chicago; rail cars — 800. **General Instrument Corp.** (Chicago Miniature Lamp Works Div.); Chicago; incandescent lamps — 700. **General Signal Corp.** (Marsh Instrument Unit); Skokie; industrial measuring instruments — 700. **Inryco Inc.** (HQ); Melrose Park; sheet metal work — 700. **Reliance Electric Co.** (Electric Div.); Franklin Park; telephone apparatus — 700. **TRW Inc.** (C. E. Niehoff & Co. Div.); Chicago; electrical equipment for internal combustion engines — 700. **W. W. Grainger Inc.**; Chicago; electric supplies wholesalers — 650. **ITT Continental Baking Co. Inc.** (Hostess Cake); Schiller Park; bakery products — 650. **Illinois Glove Co.** (Goodluck Glove Div.); Chicago; gloves — 625. **Searle Pharmaceuticals Inc.**; Skokie; pharmaceuticals — 620. **Mark Control Corp.** (Powers Div.); Skokie; automatic controls — 600. **Rego Co.**; Chicago; valves, controls — 600. **Sloan Valve Co.** (Railroad Products Div. - HQ); Franklin Park; plumbing fixture fittings, valves — 600.

O'Hare International Tower Hotel; Chicago; hotel — 575. **Skil Corp.**; Chicago; power hand tools — 570. **International Telephone & Telegraph Corp.** (Harper Div.); Morton Grove; bolts, screws, rivets — 550. **National Can Corp.** (HQ); Chicago; metal, glass, plastic containers — 530. **Allstate Insurance Co.**; Skokie; life, health, casualty insurance — 525. **Salerno-Megowen Biscuit Co.** (HQ); Chicago; cookies — 525. **Beltone Electronics Corp.**; Chicago; hearing aids — 500. **Burns International Security Service**; Chicago; security services — 500. **Federal Mogul Corp.** (Metal Removal Tooling Div.); Chicago; carbide cutting tools — 500. **GTE Automatic Electric Labs** (HQ); Northlake; research laboratory — 500. **Illinois Tool Works Inc.** (Licon Div.);

Chicago; semiconductors — 500. **Pittway Corp.** (Barr Co. Div.); Chicago; communications equipment — 500. **Wells Mfg. Co.** (HQ); Skokie; iron foundries — 500.

12th District

Far Northwest Suburbs — Palatine

The new district contains only 46 percent of the people who lived in the old 12th, but the new 12th is even more Republican than the old one, which cast 62 percent of its votes for Ronald Reagan in 1980.

The new alignment all but removes the district from the metropolitan Chicago political orbit. The population center of the new district still is in the outer suburban area of Chicago, including Palatine and most of Hoffman Estates, which have grown dramatically during the past 20 years. But the boundary of the district has been totally revised. During the 1970s the district contained the populous southern portion of Lake County, including wealthy lakefront suburbs such as Highland Park and Deerfield. For the 1980s, it was moved north and west, taking on most of semi-rural McHenry County and only the western two-thirds of Lake. Most of Arlington Heights, the largest city in the old 12th was shifted to the new 10th District; a small part remains in the 12th.

The new 12th has both suburban and farm-oriented voting blocs. The western part of McHenry County still has dairy farms and small market towns. The largest city in McHenry is Woodstock, with fewer than 12,000 residents. But suburbia encroached on the county in the 1970s, and should continue to do so. McHenry, which gave Reagan 65 percent of its vote in 1980, has 27 percent of the district's residents.

Election Returns

12th District		Democrat		Republican	
1976	President	66,018	(30.5%)	146,331	(67.7%)
	Governor	35,151	(16.4%)	178,651	(83.3%)
	House	36,076	(19.4%)	147,344	(79.4%)
1978	Governor	32,713	(23.4%)	105,998	(75.8%)
	Senate	43,623	(31.7%)	92,160	(67.0%)
	House	32,702	(25.0%)	97,970	(75.0%)
1980	President	50,189	(24.4%)	131,495	(64.0%)
	Senate	86,437	(42.3%)	114,860	(56.2%)
	House	60,174	(25.0%)	180,169	(75.0%)
1982	Governor	36,645	(27.3%)	95,143	(70.9%)
	House	40,108	(30.7%)	86,487	(66.2%)

Demographics

Population: 519,181. **Percent Change from 1970:** 39.0%.

Land Area: 966 square miles. **Population per Square Mile:** 537.5.

Counties, 1980 Population: Cook (Pt.) — 219,535; Lake (Pt.) — 155,408; McHenry (Pt.) — 144,238.

Cities, 1980 Population: Arlington Heights (Pt.) — 11,190; Bartlett (Pt.) — 4,705; Crystal Lake — 18,590; Elgin (Pt.) — 9,010; Elk Grove Village (Pt.) — 228; Hanover Park (Pt.) — 8,059; Hoffman Estates (Pt.) — 33,807; Libertyville (Pt.) — 1; McHenry — 10,908; Mount

Prospect (Pt.) — 20,885; Mundelein (Pt.) — 7,984; North Chicago (Pt.) — 0; Palatine — 32,166; Rolling Meadows (Pt.) — 20,156; Round Lake Beach — 12,921; Schaumburg (Pt.) — 16,538; Streamwood — 23,456; Waukegan (Pt.) — 1,311; Woodstock — 11,725.

Race and Ancestry: White — 96.4%; Black — 0.8%; American Indian, Eskimo and Aleut — 0.1%; Asian and Pacific Islander — 1.6%. Spanish Origin — 3.0%. English — 4.1%; French — 0.5%; German — 13.2%; Irish — 4.3%; Italian — 3.0%; Norwegian — 0.9%; Polish — 4.7%; Swedish — 1.4%.

Newspapers, Circulation: *Crystal Lake Morning Herald* (m), Crystal Lake — 8,424; *Daily Sentinel* (e), Woodstock — 8,669. Chicago *Sun-Times*, *Chicago Tribune*, Chicago *Daily Herald* and Waukegan-North Chicago *News-Sun* also circulate in the district.

Universities, Enrollment: College of Lake County, Grayslake — 11,266; McHenry County College, Crystal Lake — 3,354; William Rainey Harper College, Palatine — 17,917.

Commercial Television Stations, Affiliation: Entire district is located in Chicago ADI.

Industries:

Motorola Inc.; Schaumburg; auto parts wholesaling — 8,000. **Kemper Corp.** (HQ); Long Grove; casualty, life, health insurance — 2,000. **Intermatic Inc.** (HQ); Spring Grove; appliance timers — 950. **American Data Centre Inc.;** Palatine; systems analysis services — 838. **Oak Technology Inc.** (HQ); Crystal Lake; electronic components — 800.

Eltra Corp. (Woodstock Die Casting Div.); Woodstock; zinc, aluminum castings — 700. **Arnold Engineering Co.** (HQ); Marengo; permanent magnets — 679. **Sun Electric Corp.** (HQ); Crystal Lake; automatic testing equipment — 670. **Union Special Corp.;** Huntley; sewing machines — 650. **Warner Electric Brake & Clutch Co.** (Motion Controls Div.); Marengo; electro-magnetic brakes, clutches — 550. **Recon/Optical Inc.** (CAI Div. - HQ); Barrington; aerial cameras — 540. **Echlin Mfg. Co.** (Brake Parts Co. Div.); McHenry; brakes — 500. **Precision Twist Drill Machine Co.** (HQ); Crystal Lake; machine tool accessories — 500. **T. C. Industries Inc.** (American Steel Treating Div.); Crystal Lake; steel heat treating — 500. **UOP Inc.** (Flexonics Div.); Bartlett; thin-walled metal products — 500.

13th District

Southwest Chicago Suburbs — Downers Grove

Once concentrated almost entirely within Du Page County, the 13th now draws 44 percent of its population from the Cook County suburbs nearer Chicago. It remains one of the most affluent districts in the country and one of the most Republican.

GOP strength in Du Page is formidable. Since 1952 no Republican presidential nominee has drawn less than 60 percent of the vote in Du Page County. And in the 1982 gubernatorial election, in which incumbent Republican James R. Thompson barely squeaked by Democrat Adlai E. Stevenson III, the county gave the Republican 71 percent of its vote.

The most densely populated areas of the new district are clustered along the old Burlington Northern tracks that extend west from the city to Riverside, Western Springs, Hinsdale, Clarendon Hills and Downers Grove. The cul-de-sacs of Riverside, one of the first planned suburban developments in the area, were copied again and again as suburbia crept along the railroad line, out from Cook County into Du Page. By shifting the district to the east, closer to the city, the remap gives up a set of 1960s suburbs and takes on an older group.

The only blue-collar territory in the new 13th is in Broadview, Lisle and Westmont, prewar industrial suburbs. But any Democratic votes in these areas are canceled out by the affluent communities surrounding them.

In the geographic center of the new district is the Argonne National Laboratory, a federal energy research center that employs about 5,000 people. At the southern end of Cook County, the district opens up to rolling countryside, with pockets of new residential developments. Much of the Cook County park system is located in this area. The district also includes a corner of Will County, located between Joliet and Chicago, which is largely undeveloped. Only 8 percent of the vote is cast in Will County.

Election Returns

13th District		Democrat		Republican	
1976	President	69,653	(29.1%)	164,697	(68.7%)
	Governor	58,250	(23.0%)	192,904	(76.1%)
	House	73,566	(32.8%)	150,451	(67.1%)
1978	Governor	24,057	(16.5%)	119,578	(82.0%)
	Senate	43,771	(30.1%)	99,572	(68.4%)
	House	43,877	(30.6%)	99,666	(69.4%)
1980	President	68,726	(26.0%)	164,990	(62.4%)
	Senate	100,771	(49.2%)	100,864	(49.3%)
	House	65,989	(26.7%)	181,395	(73.3%)
1982	Governor	50,094	(29.5%)	116,669	(68.7%)
	House	49,105	(30.2%)	113,423	(69.8%)

Demographics

Population: 519,441. **Percent Change from 1970:** 33.5%.

Land Area: 591 square miles. **Population per Square Mile:** 878.9.

Counties, 1980 Population: Cook (Pt.) — 227,542; Du Page (Pt.) — 249,872; Will (Pt.) — 42,027.

Cities, 1980 Population: Alsip (Pt.) — 4,244; Bellwood (Pt.) — 5,593; Bolingbrook (Pt.) — 29,362; Brookfield (Pt.) — 11,147; Crestwood (Pt.) — 4,602; Darien — 14,536; Downers Grove (Pt.) — 40,161; Elmhurst (Pt.) — 2,060; Forest Park (Pt.) — 10,258; Glen Ellyn (Pt.) — 3,882; Hinsdale — 16,726; La Grange (Pt.) — 12,855; La Grange Park — 13,359; Lisle — 13,625; Lombard (Pt.) — 422.

Naperville (Pt.) — 26,494; Northlake (Pt.) — 1,897; Orland Park (Pt.) — 23,045; Palos Heights — 11,096; Palos Hills — 10,097; Tinley Park (Pt.) — 12,479; Villa Park (Pt.) — 1,678; Westchester — 17,730; Western Springs — 12,876; Westmont — 16,718; Wheaton (Pt.) — 11,571; Woodridge — 22,322; Worth (Pt.) — 8,720.

Race and Ancestry: White — 95.2%; Black — 1.5%; American Indian, Eskimo and Aleut — 0.1%; Asian and Pacific Islander — 2.5%. Spanish Origin — 1.8%. Dutch — 1.2%; English — 3.6%; German — 8.5%; Greek — 0.8%; Irish — 5.6%; Italian — 4.6%; Polish — 6.4%; Swedish — 1.1%.

Universities, Enrollment: Bethany Theological Seminary, Oak Brook — 137; DeAndreis Seminary, Lemont — 48; George Williams College, Downers Grove — 1,265; Illinois Benedictine College, Lisle — 1,834; Moraine Valley Community College, Palos Hills — 10,917; North Central College, Naperville — 1,296; Trinity Christian College, Palos Heights — 404.

Newspapers, Circulation: Chicago *Daily Herald*, Chicago *Sun-Times*, *Chicago Tribune* and Joliet *Herald-News* circulate in the district.

Commercial Television Stations, Affiliation: Entire district is located in Chicago ADI.

Industries:

Bell Telephone Laboratories; Naperville; research labs — 4,000. **Hinsdale Sanitarium & Hospital;** Hinsdale; hospital — 1,700. **Wescom**

Inc. (HQ); Downers Grove; telephone, telegraph equipment — 1,700. **The St. George Corp.;** Palos Heights; hospital — 1,300. **Good Samaritan Hospital;** Downers Grove; hospital — 1,250.

Evangelical Hospital Assn.; Downers Grove; hospital — 1,100. **McDonald's Corp.** (HQ); Oak Brook; fast food operations — 950. **Amsted Industries Inc.** (Griffin Pipe Products Div.); Oak Brook; business services — 800.. **Andrew Corp.** (HQ); Orland Park; electronic communications equipment — 800. **Don Edward & Co.;** Riverside; restaurant equipment wholesaling — 700. **International Harvester Co. Inc.** (Engineering Research); Hinsdale; engineering services — 700. **Pepperidge Farm Inc.;** Downers Grove; bakery products — 700. **Molex Inc.** (HQ); Lisle; current-carrying wiring devices — 650. **Nalco Chemical Co.** (HQ); Oak Brook; specialized chemicals — 625.

Chicago Bridge & Iron Co. (HQ); Oak Brook; structural metal, plate fabrication — 600. **Eastman Kodak Co.;** Oak Brook; photographic supplies wholesaling — 600. **Spiegel Inc.** (HQ); Oak Brook; mail-order house — 600. **Union Oil Co. of California** (Union 76 Div.); Lemont; petroleum refining — 600. **Packard Instrument Co. Inc.** (HQ); Downers Grove; scientific instruments — 550. **Grayhill Inc.** (HQ); La Grange; electronic switches — 500. **Hendrickson MacMeekin Associates** (Wilton Enterprises Div.); Woodridge; plastic products — 500. **Rexnord Inc.** (Bearing Div.); Downers Grove; mechanical power transmission equipment — 500. **Waste Management Inc.;** Oak Brook; waste collection, storage, processing, recovery — 500.

14th District

North Central — De Kalb, Elgin

The new 14th stretches from Naperville, whose commuters hop the train for Chicago, south to Wenona, a crossroads farm town that serves the surrounding agricultural community in Marshall County. In between, in the valleys of the Illinois and Fox rivers, are a host of light industrial plants, including two large glassworks.

The semi-industrial character of the district does not interfere with its Republican loyalties; the five counties that cast most of the vote — Kane, De Kalb, Du Page, Kendall and La Salle — all went for Ronald Reagan easily in 1980. All but La Salle even went for the badly beaten GOP Senate nominee, Dave O'Neal.

Located on the Fox River is Elgin, the largest city in the district. Elgin began as an industrial center; its name is on many of the country's street sweepers. In recent years, however, it has become a suburban outpost for white-collar Chicagoans who have settled on its east side, within Cook County. The 14th also includes the portion of industrial Aurora on the western side of the Fox River, which contains the city's white-collar residential section. Elgin and Aurora together give Kane County about 40 percent of the district's population.

The only other large city in the district is De Kalb, an agricultural research center and site of Northern Illinois University, which has 26,000 students. Reagan's 1980 showing was weaker in De Kalb than in any of the district's other counties, not because Jimmy Carter was strong but because independent candidate John B. Anderson drew nearly 10 percent of the vote.

The 14th is a mixture of suburban and agricultural interests. Corn and soybeans remain important to the economy in De Kalb and La Salle counties, where the farm land is among the richest in the country. But there is a new orientation toward Chicago with the added territory in Du Page and Kane counties.

Redistricting complicated the geography of the district. The new 14th has only one complete county and parts

of eight others. Cook, McHenry, Boone and Marshall counties are new to the district, but each has less than 1 percent of the overall population. The district line cuts right through Aurora and Elgin.

Election Returns

14th District		Democrat		Republican	
1976	President	76,024	(38.3%)	118,335	(59.7%)
	Governor	45,252	(23.2%)	149,109	(76.3%)
	House	79,022	(41.5%)	109,879	(57.8%)
1978	Governor	36,457	(29.5%)	85,823	(69.5%)
	Senate	50,333	(39.7%)	74,566	(58.8%)
	House	47,854	(38.4%)	76,659	(61.6%)
1980	President	61,516	(27.6%)	136,573	(61.4%)
	Senate	98,979	(44.5%)	117,660	(52.9%)
	House	48,963	(24.8%)	148,851	(75.2%)
1982	Governor	53,575	(33.2%)	105,097	(65.0%)
	House	53,914	(35.4%)	98,262	(64.6%)

Demographics

Population: 521,909. **Percent Change from 1970:** 17.7%.

Land Area: 2,806 square miles. **Population per Square Mile:** 186.0.

Counties, 1980 Population: Boone (Pt.) — 950; Cook (Pt.) — 2,013; De Kalb — 74,624; Du Page (Pt.) — 83,259; Kane (Pt.) — 210,202; Kendall (Pt.) — 33,336; La Salle (Pt.) — 109,143; Marshall (Pt.) — 4,723; McHenry (Pt.) — 3,659.

Cities, 1980 Population: Aurora (Pt.) — 26,536; Bartlett (Pt.) — 8,549; Batavia — 12,574; Carol Stream (Pt.) — 2,628; Carpentersville — 23,272; De Kalb — 33,099; Elgin (Pt.) — 54,788; Hanover Park (Pt.) — 5,420; La Salle — 10,347; Naperville (Pt.) — 15,208; Ottawa — 18,166; Peru — 10,886; St. Charles — 17,492; Streator (Pt.) — 14,714; West Chicago — 12,550; Wheaton (Pt.) — 6,950.

Race and Ancestry: White — 95.2%; Black — 1.9%; American Indian, Eskimo and Aleut — 0.1%; Asian and Pacific Islander — 1.1%. Spanish Origin — 3.9%. English — 5.9%; French — 0.6%; German — 13.1%; Irish — 3.8%; Italian — 2.2%; Norwegian — 1.4%; Polish — 2.6%; Swedish — 1.7%.

Universities, Enrollment: Aurora College, Aurora — 1,230; Elgin Community College, Elgin — 5,160; Illinois Valley Community College, Oglesby — 4,250; Judson College, Elgin — 451; Kishwaukee College, Malta — 4,251; Northern Illinois University, De Kalb — 26,064; Waubonsee Community College, Sugar Grove — 6,008.

Newspapers, Circulation: *Courier News* (eS), Elgin — 37,154; *Daily Chronicle* (e), De Kalb — 11,684; *The Daily Journal* (e), Wheaton — 6,417; *The Daily Times* (e), Ottawa — 13,830; *News-Tribune* (e), La Salle — 21,134; *Streator Times-Press* (e), Streator — 11,602. Aurora *Beacon-News, Chicago Tribune* and Joliet *Herald-News* also circulate in the district.

Commercial Television Stations, Affiliation: Most of district is located in Chicago ADI. Portions are in Rockford ADI and Peoria ADI.

Industries:

Caterpillar Tractor Corp.; Aurora; construction machinery — 3,800. **Universities Research Associates** (Fermi National Accelerator Lab); Batavia; atomic research — 1,940. **All-Steel Inc.** (HQ); Aurora; metal office furniture — 1,700. **Barber-Greene Co.** (HQ); Aurora; asphalt machinery — 1,650. *(Note: plant straddles 14th and 4th districts.)* **Standard Oil Co. of Indiana** (Amoco Research Center); Naperville; research, development laboratories — 1,500.

Sherman Hospital; Elgin; hospital — 1,490. **Central Du Page Hospital Assn.;** Winfield; hospital — 1,200. **Owens-Illinois Inc.;** Streator; glass containers — 1,200. **Elgin Mental Health Center;** Elgin; state mental hospital — 1,050. **Chicago Rawhide Mfg. Co.** (HQ); Elgin; gaskets — 1,000. **GTE Automatic Electric Inc.;** Genoa; switchboards — 1,000. **Metropolitan Life Insurance Co.;** Aurora; life insurance — 980. **Lyon Metal Products Inc.** (HQ); Aurora; metal shelving — 975. **Furnas Electric Co.** (HQ); Batavia; industrial controls — 950. **First National Bank of Chicago;** Elgin; credit card operations — 850. **Hills-McCanna Co.** (HQ); Carpentersville; valves, pumps — 825.

General Electric Co. Inc. (Appliance Motor Dept.); De Kalb; motors — 800. **Dart Industries** (Thatcher Glass Mfg. Div.); Streator; glass containers — 750. **General Mills Inc.** (Package Foods Operating Div.); West Chicago; breakfast cereals — 750. **Illinois Tool Works Inc.** (Shake-Proof Div.); Elgin; metal fasteners — 750. **Morrison Construction Co.;** Marseilles; general contracting — 700. **Amsted Industries Inc.** (Burgess-Norton Mfg. Co. Div.); Geneva; screw machine products — 650. **Farmers Insurance;** North Aurora; life insurance — 650. **Howard P. Foley Co.;** Marseilles; electrical contracting — 650. **Sundstrand Corp.;** La Salle; hydro transmissions — 650. **CTS Knights Inc.;** Sandwich; electronic components — 625. **Dukane Corp.** (HQ); St. Charles; audio-visual equipment — 625.

American Gage & Machine Co. (HQ); Elgin; electrical measuring devices, machine tools — 600. **Anaconda-Ericsson Inc.;** Sycamore; wire, cables — 600. **Consolidated Freight Corp.;** Peru; trucking — 600. **De Kalb Agresearch Inc.** (HQ); De Kalb; farm supply wholesaling, commodity brokers — 600. **Katy Industries Inc.** (HQ); Elgin; special industrial machinery — 600. **Swift Processed Meats;** St. Charles; processed meats — 550. **Continental Can Co. Inc.** (Equipment Div.); West Chicago; business services — 500. **General Signal Corp.** (Aurora Pump Div.); North Aurora; pumps, pumping equipment — 500. **A. O. Smith Harvestore;** De Kalb; prefabricated metal buildings — 500. **Stephens-Adamson Inc.** (HQ); Aurora; conveyor systems — 500.

15th District

Central — Bloomington, Kankakee

The 15th District, which sprawls north from Lincoln in the center of the state all the way to the edge of Chicago's suburbs, is an amalgamation of parts of three former districts. Redistricting essentially dismantled the old 21st District.

After carving away the population centers of Decatur and Champaign/Urbana, the map makers combined the remainder of the 21st with the southern sections of the old 17th and 15th districts, most of them sparsely populated.

Like the old 15th, however, the new district is traditional Republican farm country. Corn and soybean counties such as Iroquois and Ford are among the most Republican in the state; both gave Ronald Reagan more than two-thirds of their 1980 vote. Republican Gov. James R. Thompson won 73 percent in Iroquis and 72 percent in Ford in his razor-close 1982 re-election.

The Will and Kankakee County portions of the district include numerous truck farms whose products are sold at Chicago area markets.

Bloomington, with about 44,000 residents, and nearby Normal, with about 36,000, comprise the major population centers in the new district. They are linked by Illinois State University and Illinois Wesleyan University. Also in Bloomington is the national headquarters of State Farm Insurance, the largest car insurer in the world. Rantoul, with about 20,000 residents, is dominated by the Chanute Air Force Base.

The incumbent will find it prudent to take an interest in nuclear power. Several nuclear power plants line the Illinois River and there is a major nuclear-waste storage facility in Morris.

Election Returns

15th District		Democrat		Republican	
1976	President	81,858	(39.2%)	123,957	(59.3%)
	Governor	48,720	(23.6%)	156,621	(76.0%)
	House	64,594	(32.3%)	135,094	(67.7%)
1978	Governor	51,548	(30.9%)	114,248	(68.5%)
	Senate	69,482	(41.4%)	97,045	(57.8%)
	House	42,712	(26.0%)	121,359	(74.0%)
1980	President	60,415	(28.7%)	134,660	(63.9%)
	Senate	88,839	(43.0%)	115,687	(56.0%)
	House	70,478	(30.3%)	162,116	(69.7%)
1982	Governor	55,627	(35.2%)	100,286	(63.4%)
	House	53,303	(33.7%)	105,038	(66.3%)

Demographics

Population: 518,995. **Percent Change from 1970:** 8.4%.

Land Area: 7,477 square miles. **Population per Square Mile:** 69.4.

Counties, 1980 Population: Champaign (Pt.) — 47,524; De Witt — 18,108; Ford — 15,265; Grundy — 30,582; Iroquois — 32,976; Kankakee — 102,926; La Salle (Pt.) — 1,545; Livingston — 41,381; Logan (Pt.) — 22,616; McLean — 119,149; Piatt — 16,581; Will (Pt.) — 59,841; Woodford (Pt.) — 10,501.

Cities, 1980 Population: Bloomington — 44,189; Bourbonnais — 13,280; Bradley — 11,008; Joliet (Pt.) — 18; Kankakee — 30,141; Lincoln — 16,327; Normal — 35,672; Park Forest (Pt.) — 3,311; Pontiac — 11,227; Rantoul — 20,161; Streator (Pt.) — 77.

Race and Ancestry: White — 93.1%; Black — 5.7%; American Indian, Eskimo and Aleut — 0.1%; Asian and Pacific Islander — 0.5%. Spanish Origin — 1.2%. Dutch — 0.8%; English — 8.8%; French — 1.8%; German — 14.6%; Irish — 4.4%; Italian — 1.2%; Norwegian — 0.6%; Polish — 1.1%; Swedish — 0.8%.

Universities, Enrollment: Governors State University, Park Forest South — 4,853; Illinois State University, Normal — 19,717; Illinois Wesleyan University, Bloomington — 1,692; Kankakee Community College, Kankakee — 3,691; Lincoln Christian College, Lincoln — 591; Lincoln College, Lincoln — 968; Olivet Nazarene College, Kankakee — 2,116.

Newspapers, Circulation: *Clinton Daily Journal* (e), Clinton — 4,448; *The Daily Leader* (e), Pontiac — 8,889; *The Daily Pantagraph* (mS), Bloomington — 51,539; *Daily Times-Republic* (e), Watseka — 3,027; *Herald* (e), Morris — 7,456; *Journal* (eS), Kankakee — 33,422; *Lincoln Courier* (e), Lincoln — 6,882; *Paxton Daily Record* (e), Paxton — 1,530. *Champaign-Urbana News-Gazette, Chicago Tribune,* and Joliet *Herald-News* also circulate in the district.

Commercial Television Stations, Affiliation: WBLN, Bloomington (None). District is divided among Chicago ADI, Peoria ADI and Springfield-Decatur-Champaign ADI.

Military Installations: Chanute Air Force Base, Rantoul — 4,602.

Nuclear Power Plants: Braidwood 1 and 2, Braidwood (Westinghouse, Commonwealth Edison); Clinton 1 and 2, Clinton (General Electric, Baldwin); Dresden 1, Morris (General Electric, Bechtel), July 1960, shut down; Dresden 2, Morris (General Electric, United Engineers and Constructors), June 1970; Dresden 3, Morris (General Electric, United Engineers and Constructors), November 1971; Lasalle 1, Seneca (General Electric, Commonwealth Edison); Lasalle 2, Seneca (General Electric, Commonwealth Edison).

Industries:

State Farm Mutual Automobile Insurance Co. (HQ); Bloomington; casualty insurance — 3,300. **National Union Electric Corp.** (The Eureka Co. Div. - HQ); Bloomington; vacuum cleaners — 2,500. **General Electric Co.;** Bloomington; electric motors — 1,500. **A. O. Smith Corp.** (Consumer Products Div.); Kankakee; water heaters — 1,200. **General Foods Corp.;** Kankakee; pet food — 1,100. **Lincoln Development Center;** Lincoln; state mental hospital — 1,100.

Roper Corp. (Outdoor Products Div.); Bradley; garden tractors — 804. **Armour Pharmaceutical Co.** (Blood Plasma Services); Bradley; pharmaceuticals — 700. **Eaton Corp.** (Circuit Protective Devices Div.); Lincoln; electrical switchgears — 700. **Country Mutual Insurance Co.** (HQ); Bloomington; auto, fire, casualty insurance — 674. **R. R. Donnelley & Sons Co.;** Dwight; printing — 650. **Growmark Inc.** (HQ); Bloomington; grain wholesaling — 600. **Northern Petrochemical Co. Inc.;** Morris; industrial inorganic chemicals — 600. **Sterling Drugs Inc.;** Lincoln; insecticides, perfumes — 600. **Uarco Inc.;** Watseka; manifold business forms — 560. **Johnson & Johnson Inc.** (Personal Products Co. Div.); Wilmington; sanitary paper products — 525. **Caterpillar Tractor Co.;** Pontiac; earth moving equipment — 500. **MSL Industries Inc.** (Howard Industries Div.); Milford; electric motors — 500.

16th District

Northwest — Rockford

Even though it includes the industrial city of Rockford, the 16th has not elected a Democrat to the House in this century, and redistricting changed it very little. While districts all around it were undergoing major surgery, the 16th was preserved virtually intact. It nestles compactly in the northwest corner of the state, much as it did in the 1950s.

The district does take in two new counties, Carroll and Whiteside, which border the Mississippi River. They replace McHenry and part of Boone counties, which were pared away. But about 90 percent of the population was carried over from the old 16th. The most populous county is Winnebago, where about 50 percent of the district's vote is cast. Rockford, the seat of Winnebago County, is the second largest city in Illinois.

There is substantial industry in the district. Rockford has a large blue-collar population that is unionized in plants making machine tools, agricultural implements and defense-related aviation equipment. Nearby Belvidere in Boone County has a Chrysler plant. Freeport, just west of Rockford in Stephenson County, produces computer parts. But all three of these industrial counties vote consistently Republican in most state elections.

The rest of the district is largely rural, settled by Germans, Swedes and Yankees transplanted from New England. It ranks first in the state in dairy farming. The northwest corner of the district is a popular vacation area with antique stores and state parks scattered throughout hilly Jo Daviess County.

Two small towns in the 16th District were home to Ronald Reagan; he was born in Tampico and grew up in Dixon. John B. Anderson, who is from Rockford, represented the 16th as a Republican in the House of Representatives for two decades until he ran for president in the 1980 election. Anderson's neighbors in Winnebago County gave him about 22 percent of their presidential vote — his second-best countywide showing in the country.

Election Returns

16th District		Democrat		Republican	
1976	President	84,993	(41.6%)	115,618	(56.6%)
	Governor	43,944	(21.9%)	155,257	(77.5%)
	House	59,561	(32.2%)	125,303	(67.8%)

16th District		Democrat		Republican	
1978	Governor	41,350	(36.9%)	69,416	(62.0%)
	Senate	49,151	(43.9%)	61,136	(54.6%)
	House	36,657	(33.6%)	72,434	(66.3%)
1980	President	60,910	(28.4%)	117,600	(54.9%)
	Senate	98,591	(46.9%)	108,706	(51.7%)
	House	60,307	(32.7%)	124,355	(67.3%)
1982	Governor	69,250	(44.0%)	85,506	(54.3%)
	House	66,877	(42.8%)	89,405	(57.2%)

Demographics

Population: 519,035. **Percent Change from 1970:** 2.8%.

Land Area: 4,539 square miles. **Population per Square Mile:** 114.4.

Counties, 1980 Population: Boone (Pt.) — 27,680; Carroll — 18,779; Jo Daviess — 23,520; Lee — 36,328; Ogle — 46,338; Stephenson — 49,536; Whiteside — 65,970; Winnebago — 250,884.

Cities, 1980 Population: Belvidere — 15,176; Dixon — 15,701; Freeport — 26,266; Loves Park — 13,192; Rock Falls — 10,633; Rockford — 139,712; Sterling — 16,281.

Race and Ancestry: White — 93.3%; Black — 4.8%; American Indian, Eskimo and Aleut — 0.2%; Asian and Pacific Islander — 0.5%. Spanish Origin — 2.6%. Dutch — 1.5%; English — 6.6%; French — 0.5%; German — 16.1%; Irish — 3.4%; Italian — 2.1%; Norwegian — 1.1%; Polish — 0.8%; Swedish — 3.4%.

Universities, Enrollment: Highland Community College, Freeport — 1,765; Morrison Institute of Technology, Morrison — 194; Rockford College, Rockford — 1,233; Rock Valley College, Rockford — 9,289; Sauk Valley College, Dixon — 3,177.

Newspapers, Circulation: *Belvidere Daily Republican* (e), Belvidere — 5,284; *The Daily Gazette* (e), Sterling — 13,992; *Dixon Evening Telegraph* (e), Dixon — 11,358; *Freeport Journal-Standard* (e), Freeport — 18,351; *Rockford Register Star* (mS), Rockford — 77,101.

Commercial Television Stations, Affiliation: WIFR-TV, Freeport (CBS); WQRF-TV, Rockford (None); WREX-TV, Rockford (ABC); WTVO, Rockford (NBC). District is divided between Rockford ADI and Davenport (Iowa)-Rock Island-Moline ADI.

Military Installations: Savanna Army Depot Activity (Army), Savanna — 566.

Nuclear Power Plants: Byron 1 and 2, Byron (Westinghouse, Commonwealth Edison).

Industries:

Honeywell Inc. (Micro Switch Div.); Freeport; switches — 4,500. **Chrysler Corp.** (Belvidere Assembly Plant); Belvidere; auto assembly — 3,786. **Sundstrand Corp.** (HQ); Rockford; generators — 3,500. **Ingersoll Milling Machine Co.** (HQ); Rockford; metal-cutting machines — 2,200. **General Electric Co.;** Morrison; automatic appliance controls — 2,000.

Rockford Memorial Hospital Assn.; Rockford; hospital — 1,700. **Rockford Products Corp.** (HQ); Rockford; bolts, screws, rivets — 1,600. **Amerock Corp.** (HQ); Rockford; metal cabinet hardware — 1,500. **Barber-Colman Co.;** Rockford; aircraft products, environmental controls, industrial measuring instruments — 1,500. **Kelly-Springfield Tire Co.;** Freeport; tires, inner tubes — 1,500. **Northwestern Steel & Wire Co.** (HQ); Sterling; steel, wire products — 1,400. **Swedish American Hospital Assn.;** Rockford; hospital — 1,200. **Atwood Vacuum Machine Co.** (Mobile Products Div. - HQ); Rockford; auto, recreational vehicle hardware — 1,000. **Caron International Inc.** (HQ); Rochelle; yarn mills — 1,000. **Elco Industries Inc.** (HQ); Rockford; bolts, screws, rivets — 1,000.

Kelsey-Hayes Co. Inc. (Gunite Div.); Rockford; iron, steel foundries — 1,000. **Warner-Lambert Co.** (Consumer Products Group); Rockford; gum, pharmaceuticals, drugs — 1,000. **Woodward Governor Co.** (HQ); Rockford; aircraft governors, engines, generators, parts —

1,000. **White Consolidated Industries** (White-Sundstrand Machine Tool Co. Div); Belvidere; machine tools — 900. **Del Monte Corp.** (Midwest Div.); Rochelle; canned fruits, vegetables — 800. **Newell Companies Inc.** (HQ); Freeport; drapery hardware, paint brushes, scales — 800. **Warner Electric Brake & Clutch Co.** (HQ); South Beloit; vehicle brakes, clutches — 800. **Barber-Colman Co.**; Rockford; environmental controls, textile machinery — 750. **Borg-Warner Corp.**; Rockford; clutches — 703. **Ex-Cell-O Corp.** (Greenlee Machine & Foundry Div.); Rockford; machine tools — 650.

Barber-Colman Co. (Machines Tool Div.); Rockford; machine tools — 600. **J. L. Clark Mfg. Co.** (HQ); Rockford; metal, plastic, fiber containers — 600. **Economy Fire & Casualty Co.** (HQ); Freeport; casualty insurance — 600. **National Mfg. Co.** (HQ); Sterling; hardware — 600. **Ex-Cell-O Corp.** (Greenlee Tool Div.); Rockford; power hand tools — 591. **Babcock & Wilcox Co.** (W. F. & John Barnes Co. Div.); Rockford; machine tools — 510. **Kable Printing Co.**; Mount Morris; commercial printing — 500. **Mattison Machine Works Inc.**; Rockford; machine tools — 500. **Warner Electric Brake & Clutch Co.**; Roscoe; clutches, brakes — 500.

17th District

West — Rock Island, Moline, Galesburg

Cradled between the Mississippi and Illinois rivers, the 17th is prime farm land where most corn and soybean growers can survive even bad years. In the northern part of the district, in Bureau and Henry counties, billboards proclaim the area the "Hog Capital of the World."

The urban center of the district is at its northwestern edge, in Rock Island County, where Rock Island and Moline make up the Illinois half of the "Quad Cities." (The Iowa cities are Davenport and Bettendorf.) Together, Rock Island and Moline have more than 90,000 residents.

The Rock Island Arsenal employs 8,000 defense workers who produce guns and bullets for the U.S. government, continuing an activity begun in 1862. Also in Rock Island and Moline is one of the country's most intensive concentrations of farm equipment manufacturing. Deere & Company is headquartered at Moline, and, along with International Harvester, has several plants elsewhere in the district. New to the redrawn 17th are a plant and two foundries operated by the Caterpillar Tractor Company outside of Peoria.

However, times were bad for the agricultural implement industry in the early 1980s, and unemployment in the area was high.

The new 17th tilts Republican, although there is more competition between the parties than in other downstate districts. Labor in Rock Island County provides a substantial Democratic base, but the rural areas usually outvote the industrial cities.

Election Returns

17th District		Democrat		Republican	
1976	President	100,760	(45.0%)	119,970	(53.6%)
	Governor	65,404	(29.6%)	154,238	(69.9%)
	House	75,354	(35.3%)	138,002	(64.7%)
1978	Governor	48,996	(38.6%)	76,684	(60.5%)
	Senate	55,741	(44.0%)	69,359	(54.7%)
	House	8,329	(8.4%)	91,155	(91.6%)
1980	President	80,889	(35.9%)	125,591	(55.7%)

17th District		Democrat		Republican	
1980	Senate	111,048	(50.8%)	104,559	(47.8%)
	House	56,486	(28.3%)	143,458	(71.7%)
1982	Governor	84,825	(48.0%)	89,297	(50.5%)
	House	94,483	(52.8%)	84,347	(47.2%)

Demographics

Population: 519,333. **Percent Change from 1970:** 4.0%.

Land Area: 6,391 square miles. **Population per Square Mile:** 81.3.

Counties, 1980 Population: Bureau — 39,114; Fulton (Pt.) — 31,292; Henderson — 9,114; Henry — 57,968; Knox — 61,607; La Salle (Pt.) — 1,345; Marshall (Pt.) — 9,756; McDonough (Pt.) — 31,971; Mercer — 19,286; Peoria (Pt.) — 56,495; Putnam — 6,085; Rock Island — 165,968; Stark — 7,389; Warren — 21,943.

Cities, 1980 Population: Canton — 14,626; East Moline — 20,907; Galesburg — 35,305; Kewanee — 14,508; Macomb — 19,863; Moline — 45,709; Monmouth — 10,706; Pekin (Pt.) — 4; Rock Island — 47,036.

Race and Ancestry: White — 95.6%; Black — 2.7%; American Indian, Eskimo and Aleut — 0.1%; Asian and Pacific Islander — 0.4%. Spanish Origin — 2.2%. Dutch — 0.6%; English — 9.3%; French — 0.6%; German — 10.7%; Irish — 4.3%; Italian — 1.1%; Polish — 0.6%; Swedish — 3.6%.

Universities, Enrollment: Augustana College, Rock Island — 2,434; Black Hawk College, East Campus, Kewanee — 1,069; Black Hawk College, Quad Cities Campus, Moline — 6,381; Carl Sandburg College, Galesburg — 3,542; Knox College, Galesburg — 972; Monmouth College, Monmouth — 680; Spoon River College, Canton — 2,408; Western Illinois University, Macomb — 11,904.

Newspapers, Circulation: *The Argus* (eS), Rock Island — 23,141; *The Daily Dispatch* (eS), Moline — 35,688; *Daily Ledger* (e), Canton — 9,236; *Daily Review Atlas* (e), Monmouth — 5,923; *Macomb Daily Journal* (e), Macomb — 10,845; *The Register-Mail* (e), Galesburg — 21,669; *Star-Courier* (e), Kewanee — 9,529. Peoria *Journal Star* also circulates in the district.

Commercial Television Stations, Affiliation: WHBF-TV, Rock Island (CBS); WQAD-TV, Moline (ABC). Most of district is located in Davenport (Iowa)-Rock Island-Moline (Ill.) ADI. Portions are in Quincy-Hannibal (Mo.) ADI and Springfield-Decatur-Champaign ADI.

Military Facilities: Greater Peoria Airport (Air National Guard), Bartonville — 654; Rock Island Arsenal (Army), Rock Island — 8,027.

Nuclear Power Plants: Quad Cities 1, Cordova (General Electric, United Engineers and Constructors), February 1973; Quad Cities 2, Cordova (General Electric, United Engineers and Constructors), March 1973.

Industries:

Caterpillar Tractor Co. Inc.; Mapleton; foundry — 2,200. **Magic Chef Inc.** (Admiral Div.); Galesburg; refrigerators — 2,000. **International Harvester Co. Inc.**; East Moline; farm machinery — 1,800. **Deere & Co.**; Milan; warehouse, parts distributing — 1,424. **Butler Mfg. Co.**; Galesburg; metal buildings — 1,200.

Burlington Northern Inc.; Galesburg; railroad terminal operations — 1,100. **Galesburg Mental Health Center**; Galesburg; state mental hospital — 1,070. **Harper-Wyman Co.**; Princeton; cooking equipment — 900. **J. I. Case Co.**; Rock Island; diesel cylinders — 850. **Jones & Laughlin Steel Corp.**; Hennepin; steel sheet, strip, bars — 850. **The Gates Rubber Co.**; Galesburg; rubber hose — 752. **Chromalloy-American Corp.** (Servus Rubber Co. Div.); Rock Island; rubber, vinyl — 720. **Federal-Mogul Corp.**; Macomb; roller bearings — 650. **Wilson Foods Corp.**; Monmouth; meatpacking — 600. **CNF Distributors Inc.**; Rock Island; pharmaceutical wholesaling — 500. **King-Seeley Thermos Co.**; Macomb; metal cans, plastics — 500. **Deere & Co.** (HQ); Moline; farm, construction machinery — more than 500. **Deere & Co.** (John Deere Foundry); East Moline; iron foundry — more than 500.

International Harvester Co. Inc.; Rock Island; farm machinery — more than 500.

18th District

Central — Peoria

The 18th zigs and zags from Peoria south to the outskirts of Decatur and Springfield and west to Hancock County on the Mississippi. A mostly rural area, it is linked by the broad Illinois River basin, ideal for growing corn. The only major urban area is Peoria with 124,160 residents and neighboring Pekin, Everett M. Dirksen's hometown, with 33,963.

The district traditionally is Republican. The GOP even may be a bit stronger within the new district lines than in the old ones; Ronald Reagan's 1980 vote was 60 percent in the old 18th, and 61.2 percent in the new one. But a strong challenge by a Democrat, coupled with the economic misfortunes of the district, gave House Minority Leader Robert H. Michel a scare in 1982. He won re-election with only 51.6 percent of the vote.

Peoria is a troubled industrial city. It is dominated by the international headquarters of the Caterpillar Tractor Company, which employs more than 26,000 people in the district. Moreover, Peoria has lost much of its other industry during the 1970s, including a once-thriving brewery. Pekin is a grain processing and shipping center; it produces ethanol, both for fuel and for drink.

Outside the Peoria environs, the 18th was drastically rearranged. In the 1960s Peoria anchored the southern end of the district; in the 1970s it was in the center. For the 1980s it is perched at the northern tip. The district contains eight complete counties and parts of eight more.

Election Returns

18th District		Democrat		Republican	
1976	President	92,613	(44.3%)	114,120	(54.6%)
	Governor	60,688	(29.4%)	145,213	(70.3%)
	House	74,972	(38.6%)	119,329	(61.4%)
1978	Governor	63,949	(38.0%)	103,375	(61.4%)
	Senate	76,323	(45.5%)	89,473	(53.3%)
	House	50,741	(30.7%)	114,621	(69.3%)
1980	President	71,861	(32.0%)	137,198	(61.2%)
	Senate	106,402	(39.7%)	159,957	(59.6%)
	House	92,612	(36.2%)	163,281	(63.8%)
1982	Governor	80,556	(43.8%)	101,715	(55.3%)
	House	91,281	(48.4%)	97,406	(51.6%)

Demographics

Population: 519,026. **Percent Change from 1970:** 8.3%.

Land Area: 6,416 square miles. **Population per Square Mile:** 80.9.

Counties, 1980 Population: Brown — 5,411; Cass — 15,084; Fulton (Pt.) — 12,395; Hancock — 23,877; Logan (Pt.) — 9,186; Macon (Pt.) — 30,699; Mason — 19,492; McDonough (Pt.) — 5,496; Menard — 11,700; Morgan — 37,502; Peoria (Pt.) — 143,971; Sangamon (Pt.) — 35,083; Schuyler (Pt.) — 8,091; Scott — 6,142; Tazewell — 132,078; Woodford (Pt.) — 22,819.

Cities, 1980 Population: Decatur (Pt.) — 14,581; East Peoria — 22,385; Jacksonville — 20,284; Morton — 14,178; Pekin (Pt.) — 33,963; Peoria — 124,160; Washington — 10,364.

Race and Ancestry: White — 94.5%; Black — 4.6%; American Indian, Eskimo and Aleut — 0.1%; Asian and Pacific Islander — 0.5%. Spanish Origin — 0.7%. Dutch — 0.6%; English — 11.2%; French — 0.7%; German — 14.8%; Irish — 4.3%; Italian — 0.9%; Scottish — 0.5%; Swedish — 0.6%.

Universities, Enrollment: Bradley University, Peoria — 5,647; Eureka College, Eureka — 461; Illinois Central College, East Peoria — 14,223; Illinois College, Jacksonville — 798; MacMurray College, Jacksonville — 736; Midstate College, Peoria — 295; Robert Morris College, Carthage — 1,328.

Newspapers, Circulation: *Courier* (eS), Jacksonville — 8,911; *Illinoian-Star* (e), Beardstown — 2,671; *Journal* (mS), Jacksonville — 8,600; *The Journal Star* (all day, S), Peoria — 102,939; *Pekin Daily Times* (e), Pekin — 21,870. Springfield *State Journal-Register* also circulates in the district.

Commercial Television Stations, Affiliation: WEEK-TV, Peoria (NBC); WMBD-TV, Peoria (CBS); WRAV-TV, Peoria (ABC). District is divided among Peoria ADI, Quincy-Hannibal (Mo.) ADI, and Springfield-Decatur-Champaign ADI.

Industries:

Caterpillar Tractor Co. (HQ); Peoria; construction equipment — 23,300. **Caterpillar Tractor Co.;** Decatur; tractors, road equipment — 3,400. *(Note: plant straddles 18th and 20th districts.)* **St. Francis Hospital-Medical Center;** Peoria; hospital — 3,100. **Keystone Consolidated Industries** (HQ); Peoria; steel, wire products — 2,000. **Methodist Medical Center;** Peoria; hospital — 2,000.

American Standard Inc. (Wabco Construction & Mining Equipment Control); Peoria; construction machinery — 1,650. **Oscar Mayer & Co. Inc.;** Beardstown; pork processing — 938. **Mobil Oil Corp.** (Plastics Div.); Jacksonville; house furnishings — 900. **Dickey-John Corp.;** Auburn; measuring devices — 850. **Capitol Records Inc.;** Jacksonville; phonograph records — 750. **Fleming-Potter Co.;** Peoria; commercial printing — 700. **The Peoria Journal Star Inc.** (HQ); Peoria; newspaper publishing — 550. **Guard Services Inc.;** Peoria; security services — 500. **Pinkerton's Inc.;** Peoria; security services — 500.

19th District

Southeast — Danville, Champaign-Urbana

The new 19th is part of the Midwest Corn Belt on the north and strictly southern Illinois on the south. The corn-growing areas are fertile and the farms profitable. The southern counties are less prosperous and devoted more to general farming.

Politically the district tends to divide along the same lines. Yankee Republicans settled the northern portion of the district, while conservative Democrats migrating from below the Mason-Dixon Line settled the southern part.

The district lost four counties in the center of the state — Christian, Fayette, Shelby and Moultrie — all traditionally Democratic. Christian, a coal-mining county, has a strong Democratic organization. To make up for the loss of population, the district picked up Hamilton and White counties in the south and the urban portion of Champaign County around the University of Illinois. Champaign and Urbana together have about 95,000 people, and the university influence leads them into the Democratic column in most contests. Remaining in the district is Danville, an industrial and farm market center. Danville has significant Democratic strength; General Motors is a major employer there.

Hamilton and White counties, on the district's new southern border, are laced with stripper oil wells. White is the major oil-producing county in the state, and Hamilton is not far behind. A huge coal mine is also located in White County.

Election Returns

19th District		Democrat		Republican	
1976	President	101,969	(45.8%)	117,017	(52.7%)
	Governor	68,726	(31.4%)	148,988	(68.1%)
	House	115,376	(52.4%)	105,014	(47.6%)
1978	Governor	46,606	(36.2%)	81,456	(63.2%)
	Senate	56,991	(44.6%)	69,569	(54.4%)
	House	58,029	(44.7%)	71,881	(55.3%)
1980	President	78,359	(34.2%)	131,504	(57.4%)
	Senate	110,784	(49.4%)	109,536	(48.9%)
	House	54,375	(30.5%)	123,455	(69.2%)
1982	Governor	73,054	(40.8%)	104,169	(58.2%)
	House	87,231	(47.9%)	94,833	(52.1%)

Demographics

Population: 518,350. Percent Change from 1970: 4.9%.

Land Area: 8,364 square miles. Population per Square Mile: 62.0.

Counties, 1980 Population: Champaign (Pt.) — 120,868; Clark — 16,913; Clay — 15,283; Coles — 52,260; Crawford — 20,818; Cumberland — 11,062; Douglas — 19,774; Edgar — 21,725; Edwards — 7,961; Effingham — 30,944; Hamilton — 9,172; Jasper — 11,318; Lawrence — 17,807; Richland — 17,587; Vermilion — 95,222; Wabash — 13,713; Wayne — 18,059; White — 17,864.

Cities, 1980 Population: Champaign — 58,133; Charleston — 19,355; Danville — 38,985; Effingham — 11,270; Mattoon — 19,055; Urbana — 35,978.

Race and Ancestry: White — 94.8%; Black — 3.9%; American Indian, Eskimo and Aleut — 0.1%; Asian and Pacific Islander — 0.8%. Spanish Origin — 0.8%. Dutch — 0.7%; English — 14.9%; French — 0.8%; German — 13.7%; Irish — 4.5%; Italian — 0.6%; Polish — 0.6%; Scottish — 0.5%.

Universities, Enrollment: Danville Area Community College, Danville — 3,536; Eastern Illinois University, Charleston — 9,989; Lake Land College, Mattoon — 4,093; Lincoln Trail College, Robinson — 1,795; Olney Central College, Olney — 2,381; Parkland College, Champaign — 7,952; University of Illinois at Urbana-Champaign, Urbana — 34,792; Wabash Valley College, Mount Carmel — 3,269.

Newspapers, Circulation: *Champaign-Urbana News-Gazette* (all day, S), Champaign — 48,736; *Coles County Daily Times-Courier* (m), Charleston — 6,687; *Commercial-News* (eS), Danville — 30,902; *The Daily Clay County Advocate-Press* (e), Flora — 3,365; *The Daily Record* (e), Lawrenceville — 5,124; *Daily Reporter* (e), Casey — 2,843; *Daily Republican-Register* (e), Mount Carmel — 4,681; *Effingham Daily News* (e), Effingham — 13,761; *Mattoon Journal-Gazette* (e), Mattoon — 12,170; *Olney Daily Mail* (e), Olney — 3,350; *Paris Beacon-News* (e), Paris — 7,100; *Robinson Daily News* (e), Robinson — 7,757; *Times* (e), Carmi — 2,900.

Commercial Television Stations, Affiliation: WCIA, Champaign (CBS); WICD, Champaign (NBC). District is divided among Springfield-Decatur-Champaign ADI, Evansville (Ind.) ADI, and Terre Haute (Ind.) ADI. Portion is in Paducah (Ky.)-Cape Girardeau (Mo.)-Harrisburg ADI.

Industries:

General Motors Corp. (Central Foundry Div.); Danville; iron foundries — 1,750. **World Color Press Inc.** (HQ); Effingham; commercial printing — 1,230. **Mercy Hospital;** Urbana; hospital — 1,100. **Hyster Co. Inc.;** Danville; fork lifts — 1,050. **Carle Foundation** (HQ); Urbana; hospital — 1,000. **Fedders Corp.;** Effingham; air conditioners — 1,000. **General Electric Co.;** Mattoon; electric lamps — 1,000. **Roadmaster Inc.** (Wheel Good); Olney; children's vehicles — 1,000.

United Industrial Syndicate (Airtex Products Div.); Fairfield; automotive parts — 950. **Tee-Pak Inc.;** Danville; sausage casings — 924. **Snap-On Tools Corp.;** Mount Carmel; hand tools — 830. **R. R. Donnelley & Sons. Co.;** Mattoon; commercial printing — 805. **National Distillers & Chemical Corp.;** Tuscola; petroleum refining — 800. **Gulf & Western Mfg. Co.** (Bohn Heat Transfer Div.); Danville; air conditioning — 750.

Amax Inc. (Coal Div.); Keensburg; coal mining — 733. **Carnation Co.** (Collegiate Cap & Gown Co.); Champaign; apparel — 635. **Champion Laboratories Inc.** (Pyroil Div. - HQ); West Salem; motor vehicle parts — 600. **Decatur Garment Co. Inc.;** McLeansboro; women's dresses — 600. **General Electric Co.;** Danville; generators — 600. **J. M. Jones Co. Inc.;** Urbana; grocery wholesaling — 600. **Kraft Foods** (Humko); Champaign; vegetable oil, shortening — 520. **Southland Corp.** (Midwest Distribution Center); Champaign; food distributing — 500. **White Consolidated Industries** (Blaw-Knox Construction Equipment Div.); Mattoon; asphalt paving machinery — 500.

20th District

Central — Springfield, Decatur, Quincy

The new map drawn up by Democrats weakened the Republican incumbent by expanding the district east to Christian, Shelby and Moultrie counties — traditional Democratic territory where southern folksiness traditionally has played better than Yankee politics of issues and moral principle. It also includes four-fifths of Decatur, an industrial city of nearly 100,000 that often votes Democratic.

Meanwhile, the 20th lost the reliably Republican suburbs of Springfield, and nearby Scott and Morgan counties. The result is a marginal district, won in 1982 by a Democrat with 50.4 percent of the vote. A Democrat last won in 1940.

The district kept the town of Quincy, on the Mississippi River, and the city of Springfield, with the state capitol and a substantial bloc of white-collar workers in state government. Springfield in Sangamon County is the district's largest city, and altogether the portion of Sangamon County included in the district casts more than a quarter of the vote.

Agriculture remains the economic base of the district, thanks to the rich bottom lands of the Illinois and Mississippi rivers. Hogs, corn and soybeans are important; the soybean market in Decatur sets prices for a large area of the Midwest. But coal takes on additional importance in the new 20th, with the addition of the mining counties of Christian, Shelby and Moultrie.

Election Returns

20th District		Democrat		Republican	
1976	President	114,032	(48.2%)	119,329	(50.5%)
	Governor	73,906	(31.6%)	159,008	(68.0%)
	House	92,133	(41.1%)	131,896	(58.9%)
1978	Governor	81,441	(42.4%)	109,580	(57.1%)
	Senate	98,278	(51.5%)	91,153	(47.8%)
	House	63,927	(33.3%)	127,875	(66.7%)

20th District		Democrat		Republican	
1980	President	89,095	(38.0%)	132,407	(56.5%)
	Senate	123,294	(53.4%)	105,466	(45.7%)
	House	113,822	(42.0%)	157,420	(58.0%)
1982	Governor	68,923	(44.9%)	83,790	(54.6%)
	House	100,758	(50.4%)	99,348	(49.6%)

Demographics

Population: 519,015. **Percent Change from 1970:** 3.2%.

Land Area: 6,635 square miles. **Population per Square Mile:** 78.2.

Counties, 1980 Population: Adams — 71,622; Calhoun — 5,867; Christian — 36,446; Fayette (Pt.) — 876; Greene — 16,661; Jersey — 20,538; Macon (Pt.) — 100,676; Macoupin — 49,384; Montgomery (Pt.) — 18,300; Moultrie — 14,546; Pike — 18,896; Sangamon (Pt.) — 141,006; Schuyler (Pt.) — 274; Shelby — 23,923.

Cities, 1980 Population: Decatur (Pt.) — 79,500; Quincy — 42,554; Springfield — 99,637; Taylorville — 11,386.

Race and Ancestry: White — 94.2%; Black — 5.1%; American Indian, Eskimo and Aleut — 0.1%; Asian and Pacific Islander — 0.3%. Spanish Origin — 0.5%. Dutch — 0.5%; English — 11.5%; French — 0.8%; German — 16.0%; Irish — 4.7%; Italian — 1.3%; Scottish — 0.5%.

Universities, Enrollment: Blackburn College, Carlinville — 516; Gem City College - School of Horology, Quincy — 170; John Wood Community College, Quincy — 3,140; Lincoln Land Community College, Springfield — 6,071; Millikin University, Decatur — 1,523; Principia College, Elsah — 911; Quincy College, Quincy — 983; Richland Community College, Decatur — 2,984; Sangamon State University, Springfield — 3,683; Springfield College in Illinois, Springfield — 438.

Newspapers, Circulation: *Daily Union* (e), Shelbyville — 4,550; *Herald and Review* (meS), Decatur — 34,497; *News-Herald* (e), Litchfield — 5,450; *The Quincy Herald-Whig* (eS), Quincy — 30,818; *The State Journal-Register* (meS), Springfield — 71,540; *The Taylorville Daily Breeze-Courier* (e), Taylorville — 8,759.

Commercial Television Stations, Affiliation: WAND, Decatur (ABC); WBHW, Springfield (None); WGEM-TV, Quincy (NBC, ABC); WICS, Springfield (NBC). Most of district is divided between Springfield-Decatur-Champaign ADI and St. Louis (Mo.) ADI. Portion is in Quincy-Hannibal (Mo.) ADI.

Military Installations: Capital Municipal Airport (Air Force), Springfield — 1,234.

Industries:
Caterpillar Tractor Co.; Decatur; tractors, road equipment — 3,400. *(Note: plant straddles 18th and 20th districts.)* **St. John's Hospital;** Springfield; hospital — 2,600. **A. E. Staley Mfg. Co.** (HQ); Decatur; corn, soybean products, cleansers — 2,560. **Cooper Industries Inc.** (Machinery Group); Quincy; pumps — 2,300. **Memorial Medical Center;** Springfield; hospital — 2,300.

Firestone Tire & Rubber Co.; Decatur; tires — 2,000. **Horace Mann Educators Corp.** (HQ); Springfield; insurance — 1,540. **Franklin Life Insurance Co.** (HQ); Springfield; life insurance — 1,460. **St. Mary's Hospital;** Decatur; hospital — 1,390. **Wagner Castings Co.;** Decatur; nodular iron foundries — 1,350. **Decatur Memorial Hospital;** Decatur; hospital — 1,240. **Firestone Tire & Rubber Co. Inc.** (Electric Wheel Co.); Quincy; auto parts — 1,200. **Norfolk & Western Railway Co.;** Decatur; railway operations — 1,200.

Mueller Co. (HQ); Decatur; brass, iron valves and fittings — 900. **Peabody Coal Co.;** Pawnee; coal mining — 900. **Fiat-Allis Construction;** Springfield; heavy construction machinery — 850. **Harris Corp.** (Broadcasting Products Div.); Quincy; communications equipment — 850. **Borg-Warner Corp.** (York Automotive Div.); Decatur; auto parts — 800. **Harris Corp.** (Broadcasting Products Div.); Quincy; communications equipment — 750. **Borg-Warner Corp.** (Marvel-Schebler-Illotson Div.); Decatur; aircraft parts — 650. **Pillsbury Co. Inc.;** Springfield; flour — 500.

21st District

Southwest — East St. Louis, Alton

The new 21st is dominated by the grimy industrial region located across the Mississippi River from St. Louis, Mo. Steel and petroleum refining are the dominant industries although they are in serious decline. Southern St. Clair County has an active coal industry with major strip-mining operations. East of the river are rural areas devoted to dairy farming, wheat, soybeans and corn.

East St. Louis is still the largest city in the district, but it is a shell of its former self. Abandoned by manufacturing firms, the city is also losing most of its remaining retail stores. About 21 percent of its population moved during the 1970s, leaving the city about the size it was in 1910.

East St. Louis is overwhelmingly black (96 percent), while neighboring Belleville to the south and Granite City to the north are predominantly white. Of the three blue-collar communities, Belleville is the most viable; many of its residents commute to work in St. Louis. Further north is the old river port of Alton, now an industrial community producing steel.

Previously composed only of St. Clair County and half of neighboring Madison, the 21st had to expand significantly to make up its population deficit. For the 1980s it includes all of Madison and Bond, all but two townships in St. Clair, and sections of Montgomery and Clinton counties. Thanks largely to St. Clair County, the 21st remains the only rock-solid Democratic district outside the Chicago area. St. Clair was one of only three Illinois counties that voted for Jimmy Carter in 1980.

Election Returns

21st District		Democrat		Republican	
1976	President	120,941	(56.0%)	92,047	(42.6%)
	Governor	90,495	(42.8%)	120,032	(56.8%)
	House	138,782	(71.4%)	55,636	(28.6%)
1978	Governor	62,859	(50.2%)	61,248	(48.9%)
	Senate	71,848	(57.7%)	51,561	(41.4%)
	House	81,704	(66.5%)	41,244	(33.5%)
1980	President	93,309	(44.9%)	104,414	(50.3%)
	Senate	114,485	(56.2%)	87,870	(43.0%)
	House	120,941	(59.9%)	80,882	(40.0%)
1982	Governor	73,406	(51.8%)	67,147	(47.4%)
	House	89,500	(63.6%)	46,764	(33.3%)

Demographics

Population: 521,036. **Percent Change from 1970:** -2.0%.

Land Area: 2,203 square miles. **Population per Square Mile:** 236.5.

Counties, 1980 Population: Bond — 16,224; Clinton (Pt.) — 18,768; Madison — 247,691; Montgomery (Pt.) — 13,386; St. Clair (Pt.) — 224,967.

Cities, 1980 Population: Alton — 34,171; Belleville — 41,580; Collinsville — 19,613; East St. Louis — 55,200; Edwardsville — 12,480; Fairview Heights — 12,414; Granite City — 36,815; O'Fallon — 12,241; Wood River — 12,449.

Race and Ancestry: White — 84.3%; Black — 14.7%; American Indian, Eskimo and Aleut — 0.2%; Asian and Pacific Islander — 0.5%. Spanish Origin — 1.1%. English — 8.0%; French — 1.1%; German — 17.8%; Irish — 3.8%; Italian — 1.1%; Polish — 1.0%.

Universities, Enrollment: Belleville Area College, Belleville — 11,840; Greenville College, Greenville — 858; Lewis and Clark Community College, Godfrey — 5,741; McKendree College, Lebanon — 620; Southern Illinois University (Edwardsville campus), Edwardsville — 9,832; State Community College of East St. Louis, East St. Louis — 1,884.

Newspapers, Circulation: *Alton-Telegraph* (e), Alton — 38,374; *Edwardsville Intelligencer* (e), Edwardsville — 7,530; *News-Democrat* (eS), Belleville — 41,812. *St. Louis Globe-Democrat* (Mo.) and *St. Louis Post-Dispatch* (Mo.) also circulate in the district.

Commercial Television Stations, Affiliation: Entire district is located in St. Louis (Mo.) ADI.

Military Installations: Scott Air Force Base, Belleville — 18,734; St. Louis Area Support Center (Army), Granite City — 461.

Industries:

Olin Corp. (Signal Products Operation); East Alton; copper, brass strip — 4,000. **National Steel Corp.;** Granite City; steel mill — 3,900. **Laclede Steel Co.;** Alton; steel mill, fabricated steel — 2,700. **Shell Oil Co.;** Roxana; petroleum refining — 1,700. **St. Elizabeth's Hospital;** Belleville; hospital — 1,600.

Memorial Hospital & Convalescent Center; Belleville; hospital — 1,560. **Amsted Industries Inc.** (American Steel Foundries Div.); Granite City; iron, steel forgings — 1,300. **Monsanto Co.** (Industrial Chemicals Co.); Sauget; chemicals — 1,200. **St. Elizabeth Hospital;** Granite City; hospital — 1,100. **Cerro Copper Products Co.;** East St. Louis; copper tubing — 1,000. **Jefferson Smurfit Inc.;** Alton; corrugated boxes, printing — 700. **Illinois Central Gulf Railroad;** East St. Louis; railroad operations — 650. **Owens-Illinois Inc.;** Godfrey; machine shop — 633. **Consolidation Coal Co. Inc.** (Hillsboro Mine); Coffeen; coal mining — 601. **Consolidated Aluminum Corp.;** Madison; aluminum products — 550. **Alton & Southern Railway Co.;** East St. Louis; railroad operations — 540. **Swift Independent Packing Co.;** National Stock Yards; meatpacking, processed hams — 500. **Thacker Construction Co. Inc.;** Godfrey; heavy construction — 500.

22nd District

South — Carbondale

At the southern tip of Illinois the prairies give way to hilly countryside, and coal replaces large-scale farming as a dominant economic activity. About 15,000 miners work in the Illinois Basin, a coal vein that runs under Franklin, Williamson, Saline, Perry and Jefferson counties. The people here are descendants of 19th century settlers from Kentucky, Tennessee and other parts of the South; they are traditional Democrats, although those loyalties are gradually changing.

The new 22nd is similar in outline to the old 24th, but it has been redrawn for the benefit of its liberal Democratic incumbent, who escaped defeat by fewer than 2,000 votes in 1980. The most important change is the addition of heavily Democratic territory in St. Clair County. The district takes on Centreville and Sugar Loaf townships on the southern outskirts of East St. Louis, urbanized blue-collar areas that had been in the old 23rd District.

The district also lost two counties — Hamilton and White — that are historically Democratic but opposed the incumbent in 1980. In a separate exchange, marginal Bond County was moved to the 21st, and Fayette, slightly more Democratic, was given to the 22nd in replacement.

Carbondale and the other small cities of the 22nd lie along the Main Street of the district: State Route 13. Carbondale is dominated by Southern Illinois University, with 23,000 students.

At the southern tip of the district is Alexander County, in the region called "Little Egypt." The depressed river town of Cairo is its county seat. Alexander County gave Jimmy Carter 51 percent of its vote in 1980, making it second only to Cook County in its Democratic presidential showing.

Election Returns

22nd District		Democrat		Republican	
1976	President	127,388	(54.4%)	103,843	(44.4%)
	Governor	91,812	(39.9%)	137,191	(59.7%)
	House	153,347	(68.7%)	69,844	(31.3%)
1978	Governor	79,016	(48.1%)	84,490	(51.4%)
	Senate	85,725	(53.0%)	74,875	(46.3%)
	House	106,864	(65.5%)	56,264	(34.5%)
1980	President	96,562	(41.6%)	125,032	(53.9%)
	Senate	120,981	(54.3%)	99,636	(44.7%)
	House	104,830	(51.6%)	93,945	(46.2%)
1982	Governor	112,999	(49.8%)	112,421	(49.5%)
	House	123,693	(66.2%)	63,279	(33.8%)

Demographics

Population: 521,303. **Percent Change from 1970:** 9.3%.

Land Area: 8,201 square miles. **Population per Square Mile:** 63.6.

Counties, 1980 Population: Alexander — 12,264; Clinton (Pt.) — 13,849; Fayette (Pt.) — 21,291; Franklin — 43,201; Gallatin — 7,590; Hardin — 5,383; Jackson — 61,522; Jefferson — 36,552; Johnson — 9,624; Marion — 43,523; Massac — 14,990; Monroe — 20,117; Perry — 21,714; Pope — 4,404; Pulaski — 8,840; Randolph — 35,652; Saline — 28,448; St. Clair (Pt.) — 42,564; Union — 17,765; Washington — 15,472; Williamson — 56,538.

Cities, 1980 Population: Cahokia — 18,904; Carbondale — 26,287; Centralia — 15,126; Harrisburg — 10,410; Herrin — 10,549; Marion — 14,031; Mount Vernon — 17,193.

Race and Ancestry: White — 92.7%; Black — 6.5%; American Indian, Eskimo and Aleut — 0.1%; Asian and Pacific Islander — 0.4%. Spanish Origin — 0.6%. Dutch — 0.5%; English — 13.2%; French — 1.0%; German — 13.9%; Irish — 5.4%; Italian — 1.0%; Polish — 1.0%.

Universities, Enrollment: John A. Logan College, Carterville — 2,061; Kaskaskia College, Centralia — 2,930; Parks College of Aeronautical Technology, Cahokia — 1,044; Rend Lake College, Ina — 2,597; Shawnee College, Ullin — 2,360; Southeastern Illinois College, Harrisburg — 2,064; Southern Illinois University (Carbondale campus), Carbondale — 23,236.

Newspapers, Circulation: *Cairo Evening Citizen* (e), Cairo — 5,132; *Call* (e), Du Quoin — 4,703; *Centralia Sentinel* (eS), Centralia — 18,056; *The Daily American* (e), West Frankfort — 4,344; *The Daily Register* (e), Harrisburg — 7,342; *Eldorado Daily Journal* (e), Eldorado — 2,731; *The Marion Daily Republican* (e), Marion — 5,250; *News* (e), Benton — 6,716; *Register-News* (e), Mount Vernon — 12,911; *Southern Illinoisan* (e), Carbondale — 30,209. *St. Louis Globe-Democrat* (Mo.) and *St. Louis Post-Dispatch* (Mo.) also circulate in the district.

Commercial Television Stations, Affiliation: WDDD-TV, Marion (None); WSIL-TV, Harrisburg (ABC). District is divided between Paducah (Ky.)-Cape Girardeau (Mo.)-Harrisburg ADI and St. Louis (Mo.) ADI.

Industries:

Magic Chef Inc. (Norge Div.); Herrin; laundry equipment — 1,600. **Spartan Printing Co.;** Sparta; magazine printing — 1,600. **Sohio Alaska Petroleum Co.** (Old Ben Coal Co.); Sesser; coal mining — 1,210. **Illinois Central Gulf Railroad Co.;** Centralia; railroad operations — 1,200. **Inland Steel Corp.;** Sesser; coal mining — 1,180.

Consolidation Coal Co. (Illinois Surface Operations); Pinckneyville; coal mining — 1,150. **General Tire & Rubber Co. Inc.;** Mount Vernon; tires — 900. **The Singer Co.** (Climate Control Div.); Red Bud; heating, air conditioning equipment — 850. **Koppers Co. Inc.** (Treated Wood Products Div.); Carbondale; gum & wood chemicals — 650. **John Crane-Houdaille Inc.;** Vandalia; industrial machinery — 600. **Sohio Alaska Petroleum Co.** (Old Ben Coal Co.); Benton; coal mining — 562. **Allen Industries Inc.;** Herrin; cotton, padding — 500. **Allied Chemical Corp.** (Specialty Chemical Div.); Metropolis; industrial chemicals — 500.

Gilster-Mary Lee Corp.; Steeleville; blended flour mixes — 500. **MCA Inc.;** Pinckneyville; phonograph records — 500. **Missouri Railroad Co.;** Dupo; railroad operations — 500. **Peabody Coal Co.;** Sparta; coal mining — 500. **Sahara Coal Co. Inc.;** Harrisburg; coal mining — 500. **Smoler Bros. Inc.;** Herrin; women's dresses — 500. **Tuck Industries Inc.;** Carbondale; paper coating — 500.

Indiana

Gerrymandering was resurrected in Indiana in 1981 when the Republican Party, in complete control of the Legislature and the governor's office, redrew congressional district lines in a way that seriously jeopardized three of the state's six Democratic incumbents.

Forced to drop one of the state's 11 districts, Indiana Republicans carefully carved through counties and townships to concentrate most of the Democratic vote in three constituencies and spread the Republican vote thickly and evenly across the rest of the state.

The GOP thought the plan might shift the state's House delegation from its 6-to-5 Democratic majority to at least a 6-to-4 majority for Republicans, and possibly 7-to-3. The uncertainty revolved around the new 2nd District, where the Democratic incumbent lost much of his old district and had several new Republican areas added. The incumbent, however, won a sixth term in 1982.

Redistricting seriously hurt two other Democrats as well. One decided to run for the Senate, where his challenge against the Republican incumbent was unsuccessful. The second had his district divided among four other districts and finally decided to run against the Democratic incumbent in the new 10th. He lost in the primary.

Even though the state lost a district, Republicans were able to carve out a new constituency north of Indianapolis without a resident incumbent. This 6th District had the highest GOP vote of any new district in the state. Winning agreement on the exact location of the new 6th was difficult because several ambitious Republican politicians lived in the area and wanted to have the option of running there in 1982.

The partisan map, drawn up by Allan Sutherlin, former executive director of the state Republican Party, was not shown to the legislators until the last day of the legislative session, April 30, 1981. It was attached to an unrelated bill and presented to the Indiana House.

Although the plan had received final approval the night before from the state's Republican congressmen and GOP legislative leaders, many state Republican legislators were upset by the last-minute timing. As a result, the plan was initially rejected in the House by a 47-51 vote. The Republican leadership hastily called a caucus, explained the new map and assured legislators that Republican House members were pleased with their new district lines.

Democrats introduced an alternative plan that had a smaller population deviation than the Republican version and that split only one county. But it was quickly rejected when Republican legislators fell back into line. The House then adopted by a 53-42 vote the Republican plan it had earlier rejected. The bill was sent the same day to the Senate, where it won quick approval on a 32-13 vote. It was signed May 5, 1981, by Gov. Robert D. Orr.

The population difference between the new districts is 3.1 percent, compared with just over 0.2 percent for the plan that was adopted in 1971. The largest district, the 3rd, is 1.7 percent above the ideal, and the smallest, the newly created 6th, is 1.4 percent below the ideal.

Democrats, labor leaders and some civic groups talked about filing a suit against the plan charging that the population variance was too large and that the lines were drawn with purely political motives. However, in late September 1981 the state's Democratic congressional delegation opted against a suit. By then most of the incumbents were already running in their new districts and did not welcome the added uncertainty of a court case.

As it turned out, Republicans did not do as well as they had hoped in the 1982 elections. While the GOP took the new 6th District, a Republican incumbent lost to his Democratic challenger, making the line-up for the 98th Congress 5-5.

Age of Population

District	Population Under 18	Voting Age Population	Population 65 & Over (% of VAP)	Median Age
1	171,237	375,863	47,696 (12.7%)	28.2
2	162,529	390,981	58,462 (15.0%)	29.5
3	162,979	395,121	62,682 (15.9%)	29.6
4	171,548	382,150	58,015 (15.2%)	28.8
5	168,009	380,248	55,952 (14.7%)	29.2
6	159,106	381,833	54,972 (14.4%)	30.7
7	152,053	403,139	62,715 (15.6%)	28.8
8	151,593	395,151	70,673 (17.9%)	30.8
9	161,855	383,018	56,470 (14.7%)	28.4
10	157,409	384,402	57,747 (15.0%)	28.4
State	1,618,318	3,871,906	585,384 (15.1%)	29.2

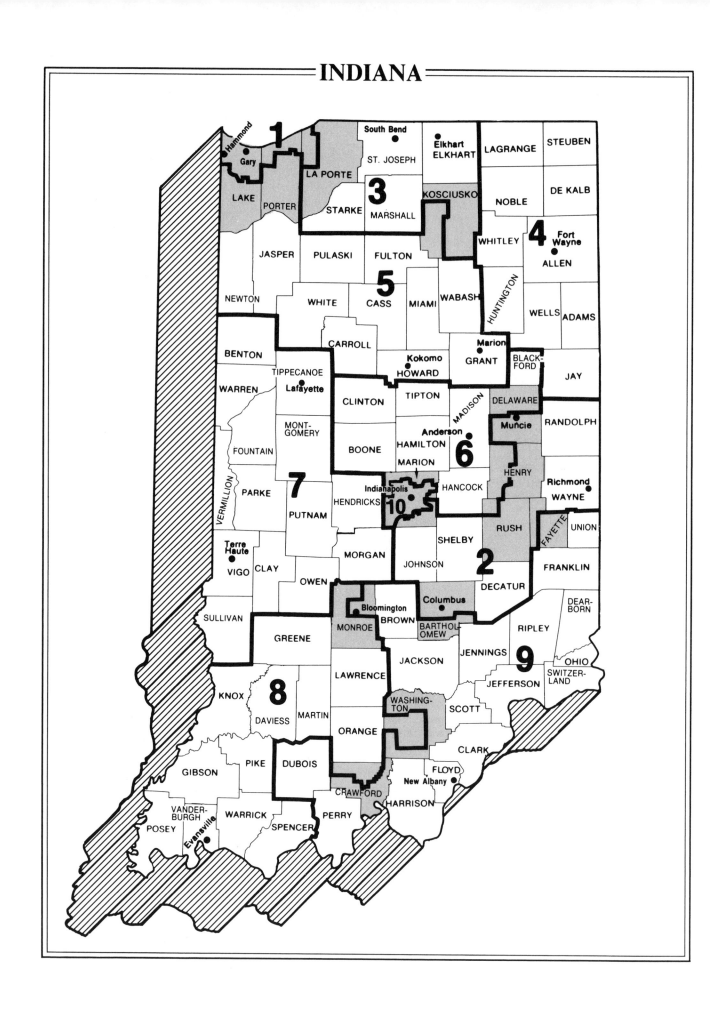

INDIANA

Income and Occupation

District	Median Family Income	White Collar Workers	Blue Collar Workers	Service Workers	Farm Workers
1	$ 23,599	42.4%	43.6%	13.6%	0.4%
2	20,438	48.9	35.3	12.7	3.1
3	20,199	47.2	38.1	12.4	2.4
4	20,841	45.8	38.4	12.3	3.5
5	21,434	41.1	41.8	12.7	4.4
6	23,466	55.6	31.2	10.8	2.3
7	20,027	47.5	34.9	13.8	3.7
8	18,612	44.2	38.8	13.4	3.6
9	18,497	42.3	41.1	12.7	3.9
10	18,392	50.0	33.7	15.7	0.5
State	$ 20,535	46.6%	37.6%	13.0%	2.8%

Education: School Years Completed

District	8 Years or Fewer	4 Years of High School	4 Years of College or More	Median School Years
1	18.3%	41.0%	9.5%	12.3
2	16.0	43.2	12.2	12.4
3	15.7	41.3	12.9	12.4
4	14.2	44.0	11.9	12.5
5	14.6	46.1	11.0	12.4
6	11.5	41.1	19.6	12.6
7	14.3	43.6	14.4	12.5
8	20.3	40.2	11.5	12.3
9	22.4	40.2	10.5	12.3
10	18.4	36.7	11.2	12.3
State	16.6%	41.7%	12.5%	12.4

Housing and Residential Patterns

District	Owner Occupied	Renter Occupied	Urban	Rural
1	67.3%	32.7%	96.4%	3.6%
2	72.0	28.0	65.5	34.5
3	75.1	24.9	63.2	36.8
4	75.6	24.4	57.8	42.2
5	75.6	24.4	48.7	51.3
6	72.4	27.6	63.5	36.5
7	73.8	26.2	46.6	53.4
8	73.9	26.1	54.9	45.1
9	74.8	25.2	46.2	53.8
10	57.0	43.0	100.0	0.0
State	71.7%	28.3%	64.2%	35.8%

1st District

Industrial Belt — Gary, Hammond

For the first time in half a century, redistricting pushed the 1st District beyond the borders of Lake County. Stretching from the Illinois border at Hammond to Michigan City 40 miles to the east, the new district covers the entire Indiana shore line along Lake Michigan. It extends inland only slightly beyond the congested and polluted lakefront industrial area.

The district's industrial base and large black population in Gary make it the state's most Democratic territory.

Although Jimmy Carter drew only 50 percent of the vote in 1980 within the new district lines, this was still a higher percentage than he received in any other district in the state.

The Democratic strength in the new district lies principally within Lake County, which casts more than 80 percent of the vote. Centered on Gary, the state's third largest city with nearly 152,000 people, and Hammond, with a population just under 100,000, the new district carefully avoids the increasingly Republican parts of the county found roughly south of U. S. Route 30.

Although not as strongly Democratic as the Lake County portion of the district, northern Porter County and Michigan City in La Porte County are heavily industrial and blue-collar oriented. Porter County contains Burns Harbor, the state's only shipping port. There are also several steel mills and the state prison in the area. Many of the steel and oil refinery workers from Gary and Hammond have moved out to this area.

Election Returns

1st District		Democrat		Republican	
1976	President	127,309	(56.8%)	94,741	(42.2%)
	Governor	121,458	(56.7%)	91,850	(42.9%)
	Senate	119,281	(55.5%)	94,336	(43.9%)
	House	147,144	(68.7%)	66,946	(31.2%)
1978	House	87,171	(73.1%)	27,974	(23.5%)
1980	President	106,716	(49.9%)	95,848	(44.8%)
	Governor	111,773	(56.4%)	85,659	(43.2%)
	Senate	123,024	(60.1%)	81,602	(39.9%)
	House	137,525	(68.2%)	64,153	(31.8%)
1982	Senate	104,396	(65.7%)	53,518	(33.7%)
	House	87,369	(56.3%)	66,921	(43.1%)

Demographics

Population: 547,100. **Percent Change from 1970:** -5.9%.

Land Area: 369 square miles. **Population per Square Mile:** 1,482.7.

Counties, 1980 Population: La Porte (Pt.) — 41,682; Lake (Pt.) — 447,031; Porter (Pt.) — 58,387.

Cities, 1980 Population: Crown Point (Pt.) — 1; East Chicago — 39,786; Gary — 151,953; Griffith — 17,026; Hammond — 93,714; Highland — 25,935; Hobart — 22,987; Lake Station — 14,294; Merrillville — 27,677; Michigan City (Pt.) — 30,627; Munster — 20,671; Portage — 27,409; Schererville (Pt.) — 8,732.

Race and Ancestry: White — 71.3%; Black — 24.2%; American Indian, Eskimo and Aleut — 0.1%; Asian and Pacific Islander — 0.4%. Spanish Origin — 8.2%. Dutch — 0.7%; English — 5.2%; German — 5.8%; Greek — 0.7%; Hungarian — 0.9%; Irish — 3.0%; Italian — 1.0%; Polish — 5.1%; Swedish — 0.6%.

Universities, Enrollment: Calumet College, Whiting — 1,374; Indiana University Northwest, Gary — 4,446; Purdue University (Calumet campus), Hammond — 7,229; Purdue University (North Central campus), Westville — 2,183.

Newspapers, Circulation: *The News-Dispatch* (e), Michigan City — 18,278; *Post-Tribune* (eS), Gary — 83,180; *The Times* (eS), Hammond — 66,653; *Tribune* (e), Chesterton — 4,318. *Chicago Tribune* also circulates in the district.

Commercial Television Stations, Affiliation: Entire district is located in Chicago (Ill.) ADI.

Industries:

Inland Steel Co.; East Chicago; steel mill — 22,000. **United States Steel Corp.;** Gary; steel foundries — 15,500. **Jones & Laughlin Steel Corp.** (Indiana Harbor Works); East Chicago; steel mill — 7,500. **Bethlehem Steel Corp.** (Burns Harbor Plant); Portage; steel mill — 6,500. **Amoco Oil Co.;** Whiting; crude oil, natural gas — 2,000. **National Steel Corp.** (Midwest Steel Div.); Portage; galvanized steel — 2,000.

United States Steel Corp. (Tubing Specialties); Gary; tubing — 1,700. **St. Mary Medical Center Inc.;** Hobart; hospital — 1,550. **St. Margaret's Hospital;** Hammond; hospital — 1,500. **Union Tank Car Co.;** East Chicago; tank cars — 1,500. **Indiana Harbor Belt Railroad Co.;** Hammond; railroad operations — 1,450. **St. Catherine Hospital;** East Chicago; hospital — 1,240. **Emcor Inc.;** Hammond; heavy construction — 1,200. **Lever Bros. Co.;** Hammond; soap products — 1,200. **Methodist Northlake Hospital;** Gary; hospital — 1,200. **White Consolidated Industries** (Blaw-Knox Foundry Mill Machinery Div.); East Chicago; metal working machinery — 972. **American Maize-Products Co.;** Hammond; wet corn milling — 834.

Anderson Co. of Indiana (HQ); Gary; motor vehicle parts — 800. **Joy Mfg. Co.;** Michigan City; air compressors — 750. **Energy Cooperative Inc.;** East Chicago; petroleum refining — 650. **Jaymar-Ruby Inc.** (HQ); Michigan City; men's, boys' clothing — 600. **La Salle Steel Co. Inc.;** Hammond; steel sheet, bars — 600. **The Marley-Wylain Co. Inc.** (Weil-McLain Div.); Michigan City; heating equipment — 600. **McAuliffe Mechanical Contractors;** East Chicago; plumbing, heating contracting — 600. **Union Carbide Corp.** (Chemical Div.); Whiting; synthetic resins — 580. **Combustion Engineering Co.;** East Chicago; grinders — 550. **International Mill Service Inc.;** Whiting; steel wholesaling — 502. **First United Life Insurance Co.;** Gary; life, health insurance — 500.

2nd District

East Central — Muncie, Richmond

Shaped like the letter "J," this district runs through a collection of areas with virtually nothing in common — Indianapolis suburbs, lightly populated farm lands and three industrial cities.

Two-thirds of the vote is cast in the vicinities of Indianapolis, Muncie, Richmond and Columbus. Voters in those cities read different newspapers and watch different television stations. The only economic thread common to the cities is a dependence on the auto industry.

Muncie, the model for *Middletown*, the sociological study of small-town American life in the 1920s, is the largest city in the district, with a population of 77,216. It was settled largely by Southerners and tends to be more Democratic than the other cities in the district. Auto parts factories are crucial to its livelihood, which is why times were so hard in the early 1980s.

Columbus, the smallest of the major cities in the district, is the home of Cummins Engine Company, the world's largest manufacturer of diesel engines. Added to the 2nd District in the 1981 remap, Columbus usually yields higher Republican percentages than either Richmond or Muncie.

The portions of metropolitan Indianapolis placed in the 2nd are primarily conservative, middle-income suburban areas. The suburban part of the 2nd also extends south of Indianapolis into Johnson County, which is just as conservative. In 1980 Democratic Sen. Birch Bayh won only 35 percent of the vote in the Indianapolis and Johnson County portions of the 2nd District. These account for just under a third of the district's total vote.

The corn and hog farmers of the district usually vote Republican — GOP Sen. Richard G. Lugar carried every county in the district in 1982. But the farmers also have demonstrated a willingness to back House Democrats who pay attention to them.

Election Returns

2nd District		Democrat		Republican	
1976	President	92,744	(41.9%)	126,543	(57.2%)
	Governor	86,714	(39.8%)	130,193	(59.7%)
	Senate	79,676	(36.5%)	136,180	(62.4%)
	House	127,653	(61.9%)	78,334	(38.0%)
1978	House	82,480	(54.4%)	68,174	(45.0%)
1980	President	76,120	(33.5%)	138,118	(60.9%)
	Governor	79,723	(36.1%)	140,205	(63.5%)
	Senate	92,016	(40.9%)	132,775	(59.1%)
	House	119,837	(54.8%)	98,675	(45.2%)
1982	Senate	75,749	(39.2%)	116,496	(60.3%)
	House	107,298	(56.2%)	83,593	(43.8%)

Demographics

Population: 553,510. **Percent Change from 1970:** 7.8%.

Land Area: 3,193 square miles. **Population per Square Mile:** 173.4.

Counties, 1980 Population: Bartholomew (Pt.) — 54,951; Decatur — 23,841; Delaware (Pt.) — 105,981; Fayette (Pt.) — 1,844; Henry (Pt.) — 39,714; Johnson — 77,240; Marion (Pt.) — 86,381; Randolph — 29,997; Rush (Pt.) — 17,616; Shelby — 39,887; Wayne — 76,058.

Cities, 1980 Population: Beech Grove (Pt.) — 7,237; Columbus (Pt.) — 30,567; Franklin — 11,563; Greenwood — 19,327; Indianapolis (Pt.) — 76,047; Muncie — 77,216; New Castle — 20,056; Richmond — 41,349; Shelbyville — 14,989.

Race and Ancestry: White — 96.7%; Black — 2.6%; American Indian, Eskimo and Aleut — 0.1%; Asian and Pacific Islander — 0.3%. Spanish Origin — 0.6%. Dutch — 0.7%; English — 16.8%; French — 0.8%; German — 12.5%; Irish — 4.8%; Italian — 0.5%; Scottish — 0.5%.

Universities, Enrollment: Ball State University, Muncie — 18,490; Columbus Technical Institute, Columbus — 1,612; Earlham College, Richmond — 1,202; Eastcentral Technical Institute, Muncie — 2,228; Franklin College of Indiana, Franklin — 633; Indiana University East, Richmond — 1,369; Whitewater Technical Institute, Richmond — 925.

Newspapers, Circulation: *The Courier Times* (e), New Castle — 14,146; *Daily Journal* (e), Franklin — 13,337; *Greensburg Daily News* (e), Greensburg — 6,536; *The Muncie Evening Press* (e), Muncie — 17,931; *The Muncie Star* (mS), Muncie — 29,369; *News-Gazette* (e), Winchester — 5,257; *Palladium-Item* (eS), Richmond — 22,270; *The Republic* (e), Columbus — 22,183; *Rushville Daily Republican* (e), Rushville — 4,292; *The Shelbyville News* (e), Shelbyville — 10,747. *The Indianapolis News* and *The Indianapolis Star* also circulate in the district.

Commercial Television Stations, Affiliation: WKOI, Richmond (None). Most of district is located in Indianapolis ADI. Small portions are in Cincinnati (Ohio) ADI and Dayton (Ohio) ADI.

Industries:

General Motors Corp.; Muncie; motor vehicle parts — 2,440. **Ball Memorial Hospital Assn.;** Muncie; hospital — 1,950. **Belden Corp.;** Richmond; electronic cable — 1,600. **Borg-Warner Corp.** (Warner Gear Div.); Muncie; motor vehicle parts — 1,440. **Bartholomew County Hospital;** Columbus; hospital — 1,250.

National Railroad Passenger Corp. (AMTRAK); Beech Grove; railroad operations — 1,200. **Westinghouse Electric Corp.** (Large Power Transformer Div.); Muncie; transformers — 1,200. **Arvin Industries Inc.** (Automotive Products Div.); Franklin; auto parts — 1,100. **Reid Memorial Hospital**; Richmond; hospital — 1,050. **Anchor Hocking Corp.**; Winchester; glass containers — 1,000. **Cosco Inc.** (Home Products Div. - HQ); Columbus; metal household furniture — 1,000. **Wayne Corp.** (Transportation Div. - HQ); Richmond; bus bodies — 1,000. **Chrysler Corp.**; New Castle; motor vehicle parts — 922.

Ball Corp. (HQ); Muncie; glass, metal containers — 900. **Textron Inc.** (Golden Operations); Columbus; gray iron castings — 900. **Burger Chef Systems Inc.** (HQ); Indianapolis; fast food restaurant chain — 757. **Cummins Engine Co. Inc.** (HQ); Columbus; diesel engines — 700. **Harsco Corp.** (Broderick Co. Div.); Muncie; steel forgings — 700. **Marsh Supermarkets Inc.** (HQ); Yorktown; grocery chain — 700. **Wavetek Indiana Inc.**; Beech Grove; electronic measuring devices — 630. **Aluminum Co. of America**; Richmond; aluminum, plastic — 600. **Arvin Industries Inc.** (Arvinyl Div. - HQ); Columbus; automotive parts — 600.

Tappan Co. Inc. (Kemper Div.); Richmond; kitchen cabinets — 600. **Union City Body Co. Inc.** (HQ); Union City; truck bodies — 595. **General Motors Corp.** (Delco Remy Div.); Muncie; electrical auto parts 560. **Richmond Recording Corp.** (PRC Recording Co. Div.); Richmond; records — 515. **Design and Mfg. Corp.**; Richmond; dishwashers — 500. **Knauf Fiberglass**; Shelbyville; fiberglass — 500. **Masco Corp. of Indiana** (Electra Div.); Indianapolis; electronic scanners — 500. **Norfolk & Western Railway Co. Inc.**; Muncie; railroad operations — 500. **Sheller-Globe Corp.** (Hardy Div.); Union City; die castings — 500.

3rd District

North Central — South Bend

Anchored by the industrial cities of South Bend and Elkhart, the 3rd is a swing district. In 1980 and 1982 it sent a Republican to the House. For 11 terms prior to that, it elected a Democrat but only twice gave him 60 percent of the vote.

South Bend, besides being the home of Notre Dame University, has an American Motors assembly plant and several Bendix facilities that make automobile and airplane parts. With a population of 109,727, it is a mixture of blue-collar workers and university-related professionals. St. Joseph County, which includes South Bend, often supports Democrats at the state and local level, but the margins fluctuate considerably.

Elkhart's economy is less closely tied to the auto industry and therefore is healthier than South Bend's. The city is headquarters for Miles Laboratories.

The more prosperous voters of Elkhart — combined with a Mennonite community based in Goshen, the seat of Elkhart County — give the county a Republican flavor. Republicans routinely draw more than 60 percent of the Elkhart County vote in local and statewide elections.

Elkhart County comprises about a quarter of the district's population; St. Joseph County contributes about 45 percent. The large Republican pluralities from Elkhart frequently offset the smaller Democratic margins from St. Joseph, particularly when combined with GOP strength among the district's farmers.

About a third of the vote comes from four rural counties to the south and west of South Bend and Elkhart. The cattle and dairy farmers of Kosciusko, Marshall and La Porte counties traditionally vote a strong Republican ticket. In Starke County, where potatoes are a major crop, the voters sometimes side with the Democrats.

The 3rd gained Starke, Marshall and much of Kosciusko in redistricting; it transferred to the 1st the northwest portion of La Porte County including more than 80 percent of Michigan City.

Election Returns

3rd District		Democrat		Republican	
1976	President	95,289	(44.0%)	118,782	(54.9%)
	Governor	72,581	(34.1%)	138,858	(65.3%)
	Senate	77,443	(36.7%)	132,170	(62.7%)
	House	118,148	(56.0%)	92,545	(43.8%)
1978	House	78,507	(56.4%)	58,556	(42.1%)
1980	President	81,627	(36.6%)	124,750	(55.9%)
	Governor	86,832	(39.9%)	129,675	(59.6%)
	Senate	97,676	(44.5%)	121,940	(55.5%)
	House	103,819	(46.9%)	117,684	(53.1%)
1982	Senate	76,728	(44.7%)	93,933	(54.7%)
	House	83,046	(48.8%)	86,958	(51.2%)

Demographics

Population: 558,100. **Percent Change from 1970:** 5.5%.

Land Area: 2,577 square miles. **Population per Square Mile:** 216.6.

Counties, 1980 Population: Elkhart — 137,330; Kosciusko (Pt.) — 51,051; La Porte (Pt.) — 66,950; Marshall — 39,155; St. Joseph — 241,617; Starke — 21,997.

Cities, 1980 Population: Elkhart — 41,305; Goshen — 19,665; La Porte — 21,796; Michigan City (Pt.) — 6,223; Mishawaka — 40,201; South Bend — 109,727; Warsaw — 10,647.

Race and Ancestry: White — 93.4%; Black — 5.3%; American Indian, Eskimo and Aleut — 0.2%; Asian and Pacific Islander — 0.4%. Spanish Origin — 1.4%. Dutch — 1.0%; English — 7.7%; French — 0.7%; German — 16.0%; Hungarian — 1.3%; Irish — 3.6%; Italian — 1.0%; Polish — 4.3%; Swedish — 0.6%.

Universities, Enrollment: Ancilla College, Donaldson — 422; Bethel College, Mishawaka — 487; Goshen Biblical Seminary, Elkhart — 140; Goshen College, Goshen — 1,291; Grace College, Winona Lake — 1,172; Indiana University (South Bend campus), South Bend — 6,299; La Porte Business College, La Porte — 119; Mennonite Biblical Seminary, Elkhart — 72; Michiana College of Commerce, South Bend — 158; Northcentral Technical Institute, South Bend — 2,018; St. Mary's College, Notre Dame — 1,816; University of Notre Dame, Notre Dame — 8,925.

Newspapers, Circulation: *The Elkhart Truth* (e), Elkhart — 29,851; *The Goshen News* (e), Goshen — 13,868; *La Porte Herald-Argus* (e), La Porte — 13,587; *The Pilot-News* (e), Plymouth — 9,177; *South Bend Tribune* (eS), South Bend — 106,171; *Times-Union* (e), Warsaw — 12,614.

Commercial Television Stations, Affiliation: WHME-TV, South Bend (None); WNDU-TV, South Bend (NBC); WSBT-TV, South Bend (CBS); WSJV, Elkhart (ABC). Most of district is located in South Bend-Elkhart ADI. Portion is located in Chicago (Ill.) ADI.

Industries:

Miles Laboratories Inc. (HQ); Elkhart; pharmaceuticals, medical supplies — 3,000. **The Bendix Corp.** (Automotive Div.); South Bend; engine components — 3,300. **Uniroyal Inc.**; Mishawaka; rubber, plastic products — 1,371. **Memorial Hospital of South Bend**; South Bend; hospital — 1,300. **Wheelabrator-Frye Inc.** (Materials Cleaning Systems Div.); Mishawaka; industrial cleaning equipment — 1,300.

American Motors Corp.; (General Corp.); South Bend; motor vehicle assembly — 1,200. **Johnson Controls Inc.** (Control Products

Div.); Goshen; automatic controls — 1,200. **Zimmer USA Inc.** (HQ); Warsaw; orthopedic supplies — 1,200. **St. Joseph's Hospital of South Bend;** South Bend; hospital — 1,100. **Howmet Turbine Components Corp.;** La Porte; engine components — 1,000. **The Torrington Co.;** South Bend; bearings — 1,060. **CTS Corp.;** Elkhart; resistors — 1,050. **R. R. Donnelly & Sons Co.** (Warsaw Mfg. Div.); Warsaw; commercial printing — 1,010. **The Bendix Corp.** (Aircraft Brake & Strut Div.); South Bend; aircraft parts — 1,000. **Elkhart General Hospital;** Elkhart; hospital — 1,000.

Raco Inc.; South Bend; wiring devices — 800. **The Dalton Foundries Inc.** (Warsaw Foundry Div. - HQ); Warsaw; gray ductile iron — 775. **Coachmen Industries Inc.** (HQ); Middlebury; recreational vehicles — 746. **Goshen Rubber Co. Inc.** (HQ); Goshen; industrial rubber products — 700. **American Home Foods Inc.;** La Porte; canned snack foods — 650. **American Home Products Corp.** (Whitehall Laboratories Div.); Elkhart; pharmaceuticals — 600. **Fairmont Homes Inc.** (HQ); Nappanee; mobile homes — 550. **Allied Products Corp.;** South Bend; metal stampings — 525. **Reliance Electric Co.** (Dodge Mfg. Div.); Mishawaka; high speed gears — 500. **Whirlpool Corp.** (Parts Distribution Center); La Porte; appliance parts wholesaling — 500.

4th District

Northeast — Fort Wayne

Firmly planted in the northeastern corner of the state, the 4th is dominated politically and economically by Fort Wayne. Allen County, which includes Fort Wayne, has 53 percent of the district's population.

With 172,196 residents, Fort Wayne is Indiana's second largest city; it is the only community in the 4th with more than 20,000 people. Voters in the nine counties surrounding Allen look to Fort Wayne for their news and commercial needs.

Located where the St. Marys and St. Joseph rivers meet to form the Maumee, Fort Wayne has been a transportation and manufacturing center since the time when John Chapman, better known as Johnny Appleseed, lived and died there during the first half of the 19th century. In more recent times General Electric and International Harvester have been the two leading employers there. Harvester's decision in 1982 to pull out of Fort Wayne entirely, idling more than 4,000 workers, was a crippling blow to the city's economy.

With a large German ethnic population, Fort Wayne is a strongly Republican town dominated by two conservative newspapers. Only once in the last 40 years — in 1964 — has Allen County failed to support the GOP presidential nominee. The surrounding farm counties usually vote as consistently for the GOP as Fort Wayne does.

Between 1950 and 1980 only one Democrat won election from the Fort Wayne district; he held the seat for three terms. In 1980 and 1982, every county in the 4th voted Republican for all major contests. Adams is the only rural county Democrats occasionally manage to carry.

The district was little changed by the remap. The 4th lost Wabash County in the southwest but gained the rest of Adams County and all of Wells and Jay counties.

Election Returns

4th District		Democrat		Republican	
1976	President	88,170	(40.3%)	127,446	(58.3%)
	Governor	82,079	(38.4%)	129,975	(60.7%)
1976	Senate	74,526	(34.9%)	136,123	(63.8%)
	House	101,539	(47.1%)	112,123	(52.0%)
1978	House	52,720	(38.0%)	83,573	(60.2%)
1980	President	73,699	(33.1%)	128,189	(57.7%)
	Governor	84,495	(38.9%)	131,475	(60.6%)
	Senate	92,240	(42.2%)	126,333	(57.8%)
	House	90,372	(41.6%)	126,137	(58.1%)
1982	Senate	82,327	(40.0%)	121,495	(59.1%)
	House	60,054	(35.1%)	110,155	(64.3%)

Demographics

Population: 553,698. **Percent Change from 1970:** 7.2%.

Land Area: 3,919 square miles. **Population per Square Mile:** 141.3.

Counties, 1980 Population: Adams — 29,619; Allen — 294,335; De Kalb — 33,606; Huntington — 35,596; Jay — 23,239; La Grange — 25,550; Noble — 35,443; Steuben — 24,694; Wells — 25,401; Whitley — 26,215.

Cities, 1980 Population: Fort Wayne — 172,196; Huntington — 16,202.

Race and Ancestry: White — 93.9%; Black — 4.8%; American Indian, Eskimo and Aleut — 0.2%; Asian and Pacific Islander — 0.4%. Spanish Origin — 1.3%. Dutch — 0.8%; English — 10.1%; French — 1.2%; German — 22.2%; Irish — 3.2%; Italian — 0.5%; Polish — 0.5%.

Universities, Enrollment: Concordia Theological Seminary, Fort Wayne — 571; Fort Wayne Bible College, Fort Wayne — 484; Huntington College, Huntington — 545; Indiana Institute of Technology, Fort Wayne — 544; Indiana University-Purdue University (Fort Wayne campus), Fort Wayne — 10,182; Northeast Technical Institute, Fort Wayne — 2,756; International Business College, Fort Wayne — 413; ITT Technical Institute, Fort Wayne — 920; St. Francis College, Fort Wayne — 1,293; Tri-State University, Angola — 1,261.

Newspapers, Circulation: *The Auburn Evening Star* (e), Auburn — 6,062; *The Commercial Mail & Columbia City Post* (e), Columbia City — 5,846; *The Commercial Review* (e), Portland — 6,266; *Decatur Daily Democrat* (e), Decatur — 5,755; *Huntington Herald-Press* (eS), Huntington — 9,216; *The Kendallville News-Sun* (e), Kendallville — 6,618; *The Journal-Gazette* (mS), Fort Wayne — 60,471; *News-Banner* (e), Bluffton — 5,553; *The News-Sentinel* (e), Fort Wayne — 72,019.

Commercial Television Stations, Affiliation: WANE-TV, Fort Wayne (CBS); WFFT-TV, Fort Wayne (None); WKJG, Fort Wayne (NBC); WPTA, Fort Wayne (ABC); WXJC-TV, Angola (None). Most of district is located in Fort Wayne ADI. Portion is in South Bend-Elkhart ADI.

Military Installations: Fort Wayne Municipal Airport (Air Force), Fort Wayne — 1,191.

Industries:

Lincoln National Life Insurance Co. (HQ); Fort Wayne; life insurance — 3,000. **General Electric Co.;** Fort Wayne; electric motors — 2,800. **Lutheran Hospital;** Fort Wayne; hospital — 2,230. **Parkview Memorial Hospital;** Fort Wayne; hospital — 2,200. **B. F. Goodrich Co.;** Woodburn; tires — 1,800.

Dana Corp. (Spicer Axle Div.); Fort Wayne; axles — 1,700. **Zollner Corp.** (HQ); Fort Wayne; pistons — 1,600. **General Electric Co.** (Component Motor Div.); Fort Wayne; electronic components — 1,500. **Phelps Dodge Industries Inc.** (Phelps Dodge Magnet Wire Co.); Fort Wayne; aluminum, copper wire — 1,500. **The Indiana Glass Co.** (HQ); Dunkirk; pressed, blown glassware — 1,300. **Ancilla Domini Sisters Inc.;** Fort Wayne; hospital — 1,200. **North American Van Lines Inc.** (HQ); Fort Wayne; trucking — 1,200. **Fort Wayne State Hospital;** Fort Wayne; state mental hospital — 1,000. **Magnavox Government Industrial Electronics;** Fort Wayne; technical center — 1,000. **Franklin**

Electric Co. Inc. (HQ); Bluffton; electric motors — 983.
CTS of Berne Inc. (HQ); Berne; electronic resistors — 975. **General Electric Co.**; Fort Wayne; transformers — 950. **King-Seeley Thermos Co. Inc.**; Kendallville; automatic controls — 800. **General Electric Co.**; Decatur; motors — 790. **Litton Systems Inc.** (Triad-Utrad Div.); Huntington; electronic inductors — 750. **Dana Corp.**; Columbia City; motor vehicle parts — 700. **E-Systems Inc.** (Memcor Div.); Huntington; electronic equipment — 700. **General Electric Co.**; Fort Wayne; motors — 700. **International Telephone & Telegraph Corp.** (Aerospace/Optical Div.); Fort Wayne; transmitting equipment — 700.

Central Soya Co. Inc. (HQ); Fort Wayne; animal feed, soy oil — 670. **Borg-Warner Corp.** (Warner Gear Div.); Auburn; motor vehicle parts — 600. **Dana Corp.**; Angola; valves, motor vehicle parts — 600. **K Mart Corp.**; Fort Wayne; warehousing — 600. **Monsanto Co.** (FAB Products); Ligonier; plastic bottles — 580. **Peter Eckrich & Sons Inc.**; Fort Wayne; meat products — 575. **Kerr Glass Mfg. Corp.**; Dunkirk; glass containers — 550. **Kraft Inc.** (Kraft Foods Div.); Kendallville; candy — 550. **Teledyne Inc.**; Portland; steel mill — 550. **Our Sunday Visitor Inc.** (HQ); Huntington; commercial printing — 530.

American Standard Inc. (Majestic Co. Div.); Huntington; concrete products — 500. **Central Soya Co. Inc.** (Master Mix); Decatur; soy oil mills, animal feed — 500. **Dana Corp.** (Spicer Clutch Div.); Auburn; clutches — 500. **Eagle-Picher Industries Inc.** (Plastics Div.); Grabill; custom plastic products — 500. **Fort Wayne Newspapers Inc.** (HQ); Fort Wayne; newspaper publishing — 500. **Fruehauf Corp.**; Fort Wayne; truck trailers — 500. **General Electric Co.** (General Purpose Motor Div.); Fort Wayne; small motors — 500. **REA Magnet Wire Co. Inc.** (HQ); Fort Wayne; copper, aluminum wire — 500. **Slater Steel Inc.** (Joslyn Stainless Steel Div.); Fort Wayne; stainless steel — 500. **Super Value Stores Inc.** (Food Marketing Div.); Fort Wayne; grocery wholesaling — 500.

5th District

North Central, Northwest — Kokomo

The 5th travels northwest from Kokomo, a small industrial center in Howard County, to the suburbs of Chicago in Lake County. It includes three distinct political worlds that share one common element — they vote Republican.

The segment friendliest to Republicans is in the southeast corner of the district near Kokomo and Marion, a nearby industrial city in Grant County. Both have numerous small factories and a few very large ones, most of them related to the automobile industry. The cities also serve as major distribution points for the area's agricultural output. The decline in the auto industry had as serious an effect on these communities as on any in the nation, with unemployment exceeding 15 percent in 1982 in several places.

Troubled or not, Howard and Grant counties vote a nearly straight GOP line. Almost a third of the district's vote comes from these two counties, neither of which has backed a major statewide Democratic candidate since 1974 when Grant gave Democrat Sen. Birch Bayh a 780-vote plurality.

Ninety miles to the northwest are the residents of southern Lake and Porter counties. These fast-growing suburban areas are attracting some employees from the steel mills along Lake Michigan as well as former Chicago residents who are escaping to what they hope will be a slower-paced life.

Voters in these two counties are separate from the rest of the district psychologically as well as geographically. They watch Chicago television stations and read newspapers from Chicago and Gary. Although they hold more than a quarter of the district's voting-age population, these counties accounted for only a fifth of the district vote in 1982. The area went strongly for Ronald Reagan in 1980.

In between the small industrial cities and the burgeoning outer suburban fringe, among the corn and soybean fields, live farmers who tend to vote a straight Republican ticket. Just under half of the district's vote in 1982 came from the 10 rural counties; all 10 supported the GOP House and Senate candidates.

Election Returns

5th District		Democrat		Republican	
1976	President	81,118	(40.9%)	114,774	(57.9%)
	Governor	73,513	(37.5%)	121,173	(61.8%)
	Senate	70,755	(36.2%)	122,720	(62.8%)
	House	89,698	(47.6%)	97,997	(52.0%)
1978	House	54,169	(41.4%)	71,900	(55.0%)
1980	President	68,760	(31.0%)	140,368	(63.3%)
	Governor	79,355	(36.7%)	135,777	(62.8%)
	Senate	89,961	(41.1%)	128,931	(58.9%)
	House	90,354	(41.8%)	125,873	(58.2%)
1982	Senate	76,055	(42.5%)	101,826	(56.9%)
	House	67,238	(38.9%)	105,469	(61.1%)

Demographics

Population: 548,257. **Percent Change from 1970:** 13.2%.

Land Area: 5,327 square miles. **Population per Square Mile:** 102.9.

Counties, 1980 Population: Carroll — 19,722; Cass — 40,936; Fulton — 19,335; Grant — 80,934; Howard — 86,896; Jasper — 26,138; Kosciusko (Pt.) — 8,504; Lake (Pt.) — 75,934; Miami — 39,820; Newton — 14,844; Porter (Pt.) — 61,429; Pulaski — 13,258; Wabash — 36,640; White — 23,867.

Cities, 1980 Population: Crown Point (Pt.) — 16,454; Kokomo — 47,808; Logansport — 17,899; Marion — 35,874; Peru — 13,764; Schererville (Pt.) — 4,477; Valparaiso — 22,247; Wabash — 12,985.

Race and Ancestry: White — 96.8%; Black — 2.2%; American Indian, Eskimo and Aleut — 0.2%; Asian and Pacific Islander — 0.4%. Spanish Origin — 1.1%. Dutch — 1.2%; English — 11.1%; French — 0.8%; German — 12.9%; Irish — 3.8%; Italian — 0.7%; Polish — 1.3%.

Universities, Enrollment: Indiana University (Kokomo campus), Kokomo — 2,543; Kokomo Technical Institute, Kokomo — 1,691; Manchester College, North Manchester — 1,253; Marion College, Marion — 1,108; St. Joseph's College, Rensselaer — 1,002; Taylor University, Upland — 1,582; Valparaiso University, Valparaiso — 4,532.

Newspapers, Circulation: *Chronicle-Tribune* (mS), Marion — 23,748; *Herald Journal* (e), Monticello — 5,829; *The Kokomo Tribune* (eS), Kokomo — 29,654; *The Peru Daily Tribune* (e), Peru — 9,162; *Pharos-Tribune* (eS), Logansport — 16,171; *Republican* (e), Rensselaer — 3,794; *The Rochester Sentinel* (e), Rochester — 4,665; *The Vidette-Messenger* (e), Valparaiso — 13,246; *Wabash Plain Dealer* (e), Wabash — 8,376. Gary *Post-Tribune* and Hammond *Times* also circulate in the district.

Commercial Television Stations, Affiliation: District is divided among Fort Wayne ADI, Indianapolis ADI, South Bend-Elkhart ADI and Chicago (Ill.) ADI.

Military Installations: Grissom Air Force Base, Bunker Hill — 4,339.

Industries:

General Motors Corp. (Delco Electronics Div.); Kokomo; motor vehicle parts — 10,790. **Chrysler Corp.;** Kokomo; transmissions — 3,200. **General Motors Corp.** (Fisher Body Div.); Marion; auto assembly — 2,800. **RCA Corp.;** Marion; TV picture tubes — 2,300. **Cabot Corp.** (HI Technology Div.); Kokomo; special alloys — 1,500.

Continental Steel Corp. (HQ); Kokomo; steel — 1,318. **General Tire & Rubber Co.** (Industrial Div.); Wabash; industrial tires — 1,300. **National Can Corp.** (Foster Forbes Glass Div.); Marion; glass containers — 1,200. **Essex Group Inc.** (Controls Div.); Logansport; industrial controls — 1,000. **Marion General Hospital;** Marion; hospital — 1,000. **Wilson Foods Corp.;** Logansport; meatpacking — 1,000. **RCA Corp.** (Consumer Electronics Div.); Monticello; radio cabinets — 988.

McGill Mfg. Co. Inc. (HQ); Valparaiso; ball, roller bearings — 900. **Evans Transportation Co.** (Monon Trailer Div.); Monon; truck trailers — 800. **Chrysler Corp.** (Kokomo Casting Div.); Kokomo; die casting — 670. **Electronic Memories Magnetics** (Indiana General Div.); Valparaiso; fabricated metal, motors — 640. **Ericsson Inc.** (Anaconda Wire and Cable Div.); Marion; copper, aluminum cable — 600. **Essex Group Inc.** (Power Conductor Div.); Marion; wire — 600. **Dana Corp.;** Marion; motor vehicle parts — 550. **Square D Co.;** Peru; electrical switchgears — 500.

6th District

Central — Northern Indianapolis, Anderson

The 6th was designed by GOP cartographers to be a guaranteed Republican seat. A quarter of its vote is cast within Indianapolis, and most of that is in affluent areas of Washington Township, which includes some of the most Republican turf in the state. In 1980 Jimmy Carter received only 23 percent of the vote in the Indianapolis portion of the new 6th District.

But Hamilton County, directly to the north, outdoes even Washington Township in its partisan loyalty. It is the single most Republican county in Indiana as well as the fastest-growing. In 1980 it gave the Republican Senate candidate 74 percent of the vote.

Anderson, with a population of 65,000, is the district's only city of any size other than Indianapolis. It and surrounding Madison County contribute a quarter of the vote in the new district. Although two General Motors auto plants in Anderson give it a large United Auto Workers base and a solid Democratic vote, surrounding Madison County has been going Republican in recent statewide elections. Since 1948, Madison has supported only one Democratic presidential candidate — Lyndon B. Johnson in 1964.

The rest of the new district is primarily rural. Farmers in the smaller counties north and east of Indianapolis are upset that they were included in a predominantly urban and suburban district. But conservative farmers and conservative middle-class suburban homeowners have enough in common politically to make for relatively homogenous district politics.

Election Returns

6th District		Democrat		Republican	
1976	President	86,898	(38.1%)	139,352	(61.1%)
	Governor	81,998	(36.3%)	142,660	(63.2%)
	Senate	75,631	(33.6%)	147,952	(65.7%)
	House	99,922	(42.7%)	134,014	(57.2%)
1978	House	66,664	(42.1%)	91,235	(57.7%)

6th District		Democrat		Republican	
1980	President	73,070	(29.3%)	161,358	(64.7%)
	Governor	75,459	(32.0%)	159,875	(67.8%)
	Senate	89,414	(36.3%)	157,171	(63.7%)
	House	101,437	(43.9%)	129,064	(55.9%)
1982	Senate	64,471	(32.9%)	130,664	(66.6%)
	House	70,764	(35.1%)	131,100	(64.9%)

Demographics

Population: 540,939. **Percent Change from 1970:** 16.1%.

Land Area: 2,922 square miles. **Population per Square Mile:** 185.1.

Counties, 1980 Population: Blackford — 15,570; Boone — 36,446; Clinton — 31,545; Delaware (Pt.) — 22,606; Hamilton — 82,027; Hancock — 43,939; Henry (Pt.) — 13,622; Madison — 139,336; Marion (Pt.) — 137,041; Rush (Pt.) — 1,988; Tipton — 16,819.

Cities, 1980 Population: Anderson — 64,695; Carmel — 18,272; Elwood — 10,867; Frankfort — 15,168; Greenfield — 11,439; Indianapolis (Pt.) — 123,517; Lawrence (Pt.) — 6,875; Lebanon — 11,456; Noblesville — 12,056.

Race and Ancestry: White — 96.2%; Black — 3.0%; American Indian, Eskimo and Aleut — 0.1%; Asian and Pacific Islander — 0.5%. Spanish Origin — 0.6%. Dutch — 0.7%; English — 15.3%; French — 0.8%; German — 10.9%; Irish — 4.5%; Italian — 0.5%; Polish — 0.5%; Scottish — 0.5%.

Universities, Enrollment: Anderson College, Anderson — 2,005.

Newspapers, Circulation: *Anderson Daily Bulletin* (e), Anderson — 16,752; *The Anderson Herald* (mS), Anderson — 21,471; *The Call-Leader* (e), Elwood — 5,021; *The Daily Reporter* (e), Greenfield — 6,036; *The Lebanon Reporter* (e), Lebanon — 6,718; *News-Times* (e), Hartford City — 3,443; *Noblesville Daily Ledger* (e), Noblesville — 8,337; *The Times* (e), Frankfort — 8,052; *Tribune* (e), Tipton — 3,859. *The Indianapolis News, The Indianapolis Star* and *The Muncie Star* also circulate in the district.

Commercial Television Stations, Affiliation: WHMB-TV, Noblesville (None). Entire district is located in Indianapolis ADI.

Industries:

General Motors Corp. (Delco Remy Div.); Anderson; storage batteries — 9,960. **General Motors Corp.** (Guide Div.- HQ); Anderson; auto parts — 4,300. **St. Vincent's Hospital;** Indianapolis; hospital — 2,300. **Chrysler Corp.;** Indianapolis; engine components — 1,500. **RCA Corp.;** Indianapolis; administrative offices — 1,000.

Firestone Tire & Rubber Co. (Industrial Products Co. Div.); Noblesville; rubber products — 817. **Dow Chemical Co.;** Indianapolis; pharmaceuticals — 700. **Eli Lilly & Co.** (Greenfield Laboratories); Greenfield; biological products — 650. **Federal-Mogul Corp.** (National Seal Div.); Frankfort; auto sealants — 650. **Minnesota Mining & Mfg. Co.;** Hartford City; rubber products, boxes — 600. **Best Lock Corp.;** Indianapolis; locks — 580. **Ex-Cell-O Corp.;** Elwood; aircraft parts — 575. **Mayflower Corp.** (HQ); Carmel; trucking — 564.

7th District

West Central — Terre Haute, Lafayette

The 7th District was shifted northward by redistricting, further from the Democratic traditions of the southern hill country and closer to the Republican-dominated corn and soybean belt.

Retained in the district is the Wabash River, a broad tributary of the Ohio that Hoosier chauvinists still rhapsodize about when they sing "My Indiana Home." The Wa-

Indianapolis

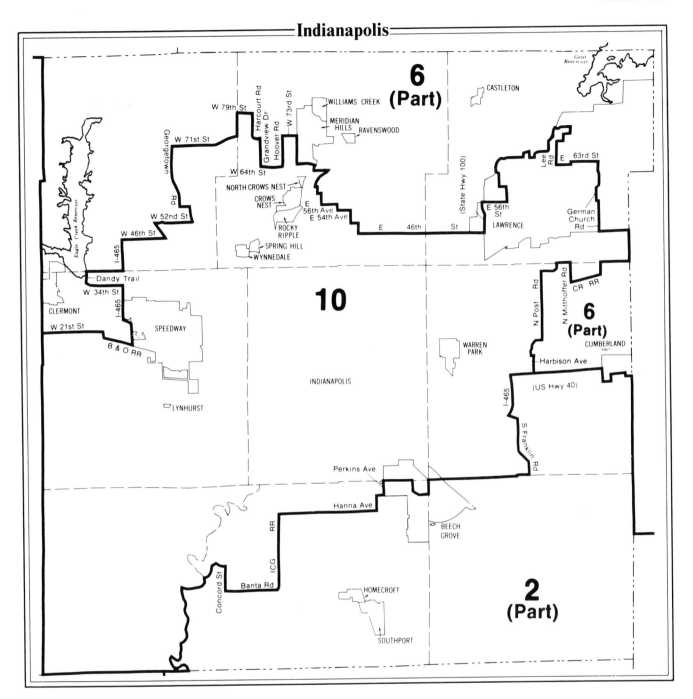

bash flows through six of the district's 14 counties. It is the state's longest river and was responsible for the rapid development of the area in the early 19th century, when newcomers arrived in Indiana via flatboats and steamers.

The Wabash crosses some of the richest glaciated farm land in the Midwest, land used primarily for grain and livestock farming. The voters here are the kind of solid Republican farmers whose opinions have determined the course of state politics over most of this century.

The most significant change brought about by redistricting involved trading one university community for another. The 7th District gave up Bloomington, the home of Indiana University, and obtained West Lafayette, the site of Purdue. Although both institutions have about 32,000 students, Purdue, with its stronger emphasis on agriculture and engineering, has a more conservative and Republican academic community that nearly always places surrounding Tippecanoe County in the Republican column.

At the southern end of the district is Terre Haute in Vigo County. Once part of a small coal-mining region that has since turned to light industry, Terre Haute has Democratic roots that it is only slowly forgetting. Flanking Vigo County on the north and south are Vermillion and Sullivan counties, which also have supported Democrats.

The most Republican counties in the district are Hendricks and Morgan near Indianapolis. Here almost any GOP candidate can expect to receive at least twice as many votes as any Democrat.

Hendricks, Morgan and rural Benton County were added to the 7th by redistricting. In addition to the Bloomington portion of Monroe County, the 7th also gave up the portion of Greene County it had during the 1970s.

Election Returns

7th District		Democrat		Republican	
1976	President	98,966	(43.5%)	126,314	(55.5%)
	Governor	88,379	(39.5%)	134,001	(59.9%)
	Senate	84,884	(37.9%)	137,223	(61.3%)
	House	97,080	(43.3%)	126,687	(56.6%)
1978	House	75,948	(47.6%)	82,858	(51.9%)
1980	President	77,802	(33.9%)	136,445	(59.4%)
	Governor	89,007	(39.7%)	134,582	(60.0%)
	Senate	98,702	(43.3%)	129,363	(56.7%)
	House	89,661	(39.7%)	135,559	(59.9%)
1982	Senate	79,419	(42.2%)	107,436	(57.1%)
	House	70,249	(37.7%)	115,884	(62.3%)

Demographics

Population: 555,192. **Percent Change from 1970:** 9.2%.

Land Area: 5,785 square miles. **Population per Square Mile:** 96.0.

Counties, 1980 Population: Benton — 10,218; Clay — 24,862; Fountain — 19,033; Hendricks — 69,804; Montgomery — 35,501; Morgan — 51,999; Owen — 15,841; Parke — 16,372; Putnam — 29,163; Sullivan — 21,107; Tippecanoe — 121,702; Vermillion — 18,229; Vigo — 112,385; Warren — 8,976.

Cities, 1980 Population: Crawfordsville — 13,325; Lafayette — 43,011; Martinsville — 11,311; Terre Haute — 61,125; West Lafayette — 21,247.

Race and Ancestry: White — 97.3%; Black — 1.7%; American Indian, Eskimo and Aleut — 0.1%; Asian and Pacific Islander — 0.6%. Spanish Origin — 0.6%. Dutch — 0.8%; English — 13.5%; French — 0.9%; German — 10.0%; Irish — 3.9%; Italian — 0.6%; Scottish — 0.5%.

Universities, Enrollment: DePauw University, Greencastle — 2,503; Indiana State University, Terre Haute — 12,362; Lafayette Technical Institute, Lafayette — 1,015; Purdue University, West Lafayette — 32,983; Rose-Hulman Institute of Technology, Terre Haute — 1,268; St. Mary-of-the-Woods College, St. Mary-of-the-Woods — 707; Wabash College, Crawfordsville — 774; Wabash Valley Technical Institute, Terre Haute — 1,355.

Newspapers, Circulation: *Banner-Graphic* (e), Greencastle — 5,982; *The Brazil Times* (e), Brazil — 5,569; *The Daily Clintonian* (e), Clinton — 5,087; *Journal and Courier* (eS), Lafayette — 40,041; *Journal-Review* (e), Crawfordsville — 11,011; *Reporter* (e), Martinsville — 7,417; *Spencer Evening World* (e), Spencer — 3,657; *The Star* (mS), Terre Haute — 24,260; *Sullivan Daily Times* (e), Sullivan — 5,150; *The Tribune* (eS), Terre Haute — 21,448. *The Indianapolis News* and *The Indianapolis Star* also circulate in the district.

Commercial Television Stations, Affiliation: WBAK-TV, Terre Haute (ABC); WLFI-TV, Lafayette (CBS); WTHI-TV, Terre Haute (CBS); WTWO, Terre Haute (NBC). District is divided among Indianapolis ADI, Lafayette ADI and Terre Haute ADI.

Military Installations: Hulman Field (Air Force), Terre Haute — 1,074; Newport Army Ammunition Plant, Newport — 300.

Industries:

R. R. Donnelly & Sons Inc.; Crawfordsville; book printing — 1,900. **Aluminum Co. of America Inc.;** Lafayette; elevators, escalators — 1,700. **Eli Lilly & Co. Inc.** (Tippecanoe Laboratories); Lafayette; pharmaceuticals — 1,550. **St. Elizabeth Hospital Medical Center Inc.;** Lafayette; hospital — 1,300. **Lafayette Home Hospital Inc.;** Lafayette; hospital — 1,200.

International Business Machines Corp.; Greencastle; paper, paperboard — 1,000. **Eli Lilly & Co.;** Clinton; research — 825. **Duncan Electric Co. Inc.** (HQ); Lafayette; electrical meters — 800. **Fairfield Mfg. Co.** (HQ); Lafayette; auto gears — 800. **J. I. Case Co. Inc.;** Terre Haute; construction machinery — 700. **TRW Inc.** (Ross Gear Div.); Lafayette; motor vehicle parts — 641. **Allen-Bradley Co.** (Rostone Div.); Lafayette; insulation — 600. **Emhart Industries Inc.** (Mallory Capacitor Co.); Greencastle; capacitors — 600.

General Foods Corp.; Lafayette; food specialties — 600. **General Housewares Corp.;** Terre Haute; metal stampings — 600. **Pfizer Inc.** (Vigo Plant); Terre Haute; medicinal chemicals — 600. **Harrison Steel Castings Co. Inc.;** Attica; steel castings — 599. **Raybestos-Manhattan Inc.** (Friction Material Div.); Crawfordsville; asbestos products — 505. **Great Dane Trailers;** Brazil; truck trailers — 500. **Green Giant Co. Inc.;** Lafayette; frozen foods — 500.

8th District

Southwest — Evansville

During the 1970s the 8th District was the most marginal district in the state. It elected four different people to Congress, none of whom remained in office for more than two terms.

In an unsuccessful attempt to overcome that tradition and keep a Republican incumbent in office, GOP map makers carefully excised two key Democratic counties — Dubois and Perry. Left intact was Evansville (Vanderburgh County), the economic center of the district and southern Indiana.

With a population of 130,496, Evansville is the fourth largest city in the state. From the time when former U.S. Sen. Vance Hartke was mayor in the 1950s, the city has tried to entice new industry to replace major corporations that pulled out after World War II. But since 1960, when the population peaked at 142,000, Evansville has been losing residents.

The political influence of Evansville, however, spreads throughout the southern half of the district. More than one-half of the district's voters watch Evansville television stations, and the city's diversified economic base provides employment for a large area along the Ohio River.

Over the last several decades the 8th District has gradually shifted its geography. Before 1966, the district stretched nearly the entire width of the state along the Ohio River. The Democratic heritage of the rural river counties, which dates back to the original settlement of the area 150 years ago, made the 8th a rural, Democratic district.

In the four remaps that have taken place since 1966, the number of river counties has decreased from nine to just four. At the same time the district has continued to move north into more prosperous, more Republican agricultural territory.

The 1981 remap extended the 8th District north all the way to Bloomington, taking in the southern, most prosperous third of the city and about four-fifths of the surrounding Monroe County suburbs.

This area normally votes Republican, although it does include some students and faculty from Indiana University. The main portion of the university community is in the 9th District.

Election Returns

8th District		Democrat		Republican	
1976	President	115,188	(49.0%)	118,212	(50.3%)
	Governor	104,500	(45.5%)	124,511	(54.2%)
	Senate	93,399	(40.9%)	133,632	(58.5%)
	House	110,638	(49.1%)	114,476	(50.9%)
1978	House	79,273	(47.5%)	87,542	(52.5%)
1980	President	95,833	(40.4%)	127,427	(53.7%)
	Governor	105,596	(45.6%)	125,249	(54.1%)
	Senate	115,203	(51.0%)	110,636	(49.0%)
	House	101,131	(43.8%)	129,710	(56.1%)
1982	Senate	94,007	(47.3%)	103,574	(52.1%)
	House	100,592	(51.4%)	94,127	(48.1%)

Demographics

Population: 546,744. **Percent Change from 1970:** 9.3%.

Land Area: 5,547 square miles. **Population per Square Mile:** 98.6.

Counties, 1980 Population: Crawford (Pt.) — 4,744; Daviess — 27,836; Gibson — 33,156; Greene — 30,416; Knox — 41,838; Lawrence — 42,472; Martin — 11,001; Monroe (Pt.) — 56,016; Orange — 18,677; Pike — 13,465; Posey — 26,414; Spencer — 19,361; Vanderburgh — 167,515; Warrick — 41,474; Washington (Pt.) — 12,359.

Cities, 1980 Population: Bedford — 14,410; Bloomington (Pt.) — 18,938; Evansville — 130,496; Vincennes — 20,857; Washington — 11,325.

Race and Ancestry: White — 96.7%; Black — 2.7%; American Indian, Eskimo and Aleut — 0.1%; Asian and Pacific Islander — 0.3%. Spanish Origin — 0.5%. Dutch — 0.6%; English — 16.8%; French — 1.1%; German — 16.9%; Irish — 5.2%; Scottish — 0.5%.

Universities, Enrollment: Indiana State University (Evansville campus), Evansville — 3,251; ITT Technical Institute, Evansville — 252; Lockyear College, Evansville — 700; Northwood Institute (West Baden campus), West Baden Springs — 123; Oakland City College, Oakland City — 610; St. Meinrad College, St. Meinrad — 209; St. Meinrad School of Theology, St. Meinrad — 162; Southwest Technical Institute, Evansville — 1,373; University of Evansville, Evansville — 5,180; Vincennes University, Vincennes — 4,259.

Newspapers, Circulation: *The Evansville Courier* (mS), Evansville — 62,849; *The Evansville Press* (eS), Evansville — 44,060; *The Evening World* (e), Bloomfield — 3,169; *Herald-Telephone* (eS), Bloomington — 40,454; *Knox County Daily News* (e), Bicknell — 2,700; *Linton Daily Citizen* (e), Linton — 6,410; *Mount Vernon Democrat* (m), Mount Vernon — 3,520; *Princeton Daily Clarion* (e), Princeton — 6,824; *The Times-Mail* (eS), Bedford — 11,449; *Vincennes Sun-Commercial* (eS), Vincennes — 14,618; *The Washington Times-Herald* (e), Washington — 11,168.

Commercial Television Stations, Affiliation: WEHT, Evansville (CBS); WFIE-TV, Evansville (NBC); WTTV, Bloomington (None); WTVW, Evansville (ABC). District is divided among Evansville ADI, Indianapolis ADI, Terre Haute ADI and Louisville (Ky.) ADI.

Military Installations: Crane Naval Weapons Support Center, Crane — 3,871.

Industries:

Aluminum Co. of America (Warrick Operations); Newburgh; rigid containers — 3,500. **RCA Corp.** (Consumer Electronic Div.); Bloomington; radios, televisions — 3,500. **Whirlpool Corp.**; Evansville; household refrigerators — 3,200. **Mead Johnson & Co. Inc.** (HQ); Evansville; food, pharmaceuticals — 2,950. **Deaconess Hospital Inc.**; Evansville; hospital — 2,200.

Louisville & Nashville Railroad Co.; Evansville; railroad operations — 2,000. **St. Mary's Medical Center**; Evansville; hospital — 1,600. **Welborn Memorial Baptist Hospital Inc.**; Evansville; hospital — 1,280. **General Electric Co. Inc.**; Bloomington; household cooking equipment — 1,200. **General Motors Corp.** (Central Foundry Div.); Bedford; aluminum foundry — 1,177. **Bloomington Hospital**; Bloomington; hospital — 1,150. **General Electric Co. Inc.** (Plastics Div.); Mount Vernon; plastic materials — 1,000.

Zenith Electronics Corp. of Indiana; Evansville; televisions — 1,200. **Bucyrus-Erie Co.**; Evansville; construction machinery — 990. **Westinghouse Electric Corp.**; Bloomington; electrical industrial appliances — 950. **Bliss & Laughlin Industries**; Evansville; casters, wheels — 850. **Otis Elevator Co. Inc.**; Bloomington; elevators, escalators — 800. **Sohio Petroleum Inc.** (Old Ben Coal Div.); Oakland City; coal mining — 800. **Smith Cabinet Mfg. Co. Inc.** (Child Craft Div); Salem; radio cabinets — 650. **American Standard Inc.** (Keller-Crescent Div.); Evansville; advertising agency — 600.

Carpenter Body Works Inc.; Mitchell; bus bodies — 600. **Emge Packing Co. Inc.** (HQ); Fort Branch; meatpacking — 600. **Princeton Industries Corp.** (HQ); Princeton; specialty manufacturing — 590. **Cox Hotel Corp.**; French Lick; resort — 550. **Peabody Coal Co.**; Lynnville; coal mining — 502. **Evansville Printing Corp.**; Evansville; commercial printing — 500. **International Steel Co.** (International Revolving Door Div. - HQ); Evansville; revolving doors — 500. **Mid Valley Inc.**; Evansville; highway contracting — 500.

9th District

Southeast — Bloomington, New Albany

This is the largest and least urbanized district in the state. The hilly forests and farm lands are more akin to Kentucky and parts of southern Ohio and Illinois than to the flat Hoosier farm lands farther north. Many of those who settled here came from the South and brought with them their Democratic allegiances.

Poultry and cattle are the major agricultural commodities of the area, which also is the site of some of the nation's finest and most abundant limestone quarries. Stonecutters here excavate rock that is used for building material throughout the country.

The Indiana suburbs of Louisville, Ky., along the Ohio River make up the district's largest concentration of voters. Centered on New Albany, the district's largest city with just 37,000 people, this area is experiencing a minor population boom. With the counties along the Ohio River leading the way, the 9th grew faster in the 1970s than all but one district in the state.

In the days of the steamboats when Indiana's economy depended upon the cargoes that came up the Ohio River, New Albany was the state's largest city. Although the river's contribution to the local livelihood has dropped off considerably since then, the 9th District still depends on the river traffic and the industries located along the river bank for many of its jobs.

In its northwest corner, the 9th took on most of Bloomington, the home of Indiana University. The district boundary runs along 3rd Street in Bloomington, placing the northern two-thirds of the city's 52,000 residents in the 9th. Included in that area is all of Indiana University's campus and most of the off-campus housing.

Redistricting also gave the 9th the Democratic counties of Dubois and Perry and part of Crawford County, all formerly in the 8th District.

Conceding that the Democratic incumbent was unbeatable, the Republican Legislature made no effort to weaken him in the 1981 redistricting, although they moved his hometown into another district. He switched residence and was re-elected with 67 percent of the vote.

Election Returns

9th District		Democrat		Republican	
1976	President	109,023	(51.9%)	98,908	(47.1%)
	Governor	99,985	(49.2%)	102,365	(50.4%)
	Senate	93,406	(45.9%)	109,051	(53.6%)
	House	131,934	(87.6%)	18,675	(12.4%)
1978	House	96,103	(64.1%)	53,887	(35.9%)
1980	President	92,931	(42.7%)	112,568	(51.7%)
	Governor	102,146	(49.0%)	105,465	(50.6%)
	Senate	108,493	(50.8%)	105,014	(49.2%)
	House	133,378	(63.3%)	76,946	(36.6%)
1982	Senate	77,799	(50.8%)	74,639	(48.7%)
	House	121,094	(67.1%)	58,532	(32.4%)

Demographics

Population: 544,873. **Percent Change from 1970:** 14.2%.

Land Area: 6,107 square miles. **Population per Square Mile:** 89.2.

Counties, 1980 Population: Bartholomew (Pt.) — 10,137; Brown — 12,377; Clark — 88,838; Crawford (Pt.) — 5,076; Dearborn — 34,291; Dubois — 34,238; Fayette (Pt.) — 26,428; Floyd — 61,169; Franklin — 19,612; Harrison — 27,276; Jackson — 36,523; Jefferson — 30,419; Jennings — 22,854; Monroe (Pt.) — 42,769; Ohio — 5,114; Perry — 19,346; Ripley — 24,398; Scott — 20,422; Switzerland — 7,153; Union — 6,860; Washington (Pt.) — 9,573.

Cities, 1980 Population: Bloomington (Pt.) — 33,106; Clarksville — 15,164; Columbus (Pt.) — 47; Connersville — 17,023; Jeffersonville — 21,220; Madison — 12,472; New Albany — 37,103; Seymour — 15,050.

Race and Ancestry: White — 97.3%; Black — 1.9%; American Indian, Eskimo and Aleut — 0.1%; Asian and Pacific Islander — 0.4%. Spanish Origin — 0.6%. English — 14.8%; French — 1.1%; German — 19.7%; Irish — 5.4%.

Universities, Enrollment: Hanover College, Hanover — 1,011; Indiana University (Bloomington campus), Bloomington — 31,877; Indiana University (Southeast campus), New Albany — 4,336; Southcentral Technical Institute, Sellersburg — 1,231.

Newspapers, Circulation: *Connersville News-Examiner* (e), Connersville — 8,010; *The Evening News* (e), Jeffersonville — 17,212; *The Herald* (e), Jasper — 11,160; *The Madison Courier* (e), Madison — 9,405; *Seymour Daily Tribune* (e), Seymour — 9,655; *Tribune* (eS), New Albany — 10,640. Columbus *Republic* also circulates in the district.

Commercial Television Stations, Affiliation: District is divided among Evansville ADI, Indianapolis ADI, Cincinnati (Ohio) ADI and Louisville (Ky.) ADI.

Military Installations: Indiana Army Ammunition Plant, Charlestown — 1,695; Jefferson Proving Ground (Army), Madison — 519.

Nuclear Power Plants: Marble Hill 1 and 2, Madison (Westinghouse, Public Service Co. of Indiana).

Industries:

Hillenbrand Industries Inc. (HQ); Batesville; burial caskets, hospital equipment — 2,700. **Ford Electronic & Refrigeration Corp.** (Refrigeration Products Div.); Connersville; automotive climate control systems — 2,600. **Design & Mfg. Corp.** (HQ); Connersville; dishwashers — 1,500. **ICI Americas Inc.** (Indiana Army Ammunition Depot); Charlestown; ammunition — 1,200. **Kimball International Inc.** (HQ); Jasper; musical instruments — 1,200.

Joseph A. Seagram & Sons Inc.; Lawrenceburg; distillery — 1,100. **Muscatatuck State Hospital;** Butlerville; state mental hospital — 1,000. **Colgate-Palmolive Co.;** Jeffersonville; soap, toiletries — 950. **Tell City Chair Co.;** Tell City; wooden household furniture — 820. **General Electric Co.;** Tell City; electric motors — 655. **Dart Industries**

Inc. (Thatcher Glass & Mfg. Co.); Lawrenceburg; glass containers — 650. **Stant Mfg. Co.** (HQ); Connersville; automobile parts — 645. **Beatrice Foods Co.** (Arist-O-Kraft Div.); Jasper; wooden kitchen cabinets — 600. **Dresser Industries Inc.** (Roots Blower Operation); Connersville; oil field machinery — 600.

Morgan Packing Co. Inc. (HQ); Austin; vegetable canning, packing — 600. **Reliance Electric Co.;** Madison; electric motors — 600. **DMI Furniture Inc.** (HQ); Huntingburg; household furniture — 550. **Inland Tugs Co.;** Jeffersonville; marine towing — 550. **Kimball International Inc.;** Jasper; wooden furniture — 550. **Jeffboat Inc.;** Jeffersonville; shipbuilding — 540. **Kayser-Roth Corp.** (Excello Div.); Seymour; men's shirts — 525. **The Pillsbury Co.;** New Albany; flour mill — 525. **Amoco Container Co.;** Seymour; plastic products — 500. **International Telephone & Telegraph Corp.;** North Vernon; automotive stampings — 500.

10th District

Indianapolis

Indianapolis has a larger population than San Francisco or Washington, D.C., but it has retained a small city flavor. It does not have the ethnic mixture of other industrial cities in the Midwest; most of its white residents are Protestants with small-town roots in Indiana or neighboring states, and they still reflect those roots after a generation or more of urban life.

The city's diversified economy ranges from pharmaceuticals to automotive plants. The state government and an army base also contribute to the local economy.

The 10th includes about 70 percent of Indianapolis' population, leaving out the heavily Republican section in northern Washington Township. The major Democratic strength in the district lies in Center Township, which is about 40 percent black and contributes more than a third of the district's vote. Center Township is large enough to tilt the 10th Democratic even though Indianapolis' white population is more conservative than in most cities of comparable size.

North of the downtown area behind the old mansions that line Meridian Street are middle-income, integrated neighborhoods with large trees and broad streets. This area, in the southern part of Washington Township, has been loyal to Democratic House candidates.

The western side of the district features the nationally famous town of Speedway and its Memorial Day classic, the "Indianapolis 500." When not overrun with racing enthusiasts, this is a white-collar, middle-income area that often votes Republican.

Election Returns

10th District		Democrat		Republican	
1976	President	120,009	(49.8%)	118,886	(49.4%)
	Governor	116,034	(48.7%)	120,887	(50.8%)
	Senate	109,521	(46.1%)	126,446	(53.2%)
	House	142,612	(61.1%)	90,105	(38.6%)
1978	House	78,905	(58.7%)	54,814	(40.8%)
1980	President	97,427	(49.1%)	90,132	(45.4%)
	Governor	98,459	(47.4%)	108,940	(52.4%)
	Senate	108,914	(55.2%)	88,349	(44.8%)
	House	118,994	(55.5%)	95,470	(44.5%)
1982	Senate	97,449	(56.4%)	74,720	(43.3%)
	House	114,674	(66.7%)	56,992	(33.2%)

Demographics

Population: 541,811. **Percent Change from 1970:** -12.4%.

Land Area: 187 square miles. **Population per Square Mile:** 2,897.4.

Counties, 1980 Population: Marion (Pt.) — 541,811.

Cities, 1980 Population: Beech Grove (Pt.) — 5,959; Indianapolis (Pt.) — 501,243; Lawrence (Pt.) — 18,716; Speedway — 12,641.

Race and Ancestry: White — 71.4%; Black — 27.4%; American Indian, Eskimo and Aleut — 0.2%; Asian and Pacific Islander — 0.5%. Spanish Origin — 1.0%. English — 12.1%; French — 0.7%; German — 7.6%; Irish — 4.3%; Italian — 0.6%.

Universities, Enrollment: Butler University, Indianapolis — 3,906; Central Indiana Technical Institute, Indianapolis — 4,253; Christian Theological Seminary, Indianapolis — 306; Clark College, Indianapolis — 619; Indiana Central University, Indianapolis — 3,176; Indiana University-Purdue University (Indianapolis campus), Indianapolis — 22,797; ITT Technical Institute, Indianapolis — 918; Marian College, Indianapolis — 845.

Newspapers, Circulation: *The Indianapolis News* (e) — 143,141; *The Indianapolis Star* (mS), Indianapolis — 220,463.

Commercial Television Stations, Affiliation: WISH-TV, Indianapolis (CBS); WRTV, Indianapolis (ABC); WTHR, Indianapolis (NBC). Entire district is located in Indianapolis ADI.

Military Installations: Fort Benjamin Harrison, Indianapolis — 6,900; Naval Avionics Center, Indianapolis — 2,242.

Industries:

General Motors Corp. (Detroit Diesel Allison Div.); Indianapolis; transmissions — 13,900. **Eli Lilly & Co.** (Elanco Products Co. Div. - HQ); Indianapolis; pharmaceuticals — 7,960. **Western Electric Co. Inc.;** Indianapolis; telephones — 6,100. **Methodist Hospital of Indiana;** Indianapolis; hospital — 4,710. **General Motors Corp.** (Chevrolet Motor Div.); Indianapolis; auto stampings — 3,500.

Community Hospital of Indianapolis Inc.; Indianapolis; hospital — 3,300. **Ford Motor Co.** (Chassis Div.); Indianapolis; auto parts — 3,000. **RCA Corp.;** Indianapolis; televisions — 2,500. **Blue Cross-Blue Shield of Indiana;** Indianapolis; health insurance — 2,300. **Mutual Hospital Insurance Inc.** (HQ); Indianapolis; health insurance — 2,300. **American Fletcher Corp.;** Indianapolis; bank holding company — 2,160. **Indiana National Corp.;** Indianapolis; bank holding company — 2,100. **Sisters of St. Francis Health Service;** Beech Grove; hospital — 1,850.

Consolidated Rail Corp.; Indianapolis; railroad operations — 1,600. **Indianapolis Newspapers Inc.;** Indianapolis; newspaper publishing — 1,600. **Merchants National Corp.;** Indianapolis; bank holding company — 1,600. **American States Insurance Co.** (HQ); Indianapolis; casualty insurance — 1,500. **Chrysler Corp.;** Indianapolis; engine components — 1,500. **International Harvester Co.;** Indianapolis; engines — 1,500. **Carrier Corp.** (BDP Div.); Indianapolis; air conditioning, heating equipment — 1,330. **P. T. Components;** Indianapolis; bearings, chains — 1,300. **National Distillers & Chemical Corp.** (Bridgeport Brass); Indianapolis; brass castings — 1,217.

Emhart Industries Inc. (Mallory Components Group); Indianapolis; batteries, controls — 1,200. **Stewart-Warner Corp.** (South Wind Div.); Indianapolis; heat transfer equipment — 1,150. **Amsted Industries Inc.** (Diamond Chain Co. Div.); Indianapolis; power transmissions — 1,000. **Jenn-Air Corp.** (HQ); Indianapolis; cooking equipment — 1,000. **Veterans Administration;** Indianapolis; veterans' hospital — 1,000. **William H. Block Co. Inc.** (HQ); Indianapolis; department store chain — 1,000. **The Hunt Corp.;** Indianapolis; general building contracting — 900. **Indiana Group Inc.;** Indianapolis; casualty, life insurance — 812. **Carnation Co.** (Herff Jones Jewelry Div.); Indianapolis; jewelry — 800.

Pinkerton's Inc.; Indianapolis; security services — 800. **Richardson Co. Inc.** (Storage Battery Parts Div.); Indianapolis; plastic, rubber products — 800. **Schwitzer-Wallace-Murray Corp.** (Engine Components Group); Indianapolis; fabricated metal products — 793. **Chrysler Corp.** (Indianapolis Chrysler Foundry); Indianapolis; engine foundry — 700. **Yellow Freight Systems Inc.;** Indianapolis; trucking — 700. **Northwestern Mutual Life Insurance;** Indianapolis; life insurance — 660. **American United Life Insurance Co.** (HQ); Indianapolis; life insurance — 650. **McLean Trucking Co. Inc.;** Indianapolis; trucking — 650. **Roadway Express Inc.;** Indianapolis; truck terminal — 625.

Dow Chemical Co.; Indianapolis; pharmaceuticals — 600. **National Starch & Chemical Corp.;** Indianapolis; corn oils — 600. **Indianapolis Rubber Co.;** Indianapolis; tubes — 550. **Howard W. Sams & Co. Inc.** (ITT Publishing - HQ); Indianapolis; publishing — 550. **Stokely-Van Camp Inc.** (HQ); Indianapolis; food processing, packing — 525. **Hyatt Corp.;** Indianapolis; hotel — 520. **Amax Inc.** (Coal Co. Div.- HQ); Indianapolis; coal mining operations — 500. **Regency Electronics Inc.** (HQ); Indianapolis; communications equipment — 500. **Union Carbide Corp.** (Linde Div.); Indianapolis; special industrial machinery — 500.

Iowa

Republicans were in full control of Iowa state government, but they avoided the temptation to gerrymander and instead adopted a congressional redistricting plan that respects Iowa's tradition of competitive two-party politics. Gov. Robert Ray signed the new boundaries into law Aug. 20, 1981.

Under a law that Republicans pushed through the Legislature in 1980, the state's non-partisan Legislative Service Bureau was given the task of presenting proposals for new congressional and state legislative districts. The bureau's mandate was to follow "objective" criteria in drawing the boundaries — population equality, compactness, contiguity and preservation of local boundaries — and to ignore partisan concerns or the wishes of incumbents.

When the bureau's non-partisan map was presented in April, it caused a highly partisan uproar. "It looks like a Democratic computer wrote it," said an aide to GOP Gov. Robert Ray. Two of the state's three Republican representatives were placed in the same district.

On its second try, the bureau's computer gave the two Republicans separate districts, but made one of those districts substantially more Democratic.

State law stipulated that the bureau's first two proposals could not be amended. But they could be rejected outright. The state Senate killed the first plan May 14 and the second one June 25, 1981.

In July 1981, the bureau offered another proposal. The law allowed the Legislature to make changes in this version, but none was made, and it was enacted verbatim. The person most upset by that action was the Republican incumbent in the 3rd District, which gained Democratic Johnson County and lost several GOP counties under the proposal.

GOP leaders essentially ignored the incumbent's protests. They sensed that the public was becoming annoyed with the money and time consumed in the redistricting process and feared that changing the third plan to suit their partisan interests would be viewed as a violation of the "good government" principle embodied in the basic redistricting law.

The Senate considered and rejected a number of amendments to the third plan, including a totally redrafted version prepared by the Republican State Central Committee. The bill passed the Senate Aug. 12, 1981, by a 39-10 vote, and the next day the House approved the package 92-5. Ray signed it into law a week later.

Iowa's overall population growth in the 1970s was only 3.1 percent, and the population disparity among the old districts was not great. Population deviations among the redrawn districts are virtually non-existent. The district farthest out of line is the 2nd, which is 144 people over the ideal population of 485,564, a deviation of .030 percent.

Age of Population

District	Population Under 18	Voting Age Population	Population 65 & Over (% of VAP)	Median Age
1	140,421	345,540	64,556 (18.7%)	30.4
2	147,436	338,272	58,801 (17.4%)	29.2
3	133,074	352,455	60,717 (17.2%)	28.8
4	129,253	356,227	53,382 (15.0%)	29.0
5	138,839	346,800	75,869 (21.9%)	32.1
6	136,850	348,641	74,259 (21.3%)	31.6
State	825,873	2,087,935	387,584 (18.6%)	30.0

Income and Occupation

District	Median Family Income	White Collar Workers	Blue Collar Workers	Service Workers	Farm Workers
1	$ 20,097	45.1%	34.4%	13.4%	7.0%
2	21,172	44.6	33.1	13.0	9.3
3	20,496	46.0	29.5	14.6	9.9
4	21,791	58.2	24.8	13.4	3.5
5	18,095	42.4	29.2	14.3	14.2
6	18,616	42.9	28.3	14.0	14.7
State	$ 20,052	46.8%	29.8%	13.8%	9.6%

Education: School Years Completed

District	8 Years or Fewer	4 Years of High School	4 Years of College or More	Median School Years
1	17.5%	42.2%	13.0%	12.5
2	17.1	44.2	13.2	12.5
3	16.9	41.6	16.5	12.5

IOWA

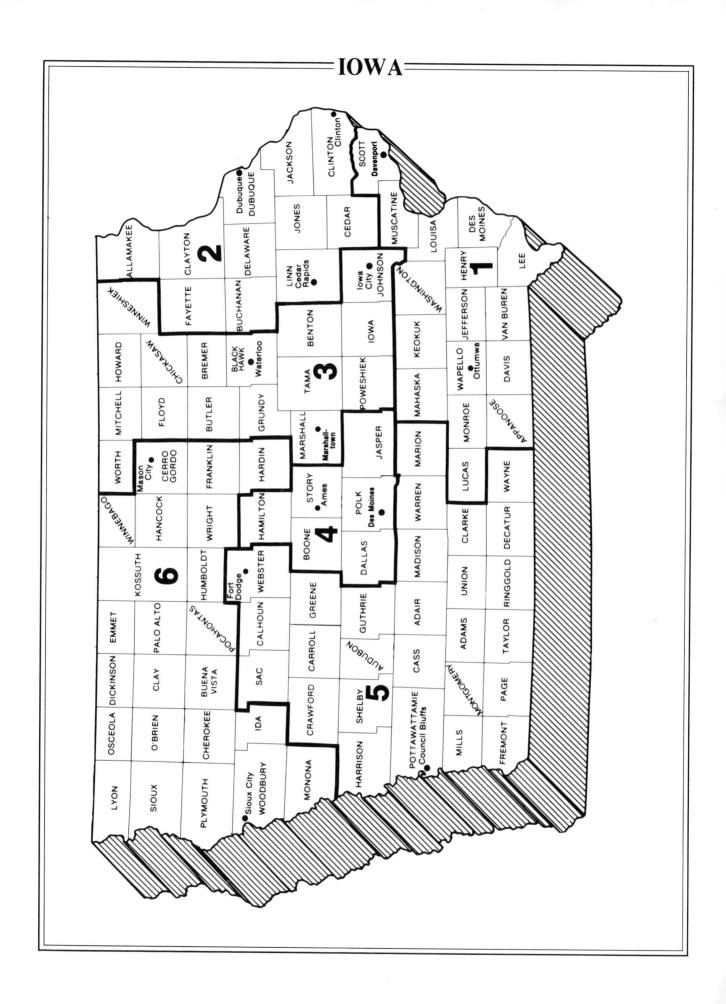

District	8 Years or Fewer	4 Years of High School	4 Years of College or More	Median School Years
4	10.3	41.9	19.1	12.7
5	19.2	45.4	10.1	12.4
6	19.0	42.1	12.1	12.5
State	16.7%	42.9%	13.9%	12.5

Housing and Residential Patterns

District	Owner Occupied	Renter Occupied	Urban	Rural
1	72.8%	27.2%	63.6%	36.4%
2	73.4	26.6	60.7	39.3
3	70.8	29.2	54.8	45.2
4	67.5	32.5	78.3	21.7
5	73.8	26.2	44.1	55.9
6	72.9	27.1	50.4	49.6
State	71.8%	28.2%	58.6%	41.4%

1st District

Southeast — Davenport

Redistricting made the 1st even safer for Republicans. The 1st District lost heavily Democratic Johnson County and gained several rural counties where the Republican Party plays a dominant role. Although the district takes in a total of 16 southeastern Iowa counties, 60 percent of the constituents are in four counties strung along the Mississippi River.

With a population of 160,000, Scott County (Davenport) is by far the largest population center of the district. It is a heavily industrialized area with a sizable blue-collar vote. Republicans gained ground in Scott County during the 1970s; in 1982, the Republican incumbent took 63 percent of the county's vote. Scott was the largest county in Iowa to vote Republican in the hotly-contested U. S. Senate races of 1978 and 1980.

Davenport is part of the Quad-Cities metropolitan area (with nearby Bettendorf, Iowa, and Rock Island and Moline, Ill.). Down the river from Davenport in the new 1st District are three other major shipping and manufacturing counties, each containing approximately 40,000 residents. Of the three, Muscatine County votes consistently Republican, but Democratic candidates running statewide often win Des Moines County (Burlington) and Lee County (Keokuk).

In addition to moving Democratic Johnson County from the 1st District to the 3rd, the remap also removed three Republican-dominated counties: Benton, Poweshiek and Iowa. But at the same time it added five Republican farming counties: Mahaska, Appanoose, Keokuk, Lucas and Davis.

Democrats have respectable strength in two other counties added in redistricting — Wapello and Monroe. Ottumwa, a city with a population of 27,000 in Wapello County, produces farm machinery and is a trade center for area farm lands.

Republicans prevail in the rural portions of the district, where farmers depend largely on corn, livestock and poultry for their livelihood.

Election Returns

1st District		Democrat		Republican	
1976	President	100,738	(49.6%)	99,128	(48.8%)
	House	102,394	(51.7%)	95,346	(48.1%)
1978	Governor	52,818	(41.3%)	74,456	(58.2%)
	Senate	57,297	(47.1%)	63,148	(51.9%)
	House	51,629	(42.8%)	68,803	(57.0%)
1980	President	85,545	(41.3%)	104,062	(50.2%)
	Senate	95,134	(47.3%)	103,673	(51.5%)
	House	72,751	(37.6%)	119,332	(61.7%)
1982	Governor	76,386	(48.4%)	80,435	(51.0%)
	House	61,734	(40.8%)	89,585	(59.2%)

Demographics

Population: 485,961. **Percent Change from 1970:** 5.0%.

Land Area: 7,622 square miles. **Population per Square Mile:** 63.8.

Counties, 1980 Population: Appanoose — 15,511; Davis — 9,104; Des Moines — 46,203; Henry — 18,890; Jefferson — 16,316; Keokuk — 12,921; Lee — 43,106; Louisa — 12,055; Lucas — 10,313; Mahaska — 22,867; Monroe — 9,209; Muscatine — 40,436; Scott — 160,022; Van Buren — 8,626; Wapello — 40,241; Washington — 20,141.

Cities, 1980 Population: Bettendorf — 27,381; Burlington — 29,529; Davenport — 103,264; Fort Madison — 13,520; Keokuk — 13,536; Muscatine — 23,467; Oskaloosa — 10,989; Ottumwa — 27,381.

Race and Ancestry: White — 96.6%; Black — 2.0%; American Indian, Eskimo and Aleut — 0.2%; Asian and Pacific Islander — 0.4%. Spanish Origin — 1.6%. Dutch — 1.8%; English — 9.2%; French — 0.7%; German — 17.3%; Irish — 4.7%; Italian — 0.5%; Norwegian — 0.5%; Swedish — 1.4%.

Universities, Enrollment: American Institute of Commerce, Bettendorf — 429; A. R. T. Technical College, Davenport — 150; Indian Hills Community College (main campus), Ottumwa — 1,589; Indian Hills Community College (Centerville Campus), Centerville — 296; Iowa Wesleyan College, Mount Pleasant — 813; Maharishi International University, Fairfield — 531.

Marycrest College, Davenport — 1,196; Muscatine Iowa Community College, Muscatine — 925; Palmer College of Chiropractic, Davenport — 1,861; St. Ambrose College, Davenport — 1,993; Scott Community College, Bettendorf — 1,985; Southeastern Community College, West Burlington — 1,761; Vennard College, University Park — 219; William Penn College, Oskaloosa — 57.

Newspapers, Circulation: *The Daily Democrat* (e), Fort Madison — 7,855; *Daily Gate City* (e), Keokuk — 7,888; *The Fairfield Ledger* (e), Fairfield — 5,650; *The Hawk Eye* (eS), Burlington — 20,025; *Iowegian & Citizen* (m), Centerville — 5,004; *Mount Pleasant News* (e), Mount Pleasant — 4,180; *Muscatine Journal* (e), Muscatine — 11,918; *Oskaloosa Herald* (e), Oskaloosa — 6,466; *Ottumwa Courier* (e), Ottumwa — 17,781; *Quad City Times* (all day, S), Davenport — 64,474; *The Washington Evening Journal* (e), Washington — 5,683. *The Des Moines Register* and *Des Moines Tribune* also circulate in the district.

Commercial Television Stations, Affiliation: WOC-TV, Davenport (NBC). District is divided among Cedar Rapids-Waterloo ADI, Davenport-Rock Island (Ill.)-Moline (Ill.) ADI, Des Moines ADI, Ottumwa-Kirksville (Mo.) ADI and Quincy (Ill.)-Hannibal (Mo.) ADI.

Military Installations: Iowa Army Ammunition Plant, Middletown — 940.

Industries:

Aluminum Co. of America; Bettendorf; aluminum extruded products — 2,800. **Caterpillar Tractor Co.;** Davenport; earthmoving equipment — 1,575. **Deere & Co.;** Ottumwa; farm implements — 1,500. **Textron Inc.** (Sheaffer Eaton Div.); Fort Madison; pens, pencils — 1,500. **J. I. Case Co.;** Burlington; construction machinery — 1,240.

Deere & Co.; Davenport; construction machinery — 1,200. **Sheller-Globe Corp.;** Keokuk; molded rubber products — 1,100. **Oscar Mayer & Co. Inc.;** Davenport; meatpacking — 1,060. **General Electric Co.;** Burlington; switchgears — 900. **J. I. Case Co.;** Bettendorf; construction, farm machinery — 850. **Grain Processing Corp.** (HQ); Muscatine; wet corn milling, organic chemicals — 850. **H. J. Heinz Co. Inc.;** Muscatine; canned fruits, vegetables — 850. **Mason & Hanger-Silas Mason Co.;** Middletown; ammunition — 850. **Bandag Inc.** (HDP Div. - HQ); Muscatine; tire retreading products — 600. **Bendix Corp.;** Davenport; aircraft parts — 600.

Per Mar Security & Research (Per Mar Alarm Systems - HQ); Davenport; security services — 600. **Ralston Purina Co.;** Davenport; cereals — 600. **Stanley Consultants Inc.** (HQ); Muscatine; engineering services — 600. **Gulf & Western Industries Inc.;** Davenport; industrial controls — 550. **Fruehauf Corp.;** Fort Madison; truck trailers — 500. **Hon Industries Inc.** (HQ); Muscatine; metal office furniture — 500. **The Hubinger Co.** (HQ); Keokuk; corn syrup, starch — 500. **Kast Metals Corp.;** Keokuk; steel foundries — 500. **Monsanto Co.;** Muscatine; agricultural chemicals — 500.

2nd District

Northeast — Cedar Rapids

This district remains what it has been for decades: a triangle of interdependent industrial cities surrounded by corn, livestock and dairy farms.

All redistricting did was trade Winneshiek County to the 3rd in return for Buchanan County. Buchanan and Winnishiek cast fewer than 10,000 votes apiece in 1980 and gave GOP candidates 53 percent of the vote or better.

The population centers in the district are Cedar Rapids, Dubuque and Clinton. Cedar Rapids, the second largest city in Iowa, is a center for meatpacking, grain processing and manufacturing of farm hardware and radio equipment. Traditionally Republican, it swung to the Democratic side in statewide contests during the early 1970s but by 1980 seemed to be swinging back again.

Dubuque, with slightly more than 60,000 people, is largely Catholic and historically friendlier to Democrats. It is a processing point for the dairy industry; it also builds tractors and other farm implements. In 1980, Dubuque County was one of four Iowa counties carried by Jimmy Carter.

The city of Clinton, about half the size of Dubuque, is another local manufacturing center on the west bank of the Mississippi River. Democratic strength in Clinton County dropped dramatically during the 1970s, and the area is only slightly less Republican than the district's eight rural counties, where Republican candidates often receive more than 55 percent of the total vote.

The only 2nd District county that lost population in the 1970s was Fayette County. Every other Iowa congressional district contains at least two counties where population declined in the 1970s.

Election Returns

2nd District		Democrat		Republican	
1976	President	101,630	(48.5%)	103,412	(49.4%)
	House	103,191	(50.5%)	99,995	(48.9%)
1978	Governor	60,267	(42.7%)	79,807	(56.6%)
	Senate	65,062	(47.1%)	71,354	(51.7%)
	House	64,841	(46.4%)	74,074	(53.0%)

2nd District		Democrat		Republican	
1980	President	86,085	(40.0%)	106,157	(49.4%)
	Senate	100,577	(47.9%)	107,698	(51.3%)
	House	94,816	(45.8%)	110,419	(53.3%)
1982	Governor	75,359	(44.1%)	94,424	(55.3%)
	House	69,539	(41.1%)	99,478	(58.9%)

Demographics

Population: 485,708. Percent Change from 1970: 2.9%.

Land Area: 7,116 square miles. Population per Square Mile: 68.3.

Counties, 1980 Population: Allamakee — 15,108; Buchanan — 22,900; Cedar — 18,635; Clayton — 21,098; Clinton — 57,122; Delaware — 18,933; Dubuque — 93,745; Fayette — 25,488; Jackson — 22,503; Jones — 20,401; Linn — 169,775.

Cities, 1980 Population: Cedar Rapids — 110,243; Clinton — 32,828; Dubuque — 62,321; Marion — 19,474.

Race and Ancestry: White — 98.5%; Black — 0.8%; American Indian, Eskimo and Aleut — 0.1%; Asian and Pacific Islander — 0.3%. Spanish Origin — 0.6%. Dutch — 0.6%; English — 5.6%; French — 0.5%; German — 27.3%; Irish — 5.1%; Norwegian — 1.4%; Swedish — 0.6%.

Universities, Enrollment: Clarke College, Dubuque — 817; Coe College, Cedar Rapids — 1,426; Cornell College, Mount Vernon — 933; Divine Word College, Epworth — 86; Clinton Community College, Clinton — 825; Kirkwood Community College, Cedar Rapids — 5,011; Loras College, Dubuque — 1,868; Mount Mercy College, Cedar Rapids — 1,066; Mount St. Clare College, Clinton — 392; University of Dubuque-College of Liberal Arts, Dubuque — 1,064; University of Dubuque-Theological Seminary, Dubuque — 144; Upper Iowa University, Fayette — 404; Wartburg Theological Seminary, Dubuque — 248.

Newspapers, Circulation: *The Cedar Rapids Gazette* (mS), Cedar Rapids — 68,860; *Clinton Herald* (e), Clinton — 22,384; *Register* (e), Oelwein — 7,248; *Telegraph-Herald* (eS), Dubuque — 39,073.

Commercial Television Stations, Affiliation: KCRG-TV, Cedar Rapids (ABC); KDUB-TV, Dubuque (ABC); KGAN-TV, Cedar Rapids (CBS). Most of district is located in Cedar Rapids-Waterloo ADI. Portion is in Davenport-Rock Island (Ill.)-Moline (Ill.) ADI.

Nuclear Power Plants: Duane Arnold, Palo (General Electric, Bechtel), February 1975.

Industries:

Deere & Co.; Dubuque; tractors, industrial equipment — 4,100. **Rockwell International Corp.** (Collins Telecommunications Products Div.); Cedar Rapids; electronic communications equipment — 2,930. **Wilson Foods Corp.;** Cedar Rapids; meat, poultry products — 2,000. **FMC Corp.** (Cable Crane & Excavator Div.); Cedar Rapids; construction machinery — 1,800. **St. Luke's Methodist Hospital;** Cedar Rapids; hospital — 1,800.

Rockwell International Corp. (Collins Air Transport Div.); Cedar Rapids; electronic communications equipment — 1,654. **Rockwell International Corp.** (Collins Government Avionics Div.); Cedar Rapids; electronic communications equipment — 1,445. **Dubuque Packing Co.** (HQ); Dubuque; meatpacking — 1,400. **Mercy Hospital;** Cedar Rapids; hospital — 1,400. **Quaker Oats Co.;** Cedar Rapids; cereals — 1,400. **Standard Brands Inc.** (Clinton Corn Processing Co.); Clinton; wet corn milling — 1,300. **Sisters of Mercy Health Corp.;** Dubuque; hospital — 1,290. **Harnischfeger Corp.;** Cedar Rapids; hoists, industrial cranes — 1,200. **Walter Kidde & Co. Inc.** (Le Febure Div.); Cedar Rapids; metal office furniture — 1,200.

Rockwell International Corp. (Collins General Aviation); Cedar Rapids; electronic communications equipment — 1,185. **E. I. du Pont de Nemours & Co. Inc.;** Camanche; cellulosic man-made fibers — 1,100. **Rockwell International Corp.** (Graphic Systems Div.); Cedar Rapids; printing trades machinery — 705. **Cherry-Burrell** (HQ); Cedar Rapids; food products machinery — 700. **Flexsteel Industries Inc.**

(HQ); Dubuque; wooden furniture — 650. **Chicago & North Western Transportation Co.**; Clinton; railroad operations — 600. **A. C. Nielsen Co.** (Nielsen Clearinghouse); Clinton; market research services — 600. **Walter Kidde & Co. Inc.** (Vanity Fair); Dyersville; children's toys, aluminum castings — 500.

3rd District

North Central — Waterloo, Iowa City

Johnson County, shifted into the 3rd from the 1st, added Democratic strength to this Republican territory. It is a fast-growing county with a population of 81,717, and in 1980 it gave Ronald Reagan a meager 32 percent of the vote. Independent candidate John B. Anderson received nearly 19 percent of the county's presidential vote. Johnson County has a strong liberal influence from the University of Iowa in Iowa City (population 50,508). The university has about 25,000 students.

Still, Johnson County's population amounts to less than one-fifth of the district's total. The largest bloc of 3rd District votes — nearly 30 percent — is cast in Black Hawk County.

With the twin cities of Waterloo and Cedar Falls, Black Hawk County is Iowa's fourth-largest metropolitan area. Meatpacking and the farm implement industry are crucial, and labor unions have demonstrated political strength here. But there is a long Republican tradition in House voting. Waterloo is the only major city in Iowa that has not been represented by a Democrat since World War II.

In addition to Johnson County, the district gained four other counties: Benton, Poweshiek and Iowa, all on the district's southern border, and Winneshiek, at its northeast corner. All four favor Republicans; none contains a major city.

Those four counties only partially compensate for Republican territory the district lost. Gone are six counties on the western side of the 3rd District: Cerro Gordo, Hardin, Hamilton, Wright, Hancock and Franklin. All except Cerro Gordo County are solidly Republican, rural and small-town counties. On its eastern side, the 3rd District lost Republican Buchanan County to the 2nd District.

Election Returns

3rd District		Democrat		Republican	
1976	President	105,877	(48.0%)	108,818	(49.4%)
	House	99,521	(45.1%)	120,750	(54.8%)
1978	Governor	54,934	(37.9%)	88,267	(61.0%)
	Senate	69,371	(47.8%)	74,160	(51.1%)
	House	41,809	(30.0%)	97,018	(69.5%)
1980	President	91,217	(39.8%)	111,226	(48.5%)
	Senate	100,339	(44.5%)	123,580	(54.8%)
	House	98,709	(45.2%)	118,581	(54.3%)
1982	Governor	84,658	(44.6%)	103,685	(54.6%)
	House	83,581	(44.5%)	104,072	(55.5%)

Demographics

Population: 485,529. **Percent Change from 1970:** 3.9%.

Land Area: 8,934 square miles. **Population per Square Mile:** 54.3.

Counties, 1980 Population: Benton — 23,649; Black Hawk — 137,961; Bremer — 24,820; Butler — 17,668; Chickasaw — 15,437; Floyd — 19,597; Grundy — 14,366; Howard — 11,114; Iowa — 15,429; Johnson — 81,717; Marshall — 41,652; Mitchell — 12,329; Poweshiek — 19,306; Tama — 19,533; Winneshiek — 21,876; Worth — 9,075.

Cities, 1980 Population: Cedar Falls — 36,322; Iowa City — 50,508; Marshalltown — 26,938; Waterloo — 75,985.

Race and Ancestry: White — 96.7%; Black — 2.1%; American Indian, Eskimo and Aleut — 0.3%; Asian and Pacific Islander — 0.6%. Spanish Origin — 0.6%. Dutch — 0.9%; English — 6.3%; French — 0.5%; German — 24.8%; Irish — 3.7%; Norwegian — 2.9%; Swedish — 0.7%.

Universities, Enrollment: Grinnell College, Grinnell — 1,260; Hawkeye Institute of Technology, Waterloo — 2,116; Luther College, Decorah — 2,085; Marshalltown Community College, Marshalltown — 1,211; Northeast Iowa Technical Institute, Calmar — 1,026; University of Iowa, Iowa City — 25,100; University of Northern Iowa, Cedar Falls — 11,020; Wartburg College, Waverly — 1,108.

Newspapers, Circulation: *Cedar Valley Times* (e), Vinton — 3,642; *Charles City Press* (e), Charles City — 4,212; *Iowa City Press-Citizen* (e), Iowa City — 17,349; *The Record* (m), Cedar Falls — 4,508; *Times-Republican* (e), Marshalltown — 15,821; *Waterloo Courier* (eS), Waterloo — 54,337. *The Des Moines Register* and *Des Moines Tribune* also circulate in the district.

Commercial Television Stations, Affiliation: KWWL-TV, Waterloo (NBC). Most of district is located in Cedar Rapids-Waterloo ADI. Portions are in Des Moines ADI and Rochester (Minn.)-Mason City ADI.

Industries:

Deere & Co. Inc.; Waterloo; farm machinery, equipment — 6,300. **Fisher Controls Co. Inc.** (HQ); Marshalltown; control valves, electricity measuring devices — 3,200. **Amana Refrigeration Inc.** (HQ); Amana; freezers, refrigerators — 2,700. **Deere & Co. Inc.;** Waterloo; tractors — 2,100. **The Rath Packing Co.** (HQ); Waterloo; meatpacking — 2,000.

White Farm Equipment; Charles City; farm machinery — 1,500. **Deere & Co. Inc.;** Cedar Falls; engineering center — 1,300. **Veterans Administration;** Iowa City; veterans' hospital — 1,000. **Deere & Co. Inc.;** Waterloo; engines — 925. **Houdaille Industries Inc.** (Viking Pump Div.); Cedar Falls; pumps, pumping equipment — 900. **Waterloo Industries Inc.** (HQ); Waterloo; metal tools — 750. **Luthern Mutual Life Insurance;** Waverly; life insurance — 708. **Koehring Co.** (Bantam Div.); Waverly; construction machinery — 700. **American College Testing;** Iowa City; educational testing — 580. **Cooper Labs Inc.** (Owens Brush Div.); Iowa City; toothbrushes, hair brushes — 550. **Sheller-Globe Corp.;** Iowa City; plastics products — 549. **Eltra Corp.** (Marshalltown Instruments Div.); Marshalltown; industrial measuring instruments — 500.

4th District

Central — Des Moines, Ames

More than 60 percent of the 4th District's voters are in Polk County, most of them in Des Moines, Iowa's big city. Surrounding farms and smaller industrial towns look to Des Moines as a commercial, financial and governmental center and, because Des Moines is the capital, state government contributes to the white-collar work force.

The city also depends on grain marketing, publishing and the manufacture of farm equipment. The United Auto Workers is a significant political presence. Des Moines is predominantly white, Protestant and middle-class with less ethnic flavor than other Midwestern industrial cities.

Polk is the state's crucial Democratic county, but

Democrats may be growing weaker here as the central city's population declines. Many fast-growing communities around Des Moines show a preference for Republicans. Areas such as suburban West Des Moines, where the population expanded 33 percent in the 1970s, were largely responsible for Ronald Reagan's slim margin of victory in Polk County's 1980 presidential vote.

Redistricting removed eight counties southeast of Des Moines: Marion, Mahaska, Appanoose, Keokuk, Lucas, Davis, Wapello and Monroe. Republicans hold the advantage in all but the last two.

The district gains four central Iowa counties: Story, Dallas, Boone and Hamilton. Story is the most important. It includes Ames (population 45,775), the home of Iowa State University's 24,000 students. With most of the college students eligible to vote, Story County has generally backed liberal Democrats for statewide office. But no Democrat running for president has carried the county since Lyndon B. Johnson in 1964.

Election Returns

4th District		Democrat		Republican	
1976	President	113,687	(51.1%)	103,091	(46.3%)
	House	149,467	(69.7%)	64,296	(30.0%)
1978	Governor	64,764	(44.3%)	80,052	(54.7%)
	Senate	79,144	(55.2%)	62,559	(43.6%)
	House	89,217	(64.0%)	50,100	(36.0%)
1980	President	95,948	(41.5%)	105,044	(45.4%)
	Senate	121,561	(53.9%)	101,258	(44.9%)
	House	128,650	(57.9%)	93,174	(41.1%)
1982	Governor	103,192	(55.2%)	82,060	(43.9%)
	House	118,849	(66.1%)	60,534	(33.6%)

Demographics

Population: 485,480. **Percent Change from 1970:** 6.6%.

Land Area: 3,627 square miles. **Population per Square Mile:** 133.9.

Counties, 1980 Population: Boone — 26,184; Dallas — 29,513; Hamilton — 17,862; Jasper — 36,425; Polk — 303,170; Story — 72,326.

Cities, 1980 Population: Ames — 45,775; Ankeny — 15,429; Boone — 12,602; Des Moines — 191,003; Newton — 15,292; Urbandale — 17,869; West Des Moines — 21,894.

Race and Ancestry: White — 95.1%; Black — 3.0%; American Indian, Eskimo and Aleut — 0.2%; Asian and Pacific Islander — 1.0%. Spanish Origin — 1.2%. Dutch — 2.1%; English — 9.3%; French — 0.7%; German — 11.8%; Irish — 4.4%; Italian — 1.3%; Norwegian — 2.5%; Scottish — 0.5%; Swedish — 1.8%.

Universities, Enrollment: American Institute of Business, Des Moines — 1,034; College of Osteopathic Medicine and Surgery, Des Moines — 545; Des Moines Area Community College, Ankeny — 6,347; Drake University, Des Moines — 6,592; Faith Baptist Bible College, Ankeny — 440; Grand View College, Des Moines — 1,193; Iowa State University, Ames — 24,754; Open Bible College, Des Moines — 95; United Electronics Institute, West Des Moines — 340.

Newspapers, Circulation: *Ames Daily Tribune* (e), Ames — 10,658; *The Daily Freeman-Journal* (e), Webster City — 30,410; *The Des Moines Register* (mS), Des Moines — 208,413; *Des Moines Tribune* (eS), Des Moines — 81,753; *Nevada Evening Journal* (e), Nevada — 3,185; *News-Republican* (eS), Boone — 6,126; *The Newton Daily News* (e), Newton — 7,901; *Perry Daily Chief* (e), Perry — 3,458.

Commercial Television Stations, Affiliation: KCCI-TV, Des Moines (CBS); WHO-TV, Des Moines (NBC); WOI-TV, Ames (ABC). Entire district is located in Des Moines ADI.

Military Installations: Des Moines Municipal Airport (Air Force), Des Moines — 1,123; Fort Des Moines, Des Moines — 1,106.

Industries:

The Maytag Co. (HQ); Newton; washing machines — 2,900. **Deere & Co.**; Ankeny; farm machinery — 2,500. **Iowa Methodist Medical Center;** Des Moines; hospital — 2,500. **Mercy Hospital & Medical Center;** Des Moines; hospital — 2,000. **Meredith Corp.** (HQ); Des Moines; publishing, broadcasting — 2,000.

Firestone Tire & Rubber Co.; Des Moines; tires, inner tubes — 1,750. **Iowa Lutheran Hospital;** Des Moines; hospital — 1,600. **Bankers Life Co. Inc.** (HQ); Des Moines; life insurance — 1,500. **Sundstrand Corp.** (Sundstrand Hydro Transmission); Ames; transmissions — 1,500. **Des Moines Register & Tribune Co.** (HQ); Des Moines; newspaper publishing, broadcasting — 1,400. **The Armstrong Rubber Co.;** Des Moines; tires, inner tubes — 1,100. **AMF Inc.** (Lawn & Garden Div.); Des Moines; lawn, garden equipment — 1,000. **Blue Cross of Iowa;** Des Moines; health insurance — 1,000. **Roan Transport Corp.** (Arizona Tank Lines - HQ); Des Moines; trucking — 1,000. **Chicago & North Western Transportation Co.;** Boone; railroad operations — 800. **Oscar Mayer & Co.;** Perry; meat wholesaling — 750. **The Vernon Co. Inc.** (Specialty Counselors Div. - HQ); Newton; advertising signs — 675. **Bourns Inc.;** Ames; musical instruments — 650.

Pittsburgh-Des Moines Steel Co. (Sola-Flex); Des Moines; fabricated structural metal — 650. **Equitable of Iowa Companies** (HQ); Des Moines; life insurance — 604. **Employers Mutual Casualty Co.** (HQ); Des Moines; accident, health insurance — 602. **Iowa Des Moines National Bank** (HQ); Des Moines; banking — 600. **Super Value Stores Inc.;** Des Moines; grocery wholesaling — 600. **White Consolidated Industries Inc.** (Webster City Products Co.); Webster City; laundry equipment — 600. **Charter Data Services Inc.** (HQ); Des Moines; magazine business services — 550. **Farmers Mutual Hail Insurance;** Des Moines; fire, marine, casualty insurance — 502. **Amoco Oil Co.;** Des Moines; credit card center — 500. **Minnesota Mining & Mfg. Co.;** Ames; abrasive products — 500. **Preferred Risk Mutual Insurance** (HQ); Des Moines; automobile, fire insurance — 500. **Swift Independent Packing Co.;** Des Moines; meatpacking — 500.

5th District

Southwest — Council Bluffs, Fort Dodge

The 5th District expands north to take in Crawford, Sac and Calhoun counties, all of which are small-town, rural and Republican, and Webster County, which delivers a generally reliable Democratic majority and makes up just under 10 percent of the 5th District's total population.

Also new to the district is Marion County, with nearly 30,000 residents and a preference for the GOP. Marion County is actually southeast of Des Moines, testimony to the far-ranging nature of the 5th. Marion adjoins Warren County, which contains the outlying southern suburbs of Des Moines and leans Democratic. Warren, Iowa's fastest growing county in the 1970s, experienced a population boom of 27 percent.

The district's most steadfastly Republican counties are Pottawattamie, Page, Montgomery, Mills and Fremont. Clustered in the extreme southwest corner of the district, they make up about 30 percent of the district's population. Pottawattamie County contains the district's largest city: industrial Council Bluffs, which stands across the Missouri River from Omaha and is part of its metropolitan area.

The 5th District's sparsely-populated central counties are dependent on agriculture — livestock, poultry, feed grains and soybeans. The terrain in much of this area of the state is not as favorable for farming as in other parts of the state. Iowa's southwest tier of counties is largely hilly and rocky, especially along the Iowa-Missouri border. The small towns and farms here almost always favor statewide Republican candidates by wide margins.

Election Returns

5th District		Democrat		Republican	
1976	President	101,119	(48.6%)	103,428	(49.7%)
	House	126,953	(63.2%)	72,234	(36.0%)
1978	Governor	59,289	(42.5%)	79,780	(57.1%)
	Senate	63,670	(46.5%)	72,420	(52.9%)
	House	79,638	(59.4%)	54,385	(40.6%)
1980	President	74,675	(34.8%)	123,622	(57.5%)
	Senate	82,298	(40.2%)	120,386	(58.8%)
	House	120,210	(58.9%)	83,949	(41.1%)
1982	Governor	74,494	(44.9%)	90,497	(54.6%)
	House	93,333	(58.9%)	65,200	(41.1%)

Demographics

Population: 485,639. **Percent Change from 1970:** 1.5%.

Land Area: 15,157 square miles. **Population per Square Mile:** 32.0.

Counties, 1980 Population: Adair — 9,509; Adams — 5,731; Audubon — 8,559; Calhoun — 13,542; Carroll — 22,951; Cass — 16,932; Clarke — 8,612; Crawford — 18,935; Decatur — 9,794; Fremont — 9,401; Greene — 12,119; Guthrie — 11,983; Harrison — 16,348; Madison — 12,597; Marion — 29,669; Mills — 13,406; Montgomery — 13,413; Page — 19,063; Pottawattamie — 86,561; Ringgold — 6,112; Sac — 14,118; Shelby — 15,043; Taylor — 8,353; Union — 13,858; Warren — 34,878; Wayne — 8,199; Webster — 45,953.

Cities, 1980 Population: Council Bluffs — 56,449; Fort Dodge — 29,423; Indianola — 10,843.

Race and Ancestry: White — 99.0%; Black — 0.3%; American Indian, Eskimo and Aleut — 0.1%; Asian and Pacific Islander — 0.2%. Spanish Origin — 0.6%. Dutch — 2.0%; English — 9.2%; French — 0.6%; German — 19.2%; Irish — 4.4%; Norwegian — 0.9%; Swedish — 1.8%.

Universities, Enrollment: Central University of Iowa, Pella — 1,541; Graceland College, Lamoni — 1,304; Iowa Central Community College, Fort Dodge — 2,940; Iowa Western Community College, Council Bluffs — 2,510; Simpson College, Indianola — 829; Southwestern Community College, Creston — 569.

Newspapers, Circulation: *Atlantic News-Telegraph* (e), Atlantic — 7,725; *Carroll Daily Times-Herald* (e), Carroll — 7,005; *Creston News-Advertiser* (e), Creston — 6,831; *The Daily Nonpareil* (eS), Council Bluffs — 19,731; *The Messenger* (e), Fort Dodge — 30,410; *Sentinel* (e), Shenandoah — 3,783. *The Des Moines Register, Des Moines Tribune* and *Omaha World-Herald* (Neb.) also circulate in the district.

Commercial Television Stations, Affiliation: KVFD-TV, Fort Dodge (NBC). Most of district is divided between Des Moines ADI and Omaha (Neb.) ADI. Portion is in Sioux City ADI.

Military Installations: Fort Dodge Facility (Air Force), Fort Dodge — 183.

Industries:
Rolscreen Co. (HQ); Pella; windows — 1,750. **Iowa State Hospital;** Glenwood; psychiatric hospital — 1,330. **Veterans Administration;** Knoxville; veterans' psychiatric hospital — 1,000. **Vermeer Mfg. Co.** (HQ); Pella; agricultural equipment — 825. **Farmland Foods Inc.;** Denison; meatpacking — 800.

Land O'Lakes Inc. (Felco Div.); Fort Dodge; feeds, farm supplies — 600. **Union Carbide Corp.** (Consumer Products); Red Oak; batteries — 600. **Eaton Corp.** (Transmission Div.); Shenandoah; motor vehicle parts — 550. **General Electric Co.;** Carroll; automated control devices — 550. **Centralab Inc.;** Fort Dodge; electronic components — 500. **Chicago & North Western Transportation Co.;** Council Bluffs; railroad operations — 500.

6th District

Northwest — Sioux City

Northwestern Iowa's flat, rich soil makes it one of the most agriculturally productive areas of the nation, with consistently impressive corn and soybean yields. But as farming has become more costly and technologically more complex, many small-scale farmers have sold their land to agribusiness operations, eliminating jobs and causing migration from the 6th District. Of the 23 counties in the 6th, all but seven lost population in the 1970s.

Some of the more industrialized pockets of the district were hard hit by the recession in the early 1980s. Emmet County, for example, saw its unemployment soar to 16 percent in 1982, the result of meatpacking plant closings.

Sioux City, western Iowa's largest city, is the political core of the 6th District. An old meatpacking town on the Missouri River, Sioux City has grown into an urban center with a massive downtown urban renewal project that includes a regional shopping center.

The city and surrounding Woodbury County have about a fifth of the district's population and generally vote Republican, although they support the Democratic House incumbent. In 1980 Ronald Reagan won every county in the 6th.

In the remap the 6th District lost Democratic Webster County and picked up Cerro Gordo County, comparable in population to Webster but usually favorable to Republicans. Mason City (population 30,144), seat of Cerro Gordo County, is also the town that inspired Meredith Willson, a native son, to write *The Music Man*.

Also joining the 6th District are Hardin, Wright, Hancock and Franklin counties, formerly in the 3rd District. They cast fewer than 10,000 votes each and are Republican-dominated.

Crawford, Sac and Calhoun counties, which vote GOP in statewide races, were moved out of the 6th District into the 5th.

Election Returns

6th District		Democrat		Republican	
1976	President	96,880	(44.9%)	114,986	(53.3%)
	House	127,909	(61.2%)	79,112	(37.8%)
1978	Governor	53,445	(37.2%)	89,353	(62.3%)
	Senate	60,522	(43.3%)	77,957	(55.8%)
	House	76,231	(55.2%)	61,868	(44.8%)
1980	President	75,202	(34.2%)	125,915	(57.2%)
	Senate	81,636	(38.9%)	126,419	(60.2%)
	House	127,627	(61.6%)	79,448	(38.4%)
1982	Governor	69,202	(41.4%)	97,212	(58.2%)
	House	101,690	(64.3%)	56,487	(35.7%)

Demographics

Population: 485,491. **Percent Change from 1970:** -0.8%.

Land Area: 13,511 square miles. **Population per Square Mile:** 35.9.

Counties, 1980 Population: Buena Vista — 20,774; Cerro Gordo — 48,458; Cherokee — 16,238; Clay — 19,576; Dickinson — 15,629; Emmet — 13,336; Franklin — 13,036; Hancock — 13,833; Hardin — 21,776; Humboldt — 12,246; Ida — 8,908; Kossuth — 21,891; Lyon — 12,896; Monona — 11,692; O'Brien — 16,972; Osceola — 8,371; Palo Alto — 12,721; Plymouth — 24,743; Pocahontas — 11,369; Sioux — 30,813; Winnebago — 13,010; Woodbury — 100,884; Wright — 16,319.

Cities, 1980 Population: Mason City — 30,144; Sioux City — 82,003; Spencer — 11,726.

Race and Ancestry: White — 98.8%; Black — 0.3%; American Indian, Eskimo and Aleut — 0.3%; Asian and Pacific Islander — 0.2%. Spanish Origin — 0.7%. Dutch — 6.0%; English — 4.9%; French — 0.7%; German — 23.0%; Irish — 2.9%; Norwegian — 4.0%; Swedish — 1.6%.

Universities, Enrollment: Briar Cliff College, Sioux City — 1,272; Buena Vista College, Storm Lake — 1,368; Dordt College, Sioux Center — 1,160; Ellsworth Community College, Iowa Falls — 959; Iowa Lakes Community College, Estherville — 1,783; Morningside College, Sioux City — 1,428; North Iowa Area Community College, Mason City — 2,163; Northwest Iowa Technical College, Sheldon — 434; Northwestern College, Orange City — 955; Waldorf College, Forest City — 400; Western Iowa Tech Community College, Sioux City — 1,323; Westmar College, Le Mars — 652.

Newspapers, Circulation: *Cherokee Daily Times* (m), Cherokee — 4,652; *Daily Reporter* (e), Spencer — 4,211; *Globe-Gazette* (e), Mason City — 22,585; *Le Mars Daily Sentinel* (e), Le Mars — 5,642; *News* (e), Estherville — 3,172; *Sioux City Journal* (mS), Sioux City — 58,049. *The Des Moines Register* and *The Des Moines Tribune* also circulate in the district.

Commercial Television Stations, Affiliation: KCAU-TV, Sioux City (ABC); KIMT, Mason City (CBS); KMEG, Sioux City (CBS); KTIV-TV, Sioux City (NBC). Most of district is located in Sioux City ADI. Portions are in Des Moines ADI, Mankato (Minn.) ADI, Rochester (Minn.)-Mason City ADI and Sioux Falls (S.D.)-Mitchell (S.D.) ADI.

Military Installations: Sioux City Municipal Airport (Air Force), Sergeant Bluff — 961.

Industries:

St. Luke's Medical Center; Sioux City; hospital — 1,450. **Winnebago Industries Inc.** (HQ); Forest City; motor homes, truck bodies — 1,200. **Berkley & Co. Inc.** (HQ); Spirit Lake; fishing tackle — 600. **Wilson Foods Corp.;** Cherokee; meatpacking — 600. **Iowa Beef Processors Inc.;** Storm Lake; meatpacking — 575. **Eaton Corp.;** Spencer; lubricating oils, greases — 500. **Snap-On Tools Corp.** (Weindenhoff Div.); Algona; tool chests — 500. **Western Contracting Corp.;** Sioux City; heavy construction — 500.

Kansas

Outnumbered by Republicans in both chambers of the Kansas Legislature, Democrats managed to force redistricting into federal court and emerged with a decision that in 1982 gave them a second seat in the state's U.S. House delegation.

The court-approved plan, announced June 2, 1982, pleased Democratic Gov. John Carlin, who vetoed two congressional maps passed by the GOP Legislature in 1982. Carlin said he could not accept the legislative efforts because they split Sedgwick County (Wichita) and Wyandotte County (Kansas City) between two districts. Another goal for Carlin and the Democrats, however, was to weaken the delegation's one vulnerable Republican in the 2nd District.

The first attempt at a remap was passed by the state Senate on Feb. 9, 1982, by a 24-15 margin, and by the state House the following day, 77-47. It was vetoed by Carlin on Feb. 18. The second try, approved by nearly identical margins, was vetoed on April 22. By blocking the plan, Carlin and the Democrats were able to send the question to a three-judge federal panel, two of whose members were Democratic appointees.

The federal panel had few difficult choices to make. Kansas kept its five House seats, and population differences among the districts were small. The only important political issue focused on Douglas County, location of the University of Kansas at Lawrence and a center for liberal Democrats and moderate Republicans. Adding it to the 2nd would have posed serious political problems for the New Right Republican incumbent; placing it in any of the other nearby districts was unlikely to have any political impact.

The court decided to put Douglas County in the 2nd and unite all of Sedgwick County in the 4th and all of Wyandotte County in the 3rd, eliminating the division of counties Carlin objected to in his vetoes.

Nine days after the new map was approved, the 2nd District incumbent announced his retirement from the House. His seat was won by a Democrat in 1982.

Aside from the 2nd, the only district to change its political character significantly was the 4th, centered around Wichita. By unifying Sedgwick County within the 4th and trading some outlying agricultural counties with the neighboring 5th, the remap strengthened the Democratic incumbent.

Age of Population

District	Population Under 18	Voting Age Population	Population 65 & Over (% of VAP)	Median Age
1	129,700	342,439	75,593 (22.1%)	32.2
2	123,994	348,994	51,790 (14.8%)	27.5
3	138,303	334,153	45,786 (13.7%)	30.1
4	131,462	341,718	51,611 (15.1%)	29.4
5	125,576	347,340	81,483 (23.5%)	32.8
State	649,035	1,714,644	306,263 (17.9%)	30.1

Income and Occupation

District	Median Family Income	White Collar Workers	Blue Collar Workers	Service Workers	Farm Workers
1	$ 17,491	42.5%	29.0%	13.7%	14.8%
2	19,151	54.2	26.2	14.5	5.2
3	23,821	62.9	25.7	10.2	1.2
4	20,970	52.0	34.1	11.5	2.5
5	17,495	42.2	36.3	13.6	7.9
State	$ 19,707	50.9%	30.3%	12.6%	6.2%

Education: School Years Completed

District	8 Years or Fewer	4 Years of High School	4 Years of College or More	Median School Years
1	18.2%	40.8%	13.2%	12.5
2	12.6	40.9	20.0	12.6
3	11.0	35.8	23.1	12.8
4	12.0	39.2	17.0	12.6
5	19.1	39.3	12.3	12.4
State	14.6%	39.2%	17.0%	12.6

Housing and Residential Patterns

District	Owner Occupied	Renter Occupied	Urban	Rural
1	74.7%	25.3%	44.6%	55.4%
2	64.1	35.9	67.5	32.5

KANSAS

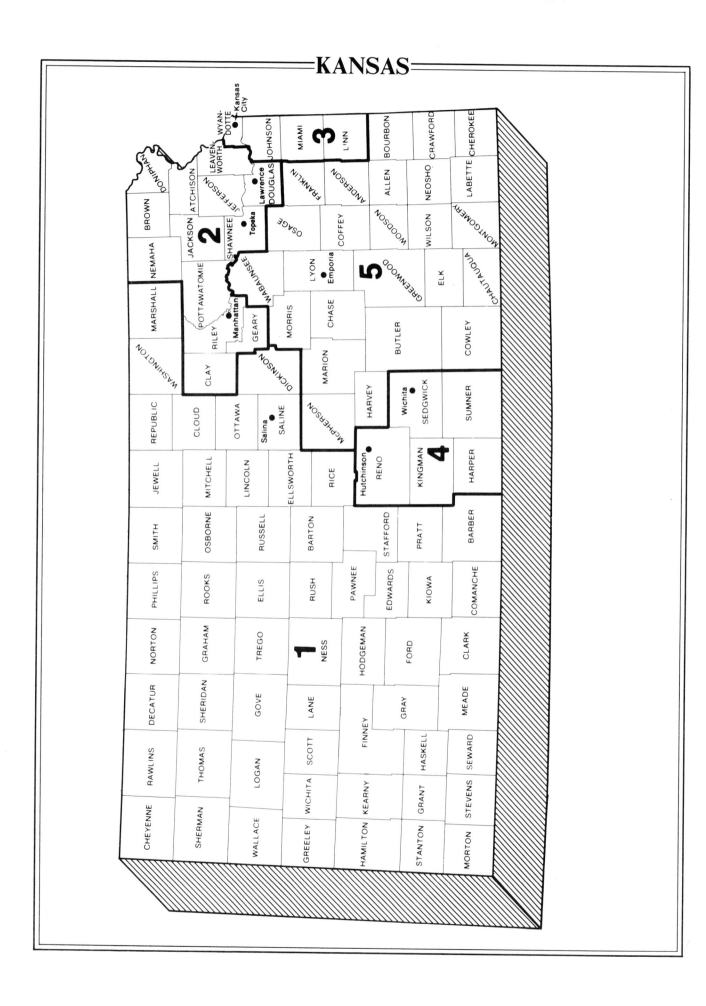

District	Owner Occupied	Renter Occupied	Urban	Rural
3	71.0	29.0	89.9	10.1
4	66.1	33.9	80.6	19.4
5	74.8	25.2	50.8	49.2
State	70.2%	29.8%	66.7%	33.3%

1st District

West — Salina, Dodge City

The "big first" grows bigger with each census, as its wheat farms and market towns lose population and force the lines farther east. For the 1980s the district stretches across 58 counties and two-thirds of the state's land area, marching east to within 50 miles of the Missouri border.

Population decline during the 1970s did not change the demographics of the 1st. It is still dominated by grain-growing and livestock interests. Bountiful harvests of hardy winter wheat grown by western Kansas farmers help make the state the leading wheat producer in the nation, far outpacing its nearest rival, North Dakota.

Gaining Dickinson and Marshall counties in the 1982 remap and yielding Clay County to the neighboring 2nd, the 1st retained its solidly rural and conservative character. Firmly Republican, the area has been represented in the House by the GOP since 1963. Republicans outnumber Democrats in the district's voter registration by 115,204 to 70,894.

Farmers and ranchers in western Kansas generally are suspicious of federal involvement in agriculture and in normal years can be counted on to back candidates who endorse a free market approach. But like their counterparts in Nebraska and the Dakotas, they can turn ornery in hard times, as witnessed by the defection of 15 Republican counties in the 1976 presidential election.

Around the turn of the century, western Kansas was a hotbed of populism, boasting among its political characters "Sockless" Jerry Simpson, who vowed that populism would never die. But populism has all but died in western Kansas; it thrived among the area's poorer and more marginal farmers, most of whom had simply given up and moved away by the 1930s, leaving more prosperous and more conservative wheat growers in control.

The 1st has no major population center. Salina, near the eastern edge of the district, is the largest city in the territory. In contrast to the stagnation common in other parts of the 1st, Salina grew by a healthy 10.9 percent in the 1970s, thanks to the growth of manufacturing jobs at plants operated by Beech Aircraft and Tony's Pizza, a frozen-food company.

Nearby, in Dickinson County, is Abilene, where tourism is centered on Dwight D. Eisenhower's birthplace, gravesite and presidential memorial. Abilene is new to the 1st, but it fits in well with the overall Republican character. In 1980 Ronald Reagan took Dickinson County with 67.6 percent.

Farther west, the ranches grow larger and the population more sparse. The largest cities in the western part of the 1st are Dodge City, which began as a boom town during 19th-century cattle drives, and Garden City, whose emergence as a meatpacking center led to rapid growth in the 1970s. In 1976 farm discontent allowed Jimmy Carter to carry normally Republican Dodge City and surrounding Ford County, but Reagan won them easily in 1980.

Election Returns

1st District		Democrat		Republican	
1976	President	96,421	(45.3%)	111,433	(52.4%)
	House	58,756	(28.6%)	146,292	(71.3%)
1978	Governor	82,753	(49.3%)	81,531	(48.6%)
	Senate	60,640	(35.7%)	102,072	(60.1%)
	House	5,055	(3.6 %)	135,538	(96.4%)
1980	President	56,219	(26.4%)	140,375	(66.0%)
	Senate	66,826	(31.7%)	143,706	(68.3%)
	House	78,128	(38.2%)	126,461	(61.8%)
1982	Governor	72,725	(42.5%)	94,762	(55.4%)
	House	51,079	(30.2%)	115,749	(68.4%)

Demographics

Population: 472,139. **Percent Change from 1970:** 0.2%.

Land Area: 49,399 square miles. **Population per Square Mile:** 9.6.

Counties, 1980 Population: Barber — 6,548; Barton — 31,343; Cheyenne — 3,678; Clark — 2,599; Cloud — 12,494; Comanche — 2,554; Decatur — 4,509; Dickinson — 20,175; Edwards — 4,271; Ellis — 26,098; Ellsworth — 6,640; Finney — 23,825; Ford — 24,315; Gove — 3,726; Graham — 3,995; Grant — 6,977; Gray — 5,138; Greeley — 1,845; Hamilton — 2,514; Haskell — 3,814; Hodgeman — 2,269; Jewell — 5,241; Kearny — 3,435; Kiowa — 4,046; Lane — 2,472; Lincoln — 4,145; Logan — 3,478; Marshall — 12,787; Meade — 4,788; Mitchell — 8,117; Morton — 3,454; Ness — 4,498; Norton — 6,689; Osborne — 5,959; Ottawa — 5,971; Pawnee — 8,065; Phillips — 7,406; Pratt — 10,275; Rawlins — 4,105; Republic — 7,569; Rice — 11,900; Rooks — 7,006; Rush — 4,516; Russell — 8,868; Saline — 48,905; Scott — 5,782; Seward — 17,071; Sheridan — 3,544; Sherman — 7,759; Smith — 5,947; Stafford — 5,694; Stanton — 2,339; Stevens — 4,736; Thomas — 8,451; Trego — 4,165; Wallace — 2,045; Washington — 8,543; Wichita — 3,041.

Cities, 1980 Population: Dodge City — 18,001; Garden City — 18,256; Great Bend — 16,608; Hays — 16,301; Liberal — 14,911; Salina — 41,843.

Race and Ancestry: White — 96.7%; Black — 0.9%; American Indian, Eskimo and Aleut — 0.3%; Asian and Pacific Islander — 0.3%. Spanish Origin — 3.1%. Dutch — 1.3%; English — 10.1%; French — 1.5%; German — 25.3%; Irish — 4.1%; Scottish — 0.6%; Swedish — 1.5%.

Universities, Enrollment: Barton County Community College, Great Bend — 2,218; Cloud County Community College, Concordia — 1,826; Colby Community College, Colby — 1,363; Dodge City Community College, Dodge City — 1,038; Fort Hays State University, Hays — 5,863; Friends Bible College, Haviland — 152; Garden City Community College, Garden City — 1,213; Kansas Technical Institute, Salina — 450; Kansas Wesleyan University, Salina — 490; Marymount College, Salina — 844; Pratt Community College, Pratt — 1,166; St. Mary of the Plains College, Dodge City — 698; Seward County Community College, Liberal — 1,100; Sterling College, Sterling — 489.

Newspapers, Circulation: *Abilene Reflector-Chronicle* (e), Abilene — 5,279; *Beloit Daily Call* (e), Beloit — 3,004; *Blade-Empire* (e), Concordia — 3,790; *Colby Free Press* (m), Colby — 3,176; *Dodge City Daily Globe* (e), Dodge City — 8,886; *The Garden City Telegram* (e), Garden City — 9,676; *Goodland Daily News* (eS), Goodland — 3,075; *Great Bend Tribune* (eS), Great Bend — 11,826; *The Hays Daily News* (eS), Hays — 12,909; *The Lyons Daily News* (e), Lyons — 3,232; *The Russell Daily News* (e), Russell — 3,632; *The Salina Journal* (eS), Salina — 32,540; *Southwest Daily Times* (e), Liberal —

9,164; *Telegram* (e), Norton — 3,749; *The Tiller & Toiler* (e), Larned — 3,018; *Tribune* (e), Pratt — 4,117. *The Hutchinson News* also circulates in the district.

Commercial Television Stations, Affiliation: KAYS, Hays (CBS, ABC); KLOE-TV, Goodland (CBS, ABC); KSNG, Garden City (NBC); KTVC, Ensign (CBS); KUPK-TV, Garden City (ABC). Most of district is located in Wichita-Hutchinson ADI. Portions are in Amarillo (Tex.) ADI and Lincoln (Neb.)-Hastings (Neb.)-Kearney (Neb.) ADI.

Military Installations: Smokey Hill Air National Guard Range, Brookville — 47.

Industries:

Iowa Beef Processors Inc.; Garden City; beef products — 2,000. **Schwans Sales Enterprises Inc.** (Tony's Pizza Service); Salina; frozen foods — 1,200. **Travenol Laboratories Inc.;** Hays; pharmaceutical preparations — 921. **Beech Aircraft Corp.;** Salina; aircraft — 900. **National Beef Packing Co. Inc.** (HQ); Liberal; meatpacking — 800. **XL Corp.;** Dodge City; meats, meat products — 560. **The Fuller Brush Co. Inc.** (Mohawk Brush Co. - HQ); Great Bend; brushes, cleaning agents — 548. **North American Philips Lighting Corp.;** Salina; fluorescent lamps — 500.

2nd District

Topeka, Lawrence

The character of the 2nd, in the northeast corner of the state, was changed markedly by the remap. Nevertheless, the GOP retains a lopsided voter registration edge within the new lines.

The most important changes were in the eastern part of the district. The 2nd lost the Kansas City suburbs of Wyandotte County to the 3rd. This is blue-collar suburban territory, Democratic by registration. The impact of that change was more than canceled, however, by the addition of Douglas County with its University of Kansas population. Douglas was one of three Kansas counties to deny Ronald Reagan an absolute majority in 1980, although he carried it by 4,700 votes. In addition, the academic community tends to prefer moderate Republican politics, shifting the district's balance slightly to the left within the Republican Party as well.

Douglas County is a more consistent liberal influence on the district than Riley County (Manhattan), home of Kansas State University. Kansas State is an agriculture-oriented school, and there is a solid Republican farm vote in rural Riley County. But Riley can be dangerous territory for Republicans; it provided the political base for Democrat Martha Keys, who won the 2nd twice in the 1970s.

Although most of the redistricting argument was over the placement of two academic centers in the 2nd, the district's dominant city is Topeka, the state capital, with a population of 115,266. State government is among the largest employers in Topeka and surrounding Shawnee County, but a substantial industrial base exists as well. Layoffs in the early 1980s at Topeka's large Goodyear tire plant where fortunes waned along with the national automobile industry, battered the area's economy.

Democrats are somewhat stronger in Shawnee County than in less urbanized parts of the state. But both Gerald R. Ford and Reagan won Shawnee County easily. So has every other Republican nominee since Warren G. Harding, except Alf Landon and Barry Goldwater.

The 2nd has a considerable presence of federal instal-

lations. In Leavenworth, along with the legendary federal penitentiary, is the Army's Command and General Staff College at Fort Leavenworth. Junction City is home to Fort Riley, and much of Jackson County's territory consists of the Pottawatomie Indian Reservation.

In addition to the more controversial changes, the constituency gave up three very conservative counties — Marshall and Dickinson to the 1st and Wabaunsee to the 5th — while picking up conservative, rural Clay County.

Election Returns

2nd District		Democrat		Republican	
1976	President	76,297	(42.6%)	97,716	(54.5%)
	House	81,687	(47.2%)	88,425	(51.1%)
1978	Governor	68,935	(48.1%)	70,302	(49.1%)
	Senate	73,338	(50.6%)	67,959	(46.9%)
	House	58,007	(41.6%)	81,467	(58.4%)
1980	President	61,150	(33.9%)	100,343	(55.6%)
	Senate	68,989	(39.1%)	107,633	(60.9%)
	House	79,779	(46.3%)	92,149	(53.5%)
1982	Governor	86,932	(57.8%)	60,656	(40.3%)
	House	86,286	(57.4%)	63,942	(42.6%)

Demographics

Population: 472,988. **Percent Change from 1970:** 5.8%.

Land Area: 7,203 square miles. **Population per Square Mile:** 65.7.

Counties, 1980 Population: Atchison — 18,397; Brown — 11,955; Clay — 9,802; Doniphan — 9,268; Douglas — 67,640; Geary — 29,852; Jackson — 11,644; Jefferson — 15,207; Leavenworth — 54,809; Nemaha — 11,211; Pottawatomie — 14,782; Riley — 63,505; Shawnee — 154,916.

Cities, 1980 Population: Atchison — 11,407; Junction City — 19,305; Lawrence — 52,738; Leavenworth — 33,656; Manhattan — 32,644; Topeka — 115,266.

Race and Ancestry: White — 88.5%; Black — 7.3%; American Indian, Eskimo and Aleut — 1.2%; Asian and Pacific Islander — 1.2%. Spanish Origin — 3.0%. Dutch — 0.6%; English — 9.6%; French — 0.9%; German — 13.8%; Irish — 3.8%; Scottish — 0.5%; Swedish — 1.1%.

Universities, Enrollment: Baker University, Baldwin City — 920; Benedictine College, Atchison — 1,082; Haskell Indian Junior College, Lawrence — 1,028; Highland Community College, Highland — 1,233; Kansas State University, Manhattan — 19,547; Manhattan Christian College, Manhattan — 260; St. Mary College, Leavenworth — 864; University of Kansas, Lawrence — 26,745; Washburn University of Topeka, Topeka — 6,031.

Newspapers, Circulation: *Atchison Daily Globe* (e), Atchison — 6,233; *The Clay Center Dispatch* (e), Clay Center — 3,934; *The Daily Union* (eS), Junction City — 8,560; *Hiawatha Daily World* (e), Hiawatha — 3,426; *Journal-World* (eS), Lawrence — 19,107; *The Leavenworth Times* (eS), Leavenworth — 9,702; *The Manhattan Mercury* (eS), Manhattan — 12,960; *Topeka Capital Journal* (mS), Topeka — 69,104.

Commercial Television Stations, Affiliation: KSNT, Topeka (NBC); WIBW-TV, Topeka (CBS, ABC). District is divided between Topeka ADI and Kansas City (Mo.) ADI.

Military Installations: Forbes Airport (Air Force), Pauline — 959; Fort Leavenworth, Leavenworth — 4,491; Fort Riley, Junction City — 22,589.

Industries:

Atchison, Topeka & Santa Fe Railroad; Topeka; railroad operations — 2,800. **Goodyear Tire & Rubber Co. Inc.;** Topeka; tires, inner tubes — 2,008. **Stormont-Vail Hospital;** Topeka; hospital — 1,470. **St. Francis Hospital & Medical Center;** Topeka; hospital — 1,340. **Veterans Administration;** Topeka; veterans' hospital — 1,260.

American Yearbook Co. (HQ); Topeka; book publishing, printing — 1,150. **Hallmark Cards Inc.;** Lawrence; greeting cards — 1,000. **The Menninger Foundation;** Topeka; psychiatric hospital — 1,000. **Hallmark Cards Inc.;** Leavenworth; gift wrap, writing paper — 930. **Hallmark Cards Inc.;** Topeka; greeting cards — 850. **E. I. du Pont de Nemours & Co. Inc.;** Topeka; plastics materials — 520. **Security Benefits Life Insurance Co.;** Topeka; life insurance — 509. **McCall Pattern Co.;** Manhattan; home sewing patterns — 500.

3rd District

East — Kansas City

When Rodgers and Hammerstein wrote that "Everything's up-to-date in Kansas City," they meant Kansas City, Mo. Kansas City, Kan., on the western bank of the Missouri River, has long lived in the shadow of its larger and more bustling namesake. Many Kansans in the metropolitan area read Missouri newspapers, travel through a Missouri airport and railroad terminal and cheer the Missouri baseball and football teams they watch on Missouri-based television stations.

The 3rd District, centered around blue-collar Kansas City and its affluent suburbs, is not totally dependent on its proximity to the Missouri metropolis; yet it remains within the orbit of Missouri's economy. The 3rd's suburbs, where stately homes and manicured lawns attest to some of the highest per-capita incomes among any counties in the nation, are home to many Trans World Airlines pilots and executives who commute to the company's Missouri offices.

Johnson County, which has the most affluent Kansas City, Mo., suburbs on the Kansas side, is strongly Republican and growing in population and political influence. Urbanized Kansas City, Kan., the other population center in the 3rd, is declining in both. Johnson accounts for about 60 percent of the district vote; Wyandotte County, which contains Kansas City, Kan., about 30 percent.

Once one of the Great Plains' major stockyard centers, Kansas City, Kan., has taken advantage of its railroad links to diversify its economy in the post-World War II years with food-processing plants, soap products and some electronics manufacturers; a General Motors assembly plant is among Wyandotte County's largest employers. But the urban-based population shrunk significantly in the 1970s, with Kansas City's 4.2 percent loss pacing Wyandotte County's 7.8 percent drop. With a black population of more than 25 percent, Kansas City has the largest concentration of minority voters in Kansas.

Despite its shrinking population Wyandotte County remains the state's most important Democratic outpost. It gave Jimmy Carter 59.9 percent in 1976 and 54.4 percent in 1980. But the voting power of urban Democrats is more than offset by voters in the 3rd's solidly Republican suburbs. Gerald R. Ford in 1976 and Ronald Reagan in 1980 defeated Carter by better than 2-to-1 in Johnson County.

The 1982 remap saw Wyandotte County reunified within the 3rd District boundaries. The 3rd yielded Douglas County to the 2nd and Franklin County to the 5th and gained largely rural Linn County and semi-rural Miami County from the 5th. Within the new boundaries of the

3rd, there are 87,667 registered Republicans, 73,140 registered Democrats and 87,237 unaffiliated or third-party voters.

Election Returns

3rd District		Democrat		Republican	
1976	President	78,764	(41.8%)	104,811	(55.6%)
	House	53,240	(31.2%)	112,932	(66.2%)
1978	Governor	57,008	(43.6%)	68,862	(52.7%)
	Senate	57,175	(43.1%)	68,315	(51.5%)
	House	9,852	(9.7%)	91,735	(90.2%)
1980	President	70,201	(35.8%)	108,207	(55.1%)
	Senate	66,370	(36.2%)	117,172	(63.8%)
	House	75,874	(40.9%)	104,912	(56.5%)
1982	Governor	85,769	(60.8%)	50,870	(36.0%)
	House	53,140	(38.3%)	82,117	(59.2%)

Demographics

Population: 472,456. **Percent Change from 1970:** 8.9%.

Land Area: 1,818 square miles. **Population per Square Mile:** 259.9.

Counties, 1980 Population: Johnson — 270,269; Linn — 8,234; Miami — 21,618; Wyandotte — 172,335.

Cities, 1980 Population: Kansas City — 161,087; Leawood — 13,360; Lenexa — 18,639; Merriam — 10,794; Olathe — 37,258; Overland Park — 81,784; Prairie Village — 24,657; Shawnee — 29,653.

Race and Ancestry: White — 88.1%; Black — 9.6%; American Indian, Eskimo and Aleut — 0.3%; Asian and Pacific Islander — 0.8%. Spanish Origin — 2.6%. Dutch — 0.5%; English — 10.2%; French — 0.7%; German — 9.6%; Irish — 4.4%; Italian — 0.7%; Polish — 0.8%; Scottish — 0.5%; Swedish — 0.8%.

Universities, Enrollment: Central Baptist Theological Seminary, Seminary Heights — 136; Donnelly College, Kansas City — 495; Johnson County Community College, Overland Park — 6,358; Kansas City Kansas Community College, Kansas City — 3,580; Mid-America Nazarene College, Olathe — 1,354.

Newspapers, Circulation: *The Daily News of Johnson County* (mS), Olathe — 10,345; *The Kansas City Kansan* (eS), Kansas City — 20,667. Kansas City (Mo.) *Times* and Kansas City (Mo.) *Star* also circulate in the district.

Commercial Television Stations, Affiliation: KCMO-TV, Kansas City (CBS); KFYC, Kansas City (None). Entire district is located in Kansas City (Mo.) ADI. *(For other Kansas City stations, see 5th district in Missouri.)*

Military Installations: Sunflower Army Ammunition Plant, Desoto — 581.

Industries:

University of Kansas Medical Center; Kansas City; hospital — 5,000. **General Motors Corp.** (GM Assembly Div.); Kansas City; motor vehicle bodies — 4,800. **Atchison, Topeka & Santa Fe Railroad;** Kansas City; railroad operations — 1,500. **J. C. Penney Co. Inc.;** Shawnee Mission; warehouse, storage — 1,500. **Shawnee Mission Medical Center;** Shawnee Mission; hospital — 1,420.

King Radio Corp. (HQ); Olathe; aircraft radio transmitting equipment — 1,350. **Bethany Medical Center;** Kansas City; hospital — 1,300. **Owens-Corning Fiberglas Corp.;** Kansas City; insulation — 1,250. **Certain-Teed Corp.;** Kansas City; asbestos products — 1,100. **Owens-Corning Fiberglas Corp.** (Power & Process Contracting Div.); Shawnee Mission; special trade contracting — 1,000. **United Telecommunications** (HQ); Shawnee Mission; telecommunications equipment, technology — 780. **Associated Wholesale Grocers** (HQ); Kansas City; grocery wholesaling — 700. **Colgate-Palmolive Co.;** Kansas City; soaps, cosmetics — 680. **North Supply Co.** (HQ); Shawnee Mission; communications wiring supplies — 645.

Farmers Insurance Group; Shawnee Mission; insurance — 600. **General Motors Corp.** (Delco-Remy Div.); Olathe; electrical equipment for internal combustion engines — 600. **Sunshine Biscuits Inc.;** Kansas City; biscuits — 600. **Colt Industries Operating Corp.** (Fairbanks Morse Pump Div.); Kansas City; pumps, pumping equipment — 550. **Yellow Freight System Inc.;** Shawnee Mission; trucking — 550. **SFE Technologies** (Electro Dynamics Corp.); Shawnee Mission; electronic components — 520. **Allstate Insurance Co. Inc.;** Shawnee Mission; life insurance — 500. **Mid-West Conveyor Co. Inc.** (HQ); Kansas City; conveyors — 500. **Procter & Gamble Mfg. Co. Inc.;** Kansas City; soaps, detergents — 500.

4th District

South Central — Wichita

The Wichita-based 4th has new boundaries that help the Democrats. That party's slim registration advantage of 1,078 voters over the GOP — 87,886 to 86,809, with 87,872 independents — is an improvement for them over the old lines, and results from adding portions of Sedgwick County previously in the 5th District.

Despite the blue-collar Democratic presence in Wichita, provided by aircraft workers with Southern roots, Sedgwick County often is tilted into the GOP column by its rural outer precincts. Gerald R. Ford in 1976 and Ronald Reagan in 1980 both carried Sedgwick.

Since World War II, Wichita has tied its fortunes to the general-aviation and aerospace industries. The city once built 60 percent of the private airplanes in the nation, with such firms as Cessna, Beech and Gates Learjet employing thousands on assembly lines. But with orders for new planes declining in the early 1980s, the small airplane firms and the area subcontractors that depend on them have furloughed several thousand workers.

The steadiest economic influence in Wichita has been Boeing's military equipment plant, which, with the prospect of increased Pentagon spending, has not suffered severely during the early 1980s. McConnell Air Force Base, outside Wichita, is home to aging Titan intercontinental ballistic missiles. The presence of the Titans raised a storm of controversy in 1978 after a chemical leak resulted in the death of a serviceman.

In addition to the aviation industry, Wichita retains an identity as a corporate base for Kansas' oil industry, which played an important role in the city's early development. Oil has a modest impact in Kansas now, with most of the wells only marginally productive.

In the remap, the 4th gained Harper, Sumner and the remainder of Sedgwick counties from the 5th in return for McPherson, Marion and Harvey counties.

Election Returns

4th District		Democrat		Republican	
1976	President	87,817	(48.2%)	89,301	(49.0%)
	House	84,747	(48.5%)	85,689	(49.1%)
1978	Governor	78,627	(55.3%)	57,320	(40.3%)
	Senate	61,922	(41.7%)	80,620	(54.3%)
	House	94,075	(66.0%)	48,173	(33.8%)

4th District		Democrat		Republican	
1980	President	70,871	(37.2%)	100,757	(52.8%)
	Senate	67,697	(38.6%)	107,574	(61.4%)
	House	109,608	(61.7%)	67,188	(37.8%)
1982	Governor	79,996	(54.6%)	62,482	(42.7%)
	House	107,326	(73.9%)	35,478	(24.5%)

Demographics

Population: 473,180. **Percent Change from 1970:** 4.7%.

Land Area: 5,117 square miles. **Population per Square Mile:** 92.5.

Counties, 1980 Population: Harper — 7,778; Kingman — 8,960; Reno — 64,983; Sedgwick — 366,531; Sumner — 24,928.

Cities, 1980 Population: Hutchinson — 40,284; Wichita — 279,272.

Race and Ancestry: White — 89.2%; Black — 7.1%; American Indian, Eskimo and Aleut — 0.8%; Asian and Pacific Islander — 1.2%. Spanish Origin — 3.0%. Dutch — 0.7%; English — 11.2%; French — 0.9%; German — 13.4%; Irish — 4.0%; Swedish — 0.6%.

Universities, Enrollment: Friends University, Wichita — 935; Hutchinson Community College, Hutchinson — 2,594; Kansas Newman College, Wichita — 717; Wichita State University, Wichita — 16,621.

Newspapers, Circulation: *The Hutchinson News* (all day, S), Hutchinson — 44,564; *Wellington Daily News* (e), Wellington — 4,898; *The Wichita Eagle-Beacon* (mS), Wichita — 123,525.

Commercial Television Stations, Affiliation: KAKE-TV, Wichita (ABC); KSNW-TV, Wichita (NBC); KTVH, Hutchinson (CBS). Entire district is located in Wichita-Hutchinson ADI.

Military Installations: McConnell Air Force Base, Wichita — 5,223.

Industries:

The Boeing Co. Inc.; Wichita; aircraft parts — 17,600. **Beech Aircraft Corp.** (HQ); Wichita; aircraft — 6,319. **The Cessna Aircraft Co.** (HQ); Wichita; aircraft — 5,735. **St. Francis Hospital;** Wichita; hospital — 3,100. **Wesley Medical Center Inc.;** Wichita; hospital — 2,600.

St. Joseph Medical Center; Wichita; hospital — 1,950. **Eby & Associates of Alabama;** Wichita; dam construction — 1,200. **Cessna Aircraft Co.** (Fluid Power Div.); Hutchinson; hydraulic pumps — 1,138. **Gates Learjet Corp.** (HQ); Wichita; aircraft — 1,120. **Koch Industries Inc.** (Koch Oil Co. - HQ); Wichita; crude oil extraction, production — 1,100. **NCR Corp.** (Engineering & Mfg.); Wichita; minicomputers — 1,000. **J. I. Case Co.** (Light Equipment Div.); Wichita; light construction, farm equipment — 850. **Coleman Co. Inc.** (HQ); Wichita; outdoor electrical equipment — 800.

Derby Refining Co.; Wichita; petroleum refining — 800. **Superior Building Maintenance Inc.;** Wichita; janitorial services — 750. **Fourth Financial Corp.;** Wichita; banking — 714. **Wichita Eagle & Beacon Publishing;** Wichita; newspaper publishing — 675. **Vulcan Materials Co.** (Chemical Div.); Wichita; industrial inorganic chemicals — 620. **Pizza Hut Inc.** (HQ); Wichita; fast food restaurants — 565. **Tweco Products Inc.** (HQ); Wichita; electric welding apparatus — 525. **Trailways Inc.** (American Bus Lines); Wichita; intercity bus operations — 500.

5th District

Southeast — Emporia, Pittsburg

The 5th, in the southeast corner of the state, has a hilly landscape that belies the image of Kansas as a flat expanse of wheat and an ethnic population at variance with the other regions. The area is still called the Balkans, a reference to the Eastern Europeans who came to work in the area's mines at the turn of the century.

Recent remaps have stretched the district north and west, blurring its regional identity somewhat. In the 1980s the 5th's borders reach closer than ever toward central Kansas' wheat-growing plains.

While a Democrat has not represented the 5th in Congress since 1958, southeastern Kansas historically has been among the areas of the state most partial to Democrats. Aside from the Eastern European ethnic influence, there is a strong Southern contingent and few of the Yankee Republicans who dominate politics in the rest of the state. But this is a conservative area, one that has consistently preferred Republican state and national candidates in recent years. Redistricting will probably make the Republican habit stronger.

With the decline of the region's once-booming lead, zinc and coal mines after the early 1960s, the area has tried — with only limited success — to diversify its economy. Agriculture, primarily soybeans and wheat, remains a major industry. Manufacturing plants are scattered through the district, and there is some natural-gas drilling in the south, along the Oklahoma border.

Emporia, with a population of 25,287 the largest city in the district, is at the center of the Flint Hills that run the length of eastern Kansas. Growing from its start as a stockyard center at the railway junction of Santa Fe lines, Emporia is the major commercial center of the district. Some of its large population of Welsh extraction still celebrate St. David's Day, honoring the patron saint of Wales. Emporia and Lyon County lean Republican, although not by as much as most of the wheat-growing counties farther west.

The small industrial city of Pittsburg has a sizable number of blue-collar Democrats who work in the area's lead and zinc mines and manufacturing plants. Pittsburg is the largest city in Crawford County, which gave Jimmy Carter 54.7 percent of the vote in 1976. In 1980 Carter received 45.4 percent in Crawford, two percentage points behind Ronald Reagan.

In the remap, the 5th yielded Harper, Sumner and part of Sedgwick counties to the 4th and gave up Miami and Linn counties to the 3rd. The 5th gained Harvey, McPherson and Marion counties from the 4th, Wabaunsee County from the 2nd and Franklin County from the 3rd.

Election Returns

5th District		Democrat		Republican	
1976	President	91,122	(46.8%)	99,491	(51.1%)
	House	70,191	(37.8%)	111,848	(60.2%)
1978	Governor	76,502	(50.2%)	70,000	(46.0%)
	Senate	64,527	(42.1%)	84,388	(55.0%)
	House	66,012	(43.6%)	83,673	(55.2%)
1980	President	67,709	(33.9%)	117,130	(58.7%)
	Senate	70,389	(36.5%)	122,601	(63.5%)
	House	61,160	(31.7%)	129,164	(67.0%)
1982	Governor	80,350	(52.1%)	70,586	(45.8%)
	House	47,676	(31.1%)	103,551	(67.6%)

Demographics

Population: 472,916. **Percent Change from 1970:** 6.2%.

Land Area: 18,243 square miles. **Population per Square Mile:** 25.9.

Counties, 1980 Population: Allen — 15,654; Anderson — 8,749; Bourbon — 15,969; Butler — 44,782; Chase — 3,309; Chautauqua — 5,016; Cherokee — 22,304; Coffey — 9,370; Cowley — 36,824; Crawford — 37,916; Elk — 3,918; Franklin — 22,062; Greenwood — 8,764; Harvey — 30,531; Labette — 25,682; Lyon — 35,108; Marion — 13,522; McPherson — 26,855; Montgomery — 42,281; Morris — 6,419; Neosho — 18,967; Osage — 15,319; Wabaunsee — 6,867; Wilson — 12,128; Woodson — 4,600.

Cities, 1980 Population: Arkansas City — 13,201; Chanute 10,506; Coffeyville — 15,185; El Dorado — 10,510; Emporia — 25,287; Independence — 10,598; McPherson — 11,753; Newton — 16,332; Ottawa — 11,016; Parsons — 12,898; Pittsburg — 18,770; Winfield — 10,736.

Race and Ancestry: White — 96.2%; Black — 1.8%; American Indian, Eskimo and Aleut — 0.7%; Asian and Pacific Islander — 0.3%. Spanish Origin — 1.7%. Dutch — 1.0%; English — 11.5%; French — 0.9%; German — 13.3%; Irish — 3.6%; Italian — 0.6%; Swedish — 1.2%.

Universities, Enrollment: Allen County Community College, Iola — 848; Bethany College, Lindsborg — 840; Bethel College, North Newton — 755; Butler County Community College, El Dorado — 2,153; Central College, McPherson — 288; Coffeyville Community College, Coffeyville — 1,496; Cowley County Community College, Arkansas City — 1,910; Emporia State University, Emporia — 6,411; Fort Scott Community College, Fort Scott — 1,077; Hesston College, Hesston — 653; Independence Community College, Independence — 1,076; Labette Community College, Parsons — 1,554; McPherson College, McPherson — 542; Neosho County Community College, Chanute — 713; Ottawa University, Ottawa — 530; Pittsburg State University, Pittsburg — 5,468; St. John's College, Winfield — 212; Southwestern College, Winfield — 652; Tabor College, Hillsboro — 478.

Newspapers, Circulation: *Arkansas City Traveler* (e), Arkansas City — 6,905; *The Augusta Daily Gazette* (e), Augusta — 2,953; *The Coffeyville Journal* (eS), Coffeyville — 8,895; *The Columbus Daily Advocate* (e), Columbus — 3,273; *The Daily Republican* (e), Burlington — 2,674; *The El Dorado Times* (e), El Dorado — 5,460; *The Emporia Gazette* (e), Emporia — 11,789; *The Fort Scott Tribune* (e), Fort Scott — 5,918; *Herald* (e), Ottawa — 6,262; *Independence Daily Reporter* (eS), Independence — 8,166; *Iola Register* (e), Iola — 5,408; *McPherson Sentinel* (e), McPherson — 6,000; *Morning Sun* (mS), Pittsburg — 13,402; *Newton Kansan* (e), Newton — 8,623; *The Parsons Sun* (e), Parsons — 9,119; *Republican* (e), Council Grove — 3,010; *The Tribune* (e), Chanute — 5,940; *Winfield Daily Courier* (e), Winfield — 6,315.

Commercial Television Stations, Affiliation: KOAM-TV, Pittsburg (NBC). District is divided among Topeka ADI, Wichita-Hutchinson ADI, Joplin (Mo.)-Pittsburg ADI, Kansas City (Mo.) ADI and Tulsa (Okla.) ADI.

Military Installations: Kansas Army Ammunition Plant, Parsons — 745.

Nuclear Power Plants: Wolf Creek 1, Wolf Creek (Westinghouse, Daniel International).

Industries:

Hesston Corp. (HQ); Hesston; farm equipment — 1,200. **Automotive Controls** (ACC Electronics); Independence; transformers — 900. **Western Casualty and Surety Co.** (HQ); Fort Scott; casualty insurance — 860. **Didde Graphic Systems Corp.** (HQ); Emporia; graphic arts machinery — 700. **Day & Zimmerman Inc.** (Kansas Army Munition Plant); Parsons; ammunition — 690.

The Cessna Aircraft Co.; Winfield; aircraft parts — 650. **Emerson Electric Co.**; Independence; electric motors — 600. **Interstate Brands Corp.** (Dolly Madison Cakes); Emporia; bakery products — 550. **Sterling Drug Inc.** (Pharmaceutical Production Group); McPherson; pharmaceutical preparations — 525. **Getty Refining & Marketing Co.**; El Dorado; petroleum refining — 500. **Yellow Freight System Inc.**; Baxter Springs; trucking — 500.

Kentucky

Working its way around complaints of interference from Washington, Kentucky's Democratic-controlled Legislature approved a congressional map that redrew the lines in the populous northern and central counties while leaving the rest of the state's districts basically intact. Democratic Gov. John Y. Brown signed the bill on March 10, 1982.

The most important alterations provoked little controversy, since each incumbent was able to retain the heart of his old district. There was unexpected legislative turmoil, however, over the fate of small Jessamine County in central Kentucky.

Jessamine's 27,000 residents make up less than 1 percent of the state population. But the county, split between the 5th and 6th districts in the 1970s, was a political hot potato throughout the redistricting process. Legislative leaders finally placed it in the sprawling, poverty-stricken 5th District over the objections of county officials, who contended that Jessamine was economically and culturally tied to nearby Lexington in the Bluegrass 6th.

The county drew many legislative allies. But during final floor consideration of the redistricting plan, Democratic Rep. Carl D. Perkins of the 7th District opposed any efforts to take Jessamine out of the 5th. Perkins feared that the shift of Jessamine would force other changes that could cost him part of his base in the southern portion of the mountainous 7th.

As the dean of the congressional delegation, Perkins had considerable clout. With the help of the legislative leadership, his forces defeated amendments that would have placed Jessamine in the 6th. The margin was one vote in both the state House and Senate.

Each chamber subsequently approved the redistricting plan by lopsided margins. The House passed the final plan Jan. 27, 1982, by an 85-9 vote. The Senate approved the remap by a vote of 34 to 3 on Feb. 24.

Kentucky grew moderately in the 1970s — slightly more than the national average. But the major changes in district lines were forced by population losses in the Louisville area. The predominantly urban 3rd District was forced to expand into GOP suburbs. In turn, the neighboring 4th District had to move into rural northern Kentucky to regain the population lost to the 3rd. The adjoining Lexington-based 6th District moved south and east. All three incumbents were thought to be weakened by the changes, but they handily won re-election in 1982.

Age of Population

District	Population Under 18	Voting Age Population	Population 65 & Over (% of VAP)	Median Age
1	146,833	379,011	72,755 (19.2%)	30.7
2	159,405	361,229	52,022 (14.4%)	27.4
3	140,460	381,792	63,347 (16.6%)	30.1
4	160,015	363,075	50,877 (14.0%)	29.5
5	164,151	359,513	63,341 (17.6%)	29.4
6	141,760	377,249	53,093 (14.1%)	28.8
7	170,106	356,178	54,393 (15.3%)	28.1
State	1,082,730	2,578,047	409,828 (15.9%)	29.1

Income and Occupation

District	Median Family Income	White Collar Workers	Blue Collar Workers	Service Workers	Farm Workers
1	$ 16,457	39.1%	42.2%	12.9%	5.7%
2	15,815	40.6	40.3	12.3	6.9
3	18,437	51.5	32.9	15.0	0.5
4	21,251	53.8	32.2	11.6	2.4
5	11,578	35.6	44.8	11.8	7.8
6	17,767	53.1	28.5	13.0	5.5
7	14,311	39.0	46.3	11.4	3.3
State	$ 16,444	45.6%	37.3%	12.7%	4.4%

Education: School Years Completed

District	8 Years or Fewer	4 Years of High School	4 Years of College or More	Median School Years
1	31.1%	34.0%	8.4%	12.1
2	31.0	33.9	9.6	12.1
3	21.3	34.1	12.8	12.3
4	20.9	35.5	14.9	12.4
5	48.6	24.1	6.9	11.5
6	24.4	30.6	17.4	12.4
7	42.8	26.8	7.3	11.7
State	31.3%	31.3%	11.1%	12.1

KENTUCKY

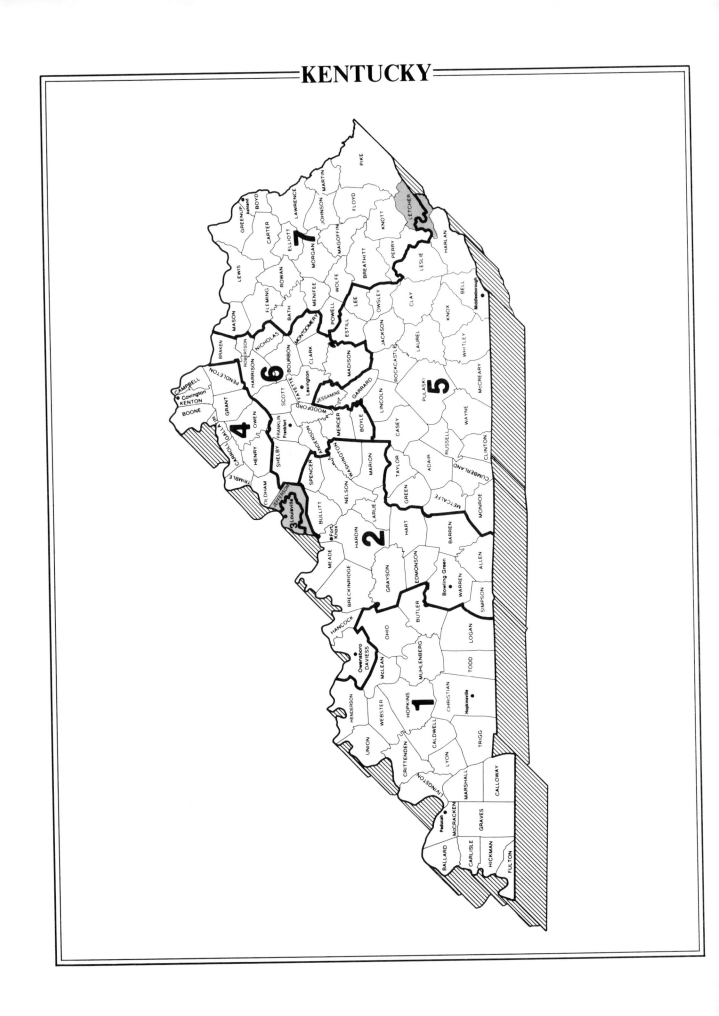

Housing and Residential Patterns

District	Owner Occupied	Renter Occupied	Urban	Rural
1	74.2%	25.8%	39.8%	60.2%
2	72.0	28.0	44.3	55.7
3	61.9	38.1	99.5	0.5
4	73.4	26.6	68.7	31.3
5	73.8	26.2	18.9	81.1
6	61.3	38.7	64.2	35.8
7	74.9	25.1	21.2	78.8
State	70.0%	30.0%	50.9%	49.1%

1st District

West — Paducah

The birthplace of Jefferson Davis, Kentucky's 1st District votes more like the Deep South than like other parts of the state. In contests for governor and for the U.S. Senate, the 1st generally turns in the highest Democratic majorities in Kentucky. Jimmy Carter won it in 1976 with 65 percent of the vote, his highest share in the state. Except for the three years following the expulsion of Democrat Henry C. Burnett in 1861 for support of rebellion, this area of Kentucky has never had Republican representation in the U.S. House.

But the district's tradition is also conservative. The western lowlands near the Mississippi River — known as the Jackson Purchase — were once slaveholding territory. This is the only part of Kentucky where cotton is grown.

The district does not have a massive black population; only one of the 24 counties in the 1st is more than 20 percent black. But the heritage of the district and its relative poverty made it fertile ground for the rural populism of independent presidential candidate George C. Wallace in 1968.

Four of the five counties Wallace carried in Kentucky are in the 1st. Two were in the Purchase area. The other two —Christian County (Hopkinsville) and Todd County (Elkton) — are located further east along the Tennessee border.

No city in the 1st District has more than 30,000 people. Most of the area is closely tied to agriculture; soybeans and dark-fired (or smokeless) tobacco are major crops. Coal fields provide employment in the northeastern part of the district. Several small chemical factories are prominent in small cities such as Paducah and Calvert City.

The Ohio River port of Paducah long has been the population center and political capital of western Kentucky. It was the home of Alben W. Barkley, longtime Democratic senator and vice president under Harry S Truman. Barkley helped provide an economic shot-in-the-arm to Paducah by steering an Atomic Energy Commission plant to the area. But the city has lost population since 1950. Recent growth in the Paducah area has been in neighboring Livingston and Marshall counties, which both enjoyed population gains of more than 20 percent in the 1970s.

About 60 miles southeast of Paducah and 10 miles north of Clarksville, Tenn., is bustling Hopkinsville, an agricultural market and trade center for the nearby Fort Campbell military base. With its highly mobile population, the Hopkinsville area has developed more independent voting habits than the rest of the district.

Christian was one of only four counties in the 1st that Reagan carried in 1980. The others were traditionally Republican counties in the northern hills. But together these three GOP bastions — Butler, Crittenden and Ohio counties — have less than 10 percent of the district population.

Redistricting made only one small change in the 1st. Rural Ohio County, formerly split between the 1st and 2nd districts, is now entirely in the 1st, bringing in about 8,700 new constituents.

Election Returns

1st District		Democrat		Republican	
1976	President	114,194	(64.8%)	59,226	(33.6%)
	House	120,411	(81.6%)	27,209	(18.4%)
1978	Senate	37,126	(66.6%)	17,431	(31.3%)
	House	44,664	(100.0%)	—	
1979	Governor	82,909	(65.3%)	44,146	(34.7%)
1980	President	102,503	(53.9%)	83,296	(43.8%)
	Senate	106,063	(73.8%)	37,802	(26.3%)
	House	120,491	(99.0%)	1,201	(1.0%)
1982	House	x[1]		—[1]	

[1] *No votes tabulated where candidate was unopposed; x indicates winner.*

Demographics

Population: 525,844. **Percent Change from 1970:** 12.3%.

Land Area: 9,132 square miles. **Population per Square Mile:** 57.6.

Counties, 1980 Population: Ballard — 8,798; Butler — 11,064; Caldwell 13,473; Calloway 30,031; Carlisle — 5,487; Christian — 66,878; Crittenden — 9,207; Fulton — 8,971; Graves — 34,049; Henderson — 40,849; Hickman — 6,065; Hopkins — 46,174; Livingston — 9,219; Logan — 24,138; Lyon — 6,490; Marshall — 25,637; McCracken — 61,310; McLean — 10,090; Muhlenberg — 32,238; Ohio — 21,765; Todd — 11,874; Trigg — 9,384; Union — 17,821; Webster — 14,832.

Cities, 1980 Population: Henderson — 24,834; Hopkinsville — 27,318; Madisonville — 16,979; Mayfield — 10,705; Murray — 14,248; Paducah — 29,325.

Race and Ancestry: White — 90.5%; Black — 8.8%; American Indian, Eskimo and Aleut — 0.1%; Asian and Pacific Islander — 0.3%. Spanish Origin — 0.9%. English — 24.9%; French — 0.7%; German — 4.1%; Irish — 6.3%.

Universities, Enrollment: Draughon's Business College, Paducah — 287; Institute of Electronic Technology, Paducah — 175; Murray State University, Murray — 8,061; Henderson Community College, Henderson — 843; Hopkinsville Community College, Hopkinsville — 1,089; Madisonville Community College, Madisonville — 843; Paducah Community College, Paducah — 1,850.

Newspapers, Circulation: *Fulton Daily Leader* (e), Fulton — 3,225; *The Gleaner* (mS), Henderson — 10,963; *Kentucky New Era* (e), Hopkinsville — 15,561; *Mayfield Messenger* (e), Mayfield — 7,251; *Messenger* (e), Madisonville — 10,928; *The Murray Ledger and Times* (e), Murray — 7,629; *The Paducah Sun* (eS), Paducah — 30,663.

Commercial Television Stations, Affiliation: WPSD-TV, Paducah (NBC). District is divided among Evansville (Ind.) ADI, Nashville (Tenn.) ADI and Paducah-Cape Girardeau (Mo.)-Harrisburg (Ill.) ADI.

Military Installations: Fort Campbell, see Tennessee Congressional District 7.

Industries:

Union Carbide Corp. (Nuclear Div.); Paducah; inorganic chemicals — 1,810. **General Tire & Rubber Co.;** Mayfield; tires — 1,500. **Pyro Mining Co. Inc.;** Sturgis; coal mining — 1,150. **Island Creek Coal Co.** (West Kentucky Coal Div.); Madisonville; coal mining — 1,142. **Regional Medical Center;** Madisonville; hospital — 1,100. **Illinois Central Gulf Railroad** (Paducah Shops Div.); Paducah; engine repairing — 1,000. **Lourdes Hospital Inc.;** Paducah; hospital — 1,000.

ARCO Aluminum Co.; Henderson; aluminum smelting — 970. **Quaker Oats Co.** (Fisher-Price Toys Div.); Murray; toys — 800. **Borg-Warner Corp.** (York Div.); Madisonville; air conditioners — 700. **B. F. Goodrich Co.;** Calvert City; synthetic rubber — 680. **S. K. W. Alloys Inc.;** Calvert City; ferroalloys — 650. **Air Products & Chemicals Inc.;** Calvert City; industrial chemicals — 600. **Peabody Coal Co.;** Morganfield; coal mining — 600.

Pennwalt Corp.; Calvert City; industrial chemicals — 600. **Westvaco Corp.;** Wickliffe; pulp, paper mill — 550. **Emerson Electric Co.;** Russellville; electrical motors, generators — 500. **E. R. Carpenter Co. Inc.;** Russellville; urethane foam — 500. **Peabody Coal Co.;** Morganfield; coal mining — 500. **Pennwalt Corp.** (Industrial Chemical Div.); Calvert City; alkalies, acids — 500. **Thomas Industries Inc.** (Residential Lighting Div.); Hopkinsville; lighting fixtures — 500.

2nd District

West Central — Owensboro

Perched between the staunchly Democratic 1st and the reliably Republican 5th, the 2nd is a swing district in state and national elections.

Republicans are consistent winners in only three small counties in the 18-county district. The three — Allen, Edmonson and Grayson — were hotbeds of Union support in west central Kentucky during the Civil War. The district includes Abraham Lincoln's birthplace and boyhood home, both near Hodgensville, in Larue County.

But GOP candidates often carry the three major population centers — Daviess County (Owensboro), Hardin County (Elizabethtown) and Warren County (Bowling Green). Together they cast nearly half the district vote. Ronald Reagan won all but Daviess in 1980, affording him a narrow plurality in the 2nd.

The T-shaped district is diverse. Primarily agricultural, it has some industry in Owensboro and Bowling Green. The 2nd takes in some of the Bluegrass region in the east, touches the Louisville suburbs in the north and includes the rolling hill country of the Pennyrile region in the southwest. The geographic heart of the district is the Knobs area, a region of sinkholes and caves that includes the Mammoth Cave National Park.

Warren County's 24 percent growth rate in the 1970s was the highest of the district's major population centers. Bowling Green is the home of Western Kentucky University, the largest college in the state west of Louisville.

The fastest growth in the 1970s outside the district's population centers was in Bullitt County, a part of the Louisville suburbs. A controversial busing plan in metropolitan Jefferson County helped fuel a 66 percent growth rate in neighboring Bullitt, the second largest population increase in the state. With a sizable blue-collar element that frequently bolts the Democratic ticket, Bullitt was the only Kentucky county outside the 1st to vote for George C. Wallace in his 1968 presidential bid.

Along the Ohio River in the northwest corner of the district is Owensboro, the largest city in the 2nd and the

third largest in the state. Nearby oil and coal fields and a large General Electric plant provide an industrial base.

Between Owensboro and Louisville is Hardin County, the home of Fort Knox. The large military presence makes it the most populous county in the 2nd. But many of the military personnel do not vote in the district, and Hardin regularly has a lower turnout than either Daviess or Warren counties.

The rest of the district is rural. Tobacco and livestock are mainstays of the economy. Republicans are strongest in the poorer farm counties in the center of the district; Democrats run best in the outer Bluegrass counties to the northeast.

Because it had about 19,000 more residents in 1980 than the ideal district population, the 2nd shed rural Anderson County in the northeast and half of rural Ohio County in the west. The changes did not alter the political complexion of the district. Ohio County is reliably Republican and Anderson County usually votes Democratic.

Election Returns

2nd District		Democrat		Republican	
1976	President	75,633	(54.9%)	60,030	(43.6%)
	House	75,424	(60.3%)	49,683	(39.7%)
1978	Senate	33,573	(61.0%)	20,322	(36.9%)
	House	34,774	(100.0%)	—	
1979	Governor	71,112	(58.0%)	51,452	(42.0%)
1980	President	78,356	(47.0%)	83,861	(50.3%)
	Senate	99,776	(67.2%)	48,788	(32.8%)
	House	94,940	(65.7%)	49,631	(34.3%)
1982	House	49,571	(73.8%)	17,561	(26.2%)

Demographics

Population: 520,634. **Percent Change from 1970:** 17.5%.

Land Area: 6,790 square miles. **Population per Square Mile:** 76.7.

Counties, 1980 Population: Allen — 14,128; Barren — 34,009; Breckinridge — 16,861; Bullitt — 43,346; Daviess — 85,949; Edmonson — 9,962; Grayson — 20,854; Hancock — 7,742; Hardin — 88,917; Hart — 15,402; Larue — 11,922; Marion — 17,910; Meade — 22,854; Nelson — 27,584; Simpson — 14,673; Spencer — 5,929; Warren — 71,828; Washington — 10,764.

Cities, 1980 Population: Bowling Green — 40,450; Elizabethtown — 15,380; Glasgow — 12,958; Owensboro — 54,450; Radcliff — 14,519.

Race and Ancestry: White — 92.9%; Black — 6.1%; American Indian, Eskimo and Aleut — 0.1%; Asian and Pacific Islander — 0.5%. Spanish Origin — 1.0%. English — 24.9%; French — 0.8%; German — 5.4%; Irish — 6.5%.

Universities, Enrollment: Bowling Green Business College, Bowling Green — 288; Brescia College, Owensboro — 860; Elizabethtown Community College, Elizabethtown — 1,946; Kentucky Wesleyan College, Owensboro — 925; Owensboro Business College, Owensboro — 453; St. Catharine College, St. Catharine — 243; Western Kentucky University, Bowling Green — 13,332.

Newspapers, Circulation: *Messenger-Inquirer* (mS), Owensboro — 32,711; *The News Enterprise* (e), Elizabethtown — 12,205; *Park City Daily News* (eS), Bowling Green — 18,648; *Times* (eS), Glasgow — 7,159. Louisville *Courier-Journal* also circulates in the district.

Commercial Television Stations, Affiliation: WBKO, Bowling Green (ABC). Most of district is located in Louisville ADI. Portions are in Bowling Green ADI, Evansville (Ind.) ADI and Nashville (Tenn.) ADI.

Military Installations: Fort Knox, Radcliff — 21,571.

Industries:

Union Underwear Co. Inc. (HQ); Bowling Green; men's, boys' underwear — 1,500. Union Underwear Co. Inc.; Bowling Green; men's, boy's underwear — 1,300. Martin Marietta Aluminum Co.; Lewisport; rolling mill — 1,200. General Electric Co. (Electronic Components Div.); Owensboro; television tubes — 1,180. Owensboro-Daviess County. Hospital; Owensboro; hospital — 1,150.

Colt Industries Inc. (Holly Carburetor Div.); Bowling Green; engine carburetors — 1,130. National Southwire Aluminum Inc.; Hawesville; aluminum smelting — 1,070. R. R. Donnelley & Sons. Co.; Glasgow; publishing — 926. The Kendall Co. Inc. (Fabricating Div.); Franklin; surgical supplies — 900. Eaton Corp. (Standard Power Control Div.); Bowling Green; electric controls — 866. Sorenson Mfg. Co. Inc.; Glasgow; auto engine parts — 800. The Gates Rubber Co. Inc.; Elizabethtown; rubber auto products — 669. Green River Steel Inc.; Owensboro; steel — 660. FMC Corp. (Crane & Excavator Div.); Bowling Green; industrial machinery — 600. James B. Beam Distilling Co. (Glen Spey Ltd.); Clermont; distillery — 600. S. K. F. Industries Inc. (Tyson Bearing Co. Div.); Glasgow; tapered roller bearings — 600. Koehring Co. (Atomaster Div.); Bowling Green; space heaters — 590.

Owens-Illinois Inc. (Lily Div.); Bardstown; paper, plastic containers — 550. Eaton Corp.; Glasgow; axles — 525. General Electric Co. (Hermetic Motor Dept.); Scottsville; hermetic motors — 519. AMF Inc. (Potter & Brumfield Div.); Franklin; electric relays — 500. Colt Industries Inc. (Crucible Magnetics Div.); Elizabethtown; magnets — 500. Field Packing Co.; Owensboro; meatpacking — 500. General Electric Co.; Owensboro; motors — 500. General Motors Corp. (Assembly Div.); Bowling Green; auto assembly — 500. Olin Corp. (Chemical Div.); Brandenburg; liquefied industrial gases — 500. Scotty's Construction Inc.; Bowling Green; highway construction — 500. Texas Gas Transmission Corp. (HQ); Owensboro; gas transmission — 500.

3rd District

Louisville and Suburbs

Although the 3rd still is based in Louisville, the district's 15 percent population loss in the 1970s necessitated the addition of about 130,000 new suburban constituents.

The old district, made up of only Louisville and a few inner suburbs, was reliably Democratic. It gave Jimmy Carter a 23,438-vote majority in 1980. But the territory added to the district has a slight Republican tilt. It favored Ronald Reagan by about 6,000 votes.

Most of the new voters live south and southeast of the city in such blue-collar communities as Buechel, Fern Creek and Jeffersontown. Many of the new constituents work in suburban Louisville's General Electric and Ford plants. While a large share are registered Democrats, they are swing voters. Their support for Republican candidates frequently puts metropolitan Jefferson County in the GOP column.

The new 3rd takes in very few of the more affluent suburbs east and northeast of the city. A portion of St. Matthews, home to young professionals and retirees, is the only major addition to the 3rd from this part of the metropolitan area.

Louisville with its large black and Catholic constituencies contains 57 percent of the district population. Many of the Catholics are descendants of German immigrants. But in its social history, Louisville has faced South. Its public places were not fully desegregated until well after World War II. In recent years court-ordered busing has been a major problem, particularly in blue-collar neighborhoods in the South End and in neighboring Shively. The right-to-

life movement is strong within the conservative Catholic constituency.

Blacks comprise 28 percent of the city population, a larger share than in any other population center in the state. Most blacks live near downtown in the West End, an area that regularly turns in heavy Democratic majorities.

The Republican East End features some remaining mansions on the bluffs overlooking the Ohio River. Slightly inland from the river is the Cherokee triangle, a bastion of liberalism where young professionals live in old houses that have been restored. The South End is predominantly white, blue-collar and Democratic.

The busing furor and a depressed economy spurred a population exodus from both the city and its suburbs in the late 1970s. The countywide busing plan took effect in 1975. On its heels came economic problems that idled thousands of workers throughout the Louisville area.

Election Returns

3rd District		Democrat		Republican	
1976	President	106,071	(54.0%)	83,972	(42.7%)
	House	106,903	(57.2%)	77,649	(41.6%)
1978	Senate	43,296	(57.1%)	31,342	(41.3%)
	House	44,327	(57.5%)	30,990	(40.2%)
1979	Governor	104,492	(68.3%)	48,606	(31.7%)
1980	President	101,315	(52.3%)	83,848	(43.3%)
	Senate	113,138	(64.8%)	61,497	(35.2%)
	House	103,120	(56.7%)	76,477	(42.1%)
1982	House	92,849	(65.1%)	45,900	(32.2%)

Demographics

Population: 522,252. **Percent Change from 1970:** -9.3%.

Land Area: 159 square miles. **Population per Square Mile:** 3,284.6.

Counties, 1980 Population: Jefferson (Pt.) — 522,252.

Cities, 1980 Population: Jeffersontown (Pt.) — 8,371; Louisville — 298,451; Shively — 16,819; St. Matthews (Pt.) — 9,030.

Race and Ancestry: White — 79.2%; Black — 20.0%; American Indian, Eskimo and Aleut — 0.1%; Asian and Pacific Islander — 0.4%. Spanish Origin — 0.6%. English — 12.5%; French — 0.8%; German — 9.9%; Irish — 6.0%; Italian — 0.5%.

Universities, Enrollment: Bellarmine College, Louisville — 2,284; Jefferson Community College, Louisville — 6,595; Kentucky College of Technology, Louisville — 981; Louisville Presbyterian Theological Seminary, Louisville — 168; Louisville Technical Institute, Louisville — 341; Southern Baptist Theological Seminary, Louisville — 2,014; Spalding College, Louisville — 1,048; Spencerian College, Louisville — 252; Sullivan Junior College of Business, Louisville — 1,325; University of Louisville, Louisville — 20,640; Watterson College, Louisville — 1,035.

Newspapers, Circulation: *The Courier Journal* (mS), Louisville — 188,625; *The Louisville Times* (e), Louisville — 150,645.

Commercial Television Stations, Affiliation: WAVE-TV, Louisville (NBC); WDRB-TV, Louisville (None); WHAS-TV, Louisville (CBS); WLKY-TV, Louisville (ABC). Entire district is located in Louisville ADI.

Military Installations: Louisville Naval Ordnance Station, Louisville — 2,416; Standiford Field (Air Force), Louisville — 887.

Industries:

General Electric Co. (Major Appliance Group); Louisville; refrigerators, electric ranges, air conditioners, washers & dryers — 13,500.

Philip Morris Inc.; Louisville; tobacco products — 4,372. **Ford Motor Co. Inc.;** Louisville; auto assembly — 3,700. **Philip Morris Inc.** (Philip Morris Stemming); Louisville; tobacco products — 3,200. **Baptist Hospital Inc.;** Louisville; hospital — 2,800.

Brown & Williamson Tobacco (HQ); Louisville; cigarettes — 2,700. **Brown-Forman Distillers Corp.** (Early Times Distillery Co. - HQ); Louisville; distillery — 2,420. **N. K. C. Inc.;** Louisville; hospital — 1,800. **First Kentucky National Corp.** (HQ); Louisville; banking — 1,600. **Loews Theatres Inc.** (Lorillard Div.); Louisville; cigarettes — 1,600. **American Standard Inc.** (United States Plumbing Products Div.); Louisville; plumbing fixtures — 1,500. **Jewish Hospital Assn.;** Louisville; hospital — 1,450. **Courier Journal & Louisville Times Co.** (HQ); Louisville; newspaper publishing — 1,400. **E. I. du Pont de Nemours & Co.** (Elastomer Chemicals Dept.); Louisville; neoprene — 1,350. **Henry Vogt Machine Co.** (HQ); Louisville; valves, fittings — 1,300. **Belknap Inc.** (HQ); Louisville; hardware wholesaler — 1,220. **Grow Group Inc.** (Devoe & Raynolds Co. Div.); Louisville; paint coatings — 1,200.

Humana of Kentucky Inc. (Audubon Hospital); Louisville; hospital — 1,110. **Humana of Kentucky Inc.** (Suburban Hospital); Louisville; hospital — 1,080. **Methodist Evangelical Hospital;** Louisville; hospital — 1,080. **Saints Mary & Elizabeth Hospital;** Louisville; hospital — 1,000. **Veterans Administration;** Louisville; veterans' hospital — 1,000. **Citizens Fidelity Corp.** (HQ); Louisville; banking — 950. **Liberty National Bancorp Inc.** (HQ); Louisville; banking — 942. **International Harvester Co.;** Louisville; engines — 900. **Capital Holding Corp.** (HQ); Louisville; life, casualty insurance — 879. **Armour & Co.** (Armour Foods Co.); Louisville; meatpacking — 850. **Reynolds Metals Co.** (Flexible Packaging Div.); Louisville; aluminum foil — 820. **Chemetron Corp.** (Tube-Turns Div.); Louisville; valves, industrial chemicals — 800.

Standard Gravure Corp. (HQ); Louisville; rotogravure printing — 750. **Allis-Chalmers Corp.;** Louisville; blowers, ventilation fans — 700. **The Enro Shirt Co. Inc.** (Wilson Bros.); Louisville; men's shirts — 700. **Smith's Transfer Corp.;** Louisville; trucking — 700. **American Printing House for the Blind;** Louisville; book publishing — 620. **Rohm & Haas Kentucky Inc.;** Louisville; plastics — 550. **Dover Corp.** (C. Lee Cook Div.); Louisville; metallic packing — 525. **Corning Glass Works** (Corhart Refractories Co. Div.); Louisville; refractory — 500. **First National Bank Louisville;** Louisville; banking — 500. **Joseph E. Seagram Sons Inc.** (Calvert Distillers); Louisville; distillery — 500. **Webb Mechanical Enterprises;** Louisville; plumbing, heating, cooling contractors — 500. **Whayne Supply Co.** (HQ); Louisville; mining machinery wholesalers — 500. **R. L. White Co. Inc.** (HQ); Louisville; publishing, printing 500.

4th District

Louisville Suburbs; Covington, Newport

Although the expansion of the 3rd District has forced the neighboring 4th to extend into rural northern Kentucky, the district remains predominantly suburban and Republican.

The population is concentrated at each end. Four out of every five district voters live either in the suburbs of Louisville in the west or in those of Cincinnati in the east. Both areas are reliably Republican and have made the district the most consistent GOP bastion outside the mountainous 5th.

Redistricting shifted the balance of power within the district from Jefferson County to suburban northern Kentucky. Some 55 percent of the population of the old 4th lived in the Louisville suburbs. With the remap, 51 percent live in Boone, Campbell and Kenton counties near Cincinnati. Along the Ohio River between the two population centers are four predominantly rural Democratic counties.

To compensate the 4th for the loss of some Louisville

suburbs, four rural Bluegrass counties were added from the 6th, plus the southern portions of Campbell and Kenton counties.

The new rural terrain gives the Democrats a bigger toehold in the 4th, but probably not enough to threaten the Republicans. The portion of the Jefferson County remaining in the 4th gave Ronald Reagan 61 percent of the vote in 1980. There is a largely blue-collar constituency at the southern end of the county. But in the northeastern sector are some of the wealthiest communities in the United States.

Populous northern Kentucky is not so affluent, but the suburban commuters and factory workers who live there regularly turn in GOP majorities. Reagan carried Boone, Campbell and Kenton counties in 1980 with at least 56 percent of the vote in each.

Covington and Newport are old factory towns directly across the Ohio River from Cincinnati. Like the Louisville area, they have a large Catholic population of German extraction. Anti-abortion candidate Ellen McCormack ran a close second to Jimmy Carter there in the 1976 Democratic presidential primary.

The major population growth in northern Kentucky has been in Boone County. Attracting suburban spillover from Campbell and Kenton counties, it grew 40 percent in the 1970s. Oldham County, at the other end of the district, had an even higher growth rate. Thanks largely to the busing furor in neighboring Jefferson County, it grew 91 percent in the 1970s, the largest growth rate in the state. Oldham, however, contains only 5 percent of the district population.

Election Returns

4th District		Democrat		Republican	
1976	President	71,300	(41.3%)	99,199	(57.5%)
	House	69,256	(46.5%)	77,863	(52.2%)
1978	Senate	54,006	(60.1%)	34,211	(38.1%)
	House	35,706	(37.5%)	58,063	(60.9%)
1979	Governor	68,993	(57.4%)	51,266	(42.6%)
1980	President	77,599	(39.7%)	108,825	(55.7%)
	Senate	98,330	(58.3%)	70,449	(41.7%)
	House	60,172	(34.2%)	115,834	(65.8%)
1982	House	61,937	(45.3%)	74,109	(54.2%)

Demographics

Population: 523,090. **Percent Change from 1970:** 18.6%.

Land Area: 2,540 square miles. **Population per Square Mile:** 205.9.

Counties, 1980 Population: Boone — 45,842; Campbell — 83,317; Carroll — 9,270; Gallatin — 4,842; Grant — 13,308; Henry — 12,740; Jefferson (Pt.) — 162,752; Kenton — 137,058; Oldham — 27,795; Owen — 8,924; Pendleton — 10,989; Trimble — 6,253.

Cities, 1980 Population: Covington — 49,563; Erlanger — 14,433; Florence — 15,586; Fort Thomas — 16,012; Jeffersontown (Pt.) — 7,424; Newport — 21,587; St. Matthews (Pt.) — 4,324.

Race and Ancestry: White — 97.0%; Black — 2.4%; American Indian, Eskimo and Aleut — 0.1%; Asian and Pacific Islander — 0.4%. Spanish Origin — 0.6%. Dutch — 0.5%; English — 16.4%; French — 0.7%; German — 15.4%; Irish — 6.4%; Italian — 0.6%.

Universities, Enrollment: Northern Kentucky University, Highland Heights — 8,375; R. E. T. S. Electronic Institute, Louisville — 450;

Seminary of St. Pius X, Erlanger — 104; Thomas More College, Fort Mitchell — 1,316.

Newspapers, Circulation: *The Kentucky Post* (e), Covington — 51,380. *The Cincinnati* (Ohio) *Enquirer*, Louisville *Courier-Journal* and *The Louisville Times* also circulate in the district.

Commercial Television Stations, Affiliation: WXIX-TV, Newport (None). District is divided between Louisville ADI and Cincinnati (Ohio) ADI.

Industries:

Ford Motor Co. (Kentucky Truck Plant); Fincastle; truck assembly — 2,162. **Blue Cross & Blue Shield of Kentucky** (HQ); Jeffersontown; health insurance — 1,100. **Seaboard Systems;** Covington; railroad operations — 750. **Litton Systems Inc.;** Florence; conveyors — 600. **Interlake Steel;** Newport; steel pipes — 572. **Square D Co.;** Florence; warehousing — 550.

5th District

Southeast

Rural and poor, the 5th District is worlds apart from the suburban 4th. But it equals and usually exceeds the 4th in its Republicanism. The mountain counties have been voting the GOP ticket for more than a century.

Since the Civil War — when its small-scale farmers were hostile to slaveholding secessionist Democrats elsewhere in Kentucky — southeast Kentucky has been one of the most loyal GOP strongholds in the nation. Alfred M. Landon carried nearly all its counties in 1936. Barry Goldwater won the 5th in 1964, the only district in Kentucky he carried.

The only significant sources of Democratic votes are Bell and Harlan counties, in the coal-producing southeast corner of the district. Bell and Harlan were the only counties in the district to back Jimmy Carter in 1980, but together they have only 15 percent of the district's population. Every place else in the 5th was Reagan territory. In nine counties, the Republican nominee drew more than 70 percent of the vote.

Despite some of the richest coal deposits in the nation along the district's eastern border, the 5th is the poorest district in Kentucky and one of the poorest in the nation. In 1980 nearly half the residents had not gone past the eighth grade in school. The recent revival in the coal industry has helped end decades of population decline, but none of the counties in the district has a per-capita income that approaches the statewide level.

Tobacco, apples, poultry and livestock are mainstays of the farm economy in the rolling hill country in the central and western parts of the district. Poor transportation and the absence of major population centers have curtailed industrial development. The new 5th is the only district in the state — and may turn out to be the only one in the country in the 1980s — without a city of 15,000 population. Its largest community, Middlesborough, has 12,251 residents.

Madison County (Richmond) was the most populous in the old 5th, but redistricting moved its 53,000 residents into the 6th. Other changes in the district lines were comparatively minor. Jessamine County, which was split between the 5th and 6th districts, is now entirely in the 5th. And the 5th District's share of Letcher County along the Virginia border has been expanded to include a few more

precincts from the old 7th. Together the two additions give the 5th District about 20,000 new constituents.

Election Returns

5th District		Democrat		Republican	
1976	President	67,794	(42.0%)	92,134	(57.1%)
	House	45,475	(32.3%)	94,023	(66.8%)
1978	Senate	34,338	(52.8%)	29,450	(45.3%)
	House	15,403	(21.0%)	57,782	(78.9%)
1979	Governor	63,534	(43.9%)	81,175	(56.1%)
1980	President	69,640	(36.9%)	116,015	(61.4%)
	Senate	90,633	(54.1%)	76,809	(45.9%)
	House	48,566	(30.9%)	108,392	(69.0%)
1982	House	28,285	(34.8%)	52,928	(65.2%)

Demographics

Population: 523,664. **Percent Change from 1970:** 22.4%.

Land Area: 9,473 square miles. **Population per Square Mile:** 55.3.

Counties, 1980 Population: Adair — 15,233; Bell — 34,330; Casey — 14,818; Clay — 22,752; Clinton — 9,321; Cumberland — 7,289; Estill — 14,495; Garrard — 10,853; Green — 11,043; Harlan — 41,889; Jackson — 11,996; Jessamine — 26,146; Knox — 30,239; Laurel — 38,982; Lee — 7,754.

Leslie — 14,882; Letcher (Pt.) — 4,329; Lincoln — 19,053; McCreary — 15,634; Metcalfe — 9,484; Monroe — 12,353; Owsley — 5,709; Pulaski — 45,803; Rockcastle — 13,973; Russell — 13,708; Taylor — 21,178; Wayne — 17,022; Whitley — 33,396.

Cities, 1980 Population: Middlesborough — 12,251; Nicholasville — 10,400; Somerset — 10,649.

Race and Ancestry: White — 97.7%; Black — 2.1%; American Indian, Eskimo and Aleut — 0.1%; Asian and Pacific Islander — 0.1%. Spanish Origin — 0.8%. English — 35.7%; French — 0.5%; German — 3.2%; Irish — 6.3%.

Universities, Enrollment: Asbury College, Wilmore — 1,224; Asbury Theological Seminary, Wilmore — 715; Campbellsville College, Campbellsville — 698; Cumberland College, Williamsburg — 2,162; Lindsey Wilson College, Columbia — 408; Sue Bennett College, London — 280; Union College, Barbourville — 894; Somerset Community College, Somerset — 980; Southeast Community College, Cumberland — 578.

Newspapers, Circulation: *The Commonwealth-Journal* (e), Somerset — 11,902; *Harlan Daily Enterprise* (e), Harlan — 7,421; *Middlesboro Daily News* (e), Middlesborough — 6,960; *Times-Tribune* (eS), Corbin — 8,194.

Commercial Television Stations, Affiliation: District is divided between Lexington ADI and Knoxville (Tenn.) ADI. Portions are in Bowling Green ADI, Louisville ADI, Bristol (Va.)-Kingsport (Tenn.)-Johnson City (Tenn.) ADI and Nashville (Tenn.) ADI.

Industries:

Union Underwear Co. Inc.; Campbellsville; men's, boys' underwear — 4,000. **American Greeting Corp.;** Corbin; greeting cards — 1,100. **Palm Beach Co.;** Somerset; men's coats — 1,000. **United States Steel Corp.;** Lynch; coal mining — 1,000. **Tecumseh Products Co.;** Somerset; air conditioner compressors — 900.

Russell Sportswear Corp.; Russell Springs; ladies' blouses, sportswear — 725. **Greenwood Lead & Mining Co.;** Parkers Lake; coal mining — 700. **Caron International Inc.** (Spinning Co. Div.); London; worsted yarns — 650. **Marlene Industries Corp.** (Liberty Sportswear Div.); Liberty; women's blouses, sportswear — 650. **Sutton Shirt Corp.;** Albany; men's, boys' shirts — 565. **Mellco & Greer;** London; road contractors — 500. **Scotia Coal Co.;** Partridge; coal mining — 500.

6th District

North Central — Lexington, Frankfort

The 6th is Kentucky as the rest of the nation pictures it. Horses, tobacco and whiskey are the mainstays of its culture and economy.

The population of the 6th was fairly evenly divided in the 1970s between Republican Fayette County (Lexington) and the Democratic countryside. But the ripple effect from the extensive redistricting in the Louisville area has forced the 6th to move south and east.

The Democratic Legislature removed from the 6th four rural counties in northern Kentucky and replaced them with five small counties on the district's eastern and western flanks. It also took out areas near Cincinnati (in the southern portions of Campbell and Kenton counties) and near Lexington (the northern portion of Jessamine County) and put in a populous swing county (Madison).

The centerpiece of the 6th remains Fayette County, home for 40 percent of district residents. Lexington is best known for its thoroughbred horse farms. But a diverse economic base has made it the most prosperous part of the state outside Louisville.

A large white-collar element enables GOP candidates to carry the Lexington area. However, Fayette is no bastion of conservatism. Ronald Reagan's 49 percent share of the 1980 presidential vote in the county was 5 percentage points below Gerald R. Ford's showing four years earlier. Many of the defectors in 1980 went to independent John B. Anderson, who drew 7 percent there, his highest vote in Kentucky.

The attraction of new businesses to the Lexington area produced a postwar population boom. But during the 1970s the county began to curb residential and industrial expansion, spurring population and manufacturing growth in rural Bluegrass counties within commuting distance of Lexington.

The most populous of the adjoining counties is Madison, transferred in 1982 from the 5th. Madison voted for Reagan in 1980, while also backing the Democratic congressional candidate.

The northern portion of the county is dotted with bedroom communities whose residents work in the nearby city of Lexington. The southern portion revolves around Richmond, a tobacco market and site of Eastern Kentucky University. Ten percent of the district population lives in Madison, making it the second largest county in the 6th District.

The five Democratic counties added to the district on its eastern and western borders represent 10 percent of the district vote. Anderson County, on the western end, was moved over from the 2nd District. Bracken, Montgomery, Nicholas and Robertson counties are on the eastern flank and were switched from the fast-growing 7th.

The district's other major population center is Franklin County, which includes the state capital of Frankfort. The long heritage of Democratic governors has produced a loyal pool of state workers who help keep the county in the Democratic column. Jimmy Carter won it in 1980 with 60 percent of the vote, his top showing in the district.

Despite redistricting favorable to the Democrats, the Republican House incumbent in 1982 retained the seat he had first won in 1978.

Election Returns

6th District		Democrat		Republican	
1976	President	83,835	(51.9%)	74,110	(45.9%)
	House	84,513	(85.6%)	9,299	(9.4%)
1978	Senate	51,665	(66.0%)	23,928	(30.6%)
	House	41,316	(46.6%)	45,626	(51.5%)
1979	Governor	87,957	(64.1%)	49,170	(35.9%)
1980	President	90,271	(49.1%)	83,127	(45.3%)
	Senate	110,643	(71.2%)	44,701	(28.8%)
	House	73,298	(44.4%)	90,774	(55.0%)
1982	House	49,839	(41.4%)	68,418	(56.8%)

Demographics

Population: 519,009. **Percent Change from 1970:** 18.5%.

Land Area: 3,993 square miles. **Population per Square Mile:** 130.0.

Counties, 1980 Population: Anderson — 12,567; Bourbon — 19,405; Boyle — 25,066; Bracken — 7,738; Clark — 28,322; Fayette — 204,165; Franklin — 41,830; Harrison — 15,166; Madison — 53,352; Mercer — 19,011; Montgomery — 20,046; Nicholas — 7,157; Robertson — 2,265; Scott — 21,813; Shelby — 23,328; Woodford — 17,778.

Cities, 1980 Population: Danville — 12,942; Frankfort — 25,973; Georgetown — 10,972; Lexington — 194,093; Richmond — 21,705; Winchester — 15,216.

Race and Ancestry: White — 90.0%; Black — 9.3%; American Indian, Eskimo and Aleut — 0.1%; Asian and Pacific Islander — 0.5%. Spanish Origin — 0.6%. English — 25.8%; French — 0.7%; German — 5.3%; Irish — 6.5%; Italian — 0.5%; Scottish — 0.6%.

Universities, Enrollment: Berea College, Berea — 1,434; Centre College of Kentucky, Danville — 749; Eastern Kentucky University, Richmond — 14,081; Fugazzi College, Lexington — 255; Georgetown College, Georgetown — 1,270; Kentucky Junior College of Business, Lexington — 1,582; Kentucky State University, Frankfort — 2,342; Lexington Technical Institute, Lexington — 2,111; Lexington Theological Seminary, Lexington — 106; Midway College, Midway — 316; Transylvania University, Lexington — 810; University of Kentucky, Lexington — 23,130.

Newspapers, Circulation: *The Advocate Messenger* (eS), Danville — 11,017; *The Lexington Herald* (mS), Lexington — 70,151; *The Lexington Leader* (eS), Lexington — 33,963; *The Richmond Register* (e), Richmond — 8,770; *The State Journal* (eS), Frankfort — 10,451; *The Winchester Sun* (e), Winchester — 6,596.

Commercial Television Stations, Affiliation: WKYT-TV, Lexington (CBS); WLEX-TV, Lexington (NBC); WTVQ-TV, Lexington (ABC). Most of district is located in Lexington ADI. Portions are in Louisville ADI and Cincinnati (Ohio) ADI.

Military Installations: Lexington Bluegrass Army Depot Activity, Lexington — 1,471; Bluegrass Army Depot Activity, Richmond — 780; Richmond Bomb Scoring Site (Air Force), Richmond — 86.

Industries:

International Business Machines Corp. (Office Products Div.); Lexington; electric typewriters, copiers — 6,200. **Square D Co.** (Distribution Equipment Div.); Lexington; switches — 1,600. **GTE Products Corp.** (Lighting Products Group); Winchester; lamps — 1,040. **A. O. Smith Corp.** (Hermetic Motor Div.); Mount Sterling; electric motors — 1,000. **Union Underwear Co. Inc.;** Frankfort; underwear mills — 1,000.

Rand McNally Co.; Versailles; printing — 900. **Hobart Corp.** (KitchenAid Div.); Mount Sterling; dishwashers — 800. **The Trane Co.;** Lexington; heating, cooling equipment — 800. **FMC Corp.;** Lexington; hydraulic cranes — 750. **Rockwell International Corp.** (Truck Axle Div.); Winchester; truck axles — 705. **American Greeting Corp.;**

Danville; greeting cards — 700. **National Distillers & Chemical Corp.;** Frankfort; distillery — 700. **Whirlpool Corp.;** Danville; trash compactors — 680. **Blue Grass Industries Inc.** (HQ); Carlisle; men's woven underwear — 650. **Medusa Aggregates Co. Inc.** (State Contracting & Stone Co.); Lexington; road construction — 650. **Kentucky Central Flood Insurance Co.;** Lexington; life insurance — 618. **Blue Grass Industries Inc.;** Mount Sterling; men's woven underwear — 600.

Kentucky Central Life Insurance Co. (HQ); Lexington; life insurance — 550. **Parker-Hannifin Corp.** (Parker Seal Co.); Berea; fabricated rubber products — 550. **First Security National Bank & Trust** (HQ); Lexington; banking — 513. **American Standard Inc.** (Wabco Fluid Power Div.); Lexington; hydraulic machinery — 500. **Bundy Corp.** (Tubing Div.); Winchester; metal tubing —500. **Clark Equipment Co.;** Georgetown; construction machinery — 500. **Corning Glass Works;** Harrodsburg; optical glass — 500. **Ladish Co.** (Kentucky Div.); Cynthiana; valves — 500. **Langley Trucking Co.;** Lexington; trucking — 500. **Southwestern Tobacco Co. Inc.;** Lexington; tobacco storage — 500.

7th District

East — Ashland

The 7th District reaches into poverty-stricken Appalachia. Major products in the hill country along the district's northern boundary include tobacco, cattle and fruit. Natural gas and coal are mined in the mountains of the southeast. Ashland, the district's only population center, is home to petrochemical and steel plants.

The 7th is one of the poorest districts in the United States, yet in the 1970s it grew faster than any other Kentucky district. The population grew by 23 percent in the decade, as many former residents were lured back to their hometowns by a revival of the coal industry and a decline in automobile industry jobs in the urban Midwest.

With the United Mine Workers (UMW) a major force in politics, the 7th is Democratic. Between 1960 and 1982 it failed to support the Democratic presidential nominee only in 1972. Even then, seven of the eight Kentucky counties won by George McGovern were in the district.

Democratic strength is greatest in the southern two-thirds of the district, the rugged area that is one of the nation's leading producers of bituminous coal. Since the New Deal and the UMW transformed politics in the region, the coal counties have regularly turned in some of the highest Democratic percentages in the state. Four counties gave Jimmy Carter more than 70 percent of the vote in 1980.

Pike County anchors the eastern tip of the 7th District. In land area, Pike is the largest county in Kentucky. In population, it is first in the district — Pike County residents make up about 15 percent of the voters in the 7th. And in recent years, Pike has been the leading county in the country in coal production.

Coal and poverty go hand in hand. Some of the poorest counties in the nation are deep in the Kentucky coal country, which dominates the 7th and stretches over into the neighboring 5th District. Many of the counties in this part of the state have per-capita incomes less than half the national level.

Within the 7th, the standard of living is highest in the area around Ashland. The Ohio River city lies just across the border from Huntington, W. Va., and is headquarters for the Ashland Oil Company. Although layoffs have hurt the local economy, strong unions help keep the Ashland

area — industrialized Boyd and Greenup counties — in the Democratic column. Along with oil refineries, there are railroad maintenance facilities and steel plants that provide employment for a large blue-collar work force. Residents of the Ashland area account for about one-sixth of the district vote.

The northern portion of the 7th District, stretching from the West Virginia boundary northwestward into the Ohio River Valley, is primarily agricultural. But compared to the fertile Bluegrass region, it is mediocre land dominated by small-scale and subsistence farming.

Redistricting switched four small counties in the northwest corner into the 6th District. Several precincts in Letcher County were moved into the 5th District.

Election Returns

7th District		Democrat		Republican	
1976	President	97,090	(60.3%)	62,781	(39.0%)
	House	103,728	(73.0%)	38,360	(27.0%)
1978	Senate	36,726	(64.4%)	19,082	(33.5%)
	House	48,608	(76.3%)	15,107	(23.7%)
1979	Governor	79,091	(58.8%)	55,463	(41.2%)
1980	President	97,733	(55.2%)	76,302	(43.1%)
	Senate	102,308	(69.0%)	45,983	(31.0%)
	House	109,826	(100.0%)	—	
1982	House	82,463	(79.4%)	21,436	(20.6%)

Demographics

Population: 526,284. **Percent Change from 1970:** 23.4%.

Land Area: 7,585 square miles. **Population per Square Mile:** 69.4.

Counties, 1980 Population: Bath — 10,025; Boyd — 55,513; Breathitt — 17,004; Carter — 25,060; Elliott — 6,908; Fleming — 12,323; Floyd — 48,764; Greenup — 39,132; Johnson — 24,432; Knott — 17,940; Lawrence — 14,121; Letcher (Pt.) — 26,358; Lewis — 14,545; Magoffin — 13,515; Martin — 13,925; Mason — 17,765; Menifee — 5,117; Morgan — 12,103; Perry — 33,763; Pike — 81,123; Powell — 11,101; Rowan — 19,049; Wolfe — 6,698.

Cities, 1980 Population: Ashland — 27,064.

Race and Ancestry: White — 98.8%; Black — 1.0%; American Indian, Eskimo and Aleut — 0.1%; Asian and Pacific Islander — 0.1%. Spanish Origin — 0.7%. Dutch — 0.5%; English — 37.9%; French — 0.6%; German — 3.6%; Irish — 6.2%.

Universities, Enrollment: Alice Lloyd College, Pippa Passes — 231; Ashland Community College, Ashland — 1,472; Hazard Community College, Hazard — 326; Kentucky Christian College, Grayson — 495; Lees Junior College, Jackson — 304; Maysville Community College, Maysville — 513; Morehead State University, Morehead — 7,195; Pikeville College, Pikeville — 616; Prestonsburg Community College, Prestonsburg — 751.

Newspapers, Circulation: *Ashland Daily Independent* (eS), Ashland — 25,479; *The Ledger Independent* (m), Maysville — 8,326.

Commercial Television Stations, Affiliation: WKYH-TV, Hazard (NBC); WTSF, Ashland (None). Most of district is in Lexington ADI and Charleston-Huntington (W.Va.) ADI. Portions are in Bristol (Va.)-Kingsport (Tenn.)-Johnson City (Tenn.) ADI and Cincinnati (Ohio) ADI.

Industries:

Armco Steel Corp.; Ashland; steel sheets — 4,284. **Ashland Oil Inc.** (HQ); Ashland; petroleum refining — 2,000. **Chesapeake & Ohio Railroad Co.** (Raceland Car Shop); Russell; freight cars — 2,000.

Emerson Electric Co. (Browning Mfg. Co.); Maysville; power equipment — 1,300. Falcon Coal Co. Inc.; Jackson; consulting engineers — 1,000.

Beth-Elkhorn Corp.; Jenkins; coal mining — 950. National Mines Corp. (Beaver Creek Div.); Wayland; coal mining — 750. Ashland Oil Inc.; Catlettsburg; petroleum refining — 675. National Mine Service Co. Inc.; Ashland; mining equipment, machinery — 661. Blue Diamond Mining Co. Inc.; Leatherwood; coal mining — 650. Allied Chemical Corp. (Semet-Solvay Div.); Ashland; coke products — 550. South-East Coal Co.; Whitesburg; coal mining — 525. American Standard Co.; Paintsville; plumbing fixtures — 500. Kentland-Elkhorn Coal Corp.; Mouthcard; coal mining — 500. Kentucky Carbon Corp.; Phelps; coal mining — 500. Martiki Coal Corp.; Lovely; coal mining — 500.

Louisiana

Unlike its counterparts in most of the Deep South, Louisiana's Legislature managed to come up with a redistricting plan that pleased the governor, the congressional delegation and the Justice Department. The state's new map was passed by the Legislature in November 1981 and was approved by Justice June 18, 1982.

Disappointed that the remap did not create a black-majority district in New Orleans, state black leaders filed suit in federal district court to overturn the plan. On Sept. 24, 1983, the court threw out the two New Orleans districts and gave the Legislature until Jan. 31, 1984, to draw new ones. Meanwhile, the original lines took effect for the 1982 elections.

Louisiana kept its allotment of eight congressional districts. Boundary changes outside the New Orleans area were limited to minor adjustments for population balance. Around New Orleans, however, more significant alterations were necessary because the city lost population in the 1970s while the surrounding suburbs gained substantially.

During the legislative maneuvering in early November 1981, the Democratic majority in Louisiana's House and Senate had proposed more radical changes. Both chambers passed similar bills that would have made the New Orleans 2nd a black-majority district, enhancing the prospect that it would elect Louisiana's first black House member in this century.

But Republican Gov. David C. Treen threatened to veto the legislation, claiming that the GOP incumbent in the neighboring 1st District would have to absorb too much unfavorable terrain. Subsequently, the Legislature adopted a plan that made more modest changes, preserving the majority-white constituency of the 2nd District.

After extensive lobbying by Treen and members of Louisiana's House delegation, the Justice Department approved the redistricting plan in June. Black leaders lambasted the decision, claiming that a Republican administration had helped a Republican governor save a Republican House seat.

Treen defended the decision on the basis of history and demographics. New Orleans has been divided between two districts since the mid-19th century. Blacks, said Treen, exert a strong influence in both. He added that on the basis of population trends, blacks were expected to comprise 50.4 percent of the 2nd District population by 1986.

Age of Population

District	Population Under 18	Voting Age Population	Population 65 & Over (% of VAP)	Median Age
1	157,347	367,614	50,290 (13.7%)	28.5
2	162,585	364,679	52,459 (14.4%)	27.9
3	174,501	351,768	35,567 (10.1%)	26.4
4	161,510	363,684	58,547 (16.1%)	28.2
5	166,533	360,687	66,071 (18.3%)	28.1
6	162,518	362,252	41,937 (11.6%)	26.6
7	169,790	355,571	46,188 (13.0%)	26.7
8	175,684	349,177	53,220 (15.2%)	26.7
State	1,330,468	2,875,432	404,279 (14.1%)	27.4

Income and Occupation

District	Median Family Income	White Collar Workers	Blue Collar Workers	Service Workers	Farm Workers
1	$ 19,796	58.1%	28.3%	12.6%	1.1%
2	16,522	49.3	33.1	16.8	0.8
3	21,793	52.2	35.8	10.1	1.9
4	16,862	48.3	35.0	14.6	2.0
5	14,579	45.3	35.2	13.7	5.8
6	20,069	55.8	30.8	11.7	1.7
7	19,622	47.0	37.9	12.1	3.0
8	15,587	41.7	38.3	16.2	3.7
State	$ 18,088	50.0%	34.2%	13.3%	2.4%

Education: School Years Completed

District	8 Years or Fewer	4 Years of High School	4 Years of College or More	Median School Years
1	20.4%	31.3%	18.3%	12.5
2	25.8	30.9	12.2	12.2
3	25.2	32.8	14.4	12.3
4	21.2	32.6	13.1	12.3
5	28.2	29.4	11.7	12.1
6	17.6	31.5	19.1	12.5
7	28.9	29.1	13.1	12.1
8	32.5	29.8	9.1	12.0
State	24.9%	30.9%	13.9%	12.2

LOUISIANA

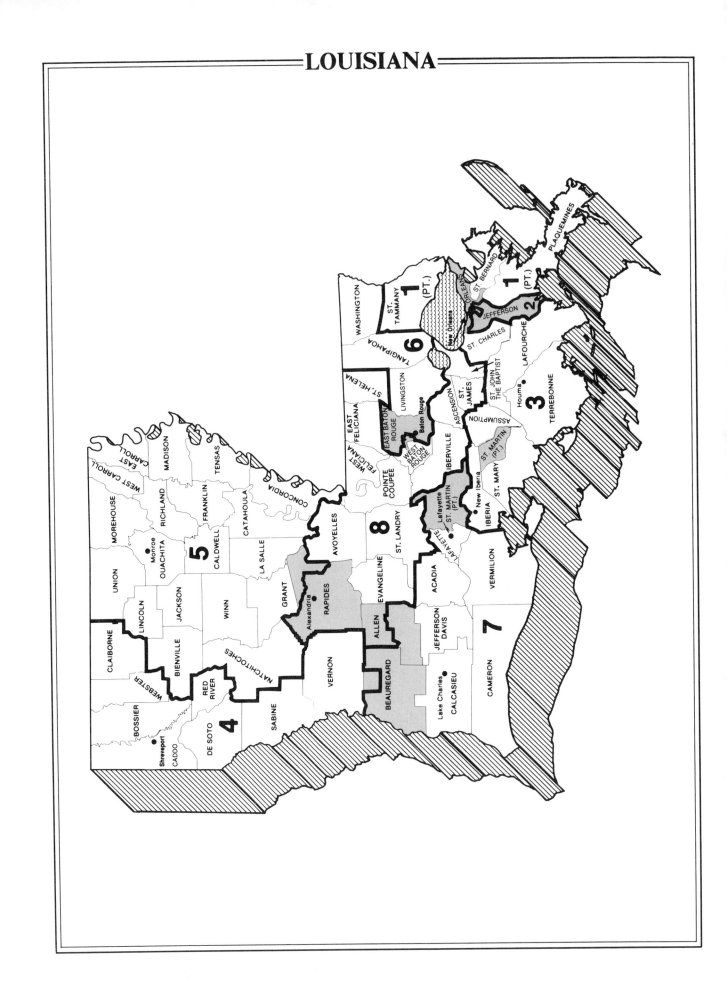

Housing and Residential Patterns

District	Owner Occupied	Renter Occupied	Urban	Rural
1	60.0%	40.0%	85.0%	15.0%
2	46.8	53.2	99.1	0.9
3	67.7	32.3	71.7	28.3
4	68.4	31.6	65.3	34.7
5	73.3	26.7	47.6	52.4
6	67.4	32.6	70.6	29.4
7	71.5	28.5	62.6	37.4
8	71.0	29.0	47.4	52.6
State	65.5%	34.5%	68.6%	31.4%

1st District

Southeast — New Orleans

New Orleans casts more than 60 percent of the 1st District vote. While the district has some of the fashionable neighborhoods along Lake Pontchartrain and around Loyola, Tulane and Xavier universities, it includes few of the city's tourist spots; most of the district's New Orleans portion is in middle- to lower-income neighborhoods.

Some of this territory is in the northern and eastern parts of the city; the rest is along the west bank of the Mississippi River in a section known as Algiers. Much of the district is below sea level but is protected from flooding by a system of levees.

These are ethnic communities, populated by Italians, Irish, Cubans and the largest number of Hondurans outside Central America. But the ethnicity is not always easy to notice. Rather than living in separate communities, the different groups are scattered throughout the city in "marble cake" fashion.

Although New Orleans is 55 percent black, whites form a majority in the city's 1st District sector. Redistricting transferred about 40,000 residents of predominantly black neighborhoods east of the French Quarter from the 1st to the 2nd District, while moving about 40,000 residents in the predominantly white Uptown area around the three universities from the 2nd to the 1st. With the remap reducing the black share of 1st District population from 37 to 29 percent, Republican candidates should benefit.

About 62 percent of the new district population lives in New Orleans. Of the rest, 21 percent lives in St. Tammany Parish, 12 percent in St. Bernard Parish and 5 percent in Plaquemines Parish.

Twenty-five miles north of New Orleans across Lake Pontchartrain, St. Tammany is a booming suburban haven. Once an isolated vacation area for residents escaping the heat and humidity of New Orleans, it has become a popular home for New Orleans oil executives. The construction of the Lake Pontchartrain Causeway and Interstate 10, a thoroughfare that links New Orleans with the Mississippi Gulf Coast, has made the parish accessible.

Pine forests cover much of the St. Tammany landscape. But near the lake in communities like Slidell (population 26,718) and Mandeville (population 6,076), new subdivisions have sprouted. During the 1970s St. Tammany showed a 74 percent population increase, the largest of any parish in the state. Many of the newcomers are refugees from the North and Midwest who have maintained their Republican voting habits. St. Tammany gave Ronald Reagan 63.7 percent of the vote in 1980, his second best showing in Louisiana.

Southeast of New Orleans is the low, flat marshland of Plaquemines and St. Bernard parishes. Jutting into the Gulf of Mexico, the two parishes are flooded frequently and the land is being steadily repossessed by the gulf. Some scientists speculate that Plaquemines may be submerged by the year 2000.

The disappearance of Plaquemines parish into the gulf would not be bad news for the more liberal-minded Louisiana politicians. For generations the sleepy parish has been a world of its own, ruled with an iron hand by segregationist Leander Perez until his death in 1969. Reflecting Perez' wishes, Plaquemines cast more than 75 percent of its ballots for Dixiecrat Strom Thurmond in 1948, Barry Goldwater in 1964 and George C. Wallace in 1968. But Perez' descendants have not been able to sustain his brand of autocratic rule; they played a minor role in the 1980 campaign. Reagan carried the parish with only 54 percent of the vote.

Plaquemines has maintained its basic suspicion of outsiders. During the 1970s it grew at a rate of only 3 percent, the smallest of any parish along the Gulf Coast.

Lying closer to New Orleans, St. Bernard is less inbred. The parish has a growing blue-collar population that is similar to the expanding working-class neighborhoods on the marshy, largely undeveloped east side of the city. The blue-collar element often votes Democratic in closely contested statewide races. Jimmy Carter carried the parish narrowly in 1976, although Reagan won it comfortably in 1980 with 60 percent of the vote.

Election Returns

1st District		Democrat		Republican	
1976	President	79,056	(49.6%)	75,879	(47.6%)
	House	64,239	(50.4%)	50,927	(40.0%)
1978	Senate	66,368	(67.3%)	—	
	House	19,623	(19.2%)	81,548	(80.0%)
1979	Governor	67,704	(42.5%)	91,467	(57.5%)
1980	President	79,279	(41.8%)	103,597	(54.7%)
	Senate	54,060	(57.3%)	—	
	House	5,204	(5.7 %)	76,924	(84.1%)
1982	House	—[1]		x[1]	

[1] *No votes tabulated where candidate was unopposed; x indicates winner.*

Demographics

Population: 525,337. **Percent Change from 1970:** 14.9%.

Land Area: 2,577 square miles. **Population per Square Mile:** 203.7.

Counties, 1980 Population: Orleans (Pt.) — 323,946; Plaquemines — 26,049; St. Bernard — 64,097; St. Tammany — 110,869.

Cities, 1980 Population: New Orleans (Pt.) — 323,946; Slidell — 26,718.

Race and Ancestry: White — 68.2%; Black — 29.4%; American Indian, Eskimo and Aleut — 0.2%; Asian and Pacific Islander — 1.4%. Spanish Origin — 3.9%. English — 7.3%; French — 7.0%; German — 4.1%; Irish — 3.2%; Italian — 3.2%.

Universities, Enrollment: Delgado Community College, New Orleans — 8,423; Loyola University, New Orleans — 4,616; New Orleans

Baptist Theological Seminary, New Orleans — 1,243; Notre Dame Seminary-Graduate School of Theology, New Orleans — 69; Our Lady of Holy Cross College, New Orleans — 816; St. Joseph Seminary College, St. Benedict — 100; St. Mary's Dominican College, New Orleans — 830; Southern University in New Orleans, New Orleans — 2,574; Tulane University, New Orleans — 10,040; University of New Orleans, Lakefront — 14,897; Xavier University of Louisiana, New Orleans — 2,003.

Newspapers, Circulation: *Daily Times* (eS), Slidell — 10,146; *Sentry-News* (mS), Slidell — 6,137; *The Times-Picayune/The States-Item* (all day), New Orleans — 275,376.

Commercial Television Stations, Affiliation: WGNO-TV, New Orleans (None); WVUE, New Orleans (ABC). Entire district is located in New Orleans ADI. *(For other New Orleans stations, see 2nd district.)*

Military Installations: Jackson Barracks Air National Guard Station, New Orleans — 388; New Orleans Naval Air Station, New Orleans — 1,710; New Orleans Naval Support Activity, New Orleans — 4,794; Slidell Radar Site (Air Force), Slidell — 7.

Industries:

Martin Marietta Corp. (Aerospace-Michoud Div.); New Orleans; guided missiles, space vehicles — 3,200. **Boh Bros. Construction Co. Inc.** (HQ); New Orleans; highway, bridge construction — 1,600. **Amstar Corp.**; Arabi; cane sugar refining — 800. **Amax Nickel Refining Inc.**; Braithwaite; nickel, copper refining — 700. **Tenneco Oil Co.**; Chalmette; petroleum refining — 630.

Louisiana Coca-Cola Bottling Co. (HQ); New Orleans; soft drink bottling — 600. **Wembley Industries Inc.** (Enchino Fine Neckwear Div. - HQ); New Orleans; men's neckwear — 600. **Western Electric Co. Inc.**; New Orleans; electrical apparatus wholesaling — 550. **American Marine Corp.** (HQ); New Orleans; shipbuilding, marine services — 500. **Todd Shipyards Corp.**; New Orleans; shipbuilding — 500.

2nd District

Jefferson Parish — New Orleans

Redistricting has transformed the 2nd from a substantially urban to a predominantly suburban district. But because the district contains the heart of Democratic New Orleans, it remains one of the most liberal constituencies in the Deep South.

Although only 44 percent of the residents of the redrawn district live in New Orleans, the city portion is 75 percent black and gave Jimmy Carter nearly 80 percent of the vote in 1980. Those votes should be enough to outweigh those cast in the Republican suburbs of Jefferson Parish.

Map makers moved the affluent and generally Republican Uptown area near Loyola, Tulane and Xavier universities into the 1st District. They transferred the heavily black Lower 9th Ward, just east of the French Quarter, and the adjacent Fairgrounds section near predominantly black Dillard University into the 2nd.

The district retained the French Quarter, the Garden District with its historic mansions, downtown New Orleans and the Carrollton section. Carrollton is an area of middle-class whites on the west side that is separated from the rest of the newly drawn district by the Uptown sector.

The 75,000-seat Louisiana Superdome is the centerpiece of the construction boom the downtown area has undergone in the 1970s. Along nearby Poydras Avenue, many major oil companies have built large office towers. Across the Mississippi River is the site of the 1984 World's Fair.

Despite the bustle, New Orleans is more like the older cities of the North than the young boom towns of the Sun

Belt; it lost population in recent decades, in particular, its white population. Redistricting increased the black share of the 2nd District population from 41 to 44.5 percent, the largest of any district in Louisiana. But the old district's growth rate of only 2 percent in the 1970s forced its lines to be drawn deeper into suburban Jefferson Parish.

Few changes were made on the west bank of the Mississippi. There the 2nd lost only Grand Isle, a tiny island of 2,000 residents in the Gulf of Mexico that is reached only through Lafourche Parish in the 3rd District.

But on the populous east bank (which is actually to the north), the boundary was moved roughly a mile and a half north from the ugly, warehouse-lined Airline Highway (U.S. Route 61) to Interstate 10. That change brought about 60,000 new suburban residents into the district.

On the eastern end of the parish the 2nd picked up Old Metairie, an unincorporated area that was New Orleans' original suburb. It is a community of established wealth. To the west are newer, middle-class suburbs. Redistricting gave the 2nd the New Orleans International Airport and a third of Kenner, an area of new subdivisions that doubled its population in the 1970s.

The populous east bank of Jefferson Parish is more white-collar, affluent and Republican than the west bank. It gave Ronald Reagan 65 percent of the vote in 1980. The more black and heavily blue-collar west bank gave Reagan only 52 percent.

Shipbuilding and offshore oil supply companies line the Harvey Canal on the west bank. Avondale is one of the largest shipyards in the country. Many workers live in Gretna (population 20,615) and Westwego (population 12,663), the most populous towns on the west bank. Both began as railheads but have shown little growth in recent years.

Election Returns

2nd District		Democrat		Republican	
1976	President	82,140	(53.5%)	68,333	(44.5%)
	House	86,904	(76.8%)	19,471	(17.2%)

2nd District		Democrat		Republican	
1978	Senate	54,979	(68.9%)	—	
	House	51,457	(76.8%)	7,921	(11.8%)
1979	Governor	77,410	(52.3%)	70,527	(47.7%)
1980	President	94,646	(53.7%)	75,920	(43.1%)
	Senate	56,575	(67.9%)	—	
	House	49,047	(56.7%)	30,374	(35.1%)
1982	House	x[1]		—[1]	

[1] No votes tabulated where candidate was unopposed; x indicates winner.

Demographics

Population: 526,888. **Percent Change from 1970:** 1.4%.

Land Area: 319 square miles. **Population per Square Mile:** 1,652.9.

Counties, 1980 Population: Jefferson (Pt.) — 293,695; Orleans (Pt.) — 233,569.

Cities, 1980 Population: Gretna — 20,615; Harahan — 11,384; Kenner (Pt.) — 21,981; Metairie (CDP) (Pt.) — 49,657; New Orleans (Pt.) — 233,569; Westwego — 12,663.

Race and Ancestry: White — 53.7%; Black — 44.5%; American Indian, Eskimo and Aleut — 0.2%; Asian and Pacific Islander — 0.9%. Spanish Origin — 3.5%. English — 5.5%; French — 8.7%; German — 2.9%; Irish — 2.2%; Italian — 2.5%.

Newspapers, Circulation: New Orleans *Times-Picayune/The States-Item* circulates in the district.

Universities, Enrollment: Dillard University, New Orleans — 1,208; Louisiana State University Medical Center at New Orleans, New Orleans — 2,529.

Commercial Television Stations, Affiliation: WDSU-TV, New Orleans (NBC); WULT, New Orleans (None); WWL-TV, New Orleans (CBS). Entire district is located in New Orleans ADI. *(For other New Orleans stations, see 1st district.)*

Industries:

Avondale Shipyards Inc. (HQ); Westwego; shipbuilding — 5,100. **Charity Hospital at New Orleans** (HQ); New Orleans; hospital — 4,500. **Motion Industries Inc.;** Harahan; industrial supplies wholesaling — 2,900. **Shell Oil Co.;** New Orleans; offshore oil production — 2,630. **Alton Ochsner Medical Foundation;** Jefferson; hospital — 2,500.

Great Atlantic & Pacific Tea Co. (Southern Group); Jefferson; warehousing — 1,750. **Touro Infirmary;** New Orleans; hospital — 1,700. **Ingram Corp.** (Ingram Marine Constructors Div. - HQ); New Orleans; petroleum marketing, marine transportation, pipeline construction — 1,500. **Veterans Administration;** New Orleans; veterans' hospital — 1,500. **D.H. Holmes Co. Ltd.** (HQ); New Orleans; department store chain — 1,400. **Gulf Oil Corp.** (Gulf Energy & Minerals Co.); New Orleans; oil, gas field exploratory services — 1,310. **Hilton Hotel Corp.;** New Orleans; hotel — 1,300. **West Jefferson General Hospital;** Marrero; hospital — 1,300. **Delta Airlines Inc.;** New Orleans; commercial airline — 1,160. **Hyatt Corp.;** New Orleans; hotel — 1,100. **Times-Picayune Publishing Corp.;** New Orleans; newspaper publishing — 1,000. **First Commerce Corp.** (HQ); New Orleans; bank holding company — 960. **American Cyanamid Co. Inc.;** Westwego; industrial chemicals — 950. **Fairmont Roosevelt Hotel Inc.;** New Orleans; hotel — 850. **Hotel Dieu Inc.;** New Orleans; hospital — 850. **Marriott Corp.;** New Orleans; hotel — 850. **Whitney National Bank of New Orleans** (HQ); New Orleans; banking — 760. **Mobil Oil Corp.;** New Orleans; oil field exploratory services — 750. **Bourbon Orleans Inc.;** New Orleans; hotel — 700. **Exxon Co. U.S.A. Inc.;** New Orleans; oil production — 700. **Lykes Bros. Steamship Co. Inc.** (HQ); New Orleans; deep sea carrier — 687. **Gaffney Inc.;** Kenner; industrial contracting — 650. **Chevron Oil Co. Inc.;** New Orleans; oil production — 600. **Sonesta International Hotels;** New Orleans; hotel — 600. **Texaco Inc.;** Harvey; oil production — 600. **Texaco Inc.;** New Orleans; oil production — 600. **Vinson Guard Service Inc.** (HQ); New Orleans; security services — 600. **Avondale Shipyards Inc.** (Harvey Quick Repair Div.); Harvey; metal castings — 560. **McDermott Inc.** (McDermott Fabricators Div. - HQ); New Orleans; steam generating equipment — 550. **New Hotel Monteleone Inc.;** New Orleans; hotel — 540.

Pellerin Milnor Corp. (HQ); Kenner; laundry, dry cleaning machinery — 524. **Louisiana Land Exploration Co.** (HQ); New Orleans; oil production — 509. **Amoco Production Co.;** New Orleans; crude oil extraction — 500. **Bean Dredging Corp.;** New Orleans; heavy construction — 500. **Deansgate Inc.;** New Orleans; men's suits, trousers — 500. **Geosource Inc.** (Oilfield Services Div.); Harvey; oil field machinery — 500. **T. L. James & Co. Inc.;** Kenner; highway construction — 500. **Louisiana Paving Co. Inc.;** Kenner; highway construction — 500. **Pendleton Guard & Security Service** (HQ); New Orleans; security services — 500.

3rd District

South Central — Part of Metairie, New Iberia

Just west of metropolitan New Orleans is Acadiana, or Cajun Louisiana. Acadiana covers roughly the southern half of Louisiana west of the Mississippi River — and much of the 3rd District. French is still the primary language in some parts of southern Louisiana, although its use is fading among the younger generation. This area is predominantly Catholic, one of the few in the Deep South, and there is a historic antagonism to the hard-shell Protestantism of north Louisiana and neighboring states.

This area is unique politically as well as culturally. There are relatively few blacks, and race has always been a less important issue here than in other parts of the state. There is more loyalty to the national Democratic Party than elsewhere in Louisiana. In 1980 Ronald Reagan was able to carry only three of the district's seven Cajun parishes outside the New Orleans area.

During the 1970s the 3rd was divided nearly evenly between the conservative suburbs of Jefferson Parish and the more moderate Cajun parishes. The district's 25 percent growth rate during that decade required the Legislature to move about 60,000 New Orleans suburbanites in Jefferson Parish to the underpopulated 2nd. To even out the numbers the map makers added about 25,000 more residents of Cajun country — all of rural Assumption Parish plus Grand Isle, a beach and recreation area on the gulf.

As a result of those changes more than two-thirds of the district voters now live in the Cajun parishes, most of them within several miles of U.S. 90, the thoroughfare that runs through the south Louisiana "oil patch" connecting New Orleans and Lafayette. Houma, Morgan City and New Iberia are the major towns along this corridor. Dotted with marshland, bayous and waterways, this part of Louisiana for generations was valued for its sugar cane, salt, muskrat pelts and shrimp. But the dominant feature of the economy in recent years has been oil. Deposits are centered in St. Mary and Terrebonne parishes, as well as offshore. A large super-port for tankers has been built about 12 miles off Lafourche Parish in the Gulf of Mexico.

With oil work commanding high wages, a great many workers from outside Louisiana flocked to the coastal parishes. But the rising cost of exploration and production is slowing down the oil boom, and the region may regain its tranquility. Because jobs here required few references, the area had become a haven for fugitives, runaways and illegal aliens.

The district retained about 160,000 constituents in suburban New Orleans, along the fast-growing east bank of Jefferson Parish near Lake Pontchartrain, including affluent portions of Kenner and new Metairie. While there are some small office buildings in these suburbs, most residents commute to white-collar jobs in New Orleans.

Suburbanization, however, has helped clean up the parish's freewheeling image. For decades, it was known as the "Free State of Jefferson" because of its tolerance for casinos, slot machines and cock fights. Gambling in recent years has been restricted to horse races.

Election Returns

3rd District		Democrat		Republican	
1976	President	71,103	(44.6%)	84,197	(52.9%)
	House	40,183	(29.6%)	95,416	(70.3%)
1978	Senate	42,407	(62.8%)	—	
	House	2,094	(85.4%)	334	(13.6%)
1979	Governor	61,807	(35.8%)	110,931	(64.2%)
1980	President	71,911	(37.2%)	113,731	(58.9%)
	Senate	47,700	(50.8%)	—	
	House	74,645	(85.4%)	448	(0.5%)
1982	House	x[1]		—[1]	

[1] *No votes tabulated where candidate was unopposed; x indicates winner.*

Demographics

Population: 526,269. **Percent Change from 1970:** 29.1%.

Land Area: 4,528 square miles. **Population per Square Mile:** 116.2.

Counties, 1980 Population: Assumption — 22,084; Iberia — 63,752; Jefferson (Pt.) — 160,897; Lafourche — 82,483; St. Charles — 37,259; St. Martin (Pt.) — 1,148; St. Mary — 64,253; Terrebonne — 94,393.

Cities, 1980 Population: Houma — 32,602; Kenner (Pt.) — 44,401; Metairie (CDP) (Pt.) — 114,503; Morgan City — 16,114; New Iberia — 32,766; Thibodaux — 15,810.

Race and Ancestry: White — 82.7%; Black — 15.2%; American Indian, Eskimo and Aleut — 0.9%; Asian and Pacific Islander — 0.6%. Spanish Origin — 3.5%. English — 6.9%; French — 21.2%; German — 2.8%; Irish — 2.3%; Italian — 2.4%.

Universities, Enrollment: Nicholls State University, Thibodaux — 6,542; Phillips College of Greater New Orleans, Metairie — 286.

Newspapers, Circulation: *The Daily Comet* (e), Thibodaux — 10,608; *The Daily Iberian* (eS), New Iberia — 15,799; *The Daily Review* (e), Morgan City — 6,822; *Houma Daily Courier-The Terrebonne Press* (eS), Houma — 19,108; *St. Mary and Franklin Bannner-Tribune* (e), Franklin — 3,900. New Orleans *Times-Picayune/The States-Item* also circulates in the district.

Commercial Television Stations, Affiliation: District is divided among Baton Rouge ADI, Lafayette ADI and New Orleans ADI.

Nuclear Power Plants: Waterford 3, Taft (Combustion Engineering, Ebasco Services Inc.).

Industries:

Ebasco Services Inc.; Killona, engineering services, construction — 2,000. **Newpark Resources Inc.;** Metairie; oilfield contracting — 2,000. **Shell Oil Co. Inc.** (Norco Mfg. Complex); Norco; petroleum products — 2,000. **Delta Service Industries** (Delta Construction Div. - HQ); Houma; pipeline contracting — 1,500. **East Jefferson General Hospital;** Metairie; hospital — 1,360.

McDermott Inc.; Amelia; crude oil extracting — 1,000. **Tidewater Inc.;** Morgan City; marine transport services — 1,000. **Avondale Shipyards Inc.** (Offshore Div.); Morgan City; offshore oil, gas equipment — 950. **Monsanto Co.;** Luling; synthetic fibers — 900. **Martin Mills Inc.;** Jeanerette; men's, boys' underwear — 878. **Loffland Bros. Co. Inc.;** New Iberia; oil well drilling — 729. **Seahorse Inc.;** Morgan City; marine transport services — 700. **Offshore Logistic Inc.;** New Iberia; air transportation — 650. **Garber Industries Inc.;** Berwick; offshore oil well services — 600.

The Service Machine Group (HQ); Amelia; shipyard — 598. **Gonsoulin Industries Inc.;** Houma; shipbuilding, marine towing — 550. **Tompkins-Beckwith Inc.;** Hahnville; plumbing, heating contracting — 550. **Progress Drilling & Marine Inc.;** Amelia; oil drilling — 540. **Danos Bros. Inc.;** Larose; oil field services — 500. **Service Equipment & Engineering;** Houma; oil well drilling — 500. **Tide X Inc.** (HQ); Morgan City; marine transport services — 500. **H. B. Zachry;** St. Rose; general contracting — 500.

4th District

Northwest — Shreveport

The 4th is dominated by Shreveport, the conservative stronghold that fought Huey P. Long in the 1930s and became a center of Republican voting in the 1970s.

Shreveport once conducted its battles against the rest of the state from a position of wealth and prominence made possible by the presence of the oil industry. But these days, the money and power are going south. The oil and gas boom in northwest Louisiana has long since faded, and, while Shreveport remains a branch-office town for oil companies, it has relatively few new, high-paying jobs to attract people. The population growth in Shreveport and surrounding upcountry parishes has been much slower than in the rest of the state.

Shreveport has helped itself by diversifying. Western Electric is the major employer now, and General Motors has opened a large plant to produce light trucks. Diversification has maintained the influence of non-Southerners that began with the oil boom early this century.

The city's strong middle class and the military presence in nearby Bossier Parish have been reliably Republican in state and national elections. Gerald R. Ford in 1976, Republican Gov. David C. Treen in 1979 and Ronald Reagan in 1980 all carried populous Shreveport and surrounding Caddo Parish with at least 55 percent of the vote. Blacks comprise 41 percent of Shreveport's population and industrialization has given organized labor a toehold, but their influence is far outweighed by conservative sentiments. The district remains in Democratic hands only because its recent Democratic incumbents have been willing to talk its language.

Across the Red River from Shreveport is Bossier City, the site of Barksdale Air Force Base, headquarters for a unit of the Strategic Air Command. Many military retirees have settled in the area, drawn by the low taxes and recreational lakes nearby. Another source of recreation is Louisiana Downs, a lucrative race track that was located in Bossier City after Shreveport's more conservative city fathers rejected it.

Nearly half of the district population lives in Caddo Parish. Another 15 percent resides in Bossier Parish. The rest of the voters are scattered in rural parishes to the south and east.

The eastern parishes along the Arkansas border —

Claiborne and Webster — are part of the rural upcountry and home for about 12 percent of the district population. An area of small cotton, poultry and livestock farms, Claiborne and Webster are increasingly Republican. Minden (population 15,084) is the largest town in the eastern parishes.

The district's four southern parishes, with nearly one-quarter of the district vote, form a transitional area between the Louisiana upcountry and the Cajun parishes to the south. They usually vote Democratic. All of the southern parishes backed Carter in both 1976 and 1980. Timber and cattle are important here, with cotton still grown in the bottomlands of the Red River.

For population balance, the southern end of the district was expanded to inclu ³e the northern portion of Beauregard Parish. Most of the district's 16,500 new constituents live in the county sea⁺ of De Ridder.

Election Returns

4th District		Democrat		Republican	
1976	President	68,876	(45.5%)	80,007	(52.8%)
	House	79,251	(99.1%)	743	(0.9%)
1978	Senate	76,060	(58.4%)	—	
	House	37,313	(27.9%)	36,019	(26.9%)
1979	Governor	71,113	(46.9%)	80,383	(53.1%)
1980	President	81,619	(44.3%)	99,476	(54.0%)
	Senate	74,830	(60.1%)	—	
	House	33,049	(26.8%)	29,992	(24.4%)
1982	House	x¹		—¹	

¹ *No votes tabulated where candidate was unopposed; x indicates winner.*

Demographics

Population: 525,194. **Percent Change from 1970:** 11.3%.

Land Area: 6,666 square miles. **Population per Square Mile:** 78.8.

Counties, 1980 Population: Beauregard (Pt.) — 16,474; Bossier — 80,721; Caddo — 252,358; Claiborne — 17,095; De Soto — 25,727; Red River — 10,433; Sabine — 25,280; Vernon — 53,475; Webster — 43,631.

Cities, 1980 Population: Bossier City — 50,817; De Ridder — 11,057; Minden — 15,084; Shreveport — 205,820.

Race and Ancestry: White — 67.0%; Black — 31.6%; American Indian, Eskimo and Aleut — 0.3%; Asian and Pacific Islander — 0.5%. Spanish Origin — 2.0%. English — 13.4%; French — 1.9%; German — 2.6%; Irish — 4.8%; Italian — 0.7%.

Universities, Enrollment: Centenary College of Louisiana, Shreveport — 1,014; Louisiana State University in Shreveport, Shreveport — 3,755; Southern University at Shreveport, Shreveport — 723.

Newspapers, Circulation: *Minden Press-Herald* (e), Minden — 4,016; *Shreveport Journal* (e), Shreveport — 33,493; *The Times* (m), Shreveport — 86,508.

Commercial Television Stations, Affiliation: KSLA-TV, Shreveport (CBS); KTBS-TV, Shreveport (ABC). Most of district is located in Shreveport ADI. Portions are in Alexandria ADI and Lake Charles ADI.

Military Installations: Barksdale Air Force Base, Bossier City — 7,543; Fort Polk, Leesville — 15,424; Louisiana Army Ammunition Plant, Minden — 934.

Industries:

Western Electric Co. Inc.; Shreveport; telephone apparatus — 4,886. **Louisiana State University Medical Center;** Shreveport; hospital

— 2,000. **Schumpert Medical Center;** Shreveport; hospital — 2,000. **General Motors Corp.** (Assembly Div.); Shreveport; pickup trucks — 1,500. **United States Riley Corp.** (Riley-Beaird Div.); Shreveport; special industrial machinery — 1,340.

Owens-Illinois Inc. (Libbey Glass Co. Div.); Shreveport; glass tableware — 975. **International Paper Co.;** Shreveport; woodlands management — 774. **Thiokol Corp.** (Louisiana Div.); Shreveport; special chemical preparations — 750. **Thiokol Corp.** (Louisiana Army Ammunition Plant Div.); Minden; ammunition — 700. **Vancouver Plywood Co. Inc.** (HQ); Florien; pine plywood — 650. **First National Bancorp Inc.;** Shreveport; bank holding company — 600. **Gould Inc.** (Automotive Battery Div.); Shreveport; wet primary batteries — 500.

5th District

North — Monroe

The rural 5th District is one of the poorest areas of Louisiana. Small farms predominate, with cotton and soybeans the major crops, especially in the lands along the Mississippi River in the east and the Red River in the west. Cattle and poultry provide additional income.

Forests cover much of the district and what little industry exists is timber related. Lumber mills and paper manufacturers are scattered throughout the district.

The early settlers in the upcountry were small farmers and enemies of the wealthy cotton and sugar planters elsewhere in Louisiana. They spawned the populism that early this century molded the thinking of Huey Long, a native of Winn Parish. But after World War II, the region became a bulwark of states' rights and opposition to integration. Both Barry Goldwater in 1964 and George C. Wallace in 1968 drew a higher share of the vote in the old 5th District than in any other Louisiana district. Although the district normally votes Republican now in presidential contests, it still prefers Democrats at the congressional level.

Republican strength is concentrated in the district's only major population center, Ouachita Parish (Monroe), home for about one-quarter of the district's voters. Monroe (population 57,597) is at the center of a large gas field and long has been the trading hub of northeast Louisiana. The opening of Interstate 20 has pumped new life into the city, making it a convention center and overnight stop for motorists along the heavily traveled thoroughfare from Atlanta to Dallas.

Monroe is nearly one-half black. Across the Ouachita River is its more affluent, predominantly white sister city of West Monroe (population 14,993). One of the district's major employers, the Manville Forest Products Corp. (a subsidiary of the Johns-Manville Corp.), has its regional administrative headquarters in West Monroe.

Ouachita Parish gave Ronald Reagan 63 percent of the vote in 1980, his best showing in north Louisiana. The smaller parishes adjoining it are nearly as Republican. The most reliable is neighboring Lincoln Parish, one of Louisiana's leading peach-growing centers.

The Democratic strongholds in the 5th are along the Mississippi and Red rivers, where the concentration of blacks is the heaviest. In three of the four parishes that adjoin the Mississippi, blacks comprise a majority of the population. Two of them — East Carroll and Madison — were the only parishes in north Louisiana to buck Wallace and vote for Hubert H. Humphrey in 1968.

While the river parishes boast some of the richest farm land in Louisiana, this is a poverty-stricken area. Remnants of the plantation system still exist in some places, and many of the poorer residents remain sharecroppers. Incomes are less than half those in Louisiana's major urban centers. With few employment alternatives, the area has been losing population.

For population balance, the 5th was extended deeper into the northeast corner of Rapides Parish. The district added about 18,000 rural residents and the Tioga campground, site of a large Pentecostal gathering every July 4 that is a required stop for Louisiana office-seekers.

Election Returns

5th District		Democrat		Republican	
1976	President	83,034	(48.1%)	85,900	(49.8%)
	House	85,541	(53.0%)	75,456	(46.8%)
1978	Senate	73,293	(55.6%)	—	
	House	68,440	(52.5%)	1,025	(0.8%)
1979	Governor	109,553	(50.2%)	108,731	(49.8%)
1980	President	83,040	(41.7%)	110,824	(55.7%)
	Senate	65,235	(54.7%)	—	
	House	94,381	(86.8%)	2,420	(2.2 %)
1982	House	x[1]		—[1]	

[1] No votes tabulated where candidate was unopposed; x indicates winner.

Demographics

Population: 527,220. **Percent Change from 1970:** 12.6%.

Land Area: 13,174 square miles. **Population per Square Mile:** 40.0.

Counties, 1980 Population: Bienville — 16,387; Caldwell — 10,761; Catahoula — 12,287; Concordia — 22,981; East Carroll — 11,772; Franklin — 24,141; Grant — 16,703; Jackson — 17,321; La Salle — 17,004; Lincoln — 39,763; Madison — 15,975; Morehouse — 34,803; Natchitoches — 39,863; Ouachita — 139,241; Rapides (Pt.) — 26,164; Richland — 22,187; Tensas — 8,525; Union — 21,167; West Carroll — 12,922; Winn — 17,253.

Cities, 1980 Population: Bastrop — 15,527; Monroe — 57,597; Natchitoches — 16,664; Pineville (Pt.) — 101; Ruston — 20,585; Tallulah — 11,634; West Monroe — 14,993.

Race and Ancestry: White — 68.2%; Black — 31.2%; American Indian, Eskimo and Aleut — 0.1%; Asian and Pacific Islander — 0.2%. Spanish Origin — 1.0%. English — 19.8%; French — 2.5%; German — 1.5%; Irish — 6.2%; Italian — 0.5%.

Universities, Enrollment: Grambling State University, Grambling — 3,549; Louisiana Tech University, Ruston 9,979; Northeast Louisiana University, Monroe — 10,037; Northwestern State University of Louisiana, Natchitoches — 5,919.

Newspapers, Circulation: *Bastrop Daily Enterprise* (e), Bastrop — 6,473; *Leader* (e), Ruston — 6,627; *News-Star-World* (mS), Monroe — 43,211. *Alexandria Daily Town Talk* also circulates in the district.

Commercial Television Stations, Affiliation: KLAA, West Monroe (NBC); KNOE-TV, Monroe (CBS). Most of district is located in Monroe ADI. Portions are in Alexandria ADI and Shreveport ADI.

Industries:

Manville Forest Products Corp. (regional headquarters); West Monroe; paper, paper products — 1,800. **International Paper Co.** (White Papers Group); Bastrop; stationery — 1,300. **Continental Forest Products** (Continental Forest Industries); Hodge; kraft paper — 1,200. **St. Francis Medical Center;** Monroe; hospital — 1,200. **Ford, Bacon & Davis Construction;** Monroe; general contracting — 1,100.

General Motors Corp. (Guide Lamp Div.); Monroe; vehicular lighting equipment — 700. **State Farm Insurance Co.;** Monroe; casualty insurance — 700. **Dresser Industries Inc.** (Industrial Valve Div.); Tioga; industrial valves — 650. **Great Plains Bag Corp.;** Hodge; paper — 650. **Glenwood Regional Medical Center;** West Monroe; hospital — 566. **International Paper Co.;** Bastrop; sanitary paper products — 500. **Louisiana Pacific Corp.** (Plywood Div.); Urania; particle board, plywood — 500.

6th District

East Central — Baton Rouge

The 6th is a diverse district. It extends from the state capital and university community of Baton Rouge on the west to Bogalusa, a town known for racial turmoil, on the east. The territory in between is primarily rural, with pine forests and small farms providing the base for lumbering and agriculture. But there has been increasing suburbanization, as commuters from Baton Rouge and New Orleans have moved out to get more breathing space.

The suburban expansion and Louisiana's oil and natural gas boom enabled the old 6th to grow at a faster rate, 26.5 percent, in the 1970s than any other district in the state. Some of the gas came from the newly developed Tuscaloosa Trend just north of Baton Rouge. But most of the oil is pumped from fields in other parts of Louisiana to refineries and chemical plants that line the Mississippi River around Baton Rouge.

Baton Rouge itself grew 32 percent in the 1970s, reaching a population of 219,419 and becoming the second largest city in Louisiana. All but about 5 percent of the city is in the 6th; the rest is in the 8th. State government employees and service workers in Baton Rouge provide a large white-collar base that has made Republicans dominant in state and national elections. But the large academic communities at Louisiana State University (enrollment 27,000) and predominantly black Southern University (enrollment 9,000 and located in the 8th District portion of Baton Rouge), the extensive labor activity in local industry and the city's 37 percent black population put Democrats in a competitive position. Gerald R. Ford in 1976, Gov. David C. Treen in 1979 and Ronald Reagan in 1980 all carried East Baton Rouge Parish, but with less than 54 percent of the vote.

The 34-story state Capitol, built by Gov. Huey Long in the 1930s, remains the city's symbol and leading tourist attraction. Long was assassinated in a Capitol corridor in 1935 and is buried in a sunken garden in front of the building, under a statue for whom the model was his son, Russell, a U. S. Senator since 1949.

Baton Rouge assumes even greater importance in the 6th with redistricting. Transferred to the 8th District were about 53,000 voters from areas north of the city. About 25,000 live in the Scotlandville section of populous East Baton Rouge Parish. The rest live in rural East Feliciana and St. Helena parishes and the eastern part of West Feliciana Parish.

About two-thirds of district voters now reside in the Baton Rouge area. The rest are to the east in the Florida parishes, so named because they were part of Spanish Florida until 1810. Loyalty to the Democratic Party remains strong here, although in 1968 Wallace drew 81 percent of the vote in Livingston Parish, his top showing in the state. Suburbanization has tempered the political climate in Livingston Parish somewhat since then.

Farther east is Tangipahoa Parish. Its leading town, Hammond (population 15,043), is the trade center for the Florida parishes. The Hammond area is one of the nation's leading suppliers of strawberries. There is a large Italian-American community, descendants of immigrants brought to the area in the 19th century by the Illinois Central Railroad, the major landowner, specifically to raise strawberries. Washington Parish, on the eastern end of the district, is a heavily forested rural backwater bounded on the north and east by Mississippi.

Election Returns

6th District		Democrat		Republican	
1976	President	73,695	(53.2%)	61,253	(44.2%)
	House	42,960	(34.3%)	82,239	(65.7%)
1978	Senate	54,772	(56.2%)	—	
	House	603	(0.6%)	85,336	(90.4%)
1979	Governor	85,639	(53.0%)	76,016	(47.0%)
1980	President	85,067	(43.5%)	103,932	(53.2%)
	Senate	63,755	(57.8%)	—	
	House	541	(0.5%)	96,425	(90.6%)
1982	House	—[1]		x[1]	

[1] *No votes tabulated where candidate was unopposed; x indicates winner.*

Demographics

Population: 524,770. **Percent Change from 1970:** 29.5%.

Land Area: 2,559 square miles. **Population per Square Mile:** 205.1.

Counties, 1980 Population: East Baton Rouge (Pt.) — 341,059; Livingston — 58,806; Tangipahoa — 80,698; Washington — 44,207.

Cities, 1980 Population: Baker — 12,865; Baton Rouge (Pt.) — 208,293; Bogalusa — 16,976; Hammond — 15,043.

Race and Ancestry: White — 73.8%; Black — 25.1%; American Indian, Eskimo and Aleut — 0.1%; Asian and Pacific Islander — 0.6%. Spanish Origin — 1.6%. English — 12.8%; French — 7.4%; German — 2.7%; Irish — 4.3%; Italian — 2.6%.

Universities, Enrollment: Louisiana State University and Agricultural and Mechanical College, Baton Rouge — 27,236; Southeastern Louisiana University, Hammond — 7,707.

Newspapers, Circulation: *Advocate* (mS), Baton Rouge — 74,252; *Daily News* (eS), Bogalusa — 8,521; *The Daily Star* (e), Hammond — 7,502; *State Times* (e), Baton Rouge — 40,841.

Commercial Television Stations, Affiliation: WAFB-TV, Baton Rouge (CBS); WBRZ, Baton Rouge (ABC); WRBT, Baton Rouge (NBC). District is divided between Baton Rouge ADI and New Orleans ADI.

Military Installations: Hammond Air National Guard Communications Station, Hammond — 156.

Industries:

Crown Zellerbach Corp. (Mill Div.); Bogalusa; paper, fiberboard — 2,500. **Payne & Keller of Louisiana;** Baton Rouge; heavy industrial construction — 2,500. **Jacobs/Wiese Constructors Inc.** (HQ); Baton Rouge; heavy industrial construction — 1,700. **Our Lady of the Lake Regional Medical Center;** Baton Rouge; hospital — 1,400. **Baton Rouge General Hospital;** Baton Rouge; hospital — 1,200. **Charter Marketing Co. Inc.** (HQ); Hammond; petroleum marketing — 1,200.

American Bank of Baton Rouge (HQ); Baton Rouge; bank holding company — 800. **Universal Corp.** (HQ); Baton Rouge; industrial contracting —800. **Fidelity National Bank of Baton Rouge;** Baton Rouge; bank holding company — 700. **Capital City Press Inc.;** Baton Rouge; newspaper publishing — 550. **Louisiana National Bank of Baton Rouge;** Baton Rouge; bank holding company — 550. **Davis International Corp.;** Baton Rouge; electrical contracting — 500. **Georgia-Pacific Corp.;** Zachary; pulp mill — 500.

7th District

Southwest — Lake Charles, Lafayette

South Louisiana's oil boom is altering the 7th District's traditional balance between rural Cajun country in the east and heavy industry along the Texas border in the west. Oil discoveries brought rapid change to the Cajun parishes in the 1970s, and the city of Lafayette, traditional center for Cajun culture in Louisiana, is beginning to reflect the values and politics of the oil industry.

Founded by Acadian refugees, Lafayette still maintains much of its ethnic flavor. Many of the street signs are in French and the city is headquarters for an organization seeking to encourage bilingualism in Louisiana. But the recent offshore oil discoveries have transformed it into a mini-Houston. Many Texas-based companies have established branch offices in Lafayette and oil support services ring the city. No longer a slow-paced Cajun market town, Lafayette is a bustling stronghold of white-collar Republicanism. Lafayette Parish led the state's conversion to Republican voting habits, giving Ronald Reagan 59 percent of the vote.

Although the boom had ebbed somewhat by 1982, profits in the Lafayette area were high and unemployment was low. The city is said to have more millionaires per capita than any other place in the country.

Smaller towns dot the rest of this part of Acadiana. Although less prosperous than Lafayette, these towns have been more successful in protecting their Cajun heritage. To the east in St. Martin Parish along the winding Bayou Teche is St. Martinville, once known as Le Petit Paris because it was a haven for Royalists after the French Revolution.

To the south of Lafayette in coastal Vermilion Parish is Abbeville, a rice-trading center and fishing port, and the small town of Kaplan, which every July 14 celebrates Bastille Day. To the west the farm land in Acadia Parish is one of the nation's leading sources of rice. Sugar cane and sweet potatoes are also major cash crops. Hunting, fishing and trapping are popular in the marshlands along the gulf.

Beyond the rice fields lies a much different part of the 7th, a grimy concentration of heavy industry that centers on Lake Charles and extends into Texas. This region was dependent on oil and petrochemicals long before the industry came to Lafayette, but the oil people here are blue-collar workers, some of whom live as transients in Lake Charles waiting for their next assignment on offshore drilling rigs. With more than 30 petrochemical plants, Lake Charles is one of the most unionized cities in Louisiana, and it is heavily Democratic.

Redistricting made only one small change in the 7th. The northwest corner of rural Beauregard Parish was transferred to the 4th District.

Election Returns

7th District		Democrat		Republican	
1976	President	95,887	(59.0%)	62,691	(38.3%)
	House	111,181	(83.4%)	22,149	(16.6%)

7th District		Democrat		Republican	
1978	Senate	64,712	(56.5%)	—	
	House	75,632	(60.3%)	40,945	(32.7%)
1979	Governor	82,767	(45.7%)	98,304	(54.3%)
1980	President	96,448	(47.6%)	98,749	(48.8%)
	Senate	46,898	(54.9%)	—	
	House	x[1]		—[1]	
1982	House	x[1]		—[1]	

[1] No votes tabulated where candidate was unopposed; x indicates winner.

Demographics

Population: 525,361. **Percent Change from 1970:** 19.6%.

Land Area: 7,397 square miles. **Population per Square Mile:** 71.0.

Counties, 1980 Population: Acadia — 56,427; Allen (Pt.) — 9,448; Beauregard (Pt.) — 13,218; Calcasieu — 167,223; Cameron — 9,336; Jefferson Davis — 32,168; Lafayette — 150,017; St. Martin (Pt.) — 39,066; Vermilion — 48,458.

Cities, 1980 Population: Abbeville — 12,391; Crowley — 16,036; Eunice (Pt.) — 221; Jennings — 12,401; Lafayette — 81,961; Lake Charles — 75,226; Sulphur — 19,709.

Race and Ancestry: White — 79.2%; Black — 20.1%; American Indian, Eskimo and Aleut — 0.2%; Asian and Pacific Islander — 0.3%. Spanish Origin — 1.7%. English — 8.0%; French — 25.6%; German — 2.3%; Irish — 2.1%; Italian — 0.6%.

Universities, Enrollment: Louisiana State University at Eunice, Eunice — 1,430; McNeese State University, Lake Charles — 5,391; University of Southwestern Louisiana, Lafayette — 13,851.

Newspapers, Circulation: *The Crowley Post-Signal* (eS), Crowley — 5,165; *The Daily Advertiser* (eS), Lafayette — 29,587; *Jennings Daily News* (e), Jennings — 5,495; *Lake Charles American Press* (mS), Lake Charles — 39,476; *Meridional* (eS), Abbeville — 6,398.

Commercial Television Stations, Affiliation: KADN, Lafayette (None); KATC, Lafayette (ABC); KLFY-TV, Lafayette (CBS); KPLC-TV, Lake Charles (NBC). District is divided between Lafayette ADI and Lake Charles ADI.

Military Installations: Lake Charles Air Force Station, Lake Charles — 7.

Industries:

Cities Service Co. (Petroleum Products Group); Lake Charles; petroleum products — 3,200. **PPG Industries Inc.** (Chemical Div.); Lake Charles; chlorine — 2,400. **Martin Mills Inc.** (HQ); St. Martinville; men's, boys' underwear — 1,800. **Bechtel Inc.;** Westlake; engineering services — 1,200. **Olin Corp.** (Olin Chemical Group); Lake Charles; industrial chemicals — 925.

Conoco Inc. (Chemical Div.); Westlake; inorganic chemicals — 860. **CRC-Mallard Inc.;** Lafayette; oil well drilling — 750. **Firestone Tire & Rubber Co.;** Lake Charles; synthetic rubber — 670. **Reading & Bates Drilling Co.;** Lafayette; oil well drilling — 600. **Cit-Con Oil Corp.;** Lake Charles; petroleum refining — 558. **Transworld Drilling Co. Ltd.;** Lafayette; offshore oil drilling — 550. **Hercules Inc.;** Lake Charles; plastics — 525. **Louisiana Paving Co. Inc.;** Lafayette; paving contracting — 500. **NL Industries Inc.** (NL Inland Well Service Div.); Abbeville; oil well services — 500.

8th District

Central — Alexandria

In some ways, the redrawn 8th is a microcosm of Louisiana. It starts in the piney woods of the north, moves southeastward to include parts of the Cajun and Florida parishes and ends up on the outskirts of metropolitan New Orleans.

But the district is poorer, more rural and more loyally Democratic than the state as a whole. Jimmy Carter carried it in both 1976 and 1980 with a percentage higher than he received in any other district in Louisiana.

About 18,000 constituents in the rural and conservative northeast corner of Rapides Parish (Alexandria) were transferred to the 5th and about 53,000 residents of the Florida parishes, most of them black, were annexed from the 6th. The new 8th has a black population of 38 percent, compared with 33 percent in the old district.

Under the new map, the district gained most of the Scotlandville section of East Baton Rouge Parish, the eastern portion of West Feliciana Parish and the entire parishes of East Feliciana and St. Helena. A moderate Democratic voting record is no handicap here. West Feliciana was the only parish in Louisiana to back George McGovern in 1972.

The 8th retained most of Rapides Parish, including Alexandria (population 51,565), the district's major population center and its conservative keystone. With neighboring Pineville, it is the commercial and military center of central Louisiana. Nearby forests fuel lumber mills. Just outside town is England Air Force Base.

Rapides, Avoyelles and Evangeline parishes together cast 35 percent of the district vote. These three parishes constitute a border where the Protestant north and the Cajun Catholic south meet. Cotton, a leading crop of north Louisiana, is grown along the Red River. Rice and sugar cane, major crops of the South, are grown nearby.

The 8th takes in sections of Cajun country beginning just south of Rapides Parish and extending south and east toward Baton Rouge. This area is racially more tolerant than the rest of the district, and it is reliably Democratic in its voting habits. St. Landry, a Cajun parish, is the most populous parish in the district outside Rapides, holding 16 percent of the population. The county seat of Opelousas was briefly the capital of Louisiana during the Civil War. Its annual Yambilee festival testifies to its claim of being the sweet potato capital of Louisiana.

Farther east are the Mississippi River parishes, the center of Louisiana's productive "sugar bowl." Along the river south of Baton Rouge are a number of old plantations, a reminder of the wealth and power of the antebellum planters. The plantation buildings coexist incongruously with modern petrochemical plants, a source of jobs and Democratic votes.

The combination of organized labor and blacks — about 40 percent of the population in the six river parishes — makes this area one of the most Democratic in the state. In 1979 Democratic gubernatorial candidate Louis Lambert swept all six with at least 60 percent of the vote. Carter did nearly as well the next year in the presidential race, drawing at least 60 percent in all the river parishes except St. John the Baptist, where he won 55 percent.

The remap also shifted about 22,000 residents of Assumption Parish to the 3rd.

Election Returns

8th District		Democrat		Republican	
1976	President	107,574	(59.4%)	69,186	(38.2%)
	House	113,839	(82.4%)	18,181	(13.2%)

8th District		Democrat		Republican	
1978	Senate	66,182	(55.2%)	—	
	House	76,516	(66.7%)	36,406	(31.7%)
1979	Governor	125,141	(69.7%)	54,332	(30.7%)
1980	President	116,443	(55.9%)	86,624	(41.6%)
	Senate	75,717	(58.1%)	—	
	House	70,680	(56.0%)	47,063	(37.3%)
1982	House	x[1]		—[1]	

[1] *No votes tabulated where candidate was unopposed; x indicates winner.*

Demographics

Population: 524,861. **Percent Change from 1970:** 10.4%.

Land Area: 7,303 square miles. **Population per Square Mile:** 71.9.

Counties, 1980 Population: Allen (Pt.) — 11,942; Ascension — 50,068; Avoyelles — 41,393; East Baton Rouge (Pt.) — 25,132; East Feliciana — 19,015; Evangeline — 33,343; Iberville — 32,159; Pointe Coupee — 24,045; Rapides (Pt.) — 109,118; St. Helena — 9,827; St. James — 21,495; St. John The Baptist — 31,924; St. Landry — 84,128; West Baton Rouge — 19,086; West Feliciana — 12,186.

Cities, 1980 Population: Alexandria — 51,565; Baton Rouge (Pt.) — 11,126; Eunice (Pt.) — 12,258; Opelousas — 18,903; Pineville (Pt.) — 11,933.

Race and Ancestry: White — 61.1%; Black — 38.3%; American Indian, Eskimo and Aleut — 0.1%; Asian and Pacific Islander — 0.2%. Spanish Origin — 1.6%. English — 10.1%; French — 17.2%; German — 1.4%; Irish — 2.3%; Italian — 0.9%.

Universities, Enrollment: Louisiana College, Pineville — 1,149; Louisiana State University at Alexandria, Alexandria — 1,408; Southern University and Agricultural and Mechanical College, Baton Rouge — 8,458.

Newspapers, Circulation: *Alexandria Daily Town Talk* (eS), Alexandria — 34,646; *The Daily World* (eS), Opelousas — 14,174. Baton Rouge *Advocate* and Baton Rouge *State Times* also circulate in the district.

Commercial Television Stations, Affiliation: KALB-TV, Alexandria (NBC, ABC); KLAX-TV, Alexandria (None). Most of district is divided among Alexandria ADI, Baton Rouge ADI and Lafayette ADI. Portion is in New Orleans ADI.

Military Installations: England Air Force Base, Alexandria — 3,502.

Nuclear Power Plants: River Bend 1 and 2, St. Francisville (General Electric, Stone & Webster).

Industries:

Exxon Corp. (Exxon Co. U.S.A. Inc.); Baton Rouge; petroleum refining — 2,400. **Ethyl Corp.;** Baton Rouge; chemicals — 2,400. **Exxon Corp.** (Exxon Chemical Americas); Baton Rouge; chemicals — 1,600. **East Louisiana State Hospital;** Jackson; mental hospital — 1,500. **Central Louisiana State Hospital;** Pineville; hospital — 1,100.

Crown Zellerbach Corp.; St. Francisville; paper mill — 1,080. **Dresser Industries Inc.;** Alexandria; industrial valves — 1,000. **Kaiser Aluminum & Chemical Corp.;** Gramercy; chlorine — 986. **Ciba-Geigy Corp.;** St. Gabriel; herbicides — 800. **Matthews-McCracken-Rutland** (HQ); Baton Rouge; electrical contracting — 800. **Standard Fittings Co.** (HQ); Opelousas; metal fittings — 800. **Kaiser Aluminum & Chemical Corp.;** Baton Rouge; aluminum production — 775. **Copolymer Rubber & Chemical Corp.** (HQ); Baton Rouge; synthetic rubber — 735. **Georgia-Pacific Corp.;** Plaquemine; inorganic chemicals — 650.

BASF Wyandotte Chemical Corp.; Geismar; industrial inorganic chemicals — 600. **Chevron Oil Co. Inc.;** Lakeland; crude oil extraction — 600. **J. A. Jones Construction Co.;** Vick; heavy construction — 600. **Security Industrial Insurance;** Donaldsonville; life, casualty insurance — 600. **Godchaux Henderson Sugar Co.;** Reserve; sugar refining — 580. **Shell Oil Co. Inc.** (Shell Chemical Co. Div.); Geismar; inorganic pigments, pesticides — 554. **Port Allen Marine Service Inc.** (HQ); Port Allen; marine repair, shipbuilding — 525. **E. I. du Pont de Nemours & Co.** (Pontchartrain Works); Laplace; inorganic chemicals, synthetic rubber — 515. **Brown & Root Inc.;** Boyce; construction — 500. **Freeport Mineral Co.** (Freeport Chemical Co.); Uncle Sam; phosphoric acid — 500. **Ormet Corp.;** Gonzalez; industrial inorganic chemicals — 500.

Maine

The Maine Legislature did not consider new boundaries for the state's two congressional districts until 1983, when it approved a plan unlikely to jeopardize either of the two Republican incumbents. Maine law allows up to two years after completion of the census for district lines to be redrawn.

The map in effect for the 1984 elections simply transferred 18,000 people in rural Waldo County from the 1st to the 2nd District. It was the first time that a Maine county had ever been split between two districts. The population variation between the two districts was just eight people.

Democrats, who controlled the Legislature, initially had threatened to place the hometown of the 2nd District incumbent in the 1st District. But in exchange for a two-seat expansion of the state Senate, Democrats agreed to drop that idea.

The state redistricting commission then drew up the map dividing Waldo County. Both the House and Senate approved that map March 30, 1983, by two-thirds majorities. It did not require Democratic Gov. Joseph E. Brennan's signature.

The profiles below are for the two districts in effect for the 1982 elections. The parts of Waldo transferred to the 2nd District do not contain any of the universities, newspapers, television stations, military installations or industries listed below.

Age of Population

District	Population Under 18	Voting Age Population	Population 65 & Over (% of VAP)	Median Age
1	162,825	418,360	74,665 (17.8%)	31.0
2	158,562	384,913	66,253 (17.2%)	29.8
State	321,387	803,273	140,918 (17.5%)	30.4

Income and Occupation

District	Median Family Income	White Collar Workers	Blue Collar Workers	Service Workers	Farm Workers
1	$ 17,146	49.8%	34.5%	12.9%	2.9%
2	15,126	42.3	39.4	13.4	4.9
State	$ 16,167	46.3%	36.8%	13.1%	3.8%

Education: School Years Completed

District	8 Years or Fewer	4 Years of High School	4 Years of College or More	Median School Years
1	14.5%	38.6%	16.6%	12.5
2	18.8	40.1	12.0	12.4
State	16.6%	39.3%	14.4%	12.5

Housing and Residential Patterns

District	Owner Occupied	Renter Occupied	Urban	Rural
1	69.9%	30.1%	51.0%	49.0%
2	72.1	27.9	43.8	56.2
State	70.9%	29.1%	47.5%	52.5%

1st District

South — Portland; Augusta

Maine's industrial Democratic core follows Interstate 95 from Biddeford in the south to Waterville in the north, right through the heart of the 1st. With the exception of Androscoggin County (Lewiston), all the state's most populous and Democratic counties lie in the district. The 1st is made competitive for Republicans by the small coastal towns that stretch northeast from Portland and by a consensus in the state Legislature that heavily Democratic Lewiston should be kept in the 2nd.

Powered by the waters of Maine's rivers, the industries here have made shoes, ships, textiles, lumber and paper throughout the 20th century. The low wages and high unemployment afflicting the area in the postwar years made southern Maine a fertile recruiting ground for Edmund S. Muskie and other Democratic leaders in the 1950s.

Portland is Maine's largest city with 61,572 people, and its Irish and Franco-American communities, combined with a large environmentalist white-collar vote, have kept

MAINE

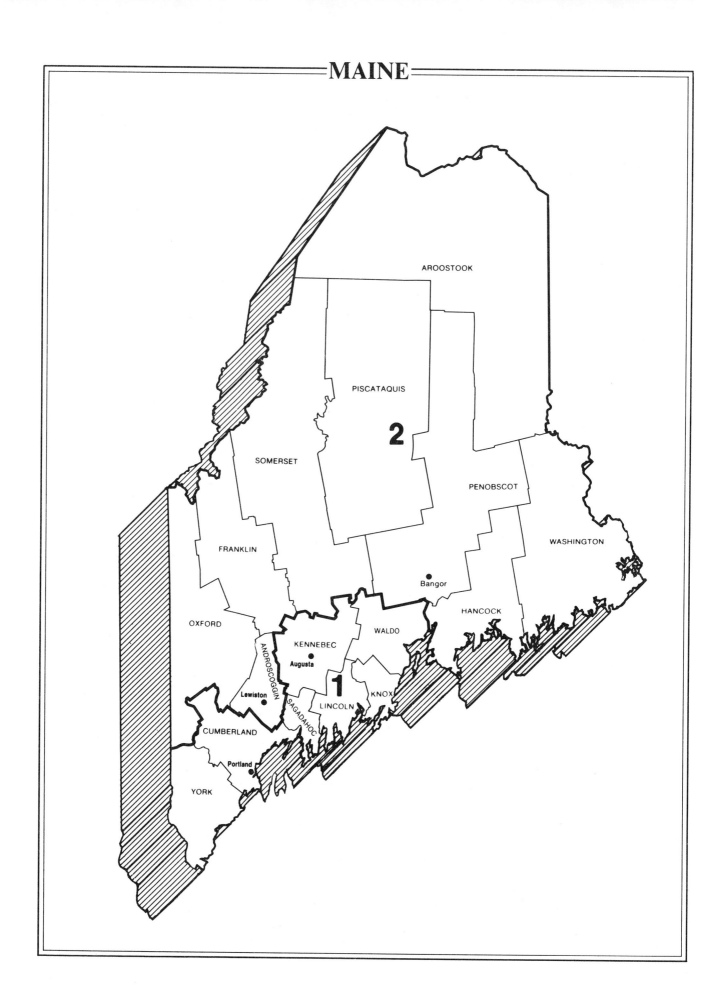

surrounding Cumberland County in the Democratic column in most contests. The spread of high-technology industry up the coast from Boston has brought a modest boom to Portland in recent years; its unemployment rate is low and its downtown streets are home to trendy boutiques and restaurants.

Biddeford and Saco, heavily Franco-American factory towns south of Portland, and Waterville, a textile city at the northern edge of Kennebec County, are other Democratic strongholds. Nearby Augusta, the state capital, has a smaller Franco-American population than any of the others and is more evenly split between factory workers and white-collar government employees.

The district's Republican heartland lies along the coast south and east of the Democratic industrial core. Lincoln, Knox and Waldo counties consist mainly of coastal Republican towns that help make Maine the No. 1 lobster state as well as the "Vacation State." There also are a number of inland farms in these counties.

Election Returns

1st District		Democrat		Republican	
1976	President	123,598	(47.9%)	127,019	(49.2%)
	Senate	159,119	(61.2%)	100,806	(38.8%)
	House	108,105	(42.6%)	145,523	(57.4%)
1978	Governor	94,454	(47.7%)	72,511	(36.6%)
	Senate	66,823	(33.5%)	112,466	(56.5%)
	House	70,348	(35.8%)	120,791	(61.5%)
1980	President	117,613	(41.9%)	126,274	(45.0%)
	House	86,819	(31.5%)	188,667	(68.5%)
1982	Governor	159,449	(63.0%)	89,901	(35.5%)
	Senate	152,289	(60.2%)	100,661	(39.8%)
	House	118,884	(47.9%)	124,850	(50.4%)

Demographics

Population: 581,185. **Percent Change from 1970:** 17.2%.

Land Area: 4,575 square miles. **Population per Square Mile:** 127.0.

Counties, 1980 Population: Cumberland — 215,789; Kennebec — 109,889; Knox — 32,941; Lincoln — 25,691; Sagadahoc — 28,795; Waldo — 28,414; York — 139,666.

Cities, 1980 Population: Augusta — 21,819; Bath — 10,246; Biddeford — 19,638; Brunswick — 17,366; Gorham — 10,101; Portland — 61,572; Saco — 12,921; Sanford — 18,020; Scarborough — 11,347; South Portland — 22,712; Waterville — 17,779; Westbrook — 14,976; Windham — 11,282.

Race and Ancestry: White — 99.0%; Black — 0.3%; American Indian, Eskimo and Aleut — 0.2%; Asian and Pacific Islander — 0.3%. Spanish Origin — 0.5%. English — 20.8%; French — 10.2%; German — 2.0%; Irish — 4.9%; Italian — 1.6%; Polish — 0.6%; Scottish — 1.4%; Swedish — 0.5%.

Universities, Enrollment: Andover College, Portland — 346; Bowdoin College, Brunswick — 1,385; Casco Bay College, Portland — 206; Colby College, Waterville — 1,705; Kennebec Valley Vocational-Technical Institute, Waterville — 503; Nasson College, Springvale — 562; Portland School of Art, Portland — 357; St. Joseph's College, North Windham — 497; Southern Maine Vocational Technical Institute, South Portland — 1,572; Thomas College, Waterville — 852; Unity College, Unity — 652; University of Maine at Augusta, Augusta — 3,420; University of New England, Biddeford — 548; University of Southern Maine, Portland — 8,203; Westbrook College, Portland — 920.

Newspapers, Circulation: *Central Maine Morning Sentinel* (m), Waterville — 25,664; *Evening Express* (e), Portland — 30,030; *Journal Tribune* (e), Biddeford — 14,262; *Kennebec Journal* (m), Augusta — 18,599; *Portland Press Herald* (m), Portland — 55,188; *Times Record* (e), Brunswick — 13,458.

Commercial Television Stations, Affiliation: WCSH-TV, Portland (NBC); WGAN-TV, Portland (CBS). Most of district is in Portland-Poland Spring ADI. Portion is in Bangor ADI.

Military Installations: Brunswick Naval Air Station, Brunswick — 3,916; Portsmouth Naval Shipyard, Kittery — 9,503; South Portland Air National Guard Station, South Portland — 243.

Nuclear Power Plants: Maine Yankee, Wiscasset (Combustion Engineering, Stone & Webster), December 1972.

Industries:

Bath Iron Works Corp.; Bath; shipbuilding — 5,000. **Maine Medical Center Inc.;** Portland; hospital — 3,010. **Scott Paper Co.** (S. D. Warren Co. Div.); Westbrook; paper mills — 2,000. **Maine Central Railroad Co.;** Portland; railroad operations — 1,650. **Union Mutual Life Insurance Co.** (HQ); Portland; health, life, accident insurance — 1,400.

Nike Inc.; Saco; athletic shoes — 1,200. **United Technologies Corp.** (Pratt & Whitney Aircraft Group Div.); North Berwick; aircraft parts — 1,200. **Fairchild Camera & Instruments** (Semiconductor Div.); South Portland; electronic components — 1,100. **L. L. Bean Inc.** (HQ); Freeport; mail-order house — 1,100. **Maremont Corp.** (Saco Defense Systems Div.); Saco; machine guns — 1,000. **Sprague Electric Co.;** Sanford; electronic components — 1,000. **Veterans Administration;** Augusta; veterans' hospital — 1,000. **Keyes Fibre Co.;** Waterville; pulp, paperboard mills — 929. **Scott Paper Co.;** Winslow; pulp, paper mills — 900. **Edwards Mfg. Co.;** Augusta; cotton fabric — 795.

Sebago Inc. (HQ); Westbrook; men's, women's footwear — 750. **Digital Equipment Corp.;** Augusta; electronic computing equipment — 687. **Duchess Footwear Corp.;** South Berwick; women's shoes — 627. **GTE Products Corp.;** Standish; power distributing & control devices — 600. **Hannaford Bros. Co.** (Wellby Super Drug Stores - HQ); South Portland; general grocery & drug stores — 550. **Prime Tanning Co. Inc.** (HQ); Berwick; leather tanning, finishing — 550. **West Point-Pepperell Inc.;** Biddeford; cotton mills — 550. **General Electric Co.;** South Portland; metal doors, frames — 500. **Statler Industries Inc.** (Tissue Co. Div.); Augusta; sanitary paper products — 500.

2nd District

North — Lewiston; Bangor

America's largest congressional district east of the Mississippi, the 2nd accounts for the vast bulk of Maine's territory. Across its northern reaches stretch the pine forests that have fueled the northwoods economy since the 18th century. Its people are clustered at the southern end, closer to the state's industrial core, which lies mainly in the 1st District.

The one portion of the 2nd actually within Maine's industrial belt is Androscoggin County, anchored by the twin cities of Lewiston (population 40,481) and Auburn (population 23,128). Old factory towns — Auburn claims to be the home of the shoe industry in Maine — the cities are the main source of Democratic votes in the 2nd. Lewiston, the state's second largest city, is the more Democratic of the two, but both voted for Jimmy Carter in 1980; Androscoggin was the only county in the district to go for Carter that year.

The only other city of any size in the 2nd is Bangor (Penobscot County), the third largest city in the state. Bangor's heyday as a ship-making center is over, as are the days when woodsmen from the north came to the city to squander their paychecks in the neighborhood known as the "Devil's Half-Acre." Although diminished, Bangor's wood-products industry and modest port remain in operation.

Unlike the industrial towns farther south, Bangor occasionally votes Republican; in 1980 Ronald Reagan carried it by 50 votes. Still, two years later, Democratic Sen. George J. Mitchell won 63 percent of the vote in Penobscot County.

The rest of the district is rural, much of it covered with forests that supply trees for huge lumber and paper mills. The remaining land is turned to blueberries, apples, corn, chickens and Maine's biggest cash crop, potatoes. The potatoes are grown largely in northern Aroostook County.

Yankee Republican farmers form a solid majority outside the industrial cities, and their votes keep the district Republican in most elections. Still, the chronic poverty that afflicts the area is gradually bringing some of its residents into the Democratic column as they turn to the government for assistance. Pockets of severe poverty are found in the woodlands in Aroostook County and in coastal Washington County, which lacks the tourist attraction of the more accessible coastal regions. With the help of a large Franco-American population, Democrats often prevail in Washington County.

Election Returns

2nd District		Democrat		Republican	
1976	President	108,681	(48.3%)	109,301	(48.5%)
	Senate	133,585	(59.0%)	92,683	(41.0%)
	House	43,150	(19.7%)	169,292	(77.1%)
1978	Governor	82,039	(47.6%)	54,351	(31.5%)
	Senate	60,504	(34.4%)	99,828	(56.7%)
	House	70,691	(40.8%)	87,939	(50.8%)
1980	President	103,361	(42.6%)	112,248	(46.3%)
	House	51,026	(21.5%)	186,406	(78.5%)
1982	Governor	121,617	(58.7%)	83,048	(40.1%)
	Senate	127,530	(61.7%)	79,221	(38.3%)
	House	68,086	(33.4%)	136,075	(66.6%)

Demographics

Population: 543,475. **Percent Change from 1970:** 9.1%.

Land Area: 26,420 square miles. **Population per Square Mile:** 20.6.

Counties, 1980 Population: Androscoggin — 99,657; Aroostook — 91,331; Franklin — 27,098; Hancock — 41,781; Oxford — 48,968; Penobscot — 137,015; Piscataquis — 17,634; Somerset — 45,028; Washington — 34,963.

Cities, 1980 Population: Auburn — 23,128; Bangor — 31,643; Lewiston — 40,481; Orono — 10,578; Presque Isle — 11,172.

Race and Ancestry: White — 98.3%; Black — 0.3%; American Indian, Eskimo and Aleut — 0.6%; Asian and Pacific Islander — 0.2%. Spanish Origin — 0.4%. English — 25.5%; French — 16.1%; German — 1.6%; Irish — 5.2%; Italian — 0.8%; Scottish — 1.7%; Swedish — 0.7%.

Universities, Enrollment: Bangor Theological Seminary, Bangor — 94; Bates College, Lewiston — 1,488; Beal College, Bangor — 429; Central Maine Medical Center School of Nursing, Lewiston — 88; Central Maine Vocational-Technical Institute, Auburn — 436; College of the Atlantic, Bar Harbor — 178; Eastern Maine Vocational-Technical Institute, Bangor — 463; Husson College, Bangor — 1,416; Maine Maritime Academy, Castine — 643; Northern Maine Vocational-Technical Institute, Presque Isle — 1,057; University of Maine at Farmington, Farmington — 1,967; University of Maine at Fort Kent, Fort Kent — 606; University of Maine at Machias, Machias — 626; University of Maine at Orono, Orono — 11,262; University of Maine at Presque Isle, Presque Isle — 1,416.

Newspapers, Circulation: *Bangor Daily News* (m), Bangor — 81,061; *The Lewiston Daily Sun* (m), Lewiston — 34,734; *Lewiston Journal* (e), Lewiston — 13,727.

Commercial Television Stations, Affiliation: WABI-TV, Bangor (CBS); WAGM-TV, Presque Isle (CBS, ABC, NBC); WLBZ-TV, Bangor (NBC); WMTW, Poland Spring (ABC); WVII-TV, Bangor (ABC). Most of district is in Bangor ADI. Portions are in Presque Isle ADI and Portland-Poland Spring ADI.

Military Installations: Bangor International Airport (Air Force), Bangor — 983; Caswell Air Force Station, Caswell — 5; Cutler Naval Communications Center, East Machias — 209; Loring Air Force Base, Limestone — 4,011; Winter Harbor Naval Security Group Activity, Winter Harbor — 362.

Industries:

Eastern Maine Medical Center; Bangor; hospital — 1,860. **G. H. Bass & Co.** (HQ); Wilton; women's footwear — 1,750. **Boise Cascade Corp.;** Rumford; paper mills — 1,700. **Great Northern Nekoosa Corp.;** Millinocket; paper mills — 1,647. **International Paper Co.** (Pulp & Paper); Jay; paper mills — 1,350.

Georgia-Pacific Corp.; Princeton; logging — 1,200. **St. Regis Paper Co.;** Bucksport; paper mills — 1,200. **AKF Foods Inc.** (HQ); Presque Isle; frozen potato products — 1,190. **Georgia-Pacific Corp.;** Woodland; paper mills — 1,150. **Dexter Shoe Co.** (HQ); Dexter; men's, women's casual footwear — 1,100. **Fraser Paper Ltd.;** Madawaska; paper mills — 1,100. **Guilford Industries Inc.** (HQ); Guilford; synthetic fabric mills — 971. **Great Northern Nekoosa Corp.;** East Millinocket; paper mills — 883. **Bates Fabrics Inc.** (HQ); Lewiston; fabric mills — 750. **Acton Food Service Corp.** (DeCoster Egg Farms Div.); Turner; eggs, poultry wholesaling — 700. **Diamond International Corp.** (New England Land & Timber Div.); Old Town; pulp mills — 700. **Lincoln Pulp & Paper Co. Inc.;** Lincoln; pulp mill — 700. **L. O. F. Plastics Inc.** (Pioneer Plastics); Auburn; plastics, chemicals — 700. **Pure I Inc.** (HQ); Lewiston; poultry dressing — 700. **Knapp King-Size Corp.** (Barker Div.); Lewiston; fabricated textile products — 675. **Eastland Woolen Mill Inc.;** Corinna; fabric mills — 672. **Cianbro Corp.;** Madison; industrial building contracting — 634. **Etonic Inc.;** Auburn; athletic shoes — 630. **Dori Shoe Co. Inc.** (Adores-Geppetto Div.); Lewiston; women's shoes — 525. **Irving Tanning Co.;** Hartland; leather tanning, finishing — 525. **The Jackson Laboratory Inc.** (HQ); Bar Harbor; biomedical research laboratory — 505.

Maryland

One Democrat was pleased and another unhappy at the craftsmanship of Maryland's solidly Democratic Legislature, which had to rearrange the state's eight existing congressional districts to reflect the 13 percent population decline in the city of Baltimore during the 1970s.

The 2nd District gave up Pikesville, a predominantly Jewish suburban area. In exchange, the district got a portion of Republican-leaning Harford County. The district's Democratic incumbent survived the shift, but it could pose problems for any Democrat who wants to succeed him.

This change was needed to make way for the underpopulated 3rd, which had to expand out of Baltimore. After redistricting the 3rd included Pikesville as well as the similarly liberal new town of Columbia.

The redistricting plan was created by a five-member commission appointed by Democratic Gov. Harry R. Hughes. Three prominent Democrats — the leaders of the Legislature's two chambers and the state treasurer — dominated the panel. The commission reported to Hughes in January 1982, then passed its recommendations on to the Legislature for review.

The state Senate's Constitution and Administrative Law Committee wanted to change the plan to return Pikesville to the 2nd, accommodating that district's incumbent. But it backed down under pressure from the Senate leadership and from the 3rd District's Democratic incumbent, who said that if they deprived her of Pikesville, she would fight to get another piece of the 2nd's Democratic turf, blue-collar Dundalk. The committee acquiesced and stuck with the commission version. With that problem out of the way, the Senate voted the plan through April 2, 1982, by 40-5 and the House April 9 by 102-15.

Age of Population

District	Population Under 18	Voting Age Population	Population 65 & Over (% of VAP)	Median Age
1	156,485	369,721	54,049 (14.6%)	29.9
2	137,566	388,788	46,971 (12.1%)	31.4
3	128,680	399,019	73,372 (18.4%)	32.8
4	152,553	372,900	32,775 (8.8%)	28.9
5	152,732	374,737	29,585 (7.9%)	27.5
6	151,763	376,405	54,034 (14.4%)	31.1
7	151,024	376,566	56,465 (15.0%)	29.0
8	136,727	391,309	48,358 (12.4%)	32.3
State	1,167,530	3,049,445	395,609 (13.0%)	30.3

Income and Occupation

District	Median Family Income	White Collar Workers	Blue Collar Workers	Service Workers	Farm Workers
1	$ 19,978	48.0%	32.8%	14.0%	5.3%
2	24,190	58.4	29.8	10.7	1.1
3	21,444	62.9	25.1	11.6	0.4
4	24,892	62.3	25.0	11.8	0.9
5	25,635	66.6	20.7	12.0	0.7
6	22,043	52.7	31.8	12.4	3.1
7	15,072	48.7	29.6	21.2	0.5
8	33,404	78.3	11.9	9.1	0.6
State	$23,112	60.5%	25.4%	12.6%	1.5%

Education: School Years Completed

District	8 Years or Fewer	4 Years of High School	4 Years of College or More	Median School Years
1	20.4%	34.1%	12.5%	12.3
2	16.1	36.0	16.9	12.5
3	20.9	28.9	19.9	12.4
4	12.7	37.4	19.0	12.6
5	9.4	37.5	21.9	12.7
6	18.9	35.6	16.7	12.4
7	27.8	26.4	11.4	12.0
8	5.8	25.1	43.0	13.5
State	16.5%	32.5%	20.4%	12.5

Housing and Residential Patterns

District	Owner Occupied	Renter Occupied	Urban	Rural
1	71.9%	28.1%	27.7%	72.3%
2	65.3	34.7	86.1	13.9

MARYLAND

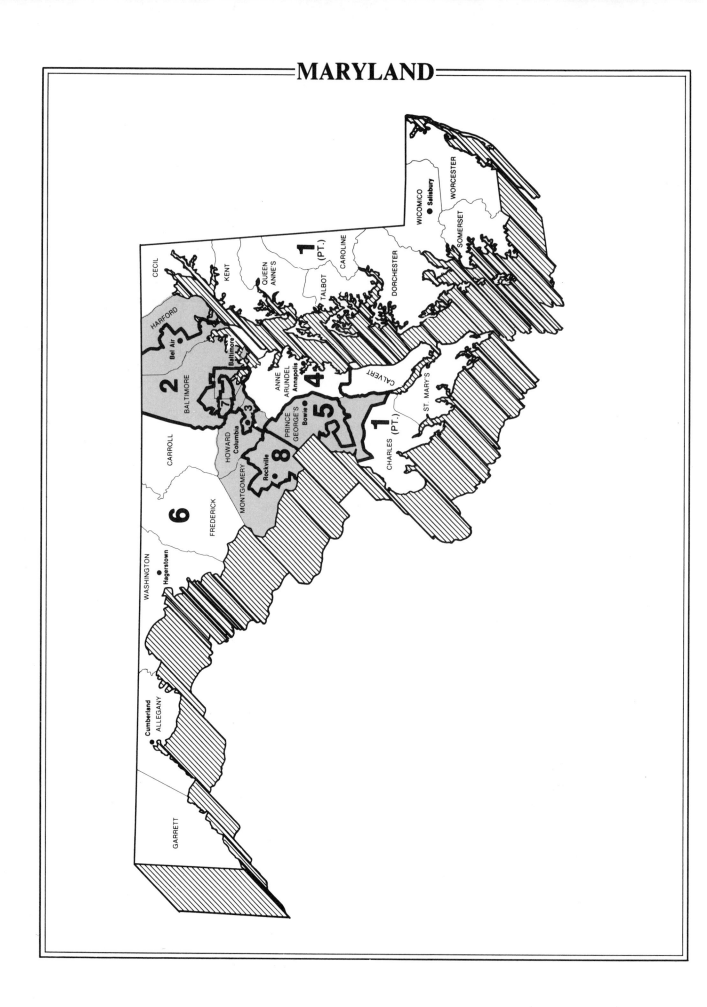

District	Owner Occupied	Renter Occupied	Urban	Rural
3	61.1	38.9	98.9	1.1
4	64.7	35.3	89.0	11.0
5	55.9	44.1	96.5	3.5
6	72.6	27.4	45.5	54.5
7	41.9	58.1	99.9	0.1
8	62.9	37.1	98.8	1.2
State	62.0%	38.0%	80.3%	19.7%

1st District

Eastern Shore, Southern Maryland

The stubborn, independent Chesapeake Bay watermen symbolize the conservatism of the 1st District and Maryland's Eastern Shore. Grumbling about government limits on their catches, they set off every day in small, old boats to bring back bushels of crabs and oysters from the bay.

Sitting on either side of Chesapeake Bay, this Southern-oriented district has a 3-to-1 Democratic registration, but its deep-seated conservatism generally gives it to the GOP in federal elections.

Jimmy Carter lost the district to Gerald R. Ford and Ronald Reagan in 1976 and 1980. In 1968 George C. Wallace made a strong showing, gaining more than a quarter of the vote in three Eastern Shore counties and swinging the 1st to Richard Nixon. From 1962 through 1978 the area sent Republicans to the House. That streak was broken in 1980 when a Democrat won election.

Redistricting changed the politics of the 1st very little, even though its 24-percent population growth in the 1970s was more than three times the statewide average. The bulk of the population is on the Eastern Shore, with the rest in three counties of southern Maryland across the bay.

The map makers made the necessary population cuts by dividing fast growing Harford County in half. The suburban area around Bel Air went to the 2nd District. The 1st kept the more rural eastern section of Harford that includes the Aberdeen Proving Grounds. Two other military installations are in this district — the Patuxent Naval Air Center and the Indian Head Naval Ordnance Station, both in southern Maryland.

Southern Maryland has the same rural ambiance as the Eastern Shore. Tobacco farming predominates throughout this region. Charles County, however, is being drawn gradually into the orbit of suburban Washington, D.C. Shopping centers and subdivisions have sprung up in Waldorf, the largest town in Charles County, causing Waldorf to double in size over the last decade.

On either side of the bay, shellfish have a special place in Maryland life and politics. The Chesapeake's yield makes possible that celebrated Maryland event, the crab feast, conducted around long tables covered with newspapers and laden with crustaceans, corn on the cob and beer. Crab feasts are vital stops for local politicians.

The once-isolated Eastern Shore has experienced substantial growth in the 30 years since the Chesapeake Bay Bridge linked it conveniently to the rest of Maryland, but on the whole it remains farm country. The shore raises tomatoes, strawberries and poultry. Frank Perdue houses the headquarters of his chicken business there. Salisbury, the market center for much of the eastern shore, is the largest city in the district with 16,429 residents.

The area of fastest growth is along the Atlantic Ocean. Condominium towers give Ocean City, which tripled in population during the 1970s, a Miami Beach appearance. Tourism animates the beach town's economy, although there has been an increase in year-round residence.

Blacks, many of whom work on the farms, make up a sizable proportion of the residents in most counties of the district. But while they comprise nearly 20 percent of the population districtwide, they are rarely a decisive force politically.

Election Returns

1st District		Democrat		Republican	
1976	President	76,207	(49.4%)	78,180	(50.6%)
	Senate	70,297	(49.6%)	65,389	(46.1%)
	House	65,828	(46.2%)	76,707	(53.8%)
1978	Governor	86,140	(70.5%)	36,050	(29.5%)
	House	41,715	(36.5%)	72,453	(63.5%)
1980	President	75,300	(41.6%)	94,343	(52.1%)
	Senate	46,236	(32.1%)	97,746	(67.9%)
	House	87,920	(51.9%)	81,506	(48.1%)
1982	Governor	80,375	(71.4%)	32,185	(28.6%)
	Senate	74,187	(57.1%)	55,668	(42.9%)
	House	89,503	(69.3%)	39,656	(30.7%)

Demographics

Population: 526,206. **Percent Change from 1970:** 21.7%.

Land Area: 4,653 square miles. **Population per Square Mile:** 113.1.

Counties, 1980 Population: Calvert — 34,638; Caroline — 23,143; Cecil — 60,430; Charles — 72,751; Dorchester — 30,623; Harford (Pt.) — 62,302; Kent — 16,695; Queen Anne's — 25,508; Somerset — 19,188; St. Mary's — 59,895; Talbot — 25,604; Wicomico — 64,540; Worcester — 30,889.

Cities, 1980 Population: Aberdeen — 11,533; Cambridge — 11,703; Lexington Park (CDP) — 10,361; Salisbury — 16,429.

Race and Ancestry: White — 80.4%; Black — 18.6%; American Indian, Eskimo and Aleut — 0.2%; Asian and Pacific Islander — 0.5%. Spanish Origin — 1.0%. Dutch — 0.5%; English — 19.7%; French — 0.6%; German — 6.1%; Irish — 4.7%; Italian — 1.2%; Polish — 0.7%; Scottish — 0.6%.

Universities, Enrollment: Cecil Community College, North East — 1,184; Charles County Community College, La Plata — 3,831; Chesapeake College, Wye Mills — 1,631; St. Mary's College of Maryland, St. Mary's City — 1,349; Salisbury State College, Salisbury — 4,318; University of Maryland Eastern Shore, Princess Anne — 1,073; Washington College, Chestertown — 799; Wor-Wic Technical Community College, Salisbury — 627.

Newspapers, Circulation: *The Banner* (e), Cambridge — 7,690; *The Daily Times* (eS), Salisbury — 27,120; *The Star-Democrat* (m), Easton — 10,308.

Commercial Television Stations, Affiliation: WBOC-TV, Salisbury (CBS, NBC); WMDT, Salisbury (ABC, NBC). District is divided among Baltimore ADI, Salisbury ADI and Washington, D.C. ADI.

Military Installations: Aberdeen Proving Ground, Aberdeen — 13,543; Indian Head Naval Ordnance Station, Indian Head — 2,824; Patuxent River Naval Air Test Center, Lexington Park — 9,513.

Nuclear Power Plants: Calvert Cliffs 1, Lusby (Combustion Engineering, Bechtel), May 1975; Calvert Cliffs 2, Lusby (Combustion Engineering, Bechtel), April 1977.

Industries:

Purdue Inc. (HQ); Salisbury; poultry dressing, processing; soy bean oil, grain — 8,000. **Preston Trucking Co.;** Preston; trucking — 4,175. **Bata Shoe Co. Inc.** (HQ); Belcamp; rubber, canvas shoes — 1,600. **North American Philips Corp.** (Airpax Div.); Cambridge; switch gear apparatus — 1,500. **Peninsula General Hospital & Medical Center Inc.;** Salisbury; hospital — 1,200.

Amca International Corp. (Wiley Mfg. Div.); Port Deposit; hatch fabricating — 900. **Showell Farms Inc.** (HQ); Showell; poultry dressing — 900. **The Black & Decker Mfg. Co.;** Easton; electric lawn tools — 691. **Campbell Soup Co.;** Salisbury; frozen foods — 600. **Dresser Industries Inc.** (Petroleum Equipment Div.); Salisbury; measuring, dispensing pumps — 600. **Country Pride Food Ltd.;** Hurlock; poultry dressing, animal feed — 600. **English Co.;** Easton; food service, bakery products — 560. **Chesapeake Foods Inc.;** Berlin; poultry processing — 558. **Cold Water Seafood Corp.;** Cambridge; seafood processing — 500. **Waverly Press;** Easton; scientific, medical book printing — 500.

2nd District

Baltimore Suburbs

Democratic politics in the old 2nd stood on two pillars: the liberal Jewish area around Pikesville and the blue-collar neighborhoods clustered around Dundalk. The loss of Pikesville to the 3rd District is not fully compensated by the addition of burgeoning western Harford County. While Democratic by registration, western Harford often favors Republicans. The last time the county as a whole supported a Democrat for president was in 1964.

Western Harford used to be farm land, but people have followed Interstate 95 out of Baltimore and turned the pastures into subdivisions. Comfortable old Bel Air, once a trading center for the farmers, grew by 23.9 percent during the 1970s.

Baltimore County, which still constitutes the bulk of the district, is affluent and generally Republican in its northern reaches, beyond the Baltimore beltway, but it is blue-collar and Democratic closer to the city. In such prosperous towns as Towson, Lutherville and Cockeysville sit the spacious homes of Baltimore's business establishment.

Northern Baltimore County is careful to point out that it has nothing to do with Baltimore city, although many of its residents grew up in Baltimore. Former Vice President Spiro T. Agnew moved out of the city to the northern suburbs, switched to the Republican Party and began his political career here.

Baltimore County grew much faster in the 1950s and 1960s — when Agnew served on the county zoning board, as county executive and as governor — than it did in the 1970s, when its population grew only 5.7 percent. The robust building industry in the county found a friend in Agnew, who took kickbacks in return for favors. Disclosure of this practice led to his resignation from the vice presidency in 1973.

The southern area of the county, inside the beltway, is a political extension of Baltimore. Dundalk, just east of the city, is largely Polish and firmly Democratic. The Bethlehem Steel mill at Sparrows Point serves as its major employer, though the industry's hard times have led to layoffs.

With Pikesville out and western Harford in, the new 2nd is shoved one step closer to national Republican voting habits. The old 2nd favored Ronald Reagan by one percentage point in 1980; within the territory of the new 2nd, the margin was four points.

Election Peturns

2nd District		Democrat		Republican	
1976	President	87,295	(46.1%)	102,243	(53.9%)
	Senate	98,892	(54.4%)	74,662	(41.2%)
	House	117,076	(66.3%)	41,219	(23.3%)
1978	Governor	108,230	(75.1%)	35,972	(24.9%)
	House	83,888	(62.9%)	49,563	(37.1%)
1980	President	98,946	(43.5%)	107,701	(47.3%)
	Senate	59,713	(34.9%)	111,560	(65.1%)
	House	106,913	(55.0%)	87,534	(45.0%)
1982	Governor	77,697	(48.3%)	83,170	(51.7%)
	Senate	85,101	(54.9%)	69,841	(45.1%)
	House	83,318	(52.6%)	75,062	(47.4%)

Demographics

Population: 526,354. **Percent Change from 1970:** 13.6%.

Land Area: 722 square miles. **Population per Square Mile:** 729.0.

Counties, 1980 Population: Baltimore (Pt.) — 442,726; Harford (Pt.) — 83,628.

Cities, 1980 Population: Carney (CDP) — 21,488; Cockeysville (CDP) — 17,013; Dundalk (CDP) — 71,293; Edgewood (CDP) (Pt.) — 18,710; Essex (CDP) — 39,614; Joppatowne (CDP) — 11,348; Lutherville-Timonium (CDP) — 17,854; Middle River (CDP) — 26,756; Overlea (CDP) — 12,965; Parkville (CDP) — 35,159; Perry Hall (CDP) — 13,455; Randallstown (CDP) (Pt.) — 16,158; Reisterstown (CDP) — 19,385; Rosedale (CDP) — 19,956; Towson (CDP) (Pt.) — 23,835.

Race and Ancestry: White — 92.9%; Black — 5.4%; American Indian, Eskimo and Aleut — 0.1%; Asian and Pacific Islander — 1.3%. Spanish Origin — 0.8%. English — 8.6%; French — 0.6%; German — 13.2%; Greek — 0.6%; Irish — 4.9%; Italian — 3.2%; Polish — 3.4%; Russian — 0.7%; Scottish — 0.5%.

Universities, Enrollment: Dundalk Community College, Dundalk — 2,213; Essex Community College, Rossville — 9,413; Goucher College, Towson — 1,087; Harford Community College, Bel Air — 4,180.

Newspapers, Circulation: Baltimore *Sun* , Baltimore *Evening Sun* and Baltimore *News-American* circulate in the district.

Commercial Television Stations, Affiliation: Entire district is located in Baltimore ADI.

Military Installations: Glenn L. Martin Airport (Air Force), Middle River — 1,702.

Industries:

Bethlehem Steel Corp.; Sparrows Point; steel production — 12,300. **Westinghouse Electric Corp.;** Hunt Valley; electronic testing equipment — 2,300. **A. A. I. Corp.** (HQ); Cockeysville; weapons, munitions 2,050. **Franklin Square Hospital;** Rossville; hospital — 1,800. **Western Electric Co. Inc.;** Cockeysville; communication services — 1,700.

Eastmet Corp. (Eastern Stainless Steel Co.); Eastpoint; steel — 1,500. **The Flintkote Co.** (Campbell-Grove Div.); Hunt Valley; concrete products — 1,500. **Rosewood Center;** Owings Mills; state psychiatric hospital — 1,450. **Pinkerton's Inc.;** Hillendale; security services — 1,400. **Maryland Blue Cross Inc.;** Towson; health insurance — 1,000. **Whiting Turner Contracting Co.** (HQ); Towson; general contracting — 1,000. **Black & Decker Mfg. Co.** (HQ); Towson; power tools — 850. **Becton Dickinson & Co.** (Microbiology Systems Div.); Hunt Valley; microbiology services — 750. **The Bendix Corp.** (Communications Div.); Towson; electronic communications systems — 700. **Noxell Corp.** (HQ); Cockeysville; cosmetics — 650. **National Wire Products Corp.;** Eastpoint; wire mesh — 600. **Ensec Service Corp.;** Lutherville-Timonium; security services — 500. **Maryland Cup Corp.** (HQ); Owings Mills; food containers — 500.

3rd District

Baltimore; Northern and Southern Suburbs

From knishes to kielbasa to quiche, office-seekers who stop for a snack in the 3rd District will be struck by its culinary — and ethnic — diversity.

Underpopulated by nearly 100,000, the 3rd was forced into a suburban expansion to make up its deficit. It was redrawn to take in Jewish Pikesville and northwest Baltimore, blue-collar East Baltimore, with its huge Polish community, and the planned community of Columbia, in Howard County, an enclave of affluent liberal Democrats.

Suburban Pikesville absorbed much of the Jewish population that fled northwest Baltimore as the city's black ghetto expanded. In religious observance, Pikesville is more traditional than most suburban Jewish communities in other parts of the country. Many of the delicatessens and other shops in Pikesville close on Saturday. Israel is the dominant political issue.

Inside the Baltimore city line, less prosperous Jews — the elderly and recent Russian immigrants — live in the Mount Washington section, along with young professionals who display liberal sympathies similar to those of their neighbors.

The most firmly Republican part of the 3rd is Roland Park, an affluent and tradition-bound neighborhood. The vote from this elegant community is drowned in the huge Democratic tide from the rest of the district.

Blue-collar Democrats in East Baltimore provide much of the Democratic margin. Home to many workers in heavy industry, Little Italy, Greektown, Canton and Hamilton are the parts of town where the "Bawlamer" accent is strongest and the attachment to baseball's Orioles deepest.

East Baltimore contains the state's industrial heart, producing soap, steel, autos and cable. It also has the city's busy port, which handles everything from delicate electronic parts to coal. Yet the most celebrated aspect of the harbor is not the port but Harborplace, a stretch of trendy shops and restaurants where decaying warehouses once stood. Harborplace's pleasure-boat dock, aquarium and convention hall and the nation's oldest warship, the *Constellation*, attract large crowds to the revitalized Inner Harbor.

This project has sparked the renewal of the adjacent Otterbein neighborhood where young professionals of liberal persuasion have restored old brick town houses. To the south near the city line is the district's largest community of blacks. Some 16 percent of the new district's constituents are black, most of them in this area.

Moving southwest into the suburbs, the 2nd picks up most of Catonsville, a middle-class ethnic town whose residents worked their way up the social ladder from blue-collar Baltimore. When the Berrigan brothers, two radical priests, poured blood on the files of the Catonsville draft board during the Vietnam War, the resulting trial brought national attention to the quiet community. Catonsville is politically marginal.

Columbia is firmly on the liberal side. Designed by James W. Rouse, the same developer who created Harborplace, Columbia has grown rapidly since it opened in the mid-60s. Rouse's idealistic social and environmental goals for Columbia attracted like-minded people. The town, about one-fifth black, has its own subsidized housing scattered about to avoid segregated neighborhoods.

Election Returns

3rd District		Democrat		Republican	
1976	President	108,801	(51.5%)	102,500	(48.5%)
	Senate	130,972	(64.5%)	65,098	(32.0%)
	House	134,990	(73.8%)	44,551	(24.4%)
1978	Governor	112,043	(79.6%)	28,704	(20.4%)
	House	115,163	(92.3%)	9,160	(7.3%)
1980	President	105,804	(54.0%)	72,565	(37.1%)
	Senate	60,942	(36.7%)	105,283	(63.3%)
	House	135,590	(74.2%)	47,072	(25.8%)
1982	Governor	94,274	(54.5%)	78,733	(45.5%)
	Senate	107,144	(71.4%)	42,836	(28.6%)
	House	110,042	(74.2%)	38,259	(25.8%)

Demographics

Population: 527,699. **Percent Change from 1970:** -3.3%.

Land Area: 154 square miles. **Population per Square Mile:** 3,426.6.

Counties, 1980 Population: Baltimore (Pt.) — 157,718; Howard (Pt.) — 55,625.

Cities, 1980 Population: Arbutus (CDP) — 20,163; Baltimore (Pt.) — 314,356; Catonsville (CDP) — 33,208; Columbia (CDP) (Pt.) — 47,394; Lansdowne-Baltimore Highlands (CDP) — 16,759; Lochearn (CDP) (Pt.) — 6,482; Milford Mill (CDP) (Pt.) — 15,081; Pikesville (CDP) — 22,555; Randallstown (CDP) (Pt.) — 9,769; Security (CDP) (Pt.) — 495; Towson (CDP) (Pt.) — 27,248.

Race and Ancestry: White — 82.2%; Black — 16.0%; American Indian, Eskimo and Aleut — 0.3%; Asian and Pacific Islander — 1.1%. Spanish Origin — 1.1%. English — 6.8%; French — 0.5%; German — 10.6%; Greek — 0.8%; Irish — 4.7%; Italian — 3.0%; Polish — 4.3%; Russian — 3.2%.

Universities, Enrollment: Baltimore Hebrew College, Baltimore — 204; Catonsville Community College, Catonsville — 10,301; College of Notre Dame of Maryland, Baltimore — 1,446; Howard Community College, Columbia — 3,043; Loyola College, Baltimore — 5,926; Morgan State University, Baltimore — 5,034; St. Mary's Seminary and University, Baltimore — 318; Towson State University, Towson — 271; University of Maryland, Baltimore County, Catonsville — 6,256; Villa Julie College, Stevenson — 729.

Newspapers, Circulation: *News-American* (eS), Baltimore — 142,547. Baltimore *Sun* and Baltimore *Evening Sun* also circulate in the district.

Commercial Television Stations, Affiliation: WMAR-TV, Baltimore (NBC); WNUV-TV, Baltimore (None). Entire district is located in Baltimore ADI. *(For other Baltimore stations, see 7th District.)*

Industries:

Western Electric Co.; Baltimore; cables, cords, plugs — 4,800. **Maryland National Bank** (HQ); Baltimore; banking — 4,310. **Baltimore & Ohio Railroad Co.** (HQ); Baltimore; railroad operations — 4,000. **General Motors Corp.** (GM Assembly Div.); Baltimore; auto, truck assembly — 2,900. **Baltimore City Hospital;** Baltimore; hospital — 2,500.

Equitable Bancorporation (HQ); Baltimore; banking — 2,467. **Sinai Hospital of Baltimore;** Baltimore; hospital — 2,300. **St. Agnes Hospital;** Baltimore; hospital — 2,200. **Bethlehem Steel Corp.** (Ship Repair Div.); Baltimore; shipbuilding — 2,000. **Chesapeake & Ohio Railway Co.;** Baltimore; railway — 2,000. **Montgomery Ward & Co. Inc.** Baltimore; credit operations — 2,000. **Greater Baltimore Medical Center;** Baltimore; hospital — 1,900. **I. C. Isaacs Co.** (HQ); Baltimore; men's clothing — 1,740. **St. Joseph Hospital Inc.;** Baltimore; hospital — 1,530. **Maryland Shipbuilding & Drydock Co.** (HQ); Baltimore; shipbuilding — 1,500. **South Baltimore General Hospital;** Baltimore; hospital — 1,400. **Armco Inc.** (Stainless Steel Div.); Baltimore; steel — 1,300. **First Maryland Bancorp** (HQ); Baltimore; banking — 1,300. **Mercy Hospital Inc.;** Baltimore; hospital — 1,300. **Anchor Hocking**

Corp. (Carr Lowery Glass Co.); Baltimore; glass containers — 1,250. **Koppers Co. Inc.** (Piston Ring and Seal Div.); Baltimore; piston rings — 1,250.

Martin Marietta Corp. (Baltimore Div.); Baltimore; aircraft, aerospace equipment — 1,200. **Hearst Corp.;** Baltimore; newspaper publishing — 1,030. **Joseph A. Bank Clothiers Inc.;** Baltimore; men's wear — 1,000. **Lever Bros. Co. Inc.;** Baltimore; detergents — 1,000. **Schluderburg-Kurdle Co. Inc.** (HQ); Baltimore; meatpacking — 995. **McCormick & Co. Inc.;** Baltimore; teas, spices, extracts — 900. **L. Gordon & Son Inc.;** Baltimore; memo pads — 750. **W. R. Grace & Co.** (Davison Chemical Div.); Baltimore; industrial inorganic chemicals — 750. **Amstar Corp.** (Domino); Baltimore; sugar cane refining — 700. **SCM Corp.;** Baltimore; pigments, colors — 700. **Joseph E. Seagram & Sons Inc.** (Calvert Plant); Baltimore; distilling — 700. **Sun Life Insurance Co.** (HQ); Baltimore; life, accident insurance — 700. **Mercantile Bankshares Corp.** (HQ); Baltimore; banking — 680. **Atlantic & Gulf Stevedores Inc.;** Baltimore; stevedoring — 615.

Baltimore Contractors Inc.; Baltimore; general contracting — 600. **Crown Cork & Seal Co. Inc.** (Machinery Div.); Baltimore; food packaging equipment — 600. **Northeast Foods Inc.;** Baltimore; bakery products — 600. **The Rouse Co.** (HQ); Columbia; real estate developing — 600. **Environmental Elements Corp.** (HQ); Baltimore; blowers, ventilating fans — 572. **Locke Insulators Inc.;** Baltimore; porcelain electrical supplies — 570. **Western Maryland Railway Co.** (HQ); Baltimore; railroad operations — 550. **Dresser Industries Inc.** (Harbison-Walker Refractors Div.); Baltimore; warehousing — 510. **American Can Co. Inc.;** Baltimore; cans — 500. **Bethlehem Steel Corp.;** Baltimore; fabricated structural metal — 500. **Great Atlantic/Pacific Tea Co.;** Baltimore; food distributing — 500. **International Business Machines Corp.;** Baltimore; equipment rental — 500. **Procter & Gamble Mfg. Co.;** Baltimore; soap, detergents — 500. **Riggs Distler & Co. Inc.** (HQ); Baltimore; plumbing, heating, electrical contracting — 500.

4th District

Anne Arundel, Southern Prince George's Counties

The 4th, which underwent only minor changes in redistricting, continues to unite Baltimore and Washington D.C. suburbia. In spite of its 3-to-1 Democratic registration advantage, the middle-class constituency has a volatile political nature. Gerald R. Ford took it in 1976 and Ronald Reagan in 1980, both by small margins. Democratic Sen. Paul S. Sarbanes carried it in 1976 and 1982, as did his GOP colleague, Charles McC. Mathias Jr., in both 1974 and 1980.

The overpopulated 4th gave up several generally liberal Prince George's County precincts to the 5th. The district gained a small piece of Howard County — the towns of Savage and Jessup, which hold Maryland's state prison complex.

Southern Prince George's County, with a large contingent of federal workers and blacks, remains the more liberal part of the 4th. The blacks moved out of Washington during the 1970s, settling in suburbs such as Oxon Hill and Hillcrest Heights. The ensuing racial tensions have made some of the whites more conservative.

Andrews Air Force Base is in the 4th; the military vote, concentrated outside the Andrews facility in Camp Springs, tends to go Republican. The district also has Fort Meade and the National Security Agency.

Across the Patuxent River, Anne Arundel has 70 percent of the new district's population, and it outvotes the Washington suburbs in Prince George's. In southern Anne Arundel, tobacco farmers and watermen display ideological kinship with the Eastern Shore.

Annapolis, both the state capital and county seat, is located mid-county. In addition to a sizable number of government employees, it contains a large black community, which has been there three centuries and composes a third of the town; Kunta Kinte, Alex Haley's forebear in the book *Roots*, landed there as a slave. Annapolis also has a growing population of young professionals who find the quaint old seaport a chic place to live; it also is the home of the U.S. Naval Academy.

Just north of Annapolis, suburban Baltimore begins and the Republican vote increases. In Severna Park, where corporate executives live in homes fronting Chesapeake Bay, Republicans are in firm control. Nearby sits Gibson Island, whose guarded causeway keeps outsiders away from the rich people's enclave. Farther inland, the new town of Crofton, a bedroom community founded in the late 1960s, stays loyally Republican as well.

The suburbs closest to Baltimore are not as wealthy. Glen Burnie and Linthicum, near Baltimore-Washington International Airport, are middle-income suburbs that often favor Republicans. A band of blue-collar Democratic towns occupies the northernmost end of the district.

Election Returns

4th District		Democrat		Republican	
1976	President	80,239	(49.9%)	80,601	(50.1%)
	Senate	79,050	(51.8%)	66,065	(43.3%)
	House	65,487	(42.7%)	87,872	(57.3%)
1978	Governor	79,543	(69.9%)	34,243	(30.1%)
	House	41,337	(38.6%)	65,838	(61.4%)
1980	President	73,667	(41.4%)	89,510	(50.3%)
	Senate	50,391	(33.9%)	98,037	(66.1%)
	House	46,115	(29.2%)	111,676	(70.8%)
1982	Governor	66,267	(50.6%)	64,568	(49.3%)
	Senate	72,801	(57.7%)	53,324	(42.3%)
	House	47,947	(38.8%)	75,617	(61.2%)

Demographics

Population: 525,453. **Percent Change from 1970:** 17.7%.

Land Area: 624 square miles. **Population per Square Mile:** 842.1

Counties, 1980 Population: Anne Arundel — 370,775; Howard (Pt.) — 17,076; Prince George's (Pt.) — 137,602.

Cities, 1980 Population: Andrews AFB (CDP) — 10,064; Annapolis — 31,740; Arnold (CDP) — 12,285; Brooklyn Park (CDP) — 11,508; Camp Springs (CDP) (Pt.) — 10,022; Clinton (CDP) (Pt.) — 852; Columbia (CDP) (Pt.) — 3,555; Crofton (CDP) — 12,009; Ferndale (CDP) — 14,314; Fort Meade (CDP) — 14,083; Glen Burnie (CDP) — 37,263; Hillcrest Heights (CDP) — 17,021; Lake Shore (CDP) — 10,181; Odenton (CDP) — 13,270; Oxon Hill (CDP) — 36,267; Severn (CDP) — 20,147; Severna Park (CDP) — 21,253; South Gate (CDP) — 24,185; Suitland-Silver Hill (CDP) (Pt.) — 17,755.

Race and Ancestry: White — 77.0%; Black — 20.7%; American Indian, Eskimo and Aleut — 0.2%; Asian and Pacific Islander — 1.8%. Spanish Origin — 1.4%. English — 9.3%; French — 0.6%; German — 8.0%; Irish — 4.5%; Italian — 2.0%; Polish — 1.5%; Scottish — 0.5%.

Universities, Enrollment: Anne Arundel Community College, Arnold — 7,388; St. John's College, Annapolis — 365; United States Naval Academy, Annapolis — 4,528.

Newspapers, Circulation: *The Capital* (e), Annapolis — 30,016. Baltimore *Evening Sun* and *The Washington Post* also circulate in the district.

Commercial Television Stations, Affiliation: District is divided between Baltimore ADI and Washington, D.C., ADI.

Military Installations: Andrews Air Force Base, Camp Springs — 10,778; Brandywine Communications Station (Air Force), Brandywine — 1; Fort George G. Meade, Laurel — 14,241; U.S. Naval Academy, Annapolis — 2,669.

Industries:

Westinghouse Electric Corp. (Defense & Electronics Systems); Linthicum Heights; electronic defense systems development — 10,500. **General Electric Co.**; Columbia; appliances — 1,900. **Roper Corp.** (Roper-Eastern Group Div.); Columbia; drapery hardware, garden tractors — 1,800. **Giant Food Inc.** (Giant Distribution - HQ); Landover; groceries — 1,500. **North Arundel Hospital Assn.**; Glen Burnie; hospital — 1,100.

The Anne Arundel General Hospital Inc.; Annapolis; hospital — 1,000. **Westinghouse Electric Corp.** (Ocean Research & Engineering Center); Annapolis; research laboratory — 800. **Gould Inc.** (Chesapeake Instrument Div.); Glen Burnie; sonar equipment — 720. **IIT Research Institute Inc.**; Annapolis; research — 683. **Baltimore Aircoil Co.** (PACO Div. - HQ); Jessup; fabricated platework — 560.

5th District

Northern Prince George's County

This is the land of the inconspicuous bureaucrats, the lower- and middle-level federal employees who work behind the green walls and glass partitions of Washington, D.C. Each morning, they jam into subway trains or inch down New York Avenue in their cars, heading for one of the many agencies in the capital. At night, they return to a suburbia of postwar tract housing.

Prince George's is a few status rungs down from its wealthy neighbor, Montgomery County, which holds "Pee-Gee" in disdain. The fact is, however, that Prince George's has a relatively high median income and many comfortable old neighborhoods that belie its tacky reputation.

Prince George's was where Washington's white working class moved after World War II, as the city itself became increasingly black. Since the mid-1960s there has been a second migration, as middle-class blacks have spread out from Washington's southeast section. Many of the black newcomers work in the same agencies as the earlier white arrivals. Still, there has been frequent racial tension and constant argument over integration of the county school system, a problem aggravated by the Southern origins of many of the whites.

The black population of Prince George's County doubled over the last decade; in 1980 a third of the residents of the 5th District were black. Blacks are concentrated in the southern end of the district near the solidly black and impoverished Anacostia section of Washington. More prosperous blacks have moved farther out, past the Capital Beltway, to Glenn Dale and Mitchellville, home of boxer Sugar Ray Leonard, the former world welterweight champion.

The county's white voters began growing more conservative in the 1960s, and an older version of the 5th elected a Republican in 1968, 1970 and 1972. But by mid-decade the black population had grown so large that Democratic tendencies began to reassert themselves. In the years since then, Republican assaults on the federal bureaucracy have driven many white employees back to the Democratic Party as well. The 5th backed Jimmy Carter in 1976 and 1980.

Redistricting changed the 5th very little, unlike the major remap of a decade earlier that removed most of its vestigial rural territory. Most of the 1982 revisions serve to make up the district's population deficit of about 50,000. One area gained from the 4th District is Suitland, home of the U.S. Census Bureau and of a bumper crop of federal workers, who support the Democrats. The other big addition was District Heights, nearly half-black and equally Democratic. Upper Marlboro, the county seat, also moved into the 5th.

Thanks to a second minor change at its northwestern border, the district now lies entirely within Prince George's. Map makers sent a small slice of Montgomery County, which had been in the 5th during the 1970s, to the neighboring 8th.

Election Returns

5th District		Democrat		Republican	
1976	President	88,033	(57.9%)	63,897	(42.1%)
	Senate	83,190	(58.2%)	52,640	(36.8%)
	House	81,611	(56.1%)	63,876	(43.9%)
1978	Governor	68,593	(75.4%)	22,341	(24.6%)
	House	65,295	(73.0%)	24,128	(27.0%)
1980	President	78,156	(50.9%)	61,644	(40.2%)
	Senate	63,699	(48.1%)	68,772	(51.9%)
	House	106,237	(74.9%)	35,600	(25.1%)
1982	Governor	81,021	(76.0%)	25,571	(24.0%)
	Senate	73,860	(69.2%)	32,821	(30.8%)
	House	83,937	(79.6%)	21,533	(20.4%)

Demographics

Population: 527,469. **Percent Change from 1970:** 0.5%.

Land Area: 308 square miles. **Population per Square Mile:** 1,712.6.

Counties, 1980 Population: Prince George's (Pt.) — 527,469.

Cities, 1980 Population: Adelphi (CDP) — 12,530; Beltsville (CDP) — 12,760; Bowie — 33,695; Camp Springs (CDP) (Pt.) — 6,096; Chillum (CDP) — 32,775; Clinton (CDP) (Pt.) — 15,586; College Park — 23,614; Coral Hills (CDP) — 11,602; East Riverdale (CDP) — 14,117; Forestville (CDP) — 16,401; Greenbelt — 17,332; Hyattsville — 12,709; Langley Park (CDP) (Pt.) — 11,114; Lanham-Seabrook (CDP) — 15,814; Laurel — 12,103; New Carrollton — 12,632; South Laurel (CDP) — 18,034; Suitland-Silver Hill (CDP) (Pt.) — 14,409; Takoma Park (Pt.) — 4,900; Walker Mill (CDP) — 10,651.

Race and Ancestry: White — 61.2%; Black — 34.9%; American Indian, Eskimo and Aleut — 0.2%; Asian and Pacific Islander — 2.4%. Spanish Origin — 2.2%. English — 7.7%; French — 0.7%; German — 4.8%; Irish — 4.2%; Italian — 2.3%; Polish — 0.9%; Russian — 0.6%.

Universities, Enrollment: Bowie State College, Bowie — 2,756; De Sales Hall School of Theology, Hyattsville — 23; Prince George's Community College, Largo — 13,747; University of Maryland at College Park, College Park — 37,864; University of Maryland, University College, College Park — 11,283; Washington Bible College, Lanham — 602.

Newspapers, Circulation: *Prince George's Journal* (m), College Park — 40,290. *The Washington Post* also circulates in the district.

Commercial Television Stations, Affiliation: Entire district is located in Washington, D.C. ADI.

Military Installations: Harry Diamond Laboratories (Army), Adelphi — 1,310; Harry Diamond Laboratories Test Area (Army), Adelphi — 85; Washington Naval Communications Unit, Cheltenham — 425.

Industries:

Prince Georges General Hospital; Hyattsville; hospital` — 1,950. **Litton Systems Inc.** (Amecon Div.); College Park; electronic communications equipment — 1,200. **Capitol Milk Producers Co-op** (HQ); Laurel; ice cream, frozen desserts — 900. **Suburban Bancorporation** (HQ); Hyattsville; bank holding company — 800.

Chesapeake Investors Inc.; Seabrook; investments — 700. **M. S. Ginn & Co.** (HQ); Hyattsville; office supplies wholesaling — 600. **The Macke Co.** (HQ); Hyattsville; vending machine operators — 600. **District Photo Inc.** (Clark Color Labs - HQ); Beltsville; photo finishing — 500. **Hechinger Co.** (HQ); Landover; hardware retailing — 500. **Kiplinger Washington Editors Inc.;** Hyattsville; publishing — 500. **Science Management Corp.;** Landover; management services — 500. **Dart Drug Corp.** (HQ); Landover; drug retailing — more than 500.

6th District

West — Hagerstown, Cumberland

Moving from the Baltimore and Washington suburbs over rolling farm land to the Appalachian Mountains, this elongated district displays a basic conservatism. Lopsidedly Democratic by registration, it nevertheless has a Republican voting pattern that its population growth has reinforced. Ronald Reagan rolled up a 58 percent share of the vote there in 1980, his best in the state.

Most of the growth during the 1970s occurred in the district's outer suburban belt in Howard, Frederick and Carroll counties. So many people had moved to those counties that more than 100,000 residents had to be shifted into other districts. The 6th shed its excess population by sending the liberal new town of Columbia to the 3rd.

The 6th also moved entirely out of Baltimore County, but picked up a small rural area at the extreme western end of Montgomery County. These two changes were not expected to have any significant political effect.

The major town in the part of the district closest to Baltimore and Washington is Frederick, an 18th century museum piece that has begun to arrest its economic decline by courting a new identity as a restaurant and boutique center. Frederick County is best known nationally for Camp David, the presidential retreat in its mountainous northern reaches.

Just east of Frederick, the Baltimore suburban sprawl has moved out Interstate 70 into Carroll County, bringing a surge of subdivisions to once sleepy small towns such as Sykesville and Eldersburg. Growth was less brisk in Washington County on Frederick's western border, where blue-collar Hagerstown has been troubled by recession. Layoffs have crippled the labor force at the Mack Truck works and the Fairchild aircraft plant in Hagerstown. Fairchild announced in late August 1983 that it was closing its Hagerstown plant by the end of the year.

Economic woes also beset Allegany County in the Appalachian foothills. This is the only county in the district that lost population in the 1970s. Much of the loss came in the decaying old manufacturing city of Cumberland, which industry has been leaving. Employment has plummeted at the Celanese textile fiber factory and the Kelly-Springfield tire plant on which the city depends.

Elsewhere in Allegany, there is a mountain Republican vote similar to that found up and down the Appalachian chain. By registration, the county is evenly split. In actual voting patterns, however, Allegany shows a Republican

fealty rivaled in the district only by the westernmost county, mountainous Garrett.

Rural Garrett has a year-round tourist economy, hosting skiers in the winter and boaters in the summer. It boasts the only Republican registration advantage of any county in the 6th — or in the state, for that matter.

Election Returns

6th District		Democrat		Republican	
1976	President	71,206	(43.7%)	91,657	(56.3%)
	Senate	59,374	(38.4%)	87,327	(56.4%)
	House	103,773	(71.5%)	41,267	(28.5%)
1978	Governor	78,295	(55.8%)	62,117	(44.2%)
	House	103,378	(89.1%)	12,662	(10.9%)
1980	President	64,800	(34.5%)	108,821	(58.0%)
	Senate	45,269	(28.5%)	113,727	(71.5%)
	House	118,296	(69.0%)	53,092	(31.0%)
1982	Governor	75,977	(51.3%)	72,231	(48.7%)
	Senate	68,922	(48.5%)	73,331	(51.5%)
	House	102,596	(74.4%)	35,321	(25.6%)

Demographics

Population: 528,168. **Percent Change from 1970:** 24.3%.

Land Area: 3,116 square miles. **Population per Square Mile:** 169.5.

Counties, 1980 Population: Allegany — 80,548; Carroll — 96,356; Frederick — 114,792; Garrett — 26,498; Howard (Pt.) — 45,871; Montgomery (Pt.) — 51,017; Washington — 113,086.

Cities, 1980 Population: Columbia (CDP) (Pt.) — 1,569; Cumberland — 25,933; Ellicott City (CDP) — 21,784; Frederick — 28,086; Hagerstown — 34,132; Potomac (CDP) (Pt.) — 12,018; Redland (CDP) (Pt.) — 231.

Race and Ancestry: White — 95.2%; Black — 3.8%; American Indian, Eskimo and Aleut — 0.1%; Asian and Pacific Islander — 0.8%. Spanish Origin — 0.8%. Dutch — 0.6%; English — 11.8%; French — 0.6%; German — 18.2%; Irish — 4.4%; Italian — 1.4%; Polish — 0.7%; Scottish — 0.7%.

Universities, Enrollment: Allegany Community College, Cumberland — 1,777; Frederick Community College, Frederick — 2,116; Frostburg State College, Frostburg — 3,662; Garrett Community College, McHenry — 652; Hagerstown Business College, Hagerstown — 232; Hagerstown Junior College, Hagerstown — 2,242; Hood College, Frederick — 1,097; Maryland Medical Secretarial School, Hagerstown — 267; Montgomery College (Germantown campus), Germantown — 1,924; Mount St. Mary's College, Emmitsburg — 1,649; Western Maryland College, Westminster — 1,947.

Newspapers, Circulation: *Carroll County Times* (m), Westminster — 18,994; *The Daily Mail* (e), Hagerstown — 25,592; *The Frederick Post* (m), Frederick — 19,540; *The Morning Herald* (m), Hagerstown — 19,085; *News* (m), Cumberland — 14,103; *The News* (e), Frederick — 13,582; *Times* (eS), Cumberland — 20,453.

Commercial Television Stations, Affiliation: WHAG-TV, Hagerstown (NBC). Most of district is located in Washington, D.C., ADI. Portions are in Baltimore ADI and Pittsburgh (Pa.) ADI.

Military Installations: D.W. Taylor Naval Ship Research and Development Center, Potomac — 2,591; Fort Ritchie, Cascade — 2,069.

Industries:

The Black & Decker Mfg. Co.; Hampstead; portable power tools — 3,000. **The Kelly-Springfield Tire Co.** (Star Rubber Co. Div. - HQ); Cumberland; tires, inner tubes — 2,400. **Mack Trucks Inc.;** Hagerstown; transmissions — 2,333. **Westvaco Corp.;** Luke; printing papers — 1,860. **Fairchild Industries Inc.** (Fairchild Republic Div.); Hagerstown; aircraft — 1,748.

Springfield State Hospital; Sykesville; state psychiatric hospital — 1,600. Washington County Hospital Assn.; Hagerstown; hospital — 1,200. Eastalco Aluminum Co. (HQ); Frederick; aluminum reduction — 1,000. Bendix Field Engineering Corp. (HQ); Columbia; communications services — 900. Standard Oil Co. of Ohio; (Pangborn Div.); Hagerstown; industrial machinery — 900. Bionetics Research Labs Inc. (Frederick Cancer Research Center); Frederick; research laboratory — 800. Hercules Inc. (Aerospace Div.); Cumberland; research laboratory — 800. Random House Inc.; Westminster; book publishing — 700.

S. J. Groves & Sons; Bloomington; heavy construction contractors — 600. Londontown Corp. (HQ); Sykesville; raincoats — 600. PPG Industries Inc.; Cumberland; glass — 600. Mapco Inc. (Mettiki Coal Corp.); Oakland; coal mining — 596. Communications Satellite Corp.; Clarksburg; commercial research lab — 580. Bausch & Lomb Inc.; Oakland; optical lens — 550. Fairchild Industries Inc. (Communications and Electronics Div. - HQ); Germantown; communications equipment — 549. Claire Frock Co. Inc.; Thurmont; women's dresses — 530. Ryder Truck Lines Inc.; Hagerstown; trucking — 500.

7th District

Baltimore — West and Central

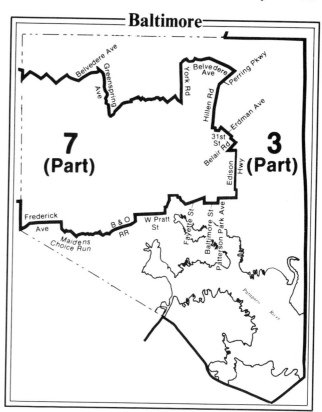

Overwhelmingly black, the Baltimore inner-city 7th gave Jimmy Carter his best Maryland vote in 1980, allowing him to carry the state. The district suffered the steepest population drop in the state during the 1970s, and the Legislature had no choice but to expand it to the west into the suburbs. While that made the 7th slightly less black, the change was not enough to alter its basic nature. It dropped from 79 percent black to 73.3 percent — the 4th largest black percentage of any congressional district in the United States.

The district picked up the huge Social Security complex in suburban Woodlawn and the many federal workers, white but mostly Democratic, who live around it. The rest of the suburban additions — Catonsville Manor, Lochearn, Milford and Woodmoore — often go Republican, but they are overwhelmed by the urban Democratic vote. Within Baltimore, the lines were adjusted to make room for the radically readjusted 3rd District. The 7th lost a chunk of North Baltimore to the 3rd, including affluent, Republican Roland Park and blue-collar Democratic Hampden.

Meanwhile, the 7th gained the Johns Hopkins University community and the adjacent liberal academic enclave of Waverly. Other pickups were the racially mixed working-class neighborhoods around Memorial Stadium, home of the Orioles baseball team and the Colts football team.

The 7th kept the gentrified areas of Bolton Hill and Druid Hill Park, where white liberals live among the brick sidewalks, marble stoops and gas lamps. Also retained was downtown Baltimore, rejuvenated by the construction of new office buildings in the 1970s. With the help of the new Harborplace, in the 3rd District, downtown Baltimore has developed a brisk tourist trade.

But the core of the district lies in West Baltimore, where blacks are concentrated. The city has long had a significant black population, dating back to the early 1800s when blacks were freed by Maryland tobacco plantations losing out to competitors farther south. The poorest parts of the district lie closest to the city's center. Moving west out Liberty Heights Avenue, the tenements give way to neat row houses where middle-class blacks live.

The 7th District's solid Democratic vote can be decisive in close statewide contests such as the 1980 presidential balloting. But its impact is limited by low participation; the 7th traditionally generates the lowest turnout in the state.

Election Returns

7th District		Democrat		Republican	
1976	President	120,831	(77.1%)	35,937	(22.9%)
	Senate	120,346	(81.6%)	23,964	(16.2%)
	House	118,247	(90.1%)	7,276	(5.5 %)
1978	Governor	71,574	(77.4%)	20,891	(22.6%)
	House	69,843	(89.1%)	2,335	(2.0%)
1980	President	127,824	(78.3%)	27,659	(16.9%)
	Senate	50,908	(42.6%)	68,480	(57.4%)
	House	115,908	(84.6%)	21,177	(15.4%)
1982	Governor	102,661	(82.7%)	21,466	(17.3%)
	Senate	106,496	(87.2%)	15,589	(12.8%)
	House	103,496	(87.9%)	14,203	(12.1%)

Demographics

Population: 527,590. **Percent Change from 1970:** -11.2%.

Land Area: 49 square miles. **Population per Square Mile:** 10,767.1.

Counties, 1980 Population: Baltimore (Pt.) — 55,171.

Cities, 1980 Population: Baltimore (Pt.) — 472,419; Lochearn (CDP) (Pt.) — 20,426; Milford Mill (CDP) (Pt.) — 5,273; Security (CDP) — 28,958.

Race and Ancestry: White — 25.4%; Black — 73.3%; American Indian, Eskimo and Aleut — 0.2%; Asian and Pacific Islander — 0.7%. Spanish Origin — 0.9%. English — 3.4%; German — 3.2%; Irish — 1.8%; Italian — 0.8%; Polish — 0.6%.

Universities, Enrollment: Community College of Baltimore, Baltimore — 9,410; Coppin State College, Baltimore — 2,265; John Hopkins University, Baltimore — 9,853; Maryland Institute College of Art, Baltimore — 1,023; Peabody Conservatory of Music, Baltimore — 419; Sojourner-Douglass College, Baltimore — 170; University of Baltimore, Baltimore — 5,338; University of Maryland at Baltimore, Baltimore — 4,777.

Newspapers, Circulation: *The Evening Sun* (eS), Baltimore — 170,585; *The Sun* (mS), Baltimore — 178,960. Baltimore *News-American* also circulates in the district.

Commercial Television Stations, Affiliation: WBAL-TV, Baltimore (CBS); WBFF, Baltimore (None); WJZ-TV, Baltimore (ABC). Entire district is located in Baltimore ADI. *(For other Baltimore stations, see 3rd District.)*

Industries:

Johns Hopkins Hospital Inc.; Baltimore; hospital — 4,500. **A. S. Abell Co.** (HQ); Baltimore; publishing, broadcasting — 1,800. **The Union Memorial Hospital;** Baltimore; hospital — 1,800. **Monumental Corp.** (HQ); Baltimore; life insurance — 1,620. **Abacus Corp.** (HQ); Baltimore; janitorial services — 1,380.

Maryland General Hospital; Baltimore; hospital — 1,300. **Allegheny Beverage Corp.** (HQ); Baltimore; soft drink bottling — 1,290. **Publication Press Inc.;** Baltimore; book printing — 1,000. **Maryland Casualty Co.** (HQ); Baltimore; insurance — 800. **Union Trust Company of Maryland** (HQ); Baltimore; banking — 800. **CGR Medical Corp.** (HQ); Baltimore; X-ray equipment — 700. **J & L Janitorial Service Inc.;** Baltimore; janitorial services — 620. **Janitorial Maintenance Inc.;** Baltimore; janitorial services — 500.

8th District

Montgomery County

During the 1979 energy crisis, Montgomery County vendors walked along the gas lines selling hot croissants rather than hot dogs or pretzels. Affluent and sophisticated, Montgomery County has the highest median family income of any county in the nation. It prides itself on its discriminating taste in what it eats and whom it elects.

As a result, the 8th has a history of ticket splitting. In 1976 Jimmy Carter carried it for president, and a Republican won the House seat. Four years later Ronald Reagan won easily but the district gave a second term to its Democratic House incumbent. Independent John B. Anderson ran up his biggest Maryland margin here (12.5 percent).

The district has a 2-to-1 Democratic registration, but Democrats often splinter over matters of personality and ideology. For that reason, the three House members elected before 1978 were Republicans, albeit moderates.

Trade association executives, lawyers and high-level government employees reside in Montgomery County, along with much of Congress. Physicians, statisticians and other well-paid experts also live in the 8th and work in such Montgomery-based federal installations as the National Institutes of Health and the National Bureau of Standards or in private think tanks along I-495 and I-270.

Slightly overpopulated by 1980, the 8th lost some of the wealthy community of Potomac and rural western Montgomery County to the 6th, further diminishing its Republican vote. It gained Takoma Park, a lower-middle-class section of the county that had been in the 5th.

Silver Spring has traditionally had the county's largest Jewish population, reflecting the urban migration of Jews a generation ago up Washington's 16th Street and past the Maryland line. But its Jewish community now is dominated by the elderly, and Silver Spring's newer residents include Hispanics and a growing Vietnamese group. The more affluent Jewish voters are in Bethesda and Chevy Chase, otherwise wealthy WASP enclaves. Rockville, the Montgomery County seat and, at 43,811, the second largest incorporated city in Maryland, is a step down the status scale.

Election Returns

8th District		Democrat		Republican	
1976	President	125,996	(52.1%)	116,064	(47.9%)
	Senate	128,827	(54.0%)	94,078	(39.4%)
	House	100,824	(42.8%)	109,337	(46.4%)
1978	Governor	113,020	(68.2%)	52,792	(31.8%)
	House	83,026	(52.1%)	76,299	(47.9%)
1980	President	100,363	(40.1%)	116,514	(46.6%)
	Senate	57,207	(23.7%)	184,548	(76.3%)
	House	146,907	(60.0%)	98,014	(40.0%)
1982	Governor	122,028	(70.1%)	51,764	(29.7%)
	Senate	113,237	(65.1%)	60,771	(34.9%)
	House	121,761	(71.3%)	48,910	(28.7%)

Demographics

Population: 528,036. **Percent Change from 1970:** 7.3%.

Land Area: 213 square miles. **Population per Square Mile:** 2,479.0.

Counties, 1980 Population: Montgomery (Pt.) — 528,036.

Cities, 1980 Population: Aspen Hill (CDP) — 47,455; Bethesda (CDP) — 62,736; Chevy Chase (CDP) — 12,232; Colesville (CDP) — 14,359; Gaithersburg — 26,424; Langley Park (CDP) (Pt.) — 2,924; Montgomery Village (CDP) — 18,725; North Bethesda (CDP) — 22,671; Olney (CDP) — 13,026; Potomac (CDP) (Pt.) — 28,384; Redland (CDP) (Pt.) — 10,528; Rockville — 43,811; Silver Spring (CDP) — 72,893; Takoma Park (Pt.) — 11,331; Wheaton-Glenmont (CDP) — 48,598; White Oak (CDP) — 13,700.

Race and Ancestry: White — 85.0%; Black — 9.1%; American Indian, Eskimo and Aleut — 0.2%; Asian and Pacific Islander — 4.3%. Spanish Origin — 4.1%. English — 9.0%; French — 0.8%; German — 5.4%; Greek — 1.1%; Hungarian — 0.5%; Irish — 5.1%; Italian — 2.3%; Polish — 1.7%; Russian — 3.2%; Scottish — 0.7%.

Universities, Enrollment: Capitol Institute of Technology, Kensington — 681; Columbia Union College, Takoma Park — 872; Montgomery College (Rockville campus), Rockville — 12,054; Montgomery College (Takoma Park campus), Takoma Park — 3,737; Uniformed Services University of the Health Sciences School of Medicine, Bethesda — 30; Washington Theological Union, Silver Spring — 281.

Newspapers, Circulation: *The Montgomery Journal* (m), Chevy Chase — 36,491. *The Washington Post* also circulates in the district.

Commercial Television Stations, Affiliation: Entire district is located in Washington, D.C. ADI.

Military Installations: Defense Mapping Agency Hydro/Topographic Center, Brookmont — 3,176; National Naval Medical Center, Bethesda — 5,687; White Oak Naval Surface Weapons Center, Silver Spring — 1,958.

Industries:

Automation Industries Inc. (Vitro Labs); Silver Spring; systems engineering — 6,000. **Bechtel Power Corp.;** Gaithersburg; power plant constructing — 2,800. **Marriott Corp.** (HQ); North Bethesda; hotel, restaurant operations — 1,800. **International Business Machines Corp.** (Federal Systems Div.); Gaithersburg; research laboratory — 1,450.

Red Coats Inc. (Admiral Security Service); Bethesda; janitorial services — 1,400.

Computer Sciences Corp. (System Sciences Div.); Silver Spring; computer systems services — 1,300. **Holy Cross Hospital of Silver Spring Inc.;** Silver Spring; hospital — 1,300. **Suburban Hospital Assn.;** Bethesda; hospital — 1,300. **Electronic Data Systems Corp.;** Bethesda; data processing services — 1,250. **General Electric Co.** (Information Services Business Div.); Rockville; consulting, public relations services — 1,200. **Litton Bionetics Inc.** (HQ); Kensington; research laboratory — 1,090. **Singer Co. Inc.** (Aerospace Systems Group); Silver Spring; aerospace equipment — 900. **Miller & Long Co. Inc.** (HQ); Bethesda;

concrete construction contracting — 830. **Watkins-Johnson Co.** (CEI Div.); Gaithersburg; electronic communications systems — 800.

Rixon Inc. (HQ); Silver Spring; electronic communications equipment — 750. **International Business Machines Corp.** (Data Processing Div.); Bethesda; data processing — 650. **NUS Corp.** (HQ); Rockville; environmental engineering services — 600. **Computer Data Systems Inc.** (Electronic Composition Div.); Bethesda; computer systems services — 550. **Local Digital Distribution;** Germantown; telecommunication services — 500. **Martin Marietta Corp.** (Aerospace Div.); Bethesda; guided missiles, defense-related products — 500. **Resicon Building Corp.;** Bethesda; concrete contracting — 500. **Tracor Inc.** (Systems Technology Div.); Rockville; research laboratory — 500.

Massachusetts

Even though they held the governorship and controlled the state Legislature by overwhelming margins, Massachusetts Democrats quarreled with each other rather than the GOP in the state's redistricting process.

With a population that grew by only 0.8 percent during the 1970s, Massachusetts was forced to drop from 12 House seats to 11. At first, it seemed that the Democrats would pick on the Republican incumbent in the 10th District, sacrificing her district and using the boundary changes to help the weak Democratic incumbent in the neighboring 4th District.

But any such plans fell victim to internal Democratic warfare. The 10th was in fact merged into the old 4th District, but in a way that stood to benefit the Republican, not the Democrat. The Democrat's iconoclastic style had irked the leadership during his four terms in the state House, and his failure to endorse the full statewide Democratic ticket in 1978 added to the displeasure. When the lines were redrawn, the Republican found that the new district contained more than three times as many of her old constituents as it did of the Democrat's. Much of the old 4th was parceled out among the neighboring 2nd, 3rd and 5th districts.

U.S. House Speaker Thomas P. O'Neill Jr., other safe Democratic incumbents and the state's two Democratic senators tried to persuade the state's legislative leaders to change the lines but to no avail. Their pleas turned out to be unnecessary. The two incumbents faced each other in the 1982 general election and the Democrat won 59 percent of the vote.

The Special Commission on Congressional Redistricting, led by House Majority Leader George Keverian of Everett and Senate President William M. Bulger of South Boston, unveiled its new map on Dec. 9, 1981. The plan was approved by voice vote in the Senate and by a vote of 122 to 32 in the House. Gov. Edward J. King signed it Dec. 16, 1981. No newly drawn district exceeded the statewide average by more than 1,997 people or fell short of the target by more than 2,708.

Massachusetts is one of the most Democratic states in the nation. In 1983, the Democrats held the governorship, both chambers of the state Legislature, both U.S. Senate seats and 10 of the 11 U.S. House seats. Never in the state's history have the Republicans had such minimal influence in the congressional delegation.

Age of Population

District	Population Under 18	Voting Age Population	Population 65 & Over (% of VAP)	Median Age
1	131,532	391,008	66,994 (17.1%)	30.6
2	144,151	377,798	66,787 (17.7%)	31.4
3	144,713	376,641	61,279 (16.3%)	30.5
4	135,750	386,245	66,544 (17.2%)	32.1
5	149,388	368,925	53,808 (14.6%)	30.1
6	135,650	383,191	68,157 (17.8%)	32.6
7	136,765	387,217	65,637 (17.0%)	32.1
8	87,439	434,109	67,920 (15.6%)	29.3
9	138,239	380,987	63,703 (16.7%)	30.7
10	144,561	377,639	77,422 (20.5%)	33.1
11	142,201	382,888	68,280 (17.8%)	31.1
State	1,490,389	4,246,648	726,531 (17.1%)	31.2

Income and Occupation

District	Median Family Income	White Collar Workers	Blue Collar Workers	Service Workers	Farm Workers
1	$ 19,567	52.4%	31.1%	14.8%	1.7%
2	19,648	49.7	36.2	13.2	0.9
3	21,847	55.2	31.2	12.9	0.8
4	22,758	61.3	27.2	10.9	0.7
5	23,489	59.7	28.7	11.0	0.7
6	22,131	56.6	29.0	13.4	1.1
7	23,088	61.4	26.3	11.8	0.5
8	19,973	66.7	18.7	14.2	0.4
9	19,938	58.4	25.1	15.9	0.6
10	19,577	54.1	29.5	14.3	2.1
11	20,955	57.2	27.4	15.0	0.4
State	$ 21,166	57.7%	28.1%	13.4%	0.9%

Education: School Years Completed

District	8 Years or Fewer	4 Years of High School	4 Years of College or More	Median School Years
1	14.6%	37.5%	17.6%	12.5
2	18.5	36.9	13.7	12.4
3	14.8	35.6	18.2	12.6
4	17.1	29.1	27.4	12.7

MASSACHUSETTS

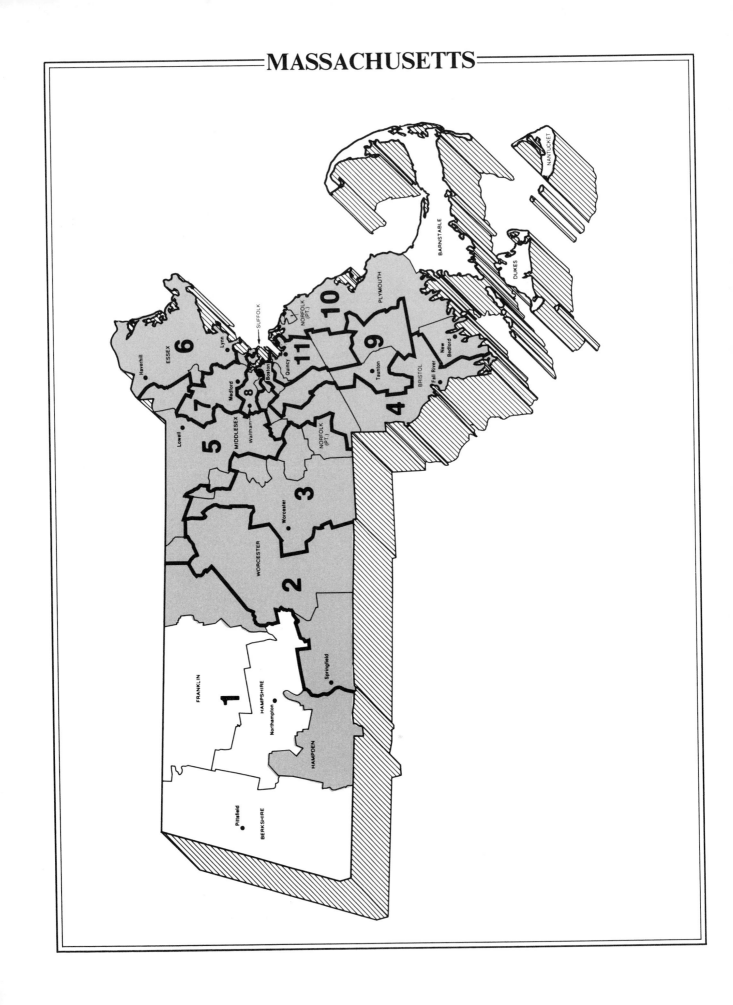

District	8 Years or Fewer	4 Years of High School	4 Years of College or More	Median School Years
5	13.6	33.3	24.9	12.7
6	11.4	38.5	18.9	12.7
7	11.2	41.8	17.7	12.6
8	13.8	30.3	30.1	12.8
9	16.1	37.0	18.5	12.5
10	16.1	35.6	19.5	12.6
11	10.9	44.7	13.8	12.5
State	14.4%	36.4%	20.0%	12.6

Housing and Residential Patterns

District	Owner Occupied	Renter Occupied	Urban	Rural
1	62.5%	37.5%	69.0%	31.0%
2	61.5	38.5	79.3	20.7
3	61.5	38.5	76.0	24.0
4	60.8	39.2	83.4	16.6
5	60.0	40.0	82.5	17.5
6	61.5	38.5	88.9	11.1
7	61.1	38.9	98.9	1.1
8	30.9	69.1	100.0	0.0
9	48.5	51.5	91.1	8.9
10	70.5	29.5	54.5	45.5
11	57.8	42.2	98.1	1.9
State	57.5%	42.5%	83.8%	16.2%

1st District

West — Berkshire Hills, Pioneer Valley

Extending over parts of five counties, the 1st is the closest thing to a rural district remaining in Massachusetts. It is dominated by small manufacturing centers and placid hill towns set amid woodland. The only heavily developed patch is a string of small cities along the winding Connecticut River, running through the Pioneer Valley on Interstate 91.

While there are significant Italian, Irish, Polish and French-Canadian enclaves, the 1st as a whole is not as heavily ethnic as eastern Massachusetts. Residents of the area west of the Connecticut River often feel cut off from Boston's influence, and it is one of the few parts of New England where as many baseball fans cheer for the New York Yankees as for the Boston Red Sox. An area of the state where Republicans often run well, the 1st has been protected from Democrats' redistricting schemes by its isolated western location.

All of the territory's cities, primarily red-brick mill towns with industry based on textiles, electrical equipment and light manufacturing, have lost residents since the 1970 census. The one center of population growth in the 1970s was Hampshire County, which grew by a robust 12 percent. Hampshire includes the youth-oriented "five college" area that is home to the University of Massachusetts, Smith, Mount Holyoke, Amherst and Hampshire colleges.

The district's largest employer, the sprawling General Electric installation in Pittsfield, produces electrical transformers, plastics and weapons guidance systems. The plant's reliance on cyclical military contracts and the grad-

ual shift of GE operations to the Sun Belt keep the local economy alternating between periods of stability and decline. The second-oldest commercial nuclear power plant in the nation, the Yankee Atomic plant in isolated Rowe near the Vermont border, has eased the energy-starved area's dependence on OPEC oil, although it has been the focus of a local controversy over waste disposal.

Outside the cities, dairy farming remains important to the western Massachusetts economy, although the number of farms is comparatively small. There is also some tobacco growing along the Connecticut border.

Pittsfield, the largest city in the 1st, leans Democratic but sometimes splits its ticket to support liberal Republicans. In the closely fought 1978 governor's race, Pittsfield and Berkshire County bucked the statewide trend and supported a liberal Republican, Francis W. Hatch, over the conservative Democrat Edward J. King. At the same time, the county gave strong margins to liberal Democrat Paul E. Tsongas over Republican Edward W. Brooke. In that election, Berkshire County's vote was within one-tenth of a percentage point of the statewide outcome; the county is often viewed as a bellwether of Massachusetts political trends.

The remap added to the 1st the town of Orange, unifying all of Franklin County within the district. The new boundaries also extend the 1st into Worcester County, adding the towns of Athol, Royalston, Winchendon, Templeton, Philipston and Petersham.

Although the 1st District is generally as Democratic as the state as a whole, it has never sent a Democrat to the U.S. House.

Election Returns

1st District		Democrat		Republican	
1976	President	131,832	(56.2%)	94,134	(40.2%)
	Senate	158,843	(69.3%)	65,985	(28.8%)
	House	86,703	(37.8%)	141,781	(61.8%)
1978	Governor	73,029	(43.6%)	94,239	(56.2%)
	Senate	93,343	(55.1%)	75,907	(44.8%)
	House	6,474	(4.6%)	134,936	(95.3%)
1980	President	98,141	(42.6%)	92,388	(40.1%)
	House	58,782	(26.5%)	159,816	(72.1%)
1982	Governor	104,773	(58.9%)	46,984	(36.5%)
	Senate	101,394	(52.5%)	76,617	(41.2%)
	House	—[1]		x[1]	

[1] *No votes tabulated where candidate was unopposed; x indicates winner.*

Demographics

Population: 522,540. **Percent Change from 1970:** 4.1%.

Land Area: 2,715 square miles. **Population per Square Mile:** 192.5.

Counties, 1980 Population: Berkshire — 145,110; Franklin — 64,317; Hampden (Pt.) — 147,645; Hampshire — 138,813; Worcester (Pt.) — 26,655.

Cities, 1980 Population: Adams — 10,381; Agawam — 26,271; Amherst — 33,229; Athol — 10,634; Easthampton — 15,580; Greenfield — 18,436; Holyoke — 44,678; North Adams — 18,063; Northampton — 29,286; Pittsfield — 51,974; South Hadley — 16,399; Westfield — 36,465; West Springfield — 27,042.

Race and Ancestry: White — 96.8%; Black — 1.2%; American Indian, Eskimo and Aleut — 0.1%; Asian and Pacific Islander — 0.5%.

Spanish Origin — 2.0%. English — 9.1%; French — 8.4%; German — 2.6%; Irish — 7.2%; Italian — 4.7%; Polish — 7.2%; Russian — 0.7%; Scottish — 0.9%; Swedish — 0.5%.

Universities, Enrollment: Amherst College, Amherst — 1,541; Berkshire Christian College, Lenox — 146; Berkshire Community College, Pittsfield — 1,814; Business Education Institute, West Springfield — 297; Greenfield Community College, Greenfield — 1,461; Hampshire College, Amherst — 1,227; Holyoke Community College, Holyoke — 5,315; Mount Holyoke College, South Hadley — 2,002.

North Adams State College, North Adams — 2,917; St. Hyacinth College and Seminary, Granby — 51; Simon's Rock of Bard College, Great Barrington — 261; Smith College, Northampton — 2,969; University of Massachusetts at Amherst, Amherst — 24,737; Westfield State College, Westfield — 2,944; Williams College, Williamstown — 1,999.

Newspapers, Circulation: *Athol Daily News* (e), Athol — 5,556; *The Berkshire Eagle* (m), Pittsfield — 31,026; *Daily Hampshire Gazette* (e), Northampton — 18,928; *Greenfield Recorder* (e), Greenfield — 15,143; *The Transcript* (e), North Adams — 12,972; *Transcript-Telegram* (e), Holyoke — 29,077; *Westfield Evening News* (e), Westfield — 7,000.

Commercial Television Stations, Affiliation: WCDC, Adams (ABC). Most of district is located in Springfield ADI. Portions are in Boston ADI and Albany (N.Y.)-Schenectady (N.Y.)-Troy (N.Y.) ADI.

Military Installations: Barnes Municipal Airport (Air Force), Westfield — 708.

Nuclear Power Plants: Yankee-Rowe 1, Rowe (Westinghouse, Stone & Webster), July 1961.

Industries:

General Electric Co.; Pittsfield; electrical equipment — 7,000. **Digital Equipment Corp.;** Westfield; semiconductors — 1,800. **Sprague Electric Co.** (HQ); North Adams; electronic capacitors — 1,800. **Dennison National Co.** (HQ); Holyoke; notebooks — 1,500. **L. S. Starrett Co. Inc.** (Webber Gage Div. - HQ); Athol; precision tools — 1,500.

Berkshire Medical Center Inc.; Pittsfield; hospital — 1,400. **Beatrice Foods Co.** (Buxton Div.); Agawam; leather goods — 1,100. **Holyoke Hospital;** Holyoke; hospital — 1,000. **Veterans Administration;** Northampton; veterans' hospital — 1,000. **Litton Industrial Products Inc.** (Union Butterfield Div.); Athol; precision tools — 900. **MTD Products Inc.** (Columbia Mfg. Co. Div.); Westfield; bicycles — 800. **James River-Graphics Inc.** (HQ); South Hadley; sensitized paper — 760. **The Pro Corp.;** Florence; brooms, brushes — 700. **Textron Inc.** (Sheaffer-Eaton Div.); Pittsfield; stationery — 700. **TRW Inc.** (United-Greenfield Div.); Greenfield; industrial machinery — 700.

Beloit Corp. (Jones-Plastic Div.); Dalton; woodworking machinery — 650. **Adams Print Works Inc.** (HQ); Adams; fabric printing, finishing — 600. **General Electric Co.** (Plastic Business Div.); Pittsfield; plastic sheeting — 600. **Hammermill Paper Co.** (Strathmore Paper Co. Div.); Westfield; paper mills — 600. **Ingersoll-Rand Co. Inc.** (Miller Falls Co. Div.); South Deerfield; machine, hand tools — 600. **Kimberly-Clark Corp.** (Schweitzer Div.); Lee; paper, paperboard products — 600. **Stanley Home Products Inc.;** East Hampton; brushes — 600. **Crane & Co. Inc.;** Dalton; paper mills — 575. **Hammermill Paper Co.** (Old Colony Envelope Co. Div.); Westfield; envelopes — 550. **Savage Industries Inc.;** Westfield; small arms — 513. **Eltra Corp.;** West Springfield; electrical equipment — 500.

2nd District

West Central — Springfield

The economic woes of the 1970s badly hurt Springfield and Chicopee, in the center of the industrial corridor that runs along the Connecticut River. The old 2nd District as a whole lost 1.3 percent of its population between 1970 and 1980, forcing it to move east to pick up additional territory in northern Worcester County.

Springfield is the population base of the 2nd District as well as the commercial center of the western part of the state. The city has significant French-Canadian and Polish populations, and is 16 percent black and 9 percent Puerto Rican. Among the largest Springfield employers are Smith and Wesson, the firearms manufacturers, and the Massachusetts Mutual Life Insurance offices. Springfield has diversified its economy since the mid-70s' recession and was showing signs of renewal when the early 1980s economic downturn began.

Chicopee, the second-largest city in the district, suffered a 17.3 percent loss of population during the past decade. The closure of rubber and metal companies eliminated about 5,600 jobs, and the Strategic Air Command closed its Westover Air Force Base bomber field — once the largest on the East Coast — in 1973. Westover remains a reserve base. In the last few years, however, the city has attracted some new high-technology industries.

The Democratic voters in Springfield and Chicopee usually outvote the Republicans in the territory's smaller towns. Of the cities in the newly drawn 2nd, only suburban Westfield and Leominster voted for Ronald Reagan in 1980.

The addition of the medium-sized cities of Gardner, Fitchburg and Leominster, and the town of Westminster, all of which had been in the old 4th District, preserves the 2nd's character as a center for light industry. The district lost Orange, Athol, Royalston, Winchendon, Templeton, Philipston and Petersham to the 1st. It lost Ashburnham to the 5th District and Douglas to the 3rd.

Election Returns

2nd District		Democrat		Republican	
1976	President	135,571	(61.1%)	80,355	(36.2%)
	Senate	153,605	(69.7%)	60,099	(27.3%)
	House	147,302	(69.7%)	55,395	(26.2%)
1978	Governor	81,928	(50.9%)	78,636	(48.8%)
	Senate	91,358	(55.7%)	72,458	(44.2%)
	House	125,745	(78.8%)	33,873	(21.2%)
1980	President	100,089	(45.3%)	88,677	(40.1%)
	House	128,761	(64.2%)	55,749	(27.8%)
1982	Governor	99,391	(57.9%)	61,971	(36.1%)
	Senate	100,901	(57.1%)	73,867	(41.8%)
	House	118,215	(72.6%)	44,544	(27.4%)

Demographics

Population: 521,949. **Percent Change from 1970:** -2.2%.

Land Area: 999 square miles. **Population per Square Mile:** 522.5.

Counties, 1980 Population: Hampden (Pt.) — 295,373; Worcester (Pt.) — 226,576.

Cities, 1980 Population: Chicopee — 55,112; East Longmeadow — 12,905; Fitchburg — 39,580; Gardner — 17,900; Holden — 13,336; Leominster — 34,508; Longmeadow — 16,301; Ludlow — 18,150; Oxford — 11,680; Palmer — 11,389; Southbridge — 16,665; Spencer — 10,774; Springfield — 152,319; Webster — 14,480; Wilbraham — 12,053.

Race and Ancestry: White — 91.8%; Black — 5.3%; American Indian, Eskimo and Aleut — 0.1%; Asian and Pacific Islander — 0.4%.

Spanish Origin — 3.7%. English — 6.4%; French — 12.6%; German — 1.5%; Greek — 0.8%; Irish — 6.5%; Italian — 5.0%; Polish — 6.8%; Portuguese — 1.4%; Russian — 0.6%; Scottish — 0.7%; Swedish — 1.0%.

Universities, Enrollment: American International College, Springfield — 2,037; Anna Maria College, Paxton — 1,503; Bay Path Junior College, Longmeadow — 677; College of Our Lady of the Elms, Chicopee — 631; Fitchburg State College, Fitchburg — 5,670; Mount Wachusett Community College, Gardner — 1,613; Nichols College, Dudley — 1,076; Springfield College, Springfield — 2,725; Springfield Technical Community College, Springfield — 3,785; Western New England College, Springfield — 5,310.

Newspapers, Circulation: *Fitchburg-Leominster Sentinel and Enterprise* (e), Fitchburg — 23,698; *The Gardner News* (e), Gardner — 7,852; *The News* (e), Southbridge — 6,070; *News* (eS), Springfield — 75,619; *Union* (mS), Springfield — 72,495.

Commercial Television Stations, Affiliation: WGGB-TV, Springfield (ABC); WWLP, Springfield (NBC). Most of district is located in Boston ADI. Portion is in Springfield ADI.

Military Installations: Westover Air Force Base, Chicopee — 2,020.

Industries:

Baystate Medical Center Inc.; Springfield; hospital — 3,820. **American Optical Corp.** (HQ); Southbridge; ophthalmic goods — 3,000. **Massachusetts Mutual Life Insurance Co.** (HQ); Springfield; life, accident insurance — 2,800. **Bangor Punta Corp.** (Smith & Wesson Div.); Springfield; firearms — 2,600. **Milton Bradley Co.;** East Longmeadow; games — 2,000.

American Hoechst Corp. (Foster Grant Div.); Leominster; plastics products — 1,700. **Digital Equipment Corp.;** Westminster; computers — 1,650. **Questor Corp.** (Spalding North America Div.); Chicopee; sporting goods — 1,500. **Wallace-Murray Corp.** (Simonds Cutting Tools Div.); Fitchburg; hand tools — 1,460. **Simplex Time Recorder Co.** (HQ); Gardner; time recording machines — 1,400. **Monsanto Co.;** Springfield; resin, plastics — 1,300. **Easco Tools Inc.** (HQ); Springfield; wrenches — 1,250. **Mercy Hospital Corp.;** Springfield; hospital — 1,200. **Ambac Industries Inc.** (American Bosch Div.); Springfield; diesel motors — 1,100. **Consolidated Rail Corp.;** Springfield; railroad operations — 1,000. **General Electric Co.;** Fitchburg; turbines — 1,000. **W. E. Wright Co. Inc.** (Trimtex Div. - HQ); West Warren; apparel trimmings — 800.

Cranston Print Works Co.; Webster; textile printing — 700. **Monarch Life Insurance Co.** (HQ); Springfield; life, health insurance — 700. **Package Machinery Co.** (HQ); East Longmeadow; food packaging machinery — 691. **Crane Co.;** Indian Orchard; valves — 650. **James River-Massachusetts Inc.;** Fitchburg; paper mill — 650. **The Republican Co. Inc.;** Springfield; newspaper publishing — 620. **Titeflex Corp.;** Springfield; machinery, plastic products — 600. **Monsanto Co.** (Resins Products Div.); Indian Orchard; plastic resins — 580. **Harrington & Richardson Inc.** (Harrich International); Gardner; firearms — 575. **Anglo Fabrics Co. Inc.;** Webster; woolen mills — 570. **American Saw & Mfg. Co.;** East Longmeadow; hand saws, cutlery — 500. **Brookfield Athletic Shoe Co.** (Braun-Bilt - HQ); East Brookfield; ice skates, athletic shoes — 500. **Rexnord Inc.** (Roller Chain Div.); Springfield; fabricated wire products — 500.

3rd District

Central — Worcester

The 3rd District is built around the city of Worcester, the state's second-largest city. Worcester's total population declined substantially during the 1970s; however, its economy showed signs of health.

Among the nation's first major industrial centers not built on a natural waterway, Worcester started as a center for the manufacturing of textiles and wire. Now it has a broadly based economy centered around the metals and machine-tool industries, which in the early 1980s gave it an unemployment figure below the statewide average and far below the national unemployment rate. The Norton Company, the world's largest maker of grinding wheels, leads the list of Worcester employers.

Computer manufacturers have been attracted in recent years to the Marlborough area and other communities east of Worcester on Interstate 495, the outer highway surrounding Boston. Digital Equipment Corp. is in Marlborough; Data General has located its headquarters in Westborough.

Worcester is also a major educational center. The Public Affairs Research Center affiliated with Clark University has emerged as a major political science institute. Holy Cross College, founded in 1843 as the first Catholic college in New England, towers over the city from a scenic hillside.

The area within the new 3rd District gave a 43-to-40-percent plurality to Jimmy Carter in 1980, but showed little enthusiasm for him. While the city of Worcester gave Carter a 7,841-vote plurality, Ronald Reagan carried Worcester County by 2,774 votes. In 1978, the city of Worcester produced almost identical Democratic margins for conservative Edward J. King for governor and liberal Paul E. Tsongas for senator.

Redistricting added Douglas from the 2nd; Sherborn, Millis and Norfolk from the old 10th; and Lunenburg, Shirley, Lancaster, Bolton and Stow from the old 4th. The changes should make the district slightly more Republican, but probably will not pose a significant counterweight to Worcester's usual Democratic turnout.

Election Returns

3rd District		Democrat		Republican	
1976	President	135,116	(58.0%)	91,022	(39.1%)
	Senate	165,117	(71.4%)	63,109	(27.3%)
	House	173,707	(92.6%)	13,739	(7.3%)
1978	Governor	93,542	(53.0%)	82,251	(46.6%)
	Senate	95,750	(53.3%)	83,707	(46.6%)
	House	127,494	(74.3%)	43,916	(25.6%)
1980	President	91,764	(40.7%)	98,707	(43.8%)
	House	149,044	(68.6%)	67,992	(31.3%)
1982	Governor	105,820	(58.3%)	69,671	(38.4%)
	Senate	106,065	(58.5%)	73,930	(40.7%)
	House	x[1]		—[1]	

[1] *No votes tabulated where candidate was unopposed; x indicates winner.*

Demographics

Population: 521,354. **Percent Change from 1970:** 2.2%.

Land Area: 729 square miles. **Population per Square Mile:** 715.2.

Counties, 1980 Population: Middlesex (Pt.) — 90,243; Norfolk (Pt.) — 54,235; Worcester (Pt.) — 376,876.

Cities, 1980 Population: Auburn — 14,845; Bellingham — 14,300; Clinton — 12,771; Franklin — 18,217; Grafton — 11,238; Holliston — 12,662; Hudson — 16,408; Marlborough — 30,617; Milford — 23,390; Millbury — 11,808; Northborough — 10,568; Northbridge — 12,246; Shrewsbury — 22,674; Westborough — 13,619; Worcester — 161,799.

Race and Ancestry: White — 96.8%; Black — 1.5%; American Indian, Eskimo and Aleut — 0.1%; Asian and Pacific Islander — 0.5%. Spanish Origin — 2.1%. English — 7.4%; French — 7.8%; German —

1.5%; Greek — 0.8%; Irish — 10.4%; Italian — 7.1%; Polish — 3.1%; Portuguese — 1.1%; Russian — 0.8%; Scottish — 0.8%; Swedish — 1.7%.

Universities, Enrollment: Assumption College, Worcester — 2,802; Atlantic Union College, South Lancaster — 675; Becker Junior College, Worcester — 749; Central New England College of Technology, Worcester — 295; Clark University, Worcester — 2,495; College of The Holy Cross, Worcester — 2,663; Dean Junior College, Franklin — 1,856; Quinsigamond Community College, Worcester — 2,275; The Salter School, Worcester — 150; School of the Worcester Art Museum, Worcester — 103; Worcester Junior College, Worcester — 1,104; Worcester Polytechnic Institute, Worcester — 3,124; Worcester State College, Worcester — 6,314.

Newspapers, Circulation: *Clinton Daily Item* (e), Clinton — 4,060; *The Evening Gazette* (eS), Worcester — 88,910; *Hudson Daily Sun* (e), Hudson — 2,582; *Marlboro Enterprise* (e), Marlborough — 6,827; *Milford Daily News* (e), Milford — 14,138; *Worcester Telegram* (mS), Worcester — 56,119. *The Boston Globe* also circulates in the district.

Commercial Television Stations, Affiliation: WGTR-TV, Marlborough, (None); WSMW-TV, Worcester (None). Entire district is located in Boston ADI.

Military Installations: Worcester Air National Guard Station, Worcester — 408.

Industries:

Norton Co. (HQ); Worcester; grinding wheels — 3,200. **Data General Corp. (HQ);** Westborough; digital equipment — 3,000. **St. Vincent Hospital Corp.;** Worcester; hospital — 2,200. **Wyman-Gordon Co. (HQ);** Worcester; forgings — 2,100. **Hanover Insurance Companies Inc.;** Worcester; casualty insurance — 2,050.

Data General Corp.; Southborough; digital computers — 1,700. **The Memorial Hospital;** Worcester; hospital — 1,700. **Riley Stoker Corp.;** Worcester; boilers, steam turbines — 1,700. **Wyman-Gordon Co.;** North Grafton; forgings — 1,700. **State Mutual Life Insurance Co. of America** (HQ); Worcester; life, health, accident insurance — 1,600. **Digital Equipment Corp.;** Marlborough; digital computers — 1,500. **Cincinnati Milicron-Heald Machine Tool Co.;** Worcester; grinding, boring tools — 1,300. **Dresser Industries Inc.** (Bay State Abrasives Div.); Westborough; abrasive products — 1,200. **Jamesbury Corp.** (HQ); Worcester; ball valves — 1,200. **Worcester Hahnemann Hospital;** Worcester; hospital — 1,200. **Paul Revere Life Insurance Co.** (HQ); Worcester; life, health insurance — 1,050. **Walter Kidde & Co. Inc.** (Fenwal Div.); Ashland; thermostats — 1,000. **Sylvania GTE** (Strategic Systems Div.); Westborough; weapons systems — 920. **Digital Equipment Corp.;** Hudson; digital computers — 800.

Timex Corp. (Timex Clock Co.); Ashland; clocks, timers — 800. **NYPRO Inc.** (HQ); Clinton; custom plastic products — 700. **White Consolidated Industries** (A. T. F. Davidson Co.); Whitinsville; offset printing presses — 700. **Waters Associates Inc.** (HQ); Milford; laboratory instruments — 657. **Springfield Sugar & Products Co.** (New England Grocers); Northborough; grocery wholesaling — 650. **Worcester Telegram & Gazette** (HQ); Worcester; newspaper publishing, radio broadcasting — 650. **Morgan Construction;** Worcester; machinery construction — 628. **The Warner & Swasey Co.;** Worcester; abrasive products — 614. **International Telephone & Telegraph Corp.;** Clinton; wire, cable — 500. **Sprague Electric Co.;** Worcester; electronic components — 500. **Van Brode Milling Co.** (HQ); Clinton; plastic products — 500. **Wright Line Inc.** (HQ); Worcester; filing cabinets — 500.

4th District

Boston Suburbs, Fall River

The new 4th, built out of portions of the old 4th and 10th districts, favors the Democrats. The voter registration figures show 115,000 Democrats, 44,000 Republicans and 119,000 Independents. As presently drawn, the 4th opted for Jimmy Carter in 1980 by a 42-to-40-percent margin.

The new 4th included only two towns from the old 4th — Brookline, a suburb with a large Jewish population, and Newton. Both towns are longtime Democratic strongholds; both towns gave 60 percent margins to George McGovern in 1972.

The new 4th District extends south from the Boston suburbs all the way to the Rhode Island boundary. The industrial town of Fall River, located on the border of the two states, is traditionally Democratic, populated by the blue-collar workers in the city's needle trades. The city is trying to diversify beyond its garment industry base. A pilot plant for synthetic fuels development is expected to boost the area's economy.

Although Fall River supported its Republican House incumbent for several elections, it voted Democratic in 1982. The city's Democratic leanings have shown up clearly in other contests. In 1978, Fall River gave a 71.1 percent majority to Gov. Edward J. King and a 63.5 percent victory to Sen. Paul E. Tsongas. In 1972, it gave McGovern 63.0 percent of its vote.

One of the 19 towns from the old 10th is Wellesley, an affluent western suburb with a population of 27,209, which usually favors Republicans. Attleboro, a city of 34,000, also is generally good territory for any Republican candidate; the Republican House candidate carried it in 1982. Its traditional jewelry trade is now giving way to high-technology industries, symbolized by its Texas Instruments plant. While surrounding Bristol County was giving Carter a 6,000-vote victory in the 1980 election, Attleboro gave a plurality to Ronald Reagan. Both King and Tsongas carried the city in 1978, but by margins smaller than they enjoyed statewide.

Election Returns

4th District		Democrat		Republican	
1976	President	130,677	(54.3%)	101,713	(42.3%)
	Senate	166,106	(70.5%)	66,167	(28.1%)
	House	49,714	(23.9%)	158,148	(75.9%)
1978	Governor	85,764	(46.7%)	97,487	(53.1%)
	Senate	94,681	(51.2%)	89,896	(48.7%)
	House	91,601	(55.9%)	71,573	(43.7%)
1980	President	101,534	(42.6%)	95,429	(40.0%)
	House	113,347	(49.6%)	115,122	(50.4%)
1982	Governor	129,594	(63.6%)	67,724	(33.2%)
	Senate	131,451	(64.4%)	70,762	(34.7%)
	House	121,802	(59.5%)	82,804	(40.5%)

Demographics

Population: 521,995. **Percent Change from 1970:** 1.8%.

Land Area: 501 square miles. **Population per Square Mile:** 1,041.9.

Counties, 1980 Population: Bristol (Pt.) — 251,673; Middlesex (Pt.) — 113,083; Norfolk (Pt.) — 157,239.

Cities, 1980 Population: Attleboro — 34,196; Brookline — 55,062; Fall River — 92,574; Foxborough — 14,148; Mansfield — 13,453; Medfield — 10,220; Natick — 29,461; Newton — 83,622; North Attleborough — 21,095; Norton — 12,690; Seekonk — 12,269; Sharon — 13,601; Somerset — 18,813; Swansea — 15,461; Walpole — 18,859; Wellesley — 27,209; Westport — 13,763.

Race and Ancestry: White — 97.2%; Black — 1.0%; American Indian, Eskimo and Aleut — 0.1%; Asian and Pacific Islander — 1.3%. Spanish Origin — 1.4%. English — 8.2%; French — 5.7%; German — 1.6%; Greek — 0.5%; Irish — 8.8%; Italian — 4.7%; Polish — 2.2%; Portuguese — 10.7%; Russian — 3.3%; Scottish — 0.8%; Swedish — 0.6%.

Universities, Enrollment: Andover Newton Theological School, Newton Centre — 463; Aquinas Junior College, Newton — 316; Babson College, Babson Park — 3,115; Boston College, Chestnut Hill — 14,430; Bristol Community College, Fall River — 2,405; Hebrew College, Brookline — 134; Hellenic College/Holy Cross Greek Orthodox Theological School, Brookline — 182; Lasell Junior College, Newton — 673; Massachusetts Bay Community College, Wellesley Hills — 4,415; Mount Ida Junior College, Newton Centre — 825; Pine Manor College, Chestnut Hill — 585; Wellesley College, Wellesley — 2,164; Wheaton College, Norton — 1,208.

Newspapers, Circulation: *Herald-News* (e), Fall River — 40,620; *The Sun Chronicle* (e), Attleboro — 22,127. *The Boston Globe* also circulates in the district.

Commercial Television Stations, Affiliation: District is divided between Boston ADI and Providence (R.I.)-New Bedford ADI.

Military Installations: Natick Research and Development Laboratories (Army), Natick — 1,455; Wellesley Air National Guard Station, Wellesley — 188.

Industries:

The Foxboro Co. (HQ); Foxborough; industrial measuring instruments — 5,500. **Texas Instruments Inc.;** Attleboro; industrial controls — 5,500. **Codex Corp.** (HQ); Mansfield; digital radio, television equipment — 1,900. **L. G. Balfour Co.** (HQ); Attleboro; precious metals — 1,800. **Charlton Memorial Hospital Inc.;** Fall River; hospital — 1,800.

Newton Wellesley Hospital Corp.; Newton; hospital — 1,600. **Prime Computer Inc.** (HQ); Natick; mini-computers — 1,400. **Leonard Morse Hospital;** Natick; hospital — 1,280. **Quaker Fabric Corp.** (HQ); Fall River; upholstery fabric — 1,200. **Swank Inc.** (Prince Gardner Div. - HQ); Attleboro; leather goods — 1,100. **Honeywell Information Systems;** Wellesley; computers — 1,000. **Sun Life Assurance Co. of Canada** (U. S. A. - HQ); Wellesley; life insurance — 900. **ITT Continental Baking Co. Inc.;** Natick; bakery products — 780. **Aetna Life & Casualty Co. Inc.;** Fall River; insurance — 750. **Aluminum Processing Corp.;** Fall River; aluminum processing — 700.

Bird Machine Co. Inc. (HQ); South Walpole; general machinery — 700. **Leach & Garner Co.** (HQ); Attleboro; precious metals — 655. **Corning Glass Works** (Medical Products Div.); Medfield; medical diagnostic equipment — 650. **Engelhard Corp.;** Plainville; non-ferrous metal products — 625. **Crosby Valve & Gage** (HQ); Wrentham; valves, gauges — 616. **Intersil Inc.** (The Datel Intersil Div.); Mansfield; data conversion equipment — 565. **Marriott Corp.;** Newton; hotel — 550. **Honeywell Information Systems** (Field Engineering Div.); Newton; computer equipment — 500. **Shelburne Shirt Co. Inc.;** Fall River; men's shirts — 500.

5th District

North — Lowell, Lawrence

A district centered around two gritty mill towns where the American textile industry got its start in the early 19th century, the 5th has seen gradual economic decline followed by modest renewal.

The long-running rivalry of Lowell and Lawrence, the population centers of the district, springs from their different histories as textile centers: Lowell, the model "company town," was carefully watched over by paternal Yankee Protestants, while Lawrence's unsafe work places and substandard living conditions gave rise to immigrant workers' resentment of the city's planners, Boston's State Street

financiers. Soon after mill workers won Lawrence's strike of 1912 — in which agitation for wage increases led to one of the sharpest confrontations in labor history — textile companies began leaving the Merrimack Valley, looking for cheaper labor in the South.

Both towns were in sad economic shape. Since 1975, however, Lowell has seen its economy revitalized by the arrival of high-technology firms. Wang, a computer company, is the city's largest employer. The nation's first urban historical park has been established in Lowell around the Merrimack River's system of canals.

Lawrence has been slower to profit from the technology boom, but in the late 1970s a paint company and other light manufacturing firms began moving into abandoned mill space downtown. The recession of the early 1980s slowed that activity somewhat. Both cities are solidly Democratic.

There is more to the 5th than Lowell and Lawrence. More than 50 percent of the district was suburban in the 1970s, and territory newly added to the district includes the well-to-do suburbs of Weston and Wayland, upper-crust Lincoln and bucolic Sudbury. All four towns gave pluralities to Ronald Reagan in 1980, as did Andover and Concord, which remain in the district. But all these suburbs have strong liberal factions and go Democratic in most contests. Concord gave 22.5 percent of its ballots to independent presidential candidate John B. Anderson in 1980, the main reason Ronald Reagan came in first there.

Framingham, which blends light manufacturing and middle-class neighborhoods, was shifted into the 5th from the old 4th. In the 1980 election Framingham went narrowly for Jimmy Carter. Republican voters in the smaller towns helped Reagan in 1980 carry the district with just 44 percent, while Jimmy Carter and Anderson were splitting the majority.

In the 1981 remap, the 5th gained Maynard, Sudbury, Framingham, Ayer, Weston, Wayland, Lincoln and Harvard from the 4th, and Ashburnham from the 2nd. It lost North Reading to the 6th, and Lexington, Wilmington, Billerica and Tewksbury to the 7th.

Election Returns

5th District		Democrat		Republican	
1976	President	126,779	(55.1%)	96,540	(42.0%)
	Senate	157,006	(69.0%)	67,385	(29.6%)
	House	136,824	(60.6%)	88,913	(39.4%)
1978	Governor	94,777	(53.0%)	83,334	(46.6%)
	Senate	111,656	(61.5%)	69,745	(38.4%)
	House	93,325	(61.1%)	36,382	(23.8%)
1980	President	89,068	(39.1%)	100,189	(44.0%)
	House	130,658	(60.0%)	85,736	(39.5%)
1982	Governor	104,733	(57.2%)	72,627	(39.6%)
	Senate	103,147	(56.8%)	76,694	(42.3%)
	House	140,177	(84.7%)	—	

Demographics

Population: 518,313. **Percent Change from 1970:** 3.3%.

Land Area: 575 square miles. **Population per Square Mile:** 901.4.

Counties, 1980 Population: Essex (Pt.) — 126,246; Middlesex (Pt.) — 375,822; Worcester (Pt.) — 16,245.

Cities, 1980 Population: Acton — 17,544; Andover — 26,370; Bedford — 13,067; Chelmsford — 13,174; Concord — 16,293; Dracut — 21,249; Framingham — 65,113; Harvard — 12,170; Lawrence — 63,175; Lowell — 92,418; Methuen — 36,701; Sudbury — 14,027; Wayland — 12,170; Westford — 13,434; Weston — 11,169.

Race and Ancestry: White — 95.4%; Black — 1.5%; American Indian, Eskimo and Aleut — 0.1%; Asian and Pacific Islander — 0.8%. Spanish Origin — 3.9%. English — 8.5%; French — 7.9%; German — 2.0%; Greek — 1.4%; Irish — 10.0%; Italian — 5.9%; Polish — 2.0%; Portuguese — 1.6%; Russian — 1.2%; Scottish — 0.9%; Swedish — 0.6%.

Universities, Enrollment: Framingham State College, Framingham — 6,093; Middlesex Community College, Bedford — 1,433; Regis College, Weston — 1,277; University of Lowell, Lowell — 8,398.

Newspapers, Circulation: *Lawrence Eagle-Tribune* (e), Lawrence — 51,575; *The Middlesex News* (eS), Framingham — 49,798; *The Sun* (e), Lowell — 56,127. *The Boston Globe* also circulates in the district.

Commercial Television Stations, Affiliation: Entire district is located in Boston ADI.

Military Installations: Fort Devens, Ayer — 10,407; Hanscom Air Force Base, Bedford — 4,798.

Industries:

Raytheon Co.; Andover; military electronic equipment — 5,600. **Digital Equipment Corp.** (HQ); Maynard; digital computers — 5,093. **Raytheon Co.;** Bedford; missile research, development — 3,800. **Wang Laboratories Inc.** (HQ); Lowell; computers — 3,500. **General Motors Corp.** (Assembly Div.); Framingham; automobiles — 2,000.

Computervision Corp. (HQ); Bedford; computers, computer programs — 2,600. **Dennison Mfg. Co.** (HQ); Framingham; stationery — 2,500. **Raytheon Co.** (Equipment Div.); Wayland; guided missile parts — 2,500. **Data Terminal Systems Inc.;** Maynard; electronic cash registers — 2,000. **Genrad Inc.** (HQ); Concord; electronic testing devices — 2,000. **The Mitre Corp.** (HQ); Bedford; systems engineering — 2,000. **Raytheon Co.;** Lowell; missiles — 2,000. **Raytheon Co.;** Sudbury; electronic equipment — 2,000. **Zayre Corp.** (HQ); Framingham; department store chain — 2,000. **Framingham Union Hospital Inc.;** Framingham; hospital — 1,560. **Lawrence General Hospital;** Lawrence; hospital — 1,400. **Veterans Administration;** Bedford; veterans' hospital — 1,400.

Gould Inc. (Modicon Div.); Andover; industrial measuring instruments — 1,250. **Courier Corp.** (HQ); Lowell; printing — 1,100. **Millipore Corp.** (HQ); Bedford; industrial machinery — 1,100. **Kratos Inc.** (Schoeffel International); Acton; scientific instruments — 1,090. **BASF Wyandotte Corp.** (Systems Div.); Bedford; electronic components — 1,000. **Emerson Hospital Inc.;** Concord; hospital — 1,000. **Honeywell Information Systems Inc.;** Lawrence; computers — 1,000. **Malden Mills Industries Inc.** (HQ); Lawrence; fabric mills — 1,000. **Prime Computer Inc.;** Framingham; computers — 1,000. **The Gillette Co. Inc.;** Andover; toiletries — 800. **Bose Corp.** (HQ); Framingham; loudspeakers — 734.

Acton Food Service Corp. (DeCoster Egg Farm); Acton; eggs — 700. **Grieco Bros. Inc.** (HQ); Lawrence; men's suits — 700. **Hewlett-Packard Co.;** Andover; X-ray, electromedical equipment — 700. **Murray Printing Co. Inc.;** Westford; lithograph offset printing — 700. **International Telephone & Telegraph Corp.;** Lawrence; semiconductors — 650. **Joan Fabrics Corp.** (HQ); Lowell; broad-woven fabrics — 650. **Apollo Computers** (HQ); Chelmsford; computing equipment, software — 575. **Baird Corp.** (HQ); Bedford; laboratory, medical equipment — 525. **Holmes Transportation Inc.;** Framingham; trucking — 500. **Nickerson Seafoods Co. Inc.;** Nabnasset; warehousing — 500. **Wang Laboratories Inc.;** Lawrence; computer-related services — 500.

6th District

North Shore — Lynn, Peabody

An area of geographical variety and economic contrast, the 6th contains chronically depressed mill towns, worka-

day factory cities, comfortable suburbs, pockets of aristocratic wealth and scenic ocean-front villages. Its vote-heavy areas are at the southern end of Essex County, and are strongly Democratic. But the district's strong 1980 vote for independent John B. Anderson helped Ronald Reagan carry the 6th, and Essex County as a whole, by a plurality.

Lynn, historically a shoe-manufacturing center but now home of a large General Electric aircraft engine plant, suffered a 13 percent population loss between 1970 and 1980, but remains the 6th's largest city. Lynn gave Jimmy Carter only a 3,800-vote margin in 1980, about half the edge it had given conservative Democrat Edward J. King in the 1978 governor's race. Nearby Peabody, once the largest leather-processing city in the world, gave Carter a 600-vote edge in 1980, also far less than King's margin. Similarly Democratic is Salem, on the northern end of this industrial tier. It gave comfortable margins to Carter.

North of Salem are areas of Essex County where the aristocratic tradition of Yankee Protestantism provides GOP votes but now tends to favor liberal Republicans. Beverly and nearby Gloucester provided sizable Republican margins in both 1978 and 1980. Suburban Wenham was one of only three towns in the commonwealth where Anderson outpolled Carter.

On the northern coast, maritime interests are central to Gloucester, home of the Fisherman's Memorial landmark, and Rockport, a historic fishing village deluged with tourists and artists in the summer. Newburyport, whose 19th century clipper ship economy gave way to light manufacturing, is the "Yankee City" singled out for study by sociologists in the 1920s. It has attracted some emigrants from urban areas and was one of the few Bay State cities to grow, albeit slowly, in the 1970s. A major northern coast political issue is the siting of the Seabrook nuclear power plant, just across the New Hampshire line.

Haverhill won the dubious distinction in a 1981 survey of being the nation's metropolitan area with the least desirable "quality of life." The town's economic base in the shoe industry has long since disappeared and there has been no comparable successor.

In the remap, the 6th gained North Reading from the 5th, and Lynnfield and Saugus from the 7th.

Election Returns

6th District		Democrat		Republican	
1976	President	132,384	(53.1%)	109,094	(43.7%)
	Senate	168,884	(69.0%)	72,751	(29.7%)
	House	137,872	(56.2%)	97,811	(39.9%)
1978	Governor	96,487	(47.9%)	103,950	(51.7%)
	Senate	103,229	(50.6%)	100,411	(49.3%)
	House	110,804	(55.6%)	84,897	(42.6%)
1980	President	94,549	(37.9%)	109,933	(44.1%)
	House	126,667	(53.5%)	105,241	(44.5%)
1982	Governor	118,776	(57.8%)	78,536	(38.2%)
	Senate	123,650	(60.2%)	80,029	(39.0%)
	House	117,723	(57.8%)	85,849	(42.2%)

Demographics

Population: 518,841. **Percent Change from 1970:** -0.8%.

Land Area: 447 square miles. **Population per Square Mile:** 1,160.7.

Counties, 1980 Population: Essex (Pt.) — 507,386; Middlesex (Pt.) — 11,455.

Cities, 1980 Population: Amesbury — 13,971; Beverly — 37,655; Danvers — 24,100; Gloucester — 27,768; Haverhill — 46,865; Ipswich — 11,158; Lynn — 78,471; Lynnfield — 11,267; Marblehead — 20,126; Newburyport — 15,900; North Andover — 20,129; North Reading — 11,455; Peabody — 45,976; Salem — 38,220; Saugus — 24,746; Swampscott — 13,837.

Race and Ancestry: White — 97.9%; Black — 1.0%; American Indian, Eskimo and Aleut — 0.1%; Asian and Pacific Islander — 0.4%. Spanish Origin — 1.1%. English — 10.8%; French — 5.7%; German — 1.3%; Greek — 2.1%; Irish — 10.5%; Italian — 7.4%; Polish — 2.5%; Portuguese — 1.2%; Russian — 1.3%; Scottish — 1.0%; Swedish — 0.7%.

Universities, Enrollment: Bradford College, Bradford — 378; Endicott College, Beverly — 840; Essex Agricultural and Technical Institute, Hawthorne — 673; Gordon College, Wenham — 1,077; Gordon-Conwell Theological Seminary, South Hamilton — 684; Marian Court Junior College of Business, Swampscott — 149; Merrimack College, North Andover — 3,759; North Shore Community College, Beverly — 2,651; Northern Essex Community College, Haverhill — 6,534; Salem State College, Salem — 8,607.

Newspapers, Circulation: *Beverly Times* (e), Beverly — 10,701; *Daily Evening Item* (e), Lynn — 29,854; *The Daily News* (e), Newburyport — 10,659; *The Daily Peabody Times* (e), Peabody — 5,238; *Daily Times* (e), Gloucester — 11,772; *The Gazette* (e), Haverhill — 18,462; *The Salem Evening News* (e), Salem — 30,813. *The Boston Globe* also circulates in the district.

Commercial Television Stations, Affiliation: Entire district is located in Boston ADI.

Industries:

Western Electric Co. Inc.; North Andover; telephones — 8,192. General Electric Co. (Aircraft Engine Group); Lynn; aircraft jet engines — 7,000. General Electric Co. (Industrial Marine Steam Turbine Div.); Lynn; turbines, generators — 5,000. The Salem Hospital Inc.; Salem; hospital — 1,400. Lynn Hospital Corp.; Lynn; hospital — 1,370.

General Electric Co. (Medium Steam Turbine Div.); Lynn; turbines, generators — 1,300. USM Corp. (Emhart Corp.); Beverly; electronic machinery — 1,200. Beverly Hospital Corp.; Beverly; hospital — 1,100. GTE Products Corp.; Salem; incandescent lamps — 1,000. General Mills Inc. (The Gorton Group); Gloucester; seafood — 900. Varian Associates (Varian Extrion); Gloucester; ion implantation equipment — 900. GTE Products Corp.; Danvers; fluorescent lights — 730. North American Philips Lighting (Norelco); Lynn; electric lamps — 725.

Varian Associates; Beverly; microwave tubes — 700. GTE Products Corp.; Danvers; fluorescent lighting — 675. EG & G Inc. (Technical Products Group); Salem; electronic components — 650. Gould Inc. (Electric Fuse Div.); Newburyport; electrical equipment — 616. Bell Telephone Labs Inc.; North Andover; research, development — 550. Gloucester Engineering Co. Inc. (HQ); Gloucester; special industrial machinery — 500. USM Corp. (Dyna-Pert); Beverly; electronic pipes — 500.

7th District

Northern Suburbs — Medford, Malden

Primarily a collection of medium-sized cities on the edge of metropolitan Boston, the 7th had to expand north and west through Middlesex County to make up its population deficit. While the newly added areas give the 7th a slightly more suburban character, the district remains solidly Democratic.

The communities north of Boston are heavily urbanized and town boundaries are almost invisible. All the blue-collar towns close to the Boston city limits have lost population since 1970, some of them sharply. Chelsea declined by 17.0 percent, Everett by 12.5 percent, Melrose by 9 percent. Energetic urban improvement efforts have slowed the decline of Malden, where Italians are the dominant ethnic group. Jimmy Carter handily won all these cities in 1980 except Melrose, where Ronald Reagan had a 1,855-vote edge.

Woburn, situated along the Route 128 beltway, the core of Massachusetts' high-technology industry, experienced slight growth during the 1970s. It was one of only nine of the state's 39 cities that underwent any expansion at all. Woburn's residents gave Carter a 447-vote margin. Independent John B. Anderson was popular in Woburn too, gaining nearly 2,500 votes.

Most of the suburban areas added by the remap have also grown since 1970. Within the orbit of Lowell's rebounding economy, Billerica's 16.0 percent growth paced Tewksbury's 8.3 percent and Wilmington's 2.2 percent. All three towns went narrowly for Reagan in 1980, with the vote for Anderson denying Carter victory in all of them.

The comfortable, upper-middle-class suburb of Lexington, added from the 5th District, went overwhelmingly for liberal Republican Francis Hatch in the 1978 governor's race. However, the onetime stronghold of Yankee Republicanism now can be depended upon to back liberal Democrats against most opponents from the more conservative side of the GOP.

In the remap, the 7th yielded Lynnfield and Saugus to the 6th and gained Billerica, Tewksbury, Wilmington and Lexington from the 5th.

Election Returns

7th District		Democrat		Republican	
1976	President	138,724	(57.9%)	91,541	(38.2%)
	Senate	167,884	(73.4%)	59,917	(26.2%)
	House	181,524	(76.4%)	45,852	(19.3%)
1978	Governor	115,729	(60.8%)	74,175	(39.0%)
	Senate	117,065	(59.9%)	78,337	(40.1%)
	House	146,837	(92.4%)	12,114	(7.6%)
1980	President	103,873	(42.1%)	103,704	(42.1%)
	House	168,465	(91.9%)	14,895	(8.1%)
1982	Governor	122,072	(60.8%)	70,109	(34.9%)
	Senate	128,269	(63.9%)	70,431	(35.1%)
	House	151,305	(77.8%)	43,063	(22.2%)

Demographics

Population: 523,982. **Percent Change from 1970:** -3.7%.

Land Area: 162 square miles. **Population per Square Mile:** 3,234.5.

Counties, 1980 Population: Middlesex (Pt.) — 436,834; Suffolk (Pt.) — 87,148.

Cities, 1980 Population: Billerica — 36,727; Burlington — 23,486; Chelsea — 25,431; Everett — 37,195; Lexington — 29,479; Malden — 53,386; Medford — 58,076; Melrose — 30,055; Reading — 22,678; Revere — 42,423; Stoneham — 21,424; Tewksbury — 24,635; Wakefield — 24,895; Wilmington — 17,471; Winchester — 20,701; Winthrop — 19,294; Woburn — 36,626.

Race and Ancestry: White — 97.6%; Black — 1.1%; American Indian, Eskimo and Aleut — 0.1%; Asian and Pacific Islander — 0.7%. Spanish Origin — 1.4%. English — 7.2%; French — 2.1%; German — 1.3%; Greek — 0.7%; Irish — 14.7%; Italian — 18.1%; Polish — 1.5%; Portuguese — 0.8%; Russian — 1.2%; Scottish — 0.9%; Swedish — 0.6%.

Universities, Enrollment: Tufts University, Medford — 6,774.

Newspapers, Circulation: *Daily Times & Chronicle* (e), Woburn — 16,625; *Item* (e), Wakefield — 6,605; *Medford Daily Mercury* (e), Medford — 6,458; *Melrose Evening News* (e), Melrose — 1,907; *News* (e), Malden — 7,829; *Record* (e), Chelsea — 4,850. *The Boston Globe* also circulates in the district.

Commercial Television Stations, Affiliation: Entire district is located in Boston ADI.

Industries:

Avco Corp. (Systems Div.); Wilmington; aerospace engineering — 3,100. **Lahey Clinic Foundation Inc.** (HQ); Burlington; hospital — 1,800. **RCA Corp.** (Government Systems Div.); Burlington; laser equipment — 1,600. **Marshalls Inc.** (HQ); Woburn; department stores — 1,400. **Sweetheart Plastics Inc.** (Guild Machine Div. - HQ); Wilmington; disposable plastic products — 1,400.

New England Memorial Hospital; Stoneham; hospital — 1,300. **The Malden Hospital Inc.;** Malden; hospital — 1,220. **Itek Corp.** (Optical Systems Div.); Lexington; electrical specialties — 1,150. **RCA Corp.** (Automated Systems); Burlington; scientific equipment — 1,120. **Honeywell Inc.;** Lexington; electro-optical equipment — 1,100. **Tewksbury State Hospital;** Tewksbury; hospital — 1,030. **General Electric Co.;** Wilmington; aerospace instruments — 1,000. **Raytheon Service Co.** (HQ); Burlington; engineering services — 1,000. **Itek Corp.** (HQ); Lexington; graphic products — 925. **American Mutual Insurance Co. of Boston** (HQ); Wakefield; fire, casualty insurance — 900. **Analog Devices Inc.;** Wilmington; semiconductors — 810. **Analogic Corp.** (HQ); Wakefield; digital instruments — 800. **Digital Equipment Corp.;** Woburn; computers — 800.

Wang Laboratories Inc.; Tewksbury; computers — 800. **Instrumentation Laboratory Inc.** (HQ); Lexington; medical instruments — 750. **New England Nuclear Corp.** (Nuclear Medicine Technology Center); North Billerica; pharmaceuticals — 750. **Nixdorf Computer Corp.** (HQ); Burlington; data entry computers — 750. **Dynamics Research Corp.** (HQ); Wilmington; computer systems — 720. **C. R. Bard Inc.;** Billerica; surgical, medical instruments — 700. **Digital Equipment Corp.;** Tewksbury; digital computers — 700. **Compugraphics Corp.** (HQ); Wilmington; printing equipment — 650. **Applicon Inc.** (HQ); Burlington; electronic computing equipment — 600. **Data Printer Corp.;** Malden; computers — 600. **Avco Everett Research Laboratory Inc.** (HQ); Everett; research — 570. **High Voltage Engineering Corp.** (HQ); Burlington; scientific equipment — 550. **Armatron International Inc.** (HQ); Melrose; electronic detection equipment — 500. **Raytheon Co.** (HQ); Lexington; electronic equipment — 500.

8th District

Boston and Suburbs — Cambridge

Ethnic, working-class Cambridge coexists peacefully, if not always sympathetically, with the Harvard-MIT colossus that surrounds it. There is a political cohesiveness that transcends cultural differences — both segments of the 8th District are Democratic and liberal on economic issues.

The cultural divisions, however, are real. Outside the university precincts exists a crowded, grimy city. The proximity of trendy Harvard Square and seedy Central Square makes Cambridge no stranger to town-vs.-gown tensions. One city councilman has practically made a career of baiting the Ivy League school, suggesting repeatedly that Har-

vard Yard be paved over to relieve the city's parking problems.

With a straight-ticket Democratic voting history, Cambridge gave 74 percent of its vote to George McGovern in 1972 — his majority statewide was 54 percent — and it gave Jimmy Carter a 61-to-20-percent victory in 1980. But Cambridge voters sometimes cross party lines to seek out liberals. In the 1978 gubernatorial race, liberal Republican Francis Hatch beat conservative Democrat Edward J. King in the city by 59 to 41 percent.

The 8th extends across the Charles River to include a large segment of Boston. Allston and Brighton, historically centers for Boston's Jewish community, today have a large transient student population. Harvard Business School, Boston University and part of Boston College are within the boundaries of the district in Boston's 21st and 22nd wards. Joined to the territory is Boston's 4th Ward, which adds Northeastern University and Harvard Medical School and unifies the Back Bay and the Fenway in the 8th.

The affluent Back Bay has become a symbol of high-income urban "gentrification." Beacon Hill, where the 23-carat gold statehouse dome dominates elegant 18th- and 19th-century homes built by Federalists, is now predominantly liberal and Democratic. Irish working-class Charlestown and heavily Italian East Boston are also in the 8th.

To the west, the district includes the working-class city of Somerville and the middle-class towns of Arlington and Watertown. All three gave large margins to the Democratic Senate and gubernatorial candidates in 1978 and distinctly narrower pluralities to Carter in 1980. Suburban Belmont, the home of the John Birch Society's national headquarters, does not have much in common with Birch Society politics; it favored liberals Hatch for the 1978 governorship and Paul E. Tsongas for the Senate. Independent John B. Anderson's 16.8 percent showing tilted the town to Ronald Reagan in 1980.

The remap joined the medium-sized city of Waltham to the 8th. Waltham has its own town-and-gown problems. It has a blue-collar majority, largely Italian, and is also the home of Brandeis University, with an aggressively liberal student and faculty community.

Election Returns

8th District		Democrat		Republican	
1976	President	134,941	(61.5%)	73,957	(33.7%)
	Senate	160,440	(75.2%)	46,462	(21.8%)
	House	147,659	(71.4%)	46,216	(22.4%)
1978	Governor	86,451	(52.2%)	78,795	(47.6%)
	Senate	94,538	(56.5%)	72,544	(43.4%)
	House	115,337	(76.5%)	28,566	(19.0%)
1980	President	106,217	(50.6%)	67,209	(32.0%)
	House	140,702	(74.4%)	48,410	(25.6%)
1982	Governor[1]	120,543	(67.9%)	50,879	(28.7%)
	Senate	125,170	(70.8%)	49,854	(28.2%)
	House	123,296	(74.9%)	41,370	(25.1%)

[1] *Boston returns for the 1982 gubernatorial and Senate races were estimated; final 1982 returns from Boston were unavailable at publication time.*

Demographics

Population: 521,548. **Percent Change from 1970:** -7.1%.

Land Area: 54 square miles. **Population per Square Mile:** 9,658.3.

Counties, 1980 Population: Middlesex (Pt.) — 339,597; Suffolk (Pt.) — 181,951.

Cities, 1980 Population: Arlington — 48,219; Belmont — 26,100; Boston (Pt.) — 181,951; Cambridge — 95,322; Somerville — 77,372; Waltham — 58,200; Watertown — 34,384.

Race and Ancestry: White — 90.9%; Black — 4.6%; American Indian, Eskimo and Aleut — 0.1%; Asian and Pacific Islander — 2.9%. Spanish Origin — 3.0%. English — 6.5%; French — 2.0%; German — 1.9%; Greek — 1.6%; Irish — 14.2%; Italian — 12.5%; Polish — 1.4%; Portuguese — 2.5%; Russian — 2.1%; Scottish — 1.0%; Swedish — 0.5%.

Universities, Enrollment: The Art Institute of Boston, Boston — 602; Arthur D. Little Management Education Institute, Cambridge — 67; Bay State Junior College, Boston — 705; Bentley College, Waltham — 7,150; Berklee College of Music, Boston — 2,643; Boston Architectural Center, Boston — 550; Boston College *(See 4th District);* Boston Conservatory of Music, Boston — 379; Boston State College, Boston — 9,042; Boston University, Boston — 28,165; Brandeis University, Waltham — 2,831; Bunker Hill Community College, Charlestown — 2,739.

Chamberlayne Junior College, Boston — 973; Emerson College, Boston — 2,110; Emmanuel College, Boston — 1,090; Episcopal Divinity School, Cambridge — 117; Fisher Junior College — 3,666; Franklin Institute of Boston, Boston — 664; Harvard University, Cambridge — 16,132; Harvard University (Radcliffe College campus), Cambridge — 2,320; Katherine Gibbs School, Boston — 552; Lesley College, Cambridge — 2,807; Massachusetts College of Art, Boston — 2,144; Massachusetts College of Pharmacy and Allied Health Sciences, Boston — 1,379; Massachusetts Institute of Technology, Cambridge — 13,058.

New England College of Optometry, Boston — 359; New England Conservatory of Music, Boston — 789; New England Institute of Applied Arts and Sciences, Boston — 147; New England School of Law, Boston — 1,076; Newbury Junior College, Boston — 2,521; Northeastern University, Boston — 43,184; St. John's Seminary, Brighton — 244; School of the Museum of Fine Arts, Boston — 619; Simmons College, Boston — 2,803; Wentworth Institute of Technology, Boston — 2,999; Weston College School of Theology, Cambridge — 216; Wheelock College, Boston — 981.

Newspapers, Circulation: *The Christian Science Monitor* (m), Boston — 151,823; *The News-Tribune* (e), Waltham — 11,755. *The Boston Globe* and *Boston Herald American* also circulate in the district. Foreign language newspapers: *Baikar* (Armenian), Watertown — 2,300; *Hairenik* (Armenian), Boston — 3,400.

Commercial Television Stations, Affiliation: WBZ-TV, Boston (NBC); WLVI-TV, Cambridge (None); WQTV, Boston (None); WSBK-TV, Brighton (None). Entire district is located in Boston ADI. *(For other Boston stations, see 9th district.)*

Military Installations: Material and Mechanical Research Center (Army), Watertown — 624.

Industries:

John Hancock Mutual Life Insurance Co. (HQ); Boston; insurance — 6,000. **Polaroid Corp.** (HQ); Cambridge; photographic equipment, supplies — 3,000. **Liberty Mutual Insurance Co.** (HQ); Boston; casualty insurance — 2,700. **Beth Israel Hospital Assn.;** Boston; hospital — 2,500. **Polaroid Corp.;** Waltham; photographic equipment, supplies — 2,500.

Raytheon Co.; Waltham; electronic components — 2,400. **Delta Airlines Inc.;** Boston; commercial airline — 2,200. **New England Mutual Life Insurance Co.** (HQ); Boston; insurance — 2,000. **North American Philips Electronic Corp.;** Waltham; hospital communication equipment services — 1,800. **Charles Stark Draper Laboratory** (HQ); Cambridge; research — 1,760. **Honeywell Information Systems Inc.;** Boston; computers — 1,600. **Mount Auburn Hospital;** Cambridge; hospital — 1,600. **Raytheon Co.** (Microwave & Power Tube Div.); Waltham; electronic devices — 1,600. **St. Elizabeth's Hospital of Boston Inc.;** Boston; hospital — 1,600. **McLean Hospital Corp.;** Belmont; psychiatric hospital — 1,500. **Prudential Insurance Co. of America;** Boston; health, life insurance — 1,500.

= Boston =

Arthur D. Little Inc. (HQ); Cambridge; management consulting, engineering services — 1,350. **Charles T. Main Inc.;** Boston; engineering services — 1,300. **American Airlines Inc.;** Boston; commercial airline — 1,200. **Badger America Inc.** (HQ); Cambridge; engineering services — 1,200. **Eastern Air Lines Inc.;** Boston; commercial airline — 1,200. **The Gillette Co.** (HQ); Boston; safety razors, toiletries — 1,200. **Hewlett-Packard Co. Inc.;** Waltham; electronic medical equipment — 1,200. **Honeywell Information Systems Inc.;** Waltham; computers — 1,100. **Waltham Hospital;** Waltham; hospital — 1,050. **Automatic Data Processing of New England Inc.** (HQ); Waltham; data processing — 1,000. **H. P. Hood Inc.** (HQ); Boston; dairy, citrus products — 1,000.

Standard-Thomson Corp.; Waltham; heating, cooling controls — 1,000. **U. S. Air Inc.;** Boston; commercial airline — 1,000. **Bolt, Beranek & Newman Inc.** (HQ); Cambridge; engineering consulting services — 989. **American Biltrite Inc.** (Boston Industrial Products); Cambridge; rubber hose, belting — 900. **The Schrafft Candy Co. Inc.;** Boston; candy — 900. **Sheraton Boston Corp.;** Boston; hotel — 900. **Western Electric Co. Inc.;** Watertown; construction, warehousing — 900. **ABT Associates Inc.** (HQ); Cambridge; research — 800. **Checker Taxi Co. Inc.;** Boston; taxicab operations — 800. **Raytheon Co.** (Microwave & Power Tube Div.); Waltham; tubes — 800. **GTE Laboratories Inc.;** Waltham; research — 760.

Boston Park Plaza Hotel Operating Co.; Boston; hotel — 750. **Electronics Corp. of America** (HQ); Cambridge; electronic controls — 600. **New Balance Inc.;** Boston; athletic shoes — 600. **P & L Sportswear Co. Inc.;** Boston; women's suits, skirts — 600. **Bethlehem Steel Corp.;** Boston; ship repairing — 550. **Hotel Management Associates;** Boston; hotel — 550. **Hyatt Corp.;** Cambridge; hotel — 550. **C. E. Maguire Inc.** (HQ); Waltham; engineering services — 500. **The Stride Rite Corp.** (HQ); Cambridge; babies', children's shoes — 500. **TRW Inc.;** Cambridge; motor vehicle parts — 500.

9th District

Boston and Southern Suburbs

If the 8th District has many of the fashionable and historical areas that attract tourist guidebook superlatives, it is the 9th that contains most of Boston's workaday precincts. The old 9th suffered a 10.1 percent population loss between 1970 and 1980 — the steepest drop in the state — and its boundaries had to be stretched south from its 12 Boston wards to include several smaller cities and towns.

The population of Boston itself has dipped below the 600,000 mark, and the ethnic character of the city is changing dramatically. While white population has dropped by 24.9 percent since the 1970 count, blacks have increased by 20.6 percent and now account for 22.4 percent of Boston's population. Blacks and Hispanics together comprise about 30 percent of the city.

Boston has long been thoroughly Democratic. But the city showed some reluctance to support Jimmy Carter in the 1980 presidential election; it gave the incumbent president only a 53.3-percent showing, far less than the 66.2 percent George McGovern compiled in 1972. Carter's plurality within the boundaries of the new 9th District was less than 5,000 votes.

The inner-city part of the 9th includes the heavily Italian North End; the trendy Waterfront area, where young government workers and other professionals are moving; the West End, where towering high-rises replaced a thriving ethnic community in the 1950s; the Government Center complex; and most of the downtown shopping district. Conversion of the historic Quincy Market into a glittery emporium of upscale merchandise has injected new life into the historic area.

Beyond these areas lies a group of communities that have experienced serious racial tensions in the past decade. South Boston, still 98.5 percent white and overwhelmingly Irish, was the center of bitter opposition to school busing in the 1970s. Substantial support in South Boston allowed George C. Wallace to carry the old 9th when he ran in the 1976 Democratic presidential primary.

Roxbury and Mission Hill, whose census tract is 69.1 percent black, border on Jamaica Plain, still a predominantly white community but changing rapidly. Since the 1970 census more than one-third of the white population of this area left, the black population more than doubled in size and Hispanics came to make up 21 percent of the residents. Part of the South End, an area of urban restoration, is also in the 9th District, as is racially mixed Dorchester.

Southern suburbs added by the remapping include Stoughton, Easton, Raynham, Dighton, Taunton, Bridgewater, Halifax, Middleborough and Lakeville. Together they have 148,000 people, and all but one of the towns went for Ronald Reagan in 1980. But the town of Taunton, which has more than a quarter of the new population, voted for Carter and is generally Democratic. The 9th District yielded Boston's 4th Ward to the 8th District and the towns of Walpole and Dover to the 4th District.

Election Returns

9th District		Democrat		Republican	
1976	President	118,663	(54.4%)	91,849	(42.1%)
	Senate	135,462	(64.3%)	71,357	(33.9%)
	House	100,465	(55.2%)	71,044	(39.1%)
1978	Governor	100,049	(57.3%)	73,994	(42.4%)
	Senate	94,719	(54.0%)	80,544	(45.9%)
	House	125,285	(80.0%)	21,589	(13.8%)
1980	President	89,233	(43.7%)	84,915	(41.6%)
	House	127,815	(81.9%)	28,129	(18.0%)
1982	Governor[1]	100,684	(58.8%)	63,536	(37.1%)
	Senate	105,251	(61.6%)	64,181	(37.6%)
	House	102,665	(64.1%)	55,030	(34.3%)

[1] Boston returns for the 1982 gubernatorial and Senate races were estimated; final 1982 returns from Boston were unavailable at publication time.

Demographics

Population: 519,226. **Percent Change from 1970:** -5.2%.

Land Area: 362 square miles. **Population per Square Mile:** 1,434.3.

Counties, 1980 Population: Bristol (Pt.) — 76,061; Norfolk (Pt.) — 141,014; Plymouth (Pt.) — 45,050; Suffolk (Pt.) — 257,101.

Cities, 1980 Population: Boston (Pt.) — 257,101; Bridgewater — 17,202; Canton — 18,182; Dedham — 25,298; Easton — 16,623; Middleborough — 16,404; Needham — 27,901; Norwood — 29,711; Stoughton — 26,710; Taunton — 45,001; Westwood — 13,212.

Race and Ancestry: White — 78.6%; Black — 16.0%; American Indian, Eskimo and Aleut — 0.2%; Asian and Pacific Islander — 1.5%. Spanish Origin — 5.0%. English — 6.1%; French — 1.8%; German — 1.4%; Greek — 1.0%; Irish — 15.6%; Italian — 6.2%; Polish — 1.6%; Portuguese — 4.1%; Russian — 1.1%; Scottish — 0.8%; Swedish — 0.6%.

Universities, Enrollment: Blue Hills Regional Technical Institute, Canton — 526; Bridgewater State College, Bridgewater — 4,472; Stonehill College, North Easton — 2,643; Suffolk University, Boston — 6,136; University of Massachusetts at Boston, Boston — 8,460.

Newspapers, Circulation: The Boston Globe (all day, S), Boston — 487,075; Boston Herald American (mS), Boston — 252,483; The Daily Transcript (e), Dedham — 9,779; Taunton Daily Gazette (e), Taunton — 14,436.

Commercial Television Stations, Affiliation: WCVB-TV, Boston (ABC); WNAC-TV, Boston (CBS); WXNE-TV, Boston (None). District is divided between Boston ADI and Providence (R.I.)-New Bedford ADI. (For other Boston stations, see 8th District.)

Military Installations: South Boston Support Activity (Army), South Boston — 546.

Industries:

Massachusetts General Hospital (HQ); Boston; hospital — 9,000. **First National Boston Corp.** (HQ); Boston; banking — 5,900. **Stone & Webster Engineering Corp.** (HQ); Boston; engineering — 4,000. **Boston City Hospital;** Boston; hospital — 3,090. **Commercial Union Corp.** (HQ); Boston; life, property, fire, casualty insurance — 3,000. **Veterans Administration;** Boston; veterans' hospital — 3,000.

GTE Products Corp.; Needham Heights; communications equipment — 2,800. **New England Medical Center Inc.** (HQ); Boston; hospital — 2,500. **Affiliated Publications Inc.** (HQ); Boston; newspaper publishing — 2,000. **Blue Shield of Massachusetts Inc.** (HQ); Boston; health insurance — 2,000. **Raytheon Co.;** Norwood; data systems — 2,000. **University Hospital Inc.;** Boston; hospital — 2,000. **Federal Reserve Bank of Boston;** Boston; banking — 1,500. **New England Merchants Co.** (HQ); Boston; bank holding company — 1,500. **Polaroid Corp.;** Norwood; cameras, ophthalmic goods — 1,500. **Shawmut Corp.** (HQ); Boston; bank holding company — 1,500. **Teradyne Inc.** (HQ); Boston; electronic testing devices — 1,400. **Hearst Corp.;** Boston; newspaper publishing — 1,300.

Faulkner Hospital Corp.; Boston; hospital — 1,200. **Jordan Marsh Co.** (HQ); Boston; department stores — 1,200. **Norwood Hospital;** Norwood; hospital — 1,200. **Analog Devices Inc.;** Norwood; research — 1,130. **Veterans Administration;** Boston; veterans' hospital — 1,050. **New England Baptist Hospital;** Boston; hospital — 1,000. **Princess House Inc.;** North Dighton; gift items — 950. **First Security Services** (JAB Uniform Co. Div. - HQ); Boston; security services — 900.

Northrop Corp.; Norwood; precision equipment — 900. **State Street Bank & Trust Co.** (HQ); Boston; banking — 860. **Allied Maintenance Corp.**; Boston; janitorial services — 850. **Edison International Inc.** (Masoneilan Div.); Norwood; valves, controls — 832.

Analog Devices Inc. (HQ); Norwood; semiconductors — 823. **Plymouth Rubber Co. Inc.**; Canton; rubber, plastic products — 800. **Dart Industries Inc.** (Coppercraft Guild Div.); Taunton; copper products — 750. **Reed & Barton Corp.** (HQ); Taunton; silverware — 750. **Morse Shoe Inc.** (HQ); Canton; shoes — 700. **A. F. Publicover Co. Inc.** (HQ); Boston; security services — 690. **Boston Safe Deposit & Trust Co.**; Boston; banking — 660. **The Kendall Co.** (HQ); Boston; cotton goods — 650. **CDI Corp.**; Needham; drafting — 600. **Linsco Corp.**; Boston; securities brokers — 600. **United Engineers & Constructors** (Jackson & Moreland International); Boston; engineering services — 600. **Colonial Provision Co. Inc.** (HQ); Boston; prepared meat products — 550.

Delmed Inc.; Canton; plastic products — 550. **Camp Dresser & McKee Inc.** (HQ); Boston; environmental engineering services — 533. **New England Nuclear Corp.**; Boston; medicinal products — 514. **Coca-Cola Bottling Co., New England** (HQ); Needham Heights; soft drink bottling — 500. **Coopers & Lybrand**; Boston; accounting services — 500. **Excelon Security Services Inc.**; Boston; security services — 500. **Factory Mutual Engineering** (Factory Mutual Insurance); Norwood; accounting services — 500. **Hersey Products Inc.**; Dedham; fluid meters — 500. **Houghton Mifflin Co.** (HQ); Boston; book publishing — 500. **Metcalf & Eddy Inc.** (HQ); Boston; engineering services — 500. **Sheraton Boston Corp.**; Boston; hotel — 500. **XTRA Corp.**; Boston; bookkeeping services — 500.

10th District

South Shore, Southeast and Cape Cod

With a brisk 23.0 percent population increase since the 1970 census, the old southeastern district was the only area of the state that experienced rapid growth during the 1970s. Numbered as the 12th for the past two decades, it was given a new designation as the 10th with the state's reduction to 11 districts.

Paced by the fast-growing South Shore suburbs that send commuters to downtown Boston, Plymouth County grew by 21.6 percent. Further out, the boom that has transformed scenic Cape Cod from a summertime retreat to a year-round residence helped Barnstable County's population to surge by 53.0 percent.

The area is the most Republican in the Democratic-dominated state. Three of the four Bay State counties that Richard Nixon carried in 1972 — Barnstable, Nantucket and Dukes (Martha's Vineyard) — are in the new 10th. The district was also Ronald Reagan's strongest and Jimmy Carter's weakest district in 1980, with a 47-to-35-percent Reagan plurality within the new boundaries.

The town of Plymouth has seen its population almost double since 1970. The site of a historic district around Plymouth Rock, the town is also home to the controversial Pilgrim nuclear power plant. In 1980, the town was tilted narrowly to Reagan by independent John B. Anderson's 2,500-vote showing.

To the southwest, on Bristol County's Buzzards Bay coast, lies New Bedford, which was the world's largest whaling center in the early 19th century and which retains its orientation toward the fishing industry. The city was a pre-Civil-War way-station along the "Underground Railroad" spiriting runaway slaves to safety, and now is home to a large number of illegal immigrants amid its significant

legal migrations from Portugal and the Cape Verde Islands. New Bedford is Democratic.

Cape Cod is all in Barnstable County, where every town enjoyed at least modest growth during the decade. Environmentalists, fearful of despoiling the area's sandy shores and fragile marine life, have fought to keep oil-drilling exploration in offshore Georges Bank under strict controls. Along the curve of the cape lies a sandy national seashore preserve, a mecca for summer tourists but a lonely winter outpost for seamen in a still vigorous fishing trade. Provincetown, an artists' retreat at the tip of the cape, is the only town in this solidly Republican county where Carter outpolled Reagan in 1980.

The 10th also includes the islands of Nantucket and Martha's Vineyard, where a strong sense of independence reigns. When the recent reorganization of the state Legislature sought to deprive the islands of their own legislative seats, there was considerable discussion of seceding from the Bay State to join Vermont or becoming sovereign states on their own.

In the remap, the district lost Rockland and Weymouth to the 11th, and gained Hanson from the 10th.

Election Returns

10th District		Democrat		Republican	
1976	President	120,609	(50.5%)	110,035	(46.1%)
	Senate	146,650	(64.2%)	78,390	(34.3%)
	House	195,007	(98.7%)	2,532	(1.3%)
1978	Governor	88,532	(48.4%)	93,523	(51.1%)
	Senate	92,095	(50.5%)	89,962	(49.3%)
	House	156,046	(99.0%)	1,437	(0.9%)
1980	President	86,914	(35.0%)	118,065	(47.5%)
	House	173,233	(72.0%)	67,407	(28.0%)
1982	Governor	110,394	(54.6%)	84,840	(42.0%)
	Senate	115,167	(56.9%)	85,679	(42.4%)
	House	138,418	(68.7%)	63,014	(31.3%)

Demographics

Population: 522,200. **Percent Change from 1970:** 26.6%.

Land Area: 1,099 square miles. **Population per Square Mile:** 475.2.

Counties, 1980 Population: Barnstable — 147,925; Bristol (Pt.) — 146,907; Dukes — 8,942; Nantucket — 5,087; Norfolk (Pt.) — 7,174; Plymouth (Pt.) — 206,165.

Cities, 1980 Population: Barnstable — 30,898; Bourne — 13,847; Dartmouth — 23,966; Dennis — 12,360; Duxbury — 11,807; Fairhaven — 15,759; Falmouth — 23,640; Hanover — 11,358; Hingham — 20,339; Marshfield — 20,916; New Bedford — 98,478; Pembroke — 13,487; Plymouth — 35,913; Scituate — 17,317; Wareham — 18,457; Yarmouth — 18,449.

Race and Ancestry: White — 95.5%; Black — 1.4%; American Indian, Eskimo and Aleut — 0.3%; Asian and Pacific Islander — 0.3%. Spanish Origin — 1.5%. English — 12.0%; French — 4.2%; German — 1.9%; Irish — 10.4%; Italian — 3.5%; Polish — 1.5%; Portuguese — 12.0%; Scottish — 1.2%; Swedish — 0.9%.

Universities, Enrollment: Cape Cod Community College, West Barnstable — 4,464; Massachusetts Maritime Academy, Buzzards Bay — 932; Southeastern Massachusetts University, North Dartmouth — 5,511.

Newspapers, Circulation: *Cape Cod Times* (eS), Hyannis — 35,793; *The Standard-Times* (eS), New Bedford — 48,489. *The Boston Globe* also circulates in the district.

Commercial Television Stations, Affiliation: WLNE, New Bedford (CBS). Most of district is located in Boston ADI. Portion is in Providence (R.I.)-New Bedford ADI.

Military Installations: Camp Edwards, Bourne — 3,338; Otis Air Force Base, Falmouth — 1,597; North Truro Air Force Station, North Truro — 115.

Nuclear Power Plants. Pilgrim 1, Plymouth (General Electric, Bechtel), December 1972.

Industries:

St. Luke's Hospital Inc.; New Bedford; hospital — 1,640. **Cape Cod Hospital;** Hyannis; hospital — 1,030. **Arcata National Corp.** (Halliday Lithographic Corp.); West Hanover; book printing — 1,000. **Chamberlain Mfg. Corp.;** New Bedford; firearms — 1,000. **Berkshire Hathaway Inc.** (HQ); New Bedford; insurance — 900.

Gulf & Western Mfg. Co.; New Bedford; cutting tools — 800. U. S. Industries Inc. (Shepard Clothing Div.); New Bedford; boys', men's clothing — 800. **Aerovox Inc.;** New Bedford; coated paper — 750. **Calvin Clothing Corp.;** New Bedford; boys', men's clothing — 750. **Cornell-Dubilier Electric Corp.;** New Bedford; capacitors — 625. **Acushnet Co. Inc.** (Titleist Golf Div.); Acushnet; sporting goods — 600. **Arcata Corp.;** Plympton; bookbinding — 600. **Polaroid Corp.;** New Bedford; photographic film — 500.

11th District

South Shore Suburbs — Quincy, Brockton

The 11th includes the southern wards of Boston and the city's southern suburbs. Its closer-in communities declined slightly in population during the 1970s, but its more distant Boston suburbs gained slightly.

The area is usually Democratic — George McGovern won it in 1972 and Jimmy Carter carried it in 1976 — but the new district gave Ronald Reagan a 44-to-41-percent victory in 1980. Independent candidate John B. Anderson pulled only 13.1 percent here, his lowest statewide share.

All four of the district's Boston wards, which hold about one-third of the 11th's population, lost residents during the decade: Dorchester was down by 26 percent, Hyde Park by 15 percent and Neponset and Mattapan by 18.5 percent. Moreover, all these areas — like Boston and Suffolk County as a whole — showed substantial losses of white residents while the black population soared. The Neponset-Mattapan census tract in Boston, now evenly balanced racially, showed a 50 percent decline among whites as the black population nearly doubled. Hyde Park's black population has multiplied nearly tenfold since 1970.

Quincy, at the end of the MBTA Red Line that brings commuters home to the South Shore from Boston, is the largest community in Norfolk County. It has a heavy concentration of ethnics, with Irish, Italian and French-Canadian pockets. The Quincy shipyards along the Fore River turn out liquefied-natural-gas tankers that bring the highly volatile cargo from the Middle East to energy-starved New England. Quincy gave 60 percent margins to the Democratic candidates for Senate and governor in 1978, but Reagan eked out a 61-vote victory in the city in 1980.

Brockton, with 95,000 residents the largest city in Plymouth County, was long the shoe-making center of the nation. Then named North Bridgewater, it shod half the Union Army in the Civil War. But the city's footwear industry has been in decline for a generation. Brockton remains solidly Democratic.

In the remapping process, the 11th District gained the towns of East Bridgewater, West Bridgewater, Rockland and Weymouth.

Election Returns

11th District		Democrat		Republican	
1976	President	124,179	(55.8%)	90,036	(40.4%)
	Senate	146,660	(66.1%)	71,019	(32.0%)
	House	152,744	(71.5%)	1,688	(0.8%)
1978	Governor	114,006	(63.3%)	65,688	(36.5%)
	Senate	104,849	(57.6%)	77,073	(42.3%)
	House	150,363	(91.2%)	2,472	(1.5%)
1980	President	92,420	(41.6%)	98,415	(44.3%)
	House	155,815	(94.3%)	9,331	(5.6%)
1982	Governor[1]	102,331	(58.5%)	64,802	(37.0%)
	Senate	106,619	(61.1%)	66,558	(38.1%)
	House	x[2]		—[2]	

[1] *Boston returns for the 1982 gubernatorial and Senate races were estimated; final 1982 returns from Boston were unavailable at publication time.*

[2] *No votes tabulated where candidate was unopposed; x indicates winner.*

Demographics

Population: 525,089. **Percent Change from 1970:** -2.8%.

Land Area: 183 square miles. **Population per Square Mile:** 2,869.3.

Counties, 1980 Population: Norfolk (Pt.) — 246,925; Plymouth (Pt.) — 154,222; Suffolk (Pt.) — 123,942.

Cities, 1980 Population: Abington — 13,517; Boston (Pt.) — 123,942; Braintree — 36,337; Brockton — 95,172; Holbrook — 11,140; Milton — 25,860; Quincy — 84,743; Randolph — 28,218; Rockland — 15,695; Weymouth — 55,601; Whitman — 13,534.

Race and Ancestry: White — 89.8%; Black — 8.1%; American Indian, Eskimo and Aleut — 0.2%; Asian and Pacific Islander — 0.6%. Spanish Origin — 1.8%. English — 6.3%; French — 1.8%; German — 1.2%; Greek — 0.8%; Irish — 19.5%; Italian — 7.5%; Polish — 1.4%; Portuguese — 0.9%; Russian — 1.2%; Scottish — 1.2%; Swedish — 1.0%.

Universities, Enrollment: Aquinas Junior College, Milton — 416; Curry College, Milton — 868; Eastern Nazarene College, Wollaston — 832; Laboure Junior College, Boston — 484; Massasoit Community College, Brockton — 6,397; Quincy Junior College, Quincy — 4,118.

Newspapers, Circulation: *The Enterprise* (e), Brockton — 60,651; *The Patriot Leader* (e), Quincy — 83,608. *The Boston Globe* also circulates in the district.

Commercial Television Stations, Affiliation: Entire district is located in Boston ADI.

Military Installations: South Weymouth Naval Air Station, South Weymouth — 991.

Industries:

New England Deaconess Hospital; Boston; hospital — 3,000. **The Foxboro Co.;** East Bridgewater; flow control devices — 2,200. **General Dynamics Corp.** (Quincy Shipbuilding Div.); Quincy; shipyard — 2,116. **Multibank Financial Corp.;** Quincy; bank holding company — 1,560. **State Street Bank & Trust Co.;** Quincy; operation center — 1,500.

Veterans Administration; Brockton; veterans' hospital — 1,400. **Brockton Hospital Co.;** Brockton; hospital — 1,300. **Cardinal Cushing General Hospital;** Brockton; hospital — 1,100. **South Shore Hospital;** South Weymouth; hospital — 1,100. **The Carney Hospital Inc.** (HQ); Boston; hospital — 1,000. **Suburban Contract Cleaning Co.;** South Weymouth; janitorial services — 900. **Incom International Inc.** (Boston

Gear); Quincy; industrial gears — 850. **Raytheon Co.** (Microwave & Power Tube Div.); Quincy; tubes — 850.

Jordan Marsh Co.; Quincy; warehousing — 700. **Westinghouse Electric Corp.** (Sturtevant Div.); Boston; blowers, exhaust fans — 700.

Sigma Instruments Inc. (HQ); Braintree; transformers — 650. **Armstrong World Industries Inc.;** Braintree; industrial rubber — 600. **Pneumatic Scale Corp.;** Quincy; food, beverage packaging machinery — 550. **Electro Signal Lab Inc.;** Rockland; detection devices — 500.

Michigan

Michigan Democrats lost a redistricting battle in 1982 when GOP Gov. William G. Milliken vetoed the congressional map that emerged from the Democratic Legislature, but they won the war when a federal court ordered the state to adopt the bulk of the remap as it had been passed. Because Michigan's cities lost heavily in population during the 1970s, Republicans had been hoping for a plan that would reduce urban Democratic representation. The court version, handed down May 17, 1982, generally favored incumbents of both parties.

Under reapportionment, Michigan was forced to give up one of its 19 districts. Democrats in the Legislature initially proposed a map that would have erased the 2nd District seat, held by a moderate Republican, but the Legislature's final decision was to sacrifice the Democratic 18th District in the suburbs north of Detroit. The surgery was done with little pain because the incumbent had announced he was leaving Congress to run for governor.

The Legislature's compromise map was passed by the Michigan House on a near party-line vote on March 30 and by the Senate a week later. On April 27 Milliken vetoed it, asserting that it would give Democrats at least 12 of 18 seats, "a distortion of the views of the Michigan electorate." But the three-judge federal panel in Flint, two of its members Democratic appointees, ruled in favor of the basic Democratic plan. The judges chose the Legislature's map over GOP-drawn lines and over the first Democratic plan dissolving the 2nd District.

The only changes made in the Legislature's map were in the 5th District, which had been drawn to damage seriously the Republican incumbent's chances for re-election. Instead the court gave the 5th a constituency barely changed from the previous decade.

Redistricting contributed to the defeat of the Republican incumbent in the 6th District, who in 1982 lost to the man he had bested in 1980. Previously based in Lansing, the 6th took on extensive new territory in Oakland County, including the Democratic stronghold of Pontiac.

Substantial changes were made in some of the other districts, but they did not threaten the incumbents. Although Detroit lost a fifth of its population during the 1970s, legislators were determined to keep the two inner-city districts in the hands of their black Democratic incumbents. As a result, the 1st and 13th districts changed their characters only marginally, while districts on the edges of

the city added substantial territory. The 2nd picked up a wide stretch of farm land west and south of Ann Arbor, while the 16th moved beyond the industrial corridor south of Detroit into the countryside.

Age of Population

District	Population Under 18	Voting Age Population	Population 65 & Over (% of VAP)	Median Age
1	165,378	349,182	47,777 (13.7%)	27.8
2	138,649	375,911	45,010 (12.0%)	28.7
3	147,048	367,512	49,244 (13.4%)	28.2
4	158,814	355,746	56,287 (15.8%)	29.6
5	154,949	359,611	52,190 (14.5%)	28.0
6	153,598	360,961	36,341 (10.1%)	26.3
7	167,692	346,868	40,344 (11.6%)	27.5
8	163,983	350,577	53,116 (15.2%)	28.5
9	157,664	356,896	58,147 (16.3%)	29.1
10	157,191	357,369	52,523 (14.7%)	27.8
11	146,781	367,779	70,884 (19.3%)	30.3
12	152,525	362,035	45,200 (12.5%)	29.3
13	154,319	360,241	67,365 (18.7%)	29.0
14	142,137	372,422	58,019 (15.6%)	30.9
15	158,307	356,253	30,909 (8.7%)	27.2
16	146,971	367,589	52,476 (14.3%)	30.2
17	132,146	382,414	60,307 (15.8%)	31.4
18	153,834	360,726	36,119 (10.0%)	30.6
State	2,751,986	6,510,092	912,258 (14.0%)	28.8

Income and Occupation

District	Median Family Income	White Collar Workers	Blue Collar Workers	Service Workers	Farm Workers
1	$ 18,689	46.5%	35.6%	17.7%	0.2%
2	24,567	58.0	27.5	12.7	1.8
3	21,555	52.1	31.9	14.3	1.7
4	19,564	44.6	38.6	12.9	3.9
5	21,384	49.6	35.9	12.8	1.7
6	24,021	53.6	30.2	14.7	1.5
7	23,783	43.2	42.4	13.3	1.1
8	20,955	43.4	38.5	14.3	3.8
9	18,799	44.1	38.4	13.9	3.6
10	18,614	46.3	35.2	14.5	3.9
11	16,133	45.5	33.3	17.9	3.3
12	24,991	50.8	35.2	13.1	0.8
13	12,825	45.7	33.4	20.5	0.3

MICHIGAN

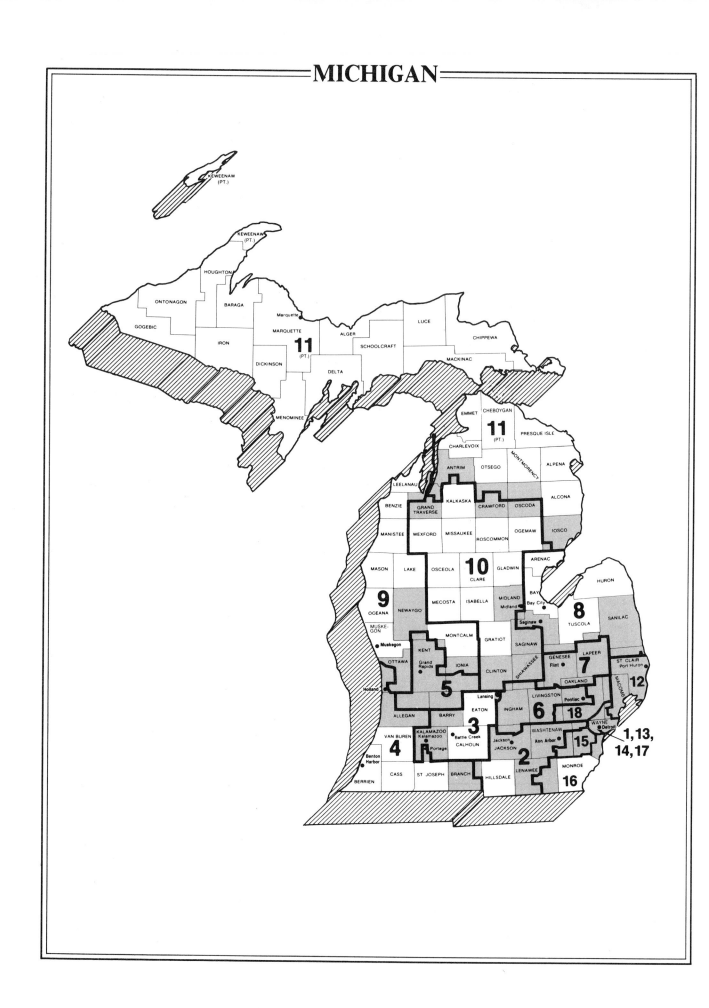

District	Median Family Income	White Collar Workers	Blue Collar Workers	Service Workers	Farm Workers
14	24,862	53.2	33.1	13.4	0.3
15	25,687	47.8	38.1	13.5	0.6
16	24,996	48.3	37.2	13.5	1.0
17	25,853	60.3	27.1	12.3	0.3
18	33,080	68.0	21.5	10.0	0.5
State	$ 22,107	50.6%	33.8%	13.9%	1.7%

Education: School Years Completed

District	8 Years or Fewer	4 Years of High School	4 Years of College or More	Median School Years
1	19.3%	33.2%	8.8%	12.3
2	9.5	35.2	24.8	12.8
3	12.1	38.4	16.6	12.6
4	17.7	38.8	12.6	12.4
5	13.5	37.9	15.3	12.5
6	10.8	37.7	19.2	12.6
7	14.0	40.9	10.8	12.4
8	18.8	41.2	9.6	12.3
9	17.0	39.5	11.5	12.4
10	16.1	41.7	12.3	12.4
11	17.9	41.4	11.7	12.4
12	13.8	42.9	9.9	12.4
13	26.9	27.2	8.5	11.9
14	17.0	38.0	11.9	12.4
15	13.0	40.0	12.6	12.5
16	16.6	40.3	11.4	12.4
17	11.2	37.5	17.7	12.6
18	6.2	33.0	30.8	13.0
State	15.1%	38.0%	14.3%	12.5

Housing and Residential Patterns

District	Owner Occupied	Renter Occupied	Urban	Rural
1	67.0%	33.0%	100.0%	0.0%
2	69.3	30.7	65.0	35.0
3	68.0	32.0	68.9	31.1
4	75.6	24.4	38.6	61.4
5	73.2	26.8	72.7	27.3
6	70.0	30.0	66.9	33.1
7	75.6	24.4	68.3	31.7
8	78.0	22.0	47.5	52.5
9	79.1	20.9	41.2	58.8
10	79.9	20.1	28.5	71.5
11	77.2	22.8	36.6	63.4
12	77.9	22.1	84.2	15.8
13	40.9	59.1	100.0	0.0
14	79.2	20.8	100.0	0.0
15	71.4	28.6	90.8	9.2
16	76.0	24.0	79.2	20.8
17	74.6	25.4	100.0	0.0
18	78.0	22.0	84.8	15.2
State	72.7%	27.3%	70.7%	29.3%

1st District

Detroit — North Central; Highland Park

Detroit was not all that special at the turn of the century. It brewed beer and turned out carriages and stoves, and its complacent citizens took to calling it "the most beautiful city in America." But Henry Ford's first large factory in Highland Park was followed by others, plants put up by Buick, R. E. Olds and the Fisher brothers. The north side of Detroit became a sea of single- and double-family houses for the workers who flocked to the assembly lines from rural Michigan, Appalachia and Eastern Europe.

The neighborhoods within the 1st District, northwest of downtown Detroit, have changed character as the economic forces driving the auto industry and the city of Detroit have changed. When the 1st District was created in 1964, it was about 50 percent black. By the end of the 1970s, more than 80 percent of its residents were black, reflecting both white flight and the arrival of blacks from poorer areas of the city and from the South. Although the 1982 redistricting reduced the black majority, it did not make a substantial difference in the demography or the overwhelmingly Democratic politics of the district.

The 1st is generally better off than its inner-city neighbor, the 13th. More of its homes are owner-occupied, and its residents are better educated. The racially mixed communities north of Seven Mile Road have a high percentage of professionals and professional city employees living in well-preserved prewar houses. The district also edges up against Rosedale Park, a gentrified area most of which is in the 17th District.

East of Southfield Road, the neighborhoods grow more black, moving from middle- to lower-middle class. Both skilled and unskilled blacks live in Highland Park and in the area north of the University of Detroit, as well as toward the south and east of the district.

Highland Park, a city entirely surrounded by Detroit, is the home of Chrysler Corp. Once a white ethnic bastion, the city is now 84 percent black. Although Highland Park retained its middle-class character through most of the 1960s and early 1970s, hard times and rising unemployment have hurt its increasingly marginal neighborhoods.

Even before redistricting, the 1st had several white enclaves, and more were added. The Poles living in the northeast corner of the district, north of Hamtramck, have been joined by a middle-class ethnic community around the Southfield Freeway in the southwest. These new voters tend to be older and conservative on social issues, uncomfortable with the liberal activism that has dominated local politics since the district's creation in 1964.

Also added were working-class neighborhoods that surround Patton Park, on the eastern edge of Dearborn. Most of the people here are Eastern European ethnics and Southern whites, but there are substantial numbers of Hispanics.

Election Returns

1st District		Democrat		Republican	
1976	President	148,065	(83.5%)	27,136	(15.3%)
	Senate	142,687	(85.7%)	22,216	(13.4%)
	House	142,854	(85.7%)	21,711	(13.0%)
1978	Governor	79,083	(62.8%)	46,869	(37.2%)
	Senate	100,339	(81.1%)	23,325	(18.9%)
	House	105,641	(91.7%)	8,483	(7.4%)
1980	President	143,653	(85.6%)	19,341	(11.5%)
	House	139,709	(88.5%)	16,763	(10.6%)

1st District		Democrat		Republican	
1982	Governor	94,616	(66.6%)	43,845	(30.8%)
	Senate	100,910	(71.8%)	37,829	(26.9%)
	House	125,517	(96.7%)	—	

Demographics

Population: 514,560. **Percent Change from 1970:** -10.0%.

Land Area: 58 square miles. **Population per Square Mile:** 8,871.1.

Counties, 1980 Population: Wayne (Pt.) — 514,560.

Cities, 1980 Population: Detroit (Pt.) — 486,651; Highland Park — 27,909.

Race and Ancestry: White — 26.8%; Black — 70.7%; American Indian, Eskimo and Aleut — 0.2%; Asian and Pacific Islander — 0.5%. Spanish Origin — 2.1%. English — 2.2%; German — 1.6%; Irish — 1.2%; Italian — 0.6%; Polish — 4.8%; Ukranian — 0.5%.

Universities, Enrollment: Highland Park Community College, Highland Park — 2,654; Lewis College of Business, Detroit — 455; Marygrove College, Detroit — 1,025; Mercy College of Detroit, Detroit — 2,490; University of Detroit, Detroit — 6,610.

Newspapers, Circulation: *Detroit Free Press* and *The Detroit News* circulate in the district.

Commercial Television Stations, Affiliation: Entire district is located in Detroit ADI.

Industries:

General Motors Corp. (Detroit Diesel Allison Div.); Detroit; internal combustion engines — 9,700. **Chrysler Corp.** (HQ); Highland Park; motor vehicles — 9,000. **Sinai Hospital of Detroit Inc.;** Detroit; hospital — 2,500. **Grace Hospital;** Detroit; hospital — 1,500. **Ford Motor Co.** (Ford Tractor Div.); Detroit; farm tractors — 1,200.

Guardian Protective Service (Centurian Uniforms); Detroit; security services — 800. **Michigan Wisconsin Pipeline Co.** (HQ); Detroit; natural gas transmission, extraction — 800. **Total Building Services Inc.;** Detroit; janitorial services — 800. **Shatterproof Glass Corp.** (HQ); Detroit; glass products — 700. **Fred Sanders** (HQ); Highland Park; bakery products — 600. **American Bakeries Co.** (Taystee Bread Div.); Detroit; bakery products — 531. **Allied Supermarkets Inc.** (HQ); Detroit; grocery chain — 500. **Bonded Guard Services Inc.;** Detroit; security services — 500. **Chrysler Corp.** (McGraw Glass Plant); Detroit; auto glass — 500.

2nd District

Southeast — Ann Arbor, Jackson

The newly drawn 2nd reaches south and west from the Detroit suburbs to the northern edge of the nation's Corn Belt. A 90-mile stretch that takes in portions of six counties and the cities of Ann Arbor and Jackson, it is very different from the compact, more urbanized 2nd District of the 1970s.

But while the bulk of the territory and a little more than half the people are new, the 2nd is still home to the same uneasy mix of academics, blue-collar workers and conservative farmers it has held since the 1950s. Moderate Republicanism seems to be the only politics that works districtwide; both the incumbent in 1982 and his predecessor used a Ripon Republican approach to defeat a diverse array of Democratic challengers.

The old 2nd needed only 9,000 people to reach its ideal size, but it became a victim of the broad population losses in the Detroit area. With the 16th District moving into Monroe County to allow the Detroit city districts to expand, the 2nd had nowhere to go but into the rural counties to the west. It gained Republican voters in western Washtenaw County, most of Jackson and Lenawee counties, all of Hillsdale County and two townships in Branch County.

In exchange, it gave up the more Democratic portions of the Detroit suburb of Livonia, all of Monroe County and the southeastern part of Washtenaw County, including staunchly Democratic Ypsilanti. The net result is a solid edge for Republicans districtwide.

The GOP dominates the rural townships that make up most of the new territory. The small towns and corn and dairy farms that dot the flat land of Hillsdale, Lenawee, Jackson and Branch counties are a steady source of Republican votes; the last time any of those counties voted for a Democratic presidential candidate was in 1964. Hillsdale County, home of conservative Hillsdale College, has given at least 62 percent of its votes to every GOP presidential candidate since then.

The other block of Republican votes comes from the Detroit suburbs. About a fifth of the district's residents live in a sliver of Wayne County that begins only a mile and a half west of Detroit, in the mostly upper-middle class Livonia neighborhoods north of I-96. Professionals and middle-level managers from the area's auto plants give northern Livonia its Republican character, although some blue-collar Democrats live in the older northeast corner of the city. Republicans also hold sway to the west, in the small cities of Northville and Plymouth and the newer subdivisions in the townships that surround them.

Nowhere is the 2nd's volatile combination of residents more evident than in Washtenaw County, which holds close to a third of the district's population. The students and academic community centered around the University of Michigan in Ann Arbor give that city a bohemian image that stands in marked contrast to the conservatism found on the sheep and vegetable farms to the south and west. The two poles of the county — the rural west and urban east — have swung Washtenaw from Republican to Democratic and back in each presidential election since 1960; it was the only county in the nation to support George McGovern in 1972 and Gerald R. Ford in 1976.

Ann Arbor has a relatively small blue-collar presence and a somewhat tenuous Democratic base — the student wards provide its only consistently liberal Democratic vote. With much of the city's economy based on the university and high technology industries, its electorate tends as a whole to take a more independent line. John B. Anderson pulled in one of his highest margins in the state here in 1980, garnering 15 percent of the vote.

Much of the rest of the 2nd District's Democratic vote comes from Jackson, a small industrial city caught up in the auto industry's difficulties. Jackson's Democratic vote is cast largely by workers in the tool-and-die and auto parts industries. But many of these workers grew up in the surrounding Republican countryside and sometimes reflect that background in statewide and national elections.

Election Returns

2nd District		Democrat		Republican	
1976	President	90,250	(40.7%)	126,141	(56.9%)

2nd District		Democrat		Republican	
1976	Senate	93,962	(43.9%)	118,305	(55.3%)
	House	98,014	(46.3%)	112,344	(53.1%)
1978	Governor	59,184	(33.3%)	118,029	(66.5%)
	Senate	80,219	(45.2%)	97,091	(54.8%)
	House	63,276	(36.3%)	109,951	(63.1%)
1980	President	88,499	(36.8%)	125,724	(52.2%)
	House	85,827	(38.4%)	135,844	(60.8%)
1982	Governor	90,635	(51.3%)	79,894	(45.2%)
	Senate	99,167	(57.1%)	72,035	(41.5%)
	House	53,040	(32.5%)	106,960	(65.4%)

Demographics

Population: 514,560. **Percent Change from 1970:** 10.1%.

Land Area: 2,346 square miles. **Population per Square Mile:** 219.3.

Counties, 1980 Population: Branch (Pt.) — 4,989; Hillsdale — 42,071; Jackson (Pt.) — 141,448; Lenawee (Pt.) — 46,997; Washtenaw (Pt.) — 168,243; Wayne (Pt.) — 110,812.

Cities, 1980 Population: Adrian (Pt.) — 2,839; Ann Arbor — 107,966; Jackson — 39,739; Livonia (Pt.) — 61,898.

Race and Ancestry: White — 92.9%; Black — 4.7%; American Indian, Eskimo and Aleut — 0.2%; Asian and Pacific Islander — 1.4%. Spanish Origin — 1.3%. Dutch — 0.8%; English — 10.5%; French — 1.0%; German — 10.0%; Irish — 3.4%; Italian — 1.3%; Polish — 3.2%; Russian — 0.6%; Scottish — 0.8%.

Universities, Enrollment: Concordia College, Ann Arbor — 526; Hillsdale College, Hillsdale — 1,006; Jackson Community College, Jackson — 7,542; Madonna College, Livonia — 3,213; St. John's Provincial Seminary, Plymouth — 161; Schoolcraft College, Livonia — 8,077; Spring Arbor College, Spring Arbor — 842; University of Michigan, Ann Arbor — 36,311; Washtenaw Community College, Ann Arbor — 8,455.

Newspapers, Circulation: *The Ann Arbor News* (eS), Ann Arbor — 42,250; *The Hillsdale Daily News* (e), Hillsdale — 8,210; *Jackson Citizen Patriot* (eS), Jackson — 38,227. *Detroit Free Press* and *The Detroit News* also circulate in the district.

Commercial Television Stations, Affiliation: WIHT, Ann Arbor (None). District is divided among Detroit ADI, Grand Rapids-Kalamazoo-Battle Creek ADI, Lansing ADI and Toledo (Ohio) ADI.

Industries:

Hoover Universal Inc.; Ann Arbor; plastics, industrial machinery — 6,500. **University Hospital;** Ann Arbor; hospital — 4,960. **Bechtel Power Corp.;** Ann Arbor; engineering services — 2,253. **Tecumseh Products Co.** (HQ); Tecumseh; refrigeration compressors, small engines — 1,540. **St. Mary Hospital of Livonia Inc.;** Livonia; hospital — 1,200.

Commonwealth Associates Inc. (HQ); Jackson; engineering services — 1,100. **W. A. Foote Memorial Hospital;** Jackson; hospital — 1,000. **General Motors Corp.** (Fisher Body Div.); Tecumseh; automotive stampings — 1,000. **Plymouth Center for Human Development;** Northville; state psychiatric hospital — 1,000. **Veterans Administration;** Ann Arbor; veterans' hospital — 1,000. **Aeroquip Corp.;** Jackson; engineering services — 900. **Addison Products Co.;** Jonesville; refrigeration equipment — 800. **Aeroquip Corp.** (HQ); Jackson; rubber hoses, hardware — 800. **Acorn Building Components Inc.;** Quincy; metal doors, frames — 600. **Goodyear Tire & Rubber Co.;** Jackson; tires, inner tubes — 600. **Jackson Crankshaft Co.** (HQ); Jackson; industrial metal machinery — 600. **Tecumseh Products Co.** (Peerless Gear & Machine Div.); Clinton; speed changers, gears — 600. **Chrysler Corp.;** Chelsea; commercial testing laboratories — 570. **Hoover-NSK Bearing Co.** (HQ); Ann Arbor; ball bearings — 550. **Parke, Davis & Co.;** Ann Arbor; research — 550. **Ford Motor Co.** (Climate Control Div.); Plymouth; motor vehicle parts — 500. **Hayes-Albion Corp.** (HQ); Jackson; automobile parts, iron hardware — 500. **Kelsey-Hayes Co. Inc.;** Jackson; motor vehicle parts — 500. **Sparton Corp.** (Electronics Div. - HQ); Jackson; military electronics — 500. **Xerox Corp.** (University Microfilms); Ann Arbor; micropublishing — 500.

3rd District

South Central — Lansing, Kalamazoo

Although the 3rd is anchored by the medium-sized industrial cities of Kalamazoo and Battle Creek, votes from the surrounding farm land have traditionally defined district politics as Republican. The Democratic incumbent's 1978 victory made him only the second member of his party elected from the district in this century. He won in 1980 with the smallest margin of any re-elected incumbent in the state but increased his margin in 1982.

The Legislature tried to shore up Democratic strength by removing from the district portions of six rural Republican counties plus the northern — and more Republican — half of rural Barry County. Democratic legislators also took out a chunk of Kalamazoo County, moving the suburban Republican community of Portage into the 4th District.

In place of the excised territory, the legislators added much of downtown and western Lansing. Drawing the line through the city to include the state Capitol and several General Motors plants, they gave the 3rd Lansing's most Democratic precincts, including many of its blue-collar, Hispanic and black neighborhoods. Added together, the changes in the district lower the Republican vote considerably, although Democrats still have only an estimated 46 percent of the registered voters.

There remain large patches of rural and suburban Republican territory between the major cities. White-collar suburbs like Delta Township, west of Lansing, and Battle Creek Township, home to Kellogg Company executives, provide Republicans with overwhelming electoral margins. The small towns and rolling fields of Eaton, Kalamazoo and Calhoun counties, which are given over to wheat and corn, or to celery and mint in the wet lower-lying areas, support a strong conservative presence. Only in southern Barry County, settled over the years by workers from Battle Creek and Kalamazoo, do Democrats find a welcome in the countryside.

Apart from Lansing, much of the 3rd's Democratic population lives in three industrial cities lined up along I-94, the major Detroit-Chicago highway: Kalamazoo, Battle Creek and Albion.

Kalamazoo is the most politically balanced of the three. Its paper mills and automobile assembly plants are the base for a powerful union presence and blue-collar Democratic vote, while four colleges bring a liberal academic cast to city politics. But the pharmaceutical workers at the Upjohn Company, the corporate managers who live in and around the southern half of the city and the area's Dutch residents give Kalamazoo a strong moderate-to-conservative Republican vote.

Battle Creek was known in the early decades of this century as the "health city" because of its sanitariums emphasizing grain and cereal products. Now it is more widely recognized, especially among legions of morning cereal-box readers, as the headquarters for both Kellogg and Post breakfast cereals.

Election Returns

3rd District		Democrat		Republican	
1976	President	77,860	(39.6%)	114,346	(58.2%)
	Senate	88,526	(47.1%)	97,979	(52.2%)
	House	95,979	(49.8%)	94,859	(49.3%)
1978	Governor	59,790	(37.9%)	97,858	(62.0%)
	Senate	70,414	(45.2%)	85,282	(54.8%)
	House	83,612	(52.5%)	75,543	(47.5%)
1980	President	79,581	(36.8%)	112,115	(51.9%)
	House	110,895	(52.7%)	98,101	(46.6%)
1982	Governor	80,599	(47.0%)	85,549	(49.8%)
	Senate	93,475	(55.8%)	71,972	(43.0%)
	House	96,842	(56.3%)	73,315	(42.6%)

Demographics

Population: 514,560. **Percent Change from 1970:** 3.7%.

Land Area: 2,095 square miles. **Population per Square Mile:** 245.6.

Counties, 1980 Population: Barry (Pt.) — 18,973; Calhoun — 141,557; Eaton — 88,337; Ingham (Pt.) — 79,977; Kalamazoo (Pt.) — 185,716.

Cities, 1980 Population: Albion — 11,059; Battle Creek — 35,724; Kalamazoo — 79,722; Lansing (Pt.) — 77,999; Portage (Pt.) — 17,930.

Race and Ancestry: White — 88.7%; Black — 8.8%; American Indian, Eskimo and Aleut — 0.4%; Asian and Pacific Islander — 0.6%. Spanish Origin — 2.4%. Dutch — 3.5%; English — 11.6%; French — 1.0%; German — 8.1%; Irish — 3.1%; Italian — 0.8%; Polish — 1.3%; Scottish — 0.6%; Swedish — 0.5%.

Universities, Enrollment: Albion College, Albion — 1,936; Argubright Business College, Battle Creek — 85; Great Lakes Bible College, Lansing — 182; Kalamazoo College, Kalamazoo — 1,452; Kalamazoo Valley Community College, Kalamazoo — 6,050; Kellogg Community College, Battle Creek — 4,941; Lansing Community College, Lansing — 19,424; Nazareth College at Kalamazoo, Nazareth — 541; Olivet College, Olivet — 665; Thomas M. Cooley Law School, Lansing — 1,052; Western Michigan University, Kalamazoo — 20,698.

Newspapers, Circulation: *Albion Evening Recorder* (e), Albion — 4,085; *Enquirer and News* (eS), Battle Creek — 33,446; *Kalamazoo Gazette* (eS), Kalamazoo — 60,422; *Lansing State Journal* (eS), Lansing — 74,025; *Marshall Evening Chronicle* (e), Marshall — 2,639.

Commercial Television Stations, Affiliation: WKZO-TV, Kalamazoo (CBS); WUHQ-TV, Battle Creek (ABC). District is divided between Grand Rapids-Kalamazoo-Battle Creek ADI and Lansing ADI.

Military Installations: W. K. Kellogg Regional Airfield (Air Force), Springfield — 715.

Industries:

General Motors Corp. (Oldsmobile Div.); Lansing; motor vehicle bodies — 18,000. **The Upjohn Co.** (HQ); Kalamazoo; pharmaceutical preparations, medical laboratories — 6,000. **General Motors Corp.** (Fisher Body Div.); Lansing; auto bodies — 4,900. **Kellogg Co.** (HQ); Battle Creek; breakfast cereals, related foods — 4,600. **General Motors Corp.** (Fisher Body Div.); Kalamazoo; motor vehicle parts — 3,240.

Borgess Medical Center Inc.; Kalamazoo; hospital — 2,600. **General Foods Corp.** (Post Cereals Div.- HQ); Battle Creek; breakfast cereals — 2,000. **Bronson Methodist Hospital;** Kalamazoo; hospital — 1,760. **Motor Wheel Corp.** (HQ); Lansing; motor vehicle parts — 1,600. **Veterans Administration;** Battle Creek; veterans' hospital — 1,300. **James River Corp.;** Kalamazoo; paper mills — 1,250. **State Farm Fire & Casualty Co.;** Marshall; casualty insurance — 1,110. **Pneumo Corp.** (NWL Control Systems Div.); Kalamazoo; aircraft parts — 1,100. **Kalamazoo State Hospital;** Kalamazoo; state psychiatric hospital — 1,090. **Asgrow Seed Co.;** Richland; nursery, farm supplies — 1,000. **Eagle-Picher Industries Inc.** (Union Steel Products Div.); Albion; conveying equipment — 1,000. **Eaton Corp.** (Fluid Power Operations); Marshall; automotive parts — 1,000. **Michigan National Bank** (HQ); Lansing; banking — 900.

General Motors Corp.; Lansing; auto parts, supplies wholesaling — 850. **Owens-Illinois Inc.;** Charlotte; glass containers — 800. **St. Regis Paper Co.** (Folding Carton Div.); Battle Creek; paper mill — 780. **Michigan National Bank** (Michigan Bankard Div.); Lansing; banking — 700. **Transamerican Insurance;** Battle Creek; life, accident, medical insurance — 700. **Allied Paper Inc.;** Kalamazoo; paper mill — 600. **Hoover Universal Inc.** (Aluminum Div.); Charlotte; aluminum rolling, drawing — 595. **Union Pump Co.** (HQ); Battle Creek; pumps, pumping equipment — 550. **Allied Paper Inc.** (HQ); Kalamazoo; paper mill — 525. **C & J Commercial Driveaway Inc.;** Lansing; trucking — 500. **Grand Trunk Western Railroad;** Battle Creek; railroad operations — 500. **Shakespeare Co.** (Shakespeare Products Div.); Kalamazoo; motor vehicle parts — 500. **Stryker Corp.** (HQ); Kalamazoo; surgical, medical equipment — 500.

4th District

Southwest — Benton Harbor/St. Joseph; Holland

Stretching 100 miles along the eastern shore of Lake Michigan and another 100 miles on the Indiana border, the L-shaped 4th District is among the most Republican constituencies in the country. In only one of its counties did Republican Robert P. Griffin receive less than 60 percent of the vote in his losing Senate race in 1978 against Democrat Carl Levin, and in 1980 Ronald Reagan came close to that record, falling below 61 percent in just two counties.

Redistricting barely changed the nature of the 4th, which needed to shed just 600 people to reach ideal size. It remains overwhelmingly agricultural; fewer than a fifth of its residents live in its five small cities. The district lost the farms of Hillsdale and Lenawee counties and the small industrial city of Adrian, picking up in their stead about half the suburban Kalamazoo community of Portage, two-thirds of Allegan County and most of the western edge of Ottawa County. With the last two counties came the shore city of Grand Haven and three-fourths of Holland.

Cass, St. Joseph and Branch counties form the northeastern edge of the Corn Belt, their rolling terrain covered with feed grains, wheat, corn and pasture land. The Republican majorities in the three counties are only slightly diluted by the conservative Democratic vote coming from the workers in the plants and foundries of Dowagiac, Three Rivers and Coldwater.

The gentle climate produced by the lake has made fruits and berries the chief crop of the four lake shore counties: peaches, tomatoes and plums in Berrien, blueberries in Van Buren and apples and grapes in Ottawa and Allegan. A small food processing industry has grown up in Berrien County, and several wineries dot the fields around Paw Paw in Van Buren County. The shoreline is also a powerful retirement and tourist draw, and every summer towns from Grand Haven to Grand Beach host visitors and part-time residents from Chicago, Gary and South Bend.

Some of the strongest Republican precincts in the state are in Allegan and Ottawa counties, at the northern end of the 4th District. Allegan County was the political base of Clare Hoffman, a resolutely anti-New Deal Republican who represented the 4th in the House for close to 30 years.

Holland, on the line between Ottawa and Allegan counties, is the other GOP stronghold. Holland is the westernmost point of the "Dutch Triangle," with Grand Rapids and Kalamazoo as the two other sides. This area was settled by immigrants from the Netherlands beginning in the mid-19th century. Holland's Dutch character goes beyond its name and its wooden shoe factory, tidy houses and famous Tulip Festival to a Calvinist religious style. It also practices a scrupulous Republicanism. The city's small-business executives tend to be conservative on economic issues but marginally less so on other questions than the rest of the district; in the 1980 GOP presidential primary, Holland and the rest of Ottawa County supported George Bush.

The major chunk of Democratic votes in the district comes from the Benton Harbor-St. Joseph area, although most of surrounding Berrien County is as Republican as the rest of the district. Benton Harbor once offered a haven to runaway slaves on the underground railroad. Today it is almost 90 percent black, an auto industry city in the throes of precipitous decline.

St. Joseph, once a bedroom community for Benton Harbor, now has a significant manufacturing base of its own, with both the Whirlpool Corp. and Leco Corp. head-quartered there. The blue-collar workers in St. Joseph and in towns to the south vote for conservative Democrats, as do retirees from industrial Illinois and Indiana who now live in shore cottages in towns such as New Buffalo.

Election Returns

4th District		Democrat		Republican	
1976	President	72,586	(37.4%)	119,110	(61.3%)
	Senate	73,603	(40.2%)	108,684	(59.3%)
	House	67,297	(36.5%)	114,837	(62.3%)
1978	Governor	56,652	(39.5%)	86,841	(60.5%)
	Senate	53,394	(37.9%)	87,350	(62.1%)
	House	40,003	(28.7%)	98,444	(70.5%)
1980	President	66,585	(31.9%)	126,001	(60.3%)
	House	41,744	(21.2%)	152,374	(77.3%)
1982	Governor	61,251	(40.0%)	87,877	(57.4%)
	Senate	66,613	(44.2%)	82,162	(54.5%)
	House	56,877	(38.8%)	87,489	(59.7%)

Demographics

Population: 514,560. **Percent Change from 1970:** 12.8%.

Land Area: 3,374 square miles. **Population per Square Mile:** 152.5.

Counties, 1980 Population: Allegan (Pt.) — 59,793; Berrien — 171,276; Branch (Pt.) — 35,199; Cass — 49,499; Kalamazoo (Pt.) — 26,662; Ottawa (Pt.) — 49,234; St. Joseph — 56,083; Van Buren — 66,814.

Cities, 1980 Population: Benton Harbor — 14,707; Grand Haven — 11,763; Holland (Pt.) — 16,720; Niles — 13,115; Portage (Pt.) — 20,227.

Race and Ancestry: White — 91.1%; Black — 7.3%; American Indian, Eskimo and Aleut — 0.4%; Asian and Pacific Islander — 0.5%. Spanish Origin — 1.6%. Dutch — 5.7%; English — 9.3%; French — 0.9%; German — 12.0%; Irish — 3.1%; Italian — 0.8%; Polish — 1.9%; Swedish — 0.7%.

Universities, Enrollment: Andrews University, Berrien Springs — 3,018; Glen Oaks Community College, Centreville — 1,224; Lake Michigan College, Benton Harbor — 3,602; Southwestern Michigan College, Dowagiac — 2,133.

Newspapers, Circulation: *Coldwater Daily Reporter* (e), Coldwater — 8,851; *The Daily Star* (e), Niles — 7,436; *Dowagiac News* (m), Dowagiac — 3,125; *Grand Haven Tribune* (e), Grand Haven — 9,856; *The Herald-Palladium* (e), Benton Harbor — 36,314; *South Haven Daily Tribune* (m), South Haven — 2,705; *Sturgis Journal* (e), Sturgis — 10,278; *Three Rivers Commercial* (e), Three Rivers — 4,789. *Kalamazoo Gazette* also circulates in the district.

Commercial Television Stations, Affiliation: District is divided between Grand Rapids-Kalamazoo-Battle Creek ADI and South Bend (Ind.)-Elkhart (Ind.) ADI.

Nuclear Power Plants: Cook 1, Bridgeman (Westinghouse, American Electric Power Service Corp.), August 1975; Cook 2, Bridgeman (Westinghouse, J. A. Jones Construction), July 1978; Palisades, South Haven (Combustion Engineering, Bechtel), December 1971.

Industries:

General Motors Corp. (Hydra-matic Div.); Three Rivers; motor vehicle bodies — 1,850. **Whirlpool Corp.** (St. Joseph Div.); St. Joseph; laundry equipment — 1,685. **Heath Co.** (HQ); St. Joseph; electronic testing equipment, radio & television receivers — 1,200. **Whirlpool Corp.** (HQ); Benton Harbor; household appliances — 1,000. **Hayworth Industries Inc.** (HQ); Holland; office, store shelving — 900.

Simplicity Pattern Co. Inc.; Niles; garment pattern publishing — 852. **Bendix Corp.** (Hydraulic Div.); St. Joseph; motor vehicle parts — 800. **National-Standard Co.** (Machinery Div. - HQ); Niles; wire products — 800. **Kirsch Co.** (HQ); Sturgis; drapery, furniture hardware — 750. **Life Savers Inc.;** Holland; candy, gum — 750. **L. Perrigo Co.** (HQ); Allegan; pharmaceutical preparations — 720. **Leco Corp.** (Tem-Press Div. - HQ); St. Joseph; laboratory instruments — 700. **Rockwell International Corp.** (Universal Joint Plant); Allegan; motor vehicle parts — 700. **Sundstrand Heat Transfer Inc.;** Dowagiac; refrigeration equipment — 700.

Donnelly Mirrors Inc. (HQ); Holland; flat glass products — 650. **Cooper Industries Inc.** (Gardner-Denver Div.); Grand Haven; power driven hand tools — 635. **Canonie Construction Co.** (HQ); South Haven; heavy construction — 600. **Clark Equipment Co.** Buchanan; industrial trucks, machinery — 600. **Auto Specialties Mfg. Co. Inc.** (HQ); St. Joseph; malleable iron foundry, automobile parts — 550. **International Research & Development;** Mattawan; research — 515. **Bastian-Blessing Food Service Equipment Co.;** Grand Haven; air conditioning, heating equipment — 508. **The Marmon Group Inc.** (Midwest Foundry); Coldwater; grey iron foundry — 500. **Parker-Hannifin Corp.** (Brass Div.); Otsego; brass fittings — 500.

5th District

West Central — Grand Rapids

Gerald Ford probably would not have recognized his old district if the Legislature's initial plan to extend it to the Lake Michigan shore had stood. But the lines the federal court finally allowed left the 5th with about 90 percent of its population intact and its Republican-leaning political makeup virtually unchanged.

The district, which grew by 9 percent in the 1970s but still needed to expand slightly to reach its ideal size, picked up safely Republican territory in rural northern Barry County and politically marginal areas in northeast Allegan County. It also gained two small agricultural townships in Newaygo County. In exchange, it had to give up the northern half of Ionia County, including the manufacturing towns of Ionia and Belding and their blue-collar voters. It added scattered townships in Montcalm, Clinton and Eaton counties, all solidly GOP-oriented.

The 5th is centered on Grand Rapids and the towns immediately surrounding it, which together account for 60 percent of the district's population. Michigan's second-largest city, Grand Rapids attained an image during the Ford presidency of a clean-cut, all-American middle-class Republican community. The high-tech and service industries that have located there — aircraft instrumentation firms, a Keebler cookie distribution center and, a ten-minute drive to the east, the national headquarters of the Amway household products corporation — have brought in technicians, managers and professionals whose neat houses, manicured lawns and Republican votes reinforce that picture.

But Grand Rapids' heavy industry, including several auto parts factories, General Motors plants and firms making auditorium seats and metal office furniture, have given it an equally important working-class and union presence. Grand Rapids has the largest black population outside the auto corridor between Detroit and Bay City. The blue-collar workers clustered in the central and western parts of the city helped the 1982 Democratic House challenger take Grand Rapids with 56 percent of the vote. Blue-collar suburbs such as Wyoming and Walker reinforce the core city's Democratic strength, although in recent years younger union members have tended to split their tickets to a degree unheard of among their older colleagues.

The area's GOP is divided. The conservative community clustered around Calvin College and the small-business owners in southeast Grand Rapids are largely descendants of the Dutch craftsmen brought in by the city's once-famous furniture industry. This is the "Dutch Wing" that controls local affairs. The wealthier executives and younger professionals to the northeast and in East Grand Rapids and Kentwood make up the more cosmopolitan "Ford Wing."

Outside the Grand Rapids metropolitan area stretch miles of farm land peppered with developments that have sprung up in recent decades. The medium-sized family farms of the district's five counties produce fruit, feed grains and dairy products, and their owners, like small-scale farmers throughout the state, are suffering from the credit crunch that has gripped them for the past several years.

The rural towns are politically mixed. Townships along Route 131 north and south of Grand Rapids have attracted blue-collar Democrats who moved out from the west side of the city. Polish Catholics live in the eastern townships of Allegan County, while the small towns of northern Kent County have been settled by Irish Catholic workers in the plants of Grand Rapids, Belding and Greenville. By contrast, conservative Dutch influence is strong in the Allegan County towns near Holland, and white-collar subdivisions have sprung up along Barry County's Thornapple River and near its lakes.

Election Returns

5th District		Democrat		Republican	
1976	President	66,634	(31.7%)	140,552	(66.8%)
	Senate	78,766	(38.9%)	122,642	(60.6%)
	House	92,171	(45.4%)	110,130	(54.2%)
1978	Governor	71,181	(42.7%)	95,291	(57.2%)
	Senate	74,285	(44.8%)	91,426	(55.2%)
	House	79,555	(48.3%)	82,243	(49.9%)
1980	President	80,701	(34.7%)	128,842	(55.4%)
	House	98,196	(44.7%)	119,054	(54.2%)

5th District		Democrat		Republican	
1982	Governor	78,154	(41.9%)	103,220	(55.3%)
	Senate	89,675	(48.8%)	91,765	(50.0%)
	House	87,229	(46.9%)	98,650	(53.1%)

Demographics

Population: 514,560. **Percent Change from 1970:** 9.5%.

Land Area: 1,729 square miles. **Population per Square Mile:** 297.6.

Counties, 1980 Population: Allegan (Pt.) — 21,762; Barry (Pt.) — 26,808; Ionia (Pt.) — 21,953; Kent (Pt.) — 440,302; Newaygo (Pt.) — 3,735.

Cities, 1980 Population: East Grand Rapids — 10,914; Grand Rapids — 181,843; Grandville — 12,412; Kentwood — 30,438; Walker — 15,088; Wyoming — 59,616.

Race and Ancestry: White — 91.8%; Black — 6.2%; American Indian, Eskimo and Aleut — 0.5%; Asian and Pacific Islander — 0.6%. Spanish Origin — 1.9%. Dutch — 14.8%; English — 7.0%; French — 0.8%; German — 7.4%; Irish — 2.7%; Italian — 0.8%; Polish — 3.3%; Swedish — 0.7%.

Universities, Enrollment: Aquinas College, Grand Rapids — 2,529; Calvin College, Grand Rapids — 4,058; Calvin Theological Seminary, Grand Rapids — 190; Davenport College of Business, Grand Rapids — 3,047; Grace Bible College, Grand Rapids — 177; Grand Rapids Baptist College and Seminary, Grand Rapids — 1,216; Grand Rapids Junior College, Grand Rapids — 8,871; Kendall School of Design, Grand Rapids — 482; Reformed Bible College, Grand Rapids — 212; R.E.T.S. Electronic School, Wyoming — 256.

Newspapers, Circulation: *The Grand Rapids Press* (eS), Grand Rapids — 127,346; *Sentinel-Standard* (m), Ionia — 4,422.

Commercial Television Stations, Affiliation: WOTV, Grand Rapids (NBC); WWMA-TV, Grand Rapids (None); WZZM-TV, Grand Rapids (ABC). Entire district is located in Grand Rapids-Kalamazoo-Battle Creek ADI.

Industries:

Steelcase Inc. (HQ); Grand Rapids; office furniture — 6,000. **Amway Corp.** (HQ); Ada; cleaning products — 4,500. **General Motors Corp.** (Fisher Body Div.); Grand Rapids; automotive stampings — 3,050. **General Motors Corp.** (Rochester Products Div.); Grand Rapids; engine parts — 2,550. **Butterworth Hospital;** Grand Rapids; hospital — 2,250.

White Consolidated Industries (Kelvinator Compressor Co. Div.); Grand Rapids; household appliances — 2,200. **Lear Siegler Inc.** (Instrument Div.); Grand Rapids; electronic communications equipment — 2,052. **General Motors Corp.** (Fisher Body Div.); Grand Rapids; automotive stampings — 1,900. **Blodgett Memorial Medical Center;** Grand Rapids; hospital — 1,700. **Sisters of Mercy Health Corp.;** Grand Rapids; hospital — 1,600. **Chesapeake & Ohio Railway Co.;** Grand Rapids; railroad operations — 1,500. **Lear Siegler Inc.** (Rapistan Div.); Grand Rapids; conveyors — 1,340. **American Seating Co.** (HQ); Grand Rapids; institutional furniture — 1,250. **IMFS Inc.** (HQ); Grand Rapids; trucking — 1,170. **Westinghouse Electric Corp.** (Architectural Systems Div.); Grand Rapids; office furniture — 1,000. **Wolverine World Wide Inc.** (HQ); Rockford; leather footwear — 1,000. **Meijer Inc.** (HQ); Grand Rapids; grocery, department store chain — 900. **Spartan Stores Inc.** (HQ); Grand Rapids; groceries — 850. **Keebler Co.** (Grand Rapids Distribution Center); Grand Rapids; cookies — 800. **Keeler Corp.;** Grand Rapids; hardware, metal stampings — 800.

Hastings Mfg. Co. (HQ); Hastings; non-electrical machinery — 775. **Bradford-White Corp.;** Middleville; household appliances — 750. **Reynolds Metals Co.;** Grand Rapids; secondary aluminum smelting — 750. **Foremost Insurance Co.** (HQ); Grand Rapids; casualty, title, life insurance — 700. **Keeler Corp.** (Keeler Brass - HQ); Grand Rapids; automotive stampings — 700. **Pinkerton's Inc.;** Grand Rapids; electronic communications equipment — 659. **Goetze Corp. of America;** Sparta; gray iron foundry — 650. **Gulf & Western Industries Inc.;**

Hastings; machine tools — 650. **Jet Electronics & Technology;** Grand Rapids; scientific instruments — 625. **Pepsico Inc.** (Wilson Sporting Goods Co. Div.); Grand Rapids; sporting goods — 623. **World Book-Childcraft International;** Grand Rapids; marketing operations — 600. **Knape & Vogt Mfg. Co.** (HQ); Grand Rapids; hardware — 560. **Old Kent Financial Corp.** (HQ); Grand Rapids; banking — 548. **Airco Inc.** (Jackson Products/Aden Safety Div.); Belmont; ophthalmic goods — 500. **Amway Hotel Corp.;** Grand Rapids; hotel — 500.

6th District

Central — Part of Lansing, Pontiac

Altered substantially by the 1970 redistricting, the 6th changed significantly again under the new lines. Trying to recoup their loss of the district to a Republican in 1980 and to strengthen the Democratic incumbent in the 3rd at the same time, Democratic legislators walked through a delicate political balancing act. Their gamble paid off in 1982 when the Democrat who lost his seat in 1980 regained it, but he won just 51 percent of the vote.

In the 1970s the 6th had included all of Jackson and virtually all of Lansing, the state capital; these cities were the basis of the Democratic vote. The new map removed half of Lansing and all of Jackson, but also took out the Republicans of rural Jackson County and the 6th's portions of GOP-leaning western Washtenaw County. For the 1980s the district extends farther eastward than ever, through the Detroit exurbs of northwestern Oakland County to Pontiac, which has the fourth-largest concentration of black voters in the state.

What remains of Lansing in the 6th is politically marginal. The upper-level professionals and executives who live in the posh houses along Tecumseh River Drive in the northwest and in the Groesbeck section along Lansing's eastern edge turn in solid GOP votes, while state employees and younger professionals in some of the neighborhoods south of the Grand River are more independent. Democratic votes come from Eastern European and Hispanic blue-collar neighborhoods in the northeast and southeast sections of the city.

East Lansing, with a student population of more than 40,000 at Michigan State University, remains in the district and is an important source of Democratic votes. State government workers and university faculty in the suburban communities of Meridian Township and Okemos give those areas a Democratic tilt, although the business people and company managers who also live there exert a strong Republican influence. The rest of Ingham County, except blue-collar Delhi Township, is rural and strongly Republican.

The truck farms of eastern Ingham County also stretch into neighboring Livingston County, the state's second fastest-growing county during the 1970s. One of Michigan's most conservative areas, Livingston was settled by German Protestant farmers who made it a center of German-American Bund activism in the 1930s and a GOP stronghold; Democrats trying for local office still run as nominal Republicans. But eastern Livingston County has changed, its farm land eaten up by development spurred on by white flight from Lansing, Detroit, Flint and Pontiac. Townships like Hartland and Hamburg more than doubled in size in the late 1970s, and the newcomers have begun to leaven the conservative makeup of the county.

Democratic legislators hoped to balance the loss of western Lansing and Jackson by bringing in Pontiac. Made up of low-income blacks, Hispanics and socially conservative Southern whites — George C. Wallace got 51 percent of the vote there in the 1972 presidential primary — Pontiac has been devastated by the slump in the auto industry. Its unemployment reached 29.6 percent in April 1982, the highest in the country for any city with more than 50,000 residents.

But while the Pontiac electorate may be Democratic, it is also largely unmobilized and consistently turns out in low numbers. Pontiac is not an automatic windfall for a Democratic candidate unless he is willing to court it assiduously.

To extend the new 6th to Pontiac, map makers had to cut a path through the farms and suburbs of western Oakland County. The trailer parks and modern subdivisions of Waterford Township, built wherever farmers decided to sell off their land, are overwhelmingly white and middle-class. Pickup trucks with gun racks, owned by blue-collar families that moved out of Pontiac, are a common sight. These new suburbanites are the auto workers with Southern roots whose law-and-order outlook led them to vote for Wallace in 1972. Like Pontiac, Waterford Township may be troublesome in the coming years to Democratic candidates who take it for granted.

Election Returns

6th District		Democrat		Republican	
1976	President	80,770	(39.0%)	120,518	(58.2%)
	Senate	94,293	(47.3%)	102,497	(51.4%)
	House	90,309	(46.2%)	103,565	(52.9%)
1978	Governor	54,469	(31.8%)	116,416	(68.0%)
	Senate	79,536	(46.4%)	91,910	(53.6%)
	House	78,744	(48.2%)	84,602	(51.8%)
1980	President	85,927	(37.5%)	114,729	(50.1%)
	House	91,068	(42.3%)	123,140	(57.1%)
1982	Governor	80,188	(46.5%)	83,207	(48.3%)
	Senate	94,414	(55.6%)	72,138	(42.4%)
	House	84,778	(51.4%)	78,388	(47.5%)

Demographics

Population: 514,559. **Percent Change from 1970:** 19.0%.

Land Area: 1,517 square miles. **Population per Square Mile:** 339.2.

Counties, 1980 Population: Clinton (Pt.) — 5,746; Genesee (Pt.) — 3,459; Ingham (Pt.) — 195,543; Jackson (Pt.) — 10,047; Livingston (Pt.) — 73,997; Oakland (Pt.) — 215,136; Shiawassee (Pt.) — 10,631.

Cities, 1980 Population: East Lansing — 51,392; Lansing (Pt.) — 52,415; Pontiac — 76,715.

Race and Ancestry: White — 90.3%; Black — 7.2%; American Indian, Eskimo and Aleut — 0.4%; Asian and Pacific Islander — 0.8%. Spanish Origin — 2.4%. Dutch — 0.8%; English — 10.7%; French — 1.3%; German — 7.9%; Irish — 3.3%; Italian — 1.2%; Polish — 2.1%; Scottish — 0.7%; Swedish — 0.5%.

Universities; Enrollment: Michigan State University, East Lansing — 47,316; Pontiac Business Institute, Pontiac — 1,653.

Newspapers, Circulation: *The Oakland Press* (eS), Pontiac — 73,462. *Detroit Free Press,* *The Detroit News* and *Lansing State Journal* also circulate in the district.

Commercial Television Stations, Affiliation: WILX-TV, Onondaga (NBC); WJIM-TV, Lansing (CBS). District is divided between Detroit ADI and Lansing ADI. A small portion is in Flint-Saginaw-Bay City ADI.

Industries:

General Motors Corp. (Truck and Bus Mfg. Div.); Pontiac; motor vehicles — 12,039. General Motors Corp. (Pontiac Motor Div.); Pontiac; motor vehicles — 11,500. General Motors Corp. (Pontiac Motor Div.); Pontiac; motor vehicles — 2,460. Edward W. Sparrow Hospital; Lansing; hospital — 2,200. General Motors Corp. (Central Foundry Div.); Pontiac; gray iron foundry — 2,124.

Sisters of Mercy Health Corp.; Pontiac; hospital — 2,000. Ingham Medical Center; Lansing; hospital — 1,200. General Motors Corp. (Parts Div.); Pontiac; warehousing — 1,110. Pontiac Osteopathic Hospital (HQ); Pontiac; hospital — 1,000. Aeroquip Corp. (Industrial Div.); Leslie; screw machine products — 710. General Motors Corp. (Parts Div.); Drayton Plains; warehousing — 600.

7th District

East Central — Flint

The Flint-centered 7th grew by little more than 2 percent in the 1970s and had to expand into areas bound to dilute its Democratic character. For the 1980s the 7th looks much like the district in which Democratic Sen. Donald W. Riegle Jr. first launched his congressional career in 1966 — as a Republican.

Nearly all of Lapeer County, which was in the district during the 1960s but was removed for the 1970s, is back in now, adding 67,000 people. Much of the county is agricultural, with a variety of vegetables grown on its moderately fertile soil, including onions around Imlay City and mushrooms near Attica and Dryden. The farmers in the area used migrant labor until several years ago, and the county now has small enclaves of Indochinese and Hispanic residents.

Some of suburban Flint's development has spilled over into western Lapeer County, along Route 21. While the county went for Republican Robert P. Griffin in his unsuccessful 1978 Senate re-election bid, Elba and Oregon townships, with their new subdivisions housing young professionals and United Auto Workers union (UAW) members from the automobile plants in Flint, gave Griffin's Democratic challenger close to 54 percent of their votes. The GOP margin came from farther east and north, where rural Republican influence is strongest.

The major difference between the district that went Republican for Riegle in 1966 and the new one is a tier of four northern Oakland County townships that are in the 7th for the first time. Their 32,000 residents are a mix of small-business people, farmers and auto workers employed in the factories of Flint and Pontiac; the area leans Republican on the strength of the vote from the first two groups.

Even with the 7th's new additions, however, Republicans will have a hard time winning what probably remains the most Democratic district in the state outside the Detroit area. About 80 percent of the vote is cast in Flint and surrounding Genesee County, and, while the outer portions of Genesee County are politically mixed, Flint leaves no doubt about its partisan leanings. In 1980 it backed Jimmy Carter by more than 2-to-1.

Flint has always made its living from General Motors and its Chevrolet and Buick, AC Spark Plug and Fisher

Body plants. The UAW is the most potent political force in the city; if the union's endorsement no longer translates directly into rank-and-file votes, it does guarantee volunteers and financial support that boost a campaign immeasurably. Much of the white working class came to Flint from the South after World War II; George C. Wallace took 15 percent in Genesee County in 1968, his best performance in any of Michigan's urban areas.

Flint has been hurt by its overwhelming reliance on the auto industry. While the well-to-do professionals have stayed put, the empty houses and broken windows of Flint's north side reflect a gloomy statistic: the city lost almost 34,000 of its residents during the 1970s.

Much of the area encircling Flint consists of Democratic and racially mixed blue-collar communities, particularly in Mount Morris and Genesee townships. The GOP is strongest in the southeast corner of the county, around the white-collar suburbs of Atlas and Goodrich and in the wealthy developments of Grand Blanc Township.

Election Returns

7th District		Democrat		Republican	
1976	President	95,588	(50.3%)	91,817	(48.3%)
	Senate	111,040	(60.4%)	71,753	(39.0%)
	House	124,873	(67.3%)	57,667	(31.1%)
1978	Governor	70,975	(47.7%)	77,695	(52.3%)
	Senate	82,701	(55.6%)	66,028	(44.4%)
	House	106,298	(72.3%)	38,773	(26.4%)
1980	President	98,309	(46.7%)	94,845	(45.1%)
	House	147,590	(82.7%)	19,856	(11.1%)
1982	Governor	88,777	(57.7%)	62,630	(40.7%)
	Senate	105,425	(65.9%)	53,811	(33.7%)
	House	118,538	(75.4%)	36,303	(23.1%)

Demographics

Population: 514,560. **Percent Change from 1970:** 5.0%.

Land Area: 1,262 square miles. **Population per Square Mile:** 407.7.

Counties, 1980 Population: Genesee (Pt.) — 410,783; Lapeer (Pt.) — 67,227; Oakland (Pt.) — 32,695; Sanilac (Pt.) — 582; Shiawassee (Pt.) — 3,273.

Cities, 1980 Population: Burton — 29,976; Flint — 159,611.

Race and Ancestry: White — 82.8%; Black — 15.3%; American Indian, Eskimo and Aleut — 0.5%; Asian and Pacific Islander — 0.5%. Spanish Origin — 1.7%. Dutch — 0.5%; English — 9.6%; French — 1.6%; German — 6.8%; Hungarian — 0.7%; Irish — 3.0%; Italian — 0.8%; Polish — 1.8%; Scottish — 0.6%.

Universities, Enrollment: Baker Junior College of Business, Flint — 1,311; Charles Stewart Mott Community College, Flint — 9,751; General Motors Institute, Flint — 2,327; Ross Business Institute, Flint — 219; University of Michigan (Flint campus), Flint — 4,410.

Newspapers, Circulation: *The Flint Journal* (eS), Flint — 107,747. *Detroit Free Press*, *The Detroit News* and *The Oakland Press* also circulate in the district.

Commercial Television Stations, Affiliation: WJRT-TV, Flint (ABC). District is divided between Detroit ADI and Flint-Saginaw-Bay City ADI.

Industries:

General Motors Corp. (Buick Motor Div.); Flint; motor vehicle bodies — 18,000 General Motors Corp. (AC Spark Plug Div.); Flint; auto parts — 11,230. General Motors Corp. (Chevrolet Motor Div.);

Flint; automobiles — 6,280. **General Motors Corp.** (Truck &˙Bus Mfg. Div.); Flint; motor vehicles — 6,200. **General Motors Corp.** (Fisher Body Div.); Flint; motor vehicle bodies — 5,600.

General Motors Corp. (Chevrolet Motor Div.); Flint; motor vehicle bodies — 4,500. **General Motors Corp.** (Fisher Body Div.); Grand Blanc; motor vehicle parts — 3,340. **General Motors Corp.** (Fisher Body Div.); Flint; auto bodies, parts — 3,300. **General Motors Corp.** (Chevrolet-Flint Engine Plant); Flint; auto parts — 3,200. **General Motors Corp.** (Parts Div.); Grand Blanc; warehousing, storage — 3,200. **Hurley Medical Center;** Flint; hospital — 2,520. **St. Joseph Hospital Corp.;** Flint; hospital — 1,720.

McClaren General Hospital; Flint; hospital — 1,700. **Flint Osteopathic Hospital Inc.;** Flint; hospital — 1,460. **Citizens Commercial and Savings Bank** (HQ); Flint; banking — 625. **Complete Auto Transit Inc.;** Flint; trucking — 558. **Firestone Tire & Rubber Co.** (Hamill Div.); Imlay City; fabricated textile products — 500. **Genesee Merchants Bank & Trust Co.** (HQ); Flint; banking — 500. **United Michigan Corp.** (HQ); Flint; bank holding company — 500.

8th District

East — Bay City, Saginaw

When singer-songwriter Paul Simon took off to look for America in the late 1960s, he began in Saginaw, taking four days to hitchhike east. In more recent, less prosperous days, entire families have been leaving Saginaw, but they have headed south looking for work, not east looking for America.

What redistricting did to the 8th in the 1970s, putting Saginaw and Bay City together to make it possible for a Democrat to win there, time and a changing economy could undo by the end of the 1980s. The two cities, centers of Democratic strength in the 8th, lost 16 percent of their populations during the 1970s, while the Republican rural counties to the east were growing. The Bay City-Saginaw corridor now has fewer than one-third of the 8th's residents.

The 1982 redistricting helped the Democrats, but only slightly. The district lost most of rural Lapeer County, which votes Republican in most races. It picked up Arenac County in the north, a small, forested area whose proximity both to I-75 and Lake Huron has made it a popular vacation spot and home for retired auto workers. The UAW influence in Arenac County put it in the Democratic column in the 1978 contests for U.S. Senate and governor.

The 8th also lost some of the less crowded suburbs southwest of Saginaw, replacing them with a sliver of Midland, a tier of blue-collar townships north of Flint that had been going Republican, and conservative farm territory in St. Clair and Sanilac counties.

The gray industrial corridor of auto plants, chemical and cement factories, tool and die shops and port facilities lining the banks of the Saginaw River from Bay City to Saginaw is the district Democratic stronghold. White ethnics, blacks and Hispanics in Saginaw gave Jimmy Carter 58 percent of the vote in 1980 at the same time that Saginaw County as a whole went for Ronald Reagan. Bay City's politically active Polish working class joins with the steel and chemical workers between there and Midland to anchor Democratic strength in Bay County.

While northern Bay County's generally poor farm land gave rise to a Democratic-leaning impoverished rural sector, the rich soil of the Saginaw Valley south of Saginaw produced just the opposite: a well-off and conservative

agricultural community specializing in potatoes, dry beans and soft white winter wheat. German Lutheran influence is strong in the eastern part of the county, particularly around the well-kept town of Frankenmuth, whose prosperous burghers live in neat, brown-trimmed Bavarian-style houses adorned with flower boxes.

Once heavily forested, the vast flat reaches of Michigan's Thumb now bear sugar beets and dry beans, corn and wheat. The state's top two dairy counties are Sanilac and Huron; the latter has more than twice as many cows as it does people. The long Lake Huron coastline stretching around the Thumb is dotted with small fishing villages and lakeside resorts such as Caseville and Port Austin. The only heavy industry is in the western end of Huron County, where huge tool and die plants at Sebewaing and Elkton supply the factories across Saginaw Bay.

The Thumb is Republican territory. Sanilac County led the state in supporting Richard Nixon in 1972 and was second in its backing for Reagan in 1980, with the other counties not far behind.

Election Returns

8th District		Democrat		Republican	
1976	President	88,638	(44.6%)	107,682	(54.2%)
	Senate	97,239	(51.3%)	91,525	(48.3%)
	House	113,761	(59.1%)	77,547	(40.3%)
1978	Governor	75,717	(46.8%)	85,961	(53.2%)
	Senate	80,371	(50.1%)	80,101	(49.9%)
	House	106,736	(67.0%)	52,379	(32.9%)
1980	President	88,369	(40.5%)	113,128	(51.9%)
	House	128,941	(63.0%)	72,131	(35.2%)
1982	Governor	87,458	(50.7%)	77,907	(45.1%)
	Senate	100,408	(59.3%)	67,016	(39.6%)
	House	113,515	(91.0%)	—	

Demographics

Population: 514,560. **Percent Change from 1970:** 8.3%.

Land Area: 4,194 square miles. **Population per Square Mile:** 122.7.

Counties, 1980 Population: Arenac — 14,706; Bay — 119,881; Genesee (Pt.) — 36,207; Huron — 36,459; Lapeer (Pt.) — 2,811; Midland (Pt.) — 4,683; Saginaw (Pt.) — 194,274; Sanilac (Pt.) — 40,207; St. Clair (Pt.) — 8,371; Tuscola — 56,961.

Cities, 1980 Population: Bay City — 41,593; Midland (Pt.) — 1,906; Saginaw — 77,508.

Race and Ancestry: White — 90.0%; Black — 7.2%; American Indian, Eskimo and Aleut — 0.4%; Asian and Pacific Islander — 0.3%. Spanish Origin — 3.4%. Dutch — 0.5%; English — 7.2%; French — 2.6%; German — 14.3%; Hungarian — 0.5%; Irish — 2.3%; Italian — 0.6%; Polish — 5.5%; Scottish — 0.6%.

Universities, Enrollment: Delta College, University Center — 9,865; Saginaw Valley State College, University Center — 4,331.

Newspapers, Circulation: *The Bay City Times* (eS), Bay City — 40,127; *The Huron Daily Tribune* (e), Bad Axe — 9,291; *The Saginaw News* (eS), Saginaw — 54,256. *The Flint Journal* and Port Huron *Times Herald* also circulate in the district.

Commercial Television Stations, Affiliation: WEYI-TV, Saginaw (CBS); WNEM-TV, Bay City (NBC). Most of district is located in Flint-Saginaw-Bay City ADI. Portion is in Detroit ADI.

Military Installations: Port Austin Air Force Station, Port Austin — 117.

Industries:

General Motors Corp. (Steering Gear Div.); Saginaw; motor vehicle parts — 8,820. **General Motors Corp.** (Chevrolet Motor Div.); Saginaw; motor vehicles — 4,500. **General Motors Corp.** (Central Foundry Div.); Saginaw; malleable iron foundries — 2,606. **General Motors Corp.** (Chevrolet Motor Div.); Bay City; motor vehicles — 2,580. **General Motors Corp.** (Chevrolet Div.); Saginaw; motor vehicle parts — 1,800.

Saginaw General Hospital; Saginaw; hospital — 1,150. **General Motors Corp.** (Chevrolet Motor Div.); Saginaw; motor vehicles — 1,070. **Eaton Corp.** (Engine Components Div.); Saginaw; motor vehicle parts — 787. **Eltra Corp.** (Prestolite Motor Div.); Bay City; electrical engine equipment — 680. **Chesapeake & Ohio Railway Co.;** Saginaw; railroad operations — 600. **General Motors Corp.** (Chevrolet Motor Div.); Saginaw; motor vehicle parts — 600. **Second National Corp.;** Saginaw; bank holding company — 500.

9th District

West — Muskegon, Traverse City

The 9th has grown longer and narrower over the years, expanding up and down the Lake Michigan coast, but the 1982 redistricting drew it in a little to trim some excess population. The third fastest-growing district in Michigan during the 1970s, it had to lose 23,000 people to come down to ideal size. The Legislature removed two of the areas of greatest increase, safely Republican Allegan County and the southwestern third of equally Republican Ottawa County, and added 77,000 people from rural Montcalm and Ionia counties. It also tacked on Traverse City and three surrounding townships in Grand Traverse County. The traditional GOP majority remains intact.

The district's political poles are set in its two southernmost lake shore counties, Muskegon and Ottawa, which together hold more than half its residents. Ottawa County remains the Republican anchor, even with part of it transferred to the 4th. Ottawa gave Ronald Reagan and Gerald R. Ford their highest percentages in the state in 1980 and 1976, and in 1964 was one of three counties in Michigan to back Barry Goldwater. Redistricting removed most of Holland, the county's largest city, but kept conservative Dutch towns such as white-collar Zeeland and Vriesland. Fruit and grain farmers north of Holland turn in reliably Republican percentages, as do the middle-class suburbanites in the fast-growing towns west of the border with Grand Rapids.

The Democratic Party's strongest constituency is in and around the city of Muskegon, a community of 40,000 that first rose out of the sawdust of Michigan's lumbering era. More recently, Muskegon has built up one of western Michigan's heaviest manufacturing bases, turning out auto parts, tank engines, cranes and hoists, paper, bowling equipment and office furniture. Consequently the city was badly hit by the depression of the early 1980s.

Democratic strength is highest in the city's ethnic blue-collar neighborhoods, in the black precincts and in black-majority Muskegon Heights, which gave Jimmy Carter 75 percent of its vote in 1980. But the party's vote in the city is generally offset by GOP margins from the large old houses of North Muskegon, upper-middle class suburbs like Norton Shores and Roosevelt Park and farm areas to the north of Muskegon.

The rest of the 9th District consists of sparsely populated counties whose chief industries are farming, tourism and food processing. Fremont, in Newaygo County, is international headquarters for Gerber baby foods, while Oceana County's fruits and asparagus are processed in towns such as Pentwater and Shelby. The orchards in Leelanau and Benzie counties produce 40 percent of the country's tart cherries and a quarter of its sweet cherries. Towns all along the shore draw retirees and summertime residents from downstate Michigan, and from Wisconsin, Illinois and Indiana as well. The lakes and forests inland pull in hikers and hunters year-round.

Most of the rural counties are solidly Republican, although there are Democratic pockets. Traverse City has drawn unionized state employees and immigrants from downstate; both groups provide generally liberal votes. Greenville, Belding and Manistee are blue-collar communities with a bread-and-butter Democratic vote. Blacks who settled around the 1930s black resort town of Idlewild form depressed Lake County's Democratic base.

Election Returns

9th District		Democrat		Republican	
1976	President	78,806	(37.0%)	131,374	(61.7%)
	Senate	83,281	(40.8%)	120,090	(58.8%)
	House	65,870	(32.5%)	135,326	(66.8%)
1978	Governor	76,567	(43.8%)	98,041	(56.1%)
	Senate	75,525	(43.4%)	98,323	(56.6%)
	House	58,983	(34.5%)	111,657	(65.4%)
1980	President	77,925	(33.4%)	136,272	(58.5%)
	House	21,693	(12.2%)	150,890	(84.6%)
1982	Governor	73,106	(41.0%)	99,444	(55.8%)
	Senate	81,745	(46.4%)	92,313	(52.4%)
	House	60,932	(35.1%)	112,504	(64.9%)

Demographics

Population: 514,560. **Percent Change from 1970:** 13.9%.

Land Area: 5,672 square miles. **Population per Square Mile:** 90.7.

Counties, 1980 Population: Benzie — 11,205; Grand Traverse (Pt.) — 31,919; Ionia (Pt.) — 29,862; Kent (Pt.) — 4,204; Lake — 7,711; Leelanau — 14,007; Manistee — 23,019; Mason — 26,365; Montcalm — 47,555; Muskegon — 157,589; Newaygo (Pt.) — 31,182; Oceana — 22,002; Ottawa (Pt.) — 107,940.

Cities, 1980 Population: Holland (Pt.) — 9,561; Muskegon — 40,823; Muskegon Heights — 14,611; Norton Shores — 22,025; Traverse City — 15,516.

Race and Ancestry: White — 93.6%; Black — 4.5%; American Indian, Eskimo and Aleut — 0.6%; Asian and Pacific Islander — 0.3%. Spanish Origin — 1.9%. Dutch — 10.5%; English — 7.6%; French — 1.4%; German — 8.5%; Irish — 2.5%; Italian — 0.5%; Norwegian — 0.5%; Polish — 2.6%; Swedish — 1.3%.

Universities, Enrollment: Grand Valley State Colleges, Allendale — 7,142; Hope College, Holland — 2,464; Montcalm Community College, Sidney — 1,559; Muskegon Business College, Muskegon — 1,125; Muskegon Community College, Muskegon — 5,173; Northwestern Michigan College, Traverse City — 3,389; Western Theological Seminary, Holland — 117; West Shore Community College, Scottville — 1,011.

Newspapers, Circulation: *The Daily News* (e), Greenville — 7,692; *The Holland Sentinel* (e), Holland — 17,371; *The Muskegon Chronicle* (eS), Muskegon — 44,496; *News* (e), Ludington — 8,596; *News-Advocate* (e), Manistee — 5,640; *Traverse City Record-Eagle* (e), Traverse City — 23,758. *The Grand Rapids Press* also circulates in the district.

Commercial Television Stations, Affiliation: WGTU, Traverse City (ABC); WPBN-TV, Traverse City (NBC). District is divided between Grand Rapids-Kalamazoo-Battle Creek ADI and Traverse City-Cadillac ADI.

Industries:

Herman Miller Inc. (HQ); Zeeland; office furniture — 2,400. **White Consolidated Industries** (Greenville Products Co. Div.); Greenville; household refrigerators, freezers — 2,000. **White Consolidated Industries** (Gibson Appliance Div.); Greenville; household refrigerators, freezers, washing machines — 1,500. **Chef Pierre Inc.**; Traverse City; frozen pies — 1,200. **Gerber Products Co.** (HQ); Fremont; baby food, infant clothing — 1,200. **Hackley Hospital Inc.**; Muskegon; hospital — 1,200.

Munson Medical Center; Traverse City; hospital — 1,150. **Teledyne Industries Inc.** (Continental Motors Div.); Muskegon; internal combustion engines — 1,110. **Goetze Corp. of America** (HQ); Muskegon; piston rings — 1,000. **Scott Paper Co.** (S. D. Warren Div.); Muskegon; paper mills — 1,000. **The Shaw-Walker Co.** (HQ); Muskegon; metal office furniture, machinery — 1,000. **White Consolidated Industries** (Belding Products Div.); Belding; air conditioning equipment — 1,000. **General Tire & Rubber Co. Inc.** (Chemical Plastic Div.); Ionia; automobile parts — 950. **Textron Inc.** (CWC Castings Div.); Muskegon; gray iron foundry — 944. **Bil Mar Foods Inc.** (HQ); Zeeland; poultry processing — 800. **Howmet Turbine Components Corp.;** Whitehall; steel investment foundries — 800.

General Electric Co. Holland; hermetic motors — 750. **McGraw-Edison Co.** (Clarke Div.); Muskegon; service industry machinery — 729. **Brunswick Corp.;** Muskegon; sporting goods — 700. **Dresser Industries Inc.;** Muskegon; cranes, hoists — 700. **Interspace Corp.** (Hart & Cooley Div.); Holland; ornamental metal work — 675. **Federal-Mogul Corp.;** Greenville; motor vehicle parts — 580. **Kysor Industrial Corp.;** Rothbury; motor vehicle parts — 580. **Hitachi Magnetics Corp.** (HQ); Edmore; fabricated metal products — 575. **United Technologies Corp.** (Essex Wire Co.); Traverse City; electrical engine equipment — 550. **Ex-Cell-O Corp.** (Cone Drive Operations); Traverse City; speed changers — 500. **Keene Corp.** (Kaydon Bearing Div.); Muskegon; ball, roller bearings — 500. **Teledyne Industries Inc.** (Continental Motors); Muskegon; internal combustion engines — 500. **Westran Corp.** (HQ); Muskegon; steel castings — 500.

10th District

North Central — Midland

Sprawling through 23 counties in the heart of the Lower Peninsula, the old 10th was the state's fastest-growing district during the 1970s, as urban refugees built year-round homes on land that once was empty most of the time.

Because of the population growth, 113,000 people had to be moved out of the 10th to bring it down to ideal size. But the redrawn district still comprises 20 counties, carving out a chunk of Michigan woods and farm land so big that it presents political candidates with enormous campaign problems. To reach most of the voters in the 10th, a candidate has to advertise in four cities outside its borders — Lansing, Flint, Saginaw and Bay City. The northern counties, where most of the district's growth occurred, are the least accessible of all.

Dropped from the district of the 1970s were part of the city of Midland, plus Montcalm and Arenac counties, the northern townships of Grand Traverse County and an area east of Lansing. Newly added were some northern Lansing suburbs in Clinton County, farm land in Shiawassee and Saginaw counties and five small townships in the forests of Crawford and Oscoda counties.

Outdoor enthusiasts are an important source of income

for the hilly counties in the northern part of the district. Where towering, silent stands of white pines once stood, offering their lumber to home builders all over the Midwest, second-growth forests now draw hikers, skiers and snowmobilers. The hotels and motels that fill the towns of Grayling and Roscommon are booked year-round.

Much of the 10th District's growth and most of its political change has come along the corridor of I-75, the highway that runs north from Detroit all the way to the Mackinac Straits. Retirees have followed I-75 out of the grime of Michigan's industrial southeast. Many of them are UAW members who once spent their vacations by the lakes or in the woods of the district's northeastern counties. Their new year-round homes are on Houghton and Higgins lakes and in towns such as Harrison and West Branch.

These people have brought with them the political and social concerns they developed as urban dwellers, forcing a gradual shift in the political direction of the area. Counties such as Clare, Gladwin and Roscommon voted solidly Republican in 1970; by 1978 they were voting for Democrats.

Kalkaska County, farther west, was the fastest-growing county in the state in the 1970s, more than doubling in size with the expansion of its independent oil industry. Missaukee County, just below it, has had some spillover development in the area near Houghton Lake, but farther west its hilly terrain is still given over to dairy cattle and a bedrock conservative population that in 1964 gave Barry Goldwater his highest percentage in the state. The depressed industrial city of Cadillac, in Wexford County, is the area's largest population center and its only traditional source of Democratic voters.

The 10th's southern half, where some 70 percent of its residents live, is a jumble of small cities surrounded by farm land. Midland, with 37,000 residents, is the largest city in the district. The Dow Chemical Company's international headquarters and Dow Corning headquarters face each other across Midland Road, dominating the city's economy and setting the tone for its Republican politics.

Owosso and Alma are more traditional manufacturing cities, reliant on the auto industry and hospitable ground for Democrats. Some of the blue-collar workers here and in Saginaw and Flint also work small farms in Shiawassee, Saginaw and Gratiot counties, giving the countryside a more Democratic flavor than is found elsewhere in Michigan. A similar tendency marks the blue-collar suburbs of Clinton County, just north of Lansing, and Isabella County's seat of Mount Pleasant, where the faculty of Central Michigan State University plays a major role in the local Democratic Party.

But most of the area's land is agricultural. Sugar beets are grown in Gratiot County, and the flatter terrain of Isabella County is used for corn and soybeans. Dairying is an important source of income in the west central counties; Reed City in Osceola County has both dairy processing plants and a Yoplait yogurt plant.

It was in Gratiot County that the flame-retardant chemical PBB was manufactured. In 1973 PBB was mixed by mistake into farm livestock feed, and the cows of the surrounding counties and as far north as Missaukee County were contaminated, many of them giving birth to stillborn calves and dying in the process. The experience proved a nightmare for the area's farmers; chemical contaminants became a raging political issue, recently rekindled when it was discovered that the chemical has been seeping into the area's water table from the landfills in which thousands of dead cows were buried.

Election Returns

10th District		Democrat		Republican	
1976	President	81,184	(40.8%)	114,855	(57.7%)
	Senate	86,038	(45.2%)	103,111	(54.2%)
	House	81,753	(43.5%)	104,676	(55.7%)
1978	Governor	74,425	(44.6%)	92,256	(55.3%)
	Senate	77,717	(47.1%)	87,317	(52.9%)
	House	84,715	(51.8%)	78,618	(48.1%)
1980	President	81,232	(36.1%)	122,741	(54.5%)
	House	111,887	(52.6%)	97,604	(45.9%)
1982	Governor	76,888	(44.6%)	87,968	(51.0%)
	Senate	89,171	(52.4%)	78,854	(46.3%)
	House	102,048	(60.1%)	66,080	(39.0%)

Demographics

Population: 514,560. **Percent Change from 1970:** 23.5%.

Land Area: 8,991 square miles. **Population per Square Mile:** 57.2.

Counties, 1980 Population: Antrim (Pt.) — 490; Clare — 23,822; Clinton (Pt.) — 50,147; Crawford (Pt.) — 7,652; Gladwin — 19,957; Grand Traverse (Pt.) — 18,662; Gratiot — 40,448; Iosco (Pt.) — 1,199; Isabella — 54,110; Kalkaska — 10,952; Mecosta — 36,961; Midland (Pt.) — 68,895; Missaukee — 10,009; Ogemaw — 16,436; Osceola — 18,928; Oscoda (Pt.) — 3,395; Roscommon — 16,374; Saginaw (Pt.) — 33,785; Shiawassee (Pt.) — 57,236; Wexford — 25,102.

Cities, 1980 Population: Big Rapids — 14,361; Cadillac — 10,199; Lansing (Pt.) — 0; Midland (Pt.) — 35,344; Mount Pleasant — 23,746; Owosso — 16,455.

Race and Ancestry: White — 98.1%; Black — 0.5%; American Indian, Eskimo and Aleut — 0.5%; Asian and Pacific Islander — 0.3%. Spanish Origin — 1.2%. Dutch — 1.7%; English — 11.0%; French — 1.7%; German — 13.1%; Irish — 3.2%; Italian — 0.6%; Polish — 1.9%; Scottish — 0.6%; Swedish — 0.7%.

Universities, Enrollment: Alma College, Alma — 1,201; Central Michigan University, Mount Pleasant — 18,269; Ferris State College, Big Rapids — 11,112; Kirtland Community College, Roscommon — 1,395; Mid-Michigan Community College, Harrison — 2,161; Northwood Institute (Midland campus), Midland — 1,945.

Newspapers, Circulation: *The Argus-Press* (e), Owosso — 14,615; *Cadillac News* (e), Cadillac — 8,433; *Midland Daily News* (e), Midland — 17,534; *Morning Sun* (m), Mount Pleasant — 7,826; *The Pioneer* (m), Big Rapids — 5,028. *The Saginaw News* and *Traverse City Record-Eagle* also circulate in the district.

Commercial Television Stations, Affiliation: WWTV, Cadillac (CBS). District is divided between Flint-Saginaw-Bay City ADI and Traverse City-Cadillac ADI. Portions are in Grand Rapids-Kalamazoo-Battle Creek ADI and Lansing ADI.

Nuclear Power Plants: Midland 1 and 2, Midland (Babcock & Wilcox, Bechtel).

Industries:

The **Dow Chemical Co.** (HQ); Midland; chemicals, plastics — 8,100. **Midland Hospital Assn.;** Midland; hospital — 1,400. **Universal Electric Co.** (HQ); Owosso; electric motors, generators — 900. **Evart Products Co.;** Evart; plastic products — 754. **Cadillac Rubber & Plastics Inc.** (HQ); Cadillac; fabricated rubber products — 600.

Midland-Ross Corp. (Power Controls Div.); Owosso; motor vehicle parts — 600. **Federal-Mogul Corp.;** St. Johns; ball bearings — 540. **Bechtel Power Corp.;** Midland; heavy construction — 509. **Dow Corning Corp.** (HQ); Midland; plastics materials — 500. **Lobdell-Emery Mfg. Co.** (Greencastle Mfg. Co. Div. - HQ); Alma; auto parts, stampings — 500. **Total Petroleum Inc.** (Vickers Petroleum Div. - HQ); Alma; petroleum refining — 500.

11th District

Upper Peninsula; Northern Lower Peninsula

The vast, empty forests that cover the 470 miles from Ironwood on the Wisconsin border to Tawas City on Lake Huron loom over a district rich in natural resources, sparse in settlement and low in its standard of living. The 11th has only one city of over 15,000; of the eight counties in Michigan that lost population during the 1970s, six are in the district.

The 11th is contiguous with the rest of the state only because of the Mackinac Bridge. The third-longest suspension bridge on the continent, it crosses the point where Lake Michigan and Lake Huron meet, joining Michigan's Upper and Lower peninsulas. The Upper Peninsula (UP), attached by land to Wisconsin, has 62 percent of the district's residents, the bulk of its Democrats and a rough-hewn pride of place that induces occasional secessionist grumblings among its partisans. People in the western UP root for the Green Bay Packers, not the Detroit Lions.

The lakes and rivers, pine and hardwood forests and trackless miles of coastline on three Great Lakes have inspired a quiet passion among people who know the UP. It was to the seclusion of a river in Schoolcraft County that Ernest Hemingway came to mend the spirit and body tattered by his experiences in Italy during World War I. The UP's brilliantly colored autumn forests, its fish and game, ski slopes and campgrounds are some of the Midwest's most powerful vacation magnets.

The UP's once busy mining industry is in a slump. The only industries still prospering are part of the new high technology enclave around Michigan Technological University in Houghton, and those dealing with lumber and wood products, which feed mills in Escanaba and Manistique.

The western UP has generally been the Democratic stronghold of Michigan north of Saginaw. Eastern European and Scandinavian immigrants brought in to mine copper gave it a liberal, union-oriented tradition; their descendants and other miners, millworkers, loggers and longshoremen still dominate the politics of the UP's western counties. Five of the nine counties in the state won by Jimmy Carter in 1980 are here.

The eastern UP is far more Republican and representative of the part of the district "below the bridge." Mackinac Island, a tourist retreat preserved much as it was at the turn of the century, plays host every two years to the state GOP's Mackinac Leadership Conference. The only major city in the eastern part of the UP is Sault Ste. Marie, whose Soo Locks send grain, ores and pulpwood eastward from the port cities of Lake Superior. But much of the city's labor force is on the federal payroll, working for the Corps of Engineers or the Coast Guard. Most of Chippewa and Mackinac counties are heavily dependent on tourism and farming, with little of the industrial presence that creates Democratic sympathies farther west.

The migration of former city-dwellers that has begun to transform the 10th District is also evident in the 11th below the Mackinac Bridge. Retired auto workers have settled in Emmet, Presque Isle and Cheboygan counties, and Democrats have begun to make inroads in local elections.

But this area remains mostly as it has been, its communities conservative and spread far apart. Most of the development in the far north of the Lower Peninsula has been along its edges, where the lakes have allowed factories to ship their products out. The immense limestone quarry of Rogers City and cement and paper plants of Alpena give those Lake Huron cities the most solidly blue-collar population in the southern 11th. But elsewhere the emphasis is on farming and tourism, with only small industries in such Lake Michigan tourist cities as Charlevoix and Petoskey.

Election Returns

11th District		Democrat		Republican	
1976	President	108,130	(48.4%)	112,569	(50.3%)
	Senate	110,758	(53.8%)	94,256	(45.8%)
	House	96,571	(44.9%)	117,669	(54.7%)
1978	Governor	90,986	(50.5%)	89,142	(49.5%)
	Senate	96,959	(55.1%)	78,923	(44.9%)
	House	78,736	(45.3%)	94,991	(54.7%)
1980	President	99,755	(41.9%)	119,100	(50.0%)
	House	75,941	(34.4%)	143,392	(65.0%)
1982	Governor	95,846	(51.8%)	84,441	(45.6%)
	Senate	91,796	(49.7%)	90,582	(49.1%)
	House	69,181	(39.5%)	106,039	(60.5%)

Demographics

Population: 514,560. **Percent Change from 1970:** 10.9%.

Land Area: 22,561 square miles. **Population per Square Mile:** 22.8.

Counties, 1980 Population: Alcona — 9,740; Alger — 9,225; Alpena — 32,315; Antrim (Pt.) — 15,704; Baraga — 8,484; Charlevoix — 19,907; Cheboygan — 20,649; Chippewa — 29,029; Crawford (Pt.) — 1,813; Delta — 38,947; Dickinson — 25,341; Emmet — 22,992; Gogebic — 19,686; Grand Traverse (Pt.) — 4,318; Houghton — 37,872; Iosco (Pt.) — 27,150; Iron — 13,635; Keweenaw — 1,963; Luce — 6,659; Mackinac — 10,178; Marquette — 74,101; Menominee — 26,201; Montmorency — 7,492; Ontonagon — 9,861; Oscoda (Pt.) — 3,463; Otsego — 14,993; Presque Isle — 14,267; Schoolcraft — 8,575.

Cities, 1980 Population: Alpena — 12,214; Escanaba — 14,355; Marquette — 23,288; Menominee — 10,099; Sault Ste. Marie — 14,448.

Race and Ancestry: White — 97.3%; Black — 0.6%; American Indian, Eskimo and Aleut — 1.6%; Asian and Pacific Islander — 0.3%. Spanish Origin — 0.4%. Dutch — 1.0%; English — 7.1%; French — 6.4%; German — 10.5%; Irish — 3.3%; Italian — 2.2%; Norwegian — 0.8%; Polish — 4.1%; Scottish — 0.9%; Swedish — 3.1%.

Universities, Enrollment: Alpena Community College, Alpena — 2,082; Bay de Noc Community College, Escanaba — 1,480; Gogebic Community College, Ironwood — 1,130; Lake Superior State College, Sault Ste. Marie — 2,501; Michigan Technological University, Houghton — 7,865; North Central Michigan College, Petoskey — 1,881; Northern Michigan University, Marquette — 9,361; Suomi College, Hancock — 578.

Newspapers, Circulation: *The Alpena News* (e), Alpena — 12,971; *Cheboygan Daily Tribune* (e), Cheboygan — 4,340; *The Daily Mining Gazette* (e), Houghton — 11,928; *The Daily News* (e), Iron Mountain — 9,747; *The Daily Press* (e), Escanaba — 9,648; *The Evening News* (e), Sault Ste. Marie — 8,749; *The Herald Leader* (e), Menominee — 4,874; *The Ironwood Daily Globe* (e), Ironwood — 9,988; *The Mining Journal* (e), Marquette — 17,681; *Petoskey News-Review* (e), Petoskey — 10,607.

Commercial Television Stations, Affiliation: WBKB, Alpena (CBS); WGTQ, Sault Ste. Marie (None); WJMN-TV, Escanaba (NBC); WLUC-TV, Marquette (CBS, ABC); WTOM-TV, Cheboygan (NBC);

WWUP, Sault Ste. Marie (CBS). District is divided among Marquette ADI, Traverse City-Cadillac ADI, and Green Bay (Wis.) ADI. Portions are in Alpena ADI, Flint-Saginaw-Bay City ADI and Duluth (Minn.)-Superior (Wis.) ADI.

Military Installations: Bayshore Bomb Scoring Site (Air Force), Bayshore — 51; Calumet Air Force Station, Calumet City — 90; Phelps Collins Airport (Air Force), Alpena — 85; K. I. Sawyer Air Force Base, Gwinn — 4,277; Wurtsmith Air Force Base, Oscoda — 3,200.

Nuclear Power Plants: Big Rock Point 1, Charlevoix (General Electric, Bechtel), March 1963.

Industries:

Cleveland Cliffs Iron Co. (Empire & Tilden Iron Mines); Ishpeming; iron ore mining — 2,300. **The Mead Corp.** (Publishing Paper Div.); Escanaba; paper mill — 1,450. **Besser Co.** (HQ); Alpena; special industrial machinery — 625. **Procter & Gamble Paper Products Co.** (Charmin Paper Products Div.); Cheboygan; paper mills — 550. **American Motors Corp.** (Coleman Products Co.); Iron River; wiring harnesses — 537. **Grede Foundries Inc.;** Iron Mountain; grey iron foundry — 520. **Abitibi Corp.;** Alpena; wood products — 500. **Kimberly-Clark Corp.;** Munising; paper mill — 500.

12th District

Southeast — Macomb County, Port Huron

The 12th is one of the few districts in the Detroit area that occupies less territory after redistricting than it did before. Its population in 1980 was 30,000 over the ideal, in large part because of the tremendous growth of a second ring of suburbs that sprung up in outer Macomb County.

As a result of the district's growth, legislators pulled it back out of Oakland and Sanilac counties, into which it had been moved a decade earlier. They also trimmed off the top of St. Clair County, and took out three mixed rural and working-class suburban townships in northeastern Macomb County. The only new ground gained by the 12th was in the northeast corner of the city of Warren, where 67,000 residents were added. Politically the district remains the same — a minority of farmers and small-town dwellers, usually Republican, dominated by a Democratic bastion of blue-collar ethnicity in southeastern Macomb County.

The heart of the 12th is in the six-mile stretch from Detroit north to Fraser. More than 40 percent of the vote is cast there, virtually all by blue-collar ethnics.

The suburbs of southern Macomb County were built on the rising incomes of the Poles and Italians, Belgians, Germans and Slovenes who first settled on the east side of Detroit in the early decades of the century. The neighborhoods in the first miles out from the city retain their lower-middle class character, but farther out, in Fraser and the northern parts of Roseville, Warren and St. Clair Shores, the lawns are a bit larger and the houses more expensive.

The inner suburbs all lost population during the 1970s as the migration outward gathered steam. The townships north of Fraser — Clinton, Harrison and Macomb — exploded with new subdivisions. The population there remains mostly blue-collar, but middle-level managers have moved into the classier developments.

Especially in the older neighborhoods close to Detroit, most of the wage-earners are auto workers and UAW members. Roots are still important, and Polish and Italian clubs thrive. But the old social welfare values that made the

Democratic Party home for the first generation are not so strong in the second. While respect for the union and the party continues, blind allegiance does not, especially on issues such as busing. Southern Macomb County is moving toward the Republican Party in statewide and national elections.

St. Clair Shores is the wealthiest of the Macomb County towns; its streets near Lake St. Clair are lined with large houses. The shore front is packed with marinas, and looks out on what is said to be the busiest waterway for weekend pleasure boats in the world. Voters in St. Clair Shores are the most Republican bloc in the district.

The only sizable city in Macomb outside the immediate Detroit area is Mount Clemens, whose 19,000 residents are a curious jumble of rich and poor, black and white. Fifty years ago Mount Clemens was a resort town renowned for its mineral baths and racy entertainment. Babe Ruth made it a point to visit when the Yankees were in Detroit. Today it has a small manufacturing base and is the commercial center for the suburban developments that surround it. It is also safely Democratic territory.

The land stretching from Mount Clemens up to Port Huron, at the northern end of St. Clair County, is rural. Small truck farms in the south give way to fields of sugar beets and soybeans farther north and to a dairy industry.

St. Clair County, at the base of Michigan's Thumb, is as Republican as the rest of the Thumb area. Only in Port Huron, its county seat, do concentrations of blue-collar workers live. Port Huron votes Democratic, although its politics are far to the right of the famous "Port Huron Statement" issued there by the Students for a Democratic Society in the early 1960s.

Election Returns

12th District		Democrat		Republican	
1976	President	93,854	(45.3%)	109,186	(52.8%)
	Senate	105,949	(53.4%)	91,053	(45.9%)
	House	108,107	(56.5%)	82,059	(42.9%)
1978	Governor	71,931	(42.5%)	97,458	(57.5%)
	Senate	87,154	(51.9%)	80,799	(48.1%)
	House	95,414	(59.8%)	63,684	(39.9%)
1980	President	89,069	(38.5%)	124,419	(53.7%)
	House	124,866	(57.5%)	91,350	(42.1%)
1982	Governor	91,629	(49.7%)	85,384	(46.3%)
	Senate	107,533	(60.0%)	69,043	(38.5%)
	House	103,851	(65.9%)	52,312	(33.2%)

Demographics

Population: 514,560. **Percent Change from 1970:** 9.4%.

Land Area: 905 square miles. **Population per Square Mile:** 568.6.

Counties, 1980 Population: Macomb (Pt.) — 384,129; St. Clair (Pt.) — 130,431.

Cities, 1980 Population: Fraser — 14,560; Mount Clemens — 18,806; Port Huron — 33,981; Roseville — 54,311; St. Clair Shores — 76,210; Warren (Pt.) — 67,425.

Race and Ancestry: White — 96.6%; Black — 2.1%; American Indian, Eskimo and Aleut — 0.3%; Asian and Pacific Islander — 0.5%. Spanish Origin — 1.1%. English — 6.0%; French — 1.9%; German — 10.4%; Greek — 0.5%; Irish — 2.9%; Italian — 6.0%; Polish — 7.0%; Scottish — 0.8%.

Universities, Enrollment: Macomb County Community College, Warren — 25,619; St. Clair County Community College, Port Huron — 3,634.

Newspapers, Circulation: *The Macomb Daily* (e), Mount Clemens — 55,687; *The Times Herald* (eS), Port Huron — 31,050. *Detroit Free Press* and *The Detroit News* also circulate in the district.

Commercial Television Stations, Affiliation: Most of district is located in Detroit ADI. Portion is in the Flint-Saginaw-Bay City ADI.

Military Installations: Selfridge Air National Guard Base, Mount Clemens — 3,933.

Industries:

Ford Motor Co. (Chesterfield Trim Plant); Mount Clemens; motor vehicle parts — 1,570. **Detroit Macomb Hospital Assn.;** Warren; hospital — 1,500. **Mueller Brass Co.** (HQ); Port Huron; copper rolling, drawing — 1,200. **Diamond Crystal Salt Co.;** St. Clair; salt producing — 1,100. **Mount Clemens General Hospital;** Mount Clemens; hospital — 1,100. **Campbell-Ewald Co.** (HQ); Warren; advertising — 500. **Ford Motor Co.** (Plastics, Paint & Vinyl Div.); Mount Clemens; paints, varnishes — 500.

13th District

Downtown Detroit

After their first settlement burned to the ground in 1805, Detroiters coined the motto, "It shall rise again from the ashes." That is what the city has been trying to do since the 1967 riots desolated Detroit's inner core, leaving physical and emotional scars that have proved resistant to quick cure. One need only wander through the 13th District, where blocks of burned out buildings stand close to the glittering symbols of Detroit's hoped-for renaissance, to see the rising and the ashes all at once.

The 13th lost 174,000 residents between 1970 and 1980, a record beaten only by the old New York 21st. To keep the 13th in existence for the 1980s, map makers extended its border in every direction but south, where the Detroit River flows.

The changes did not affect the black representation the district has had since 1954. Although the new lines reduce the overwhelming majority blacks have held in the 13th since massive white flight took place in the 1960s and 1970s, blacks remain the clearly dominant political force.

Most of the district is a mix of working-class and poverty-level black neighborhoods, largely clustered south of Ford Freeway. The heart of the ghetto is east of Woodward Avenue, which bisects the city, heading northwest through successively wealthier suburbs until it reaches Pontiac. The area east of Woodward and south of Gratiot Avenue was tagged "Black Bottom" even before World War II. Blacks crowded into that section as they moved to Detroit for jobs in the auto industry, then found themselves trapped there by segregated housing patterns in the rest of the city.

"Black Bottom" no longer exists — it has been taken over by high-rises and other middle-class housing. But Detroit's poorest neighborhoods still fill the area to the north and spread east toward the Grosse Pointes. Some areas, while depressed, continue to show the vibrant street life that gave root to the "Motown Sound" of the 1960s. Others have yet to emerge from the devastation of the riots.

Outside the inner-city core are moderate-income areas, black and racially mixed, such as Chandler Park and the

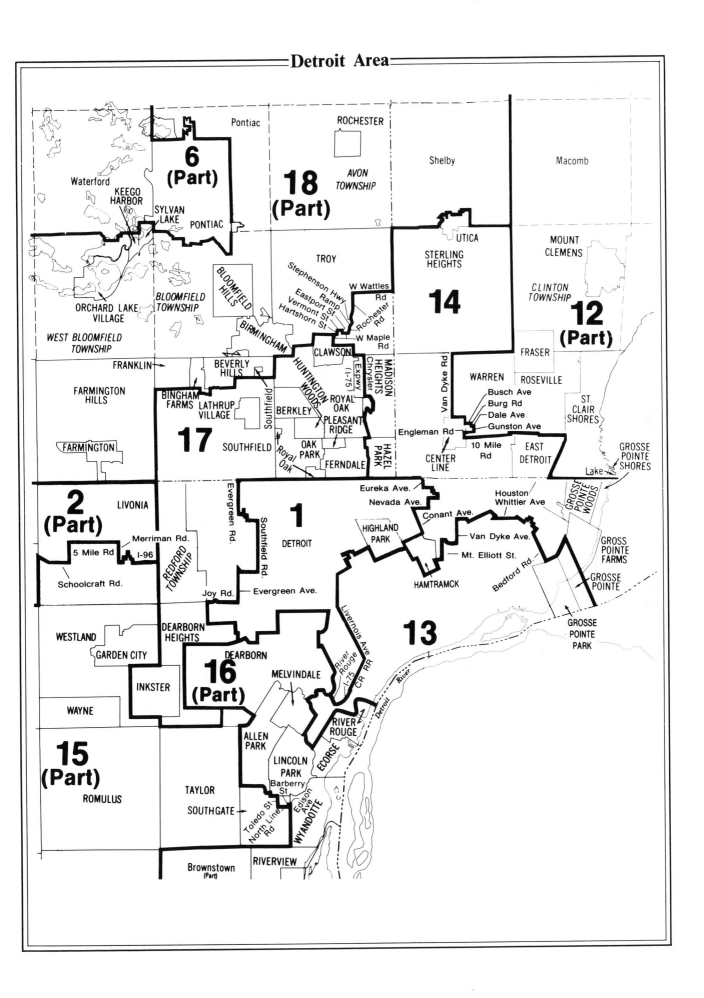

Detroit Area

community around Wayne State University. Blue-collar ethnics still live in the northeast end of the district, around the Detroit City Airport, and more were added by redistricting. The price difference between housing in the suburbs and in Detroit has begun to bring young whites back to the city.

Downtown Detroit stands like a denial of its surroundings. Deserted during the "Murder City" days of the early 1970s, it is very much alive today, but within well-fortified glass towers. The 73-story Renaissance Center symbolizes the attempt at revitalizing the city's commercial core, and the looming presences of General Motors, Burroughs Corp. and United Auto Workers headquarters still keep the business district ticking. Hart Plaza and the area along the riverfront are jammed every weekend with festivals celebrating one ethnic group or holiday after another.

But the decay against which Detroit is struggling still threatens to overcome it: J. L. Hudson's, the downtown area's last large department store, announced in mid-July 1982 that it was closing, and the Renaissance Center was recently sold at a loss by its original owners.

Redistricting brought in a diverse and interesting group of communities. In the southwest, the 13th picked up many of Detroit's Hispanic neighborhoods, while farther south is an edge of the Arab section that spilled over from Dearborn. The southern tip of the district, which juts north of River Rouge and Ecorse, houses blacks working in the plants that line the "downriver" communities of the 16th District.

Standing in sharp contrast to most of the district is its far eastern end, where Grosse Pointe Park and Grosse Pointe were tacked on for the 1980s. Although not as ritzy as their neighbors to the north, these two are upper middle-class communities of corporate managers and professionals, and the sole concentrated source of Republican votes in the district.

Election Returns

13th District		Democrat		Republican	
1976	President	127,666	(80.1%)	29,140	(18.3%)
	Senate	125,129	(83.8%)	22,026	(14.8%)
	House	121,510	(86.5%)	17,316	(12.3%)
1978	Governor	72,958	(66.7%)	36,247	(33.1%)
	Senate	93,308	(86.1%)	15,011	(13.9%)
	House	72,364	(79.7%)	18,290	(20.2%)
1980	President	123,194	(91.4%)	8,190	(6.1%)
	House	114,196	(86.9%)	16,022	(12.2%)
1982	Governor	89,489	(66.6%)	41,469	(30.8%)
	Senate	95,442	(71.8%)	35,780	(26.9%)
	House	108,351	(88.0%)	13,732	(11.1%)

Demographics

Population: 514,560. **Percent Change from 1970:** -30.8%.

Land Area: 65 square miles. **Population per Square Mile:** 7,916.3.

Counties, 1980 Population: Wayne (Pt.) — 514,560.

Cities, 1980 Population: Detroit (Pt.) — 495,020; Grosse Pointe Park — 13,639.

Race and Ancestry: White — 26.0%; Black — 71.1%; American Indian, Eskimo and Aleut — 0.3%; Asian and Pacific Islander — 0.7%.

Spanish Origin — 3.1%. English — 3.2%; French — 0.5%; German — 2.2%; Irish — 1.5%; Italian — 1.0%; Polish — 2.5%.

Universities, Enrollment: Center for Creative Studies, Detroit — 1,086; Detroit College of Law, Detroit — 848; Detroit Institute of Technology, Detroit — 611; Sacred Heart Seminary, Detroit — 114; Wayne County Community College, Detroit — 18,386; Wayne State University, Detroit — 33,408.

Newspapers, Circulation: *Detroit Free Press* (mS), Detroit — 605,156; *The Detroit News* (all day, S), Detroit — 629,553. Foreign language newspaper: *Dziennik Polski* (Polish), Detroit — 11,500.

Commercial Television Stations, Affiliation: WDIV, Detroit (NBC); WGPR-TV, Detroit (None). Entire district is located in Detroit ADI. *(For other Detroit stations, see 17th District.)*

Industries:

General Motors Corp. (Cadillac Motors Div.); Detroit; automobiles — 7,400. **Blue Cross & Blue Shield of Michigan** (HQ); Detroit; health insurance — 5,300. **Henry Ford Hospital** (HQ); Detroit; hospital — 5,200. **Chrysler Corp.** (Jefferson Assembly Plant); Detroit; automobiles — 4,800. **General Motors Corp.** (HQ); Detroit; motor vehicles — 4,000.

The Budd Co. Inc. (Wheel & Brake Div.); Detroit; special automotive machine tools — 3,500. **Manufacturers National Corp.** (HQ); Detroit; bank holding company — 3,400. **General Motors Corp.** (Fisher Body Ternsted Div.); Detroit; motor vehicles — 3,300. **American Natural Resources Co.** (HQ); Detroit; natural gas extraction, transmission; coal mining — 2,500. **Evening News Assn.;** Detroit; newspaper publishing; television, radio broadcasting — 2,500. **Harper Hospital** (HQ); Detroit; hospital — 2,300. **Hutzel Hospital Inc.;** Detroit; hospital — 1,700. **General Motors Corp.** (Fisher Body Div.); Detroit; motor vehicle parts — 1,600. **Detroit Free Press Inc.** (HQ); Detroit; newspaper publishing — 1,550. **Children's Hospital of Michigan** (HQ); Detroit; children's hospital — 1,540.

Burroughs Corp. (HQ); Detroit; computing equipment — 1,500. **General Motors Corp.** (AC-Delco Div.); Detroit; automotive parts wholesaling — 1,500. **Stroh Brewery Co.** (HQ); Detroit; brewery — 1,420. **Ford Motor Co.;** Detroit; administrative offices — 1,400. **Chrysler Corp.** (Axle Div.); Detroit; motor vehicle parts — 1,300. **Parke, Davis & Co.;** Detroit; pharmaceutical, chemical preparations — 1,200. **Bon Secours Hospital;** Detroit; hospital — 1,100. **Northern States Bancorp.** (HQ); Detroit; bank holding company — 1,100. **Champion Spark Plug Co. Inc.** (Ceramic Div.); Detroit; spark plugs — 1,000. **NBD Bancorp Inc.** (HQ); Detroit; bank holding company — 1,000. **Western Renaissance Center;** Detroit; hotel — 1,000. **Chrysler Corp.** (Vernor Tool & Die); Detroit; motor vehicle bodies, parts — 900. **Bank of the Commonwealth** (HQ); Detroit; banking — 865.

Chrysler Transport Inc. (Lynch Road Terminal - HQ); Detroit; trucking — 806. **Detroit Bank Corp.** (HQ); Detroit; bank holding company — 800. **General Motors Corp.** (Fisher Body Div.); Detroit; motor vehicle parts — 800. **Grand Trunk Western Railroad Co.** (HQ); Detroit; railroad operations — 800. **Fruehauf Corp.** (HQ); Detroit; transportation equipment — 700. **General Motors Overseas Distribution;** Detroit; automobile distributing — 700. **Chrysler Corp.** (Mack Avenue Stamping Plant); Detroit; automotive stampings — 600. **Frederick & Herrud Inc.;** Detroit; meatpacking — 600. **General Motors Corp.** (Truck & Bus Mfg. Div.); Detroit; motor vehicles — 600. **The Smith Group** (HQ); Detroit; architectural services — 590. **Stecher-Traung-Schmidt Corp.** (HQ); Detroit; commercial printing — 550. **McLouth Steel Corp.** (HQ); Detroit; steel mills, trucking — 510. **Cadillac Overall Supply Co.** (HQ); Detroit; industrial laundering — 500. **Charge Card Assn.;** Detroit; business services — 500. **General Motors Acceptance Corp.** (HQ); Detroit; automotive financing, insurance — 500.

14th District

Detroit Suburbs — Warren

The redrawn 14th is a 15-mile corridor with an ethnic and social diversity that takes in the rumbling auto plants of Warren, the graceful old mansions of the Grosse Pointes, the kielbasa of Hamtramck and the *pétanque* games of Detroit's Belgian neighborhoods.

The 14th lost 55,000 residents during the 1970s. With most of that decline in the northeast Detroit sections of the district, redistricting had to change the urban-suburban balance of the 14th. The bulk of the district was shifted out of Detroit and Wayne County — only 38 percent of the new population lives below Eight Mile Road, the city's northern boundary. The added areas, brought in from the dismembered 18th District, are in northern Warren, Sterling Heights and the southeastern edge of Oakland County. With the loss of the two southern Grosse Pointes and the addition of what are generally blue-collar suburbs, an already Democratic district becomes marginally more Democratic.

The new 14th includes six different cities or villages in the area south of the Detroit city limits, some encircled by the city, some not. At the far eastern end Grosse Pointe Shores and Grosse Pointe Farms boast the kind of Republicanism associated with corporate board rooms and casual access to political power. Farther inland, in Grosse Pointe Woods and Harper Woods, are three-bedroom ranch houses and middle-level managers whose national and statewide allegiance is usually to the GOP, but who are comfortable splitting their tickets in local contests.

To the west stretches northeast Detroit, an ethnic quilt of solid working-class neighborhoods where a Democrat stumping for votes can spend his time productively at the corner bar. Poles, Germans, Italians and Belgians all settled here, drawn by the auto industry. Ties to the old country are kept alive, a generation and more later, by local religious observance, bicycle races organized in the Belgian community and waterfront festivals put on by German and Italian clubs.

The center of Polish activity is Hamtramck, a city wholly surrounded by Detroit. Its neat streets of two-story frame houses, broken only by the spires of Catholic churches, were once home to 50,000 people. Most of them worked at the huge Dodge plant at the southern end of town. Now down to 21,000, Hamtramck is dependent these days on jobs at smaller factories.

North of Eight Mile Road, the 14th takes in a small part of Oakland County and southeastern Macomb County, and these areas have nearly half the district residents. Middle-class ethnics live in East Detroit, Hazel Park and northern Warren, and lower middle-class Appalachians reside in the shadow of steel plants and auto parts factories in southern Warren. The combination makes this area the socially conservative heart of Democratic strength in the northeastern Detroit suburbs.

Warren, now the third largest city in the state, became a national symbol in the 1970s for its militant opposition to school busing and integrated public housing. In 1980 Warren supported Democratic candidates for congressional and state offices, but gave Ronald Reagan a clear margin over Jimmy Carter.

There is a Republican vote in the northern end of the 14th, around Troy, Sterling Heights and Utica. Although Ford and Chrysler plants in Sterling Heights and Utica have brought the area Democratic auto workers, the towns also have high concentrations of white-collar voters who tend to side with the GOP. The same ethnic diversity that marks the rest of the district holds here as well, and Sterling Heights plays host to a different ethnic festival every weekend during the summer.

Election Returns

14th District		Democrat		Republican	
1976	President	99,782	(45.7%)	114,792	(52.5%)
	Senate	111,130	(53.2%)	96,522	(46.2%)
	House	127,950	(66.5%)	62,778	(32.6%)
1978	Governor	68,428	(40.2%)	101,641	(59.8%)
	Senate	90,316	(53.8%)	77,406	(46.2%)
	House	106,042	(69.6%)	45,582	(29.9%)
1980	President	97,621	(42.8%)	114,356	(50.0%)
	House	118,733	(57.0%)	87,738	(42.0%)
1982	Governor	84,842	(57.7%)	57,151	(38.9%)
	Senate	94,185	(52.5%)	47,151	(26.3%)
	House	116,421	(95.0%)	—	

Demographics

Population: 514,559. **Percent Change from 1970:** -1.2%.

Land Area: 107 square miles. **Population per Square Mile:** 4,809.0.

Counties, 1980 Population: Macomb (Pt.) — 255,563; Oakland (Pt.) — 65,685; Wayne (Pt.) — 193,311.

Cities, 1980 Population: Detroit (Pt.) — 123,201; East Detroit — 38,280; Grosse Pointe Farms — 10,551; Grosse Pointe Woods — 18,886; Hamtramck — 21,300; Harper Woods — 16,361; Hazel Park — 20,914; Madison Heights (Pt.) — 29,000; Sterling Heights — 108,999; Troy (Pt.) — 15,771; Warren (Pt.) — 93,709.

Race and Ancestry: White — 93.1%; Black — 4.9%; American Indian, Eskimo and Aleut — 0.3%; Asian and Pacific Islander — 1.1%. Spanish Origin — 1.0%. English — 5.0%; French — 1.3%; German — 7.5%; Greek — 0.6%; Irish — 3.0%; Italian — 6.2%; Polish — 13.4%; Scottish — 0.8%; Ukranian — 0.9%.

Newspapers, Circulation: *Detroit Free Press*, *The Detroit News*, Mount Clemens *Macomb Daily* and Royal Oak *Daily Tribune* circulate in the district.

Commercial Television Stations, Affiliation: Entire district is located in Detroit ADI.

Military Installations: Detroit Arsenal (Army), Warren — 5,944; Detroit Arsenal Tank Plant (Army), Warren — 2,202.

Industries:

General Motors Corp. (Chevrolet Motor Div.); Warren; motor vehicle bodies — 7,130. **General Motors Corp.** (Fisher Body Div.); Warren; auto bodies — 6,100. **General Motors Corp.** (Chevrolet Motor Div.); Detroit; motor vehicles — 6,000. **Chrysler Corp.** (Stamping Plant); Sterling Heights; auto stampings — 3,400. **Ford Motor Co.**; Sterling Heights; motor vehicle parts — 3,000.

General Motors Corp. (Hydra-matic Div.); Warren; motor vehicle parts — 2,660. **Chrysler Corp.** (Truck Assembly Plant); Sterling Heights; trucks — 2,600. **Chrysler Corp.**; Warren; automotive stampings — 2,500. **Ford Motor Co.**; Utica; automotive stampings — 2,500. **St. John Hospital Corp.**; Detroit; hospital — 2,000. **General Motors Corp.** (Chevrolet Motor Div.); Detroit; motor vehicles — 1,800. **Ford Motor Co.**; Troy; general warehousing — 1,680. **Ford Motor Co.**; Utica; motor vehicle parts — 1,600. **The Evening News Assn.**; Utica; newspaper publishing — 1,500. **TRW Inc.** (Michigan Hydraulics Div.); Utica; motor vehicle parts — 1,500. **Chrysler Corp.**; Detroit; automotive engines, parts — 1,300. **Chrysler Corp.** (Axle Div.); Detroit; motor vehicle parts — 1,300. **Ford Motor Co.** (Tractor Div.); Troy; tractors — 1,200. **General Electric Co.** (Carboloy Systems); Warren; machine tool accessories — 1,200. **Holy Cross Hospital**; Detroit; hospital — 1,200.

General Motors Corp. (Assembly Div.); Warren; motor vehicles — 1,090. **North Detroit General Hospital**; Detroit; hospital — 1,000. **Colt Industries Operating Corp.** (Holley Carburetor Div.); Warren; metal automobile hardware — 950. **Chrysler Corp.**; Detroit; motor vehicle parts — 900. **Borg-Warner Corp.** (Borg and Beck); Utica; motor vehicle parts — 800. **Expert Automation Inc.;** Utica; welding machines — 800. **Bendix Machine Tool Corp.** (HQ); Warren; machine tools — 650. **General Motors Corp.** (Assembly Div.); Warren; administrative offices — 600. **Chrysler Defense Inc.** (HQ); Utica; small arms ammunition — 550. **General Motors Corp.** (Technical Center Service Div.) Warren; engineering services — 518. **Parker-Hannifin Corp.** (Detroit Fluid Power Sales Div.); Troy; industrial machinery wholesaling — 505. **Bundy Corp.** (Bundy Tubing Div.); Warren; steel pipes, tubes — 500. **Olsonite Corp.** (HQ); Detroit; plastic products — 500.

15th District

Southwestern Wayne County

The Industrial Expressway heading west from Detroit is the 15th District's spine. Lining the ribs that branch from it on its way out toward the airport are automobile and chemical plants, trucking firms and auto parts factories. In the distance squat retreating rows of suburban tract houses, home to more than a quarter of the district's voters.

Previously made up almost entirely of western Wayne County, the 15th had to join the other Detroit-area districts in moving outward. Wayne County still holds more than 80 percent of the 15th's voters.

But the district has been pushed west into Washtenaw County, out of the towns at the mouth of the Detroit River and the close-in communities of Inkster and Dearborn Heights. Taking their place are Ypsilanti and its neighboring townships and a hook south of Ann Arbor around the small city of Saline.

Most of the towns along the Industrial Expressway are lower middle-class communities. Almost entirely white and heavily settled by Eastern Europeans and migrants from the hills of Kentucky and Tennessee, they are unreservedly Democratic, socially conservative and often unfriendly to blacks.

Politics is volatile, sometimes marked by a "throw the bums out" attitude that shortens the careers of local officeholders trying to deal with declining tax bases and poverty-stricken school systems.

Farther out in Wayne County, things are less crowded. Small farms are scattered around suburban townships inhabited by auto workers who were prosperous enough to move out from the central suburban ring. Canton Township is the district's only substantially Republican community, a white-collar suburb of split-level ranch houses whose gradual encroachment into the surrounding farm land has been slowed by the recession.

Visitors familiar with the decaying inner cities of the auto corridor north of Detroit would instantly recognize Ypsilanti. Downtown "Ypsi City" is empty, the huge auto plants of the Willow Run section unable to continue breathing life into it. The 19,000 students of Eastern Michigan University, at the city's northwestern end, spend their money and their time in Ann Arbor, a ten-minute drive away.

The district's largest concentration of blacks is in Ypsilanti and Ypsilanti Township. Many of the white auto workers living there moved up from the South, and relations between the two communities sometimes have been tense. But together they give Democrats a grip on the area that far outweighs the small Republican margins turned in by the farms nearby.

Election Returns

15th District		Democrat		Republican	
1976	President	95,762	(50.2%)	91,237	(47.8%)
	Senate	105,697	(57.5%)	76,833	(41.8%)
	House	120,605	(68.2%)	54,138	(30.6%)
1978	Governor	60,347	(42.4%)	81,993	(57.6%)
	Senate	78,667	(55.2%)	63,882	(44.8%)
	House	88,471	(70.1%)	36,523	(28.9%)
1980	President	89,641	(43.0%)	101,740	(48.8%)
	House	114,316	(61.5%)	69,583	(37.4%)
1982	Governor	92,040	(64.7%)	46,293	(32.6%)
	Senate	98,213	(69.8%)	40,625	(28.9%)
	House	94,950	(72.8%)	33,904	(26.0%)

Demographics

Population: 514,560. **Percent Change from 1970:** 11.1%.

Land Area: 395 square miles. **Population per Square Mile:** 1,302.7.

Counties, 1980 Population: Washtenaw (Pt.) — 96,505; Wayne (Pt.) — 418,055.

Cities, 1980 Population: Dearborn Heights (Pt.) — 10,161; Garden City — 35,640; Livonia (Pt.) — 42,916; Romulus — 24,857; Southgate (Pt.) — 29,268; Taylor — 77,568; Wayne — 21,159; Westland — 84,603; Ypsilanti — 24,031.

Race and Ancestry: White — 92.5%; Black — 5.5%; American Indian, Eskimo and Aleut — 0.3%; Asian and Pacific Islander — 1.0%. Spanish Origin — 1.5%. English — 7.9%; French — 1.5%; German — 7.3%; Hungarian — 1.0%; Irish — 3.8%; Italian — 1.9%; Polish — 5.3%; Scottish — 0.8%.

Universities, Enrollment: Cleary College, Ypsilanti — 765; Detroit Institute of Aeronautics, Ypsilanti — 50; Eastern Michigan University, Ypsilanti — 19,323.

Newspapers, Circulation: *The Ypsilanti Press* (eS), Ypsilanti — 16,037. *The Ann Arbor News, Detroit Free Press* and *The Detroit News* also circulate in the district.

Commercial Television Stations, Affiliation: Entire district is located in Detroit ADI.

Industries:

General Motors Corp. (Hydra-Matic Div.); Ypsilanti; motor vehicle bodies — 10,500. **General Motors Corp.** (Assembly Div.); Ypsilanti; auto assembly — 5,300. **Ford Motor Co.** (Automotive Assembly Div.); Wayne; auto assembly — 3,700. **General Motors Corp.** (Fisher Body Div.); Livonia; automotive stampings — 3,400. **Ford Motor Co.** (Livonia Automatic Transmission Plant); Livonia; auto transmissions — 3,200.

General Motors Corp. (Chevrolet Motor Div.) Livonia; motor vehicle parts — 2,700. **Sisters of Mercy Health Corp.;** Ypsilanti; hospital — 2,600. **Ford Motor Co.** (Rawsonville Plant); Ypsilanti; motor vehicles — 2,500. **Hoover Universal Inc.** (Automotive Products Group); Saline; auto seats — 2,300. **Ford Motor Co.** (Plastics Paint & Vinyl Div.); Saline; motor vehicle parts — 2,200. **American Motors Corp.** Detroit; motor vehicle bodies — 1,984. **General Motors Corp.** (Detroit Diesel Allison Div.); Romulus; auto engines — 1,900. **Ford Motor Co.** (Electrical & Electronic Div.); Ypsilanti; motor vehicle parts — 1,800. **Ford Motor Co. Inc.** (Parts Redistribution Center); Romulus; auto parts warehousing — 1,350. **Ford Motor Co.;** Wayne; trucks — 1,100.

Kelsey-Hayes Co. Inc. (HQ); Romulus; auto parts — 1,100. **Garden City Osteopathic Hospital;** Garden City; hospital — 1,070. **General Motors Corp.** (Cadillac Motor Car Div.); Livonia; motor vehicles — 970. **Massey-Ferguson Inc.;** Detroit; motor vehicle parts — 705. **R. L. Polk Co.** (Marketing Services Div.); Taylor; warehousing, direct mailing services — 650. **Michigan National Bank;** Livonia; computer programming services — 600. **General Motors Corp.** (Distribution Center); Belleville; automotive parts, supplies — 550. **Burroughs Corp.;** Wayne; calculating, accounting machines — 525. **GTE Products Corp.** (Unistrut Div.); Wayne; fabricated metal distribution center — 500. **Zantop International Airlines** (HQ); Ypsilanti; air freight carriers — 500.

16th District

Southeast Wayne County; Monroe County

Several years ago, *The Detroit News* called the 16th "the most polluted congressional district in the nation." Redistricting probably will cost it that distinction, not because great strides have been made in cleaning its air or rivers, but because the district has been pushed down the Lake Erie shoreline into the small towns and spread-out farms of southeastern Michigan.

The 16th lost close to 15 percent of its population in the 1970s. To give the two Detroit districts room to expand, Democratic legislators moved the 16th entirely out of the city. It was extended south through Monroe County and into Lenawee County, taking in at its western end most of the city of Adrian.

Despite the changes, the 16th remains an overwhelmingly industrialized constituency. At the district's northern end is Dearborn, home of the Ford Motor Company and site of Ford's immense River Rouge complex. The haze-covered stretch of communities along the Detroit River in Wayne County, from River Rouge to Gibraltar, is a conglomeration of steel mills, foundries, automobile factories, tool-and-die shops and chemical plants; they loom over a broken sea of apartments, tract homes on uniform lots and one- and two-family frame houses.

The Wayne County portion of the district, which accounts for about two-thirds of its population, is one of the most Democratic areas in Michigan. The eastern end of Dearborn, with its dilapidated prewar housing, is home to the country's largest single community of Arab-Americans, who join with the city's auto workers in solid support of Democratic candidates. Similar sentiments hold among the auto workers and steelworkers, many of them black, who fill the duplexes of River Rouge and Ecorse, and among the tool-and-die and foundry workers of Melvindale, the transplanted Appalachians living in postwar tract homes in Lincoln Park and Southgate, the Polish auto and chemical workers of Wyandotte and the Eastern Europeans of Allen Park.

The industrial and suburban towns of southern Wayne County — Gibraltar, Rockwood, and Flat Rock — are harder to categorize. Their residents are a mix of loyal union members and middle-class blue-collar workers to whom GOP tax policies are appealing.

Republicans also do well among the white-collar residents of Riverview and the company managers of Lincoln Park, many of them reaching retirement age. The shaded streets of western Dearborn and Grosse Ile pass by large old homes whose owners — executives and wealthy professionals — cast the most solid Republican votes in the area.

Monroe County, south of Wayne County, brings 135,000 new people to the 16th. It is politically marginal territory. The factories in Dundee and in the city of Monroe give the county a firm union presence, but the rural western portions are conservative enough to support active chapters of the John Birch Society. The county's Lake Erie shoreline has attracted a large retired population from Detroit and Toledo, Ohio. These retirees' varied economic backgrounds mirror equally diverse political leanings.

The only substantial blue-collar vote outside Wayne County comes from Adrian. Democrats are well organized in the city, but their strength is minimal among the farmers growing corn and other feed grains in the rest of eastern Lenawee County.

Election Returns

16th District		Democrat		Republican	
1976	President	114,987	(53.1%)	97,607	(45.1%)
	Senate	121,663	(58.4%)	85,033	(40.8%)
	House	138,770	(70.1%)	56,827	(28.7%)
1978	Governor	77,542	(47.3%)	86,479	(52.7%)
	Senate	93,461	(57.4%)	69,314	(42.6%)
	House	100,982	(67.1%)	47,597	(31.6%)
1980	President	95,357	(44.3%)	103,367	(48.0%)
	House	121,173	(61.1%)	72,230	(36.7%)
1982	Governor	103,657	(61.6%)	59,256	(35.2%)
	Senate	113,052	(68.0%)	51,059	(30.7%)
	House	114,006	(73.7%)	39,227	(25.3%)

Demographics

Population: 514,560. **Percent Change from 1970:** -0.7%.

Land Area: 960 square miles. **Population per Square Mile:** 536.0.

Counties, 1980 Population: Lenawee (Pt.) — 42,951; Monroe — 134,659; Wayne (Pt.) — 336,950.

Cities, 1980 Population: Adrian (Pt.) — 18,347; Allen Park — 34,196; Dearborn — 90,660; Ecorse — 14,447; Lincoln Park — 45,105; Melvindale — 12,322; Monroe — 23,531; River Rouge — 12,912; Riverview — 14,569; Southgate (Pt.) — 2,790; Trenton — 22,762; Woodhaven — 10,902; Wyandotte — 34,006.

Race and Ancestry: White — 95.5%; Black — 2.7%; American Indian, Eskimo and Aleut — 0.3%; Asian and Pacific Islander — 0.5%. Spanish Origin — 2.4%. English — 6.9%; French — 2.4%; German — 9.0%; Hungarian — 1.8%; Irish — 3.5%; Italian — 3.0%; Polish — 6.0%; Scottish — 0.7%.

Universities, Enrollment: Adrian College, Adrian — 1,116; Detroit College of Business, Dearborn — 2,368; Henry Ford Community College, Dearborn — 16,236; Monroe County Community College, Monroe — 2,151; Siena Heights College, Adrian — 1,456; University of Michigan (Dearborn campus), Dearborn — 6,360.

Newspapers, Circulation: *The Daily Telegram* (e), Adrian — 16,974; *Monroe Evening News* (e), Monroe — 27,135. *Detroit Free Press* and *The Detroit News* also circulate in the district.

Commercial Television Stations, Affiliation: District is divided between Detroit ADI and Toledo (Ohio) ADI.

Nuclear Power Plants: Enrico Fermi 2, Laguna Beach (General Electric, Daniel International).

Industries:

Ford Motor Co.; Dearborn; auto bodies, parts, engines, frames, glass & auto stampings — 10,800. **Ford Motor Co.** (Body & Assembly Div.); Allen Park; administrative offices — 9,650. **National Steel Corp.** (Great Lakes Steel Div.); Ecorse; steel works — 5,600. **Ford Motor Co.** (Rouge Steel Co.); Dearborn; steel foundries — 4,400. **Ford Motor Co.** (Woodhaven Stamping Plant); Trenton; automotive stampings — 2,500.

Oakwood Hospital; Dearborn; hospital — 2,300. **Chrysler Corp.** (Trenton Engine Plant); Trenton; internal combustion engines — 1,900.

Ford Motor Co. (HQ); Dearborn; motor vehicle parts, bodies — 1,800. **Ford Motor Co.** (Stamping Plant); Monroe; automotive stampings — 1,700. **McLouth Steel Corp.;** Trenton; steel mill — 1,676. **Veterans Administration;** Allen Park; veterans' hospital — 1,500. **Wyandotte General Hospital;** Wyandotte; hospital — 1,130. **Ford Motor Credit Co.** (HQ); Dearborn; auto financing operations — 1,000. **Ford Motor Co.** (Research & Engineering Div.); Dearborn; engineering services — 1,000. **Ford Motor Co.** (Parts & Service Div.); Dearborn; auto service, parts — 850.

Hyatt Corp.; Dearborn; hotel operations — 800. **United Technology Corp.;** Dearborn; electrical engine equipment — 800. **World Book-Childcraft International;** Lincoln; marketing operations — 750. **BASF Wyandotte Corp.;** Wyandotte; shipbuilding, repairing — 700. **Guardian Industries Corp.** (Glass Mfg. Corp.); Carleton; flat glass — 650. **Wismer & Beck Engineering Contractors;** Newport; engineering services — 637. **Essex Group Inc.** (Automotive Products Div.); Dearborn; electrical engine equipment — 600. **Monsanto Co.** (Detergent & Fine Chemical Div.); Trenton; detergents, chemicals — 550. **Pennwalt Corp.;** Wyandotte; inorganic chemicals — 500.

17th District

Northwest Detroit; Southeast Oakland County

The 17th remains a uniformly white-collar district even though it was forced by Detroit's population loss to expand the suburban beachhead it first established in 1972. Over half of its territory is new, and Detroit residents, who used to cast more than 50 percent of its votes, now contribute less than a fifth. More than half the ballots come from Oakland County.

To make room for the 1st District, the 17th was pulled out of most of its northwestern Detroit neighborhoods. It picked up Dearborn Heights and Inkster, two Wayne County communities along the western edge of Dearborn, but otherwise all its growth was in the Oakland County suburbs. It inherited the southwestern portion of the dissolved 18th.

The area of Detroit left in the district is the far western end of the city. It includes the black neighborhoods close to the city line, and racially mixed Brightmoor, with its large numbers of Appalachian blue-collar workers. The civil servants of Rosedale Park and the police families of "Coppers' Corner" — the northwestern city neighborhood where many of Detroit's white police officers cluster — give the city portion of the new 17th a relatively conservative Democratic presence.

The only urban addition to the 17th is black-majority Inkster, which bulges out of the district's southern tip. Once home to workers drawn by Detroit's pre-Depression industrial boom, it is still an overwhelmingly Democratic blue-collar city. Dearborn Heights is politically mixed, with the wealthy neighborhoods just north and east of Inkster leaning Republican while the blue-collar workers in the bungalows north of Ford Road are more sympathetic to Democrats. The generally liberal young professionals of the eastern tip of Dearborn Heights reinforce the Democratic vote.

Redford Township, which stretches between Dearborn Heights and the Oakland County line, is also divided. The lower middle-class workers living along the unpaved roads in the north are Democrats although their turnout tends to be low. The politically active and well-off Moose and Elks members to the south, many of them Polish, are more open to splitting their tickets.

The addition of so much of Oakland County means an inevitable weakening of the district's Democratic margins, although the 17th still has some of the county's most consistent Democratic voters. The largest of the suburban towns is Southfield, just north of Redford Township, one of two centers for corporate headquarters and professionals' offices in the suburbs northwest of Detroit. Its 40-story high-rises lining the Northwestern Highway house a substantial population of Jewish senior citizens, while younger middle-class Jewish people live in the single-family houses away from the expressway. Coupled with the black community in the southern half of Southfield, the Jewish vote puts the city solidly behind Democratic candidates.

Oak Park, where the Jewish community that left northwestern Detroit first settled, is just to the east of Southfield. Its many Orthodox Jews have tended to vote more conservatively in recent years, but thanks to the more liberal Jewish voters in the western part of the city, Jimmy Carter still managed a 62-38 point citywide margin over Reagan in 1980. Next door to Oak Park are the middle-class blue-collar neighborhoods of Ferndale, which Carter also carried.

The core of the GOP's strength is in the Catholic neighborhoods that stand in the shadow of Royal Oak's Shrine of the Little Flower, where Father Charles Coughlin, the right-wing radio commentator, preached in the 1930s. Solid Republican votes also come from the ranch homes of Lathrup Village, entirely surrounded by Southfield, and Pleasant Ridge, a small town on the northern edge of Ferndale. Although the younger couples in the built-up section of Huntington Woods tend to be more liberal, wealthy professionals and executives living along the elm-shaded streets above the Detroit Zoo keep Huntington Woods in the GOP column as well.

Election Returns

17th District		Democrat		Republican	
1976	President	97,333	(45.2%)	114,031	(52.9%)
	Senate	111,264	(53.4%)	95,453	(45.8%)
	House	130,414	(65.5%)	66,219	(33.3%)
1978	Governor	61,580	(37.1%)	104,582	(62.9%)
	Senate	94,370	(56.6%)	72,488	(43.4%)
	House	118,429	(84.4%)	17,992	(12.8%)
1980	President	104,307	(47.7%)	94,266	(43.1%)
	House	142,203	(70.0%)	57,744	(28.4%)
1982	Governor	117,855	(62.6%)	65,792	(34.9%)
	Senate	123,622	(66.3%)	60,166	(32.3%)
	House	116,901	(66.6%)	55,620	(31.7%)

Demographics

Population: 514,560. **Percent Change from 1970:** -11.7%.

Land Area: 101 square miles. **Population per Square Mile:** 5,094.7.

Counties, 1980 Population: Oakland (Pt.) — 264,917; Wayne (Pt.) — 249,643.

Cities, 1980 Population: Berkley — 18,637; Clawson — 15,103; Dearborn Heights (Pt.) — 57,545; Detroit (Pt.) — 98,467; Ferndale — 26,227; Inkster — 35,190; Madison Heights (Pt.) — 6,375; Oak Park — 31,537; Royal Oak — 70,893; Southfield — 75,568.

Race and Ancestry: White — 85.6%; Black — 12.8%; American Indian, Eskimo and Aleut — 0.2%; Asian and Pacific Islander — 0.9%.

Spanish Origin — 1.1%. English — 6.3%; French — 1.2%; German — 5.7%; Greek — 0.5%; Hungarian — 0.9%; Irish — 3.5%; Italian — 2.3%; Polish — 6.5%; Russian — 2.2%; Scottish — 1.0%; Ukranian — 0.5%.

Universities, Enrollment: Lawrence Institute of Technology, Southfield — 5,260.

Newspapers, Circulation: *The Daily Tribune* (e), Royal Oak — 47,983. *Detroit Free Press*, the *Detroit News* and Pontiac *Oakland Press* also circulate in the district.

Commercial Television Stations, Affiliation: WJBK-TV, Detroit (CBS); WKBD-TV, Detroit (None); WXON, Southfield (None); WXYZ-TV, Detroit (ABC). Entire district is located in Detroit ADI. *(For other Detroit stations, see 13th District.)*

Industries:

William Beaumont Hospital; Royal Oak; hospital — 4,160. **Providence Hospital;** Southfield; hospital — 2,650. **International Business Machines Corp.;** Southfield; information systems — 1,000. **Martin Place Hospital Inc.;** Royal Oak; hospital — 1,000. **Burns International Security Service;** Oak Park; security services — 900.

Federal-Mogul Corp. (HQ); Southfield; engine parts, tools, accessories — 800. **De Vlieg Machine Co.** (Microbore Div. - HQ); Royal Oak; machine tools — 750. **Giffels Associates Inc.** (HQ); Southfield; architectural services — 690. **American Motors Corp.** (HQ); Southfield; motor vehicles — 677. **The Development Group;** Southfield; real estate developing — 600. **Natkin & Co.;** Oak Park; plumbing, heating construction — 600. **Beverage Management Inc.** (Seven-Up/Canada Dry Bottling Co.); Detroit; soft drink distributing — 500.

18th District

Oakland County

Republicans should have no problems in holding the 18th District. It is basically the old 19th, much of it territory that has been represented by the same Republican incumbent for over a quarter of a century. The district gave Richard Nixon his highest statewide percentage in 1972 and is the one GOP bastion in metropolitan Detroit.

The new lines make it even more Republican. It lost Pontiac, the only large concentration of poor voters it had, and picked up Republican sections of the old 18th District, including much of Troy.

The district's Republican core is in the cluster of towns on both sides of suburban Woodward Avenue, along which Detroit's wealthy first escaped the city. In 1980 Ronald Reagan carried most of this area by at least 2-to-1, taking 75 percent of the vote in Bloomfield Hills and in some Troy precincts.

Bloomfield Hills and Birmingham are much like the Grosse Pointes, dotted with the 1920s mansions and newer ranch houses of top-level auto executives and professionals. Bloomfield Hills was former Republican Gov. George Romney's hometown in his days as an auto executive.

To the west are the only slightly more modest, shaded streets of Farmington Hills, a town of lawyers, doctors and business executives. Troy, to the east, is a gathering ground for gleaming suburban business headquarters and professionals' offices; off the main roads live WASPish upper middle-class voters. Younger auto executives have begun moving into expensive new homes in Avon Township, to the north, which is emerging as the new Bloomfield Hills.

The southwestern end of the 18th is a jumble of suburbs whose exploding populations helped make the district the second fastest-growing constituency in the state in the

1970s. At its far western end it jabs into two Livingston County townships: the older blue-collar suburbs of Green Oak Township, many of its houses sporting two or three rusting cars in front; and Brighton Township, whose newer subdivisions have attracted a mix of factory workers and professionals from Ann Arbor and the Detroit area.

The horse country of western Oakland County over the years has been squeezed by development, and the countryside has taken on a decidedly blue-collar cast around South Lyon and in more ethnic Commerce Township. The small apartments and trailer parks of Wixom and Walled Lake house factory workers who tend toward conservatism on social issues.

The northern end of the district is less wealthy. Pontiac Township, just east of Pontiac, is a melting pot into whose 20-year-old subdivisions the surrounding area's auto workers, mid-level managers and small-business men have poured. The district's outlying townships in northeastern Oakland County are rural and strongly Republican, although much of the farm land north of Rochester has been sold off for shopping centers and suburban developments.

The 18th also gained three Macomb County townships. Two are basically rural, but Shelby Township, just north of Utica, is more in line with the rest of Macomb, its small postwar brick houses holding blue-collar workers from Utica and Warren who give Democrats one of their few toeholds in the district.

Election Returns

18th District		Democrat		Republican	
1976	President	76,445	(36.8%)	127,570	(61.4%)
	Senate	87,525	(43.7%)	111,190	(55.6%)
	House	81,433	(41.5%)	113,446	(57.8%)
1978	Governor	55,441	(32.4%)	115,686	(67.6%)
	Senate	75,457	(44.0%)	96,189	(56.0%)
	House	70,921	(45.0%)	85,143	(54.1%)
1980	President	67,833	(28.0%)	150,366	(62.1%)
	House	88,357	(39.0%)	135,285	(59.7%)
1982	Governor	74,261	(37.2%)	118,255	(59.2%)
	Senate	83,947	(42.9%)	108,987	(55.7%)
	House	46,545	(25.7%)	132,902	(73.3%)

Demographics

Population: 514,560. **Percent Change from 1970:** 31.4%.

Land Area: 623 square miles. **Population per Square Mile:** 825.9.

Counties, 1980 Population: Livingston (Pt.) — 26,292; Macomb (Pt.) — 54,908; Oakland (Pt.) — 433,360.

Cities, 1980 Population: Beverly Hills — 11,598; Birmingham — 21,689; Farmington — 11,022; Farmington Hills — 58,056; Novi — 22,525; Troy (Pt.) — 51,331.

Race and Ancestry: White — 97.2%; Black — 0.8%; American Indian, Eskimo and Aleut — 0.2%; Asian and Pacific Islander — 1.4%. Spanish Origin — 0.9%. Dutch — 0.5%; English — 8.6%; French — 1.2%; German — 8.0%; Hungarian — 0.6%; Irish — 3.8%; Italian — 2.6%; Polish — 4.6%; Russian — 1.1%; Scottish — 1.0%; Swedish — 0.5%.

Universities, Enrollment: Cranbrook Academy of Art, Bloomfield Hills — 148; Michigan Christian College, Rochester — 353; Oakland Community College, Bloomfield Hills — 23,554; Oakland University, Rochester — 12,006; St. Mary's College, Orchard Lake — 313; Walsh

College of Accountancy and Business Administration, Troy — 1,543; William Tyndale College, Farmington Hills — 377.

Newspapers, Circulation: *Detroit Free Press*, *The Detroit News*, Mount Clemens *Macomb Daily* and Pontiac *Oakland Press* circulate in the district.

Commercial Television Stations, Affiliation: Entire district is located in Detroit ADI.

Industries:

K-Mart Corp. (HQ); Troy; department store chain — 3,700. **Ford Motor Co.** (Automotive Assembly Plants); Wixom; motor vehicles — 2,600. **General Motors Corp.** (Proving Grounds); Milford; automotive testing — 2,580. **Zieger Osteopathic Hospital;** Farmington; specialized hospital — 1,400. **Crittenton Hospital Inc.;** Rochester; hospital — 1,300. **Ford Motor Co.;** Romeo; auto equipment, tractors — 1,300.

Computer Peripherals Inc.; Rochester; electronic computing equipment — 1,100. **Lear Siegler Inc.** (National Twist Drill Tool Div.); Rochester; machine tool accessories — 1,000. **Rockwell International Corp.** (Automotive Operations Div.); Troy; automotive stampings — 1,000. **Williams International Corp.** (HQ); Walled Lake; turbine research — 950. **Sperry Corp.** (Vickers Div.); Troy; machinery, aircraft parts — 900. **Consumer Pulse of Detroit Inc.** (HQ); Birmingham; public relations services — 850. **Ford Export Corp.;** Wixom; sales, exporting services — 750.

The Bendix Corp. (HQ); Southfield automobile parts — 600 **Darcy-MacManus & Masius Inc.** (HQ); Bloomfield Hills; advertising — 600. **Quanex Corp.** (Michigan Seamless Tube Div.); South Lyon; seamless steel tubing — 550. **Ex-Cell-O Corp.** (Packaging Systems Div.); Walled Lake; research laboratories — 500. **Holloway Construction Co.;** Wixom; heavy highway construction — 500. **Parke, Davis & Co.** (Parkdale Sterile Products); Rochester; biological products — 500. **Jervis B. Webb Co.** (HQ); Farmington; conveyors, hoists — 500.

Minnesota

A technically non-partisan, three-judge federal panel gave Minnesota Democrats exactly what they wanted in congressional redistricting in 1982, breaking with tradition to draw a "four-four" map — four largely rural districts and four within the seven-county Minneapolis-St. Paul metropolitan area.

Previous maps had allowed rural votes to dominate five of the state's eight districts. The immediate political result was a reversal in 1982 of the 5-to-3 Republican edge in the state's eight-member congressional delegation.

In drawing the plan, the federal judges largely ignored the interests of incumbents — particularly Republicans. Drastically realigning the districts in the southern half of the state and around the Twin Cities suburbs, the judges created a new Democratic-leaning 6th District in the suburbs north of Minneapolis and St. Paul.

Two Republican incumbents were thrown together in a new rural constituency in southern Minnesota, and one GOP representative found his home placed in a district safely controlled by a Democrat. Two of these incumbents, forced to move in order to run in the 1st and 6th districts, lost their re-election bids in 1982.

Redistricting chores were turned over to the three-judge federal panel following an impasse in the state legislature. On March 11, the court handed down a map similar to a "four-four" plan passed in the state Senate but opposed by both the House and GOP Gov. Albert H. Quie. The court justified the redistricting plan on the grounds that the Twin Cities area had nearly half the state's population and deserved four full districts. The panel divided 2-1.

The court said the plan proposed by the state's Republicans, which would have made only minor changes to reflect slight population shifts, would disperse Twin Cities interests among five districts dominated by rural interests.

In their appeal to the U.S. Supreme Court, Republicans charged the lower court's "four-four" plan constituted a policy decision that went beyond the court's purview. But on May 17, 1982, the high court upheld the plan without issuing an opinion.

The federal judges followed the "one-person, one-vote" dictum to an extreme. The two largest districts — the 5th and 8th — were just 10 people over the ideal district population of 509,496. The smallest district — the 1st — was only 46 short.

Age of Population

District	Population Under 18	Voting Age Population	Population 65 & Over (% of VAP)	Median Age
1	146,834	362,626	66,631 (18.4%)	29.1
2	146,413	363,087	82,298 (22.7%)	31.5
3	156,817	352,682	36,066 (10.2%)	29.2
4	133,610	375,922	59,518 (15.8%)	29.3
5	108,125	401,381	69,437 (17.3%)	30.0
6	177,143	332,303	27,040 (8.1%)	26.6
7	153,889	355,632	68,572 (19.3%)	28.2
8	148,977	360,529	70,002 (19.4%)	30.5
State	1,171,808	2,904,162	479,564 (16.5%)	29.2

Income and Occupation

District	Median Family Income	White Collar Workers	Blue Collar Workers	Service Workers	Farm Workers
1	$ 19,869	47.1%	28.0%	15.1%	9.7%
2	16,935	39.7	28.1	14.2	18.0
3	28,447	66.3	21.5	10.9	1.3
4	23,472	60.6	24.7	14.2	0.6
5	21,500	60.8	23.8	15.0	0.5
6	25,146	53.7	32.9	11.7	1.6
7	16,468	44.2	26.2	16.0	13.6
8	18,905	45.5	34.2	16.3	4.0
State	$ 21,185	53.2%	27.1%	14.0%	5.7%

Education: School Years Completed

District	8 Years or Fewer	4 Years of High School	4 Years of College or More	Median School Years
1	20.2%	38.7%	15.0%	12.5
2	27.8	38.5	10.2	12.3
3	7.0	36.6	27.9	13.0
4	12.4	38.3	21.9	12.7
5	11.7	35.7	21.6	12.7
6	9.0	45.2	17.2	12.7
7	27.2	35.5	12.3	12.4
8	18.2	40.4	12.4	12.5
State	16.7%	38.6%	17.4%	12.6

MINNESOTA

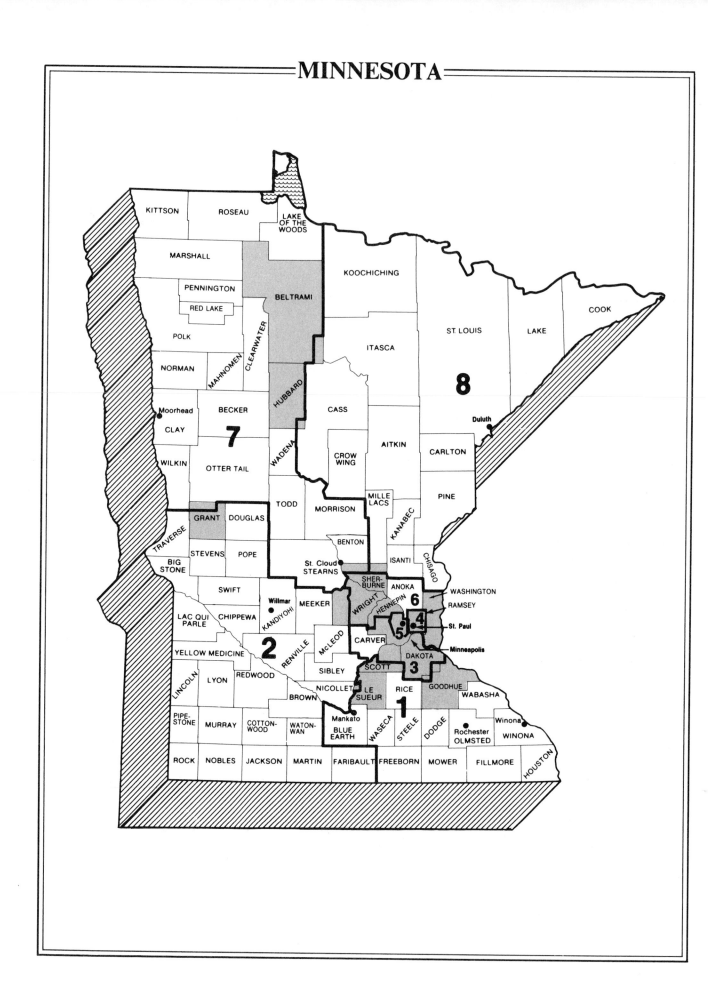

Housing and Residential Patterns

District	Owner Occupied	Renter Occupied	Urban	Rural
1	75.3%	24.7%	51.2%	48.8%
2	76.6	23.4	33.8	66.2
3	75.1	24.9	91.4	8.6
4	62.5	37.5	99.7	0.3
5	54.2	45.8	100.0	0.0
6	79.4	20.6	80.2	19.8
7	77.3	22.7	35.2	64.8
8	78.0	22.0	43.4	56.6
State	71.7%	28.3%	66.9%	33.1%

1st District

Southeast — Rochester, Mankato

The staunchly Republican corn and hog farmers who populate the southeastern corner of Minnesota can put to rest their fears that working-class suburbanites will take over political control in the 1st District.

In keeping with the objective of creating four metropolitan and four rural districts, a court ordered redistricting plan eliminated from the 1st the rapidly growing St. Paul suburbs in Washington and Dakota counties. In 1980 those counties accounted for nearly 40 percent of the congressional vote. By the end of the 1980s, given existing growth rates, the old district most likely would have had a suburban majority.

But with suburban Washington and most of Dakota out and five largely rural counties added, the 1st was expected to revert to its historic rural and Republican orientation. Ironically, the district in 1982 promptly elected a Democrat to the House for the first time since 1890. GOP leaders blamed a divisive nomination battle between two Republican incumbents for the Democrat's victory.

German Protestants settled this area just north of Iowa before the Civil War. The rolling hills that extend from the Mississippi to the great bend in the Minnesota River offer some of the state's richest and most productive farm land. With the exception of Rochester and some Mississippi River towns, the population centers in the district were devoted to serving the surrounding farms, or in the case of the meatpacking city of Austin, processing the primary local product — hogs. Austin, where the meatpacking industry is heavily unionized, is the only consistently Democratic area in the district.

Rochester, the state's fifth largest city with 57,890 people, is the district's largest city, although its influence does not extend far beyond surrounding Olmsted County. Rochester has a much more white-collar, professional work force than the rest of the district due to the presence of the Mayo clinic and a large IBM facility. Politically, however, its voters are as Republican as the farmers.

Election Returns

1st District		Democrat		Republican	
1976	President	115,365	(48.3%)	117,325	(49.1%)
	Senate	149,221	(63.8%)	70,801	(30.3%)
	House	70,088	(30.4%)	157,568	(68.3%)

1st District		Democrat		Republican	
1978	Governor	65,624	(34.1%)	124,283	(64.7%)
	Senate[1]	70,802	(36.2%)	120,476	(61.6%)
	Senate[2]	59,406	(30.6%)	128,774	(66.3%)
	House	72,574	(37.9%)	117,233	(61.3%)
1980	President	81,000	(35.8%)	120,765	(53.4%)
	House	73,068	(31.0%)	162,884	(69.0%)
1982	Governor	108,578	(51.6%)	98,896	(47.0%)
	Senate	84,695	(40.0%)	125,107	(59.1%)
	House	109,257	(51.2%)	102,298	(47.9%)

[1] Election for a full six-year term.
[2] Election for the remaining four years of the term of Hubert H. Humphrey who died Jan. 13, 1978.

Demographics

Population: 509,460. **Percent Change from 1970:** 5.2%.

Land Area: 8,599 square miles. **Population per Square Mile:** 59.2.

Counties, 1980 Population: Blue Earth — 52,314; Dakota (Pt.) — 793; Dodge — 14,773; Fillmore — 21,930; Freeborn — 36,329; Goodhue (Pt.) — 37,831; Houston — 18,382; Le Sueur (Pt.) — 23,058; Mower — 40,390; Olmsted — 92,006; Rice — 46,087; Scott (Pt.) — 11,200; Steele — 30,328; Wabasha — 19,335; Waseca — 18,448; Winona — 46,256.

Cities, 1980 Population: Albert Lea — 19,200; Austin — 23,020; Faribault — 16,241; Mankato (Pt.) — 28,642; Northfield (Pt.) — 12,549; Owatonna — 18,632; Red Wing — 13,736; Rochester — 57,890; Winona — 25,075.

Race and Ancestry: White — 98.8%; Black — 0.2%; American Indian, Eskimo and Aleut — 0.2%; Asian and Pacific Islander — 0.5%. Spanish Origin — 0.7%. Dutch — 0.6%; English — 3.2%; French — 0.5%; German — 21.9%; Irish — 2.6%; Norwegian — 8.6%; Polish — 1.0%; Swedish — 1.6%.

Universities, Enrollment: Austin Community College, Austin — 893; Bethany Lutheran College, Mankato — 283; Carleton College, Northfield — 1,854; College of St. Teresa, Winona — 646; Mankato State University, Mankato — 11,424; Mayo Medical School, Rochester — 162; Minnesota Bible College, Rochester — 101; Rochester Community College, Rochester — 3,113; St. Mary's College, Winona — 1,303; St. Olaf College, Northfield — 3,047; University of Minnesota Technical College (Waseca campus), Waseca —1,123; Winona State University, Winona — 5,353.

Newspapers, Circulation: *Austin Daily Herald* (e), Austin — 10,625; *Faribault Daily News* (e), Faribault — 9,230; *Free Press* (e), Mankato — 26,579; *People's Press* (mS), Owatonna — 8,119 *Republican-Eagle* (e), Red Wing — 9,332; *Rochester Post-Bulletin* (e), Rochester — 37,766; *Tribune* (eS), Albert Lea — 10,423; *Waseca Daily Journal* (e), Waseca — 4,709; *Winona Daily News* (mS), Winona — 17,709. The *Minneapolis Star and Tribune* also circulates in the district.

Commercial Television Stations, Affiliation: KAAL, Austin (ABC); KEYC-TV, Mankato (CBS); KTTC, Rochester (NBC). District is divided among Mankato ADI, Minneapolis-St. Paul ADI, La Crosse (Wis.)-Eau Claire (Wis.) ADI and Rochester-Mason City (Iowa)-Austin ADI.

Nuclear Power Plants: Prairie Island 1, Red Wing (Westinghouse, Northern States Power), December 1973; Prairie Island 2, Red Wing (Westinghouse, Northern States Power), December 1974.

Industries:

Mayo Foundation; Rochester; medical clinic — 6,860. **International Business Machines Corp.;** Rochester; electronic computing equipment — 6,000. **George A. Hormel & Co.** (HQ); Austin; meatpacking — 3,800. **St. Mary's Hospital;** Rochester; hospital — 3,500. **Rochester Methodist Hospital;** Rochester; hospital — 1,780.

Wilson Foods Corp.; Albert Lea; meatpacking — 1,500. **Brown Printing Co. Inc.** (HQ); Waseca; commercial printing — 1,300. **E. F.**

Johnson Co. (HQ); Waseca; electronic communications equipment — 1,100. **Owatonna Tool Co.** (Command Products Div. - HQ); Owatonna; hand tools, hardware — 1,100. **The Kahler Corp.** (HQ); Rochester; hotel operations — 800. **Sheldahl Inc.;** Northfield; electronic components, plastic products — 700.

Federated Mutual Insurance Co. (HQ); Owatonna; accident, health, life insurance — 670. **Taylor Corp.** (Carlson Craft Div.); Mankato; commercial printing — 600. **Fiberite Corp.** (HQ); Winona; plastics materials — 500. **Gould Inc.** (Engine Parts Div.); Lake City; motor vehicle parts — 500. **Jostens Inc.** (Engraving Div.); Owatonna; jewelry and metal engraving — 500. **Litton Business Systems Inc.** (Streater Div.); Albert Lea; store fixtures — 500. **Pillsbury Co.** (Green Giant Co.); Le Sueur; canned, frozen vegetables — 500.

2nd District

Southwest — Willmar

The landscape of the new 2nd District is dotted for mile upon mile with silos and grain elevators, broken up occasionally by small market centers located at country crossroads. The district's largest town, Willmar, has only 15,895 residents.

Bisected by the broad Minnesota River, the sprawling 31-county district includes some of the best farm land in the state and some that is not so productive. Accordingly, the political outlook of the district's farmers tends to reflect their short-term economic well-being.

The well-to-do farmers in the south along the Iowa border enjoy bountiful harvests of corn and soybeans. Worthington, located in Nobles county, claims to be the "Turkey Capital of the World." Many voters in the southern two tiers of counties are of German ethnic stock. Like those in the adjoining 1st, they share a strong Republican tradition and an allegiance to the Farm Bureau, the most conservative of the state's three major farm organizations.

As one moves north along the Minnesota River, dairy farms become more common. The flat farm lands yield to a more rolling terrain broken up by lakes. Until one reaches the prairie counties north of the Minnesota River, the political flavor remains largely Republican.

Above the river, north of Renville and Yellow Medicine counties, the land is sandy and rocky and the politics unpredictable. Farmers here have to work harder to scratch out an existence, and they display a frequent dissatisfaction with any party that holds power.

At the turn of the century the Scandinavian settlers in this area battled constantly with the railroads, bankers and grain merchants. Disillusioned by Republicans and Democrats alike, they were ripe for third-party alternatives. The Farmer-Labor Party found early support in this region, as did presidential candidate Robert LaFollette in 1924, when his Progressive Party carried nine of the 13 counties wholly contained in the district north of the Minnesota.

Today, with strong support from the National Farmers Union, Democrats often run well in this part of the district. But the population is not large enough to overcome the more heavily Republican areas to the south and east.

The remap gave the district five new counties and most of a sixth in this northern, more Democratic region. However, the other redistricting changes were likely to strengthen Republican candidates running in the new 2nd. The group of solidly Republican counties on the Iowa border, previously split among the old 1st, 2nd and 6th districts, were divided only two ways, with the 2nd getting

five of the nine.

Running a campaign in the new 2nd District is likely to be an exhausting and expensive exercise. To reach voters via television, a candidate has to buy time not only in the Twin Cities but also in Mankato and Alexandria, Minn., and in Sioux Falls, S.D. Some might prefer to run their campaigns by mail order in the tradition of one of the district's most famous sons, R. W. Sears, who began shipping watches from Redwood in 1886 with the help of his partner, Alvah Roebuck.

Election Returns

2nd District		Democrat		Republican	
1976	President	128,804	(53.2%)	107,252	(44.3%)
	Senate	153,148	(64.2%)	67,553	(28.3%)
	House	126,527	(53.2%)	111,181	(46.8%)
1978	Governor	96,310	(43.2%)	120,934	(54.2%)
	Senate[1]	85,337	(38.4%)	131,076	(58.9%)
	Senate[2]	79,217	(36.1%)	131,438	(59.8%)
	House	103,862	(47.1%)	116,038	(52.6%)
1980	President	101,134	(39.1%)	135,287	(52.3%)
	House	120,227	(44.6%)	149,548	(55.4%)
1982	Governor	129,967	(56.5%)	97,377	(42.3%)
	Senate	96,460	(42.3%)	129,729	(57.0%)
	House	103,243	(45.5%)	123,508	(54.5%)

[1] *Election for a full six-year term.*
[2] *Election for the remaining four years of the term of Hubert H. Humphrey who died Jan. 13, 1978.*

Demographics

Population: 509,500. **Percent Change from 1970:** 2.1%.

Land Area: 18,741 square miles. **Population per Square Mile:** 27.2.

Counties, 1980 Population: Big Stone — 7,716; Brown — 28,645; Chippewa — 14,941; Cottonwood — 14,854; Douglas — 27,839; Faribault — 19,714; Grant (Pt.) — 6,435; Jackson — 13,690; Kandiyohi — 36,763; Lac Qui Parle — 10,592; Le Sueur (Pt.) — 376; Lincoln — 8,207; Lyon — 25,207; Martin — 24,687; McLeod — 29,657; Meeker — 20,594; Murray — 11,507; Nicollet — 26,929; Nobles — 21,840; Pipestone — 11,690; Pope — 11,657; Redwood — 19,341; Renville — 20,401; Rock — 10,703; Sibley — 15,448; Stevens — 11,322; Swift — 12,920; Traverse — 5,542; Watonwan — 12,361; Wright (Pt.) — 14,269; Yellow Medicine — 13,653.

Cities, 1980 Population: Fairmont — 11,506; Mankato (Pt.) — 9; Marshall — 11,161; New Ulm — 13,755; Willmar — 15,895; Worthington — 10,243.

Race and Ancestry: White — 99.2%; Black — 0.1%; American Indian, Eskimo and Aleut — 0.2%; Asian and Pacific Islander — 0.4%. Spanish Origin — 0.5%. Dutch — 2.1%; English — 2.1%; German — 29.4%; Irish — 1.4%; Norwegian — 8.1%; Polish — 0.7%; Swedish — 3.4%.

Universities, Enrollment: Alexandria Area Technical Institute, Alexandria — 1,279; Dr. Martin Luther College, New Ulm — 808; Gustavus Adolphus College, St. Peter — 2,315; Southwest State University, Marshall — 2,131; University of Minnesota (Morris campus) Morris — 1,624; Willmar Community College, Willmar — 868; Worthington Community College, Worthington — 657.

Newspapers, Circulation: *Independent* (m), Marshall — 8,212; *The Journal* (m), New Ulm — 11,129; *Sentinel* (m), Fairmont — 12,290; *West Central Tribune* (e), Willmar — 16,779; *Worthington Daily Globe* (e), Worthington — 17,757. The Mankato *Free Press* and *Minneapolis Star and Tribune* also circulate in the district.

Commercial Television Stations, Affiliation: KCMT, Alexandria (NBC, ABC). District is divided among Alexandria ADI, Mankato ADI, Minneapolis-St. Paul ADI, Fargo (N.D.) ADI, Rochester-Mason City (Iowa)-Austin ADI and Sioux Falls (S.D.)-Mitchell (S.D.) ADI.

Industries:

Minnesota Mining & Mfg. Co.; Hutchinson; electronic components — 2,000. Campbell Soup Co. Inc.; Worthington; poultry processing — 825. Minnesota Mining & Mfg. Co. (Electro Products Div.); New Ulm; electronic components — 700. Schwans Sales Enterprises Inc. (HQ); Marshall; frozen specialties — 650. Kraftco Corp. (Kraft Foods); New Ulm; cheese processing — 600. Magnetic Peripherals Inc.; Redwood Falls; electronic computing equipment — 600.

Harsco Corp. (Fairmont Railway Motors Div.); Fairmont; hydraulic tools — 580. Minnesota Mining & Mfg. Co.; New Ulm; photographic equipment and supplies — 575. Stokely-Van Camp Inc.; Fairmont; frozen, canned fruits, vegetables — 550. Jennie-O-Foods Inc. (HQ); Willmar; turkey processing plant — 500. The Toro Co. Inc.; Windom; lawn mowers — 500.

3rd District

Southern and Western Twin Cities Suburbs

As affluent suburban voters have moved farther and farther from the Twin Cities, the 3rd District has doggedly followed them. Once confined only to the inner core of Minneapolis suburbs within Hennepin County, the 3rd now ranges into five counties, reaching the western and southern extremities of the metropolitan area. Although western Carver County and southern Dakota County still appear largely rural, they are among the fastest growing parts of the state and likely will be suburbanized by the end of the 1980s.

In all, 42 percent of the voters in the new 3rd District were not residents of the old 3rd District at the time of the 1980 census. However, many of those living in the newly added part of the district have only recently moved out from closer-in portions removed by the remap, and, for that reason, the district was expected to continue to support its moderate Republican incumbent.

The heart of the district remains the upper-class suburbs just west of Minneapolis, such as Edina, St. Louis Park and Golden Valley. No fewer than nine golf courses service the white-collar professionals in these three suburbs alone. Many of these weekend golfers spend their weekdays working for high-technology firms such as Control Data and Honeywell, which are headquartered in the Twin Cities area. The Republican vote here and in Minnetonka, just to the west, is overwhelming. In some precincts the Carter-Mondale team drew less than 25 percent in 1980.

Bloomington, the district's largest suburb and the state's fourth largest city, was divided in the remap between the 3rd and 5th districts. The 3rd District part, west of Interstate 35W, contains about 70 percent of the city's 82,000 residents and is considerably more Republican than the eastern portion.

In addition to losing part of Bloomington, the district lost neighboring Richfield, an older, less affluent suburb that votes Democratic. Also removed were four suburbs to the north, where the voters often split their tickets but remained loyal to the Republican incumbent.

The 3rd District's quest for new suburban voters extended in three directions — everywhere but north. The major addition was to the east in the less Democratic lower reaches of Dakota County south of St. Paul. Nearly 145,000 people live in the 3rd District portion of Dakota County, the fastest growing part of the district.

The Dakota County voters placed in the newly drawn 3rd narrowly went for Ronald Reagan in 1980, while those moved to the 4th backed Jimmy Carter. In 1978 the county as a whole broke with its past allegiance to the Democrats and supported Republicans in all but two of the seven statewide partisan contests.

Election Returns

3rd District		Democrat		Republican	
1976	President	105,384	(45.0%)	122,673	(52.4%)
	Senate	144,466	(62.3%)	69,601	(30.0%)
	House	69,355	(31.6%)	145,858	(66.4%)
1978	Governor	81,323	(39.3%)	124,060	(60.0%)
	Senate[1]	71,042	(35.0%)	130,095	(64.1%)
	Senate[2]	42,562	(21.9%)	147,843	(76.1%)
	House	62,905	(31.1%)	139,024	(68.7%)
1980	President	122,756	(40.7%)	141,887	(47.0%)
	House	71,076	(27.6%)	186,325	(72.4%)
1982	Governor	113,322	(47.0%)	124,029	(51.5%)
	Senate	85,909	(35.4%)	154,547	(63.8%)
	House	60,993	(26.4%)	166,891	(72.1%)

[1] Election for a full six-year term.
[2] Election for the remaining four years of the term of Hubert H. Humphrey who died Jan. 13, 1978.

Demographics

Population: 509,499. Percent Change from 1970: 25.3%.

Land Area: 1,213 square miles. Population per Square Mile: 420.0.

Counties, 1980 Population: Carver — 37,046; Dakota (Pt.) — 143,684; Goodhue (Pt.) — 918; Hennepin (Pt.) — 295,267; Scott (Pt.) — 32,584.

Cities, 1980 Population: Apple Valley — 21,818; Bloomington (Pt.) — 57,821; Burnsville — 35,674; Crystal (Pt.) — 256; Eagan — 20,700; Eden Prairie — 16,263; Edina — 46,073; Golden Valley — 22,775; Hastings (Pt.) — 12,811; Hopkins — 15,336; Inver Grove Heights (Pt.) — 14,629; Lakeville — 14,790; Minnetonka — 38,683; New Hope — 23,087; Northfield (Pt.) — 13; Plymouth — 31,615; South St. Paul (Pt.) — 770; St. Louis Park — 42,931.

Race and Ancestry: White — 97.9%; Black — 0.6%; American Indian, Eskimo and Aleut — 0.2%; Asian and Pacific Islander — 1.0%. Spanish Origin — 0.6%. Dutch — 0.5%; English — 3.4%; French — 0.7%; German — 15.8%; Irish — 2.8%; Norwegian — 4.7%; Polish — 1.0%; Russian — 0.9%; Swedish — 3.5%.

Universities, Enrollment: Golden Valley Lutheran College, Golden Valley — 590; Inver Hills Community College, Inver Grove Heights — 3,785; Normandale Community College, Bloomington — 4,953; Northwest Technical Institute, St. Louis Park — 46; St. Paul Bible College, Bible College — 661.

Newspapers, Circulation: The Minneapolis Star and Tribune circulates in the district.

Commercial Television Stations, Affiliation: KMSP-TV, Edina (None); WTCN-TV, Golden Valley (NBC). Entire district is located in Minneapolis-St. Paul ADI.

Industries:

Honeywell Inc. (Defense Systems Div.); Hopkins; munitions — 4,500. Sperry Corp. (Defense Systems Div. - HQ); Eagan; administrative offices — 3,300. Prudential Insurance Co. of America (North Central Home Office); Minneapolis; life insurance — 2,100.

Rosemount Inc. (HQ); Hopkins; temperature controls — 2,100. **Methodist Hospital;** St. Louis Park; hospital — 2,000. **Litton Systems Inc.;** Plymouth; administrative offices — 1,800.

General Mills Inc. (HQ); Golden Valley; cereals — 1,550. **Honeywell Inc.** (Residential Div.); Hopkins; electronic communications equipment — 1,500. **Northern Telecom Inc.** (Electronic Office Systems); Minnetonka; computing equipment — 1,400. **Safco Products Co.;** New Hope; paper products wholesaling — 1,100. **National Car Rental Systems** (HQ); Edina; auto, truck rental — 1,000. **Gelco Corp.** (HQ); Eden Prairie; truck leasing — 950. **Lieberman Enterprises Inc.;** Bloomington; phonograph record wholesaling — 900. **Tennant Co.** (HQ); Minneapolis; service industry machinery — 856. **Liberty Diversified Industries;** Plymouth; corrugated boxes, plastics products — 850. **Smead Mfg. Co.** (HQ); Hastings; paper, paperboard products — 850. **Continental Machines Inc.;** Savage; machine tools — 765. **Eaton Corp.** (Fluid Power Operations); Eden Prairie; motor vehicle parts — 750.

MTS Systems Corp. (HQ); Hopkins; laboratory equipment — 720. **Magnetic Controls Co.** (HQ); Bloomington; electricity testing equipment — 720. **Donaldson Co. Inc.** (HQ); Bloomington; air filters — 700. **Nortronics Co. Inc.** (Recorder Care Div. - HQ); Golden Valley; magnetic recording equipment — 700. **Pinkerton's Inc.;** Edina; protection services — 700. **B. Dalton Co.** (HQ); Edina; bookstore chain — 668. **M. A. Mortenson Co.;** Golden Valley; general contracting — 600. **American Family Mutual Insurance Co.;** Eden Prairie; life insurance — 550. **Pepsi-Cola Bottling Co. of Minneapolis-St. Paul;** Burnsville; soft drink bottling — 530. **CPT Corp.** (HQ); Eden Prarie; word processing equipment — 500. **Carlson Marketing Group Inc.** (HQ); Plymouth; marketing services — 500. **Erickson Petroleum Corp.;** Bloomington; petroleum wholesaling — 500. **Pickwick International Inc.** (HQ); St. Louis Park; phonograph records — 500.

4th District

St. Paul and Suburbs

St. Paul is a Democratic city with a German- and Irish-Catholic population and a strong labor tradition that developed in the days when it was a major port and railroading hub. In every aspect except its Democratic loyalties, it differs from its supposed twin, Minneapolis.

The working-class neighborhoods on St. Paul's East Side are solidly Democratic. These precincts have routinely supported every major statewide Democratic candidate of recent years except one — 1978 Senate nominee Robert Short, whom they deserted in favor of Republican David Durenberger.

West of Lexington Parkway, where the houses and the spaces between them are larger, Republicans usually do slightly better, but only occasionally do they prevail. Various colleges and the University of Minnesota's School of Agriculture give this area a young and culturally vibrant quality that is missing elsewhere in the 4th District.

In the 1950s when Eugene J. McCarthy represented St. Paul in the U.S. House, nearly 90 percent of the 4th District vote came from the city. But with the growth of the suburbs and a decline in St. Paul's population from its 1960 peak of 313,000 to 270,000 in 1980, St. Paul made up just half the redrawn district.

Most of the suburban vote lies north of the city in Ramsey County. There nearly 190,000 people live in a collection of prefabricated postwar suburbs that tend to be about 10 percent less Democratic than St. Paul.

Slightly more that 50,000 people were added to the district in a modest redistricting change that was likely to benefit the already secure incumbent. The northern communities of Dakota County — South St. Paul, West St.

Paul and Mendota Heights — were added to bring the district up to the ideal population.

St. Paul serves as headquarters for several large companies, including 3-M and American Hoist and Derrick. South St. Paul, a well-worn community of 20,000, is known for its stockyards. West St. Paul is not quite as Democratic as South St. Paul, but still supported the Carter-Mondale ticket in 1980 by a convincing margin.

Mendota Heights, the smallest of the three newly added suburbs, is the only one that votes Republican.

Election Returns

4th District		Democrat		Republican	
1976	President	148,298	(58.4%)	97,026	(38.2%)
	Senate	172,478	(70.3%)	54,306	(22.1%)
	House	143,096	(63.9%)	73,397	(32.8%)
1978	Governor	87,857	(44.3%)	108,756	(54.8%)
	Senate[1]	81,706	(42.2%)	109,231	(56.5%)
	Senate[2]	57,878	(30.6%)	125,835	(66.6%)
	House	104,572	(56.7%)	79,744	(43.2%)
1980	President	137,337	(53.3%)	88,633	(34.4%)
	House	127,004	(56.6%)	95,448	(42.5%)
1982	Governor	132,664	(59.9%)	85,117	(38.5%)
	Senate	113,687	(50.4%)	109,412	(48.5%)
	House	153,494	(73.2%)	56,248	(26.8%)

[1] *Election for a full six-year term.*
[2] *Election for the remaining four years of the term of Hubert H. Humphrey who died Jan. 13, 1978.*

Demographics

Population: 509,532. **Percent Change from 1970:** -3.4%.

Land Area: 181 square miles. **Population per Square Mile:** 2,815.1.

Counties, 1980 Population: Dakota (Pt.) — 49,802; Ramsey (Pt.) — 457,422; Washington (Pt.) — 2,308.

Cities, 1980 Population: Blaine (Pt.) — 0; Inver Grove Heights (Pt.) — 2,542; Maplewood — 26,990; Mounds View — 12,593; New Brighton — 23,269; North St. Paul — 11,921; Roseville — 35,820; Shoreview — 17,300; South St. Paul (Pt.) — 20,465; St. Paul — 270,230; West St. Paul — 18,527; White Bear Lake (Pt.) — 22,528.

Race and Ancestry: White — 93.4%; Black — 2.9%; American Indian, Eskimo and Aleut — 0.6%; Asian and Pacific Islander — 1.6%. Spanish Origin — 2.0%. English — 2.5%; French — 1.1%; German — 13.6%; Irish — 3.5%; Italian — 1.1%; Norwegian — 3.1%; Polish — 1.7%; Russian — 0.5%; Swedish — 3.6%.

Universities, Enrollment: Bethel College, St. Paul — 2,055; Bethel Theological Seminary, St. Paul — 461; College of St. Catherine, St. Paul — 2,387; College of St. Thomas, St. Paul — 5,281; Concordia College, St. Paul — 700; Hamline University, St. Paul — 1,802; Lakewood Community College, White Bear Lake — 3,809; Luther/Northwestern Theological Seminaries, St. Paul — 880; Macalester College, St. Paul — 1,728; Metropolitan State University, St. Paul — 2,146 Northwestern College, Roseville — 825; Northwestern College of Chiropractic, St. Paul — 410; St. Paul Seminary, St. Paul — 107; School of the Associated Arts, St. Paul — 104; United Theological Seminary of the Twin Cities, New Brighton — 192; William Mitchell College of Law, St. Paul — 1,157.

Newspapers, Circulation: *St. Paul Dispatch* (e), St. Paul — 115,218; *St. Paul Pioneer Press* (mS), St. Paul — 101,250. *Minneapolis Star and Tribune* also circulates in the district.

Commercial Television Stations, Affiliation: KSTP-TV, St. Paul (ABC). Entire district is located in Minneapolis-St. Paul ADI.

Minneapolis - St. Paul Area

Industries:

Minnesota Mining & Mfg. Co. (HQ); St. Paul; abrasives; adhesives; recording and photographic materials; tape — 11,600. **Sperry Corp.** Roseville; computers — 5,000. **United Hospitals Inc.**; St. Paul; hospital — 2,500. **American Hoist & Derrick Co.** (HQ); St. Paul; cranes, hoists — 1,800. **Whirlpool Corp.**; St. Paul; appliances — 1,800.

Ford Motor Co. (Twin City Assembly Plant); St. Paul; truck assembly — 1,750. **Sperry Corp.**; St. Paul; computers — 1,600. **Honeywell Inc.** (Defense System Div.); St. Paul; munitions — 1,500. **West Publishing Co.** (HQ); St. Paul; law book publishing — 1,460. **St. Joseph's Hospital Inc.**; St. Paul; hospital — 1,400. **St. John's Lutheran Hospital Assn.**; St. Paul; hospital — 1,350. **St. Paul Companies Inc.** (HQ); St. Paul; insurance holding company — 1,270. **Brown & Bigelow Inc.**; St. Paul; calendars — 1,090. **Burlington Northern Inc.** (HQ); St. Paul; railroad operations, lumber mills — 1,000. **Economics Laboratory Inc.** (Klenzade Div. - HQ); St. Paul; cleaners — 1,000. **State Farm Mutual Insurance Co.**; St. Paul; accident insurance —

1,000. **Marsden Building Maintenance Co.**; St. Paul; janitorial services — 950.

Champion International Corp. (Packaging Div.); St. Paul; paperboard — 900. **Control Data Corp.**; St. Paul; computers — 900. **Northwest Publications Inc.** (HQ); St. Paul; newspaper publishing — 900. **Paper Calmenson & Co.** (Pacal Steel - HQ); St. Paul; metal work — 900. **First National Bank of St. Paul**; St. Paul; banking — 871. **Cardiac Pacemakers Inc.** (HQ); St. Paul; pacemakers — 850. **The Gillette Co. Inc.** (St. Paul Mfg. Div.); St. Paul; toiletries — 850. **NCR Comten Inc.** (Comress Div. - HQ); St. Paul; computer equipment — 850. **Mutual Service Life Insurance Co.** (HQ); St. Paul; life, accident insurance — 837. **Olympia Brewing Co.** (Theodore Hamm Co.); St. Paul; brewery — 800. **Farmers Union Central Exchange** (HQ); St. Paul; farm supply wholesaling — 750. **Land O' Lakes Inc.** (Bridgeman Div. - HQ); St. Paul; meatpacking, dairy products — 750. **Mutual Service Casualty Insurance Co.** (HQ); St. Paul; casualty insurance — 750.

Minnesota Mutual Life Insurance Co. (HQ); St. Paul; life insurance — 739. **The Webb Co.** (HQ); St. Paul; publishing, printing — 700. **Harris-Stewart Companies Inc.** (Harris Mechanical Contracting - HQ); St. Paul; mechanical contractors — 600. **Control Data Corp.** (Syntonic Technology); St. Paul; radio maintenance — 600. **Farmers Union Grain Terminal Assn.** (Amber Milling Div. - HQ); St. Paul; grain milling, marketing — 570. **American Security Corp.**; St. Paul; security services — 500. **Buckbee-Mears Co.** (Beissil Div.); St. Paul; printing, photoengraving — 500. **Chicago & North Western Transportation Co.** (Northwest Chemco); St. Paul; rail terminal operations — 500. **First Computer Corp.** (HQ); St. Paul; data processing services — 500. **Gould Inc.**; St. Paul; storage batteries — 500. **Murphy Motor Freight Lines Inc.** (HQ); St. Paul; trucking — 500. **Pearson Candy Co.**; St. Paul; candy — 500. **Farmers Union Central Exchange;** Inver Grove Heights; farm supply wholesaling — more than 500.

5th District

Minneapolis and Suburbs

This is one of the few districts in the country where candidates are not afraid to refer to themselves as liberals. Minneapolis residents account for nearly three-fourths of the district's voters, and except for those on the city's southwest side, they predictably choose liberal candidates over conservatives.

Minneapolis, with its large Scandinavian population, saw early prosperity as a wheat-milling center. Although many of the flour mills that once lined the Mississippi River at St. Anthony's Falls have moved away, the milling companies that settled in Minneapolis have remained and diversified. They are major employers in the Twin Cities, along with the new "brain power" firms that find Minneapolis ideally suited to their needs.

Honeywell and Control Data have their worldwide headquarters in Minneapolis; the headquarters for 3M is in St. Paul, just over the river. The highly skilled, white-collar professionals who have been attracted by these "clean" industries help to give the city a clean-cut image that is reflected in the glistening towers of its new downtown area.

But Minneapolis is not just parks, lakes, glass and chrome. Northwest of the elegant downtown office towers are some poor neighborhoods. The city's Chippewa Indian population lives Southeast of downtown. East of the Mississippi River are older, more traditional blue-collar areas adjoining the main campus of the University of Minnesota. Although the city gives off an aura of prosperity and growth, the population is declining at a swift pace. Having peaked in 1950 at 522,000 inhabitants, Minneapolis was down to 371,000 in 1980.

To make up for the declining population, the boundaries of the 5th District were expanded slightly. The southern border, which formerly coincided with the Minneapolis city limits, was extended to include about 60,000 people in Richfield and the eastern portion of Bloomington. Although the southern addition is not as Democratic as Minneapolis, the map was drawn to keep the most Republican parts of Bloomington in the 3rd District.

On the northern side of the district, three solidly Democratic suburbs from Anoka County were removed, and three larger communities in Hennepin County added. Robbinsdale, Brooklyn Center and Crystal are not quite as Democratic as the rest of the district, but Democrats should have little trouble carrying them. In 1982 Hubert H. "Skip" Humphrey III represented much of that area as a Democrat in the Minnesota Senate.

Election Returns

5th District		Democrat		Republican	
1976	President	161,266	(60.9%)	94,618	(35.7%)
	Senate	181,265	(72.2%)	52,603	(21.0%)
	House	147,283	(64.0%)	76,137	(33.1%)
1978	Governor	106,710	(54.5%)	86,884	(44.3%)
	Senate[1]	97,266	(50.1%)	94,293	(48.6%)
	Senate[2]	57,575	(29.6%)	131,019	(67.3%)
	House	103,074	(57.4%)	76,629	(42.6%)
1980	President	163,443	(59.6%)	77,062	(28.1%)
	House	128,432	(60.5%)	78,110	(36.8%)
1982	Governor	142,375	(63.4%)	78,871	(35.1%)
	Senate	124,587	(54.9%)	100,411	(44.3%)
	House	136,634	(65.5%)	61,184	(29.4%)

[1] *Election for a full six-year term.*
[2] *Election for the remaining four years of the term of Hubert H. Humphrey who died Jan. 13, 1978.*

Demographics

Population: 509,506. **Percent Change from 1970:** -15.3%.

Land Area: 89 square miles. **Population per Square Mile:** 5,724.8.

Counties, 1980 Population: Hennepin (Pt.) — 509,506.

Cities, 1980 Population: Bloomington (Pt.) — 24,010; Brooklyn Center — 31,230; Crystal (Pt.) — 25,287; Minneapolis — 370,951; Richfield — 37,851; Robbinsdale — 14,422.

Race and Ancestry: White — 90.0%; Black — 5.8%; American Indian, Eskimo and Aleut — 1.9%; Asian and Pacific Islander — 1.4%. Spanish Origin — 1.1%. English — 3.0%; French — 0.9%; German — 10.1%; Irish — 2.8%; Italian — 0.6%; Norwegian — 6.0%; Polish — 2.0%; Russian — 0.5%; Swedish — 5.5%.

Universities, Enrollment: Augsburg College, Minneapolis — 1,501; Brown Institute, Minneapolis — 940; Medical Institute of Minnesota, Minneapolis — 206; Minneapolis College of Art and Design, Minneapolis — 579; Minneapolis Community College, Minneapolis — 3,003; North Central Bible College, Minneapolis — 701; Northwestern Electronics Institute, Minneapolis — 712; St. Mary's Junior College, Minneapolis — 730; University of Minnesota, Minneapolis — 65,678.

Newspapers, Circulation: *Minneapolis Star and Tribune* (all day, S), Minneapolis — 362,015.

Commercial Television Stations, Affiliation: KTMA-TV, Minneapolis (None); WCCO-TV, Minneapolis (CBS). Entire district is located in Minneapolis-St. Paul ADI.

Military Installations: Minneapolis-St. Paul International Airport (Air Force), Minneapolis — 2,145.

Industries:

Fairview Community Hospitals; Minneapolis; hospital — 4,200. **Northwest Airlines Inc.** (Northwest Orient Airlines - HQ); Minneapolis; commercial airline — 4,000. **Abbott Hospital;** Minneapolis; hospital — 3,200. **Republic Airlines Inc.** (HQ); Minneapolis; commercial airline — 3,070. **Corroon & Black of Minnesota;** Minneapolis; casualty, life insurance, surety company — 2,800.

Control Data Corp. (HQ); Minneapolis; computers — 2,500. **Veterans Administration;** Minneapolis; veterans' hospital — 2,500. **Metropolitan Medical Center;** Minneapolis; hospital — 2,200. **North Memorial Medical Center;** Minneapolis; hospital — 2,100. **Honeywell Inc.** (HQ); Minneapolis; electronic computing equipment — 2,000. **The Pillsbury Co.** (HQ); Minneapolis; prepared baking mixes; canned, frozen vegetables — 2,000. **Investors Diversified Services** (HQ); Minneapolis; investment company — 1,580. **First National Bank of Minnesota** (HQ); Minneapolis; banking — 1,500. **Honeywell Inc.** (Avionics Div.); Minneapolis; electronic communications equipment — 1,500. **Northwestern National Bank of Minneapolis** (HQ); Minneapolis; banking — 1,500. **Inter-Regional Financial Group;** Minneapolis; investment banking — 1,450.

St. Mary's Hospital; Minneapolis; hospital — 1,400. **Graco Inc.** (HQ); Minneapolis; pumps — 1,200. **Federal Reserve Bank of Minnesota** (HQ); Minneapolis; banking — 1,140. **Shamrock Industries Inc.;** Minneapolis; plastic products — 1,100. **Thermo King Corp.** (HQ); Minneapolis; commercial refrigeration equipment — 1,000. **Northwestern National Life Insurance** (HQ); Minneapolis; life, health insurance — 995. **Bureau of Engraving Inc.** (HQ); Minneapolis; electronic components, commercial printing — 900. **The Toro Co. Inc.** (HQ); Minneapolis; lawn mowers — 875. **Allied Central Stores Inc.** (HQ); Minneapolis; department stores — 820. **International Multifoods Corp.** (HQ); Minneapolis; flour, animal feed — 680. **Moore Business Forms Inc.** (International Graphics Corp.); Minneapolis; commercial printing — 600. **Piper Jaffray Inc.** (HQ); Minneapolis; securities brokerage — 595.

United Air Lines Inc.; Minneapolis; commercial airline — 590 **Ellerbe Inc.** (HQ); Minneapolis; architectural services — 570. **Gresen Mfg. Co.** (HQ); Minneapolis; hydraulic industrial machinery — 559. **Hayes Contractors Inc.** (Lamb Plumbing & Heating); Minneapolis; mechanical contracting — 550. **Hitchcock Industries Inc.** (Texas Foundry Div. - HQ); Minneapolis; non-ferrous foundry — 550. **Twin City Federal Savings & Loan Assn.** (HQ); Minneapolis; savings and loan association — 550. **Knutson Construction Co.;** Minneapolis; general contracting — 500. **Kraus-Anderson Construction Co.;** Minneapolis; commercial construction — 500. **Peavey Co.** (HQ); Minneapolis; flour, animal feed — 500.

6th District

Northern and Eastern Twin Cities Suburbs

Even though Minnesota did not gain any new districts through reapportionment, the 6th is essentially a brand new constituency. Made up of one entire county (Anoka) and parts of five others, the new 6th includes voters from all but two of the state's eight old districts. The 6th sits atop the Twin Cities like a magnet, collecting nearly all of the suburban fringe areas on the north, east and west, as well as some rural farm land just beyond the most distant suburbs.

Unlike the more conservative southern suburbs in the 3rd District, the new turf in the 6th includes many marginally Democratic areas and a few hard-core Democratic strongholds. It was these votes that helped a Democratic challenger win the House seat in 1982 over the Republican incumbent who moved into the district after his home was placed in a district represented by an unbeatable Democrat.

The only part of the new 6th the Republican had represented previously was Washington County, wedged on the eastern side of the district between St. Paul and the St. Croix River. Fewer than a quarter of the district's voters live in Washington County. The old 1st extended south from Washington County into conservative rural territory. The new 6th moves north and west from Washington into much more Democratic areas.

Anoka County, with nearly 200,000 people, is likely to become the power base of the district. It is also the district's strongest Democratic area. In 1980 Jimmy Carter easily outpolled Ronald Reagan in Anoka, 52-38 percent. Even in the Democrats' 1978 statewide debacle, in which Republicans took both U.S. Senate seats and the governorship, Democratic Gov. Rudy Perpich and most of his ticket carried Anoka County.

Representing nearly 40 percent of the district's popu-

lation, Anoka is a mix of new suburbs, farms and small towns. Lake Wobegon, the mythical sleepy town in Garrison Keilor's weekly radio program, "A Prairie Home Companion," is modeled after Keilor's boyhood home in Anoka County. But the Lake Wobegons of this part of Minnesota are quickly disappearing as the Twin Cities metropolitan area continues to expand into the rolling countryside of the surrounding counties.

Changing even more rapidly than Anoka are Wright and Sherburne counties, the two largest growth areas in the state during the 1970s. Both are Democratic and willing to support liberals although they gave only tepid support to Carter in 1980.

The only portion of the new district that supported Reagan in 1980 was the northwest quarter of Hennepin County. This includes the affluent area around Lake Minnetonka, which came from the old 2nd District and is among the most reliably Republican parts of the state. In the portions of northwest Hennepin closest to Anoka County, such as Brooklyn Park and Osseo, the voters often split their tickets, telling pollsters they "vote for the man, not the party."

Election Returns

6th District		Democrat		Republican	
1976	President	85,390	(53.4%)	70,450	(44.0%)
	Senate	107,438	(67.4%)	38,281	(24.0%)
	House	76,888	(51.6%)	72,027	(48.4%)
1978	Governor	51,464	(40.4%)	66,040	(51.9%)
	Senate[1]	46,388	(36.2%)	68,303	(53.3%)
	Senate[2]	37,235	(29.4%)	76,132	(60.1%)
	House	56,340	(48.9%)	58,470	(50.7%)
1980	President	73,786	(46.0%)	68,292	(42.6%)
	House	63,644	(42.1%)	87,481	(57.9%)
1982	Governor	121,034	(57.2%)	87,696	(41.5%)
	Senate	97,308	(45.6%)	114,612	(53.7%)
	House	109,246	(50.8%)	105,734	(49.2%)

[1] *Election for a full six-year term.*
[2] *Election for the remaining four years of the term of Hubert H. Humphrey who died Jan. 13, 1978.*

Demographics

Population: 509,446. **Percent Change from 1970:** 38.8%.

Land Area: 1,788 square miles. **Population per Square Mile:** 284.9.

Counties, 1980 Population: Anoka — 195,998; Hennepin (Pt.) — 136,638; Ramsey (Pt.) — 2,362; Sherburne (Pt.) — 18,773; Washington (Pt.) — 111,263; Wright (Pt.) — 44,412.

Cities, 1980 Population: Anoka — 15,634; Blaine (Pt.) — 28,558; Brooklyn Park — 43,332; Columbia Heights — 20,029; Coon Rapids — 35,826; Cottage Grove — 18,994; Fridley — 30,228; Hastings (Pt.) — 16; Maple Grove — 20,525; Oakdale — 12,123; Ramsey — 10,093; Stillwater — 12,290; White Bear Lake (Pt.) — 10; Woodbury — 10,297.

Race and Ancestry: White — 98.1%; Black — 0.4%; American Indian, Eskimo and Aleut — 0.4%; Asian and Pacific Islander — 0.7%. Spanish Origin — 0.7%. English — 2.5%; French — 1.1%; German — 14.1%; Irish — 1.9%; Norwegian — 4.0%; Polish — 1.7%; Swedish — 3.8%.

Universities, Enrollment: Anoka-Ramsey Community College, Coon Rapids — 3,858; North Hennepin Community College, Brooklyn Park — 4,101.

Newspapers, Circulation: *Stillwater Gazette* (e), Stillwater — 5,119. The *Minneapolis Star and Tribune, St. Paul Dispatch* and *St. Paul Pioneer Press* also circulate in the district.

Commercial Television Stations, Affiliation: WFBT-TV, Brooklyn Park (None). Entire district is located in Minneapolis-St. Paul ADI.

Military Installations: Twin Cities Army Ammunition Plant, New Brighton — 188.

Nuclear Power Plants: Monticello, Monticello (General Electric, Bechtel), June 1971.

Industries:

FMC Corp. (Northern Ordnance Div.); Fridley; ordnance equipment — 3,820. **Andersen Corp.;** Bayport; wood and metal millwork — 2,500. **Federal Cartridge Corp.** (Hoffman Engineering Co. Div.); Anoka; small arms ammunition — 2,500. **Medtronic Inc.;** Fridley; pacemakers — 2,500. **Onan Corp.** (HQ); Fridley; generators — 1,710.

The Cornelius Co.; Anoka; refrigeration equipment — 1,000. **Health Central Inc.;** Anoka; hospital — 750. **Advance Machine Co.** (HQ); Spring Park; service industry machines — 725. **Cea-Carter-Day Co. Inc.** (HQ); Fridley; dust control equipment — 550. **Ball Corp.** (Ball Electronic Display); Circle Pines; closed circuit television equipment — 500. **Consolidated Freightways Corp.;** Blaine; trucking — 500. **Minneapolis Electric Steel Castings Co.;** Robbinsdale; steel castings — 500.

7th District

Northwest — St. Cloud, Moorhead

From the prairie wheat fields along the Red River of the North to the hills, forests and lakes in the middle of the state, this is Minnesota's most marginal district — both politically and economically.

The farmers struggle each year to meet their high operating costs on land that does not match the quality of the soil to the south. Those living in the chilly central section try to eke out a living almost any way they can. A few dollars can usually be made from the sportsmen who hunt and fish in the region, and there is some money in the region's lumber business, which once was an economic mainstay but now is in decline. The snowmobile industry, a more recent economic boon to the area, was hurt by the recession and several dry winters and has been slow to recover. In 1982 the per-capita income in the 7th District was the lowest in the state.

Politically the district has been in the marginal category ever since popular Democrat Rep. Bob Bergland left in 1977 to become agriculture secretary in the Carter administration. Bergland's successor, a Republican, won reelection twice with just 53 percent of the vote. Changes made by the remap made the district even more marginal; the incumbent was returned to office in 1982 with just slightly more than 50 percent of the vote.

The 7th retained two of the GOP's strongest areas — Clay and Otter Tail counties in the center of the district. But three counties on the eastern side of the district and six on the south were removed, taking with them more than 150,000 people. In exchange, 141,000 people were added from Stearns, Benton and part of Sherburne counties. Stearns and Benton gave Ronald Reagan small margins in 1980; Sherburne voted for Jimmy Carter.

St. Cloud, the seat of Stearns County with 43,000 residents, replaced Moorhead, with 30,000, as the district's largest city. For years a major center for granite quarrying,

St. Cloud attracted a diverse ethnic population that German Catholics dominated. In the early 1980s the descendants of the old stone cutters shared their ancestors' support of the Democratic Party on economic issues, but they often strayed to the GOP when social issues, especially abortion, become paramount.

Apart from St. Cloud and Moorhead, there are few population centers in the district. The wheat-growing central sections of the district are slightly more populous than the rest, and also more Republican. Farther north, near the Canadian border, the land supports fewer people, and the vote is usually Democratic. Red Lake County, situated between the Red Lake and White Earth Indian reservations, is one of only two counties in the state that voted Democratic in 1978 for both Senate candidates and for governor.

Election Returns

7th District		Democrat		Republican	
1976	President	140,207	(54.1%)	109,051	(42.0%)
	Senate	165,907	(64.3%)	68,050	(26.4%)
	House	171,725	(67.4%)	79,897	(31.4%)
1978	Governor	87,327	(44.9%)	100,142	(51.4%)
	Senate[1]	74,863	(37.8%)	116,108	(58.6%)
	Senate[2]	79,139	(40.2%)	108,204	(54.9%)
	House	87,832	(45.1%)	102,952	(52.9%)
1980	President	103,081	(41.5%)	123,905	(49.9%)
	House	117,757	(47.4%)	130,705	(52.6%)
1982	Governor	123,277	(59.4%)	81,396	(39.2%)
	Senate	92,069	(42.5%)	123,000	(56.7%)
	House	107,062	(49.7%)	108,254	(50.3%)

[1] *Election for a full six-year term.*
[2] *Election for the remaining four years of the term of Hubert H. Humphrey who died Jan. 13, 1978.*

Demographics

Population: 509,521. **Percent Change from 1970:** 10.8%.

Land Area: 24,259 square miles. **Population per Square Mile:** 21.0.

Counties, 1980 Population: Becker — 29,336; Beltrami (Pt.) — 30,561; Benton — 25,187; Clay — 49,327; Clearwater — 8,761; Grant (Pt.) — 736; Hubbard (Pt.) — 14,000; Kittson — 6,672; Lake of the Woods — 3,764; Mahnomen — 5,535; Marshall — 13,027; Morrison — 29,311; Norman — 9,379; Otter Tail — 51,937; Pennington — 15,258; Polk — 34,844; Red Lake — 5,471; Roseau — 12,574; Sherburne (Pt.) — 8,043; Stearns — 108,161; Todd — 24,991; Wadena — 14,192; Wilkin — 8,454.

Cities, 1980 Population: Bemidji — 10,949; Fergus Falls — 12,519; Moorhead — 29,998; St. Cloud — 42,566.

Race and Ancestry: White — 97.6%; Black — 0.1%; American Indian, Eskimo and Aleut — 1.7%; Asian and Pacific Islander — 0.3%. Spanish Origin — 0.5%. English — 2.0%; French — 1.3%; German — 22.9%; Irish — 1.6%; Norwegian — 12.4%; Polish — 2.5%; Swedish — 3.2%.

Universities, Enrollment: Bemidji State University, Bemidji — 5,609; College of St. Benedict, St. Joseph — 2,177; Concordia College, Moorhead — 2,625; Fergus Falls Community College, Fergus Falls — 589; Moorhead State University, Moorhead — 6,052; Northland Community College, Thief River Falls — 580; St. Cloud State University, St. Cloud — 12,511; St. John's University, Collegeville — 2,063; Tri-College University, Moorhead — 215; University of Minnesota Technical College (Crookston campus), Crookston — 1,179.

Newspapers, Circulation: *Crookston Daily Times* (e), Crookston — 5,370; *Daily Journal* (e), Fergus Falls — 13,635; *Little Falls Daily Transcript* (e), Little Falls — 3,678; *The Pioneer* (mS), Bemidji — 6,861; *St. Cloud Daily Times* (e), St. Cloud — 27,299.

Commercial Television Stations, Affiliation: KXLI, St. Cloud (None). District is divided among Alexandria ADI, Minneapolis-St.Paul ADI and Fargo (N.D.) ADI.

Industries:

St. Cloud Hospital Inc.; St. Cloud; hospital — 1,560. **White Consolidated Industries** (Franklin Mfg. Co.); St. Cloud; refrigeration equipment — 1,200. **Marvin Lumber & Cedar Co.** (HQ); Warroad; lumber millwork — 850. **General Signal Manufacturers** (De Zurik Div.); Sartell; industrial valves, pipe fittings — 750. **Brown Boveri Turbomachinery**; St. Cloud; gas, steam, hydraulic turbines — 600. **Vision-Ease Corp.**; St. Cloud; glass, glassware — 520. **Cold Spring Granite Co.** (HQ); Cold Spring; granite extraction — 500. **Swift & Co.**; Detroit Lakes; turkey processing — 500.

8th District

Northeast — Duluth

Based in the barren and remote northern reaches of Minnesota, the 8th District has a long Democratic tradition. Immigrants from Sweden, Finland and Eastern Europe settled here after the turn of the century to work in the iron ore mines scattered throughout the Mesabi and Vermillion Iron ranges located in the center of the district. Strongly allied with unions, the workers on the iron range are unswerving in their allegiance to the Democrats. Within the party, however, bitter factional feuds fester.

Life on the Range, as it is called, has not been easy in recent decades. By the end of World War II the high quality iron ore mines were largely depleted. Only the discovery of new taconite mining technology saved the local economy from collapse. Taconite, however, is pulled from the earth in huge open-pit mines that require far fewer people to operate than the old underground mines. By 1982 the recession in the steel and auto industries had created additional job shortages in towns such as Hibbing, Eveleth, Mountain Iron, Virginia and Chisholm. In some, unemployment exceeded 40 percent.

The only other significant economic activity in the area is related to its scenic beauty. A favorite of hunters, fishers, backwoods campers and canoe enthusiasts, northeastern Minnesota attracts a large tourist population every summer. In the winter, snowmobiling and ice fishing keep the tourist dollars flowing, although the sale of gasoline, bait and insect repellent to the van loads of vacationers does not make anyone rich on the Iron Range.

Democrats here have little patience with those who want to protect the wilderness areas from development. In his 1978 Senate primary against liberal Democrat Donald Fraser, Robert Short ran up large pluralities in the area by campaigning against restrictions on motorboats and snowmobiles in the Boundary Waters Canoe Area. Short's margin here allowed him to defeat Fraser in the primary, and this was the only area he won in the general election against Republican David Durenberger.

The district's only major population center is the port city of Duluth, the state's third largest city. With some 93,000 people, it accounts for about a fifth of the district's vote. From Duluth's steep bluffs, 800 feet above Lake Superior, one can see the active port below where much of

the grain from the Plains States is shipped east. Iron ore and other raw materials for heavy industry also pass through the port, although in diminishing amounts.

Duluth and surrounding St. Louis County, which extends to the Canadian border and includes most of the Iron Range population, are firmly Democratic. In 1978, when Democrats were being defeated almost everywhere else in the state, the Democratic Senate and gubernatorial candidates both received more than 60 percent of the major party vote in St. Louis County.

Redistricting added nearly 100,000 new voters in four counties on the district's western border. Cass and Crow Wing counties often vote Republican, but they are not large enough to overcome the Democratic strength in the rest of the district. The district lost Anoka County at the southern end of the district, near the Twin Cities.

Election Returns

8th District		Democrat		Republican	
1976	President	185,726	(62.7%)	101,000	(34.1%)
	Senate	216,813	(73.7%)	57,416	(19.5%)
	House	235,037	(94.6%)	13,512	(5.4%)
1978	Governor	141,629	(57.3%)	98,920	(40.0%)
	Senate[1]	110,771	(45.1%)	124,510	(50.7%)
	Senate[2]	125,663	(51.3%)	108,663	(44.3%)
	House	188,127	(88.6%)	22,180	(10.4%)
1980	President	171,636	(53.9%)	117,437	(36.9%)
	House	204,585	(67.0%)	96,646	(31.6%)
1982	Governor	177,887	(74.4%)	58,414	(24.4%)
	Senate	145,686	(60.6%)	92,389	(38.5%)
	House	176,392	(76.7%)	53,467	(23.3%)

[1] *Election for a full six-year term.*
[2] *Election for the remaining four years of the term of Hubert H. Humphrey who died Jan. 13, 1978.*

Demographics

Population: 509,506. **Percent Change from 1970:** 10.7%.

Land Area: 24,680 square miles. **Population per Square Mile:** 20.6.

Counties, 1980 Population: Aitkin — 13,404; Beltrami (Pt.) — 421; Carlton — 29,936; Cass — 21,050; Chisago — 25,717; Cook — 4,092; Crow Wing — 41,722; Hubbard (Pt.) — 98; Isanti — 23,600; Itasca — 43,069; Kanabec — 12,161; Koochiching — 17,571; Lake — 13,043; Mille Lacs — 18,430; Pine — 19,871; Sherburne (Pt.) — 3,092; St. Louis — 222,229.

Cities, 1980 Population: Brainerd — 11,489; Cloquet — 11,142; Duluth — 92,811; Hibbing — 21,193; Virginia — 11,056.

Race and Ancestry: White — 97.5%; Black — 0.3%; American Indian, Eskimo and Aleut — 1.7%; Asian and Pacific Islander — 0.4%. Spanish Origin — 0.3%. Dutch — 0.6%; English — 2.8%; French — 1.6%; German — 11.0%; Irish — 2.3%; Italian — 1.2%; Norwegian — 5.7%; Polish — 1.8%; Swedish — 7.4%.

Universities, Enrollment: Brainerd Community College, Brainerd — 630; College of St. Scholastica, Duluth — 1,115; Crosier Seminary Junior College, Onamia — 35; Hibbing Community College, Hibbing — 812; Itasca Community College, Grand Rapids — 996; Mesabi Community College, Virginia — 949; Rainy River Community College, International Falls — 516; Vermillion Community College, Ely — 545; University of Minnesota (Duluth campus), Duluth — 7,393.

Newspapers, Circulation: *The Brainerd Daily Dispatch* (eS), Brainerd — 13,924; *The Daily Journal* (e), International Falls — 5,485; *Duluth Herald* (e), Duluth — 20,183; *Duluth News-Tribune* (mS), Duluth —

51,754; *Hibbing Daily Tribune* (eS), Hibbing — 10,512; *Mesabi Daily News* (eS), Virginia — 15,216.

Commercial Television Stations, Affiliation: KBJR-TV, Duluth (NBC); KDLH, Duluth (CBS); KNMT, Walker (NBC); WDIO-TV, Duluth (ABC); WIRT, Hibbing (ABC). Most of district is located in Duluth ADI. Portions are in Alexandria ADI and Minneapolis-St. Paul ADI.

Military Installations: Duluth International Airport (Air Force), Duluth — 1,404; Duluth Air National Guard Base, Duluth — 1,114.

Industries:

United States Steel Corp. (Minntac Mine); Mountain Iron; iron ore mining — 1,800. **Reserve Mining Co.;** Babbitt; iron ore mining — 1,590. **The Eveleth Taconite Co.;** Eveleth; taconite mining — 1,450. **Blandin Paper Co.** (HQ); Grand Rapids; paper mills — 1,350. **Erie Mining Co.;** Hoyt Lakes; iron ore mining — 1,350.

St. Luke's Hospital; Duluth; hospital — 1,300. **Hibbing Taconite;** Hibbing; iron ore mining — 1,200. **Potlatch Corp.** (Northwest Paper Div.); Cloquet; pulp, paper mills — 1,200. **Eveleth Expansion Co.;** Eveleth; iron ore mining — 1,170. **Conwed Corp.;** Cloquet; insulation materials — 1,050. **Hanna Mining** (National Steel Pellet Co.); Keewatin; iron ore mining — 1,000. **Reserve Mining Co.** (HQ); Silver Bay; iron ore mining — 1,000.

Boise Cascade Corp. (Paper Div.); International Falls; pulp, paper mills — 820. **Diamond Tool & Horseshoe Co.;** Duluth; metal hand tools — 700. **Potlatch Corp.** (Northwest Paper Div.); Brainerd; paper mills — 654. **Hanna Mining Co.** (Butler Taconite Co.); Nashwauk; iron ore mining — 650. **Jones & Laughlin Steel Corp.** (Northwest Ore Div.); Virginia; iron ore mining — 600. **Inland Steel Mining Co.** (Minorca Mine); Virginia; iron ore mining — 550. **Plastech Research Inc.** (HQ); Rush City; plastics products — 540.

Mississippi

Ten weeks after the U. S. Justice Department rejected Mississippi's redistricting map because it diluted the voting strength of blacks, a three-judge federal panel in Jackson June 9, 1982, accepted a temporary plan that created the state's first black majority district since 1966. Some black leaders had charged that the districts in the original remap were drawn to prevent election of a black representative. Mississippi, which has a 35 percent black population, has not sent a black to Congress since the Reconstruction era.

The heaviest concentration of blacks is in the rural Delta region along the Mississippi River. Until 1966 Mississippi had a district in the Delta region with a majority-black population, but whites controlled the seat because few blacks were registered to vote at that time.

Substantial black registration began after the passage of the Voting Rights Act in 1965. However, the Delta-based district was dismantled in 1966 when the U. S. Supreme Court ordered that Mississippi districts be redrawn so that the population would be evenly distributed among them. By dividing the Delta among the 1st, 2nd and 3rd districts, each of which stretches across the state to predominantly white counties, the Legislature could dilute the potential strength of black voters.

Mississippi's population grew by a healthy 13.7 percent from 1970 to 1980, but the increase of 303,644 residents was scattered enough to leave the five districts close in population. Thus the Legislature made only minor changes in the district lines, rejecting pleas from black state legislators to create a majority-black district.

The court-ordered map made the new 2nd, the "Delta District," the majority black district. But as drawn by the court the 2nd was less than 54 percent black, and the civil rights leaders who initiated the Jackson court suit were not satisfied with it. Declaring that they needed a 65 percent black majority in the district to elect a black candidate, these leaders wanted to extend the Delta district into the northern part of heavily black Hinds County (Jackson).

They appealed the court's plan to the Supreme Court, which remanded the case to the lower court in May 1983. No further action had been taken by mid-September 1983.

The Justice Department's rejection of the original map resulted in a postponement of Mississippi's House primaries, originally scheduled for June 1, 1982, until mid-August. Congressional candidates in 1982 stood for election in the districts outlined in the court's plan. The incumbent in the 2nd District retired, leaving the new district open. A black won the Democratic nomination, but he lost in November to a white Republican who had been a Democratic circuit court judge.

Age of Population

District	Population Under 18	Voting Age Population	Population 65 & Over (% of VAP)	Median Age
1	159,808	344,906	61,715 (17.9%)	29.0
2	177,482	327,172	64,875 (19.8%)	26.6
3	157,287	346,476	59,092 (17.1%)	28.2
4	158,110	345,780	57,893 (16.7%)	27.8
5	161,510	342,107	45,782 (13.4%)	27.0
State	814,197	1,706,441	289,357 (17.0%)	27.7

Income and Occupation

District	Median Family Income	White Collar Workers	Blue Collar Workers	Service Workers	Farm Workers
1	$ 14,359	38.8%	46.3%	10.5%	4.4%
2	12,270	43.5	34.7	12.9	8.9
3	14,833	44.5	39.3	12.0	4.2
4	15,396	51.4	32.7	13.3	2.6
5	15,900	47.4	37.0	13.1	2.5
State	$ 14,591	45.1%	38.1%	12.3%	4.4%

Education: School Years Completed

District	8 Years or Fewer	4 Years of High School	4 Years of College or More	Median School Years
1	31.3%	29.1%	9.1%	12.0
2	35.3	23.4	11.8	11.9
3	25.3	30.1	11.7	12.2
4	23.3	28.0	16.5	12.4
5	19.7	35.1	12.3	12.4
State	27.0%	29.2%	12.3%	12.2

MISSISSIPPI

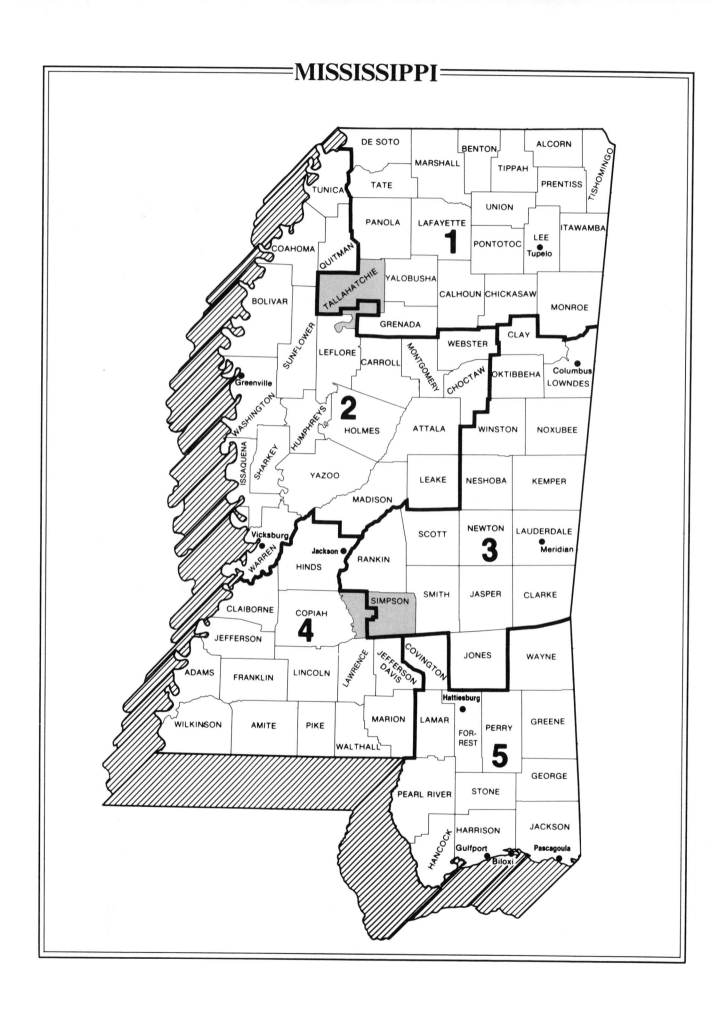

Housing and Residential Patterns

District	Owner Occupied	Renter Occupied	Urban	Rural
1	74.9%	25.1%	32.4%	67.6%
2	64.1	35.9	43.2	56.8
3	74.4	25.6	40.8	59.2
4	69.8	30.2	56.3	43.7
5	71.7	28.3	64.0	36.0
State	71.0%	29.0%	47.3%	52.7%

1st District

North — Tupelo

The 1st District stretches from the Mississippi River east to the Alabama state line, running along the northern border of the state. Overwhelmingly rural, the district takes in the flat, rich farm land on the edge of the Delta region in the northwestern part of Mississippi and the less fertile plots of the northeastern Hill Country. Although cotton was once the dominant crop, 1st District farmers now also produce soybeans, rice, corn, wheat, livestock and poultry.

The old district's population grew by nearly 14 percent in the 1970s, with the largest boom in the Memphis (Tenn.) suburbs in De Soto County. Population also increased in the eastern and central portions of the district, where the arrival of new industry and construction of the Tennessee-Tombigbee Waterway provided new jobs.

The only major population decrease was in the rural Delta county of Tallahatchie, which has a black majority. The overall black population in the old 1st declined from 35 percent in 1970 to 30 percent in the new census, as blacks moved out of the Delta and into Memphis, Tenn., and other large Southern cities. Under the lines drawn for the 98th Congress, the district's black population fell even further, to 26 percent.

The 1st is the state's most reliably Democratic district. Jimmy Carter won 60 percent of the vote here in 1976, his best district margin in Mississippi. Four years later when he lost statewide, Carter won the area within the 1st with 55 percent.

Under the court-ordered reapportionment plan, the 1st gained white-dominated Calhoun, Chickasaw and Monroe counties from the 2nd, and lost three black-majority Delta counties. That shift was not expected to change district politics much. The Democratic incumbent was elected to a twenty-second term in 1982.

Election Returns

1st District		Democrat		Republican	
1976	President	90,084	(60.0%)	56,837	(37.8%)
	Senate	97,378	(100.0%)	—	
	House	92,687	(96.2%)	3,578	(3.7%)
1978	Senate	35,225	(40.3%)	41,493	(47.5%)
	House	55,315	(66.7%)	25,889	(31.2%)
1979	Governor	84,041	(65.3%)	44,616	(34.7%)
1980	President	93,980	(54.7%)	73,075	(42.5%)
	House	99,985	(62.9%)	58,896	(37.1%)

1st District		Democrat		Republican	
1982	Senate	80,329	(70.1%)	34,318	(29.9%)
	House	79,726	(70.9%)	32,750	(29.1%)

Demographics

Population: 504,714. **Percent Change from 1970:** 17.7%.

Land Area: 10,247 square miles. **Population per Square Mile:** 49.3.

Counties, 1980 Population: Alcorn — 33,036; Benton — 8,153; Calhoun — 15,664; Chickasaw — 17,853; De Soto — 53,930; Grenada — 21,043; Itawamba — 20,518; Lafayette — 31,030; Lee — 57,061; Marshall — 29,296; Monroe — 36,404; Panola — 28,164; Pontotoc — 20,918; Prentiss — 24,025; Tallahatchie (Pt.) — 15,447; Tate — 20,119; Tippah — 18,739; Tishomingo — 18,434; Union — 21,741; Yalobusha — 13,139.

Cities, 1980 Population: Corinth — 13,839; Grenada — 12,641; Tupelo — 23,905.

Race and Ancestry: White — 73.8%; Black — 26.0%; American Indian, Eskimo and Aleut — 0.1%; Asian and Pacific Islander — 0.2%. Spanish Origin — 0.8%. English — 24.6%; French — 0.5%; German — 1.8%; Irish — 8.1%.

Universities, Enrollment: Blue Mountain College, Blue Mountain — 375; Itawamba Junior College, Fulton — 2,407; Northeast Mississippi Junior College, Booneville — 2,048; Northwest Mississippi Junior College, Senatobia — 3,306; Rust College, Holly Springs — 715; University of Mississippi, University — 9,607.

Newspapers, Circulation: *The Daily Corinthian* (e), Corinth — 7,540; *The Daily Sentinel Star* (e), Grenada — 4,924; *Northeast Mississippi Daily Journal* (m), Tupelo — 34,134; *The Oxford Eagle* (e), Oxford — 3,912.

Commercial Television Stations, Affiliation: WTVA, Tupelo (NBC, ABC). District is divided between Columbus-Tupelo ADI and Memphis (Tenn.) ADI. Portion is in Greenwood-Greenville ADI.

Nuclear Power Plants: Yellow Creek 1 and 2, Corinth (Combustion Engineering, Tennessee Valley Authority).

Industries:

North Mississippi Medical Center Inc. (HQ); Tupelo; hospital — 1,750. **International Telephone & Telegraph Corp.**; Corinth; telephone apparatus — 1,500. **Colt Industries Inc.** (Holley Carburetor Div.); Water Valley; carburetors — 1,277. **International Playtex Inc.** (Pennaco Hosiery Div.); Grenada; women's hosiery — 925. **Emerson Electric Co.** (Motor Div.); Oxford; electric motors — 900. **McQuay-Perfex Inc.**; Grenada; air conditioning equipment — 900.

Panola Mills Inc.; Batesville; men's underwear — 800. **The Wurlitzer Co.**; Holly Springs; pianos — 800. **Amory Garment Co.**; Amory; men's, boys' trousers — 750. **Futorian Corp.**; Okolona; upholstered furniture — 750. **Mid-South Packers**; Tupelo; meatpacking — 750. **Dover Corp.** (Elevator Div.); Horn Lake; elevators — 700. **Hall of Mississippi Inc.**; Corinth; commercial printing — 700. **Sunbeam Corp.** (Aircap Manufacturers Div.); Tupelo; power mowers — 700. **Prentiss Mfg. Co.**; Booneville; men's shirts — 675. **Emerson Electric Co.** (Day-Brite Lighting Co.); Tupelo; electric lamps — 665. **Rockwell International Corp.**; Tupelo; power tools — 650.

U. S. Industries Inc. (Brookwood Furniture Div.); Pontotoc; upholstered furniture — 650. **Arvin Industries Inc.** (Electric Housewares Div.); Verona; electric appliances — 600. **Purnell's Pride Inc.** (HQ); Tupelo; poultry, egg wholesaling — 580. **Action Industries Inc.** (HQ); Tupelo; reclining chairs — 550. **Tecumseh Products Co.**; Verona; refrigeration — 540. **International Telephone & Telegraph Corp.** (Lighting Fixture Div.); Southaven; outdoor lighting fixtures — 520. **The William Carter Co.**; Senatobia; women's, men's underwear — 500. **Chambers Corp.**; Oxford; household cooking equipment — 500. **Intex Plastics**; Corinth; plastics — 500. **Kellwood Co.** (Calford Group-Pants Div.); Calhoun City; boys' trousers — 500. **Oxford Industries Inc.** (Lanier Clothes Div.); Tupelo; men's, boys' coats — 500. **Tenneco Inc.** (Walker Mfg. Div.); Aberdeen; automobile parts — 500.

2nd District

Mississippi Delta — Greenville, Vicksburg

Known as the home of Mississippi's wealthiest cotton planters, the 2nd District has always had a far larger population of poor rural blacks. By 1980 most of the plantations were gone, but the rural poverty remained.

The 2nd was altered substantially by the federal judges' plan, becoming the modern counterpart to the "Delta district" that existed until 1966. It took in three Delta counties from the 1st District to the north, and another five from the 3rd and 4th. With the new Delta counties also came several counties rooted in the red clay of the Hill Country, a predominantly white region. The two segments of the district once had a fierce regional rivalry, traced back to the divergent economic interests of the landed gentry in the Delta and the small farmers in the hills.

In the past generation, thousands of the Delta's blacks were pushed out of work by mechanization on the farms and moved on to Chicago, St. Louis and closer Sun Belt cities such as Little Rock, Ark., and Memphis, Tenn. Nonetheless, the new 2nd District is 54 percent black and came within 3,000 votes of electing a black to the U.S. House in 1982.

Greenville, an old river port and cotton market, is the largest city in the Delta and one of the few areas in the region to gain population in the 1970s. It has a reputation as one of the most racially tolerant communities in the state.

The hill region is more industrialized than the Delta area, although it also contains pockets of poverty. The growing industries here are paper and pulp mills and furniture manufacturing.

Although it elected a Republican to the House in 1982, the new 2nd District is nearly as consistent in its Democratic voting habits as the 1st. Its Republican enclaves in Oktibbeha and Lowndes counties, toward the Alabama line, were removed in redistricting. Only one of the eleven counties it picked up, Warren County (Vicksburg), supported Ronald Reagan in 1980.

Election Returns

2nd District		Democrat		Republican	
1976	President	77,279	(50.1%)	72,508	(47.0%)
	Senate	108,494	(100.0%)	—	
	House	89,929	(69.6%)	38,065	(29.5%)
1978	Senate	34,870	(27.1%)	51,518	(40.0%)
	House	74,180	(66.9%)	33,610	(30.3%)
1979	Governor	87,200	(64.9%)	47,071	(35.1%)
1980	President	110,364	(55.1%)	84,742	(42.3%)
	House	109,766	(72.7%)	36,842	(24.4%)
1982	Senate	85,514	(61.3%)	53,964	(38.7%)
	House	71,536	(48.4%)	74,450	(50.3%)

Demographics

Population: 504,654. **Percent Change from 1970:** 1.3%.

Land Area: 11,982 square miles. **Population per Square Mile:** 42.1.

Counties, 1980 Population: Attala — 19,865; Bolivar — 45,965; Carroll — 9,776; Choctaw — 8,996; Coahoma — 36,918; Holmes — 22,970; Humphreys — 13,931; Issaquena — 2,513; Leake — 18,790; Leflore — 41,525; Madison — 41,613; Montgomery — 13,366; Quitman — 12,636; Sharkey — 7,964; Sunflower — 34,844; Tallahatchie (Pt.) — 1,710; Tunica — 9,652; Warren — 51,627; Washington — 72,344; Webster — 10,300; Yazoo — 27,349.

Cities, 1980 Population: Canton — 11,116; Clarksdale — 21,137; Cleveland — 14,524; Greenville — 40,613; Greenwood — 20,115; Vicksburg — 25,434; Yazoo City — 12,426.

Race and Ancestry: White — 45.7%; Black — 53.7%; American Indian, Eskimo and Aleut — 0.2%; Asian and Pacific Islander — 0.3%. Spanish Origin — 1.1%. English — 16.3%; French — 0.5%; German — 1.2%; Irish — 5.4%; Italian — 0.6%.

Universities, Enrollment: Coahoma Junior College, Clarksdale — 1,520; Delta State University, Cleveland — 3,172; Holmes Junior College, Goodman — 1,052; Mississippi Delta Junior College, Moorhead — 1,702; Mississippi Valley State University, Itta Bena — 2,574; Wood Junior College, Mathiston — 435.

Newspapers, Circulation: *The Bolivar Commercial* (e), Cleveland — 6,020; *Daily Morning People's Press* (m), Yazoo City — 3,198; *Delta Democrat-Times* (eS), Greenville — 15,597; *The Greenwood Commonwealth* (eS), Greenwood — 8,769; *Press Register* (eS), Clarksdale — 7,321; *Vicksburg Evening Post* (eS), Vicksburg — 15,580.

Commercial Television Stations, Affiliation: WABG-TV, Greenwood (ABC); WXVT, Greenville (CBS). District is divided between Greenwood-Greenville ADI and Jackson ADI. Portions are in Columbus-Tupelo ADI and Memphis (Tenn.) ADI.

Industries:

Travenol Laboratories Inc.; Cleveland; pharmaceuticals — 1,000. **Marathon Le Tourneau Co. Inc.;** Vicksburg; construction machinery — 900. **D. H. Baldwin Co.** (Baldwin Piano & Organ Co.); Greenwood; pianos, organs — 950. **Mohasco Corp.;** Greenville; carpets, rugs — 900. **Anderson-Tully Co.;** Vicksburg; hardwood, flooring — 800.

Mississippi Chemical Corp. (HQ); Yazoo City; fertilizers — 737. **U. S. Industries Inc.** (Belwood Div.); Ackerman; millwork — 600. **Westinghouse Electric Corp.** (Lighting Div.); Vicksburg; lighting fixtures — 550. **The Carthage Corp.;** Carthage; men's slacks — 500. **United States Gypsum Co.;** Greenville; insulation — 500.

3rd District

South Central — Meridian

Until the court's remap, the 3rd was geographically the largest of Mississippi's districts. It is still mostly agricultural, but includes sections with a burgeoning timber industry, outlying suburbs of Jackson, and the air force base at Columbus in newly-added Lowndes County. The district was removed entirely from the Delta region and centered in the Hill Country along the eastern edge of Mississippi.

Lauderdale County, located on the Alabama border, is the district's major population center. Meridian, Lauderdale's county seat, is an increasingly Republican industrial town.

The addition of Columbus, with its military-related residents from the North and Midwest, contributes significantly to the Republican presence in the 3rd. Another population center is Laurel. The seat of Jones County on the district's southern edge, Laurel is home to a timber-related industry fueled by its proximity to Mississippi's Piney Woods. Oil and gas drilling in southern Mississippi has spawned oil-related industries in the area. Laurel has been shifting in a Republican direction in recent national elections.

To the south and west in the district is another Republican stronghold, Rankin County, home to more than 50,000 suburbanites oriented toward metropolitan Jackson. In 1980 Ronald Reagan led Jimmy Carter by a 2-1 margin in Rankin County, one of the fastest growing areas in the state.

The redistricting plan added four counties to the top of the district (Clay, Winston, Oktibbeha, and Lowndes) and one to the bottom (Jones) — the last three all supported Reagan in 1980. It also removed seven counties to the west, all but one of them majority-black and solidly Democratic. Four counties and half of a fifth at the bottom of the 3rd (Marion, Lawrence, Jefferson Davis, Covington, and Simpson) were also dropped — most of them were heavily black and Democratic as well.

Election Returns

3rd District		Democrat		Republican	
1976	President	76,461	(48.4%)	77,617	(49.2%)
	Senate	117,241	(100.0%)	—	
	House	103,510	(76.2%)	31,925	(23.5%)
1978	Senate	41,623	(34.9%)	53,104	(44.5%)
	House	75,650	(71.2%)	30,665	(28.8%)
1979	Governor	84,397	(57.9%)	61,282	(42.1%)
1980	President	74,295	(41.3%)	102,116	(56.7%)
	House	117,755	(79.1%)	31,035	(20.9%)
1982	Senate	87,188	(66.3%)	44,284	(33.7%)
	House	114,530	(93.1%)	—	

Demographics

Population: 503,763. **Percent Change from 1970:** 17.0%.

Land Area: 9,827 square miles. **Population per Square Mile:** 51.3.

Counties, 1980 Population: Clarke — 16,945; Clay — 21,082; Jasper — 17,265; Jones — 61,912; Kemper — 10,148; Lauderdale — 77,285; Lowndes — 57,304; Neshoba — 23,789; Newton — 19,944; Noxubee — 13,212; Oktibbeha — 36,018; Rankin — 69,427; Scott — 24,556; Simpson (Pt.) — 20,325; Smith — 15,077; Winston — 19,474.

Cities, 1980 Population: Columbus — 27,383; Jackson (Pt.) — 2; Laurel — 21,897; Meridian — 46,577; Pearl — 20,778; Starkville — 15,169.

Race and Ancestry: White — 67.6%; Black — 31.3%; American Indian, Eskimo and Aleut — 0.7%; Asian and Pacific Islander — 0.3%. Spanish Origin — 0.8%. English — 21.8%; French — 0.6%; German — 2.2%; Irish — 7.2%; Scottish — 0.5%.

Universities, Enrollment: Clarke College, Newton — 201; East Central Junior College, Decatur — 785; East Mississippi Junior College, Scooba — 1,049; Jones County Junior College, Ellisville — 2,402; Mary Holmes College, West Point — 472; Meridian Junior College, Meridian — 2,877; Mississippi State University, Mississippi State — 11,409; Mississippi University for Women, Columbus — 2,070; Wesley College, Florence — 91.

Newspapers, Circulation: *The Commercial Dispatch* (eS), Columbus — 13,708; *Daily Times Leader* (e), West Point — 4,325; *Laurel Leader-Call* (e), Laurel — 10,292; *The Meridian Star* (eS), Meridian — 23,910; *Starkville Daily News* (m), Starkville — 6,440.

Commercial Television Stations, Affiliation: WCBI-TV, Columbus (CBS); WDAM-TV, Laurel (NBC); WHTV, Meridian (CBS, NBC); WTDK-TV, Meridian (ABC). District is divided among Columbus-Tupelo ADI, Jackson ADI, Laurel-Hattiesburg ADI and Meridian ADI.

Military Installations: Allen C. Thompson Field (Air Force), Flowood — 660; Columbus Air Force Base, Columbus — 2,970; Key Field (Air Force), Meridian — 1,341; Naval Air Station, Meridian — 1,900.

Industries:

Bryan Foods Inc. (Flavo Tech Co. - HQ); West Point; meatpacking — 1,660. **Mississippi State Hospital;** Pearl; state psychiatric hospital — 1,650. **Universal Mfg. Corp.** (Northwest Industries); Mendenhall; transformers — 1,450. **United Technologies Corp.** (Electro Systems Div.); Columbus; electrical equipment for internal combustion engines — 1,400. **Masonite Corp.** (Central Hardboard Div.); Laurel; saw mill — 1,400.

McCarty-State Pride Farms Inc.; Magee; hatchery, poultry processing — 1,200. **Babcock & Wilcox Co. Inc.;** West Point; industrial process furnaces — 1,120. **Spartus Corp.;** Louisville; clocks — 1,000. **Kayser-Roth Corp.;** Quitman; knit underwear mills — 975. **Burlington Industries Inc.;** Stonewall; cotton fabric — 900. **Peavey Electronic Corp.;** Meridian; radio, television receiving sets — 900. **Howard Industries Inc.;** Laurel; transformers — 820. **Emerson Electric Co.** (U.S. Electrical Motors Div.); Philadelphia; motors — 775. **Stevens Sportswear Co. Inc.** (HQ); Taylorsville; women's, children's clothing — 750. **Taylor Machine Works Inc.** (HQ); Louisville; forklifts, large equipment — 731. **Beatrice Foods Co.** (Magnolia Products Div.); Columbus; toilet seats — 700.

Johnston-Tombigbee Furniture Mfg. Co.; Columbus; wooden household furniture — 650. **Midland Shirt Co. Inc.** (HQ); Union; men's shirts — 650. **Georgia-Pacific Corp.;** Taylorsville; plywood, particle board — 595. **Seminole Mfg. Co.** (American Trouser Div. - HQ); Columbus; men's, boys' slacks, suits — 550. **The Marmon Group Inc.** (Wells Lamont Div.); Philadelphia; cotton gloves — 530. **General Tire & Rubber Co.;** Columbus; rubber carpet — 525. **The Raleigh Corp.;** Raleigh; men's, women's clothing — 525. **Georgia-Pacific Corp.;** Louisville; plywood, wood products — 517. **The Boys-Tone Shirt Co. Inc.;** Decatur; boys' shirts — 500. **B. C. Rogers Poultry Inc.** (HQ); Morton; poultry processing — 500. **Weyerhaeuser Co.;** Philadelphia; sawmill — 500.

4th District

Southwest — Jackson

The 4th is dominated by Jackson, the state capital and Mississippi's largest city, with a population of more than 200,000. It is the one largely urban district in Mississippi.

Jackson and surrounding Hinds County give the GOP a strong political base. An increasingly prosperous commercial and financial center, Jackson grew by nearly one-third in the 1970s. Together with its suburbs, it now casts about one-half the 4th District vote.

But Jackson is also 47 percent black, and the votes from its black community, combined with those in the rural counties to the south, make Democrats competitive in congressional elections. The 4th was Republican for most of the 1970s, but it turned Democratic in 1981 in a special election and remained Democratic after the 1982 election.

Altogether the district is 45 percent black, and it was this independent black vote that oddly enough accounted for the district's GOP leanings in the 1970s. Blacks ran independent House candidates in 1972, 1978 and 1980. They siphoned votes from the Democratic nominees, enabling Republicans to win the House seat.

With the removal of Vicksburg, the only other city of any size in the 4th is Natchez. Known chiefly for its antebellum mansions and Civil War history, Natchez blossomed in recent years with light manufacturing and as a center for local oil activity. It tilts Adams County toward the GOP in most statewide races, although in 1976, while

Hinds County was delivering the district as a whole to Gerald R. Ford, Adams gave Jimmy Carter a 188-vote margin.

Redistricting changed the 4th only slightly, giving it half of Simpson County and Lawrence, Jefferson Davis, and Marion counties. Simpson and Lawrence counties went Republican in the 1980 presidential election. In national elections, their addition is likely to offset the loss of Warren County and Vicksburg, which went into the new 2nd District.

Election Returns

4th District		Democrat		Republican	
1976	President	73,727	(44.3%)	88,497	(53.1%)
	Senate	118,198	(100.0%)	—	
	House	42,057	(30.5%)	93,154	(67.5%)
1978	Senate	29,579	(20.6%)	69,341	(48.2%)
	House	43,313	(32.8%)	62,234	(47.2%)
1979	Governor	92,843	(64.0%)	52,169	(36.0%)
1980	President	94,597	(48.3%)	96,515	(49.3%)
	House	56,895	(33.2%)	62,654	(36.6%)
1982	Senate	90,436	(60.1%)	60,021	(39.9%)
	House	79,977	(52.6%)	69,469	(45.6%)

Demographics

Population: 503,890. **Percent Change from 1970:** 12.1%.

Land Area: 8,075 square miles. **Population per Square Mile:** 62.4.

Counties, 1980 Population: Adams — 38,035; Amite — 13,369; Claiborne — 12,279; Copiah — 26,503; Franklin — 8,208; Hinds — 250,998; Jefferson — 9,181; Jefferson Davis — 13,846; Lawrence — 12,518; Lincoln — 30,174; Marion — 25,708; Pike — 36,173; Simpson (Pt.) — 3,116; Walthall — 13,761; Wilkinson — 10,021.

Cities, 1980 Population: Brookhaven — 10,800; Clinton — 14,660; Jackson (Pt.) — 202,893; McComb — 12,331; Natchez — 22,015.

Race and Ancestry: White — 54.4%; Black — 45.2%; American Indian, Eskimo and Aleut — 0.1%; Asian and Pacific Islander — 0.2%. Spanish Origin — 0.8%. English — 17.7%; French — 0.8%; German — 1.5%; Irish — 5.0%.

Universities, Enrollment: Alcorn State University, Lorman — 2,341; Belhaven College, Jackson — 917; Copiah-Lincoln Junior College, Wesson — 1,617; Hinds Junior College, Raymond — 6,697; Jackson State University, Jackson — 7,099; Millsaps College, Jackson — 1,099; Mississippi College, Clinton — 3,055; Phillips College, Jackson — 352; Reformed Theological Seminary, Jackson — 238; Southwest Mississippi Junior College, Summit — 1,135; Tougaloo College, Tougaloo — 886; Utica Junior College, Utica — 845.

Newspapers, Circulation: *Clarion Ledger* (mS), Jackson — 65,012; *Daily Leader* (e), Brookhaven — 7,499; *Enterprise Journal* (eS), McComb — 12,450; *Jackson Daily News* (eS), Jackson — 40,320; *Natchez Democrat* (mS), Natchez — 13,407.

Commercial Television Stations, Affiliation: WAPT, Jackson (ABC); WJTV, Jackson (CBS); WLBT, Jackson (NBC). Most of district is located in Jackson ADI. Portions are in Laurel-Hattiesburg ADI and Baton Rouge (La.) ADI.

Nuclear Power Plants: Grand Gulf 1 and 2, Port Gibson (General Electric, Bechtel).

Industries:

International Paper Co. (Consumer Packing Group); Natchez; pulp mill — 12,000. **Desoto Inc.** (Jackson Furniture Div.); Jackson; furniture — 1,800. **Mississippi Baptist Medical Center;** Jackson; hospital — 1,750. **Croft Metals Inc.** (HQ); McComb; aluminum doors — 1,400. **General Motors Corp.** (Packard Electric Co. Div.); Clinton; vehicle wiring systems — 1,398.

Veterans Administration; Jackson; veterans' hospital — 1,200. **St. Dominic Jackson Memorial Hospital;** Jackson; hospital — 1,100. **First Mississippi Corp.** (HQ); Jackson; fertilizers, dyes, pigments — 1,000. **Hinds General Hospital;** Jackson; hospital — 1,000. **Irby Construction Co.;** Jackson; heavy construction — 975. **Allstate Insurance Co.;** Jackson; life insurance — 900. **Armstrong Rubber Co. Inc.;** Natchez; tires — 900. **Sperry Corp;** Jackson; hydraulic pumps — 900. **First Capital Corp.** (HQ); Jackson; bank holding company — 750. **Capital Security Service Inc.** (HQ); Jackson; security services — 740.

Bechtel Power Corp.; Port Gibson; industrial construction — 615. **American Public Life Insurance Co.;** Jackson; health, life insurance — 608. **Day Detectives Inc.** (HQ); Jackson; security services — 600. **Deposit Guaranty National Bank** (HQ); Jackson; banking — 600. **New Orleans Furniture Mfg. Co.** (Oklahoma Furniture Mfg. Co. Div. - HQ); Columbia; upholstered furniture — 570. **St. Regis Paper Co.;** Monticello; paper mill — 565. **McRaes Inc.** (HQ); Jackson; department stores — 500. **Mississippi Publishers Corp.;** Jackson; newspaper publishing — 500. **Palm Beach Co.** (Haspel Bros. Div.); Tylertown; men's clothing — 500. **Presto Mfg. Co.** (HQ); Jackson; household appliances — 500.

5th District

Southeast — Gulf Coast, Hattiesburg

Mississippi's long-dormant Republican Party has made its greatest inroads in the 5th District, a solidly conservative region where Democrats are no longer even competitive in national elections. Ronald Reagan carried Mississippi in 1980 only because of a 28,596-vote edge in the 5th District. Of his top three counties in the state that year, the 5th has two — Lamar and Jackson.

On the map, the 5th gave up Jones County in exchange for Covington County, previously located in the 3rd District. By moving Jones County, which includes the city of Laurel, into the 3rd, the new map divided the Laurel-Hattiesburg metropolitan area between two districts for the first time.

The change made no difference in the political character of the 5th. In 1980 Covington County gave Reagan 53.1 percent to Jimmy Carter's 45.3 percent; Jones gave Reagan the same percentage, and 45.8 percent to Carter.

The political heart of the district is the Mississippi Gulf Coast, with the fast-growing cities of Gulfport, Biloxi and Pascagoula. Shipbuilding is big business in this region, especially in Pascagoula, where a Litton Industries shipyard handles major Navy contracts. The coastal counties are home for many gulf shrimpers and seafood processing plants, as well as government and military installations.

The tier of counties above the coast are part of the poorer Piney Woods region, where the economy is centered on wood products. The land is not particularly good for agriculture, but there is some dairy and poultry farming.

Hattiesburg, the seat of Forrest County, is a white-collar town whose leading employer is the University of Southern Mississippi. The absence of a big blue-collar population has made the city fertile GOP territory for 20 years.

Blacks comprise only 20 percent of the population in the 5th District, a far smaller percentage than in other parts of the state, and racial issues have never been an overriding preoccupation.

Election Returns

5th District		Democrat		Republican	
1976	President	63,758	(46.1%)	71,387	(51.6%)
	Senate	113,122	(100.0%)	—	
	House	47,146	(34.4%)	89,886	(65.6%)
1978	Senate	44,157	(42.2%)	47,633	(45.5%)
	House	3,100	(3.6%)	83,876	(96.4%)
1979	Governor	65,139	(52.7%)	58,554	(47.3%)
1980	President	56,045	(38.7%)	84,641	(58.5%)
	House	43,374	(27.4%)	115,045	(72.6%)
1982	Senate	70,632	(64.8%)	38,340	(35.2%)
	House	22,634	(21.5%)	82,884	(78.5%)

Demographics

Population: 503,617. **Percent Change from 1970:** 22.9%.

Land Area: 7,103 square miles. **Population per Square Mile:** 70.9.

Counties, 1980 Population: Covington — 15,927; Forrest — 66,018; George — 15,297; Greene — 9,827; Hancock — 24,537; Harrison — 157,665; Jackson — 118,015; Lamar — 23,821; Pearl River — 33,795; Perry — 9,864; Stone — 9,716; Wayne — 19,135.

Cities, 1980 Population: Biloxi — 49,311; Gulfport — 39,676; Hattiesburg — 40,829; Moss Point — 18,998; Ocean Springs — 14,504; Pascagoula — 29,318; Picayune — 10,361.

Race and Ancestry: White — 79.0%; Black — 19.8%; American Indian, Eskimo and Aleut — 0.2%; Asian and Pacific Islander — 0.6%. Spanish Origin — 1.4%. English — 18.1%; French — 3.7%; German — 3.4%; Irish — 5.4%; Italian — 0.8%; Scottish — 0.5%.

Universities, Enrollment: Mississippi Gulf Coast Junior College, Perkinston — 6,315; Pearl River Junior College, Poplarville — 1,508; Phillips College, Gulfport — 1,016; University of Southern Mississippi, Hattiesburg — 12,512; William Carey College, Hattiesburg — 1,703.

Newspapers, Circulation: *The American* (eS), Hattiesburg — 24,527; *The Daily Herald* (eS), Biloxi — 35,861; *The Mississippi Press* (eS), Pascagoula — 22,312; *Picayune Item* (eS), Picayune — 5,330; *South Mississippi Sun* (mS), Biloxi — 9,189. Mobile (Ala.) *Press* also circulates in the district.

Commercial Television Stations, Affiliation: WLHT, Hattiesburg (None); WLOX-TV, Biloxi (ABC). District is divided among Biloxi ADI, Laurel-Hattiesburg ADI, Mobile (Ala.) ADI and New Orleans (La.) ADI.

Military Installations: Gulfport Naval Construction Battalion Center, Gulfport — 5,136; Keesler Air Force Base, Biloxi — 9,278; Mississippi Army Ammunition Plant, Picayune — 206; Naval Oceanographic Office, Bay St. Louis — 1,378.

Industries:

Litton Systems Inc. (Ingalls Shipbuilding Div.); Pascagoula; shipbuilding — 10,000. **International Paper Co.;** Moss Point; paper, paper products — 1,250. **Forrest County General Hospital;** Hattiesburg; hospital — 1,220. **Chevron USA Inc.;** Pascagoula; petroleum refining — 970. **Hercules Inc.;** Hattiesburg; gum, wood chemicals — 863.

Big Yank Corp.; Hattiesburg; work clothing — 800. **MFC Services** (Collinswood Poultry Div.); Collins; poultry processing — 600. **Mississippi Chemical Corp.;** Pascagoula; fertilizer — 525. **Combustion Engineering Inc.** (National Tank Co. Div.); Gulfport; heating equipment — 500. **E. I. du Pont de Nemours & Co. Inc.;** Pass Christian; industrial inorganic chemicals — 500. **Sealand Terminal Corp.;** Gulfport; marine cargo handling — 500. **Sunbeam Corp.** (Northern Electric Co. Div.); Hattiesburg; electric housewares — 500. **Sunbeam Corp.** (Northern Electric Co. Div.); Waynesboro; electric blankets — 500.

Missouri

Forced by reapportionment to drop one of 10 House seats, a three-judge federal panel in Missouri decided to preserve a black-majority district in St. Louis at the expense of a district held by a freshman Republican.

Under the redistricting plan, announced Dec. 28, 1981, by the federal panel, the 8th District was dismembered, which threw the GOP incumbent into a district held by a well-established Democrat. A second Republican incumbent's home was cut off from his southeast Missouri district.

The 1st District, whose mostly black population was represented by a black, lost more than one-fourth of its population during the 1970s and was often suggested as a target for elimination. But the court chose to keep a district similar to the 1st, giving it an expanded territory with a narrow black majority, and place the reapportionment burden on the state's rural areas, where significant growth took place.

The remap saved the 1st District's black incumbent but cost one Republican incumbent his seat.

The federal judges acted after the state Legislature failed to produce a new district map in two attempts — once during the regular 1981 session and again in a special redistricting session, called by Republican Gov. Christopher S. "Kit" Bond, which adjourned Dec. 17, 1981.

Legislators could not agree on a way to drop one district as required by reapportionment. The suggestions included a plan to combine the 1st District and the 3rd District in St. Louis and a proposal to establish a new northern Missouri district incorporating parts of the 6th and 9th districts. But a majority could not be found for either of those ideas.

Missouri has been slower than some of the border states to break out of its historic voting patterns. Without substantial growth to disrupt its political habits or a major statewide racial crisis to turn white voters to the right, it has basically kept its Democratic orientation.

The 1982 elections essentially preserved the status quo. But the Democrats' urban constituency is shrinking at the same time the suburbs around St. Louis and Kansas City are growing and showing more affection for the GOP. And traditionally Democratic rural areas also have demonstrated that they will vote Republican; Ronald Reagan carried 98 of the state's 114 counties in 1980, including counties in Little Dixie and the Bootheel.

Age of Population

District	Population Under 18	Voting Age Population	Population 65 & Over (% of VAP)	Median Age
1	153,062	393,146	74,588 (19.0%)	29.7
2	159,528	386,511	46,702 (12.1%)	30.5
3	142,456	403,646	76,186 (18.9%)	32.3
4	156,222	390,415	70,341 (18.0%)	30.1
5	141,619	405,263	71,266 (17.6%)	31.1
6	150,107	396,507	78,169 (19.7%)	32.1
7	146,311	399,610	81,401 (20.4%)	32.1
8	158,326	387,786	81,160 (20.9%)	31.4
9	154,852	391,319	68,313 (17.5%)	29.0
State	1,362,483	3,554,203	648,126 (18.2%)	30.9

Income and Occupation

District	Median Family Income	White Collar Workers	Blue Collar Workers	Service Workers	Farm Workers
1	$ 18,108	54.3%	26.9%	18.3%	0.5%
2	26,519	66.3	22.2	10.9	0.6
3	21,602	55.2	31.7	12.3	0.8
4	17,145	45.2	34.4	13.1	7.3
5	20,462	56.3	28.4	14.6	0.6
6	18,610	46.5	32.1	12.8	8.6
7	15,056	44.0	36.3	13.2	6.4
8	13,733	39.7	38.6	14.0	7.6
9	18,826	45.9	33.5	13.4	7.1
State	$ 18,784	51.0%	31.3%	13.6%	4.2%

Education: School Years Completed

District	8 Years or Fewer	4 Years of High School	4 Years of College or More	Median School Years
1	23.6%	29.7%	14.9%	12.3
2	12.1	34.2	25.6	12.8
3	24.0	35.0	13.0	12.3
4	21.8	40.4	11.1	12.3
5	14.6	37.3	15.8	12.5
6	19.0	41.9	11.7	12.4
7	21.8	38.4	11.1	12.3

MISSOURI

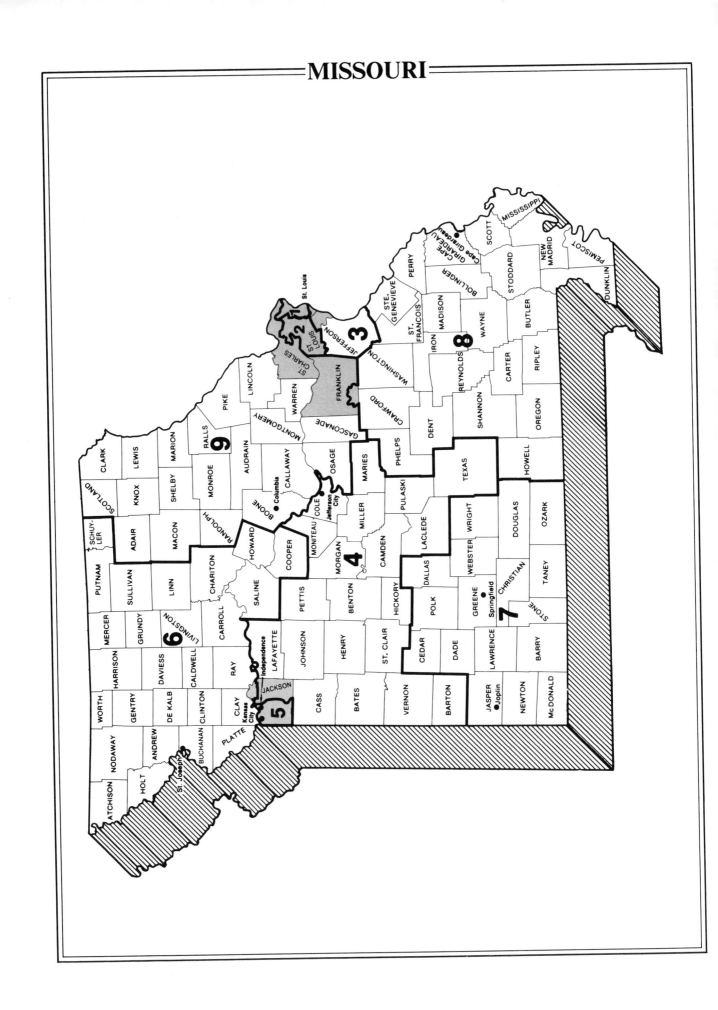

District	8 Years or Fewer	4 Years of High School	4 Years of College or More	Median School Years
8	35.6	31.9	8.3	12.0
9	23.5	37.7	13.6	12.3
State	21.7%	36.3%	13.9%	12.4

Housing and Residential Patterns

District	Owner Occupied	Renter Occupied	Urban	Rural
1	54.4%	45.6%	99.3%	0.7%
2	75.7	24.3	97.1	2.9
3	68.8	31.2	84.1	15.9
4	74.5	25.5	44.8	55.2
5	59.8	40.2	99.3	0.7
6	72.8	27.2	56.6	43.4
7	74.3	25.7	48.8	51.2
8	73.7	26.3	37.9	62.1
9	74.2	25.8	45.2	54.8
State	69.6%	30.4%	68.1%	31.9%

1st District

North St. Louis, Northeast St. Louis County

St. Louis' postwar story is one of retreat rather than advance. Blacks and whites alike have fled the once-great city — the well-off to distant suburbia and the less affluent to neighborhoods just outside the independent city's borders. Numerous factories and businesses have closed; the downtown area has declined to an extent that shocks even those visitors accustomed to inner-city blight.

Reflecting the exodus, the 1st District lost over one-quarter of its people during the 1970s, more than any other Missouri district. To survive for the 1980s the district had to be stretched south to pick up urban territory as well as west and north into the suburbs of St. Louis County. Fifty-two percent of the district's residents live outside the city limits.

Although newly added communities such as University City are among the most liberal in Missouri, much of the territory brought in by redistricting is populated by working-class conservatives who find jobs in the auto assembly and aerospace manufacturing facilities ringing St. Louis. In predominantly white communities such as Ferguson, Bellefontaine Neighbors and Jennings, the blue-collar voters are fiercely opposed to busing and abortion. Republicans often win here in statewide elections.

But GOP sentiments are drowned in a tide of Democratic votes from the city portion of the 1st. Most of the redrawn district's black population — comprising 52 percent of its total — lives within the city limits, north of Interstate 44. The old 1st was two-thirds black. The poverty of the Near North and Near South sides contrasts with parts of the West End, where some of the city's remaining white-collar professionals live.

Although St. Louis' manufacturing economy today is overshadowed by the plants outside its limits, the 1st District is not without an industrial presence. Ralston-Purina, the cereal company to which Missouri Sen. John C. Danforth is heir, is headquartered here. A corridor of light manufacturing is located toward the city's northern end.

Election Returns

1st District		Democrat		Republican	
1976	President	116,330	(56.4%)	82,828	(40.4%)
	Governor	112,627	(56.7%)	85,892	(43.2%)
	Senate	107,426	(51.0%)	100,404	(47.7%)
	House	122,428	(59.6%)	83,088	(40.4%)
1978	House	101,349	(65.2%)	52,188	(33.6%)
1980	President	142,545	(64.6%)	68,196	(30.9%)
	Governor	125,084	(61.7%)	77,409	(38.2%)
	Senate	144,791	(73.3%)	51,717	(26.2%)
	House	152,731	(72.2%)	58,780	(27.8%)
1982	Senate	107,345	(66.5%)	53,979	(33.5%)
	House	102,656	(66.1%)	52,599	(33.9%)

Demographics

Population: 546,208. **Percent Change from 1970:** -20.7%.

Land Area: 131 square miles. **Population per Square Mile:** 4,169.5.

Counties, 1980 Population: St. Louis (Pt.) — 285,178.

Cities, 1980 Population: Bellefontaine Neighbors — 12,082; Berkeley (Pt.) — 2,681; Clayton — 14,219; Ferguson — 24,740; Florissant (Pt.) — 2,546; Jennings — 17,026; Maplewood — 10,960; Overland (Pt.) — 82; Richmond Heights (Pt.) — 8,632; Spanish Lake — 20,632; St. Louis (Pt.) — 261,030; University City — 42,738.

Race and Ancestry: White — 47.5%; Black — 51.5%; American Indian, Eskimo and Aleut — 0.1%; Asian and Pacific Islander — 0.6%. Spanish Origin — 0.9%. English — 4.1%; French — 0.5%; German — 8.2%; Irish — 3.2%; Italian — 1.3%; Polish — 0.9%; Russian — 0.7%.

Universities, Enrollment: Aquinas Institute, St. Louis — 111; Bailey Technical School, St. Louis — 950; Christ Seminary - Seminex, St. Louis — 204; Concordia Seminary, St. Louis — 724; Fontbonne College, St. Louis — 866; Harris-Stowe State College, St. Louis — 1,175; St. Louis College of Pharmacy, St. Louis — 684; St. Louis Community College at Florissant Valley, St. Louis — 11,484; St. Louis Community College at Forest Park, St. Louis — 7,344; St. Louis Conservatory of Music, St. Louis — 108; St. Louis University, St. Louis — 10,712; University of Missouri (St. Louis campus), St. Louis — 11,344; Washington University, St. Louis — 10,804.

Newspapers, Circulation: *St. Louis Globe-Democrat* (mS), St. Louis — 259,355; *St. Louis Post-Dispatch* (eS), St. Louis — 241,861.

Commercial Television Stations, Affiliation: KDNL-TV, St. Louis (None); KMOX-TV, St. Louis (CBS); KNLC, St. Louis (None); KPLR-TV, St. Louis (None); KSDK, St. Louis (NBC); KTVI, St. Louis (ABC). Entire district is located in St. Louis ADI.

Military Installations: St. Louis Army Ammunition Plant, St. Louis — 16.

Industries:

Emerson Electric Co. (Emerson Motors Div.); St. Louis; industrial controls — 5,000. **Barnes Hospital Inc.;** St. Louis; hospital — 3,700. **General Motors Corp.** (Assembly Div.); St. Louis; vehicle assembly — 3,000. **Ralston Purina Co.** (Checkerboard Grain Co. - HQ); St. Louis; animal feeds — 3,000. **McGraw-Edison Co. Inc.** (Bussman Mfg. Div.); St. Louis; vehicle parts — 2,750.

Emerson Electric Co. (HQ); St. Louis; electric motors, allied products — 2,500. **Edison International Inc.** (Wagner Div.); St. Louis; motors, transformers — 2,300. **First Union Bancorp.** (HQ); St. Louis; banking — 2,300. **St. Anthony's Medical Center Inc.;** St. Louis; hospital — 2,080. **Christian Hospital Northeast-Northwest** (Northeast Div.); Spanish Lake; hospital — 2,000. **Jewish Hospital of St. Louis;** St. Louis; hospital — 2,000. **Missouri Pacific Railroad Co.** (HQ); St. Louis; railroad, trucking operations — 2,000. **Ralston Purina Co.** (Consumer Products Div.); St. Louis; animal feeds — 2,000. **Boatmen's Bancshares Inc.;** St. Louis; bank holding company — 1,700. **Mercantile Bancorporation Inc.** (HQ); St. Louis; banking — 1,680.

Brown Group Inc. (Shoe Div. - HQ); St. Louis; shoes — 1,600. **Pulitzer Publishing Co.** (HQ); St. Louis; newspaper publishing — 1,500. **General Bancshares Corp.** St. Louis; banking — 1,350. **UMC Industries Inc.** (National Vendors); St. Louis; vending machines — 1,250. **Evangelical Deaconess Society**; St. Louis; hospital — 1,200. **Lincoln Engineering Co.** (HQ); St. Louis; industrial machinery wholesalers — 1,200. **McNeil Corp.**; St. Louis; motor vehicle parts — 1,200. **Cardinal Glennon Memorial Hospital for Children**; St. Louis; children's hospital — 1,030. **Chase Hotel Redevelopment Corp.**; St. Louis; hotel — 1,000. **Emerson Electric Co.** (Day Brite Lighting Div.); St. Louis; electric lighting fixtures — 1,000.

Emerson Electric Co. (Electronics & Space Div.); St. Louis; electronic communications equipment — 1,000. **Emerson Electric Co.** (Special Products Div.); St. Louis; power driven hand tools — 1,000. **Laclede Gas Co.** (Midwest Missouri Gas Div. - HQ); St. Louis; natural gas distribution — 1,000. **St. Luke's Episcopal Presbyterian Hospital**; St. Louis; hospital — 1,000. **Blue Cross Hospital Service of Missouri** (HQ); St. Louis; health insurance — 965. **The Sverdrup Corp.** (HQ); St. Louis; engineering services — 950. **Mallinckrodt Inc.** (Chemical Group); St. Louis; medicinal, industrial chemicals — 900. **Scullin Steel Co.**; St. Louis; steel castings — 900. **Wohl Shoe Co. Inc.** (Regal Div. - HQ); St. Louis; shoe marketing — 900. **Federal Reserve Bank of St. Louis** (HQ); St. Louis; banking — 894. **Sunnen Products Co.**; St. Louis; industrial machine tools — 850. **Baker Protective Services Inc.**; St. Louis; security services — 800.

Combustion Engineering Inc. (Power Systems); St. Louis; steel fabrication — 800. **Emerson Electric Co.** (Corporate Div.); St. Louis; accounting services — 800. **Moog Automotive Inc.** (HQ); St. Louis; auto parts — 800. **Process Piping Co.**; St. Louis; heavy construction — 790. **Norfolk & Western Railway Co.**; St. Louis; railroad operations — 784. **American Can Co.** (Mfg.-Packaging Div.); St. Louis; metal cans — 700. **General Electric Co.** (Lamp Business Div.); St. Louis; electric lamps — 700. **National Industrial Security**; St. Louis; security services — 700. **ITT Continental Baking Co.**; St. Louis; bread, other bakery products — 600. **International Telephone & Telegraph Corp.** (Weaver Mfg. Div.); St. Louis; pole line hardware — 600. **Lever Bros. Co.**; St. Louis; detergents — 600.

H. H. Robertson Co. (Cupples Products Div.); St. Louis; sheet metal work — 600. **The Stouffer Corp.**; St. Louis; hotel — 600. **Sigma-Aldrich Corp.** (HQ); St. Louis; biochemicals, metal partitions — 550. **Burlington Northern Inc.** (Frisco Region); St. Louis; railroad operations — 500. **A. G. Edwards & Sons Inc.** (HQ); St. Louis; securities, commodities brokers — 500. **May Department Stores Co.** (Famous Barr Co. - HQ); St. Louis; department stores — 500. **McCabe-Powers Body Co.**; St. Louis; truck bodies — 500. **Pepsi-Cola Bottling Co. Inc.** (HQ); St. Louis; soft drink bottler — 500. **Procter & Gamble Mfg. Co.**; St. Louis; soap, detergents — 500. **Rexall Corp.** (HQ); St. Louis; pharmaceuticals — 500. **Spann Building Maintenance Co.** (HQ); St. Louis; janitorial services — 500. **Alton & Southern Railway Co.**; St. Louis; railroad operations — 500.

2nd District

Western St. Louis County, St. Charles

The 2nd District contains the high- and middle-income suburbs of St. Louis, a significant blue-collar population and a few low-income neighborhoods. Net population change in the old district during the 1970s was negligible; growth of outlying suburban areas in St. Louis County was negated by declines in areas closer to the city.

The district's vote tilts toward the Republican Party in statewide elections, although it sent a Democrat to the House in the late 1970s and early 1980s.

The new map reinforces the district's tendency to vote Republican, and it may improve the chances of a Republican challenger. Shifted out of the 2nd into the 1st were blue-collar communities such as Ferguson and St. Ferdi-

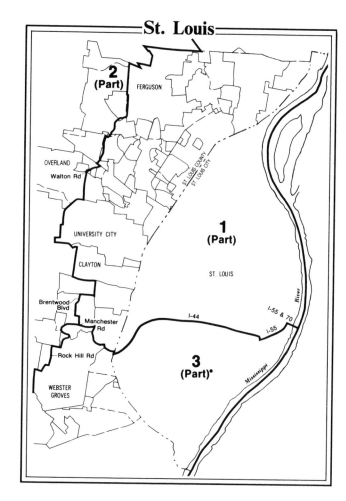

nand, which tended to vote Democratic.

The 2nd took in the old 8th District's share of western St. Louis County, with about 58,000 residents who are for the most part affluent and Republican. From the 9th, north of the city, it picked up nearly 53,000 residents of heavily Democratic Florissant plus 65,185 residents of politically marginal St. Charles County.

The 2nd holds many of the manufacturing and assembly plants that overshadow the industrial activity remaining within the city. McDonnell Douglas, Emerson Electric and Monsanto are among the district's major employers.

Election Returns

2nd District		Democrat		Republican	
1976	President	97,561	(44.0%)	120,324	(54.2%)
	Governor	100,239	(45.5%)	119,626	(54.3%)
	Senate	80,456	(36.9%)	136,313	(62.5%)
	House	133,525	(51.8%)	105,592	(48.2%)
1978	House	108,898	(59.2%)	75,051	(40.8%)
1980	President	93,845	(36.9%)	153,176	(60.3%)
	Governor	97,715	(37.7%)	160,554	(62.0%)
	Senate	124,600	(43.8%)	159,126	(55.9%)
	House	136,679	(56.3%)	106,116	(43.7%)
1982	Senate	65,468	(36.4%)	114,444	(63.6%)
	House	100,770	(56.5%)	77,433	(43.5%)

Demographics

Population: 546,039. **Percent Change from 1970:** 11.4%.

Land Area: 367 square miles. **Population per Square Mile:** 1,487.8.

Counties, 1980 Population: St. Charles (Pt.) — 65,185; St. Louis (Pt.) — 480,854.

Cities, 1980 Population: Ballwin — 12,656; Berkeley (Pt.) — 13,465; Bridgeton — 18,445; Creve Coeur — 11,757; Florissant (Pt.) — 52,826; Hazelwood — 12,935; Kirkwood (Pt.) — 26,407; Overland (Pt.) — 19,538; Richmond Heights (Pt.) — 2,884; St. Ann — 15,523; St. Charles (Pt.) — 37,323; St. Peters (Pt.) — 8,142; Webster Groves (Pt.) — 1,711.

Race and Ancestry: White — 93.3%; Black — 5.3%; American Indian, Eskimo and Aleut — 0.1%; Asian and Pacific Islander — 0.9%. Spanish Origin — 0.9%. English — 7.4%; French — 1.0%; German — 15.9%; Irish — 4.8%; Italian — 1.6%; Polish — 1.1%; Russian — 1.3%.

Universities, Enrollment: Covenant Theological Seminary, Creve Coeur — 164; The Lindenwood Colleges, St. Charles — 1,678; Logan College of Chiropractic, Chesterfield — 654; Maryville College, Bellefontaine — 1,423; Missouri Baptist College, Creve Coeur — 459; St. Louis Christian College, Florissant — 172; St. Louis Community College at Meramec, Kirkwood — 11,076; St. Mary's College of O'Fallon, O'Fallon — 496.

Newspapers, Circulation: *St. Louis Globe-Democrat* and *St. Louis Post-Dispatch* circulate in the district.

Commercial Television Stations, Affiliation: Entire district is located in St. Louis ADI.

Military Installations: Lambert St. Louis International Airport (Air National Guard), St. Ann — 1,375; St. Louis Air Force Station, St. Ann — 19.

Industries:

McDonnell Douglas Corp. (McDonnell Aircraft Co. - HQ); Hazelwood; aircraft, missiles — 24,000. **Monsanto Co.** (HQ); Ladue; administrative offices, research labs — 5,200. **McDonnell Douglas Corp.** (Automation Corp. - HQ); Hazelwood; data processing — 5,000. **McGraw-Edison Co. Inc.** (Bussmann Mfg. Div.); Hazelwood; switchgear apparatus — 2,750. **Western Electric Co. Inc.**; Ballwin; engineering services — 2,200.

St. John's Mercy Medical Center; Creve Coeur; hospital — 1,850. **Ozark Airlines Inc.** (HQ); Hazelwood; air transportation — 1,800. **Missouri Baptist Hospital;** Town and Country; hospital — 1,600. **Ford Motor Co.;** Hazelwood; auto assembly — 1,410. **McDonnell Douglas Corp.** (Electronic Div.); St. Charles; aircraft parts — 1,400. **Sisters of St. Mary Inc.;** St. Charles; acute care hospital — 1,370. **DePaul Community Health Center** (HQ); Hazelwood; hospital — 1,300. **St. Joseph Hospital of Kirkwood;** Kirkwood; hospital — 1,200. **St. Luke's Episcopal Presbyterian Hospital;** Chesterfield; hospital — 1,020. **Christian Hospital Northeast-Northwest** (Northwest Div.); Florissant; hospital — 1,000. **McDonnell Douglas Corp.** (Automation Corp.); Hazelwood; data processing services — 1,000. **Emerson Electric Co. Inc.** (Alco Controls Div.); Hazelwood; industrial controls — 800.

Emerson Electric Co. (Environmental Products Div.); Hazelwood; industrial controls — 800. **McCarthy Bros. Co.** (Construction Management Div.- HQ); Ladue; general construction — 800. **ACF Industries** (Shippers Coreline Div.); St. Charles; railroad equipment — 750. **International Telephone & Telegraph Corp.** (Blackburn Div.); Overland; electrical fittings — 750. **General Motors Corp.** (Parts Div.); Hazelwood; auto parts wholesalers — 659. **Ramsey Corp.** (TRW Piston Ring Div. - HQ); Ballwin; piston rings — 650. **Boise Cascade Corp.** (Complete Can Div.); Hazelwood; fiber cans, tubes, drums — 600. **H. B. E. Corp.** (Hospital Building & Equipment Co. - HQ); Ladue; general contracting — 600. **Mallinckrodt Inc.** (HQ); Hazelwood; administrative offices, research labs — 600. **Alert Security Service Inc.;** Creve Coeur; security services — 525. **Marriott Corp.;** St. Ann; hotel — 500. **Trans World Airlines Inc.;** St. Ann; administrative offices — 500. **Westinghouse Electric Corp.** (Distribution Equipment Div.); Kirkwood; telephone equipment distribution — 500.

3rd District

South St. Louis, Southeast St. Louis County and Jefferson County

The new 3rd District gained more than 150,000 new constituents, many of whom tend to vote Republican. The new people were brought in to make up for the old district's 13 percent population decline during the 1970s.

To accommodate southward expansion of the underpopulated 1st District, the 3rd also moved south, and all of it is located below Interstate 44 in St. Louis. That cost the Democratic incumbent some of his working-class ethnic communities in south St. Louis, but city residents still make up more than one-third of the district's population.

South St. Louis voters were once firmly rooted in the New Deal coalition, but they have become increasingly concerned about taxes, government spending, abortion and busing. Nonetheless, Democratic ties persist — Jimmy Carter won 52 percent in 1980 in the city portions of the old 3rd.

Nearly 40 percent of the voters in the new 3rd District are in St. Louis County, outside the city. The 3rd picked up all or part of several communities from the 2nd, among them Webster Groves and Sunset Hills. Some of the county voters grew up on St. Louis' South Side and moved out during the 1970s; others are affluent, veteran suburbanites. Both groups are inclined to vote Republican in statewide elections; successful Democrats must appeal to suburban voters with a philosophy blending conservative and progressive elements.

The residents of Jefferson County are the largest bloc of newcomers to the 3rd; they make up more than a quarter of the redrawn district's population. Jefferson has come under the umbrella of metropolitan St. Louis in recent years, but much of the county is still rural. Democrats can win Jefferson with a conservative pitch, but the GOP is always a threat. Carter won Jefferson in 1976, but Ronald Reagan took it four years later.

Election Returns

3rd District		Democrat		Republican	
1976	President	118,403	(50.0%)	114,390	(48.3%)
	Governor	124,423	(52.9%)	110,310	(46.9%)
	Senate	103,567	(44.6%)	127,615	(54.9%)
	House	150,795	(64.9%)	81,681	(35.1%)
1978	House	153,994	(77.7%)	43,968	(22.2%)
1980	President	94,314	(40.4%)	127,018	(54.4%)
	Governor	117,539	(46.4%)	133,999	(52.9%)
	Senate	100,459	(43.2%)	131,047	(56.4%)
	House	168,109	(67.8%)	79,916	(32.2%)
1982	Senate	70,041	(40.8%)	101,529	(59.2%)
	House	131,566	(77.9%)	37,388	(22.1%)

Demographics

Population: 546,102. **Percent Change from 1970:** 0.3%.

Land Area: 768 square miles. **Population per Square Mile:** 711.1.

Counties, 1980 Population: Jefferson — 146,183; St. Louis (Pt.) — 207,864.

Cities, 1980 Population: Arnold — 19,141; Crestwood — 12,815; Kirkwood (Pt.) — 1,580; St. Louis (Pt.) — 192,055; Webster Groves (Pt.) — 21,386.

Race and Ancestry: White — 97.8%; Black — 1.4%; American Indian, Eskimo and Aleut — 0.2%; Asian and Pacific Islander — 0.5%. Spanish Origin — 1.0%. English — 6.4%; French — 1.5%; German — 20.0%; Irish — 5.3%; Italian — 2.6%; Polish — 1.0%.

Universities, Enrollment: Basic Institute of Technology, St. Louis — 280; Cardinal Glennon College, St. Louis — 83; Eden Theological Seminary, St. Louis — 149; Jefferson College, Hillsboro — 2,361; Kenrick Seminary, St. Louis — 125; Webster College, St. Louis — 3,658.

Newspapers, Circulation: *Jefferson County Democrat Rocket* (m), Festus — 8,043. *St. Louis Globe-Democrat* and *St. Louis Post-Dispatch* also circulate in the district.

Commercial Television Stations, Affiliation: Entire district is located in St. Louis ADI.

Military Installations: Defense Mapping Agency Aerospace Center, St. Louis — 3,658; Gateway Army Ammunition Plant, St. Louis — 16; Jefferson Barracks Air National Guard Station, St. Louis — 474.

Industries:

Anheuser-Busch Companies Inc. (HQ); St. Louis; brewery, metal cans — 6,000. **Chrysler Corp.;** Fenton; auto assembly — 5,600. **Veterans Administration;** St. Louis; veterans' hospital — 2,800. **ACF Industries Inc.;** St. Louis; railroad cars — 2,500. **Maritz Inc.** (HQ); Fenton; management consulting, public relations services — 1,600.

Nooter Corp. (Missouri Boiler & Tank Co. Div. - HQ); St. Louis; fabricated plate work — 1,300. **St. Louis State Hospital;** St. Louis; state hospital — 1,240. **Swank Inc.** (Prince Gardner Div.); St. Louis; women's handbags — 1,200. **Lutheran Charities Assn.** (HQ); St. Louis; hospital — 1,190. **Monsanto Co.** (Industrial Chemicals Co.); St. Louis; chemicals — 1,000. **Emerson Electric Co.** (White Rodgers Div.); St. Louis; automatic equipment controls — 800. **Yellow Freight System Inc.;** St. Louis; trucking — 800.

St. Joe Minerals Corp. (Lead Smelting Div.); Herculaneum; lead smelting — 750. **PPG Industries Inc.;** Crystal City; glass — 700. **United Van Lines Inc.** (HQ); Fenton; trucking — 605. **Spielberg Mfg. Co.** (Toni Handbags/Anton Designs Handbags); Barnhart; women's handbags — 600. **Sigma Chemical Co.** (HQ); St. Louis; biochemical products — 525. **The Macke Co. Inc.** (Macke Building Services); St. Louis; janitorial services — 500. **Von Hoffmann Corp.** (HQ); St. Louis; book publishing — 500.

4th District

West — Kansas City Suburbs, Jefferson City

Redistricting enhanced the rural character of the 4th District by removing some of its metropolitan Kansas City areas and extending the district's boundaries into the heart of south-central Missouri.

Many of the rural counties gained in redistricting are solidly Republican, and this could cause Democratic candidates some trouble. Shifted into the 4th from the dismembered 8th were seven counties: Cole, Moniteau, Miller, Maries, Camden, Pulaski and Texas. Six of those counties voted for the Republican House candidate in 1980; all seven voted Republican in the presidential and Senate contests. Also placed in the 4th was Laclede County, a GOP bastion formerly part of the 7th District.

Despite the Republican influx, the district retained many of its rural counties south and east of Kansas City, plus solidly Democratic areas of Jackson County east of the city. The 4th gave up a slice of Jackson County to the 6th

District, along with three rural counties in its northeastern corner. It lost most of Independence to the underpopulated 5th.

The district's farms raise corn, soybeans, wheat and some livestock. Outside Jackson County, the largest population center is Jefferson City (Cole County), the state capital. The redrawn 4th contains all the tourist territory around the Lake of the Ozarks on Camden County's northern border. It also contains Missouri's largest military facilities — the Whiteman and Richards-Gebaur Air Force bases, and Fort Leonard Wood.

Election Returns

4th District		Democrat		Republican	
1976	President	97,502	(48.2%)	103,436	(51.2%)
	Governor	94,581	(47.0%)	106,529	(52.9%)
	Senate	79,866	(39.8%)	120,022	(59.8%)
	House	128,635	(63.2%)	74,848	(36.7%)
1978	House	121,169	(70.0%)	51,956	(30.0%)
1980	President	90,030	(40.4%)	125,179	(56.1%)
	Governor	94,632	(43.3%)	123,710	(56.5%)
	Senate	106,131	(48.4%)	112,744	(51.4%)
	House	133,800	(58.3%)	95,700	(41.7%)
1982	Senate	82,358	(46.8%)	93,663	(53.2%)
	House	96,388	(54.8%)	79,565	(45.2%)

Demographics

Population: 546,637. **Percent Change from 1970:** 19.7%.

Land Area: 13,627 square miles. **Population per Square Mile:** 40.1.

Counties, 1980 Population: Barton — 11,292; Bates — 15,873; Benton — 12,183; Camden — 20,017; Cass — 51,029; Cole — 56,663; Henry — 19,672; Hickory — 6,367; Jackson (Pt.) — 80,389; Johnson — 39,059; Laclede — 24,323; Lafayette — 29,925; Maries — 7,551; Miller — 18,532; Moniteau — 12,068; Morgan — 13,807; Pettis — 36,378; Pulaski — 42,011; St. Clair — 8,622; Texas — 21,070; Vernon — 19,806.

Cities, 1980 Population: Belton — 12,708; Blue Springs — 25,927; Independence (Pt.) — 23,346; Jefferson City (Pt.) — 33,594; Lee's Summit (Pt.) — 5,182; Sedalia — 20,927; Warrensburg — 13,807.

Race and Ancestry: White — 96.0%; Black — 2.7%; American Indian, Eskimo and Aleut — 0.3%; Asian and Pacific Islander — 0.5%. Spanish Origin — 1.0%. Dutch — 0.7%; English — 12.4%; French — 0.9%; German — 14.4%; Irish — 4.8%; Italian — 0.5%.

Universities, Enrollment: Central Missouri State University, Warrensburg — 9,989; Cottey College, Nevada — 311; Lincoln University, Jefferson City — 2,657; St. Paul's College, Concordia — 124; State Fair Community College, Sedalia — 1,543; Wentworth Military Academy and Junior College, Lexington — 92.

Newspapers, Circulation: *Capital News* (mS), Jefferson City — 5,077; *Daily Fort Gateway Guide* (e), Waynesville — 4,118; *Democrat* (e), Clinton — 4,131; *Democrat* (e), Sedalia — 15,816; *Lamar Democrat* (e), Lamar — 3,144; *Lebanon Daily Record* (e), Lebanon — 6,854; *The Nevada Daily Mail* (eS), Nevada — 5,681; *Post-Tribune* (eS), Jefferson City — 16,831; *State-Journal* (e), Warrensburg — 4,980. *Kansas City Star* and *Kansas City Times* also circulate in the district.

Commercial Television Stations, Affiliation: KRCG, Jefferson City (CBS). District is divided among Columbia-Jefferson City ADI, Kansas City ADI, Springfield ADI and Joplin-Pittsburg (Kan.) ADI.

Military Installations: Fort Leonard Wood, Jefferson City — 10,476; Lake City Army Ammunition Plant, Independence — 1,853; Richards-Gebaur Air Force Base, Grandview — 1,652; Whiteman Air Force Base, Knob Noster — 3,561.

Industries:

Remington Arms Co. Inc. (Lake City Army Ammunition Plant Div.) Independence; small arms ammunition — 1,400. The H. D. Lee Co. Inc. (Lebcut); Lebanon; men's shirts — 1,100. Nevada State School & Hospital; Nevada; state mental hospital — 1,010. Westinghouse Electric Corp.; Jefferson City; transformers — 1,000. Chesebrough-Pond's Inc.; Jefferson City; cosmetics — 900.

Fasco Industries Inc.; Eldon; motors, generators — 750. Marriott Corp.; Osage Beach; resort — 750. O'Sullivan Industries Inc.; Lamar; wooden household furniture — 643. Von Hoffmann Press Inc.; Jefferson City; book printing — 600. Cargill Inc. (Poultry Products Inc.); California; turkey production — 500. Chase Resorts Inc.; Lake Ozark; hotel — 500. Ozark Fisheries Inc.; Richland; fish hatchery — 500.

5th District

Most of Kansas City, Eastern Suburbs

Though Kansas City has not suffered the massive, St. Louis-like flight of people and businesses, its population had shrunk to less than 450,000 by 1980 — fewer than lived in the city 30 years earlier. The old 5th, which included most of Kansas City plus suburban Grandview and part of Raytown, was expanded under the remap to take in 146,000 additional people, most of them in suburbs east of the city. This is sure to increase the Republican vote, making the GOP a bit more competitive in a district that has seen little action in recent years.

The eastern boundary of the redrawn district follows the route of Missouri 291, which cuts through the eastern sections of Independence and Lee's Summit, dividing those towns between the 4th and 5th districts. Partisan allegiances are much more closely divided in these suburbs than in Kansas City itself; Lee's Summit has leaned to Republicans while Independence, the home of Harry S Truman, usually gives Democrats an edge.

Despite the remap, the 5th was expected to remain primarily Democratic in most elections. Jimmy Carter won 60 percent of the Kansas City vote in 1980, offsetting Ronald Reagan's narrower advantage in suburban Jackson County.

In 1982 the district elected the state's second black U.S. House member. Blacks make up about one-fourth of the district's population.

Kansas City still depends to a great extent on grain; it is the marketing center for a surrounding six-state agricultural region. Meatpacking continues, though the stockyards are far less important economically in the 1980s than they were in the city's cow-town heyday. Hallmark, a greeting card company, ranks as the second largest employer, with 6,000 workers.

Election Returns

5th District		Democrat		Republican	
1976	President	119,296	(57.4%)	84,849	(40.8%)
	Governor	124,819	(60.5%)	80,284	(38.9%)
	Senate	99,767	(49.1%)	101,298	(49.8%)
	House	123,725	(64.2%)	63,311	(32.8%)
1978	House	108,068	(72.3%)	39,692	(26.6%)
1980	President	122,645	(54.6%)	89,058	(39.6%)
	Governor	122,195	(56.2%)	94,247	(43.3%)

5th District		Democrat		Republican	
1980	Senate	146,905	(66.1%)	73,966	(33.3%)
	House	144,179	(69.3%)	63,863	(30.7%)
1982	Senate	98,332	(59.4%)	67,222	(40.6%)
	House	96,059	(57.9%)	66,664	(40.1%)

Demographics

Population: 546,882. **Percent Change from 1970:** -10.3%.

Land Area: 267 square miles. **Population per Square Mile:** 2,048.2.

Counties, 1980 Population: Jackson (Pt.) — 546,882.

Cities, 1980 Population: Grandview — 24,502; Independence (Pt.) — 88,460; Kansas City (Pt.) — 371,991; Lee's Summit (Pt.) — 23,559; Raytown — 31,759.

Race and Ancestry: White — 74.6%; Black — 22.9%; American Indian, Eskimo and Aleut — 0.4%; Asian and Pacific Islander — 0.7%. Spanish Origin — 2.8%. Dutch — 0.5%; English — 9.4%; French — 0.7%; German — 7.3%; Irish — 4.6%; Italian — 1.7%; Polish — 0.5%; Swedish — 0.5%.

Universities, Enrollment: Avila College, Kansas City — 2,125; Calvary Bible College, Kansas City — 472; Kansas City Art Institute, Kansas City — 588; Longview Community College, Lee's Summit — 4,456; Missouri Institute of Technology, Kansas City — 1,540; Nazarene Theological Seminary, Kansas City — 458; Penn Valley Community College, Kansas City — 5,096; Pioneer Community College, Kansas City — 479; Rockhurst College, Kansas City — 3,224; St. Paul School of Theology Methodist, Kansas City — 133; University of Health Sciences/College of Osteopathic Medicine, Kansas City — 616; University of Missouri (Kansas City campus), Kansas City — 11,416.

Newspapers, Circulation: *The Examiner* (e), Independence — 15,742; *Kansas City Star* (eS), Kansas City — 277,157; *Kansas City Times* (m), Kansas City — 315,359.

Commercial Television Stations, Affiliation: KMBC-TV, Kansas City (ABC); KSHB-TV, Kansas City (None); WDAF-TV, Kansas City (NBC). Entire district is located in Kansas City ADI. *(For other Kansas City stations, see 3rd district in Kansas.)*

Industries:

Bendix Corp.; Kansas City; electrical industrial appliances — 7,250. Hallmark Cards Inc. (HQ); Kansas City; greeting cards — 6,000. ITT Continental Baking Co. Inc.; Kansas City; bakery — 5,400. General Motors Corp.; Kansas City; auto assembly — 5,000. Western Electric Co. Inc.; Lee's Summit; communications equipment — 5,000.

Armco Steel Corp. (Construction Products Co.); Kansas City; steel, steel wire, nails — 4,200. St. Luke's Hospital of Kansas City; Kansas City; hospital — 2,900. Black & Veatch (HQ); Kansas City; engineering services — 2,450. Allis-Chalmers Corp. (Combine Div.); Independence; farm machinery — 2,000. Missouri Pacific Railroad Co.; Kansas City; railroad operations — 2,000. Research Hospital & Medical Center; Kansas City; hospital — 2,000. First National Charter Corp.; Kansas City; bank holding company — 1,970. The Kansas City Star Co. (HQ); Kansas City; newspaper publishing — 1,470. Menorah Medical Center; Kansas City; hospital — 1,450. Mobay Chemical Corp.; Kansas City; agricultural chemicals — 1,300.

Baptist Memorial Hospital; Kansas City; hospital — 1,200. Truman Medical Center Inc.; Kansas City; hospital — 1,200. Veterans Administration; Kansas City; veterans' hospital — 1,200. St. Joseph Hospital Inc.; Kansas City; hospital — 1,160. Burns & McDonnell Engineering Co. (HQ); Kansas City; engineering, architectural services — 1,150. Children's Mercy Hospital; Kansas City; hospital — 1,000. Commerce Bank of Kansas City (HQ); Kansas City; banking — 1,000. Paccar Inc. (Kenworth Truck Div.); Kansas City; trucks — 1,000. St. Mary's Hospital; Kansas City; hospital — 1,000. United Missouri Bank of Kansas City (HQ); Kansas City; banking — 934. Federal Reserve Bank of Kansas City (HQ); Kansas City; banking — 900.

First National Bank of Kansas City (HQ); Kansas City; banking — 865. Cook Paint & Varnish Co. (HQ); Kansas City; paints, allied products — 800. **International Business Machines Corp.;** Kansas City; sales, service — 800. **Pinkerton's Inc.;** Kansas City; security services — 797. **Western Auto Supply Co.** (HQ); Kansas City; household, auto supply wholesaler — 750. **Western Crown Plaza Inc.;** Kansas City; hotel — 750. **Mobil Oil Credit Corp.;** Kansas City; credit card operations — 705. **Business Men's Assurance Co. of America** (HQ); Kansas City; life, health insurance — 700. **Hyatt Corp.;** Kansas City; hotel — 700. **International Telephone & Telegraph Corp.** (Apcoa Div.); Kansas City; taxi, car rental services — 700. **Mutual Benefit Life Insurance Co.;** Kansas City; life insurance — 700.

Panhandle Eastern Pipe Line Co.; Kansas City; natural gas transmission — 700. **Yellow Freight System Inc.;** Kansas City; trucking — 700. **Amoco Oil Co.;** Kansas City; data processing services — 550. **Kansas City Life Insurance Co.** (HQ); Kansas City; life insurance — 525. **Armco Steel Corp.;** Kansas City; steel mill — 500. **Blue Cross of Kansas City** (HQ); Kansas City; health insurance — 500. **Consolidated Freightways Corp.;** Kansas City; trucking — 500. **Emerson Electric Co.** (Pitman Div.); Grandview; hydraulic construction machinery — 500. **Jones Store Co.** (HQ); Kansas City; department stores — 500. **Midwest Research Institute** (HQ); Kansas City; research organization — 500. **Tension Envelope Corp.** (HQ); Kansas City; envelopes — 500.

6th District

Northwest — St. Joseph, Part of Kansas City

A vast stretch of northwestern Missouri, the 6th covers 27 whole counties, encompassing some of the most fertile agricultural areas in the state. But half the district's residents live in a three-county patch of urbanized territory in the 6th's southwest corner.

Although residents of the portions of Kansas City in Clay and Platte counties consider themselves "northlanders" and seek an identity distinct from the residents of the city south of the Missouri River, many of them find work in its industries and businesses. A Trans World Air Lines facility in this area serves as the district's largest employer.

The city of St. Joseph makes Buchanan County the third urbanized county in the district. A booming supply depot for prospectors heading to California in search of gold in the 1800s, St. Joseph gained a place in history as the eastern end of the Pony Express. The city today is a flour-milling and agribusiness center.

After backing Jimmy Carter for president in 1976, Clay, Platte and Buchanan counties moved somewhat tentatively to the GOP column in 1980. Ronald Reagan carried each with about 54 percent of the vote. But the picture of partisan preference is still blurred here. Democratic Sen. Thomas F. Eagleton won solid support in this area in his 1980 re-election.

The rest of the 6th's counties are rural and generally conservative. Parts of the rolling north Missouri prairie resemble the Iowa breadbasket; cattle and feed grains dominate the economy. Boosted by a strong showing in the rural counties, Reagan carried the redrawn 6th by about 19,000 votes in 1980.

Though population in suburban Platte County expanded rapidly during the 1970s, most counties in the 6th either saw modest growth or slight decline. Redistricting added five new rural counties and part of another: Saline, Cooper and Howard in the central part of the state, Putnam and Schuyler on the Iowa border, and a small slice of northeast Jackson County.

Transferred from the 6th to the 9th under the remap was Adair County.

Election Returns

6th District		Democrat		Republican	
1976	President	119,405	(52.2%)	107,314	(46.9%)
	Governor	112,323	(49.4%)	114,585	(50.4%)
	Senate	91,629	(41.0%)	130,655	(58.4%)
	House	96,451	(43.1%)	126,063	(56.4%)
1978	House	88,482	(47.6%)	97,277	(52.4%)
1980	President	102,849	(42.1%)	122,321	(50.0%)
	Governor	111,983	(45.9%)	131,291	(53.8%)
	Senate	130,124	(56.3%)	100,305	(43.4%)
	House	78,024	(34.1%)	150,517	(65.9%)
1982	Senate	88,834	(49.7%)	89,848	(50.3%)
	House	79,053	(44.7%)	97,993	(55.3%)

Demographics

Population: 546,614. **Percent Change from 1970:** 7.2%.

Land Area: 14,260. square miles. **Population per Square Mile:** 38.3.

Counties, 1980 Population: Andrew — 13,980; Atchison — 8,605; Buchanan — 87,888; Caldwell — 8,660; Carroll — 12,131; Chariton — 10,489; Clay — 136,488; Clinton — 15,916; Cooper — 14,643; Daviess — 8,905; De Kalb — 8,222; Gentry — 7,887; Grundy — 11,959; Harrison — 9,890; Holt — 6,882; Howard — 10,008; Jackson (Pt.) — 1,995; Linn — 15,495; Livingston — 15,739; Mercer — 4,685; Nodaway — 21,996; Platte — 46,341; Putnam — 6,092; Ray — 21,378; Saline — 24,919; Schuyler — 4,979; Sullivan — 7,434; Worth — 3,008.

Cities, 1980 Population: Excelsior Springs — 10,424; Gladstone — 24,990; Independence (Pt.) — 0; Kansas City (Pt.) — 76,168; Liberty — 16,251; Marshall — 12,781; St. Joseph — 76,691.

Race and Ancestry: White — 97.3%; Black — 1.8%; American Indian, Eskimo and Aleut — 0.2%; Asian and Pacific Islander — 0.3%. Spanish Origin — 1.0%. Dutch — 0.7%; English — 13.2%; French — 0.8%; German — 11.2%; Irish — 5.0%; Italian — 0.8%; Scottish — 0.5%; Swedish — 0.5%.

Universities, Enrollment: Central Methodist College, Fayette — 648; Conception Seminary College, Conception — 95; Kemper Military School and College, Boonville — 125; Maple Woods Community College, Kansas City — 2,279; Midwestern Baptist Theological Seminary, Kansas City — 397; Missouri Valley College, Marshall — 497; Missouri Western State College, St. Joseph — 4,061; Northwest Missouri State University, Maryville — 4,943; Park College, Parkville — 471; Platt College, St. Joseph — 1,340; Tarkio College, Tarkio — 253; William Jewell College, Liberty — 1,687.

Newspapers, Circulation: *Boonville Daily News & Advertiser* (e), Boonville — 4,120; *Constitution-Tribune* (e), Chillicothe — 6,710; *The Daily Forum* (e), Maryville — 5,189; *The Daily News* (e), Richmond — 3,245; *Democrat* (e), Carrollton — 3,443; *The Democrat-News* (e), Marshall — 5,520; *Gazette* (m), St. Joseph — 45,655; *News-Bulletin* (e), Brookfield — 5,380; *News-Press* (eS), St. Joseph — 29,886; *Republican-Times* (e), Trenton — 4,751; *Standard* (e), Excelsior Springs — 2,595. *Kansas City Star* and *Kansas City Times* also circulate in the district.

Commercial Television Stations, Affiliation: KQTV, St. Joseph (ABC). Most of district is located in Kansas City ADI. Portions are in Columbia-Jefferson City ADI, St. Joseph ADI, and Ottumwa (Iowa)-Kirksville ADI.

Military Installations: Rosecrans Memorial Airport (Air National Guard), Elwood — 612.

Industries:

Trans World Air Lines Inc.; Kansas City; airline operations — 7,500. **Ford Motor Co.;** Kansas City; auto assembly — 4,100. **Missouri Methodist Hospital Assn.;** St. Joseph; hospital — 1,520. **North Kansas City Memorial Hospital;** Kansas City; hospital — 1,200. **Hallmark**

Cards Inc.; Liberty; distribution center — 1,000. **St. Joseph State Hospital**; St. Joseph; state mental health hospital — 1,000.

Farmland Industries Inc. (HQ); Kansas City; petroleum refining, animal feed — 950. **Wilcox Electric Inc.**; Kansas City; electronic components — 900. **Wilson Food Corp.**; Marshall; hog processing — 870. **Banquet Foods Corp.**; Marshall; frozen fruits, vegetables — 800. **Mead Corp.**; St. Joseph; paper — 800. **Quaker Oats Co.**; St. Joseph; cereal — 800.

Walsworth Publishing Co. Inc.; Marceline; yearbook wholesaling — 700. **Wire Rope Corp. of America Inc.** (HQ); St. Joseph; wire rope — 600. **CPC International Inc.**; Kansas City; sweeteners — 510. **Banquet Foods Corp.**; Carrollton; frozen foods — 500. **Banquet Foods Corp.**; Milan; poultry dressing — 500. **Churchill Truck Lines Inc.** (HQ); Chillicothe; trucking — 500. **Sherwood Medical Instruments**; St. Joseph; medical instruments — 500.

7th District

Southwest — Springfield, Joplin

Long a poor, isolated area resembling Appalachia, the scenic Ozark highlands have been discovered by tourists, retirees and new industry. Newcomers streamed into the 7th during the 1970s, boosting the population 22.2 percent, the fastest growth rate in any Missouri district. But there is little change in the district's Republican character.

The tourist and retiree presence is most obvious in the south-central part of the district, around Table Rock Reservoir and Bull Shoals Lake. Stone and Taney counties there each grew 57 percent during the 1970s.

More than a third of the district's residents live in Springfield and surrounding Greene County, the region's industrial and commercial center. Kraft, Litton and Zenith are major employers. The other population center in the district is Joplin, an old lead- and zinc-mining town turned to manufacturing.

However, the rural and agricultural character of the Ozarks has not yielded completely to development and modernization. There are still many small, isolated communities, the legacy of the Ozarks' original settlers — Scots-Irish mountaineers who relocated from eastern Tennessee, western Virginia and Kentucky and who generally kept to themselves and coaxed their crops from the rocky soil. The international headquarters of the Assemblies of God is in Springfield, reflecting the traditional importance of fundamentalism in the Ozarks.

Political attitudes here have changed little in the past century. The Ozarks had no use for slavery on their small, hilly farms; most were pro-Union in the Civil War and have voted Republican ever since. GOP candidates regularly take more than 60 percent of the vote in southwest Missouri; Ronald Reagan swept every county in the 7th in the 1980 presidential contest.

Redistricting barely altered the 7th, shifting only one county, Laclede, into the 4th District.

Election Returns

7th District		Democrat		Republican	
1976	President	98,916	(46.9%)	110,814	(52.5%)
	Governor	83,511	(39.9%)	125,477	(59.9%)
	Senate	70,334	(33.9%)	135,953	(65.5%)

7th District		Democrat		Republican	
1976	House	78,703	(38.0%)	128,452	(62.0%)
1978	House	64,141	(38.9%)	100,924	(61.1%)
1980	President	85,364	(36.4%)	141,329	(60.2%)
	Governor	97,613	(41.9%)	134,918	(57.9%)
	Senate	93,937	(40.9%)	135,139	(58.8%)
	House	73,029	(32.0%)	155,374	(68.0%)
1982	Senate	83,725	(46.4%)	96,653	(53.6%)
	House	89,549	(49.5%)	91,391	(50.5%)

Demographics

Population: 545,921. **Percent Change from 1970:** 22.2%.

Land Area: 10,456 square miles. **Population per Square Mile:** 52.2.

Counties, 1980 Population: Barry — 24,408; Cedar — 11,894; Christian — 22,402; Dade — 7,383; Dallas — 12,096; Douglas — 11,594; Greene — 185,302; Jasper — 86,958; Lawrence — 28,973; McDonald — 14,917; Newton — 40,555; Ozark — 7,961; Polk — 18,822; Stone — 15,587; Taney — 20,467; Webster — 20,414; Wright — 16,188.

Cities, 1980 Population: Carthage — 11,104; Joplin — 38,893; Springfield — 133,116.

Race and Ancestry: White — 98.1%; Black — 0.8%; American Indian, Eskimo and Aleut — 0.6%; Asian and Pacific Islander — 0.3%. Spanish Origin — 0.6%. Dutch — 0.8%; English — 16.5%; French — 1.0%; German — 8.1%; Irish — 5.6%; Scottish — 0.5%; Swedish — 0.5%.

Universities, Enrollment: Assemblies of God Graduate School, Springfield — 212; Baptist Bible College, Springfield — 1,721; Central Bible College, Springfield — 1,094; Crowder College, Neosho — 1,183; Drury College, Springfield — 2,922; Evangel College, Springfield — 1,851; Missouri Southern State College, Joplin — 4,013; School of the Ozarks, Point Lookout — 1,259; Southwest Baptist College, Bolivar — 1,592; Southwest Missouri State University, Springfield — 15,137; Water & Wastewater Technical School, Neosho — 160.

Newspapers, Circulation: *Advertiser* (e), Aurora — 3,890; *Carthage Press* (e), Carthage — 5,684; *The Joplin Globe* (mS), Joplin — 40,352; *Neosho Daily News* (eS), Neosho — 6,517; *The Springfield Daily News* (mS), Springfield — 37,473; *The Springfield Leader & Press* (eS), Springfield — 38,306; *Times* (e), Monett — 4,246.

Commercial Television Stations, Affiliation: KMTC, Springfield (ABC); KODE-TV, Joplin (ABC); KOLR-TV, Springfield (CBS); KSPR, Springfield (None); KTVJ, Joplin (CBS); KYTV, Springfield (NBC). Most of district is located in Springfield ADI. Portion is in Joplin-Pittsburg (Kan.) ADI.

Military Installations: Air Force Plant 65, Neosho — 12.

Industries:

Zenith Electronics Corp.; Springfield; televisions — 2,300. **Lester E. Cox Medical Center** (HQ); Springfield; hospital — 2,280. **St. John's Regional Health Center** (HQ); Springfield; hospital — 1,770. **Burlington Northern Inc.**; Springfield; railroad operations — 1,500. **St. John's Hospital**; Joplin; hospital — 1,100.

Kraft Inc.; Springfield; food processing, packaging — 1,050. **Litton Systems Inc.**; Springfield; printed wiring — 1,000. **Paul Mueller Co.** (HQ); Springfield; milk tanks, vats — 1,000. **Prime Inc.** (HQ); Springfield; trucking — 975. **General Electric Co. Inc.**; Springfield; electric motors — 930. **Dayco Corp.**; Springfield; rubber belting — 826 **Fasco Industries Inc.**; Ozark; motors — 801.

Sperry Corp. (Vickers Div.); Joplin; hydraulic pumps — 800. **La-Z-Boy Chair Co.** (Midwest Div.); Neosho; upholstered furniture — 730. **Associated Wholesale Groceries**; Springfield; frozen foods wholesaling — 725. **Emerson Electric Co.** (Motor Div.); Ava; motors, generators — 679. **Juvenile Shoe Corp. of America** (HQ); Aurora; women's, children's shoes — 675. **Foremost-McKesson Inc.** (Foremost Food Group); Springfield; dairy products — 658. **Eagle-Picher Industries Inc.** (Electronic Div.); Joplin; power batteries — 650.

Teledyne Inc. (Continental Aviation & Engineering Div.); Neosho; aircraft engine overhauls — 604. **Jumping-Jacks Shoes Inc.** (HQ); Monett; children's shoes — 555. **Tyson Foods Inc.** (Honeybear Foods); Neosho; poultry processing — 525. **L. D. Schreiber Cheese Co.;** Carthage; cheese processing — 516. **Brown Group Inc.** (Brown Shoe Co. Div.); Mountain Grove; shoes — 506. **Atlas Powder Co.;** Joplin; explosives — 500. **Fasco Industries Inc.;** Cassville; electric motors — 500. **Hudson Foods Inc.;** Noel; poultry processing — 500.

8th District

Southeast — Cape Girardeau

The redrawn 8th merges 18 counties from the old 10th District with seven counties from the old 8th. The remap diminished Republican strength by moving Jefferson County and its 146,183 people, many of whom tended to vote Republican, to the 3rd District. In the new 8th the largest block of GOP votes is in Cape Girardeau County, which has just under 59,000 people. That county and neighboring Perry County both voted Republican in the 1976 and 1980 presidential contests.

At the opposite end of the partisan spectrum are the Bootheel counties in the extreme southeast corner of the district. This area still looks and votes like the old South. Although Ronald Reagan's philosophy appealed to conservative Democrats throughout Missouri, four Bootheel counties with a total population of nearly 100,000 — Dunklin, Pemiscot, New Madrid and Mississippi — voted for Jimmy Carter and the rest of the statewide Democratic ticket in November 1980.

Republicans, however, have gained ground in recent elections in traditionally Democratic counties elsewhere in the 8th. Iron County, for example, voted only narrowly for Carter in 1980.

On the western border of the redrawn 8th are the seven counties with 131,363 people formerly in the old 8th: Phelps, Howell, Crawford, Washington, Dent, Oregon and Shannon. The most populous of those is Phelps County (population 33,633). The Democratic Party is strongest in Oregon and Shannon counties, but those two together contain fewer than 19,000 people.

Election Returns

8th District		Democrat		Republican	
1976	President	109,866	(56.3%)	84,280	(43.2%)
	Governor	99,480	(51.8%)	92,467	(48.1%)
	Senate	97,047	(50.7%)	94,027	(49.1%)
	House	133,391	(70.9%)	54,494	(29.0%)
1978	House	93,797	(62.6%)	56,025	(37.4%)
1980	President	94,184	(44.0%)	114,559	(53.5%)
	Governor	100,420	(47.4%)	111,176	(52.5%)
	Senate	102,136	(49.4%)	104,186	(50.4%)
	House	91,475	(43.7%)	118,080	(56.3%)
1982	Senate	86,427	(52.7%)	77,626	(47.3%)
	House	76,413	(46.9%)	86,493	(53.1%)

Demographics

Population: 546,112. **Percent Change from 1970:** 14.3%.

Land Area: 16,142 square miles. **Population per Square Mile:** 33.8.

Counties, 1980 Population: Bollinger — 10,301; Butler — 37,693; Cape Girardeau — 58,837; Carter — 5,428; Crawford — 18,300; Dent — 14,517; Dunklin — 36,324; Franklin (Pt.) — 6,514; Howell — 28,807; Iron — 11,084; Madison — 10,725; Mississippi — 15,726; New Madrid — 22,945; Oregon — 10,238; Pemiscot — 24,987; Perry — 16,784; Phelps — 33,633; Reynolds — 7,230; Ripley — 12,458; Scott — 39,647; Shannon — 7,885; St. Francois — 42,600; Ste. Genevieve — 15,180; Stoddard — 29,009; Washington — 17,983; Wayne — 11,277.

Cities, 1980 Population: Cape Girardeau — 34,361; Kennett — 10,145; Poplar Bluff — 17,139; Rolla — 13,303; Sikeston — 17,431.

Race and Ancestry: White — 95.1%; Black — 4.4%; American Indian, Eskimo and Aleut — 0.2%; Asian and Pacific Islander — 0.2%. Spanish Origin — 0.5%. Dutch — 0.6%; English — 15.5%; French — 1.9%; German — 11.5%; Irish — 6.4%.

Universities, Enrollment: Mineral Area College, Flat River — 1,397; St. Mary's Seminary College, Perryville — 71; Southeast Missouri State University, Cape Girardeau — 9,135; Three Rivers Community College, Poplar Bluff — 1,689; University of Missouri (Rolla campus), Rolla — 6,659.

Newspapers, Circulation: *Daily American Republic* (e), Poplar Bluff — 16,221; *The Daily Dunklin Democrat* (e), Kennett — 6,266; *The Daily Journal* (e), Flat River — 9,349; *Daily Standard* (eS), Sikeston — 11,098; *Daily Statesman-Messenger* (e), Dexter — 4,479; *Rolla Daily News* (eS), Rolla — 8,255; *The Southeast Missourian* (eS), Cape Girardeau — 16,792; *West Plains Daily Quill* (e), West Plains — 8,799.

Commercial Television Stations, Affiliation: KFVS-TV, Cape Girardeau (CBS); KPOB-TV, Poplar Bluff (ABC). District is divided among St. Louis ADI, Springfield ADI and Paducah (Ky.)-Cape Girardeau-Harrisburg (Ill.) ADI. Portions are in Jonesboro (Ark.) ADI and Memphis (Tenn.) ADI.

Industries:

Procter & Gamble Co.; Cape Girardeau; sanitary paper products — 1,350. **Noranda Aluminum Inc.;** New Madrid; aluminum production — 1,030. **Emerson Electric Co.** (Motor Div.); Kennett; motors — 1,000. **St. Joe Minerals Corp.;** Steelville; lead mining — 1,000. **Amax Lead Co. of Missouri;** Boss; lead mining — 970.

Mississippi Lime Co.; Ste. Genevieve; lime, limestone — 750. **Interco Inc.;** Cape Girardeau; shoes — 679. **Arvin Industries Inc.;** Dexter; auto exhaust equipment — 600. **Flat River Glass Co.;** Flat River; glass bottles — 573. **Brown Group Inc.;** Bernie; footwear — 500. **Federal-Mogul Corp.;** Malden; motor vehicle parts — 500. **Inland Shoe Mfg. Co. Inc.;** Advance; children's, women's shoes — 500.

9th District

Northeast — Columbia

Pushed north by the underpopulated St. Louis districts reaching outward for people, the 9th District drew away from metropolitan St. Louis and nearby St. Charles, taking on more of a small-town identity. Hannibal, Mississippi River boyhood home of Mark Twain, Huck Finn and Tom Sawyer, is the second largest city in the district, with 18,811 people.

The district lost about 65,000 people in part of St. Louis and St. Charles counties, both GOP-leaning areas. Some 79,000 St. Charles residents were kept in the district; most are in rural portions of the county and are likely to vote Democratic.

Having shed population in the St. Louis area, the redrawn 9th annexed the northern section of the old 8th

District, beginning with Boone County (Columbia), whose 100,376 people make it the largest voting bloc in the new 9th.

The moderate-to-liberal University of Missouri community in Columbia lends an element of uncertainty to Boone County elections. Republicans carried Boone in the 1976 and 1980 gubernatorial contests, but Jimmy Carter won the county's presidential vote in both those years. Independent presidential candidate John B. Anderson received 9 percent there in 1980, his best showing in the state.

The 9th crosses the Missouri River to take in Franklin, Osage and Gasconade counties. In a transfer with the 6th District, the 9th gave up Putnam and Schuyler counties and took in Adair County.

The remap enhanced Republican strength in the 9th District, but surviving intact is the heart of the district's Democratic strength — northeast Missouri's "Little Dixie," a traditionally Democratic corn-and-cattle-raising area first settled by pro-slavery planters from Virginia and Kentucky. Though Ronald Reagan's conservative themes helped him carry all but two counties in this region in the 1980 election, Little Dixie is still a reliable supporter of most Democrats.

Election Returns

9th District		Democrat		Republican	
1976	President	113,745	(49.6%)	112,799	(49.2%)
	Governor	112,336	(49.0%)	116,732	(50.9%)
	Senate	89,884	(39.5%)	136,586	(60.0%)
	House	133,154	(58.8%)	90,075	(39.8%)
1978	House	126,655	(68.4%)	58,500	(31.6%)
1980	President	97,269	(41.5%)	126,289	(53.9%)
	Governor	106,148	(45.9%)	124,225	(53.7%)
	Senate	116,565	(51.2%)	110,429	(48.5%)
	House	132,034	(54.1%)	112,170	(45.9%)
1982	Senate	75,307	(45.8%)	89,024	(54.2%)
	House	99,228	(60.8%)	63,942	(39.2%)

Demographics

Population: 546,171. **Percent Change from 1970:** 20.6%.

Land Area: 12,927 square miles. **Population per Square Mile:** 42.3.

Counties, 1980 Population: Adair — 24,870; Audrain — 26,458; Boone — 100,376; Callaway — 32,252; Clark — 8,493; Franklin (Pt.) — 64,719; Gasconade — 13,181; Knox — 5,508; Lewis — 10,901; Lincoln — 22,193; Macon — 16,313; Marion — 28,638; Monroe — 9,716; Montgomery — 11,537; Osage — 12,014; Pike — 17,568; Ralls — 8,911; Randolph — 25,460; Scotland — 5,415; Shelby — 7,826; St. Charles (Pt.) — 78,922; Warren — 14,900.

Cities, 1980 Population: Columbia — 62,061; Fulton — 11,046; Hannibal — 18,811; Jefferson City (Pt.) — 25; Kirksville — 17,167; Mexico — 12,276; Moberly — 13,418; St. Charles (Pt.) — 56; St. Peters (Pt.) — 7,558.

Race and Ancestry: White — 95.8%; Black — 3.3%; American Indian, Eskimo and Aleut — 0.1%; Asian and Pacific Islander — 0.5%. Spanish Origin — 0.6%. Dutch — 0.5%; English — 11.6%; French — 1.0%; German — 19.3%; Irish — 4.6%; Italian — 0.5%.

Universities, Enrollment: Columbia College, Columbia — 808; Culver-Stockton College, Canton — 586; East Central Junior College, Union — 2,060; Hannibal-LaGrange College, Hannibal — 432; Kirksville College of Osteopathic Medicine, Kirksville — 516; Moberly Junior College, Moberly — 900; Northeast Missouri State University, Kirksville — 6,366; Stephens College, Columbia — 1,390; University of Missouri (Columbia campus), Columbia — 24,306; Westminster College, Fulton — 674; William Woods College, Fulton — 1,316.

Newspapers, Circulation: *The Columbia Daily Tribune* (eS), Columbia — 17,986; *Columbia Missourian* (mS), Columbia — 6,861; *Hannibal Courier-Post* (e), Hannibal — 12,167; *Kingdom Daily Sun-Gazette* (mS), Fulton — 3,699; *Kirksville Daily Express & News* (eS), Kirksville — 9,960; *Macon Chronicle-Herald* (e), Macon — 4,549; *Mexico Ledger* (e), Mexico — 12,319; *Moberly Monitor-Index & Democrat* (eS), Moberly — 9,515.

Commercial Television Stations, Affiliation: KCBJ-TV, Columbia (ABC); KHQA-TV, Hannibal (CBS); KOMU-TV, Columbia (NBC); KTVO, Kirksville (ABC). District is divided among Columbia-Jefferson City ADI, St. Louis ADI and Quincy (Ill.)-Hannibal ADI. A portion is in Ottumwa (Iowa)-Kirksville ADI.

Nuclear Power Plants: Callaway 1, Fulton (Westinghouse, Daniel International).

Industries:

Daniel International Corp.; Fulton; general contracting — 3,700. **A. P. Green Refractories Co.;** Mexico; refractories — 1,500. **Fulton State Hospital;** Fulton; state mental hospital — 1,400. **Monsanto Co.** (Electronics Materials Co.); St. Peters; semiconductors — 1,400. **Boone County Hospital;** Columbia; hospital — 1,350.

Veterans Administration; Columbia; veterans' hospital — 1,120. **A. B. Chance Co.** (HQ); Centralia; pole line hardware — 1,000. **Shelter Mutual Insurance Co.** (HQ); Columbia; accident, health insurance — 774. **State Farm Life Insurance Co.;** Columbia; fire, casualty insurance — 719. **Hazel Bindery Inc.** (HQ); Washington; specialty advertising products — 646. **The Binkley Co.** (HQ); Warrenton; motor vehicle, railroad, farm machinery parts — 600. **Kaiser Aluminum & Chemical Corp.** (Refractories Div.); Mexico; clay refractories — 600.

Minnesota Mining & Mfg. Co.; Columbia; semiconductors — 600. **Trans-Fleet Enterprises Inc.** (HQ); Columbia; management services — 560. **Banquet Foods Corp.;** Macon; frozen fruits, vegetables — 500. **Beacon Shoe Co. Inc.;** Jonesburg; women's shoes — 500. **Norfolk & Western Railroad;** Moberly; terminal operations — 500. **Orbco Inc.;** Moberly; automotive parts — 500. **Toastmaster Inc.;** Macon; electric housewares — 500.

Montana

Montana, like Maine, did not redistrict until 1983 when it made only slight changes in the line dividing its two congressional districts. The map in place for the 1984 elections shifted just 16,773 people in four counties from the western 1st District to the eastern 2nd District. The four counties were Toole, Pondera, Liberty and Meagher.

The map was drawn by the state's five-member bipartisan Districting and Apportionment Commission. Final approval of the plan was delayed until 1983 because the state constitution requires that redistricting changes be reviewed by the state Legislature in a regularly scheduled session. Those sessions occur only in odd-numbered years, and because census data was not made available in 1981 until after the regular session had ended, lawmakers did not officially receive the plan until Jan. 5, 1983. The Legislature returned the map unchanged to the commission Feb. 4. After a required 28-day waiting period, the map became official March 4.

The profiles below are for the districts in effect for the 1982 elections. The 1983 redistricting did not affect any of the universities, newspapers, television stations, military facilities or industries listed below.

Age of Population

District	Population Under 18	Voting Age Population	Population 65 & Over (% of VAP)	Median Age
1	118,262	291,809	43,858 (15.0%)	29.0
2	113,633	262,986	40,701 (15.5%)	29.0
State	231,895	554,795	84,559 (15.2%)	29.0

Income and Occupation

District	Median Family Income	White Collar Workers	Blue Collar Workers	Service Workers	Farm Workers
1	$ 18,410	51.6%	26.0%	15.5%	6.9%
2	18,417	48.6	25.1	14.6	11.7
State	$ 18,413	50.1%	25.6%	15.1%	9.3%

Education: School Years Completed

District	8 Years or Fewer	4 Years of High School	4 Years of College or More	Median School Years
1	12.8%	37.8%	18.7%	12.7
2	15.9	38.1	16.1	12.6
State	14.3%	38.0%	17.5%	12.6

Housing and Residential Patterns

District	Owner Occupied	Renter Occupied	Urban	Rural
1	68.8%	31.2%	50.6%	49.4%
2	68.3	31.7	55.4	44.6
State	68.6%	31.4%	52.9%	47.1%

1st District

Western Mountains — Helena; Missoula

As the Montana plains climb west into the Rocky Mountains, the 1st District electorate becomes more heavily unionized and more Democratic.

The two most predictably Democratic counties in the state sit on the Continental Divide, just south of the state capital, Helena. Silver Bow County (Butte) and neighboring Deer Lodge County were the only two counties in the state to vote for the Democratic presidential candidates in 1972 and 1980. As huge shovels continue to dig away at the copper, zinc and lead from the "richest hill on Earth," the manpower needs continue to shrink, forcing many miners out of work. Deer Lodge County lost 20 percent of its population in the 1970s; Silver Bow, 9 percent.

Missoula, the home of the University of Montana, also is a center for the lumber industry. The political strength of the university community often gives Missoula County a strong Democratic bent. Although Jimmy Carter did not win the county in 1980, it was one of the few in Montana where Ronald Reagan received less than 50 percent of the vote.

MONTANA

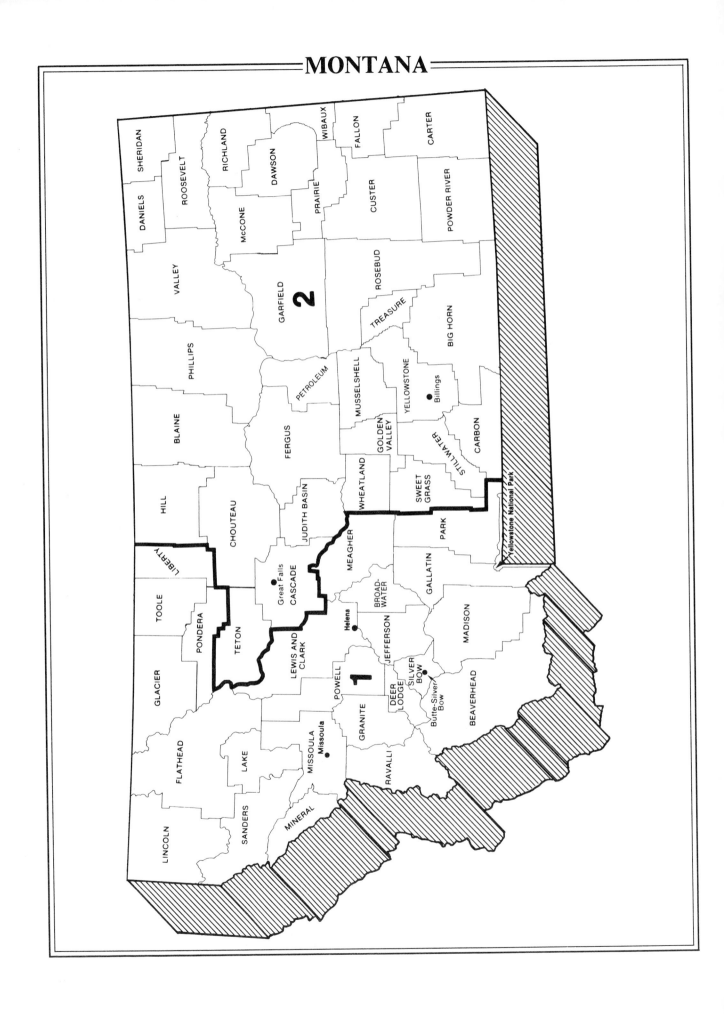

North of Missoula is a mixture of Democratic logging areas and Republican counties devoted to ranching and growing cherries. The counties south of Missoula tend to be Democratic.

The redistricting scheduled to take effect with the 99th Congress simply transferred out of the 1st District four rural wheat-growing counties — Liberty, Meagher, Pondera and Toole — with a population of less than 17,000. The shift does not change the political balance between the two districts.

Election Returns

1st District		Democrat		Republican	
1976	President	77,885	(45.6%)	90,124	(52.7%)
	Governor	99,859	(60.8%)	62,422	(38.0%)
	Senate	102,973	(62.3%)	62,184	(37.7%)
	House	111,487	(66.4%)	56,297	(33.6%)
1978	Senate	88,319	(57.7%)	64,704	(42.3%)
	House	86,016	(57.3%)	64,093	(42.7%)
1980	President	64,393	(33.1%)	107,574	(55.3%)
	Governor	106,897	(55.4%)	85,885	(44.6%)
	House	112,866	(61.4%)	70,874	(38.6%)
1982	Senate	87,832	(52.0%)	72,941	(43.2%)
	House	100,087	(59.7%)	62,402	(37.2%)

Demographics

Population: 410,071. **Percent Change from 1970:** 18.0%.

Land Area: 55,841 square miles. **Population per Square Mile:** 7.3.

Counties, 1980 Population: Beaverhead — 8,186; Broadwater — 3,267; Deer Lodge — 12,518; Flathead — 51,966; Gallatin — 42,865; Glacier — 10,628; Granite — 2,700; Jefferson — 7,029; Lake — 19,056; Lewis and Clark — 43,039; Liberty — 2,329; Lincoln — 17,752; Madison — 5,448; Meagher — 2,154; Mineral — 3,675; Missoula — 76,016; Park — 12,660; Pondera — 6,731; Powell — 6,958; Ravalli — 22,493; Sanders — 8,675; Silver Bow — 38,092; Toole — 5,559; Yellowstone National Park — 275.

Cities, 1980 Population: Anaconda-Deer Lodge County — 12,518; Bozeman — 21,645; Butte-Silver Bow — 37,205; Helena — 23,938; Kalispell — 10,648; Missoula — 33,388.

Race and Ancestry: White — 95.6%; Black — 0.1%; American Indian, Eskimo and Aleut — 3.4%; Asian and Pacific Islander — 0.4%. Spanish Origin — 1.0%. Dutch — 1.4%; English — 9.1%; French — 1.9%; German — 12.9%; Irish — 6.9%; Italian — 1.1%; Norwegian — 4.2%; Polish — 0.6%; Scottish — 1.3%; Swedish — 1.9%.

Universities, Enrollment: Carroll College, Helena — 1,326; Flathead Valley Community College, Kalispell — 1,778; Montana College of Mineral Science and Technology, Butte — 1,387; Montana State University, Bozeman — 10,745; University of Montana, Missoula — 8,884; Western Montana University, Dillon — 767.

Newspapers, Circulation: *Bozeman Daily Chronicle* (eS), Bozeman — 8,918; *The Daily Inter Lake* (eS), Kalispell — 10,337; *Enterprise* (e), Livingston — 3,624; *Independent Record* (eS), Helena — 12,145; *Missoulian* (mS), Missoula — 31,397; *The Montana Standard* (mS), Butte — 19,646; *Ravalli Republic* (m), Hamilton — 3,960.

Commercial Television Stations, Affiliation: KCFW-TV, Kalispell (NBC, CBS); KECI-TV, Missoula (NBC, CBS); KPAX-TV, Missoula (ABC, CBS); KTVG, Helena (NBC); KTVM, Butte (NBC, CBS); KXLF-TV, Butte (ABC, CBS). Most of district is located in Missoula-Butte ADI. Portions are in Billings-Hardin ADI, Great Falls ADI, Helena ADI and Spokane (Wash.) ADI.

Industries:

Champion International Corp. (Champion Building Products); Bonner; plywood mill — 1,000. **St. Regis Paper Co.;** Libby; lumber, plywood mills — 900. **Plum Creek Lumber Co.** (HQ); Columbia Falls; lumber, plywood mills — 700. **Champion International Corp.** (Champion Packaging Div.); Missoula; pulp, paper mills — 682. **Arco Metals Co.** (Arco Aluminum Co. Div.); Columbia Falls; aluminum production — 590. **Burlington Northern Inc.** (Timber & Land Dept.); Missoula; railroad operations — 550. **Evans Products Co.;** Missoula; lumber, plywood mills — 550.

2nd District

East — Billings; Great Falls

This is flat country — a land of sizzling summer heat and numbing winter cold, given over to wheat growing, cattle raising and, more recently, energy development. Covering three-quarters of the state, the 2nd tends to favor Republicans or conservative Democrats.

Billings, with a population of 66,798, is the state's largest city. Originally a farm market center, today it is headquarters for the many energy ventures sprouting across the plains. It is a Republican town, although in 1982 it supported Democratic Sen. John Melcher in his re-election bid.

Great Falls, Montana's second population center with 56,725 residents, also is in the 2nd District. Cheap hydroelectric power drawn from the nearby falls on the Missouri River spurred the city's industrial development in the early 1900s, and it retains a large blue-collar population. With a tradition of union activism since the turn of the century — including one of the first Newspaper Guild locals in the Northwest — the city often turns in Democratic majorities, except at the presidential level.

Coal discoveries in Rosebud County, east of Billings, have brought in many newcomers. The county grew 64 percent in the 1970s, the largest increase of any county in the state. The political result has been to render this former GOP bastion into a marginal political area. After giving nearly 55 percent of its vote to Ronald Reagan in the 1980 presidential election, the county delivered 69 percent to Democrat Melcher in the 1982 Senate race.

The sparsely populated ranching counties in the southeast corner, most of them losing population, are among the most Republican in the state. This area went for Barry Goldwater in 1964 and backed losing GOP state candidates through the 1970s. Between the Canadian border and the Missouri River are the eight wheat-growing "High Line" counties. While they usually vote Republican in presidential contests the wheat farmers sometimes side with local Democratic candidates.

As a result of the 1983 redistricting four more counties — Liberty, Meagher, Pondera and Toole — were added to the 2nd for the 99th Congress. The change is not expected to have any political effect.

Election Returns

2nd District		Democrat		Republican	
1976	President	71,374	(45.2%)	83,579	(53.0%)
	Governor	95,561	(62.7%)	53,426	(35.0%)
	Senate	103,259	(66.1%)	53,029	(33.9%)
	House	68,972	(45.0%)	84,149	(55.0%)

2nd District		Democrat		Republican	
1978	Senate	72,034	(53.4%)	62,885	(46.6%)
	House	57,480	(43.1%)	75,766	(56.9%)
1980	President	53,639	(31.6%)	99,240	(58.6%)
	Governor	92,677	(55.3%)	75,007	(44.7%)
	House	63,370	(40.9%)	91,431	(59.1%)
1982	Senate	87,029	(57.2%)	60,848	(40.0%)
	House	65,815	(44.2%)	79,968	(53.7%)

Demographics

Population: 376,619. **Percent Change from 1970:** 8.5%.

Land Area: 89,548 square miles. **Population per Square Mile:** 4.2.

Counties, 1980 Population: Big Horn — 11,096; Blaine — 6,999; Carbon — 8,099; Carter — 1,799; Cascade — 80,696; Chouteau — 6,092; Custer — 13,109; Daniels — 2,835; Dawson — 11,805; Fallon — 3,763; Fergus — 13,076; Garfield — 1,656; Golden Valley — 1,026; Hill — 17,985; Judith Basin — 2,646; McCone — 2,702; Musselshell — 4,428; Petroleum — 655; Phillips — 5,367.

Powder River — 2,520; Prairie — 1,836; Richland — 12,243; Roosevelt — 10,467; Rosebud — 9,899; Sheridan — 5,414; Stillwater — 5,598; Sweet Grass — 3,216; Teton — 6,491; Treasure — 981; Valley — 10,250; Wheatland — 2,359; Wibaux — 1,476; Yellowstone — 108,035.

Cities, 1980 Population: Billings — 66,798; Great Falls — 56,725; Havre — 10,891.

Race and Ancestry: White — 92.4%; Black — 0.4%; American Indian, Eskimo and Aleut — 6.2%; Asian and Pacific Islander — 0.3%. Spanish Origin — 1.6%. Dutch — 0.6%; English — 5.6%; French — 1.0%; German — 14.8%; Irish — 3.3%; Italian — 0.7%; Norwegian — 5.1%; Polish — 0.6%; Scottish — 0.8%; Swedish — 1.2%.

Universities, Enrollment: College of Great Falls, Great Falls — 1,253; Dawson College, Glendive — 432; Eastern Montana College, Billings — 3,779; Miles Community College, Miles City — 746; Northern Montana College, Havre — 1,473; Rocky Mountain College, Billings — 441.

Newspapers, Circulation: *The Billings Gazette* (mS), Billings — 59,164; *Great Falls Tribune* (mS), Great Falls — 37,588; *The Havre Daily News* (e), Havre — 4,810; *Miles City Star* (eS), Miles City — 4,304.

Commercial Television Stations, Affiliation: KFBB-TV, Great Falls (ABC, NBC); KOUS-TV, Hardin (NBC); KRTV, Great Falls (NBC, CBS); KTVQ, Billings (CBS); KULR-TV, Billings (ABC); KXGN, Glendive (CBS, NBC); KYUS-TV, Miles City (NBC). Most of district is located in Billings-Hardin ADI and Great Falls ADI. Portions are in Miles City-Glendive ADI, Minot (N.D.)-Bismarck (N.D.)-Dickinson (N.D.) ADI, and Rapid City (S.D.) ADI.

Military Installations: Great Falls International Airport (Air Force), Great Falls — 1,078; Malmstrom Air Force Base, Great Falls — 4,887.

Industries:

Burlington Northern Inc.; Billings; railroad operations — 980. **Leonard Pipeline Contractors;** Glasgow; pipeline construction — 850. **Decker Coal Co.;** Decker; coal mining — 650. **Peter Kiewit Sons Co.;** Decker; highway construction, coal mining — 540.

Nebraska

If Nebraska Republicans had had their way, the state's three congressional districts would have remained unchanged in the 1980s. But under the threat of a Democratic lawsuit charging that the 2.4 percent population variance between the districts was too great, the GOP reluctantly made two minor changes that brought the variance to 0.23 percent.

The political impact of the revisions was minimal. Fewer than 8,000 of the state's 856,000 registered voters were affected by the changes, which moved six townships in Cass County from the 2nd District to the 1st and all of rural Thayer County from the 1st to the 3rd.

Democrats in Nebraska's unicameral Legislature introduced a more elaborate plan in 1981 that featured a population variance of just 0.01 percent (57 people). It was designed to strengthen the party's chances in the 1st, which had elected a Democrat only once in its 20-year history.

The Democratic plan, proposed in late April, would have dropped three heavily Republican counties from the 1st (Knox, Pierce and Madison) and replaced them with three marginal counties in the 3rd. Republicans called this a "drastic and unnecessary change" and a blatant effort at political gerrymandering.

Although the single-chamber Legislature is officially non-partisan, senators registered in the Republican Party outnumber registered Democrats by about a two-to-one margin. So Democrats knew their plan had no chance of winning on a roll call. But they thought a federal court might approve it because its population variance was so much lower than that of the original GOP status-quo idea.

Republicans asked the state attorney general if the map in place during the 1970s would stand up in court and were told it might be vulnerable to challenge. So they reluctantly drew their own plan altering the boundaries slightly to equalize population. That map was finally approved May 27, 1981, on a 37-6 vote, and Republican Gov. Charles Thone signed it May 28, 1981.

Age of Population

District	Population Under 18	Voting Age Population	Population 65 & Over (% of VAP)	Median Age
1	139,092	383,987	74,959 (19.5%)	30.0
2	157,921	364,998	50,168 (13.7%)	28.3
3	150,157	373,670	80,557 (21.6%)	31.3
State	447,170	1,122,655	205,684 (18.3%)	29.7

Income and Occupation

District	Median Family Income	White Collar Workers	Blue Collar Workers	Service Workers	Farm Workers
1	$ 18,803	46.4%	28.0%	14.3%	11.3%
2	21,400	59.1	25.1	13.8	2.0
3	17,305	40.9	28.3	13.2	17.6
State	$ 19,122	48.8%	27.1%	13.8%	10.3%

Education: School Years Completed

District	8 Years or Fewer	4 Years of High School	4 Years of College or More	Median School Years
1	17.4%	40.1%	14.9%	12.5
2	10.5	39.4	19.7	12.7
3	17.1	42.2	12.2	12.5
State	15.1%	40.6%	15.5%	12.6

Housing and Residential Patterns

District	Owner Occupied	Renter Occupied	Urban	Rural
1	68.9%	31.1%	57.1%	42.9%
2	64.3	35.7	88.5	11.5
3	71.9	28.1	43.2	56.8
State	68.4%	31.6%	62.9%	37.1%

1st District

East Central — Lincoln

The state capital, Lincoln, gives the 1st District a modest urban flavor, but the city does not dominate the district the way Omaha influences the neighboring 2nd.

NEBRASKA

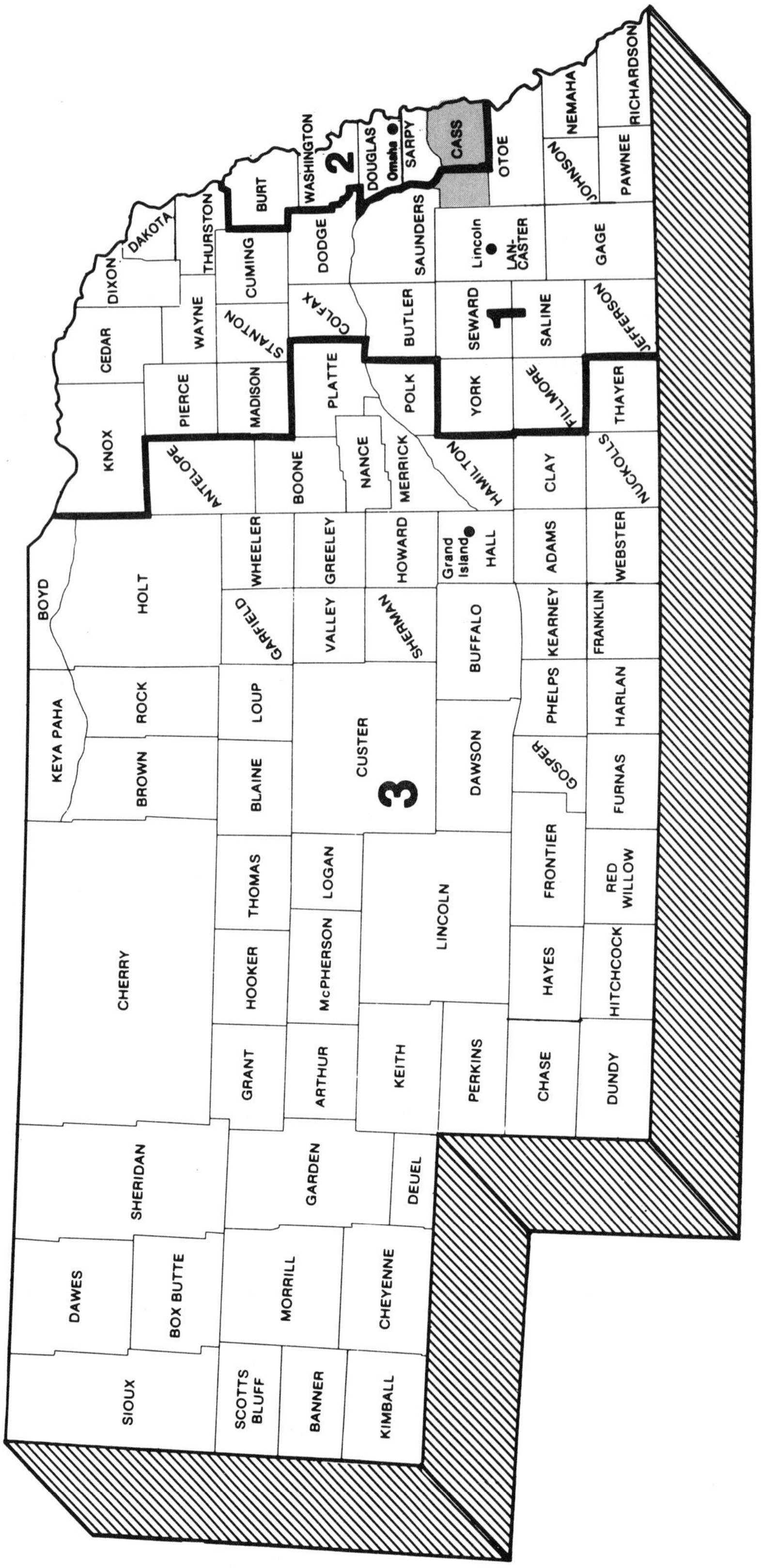

DAKOTA
DIXON
CEDAR
KNOX
BOYD
KEYA PAHA

WASHINGTON
2
BURT
THURSTON
CUMING
WAYNE
STANTON
PIERCE
MADISON
ANTELOPE
WHEELER
GARFIELD
LOUP
BLAINE
THOMAS
HOOKER
GRANT
ARTHUR

DODGE
COLFAX
PLATTE
BOONE
NANCE
GREELEY
VALLEY
CUSTER
3
LOGAN
McPHERSON
KEITH

DOUGLAS
Omaha
SARPY
SAUNDERS
BUTLER
POLK
MERRICK
HOWARD
SHERMAN
BUFFALO
DAWSON
LINCOLN
PERKINS

CASS
OTOE
Lincoln
LAN-CASTER
SEWARD
1
YORK
HAMILTON
Grand Island
HALL
ADAMS
KEARNEY
PHELPS
GOSPER
FRONTIER
HAYES
CHASE
DUNDY

NEMAHA
RICHARDSON
JOHNSON
PAWNEE
GAGE
SALINE
FILLMORE
THAYER
CLAY
NUCKOLLS
WEBSTER
FRANKLIN
HARLAN
FURNAS
RED WILLOW
HITCHCOCK
JEFFERSON

CHERRY
ROCK
BROWN

SHERIDAN
GARDEN
DEUEL

DAWES
BOX BUTTE
MORRILL
CHEYENNE

SIOUX
SCOTTS BLUFF
BANNER
KIMBALL

Lancaster County, which includes Lincoln and its few surrounding suburbs, makes up 37 percent of the new 1st District's population. Essentially a white-collar town, Lincoln is dominated by the state government and the University of Nebraska located there. Partisan registration in the county is nearly evenly split between the two major parties and Lancaster County can go either way in a close statewide election.

The rest of the district is made up largely of prosperous, predominantly Republican farming areas where corn is the major crop. The few small cities such as Fremont, Norfolk and Beatrice are market centers closely tied to farming.

The counties located along the Platte River (Colfax, Dodge, Butler and Saunders) occasionally support Democrats, along with Saline County, southwest of Lincoln, and Dakota County, a meatpacking area situated along the Missouri River that is becoming a suburb of Sioux City, Iowa.

The rest of the 1st District's 27 counties, particularly those located toward the northern border, cast an overwhelming Republican vote. Ronald Reagan, who took 62 percent of the vote districtwide in 1980, won 72 percent of the vote in the northern 10 counties of the 1st District.

In the remap, the district lost rural Thayer County while gaining six townships on the western side of Cass County. These counties are geographically located midway between Lincoln and Omaha but are politically closer to Lincoln. Two of the six townships have Democratic registration advantages, but all six have been voting as Republican as the rest of the 1st District.

Election Returns

1st District		Democrat		Republican	
1976	President	82,128	(40.5%)	116,065	(57.3%)
	Senate	104,382	(52.0%)	96,253	(48.0%)
	House	53,631	(27.0%)	145,011	(73.0%)
1978	Governor	62,592	(38.1%)	101,685	(61.9%)
	Senate	113,352	(68.9%)	51,139	(31.1%)
	House	70,931	(42.0%)	97,938	(58.0%)
1980	President	57,724	(27.9%)	129,333	(62.4%)
	House	43,673	(21.6%)	158,898	(78.4%)
1982	Governor	99,960	(52.8%)	89,115	(47.1%)
	Senate	124,729	(66.3%)	51,873	(27.6%)
	House	45,676	(24.9%)	137,675	(75.1%)

Demographics

Population: 523,079. **Percent Change from 1970:** 6.6%.

Land Area: 14,989 square miles. **Population per Square Mile:** 34.9.

Counties, 1980 Population: Butler — 9,330; Cass (Pt.) — 4,752; Cedar — 11,375; Colfax — 9,890; Cuming — 11,664; Dakota — 16,573; Dixon — 7,137; Dodge — 35,847; Fillmore — 7,920; Gage — 24,456; Jefferson — 9,817; Johnson — 5,285; Knox — 11,457; Lancaster — 192,884; Madison — 31,382; Nemaha — 8,367; Otoe — 15,183; Pawnee — 3,937; Pierce — 8,481; Richardson — 11,315; Saline — 13,131; Saunders — 18,716; Seward — 15,789; Stanton — 6,549; Thurston — 7,186; Wayne — 9,858; York — 14,798.

Cities, 1980 Population: Beatrice — 12,891; Fremont — 23,979; Lincoln — 171,932; Norfolk — 19,449.

Race and Ancestry: White — 97.4%; Black — 0.8%; American Indian, Eskimo and Aleut — 0.9%; Asian and Pacific Islander — 0.5%. Spanish Origin — 0.9%. Dutch — 0.7%; English — 5.6%; French — 0.6%; German — 27.4%; Irish — 2.9%; Norwegian — 0.5%; Polish — 0.6%; Swedish — 1.9%.

Universities, Enrollment: Concordia Teachers College, Seward — 1,085; Doane College, Crete — 659; Lincoln School of Commerce, Lincoln — 841; Midland Lutheran College, Fremont — 861; Nebraska Wesleyan University, Lincoln — 1,165; Northeast Technical Community College, Norfolk — 1,554; Peru State College, Peru — 856; Southeast Community College (Lincoln campus), Lincoln — 2,585; Southeast Community College (Milford campus), Milford — 1,053; Union College, Lincoln — 888; University of Nebraska (Lincoln campus), Lincoln — 24,128; Wayne State College, Wayne — 2,312; York College, York — 360.

Newspapers, Circulation: *Beatrice Daily Sun* (e), Beatrice — 11,045; *Fremont Tribune* (e), Fremont — 13,664; *Journal* (e), Falls City — 5,299; *Lincoln Journal* (eS), Lincoln — 44,300; *Lincoln Star* (mS), Lincoln — 30,447; *Nebraska City News-Press* (eS), Nebraska City — 4,246; *The Norfolk Daily News* (e), Norfolk — 21,954; *York News-Times* (e), York — 6,270. *Omaha World-Herald* also circulates in the district.

Commercial Television Stations, Affiliation: KOLN-TV, Lincoln (CBS). District is divided among Lincoln-Hastings-Kearney ADI, Omaha ADI and Sioux City (Iowa) ADI.

Military Installations: Lincoln Municipal Airport (Air Force), Lincoln — 1,183.

Nuclear Power Plants: Cooper Station, Brownville (General Electric, Burns & Roe), July 1974.

Industries:

Iowa Beef Processors Inc. (HQ); Dakota City; meatpacking — 2,800. **Burlington Northern Inc.;** Lincoln; railroad operations — 2,300. **Goodyear Tire & Rubber Co.;** Lincoln; tires — 1,500. **Bryan Memorial Hospital Inc.;** Lincoln; hospital — 1,250. **George A. Hormel & Co.;** Fremont; meatpacking — 1,150.

Campbell Soup Co.; Tecumseh; poultry processing — 800. **Dale Electronics Inc.;** Norfolk; electrical switchgear apparatus — 780. **Kawasaki Motor Corp.;** Lincoln; motor vehicle bodies — 700. **Outboard Marine Corp.;** Lincoln; lightweight industrial vehicles — 610. **Miller & Paine Inc.** (HQ); Lincoln; department stores — 600. **Petersen Mfg. Co. Inc.** (HQ); DeWitt; hand tools — 597.

Farmland Foods Inc.; Crete; pork processing — 580. **Sandoz Inc.** (Dorsey Laboratories); Lincoln; pharmaceutical preparations — 550. **Sherwood Medical Industries** (Monoject Div.); Norfolk; disposable medical instruments — 550. **Nucor Corp.** (Steel Div.); Norfolk; steel foundries — 535. **First National Bank & Trust Co.;** Lincoln; banking — 507. **Square D Co.;** Lincoln; circuit breakers — 500.

2nd District

East — Omaha

The 2nd is dominated by Omaha, whose metropolitan area holds 60 percent of the district's population and whose newspapers and television stations provide nearly all of its information.

Omaha is famous for the stockyards that traditionally have served the cattle, hog and sheep growers of Nebraska. Omaha has a diversified economy. Its major industries are meatpacking, railroading, dairy products and food processing, and the city is an insurance center.

Although it is an ethnic, industrial city and nominal Democratic territory, Omaha votes for conservatives. The blue-collar electorate, heavily Irish and Slavic, resembles that of ethnic areas in other Midwestern cities but has weaker Democratic Party ties. Omaha's 12 percent black population helps boost the Democratic vote.

In gubernatorial races Democrats usually win in Omaha. They have carried it and surrounding Douglas County in eight of the last nine elections. But the county has gone Republican for president every time but once in the post-Roosevelt era and has had Republican representation in the House for all but four of the past 30 years. With Omaha's suburbs doubling in size in the 1970s and the city losing more than 10 percent of its population, Douglas County's Democratic identification is becoming even weaker.

While Democrats maintained roughly a 50-40 registration advantage in the district's three southern counties during the 1970s, voters there have been splitting their tickets for nearly a generation. The two smaller counties to the north of Omaha are part of the Nebraska corn belt and solidly Republican.

Election Returns

2nd District		Democrat		Republican	
1976	President	75,218	(38.8%)	114,370	(59.0%)
	Senate	118,417	(62.8%)	70,092	(37.1%)
	House	105,618	(54.7%)	87,268	(45.2%)
1978	Governor	72,943	(50.3%)	71,883	(49.6%)
	Senate	102,081	(70.3%)	42,885	(29.5%)
	House	76,337	(52.3%)	69,633	(47.7%)
1980	President	61,075	(30.1%)	123,845	(61.0%)
	House	88,167	(43.8%)	106,600	(53.0%)
1982	Governor	87,662	(53.3%)	76,738	(46.6%)
	Senate	120,686	(73.5%)	35,718	(21.7%)
	House	70,431	(43.1%)	92,639	(56.7%)

Demographics

Population: 522,919. **Percent Change from 1970:** 6.2%.

Land Area: 1,820 square miles. **Population per Square Mile:** 287.3.

Counties, 1980 Population: Burt — 8,813; Cass (Pt.) — 15,545; Douglas — 397,038; Sarpy — 86,015; Washington — 15,508.

Cities, 1980 Population: Bellevue — 21,813; Omaha — 314,255.

Race and Ancestry: White — 89.4%; Black — 8.4%; American Indian, Eskimo and Aleut — 0.4%; Asian and Pacific Islander — 0.8%. Spanish Origin — 2.1%. English — 5.3%; French — 0.7%; German — 12.6%; Irish — 4.6%; Italian — 1.7%; Norwegian — 0.5%; Polish — 2.1%; Swedish — 1.5%.

Universities, Enrollment: Bellevue College, Bellevue — 2,380; College of St. Mary, Omaha — 751; Creighton University, Omaha — 5,614; Dana College, Blair — 564; Grace College of the Bible, Omaha — 457; Metropolitan Technical Community College, Omaha — 5,782; Nebraska College of Business, Omaha — 810; Omaha College of Health Careers, Omaha — 350; University of Nebraska (Omaha campus), Omaha — 13,546; University of Nebraska Medical Center, Omaha — 2,499.

Newspapers, Circulation: *Omaha World-Herald* (meS), Omaha — 234,942.

Commercial Television Stations, Affiliation: KETV, Omaha (ABC); KMTV, Omaha (NBC); WOWT, Omaha (CBS). Entire district is located in the Omaha ADI.

Military Installations: Offutt Air Force Base, Bellevue — 14,241.

Nuclear Power Plants: Fort Calhoun 1, Fort Calhoun (Combustion Engineering, Gibbs & Hill), June 1974.

Industries:

Mutual of Omaha Insurance Co. (HQ); Omaha; insurance —

4,620. **Western Electric Co. Inc.;** Omaha; telephone cable — 4,500. **Union Pacific Railroad Co. Inc.;** Omaha; railroad operations — 3,900. **Creighton Omaha Regional Health Center;** Omaha; hospital — 2,600. **Archbishop Bergan Mercy Hospital;** Omaha; hospital — 1,930.

Bishop Clarkson Memorial Hospital; Omaha; hospital — 1,600. **Peter Kiewit Sons Inc.** (Contractors Equipment Co. - HQ); Omaha; general contracting — 1,500. **Immanuel Inc.;** Omaha; hospital — 1,430. **United Benefit Life Insurance Co.** (United of Omaha); Omaha; life insurance — 1,400. **Valmont Industries Inc.** (HQ); Valley; irrigation equipment — 1,400. **Lozier Corp.;** Omaha; store fixtures, shelvings — 1,200. **Internorth Inc.** (Northern Natural Gas Co. - HQ); Omaha; natural gas distribution — 1,100. **Sperry Corp.** (Sperry-Vickers Div.); Omaha; hydraulic pumps — 1,100. **Nebraska Methodist Hospital;** Omaha; hospital — 1,080. **Control Data Corp.** (Sales Div.); Omaha; computing equipment — 1,000. **Kellogg Co.;** Omaha; cereals — 975.

First Data Resources Inc. (Proven Products Div. - HQ); Omaha; data processing services — 900. **Floor Brite Inc.** (HQ); Omaha; janitorial services — 900. **Omaha World Herald;** Omaha; newspaper publishing — 850. **Omaha National Corp.;** Omaha; banking — 784. **Campbell Soup Co.;** Omaha; food processing — 600. **Continental Can Co. Inc.;** Omaha; metal cans — 600. **Fabergé Inc.** (Tip Top Div.); Omaha; hair care products — 600. **Fruehauf Corp.** (Liquid Bulk Tank Div.); Omaha; trucking — 500. **Inter Micor Systems Inc.** (Reservation Center); Omaha; business services — 500.

3rd District

Central and West — Grand Island

Covering three-quarters of the state's land area, this is a rural district that runs from the corn belt at its eastern end to the wheat and ranching highlands west of the 100th meridian. One can drive for hours along some of the district's straight, flat roads without passing any community larger than a village. Many of the counties have one market town and little else but pasture.

The 3rd is the most Republican district in the state. It gave more than 70 percent of its vote to Ronald Reagan in 1980. In strong Democratic years, Republicans are occasionally vulnerable in this area. But the huge GOP registration advantage — exceeding 70 percent in some smaller counties — is usually more than enough to keep Republican incumbents in office. Democrats last won this seat in 1958 for only the sixth time since Nebraska gained statehood in 1867.

The only city with more than 25,000 people in the district is Grand Island, largely a service center for the surrounding farm areas. Smaller population clusters such as Kearney, North Platte and Scottsbluff are strung along the Platte River west of Grand Island.

North of Grand Island are three Democratic counties: Sherman, Greeley and Howard. Two others (Nance and Platte) have slimmer Democratic registration edges. During the 1970s Democratic Senate and gubernatorial candidates usually won these counties, but in recent years they have supported the Republican House incumbent, who was first elected in 1974.

During the 1970s more than one-half of the 61 counties in the 3rd District lost population. Most were in cattle lands just beyond the Platte River or in the western panhandle. As a result, the 3rd was the only district in Nebraska that needed to gain people in redistricting. The addition of Republican Thayer County makes the GOP even less vulnerable.

Election Returns

3rd District		Democrat		Republican	
1976	President	76,346	(36.2%)	129,270	(61.2%)
	Senate	91,010	(43.6%)	117,939	(56.4%)
	House	51,758	(24.6%)	153,351	(73.0%)
1978	Governor	81,219	(44.3%)	101,905	(55.6%)
	Senate	118,843	(64.4%)	65,782	(35.6%)
	House	36,549	(20.3%)	143,348	(79.7%)
1980	President	48,052	(20.8%)	166,759	(72.4%)
	House	35,575	(16.1%)	185,830	(83.9%)
1982	Governor	89,725	(46.3%)	104,232	(53.7%)
	Senate	117,935	(61.0%)	68,169	(35.5%)
	House	—[1]		x[1]	

[1] *No votes tabulated where candidate was unopposed; x indicates winner.*

Demographics

Population: 523,827. **Percent Change from 1970:** 4.2%.

Land Area: 59,836 square miles. **Population per Square Mile:** 8.8.

Counties, 1980 Population: Adams — 30,656; Antelope — 8,675; Arthur — 513; Banner — 918; Blaine — 867; Boone — 7,391; Box Butte — 13,696; Boyd — 3,331; Brown — 4,377; Buffalo — 34,797; Chase — 4,758; Cherry — 6,758; Cheyenne — 10,057; Clay — 8,106; Custer — 13,877; Dawes — 9,609; Dawson — 22,304; Deuel — 2,462; Dundy — 2,861; Franklin — 4,377.
Frontier — 3,647; Furnas — 6,486; Garden — 2,802; Garfield — 2,363; Gosper — 2,140; Grant — 877; Greeley — 3,462; Hall — 47,690; Hamilton — 9,301; Harlan — 4,292; Hayes — 1,356; Hitchcock — 4,079; Holt — 13,552; Hooker — 990; Howard — 6,773; Kearney — 7,053; Keith — 9,364; Keya Paha — 1,301; Kimball — 4,882; Lincoln — 36,455; Logan — 983; Loup — 859.
McPherson — 593; Merrick — 8,945; Morrill — 6,085; Nance — 4,740; Nuckolls — 6,726; Perkins — 3,637; Phelps — 9,769; Platte — 28,852; Polk — 6,320; Red Willow — 12,615; Rock — 2,383; Scotts Bluff — 38,344; Sheridan — 7,544; Sherman — 4,226; Sioux — 1,845; Thayer — 7,582; Thomas — 973; Valley — 5,633; Webster — 4,858; Wheeler — 1,060.

Cities, 1980 Population: Columbus — 17,328; Grand Island — 33,180; Hastings — 23,045; Kearney — 21,158; North Platte — 24,479; Scottsbluff — 14,156.

Race and Ancestry: White — 98.0%; Black — 0.1%; American Indian, Eskimo and Aleut — 0.4%; Asian and Pacific Islander — 0.2%; Spanish Origin — 2.4%. Dutch — 0.8%; English — 6.8%; French — 1.0%; German — 27.4%; Irish — 4.3%; Norwegian — 0.5%; Polish — 1.8%; Scottish — 0.5%; Swedish — 3.1%.

Universities, Enrollment: Central Technical Community College, Grand Island — 5,134; Chadron State College, Chadron — 1,921; Grand Island School of Business, Grand Island — 128; Hastings College, Hastings — 832; Kearney State College, Kearney — 6,948; McCook Community College, McCook — 516; Nebraska Western College, Scottsbluff — 1,210.

Newspapers, Circulation: *The Alliance Times-Herald* (e), Alliance — 4,669; *Columbus Telegram* (e), Columbus — 11,723; *Hastings Daily Tribune* (e), Hastings — 18,044; *Holdrege Daily Citizen* (e), Holdrege — 3,991; *Independent* (eS), Grand Island — 25,507; *Kearney Daily Hub* (e), Kearney — 10,907; *McCook Daily Gazette* (e), McCook — 10,651; *North Platte Telegraph* (mS), North Platte — 17,414; *Star-Herald* (mS), Scottsbluff — 17,824. *Omaha World-Herald* also circulates in the district.

Commercial Television Stations, Affiliation: KCNA-TV, Albion (ABC); KDUH-TV, Scottsbluff (NBC, ABC); KGIN-TV, Grand Island (CBS); KHAS-TV, Hastings (NBC); KHGI-TV Kearney (ABC); KNOP-TV, North Platte (NBC); KOMC, McCook (NBC); KSNB-TV, Superior (ABC); KSTF, Scottsbluff (CBS, ABC); KWNB-TV, Hayes Center (ABC). Most of district is located in Lincoln-Hastings-Kearney ADI. Portions are in North Platte ADI, Cheyenne (Wyo.) ADI, Denver (Colo.) ADI, Rapid City (S.D.), Sioux Falls (S.D.)-Mitchell (S.D.) ADI and Wichita (Kan.)-Hutchinson (Kan.) ADI.

Military Installations: Cornhusker Army Ammunition Plant, Grand Island — 184; Hastings Bomb Scoring Site (Air Force), Hastings — 81.

Industries:

Western Electric Co. Inc.; Grand Island; power line construction — 4,500. **Union Pacific Railroad Co.;** North Platte; railroad operations — 2,100. **Dale Electronics Inc.** (HQ); Columbus; electronic equipment — 1,000. **Monfort of Colorado;** Grand Island; beef processing — 1,000. **The Wickes Corp.** (Behlen Mfg. Div.); Columbus; farm machinery, grain storage buildings — 1,000.

Becton Dickinson & Co.; Columbus; medical instruments — 850. **J. A. Baldwin Mfg. Co.;** Kearney; motor vehicle filters — 800. **Sperry Corp.** (Sperry New Holland Div.); Lexington; farm equipment — 750. **Becton Dickinson & Co.;** Holdrege; medical instruments — 725. **Monroe Auto Equipment Inc.;** Cozad; auto parts — 700. **Lindsay Mfg. Co.** (Lindsay Irrigation - HQ); Lindsay; farm machinery — 600. **Lockwood Corp.** (HQ); Gering; agricultural machinery — 600. **Chief Industries Inc.** (Bellavista Mobile Homes Div. - HQ); Grand Island; mobile homes — 575. **TRW Inc.;** Ogallala; electrical industrial appliances — 560. **Burlington Northern Inc.;** Alliance; railroad operations — 550. **Eaton Corp.** (Engine Component Div.); Kearney; valves — 550.

Nevada

Regional loyalties prevailed over partisanship as Nevada's Legislature debated where to put the state's newly acquired second House district.

Conservative Democrats from northern Nevada joined with Republicans to thwart a proposal by Las Vegas Democrats that would have split moderate-to-liberal Las Vegas (Clark County), enabling it to dominate both districts. The bipartisan state coalition passed a remap that concentrated Clark County voting strength in a single district, leaving northern Nevada dominant in the state's other district.

Because its population grew 63.5 percent during the 1970s, Nevada earned a second House seat in 1980 reapportionment. The state had been limited to one at-large seat since its admission to the Union in 1864.

The intervention of GOP Gov. Robert List was critical to passage of the coalition plan. Democrats had majorities in Nevada's Assembly and Senate, and both chambers initially approved the Las Vegas Democrats' plan.

But List vowed to veto their work and threatened to call lawmakers into a special session. Pressured because the regular legislative session was dragging on to record length, the Assembly reversed itself May 30, 1981, and adopted the coalition plan by a 21-19 vote. After more pressure from the governor, the Senate June 3, 1981, followed suit, by a vote of 11-8. Gov. List signed the bill into law that evening.

Age of Population

District	Population Under 18	Voting Age Population	Population 65 & Over (% of VAP)	Median Age
1	107,766	292,870	32,739 (11.2%)	30.4
2	108,033	291,824	33,017 (11.3%)	30.0
State	215,799	584,694	65,756 (11.2%)	30.2

Income and Occupation

District	Median Family Income	White Collar Workers	Blue Collar Workers	Service Workers	Farm Workers
1	$ 21,270	49.3%	19.9%	30.0%	0.8%
2	21,349	51.3	25.0	21.2	2.4
State	$ 21,311	50.3%	22.5%	25.6%	1.6%

Education: School Years Completed

District	8 Years or Fewer	4 Years of High School	4 Years of College or More	Median School Years
1	9.9%	40.6%	13.1%	12.6
2	9.2	40.2	15.8	12.7
State	9.6%	40.4%	14.4%	12.6

Housing and Residential Patterns

District	Owner Occupied	Renter Occupied	Urban	Rural
1	57.7%	42.3%	96.3%	3.7%
2	61.5	38.5	74.3	25.7
State	59.6%	40.4%	85.3%	14.7%

1st District

South — Las Vegas

Las Vegas has come a long way from its days as a Mormon mission in the mid-1800s. In the 50 years since legalized gambling and the building of the Boulder Dam brought a construction boom to the city, it has developed from a dusty town of fewer than 10,000 people to a neon extravaganza with 164,674 full-time residents. Clark County, including Las Vegas and its suburbs, grew by nearly 70 percent during the 1970s. Just over half of all Nevadans live in the new 1st District, which takes in most of Las Vegas and the southeastern half of Clark County.

The "Strip" of casinos, nightclubs and hotels that gives Las Vegas its vaguely disreputable image is actually outside the city limits. But the Strip is the economic focal point of the area. Most of the 1st District's residents are connected in some way to the gaming, entertainment and tourism industries; with the recession cutting sharply into the number of visitors looking for a piece of the action, Las Vegas' unemployment rate hit 13 percent early in 1983.

Most voters in the 1st are registered Democrats, but in general elections party affiliation tends to be less impor-

NEVADA

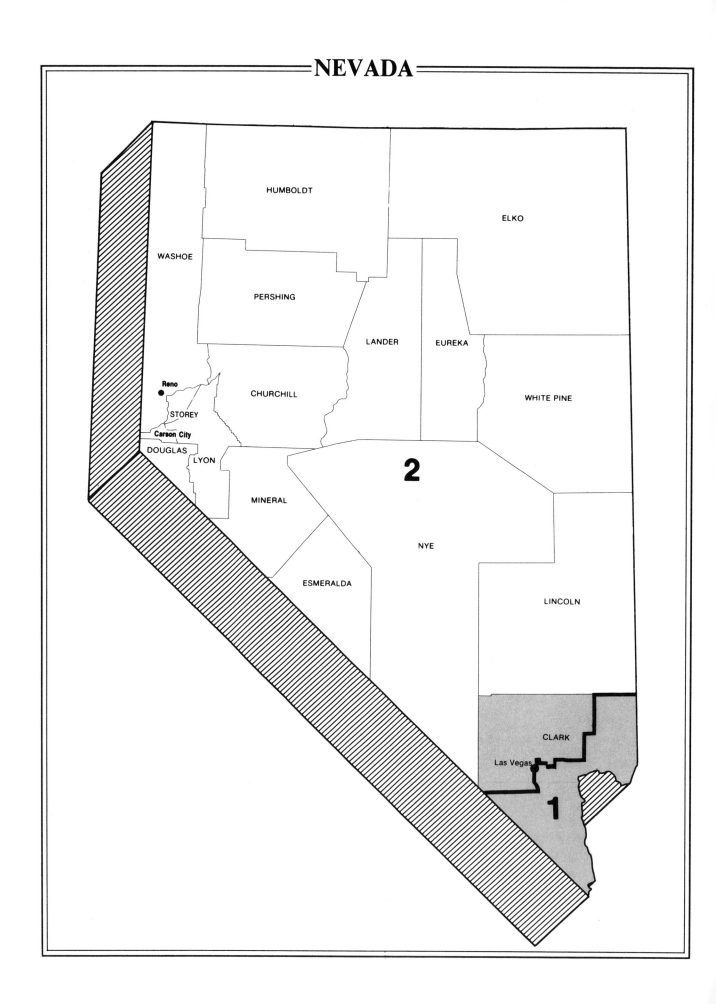

tant than ideology. Las Vegas' large Mormon community has long been a potent force for conservatism; government workers employed at nearby Nellis Air Force Base and the Department of Energy's Nevada Test Range also help Republican candidates in Clark County.

The bulk of the vote comes from the area's service workers, many of whom are unionized. This group includes a sizable black population. North Las Vegas, whose portion of the 1st is 42 percent black, and Las Vegas' West Side — its slum area — hold most of the district's 40,000 blacks.

Election Returns

1st District		Democrat		Republican	
1976	President	43,872	(51.3%)	40,483	(47.3%)
	Senate	64,961	(76.0%)	18,595	(21.7%)
	House	71,393	(85.2%)	8,406	(10.0%)
1978	Governor	45,905	(55.3%)	34,993	(42.2%)
	House	58,482	(71.1%)	17,807	(21.6%)
1980	President	32,778	(30.4%)	64,073	(59.4%)
	Senate	45,895	(43.0%)	57,745	(54.1%)
	House	74,053	(69.6%)	24,859	(23.4%)
1982	Governor	64,124	(62.0%)	37,801	(36.5%)
	Senate	57,770	(55.1%)	46,983	(44.9%)
	House	61,901	(57.5%)	45,675	(42.5%)

Demographics

Population: 400,636. **Percent Change from 1970:** 69.5%.

Land Area: 4,034 square miles. **Population per Square Mile:** 99.3.

Counties, 1980 Population: Clark (Pt.) — 400,636.

Cities, 1980 Population: Henderson — 24,363; Las Vegas (Pt.) — 149,612; North Las Vegas (Pt.) — 31,505.

Race and Ancestry: White — 84.5%; Black — 9.9%; American Indian, Eskimo and Aleut — 0.6%; Asian and Pacific Islander — 2.2%. Spanish Origin — 7.6%. Dutch — 0.5%; English — 9.5%; French — 1.2%; German — 6.2%; Irish — 4.2%; Italian — 4.0%; Norwegian — 0.5%; Polish — 1.1%; Russian — 0.7%; Scottish — 0.6%; Swedish — 0.6%.

Universities, Enrollment: University of Nevada (Las Vegas campus), Las Vegas — 9,804.

Newspapers, Circulation: *Las Vegas Review-Journal* (eS), Las Vegas — 81,045; *Sun* (mS), Las Vegas — 57,051; *The Valley Times* (mS), North Las Vegas — 13,870.

Commercial Television Stations, Affiliation: KLAS-TV, Las Vegas (CBS); KTNV-TV, Las Vegas (ABC); KVBC, Las Vegas (NBC); KVVU-TV, Henderson (None). Entire district is located in Las Vegas ADI.

Industries:

MGM Grand Hotels Inc. (HQ); Las Vegas; casino, hotel holding company — 5,000. **Reynolds Electrical & Engineering Co.**; Las Vegas; management services — 4,200. **Hilton Hotels Corp.** (Las Vegas Hilton); Las Vegas; hotel, casino — 3,000. **Desert Palace Inc.** (Caesar's Palace); Las Vegas; resort, casino — 2,900. **Karat Inc.**; Las Vegas hotel, casino — 2,800.

Trans-Sterling Inc. (HQ); Las Vegas; casinos, hotels — 2,700. **Dunes Hotels & Casinos Inc.** (HQ); Las Vegas; casinos, hotels — 2,600. **N & T Associates Inc.** (Aladdin Hotel); Las Vegas; casino, hotel — 2,300. **Hilton Hotels Corp.** (Flamingo Hotel); Las Vegas; hotel — 2,000. **Sunrise Hospital Inc.**; Las Vegas; hospital — 2,000. **Hotel Riviera Inc.** (HQ); Las Vegas; hotel, casino — 1,740. **Summa Corp.** (Sands Hotel); Las Vegas; hotel — 1,650. **Circus Circus Hotels Inc.** (Circus Circus); Las Vegas; hotel, casino — 1,600. **Summa Corp.**

(Desert Inn Hotel); Las Vegas; hotel, casino — 1,600. **El Rancho Hotel & Casino**; Las Vegas; hotel, casino — 1,500. **Hotel Ramada of Nevada** (Tropicana Hotel); Las Vegas; hotel, casino — 1,460. **Imperial Palace Inc.**; Las Vegas; hotel, casino — 1,400.

Golden Nugget Inc. (HQ); Las Vegas; casino, hotel — 1,330. **NLV Casino Corp.** (Silver Nugget); Las Vegas; casino, hotel — 1,300. **Hughes Properties Inc.**; Las Vegas; real estate holding company — 1,290. **River Boat Casino Inc.** (Holiday Casino); Las Vegas; casino — 1,250. **Southern Nevada Memorial Hospital**; Las Vegas; hospital — 1,150. **Scott Corp.** (HQ); Las Vegas; casino, hotel — 1,050. **Horseshoe Club Operating Co.**; Las Vegas; casino, hotel — 1,000. **Baby Grand Corp.** (Maxim Hotel); Las Vegas; casino, hotel — 950. **Showboat Operating Co.** (HQ); Las Vegas; casino, hotel — 943. **Elsinore Corp.** (HQ); Las Vegas; casino, hotel — 900. **Casino Properties Inc.** (Las Vegas Hacienda Hotel); Las Vegas; hotel, casino — 850. **California Hotel & Casino** (HQ); Las Vegas; casino, hotel — 800. **Sundance Hotel & Casino Inc.**; Las Vegas; casino, hotel — 800.

Titanium Metals Corp. of America; Henderson; titanium metals — 800. **Barbary Coast Hotel Casino Inc.**; Las Vegas; casino, hotel — 700. **Riverside Resort & Casino**; Searchlight; casino, motel — 683. **Mini-Price Motor Inn Casino**; Las Vegas; casino, hotel — 630. **E G & G Inc.**; Las Vegas; commercial testing labs — 620. **Summa Corp.** (Silver Slipper); Las Vegas; casino — 600. **The Golden Gate**; Las Vegas; casino, hotel — 530. **Mark III Corp.** (Landmark Hotel); Las Vegas; hotel, casino — 500. **NLV Casino Corp.** (Silver City); Las Vegas; casino — 500. **Republic Airlines West Inc.** (Hughes Airwest); Las Vegas; commercial airline — 500.

2nd District

North — Reno and the Cow Counties

Although 15 percent of the people in the new 2nd live in North Las Vegas and northern Clark County, the 2nd is referred to as the "non-Las Vegas" district. It is dominated by northwestern Nevada's Washoe County (Reno), a Republican stronghold containing nearly one-half of the district's voters.

Gambling is an all-important component of the Washoe County economy, but Reno and Lake Tahoe take pains to differentiate themselves from Las Vegas. This is "old Nevada," the part of the state that was built on mining in the 19th century and dominated the state politically until Las Vegas overshadowed it in the 1950s. Republicans have a registration advantage in Washoe County and nearby Douglas County and Carson City. Those three areas each gave Ronald Reagan at least 64 percent of the vote in 1980.

About one-fourth of the district's residents are dispersed through the Cow Counties, a huge expanse of mountain and desert that occupies most of the state. Cattle- and sheep-raising are the main economic activities here, but silver and gold mining are mounting a comeback as technological improvements make it profitable to extract and process low-grade ore.

The Cow Counties were populist and Democratic for most of this century, but their voters are gradually turning Republican in frustration over national Democratic liberalism, especially the party's land and water policies. (Nearly all of the land in the 2nd District is federally owned.) Most residents thought President Carter's plan to place a mobile MX missile system in this region would strain the meager water supply, and there was rejoicing when President Reagan decided to deploy the MX outside Nevada.

In 1982 a Republican became the first person to represent the new district, winning 55.5 percent of the vote.

Election Returns

2nd District		Democrat		Republican	
1976	President	46,521	(43.8%)	57,957	(54.5%)
	Senate	58,958	(55.5%)	43,420	(40.9%)
	House	79,148	(75.8%)	14,673	(14.1%)
1978	Governor	60,721	(57.4%)	39,163	(37.1%)
	House	71,574	(68.3%)	25,642	(24.5%)
1980	President	32,358	(24.2%)	86,565	(64.8%)
	Senate	44,462	(33.4%)	81,961	(61.6%)
	House	87,295	(66.1%)	36,146	(37.5%)
1982	Governor	61,478	(49.3%)	60,263	(48.3%)
	Senate	54,378	(43.3%)	71,239	(56.7%)
	House	52,265	(41.3%)	70,188	(55.5%)

Demographics

Population: 399,857. **Percent Change from 1970:** 58.5%.

Land Area: 105,860 square miles. **Population per Square Mile:** 3.8.

Counties, 1980 Population: Churchill — 13,917; Clark (Pt.) — 62,451; Douglas — 19,421; Elko — 17,269; Esmeralda — 777; Eureka — 1,198; Humboldt — 9,434; Lander — 4,076; Lincoln — 3,732; Lyon — 13,594; Mineral — 6,217; Nye — 9,048; Pershing — 3,408; Storey — 1,503; Washoe — 193,623; White Pine — 8,167.

Cities, 1980 Population: Carson City — 32,022; Las Vegas (Pt.) — 15,062; North Las Vegas (Pt.) — 11,234; Reno — 100,756; Sparks — 40,780.

Race and Ancestry: White — 90.4%; Black — 2.8%; American Indian, Eskimo and Aleut — 2.7%; Asian and Pacific Islander — 1.7%. Spanish Origin — 5.9%. Dutch — 0.6%; English — 10.1%; French — 1.4%; German — 7.4%; Irish — 4.5%; Italian — 3.0%; Norwegian — 0.8%; Polish — 0.6%; Portuguese — 0.5%; Scottish — 0.9%; Swedish — 1.0%.

Universities, Enrollment: Clark County Community College, North Las Vegas — 8,954; Northern Nevada Community College, Elko — 1,133; Reno Business College, Reno — 235; Sierra Nevada College, Incline Village — 174; Truckee Meadows Community College, Reno — 7,200; University of Nevada (Reno campus), Reno — 9,161; Western Nevada Community College, Carson City — 3,209.

Newspapers, Circulation: *Elko Daily Free Press* (e), Elko — 3,717; *Ely Daily Times* (e), Ely — 2,509; *Nevada Appeal* (eS), Carson City — 8,989; *Nevada State Journal* (mS), Reno — 32,252; *Reno Evening Gazette* (e), Reno — 24,286. The *Las Vegas Review-Journal* also circulates in the district.

Commercial Television Stations, Affiliation: KAME-TV, Reno (None); KCRL-TV, Reno (NBC); KOLO-TV, Reno (ABC); KTVN, Reno (CBS). District is divided among Las Vegas ADI, Reno ADI and Salt Lake City (Utah) ADI.

Military Installations: Fallon Naval Air Station, Fallon — 1,749; Hawthorne Army Ammunition Plant, Hawthorne — 663; Hawthorne Bomb Scoring Site (Air Force), Babbitt — 97; Indian Springs Auxiliary Air Field, Indian Springs — 291; Nellis Air Force Base, Las Vegas — 9,269; Reno International Airport (Air Force), Reno — 294.

Industries:

MGM Grand Hotel Reno Inc.; Reno; casino, hotel — 3,500. **Harrah's Club** (HQ); Reno; casino, hotel — 3,000. **Harrahs Club;** Stateline; casino — 2,500. **Washoe Medical Center;** Reno; hospital — 2,100. **Desert Palace Inc.** (Caesar's Tahoe); Stateline; hotel, casino — 1,750.

Sparks Nuggett Inc. (HQ); Sparks; casino, hotel — 1,700. **Harolds Club;** Reno; casino — 1,500. **Sierra Development Co.;** Reno; casino — 1,500. **Sahara-Tahoe Corp.;** Stateline; hotel — 1,400. **Speidel Newspapers Inc.** (Gannett West); Reno; newspaper publishing — 1,350. **St. Mary's Hospital Inc.;** Reno; hospital — 1,200. **Hilton Hotel Inc.** (HQ); Reno; casino, hotel — 975. **Bentley Nevada Corp.** (HQ); Minden; machinery protection systems — 870. **Comstock Hotel & Casino;** Reno; hotel, casino — 800. **El Dorado Hotel & Casino;** Reno; hotel — 775. **Harvey's Wagon Wheel Inc.** (HQ); Stateline; casino, hotel — 750. **Boomtown Inc.;** Verdi; casino — 650.

Nevada Properties — Reno; hotel, casino — 600. **Camill Solari & Sons Inc.** (HQ); Reno; contracting — 593. **Cactus Pete Inc.;** Jackpot; casino, hotel — 560. **Lynch Communication Systems** (HQ); Reno; communications equipment — 550. **Cloud's California-Nevada Lodge;** Crystal Bay; casino, hotel — 500. **Day and Zimmermann/Basil Corp.;** Hawthorne; warehousing — 500. **Robert L. Helms Construction Development;** Sparks; highway construction — 500. **Loftin Associates Inc.** (Ormsby House); Carson City; casino, hotel — 500. **Sundowner Hotel-Casino;** Reno; hotel, casino — 500. **J. C. Penney & Co.;** Reno; catalogue distribution center — more than 500.

New Hampshire

Although New Hampshire's population grew 24.8 percent in the 1970s — the swiftest pace of any state outside the South and West — the Granite State fell short of gaining a third House seat. The 1982 redistricting process thus stirred little controversy, as the state Legislature needed only to balance the populations of the state's two districts.

The new boundaries shifted just two towns, both in booming Rockingham County, from the eastern 1st District to the western 2nd. The two towns, both suburbs of Salem, are Windham, whose population grew by 88.3 percent since 1970, and Atkinson, with a 91.9 percent growth rate. In the 1972 redistricting, Salem had been moved from the 1st to the 2nd. Reuniting the city and its suburbs within the 2nd was a solution readily accepted by both parties in the 1982 remap. The shift of the two towns was unlikely to have a major impact on either district's voting patterns.

The state Legislature approved the new map with little wrangling. The bill passed by voice votes in the state Senate on Jan. 20, 1982, and in the House on Feb. 16. The governor signed the bill into law March 4.

The remap, which shifted a total of about 10,000 people, narrowed the population spread between the districts to 1,616.

Age of Population

District	Population Under 18	Voting Age Population	Population 65 & Over (% of VAP)	Median Age
1	128,365	332,498	51,279 (15.4%)	30.0
2	129,717	330,030	51,688 (15.7%)	30.3
State	258,082	662,528	102,967 (15.5%)	30.1

Income and Occupation

District	Median Family Income	White Collar Workers	Blue Collar Workers	Service Workers	Farm Workers
1	$ 19,665	51.8%	35.1%	11.9%	1.2%
2	19,780	52.3	34.6	11.2	1.9
State	$ 19,723	52.1%	34.8%	11.5%	10.3%

Education: School Years Completed

District	8 Years or Fewer	4 Years of High School	4 Years of College or More	Median School Years
1	15.1%	37.0%	17.5%	12.6
2	14.2	37.4	18.9	12.6
State	14.7%	37.2%	18.2%	12.6

Housing and Residential Patterns

District	Owner Occupied	Renter Occupied	Urban	Rural
1	66.2%	33.8%	54.0%	46.0%
2	69.1	30.9	50.3	49.7
State	67.6%	32.4%	52.2%	47.8%

1st District

East — Manchester

The eastern district, extending from New Hampshire's coast to the granite peaks of the White Mountains, is an area of rich geographical and political variation. The southern tier of the district is dominated by blue-collar, ethnic, industrial cities that produce Democratic majorities, while the rugged northern territory is home to small Yankee towns that are Republican bastions. Although a Democrat represented the 1st in the early 1980s, the territory often backed Republicans in national and statewide races.

The state's largest concentration of voters is in the city of Manchester, a heavily ethnic city where the arch-conservative *Manchester Union Leader* commands considerable statewide attention. Textile mills came to Manchester in the 19th century to take advantage of the hydropower of the Merrimack River. They drew large numbers of immigrant workers, especially French Canadians. But the Depression paralyzed the region's economy. Some of the long-abandoned redbrick mills are finding new life as light-manufacturing or retail space, but many still stand empty.

NEW HAMPSHIRE

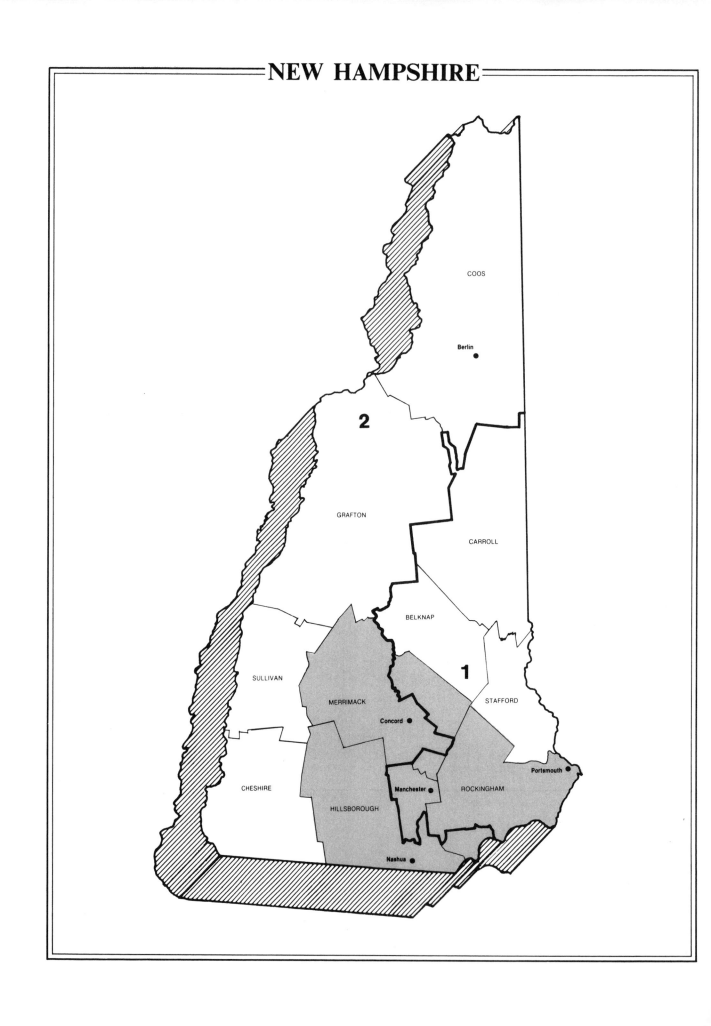

The huge Franco-American vote in Manchester is Democratic but conservative, and it has been influenced at times by the *Union Leader's* blistering editorials to abandon Democratic candidates accused of liberalism or worse. But the city is available to most mainstream Democratic candidates. In 1980 Manchester gave Jimmy Carter a humiliating 28.9 percent of the vote, but handed a majority to Democrat John A. Durkin in his unsuccessful bid for a second Senate term.

The coastal region retains its traditional shipping and maritime interests; it also experiences annually a large influx of summer tourists. Large numbers of anti-nuclear demonstrators have been attracted to the site of the controversial twin nuclear reactors at Seabrook. Homegrown environmentalists blocked a proposal in the mid-1970s to construct an oil refinery complex on the coast.

The major coastal town is Portsmouth, home to wealthy sea captains two centuries ago. It has been in decline most of this century, but its architectural grace and convenience to Boston make it a fashionable day-trip tourist center. Although the Portsmouth Naval Shipyard is centered across the river estuary in Kittery, Maine, many shipyard workers live in New Hampshire, where they generally cast Democratic votes. Outside of Portsmouth is Pease Air Force Base, a Strategic Air Command bomber field.

In Strafford County the University of New Hampshire, with 12,624 students, dominates the town of Durham and leads the area in supporting liberal candidates. Both Eugene J. McCarthy in 1968 and George McGovern in 1972 swept the Democratic presidential primary vote on antiwar platforms. Strafford County is among only five counties in the nation that have voted, with only one exception, for the winner of the presidential contest in every election since 1892. Strafford County's one lapse came in 1968, when it backed Hubert H. Humphrey.

Sparsely populated Carroll County to the north is among the most Republican counties in the nation. It has provided overwhelming margins for the GOP in every statewide race since World War II. Carroll was the only county in the state to support Barry Goldwater for president in 1964, although it gave the GOP ticket an uncharacteristically low 55.0 percent. That year Goldwater's statewide share was only 36.1 percent.

Neighboring Belknap County, in the center of the state's Lakes District and dominated by Lake Winnipesaukee, is another Republican area. To the north, the 1st includes part of the White Mountain National Forest, with many mountain ski areas around the resort cities of Conway and North Conway.

Election Returns

1st District		Democrat		Republican	
1976	President	71,632	(42.7%)	93,141	(55.5%)
	Governor	66,139	(39.3%)	102,191	(60.7%)
	House	106,237	(68.3%)	46,780	(30.0%)
1978	Governor	64,226	(46.6%)	66,526	(48.3%)
	Senate	66,342	(49.3%)	67,135	(49.9%)
	House	81,417	(61.7%)	48,085	(36.5%)
1980	President	53,617	(27.3%)	115,356	(59.8%)
	Governor	107,762	(55.9%)	84,515	(43.8%)
	Senate	91,645	(48.5%)	97,372	(51.5%)
	House	111,809	(60.9%)	71,738	(39.1%)

1st District		Democrat		Republican	
1982	Governor	59,592	(44.3%)	72,662	(54.0%)
	House	76,281	(54.9%)	61,876	(44.6%)

Demographics

Population: 460,863. **Percent Change from 1970:** 27.4%.

Land Area: 4,515 square miles. **Population per Square Mile:** 102.1.

Counties, 1980 Population: Belknap — 42,884; Carroll — 27,931; Hillsborough (Pt.) — 127,138; Merrimack (Pt.) — 21,342; Rockingham (Pt.) — 156,160; Strafford 85,408.

Cities, 1980 Population: Derry — 18,875; Dover — 22,377; Durham — 10,652; Exeter — 11,024; Goffstown — 11,315; Hampton — 10,493; Laconia — 15,575; Londonderry — 13,598; Manchester — 90,936; Merrimack — 15,406; Portsmouth — 26,254; Rochester — 21,560; Somersworth — 10,350.

Race and Ancestry: White — 98.8%; Black — 0.5%; American Indian, Eskimo and Aleut — 0.2%; Asian and Pacific Islander — 0.4%. Spanish Origin — 0.7%. English — 14.4%; French — 12.5%; German — 2.1%; Greek — 1.1%; Irish — 6.4%; Italian — 2.0%; Polish — 1.7%; Scottish — 1.1%; Swedish — 0.6%.

Universities, Enrollment: Hesser College, Manchester — 2,302; McIntosh College, Dover — 254; New Hampshire College, Manchester — 5,086; New Hampshire Vocational-Technical College, Laconia — 252; New Hampshire Vocational-Technical College, Manchester — 366; New Hampshire Vocational-Technical College, Portsmouth — 239; Notre Dame College, Manchester — 770; St. Anselms College, Manchester — 1,936; University of New Hampshire, Durham — 12,624; White Pines College, Chester — 82.

Newspapers, Circulation: *Citizen* (e), Laconia — 8,535; *Foster's Democrat* (e), Dover — 20,080; *Manchester Union Leader* (mS), Manchester — 63,760; *The Portsmouth Herald* (e), Portsmouth — 18,572. *Nashua Telegraph* also circulates in the district.

Commercial Television Stations, Affiliation: WMUR-TV, Manchester (ABC). District is divided between Boston (Mass.) ADI and Portland (Maine)-Poland Spring (Maine) ADI.

Military Installations: Pease Air Force Base, Newington — 4,740.

Nuclear Power Plants: Seabrook 1 and 2, Seabrook (Westinghouse, United Engineers and Constructors).

Industries:

Perini Power Construction Inc.; Seabrook; construction — 2,500. **Digital Equipment Corp.** (Computer Products Group Div.); Merrimack; minicomputers — 2,200. **General Electric Co.**; Somersworth; transformers — 2,000. **Sun Chemical Corp.** (Kollsman Instrument Div.); Merrimack; avionics — 1,700. **Ex-Cell-0 Corp.** (Davidson Rubber Div.); Dover; molded urethane — 1,300.

Catholic Medical Center; Manchester; hospital — 1,050. **Groveton Papers Co. Inc.** (Campbell Stationery - HQ); Groveton; paper mill — 1,000. **Raytheon Co. Inc.** (Raytheon Marine Co.); Manchester; transmitters, detection devices — 1,000. **Somersworth Inc.** (Roberts Shoe Div.); Somersworth; women's footwear — 900. **Data General Corp.**; Portsmouth; electronic computing equipment — 800. **Diamond International Corp.**; Groveton; paper mill — 800. **Kingston Warren Corp.** (HQ); Newfields; automotive stampings — 800. **Pandora Industries Inc.** (HQ); Manchester; women's knitwear — 800. **Hadco Printed Circuits Inc.**; Derry; printed electronic components — 780. **Velcro USA Inc.**; Manchester; nylon fasteners — 640. **Prevue Products Inc.** (HQ); Manchester; footwear — 625.

K. W. Thompson Tool Co. Inc.; Rochester; pistols — 615. **Harris Corp.**; Dover; printing equipment — 579. **GTE Products Corp.** (Lighting Products Div.); Manchester; lamps — 525. **Anheuser-Busch Inc.**; Merrimack; brewery — 500. **Moore Business Forms Inc.**; Dover; printing, business machinery — 500. **Sanders Associates Inc.**; Manchester; electronic components — 500. **Davison Construction Co.**; Manchester; general contracting — 500.

2nd District

West — Concord, Nashua

From the Connecticut River Valley to the Presidential Range of the White Mountains, the heavily forested western district of New Hampshire contains some of the most scenic areas of the Northeast. Most of the 2nd is very lightly populated, with few population centers outside the fast-growing southern tier that borders Massachusetts; some residents in the southern part of the state consider themselves outer-ring Boston suburbanites.

Nashua, the largest city in the 2nd, grew to nearly 68,000 people in the 1970s. Spurred by the arrival of high-technology firms, Nashua feeds into the belt of electronics-oriented industry that straddles the Bay State border. Although the traditional textile-mill economic base once attracted French-Canadian immigrants in large numbers, the newcomers tend to be well-educated, upwardly mobile refugees from "Taxachusetts." Usually a Democratic stronghold, Nashua in 1968 was one of the few New Hampshire towns that backed Lyndon B. Johnson against Eugene J. McCarthy's primary insurgency.

Nearby Salem has shared in the southern tier's boom, growing by 19.8 percent in the 1970s. Salem usually favors Republicans, although in 1980 it backed Democrats for Senate and governor. The Salem suburbs of Windham and Atkinson, the only towns shifted in the 1982 remap, also generally back GOP candidates.

State government workers dominate the capital city, Concord, but New Hampshire does not have a large or politically influential bureaucracy. Concord grew just 1.3 percent in the 1970s, the smallest growth recorded by any city in the state. Concord's textile-mill economic base has faded and with it the city's old blue-collar Democratic vote. The city's electorate is generally liberal but independent. Outside the Concord-Nashua corridor, the district is largely bedrock Republican territory. The small city of Keene is the center of the hilly Monadnock region, and Peterborough's Macdowell Colony is a haven for writers and artists. Grafton County's population center is around the scenic valley's three-city nexus: Hanover and Lebanon in New Hampshire and White River Junction in Vermont. Hanover is home to Dartmouth College; a heavy turnout among students often tilts the county toward liberals.

Coos County is New Hampshire's "North Country," an isolated woodland where voters must brave severe winter weather to take part in the state's presidential primary. The only town of any size in the North Country is Berlin, a lonely Democratic outpost in a solidly Republican area. In 1976 Carter carried only four communities in Coos County, but his sweep of Berlin provided him his winning county margin.

Election Returns

2nd District		Democrat		Republican	
1976	President	76,003	(44.2%)	92,794	(54.0%)
	Governor	78,576	(45.2%)	95,398	(54.8%)
	House	67,361	(39.7%)	102,218	(60.3%)
1978	Governor	68,907	(52.3%)	55,938	(42.5%)
	Senate	61,603	(47.6%)	66,610	(51.5%)
	House	40,826	(32.3%)	85,581	(67.7%)

2nd District		Democrat		Republican	
1980	President	70,171	(30.7%)	124,612	(54.5%)
	Governor	118,674	(62.1%)	71,663	(37.5%)
	Senate	87,810	(47.2%)	98,191	(52.8%)
	House	65,602	(36.3%)	115,131	(63.7%)
1982	Governor	72,725	(49.2%)	72,727	(49.2%)
	House	37,906	(29.2%)	92,098	(70.8%)

Demographics

Population: 459,747. **Percent Change from 1970:** 22.3%.

Land Area: 4,478 square miles. **Population per Square Mile:** 102.7.

Counties, 1980 Population: Cheshire — 62,116; Coos — 35,147; Grafton — 65,806; Hillsborough (Pt.) — 149,470; Merrimack (Pt.) — 76,960; Rockingham (Pt.) — 34,185; Sullivan — 36,063.

Cities, 1980 Population: Berlin — 13,084; Claremont — 14,557; Concord — 30,400; Hudson — 14,022; Keene — 21,449; Lebanon — 11,134; Nashua — 67,865; Salem — 24,124.

Race and Ancestry: White — 98.9%; Black — 0.4%; American Indian, Eskimo and Aleut — 0.1%; Asian and Pacific Islander — 0.3%. Spanish Origin — 0.6%. English — 14.6%; French — 11.9%; German — 2.3%; Greek — 0.5%; Irish — 5.1%; Italian — 1.9%; Polish — 1.3%; Scottish — 1.1%; Swedish — 0.6%.

Universities, Enrollment: Castle Junior College, Windham — 117; Colby-Sawyer College, New London — 604; Daniel Webster College, Nashua — 720; Dartmouth College, Hanover — 4,379; Franklin Pierce College, Rindge — 991; Keene State College, Keene — 3,265; Nathaniel Hawthorne College, Antrim — 472; New England College, Henniker — 1,272; New Hampshire Technical Institute, Concord — 907; New Hampshire Vocational-Technical College, Berlin — 401; New Hampshire Vocational-Technical College, Claremont — 388; New Hampshire Vocational-Technical College, Nashua — 1,028; Plymouth State College, Plymouth — 3,356; Rivier College, Nashua — 1,920.

Newspapers, Circulation: *Concord Monitor* (e), Concord — 19,777; *Eagle-Times* (eS), Claremont — 9,773; *The Keene Sentinel* (e), Keene — 12,633; *Nashua Telegraph* (e), Nashua — 26,824; *Valley News* (e), Lebanon — 13,216. *Manchester Union Leader* also circulates in the district.

Commercial Television Stations, Affiliation: District is divided between Boston (Mass.) ADI and Portland (Maine)-Poland Spring (Maine) ADI.

Industries:

Nashua Corp. (HQ); Nashua; photographic equipment — 2,258. **Mary Hitchcock Memorial Hospital;** Hanover; hospital — 1,950. **James River Corp.** (Berlin-Gorham Group); Berlin; pulp, paper mill — 1,800. **Sanders Associates Inc.** (HQ); Nashua; transmitters, electronic components — 1,742. **New Hampshire Ball Bearings** (HQ); Peterborough; ball bearings — 1,500.

Centronics Data Computer Corp. (HQ); Hudson; computers — 1,360. **International Packings Corp.** (Transtec - HQ); Bristol; packing, sealing devices — 1,160. **Ingersoll-Rand Co.** (Impco Div.); Nashua; paper industries machinery — 1,150. **Kingsbury Machine Tool Corp.** (HQ); Keene; metal-cutting machine tools — 1,000. **Joy Mfg. Co.;** Claremont; construction machinery — 900. **Hitchiner Mfg. Co. Inc.** (HQ); Milford; steel, aluminum — 800. **Sturm-Ruger & Co. Inc.;** Newport; firearms — 750. **Rumford National Graphics Inc.** (Rumford Press Div. - HQ); Concord; commercial printing, photography — 700. **Sprague Electric Co. Inc.** (Semiconductor Div.); Concord; transistors — 700. **Teradyne Connection Systems Inc.** (HQ); Nashua; electronic components — 700. **Markem Corp.** (HQ); Keene; labeling machinery — 650. **M. P. B. Corp.** (HQ); Keene; ball bearings — 600. **M. P. B. Corp.** (New Hampshire Industries); Lebanon; split ball bearings — 600. **Digital Equipment Corp.;** Nashua; computer programming — 524. **Watts Regulator Co.** (Webster Valve Co.); Franklin; valves — 500.

New Jersey

In a decision with sweeping implications for redistricting politics across the country, the Supreme Court June 22, 1983, struck down New Jersey's new congressional district map. In a 5-4 vote, the court ruled that states must adhere as closely as possible to the "one man, one vote" standard of reapportionment — and ultimately bear the burden of providing that deviations from precise population equality were made in pursuit of a legitimate goal.

The ruling upheld a three-judge federal court ruling on March 3, 1982, overturning the New Jersey map because the state's 0.69 percent deviation between the most and least populated districts violated the "one man, one vote" principle first set down in 1964. *(Details of Supreme Court rulings on redistricting, p. 618)*

The court did not rule on the underlying issue in the New Jersey case — the fact that the New Jersey Legislature drew district lines to benefit Democrats. As a partisan gerrymander, the 1982 New Jersey remap had few peers. One new constituency reached from the New York City suburbs down the Delaware River to the outskirts of Trenton. Another began in the Philadelphia suburbs and ended up just across the bay from Staten Island. Still another twisted and curled through industrial mid-Jersey in search of as many Democrats as it could crowd within its borders.

The Democratic Legislature shoved the new plan through Jan. 18, 1982 — by a vote of 42-34 in the Assembly and 21-18 in the Senate. Democratic Gov. Brendan T. Byrne signed it the next day, shortly before the inauguration of his Republican successor, Thomas H. Kean.

New Jersey had to lose one of its 15 seats. The obvious casualty was Republican Rep. Millicent Fenwick's old 5th District, a painless choice because Fenwick chose to run for the Senate.

Although Fenwick's decision gave the Legislature a district for easy removal, Democrats still were determined to make mischief for the other party. As drawn by the Legislature, the new map paired two Republican incumbents, created an open 7th District that leaned Democratic, removed troublesome Republican territory from the 3rd and added Democrats to the marginally Republican 9th.

The Republican incumbent in the 9th lost his re-election bid. Republicans managed to avoid complete disaster by shifting players. One of the GOP incumbents in the 5th decided to run in the 12th; both incumbents were re-elected in 1982. The 12th's Republican incumbent moved to the open 7th, which he won easily.

It was the Republicans who brought suit in federal court, persuading the three GOP appointees to overturn the Democratic remap. But U.S. Supreme Court Justice William J. Brennan Jr. imposed a stay on the lower court ruling March 15, 1982, to allow a Democratic appeal to the full court. The Supreme Court did not consider the appeal until early 1983, which left the Democratic boundaries in place for the 1982 elections.

As of September 1983, the Legislature had not completed action on a new redistricting measure. Democrats hoped to pass a remap that made only minor adjustments in the 1982 boundaries. Republicans wanted to reshape substantially some of the districts to undo some of the Democrats' political damage as well as even the population.

The profiles below are for those districts in place for the 1982 elections.

Age of Population

District	Population Under 18	Voting Age Population	Population 65 & Over (% of VAP)	Median Age
1	159,634	366,423	49,168 (13.4%)	29.0
2	144,309	381,970	79,068 (20.7%)	32.8
3	145,152	379,673	70,476 (18.6%)	32.2
4	144,727	382,745	53,209 (13.9%)	30.9
5	154,773	371,594	48,949 (13.2%)	32.0
6	131,333	392,465	48,773 (12.4%)	31.1
7	138,133	387,430	57,887 (14.9%)	32.3
8	142,987	383,151	61,931 (16.2%)	31.9
9	117,987	409,362	69,751 (17.0%)	35.9
10	164,870	360,962	52,640 (14.6%)	28.7
11	124,041	401,249	67,296 (16.8%)	34.7
12	141,039	385,868	58,407 (15.1%)	34.1
13	145,497	380,671	75,583 (19.9%)	33.2
14	136,379	390,399	66,633 (17.1%)	32.2
State	1,990,861	5,373,962	859,771 (16.0%)	32.2

Income and Occupation

District	Median Family Income	White Collar Workers	Blue Collar Workers	Service Workers	Farm Workers
1	$ 20,273	53.2%	33.4%	12.5%	0.9%
2	18,439	48.0	32.8	17.3	1.9

NEW JERSEY

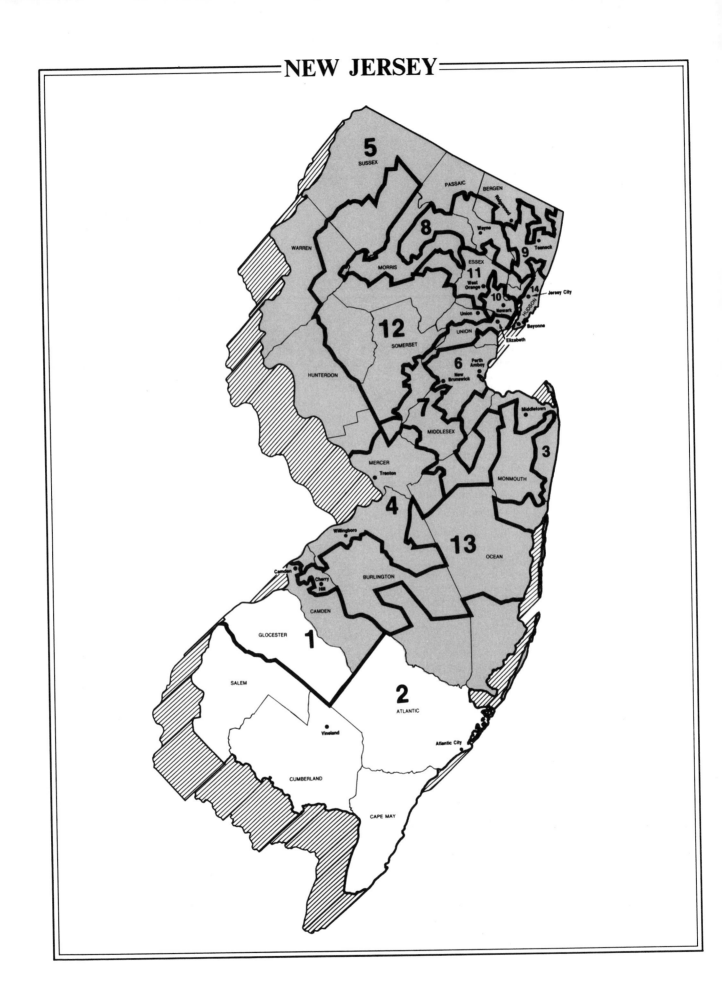

District	Median Family Income	White Collar Workers	Blue Collar Workers	Service Workers	Farm Workers
3	22,575	60.9	26.1	12.3	0.7
4	22,152	59.2	27.4	12.7	0.7
5	27,809	64.5	24.5	9.6	1.4
6	25,193	56.3	32.4	10.8	0.5
7	25,322	59.2	29.7	10.5	0.7
8	21,694	53.6	35.4	10.6	0.4
9	26,649	67.1	23.1	9.3	0.5
10	14,729	46.0	37.9	15.7	0.3
11	26,237	66.1	23.3	10.2	0.5
12	30,287	68.8	20.9	9.3	1.0
13	23,040	64.1	23.7	11.2	1.1
14	17,463	50.8	37.1	11.9	0.2
State	$ 22,906	58.8%	28.9%	11.6%	0.8%

Education: School Years Completed

District	8 Years or Fewer	4 Years of High School	4 Years of College or More	Median School Years
1	18.0%	38.3%	12.7%	12.3
2	21.4	37.1	11.2	12.3
3	14.1	37.9	18.3	12.6
4	15.9	38.0	16.2	12.5
5	10.6	36.5	26.1	12.8
6	17.4	39.5	16.2	12.5
7	16.2	35.3	22.4	12.6
8	24.4	33.4	14.6	12.3
9	14.9	36.0	22.4	12.6
10	27.5	32.0	9.8	12.1
11	14.9	35.7	23.1	12.6
12	11.0	34.1	29.5	12.9
13	13.4	37.1	20.6	12.6
14	29.7	31.1	11.6	12.1
State	17.7%	35.9%	18.3%	12.5

Housing and Residential Patterns

District	Owner Occupied	Renter Occupied	Urban	Rural
1	69.8%	30.2%	87.9%	12.1%
2	69.5	30.5	67.6	32.4
3	67.1	32.9	97.7	2.3
4	67.8	32.2	89.1	10.9
5	80.0	20.0	65.6	34.4
6	66.0	34.0	100.0	0.0
7	61.7	38.3	91.7	8.3
8	54.3	45.7	99.2	0.8
9	61.9	38.1	100.0	0.0
10	27.7	72.3	100.0	0.0
11	60.9	39.1	100.0	0.0
12	77.2	22.8	72.5	27.5
13	80.9	19.1	75.2	24.8
14	28.6	71.4	100.0	0.0
State	62.0%	38.0%	89.0%	11.0%

1st District

Southwest — Camden

The 1st, which encompasses Camden and Gloucester counties, is an amalgam of decaying urban areas, older suburbs and a rapidly developing countryside once covered by tomato patches but now sprouting subdivisions. Many of the new suburbanites moved into the district from Philadelphia and retain their Democratic loyalties. The Philadelphians were largely responsible for the district's switch in representation in 1974, when it elected a Democrat after choosing only Republicans for three-quarters of a century.

Democrats long have prevailed in the industrial region near the Delaware River — in Camden, the other river towns such as Logan, and the layer of blue-collar suburbs beyond them. The electorate is hardly changed by redistricting. It continues to mirror blue-collar disaffection with national Democratic tickets, as it did in 1980, when Ronald Reagan carried it with 47 percent of the vote.

Numerous businesses and residents have fled depressed Camden, leaving block after block of boarded-up and burnt-out buildings. Camden lost 17.2 percent of its population during the 1970s. Campbell Soup Co., RCA and the Camden County government complex keep the city alive economically. Despite its dwindling population base, Camden remains the district's largest city. Slightly more than half its residents are black, with the rest blue-collar whites, most of them Italian-American.

Of the suburbs close to Camden, wealthy Haddonfield is the major Republican enclave. The prominence of its residents sometimes makes up for their lack of numbers. In the late 1940s Haddonfield's influence changed the path of the New Jersey Turnpike, then under construction, to avoid the town. The other close-in suburbs lean Democratic. In these older communities along the Black Horse Pike, Italian-Americans have a strong influence.

Farther east, in what was recently farm country, are the newer, fast-developing suburbs such as Winslow Township, which grew by nearly 80 percent in the 1970s. Republican votes can be found there, but the political complexion of these newer suburbs is marginal, thanks to the residual partisan ties of their many expatriate Philadelphians.

Election Returns

1st District		Democrat		Republican	
1976	President	112,618	(56.4%)	82,826	(41.5%)
	Senate	120,230	(65.3%)	61,792	(33.6%)
	House	135,917	(69.8%)	57,008	(29.3%)
1977	Governor	88,977	(63.2%)	46,358	(32.9%)
1978	Senate	77,303	(60.5%)	48,384	(37.8%)
	House	105,325	(79.0%)	27,282	(20.5%)
1980	President	84,799	(43.0%)	92,494	(46.9%)
	House	146,876	(76.4%)	42,731	(22.2%)
1981	Governor	115,439	(71.4%)	46,273	(28.6%)
1982	Senate	82,261	(56.3%)	61,879	(42.3%)
	House	110,570	(73.3%)	39,501	(26.2%)

Demographics

Population: 526,057. **Percent Change from 1970:** 9.4%.

Land Area: 508 square miles. **Population per Square Mile:** 1,035.5.

Counties, 1980 Population: Camden (Pt.) — 326,140; Gloucester — 199,917.

Cities, 1980 Population: Bellmawr — 13,721; Camden — 84,910; Deptford — 23,473; Franklin — 12,396; Glassboro — 14,574; Gloucester — 45,156; Gloucester City — 13,121; Haddonfield — 12,337; Lindenwold — 18,196; Monroe — 21,639; Vorhees — 12,919; Washington — 27,878; West Deptford — 18,002; Winslow — 20,034; Woodbury — 10,353.

Race and Ancestry: White — 81.6%; Black — 14.6%; American Indian, Eskimo and Aleut — 0.1%; Asian and Pacific Islander — 0.7%. Spanish Origin — 4.1%. English — 5.5%; German — 6.2%; Irish — 7.2%; Italian — 10.4%; Polish — 2.6%; Russian — 0.5%; Scottish — 0.5%.

Universities, Enrollment: Camden County College, Blackwood — 8,360; Glassboro State College, Glassboro — 10,112; Gloucester County College, Sewell — 3,068; New Jersey School of Osteopathic Medicine, Camden — 117; Rutgers, The State University of New Jersey (Camden Campus), Camden — 5,143.

Newspapers, Circulation: *Courier-Post* (eS), Camden — 122,363; *The Gloucester County Times* (eS), Woodbury — 25,840. *Philadelphia Daily News* and *The Philadelphia Inquirer* also circulate in the district.

Commercial Television Stations, Affiliation: Entire district is located in Philadelphia (Pa.) ADI.

Military Installations: Gibbsboro Air Force Station, Gibbsboro — 87.

Industries:

RCA Corp.; Camden; radios, televisions — 4,000. **Cooper Medical Center;** Camden; hospital — 1,600. **Our Lady of Lourdes Hospital;** Camden; hospital — 1,400. **Campbell Soup Co.** (HQ); Camden; canned foods — 1,300. **CBS Inc.** (CBS Records); Pitman; phonograph records — 1,200. **Owens-Corning Fiberglas Corp.;** Barrington; insulation — 1,200.

Camden County Health Services Center; Blackwood; hospital — 1,100. **Underwood Memorial Hospital;** Woodbury; hospital — 1,100. **West Jersey Hospital System;** Camden; hospital — 1,000. **Campbell Sales Co. Inc.** (HQ); Camden; canned goods wholesaling — 900. **Mobil Research & Development;** Paulsboro; research — 900. **Texaco Inc.** (Refining Dept.); Westville; oil products wholesaling — 750. **Owens-Illinois Inc.** (Closure Div.); Glassboro; high-speed drives, gears — 700. **RCA Corp.** (Distributor & Special Products Div.); Deptford; electronic parts wholesaling — 500.

2nd District

South — Atlantic City, Vineland

Atlantic City, the saying went, was built on "ocean, emotion and promotion." The faded old resort town has seen better days — it lost 14 percent of its population during the 1970s — but casino gambling has helped stem the exodus.

Elsewhere in the 2nd, the story is one of growth; the small communities outside Atlantic City, once summer towns, are attracting thousands of new year-round residents, many of them refugees from older, urban parts of the state. Retirement communities also have sprung up inland. Before redistricting trimmed it back, the 2nd was the most populous district in the state. It grew 28 percent during the 1970s.

The areas within the newly drawn 2nd overwhelmingly favored Ronald Reagan in 1980. Republicans have impressive strength in two of the district's shore counties, Ocean and Cape May. The third shore county, Atlantic, is marginal.

The 1982 redistricting placed the entire northern half of Ocean County beyond the 2nd District boundaries; the burgeoning Republican population in that portion of the county might have posed a threat to Democrats in coming

years. The parts of Ocean retained in the 2nd include resort-oriented Long Beach Island and such rural pinelands townships as Bass River.

Cape May County is vacation-oriented but diverse. At the northern tip of its coast lies Ocean City, a family town where liquor sales are illegal. Farther south are wealthy Avalon and Stone Harbor and honky-tonk Wildwood. The elegant Victorian homes of Cape May city are at the southern tip.

Atlantic County once had a pronounced Republican tilt, but that ended in the early 1970s when the political machine of the late state Sen. Frank S. "Hap" Farley lost its grip. The sole remaining tribute to the organization's three-decade rule is the Farley rest stop on the Atlantic City Expressway.

Atlantic City, a bastion of Democratic votes, dominates the county. Nearly half black, with a large contingent of low-paid service workers, the resort had been losing its tourist trade until the advent of casinos. Gambling palaces now line the famed boardwalk, where the biggest thrills previously came from the diving horse of the Steel Pier and the annual Miss America pageant. The other Atlantic County vacation towns offer a quieter atmosphere and Republican allegiances.

Salem and Cumberland, are a mix of industrial and rural. People who spend their weekdays working in the garment factories and glass plants of these counties head for the marshes on weekends to hunt muskrats. On Election Day, they usually vote Democratic.

Election Returns

2nd District		Democrat		Republican	
1976	President	107,139	(51.1%)	98,480	(47.0%)
	Senate	113,874	(60.4%)	72,771	(38.6%)
	House	125,090	(63.3%)	72,383	(36.7%)
1977	Governor	88,723	(55.0%)	68,636	(42.3%)
1978	Senate	74,078	(51.7%)	66,823	(46.6%)
	House	97,487	(68.6%)	44,557	(31.4%)
1980	President	81,115	(38.4%)	112,079	(53.0%)
	House	117,288	(60.3%)	74,279	(38.2%)
1981	Governor	79,367	(46.6%)	90,822	(53.4%)
1982	Senate	79,379	(49.6%)	76,557	(47.9%)
	House	102,826	(68.0%)	47,069	(31.2%)

Demographics

Population: 526,279. **Percent Change from 1970:** 19.5%.

Land Area: 2,081 square miles. **Population per Square Mile:** 252.9.

Counties, 1980 Population: Atlantic — 194,119; Burlington (Pt.) — 8,388; Cape May — 82,266; Cumberland — 132,866; Ocean (Pt.) — 43,964; Salem — 64,676.

Cities, 1980 Population: Atlantic City — 40,199; Bridgeton — 18,795; Egg Harbor — 19,381; Galloway — 12,176; Hammonton — 12,298; Lower Twp. — 17,105; Middle Twp. — 11,373; Millville — 24,815; Ocean City — 13,949; Pennsville — 13,848; Pleasantville — 13,435; Somers Point — 10,330; Stafford — 10,385; Ventnor City — 11,704; Vineland — 53,753.

Race and Ancestry: White — 83.6%; Black — 13.2%; American Indian, Eskimo and Aleut — 0.3%; Asian and Pacific Islander — 0.5%. Spanish Origin — 4.4%. English — 8.0%; French — 0.5%; German — 6.7%; Irish — 6.0%; Italian — 9.2%; Polish — 1.7%; Russian — 1.1%; Scottish — 0.5%.

Universities, Enrollment: Atlantic Community College, Mays Landing — 3,827; Cumberland County College, Vineland — 2,569; Salem Community College, Penns Grove — 1,228; Stockton State College, Pomona — 4,919.

Newspapers, Circulation: *Bridgeton Evening News* (e), Bridgeton — 12,071; *The Millville Daily* (e), Millville — 23,982; *The Press* (mS), Atlantic City — 73,309; *Today's Sunbeam* (m), Salem — 11,365; *Vineland Times Journal* (e), Vineland — 23,982. *The Philadelphia Inquirer* also circulates in the district.

Commercial Television Stations, Affiliation: WAAT, Wildwood (NBC); WRBV, Vineland (None); WWAC-TV, Atlantic City (None). Most of district is located in Philadelphia (Pa.) ADI. Portion is in New York (N.Y.) ADI.

Military Installations: Earle Naval Weapons Station, Colts Neck — 1,508; Atlantic City Airport (Air National Guard), Pleasantville — 1,054.

Nuclear Power Plants: Hope Creek 1, Lower Alloways Creek (General Electric, Bechtel); Salem 1, Lower Alloways Creek (Westinghouse, United Engineers & Constructors), June 1977; Salem 2, Lower Alloways Creek (Westinghouse, United Engineers & Constructors), October 1981.

Industries:

Resorts International Hotel; Atlantic City; casino, hotel — 4,200. **E. I. du Pont de Nemours & Co.** (Chambers Works); Deepwater; organic materials — 4,000. **Marina Associates;** Atlantic City; casino, hotel — 3,600. **Adamar of New Jersey Inc.;** Atlantic City; casino, hotel — 3,000. **Bally's Park Place Inc.** (HQ); Atlantic City; casino, hotel — 3,000. **Caesar's New Jersey Inc.;** Atlantic City; casino, hotel — 3,000. **Wheaton Industries Inc.** (HQ); Millville; glass containers — 3,000.

Claridge Ltd.; Atlantic City; casino, hotel — 2,700. **GNAC Corp.;** Atlantic City; casino, hotel — 2,500. **Greate Bay Hotel & Casino Inc.;** Atlantic City; casino, hotel — 2,500. **Hi-Ho Casino;** Atlantic City; casino, hotel — 2,500. **Owens-Illinois Inc.** (Kimble Div.); Vineland; pressed, blown glass — 2,000. **Lenox China Inc.;** Pomona; china — 1,500. **Atlantic City Medical Center;** Atlantic City; hospital — 1,050. **Anchor Hocking Corp.;** Salem; glass containers — 1,100. **Ancora Psychiatric Hospital;** Hammonton; state psychiatric hospital — 1,000. **Kerr Glass Mfg. Corp.;** Millville; glass containers — 1,000. **Owens-Illinois Inc.;** Bridgeton; glass containers — 1,000. **Mannington Mills Inc.** (HQ); Salem; linoleum floor coverings — 800. **Prudential Property & Casualty Insurance Co.;** Linwood; casualty insurance — 760. **William B. Kessler Inc.** (HQ); Hammonton; men's clothing — 750. **Wheaton Industries Inc.** (Wheaton Plastic Co.); Mays Landing; plastic products — 700. **Wheaton Industries Inc.** (Scientific Div.); Millville; glass containers — 600. **American Home Products Corp.** (Whitehall Laboratories Div.); Hammonton; pharmaceutical preparations — 550. **Calvi Electric Co.;** Atlantic City; electrical contracting — 500. **Prudential Insurance Co. of America;** Linwood; life, health insurance — 500.

3rd District

Central Coast — Asbury Park, Long Branch

When the Legislature created this district in 1982, some members complained that at high tide it would cease to exist. Crafted to help the Democratic incumbent, the new 3rd hugs the coastline in search of Democratic votes, avoiding inland Republican areas of Monmouth County. But the new 3rd hardly stacks up as a Democratic bastion. Ronald Reagan carried the region with 56.5 percent of the vote in 1980.

One dependable source of Democratic votes is along the Lower New York Bay shore. The chain of blue-collar towns there includes Keyport, Union Beach, Keansburg and Belford.

Two faded resort towns, Long Branch and Asbury Park, also harbor Democratic votes. Long Branch has sizable white ethnic and black populations; Asbury Park, with a grimy old boardwalk dominated by thrill rides, has a black majority.

Outside those communities, the district is mostly Republican. Deal, with its mansions and quiet elegance, typifies the well-to-do Republicanism that prevails along some parts of the 3rd's Atlantic Coast.

Inland Eatontown is politically marginal. It houses technologically oriented Fort Monmouth; GOP votes come from the military personnel there and the people working in the electronics and computer industries that have spun off from the base. But the high number of other federal workers and the young apartment dwellers in Eatontown serve as a Democratic counterweight.

The other inland towns, such as Old Bridge and Manalapan, contain New York commuters who embody the usual suburban loyalty to the Republican Party. Middletown Township, the 3rd's largest political entity, votes firmly Republican. Across the Navesink River in working-class Red Bank Democrats have their strongest inland bastion.

The district received a few Republican shore towns when a northern segment of Ocean County was added. Fast-growing Brick Township is a haven for retirees from New York and New Jersey. Local Republican candidates are able to perform well there, although many of them have residual Democratic loyalties.

Lakewood has acres of pine trees and a Democratic tradition. Before World War II it contained many resorts for the well-off, who were attracted by its clean air and mineral-rich water. When the resorts folded, the black servants stayed — and the town, now 20.1 percent black, has the highest minority population in Ocean County. It also has a large Jewish community.

Election Returns

3rd District		Democrat		Republican	
1976	President	90,107	(43.5%)	113,163	(54.7%)
	Senate	112,402	(55.8%)	86,799	(43.1%)
	House	115,270	(62.5%)	67,102	(36.4%)
1977	Governor	84,132	(56.3%)	61,797	(41.4%)
1978	Senate	83,917	(54.8%)	67,340	(44.0%)
	House	76,495	(54.6%)	62,336	(44.5%)
1980	President	74,656	(34.3%)	122,879	(56.5%)
	House	99,528	(48.9%)	100,304	(49.3%)
1981	Governor	74,777	(45.3%)	90,275	(54.7%)
1982	Senate	82,860	(49.7%)	81,857	(49.1%)
	House	104,055	(62.3%)	60,515	(36.2%)

Demographics

Population: 524,825. **Percent Change from 1970:** 12.1%.

Land Area: 241 square miles. **Population per Square Mile:** 2,177.7.

Counties, 1980 Population: Middlesex (Pt.) — 51,515; Monmouth (Pt.) — 356,282; Ocean (Pt.) — 117,028.

Cities, 1980 Population: Aberdeen — 17,235; Asbury Park — 17,015; Brick — 53,629; Eatontown — 12,703; Hazlet — 23,013; Keansburg — 10,613; Lakewood — 38,464; Long Branch — 29,819; Manalapan

— 18,914; Middletown — 62,574; Neptune — 28,366; Ocean — 23,570; Old Bridge — 51,515; Point Pleasant — 17,747; Red Bank — 12,031.

Race and Ancestry: White — 89.7%; Black — 8.1%; American Indian, Eskimo and Aleut — 0.1%; Asian and Pacific Islander — 1.0%. Spanish Origin — 3.1%. English — 4.3%; French — 0.5%; German — 5.6%; Greek — 0.5%; Hungarian — 0.8%; Irish — 9.1%; Italian — 10.4%; Polish — 3.3%; Russian — 1.7%; Scottish — 0.8%.

Universities, Enrollment: Brookdale Community College, Lincroft — 10,789; Georgian Court College, Lakewood — 1,385; Monmouth College, West Long Branch — 3,826.

Newspapers, Circulation: *Asbury Park Press* (eS), Asbury Park — 106,525; *The Daily Register* (e), Red Bank — 31,406. New Brunswick *Home News*, *New York Daily News*, *The New York Times*, Perth Amboy *News Tribune* and Newark *Star-Ledger* also circulate in the district.

Commercial Television Stations, Affiliation: Entire district is in New York (N.Y.) ADI.

Military Installations: Fort Monmouth, Red Bank — 11,309.

Industries:

Monmouth Medical Center; Long Branch; hospital — 1,900. **Jersey Shore Medical Center;** Neptune; hospital — 1,470. **Riverview Hospital;** Red Bank; hospital — 1,400. **Perkin-Elmer Corp.** (Computer Operations Div.); Oceanport; electronic computing equipment — 1,200. **Point Pleasant Hospital Inc.;** Point Pleasant Beach; hospital — 1,200.

Continental Insurance Co. (Insco Systems Div.); Neptune; data processing — 950. **Midland Glass Co. Inc.** (HQ); Cliffwood; glass containers — 750. **Paco Pharmaceutical Services;** Lakewood; drug, cosmetic packaging — 700. **Electronic Associates Inc.** (HQ); West Long Branch; electronic computing equipment — 660. **Bendix Corp.;** Eatontown; radio, TV transmitting equipment — 650. **Asbury Park Press Inc.** (HQ); Asbury Park; newspaper publishing — 600. **Excel Wood Products Co. Inc.** (HQ); Lakewood; wood kitchen cabinets — 500.

4th District

Central — Trenton

"Trenton Makes, the World Takes" is the motto of the city that forms the core of the 4th district. A historical old town, New Jersey's capital chooses to identify itself with its industrial base rather than its history. While many state capital cities now have post-industrial economies based on professional employment, Trenton is still dependent on metal products, auto parts and electrical wiring. It has a third of the population of Mercer County, and the people who work in its factories vote Democratic in most elections.

In 1982 the Legislature reinforced Democratic strength in a bid to damage the Republican incumbent whose 1980 election was regarded as a fluke brought on by the conviction of veteran Democratic Rep. Frank Thompson Jr. in the FBI's Abscam corruption probe. The map makers dropped from the 4th Republican and marginal towns in southern Middlesex County. The scheme proved futile as the incumbent was re-elected by a 10,000 vote margin.

To add Democrats the district dipped down along the Delaware to encompass several working-class river communities in Burlington County and one in Camden County. Jimmy Carter came within about 3,000 votes of carrying what is now the new 4th in 1980; he trailed by nearly twice that much in the old version.

The new Camden County town in the 4th is Pennsau-ken, which sprawls on either side of the garish commercial strip of Route 130, heading north from Camden. Many of Camden's ethnic whites followed the road out of their decaying city to Pennsauken, taking their Democratic habits with them. Farther north on 130 in Burlington County are similar ethnic towns such as Edgewater Park.

The biggest new town brought in from Burlington County is Willingboro, a white-collar enclave that votes Democratic because of the middle-class black element that makes up more than a third of its population. Started after World War II as one of the Levittowns, it changed its name because its mail was going to the Levittown across the river in Pennsylvania.

With a fifth of the new 4th's population, Trenton continues to dominate the district. Almost half black, Trenton votes solidly Democratic. Blacks have begun to advance in local political offices, although Italians remain the dominant ethnic group. The city lost 12.1 percent of its population from 1970 to 1980 as ethnic whites left for Hamilton and other suburbs. Italians cluster in the Chambersburg section of town. Near that neighborhood is the legendary Lorenzo's Restaurant, where politicians from around the state congregate.

Much of Mercer's suburban blue-collar vote can be found in Hamilton, which has just 10,000 fewer people than Trenton. Democrats can count on Hamilton in state and national elections, but Republicans control the township on the local level.

Election Returns

4th District		Democrat		Republican	
1976	President	109,678	(54.4%)	87,757	(43.5%)
	Senate	121,304	(63.8%)	67,226	(35.4%)
	House	112,436	(57.9%)	78,748	(40.5%)
1977	Governor	97,165	(64.2%)	50,928	(33.6%)
1978	Senate	75,731	(56.5%)	56,906	(42.5%)
	House	67,926	(52.7%)	58,997	(45.8%)
1980	President	94,146	(43.9%)	97,451	(45.4%)
	House	83,588	(43.8%)	103,757	(54.4%)
1981	Governor	91,859	(58.3%)	65,602	(41.7%)
1982	Senate	88,146	(56.1%)	67,093	(42.7%)
	House	75,658	(46.5%)	85,660	(52.7%)

Demographics

Population: 527,472. **Percent Change from 1970:** 4.0%.

Land Area: 433 square miles. **Population per Square Mile:** 1,218.2.

Counties, 1980 Population: Burlington (Pt.) — 211,431; Camden (Pt.) — 37,747; Mercer (Pt.) — 267,142; Middlesex (Pt.) — 5,605; Monmouth (Pt.) — 5,547.

Cities, 1980 Population: Burlington — 10,246; Burlington Twp. — 11,527; Cinnaminson — 16,072; Delran — 14,811; East Windsor — 21,041; Ewing — 34,842; Hamilton — 82,801; Lawrence — 19,724; Maple Shade — 20,525; Pemberton — 29,720; Pennsauken — 33,912; Trenton — 92,124; Willingboro — 39,912.

Race and Ancestry: White — 79.7%; Black — 17.3%; American Indian, Eskimo and Aleut — 0.1%; Asian and Pacific Islander — 1.3%. Spanish Origin — 3.0%. English — 5.5%; German — 5.7%; Hungarian — 1.3%; Irish — 5.3%; Italian — 9.2%; Polish — 3.9%; Russian — 1.0%; Scottish — 0.5%; Ukranian — 0.5%.

Universities, Enrollment: Burlington County College, Pemberton — 6,619; Mercer County Community College, Trenton — 8,091; Rider College, Lawrenceville — 5,729; Thomas A. Edison State College, Trenton — 3,619; Trenton State College, Trenton — 10,534.

Newspapers, Circulation: *Burlington County Times* (eS), Willingboro — 41,631; *Trenton Times* (e), Trenton — 69,303; *The Trentonian* (m), Trenton — 65,838. Camden *Courier-Post*, *Philadelphia Daily News* and *The Philadelphia Inquirer* also circulate in the district.

Commercial Television Stations, Affiliation: WKBS-TV, Burlington (None). Most of district is located in Philadelphia (Pa.) ADI. Portion is in New York (N.Y.) ADI.

Military Installations: Fort Dix, Fort Dix — 10,084; Naval Air Propulsion Center, Trenton — 602.

Industries:

General Motors Corp. (Fisher Body Div.); Trenton; automotive hardware — 3,910. **McGraw-Hill Inc.;** Hightstown; book distributing — 1,800. **RCA Corp.** (Astro-Electronics Div.); Hightstown; research — 1,500. **GTE Products Corp.** (Wiring Devices Div.); Trenton; wire products — 1,300. **Emhart Industries Inc.** (Hill Refrigeration Div.); Trenton; commercial refrigeration equipment — 1,250.

Lenox China Inc. (HQ); Trenton; china — 1,200. **St. Francis Medical Center;** Trenton; hospital — 1,200. **Helene Fuld Medical Center;** Trenton; hospital — 1,100. **GTE Satellite Corp.** (Sylvania-Circle F Div.); Trenton; telephone communications — 1,000. **Inductotherm Industries Inc.** (HQ); Rancocas; industrial furnaces — 1,000. **Mercer Medical Center;** Trenton; hospital — 1,000. **River Road Corp.;** Delair; aluminum products — 875. **New Jersey Manufacturers Insurance Co.** (HQ); Trenton; casualty, property insurance — 807. **General Electric Co.;** Trenton; heating equipment — 700. **Goodall Rubber Co.** (HQ); Trenton; industrial rubber products — 650. **Broken Lance Enterprises Inc.;** Pemberton; janitorial services — 630.

Heinemann Electric Co. Inc.; Trenton; switchgear equipment — 600. **NL Industries Inc.** (Industrial Chemical Div.); Hightstown; research — 600. **Hoeganaes Corp.;** Riverton; blast furnace — 585. **AFG Industries Inc.;** Riverton; flat glass — 500. **Globe Security System Inc.;** Beverly; security services — 500. **Hooker Chemical & Plastic Corp.** (Ruco Div.); Florence; plastic products — 500. **New Jersey National Bank** (HQ); Trenton; banking — 500. **North American Philips Lighting Corp.** (Norelco Div. - HQ); Hightstown; electric lamps — 500. **TRW Inc.** (Crescent Insulator Wire); Trenton; wire, cable — 500. **United States Pipe & Foundry Co.;** Burlington; cast iron — 500.

5th District

North and West — Ridgewood, Phillipsburg

In a flight of cartographic fancy, the Legislature in 1982 packed North Jersey Republicans into a new district many call "the Swan." Its long neck and twisted body stretch from the New York suburbs to the rural upper reaches of the Delaware River. One wing covers the affluent GOP towns in northern Bergen County; its head pokes into the equally Republican suburbia of Morris County; the second wing follows the Delaware to the outskirts of Trenton.

Democrats form a decided minority in the new 5th. They have a small stronghold in the manufacturing center of Phillipsburg, the home of a large Ingersoll-Rand plant in otherwise Republican Warren County. Hackettstown has an M&M/Mars candy factory and other blue-collar employment sources that make it politically marginal. Elsewhere Democrats are hard to find.

Along the Delaware in Hunterdon, Warren and Sussex counties, one finds rural values, farming and Republican loyalties. New Jersey is the most densely populated state in the Union, but travelers to this part of the state are amazed to find large swatches of sparsely populated countryside.

Close to the New York border the terrain is mountainous and even less populous. The Ramapo Mountains extend into upper Passaic County, where a hillbilly-like group called the "Jackson Whites" lives in cultural isolation. They are descendants of miners, a symbol of the old Ringwood ironworks that made cannonballs for the American Revolutionary War. The flatter land of Ringwood and West Milford, the 5th's other Passaic town, is developing suburbia.

The Morris County appendage of the 5th is comprised of middle-income suburbs. Bergen County has the district's most important single voting bloc. While the county's 35 percent share of the district's population does not dominate the 5th numerically, the Bergen towns are politically well organized and Republicans there are willing to help local candidates. The Morris segment claims 23 percent of the population, followed by Warren with 13 percent.

Upper Bergen has the most money, too. It is a homogeneous collection of leafy towns where upper-income Republicans live in large houses. Former president Richard Nixon resides in one such suburb, Saddle River.

Election Returns

5th District		Democrat		Republican	
1976	President	95,534	(41.4%)	130,956	(56.7%)
	Senate	119,076	(55.5%)	92,936	(43.3%)
	House	115,264	(52.7%)	100,353	(45.9%)
1977	Governor	84,005	(52.6%)	72,323	(45.3%)
1978	Senate	78,000	(51.1%)	72,093	(47.2%)
	House	74,702	(48.6%)	75,119	(48.8%)
1980	President	67,817	(28.9%)	139,235	(59.4%)
	House	74,276	(33.9%)	139,649	(63.7%)
1981	Governor	56,103	(33.4%)	111,939	(66.6%)
1982	Senate	62,315	(36.5%)	106,456	(62.3%)
	House	53,659	(33.5%)	104,695	(65.3%)

Demographics

Population: 526,367. **Percent Change from 1970:** 12.2%.

Land Area: 1,322 square miles. **Population per Square Mile:** 398.2.

Counties, 1980 Population: Bergen (Pt.) — 187,942; Hunterdon (Pt.) — 51,586; Mercer (Pt.) — 15,003; Morris (Pt.) — 120,006; Passaic (Pt.) — 35,375; Sussex (Pt.) — 44,630; Warren (Pt.) — 71,825.

Cities, 1980 Population: Denville — 14,380; Hopewell — 10,893; Jefferson — 16,413; Mahwah — 12,127; Montville — 14,290; Mount Olive — 18,748; Phillipsburg — 16,647; Ramsey — 12,899; Randolph — 17,828; Ridgewood — 25,208; Ringwood — 12,625; River Edge — 11,111; Roxbury — 18,878; Vernon — 16,302; Waldwick 10,802; West Milford — 22,750; Wyckoff — 15,500.

Race and Ancestry: White — 97.3%; Black — 0.9%; American Indian, Eskimo and Aleut — 0.1%; Asian and Pacific Islander — 1.4%. Spanish Origin — 1.5%. Dutch — 1.9%; English — 5.7%; French — 0.6%; German — 8.2%; Greek — 0.5%; Hungarian — 1.1%; Irish — 6.9%; Italian — 9.2%; Norwegian — 0.5%; Polish — 2.9%; Russian — 1.0%; Scottish — 0.7%; Swedish — 0.5%; Ukranian — 0.5%.

Universities, Enrollment: Centenary College, Hackettstown — 939; Immaculate Conception Seminary, Mahwah — 217; Ramapo College of New Jersey, Mahwah — 4,574.

Newspapers, Circulation: Morristown *Daily Record, New York Daily News, The New York Times*, Hackensack *Record*, Newark *Star-Ledger, Trenton Times* and *The Trentonian* circulate in the district.

Commercial Television Stations, Affiliation: Most of district is located in New York (N.Y.) ADI. Small portion is in Philadelphia (Pa.) ADI.

Industries:

Ingersoll-Rand Co.; Phillipsburg; machine parts, foundry — 2,400. **Butler Service Group** (HQ); Montvale; engineering services — 1,800. **Society Valley Hospital;** Ridgewood; hospital — 1,300. **Mobil Oil Corp.** (Mobil Telecommunications Dept.); Pennington; research — 950. **Hoffmann-La Roche Inc.;** Belvidere; pharmaceuticals — 882.

Abex Corp. (Railroad Products Div.); Mahwah; castings — 800. **Prentice-Hall Inc.;** Old Tappan; administrative offices — 800. **Playboy of Sussex** (Playboy at Great Gorge); McAfee; resort — 750. **SRI Corp.** (HQ); Branchville; casualty, health insurance — 750. **Amerace Corp.** (Elastimold Div.); Hackettstown; electrical wire — 700. **Cessna Aircraft Co. Inc.** (Aircraft Radio & Control Div.); Boonton; automatic pilots — 700. **Mars Inc.** (M & M Mars Div.); Hackettstown; candy — 700. **Pan American World Airways Inc.;** Northvale; management, public relations — 700. **Burroughs Corp.** (Terminal Systems Group); Flemington; electronic display equipment — 650. **Hoke Inc.** (HQ); Cresskill; metal valves — 600.

Sterling Drug Inc. (Ogilvie Products Div.); Montvale; household pesticides, cleaners — 600. **Volvo North America Corp.;** Northvale; auto, truck parts wholesaling — 549. **American Can Co.;** Washington; plastic, metal containers — 500. **J. T. Baker Chemical Co.** (HQ); Phillipsburg; industrial chemicals — 500. **The Bates Mfg. Co. Inc.;** Hackettstown; office machines — 500. **Dynamit Nobel of America Inc.** (Sporting Arms Div. - HQ); Northvale; plastics, shotguns, ammunition — 500. **Thomas J. Lipton Inc.;** Flemington; dehydrated foods — 500. **Litton Industries Inc.** (Sweda International Div.); Pine Brook; administrative offices — 500. **MEM Co. Inc.** (HQ); Northvale; cosmetics, boxes, plastics products — 500. **Western Electric Co. Inc.;** Hopewell; research center — 500. **Western Union Corp.** (HQ); Saddle River; telegraph communications — 500.

6th District

Central — New Brunswick, Perth Amboy

Exxon's giant Bayway refinery, with its flaring gas and oppressive stench, is responsible for much of New Jersey's image problem. Travelers who see the refinery from the turnpike wonder why anyone would live near it. But thousands of the voters of the 6th District do. They are predominantly white ethnics and Hispanics, many of them living within sight and smell of the refinery complex.

The 6th actually extends for miles beyond the refinery and the turnpike. Covering most of industrial Middlesex County, the 6th traditionally has been a rich source of votes for the Democratic Party. On the congressional level, the Middlesex constituency has been reliably Democratic since 1961. Before that, the county was split between two Republican districts.

In statewide and national races, however, that partisanship is far from unshakable. Middlesex, which solidly supported John F. Kennedy in 1960, barely went for Jimmy Carter in 1976 and voted for Ronald Reagan in 1980.

The 1982 redistricting made the 6th slightly more Democratic. The map makers pared away GOP and marginal towns in southern Middlesex, rounding out the 6th with industrial Rahway in Union County and Democratic-leaning East Brunswick, which had been in the 4th District. Democrats have at least a nominal advantage nearly everywhere in the new district.

Middlesex is a place where things are made. The closer one gets to the Arthur Kill, separating New Jersey and Staten Island, the heavier and dirtier the industry becomes. Bleak Perth Amboy, now 40 percent Hispanic, illustrates the economic problems troubling this industrial belt. A Canadian company opened a new steel plant there in 1977, but recent layoffs have dashed any hopes it would spark a resurgence.

The massive petrochemical industry quartered in the eastern half of the 6th has provided a more stable employment picture, although its contribution to air quality and aesthetics remains slight. Linden (home of Bayway), Sayreville and South Amboy house chemical works.

In Edison Township people work in less grimy electronics plants, a legacy of Thomas A. Edison, who developed many of his inventions there. The presence of Rutgers University and a one-quarter black population keep New Brunswick thoroughly Democratic. Johnson & Johnson, the medical supply manufacturer, is leading an effort to revitalize New Brunswick by building its new headquarters downtown.

Republicans rule in white-collar suburban South Plainfield. They also can be found among the New York commuters in Woodbridge, the district's largest town, but a sizable blue-collar group keeps that town competitive.

Election Returns

6th District		Democrat		Republican	
1976	President	113,745	(51.7%)	101,923	(46.4%)
	Senate	132,272	(67.7%)	60,375	(30.9%)
	House	112,156	(56.5%)	67,198	(33.9%)
1977	Governor	90,053	(56.4%)	65,032	(40.7%)
1978	Senate	82,977	(61.3%)	49,807	(36.8%)
	House	62,561	(48.5%)	60,125	(46.6%)
1980	President	87,553	(41.1%)	107,163	(50.4%)
	House	94,310	(49.1%)	93,079	(48.5%)
1981	Governor	79,394	(52.9%)	70,571	(47.1%)
1982	Senate	86,167	(56.1%)	66,177	(43.1%)
	House	100,418	(68.1%)	46,093	(31.3%)

Demographics

Population: 523,798. **Percent Change from 1970:** -2.5%.

Land Area: 171 square miles. **Population per Square Mile:** 3,063.1.

Counties, 1980 Population: Middlesex (Pt.) — 457,454; Union (Pt.) — 66,344.

Cities, 1980 Population: Carteret — 20,598; East Brunswick — 37,711; Edison — 70,193; Highland Park — 13,396; Linden — 37,836; Metuchen — 13,762; New Brunswick — 41,442; Perth Amboy — 38,951; Piscataway — 42,223; Rahway — 26,723; Sayreville — 29,969; South Plainfield — 20,521; South River — 14,361; Woodbridge — 90,074.

Race and Ancestry: White — 87.5%; Black — 8.1%; American Indian, Eskimo and Aleut — 0.1%; Asian and Pacific Islander — 1.9%. Spanish Origin — 6.4%. English — 2.2%; German — 4.2%; Greek — 0.6%; Hungarian — 3.4%; Irish — 5.5%; Italian — 9.4%; Polish — 8.1%; Portuguese — 0.5%; Russian — 1.9%; Ukranian — 1.2%.

Universities, Enrollment: College of Medicine and Dentistry of New Jersey (Rutgers Medical School), Piscataway — 426; Middlesex County College, Edison — 11,939; New Brunswick Theological Seminary, New Brunswick — 112; Rutgers, The State University of New Jersey (New Brunswick campus), New Brunswick — 33,372.

Newspapers, Circulation: *The Home News* (eS), New Brunswick — 58,501; *The News Tribune* (e), Perth Amboy — 53,765. Elizabeth *Daily Journal, New York Daily News* and *The New York Times* also circulate in the district.

Commercial Television Stations, Affiliation: WNJU-TV, Linden (None, Spanish). Entire district is located in New York (N.Y.) ADI.

Industries:

General Motors Corp. (Assembly Div.); Linden; auto assembly — 5,200. **Johnson & Johnson** (HQ); New Brunswick; surgical dressings, pharmaceuticals, toiletries — 3,500. **Merck & Co. Inc.** (HQ); Rahway; pharmaceuticals — 3,500. **E. R. Squibb & Sons Inc.;** New Brunswick; pharmaceuticals — 3,000. **Revlon Inc.;** Edison; cosmetics — 2,400.

Exxon Research & Engineering Co.; Linden; research — 2,000. **Bell Telephone Labs Inc.;** Piscataway; communications — 1,900. **Community Hospital Group Inc.** (John F. Kennedy Medical Center); Edison; hospital — 1,800. **Amerada Hess Corp.** (Hess Oil Virgin Islands Corp.); Woodbridge; petroleum refining — 1,750. **Raritan Bay Health Services;** Perth Amboy; hospital — 1,700.

Ford Motor Co.; Edison; autos — 1,600. **United States Metal;** Carteret; copper refining — 1,600. **E. I. du Pont de Nemours & Co.;** Parlin; photo products — 1,500. **Fedders Corp.** (Fedders Solar Products Co. - HQ); Edison; heating, cooling equipment — 1,500. **St. Peter's Medical Center;** New Brunswick; hospital — 1,400. **NL Industries Inc.** (Titanium Pigment Div.); Sayreville; titanium dioxide — 1,250. **Exxon Corp.** (Exxon Co. USA); Linden; petroleum refining — 1,200. **ITT Autowiz Inc.;** Piscataway; auto parts wholesaling — 1,200. **Eastern Airlines Inc.** (Reservations & Telephone Div.); Iselin; airline operations — 1,160. **Middlesex General Hospital Inc.;** New Brunswick; hospital — 1,100. **Personal Products Co.** (HQ); Milltown; sanitary napkins — 1,100. **Triangle PWC Inc.** (HQ); New Brunswick; insulated electrical wire — 1,000.

American Telephone & Telegraph (Stock & Bond Div.); Piscataway; management consulting — 900. **Sunshine Biscuits Inc.;** Sayreville; biscuits, crackers — 900. **White Consolidated Industries;** Edison; air conditioners — 900. **Chevron USA Inc.;** Perth Amboy; petroleum refining — 800. **Standard Plastic Products Inc.** (HQ); South Plainfield; plastic dolls — 800. **Twin County Grocers Inc.;** Edison; grocery wholesaling — 760. **Siemens Corp.** (HQ); Iselin; medical, industrial equipment — 750. **American Cyanamid Co.** (Warners Plant); Linden; chemicals — 725. **Hercules Inc.;** Parlin; chemical products — 725. **General Signal Appliance Corp.** (Regina Co. Div.); Rahway; floor polishing machines — 700. **Emerson Quiet Kool Corp.;** Woodbridge; air conditioners — 675.

Mattel Inc.; South Plainfield; dolls, plastic products — 650. **Royal Food Distributors Inc.;** Woodbridge; meat, dairy wholesaling — 650. **Continental Copper & Steel Industries** (Hatfield Wire & Cable Div.); Linden; wire, cable — 600. **Kimberly-Clark Corp.** (Schweitzer Co.); Spotswood; cigarette paper — 580. **General Motors Corp.** (Delco Remy Div.); New Brunswick; batteries — 560. **General Dynamics Corp.** (Electro Dynamic); Avenel; generators — 550. **Engelhard Corp.** (Engelhard Industries Div. - HQ); Edison; metal refining — 546. **Beatrice Foods Co.** (Dri-Print Foils Div.); Rahway; hot stamping foils — 500. **Hatco Chemical Corp.;** Fords; plasticizers — 500. **Johnson & Johnson Inc.** (Permacel Tape Div.); New Brunswick; adhesive tape — 500.

7th District

North and Central — Elizabeth

In an effort to create a new Democratic district, the Legislature in 1982 traced a curving partisan path through industrial Elizabeth, liberal, academic Princeton and largely Jewish Marlboro in Monmouth County. The resulting congressional district was called "the Fishhook" by detractors. It had no resident incumbent and seemed a likely Democratic pickup for 1982. But the Republican incumbent whose old district was divided between the 7th and the 12th decided to run in the 7th and won in 1982 with 56 percent of the vote.

Elizabeth found its place on the 19th century industrial map as a manufacturing town for Singer Sewing Machines and became an ethnic working-class city. Today it houses a fifth of the district's population and retains an ethnic diversity reinforced by an infusion of blacks and Hispanics. In most elections it is heavily Democratic. The petrochemical industry and other heavy manufacturing make Elizabeth a dingy place. The city is the site of the notorious Kin-Buc toxic waste dump, closed because of the peril it posed to groundwater.

Strung along the narrow upper neck of the 7th in northern Union County are pleasant suburban towns such as Westfield and Cranford. While Republican, these towns have sizable groups of liberal young professionals who sometimes elect Democrats to local office.

In the southwest corner of the county is predominantly black Plainfield, which votes Democratic. The same party leanings are found in the Somerset County industrial boroughs just to the west, Bound Brook and Manville. The latter town is an asbestos-making center.

Beyond the Union County line, the district slices southwest into Middlesex County, where rapid growth has brought fluid politics to Monroe, North Brunswick and South Brunswick. All nearly doubled in population during the 1970s as new industrial parks popped up among the farm land. Of the three, Monroe figures as the best Republican bet. Two large retirement villages there, Rossmoor and Clearbrook, have helped GOP office-seekers.

The next chunk of territory south includes Princeton Borough and surrounding Princeton Township, stitched onto the 7th from Mercer County. This area combines liberal academics with moderate Republican business people. When the Republican candidate is a conservative, a Democrat usually carries this portion of the district. Carter took both the borough and the township in 1980.

At its extreme southern end, the new 7th reaches into a developing part of Monmouth County. It runs through politically marginal Millstone, Republican Freehold Township and Marlboro, whose sizable Jewish community tilts it toward the Democrats.

Election Returns

7th District		Democrat		Republican	
1976	President	102,139	(46.5%)	113,207	(51.5%)
	Senate	124,779	(61.3%)	75,807	(37.4%)
	House	72,967	(35.6%)	128,239	(62.5%)
1977	Governor	83,121	(51.1%)	74,925	(46.1%)
1978	Senate	70,555	(50.5%)	66,330	(47.5%)
	House	46,152	(32.9%)	93,265	(66.5%)
1980	President	87,901	(40.8%)	106,066	(49.2%)
	House	58,760	(29.9%)	132,995	(67.7%)
1981	Governor	77,136	(46.3%)	89,631	(53.7%)
1982	Senate	79,518	(48.0%)	83,556	(50.5%)
	House	70,978	(43.2%)	91,837	(56.0%)

Demographics

Population: 525,563. **Percent Change from 1970:** -0.4%.

Land Area: 341 square miles. **Population per Square Mile:** 1,541.2.

Counties, 1980 Population: Mercer (Pt.) — 25,718; Middlesex (Pt.) — 81,319; Monmouth (Pt.) — 50,708; Somerset (Pt.) — 77,032; Union (Pt.) — 290,786.

Cities, 1980 Population: Clark — 16,699; Cranford — 24,573; Elizabeth — 106,201; Franklin — 31,358; Freehold — 10,020; Freehold Twp. — 19,202; Manville — 11,278; Marlboro — 17,560; Middlesex — 13,480; Monore — 15,858; North Brunswick — 22,220; North Plainfield — 19,108; Plainfield — 45,555; Princeton — 12,035; Princeton Twp. — 13,683; Roselle — 20,641; Roselle Park — 13,377; Scotch Plains — 20,774; South Brunswick — 17,127; Westfield — 30,447.

Race and Ancestry: White — 82.1%; Black — 14.1%; American Indian, Eskimo and Aleut — 0.1%; Asian and Pacific Islander — 1.7%. Spanish Origin — 7.7%. English — 3.7%; German — 4.9%; Greek — 0.5%; Hungarian — 1.4%; Irish — 5.2%; Italian — 9.7%; Polish — 5.1%; Portuguese — 1.1%; Russian — 2.0%; Scottish — 0.6%; Ukrainian — 0.8%.

Universities, Enrollment: Princeton Theological Seminary, Princeton — 871; Princeton University, Princeton — 6,166; Union College, Cranford — 6,251; Westminster Choir College, Princeton — 470.

Newspapers, Circulation: *Daily Journal* (e), Elizabeth — 40,776. Bridgewater *Courier-News*, New Brunswick *Home News*, *New York Daily News*, *The New York Times* and Newark *Star-Ledger* also circulate in the district.

Commercial Television Stations, Affiliation: Most of district is located in New York (N.Y.) ADI. Portion is in Philadelphia (Pa.) ADI.

Industries:

Educational Testing Service; Princeton; educational testing — 2,880. **American Cyanamid Co.** (Organic Chemical Div.); Bound Brook; industrial chemicals — 2,730. **Hyatt Clark Industries Inc.;** Clark; motor vehicle parts — 2,500. **Singer Co.** (Industrial Products Div.); Elizabeth; sewing machines — 2,400. **Wakefern Food Corp.** (Shop-Rite - HQ); Elizabeth; grocery wholesaling — 2,340.

Johns-Manville Sales Corp.; Manville; asbestos building products — 2,200. **Transco Group Inc.;** Somerset; management services — 2,000. **Union Carbide Corp.;** Bound Brook; adhesives — 1,800. **Muhlenberg Hospital;** Plainfield; hospital — 1,700. **L.I.G. America Inc.;** Freehold; metal refining — 1,500. **RCA Corp.** (Astro Electronics Systems); Princeton; electronics systems — 1,350. **Lockheed Electronics Co.** (HQ); Plainfield; radar weapons — 1,300. **Rhone-Poulenc Inc.** (Chipman Chemicals Div.); Monmouth Junction; agricultural chemicals — 1,300. **Elizabeth General Hospital;** Elizabeth; hospital — 1,100. **Marlboro Psychiatric Hospital;** Marlboro; psychiatric hospital — 1,100.

Burry-Lu Inc.; Elizabeth; cookies, crackers — 1,000. **International Business Machines Corp.** (Information Records Div.); Dayton; data processing supplies — 1,000. **E. R. Squibb & Sons Inc.** (HQ); Princeton; pharmaceuticals — 1,000. **J. B. Williams Co. Inc.;** Cranford; drugs, toiletries — 1,000. **Cosmair Inc.** (HQ); Clark; hair care products — 900. **Carter-Wallace Inc.** (Lambert Kay Div.); Cranbury; pet food — 850. **Carter-Wallace Inc.** (Wampole Labs); Cranbury; pharmaceuticals — 850. **E & P Enterprises** (Port Side Industrial Park); Elizabeth; industrial real estate — 800. **Knickerbocker Toy Co. Inc.** (HQ); Middlesex; toys — 750. **Brockway Glass Co. Inc.;** Freehold; glass containers — 725. **Sea Land Freight Service Inc.;** Elizabeth; freight handlers — 700.

Phelps Dodge Copper Co.; Elizabeth; copper alloy products — 670. **Midland-Ross Corp.** (Cameron-Waldron Div.); Somerset; paper industries machinery — 580. **The Nestlé Co. Inc.;** Freehold; instant coffee — 550. **Simmons USA Corp.;** Elizabeth; bedding — 550. **Acme Building Service Co. Inc.** (HQ); Plainfield; janitorial services — 500. **Alpha Wire Corp.;** Elizabeth; wire, cable, tubing — 500. **Hayward Mfg. Co. Inc.** (HQ); Elizabeth; swimming pools — 500. **Minnesota Mining & Mfg. Co.** (Magnetic Audio/Video Div.); Freehold; electronic computing equipment — 500. **RCA American Communications;** Princeton; satellite communications — 500. **United States Lines Inc.** (HQ); Cranford; ocean liner operations — 500. **Wilson Jones Co.;** Elizabeth; looseleaf binders — 500.

8th District

North — Paterson

To Alexander Hamilton, the Great Falls of the Passaic River was an ideal location for a factory town. Then Treasury secretary, he set up the Society for Establishing Useful Manufactures in 1791 to build Paterson.

In time the thriving "Silk City" became one of the world's leading textile producers, attracting Irish, Polish, Italian and Russian craftsmen to work the looms. It also played out a history of labor strife and strong unions whose influence lives on.

Nowadays much of the industry is gone, leaving widespread unemployment and unsavory slums. A majority of the population is black or Hispanic, and there is chronic racial tension. In 1967 black boxer Rubin "Hurricane" Carter was found guilty of killing three white patrons in the Lafayette Grill, and his conviction nearly provoked a riot. A decade later the Lafayette Grill was called the Zodiac Lounge, and its clientele and neighborhood were exclusively black.

Paterson still contains 25 percent of the district's electorate, despite its severe population decline, and it is firmly Democratic. The only recent exception has been the success of moderate Republican Lawrence "Pat" Kramer, the city's mayor for the late 1960s and much of the 1970s. Kramer retired after losing the 1981 GOP gubernatorial primary and was replaced by a Democrat.

Paterson and the rest of southern Passaic County provide the Democratic vote in the 8th. The Passaic County suburbs next to Paterson, such as Clifton and Haledon, are where the white ethnics went when they fled the city. They still vote Democratic. Down the Passaic River lies the city of Passaic, a smaller but equally troubled version of Paterson. As in Paterson, the textile industry here also has evaporated.

In the northern half of the hourglass-shaped county, the terrain is more suburban. The subdivisions of Wayne Township usually vote Republican but make an exception for the Democratic House incumbent, a former mayor. Proceeding northwest from Wayne, however, suburban Bloomingdale and other suburbs cast a predictably solid Republican vote.

In Bergen County the 8th District includes Garfield and Wallington, two old mill towns with few minorities and little poverty. These communities have more in common with the blue-collar neighborhoods of Passaic County than with affluent Bergen.

The 1982 remap gave the 8th several developing suburbs in Morris County, such as Rockaway, and two firmly Republican towns from Bergen County, Oakland and Franklin Lakes. The district gave up the Republican communities of Ringwood and West Milford in Passaic County.

Election Returns

8th District		Democrat		Republican	
1976	President	85,379	(44.7%)	100,718	(52.7%)
	Senate	100,610	(58.8%)	67,352	(39.4%)
	House	114,571	(66.3%)	57,720	(33.4%)
1977	Governor	58,644	(46.3%)	64,894	(51.2%)

8th District		Democrat		Republican	
1978	Senate	59,825	(53.1%)	50,476	(44.8%)
	House	73,787	(67.8%)	34,960	(32.1%)
1980	President	67,435	(36.6%)	100,672	(54.6%)
	House	91,125	(55.7%)	69,574	(42.6%)
1981	Governor	78,087	(43.5%)	101,454	(56.5%)
1982	Senate	71,454	(54.2%)	57,423	(43.5%)
	House	89,980	(70.7%)	36,317	(28.5%)

Demographics

Population: 526,138. **Percent Change from 1970:** -4.1%.

Land Area: 181 square miles. **Population per Square Mile:** 2,906.8.

Counties, 1980 Population: Bergen (Pt.) — 59,756; Morris (Pt.) — 88,409; Passaic (Pt.) — 377,973.

Cities, 1980 Population: Clifton — 74,388; Dover — 14,681; Garfield — 26,803; Hawthorne — 18,200; Oakland — 13,443; Passaic — 52,463; Paterson — 137,970; Pequannock — 13,776; Pompton Lakes — 10,660; Rockaway — 19,850; Wallington — 10,741; Wanaque — 10,025; Wayne — 46,474.

Race and Ancestry: White — 81.6%; Black — 11.5%; American Indian, Eskimo and Aleut — 0.1%; Asian and Pacific Islander — 1.0%. Spanish Origin — 12.9%. Dutch — 2.2%; English — 2.9%; German — 4.2%; Hungarian — 1.0%; Irish — 4.1%; Italian — 13.0%; Polish — 5.6%; Russian — 1.5%; Scottish — 0.5%; Ukranian — 0.9%.

Universities, Enrollment: County College of Morris, Dover — 10,663; Passaic County Community College, Paterson — 4,108; William Paterson College of New Jersey, Wayne — 12,517.

Newspapers, Circulation: *The Daily Advance* (eS), Dover — 15,270; *The Herald-News* (eS), Passaic — 71,146; *The News* (m), Paterson — 49,257. Morristown *Daily Record*, *New York Daily News*, *The New York Times*, Newark *Star-Ledger* and Hackensack *Record* also circulate in the district.

Commercial Television Stations, Affiliation: WXTV, Paterson (None, Spanish). Entire district is located in New York (N.Y.) ADI.

Military Installations: Picatinny Arsenal, Dover — 6,113.

Industries:

St. Joseph's Hospital/Medical Center Inc.; Paterson; hospital — 1,900. **American Cyanamid Co. Inc.** (HQ); Wayne; industrial chemicals — 1,500. **International Business Machines Corp.** (Office Products Div.); Franklin Lakes; consulting services — 1,500. **International Telephone & Telegraph Corp.** (Avionics Div.); Clifton; navigation communications equipment — 1,200. **Dover General Hospital & Medical Center;** Dover; hospital — 1,070.

General Instrument Corp. (HQ); Clifton; electronic components — 1,000. **Howmet Turbine Components Corp.** (Austenal Dover Div.); Dover; die castings — 1,000. **Shulton Inc.** (HQ); Clifton; toiletries — 1,000. **Vornado Inc.** (Two Guys - HQ); Garfield; department stores — 1,000. **State Farm Fire and Casualty Co.;** Wayne; casualty insurance — 900. **Dart Industries Inc.** (Thatcher Glass Mfg. Co. Div.); Wharton; glass — 850. **GAF Corp.;** Wayne; administrative, research offices — 800. **Hewlett-Packard Co. Inc.;** Rockaway; electronic components — 800. **Prudential Insurance Co. of America;** Wayne; casualty insurance — 800. **Westinghouse Electric Corp.;** Dover; elevators — 743. **Givaudan Corp.;** Clifton; synthetic fragrances — 725.

Beecham Inc. (HQ); Clifton; toiletries — 700. **Meyer Brothers** (HQ); Paterson; department stores — 650. **Burlington Industries Inc.** (Westwood Industries Div.); Paterson; lamps — 625. **American Standard Inc.;** Wayne; pneumatic tubes — 600. **Borden Inc.** (Drake Bakeries); Wayne; baking products — 600. **American District Telegraph Co.** (ADT Security Systems); Clifton; electronic alarms — 500. **C. N. Burman Co.** (Paterson Shade Co.); Paterson; lamp wholesaling — 500. **E. I. du Pont de Nemours & Co.;** Pompton Lakes; explosives — 500. **The Mosler Safe Co.;** Wayne; iron safes — 500. **Union Camp Corp.** (HQ); Wayne; paper, paperboard — 500.

9th District

North — Fort Lee, Hackensack

The George Washington Bridge, connecting Manhattan's 181st Street and the New Jersey Palisades, is a fitting symbol for the 9th. Opened in 1931, the majestic span spurred the growth of suburban Bergen County. But in recent years the old, pothole-strewn bridge has carried fewer New York expatriates to the New Jersey side and the population of southern Bergen County, part of the 9th District, has slumped considerably.

As a result of the 1982 redistricting the district lies completely within Bergen. During the 1970s it included a chunk of Hudson County — which, while firmly Democratic, frustrated Bergen Democrats because they were forced to appease Hudson party leaders wanting a say in selecting the House nominee.

The 9th is a swing district. Ronald Reagan took the territory inside it with 55 percent of the vote in 1980, but Democrat James J. Florio carried it narrowly in his losing campaign for governor in 1981.

South Bergen is a series of towns sitting in the Hackensack Meadowlands, a large marsh that also contains warehouses, truck depots, factories and the Meadowlands sports complex. Several New York teams, including the football Giants, have crossed the river to play in the Meadowlands. The complex also has an auditorium named after former Gov. Brendan Byrne, who drew a barrage of criticism for allowing his political allies to create a personal monument to him while he was still in office.

The area closest to the George Washington Bridge is Democratic and solidly liberal. Apartments in Fort Lee, Cliffside Park and Edgewater line the Hudson River Palisades and house single professionals who work in New York City. Academics who teach at New Jersey colleges have an enclave in Leonia and also vote Democratic. Democrats perform well in Englewood, which is 40.6 percent black.

Farther north along the Palisades are affluent communities such as Alpine, Tenafly and Norwood. Many of the business executives who live there commute to New York; others work in one of Bergen's many corporate headquarters, such as those of CPC International Inc. and Prentice-Hall.

To the west out Route 4 are the large Democratic towns added to the 9th — blue-collar Hackensack and largely Jewish Teaneck and Fair Lawn. Another is Paramus, the county's commercial hub, which has a mix of young professionals and older suburbanites. It alternates between the parties.

Redistricting joins to the 9th a small Republican segment in the middle of Bergen County. But sylvan towns such as Woodcliff Lake, with their corporate offices, are hardly enough to disturb the political marginality.

Election Returns

9th District		Democrat		Republican	
1976	President	114,065	(42.2%)	151,636	(56.1%)
	Senate	142,737	(56.6%)	105,575	(41.9%)
	House	128,834	(50.5%)	123,787	(48.6%)
1977	Governor	97,650	(56.9%)	71,206	(41.5%)

9th District		Democrat		Republican	
1978	Senate	97,376	(53.4%)	82,909	(45.5%)
	House	78,478	(43.3%)	89,864	(49.6%)
1980	President	97,532	(36.1%)	148,238	(54.8%)
	House	118,787	(47.0%)	127,802	(50.6%)
1981	Governor	100,789	(50.2%)	99,912	(49.8%)
1982	Senate	100,506	(53.3%)	86,746	(46.0%)
	House	99,090	(53.0%)	86,022	(46.0%)

Demographics

Population: 527,349. **Percent Change from 1970:** -6.6%.

Land Area: 105 square miles. **Population per Square Mile:** 5,022.4.

Counties, 1980 Population: Bergen (Pt.) — 527,349.

Cities, 1980 Population: Bergenfield — 25,568; Cliffside Park — 21,464; Dumont — 18,334; Elmwood Park — 18,377; Englewood — 23,701; Fair Lawn — 32,229; Fairview — 10,519; Fort Lee — 32,449; Glen Rock — 11,497; Hackensack — 36,039; Hasbrouck Heights — 12,166; Hillsdale — 10,495; Lodi — 23,956; New Milford — 16,876; Paramus — 26,474; Ridgefield Park — 12,738; Rutherford — 19,068; Saddle Brook — 14,084; Teaneck — 39,007; Tenafly — 13,552; Westwood — 10,714.

Race and Ancestry: White — 90.4%; Black — 5.8%; American Indian, Eskimo and Aleut — 0.1%; Asian and Pacific Islander — 2.7%. Spanish Origin — 4.1%. Dutch — 0.7%; English — 2.4%; French — 0.5%; German — 6.4%; Greek — 1.2%; Hungarian — 0.9%; Irish — 7.1%; Italian — 17.2%; Polish — 3.9%; Russian — 2.7%.

Universities, Enrollment: Bergen Community College, Paramus — 11,533; Fairleigh Dickinson University, Rutherford — 20,195; Felician College, Lodi — 402.

Newspapers, Circulation: *The Record* (e), Hackensack — 149,210. Passaic *Herald-News*, *New York Daily News* and *The New York Times* also circulate in the district.

Commercial Television Stations, Affiliation: Entire district is located in New York (N.Y.) ADI.

Industries:

Bendix Corp. (Navigation & Control Group); Teterboro; communications equipment — 3,000. **Curtiss-Wright Corp.** (HQ); Wood-Ridge; aircraft parts — 2,336. **Becton Dickinson & Co.** (HQ); Paramus; surgical instruments — 1,800. **Bergen Pines County Hospital;** Paramus; hospital — 1,800. **Hackensack Medical Center;** Hackensack; hospital — 1,700.

Nabisco Inc.; Fair Lawn; biscuits, bakery products — 1,500. **Englewood Hospital Assn.;** Englewood; hospital — 1,400. **Prentice-Hall Inc.** (HQ); Englewood Cliffs; publishing — 1,400. **Bergen Evening Record Corp.;** Hackensack; newspaper publishing — 1,000. **Holy Name Hospital Inc.;** Teaneck; hospital — 1,000. **Thomas J. Lipton Inc.** (HQ); Englewood Cliffs; teas — 1,000. **Universal Coordinators Inc.;** Elmwood Park; truck leasing — 1,000. **Marcal Paper Mills Inc.** (HQ); Elmwood Park; sanitary paper products — 900. **Metpath Inc.;** Teterboro; medical laboratory — 850. **American Book-Stratford Press;** Saddle Brook; book printing — 800. **Frier Industries Inc.;** Carlstadt; house slippers — 800. **Universal Mfg. Corp.;** Paramus; transformers — 800. **CPC International Inc.** (HQ); Englewood Cliffs; corn products — 750. **Clark O'Neill Inc.;** Fairview; direct-mail services — 700. **Flexi-Van Financial Service;** Hackensack; accounting services — 700. **Howmedica Inc.;** Rutherford; orthopedic supplies — 650.

Becton Dickinson & Co.; East Rutherford; medical instruments — 600. **Bradford Securities Operations** (HQ); Fort Lee; securities services — 600. **Brevel Motors Inc.;** Carlstadt; small motors — 550. **Agfa-Gevaert Inc.** (HQ); Teterboro; photo equipment importers — 500. **Arrow Fastener Co. Inc.;** Saddle Brook; stapling machines — 500. **Beatrice Foods Co.** (Melnor Industries Div.); Moonachie; gardening tools — 500. **Dial America Marketing Inc.** (HQ); Teaneck; telephone marketing — 500. **The Inventory Co. Inc.;** Fort Lee; inventory comput-

ing — 500. **Maplewood Equipment Co.;** Fairview; interstate bus line — 500. **Power Mat Corp.;** Hackensack; generators, motors — 500. **Sandvik Inc.** (Coromant - HQ); Fair Lawn; metal cutting tools — 500. **Sharp Electronics Corp.** (Sharp Mfg. Co. - HQ); Paramus; electrical machine wholesaling — 500.

10th District

North — Newark

A generation ago, Newark was a city of nearly half a million people in which Irish and Italians competed for political power. By 1980 it had only 329,000, and there was no dispute over who held political power. Blacks make up 58 percent of the population, and Kenneth Gibson, elected in 1971 as the city's first black mayor, has remained in office ever since.

The 10th was underpopulated by nearly 100,000, so it was expanded beyond Newark's borders, and the city now has only about 60 percent of the district's electorate. But the 1982 redistricting preserved the black majority and the Democratic tilt. The area within the redrawn 10th gave Jimmy Carter 68.3 percent of its presidential vote in 1980.

"Wherever America's cities are going," Mayor Gibson once said, "Newark will get there first." Gibson's city did in fact foreshadow many of the urban problems that spread throughout the Northeast in the 1970s. Its Central Ward, devastated by riot in 1967, had not recovered more than 15 years later.

Despite a population loss of nearly 14 percent in the 1970s, Newark remains the largest city in the state, and the corporate headquarters of Prudential Insurance and other companies keep the central business area alive by day. Newark Airport and the busy docks provide other economic mainstays.

Newark's ethnic population breaks down this way: blacks in the Central and South Wards; Irish and blacks in the West Ward; Hispanics in the industrial East Ward, with Puerto Ricans more toward the center of town and Portuguese in the Ironbound section; and Italians in the North Ward.

Under the 1982 map, the underpopulated 10th was fleshed out with Hillside, Irvington and South Orange. The first two resemble Newark — blue-collar whites living in uneasy coexistence with blacks. Heavily Jewish South Orange is affluent and professional.

The 10th kept East Orange, whose stock brokerage houses have earned it the nickname "Wall Street of New Jersey." Despite the commercial strips along Central Avenue and Evergreen Place, however, East Orange has its own problems with poverty; it has a higher share of blacks than Newark, 83 percent.

Wealthy Glen Ridge, an anomaly in the district with its business executives, stayed in the 10th; its GOP votes continue to be drowned in the Democratic tide. Another holdover is Harrison, in Hudson County across the Passaic River from Newark. Virtually all-white, this blue-collar factory town is loyally Democratic.

Political intrigue and corruption are constant issues in Newark and environs. Gibson's predecessor, Hugh Addonizio, was convicted in 1970 of extorting payments from municipal contractors. Gibson, who defeated Addonizio for mayor that year, has his own problems with the law — a grand jury indicted him in 1982 for giving an ally an alleged no-show city job, even though this is common practice in New Jersey politics. Gibson subsequently was cleared when, acting on a motion from the local county prosecutor, a state court judge dismissed the case.

Election Returns

10th District		Democrat		Republican	
1976	President	101,273	(66.9%)	47,087	(31.1%)
	Senate	104,440	(76.6%)	29,634	(21.7%)
	House	110,836	(79.6%)	26,587	(19.1%)
1977	Governor	55,850	(57.6%)	39,215	(40.4%)
1978	Senate	62,354	(73.1%)	21,707	(25.4%)
	House	70,086	(82.5%)	14,001	(16.5%)
1980	President	90,610	(68.3%)	34,952	(26.4%)
	House	96,242	(81.7%)	19,334	(16.4%)
1981	Governor	76,282	(74.6%)	25,933	(25.4%)
1982	Senate	73,006	(75.1%)	22,710	(23.4%)
	House	76,684	(82.6%)	14,551	(15.7%)

Demographics

Population: 525,832. **Percent Change from 1970:** -8.7%.

Land Area: 39 square miles. **Population per Square Mile:** 13,482.9.

Counties, 1980 Population: Essex (Pt.) — 492,150; Hudson (Pt.) — 12,242; Union (Pt.) — 21,440.

Cities, 1980 Population: East Orange — 77,690; Harrison — 12,242; Hillside — 21,440; Irvington — 61,493; Newark — 329,248; South Orange — 15,864.

Race and Ancestry: White — 36.9%; Black — 54.8%; American Indian, Eskimo and Aleut — 0.2%; Asian and Pacific Islander — 1.0%. Spanish Origin — 13.8%. English — 1.7%; German — 1.6%; Irish — 2.2%; Italian — 6.6%; Polish — 2.0%; Portuguese — 3.9%; Russian — 0.7%; Ukranian — 0.6%.

Universities, Enrollment: College of Medicine and Dentistry of New Jersey (New Jersey Dental School and New Jersey Medical School), Newark — 1,920; Essex County College, Newark — 6,318; New Jersey Institute of Technology, Newark — 6,201; Rutgers, The State University of New Jersey (Newark Campus), Newark — 9,929; Seton Hall University, South Orange — 10,420; Upsala College, East Orange — 1,737.

Newspapers, Circulation: *The Star-Ledger* (mS), Newark — 407,331. *New York Daily News* and *The New York Times* also circulate in the district.

Commercial Television Stations, Affiliation: WWHT, Newark (None). Entire district is located in New York (N.Y.) ADI.

Industries:

Prudential Insurance Co. of America (HQ); Newark; life, health, casualty insurance — 3,200. **Foster Wheeler Corp.** (HQ); Livingston; industrial engineering — 2,300. **Mutual Benefit Life Insurance** (HQ); Newark; life insurance — 2,060. **Federal Pacific Electric Co.** (HQ); Newark; circuit breakers — 1,700. **United Hospitals Medical Center;** Newark; hospital — 1,700.

First National State Bancorp (HQ); Newark; banking — 1,600. **Newark Beth Israel Medical Center;** Newark; hospital — 1,600. **New Jersey Blue Cross Plan** (HQ); Newark; health insurance — 1,500. **Anheuser Busch Inc.;** Newark; brewery — 1,400. **Eastern Airlines Inc.;** Newark; commercial airline — 1,400. **St. Michael's Medical Center;** Newark; hospital — 1,150. **Bristol-Meyers Inc.;** Hillside; toiletries — 1,000. **The Hartz Mountain Corp.** (HQ); Harrison; pet foods, pet supplies — 1,000. **United Airlines Inc.;** Newark; commercial airline — 1,000. **Pabst Brewing Co.;** Newark; brewery — 800. **Phibro Corp.**

(Engelhard Industries Div.); Newark; inorganic chemicals — 800.

Sangamo Weston Inc. (Weston Instruments Div.); Newark; electronic testing equipment — 800. **Fidelity Union Bank** (HQ); Newark; banking — 700. **International Services Inc.** (HQ); Irvington; janitorial services — 700. **Newark Morning Ledger Co.;** Newark; newspaper publishing — 700. **McGraw Edison Co. Inc.** (Worthington Pump Div.); Harrison; bronze, steel — 625. **All State Cleaning Contractors;** Newark; janitorial services — 600.

Charles Beseler Co. Inc.; East Orange; projection equipment — 500. **McGraw Edison Co. Inc.** (Worthington Pump Corp.); East Orange; pumps 500. **People Express Airlines Inc.;** Newark; commercial airline — 550. **Westinghouse Electric Corp.** (Relay Instrument Div.); Newark; electric relays — 500.

11th District

North — Newark Suburbs

Democrats retain a modest but dependable edge in the new 11th. The 1982 redistricting preserved the basic geographic character of the district: Republicans in the west and Democrats in the east, closer to Newark.

The 11th was slightly underpopulated before redistricting, and fast-growing Parsippany-Troy Hills and East Hanover were taken from Republican Morris County to help pad out the district. Politically marginal Livingston in Essex County was another addition. The home of well-to-do WASPs, it also has a large Jewish community that votes Democratic.

To the north, Totowa joined the two other Passaic County towns already in the 11th, West Paterson and Little Falls. All three are politically competitive, filled with blue-collar ethnics who fled decaying Paterson and are gradually dropping their residual Democratic ties. But the district lost dependably Democratic Hillside, Irvington and South Orange to Newark's badly underpopulated 10th District.

The remap sought to redress the imbalance in part by grafting onto the 11th industrial Kearny and Secaucus in Hudson County. Secaucus' firm Democratic habits have been slightly eroded by an up-scale housing development at the periphery of the Hackensack Meadowlands, popular with Republican business executives. Called Harmon Cove, it has changed Secaucus' old image as an eyesore. The new district also picked up Lyndhurst, a slice of blue-collar Bergen County. Like Totowa, Lyndhurst votes Republican at times.

Remaining in the 11th are the Caldwells, Fairfield and Essex Fells, all places with Republican tendencies. But votes from those communities are generally canceled out by those in the towns closest to Newark, where Democrats have a sizable lead.

The path of white flight from Newark determined the ethnic distribution of these close-in suburbs. Fed by the heavily Italian North Ward of Newark, Verona and Belleville have large Italian contingents. West Orange is home to Jews who lived in Newark's South Ward a generation ago.

Affluent Montclair, with its mansions built as summer places by the 19th-century New York rich, is marginal, thanks to its mixture of wealthy Democratic Jews and Republican WASPs.

Montclair and the Oranges are centers of the Essex Democratic Party's liberal wing.

Election Returns

11th District		Democrat		Republican	
1976	President	104,074	(43.3%)	130,443	(54.2%)
	Senate	128,943	(59.2%)	85,825	(39.4%)
	House	123,871	(58.1%)	87,735	(41.1%)
1977	Governor	92,903	(56.0%)	69,574	(42.0%)
1978	Senate	84,734	(54.0%)	70,554	(45.0%)
	House	93,206	(62.2%)	53,541	(35.7%)
1980	President	83,798	(38.0%)	110,742	(50.2%)
	House	105,947	(52.4%)	91,236	(45.1%)
1981	Governor	79,459	(50.2%)	78,876	(49.8%)
1982	Senate	86,724	(50.0%)	84,732	(48.8%)
	House	105,607	(64.3%)	57,099	(34.8%)

Demographics

Population: 525,290. **Percent Change from 1970:** -7.0%.

Land Area: 154 square miles. **Population per Square Mile:** 3,411.0.

Counties, 1980 Population: Bergen (Pt.) — 36,913; Essex (Pt.) — 339,423; Hudson (Pt.) — 51,377; Morris (Pt.) — 63,340; Passaic (Pt.) — 34,237.

Cities, 1980 Population: Belleville — 35,367; Bloomfield — 47,792; Cedar Grove — 12,600; Kearny — 35,735; Little Falls — 11,496; Livingston — 28,040; Lyndhurst — 20,326; Maplewood — 22,950; Montclair — 38,321; North Arlington — 16,587; Nutley — 28,998; Orange — 31,136; Parsippany-Troy Hills — 49,868; Secaucus — 13,719; Totowa — 11,448; Verona — 14,166; West Caldwell — 11,407; West Orange — 39,510; West Paterson — 11,293.

Race and Ancestry: White — 90.4%; Black — 6.9%; American Indian, Eskimo and Aleut — 0.1%; Asian and Pacific Islander — 1.9%. Spanish Origin — 2.8%. Dutch — 0.5%; English — 3.3%; German — 4.7%; Greek — 0.6%; Hungarian — 0.7%; Irish — 7.2%; Italian — 20.9%; Polish — 4.3%; Portuguese — 0.7%; Russian — 2.1%; Scottish — 1.0%; Ukranian — 0.5%.

Universities, Enrollment: The Berkeley School, Little Falls — 632; Bloomfield College, Bloomfield — 2,092; Caldwell College, Caldwell — 717; Montclair State College, Upper Montclair — 15,829; Northeastern Bible College, Essex Fells — 319.

Newspapers, Circulation: Union City *Dispatch*, Passaic *Herald-News*, Jersey City *Journal*, Paterson *News*, *New York Daily News*, *The New York Times* and Newark *Star-Ledger* circulate in the district.

Commercial Television Stations, Affiliation: Entire district is located in New York (N.Y.) ADI.

Industries:

Hoffmann-La Roche Inc. (HQ); Nutley; pharmaceuticals — 6,000. **Western Electric Co. Inc.;** Kearny; telephones — 6,000. **The Singer Co.** (Kearfott Div.); Little Falls; electronic transmitters — 6,000. **Nabisco Brands Inc.** (HQ); Parsippany; margarine, cookies, crackers — 5,000. **Lummus Group Inc.** (HQ); Bloomfield; construction engineering designers — 1,900. **Congoleum Corp.** (Resilient Flooring Div.); Kearny; administrative offices — 1,900.

St. Barnabas Medical Center; Livingston; hospital — 1,700. **Essex County Hospital Center;** Cedar Grove; psychiatric hospital — 1,600. **Goody Products Inc.** (HQ); Kearny; hair care products — 1,500. **Mountainside Hospital;** Montclair; hospital — 1,500. **Westinghouse Electric Corp.** (Lamp Div.); Bloomfield; electric bulbs — 1,500. **Clara Maass Memorial Hospital;** Belleville; hospital — 1,340. **International Telephone & Telegraph Corp.** (Avionics Div.); Nutley; navigation communications equipment — 1,320. **S. B. Thomas Inc.** (HQ); Totowa; specialty bakery products — 1,100. **Pennwalt Corp.** (Wallace & Tiernan Div.); Belleville; chlorine — 1,000. **Prudential Insurance Co. of America;** Roseland; life insurance — 1,000. **Spartan Security Services Inc.;** Montclair; protective services — 1,000. **Matsushita Electric Corp.** (HQ); Secaucus; television, radio importing — 960. **American Insurance Co. Inc.** (HQ); Parsippany; health, casualty insurance — 800. **Walter Kidde & Co. Inc.;** Belleville; aircraft parts — 800.

Schiavone Construction Co. (HQ); Secaucus; highway, heavy construction — 800. **Biderman Industries USA Inc.** (Calvin Klein - HQ); Secaucus; clothing wholesaling — 750. **Conrac Corp.** (Systems East Div.); Caldwell; precision instruments — 750. **Peerless Tube Co. Inc.** (HQ); Bloomfield; metal, plastic tubing — 750. **Ebasco Services Inc.;** Lyndhurst; engineering services — 700. **Nelson Distribution Corp.** (Tri-State Bradley - HQ); Secaucus; trucking — 625. **Brinks Warehousing Inc.** (HQ); Secaucus; trucking — 600. **Danielle Men's Clothing Inc.** (Don Robbie - HQ); Secaucus; men's wear wholesaling — 600. **New Jersey Bank** (HQ); West Paterson; banking — 600. **Pinkerton's Inc.;** Maplewood; protection services — 600. **Resistoflex Corp.** (HQ); Roseland; valves, pipe fittings — 550. **Atlantic Window Cleaning Co.;** West Orange; janitorial services — 500. **David's Specialty Shops Inc.** (HQ); Secaucus; women's clothing stores — 500. **Maislin Transport of Delaware;** Kearny; truck terminal — 500. **NPS Corp.** (HQ); Secaucus; plumbing, heating, air conditioning contracting — 500.

12th District

North and Central — Morristown

From the mansions of Far Hills to the two-story Tudor houses of Morris Plains, the ambiance of the new 12th is Republican, but not deeply conservative. Presidential candidate John B. Anderson made his second best New Jersey showing here in 1980, winning 9.4 percent of the vote. At the same time the district's party loyalties made it first in the state for Ronald Reagan, who garnered 60.7 percent of its ballots.

The pieces of Somerset, Morris and Union counties placed in the new 12th have almost equal populations, so no one county dominates. The Union County section (covering such towns as Union, Springfield and Mountainside) and eastern Morris County (Harding, Morristown, Hanover) are affluent bedroom suburbia, home for Republican business executives. The portions of western Morris in the 12th (Washington, Chester) are more rural, with middle-class subdivisions springing up. Hunt country nestles in northern Somerset, with the farms in the southern half of the county giving way to tract housing. Some of Manhattan's largest corporations have moved their headquarters to the rolling greenery of Morris and Somerset counties. Ortho and Allied Chemical are among those shifting operations there.

Farming occupies the district's Hunterdon County segment as well as its lake-dotted Warren and Sussex County portions. In this rural territory conservatism is more intense than in other parts of the district.

Pockets of Democrats can be found in Somerset County in industrial Raritan and Somerville, with their chemical and pharmaceutical works, and in Kenilworth, a blue-collar suburb near Elizabeth. Elsewhere, the 12th is uniformly Republican.

According to an old saying, there are more millionaires within a one-mile radius of Morristown Green than anywhere else on Earth. That is no longer true, if it ever was. The millionaires have moved to the hunt country farther south in the 12th. Jacqueline Kennedy Onassis maintains a mansion in Peapack. Quaint Morristown nowadays must content itself with a community of commuters who work on Wall Street and elsewhere in the everyday Manhattan business world.

Election Returns

12th District		Democrat		Republican	
1976	President	100,389	(40.6%)	141,684	(57.3%)
	Senate	124,373	(54.4%)	101,212	(44.3%)
	House	88,879	(36.3%)	152,301	(62.1%)
1977	Governor	85,741	(46.4%)	94,612	(51.2%)
1978	Senate	72,831	(45.5%)	84,194	(52.6%)
	House	50,521	(31.5%)	109,945	(68.5%)
1980	President	70,340	(20.3%)	151,143	(60.7%)
	House	42,601	(18.4%)	183,734	(79.5%)
1981	Governor	60,378	(32.8%)	123,801	(67.2%)
1982	Senate	57,456	(31.9%)	121,142	(67.2%)
	House	57,049	(32.3%)	117,793	(66.8%)

Demographics

Population: 526,907. **Percent Change from 1970:** 7.3%.

Land Area: 891 square miles. **Population per Square Mile:** 591.4.

Counties, 1980 Population: Essex (Pt.) — 19,543; Hunterdon (Pt.) — 35,775; Morris (Pt.) — 135,875; Somerset (Pt.) — 126,097; Sussex (Pt.) — 71,489; Union (Pt.) — 125,524; Warren (Pt.) — 12,604.

Cities, 1980 Population: Berkeley Heights — 12,549; Bernards — 12,920; Bridgewater — 29,175; Hanover — 11,846; Hillsborough — 19,061; Hopatcong — 15,531; Madison — 15,357; Millburn — 19,543; Morris — 18,486; Morristown — 16,614; New Providence — 12,426; Readington — 10,855; Somerville — 11,973; Sparta — 13,333; Springfield — 13,955; Summit — 21,071; Union — 50,184; Washington — 11,402.

Race and Ancestry: White — 95.2%; Black — 3.1%; American Indian, Eskimo and Aleut — 0.1%; Asian and Pacific Islander — 1.2%. Spanish Origin — 1.5%. Dutch — 0.8%; English — 6.3%; French — 0.6%; German — 7.8%; Greek — 0.5%; Hungarian — 1.0%; Irish — 6.2%; Italian — 10.3%; Polish — 3.8%; Russian — 1.6%; Scottish — 0.8%; Swedish — 0.5%; Ukranian — 0.7%.

Universities, Enrollment: Assumption College for Sisters, Mendham — 31; College of Saint Elizabeth, Convent Station — 851; Don Bosco College, Newton — 83; Drew University, Madison — 2,331; Kean College of New Jersey, Union — 13,237; Somerset County College, Somerville — 4,509.

Newspapers, Circulation: *The Courier-News* (e), Bridgewater — 58,596; *Daily Record* (mS), Morristown — 56,021; *New Jersey Herald* (eS), Newton — 17,515. Newark *Star-Ledger* and *The New York Times* also circulate in the district.

Commercial Television Stations, Affiliation: Entire district is located in New York (N.Y.) ADI.

Industries:

Bell Telephone Laboratories (HQ); Murray Hill; research, development — 3,985. **Bell Telephone Laboratories;** Whippany; research, development — 2,732. **Research-Cottrell Inc.** (HQ); Somerville; ventilation systems — 2,700. **Allied Corp.** (HQ); Morristown; oil, gas producing — 2,000. **Ethicon Inc.** (HQ); Somerville; surgical supplies — 2,000. **Warner-Lambert Co. Inc.** (HQ); Morris Plains; pharmaceuticals, chewing gum, medical supplies — 2,000.

Overlook Hospitals Assn.; Summit; hospital — 1,900. **Veterans Administration;** Basking Ridge; veterans' hospital — 1,850. **Ciba-Geigy Corp.;** Summit; pharmaceuticals — 1,700. **AM International Inc.** (Varityper Div.); Hanover; computerized typesetting machines — 1,670. **Sandoz Inc.** (HQ); Hanover; dye, chemical importing — 1,600. **Morristown Memorial Hospital;** Morristown; hospital — 1,560. **Exxon Research & Engineering Co.** (HQ); Florham Park; research, development — 1,500. **International Insurance Co.** (HQ); Morristown; insurance — 1,500. **RCA Corp.** (Solid State Div.); Somerville; television picture tubes — 1,500. **Pirelli Enterprises Corp.** (HQ); Union; insulat-ing wire — 1,400. **Schering Corp.;** Union; pharmaceuticals — 1,400.

American Hoechst Corp. (HQ); Somerville; organic chemicals — 1,300. **Ortho Pharmaceutical Corp.** (HQ); Raritan; pharmaceuticals — 1,300. **The Mennen Co.** (HQ); Morristown; toiletries — 1,200. **Somerset Hospital;** Somerville; hospital — 1,200. **Automatic Switch Co.** (HQ); Florham Park; solenoid valves — 1,150. **Nabisco Inc.** (HQ); Hanover; cookies — 1,000. **C. R. Bard Inc.** (HQ); Murray Hill; surgical equipment wholesalers — 900. **Lumbermen's Mutual Casualty Co.** (American Motorists Insurance Co.); Summit; insurance — 800. **Ortho Diagnostics Inc.** (Instrument Div. - HQ); Raritan; pharmaceuticals — 800. **Western Electric Co. Inc.;** Union; warehousing — 700. **American Hoechst Corp.** (Azoplate Div.); Somerville; lithographic plates, inks — 650. **Western Electric Co. Inc.;** Morristown; testing instruments — 650. **Burroughs OEM Corp.;** Warren; electronic compounds — 638. **Allstate Insurance Co.;** Murray Hill; health insurance — 600.

Corporate Building Maintenance; Somerville; janitorial service — 600. **Litton Business Systems Inc.** (Monroe Calculator Div.); Morris Plains; business systems — 600. **Mack Trucks Inc.;** Bridgewater; truck part wholesaling — 550. **Beneficial Management Corp.;** Morristown; management, accounting services — 540. **Celanese Corp.** (Summit Technical Center); Summit; research, plastics — 525. **Tuscan Dairy Farms Inc.** (HQ); Union; milk processors — 510. **Roche Clinical Laboratories** (HQ); Raritan; medical laboratory — 505. **A. E. G. Telefunken Corp.** (HQ); Somerville; power tool wholesaling — 500. **Aetna Maintenance Inc.;** Hanover; janitorial service — 500. **Amerace Corp.** (ESNA Div.); Union; industrial fasteners — 500. **American Hoechst Corp.** (Azoplate Div.); Murray Hill; pre-sensitized photo supplies — 500. **Johnson & Johnson Inc.** (Baby Products Inc.); Skillman; medical supplies — 500. **Keuffel & Esser Co.** (HQ); Morristown; engineering instruments — 500. **Schering-Plough Corp.** (HQ); Kenilworth; pharmaceuticals, cosmetics — 500.

13th District

South and Central

In an effort to create a "dumping ground" for Republican votes troubling to Democrats in neighboring districts, the Legislature established a 13th District in 1982 that stretches all over the map, from the Philadelphia suburbs in Camden County to the New York suburbs in Monmouth County.

While the elongated district may be difficult to represent, it is strong GOP territory. The new 13th gave Ronald Reagan his second highest percentage in the state in 1980.

The 1982 remap shifted blue-collar Democratic towns along the Delaware River to the 4th District and placed much of the central section of Monmouth in the 13th. Affluent suburbs such as Rumson, Little Silver, Shrewsbury and Holmdel are part of the artfully drawn salient that reaches into Monmouth.

During the 1970s these towns enjoyed substantial growth because business executives and retirees, looking for less bustle and more space, arrived from New York and its older, close-in suburbs. Holmdel, for example, grew 38.1 percent.

The tale of growth is similar in the Toms River region in northern Ocean County, part of which the 13th possessed during the 1970s. Less affluent than the district's Monmouth constituents, many of these people have working-class roots and origins in New York and North Jersey. They sometimes reassert their Democratic heritage on the local-office level, but tend to vote Republican in state and national elections. Across the inland waterway, the string of small shore communities, such as Lavalette, remains firmly Republican.

Away from the sea are the Pine Barrens of Ocean and Burlington counties — a sparsely settled wilderness in the midst of the most densely populated state in the Union. Two centuries ago iron smelters abounded in the vast forest where the ferrous soil was turned into cannonballs and metal fixtures. The forges have long departed, leaving cranberry and blueberry farming as the chief enterprises, along with housing and commercial development, halted now by the recession. Eager for extra tax money, the GOP politicians who dominate the pine lands have fought federal and state efforts to protect the wilderness from builders.

This area has a long association with the armed forces. Fort Dix and Maguire Air Force Base, with their Republican-leaning military votes, have both an economic and political influence.

The population center of the district remains in the Philadelphia suburbs of Burlington and Camden Counties. By design, it is difficult to find apartment buildings or low-income housing in this collection of suburbs. One of them, Mount Laurel, has been fighting the state over implementing a 1975 New Jersey Supreme Court decision striking down its ordinance that homes be built on lots of a quarter acre or larger. Such residential patterns help keep this area's politics firmly Republican.

The district's single largest community, however, shows a more marginal cast. In Cherry Hill, one of the first New Jersey suburbs to develop after World War II, the parties regularly trade local and state legislative offices. Cherry Hill has a large number of young professionals in its apartment buildings, as well as a sizable number of Jews — both strong Democratic blocs. Otherwise, the township possesses a suburban ambiance.

Election Returns

13th District		Democrat		Republican	
1976	President	97,819	(44.0%)	120,508	(54.2%)
	Senate	110,252	(55.0%)	87,987	(43.9%)
	House	93,426	(44.3%)	115,380	(54.7%)
1977	Governor	94,101	(58.6%)	62,259	(38.8%)
1978	Senate	68,509	(49.3%)	68,390	(49.3%)
	House	67,239	(45.4%)	79,529	(53.7%)
1980	President	69,598	(30.7%)	136,288	(60.1%)
	House	88,339	(40.8%)	123,646	(57.1%)
1981	Governor	80,052	(44.4%)	100,133	(55.6%)
1982	Senate	75,452	(44.8%)	92,063	(54.6%)
	House	65,820	(39.1%)	100,061	(59.5%)

Demographics

Population: 526,168. **Percent Change from 1970:** 26.0%.

Land Area: 967 square miles. **Population per Square Mile:** 544.1.

Counties, 1980 Population: Burlington (Pt.) — 142,723; Camden (Pt.) — 107,763; Monmouth (Pt.) — 90,636; Ocean (Pt.) — 185,046.

Cities, 1980 Population: Berkeley — 23,151; Cherry Hill — 68,785; Collingswood — 15,838; Dover — 64,455; Evesham — 21,508; Haddon — 15,875; Howell — 25,065; Jackson — 25,644; Lacey — 14,161; Manchester — 27,987; Medford — 17,622; Moorestown — 15,596; Mount Holly — 10,818; Mount Laurel — 17,614; New Hanover — 14,258; Wall — 18,952.

Race and Ancestry: White — 93.7%; Black — 4.3%; American Indian, Eskimo and Aleut — 0.1%; Asian and Pacific Islander — 1.2%. Spanish Origin — 1.8%. Dutch — 0.6%; English — 6.4%; French — 0.6%; German — 7.8%; Hungarian — 0.7%; Irish — 7.3%; Italian — 9.6%; Polish — 3.0%; Russian — 1.8%; Scottish — 0.7%.

Universities, Enrollment: Ocean County College, Toms River — 5,587.

Newspapers, Circulation: *Ocean County Times-Observer* (mS), Toms River — 24,848. *Asbury Park Press, Burlington County Times, New York Daily News* and Newark *Star-Ledger* also circulate in the district.

Commercial Television Stations, Affiliation: District is divided between Philadelphia (Pa.) ADI and New York (N.Y.) ADI.

Military Installations: Fort Dix, *(See 4th District)*; Lakehurst Naval Air Engineering Center, Lakehurst — 2,924; McGuire Air Force Base, Wrightstown — 11,628.

Nuclear Power Plants: Oyster Creek 1, Toms River (General Electric, Burns and Roe), December 1969.

Industries:

Bell Telephone Laboratories; Holmdel; research — 3,844. **RCA Corp.** (Government Systems Div. - HQ); Moorestown; electronics, radar systems — 3,400. **Stone & Webster Engineering;** Cherry Hill; engineering services — 2,000. **Heritage Bancorporation;** Cherry Hill; banking — 1,500. **RCA Corp.** (RCA Service Co.); Cherry Hill; installing, servicing electronic products — 1,500.

Prudential Property & Casualty Insurance Co. (HQ); Holmdel; casualty insurance — 1,270. **Siemens Corp.;** Cherry Hill; electronic components — 1,200. **Burlington County Memorial Hospital** (HQ); Mount Holly; hospital — 1,150. **Toms River Chemical Corp.;** Toms River; dyes — 1,100. **John Maneely Co. Inc.** (HQ); Collingswood; metal tubing — 900. **Charles of the Ritz Group Ltd.;** Holmdel; cosmetics — 800. **Insurance Co. of North America** (Electronic Insurance Systems Div.); Cherry Hill; data processing — 775. **Lily-Tulip Inc.;** Holmdel; paper cups — 717. **Siemens Corp.** (Telecommunication & Engineering Div.); Cherry Hill; electronic components — 700. **Molins Machine Co. Inc.** (Langston Div.); Cherry Hill; paper industries machinery — 600. **Northern Telecom Inc.** (Spectron Div.); Moorestown; data processing equipment — 550. **J. J. Henry Co. Inc.;** Moorestown; marine engineering services — 500. **Tyco Industries Inc.** (HQ); Moorestown; toys — 500.

14th District

North — Jersey City

Urban Hudson County takes politics seriously. On Election Day the row houses are adorned with campaign posters, bunting and flags. People follow the ups and downs of local politicians with all the passion others reserve for sports stars. Tales of Byzantine local political intrigue spice the talk at neighborhood taprooms.

But Hudson County politics, a kaleidoscope of shifting factions, also can be rough. From 1917 to the late 1940s, legendary political boss Frank Hague ruled the county by sending his opponents to jail or the hospital.

Unions are strong in Hudson, especially along the docks, which remain central to the county's economy; the 1954 film,"On The Waterfront" was set in Hoboken.

The 1982 redistricting did little to alter the deep-seated Democratic ways of blue-collar Hudson. In 1980 it was one of only three New Jersey counties to vote for Jimmy Carter. And while population decline (8.4 percent in the 1970s) has lessened Hudson's once formidable clout, it still remains a vital county for a Democratic statewide candidate to win big.

Under the 1982 district map, the 14th lost Kearny, which went to strengthen Democrats in the 11th District. To make up for its population deficit, the 14th picked up two Hudson towns from the 9th — North Bergen and Union City. The district also added three of the 9th's Bergen County communities — Ridgefield, Little Ferry and Palisades Park.

While mainly blue-collar in makeup, the new Bergen County towns in the district are more suburban than the Hudson towns and swing between the two parties. North Bergen and Union City vote reliably Democratic, although the growing Cuban community in Union City shows occasional Republican inclinations. The Cubans, many of them professionals and merchants, have helped stabilize a deteriorating urban area; their shops now crowd Bergenline Avenue.

Weehawken typifies the economic woes of Hudson County. Its unemployment surged when Seatrain, the shipping firm, went out of business. In 1982 the state assumed fiscal supervision of the town's financially troubled local government.

Neighboring Hoboken, however, shows signs of economic vitality. Its proximity to Manhattan and its fine old brownstones have attracted a new class of singles and young professional couples. Most of the newcomers have liberal leanings. Famous as the birthplace of singer Frank Sinatra, Hoboken is better known to North Jersey train commuters for its picturesque Lackawanna Terminal, where they board the Port Authority Trans Hudson line (known as PATH) to New York.

Bayonne, the home of the giant Military Ocean Terminal, has a longstanding political rivalry with equally Democratic Jersey City. Because it is second in the county in size, with only a third of Jersey City's population, Bayonne often loses out politically.

Although it lost 14.1 percent of its population in the 1970s, Jersey City nevertheless continues to dominate the district. It still contains half of Hudson County's population. About 40 percent black and Hispanic, Jersey City has its problems with poverty, much of it concentrated in the run-down Paulus Hook section. As Jersey City lovers are fond of pointing out, the Statue of Liberty actually stands within their city limits, not New York's; unfortunately, the statue has its back to Jersey City.

Election Returns

14th District		Democrat		Republican	
1976	President	110,694	(54.4%)	89,300	(43.9%)
	Senate	126,348	(67.1%)	59,217	(31.5%)
	House	89,141	(49.3%)	83,391	(46.1%)
1977	Governor	83,389	(62.0%)	47,059	(35.0%)
1978	Senate	94,770	(70.0%)	38,287	(28.3%)
	House	79,782	(60.0%)	34,262	(25.8%)
1980	President	90,064	(47.8%)	87,155	(46.3%)
	House	98,433	(58.2%)	66,861	(39.6%)

14th District		Democrat		Republican	
1981	Governor	95,083	(65.2%)	50,782	(34.8%)
1982	Senate	92,305	(69.3%)	39,235	(29.4%)
	House	94,021	(74.3%)	28,257	(22.3%)

Demographics

Population: 526,778. **Percent Change from 1970:** -8.7%.

Land Area: 34 square miles. **Population per Square Mile:** 15,493.5.

Counties, 1980 Population: Bergen (Pt.) — 33,425; Hudson (Pt.) — 493,353.

Cities, 1980 Population: Bayonne — 65,047; Hoboken — 42,460; Jersey City — 223,532; North Bergen — 47,019; Palisades Park — 13,732; Ridgefield — 10,294; Union City — 55,593; Weehawken — 13,168; West New York — 39,194.

Race and Ancestry: White — 75.1%; Black — 13.3%; American Indian, Eskimo and Aleut — 0.1%; Asian and Pacific Islander — 3.1%. Spanish Origin — 26.6%. English — 1.5%; German — 3.1%; Greek — 0.7%; Irish — 6.5%; Italian — 13.7%; Polish — 4.5%; Russian — 0.8%; Ukranian — 0.5%.

Universities, Enrollment: Hudson County Community College Commission, North Bergen — 2,532; Jersey City State College, Jersey City — 9,044; St. Peter's College, Jersey City — 4,090; Stevens Institute of Technology, Hoboken — 2,830.

Newspapers, Circulation: *The Dispatch* (m), Union City — 40,705; *The Jersey Journal* (e), Jersey City — 70,378. *New York Daily News* also circulates in the district. Foreign language newspaper: *Svoboda* (Ukrainian), Jersey City — 17,000.

Commercial Television Stations, Affiliation: Entire district is located in New York (N.Y.) ADI.

Military Installations: Bayonne Military Ocean Terminal (Army), Bayonne — 2,268.

Industries:

Colgate Palmolive Co. Inc.; Jersey City; toiletries — 2,000. **United Terminal Inc.;** Bayonne; stevedoring — 2,000. **Jersey City Medical Center;** Jersey City; hospital — 1,800. **K-Mart Apparel Corp.** (HQ); North Bergen; women's, teens clothing retailing — 1,500. **General Foods Corp.** (Maxwell House Div.); Hoboken; coffee — 1,200.

Prudential Building Services Corp. (HQ); Jersey City; janitorial services — 1,150. **Christ Hospital Inc.;** Jersey City; hospital — 1,000. **Stamm International Inc.;** Palisades Park; heating equipment — 1,000. **Maidenform Inc.;** Bayonne; women's lingerie — 900. **Palm Beach Co.** (Evan Picone); North Bergen; women's suits, skirts — 825. **Bethlehem Steel Corp.;** Hoboken; ship repairing — 817. **Jaclyn Inc.;** North Bergen; warehousing — 800. **Owens-Illinois Inc.;** North Bergen; glass containers — 750. **First Jersey National Corp.** (HQ); Jersey City; banking — 700. **Soundesign Corp.** (HQ); Jersey City; audio systems — 700.

Houbigant Inc.; Ridgefield; perfumes, toiletries — 650. **A-P-A Truck Leasing Corp.** (HQ); North Bergen; trucking — 600. **Levolor Lorentzen Inc.;** Hoboken; venetian blinds — 600. **Olla Industries Inc.** (HQ); Weehawken; women's handbags — 600. **CPC International Inc.** (Best Foods Div.); Bayonne; mayonnaise, salad dressing — 550. **Block Drug Co. Inc.** (HQ); Jersey City; dental supplies, dentures — 510. **Joseph Dixon Crucible Co.** (HQ); Jersey City; pencils, crayons — 500. **Jaclyn Inc.** (HQ); West New York; women's handbags — 500. **Walsh Trucking Co. Inc.;** North Bergen; trucking — 500.

New Mexico

Rejecting conservative appeals for a drastic revision of district lines, New Mexico legislators approved a remap that created a new seat in the Albuquerque area while leaving the two existing districts essentially intact. The plan was signed Jan. 19, 1982, by Democratic Gov. Bruce King.

New Mexico's 28 percent population growth during the 1970s entitled the state to a third congressional seat. That windfall gave rise to a year of squabbling among New Mexico politicians. Both parties quickly agreed that one district would be dominated by Bernalillo County (Albuquerque). But they were divided on how to redraw the rest of the state.

The ruling conservative coalition in the New Mexico House won passage of a plan to scrap the existing northern and southern districts in favor of an eastern and western configuration that would have divided the Democratic Hispanic vote in northern New Mexico, possibly allowing conservatives to take three seats.

But the Democratic-controlled Senate and the state's two Republican congressional incumbents objected to the House plan. The incumbents argued that cultural and economic ties favored retention of northern and southern districts outside the Albuquerque area. They also were concerned that the House plan would disrupt their re-election efforts. One had been gearing up to run in the new Albuquerque district, while the other wanted to retain his base in conservative southern New Mexico.

Thanks to active lobbying by both incumbents during the state Legislature's special January 1982 session, a north-south plan was approved by votes of 54-12 in the House and 32-9 in the Senate. Both incumbents won re-election in 1982. A Democrat was elected to the open seat in the northern district.

Age of Population

District	Population Under 18	Voting Age Population	Population 65 & Over (% of VAP)	Median Age
1	126,494	307,647	35,961 (11.7%)	28.3
2	139,103	297,158	45,900 (15.4%)	27.5
3	152,310	280,182	34,045 (12.2%)	26.3
State	417,907	884,987	115,906 (13.1%)	27.4

Income and Occupation

District	Median Family Income	White Collar Workers	Blue Collar Workers	Service Workers	Farm Workers
1	$ 18,951	62.0%	24.2%	12.6%	1.2%
2	15,722	47.8	32.4	13.8	6.1
3	16,409	52.1	30.6	14.4	3.0
State	$ 16,928	54.4%	28.8%	13.5%	3.3%

Education: School Years Completed

District	8 Years or Fewer	4 Years of High School	4 Years of College or More	Median School Years
1	12.4%	33.9%	22.3%	12.8
2	20.4	35.1	13.6	12.4
3	20.6	33.4	16.7	12.5
State	17.7%	34.1%	17.6%	12.6

Housing and Residential Patterns

District	Owner Occupied	Renter Occupied	Urban	Rural
1	63.7%	36.3%	93.2%	6.8%
2	68.3	31.7	70.8	29.2
3	72.8	27.2	52.3	47.7
State	68.1%	31.9%	72.1%	27.9%

1st District

Central — Albuquerque

After a decade as part of New Mexico's sprawling northern district, the fast-growing Albuquerque area dominates a constituency of its own in the 1980s.

The new 1st District has a GOP flavor. Albuquerque and surrounding Bernalillo County have voted Republican in all but one presidential election between 1952 and 1980 and have provided a fairly solid base for the Republican

NEW MEXICO

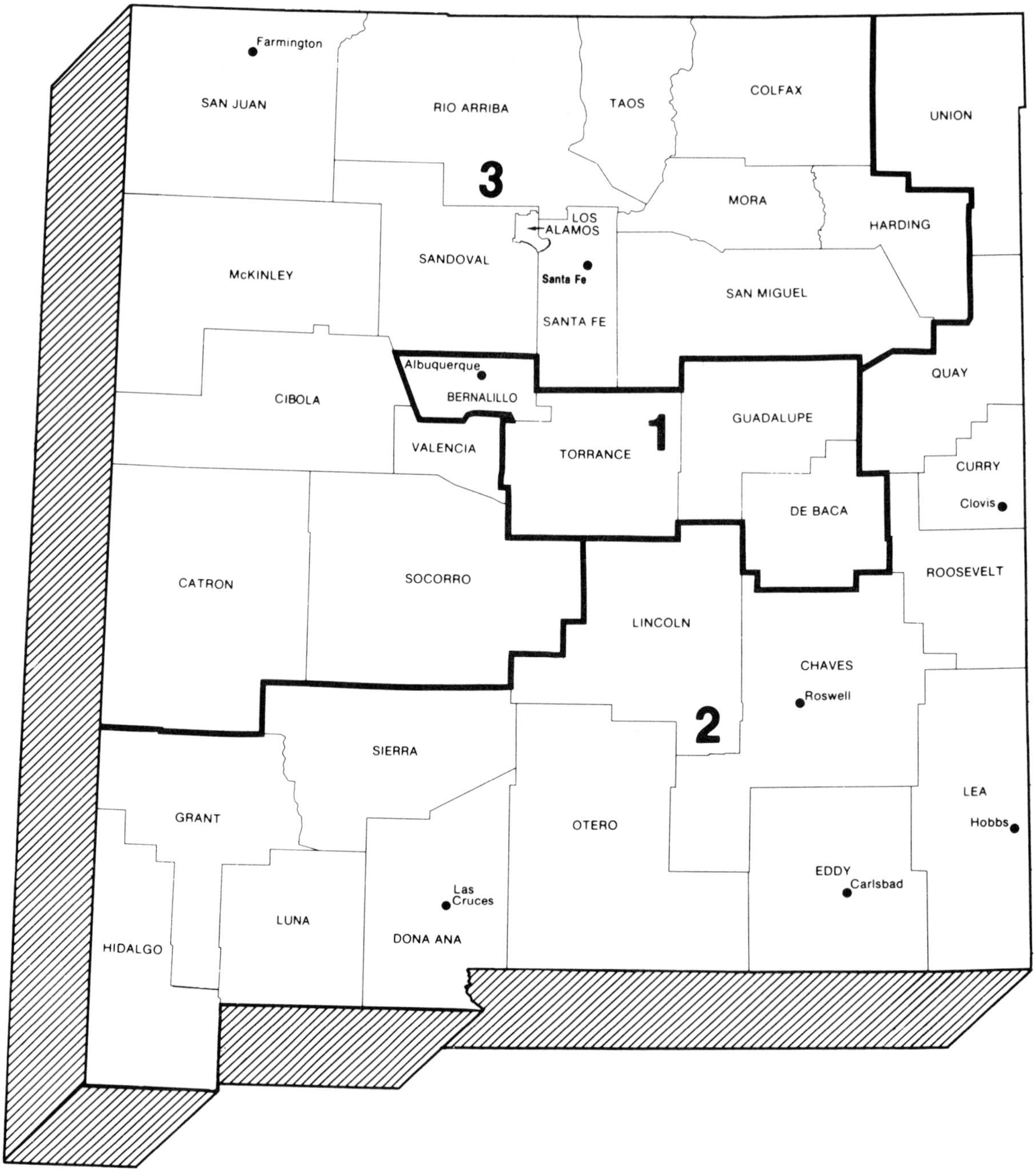

SAN JUAN
Farmington

RIO ARRIBA

TAOS

COLFAX

UNION

3

MORA

HARDING

McKINLEY

SANDOVAL

LOS
ALAMOS

Santa Fe

SAN MIGUEL

SANTA FE

CIBOLA

Albuquerque
BERNALILLO

QUAY

VALENCIA

TORRANCE

1

GUADALUPE

CURRY

Clovis

DE BACA

ROOSEVELT

CATRON

SOCORRO

LINCOLN

CHAVES

Roswell

2

SIERRA

LEA

Hobbs

GRANT

OTERO

LUNA

Las
Cruces

EDDY
Carlsbad

HIDALGO

DONA ANA

incumbent who also represented the county when it was part of the old 1st District.

Originally a health resort and trade center, Albuquerque had fewer than 40,000 residents in 1940. Its postwar emergence as a Republican stronghold was fueled by the development of a prosperous military-aerospace industry. By 1960 the population exceeded 200,000. During the next two decades a diversified economy sustained the boom. The city's population grew 36 percent in the 1970s, enhancing its position as New Mexico's commercial hub and major population center. Including the Bernalillo County suburbs, the Albuquerque area is home for nearly one-third of New Mexico's 1.3 million residents.

Electronics firms have provided the impetus for Albuquerque's latest round of population growth. Young engineers and scientists attracted by jobs and retirees attracted by the weather have helped in recent years to retain the county's Republican slant.

But Albuquerque is not as stridently conservative as many other Sun Belt population centers. Ronald Reagan's 53 percent share of the 1980 vote in Bernalillo County was two percentage points below his statewide figure and no better than Gerald R. Ford's showing in the Albuquerque area four years earlier.

The county's large minority population provides Democrats a potentially strong base. Hispanics alone comprise 37 percent of the county population. Indians, blacks and Asians make up another 6 percent. In addition, the newest generation of white-collar migrants exhibits some liberal tendencies. Independent presidential candidate John B. Anderson drew 10 percent of the county vote in 1980, well above his statewide mark of 6 percent.

Three sparsely populated counties east of Albuquerque are also included in the new 1st District. Together the three — De Baca, Guadalupe and Torrance counties — hold only 3 percent of the district population. Ranching is the mainstay of the economy in De Baca and Guadalupe counties, both of which lost population in the 1970s.

Election Returns

1st District		Democrat		Republican	
1976	President	67,451	(45.4%)	79,679	(53.6%)
	Senate	55,282	(37.3%)	92,069	(62.1%)
	House	37,607	(25.2%)	110,833	(74.3%)
1978	Governor	59,418	(49.0%)	61,745	(51.0%)
	Senate	57,511	(47.4%)	63,811	(52.6%)
	House	43,228	(37.3%)	72,695	(62.7%)
1980	President	57,566	(35.2%)	87,583	(53.5%)
	House	74,807	(47.2%)	83,579	(52.7%)
1982	Governor	76,539	(53.0%)	67,851	(47.0%)
	Senate	77,966	(54.2%)	65,802	(45.8%)
	House	67,534	(47.6%)	74,459	(52.4%)

Demographics

Population: 434,141. **Percent Change from 1970:** 32.1%.

Land Area: 9,859 square miles. **Population per Square Mile:** 44.0.

Counties, 1980 Population: Bernalillo — 419,700; De Baca — 2,454; Guadalupe — 4,496; Torrance — 7,491.

Cities, 1980 Population: Albuquerque — 331,767.

Race and Ancestry: White — 79.7%; Black — 2.3%; American Indian, Eskimo and Aleut — 2.6%; Asian and Pacific Islander — 1.0%. Spanish Origin — 37.4%. English — 8.0%; French — 0.7%; German — 4.9%; Irish — 3.1%; Italian — 1.2%; Polish — 0.6%; Scottish — 0.5%.

Universities, Enrollment: University of Albuquerque, Albuquerque — 1,869; University of New Mexico, Albuquerque — 22,405.

Newspapers, Circulation: *Albuquerque Journal* (mS), Albuquerque — 80,266; *The Albuquerque Tribune* (e), Albuquerque — 40,734.

Commercial Television Stations, Affiliation: KGGM-TV, Albuquerque (CBS); KGSW, Albuquerque (None); KLKK-TV, Albuquerque (None); KOAT-TV, Albuquerque (ABC); KOB-TV, Albuquerque (NBC). Most of district is located in Albuquerque ADI. Portion is in Lubbock (Texas) ADI.

Military Installations: Kirtland Air Force Base, Albuquerque — 11,853.

Industries:

Sandia Corp. (Sandia Laboratories - HQ); Albuquerque; research labs — 6,250. **General Electric Co.**; Albuquerque; jet engines — 1,800. **Southwest Community Health Services**; Albuquerque; hospital — 1,700. **Dynalectron Corp.** (Facility Services Div.); Albuquerque; airport operations — 1,500. **GTE Lenkurt Inc.** (Lenkurt Electric Inc.); Albuquerque; electronic components — 1,460.

St. Joseph Hospital; Albuquerque; hospital — 1,420. **Veterans Administration**; Albuquerque; veterans' hospital — 1,200. **Lovelace Medical Foundation**; Albuquerque; hospital — 1,100. **Intel Corp.**; Rio Rancho Estates; semiconductors — 1,000. **Albuquerque Publishing Co. Inc.** (HQ); Albuquerque; newspaper publishing — 650. **Levi Strauss & Co.**; Albuquerque; men's, women's clothing — 600. **BDM Corp.** (Technology Operations Center); Albuquerque; professional services company — 580. **Kent Nowlin Construction Inc.** (HQ); Albuquerque; heavy construction — 500.

2nd District

South and East — Las Cruces, Roswell

The redistricting plan removed energy-rich northwestern New Mexico with its large Indian population from the 2nd District and added lightly populated Union and Quay counties in the northeast. But the sprawling district remains politically homogeneous. It is mostly rural and very conservative.

The election of a Republican who ran as a write-in candidate in 1980 was evidence of crumbling party ties in southern New Mexico, territory that was once firmly Democratic. During the 1970s the district developed a strong habit of voting Republican in statewide contests, in part because ranchers and other Southern-style Democrats resented their party's liberal national program. The district kept its Democratic House representation only because incumbent Harold E. Runnels maintained a strictly conservative voting record. Runnels encountered little opposition during his decade in office, but Democrats could not hold on after his death in 1980. In 1982 the Republican incumbent won re-election with more than 58 percent of the vote.

The centerpiece of the 2nd is "Little Texas," the southeastern corner of the state. Settled by Texans early in the 20th century, the region is economically, culturally and politically similar to the adjoining Texas plains. Most of the land here is devoted to grazing cattle or sheep. But oil and military projects have increased the standard of living and reshaped voting habits in a Republican direction.

Nearly one-half of the vote in the 14-county district is

concentrated in the four counties that make up Little Texas. The oil- and gas-producing centers of Chaves County (Roswell) and Lea County (Hobbs) are bastions of conservatism. Each gave Ronald Reagan more than 65 percent of the vote in 1980. So did Curry County (Clovis), which is the site of a large Air Force base.

Eddy County is less conservative. Near Carlsbad are the nation's most productive potash mines, and the area's unionized miners occasionally give Democrats enough votes to carry the county. Nonetheless Reagan won it in 1980 with 56 percent of the vote.

Located to the west are Otero County and Dona Ana County. Together they include nearly one-third of the 2nd District population. The city of Alamogordo, located in Otero County across the Sacramento Mountains from Little Texas, is culturally and politically in step with the region.

Dona Ana County is located further west in the Rio Grande Valley. Most of the county's population lives around Las Cruces, the largest city in New Mexico south of Albuquerque. Cotton, pecans and green chilies (the official state vegetable) are grown in profusion on the valley's irrigated farms. The county has a Hispanic majority, giving the Democrats a substantial base, but Republicans generally carry it. Reagan drew 54 percent of the Dona Ana vote in 1980. Parts of Dona Ana, Otero and Sierra counties hold the sprawling White Sands Missile Range.

The district's only Democratic strongholds are in the Mexican Highlands, along the Arizona border, where copper and lead mines have attracted a unionized work force. But less than 10 percent of the district's voters live in this semi-arid region of desert and mountains.

Election Returns

2nd District		Democrat		Republican	
1976	President	60,392	(46.4%)	68,581	(52.7%)
	Senate	54,212	(40.4%)	79,536	(59.3%)
	House	87,214	(67.3%)	42,436	(32.7%)
1978	Governor	49,082	(45.2%)	59,434	(54.8%)
	Senate	41,877	(39.2%)	65,004	(60.8%)
	House	68,060	(95.3%)	3,337	(4.7%)
1980	President	50,472	(35.1%)	86,337	(60.1%)
	House	38,796	(32.9%)	48,482	(41.1%)
1982	Governor	54,046	(42.9%)	71,958	(52.1%)
	Senate	56,464	(45.3%)	68,245	(54.7%)
	House	50,599	(41.6%)	71,021	(58.4%)

Demographics

Population: 436,261. **Percent Change from 1970:** 17.9%.

Land Area: 55,038 square miles. **Population per Square Mile:** 7.9.

Counties, 1980 Population: Chaves — 51,103; Curry — 42,019; Dona Ana — 96,340; Eddy — 47,855; Grant — 6,204; Hidalgo — 6,049; Lea — 55,993; Lincoln — 10,997; Luna — 15,585; Otero — 44,665; Quay — 10,577; Roosevelt — 15,695; Sierra — 8,454; Union — 4,725.

Cities, 1980 Population: Alamogordo — 24,024; Artesia — 10,385; Carlsbad — 25,496; Clovis — 31,194; Hobbs — 29,153; Las Cruces — 45,086; Roswell — 39,676.

Race and Ancestry: White — 82.4%; Black — 2.8%; American Indian, Eskimo and Aleut — 1.0%; Asian and Pacific Islander — 0.5%; Spanish Origin — 33.6%. Dutch — 0.7%; English — 12.7%; French —

1.0%; German — 5.7%; Irish — 5.2%; Italian — 0.6%; Scottish — 0.6%.

Universities, Enrollment: College of the Southwest, Hobbs — 216; Eastern New Mexico University (main campus), Portales — 3,701; Eastern New Mexico University (Roswell campus), Roswell — 1,011; New Mexico Junior College, Hobbs — 1,459; New Mexico Military Institute, Roswell — 750; New Mexico State University (main campus), Las Cruces — 12,347; New Mexico State University (Alamogordo campus), Alamogordo — 1,182; New Mexico State University (Carlsbad campus), Carlsbad — 703; Western New Mexico University, Silver City — 1,489.

Newspapers, Circulation: *Alamogordo Daily News* (eS), Alamogordo — 9,016; *Artesia Daily Press* (eS), Artesia — 3,505; *Carlsbad Current-Argus* (eS), Carlsbad — 7,856; *Clovis News Journal* (eS), Clovis — 10,125; *Deming Headlight* (e), Deming — 3,650; *Hobbs Daily News-Sun* (eS), Hobbs — 9,925; *Las Cruces Sun-News* (eS), Las Cruces — 14,719; *Lovington Daily Leader* (eS), Lovington — 3,225; *Portales News Tribune* (eS), Portales — 3,819; *Press & Independent* (e), Silver City — 6,710; *Roswell Daily Record* (eS), Roswell — 13,505.

Commercial Television Stations, Affiliation: KAVE-TV, Carlsbad (ABC); KBIM, Roswell (CBS); KMCC, Clovis (ABC); KSWS-TV, Roswell (NBC). District is divided among Albuquerque ADI, Roswell ADI, Amarillo (Texas) ADI, El Paso (Texas) ADI, Lubbock (Texas) ADI, Odessa (Texas)-Midland (Texas) ADI and Tucson (Ariz.) ADI.

Military Installations: Cannon Air Force Base, Clovis — 4,317; Holloman Air Force Base, Alamogordo — 7,270; White Sands Missile Range, Las Cruces — 7,558.

Industries:

Chino Mines Co.; Hurley; copper mining, smelting — 1,000. **Hanes Corp.** (L'eggs Products); Mesilla Park; women's hosiery — 950. **Phelps Dodge Corp.;** Tyrone; copper mining — 870. **International Minerals & Chemicals Corp.;** Carlsbad; potash mining — 650. **Transportation Mfg. Corp.;** Roswell; buses — 650.

Ideal Basic Industries Inc. (Potash Co. of America Div.); Carlsbad; potash mining — 560. **Bechtel Power Corp.;** Bayard; industrial contracting — 550. **Phelps Dodge Corp.;** Lordsburg; smelting — 535. **Dynalectron Corp.** (Land Air Div.); Holloman Air Force Base; electronic components — 508.

3rd District

North and West — Farmington, Santa Fe

The new 3rd covers nearly half the land area of New Mexico. With three out of every five residents either Hispanic or Indian, it is decidedly more liberal and Democratic than either of the state's other constituencies.

The population of the 3rd is almost equally divided between the predominantly Hispanic counties of northern New Mexico and the energy-rich Indian lands along the Arizona border. Northern New Mexico was in the old 2nd District during the 1970s, while the Indian lands were in the 1st.

Of the two regions, the Hispanic north is the most loyally Democratic. It includes the only five New Mexico counties carried by Jimmy Carter in 1980. The capital city of Santa Fe is the center of the region. Its nearly 50,000 residents make it the second largest city in the state. A pleasant mixture of Spanish and Indian cultures in Santa Fe has attracted a steady influx of young Anglos. Santa Fe County comprises 17 percent of the district population, far more than any other county in the region.

The rest of the Hispanic north is primarily mountainous, semi-arid grazing land, with much poverty and subsistence farming. By the end of 1981 the unemployment rate had topped 10 percent in four rural counties, with a staggering 31 percent of the population unemployed in Mora County.

An economic oasis is the Anglo community of Los Alamos, where the atomic bomb was developed during World War II. Los Alamos is one of the most prosperous counties in the country; its voters — well educated and scientifically inclined — largely vote the Republican ticket. But Los Alamos County comprises only 4 percent of the district population. And its voters have an independent streak, exhibited in 1980 when John B. Anderson drew 15 percent there, his highest vote in the state.

The Indian country divides more closely at the polls. The Indians, most of them Navajo, usually vote Democratic. But they turn out in small numbers and occasionally bolt to the Republicans. The council for the Pueblo tribes endorsed Ronald Reagan in 1980, and McKinley County — the only county in the state with an Indian majority — gave Reagan 57 percent of the vote. Republican beachheads also have been established in the towns of Gallup and Grants, which have growing Anglo populations.

The region's largest GOP stronghold, however, is San Juan County, where a conservative Anglo population has settled around Farmington to tap the vast supply of oil, gas and coal in the Four Corners area. San Juan gave Reagan 66 percent of the vote in 1980.

San Juan was one of three New Mexico counties with a population growth of more than 50 percent in the 1970s. The other two counties, Sandoval and Valencia, are also in the new 3rd District. Valencia County was divided by the state Legislature in 1981. The more conservative western portion, centered in the one-time uranium boom town of Grants, became a new entity called Cibola County, taking its name from the Spanish word for female bison. The eastern portion, near Albuquerque, remained in Valencia County. Both it and Sandoval abut Bernalillo County and are combinations of Indian villages and growing suburban communities. Together, Sandoval, Valencia and the new Cibola County comprise 15 percent of the district population.

Election Returns

3rd District		Democrat		Republican	
1976	President	73,305	(53.1%)	63,159	(45.8%)
	Senate	66,888	(51.2%)	63,076	(48.3%)
	House	60,542	(49.4%)	61,449	(50.2%)
1978	Governor	66,131	(57.1%)	49,669	(42.9%)
	Senate	60,657	(52.6%)	54,627	(47.4%)
	House	55,183	(56.8%)	42,043	(43.2%)
1980	President	59,788	(40.2%)	76,859	(51.6%)
	House	62,385	(47.2%)	55,413	(41.9%)
1982	Governor	85,255	(62.2%)	51,817	(37.8%)
	Senate	83,252	(61.1%)	53,081	(38.9%)
	House	84,669	(64.5%)	46,466	(35.4%)

Demographics

Population: 432,492. **Percent Change from 1970:** 35.8%.

Land Area: 56,438 square miles. **Population per Square Mile:** 7.7.

Counties, 1980 Population: Catron — 2,720; Colfax — 13,667; Harding — 1,090; Los Alamos — 17,599; McKinley — 56,449; Mora — 4,205; Rio Arriba — 29,282; San Juan — 81,433; San Miguel — 22,751; Sandoval — 34,799; Santa Fe — 75,360; Socorro — 12,566; Taos — 19,456; Valencia — 61,115.

Cities, 1980 Population: Farmington — 31,222; Gallup — 18,161; Grants — 11,439; Las Vegas — 14,322; Santa Fe — 48,953.

Race and Ancestry: White — 62.9%; Black — 0.5%; American Indian, Eskimo and Aleut — 20.9%; Asian and Pacific Islander — 0.3%. Spanish Origin — 39.0%. English — 6.9%; French — 0.5%; German — 3.6%; Irish — 2.1%; Italian — 0.9%.

Universities, Enrollment: College of Santa Fe, Santa Fe — 1,074; New Mexico Highlands University, Las Vegas — 2,259; New Mexico Institute of Mining and Technology, Socorro — 1,334; New Mexico State University (San Juan campus), Farmington — 1,198; St. John's College, Santa Fe — 341.

Newspapers, Circulation: *Farmington Daily Times* (eS), Farmington — 14,411; *Gallup Independent* (e), Gallup — 10,818; *Grants Daily Beacon* (e), Grants — 4,656; *Los Alamos Monitor* (eS), Los Alamos — 4,556; *The New Mexican* (eS), Santa Fe — 17,664; *Optic* (e), Las Vegas — 4,320; *Raton Range* (e), Raton — 3,260.

Commercial Television Stations, Affiliation: KIVA-TV, Farmington (NBC). Most of district is located in the Albuquerque ADI. Portions are in Farmington ADI and Tucson (Ariz.) ADI.

Military Installations: Fort Wingate Depot Activity, Gallup — 91.

Industries:

Stearns-Roger Inc.; Waterflow; general contracting — 2,000. **Kerr-McGee Nuclear Corp.;** Grants; uranium mining — 1,400. **Zia Co.** (Los Alamos Constructors); Los Alamos; general contracting — 1,200. **Utah International Inc.;** Navajo; coal mining — 700. **Gulf Oil Co. Inc.** (Gulf Mineral Resources Div.); Grants; uranium mining — 650. **Kaiser Steel Corp.;** Raton; coal mining — 525. **Molycorp Inc.;** Questa; mining — 500. **United Nuclear Corp.;** Gallup; uranium mining — 500.

New York

After prolonged judicial prodding and complaints from the Justice Department, New York's divided Legislature finally managed to work out a compromise congressional map that eliminated five U.S. House districts, as required by the 1980 Census, and spread the damage as evenly as possible between the two parties. The final redistricting product cleared the Republican Senate and the Democratic Assembly on the last day of the 1982 session. It demanded more than token sacrifices by Republicans throughout the state even though most of New York's population losses were in urban Democratic districts.

The new map paired two sets of GOP incumbents and one set of Democratic incumbents. It also set a Democratic incumbent against a Republican seatholder in Brooklyn in a configuration that favored the Republican. The Legislature made those pairings with the assumption that they would cost each party two seats. To make the fifth sacrifice, map makers created what they called a "fair fight" in the northern New York suburbs between a Democrat and a Republican incumbent.

The intention was to keep change to a minimum in the delegation's proportional partisan breakdown, which stood at 22 Democrats and 17 Republicans. The Legislature was successful; after the 1982 elections, the New York delegation included 20 Democrats and 14 Republicans.

Pushing the two parties together in the Legislature was a three-judge federal panel, which appointed a special master to draw up his own set of lines. Manhattan lawyer Robert L. Patterson Jr., a Republican, devised a plan that paired several sets of senior incumbents — something both parties wanted to avoid.

Patterson's presence gave the Legislature more than enough incentive to compromise partisan differences and enact a redistricting bill. Its first version easily passed both chambers May 11 (Senate, 47-11; Assembly, 114-35), and Democratic Gov. Hugh L. Carey promptly signed it. That map was generally similar to the final one, although it made slightly different incumbent pairings and created a new Hispanic district that stretched from Brooklyn to East Harlem in Manhattan.

It was the favorable treatment of the Hispanic constituency at the expense of the black community that displeased the Justice Department, which has jurisdiction over New York districts under the Voting Rights Act of 1965. Justice argued that the strength of the black vote in

Brooklyn had been diluted by placing most black voters in the 12th District.

The Legislature was able to meet these objections without unraveling the entire statewide ball of cartographic string. It lopped off the Manhattan parts of the new 11th, thus giving blacks a near-majority in the 11th. That set up an unavoidable chain reaction in Brooklyn and Queens, creating one open district and pairing two Democrats. One of the incumbents solved the problem by moving to the open district where he had party support.

Once again, the divided Legislature managed to pass the redistricting bill without difficulty. It cleared the Senate 53-5 and the Assembly 96-43 on July 2, and Carey signed it immediately. The plan was approved by the Justice Department the next day and by the overseeing federal court July 6.

Age of Population

District	Population Under 18	Voting Age Population	Population 65 & Over (% of VAP)	Median Age
1	165,420	350,987	55,046 (15.7%)	29.8
2	164,540	351,055	40,282 (11.5%)	29.0
3	138,950	379,111	53,483 (14.1%)	33.9
4	140,402	377,969	42,082 (11.1%)	32.9
5	129,621	383,910	62,601 (16.3%)	34.3
6	147,941	368,903	61,592 (16.7%)	31.9
7	109,665	409,287	81,383 (19.9%)	35.1
8	112,691	399,706	81,333 (20.3%)	36.3
9	108,723	407,420	87,148 (21.4%)	36.8
10	114,325	398,815	85,827 (21.5%)	35.7
11	185,553	332,612	38,422 (11.6%)	25.6
12	168,434	348,549	37,671 (10.8%)	27.6
13	128,962	389,944	86,149 (22.1%)	33.7
14	136,765	379,098	66,600 (17.6%)	32.5
15	72,014	444,395	78,336 (17.6%)	36.6
16	134,681	381,724	66,773 (17.5%)	32.3
17	74,179	442,060	79,933 (18.1%)	34.9
18	189,780	328,326	35,232 (10.7%)	24.9
19	116,828	394,974	89,499 (22.7%)	35.4
20	129,029	392,174	69,817 (17.8%)	34.7
21	151,718	365,060	53,214 (14.6%)	31.1
22	153,441	363,184	52,470 (14.4%)	31.8
23	126,960	389,983	73,332 (18.8%)	31.8
24	151,567	364,047	62,425 (17.1%)	31.1
25	141,217	373,822	68,623 (18.4%)	30.8

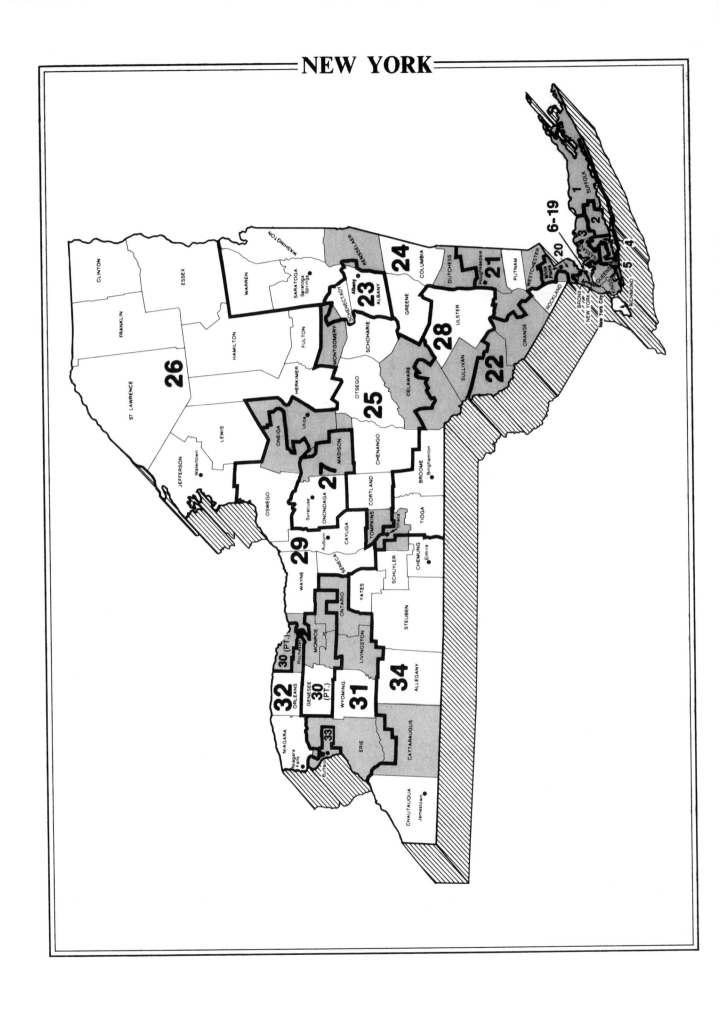

NEW YORK

District	Population Under 18	Voting Age Population	Population 65 & Over (% of VAP)	Median Age
26	152,026	364,170	62,928 (17.3%)	29.2
27	143,489	372,734	55,611 (14.9%)	29.4
28	134,215	382,593	63,593 (16.6%)	30.4
29	149,749	366,552	59,738 (16.3%)	30.1
30	145,721	371,098	54,869 (14.8%)	30.1
31	146,661	368,360	56,240 (15.3%)	31.1
32	141,222	375,165	60,874 (16.2%)	30.8
33	133,136	383,256	69,957 (18.3%)	31.4
34	148,238	369,166	67,684 (18.3%)	30.6
State	4,687,863	12,870,209	2,160,767 (16.8%)	31.9

Income and Occupation

District	Median Family Income	White Collar Workers	Blue Collar Workers	Service Workers	Farm Workers
1	$ 22,292	58.4%	25.7%	14.0%	1.9%
2	23,647	52.3	32.9	13.8	1.0
3	30,726	70.0	18.5	10.4	1.0
4	28,342	65.7	22.6	11.1	0.6
5	26,789	66.0	21.0	12.1	0.8
6	19,656	55.5	26.2	17.9	0.4
7	21,047	66.0	22.0	11.6	0.3
8	21,848	67.7	20.6	11.4	0.3
9	18,480	56.6	28.5	14.6	0.3
10	19,677	68.4	21.7	9.7	0.2
11	9,542	46.4	34.5	18.8	0.3
12	12,690	52.4	24.8	22.7	0.2
13	15,523	59.7	29.0	11.0	0.3
14	22,083	62.9	22.9	13.8	0.4
15	24,237	79.0	10.2	10.7	0.1
16	10,720	50.3	27.4	21.8	0.4
17	20,688	76.7	11.8	11.3	0.2
18	8,448	44.6	32.2	22.8	0.4
19	18,985	60.5	24.9	14.2	0.4
20	27,379	67.8	18.3	13.0	0.9
21	24,546	60.3	25.0	13.6	1.1
22	25,590	62.4	22.3	14.1	1.2
23	20,347	62.6	22.4	14.1	0.9
24	19,300	53.7	29.5	13.7	3.1
25	17,329	49.7	30.3	14.9	5.1
26	16,291	44.5	33.5	15.9	6.0
27	20,975	58.9	26.6	13.0	1.4
28	18,994	55.5	27.9	14.8	1.9
29	20,491	51.5	32.7	12.8	2.9
30	24,034	55.8	30.8	11.8	1.6
31	22,506	55.4	29.2	12.9	2.6
32	21,004	48.7	35.9	14.0	1.5
33	17,724	48.2	35.5	16.0	0.4
34	17,363	46.3	34.9	14.2	4.6
State	$ 20,180	59.2%	25.7%	13.9%	1.3%

Education: School Years Completed

District	8 Years or Fewer	4 Years of High School	4 Years of College or More	Median School Years
1	12.2%	38.9%	18.0%	12.6
2	13.5	42.9	12.2	12.5
3	10.7	33.0	30.1	12.9
4	9.5	41.6	20.5	12.7
5	12.5	38.1	21.0	12.7
6	20.2	36.8	9.6	12.3
7	19.2	31.8	20.6	12.5
8	18.4	34.6	18.8	12.5
9	27.5	32.5	11.9	12.2
10	20.7	34.2	16.7	12.4
11	34.8	26.2	7.3	11.7
12	21.2	36.5	9.2	12.3
13	30.3	30.8	11.6	12.1
14	19.3	37.3	13.7	12.4
15	14.8	19.1	42.3	13.4
16	32.7	25.1	11.5	11.9
17	14.9	21.4	38.8	13.2
18	35.0	26.5	4.1	11.6
19	24.4	34.8	12.7	12.2
20	13.6	31.4	28.7	12.8
21	13.8	35.7	21.1	12.6
22	13.6	34.0	24.0	12.7
23	15.9	35.3	19.4	12.6
24	15.8	37.5	15.4	12.5
25	17.5	37.2	14.1	12.4
26	19.3	37.1	11.8	12.4
27	13.1	36.7	19.1	12.6
28	15.6	36.5	17.6	12.5
29	16.1	35.4	17.3	12.5
30	12.5	36.5	19.2	12.6
31	12.8	37.4	18.9	12.6
32	15.7	39.1	13.1	12.4
33	22.9	33.3	10.2	12.2
34	15.8	40.0	12.3	12.4
State	18.3%	34.1%	17.9%	12.5

Housing and Residential Patterns

District	Owner Occupied	Renter Occupied	Urban	Rural
1	78.5%	21.5%	91.3%	8.7%
2	78.6	21.4	99.8	0.2
3	79.9	20.1	98.8	1.2
4	85.8	14.2	100.0	0.0
5	74.4	25.6	100.0	0.0
6	55.2	44.8	100.0	0.0
7	29.8	70.2	100.0	0.0
8	37.5	62.5	100.0	0.0
9	28.0	72.0	100.0	0.0
10	33.9	66.1	100.0	0.0
11	16.5	83.5	100.0	0.0
12	16.8	83.2	100.0	0.0
13	22.6	77.4	100.0	0.0
14	49.5	50.5	100.0	0.0
15	10.7	89.3	100.0	0.0
16	4.0	96.0	100.0	0.0
17	10.2	89.8	100.0	0.0
18	5.6	94.4	100.0	0.0
19	26.3	73.7	100.0	0.0
20	50.6	49.4	97.9	2.1
21	68.6	31.4	66.2	33.8
22	68.5	31.5	78.5	21.5
23	57.7	42.3	88.7	11.3
24	73.1	26.9	36.9	63.1
25	67.4	32.6	45.6	54.4
26	70.5	29.5	37.5	62.5
27	63.2	36.8	77.5	22.5
28	66.3	33.7	52.1	47.9
29	68.3	31.7	51.5	48.5
30	68.6	31.4	72.3	27.7
31	74.7	25.3	61.3	38.7
32	67.5	32.5	79.9	20.1
33	52.5	47.5	97.8	2.2
34	72.7	27.3	43.5	56.5
State	48.6%	51.4%	84.6%	15.4%

1st District

Long Island — Eastern Suffolk County

The potato fields are giving way to housing developments in eastern Suffolk County, and commercial fishing grounds are now dominated by pleasure boats. While New York as a whole lost 3.8 percent of its population during the 1970s, the 1st expanded 29.1 percent, making it the most populous district in the state before the remap.

The departure of more than 100,000 people from the old 1st did not alter the district's solid Republican character. Map makers moved the boundary farther east, away from the Nassau County border.

The middle-class Republican towns of Ronkonkoma, Kings Park and Commack were shifted out of the 1st, along with the Democratic bastion of Dix Hills, home to affluent Jews. The most significant remaining patch of Democrats is around the state university at Stony Brook. The large gay enclave in Fire Island's Cherry Grove would be a liberal force if it stayed year-round, but it is primarily a summer community that by election time is back in Manhattan.

For 18 years prior to 1978, Democrat Otis G. Pike represented the 1st. Pike's outspoken independent style appealed to Republicans, but after his departure the area's normal voting pattern revived. The last time this area went Democratic for president was in 1964.

Republicans come in three varieties here: the longtime residents who fish and farm, the landed gentry living on inherited wealth and the middle-income ethnics moving farther and farther from the city.

The fishermen generally work out of Montauk, while the remaining farmers are mostly found around Southold. The rich live in Sag Harbor and Shelter Island; the adjacent Hamptons also have wealthy residents, but they tend to live there only in the summer. Shirley, Mastic and the Moriches host large numbers of ethnic newcomers, especially retired New York City policemen. Many of the ethnics are Italian, and they are receptive to Republican candidates.

Advanced technology, particularly related to defense, plays a major role in the district's economy. Grumman builds military aircraft at its Calverton facility. Nearby is Brookhaven National Laboratory, where military-oriented research takes place. And the Shoreham nuclear plant — controversial because of cost overruns and safety concerns — sits on the North Shore, awaiting federal permission to begin operations.

Election Returns

1st District		Democrat		Republican	
1976	President	85,138	(45.7%)	100,390	(53.9%)
	Senate	83,505	(45.9%)	97,194	(53.4%)
	House	116,012	(65.3%)	52,790	(29.7%)
1978	Governor	58,788	(40.6%)	80,279	(55.4%)
	House	57,507	(41.9%)	77,138	(56.2%)
1980	President	61,867	(33.2%)	105,748	(56.7%)
	Senate	68,335	(37.1%)	99,677	(54.1%)
	House	73,298	(41.9%)	98,622	(56.3%)
1982	Governor	65,019	(43.5%)	81,307	(54.4%)
	Senate	79,235	(54.8%)	64,566	(44.7%)
	House	49,787	(36.1%)	88,234	(63.9%)

Demographics

Population: 516,407. **Percent Change from 1970:** 36.7%.

Land Area: 633 square miles. **Population per Square Mile:** 815.8.

Counties, 1980 Population: Suffolk (Pt.) — 516,407.

Cities, 1980 Population: Centereach (CDP) — 30,136; Coram (CDP) — 24,752; East Patchogue (CDP) — 18,139; Farmingville (CDP) — 13,398; Hauppauge (CDP) (Pt.) — 6,719; Holbrook (CDP) (Pt.) — 4,899; Holtsville (CDP) (Pt.) — 11,073; Lake Ronkonkoma (CDP) (Pt.) — 18,644; Mastic (CDP) — 10,413; Medford (CDP) — 20,418; Nesconset (CDP) — 10,706; Patchogue — 11,291; Port Jefferson Station (CDP) — 17,009; Selden (CDP) — 17,259; Setauket-East Setauket (CDP) — 10,176; Shirley — 18,072; Smithtown (CDP) (Pt.) — 14,653; St. James (CDP) — 12,122; Stony Brook (CDP) — 16,155.

Race and Ancestry: White — 94.1%; Black — 3.9%; American Indian, Eskimo and Aleut — 0.2%; Asian and Pacific Islander — 0.9%. Spanish Origin — 3.6%. English — 3.7%; French — 0.5%; German — 6.5%; Greek — 0.6%; Hungarian — 0.5%; Irish — 7.3%; Italian — 14.0%; Norwegian — 0.6%; Polish — 3.4%; Russian — 1.2%; Scottish — 0.5%.

Universities, Enrollment: Long Island University (Southhampton center), Southampton — 1,441; State University of New York at Stony Brook, Stony Brook — 14,870; Suffolk County Community College (Selden campus), Selden — 21,505.

Newspapers, Circulation: Melville *Newsday*, *New York Daily News* and *The New York Times* circulate in the district.

Commercial Television Stations, Affiliation: WSNL-TV (None), Smithtown. Entire district is located in New York ADI.

Military Installations: Montauk Air Force Station, Montauk — 11; Suffolk County Airport (Air Force), Westhampton Beach — 792.

Nuclear Power Plants: Shoreham, Brookhaven (General Electric, Stone & Webster).

Industries:
Brookhaven National Laboratory; Upton; research — 3,220. **Grumman Aerospace Corp.;** Calverton; aircraft — 2,606. **Brookhaven Memorial Hospital & Medical Center;** East Patchogue; hospital — 1,200.

2nd District

Long Island — Western Suffolk County

Defense is a big industry in the 2nd District, and the remap has made it even bigger. The 1st picks up the Fairchild-Republic aviation plant in Farmingdale and its spinoff companies along the Route 110 industrial corridor.

But defense is not the only major industry. As with the 1st, this district's proximity to the water has spawned a big vacation industry. Many residents have boat slips on the Great South Bay. Each Saturday morning in the warm weather, the ferry is full from Bay Shore to Ocean Beach on Fire Island. Cars are banned on Fire Island, where summer people run errands with toy wagons in tow. Bay Shore also hosts a strong commercial fishing industry.

Redistricting dilutes the 2nd's Republican character only slightly. The area within the new 2nd went for former GOP Sen. James L. Buckley in 1976 while Buckley was losing badly in most of the state to Democrat Daniel Patrick Moynihan.

But there is a significant influx of Democrats from liberal Dix Hills, which had been in the 1st, and a small one from the old 4th's North Amityville, with a population of low-income blacks whose ancestors moved to Long Island

New York 365

to work as servants in the mansions of South Amityville. The district retains two Democratic towns: Central Islip, which has significant numbers of low-income blacks, and Brentwood, a mix of blue-collar whites and Hispanics.

The heavy Republican vote comes from such well-to-do towns as Babylon village and Sayville located on the stretch of waterfront along the South Shore. Italian-American Copiague is a bastion of blue-collar Republican voting. North Babylon and Deer Park have high Republican enrollments, but the Democrats have made inroads there by appealing to the numerous technicians and executives who are employed in the defense industry. Another of the district's swing areas is blue-collar Lindenhurst, once a German community.

Election Returns

2nd District		Democrat		Republican	
1976	President	78,810	(45.2%)	94,673	(54.3%)
	Senate	78,717	(46.3%)	90,177	(53.1%)
	House	95,801	(57.2%)	70,653	(42.2%)
1978	Governor	56,406	(39.3%)	81,191	(56.5%)
	House	75,132	(54.7%)	62,131	(45.3%)
1980	President	61,484	(33.6%)	106,088	(57.9%)
	Senate	66,969	(37.1%)	97,686	(54.1%)
	House	97,411	(56.2%)	75,909	(43.8%)
1982	Governor	59,654	(36.1%)	102,741	(62.1%)
	Senate	70,747	(55.4%)	56,747	(44.4%)
	House	80,951	(63.9%)	42,790	(33.8%)

Demographics

Population: 515,595. **Percent Change from 1970:** 5.1%.

Land Area: 166 square miles. **Population per Square Mile:** 3,106.0.

Counties, 1980 Population: Suffolk (Pt.) — 515,595.

Cities, 1980 Population: Babylon — 12,388; Bay Shore (CDP) — 10,784; Brentwood (CDP) — 44,321; Central Islip (CDP) — 19,734; Copiague (CDP) — 20,132; Deer Park (CDP) — 30,394; Dix Hills (CDP) (Pt.) — 12,716; East Islip (CDP) — 13,852; Hauppauge (CDP) (Pt.) — 10,196; Holbrook (CDP) (Pt.) — 19,483; Holtsville (CDP) (Pt.) — 2,442; Islip (CDP) — 13,438; Lake Ronkonkoma (CDP) (Pt.) — 19,692; Lindenhurst — 26,919; North Amityville (CDP) — 13,140; North Babylon (CDP) — 19,019; North Bay Shore (CDP) — 35,020; North Great River (CDP) — 11,416; North Lindenhurst (CDP) — 11,511; Sayville (CDP) — 12,013; West Babylon (CDP) — 41,699; West Islip (CDP) — 29,533; Wyandanch (CDP) — 13,215.

Race and Ancestry: White — 88.8%; Black — 8.6%; American Indian, Eskimo and Aleut — 0.2%; Asian and Pacific Islander — 0.7%. Spanish Origin — 6.7%. English — 2.3%; German — 6.3%; Hungarian — 0.5%; Irish — 8.3%; Italian — 18.4%; Polish — 2.0%; Russian — 1.0%.

Universities, Enrollment: Dowling College, Oakdale — 2,320.

Newspapers, Circulation: Melville, *Newsday, New York Daily News, The New York Times* and *New York Post* also circulate in the district.

Commercial Television Stations, Affiliation: Entire district is located in New York ADI.

Industries:

Fairchild Republic Co.; Farmingdale; aircraft — 3,500. **Eaton Corp.** (Cutler Hammer Div.); Deer Park; electronic scientific instruments — 2,600. **Entenmann's Inc.** (HQ); Bay Shore; bakery products — 2,200. **Southside Hospital Inc.;** Bay Shore; hospital — 1,500. **Brunswick Hospital Center Inc.;** Amityville; hospital — 1,450. **Good Samaritan Hospital;** West Islip; hospital — 1,450. **I L C Industries Inc.** (HQ); Bohemia; data processing equipment — 550. **Walbaum Inc.** (HQ); Islip; warehousing — 550. **Sperry Systems** (Electronic Systems Operations); Ronkonkoma; electronic defense equipment — 500.

3rd District

Long Island — Parts of Nassau and Suffolk Counties

The new 3rd District encompasses the most dramatically reworked constituency on Long Island. Starting at the New York City line, the district covers northern Nassau County and reaches into northwestern Suffolk County as far as the Nissequogue River. The population division between the two counties is almost even, with 51 percent from Nassau and 49 percent from Suffolk. New territory was added from Suffolk's overpopulated 1st.

The new 3rd is a combination of the old 6th District, which extended into New York City, and the old 3rd, which straddled the Nassau-Suffolk border but extended south all the way to the ocean. Overall, the redrawn 3rd tilts Republican, but Democrats can do well there, as was illustrated by the Democratic defeat of the Republican incumbent in 1982.

Defense remains the crucial industry, although the remap deprives the 3rd of some major Grumman and Fairchild-Republic installations. The district keeps the Hazeltine works in Greenlawn and the Sperry operation in Great Neck. Many of the residents who are not involved in defense commute to jobs in New York City.

The Nassau part of the district is a partisan patchwork. Northern Oyster Bay contains Republican corporate executives in such prosperous communities as Bayville and Muttontown. North Hempstead turns in a heavy Democratic vote; the liberal Jewish influence is strong in New Hyde Park, Manhasset and Roslyn. These crowded older suburbs lost population in the 1970s.

F. Scott Fitzgerald set "The Great Gatsby" on Long Island's mansion-dotted North Shore, on the Nassau side, but he would probably have to set it somewhere else today. While rich people still live in Gatsby's Glen Cove, some of the estates have been turned into museums, and a small garment manufacturing industry is attracting new Hispanic residents. The Hispanics vote Democratic and help keep the community politically marginal.

The Suffolk portion of the district displays a more uniform Republican cast, although Democrats have made inroads in local offices. Huntington is home to many ethnic Irish and Italian Republicans. Smithtown, another ethnic area farther east, is new to the district. Both towns, in the earlier-settled parts of burgeoning Suffolk, grew minimally in the 1970s.

Election Returns

3rd District		Democrat		Republican	
1976	President	128,327	(46.5%)	146,614	(53.1%)
	Senate	136,721	(50.3%)	133,281	(49.0%)
	House	146,320	(56.3%)	107,365	(41.3%)
1978	Governor	87,145	(46.1%)	92,435	(49.0%)
	House	94,226	(50.9%)	83,970	(45.4%)

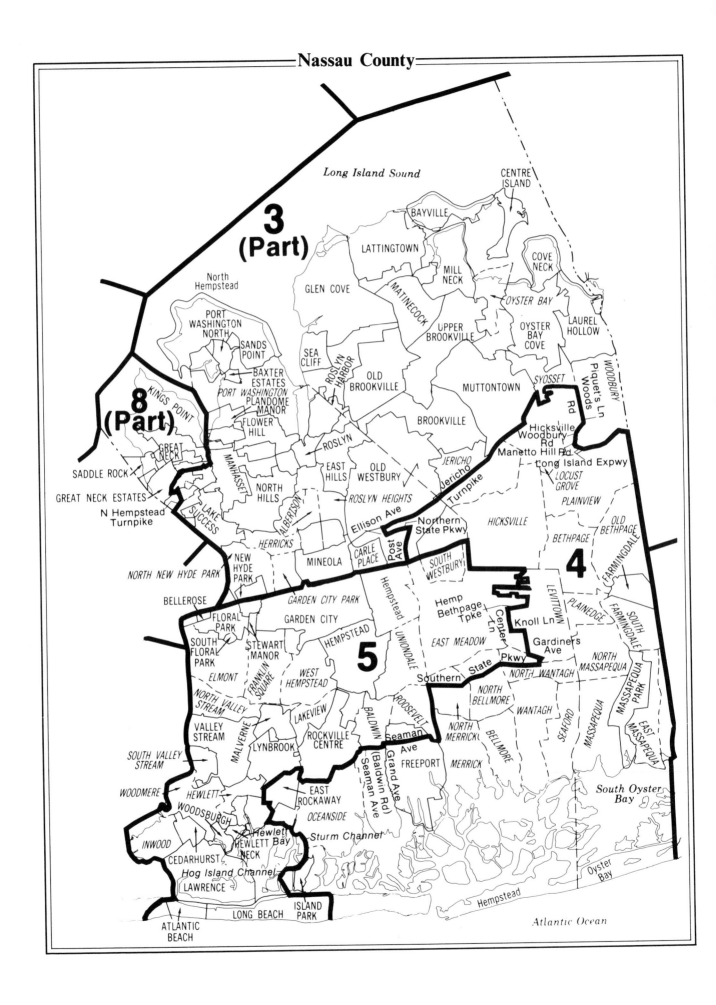

Nassau County

3rd District		Democrat		Republican	
1980	President	82,250	(34.3%)	132,779	(55.4%)
	Senate	99,577	(41.1%)	117,911	(48.7%)
	House	109,628	(46.9%)	120,670	(51.6%)
1982	Governor	10,643	(58.0%)	77,811	(41.5%)
	Senate	95,248	(55.2%)	72,912	(42.2%)
	House	93,846	(51.8%)	83,238	(46.0%)

Demographics

Population: 518,061. **Percent Change from 1970:** -3.4%.

Land Area: 222 square miles. **Population per Square Mile:** 2,333.6.

Counties, 1980 Population: Nassau (Pt.) — 265,832; Suffolk (Pt.) — 252,229.

Cities, 1980 Population: Commack (CDP) — 34,719; Dix Hills (CDP) (Pt.) — 13,977; East Northport (CDP) — 20,187; Elwood (CDP) — 11,847; Floral Park (Pt.) — 2,327; Glen Cove — 24,618; Greenlawn (CDP) — 13,869; Hauppauge (CDP) (Pt.) — 4,045; Huntington (CDP) — 21,727; Huntington Station (CDP) — 28,769; Jericho (CDP) (Pt.) — 99; Kings Park (CDP) — 16,131; Mineola (Pt.) — 20,705; North New Hyde Park (CDP) — 15,114; Port Washington (CDP) — 14,521; Smithtown (CDP) (Pt.) — 16,253; South Huntington (CDP) — 14,854; Westbury (Pt.) — 7,734.

Race and Ancestry: White — 95.1%; Black — 2.8%; American Indian, Eskimo and Aleut — 0.1%; Asian and Pacific Islander — 1.5%. Spanish Origin — 2.7%. English — 3.2%; French — 0.5%; German — 6.5%; Greek — 1.0%; Hungarian — 0.7%; Irish — 8.0%; Italian — 15.4%; Polish — 3.7%; Portuguese — 0.6%; Russian — 3.5%; Scottish — 0.5%.

Universities, Enrollment: Adelphi Business School, Mineola — 1,208; Katherine Gibbs School, Huntington — 356; Long Island University (C. W. Post Center), Greenvale — 12,927; New York Chiropractic College, Glen Head — 738; New York Institute of Technology, Old Westbury — 10,667; Seminary of the Immaculate Conception, Huntington — 341; State University College at Old Westbury, Old Westbury — 3,123; Webb Institute of Naval Architecture, Glen Cove — 74.

Newspapers, Circulation: *Newsday* (eS), Melville — 491,221. *New York Daily News*, *The New York Times* and *New York Post* also circulate in the district.

Commercial Television Stations, Affiliation: Entire district is located in New York ADI.

Military Installations: Roslyn Air National Guard Station, Roslyn — 461.

Industries:

Sperry Systems (Electronic Systems Operations - HQ); Great Neck; electronic defense equipment — 5,100. **North Shore University Hospital;** Manhasset; hospital — 2,750. **Newsday Inc.** (HQ); Melville; newspaper publishing — 2,300. **Hazeltine Corp.** (HQ); Greenlawn; electronic equipment — 2,200. **Kings Park Psychiatric Center;** Kings Park; mental hospital — 2,050.

Chase Manhattan Bank (Consumer Banking Div.); New Hyde Park; banking — 2,000. **Pergament Distributors Inc.;** Melville; paint wholesaling — 2,000. **Nassau Hospital Assn. Corp.;** Mineola; hospital — 1,850. **Esteé Lauder Inc.** (HQ); Melville; cosmetics — 1,800. **Veterans Administration;** Northport; veterans' hospital — 1,800. **Park Lane Hosiery** (HQ); New Hyde Park; hosiery — 1,700. **Huntington Hospital Assn.;** Huntington; hospital — 1,350. **Alarm Device Mfg.** (Ademco - HQ); Syosset; alarm devices — 1,200. **Fotocircuits Corp.** (HQ); Glen Cove; photographic products — 1,200. **PRD Electronics;** Syosset; electronic communications equipment — 1,200. **National Bank of North America;** Melville; data processing services — 1,100.

Veeco Instruments Inc. (Lambda Electronics Div. - HQ); Melville; electronic communications equipment — 1,100. **St. John's Episcopal Hospital;** Smithtown; hospital; 1,080. **Glen Cove Community Hospital;** Glen Cove; hospital — 1,036. **Cablevision Systems Development Co.;** Woodbury; cable television — 1,000. **Geico Insurance Corp.** (Northeast Div.); Woodbury; insurance; 1,000. **Canon USA** (HQ); Lake Success; cameras; electronic and optical equipment — 900. **Databit Inc.** (HQ); Hauppauge; telecommunications systems — 800. **Kollmorgan Corp.** (Photocircuits Div.); Glen Cove; motors, generators — 760. **Powers Chemco Inc.** (Chemco Photo Products Co. Div. - HQ); Glen Cove; photographic equipment, supplies — 700. **Applied Digital Data Systems** (HQ); Hauppauge; electronic data systems — 660. **Telephonics Corp.** (HQ); Huntington; electronic communications equipment — 610.

Comtech Telecommunications (HQ); Hauppauge; electronic communications equipment — 600. **Gould Inc.** (Simulation Systems Div.); Melville; aircraft training devices — 600. **Publishers Clearinghouse;** Port Washington; magazine marketing — 600. **Norden Systems Inc.;** Melville; electronic communications equipment — 550. **The Singer Co. Inc.** (Sewing Products Div.); Syosset; management services — 550. **Deutsch Relays Inc.;** East Northport; electronic components — 500. **Eastern States Bankcard Assn.;** New Hyde Park; data processing services — 500. **Slater Electric Inc.** (HQ); Glen Cove; electrical wiring devices — 500. **Underwriters Laboratories Inc.;** Melville; commercial testing laboratory — 500. **Lackman Food Service;** Jericho; food services — more than 500.

4th District

Long Island — Southeastern Nassau County

In 1947 row after row of inexpensive Cape Cod homes began sprouting on what had been Long Island farm land. Levittown was under way. For the hordes of returning GIs these low-cost houses were the next best thing to the vine-covered cottages of their dreams.

Today the last farm land is long since developed. Levittown and the surrounding middle-income suburbs of the 4th District have the settled, comfortable look of established suburbia — conditions that make the constituency safe for the Republicans.

This is an overwhelmingly white middle-class area. The district contains a black population of 3.7 percent, smaller than in the 1970s because the largely black areas in run-down North Freeport were moved to the 5th District.

Already loaded with aerospace workers, the 4th gets more with the addition of the huge Grumman plant at Bethpage, where 16,000 people are employed. As elsewhere in Nassau, the railroad platforms are filled each morning with commuters clutching their early editions of *Newsday*, the local paper.

While thousands of the district's residents may stream into New York City on weekdays, thousands of city dwellers head for the 4th on summer weekends — in particular to Jones Beach, a state park known for its miles of clean white sand.

Redistricting changed the partisan character of the district very little. The district was once much more competitive; anti-war Democrat Allard K. Lowenstein managed to win a term in it in 1968. But a 1970 court order reshaped the district, removing the Democratic "Five Towns" area and allowing the Republicans to take over.

In the 1982 remap, the lawmakers made up the 4th's population deficit by attaching the southern half of generally Republican Oyster Bay. The new area includes not only Bethpage but also Massapequa, whose postwar development attracted a combination of Italian and Jewish homeowners and led wags to refer to it as "Matzo-Pizza." Massapequa today is largely Italian and increasingly Republican. The lone Democratic bastion in south Oyster Bay is Plainview, a middle-income Jewish suburb.

All of Levittown except the western area is in the 4th. The town shows clear Republican leanings but supports statewide Democrats on a selective basis.

Closer to the water, identification with the Republican Party is stronger. Alfonse D'Amato, one-time local GOP municipal official who was elected to the U.S. Senate in 1980, comes from this section of the 4th District. The now-faded older suburbs that boomed in the postwar years — Baldwin, Oceanside and Freeport, a commercial fishing center — are Irish and Italian strongholds and solid D'Amato territory.

Bellmore, Merrick and Seaford have a more prosperous look and equally firm GOP ties. The same can be said for the half of Long Beach Island in the 4th, containing Lido Beach.

Election Returns

4th District		Democrat		Republican	
1976	President	99,242	(47.8%)	107,420	(51.8%)
	Senate	104,812	(51.3%)	98,382	(48.1%)
	House	87,459	(45.3%)	105,000	(54.4%)
1978	Governor	72,769	(44.4%)	82,731	(50.5%)
	House	52,739	(35.9%)	93,905	(63.8%)
1980	President	70,189	(34.0%)	117,359	(56.8%)
	Senate	78,287	(38.8%)	106,045	(52.6%)
	House	63,860	(34.6%)	117,151	(63.4%)
1982	Governor	100,722	(47.2%)	107,155	(50.2%)
	Senate	126,917	(58.7%)	88,454	(40.9%)
	House	63,390	(36.3%)	105,241	(60.4%)

Demographics

Population: 518,371. **Percent Change from 1970:** -9.0%.

Land Area: 96 square miles. **Population per Square Mile:** 5,399.7.

Counties, 1980 Population: Nassau (Pt.) — 518,371.

Cities, 1980 Population: Baldwin (CDP) (Pt.) — 18,866; Bellmore (CDP) — 18,106; Bethpage (CDP) — 16,840; East Massapequa (CDP) — 13,987; East Rockaway — 10,917; Freeport (Pt.) — 32,108; Hicksville (CDP) — 43,245; Jericho (CDP) (Pt.) — 12,640; Levittown (CDP) (Pt.) — 37,427; Massapequa (CDP) — 24,454; Massapequa Park — 19,779.

Merrick (CDP) — 24,478; North Bellmore (CDP) (Pt.) — 14,214; North Massapequa (CDP) — 21,385; North Merrick (CDP) (Pt.) — 8,859; North Wantagh (CDP) (Pt.) — 8,699; Oceanside (CDP) — 33,639; Plainview (CDP) — 28,037; Seaford (CDP) — 16,117; South Farmingdale (CDP) — 16,439; Wantagh (CDP) — 19,817; Westbury (Pt.) — 6,137.

Race and Ancestry: White — 94.7%; Black — 3.7%; American Indian, Eskimo and Aleut — 0.1%; Asian and Pacific Islander — 0.9%; Spanish Origin — 3.0%. English — 2.2%; German — 6.4%; Greek — 0.9%; Hungarian — 0.9%; Irish — 9.0%; Italian — 16.3%; Polish — 3.4%; Russian — 4.0%.

Universities, Enrollment: Berkeley-Claremont School, Hicksville — 415; State University of New York Agricultural and Technical College at Farmingdale, Farmingdale — 13,834.

Newspapers, Circulation: Melville, *Newsday*, *New York Daily News*, *The New York Times* and *New York Post* circulate in the district.

Commercial Television Stations, Affiliation: Entire district is located in New York ADI.

Industries:

Grumman Aerospace Corp. (HQ); Bethpage; aircraft, parts — 16,000. **Fairchild Industries Inc.** (Fairchild Republic Co.); Farmingdale; aircraft — 4,292. **Grumman Data Systems Corp.** (HQ); Bethpage; computer services — 1,200. **South Nassau Communities Hospital;** Oceanside; hospital — 1,200. **Sangamo Weston Inc.** (Fairchild Weston Div.); Syosset; photographic equipment — 1,000.

K-Security Guard Corp. (HQ); Bellmore; security services — 650. **Alsy Mfg. Inc.** (V R Div.); Hicksville; electric lamps — 600. **Ebasco Services Inc.;** Jericho; engineering services — 600. **Ontel Corp.** (HQ); Woodbury; electronic components — 600. **Gil Rosenberg Inc.;** Syosset; liquors wholesaling — 600. **White Rose Food Corp.** (HQ); Farmingdale; grocery wholesalers — 600. **Del Laboratories Inc.** (HQ); Farmingdale; cosmetics, drugs — 570. **General Signal Corp.** (Cardion Electronics Div.); Woodbury; electronics communications equipment — 520. **Executone Inc.** (HQ); Jericho; communications equipment — 500.

5th District

Long Island — Southwestern Nassau County

The horse races here are at Belmont Park, not at the polls. Politics in the home district of Nassau GOP boss Joseph Margiotta are usually placid. Republicans have held the seat since its creation in 1962 as the old 4th, thanks in large part to Margiotta's effective GOP organization.

Margiotta's machine functions even under adversity. After his 1982 conviction on federal mail fraud and extortion charges, Margiotta remained active in local Nassau politics. Throughout the 1970s Margiotta's apparatus displayed a reach rivaling that of the late Mayor Richard J. Daley of Chicago. The core of Margiotta's support is the town of Hempstead, most of which is in the 5th District and which has been organized down to the block level.

So important is Hempstead to Margiotta — and so complete is his control there — that he pushed through a change in party bylaws allowing him to remain Hempstead GOP leader even after he moved away to the more fashionable North Shore.

Aside from those in wealthy Atlantic Beach on Long Beach Island, most of the district's Republicans can be found inland. One group of them, mostly Irish and Italian homeowners a generation removed from the city, occupies such towns as Elmont and Valley Stream. Moneyed Garden City is home to many business executives.

The under-populated 5th had to expand to take in most of the town of Hempstead. It was moved east to cover a slice of Levittown, Baldwin and North Freeport. Discounting black North Freeport, these additions bring more Republicans into an already GOP-oriented district.

North Freeport joins the sizable black populations in Roosevelt and Hempstead Village that vote predictably Democratic. Other Democratic pockets are Long Beach, a run-down seaside resort given over to senior-citizen residential hotels, and the "Five Towns" in Nassau's southwestern corner. These communities — Woodmere, Cedarhurst, Inwood, Lawrence and Hewlett — have the district's largest concentration of Jews. Jewish voters provide the backbone of the Democrats' strength here, making up 30 percent of the 5th's population.

Election Returns

5th District		Democrat		Republican	
1976	President	111,254	(48.1%)	118,897	(51.5%)
	Senate	118,129	(52.0%)	107,762	(47.4%)
	House	96,769	(44.3%)	121,608	(55.7%)
1978	Governor	77,900	(45.6%)	84,296	(49.3%)
	House	61,272	(38.3%)	94,665	(59.1%)
1980	President	76,701	(36.2%)	117,106	(55.3%)
	Senate	85,692	(40.6%)	106,129	(50.3%)
	House	82,735	(40.3%)	117,001	(57.0%)
1982	Governor	72,146	(45.1%)	83,442	(52.2%)
	Senate	87,247	(56.8%)	65,843	(42.8%)
	House	67,002	(38.8%)	100,485	(58.1%)

Demographics

Population: 513,531. **Percent Change from 1970:** -7.5%.

Land Area: 75 square miles. **Population per Square Mile:** 6,847.1.

Counties, 1980 Population: Nassau (Pt.) — 513,531.

Cities, 1980 Population: Baldwin (CDP) (Pt.) — 12,764; East Meadow (CDP) — 39,317; Elmont (CDP) — 27,592; Floral Park (Pt.) — 14,478; Franklin Square (CDP) — 29,051; Freeport (Pt.) — 6,164; Garden City — 22,927; Hempstead — 40,404; Levittown (CDP) (Pt.) — 19,618; Long Beach — 34,073; Lynbrook — 20,424; Mineola (Pt.) — 52; North Bellmore (CDP) (Pt.) — 6,416; North Merrick (CDP) (Pt.) — 3,989; North Valley Stream (CDP) — 14,530; North Wantagh (CDP) (Pt.) — 3,978; Rockville Centre — 25,412; Roosevelt (CDP) — 14,109; Uniondale (CDP) — 20,016; Valley Stream — 35,769; West Hempstead (CDP) — 18,536; Woodmere (CDP) — 17,205.

Race and Ancestry: White — 85.6%; Black — 12.3%; American Indian, Eskimo and Aleut — 0.1%; Asian and Pacific Islander — 1.0%. Spanish Origin — 3.7%. English — 2.1%; German — 5.9%; Greek — 0.9%; Hungarian — 0.8%; Irish — 8.2%; Italian — 16.6%; Polish — 3.2%; Russian — 4.0%.

Universities, Enrollment: Adelphi University, Garden City — 11,833; Hofstra University, Hempstead — 10,989; Molloy College, Rockville Centre — 1,501; Nassau Community College, Garden City — 20,590.

Newspapers, Circulation: *New York Daily News*, *New York Post* and *The New York Times* circulate in the district.

Commercial Television Stations, Affiliation: Entire district is located in New York ADI.

Industries:
Doubleday & Co. Inc. (HQ); Garden City; book publishing — 1,600. **Deutsche Lufthansa A.G.** (HQ); East Meadow; commercial airline — 1,500. **Mercy Hospital Assn. Inc.**; Rockville Centre; hospital — 1,250. **Bulova System & Instruments** (HQ); Valley Stream; ammunition — 900. **Esselte Pendaflex Corp.** (HQ); Garden City; filing folders — 500. **Studley Paper Co. Inc.**; Inwood; paper bags — 500.

6th District

Southern Queens — Ozone Park, Jamaica

New York's burgeoning Catholic middle class settled this part of Queens a generation ago as it expanded outward from homes closer to the inner city. Now Queens is part of the inner city, and people are leaving for outer suburbs or other states. The old district lost nearly 10 percent of its population in the 1970s.

The old 7th District was 45 percent black by 1980. The areas added by redistricting bring the proportion up to 50 percent in the new version of the district, renumbered the 6th. Whatever the racial divisions, the new 6th is a safe Democratic district. The area within the redrawn 6th backed Jimmy Carter with 58 percent of the vote.

Middle-class blacks increasingly have moved into the quiet, tree-lined sections near the Nassau County line, such as Rosedale, Springfield Gardens and Laurelton. To the west in Jamaica, a major terminal for Long Island trains, the landscape becomes more urban and the blacks poorer. By coincidence, Jamaica in Queens has become a home for significant numbers of blacks from the island of Jamaica in the Caribbean.

The district has seen occasional conflict between the races. White parents in Rosedale staged demonstrations in 1981 over a court order to transfer their children to a mostly black school. With blacks accounting for a majority of the 6th's population, local politicians have to be careful to seem responsive to both black and white voters.

South of Jamaica lie Ozone Park and Howard Beach, white working-class areas populated by Italians and Jews. Aqueduct Race Track ("the Big A") is in this part of the district.

The 6th picks up the Rockaways, a narrow peninsula that commuters reach via an elevated train across Jamaica Bay. Popular with beach-goers, the Rockaways have a diverse mix of year-round residents. Far Rockaway has many elderly Jews. Arverne is poor and largely black and Neponsit is largely populated by wealthy Jews and WASPs.

Aside from the demographic changes, the abiding concern of the 6th is its John F. Kennedy International Airport. JFK provides employment for the district but also a great deal of jet noise. In the early 1970s local residents unsuccessfully sought to stop the supersonic Concorde from landing at JFK. Flight routes and hours continue to preoccupy community groups.

Election Returns

6th District		Democrat		Republican	
1976	President	115,346	(69.3%)	50,369	(30.3%)
	Senate	114,362	(70.9%)	45,363	(28.1%)
	House	120,591	(85.1%)	10,680	(7.5%)
1978	Governor	78,642	(69.0%)	32,658	(28.7%)
	House	84,080	(85.0%)	11,824	(11.9%)
1980	President	89,495	(58.1%)	55,064	(35.7%)
	Senate	76,249	(50.5%)	58,054	(38.5%)
	House	105,100	(83.0%)	18,297	(14.5%)
1982	Governor	85,173	(70.7%)	33,849	(28.1%)
	Senate	87,060	(79.8%)	21,333	(19.5%)
	House	95,483	(95.9%)	—	

Demographics

Population: 516,844. **Percent Change from 1970:** -5.7%.

Land Area: 41 square miles. **Population per Square Mile:** 12,606.0.

Counties, 1980 Population: Queens (Pt.) — 516,844.

Cities, 1980 Population: New York (Pt.) — 516,844.

Race and Ancestry: White — 44.1%; Black — 50.3%; American Indian, Eskimo and Aleut — 0.2%; Asian and Pacific Islander — 1.4%.

New York City and Nassau County

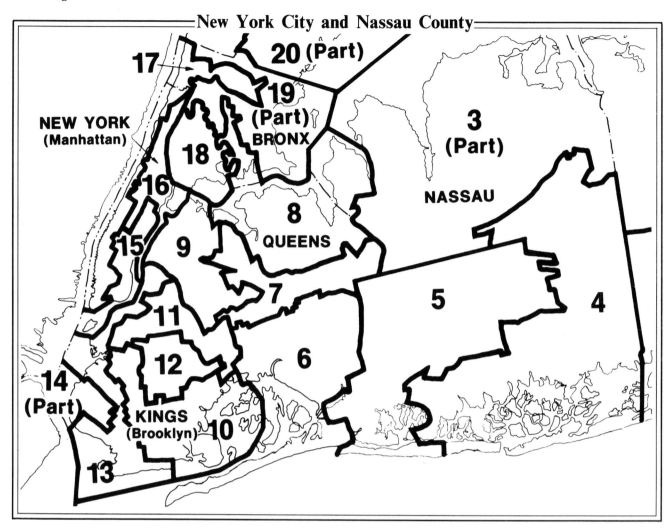

Spanish Origin — 9.4%. English — 1.3%; German — 2.2%; Irish — 4.2%; Italian — 10.8%; Polish — 1.9%; Russian — 1.7%.

Newspapers, Circulation: *New York Daily News*, *New York Post* and *New York Times* circulate in the district.

Commercial Television Stations, Affiliation: Entire district is located in New York ADI.

Industries:

Pan American World Airways Inc.; Jamaica; commercial airline — 1,400. **United Airlines Inc.;** Jamaica; commercial airline — 1,400. **American Airlines Inc.;** Jamaica; commercial airline — 1,000. **Eastern Air Lines Inc.;** Jamaica; commercial airline — 1,000. **Port Authority of New York & New Jersey** (JFK International Airport); Jamaica; airport operations — 800. **Capitol International Airways;** Jamaica; commercial airline — 700. **Allied New York Services;** Jamaica; aviation refueling — 600. **British Airways** (British Overseas Div.); Jamaica; commercial airline — 600. **Ideal Toy Corp.** (HQ); Jamaica; toys, games — 550.

7th District

Central Queens — Hollis, Kew Gardens

This district extends from the semi-suburban neighborhoods near the Nassau border to the apartment towers at the borough's heart. Mostly white and largely Jewish, it casts a solidly Democratic vote.

The one Republican enclave is near the Queens-Nassau line in tree-shaded Bellerose and Queens Village. The suburban-oriented homeowners there regularly flout their Democratic registration and vote Republican in state and national elections.

Besides its expansion into eastern Queens, the 7th moved slightly south to take in East Elmhurst, Kew Gardens and part of Jamaica — adding blacks in the process. Some Democratic votes were lost, however, with the removal of Jackson Heights, with its substantial Hispanic population.

Another concentration of minorities can be found in Corona's massive Lefrak City complex. Middle-income whites have been leaving the twenty-building development off the Long Island Expressway, and blacks and Hispanics have been replacing them.

Rego Park, an area developed in the 1920s, typifies the middle-class Jewish portion of the district. This is a community of six-story apartment buildings and tightly spaced brick houses. Some of its residents had turned more conservative on social issues by the early 1980s, but most remained loyal Democrats.

Like the rest of Queens, the 7th is a bedroom community rather than a core city area. There is no major industrial activity in the district.

Election Returns

7th District		Democrat		Republican	
1976	President	110,300	(62.5%)	65,412	(37.0%)
	Senate	115,073	(66.7%)	55,857	(32.4%)
	House	122,875	(80.2%)	24,858	(16.2%)
1978	Governor	76,208	(64.9%)	37,987	(32.3%)
	House	82,928	(76.5%)	18,576	(17.1%)
1980	President	75,859	(48.5%)	68,309	(43.7%)
	Senate	77,274	(50.5%)	58,833	(38.5%)
	House	95,511	(72.3%)	34,552	(26.2%)
1982	Governor	77,205	(59.5%)	50,668	(39.1%)
	Senate	91,717	(75.2%)	29,456	(24.2%)
	House	84,013	(77.2%)	24,832	(22.8%)

Demographics

Population: 518,952. **Percent Change from 1970:** -2.6%.

Land Area: 22 square miles. **Population per Square Mile:** 23,588.7.

Counties, 1980 Population: Queens (Pt.) — 518,952.

Cities, 1980 Population: New York (Pt.) — 518,952.

Race and Ancestry: White — 73.2%; Black — 11.8%; American Indian, Eskimo and Aleut — 0.1%; Asian and Pacific Islander — 7.2%. Spanish Origin — 19.7%. English — 1.5%; French — 0.6%; German — 4.3%; Greek — 1.6%; Hungarian — 1.4%; Irish — 4.4%; Italian — 8.4%; Polish — 3.9%; Russian — 4.7%; Ukranian — 0.5%.

Universities, Enrollment: St. John's University, Jamaica — 17,945; York College, Jamaica — 3,801.

Newspapers, Circulation: *New York Daily News, The New York Times* and *New York Post* circulate in the district.

Commercial Television Stations, Affiliation: Entire district is located in New York ADI.

Industries:

Long Island Jewish Hillside Medical Center; New Hyde Park; hospital — 4,300. **Creedmore State Hospital;** Queens Village; state psychiatric hospital — 2,500. **Queens Hospital Center;** Jamaica; hospital — 2,500. **Mary Immaculate Hospital;** Jamaica; hospital — 1,020.

8th District

Northern Queens; Eastern Bronx

The new 8th is centered in northeast Queens, a middle- to upper middle-class residential area. With its single-family homes and broad streets it resembles a Long Island suburb more than it does the parts of Queens closer to Manhattan. Large homes front Little Neck Bay and Long Island Sound.

Flushing has more closely packed housing and a more urban feel. This old section was a Dutch settlement as early as 1645 and its downtown area is a priceless historic district.

Flushing grew rapidly after Queens' first gas line opened there in 1855. It was the site of world's fairs in 1939 and 1964 and holds both Shea Stadium and La Guardia Airport. As in the territory around Kennedy Airport farther out in Queens, noise is a perennial political issue.

In all, the Queens portion of the district has about 66 percent of the population. Five percent is across the city line in Nassau County and 20 percent is across the East River in the Bronx.

The Nassau portion of the new 8th takes in suburban Great Neck, a community of affluent, liberal Jews. Jutting into Long Island Sound, Great Neck is the site of the U.S. Merchant Marine Academy at Kings Point.

On the other side of Flushing Bay, in the Bronx, the 8th reaches north from the East River almost up to the Bronx Zoo. Jews, many of them elderly, dominate the quiet neighborhoods of Parkchester, Van Ness and Pelham Parkway.

South of the Cross Bronx Expressway, the 8th has its main concentration of blacks and Hispanics in Soundview.

Election Returns

8th District		Democrat		Republican	
1976	President	105,219	(58.8%)	72,954	(40.7%)
	Senate	111,314	(63.8%)	61,700	(35.3%)
	House	119,268	(74.8%)	33,649	(21.1%)
1978	Governor	74,363	(61.4%)	42,889	(35.4%)
	House	83,719	(75.1%)	20,780	(18.6%)
1980	President	71,229	(45.2%)	73,444	(46.6%)
	Senate	79,027	(51.8%)	56,827	(37.2%)
	House	91,343	(67.2%)	42,914	(31.5%)
1982	Governor	94,134	(60.9%)	58,402	(37.8%)
	Senate	108,068	(75.3%)	34,737	(24.2%)
	House	91,830	(89.5%)	—	

Demographics

Population: 512,397. **Percent Change from 1970:** -6.5%.

Land Area: 36 square miles. **Population per Square Mile:** 14,233.3.

Counties, 1980 Population: Bronx (Pt.) — 149,163; Nassau (Pt.) — 23,848; Queens (Pt.) — 339,386.

Cities, 1980 Population: New York (Pt.) — 488,549.

Race and Ancestry: White — 78.9%; Black — 10.0%; American Indian, Eskimo and Aleut — 0.1%; Asian and Pacific Islander — 5.2%. Spanish Origin — 13.9%. English — 1.3%; German — 3.6%; Greek — 2.1%; Hungarian — 1.2%; Irish — 6.1%; Italian — 13.9%; Polish — 4.0%; Russian — 4.9%; Ukranian — 0.5%.

Universities, Enrollment: Academy of Aeronautics, Flushing — 1,932; Cathedral College of the Immaculate Conception, Douglaston — 115; Queens College, Flushing — 18,127; Queensborough Community College, Bayside — 11,814; United States Merchant Marine Academy, Kings Point — 1,144.

Newspapers, Circulation: Melville *Newsday, New York Daily News, New York Post* and *The New York Times* circulate in the district.

Commercial Television Stations, Affiliation: Entire district is located in New York ADI.

Industries:

Booth Memorial Medical Center; Flushing; hospital — 1,600. **American Airlines Inc.;** Flushing; commercial airline — 1,500. **Flushing Hospital;** Flushing; hospital — 1,200. **Electro Audio Dynamics Inc.** (HQ); Great Neck; high fidelity speakers — 1,161. **Western Electric Co. Inc.;** Whitestone; distribution, repair center — 1,000.

Bulova Watch Co. Inc. (HQ); Flushing; watches, clocks — 800. **New York Airlines Inc.;** Flushing; commercial airline — 780. **Port Authority of New York & New Jersey** (La Guardia Airport); Flushing; airport operations — 600. **American Bakeries Co.;** Flushing; bread — 500. **Eastern Air Lines Inc.;** Flushing; commercial airline — 500.

New York City — Queens

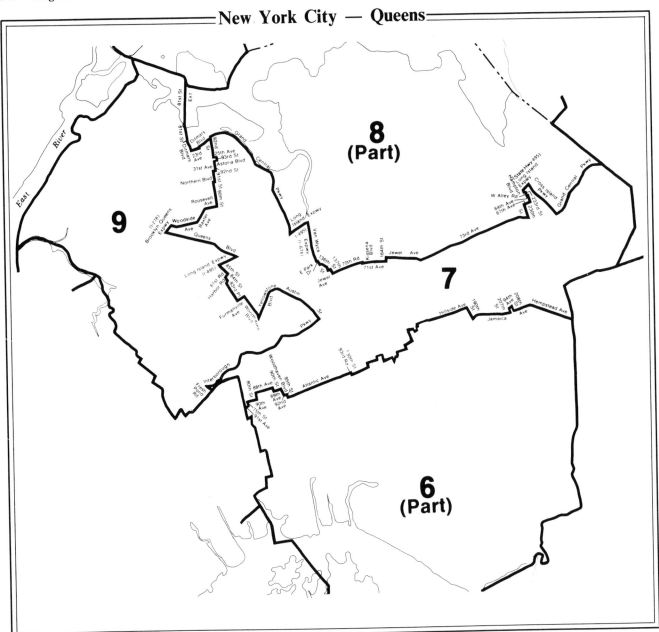

9th District

Western Queens — Astoria, Jackson Heights

The most diverse district in Queens, the melting-pot 9th encompasses old factories, drug-ridden slums, world-class tennis courts and Archie Bunker's home.

Bunker's televised opinions on race, drugs and modern morality generally found wide agreement inside the row houses of Astoria. The neighborhood shown in the "All in the Family" program was on Astoria's Steinway Street.

The proximity of urban decay and impoverished minorities helped push the old district to Richard Nixon by a large margin in 1972, and when Gerald R. Ford carried it in 1976 there was a widespread feeling that it would elect a

Republican to the House after the eventual retirement of veteran conservative Democrat James J. Delaney. The election of a Democrat thus surprised and disappointed many national Republicans. The district further proved its independence by choosing Ronald Reagan over Jimmy Carter in 1980.

Aging industrial loft buildings are clustered in Long Island City and Sunnyside. Former occupants, light manufacturers for the most part, gradually have been moving to more modern facilities in the suburbs. But Long Island City has taken on a new identity as young professionals restore its old living quarters, a development that the blue-collar residents do not always applaud.

Generally liberal Democratic politics prevail in Forest Hills, where affluent Jews and WASPs live in elegant Tudor-style homes. The West Side Tennis Club in Forest

Hills hosted the United States Open Tennis Championships from 1915 until 1977. The Open moved to a refurbished stadium in Flushing Meadow Park in 1978. In the early 1970s Forest Hills displayed its own streak of conservatism, objecting to the construction of public housing within its borders.

The district keeps the same share of whites it had before (82 percent) by expanding north and east. The newly added whites from Astoria balance out the Hispanics and blacks brought in from Jackson Heights.

Until the 1970s Jackson Heights was mostly white and middle-class. Then low-income minorities moved in, many of them from South America. Some of the neighborhoods have deteriorated. Police know Jackson Heights as a cocaine center of the Northeast. Among the whites, Jews and Italians predominate, many of them elderly.

Election Returns

9th District		Democrat		Republican	
1976	President	82,228	(50.5%)	79,869	(49.0%)
	Senate	87,893	(55.6%)	68,814	(43.6%)
	House	125,527	(91.8%)	4,680	(3.4%)
1978	Governor	60,928	(52.1%)	51,894	(44.4%)
	House	67,162	(62.6%)	37,384	(34.9%)
1980	President	57,779	(40.0%)	76,761	(53.1%)
	Senate	71,380	(50.5%)	54,345	(38.5%)
	House	82,380	(65.6%)	41,184	(32.8%)
1982	Governor	65,528	(55.3%)	51,086	(43.1%)
	Senate	74,166	(68.8%)	32,852	(30.5%)
	House	75,286	(73.2%)	20,352	(19.8%)

Demographics

Population: 516,143. **Percent Change from 1970:** -4.5%.

Land Area: 21 square miles. **Population per Square Mile:** 24,578.2.

Counties, 1980 Population: Queens (Pt.) — 516,143.

Cities, 1980 Population: New York (Pt.) — 516,143.

Race and Ancestry: White — 84.1%; Black — 3.7%; American Indian, Eskimo and Aleut — 0.1%; Asian and Pacific Islander — 5.9%. Spanish Origin — 16.6%. English — 1.3%; French — 0.7%; German — 6.9%; Greek — 5.4%; Hungarian — 0.8%; Irish — 7.7%; Italian — 16.1%; Polish — 2.8%; Russian — 1.4%; Ukranian — 0.8%.

Universities, Enrollment: La Guardia Community College, Long Island City — 6,563.

Newspapers, Circulation: *New York Daily News, New York Post* and *The New York Times* circulate in the district.

Commercial Television Stations, Affiliation: Entire district is located in New York ADI.

Industries:

Queens Hospital Center at Elmhurst; Elmhurst; hospital — 3,000. **Standard Motor Products Inc.** (HQ); Long Island City; electrical equipment for internal combustion engines — 1,200. **Swingline Inc.** (HQ); Long Island City; stapling equipment — 1,000. **Broadway Maintenance Corp.** (HQ); Long Island City; special trade contracting, electrical repairing — 700. **Brookfield Clothes Inc.** (HQ); Long Island City; men's suits — 694.

Slattery Associates Inc. (HQ); Maspeth; heavy construction — 600. **Equitable Bag Co. Inc.;** (HQ); Long Island City; paper bags — 550. **Warner-Lambert Co. Inc.** (Consumer Products Group); Long Island City; chewing gum — 544. **Armor Elevator Co. Inc.;** Jackson Heights; elevators — 500. **Carisbrook Industries Inc.** (Longwood Machine Works Div.); Woodside; cotton, tire cord — 500. **I B I Security Service Inc.** (HQ); Long Island City; security services — 500. **Kraftco Corp.** (Breyers Sealtest Ice Cream Div.); Long Island City; ice cream — 500. **Russ Togs Inc.** (Juniorite Div.); Long Island City; general warehousing — 500.

10th District

Central and Southern Brooklyn — Flatbush

The new 10th is a loose descendant of the heavily Jewish Flatbush-based district that sent Democrat Emanuel Celler to Congress for 50 years before his primary loss in 1972. The old district changed dramatically in the 1970s, with Jews moving out and blacks coming to constitute a majority.

The 1982 remap essentially restored the district's earlier ethnic complexion. Map makers shifted black areas in the district's northern half to the two Brooklyn districts designed for black representation. Once again, more than 8 percent of the people in the 10th are white. Jews predominate, although Italians are a significant presence.

The 10th retains its solidly Democratic cast. The territory within the redrawn district favored Jimmy Carter with 68 percent of the vote in 1976; four years later Carter still carried the area by a narrow margin.

Flatbush today is an amalgamation of single family homes, run-down apartment buildings and rooming houses such as the one on Marlboro Street where portions of the motion picture "Sophie's Choice" were filmed. The yeshivas and bagel bakeries along Ocean Parkway testify to the area's ethnic character.

Blue-collar Canarsie and Sheepshead Bay contain a mixture of Italians and Jews. Many residents work in the small factories, turning out plastics and electrical parts. An entirely different breed of Democrat inhabits Park Slope, where the town houses are elegant and the politics liberal.

Election Returns

10th District		Democrat		Republican	
1976	President	105,965	(68.0%)	49,084	(31.5%)
	Senate	112,176	(73.9%)	38,157	(25.1%)
	House	108,272	(79.0%)	25,446	(18.6%)
1978	Governor	66,995	(68.6%)	27,854	(28.5%)
	House	99,203	(80.0%)	20,759	(16.7%)
1980	President	64,034	(49.8%)	56,294	(43.8%)
	Senate	73,699	(59.5%)	38,386	(31.0%)
	House	81,180	(73.9%)	26,723	(24.3%)
1982	Governor	101,381	(67.7%)	46,239	(30.9%)
	Senate	107,226	(80.3%)	25,229	(18.9%)
	House	89,852	(79.2%)	21,726	(19.1%)

Demographics

Population: 513,140. **Percent Change from 1970:** -6.9%.

Land Area: 23 square miles. **Population per Square Mile:** 22,310.4.

Counties, 1980 Population: Kings (Pt.) — 513,140.

Cities, 1980 Population: New York (Pt.) — 513,140.

Race and Ancestry: White — 88.2%; Black — 5.2%; American Indian, Eskimo and Aleut — 0.1%; Asian and Pacific Islander — 2.9%. Spanish Origin — 8.8%. English — 1.5%; German — 1.8%; Greek — 0.9%; Hungarian — 1.2%; Irish — 5.9%; Italian — 17.3%; Polish — 6.6%; Russian — 8.1%.

Newspapers, Circulation: *New York Daily News, New York Post* and *The New York Times* circulate in the district.

Commercial Television Stations, Affiliation: Entire district is located in New York ADI.

Industries:
   Methodist Hospital of Brooklyn Inc.; Brooklyn; hospital — 1,850.

11th District

Northern Brooklyn — Bedford-Stuyvesant

The 11th in its current form was not part of the Legislature's original remap but the fruit of the Justice Department's refusal to accept a single Hispanic-oriented constituency that stretched from Brooklyn to the Lower East Side and East Harlem in Manhattan.

To redress the Justice Department's claim that the first version diluted the voting strength of Brooklyn's black community, map makers removed the Manhattan portions of the 11th. As redrawn a second time for the 1982 election, the 11th combined territory from the old 12th and 14th districts. That made the district 38 percent Hispanic and 47 percent black.

The addition of more blacks turned out to be a piece of good luck for the black who wanted to run for the House in the new district. Two Hispanics also vied for the Democratic nomination, splitting the Hispanic vote. The black won the primary with just under 50 percent of the vote and had only token Republican opposition in the general election.

In the House he succeeded Democrat Frederick W. Richmond, a white millionaire who was forced to resign his seat in 1982 after pleading guilty to charges that included income tax evasion and possession of marijuana.

Brooklyn Heights and Park Slope were removed from the district, taking with them their liberal white residents. The whites remaining — about 30 percent of the population — are not upper middle-class liberals but largely Italian working-class people in old neighborhoods on the edges of Williamsburg and Greenpoint.

Bedford-Stuyvesant is the oldest black section in the 11th. Once a fashionable white area, large parts of Bed-Stuy now resemble the devastated South Bronx. But the area also boasts a modest effort at rejuvenation. In the late 1960s Sen. Robert F. Kennedy helped establish a shopping mall and office complex. International Business Machines Corp. opened a typewriter assembly plant. Still, there is little major industry anywhere in this district; like most of the city, it is mainly residential.

East New York has not enjoyed even a modest revitalization. Until the 1960s this was an Italian and Jewish neighborhood.

But since then low-income blacks and Hispanics have moved there from Bedford-Stuyvesant seeking better housing, and the whites have fled. A small section of overwhelmingly black Brownsville, one of the most blighted areas anywhere in the nation, is in the 11th District.

Election Returns

11th District		Democrat		Republican	
1976	President	88,151	(75.8%)	27,437.	(23.6%)
	Senate	79,033	(73.6%)	26,776	(24.9%)
	House	78,819	(82.0%)	14,022	(14.6%)
1978	Governor	59,864	(72.6%)	20,509	(24.9%)
	House	47,250	(78.2%)	10,258	(17.0%)
1980	President	71,142	(69.7%)	25,844	(25.3%)
	Senate	58,343	(59.0%)	30,387	(30.7%)
	House	63,979	(78.0%)	13,651	(16.6%)
1982	Governor	41,797	(67.7%)	19,063	(30.9%)
	Senate	44,207	(80.3%)	10,401	(18.9%)
	House	39,357	(83.7%)	4,449	(9.5%)

Demographics

Population: 518,165. **Percent Change from 1970:** -26.5%.

Land Area: 15 square miles. **Population per Square Mile:** 34,544.3.

Counties, 1980 Population: Kings (Pt.) — 518,165.

Cities, 1980 Population: New York (Pt.) — 518,165.

Race and Ancestry: White — 29.6%; Black — 47.1%; American Indian, Eskimo and Aleut — 0.2%; Asian and Pacific Islander — 1.0%. Spanish Origin — 38.0%. English — 1.5%; German — 0.8%; Irish — 1.0%; Italian — 5.8%; Polish — 0.5%.

Universities, Enrollment: Long Island University (Brooklyn center), Brooklyn — 8,920; Pratt Institute, Brooklyn — 4,500; St. Joseph's College, Brooklyn — 1,225.

Newspapers, Circulation: *New York Daily News, New York Post* and *The New York Times* circulate in the district.

Commercial Television Stations, Affiliation: Entire district is located in New York ADI.

Industries:
   Brooklyn Cumberland Medical Center; Brooklyn; hospital — 1,500. **J. W. Mays Inc. (HQ);** Brooklyn; department stores — 1,200. **Wyckoff Heights Hospital;** Brooklyn; hospital — 1,200. **Pfizer Inc.;** Brooklyn; pharmaceuticals — 1,070. **Amstar Corp.;** Brooklyn; sugar refinery — 700. **Barouh Eaton Allen Corp. (HQ);** Brooklyn; carbon paper — 600. **Kentile Floors Inc. (HQ);** Brooklyn; vinyl flooring — 500.

12th District

Central Brooklyn — Crown Heights

The 12th is the city's most solidly black district. The new 12th is 80.1 percent black and 10.1 percent Hispanic — and thoroughly Democratic. It is second only to Chicago's 1st District in percentage of blacks. The previous district was just 54 percent black and had lost a third of its population during the 1970s.

The district would have had an even higher black population had the Justice Department not complained that it was being packed with blacks to keep them out of the 11th, designed for Hispanic representation. At the behest of Justice, map makers remolded the 12th substantially. Chunks of Bedford-Stuyvesant and other black neighborhoods were switched into the 11th, pushing the 12th south.

The courts have been the crucible of Brooklyn's black

New York City — Brooklyn

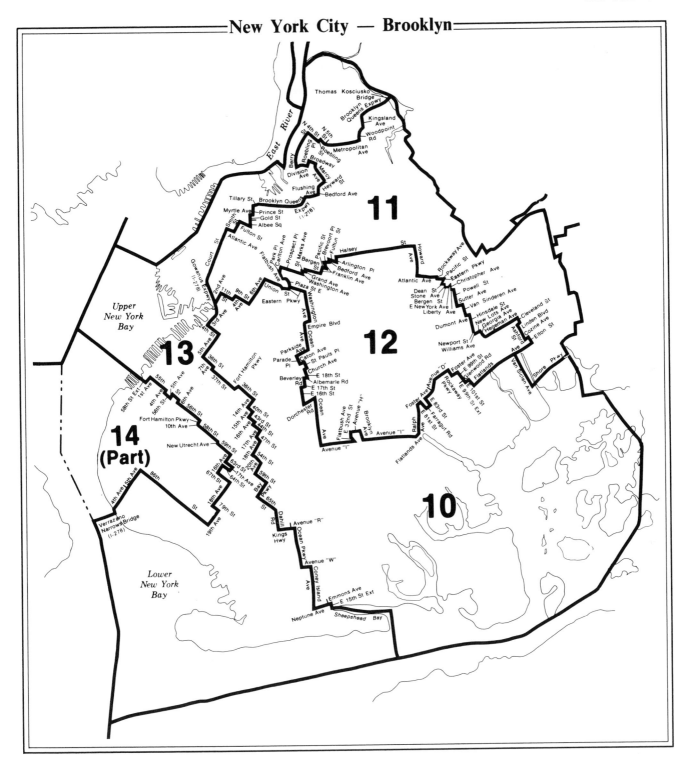

congressional representation. Pressured by the Supreme Court, the Legislature in 1968 made the 12th the city's second black district; the first was the traditional one in Harlem.

Urban blight and poverty characterize most of the 12th, as they do the 11th next door. Devastated slices of black Bedford-Stuyvesant and Brownsville and Hispanic East New York make urban economic survival the one

crucial concern of whoever represents the district. Large public housing projects and a sizable welfare clientele are basic parts of the constituency.

Most of the district's whites come from the northern part of Flatbush, a longstanding middle-class Jewish community in which Brooklyn College is located.

Crown Heights, just north of Flatbush, once contained a large Jewish population. Now it is largely home to blacks and Hispanics, although tightly knit communities of orthodox Jews remain. Run-down in some of its neighborhoods, Crown Heights has been able to achieve a middle-class stability in others.

Ebbets Field, home of the Brooklyn Dodgers, was in Crown Heights. After the Dodgers left for Los Angeles in 1958, an apartment complex replaced the ball park.

Election Returns

12th District		Democrat		Republican	
1976	President	99,093	(72.6%)	36,579	(26.8%)
	Senate	97,325	(75.0%)	30,895	(23.8%)
	House	99,161	(82.7%)	19,552	(16.3%)
1978	Governor	53,091	(72.9%)	18,115	(24.9%)
	House	31,654	(80.7%)	6,607	(16.8%)
1980	President	68,133	(59.6%)	39,400	(34.5%)
	Senate	65,025	(58.9%)	33,868	(30.7%)
	House	74,196	(76.7%)	17,793	(18.4%)
1982	Governor	43,873	(67.7%)	20,009	(30.9%)
	Senate	46,402	(80.3%)	10,918	(18.9%)
	House	44,586	(90.5%)	3,215	(6.5%)

Demographics

Population: 516,983. **Percent Change from 1970:** -12.5%.

Land Area: 11 square miles. **Population per Square Mile:** 46,998.5.

Counties, 1980 Population: Kings (Pt.) — 516,983.

Cities, 1980 Population: New York (Pt.) — 516,983.

Race and Ancestry: White — 12.9%; Black — 80.1%; American Indian, Eskimo and Aleut — 0.2%; Asian and Pacific Islander — 1.7%. Spanish Origin — 10.1%. English — 2.3%; French — 0.7%; Irish — 1.1%; Italian — 1.3%; Polish — 0.7%; Russian — 1.0%.

Universities, Enrollment: Brooklyn College, Brooklyn — 16,691; Downstate Medical Center, Brooklyn — 1,432; Medgar Evers College, Brooklyn — 2,988.

Newspapers, Circulation: *New York Daily News, New York Post* and *The New York Times* circulate in the district.

Commercial Television Stations, Affiliation: Entire district is located in New York ADI.

Industries:
  Kings County Hospital; Brooklyn; hospital — 7,000. **Brookdale Hospital & Medical Center;** Brooklyn; hospital — 3,100. **Kingsbrook Jewish Medical Hospital Center;** Brooklyn; hospital — 2,030. **Jewish Hospital & Medical Center of Brooklyn;** Brooklyn; hospital — 2,000. **Kingsboro Psychiatric Center;** Brooklyn; state psychiatric hospital — 1,800. **St. Mary's Hospital of Brooklyn;** Brooklyn; hospital — 1,100.

13th District

Western and Southern Brooklyn — Bensonhurst

This elongated district reaches north from Brooklyn's Atlantic beaches to the East River waterfront. It is overwhelmingly white. Already believed to have the largest percentage of Jewish residents in the country, the 13th now also includes Williamsburg, center of Hasidic Jewish life in America.

The heart of the district remains in middle-class Bensonhurst, whose Jewish delicatessens and Italian open-air markets signal its ethnic makeup. The Jews generally live in Bensonhurst's apartment buildings, the Italians in its row houses. Brighton Beach, south of Bensonhurst, has become a magnet for Soviet Jews who have been allowed to emigrate. Russian is spoken routinely on its business streets.

Coney Island is the 13th's best known section. At one time New Yorkers of all races and incomes flocked to Coney's beaches, thrill rides and hot dog stands. Now the city's fun center attracts mostly low-income minorities, and the beaches and amusements are run-down. Puerto Ricans, blacks and elderly Jews live in uneasy coexistence.

The district picked up the Brooklyn Navy Yard, once a federal facility and now owned by the city. Some ships are repaired there but light manufacturing firms occupy most of it. Many Brooklyn docks have lost out in competition with newer Southern ports. A Norwegian community, descended from merchant seamen, lives on in otherwise Hispanic Sunset Park.

Brooklyn Heights, where expensive co-ops and town houses abound, displays upper-crust liberalism. Writer Norman Mailer and other celebrities have moved there, lured by the elegant brownstones and the spectacular views of the Lower Manhattan skyline.

Farther north up the East River is the nation's largest concentration of Hasidic Jews. The Hasidim in Williamsburg are an insular community not often involved in politics, but they have been known to favor the more conservative candidates in Democratic primaries, and Ronald Reagan drew surprising support among them. Hispanics are also numerous in Williamsburg. North from there into Greenpoint, Catholic parishes replace the synagogues. Poles and Italians inhabit the neatly kept row houses.

The district is usually Democratic. In 1980 the Democratic Senate candidate won 61 percent of the vote in her unsuccessful race. Jimmy Carter came within 1,000 votes of carrying the 13th that same year.

Election Returns

13th District		Democrat		Republican	
1976	President	101,302	(65.4%)	52,759	(34.0%)
	Senate	106,023	(70.8%)	41,783	(27.9%)
	House	103,542	(77.6%)	26,999	(20.2%)
1978	Governor	75,610	(65.4%)	37,348	(32.3%)
	House	65,765	(77.1%)	18,538	(21.7%)
1980	President	65,323	(50.4%)	55,585	(42.9%)
	Senate	73,468	(60.6%)	38,131	(31.5%)
	House	77,403	(69.5%)	30,356	(27.2%)
1982	Governor	75,888	(67.7%)	34,611	(30.9%)
	Senate	80,263	(80.3%)	18,885	(18.9%)
	House	68,549	(80.5%)	14,257	(16.8%)

Demographics

Population: 518,906. **Percent Change from 1970:** -9.8%.

Land Area: 17 square miles. **Population per Square Mile:** 30,523.9.

Counties, 1980 Population: Kings (Pt.) — 518,906.

Cities, 1980 Population: New York (Pt.) — 518,906.

Race and Ancestry: White — 82.2%; Black — 7.2%; American Indian, Eskimo and Aleut — 0.1%; Asian and Pacific Islander — 2.3%.

Spanish Origin — 15.9%. English — 1.5%; German — 1.4%; Greek — 0.7%; Hungarian — 2.9%; Irish — 2.8%; Italian — 24.3%; Polish — 6.9%; Russian — 4.9%.

Universities, Enrollment: Brooklyn Law School, Brooklyn — 1,169; Kingsborough Community College, Brooklyn — 8,425; New York City Technical College, Brooklyn — 13,199; Polytechnic Institute of New York, Brooklyn — 4,747; St. Francis College, Brooklyn — 2,996.

Newspapers, Circulation: *Brooklyn Daily Bulletin* (m), Brooklyn — 3,080; *The Daily Challenge* (mS) — 72,500. *New York Daily News, New York Post* and *The New York Times* circulate in the district.

Commercial Television Stations, Affiliation: Entire district is located in New York ADI.

Military Installations: Brooklyn Naval Station, Brooklyn — 611; Fort Hamilton, Brooklyn — 1.068.

Industries:
Maimonides Medical Center Inc.; Brooklyn; hospital — 2,900. **Long Island College Hospital;** Brooklyn; hospital — 2,230. **Watchtower Bible & Tract Society of New York** (HQ); Brooklyn; periodicals publishing — 2,210. **Coney Island Hospital;** Brooklyn; hospital — 2,100. **Coastal Dry Dock & Repair Corp.;** Brooklyn; ship repairing — 1,000.

Northeast Marine Terminal Co.; Brooklyn; marine cargo handling — 900. **Peerless Importers Inc.;** Brooklyn; wine, liquor wholesaling — 800. **Triple A Maintenance Corp.;** Brooklyn; janitorial services — 800. **Williamsburg Steel Products Co.;** Brooklyn; hollow metal doors, elevator cabs — 620. **Marsel Mirror & Glass Products;** Brooklyn; mirrors — 520. **Intensive Security Guards Inc.;** Brooklyn; security services — 500.

14th District

Staten Island; Southwest Brooklyn

Politically as well as demographically, Staten Island has been moving in a different direction from the rest of New York City. After the Verrazano Narrows Bridge opened in 1964, hordes of Brooklyn ethnics surged across in search of suburban greenery. While the city's population dropped 10.4 percent in the 1970s, Staten Island's grew 19.2 percent as suburban developments replaced farm land. In 1980, while the rest of the city voted Democratic for president and the U.S. Senate, Staten Island supported Republican candidates for both offices. Democrats here display little party loyalty.

The remap makes the 14th District politically more homogeneous than it had been. Staten Island provides 68 percent of the vote, but, as in the past, it is too small for a full district of its own and has to share its congressional representation with residents of one of the other boroughs. During the 1970s it was linked with liberal Lower Manhattan. But the new map ties Staten Island to Brooklyn's Bay Ridge, a conservative community culturally similar to the island itself.

With its row houses and brownstones, Bay Ridge displays a more urban character than Staten Island. Overwhelmingly white and largely Italian, Bay Ridge also has a distinctive Scandinavian presence.

On Staten Island, the few blacks (7 percent) and Hispanics (5 percent) cluster in the north near the water. They live in low-income housing in such places as Stapleton and Port Richmond. Generally, incomes are higher south of the Staten Island Expressway. In the large homes of Todt Hill and Emerson Hill one can find many registered Republi-

cans. The South Shore and the Tottenville area are more middle income.

Many Staten Islanders work in factories and container ports that line the Kill Van Kull and the Arthur Kill. Others commute to Manhattan on the renowned ferry, whose 400 percent price increase during the 1970s lifted its cost to a quarter. The island has many of the growing pains of expanding suburbs as homeowners fight developers over land use and sewer hookups.

Election Returns

14th District		Democrat		Republican	
1976	President	72,736	(46.8%)	81,884	(52.7%)
	Senate	81,013	(53.4%)	69,561	(45.8%)
	House	92,072	(65.0%)	35,270	(24.9%)
1978	Governor	55,640	(47.7%)	55,918	(47.9%)
	House	57,708	(57.7%)	35,607	(35.6%)
1980	President	55,789	(36.1%)	87,135	(56.4%)
	Senate	62,428	(39.8%)	74,643	(47.5%)
	House	54,894	(38.1%)	78,246	(54.3%)
1982	Governor	80,086	(56.3%)	59,636	(41.9%)
	Senate	89,112	(68.5%)	40,245	(30.9%)
	House	51,728	(42.9%)	67,626	(56.1%)

Demographics

Population: 515,863. **Percent Change from 1970:** 8.7%.

Land Area: 64 square miles. **Population per Square Mile:** 8,060.4.

Counties, 1980 Population: Kings (Pt.) — 163,742; Richmond — 352,121.

Cities, 1980 Population: New York (Pt.) — 515,863.

Race and Ancestry: White — 90.0%; Black — 5.1%; American Indian, Eskimo and Aleut — 0.1%; Asian and Pacific Islander — 2.5%. Spanish Origin — 6.6%. English — 1.7%; German — 2.5%; Greek — 1.6%; Irish — 9.1%; Italian — 30.0%; Norwegian — 1.6%; Polish — 2.2%; Russian — 1.0%.

Universities, Enrollment: College of Staten Island, Staten Island — 10,608; Wagner College, Staten Island — 2,454.

Newspapers, Circulation: *Staten Island Advance* (eS), Staten Island — 73,119. *New York Daily News, New York Post* and *The New York Times* circulate in the district.

Commercial Television Stations, Affiliation: Entire district is located in New York ADI.

Industries:
Staten Island Development Center; Staten Island; state psychiatric hospital — 3,100. **Lutheran Medical Center Corp.;** Brooklyn; hospital — 2,400. **St. Vincent's Medical Center;** Staten Island; hospital — 2,130. **Staten Island Hospital;** Staten Island; hospital — 1,400. **Bayley Seton Hospital;** Staten Island; hospital — 1,070. **South Beach Psychiatric Center;** Staten Island; state psychiatric hospital — 1,000. **Procter & Gamble Mfg. Co.** (Port Ivory Div.); Staten Island; soap, shortening — 925.

15th District

Manhattan — East Side

In the 1930s the "Silk Stocking District" on Manhattan's East Side was a bastion of aristocratic Republicans who disdained the New Deal. In the early 1980s a mere 16 percent of the district was Republican by registration. The East Side may remain a place of elegant town houses and chauffeured limousines, but it harbors great sympathy for the downtrodden, at least from a distance: It is where the phrase "limousine liberal" was born. The 15th is the smallest district in the nation in land area, seven square miles, and the nation's most densely populated — 73,772.7 people per square mile. Its area is 280 times smaller than Delaware.

Signs of the area's changing political climate were evident in 1968 when Edward I. Koch, later New York's mayor, became the first Democrat to win the seat since 1936. George McGovern carried the district handily in 1972, as did Jimmy Carter in 1976 and 1980.

The 15th offers surprising diversity despite its affluence. Trendy discos and chic stores cater to its population of young single professionals. The Turtle Bay area around the United Nations contains many foreign missions. There is still some Hungarian and German influence in the old Yorkville section just west of Gracie Mansion, the mayor's residence along the East River.

The 15th moved south to make up a population deficit and further enriched its ethnic mix. The district takes in Chinatown, Little Italy and the Lower East Side, which is now heavily Hispanic. Nevertheless, the district retains an overwhelming white majority, 71 percent. The one thing the district does not have is a sizable middle class. Most of the people who are not rich are poor.

Apart from the deteriorated Lower East Side, however, this district has seen an economic surge that the current recession has failed to stop. Office tower construction is crowding midtown Manhattan, threatening to block the sun entirely from its streets. While some corporate headquarters have left town, myriad consulting and other service-related firms have moved in to replace them, giving midtown Manhattan a reason for cautious optimism that few would have expressed a decade earlier.

Election Returns

15th District		Democrat		Republican	
1976	President	118,721	(64.7%)	62,931	(34.3%)
	Senate	126,361	(71.2%)	46,356	(26.1%)
	House	115,228	(74.1%)	29,516	(19.0%)
1978	Governor	89,589	(69.1%)	36,486	(28.1%)
	House	58,302	(47.1%)	56,396	(45.6%)
1980	President	94,130	(51.7%)	64,562	(35.5%)
	Senate	122,155	(69.3%)	27,032	(15.3%)
	House	74,047	(45.9%)	83,900	(52.0%)
1982	Governor	91,177	(64.9%)	47,239	(33.6%)
	Senate	108,957	(80.6%)	24,673	(18.2%)
	House	55,483	(44.8%)	66,262	(53.6%)

Demographics

Population: 516,409. **Percent Change from 1970:** -3.2%.

Land Area: 7 square miles. **Population per Square Mile:** 73,772.7.

Counties, 1980 Population: New York (Pt.) — 516,409.

Cities, 1980 Population: New York (Pt.) — 516,409.

Race and Ancestry: White — 77.3%; Black — 5.2%; American Indian, Eskimo and Aleut — 0.1%; Asian and Pacific Islander — 10.3%.

Spanish Origin — 14.6%. English — 5.1%; French — 1.2%; German — 4.0%; Greek — 0.7%; Hungarian — 1.5%; Irish — 4.8%; Italian — 4.9%; Polish — 2.9%; Russian — 5.6%; Scottish — 0.5%; Ukranian — 0.6%.

Universities, Enrollment: Berkeley-Claremont School, New York — 785; Bernard M. Baruch College, New York — 14,592; College of Optometry, New York — 261; City University of New York Graduate School and University Center, New York — 3,047; Hunter College, New York — 17,510; Interboro Institute, New York — 515; Katharine Gibbs School, New York — 598; Laboratory Institute of Merchandising, New York — 275; Mannes College of Music, New York — 161; Marymount Manhattan College, New York — 2,249; New York School of Interior Design, New York — 782; School of Visual Arts, New York — 5,144; Tobe-Coburn School for Fashion Careers, New York — 218; Touro College, New York — 1,958; The Wood School, New York — 450.

Newspapers, Circulation: *New York Daily News* (mS), Manhattan — 1,539,481; *New York Post* (e), Manhattan — 646,854; *The New York Times* (mS), Manhattan — 894,687; *The News World* (mS), Manhattan — 72,510. Foreign language newspapers: *China Post* (Chinese), Manhattan — 22,700; *China Tribune* (Chinese), Manhattan — 9,854; *Jewish Daily Forward* (Yiddish), Manhattan — 35,000; *National Herald* (Greek), Manhattan — 20,000; *Novoye Russkoye Slovo* (Russian), Manhattan — 29,087; *The Reimei News* (Chinese), Manhattan — 20,000; *United Journal* (Chinese), Manhattan — 7,035.

Commercial Television Stations, Affiliation: WNBC-TV, New York (NBC); WNEW-TV, New York (None); WOR-TV, New York (None); WPIX, New York (None). Entire district is located in New York ADI. *(For other New York stations, see 17th District.)*

Industries:

Metropolitan Life Insurance Co. (HQ); New York; life, accident, casualty insurance — 8,730. **R. H. Macy & Co. Inc.** (HQ); New York; department stores — 6,570. **Equitable Life Assurance Society** (HQ); New York; life, accident insurance — 5,800. **Metro North Commuter Railroad Co.** (HQ); New York; railroad operations —5,500. **New York Life Insurance Co.** (HQ); New York; life, health insurance — 5,000.

J. C. Penney Co. Inc. (HQ); New York; department store chain — 4,500. **Blue Cross & Blue Shield of Greater New York** (HQ); New York; health insurance — 4,180. **Beth Israel Medical Center** (HQ); New York; hospital — 3,970. **Mobil Corp.** (HQ); New York; petroleum production — 3,500. **National Broadcasting Co. Inc.** (HQ); New York; television, radio broadcasting — 3,500. **New York News Inc.** (HQ); New York; newspaper publishing, radio, television broadcasting — 3,500. **Society of New York Hospital Inc.** (HQ); New York; hospital — 3,500. **B. Altman & Co. Inc.** (HQ); New York; department stores — 3,000. **Prudential Building Maintenance** (HQ); New York; janitorial services — 3,000. **Union Carbide Corp.** (HQ); New York; chemicals, carbon products, batteries — 3,000. **CBS Inc.** (HQ); New York; television, radio broadcasting, phonograph records — 2,900. **McGraw-Hill Inc.** (HQ); New York; book, magazine publishing — 2,898. **Charles of the Ritz Group Ltd.;** New York; cosmetics — 2,700.

Simplicity Pattern Co. Inc. (HQ); New York; garment sewing patterns — 2,500. **Time Inc.** (HQ); New York; magazine, book publishing — 2,500. **Memorial Sloan-Kettering Cancer Center;** New York; hospital — 2,450. **Young & Rubicam Inc.** (HQ); New York; advertising agency — 2,320. **Lenox Hill Hospital;** New York; hospital — 2,300. **American Broadcasting Companies** (HQ); New York; television, radio broadcasting, publishing — 2,000. **The Associated Press Inc.** (HQ); New York; news service — 2,000. **Avon Products Inc.** (HQ); New York; cosmetics, jewelry — 2,000. **Bankers Trust Co.** (HQ); New York; banking — 2,000. **Mann, Judd & Landau** (HQ); New York; accounting services — 2,000. **Marsh & McLennan Companies** (HQ); New York; insurance brokerage — 2,000. **Owners Maintenance Corp.;** New York; janitorial services — 2,000. **Pan American World Airways Inc.** (HQ); New York; commercial airline — 2,000. **Smith Barney, Harris Upman Co. Inc.** (HQ); New York; securities dealers — 2,000.

Exxon Corp. (HQ); New York; petroleum production, refining — 1,900. **Aberdeen Mfg. Corp.** (HQ); New York; curtains, housewares — 1,800. **Gotham Building Maintenance** (HQ); New York; janitorial services — 1,800. **Hilton Hotels Corp.** (The Waldorf Astoria); New York;

hotel — 1,800. **News Group Publication Inc.** (HQ); New York; newspaper, periodical publishing — 1,800. **Pfizer Inc.** (HQ); New York; pharmaceuticals, hospital products, cosmetics — 1,700. **Hilton Hotel Corp.**; (New York Hilton Hotel); New York; hotel — 1,600. **International Paper Co.** (HQ); New York; packaging materials, paper — 1,600. **Teachers Insurance & Annuity Assn. of America** (HQ); New York; life insurance — 1,600. **Arcade Cleaning Contractors** (HQ); New York; janitorial services — 1,570. **American Argo Corp.** (Tulip Tops Div. - HQ); New York; women's knitwear — 1,500. **American Home Products Corp.** (Wyeth Laboratories - HQ); New York; drugs, biological products — 1,500. **American Yvette Co. Inc.** (HQ); New York; management services — 1,500. **Harcourt Brace Jovanovich Inc.** (HQ); New York; book publishing — 1,500.

The New York Times Co. Inc. (HQ); New York; publishing; radio, television broadcasting — 1,500. **Benton & Bowles Inc.** (HQ); New York; advertising agency — 1,440. **Ballantine Books Inc.**; New York; book publishing — 1,400. **Bergdorf Goodman Inc.** (HQ); New York; women's clothing stores — 1,400. **Cabrini Medical Center** (HQ); New York; hospital — 1,400. **Coopers & Lybrand** (HQ); New York; accounting services — 1,400. **Esso Standard Libya Inc.**; New York; petroleum production — 1,400. **Westin Hotel Co.**; New York; hotel — 1,350. **Guardian Life Insurance Co. of America**; New York; life, health insurance — 1,300. **International Telephone & Telegraph Corp.** (HQ); New York; telecommunications, electronic equipment — 1,300. **Mutual Life Insurance Co. of New York** (HQ); New York; life, health insurance — 1,300. **Grey Advertising Inc.** (HQ); New York; advertising agency — 1,250. **Philip Morris Inc.** (HQ); New York; cigarettes, beer, soft drinks — 1,250. **Bristol-Myers Co. Inc.** (HQ); New York; pharmaceutical, medical, cosmetic products — 1,200.

Colgate-Palmolive Co. (HQ); New York; soaps, cleansers, toiletries — 1,200. **General Electric Technical Service Inc.**; New York; repair services — 1,200. **The Hertz Corp.** (HQ); New York; auto, truck rental — 1,200. **Ohrbachs Inc.** (HQ); New York; women's clothing stores — 1,200. **Sterling Drug Inc.** (HQ); New York; household cleansers, toiletries, drugs — 1,200. **C. I. T. Financial Corp.** (HQ); New York; consumer, industrial financing — 1,100. **Doyle Dane Bernbach International Inc.** (HQ); New York; advertising agency — 1,100. **Ogilvy & Mather International** (HQ); New York; advertising agency — 1,100. **Joseph E. Seagram & Sons.** (HQ); New York; distillery — 1,100. **Arthur Young & Co.** (HQ); New York; accounting services — 1,100. **Knoll International Inc.** (HQ); New York; office furniture — 1,080. **Arthur Andersen & Co.**; New York; accounting, auditing services — 1,050. **Ayerst International Inc.**; New York; pharmaceutical preparations — 1,000. **Citicorp** (HQ); New York; banking — 1,000.

Consolidated Rail Corp.; New York; railroad regional office — 1,000. **General Mills Inc.** (David Crystal Div.); New York; administrative offices — 1,000. **W. R. Grace & Co.** (Baker & Taylor Div.); New York; wholesale book distributing — 1,000. **M. Lowenstein Corp.** (HQ); New York; fabric — 1,000. **Macmillan Inc.** (HQ); New York; book publishing — 1,000. **Revlon Inc.** (HQ); New York; cosmetics, perfumes — 1,000. **Target Sportswear Inc.** (Benton Limited Div. - HQ); New York; men's, women's coats — 1,000. **J. Walter Thompson Co.** (HQ); New York; advertising agency — 1,000. **Ziff Corp.** (HQ); New York; periodicals publishing — 1,000. **Holmes Protection Inc.** (HQ); New York; security services — 950. **A S A G Inc.**; New York; industrial organic chemicals, medical chemicals, pesticides — 930. **American Brands Inc.** (American Tobacco Co. Div. - HQ); New York; tobacco — 900. **Batten, Barton, Durstine & Osborn Inc.** (HQ); New York; advertising agency — 900. **Conde Nast Publications Inc.** (HQ); New York; magazine publishing — 900.

Ernst & Whinney; New York; accounting services — 900. **Ferlin Service Industries Inc.**; New York; janitorial services — 900. **John C. Mandel Security Bureau Inc.** (HQ); New York; security services — 900. **PRC Harris Inc.**; New York; engineering services — 900. **Touche Ross & Co.** (HQ); New York; accounting services — 900. **W. R. Grace & Co. Inc.** (HQ); New York; chemicals, fertilizers — 850. **Eastman Kodak Co.**; New York; administrative offices — 800. **Empire Speedy Messenger Service**; New York; messenger services — 800. **Lever Bros. Co.** (HQ); New York; detergents, toiletries — 800. **L T R Holding Corp.** (HQ); New York; watches, clocks — 800. **PLX Group Inc.**; New York; holding company — 800. **John Wiley & Sons Inc.** (HQ); New York; textbook publishing — 800. **Warner Communications Inc.** (HQ); New York; records, tapes, music publishing, movie production — 800.

N. W. Ayer ABH International Inc. (HQ); New York; advertising agency — 750.

Ted Bates Worldwide Inc. (HQ); New York; advertising agency — 750. **Dancer-Fitzgerald-Sample Inc.** (HQ); New York; advertising agency — 750. **Penntech Papers Inc.**; New York; uncoated paper — 750. **Home Box Office Inc.**; New York; cable television service — 750. **USI Credit Corp.**; New York; finance company — 717. **RCA Corp.** (HQ); New York; televisions, phonograph records; television, radio broadcasting — 708. **M R A Associates Inc.** (HQ); New York; security services — 700. **Main Hurdman** (HQ); New York; accounting services — 700. **National Distillers & Chemical Corp.** (HQ); New York; alcoholic beverages — 700. **Newsweek Inc.** (HQ); New York; magazine, book publishing — 700. **RKO General Inc.** (HQ); New York; radio, television broadcasting — 700. **Rockefeller Center Inc.** (HQ); New York; real estate management — 700. **Skadden, Arps, Slate, Meagher & Flom** (HQ); New York; law firm — 700.

J. P. Stevens & Co. Inc. (HQ); New York; apparel fabrics, home furnishings — 700. **United Artists Corp.** (HQ); New York; motion picture production — 700. **Bell Security Inc.** (HQ); New York; security services — 675. **Tiffany & Co.** (HQ); New York; jewelry, silverware retailing, manufacturing — 675. **Trans World Corp.** (HQ); New York; commercial airline — 671. **Galbreath-Ruffin Corp.** (HQ); New York; real estate management — 650. **Temco Service Industries Inc.** (HQ); New York; janitorial services — 650. **Toshoku America Inc.**; New York; import-export operations — 650. **United Merchants & Manufacturers Inc.** (HQ); New York; fabrics — 650. **Compton Advertising Inc.** (HQ); New York; advertising agency — 640. **Kaye, Scholer, Fierman, Hays & Handler** (HQ); New York; law firm — 640. **Pat Fashions Industries**; New York; women's shirts wholesaling — 640. **Alitalia Air Lines**; New York; commercial airline — 626.

Caltex Petroleum Corp. (HQ); New York; petroleum production, refining — 623. **Varig Brazilian Airlines**; New York; commercial airline — 602. **Blyth Eastman Paine Webber Inc.** (HQ); New York; investment banking — 600. **Celanese Corp.** (HQ); New York; synthetic fibers — 600. **William Esty Co. Inc.**; New York; advertising agency — 600. **Glenville Lingerie Corp.** (HQ); New York; women's underwear — 600. **Harper & Row Publishers Inc.** (HQ); New York; publishing — 600. **J M S Mfg. Corp.**; New York; men's, boys' clothing — 600. **Loews Corp.** (HQ); New York; casualty, life insurance, cigarettes, hotels, movie theaters — 600. **Space Control Corp.**; New York; inventory control services — 600. **Sperry & Hutchinson Co.** (HQ); New York; household furniture; trading stamp services — 600. **Squibb Corp.** (HQ); New York; pharmaceuticals, hospital products, gum, candy — 600. **Tishman Real Estate & Construction Co.**; New York; general contracting — 600.

Val Mode Lingerie Inc. (HQ); New York; women's underwear — 600. **Allied Stores Marketing Corp.** (HQ); New York; general merchandise wholesaling — 590. **Bowery Savings Bank** (HQ); New York; banking — 587. **Capitol Messenger Service**; New York; messenger services — 578. **The Sheraton Corp.** (Sheraton Center); New York; hotel — 575. **Trust House Forte Inc.**; New York; hotel — 570. **B T Credit Co. Inc.**; New York; credit card service — 550. **Montrose Realty Corp.**; New York; real estate managers — 550. **Gold Mills Inc.**; New York; synthetic fabric — 530. **Marsteller Inc.** (Burson-Marsteller); New York; public relations — 526. **The Sheraton Corp.** (New York Sheraton Hotel); New York; hotel — 525. **The Roosevelt Hotel**; New York; hotel — 512.

American Building Maintenance Co.; New York; janitorial services — 500. **Burlington Industries Inc.** (Catlin Farish Co. Div.); New York; administrative offices — 500. **Chartcom Inc.** (HQ); New York; radio broadcasting — 500. **Columbia Pictures Industries Inc.** (HQ); New York; motion picture production, coin-operated machines, broadcasting — 500. **Correspondent Resources Inc.**; New York; consulting services — 500. **Diamond International Corp.** (HQ); New York; packaging materials — 500. **Educational Broadcasting Corp.** (HQ); New York; television broadcasting — 500. **Feature Ring Co. Inc.** (HQ); New York; gold rings — 500. **Formfit Rogers Inc.** (HQ); New York; women's underwear — 500. **GAF Corp.** (HQ); New York; building materials, chemicals, photographic supplies — 500. **Graphic Rehabilitation Corp.**; New York; carpentry — 500. **Greater New York Mutual Insurance Co.** (HQ); New York; mutual insurance — 500. **Hotel St. Moritz Inc.**; New York; hotel — 500. **Management Safeguards Inc.** (HQ); New York; management consulting services — 500.

McCann-Erickson Inc. (HQ); New York; advertising agency —
500. **Mego International Inc.** (HQ); New York; toys — 500. **Milliken
& Co.** (HQ); New York; fabric — 500. **Nabisco Brands Inc.;** New
York; margerine, cookies, crackers — 500. **Page Boy Inc.;** New York;
radio paging service — 500. **Paul Weiss, Rifkind, Wharton & Garrison;** New York; law firm — 500. **Penn Industries Inc.** (HQ); New York;
freight car loading — 500. **Penn Protective Service Inc.;** New York;
security services — 500. **Petrocelli Clothes Inc.** (HQ); New York;
men's suits — 500. **Proskauer, Rose, Goetz & Mendelsohn;** New York;
law firm — 500. **Random House Inc.** (HQ); New York; book publishing
— 500. **Schenley Industries Inc.** (HQ); New York; liquor, wine — 500.
Wells Rich Greene Inc. (HQ); New York; advertising agency — 500.

16th District

Manhattan — Harlem

Created in 1944 as New York's first black district, the
16th has seen its black majority eroded somewhat by redistricting. A large population decline in the 1970s forced it
to expand north to the tip of Manhattan, taking in many
Hispanics.

After the 1972 remap the black share of the population
stood at 58.7 percent. In the new 16th, this share dwindled
to 48.5 percent, with Hispanics composing more than a
third. The district has had only two representatives, both
black, since it was created in 1944; the first was the legendary Adam Clayton Powell Jr.

Defense of social programs, both national and local, is
the first priority for any Harlem politician. The city's budget austerity plans have drawn the wrath of Harlem's community groups and created friction between the incumbent
and City Hall.

In the 19th century, Harlem contained the large homes
of wealthy whites. Later it attracted a Jewish community
from the Lower East Side. But after World War I, blacks
began arriving from the South in great numbers, attracted
by jobs and a large stock of low-rent housing. Musicians
such as Cab Calloway and Duke Ellington and writers such
as James Baldwin and Ralph Ellison made it the center of
American black cultural life. Clergymen such as Powell,
who succeeded his father as pastor at the huge Abyssinian
Baptist Church, influenced black opinion around the country.

Harlem's crime and drug problems are well known. Its
central business district along 125th Street is seedy. Polo
Ground Towers and other low-income projects house many
of the residents. The Sugar Hill neighborhood, once the
elegant address of prominent black professionals, has faded
now that blacks have legal and financial access to housing
in other parts of the metropolitan area.

East Harlem, Italian until mid-century, produced one
of the most controversial House members of the 1940s in
Vito Marcantonio, a fiery liberal renowned for his par-
liamentary skill. Today East Harlem has the largest population of Puerto Ricans outside of Puerto Rico. Beneath the
elevated railroad tracks on Park Avenue is La Marquetta,
an open retail market; its stalls sell everything from plan-
tains to pinafores.

West of Harlem, across Morningside Park, lies Columbia University. Columbia's violent student revolt in 1968
was sparked by the university's plans to build a gymnasium
in the park and share its facilities with Harlem residents.

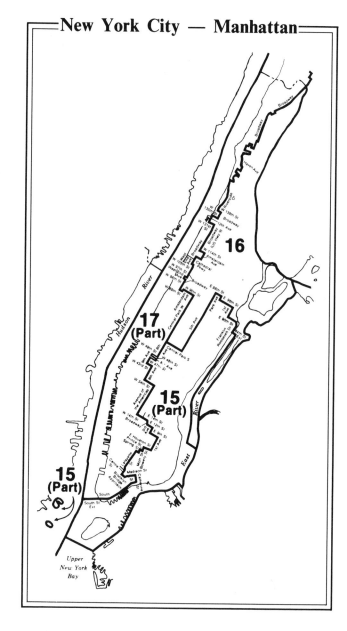

New York City — Manhattan

Today Columbia largely remains aloof from the black community.

The 16th's new Hispanic areas at the northern end of
Manhattan lie east of Broadway in the Washington
Heights and Inwood sections. Many of the residents come
from South America; a substantial number are illegal
aliens.

Election Returns

16th District		Democrat		Republican	
1976	President	129,187	(82.3%)	26,088	(16.6%)
	Senate	116,148	(79.8%)	24,591	(16.9%)
	House	116,199	(91.8%)	6,121	(4.8%)
1978	Governor	83,308	(81.3%)	16,663	(16.3%)
	House	77,335	(91.8%)	5,063	(6.0%)

16th District		Democrat		Republican	
1980	President	108,892	(74.7%)	24,017	(16.5%)
	Senate	97,946	(69.3%)	21,675	(15.3%)
	House	112,752	(90.4%)	7,706	(6.2%)
1982	Governor	86,258	(85.9%)	12,146	(12.1%)
	Senate	73,609	(89.4%)	7,455	(9.1%)
	House	76,626	(97.5%)	—	

Demographics

Population: 516,405. **Percent Change from 1970:** -16.7%.

Land Area: 8 square miles. **Population per Square Mile:** 64,550.6.

Counties, 1980 Population: New York (Pt.) — 516,405.

Cities, 1980 Population: New York (Pt.) — 516,405.

Race and Ancestry: White — 24.5%; Black — 48.5%; American Indian, Eskimo and Aleut — 0.3%; Asian and Pacific Islander — 1.5%. Spanish Origin — 37.9%. English — 1.5%; German — 1.2%; Greek — 0.7%; Irish — 1.4%; Italian — 1.0%; Polish — 0.6%; Russian — 0.9%.

Universities, Enrollment: Boricua College, New York — 869; City College, New York — 12,341; Columbia University, New York — 17,119; Jewish Theological Seminary of America, New York — 475; Mount Sinai School of Medicine, New York — 453; New York College of Podiatric Medicine, New York — 453; Teachers College — Columbia University, New York — 4,687; Yeshiva University, New York — 4,262.

Newspapers, Circulation: *New York Daily News*, New York *News World*, *New York Post* and *The New York Times* circulate in the district. Foreign language newspaper: *Il Progresso Italo-Americano* (Italian), Manhattan — 66,444.

Commercial Television Stations, Affiliation: Entire district is located in New York ADI.

Industries:
Presbyterian Hospital of New York; New York; hospital — 6,000.
The Mount Sinai Hospital; New York; hospital — 5,000.

17th District

West Side Manhattan; Part of the Bronx

The West Side story is one of Byzantine politics and unmitigated liberalism. Some of the most active members of the district's aging Jewish community have lifelong roots in left-wing politics, and the one-quarter of the district that is black and Hispanic reinforces that tradition. The "reform" wing of the party long ago won its fight with the Tammany Hall regulars here, so the factional arguments are waged among the various Democratic clubs.

The West Side has been upgraded significantly from its slum condition in the late 1940s. In recent years its roomy old apartments have attracted those tired of the cramped and more expensive quarters closer to the East River. The Clinton section, which runs from 37th Street up to 57th and from 8th Ave. to the Hudson, can hardly be called "Hell's Kitchen," as it was in the Depression. Central Park West contains some of the most graceful apartment buildings in the city. The century-old Dakota is popular among celebrities; former Beatle John Lennon resided there until his 1980 assassination at its front door.

Many more unknown performers and artists live in the district, waiting tables and hoping for a break. Although

the Broadway theaters and most of the city's cultural institutions are within the 15th's boundaries, the 17th has the Lincoln Center for the Performing Arts in its territory.

Above the Upper West Side, the 17th threads along the Hudson and includes the parts of Inwood and Washington Heights west of Broadway. Jews, many of them elderly, live here, and there are large numbers of Puerto Ricans.

In the 1970s the district extended into the Bronx to include Riverdale, that borough's one remaining center of old-fashioned elegance. Due to the remap, the Bronx plays a far greater political role in the 17th than it did during the 1970s. To make up population deficits, the 17th was moved farther into the northern part of the Bronx to Williamsbridge, a middle-class black section.

The 17th also dropped south to cover Greenwich Village and the Wall Street area. The Village's bohemian culture has not been diluted by the upper-income people who have moved in and made it fashionable during the 1960s and 1970s. The Village was once an Italian political stronghold (it borders on Manhattan's Little Italy) and Carmine DeSapio, the last powerful Tammany Hall boss in the city during the 1950s, lived in the Village in retirement. Local politics in the 1980s are a far cry from the DeSapio era; gays are a more important political faction than any European ethnic group. One thing that unites many of the strands in this part of the district, however, is opposition to Westway, the proposed interstate highway slated to be built nearby.

Few people live around Wall Street, but a large residential-office complex being built on an adjacent landfill in the Hudson will change that. Under construction next to the World Trade Center, Battery Park City will have 16,000 living units.

Election Returns

17th District		Democrat		Republican	
1976	President	131,226	(72.2%)	48,786	(26.8%)
	Senate	128,523	(74.0%)	40,417	(23.3%)
	House	114,009	(76.5%)	27,952	(18.8%)
1978	Governor	75,429	(74.4%)	22,632	(22.3%)
	House	74,520	(70.9%)	25,575	(24.3%)
1980	President	104,832	(62.1%)	47,241	(28.0%)
	Senate	107,321	(66.5%)	31,765	(19.7%)
	House	85,094	(63.4%)	40,274	(30.0%)
1982	Governor	116,939	(74.7%)	35,989	(23.0%)
	Senate	122,320	(84.6%)	79,765	(13.7%)
	House	113,172	(85.0%)	19,928	(15.0%)

Demographics

Population: 516,239. **Percent Change from 1970:** 0.3%.

Land Area: 13 square miles. **Population per Square Mile:** 39,710.7.

Counties, 1980 Population: Bronx (Pt.) — 120,768; New York (Pt.) — 395,471.

Cities, 1980 Population: New York (Pt.) — 516,239.

Race and Ancestry: White — 73.0%; Black — 15.8%; American Indian, Eskimo and Aleut — 0.2%; Asian and Pacific Islander — 3.4%. Spanish Origin — 15.5%. English — 4.0%; French — 0.7%; German — 4.1%; Greek — 0.9%; Hungarian — 1.1%; Irish — 5.2%; Italian — 5.5%; Polish — 3.0%; Russian — 5.6%; Ukranian — 0.6%.

Universities, Enrollment: Bank Street College of Education, New York — 596; Barnard College, New York — 2,524; Borough of Manhattan Community College, New York — 8,568; College of Insurance, New York — 1,944; College of Mount Saint Vincent, Riverdale — 1,226; Columbia University *(see 16th District)*; Cooper Union, New York — 871; Fashion Institute of Technology, New York — 9,819; Fordham University *(see 19th District)*; General Theological Seminary, New York — 186; Germain School of Photography, New York — 264; Hebrew Union College - Jewish Institute of Religion, New York — 147; John Jay College of Criminal Justice, New York — 6,172.

The Juilliard School, New York — 1,269; Manhattan College, Riverdale Bronx — 5,006; Manhattan School of Music, New York — 712; New School for Social Research, New York — 4,216; New York Law School, New York — 1,364; New York University, New York — 32,554; Pace University, New York — 11,950; Parsons School of Design, New York — 2,502; Taylor Business Institute, New York — 1,432; Technical Career Institutes, New York — 2,037; Union Theological Seminary, New York — 385.

Newspapers, Circulation: *Daily World* (m), Manhattan — 50,000; *The Journal of Commerce and Commercials* (m), 22,502; *The Wall Street Journal* (m), Manhattan — 1,700,848. *New York Daily News,* New York *News World, New York Post* and *The New York Times* also circulate in the district. Foreign language newspapers: *World Journal* (Chinese), Manhattan — 50,000; *El Diario-La Prensa* (Spanish), Manhattan — 68,979.

Commercial Television Stations, Affiliation: WABC-TV, New York (ABC); WCBS-TV, New York (CBS). Entire district is located in New York ADI. *(For other New York stations, see 15th District.)*

Industries:

J. P. Morgan & Co. Inc. (HQ); New York; banking — 8,986. Merrill Lynch & Co. Inc. (HQ); New York; securities dealers — 7,500. Irving Trust Co. (HQ); New York; banking — 6,700. **American Express Co.** (HQ); New York; insurance, credit operations — 6,000. Allied Building & Airport Services; New York; janitorial services — 4,102.

New York City Health & Hospital (HQ); New York; hospital — 3,800. Ebasco Services Inc. (HQ); New York; general contracting — 3,500. St. Luke's-Roosevelt Hospital Center (HQ); New York; hospital — 3,500. Associates Corp. of North America (HQ); New York; consumer, commercial financing — 3,000. Bank of New York Co. Inc. (HQ); New York; banking — 3,000. Chase Manhattan Bank (HQ); New York; banking — 2,800. Federal Reserve Bank of New York (HQ); New York; banking — 2,800. St. Vincent's Hospital & Medical Center of New York (HQ); New York; hospital — 2,700. The E. F. Hutton Group Inc. (HQ); New York; securities dealers — 2,600. American International Group Inc. (HQ); New York; life, health, casualty insurance — 2,500. City Insurance Co.; New York; casualty insurance — 2,500. Farrell Lines Inc.; New York; ocean transportation — 2,500. Port Authority of New York (HQ); New York; transportation facilities operations — 2,500.

City Center of Music & Drama (HQ); New York; theater producers — 2,490. Bear Stearns & Co.; New York; securities dealers — 2,400. Marine Insurance Co. Ltd. (HQ); New York; casualty insurance — 2,100. Newark Insurance Co. (HQ); New York; fire, casualty insurance — 2,100. Western Electric Co. Inc. (HQ); New York; telephone apparatus — 2,030. A I G Risk Management Inc.; New York; insurance risk management — 2,000. Bache Group Inc. (HQ); New York; securities dealers — 2,000. The Continental Corp. (HQ); New York; life, accident, casualty insurance — 2,000. Firemen's Insurance Co. of Newark (HQ); New York; life, accident insurance — 2,000. Globe Indemnity Co.; New York; fire, casualty insurance — 2,000. Misericordia Hospital & Medical Center; Bronx; hospital — 2,000. Fidelity & Casualty Co. of New York (HQ); New York; casualty insurance — 1,950. Home Insurance Co. Inc. (HQ); New York; life, accident, casualty insurance — 1,900.

Manufacturers Hanover Trust Co. (HQ); New York; banking — 1,900. The State Insurance Fund (HQ); New York; health, accident insurance — 1,900. New York Stock Exchange Inc. (HQ); New York; stock exchange — 1,850. Lawrence Shipping Corp.; New York; ocean transportation — 1,700. Lehman Bros. Kuhn Loeb Inc. (HQ); New York; securities dealers — 1,600. Lerner Stores Corp. (HQ); New

York; women's, children's clothing stores — 1,500. **1860 Broadway Inc.;** New York; real estate agents, managers — 1,500. **Depository Trust Co. Inc.;** New York; stock transfer agency — 1,460. **RCA Global Communications Inc.** (HQ); New York; international communications services — 1,400. **Royal Prudential Industries;** New York; janitorial services — 1,400. **Stone & Webster Engineering Corp.;** New York; administrative offices — 1,400. **Kidder, Peabody & Co. Inc.** (HQ); New York; investment banking — 1,300. **Gibbs & Hill Inc.** (HQ); New York; engineering services — 1,270. **Crum & Forster** (HQ); New York; health, casualty insurance — 1,200. **Drexel Burnham Lambert Group** (HQ); New York; securities dealers — 1,200.

Gulf & Western Industries Inc. (HQ); New York; financial services, apparel, valves, auto parts — 1,200. St. Clare's Hospital & Health Center (HQ); New York; hospital — 1,200. Wackenhut Corp.; New York; security services — 1,100. A. G. Becker - Warburg Paribas Becker Inc.; New York; securities dealers — 1,000. Chemical New York Corp. (HQ); New York; banking — 1,000. Empire Mutual Insurance Co. (HQ); New York; property, casualty insurance — 1,000. The First Boston Corp. (HQ); New York; securities dealers — 1,000. Johnson & Higgins (HQ); New York; insurance brokers — 1,000. Olympic Security Systems Inc.; New York; security services — 1,000. Pinkerton's Inc. (HQ); New York; security services — 1,000. Western Union International (HQ); New York; telegraph communications — 1,000. Bank of America National Trust & Savings Assn. (Bank America International New York); New York; international banking — 992. KMGA Inc. (HQ); New York; costume jewelry wholesaling — 980. American Cable & Radio Corp. (HQ); New York; radio telephone, telegraph communications — 900. ITT World Communications Inc. (HQ); New York; international communications — 900. Brown Bros. Harriman & Co. (HQ); New York; commercial banking, security brokers — 886.

Rothschild L F Unterberg Towbin (HQ); New York; securities dealers — 860. International Business Machines Corp.; New York; administrative offices — 850. Swiss Bank Corp., New York Agency; New York; foreign banking agency — 810. Goldman Sachs & Co. (HQ); New York; securities dealers — 800. Capital Cities Media Inc. (Fairchild Publications Div.); New York; publishing — 750. D P S Protective Systems Inc. (HQ); New York; security services — 750. **195 Broadway Corp.** (HQ); New York; real estate management, leasing services — 740. Group Health Inc.; New York; health insurance — 703. American Express International Banking; (HQ); New York; international banking — 700. Anchor Cleaning Services Inc.; New York; janitorial services — 700. Birmingham Fire Insurance Co. of Pennsylvania Inc.; New York; fire, casualty insurance — 700. Columbia Operating Co. Inc.; New York; taxi cab services — 700. Metropolitan Opera Assn.; New York; opera companies — 700. Schroders Inc. (Schroder Naess & Thomas Div. - HQ); New York; banking, securities — 700.

USLIFE Corp. (HQ); New York; life insurance, finance company — 700. Shearson/American Express Inc. (HQ); New York; securities dealers — 650. McAllister Bros. Inc. (HQ); New York; tugboat services — 625. Oppenheimer & Co. Inc. (HQ); New York; securities dealers — 620. Aetna Casualty & Surety Co.; New York; casualty insurance — 600. Allcity Insurance Co. Inc. (HQ); New York; casualty insurance — 600. Donaldson, Lufkin & Jenrette Inc. (HQ); New York; securities dealers — 600. F. W. Woolworth Co. (HQ); New York; general variety stores — 600. Galeries Anspach New York Inc. (HQ); New York; department store chain — 600. Home Life Insurance Co. (HQ); New York; life, health insurance — 600. Madison Detective Bureau Inc.; New York; security services — 600. Madison Square Garden Center; New York; real estate management — 600. Securities Industry Automation Corp. (HQ); New York; data processing services — 600. Standard & Poor's Corp. (HQ); New York; financial publishing — 600. U.S. Trust Corp. (HQ); New York; banking — 600.

Weil Gotshal & Manges (HQ); New York; law firm — 587. Sullivan & Cromwell (HQ); New York; law firm — 586. Alliance Assurance Co. Ltd. (HQ); New York; casualty insurance — 550. Barclays Bank International; New York; international banking — 550. Guy Carpenter & Co. Inc. (HQ); New York; reinsurance brokers — 550. Dover Garage Inc.; New York; taxi services — 550. Pandick Press Inc. (J. F. Newcomb Div. - HQ); New York; commercial printing — 550. Cravath Swaine Moore (HQ); New York; law firm — 535. Cahill, Gordon & Reindel (HQ); New York; law firm — 515. Shearman & Sterling (HQ); New York; law firm — 512. Bank of Montreal; New

York; international banking — 500. **Dow Jones & Co. Inc.** (HQ); New York; publishing — 500. **First Investors Consolidated Corp.** (HQ); New York; securities dealers — 500. **Ford, Bacon & Davis Inc.**; New York; industrial engineering services — 500. **Harlyn Industries Inc.** (Semon Bachev Co. Div.); New York; glass products — 500.

Hudson-Shatz Painting Co. Inc. (HQ); New York; painting contractors — 500. **ISCI Ltd.** (HQ); New York; security, janitorial services — 500. **Walter Kidde Constructors International**; New York; engineering services, general contracting — 500. **Milbank, Tweed, Hadley & McCloy** (HQ); New York; law firm — 500. **National Bank of North America** (HQ); New York; banking — 500. **Public Service Mutual Insurance Co.** (HQ); New York; casualty insurance — 500. **Pyramid Belt Co. Inc.** (Esta Novelties Div.); New York; women's, children's belts — 500. **Rapid Exterminating Co. Inc.**; New York; exterminators — 500. **Security Messenger Service Inc.**; New York; messenger services — 500. **Securities Settlement Corp.**; New York; securities clearing services — 500. **Stella D'Oro Biscuit Co.**; Bronx; biscuits — 500. **Superior Building Maintenance Co.**; New York; janitorial services — 500. **Thomson McKinnon Inc.** (HQ); New York; securities dealers — 500. **TRW Inc.** (United Transformer Co. Div.); New York; electric transformers — 500. **Universal Maintenance Corp.**; New York; janitorial services — 500.

18th District

South Bronx

The acres of abandoned and vandalized buildings in the South Bronx have made it the nation's symbol of contemporary urban decay. A 1980 film about the local police station was called "Fort Apache, the Bronx." In the most blighted sections, Mott Haven and Melrose, one can sometimes walk for blocks meeting no one but the occasional stray dog.

Although Presidents Carter and Reagan pledged to help the South Bronx, little has happened. Community self-help organizations exercise some political power, but this is limited because of the low voting participation among the Puerto Ricans and other Hispanic groups who live here. In addition, large numbers of illegal aliens have arrived in the South Bronx from Latin America and the Caribbean, further reducing the political power of Hispanics in the district.

Moreover, the South Bronx was the scene of a mass exodus during the 1970s. By the time of the 1980 Census the district population was down to 233,787, less than half its 1970 population. Ordinarily a population drop of that magnitude would make the district a prime candidate for elimination in redistricting. But because the incumbent was the only Hispanic member of the state's House delegation, and because the South Bronx is covered under the Voting Rights Act, the Legislature was careful to craft a district in which he could continue to win. Keeping the district's population homogeneous was not difficult because there were substantial numbers of Hispanics in adjoining constituencies.

Hispanics make up 51 percent of the population in the newly drawn 18th, down from 54 percent, but seemingly enough to ensure Hispanic political control. Most are blue-collar workers. Part of the Hispanic population is made up of refugees who came to the United States in the April-to-August 1980 mass emigration from Cuba. Blacks make up 43.7 percent of the new constituency.

The additions to the district give it slightly more middle-class territory. Fordham Heights has a considerable

Italian population remaining, and Jews still live in East Tremont.

Election Returns

18th District		Democrat		Republican	
1976	President	104,520	(79.0%)	27,059	(20.5%)
	Senate	93,834	(77.7%)	25,457	(21.1%)
	House	101,358	(91.6%)	5,854	(5.3%)
1978	Governor	62,112	(70.5%)	24,027	(27.3%)
	House	63,575	(90.4%)	4,503	(6.4%)
1980	President	79,399	(73.1%)	24,351	(22.4%)
	Senate	60,752	(60.4%)	29,402	(29.2%)
	House	77,519	(90.8%)	5,230	(6.1%)
1982	Governor	62,677	(86.6%)	7,910	(10.9%)
	Senate	50,749	(89.6%)	5,240	(9.3%)
	House	57,009	(98.9%)		

Demographics

Population: 518,106. **Percent Change from 1970:** -37.0%.

Land Area: 13 square miles. **Population per Square Mile:** 39,854.3.

Counties, 1980 Population: Bronx (Pt.) — 518,106.

Cities, 1980 Population: New York (Pt.) — 518,106.

Race and Ancestry: White — 24.5%; Black — 43.7%; American Indian, Eskimo and Aleut — 0.3%; Asian and Pacific Islander — 1.1%. Spanish Origin — 51.3%. English — 1.4%; Irish — 1.0%; Italian — 1.0%.

Universities, Enrollment: Bronx Community College, Bronx — 6,885; Hostos Community College, Bronx — 2,852; Monroe Business Institute, Bronx — 1,025.

Newspapers, Circulation: *New York Daily News*, *New York Post* and *The New York Times* circulate in the district.

Commercial Television Stations, Affiliation: Entire district is located in New York ADI.

Industries:

Lincoln Medical Center; Bronx; hospital — 2,300. **Bronx Lebanon Hospital Center** (HQ); Bronx; hospital — 1,200. **Santini Bros.**; Bronx; moving, storage — 1,000. **St. Barnabas Hospital**; Bronx; hospital — 1,000. **Celebrity Inc.** (HQ); Bronx; leather goods — 950. **American Bank Note Co.**; Bronx; engraving; security printing — 900. **Dollar Savings Bank of New York** (HQ); Bronx; banking — 700. **H. W. Wilson Co.**; Bronx; reference book publishing — 600.

19th District

South Yonkers; Eastern Bronx

The 19th district was altered substantially, moving out of Queens and reaching into Yonkers in Westchester County. But its character remains the same. It is a collection of Catholic ethnic neighborhoods, most of them with single-family homes, strong community ties and conservative views on social issues.

While the 19th votes loyally Democratic (Jimmy Carter carried it both in 1976 and 1980), it traditionally has sent some Republicans to the Legislature in Albany. The white population declined with redistricting — from 80

New York City — Bronx

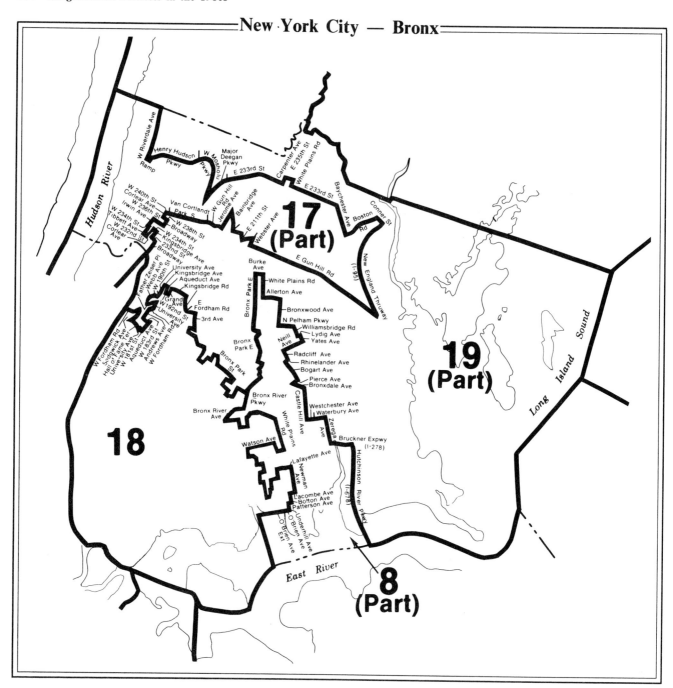

percent to 66 percent — but the Democratic incumbent was considered to be safe.

The newly drawn 19th has three separate arms that reach out for blue-collar Democratic votes. One goes south to Throg's Neck, another west to Belmont and the third north into Yonkers across the Westchester County line. Yonkers does not fit the Westchester County suburban stereotype; it is urbanized and heavily ethnic. The Italian community there does have Republican leanings, but should support socially conservative Democrats.

The district has a substantial Jewish vote in Co-op City, a huge high-rise project — 35 buildings housing more than 35,000 residents — built in the late 1960s on landfill between the Hutchinson River and the New England Thru-

way. Blacks and Hispanics have been making inroads in Co-op City, however, and now comprise 40 percent of it. Minorities populate Baychester in the low-income housing area north of Gun Hill Road.

Election Returns

19th District		Democrat		Republican	
1976	President	86,329	(60.4%)	55,862	(39.1%)
	Senate	86,846	(63.4%)	48,647	(35.5%)
	House	97,455	(76.2%)	25,188	(19.7%)
1978	Governor	48,431	(50.8%)	43,631	(45.8%)
	House	70,024	(76.3%)	18,756	(20.4%)

19th District		Democrat		Republican	
1980	President	64,980	(51.0%)	54,709	(42.9%)
	Senate	63,715	(52.9%)	44,392	(36.9%)
	House	82,321	(76.9%)	21,418	(20.0%)
1982	Governor	84,656	(60.0%)	53,799	(38.2%)
	Senate	93,220	(71.6%)	36,122	(27.8%)
	House	118,803	(93.7%)	—	

Demographics

Population: 511,802. **Percent Change from 1970:** 1.4%.

Land Area: 32 square miles. **Population per Square Mile:** 15,993.8.

Counties, 1980 Population: Bronx (Pt.) — 380,935; Westchester (Pt.) — 130,867.

Cities, 1980 Population: New York (Pt.) — 380,935; Yonkers (Pt.) — 130,867.

Race and Ancestry: White — 77.1%; Black — 13.2%; American Indian, Eskimo and Aleut — 0.1%; Asian and Pacific Islander — 1.7%. Spanish Origin — 15.9%. English — 1.5%; German — 2.8%; Greek — 0.9%; Hungarian — 0.9%; Irish — 9.8%; Italian — 21.5%; Polish — 2.8%; Russian — 2.5%; Ukranian — 0.6%.

Universities, Enrollment: Fordham University, Bronx — 14,653; Herbert H. Lehman College, Bronx — 9,248; Maritime College, Bronx — 1,070; St. Joseph's Seminary, Yonkers — 180; Sarah Lawrence College, Bronxville — 1,109.

Newspapers, Circulation: *New York Daily News*, *New York Post* and *The New York Times* circulate in the district.

Commercial Television Stations, Affiliation: Entire district is located in New York ADI.

Industries:

Montefiore Hospital & Medical Center (HQ); Bronx; hospital — 4,500. **Bronx Municipal Hospital Center;** Bronx; hospital — 3,500. **Polychrome Corp.** (HQ); Yonkers; printing equipment, supplies — 1,800. **Yonkers Contracting Co. Inc;** Yonkers; general contracting — 1,500. **Loral Corp.** (Loral Electronic Systems); Yonkers; electronic equipment — 800.

E & B Supermarkets (HQ); Bronx; supermarket — 700. **World Book-Childcraft International;** Yonkers; educational materials wholesaling — 677. **Circle Industries Corp.** (HQ); Bronx; flooring contracting — 600. **Art Steel Co. Inc.** (HQ); Bronx; metal office furniture — 500. **Insilco Corp.** (Stewart Stamping Div.); Yonkers; metal stamping — 500. **Precision Valve Corp.** (HQ); Yonkers; aerosol valves — 500. **White Swan Uniforms Inc.** (HQ); Yonkers; women's uniforms — 500.

20th District

Central and Southern Westchester County

The stereotyped WASPy Westchester that John Cheever wrote about still exists, replete with fieldstone patios, gin-and-tonics and Republican loyalties. But the county has always been more varied than that picture implies. Its politics are determined at least as much by liberal Jewish suburbanites and more conservative middle-class Italian neighborhoods as by WASP enclaves. The mix that keeps New Rochelle politically volatile characterizes the district overall.

Republicans had a small registration advantage in the old district and the remap increased it slightly. The new 20th picked up Republican towns from the old 23rd District, notably Eastchester, Mount Pleasant and the half of

Mount Kisco that was not previously in the district.

Yet the GOP is not as well organized here as in Nassau County on Long Island, the other huge suburban county adjoining the city. Westchester's large corps of well-educated independents has proved hospitable to the Democratic incumbent. Moreover, Democrats have benefited from an influx of minorities migrating from the city. Partly because of minority arrivals, Democrat Alfred B. DelBello cracked the long Republican hold on the county executive's office in 1973.

Like the closer-in parts of Nassau, the old Westchester suburbs lost population during the 1970s as children grew up and left and new homeowners settled farther out on the metropolitan area's fringe. These towns are marked by competitive politics. In the old mill town of Mount Vernon, which suffered an 8.3-percent population drop during the 1970s, black Democrats compete with Italian Republicans for political power. Jews dilute the Republican vote in wealthy Scarsdale, where the population fell 8.2 percent. Conservative Italian Republicans are a potent influence in White Plains, where more moderate WASP Republicans are the other key faction. White Plains registered a 6.6-percent population decrease in the 1970s.

The district gave up ethnic southern Yonkers and received the northern section of the city, which has more Jews and blacks and fewer Italians.

Republicans have their strongholds in Larchmont, Pelham and New Castle. GOP strength was reinforced in redistricting by the addition of several similar suburban enclaves — Bronxville, Tuckahoe, Pleasantville, Briarcliff Manor and North Tarrytown. The business executives who live in these towns either commute into the city or work in one of the county's many corporate headquarters, such as Pepsico and IBM. But Republicans generally need to nominate a moderate candidate to have a chance at the congressional level.

Election Returns

20th District		Democrat		Republican	
1976	President	89,956	(46.5%)	102,539	(53.0%)
	Senate	98,335	(52.1%)	88,671	(47.0%)
	House	96,669	(53.1%)	83,327	(45.8%)
1978	Governor	68,539	(50.3%)	63,077	(46.3%)
	House	72,384	(54.8%)	58,187	(44.0%)
1980	President	65,774	(37.0%)	92,933	(52.3%)
	Senate	76,507	(44.1%)	73,948	(42.6%)
	House	97,292	(58.2%)	68,404	(40.9%)
1982	Governor	97,911	(52.1%)	86,829	(46.2%)
	Senate	113,601	(62.6%)	66,797	(36.8%)
	House	98,425	(56.5%)	72,005	(41.3%)

Demographics

Population: 512,203. **Percent Change from 1970:** -5.0%.

Land Area: 171 square miles. **Population per Square Mile:** 3,048.0.

Counties, 1980 Population: Westchester (Pt.) — 521,203.

Cities, 1980 Population: Eastchester (CDP) — 20,305; Harrison — 23,046; Mamaroneck — 17,616; Mount Vernon — 66,713; New Rochelle — 70,794; Ossining — 20,196; Port Chester — 23,565; Rye — 15,083; Scarsdale — 17,650; White Plains — 46,999; Yonkers (Pt.) — 64,484.

Race and Ancestry: White — 80.8%; Black — 15.5%; American Indian, Eskimo and Aleut — 0.1%; Asian and Pacific Islander — 1.9%. Spanish Origin — 5.6%. English — 3.4%; French — 0.5%; German — 3.8%; Hungarian — 0.6%; Irish — 6.4%; Italian — 18.6%; Polish — 1.9%; Portuguese — 0.7%; Russian — 2.8%; Scottish — 0.5%.

Universities, Enrollment: Berkeley School, White Plains — 690; College of New Rochelle, New Rochelle — 4,485; Concordia College, Bronxville — 389; Elizabeth Seton College, Yonkers — 1,249; Iona College, New Rochelle — 6,139; The King's College, Briarcliff Manor — 852; Manhattanville College, Purchase — 1,320; Maryknoll School of Theology, Maryknoll — 252; New York Medical College, Valhalla — 1,062.

Pace University at White Plains, White Plains — 3,949; St. Vladimir's Orthodox Theological Seminary, Crestwood — 105; State University College at Purchase, Purchase — 3,653; University College of Pace University, Pleasantville — 4,153; Westchester Business Institute, White Plains — 953; Westchester Community College, Valhalla — 8,198.

Newspapers, Circulation: *The Mamaroneck Daily Times* (eS), Mamaroneck — 8,131; *The Mount Vernon Daily Argus* (eS), Mount Vernon — 11,645; *New Rochelle Standard-Star* (eS), New Rochelle — 15,074; *The Ossining Citizen Register* (eS), Ossining — 7,909; *Patent Trader* (all day), Mount Kisco — 13,816; *The Port Chester Daily Item* (eS), Port Chester 12,585; *Today* (m), White Plains — 34,783; *The White Plains Reporter-Dispatch* (eS), White Plains — 43,547; *The Yonkers Herald Statesman* (eS), Yonkers — 34,797. *New York Daily News* and *The New York Times* also circulate in the district.

Commercial Television Stations, Affiliation: Entire district is located in New York ADI.

Military Installations: Westchester County Municipal Airport (Air National Guard), White Plains — 651.

Industries:

ARA Services Inc. (Food Service Div.); White Plains; administrative offices — 8,000. **Readers Digest Assn. Inc.** (HQ); Chappaqua; magazine, book publishing — 3,400. **Bank of New York**; Harrison; banking — 3,000. **General Foods Corp.** (HQ); White Plains; food processing — 3,000. **General Motors Corp.** (Assembly Div.); Tarrytown; automobiles — 2,600.

International Business Machines Corp. (Data Processing Div.); White Plains; data processing services — 2,000. **Texaco Inc.** (HQ); White Plains; petroleum production — 1,700. **Pepsico Inc.** (HQ); Purchase; soft drinks — 1,500. **T I United States Ltd.**; Larchmont; steel wholesaling — 1,500. **Westchester County Medical Center**; Valhalla; hospital — 1,210. **International Business Machines Corp.** (HQ); Armonk; computers, office machines — 1,200. **United Hospital**; Port Chester; hospital — 1,100. **New York Hospital**; White Plains; psychiatric hospital — 1,050.

New Rochelle Hospital & Medical Center; New Rochelle; hospital — 1,020. **Nestlé Enterprises Inc.** (HQ); White Plains; chocolate, coffee, food products — 1,000. **St. John's Riverside Hospital Inc.**; Yonkers; hospital — 1,000. **Tuck Industries Inc.**; New Rochelle; pressure sensitive tapes — 1,000. **Neptune World-Wide Moving Inc.** (HQ); New Rochelle; moving company — 800. **Phelps Industries** (Phelps Dodge Copper Products Div.); Yonkers; copper wire — 800. **Otis Elevator Co. Inc.**; Yonkers; elevators — 750.

Berkey Photo Inc. (HQ); White Plains; film processing, wholesaling — 700. **Carlin-Atlas**; New Rochelle; general contracting — 700. **Sealectro Corp.** (HQ); Mamaroneck; insulated electricity terminals — 700. **Exquisite Form Industries Inc.** (HQ); Pelham; women's underwear — 600. **ITT Continental Baking Co. Inc.** (HQ); Rye; bakery products, frozen specialties — 600. **Sturman Organization Ltd.**; Mount Vernon; building operators — 600. **International Business Machines Corp.**; Harrison; administrative offices — 550. **Baker Instruments Corp.**; Pleasantville; professional equipment wholesaling — 500. **Joyce Beverages Inc.** (HQ); New Rochelle; soft drink bottling — 500. **Longines-Wittnauer Watch Co. Inc.**; New Rochelle; watches — 500. **Daniel Starch & Staff Inc.**; Mamaroneck; management consulting — 500. **USV Pharmaceutical Corp.** (Medical Device Lab - HQ); Tuckahoe; medicinal chemicals — 500. **Westchester-Rockland Newspapers** (HQ); White Plains; newspaper publishing — 500.

21st District

Hudson Valley — Poughkeepsie

Redistricting accomplished something in 1982 that Franklin Delano Roosevelt would have liked to have done in his time. It removed the Roosevelt family home of Hyde Park from the constituency represented in the 1930s by Hamilton Fish Jr., FDR's loudest congressional opponent. In 1982, the 21st was still represented by a Hamilton Fish Jr., but he is more inclined toward moderate Republicanism than was his conservative father.

Hyde Park's removal did not change the partisan nature of the district much. Most of the communities are as solidly Republican as they were in the 1930s. But like the son, the district's Republicanism is more moderate.

The district starts in the New York suburbs of upper Westchester County, where moderate GOP politics gets a good response from "Rockefeller Republicans" in Bedford and other comfortable towns. To the north, among the housing developments of fast-growing Putnam County, is another wellspring of GOP votes. Above that lies still another Republican county, rural Dutchess, with its country mansions along the Hudson River and the Connecticut border.

Poughkeepsie is the district's largest population center. An important river port and conduit for Dutchess County farm products in the late 18th and early 19th centuries, Poughkeepsie in the early 1980s relied more on the electronics equipment industry. The city is a blend of ethnic Democrats and academic liberals from Vassar College.

In redistricting the 21st picked up some additional Democratic voters in the depressed mill town of Newburgh in Orange County, previously in the old 26th. Southeast of Newburgh lies Beacon, a dying town that never recovered from the loss of its hat industry.

Environmental concerns animate the politics of this district on the fringe of a vast metropolitan region. The Hudson River gentry united in the early 1970s to stop a planned hydropower project at Storm King. And controversy plagues the nuclear power complex at Indian Point on the Hudson.

Election Returns

21st District		Democrat		Republican	
1976	President	80,741	(42.0%)	110,434	(57.4%)
	Senate	81,068	(42.9%)	106,372	(56.3%)
	House	55,089	(29.9%)	128,475	(69.8%)
1978	Governor	59,955	(40.9%)	80,112	(54.6%)
	House	30,371	(22.4%)	102,995	(76.0%)
1980	President	60,495	(30.7%)	115,998	(58.8%)
	Senate	69,815	(36.3%)	101,051	(52.5%)
	House	36,007	(19.6%)	146,297	(79.8%)
1982	Governor	61,019	(37.9%)	97,116	(60.3%)
	Senate	81,222	(51.9%)	74,136	(47.4%)
	House	38,664	(24.8%)	117,460	(75.2%)

Demographics

Population: 516,778. **Percent Change from 1970:** 11.3%.

Land Area: 1,154 square miles. **Population per Square Mile:** 447.8.

Counties, 1980 Population: Dutchess (Pt.) — 188,525; Orange (Pt.) — 119,412; Putnam — 77,193; Westchester (Pt.) — 131,648.

Cities, 1980 Population: Arlington (CDP) — 11,305; Beacon — 12,937; Jefferson Valley-Yorktown (CDP) — 13,380; Newburgh — 23,438; Peekskill — 18,236; Poughkeepsie — 29,757.

Race and Ancestry: White — 91.2%; Black — 6.6%; American Indian, Eskimo and Aleut — 0.1%; Asian and Pacific Islander — 0.9%. Spanish Origin — 3.1%. Dutch — 0.6%; English — 5.2%; French — 0.9%; German — 5.8%; Greek — 0.5%; Hungarian — 0.7%; Irish — 8.9%; Italian — 12.0%; Polish — 2.1%; Russian — 1.2%; Scottish — 0.6%.

Universities, Enrollment: Dutchess Community College, Poughkeepsie — 6,673; Marist College, Poughkeepsie — 2,774; Mount St. Mary College, Newburgh — 1,079; United States Military Academy, West Point — 4,300; Vassar College, Poughkeepsie — 2,364.

Newspapers, Circulation: *The Evening Star* (eS), Peekskill — 11,645; *Newburgh Beacon-News* (eS), Newburgh — 23,580; *Poughkeepsie Journal* (mS), Poughkeepsie — 39,612. Middletown *Times Herald-Record*, *New York Daily News* and *The New York Times* also circulate in the district.

Commercial Television Stations, Affiliation: WFTI-TV, Poughkeepsie (None). Entire district is located in New York ADI.

Military Installations: West Point Military Reservation (Army), Newburgh — 4,613.

Nuclear Power Plants: Indian Point 2, Buchanan (Westinghouse, WEDCO), August 1974. Indian Point 3, Buchanan (Westinghouse, WEDCO), August 1976.

Industries:

International Business Machines Corp. (Data Systems Div.); Poughkeepsie; business machines; electronic equipment — 12,000. **International Business Machines Corp.** (East Fishkill Facility Purchasing); Hopewell Junction; computer components wholesaling — 11,000. **Veterans Administration;** Montrose; veterans' hospital — 1,650. **Hudson River Psychiatric Center;** Poughkeepsie; state psychiatric hospital — 1,200. **International Business Machines Corp.** (Research Div.); Yorktown Heights; research, development — 1,200.

Harlem Valley State Hospital; Wingdale; state psychiatric hospital — 1,140. **Texaco Inc.** (Research Center); Beacon; petroleum research — 1,000. **Vassar Bros. Hospital;** Poughkeepsie; hospital — 1,000. **Automatic Systems Developers Inc.** Poughkeepsie; electronic equipment — 517.

22nd District

Lower Hudson Valley

This was the "fair fight" district that New York legislators created, throwing a Democratic and Republican incumbent into a district that either one had a good chance to win. Although the Democrat had the registration advantage (55-45), the Republican had the geographic advantage. Only a fifth of the population came from the Democrat's old district in Westchester County while two thirds came from the Republican's Hudson Valley constituency.

The diverse 22nd covers three worlds. Starting in a patch of graceful old Westchester suburbs, the district crosses the Hudson River and moves west through the growing outer suburbia of Orange and Rockland counties to the Catskill Mountain resorts in lower Sullivan.

The Westchester section, a place of wide, tree-lined streets, contains white-collar city commuters and ethnic blue-collar families that have fled New York. A solid Jewish element gives the Democrats a slight advantage. These

suburbs — Hastings, Irvington, Tarrytown — have been densely populated for decades.

Once bucolic, Rockland and Orange grew substantially in the 1970s. Farming still exists in Orange, the more distant of the two from the city. The GOP enjoys almost a 3-to-2 lead there.

In Rockland, the registration ratio is reversed because of a big blue-collar population. Still, the county backed Ronald Reagan in his 1980 presidential bid with 56 percent of its vote. Rockland contributes by far the biggest bloc of votes in the merged district: it accounts for approximately half the population of the new 22nd.

Jewish retirees help keep Sullivan in the Democratic column in some elections, although not all. The lower end of the Catskill Borscht Belt along Route 17 in the southern part of the county contains the Concord Hotel and other noted resorts.

Election Returns

22nd District		Democrat		Republican	
1976	President	123,237	(46.0%)	142,770	(53.3%)
	Senate	131,936	(50.3%)	128,277	(48.9%)
	House	98,282	(39.1%)	149,873	(59.7%)
1978	Governor	97,504	(45.2%)	109,170	(50.6%)
	House	78,113	(40.8%)	102,945	(53.8%)
1980	President	91,403	(34.3%)	147,407	(55.4%)
	Senate	108,201	(42.6%)	115,445	(45.3%)
	House	85,432	(35.2%)	148,003	(61.0%)
1982	Governor	85,369	(47.6%)	91,096	(50.8%)
	Senate	109,251	(62.4%)	64,622	(36.9%)
	House	73,124	(42.0%)	92,266	(52.9%)

Demographics

Population: 516,625. **Percent Change from 1970:** 14.4%.

Land Area: 1,319 square miles. **Population per Square Mile:** 391.7.

Counties, 1980 Population: Orange (Pt.) — 140,191; Rockland — 259,530; Sullivan (Pt.) — 34,023; Westchester (Pt.) — 82,881.

Cities, 1980 Population: Dobbs Ferry — 10,053; Hartsdale (CDP) — 10,216; Middletown — 21,454; Monsey (CDP) — 12,380; Nanuet (CDP) — 12,578; New City (CDP) — 35,859; Pearl River (CDP) — 15,893; Spring Valley — 20,537; Suffern — 10,794; Tarrytown — 10,648.

Race and Ancestry: White — 90.0%; Black — 6.8%; American Indian, Eskimo and Aleut — 0.2%; Asian and Pacific Islander — 1.7%. Spanish Origin — 4.1%. Dutch — 0.7%; English — 3.6%; French — 0.5%; German — 5.3%; Greek — 0.5%; Hungarian — 1.3%; Irish — 8.3%; Italian — 10.8%; Polish — 3.3%; Russian — 3.1%; Scottish — 0.5%.

Universities, Enrollment: Dominican College of Blauvelt, Orangeburg — 1,386; Marymount College, Tarrytown — 1,269; Mercy College, Dobbs Ferry — 7,946; Nyack College, Nyack — 727; Orange County Community College, Middletown — 4,981; Rockland Community College, Suffern — 7,798; St. Thomas Aquinas College, Sparkill — 1,245.

Newspapers, Circulation: The Rockland Journal-News (eS), Nyack — 46,407; The Tarrytown Daily News (eS) — 5,498; Times Herald-Record (mS), Middletown — 66,988; The Union-Gazette (e), Port Jervis — 5,085. *New York Daily News* and *The New York Times* also circulate in the district.

Commercial Television Stations, Affiliation: Entire district is located in New York ADI.

Industries:

Letchworth Village; Thiells; state psychiatric hospital — 3,000. **Technicon Instruments Corp.** (HQ); Tarrytown; analytical instruments — 1,500. **Middletown State Hospital;** Middletown; state psychiatric hospital — 1,300. **Ciba-Geigy Corp.** (HQ); Ardsley; agricultural chemicals, plastics, pharmaceuticals — 1,200. **Gleason Security Services** (HQ); Hartsdale; security services — 1,200. **Kolmar Laboratories Inc.** (HQ); Port Jervis; cosmetics — 1,200.

Horton Memorial Hospital; Middletown; hospital — 1,180. **Good Samaritan Hospital;** Suffern; hospital — 1,050. **Avon Products Inc.;** Suffern; cosmetics — 1,000. **Nyack Hospital Inc.;** Nyack; hospital — 1,000. **General Foods Corp.;** Tarrytown; research — 900. **Burns International Security Service;** Hartsdale; security services — 750. **Chromalloy-American Corp.** (Research & Technology Div.); Orangeburg; aircraft parts — 700. **Stauffer Chemical Co.** (Corporate Engineering Dept.); Dobbs Ferry; research — 600. **Building Services of Rockland Ltd.;** Monsey; janitorial services — 500. **Louis Hornick & Co. Inc.;** Haverstraw; lace curtains — 500.

23rd District

Hudson and Mohawk Valleys — Albany, Schenectady

The focus of the 23rd is on the declining industrial towns that line the banks of the Hudson and Mohawk rivers. The blue-collar vote combines with that of the state government community in Albany to make the district safe for the Democrats.

The district's identity is reinforced by the addition of Troy, the mid-19th century industrial museum piece that makes shirts, contains Rensselaer Polytechnic Institute and leans Democratic. Troy lost 10 percent of its population over the 1970s, about the same as the other industrial cities that form the district's Democratic foundation.

Amsterdam never has recovered from the closing of its Mohawk Carpet plant in the early 1960s. It hangs on economically with the help of small industries, such as the manufacture of video games. Schenectady remains a one-company town. Almost a third of its people work for General Electric, assembling turbines and generators. GOP sympathies among the significant number of Italian-Americans in Amsterdam and Schenectady make Republicans competitive for local offices. Both cities have Republican mayors.

In Albany, however, Republicans are not so lucky. Party registration in the state capital goes 10-to-1 against them. Albany has had Democratic congressional representation for all but four years since 1922. Albany County was one of just four upstate counties to back Jimmy Carter in 1980.

Democrat Erastus Corning, mayor of Albany from 1942 until his death in 1983, was boss of one of the nation's few surviving political machines and chaired the county party. The Corning machine began in the 1920s, when his Yankee family formed an alliance with the Irish Catholic O'Connell family, which held the informal political power.

The 14-year rule of the late Gov. Nelson A. Rockefeller created a corps of Republican stalwarts, many still working for the state, who live in the Albany suburbs of Colonie, Guilderland and Bethlehem. But the Democratic strength elsewhere in the district regularly overwhelms them.

State government is the 23rd's largest employer and has been increasingly concentrated in downtown Albany since the opening of the mammoth state office complex there in the 1970s. Before that, many state offices had

moved to the suburbs. The Rockefeller Empire State Plaza, named after its originator, was designed to revitalize the city. The long-awaited project has succeeded to an extent. Young professionals are restoring the old neighborhood around Center Square. Aside from this white-collar influence, the Albany area still has heavy industry and a thriving port, providing ample blue-collar jobs.

Election Returns

23rd District		Democrat		Republican	
1976	President	121,113	(47.2%)	133,750	(52.1%)
	Senate	131,603	(52.0%)	117,800	(46.8%)
	House	180,928	(75.6%)	55,876	(23.3%)
1978	Governor	105,322	(50.7%)	91,455	(44.0%)
	House	149,337	(73.0%)	47,735	(23.3%)
1980	President	120,535	(48.4%)	98,824	(39.7%)
	Senate	113,135	(47.1%)	93,818	(39.0%)
	House	172,750	(73.6%)	52,659	(22.4%)
1982	Governor	116,855	(54.2%)	96,556	(55.8%)
	Senate	151,265	(68.9%)	66,565	(30.3%)
	House	164,427	(76.1%)	41,386	(19.2%)

Demographics

Population: 516,943. **Percent Change from 1970:** -4.0%.

Land Area: 798 square miles. **Population per Square Mile:** 647.8.

Counties, 1980 Population: Albany — 285,909; Montgomery (Pt.) — 24,450; Rensselaer (Pt.) — 56,638; Schenectady — 149,946.

Cities, 1980 Population: Albany — 101,727; Amsterdam — 21,872; Cohoes — 18,144; Latham (CDP) — 11,182; Loudonville (CDP) — 11,480; Roessleville (CDP) — 11,685; Rotterdam (CDP) — 22,933; Schenectady — 67,972; Troy — 56,638; Watervliet — 11,354.

Race and Ancestry: White — 93.2%; Black — 5.2%; American Indian, Eskimo and Aleut — 0.1%; Asian and Pacific Islander — 0.9%. Spanish Origin — 1.2%. Dutch — 0.9%; English — 5.4%; French — 2.6%; German — 5.3%; Irish — 8.1%; Italian — 10.1%; Polish — 4.7%; Russian — 1.0%; Scottish — 0.6%; Ukranian — 0.6%.

Universities, Enrollment: Albany Business College, Albany — 849; Albany College of Pharmacy, Albany — 585; Albany Law School, Albany — 688; Albany Medical College, Albany — 577; College of St. Rose, Albany — 2,916; Hudson Valley Community College, Troy — 7,279; Maria College, Albany — 661; Rensselaer Polytechnic Institute, Troy — 6,308.

Russell Sage College, Troy — 2,651; Schenectady County Community College, Schenectady — 2,750; Siena College, Loudonville — 3,066; State University of New York at Albany, Albany — 16,069; Union College, Schenectady — 3,394; University of the State of New York Regents External Degree Program, Albany — 30,463.

Newspapers, Circulation: *Knickerbocker News* (e), Albany — 50,890; *The Recorder* (e), Amsterdam — 14,423; *The Times Record* (eS), Troy — 46,351; *Times-Union* (mS), Albany — 82,628; Schenectady Gazette (m), Schenectady — 70.021.

Commercial Television Stations, Affiliation: WNYT, Albany (NBC); WTEN, Albany (ABC); WXXA-TV, Albany (None); WRGB, Schenectady (CBS). Entire district is located in Albany-Schenectady-Troy ADI.

Military Installations: Schenectady Airport (Air Force), Schenectady — 902; Watervliet Arsenal (Army), Watervliet — 2,184.

Industries:

General Electric Co.; Schenectady; gas turbines, transmission tubes, motors — 18,500. **Albany Medical Center Hospital;** Albany; hospital — 3,700. **General Electric Co.** (Knolls Atomic Power Lab);

Schenectady; atomic research — 3,000. **United Bank Corp. of New York;** Albany; bank holding company — 2,460. **General Electric Co;** (Research and Development Center); Schenectady; research — 2,100.

St. Peter's Hospital; Albany; hospital — 1,910. **Ellis Hospital Inc.;** Schenectady; hospital — 1,590. **Veterans Administration;** Albany; veterans' hospital — 1,500. **Bendix Corp.** (Friction Material Div.); Troy; friction materials — 1,200. **Penn Central Co.;** Selkirk; railroad operations — 1,200. **St. Clare's Hospital of Schenectady, Inc.;** Schenectady; hospital — 1,200. **Samaritan Hospital;** Troy; hospital — 1,030. **Norton Co. Inc.** (Coated Abrasive Div.); Watervliet; abrasive products — 1,000. **Mechanical Technology Inc.** (Research & Development Div. - HQ); Latham; research, machine tools — 934. **Ford Motor Co.;** Troy; vehicle radiators — 900.

Cluett Peabody & Co. Inc. (Arrow Co. Div.); Troy; men's shirts — 800. **The Hearst Corp.;** Albany; newspaper publishing — 750. **Burns International Security Service;** Albany; security services — 600. **Garden Way Inc.;** Troy; garden equipment — 600. **McDonnell Douglass Corp.** (McDonnell Douglass Automation Co.); Albany; data processing services — 600. **Blue Shield of Northeastern New York Inc.;** Slingerlands; health insurance — 535. **Callanan Industries Inc.** (HQ); South Bethlehem; paving mixtures — 500. **Key Bank** (HQ); Albany; banking — 500.

24th District

Upper Hudson Valley — Saratoga Springs

This traditionally Republican district has been made safer with the shift of industrial Troy to the 23rd. Much of the GOP vote comes from the developing suburbia of the Albany-Troy-Schenectady area, which made the 24th one of only six old New York districts that registered a population increase during the 1970s. Such towns as Greenbush, Half Moon and Clifton Park contribute a solid Republican vote, buttressed by the rural reaches of the 24th.

Troy's departure leaves as the lonely Democratic enclaves the declining industrial towns of Glens Falls in Warren County, Hudson in Columbia County and Rensselaer in Rensselaer County. All three communities lost more than 7 percent in population in the 1970s.

For the 1980s the district expanded south to rope in the upper part of Dutchess County, where the landed gentry maintain their estates. Agricultural pursuits are conspicuous in much of the 24th. Dairy farming — a mainstay of the local economy — thrives throughout much of the district. Columbia County, in the district's southern arm, specializes in horse breeding.

The leisure industry also plays a large role in the local economic life. The Catskill Mountains of Greene County and the Adirondacks of Warren County are year-round resort areas. Lake George, in the district's northern end, is popular for boating and fishing.

But Saratoga Springs attracts the most notice from the outside world. Known far and wide for its mineral spas, elegant architecture and beautiful race track, the resort also has developed into a regional winter sports center. Speed skating, cross-country skiing and snowshoe competitions lure crowds of sports fans during the cold months.

Election Returns

24th District		Democrat		Republican	
1976	President	85,243	(38.6%)	134,171	(60.8%)
	Senate	85,610	(40.1%)	126,505	(59.3%)
	House	93,303	(44.2%)	102,238	(48.5%)

24th District		Democrat		Republican	
1978	Governor	71,813	(39.7%)	102,236	(56.6%)
	House	76,051	(42.6%)	102,365	(57.4%)
1980	President	79,593	(35.2%)	121,819	(53.9%)
	Senate	74,239	(34.0%)	114,067	(52.3%)
	House	64,103	(30.6%)	145,622	(69.4%)
1982	Governor	76,153	(36.2%)	131,733	(62.7%)
	Senate	100,110	(51.1%)	90,858	(46.4%)
	House	49,441	(26.1%)	140,296	(73.9%)

Demographics

Population: 515,614. **Percent Change from 1970:** 15.8%.

Land Area: 4,810 square miles. **Population per Square Mile:** 107.2.

Counties, 1980 Population: Columbia — 59,487; Dutchess (Pt.) — 56,530; Greene — 40,861; Rensselaer (Pt.) — 95,328; Saratoga — 153,759; Warren — 54,854; Washington — 54,795.

Cities, 1980 Population: Brunswick — 10,974; Catskill — 11,453; Clifton Park — 23,989; East Greenbush — 12,913; Glens Falls — 15,897; Halfmoon — 11,860; Hyde Park — 20,768; Kingsbury — 11,660; Milton — 12,876; Moreau — 11,188; North Greenbush — 10,396; Queensbury — 18,978; Schodack — 11,345; Saratoga Springs — 23,906.

Race and Ancestry: White — 97.8%; Black 1.5%; Indian, Eskimo and Aleut — 0.1%; Asian and Pacific Islander — 0.3%. Spanish Origin — 0.8%. Dutch — 1.2%; English — 8.4%; French — 3.3%; German — 5.9%; Irish — 7.0%; Italian — 5.5%; Polish — 2.1%; Scottish — 0.7%.

Universities, Enrollment: Adirondack Community College, Glens Falls — 2,770; Bard College, Annandale-on-Hudson — 688; Columbia-Greene Community College, Hudson — 1,234; Empire State College, Saratoga Springs — 4,769; Skidmore College, Saratoga Springs — 2,432.

Newspapers, Circulation: *Daily Mail* (e), Catskill — 4,627; *The Post-Star* (m), Glens Falls — 32,228; *Register-Star* (e), Hudson — 34,658; *Saratogian-Tri-County News* (eS), Saratoga Springs — 12,003. Albany *Knickerbocker News*, Albany *Times-Union* and Troy *Times-Record* also circulate in the district.

Commercial Television Stations, Affiliation: Most of district is located in Albany-Schenectady-Troy ADI. Portion is in New York ADI.

Military Installations: Saratoga Air Force Station, Saratoga Springs — 5.

Industries:

General Electric Co.; Hudson Falls; industrial appliances — 1,200. **Glens Falls Hospital;** Glens Falls; hospital — 1,700. **General Electric Co. Inc.** (Silicone Products Dept.); Waterford; silicone — 1,600. **Finch Pruyn & Co. Inc.;** Glens Falls; paper mills — 869. **Ciba-Geigy Corp.;** Glens Falls; chemical preparations — 700. **Oak Materials Group Inc.** (Circuit Materials Div. - HQ); Hoosick Falls; synthetic organic fibers — 700.

International Paper Co. (Hudson River Mill); Corinth; paper mill — 600. **Scott Paper Co. Inc.;** Fort Edward; paper products — 600. **Mallinckrodt Inc.** (National Catheter Co.); Argyle; catheters — 580. **C. R. Bard Inc.** (USCI Div.); Glens Falls; catheters — 500. **Huyck Corp.;** Rensselaer; felt — 500.

25th District

Central — Rome, Utica

A GOP patchwork, the brand-new 25th was stitched together mainly from the old 31st with scraps from the former 27th, 32nd and 33rd. The district now reaches from the outskirts of Ithaca to the Albany suburbs, jutting north to include a section of the Mohawk Valley.

The Mohawk Valley's Oneida County, which has slightly under half of the district's population, dominates the district politically. Outside of the Democratic Rome-Utica corridor, Oneida has a diverse but reliable Republican majority. Traditionally German Schoharie County, west of Albany, has seen rapid suburban development. People moving out of Schenectady and the state capital gave Schoharie a 20 percent growth rate in the 1970s, as once-quiet villages like Cobleskill welcomed the construction bulldozers.

The rest of the district retains its rural character. Cooperstown village is the perfect symbol for this woodsy part of the 25th. A slice of small-town America founded in 1785 by William Cooper, father of James Fenimore Cooper, it contains the National Baseball Hall of Fame and the Farmers' Museum.

The 25th's country and suburban vote should overcome the Democratic industrial bastions in the Mohawk Valley. Utica, the largest town, hosts a General Electric factory that manufactures aircraft parts. In blue-collar Utica, a Republican has won a two-year mayoral term only once in the last two decades.

The GOP fares somewhat better in nearby Rome, whose factory-worker Democratic nature is watered down by the military vote associated with adjacent Griffiss Air Force Base. But Democrats usually prevail locally. Rome makes wire, cable and cookware.

Election Returns

25th District		Democrat		Republican	
1976	President	87,132	(41.8%)	120,009	(57.6%)
	Senate	81,524	(39.0%)	126,529	(60.5%)
	House	81,533	(39.0%)	126,251	(60.4%)
1978	Governor	75,314	(41.9%)	98,190	(54.6%)
	House	30,178	(22.3%)	104,159	(77.1%)
1980	President	79,689	(38.5%)	105,701	(51.1%)
	Senate	66,467	(33.0%)	113,677	(56.5%)
	House	57,723	(31.0%)	124,978	(67.1%)
1982	Governor	72,489	(39.9%)	106,675	(58.8%)
	Senate	104,956	(59.2%)	70,661	(39.9%)
	House	70,793	(42.4%)	93,071	(55.8%)

Demographics

Population: 515,039. **Percent Change from 1970:** -0.4%.

Land Area: 5,301 square miles. **Population per Square Mile:** 97.2.

Counties, 1980 Population: Chenango — 49,344; Cortland — 48,820; Delaware (Pt.) — 37,389; Madison (Pt.) — 12,847; Montgomery (Pt.) — 28,989; Oneida (Pt.) — 223,179; Otsego — 59,075; Schoharie — 29,710; Tompkins (Pt.) — 25,686.

Cities, 1980 Population: Cortland — 20,138; Dryden — 12,156; Kirkland — 10,334; New Hartford — 21,286; Oneida — 10,810; Oneonta — 14,933; Rome — 43,826; Utica — 75,632; Whitestown — 20,150.

Race and Ancestry: White — 97.3%; Black — 1.8%; American Indian, Eskimo and Aleut — 0.2%; Asian and Pacific Islander — 0.4%. Spanish Origin — 0.9%. Dutch — 1.1%; English — 10.6%; French — 1.3%; German — 5.9%; Irish — 5.0%; Italian — 8.3%; Polish — 4.0%; Scottish — 0.7%.

Universities, Enrollment: College of Technology, Utica — 3,563; Hamilton College, Clinton — 1,661; Hartwick College, Oneonta — 1,447; Mohawk Valley Community College, Utica — 6,611; State University College at Cortland, Cortland — 6,080; State University College at Oneonta, Oneonta — 6,320.

State University of New York Agricultural and Technical College at Cobleskill, Cobleskill — 2,692; State University of New York Agricultural and Technical College at Delhi, Delhi — 2,713; Tompkins Cortland Community College, Dryden — 3,092; Utica College of Syracuse University, Utica — 2,078; Utica School of Commerce, Utica — 274.

Newspapers, Circulation: *Cortland Standard* (e), Cortland — 13,105; *Daily Press* (m), Utica — 28,560; *Daily Sentinel* (e), Rome — 19,712; *The Daily Star* (m), Oneonta — 18,700; *The Evening Sun* (e), Norwich — 7,406; *Observer-Dispatch* (eS), Utica — 37,545; *Oneida Daily Dispatch* — 10,767.

Commercial Television Stations, Affiliation: WKTV, Utica (NBC); WUTR, Utica (ABC). District is divided among Albany-Schenectady-Troy ADI, Binghamton ADI, Syracuse ADI and Utica ADI.

Military Installations: Griffiss Air Force Base, Rome — 6,845; Stockbridge Test Annex (Air Force), Merrillsville — 2.

Industries:

General Electric Co. (Aerospace Electronics Div.); Utica; aircraft equipment — 3,000. **Oneida Ltd.** (HQ); Oneida; stainless steelware — 2,300. **Bendix Corp.** (Electrical Components Div.); Sidney; electrical equipment for internal combustion engines — 2,078. **Oneida Ltd.;** Sherrill; stainless steel ware — 2,040. **Rome Developmental Center;** Rome; state psychiatric hospital — 1,810.

Chicago Pneumatic Tool Co.; Utica; machine tools — 1,800. **Marcy Psychiatric Center;** Marcy; state psychiatric hospital — 1,600. **Utica National Insurance Group** (HQ); New Hartford; life, health, casualty insurance — 1,535. **SCM Corp.** (Smith Corona Div.); Cortland; typewriters, business equipment — 1,410. **Revere Copper & Brass Inc.;** Rome; fabricated copper, brass — 1,350. **Morton-Norwich Products Inc.;** Norwich; pharmaceuticals — 1,320. **St. Luke's Memorial Hospital Center;** New Hartford; hospital — 1,200. **Nabisco Brands Inc.** (Life Savers Inc.); Canajoharie; candy — 1,100. **Mary Imogene Bassett Hospital;** Cooperstown; hospital — 1,000. **Kelsey Hayes Co. Inc.;** Utica; auto, aircraft engines parts, turbines, mechanical power transmission equipment — 1,000. **The Raymond Corp.** (HQ); Greene; material handling systems — 1,000. **Rome Cable Corp.** (HQ); Rome; cables — 985.

SCM Corp.; Groton; office machines — 900. **Nestlé Enterprises Inc.** (Beech-Nut Foods Corp.); Canajoharie; baby food — 800. **ICL Inc.;** Utica; electronic computing equipment — 730. **Special Metals Corp.;** New Hartford; electrometallurgical products — 650. **The Bendix Corp.** (Fluid Power Div.); Utica; aircraft components — 612. **Abelove Holding Corp.;** Utica; linen supply service — 600. **Norwich Shoe Co. Inc.;** Norwich; shoes — 600. **Simmonds Precision Engine Systems Inc.** (HQ); Norwich; aircraft ignitions — 588. **Mele Mfg. Co. Inc.** (HQ); Utica; wooden frames — 527. **Pall Trinity Micro Corp.;** Cortland; filters — 500.

26th District

North — Plattsburgh, Watertown

The winds blow cold from Canada into the North Country of the Adirondacks, but they fail to chill the Republican loyalty of the region's voters, who by 1983 had not elected a Democrat to Congress in this century.

Democrats can be found scattered throughout this sparsely populated land of forest and water, geographically the state's largest district. But even though the largely desolate 26th — akin to parts of poverty-stricken Appalachia — contains some of the most economically depressed areas in the state outside New York City, wholesale defections from the GOP have never occurred.

Bounded by Canada to the north and the Adirondacks to the east, the northern reaches of the 26th are far from major transportation routes, making the district less than attractive to large-scale industry. The small amount of industrial activity here is in wood and paper products.

The North Country's traditional Democratic voters — French-Canadian loggers and autoworkers at Massena's General Motors foundry — have little political impact. Nor will the addition of a piece of the industrial Mohawk Valley affect the political balance.

In the district's rural counties, Yankee Republican dairy farmers manage to survive despite the harsh winters and soil of only modest fertility. Tourism provides a steadier economic base. Lake Placid in Essex County hosted the 1980 Winter Olympics. The Adirondacks, Lake Champlain and the Thousand Islands attract hordes of vacationers every summer. Moderating the district's conservatism is an environmental consciousness brought on by the fear that acid rain will harm the fish in the Adirondack lakes and keep sport fishermen away.

The St. Lawrence Seaway, opened in the 1950s, helps the North Country's economy. Billions of dollars of minerals and manufactured goods move through its locks each year. At Massena on the St. Lawrence River, an immense hydropower project has spawned an aluminum industry.

Watertown, the North Country's largest city, has a small-scale manufacturing base and Republican loyalties. Long the area's commercial center, Watertown was where F. W. Woolworth in 1878 introduced the idea of selling a fixed-price line of goods in a department store.

The military is important here as well. Strategic Air Command bombers fly out of Plattsburgh Air Force Base, a major local employer. In summer thousands of Army reservists and National Guardsmen train at Fort Drum; in winter active duty units perform cold-weather maneuvers.

The district gave up agricultural Oswego County, site of a large nuclear complex, to the 29th District and added rural Herkimer, Hamilton and Fulton counties. These last three have a combined population of 127,000 and a GOP voter registration advantage of 2-to-1. Herkimer is devoted to dairy farming, Hamilton is a popular recreation area and Fulton is home to a leather-products industry.

Election Returns

26th District		Democrat		Republican	
1976	President	62,609	(35.8%)	103,830	(59.3%)
	Senate	67,112	(39.2%)	101,942	(59.5%)
	House	66,174	(39.3%)	102,305	(60.7%)
1978	Governor	61,779	(41.6%)	80,661	(54.3%)
	House	50,794	(33.1%)	102,630	(66.9%)
1980	President	79,352	(42.6%)	91,909	(49.3%)
	Senate	51,197	(28.5%)	102,787	(57.3%)
	House	48,699	(27.3%)	127,279	(71.5%)
1982	Governor	46,285	(29.8%)	105,193	(67.8%)
	Senate	103,413	(60.5%)	72,582	(42.5%)
	House	43,208	(28.4%)	108,962	(71.6%)

Demographics

Population: 516,196. **Percent Change from 1970:** 3.1%.

Land Area: 13,410 square miles. **Population per Square Mile:** 38.5.

Counties, 1980 Population: Clinton — 80,750; Essex — 36,176; Franklin — 44,929; Fulton — 55,153; Hamilton — 5,034; Herkimer — 66,714; Jefferson — 88,151; Lewis — 25,035; St. Lawrence — 114,254.

Cities, 1980 Population: Canton — 11,568; German Flatts — 14,981; Gloversville — 17,836; Herkimer — 11,027; Malone — 11,276; Massena — 14,856,; Ogdensburg — 12,375; Plattsburgh — 21,057; Potsdam — 17,411; Watertown — 27,861.

Race and Ancestry: White — 98.1%; Black — 0.7%; American Indian, Eskimo and Aleut — 0.6%; Asian and Pacific Islander — 0.3%. Spanish Origin — 0.7%. Dutch — 0.6%; English — 10.7%; French — 9.0%; German — 4.1%; Irish — 5.0%; Italian — 3.5%; Polish — 1.4%; Scottish — 0.6%.

Universities, Enrollment: Clarkson College of Technology, Potsdam — 3,830; Clinton Community College, Plattsburgh — 1,510; Fulton-Montgomery Community College, Johnstown — 1,633; Herkimer County Community College, Herkimer — 2,199; Jefferson Community College, Watertown — 1,751; Mater Dei College, Ogdensburg — 310; North Country Community College, Saranac Lake — 1,449.

Paul Smith's College of Arts and Sciences, Paul Smiths — 1,223; St. Lawrence University, Canton — 2,418; State University College at Plattsburgh, Plattsburgh — 6,320; State University College at Potsdam, Potsdam — 4,678; State University of New York Agricultural and Technical College at Canton, Canton — 2,593; Wadhams Hall, Ogdensburg — 62.

Newspapers, Circulation: *Adirondack Enterprise* (e), Saranac Lake — 4,902; *The Evening Times* (e), Little Falls — 6,478; *Herkimer Evening Telegram* (e), Herkimer — 7,619; *The Journal* (eS), Ogdensburg — 5,507; *The Leader-Herald* (e), Gloversville — 13,751; *Malone Telegram* (e), Malone — 6,034; *Press Republican* (m), Plattsburgh — 21,698; *Watertown Daily Times* (e), Watertown — 42,521.

Commercial Television Stations, Affiliation: WPTZ, North Pole (NBC); WWNY-TV, Carthage (CBS, ABC, NBC). District is divided among Albany-Schenectady-Troy ADI, Utica ADI, Watertown-Carthage ADI and Burlington (Vt.)-Plattsburgh ADI.

Military Installations: Fort Drum, Watertown — 8,418; Great Bend Bomb Scoring Site, Great Bend — 45; Plattsburgh Air Force Base, Plattsburgh — 4,340; Watertown Air Force Station, Watertown — 11.

Industries:

Aluminum Co. of America Inc.; Massena; aluminum — 2,500. **Remington Arms Co. Inc.;** Ilion; firearms — 2,400. **Mohawk Data Sciences Corp.;** Herkimer; electronic computing equipment — 1,250. **General Motors Corp.** (Central Foundry Div.); Massena; aluminum foundry — 1,235. **Wolverine World Wide Inc.** (Tru Stitch Footwear Div.); Malone; leather footwear — 1,100.

General Signal Corps (New York Air Brake Co. Unit); Watertown; railroad car rental — 1,085. **Schine Enterprises Inc.;** Gloversville; hotel management — 1,000. **International Paper Co.;** Ticonderoga; paper mill — 900. **Reynolds Metals Co. Inc.;** Massena; aluminum — 850. **Ayerst Laboratories Inc.;** Rouses Point; pharmaceuticals — 825. **St. Regis Paper Co. Inc.;** Deferiet; paper mill — 750. **Georgia-Pacific Corp.** (Northeast Div.); Plattsburgh; tissue products — 665. **Daniel Green Co.;** Dolgeville; slippers — 650. **Harris Corp.** (Bindery Systems Div.); Champlain; book binding equipment — 650. **St. Joe Zinc Co.;** Balmat; zinc mining — 600. **Newton Falls Paper Mills Inc.** (HQ); Newton Falls; paper mill — 520.

27th District

Central — Syracuse

For a manufacturing city of its size Syracuse has shown an unusual affection for the GOP. Despite a Democratic registration lead, it has a majority of Republicans on its City Council. One important reason is the defection of Italian blue-collar workers from the Democratic Party.

During the 1970s the city was divided between two congressional districts, fragmenting the Democratic strength that does exist in Syracuse. In 1982, with population declining in Syracuse and surrounding Onondaga County, the Legislature reunited the city in one constituency. However, map makers added enough rural and suburban territory to the Syracuse part of the district to create a 3-to-2 Republican registration advantage.

A diversified industrial base and ethnicity characterize Syracuse. Its factories make steel, chemicals, electronic equipment and auto parts. The city's Italians, blacks, Poles, Jews, Lithuanians and Irish traditionally have had their own well-defined neighborhoods. In the Irish section, Tipperary Hill, the traffic signals are reversed, with green at the top. The eastern part of town, the site of Syracuse University, is white-collar and Republican.

In Onondaga County outside Syracuse, Democrats do well in Salina, whose name comes from the days when the area had large salt mines. The suburban Syracuse vote from Baldwinsville and Skaneateles is predictably Republican.

Cows dot the rolling hills of the other county in the district, Madison, whose population comprises just 10 percent of the district. Madison is solidly Republican.

Election Returns

27th District		Democrat		Republican	
1976	President	83,172	(39.2%)	128,045	(60.4%)
	Senate	74,581	(36.3%)	129,754	(63.1%)
	House	93,717	(46.0%)	105,056	(51.5%)
1978	Governor	66,246	(41.5%)	88,091	(55.2%)
	House	83,313	(52.1%)	71,832	(45.0%)
1980	President	78,189	(37.4%)	107,128	(51.2%)
	Senate	67,285	(33.0%)	111,155	(54.6%)
	House	50,746	(25.4%)	137,321	(68.6%)
1982	Governor	83,294	(45.3%)	97,540	(53.0%)
	Senate	109,530	(61.4%)	67,390	(37.8%)
	House	79,209	(44.2%)	95,290	(53.2%)

Demographics

Population: 516,223. **Percent Change from 1970:** -1.1%.

Land Area: 1,339 square miles. **Population per Square Mile:** 385.5.

Counties, 1980 Population: Madison (Pt.) — 52,303; Onondaga — 463,920.

Cities, 1980 Population: Camillus — 24,333; Cicero — 24,689; Clay — 52,838; De Witt — 26,868; Geddes — 18,528; Lysander — 13,897; Manlius — 28,489; Onondaga — 17,824; Salina — 37,400; Sullivan — 13,371; Syracuse — 170,105; Van Buren — 12,585.

Race and Ancestry: White — 92.3%; Black — 5.9%; American Indian, Eskimo and Aleut — 0.7%; Asian and Pacific Islander — 0.6%. Spanish Origin — 1.0%. Dutch — 0.5%; English — 8.6%; French — 1.6%; German — 5.9%; Irish — 6.4%; Italian — 8.9%; Polish — 3.4%; Russian — 0.7%; Scottish — 0.6%; Ukranian — 0.6%.

Universities, Enrollment: Cazenovia College, Cazenovia — 547; Colgate University, Hamilton — 2,550; College of Environmental Science and Forestry, Syracuse — 1,759; Le Moyne College, Syracuse — 1,838; Maria Regina College, Syracuse — 505; Onondaga Community College, Syracuse — 7,318; Powelson Business Institute, Syracuse — 600; State University of New York Agricultural and Technical College at Morrisville, Morrisville — 3,179; Syracuse University, Syracuse — 22,997; Upstate Medical Center, Syracuse — 937.

Newspapers, Circulation: *The Post Standard* (mS), Syracuse — 83,585; *Syracuse Herald Journal* (eS), Syracuse — 115,573.

Commercial Television Stations, Affiliation: WIXT, Syracuse (ABC); WSTM-TV, Syracuse (NBC); WTVH, Syracuse (CBS). Entire district is located in Syracuse ADI.

Military Installations: Hancock Field (Air Force), Syracuse — 2,026; Stockbridge Test Annex *(See 25th District)*

Industries:

General Electric Co. Inc. (Electric Systems Div.); Syracuse; electronic machinery components — 6,800. **State University of New York Upstate Medical Center;** Syracuse; hospital — 2,600. **Irving Crouse Memorial Hospital;** Syracuse; hospital — 2,120. **Chrysler Corp.** (New Process Gear Corp.); East Syracuse — auto transmissions — 2,100. **Crouse-Hinds Co.** (HQ); Syracuse; electrical construction materials, lighting fixtures — 2,058.

Allied Chemical Corp. (Semet-Solvay Div.); Solvay; soda ash, caustic chemicals — 2,000. **Bristol Myers Co.** (Bristol Laboratories Div.); Syracuse; cosmetics, pharmaceutical preparations — 2,000. **St. Joseph's Hospital & Health Center;** Syracuse; hospital — 1,800. **General Motors Corp.** (Fisher Body Div.); Syracuse; automotive plastic parts — 1,550. **Colt Industries Inc.** (Crucible Specialty Metals Div.); Syracuse; steel — 1,450. **General Electric Co.** (Television Component Products Dept.); Liverpool; television picture tubes — 1,300. **Veterans Administration;** Syracuse; veterans' hospital — 1,300. **Carrier Corp.** (Carlyle Compressor Div.); East Syracuse; refrigeration equipment — 1,200. **Community General Hospital of Greater Syracuse;** Syracuse; hospital — 1,200. **Agway Inc.** (HQ); Dewitt; animal feeds, fertilizers, petroleum distributing — 1,000.

Consolidated Rail Corp.; East Syracuse; railroad terminal — 1,000. **Syroco Inc.** (HQ); Baldwinsville; plastic giftware — 726. **Syracuse China Corp.** (HQ); Syracuse; china — 725. **Magnavox CATV Systems Inc.;** Manlius; cable television equipment — 700. **Marine Midland Bank;** Syracuse; banking — 600. **Lipe-Rollway Corp.** (Lipe Clutch Products Div. - HQ); Liverpool; roller bearings — 550. **Pass & Seymour Inc.** (Sierra Electric Co. Div. - HQ); Syracuse; electrical wiring devices — 550. **Nationwide Mutual Insurance Co.;** North Syracuse; life insurance — 540. **The Herald Co. Inc.;** Syracuse; newspaper publishing — 525. **P & C Food Markets Inc.** (HQ); Syracuse; grocery chain — 500.

28th District

Southern Tier — Binghamton, Ithaca

Reaching from high above Cayuga's waters to high above those of the Hudson, the elongated 28th kept its 5-to-3 Republican registration edge. It also kept its Democratic incumbent, who won re-election in 1982 with 56.4 percent of the vote. The 1982 redistricting took away southern Sullivan County, which is marginally Democratic, but compensated for that with the blue-collar town of Kingston on the Hudson River.

The Triple Cities of Binghamton, Johnson City and Endicott are industrial but politically marginal. This is the area in which Thomas J. Watson located his first IBM plant, and it still reflects some of the corporate paternalism the Watson family practiced for generations. Of the three, only Binghamton has a Democratic advantage in registration, and the difference there is small. In all three cities, conservative working-class voters, many of them Italian, join with white-collar technicians and professionals to form a potent bloc for the GOP. Binghamton elects Democrats to the New York Assembly but in 1982 its state senator was the Senate's Republican leader.

The small towns and farms of rural Delaware and Tioga counties add to the Republican totals. Tioga is out of the way enough that organized crime chieftains held their now-famous 1957 national conclave in the hamlet of Apalachin.

Tompkins County is the site of Cornell University in Ithaca. Cornell dominates Ithaca economically and politically. The picturesque Ivy League school, sitting on a hill overlooking Lake Cayuga, keeps the city Democratic and relatively liberal. In contrast the rural parts of the county have a Republican tilt.

Sullivan County, the northern portion of which remains in the new 28th, is the only place in the district with a Democratic registration majority, although it frequently votes for statewide and national Republican candidates. Heavily Jewish, it contains many resort hotels, including Grossinger's, the famous launching pad for comedians. Sullivan County grew at a rate of nearly 24 percent in the 1970s.

Before redistricting, the 28th included the more Republican Catskill areas of Ulster County. Redistricting brought in the rest of Ulster, including Kingston, with its small textile industry. The county's other Democratic pocket — a small one — lies in Woodstock, an artists' colony. The celebrated 1969 rock festival was named after the village but actually occurred at Bethel, also in the district, in Sullivan County.

Election Returns

28th District		Democrat		Republican	
1976	President	110,702	(47.5%)	121,263	(52.0%)
	Senate	93,049	(43.6%)	118,310	(55.5%)
	House	125,337	(59.3%)	85,784	(40.6%)
1978	Governor	75,136	(44.2%)	89,855	(52.8%)
	House	80,997	(49.1%)	83,606	(50.7%)
1980	President	83,039	(37.6%)	108,287	(49.1%)
	Senate	83,731	(39.4%)	107,602	(50.6%)
	House	100,587	(48.2%)	106,457	(51.0%)
1982	Governor	74,845	(41.8%)	101,476	(56.7%)
	Senate	102,774	(58.7%)	70,162	(40.1%)
	House	100,665	(56.4%)	75,991	(42.5%)

Demographics

Population: 516,808. **Percent Change from 1970:** 4.1%.

Land Area: 3,542 square miles. **Population per Square Mile:** 145.9.

Counties, 1980 Population: Broome — 213,648; Delaware (Pt.) — 9,435; Sullivan (Pt.) — 31,132; Tioga — 49,812; Tompkins (Pt.) — 54,623; Ulster — 158,158.

Cities, 1980 Population: Binghamton — 55,860; Chenango — 12,223; Endicott — 14,457; Ithaca — 28,732; Johnson City — 17,126; Kingston — 24,481; New Paltz — 10,183; Owego — 20,471; Saugerties — 17,975; Ulster — 12,319; Union — 61,179; Vestal — 27,238; Warwarsing — 12,956.

Race and Ancestry: White — 95.4%; Black — 2.8%; American Indian, Eskimo and Aleut — 0.1%; Asian and Pacific Islander — 0.9%. Spanish Origin — 1.8%. Dutch — 1.2%; English — 9.2%; French — 0.7%; German — 6.7%; Hungarian — 0.5%; Irish — 6.1%; Italian — 6.2%; Polish — 2.4%; Russian — 1.4%; Scottish — 0.6%; Ukranian — 0.5%.

Universities, Enrollment: Broome Community College, Binghamton — 6,267; Cornell University, Ithaca — 17,641; Ithaca College, Ithaca — 4,975; Mount Saint Alphonsus Seminary, Esopus — 57; State University College at New Paltz, New Paltz — 7,204; State University of New York at Binghamton, Binghamton — 11,280; Sullivan County Community College, Loch Sheldrake — 1,662; Ulster County Community College, Stone Ridge — 3,061.

Newspapers, Circulation: *The Evening Press* (eS), Binghamton — 66,993; *The Daily Freeman* (eS), Kingston — 20,920; *The Ithaca Journal* (e), Ithaca — 20,364; *The Sun-Bulletin* (m), Binghamton — 27,735.

Commercial Television Stations, Affiliation: WBNG-TV, Binghamton (CBS); WICZ-TV, Binghamton (NBC); WMGC-TV, Binghamton (ABC). District is divided between Binghamton ADI and New York ADI. Portion is in Syracuse ADI.

Industries:

International Business Machines Corp.; Endicott; electronic computing equipment — 10,000. **International Business Machines Corp.;** Kingston; data processing equipment — 5,200. **International Business Machines Corp.** (Federal Systems Div.); Owego; data processing equipment — 5,000. **The Singer Co.** (Link Flight Simulation Div.); Binghamton; flight training devices — 4,000. **Endicott Johnson Corp.** (HQ); Endicott; men's, children's footwear — 2,000.

Borg-Warner Corp. (Morse Chain Div.); Ithaca; power transmission equipment — 1,950. **United Health Services Inc.** (HQ); Johnson City; hospital — 1,800. **GAF Corp.;** Binghamton; photographic equipment — 1,700. **General Electric Co.** (Aircraft Equipment Div.); Johnson City; transformers — 1,700. **NCR Corp.** (Terminal Systems Div.); Ithaca; data processing services — 1,400. **Our Lady of Lourdes Memorial Hospital;** Binghamton; hospital — 1,300. **Universal Instruments Corp.** (HQ); Binghamton; special industrial machinery — 1,300. **Rotron Inc.** (HQ); Woodstock; cooling devices — 1,200. **GAF Corp.;** Binghamton; photographic equipment — 1,080.

Antitec Image Corp.; Binghamton; photographic equipment — 700. **Becton Dickinson & Co.** (Bard Parker Div.); Hancock; surgical instruments — 600. **Frito Lay Inc.;** Binghamton; snack foods — 600. **Amperex Electronics Corp.** (Amperex Ferroxcube Corp.); Saugerties; ferrite components — 550. **Bunker Ramo Corp.** (Cadre Operations); Endicott; electronic parts — 550. **Stow Mfg. Co.** (Components Assembly Div. - HQ); Binghamton; construction machinery — 520. **Avnet Inc.** (Channel Master Div.); Ellenville; television equipment — 500. **Binghamton Press Co. Inc.;** Binghamton; newspaper publishing — 500. **Endicott Johnson Corp.** (Alpine Factory); Endicott; shoes — 500.

29th District

West — Part of Rochester

Rochester on its own would probably elect a Democrat to Congress, but the Democratic vote has traditionally been divided between two districts, with Republicans taking both. The 1982 remap did not disrupt tradition. The new 29th includes the eastern section of the city as part of its generally rural and suburban constituency. The district takes in the the poor black and Puerto Rican neighborhoods in northeastern Rochester and well-to-do Republican homes along East Avenue, which leads out to the suburbs.

Rochester's biggest employer is Eastman Kodak; the company's headquarters are in the 32nd District. Despite the generally harsh economic conditions, Kodak has been expanding. The Rochester suburbs contain a Xerox facility and many other high-tech plants that employ engineers who stay devoutly Republican. Webster, site of the Xerox factory, is an elite town for GOP-minded corporate executives.

The Monroe County section comprises only one-third of the district's population. The remainder of the 29th is rural Republican; apples and cherries lead the list of crops grown in the district.

The Monroe County portion of the 19th was reduced and the district expanded south and east. New to the district, Cayuga and Seneca counties have the Finger Lakes, which are regional tourist attractions. Seneca is made up of small, primarily agricultural towns; one of the county's largest employers is the Seneca Army Depot near Romulus. Western Oneida County joins the 29th, bringing military people who live there and work at Griffiss Air Force Base across the line in the 25th.

Another addition, Oswego County, will force the incumbent to grapple with nuclear energy issues. The township of Scriba, previously in the 30th District, has two nuclear generators in operation and one under construction.

Election Returns

29th District		Democrat		Republican	
1976	President	77,962	(41.6%)	108,699	(58.1%)
	Senate	75,162	(41.5%)	105,034	(58.0%)
	House	58,463	(32.5%)	116,134	(64.6%)
1978	Governor	67,830	(43.2%)	83,330	(53.1%)
	House	26,989	(18.2%)	110,905	(74.6%)
1980	President	83,709	(40.2%)	101,446	(48.7%)
	Senate	67,920	(34.4%)	104,794	(53.1%)
	House	43,331	(24.9%)	119,265	(68.5%)
1982	Governor	70,427	(40.0%)	102,679	(58.3%)
	Senate	97,795	(57.4%)	70,650	(41.5%)
	House	47,463	(30.2%)	104,412	(66.4%)

Demographics

Population: 516,301. **Percent Change from 1970:** 2.1%.

Land Area: 3,148 square miles. **Population per Square Mile:** 164.0.

Counties, 1980 Population: Cayuga — 79,894; Monroe (Pt.) — 173,905; Oneida (Pt.) — 30,287; Oswego — 113,901; Seneca — 33,733; Wayne — 84,581.

Cities, 1980 Population: Arcadia — 14,697; Auburn — 32,548; Brighton — 35,776; Fulton — 13,312; Geneva (Pt.) — 0; Newark — 10,017; Oswego — 19,793; Penfield — 27,201; Rochester (Pt.) — 82,003; Webster — 28,925.

Race and Ancestry: White — 93.7%; Black — 4.6%; American Indian, Eskimo and Aleut — 0.2%; Asian and Pacific Islander — 0.5%. Spanish Origin — 1.5%. Dutch — 2.0%; English — 11.2%; French — 1.7%; German — 6.5%; Irish — 4.9%; Italian — 7.6%; Polish — 2.3%; Russian — 0.7%; Scottish — 0.5%; Ukranian — 0.8%.

Universities, Enrollment: Cayuga County Community College, Auburn — 3,057; Eisenhower College of the Rochester Institute of Technology, Seneca Falls — 570; Monroe Community College, Rochester — 11,056; State University College at Oswego, Oswego — 7,554; Wells College, Aurora —527.

Newspapers, Circulation: *Citizen* (eS), Auburn — 17,315; *The Palladium-Times* (e), Oswego — 11,183.

Commercial Television Stations, Affiliation: WROC-TV, Rochester (NBC). Most of district is located in Syracuse ADI and Rochester ADI. Portion is in Utica ADI.

Military Installations: Ava Test Annex (Air Force), Ava — 2; Seneca Army Depot, Romulus — 1,340; Verona Test Annex (Air Force), Verona — 15.

Nuclear Power Plants: Fitzpatrick, Scriba (General Electric, Stone & Webster), July 1975; Nine Mile Point 1, Oswego (General Electric, Stone & Webster), December 1969; Nine Mile Point 2, Oswego (General Electric, Stone & Webster).

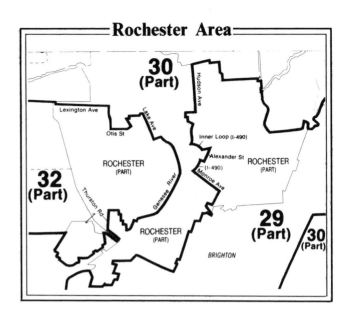

Industries:

Xerox Corp.; Webster; copiers — 8,632. **Rochester General Hospital;** Rochester; hospital — 2,640. **The Gleason Works;** Rochester; gears, machine tools — 2,300. **Goulds Pumps Inc.** (HQ); Seneca Falls; pumps — 2,000. **The Genesee Hospital;** Rochester; hospital — 2,000. **Mobil Oil Corp.** (Chemical Co., Plastics Div.); Macedon; polyethylene — 2,000.

Miller Brewing Co.; Fulton; brewery — 1,900. **The Nestlé Co. Inc.;** Fulton; chocolate — 1,350. **Garlock Inc.** (Mechanical Packing Div.); Palmyra; sealing devices — 1,200. **Harris Corp.** (RF Communications Div.); Rochester; electronic communications equipment — 1,100. **Alcan Aluminum Corp.** (Sheet & Plate Div.); Oswego; aluminum rolling — 1,000. **General Electric Co.** (Semiconductor Products Dept.); Auburn; power semiconductors — 1,000. **Alco Power Inc.** (HQ); Auburn; diesel engines — 900. **Burroughs Corp.;** Rochester; business forms — 900.

Camden Wire Co. Inc.; Camden; copper wire — 750. **USM Corp.** (Farrell Rochester Div.); Rochester; machine tools — 750. **Singer Co. Inc.** (Climate Control Div.); Auburn; heating, cooling equipment — 700. **C. H. Stuart Inc.** (HQ); Newark; costume jewelry — 700. **Gulf & Western Industries Inc.;** Union Springs; electrical equipment for internal combustion equipment — 600. **Computer Consoles Inc.** (HQ); Rochester; electronic computing equipment — 535. **Doyle Detective Bureau Inc.;** Rochester; security services — 520. **Stone & Webster Engineering;** Lycoming; engineering services — 510. **Sealright Co. Inc.;** Fulton; paper containers — 500.

30th District

West — Northwestern Rochester, Batavia

The reshaped 30th district continues to be comfortably Republican despite the loss of dependable Republican territory and the addition of part of Rochester.

Under the new plan, the district gave up rural Wyoming County and all but four towns in Livingston County to the new 31st. Both counties are Republican strongholds. The 30th already contained the predominantly Republican northwestern quarter of Rochester; the only Republican on the Rochester City Council in 1982 was from the city's northwest section. To that the remap added the central segment of the city east of the Genesee River. This addition brings in Democrats from the black neighborhoods and the academic community around the University of Rochester.

The Democratic influence was balanced by giving the district more Republican Rochester suburbs. Brisk growth in these towns will make them increasingly important in years to come. Greece, Clarkson, Hamlin and Parma were joined by Irondequoit, Perinton, Pittsford and Mendon. All the additions are white and middle-class, though Irondequoit is not as homogeneous as the others. Settled by Italians and other European groups that fled Rochester as the city's black population expanded, Irondequoit is the largest (population 57,000) of the suburbs added to the 30th.

The remap also shifted several towns in Ontario County to the 30th. Towns such as Victor and Manchester are rural communities in which Rochester commuters and dairy farmers coexist.

Most of the district's residents live in and around Rochester. The rest of the district, primarily farm land, displays firm Republican fealty. Genesee, the only county in the 30th that redistricting did not fragment, harbors industrial Batavia, which has been hurt by the departure of a Sylvania television plant. Besides its industry, dairy and vegetable farming predominate in Batavia. Through the county flows the remarkably clean Genesee River, one of the few in the country that flow northward.

Election Returns

30th District		Democrat		Republican	
1976	President	113,013	(43.7%)	143,933	(55.7%)
	Senate	123,539	(49.1%)	126,539	(50.3%)
	House	84,887	(34.5%)	156,825	(63.7%)
1978	Governor	82,190	(47.2%)	84,525	(48.6%)
	House	27,281	(16.3%)	126,107	(75.5%)
1980	President	107,324	(44.7%)	106,460	(44.4%)
	Senate	83,059	(35.9%)	119,203	(51.5%)
	House	52,255	(22.5%)	170,369	(73.3%)
1982	Governor	74,634	(40.7%)	106,314	(57.9%)
	Senate	106,247	(59.2%)	71,708	(40.0%)
	House	48,764	(27.9%)	119,105	(68.2%)

Demographics

Population: 516,819. **Percent Change from 1970:** 3.5%.

Land Area: 1,348 square miles. **Population per Square Mile:** 383.4.

Counties, 1980 Population: Genesee — 59,400; Livingston (Pt.) — 17,290; Monroe (Pt.) — 408,293; Ontario (Pt.) — 31,836.

Cities, 1980 Population: Batavia — 16,703; Chili — 23,676; Greece — 81,367; Henrietta — 36,134; Irondequoit — 57,648; Parma — 12,585; Perinton — 41,802; Pittsford — 26,743; Rochester (Pt.) — 99,006.

Race and Ancestry: White — 93.1%; Black — 4.9%; American Indian, Eskimo and Aleut — 0.3%; Asian and Pacific Islander — 0.7%. Spanish Origin — 1.8%. Dutch — 0.8%; English — 8.0%; French — 0.9%; German — 9.2%; Irish — 4.9%; Italian — 10.4%; Polish — 2.5%; Scottish — 0.6%; Ukranian — 0.7%.

Universities, Enrollment: Bryant and Stratton Business Institute, Rochester — 627; Colgate Rochester Divinity School/Croser Theological Seminary, Rochester — 206; Genesee Community College, Batavia — 2,313; Nazareth College of Rochester, Rochester — 2,778; Roberts Wesleyan College, Rochester — 617; Rochester Business Institute,

Rochester — 217; Rochester Institute of Technology, Rochester — 14,948; St. Bernard's Seminary, Rochester — 93; St. John Fisher College, Rochester — 2,303; University of Rochester, Rochester — 8,329.

Newspapers, Circulation: *The Daily News* (e), Batavia — 13,967.

Commercial Television Stations, Affiliation: WHEC-TV, Rochester (CBS); WOKR, Rochester (ABC); WUHF, Rochester (None). District is divided between Buffalo ADI and Rochester ADI.

Industries:

General Motors Corp. (Rochester Products Div.); Rochester; carburetors — 8,000. **Xerox Corp.** (Information Systems Group); Rochester; administrative offices — 2,600. **Gannett Co. Inc.** (HQ); Rochester; newspaper publishing — 1,600. **Rochester Psychiatric Center;** Rochester; state psychiatric hospital — 1,400. **Highland Hospital of Rochester;** Rochester; hospital — 1,170.

Hickey-Freeman Co. Inc. (Walter Morton Clothes - HQ); Rochester; men's suits — 1,000. **Genesee Brewing Co. Inc.** (HQ); Rochester; brewery — 900. **GTE Products Corp.;** Batavia; electronic parts wholesaling — 788. **N A P Consumer Electronics;** Batavia; electronics wholesaling — 768. **E. I. Du Pont de Nemours & Co.;** Rochester; photographic paper — 700. **Interpace Corp.** (Lapp Insulator Div.); LeRoy; high voltage insulators — 700. **Marine Midland Banks Inc.;** Rochester; banking — 700.

Rochester Hospital Service; Rochester; hospital insurance — 690. **American Can Co.;** Fairport; metal containers — 600. **Chloride Inc.** (Electro Networks Div.); Caledonia; power supplies — 600. **McCurdy & Co. Inc.** (HQ); Rochester; department stores — 600. **The Singer Co. Inc.** (Education Systems); Rochester; photographic equipment — 600. **Sybron Corp.** (Castle Co. Div.); Rochester; hospital sterilizers — 600. **Case-Hoyt Corp.** (HQ); Rochester; commercial printing — 585. **Lawyers Cooperative Publishing Co.** (HQ); Rochester; publishing — 500.

31st District

West — Buffalo Suburbs

Redistricting has greatly increased the area of the new 31st. The old 38th was entirely within Erie County. As redrawn and renumbered, the new 31st is anchored in Erie County, but extends east through parts of three rural counties. The district is overwhelmingly Republican.

Before redistricting, the Republican incumbent had run well even among blue-collar workers. Under the remap the district lost such traditionally Democratic towns as Cheektowaga and Lancaster. West Seneca and Hamburg, the two blue-collar Erie County communities that remain, have large concentrations of steel and auto workers. These towns, however, comprise only 20 percent of the district's population. More typical of the Erie County territory in the district are the upper-income suburbs of Amherst and Clarence.

In the east, the 31st picked up Wyoming County, most of Livingston County and part of Ontario County. All lean toward the Republican party. These counties, Protestant and Northern European, differ from the Erie County sections of the 31st, which are Catholic and Eastern European. Potatoes and other vegetables grow here. Apart from a boiler plant in Dansville, little industry occupies this area.

Nuclear safety is an issue that the 31st must face, thanks to the inclusion of the northern slice of Cattaraugus County in the district. This part of the county is home to the West Valley nuclear fuel reprocessing plant, along with 600,000 gallons of lethal radioactive waste.

Election Returns

31st District		Democrat		Republican	
1976	President	94,307	(43.0%)	123,578	(56.4%)
	Senate	97,349	(46.0%)	113,011	(53.4%)
	House	51,140	(24.5%)	157,033	(75.2%)
1978	Governor	57,464	(39.0%)	81,330	(55.3%)
	House	9,704	(7.7%)	109,644	(87.5%)
1980	President	89,161	(40.0%)	112,088	(50.3%)
	Senate	59,135	(29.1%)	116,487	(57.4%)
	House	39,356	(19.6%)	160,523	(79.8%)
1982	Governor	67,892	(36.6%)	114,725	(61.8%)
	Senate	100,729	(56.7%)	75,778	(42.7%)
	House	48,843	(24.7%)	133,462	(75.3%)

Demographics

Population: 515,021. **Percent Change from 1970:** 8.9%.

Land Area: 2,537 square miles. **Population per Square Mile:** 203.0

Counties, 1980 Population: Cattaraugus (Pt.) — 9,754; Erie (Pt.) — 368,583; Livingston (Pt.) — 39,716; Ontario (Pt.) — 57,073; Wyoming — 39,895.

Cities, 1980 Population: Alden — 10,093; Amherst — 108,706; Aurora — 13,872; Canandaigua — 10,419; Clarence — 18,146; Elma — 10,574; Evans — 17,961; Geneva (Pt.) — 15,133; Hamburg — 53,270; Orchard Park — 24,359; West Seneca — 51,210.

Race and Ancestry: White — 97.2%; Black — 1.3%; American Indian, Eskimo and Aleut — 0.5%; Asian and Pacific Islander — 0.7%. Spanish Origin — 0.8%. Dutch — 0.6%; English — 7.1%; French — 0.7%; German — 13.9%; Irish — 5.4%; Italian — 6.5%; Polish — 7.3%; Russian — 0.5%; Scottish — 0.5%.

Universities, Enrollment: Christ The King Seminary, East Aurora — 184; Community College of the Finger Lakes, Canandaigua — 2,869; Daemen College, Buffalo — 1,472; Erie Community College, Buffalo — 12,649; Hilbert College, Hamburg — 653; Hobart and William Smith Colleges, Geneva — 1,874; State University of New York at Buffalo, Amherst — 23,644; State University College at Geneseo, Geneseo — 5,571.

Newspapers, Circulation: *The Daily Messenger* (e), Canandaigua — 10,016; *Finger Lakes Times* (e), Geneva — 19,338. *Buffalo Evening News* also circulates in the district.

Commercial Television Stations, Affiliation: District is divided between Buffalo ADI and Rochester ADI.

Industries:

Moog Inc. (HQ); East Aurora; electrohydraulic servovalves, machine tools — 2,230. **Veterans Administration;** Canandaigua; veterans' hospital — 1,300. **Motorola Inc.;** Arcade; semiconductors — 1,000. **Manufacturers & Traders Trust Co.;** Williamsville; banking — 900. **Foster Wheeler Energy Corp.;** Dansville; fabricated plate work — 844.

Quaker Oats Co. (Fisher Price Toys Div.); Holland; toys — 700. **Houdaille Industries Inc.** (Strippit Div.); Akron; machine tools, specialties — 650. **Champion Products Inc.;** Perry; fabric finishing — 530. **S. M. Flickinger Co. Inc.** (HQ); Buffalo; grocery wholesaling, retailing — 500. **Mobil Oil Corp.** (Chemical Div.); Canandaigua; polystyrene — 500. **Transcontinent Record Sales Inc.;** Buffalo; phonographic record wholesaling — 500.

32nd District

West — Niagara Falls; Part of Rochester

The neighboring 33rd District's need to make up for its underpopulation pushed the 32nd out of much of the Buf-

falo-area Democratic turf it had occupied. In compensation the Legislature squeezed the district east to take in a section of Democratic Rochester.

That made the 32nd slightly less Republican; it dropped from 61 percent GOP registration to 58-percent. Despite the registration edge, the district was represented in 1983 by a Democrat who was first elected in 1974. Before then no Democrat had held the seat for 62 years. The incumbent's ethnic background drew support from the district's sizable Italian-American community, many of whose members otherwise vote Republican.

In Buffalo, the 32nd lost blue-collar Riverside but kept the city's Italian north section. Affluent Delaware Park votes Republican, but the overall city vote should easily favor Democratic candidates. Politically marginal Grand Island was also dropped from the district's Erie County territory.

In Rochester, the district moved into an ethnic stew that feeds only Democratic candidates. Italians, blacks and liberal young professionals populate the city's western part. The 32nd also expanded into the downtown business district, where it covers the headquarters of such famous Rochester corporations as Bausch & Lomb and Eastman Kodak. The district also picked up Republican-leaning suburbs as well.

The 32nd retained Orleans and Niagara counties. Orleans and eastern Niagara are Republican apple-growing country. Western Niagara has the Democratic mill towns of North Tonawanda, Lockport and Niagara Falls. More famous for its picturesque waterfall, Niagara Falls hosts a chemical industry, some of whose wastes allegedly poisoned the groundwater in a residential neighborhood. The state evacuated the residents of Love Canal in 1978. Some people have since returned to the area, and the cleanup continues.

Election Returns

32nd District		Democrat		Republican	
1976	President	95,793	(46.0%)	111,359	(53.5%)
	Senate	100,105	(49.9%)	99,382	(49.6%)
	House	124,451	(62.0%)	76,242	(38.0%)
1978	Governor	69,982	(47.0%)	72,261	(48.6%)
	House	98,423	(66.6%)	45,446	(30.7%)
1980	President	89,401	(45.7%)	87,703	(44.8%)
	Senate	71,015	(34.1%)	110,391	(53.1%)
	House	120,522	(64.4%)	65,698	(35.1%)
1982	Governor	78,931	(45.4%)	92,861	(53.4%)
	Senate	105,758	(64.1%)	58,272	(35.3%)
	House	116,386	(91.4%)	8,638	(6.8%)

Demographics

Population: 516,387 **Percent Change from 1970:** -6.6%.

Land Area: 1,038 square miles. **Population per Square Mile:** 497.5.

Counties, 1980 Population: Erie (Pt.) — 130,497; Monroe (Pt.) — 120,040; Niagara — 227,354; Orleans — 38,496.

Cities, 1980 Population: Buffalo (Pt.) — 20,535; Gates — 29,756; Kenmore — 18,474; Lewiston — 16,219; Lockport — 24,844; Niagara Falls — 71,384; North Tonawanda — 35,760; Ogden — 14,693; Rochester (Pt.) — 60,732; Sweden — 14,859; Tonawanda — 91,269.

Race and Ancestry: White — 90.1%; Black — 8.4%; American Indian, Eskimo and Aleut — 0.6%; Asian and Pacific Islander — 0.3%.

Spanish Origin — 1.1%. Dutch — 0.5%; English — 7.2%; French — 0.9%; German — 10.6%; Hungarian — 0.5%; Irish — 4.6%; Italian — 11.4%; Polish — 5.0%; Scottish — 0.7%.

Universities, Enrollment: Niagara County Community College, Sanborn — 4,079; Niagara University, Niagara University — 3,870; State University College at Brockport, Brockport — 8,633.

Newspapers, Circulation: *Democrat & Chronicle* (mS), Rochester — 125,569; *Journal-Register* (e), Medina — 5,740; *Niagara Gazette* (eS), Niagara Falls — 30,046; *Tonawanda News* (e), Tonawanda — 16,936; *Times-Union* (e), Rochester — 121,740; *Union-Sun & Journal* (e), Lockport — 17,689.

Commercial Television Stations, Affiliation: District is divided between Buffalo ADI and Rochester ADI.

Military Installations: Niagara Falls International Airport (Air Force), Niagara Falls — 2,065; Youngstown Test Site (Air Force), Youngstown — 1.

Industries:

Eastman Kodak Co. (HQ); Rochester; film, cameras — fewer than 10,000. **General Motors Corp.** (Harrison Radiator Div.); Lockport; auto radiators — 7,200. **General Motors Corp.** (Chevrolet Div.); Tonawanda; auto parts — 4,400. **Bausch & Lomb** (HQ); Rochester; vision care products, instruments — 3,500. **Sybron Corp.** (Taylor Instrument Co. Div.); Rochester; environmental, appliance controls — 1,925.

Union Carbide Corp. (Linde Div.); Tonawanda; cryogenic tanks — 1,800. **General Railway Signal Co. Inc.** (Genecast Div. - HQ); Rochester; railway signals — 1,600. **Niagara Falls Memorial Medical Center;** Niagara Falls; hospital — 1,200. **Quaker Oats Co.** (Fisher Price Toys Div.); Medina; toys — 1,200. **Textron Inc.** (Bell Aerospace Textron); Niagara Falls; aircraft, aircraft parts — 1,150. **St. Mary's Hospital;** Rochester; hospital — 1,060. **Hooker Chemicals & Plastics Corp.** (Durez Div.); North Tonawanda; plastic molding — 1,000. **Kenmore Mercy Hospital;** Kenmore; hospital — 1,000. **Page Holding Co.;** Rochester; aircraft sales, service — 1,000. **Union Carbide Corp.** (Carbon Products Div.); Niagara Falls; carbon, graphite electrodes — 1,000. **General Electric Co.;** Brockport; portable electric housewares — 900. **E. I. du Pont de Nemours & Co.;** Niagara Falls; industrial inorganic chemicals — 890.

Mixing Equipment Co. Inc.; Rochester; industrial machinery — 850. **Albert Elia Building Co. Inc.;** Niagara Falls; general contracting — 750. **Guterl Special Steel Corp.;** Lockport; steel — 650. **Nitec Paper Corp.** (HQ); Niagara Falls; coated paper — 648. **Pennwalt Corp.** (Pennwalt Prescription Products); Rochester; pharmaceuticals — 641. **Itek Corp.** (Graphic Products Div.); Rochester; graphic arts equipment — 600. **Union Carbide Corp.** (Mining & Metals Div.); Niagara Falls; ferro alloys — 583. **Federal-Mogul Corp.** (National Grinding Wheel Div.); North Tonawanda; grinding wheels — 550. **Brand-Rex Co.** (General Circuits Div.); Rochester; electronic components — 500. **Nabisco Inc.** (Shredded Wheat Bakery Co.); Niagara Falls; shredded wheat — 500. **Owens-Illinois Inc.** (Glass Container Div.); Brockport; glass — 500. **Wegman's Food Markets Inc.;** Rochester; grocery chain — 500.

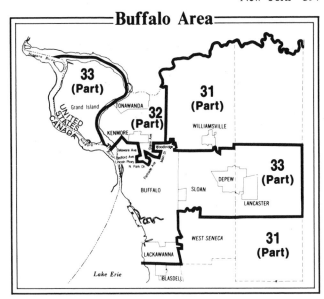

Buffalo Area

Because of its strategic location at the eastern edge of Lake Erie, Buffalo grew up as a gateway between the East and the Midwest. The Erie Barge Canal provided the link to the Great lakes early in the 19th century, a role that the railroad later assumed.

But by the early 1980s, Buffalo's economy declined as the shipbuilding, grain milling, steel and auto industries slumped.

Poles are the predominant ethnic group in the city and throughout the district. Unlike those of other Great Lakes cities, Buffalo's blacks fall far short of constituting a majority of the population and consequently have not moved into the upper echelons of political power. Few traces remain of the Germans whose culture was once pervasive in Buffalo; they have moved to the suburbs where their ethnic identity has eroded.

In this ethnic polyglot district, blue-collar Poles live in single-family houses on the eastern side of the city and in the grimy, steel-producing town of Lackawanna south of the city. Irish-Americans inhabit the south side and blacks the central city.

The 33rd picked up the Polish and very Democratic suburbs of Cheektowaga and Lancaster from the 31st as well as Grand Island from the 32nd.

33rd District

West — Buffalo

Buffalo, the state's second largest city, has a long-standing inferiority complex regarding New York City. But in the 1970s, Buffalo outdid the Big Apple in one way: its percentage of population decline was twice that of New York's.

Buffalo's 22.7 percent drop meant that the district had to take on some suburbs. The bulk of the 33rd's additions, however, were Democratic — the party the district continues to favor. Before redistricting, it voted for Jimmy Carter in both 1976 and 1980, George McGovern in 1972.

Election Returns

33rd District		Democrat		Republican	
1976	President	127,760	(57.1%)	94,722	(42.3%)
	Senate	123,157	(59.0%)	83,952	(40.2%)
	House	121,716	(61.8%)	70,995	(36.0%)
1978	Governor	92,607	(57.5%)	60,378	(37.5%)
	House	78,398	(61.4%)	45,926	(36.0%)
1980	President	126,145	(62.9%)	60,282	(30.1%)
	Senate	83,104	(42.0%)	90,753	(45.9%)
	House	116,331	(64.7%)	60,600	(33.7%)
1982	Governor	102,136	(60.3%)	64,888	(38.3%)
	Senate	121,638	(77.0%)	35,253	(22.3%)
	House	126,091	(84.1%)	19,791	(13.2%)

Demographics

Population: 516,392. **Percent Change from 1970:** -17.4%.

Land Area: 138 square miles. **Population per Square Mile:** 3,742.0.

Counties, 1980 Population: Erie (Pt.) — 516,392.

Cities, 1980 Population: Buffalo (Pt.) — 337,335; Cheektowaga — 109,442; Depew — 19,819; Grand Island — 16,770; Lackawanna — 22,701; Lancaster — 30,144.

Race and Ancestry: White — 78.7%; Black — 19.0%; American Indian, Eskimo and Aleut — 0.5%; Asian and Pacific Islander — 0.4%. Spanish Origin — 2.1%. English — 2.8%; French — 0.5%; German — 9.5%; Hungarian — 0.5%; Irish — 4.7%; Italian — 8.1%; Polish — 17.5%; Ukranian — 0.6%.

Universities, Enrollment: Bryant and Stratton Business Institute, Buffalo — 3,879; Canisius College, Buffalo — 4,226; D'Youville College, Buffalo — 1,498; Erie Community College (City campus), Buffalo — 1,293; Medaille College, Buffalo — 639; State University College at Buffalo, Buffalo — 11,749; Trocaire College, Buffalo — 849; Villa Maria College of Buffalo, Buffalo — 844.

Newspapers, Circulation: *Buffalo Evening News* (eS), Buffalo — 269,186.

Commercial Television Stations, Affiliation: WGR-TV, Buffalo (NBC); WIVB-TV, Buffalo (CBS); WKBW-TV, Buffalo (ABC); WUTV, Grand Island (None); Entire district is located in Buffalo ADI.

Industries:

Niagara Frontier Services Inc.; Buffalo; retail food distributing — 9,750. **Bethlehem Steel Corp.;** Lackawanna; steel products — 8,000. **Buffalo General Hospital** (HQ); Buffalo; hospital — 3,800. **Ford Motor Co.;** Buffalo; auto stampings — 3,400. **Westinghouse Electric Corp.;** Buffalo; electric housewares — 3,300.

Trico Products Corp. (HQ); Buffalo; auto parts — 3,000. **Marine Midland Bank Inc.** (HQ); Buffalo; bank holding company — 2,928. **American Optical Corp.** (Scientific Instrument Div.); Buffalo; optical instruments — 2,600. **General Motors Corp.** (Chevrolet Motor Div.); Buffalo; rear axles — 2,570. **National Fuel Gas Distribution Corp.** (HQ); Buffalo; natural gas distributing — 2,300. **Millard Fillmore Hospital** (HQ); Buffalo; hospital — 2,266. **First Empire State Corp.** (HQ); Buffalo; bank holding company — 2,100. **Adam Meldrum & Anderson Inc.** (HQ); Buffalo; department stores — 1,850. **Veterans Administration;** Buffalo; veterans' hospital — 1,800. **Hart Schaffner & Marx** (M. Wile & Co. Inc. - HQ); Buffalo; men's apparel — 1,750. **Manufacturers Hanover Trust Co./Western National Assn.** (HQ); Buffalo; banking — 1,727. **Sisters of Charity Hospital of Buffalo Corp.;** Buffalo; hospital — 1,673.

Children's Hospital of Buffalo Inc.; Buffalo; hospital — 1,500. **Quaker Oats Co.** (Fisher Price Toys Div. - HQ); East Aurora; toys — 1,479. **Arcata Graphics Corp.;** Depew; magazine, book printing — 1,400. **Dunlop Tire & Rubber Co.** (HQ); Buffalo; tires, sports equipment, industrial rubber products — 1,350. **Deaconess Div. of Buffalo;** Buffalo; hosptial — 1,300. **Service Systems Corp.;** Buffalo; institutional food service — 1,300. **Sierra Research Corp.;** Buffalo; airborne electronic systems — 1,125. **Buffalo Forge Co.** (HQ); Buffalo; heating, cooling equipment — 1,100. **Edison International Inc.** (Worthington Group); Buffalo; pumps, pumping equipment — 1,100. **Buffalo Evening News Inc.;** Buffalo; newspaper publishing — 1,050. **Spaulding Fibre Co., Inc.** (HQ); Buffalo; electrical materials products — 1,050. **Carborundum Co.;** Buffalo; clay refractories — 990. **Mercy Hospital;** Buffalo; hospital — 930. **Health Research Inc.** (HQ); Buffalo; business services — 900.

Roblin Industries, Inc. (HQ); Buffalo; building, steel products — 886. **Figgie International Inc.** (Scott Aviation Div.); Lancaster; health, safety products — 850. **Liberty National Bank & Trust Co.** (HQ); Buffalo; banking — 830. **General Mills Inc.;** Buffalo; flour mills — 800. **General Motors Corp.** (Harrison Radiator Div.); Buffalo; auto, truck radiators — 800. **M & G Convoy Inc.** (HQ); Buffalo; trucking — 700. **Dresser Industries Inc.** (Dresser Transportation Equipment Div.); Depew; castings — 700. **Niagara Machine & Tool Works** (HQ); Buffalo; machine tools — 660. **Blue Cross of West New York Inc.;** Buffalo; health insurance — 622. **Calspan Corp.** (Advanced Technol-

ogy Center Div. - HQ); Buffalo; aerospace, electronics research; electronic communications equipment — 602. **American Steamship Co.** (HQ); Buffalo; Great Lakes shipping — 600. **National Home Products Inc.;** Buffalo; chewing tobacco, wood furniture — 600.

South Buffalo Railway Co.; Lackawanna; railroad operations — 600. **TRW Inc.** (J. M. Williams Div.); Buffalo; hand tools — 600. **W & F Mfg. Co. Inc.** (Suny Candle Div.); Buffalo; wax specialties — 600. **Buffalo Savings Bank** (HQ); Buffalo; banking — 595. **E. I. du Pont de Nemours & Co.** (Polymer Products Dept.); Buffalo; cellulosic man-made fibers — 575. **American Precision Industries Inc.** (HQ); Buffalo; air pollution control equipment, electrical components — 569. **Westwood Pharmaceuticals Inc.** (HQ); Buffalo; pharmaceuticals — 560. **Dayton Malleable Inc.** (Pratt & Letchworth Div.); Buffalo; alloy steel casting — 550. **Merchants Mutual Insurance Co.** (HQ); Buffalo; casualty insurance — 550. **Goldome Bank for Savings;** Buffalo; banking — 548. **American Airlines Inc.;** Buffalo; commercial airline — 500. **The John W. Cowper Co. Inc.** Buffalo; general contracting — 500. **Graphic Controls Corp.** (HQ); Buffalo; recording charts — 525. **Westinghouse Electric Corp.;** Buffalo; electric motor repairing service — 500.

34th District

Southern Tier — Jamestown, Elmira

The 150-mile-long 34th reaches along the Southern Tier from Lake Erie to Elmira. Although Republicans enjoy a 5-to-3 registration advantage in the district, the Democrat who held the seat in 1983 had won re-election four times through diligent attention to the problems of the economically ailing area.

The remap slightly deepens the district's partisan hue by attaching rural Republican Schuyler and Yates counties to the 34th. Residents of these counties, which are part of the Finger Lakes region, raise dairy cows, cultivate wine grapes and work in tourism-related jobs. Tourism in Schuyler, however, has suffered since the demise in 1981 of the Grand Prix auto race at Watkins Glen.

On the western edge of the district is Chautauqua County, which contains Chautauqua Lake, a popular tourist spot. Developed in 1876 as a center for religious training, Chautauqua Institution today also offers summer programs in music, art and drama.

Democrats, although slightly outnumbered in registration, are competitive in Chautauqua County. Industrial Dunkirk and Fredonia on Lake Erie give Democrats solid support. And the Democrats have done well enough in Jamestown to help offset the Republican dairy farmers elsewhere in the county.

A similar situation prevails in Chemung County at the district's far eastern end. Arrayed against the farmers are the blue-collar Democrats of Elmira, an aging industrial city that is losing population (down 11.7 percent in the 1970s). Employment also is dropping in Elmira; Hurricane Agnes caused substantial damage in Elmira in 1972 and the city never has fully recovered.

Allegany and Cattaraugus, two farm counties with a scattering of colleges turn in lopsided Republican votes. In Steuben County, people grow grapes, blow glass and vote for the GOP. The city of Corning has a Democratic registration edge, but its longtime mayor is a Republican. The Corning Glass Works, founded in 1851, takes a paternalistic view of its city. After Hurricane Agnes destroyed the City Hall, the company financed a new one. Northern Steuben County produces the state's wines, Taylor and Great Western.

Election Returns

34th District		Democrat		Republican	
1976	President	83,721	(41.6%)	116,622	(58.0%)
	Senate	80,656	(41.4%)	113,385	(58.1%)
	House	113,017	(58.5%)	78,308	(40.6%)
1978	Governor	64,373	(42.4%)	82,190	(54.1%)
	House	81,432	(55.2%)	65,590	(44.5%)
1980	President	71,056	(36.7%)	104,050	(53.7%)
	Senate	56,209	(32.3%)	99,286	(57.1%)
	House	95,454	(51.3%)	87,777	(47.2%)
1982	Governor	54,017	(31.4%)	116,162	(67.6%)
	Senate	87,386	(53.3%)	75,499	(46.0%)
	House	99,502	(60.2%)	63,972	(38.7%)

Demographics

Population: 517,404. **Percent Change from 1970:** 1.4%.

Land Area: 5,813 square miles. **Population per Square Mile:** 89.0.

Counties, 1980 Population: Allegany — 51,742; Cattaraugus (Pt.) — 75,943; Chautauqua — 146,925; Chemung — 97,656; Schuyler — 17,686; Steuben — 99,217; Tompkins (Pt.) — 6,776; Yates — 21,459.

Cities, 1980 Population: Bath — 12,268; Corning — 12,953; Dunkirk — 15,310; Elmira — 35,327; Fredonia — 11,126; Hornell — 10,234; Horseheads — 20,238; Jamestown — 35,775; Olean — 18,207; Pomfret — 14,992; Southport — 11,586.

Race and Ancestry: White — 97.3%; Black — 1.5%; American Indian, Eskimo and Aleut — 0.5%; Asian and Pacific Islander — 0.4%. Spanish Origin — 0.8%. Dutch — 1.0%; English — 11.9%; French — 0.7%; German — 7.7%; Irish — 4.8%; Italian — 4.7%; Polish — 3.2%; Scottish — 0.5%; Swedish — 2.4%.

Universities, Enrollment: Alfred University, Alfred — 1,540; Corning Community College, Corning — 3,601; Elmira College, Elmira — 2,709; Houghton College, Houghton — 1,262; Jamestown Business College, Jamestown — 283; Jamestown Community College, Jamestown — 3,918; Keuka College, Keuka Park — 544; Olean Business Institute, Olean — 207; St. Bonaventure University, St. Bonaventure — 2,388; State University College at Fredonia, Fredonia — 5,208; State University of New York Agricultural and Technical College at Alfred, Alfred — 4,265.

Newspapers, Circulation: *Elmira Star-Gazette* (all day,S), Elmira — 40,888; *Evening Observer* (e), Dunkirk — 13,660; *The Leader* (e), Corning — 17,119; *Post-Journal* (e), Jamestown — 28,857; *Salamanca Press* (e), Salamanca — 3,684; *Times-Herald* (e) Olean — 25,186; *Tribune* (e), Hornell — 8,954; *Wellsville Daily Reporter* (eS), Wellsville — 3,919.

Commercial Television Stations, Affiliation: WENY-TV, Elmira (ABC); WETM-TV, Elmira (NBC). District is divided among Buffalo ADI, Elmira ADI and Syracuse ADI.

Industries:

Corning Glass Works (HQ); Corning; glassware, glass — 7,800. **Ingersoll-Rand Co.** (Air Power Div.); Painted Post; air, gas compressors, pumps — 2,000. **Dresser Industries Inc.** (Dresser Clark Div.); Olean; gas turbines — 1,800. **Dart Industries Inc.** (Thatcher Glass Div.); Elmira; bottles — 1,300. **Al Tech Specialty Steel Corp.** (HQ); Dunkirk; steel bars — 1,200.

Arnot Ogden Memorial Hospital; Elmira; hospital — 1,100. **Hardinge Bros. Inc.** (HQ); Elmira; machine tools — 1,100. **St. Joseph's Hospital;** Elmira; hospital — 1,030. **Acme Electric Corp.;** Olean; power supplies — 1,000. **Acme Electric Corp.** (HQ); Cuba; regulated power supplies — 1,000. **Blackstone Corp.** (HQ); Jamestown; auto radiators, heaters — 1,000. **Edison International Inc.** (McGraw Edison Co.); Wellsville; steam turbines — 1,000. **Air Preheater Co. Inc.** (HQ); Wellsville; air preheaters — 970. **AVX Corp.** (Ceramics Div.); Olean; semiconductors — 870. **ITT Grinnell Valve Co. Inc.** (Kennedy Valve Div.); Elmira; valves, hydrants — 800.

Cummins Engine Co. Inc.; Lakewood; diesel engines — 750. **Mercury Aircraft Inc.** (HQ); Hammondsport; metal stampings — 700. **Westinghouse Electric Corp.** (Industrial & Government Tube Div.); Horseheads; special electron tubes — 700. **TRW Inc.** (Bearings Div.); Jamestown; ball, roller bearings — 695. **Westinghouse Electric Corp.** (Lamp Operations Div.); Bath; high intensity lamps — 600. **Dexter Corp.** (Hysol Div.); Olean; epoxies — 593. **Shepard Niles Crane & Hoist Corp.** (HQ); Montour Falls; cranes, hoists — 555. **Facet Enterprises Inc.** (Moor Components Div.); Elmira; motor vehicle parts — 550. **Taylor Wine Co. Inc.** (Pleasant Valley Wine Co. Div.); Hammondsport; winery — 550. **Welch Foods Inc.** (HQ); Westfield; canned fruit — 550. **Corning Glass Works Inc.;** Big Flats; scientific glass products — 500. **U.S.S. Fabrications;** Elmira Heights; structural steel — 500.

North Carolina

North Carolina thought it had finished with redistricting in July 1981 when the Democratic majority in the Legislature pushed through a remap that satisfied the state GOP.

But that redistricting plan was struck down by the Justice Department in December 1981. Justice said it suspected that racial considerations caused legislators to draw a "strangely irregular" 2nd District to help the Democratic incumbent, a 29-year House veteran. The remap also was challenged by the NAACP Legal Defense and Education Fund Inc. on grounds that the plan violated blacks' voting rights.

Legislators convened in a February 1982 special session to draw new lines. Despite the objections of some conservative white Democrats, the 2nd was recast to include Durham County, which has a large and politically active black population. The revised map cleared the Legislature Feb. 11.

One month later, the Justice Department announced its approval of the legislators' second map. The Legal Defense Fund, satisfied that a black had a reasonable chance to win the revised 2nd, withdrew in early May from the suit it had filed.

Unexcited about running for re-election in a considerably reshaped district, the incumbent announced his retirement March 27.

But blacks' hopes of winning the 2nd were dashed when a Durham-based black candidate lost the Democratic primary runoff to a white former state representative who won the seat in the November election.

To ensure that no district's population deviated by more than 1 percent from the ideal size of 534,039, the Legislature in February made several other minor changes in the boundaries. None of the changes altered markedly the character of the districts as they were drawn in 1981.

Age of Population

District	Population Under 18	Voting Age Population	Population 65 & Over (% of VAP)	Median Age
1	153,797	382,422	58,247 (15.2%)	28.9
2	153,990	382,220	58,389 (15.3%)	29.5
3	156,053	379,853	48,581 (12.8%)	27.1
4	137,945	395,635	44,974 (11.4%)	28.8
5	147,206	388,006	58,381 (15.0%)	31.2
6	143,334	386,301	54,361 (14.1%)	30.8
7	167,247	371,808	40,425 (10.9%)	26.2
8	154,227	381,299	62,412 (16.4%)	31.0
9	150,476	385,849	48,307 (12.5%)	29.9
10	153,078	379,876	53,367 (14.0%)	30.2
11	140,382	390,762	75,737 (19.4%)	33.3
State	1,657,735	4,224,031	603,181 (14.3%)	29.6

Income and Occupation

District	Median Family Income	White Collar Workers	Blue Collar Workers	Service Workers	Farm Workers
1	$ 14,783	42.1%	37.0%	12.7%	8.1%
2	16,099	45.9	37.0	12.6	4.6
3	14,188	38.6	42.0	11.9	7.4
4	19,912	56.1	30.7	10.8	2.3
5	17,307	42.2	44.5	10.4	2.8
6	18,718	48.3	40.1	10.2	1.5
7	14,922	45.6	37.1	13.7	3.7
8	17,058	37.0	49.8	10.4	2.7
9	20,040	54.9	32.8	10.8	1.4
10	17,186	36.8	51.9	9.8	1.5
11	15,213	39.9	45.2	11.8	3.2
State	$ 16,792	44.6%	40.7%	11.3%	3.4%

Education: School Years Completed

District	8 Years or Fewer	4 Years of High School	4 Years of College or More	Median School Years
1	27.6%	27.5%	10.8%	12.0
2	28.3	26.2	13.0	12.0
3	26.4	30.4	8.9	12.1
4	18.0	25.7	23.0	12.6
5	27.3	27.8	12.1	12.1
6	21.3	27.4	15.7	12.3
7	21.4	32.0	12.5	12.3
8	27.3	27.6	9.6	12.0
9	16.6	27.5	18.1	12.5

NORTH CAROLINA

District	8 Years or Fewer	4 Years of High School	4 Years of College or More	Median School Years
10	29.0	25.7	9.8	11.9
11	26.7	28.6	11.8	12.1
State	24.6%	27.8%	13.2%	12.2

Housing and Residential Patterns

District	Owner Occupied	Renter Occupied	Urban	Rural
1	67.6%	32.4%	30.4%	69.6%
2	61.0	39.0	49.0	51.0
3	66.8	33.2	37.3	62.7
4	65.0	35.0	55.5	44.5
5	72.2	27.8	45.3	54.7
6	67.1	32.9	64.7	35.3
7	64.6	35.4	64.2	35.8
8	75.1	24.9	34.2	65.8
9	64.3	35.7	72.0	28.0
10	72.4	27.6	46.8	53.2
11	75.5	24.5	28.4	71.6
State	68.4%	31.6%	48.0%	52.0%

1st District

Northeast — Greenville, Kinston

The 1st begins at the ocean, passes through fishing ports and coastal swamps and ends in flat fields of soybeans, corn, peanuts and tobacco. This long has been the poorest and most agricultural region in North Carolina. Through much of the post-World War II era, out-migration was heavy; young people, especially blacks, fled the farms for urban areas. In the 1970s, however, the population increased because of rapid growth in the resort areas.

On the Outer Banks, the influx of people into oceanfront communities such as Nags Head, Hatteras and Kill Devil Hills nearly doubled the population of Dare County. Carteret County, most populous of the 1st's coastal counties, grew by 30 percent.

But away from the coast, population and industry have grown more slowly. While clothing and chemical factories are moving there, agriculture remains the major source of income. In Northampton and Hertford counties, where blacks are a majority, out-migration persists.

In the southern half of the district are the small cities of Greenville (Pitt County), Kinston (Lenoir County) and New Bern (Craven County). The counties of Pitt, Lenoir and Craven joined Dare, Carteret and Beaufort counties in Ronald Reagan's column in 1980, indicating that the district's more urbanized areas and increasingly affluent coastal counties are fertile ground for future GOP gains.

But in the early 1980s, votes from 15 rural counties were expected to keep the 1st Democratic. The Democratic ties of conservative rural whites go back to the Civil War; in 1980, Jimmy Carter won 52 percent of the overall district vote.

In the redistricting the 1st lost Jones County to the 3rd District and took in Northampton County from the 2nd. Both counties are rural and heavily Democratic.

Election Returns

1st District		Democrat		Republican	
1976	President	82,605	(60.5%)	53,042	(38.9%)
	Governor	102,944	(76.7%)	30,256	(22.5%)
	House	101,931	(76.8%)	28,811	(21.7%)
1978	Senate	44,509	(49.1%)	46,205	(50.9%)
	House	68,467	(80.2%)	16,812	(19.7%)
1980	President	84,207	(52.2%)	72,815	(45.2%)
	Governor	108,617	(69.0%)	48,087	(30.6%)
	Senate	87,460	(57.8%)	63,374	(41.8%)
	House	111,755	(99.3%)	828	(0.7%)
1982	House	79,954	(81.3%)	17,478	(17.8%)

Demographics

Population: 536,219. **Percent Change from 1970:** 13.2%.

Land Area: 9,019 square miles. **Population per Square Mile:** 59.5.

Counties, 1980 Population: Beaufort — 40,355; Bertie — 21,024; Camden — 5,829; Carteret — 41,092; Chowan — 12,558; Craven — 71,043; Currituck — 11,089; Dare — 13,377; Gates — 8,875; Greene — 16,117; Hertford — 23,368; Hyde — 5,873; Lenoir — 59,819; Martin — 25,948; Northampton — 22,584; Pamlico — 10,398; Pasquotank — 28,462; Perquimans — 9,486; Pitt — 90,146; Tyrrell — 3,975; Washington — 14,801.

Cities, 1980 Population: Elizabeth City — 14,004; Greenville — 35,740; Havelock — 17,718; Kinston — 25,234; New Bern — 14,557.

Race and Ancestry: White — 64.1%; Black — 35.3%; American Indian, Eskimo and Aleut — 0.2%; Asian and Pacific Islander — 0.3%. Spanish Origin — 1.0%. English — 27.8%; French — 0.6%; German — 2.1%; Irish — 3.1%.

Universities, Enrollment: Beaufort County Community College, Washington — 1,146; Carteret Technical College, Morehead City — 988; Chowan College, Murfreesboro — 1,108; College of the Albemarle, Elizabeth City — 1,253; Craven Community College, New Bern — 1,491; Lenoir Community College, Kinston — 1,782; Martin Community College, Williamston — 790.

Pamlico Technical Institute, Grantsboro — 155; Pitt Community College, Greenville — 2,455; Roanoke Bible College, Elizabeth City — 177; Roanoke-Chowan Technical Institute, Ahoskie — 555; East Carolina University, Greenville — 13,165; Elizabeth City State University, Elizabeth City — 1,488.

Newspapers, Circulation: *The Daily Advance* (eS), Elizabeth City — 10,982; *The Daily Reflector* (eS), Greenville — 15,502; *Kinston Daily Free Press* (eS), Kinston — 13,272; *The Sun-Journal* (e), New Bern — 14,752; *Washington Daily News* (e), Washington — 9,474.

Commercial Television Stations, Affiliation: WCTI-TV, New Bern (ABC); WITN-TV, Washington (NBC); WNCT-TV, Greenville (CBS). Most of district is located in Greenville-New Bern-Washington ADI. Portion is in Norfolk (Va.)-Portsmouth (Va.)-Newport News (Va.)-Hampton (Va.) ADI.

Military Installations: Cherry Point Marine Corps Air Station, Havelock — 14,829; Dare County Weapons Range (Air Force), Stumpy Point — 18.

Industries:

Weyerhaeuser Co. (Wood Products Div.); Plymouth; paper mills — 3,000. **E. I. du Pont de Nemours & Co. Inc.;** Kinston; synthetic organic fibers — 2,840. **Pitt County Memorial Hospital;** Greenville; hospital — 1,700. **Caswell Center;** Kinston; psychiatric hospital — 1,690. **National Spinning Co. Inc.** (Dye Masters Div.); Washington; cotton, wool yarn mills — 1,500.

Burroughs Wellcome Co.; Greenville; pharmaceutical preparations — 1,300. **Texas Gulf Inc.;** Aurora; industrial inorganic chemicals — 1,300. **Hampton Industries Inc.** (Prepshirt - HQ); Kinston; men's shirts — 1,200. **AMF Inc.** (Hatteras Yacht); New Bern; shipbuilding —

1,000. **Craven County Hospital Corp.;** New Bern; hospital — 1,000. **Kinston Shirt Co. Inc.;** Kinston; men's shirts — 1,000. **Scovill Mfg. Co. Inc.** (Hamilton Beach Div.); Washington; electric housewares — 800. **Singer Co. Inc.** (Singer Furniture Co.); Chocowinity; wood furniture — 650.

Brown & Root Inc.; Aurora; general contracting — 600. **Texfi Industries Inc.;** Kinston; warp knit fabric mills — 550. **Conner Homes Corp.** (HQ); Newport; mobile homes — 500. **Hampco Apparel Inc.;** Kinston; men's shirts — 500. **A. C. Monk Co. Inc.** (Eastern Tobacco Co. - HQ); Farmville; tobacco wholesaling — 500. **New Jersey Aluminum Co.** (Carolina Aluminum Div.); Winton; aluminum products — 500. **Perdue Farms Inc.;** Lewiston; poultry processing — 500. **Procter & Gamble Mfg. Co.;** Greenville; potato chips — 500.

2nd District

North Central — Durham, Rocky Mount

As the Legislature drew it in 1981, the 2nd was dubbed "Fountain's fishhook" because of the careful draftsmanship that allowed it to avoid Orange County, an urbanized liberal enclave influenced by the University of North Carolina at Chapel Hill.

Conservative Democratic incumbent L. H. Fountain wanted Orange County out of his mostly rural and agricultural district, and in the 1981 remap, Fountain's friends in the Legislature obliged him. To bring the district's population up to ideal size, map makers hooked the 2nd around Orange to pick up Alamance County on the west and Chatham County on the south.

But the strange shape of the 2nd prompted the Justice Department to strike down the 1981 map. When legislators convened in February to redraw district lines, they again kept Orange out of the 2nd, but they dropped Alamance and Chatham from the 2nd and gave the incumbent a county he wanted even less than Orange — Durham County in the southwestern corner of the district. The new county accounted for 28 percent of the district's people.

The city of Durham, with its politically well-organized black population and Duke University, likely would give a conservative trouble. Durham County's inclusion in the 2nd prompted Fountain to announce his retirement March 27, 1982. He said that at age 69 he did not want to bother with the trouble and expense of appealing to a large number of new constituents.

The 2nd has the largest black population of any district in the state — 40.1 percent. Although rural blacks in the past have been less politically active than their Durham counterparts, blacks all across the district were very supportive of the black Democrat who sought unsuccessfully to succeed Fountain.

The eastern part of the 2nd is on the edge of the coastal plain; cotton, peanuts and tobacco are important agricultural products. Mechanization has reduced the agricultural work force, but many small farms remain. The major cities in the east are fast-growing Rocky Mount (Nash and Edgecombe counties) and Wilson (Wilson County), centers for tobacco marketing and the manufacture of tobacco products.

In the 1976 and 1980 presidential elections, most of the district's blacks and whites found common ground in Jimmy Carter. Blacks preferred Carter's philosophy to Ronald Reagan's, and whites who saw Carter as a bit too liberal were won over by his southern roots. Reagan took

Nash and Wilson counties in 1980, but Edgecombe County and the seven other counties in the district went Democratic.

Election Returns

2nd District		Democrat		Republican	
1976	President	77,733	(57.0%)	57,761	(42.4%)
	Governor	95,622	(71.0%)	36,545	(27.2%)
	House	104,341	(87.7%)	14,473	(12.2%)
1978	Senate	37,598	(43.0%)	49,763	(57.0%)
	House	62,113	(82.8%)	11,297	(15.1%)
1980	President	80,350	(53.0%)	65,911	(43.4%)
	Governor	105,078	(69.9%)	44,103	(29.3%)
	Senate	80,300	(55.5%)	63,392	(43.8%)
	House	95,511	(68.4%)	43,353	(31.0%)
1982	House	59,617	(53.5%)	34,293	(30.8%)

Demographics

Population: 536,210. **Percent Change from 1970:** 10.4%.

Land Area: 4,481 square miles. **Population per Square Mile:** 119.7.

Counties, 1980 Population: Caswell — 20,705; Durham — 152,785; Edgecombe — 55,988; Granville — 34,043; Halifax — 55,286; Johnston (Pt.) — 4,974; Nash — 67,153; Person — 29,164; Vance — 36,748; Warren — 16,232; Wilson — 63,132.

Cities, 1980 Population: Chapel Hill (Pt.) — 383; Durham — 100,831; Henderson — 13,522; Roanoke Rapids — 14,702; Rocky Mount — 41,283; Wilson — 34,424.

Race and Ancestry: White — 59.0%; Black — 40.1%; American Indian, Eskimo and Aleut — 0.5%; Asian and Pacific Islander — 0.4%. Spanish Origin — 0.9%. English — 24.9%; German — 1.9%; Irish — 2.7%; Scottish — 0.5%.

Universities, Enrollment: Atlantic Christian College, Wilson — 1,620; Duke University, Durham — 9,587; Durham Technical Institute, Durham — 2,711; Edgecombe Technical Institute, Tarboro — 1,000; Halifax Community College, Weldon — 917; Nash Technical Institute, Rocky Mount — 1,192; North Carolina Central University, Durham — 4,917; North Carolina Wesleyan College, Rocky Mount — 736; Piedmont Technical College, Roxboro — 868; Vance-Granville Community College, Henderson — 1,131; Wilson County Technical Institute, Wilson — 1,356.

Newspapers, Circulation: *Daily Herald* (eS), Roanoke Rapids — 9,477; *Durham Morning Herald* (mS), Durham — 41,575; *The Durham Sun* (e), Durham — 21,239; *The Evening Telegram* (eS), Rocky Mount — 13,103; *Henderson Daily Dispatch* (e), Henderson — 9,131; *Southerner* (e), Tarboro — 6,140; *The Wilson Daily Times* (e), Wilson — 17,356. Raleigh *News & Observer* also circulates in the district.

Commercial Television Stations, Affiliation: WPTF-TV, Durham (NBC); WTVD, Durham (CBS). Most of district is located in Raleigh-Durham ADI. Portions are in Greensboro-Winston Salem-High Point ADI and Greenville-New Bern-Washington ADI.

Industries:

International Business Machines Corp.; Research Triangle Park; electronic computing equipment — 4,500. **Abbott Laboratories;** Rocky Mount; pharmaceuticals — 2,250. **Northern Telecommunications Inc.** Research Triangle Park; electronic equipment — 2,000. **Liggett Group Inc.** (Liggett & Myers Tobacco Co.); Durham; cigarettes — 1,600. **Collins & Aikman Corp.** (Cavel Div.); Roxboro; upholstery fabrics — 1,500. **Firestone Tire & Rubber Co.;** Wilson; tires, inner tubes — 1,500. **Harriet & Henderson Yarns Inc.** (HQ); Henderson; cotton yarn mills — 1,500.

Durham County Hospital Corp. (HQ); Durham; hospital — 1,400. **Veterans Administration;** Durham; veterans' hospital — 1,300. **Burling-**

ton Industries Inc. (Domestic Div.); Durham; cotton fabrics — 1,250. **John Umstead Hospital;** Butner; psychiatric hospital — 1,200. **Americal Corp.** (HQ); Henderson; women's hosiery — 1,000. **Blue Cross & Blue Shield of North Carolina** (HQ); Durham; health insurance — 1,000. **Burrough's Wellcome Co.;** Research Triangle Park; pharmaceutical preparations — 1,000. **Research Triangle Institute;** Research Triangle Park; research laboratories — 1,000. **Wilson Memorial Hospital Inc.;** Wilson; hospital — 1,000. **Burlington Industries Inc.** (Weaving Plant); Rocky Mount; mattress ticking — 900. **Burlington Industries Inc.;** Rocky Mount; draperies, curtains — 900.

Carolina Enterprises Inc. (Empire of Carolina); Tarboro; toys, buttons — 890. **Long Manufacturers of North Carolina Inc.** (HQ); Tarboro; agricultural machinery — 800. **Roses Stores Inc.** (HQ); Henderson; variety stores — 800. **Hardee's Food Systems Inc.** (HQ); Rocky Mount; fast food restaurant chain — 750. **Texfi-K Industries Inc.;** Rocky Mount; fabric mills — 740. **H. B. Zachry Co.;** Roxboro; construction contracting — 700. **Schlage Lock Co.;** Rocky Mount; hardware — 640. **Indian Head Inc.** (Laurens Glass Co.); Henderson; glass containers — 635. **Black & Decker Mfg. Co. Inc.;** Tarboro; power hand tools — 600. **Champion International Corp.** (Packaging Div.); Roanoke Rapids; pulp, paper mills — 600.

J. P. Stevens & Co. Inc.; Roanoke Rapids; cotton fabric mills — 600. **Rocky Mount Mills;** Rocky Mount; cotton yarns — 575. **Thorpe & Ricks Inc.** (Coastal Leaf Tobacco Co.); Rocky Mount; tobacco wholesaling — 550. **United Insurance Co. of America** (Coastal Plains Life Insurance Co.); Rocky Mount; pension, health, welfare funds — 538. **Durham Drapery Co. Inc.** (Croscill Curtain Co.); Durham; draperies, curtains — 500. **Eaton Corp.** (Air Control Div.); Roxboro; motor vehicle parts — 500. **General Electric Co.;** Durham; motors, generators, turbines — 500. **Rocky Mount Undergarment Co.** (HQ); Rocky Mount; women's wear — 500. **J. P. Taylor Co.;** Henderson; tobacco processing — 500. **Ti-Caro Inc.;** Tarboro; thread mill — 500.

3rd District

Southeast Central — Goldsboro

The 3rd is a largely flat, sandy, pine-covered area that includes the Marine Corps training center at Camp Lejeune in coastal Jacksonville. Its only noteworthy changes for the 1980s were the addition of northeastern Moore County and lightly-populated Jones County.

This is a conservative region that generally votes Democratic but which gave Republican Sen. Jesse Helms solid winning margins in his 1972 and 1978 Senate elections. In 1980, Ronald Reagan won the district's three most populous counties — Wayne (Goldsboro), Onslow (Jacksonville) and Johnston (Smithfield) — which together cast about half the vote in the 3rd.

Jimmy Carter took 57 percent of the Onslow County vote in 1976, but received just 44 percent there in 1980, a result that leads Republicans to believe they can make progress in areas where military bases are important to the local economy.

The 3rd produces more flue-cured tobacco than any district in the country, and the city of Goldsboro is a market for that crop. The district also raises poultry, hogs and sweet potatoes. Duplin County produces more turkeys than any other county in the state and ranks in the top 10 counties in the nation in total value of poultry production. At the western end of the 3rd, the town of Sanford in Lee County calls itself the brick capital of the world.

The district's new residents are the 9,705 people of Jones County, formerly in the 1st District, and the 11,105 of Moore County who were in the 8th. The addition of these people does not alter the district's political character.

Election Returns

3rd District		Democrat		Republican	
1976	President	71,701	(58.6%)	50,107	(40.9%)
	Governor	84,451	(69.5%)	35,508	(29.2%)
	House	81,007	(69.0%)	36,221	(30.9%)
1978	Senate	38,621	(42.3%)	52,625	(47.7%)
	House	57,852	(71.3%)	23,256	(28.7%)
1980	President	71,695	(51.1%)	65,996	(47.0%)
	Governor	89,723	(64.5%)	48,884	(35.1%)
	Senate	72,050	(53.1%)	62,949	(46.4%)
	House	89,370	(69.0%)	40,175	(31.0%)
1982	House	68,936	(63.5%)	39,046	(36.0%)

Demographics

Population: 535,906. **Percent Change from 1970:** 13.2%.

Land Area: 7,232 square miles. **Population per Square Mile:** 74.1.

Counties, 1980 Population: Bladen — 30,491; Duplin — 40,952; Harnett — 59,570; Johnston (Pt.) — 65,625; Jones — 9,705; Lee — 36,718; Moore (Pt.) — 11,105; Onslow — 112,784; Pender — 22,215; Sampson — 49,687; Wayne — 97,054.

Cities, 1980 Population: Goldsboro — 31,871; Jacksonville — 17,056; Sanford — 14,773.

Race and Ancestry: White — 71.1%; Black — 27.3%; American Indian, Eskimo and Aleut — 0.5%; Asian and Pacific Islander — 0.5%. Spanish Origin — 1.6%. English — 23.9%; French — 0.8%; German — 2.8%; Irish — 4.6%; Scottish — 0.8%.

Universities, Enrollment: Bladen Technical Institute, Dublin — 415; Campbell University, Buie's Creek — 2,845; Central Carolina Technical Institute, Sanford — 2,069; Coastal Carolina Community College, Jacksonville — 2,439; James Sprunt Institute, Kenansville — 746; Johnston Technical Institute, Smithfield — 1,634; Mount Olive College, Mount Olive — 405; Sampson Technical College, Clinton — 810; Sandhills Community College, Carthage — 1,729; Wayne Community College, Goldsboro — 2,403.

Newspapers, Circulation: *Daily News* (e), Jacksonville — 20,385; *The Daily Record* (e), Dunn — 8,568; *Goldsboro News-Argus* (eS), Goldsboro — 20,327; *The Sampson Independent* (e), Clinton — 7,526; *The Sanford Herald* (e), Sanford — 12,135. Raleigh *News & Observer* also circulates in the district.

Commercial Television Stations, Affiliation: District is divided among Greenville-New Bern-Washington ADI, Raleigh-Durham ADI and Wilmington ADI.

Military Installations: Camp Lejeune Marine Corps Base, Jacksonville — 41,545; Camp Lejeune Naval Regional Medical Center, Jacksonville — 935; Seymour Johnson Air Force Base, Goldsboro — 5,636.

Industries:

Burlington Industries Inc.; Erwin; cotton fabrics — 2,000. **North American Philips Corp.** (Consumer Products Div.); Smithfield; radio, television receivers — 1,750. **O. Berry Center;** Goldsboro; psychiatric hospital — 1,140. **Scovill Inc.** (Hamilton Beach Div.); Clinton; household appliances — 1,000. **J. P. Stevens & Co. Inc.;** Wallace; broadwoven knit mills — 1,000.

Data General Corp.; Clayton; electronic computing equipment — 900. **Fieldcrest Mills Inc.;** Smithfield; electric blankets — 900. **Kemp Furniture Industries Inc.** (HQ); Goldsboro; household furniture — 900. **Pfizer Corp.** (Coty Div.); Sanford; cosmetics — 900. **Young Squire Inc.;** Mount Olive; boys' clothing — 750. **Clinton Sewing Co. Inc.;** Clinton; children's outerwear — 604. **R. G. Barry Corp.;** Goldsboro; bedroom slippers — 580. **Bonders Inc.;** Dunn; children's outerwear — 500. **Eaton Corp.** (Engine Components Div.); Sanford; auto parts — 500. **Morganite Inc.;** Dunn; carbon, graphite products — 500.

4th District

Central — Raleigh, Chapel Hill

The 4th District comprises two points of the metropolitan Research Triangle area — Wake County (Raleigh) and Orange County (Chapel Hill). The Triangle's third point, Durham County, is in the 2nd.

Primary sources of employment are the University of North Carolina at Chapel Hill, North Carolina State University in Raleigh and the collection of laboratories and other research facilities run by private firms and government agencies.

Additional white-collar jobs are available in state and federal government agencies in Raleigh, North Carolina's capital. The outlying parts of Wake County are more like traditional Deep South territory; a considerable amount of tobacco is still produced there.

There is substantial Republican strength in Wake County, which has 56 percent of the district's residents and has voted Republican in the four presidential elections between 1968 and 1980. But in House races the county retains its Old South Democratic traditions.

Orange County, formerly in the 2nd, makes up 14 percent of the district's population. The university community in Chapel Hill shapes the Orange County political outlook. Orange went for George McGovern in 1972, one of only two counties in the state that did. In 1980, Ronald Reagan received only 32 percent of the vote here.

The geographic extremes of the district are also political extremes. Predominantly rural Franklin County in the northeast, formerly in the 2nd, voted for Jimmy Carter in 1976 and 1980. Randolph County in the west, containing suburbs of metropolitan Greensboro, is staunchly Republican. The district's second-most populous county, Randolph, accounts for 17 percent of the 4th's constituency.

Linking the eastern and western sections of the narrow 4th is largely rural Chatham County; it is Democratic.

Election Returns

4th District		Democrat		Republican	
1976	President	84,276	(52.7%)	74,839	(46.8%)
	Governor	99,584	(62.0%)	57,555	(35.8%)
	House	96,042	(67.7%)	45,769	(32.3%)
1978	Senate	52,079	(43.7%)	67,022	(56.3%)
	House	71,164	(89.2%)	4,599	(5.8%)
1980	President	86,907	(46.5%)	87,832	(47.0%)
	Governor	122,228	(65.2%)	62,936	(33.6%)
	Senate	94,707	(51.7%)	86,610	(47.2%)
	House	95,820	(54.9%)	76,733	(44.0%)
1982	House	70,369	(51.3%)	64,955	(47.4%)

Demographics

Population: 533,580. **Percent Change from 1970:** 27.3%.

Land Area: 3,246 square miles. **Population per Square Mile:** 164.4.

Counties, 1980 Population: Chatham — 33,415; Franklin — 30,055; Orange — 77,055; Randolph — 91,728; Wake — 301,327.

Cities, 1980 Population: Asheboro — 15,252; Cary — 21,763; Chapel Hill (Pt.) — 32,038; Garner — 10,073; High Point (Pt.) — 29; Raleigh — 150,255.

Race and Ancestry: White — 79.0%; Black — 19.9%; American Indian, Eskimo and Aleut — 0.2%; Asian and Pacific Islander — 0.6%. Spanish Origin — 0.8%. English — 24.2%; French — 0.7%; German — 4.2%; Irish — 3.8%; Italian — 0.5%; Scottish — 0.9%.

Universities, Enrollment: Asheboro College, Asheboro — 155; Hardbarger Junior College of Business, Raleigh — 995; Kings College, Raleigh — 462; Louisburg College, Salisbury — 748; Meredith College, Raleigh — 1,575; Peace College, Raleigh — 492; Randolph Technical Institute, Asheboro — 1,013; St. Augustine's College, Raleigh — 1,765.

St. Mary's College, Raleigh — 300; Shaw University, Raleigh — 1,523; Southeastern Baptist Theological Seminary, Wake Forest — 1,215; North Carolina State University at Raleigh, Raleigh — 21,225; University of North Carolina at Chapel Hill, Chapel Hill — 21,465; Wake Technical College, Raleigh — 1,806.

Newspapers, Circulation: *The Chapel Hill Newspaper* (eS), Chapel Hill — 6,642; *The Courier-Tribune* (eS), Asheboro — 14,485; *News & Observer* (mS), Raleigh — 129,520; *Times* (e), Raleigh — 34,032.

Commercial Television Stations, Affiliation: WLFL-TV, Raleigh (None); WRAL-TV, Raleigh (ABC). Most of district is located in Raleigh-Durham ADI. Portion is in Greensboro-Winston-Salem-High Point ADI.

Nuclear Power Plants: Harris 1 and 2, New Hill (Westinghouse, Daniel International).

Industries:

Wake County Hospital; Raleigh; hospital — 2,100. **International Telephone & Telegraph Corp.** (Telecommunications Corp.); Raleigh; electronic communications — 2,000. **Northern Telecommunications Inc.;** Raleigh; electronic components — 2,000. **Hukla Industries Inc.** (HQ); Asheboro; household furniture — 1,750. **Burlington Industries Inc.;** Ramseur; broad-woven fabric mills — 1,500.

Martin Marietta Corp.; Raleigh; crushed limestone, granite, gravel — 1,450. **Rex Hospital;** Raleigh; hospital — 1,200. **Westinghouse Electric Corp.;** Raleigh; meters — 1,200. **Cooper Industries Inc.;** Apex; machine tool accessories — 1,100. **Acme-McCrary Corp.** (HQ); Asheboro; women's hosiery — 1,000. **Nationwide Mutual Insurance Co.;** Raleigh; life, casualty, health insurance — 950. **Stuart Furniture Industries** (HQ); Asheboro; household furniture — 900. **Walker Shoe Co.;** Asheboro; men's shoes — 884. **Square D Co.;** Knightdale; electrical switchgears — 850. **International Business Machines Corp.;** Raleigh; research, development — 750. **Stedman Corp.** (HQ); Asheboro; knit underwear — 700. **Burlington Industries Inc.** (Klopman Div.); Wake Forest; synthetic fabrics — 650. **Laughlin Hosiery Mills Inc.** (HQ); Randleman; women's hosiery — 623.

Devil Dog Mfg. Co.; Zebulon; children's dungarees — 600. **First Citizens Bank & Trust Co.** (HQ); Raleigh; banking — 600. **Kellwood Co.** (All Sheer Inc.); Siler City; women's hosiery — 600. **Scovill Mfg. Corp.** (Schrader-Bellows Fluid Power Div.); Wake Forest; non-electrical machinery — 550. **Telex Computer Products Inc.** (Terminal Communications Div.); Raleigh; electronic computing components — 540. **Allied Chemical Corp.** (Fibers & Plastics Co.); Moncure; polyester fibers — 510. **Balfour Inc.;** Asheboro; men's, boys' socks — 500. **Carolina Coach Co.** (HQ); Raleigh; intercity bus transportation — 500. **Davidson & Jones Construction;** Raleigh; industrial construction contracting — 500. **Union Carbide Corp.;** Asheboro; dry cell batteries — 500. **Universal Polymer Products;** Fuquay-Varina; polyester yarn — 500.

5th District

Northwest — Winston-Salem

To make the district safer for its Democratic incumbent, the Democratic Legislature rid the 5th of dependably Republican Davidson County and gave it Rockingham

County, where Democratic margins, while sometimes narrow, are usually reliable.

The addition of more than 83,000 Rockingham County voters was likely to outweigh the impact of another boundary change required to bring the district's population to the ideal number. That change switched Alexander County from the 10th to the 5th. Though Alexander gave Ronald Reagan a margin above 57 percent in 1980, it cast only about 11,000 votes, a fraction of those from Democratic Rockingham.

The major city in the 5th is Winston-Salem, a tobacco-processing center that also produces textiles and communications equipment. The city and surrounding Forsyth County have 46 percent of the population in the district. Forsyth went narrowly for Reagan in the 1980 election, but the Democratic House incumbent, a Winston-Salem native, carried the county by 10,000 votes.

The Republican Party traditionally has been strong in several of the hillier counties in the western part of the district, such as Wilkes, Ashe and Alexander. Early settlers of this area set up small farms with dairy cows, poultry, apple trees and tobacco, and developed a strong antagonism toward the flatland tobacco planters, who were wealthier, politically powerful and Democratic.

Election Returns

5th District		Democrat		Republican	
1976	President	92,851	(52.1%)	84,578	(47.5%)
	Governor	105,442	(59.7%)	69,666	(39.4%)
	House	104,215	(59.6%)	69,880	(40.0%)
1978	Senate	57,051	(46.2%)	66.505	(55.8%)
	House	65,938	(53.5%)	57,288	(46.5%)
1980	President	84,718	(44.6%)	99,410	(52.4%)
	Governor	107,718	(57.0%)	80,204	(42.4%)
	Senate	86,329	(46.3%)	99,064	(53.1%)
	House	96,421	(51.5%)	90,497	(48.4%)
1982	House	87,819	(60.3%)	57,083	(39.2%)

Demographics

Population: 535,212. **Percent Change from 1970:** 16.5%.

Land Area: 3,644 square miles. **Population per Square Mile:** 146.9.

Counties, 1980 Population: Alexander — 24,999; Alleghany — 9,587; Ashe — 22,325; Forsyth — 243,683; Rockingham — 83,426; Stokes — 33,086; Surry — 59,449; Wilkes — 58,657.

Cities, 1980 Population: Eden — 15,672; Reidsville — 12,492; Winston-Salem — 131,885.

Race and Ancestry: White — 83.3%; Black — 16.2%; American Indian, Eskimo and Aleut — 0.1%; Asian and Pacific Islander — 0.2%. Spanish Origin — 0.7%. Dutch — 0.7%; English — 26.9%; French — 0.6%; German — 6.1%; Irish — 4.2%; Scottish — 0.6%.

Universities, Enrollment: Forsyth Technical Institute, Winston-Salem — 2,679; Piedmont Aerospace Institute, Winston-Salem — 155; Piedmont Bible College, Winston-Salem — 465; Rockingham Community College, Wentworth — 1,517; Rutledge College, Winston-Salem — 269; Salem College, Winston-Salem — 646; Surry Community College, Dobson — 1,938; Wake Forest University, Winston-Salem — 4,661; Wilkes Community College, Wilkesboro — 2,006; Winston-Salem State University, Winston-Salem — 2,214.

Newspapers, Circulation: *Eden Daily News* (e), Eden — 7,149; *News* (e), Mount Airy — 10,300; *The Reidsville Review* (e), Reidsville — 7,675; *The Sentinel* (e), Winston-Salem — 37,447; *Winston-Salem Journal* (mS), Winston-Salem — 71,591.

Commercial Television Stations, Affiliation: WJTM-TV, Winston-Salem (None); WXII, Winston-Salem (NBC). Most of district is located in Greensboro-Winston Salem-High Point ADI. Portions are in Charlotte ADI and Bristol (Va.)-Kingsport (Tenn.)-Johnson City (Tenn.) ADI.

Industries:

R. J. Reynolds Tobacco Co.; Winston-Salem; cigarettes — 5,000. **Western Electric Co. Inc.;** Winston-Salem; communications systems — 5,000. **Hanes Corp.** (Printables Div.); Winston-Salem; knit outerwear mills — 3,000. **North Carolina Baptist Hospital;** Winston-Salem; hospital — 3,000. **R. J. Reynolds Tobacco Co.;** Winston-Salem; cigarettes — 3,000.

Chatham Mfg. Co. (Chatham Fabric Co. - HQ); Elkin; upholstery fabric — 2,500. **R. J. Reynolds Tobacco Co.;** Winston-Salem; cigarettes — 2,500. **R. J. Reynolds Tobacco Co.;** Winston-Salem; cigarettes — 2,500. **The Wachovia Corp.** (HQ); Winston-Salem; banking — 2,250. **Pilot Freight Carriers Inc.** (HQ); Winston-Salem; trucking — 2,200. **Piedmont Aviation Inc.** (Piedmont Airlines - HQ); Winston-Salem; commercial airline — 2,140. **Forsythe County Hospital Authority;** Winston-Salem; hospital — 2,100. **Ithaca Industries Inc.** (Davsco - HQ); Wilkesboro; lingerie, pantyhose — 2,000. **R. J. Reynolds Industries Inc.** (HQ); Winston-Salem; cigarettes, cigars, canned fruits and vegetables, crude petroleum, plastic products — 2,000. **R. J. Reynolds Tobacco Co.;** Winston-Salem; smoking tobacco — 2,000.

American Brand Inc. (American Tobacco Co. Div.); Reidsville; cigarettes — 1,700. **Beatrice Foods Co. Inc.** (Krispy Kreme Doughnut Co.); Winston-Salem; bakery goods — 1,500. **ITT Grinnell Industrial Piping Co.;** Kernersville; industrial piping — 1,500. **Miller Brewing Co. Inc.;** Eden; brewery — 1,500. **Spencers Inc. of North Carolina** (HQ); Mount Airy; infants' nightwear — 1,450. **Renfro Corp.** (HQ) Mount Airy; women's hosiery — 1,140. **R. J. R. Archer Inc.** (Metals Div. - HQ); Winston-Salem; plastic, aluminum packaging — 1,100. **MacField Texturing Inc.** (Southerland Products Div. - HQ); Madison; synthetic fabric finishing — 1,000. **Westinghouse Electric Corp.;** Rural Hall; turbines — 1,000. **Integon Corp.** (HQ); Winston-Salem; life insurance — 985. **Roadway Express Inc.;** Kernersville; trucking — 900. **Sprague Electric Co.;** Lansing; electronic components — 900. **Washington Mills Co.;** Mayodan; men's underwear — 900.

Lowes Co. Inc. (HQ); North Wilkesboro; construction materials wholesaling — 815. **Modern Globe Inc.** (Shrink Stayed Fabric Div. - HQ); North Wilkesboro; knit underwear — 800. **Bahnson Co. Inc.** (HQ); Winston-Salem; air conditioning equipment — 750. **The Northwestern Bank** (HQ); North Wilkesboro; banking — 700. **Joseph Schlitz Brewing Co.;** Winston-Salem; brewery — 700. **SCM Corp.** (Proctor-Silex Div.); Mount Airy; electric housewares — 600. **Bassett Furniture Industries of North Carolina** (National Mount Airy Furniture); Mount Airy; household furniture — 560.

Carolina Mirror Corp. (HQ); North Wilkesboro; mirrors — 550. **McLean Trucking Co.** (HQ); Winston-Salem; trucking — 550. **Schneider Mills of North Carolina;** Taylorsville; women's hosiery — 550. **Adams-Millis Corp.;** Kernersville; hosiery — 548. **Fairchild Industries Inc.** (Fairchild Burns); Winston-Salem; aircraft furniture — 505. **Ballston Knitting Co. Inc.;** Mount Airy; hosiery — 500. **Brenner Co. Inc.** (Brenner Iron & Metal); Winston-Salem; structural metal — 500. **Lewittes Furniture Enterprise Inc.;** Taylorsville; household furniture — 500. **Oakdale Knitting Co. Inc.;** Mount Airy; men's, boys' hosiery — 500. **R. J. Reynolds Tobacco Co.** (HQ); Winston-Salem; tobacco products — 500. **Stoneville Furniture Co.** (HQ); Stoneville; metal dining room furniture — 500.

6th District

Central — Greensboro, High Point

The Davidson-for-Rockingham switch that benefited the 5th District incumbent was expected to make life easier for the 6th District's Republican incumbent as well. Of the counties statewide that supported Ronald Reagan, and the Republican candidates for Senate and Governor in 1980, Davidson is the most populous. Like the rest of the district, Davidson is a textile- and furniture-producing area.

Despite the addition of Davidson, the district has a 2-to-1 Democratic registration edge, and the first-term Republican seatholder lost in 1982 to his Democratic challenger.

The focal point of the 6th is Greensboro and surrounding Guilford County, home to 60 percent of the new district's residents. Greensboro, second-largest city in the state, is headquarters for several textile companies, including Burlington Industries. Guilford County also is an important furniture producer. High Point, south of Greensboro, refers to itself as the "furniture capital of the world"; visitors are directed to a building in the town that resembles a giant chest of drawers. Thomasville (Davidson County) bills itself as the "chair capital of the world" and a giant chair is the centerpiece of the town square.

Guilford County has developed an appreciable Republican vote partly because of the managerial personnel in its factories. In 1980 both Reagan and GOP Senate candidate John East carried the county.

East of Greensboro, the 6th takes in Alamance County. Conservative Democrats in Alamance have been moving to the GOP in recent years; Reagan carried the county in 1980.

Election Returns

6th District		Democrat		Republican	
1976	President	82,056	(51.3%)	76,934	(48.1%)
	Governor	97,756	(61.4%)	58,953	(37.0%)
	House	102,729	(82.4%)	18,835	(15.1%)
1978	Senate	42,608	(44.9%)	52,392	(55.1%)
	House	61,033	(64.7%)	33,275	(35.3%)
1980	President	74,137	(42.4%)	94,162	(53.8%)
	Governor	101,164	(57.2%)	74,442	(42.1%)
	Senate	76,084	(43.7%)	96,752	(55.6%)
	House	83,428	(47.6%)	91,835	(52.4%)
1982	House	68,696	(53.8%)	58,244	(45.7%)

Demographics

Population: 529,635. **Percent Change from 1970:** 10.2%.

Land Area: 1,632 square miles. **Population per Square Mile:** 324.5.

Counties, 1980 Population: Alamance — 99,319; Davidson — 113,162; Guilford — 317,154.

Cities, 1980 Population: Burlington — 37,266; Greensboro — 155,642; High Point (Pt.) — 63,351; Lexington — 15,711; Thomasville 14,144.

Race and Ancestry: White — 78.5%; Black — 20.7%; American Indian, Eskimo and Aleut — 0.3%; Asian and Pacific Islander — 0.3%; Spanish Origin — 0.7%. Dutch — 0.5%; English — 21.3%; French — 0.5%; German — 6.8%; Irish — 4.0%; Scottish — 0.8%.

Universities, Enrollment: Bennett College, Greensboro — 620; Davidson County Community College, Lexington — 2,357; Elon College, Elon College — 2,577; Greensboro College, Greensboro — 672; Guilford College, Greensboro — 1,679; Guilford Technical Institute, Jamestown — 4,190; High Point College, High Point — 1,440; Rutledge College, Greensboro — 401; Technical College of Alamance, Haw River — 1,575; North Carolina Agricultural and Technical State

University, Greensboro — 5,467; University of North Carolina at Greensboro, Greensboro — 10,390.

Newspapers, Circulation: *The Daily Times-News* (eS), Burlington — 27,898; *The Dispatch* (e), Lexington — 12,606; *Greensboro Daily News* (mS), Greensboro — 81,783; *The Greensboro Record* (e), Greensboro — 31,328; *The High Point Enterprise* (eS), High Point — 30,487; *The Times* (m), Thomasville — 7,696.

Commercial Television Stations, Affiliation: WFMY-TV, Greensboro (CBS); WGGT, Greensboro (None); WGHP-TV, High Point (ABC). Entire district is located in Greensboro-Winston Salem-High Point ADI.

Industries:

Cone Mills Corp. (HQ); Greensboro; cotton fabrics — 4,000. **Loews Theatres Inc.** (P. Lorillard Div.); Greensboro; cigarettes — 3,500. **Thomasville Furniture Industries** (Armstrong Furniture Div. - HQ); Thomasville; wooden bedroom furniture — 3,500. **Western Electric Co. Inc.;** Greensboro; communications systems — 3,200. **Burlington Industries Inc.** (HQ); Greensboro; fabrics, yarns — 2,000.

Moses H. Cone Memorial Hospital; Greensboro; hospital — 1,650. **Jefferson-Pilot Corp.** (HQ); Greensboro; life insurance, broadcasting, newspaper publishing — 1,470. **PPG Industries Inc.** (Fiber Glass Div.); Lexington; fiberglass products — 1,400. **Dart Industries Inc.** (Duracell International Div.); Lexington; batteries — 1,200. **Wesley Long Community Hospital;** Greensboro; hospital — 1,200. **General Electric Co.;** Mebane; industrial controls — 1,100. **Gilbarco Inc.;** Greensboro; gasoline pumps — 1,100. **Cone Mills Corp.** (Revolutionary Plant); Greensboro; cotton fabric mills — 1,000. **Dixie Furniture Co. Inc.** (HQ); Lexington; bedroom furniture — 1,000.

Guilford Mills Inc. (Jersey Kapwood - HQ); Greensboro; fabric mills — 1,000. **Thomas Built Buses Inc.** (HQ); High Point; bus bodies — 850. **Western Electric Co. Inc.;** Burlington; radio, television transmitting equipment — 700. **Cone Mills Corp.** (Granite Finishing Co.); Haw River; cotton fabric mills — 600. **Collins & Aikman Corp.** (Monarch Processing Div.); Graham; yarn finishing — 548. **AMF Inc.** (Hatteras Yachts); High Point; fiberglass yachts — 500. **Copland Fabrics Inc.;** Burlington; synthetic fabric mills — 500. **Glen Raven Mills Inc.;** Altamahaw; women's hosiery — 500. **Silver Knit Industries Inc.** (HQ); High Point; women's hosiery — 500.

7th District

Southeast — Fayetteville, Wilmington

Nearly one-half of the people in the 7th live in Cumberland County. With Fort Bragg and Pope Air Force Base both near Fayetteville, Cumberland is heavily oriented toward the military.

As in demographically-similar Onslow County in the 3rd District, Cumberland voters deserted the Democratic Party in droves in 1980. Jimmy Carter won 63 percent of the county vote in 1976, but tumbled to a meager 49 percent plurality the second time out. At the same time, though, Cumberland preferred Democrat Robert Morgan to Republican John P. East in Morgan's unsuccessful campaign for re-election to the Senate.

Besides Fayetteville, the only other major city in the 7th District is Wilmington (New Hanover County). The restoration of Wilmington's historic waterfront district has brought tourism and some white-collar prosperity to this old port and fishing center. Republican sentiment is strong; New Hanover County gave a majority of its vote to Ronald Reagan in 1980, the only county in the 7th District to do so.

Of North Carolina's 64,652 American Indians, 55 percent live in Robeson County, a heavily Democratic area where Carter took 70 percent of the 1980 vote. Robeson

County is about the same size as New Hanover County and more than compensates for Republican majorities on the coast.

Sweet potatoes, soybeans, corn and tobacco dominate the district's farm economy, and textiles and timber are important industries. Redistricting moved Democratic Hoke County from the 7th to the 8th.

Election Returns

7th District		Democrat		Republican	
1976	President	78,021	(65.9%)	39,640	(33.5%)
	Governor	89,722	(76.8%)	25,736	(22.0%)
	House	91,724	(81.0%)	21,571	(19.0%)
1978	Senate	37,177	(49.5%)	37,924	(50.5%)
	House	51,439	(69.4%)	22,677	(30.6%)
1980	President	70,334	(53.5%)	57,184	(43.5%)
	Governor	87,656	(66.7%)	42,627	(32.4%)
	Senate	69,903	(55.3%)	55,508	(43.9%)
	House	84,958	(68.2%)	39,551	(31.8%)
1982	House	68,529	(71.0%)	27,015	(28.0%)

Demographics

Population: 539,055. **Percent Change from 1970:** 19.5%.

Land Area: 3,590 square miles. **Population per Square Mile:** 150.2.

Counties, 1980 Population: Brunswick — 35,777; Columbus — 51,037; Cumberland — 247,160; New Hanover — 103,471; Robeson — 101,610.

Cities, 1980 Population: Fayetteville — 59,507; Lumberton — 18,241; Wilmington — 44,000.

Race and Ancestry: White — 63.1%; Black — 27.3%; American Indian, Eskimo and Aleut — 7.6%; Asian and Pacific Islander — 1.0%. Spanish Origin — 2.2%. English — 16.6%; French — 0.7%; German — 3.3%; Irish — 3.7%; Italian — 0.5%; Scottish — 0.9%.

Universities, Enrollment: Cape Fear Technical Institute, Wilmington — 1,844; Fayetteville Technical Institute, Fayetteville — 5,284; Methodist College, Fayetteville — 943; Robeson Technical Institute, Lumberton — 1,126; Rutledge College, Fayetteville — 556; Southeastern Community College, Whiteville — 2,090; Fayetteville State University, Fayetteville — 2,464; Pembroke State University, Pembroke — 2,301; University of North Carolina at Wilmington, Wilmington — 4,696.

Newspapers, Circulation: *Fayetteville Observer* (eS), Fayetteville — 42,010; *Fayetteville Times* (mS), Fayetteville — 21,663; *The Robesonian* (eS), Lumberton — 15,100; *Wilmington Morning Star* (mS), Wilmington — 37,118.

Commercial Television Stations, Affiliation: WECT, Wilmington (NBC); WKFT, Fayetteville (None); WWAY, Wilmington (ABC). Most of district is located in Wilmington ADI. Portion is in Raleigh-Durham ADI.

Military Installations: Fort Bragg, Fayetteville — 50,102; Fort Fisher Air Force Station, Kure Beach — 111; Pope Air Force Base, Springlake — 4,400; Sunny Point Military Ocean Terminal (Army), Wilmington — 441.

Nuclear Power Plants: Brunswick 1, Southport (General Electric, Brown & Root), March 1977; Brunswick 2, Southport (General Electric, Brown & Root), November 1975.

Industries:

Kelly-Springfield Tire Co.; Fayetteville; tires, inner tubes — 2,700. **E. I. du Pont de Nemours & Co. Inc.;** Wilmington; synthetic fiber — 2,300. **General Electric Co. Inc.;** Wilmington; nuclear fuel — 2,300. **Eltra Corp.** (Converse Rubber Co.); Lumberton; rubber footwear —

1,850. **Federal Paper Board Co. Inc.;** Riegelwood; pulp, paper mills — 1,500.

New Hanover Memorial Hospital; Wilmington; hospital — 1,430. **Cumberland County Hospital Systems Inc.;** Fayetteville; hospital — 1,200. **West Point-Pepperell Inc.** (Alamac Knitting Div.); Lumberton; knit outerwear mills — 1,000. **Babcock & Wilcox Co.;** Wilmington; fabricated plate work — 800. **Kayser-Roth Hosiery Inc.;** Lumberton; women's hosiery — 800. **Purolator Inc.;** Fayetteville; machinery — 800. **Croft Metals Inc. of North Carolina** (HQ); Lumber Bridge; doors, frames — 600. **National Spinning Co. Inc.;** Whiteville; knitting yarns — 600. **Ithaca Textiles Inc.;** Chadbourn; women's underwear — 575. **Pacesetter Industries Inc.** (France Neckwear Mfg. Co.); Wilmington; men's ties, belts — 500. **Singer Co. Inc.** (Coil Div.); Wilmington; air conditioning equipment — 500.

8th District

South Central — Kannapolis, Salisbury

Two changes in the boundaries of the 8th benefited Democratic office seekers. Moved from the 7th District into the 8th District was Hoke County, a rural area of the state where the 44 percent black population combines with a significant American Indian minority to deliver an overwhelming Democratic vote. Hoke makes up just 4 percent of the district population, however.

Redistricting removed from the 8th part of Republican Moore County, although the district retained affluent, GOP-voting resort communities in Moore such as Southern Pines and Pinehurst, location of the World Golf Hall of Fame.

Except for those changes, the 8th was not significantly altered by redistricting. The mountain counties in the northern part of the district and the textile factory towns in the center lean Republican; both areas voted for Reagan in 1980. The agricultural counties in the southern part of the 8th prefer Democrats; they chose Jimmy Carter in 1980.

Cotton-growing was once the major economic activity in the 8th District's southern counties, but soybeans, poultry and dairy products are playing an increasingly important role. Small cities and towns in the north such as Kannapolis, Salisbury (Rowan County) and Concord (Cabarrus County) manufacture textiles, clothing and textile machinery. Kannapolis is the district's largest population center, with 29,628 residents. Founded by Cannon Mills, the textile manufacturer, Kannapolis has never incorporated; many of the houses there still are owned by the company.

Election Returns

8th District		Democrat		Republican	
1976	President	86,180	(55.4%)	68,522	(44.1%)
	Governor	96,626	(63.2%)	55,020	(36.0%)
	House	100,426	(66.5%)	48,028	(31.8%)
1978	Senate	50,098	(45.7%)	59,464	(54.3%)
	House	63,644	(59.7%)	42,934	(40.3%)
1980	President	76,466	(45.6%)	86,672	(51.7%)
	Governor	97,469	(58.2%)	69,147	(41.3%)
	Senate	76,116	(46.1%)	88,210	(53.5%)
	House	95,687	(59.1%)	66,261	(40.9%)
1982	House	71,691	(57.4%)	52,417	(41.9%)

Demographics

Population: 535,526. **Percent Change from 1970:** 17.6%.

Land Area: 5,066 square miles. **Population per Square Mile:** 105.7.

Counties, 1980 Population: Anson — 25,649; Cabarrus — 85,895; Davie — 24,599; Hoke — 20,383; Montgomery — 22,469; Moore (Pt.) — 39,400; Richmond — 45,481; Rowan — 99,186; Scotland — 32,273; Stanly — 48,517; Union — 70,380; Yadkin (Pt.) — 21,294.

Cities, 1980 Population: Albemarle — 15,110; Concord — 16,942; Kannapolis — 29,628; Laurinburg — 11,480; Monroe — 12,639; Salisbury — 22,677.

Race and Ancestry: White — 78.5%; Black — 20.1%; American Indian, Eskimo and Aleut — 1.1%; Asian and Pacific Islander — 0.2%. Spanish Origin — 0.7%. Dutch — 0.5%; English — 21.0%; German — 7.9%; Irish — 3.6%; Scottish — 1.0%.

Universities, Enrollment: Anson Technical Institute, Ansonville — 546; Barber-Scotia College, Concord — 319; Catawba College, Salisbury — 988; Livingstone College, Salisbury — 938; Montgomery Technical Institute, Troy — 435; Pfeiffer College, Misenheimer — 814; Richmond Technical Institute, Hamlet — 1,074; Rowan Technical Institute, Salisbury — 1,884; St. Andrews Presbyterian College, Laurinburg — 754; Stanly Technical College, Albemarle — 742; Wingate College, Wingate — 1,534.

Newspapers, Circulation: *The Concord Tribune* (eS), Concord — 12,356; *The Daily Independent* (eS), Kannapolis — 13,352; *The Enquirer-Journal* (e), Monroe — 11,826; *Richmond County Daily Journal* (e), Rockingham — 7,290; *Salisbury Evening Post* (e), Salisbury — 24,591. *The Charlotte Observer* also circulates in the district.

Commercial Television Stations, Affiliation: Most of district is in Charlotte ADI. Portions are in Greensboro-Winston Salem-High Point ADI, Raleigh-Durham ADI and Florence (S.C.) ADI.

Military Installations: Fort Bragg *(See 7th District)*; Badin Air National Guard Station, Badin — 141.

Industries:

Cannon Mills Co. (HQ); Kannapolis; broad-woven fabric mills — 12,500. **Wiscassett Mills Co.;** Albemarle; yarn spinning mills — 1,800. **Linn-Corriher Corp.** (Linn Div.); Landis; yarn spinning mills — 1,270. **Burlington Industries Inc.** (Raeford Worsted Dyeing); Raeford; fabric dyeing and finishing — 1,250. **Cabarrus Memorial Hospital Inc.;** Concord; hospital — 1,200.

Burlington Industries Inc. (Richmond Plant); Cordova; fabric mills — 1,110. **Abbott Laboratories;** Laurinburg; pharmaceutical preparations — 1,000. **Allison Mfg. Co.** (HQ); Albemarle; children's shirts — 1,000. **SCM Corp.** (Proctor Silex Corp.); Southern Pines; electrical housewares — 1,000. **Hanes Corp.** (Sandhurst Plant); Rockingham; women's hosiery — 960. **Unifi Inc.;** Yadkinville; textile finishing — 960. **China Grove Cotton Mills Co.** (HQ); China Grove; yarn spinning, finishing — 950. **Cannon Mills Co. Inc.;** Concord; cotton fabrics — 900. **House of Raeford Farms Inc.;** Raeford; poultry processing — 900. **Cone Mills Corp.;** Salisbury; denim cloth — 875. **Cannon Mills Co. Inc.;** China Grove; cotton fabrics — 850. **Pinehurst Inc.** (HQ); Pinehurst; resort, real estate developing — 798. **Ingersoll-Rand Co.;** Mocksville; air compressors — 750.

Reeves Brothers Inc. (West Knitting Mills Div.); Wadesboro; knitted thermal underwear — 750. **Aluminum Co. of America;** Badin; primary aluminum production — 740. **Holly Farms Poultry Industries Inc.;** Monroe; poultry processing — 740. **Clark Equipment Co.** (Transmission Div.); Rockingham; industrial trucks, tractors — 700. **Federal Pacific Electric Co.;** Albemarle; switchgear, switchboard apparatus — 700. **Clayson Knitting Co. Inc.;** Star; men's, children's hosiery — 677. **Libbey-Owens-Ford Corp.;** Laurinburg; flat glass — 650. **M. A. N. Truck & Bus Corp.;** Cleveland; truck, bus assembly — 620. **Kayser-Roth Corp.;** Concord; women's hosiery — 617. **Fisher Supply & Engineering Co.;** Salisbury; operative builders — 608. **Fieldcrest Mills Inc.** (Karastan Laurel Hill Div.); Laurel Hill; carpets — 600. **Fieldcrest Mills Inc.** (North Carolina Finishing Co. Div.); Salisbury; cotton fabric finishers — 600.

Ithaca Industries Inc.; Robbins; women's hosiery — 600. **M. Lowenstein & Sons Inc.** (Aleo Mfg. Co. Div.); Rockingham; broad-woven cotton fabric mills — 600. **Martin Mills Inc.** (Albemarle Spinning Mills Div.); Albemarle; yarn spinning mills — 600. **Collins & Aikman Corp.** (Automotive Div.); Albemarle; auto carpeting — 570. **Waverly Mills Inc.;** Laurinburg; yarn spinning mills — 570. **Spring Mills Inc.** (Springfield Plant); Laurel Hill; broad-woven fabric mills — 564. **J. P. Stevens & Co. Inc.** (Scotland Plant); Wagram; cotton fabric — 550. **Springs Mills Inc.** (Aileen Plant); Biscoe; wooden household furniture — 550. **Faberge Inc.;** Raeford; cosmetics — 500. **McGraw-Edison Co.** (Ingraham Toastmaster Div.); Laurinburg; clocks, timers — 500. **McGregor-Doniger Inc.;** Mount Gilead; women's lingerie — 500. **Stanly Knitting Mills Inc.** (HQ); Oakboro; knit outerwear mills — 500.

9th District

West Central — Charlotte

The 9th is dominated by Mecklenburg County, location of Charlotte, the largest city of the two Carolinas. Charlotte's role as the supply, service and distribution center for the North and South Carolina Piedmont area gives it a diversified economy not dependent on the textile-and-tobacco base traditional in the region.

Large construction and trucking firms are based here, and North Carolina's major banks have built towers that give the city an impressive skyline. The blend of white-collar economic conservatism, working-class Democratic allegiances and a 26.5 percent black population make for close elections in Mecklenburg County. Ronald Reagan carried the county with 48 percent in 1980, but Republican John P. East lost it to Democrat Robert Morgan by 2,087 votes in the 1980 Senate race.

Mecklenburg County contains three-fourths of the district's population; most of the remainder is divided between Iredell and Lincoln counties, predominantly rural areas with some textile factories in the towns. Just over 7,000 residents of Republican Yadkin County fill out the 9th while the bulk of Yadkin remains in the neighboring 8th.

Situated directly above Mecklenburg, Iredell went for the GOP in the 1980 presidential and U.S. Senate races, but Democrat James B. Hunt Jr. carried it easily in his successful gubernatorial re-election bid. Yadkin County is solid GOP territory.

Election Returns

9th District		Democrat		Republican	
1976	President	86,436	(51.5%)	80,603	(48.0%)
	Governor	100,873	(61.0%)	63,075	(38.1%)
	House	71,472	(46.1%)	82,774	(53.4%)
1978	Senate	46,111	(43.8%)	59,270	(56.2%)
	House	30,214	(30.9%)	66,622	(68.3%)
1980	President	87,144	(46.0%)	93,258	(49.3%)
	Governor	122,402	(65.8%)	62,004	(33.3%)
	Senate	86,435	(48.9%)	88,705	(50.2%)
	House	72,044	(41.4%)	101,812	(58.6%)
1982	House	47,258	(41.9%)	64,297	(57.0%)

Demographics

Population: 536,325. **Percent Change from 1970:** 15.3%.

Land Area: 1,492 square miles. **Population per Square Mile:** 359.5.

Counties, 1980 Population: Iredell — 82,538; Lincoln — 42,372; Mecklenburg — 404,270; Yadkin (Pt.) — 7,145.

Cities, 1980 Population: Charlotte — 314,447; Statesville — 18,622.

Race and Ancestry: White — 75.5%; Black — 23.3%; American Indian, Eskimo and Aleut — 0.3%; Asian and Pacific Islander — 0.5%. Spanish Origin — 0.9%. Dutch — 0.5%; English — 16.4%; French — 0.6%; German — 6.2%; Irish — 4.1%; Italian — 0.5%; Scottish — 0.8%.

Universities, Enrollment: Central Piedmont Community College, Charlotte — 24,403; Davidson College, Davidson — 1,403; Johnson C. Smith University, Charlotte — 1,379; King's College, Charlotte, 375; Mitchell Community College, Statesville — 1,412; Queens College, Charlotte — 913; Rutledge College, Charlotte — 351; University of North Carolina at Charlotte, Charlotte — 9,383.

Newspapers, Circulation: *The Charlotte News* (e), Charlotte — 52,039; *The Charlotte Observer* (mS), Charlotte — 169,722; *Statesville Record & Landmark* (e), Statesville — 17,817.

Commercial Television Stations, Affiliation: WBTV, Charlotte (CBS); WCCB, Charlotte (None); WPCQ-TV, Charlotte (NBC); WSOC-TV, Charlotte (ABC). Most of district is located in Charlotte ADI. Portion is in Greensboro-Winston Salem-High Point ADI.

Military Installations: Douglas Municipal Airport (Air Force), Charlotte — 961.

Nuclear Power Plants: McGuire 1 and 2, Cowans Ford Dam (Westinghouse, Duke Power).

Industries:

Celanese Corp. (Celanese Fibers Co.); Charlotte; fibers — 3,000. **Presbyterian Hospital Inc.**; Charlotte; hospital — 1,700. **First Union Corp.** (HQ); Charlotte; bank holding company — 1,550. **Lance Inc.** (HQ); Charlotte; cookies, candies, crackers — 1,400. **NCNB Corp.** (HQ); Charlotte; banking — 1,200.

General Tire & Rubber Co.; Charlotte; tires, inner tubes — 1,100. **Charlotte Mecklenburg Hospital Inc.**; Charlotte; hospital — 1,000. **Knight Publishing Co. Inc.**; Charlotte; newspaper publishing — 1,000. **Westinghouse Corp.** (Turbine Plant); Charlotte; steam turbines — 938. **Templon Spinning Mills Inc.** (HQ); Mooresville; yarn spinning mills — 900. **United Merchants & Manufacturers Inc.** (Uniglass Industries); Statesville; fabric mills — 900.

Barclays American Corp. (Barclays Am-Fin Div. - HQ); Charlotte; banking — 857. **American Bakeries Co.** (Merita Bakery); Charlotte; bakery products — 840. **Allstate Insurance Co.**; Charlotte; life insurance — 800. **Martin Marietta Corp.** (Sodyeco); Charlotte; industrial inorganic chemicals — 800.

Reeves Brothers Inc. (Curon Div.); Cornelius; fabricated rubber products — 800. **Pinkerton's Inc.**; Charlotte; security services — 750. **Home Curtain Corp.** (Draymore Mfg. Div.); Mooresville; curtains, draperies — 700. **NL Industries Inc.** (NL Fasteners); Statesville; metal hardware — 700.

Beauty Maid Mills Inc.; Statesville; women's wear — 650. **Heritage Village Church Masonry Fellowship** (PTL Television Network - HQ); Charlotte; evangelical broadcasting — 650. **J. P. Stevens & Co. Inc.**; Lincolnton; yarn spinning mills — 650. **Radiator Specialty Co.** (HQ); Charlotte; auto parts — 625. **Charlotte Liberty Mutual Insurance Co.** (HQ); Charlotte; medical, life insurance — 575. **Clark Equipment Co.**; Statesville; motor vehicle parts — 550.

Duff-Norton Co. Inc. (HQ); Charlotte; industrial machinery — 550. **Western Electric Co. Inc.**; Charlotte; electrical wiring supplies — 502. **Belk Brothers Co.** (HQ); Charlotte; department store chain — 500. **Bernhardt Furniture Co.**; Troutman; wooden household furniture — 500. **Biggers Brothers Inc.**; Charlotte; grocery wholesaling — 500. **Blythe Industries Inc.** (Blythe Paving Co. Div. - HQ); Charlotte; heavy highway construction — 500.

Consolidated Foods Corp. (Oxford Building Services); Charlotte; janitorial services — 500. **Overnite Transportation Co.**; Charlotte; freight terminal — 500. **Security Forces Inc.** (HQ); Charlotte; security services — 500. **Thurston Motor Lines Inc.** (HQ); Charlotte; trucking — 500.

10th District

West — Gastonia, Hickory

The 10th District starts at the Tennessee line in Watauga and Avery counties, which have popular Appalachian mountain retreats, and runs south to industrial Gaston County on the border with South Carolina. It is one of two North Carolina districts in which every county gave a majority to John P. East, the Republican candidate for the Senate in 1980.

Gastonia is the seat of Gaston County, and, with 47,333 residents, the district's population center. The primary industries in the district are textiles and furniture.

The blue-collar vote, substantial in the southern and central parts of the district, is basically conservative. The blue-collar counties went for fellow-Southerner Jimmy Carter in 1976, but swung decisively to Ronald Reagan in 1980.

The remap moved nearly 10,000 people in Avery County from the 11th to the 10th. Avery and neighboring Watuaga vote strongly Republican; their economic fortunes are increasingly tied to the patronage of skiers and owners of vacation homes. The 10th lost Republican Alexander County to the 5th.

Election Returns

10th District		Democrat		Republican	
1976	President	87,054	(53.8%)	74,185	(45.8%)
	Governor	96,845	(61.1%)	61,194	(38.6%)
	House	63,918	(39.7%)	96,872	(60.2%)
1978	Senate	43,012	(43.8%)	55,169	(56.2%)
	House	698	(1.1%)	62,773	(98.9%)
1980	President	71,693	(42.1%)	93,520	(55.0%)
	Governor	91,758	(54.6%)	75,374	(44.9%)
	Senate	67,677	(41.3%)	95,378	(58.2%)
	House	49,878	(30.1%)	115,976	(69.6%)
1982	House	—		80,904	(92.7%)

Demographics

Population: 532,954. **Percent Change from 1970:** 15.6%.

Land Area: 2,680 square miles. **Population per Square Mile:** 198.9.

Counties, 1980 Population: Avery (Pt.) — 9,827; Burke — 72,504; Caldwell — 67,746; Catawba — 105,208; Cleveland — 83,435; Gaston — 162,568; Watauga — 31,666.

Cities, 1980 Population: Boone — 10,191; Gastonia — 47,333; Hickory — 20,757; Lenoir — 13,748; Morganton — 13,763; North Belmont — 10,762; Shelby — 15,310; St. Stephens — 10,797.

Race and Ancestry: White — 89.0%; Black — 10.6%; American Indian, Eskimo and Aleut — 0.1%; Asian and Pacific Islander — 0.2%. Spanish Origin — 0.5%. Dutch — 0.8%; English — 19.8%; French — 0.5%; German — 9.5%; Irish — 5.5%; Scottish — 0.7%.

Universities, Enrollment: Appalachian State University, Boone — 9,794; Belmont Abbey College, Belmont — 855; Caldwell Community College and Technical Institute, Lenoir — 1,722; Catawba Valley Technical Institute, Hickory — 2,272; Cleveland Technical College, Shelby — 1,061; Gardner-Webb College, Boiling Springs — 1,524; Gaston College, Dallas — 2,970; Lees-McRae College, Banner Elk — 730; Lenoir-Rhyne College, Hickory — 1,386; Sacred Heart College,

Belmont — 406; Western Piedmont Community College, Morganton — 1,726.

Newspapers, Circulation: *The Gastonia Gazette* (eS), Gastonia — 34,135; *The Hickory Daily Record* (e), Hickory — 26,859; *Lenoir News-Topic* (e), Lenoir — 11,166; *The News-Herald* (e), Morganton — 10,791; *The Observer-News-Enterprise* (e), Newton — 3,656; *Shelby Daily Star* (e), Shelby — 17,267. *The Charlotte Observer* also circulates in the district.

Commercial Television Stations, Affiliation: WHKY-TV, Hickory (None). Most of district is located in Charlotte ADI. Portion is in Bristol (Va.)-Kingsport (Tenn.)-Johnson City (Tenn.) ADI.

Industries:

Textron Inc. (Homelite); Gastonia; special industrial machinery — 1,800. **Bassett Furniture Industries Inc.** (Upholstery Div.); Newton; furniture — 1,600. **Carolina Freight Carriers Corp.** (HQ); Cherryville; trucking — 1,600. **Broughton Hospital;** Morganton; psychiatric hospital — 1,600. **PPG Industries;** Shelby; pressed, blown glass — 1,500.

TI-Caro Inc. (Spun-Lo Eiderilon - HQ); Gastonia; yarn, thread mills — 1,100. **Hickory Hill Furniture Co.** (Crestline Furniture Div. - HQ); Valdese; upholstered furniture — 1,050. **Gaston Memorial Hospital Inc.;** Gastonia; hospital — 1,020. **TRW Inc.;** Boone; electronic components — 1,000. **Kincaid Furniture Co. Inc.** (HQ); Hudson; wood, upholstered furniture — 900. **Henredon Furniture Industries** (HQ); Morganton; wood, upholstered furniture — 850. **Fiber Industries Inc.;** Shelby; synthetic fibers — 800. **TI-Caro Inc.** (Rex Mills Div.); Gastonia; yarn spinning mills — 800. **Tultex Corp.;** Lowell; yarn spinning mills — 800. **U. S. Industries Inc.** (Hammary Mfg. Div.); Lenoir; wooden household furniture — 800. **Coval Corp.** (HQ); Catawba; wires, cables — 750. **Union Underwear Co. Inc.** (Clevemont Mills); Kings Mountain; knit outerwear mills — 750.

Merchants Distributors Inc. (HQ); Hickory; grocery distributing — 745. **Conover Glove Mfg. Co.;** Conover; work gloves — 700. **Siecor Corp.** (Superior Cable - HQ); Hickory; telephone wire — 700. **A. M. Smyre Mfg. Co.;** Gastonia; yarn spinning mills — 700. **J. P. Stevens & Co. Inc.;** Stanley; synthetic fabric finishing — 700. **Century Furniture Co.** (HQ); Hickory; wood, upholstered furniture — 680. **Impact Furniture Inc.** (HQ); Hildebran; wooden furniture — 650. **Burlington Industries Inc.** (Sportswear Div.); Cramerton; synthetic fabric finishing — 635. **Freightliner Corp.;** Mount Holly; trucks, tractors — 610. **Lane Co. Inc.** (Hickory Chair Co.); Hickory; upholstered furniture — 600. **Skyland Textile Co.** (HQ); Morganton; children's outerwear — 600. **Ora Mill Co.;** Shelby; synthetic broad-woven fabrics — 587.

Drexel Heritage Furnishings (HQ); Drexel; wooden household furniture — 550. **Lithium Corp. of America;** Gastonia; lithium mining — 550. **Esther Mill Corp.;** Shelby; synthetic fabric mills — 549. **Broyhill Furniture Industries** (HQ); Lenoir; wooden household furniture — 500. **Eaton Corp.** (Fuller Transmissions); Kings Mountain; truck transmissions — 500. **Fasco Industries Inc.;** Shelby; industrial controls — 500. **Great Lakes Carbon Corp.** (Graphic Products Div.); Morganton; carbon, graphite products — 500. **Hickory Furniture Co.** (HQ); Hickory; wood, upholstered furniture — 500. **Hickory Mfg. Co.;** Hickory; wooden household furniture — 500. **Maiden Knitting Mills Inc.;** Maiden; knit fabrics — 500. **Parkdale Mills Inc.** (HQ); Gastonia; yarn spinning mills — 500. **Valdese Mfg. Co.;** Valdese; textile finishing, yarn mills — 500.

11th District

West — Asheville

Democrats lead comfortably in registration in the 11th District, but Republicans have been a potent minority in the mountains of western North Carolina since the Civil War. In recent years, a wave of retirees moving into picturesque Henderson and Polk counties has added to traditional GOP strength in the district. About 20 percent of the population in Polk County is 65 or older, the largest concentration of senior citizens in western North Carolina. The newcomers helped a Republican win the House seat in 1980, the first Republican since 1928 to do so.

The 11th District's sole urban center is Asheville, a resort town, home of novelist Thomas Wolfe and a regional market center whose relatively small population of 53,281 belies its commercial importance.

Along with surrounding Buncombe County, Asheville accounts for nearly one-third of the district's total population. The Democratic Party usually enjoys an edge in local Buncombe County contests, but Republican candidates carried Buncombe in the 1968, 1972 and 1980 presidential elections and in the 1978 and 1980 Senate races.

Industrial activity west of Asheville focuses on paper, pulp and textiles. Though much of the terrain is steep and rocky, there is cultivation of tobacco, corn, potatoes and oats. Some Democratic labor strength can be found in the factory towns scattered through the valleys.

Redistricting split Avery County, shifting two-thirds of its people to the 10th while keeping nearly 5,000 Avery residents in the 11th; the county is heavily Republican.

The federal government has jurisdiction over a significant share of the land in the 11th District; the Nantahala and Pisgah National Forests, the Great Smoky Mountains National Park, and the Cherokee Indian Reservation are in the 11th. Around these scenic areas, tourist dollars boost the economy.

Election Returns

11th District		Democrat		Republican	
1976	President	98,452	(54.3%)	81,747	(45.1%)
	Governor	111,428	(60.9%)	70,594	(38.6%)
	House	92,825	(51.4%)	86,176	(47.7%)
1978	Senate	67,799	(48.2%)	72,812	(51.8%)
	House	74,762	(53.7%)	64,543	(46.3%)
1980	President	87,984	(45.7%)	98,258	(51.0%)
	Governor	109,332	(56.3%)	83,641	(43.1%)
	Senate	90,592	(47.7%)	98,122	(51.7%)
	House	89,621	(46.7%)	102,123	(53.3%)
1982	House	85,410	(49.9%)	84,085	(49.2%)

Demographics

Population: 531,144. **Percent Change from 1970:** 15.6%.

Land Area: 6,763 square miles. **Population per Square Mile:** 78.5.

Counties, 1980 Population: Avery (Pt.) — 4,582; Buncombe — 160,934; Cherokee — 18,933; Clay — 6,619; Graham — 7,217; Haywood — 46,495; Henderson — 58,580; Jackson — 25,811; Macon — 20,178; Madison — 16,827; McDowell — 35,135; Mitchell — 14,428; Polk — 12,984; Rutherford — 53,787; Swain — 10,283; Transylvania — 23,417; Yancey — 14,934.

Cities, 1980 Population: Asheville — 53,583.

Race and Ancestry: White — 93.0%; Black — 5.5%; American Indian, Eskimo and Aleut — 1.2%; Asian and Pacific Islander — 0.2%. Spanish Origin — 0.7%. Dutch — 0.9%; English — 25.9%; French 0.6%; German — 4.1%; Irish — 7.0%; Scottish — 0.9%.

Universities, Enrollment: Asheville-Buncombe Technical Institute, Asheville — 2,318; Blanton's Junior College, Asheville — 206; Blue Ridge Technical Institute, Flat Rock — 947; Brevard College, Brevard — 750; Cecils Junior College of Business, Asheville — 268; Haywood

Technical Institute, Clyde — 875; Isothermal Community College, Spindale — 2,036.

Mars Hill College, Mars Hill — 1,862; Mayland Technical Institute, Spruce Pine — 603; McDowell Technical Institute, Marion — 522; Montreat-Anderson College, Montreat — 407; Southwestern Technical College, Sylva — 897; Tri-County Community College, Murphy — 653; University of North Carolina at Asheville, Asheville — 2,099; Warren Wilson College, Swannanoa — 496; Western Carolina University, Cullowhee — 6,462.

Newspapers, Circulation: *The Citizen* (mS), Asheville — 49,278; *The Daily Courier* (e), Forest — 9,865; *The Times* (eS), Asheville — 15,802; *The Times-News* (e), Hendersonville — 12,048; *The Tryon Daily Bulletin* (m), Tryon — 3,001.

Commercial Television Stations, Affiliation: WHNS, Asheville (None); WLOS-TV, Asheville (ABC). Most of district is located in Greenville (S.C.)-Spartanburg (S.C.)-Asheville ADI. Portions are in Charlotte ADI, Atlanta (Ga.) ADI, Bristol (Va.)-Kingsport (Tenn.)-Johnson City (Tenn.) ADI and Chattanooga (Tenn.) ADI.

Industries:

Travenol Laboratories (Baxter Laboratories Div.); Marion; pharmaceutical preparations — 3,500. **Olin Corp.** (Ecusta Paper & Film Group); Pisgah Forest; paper mills — 2,800. **Champion International Corp.** (Paper Div.); Canton; paper coating, glazing — 2,120. **Dayco Corp.;** Waynesville; foam rubber products — 1,950. **General Electric Co.** (Lighting Systems Dept.); Hendersonville; power transformers — 1,650.

Memorial Mission Hospital of Western North Carolina; Asheville; hospital — 1,370. **Stonecutter Mills Corp.** (HQ); Spindale; broadwoven fabric mills — 1,250. **Square D Co. Inc.** (Control Group Div.); Asheville; switchgear, switchboard apparatus — 1,200. **Cannon Mills Co.** (Beacon Mfg. Co. Div.); Swannanoa; wool blankets — 1,000. **Spindale Mills Inc.** (HQ); Spindale; synthetic woven fabric mills — 930. **Cone Mills Corp.;** Cliffside; cotton fabric mills — 900. **Henredon Furniture Industries;** Spruce Pine; upholstered furniture — 885. **American Thread Co.;** Marion; thread mills — 800. **Kimberly-Clark Corp.** (Berkley Mills Div.); Balfour; cotton fabric mills — 800. **Sylco Corp.;** Sylva; children's wear — 800. **Broyhill Furniture Industries** (Rutherford Furniture Co. Div.); Rutherfordton; wooden household furniture — 750. **Marion Mfg. Co.** (HQ); Marion; cotton fabric, yarn mills — 750.

Margaret R. Pardee Memorial Hospital; Hendersonville; hospital — 700. **Cranston Print Works Co.;** Fletcher; synthetic fabric finishing — 600. **GF Business Equipment Inc.** (General Fireproofing Co. Inc.); Forest City; furniture, fixtures — 600. **Tanner Co. Inc.** (Doncaster Div. - HQ); Rutherfordton; women's footwear — 600. **Sybron Corp.** (Sybron-Taylor Instrument Co.); Arden; industrial measuring instruments — 650. **Ethan Allen Inc.** (Pine Valley Div.); Old Fort; wooden household furniture — 550. **Sayles Biltmore Bleacheries Inc.** (HQ); Asheville; fabric finishing — 520. **Burlington Industries Inc.** (Burlington House Furniture); Robbinsville; wooden household furniture — 500. **Burlington Industries Inc.** (Greigh Fabrics Div.); Asheville; woven fabric mills — 500. **Hampshire-Designers Inc.** (Ellen Knitting Div.); Spruce Pine; women's hosiery — 500. **Mastercraft Corp.;** Spindale; cotton, synthetic fabric mills — 500.

North Dakota

The politics of North Dakota has traditionally been the politics of wheat. Former Republican Sen. Milton R. Young built his "Mr. Wheat" designation — and not much else — into a 36-year Senate career. But the state's farm community is more diverse than its political rhetoric would imply.

The Red River of the North is the center of a flat, rich, moist region that produces not only wheat but also sugar beets and potatoes. This is the most prosperous agricultural area of the state — the moisture in the soil allowed it to weather even the great dust storms of the 1930s.

The Red River valley also is the site of two of the state's largest cities, Fargo and Grand Forks. The combination of prosperous farmers and largely white-collar, service-oriented cities makes this area one of the most consistently Republican in the state.

Farther west, the farms and small towns are more likely to support Democratic candidates as inheritors of the old Non-Partisan League tradition and as champions of the declining family farm. Western North Dakota, too dry for a good wheat crop, has developed a livestock economy, newly supplemented by energy development. The dry buttes and rolling grassland attracted large cattle ranches, and this section of North Dakota is like Wyoming in appearance and commercial life.

The discovery of oil in the Williston area in the 1950s and the development of long-known coal deposits throughout the West in the 1970s gave an economic boost to the area. State and local officials have tried with some success to limit the adverse social and environmental impact of large-scale development. Generally, Democrats have backed a careful, go-slow effort, while Republicans have favored more development.

A third important component of the state's economy is the military. The Strategic Air Command has two major bases in North Dakota and there are important nuclear missile installations.

Although Democrats remain strong in many of North Dakota's rural counties, the GOP has tended to hold the balance of power in the state, thanks to a conservative following in the small cities, which are marketing rather than manufacturing centers and have no substantial blue-collar vote. Since 1936 only Lyndon B. Johnson has won the state for the Democrats in a presidential contest. Still, Democrats held the governorship between 1960 and 1980 and have sent a Democrat to the U.S. Senate since 1960.

Age of Population

District	Population Under 18	Voting Age Population	Population 65 & Over (% of VAP)	Median Age
AL	190,991	461,726	80,445 (17.4%)	28.3

Income and Occupation

District	Median Family Income	White Collar Workers	Blue Collar Workers	Service Workers	Farm Workers
AL	$ 18,023	46.3%	23.8%	15.1%	14.7%

Education: School Years Completed

District	8 Years or Fewer	4 Years of High School	4 Years of College or More	Median School Years
AL	24.8%	31.3%	14.8%	12.5

Housing and Residential Patterns

District	Owner Occupied	Renter Occupied	Urban	Rural
AL	68.7%	31.3%	48.8%	51.2%

Election Returns

At Large		Democrat		Republican	
1976	President	136,078	(45.8%)	153,470	(51.6%)
	Governor	153,309	(51.6%)	138,321	(46.5%)
	Senate	175,772	(62.1%)	103,466	(36.6%)
	House	104,263	(36.0%)	181,018	(62.4%)
1978	House	68,016	(30.9%)	147,746	(67.1%)
1980	President	79,189	(26.3%)	193,695	(64.2%)
	Governor	140,391	(46.4%)	162,230	(53.6%)
	Senate	86,658	(29.0%)	210,347	(70.3%)
	House	166,437	(56.8%)	127,707	(42.6%)
1982	Senate	164,873	(62.8%)	89,304	(34.0%)
	House	186,534	(71.6%)	72,241	(27.7%)

NORTH DAKOTA

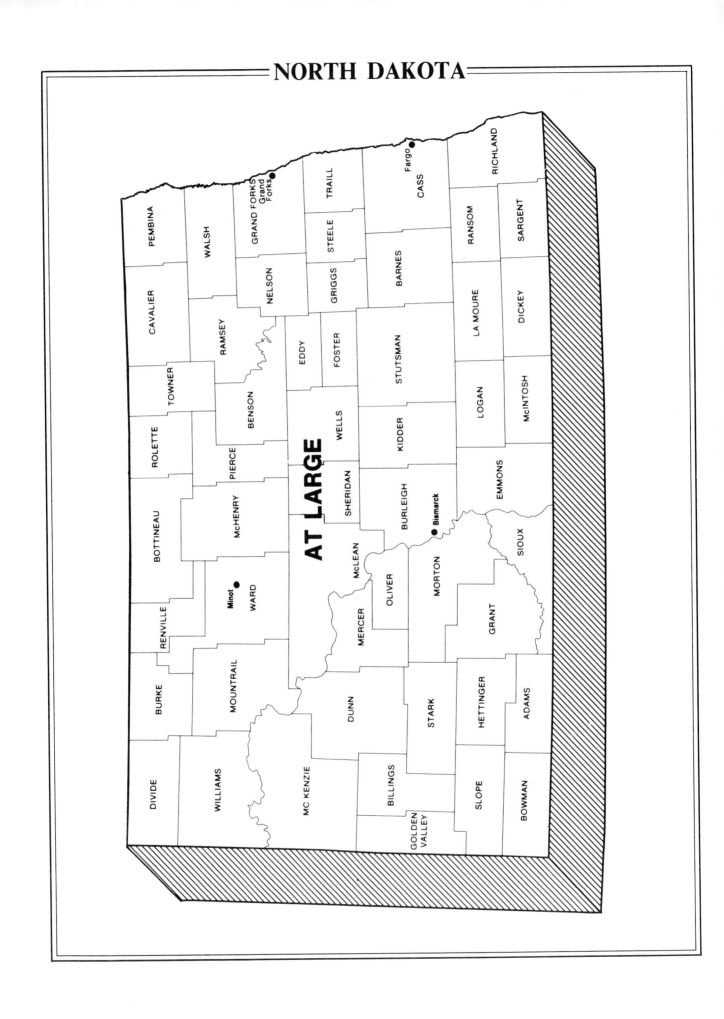

Demographics

Population: 652,717. **Percent Change from 1970:** 5.7%.

Land Area: 69,300 square miles. **Population per Square Mile:** 9.4.

Counties, 1980 Population: Adams — 3,584; Barnes — 13,960; Benson — 7,944; Billings — 1,138; Bottineau — 9,239; Bowman — 4,229; Burke — 3,822; Burleigh — 54,811; Cass — 88,247; Cavalier — 7,636; Dickey — 7,207; Divide — 3,494; Dunn — 4,627; Eddy — 3,554; Emmons — 5,877; Foster — 4,611; Golden Valley — 2,391; Grand Forks — 66,100; Grant — 4,274; Griggs — 3,714; Hettinger — 4,275; Kidder —3,833; La Moure — 6,473; Logan — 3,493; McHenry — 7,858; McIntosh — 4,800; McKenzie — 7,132; McLean — 12,383; Mercer — 9,404; Morton — 25,177; Mountrail — 7,679.

Nelson — 5,233; Oliver — 2,495; Pembina — 10,399; Pierce — 6,166; Ramsey — 13,048; Ransom — 6,698; Renville — 3,608; Richland — 19,207; Rolette — 12,177; Sargent — 5,512; Sheridan — 2,819; Sioux — 3,620; Slope — 1,157; Stark — 23,697; Steele — 3,106; Stutsman — 24,154; Towner — 4,052; Traill — 9,624; Walsh — 15,371; Ward — 58,392; Wells — 6,979; Williams — 22,237.

Cities, 1980 Population: Bismarck — 44,485; Dickinson — 15,924; Fargo — 61,383; Grand Forks — 43,765; Jamestown — 16,280; Mandan — 15,513; Minot — 32,843; West Fargo — 10,099; Williston — 13,336.

Race and Ancestry: White — 95.8%; Black — 0.4%; American Indian, Eskimo and Aleut — 3.1%; Asian and Pacific Islander — 0.4%. Spanish Origin — 0.6%. Dutch — 0.5%; English — 2.2%; French — 1.1%; German — 26.0%; Irish — 2.0%; Norwegian — 14.9%; Polish — 0.9%; Swedish — 1.5%.

Universities, Enrollment: Bismarck Junior College, Bismarck — 2,273; Dickinson State College, Dickinson — 1,143; Jamestown College, Jamestown — 615; Lake Region Junior College, Devils Lake — 615; Mary College, Bismarck — 982; Mayville State College, Mayville — 652; Minot State College, Minot — 2,529; North Dakota State School of Science, Wahpeton — 3,394; North Dakota State University (main campus), Fargo — 8,702; North Dakota State University (Bottineau campus and Institute of Forestry), Bottineau — 355; Northwest Bible College, Minot — 202; Trinity Bible Institute, Ellendale — 363; University of North Dakota (main campus), Grand Forks — 10,511; University of North Dakota (Williston Center), Williston — 646; Valley City State College, Valley City — 1,217.

Newspapers, Circulation: *The Bismarck Tribune* (e), Bismarck — 29,561; *Daily News* (e), Wahpeton — 6,587; *Devils Lake Daily Journal* (e), Devils Lake — 5,537; *Dickinson Press* (m), Dickinson — 9,023; *Forum* (all day, S), Fargo — 58,027; *Grand Forks Herald* (eS), Grand Forks — 35,287; *The Jamestown Sun* (e), Jamestown — 10,296; *The Minot Daily News* (e), Minot — 30,457; *Valley City Times-Record* (e), Valley City — 4,090; *Williston Daily Herald* (eS), Williston — 7,920.

Commercial Television Stations, Affiliation: KDIX-TV, Dickinson (CBS, ABC); KFYR-TV, Bismarck (NBC, ABC); KMOT, Minot (NBC); KQCD-TV, Dickinson (ABC, NBC); KTHI-TV, Fargo (ABC); KUMV-TV, Williston (NBC); KXJB-TV, Valley City (CBS); KXMB-TV, Bismarck (CBS, ABC); KXMC-TV, Minot (CBS, ABC); KXMD-TV, Williston (CBS, ABC); WDAY-TV, Fargo (NBC); WDAZ, Devils Lake, (NBC). District is divided between Fargo ADI and Minot-Bismarck-Dickinson ADI.

Military Installations: Bismarck Bomb Scoring Site (Air Force), Bismarck — 76; Fortuna Air Force Station, Fortuna — 13; Grand Forks Air Force Base, Emerado — 5,669; Hector Field (Air Force), Fargo — 1,113; Minot Air Force Base, Minot — 6,085; Missile Early Warning Site (Air Force), Concrete — 265.

Industries:
Kaiser Engineers Inc. (Great Plains Coal & Gasification Project); Beulah; engineering, construction — 3,189. **St. Luke's Hospital Assn.;** Fargo; hospital — 1,600. **United Hospital;** Grand Forks; hospital — 1,300. **Steiger Tractor Inc.** (HQ); Fargo; tractors — 700. **T. R. G. Drilling Corp.;** Williston; oil well drilling — 700. **American Natural Gas Co.** (Great Plains Coal & Gasification Project); Beulah; construction — 596. **Clark Equipment Co.** (Melroe Div.); Gwinner; skid steer loaders — 550.

Ohio

Democrats had some initial complaints when the Ohio Legislature, after nearly a year of partisan bickering, approved a congressional redistricting plan in late March 1982. But several weeks of reflection and one key Republican retirement convinced the two parties that neither side had gained much of an edge.

With Democrats holding the state House and Republicans controlling the Senate and governorship, a compromise had to be reached to reduce the congressional delegation by two, from 23 to 21 districts, as required by reapportionment. It was agreed that one Democratic seat would be removed from the Cleveland area — where there was a 13 percent population loss during the 1970s — and one Republican seat eliminated elsewhere in the state.

But no Democrat was willing to see his district sacrificed. While two of 13 Republican incumbents were vacating their seats to run for other office, all 10 Democrats were seeking re-election and needed districts to run in.

The Legislature ended the argument by passing a plan on March 24, the day before a federal court had threatened to take control of the matter. The bill breezed through the Ohio House by a vote of 65-30. Democratic leaders in the Senate were less enthusiastic; it won there by only two votes. Republican Gov. James A. Rhodes signed the bill the following day.

The plan gave Republicans what they were after in Ohio's rural heartland. The west central 7th District was retained for the retiring Republican incumbent's heir apparent. The Columbus-based 12th District, held by a freshman Democrat, was made more favorable to a challenge by Republicans. And the rural 4th took a strange new shape to enhance the re-election prospects of the GOP freshman there.

Democrats crafted safe districts for their incumbent in the Dayton-based 3rd and for the party's top two priorities in the Cleveland area — the delegation's only black and its only female. The Toledo and Youngstown districts, which both had Republican incumbents, retained their nominal Democratic orientation.

Democratic complaints centered on two features of the plan: the weakening of the Democrats in the 12th and the creation of a "U-shaped" district in the Cleveland suburbs in which two Democratic representatives would have had to oppose each other. That headache was unexpectedly cured in early April when the Republican in the 11th District announced his retirement. One of the Democrats, who represented a portion of the area that would become the new 11th, immediately opted to run there, avoiding a primary fight. Democrats won both districts in November and picked up the Toledo district, but they lost the 12th.

Age of Population

District	Population Under 18	Voting Age Population	Population 65 & Over (% of VAP)	Median Age
1	150,721	365,146	57,474 (15.7%)	29.2
2	144,143	370,265	59,623 (16.1%)	30.2
3	143,066	370,522	52,841 (14.3%)	30.0
4	153,931	360,765	58,804 (16.3%)	29.6
5	155,560	358,629	53,810 (15.0%)	28.3
6	155,254	359,641	56,017 (15.6%)	30.2
7	151,644	361,062	51,059 (14.1%)	29.8
8	152,584	360,843	52,001 (14.4%)	29.1
9	149,529	364,615	58,479 (16.0%)	29.4
10	151,543	362,212	57,381 (15.8%)	29.5
11	158,013	354,854	42,950 (12.1%)	28.7
12	147,519	365,406	42,538 (11.6%)	28.6
13	163,552	351,794	44,711 (12.7%)	28.5
14	140,939	373,723	57,932 (15.5%)	30.9
15	136,992	377,705	46,567 (12.3%)	28.0
16	150,753	362,462	55,285 (15.3%)	30.0
17	142,378	372,845	59,313 (15.9%)	31.6
18	146,409	367,603	66,821 (18.2%)	31.5
19	127,499	387,390	66,694 (17.2%)	34.9
20	130,938	382,556	66,051 (17.3%)	31.7
21	141,353	373,272	63,109 (16.9%)	30.6
State	3,094,320	7,703,310	1,169,460 (15.2%)	29.9

Income and Occupation

District	Median Family Income	White Collar Workers	Blue Collar Workers	Service Workers	Farm Workers
1	$ 21,445	56.8%	29.3%	13.2%	0.6%
2	21,636	54.5	31.1	13.2	1.2
3	20,011	54.5	30.6	14.2	0.7
4	19,783	43.5	39.9	12.8	3.8
5	21,155	40.9	42.5	12.8	3.8
6	18,409	45.9	38.1	12.5	3.4

OHIO

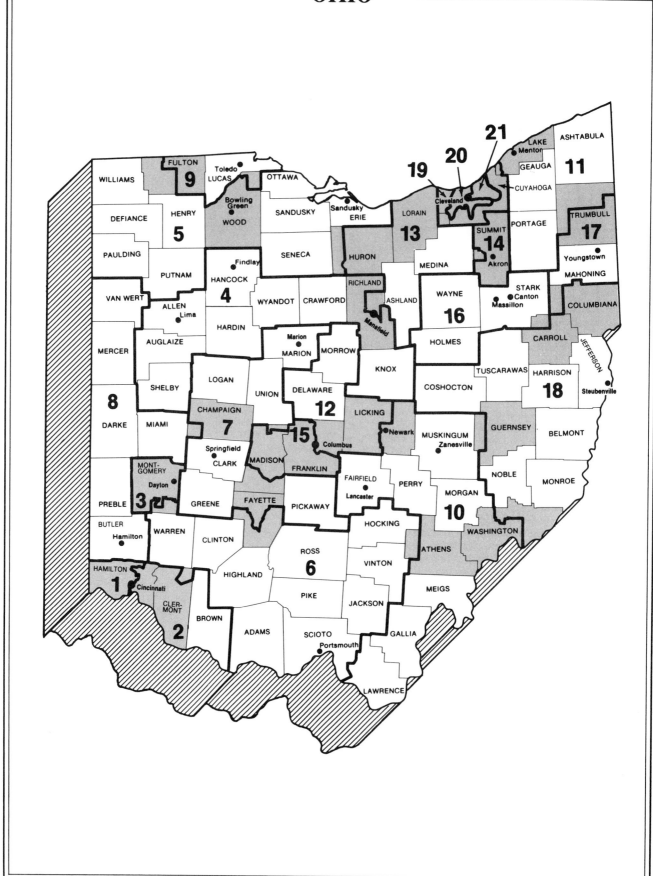

District	Median Family Income	White Collar Workers	Blue Collar Workers	Service Workers	Farm Workers
7	19,828	47.6	36.3	12.4	3.7
8	21,074	45.5	39.2	12.1	3.2
9	21,600	52.8	32.4	14.0	0.9
10	18,166	45.2	39.2	13.3	2.3
11	22,668	47.5	39.2	11.3	2.0
12	21,107	59.0	27.5	12.2	1.3
13	22,127	45.0	41.0	11.7	2.2
14	21,533	54.7	31.4	13.4	0.5
15	20,838	60.3	25.7	12.9	1.0
16	20,972	45.4	39.9	12.0	2.7
17	21,162	45.1	41.3	12.8	0.9
18	19,159	38.7	46.3	12.4	2.6
19	26,910	64.7	24.6	10.1	0.5
20	21,167	50.0	37.2	12.5	0.3
21	18,005	51.7	31.7	16.3	0.3
State	$ 20,909	50.3%	35.2%	12.7%	1.8%

Education: School Years Completed

District	8 Years or Fewer	4 Years of High School	4 Years of College or More	Median School Years
1	17.1%	34.4%	16.3%	12.4
2	17.8	32.5	18.5	12.4
3	15.5	38.7	14.2	12.5
4	14.4	46.5	10.5	12.4
5	14.8	45.7	11.1	12.4
6	21.2	38.8	11.2	12.3
7	15.1	43.3	12.5	12.4
8	17.0	42.8	11.4	12.4
9	15.4	38.6	13.6	12.4
10	17.6	43.6	10.4	12.3
11	11.7	44.0	14.1	12.5
12	10.8	40.4	17.7	12.6
13	13.5	44.0	11.6	12.4
14	13.4	39.3	15.4	12.5
15	12.6	34.2	22.2	12.6
16	16.7	43.6	11.3	12.4
17	15.0	43.6	10.6	12.4
18	19.4	45.7	7.6	12.3
19	9.3	39.8	21.3	12.7
20	17.5	39.3	9.8	12.3
21	16.9	32.1	15.3	12.4
State	15.4%	40.5%	13.7%	12.4

Housing and Residential Patterns

District	Owner Occupied	Renter Occupied	Urban	Rural
1	59.7%	40.3%	94.3%	5.7%
2	60.7	39.3	79.7	20.3
3	63.0	37.0	94.6	5.4
4	73.9	26.1	55.6	44.4
5	75.6	24.4	44.1	55.9
6	73.9	26.1	45.7	54.3
7	71.8	28.2	57.4	42.6
8	73.5	26.5	59.8	40.2
9	67.6	32.4	91.1	8.9
10	74.0	26.0	42.9	57.1
11	76.4	23.6	56.3	43.7
12	62.3	37.7	78.9	21.1
13	75.0	25.0	71.5	28.5
14	69.6	30.4	91.8	8.2
15	57.4	42.6	92.1	7.9
16	72.6	27.4	62.5	37.5

District	Owner Occupied	Renter Occupied	Urban	Rural
17	73.3	26.7	80.1	19.9
18	76.0	24.0	43.5	56.5
19	74.0	26.0	97.9	2.1
20	63.5	36.5	100.0	0.0
21	47.9	52.1	100.0	0.0
State	68.4%	31.6%	73.3%	26.7%

1st District

Hamilton County — Western Cincinnati and Suburbs

Nestled snugly in the southwestern corner of the state, the 1st stretches westward from the skyscrapers of downtown Cincinnati to the rolling farm land along the Indiana border.

GOP domination in the suburbs north and west of the city kept the district faithfully Republican during the 1970s. But the black population within Cincinnati has given the Democrats a sizable minority vote.

The western half of Cincinnati makes up 43 percent of the district's vote. Most of the other voters live in middle-class suburbs nearby. Democrats can count on about 95 percent of the vote from a few solidly black wards in Cincinnati, but the dominant political bloc is the German Catholic group that has defined the city's personality for 100 years. Once clustered in the West Side section of the city known as "Over-the-Rhine," the German-Americans have gradually moved to suburbs such as Cheviot and Green Township.

The Democratic representative, a Catholic with a fairly conservative voting record, has been able to retain the support of this crucial bloc. But in state and national contests, the German Catholics have joined with the area's sizable number of Appalachian whites — drawn from the rural hills to work in Cincinnati's industries — in voting Republican.

With a 3 percent population loss in the 1970s, the old 1st District had to gain about 65,000 new residents. But the additions were not expected to alter its basic GOP tilt. All of the new territory came from the eastern Hamilton County district that was formerly the 1st (the two Cincinnati districts switched numbers in 1982). Nearly 40,000 of the newcomers live in four suburban communities (Forest Park, Sharonville, Springdale and Glendale) straddling the Cincinnati beltway (Interstate 275) in northern Hamilton County. Usually Republican, they backed Ronald Reagan in 1980 with majorities ranging from 55 to 68 percent of the vote.

The other alterations, though minor, were likely to help the Democrats. The 1st picked up Arlington Heights and Elmwood Place, two small communities of lower- to middle-income whites that adjoin the northern portion of the city. Together they have about 4,000 residents.

The new 1st also picked up the Bond Hill and Roselawn sections of Cincinnati, which together comprise one of the city's 26 wards. Bond Hill is predominantly black; Roselawn is heavily Jewish. Both regularly turn in large Democratic majorities. Jimmy Carter carried the ward in 1980 with 66 percent of the vote, 17 percentage points better than his citywide showing.

The Cincinnati area has a diverse economy. A major

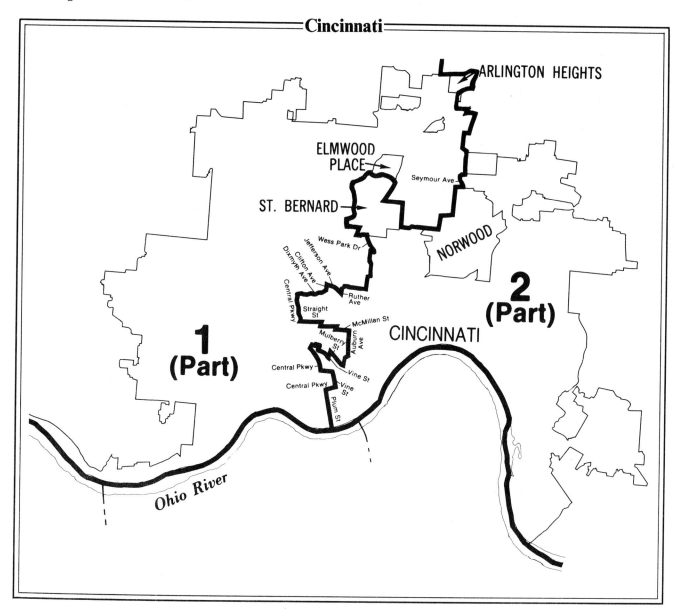

Cincinnati

Ohio River port and a regional center of commerce, the city also is headquarters for the Procter & Gamble Co. and Cincinnati Milacron, a national leader in the production of machine tools. Most of the city's plants are located within the 2nd, but provide jobs for workers from the western side of the city.

Election Returns

1st District		Democrat		Republican	
1976	President	78,416	(37.8%)	125,549	(60.4%)
	Senate	89,310	(44.9%)	104,617	(52.6%)
	House	100,245	(49.3%)	102,730	(50.5%)
1978	Governor	52,119	(38.5%)	80,477	(59.5%)
	House	72,343	(50.3%)	71,152	(49.5%)
1980	President	75,805	(35.7%)	123,757	(58.2%)
	Senate	130,422	(68.7%)	56,538	(29.8%)
	House	111,744	(54.2%)	93,650	(45.5%)
1982	Governor	75,469	(50.8%)	68,922	(46.4%)
	Senate	78,391	(51.6%)	70,892	(46.6%)
	House	99,143	(63.5%)	52,658	(33.7%)

Demographics

Population: 515,867. **Percent Change from 1970:** -2.3%.

Land Area: 262 square miles. **Population per Square Mile:** 1,969.0.

Counties, 1980 Population: Hamilton (Pt.) — 515,867.

Cities, 1980 Population: Cincinnati (Pt.) — 224,125; Forest Park — 18,675; North College Hill — 11,114; Sharonville — 10,108; Springdale — 10,111.

Race and Ancestry: White — 82.9%; Black — 16.3%; American Indian, Eskimo and Aleut — 0.1%; Asian and Pacific Islander — 0.6%. Spanish Origin — 0.6%. English — 7.4%; French — 0.5%; German — 21.3%; Irish — 4.3%; Italian — 1.4%.

Universities, Enrollment: Betz College, Cincinnati — 212; Cincinnati

Bible College, Cincinnati — 670; Cincinnati Techncial College, Cincinnati — 3,657; College of Mount St. Joseph on the Ohio, Mount St. Joseph — 1,577; Southern Ohio College, Cincinnati — 2,190.

Newspapers, Circulation: *The Cincinnati Enquirer* and *The Cincinnati Post* circulate in the district.

Commercial Stations, Affiliation: WCPO-TV, Cincinnati (CBS). Entire district is located in Cincinnati ADI. *(For other Cincinnati stations, see 2nd District.)*

Industries:

Ford Motor Co. (Transmission Div.); Cincinnati; automatic transmissions — 3,000. **The Christ Hospital;** Cincinnati; hospital — 2,600. **Procter & Gamble Co.** (Winton Hill Technical Center); Cincinnati; research — 2,500. **Merrell Dow Pharmaceutical Inc.;** Cincinnati; pharmaceuticals — 1,896. **Avon Products Inc.;** Cincinnati; cosmetics — 1,600.

St. Francis-St. George Hospital; Cincinnati; hospital — 1,200. **Providence Hospital;** Cincinnati; hospital — 1,170. **Consolidated Foods Corp.** (Kahns & Co. Div.); Cincinnati; meatpacking — 1,000. **Corporate Cleaning Systems Inc.;** Cincinnati; janitorial services — 1,000. **National Distillers Products Co.;** Cincinnati; distillery — 1,000. **Roadway Express Inc.;** Cincinnati; trucking — 1,000. **Scott & Fetzer Co.** (Campbell Hausfeld Group); Harrison; spraying equipment — 1,000. **The Stearns & Foster Co.** (Franklin Furniture Co. Div. - HQ); Cincinnati; box springs — 1,000. **Monsanto Co.** (Polymers & Resins Co.); Addyston; plastics materials — 950. **Conflo Mfg. Inc.** (The Lunkenheimer Co. Div.); Cincinnati; industrial valves — 700. **Emery Industries Inc.;** Cincinnati; industrial chemicals — 700. **The William Powell Co.** (HQ); Cincinnati; valves, pipe fittings — 700.

Procter & Gamble Co. (Miami Valley Laboratories); Cincinnati; research — 700. **Prudential Insurance Co. of America;** Cincinnati; life insurance — 700. **Cincinnati Financial Corp.** (HQ); Cincinnati; fire, casualty insurance — 650. **Federated Department Stores;** (HQ); Cincinnati; department stores — 650. **NLO Inc.;** Cincinnati; fissionable materials — 564. **Union Central Life Insurance Co.** (HQ); Cincinnati; life, accident insurance — 515. **Cincinnati Inc.** (HQ); Cincinnati; machine tools — 500. **General Signal Industries Inc.** (Time Recorder Co.); Cincinnati; time clocks — 500. **The Andrew Jergens Co.** (HQ); Cincinnati; cosmetics — 500. **The Kroger Co.** (Gold Crest Candy Co.); Cincinnati; candy — 500. **Miller Shoe Co.;** Cincinnati; women's shoes — 500. **Standex International Corp.** (Standard Publishing Div.); Cincinnati; book, miscellaneous publishing — 500.

2nd District

Hamilton County — Eastern Cincinnati and Suburbs

The 2nd is a district of political extremes. It includes the most Democratic part of Cincinnati and the most Republican suburbs around it. With the bulk of the voters outside the city, Republican candidates usually win.

Redistricting made the 2nd even more diverse. Its 8-percent population loss, coupled with the Legislature's political scalpel, pushed the 2nd eastward beyond the suburbs into the rural Ohio River Valley. The remap brought into the district about 160,000 new residents from the old 6th District. Most are suburbanites expected to swell GOP majorities.

Eighty percent of the newcomers live in fast-growing Clermont County, all of which became part of the 2nd except for rural Wayne Township in the northeast corner. While the construction of a Ford transmission plant in the county seat of Batavia has stirred development in the central part of Clermont, most of the 35 percent population boom in the 1970s was in communities to the west along the Cincinnati beltway. The increasing suburbanization of

Clermont has strengthened its Republican voting habits. Ronald Reagan carried it by a margin of 2-to-1 in 1980.

The eastern part of Clermont and all of neighboring Brown County are rural and relatively poor. Economically and politically they resemble northern Kentucky, which lies just to the south across the Ohio River. Tobacco is the major crop, and family incomes are about a third lower than in metropolitan Cincinnati. Brown County often supports Democrats — in 1976 it backed both Jimmy Carter and Democratic Sen. Howard M. Metzenbaum. But the county casts barely 6 percent of the district vote.

The eastern half of Cincinnati anchors the other end of the district and houses about one-third of its residents. Sizable black and academic communities make it the most Democratic part of the city. Blacks comprise about one-third of the total population of Cincinnati, and most live in neighborhoods such as Avondale and Walnut Hill, within the boundaries of the 2nd.

At the bottom of Walnut Hill, in the flat Ohio River basin, is downtown Cincinnati. The wharves for old sternwheelers such as the *Delta Queen*, the headquarters of the Procter & Gamble soap company and the Taft Museum are mainstays. But the area has undergone a facelift. Construction of Riverfront Stadium and Coliseum in the 1970s has symbolized a downtown renewal project designed to lure suburban dollars back to the city.

The well-to-do Republican establishment, personified by the Taft family, had a great deal of influence in the city in the past, but that influence now is felt more in the suburbs. Unlike suburban Cleveland, suburban Cincinnati is solidly in Republican hands. Indian Hills, one of the richest communities in Ohio, tops the list. It gave Reagan a staggering 88 percent of the vote.

The Cincinnati area lacks the heavy industry of the urban centers of northeastern Ohio. But manufacturing plants dot the Mill Creek Valley, which extends north from downtown into the suburbs. While the valley weaves back and forth between the 1st and 2nd districts, the 2nd includes a large Procter & Gamble plant at St. Bernard and a General Electric plant at Evendale. Norwood — a blue-collar city of 26,000 in the northeast corner of Cincinnati — is the site of a Fisher body plant.

Election Returns

2nd District		Democrat		Republican	
1976	President	76,384	(40.4%)	109,439	(57.9%)
	Senate	79,397	(44.6%)	94,219	(52.9%)
	House	62,086	(34.5%)	115,381	(64.2%)
1978	Governor	44,746	(37.7%)	71,334	(60.1%)
	House	40,925	(33.2%)	80,704	(65.5%)
1980	President	70,873	(35.7%)	115,353	(58.1%)
	Senate	119,588	(64.1%)	64,355	(34.5%)
	House	51,879	(27.9%)	131,443	(70.6%)
1982	Governor	75,933	(50.4%)	71,450	(47.5%)
	Senate	78,802	(51.6%)	71,332	(46.7%)
	House	53,169	(34.2%)	97,434	(62.7%)

Demographics

Population: 514,408. **Percent Change from 1970:** -0.5%.

Land Area: 1,067 square miles. **Population per Square Mile:** 482.1.

Counties, 1980 Population: Brown — 31,920; Clermont (Pt.) — 125,131; Hamilton (Pt.) — 357,357.

Cities, 1980 Population: Cincinnati (Pt.) — 161,332; Montgomery — 10,088; Norwood — 26,342; Reading — 12,843.

Race and Ancestry: White — 83.0%; Black — 16.2%; American Indian, Eskimo and Aleut — 0.1%; Asian and Pacific Islander — 0.5%. Spanish Origin — 0.6%. English — 10.4%; French — 0.6%; German — 14.4%; Irish — 4.7%; Italian — 1.0%; Russian — 0.5%.

Universities, Enrollment: Art Academy of Cincinnati, Cincinnati — 226; Athenaeum of Ohio, Cincinnati — 119; Chatfield College, St. Martin — 114; Cincinnati Metropolitan College, Cincinnati — 290; Hebrew Union College - Jewish Institute of Religion, Cincinnati — 136; Ohio Visual Arts Institute, Cincinnati — 140; University of Cincinnati, Cincinnati — 34,971; University of Cincinnati - Clermont General and Technical College, Batavia — 1,322; University of Cincinnati - Raymond Walters General and Technical College, Cincinnati — 3,479; Xavier University, Cincinnati — 7,267.

Newspapers, Circulation: *The Cincinnati Enquirer* (mS), Cincinnati — 188,287; *The Cincinnati Post* (e), Cincinnati — 172,062.

Commercial Television Stations, Affiliation: WBTI, Cincinnati (None); WKRC-TV, Cincinnati (ABC); WLWT, Cincinnati (NBC). Entire district is located in Cincinnati ADI. *(For other Cincinnati stations, see 1st District.)*

Military Installations: Air Force Plant 36, Evendale — 85.

Nuclear Power Plants: Zimmer 1, Moscow (General Electric, Kaiser Engineers).

Industries:

General Electric Co. (Aircraft Engine Group); Cincinnati; aircraft engines — 13,300. **Cincinnati Milacron Inc.** (HQ); Cincinnati; machine tools — 6,000. **General Motors Corp.** (GM Assembly Div.); Cincinnati; motor vehicles — 4,200. **The Procter & Gamble Co.** (HQ); Cincinnati; household, personal care products — 3,700. **The Procter & Gamble Co.** (Ivorydale Technical Center); Cincinnati; research laboratory — 2,200.

Jewish Hospital Assn.; Cincinnati; hospital — 2,100. **Children's Hospital & Medical Center Inc.**; Cincinnati; children's hospital — 2,000. **Scovill Inc.** (Nutone Div.); Cincinnati; electric housewares — 1,800. **Ford Motor Co.** (Transmission & Chassis Div.); Batavia; transmissions — 1,700. **Veterans Administration**; Cincinnati; veterans' hospital — 1,500. **Western & Southern Life Insurance Co.** (HQ); Cincinnati; life insurance — 1,500. **Bethesda Hospital Deaconess Assn.** (Bethesda Hospital); Cincinnati hospital — 1,440. **Sterling Drug Inc.** (Hilton-Davis Chemical Co. Div.); Cincinnati; cyclic crudes, organic pigments — 1,250. **Fifth Third Bank**; Cincinnati; banking — 1,220. **Formica Corp.** (Evendale Plant); Cincinnati; laminated plastic products — 1,200. **CPG Products Corp.** (Kenner Products Co. Div.); Cincinnati; toys — 1,100. **Cincinnati Milacron Inc.** (Plastics Machinery Div.); Batavia; plastic processing machinery — 1,100. **Gibson Greeting Cards Inc.** (HQ); Cincinnati; greeting cards — 1,100. **The Procter & Gamble Co. Inc.** (Sharon Woods Technical Center); Cincinnati; soaps, detergents — 1,100. **Senco Products Inc.** (HQ); Cincinnati; industrial machinery — 1,100. **United States Playing Card Co.** (Consolidated Dougherty Card Co. - HQ); Cincinnati; playing cards — 1,100. **The Cincinnati Enquirer Inc.**; Cincinnati; newspaper publishing — 1,070. **American Standard Inc.** (Steelcraft Div.); Cincinnati; steel doors — 1,000.

Bethesda Hospital Deaconess Assn. (Bethesda North Hospital); Cincinnati; hospital — 1,000. **The Central Bancorp. Inc.** (HQ); Cincinnati; bank holding company — 1,000. **Cincinnati Electronics Corp.** (HQ); Cincinnati — electronic communications equipment — 1,000. **Cincinnati General Hospital**; Cincinnati; hospital — 1,000. **Keebler Co.** Cincinnati; biscuits — 1,000. **First National Bank of Cincinnati** (HQ); Cincinnati; banking — 935. **Siemens-Allis** (Medium Motor & Generator Div.); Cincinnati; motors, generators — 898. **Henry J. Kaiser Co.**; Moscow; general contracting — 874. **United States Shoe Corp.** (HQ); Cincinnati; shoes — 800. **World Book-Childcraft International**; Cincinnati; encyclopedias — 772. **Gallenstein Bros. Inc.** Cincinnati; bridge, tunnel, highway construction — 710. **The Kroger Co.** (HQ); Cincinnati; grocery chain — 700. **Pinkerton's Inc.**; Cincinnati; security services —

650. **American Laundry Machinery Inc.**; Cincinnati; laundry, dry cleaning equipment — 630.

R. L. Polk & Co. (Cincinnati Div.); Cincinnati; miscellaneous publishing — 625. **Diamond International Corp.** (Heekin Can Div.); Cincinnati; metal cans — 600. **Le Blond Makino Machine Tool Co.** (HQ); Cincinnati; machine tools — 514. **Baldwin-United Corp.** (HQ); Cincinnati; musical instruments, insurance — 500. **Beatrice Foods Co.** (Velva Sheen Mfg. Div.); Cincinnati; silk screened fabric — 500. **Celotex Corp.** (Philip Carey Div.); Cincinnati; roofing — 500. **Coca-Cola Bottling Corp.** (HQ); Cincinnati; soft drink bottling — 500. **Great American Insurance Co.** (HQ); Cincinnati; property, casualty insurance — 500. **International Business Machines Corp.**; Cincinnati; office machine wholesaling — 500. **A. M. Kinney Inc.** (HQ); Cincinnati; engineering services — 500. **Palm Beach Co.** (Haspel Brothers Div.); Cincinnati; men's clothing — 500. **Xomox Corp.** (HQ); Cincinnati; valves, pipe fitting — 500. **Xtek Inc.**; Cincinnati; fabricated metal — 500.

3rd District

Southwest — Dayton

With a large blue-collar work force and a population that is 37 percent black, Dayton is a Democratic island in a sea of rural western Ohio Republicanism.

Most of Dayton's suburbs yield GOP majorities, but the urban vote has been large enough to keep the 3rd District marginally Democratic. Jimmy Carter carried it in both 1976 and 1980 by fewer than 3 percentage points. When liberal Republican Rep. Charles W. Whalen retired in 1978, a Democrat won the seat with 54 percent of the vote.

An 8 percent population loss during the 1970s forced the district nearly to double its land area to reach population equality, and after redistricting it covered virtually all of populous Montgomery County. That is good news for Democrats. Surrounded by Republican districts, the 3rd picks up numerous Democratic voters that the GOP districts wanted to dump.

In the east the district gained Mad River Township from the 7th. A predominantly Democratic area of 27,000 residents, it abuts the Wright-Patterson Air Force Base and is home for a number of transient federal workers.

In the west the 3rd absorbed about 60,000 new constituents from the 8th. Two-thirds of these newcomers are in Jefferson and Madison townships, mainly black and Jewish precincts adjoining Dayton that went for Carter by large margins in 1980. Farther west are three small rural townships with Republican leanings.

In the south the 3rd gained nearly all of West Carrollton and Miamisburg from the 8th. Together they have a population of about 28,000. Predominantly blue-collar, both communities voted for Ronald Reagan in 1980.

Any problems created for the Democrats by the addition of these two towns were canceled out by the removal from the district of nearby Washington Township, which went to the 6th. One of the most affluent jurisdictions in Montgomery County, suburban Washington Township is rock-ribbed Republican. It gave Reagan 70 percent of the vote in 1980.

The Dayton area claims to be the birthplace of aviation, the refrigerator, the cash register and the electrical automobile starter. Much of the high-skill industry in the region is a legacy of these local inventions. The city is the headquarters of the NCR Corp. (formerly National Cash

Register Co.), and the Mead Corp. General Motors Corp. is a major employer with several large plants in the district.

The Wright-Patterson Air Force Base northeast of the city is one of the largest military installations in the nation. It bears the name of the Wright Brothers, who had a shop in Dayton, and Lt. Frank S. Patterson of Dayton, who was killed in 1918 during a test of a device to fire a machine gun through an airplane's spinning propeller. Wright-Patterson was the site of the first human ejection from a speeding aircraft.

In the early 1970s the Dayton area was the most affluent part of Ohio outside the Cleveland suburbs. But by the early 1980s severe economic problems had arisen. GM's large Frigidaire division, Firestone Tire and Rubber and the McCall Publishing Company have all left. NCR Corp. remains, but the work force has dropped from 15,000 to 600. Without jobs, many people left the area. Dayton's population declined 16 percent in the 1970s to 200,000, its lowest level in a half-century.

Dayton's Democratic heritage predates the New Deal. During the early years of the Civil War, the local congressman was Democrat Clement L. Vallandigham. A controversial leader in the anti-Union Copperhead movement, he was exiled from the country in 1863. James M. Cox was more highly regarded nationally. A Dayton publisher, he served in Congress and as governor before winning the Democratic presidential nomination in 1920.

Blacks are the backbone of modern-day Democratic strength. With nearly unanimous support from the heavily black West Side, Carter carried the city in 1980 with 66 percent of the vote. Appalachian whites and Eastern European ethnics make up most of the rest of the city.

To the south of Dayton are the staunchly Republican white-collar suburbs of Kettering and Oakwood. Together they cast about 15 percent of the district vote, compared to Dayton's 40 percent. The fast-growing townships north of the city are largely blue-collar suburban.

Election Returns

3rd District		Democrat		Republican	
1976	President	94,213	(53.0%)	79,319	(44.6%)
	Senate	93,690	(55.0%)	70,128	(41.2%)
	House	42,087	(26.1%)	109,774	(68.0%)
1978	Governor	73,240	(60.5%)	44,960	(37.1%)
	House	66,117	(52.0%)	59,129	(46.5%)
1980	President	99,759	(47.9%)	93,754	(45.0%)
	Senate	138,994	(78.5%)	35,971	(20.3%)
	House	100,960	(54.7%)	79,288	(43.0%)
1982	Governor	88,329	(61.7%)	52,532	(36.7%)
	Senate	92,301	(63.8%)	49,991	(34.6%)
	House	119,926	(87.7%)	16,828	(12.3%)

Demographics

Population: 513,588. **Percent Change from 1970:** -7.6%.

Land Area: 399 square miles. **Population per Square Mile:** 1,287.2.

Counties, 1980 Population: Montgomery (Pt.) — 513,588.

Cities, 1980 Population: Dayton (Pt.) — 199,321; Englewood — 11,329; Huber Heights — 35,480; Kettering — 61,186; Miamisburg — 15,304; Shiloh — 11,735; Vandalia — 13,161; West Carrollton — 13,148.

Race and Ancestry: White — 80.7%; Black — 18.3%; American Indian, Eskimo and Aleut — 0.1%; Asian and Pacific Islander — 0.5%. Spanish Origin — 0.7%. Dutch — 0.5%; English — 10.6%; French — 0.8%; German — 13.0%; Hungarian — 0.6%; Irish — 4.2%; Italian — 0.9%; Polish — 0.7%.

Universities, Enrollment: ITT Technical Institute, Dayton — 600; Kettering College of Medical Arts, Kettering — 397; Miami-Jacobs Junior College of Business, Dayton — 782; Ohio Institute of Photography, Dayton — 189; RETS Tech Center, Dayton — 478; Sinclair Community College, Dayton — 17,090; Southwestern College of Business, West Carrollton — 570; United Theological Seminary, Dayton — 265; University of Dayton, Dayton — 10,311; Wright State University, Dayton —14,716.

Newspapers, Circulation: *Dayton Daily News* (eS), Dayton — 168,621; *The Journal Herald* (m), Dayton — 118,511.

Commercial Television Stations, Affiliation: WDTN, Dayton (ABC); WHIO-TV, Dayton (CBS); WKEF, Dayton (NBC). Entire district is located in Dayton ADI.

Military Establishments: Defense Electronics Supply Center, Dayton — 2,309; Wright-Patterson Air Force Base, Fairborn — 13,781 (*Base straddles line between 3rd and 7th districts*).

Industries:

General Motors Corp. (Harrison Radiator Div.); Dayton; auto parts — 4,900. **General Motors Corp.** (Delco Products Div.); Kettering; auto parts — 4,880. **General Motors Corp.** (Inland Div.); Dayton; auto parts — 4,600. **General Motors Corp.** (Delco Moraine Div.); Dayton; auto parts — 2,600. **Miami Valley Hospital;** Dayton; hospital — 2,500.

Good Samaritan Hospital & Health Center; Dayton; hospital — 2,300. **St. Elizabeth Medical Center;** Dayton; hospital — 2,050. **General Motors Corp.** (Delco Moraine Div.); Dayton; auto parts — 2,000. **Monsanto Research Corp.;** Miamisburg; research — 1,920. **Kettering Medical Center;** Dayton; hospital — 1,900. **Veterans Administration;** Dayton; veterans' hospital — 1,750. **Duriron Co. Inc.** (HQ); Dayton; special industry machinery, pumps — 1,600. **General Motors Corp.** (GM Truck & Bus Mfg. Div.); Moraine; trucks, buses — 1,400. **Dayton Osteopathic Hospital;** Dayton; hospital — 1,300. **Chrysler Corp.;** Dayton; heating, air conditioning equipment — 1,290. **The Standard Register Co.** (HQ); Dayton; business forms — 1,180. **Dayton Newspapers Inc.;** Dayton; newspaper publishing — 1,170. **Children's Medical Center** (HQ); Dayton; children's hospital — 1,000. **The Mead Corp.** (HQ); Dayton; paperboard, paper products — 1,000. **Monarch Marking Systems Inc.** (HQ); Miamisburg; tickets, tags — 1,000.

The Reynolds & Reynolds Co.; Dayton; business forms — 1,000. **Dayton Malleable Iron Co.** (G H & R Foundry Div.); Dayton; iron foundries — 913. **Bank One** (HQ); Dayton; banking — 890. **Bendix Corp.** (Automation Measurement Div.); Dayton; machine tools — 800. **The Reynolds & Reynolds Co.** (HQ); Dayton; data processing services — 800. **Metropolitan Life Insurance Co. Inc.;** Dayton; life insurance — 765. **Harris Corp.** (Business Forms Systems Div.); Dayton; printing presses, office machines — 750. **General Motors Corp.** (GM Truck & Bus Mfg. Div.); Moraine; trucks, buses — 700. **Systems Research Laboratories** (Autometrix Div. - HQ); Dayton; research, measurement instruments — 650. **NCR Corp.** (HQ); Dayton; data processing equipment — 600. **Pinkerton's Inc.;** Dayton; security services — 600. **L. M. Berry & Co.** (HQ); Dayton; advertising — 500. **Danis Industries Corp.** (B. G. Danis Div. - HQ); Dayton; general contracting — 500. **Dayton Progress Corp.** (HQ); Dayton; special dies and tools — 500. **A. O. Smith Corp.;** Dayton; electric motors — 500.

4th District

West Central — Lima, Findlay

The 4th District arches ominously in west central Ohio like a giant set of jaws about to devour Columbus. It is an imaginative design. A traveler wishing to drive directly from Shelby County on the west end of the 4th to Knox County on the east side would have to go through two other districts.

The strange shape is no accident. The 4th includes some of the strongest Republican counties in the state, placed within its borders to enhance the re-election prospects of the freshman Republican, who won a 1981 special election by only 341 votes.

Not one of the nine counties in the new 4th has supported a Democratic presidential candidate since 1964. Two of the three largest — Allen (Lima) and Hancock (Findlay) — have not deserted the GOP national ticket since 1936.

Redistricting left the incumbent nearly two-thirds of his old constituents and five of the six counties that backed him in 1981. About 150,000 residents were pared away, most of them in populous Miami County near Dayton. In their place about 180,000 new residents were added on the eastern end from the disbanded 17th District. Most of the newcomers are in Richland County, which includes Mansfield, the largest city in the old 17th. All of rural Knox County and the eastern portion of Crawford County also have been added from the old 17th.

Legislative map makers angered Mansfield's political leaders by drawing the district line down the middle of the city. The Republican-oriented southwest portion was given to the 4th, while the Democratic northeast sector joined the 13th District. The Mansfield City Council president threatened a lawsuit to overturn the redistricting plan, but ultimately desisted.

The revisions in the 4th have not changed the district's basic character. Dominated by farms and small towns, it is standard Corn Belt Republican. The fertile soil supports large farms that raise livestock, soybeans, corn and wheat. Industry is widely scattered and attracts local craftsmen rather than poor migrants.

Lima and Findlay both emerged as small manufacturing centers at the end of the 19th century when oil and gas were found nearby. Although the petroleum boom passed long ago, Findlay is the headquarters of the Marathon Oil Company and is the most prosperous part of the 4th.

Election Returns

4th District		Democrat		Republican	
1976	President	90,527	(40.2%)	128,288	(57.0%)
	Senate	86,092	(39.6%)	118,471	(54.5%)
	House	76,125	(34.6%)	144,184	(65.4%)
1978	Governor	67,411	(41.7%)	88,094	(54.6%)
	House	57,139	(34.1%)	110,377	(65.9%)
1980	President	66,747	(31.5%)	131,692	(62.2%)
	Senate	141,071	(59.5%)	89,382	(37.7%)
	House	64,125	(27.8%)	166,214	(72.2%)
1982	Governor	80,963	(49.0%)	81,408	(49.2%)
	Senate	74,984	(44.6%)	89,850	(53.4%)
	House	57,564	(35.4%)	105,087	(64.6%)

Demographics

Population: 514,696. **Percent Change from 1970:** 4.5%.

Land Area: 3,972 square miles. **Population per Square Mile:** 129.6.

Counties, 1980 Population: Allen — 112,241; Auglaize — 42,554; Crawford — 50,075; Hancock — 64,581; Hardin — 32,719; Knox —

46,304; Richland (Pt.) — 100,482; Shelby — 43,089; Wyandot — 22,651.

Cities, 1980 Population: Bucyrus — 13,433; Findlay — 35,594; Fostoria (Pt.) — 3,412; Galion — 12,391; Lima — 47,381; Mansfield (Pt.) — 40,332; Mount Vernon — 14,323; Sidney — 17,657.

Race and Ancestry: White — 95.9%; Black — 3.4%; American Indian, Eskimo and Aleut — 0.1%; Asian and Pacific Islander — 0.3%. Spanish Origin — 0.8%. Dutch — 0.8%; English — 11.1%; French — 0.8%; German — 23.1%; Irish — 3.5%; Italian — 0.8%.

Universities, Enrollment: Bluffton College, Bluffton — 640; Findlay College, Findlay — 1,062; Kenyon College, Gambier — 1,455; Lima Technical College, Lima — 1,807; Mount Vernon Nazarene College, Mount Vernon — 1,039; Northwestern Business College and Technical Center, Lima — 1,439; Ohio Northern University, Ada — 2,768; Ohio State University (Lima campus), Lima — 972; Ohio State University (Mansfield campus), Mansfield — 1,175.

Newspapers, Circulation: *The Courier* (m), Findlay — 25,575; *The Daily Chief-Union* (e), Upper Sandusky — 4,892; *The Daily Globe* (e), Shelby — 4,702; *Delphos Daily Herald* (e), Delphos — 4,082; *The Evening Leader* (e), St. Mary's — 6,609; *The Galion Inquirer* (e), Galion — 6,429; *The Lima News* (eS), Lima — 40,522; *Mount Vernon News* (e), Mount Vernon — 11,614; *News Journal* (eS), Mansfield — 38,060; *The Sidney Daily News* (e), Sidney — 12,908; *Telegraph-Forum* (e), Bucyrus — 8,456; *Times* (e), Kenton — 8,614; *Wapakoneta Daily News* (e), Wapakoneta — 4,670.

Commercial Television Stations, Affiliation: WLIO, Lima (NBC); WTLW, Lima (None). District is divided among Cleveland ADI, Columbus ADI, Dayton ADI, Lima ADI and Toledo ADI.

Military Installations: Lima Army Tank Center, Lima — 2,020.

Industries:

General Motors Corp. (Fisher Body Div.); Mansfield; stamping plant — 3,000. **General Dynamics Corp.;** Lima; artillery tanks — 2,900. **Copeland Corp.** (HQ); Sidney; refrigeration — 2,570. **Marathon Oil Co.** (HQ); Findlay; synthetic, fossil fuels — 2,500. **Westinghouse Corp.** (Small Motor Div.); Lima; motors — 2,500.

Ford Motor Co.; Lima; auto engines — 2,000. **White Consolidated Industries** (Mansfield Products Co.); Mansfield; household laundry, cooking equipment — 1,500. **St. Rita's Medical Center;** Lima; hospital — 1,400. **Whirlpool Corp.;** Findlay; clothes dryers — 1,400. **Therm-O-Disc Inc.** (HQ); Mansfield; thermostats — 1,380. **Mansfield General Hospital Corp.;** Mansfield; hospital — 1,320. **Cooper Tire & Rubber Co.** (HQ); Findlay; tires, tubes — 1,300. **Timken Co.;** Bucyrus; tapered roller bearings — 1,300. **Cooper Industries Inc.** (Cooper Energy Services); Mount Vernon; engines, compressors — 1,200. **RCA Corp.** (Solid State Div.); Findlay; solid state devices — 1,200. **Stolle Corp.;** Sidney; metal finishing — 1,200. **Lima Memorial Hospital;** Lima; hospital — 1,110.

Dresser Industries Inc.; Galion; road construction equipment — 1,100. **Peabody International Corp.;** Galion; trucks — 1,100. **Goodyear Tire & Rubber Co. Inc.;** St. Marys; molded, extruded rubber products — 1,020. **Food Franchises Inc.;** Mansfield; management services — 1,000. **ITT Telecommunications Inc.** (North Power Systems Div.); Galion; communications equipment — 1,000. **Tappan Co.** (HQ); Mansfield; microwave ovens, gas, electric ranges — 1,000. **PPG Industries Inc.;** Crestline; flat glass — 950. **Crown Controls Corp.;** New Bremen; industrial trucks — 900. **Rockwell International Corp.** (Rockwell Standard Div.); Kenton; axle parts — 899. **Teledyne Industries Inc.** (Teledyne Ohio Steel); Lima; iron, steel foundries — 850. **Westinghouse Electric Corp.;** Lima; engineering instruments — 850. **Ohio Steel Tube Co.** (Copperweld Tubing Group - HQ); Shelby; steel tubes — 797.

Ex-Cell-O Corp.; Lima; aircraft engines — 736. **Uforma Inc.** (Shelby Business Forms Div.); Shelby; business forms — 700. **Dana Corp.** (Spicer Universal Joint Div.); Lima; motor vehicle parts — 620. **Amerace Corp.** (Anchor Swan Hose Corp.); Bucyrus; rubber hose — 600. **Dresser Industries Inc.** (Le Roi Div.); Sidney; air compressors — 600. **Monarch Machine Tool Co.** (HQ); Sidney; machine tools — 600. **Standard Oil Co. of Ohio Corp.;** Lima; oil refining — 600. **Westinghouse Electric Corp.;** Upper Sandusky; electric motors — 600. **Fostoria**

Corp.; Fostoria; capital management company — 525. **Buckeye International Inc.** (Millington Plastic Co.); Upper Sandusky; plastic products — 500. **SOHIO Chemical Co.** (Chemicals Mfg.); Lima; acrylonitrile — 500.

5th District

Northwest — Bowling Green, Sandusky

On the map, the new 5th looks like a big bow tie with Wood County (Bowling Green) representing the knot. The solidly Republican district is a mixture of good, flat farm land and small towns. The Lake Erie port of Sandusky is the largest community. The second most populous is fast-growing Bowling Green, home of one of the largest academic institutions in Ohio, Bowling Green State University.

The western counties are devoted almost exclusively to agriculture. Packing plants operated by Heinz and Campbell attest to the quality of the region's tomatoes. But the Mexican-American farm workers who live in migrant camps during harvest season have added a degree of tension to the otherwise tranquil region. The 5th has the greatest concentration of Hispanics in Ohio; in two counties they comprise at least 5 percent of the population.

Previous remappings gradually brought in more territory on the east. The latest redistricting gave the district all of lakeside Erie County, all of Seneca County and a portion of rural Huron County.

With 80,000 residents, Erie County is the key addition. Located midway between Cleveland and Toledo, it has long been a major recreation area. Sandusky, the county seat, is a fishing market and coal port.

In the surrounding countryside fruit orchards and vineyards abound, and the wineries established a century ago by German immigrants in Sandusky are still a key feature of the local economy.

The sizable blue-collar element occasionally pushes Erie County into the Democratic column. But with only 15 percent of the district vote, Erie creates little more than a ripple in the large Republican pond.

The 5th lost 90,000 people with the removal of rural Van Wert County, one of the nation's premier peony farming areas; the eastern half of agricultural Fulton County; and suburban Toledo precincts in Lucas and Wood counties.

The district's proximity to Toledo, Cleveland and Detroit has given it a fair number of small-scale auto parts plants. They were hurt badly by the economic downturn in the early 1980s.

Although many areas of the 5th lost population, Wood County was a notable exception. This county, which sprawls from the outskirts of Toledo deep into the Ohio Corn Belt, had a 20 percent population surge in the 1970s. The college town of Bowling Green led the boom with a 76 percent growth rate.

Even with 22,000 residents in Lake Township and the communities of Rossford and Northwood transferred to the 9th, Wood County still has one-sixth of the 5th District voters. The county is consistently Republican, although the 18,000 students at Bowling Green provide a base for liberal contenders. Independent presidential candidate John B. Anderson drew 10 percent of the Wood County vote in 1980, his best county showing in Ohio.

Election Returns

5th District		Democrat		Republican	
1976	President	81,889	(43.2%)	103,417	(54.6%)
	Senate	74,958	(40.8%)	101,938	(55.5%)
	House	65,273	(36.0%)	115,180	(63.5%)
1978	Governor	60,251	(44.8%)	69,370	(51.6%)
	House	57,346	(41.7%)	80,305	(58.3%)
1980	President	70,292	(33.4%)	122,273	(58.1%)
	Senate	111,288	(56.7%)	80,591	(41.0%)
	House	65,685	(34.5%)	124,626	(65.5%)
1982	Governor	82,994	(53.0%)	70,329	(44.9%)
	Senate	76,249	(47.9%)	79,668	(50.0%)
	House	70,120	(44.8%)	86,450	(55.2%)

Demographics

Population: 514,189. **Percent Change from 1970:** 7.7%.

Land Area: 4,958 square miles. **Population per Square Mile:** 103.7.

Counties, 1980 Population: Defiance — 39,987; Erie — 79,655; Fulton (Pt.) — 17,720; Henry — 28,383; Huron (Pt.) — 7,538; Ottawa — 40,076; Paulding — 21,302; Putnam — 32,991; Sandusky — 63,267; Seneca — 61,901; Williams — 36,369; Wood (Pt.) — 85,000.

Cities, 1980 Population: Bowling Green — 25,728; Defiance — 16,810; Fostoria (Pt.) — 12,331; Fremont — 17,834; Perrysburg — 10,215; Sandusky — 31,360; Tiffin — 19,549; Vermilion (Pt.) — 5,634.

Race and Ancestry: White — 96.0%; Black — 2.0%; American Indian, Eskimo and Aleut — 0.1%; Asian and Pacific Islander — 0.2%. Spanish Origin — 3.2%. Dutch — 0.5%; English — 7.7%; French — 0.9%; German — 28.5%; Hungarian — 0.5%; Irish — 2.6%; Italian — 1.1%; Polish — 0.7%.

Universities, Enrollment: Bowling Green State University, Bowling Green — 17,659; Bowling Green State University Firelands College, Huron — 1,195; Defiance College, Defiance — 802; Heidelberg College, Tiffin — 761; Northwest Technical College, Archbold — 859; Terra Technical College, Fremont — 2,243; Tiffin University, Tiffin — 448.

Newspapers, Circulation: *The Advertiser-Tribune* (e), Tiffin — 11,526; *Bellevue Gazette* (e), Bellevue — 4,238; *The Bryan Times* (e), Bryan — 10,631; *The Crescent-News* (e), Defiance — 17,945; *The Daily Sentinel-Tribune* (e), Bowling Green — 13,597; *News-Herald* (e), Port Clinton — 6,252; *The News-Messenger* (e), Fremont — 15,539; *Northwest-Signal* (e), Napoleon — 5,799; *The Review Times* (e), Fostoria — 7,216; *Sandusky Register* (eS), Sandusky — 25,751. Toledo *Blade* also circulates in the district.

Commercial Television Stations, Affiliation: WGGN-TV, Sandusky (None). Most of district is located in Toledo ADI. Portions are in Cleveland ADI and Fort Wayne (Ind.) ADI.

Nuclear Power Plants: Davis-Besse 1, Oak Harbor (Babcock & Wilcox, Bechtel), July 1978.

Industries:

General Motors Corp. (Central Foundry Div.); Defiance; grey iron castings — 3,300. **Whirlpool Corp.;** Clyde; household laundry equipment — 2,400. **General Motors Corp.** (New Departure - Hyatt Bearing Div. - HQ); Sandusky; auto bearings — 2,300. **Campbell Soup Co.;** Napoleon; canned soups — 2,000. **Philips ECG Inc.;** Ottawa; cathode ray television picture tubes — 1,900.

Atlas Crankshaft Corp.; Fostoria; diesel engines — 1,600. **Bendix Autolite Corp.;** Fostoria; spark plugs — 1,600. **Ford Motor Co.** (Electrical and Electronics Div.); Sandusky; automotive hardware — 1,500. **ARO Corp.** (HQ); Bryan; pneumatic air tools — 1,370. **Chrysler Corp.** (Toledo Machining Plant); Perrysburg; auto parts — 1,100. **Owens-Illinois Inc.;** Perrysburg; packing, crating — 1,010. **General Electric Co.** (Tiffin Hermetic Motors); Tiffin; hermetic motor parts — 1,000.

Johns-Manville Sales Corp.; Defiance; insulation — 1,000. **National Machinery Co.;** Tiffin; machine tools — 1,000. **Sauder Woodworking Co. (HQ);** Archbold; household furniture — 700. **General Electric Co. (Bellevue Lamp Plant);** Bellevue; photo lamps — 650.

Brush Wellman Inc.; Elmore; beryllium — 630. **Standard Products Co. Inc.;** Port Clinton; fabricated rubber products — 600. **The Mohawk Rubber Co. (Fayette Tubular Products Div.);** Fayette; fabricated metal products — 560. **Union Carbide Corp. (Carbon Products Div.);** Fostoria; industrial carbons — 550. **American Standard Inc.;** Tiffin; vitreous china plumbing fixtures — 500. **Cedar Point Inc.;** Sandusky; amusement park — 500. **Hayes-Albion Corp.;** Tiffin; auto parts — 500. **H. J. Heinz Co.;** Fremont; tomato catsup — 500. **Imperial Clevite Inc.;** Milan; motor vehicle parts — 500.

6th District

South Central — Portsmouth, Chillicothe

The 6th is a mixture of suburbia and Appalachia. Republican majorities in the Cincinnati and Dayton suburbs and the countryside nearby enable the GOP to win most elections. But when the Democrats run well in Appalachia, as they occasionally do, the outcome can be close.

The 6th lost some of its Ohio River frontage to the 2nd in the redistricting, as the Legislature pared away all of rural Brown County and all but one small township of fast-growing Clermont County.

It gained GOP terrain north of Interstate 71, the major Cincinnati-to-Columbus artery. The district added about 50,000 new constituents in northwestern Warren County from the 8th District and about 60,000 new constituents in adjoining portions of southeastern Montgomery County. Approximately one-third of the latter live in Miami Township, which was transferred from the 8th. The rest live in affluent Washington Township, moved over from the 3rd. Nearly one-third of the voters in the new 6th live in this suburban sector between Cincinnati and Dayton.

Immediately to the east is rural Republican country. Clinton and Highland counties and the southern portion of Fayette County lie on the outer fringe of the Corn Belt. Soybeans, corn, hogs and dairy products for the nearby cities are the basis of the farm economy.

But this region of rolling hills and Republican majorities will be less influential in the district in the 1980s than it was in the 1970s. About 60,000 people in Pickaway County and the northern half of Fayette County have been transferred to the 7th.

Farther east the land is poorer, and Republican strength begins to diminish. Adams, Pike and Vinton counties are three of the four poorest in Ohio. Tobacco is grown in the Ohio River Valley, and livestock anchors the modest agricultural economy elsewhere.

Redistricting has expanded the Appalachian influence. On its eastern end, the 6th gains about 75,000 new constituents by adding all of Jackson and Hocking counties, two townships in western Athens County and the rest of Vinton County (the 6th had one township there before). All of these newcomers were formerly in the 10th District.

Nearly one-half the land area of this Appalachian portion is enclosed in the Wayne National Forest. What little industry exists is concentrated in the small cities of Portsmouth and Chillicothe. Both have lost population since 1960.

Portsmouth lies at the juncture of the Ohio and Scioto rivers. While steel and bricks have been linchpins of the local economy throughout the century, the largest employer in the district is the nearby uranium enrichment facility owned by the Atomic Energy Commission and operated by Goodyear.

Chillicothe is 44 miles due north of Portsmouth along the winding Scioto. Lumbering in nearby forests supports a large paper plant. The first state capital of Ohio, Chillicothe is dotted with early 19th-century mansions built in the Greek Revival style. The local paper, the Chillicothe *Gazette*, has been in business since 1800 and is the oldest continuously published newspaper west of the Alleghenies.

In the center of the district is Pike County, whose voters are as solidly Democratic today as they were when they sympathized with the Confederacy during the Civil War. While less dependable than Pike, the other Appalachian counties vote Democratic with varying degrees of regularity.

Election Returns

6th District		Democrat		Republican	
1976	President	85,675	(47.8%)	91,021	(50.8%)
	Senate	79,647	(46.4%)	85,903	(50.1%)
	House	61,708	(35.7%)	109,836	(63.5%)
1978	Governor	53,169	(40.8%)	74,489	(57.1%)
	House	45,323	(34.2%)	86,978	(65.6%)
1980	President	61,496	(37.6%)	93,577	(57.1%)
	Senate	122,091	(66.9%)	55,360	(30.4%)
	House	75,687	(42.1%)	103,719	(57.7%)
1982	Governor	88,440	(53.4%)	74,050	(44.7%)
	Senate	84,445	(49.9%)	81,052	(47.9%)
	House	63,435	(40.8%)	92,135	(59.2%)

Demographics

Population: 514,895. **Percent Change from 1970:** 13.0%.

Land Area: 4,930 square miles. **Population per Square Mile:** 104.4.

Counties, 1980 Population: Adams — 24,328; Athens (Pt.) — 9,063; Clermont (Pt.) — 3,352; Clinton — 34,603; Fayette (Pt.) — 13,856; Highland — 33,477; Hocking — 24,304; Jackson — 30,592; Montgomery (Pt.) — 58,109; Pike — 22,802; Ross — 65,004; Scioto — 84,545; Vinton — 11,584; Warren — 99,276.

Cities, 1980 Population: Centerville — 18,886; Chillicothe — 23,420; Franklin — 10,711; Portsmouth — 25,943; Washington (Pt.) — 7,006; Wilmington — 10,431.

Race and Ancestry: White — 97.4%; Black — 2.0%; American Indian, Eskimo and Aleut — 0.1%; Asian and Pacific Islander — 0.3%. Spanish Origin — 0.5%. Dutch — 0.8%; English — 18.7%; French — 0.8%; German — 11.5%; Irish — 5.5%; Italian — 0.6%.

Universities, Enrollment: Hocking Technical College, Nelsonville — 3,035; Ohio University (Chillicothe campus), Chillicothe — 1,227; Portsmouth Interstate Business College, Portsmouth — 1,450; Shawnee State Community College, Portsmouth — 2,111; Southern State Community College, Hillsboro — 1,531; Wilmington College, Wilmington — 1,129.

Newspapers, Circulation: *Chillicothe Gazette* (e), Chillicothe — 17,220; *The Daily Times* (e), Portsmouth — 21,366; *Greenfield Daily Times* (e), Greenfield — 4,548; *Logan Daily News* (e), Logan — 6,159; *Press Gazette* (e), Hillsboro — 4,772; *Record Herald* (e), Washington Court House — 7,240; *Wilmington News Journal* (e), Wilmington — 7,684. Dayton *Journal Herald* also circulates in the district.

Commercial Television Stations, Affiliation: Most of district is divided among Cincinnati ADI, Columbus ADI and Charleston (W.Va.)-Huntington (W.Va.) ADI. Portion is in Dayton ADI.

Industries:

Goodyear Atomic Corp.; Piketon; fissionable materials — 3,200. **The Mead Corp.** (Mead Forms Paper Div.); Chillicothe; paper, research — 2,700. **Norfolk & Western Railway Co.;** Portsmouth; railroad operations — 2,000. **Veterans Administration;** Chillicothe; veterans' hospital — 1,400. **Wear-Ever Aluminum Inc.** (HQ); Chillicothe; aluminum stampings —1,100.

The Mead Corp. (Printing & Writing Div.); Chillicothe; paper coating — 1,000. **Textron Inc.** (Randall Co. Div.); Wilmington; auto body stampings — 800. **Paccar Inc.** (Kenworth Truck Co. Div.); Chillicothe; truck bodies — 670. **Cincinnati Milacron Inc.;** Wilmington; machine parts — 600. **Plibrico Co.;** Oak Hill; clay refractory — 600. **Airborne Express Inc.;** Wilmington; air cargo services — 550. **The Irwin Auger Bit Co.;** Wilmington; auger bits — 500.

7th District

West Central — Springfield, Marion

Situated between Columbus and Dayton, the 7th district is bisected by U.S. Route 40. North of the old National Road are four solidly Republican counties that cast one-third of the district vote. Combining agriculture and small industry, they have been GOP strongholds for generations. Ronald Reagan won 62 percent in these four counties in 1980.

Marion was the hometown of Warren G. Harding and claims to be the birthplace of the steam shovel. The local Marion Power Shovel Company is still a major employer. But Marion has been hard hit by the recession. The demand for large power shovels has decreased since the strip mining boom of the 1970s, and a local steel plant has had major layoffs.

The economic picture is rosier in neighboring Union County. Its population grew by 24 percent in the 1970s, a far greater rate than that of any other county in the district. Just northwest of Columbus, it is an attractive site for industries seeking open land and low taxes. Honda has already built a motorcycle plant in the western part of the county, and the Japanese firm's first American automobile plant was being constructed nearby.

The population south of Route 40 is concentrated in Clark County (Springfield) and Greene County, which extends into the eastern suburbs of Dayton. Greene has a working-class mixture of blacks and southern whites. Wright-Patterson Air Force Base is responsible for a substantial amount of military-related employment. This area, which casts more than half the votes in the 7th, gave Reagan just 51 percent in 1980.

Springfield's site along the National Road enabled it to develop into the leading population center in the area, but it has been in an economic slump in recent years. The city has already lost a major publishing company. In 1982 the continued operation of International Harvester, the district's largest employer, was threatened. However, the company decided to keep the Springfield facility open and close its Fort Wayne, Ind., plant, instead. Since 1960 Springfield has lost 10,000 residents.

Redistricting was expected to enhance the Republican character of the district. The 7th lost Democratic Mad River Township in eastern Montgomery County to the 3rd

and a rural township in southwestern Champaign County to the 8th — about 30,000 constituents altogether.

The district gained the western part of Logan County from the 4th, all of Pickaway County and the northern half of Fayette County from the 6th and rural precincts in north and south Madison County from the 15th. All of the approximately 75,000 newcomers are from staunchly Republican counties. Each gave Reagan at least 61 percent in 1980.

Election Returns

7th District		Democrat		Republican	
1976	President	75,186	(44.6%)	88,833	(52.7%)
	Senate	76,042	(46.2%)	81,737	(49.6%)
	House	54,991	(34.6%)	104,156	(65.4%)
1978	Governor	50,312	(44.2%)	60,841	(53.5%)
	House	2,096	(2.2%)	93,499	(97.8%)
1980	President	65,353	(37.9%)	94,970	(55.1%)
	Senate	118,955	(69.4%)	49,734	(29.0%)
	House	38,970	(23.6%)	125,909	(76.4%)
1982	Governor	75,264	(48.4%)	78,155	(50.2%)
	Senate	83,018	(52.6%)	71,879	(45.6%)
	House	65,543	(42.0%)	87,842	(56.2%)

Demographics

Population: 512,706. **Percent Change from 1970:** 3.8%.

Land Area: 3,363 square miles. **Population per Square Mile:** 152.5.

Counties, 1980 Population: Champaign (Pt.) — 31,501; Clark — 150,236; Fayette (Pt.) — 13,611; Greene — 129,769; Logan — 39,155; Madison (Pt.) — 7,262; Marion — 67,974; Pickaway — 43,662; Union — 29,536.

Cities, 1980 Population: Beavercreek — 31,589; Bellefontaine — 11,888; Circleville — 11,700; Dayton (Pt.) — 4,050; Fairborn — 29,702; Marion — 37,040; Springfield — 72,563; Urbana — 10,762; Washington (Pt.) — 5,676; Xenia — 24,653.

Race and Ancestry: White — 93.8%; Black — 5.4%; American Indian, Eskimo and Aleut — 0.1%; Asian and Pacific Islander — 0.4%. Spanish Origin — 0.6%. Dutch — 0.8%; English — 14.4%; French — 0.8%; German — 12.8%; Irish — 4.4%; Italian — 0.6%; Scottish — 0.5%.

Universities, Enrollment: Air Force Institute of Technology, Wright-Patterson Air Force Base — 788; Antioch University, Yellow Springs — 4,057; Cedarville College, Cedarville — 1,500; Central State University, Wilberforce — 2,553; Circleville Bible College, Circleville — 251; Clark Technical College, Springfield — 2,670; Mansfield Business College, Marion — 115; Marion Technical College, Marion — 1,271; Ohio State University (Marion campus), Marion — 842; Urbana College, Urbana — 900; Wilberforce University, Wilberforce — 1,082; Wittenberg University, Springfield — 2,558.

Newspapers, Circulation: *Beavercreek Daily News* (e), Beaver Creek — 5,870; *Bellefontaine Examiner* (e), Bellefontaine — 10,554; *The Daily Gazette* (e), Xenia — 12,569; *The Daily News* (eS), Springfield — 27,275; *Fairborn Daily Herald* (e), Fairborn — 7,406; *Herald* (e), Circleville — 8,481; *The Marion Star* (eS), Marion — 20,062; *Marysville Journal-Tribune* (e), Marysville — 6,117; *The Sun* (mS), Springfield — 18,126; *Urbana Daily Citizen* (e), Urbana — 7,392. Dayton *Journal Herald* and *Dayton Daily News* also circulate in the district.

Commercial Television Stations, Affiliation: WTJC, Springfield (None). District is divided among Columbus ADI and Dayton ADI.

Military Installations: Springfield Municipal Airport (Air National Guard), Springfield — 1,159; Rickenbacker Air Force Base *(Base* *straddles line between 7th and 15th districts)*; Wright-Patterson Air Force Base, Fairborn — 13,781 *(Base straddles line between 3rd and 7th districts).*

Industries:

International Harvester Co. (Springfield Body Plant); Springfield; trucks — 3,600. **Dresser Industries Inc.** (Marion Power Shovel Co. Div.); Marion; excavating machinery — 2,400. **Whirlpool Corp.;** Marion; dryers, ranges — 2,200. **Tecumseh Products Co.;** Marion; refrigeration, air conditioning equipment — 1,200. **Community Hospital;** Springfield; hospital — 1,100.

Kelsey-Hayes Co. Inc.; Springfield; warehousing — 1,000. **Midland-Ross Corp.** (Grimes Div.); Urbana; vehicular lighting equipment — 1,000. **Robbins & Myers Inc.;** Springfield; industrial pumps — 1,000. **Cooper Industries Inc.** (Cooper Energy Services); Springfield; internal combustion engines — 900. **The O. M. Scott & Sons Co.** (HQ); Marysville; lawn fertilizers — 900. **General Electric Co.** (Lamp Plant); Circleville; lamps — 803. **Siemens-Allis, Inc.** (ITE Electrical Products); Bellefontaine; electrical distribution equipment — 620. **DAB Industries Inc.;** Bellefontaine; bearings, washers — 600. **B. F. Goodrich Co.** (Engineered Systems Div.); Green Camp; fabricated rubber products — 500. **Quaker Oats Co.;** Marion; pet food — 500.

8th District

Southwest — Middletown, Hamilton

In 1966 Ohio's Legislature created a new district — the 24th — to replace an old at-large seat and to accommodate rapid population growth in the corridor between Cincinnati and Dayton. Six years later the 24th was renumbered as the 8th and slightly expanded, and in 1982 it was enlarged again.

Regardless of its precise location or number, the district remains essentially Republican, with Butler County as its anchor. Butler contains two medium-sized manufacturing centers along the Great Miami River — Hamilton and Middletown. Steel, paper, automobile bodies, machine tools and a variety of other metal products are manufactured in the two cities, which have a combined population of about 106,000. As recently as the mid-1950s, Hamilton built about half of the world's safes and bank vaults.

But both cities lost population in the 1970s. Most of Butler County's 259,000 residents in 1980 lived not in Hamilton or Middletown but in suburban communities and small towns such as Oxford, the home of Miami University.

The growth in Butler County's suburban territory, just north of the Cincinnati beltway, has escalated a rightward trend in the local GOP. In recent years the county has elected some of the most conservative Republican legislators in the state. Ronald Reagan carried Butler in 1980 with 62 percent, his best showing in any of Ohio's 10 most populous counties.

Half of the residents of the new 8th live outside Butler County, in a string of fertile Corn Belt counties running north along the Indiana border. The land is flat and the roads are straight. Corn and soybeans are major cash crops in the rural counties. Poultry and livestock also are moneymakers. In the late 1970s and early 1980s, Darke and Mercer counties were the leading Ohio counties in farm income.

Mercer was settled by German Catholics and is the only county in the 8th with a strong Democratic heritage. But Mercer likes its Democrats conservative. It has not backed the party's presidential candidate since 1968.

In the 1970s the Democrats' most reliable bastion in

the 8th was the western portion of Montgomery County. But in redistricting, this area was moved to the 3rd District. The legislative scalpel also transferred the northwest corner of suburban Warren County to the 6th.

To compensate for the loss, the Legislature extended the 8th to the north and east. In the north the district was expanded to take in all of rural Van Wert County from the 5th and the rest of Mercer County from the 4th, for a total of about 65,000 new constituents. Previously the 8th had included only two small townships in the southwest corner of Mercer County.

In the east the district picked up all of Miami County from the 4th and one rural township in Champaign County from the 7th — about 92,600 new constituents altogether.

Election Returns

8th District		Democrat		Republican	
1976	President	70,042	(42.6%)	91,258	(55.5%)
	Senate	71,862	(44.2%)	85,121	(52.4%)
	House	44,464	(27.8%)	111,385	(69.7%)
1978	Governor	42,662	(41.6%)	56,933	(55.6%)
	House	28,824	(27.0%)	77,751	(73.0%)
1980	President	69,036	(34.7%)	117,158	(58.8%)
	Senate	114,942	(64.9%)	58,569	(33.1%)
	House	39,279	(22.5%)	135,509	(77.5%)
1982	Governor	74,175	(50.6%)	69,471	(47.4%)
	Senate	76,764	(51.4%)	70,315	(47.0%)
	House	49,877	(33.6%)	98,527	(66.4%)

Demographics

Population: 513,427. **Percent Change from 1970:** 11.3%.

Land Area: 2,808 square miles. **Population per Square Mile:** 182.8.

Counties, 1980 Population: Butler — 258,787; Champaign (Pt.) — 2,148; Darke — 55,096; Mercer — 38,334; Miami — 90,381; Preble — 38,223; Van Wert — 30,458.

Cities, 1980 Population: Fairfield — 30,777; Greenville — 12,999; Hamilton — 63,189; Middletown — 43,719; Oxford — 17,655; Piqua — 20,480; Troy — 19,086; Van Wert — 11,035.

Race and Ancestry: White — 96.6%; Black — 2.8%; American Indian, Eskimo and Aleut — 0.1%; Asian and Pacific Islander — 0.3%. Spanish Origin — 0.6%. Dutch — 0.6%; English — 12.6%; French — 1.0%; German — 20.4%; Irish — 3.9%; Italian — 0.7%.

Universities, Enrollment: Edison State Community College, Piqua — 2,015; Miami University, Oxford — 14,802; Miami University (Hamilton campus), Hamilton — 1,865; Miami University (Middletown campus), Middletown — 1,790; Wright State University (Western Ohio campus), Celina — 711.

Newspapers, Circulation: *Daily Advocate* (e), Greenville — 9,535; *The Daily Standard* (e), Celina — 9,805; *The Journal-News* (eS), Hamilton — 30,206; *The Middletown Journal* (eS), Middletown — 25,094; *The Piqua Daily Call* (e), Piqua — 11,426; *Times-Bulletin* (e), Van Wert — 8,036; *Troy Daily News* (eS), Troy — 10,928. Dayton *Journal Herald* and *Dayton Daily News* also circulate in the district.

Commercial Television Stations, Affiliation: Most of district is located in Dayton ADI. Portions are in Cincinnati ADI and Fort Wayne (Ind.) ADI.

Industries:

ARMCO Inc. (Middletown Works); Middletown; steel sheets — 5,000. **Hobart Corp.** (Dayton Scale Div. - HQ); Troy; food preparation equipment — 2,800. **Ohio Casualty Corp.** (HQ); Hamilton; casualty insurance — 2,500. **General Motors Corp.** (Fisher Body Div.); Hamilton; auto stampings — 2,398. **Champion International Corp.;** Hamilton; paper coating — 1,850.

Hobart Bros. Co. (Hobart Welder Sales & Service - HQ); Troy; electric welding apparatus — 1,650. **ARMCO Inc.;** (HQ); Middletown; steel sheet; oil field equipment, insurance — 1,600. **Huffy Corp.** (Ohio Bicycle Div.); Celina; bicycles — 1,520. **The Mosler Safe Co.** (Herman Safe Co. Div. - HQ); Hamilton; safes, vaults — 1,200. **A. O. Smith Corp.** (Electric Motor Div.); Tipp City; electric motors — 1,150. **Champion International Corp.;** Hamilton; paper, wood products — 1,035. **Aeroquip Corp.** (Industrial Div.); Van Wert; rubber hose lines — 900. **Somers Corp.** (Mersman Tables); Celina; tables — 800. **Celina Financial Corp.** (HQ); Celina; casualty, life insurance — 750. **Diamond International Corp.** (Packaging Products Div.); Middletown; folding cartons — 705. **Aeronca Inc.** (Aerospace Div.); Middletown; aircraft parts — 700. **Paul Revere Corp.** (Avco New Idea Farm Equipment Div.); Coldwater; farm equipment — 700.

Federal-Mogul Corp. (National Seal Div.); Van Wert; rubber products — 650. **B. F. Goodrich Co.** (Engineered Products Div.); Troy; aircraft parts — 650. **Baxter Travenol Laboratories** (Dayton Flexible Products Div.); Eaton; fabricated rubber products — 600. **Corning Glass Works;** Greenville; glassware — 600. **Square D Co.** (PE Group); Oxford; electrical equipment for internal combustion engines — 600. **The Sorg Paper Co.** (HQ); Middletown; paper mill — 587. **ARMCO Inc.;** Hamilton; coke — 581. **The Hamilton Tool Co.** (HQ); Hamilton; printing presses — 530. **The Reynolds & Reynolds Co.;** Celina; business forms — 527. **Dinner Bell Foods Inc.;** Troy; meatpacking — 500. **MSL Industries Inc.** (Miami Industries Div.); Piqua; steel pipe, tubes — 500. **Square D Co.;** Middletown; switchgears — 500.

9th District

Northwest — Toledo

Toledo is a major auto and glass manufacturing center and has one of the largest ports on the Great Lakes. But its economic picture was far from rosy in the early 1980s. As the auto industry slumped, so did the industrial city on Lake Erie. Toledo's population declined 7 percent in the 1970s.

More than two-thirds of the voters in the 9th live in Toledo, a Democratic outpost in rural Republican northwest Ohio. But the absence of a large black population keeps Democratic majorities in Toledo lower than those in Dayton or Cleveland. Jimmy Carter carried the city in 1980, but with only 49 percent of the vote.

Toledo is primarily an ethnic city. There are major concentrations of Germans, Irish, Poles and Hungarians. While traditionally Democratic, most blue-collar ethnics here pull the Republican lever at least occasionally.

In the early 20th century, Toledo elected two of the most famous mayors of the Progressive era — Samuel "Golden Rule" Jones and Brand Whitlock. Jones established one of the first municipal utilities in the country. Whitlock led the campaign for Ohio's initiative and referendum law.

About the same time, glassmakers Edward Libbey, Michael Owens and Edward Ford settled in the area. In 1930 their operations merged into Libbey-Owens-Ford that, along with Owens-Illinois and Owens-Corning Fiberglas, are major glass producers with headquarters in Toledo. Champion Spark Plug and the Willys-Overland automobile company also established their headquarters in the city in its boom years of the early 20th century. Willys-Overland went bankrupt during the Depression, but its plant was later converted into the production of jeeps.

Most of Toledo's industry was established along the west bank of the Maumee River that divides the city. To the east are blue-collar suburbs with a traditionally Democratic orientation. Republicans are concentrated in the more affluent, white-collar suburbs west of Toledo, such as Maumee and Ottawa Hills.

While Toledo dominates the 9th, the city's population loss forced the district to take in about 70,000 new rural and suburban constituents. The 9th added the rest of metropolitan Lucas County (29,000 residents), the eastern half of rural Fulton County (20,031) and the suburban northeast corner of Wood County (22,372). All of the new territory came from the 5th.

The changes were not expected to affect the marginal Democratic nature of the 9th. While Fulton is one of the most Republican counties in Ohio, the portion that joined the 9th is in the orbit of Toledo and includes most of the county's Democratic precincts. The Lucas County addition — four townships in the southwest — is a swing area. It went for Carter in 1976 and Ronald Reagan in 1980. The Wood County portion is loyally Democratic. It includes blue-collar Rossford and Northwood and neighboring Lake Township.

Election Returns

9th District		Democrat		Republican	
1976	President	112,580	(56.6%)	81,974	(41.2%)
	Senate	95,565	(51.0%)	85,545	(45.6%)
	House	99,348	(52.4%)	87,100	(46.0%)
1978	Governor	66,862	(52.0%)	58,194	(45.3%)
	House	78,595	(60.4%)	44,381	(34.1%)
1980	President	87,780	(44.1%)	91,459	(45.9%)
	Senate	120,439	(65.7%)	54,779	(29.9%)
	House	77,085	(38.9%)	114,126	(57.6%)
1982	Governor	106,278	(65.2%)	52,703	(32.3%)
	Senate	94,665	(59.0%)	60,298	(37.6%)
	House	95,162	(57.9%)	64,459	(39.3%)

Demographics

Population: 514,144. **Percent Change from 1970:** -1.1%.

Land Area: 572 square miles. **Population per Square Mile:** 898.9.

Counties, 1980 Population: Fulton (Pt.) — 20,031; Lucas — 471,741; Wood (Pt.) — 22,372.

Cities, 1980 Population: Maumee — 15,747; Oregon — 18,675; Sylvania — 15,527; Toledo — 354,635.

Race and Ancestry: White — 85.3%; Black — 12.5%; American Indian, Eskimo and Aleut — 0.2%; Asian and Pacific Islander — 0.6%. Spanish Origin — 2.6%. English — 6.0%; French — 1.3%; German — 13.8%; Hungarian — 1.2%; Irish — 3.1%; Italian — 0.9%; Polish — 6.0%.

Universities, Enrollment: Lourdes College, Sylvania — 588; Medical College of Ohio at Toledo, Toledo — 478; Michael J. Owens Technical College, Toledo — 3,216; University of Toledo, Toledo — 20,270.

Newspapers, Circulation: *The Blade* (eS), Toledo — 167,560.

Commercial Television Stations, Affiliation: WDHO-TV, Toledo (ABC); WTOL-TV, Toledo (CBS); WTVG, Toledo (NBC). Entire district is located in Toledo ADI.

Military Installations: Toledo Express Airport (Air Force), Swanton — 977.

Industries:

Jeep Corp.; Toledo; motor vehicles — 4,121. **General Motors Corp.** (Motor Div.); Toledo; automatic transmissions — 3,928. **The Toledo Hospital;** Toledo; hospital — 3,900. **Owens-Illinois Inc.** (HQ); Toledo; glass containers; corrugated shipping boxes — 2,500. **Champion Spark Plug Co.** (HQ); Toledo; spark plugs — 2,400.

St. Vincent Hospital & Medical Center; Toledo; hospital — 2,150. **Libbey-Owens-Ford. Co.;** Toledo; technical center, safety plate glass —1,900. **Owens-Corning Fiberglas Corp.** (HQ); Toledo; glass fiber products — 1,800. **Dana Corp.** (Spicer Transmission Div.); Toledo; motor vehicle parts — 1,700. **Owens-Illinois Inc.** (Libbey Glass Div.); Toledo; glass tableware — 1,700. **Consolidated Rail Corp.;** Toledo; railroad operations — 1,500. **St. Charles Hospital;** Toledo; hospital — 1,400. **Mercy Hospital of Toledo;** Toledo; hospital — 1,380. **Owens-Illinois Inc.** (Technical Center); Toledo; research, development — 1,200. **Riverside Hospital Inc.;** Toledo; hospital — 1,100. **Champion Spark Plug Co.** (DeVilbiss Co. Div.); Toledo; spray painting equipment — 1,000. **Seaway Food Town Inc.;** Toledo; grocery wholesalers — 1,000. **Ford Motor Co.** (Maumee Stamping Plant); Maumee; auto stampings — 950. **Roadway Express Inc.;** Toledo; trucking — 950. **General Mills Inc.** (Package Food Operations Div.); Toledo; cereals, food — 900.

The Toledo Blade Co.; Toledo; newspaper publishing — 800. **Johns-Manville Sales Corp.** (Fiber Glass Mfg. Div.); Waterville; fiberglass — 720. **Eltra Corp.** (Prestolite Battery Div.); Toledo; research — 650. **General Tire & Rubber Co.** (Textileather Div.); Toledo; synthetic fabrics — 600. **Sun Oil Co. of Pa.** (Toledo Refinery); Toledo; petroleum refining — 600. **Standard Oil Co. of Ohio;** Toledo; petroleum refining — 577. **Midland-Ross Corp.** (Surface Div.); Toledo; industrial furnaces — 550. **Midland-Ross Corp.** (National Cast Div.); Toledo; steel castings — 529. **Libbey-Owens-Ford Co.** (HQ); Toledo; glass, glass products — 500. **The Pilliod Cabinet Co.** (HQ); Swanton; wood furniture — 500. **Pinkerton's Inc.;** Toledo; security services — 500. **Sheller-Globe Corp.** (City Auto Stamping Div.); Toledo; stampings — 500. **Teledyne Inc.;** Toledo; turbine engines — 500.

10th District

Southeast — Lancaster, Zanesville

Nearly as large as Connecticut, the 10th District is a part of Appalachia grafted onto a Midwestern state. During the 1960s it was stagnating economically and losing population. In the 1970s, however, people began moving back to the area, in part because of the increased interest in coal mining. With a 14 percent population increase, the old 10th was second in growth among Ohio districts during the decade.

Redistricting also changed the economic character of what was the poorest district in the state for much of the 1970s. The Legislature transferred three of the poorest counties — Hocking, Jackson and Vinton — into the 6th, as well as two townships in western Athens County. The southern part of rural Noble County and the eastern part of Washington County moved into the 18th. Altogether the 10th lost about 75,000 former constituents.

The district gained about 69,000 new residents in the more prosperous eastern half of Licking County from the disbanded 17th. Three rural townships in western Guernsey County, which together have about 4,000 residents, were transferred from the 18th.

Redistricting enlarged the industrial, blue-collar base. But the 10th is Republican by tradition and remains so. It was the only district in the state that failed to elect a Democrat during the New Deal years.

Athens County, the home of Ohio University, is the only predictably Democratic part of the district. It was one of just two Ohio counties to support George McGovern in 1972. Many of the poorer voters in other counties along the Ohio River call themselves Democrats — a remnant of Civil War days — but their conservative outlook leads them toward Republican candidates in many elections.

There are no large population centers in the 10th District portion of the Ohio River Valley. Marietta and Ironton are small manufacturing towns, but neither has more than 20,000 residents. Founded in 1788, Marietta is the oldest settlement in Ohio. Ironton has integrated its economy with that of nearby Ashland, Ky.

The northern counties of the 10th have the best farm lands and the largest towns. Nearly half the district voters live in Fairfield (Lancaster), Licking (Newark) and Muskingum (Zanesville) counties. With a 28 percent population boom in the 1970s, Fairfield is the fastest-growing county in the 10th. Bedroom communities have blossomed along Route 33, a four-lane highway that connects Lancaster with Columbus, 30 miles to the northwest.

Both Lancaster and Newark, 30 miles to the northeast, are major glass-producing centers. Their counties are reliably Republican. Neighboring Muskingum occasionally strays. It includes New Concord, the boyhood home of Democratic Sen. John Glenn.

Election Returns

10th District		Democrat		Republican	
1976	President	85,488	(46.5%)	94,396	(51.4%)
	Senate	81,801	(46.1%)	90,604	(51.1%)
	House	56,021	(31.8%)	119,998	(68.2%)
1978	Governor	50,347	(38.5%)	77,081	(58.9%)
	House	34,891	(26.4%)	97,100	(73.6%)
1980	President	87,486	(38.9%)	123,853	(55.1%)
	Senate	124,988	(64.4%)	64,964	(33.5%)
	House	50,014	(26.0%)	142,074	(74.0%)
1982	Governor	77,506	(50.0%)	74,810	(48.2%)
	Senate	83,611	(52.8%)	72,802	(46.0%)
	House	57,983	(36.7%)	100,044	(63.3%)

Demographics

Population: 513,755. **Percent Change from 1970:** 12.7%.

Land Area: 4,509 square miles. **Population per Square Mile:** 113.9.

Counties, 1980 Population: Athens (Pt.) — 47,336; Fairfield — 93,678; Gallia — 30,098; Guernsey (Pt.) — 3,869; Lawrence — 63,849; Licking (Pt.) — 68,553; Meigs — 23,641; Morgan — 14,241; Muskingum — 83,340; Perry — 31,032; Washington (Pt.) — 54,118.

Cities, 1980 Population: Athens — 19,743; Columbus (Pt.) — 45; Ironton — 14,290; Lancaster — 34,953; Marietta — 16,467; Newark — 41,200; Reynoldsburg (Pt.) — 0; Zanesville — 28,655.

Race and Ancestry: White — 97.2%; Black — 2.1%; American Indian, Eskimo and Aleut — 0.1%; Asian and Pacific Islander — 0.3%. Spanish Origin — 0.5%. Dutch — 0.8%; English — 16.8%; French — 0.7%; German — 12.3%; Irish — 5.0%; Italian — 0.7%; Scottish — 0.5%.

Universities, Enrollment: Central Ohio Technical College, Newark — 1,167; Marietta College, Marietta — 1,327; Muskingum Area Technical College, Zanesville — 1,518; Muskingum College, New Concord — 1,013; Ohio State University (Newark campus), Newark — 1,160; Ohio University, Athens — 14,413; Ohio University (Lancaster campus), Lancaster — 1,512; Ohio University (Zanesville campus), Zanesville — 872; Rio Grande College and Community College, Rio Grande — 1,225; Washington Technical College, Marietta — 792.

Newspapers, Circulation: *The Advocate* (e), Newark — 23,078; *The Daily Sentinel* (eS), Pomeroy — 5,959; *Eagle-Gazette* (e), Lancaster — 18,183; *Gallipolis Daily Tribune* (eS), Gallipolis — 6,554; *The Ironton Tribune* (eS), Ironton — 9,726; *The Marietta Times* (e), Marietta — 15,218; *Messenger* (eS), Athens — 14,280; *The Times Recorder* (mS), Zanesville — 27,475.

Commercial Television Stations, Affiliation: WHIZ, Zanesville (NBC); WSFJ, Newark (None). District is divided between Columbus ADI and Charleston (W.Va.)-Huntington (W.Va.) ADI. Portions are in Zanesville ADI and Wheeling (W.Va.)-Steubenville ADI.

Military Installations: Newark Air Force Station, Heath — 2,460; Zanesville Air National Guard Station, Zanesville — 109.

Industries:

Anchor Hocking Corp. (HQ); Lancaster; glass tableware — 4,226. **Owens-Corning Fiberglas Corp.**; Newark; fiberglass — 2,400. **Ohio Power Co.** (Southern Ohio Coal); Wilkesville; coal mining — 1,883. **Rockwell International Corp.** (Truck Axle Div.); Newark; axles — 1,800. **Essex Group Inc.** (Wire Assembly Div.); Zanesville; electronic components — 1,500.

Union Carbide Corp.; Marietta; ferro alloys — 1,200. **Brockway Glass Co. Inc.**; Zanesville; glass containers — 1,150. **Babcock & Wilcox Co. Inc.** (Diamond Power Specialty Co. Div.); Lancaster; soot blowers — 1,000. **Kaiser Aluminum & Chemical Corp.**; Newark; rods, wire — 900. **Kardex Systems Inc.** (HQ); Reno; metal office furniture — 680. **B. F. Goodrich Co.**; Marietta; plastics — 650. **State Farm Fire & Casualty Co.**; Newark; casualty insurance — 650. **Burnham Corp.** (Foundry Div.); Zanesville; grey iron castings — 500. **Johns-Manville Sales Corp.** (Holophane Div.); Newark; glassware — 500. **McGraw-Edison Co.** (Power Systems Div.); Zanesville; transformers, switchgears — 500. **Robbins & Myers Inc.** (Sub-Fractional Motor Div.); Gallipolis; electric motors — 500. **Shell Oil Co.** (Shell Chemical Co. Div.); Belpre; synthetic rubber — 500.

11th District

Northeast — Ashtabula, Painesville

In recent years the 11th has been Ohio's political bellwether. It supported Jimmy Carter and Democratic Sen. Howard M. Metzenbaum in 1976. Four years later it went for Ronald Reagan. In each case, the winner's vote in the 11th came within 2 percentage points of his statewide total.

While no city in the district has a population exceeding 45,000, the area gradually has lost its rural and small-town character and has come to focus more on Cleveland. As migration from the city moved eastward between 1950 and 1970, the population of Lake and Geauga counties more than doubled. The rapid growth slowed somewhat during the 1970s, but the suburbs continue to creep further east, obliterating the truck gardens and vineyards along Lake Erie.

Geauga is the GOP mainstay in the 11th. Settled by Yankee Protestants, it was the only county in northeast Ohio to back Alf Landon in 1936. It has remained in the GOP column since then, although Republican commuters have been displacing Republican farmers.

But Geauga casts only 14 percent of the district vote. Elsewhere Republicans must scramble for support. Lake is a swing county; Republican farmers and suburbanites are canceled out by Democratic ethnics who have settled in the western part of the county. With 34 percent of the district vote, Lake County is the keystone of the 11th.

The two eastern counties — Ashtabula and Trumbull

— cast 25 percent of the vote and are usually Democratic. The coal-port cities of Ashtabula and Conneaut support a fair number of industrial plants along Lake Erie. Only a strong Republican county organization keeps GOP candidates close in Ashtabula.

Blue-collar workers whose jobs are in Warren and Youngstown, just south of the district line, boost the Democratic vote in the northern part of Trumbull County. Plant closings in the steel-making Mahoning Valley have crippled the economy in this region. In early 1982 the unemployment rate was above 15 percent in both Ashtabula and Trumbull counties.

Other voters in the 11th live to the southwest in Democratic Portage County. Sandwiched between Youngstown on the east and Akron on the west, Portage is trisected by the Ohio Turnpike and Interstate 71. The population centers of Ravenna and Kent are in the middle of the county.

The Legislature tinkered with the lines in every county of the 11th except Ashtabula. But the net effect did not alter the district's marginal status. Democrats were helped by the transfer of several Republican townships in northeastern Summit County (about 41,000 residents) to the 14th, in exchange for Kent and neighboring Brimfield Township (about 33,000). Republicans gained by adding the Republican western third of Geauga County (about 25,000) from the disbanded 22nd.

The other changes involved swing territory. Seven townships in Trumbull County were transferred to the new, 17th, while about 30,000 residents were added in western Lake County.

Election Returns

11th District		Democrat		Republican	
1976	President	89,889	(49.4%)	82,163	(45.1%)
	Senate	82,212	(52.3%)	73,844	(47.0%)
	House	64,149	(37.3%)	107,171	(62.2%)
1978	Governor	67,219	(54.0%)	53,150	(42.7%)
	House	40,159	(30.1%)	89,655	(67.2%)
1980	President	75,855	(39.9%)	97,451	(51.2%)
	Senate	128,471	(72.1%)	43,431	(24.4%)
	House	68,594	(33.9%)	127,821	(63.2%)
1982	Governor	93,483	(62.4%)	52,323	(34.9%)
	Senate	88,498	(58.0%)	59,997	(39.3%)
	House	93,302	(60.9%)	56,616	(36.9%)

Demographics

Population: 512,867. **Percent Change from 1970:** 10.0%.

Land Area: 2,088 square miles. **Population per Square Mile:** 245.6.

Counties, 1980 Population: Ashtabula — 104,215; Geauga — 74,474; Lake (Pt.) — 174,687; Portage — 135,856; Trumbull (Pt.) — 23,635.

Cities, 1980 Population: Ashtabula — 23,449; Conneaut — 13,835; Eastlake — 22,104; Kent — 26,164; Mentor — 42,065; Painesville — 16,391; Ravenna — 11,987; Willoughby — 19,329.

Race and Ancestry: White — 97.1%; Black — 2.0%; American Indian, Eskimo and Aleut — 0.1%; Asian and Pacific Islander — 0.5%. Spanish Origin — 0.6%. English — 8.2%; French — 0.5%; German — 9.2%; Hungarian — 2.1%; Irish — 3.4%; Italian — 4.0%; Polish — 2.0%; Scottish — 0.5%.

Universities, Enrollment: Hiram College, Hiram — 1,183; Kent State University, Kent — 18,936; Kent State University (Ashtabula campus), Ashtabula — 1,114; Lake Erie College, Painesville — 981; Lakeland Community College, Mentor — 7,595.

Newspapers, Circulation: *The Geauga Times Leader* (e), Chardon — 8,249; *The Lake County News-Herald* (eS), Willoughby — 32,090; *The News-Herald* (e), Conneaut — 5,000; *Record-Courier* (e), Ravenna — 26,352; *The Star-Beacon* (all day), Ashtabula — 21,358; *Star-Beacon* (m), Geneva — 2,297; *The Telegraph* (all day, S), Painesville — 18,050. Cleveland *Plain Dealer* also circulates in the district.

Commercial Television Stations, Affiliation: Most of district is located in Cleveland ADI. Portion is in Youngstown ADI.

Military Installations: Ravenna Army Ammunition Plant, Ravenna — 214.

Nuclear Power Plants: Perry 1 and 2, North Perry (General Electric, Kaiser).

Industries:

Avery Products Corp. (Fasson Products Div.); Painesville; paper coating — 1,400. **Towmotor Corp.** (HQ); Mentor; industrial forklifts — 1,250. **Robinson Memorial Hospital;** Ravenna; hospital — 1,190. **Dalton Industries Inc.** (James Kenrob Co. - HQ); Willoughby; women's knit outerwear — 1,000. **RMI Co.;** Ashtabula; sodium peroxide — 810.

The Lubrizol Corp.; Painesville; lubricant chemicals, fuel — 800. **Eagle-Picher Industries Inc.** (Ohio Rubber Co.); Willoughby; rubber products — 750. **Elkem Metals Co. Inc.;** Ashtabula; industrial inorganic chemicals — 700. **Premix Inc.** (HQ); North Kingsville; reinforced plastic — 700. **Reliance Electric Co. Inc.;** Ashtabula; electric motors — 650. **Johnson Rubber Co.** (HQ); Middlefield; fabricated rubber products — 630. **Diamond Shamrock Corp.** (T. R. Evans Research Center); Painesville; research — 600.

Rockwell International Corp. (Brake Plant); Ashtabula; motor vehicle parts — 600. **Catalytic Inc.;** Willoughby; general contracting — 500. **Eaton Corp.** (Synflex Div.); Mantua; hydraulic hose — 500. **Newport News Industrial Corp.;** Perry; nuclear power plant constructing — 500. **True Temper Corp.;** Ashtabula; hand tools — 500. **United States Concrete Pipe Co. Inc.;** Diamond; concrete sewer pipe — 500. **W. S. Tyler Inc.** (HQ); Mentor; fabricated wire products — 500.

12th District

Central — Northeastern Columbus and Suburbs

The Columbus area is one of America's great test markets. Products that succeed in this miniature of middle America usually are a hit elsewhere.

Throughout the 1970s metropolitan Franklin County was split down the middle, with the 12th carrying the eastern portion that contained most of the city's black areas. But redistricting pared away the southeastern quadrant of Franklin County and placed it in the 15th. Gone are some blue-collar and black suburbs near Lockbourne Air Force Base, plus some heavily black wards on the East Side within the shadow of Columbus' gleaming downtown skyscrapers. This move left the 12th predominanly white and middle class and appeared to cost the Democrats several thousand votes.

Also unfavorable for Democrats is the addition of about 53,000 new constituents in western Licking County, a rural Republican area brought in from the dismembered 17th. The district line was drawn just short of Newark, where the county's Democrats live. The rural expansion overshadowed the gain of some downtown Columbus neighborhoods near the Scioto River in the restored German Village area.

Blacks comprise 22 percent of Columbus' population, but they are divided nearly evenly between the 12th and

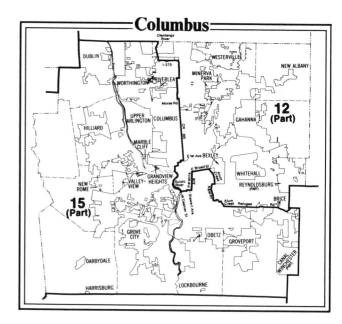

15th districts. Democratic candidates have to do very well in the inner city to carry the 12th. They sometimes succeed in contests for local office; Columbus had a Republican mayor but a Democratic council for most of the 1970s. Ticket-splitting is less frequent in state and national elections.

As one moves east from the state Capitol building along Broad Street (U.S. Route 40), the black population goes down and the Republican vote goes up. About three miles east of the Capitol is affluent Bexley, an independent community of 13,000 surrounded by the city. While normally Republican, Bexley has a large Jewish population and sometimes votes Democratic.

Two miles farther east on Broad Street is Whitehall, another independent town, population 21,000. Site of the Defense Construction Supply Center, it has a large blue-collar base and its voters are frequent ticket-splitters.

Farther out are newer suburbs. Some of these, like Reynoldsburg and Gahanna, are predominantly blue-collar. Residents are employed at large plants such as Rockwell International and Western Electric. Other communities such as Westerville are mainly white-collar. Most are reliably Republican.

Nearly three-quarters of the district voters live in Columbus or its Franklin County suburbs. A diverse array of jobs keeps the county economically healthy. Columbus has not suffered from the kind of economic collapse that afflicted most of Ohio's industrial cities in the late 1970s and early 1980s. White-collar jobs are provided by state and local government, a cluster of colleges led by Ohio State University, and commercial, banking and numerous scientific research firms. Industries have been settling in the Columbus area since World War II, attracted by its central location and the availability of a low-wage work force in nearby Appalachia.

The rest of the district is rural and Republican, with a smattering of light industry. Suburban spillover from Columbus enabled Delaware and Morrow counties to show growth rates of more than 20 percent in the 1970s.

The remap contributed to the 1982 defeat of the Democrat freshman incumbent, whose Republican challenger won with just over 50 percent of the vote.

Election Returns

12th District		Democrat		Republican	
1976	President	78,361	(42.9%)	99,828	(54.7%)
	Senate	81,538	(46.5%)	87,260	(49.8%)
	House	82,071	(44.9%)	87,507	(47.9%)
1978	Governor	59,624	(45.0%)	70,706	(53.4%)
	House	57,445	(43.1%)	75,965	(56.9%)
1980	President	80,267	(40.4%)	105,088	(52.9%)
	Senate	123,510	(65.8%)	51,844	(27.6%)
	House	100,178	(52.1%)	92,071	(47.9%)
1982	Governor	91,339	(52.5%)	78,458	(45.1%)
	Senate	91,934	(51.4%)	79,896	(44.7%)
	House	82,753	(47.3%)	88,335	(50.5%)

Demographics

Population: 512,925. **Percent Change from 1970:** 14.0%.

Land Area: 1,430 square miles. **Population per Square Mile:** 358.7.

Counties, 1980 Population: Delaware — 53,840; Franklin (Pt.) — 380,177; Licking (Pt.) — 52,428; Morrow — 26,480.

Cities, 1980 Population: Bexley — 13,405; Columbus (Pt.) — 253,357; Delaware — 18,780; Gahanna — 18,001; Reynoldsburg (Pt.) — 20,661; Westerville — 23,414; Whitehall — 21,299; Worthington (Pt.) — 17.

Race and Ancestry: White — 83.8%; Black — 15.1%; American Indian, Eskimo and Aleut — 0.1%; Asian and Pacific Islander — 0.6%. Spanish Origin — 0.7%. Dutch — 0.5%; English — 10.3%; French — 0.6%; German — 10.4%; Irish — 3.9%; Italian — 1.9%; Polish — 0.7%; Russian — 0.5%.

Universities, Enrollment: Capital University, Columbus — 2,507; Columbus Business University, Columbus — 307; Columbus College of Art and Design, Columbus — 1,119; Columbus Technical Institute, Columbus — 7,675; Denison University, Granville — 2,164; Franklin University, Columbus — 2,389; Methodist Theological School in Ohio, Delaware — 263; Ohio Institute of Technology, Columbus — 3,030; Ohio School of Career Technology, Columbus — 515; Ohio Wesleyan University, Delaware — 2,316; Otterbein College, Westerville — 1,674; Trinity Lutheran Seminary, Columbus — 290.

Newspapers, Circulation: *Columbus Citizen-Journal* (m), Columbus — 111,844; *The Columbus Dispatch* (eS), Columbus — 201,673; *The Delaware Gazette* (e), Delaware — 9,269. Newark *Advocate* also circulates in the district.

Commercial Television Stations, Affiliation: Entire district is located in Columbus ADI.

Military Installations: Defense Construction Supply Center, Whitehall — 5,080.

Industries:

Western Electric Co. Inc. (Bell Laboratories); Columbus; telephone switching equipment — 6,500. **Bancohio Corp.** (HQ); Columbus; banking — 2,500. **The Timken Co.;** Columbus; tapered roller bearings — 1,940. **Grant Hospital;** Columbus; hospital — 1,820. **J. C. Penney Co. Inc.** (Penney Catalog Distribution Center); Columbus; distribution center — 1,800.

The Dispatch Printing Co. (HQ); Columbus; newspaper publishing — 1,500. **St. Anthony Hospital;** Columbus; hospital — 1,150. **Rockwell International Corp.** (Missile Systems Div.); Columbus; electronic communications systems — 1,130. **Buckeye Union Insurance Co.** (HQ); Columbus; casualty insurance — 1,110. **Owens-Corning Fiberglas Corp.** (Fiberglas Technical Center); Granville; fiberglass — 1,010. **Abbott Laboratories** (Ross Laboratories Div.); Columbus; pharmaceuticals — 1,000. **Anheuser-Busch Inc.;** Columbus; brewery — 1,000. **Grumman Flxible Corp.** (HQ); Delaware; motor buses — 900. **J. C. Penney Casualty Insurance Co.** (HQ); Westerville; casualty insurance — 900. **Borden Inc.;** Columbus; administrative offices — 800. **The Liebert Corp.** (HQ); Columbus; air conditioners — 800. **Bell Telephone Laboratories;** Columbus; telecommunications research — 750. **Motorists Mutual Insurance Co.** (HQ); Columbus; property, casualty insurance — 725. **Kroger Co.** (Baked Foods Div.); Columbus; bakery — 710. **Continental Insurance Co.;** Columbus; insurance — 700. **Hyatt Corp.;** Columbus; hotel — 700. **Raytheon Co.** (Glenwood Range Co.); Delaware; cooking equipment — 625. **Grange Mutual Casualty Co.** (HQ); Columbus; fire, casualty insurance — 600. **HPM Corp.** (HQ); Mount Gilead; industrial machinery — 550. **Goodyear Tire & Rubber Co.;** Columbus; tire sales — 500. **International Business Machines Corp.;** Columbus; business equipment wholesaling — 500. **PPG Industries Inc.** (Coatings & Resins Div.); Delaware; industrial paints — 500. **Ranco Inc.;** Delaware; automatic environmental controls — 500. **State Mutual Insurance Co.** (HQ); Columbus; fire, casualty, life insurance — 500.

13th District

North — Lorain

Lying squarely in the midst of industrial northern Ohio, the 13th has all the problems of a declining Frost Belt economy. Heavily dependent on the automobile and steel industries, populous Lorain County was near Depression-era status in the early 1980s.

The manufacturing decline was most severe in the once-booming port town of Lorain. Although U.S. Steel's Lorain plant was more profitable than most of the company's factories in 1981, it still laid off thousands of workers.

But while the local economy has been battered, the old New Deal coalition is alive and well in Lorain County. Blue-collar ethnics, blacks and Hispanics in the cities of Lorain and Elyria combine with academics in the college town of Oberlin to produce Democratic majorities.

As one of the traditional immigration centers on the Great Lakes, Lorain has an ethnic diversity that matches the West Side of Cleveland. Fifty-six different ethnic groups have been counted within its borders. Hispanics alone comprise 14 percent of Lorain's population, a far higher share than in any other city in Ohio.

About 10 miles due south of Lorain is Oberlin, roughly the dividing point between urban, Catholic Democrats in the northern part of the district from rural, Protestant Republicans in the southern part. Founded in 1833, Oberlin College was the first coeducational institution of higher learning in the country and among the first to admit black students.

The Legislature moved two Democratic areas out of the district: Erie County (Sandusky) went to the 5th, while blue-collar Barberton and Norton townships in western Summit County went to the 14th. Together these two areas cast almost 25 percent of the district vote in 1980. The redistricting also removed two small townships in the southwestern corner of Medina County and grafted them onto the 13th.

The 13th moved south and west to annex rural Republican territory from the disbanded 17th District. Some farms in this area raise grains and livestock, but the emphasis is on producing dairy, fruit and vegetable products for nearby population centers. Most of Huron County, all of Ashland County, and the eastern portion of Richland County (Mansfield) were added to the 13th.

Democrats should do well in Mansfield — the district gains the Democratic northeastern sector of the industrial city. But Ashland regularly rewards Republican candidates with 60 percent or more of the vote.

Election Returns

13th District		Democrat		Republican	
1976	President	92,747	(49.8%)	88,539	(47.5%)
	Senate	89,955	(49.7%)	86,028	(47.6%)
	House	102,657	(58.1%)	69,791	(39.5%)
1978	Governor	70,314	(48.3%)	71.441	(49.1%)
	House	68,886	(55.0%)	56,334	(45.0%)
1980	President	75,735	(36.9%)	114,297	(55.7%)
	Senate	141,754	(69.8%)	56,812	(28.0%)
	House	99,821	(51.2%)	95,176	(48.8%)
1982	Governor	93,475	(59.8%)	58,304	(37.3%)
	Senate	87,583	(55.9%)	65,190	(41.6%)
	House	92,296	(61.2%)	53,376	(35.4%)

Demographics

Population: 515,346. Percent Change from 1970: 12.5%.

Land Area: 1,799 square miles. **Population per Square Mile:** 286.5.

Counties, 1980 Population: Ashland — 46,178; Huron (Pt.) — 47,070; Lorain (Pt.) — 268,415; Medina — 113,150; Richland (Pt.) — 30,723; Summit (Pt.) — 9,810.

Cities, 1980 Population: Amherst — 10,638; Ashland — 20,326; Avon Lake — 13,222; Brunswick — 28,104; Elyria — 57,538; Lorain — 75,416; Mansfield (Pt.) — 13,595; Medina — 15,268; North Ridgeville — 21,522; Norwalk — 14,358; Sheffield Lake — 10,484; Vermilion (Pt.) — 5,378; Wadsworth — 15,166.

Race and Ancestry: White — 92.9%; Black — 5.2%; American Indian, Eskimo and Aleut — 0.1%; Asian and Pacific Islander — 0.4%. Spanish Origin — 2.8%. Dutch — 0.5%; English — 8.6%; German — 11.9%; Hungarian — 1.9%; Irish — 3.3%; Italian — 1.8%; Polish — 2.3%; Scottish — 0.5%.

Universities, Enrollment: Ashland College, Ashland — 2,665; Lorain County Community College, Elyria — 6,233; Oberlin College, Oberlin — 2,771.

Newspapers, Circulation: *Ashland Times-Gazette* (e), Ashland — 13,067; *The Chronicle-Telegram* (eS), Elyria — 40,452; *The Journal* (eS), Lorain — 43,020; *Medina County Gazette* (m), Medina — 16,408; *Norwalk Reflector* (e), Norwalk — 8,894. Cleveland *Plain Dealer* and Mansfield *News Journal* also circulate in the district.

Commercial Television Stations, Affiliation: WUAB, Lorain (None). Entire district is located in Cleveland ADI.

Military Installations: Mansfield Lahm Airport (Air Force), Mansfield — 802.

Industries:

United States Steel Corp. (Lorain Cuyahoga Works); Lorain; steel pipes — 5,500. **Ford Motor Co.**; Lorain; motor vehicle assembly — 5,200. **General Motors Corp.** (Fisher Body Div.); Elyria; motor vehicle parts — 1,868. **Ford Motor Co.** (Ohio Truck Plant); Avon Lake; van assembly — 1,600. **The Ridge Tool Co.** (I. F. Mfg. Co. Div. - HQ); Elyria; pipe working tools — 1,400.

Ohio Farmers Insurance Co.; Westfield Center; life, casualty insurance — 1,350. **Cyclops Corp.** (Empire-Detroit Steel Div.); Mansfield; steel mill — 1,300. **Elyria Memorial Hospital Co.**; Elyria; hospital — 1,300. **Grumman Flxible Corp.**; Loudonville; buses, aircraft — 1,250. **American Ship Building Corp.** (Anship Div.); Lorain; shipbuilding — 1,200. **Ohio Brass Co.**; Mansfield; porcelain insulators — 1,000. **Gilford Instrument Laboratories Inc.**; Oberlin; analytical instruments — 900. **U-Brand Corp.** (HQ); Ashland; iron fittings — 900. **Reliance Electric Co.**; Lorain; electrical industrial appliances — 884. **B. F.**

Goodrich Co. Inc. (Chemical Group); Avon Lake; plastic — 800. **Stanadyne Inc.** (Moen Faucet Div.); Elyria; plumbing fixtures — 791.

Abbott Laboratories Inc. (Faultless Rubber Div.); Ashland; fabricated rubber products — 700. **Interpace Corp.** (Mansfield Sanitary Div.); Perrysville; vitreous china plumbing fixtures — 700. **Nordson Corp.** (HQ); Amherst; special industrial machinery — 700. **Norwalk Furniture Corp.**; Norwalk; upholstered furniture — 700. **McNeil Corp.** (F. E. Myers Co.); Ashland; pumps — 650. **MTD Products Inc.** (Midwest Industries Div.); Willard; garden tools — 600. **The Tappan Co.** (Kemper Brothers Div. - HQ); Mansfield; ranges, microwave ovens — 581. **Janitor Maintenance Inc.**; Mansfield; janitorial services — 535. **Sheller-Globe Corp.** (Norwalk Assembly Plant); Norwalk; trucks, cabs — 525.

14th District

Northeast — Akron

The 14th District is in a part of Ohio built out of rubber — tires in particular. Located within the district's confines are the corporate headquarters of the Goodyear, Goodrich, Firestone and General Tire companies. Their workers are bread-and-butter Democrats, and the 14th is one of the most Democratic districts in the state.

But the economy of the district is changing. While the major rubber companies are still the prime employers, the last quarter century has seen a steady transfer of business from the old, high-wage factories in Akron to new plants in low-wage areas of the Sun Belt. Many Akron residents have left. The city's population in 1980 was less than it was a half-century earlier.

The local economy has been kept alive by the attraction of major trucking firms and the diversification of the rubber companies into radar and aircraft parts. Much of the district's recent growth has been along the Ohio Turnpike, which used to skirt the northern end of the 14th. But to accommodate the old district's 9 percent population loss in the 1970s, the 14th was pushed north of the turnpike to take in portions of Summit County formerly in the 11th and 22nd districts. Affluent communities such as Hudson and Silver Lake give this area a slight Republican tilt. But the area casts only 15 percent of the district vote, not enough to offset the strongly Democratic character of rest of the 14th.

While some farm land exists in northern Summit County, the area increasingly is being developed for commuters whose orientation is north to Cleveland rather than south to Akron.

The rest of the 14th is within the orbit of Akron, home of nearly half the district voters. In the boom years of the rubber industry before World War II, Akron was a mecca for job-seeking Appalachians. The annual West Virginia Day was one of the city's most popular events, and it was said that more West Virginians lived in Akron than Charleston. The Appalachian descendants combine with blacks, ethnics and the academic community at the University of Akron to keep the city reliably Democratic. Jimmy Carter carried it in 1980 with 57 percent.

To the north and south of Akron are suburbs ranging from middle-class, ticket-splitting towns such as Cuyahoga Falls to solidly Republican communities like Fairlawn. These areas were cultivated by the late Ray Bliss, who learned the nuts and bolts of organizational politics in Summit County before moving on to the chairmanships of the Republican state and national committees.

But Bliss rarely found enough GOP votes in the suburbs to offset Democratic strength in Akron and Barberton, a grimy blue-collar steel-town adjoining Akron. Redistricting moved Barberton and neighboring Norton
Township from the 13th into the 14th, offsetting the loss of
the Democratic portion of Portage County (Kent) to the
11th. The new 14th includes all of Summit County except
for 10,000 residents of Copley Township.

Election Returns

14th District		Democrat		Republican	
1976	President	121,588	(60.4%)	78,475	(39.0%)
	Senate	119,426	(59.5%)	80,247	(40.0%)
	House	137,140	(69.8%)	55,684	(28.4%)
1978	Governor	86,349	(62.1%)	49,946	(35.9%)
	House	97,850	(67.4%)	44,211	(30.5%)
1980	President	100,618	(48.3%)	89,911	(43.2%)
	Senate	159,206	(78.2%)	39,191	(19.3%)
	House	117,505	(60.4%)	76,432	(39.3%)
1982	Governor	112,922	(69.8%)	46,097	(28.5%)
	Senate	101,105	(61.4%)	60,968	(37.0%)
	House	115,629	(70.5%)	48,421	(29.5%)

Demographics

Population: 514,662. **Percent Change from 1970:** -5.5%.

Land Area: 391 square miles. **Population per Square Mile:** 1,316.3.

Counties, 1980 Population: Summit (Pt.) — 514,662.

Cities, 1980 Population: Akron — 237,177; Barberton — 29,751;
Cuyahoga Falls — 43,890; Norton — 12,242; Portage Lakes —
11,310; Stow — 25,303; Tallmadge — 15,269.

Race and Ancestry: White — 88.2%; Black — 10.9%; American Indian, Eskimo and Aleut — 0.1%; Asian and Pacific Islander — 0.5%.
Spanish Origin — 0.5%. English — 8.2%; French — 0.5%; German —
9.5%; Hungarian — 1.5%; Irish — 3.6%; Italian — 3.5%; Polish —
1.5%; Scottish — 0.5%.

Universities, Enrollment: The University of Akron, Akron — 24,632.

Newspapers, Circulation: *Akron Beacon Journal* (eS), Akron —
161,955.

Commercial Television Stations, Affiliation: WAKR-TV, Akron
(ABC). Entire district is located in Cleveland ADI.

Industries:

Goodyear Tire & Rubber Co. (HQ); Akron; tires, rubber products
— 8,000. **The B. F. Goodrich Co.** (HQ); Akron; tires, tubes — 4,500.
Goodyear Aerospace Corp. (HQ); Akron; aircraft parts — 4,000.
Chrysler Corp. (Twinsburg Stamping Plant); Twinsburg; metal
stampings — 3,557. **Firestone Tire & Rubber Co.** (HQ); Akron; tires,
rubber — 2,750.

Akron City Hospital; Akron; hospital — 2,650. **Babcock &
Wilcox Co.** (Nuclear Equipment Div.); Barberton; steam generators —
2,601. **General Tire & Rubber Co.** (HQ); Akron; tires, tubes, plastic —
2,500. **Akron General Medical Center;** Akron; hospital 2,160. **Terex
Corp.** (HQ); Hudson; construction machinery — 1,700. **St. Thomas
Hospital & Medical Center;** Akron; hospital — 1,500. **Babcock &
Wilcox Co.** (Utility Power Generation Div.); Barberton; steam generators — 1,368. **Children's Hospital & Medical Center of Akron;** Akron;
children's hospital — 1,250. **The Barberton Citizens Hospital;** Barberton; hospital — 1,200. **PPG Industries Inc.** (Industrial Chemical Div.);
Barberton; inorganic chemicals — 1,129. **Alside Inc.;** Cuyahoga Falls;
siding, aluminum products — 1,000.

Consolidated Freightway; Richfield; trucking — 909. **Roadway
Express Inc.** (HQ); Akron; trucking — 750. **United Transport Indus-**
tries; Cuyahoga Falls; trucking — 750. **The Ohio Brass Co.;** Barberton;
porcelain electrical supplies — 675. **Pinkerton's Inc.;** Akron; security
services — 650. **D. S. Revco Inc.** (HQ); Twinsburg; drug store chain —
600. **McNeil-Akron Corp.;** Akron; tire curing presses — 525. **Yellow
Freight Systems Inc.;** Richfield; freight forwarding — 520. **Allstate
Insurance Co.;** Hudson; auto insurance — 500. **Babcock & Wilcox Co.;**
Akron; industrial construction contractors — 500. **Eagle-Picher Industries Inc.** (Akron Standard Div.); Akron; tire molding machinery —
500.

15th District

Central — Western Columbus and Suburbs

Of the two districts that divide Columbus, the 15th
traditionally has been the more Republican. Although it
includes most of the academic community at Ohio State,
the Democratic vote there is offset by the solid Republican
areas in northern Columbus and the rock-ribbed GOP suburbs west of the Olentangy and Scioto rivers. Upper Arlington, the largest and one of the most affluent suburbs, gave
Ronald Reagan 74 percent of its vote in 1980.

Apart from the large university vote — Ohio State has
nearly 55,000 students — the only major pocket of Democratic strength in the district is on the near west side of
Columbus. Sandwiched between the Scioto and the Ohio
State Hospital for the Insane are neighborhoods of lower-
income, Appalachian whites.

The 15th gave up the heart of downtown Columbus,
with the state Capitol and the offices of Ohio's major
banking and commercial institutions to the 12th. But with
three-quarters of the land area of Franklin County, it still
contains most of the region's expanding manufacturing
base, which includes machinery, food, fabricated metal and
printing and publishing plants.

The addition of portions of the heavily black East Side
of Columbus and blue-collar communities in the southeast
increased the Democratic vote. But these are generally low-
turnout areas.

Voters in the 15th are predominantly white-collar and
middle-class. Moderate Republicanism is the dominant political commodity in an area that continues to advertise
itself to outsiders as the "largest small town in America."
During the 1970s it was the only major urban center in
Ohio to gain population.

Within the 15th the fastest growth during the 1970s
was on the western fringe of Franklin County, where urban
commuters have been moving. Some have crossed the line
into rural Madison County. The Legislature transferred
about 8,000 residents on the county's northern and southern flanks to the 7th District.

Election Returns

15th District		Democrat		Republican	
1976	President	74,062	(40.3%)	104,096	(56.6%)
	Senate	77,090	(44.0%)	91,181	(52.0%)
	House	64,374	(36.2%)	111,275	(62.6%)
1978	Governor	55,657	(41.1%)	77,811	(57.5%)
	House	40,837	(30.0%)	95,219	(70.0%)
1980	President	70,752	(35.7%)	111,204	(56.2%)
	Senate	120,923	(64.9%)	55,335	(29.7%)
	House	56,765	(29.9%)	133,175	(70.1%)

15th District		Democrat		Republican	
1982	Governor	81,135	(49.8%)	76,818	(47.2%)
	Senate	67,534	(45.5%)	73,098	(49.2%)
	House	47,070	(29.8%)	104,678	(66.3%)

Demographics

Population: 514,697. **Percent Change from 1970:** 0.9%.

Land Area: 668 square miles. **Population per Square Mile:** 770.5.

Counties, 1980 Population: Franklin (Pt.) — 488,955; Madison (Pt.) — 25,742.

Cities, 1980 Population: Columbus (Pt.) — 311,469; Grove City — 16,816; Upper Arlington — 35,648; Worthington (Pt.) — 14,999.

Race and Ancestry: White — 87.4%; Black — 11.0%; American Indian, Eskimo and Aleut — 0.1%; Asian and Pacific Islander — 1.0%. Spanish Origin — 0.7%. Dutch — 0.5%; English — 11.4%; French — 0.7%; German — 11.0%; Irish — 4.6%; Italian — 1.9%; Polish — 0.5%.

Universities, Enrollment: Bliss College, Columbus — 1,504; Ohio State University, Columbus — 54,462; Pontifical College Josephinum, Columbus — 212.

Newspapers, Circulation: The Madison Press (e), London — 6,450. *Columbus Citizen-Journal* and *The Columbus Dispatch* also circulate in the district.

Commercial Television Stations, Affiliation: WBNS-TV, Columbus (CBS); WCMH-TV, Columbus (NBC); WTVN-TV, Columbus (ABC). Entire district is located in Columbus ADI.

Military Installations: Rickenbacker Air Force Base, Lockbourne — 3,900 *(Base straddles line between 7th and 15th districts.)*

Industries:

Nationwide Mutual Insurance Co. (HQ); Columbus; casualty, life, health insurance — 5,000. **Battelle Memorial Institute** (HQ); Columbus; scientific research — 3,270. **General Motors Corp.** (Fisher Body Div.); Columbus; fabricated metal products — 2,600. **Riverside Methodist Hospital;** Columbus; hospital — 2,800. **Hawkes Hospital of Mt. Carmel;** Columbus; hospital — 1,900.

The Children's Hospital; Columbus; hospital — 1,600. **E. I. du Pont de Nemours & Co.;** Circleville; films — 1,300. **Accuray Corp.** (HQ); Columbus; industrial measuring instruments — 1,100. **American Chemical Society** (Chemical Abstracts Service); Columbus; scientific abstracts — 1,100. **Owens-Illinois Inc.** (Consumer & Technical Products Div.); Columbus; television tubes — 983. **Ohio Medical Indemnity Mutual Corp.;** Worthington; medical insurance — 950. **Xerox Corp.** (Xerox Education Publications); Columbus; publishing — 950. **Lennox Industries Inc.;** Columbus; air conditioners — 900.

Ashland Oil Inc. (Ashland Chemical Div.); Dublin; administrative offices — 850. **Borden Inc.** (Columbus Coated Fabrics Co. Div.); Columbus; coated fabrics — 800. **Pritchard Services Inc.;** Columbus; janitorial services — 800. **Worthington Industries Inc.** (Jeffery Mfg. Div.); Worthington; mining equipment — 800. **McGraw Edison Co.** (National Electric Coil Div.); Columbus; motors — 720. **RCA Corp.;** Circleville; TV tube blanks — 700. **Celanese Corp.** (Hytrex Div.); Hilliard; plastic pipe — 550. **Robertshaw Controls Co.** (Aero Div.); Grove City; automatic environmental controls — 550. **Professional Maintenance;** Columbus; janitorial services — 500.

16th District

Northeast — Canton

Although it has undergone a variety of changes over the years, the 16th District is still centered on Stark County and the city of Canton, just as it was when William McKinley represented it a century ago.

While it is a working-class city, Canton does not share in the solidly Democratic tradition of the rest of northeastern Ohio. This difference exists because of the Republican-oriented media and the conservative mentality brought to the community by the family-run Timken Company — a large steel and roller-bearing firm that rivals Republic Steel as the district's major employer.

With a sizable black and ethnic population, Canton proper goes Democratic on occasion. But the suburbs in surrounding Stark County are solidly Republican. Since 1920 the only Democratic presidential candidates to carry the county — which accounts for nearly three-quarters of the district's population — have been Franklin D. Roosevelt and Lyndon B. Johnson.

Besides Timken, Canton is the national headquarters of the Hoover Company, the vacuum cleaner manufacturer, and Diebold Inc., a producer of bank safes and office equipment. But it is more famous as McKinley's hometown and the home of the Pro Football Hall of Fame.

The portion of the 16th outside Stark County is primarily rural and Republican. Wooster, the Wayne County seat, claims to be the site of America's first Christmas tree. Nearby Orrville is the home base of the Smucker family, makers of jams and peanut butter.

The 16th was extended south by redistricting to annex Holmes County from the old 17th. Many of Holmes' 29,000 residents are Amish, and motorists driving through the county must be careful not to plow into the back of a horse-drawn buggy. Houses without electricity are plentiful in the county and the income level is the lowest outside the Appalachian portion of the 6th. But leather and noodle factories have brought new employment to the agricultural area. Holmes County showed a 28 percent population gain in the 1970s, tying for the fourth highest growth rate in the state.

Other changes in the district lines were minor. Two small townships in the southwestern corner of Medina County were transferred to the 13th, while Brown Township in the northwest corner of Carroll County was added from the 18th.

Election Returns

16th District		Democrat		Republican	
1976	President	86,769	(47.0%)	93,751	(50.8%)
	Senate	85,260	(46.4%)	93,519	(50.9%)
	House	57,489	(32.1%)	119,567	(66.7%)
1978	Governor	59,334	(46.2%)	65,183	(50.8%)
	House	31,132	(22.4%)	108,037	(77.6%)
1980	President	74,191	(37.1%)	112,045	(56.0%)
	Senate	137,028	(69.1%)	57,757	(29.1%)
	House	41,643	(21.2%)	154,369	(78.8%)
1982	Governor	95,669	(58.1%)	65,637	(39.8%)
	Senate	88,452	(52.1%)	78,292	(46.1%)
	House	57,386	(34.2%)	110,485	(65.8%)

Demographics

Population: 513,215. **Percent Change from 1970:** 5.2%.

Land Area: 1,602 square miles. **Population per Square Mile:** 320.4.

Counties, 1980 Population: Carroll (Pt.) — 7,568; Holmes — 29,416; Stark — 378,823; Wayne — 97,408.

Cities, 1980 Population: Alliance (Pt.) — 24,315; Canton — 94,730; Massillon — 30,557; North Canton — 14,228; Wooster — 19,289.

Race and Ancestry: White — 94.4%; Black — 5.0%; American Indian, Eskimo and Aleut — 0.1%; Asian and Pacific Islander — 0.3%. Spanish Origin — 0.8%. Dutch — 0.6%; English — 7.4%; French — 0.8%; German — 16.6%; Greek — 0.5%; Hungarian — 0.6%; Irish — 2.9%; Italian — 2.9%; Polish — 0.7%; Scottish — 0.5%.

Universities, Enrollment: College of Wooster, Wooster — 1,827; Kent State University (Stark campus), Canton — 2,023; Malone College, Canton — 776; Mount Union College, Alliance — 1,097; Ohio State University - Agricultural Technical Institute, Wooster — 766; Stark Technical College, Canton — 2,691; The University of Akron - Wayne General and Technical College, Orrville — 915; Walsh College, Canton — 828.

Newspapers, Circulation: *Alliance Review* (e), Alliance — 14,278; *Daily Record* (e), Wooster — 26,746; *The Evening Independent* (e), Massillon — 18,326; *The Repository* (eS), Canton — 63,762.

Commercial Television Stations, Affiliation: WAKC, Canton (None); WJAN, Canton (None). Most of district is located in Cleveland ADI. Portion is in Wheeling (W.Va.)-Steubenville ADI.

Industries:

The Timken Co. (HQ); Canton; bearings, steel bars — 10,000. Republic Steel Corp.; Canton; steel mill — 4,500. The Hoover Co. (HQ); Canton; vacuum cleaners, electric housewares — 3,800. The Aultman Hospital Assn.; Canton; hospital — 2,500. Timken Mercy Medical Center; Canton; hospital — 2,000.

Diebold Inc. (HQ); Canton; bank equipment — 1,950. Rubbermaid Inc. (HQ); Wooster; molded rubber household products — 1,800. TRW Inc.; Minerva; metal products — 1,470. Teledyne Industries Inc. (Monarch Rubber Div.); Hartville; rubber products — 1,450. Sugardale Foods Inc.; Canton; meatpacking — 1,100. Ford Motor Co. (Transmission & Chassis Div.); Canton; transmissions chassis — 1,000. Republic Steel Corp. (Berger Mfg. Div.); Canton; metal lockers — 1,000. Standard Alliance Industries; Alliance; steel forgings — 1,000. Superiors Brand Meats Inc. (HQ); Massillon; meatpacking — 1,000. Packaging Corp. of America; Rittman; paperboard — 900. White Engines Inc. (Hercules Engine Div.); Canton; internal combustion engines — 850. AMCA International Corp. (Koehring-Morgan Engineering); Alliance; cranes — 700. Van Dorn Co.; Massillon; aluminum cans — 700.

Babcock & Wilcox Co. (Tubular Products Group); Alliance; steel pipes, tubes — 654. Gemini Mfg. Co.; Orrville; truck cabs — 650. Alliance Machine Co.; Alliance; cranes — 648. Republic Steel Corp. (Union Drawn Steel Div.); Massillon; steel bars — 600. Amsted Industries Inc. (American Steel Foundries Div.); Alliance; steel castings — 572. J. M. Smucker Co. (HQ); Orrville; jelly, fruit syrups, pickles; peanut butter — 560. Nationwide Insurance Companies; Canton; casualty, life, accident insurance — 525. Babcock & Wilcox Co. (Alliance Research Center); Alliance; research lab — 514. AM International Inc. (Data Systems Div.); Holmesville; industrial inorganic chemicals — 500. Babcock & Wilcox Co. (Industrial Power Generation Div.); Canton; metal doors, frames — 500. Eaton Corp. (Wire & Fastener Products Div.); Massillon; industrial hardware — 500. Regal Ware Inc.; Wooster; aluminum stampings — 500. Wooster Brush Co. (Buckeye Roller Co.- HQ); Wooster; paint brushes — 500.

17th District

Northeast — Youngstown, Warren

Once called America's "Little Ruhr" as a symbol of its industrial productivity, the Youngstown-Warren area has become a symbol of the nation's industrial decline. Many of the giant steel furnaces that once lighted the eastern Ohio sky are dark for good. Most of the workers have retired or left the area. Many of those who remain are looking for other jobs.

Located on the eastern border with Pennsylvania, the region was long a steel center serving both Cleveland and Pittsburgh. As late as the early 1970s the large steel plants in the Mahoning River Valley employed more than 50,000 workers. By 1982 the work force was about one-third that total. General Motors, with large facilities in Lordstown and Warren, has replaced the major steel companies as the district's largest employer.

The 17th (numbered the 19th before redistricting) has begun to diversify its economy, but the process is slow and painful. The old district lost 3 percent of its population in the 1970s, but Youngstown itself lost 18 percent.

The district's remaining blue-collar base makes the 17th one of Ohio's solidly Democratic areas in most elections. About 56 percent of the voters live in Mahoning County (Youngstown); 42 percent reside in Trumbull County (Warren). Both Mahoning and Trumbull were among the 10 Ohio counties that voted for Jimmy Carter in 1980. But the Republican House incumbent, a one-time barber with strong personal appeal in blue-collar neighborhoods, carried enough Democratic votes to win a third term in 1982 with ease.

In most elections Democratic candidates build comfortable majorities in the string of declining ethnic communities along the Mahoning River. Italians dominate in Niles and Lowellville. Eastern Europeans and Greeks are the most important groups in Campbell. In the two largest cities — Youngstown and Warren — blacks leaven the ethnic mixture.

To the south, beyond the steel mills that line the Mahoning Valley, the Republican vote increases. Homes in these suburbs are too expensive for most blue-collar workers. Typical is Boardman Township, due south of Youngstown. One of the most affluent parts of Mahoning County, it is a swing area.

The rural part of the district has been expanded with the transfer of about 8,000 residents in the western end of Columbiana County from the 18th and the addition of about 60,000 people from the portion of Trumbull County that used to be in the 11th. The new Trumbull territory is politically marginal. As in the rest of the state, the farms and small towns of the 17th are basically Republican. Apples and vegetables are major farm products in this part of Ohio.

Election Returns

17th District		Democrat		Republican	
1976	President	125,064	(59.8%)	79,749	(38.1%)
	Senate	118,346	(60.9%)	71,757	(36.9%)
	House	98,645	(49.5%)	97,402	(48.8%)
1978	Governor	85,853	(55.8%)	60,301	(39.2%)
	House	77,154	(49.0%)	79,839	(50.7%)
1980	President	105,721	(49.6%)	88,862	(41.7%)
	Senate	158,877	(79.4%)	36,419	(18.2%)
	House	87,156	(42.7%)	116,529	(57.1%)
1982	Governor	123,687	(70.8%)	45,799	(26.2%)
	Senate	123,895	(70.2%)	49,193	(27.9%)
	House	80,375	(44.9%)	98,476	(55.1%)

Demographics

Population: 515,223. **Percent Change from 1970:** -1.5%.

Land Area: 834 square miles. **Population per Square Mile:** 617.8.

Counties, 1980 Population: Columbiana (Pt.) — 7,508; Mahoning — 289,487; Trumbull (Pt.) — 218,228.

Cities, 1980 Population: Alliance (Pt.) — 0; Campbell — 11,619; Girard — 12,517; Niles — 23,088; Struthers — 13,624; Warren — 56,629; Youngstown — 115,436.

Race and Ancestry: White — 88.3%; Black — 10.7%; American Indian, Eskimo and Aleut — 0.1%; Asian and Pacific Islander — 0.3%. Spanish Origin — 1.3%. English — 5.6%; German — 6.6%; Greek — 0.9%; Hungarian — 1.4%; Irish — 3.8%; Italian — 8.3%; Polish — 1.9%; Ukranian — 0.8%.

Universities, Enrollment: A.T.E.S. Technical School, Niles — 429; Borromeo College of Ohio, Wickliffe — 96; Kent State University (Trumbull campus), Warren — 1,533; Youngstown College of Business and Professional Drafting, Youngstown — 422; Youngstown State University, Youngstown — 15,784.

Newspapers, Circulation: *Niles Daily Times* (e), Niles — 5,618; *The Tribune Chronicle* (eS), Warren — 44,719; *Vindicator* (eS), Youngstown — 102,888. *The Salem News* also circulates in the district.

Commercial Television Stations, Affiliation: WFMJ-TV, Youngstown (NBC); WKBN-TV, Youngstown (CBS); WYTV, Youngstown (ABC). Most of district is located in Youngstown ADI. Portion is in Pittsburgh (Pa.) ADI.

Military Installations: Youngstown Municipal Airport (Air Force), Vienna — 1,034.

Industries:

General Motors Corp. (Packard Electric Div.); Warren; electric cable — 10,600. **General Motors Corp.** (Assembly Div.); Lordstown; auto assembly — 5,600. **Republic Steel Corp.;** Warren; steel mill — 4,000. **St. Elizabeth Hospital & Medical Center;** Youngstown; hospital — 2,960. **General Motors Corp.** (Fisher Body Fabricating Plant); Warren; automotive stampings — 2,525.

Copperweld Steel Co.; Warren; steel mill — 2,500. **Trumbull Memorial Hospital;** Warren; hospital — 1,600. **General American Transportation Corp.;** Masury; railroad tank cars — 1,500. **Youngstown Hospital Assn.;** Youngstown; hospital — 1,500. **Youngstown Steel Door Co.;** Youngstown; railroad equipment — 1,390. **Commercial Shearing Inc.** (HQ); Youngstown; hydraulic pumps — 1,300. **Republic Steel Corp.;** Youngstown; steel — 1,100. **General Electric Co.** (Ohio Lamp Plant Div.); Warren; light bulbs — 900. **RMI Co.** (HQ); Niles; titanium — 900. **Wean United Inc.;** Warren; rolling mill machinery — 825. **Anchor Motor Freight Inc.;** Warren; trucking — 750. **W. F. W. Co. Inc.;** Youngstown; trucking — 750.

Thomas Steel Strip Corp.; Warren; cold rolled steel sheet, strips, bars — 700. **Van Huffel Tube Corp.** (HQ); Warren; welded steel pipes — 670. **Royal China Co.;** Sebring; fine earthenware china — 650. **GF Business Equipment Inc.** (HQ); Youngstown; metal office furniture, cabinets — 615. **The American Welding & Mfg. Co.** (HQ); Warren; aircraft engines — 600. **ITT Grinnell Corp.** (Pipe Hanger Div.); Warren; industrial pipe — 600. **Wean United Inc.;** Youngstown; machine tools, rolling mill equipment — 600. **The Youngstown Cartage Co.;** Youngstown; trucking — 550. **General Electric Co.;** Youngstown; lamps — 545. **General Electric Co.** (Trumbull Lamp Div.); Warren; lamps — 520. **General Electric Co.** (Lamps, Glass & Components Dept.); Niles; pressed glassware — 500. **H. K. Porter Co. Inc.;** Warren; ventilating equipment — 500.

18th District

East — Steubenville

Coal and steel have given the 18th District its polluted air, its dirty rivers, its economic livelihood and its Democratic votes.

Cramped along the steep banks of the Ohio River, Steubenville — the district's largest city with 26,400 people — long has had some of the nation's foulest air pollution. But jobs in the smoke-belching plants along a 50-mile stretch of the Ohio have taken priority over clean air, a fact that successful politicians quickly learn. With the steel industry slumping badly, the population of the Steubenville area dropped 5 percent in the 1970s.

The situation was even worse down-river in Monroe County, where aluminum plant layoffs pushed unemployment past 25 percent in 1982, the highest jobless rate in the state.

This part of Ohio resembles West Virginia and eastern Kentucky. Some cattle are raised, but the hilly terrain makes farming generally unprofitable. Under the hills, however, is extensive mineral wealth. Iron mining was once a major industry until coal took its place. In the heart of the 18th — Harrison, Jefferson, Belmont and Guernsey counties — are extensive strip mining operations. Efforts to restore the land have been largely unsuccessful. The mining activity has made this area the leading coal-producing region in Ohio. But the early 1980s recession caused unemployment to soar.

Although the steelworking and coal-mining Democrats of the district show strong party allegiance, they tend to shy away from liberals. In 1972 George McGovern was trounced in these counties. Jimmy Carter, who carried the district in 1976, lost it narrowly to Ronald Reagan in 1980. Carter carried the blue-collar communities along the Ohio, but Reagan made inroads by campaigning in Steubenville on the promise to end burdensome environmental regulations.

About half the voters in the 18th live within a few miles of the industrialized Ohio River Valley. To the west the district is less Democratic. Conservative Amish communities are scattered throughout Tuscarawas and Guernsey counties. As the land flattens, the tractors of Republican farmers replace the giant shovels of Democratic coal miners.

Republicans were helped by the addition of rural Coshocton County from the old 17th. But with only 7 percent of the district vote, the GOP-leaning county was not likely to alter the marginal character of the 18th in state and national elections.

The other changes in the district boundaries involved a trade-off of Republican areas. At its rural southern end, the 18th gained the eastern half of Washington County and the southern portion of Noble County from the 10th. Along its northern border, the district lost two townships in Columbiana County to the 17th and one township in Carroll County to the 16th. Three townships in Guernsey County were transferred to the 10th.

Election Returns

18th District		Democrat		Republican	
1976	President	110,129	(53.8%)	90,856	(44.4%)
	Senate	102,818	(52.0%)	87,786	(44.4%)
	House	119,054	(60.9%)	53,390	(27.3%)
1978	Governor	54,895	(44.5%)	64,526	(52.3%)
	House	73,597	(57.3%)	54,903	(42.7%)
1980	President	86,525	(44.7%)	94,833	(49.0%)
	Senate	130,314	(69.9%)	51,064	(27.4%)
	House	134,064	(72.3%)	51,423	(27.7%)

18th District		Democrat		Republican	
1982	Governor	99,560	(64.6%)	51,905	(33.7%)
	Senate	99,401	(62.4%)	56,668	(35.6%)
	House	x¹		—¹	

¹ *No votes tabulated where candidate was unopposed; x indicates winner.*

Demographics

Population: 514,012. **Percent Change from 1970:** 4.1%.

Land Area: 4,859 square miles. **Population per Square Mile:** 105.8.

Counties, 1980 Population: Belmont — 82,569; Carroll (Pt.) — 18,030; Columbiana (Pt.) — 106,064; Coshocton — 36,024; Guernsey (Pt.) — 38,155; Harrison — 18,152; Jefferson — 91,564; Monroe — 17,382; Noble — 11,310; Tuscarawas — 84,614; Washington (Pt.) — 10,148.

Cities, 1980 Population: Cambridge — 13,573; Coshocton — 13,405; Dover — 11,782; East Liverpool — 16,687; New Philadelphia — 16,883; Salem — 12,869; Steubenville — 26,400.

Race and Ancestry: White — 97.6%; Black — 2.0%; American Indian, Eskimo and Aleut — 0.1%; Asian and Pacific Islander — 0.2%. Spanish Origin — 0.4%. Dutch — 0.6%; English — 11.2%; French — 0.5%; German — 11.0%; Hungarian — 0.7%; Irish — 4.7%; Italian — 3.1%; Polish — 1.9%; Scottish — 0.6%.

Universities, Enrollment: Belmont Technical College, St. Clairsville — 1,271; Jefferson Technical College, Steubenville — 1,532; Kent State University (East Liverpool campus), East Liverpool — 599; Kent State University (Salem campus), Salem — 531; Kent State University (Tuscarawas campus), New Philadelphia — 914; Ohio University (Belmont County campus), St. Clairsville — 938; University of Steubenville, Steubenville — 1,003.

Newspapers, Circulation: *The Coshocton Tribune* (eS), Coshocton — 8,217; *The Daily Jeffersonian* (e), Cambridge — 15,393; *The Evening Chronicle* (e), Uhrichsville — 4,551; *The Evening Review* (e), East Liverpool — 14,785; *The Herald Star* (eS), Steubenville — 24,866; *Morning Journal* (m), Lisbon — 14,515; *The Salem News* (e), Salem — 11,316; *The Times-Leader* (eS), Martins Ferry — 24,611; *The Times-Reporter* (e), New Philadelphia — 29,929.

Commercial Television Stations, Affiliation: WTOV-TV, Steubenville (NBC, ABC). Most of district is located in Wheeling (W.Va.)-Steubenville ADI. Portions are in Cleveland ADI, Columbus ADI, Charleston (W.Va.)-Huntington (W.Va.) ADI, and Pittsburgh (Pa.) ADI.

Nuclear Power Plants: Beaver Valley 1 and 2 *(See 4th District, Pennsylvania).*

Industries:

Wheeling-Pittsburgh Steel Corp.; Steubenville; steel mill — 2,396. **North American Coal Corp.;** Powhatan Point; coal mining — 1,735. **NCR Corp.;** Cambridge; electronic components — 1,700. **Ormet Corp.** (HQ); Hannibal; aluminum — 1,400. **Consolidated Aluminum Corp.;** Hannibal; aluminum sheet — 1,300.

Wheeling-Pittsburgh Steel Corp.; Yorkville; steel processing — 979. **General Electric Co.** (Engineered Materials Group Div.); Coshocton; laminated plastic products — 850. **Central Ohio Coal Co. Inc.** (Muskingum Div.); Cumberland; coal mining — 845. **Nacco Mining Co.;** Alledonia; coal mining — 845. **Becton Dickinson & Co.** (Edmont-Wilson Div.); Coshocton; rubber, plastic-coated gloves — 800. **Titanium Metals Corp. of America** (Timet Div.); Toronto; titanium — 800. **Scio Pottery Co.;** Scio; vitreous china tableware — 700. **Crane Co.** (Deming Div.); Salem; pumps — 650.

Gulf & Western Mfg. Co. (E. W. Bliss Div.); Salem; machine tools — 650. **Clow Corp.;** Coshocton; cast iron pipes — 600. **NRM Corp.;** Columbiana; industrial machinery — 600. **Bendix Corp.** (Gradall Div.); New Philadelphia; excavating machinery — 571. **Picoma Industries Inc.** (HQ); Martins Ferry; pipe couplings — 550. **Warren Molded Plastics Inc.;** Salem; custom molded plastic — 550. **Masonite Corp.** (Commercial Div.); Dover; wood partitions — 500. **Wallace-Murray Corp.;** Salem; china, metal plumbing fixtures — 500.

19th District

Cleveland Suburbs

The 19th is the "ring around the county" district — a "U-shaped" monstrosity that merges the bulk of Cleveland's two old suburban districts into one. Critics complain that the quickest way from one end of the district to the other is by boat across Lake Erie.

This scattered terrain represents what was left for the map makers to include after they created safe districts based inside Cleveland for two Democratic incumbents. Even some of the communities that were meant for the 19th never made it all the way in. Four suburbs with at least 25,000 residents each — Euclid, Lakewood, Parma and Strongsville — were divided between the 19th and other Cleveland-area districts.

A tour around the "U" takes one through a string of diverse suburbs — some dominated by ethnic Democrats, others by white-collar Republicans. There are, however, some common threads. Nearly all these communities are overwhelmingly white and socially conservative. On the average, Cleveland's suburbs are the most affluent in Ohio.

More than 55 percent of the voters in the "U" were in the old 23rd, which surrounded Cleveland on the west and the south. Along the lake are wealthy GOP towns such as Bay Village and Rocky River. Moving inland, Democratic bowling alleys replace Republican golf clubs as centers for social contact.

Children and grandchildren of European immigrants moved out of Cleveland to inner suburbs such as Parma, due south of the city. During the 1970s many of them moved again. Parma's population declined by nearly 8,000 as residents left their ranch homes of the 1950s for the open spaces of Strongsville and other outer suburbs. But even with the population loss, Parma is still the ninth-largest city in Ohio and the largest community in the 19th. Nearby steel mills and automobile plants give this part of the district a strong union presence.

Moving east across Interstate 271, one enters suburbs that were formerly part of the 22nd District. Much of the Cleveland financial elite lives in outlying suburbs along Cuyahoga County's eastern boundary. This is solid Republican territory. Two of these affluent communities — Hunting Valley and Chagrin Falls — even voted for James E. Betts in his "sacrificial lamb" Senate candidacy against Democrat John Glenn in 1980.

Moving north toward the lake, one re-enters the world of ethnic politics. The blue-collar workers of Polish and Slovenian descent who fled the city for suburbs such as Euclid and Mayfield have retained their Democratic allegiance, although it has a conservative cast. Nearly all of the suburban 19th lies within Cuyahoga County. About 6,500 residents in eastern Lorain County and 38,000 residents in western Lake County round out the district.

Election Returns

19th District		Democrat		Republican	
1976	President	104,028	(43.1%)	130,350	(54.0%)
	Senate	112,574	(54.1%)	94,294	(45.3%)
	House	158,380	(73.3%)	54,735	(25.3%)

19th District		Democrat		Republican	
1978	Governor	74,203	(46.0%)	79,562	(49.3%)
	House	113,399	(70.8%)	39,118	(24.4%)
1980	President	87,859	(37.2%)	127,266	(53.9%)
	Senate	139,153	(69.7%)	51,977	(26.0%)
	House	153,201	(77.9%)	39,850	(20.3%)
1982	Governor	118,884	(62.8%)	67,404	(35.6%)
	Senate	112,913	(58.6%)	76,699	(39.8%)
	House	111,760	(58.8%)	72,682	(38.3%)

Demographics

Population: 514,889. **Percent Change from 1970:** -1.3%.

Land Area: 302 square miles. **Population per Square Mile:** 1,704.9.

Counties, 1980 Population: Cuyahoga (Pt.) — 470,281; Lake (Pt.) — 38,114; Lorain (Pt.) — 6,494.

Cities, 1980 Population: Bay Village — 17,846; Brecksville — 10,132; Broadview Heights — 10,920; Euclid (Pt.) — 45,689; Fairview Park — 19,311; Lakewood (Pt.) — 30,547; Lyndhurst — 18,092; Mayfield Heights — 21,550; North Olmsted — 36,486; North Royalton — 17,671; Parma (Pt.) — 49,815; Parma Heights — 23,112; Richmond Heights — 10,095; Rocky River — 21,084; Solon — 14,341; South Euclid — 25,713; Strongsville (Pt.) — 12,994; University Heights (Pt.) — 7,484; Westlake — 19,483; Wickliffe — 16,790; Willowick — 17,834.

Race and Ancestry: White — 97.2%; Black — 1.5%; American Indian, Eskimo and Aleut — 0.0%; Asian and Pacific Islander — 1.0%. Spanish Origin — 0.6%. English — 4.6%; German — 9.5%; Greek — 0.6%; Hungarian — 2.9%; Irish — 4.4%; Italian — 6.9%; Polish — 4.8%; Russian — 1.5%; Scottish — 0.5%; Ukranian — 0.8%.

Universities, Enrollment: John Carroll University, Cleveland — 3,994; Notre Dame College, Cleveland — 679; Ursuline College, Pepper Pike — 1,030; Virginia Marti School of Fashion Design, Lakewood — 76.

Newspapers, Circulation: Lorain *Journal*, Willoughby *Lake County News-Herald*, Cleveland *Plain Dealer*, and Painesville *Telegraph* circulate in the district.

Commercial Television Stations, Affiliation: Entire district is in Cleveland ADI.

Industries:

Lincoln Electric Co. (HQ); Euclid; electric arc welding apparatus — 2,600. **Veterans Administration;** Brecksville; veterans' hospital — 2,600. **Babcock & Wilcox Co.** (Bailey Meter Controls Div.); Wickliffe; fluid meters — 2,300. **Allen-Bradley Co.** (Systems Div.); Mayfield; industrial controls — 2,020. **Picker International Holdings** (HQ); High-

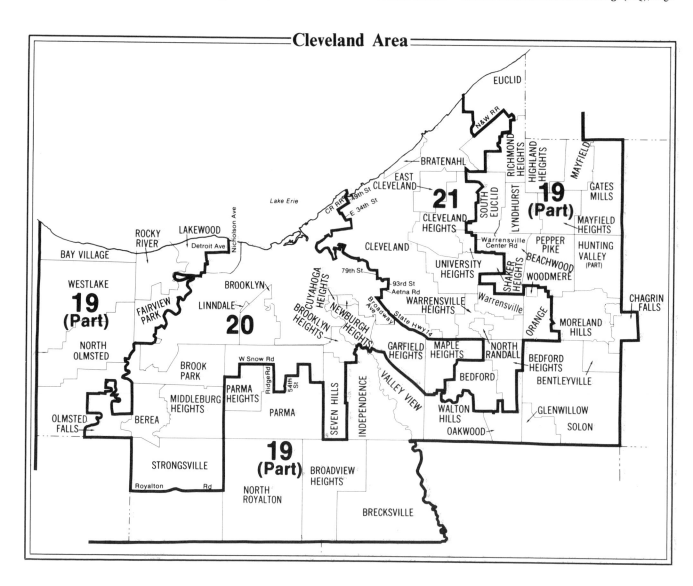

Cleveland Area

land Heights; x-ray equipment — 1,600. **Technicare Corp.** (HQ); Solon; radioisotope instruments — 1,600.

Davy McKee Corp. (HQ); Independence; engineering services — 1,500. **Parma Community General Hospital;** Parma; hospital — 1,390. **The Progressive Corp.;** Highland Heights; life, health insurance — 1,300. **The Lubrizol Corp.** (HQ); Wickliffe; fuel and lubricant additives — 1,250. **Chagrin Valley Medical Corp.;** South Euclid; hospital — 1,200. **McNeil Corp.** (Cleveland Crane & Engineering Div.); Wickliffe; monorail systems — 800. **TRW Inc.** (Replacement Div.); Independence; auto parts — 750. **B. F. Goodrich Co.** (Chemical Co.); Independence; administrative offices — 700. **General Electric Co.;** Euclid; electrometallurgical products — 631. **Norandex Inc.** (HQ); Walton Hills; aluminum storm doors — 600. **Western Electric Co. Inc.;** Solon; electrical work — 509. **Cleveland Cotton Products Co.;** Mayfield; wiping cloths wholesaling — 500.

20th District

Cleveland — Central, West, Suburbs

With blacks dominating the East Side and blue-collar ethnic voters dominating the West Side, Cleveland is essentially two cities with differing interests and values, bound together in politics only by ties to the Democratic Party.

The city's two congressional districts reflect this division. The 20th is the white district, containing the state's largest concentration of ethnic voters. Poles, Czechs, Italians, Irish and Germans are the largest groups, but there are dozens of other ethnic communities represented by at least a restaurant or two on the West Side.

The city's burgeoning steel industry fueled the ethnic influx around the turn of the century, with immigrants settling near the mills on Cleveland's West Side. Steel, automobile and aluminum plants are combined with smaller businesses to make up the employment base today.

But many of the younger ethnics who work there have bought homes in the suburbs. The West Side population declined 19 percent in the 1970s, a rate exceeded in Ohio only by the 21st on the city's East Side. Many who remain on the West Side are elderly.

The Legislature made few changes in the district's Democratic complexion. The 20th lost the town of Bedford Heights, the village of North Randall and one black ward in Garfield Heights; its 150,000 new residents are primarily conservative blue-collar Democrats from the old 23rd.

About half the newcomers live near the lake, as the 20th absorbed the far western end of Cleveland and the eastern portion of Lakewood. The other additions were near the large automobile plants southwest of the city. With Berea, Middleburgh Heights and part of Strongsville joining the 20th, the district pushed past the Ohio Turnpike, about 12 miles from downtown Cleveland.

The downtown area lies totally within the 20th. For years the center city was charitably described as a slumbering giant. Its access to the lake was blocked by docks and warehouses and its skyline was dominated by the 52-story Terminal Tower, built during the Depression.

The city's economic problems of the 1970s, notably its near-bankruptcy under former Mayor Dennis Kucinich, made it a national symbol of urban decay. But Cleveland is recovering. Its economy has successfully diversified in recent years. The new $200 million headquarters of Standard Oil of Ohio (Sohio) is spearheading a downtown construc-

tion boom that has taken some of the sting out of the auto and steel slumps.

The line that divides the city between the 20th and 21st districts remains unchanged for the 1980s, snaking a path southeastward from Lake Erie toward the inner suburbs. In parts of the city, the line runs along the notorious Cuyahoga River, a waterway once so despoiled with industrial waste that it caught fire in 1969 and nearly destroyed two railroad bridges.

Election Returns

20th District		Democrat		Republican	
1976	President	99,852	(55.1%)	75,634	(41.7%)
	Senate	88,114	(58.5%)	60,784	(40.4%)
	House	122,544	(78.3%)	14,485	(9.3%)
1978	Governor	75,669	(52.0%)	63,050	(43.3%)
	House	91,314	(91.1%)	8,916	(8.9%)
1980	President	76,209	(51.9%)	57,737	(39.3%)
	Senate	107,063	(75.4%)	27,211	(19.2%)
	House	122,265	(100.0%)	—	
1982	Governor	114,032	(74.0%)	37,213	(24.2%)
	Senate	106,403	(67.8%)	47,355	(30.2%)
	House	133,603	(85.6%)	17,675	(11.3%)

Demographics

Population: 513,494. **Percent Change from 1970:** -14.7%.

Land Area: 116 square miles. **Population per Square Mile:** 4,426.7.

Counties, 1980 Population: Cuyahoga (Pt.) — 513,494.

Cities, 1980 Population: Berea — 19,567; Brook Park — 26,195; Brooklyn — 12,342; Cleveland (Pt.) — 265,137; Garfield Heights (Pt.) — 29,374; Lakewood (Pt.) — 31,416; Maple Heights — 29,735; Middleburg Heights — 16,218; Parma (Pt.) — 42,733; Seven Hills — 13,650; Strongsville (Pt.) — 15,583.

Race and Ancestry: White — 94.6%; Black — 2.5%; American Indian, Eskimo and Aleut — 0.2%; Asian and Pacific Islander — 0.9%. Spanish Origin — 3.1%. English — 4.3%; German — 8.8%; Greek — 0.5%; Hungarian — 2.4%; Irish — 4.9%; Italian — 4.7%; Polish — 8.5%; Ukranian — 1.1%.

Universities, Enrollment: Baldwin-Wallace College, Berea — 3,505; Cleveland State University, Cleveland — 19,103; Dyke College, Cleveland — 1,416; West Side Institute of Technology, Cleveland — 628.

Newspapers, Circulation: *The Plain Dealer* (mS), Cleveland — 389,452.

Commercial Television Stations, Affiliation: WCLQ, Cleveland (None); WEWS, Cleveland (ABC); WKYC-TV, Cleveland (NBC). Entire district is located in Cleveland ADI. *(For other Cleveland stations, see 21st district.)*

Military Installations: Cleveland Naval Finance Center, Cleveland — 1,476.

Industries:

Ernst & Whinney; Cleveland; accounting services — 9,000. **General Motors Corp.** (Chevrolet Motor Div.); Cleveland; steel stampings — 5,200. **Ford Motor Co.** (Engine Plants); Cleveland; engines — 5,000. **Cuyahoga County Hospital;** Cleveland; hospital — 4,740. **Ford Motor Co.** (Casting Div.); Brook Park; auto casting — 4,400.

American Greetings Corp. (American Color Process Co. Div. - HQ); Cleveland; greeting cards, gift wrap — 3,571. **Jones & Laughlin Steel Corp.;** Cleveland; steel products — 3,500. **Standard Oil Co. of Ohio** (HQ); Cleveland; petroleum production — 2,400. **Fairview General Hospital;** Cleveland; hospital — 2,286. **National City Bank** (HQ);

Cleveland; banking — 2,200. **Stouffer Foods Corp.** (HQ); Cleveland; frozen foods — 2,200. **The Higbee Co.** (HQ); Cleveland; department stores — 1,950. **Central National Bank of Cleveland** (HQ); Cleveland; banking — 1,866. **Plain Dealer Publishing Co.;** Cleveland; newspaper publishing — 1,818. **Aluminum Co. of America;** Cleveland; aluminum forgings — 1,600. **Pittway Corp.;** Cleveland; trade journal publishing — 1,600.

The Sherwin-Williams Co. (HQ); Cleveland; paints, lacquer — 1,500. **Cook United Inc.** (HQ); Cleveland; discount department stores — 1,500. **Society Corp.** (HQ); Cleveland; banking — 1,500. **Lakewood Hospital;** Cleveland; hospital — 1,400. **Marymount Hospital Inc.;** Cleveland; hospital — 1,240. **Deaconess Hospital Cleveland;** Cleveland; hospital — 1,200. **Joseph & Feiss Co.** (HQ); Cleveland; men's clothing — 1,200. **Republic Steel Corp.** (HQ); Cleveland; steel, steel products — 1,200. **Penton/Industrial Publishing Co.** (HQ); Cleveland; periodicals publishing — 1,125. **Schweitzer-Dipple Inc.;** Cleveland; plumbing heating contracting — 1,055. **United States Steel Corp.** (Cuyahoga Plant); Cleveland; steel mill, steel wire — 1,050.

St. Alexis Hospital Assn.; Cleveland; hospital — 1,030. **Cleveland Pneumatic Co.** (HQ); Cleveland; aircraft landing equipment — 977. **Union Carbide Corp.** (Battery Products Div.); Cleveland; dry cell batteries — 950. **Hibbing Taconite Co.** (HQ); Cleveland; taconite processing — 875. **Ferro Corp.** (HQ); Cleveland; glazes, specialty coatings — 794. **PPG Industries Inc.** (Auto Finishes Div.); Cleveland; paints — 775. **Union Commerce Bank** (HQ); Cleveland; banking — 760. **H. K. Ferguson Co.** (HQ); Cleveland; general contracting — 650. **Ohio Savings Financial Corp.;** Cleveland; savings and loan — 650. **Pinkerton's Inc.;** Cleveland; security services — 650. **Lear Siegler Inc.** (Power Equipment Div.); Cleveland; electric motors — 627. **General Signal Industries Inc.** (Ceilcote Div.); Berea; corrosion proof plastics products — 600. **Gould Inc.** (Instruments Div.); Cleveland; electronic testing instruments — 600.

SCM Corp. (Glidden Coatings & Resins); Cleveland; administrative offices — 600. **National Steel Pellet Co.** (HQ); Cleveland; iron ores — 573. **Kirkwood Industries Inc.** (HQ); Cleveland; motors, generators, machinery, other electrical equipment — 565. **E. F. Hauserman Co.;** Cleveland; steel partitions — 550. **First National Supermarkets** (Finast Supermarkets Div. - HQ); Cleveland; supermarket chain — 550. **Midland Steel Products Co.** (Forest City Foundry - HQ); Cleveland; automotive parts — 550. **Public Square Hotel Co. Ltd.;** Cleveland; hotel — 550. **Diamond Shamrock Corp.;** Cleveland; administrative offices — 500. **International Business Machines Corp.;** Cleveland; administrative offices — 500. **Midland Steel Products Inc.;** Cleveland; truck frames — 500. **Oerlikon Motch Corp.** (HQ); Cleveland; machine tools — 500. **Oglebay Norton Co.** (Columbia Transportation Div.); Cleveland; Great Lakes transportation — 500.

21st District

Cleveland — East, Cleveland Heights

One of the axioms of Ohio politics is that to win statewide, a Democratic candidate must come out of Cuyahoga County with a 100,000-vote edge. Most of that lead has to be built in the 21st, which is anchored in Cleveland's heavily black East Side.

The district includes the areas devastated by riots in the 1960s, as well as middle-class neighborhoods farther from the downtown area. Heavy industries, especially automobile and machine tool plants, long have been major employers. During the 1970s the 21st was the most Democratic district in the state. In 11 East Side wards Jimmy Carter in 1980 outpolled Ronald Reagan by margins of at least 20-to-1.

To protect the one black in the Ohio congressional delegation, the heart of the old 21st was preserved intact. But to offset a 25 percent population loss, the fifth greatest decline recorded by any district in the country, the 21st was expanded to the south and east to add about 160,000 suburbanites. While most of these new constituents are white, their presence does not significantly alter the demographics of the district. The 21st remains heavily black (62 percent compared with 79 percent in the old district) and staunchly Democratic.

The new 21st juts east into working-class, white Euclid and south into Bedford, Bedford Heights and several villages. The key additions are Cleveland Heights, Shaker Heights and the western half of University Heights. With a large proportion of Jews and young professionals, these three are among the most liberal communities in Ohio. All of them voted for Carter for president in 1980, and all of them gave independent John B. Anderson at least 10 percent of the vote.

In the 1950s and 1960s Shaker Heights symbolized suburbia. But in recent years, communities farther east have replaced Shaker Heights as the county's exclusive addresses. North of Shaker Heights is Cleveland Heights. Many of its integrated neighborhoods are a short walk from University Circle, the cultural hub of Cleveland. Within several blocks of the circle is Case Western Reserve University; the city's museums of art and natural history; Severance Hall, the home of the city's renowned symphony orchestra; and the three theaters of the Cleveland Play House.

From the circle area, commuters drive along historic Euclid Avenue to their jobs downtown. While the avenue now bears the marks of poverty, it was known as "Millionaires' Row" during the city's halcyon days at the turn of the century. Few of the old mansions are left today. The one belonging to John D. Rockefeller, founder of Standard Oil, was razed to make way for a gas station.

Election Returns

21st District		Democrat		Republican	
1976	President	162,837	(70.9%)	60,922	(26.5%)
	Senate	136,872	(72.4%)	48,075	(25.4%)
	House	148,677	(80.0%)	26,591	(14.3%)
1978	Governor	93,382	(64.6%)	44,030	(30.4%)
	House	102,779	(82.1%)	18,287	(14.6%)
1980	President	138,444	(70.9%)	42,938	(22.0%)
	Senate	123,733	(82.1%)	19,789	(13.1%)
	House	131,790	(79.3%)	32,265	(19.4%)
1982	Governor	125,869	(83.6%)	22,299	(14.8%)
	Senate	126,375	(83.0%)	23,268	(15.3%)
	House	132,544	(86.1%)	21,332	(13.9%)

Demographics

Population: 514,625. **Percent Change from 1970:** -19.7%.

Land Area: 79 square miles. **Population per Square Mile:** 6,514.2.

Counties, 1980 Population: Cuyahoga (Pt.) — 514,625.

Cities, 1980 Population: Bedford — 15,056; Bedford Heights — 13,214; Cleveland (Pt.) — 308,685; Cleveland Heights — 56,438; East Cleveland — 36,957; Euclid (Pt.) — 14,310; Garfield Heights (Pt.) — 5,564; Shaker Heights — 32,487; University Heights (Pt.) — 7,917; Warrensville Heights — 16,565.

Race and Ancestry: White — 36.4%; Black — 62.3%; American Indian, Eskimo and Aleut — 0.1%; Asian and Pacific Islander — 0.6%. Spanish Origin — 1.0%. English — 3.0%; German — 2.7%; Hungarian

— 1.5%; Irish — 1.5%; Italian — 2.6%; Polish — 1.5%; Russian — 1.0%.

Universities, Enrollment: Case Western Reserve University, Cleveland — 8,416; Cleveland Institute of Art, Cleveland — 543; Cleveland Institute of Music, Cleveland — 308; Cuyahoga Community College, Cleveland — 26,335; Electronic Technology Institute, Cleveland — 800; Ohio College of Podiatric Medicine, Cleveland — 594; St. Mary Seminary, Cleveland — 64.

Newspapers, Circulation: Cleveland *Plain Dealer* circulates in the district. Foreign language newspaper: *Ameriska Domovina* (Yugoslavian), Cleveland — 9,000.

Commercial Television Stations, Affiliation: WJKW-TV, Cleveland (CBS). Entire district is located in Cleveland ADI. *(For other Cleveland stations, see 20st district.)*

Industries:

Cleveland Clinic Foundation; Cleveland; hospital — 6,000. **University Hospital of Cleveland;** Cleveland; hospital — 4,000. **Veterans Administration;** Cleveland; veterans' hospital — 2,870. **Ford Motor Co. Inc.** (Metal Stamping Div.); Bedford; automotive stampings — 2,550. **General Electric Co.** (Lighting Business Group - HQ); East Cleveland; electric lighting fixtures — 2,300.

The Mt. Sinai Hospital of Cleveland; Cleveland; hospital — 2,180. **St. Vincent Charity Hospital Inc.;** Cleveland; hospital — 1,770. **Gould Inc.** (Ocean System Div.); Cleveland; underwater communications equipment — 1,640. **TRW Inc.** (Automotive Valve Div.); Cleveland; automotive valves — 1,600. **St. Luke's Hospital Assn.;** Cleveland; hospital — 1,560. **Shelter Resources Corp.;** Cleveland; mobile homes — 1,500. **Huron Road Hospital;** East Cleveland; hospital — 1,300. **Parker-Hannifin Corp.** (HQ); Cleveland; hydraulic, pneumatic power system components — 1,300. **General Motors Corp.** (Fisher Body Div.); Cleveland; auto interiors — 1,297. **Commercial Property Service;** Cleveland; janitorial services — 1,100. **Euclid General Hospital Assn.;** Cleveland; hospital — 1,100. **Blue Cross of Northeast Ohio Inc.** (HQ); Cleveland; health insurance — 1,030. **Cleveland Twist Drill Co.** (HQ); Cleveland; twist drills — 1,000. **General Electric Co.** '(Euclid Lamp Plant); Euclid; electric lamps — 1,000. **The Richman Brothers Co.** (HQ); Cleveland; men's suits, overcoats — 1,000.

National Cleaning Contractors; Cleveland; janitorial services — 900. **Nesco Design Group Inc.;** Cleveland; engineering services — 900. **AM International Inc.** (Multigraphics Div.); Cleveland; office machines — 625. **Sheller-Globe Corp.** (Leece-Neville Div.); Cleveland; generators — 600. **S. K. Wellman Corp.** (HQ); Cleveland; fabricated metal products — 600. **Eaton Corp.** (Axle Div.); Cleveland; truck axles — 573. **Acme-Cleveland Corp.** (National Acme Div.); Cleveland; machine tools — 509. **American Seaway Foods Inc.** (HQ); Cleveland; grocery wholesaling — 500. **Barnes Group Inc.** (Bowman Distribution); Cleveland; auto wholesaling — 500. **Sherwood Refractories Inc.** (HQ); Cleveland; industrial clay — 500. **Sifco Industries** (HQ); Cleveland; forgings, plating — 500. **White Motor Corp.;** Cleveland; motor vehicle bodies — 500.

Oklahoma

Oklahoma's 1982 congressional map was a Democratic product designed to preserve the lineup of five Democrats and one Republican in the state's U.S. House delegation. The plan placed widely separated GOP cities in the 5th District, held by the state's lone GOP House member. And it divided Democratic strongholds among the five remaining districts to solidify the electoral bases of the Democratic incumbents.

An Oklahoma Supreme Court decision June 25, 1982, ended temporarily a year-long controversy over the map. The court said that the lines drawn by the Legislature would be valid for the 1982 elections, but that final approval of the plan — or an alternative map fashioned by the GOP — would be left up to the voters. In November Oklahoma voters approved the Legislature's plan by a vote of 397,142 to 379,545.

When the Legislature adopted its map on July 20, 1981, Oklahoma Republicans denounced it as a partisan gerrymander designed to protect incumbent Democrats threatened by the state's growing number of Republican voters and launched a petition drive to force a popular vote on the redistricting issue.

Democrats tried to quash the petition, arguing in court that it contained technical flaws and that there was an insufficient number of valid signatures of registered voters. But the state Supreme Court ruled June 25 that the number of signatures on the petition exceeded legal requirements.

Republicans argued that they had sufficient strength in Oklahoma to warrant a chance at winning more than one seat in the House delegation. Oklahoma Republicans have supported every GOP presidential candidate but Barry Goldwater since 1952. Another complaint was that the Legislature's map did not maintain the integrity of county lines, creating geographically sprawling districts.

Age of Population

District	Population Under 18	Voting Age Population	Population 65 & Over (% of VAP)	Median Age
1	138,733	365,006	52,774 (14.5%)	29.6
2	151,211	353,938	67,761 (19.1%)	31.8
3	138,403	365,865	77,856 (21.3%)	31.4
4	149,211	356,658	47,534 (13.3%)	27.4
5	135,344	367,630	60,357 (16.4%)	30.6
6	141,982	361,309	69,844 (19.3%)	30.6
State	854,884	2,170,406	376,126 (17.3%)	30.1

Income and Occupation

District	Median Family Income	White Collar Workers	Blue Collar Workers	Service Workers	Farm Workers
1	$ 20,138	57.3%	30.3%	11.6%	0.8%
2	15,965	45.5	37.4	12.7	4.4
3	14,125	44.2	36.8	13.6	5.3
4	17,825	51.3	31.8	13.2	3.6
5	20,839	61.2	26.4	10.7	1.7
6	17,687	44.3	34.1	13.8	7.8
State	$ 17,668	51.2%	32.5%	12.5%	3.8%

Education: School Years Completed

District	8 Years or Fewer	4 Years of High School	4 Years of College or More	Median School Years
1	12.4%	37.3%	17.1%	12.6
2	24.2	33.5	11.9	12.3
3	26.6	31.7	11.4	12.2
4	16.1	36.2	15.9	12.5
5	11.8	33.1	22.2	12.8
6	19.0	37.0	11.9	12.4
State	18.4%	34.8%	15.1%	12.5

Housing and Residential Patterns

District	Owner Occupied	Renter Occupied	Urban	Rural
1	65.7%	34.3%	88.3%	11.7%
2	77.0	23.0	40.7	59.3
3	72.4	27.6	47.1	52.9
4	69.4	30.6	73.9	26.1
5	69.2	30.8	88.2	11.8
6	70.9	29.1	65.5	34.5
State	70.7%	29.3%	67.3%	32.7%

OKLAHOMA

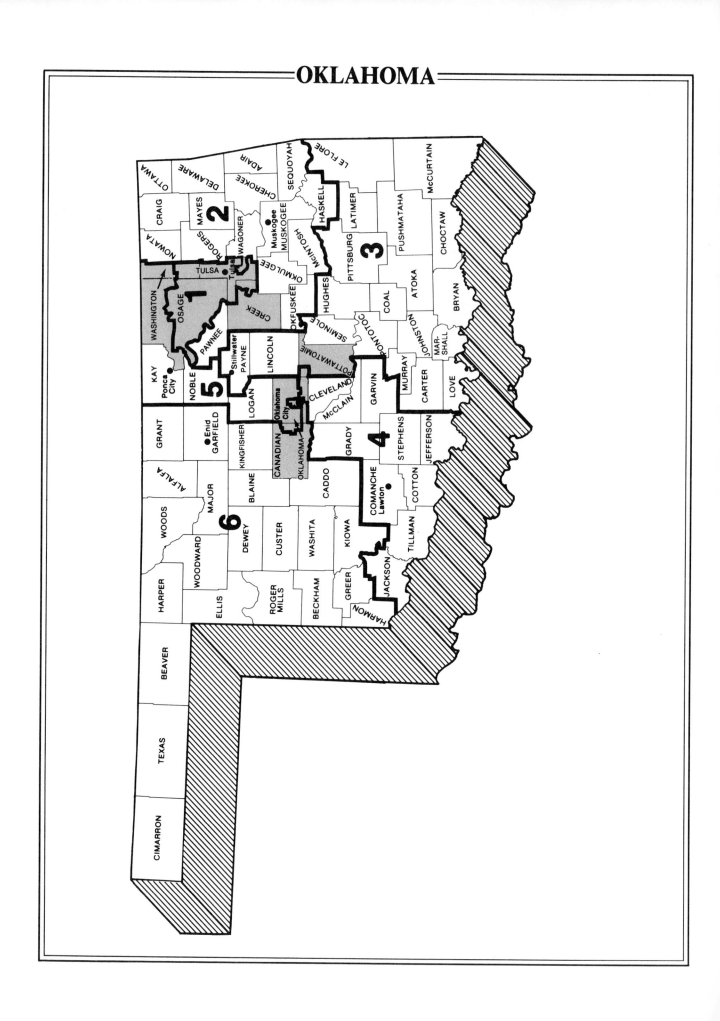

1st District

Tulsa; Parts of Osage, Creek and Washington Counties

In its white-collar Republican leanings and its antagonism to rural Democratic domination of the state, Tulsa was a forerunner of other Sun Belt cities now catching up with it. Tulsa City has gone Republican in all but two presidential elections since 1920.

The city's tendencies generally are reflected districtwide. Residents of the redrawn 1st gave both Gerald R. Ford and Ronald Reagan over 60 percent of their presidential ballots in 1976 and 1980, respectively.

Corporate headquarters for a number of petroleum companies, Tulsa calls itself "The Oil Capital of the World." Oil and gas remain of paramount importance, but Tulsa's economy has diversified considerably. With the opening of the Arkansas River Navigation System in 1971, Tulsa became a deepwater port accessible to the Gulf of Mexico. The city also maintains a thriving aeronautics industry. Its No. 1 tourist attraction is Oral Roberts University, which is the center of a large fundamentalist community.

By moving 32,000 residents in the southeastern portion of Tulsa County out of the 1st into the 2nd, map makers removed a big block of affluent Republican voters. But the portion of the city remaining in the 1st accounts for 67 percent of the district population. Southeast of Tulsa, the 1st takes in most of Broken Arrow, home to many Tulsa workers.

The new map brought in portions of Osage and Creek counties, which include some growing Tulsa suburbs. The new areas have Republican tendencies, but they are not as strong as those in the old Tulsa portion. The 1st gave up rural Pawnee County, a politically marginal area, and shed part of Washington County near the heavily Republican city of Bartlesville.

Election Returns

1st District		Democrat		Republican	
1976	President	64,514	(38.4%)	101,276	(60.3%)
	House	89,833	(53.8%)	75,571	(45.3%)
1978	Governor	56,481	(48.8%)	58,463	(50.5%)
	Senate	67,114	(60.0%)	42,997	(38.4%)
	House	66,498	(60.0%)	44,302	(40.0%)
1980	President	54,809	(30.7%)	114,517	(64.1%)
	Senate	70,785	(40.2%)	99,368	(56.4%)
	House	102,692	(58.2%)	73,875	(41.8%)
1982	Governor	78,168	(54.5%)	64,954	(45.3%)
	House	76,379	(54.1%)	64,704	(45.9%)

Demographics

Population: 503,739. **Percent Change from 1970:** 14.1%.

Land Area: 2,146 square miles. **Population per Square Mile:** 234.8.

Counties, 1980 Population: Creek (Pt.) — 29,651; Osage (Pt.) — 32,280; Tulsa (Pt.) — 437,746; Washington (Pt.) — 4,062.

Cities, 1980 Population: Broken Arrow (Pt.) — 29,531; Sand Springs — 13,246; Sapulpa — 15,853; Tulsa (Pt.) — 338,913.

Race and Ancestry: White — 84.1%; Black — 9.4%; American Indian, Eskimo and Aleut — 5.0%; Asian and Pacific Islander — 0.6%. Spanish Origin — 1.6%. Dutch — 0.6%; English — 11.1%; French — 0.8%; German — 5.1%; Irish — 4.1%; Italian — 0.5%.

Universities, Enrollment: Oklahoma College of Osteopathic Medicine and Surgery, Tulsa — 257; Oklahoma School of Business Accountancy, Law and Finance, Tulsa — 882; Spartan School of Aeronautics, Tulsa — 2,195; Tulsa Junior College, Tulsa — 12,063; University of Tulsa, Tulsa — 6,265.

Newspapers, Circulation: *Broken Arrow Daily Ledger* (e), Broken Arrow — 7,438; *Pawhuska Daily Journal-Capital* (eS), Pawhuska — 2,795; *Sapulpa Daily Herald* (eS), Sapulpa — 8,543; *The Tulsa Tribune* (e), Tulsa — 76,517; *Tulsa World* (mS), Tulsa — 124,471.

Commercial Television Stations, Affiliation: KGCT, Tulsa (None); KJRH, Tulsa (NBC); KOKI, Tulsa (None); KOTV, Tulsa (CBS); KTUL-TV, Tulsa (ABC). Entire district is located in Tulsa ADI.

Military Installations: Tulsa International Airport (Air Force), Tulsa — 974.

Industries:

Mapco International Inc.; Tulsa; petroleum brokers — 6,000. **American Airlines Inc.** (Maintenance & Engineering Center); Tulsa; airplane maintenance — 5,643. **McDonnell-Douglas Corp.;** Tulsa; aircraft — 3,200. **Rockwell International Corp.;** Tulsa; aircraft engines, communications equipment — 2,800. **Safeway Stores Inc.;** Tulsa; administrative offices — 2,730.

C C I Corp. (Crane Carrier Co. Div.); Tulsa; aircraft components, heavy vehicles — 2,500. **St. John Medical Center Inc.;** Tulsa; hospital — 2,100. **Hillcrest Medical Center Inc.;** Tulsa; hospital — 1,850. **Oklahoma Osteopathic Hospital;** Tulsa; hospital — 1,500. **Amoco Production Co.;** Tulsa; administrative offices — 1,450. **Seismograph Service Corp.** (Seismic Div. - HQ); Tulsa; seismographic surveys — 1,200. **The Telex Corp.** (HQ); Tulsa; computer equipment — 1,200. **Ford Motor Co. Inc.** (Tulsa Glass Plant); Tulsa; auto glass — 1,140. **C C I Corp.** (HQ); Tulsa; heavy machinery, guided missiles — 1,000. **Newspaper Printing Corp.;** Tulsa; business management services — 1,000. **Combustion Engineering Inc.;** Tulsa; oil field machinery — 925.

Crane Carrier Co. (HQ); Tulsa; truck trailers — 890. **Bancoklahoma Corp.;** Tulsa; banking — 850. **Tulsa Refining Inc.;** Tulsa; petroleum refining — 850. **First National Bank & Trust Co. of Tulsa** (HQ); Tulsa; banking — 805. **DM International Inc.** (Dresser Engineering Div.); Tulsa; oil refinery construction — 800. **Dover Corp.** (Norris Div.); Tulsa; pumps, pumping equipment — 800. **Unit Rig & Equipment Co.** (HQ); Tulsa; heavy trucks — 800. **John Zink Co.** (Process Systems Division - HQ); Tulsa; industrial machinery — 800. **Amoco Production Co.;** Tulsa; research center — 700. **Brunswick Corp.** (Zebco Div.); Tulsa; fishing tackle — 700. **Quarles Drilling Inc.;** Tulsa; oil drilling — 700. **Tom Inman Trucking Inc.;** Tulsa; trucking — 700 **Borg-Warner Corp.** (Byron-Jackson Pump Div.); Tulsa; pumps — 675.

General Signal Corp. (Nelson Electric Units); Tulsa; industrial controls — 650. **Group Hospital Service** (Oklahoma Blue Cross-Blue Shield - HQ); Tulsa; health insurance — 620. **HMK Industries of Texas Inc.** (Sheffield Steel); Sand Springs; steel — 610. **Geosource Inc.;** Tulsa; valves, pipefittings — 600. **Beverage Products Corp.** (HQ); Tulsa; soft drink bottling — 525. **Braden Steel Corp.;** Tulsa; structural steel — 510. **Cities Service Co.** (HQ); Tulsa; petroleum refining — 500. **Metropolitan Life Insurance Co.;** Tulsa; life insurance — 500. **Telex Computer Products Inc.** (Telex Metal Products Div. - HQ); Tulsa; computer equipment — 500. **Unit Drilling & Exploration Co.;** Tulsa; oil, gas drilling — 500.

2nd District

Northeast — Tulsa, Muskogee

This northeast Oklahoma territory has had some good fortune. Sheltered somewhat by the low-lying Ozark Mountains, it was spared the worst of the Dust Bowl winds that

Tulsa

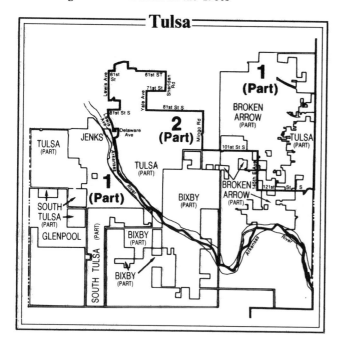

ravaged much of the state during the 1930s and 1940s. Equally important, it has attracted numerous state and federal water projects over the years — projects that have bolstered agriculture, drawn vacationers and prompted some local chambers of commerce to bill the area as "Green Country."

The growing tourism industry is crowding the area's traditional enterprises, cattle ranching and the oil and gas business. Recent oil and gas activity has been confined largely to specialized techniques for recovering from older wells.

With a 27-percent population increase, the 2nd was Oklahoma's fastest-growing district during the 1970s. Much of the growth occurred in the eastern Tulsa suburbs in Rogers and Wagoner counties, home to a substantial number of GOP voters. Muskogee, with 40,000 people the largest city wholly contained in the 2nd, dredges sand from the Arkansas River beds for use in its glass industry. Its residents harbor Democratic sentiments.

The largest Indian population in Oklahoma is concentrated within the 2nd's boundaries, in the area settled by the Five Civilized Tribes in the 19th century. The Cherokee Nation has its headquarters in Tahlequah, the seat of Cherokee County, and members of other tribes are scattered throughout the surrounding counties. There is also a modest black population in this part of the 2nd, which makes for a complex triangular pattern of race relations.

Although the 2nd had a suburban Tulsa contingent throughout the 1970s, the 1982 remap moved the district inside the city limits for the first time. The newly acquired southeastern Tulsa portion of the 2nd is a GOP haven populated by middle-rung and top-level executives from the city's corporate offices. But this Republican gain was offset by the removal of GOP-minded Bartlesville.

The 2nd thus retains a basically Democratic cast. It did vote Republican by modest margins in the 1980 presidential and Senate contests, but it has voted Democratic in most other recent statewide and national elections.

In addition to keeping the Democratic stronghold of Okmulgee County, the 2nd gained Haskell County on its

southern end and Pawnee on its western border. It lost part of Creek and all of Osage County.

Election Returns

2nd District		Democrat		Republican	
1976	President	99,467	(54.2%)	82,469	(44.9%)
	House	104,476	(57.1%)	78,256	(42.8%)
1978	Governor	81,174	(61.6%)	49,675	(37.7%)
	Senate	85,000	(66.5%)	40,827	(31.9%)
	House	70,328	(57.9%)	51,062	(42.1%)
1980	President	82,689	(41.8%)	108,520	(54.9%)
	Senate	89,295	(48.8%)	89,944	(49.2%)
	House	98,910	(56.7%)	75,434	(43.3%)
1982	Governor	102,425	(67.0%)	50,289	(32.9%)
	House	111,895	(72.6%)	42,298	(27.4%)

Demographics

Population: 505,149. **Percent Change from 1970:** 33.6%.

Land Area: 11,148 square miles. **Population per Square Mile:** 45.3.

Counties, 1980 Population: Adair — 18,575; Cherokee — 30,684; Craig — 15,014; Creek (Pt.) — 29,365; Delaware — 23,946; Haskell — 11,010; Mayes — 32,261; McIntosh — 15,562; Muskogee — 66,939; Nowata — 11,486; Okfuskee — 11,125; Okmulgee — 39,169; Ottawa — 32,870; Pawnee — 15,310; Rogers — 46,436; Sequoyah — 30,749; Tulsa (Pt.) — 32,847; Wagoner — 41,801.

Cities, 1980 Population: Broken Arrow (Pt.) — 6,230; Claremore — 12,085; Miami — 14,237; Muskogee — 40,011; Okmulgee — 16,263; Tulsa (Pt.) — 22,006.

Race and Ancestry: White — 83.3%; Black — 4.5%; American Indian, Eskimo and Aleut — 11.6%; Asian and Pacific Islander — 0.2%. Spanish Origin — 0.9%. Dutch — 0.7%; English — 13.0%; French — 0.7%; German — 4.5%; Irish — 5.3%.

Universities, Enrollment: Bacone College, Muskogee — 500; Claremore Junior College, Claremore — 1,720; Connors State College, Warner — 1,416; Northeastern Oklahoma A & M College, Miami — 2,862; Northeastern Oklahoma State University, Tahlequah — 5,743; Oklahoma State University - School of Technical Training, Okmulgee — 3,292; Oral Roberts University, Tulsa — 4,006.

Newspapers, Circulation: *The Claremore Progress* (eS), Claremore — 6,733; *The Daily Times* (eS), Pryor — 4,770; *Henryetta Daily Free-Lance* (eS), Henryetta — 3,336; *Miami News-Record* (eS), Miami — 9,620; *Nowata Daily Star* (e), Nowata — 2,983; *Phoenix & Times Democrat* (mS), Muskogee — 22,227; *Times* (mS), Okmulgee — 4,997; *Vinita Daily Journal* (e), Vinita — 3,722. *The Tulsa Tribune* and *Tulsa World* also circulate in the district.

Commercial Television Stations, Affiliation: Most of district is located in Tulsa ADI. Portions are in Fort Smith (Ark.) ADI and Joplin (Mo.)-Pittsburg (Kan.) ADI.

Industries:

St. Francis Hospital Inc.; Tulsa; hospital — 2,500. **The B. F. Goodrich Co.;** Miami; tires, inner tubes — 1,750. **Shell Oil Co. Inc.;** Tulsa; credit card center — 800. **Williams Bros. Engineering Co.** (Godsey-Earlougher Div. - HQ); Tulsa; pipeline engineering services — 700. **Brockway Glass Co. Inc.** (Glass Container Div.); Muskogee; containers — 650.

Corning Glass Works; Muskogee; glassware — 600. **Centrilift-Hughes Inc.** (HQ); Claremore; electric pumps — 550. **Acme Engineering & Mfg.;** Muskogee; fans, blowers — 500. **Colt Industries** (Holley Carburetor Div.); Sallisaw; emission control equipment — 500. **Fort Howard Paper Co.;** Muskogee; tissue paper — 500. **Stilwell Foods Inc.** (Chef-Ready Foods); Stilwell; frozen foods — 500.

3rd District

Southeast — "Little Dixie"

Situated in the region known as "Little Dixie," the 3rd has a more rural, more Southern character than any other part of the state. It was settled largely by migrants from Texas and Arkansas. Voters here are conservative, like most Oklahomans, but in their voting habits they are loyal to the Democratic Party. The 3rd has not elected a Republican to the House in the 75 years since statehood.

This loyalty remains largely because the area is far less prosperous than the rest of Oklahoma and suffers from a poor agricultural base. The "Little Dixie" region also missed out on the oil discoveries that brought wealth to the central and western sections of the state.

Wracked by rural depression, many counties lost about half their residents between 1920 and 1970. Coal County, for example, lost 68 percent of its population in that period; it began growing again only in the 1970s. The district's population increased 19 percent during the 1970s, but the main cause of the earlier exodus — failing agriculture — continues to hamper economic growth in the region.

Beef production is the source of much of the economic activity that does exist in the 3rd District, but the region lacks the expansive ranches common in western Oklahoma. There is a growing timber industry in the southeastern corner of the district, particularly in McCurtain County, where the Weyerhaeuser Co. has located a fiberboard manufacturing plant. There also is some oil exploration in the counties on the eastern side of the district.

The redistricting plan removed five rural counties from the 3rd: Garvin, Stephens, Cotton and Jefferson, near the Texas border in south-central Oklahoma; and Haskell, in Little Dixie. It added two more urbanized counties in the center of the state. One of these is Payne County, north of Oklahoma City, which includes Oklahoma State University in Stillwater. The other is Pottawatomie County, whose county seat, Shawnee, is a regional commercial center. Unlike the rest of the district, the two new counties gave Ronald Reagan solid majorities in the 1980 election.

Election Returns

3rd District		Democrat		Republican	
1976	President	110,972	(60.3%)	71,260	(38.7%)
	House	148,849	(81.6%)	31,990	(17.5%)
1978	Governor	81,052	(62.7%)	47,358	(36.6%)
	Senate	90,364	(69.8%)	36,597	(28.3%)
	House	18,574	(64.3%)	10,301	(35.7%)
1980	President	86,781	(45.9%)	95,640	(50.5%)
	Senate	101,922	(54.7%)	80,191	(43.0%)
	House	21,032	(55.7%)	16,698	(44.3%)
1982	Governor	107,304	(73.0%)	39,525	(26.9%)
	House	121,670	(82.2%)	26,335	(17.8%)

Demographics

Population: 504,268. **Percent Change from 1970:** 20.1%.
Land Area: 17,313 square miles. **Population per Square Mile:** 29.1.

Counties, 1980 Population: Atoka — 12,748; Bryan — 30,535; Carter — 43,610; Choctaw — 17,203; Coal — 6,041; Hughes — 14,338; Johnston — 10,356; Latimer — 9,840; Le Flore — 40,698; Lincoln — 26,601; Love — 7,469; Marshall — 10,550; McCurtain — 36,151; Murray — 12,147; Payne — 62,435; Pittsburg — 40,524; Pontotoc — 32,598; Pottawatomie (Pt.) — 51,178; Pushmataha — 11,773; Seminole — 27,473.

Cities, 1980 Population: Ada — 15,902; Ardmore — 23,689; Durant — 11,972; McAlester — 17,255; Oklahoma City (Pt.) — 51; Shawnee — 26,506; Stillwater — 38,268.

Race and Ancestry: White — 87.0%; Black — 4.4%; American Indian, Eskimo and Aleut — 7.6%; Asian and Pacific Islander — 0.4%. Spanish Origin — 1.1%. Dutch — 0.7%; English — 14.9%; French — 0.8%; German — 4.4%; Irish — 6.7%; Italian — 0.5%.

Universities, Enrollment: Carl Albert Junior College, Poteau — 1,858; East Central Oklahoma State University, Ada — 3,973; Eastern Oklahoma State College, Wilburton — 2,326; Murray State College, Tishomingo — 1,449; Oklahoma Baptist University, Shawnee — 1,524; Oklahoma State University, Stillwater — 22,490; St. Gregory's College, Shawnee — 341; Seminole Junior College, Seminole — 1,460; Southeastern Oklahoma State University, Durant — 4,335.

Newspapers, Circulation: *The Ada Evening News* (eS), Ada — 9,587; *Citizen* (eS), Cushing — 3,681; *The Daily Ardmoreite* (eS), Ardmore — 13,085; *Durant Daily Democrat* (eS), Durant — 7,035; *McAlester News-Capital & Democrat* (eS), McAlester — 12,041; *McCurtain Daily Gazette* (eS), Idabel — 6,045; *News* (eS), Holdenville — 2,347; *News* (e), Hugo — 3,150; *News-Press* (eS), Stillwater — 9,701; *The Seminole Producer* (eS), Seminole — 5,877; *Shawnee News-Star* (mS), Shawnee — 14,615; *Wewoka Daily Times* (eS), Wewoka — 2,318. Oklahoma City *Daily Oklahoman* also circulates in the district.

Commercial Television Stations, Affiliation: KTEN, Ada (ABC, NBC); KXII, Ardmore (CBS, NBC). District is divided among Ardmore-Ada ADI, Oklahoma City ADI, Tulsa ADI, Fort Smith (Ark.) ADI and Shreveport (La.)-Texarkana (Texas) ADI.

Military Installations: McAlester Army Ammunition Plant, McAlester — 1,055.

Industries:

Uniroyal Inc.; Ardmore; tires — 1,700. **Weyerhaeuser Co.;** Wright City; lumber, building materials — 1,700. **Blue Bell Inc.;** Seminole; work, sports clothing — 1,350. **Brunswick Corp.** (Mercury Marine #14); Stillwater; outboard motors — 800. **Stromberg-Carlson Corp.;** Ardmore; aircraft communications equipment — 650. **Holly Creek Fryers Inc.;** Broken Bow; poultry processing — 600. **Weyerhaeuser Co.;** Broken Bow; particleboard — 600. **Halliburton Co.** (Halliburton Services); Davis oil, gas field services — 555. **Weyerhaeuser Co.;** Valliant; paper products — 550.

4th District

Southwest; Part of Oklahoma City

This slice of southwestern Oklahoma has had a military flavor in the past, and it will have a stronger one in the 1980s. Already the home of Altus Air Force Base and Fort Sill, near the Texas border, the 4th District now also includes Tinker Air Force Base, just east of Oklahoma City.

The district's urban pockets are in eastern Oklahoma County around the Tinker base and extending into southeastern Oklahoma City; Cleveland County, where the University of Oklahoma in Norman is a major influence; and Lawton, the commercial center of southwest Oklahoma. Cleveland and Oklahoma counties together supply 40 percent of the voters in the district.

Oklahoma's energy boom brought new oil and gas business to the southwestern counties in the 1970s. Economic growth also is occurring in Norman, where the university is drawing high-technology industries. The remainder of the district focuses on agriculture, with cotton, wheat and livestock producers based in Garvin, Stephens, Jefferson and Cotton counties; these four counties were acquired from the 3rd through redistricting.

The population of the old district increased by 21 percent between 1970 and 1980, but the growth was lopsided. Counties close to Oklahoma City, including Cleveland, McClain and Grady, grew by as much as 63 percent, while the counties along the Texas border either held steady or lost population. The boom counties heavily favored Ronald Reagan in 1980 voting, while the low-growth areas were about evenly divided in their preferences in the national election.

Election Returns

4th District		Democrat		Republican	
1976	President	82,330	(54.3%)	67,060	(44.2%)
	House	104,021	(73.7%)	33,393	(23.6%)
1978	Governor	59,908	(55.4%)	47,219	(43.7%)
	Senate	76,306	(72.1%)	28,153	(26.6%)
	House	44,729	(58.9%)	31,163	(41.1%)
1980	President	58,544	(36.0%)	95,129	(58.6%)
	Senate	72,949	(46.8%)	77,526	(49.7%)
	House	55,411	(50.6%)	54,008	(49.4%)
1982	Governor	85,519	(65.4%)	44,849	(34.3%)
	House	84,205	(65.0%)	44,351	(34.3%)

Demographics

Population: 505,869. **Percent Change from 1970:** 24.3%.

Land Area: 8,253 square miles. **Population per Square Mile:** 61.3.

Counties, 1980 Population: Cleveland — 133,173; Comanche — 112,456; Cotton — 7,338; Garvin — 27,856; Grady — 39,490; Jackson — 30,356; Jefferson — 8,183; McClain — 20,291; Oklahoma (Pt.) — 66,848; Pottawatomie (Pt.) — 4,061; Stephens — 43,419; Tillman — 12,398.

Cities, 1980 Population: Altus — 23,101; Chickasha — 15,828; Del City (Pt.) — 0; Duncan — 22,517; Lawton — 80,054; Midwest City (Pt.) — 39,108; Moore — 35,063; Norman — 68,020; Oklahoma City (Pt.) — 38,380.

Race and Ancestry: White — 87.2%; Black — 6.3%; American Indian, Eskimo and Aleut — 3.1%; Asian and Pacific Islander — 1.2%. Spanish Origin — 3.2%. Dutch — 0.7%; English — 14.0%; French — 1.0%; German — 6.0%; Irish — 5.7%.

Universities, Enrollment: Cameron University, Lawton — 4,437; Oscar Rose Junior College, Midwest City — 8,753; University of Oklahoma, Norman — 24,289; University of Science and Arts of Oklahoma, Chickasha — 1,296; Western Oklahoma State College, Altus — 1,851.

Newspapers, Circulation: *The Altus Times* (eS), Altus — 7,791; *The Chickasha Daily Express* (eS), Chickasha — 5,715; *Daily Leader* (eS), Frederick — 2,802; *The Duncan Banner* (eS), Duncan — 11,269; *Lawton Constitution* (eS), Lawton — 18,291; *Lawton Morning Press* (mS), Lawton — 14,726; *The Norman Transcript* (eS), Norman — 15,875; *Pauls Valley Daily Democrat* (eS), Pauls Valley — 3,817. Oklahoma City *Daily Oklahoman* and *Oklahoman City Times* also circulate in the district.

Commercial Television Stations, Affiliation: KGPC, Lawton (None); KSWO-TV, Lawton (ABC). District is divided between Oklahoma City ADI and Wichita Falls (Texas)-Lawton ADI.

Military Installations: Altus Air Force Base, Altus — 4,269; Fort Sill, Lawton — 22,526; Oklahoma City Air Force Station, Midwest City — 624; Tinker Air Force Base, Midwest City — 26,130.

Industries:

Halliburton Co. (Welex); Duncan; oil field services — 3,850. **Goodyear Tire & Rubber Co. Inc.;** Lawton; tires, inner tubes — 1,150. **Maremont Corp.;** Chickasha; shock absorbers — 800. **Chromalloy American Corp.;** Oklahoma City; aircraft parts — 600. **Halliburton Co.** (Halliburton Service Div.); Duncan; oil field machinery — 500.

5th District

North Central — Part of Oklahoma City; Bartlesville

The 5th was a major point of contention in the Republican challenge to the Legislature's remap. Formerly a compact district concentrated in Oklahoma City, it was redrawn to stretch 175 miles from Oklahoma City to Bartlesville, "quarantining" Republican voters in a single constituency so they could do little harm to Democrats in other districts. It is undeniably safe for Republicans, but it will be a difficult district to represent or campaign in.

The old 5th was the state's slowest-growing district in the 1970s, and it needed 45,000 new residents to bring it up to the ideal population. To accomplish this within the confines of a partisan strategy, Democratic legislators attached Logan, Noble, Kay and parts of Osage and Washington counties to the district, running it to the Kansas border. The new counties all have Republican voting habits, but the most important GOP bastion is Washington County, where Bartlesville is located. Oil-oriented Washington County gave Ronald Reagan 74 percent of the vote in 1980.

Before redistricting, all of Oklahoma City was in the 5th. For the 1980s, however, the sprawling city is split among the 4th, 5th and 6th districts. The northern portion and the well-to-do suburbs of Nichols Hills and The Village remain in the 5th, downtown and the northeastern neighborhoods went to the 6th, and the southeastern part of town was placed in the 4th. The 5th lost much of the black population of Oklahoma City, a help to most GOP candidates.

Oil is a potent force in the 5th District as it is in the other Oklahoma City districts. The city contains the most famous symbols of the state's oil wealth: working wells on the state capitol grounds and the lawn of the governor's residence.

Logan, Noble and Osage counties are more sparsely populated than the rest of the 5th, and cattle ranching and wheat farming provide a livelihood for many of the residents in these rural counties.

Election Returns

5th District		Democrat		Republican	
1976	President	87,988	(42.0%)	117,924	(56.3%)
	House	105,778	(51.9%)	94,245	(46.3%)
1978	Governor	63,359	(42.3%)	83,723	(55.9%)
	Senate	87,483	(62.0%)	51,072	(36.2%)
	House	48,430	(38.7%)	76,826	(61.3%)
1980	President	55,490	(25.4%)	150,272	(68.9%)

Oklahoma City

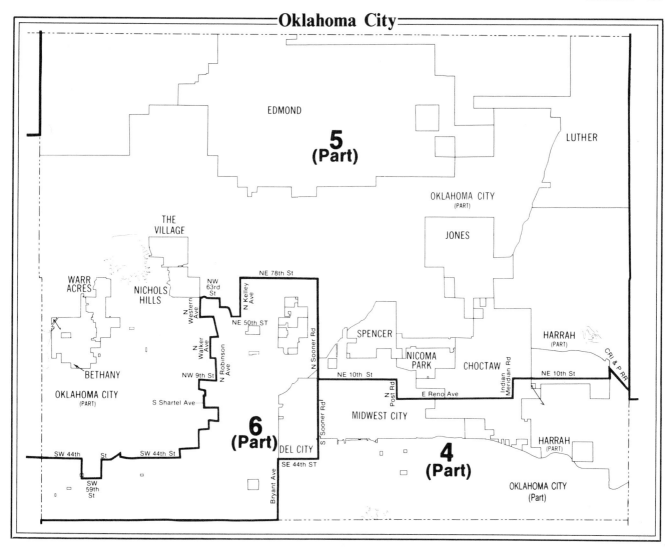

5th District		Democrat		Republican	
1980	Senate	74,526	(36.4%)	121,677	(59.4%)
	House	65,071	(37.5%)	103,604	(59.7%)
1982	Governor	79,962	(50.4%)	77,371	(48.8%)
	House	42,453	(28.9%)	98,979	(67.2%)

Demographics

Population: 502,974. **Percent Change from 1970:** 17.1%.

Land Area: 4,157 square miles. **Population per Square Mile:** 121.0.

Counties, 1980 Population: Canadian (Pt.) — 24,147; Kay — 49,852; Logan — 26,881; Noble — 11,573; Oklahoma (Pt.) — 339,423; Osage (Pt.) — 7,047; Washington (Pt.) — 44,051.

Cities, 1980 Population: Bartlesville — 34,568; Bethany — 22,130; Edmond — 34,637; Guthrie — 10,312; Midwest City (Pt.) — 10,451; Oklahoma City (Pt.) — 231,719; Ponca City — 26,238; The Village — 11,049; Yukon (Pt.) — 16,369.

Race and Ancestry: White — 88.7%; Black — 6.1%; American Indian, Eskimo and Aleut — 2.9%; Asian and Pacific Islander — 0.9%. Spanish Origin — 2.0%. Dutch — 0.7%; English — 13.6%; French — 0.8%; German — 7.0%; Irish — 4.6%.

Universities, Enrollment: Bartlesville Wesleyan College, Bartlesville —

645; Bethany Nazarene College, Bethany — 1,378; Central State University, Edmond — 11,723; Langston University, Langston — 1,322; Northern Oklahoma College, Tonkawa — 1,813; Oklahoma Christian College, Oklahoma City — 1,564; Oklahoma City Southwestern College, Oklahoma City — 835; Oklahoma City University, Oklahoma City — 2,817; Oklahoma State University - Technical Institute, Oklahoma City — 2,634.

Newspapers, Circulation: *Blackwell Journal-Tribune* (eS), Blackwell — 4,203; *Edmond Evening Sun* (eS), Edmond — 6,722; *Examiner-Enterprise* (eS), Bartlesville — 13,270; *Guthrie Daily Leader* (eS), Guthrie — 3,951; *Journal* (e), Perry — 3,423; *The Ponca City News* (eS), Ponca City — 13,725. Oklahoma City *Daily Oklahoman* and *Oklahoman City Times* also circulate in the district.

Commercial Television Stations, Affiliation: KAUT, Oklahoma City (None); KGMC, Oklahoma City (None); KOCO-TV, Oklahoma City (ABC); KOKH-TV, Oklahoma City (None); KTBO-TV, Oklahoma City (None); KTVY-TV, Oklahoma City (NBC); KWTV, Oklahoma City (None). Most of district is located in Oklahoma City ADI. Portion is in Tulsa ADI.

Industries:

Western Electric Co. Inc.; Oklahoma City; telephone equipment — 4,500. **Continental Oil Co.;** Ponca City; petroleum refining — 4,200. **Magnetic Peripherals Inc.;** Oklahoma City; computer equipment — 3,000. **Phillips Petroleum Co.** (HQ); Bartlesville; petroleum refining — 3,000. **St. Anthony Hospital;** Oklahoma City; hospital — 2,100.

Baptist Medical Center; Oklahoma City; hospital — 2,000. **Fire-**

stone Tire & Rubber Co. (Dayton Tire & Rubber Div.); Oklahoma City; tires — 1,800. **Presbyterian Hospital Inc.;** Oklahoma City; hospital — 1,600. **Conoco Exploration Ltd.;** Ponca City; oil, gas exploration — 1,440. **Gulfstream American Corp.;** Bethany; aircraft — 1,000. **Macklanburg-Duncan Co.** (The Ames Div. - HQ); Oklahoma City; metal doors, frames — 900. **LSB Industries Inc.** (Industrial Advertising Assoc. - HQ); Oklahoma City; bearings, heating, cooling equipment — 875. **The Charles Machine Works Inc.;** Perry; construction equipment — 800.

Fred Jones Mfg. Co. (HQ); Oklahoma City; automotive parts — 750. **Yellow Freight System Inc.;** Oklahoma City; trucking — 750. **C M I Corp.** (HQ); Oklahoma City; industrial machine wholesaling — 650. **Brown & Root Inc.;** Morrison; construction — 630. **American Fidelity Corp.** (HQ); Oklahoma City; accident, health insurance — 600. **The Hertz Corp.;** Oklahoma City; car rental reservation center — 600. **Huffy Corp.;** Ponca City; bicycles — 550.

6th District

Western; Part of Oklahoma City

The new 6th unites rural western Oklahoma with downtown Oklahoma City, an odd combination that creates a constituency with little common politics or sense of identity.

For decades, Oklahoma City was a Democratic center, balancing Tulsa's Republicanism. By the 1980s the city as a whole had begun to shift its allegiance to national Republican candidates. But the 40 percent of the city included in the new 6th was expected to be good Democratic territory. It includes most of Oklahoma City's 60,000 blacks.

Beyond Oklahoma City, the 6th sweeps west 300 miles across the dusty plains to the New Mexico border. Western Oklahoma was part of the Dust Bowl devastated by droughts and soil erosion in the 1930s and 1940s. It has recovered and is home to massive wheat farms and cattle ranches. Lack of water is still a chronic problem here; attempts to transport water from the lusher eastern section of the state are a regular feature of Oklahoma politics.

Western Oklahoma is the state's most conservative region; residents of this area share a general aversion to most governmental spending other than military activities and agricultural subsidies. Some of the counties gave Ronald Reagan more than 70 percent of their vote in 1980.

The new map removed Payne, Noble, Kay and Logan counties from the 6th District and brought in Harmon and Caddo counties.

Election Returns

6th District		Democrat		Republican	
1976	President	83,601	(45.6%)	97,052	(53.0%)
	House	127,640	(69.0%)	55,746	(30.1%)
1978	Governor	58,201	(42.3%)	77,844	(56.6%)
	Senate	85,268	(64.1%)	45,868	(34.5%)
	House	81,143	(65.1%)	43,433	(34.9%)
1980	President	60,622	(32.1%)	120,834	(64.0%)
	Senate	63,707	(36.0%)	109,525	(61.9%)
	House	92,910	(59.0%)	64,466	(41.0%)
1982	Governor	92,359	(63.5%)	52,649	(36.2%)
	House	102,811	(75.4%)	33,519	(24.6%)

Demographics

Population: 503,291. **Percent Change from 1970:** 4.1%.

Land Area: 25,638 square miles. **Population per Square Mile:** 19.6.

Counties, 1980 Population: Alfalfa — 7,077; Beaver — ˙6,806; Beckham — 19,243; Blaine — 13,443; Caddo — 30,905; Canadian (Pt.) — 32,305; Cimarron — 3,648; Custer — 25,995; Dewey — 5,922; Ellis — 5,596; Garfield — 62,820; Grant — 6,518; Greer — 7,028; Harmon — 4,519; Harper — 4,715; Kingfisher — 14,187; Kiowa — 12,711; Major — 8,772; Oklahoma (Pt.) — 162,662; Roger Mills — 4,799; Texas — 17,727; Washita — 13,798; Woods — 10,923; Woodward — 21,172.

Cities, 1980 Population: Del City (Pt.) — 28,424; El Reno — 15,486; Enid — 50,363; Oklahoma City (Pt.) — 133,063; Woodward — 13,610; Yukon (Pt.) — 743.

Race and Ancestry: White — 84.9%; Black — 9.8%; American Indian, Eskimo and Aleut — 3.4%; Asian and Pacific Islander — 0.5%. Spanish Origin — 2.7%. Dutch — 0.8%; English — 12.8%; French — 0.7%; German — 8.5%; Irish — 5.1%.

Universities, Enrollment: El Reno Junior College, El Reno — 1,365; Midwest Christian College, Oklahoma City — 115; Northwestern Oklahoma State University, Alva — 2,181; Oklahoma Panhandle State University, Goodwell — 1,250; Phillips University, Enid — 1,299; Sayre Junior College, Sayre — 391; South Oklahoma City Junior College, Oklahoma City — 7,345; Southwestern Oklahoma State University, Weatherford — 4,800.

Newspapers, Circulation: *The Anadarko Daily News* (eS), Anadarko — 5,959; *The Clinton Daily News* (eS), Clinton — 5,300; *The Daily Oklahoman* (mS), Oklahoma City — 181,599; *Democrat-Chief* (eS), Hobart — 2,994; *Eagle* (e), Enid — 9,870; *Elk City Daily News* (eS), Elk City — 4,911; *The El Reno Daily Tribune* (eS), El Reno — 5,270; *Herald* (eS), Guymon — 5,699; *News* (mS), Enid — 20,016; *Oklahoman City Times* (eS), Oklahoma City — 84,456; *Review-Courier* (eS), Alva — 3,985; *Weatherford Daily News* (eS), Weatherford — 3,736; *Woodward Daily Press* (eS), Woodward — 5,510.

Commercial Television Stations, Affiliation: KUIJ-TV, Sayre (ABC). Most of district is located in Oklahoma City ADI. Portions are in Amarillo (Texas) ADI, Wichita (Kan.)-Hutchinson (Kan.) ADI and Wichita Falls (Texas)-Lawton ADI.

Military Installations: Vance Air Force Base, Enid — 2,648; Will Rogers World Airport (Air Force), Oklahoma City — 1,100.

Industries:

General Motors Corp. (Assembly Div.); Oklahoma City; autos — 6,000. **Safeway Stores Inc.;** Oklahoma City; warehousing — 2,200. **Veterans Administration;** Oklahoma City; veterans' hospital — 1,400. **University Hospital;** Oklahoma City; hospital — 1,360. **First Oklahoma Bancorporation;** Oklahoma City; banking — 1,270.

Northrop Worldwide Aircraft Service Inc.; Enid; airport operations — 1,200. **Globe Life & Accident Insurance Co.;** Oklahoma City; hospital, accident insurance — 1,150. **Liberty National Corp.;** Oklahoma City; banking — 1,010. **Groendyke Investments Inc.;** Enid; trucking — 1,000. **Cooper Industries Inc.** (Demco Div.); Oklahoma City; oil field equipment — 910. **The Oklahoma Publishing Co.** (HQ); Oklahoma City; newspaper publishing; radio, television broadcasting — 900. **Transcon Lines;** Oklahoma City; trucking — 850. **Minnesota Mining & Mfg. Co.;** Weatherford; printing trades machinery — 840. **T G & Y Stores Co.** (HQ); Oklahoma City; grocery store chain — 800.

Azcon Corp. (George E. Failing Co.); Enid; drilling equipment — 750. **Champlin Petroleum Co.;** Enid; petroleum products — 700. **Chicago Rock Island Pacific Railroad Co.;** El Reno; railroad operations — 700. **Cooper Industries Inc.** (Demco Div.); Oklahoma City; oilfield equipment — 700. **Phillips Petroleum;** Oklahoma City; oil, gas exploration — 600. **Pool Well Service;** Oklahoma City; oil well service — 522. **Allied Maintenance Corp.** Oklahoma City; janitorial services — 500. **Fidelity Bank;** Oklahoma City; banking — 500. **Star Mfg. Co. of Oklahoma** (HQ); Oklahoma City; prefabricated buildings — 500.

Oregon

More than a half-million people migrated to Oregon during the 1970s, earning the state its fifth seat in the House of Representatives, a distinction that barely eluded it 10 years earlier. In the 1971 reapportionment, Oregon fell just 235 shy of the number of people needed to jump from four to five representatives.

The Democratic-controlled state Legislature approved the new redistricting bill in late July 1981. The House voted 40-20 on July 27, 1981; the Senate concurred the following day, voting 19-10. Republican Gov. Victor L. Atiyeh signed the measure Aug. 22, 1981.

Instead of trying to undermine GOP strength through gerrymandering techniques, Democratic state legislators set the less ambitious but more practical goal of drawing a redistricting map to protect the state's three House Democrats. To that end, the remap solidified Republican Party control in the 2nd District in a way that aided the 4th District Democratic incumbent. The new 5th District in the Willamette Valley was taken mostly from the western part of the old 2nd, which gave the new district a Republican tilt but tampered little with neighboring Democratic districts. In the 1982 elections the GOP held on to its one seat and picked up the new one.

Age of Population

District	Population Under 18	Voting Age Population	Population 65 & Over (% of VAP)	Median Age
1	139,445	387,395	59,440 (15.3%)	30.8
2	152,902	374,066	64,403 (17.2%)	30.8
3	132,370	394,345	68,230 (17.3%)	30.5
4	147,787	378,675	56,042 (14.8%)	29.8
5	150,553	375,567	55,221 (14.7%)	29.2
State	723,057	1,910,048	303,336 (15.9%)	30.2

Income and Occupation

District	Median Family Income	White Collar Workers	Blue Collar Workers	Service Workers	Farm Workers
1	$ 22,669	58.4%	26.3%	11.6%	3.7%
2	17,584	45.5	30.6	14.9	9.0
3	20,234	55.9	29.4	13.8	1.0
4	18,831	47.9	32.2	14.2	5.7
5	20,949	54.0	28.6	13.1	4.3
State	$ 20,027	52.7%	29.3%	13.5%	4.6%

Education: School Years Completed

District	8 Years or Fewer	4 Years of High School	4 Years of College or More	Median School Years
1	9.5%	34.2%	23.8%	12.9
2	12.8	40.0	13.6	12.6
3	11.3	36.9	16.9	12.7
4	12.2	37.6	15.9	12.6
5	11.5	37.0	19.0	12.7
State	11.5%	37.1%	17.9%	12.7

Housing and Residential Patterns

District	Owner Occupied	Renter Occupied	Urban	Rural
1	61.9%	38.1%	69.7%	30.3%
2	69.5	30.5	48.5	51.5
3	60.2	39.8	98.4	1.6
4	67.0	33.0	56.8	43.2
5	67.6	32.4	66.2	33.8
State	65.1%	34.9%	67.9%	32.1%

1st District

Western Portland and Suburbs

The new 1st District remains Democratic, but Republican strength should make Democratic candidates uneasy. The new boundaries enhance the electoral influence of west Portland and adjoining Washington County suburbs, areas where the GOP gained strength during the 1970s.

The Willamette River cuts through the city of Port-

OREGON

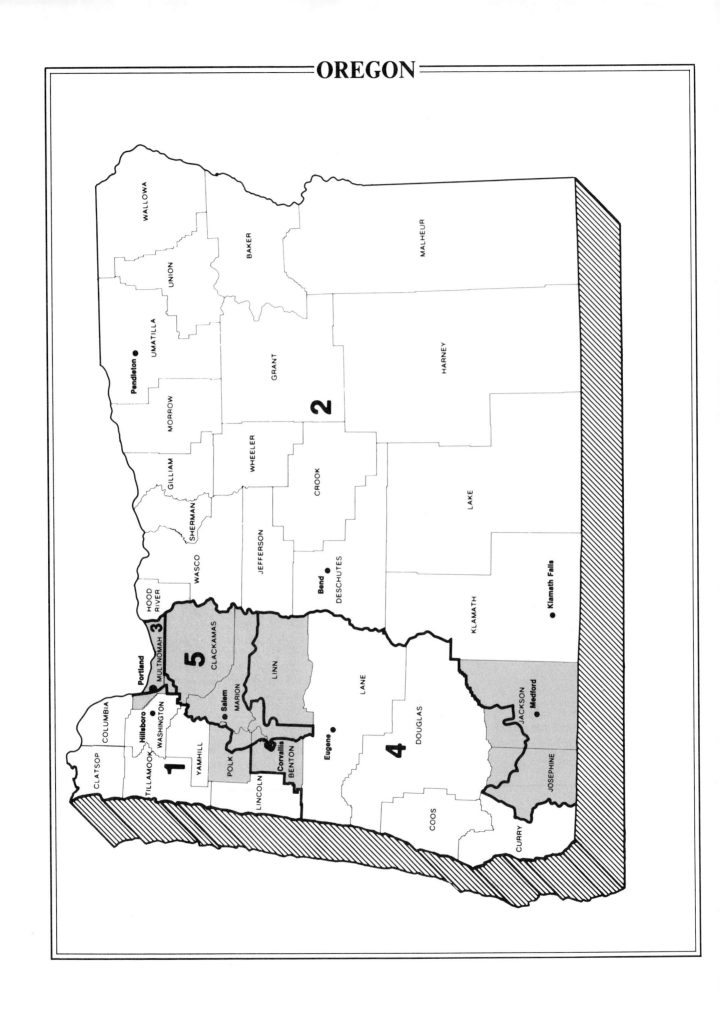

land, separating the 1st and 3rd districts. Most of Portland's population lives east of the river, in the 3rd. West of the river, in the 1st, are the downtown business district and the city's wealthier residential sections.

Downtown Portland (Multnomah County) is the hub of a metropolitan area of more than 1.2 million people, the largest between Seattle and San Francisco. Many banks, businesses and law firms are headquartered here, and their executives live in the fashionable West Hills area of the city not far from their offices.

Much of this affluent professional community identifies with the Republican Party, but Democrats have considerable strength here and independent voters wield decisive influence. In 1980 independent presidential candidate John B. Anderson won nearly 14 percent of the vote in western Multnomah County, leaving Jimmy Carter and Ronald Reagan virtually tied.

As one moves west into Washington County, GOP power increases. Republicans outnumbered Democrats in the county in 1980 for the first time. The county's population grew 55 percent during the 1970s as modest-sized bedroom communities such as Beaverton, Tigard and Hillsboro blossomed into economic satellites of Portland, with electronics and computer firms such as Intel and Tektronix providing jobs.

The strongest Democratic areas of the district are along the Columbia River and Pacific coast in the fishing and logging counties of Columbia, Clatsop, Tillamook and Lincoln. Columbia has voted for every Democratic presidential candidate since 1932; Clatsop went for Adlai E. Stevenson in 1956 and has stayed Democratic since.

Many portions of these counties are economically dependent on the lumber industry, which was hard hit by the early 1980s recession. Astoria (Clatsop County) hoped to find economic salvation by improving its harbor facilities to handle large shipments of coal from Western states to new markets in Japan, Korea and Taiwan.

Tourism props up the economy in some coastal areas, with towns such as Seaside, Cannon Beach, Lincoln City and Newport drawing visitors from Portland and other inland population centers.

Filling out the district are northern and western Polk County and Yamhill County, which are predominantly agricultural areas in the Willamette River Valley. Important crops grown and processed there are grass seed, hazelnuts and strawberries. Dropped from the 1st by redistricting were the southeast corner of Polk County and all the former district's territory in Benton County, including the city of Corvallis.

Election Returns

1st District		Democrat		Republican	
1976	President	92,985	(43.5%)	112,179	(52.5%)
	House	118,518	(59.1%)	81,905	(40.9%)
1978	Governor	86,588	(44.6%)	106,833	(55.1%)
	Senate	66,399	(34.9%)	123,544	(65.0%)
	House	121,910	(63.9%)	68,765	(36.1%)
1980	President	96,633	(38.2%)	119,438	(47.2%)
	Senate	102,740	(42.8%)	128,228	(53.4%)
	House	156,163	(66.1%)	80,186	(33.9%)
1982	Governor	72,124	(32.3%)	145,191	(65.1%)
	House	118,638	(53.8%)	101,720	(46.2%)

Demographics

Population: 526,840. **Percent Change from 1970:** 32.4%.

Land Area: 5,675 square miles. **Population per Square Mile:** 92.8.

Counties, 1980 Population: Clatsop — 32,489; Columbia — 35,646; Lincoln — 35,264; Multnomah (Pt.) — 89,596; Polk (Pt.) — 11,541; Tillamook — 21,164; Washington — 245,808; Yamhill — 55,332.

Cities, 1980 Population: Beaverton — 30,582; Forest Grove — 11,499; Hillsboro — 27,664; Lake Oswego (Pt.) — 1,214; McMinnville — 14,080; Newberg — 10,394; Portland (Pt.) — 80,185; Tigard — 14,286.

Race and Ancestry: White — 95.6%; Black — 0.5%; American Indian, Eskimo and Aleut — 0.7%; Asian and Pacific Islander — 1.8%. Spanish Origin — 2.2%. Dutch — 1.0%; English — 9.8%; French — 0.9%; German — 8.8%; Irish — 3.3%; Italian — 0.9%; Norwegian — 1.7%; Polish — 0.5%; Scottish — 1.0%; Swedish — 1.6%.

Universities, Enrollment: Bassist College, Portland — 159; Clatsop Community College, Astoria — 2,865; George Fox College, Newberg — 731; Lewis and Clark College, Portland — 3,188; Linfield College, McMinnville — 1,242; Museum Art School, Portland — 191; Oregon Graduate Center, Beaverton — 61; Oregon Polytechnic Institute, Portland — 55; Pacific University, Forest Grove — 1,101; Portland Community College, Portland — 20,458; Portland State University, Portland — 16,798; University of Oregon Health Sciences Center, Portland — 1,524.

Newspapers, Circulation: *The Daily Astorian* (e), Astoria — 9,406; *Daily Journal of Commerce* (m), Portland — 4,079; *The Oregonian* (mS), Portland — 245,623; *Oregon Journal* (e), Portland — 105,247.

Commercial Television Stations, Affiliation: KGW-TV, Portland (NBC); KOIN-TV, Portland (CBS); KPTV, Portland (None). Entire district is located in Portland ADI. *(For other Portland stations, see 3rd district.)*

Military Installations: Mount Hebo Air Force Station, Hebo — 11.

Nuclear Power Plants: Trojan, Rainier (Westinghouse, Bechtel), May 1976.

Industries:

Tektronix Inc. (HQ); Beaverton; electronic instruments — 15,000. Intel Corp.; Hillsboro; integrated circuits — 3,000. **Good Samaritan Hospital & Medical Center;** Portland; hospital — 2,800. **Burlington Northern Inc.;** Portland; railroad operations — 2,700. **Nike Inc. (HQ);** Beaverton; sporting equipment — 2,000.

St. Vincent's Hospital; Portland; hospital — 1,700. **United States National Bank of Oregon (HQ);** Portland; banking — 1,600. **Wallace Security Agency Inc.;** Portland; security services — 1,500. **ESCO Corp. (HQ);** Portland; steel foundry, construction equipment — 1,400. **Union Pacific Railroad Co.;** Portland; railroad operations — 1,300. **Veterans Administration;** Portland; veterans' hospital — 1,200. **Hoffman Construction Co.;** Portland; general contracting — 1,000. **Georgia-Pacific Corp.** (Toledo Paper Div.); Toledo; paper, paperboard mills — 900. **Crown Zellerbach Corp.** (Wauna Mill); Clatskanie; pulp, paper products — 843. **Consolidated Freightways Corp.;** Portland; accounting services — 800. **Guy F. Atkinson Co. Inc.** (Bingham Willamette); Portland; industrial measuring instruments — 750. **Georgia-Pacific Corp.** (HQ); Portland; plywood, lumber — 750.

Intel Corp.; Beaverton; integrated circuits — 750. **Floating Point Systems Inc. (HQ);** Beaverton; electronic computing equipment — 675. **First Farwest Corp.;** Portland; accident, health insurance — 670. **Southern Pacific Transportation Co.;** Portland; railroad operations — 660. **Northwest Hospital Service Inc.** (Blue Cross of Oregon - HQ); Portland; health insurance — 654. **Boise Cascade Corp.;** Saint Helens; paper mills — 635. **Wacker Siltronic Corp.;** Portland; industrial organic chemicals — 600. **A/DEC Inc.;** Newberg; dental equipment — 571. **Electro-Scientific Industries** (Esicom Group - HQ); Portland; precision measuring instruments — 544. **FMC Corp.** (Marine & Rail Equipment Div.); Portland; shipbuilding, railroad equipment — 505. **Amfac Nurseries Inc.** (Glenn Walters Nursery); Hillsboro; nursery — 500. **First Interstate Bank of Oregon (HQ);** Portland; banking — 500. **Marriott Corp.** (Marriott Portland Hotel); Portland; hotel — 500.

2nd District

East and Southwest — Bend, Medford

Eastern Oregon's "desert district" changed hands in 1980 for the first time in nearly a quarter-century, as a Republican unseated veteran Democratic Rep. Al Ullman. And the 1982 remap enhanced GOP chances of holding on to the seat. After severing the Willamette Valley from the 2nd, the Legislature added most of Josephine and Jackson counties to the 2nd District's southwest corner. Both counties usually vote Republican.

There are more jackrabbits in the new 2nd than there are voters, so any congressional candidate has to focus his efforts on the few widely scattered population centers where the overwhelming majority of the district's people live.

In the southwest, Jackson County (Medford) and Josephine County (Grants Pass) together contain one-third of the people in the 2nd. Medford is surrounded by pear, peach and apple orchards of the fruit-growing Rogue River Valley. The lumber industry also plays a prominent role in Medford, but the sawmills there are having as much difficulty surviving as those elsewhere in the state. With nearly 40,000 people, Medford is the district's largest city.

Lumbering is the main work in Grants Pass; also contributing to the economy are dairy cattle and visitors to the nearby Siskiyou National Forest. Ronald Reagan won Josephine County by a two-to-one margin in 1980.

A candidate working Jackson and Josephine counties would also schedule a stop in Klamath Falls, 75 miles east of Medford. Other than Medford and Grants Pass, it is the only sizable town in the southwest section of the district. Though the lush forests become drier and thinner on the way east to Klamath Falls, lumbering is still important there. Fishermen are drawn to Upper Klamath Lake, north of town.

The fastest growing county in Oregon during the 1970s was Deschutes; the county's largest population center is Bend, a town of 17,263 in the west central part of the district. Population in Deschutes soared 104 percent during the decade as the majestic Three Sisters Wilderness Area and the Mount Bachelor Winter Sports Area lured people to build summer homes and vacation condominiums. Many of Deschutes' newcomers are young people.

Most of eastern Oregon is a sparsely populated plateau dusted with sagebrush and dry grasses. The only towns of any significance are Baker (Baker County), Burns (Harney County) and Ontario (Malheur County). All have fewer than 9,000 people.

In the northern part of the 2nd, most people live along or near the irrigated Columbia River Valley, where wheat ripens on steep golden hillsides. The largest town in the area is Pendleton (Umatilla County), with nearly 15,000 people. Cattle and livestock are raised in the county, and Pendleton holds an annual rodeo. Like most of the counties in northern Oregon, Umatilla County is solidly Republican.

The population centers in the district's northwest corner are The Dalles and Hood River, both on the Columbia River. Wheat and grass are grown around The Dalles; Hood River processes cherries and other fruits grown in the Hood River valley to the south. Jimmy Carter won Wasco County (The Dalles) in 1976, but that was an aberration from its usual GOP allegiance.

Election Returns

2nd District		Democrat		Republican	
1976	President	87,938	(45.8%)	96,543	(50.2%)
	House	109,405	(59.4%)	64,043	(34.8%)
1978	Governor	62,512	(37.4%)	103,419	(61.8%)
	Senate	65,252	(40.1%)	96,739	(59.4%)
	House	98,635	(61.4%)	61,604	(38.3%)
1980	President	59,546	(31.8%)	108,856	(58.2%)
	Senate	80,075	(36.0%)	135,944	(61.1%)
	House	106,864	(47.8%)	111,840	(50.0%)
1982	Governor	61,704	(31.0%)	131,610	(66.1%)
	House	85,495	(44.4%)	106,912	(55.6%)

Demographics

Population: 526,968. **Percent Change from 1970:** 34.2%.

Land Area: 70,507 square miles. **Population per Square Mile:** 7.5.

Counties, 1980 Population: Baker — 16,134; Crook — 13,091; Deschutes — 62,142; Gilliam — 2,057; Grant — 8,210; Harney — 8,314; Hood River — 15,835; Jackson (Pt.) — 122,702; Jefferson — 11,599; Josephine (Pt.) — 50,348; Klamath — 59,117; Lake — 7,532; Malheur — 26,896; Morrow — 7,519; Sherman — 2,172; Umatilla — 58,861; Union — 23,921; Wallowa — 7,273; Wasco — 21,732; Wheeler — 1,513.

Cities, 1980 Population: Ashland — 14,943; Bend — 17,263; City Of The Dalles — 10,820; Grants Pass — 15,032; Klamath Falls — 16,661; La Grande — 11,354; Medford — 39,603; Pendleton — 14,521.

Race and Ancestry: White — 95.3%; Black — 0.2%; American Indian, Eskimo and Aleut — 1.8%; Asian and Pacific Islander — 0.8%. Spanish Origin — 3.4%. Dutch — 1.2%; English — 11.8%; French — 1.4%; German — 9.9%; Irish — 5.1%; Italian — 0.9%; Norwegian — 1.3%; Scottish — 1.3%; Swedish — 1.6%.

Universities, Enrollment: Blue Mountain Community College, Pendleton — 2,300; Central Oregon Community College, Bend — 1,965; Eastern Oregon State College, La Grande — 1,770; Judson Baptist College, The Dalles — 311; Oregon Institute of Technology, Klamath Falls — 2,705; Rogue Community College, Grants Pass — 3,327; Southern Oregon State College, Ashland — 4,710; Treasure Valley Community College, Ontario — 1,336.

Newspapers, Circulation: *The Bulletin* (e), Bend — 18,868; *Daily Argus Observer* (e), Ontario — 7,570; *The Daily Tidings* (e), Ashland — 5,966; *The Dalles Chronicle* (e), The Dalles — 5,433; *Democrat-Herald* (e), Baker — 3,310; *East Oregonian* (e), Pendleton — 12,731; *Grants Pass Daily Courier* (e), Grants Pass — 15,998; *Herald and News* (eS), Klamath Falls — 18,643; *Medford Mail Tribune* (eS), Medford — 27,465; *The Observer* (e), La Grande — 6,574.

Commercial Television Stations, Affiliation: KOBI, Medford (ABC, CBS); KOTI, Klamath Falls (CBS, ABC); KTVL, Medford (CBS, NBC); KTVZ, Bend (CBS, NBC). Most of district is located in Portland ADI. Portions are in Bend ADI, Medford ADI, Boise (Idaho) ADI, Spokane (Wash.) ADI and Yakima (Wash.) ADI.

Military Installations: Kingsley Field (Air Force), Klamath Falls — 197; Umatilla Army Depot Activity, Hermiston — 292.

Industries:

Weyerhaeuser Co.; Klamath Falls; lumber products — 1,700. **J. R. Simplot Co.;** Hermiston; general crop services — 1,200. **Rogue Valley Memorial Hospital;** Medford; hospital — 1,200. **Ore-Ida Foods Inc.;** Ontario; frozen vegetables — 1,100. **Boise Cascade Corp.;** Medford; lumber, plywood — 1,000.

Medford Corp. (HQ); Medford; plywood, cabinets, lumber — 725. **Harry & David** (Bear Creek Orchard - HQ); Medford; fruit growers, mail-order operation — 695. **Lamb-Weston Inc.;** Hermiston; frozen potatoes — 600. **Diamond International Corp.** (Oregon Lumber Div.); Bend; lumber, plywood — 570. **Harris Pine Mills Inc.** (HQ); Pendelton; furniture — 500.

3rd District

Eastern Portland and Suburbs

Ninety percent of the people in the redrawn 3rd are residents of Multnomah County, Oregon's most populous county and a reliable provider of votes to Democratic candidates in congressional and most state elections.

The 3rd begins in Portland at the east bank of the Willamette River, the waterway that separates west Portland from the generally less elegant eastern part of the city.

Eastern Portland has a substantial population of working class people who labor in shipping trades. The city's freshwater port has been important since the mid-19th century, when it was the funnel through which pioneers poured south into the Willamette River Valley, the end of the Oregon Trail. Today Portland's port is a major departure point for Oregon's agricultural products.

The communities of northern Portland, all part of the 3rd, have the strongest blue-collar presence. Three-fourths of Oregon's 37,000 blacks live in the city, many in the Albina section. Moving further east, away from the Willamette, light manufacturing operations give way to comfortable middle-income neighborhoods such as Parkrose, with a blend of business and professional people.

Portland's population declined nearly 4 percent in the 1970s — a loss of more than 13,000 residents — but the overall population of Multnomah County was stabilized by rapid growth in suburbs east of the city, a few of which are as sumptuous as the in-town residential areas west of the Willamette. The largest of the suburban cities in the 3rd District is Gresham, which tripled in size during the 1970s, reaching a population of 33,005. Exceeding that growth rate was Troutdale, which lies north of Gresham.

Beyond suburbia, Multnomah's population quickly thins out. There are a few farms along the Columbia River, the northern boundary of the 3rd, but Mount Hood National Forest occupies most of the eastern part of the county.

The only changes made to the 3rd District by remapping were in the small Clackamas County portion of the district. The 3rd District lost some rural Clackamas territory and gained part of Lake Oswego, an upper-income bedroom community that tends to vote Republican. Remaining in the 3rd is most of Milwaukie, a Clackamas town east of Lake Oswego with a blue-collar population and warehousing facilities.

The political character of the 3rd is not affected by the boundary changes in Clackamas, where only 10 percent of the district's people live.

Election Returns

3rd District		Democrat		Republican	
1976	President	119,325	(52.7%)	98,753	(43.6%)
	House	142,760	(82.0%)	5,288	(3.0%)
1978	Governor	101,122	(52.5%)	91,247	(47.3%)
	Senate	78,890	(41.6%)	110,324	(58.2%)
	House	145,078	(96.4%)	5,118	(3.4%)
1980	President	110,009	(46.9%)	93,356	(39.8%)
	Senate	114,064	(50.3%)	104,714	(46.2%)
	House	153,351	(71.7%)	60,220	(28.2%)
1982	Governor	89,423	(42.0%)	118,444	(55.6%)
	House	159,416	(78.3%)	44,162	(21.7%)

Demographics

Population: 526,715. **Percent Change from 1970:** 2.6%.

Land Area: 354 square miles. **Population per Square Mile:** 1,487.9.

Counties, 1980 Population: Clackamas (Pt.) — 53,671; Multnomah (Pt.) — 473,044.

Cities, 1980 Population: Gresham — 33,005; Lake Oswego (Pt.) — 15,833; Milwaukie (Pt.) — 17,334; Portland (Pt.) — 285,922.

Race and Ancestry: White — 89.6%; Black — 5.5%; American Indian, Eskimo and Aleut — 0.9%; Asian and Pacific Islander — 2.9%. Spanish Origin — 2.0%. Dutch — 0.7%; English — 8.8%; French — 1.0%; German — 9.1%; Irish — 3.5%; Italian — 1.3%; Norwegian — 1.7%; Polish — 0.5%; Scottish — 0.8%; Swedish — 1.4%.

Universities, Enrollment: Columbia Christian College, Portland — 303; Concordia College, Portland — 345; Mount Hood Community College, Gresham — 10,165; Multnomah School of the Bible, Portland — 758; Reed College, Portland — 1,132; University of Portland, Portland — 2,746; Warner Pacific College, Portland — 423; Western Conservative Baptist Seminary, Portland — 516; Western States Chiropractic College, Portland — 496.

Newspapers, Circulation: Portland *Oregonian* and Portland *Oregon Journal* circulate in the district.

Commercial Television Stations, Affiliation: KATV, Portland (ABC). Entire district is located in Portland ADI. *(For other Portland stations, see 1st district.)*

Military Installations: Portland International Airport (Air Force), Portland — 1,835.

Industries:

Emanuel Lutheran Charity Board; Portland; hospital — 1,700. **Sisters of Providence in Oregon;** Portland; hospital — 1,700. **The Boeing Co. Inc.;** Portland; aircraft parts — 1,500. **Jantzen Inc.** (HQ); Portland; men's, women's sportswear — 1,350. **Precision Castparts Corp.** (HQ); Portland; steel investment foundry — 1,300.

Portland Adventist Medical Center; Portland; hospital — 1,150. **Freightliner Corp.** (HQ); Portland; trucks — 1,050. **Reynolds Metals Co.;** Troutdale; aluminum reduction — 930. **United Grocers Inc.** (HQ); Portland; grocery wholesalers — 750. **Crown Zellerbach Corp. Inc.** (Flexible Packaging); Portland; commercial printing — 700. **Paccar Inc.** (Wagner Mining Equipment Co. Div.); Portland; mining equipment — 700. **Nabisco Inc.** (Fireside Food Products Div.); Portland; biscuits — 650.

Oeco Corp. (HQ); Portland; transformers — 550. **Owens-Illinois Inc.;** Portland; glass containers — 550. **Gilmore Steel Corp.** (Oregon Steel Mills - HQ); Portland; steel plate — 545. **United Air Lines Inc.;** Portland; airline services — 502. **Dillingham Corp.;** Portland; ship repairing — 500. **Henkels & McCoy Inc.** (West Coast Div.); Portland; engineering services — 500.

4th District

Southwest — Eugene

The transferral of most of conservative Josephine and Jackson counties to the 2nd District was designed to aid the Democrats in the 4th district. Under the remap, more than one-half of the district's residents live in Lane County

(Eugene and Springfield). The University of Oregon and the timber industry are the two most important factors in the economy of Eugene and Springfield, which lie on opposite banks of the Willamette River. Eugene has more than 105,000 people, Springfield fewer than half that.

The university, with more than 17,000 students, is located in Eugene and its influence there is easily noticed. Many of the young people who came to the school in the 1960s and 1970s stayed in Eugene after graduation, enthralled with the beauty of the Cascade Mountains to the east and the Coastal Range to the west. As those former students moved into workaday society, they learned how to influence local politics and coalesce to elect their own candidates.

The Hoedads, a 500-member tree-planting cooperative, and other liberal elements have had an interesting impact on Lane County elections. In Oregon's 1976 presidential primary, California Governor Edmund G. Brown Jr., D, won the county on a write-in vote. In 1980, Lane was the second-best county in the nation for Citizens Party presidential nominee Barry Commoner.

Matched against this environmentalist faction are the lumber industry, developers and some lumber millworkers who are concerned about growth and jobs. This conflict prompts campaigns of remarkable intensity. Conservatives have been most effective in presidential elections: Richard Nixon carried Lane County in 1968 and 1972; Ronald Reagan won it in 1980. In contests for state and congressional offices, Democrats usually prevail.

Two other counties together make up nearly a third of the district's population — Douglas County (Roseburg) and Coos County (Coos Bay). With most of Josephine County out of the new 4th, Douglas County, a farming and sheep-raising area, is the Democrats' most significant conservative problem.

Coastal Coos County occasionally supports Democratic candidates; it went for Jimmy Carter in 1976, but shifted to Reagan in 1980. Coos County was crippled in the early 1980s with an unemployment rate exceeding 20 percent. The salmon fishermen of Coos Bay were pummeled by high fuel costs and bad weather and were losing ground to huge corporate aquaculture facilities that produced higher salmon yields. The lumber situation was equally bad; in Coos Bay and other coastal towns alone, 32 mills were closed, putting 5,000 workers out of work.

Redistricting made some changes on the northern border of the 4th, but none was likely to affect election outcomes. All of western Benton County and part of northern Linn County were brought into the 4th, but the population centers in those counties are both in the new 5th.

Election Returns

4th District		Democrat		Republican	
1976	President	102,060	(51.5%)	88,526	(44.6%)
	House	98,371	(53.3%)	58,478	(31.7%)
1978	Governor	84,939	(48.4%)	90,465	(51.5%)
	Senate	68,164	(40.1%)	101,711	(59.8%)
	House	97,980	(57.9%)	71,211	(42.1%)
1980	President	107,296	(38.2%)	138,645	(49.3%)
	Senate	111,374	(48.3%)	108,637	(47.1%)
	House	125,350	(56.9%)	94,652	(43.0%)
1982	Governor	85,164	(42.0%)	111,839	(55.2%)
	House	115,448	(59.1%)	80,054	(40.9%)

Demographics

Population: 526,462. **Percent Change from 1970:** 26.9%.

Land Area: 16,024 square miles. **Population per Square Mile:** 32.9.

Counties, 1980 Population: Benton (Pt.) — 13,390; Coos — 64,047; Curry — 16,992; Douglas — 93,748; Jackson (Pt.) — 9,754; Josephine (Pt.) — 8,507; Lane — 275,226; Linn (Pt.) — 44,596; Marion (Pt.) — 202.

Cities, 1980 Population: Coos Bay — 14,424; Eugene — 105,624; Lebanon — 10,413; Roseburg — 16,644; Springfield — 41,621.

Race and Ancestry: White — 96.7%; Black — 0.4%; American Indian, Eskimo and Aleut — 1.1%; Asian and Pacific Islander — 1.0%. Spanish Origin — 1.9%. Dutch — 0.8%; English — 10.9%; French — 1.0%; German — 7.9%; Irish — 3.5%; Italian — 0.6%; Norwegian — 1.4%; Polish — 0.5%; Scottish — 0.7%; Swedish — 1.0%.

Universities, Enrollment: Lane Community College, Eugene — 7,785; Northwest Christian College, Eugene — 275; Southwestern Oregon Community College, Coos Bay — 4,642; Umpqua Community College, Roseburg — 4,943; University of Oregon, Eugene — 17,379.

Newspapers, Circulation: *Eugene Register-Guard* (eS), Eugene — 63,594; *The News Review* (eS), Roseburg — 18,913; *The World* (e), Coos-Bay — 17,513. *Albany Democrat-Herald*, The Portland *Oregonian*, Portland *Oregon Journal*, *Medford Mail Tribune* and Salem *Statesman-Journal* also circulate in the district.

Commercial Television Stations, Affiliation: KCBY-TV, Coos Bay (NBC); KEZI-TV, Eugene (ABC, CBS); KMTR-TV, Eugene (NBC); KPIC, Roseburg (None); KVAL-TV, Eugene (NBC). Most of district is located in Eugene ADI. Portions are in Medford ADI, Portland ADI and Eureka (Calif.) ADI.

Military Installations: Coos Head Naval Facility, Charleston — 126.

Industries:

Roseburg Lumber Co. Inc. (HQ); Dillard; plywood, lumber — 2,000. **Weyerhaeuser Co.;.** Springfield; lumber mill — 1,800. **Weyerhaeuser Co.;** North Bend; lumber mills — 1,650. **Health & Hospital Services Inc.;** Eugene; hospital — 1,500. **Southern Pacific Transportation Co.;** Eugene; railroad terminal — 950.

5th District

Willamette Valley — Salem, Corvallis

The newly created 5th District is hardly the dream of a meticulous mapmaker. Created from parts of the 1st, 2nd and 4th districts, it does not contain an entire county, covering instead parts of five counties that lie on either side of the Willamette River as it runs south out of Portland.

Nearly all of Marion County (Salem) is included in the 5th; it contains 39 percent of the district's population. Salem is the capital of the state, so a substantial number of the residents are on the state payroll. Another revenue producer is the processing and canning of fruits, berries and vegetables grown in Oregon's fertile Willamette river valley.

Clackamas County, with 36 percent of the new district's population, has nearly as much clout in the 5th as Marion does. Clackamas County grew at a rate of approximately 46 percent during the 1970s, thanks partly to expansion of Portland suburbs into the northwest section of the county.

One of the most affluent of those suburbs is Lake Oswego, part of which is in the new 3rd District. Democrats have a considerable edge over Republicans among registered voters in Clackamas County, but some who label themselves Democrats frequently cross party lines to elect Republicans.

The other major city in the district is Corvallis (Benton County), home of Oregon State University. The redrawn 5th District also includes the western portion of Linn County as well as southeastern Polk County.

Election Returns

5th District		Democrat		Republican	
1976	President	88,099	(45.9%)	96,119	(50.1%)
	House	130,081	(70.9%)	52,800	(28.8%)
1978	Governor	74,250	(40.9%)	106,488	(58.7%)
	Senate	62,911	(34.8%)	117,847	(65.2%)
	House	123,842	(70.6%)	51,442	(29.3%)
1980	President	83,406	(37.0%)	110,749	(49.1%)
	Senate	93,710	(42.5%)	116,767	(53.0%)
	House	115,009	(54.1%)	91,840	(43.2%)
1982	Governor	65,901	(32.3%)	132,757	(65.0%)
	House	98,952	(48.8%)	103,906	(51.2%)

Demographics

Population: 526,120. **Percent Change from 1970:** 41.1%.

Land Area: 3,625 square miles. **Population per Square Mile:** 145.1.

Counties, 1980 Population: Benton (Pt.) — 54,821; Clackamas (Pt.) — 188,248; Linn (Pt.) — 44,899; Marion (Pt.) — 204,490; Polk (Pt.) — 33,662.

Cities, 1980 Population: Albany — 26,546; Corvallis — 40,960; Lake Oswego (Pt.) — 5,821; Milwaukie (Pt.) — 597; Oregon City — 14,673; Portland (Pt.) — 276; Salem — 89,233; West Linn — 12,956; Woodburn — 11,196.

Race and Ancestry: White — 95.8%; Black — 0.5%; American Indian, Eskimo and Aleut — 0.8%; Asian and Pacific Islander — 1.3%. Spanish Origin — 3.0%. Dutch — 0.8%; English — 10.3%; French — 1.0%; German — 10.3%; Irish — 3.1%; Italian — 0.7%; Norwegian — 1.5%; Russian — 0.6%; Scottish — 0.8%; Swedish — 1.2%.

Universities, Enrollment: Chemeketa Community College, Salem — 7,584; Clackamas Community College, Oregon City — 5,289; Linn-Benton Community College, Albany — 5,531; Marylhurst College for Lifelong Learning, Marylhurst — 542; Mount Angel Seminary, St. Benedict — 114; Oregon State University, Corvallis — 17,682; Western Baptist College, Salem — 417; Western Evangelical Seminary, Portland — 171; Western Oregon State College, Monmouth — 3,129; Willamette University, Salem — 1,886.

Newspapers, Circulation: *Albany Democrat-Herald* (e), Albany — 20,448; *Corvallis Gazette-Times* (e), Corvallis — 15,056; *Enterprise-Courier* (e), Oregon City — 6,401; *Statesman-Journal* (mS), Salem — 62,407. The Portland *Oregonian* and Portland *Oregon Journal* also circulate in the district.

Commercial Television Stations, Affiliation: KECH, Salem (None). Entire district is located in Portland ADI.

Industries:

Safeway Stores Inc.; Clackamas; cold storage warehouses — 4,350. **Teledyne Industries Inc.** (WahChang); Albany; metals — 1,600. **Salem Hospital;** Salem; hospital — 1,200. **Hewlett-Packard Co.;** Corvallis; calculators — 1,120. **Omark Industries** (Orang Saw Chain Div.); Milwaukie; saw chains, hand tools — 1,000.

SAIF Corp.; Salem; accident insurance — 900. **State Farm Mutual Automobile Insurance Co.;** Salem; accident, life insurance — 900. **Crown Zellerbach Corp.;** West Linn; paper mill — 800. **Publishers Paper Co.** (HQ); Oregon City; pulp, newsprint — 630. **Oregon Metallurgical Corp.;** Albany; non-ferrous metals refining — 530.

Pennsylvania

Holding a narrow majority in the Legislature, Pennsylvania's Republicans crafted a new congressional map designed to preserve their similarly narrow edge in the state's U. S. House delegation.

Their first priority was to strengthen the 4th District's Republican incumbent, formerly a labor-oriented Democrat who switched parties in 1981, giving the GOP 13 of Pennsylvania's 25 House seats. The legislators pared away many of the old blue-collar areas that had supported the incumbent in his previous partisan incarnation and packed rural Republicans into his new district.

Because reapportionment forced the sluggishly growing Keystone State to drop from 25 to 23 House seats, two pairs of Democratic incumbents had their districts merged. In addition the new plan weakened the Democrat in the 18th District by pushing the constituency out of Democratic Pittsburgh and into the suburbs.

The ploy failed, however. After the votes were counted in November, the Democrats held 12 House seats; the Republicans 11. In the 4th the Democratic challenger won with more than 60 percent of the vote, while the Democratic incumbent in the 18th retained his seat.

With only a small majority in each legislative chamber, the state's Republican leadership had difficulty getting a new map adopted. After regional influences defeated several bills, a judicial threat finally forced the Legislature to act. Several plaintiffs had asked a federal court to impose a solution after the candidate filing period began Feb. 16, 1982, with no legislative compromise enacted.

The new map passed the state Senate March 1 by a 28-22 vote and the state House March 2, 118-73. Republican Gov. Richard Thornburgh signed it March 3, 1982.

The plan was challenged in federal court on the grounds that the population variations were so great as to be unconstitutional and that some districts had been gerrymandered. A lower federal court upheld the map, and that judgment was affirmed by the Supreme Court July 6, 1983.

Age of Population

District	Population Under 18	Voting Age Population	Population 65 & Over (% of VAP)	Median Age
1	141,099	374,046	65,470 (17.5%)	29.3
2	139,033	378,182	68,596 (18.1%)	31.0
3	124,549	391,605	80,592 (20.6%)	34.5
4	140,327	375,245	62,104 (16.6%)	30.8
5	144,972	370,556	50,556 (13.6%)	30.6
6	131,415	384,537	76,603 (19.9%)	34.3
7	128,457	387,309	68,570 (17.7%)	33.0
8	152,663	364,239	42,528 (11.7%)	30.0
9	147,099	368,331	64,934 (17.6%)	31.2
10	139,094	376,348	75,215 (20.0%)	33.1
11	126,907	388,822	83,140 (21.4%)	35.3
12	141,037	374,878	64,054 (17.1%)	32.1
13	122,179	392,167	73,644 (18.8%)	34.6
14	111,097	405,532	82,858 (20.4%)	33.1
15	129,445	385,814	65,768 (17.0%)	33.0
16	144,762	369,823	59,793 (16.2%)	30.5
17	139,460	376,440	63,411 (16.8%)	31.4
18	133,642	382,408	59,090 (15.5%)	33.5
19	139,804	376,801	59,117 (15.7%)	31.5
20	125,857	390,171	71,817 (18.4%)	34.7
21	146,031	370,614	60,943 (16.4%)	30.2
22	136,647	378,475	69,425 (18.3%)	33.2
23	137,720	378,256	62,705 (16.6%)	29.5
State	3,123,296	8,740,599	1,530,933 (17.5%)	32.1

Income and Occupation

District	Median Family Income	White Collar Workers	Blue Collar Workers	Service Workers	Farm Workers
1	$ 13,104	50.2%	33.3%	16.2%	0.3%
2	13,800	53.2	27.0	19.5	0.3
3	20,187	57.2	29.8	12.7	0.3
4	20,300	42.6	42.6	12.6	2.2
5	23,967	55.0	31.4	11.9	1.7
6	18,989	40.5	46.0	11.3	2.2
7	23,124	63.0	25.3	11.1	0.5
8	24,608	57.3	32.1	9.6	1.0
9	17,403	39.0	44.8	12.0	4.2
10	16,905	42.8	40.3	13.2	3.7
11	16,779	42.3	42.7	13.8	1.2
12	19,689	46.3	39.8	12.3	1.6
13	26,012	66.9	22.0	10.4	0.6
14	17,828	55.3	26.2	18.1	0.4
15	21,537	46.9	40.9	11.1	1.1
16	20,608	42.9	40.7	11.9	4.5
17	18,846	48.7	36.8	12.3	2.2

PENNSYLVANIA

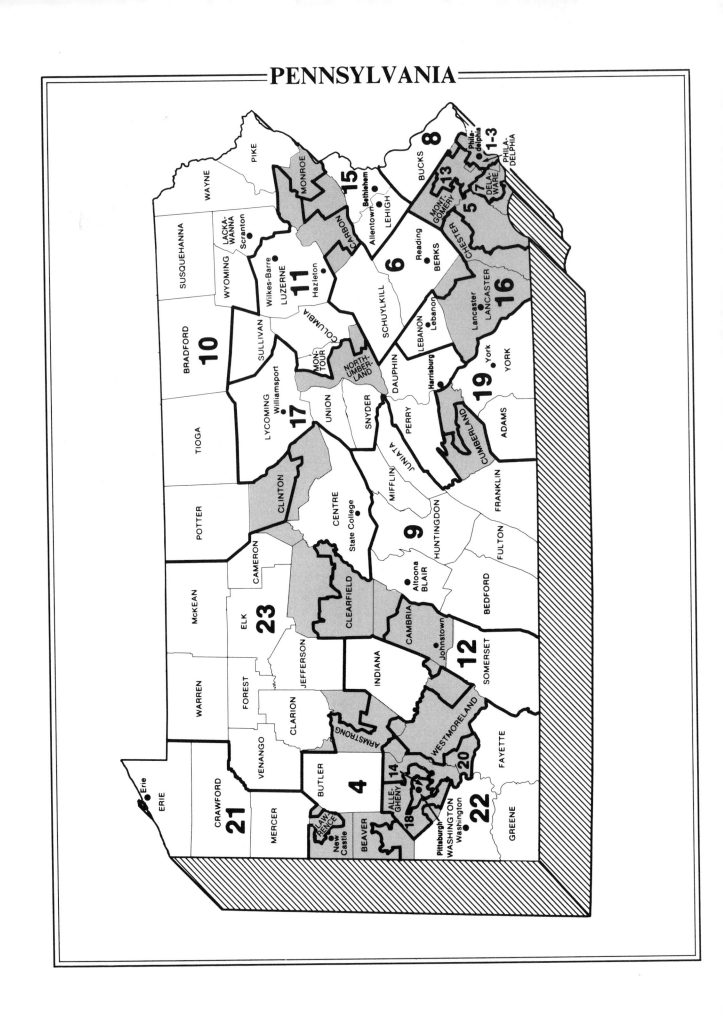

District	Median Family Income	White Collar Workers	Blue Collar Workers	Service Workers	Farm Workers
18	25,677	65.2	23.3	11.1	0.4
19	21,065	48.4	39.3	10.2	2.2
20	20,738	49.6	37.3	12.7	0.4
21	19,601	45.7	38.9	13.3	2.1
22	19,828	41.8	44.2	12.8	1.2
23	18,450	44.2	40.3	13.0	2.4
State	$ 19,995	50.1%	35.7%	12.6%	1.6%

Education: School Years Completed

District	8 Years or Fewer	4 Years of High School	4 Years of College or More	Median School Years
1	28.8%	28.2%	9.7%	11.8
2	20.2	31.7	13.2	12.2
3	18.9	40.7	9.1	12.2
4	19.1	44.5	10.2	12.3
5	14.1	37.0	20.8	12.6
6	24.0	39.9	9.3	12.2
7	12.7	40.4	19.1	12.6
8	10.7	41.6	19.1	12.6
9	22.5	43.7	8.4	12.2
10	18.3	42.6	10.5	12.3
11	22.3	42.0	9.1	12.3
12	20.7	45.1	10.9	12.3
13	11.0	34.4	27.4	12.8
14	19.0	37.2	13.8	12.3
15	19.3	38.8	13.2	12.3
16	20.8	39.4	12.8	12.3
17	16.9	44.0	11.8	12.4
18	10.3	40.0	23.9	12.7
19	19.5	40.8	13.8	12.4
20	18.2	45.4	10.6	12.4
21	14.7	45.2	12.5	12.4
22	23.5	42.5	9.1	12.2
23	18.0	44.1	12.5	12.4
State	18.4%	40.4%	13.6%	12.4

Housing and Residential Patterns

District	Owner Occupied	Renter Occupied	Urban	Rural
1	56.6%	43.4%	100.0%	0.0%
2	51.6	48.4	100.0	0.0
3	73.4	26.6	100.0	0.0
4	75.9	24.1	42.2	57.8
5	68.9	31.1	70.4	29.6
6	74.5	25.5	53.7	46.3
7	73.7	26.3	99.5	0.5
8	74.1	25.9	82.0	18.0
9	75.4	24.6	30.0	70.0
10	71.6	28.4	45.0	55.0
11	71.0	29.0	64.5	35.5
12	75.1	24.9	54.1	45.9
13	69.1	30.9	96.2	3.8
14	52.3	47.7	100.0	0.0
15	71.2	28.8	73.6	26.4
16	69.6	30.4	49.5	50.5
17	68.6	31.4	54.0	46.0
18	75.8	24.2	94.7	5.3
19	73.1	26.9	54.0	46.0
20	71.1	28.9	87.1	12.9
21	72.9	27.1	56.5	43.5
22	74.0	26.0	49.6	50.4
23	72.7	27.3	37.0	63.0
State	69.9%	30.1%	69.3%	30.7%

1st District

South and Central Philadelphia

William Penn's statue atop City Hall, the highest point in Philadelphia, looks out upon a city of distinct ethnic neighborhoods, each with the clannishness and occasional suspicion of outsiders more commonly associated with small towns. The diversity is most apparent in the 1st, which takes in the wealthy liberals of Center City, the Italians of South Philadelphia, the Irish and Poles of the "river wards" and the blacks along North Broad Street. While Ronald Reagan did well among the white ethnics in 1980, Jimmy Carter nevertheless won the area of the new 1st.

Blue-collar South Philadelphia contains most of the city's piers and the Philadelphia Navy Yard, as well as its huge sports complex — the Spectrum and Veterans and JFK stadiums. Staunchly Democratic, this section nevertheless voted for Reagan in 1980 after going for Carter in 1976. The law-and-order appeal of former Mayor Frank Rizzo, who grew up on South Philadelphia streets and walked them as a patrolman, is strong among the dock and factory workers.

The new map removed from the district nearly all of South and West Philadelphia west of the Schuylkill River. A conglomeration of blue-collar whites, blacks and Jews, these wards were not enamored of Reagan's conservatism and went for Carter in 1980. The one ward west of the river included in the merged district has most of the liberal academic community of Drexel University and the University of Pennsylvania.

Society Hill and Olde City, the sites of many of the city's historic landmarks and now affluent restoration areas, are centers of liberal Democratic activity. The gentrification of nearby Queen Village and Fairmount is displacing ethnic whites who esteem Rizzo-style politics with young professionals who disdain it.

Running north from Center City, the Frankford El railway binds together the river wards, a grimy part of town where factories and warehouses sit cheek-by-jowl with row houses. The new 1st district gave up Frankford, Bridesburg and part of Kensington to the 3rd District but kept Richmond, Fishtown, Nicetown and the rest of Kensington.

Reagan carried the river wards in 1980, but by much smaller margins than he enjoyed in South Philadelphia, where the large Italian-American population still resents Irish rule over the Democratic Party and is receptive to Republicans.

Blacks make up 32 percent of the new 1st, clustered in the rundown neighborhoods extending into North Philadelphia on either side of North Broad Street. The academic enclave of Temple University sits along Broad Street as well.

Election Returns

1st District		Democrat		Republican	
1976	President	137,596	(65.6%)	67,057	(32.0%)
	Senate	138,927	(72.5%)	51,224	(26.7%)
	House	125,699	(71.4%)	48,839	(27.7%)
1978	Governor	108,147	(57.4%)	76,991	(40.8%)
	House	116,655	(72.1%)	43,925	(27.1%)

1st District		Democrat		Republican	
1980	President	117,737	(61.3%)	60,347	(31.4%)
	Senate	94,794	(54.4%)	74,900	(43.0%)
	House	80,027	(47.1%)	42,950	(25.3%)
1982	Governor	95,324	(65.5%)	48,061	(33.0%)
	Senate	88,612	(63.4%)	48,706	(34.8%)
	House	103,626	(72.3%)	38,155	(26.6%)

Demographics

Population: 515,145. **Percent Change from 1970:** -16.6%.

Land Area: 33 square miles. **Population per Square Mile:** 15,610.5.

Counties, 1980 Population: Philadelphia (Pt.) — 515,145.

Cities, 1980 Population: Philadelphia (Pt.) — 515,145.

Race and Ancestry: White — 58.6%; Black — 32.0%; American Indian, Eskimo and Aleut — 0.2%; Asian and Pacific Islander — 2.0%. Spanish Origin — 9.8%. English — 2.6%; German — 3.5%; Irish — 6.6%; Italian — 13.5%; Polish — 2.9%; Russian — 1.3%; Ukranian — 0.9%.

Universities, Enrollment: Antonelli School of Photography, Philadelphia — 294; Community College of Philadelphia, Philadelphia — 12,838; Drexel University, Philadelphia — 11,953; Dropsie University, Philadelphia — 46; Gratz College, Philadelphia — 138; Hussian School of Art, Philadelphia — 211; Lyons Technical Institute, Philadelphia — 350; McCarrie School of Health Sciences and Technology, Philadelphia — 315.

Peirce Junior College, Philadelphia — 2,106; Pennsylvania College of Optometry, Philadelphia — 589; Pennsylvania College of Podiatric Medicine, Philadelphia — 474; Philadelphia College of the Performing Arts, Philadelphia — 364; Philadelphia College of Pharmacy and Science, Philadelphia — 1,144; Philadelphia Printing School, Philadelphia — 275; Temple University, Philadelphia — 33,158; Thomas Jefferson University, Philadelphia — 1,753; University of Pennsylvania, Philadelphia — 22,006.

Newspapers, Circulation: *The Philadelphia Inquirer* and *Philadelphia Daily News* circulate in the district. Foreign language newspaper: *"America" Ukrainian Catholic Daily* (Ukrainian), Philadelphia — 4,000.

Commercial Television Stations, Affiliation: WTAF-TV, Philadelphia (None); KYW-TV, Philadelphia (NBC). Entire district is located in Philadelphia ADI. *(For other Philadelphia stations, see 2nd and 13th districts.)*

Military Installations: Philadelphia Naval Regional Medical Center, Philadelphia — 1,055; Philadelphia Naval Shipyard, Philadelphia — 12,371; Philadephia Naval Station, Philadelphia — 7,646.

Industries:

John Wanamaker of Philadelphia (Cleland Simpson Co. - HQ); Philadelphia; department stores — 2,500. **Albert Einstein Medical Center** (Northern & Daroff Div. - HQ); Philadelphia; hospital — 2,000. **Federal Reserve Bank of Philadelphia;** Philadelphia; banking — 1,910. **Children's Hospital of Philadelphia;** Philadelphia; pediatric hospital — 1,800. **Metropolitan Hospital Inc.;** Philadelphia; osteopathic hospital — 1,800. **Penn Mutual Life Insurance Co.** (HQ); Philadelphia; life, health insurance — 1,800.

Pennsylvania Hospital; Philadelphia; hospital — 1,500. **General Accident, Fire, Life Assurance** (HQ); Philadelphia; life, health, casualty insurance — 1,300. **Episcopal Hospital;** Philadelphia; hospital — 1,200. **Rapid-American Corp.** (Botany 500 Div.); Philadelphia; men's clothing — 1,100. **Rohm & Haas Co.** (HQ); Philadelphia; plastic products — 1,000. **St. Agnes Medical Center;** Philadelphia; hospital — 1,000. **United Hospitals Inc.;** Philadelphia; hospital — 1,000. **Veterans Administration;** Philadelphia; veterans' hospital — 1,000. **Action Mfg. Co.;** Philadelphia; fuses — 900. **Blue Cross of Greater Philadelphia** (HQ); Philadelphia; health insurance — 900. **Robert Bruce Inc.** (HQ); Philadelphia; men's clothing — 850. **National Sugar Refining Co.;** Philadelphia; sugar — 800. **Pincus Bros. Inc.** (HQ); Philadelphia; men's clothing — 800. **Strawbridge & Clothier** (Clover Stores - HQ); Philadelphia; department stores — 800.

Philadelphia Saving Fund Society (HQ); Philadelphia; banking — 793. **E. I. du Pont de Nemours & Co.;** Philadelphia; paints — 750. **Amstar Corp.** (Domino Sugar); Philadelphia; sugar refining — 700. **C. Schmidt & Sons Inc.** (Christian Schmidt Brewing Co.); Philadelphia; brewery — 700. **CBS Inc.** (W. B. Saunders Co.); Philadelphia; medical book publishing — 675. **Atlantic Richfield Co. Inc.;** Philadelphia; petroleum refining — 670. **ARA Services Inc.** (HQ); Philadelphia; cafeteria chain — 600. **Philadelphia Life Insurance Co.** (HQ); Philadelphia; life insurance — 600. **Curtis Circulation Co. Inc.;** Philadelphia; marketing — 540. **Canadian Pacific Hotels Inc.** (Franklin Plaza Hotel); Philadelphia; hotel — 500. **Gulf Oil Corp.;** Philadelphia; petroleum refining — 500. **TRW Inc.;** Philadelphia; electronic components — 500.

2nd District

West Philadelphia

With an 80-percent-black population, the 2nd seems assured of black representation. Militant blacks tried to remove from the district the white wards that support the black incumbent and guarantee his renomination. But they failed and — apart from well-to-do Chestnut Hill, which went to the 13th — the white neighborhoods remained in the district. The underpopulated 2nd made up its population deficit by picking up racially mixed parts of West Philadelphia south of Market Street, which kept the district politically much as it was before.

The core of the white population in the 2nd is the neighborhood surrounding Rittenhouse Square, home of wealthy and socially conscious liberals from old Philadelphia families. Along with Society Hill in the 1st, this area forms the heart of the reform movement in Philadelphia politics. Similar in voting behavior is the small sector of the University of Pennsylvania-Drexel complex located within the 2nd.

Beyond this academic ring in West Philadelphia are black wards that mix middle-class neighborhoods and poor ones. When former Pittsburgh Mayor Peter F. Flaherty ran for governor as a Democrat in 1978 against Republican Richard L. Thornburgh, West Philadelphia blacks rejected the socially conservative Flaherty and gave a majority to Thornburgh. Then they returned to the fold to support Democrat Allen Ertel against Thornburgh in 1982.

Moving out Lancaster Avenue, past the Philadelphia Zoo and Fairmount Park, the tightly bunched row houses give way to larger homes with yards and trees. On the Philadelphia side of City Line Avenue, expensive high-rise apartment buildings look out on suburban Montgomery County. Here, in largely Jewish Wynnefield and Overbrook, Democrats predominate.

To the east of the boathouse-lined Schuylkill River lies quaint old Germantown, now only a faded reminder of its moneyed past. Many of Philadelphia's old families have fled its mansions because of an influx of blacks to proximate neighborhoods. Germantown and nearby Mount Airy are mixed communities housing middle-class blacks and young white professionals. They have strong Democratic ties, tilted toward the liberal side.

The 2nd continues to take in a slice of black North Philadelphia, with its urban blight, high crime and declining population.

Philadelphia

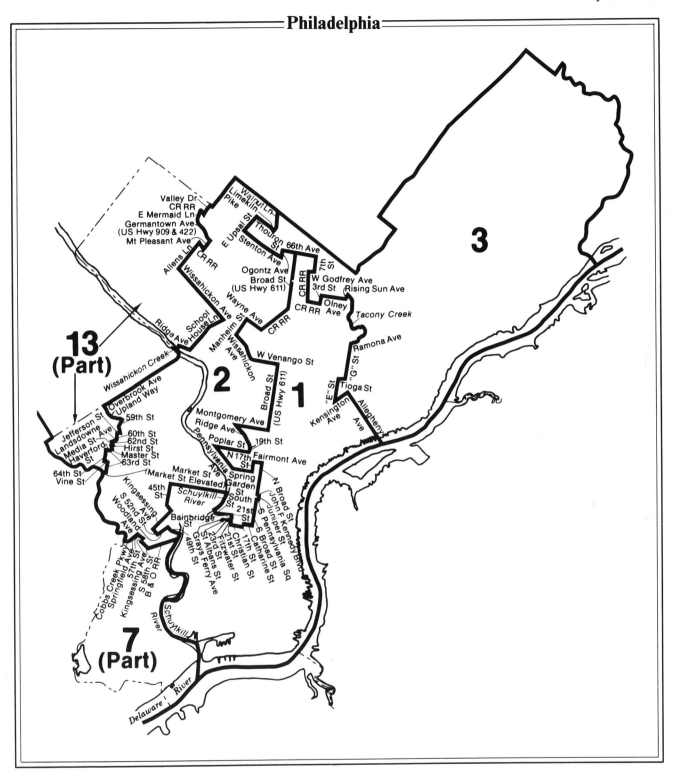

Election Returns

2nd District		Democrat		Republican	
1976	President	171,872	(82.4%)	32,849	(15.7%)
	Senate	165,478	(83.8%)	30,661	(15.5%)
	House	149,710	(79.0%)	37,692	(19.9%)
1978	Governor	94,806	(45.1%)	111,088	(52.8%)
	House	157,690	(81.8%)	30,658	(15.9%)

2nd District		Democrat		Republican	
1980	President	179,978	(86.3%)	19,058	(9.1%)
	Senate	103,572	(57.1%)	72,610	(40.0%)
	House	146,498	(86.9%)	1,758	(1.0%)
1982	Governor	122,762	(76.0%)	35,040	(21.7%)
	Senate	106,559	(71.6%)	37,179	(25.0%)
	House	120,744	(76.1%)	—	

Demographics

Population: 517,215. **Percent Change from 1970:** -17.5%.

Land Area: 29 square miles. **Population per Square Mile:** 17,835.0.

Counties, 1980 Population: Philadelphia (Pt.) — 517,215.

Cities, 1980 Population: Philadelphia (Pt.) — 517,215.

Race and Ancestry: White — 18.3%; Black — 80.0%; American Indian, Eskimo and Aleut — 0.2%; Asian and Pacific Islander — 0.7%. Spanish Origin — 1.2%. English — 1.8%; German — 1.3%; Irish — 1.9%; Italian — 1.2%; Polish — 0.5%; Russian — 1.6%.

Universities, Enrollment: Art Institute of Philadelphia, Philadelphia — 369; Berean Institute, Philadelphia — 279; Combs College of Music, Philadelphia — 111; The Curtis Institute of Music, Philadelphia — 157; Hahnemann Medical College, Philadelphia — 1,846; La Salle College, Philadelphia — 7,639; The Levitan School, Philadelphia — 66; Lutheran Theological Seminary at Philadelphia, Philadelphia — 217.

Medical College of Pennsylvania, Philadelphia — 522; Moore College of Art, Philadelphia — 677; New School of Music, Philadelphia — 79; Philadelphia College of Art, Philadelphia — 1,260; Philadelphia College of Osteopathic Medicine, Philadelphia — 822; St. Joseph's University, Philadelphia — 5,539; Tracy-Warner School, Philadelphia — 130.

Newspapers, Circulation: *The Philadelphia Inquirer* (mS), Philadelphia — 425,493; *Philadelphia Daily News* (e), Philadelphia — 230,614.

Commercial Television Stations, Affiliation: WCAV-TV, Philadelphia (CBS); WPHL-TV, Philadelphia (None); WPVI-TV, Philadelphia (ABC). Entire district is located in Philadelphia ADI. *(For other Philadelphia stations, see 1st and 13th districts.)*

Industries:

INA Corp. (HQ); Philadelphia; insurance, banking — 3,900. **Hahnemann Medical College and Hospital** (HQ); Philadelphia; hospital — 3,600. **First Pennsylvania Corp.** (HQ); Philadelphia; bank holding company — 2,800. **United Engineers & Constructors Inc.** (HQ); Philadelphia; heavy construction — 2,500. **The Budd Co.**; Philadelphia; railroad equipment — 2,400.

Provident National Corp. (HQ); Philadelphia; banking — 2,310. **Philadelphia Newspapers Inc.;** Philadelphia; newspaper publishing — 2,300. **Tasty Baking Co.** (HQ); Philadelphia; baked goods — 1,780. **Girard Trust Bank** (HQ); Philadelphia; banking — 1,200. **Presbyterian University of Pennsylvania Medical Center;** Philadelphia; hospital — 1,200. **Reliance Insurance Co.** (HQ); Philadelphia; casualty, life, health insurance — 1,200. **Stanley Blacker Inc.** (HQ); Philadelphia; men's coats — 1,150. **Catalytic Inc.** (HQ); Philadelphia; engineering services — 1,100. **Atlantic Richfield Co.** (Eastern Headquarters); Philadelphia; petroleum products — 1,000. **Colonial Penn Group Inc.** (HQ); Philadelphia; insurance — 1,000.

American Building Maintenance Co.; Philadelphia; janitorial services — 800. **FMC Corp.;** Philadelphia; chemicals wholesaling — 800. **The Franklin Consulting Co. Inc.;** Philadelphia; industrial engineering services — 800. **Provident Mutual Life Insurance of Philadelphia** (HQ); Philadelphia; life, health insurance — 792. **Atlantic Richfield Co. Inc.** (Arco Chemical Co. Div.); Philadelphia; petrochemical wholesaling — 705. **Day & Zimmermann Inc.** (Consulting Services Div. - HQ); Philadelphia; general contracting — 700. **Patgat Clothes Inc.;** Philadelphia; men's clothing — 700. **Westin Hotel Co. Inc.** Philadelphia; hotel — 700. **Hancock-Gross Inc.;** Philadelphia; rubber products — 650. **After Six Inc.** (HQ); Philadelphia; men's clothing — 600.

Chips 'n Twigs Inc. (Fashionbilt Clothes - HQ); Philadelphia; men's, boys' clothing — 600. **Commonwealth Land Title Insurance Co.** (HQ); Philadelphia; title insurance — 600. **Yoh Security Inc.** (HQ); Philadelphia; security services — 600. **Coopers & Lybrand;** Philadelphia; accounting services — 550. **Franklin Plaza Associates;** Philadelphia; real estate leasing — 500. **Hay Associates** (HQ); Philadelphia; management consultants — 500. **International Mill Service Inc.** (HQ); Philadelphia; mineral processing — 500. **National Publishing Co.** (HQ); Philadelphia; bible publishing — 500. **Realty Services Co.;** Philadelphia; janitorial services — 500. **The Sheraton Corp.** (The Sheraton Hotel); Philadelphia; hotel — 500.

3rd District

Northeast Philadelphia

Roosevelt Boulevard is the central artery of the "Great Northeast" and of the surrounding 3rd District. Nominally Democratic, the 3rd is open to the blandishments of Republicans.

Ronald Reagan won it in 1980, taking all except two wards, and a Republican won the House seat in 1978 and 1980 by appealing to his many blue-collar Catholic constituents through his advocacy of urban aid, tuition tax credits and abortion curbs.

But the Legislature added some Democratic river wards to the 3rd, and that was enough to help the Democratic challenger in 1982 who won with just more than 50 percent of the vote. The river wards were Frankford and Bridesburg, hit hard by factory layoffs. Former Philadelphia Mayor Frank Rizzo is a hero there, as he is throughout much of the 3rd.

Prevailing opinion is different in Oak Lane and West Oak Lane, two sections that line the Cheltenham Avenue border with suburban Montgomery County. In this area young professional whites and middle-class blacks prefer a more liberal kind of politics.

In much of the Great Northeast (so named because of its geographic expanse), the surroundings are more suburban than urban. In the 1950s there were still some farms here, located near North Philadelphia Airport.

Concern about crime inspires conservative social attitudes in the neat little houses along the tree-lined streets of this area. On the presidential level, the best ward for Republicans is the 66th, a favorite residence of police officers and firefighters. It barely went for Jimmy Carter even in 1976, when the rest of the city supported him by wide margins.

The Great Northeast has a large Jewish population, concentrated west of Roosevelt Boulevard. Farther east Irish and other Catholic ethnics predominate.

Election Returns

3rd District		Democrat		Republican	
1976	President	148,687	(56.3%)	110,829	(41.9%)
	Senate	167,571	(64.2%)	92,394	(35.4%)
	House	163,087	(67.0%)	80,223	(33.0%)
1978	Governor	126,763	(52.2%)	113,060	(46.6%)
	House	106,725	(47.8%)	116,617	(52.2%)
1980	President	100,811	(40.6%)	124,484	(50.1%)
	Senate	92,345	(38.5%)	144,858	(60.4%)
	House	86,167	(37.9%)	138,786	(61.0%)
1982	Governor	103,681	(52.8%)	90,914	(46.3%)
	Senate	92,004	(48.9%)	94,261	(50.1%)
	House	97,161	(50.1%)	94,497	(48.7%)

Demographics

Population: 516,154. **Percent Change from 1970:** -6.6%.

Land Area: 50 square miles. **Population per Square Mile:** 10,323.1.

Counties, 1980 Population: Philadelphia (Pt.) — 516,154.

Cities, 1980 Population: Philadelphia (Pt.) — 516,154.

Race and Ancestry: White — 91.1%; Black — 7.6%; American Indian, Eskimo and Aleut — 0.1%; Asian and Pacific Islander — 0.8%. Spanish Origin — 1.1%. English — 3.2%; German — 7.3%; Hungarian — 0.6%; Irish — 12.1%; Italian — 6.7%; Polish — 5.7%; Russian — 5.4%; Ukranian — 1.3%.

Universities, Enrollment: American Institute of Drafting, Philadelphia — 315; Holy Family College, Philadelphia — 1,279.

Newspapers, Circulation: *The Philadelphia Inquirer* and *Philadelphia Daily News* circulate in the district.

Commercial Television Stations, Affiliation: Entire district is located in Philadelphia ADI.

Military Installations: Naval Aviation Supply Office, Philadelphia — 5,803.

Industries:

The Budd Co. (Red Lion Plant); Philadelphia; railroad cars — 1,898. **Frankford Hospital;** Philadelphia; hospital — 1,500. **Nabisco Inc.;** Philadelphia; cookies, crackers — 1,400. **Whitman's Chocolates;** Philadelphia; chocolates, candy — 1,200. **Kidde Consumer Durables Corp.** (Progress Lighting Div.); Philadelphia; lighting products, housewares — 1,156.

Jeanes Hospital Inc.; Philadelphia; hospital — 1,000. **Kelsey-Hayes Co. Inc.** (Heintz Div.); Philadelphia; aerospace metals — 1,000. **Rohm & Haas Co.;** Philadelphia; chemicals — 1,000. **Brentwood Sportswear Inc.** (HQ); Philadelphia; men's sportswear — 940. **Cardo Automotive Products Inc.;** Philadelphia; auto parts — 800. **J. J. White Inc.;** Philadelphia; construction — 800. **Interco Inc.** (Devon Apparel Div.); Philadelphia; women's knit outerwear — 700. **Frankford-Quaker Grocery Co.** (HQ); Philadelphia; groceries wholesaling — 504. **Crown Cork & Seal Co. Inc.** (HQ); Philadelphia; metal cans, closings — 500. **Interco Inc.** (Devon Apparel Div.); Philadelphia; women's knit outerwear — 500. **S. K. F. Industries Inc.;** Philadelphia; ball bearings — 500.

4th District

West — New Castle

Much legislative effort went into making the 4th District more congenial to its incumbent, who was a recent Republican convert. The GOP Legislature lopped off the most strongly Democratic sections of Beaver County and shoved the district east to take in Republican turf, changing its number from the 25th to the 4th. Democrats had a registration advantage of 45,000 in the old district; that edge dwindled to 20,000 in the new but, to the Republicans' surprise, it was enough. Voters rejected the incumbent decisively.

Jimmy Carter won the old district narrowly in 1980, but Ronald Reagan took the new one. While unemployment hurt the steel communities in this part of Pennsylvania, there were not as many of these hard-hit towns in the new constituency as there were in the old. The steel-oriented county of Beaver, which went solidly for Carter in 1980, saw its clout diminished under the new map. It accounted for half of the old district's population, but makes up only 25 percent of the constituency in the new district.

Much of industrial southern Beaver was transferred to the 22nd District. The map makers carved a line that left the northern part of the county and chunks of the southeastern and southwestern corners within the 4th.

Labor union influence remains strong in the 4th District portion of Beaver county, although Republicans are more competitive there than in the south. Outside the

northern Beaver steel town of Beaver Falls, where Joe Namath grew up, lies a Republican farming region.

Lawrence and Butler, two counties that remained in the district, have much looser Democratic loyalties than Beaver. Lawrence, suffering from steel plant closings in nearby Youngstown, Ohio, went for Carter by a mere 1,102 votes in 1980, while Butler supported Reagan solidly. All of Butler is in the new 4th, as is all of Lawrence except five northern townships.

Armstrong County, a swing area, starts the chain of new territory added to the district on the east. Cartographic artistry put the Democratic mill town of Ford City into the Republican 23rd District. That left Kittanning, a Republican-leaning commercial center, as the biggest Armstrong town in the 4th.

Indiana County also was added to the 4th. The last time that the county voted Democratic in a presidential election was in 1964. A mixture of coal mines and farms, it is dominated at the polls by the rural vote. One small slice of Westmoreland County was inserted into the 4th. It is the Ligonier Valley, where the Pittsburgh elite maintain summer homes.

Election Returns

4th District		Democrat		Republican	
1976	President	92,937	(50.4%)	87,987	(47.7%)
	Senate	70,505	(40.6%)	101,835	(58.7%)
	House	87,866	(47.8%)	95,927	(52.2%)
1978	Governor	83,068	(59.7%)	55,232	(39.7%)
	House	72,496	(49.1%)	62,603	(42.4%)
1980	President	82,901	(45.3%)	87,644	(47.9%)
	Senate	109,720	(63.7%)	61,030	(35.4%)
	House	108,274	(64.1%)	60,750	(35.9%)
1982	Governor	88,123	(52.5%)	78,115	(46.6%)
	Senate	69,058	(41.2%)	96,092	(57.4%)
	House	100,481	(60.1%)	64,539	(38.6%)

Demographics

Population: 515,572. **Percent Change from 1970:** 6.1%.

Land Area: 2,672 square miles. **Population per Square Mile:** 193.0.

Counties, 1980 Population: Armstrong (Pt.) — 42,616; Beaver (Pt.) — 132,914; Butler — 147,912; Indiana — 92,281; Lawrence (Pt.) — 87,453; Westmoreland (Pt.) — 12,396.

Cities, 1980 Population: Aliquippa — 17,094; Beaver Falls — 12,525; Butler — 17,026; Butler Twp. — 18,651; Cranberry Twp. — 11,066; Indiana — 16,051; New Castle — 33,621; White Twp. — 13,177.

Race and Ancestry: White — 97.0%; Black — 2.6%; American Indian, Eskimo and Aleut — 0.1%; Asian and Pacific Islander — 0.2%. Spanish Origin — 0.4%. English — 5.4%; German — 12.7%; Hungarian — 0.7%; Irish — 4.0%; Italian — 6.8%; Polish — 2.6%; Scottish — 0.5%; Ukranian — 0.7%.

Universities, Enrollment: Butler County Community College, Butler — 1,862; Geneva College, Beaver Falls — 1,159; Indiana University of Pennsylvania, Indiana — 12,278; Lyons School of Business, New Castle — 139; Slippery Rock State College, Slippery Rock — 5,690; Vale Technical Institute, Blairsville — 620.

Newspapers, Circulation: *Beaver County Times* (eS), Beaver — 51,517; *Butler Eagle* (e), Butler — 31,043; *Ellwood City Ledger* (e), Ellwood City — 7,253; *Gazette* (e), Indiana — 21,001; *New Castle News* (e), New Castle — 22,642. *Pittsburgh Post-Gazette* and *The Pittsburgh Press* also circulate in the district.

Commercial Television Stations, Affiliation: Entire district is located in Pittsburgh ADI.

Industries:

Jones & Laughlin Steel Corp.; Aliquippa; steel mill — 7,800. **Armco Steel Corp.;** Butler; sheet, strip steel — 3,200. **Westinghouse Electric Corp.** (Industry Equipment Group); Beaver; electrical switchgears — 3,000. **Babcock & Wilcox Co.** (Tubular Products Group); Beaver Falls; seamless tubing — 2,600. **Allegheny Ludlum Steel Corp.;** Leechburg; cold rolled steel — 2,000.

Medical Center of Beaver County; Beaver; hospital — 1,700. **Anchor Hocking Corp.** (Shenango China Div.); New Castle; tableware — 1,000. **Babcock & Wilcox Co.;** Koppel; tubing, welding equipment — 1,000. **Butler County Memorial Hospital;** Butler; hospital — 1,000. **Servisco** (Columbus Services); New Castle; maintenance services — 1,000. **Rockwell International Corp.** (Rockwell-Truck Axle Div.); New Castle; truck springs — 900. **Season-All Industries Inc.** (HQ); Indiana; storm windows — 800. **Butler County Mushroom Farm** (Moonlight Mushrooms - HQ); Worthington; mushrooms — 750.

FMC Corp. (Material Handling Equipment Div.); Homer City; conveyers — 750. **Airway Industries Inc.** (HQ); Ellwood City; luggage — 600. **Mine Safety Appliances Co.;** Callery; safety equipment — 600. **McCreary Tire & Rubber Co.** (HQ); Indiana; tires — 555. **Aliquippa & Southern Railroad Co.;** Aliquippa; railroad operations — 550. **Joseph S. Finch & Co. Inc.;** Schenley; liquor wholesaling — 500. **Spang Industries Inc.** (Magnetics Div.); East Butler; electronic components — 500. **White Consolidated Industries Inc.** (Aetna Standard Engineering Div.); Ellwood City; metal-working machinery — 500.

5th District

Western Philadelphia Suburbs — Chester

Mushrooms, horses and tract houses all grow well in the outer suburbs of Philadelphia. Despite some islands of Democratic industrial territory, this is Republican turf — and burgeoning Chester County dominates it.

Farmers around the self-designated Mushroom Capital of the World in Kennett Square keep the southern part of Chester County solid for the GOP. Nearby, the Brandywine Creek meanders through estate country where the du Ponts and other Republican millionaires maintain their mansions.

A housing boom, however, has turned northern Chester County's coloration from rural Republican to suburban Republican. Exton, once a tiny farm town, received a giant shopping mall in the 1970s. Farther north the 5th covers rural northern Montgomery County — where most of the Mennonite farmers have been Republican for generations.

During the 1970s the district had Democratic enclaves in Phoenixville and Pottstown. For the 1980s these are joined by another small mill town, Coatesville. But a more significant infusion of Democrats comes from the city of Chester, a run-down part of Delaware County where the shipbuilding industry is in decline. Like the other industrial towns placed in the 5th, Chester has suffered badly from the recession. But also like them, it is consigned to a small Democratic minority in the district.

Election Returns

5th District		Democrat		Republican	
1976	President	73,374	(41.5%)	100,620	(56.9%)
	Senate	68,809	(40.4%)	100,279	(58.9%)
	House	75,904	(43.0%)	100,480	(56.9%)
1978	Governor	41,295	(33.0%)	82,823	(66.2%)
	House	35,248	(27.3%)	93,659	(72.6%)
1980	President	57,836	(31.6%)	106,938	(58.4%)
	Senate	59,268	(32.7%)	119,478	(65.9%)
	House	46,286	(27.2%)	122,468	(71.9%)
1982	Governor	44,220	(32.2%)	92,123	(67.0%)
	Senate	36,189	(26.6%)	98,122	(72.2%)
	House	44,170	(32.8%)	90,648	(67.2%)

Demographics

Population: 515,528. **Percent Change from 1970:** 9.8%.

Land Area: 700 square miles. **Population per Square Mile:** 736.5.

Counties, 1980 Population: Chester (Pt.) — 245,007; Delaware (Pt.) — 88,921; Montgomery (Pt.) — 181,600.

Cities, 1980 Population: Chester — 45,794; Coatesville — 10,698; East Goshen Twp. — 10,021; East Norriton Twp. — 12,711; Hatfield Twp. — 13,411; Lower Providence Twp. — 18,945; Phoenixville — 14,165; Pottstown — 22,729; Tredyffrin Twp. — 23,019; Upper Chichester Twp. — 14,377; West Chester Twp. — 17,435; West Goshen Twp. — 16,164; West Norriton Twp. — 14,034.

Race and Ancestry: White — 87.3%; Black — 11.2%; American Indian, Eskimo and Aleut — 0.1%; Asian and Pacific Islander — 0.7%. Spanish Origin — 1.6%. Dutch — 0.7%; English — 7.5%; German — 11.5%; Hungarian — 0.5%; Irish — 5.9%; Italian — 5.8%; Polish — 2.2%; Scottish — 0.5%; Ukranian — 0.6%.

Universities, Enrollment: Cheyney State College, Cheyney — 2,284; Immaculata College, Chester City — 1,377; Ursinus College, Collegeville — 1,139; Valley Forge Christian College, Phoenixville — 535; West Chester State College, West Chester — 8,801; Widener University, Chester — 4,343.

Newspapers, Circulation: *Daily Local News* (e), West Chester — 35,505; *The Evening Phoenix* (e), Phoenixville — 7,564; *The Pottstown Mercury* (m), Pottstown — 29,785; *The Record* (e), Coatesville — 8,394. Chester *Delaware County Daily Times*, Norristown *Times Herald* , *The Philadelphia Inquirer* and *Philadelphia Daily News* also circulate in the district.

Commercial Television Stations, Affiliation: Entire district is located in Philadelphia ADI.

Nuclear Power Plants: Limerick 1 and 2, Limerick (General Electric, Bechtel).

Industries:

Lukens Steel Co. (HQ); Coatesville; customized steel products — 2,400. **Chester Crozer Medical Center;** Chester; hospital — 2,300. **Scott Paper Co.** (Packaged Products Div.); Chester; paper mill — 1,700. **Crouse Nuclear Energy Service;** Royersford; administrative offices — 1,600. **Sun Oil Co. of Pennsylvania** (Sun Petroleum Products); Marcus Hook; petroleum refining — 1,550.

Exxon Corp. (QYX Div.); Lionville; research — 1,500. **Management Assistance Inc.** (Sorbus Service Div.); Malvern; computer services — 1,500. **Wyeth Laboratories Inc.;** Malvern; pharmaceuticals — 1,350. **Sun Ship Inc.;** Chester; shipbuilding — 1,200. **Veterans Administration;** Coatesville; veterans' psychiatric hospital — 1,200. **Dana Corp.** (Spicer Universal Joint Div.); Pottstown; universal joints — 1,100. **B. F. Goodrich Co. Inc.;** Oaks; tires — 1,100. **NL Industries Inc.** (Doehler-Jarvis Div.); Pottstown; aluminum, zinc castings — 1,000. **Pottstown Memorial Medical Center;** Pottstown; hospital — 1,000. **American Home Products Corp.** (Wyeth Laboratories Div.); West Chester; pharmaceuticals — 1,000.

Mrs. Smith's Pie Co. (HQ); Pottstown; pies, cakes — 850. **Hewlett-Packard Co.;** Avondale; optical instruments — 802. **Hooker Chemical Corp.** (Plastics Div.); Pottstown; film — 800. **B. P. Oil Inc.;** Marcus Hook; petroleum refining — 700. **Certainteed Corp.** (HQ); Valley Forge; industrial construction supplies — 700. **Congoleum Corp.;** Marcus Hook; floor covering — 700. **FMC Corp.** (Material

Handling Systems Div.); Colmar; material handling — 700. **Horace W. Longacre Inc.;** Souderton; poultry processing — 660. **Thriftway Foods Inc.** (HQ); Oaks; grocery wholesaling — 650. **Westinghouse Electric Corp.** (Combustion Turbine Systems Div.); Concordville; engineering services — 600.

National Rolling Mills Inc. (HQ); Malvern; metal products — 575. **Denney-Reyburn Co.;** West Chester; paper tags — 560. **Phoenix Steel Corp.;** Phoenixville; seamless pipes — 550. **Hatfield Packing Co.;** Hatfield; meatpacking — 510. **AMP Products Corp.** (HQ); Valley Forge; electrical supplies wholesaling — 500. **Emerson Electric Co. Inc.** (Brooks Instrument Div.); Hatfield; automatic controls — 500. **Fibre-Metal Products Co.;** Concordville; orthopedic, surgical supplies — 500. **Knoll International Inc.;** East Greenville; wooden household furniture — 500. **SMS Services Corp.;** Malvern; data processing services — 500. **The West Co.** (HQ); Phoenixville; rubber, plastic products — 500.

6th District

Southeast — Reading

The novels of this area's two most famous authors illustrate why the 6th swings back and forth between the two parties. John O'Hara's "Appointment in Samarra" and other novels focus on the wealthy families that rule the fictionalized version of his native Schuylkill County (Pottsville). In "Rabbit Run" and its sequels, John Updike explores the ethnic, working-class life of his home, Berks County (Reading). Pottsville, called Gibbsville by O'Hara, was and is Republican. In Updike's Reading (which he calls Brewer), life has a Democratic flavor.

Redistricting made few changes in the 6th. Democrats continue to have a slight registration advantage, but in statewide and national elections the district is likely to vote Republican.

A mountainous, coal-mining area, Schuylkill would seem to be prime Democratic territory. But the Eastern Europeans who worked the anthracite pits had a reason to be Republican: the O'Hara-type characters who owned the mines made that a condition of employment. Although unemployment has run high since 1950, few of these blue-collar workers blame the Republicans, and the partisan legacy lives on. The last time the county voted Democratic for president was 1964.

With a diversified economy turning out products ranging from cough drops to hosiery, Berks suffers less than Schuylkill from joblessness. The power of the unions has faded somewhat and, with it, the automatic Democratic habits of the voters. These voters stay with the Democrats for local and state legislative seats but often stray in voting for higher offices. The last time Berks voted Democratic for president also was in 1964.

Industrial Reading, also known for the factory outlets that bring bus loads of bargain hunters from far away, has diminished in political influence. It made up a third of the county's population in 1970, but contributes only one-quarter in the 1980s. At the same time the farming country and the growing suburbs have tilted increasingly Republican.

Election Returns

6th District		Democrat		Republican	
1976	President	91,016	(48.5%)	93,417	(49.7%)
	Senate	89,139	(48.1%)	94,450	(50.9%)
	House	134,458	(72.2%)	50,327	(27.0%)
1978	Governor	64,789	(43.5%)	82,867	(55.7%)
	House	105,537	(71.2%)	42,604	(28.8%)
1980	President	66,156	(35.6%)	104,703	(56.4%)
	Senate	76,270	(42.2%)	102,497	(56.7%)
	House	117,420	(64.5%)	64,696	(35.5%)
1982	Governor	75,036	(49.5%)	75,323	(49.7%)
	Senate	55,156	(37.1%)	91,645	(61.6%)
	House	108,230	(72.0%)	42,155	(28.0%)

Demographics

Population: 515,952. **Percent Change from 1970:** 3.9%.

Land Area: 1,838 square miles. **Population per Square Mile:** 280.7.

Counties, 1980 Population: Berks — 312,509; Carbon (Pt.) — 14,817; Lancaster (Pt.) — 27,996; Schuylkill — 160,630.

Cities, 1980 Population: Cumru Twp. — 11,474; Exeter Twp. — 14,419; Muhlenberg Twp. — 13,031; Pottsville — 18,195; Reading — 78,686; Spring Twp. — 17,193.

Race and Ancestry: White — 96.9%; Black — 1.6%; American Indian, Eskimo and Aleut — 0.0%; Asian and Pacific Islander — 0.4%. Spanish Origin — 1.9%. Dutch — 2.2%; English — 4.3%; German — 30.4%; Irish — 3.1%; Italian — 3.2%; Polish — 4.1%; Ukranian — 1.1%.

Universities, Enrollment: Albright College, Reading — 1,977; Alvernia College, Reading — 721; Kutztown State College, Kutztown — 5,500; McCann School of Business, Mahanoy City — 125; Pennsylvania State University (Berks campus), Reading — 1,165; Pennsylvania State University (Schuylkill campus), Schuylkill Haven — 760; Reading Area Community College, Reading — 1,441.

Newspapers, Circulation: *Eagle* (eS), Reading — 43,561; *Pottsville Republican* (e), Pottsville — 29,504; *Shenandoah Evening Herald* (e), Shenandoah — 11,602; *Times* (m), Reading — 42,474. *Lancaster New Era* also circulates in the district.

Commercial Television Stations, Affiliation: WTVE, Reading (None). District is divided between Philadelphia ADI and Wilkes-Barre—Scranton ADI. Portion is in Harrisburg-York-Lancaster-Lebanon ADI.

Industries:

Carpenter Technology Corp. (Carpenter Steel Div. - HQ); Reading; steel mill — 3,050. **Western Electric Co. Inc.;** Reading; electronic components — 3,000. **Gilbert Associates Inc.** (HQ); Reading; engineering services — 2,400. **Reading Hospital Inc.;** Reading; hospital — 2,400. **Dana Corp.** (Parish Div.); Reading; truck, auto frames — 2,000.

General Mills Inc. (David Crystal Div.); Reading; women's dresses — 1,570. **Rockwell International Corp.** (Graphic Systems Div.); Reading; printing equipment — 1,300. **The Polymer Corp.** (HQ); Reading; plastic rods — 1,110. **American Argo Corp.** (Tulip Topo Div.); Schuylkill Haven; knit outerwear mills — 1,000. **Ludens Inc.** (HQ); Reading; cough drops, candy — 1,000. **East Penn Mfg. Co. Inc.** (Deka Batteries & Cables - HQ); Lyon Station; storage batteries — 950. **Gold Mills Inc.;** Pine Grove; knit fabrics — 874. **George W. Bollman & Co.;** Adamstown; men's hats — 850. **SCM Corp.** (Glidden-C&R Div.); Reading; paint — 800. **The Bachman Co.** (HQ); Reading; pretzels — 700. **General Mills Inc.** (Fashion Flair Div.); Reading; warehousing — 700.

Raytheon Co. (Caloric Div.); Topton; household appliances — 700. **J. E. Morgan Knitting Mills Inc.** (HQ); Tamaqua; knit underwear — 613. **Baldwin Hardware Mfg. Corp.;** Reading; hardware — 600. **Itek Corp.** (Pennsylvania Optical); Reading; optical lenses — 600. **U. S. Industries Inc.** (Talbott Knitting Mill Div.); Reading; knit outerwear mills — 600. **Bally Case & Cooler Inc.** (HQ); Bally; commercial refrigeration — 550. **General Battery Corp.** (HQ); Reading; storage batteries — 550. **Bank of Pennsylvania Corp.;** (HQ); Reading; bank holding company — 520. **Reading Eagle Co.;** Reading; newspaper publishing — 510. **Birdsboro Corp.** (HQ); Birdsboro; rolling mill machinery — 500. **Blueray Systems Inc.;** Schuylkill Haven; oil burners —

500. **Inco Electroenergy Corp.** (Willson Div.); Reading; orthopedic, ophthalmic goods — 500. **McAdoo Mfg. Co. Inc.;** McAdoo; children's outerwear — 500. **The Tappan Co.** (Quaker Maid Kitchen Div.); Leesport; wooden kitchen furniture — 500. **W G M Safety Products;** Reading; prosthetic supplies — 500. **Wyomissing Corp.** (Narrow Fabric Div. - HQ); Reading; narrow woven fabric — 500.

7th District

Southwest Philadelphia Suburbs

Republicans continue to dominate Delaware County in the 1980s, although their registration edge has slipped from 3-to-1 to 2.5-to-1. That decline was not likely to help the GOP unseat the Democratic incumbent who first won the seat in 1974. In redistricting the Legislature sent Democratic Chester to the 5th District, but replaced it with comparable territory — blue-collar Ward 40 from the old 1st District in South Philadelphia. The 7th also picked up some affluent suburbs with firm Republican ties.

An amalgam of Irish, Italians and blacks, the Philadelphia part of the 7th is a workaday place that holds Philadelphia International Airport and many factories. Encompassing the Eastwick and Elmwood sections, it has staunch Democratic loyalties. While other South Philadelphia wards backed Ronald Reagan in 1980, these neighborhoods voted for Jimmy Carter.

Of the 7th's new suburban turf, the Main Line community of Radnor weighs in as the wealthiest, an old-money township where Sun Oil and *TV Guide* have their headquarters. Next door lies another addition, Haverford. Four other suburbs from the old 5th District were grafted onto the western edge of the 7th — Edgemont, Upper Providence, Middletown and Chester Heights.

Such well-off places as Marple, Newtown and Rose Valley are typical Delaware County bastions of Republicanism. Springfield, another dependably Republican community, often finds itself a center of campaign activity with candidates swarming its many shopping centers every Saturday. In adjacent Swarthmore, the academic influence of Swarthmore College makes Democrats competitive in what otherwise would be a business executives' town.

Closer to Philadelphia are blue-collar, ethnic suburbs such as Upper Darby, Yeadon and Colwyn. But the demographics of the area do not translate automatically into Democratic votes. Republicans continue to perform well in these nominally Democratic towns.

Election Returns

7th District		Democrat		Republican	
1976	President	112,341	(43.4%)	141,436	(54.6%)
	Senate	122,583	(47.8%)	132,567	(51.7%)
	House	129,774	(51.6%)	121,369	(48.3%)
1978	Governor	85,542	(40.9%)	121,565	(58.1%)
	House	95,361	(48.1%)	102,124	(51.5%)
1980	President	84,935	(34.5%)	136,488	(55.5%)
	Senate	89,008	(37.2%)	147,546	(61.6%)
	House	106,196	(44.9%)	121,666	(51.4%)
1982	Governor	68,375	(36.0%)	119,983	(63.2%)
	Senate	59,139	(31.9%)	124,447	(67.1%)
	House	105,775	(55.4%)	85,023	(44.6%)

Demographics

Population: 515,766. **Percent Change from 1970:** -8.3%.

Land Area: 140 square miles. **Population per Square Mile:** 3,684.0.

Counties, 1980 Population: Delaware (Pt.) — 466,086; Philadelphia (Pt.) — 49,680.

Cities, 1980 Population: Aston Twp. — 14,530; Darby — 11,513; Darby Twp. — 12,264; Haverford Twp. — 52,349 Lansdowne — 11,891; Marple Twp. — 23,642; Middletown Twp. — 12,463; Nether Providence Twp. — 12,730; Newtown Twp. — 11,775; Philadelphia (Pt.) — 49,680; Radnor — 27,676; Ridley Twp. — 33,771; Springfield Twp. — 25,326; Upper Darby Twp. — 84,054; Yeadon — 11,727.

Race and Ancestry: White — 92.9%; Black — 5.9%; American Indian, Eskimo and Aleut — 0.1%; Asian and Pacific Islander — 0.9%. Spanish Origin — 0.6%. English — 5.7%; German — 5.3%; Greek — 0.8%; Irish — 14.4%; Italian — 11.4%; Polish — 1.8%; Russian — 1.0%; Scottish — 0.5%; Ukranian — 0.5%.

Universities, Enrollment: Cabrini College, Radnor — 635; Delaware County Community College, Media — 6,020; Eastern College, St. Davids — 639; Haverford College, Haverford — 1,070; Keystone Secretarial and Business Administration School, Swarthmore — 162; Lyons Technical School, Upper Darby — 300; Neumann College, Aston — 766; Pennsylvania Institute of Technology, Upper Darby — 401.

Pennsylvania State University (Delaware County campus), Media — 1,380; Pennsylvania State University, Radnor Center for Graduate Studies and Continuing Education, Radnor — 397; Swarthmore College, Swarthmore — 1,316; Valley Forge Military Junior College, Wayne — 113; Villanova University, Villanova — 10,375; The Williamson Free School of Mechanical Trades, Media — 212.

Newspapers, Circulation: *Delaware County Daily Times* (m), Chester — 43,289. *The Philadelphia Inquirer* and *Philadelphia Daily News* also circulate in the district.

Commercial Television Stations, Affiliation: Entire district is located in Philadelphia ADI.

Military Installations: Philadelphia International Airport Communications Station (Air Force), Philadelphia — 13.

Industries:

The **Boeing Co. Inc.** (Vertol Div.); Ridley Park; aircraft — 4,500. **Westinghouse Electric Corp.;** Lester; metal-cutting machine tools — 2,400. **Scott Paper Co.** (Packaged Products Div. - HQ); Ridley Park; paper products — 1,800. **Franklin Mint Corp.** (HQ); Media; collectables — 1,789. **Misericordia Hospital;** Darby; hospital — 1,300.

Litton Systems Inc. (Clifton Precision Div.); Clifton Heights; electronic components — 1,200. **State Farm Fire & Casualty Co.;** Springfield; casualty insurance — 1,170. **Delaware County Memorial Hospital;** Drexel Hill; hospital — 1,100. **American Home Products Corp.** (Wyeth Laboratories Div.); Wayne; pharmaceuticals — 1,000. **Triangle Publications Inc.** (Television Publications Div. - HQ); Radnor; magazine publishing — 900. **Atlantic Richfield Co.** (Chemical & Research Center); Newtown Square; chemical research — 800. **Chilton Co.** (Consolidated Research Services - HQ); Wayne; publishing — 800. **G & H Steel Service Inc.;** Broomall; steel contractor — 700. **Computer Input Services Inc.;** Upper Darby; data processing services — 500. **Sun Co. Inc.** (HQ); Radnor; petroleum research, development — 500. **Sunroc Corp.** (HQ); Glen Riddle; heating equipment — 500.

8th District

Northern Philadelphia Suburbs

Known for its winding country lanes and 18th-century stone farmhouses, Bucks County has an image of genteel country living that suggests devout Republican loyalties. But that image is spoiled by a sizable industrial sector in

Lower Bucks and a growing suburban development that by 1982 extended north to mid-county. Blue-collar workers and independent suburbanites make Democrats competitive in the 8th. While Ronald Reagan won Bucks easily in 1980, Gerald R. Ford nearly lost it in 1976. The new 7th has a GOP registration edge of 55-45 percent, but GOP candidates have to show moderate inclinations to win.

The district includes all of Bucks and a small piece of rich and very Republican Montgomery County. It lost two Montgomery towns, Hatboro and Horsham, to the 13th District. That left mansion-dotted Bryn Athyn, Lower Moreland and part of Upper Moreland as the Montgomery appendage to the 8th.

Democratic Lower Bucks has economic problems, and they are most acute in Fairless Hills. Far from the bucolic vistas commonly associated with Bucks, this part of the county offers factories, commercial strips, tract developments and the Keystone Racetrack. Levittown's tightly spaced homes built after World War II attracted thousands of ethnic Philadelphia Democrats moving out from the inner city.

Farther north Bucks becomes more Republican. But Democrats can hold their own in the county's midsection; they win their share of local elections in communities such as Warminster and Doylestown. Democrats do especially well in and around New Hope, a quaint river town famous for its antique shops and artists' colony.

Upper Bucks, with its landed gentry and farmers, usually stays with the Republicans. Towns such as Upper Black Eddy harbor business executives who commute to Manhattan and, when home, vote Republican.

Election Returns

8th District		Democrat		Republican	
1976	President	81,782	(46.6%)	90,142	(51.4%)
	Senate	83,598	(48.0%)	88,953	(51.1%)
	House	85,782	(50.4%)	81,322	(47.8%)
1978	Governor	54,775	(40.8%)	78,208	(58.2%)
	House	81,435	(62.0%)	49,831	(38.0%)
1980	President	60,414	(32.2%)	105,284	(56.1%)
	Senate	65,595	(35.8%)	115,359	(62.9%)
	House	90,861	(49.2%)	92,614	(50.2%)
1982	Governor	60,467	(36.8%)	102,595	(62.4%)
	Senate	52,869	(32.9%)	105,874	(65.9%)
	House	83,242	(50.3%)	80,928	(48.9%)

Demographics

Population: 516,902. **Percent Change from 1970:** 14.1%.

Land Area: 626 square miles. **Population per Square Mile:** 825.7.

Counties, 1980 Population: Bucks — 479,211; Montgomery (Pt.) — 37,691.

Cities, 1980 Population: Bensalem Twp. — 52,399; Bristol — 10,867; Bristol Twp. — 58,733; Doylestown Twp. — 11,824; Falls Twp. — 36,083; Lower Makefield Twp. — 17,351; Lower Moreland Twp. — 12,472; Lower Southampton Twp. — 18,305; Middletown Twp. — 34,246; Northampton Twp. — 27,392; Upper Moreland Twp. (Pt.) — 24,272; Upper Southampton Twp. — 15,806; Warminster Twp. — 35,543; Warrington Twp. — 10,704.

Race and Ancestry: White — 96.2%; Black — 2.4%; American Indian, Eskimo and Aleut — 0.1%; Asian and Pacific Islander — 0.7%.

Spanish Origin — 1.1%. Dutch — 0.5%; English — 5.8%; German — 12.5%; Hungarian — 0.5%; Irish — 7.2%; Italian — 5.3%; Polish — 2.9%; Russian — 1.5%; Scottish — 0.6%; Ukranian — 0.6%.

Universities, Enrollment: Academy of the New Church, Bryn Athyn — 161; Bucks County Community College, Newtown — 9,104; Delaware Valley College of Science and Agriculture, Doylestown — 1,715; Pennco Tech, Bristol — 806; Philadelphia College of Bible, Langhorne — 509; Welder Training and Testing Institute, Bensalem — 150.

Newspapers, Circulation: *Bucks County Courier Times* (mS), Levittown — 63,140; *The Daily Intelligencer* (m), Doylestown — 26,698; *The Free Press* (e), Quakertown — 6,885. *The Philadelphia Inquirer* and *Philadelphia Daily News* also circulate in the district.

Commercial Television Stations, Affiliation: Entire district is located in Philadelphia ADI.

Military Installations: Naval Air Development Center, Warminster — 2,866.

Industries:

United States Steel Corp.; Morrisville; steel — 5,000. **Fischer & Porter Co.** (Lab-Crest Scientific Glass Co. - HQ); Warminster; laboratory equipment — 2,500. **Rohm & Haas Co.** (HQ); Bristol; plastics, pesticides — 1,000. **Ametek Inc.** (U. S. Gauge Div.); Sellersville; automatic controls — 965. **Pennwalt Corp.** (Sharpless Stokes Equipment Div.); Warminster; industrial machinery — 775.

Suburban Industrial Maintenance Co.; Warminster; janitorial services — 700. **Brown Boveri Corp.;** Chalfont; switchgears — 650. **Keystone Lighting Corp.;** Bristol; commercial lighting fixtures — 650. **Betz Laboratories Inc.** (HQ); Langhorne; chemicals — 600. **Minnesota Mining & Mfg. Co.;** Bristol; tape, surgical equipment — 600. **The Korman Corp.;** Langhorne; construction — 500. **Original Seafood Shantys Inc.;** Bensalem; seafood wholesaling — 500.

9th District

South Central — Altoona

To Pennsylvania Turnpike travelers, this district, which crosses the Allegheny Mountains, is a series of tunnels, long climbs and sharp descents. To Republicans, it is a predictable source of votes.

This central Pennsylvania region long has been a passageway to the West, and, other than farming, transportation has been its central focus. Before the coming of the railroad, trade and travel went the long way around the mountains, ducking south. Altoona prospered as a rail center.

With the decline of the rail system, a new travel-related culture grew up along the turnpike, the nation's first superhighway, opened in 1940. Its epitome is Breezewood, the celebrated "Town of Motels" — by night, a garish glow of neon signs amid the mountain darkness.

For the most part, the 9th is a series of small villages scattered among the mountains. It has little industry; its farmers raise cattle for beef and milk. The isolation and agricultural character of the area have bred a strong strain of conservatism. Local Republicans there boast that much of the area of the 9th has gone Republican since 1860.

Altoona, which lost 9.6 percent of its population in the 1970s, used to be a Democratic stronghold. Developed by the Pennsylvania Railroad, it has the giant Samuel Rea Railroad Shops; just to the west of it, the tracks form the famous Horseshoe Curve, an engineering marvel. But many of the railroad workers who voted Democratic have lost their jobs and left. Republicans now have a small registration lead.

The changes wrought by redistricting are of minor importance. Rural Republican Snyder and Perry counties were removed and placed in the 17th District. Brought in to replace them were Democratic coal-mining areas in southern Clearfield and northern Cambria counties, but these have too few people to make a dent in the Republican majority.

Election Returns

9th District		Democrat		Republican	
1976	President	71,159	(42.4%)	94,421	(56.2%)
	Senate	70,034	(42.0%)	95,494	(57.2%)
	House	13,423	(8.5%)	144,158	(91.5%)
1978	Governor	57,487	(42.1%)	78,022	(57.2%)
	House	40,361	(29.5%)	96,608	(70.5%)
1980	President	59,422	(35.0%)	101,766	(59.9%)
	Senate	73,514	(43.8%)	92,671	(55.2%)
	House	9,105	(5.7%)	151,155	(94.2%)
1982	Governor	63,010	(44.3%)	78,551	(55.2%)
	Senate	45,857	(32.2%)	95,121	(66.8%)
	House	49,583	(34.9%)	92,322	(65.1%)

Demographics

Population: 515,430. **Percent Change from 1970:** 8.5%.

Land Area: 5,584 square miles. **Population per Square Mile:** 92.3.

Counties, 1980 Population: Bedford — 46,784; Blair — 136,621; Cambria (Pt.) — 12,813; Clearfield (Pt.) — 41,201; Cumberland (Pt.) — 43,191; Franklin — 113,629; Fulton — 12,842; Huntingdon — 42,253; Juniata — 19,188; Mifflin — 46,908.

Cities, 1980 Population: Altoona — 57,078; Chambersburg — 16,174; Greene Twp. — 11,470; Guilford Twp. — 10,567; Logan Twp. — 12,183.

Race and Ancestry: White — 98.7%; Black — 0.9%; American Indian, Eskimo and Aleut — 0.1%; Asian and Pacific Islander — 0.2%. Spanish Origin — 0.4%. Dutch — 1.2%; English — 8.8%; French — 0.7%; German — 25.1%; Irish — 3.8%; Italian — 1.9%; Polish — 1.0%.

Universities, Enrollment: Juniata College, Huntingdon — 1,301; Pennsylvania State University (Altoona campus), Altoona — 2,133; Pennsylvania State University (Mont Alto campus), Mont Alto — 826; Shippensburg State College, Shippensburg — 5,959; Wilson College, Chambersburg — 197.

Newspapers, Circulation: *Altoona Mirror* (e), Altoona — 35,024; *Bedford Daily Gazette* (m), Bedford — 7,413; *The Daily News* (e), Huntingdon — 11,812; *Public Opinion* (e), Chambersburg — 19,813; *Record Herald* (e), Waynesboro — 10,393; *The Sentinel* (e), Lewistown — 12,799; *Tyrone Daily Herald* (e), Tyrone — 3,966. Harrisburg *Evening News* and Johnstown *Tribune-Democrat* also circulate in the district.

Commercial Television Stations, Affiliation: WOPC, Altoona (ABC); WTAJ-TV, Altoona (CBS). Most of district is located in Johnstown-Altoona ADI. Portions are in Harrisburg-York-Lancaster-Lebanon ADI and Washington, D.C. ADI.

Military Installations: Letterkenny Army Depot, Chambersburg — 6,274.

Industries:

Kidde Inc. (Grove Mfg. Co. Div.); Shady Grove; industrial trucks, hoists — 3,000. **Cluett, Peabody & Co. Inc.** (J. Shoeneman Co.); Chambersburg; men's pants — 1,703. **Consolidated Rail Corp.;** Altoona; railroad operations — 1,400. **The Altoona Hospital;** Altoona;

hospital — 1,370. **PPG Industries Inc.;** Mount Holly Springs; flat glass — 1,000.

SCM Corp.; Altoona; textile machinery — 1,000. **New Enterprise Stone & Lime Co.** (HQ); New Enterprise; limestone — 900. **Owens-Corning Fiberglas Corp.;** Huntingdon; glass fiber — 900. **Titanium Metals Corp. of America** (Standard Steel Div.); Burnham; steel products — 900. **Litton Industrial Products Inc.** (Landis Tool Co. Div.); Waynesboro; precision grinding tools — 820. **J. L. G. Industries Inc.** (HQ); McConnellsburg; hoists, cranes — 765. **American Can Co.** (Butterick Fashion Marketing); Altoona; printed patterns — 750. **Teledyne Industries Inc.** (Teledyne Landis Machine Div.); Waynesboro; machine tools — 725. **PPG Industries;** Tipton; glass products — 706. **American Can Co.;** Chambersburg; food containers — 700. **T. B. Woods Sons Co.** (HQ); Chambersburg; mechanical power transmission equipment — 656.

Frick Co. Inc. (HQ); Waynesboro; refrigeration equipment — 650. **Brown Group Recreational Industries** (Hedstrom Co. Div.); Bedford; children's toys, bicycles — 600. **Cluett, Peabody & Co. Inc.** (The Arrow Co. Div.); Lewistown; men's shirts — 600. **Corning Glass Works Inc.** (Consumer Products Div.); Greencastle; warehousing — 600. **Empire Kosher Poultry Inc.** (Dean Poultry Div. - HQ); Mifflintown; poultry processing — 600. **S. K. F. Industries Inc.** (Ball Bearing Div.); Altoona; ball bearings — 600. **Chicago Rivet & Machine Co.;** Tyrone; rivets — 550. **Jasper Textiles Inc.** (Waynesboro Knitting Co. Div.); Waynesboro; knitwear — 550. **Appleton Paper Inc.;** Roaring Spring; business forms — 520. **Avtex Fibres Inc.;** Lewistown; celluloid fiber — 500. **Elco Corp.** (Connector Div.); Huntingdon; electronic wiring devices — 500. **Sperry Corp.** (Sperry New Holland Div.); Belleville; farm machinery — 500. **U. S. Sports Inc.;** Huntingdon; sports footwear — 500. **Warnaco Inc.** (Knitwear Div.); Altoona; men's, women's outerwear — 500.

10th District

Northeast — Scranton

The city of Scranton dominated the politics of northeastern Pennsylvania in the early part of this century, but as the old coal-and-railroad town declined in population, it and Democratic Lackawanna County around it have had to speak with a quiet voice. Lackawanna is still Democratic, but its vote was too small for Jimmy Carter to carry the new 10th either in 1976 or 1980.

Moderate Republicanism sells well in Lackawanna and the party label works in the rural remainder of the district. The Scranton family remains a power in the county. William W. Scranton, known as "the Squire," served as governor in the 1960s. His son, William III, carried Democratic Lackawanna when he won the lieutenant governorship in 1978.

Despite Scranton's continuing population losses (14.2 percent in the 1970s), the growth in the outlying counties required the 10th to give up about 5,000 people in redistricting. But the district is virtually unchanged politically. It gave up two-thirds of mainly Republican Monroe County, but kept some of its Pocono Mountain resorts such as Buck Hill Falls and Camelback, plus the Democratic Stroudsburg area. Sparsely populated Potter County and part of Clinton County were tacked onto the 10th's western end. Both are Republican.

The rural counties that stayed in the 10th are, like Potter and Clinton, made up of woods, dairy farms and Republicans. Pike, a Pocono Mountain county, contains many vacation cottages and is home to business executives who commute to New York. This area experienced growth during the 1970s; Pike saw its population increase 54 percent.

Lackawanna County still has half the district's people. Its Democratic majority votes in Scranton and in blue-collar towns such as Moosic and Old Forge. The Republicans cluster in Clarks Summit, Dalton (home of the Scranton family) and other affluent suburbs. Ethnically, the scramble for political office in this polyglot county is between the Italians and the Irish.

Election Returns

10th District		Democrat		Republican	
1976	President	101,832	(48.4%)	105,197	(50.0%)
	Senate	94,752	(47.9%)	101,118	(51.2%)
	House	80,347	(38.5%)	128,331	(61.5%)
1978	Governor	58,615	(38.3%)	93,560	(61.2%)
	House	39,334	(25.4%)	115,543	(74.6%)
1980	President	79,276	(39.0%)	110,645	(54.4%)
	Senate	85,079	(44.6%)	102,923	(54.0%)
	House	43,222	(22.7%)	145,957	(76.6%)
1982	Governor	72,407	(47.2%)	79,686	(51.9%)
	Senate	53,884	(36.5%)	91,809	(62.2%)
	House	49,868	(32.5%)	103,617	(67.5%)

Demographics

Population: 515,442. **Percent Change from 1970:** 7.1%.

Land Area: 7,042 square miles. **Population per Square Mile:** 73.2.

Counties, 1980 Population: Bradford — 62,919; Clinton (Pt.) — 7,987; Lackawanna — 227,908; Monroe (Pt.) — 40,112; Pike — 18,271; Potter — 17,726; Susquehanna — 37,876; Tioga — 40,973; Wayne — 35,237; Wyoming — 26,433.

Cities, 1980 Population: Carbondale — 11,255; Dunmore — 16,781; Scranton — 88,117.

Race and Ancestry: White — 99.1%; Black — 0.4%; American Indian, Eskimo and Aleut — 0.1%; Asian and Pacific Islander — 0.3%. Spanish Origin — 0.4%. Dutch — 0.8%; English — 9.1%; German — 8.3%; Irish — 7.5%; Italian — 6.8%; Polish — 6.0%; Russian — 0.9%; Ukranian — 1.0%.

Universities, Enrollment: Baptist Bible College, Clarks Summit — 823; Center for Degree Studies, Scranton — 3,752; East Stroudsburg State College, East Stroudsburg — 3,934; Johnson School of Technology, Scranton — 570; Keystone Junior College, La Plume — 963; Lackawanna Junior College, Scranton — 1,048; Mansfield State College, Mansfield — 2,468; Marywood College, Scranton — 3,161; Pennsylvania State College (Worthington Scranton campus), Dunmore — 1,082; University of Scranton, Scranton — 4,507.

Newspapers, Circulation: *The Daily Review* (m), Towanda — 9,242; *The Evening Times* (e), Sayre — 8,400; *The Pocono Record* (mS), Stroudsburg — 18,008; *Tribune* (mS), Scranton — 40,506.

Commercial Television Stations, Affiliation: WDAV-TV, Scranton (CBS); WSWB, Scranton (None). District is divided among Wilkes-Barre—Scranton ADI, Binghamton (N.Y.) ADI, Buffalo (N.Y.) ADI, Elmira (N.Y.) ADI and New York (N.Y.) ADI.

Military Installations: Scranton Army Ammunition Plant, Scranton — 537.

Industries:

RCA Corp. (Picture Tube Div.); Dunmore; television picture tubes — 1,500. **Mercy Hospital;** Scranton; hospital — 1,370. **Ingersoll-Rand Co.;** Athens; pneumatic tools — 1,250. **Robert Packer Hospital Inc.;** Sayre; hospital — 1,250. **Sangamo Weston Inc.** (Weston Components Controls Div.); Archbald; electronic components — 1,200.

The Community Medical Center; Scranton; hospital — 1,110. **GTE Products Corp.** (Chemical & Metallurgical Div.); Towanda; chemicals — 1,048. **Masonite Corp.;** Towanda; hardboard — 790. **The Trane Co.;** Dunmore; heating, air conditioning equipment — 768. **American Technical Industries Inc.;** Peckville; computer parts — 700. **Haddon Craftsmen Inc.** (HQ); Scranton; book printing — 700. **Northeastern Educational Intermediate Unit;** Dunmore; educational films — 677.

E. I. du Pont de Nemours & Co.; Towanda; photographic supplies — 615. **Magnetic Laboratories Inc.** (Magnetics Div. - HQ); Hallstead; small electric housewares — 600. **J. P. Ward Foundries Inc.** (HQ); Blossburg; malleable iron foundry — 570. **Brook Mfg. Co. Inc.;** Old Forge; men's trousers — 500. **Chamberlain Mfg. Corp.** (Scranton Army Ammunition Plant); Scranton; shell casings — 500. **WEA Mfg. Inc.** (HQ); Olyphant; phonograph records — 500. **Whittaker Corp.** (Berwick Forge & Fabricating Div.); Renovo; railroad equipment — 500.

11th District

Northeast — Wilkes-Barre

Today it is a dubious honor to be the hard-coal center of the world. The energy crises of the 1970s spurred a modest comeback for anthracite, but mining this coal is very expensive, and no boom is on the horizon. In a town like Wilkes-Barre, unemployment and black lung disease are constant concerns of a legislator's life.

In most years this is Democratic territory. But Democratic candidates have found some of their fellow partisans to be fickle. The district went for Jimmy Carter in 1976, then turned against him four years later. Even heavily Democratic Luzerne County (Wilkes-Barre) spurned him. In that same year, the district sent a Republican to the U.S. House.

Redistricting improved the GOP's registration figure by a tiny amount, but Democrats still had 57 percent of the voters. The 11th made up its population deficit of more than 30,000 by pulling in a Democratic coal-mining section of Northumberland County and the rural Republican turf of northwestern Monroe County. The Monroe section holds the Tobyhanna Army Depot and resorts such as Mount Pocono.

Staying in the district are two politically marginal counties that mix farming, mining and light industry (Columbia and Montour) and part of a third (Carbon). Sullivan County tilts Republican.

Luzerne, with two-thirds of the district's population, anchors the district. It is a rich ethnic stew of Eastern Europeans, Italians, Irish and Welsh. Wilkes-Barre and Pittston are the county's Democratic vote centers. Another good town for the Democrats is Hazleton, in the southern part of Luzerne County. The Republicans live in more affluent Kingston, Dallas, and Forty-Fort.

Election Returns

11th District		Democrat		Republican	
1976	President	109,718	(53.7%)	92,193	(45.2%)
	Senate	106,601	(53.5%)	91,691	(46.0%)
	House	137,826	(69.4%)	60,597	(30.5%)
1978	Governor	76,221	(46.4%)	86,982	(52.9%)
	House	70,138	(56.8%)	53,299	(43.2%)
1980	President	86,508	(43.1%)	102,980	(51.3%)

11th District		Democrat		Republican	
1980	Senate	97,466	(49.0%)	98,243	(49.4%)
	House	94,916	(49.2%)	97,947	(50.8%)
1982	Governor	96,415	(56.8%)	71,911	(42.4%)
	Senate	77,660	(47.3%)	84,513	(51.4%)
	House	90,371	(53.5%)	78,485	(46.5%)

Demographics

Population: 515,729. **Percent Change from 1970:** 2.7%.

Land Area: 2,523 square miles. **Population per Square Mile:** 204.4.

Counties, 1980 Population: Carbon (Pt.) — 38,468; Columbia — 61,967; Luzerne — 343,079; Monroe (Pt.) — 11,805; Montour — 16,675; Northumberland (Pt.) — 37,386; Sullivan — 6,349.

Cities, 1980 Population: Berwick — 11,850; Bloomsburg — 11,717; Coal Twp. — 10,984; Hanover Twp. — 12,601; Hazleton — 27,318; Kingston — 15,681; Nanticoke — 13,044; Plains Twp. — 11,338; Shamokin — 10,357; Wilkes-Barre — 51,551.

Race and Ancestry: White — 99.0%; Black — 0.6%; American Indian, Eskimo and Aleut — 0.0%; Asian and Pacific Islander — 0.2%. Spanish Origin — 0.4%. Dutch — 1.7%; English — 4.9%; German — 11.3%; Hungarian — 0.7%; Irish — 5.2%; Italian — 6.0%; Polish — 11.5%; Russian — 0.9%; Ukranian — 1.3%.

Universities, Enrollment: Bloomsburg State College, Bloomsburg — 6,503; College Misericordia, Dallas — 1,114; King's College, Wilkes-Barre — 2,173; Luzerne County Community College, Nanticoke — 3,414; Pennsylvania State University (Hazleton campus), Hazleton — 1,105; Pennsylvania State University (Wilkes-Barre campus), Wilkes-Barre — 631; Wilkes College, Wilkes-Barre — 2,900.

Newspapers, Circulation: *Berwick Enterprise* (m), Berwick — 19,776; *Citizen's Voice* (m), Wilkes Barre — 46,491; *The Danville News* (e), Danville — 4,310; *The Morning Press* (m), Bloomsburg — 19,776; *The News-Item* (e), Shamokin — 15,605; *Standard-Speaker* (all day), Hazleton — 24,304; *Times-News* (e), Lehighton — 16,401; *The Wilkes-Barre Times Leader* (all day), Wilkes Barre — 51,916. Sunbury *Daily Item* also circulates in the district.

Commercial Television Stations, Affiliation: WBRE-TV, Wilkes-Barre (NBC); WNEP-TV, Avoca (ABC). Most of district is located in Wilkes-Barre—Scranton ADI. Portion is in New York (N.Y.) ADI.

Military Installations: Tobyhanna Army Depot, Tobyhanna — 4,474; Wyoming Valley Air National Guard Center, Wyoming — 6,410.

Nuclear Power Plants: Susquehanna 1 and 2, Berwick (General Electric, Bechtel).

Industries:

The Geisinger Medical Center; Danville; hospital — 2,860. **Wilkes Barre General Hospital;** Wilkes Barre; hospital — 1,480. **Leslie Fay Inc.;** Wilkes Barre; women's clothes — 1,400. **Borden Inc.** (Wise Foods); Berwick; potato chips — 1,150. **Mercy Hospital;** Wilkes Barre; hospital — 1,010.

Danville State Hospital; Danville; state psychiatric hospital — 1,000. **Topps Chewing Gum Inc.;** Duryea; chewing gum — 800. **Gulf & Western Corp.** (Consolidated Cigar Div.); Berwick; cigars — 650. **Owens-Illinois Inc.** (Kimble-Pocano Products Plant Div.); Pittston; glass face plates — 650. **RCA Corp.** (Solid State Div.); Mountaintop; semiconductors — 650. **American Brands Inc.** (American Cigar Div.); Mountaintop; cigars — 632. **Bechtel Power Corp.;** Berwick; heavy construction — 600. **Dorr-Oliver Inc.;** Hazleton; special process machinery — 600. **Humberland Dress Co.;** Mount Carmel; children's dresses — 600. **Kennedy Van Saun Corp.;** Danville; mining machinery — 600.

New Jersey Zinc Co. Inc.; Palmerton; zinc mining, smelting — 600. **Schott Optical Glass Inc.;** Duryea; ophthalmic glass — 600. **Barrett Haentjens & Co.** (HQ); Hazleton; centrifugal pumps — 550. **Mount Airy Lodge Inc.;** Mount Pocono; resort — 550. **St. Regis Paper Co.** (Flexible Package Div.); West Hazleton; polyethylene bags — 550.

Bloomsburg Mills Inc.; Bloomsburg; synthetic fiber — 500. **Luzerne Outerwear Mfg.;** Berwick; men's clothing — 500. **Metropolitan Wire Corp.** (HQ); Wilkes Barre; wire — 500. **Scotty's Fashion of Lehighton;** Lehighton; women's suits — 500.

12th District

Southwest — Johnstown

The new 12th District is drawn in nearly equal proportions from the old 12th and the old 21st. It takes in most of Westmoreland and Cambria counties; both suffer from high unemployment. Spread over the foothills of the Allegheny Mountains, Westmoreland and Cambria are similar in demographics and voting habits. Their ethnic, industrial towns, many of them nearly all white, are often dependent on one local industry. In Westmoreland County, New Stanton has a Volkswagen assembly plant. Latrobe fabricates steel; Jeannette makes steam turbines. In Cambria County, Leechburg rolls steel, Crenshaw blows glass containers and Cherry Tree holds a rail yard.

Johnstown, the biggest city in the new 12th, exemplifies the hard times felt throughout this blue-collar district. Its central business district has withered and its plants have laid off hundreds of workers. To make matters worse, a flood devastated the old city in 1977, the third deluge in the past century (although not as serious as the first two).

Cambria and Westmoreland show remarkable parallels in voting. In the 1976 presidential election, Jimmy Carter carried Westmoreland with 54.5 percent of the vote and Cambria with 53.8 percent. Four years later, the vote reflected dissatisfaction with the Democratic president; Carter won Westmoreland with 49 percent and Cambria with 50.1.

Both counties also have political histories heavy on intrigue and venality. John Torquoto ran the Cambria Democratic organization until his 1978 conviction on corruption charges. At the same time, the law caught up with Egidio "Gene" Cerilli, the Westmoreland Democratic Party chairman. Both men were convicted on charges of extorting payments from highway construction firms in their respective counties.

The remap dropped the 12th's old Republican counties — Indiana, Jefferson and most of Armstrong. It also left out a Republican area of the old 21st — the affluent Ligonier Valley. Remaining in the 12th is Somerset County, whose flat farm lands produce too few Republican votes to offset the Democratic strength.

Election Returns

12th District		Democrat		Republican	
1976	President	94,428	(50.7%)	88,982	(47.8%)
	Senate	79,146	(38.5%)	125,341	(61.0%)
	House	116,392	(63.3%)	67,398	(36.7%)
1978	Governor	106,292	(61.4%)	65,608	(37.9%)
	House	98,410	(63.1%)	57,639	(36.9%)
1980	President	87,100	(45.5%)	94,584	(49.4%)
	Senate	130,329	(63.5%)	72,563	(35.4%)
	House	126,199	(62.8%)	74,737	(37.2%)

12th District		Democrat		Republican	
1982	Governor	80,003	(49.6%)	80,055	(49.6%)
	Senate	63,254	(39.5%)	94,958	(59.3%)
	House	96,369	(61.1%)	54,212	(34.4%)

Demographics

Population: 515,915. **Percent Change from 1970:** 4.7%.

Land Area: 2,290 square miles. **Population per Square Mile:** 225.3.

Counties, 1980 Population: Armstrong (Pt.) — 9,574; Cambria (Pt.) — 170,450; Somerset — 81,243; Westmoreland (Pt.) — 254,648.

Cities, 1980 Population: Derry Twp. — 16,193; Greensburg — 17,558; Hempfield Twp. — 43,396; Jeannette — 13,106; Johnstown — 35,496; Latrobe — 10,799; Mount Pleasant Twp. — 11,851; Murrysville — 16,036; North Huntingdon Twp. — 31,517; Penn Twp. — 16,153; Richland Twp. — 12,889; Unity Twp. — 19,976.

Race and Ancestry: White — 98.4%; Black — 1.1%; American Indian, Eskimo and Aleut — 0.1%; Asian and Pacific Islander — 0.3%. Spanish Origin — 0.4%. Dutch — 0.5%; English — 5.0%; German — 14.9%; Hungarian — 1.1%; Irish — 3.2%; Italian — 5.1%; Polish — 3.9%; Scottish — 0.5%; Ukranian — 0.8%.

Universities, Enrollment: Cambria-Rowe Business College, Johnstown — 146; Mount Aloysius Junior College, Cresson — 520; St. Francis College, Loretto — 1,650; St. Vincent College, Latrobe — 880; Seton Hill College, Greensburg — 951; Triangle Institute of Technology, Greensburg — 100; University of Pittsburgh at Johnstown, Johnstown — 2,879; Westmoreland County Community College, Youngwood — 2,841.

Newspapers, Circulation: *Daily American* (m), Somerset — 9,281; *Daily Standard-Observer* (e), Irwin — 13,502; *The Latrobe Bulletin* (e), Latrobe — 11,005; *Tribune-Democrat* (mS), Johnstown — 57,398; *Tribune-Review* (mS), Greensburg — 42,424.

Commercial Television Stations, Affiliation: WJAC-TV, Johnstown (NBC); WJNL-TV, Johnstown (None); WPCB-TV, Greensburg (None). District is divided between Johnstown-Altoona ADI and Pittsburgh ADI.

Industries:

Volkswagen of America (Volkswagen Westmoreland); New Stanton; motor vehicles — 3,000. **Bethlehem Steel Corp.;** Johnstown; steel — 2,000. **United States Steel Corp.** Johnstown; steel — 2,000. **Carrier Corp.** (Elliott Co. Div.); Jeannette; turbines — 1,650. **Conemaugh Valley Memorial Hospital;** Johnstown; hospital — 1,480.

Westmoreland Hospital Assn.; Greensburg; hospital — 1,450. **Bethlehem Mines Corp.;** Ebensburg; coal mining — 1,400. **Latrobe Area Hospital Inc.;** Latrobe; hospital — 1,200. **Latrobe Steel Co.** (Cast Masters Div. - HQ); Latrobe; die casting — 1,200. **Pennsylvania Power & Light Co.** (Greenwich Collieries); Barnesboro; coal mining — 1,100. **Westinghouse Electric Corp.** (Westinghouse Advanced Reactor); Madison; research — 1,100. **Robertshaw Controls Co.** (New Stanton Div.); Youngwood; temperature controls — 1,030. **Jeannette Corp.** (HQ); Jeannette; pressed, blown glass — 1,000. **Ryder Truck Lines Inc.** (Helms Express Div.); Irwin; truck terminal — 1,000. **Florence Mining Co. Inc.;** Seward; coal mining — 978. **North American Coal Corp.** (Florence Mining Co.); Seward; coal mining — 950. **Teledyne Industries Inc.** (Teledyne Vasco); Latrobe; steel — 850. **Kennametal Inc.;** Latrobe; machine tool accessories — 710. **Westinghouse Electric Corp.** (Insulating Div.); Manor; paints, allied products — 700.

Brown Boveri Electric Inc.; Greensburg; power switching equipment — 650. **Raybestos-Manhattan Inc.** (Modulus Corp.); Mount Pleasant; industrial fasteners — 650. **Barnes & Tucker Co.;** Barnesboro; coal mining — 634. **Allegheny Power Service Corp.;** Greensburg; management consulting — 600. **Super Valu Stores Inc.** (Charley Brothers Co. Div.); Greensburg; warehousing — 560. **Champion Spark Plug Co.** (De Vilbiss Div.); Somerset; X-ray equipment — 500. **Glosser Bros. Inc.** (HQ); Johnstown; department stores — 500. **Interstate Motor Freight System** (Steel Div.); Murrysville; truck termi-

nal — 500. **PPG Industries Inc.;** Greensburg; automotive glass — 500. **Reidbord Bros. Co.;** Apollo; men's, boys' clothing — 500. **Westinghouse Electric Corp.;** Youngwood; semiconductors — 500.

13th District

Northwest Philadelphia Suburbs

In the last century the Pennsylvania Railroad developed the rolling countryside along its main line west of Philadelphia. Among the greenery grew the mansions of the city's aristocracy. The wealthy here still play tennis at the posh Merion Cricket Club and send their children to exclusive private schools such as Episcopal Academy.

The Main Line anchors the state's most affluent district. It takes a well-versed socialite to know whether a Bryn Mawr address carries more prestige than a Gladwyne one, but even a political novice knows that both towns and all the others around them vote Republican. The local brand of Republicanism is moderate.

Beyond the Main Line, north of the Schuylkill River, old towns such as Ambler and Plymouth Meeting add to the big Republican advantage. The far-north end of the district is devoted to farming and country estates.

Most of the Democrats of the 13th District gather by the river. Lined up along the Schuylkill are the old mill towns of Conshohocken and Norristown and two blue-collar sections of Philadelphia, Manayunk and Roxborough.

Redistricting bolstered the Democratic vote with the addition of another Democratic section of the city — Overbrook — and of Philadelphia's wealthiest area, Chestnut Hill, which is nominally Republican but has shown an increasing weakness for liberal Democrats. But these changes do not threaten the district's GOP majority.

Election Returns

13th District		Democrat		Republican	
1976	President	109,064	(43.0%)	139,707	(55.1%)
	Senate	119,636	(47.6%)	130,280	(51.9%)
	House	94,356	(38.9%)	147,739	(60.9%)
1978	Governor	74,460	(36.8%)	125,962	(62.3%)
	House	63,394	(33.8%)	123,849	(66.1%)
1980	President	83,825	(34.1%)	134,628	(54.8%)
	Senate	76,706	(32.7%)	154,581	(65.9%)
	House	71,295	(31.0%)	151,603	(65.9%)
1982	Governor	61,789	(35.2%)	112,129	(63.9%)
	Senate	54,725	(31.9%)	115,083	(67.0%)
	House	59,709	(35.2%)	109,198	(64.3%)

Demographics

Population: 514,346. **Percent Change from 1970:** -2.9%.

Land Area: 239 square miles. **Population per Square Mile:** 2,152.1.

Counties, 1980 Population: Montgomery (Pt.) — 424,330; Philadelphia (Pt.) — 90,016.

Cities, 1980 Population: Abington Twp. — 59,084; Cheltenham Twp. — 35,509; Horsham Twp. — 15,959; Lansdale — 16,526; Lower

Merion Twp. — 59,651; Norristown — 34,684; Philadelphia (Pt.) — 90,016; Plymouth Twp. — 17,168; Springfield Twp. — 20,344; Towamencin Twp. — 11,112; Upper Dublin Twp. — 22,348; Upper Merion Twp. — 26,138; Upper Moreland Twp. (Pt.) — 1,602; Whitemarsh Twp. — 15,101; Whitpain Twp. — 11,772.

Race and Ancestry: White — 91.8%; Black — 6.4%; American Indian, Eskimo and Aleut — 0.1%; Asian and Pacific Islander — 1.4%. Spanish Origin — 0.8%. English — 5.6%; German — 7.9%; Hungarian — 0.5%; Irish — 8.6%; Italian — 9.5%; Polish — 3.0%; Russian — 4.1%; Scottish — 0.5%; Ukranian — 0.5%.

Universities, Enrollment: American College, Bryn Mawr — 1,572; Beaver College, Glenside — 2,040; Bryn Mawr College, Bryn Mawr — 1,784; Chestnut Hill College, Philadelphia — 989; Eastern Baptist Theological Seminary, Philadelphia — 264; Gwynedd-Mercy College, Gwynedd Valley — 1,854; Harcum Junior College, Bryn Mawr — 980; Lansdale School of Business, Lansdale — 166.

Manor Junior College, Jenkintown — 304; Montgomery County Community College, Blue Bell — 7,394; Northeastern Christian Junior College, Villanova — 174; Pennsylvania State University (Ogontz campus), Abington — 2,683; Philadelphia College of Textiles and Science, Philadelphia — 2,827; Rosemont College, Rosemont — 608; Spring Garden College, Chestnut Hill — 989; St. Charles Borromeo Seminary, Overbrook — 524; Westminster Theological Seminary, Philadelphia — 391.

Newspapers, Circulation: *The Report* (e), Lansdale — 19,838; *The Times Herald* (e), Norristown — 30,756; *Today's Post* (m), King of Prussia — 7,546; *Today's Spirit* (e), Hatboro — 7,546. *The Philadelphia Inquirer, Philadelphia Daily News* and *The Pottstown Mercury* also circulate in the district.

Commercial Television Stations, Affiliation: WWSG-TV, Philadelphia (None). Entire district is located in Philadelphia ADI. *(For other Philadelphia stations, see 1st and 2nd districts.)*

Military Installations: Willow Grove Naval Air Station, Horsham — 5,956.

Industries:

Merck & Co. Inc. (Merck, Sharpe & Dohme Labs); West Point; pharmaceutical preparations — 3,800. **Sperry Corp.** (Sperry Univac Div. - HQ); Blue Bell; electronic computing equipment — 3,628. **Leeds & Northrup Co.** (HQ); North Wales; industrial instruments — 3,500. **Honeywell Inc.;** Fort Washington; industrial instruments — 3,000. **Prudential Insurance Co. of America;** Dresher; life insurance — 2,500.

Ford Aerospace Communications; Lansdale; telecommunications equipment — 2,300. **The Lankenau Hospital;** Merion; hospital — 1,700. **Norristown State Hospital;** Norristown; psychiatric hospital — 1,560. **Abington Memorial Hospital;** Abington; hospital — 1,500. **McNeil Laboratories** (HQ); Fort Washington; pharmaceuticals — 1,500. **American Electronic Labs** (HQ); Montgomeryville; electronic transmitters — 1,200. **The Macke Co.** (Building Maintenance Service Div.); Bala-Cynwyd; building maintenance — 1,200. **McNeil Laboratories;** Spring House; pharmaceutical preparations — 1,200. **Independent Publications Inc.;** Bryn Mawr; newspaper publishing, radio broadcasting — 1,110. **William H. Rorer Inc.** (HQ); Fort Washington; pharmaceuticals — 1,110. **Bryn Mawr Hospital and Rehabilitation Center;** Bryn Mawr; hospital — 1,100. **Philadelphia Gear Corp.** (HQ); King of Prussia; gears — 1,100. **American Olean Tile Co. Inc.** (Ceramic Tile Div. - HQ); Lansdale; wall, floor tile — 1,000. **Container Corp. of America** (Fibre Corrugated Div.); Philadelphia; paperboard products — 1,000.

The Girard Co. (HQ); Bala-Cynwyd; banking — 1,000. **Milez Inc.** West Point; security services — 1,000. **Montgomery Hospital;** Norristown; hospital — 1,000. **United Hospitals Inc.;** Elkins Park; hospital — 1,000. **Solid State Scientific Inc.** (HQ); Montgomeryville; semiconductors — 900. **Hatboro Industrial Park Industries;** Hatboro; men's clothing — 850. **The Williard Co. Inc.;** Jenkintown; consulting services — 836. **Computer Peripherals Inc.;** Norristown; computers — 800. **Rohm & Haas Co.;** Spring House; research — 800. **Marriott Corp.;** Bala-Cynwyd; hotel — 775. **Harleysville Mutual Insurance Co.** (HQ); Harleysville; casualty, health insurance — 739. **I. M. S. America Ltd.;** Ambler; medical consulting services — 700. **Moore Products Co.** (HQ); Spring House; controls, measuring devices — 630. **After Six Inc.**

(Ramey Tyson Shirt Co.); Norristown; men's shirts — 600. **Extracorporeal Medical Specialties** (HQ); King of Prussia; medical apparatus — 600. **Glasgow Inc.;** Glenside; road construction — 600. **Shared Medical Systems Corp.** (HQ); King of Prussia; data processing services — 600. **Stroehmann Bros. Co.;** Norristown; bread, bakery products — 550. **Yarway Corp.** (HQ); Blue Bell; pipe fittings, industrial measuring devices — 530. **Unicorn Industries Inc.;** Horsham; abrasive products — 510. **International Computaprint** (HQ); Fort Washington; computerized typesetting — 500. **Kaiser Aluminum & Chemical Corp.** (Kaiser Refractories Div.); Plymouth Meeting; non-clay refractories — 500. **Henkels & McCoy Inc.** (HQ); Blue Bell; power line construction — 500. **Kulicke & Soffa Industries Inc.** (HQ); Horsham; industrial machinery — 500. **Limitorque Corp.;** King of Prussia; valve controls — 500. **North Penn Transfer Inc.** (HQ); Lansdale; trucking — 500. **Safeguard Business Systems Inc.** (HQ); Fort Washington; business forms — 500. **Vesper Corp.;** Bala-Cynwyd; metal shelving, office fixtures — 500.

14th District

Pittsburgh

Downtown Pittsburgh has lost its pollution and griminess over the past generation; the "Golden Triangle" that forms the heart of its business district has been transformed from a train yard into a cluster of office towers and parks.

But the 14th District, redrawn to include every inch of territory within the city limits, remains a place of blast furnaces, rolling mills and smokestacks. In the city's Hazlewood section, the neighborhood is lit at night by flames from the steel mills.

Situated at the confluence of the Ohio, Allegheny and Monongahela rivers, the city is a natural industrial center. It is also a corporate headquarters town — U.S. Steel, Gulf Oil, Westinghouse Electric and Alcoa have home offices there. It has diversified widely beyond its steel economy, which helped it escape some of the ravages of recession plaguing one-industry cities.

The corporate presence has little impact on Pittsburgh's very Democratic voting habits. While some blue-collar districts showed a disdain for Jimmy Carter in 1980, the 14th did not. Carter carried the area of the new 14th by almost identical margins in 1976 and 1980. In the 1978 governor's contest, when faced with a choice between two native Pittsburghers, the voters opted for the Democrat.

Hoping to increase Republican strength in the surrounding suburban 18th district, the Legislature transferred into the 14th western Pittsburgh and such blue-collar Ohio River towns as Coraopolis and McKees Rocks.

Dumping those Democrats into the 14th made the district even more of a Democratic stronghold, increasing the registration to 82 percent Democratic. The 14th keeps two white-collar Republican suburbs east of the city, Churchill and Forest Hills.

The new district is 22 percent black, with substantial black communities in Pittsburgh's Manchester, North Side and Stanton Heights sections. Because blacks are not numerous enough to control its voting, inner-city Pittsburgh seems likely to have white congressional representation at least through the 1980s.

The south side of the city gives Pittsburgh its image as a workingman's "shot-and-beer" town. It is packed with white ethnic neighborhoods that revolve around local taverns and Catholic parishes. The inhabitants work in the many factories lining the rivers.

In the district's other residential neighborhoods, farther north, black and ethnic neighborhoods coexist with affluent, Jewish Squirrel Hill and the Oakland academic-medical complex, home of Carnegie-Mellon University, the University of Pittsburgh and Children's Hospital. All vote Democratic.

Election Returns

14th District		Democrat		Republican	
1976	President	132,719	(58.9%)	86,985	(38.6%)
	Senate	90,057	(40.5%)	129,364	(58.1%)
	House	154,317	(73.5%)	53,902	(25.7%)
1978	Governor	91,855	(52.8%)	79,163	(45.5%)
	House	99,737	(62.8%)	57,569	(36.3%)
1980	President	123,121	(58.0%)	70,994	(33.4%)
	Senate	126,529	(63.3%)	68,092	(34.1%)
	House	144,856	(73.9%)	48,475	(24.7%)
1982	Governor	100,084	(59.1%)	65,869	(38.9%)
	Senate	82,072	(48.2%)	83,648	(49.1%)
	House	120,980	(74.9%)	32,780	(20.3%)

Demographics

Population: 516,629. **Percent Change from 1970:** -17.6%.

Land Area: 79 square miles. **Population per Square Mile:** 6,539.6.

Counties, 1980 Population: Allegheny (Pt.) — 516,629.

Cities, 1980 Population: Castle Shannon — 10,164; Pittsburgh — 423,938; Wilkinsburg — 23,669.

Race and Ancestry: White — 77.1%; Black — 21.8%; American Indian, Eskimo and Aleut — 0.1%; Asian and Pacific Islander — 0.6%. Spanish Origin — 0.7%. English — 2.7%; German — 9.1%; Hungarian — 1.1%; Irish — 5.1%; Italian — 7.2%; Polish — 4.9%; Russian — 1.3%; Ukranian — 0.8%.

Universities, Enrollment: Art Institute of Pittsburgh, Pittsburgh — 2,031; Carlow College, Pittsburgh — 977; Carnegie-Mellon University, Pittsburgh — 5,415; Chatham College, Pittsburgh — 721; Community College of Allegheny County (Allegheny campus), Pittsburgh — 4,031; Community College of Allegheny County (College Center North), Pittsburgh — 3,170.

Computer Systems Institute, Pittsburgh — 293; Dean Institute of Technology, Pittsburgh — 196; Duff's Business Institute, Pittsburgh — 1,042; Duquesne University, Pittsburgh — 6,772; Electronic Institute, Pittsburgh — 402; ICM School of Business, Pittsburgh — 1,308; La Roche College, Pittsburgh — 1,346; Median School of Allied Health Careers, Pittsburgh — 550; Penn Technical Institute, Pittsburgh — 507; Pittsburgh Institute of Aeronautics, Pittsburgh — 630.

Pittsburgh Technical Institute, Pittsburgh — 317; Pittsburgh Theological Seminary, Pittsburgh — 282; Point Park College, Pittsburgh — 2,210; Robert Morris College, Coraopolis — 5,071; Triangle Institute of Technology, Pittsburgh — 145; University of Pittsburgh, Pittsburgh — 29,315; Wheeler School, Pittsburgh — 461.

Newspapers, Circulation: *Pittsburgh Post-Gazette* (m), Pittsburgh — 184,969; *The Pittsburgh Press* (eS), Pittsburgh — 267,158. McKeesport *News* also circulates in the district.

Commercial Television Stations, Affiliation: KDKA-TV, Pittsburgh (CBS); WPGH-TV, Pittsburgh (None); WPTT-TV, Pittsburgh (None); WPXI, Pittsburgh (NBC); WTAE-TV, Pittsburgh (ABC). Entire district is located in Pittsburgh ADI.

Military Installations: Greater Pittsburgh Air National Guard Base, Coraopolis — 1,303; Hays Ammunition Plant, Pittsburgh — 11.

Industries:

Mellon National Corp. (HQ); Pittsburgh; banking — 5,840. **U. S. Air Inc.;** Coraopolis; commercial airline — 5,000. **Westinghouse Electric Corp.** (Research & Development Div.); Pittsburgh; research — 3,000. **Mercy Hospital of Pittsburgh;** Pittsburgh; hospital — 2,400. **Allegheny General Hospital;** Pittsburgh; hospital — 2,300.

Western Pennsylvania Hospital; Pittsburgh; hospital — 2,200. **St. Francis General Hospital;** Pittsburgh; hospital — 2,150. **Dravo Corp.;** Pittsburgh; construction machinery — 2,104. **Aluminum Co. of America Inc.** (HQ); Pittsburgh; aluminum, aluminum products — 2,000. **American Standard Inc.** (Union Switch & Signal Div.); Pittsburgh; railroad equipment — 2,000. **Dravo Corp.** (HQ); Pittsburgh; engineering, heavy construction — 2,000. **Schneider Inc.** (HQ); Pittsburgh; plumbing, heating contracting — 2,000. **Pittsburgh Press Co.;** Pittsburgh; newspaper publishing — 1,980. **Veterans Administration;** Pittsburgh; veterans' hospital — 1,840. **Presbyterian University Hospital;** Pittsburgh; hospital — 1,800. **Shadyside Hospital;** Pittsburgh; hospital — 1,600. **Union National Bank of Pittsburgh;** Pittsburgh; banking — 1,600.

Blue Cross of Western Pennsylvania (HQ); Pittsburgh; health insurance — 1,500. **Montefiore Hospital Assn. of Western Pennsylvania;** Pittsburgh; hospital — 1,500. **South Hills Health Systems Inc.** (HQ); Pittsburgh; hospital — 1,500. **Children's Hospital;** Pittsburgh; hospital — 1,400. **H. J. Heinz Co.** (HQ); Pittsburgh; canned fruits, vegetables, preserves — 1,400. **Koppers Co. Inc.** (HQ); Pittsburgh; construction materials — 1,300. **Magee-Women's Hospital;** Pittsburgh; hospital — 1,300. **St. Clair Memorial Hospital Inc.;** Pittsburgh; hospital — 1,210. **North Hills Passavant Hospital;** Pittsburgh; hospital — 1,200. **United States Steel Corp.** (HQ); Pittsburgh; steel, steel products — 1,200. **Gulf Oil Corp.** (Research & Development Center); Pittsburgh; industrial chemical research — 1,100. **Mobay Chemical Corp.** (HQ); Pittsburgh; polyurethane products — 1,100. **Westinghouse Electric Corp.;** Pittsburgh; computers — 1,100.

Equibank (HQ); Pittsburgh; banking — 1,070. **Emerson Electric Co.** (Edwin L. Wiegand Div.); Pittsburgh; electric motors — 1,000. **M. W. Kellogg Co. Inc.** (Pullman Swindell Div.); Pittsburgh; industrial services — 1,000. **Pittsburgh-Des Moines Corp.** (HQ); Pittsburgh; structural steel — 1,000. **PPG Industries Inc.** (HQ); Pittsburgh; glass — 1,000. **Gulf Oil Corp.** (HQ); Pittsburgh; petroleum products — 900. **Jones & Laughlin Steel Inc.** (HQ); Pittsburgh; steel — 900. **Pittsburgh National Corp.** (HQ); Pittsburgh; banking — 900. **Westinghouse Electric Corp.** (HQ); Pittsburgh; electrical machinery — 900. **Pittsburgh Forgings Co.** (Riverside Div. - HQ); Pittsburgh; iron, steel forgings — 850. **Emerson Electric Co.** (E. L. Wiegand Div.); Pittsburgh; administrative offices — 800. **Mine Safety Appliances Co.** (Callery Chemical Co. Div. - HQ); Pittsburgh; safety aids — 800.

Rockwell International Corp. (Power Tool Div.); Pittsburgh; meters, power hand tools — 750. **Sargent Electric Co.** (HQ); Pittsburgh; electrical contracting — 750. **Nabisco Inc.** Pittsburgh; crackers — 725. **Allied Maintenance Corp.;** Pittsburgh; janitorial services — 700. **Calgon Corp.** (Water Management Div. - HQ); Pittsburgh; water treatment chemicals — 700. **International Business Machines Corp.;** Pittsburgh; data processing — 700. **Papercraft Corp.;** Pittsburgh; towels — 700. **Jones & Laughlin Steel Corp.;** Pittsburgh; steel blast furnace — 650. **Allied Security Inc.** (HQ); Pittsburgh; protective services — 600. **Associated Cleaning Consulting & Service;** Pittsburgh; janitorial services — 600. **Central Medical Health Services;** Pittsburgh; hospital management — 600. **Contraves Goerz Corp.** (Fecker Systems Div.); Pittsburgh; optical instruments — 600. **ITT Continental Baking Co. Inc.** (Braun Baking Co. Div.); Pittsburgh; bakery wholesaling — 600.

U. S. Air Inc.; Pittsburgh; commercial airline — 600. **Westinghouse Electric Corp.** (Tele-Computer Center); Pittsburgh; data processing — 555. **Pinkerton's Inc.;** Pittsburgh; security services — 550. **White Consolidated Industries Inc.** (Blaw-Knox Equipment Div.); Pittsburgh; industrial machinery — 550. **Consolidation Coal Co.** (HQ); Pittsburgh; coal mining — 540. **Civic Arena Corp.;** Pittsburgh; sports arena — 530. **John F. Casey Co.;** Pittsburgh; highway construction — 500. **Cities Service Co.** (Fesco Div.); McKees Rocks; plastic products — 500. **Cyclops Corp.** (Bowman Construction Products Div.); Pittsburgh; sheet metal work — 500. **Louis A. Grant Inc.;** Pittsburgh; construction — 500. **Greyhound Lines Inc.;** Pittsburgh; bus transportation — 500. **Sauer Industrial Contracting;** Pittsburgh; plumbing, heating contracting — 500. **Rockwell International Corp.** (HQ); Pittsburgh; space vehicles — 500. **Serstel Corp.;** Pittsburgh; industrial construction — 500.

15th District

East — Allentown, Bethlehem

The heavy industry, strong unions and large ethnic population of the Lehigh Valley bespeak Democratic sentiments. But disaffection with Democratic candidates, both local and national, has made the valley politically marginal; Jimmy Carter carried the area within the new 15th in 1976, but lost it in 1980. A Republican ousted the complacent Democratic House incumbent in 1978 and won re-election in 1980 and 1982.

Redistricting added to the 15th a wedge of Republican Monroe County, needed to make up the district's population deficit. Although most of Monroe is Pocono Mountain vacationland, the southwestern part moved into the 15th is largely agricultural. This addition changes very little the partisan shading of the district.

Lehigh County (Allentown) has the largest population and is politically marginal. Until 1981 Allentown had a Republican mayor. Ronald Reagan's margin in Lehigh was much higher than in the more reliably Democratic Northampton County next door. The recession did not hit Allentown as hard as some other cities because of its diversified economy that spins out trucks, appliances and clothing.

The fourth largest city in the state, Allentown has neat and pleasant residential sections, a legacy of its Pennsylvania Dutch founders. Republicans live in the prosperous West End, with blue-collar Democrats spread throughout the rest of the town.

Northampton County is grittier, thanks to the presence of heavier industry there. The smokestacks of Bethlehem Steel dominate the Bethlehem landscape, and the massive corporation dominates the city, providing its tax base and financing the urban renewal projects downtown. Nearby Easton produces paper products.

Election Returns

15th District		Democrat		Republican	
1976	President	91,229	(51.8%)	81,662	(46.3%)
	Senate	87,147	(50.5%)	84,007	(48.6%)
	House	110,798	(64.9%)	59,480	(34.8%)
1978	Governor	54,961	(42.6%)	72,798	(56.4%)
	House	59,341	(46.4%)	68,497	(53.6%)
1980	President	68,570	(38.7%)	89,260	(50.4%)
	Senate	77,432	(45.5%)	89,693	(52.7%)
	House	68,156	(39.5%)	102,907	(59.7%)
1982	Governor	62,465	(44.8%)	75,588	(54.2%)
	Senate	50,012	(37.3%)	81,947	(61.1%)
	House	58,002	(42.2%)	79,455	(57.8%)

Demographics

Population: 515,259. **Percent Change from 1970:** 7.7%.

Land Area: 921 square miles. **Population per Square Mile:** 559.5.

Counties, 1980 Population: Lehigh — 272,349; Monroe (Pt.) — 17,492; Northampton — 225,418.

Cities, 1980 Population: Allentown — 103,758; Bethlehem — 70,419; Bethlehem Twp. — 12,094; Easton — 26,027; Emmaus — 11,001; Lower Macungie Twp. — 12,958; Palmer Twp. — 13,926; Salisbury Twp. — 12,259; South Whitehall Twp. — 15,919; Whitehall Twp. — 21,538.

Race and Ancestry: White — 96.6%; Black — 1.6%; American Indian, Eskimo and Aleut — 0.1%; Asian and Pacific Islander — 0.5%. Spanish Origin — 2.8%. Dutch — 1.7%; English — 4.4%; German — 26.3%; Hungarian — 2.1%; Irish — 2.7%; Italian — 4.5%; Polish — 1.8%; Russian — 0.5%; Ukranian — 1.2%.

Universities, Enrollment: Allentown Business School, Allentown — 341; Allentown College of St. Francis de Sales, Center Valley — 731; Cedar Crest College, Allentown — 1,132; Churchman Business School, Easton — 243; Lafayette College, Easton — 2,390; Lehigh County Community College, Schnecksville — 3,312; Lehigh University, Bethlehem — 6,413; Lincoln Technical Institute, Allentown — 809; Mary Immaculate Seminary, Northampton — 53; Moravian College, Bethlehem — 1,773; Muhlenberg College, Allentown — 2,222; Northampton County Area Community College, Bethlehem — 3,728; Pennsylvania State University (Allentown campus), Fogelsville — 414; United Wesleyan College, Allentown — 213.

Newspapers, Circulation: *The Express* (eS), Easton — 51,032; *The Morning Call* (all day, S), Allentown — 118,982; *The Globe-Times* (e), Bethlehem — 34,865; *News* (e), Bangor — 3,050.

Commercial Television Stations, Affiliation: WFMZ-TV, Allentown (None). District is divided between Philadelphia ADI and New York (N.Y.) ADI.

Industries:

Bethlehem Steel Corp. (HQ); Bethlehem; steel — 6,000. **Air Products & Chemicals Inc.** (HQ); Trexlertown; industrial chemicals — 4,039. **Western Electric Co. Inc.**; Allentown; semiconductors — 4,000. **Allentown Sacred Heart Hospital Center;** Allentown; hospital — 1,400. **St. Luke's Hospital;** Bethlehem; hospital — 1,300.

Hess's Department Stores Inc. (HQ); Allentown; department stores — 1,250. **General Electric Co.** (Housewares & Audio Business Div.); Allentown; small electrical housewares — 1,200. **Genesco Inc.** (Phoenix Clothes Div.); Allentown; men's suits — 1,200. **Kraft Inc.;** Wescosville; sauces, salad dressings — 1,200. **Allentown Hospital Assn.;** Allentown; hospital — 1,150. **Easton Hospital;** Easton; hospital — 1,020. **Mack Trucks Inc.** (HQ); Allentown; heavy duty trucks — 1,000. **McGregor-Doniger Inc.** (Cross Country Clothes Div.); Northampton; men's suits — 1,000. **Fuller Co.** (HQ); Bethlehem; cement-making equipment — 870. **Atlantic Processing Inc.** (Lehigh Valley Farms); Allentown; milk processing — 750. **Call-Chronicle Newspapers Inc.;** Allentown; newspaper publishing — 750. **Mack Trucks Inc.;** Macungie; heavy duty trucks — 700. **The F. & M. Schaefer Corp.;** Fogelsville; malt beverages — 700.

Allen Products Co. Inc. (HQ); Allentown; dog food — 650. **Mack Printing Co.** (HQ); Easton; printing, binding — 650. **Lehigh Valley Industries Inc.** (Blue Ridge-Winkler); Bangor; warp knit fabrics — 630. **American Can Co.** (Dixie Products); Easton; paper cups — 600. **Bell Telephone Laboratories;** Allentown; engineering, development — 600. **Sure-Fit Products Co.** (Fashion Home Products Div. - HQ); Bethlehem; slipcovers — 550. **Victaulic Co. of America Inc.;** Easton; malleable iron — 550. **Tarkett Inc.;** Whitehall; sheet vinyl — 525. **Harsco Corp.** (I. K. G. Industries Div.); Easton; steel pipe, forgings — 510. **Paris Neckwear Co. Inc.** (Paris Handkerchief Co.); Walnutport; handkerchiefs — 500. **SCM Corp.** (Durkee Famous Foods Div.); Bethlehem; prepared foods — 500.

16th District

Southeast — Lancaster

The image of the 16th District is one of horse-drawn buggies on country lanes and black-clad "plain people" tending crops. But with the highest growth rate of any district in the state, the 16th is drawing a flock of newcomers who have little in common with the Amish farmers. The one stable element is the area's politics — the new arrivals are as conservative and Republican as the old-time residents.

The 16th had to shed a considerable amount of territory to reach population equality, but the political impact is marginal. Democratic Coatesville and some of the surrounding GOP countryside in Chester County were moved to the 5th District, and a mostly rural strip of northern Lancaster County, inhabited by cows and Republicans, was moved to the 6th. The slightly reshaped district, like the old 16th, voted heavily for Ronald Reagan in 1980.

The district encompasses all of Lebanon County, instead of just the lower half it had before redistricting. The northern section of the county contains Fort Indiantown Gap, one of the centers for Cuban refugees in 1980. Lebanon is also famous for its bologna, much of it produced by a company whose owner is a former Speaker of the Pennsylvania House. Lebanon is one of the most steadfast Republican counties in Pennsylvania. It was one of only three that Barry Goldwater carried in 1964.

Lancaster County has Democratic pockets in the city of Lancaster, which makes electrical appliances and other household items, and in the Susquehanna River town of Columbia. But it is the scenic farm country — with its oddly named hamlets, such as Bird-in-Hand and Intercourse — that sets the tone for the district.

Thirty percent of Lancaster County's population is Amish. Some of the sects cling closer to the old ways than others. They range from the Old Order Amish, who in effect live in the mid-19th century, to the "black-bumper Mennonites," who drive cars but paint the bumpers black. The excellent farm land is devoted largely to dairying, although tobacco has a niche in the agricultural economy.

Election Returns

16th District		Democrat		Republican	
1976	President	55,703	(35.8%)	97,132	(62.5%)
	Senate	54,900	(34.2%)	104,150	(64.8%)
	House	58,777	(37.2%)	98,350	(62.2%)
1978	Governor	36,559	(29.7%)	85,620	(69.5%)
	House	29,397	(24.4%)	90,848	(75.6%)
1980	President	45,062	(25.9%)	115,623	(66.4%)
	Senate	48,136	(28.4%)	119,373	(70.4%)
	House	41,455	(24.6%)	127,063	(75.3%)
1982	Governor	43,413	(32.8%)	87,988	(66.4%)
	Senate	29,054	(22.4%)	98,773	(76.3%)
	House	37,364	(28.7%)	93,034	(71.3%)

Demographics

Population: 514,585. **Percent Change from 1970:** 12.9%.

Land Area: 1,551 square miles. **Population per Square Mile:** 331.8.

Counties, 1980 Population: Chester (Pt.) — 71,653; Lancaster (Pt.) — 334,350; Lebanon — 108,582.

Cities, 1980 Population: Columbia — 10,466; East Hempfield Twp. — 15,152; Ephrata — 11,095; Lancaster — 54,725; Lancaster Twp. — 10,833; Lebanon — 25,711; Manheim Twp. — 26,042; Manor Twp. — 11,474.

Race and Ancestry: White — 96.0%; Black — 2.1%; American Indian, Eskimo and Aleut — 0.1%; Asian and Pacific Islander — 0.6%; Spanish Origin — 2.2%. Dutch — 0.7%; English — 7.0%; French —

0.5%; German — 32.6%; Irish — 2.8%; Italian — 1.4%; Polish — 0.8%.

Universities, Enrollment: Elizabethtown College, Elizabethtown — 1,738; Franklin and Marshall College, Lancaster — 2,119; Lancaster Bible College, Lancaster — 367; Lancaster Theological Seminary, Lancaster — 239; Lebanon Valley College, Annville — 1,303; Millersville State College, Millersville — 6,365.

Newspapers, Circulation: *The Columbia News* (e), Columbia — 4,730; *The Daily News* (eS), Lebanon — 29,277; *Intelligencer Journal* (mS), Lancaster — 40,611; *Lancaster New Era* (eS), Lancaster — 59,470. West Chester *Daily Local News* also circulates in the district.

Commercial Television Stations, Affiliation: WGAL-TV, Lancaster (NBC); WLYH-TV, Lancaster (CBS). Most of district is located in Harrisburg-York-Lancaster-Lebanon ADI. Portion is in Philadelphia ADI.

Military Installations: Fort Indiantown Gap, Annville — 5,467.

Industries:

Armstrong World Industries Inc. (HQ); Lancaster; floor coverings — 4,500. **Sperry Corp.**; New Holland; farm machinery — 2,053. **Lancaster General Hospital**; Lancaster; hospital — 1,800. **Victor F. Weaver Inc.** (HQ); New Holland; poultry processing — 1,400. **RCA Corp.** (Electro Optics & Devices Solid State Div.); Lancaster; television parts — 1,353.

RCA Corp. (Color Picture Tube Div.); Lancaster; television parts — 1,091. **Bethlehem Steel Corp.**; Lebanon; industrial fasteners — 1,000. **Donnelley Printing Co.**; Lancaster; commercial printing — 1,000. **Veterans Administration**; Lebanon; veterans' hospital — 1,000. **Raybestos-Manhattan Inc.** (Raybestos Friction Materials Co.); Manheim; clutch facings — 950. **Harsco Corp.** (Quaker Alloy Cast Co. Div.); Myerstown; steel alloys — 870. **ITT Grinnell Corp.**; Columbia; malleable iron foundries — 852. **General Electric Environmental Services Inc.**; Lebanon; ventilation systems — 850. **Kerr Glass Mfg. Corp.** (Packaging Products Div.); Lancaster; plastic packaging products — 820. **Howmet Corp.** (Mill Products Div.); Lancaster; aluminum sheet, foil — 773. **Yellow Freight System Inc.**; East Petersburg; trucking — 750.

Hamilton Technology Inc.; Lancaster; precision timing devices — 700. **Lebanon Steel Foundry** (HQ); Lebanon; steel castings — 700. **Sterling Drug Inc.**; Myerstown; pharmaceuticals — 635. **Armstrong Cork Co. Inc.** (Marietta Ceiling Plant); Marietta; ceiling tile — 600. **Woodstream Corp.** (HQ); Lititz; sporting goods — 600. **Walter W. Moyer Co.** (HQ); Ephrata; women's underwear — 575. **High Steel Structures Inc.** (HQ); Lancaster; structural steel — 570. **Dart Container Corp.**; Leola; plastic cups — 500. **Donnelley Printing Co.**; Lancaster; commercial printing — 500. **Jones Motor Co.** (HQ); Spring City; trucking — 500. **Warner-Lambert Co.** (Parke Davis Div.); Lititz; pharmaceuticals — 500. **Wyeth Laboratories Inc.**; Marietta; pharmaceuticals — 500.

17th District

Central — Harrisburg, Williamsport

This elongated district, which follows the Susquehanna River, amply displays the GOP affinities of central Pennsylvania. Map makers made the 17th even more Republican by joining rural Perry and Snyder counties to it.

Dauphin County (Harrisburg) has almost half the people in the 17th. Lycoming County (Williamsport) is second, with slightly more than a fourth of the population. The large state government complex and manufacturing sector in Harrisburg provide enough Democratic votes to make the party competitive for local and legislative offices. The state capital, which lost a fifth of its population during the 1970s as whites moved to the suburbs, is 43.6 percent black — a fact that enhances Democratic strength there. But

Republicans often perform well in Harrisburg.

The presence of the state government prevents life from being as placid in Dauphin as it is elsewhere in central Pennsylvania. Aside from constant political flare-ups, the county had two other disasters in the 1970s: the 1972 flood that put much of Harrisburg under water and the 1979 accident at the Three Mile Island nuclear plant.

Up the river from Dauphin, the hills and farms turn out predictably large Republican majorities. Snyder and Union were two of the three Pennsylvania counties to vote for Barry Goldwater in 1964. Democrats can be found in coal-mining Northumberland County and in Williamsport, which manufactures aircraft engines, publishes *Grit* magazine and hosts the Little League World Series.

Hershey, famed for its chocolate plant, grand old hotel and amusement park, brings out solid Republican votes, as do suburban Harrisburg towns such as Paxton Township and Lower Swatara.

Election Returns

17th District		Democrat		Republican	
1976	President	75,275	(40.1%)	108,300	(57.7%)
	Senate	71,028	(38.6%)	110,722	(60.2%)
	House	81,060	(44.9%)	98,329	(54.4%)
1978	Governor	47,659	(32.4%)	97,688	(66.5%)
	House	78,955	(54.9%)	64,782	(45.1%)
1980	President	58,724	(32.1%)	110,417	(60.4%)
	Senate	63,571	(36.0%)	110,748	(62.7%)
	House	92,086	(52.7%)	82,681	(47.3%)
1982	Governor	76,318	(50.8%)	72,766	(48.4%)
	Senate	44,424	(30.5%)	98,744	(67.9%)
	House	61,974	(42.4%)	84,291	(57.6%)

Demographics

Population: 515,900. **Percent Change from 1970:** 7.2%.

Land Area: 3,366 square miles. **Population per Square Mile:** 153.3.

Counties, 1980 Population: Dauphin — 232,317; Lycoming — 118,416; Northumberland (Pt.) — 62,995; Perry — 35,718; Snyder — 33,584; Union — 32,870.

Cities, 1980 Population: Derry Twp. — 18,115; Harrisburg — 53,264; Hershey (CDP) — 13,249; Lower Paxton Twp. — 34,830; Loyalsock Twp. — 10,763; Middletown — 10,122; Sunbury — 12,292; Susquehanna Twp. — 18,034; Swatara Twp. — 18,796; Williamsport — 33,401.

Race and Ancestry: White — 92.4%; Black — 6.6%; American Indian, Eskimo and Aleut — 0.1%; Asian and Pacific Islander — 0.4%. Spanish Origin — 0.9%. Dutch — 1.7%; English — 6.7%; French — 0.5%; German — 26.9%; Irish — 2.9%; Italian — 2.2%; Polish — 1.2%.

Universities, Enrollment: Bucknell University, Lewisburg — 3,359; Electronic Institute, Harrisburg — 160; Harrisburg Area Community College, Harrisburg — 5,521; Lycoming College, Williamsport — 1,130; Pennsylvania State University (Capitol campus), Middletown — 2,507; Pennsylvania State University (The Milton S. Hershey Medical Center), Hershey — 565; Susquehanna University, Selinsgrove — 1,830; Thompson Institute, Harrisburg — 730; Williamsport Area Community College, Williamsport — 3,280; Williamsport School of Commerce, Williamsport — 107.

Newspapers, Circulation: *The Daily Item* (e), Sunbury — 26,128; *The Evening News* (eS), Harrisburg — 63,701; *The Milton Standard* (e),

Milton — 4,855; *The Patriot* (mS), Harrisburg — 48,120; *Williamsport Sun-Gazette* (e), Williamsport — 33,969.

Commercial Television Stations, Affiliation: WHP-TV, Harrisburg (CBS); WHTM-TV, Harrisburg (ABC). Most of district is located in Wilkes-Barre—Scranton ADI. Portion is in Harrisburg-York-Lancaster-Lebanon ADI.

Military Installations: Harrisburg International Airport (Air Force), Olmsted Field, Middletown — 1,057.

Nuclear Power Plants: Three Mile Island 1, Harrisburg (Babcock & Wilcox, United Engineers & Constructors), Sept. 1974; Three Mile Island 2, Harrisburg (Babcock & Wilcox, United Engineers & Constructors), Dec. 1978. Shut down since March 28, 1979.

Industries:

Bethlehem Steel Corp.; Steelton; steel works — 3,330. **AMP Inc.** (HQ); Harrisburg; electronic components — 3,200. **Milton S. Hershey Medical Center;** Hershey; hospital — 2,500. **Avco Corp.;** Williamsport; aircraft engines — 1,900. **Harrisburg Hospital;** Harrisburg; hospital — 1,800.

American Home Foods (Chef-Boy-Ar-Dee Plant); Milton; canned specialties — 1,600. **TRW Inc.** (Harrisburg Airfoils); Harrisburg; aircraft parts — 1,600. **The Williamsport Hospital;** Williamsport; hospital — 1,450. **Polyclinic Medical Center;** Harrisburg; hospital — 1,400. **Koppers Co. Inc.** (Engineered Metal Products Group); Muncy; industrial machinery — 1,200. **Bro-Dart Inc.** (HQ); Williamsport; book printing, office furniture — 1,020. **ACF Industries Inc.** (Amcar Div.); Milton; railroad equipment — 1,000. **Fruehauf Corp.;** Middletown; truck trailers — 950. **GTE Products Corp.** (Circuit Products Div.); Williamsport; semiconductors — 950. **Bethlehem Steel Corp.;** Williamsport; steel wire, wire products — 900. **General Mills Inc.** (Pennsylvania House); Lewisburg; wooden household furniture — 900. **GTE Products Corp.;** Montoursville; photoflash lights — 842.

Nationwide Mutual Insurance Co.; Harrisburg; casualty, life insurance — 826. **AMP Inc.;** Middletown; current carrying wiring devices — 700. **Wood-Metal Industries Inc.** (HQ); Kreamer; wooden kitchen cabinets — 690. **Cluett, Peabody & Co. Inc.** (Arrow Shirt Div.); Paxinos; men's shirts — 615. **Pennsylvania National Mutual Casualty Insurance** (HQ); Harrisburg; casualty, life insurance — 560. **Merck & Co. Inc.** (Merck Chemical Mfg. Div.); Riverside; chemicals — 550. **Milton Shoe Mfg. Co.** (HQ); Milton; women's shoes — 550. **Hugh H. Wilson Corp.;** Sunbury; hair pins — 550. **Capital Blue Cross Inc.;** Harrisburg; health insurance — 542. **Cluett, Peabody & Co. Inc.** (Arrow Shirt Co. Div.); Elysburg; men's shirts — 500. **Pennsylvania National Turf Club Inc.;** Grantville; racing track — 500.

18th District

Pittsburgh Suburbs

The new 18th district is a suburban doughnut surrounding Pittsburgh, with a bite taken out of the eastern part of the ring. By transferring western Pittsburgh and Democratic suburbs such as Coraopolis to the 14th District, the Legislature hoped to give an edge to Republicans in the 18th.

The district includes prosperous Republican suburbs such as Mount Lebanon and Sewickley. Still wealthier Fox Chapel requires a minimum of four acres for building a residence. Redistricting moved another rich Republican town, Upper St. Clair, into the 18th.

The district also gained several communities where Democrats have a slight registration lead — Jefferson, South Park and Bethel Park. And it received the steelworker suburbs clustered around the Greater Pittsburgh Airport — North Fayette, Findlay, Moon and Robinson.

North of the Ohio River are wealthier suburbs on the

order of Sewickley. The upper part of Allegheny County contains Pine, Richland, McCandless and other newly developing towns that lean Republican. South of the Allegheny River another addition is Penn Hills, a sprawling and diverse township that is marginally Democratic. In the old 18th Democrats had a significant registration advantage, but the remap made the difference very small.

The area of the redrawn district went solidly for the Republicans in the 1976 and 1980 presidential elections. Republican Sen. John Heinz, who represented the 18th in the House for three terms during the 1970s, carried three-quarters of the new district's vote in his 1976 campaign for the Senate.

But the electorate knows how to split its ticket. When former Pittsburgh Mayor Pete Flaherty was the Democratic nominee for the Senate in 1980, he won the district with 55.5 percent of the vote.

The Legislature's attempt to aid Republican House candidates did not prevent the Democratic incumbent from attaining a fourth term in 1982.

Election Returns

18th District		Democrat		Republican	
1976	President	92,265	(38.7%)	141,049	(59.2%)
	Senate	55,681	(23.0%)	184,087	(76.0%)
	House	121,295	(53.7%)	104,256	(46.2%)
1978	Governor	84,043	(43.3%)	108,337	(55.8%)
	House	89,578	(50.5%)	86,501	(48.8%)
1980	President	83,343	(35.4%)	131,462	(55.8%)
	Senate	139,947	(55.5%)	108,095	(42.9%)
	House	133,997	(59.2%)	91,697	(40.5%)
1982	Governor	65,193	(34.2%)	123,086	(64.5%)
	Senate	46,204	(24.2%)	141,137	(74.0%)
	House	101,807	(54.2%)	84,428	(45.0%)

Demographics

Population: 516,050. **Percent Change from 1970:** -0.8%.

Land Area: 357 square miles. **Population per Square Mile:** 1,445.5.

Counties, 1980 Population: Allegheny (Pt.) — 516,050.

Cities, 1980 Population: Bellevue — 10,128; Bethel Park — 34,755; Carnegie — 10,099; Dormont — 11,275; Hampton Twp. — 14,260; McCandless Twp. — 26,250; Moon Twp. — 20,935; Mount Lebanon Twp. — 34,414; Penn Hills Twp. — 57,632; Ross Twp. — 35,102; Scott Twp. — 20,413; Shaler Twp. — 33,694; South Park Twp. — 13,535; Upper St. Clair Twp. — 19,023; Whitehall — 15,206.

Race and Ancestry: White — 96.8%; Black — 2.3%; American Indian, Eskimo and Aleut — 0.0%; Asian and Pacific Islander — 0.7%. Spanish Origin — 0.5%. English — 4.5%; German — 12.2%; Greek — 0.5%; Hungarian — 0.7%; Irish — 5.1%; Italian — 6.9%; Polish — 3.5%; Russian — 0.5%; Scottish — 0.6%; Ukranian — 0.7%.

Newspapers, Circulation: *Pittsburgh Post-Gazette* and *The Pittsburgh Press* circulate in the district.

Commercial Television Stations, Affiliation: Entire district is located in Pittsburgh ADI.

Military Installations: Greater Pittsburgh International Airport (Air Force), Moon — 1,516.

Industries:
Teledyne Industries Inc. (Columbia Summerill Div.); Carnegie; steel mill — 600.

19th District

South Central — York

This placid farm country has seen little to rouse it since 1863, when Robert E. Lee's army met defeat at Gettysburg. Democrats do about as well in many of these counties as Lee did. The 19th used to change hands between the parties occasionally, but it has been solidly Republican since 1974. Redistricting left its boundaries almost the same as before.

The biggest concentration of Democrats lies in the industrial city of York where turbines, hosiery and dental equipment are manufactured. But York's influence has declined along with its population (down 11.4 percent during the 1970s), and surrounding York County has an even split in terms of partisan registration.

Apart from the outlying Democratic enclave of Hanover, which makes cans, shoes and potato chips, the rest of York County is rural Republican — with a smattering of Pennsylvania Dutch influence to deepen the conservatism. The county's most popular newspaper is not the flashy and liberal *York Daily Record*, but the gray and conservative *York Dispatch*.

In fruit-growing Adams County Republicans hold sway from Gettysburg, the largest town, to the farming villages farther north. The Democrats, in the minority, are concentrated in the southeastern part of Adams. Many of them work in Hanover.

Republicans have the upper hand as well in the part of Cumberland County in the 19th, where the district's only boundary change pared away some small townships. West of the West Shore suburbs of Harrisburg, the terrain becomes more rural and more Republican. State employees and blue-collar workers who spend their days in Harrisburg live in Lemoyne and New Cumberland on the West Shore. Affluent West Shore Republicans reside in Camp Hill.

Election Returns

19th District		Democrat		Republican	
1976	President	67,964	(39.3%)	101,854	(58.9%)
	Senate	64,946	(38.2%)	103,799	(61.0%)
	House	49,714	(29.3%)	120,008	(70.7%)
1978	Governor	46,368	(35.2%)	84,183	(64.0%)
	House	27,498	(21.3%)	101,904	(78.7%)
1980	President	56,017	(31.4%)	108,392	(60.8%)
	Senate	61,895	(35.8%)	108,677	(62.8%)
	House	40,066	(23.1%)	132,112	(76.1%)
1982	Governor	56,777	(39.3%)	86,699	(60.0%)
	Senate	40,160	(28.6%)	98,578	(70.2%)
	House	41,787	(29.2%)	101,163	(70.8%)

Demographics

Population: 516,605. **Percent Change from 1970:** 14.4%.

Land Area: 1,608 square miles. **Population per Square Mile:** 321.3.

Counties, 1980 Population: Adams — 68,292; Cumberland (Pt.) — 135,350; York — 312,963.

Cities, 1980 Population: Carlisle — 18,314; Dover Twp. — 12,589;

East Pennsboro Twp. — 13,955; Fairview Twp. — 11,941; Hampden Twp. — 16,648; Hanover — 14,890; Lower Allen Twp. — 14,077; Newberry Twp. — 10,047; Springettsbury Twp. — 19,687; Spring Garden Twp. — 11,127; Upper Allen Twp. — 10,533; West Manchester Twp. — 12,728; York Twp. — 16,893; York — 44,619.

Race and Ancestry: White — 96.7%; Black — 2.3%; American Indian, Eskimo and Aleut — 0.1%; Asian and Pacific Islander — 0.6%. Spanish Origin — 0.8%. Dutch — 0.9%; English — 7.4%; French — 0.6%; German — 33.3%; Irish — 2.9%; Italian — 1.4%; Polish — 0.8%.

Universities, Enrollment: Central Pennsylvania Business School, Summerdale — 751; Dickinson College, Carlisle — 1,758; Dickinson School of Law, Carlisle — 495; Gettysburg College, Gettysburg — 1,966; Lutheran Theological Seminary at Gettysburg, Gettysburg — 244; Messiah College, Grantham — 1,304; Pennsylvania State University (York campus), York — 1,116; York College of Pennsylvania, York — 3,827.

Newspapers, Circulation: *The Evening Sentinel* (e), Carlisle — 14,999; *The Evening Sun* (e), Hanover — 26,614; *The Gettysburg Times* (m), Gettysburg — 11,181; *York Daily Record* (m), York — 34,496; *The York Dispatch* (e), York — 49,840. Harrisburg *Evening News* also circulates in the district.

Commercial Television Stations, Affiliation: WGCB-TV, Red Lion (None); WSBA-TV, York (CBS). District is divided between Harrisburg-York-Lancaster-Lebanon ADI and Baltimore (Md.) ADI.

Military Installations: Carlisle Barracks (Army), Carlisle — 1,175; Navy Ships Parts Control Center, Mechanicsburg — 6,742; New Cumberland Army Depot, New Cumberland — 5,091;

Nuclear Power Plants: Peach Bottom 2, Peach Bottom (General Electric, Bechtel), July 1974; Peach Bottom 3, Peach Bottom (General Electric, Bechtel), December 1974.

Industries:

Borg-Warner Corp.; York; heating, cooling equipment — 2,761. **York Hospital Inc.;** York; hospital — 2,750. **Caterpillar Tractor Co.;** York; construction machinery — 2,259. **Harsco Corp.** (Bowen-McLaughlin York Co. Div.); York; industrial machinery — 2,019. **Dentsply International Inc.** (F & F Koenigkramer Div. - HQ); York; dental equipment — 2,000.

Carlisle Corp. (Tire & Rubber Div.); Carlisle; tires, inner tubes — 1,500. **Danskin Inc.;** York; women's hosiery — 1,500. **Harley-Davidson Motor Co. Inc.;** York; motorcycles — 1,500. **Litton Business Systems Inc.** (Lehigh Leopold Div.); York; metal office furniture — 1,250. **E. I. du Pont de Nemours & Co.;** New Cumberland; electrical interconnections — 1,200. **McCrory Corp.** (York Distribution Co. Div.); York; durable goods wholesaling — 1,200. **Holy Spirit Hospital;** Camp Hill; hospital — 1,190. **P. H. Glatfelter Co.** (Bergstrom Paper Div. - HQ); Spring Grove; paper — 1,150. **Halls Motor Transit Co.** (HQ); Mechanicsburg; trucking — 1,100. **C. H. Masland & Sons** (Dawson Div. - HQ); Carlisle; carpets — 1,100. **Allis-Chalmers Corp.** (Hydro-Turbine Div.); York; turbines — 1,000. **Roadway Express Inc.;** Camp Hill; trucking terminal — 950. **Gannett, Fleming, Corddry & Carpenter Inc.;** Camp Hill; highway construction consultants — 930. **General Defense Corp.;** Red Lion; military ordnance — 850. **Capitol Products Corp.** (HQ); Mechanicsburg; aluminum — 800.

The Hanover Shoe Inc. (HQ); Hanover; men's footwear — 800. **Rite Aid Corp.** (Rack-Rite Distributors - HQ); Shiremanstown; drug stores — 800. **The Wickes Corp.;** Red Lion; wood, wooden furniture — 800. **Allegheny Ludlum Industries Inc.** (Alloy Rods Div.); Hanover; welding shop — 700. **Book-of-the-Month Club Inc.;** Mechanicsburg; warehousing — 700. **Harsco Corp.** (HQ); Camp Hill; steel — 700. **Acco Industries Inc.;** York; hoists, cranes — 600. **Acco Industries Inc.** (American Chain Div.); York; chains — 600. **Edison International Inc.** (Campbell Chain Div.); York; chains — 600. **Kinney Shoe Corp.;** Camp Hill; warehousing — 600. **S. K. F. Industries Inc.** (Roller Bearings Div.); Hanover; roller bearings — 600. **P. A. & S. Small Co.** (HQ); York; grocery wholesaling — 555.

Hanover Brands Inc. (HQ); Hanover; canned vegetables — 550. **Teledyne Mid America Corp.** (Teledyne McKay Div.); York; welding equipment — 550. **Westinghouse Electric Corp.;** Gettysburg; escalators

— 525. **Chemetron Corp.** (Welding Products Div.); Hanover; welding equipment — 500. **Graham Engineering Corp.** (HQ); York; plastics products — 500. **GTE Products Corp.;** York; iron, steel forgings — 500. **The Maple Press Co.;** Manchester; printing, binding — 500. **The Maple Press Co.** (HQ); York; book printing — 500. **M. F. P. Enterprises Inc.** (Musselman Fruit Products); Biglerville; canned fruit, vegetables — 500. **R. H. Sheppard Co. Inc.** (HQ); Hanover; power steering equipment — 500. **Sylvania Shoe Mfg. Co.** (Brooks Shoe Co.); McSherrystown; children's, men's shoes — 500. **G. A. & F. C. Wagman Inc.;** York; highway construction — 500.

20th District

Pittsburgh Suburbs — McKeesport

Its banks lined by steel mills, its waters crowded with barges, the Monongahela River forms the spine of this blue-collar district.

The "Mon Valley" city of Clairton was the setting for the movie "The Deer Hunter," in which young Slavic steelworkers went off to the Vietnam War. The film depicted the ethnic celebrations and male camaraderie that also animate the political life of the 20th. The wise politician here cultivates the Sons of Italy, the Polish Falcons, the Greek Catholic Union, the American Croatian Club and numerous other ethnic societies.

Although blacks make up a substantial portion of some towns — Clairton is one-quarter black — they are not concentrated enough to be a major political influence. Organized labor is a big factor in local politics and has been for a long time.

Although the Legislature reshaped the district, its firmly Democratic nature was not altered; the Democrats' registration moved from 110,000 to 130,000. Jimmy Carter carried the area of the new 20th with 58.2 percent in 1976, but only 54 percent in 1980. The difference can be traced to disaffection over unemployment in the steel industry.

Severely underpopulated before redistricting, the 20th was extended south and north in Westmoreland County, taking some of the old 21st District in the south and picking up Allegheny River towns in the north. It shed blue-collar south Pittsburgh, which went into the 14th, and Democratic-leaning South Hills communities such as Bethel Park, which were transferred to the 18th District.

The new Westmoreland territory in the district is typified by Monessen, a Mon Valley steel town. Farther east in Westmoreland County, the industries are more diverse. In the equally Democratic area along the Allegheny, the steelworks of Harrison Township round out the industrial landscape.

Election Returns

20th District		Democrat		Republican	
1976	President	126,788	(58.2%)	86,535	(39.7%)
	Senate	81,413	(37.9%)	130,499	(60.8%)
	House	147,538	(71.9%)	57,226	(27.9%)
1978	Governor	108,591	(62.5%)	63,376	(36.5%)
	House	109,681	(68.5%)	50,000	(31.2%)
1980	President	111,625	(53.8%)	81,023	(39.0%)
	Senate	134,366	(70.4%)	52,808	(27.7%)
	House	134,465	(71.6%)	53,269	(28.4%)

20th District		Democrat		Republican	
1982	Governor	100,600	(57.1%)	72,770	(41.3%)
	Senate	79,199	(45.0%)	93,421	(53.1%)
	House	127,281	(76.0%)	38,212	(22.8%)

Demographics

Population: 516,028. **Percent Change from 1970:** -8.0%.

Land Area: 464 square miles. **Population per Square Mile:** 1,112.1.

Counties, 1980 Population: Allegheny (Pt.) — 390,778; Westmoreland (Pt.) — 125,250.

Cities, 1980 Population: Baldwin — 24,598; Brentwood — 11,907; Clairton — 12,188; Duquesne — 10,094; Elizabeth Twp. — 16,269; Harrison Twp. — 13,252; Lower Burrell — 13,200; McKeesport — 31,012; Monessen — 11,928; Monroeville — 30,977; Munhall — 14,532; New Kensington — 17,660; North Versailles Twp. — 13,294; Plum — 25,390; Rostraver Twp. — 11,430; Swissvale — 11,345; West Deer Twp. — 10,897; West Mifflin — 26,279.

Race and Ancestry: White — 93.9%; Black — 5.5%; American Indian, Eskimo and Aleut — 0.1%; Asian and Pacific Islander — 0.4%. Spanish Origin — 0.5%. English — 4.5%; German — 8.2%; Hungarian — 1.8%; Irish — 3.9%; Italian — 7.0%; Polish — 5.1%; Russian — 0.6%; Scottish — 0.6%; Ukranian — 0.6%.

Universities, Enrollment: Community College of Allegheny County (Boyce campus), Monroeville — 3,571; Community College of Allegheny County (South campus), West Mifflin — 3,234; Lincoln University, Lincoln University — 1,261; New Kensington Commercial School, New Kensington — 218; Pennsylvania State University (McKeesport campus), McKeesport — 1,282; Pennsylvania State University (New Kensington campus), New Kensington — 1,041.

Newspapers, Circulation: *News* (e), McKeesport — 35,831; *The News-Citizen* (e), Vandergrift — 2,841; *Tribune* (mS), Monroeville — 7,426; *The Valley Independent* (e), Monessen — 19,252; *Valley News Dispatch* (e), Tarentum — 43,538. Greensburg *Tribune-Review*, *Pittsburgh Post-Gazette* and *The Pittsburgh Press* also circulate in the district.

Commercial Television Stations, Affiliation: Entire district is located in Pittsburgh ADI.

Industries:

United States Steel Corp. (Mon Valley Works); Homestead; steel — 6,800. **United States Steel Corp.** (Mon Valley Works); McKeesport; tubular pipes — 4,200. **United States Steel Corp.** (Mon Valley Works); Clairton; coke, chemicals — 4,100. **Allegheny Ludlum Steel Corp.**; Brackenridge; stainless steel — 3,900. **Westinghouse Electric Corp.** (Power Generation Operations Div.); East Pittsburgh; turbines — 3,900.

United States Steel Corp. (Irvin Works); Dravosburg; steel — 3,150. **American Standard Corp.** (Westinghouse Airbrake Div.); Wilmerding; air brakes — 3,000. **United States Steel Corp.** (Mon Valley Works); Duquesne; steel — 2,800. **McKeesport Hospital Inc.**; McKeesport; hospital — 2,200. **General Motors Corp.** (Fisher Body Div.); McKeesport; automobiles — 2,000. **United States Steel Corp.** (Edgar Thomson Works); Braddock; steel — 2,000. **Wheeling Pittsburgh Steel Corp.**; Monessen; steel — 2,000. **Dick Corp.** (HQ); Clairton; general contracting — 1,500. **Westinghouse Electric Corp.** (Electro-Mechanical Div.); Cheswick; nuclear power plant machinery — 1,060.

Aluminum Co. of America (Alcoa Laboratories); New Kensington; research, development — 1,000. **Forbes Health System;** Monroeville; hospital — 1,000. **PPG Industries Inc.;** Creighton; automotive, aircraft glass — 1,000. **Westinghouse Electric Corp.** (Power Circuit Breaker Div.); Trafford; power circuit breakers — 952. **Edgewater Steel Co. Inc.** (HQ); Oakmont; forged, rolled steel — 930. **United States Steel Corp.** (U. S. Steel Research Lab); Monroeville; research, development — 740. **G. C. Murphy Co.;** (HQ); McKeesport; general merchandise

stores — 600. **United States Steel Corp.;** Vandergrift; steel — 500. **Westinghouse Electric Corp.** (Advanced Energy Systems Div.); Clairton; research, development — 500.

21st District

Northwest — Erie

Although the Legislature toyed with the idea of dismantling the district and using it to pad out others needing population, Erie politicians refused to cooperate, and the district that emerged is much like the old one. The 21st gained a Republican swatch of Lawrence County — mainly farm land, but home to commuters who live in Neshannock and work in New Castle, in the 4th District. Democrats continue to enjoy a registration edge.

Politically the 21st is a sandwich. Republican Crawford County forms the center, with Democratic Erie and Mercer counties on either side. Ronald Reagan captured all of them in 1980, but Jimmy Carter won Erie and Mercer in 1976.

With slightly more than half the district's voters, Erie County is the major factor here. The city of Erie has most of the population within the county. Except for wealthy residential South Shore Drive, Erie is a working-class town, dominated by paper, metals and chemical factories, and very Democratic. The Italians live on the West Side and the Poles on the East Side.

Along Lake Erie to the east of the city lies a cherry- and grape-growing region that tends to vote Republican. To the west are loyal Democratic industrial boroughs such as Girard and Fairview.

South of Erie County dairy farmers keep Crawford County in the hands of the GOP, helped by retirees around Conneaut Lake. Titusville, in eastern Crawford, is the site of the first oil well, drilled in 1859 by Edwin L. Drake.

The steel industry in the Shenango Valley sets the Democratic tone for Mercer County. As thoroughly unionized as Erie, the mill towns of Sharon, Wheatland and Sharpsville outvote the rural stretches of Republican eastern Mercer.

Election Returns

21st District		Democrat		Republican	
1976	President	100,021	(51.0%)	92,089	(47.0%)
	Senate	84,571	(44.9%)	101,540	(53.9%)
	House	85,546	(45.0%)	103,161	(54.2%)
1978	Governor	66,863	(46.5%)	75,095	(52.2%)
	House	50,500	(35.6%)	90,599	(63.8%)
1980	President	81,616	(43.0%)	92,732	(48.9%)
	Senate	99,790	(55.3%)	77,398	(42.9%)
	House	91,249	(49.9%)	90,344	(49.4%)
1982	Governor	75,683	(47.1%)	82,752	(51.5%)
	Senate	64,968	(41.5%)	88,590	(56.6%)
	House	79,451	(49.8%)	80,180	(50.2%)

Demographics

Population: 516,645. **Percent Change from 1970:** 5.5%.

Land Area: 2,588 square miles. **Population per Square Mile:** 199.6.

Counties, 1980 Population: Crawford — 88,869; Erie — 279,780; Lawrence (Pt.) — 19,697; Mercer — 128,299.

Cities, 1980 Population: Erie — 119,123; Harborcreek Twp. — 14,644; Hermitage Twp. — 16,365; Meadville — 15,544; Milcreek Twp. — 44,303; Sharon — 19,057.

Race and Ancestry: White — 95.7%; Black — 3.7%; American Indian, Eskimo and Aleut — 0.1%; Asian and Pacific Islander — 0.3%. Spanish Origin — 0.5%. Dutch — 0.5%; English — 7.1%; French — 0.5%; German — 11.5%; Hungarian — 0.6%; Irish — 3.7%; Italian — 4.8%; Polish — 4.7%; Scottish — 0.5%; Swedish — 0.7%.

Universities, Enrollment: Allegheny College, Meadville — 1,936; Alliance College, Cambridge Springs — 261; Edinboro State College, Edinboro — 5,644; Gannon University, Erie — 3,304; Grove City College, Grove City — 2,253; Mercyhurst College, Erie — 1,364; Pennsylvania State University (Behrend College campus), Erie — 1,830; Pennsylvania State University (Shenango Valley campus), Sharon — 871; Thiel College, Greenville — 935; Triangle Institute of Technology, Erie — 408; University of Pittsburgh at Titusville, Titusville — 481; Villa Maria College, Erie — 728; Westminster College, New Wilmington — 1,784.

Newspapers, Circulation: *Corry Evening Journal* (e), Corry — 4,960; *The Erie Daily Times* (eS), Erie — 50,840; *Greenville Record Argus* (e), Greenville — 5,500; *The Herald* (e), Sharon — 26,697; *Morning News* (mS), Erie — 24,334; *The Meadville Tribune* (m), Meadville — 17,670; *The Titusville Herald* (m), Titusville — 5,137. *New Castle News* also circulates in the district.

Commercial Television Stations, Affiliation: WICU-TV, Erie (NBC); WJET-TV, Erie (ABC); WSEE, Erie (CBS). Most of district is divided between Erie ADI and Youngstown (Ohio) ADI. Portion is in Pittsburgh ADI.

Industries:

General Electric Co.; Erie; generators — 7,251. **Sharon Steel Corp.;** Farrell; steel works — 2,600. **St. Vincent Health Center;** Erie; hospital — 2,400. **Hammermill Paper Co.** (HQ); Erie; paper products — 2,020. **Hamot Medical Center;** Erie; hospital — 1,850.

Lord Corp. (Hughson Chemicals - HQ); Erie; bonded rubber — 1,200. **Zurn Industries Inc.;** Erie; steam turbines — 1,073. **Zurn Industries Inc.** (Energy Div.); Erie; high speed drives, gears — 1,000. **Erie Indemnity Co.** (HQ); Erie; management company — 935. **Westinghouse Electric Corp.** (Medium Power Transformer Div.); Sharon; transformers — 878. **Cyclops Corp.** (Sawhill Tubular Div.); Wheatland; pipes, tubing — 808. **Cooper Industries Inc.** (Energy Service Div.); Grove City; power engines — 725. **Avtex Fibers Inc.;** Meadville; acetate — 660.

Cyclops Corp. (Universal-Cyclops); Titusville; specialty steel — 628. **R. D. Werner Co. Inc.** (HQ); Greenville; aluminum products — 600. **Kaiser Aluminum & Chemical Corp.;** Erie; forgings — 591. **White Consolidated Industries** (Copes Vulcan Div.); Lake City; valves, pipe fittings — 575. **Geosource Inc.** (Flow-Measurement & Control Div.); Erie; automatic controls — 535. **Talon Inc.;** Meadville; zippers — 515. **HON Industries Inc.** (Corry Jamestown Corp. Div.); Corry; metal office furniture — 507. **PPG Industries Inc.;** Meadville; flat glass — 500.

22nd District

Southwest — Washington

This coal-rich corner of the state has fed the blast furnaces of Pittsburgh for the last century. Tales of cave-ins, strikes and cutthroat politics still embroider the talk of the miners as they down schooners of beer in the taverns that nestle among the stark hills.

The United Mine Workers (UMW) is an important force, and it has a rough history. UMW President W. A. "Tony" Boyle was convicted here in the 1969 murder of

union rival Joseph A. "Jock" Yablonski. The area's legacy of violence dates back to the Whiskey Rebellion in 1791.

Redistricting did little to alter the thoroughly Democratic character of the 22nd, which voted for Jimmy Carter in both 1976 and 1980. To make up population deficit, the legislators joined industrial and Democratic southern Beaver County to the district, taking them out of the Republican 4th. The Beaver County territory new to the 22nd includes Ohio River factory towns such as Midland and the aptly named Industry, as well as Shippingport, site of the first commercial atomic reactor.

In Allegheny County the 22nd traded Republican Upper St. Clair — sent to the 18th — for blue-collar South Fayette and Collier. Washington County has almost half the 22nd's population and dominates the district. It has a little coal mining, but the economy depends on heavy industry. Charleroi and other Monongahela River towns make steel, glass and industrial equipment.

The city of Washington, home of the county's old factory-owning families, often goes against the grain and votes Republican — as does Peters Township, a white-collar bedroom community for Pittsburgh commuters on the Allegheny County line. But these votes regularly are drowned by the Democratic tide.

Coal is the mainstay of Fayette and Greene counties. Fayette has been mined much longer than less-populous Greene; many of Fayette's deep mines are played out and strip mining has begun.

These two counties display an even firmer Democratic allegiance than Washington County. In the 1976 Senate contest between Pittsburgher John Heinz, the Republican, and Philadelphian William Green, the Democrat, Washington joined the rest of western Pennsylvania in supporting Heinz. But Fayette and Greene put aside geographical considerations and voted for the Democrat.

Election Returns

22nd District		Democrat		Republican	
1976	President	113,800	(60.0%)	72,769	(38.4%)
	Senate	86,007	(45.8%)	100,516	(53.5%)
	House	107,891	(58.2%)	76,273	(41.1%)
1978	Governor	101,520	(66.2%)	51,037	(33.3%)
	House	108,522	(72.2%)	39,395	(26.2%)
1980	President	97,195	(52.6%)	77,892	(42.2%)
	Senate	130,002	(71.6%)	49,725	(27.4%)
	House	131,854	(73.4%)	46,283	(25.8%)
1982	Governor	96,603	(60.3%)	62,316	(38.9%)
	Senate	77,635	(48.7%)	80,056	(50.2%)
	House	123,716	(78.7%)	32,176	(20.5%)

Demographics

Population: 515,122. **Percent Change from 1970:** 2.4%.

Land Area: 2,422 square miles. **Population per Square Mile:** 212.7.

Counties, 1980 Population: Allegheny (Pt.) — 26,628; Beaver (Pt.) — 71,527; Fayette — 159,417; Greene — 40,476; Washington — 217,074.

Cities, 1980 Population: Canonsburg — 10,459; Canton Twp. — 10,311; Center Twp. — 10,733; Connellsville — 10,319; Hopewell Twp. — 14,662; North Union Twp. — 15,340; Peters Twp. — 13,104; South Union Twp. — 10,992; Uniontown — 14,510; Washington — 18,363.

Race and Ancestry: White — 96.1%; Black — 3.5%; American Indian, Eskimo and Aleut — 0.1%; Asian and Pacific Islander — 0.2%. Spanish Origin — 0.5%. Dutch — 0.5%; English — 7.5%; German — 7.0%; Hungarian — 1.2%; Irish — 4.2%; Italian — 6.7%; Polish — 4.0%; Russian — 0.7%; Ukranian — 0.5%.

Universities, Enrollment: California State College, California — 4,317; Community College of Beaver County, Monaca — 1,996; Penn Commercial College, Washington — 170; Pennsylvania State University (Beaver campus), Monaca — 1,246; Pennsylvania State University (Fayette campus), Uniontown — 909; Washington and Jefferson College, Washington — 1,077; Waynesburg College, Waynesburg — 871.

Newspapers, Circulation: *The Daily Courier* (e), Connellsville — 15,080; *The Daily Herald* (e), Monongahela — 8,211; *The Democrat Messenger* (m), Waynesburg — 4,702; *Herald-Standard* (all day), Uniontown — 28,076; *Observer-Reporter* (m), Washington — 36,536; *The Telegraph* (e), Brownsville — 7,503. *Pittsburgh Post-Gazette* and *The Pittsburgh Press* also circulate in the district.

Commercial Television Stations, Affiliation: Entire district is located in Pittsburgh ADI.

Nuclear Power Plants: Beaver Valley 1, Shippingport (Westinghouse, Stone & Webster), October 1976; Beaver Valley 2, Shippingport (Westinghouse, Stone & Webster).

Industries:

Wheeling-Pittsburgh Steel Corp.; Allenport; rolling mill — 2,000. **United States Steel Corp.** (Frick Mining District); Uniontown; coal mining — 1,900. **Bethlehem Mines Corp.** (Ellsworth Div.); Eighty-Four; coal mining — 1,850. **Armco Steel Corp.** (National Supply Co.); Ambridge; steel works — 1,500. **Washington Hospital Authority;** Washington; hospital — 1,500.

McGraw-Edison Co. Inc.; Canonsburg; electrical transformers — 1,400. **Commonwealth of Pennsylvania;** Bridgeville; state hospital — 1,300. **Anchor Hocking Corp.;** Connellsville; glass containers — 1,240. **Corning Glass Works;** Charleroi; pressed, blown glass — 1,100. **Monongahela Valley Hospital;** Monongahela; hospital — 1,000. **United States Steel Corp.** (American Bridge Div.); Ambridge; fabricated steel — 1,000. **Brockway Glass Co. Inc.;** Washington; glass containers — 900. **Atlantic Richfield Co.;** Monaca; polymer plastic — 800. **Jessup Steel Co.;** Washington; stainless steel — 800. **Rockwell International Corp.;** Uniontown; meters — 800. **Fox Grocery Co. Inc.;** Belle Vernon; grocery wholesaling — 770. **Blount Inc.** (Washington Steel); Washington; stainless steel — 670. **Cyclops Corp.** (Universal Cyclops); Bridgeville; specialty steel — 640.

Combustion Engineering Inc.; Monongahela; grey iron foundry — 610. **Fruehauf Corp.** (Liquid & Bulk Tank Div.); Uniontown; bulk tanks — 600. **H. H. Robertson Co. Inc.;** Ambridge; sheet metal works — 600. **Tactec Systems Inc.** (HQ); Meadow Lands; radio equipment — 578. **Anchor Hocking Corp.** (Phoenix Glass Div.); Monaca; illuminating glass — 550. **Michael Berkowitz Co. Inc.;** Uniontown; nightwear — 550. **Hydril Co. Inc.** (Tubular Products Div.); Rochester; oil field machinery — 525. **Gateway Coal Co.;** Clarksville; coal mining — 500. **Gateway Coal Co.;** California; coal mining — 500. **GNB Corp.;** Uniontown; banking — 500. **H. B. C. Barge Inc.;** Brownsville; shipbuilding — 500.

23rd District

Northwest, Central — State College

Except when Penn State's Nittany Lions play at home or groundhog Punxsutawney Phil looks for his shadow, this remote part of the state attracts little attention. One Pennsylvania politician, opposed to building an interstate highway through it, declared that "all they have up there is a bunch of bears."

Aside from its Penn State academic complex, coal patches and small manufacturing towns, the 23rd is rural

and Republican. The remap made litle change: Republicans have a 54-46 percent registration edge.

Centre County, home of Penn State in the town of State College, is the district's population center. State College frequently votes Democratic, unlike the rest of the county. The university has spawned a small high-tech industrial complex outside town that attracts Republican-voting engineers and their families. Ronald Reagan won Centre in 1980, but he was held below 50 percent of the vote in the county because of support for independent John B. Anderson, who won 12 percent.

Elsewhere Democrats show the most strength in coal-mining Clarion and Clearfield counties, as well as in Elk County, a paper mill center and producer of the wood that goes into "Louisville Slugger" baseball bats. Elk and Clarion supported Jimmy Carter in 1976, when the rest of the district went to Gerald R. Ford.

Warren, Venango, McKean and Forest counties habitually vote Republican. Popular among hunters and canoeists, these counties grew very little in the 1970s. This region produces motor oil.

Redistricting placed a Democratic slice of Armstrong County in the 23rd. The district dips down along the west bank of the Allegheny River to take in the factory town of Ford City in Armstrong County.

Election Returns

23rd District		Democrat		Republican	
1976	President	77,107	(44.6%)	92,392	(53.4%)
	Senate	74,448	(43.2%)	96,920	(56.2%)
	House	98,707	(58.0%)	71,469	(42.0%)
1978	Governor	67,209	(46.3%)	76,777	(52.9%)
	House	68,605	(48.6%)	72,564	(51.4%)
1980	President	65,367	(37.8%)	94,528	(54.6%)
	Senate	87,057	(49.5%)	86,536	(49.2%)
	House	50,940	(29.4%)	119,447	(68.9%)
1982	Governor	63,651	(44.2%)	79,064	(54.9%)
	Senate	47,245	(33.1%)	93,380	(65.4%)
	House	49,297	(34.8%)	92,424	(65.2%)

Demographics

Population: 515,976. **Percent Change from 1970:** 6.1%.

Land Area: 7,770 square miles. **Population per Square Mile:** 66.4.

Counties, 1980 Population: Armstrong (Pt.) — 25,578; Cameron — 6,674; Centre — 112,760; Clarion — 43,362; Clearfield (Pt.) — 42,377; Clinton (Pt.) — 30,984; Elk — 38,338; Forest — 5,072; Jefferson — 48,303; McKean — 50,635; Venango — 64,444; Warren — 47,449.

Cities, 1980 Population: Bradford — 11,211; Oil City — 13,881; State College — 36,130; Warren — 12,146.

Race and Ancestry: White — 98.8%; Black — 0.5%; American Indian, Eskimo and Aleut — 0.1%; Asian and Pacific Islander — 0.4%. Spanish Origin — 0.4%. Dutch — 1.2%; English — 7.7%; French — 0.6%; German — 16.4%; Irish — 3.8%; Italian — 3.4%; Polish — 1.7%; Scottish — 0.6%; Swedish — 1.5%.

Universities, Enrollment: Clarion State College, Clarion — 5,213; DuBois Business College, DuBois — 180; Lockhaven State College, Lock Haven — 2,550; Pennsylvania State University (main campus), State College — 35,093; Pennsylvania State University (DuBois campus), DuBois — 767; University of Pittsburgh at Bradford, Bradford — 887.

Newspapers, Circulation: *The Bradford Era* (m), Bradford — 12,716; *Centre Daily Times* (e), State College — 21,479; *The Courier-Express* (e), Dubois — 11,115; *The Daily Press* (e), St. Marys — 5,698; *The Derrick* (m), Oil City — 16,578; *Express* (e), Lock Haven — 11,965; *The Kane Republican* (e), Kane — 3,011; *Leader Times* (e), Kittaning — 12,053; *The News-Herald* (e), Franklin — 8,852; *The Progress* (e), Clearfield — 18,502; *Ridgeway Record* (e), Ridgeway — 3,775; *The Spirit* (m), Punxsutawney — 6,430; *Warren Times-Observer* (m), Warren — 12,533.

Commercial Television Stations, Affiliation: District is divided between Johnstown-Altoona ADI and Pittsburgh ADI. Portions are in Erie ADI, Wilkes-Barre—Scranton ADI and Buffalo (N.Y.) ADI.

Military Installations: State College Air National Guard Station, State College — 3.

Industries:

Brockway Glass Co. Inc. (Glassware Div.); Brockway; glass, metal containers — 11,000. **The Stackpole Corp.** (HQ); St. Marys; carbon products — 1,400. **GTE Product Corp.** (Specialty Metals); Warren; precious metals — 1,200. **Keystone Carbon Co.;** St. Marys; powder — 1,150. **Owens-Illinois Inc.;** Clarion; glass containers — 1,000.

Airco Inc.; St. Marys; carbon, graphite products — 903. **Hammermill Paper Co.;** Lock Haven; paper mills — 900. **The Marmon Group Inc.** (Cerro Metal Products Div.); Bellefonte; brass castings — 900. **National Forge Co.** (HQ); Irvine; steel ingots, pipes — 900. **HRB-Singer Inc.** (HQ); State College; research, development — 850. **Joy Mfg. Co.;** Franklin; mining machinery — 850. **Dresser Industries Inc.** (Dresser Mfg. Div.); Bradford; valves, pipes — 800. **Rockwell International Corp.** (Municipal & Utility Div.); DuBois; gas meters — 800. **Penntech Papers Inc.;** Johnsonburg; pulp, paper — 735. **Piper Aircraft Corp.** (HQ); Lock Haven; aircraft — 700. **Witco Chemical** (Kendall Refining Co. Div.); Bradford; petroleum refining — 700.

Brockway Glass Co.; Crenshaw; glass containers — 650. **United States Steel Corp.** (Oil Well Div.); Oil City; oil field machinery — 650. **Struthers Wells Corp.;** Warren; heat exchangers — 620. **W. R. Case & Sons Cutlery Co.** (HQ); Bradford; cutlery — 600. **Corning Glass Works Inc.** (Electronic Products Div.); Bradford; electronic components — 600. **Esmark Inc.** (Rola Div.); Punxsutawney; radios, TVs — 600. **PPG Industries Inc.;** Ford City; plate glass — 600. **Wallace-Murray Corp.** (Eljer Plumbing Ware Div.); Ford City; vitreous china — 600. **Corning Glass Works;** State College; pressed, blown glass — 565. **Indian Head Inc.** (Pierce Glass Co. Div.); Port Allegany; bottles, jars — 550. **Erie Technological Products;** State College; electronic components — 500.

Rhode Island

Rhode Island faced a redistricting process that required only minor population shifts between its two congressional districts. Although the state's population remained at about 950,000 through the 1970s, the western 2nd District grew by 2.1 percent during the decade, while the eastern 1st declined by 2.6 percent.

A relatively simple plan to redraw the district boundaries in the northern part of the city of Providence won easy acceptance in the Legislature. The shift of about 10,600 residents from the 2nd to the 1st was likely to have little effect on congressional voting patterns.

The 1982 remap was approved by the state House on March 31 by a 71-20 vote; the state Senate approved it 35-12 on April 2. The law went into effect April 9 without the signature of the governor, who had qualms about a companion measure reapportioning the Legislature.

Age of Population

District	Population Under 18	Voting Age Population	Population 65 & Over (% of VAP)	Median Age
1	117,333	357,096	66,675 (18.7%)	32.2
2	125,518	347,207	60,247 (17.4%)	31.4
State	242,851	704,303	126,922 (18.0%)	31.8

Income and Occupation

District	Median Family Income	White Collar Workers	Blue Collar Workers	Service Workers	Farm Workers
1	$ 19,387	49.4%	36.3%	13.6%	0.7%
2	19,510	50.4	35.0	13.7	0.9
State	$ 19,448	49.9%	35.7%	13.6%	0.8%

Education: School Years Completed

District	8 Years or Fewer	4 Years of High School	4 Years of College or More	Median School Years
1	23.3%	30.8%	16.1%	12.3
2	18.1	34.7	14.7	12.4
State	20.7%	32.8%	15.4%	12.3

Housing and Residential Patterns

District	Owner Occupied	Renter Occupied	Urban	Rural
1	54.7%	45.3%	93.7%	6.3%
2	63.0	37.0	80.3	19.7
State	58.8%	41.2%	87.0%	13.0%

1st District

East — Eastern Providence; Pawtucket

Stretching around scenic Narragansett Bay on the Atlantic Ocean toward the industrial Blackstone River Valley, the 1st offers pristine coastal preserves but also some of the most densely crowded cities in the nation.

Fishing, shipping and naval operations dominate the coast. The larger towns around the bay tend to vote Democratic; Newport, Tiverton and Bristol backed Jimmy Carter by strong margins in both 1976 and 1980, although surrounding Newport County gave Ronald Reagan a narrow plurality in 1980, his best county showing in the state.

Some seacoast towns have pockets of wealthy residents and tend to favor the GOP. The towns of Compton and Middletown backed both Gerald R. Ford in 1976 and Reagan in 1980. Nearby Jamestown backed Carter by a 51-to-49-percent margin in 1976 but gave a narrow 39-to-38-percent plurality to Reagan in 1980. Independent John B. Anderson polled 22 percent in Jamestown in 1980, his highest margin in any town on the state's mainland.

The city of Newport, renowned for the ostentatious wealth of its 19th-century social elite, continues to lure tourists with its now-restored palatial mansions and its America's Cup yacht races. But Newport County and the coastal areas suffered a severe economic crisis in 1973 when the U.S. Navy removed many of its installations; the Navy pullout and the 1974-75 recession tripled the state's unemployment rate.

Later military spending increases, however, gave Newport some new vitality. The area's electronics firms, led by Raytheon, anticipate increased Pentagon contracts. Newport retains the Naval Education and Training Center complex.

RHODE ISLAND

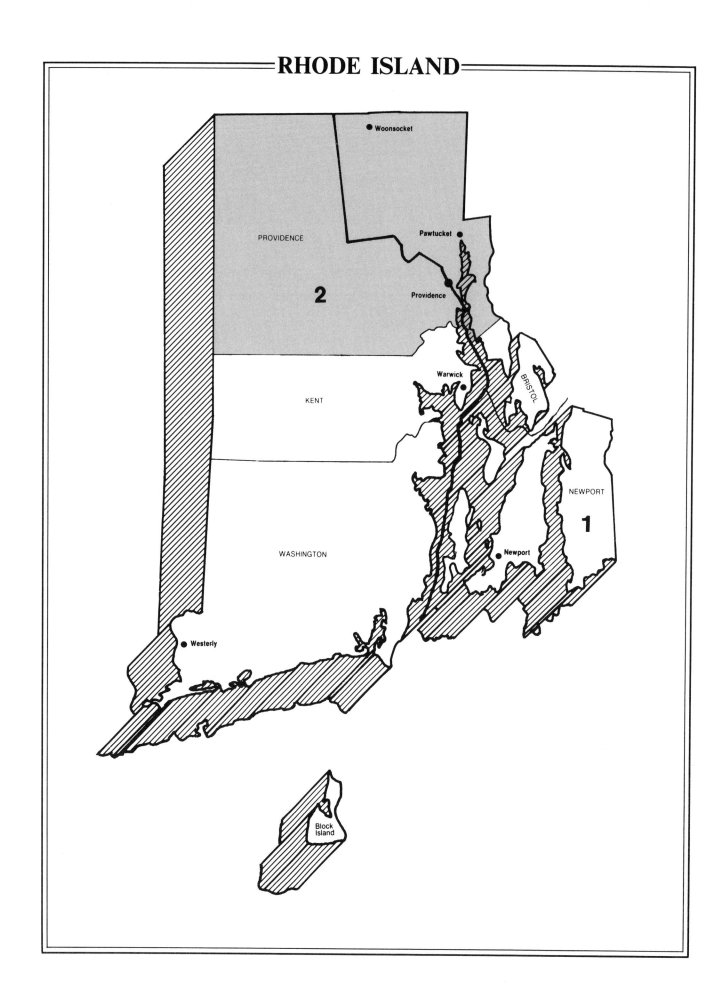

The 1st District also includes part of the Democratic stronghold of Providence, along with its smaller suburbs. Within the capital city, the 1st contains all of the heavily Italian Fourth Ward and most of the Italian Fifth Ward, both generally Democratic in statewide contests. The WASP-dominated East Side, where liberal voters around the campus of Brown University offset some of the upper-income conservatives, also has pockets of residents from Portugal and the Cape Verde Islands. The section of the city newly added to the 1st, north of Smith Street, is mostly Irish, stretching toward the Italian-accented North Providence neighborhood.

The fashionable, upper-income suburb of Barrington is a Republican enclave that gave a 46-to-35-percent plurality to Reagan in 1980; Anderson polled 19 percent in Barrington, while gaining 15.2 percent in surrounding Bristol County.

To the north the 1st includes the industrial corridor in the Blackstone Valley, including the gritty, red brick factory towns of Woonsocket, Central Falls and Pawtucket. Pawtucket was the site of the first factory in the nation, a textile mill founded in 1790 with technology pirated from British firms. The valley's economy includes metalworking and jewelry firms among much light manufacturing. The area is unshakably Democratic; even George McGovern in 1972 won all three cities. Anderson ran relatively poorly in the Blackstone Valley in 1980, which made his Providence showing one of his worst in New England.

Election Returns

1st District		Democrat		Republican	
1976	President	116,362	(57.1%)	86,772	(42.5%)
	Governor	114,720	(58.2%)	81,329	(41.3%)
	Senate	85,588	(43.2%)	112,002	(56.5%)
	House	120,224	(62.9%)	68,662	(35.9%)
1978	Governor	96,713	(63.3%)	47,643	(31.2%)
	Senate	111,254	(75.3%)	36,466	(24.7%)
	House	89,235	(61.3%)	56,383	(38.7%)
1980	President	98,522	(48.4%)	74,354	(36.5%)
	Governor	148,829	(75.2%)	49,022	(24.8%)
	House	122,965	(67.4%)	59,606	(32.6%)
1982	Governor	120,651	(75.1%)	34,758	(21.6%)
	Senate	82,253	(50.4%)	81,104	(49.6%)
	House	97,254	(60.7%)	61,253	(38.3%)

Demographics

Population: 474,429. **Percent Change from 1970:** -2.8%.

Land Area: 276 square miles. **Population per Square Mile:** 1,718.9.

Counties, 1980 Population: Bristol — 46,942; Newport — 81,383; Providence (Pt.) — 346,104.

Cities, 1980 Population: Barrington — 16,174; Bristol — 20,128; Central Falls — 16,995; Cumberland — 27,069; East Providence — 50,980; Lincoln — 16,949; Middletown — 17,216; Newport — 29,259; North Providence — 29,188; Pawtucket — 71,204; Portsmouth — 14,257; Providence (Pt.) — 60,947; Smithfield — 16,886; Tiverton — 13,526; Warren — 10,640; Woonsocket — 45,914.

Race and Ancestry: White — 95.3%; Black — 2.5%; American Indian, Eskimo and Aleut — 0.2%; Asian and Pacific Islander — 0.6%. Spanish Origin — 2.0%. English — 6.8%; French — 10.5%; German — 1.4%; Irish — 7.4%; Italian — 8.7%; Polish — 2.3%; Portuguese — 10.6%; Russian — 0.7%; Scottish — 0.7%.

Universities, Enrollment: Barrington College, Barrington — 458; Brown University, Providence — 7,045; Bryant College, Smithfield — 5,875; The Newport College-Salve Regina, Newport — 1,719; Providence College, Providence — 6,503; Rhode Island School of Design, Providence — 1,596; Roger Williams College, Bristol — 3,609.

Newspapers, Circulation: *The Evening Times* (e), Pawtucket — 29,913; *The Newport Daily News* (e), Newport — 15,523; *The Woonsocket Call and Evening Reporter* (e), Woonsocket — 32,127. Providence *Journal* and Providence *Bulletin* also circulate in the district.

Commercial Television Stations, Affiliation: WLNE, Providence (CBS); WPRI-TV, Providence (ABC); WSTG, Providence (None). Entire district is located in Providence-New Bedford (Mass.) ADI.

Military Installations: Naval Education and Training Center, Newport — 5,136; Naval Regional Medical Center, Newport — 502; Naval Underwater Systems Center, Newport — 7,074; Naval War College, Newport — 423; North Smithfield Air National Guard Facility, Slatersville — 327.

Industries:

Fram Corp. (HQ); Rumford; blowers, ventilation equipment — 5,000. **Avnet Inc.** (Carol Cable Co. Div.); Pawtucket; drawing and insulating of non-ferrous wire — 3,400. **Raytheon Co.** (Submarine Signal Div.); Portsmouth; military electronic equipment — 1,950. **American Insulated Wire Corp.** (HQ); Pawtucket; insulated wire — 1,800. **The Memorial Hospital;** Pawtucket; hospital — 1,500.

The Miriam Hospital Inc.; Providence; hospital — 1,500. **Health-Tex Inc.;** Central Falls; children's clothing — 1,400. **Hasbro Industries Inc.** (HQ); Pawtucket; toys, dolls — 1,200. **A. T. Cross Co. Inc.** (HQ); Lincoln; pens — 1,100. **Allstate Security Police Inc.;** Centerdale; security services — 900. **Worcester Textile Co.;** Centerdale; woolen fabric — 800. **Dart Industries Inc.** (Tupperware Div.); Woonsocket; plastic kitchenware — 900. **Avnet Inc.** (Miller Electric Co. Div.); Woonsocket; electrical machinery — 700. **Trifari, Krussman & Fishel Inc.** (HQ); East Providence; costume jewelry — 700.

International Telephone and Telegraph Corp. (ITT Royal Electric Div.); Pawtucket; wire cables — 650. **Fram Corp.** (Automotive Div.); East Providence; non-electrical machinery — 600. **International Packaging Corp.** (HQ); Pawtucket; plastic and metal products — 595. **Health-Tex Inc.;** Cumberland; children's clothing — 560. **Martin-Copeland Co.;** East Providence; ophthalmic goods — 560. **Amperex Electronic Corp.** (HQ); Slatersville; electrical transmitting devices — 550. **Corning Glass Works Inc.;** Central Falls; glassware — 500. **School

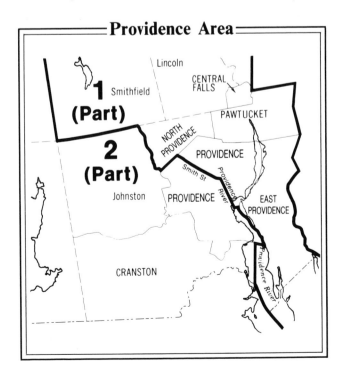

House Candy Co. (HQ); Pawtucket; candy, confectionery products — 500. **Ternor Apex Co.** (HQ); Pawtucket; synthetic resins — 500.

2nd District

West — Western Providence; Warwick

With about two-thirds of the city of Providence and its vote-heavy southern suburbs, the 2nd is largely a metropolitan district. But the area's geographical diversity — including coastal wildlife refuges, Yankee inland towns and rolling upstate hillsides — belies the image of urban bleakness a traveler sees from the swath of Amtrak rails that slices through downtown Providence.

The capital, a Democratic stronghold that suffered a 12.5 percent population loss during the 1970s, has the largest concentration of votes in the district. The 2nd includes the Providence business district where pedestrian shopping areas have had some success at reviving the downtown area; South Providence, once a mixed Irish and Jewish middle-class neighborhood that is now largely black; Federal Hill and Silver Lake where Italian-Americans predominate; and Elmwood, a traditional ethnic enclave now experiencing an influx of young white professionals.

Cranston and Warwick, the capital's largest suburbs, are middle-class areas that often split their tickets. Washington County, with coastal cities and maritime commerce as well as the inland marshes known as the "Great Swamp," registered an 8.9-percent growth rate in the 1970s, the fastest advance of any Rhode Island county. Ronald Reagan carried five of the nine towns in Washington in 1980 and took the county by 503 votes. Aided by strong showings around the University of Rhode Island, independent John B. Anderson polled 17.1 percent in the county.

Quonset Point near North Kingston is home to General Dynamics' Electric Boat Division, which assembles the hulls for the nuclear submarines that are completed in Electric Boat's Groton, Conn., facility. The submarine plant is located on the site of the sprawling old Navy installation at Quonset Point, where the phase-out of an air station and construction battalion in the mid-1970s caused economic havoc. All that is left of the military presence in North Kingstown is a storage facility and Air National Guard activities.

Plans for a nuclear power plant in Charlestown, a Washington County town, were dropped in 1979 under pressure from environmentalists. Nearby Westerly, an old shipping center that now blends light manufacturing with its fishing trade, gave a plurality to Jimmy Carter in 1980. But most of the other towns on Rhode Island's western border are Yankee enclaves that vote Republican.

Election Returns

2nd District		Democrat		Republican	
1976	President	110,037	(53.7%)	93,991	(45.9%)
	Governor	103,841	(51.5%)	96,925	(48.1%)
	Senate	82,077	(40.9%)	118,327	(58.9%)
	House	150,903	(76.3%)	44,856	(22.7%)

2nd District		Democrat		Republican	
1978	Governor	100,673	(62.3%)	48,953	(30.3%)
	Senate	118,303	(74.9%)	39,595	(25.1%)
	House	84,930	(52.4%)	77,254	(47.6%)
1980	President	98,573	(46.9%)	80,123	(38.1%)
	Governor	147,692	(72.3%)	56,566	(27.7%)
	House	90,761	(44.5%)	113,295	(55.5%)
1982	Governor	125,915	(71.6%)	44,844	(25.5%)
	Senate	85,030	(47.4%)	94,391	(51.6%)
	House	76,769	(44.4%)	96,282	(55.6%)

Demographics

Population: 472,725. **Percent Change from 1970:** 2.4%.

Land Area: 779 square miles. **Population per Square Mile:** 606.8.

Counties, 1980 Population: Kent — 154,163; Providence (Pt.) — 225,245; Washington — 93,317.

Cities, 1980 Population: Burrillville — 13,164; Coventry — 27,065; Cranston — 71,992; East Greenwich — 10,211; Johnston — 24,907; Narragansett — 12,088; North Kingstown — 21,938; Providence (Pt.) — 95,857; South Kingstown — 20,414; Warwick — 87,123; Westerly — 18,580; West Warwick — 27,026.

Race and Ancestry: White — 94.0%; Black — 3.4%; American Indian, Eskimo and Aleut — 0.4%; Asian and Pacific Islander — 0.8%. Spanish Origin — 2.2%. English — 8.4%; French — 5.8%; German — 1.5%; Irish — 7.8%; Italian — 16.4%; Polish — 1.5%; Portuguese — 2.5%; Russian — 0.6%; Scottish — 0.7%; Swedish — 0.9%.

Universities, Enrollment: Community College of Rhode Island, Warwick — 11,844; Johnson and Wales College, Providence — 4,895; New England Institute of Technology, Providence — 873; Rhode Island College, Providence — 9,260; University of Rhode Island, Kingstown — 14,579.

Newspapers, Circulation: *The Bulletin* (e), Providence — 142,022; *The Journal* (mS), Providence — 74,979; *The Pawtuxet Valley Daily Times* (e), West Warwick — 10,018; *The Westerly Sun* (eS), Westerly — 11,015. Pawtucket *Evening Times* and *The Woonsocket Call and Evening Reporter* also circulate in the district.

Commercial Television Stations, Affiliation: WJAR-TV, Providence (NBC); WSTG, Providence (None). Entire district is located in Providence-New Bedford (Mass.) ADI.

Military Installations: Coventry Air National Guard Station, Coventry — 205; Davisville Naval Construction Battalion Center, North Kingstown — 862; Quonset State Airport (Air Force), North Kingstown — 895.

Industries:

General Dynamics Corp. (Electric Boat Div.); North Kingstown; nuclear shipbuilding — 5,000. **Rhode Island Hospital;** Providence; hospital — 4,250. **Brown & Sharpe Mfg. Co.** (HQ); North Kingstown; machine tools — 2,200. **Metropolitan Property Liability Insurance Co.;** Warwick; casualty insurance — 1,910. **Leviton Mfg. Co.;** Warwick; wiring devices — 1,800.

Kent County Memorial Hospital; Warwick; hospital — 1,670. **Textron Inc.** (Bostitch Div.); East Greenwich; office machinery — 1,500. **Roger Williams General Hospital;** Providence; hospital — 1,270. **Providence Journal Co.** (HQ); Providence; newspaper publishing — 1,200. **Amica Mutual Insurance Co. Inc.** (HQ); Providence; casualty insurance — 1,120. **Davol Inc.** (HQ); Cranston; rubber, plastic products — 1,000. **Veterans Administration;** Providence; veterans' hospital — 1,000. **Blue Cross of Rhode Island;** Providence; health insurance — 990. **Imperial Knife Co. Inc.** (HQ); Providence; knives, cutlery — 990. **Harris Corp.** (Commercial Web Press Div.); Westerly; printing machinery — 900. **General Signal Corp.;** West Warwick; valves, pipe fittings — 850. **Textron Inc.** (Speidel Div.); Providence; jewelry, chains — 850. **Federal Products Corp.** (HQ); Providence; machine tool accessories — 800.

Leesona Corp. (HQ); Warwick; special industry machinery — 800. **ITT Grinnell Corp.** (HQ); Providence; pipes, valves, plumbing equipment — 700. **Allendale Mutual Insurance Co.** (HQ); Johnston; fire, marine, casualty insurance — 613. **American Hoechst Corp.;** Coventry; dyes — 600.

Elmwood Sensors Inc. (HQ); Warwick; automatic regulating controls — 600. **Gulton Industries Inc.** (Measurement Control Systems Div.); Warwick; industrial controls, transformers — 600. **Hospital Trust Corp.** (HQ); Providence; bank holding company — 600. **Ciba-Geigy Corp.;** Cranston; industrial, inorganic chemicals — 555. **Industrial National Corp.** (HQ); Providence; bank holding company — 550. **Kenney Mfg. Co.** (HQ); Warwick; drapery hardware — 550. **Colbert's Security Services Inc.** (Guardian Alarm Div. - HQ); Providence; security services — 500. **Puritan Life Insurance Co.;** Johnston; life insurance — 500. **Vargas Mfg. Co. Inc.;** Providence; precious metal jewelry — 500.

South Carolina

After a process that lasted nearly a year and required court intervention, South Carolina emerged with redrawn congressional districts only slightly different from its old ones. The new map handed down March 8, 1982, by a three-judge federal panel shifted just six of the state's 46 counties among six constituencies.

The court took up the redistricting question in February on the basis of a suit brought by the NAACP, after months of debate in the Legislature had led only to stalemate. Democrats were firmly in control of state government, but rival factions of Democratic lawmakers were unable to agree on new district boundaries.

South Carolina neither gained nor lost a district as a result of the 1980 census. The source of the maneuvering over new lines was the tremendous growth in the region around Charleston. The area's ballooning population required that the 1st District, in which Charleston's metropolitan area is located, shed about 40,000 people to come down to ideal district size.

The Legislature's two most powerful members pushed a plan taking counties from the western ends of the 1st and 2nd districts and adding them to the 3rd. The result, to the dismay of the 3rd District incumbent, would have been a district running 300 miles from the Blue Ridge Mountains in the northern part of the state to the seacoast in the south. Several maps subsequently were produced by each side only to be defeated by the other before the court stepped in.

The judges' map, which was a slightly modified version of one of the plans passed by the House, satisfied most of the principal actors. The six fastest-growing and most Republican precincts in Berkeley County, those around Charleston, were kept in the 1st District, while the rest of the county was moved to the 6th. The panel's other changes were minor, either shoring up incumbents or leaving them unharmed. Nonetheless, the first term Republican in the 6th District lost his seat to a Democratic challenger. The seat had been held by a Democrat throughout the 20th century. While incumbents were pleased by the new map, the state NAACP and black state legislators were not, believing that the state, with a one-third black population, should have at least one black representative. The NAACP appealed the lower court decision to the U.S. Supreme Court, which affirmed the lower court map Nov. 29, 1983, without opinion.

Age of Population

District	Population Under 18	Voting Age Population	Population 65 & Over (% of VAP)	Median Age
1	157,472	362,866	38,887 (10.7%)	26.2
2	150,398	372,290	41,898 (11.3%)	27.2
3	152,962	366,318	54,173 (14.8%)	29.6
4	147,510	373,015	52,400 (14.0%)	30.1
5	161,809	357,907	51,693 (14.4%)	28.7
6	171,815	347,458	48,277 (13.9%)	27.6
State	941,966	2,179,854	287,328 (13.2%)	28.1

Income and Occupation

District	Median Family Income	White Collar Workers	Blue Collar Workers	Service Workers	Farm Workers
1	$ 16,991	51.5%	32.0%	14.2%	2.3%
2	18,085	56.8	28.9	12.2	2.1
3	17,211	39.5	48.4	10.0	2.1
4	18,074	45.7	43.2	10.1	1.0
5	16,784	37.6	49.8	10.3	2.3
6	14,988	41.4	40.5	12.9	5.2
State	$ 16,978	45.4%	40.7%	11.5%	2.4%

Education: School Years Completed

District	8 Years or Fewer	4 Years of High School	4 Years of College or More	Median School Years
1	19.8%	31.8%	15.6%	12.4
2	19.1	26.5	19.1	12.5
3	28.9	26.0	11.4	11.9
4	25.4	25.6	13.9	12.1
5	30.6	25.9	10.4	11.9
6	29.8	26.9	10.4	12.0
State	25.7%	27.1%	13.4%	12.1

Housing and Residential Patterns

District	Owner Occupied	Renter Occupied	Urban	Rural
1	63.9%	36.1%	72.5%	27.5%
2	67.3	32.7	67.2	32.8

495

SOUTH CAROLINA

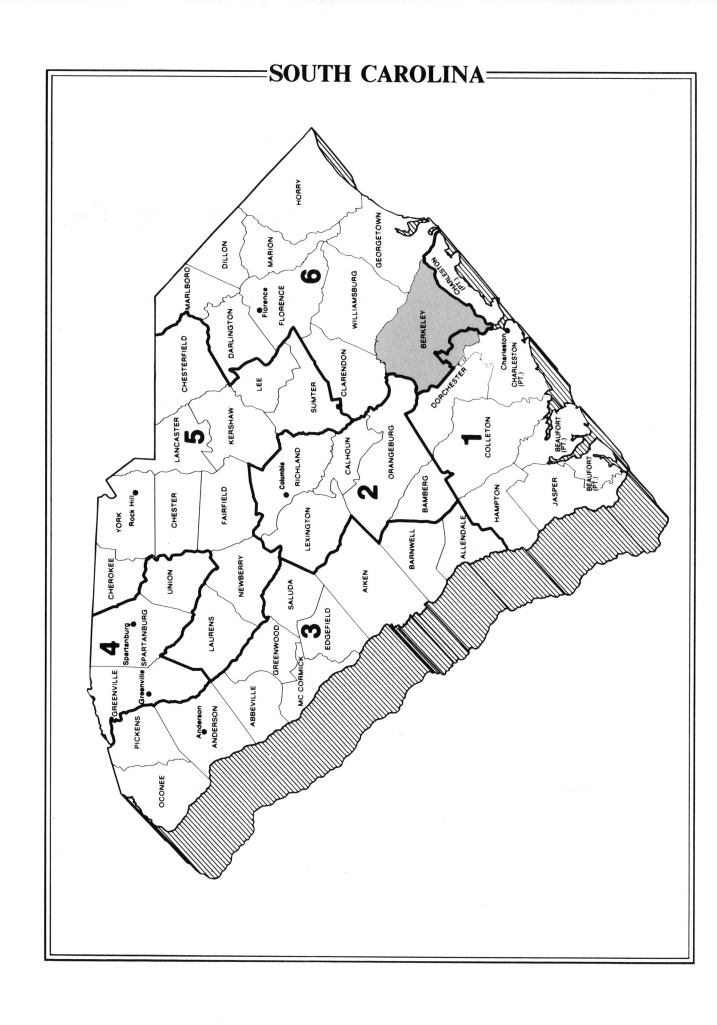

District	Owner Occupied	Renter Occupied	Urban	Rural
3	74.7	25.3	44.8	55.2
4	69.6	30.4	67.3	32.7
5	73.5	26.5	39.1	60.9
6	71.6	28.4	33.6	66.4
State	70.2%	29.8%	54.1%	45.9%

1st District

South — Charleston

Henry James, describing Charleston's listlessness at the turn of the century, disparaged the city as "effeminate." No more. While James might still recognize the carefully preserved older streets and quaint houses, the symbol of contemporary Charleston is the defense industry and the enormous postwar growth it has brought to the area. More than a fifth of South Carolina's new residents during the 1970s were attracted to Charleston.

L. Mendel Rivers, who represented the city in the House of Representatives for 30 years and chaired the Armed Services Committee for three terms, used his power to funnel vast amounts of money to the area, provoking cynics to remark that one more military base might make the city sink into the ocean. The Charleston Naval Shipyard, Charleston Air Force Base, Parris Island Marine Corps Base and numerous other military facilities place an estimated 35 percent of the district's payroll in the hands of the Defense Department and draw in private military contractors and related businesses.

Charleston's other major industries are shipping and tourism. Its wharves are lined with earthmovers and bulky air conditioning units awaiting shipment to the Middle East. The city's formal gardens, stately homes and yearly arts festival draw tourists and dollars.

Most of the people moving into the area have settled in Charleston's suburbs. North Charleston, Summerville, Hanahan and Goose Creek have exploded in population in the past decade. North Charleston, one-third the size of its parent city in 1970, was almost equal to it in population in the 1980 census. Reflecting the Northern and middle-class background of the new residents, these suburbs usually turn in solidly Republican votes at the national level — and, when offered a GOP candidate, at the local level.

The only change in the 1st District was the loss of part of Berkeley County to the 6th, reflecting an existing split in the county. While the rest of the county was giving 60 percent of its vote to Jimmy Carter in 1980, Ronald Reagan took the six metropolitan Charleston precincts in the 1st by a 74-23 margin. More than half of the district residents live in Charleston county.

In Charleston itself and in the poorer rural towns to the south, the Democratic presence remains strong. More than half of the district's residents live in Charleston County. The city, 46 percent black, is still governed by Democrats, and blacks in the precincts north of Calhoun Street turn in an overwhelmingly Democratic vote. But the white population, which is beginning to encroach on formerly black areas, is starting to tilt the area to the GOP in national elections.

The only other expanding area in the 1st lies along the coast, where Hilton Head, Kiawah and other barrier islands are being turned into playgrounds for the wealthy. Expensive developments have replaced small, dirt-poor farms, though most of the islands still are the domain of subsistence farming.

The 1st District's three small southwestern counties and northern Beaufort County remain dominated by agriculture. Oak trees and loblolly pines support a timber industry fueling pulp mills around Savannah, Ga.

Election Returns

1st District		Democrat		Republican	
1976	President	65,254	(53.4%)	56,449	(46.2%)
	House	83,295	(68.2%)	38,797	(31.8%)
1978	Governor	58,159	(55.6%)	45,622	(43.6%)
	Senate	49,581	(47.8%)	54,181	(52.2%)
	House	60,802	(60.2%)	40,250	(39.8%)
1980	President	65,690	(44.2%)	78,592	(52.9%)
	Senate	91,620	(63.0%)	53,913	(37.0%)
	House	71,574	(48.5%)	75,958	(51.5%)
1982	Governor	78,602	(66.7%)	39,325	(33.3%)
	House	52,916	(44.9%)	63,945	(54.3%)

Demographics

Population: 520,338. **Percent Change from 1970:** 25.3%.

Land Area: 4,469 square miles. **Population per Square Mile:** 116.4.

Counties, 1980 Population: Beaufort — 65,364; Berkeley (Pt.) — 54,800; Charleston — 276,974; Colleton — 31,776; Dorchester — 58,761; Hampton — 18,159; Jasper — 14,504.

Cities, 1980 Population: Charleston — 69,510; Goose Creek — 17,811; Hanahan — 13,224; Mount Pleasant — 13,838; North Charleston (Pt.) — 62,534.

Race and Ancestry: White — 66.0%; Black — 32.3%; American Indian, Eskimo and Aleut — 0.2%; Asian and Pacific Islander — 0.9%. Spanish Origin — 1.7%. English — 13.1%; French — 1.0%; German — 4.4%; Irish — 3.9%; Italian — 0.8%; Scottish — 0.6%.

Universities, Enrollment: Baptist College at Charleston, Charleston — 2,444; Beaufort Technical College, Beaufort — 1,678; The Citadel, Charleston — 3,439; College of Charleston, Charleston — 5,227; Medical University of South Carolina, Charleston — 2,157; Nielson Electronics Institute, Charleston — 292; Trident Technical College, North Charleston — 5,619; University of South Carolina at Beaufort, Beaufort — 672.

Newspapers, Circulation: *The Beaufort Gazette* (e), Beaufort — 7,304; *The Evening Post* (eS), Charleston — 36,912; *The News and Courier* (mS), Charleston — 67,057.

Commercial Television Stations, Affiliation: WCBD-TV, Charleston (ABC); WCIV, Charleston (NBC); WCSC-TV, Charleston (CBS). District is divided between Charleston ADI and Savannah (Ga.) ADI.

Military Installations: Charleston Air Force Base, Charleston — 8,498; Charleston Naval Regional Medical Center, North Charleston — 1,285; Charleston Naval Shipyard, Charleston — 8,467; Charleston Naval Station, Charleston — 39,118; Charleston Naval Supply Center, Charleston — 1,192; Charleston Naval Weapons Station, Charleston — 4,912; FBM Submarine Training Center, Charleston — 321; Fleet and Mine Warfare Training Center, Charleston — 226.; Marine Corps Air Station, Beaufort — 4,175; Parris Island Marine Corps Recruit Depot, Parris Island — 9,035.

Industries:

Westvaco Corp. (Kraft Div.); North Charleston; pulp, paper mills — 1,500. **Roper Hospital;** Charleston; hospital — 1,250. **Cummins Charleston Inc.;** Charleston Heights; diesel engines — 1,000. **Westinghouse Electric Corp.** (Micarta Div.); Hampton; plastic products — 1,000. **E. I. du Pont de Nemours & Co.** (Textile Fibers Dept.); Charleston; Dacron — 900.

Alumax of South Carolina Inc.; Goose Creek; aluminum reduction — 800. **Robert Bosch Corp.;** Charleston; diesel injection equipment — 750. **Raybestos-Manhattan Inc.** (Industrial Products); North Charleston; asbestos products — 615. **General Electric Co.** (Steam Turbine Dept.); Ladson; turbine hoods — 600. **Sea Pines Plantation Co.;** Hilton Head Island; resort — 600. **Mobay Chemical Corp.** (Dyes & Pigment Div.); Charleston; dyestuff — 580. **Detyens Shipyards Inc.;** Mount Pleasant; ship repairing — 500. **Yeargin Construction Co.;** Mount Pleasant; industrial construction — 500.

2nd District

Central — Columbia

Perched in the center of South Carolina, the 2nd is a politically diverse — some would say polarized — district that lumps together the state capital of Columbia and its fast-growing suburbs with three largely rural, black-majority counties.

Republicans in Lexington County and neighboring Richland County, which has Columbia at its western edge, dominate the constituency. The votes from these areas easily outstrip the margins given Democrats in the rural, southern portion of the district.

Lexington County provided nearly half the district's growth in the 1970s. Lexington's new inhabitants are a mix of retirees, white-collar workers who left increasingly black Columbia and employees of the glass, cement and synthetic fiber companies that have moved to the county in recent years.

Whatever brought them there, Lexington County residents are overwhelmingly white, middle-class and Republican. Lexington is one of only three counties in the state with a population less than 10 percent black, and in 1980 Ronald Reagan carried the county by a better than 2-to-1 margin. Four years earlier, when almost all of South Carolina was lining up behind Jimmy Carter, Lexington gave Gerald R. Ford 59 percent of its vote.

Neighboring Richland County is more balanced both politically and racially. The county has the largest black population in the state, most of it concentrated in inner-city Columbia. Blacks, state employees and the 28,000 students and faculty at the University of South Carolina give the city a politically liberal hue and a strong Democratic presence.

But this influence is offset in national elections by the Republican vote from Columbia's bedroom communities and portions of the surrounding county. Most of the GOP vote comes from the huge population of military personnel and retirees around Fort Jackson.

The southern portion of the district has its political and geographic center at Orangeburg, which is the site of South Carolina State College, the traditional academic center for the state's blacks. The middle-class black community that has grown up around the college has proved a potent force in local politics, and Orangeburg County and its two rural neighbors — Calhoun and Bamberg counties — have consistently gone Democratic at local and national levels. Whites in the area, reflecting a districtwide tendency, generally vote Republican.

The map shifted rural Barnwell and Allendale counties from the southern end of the 2nd into the 3rd District. The removal of these Democratic counties was expected to strengthen the Republican hold on the 2nd District.

Election Returns

2nd District		Democrat		Republican	
1976	President	70,231	(51.0%)	66,194	(48.1%)
	House	55,550	(41.2%)	78,328	(58.1%)
1978	Governor	69,062	(58.3%)	48,254	(40.7%)
	Senate	52,283	(44.0%)	66,426	(56.0%)
	House	49,838	(42.6%)	67,274	(57.4%)
1980	President	52,225	(42.5%)	66,522	(54.0%)
	Senate	85,682	(68.9%)	38,644	(31.1%)
	House	67,488	(43.5%)	88,109	(56.6%)
1982	Governor	79,301	(64.5%)	43,699	(35.5%)
	House	50,749	(41.5%)	71,569	(58.5%)

Demographics

Population: 522,688. **Percent Change from 1970:** 24.6%.

Land Area: 3,356 square miles. **Population per Square Mile:** 155.7.

Counties, 1980 Population: Bamberg — 18,118; Calhoun — 12,206; Lexington — 140,353; Orangeburg — 82,276; Richland — 269,735.

Cities, 1980 Population: Cayce — 11,701; Columbia — 101,208; Orangeburg — 14,933; West Columbia — 10,409.

Race and Ancestry: White — 64.2%; Black — 34.6%; American Indian, Eskimo and Aleut — 0.1%; Asian and Pacific Islander — 0.6%. Spanish Origin — 1.3%. English — 15.4%; French — 0.7%; German — 6.5%; Irish — 4.0%; Italian — 0.5%; Scottish — 0.6%.

Universities, Enrollment: Benedict College, Columbia — 1,422; Claflin College, Orangeburg — 739; Columbia Bible College, Columbia — 878; Columbia College, Columbia — 1,034; Columbia Junior College of Business, Columbia — 938; Denmark Technical College, Denmark — 586; Lutheran Theological Southern Seminary, Columbia — 167; Midlands Technical College, Columbia — 5,414; Orangeburg-Calhoun Technical College, Orangeburg — 1,428; South Carolina State College, Orangeburg — 3,929; University of South Carolina (main campus), Columbia — 26,135; Voorhees College, Denmark — 660.

Newspapers, Circulation: *The Columbia Record* (e), Columbia — 33,092; *The State* (mS), Columbia — 103,678; *The Times and Democrat* (mS), Orangeburg — 15,341.

Commercial Television Stations, Affiliation: WCCT-TV, Columbia (None); WIS-TV, Columbia (NBC); WLTX, Columbia (CBS); WOLO-TV, Columbia (ABC). Most of district is located in Columbia ADI. Portion is in Augusta (Ga.) ADI.

Military Installations: Fort Jackson, Columbia — 8,494; McEntire Air National Guard Base, Eastover — 1,292.

Industries:

Richland Memorial Hospital; Columbia; hospital — 2,400. **Bankers Trust of South Carolina;** Columbia; banking — 1,900. **Nassau Recycle Corp.;** Gaston; scrap metal refining — 1,780. **Allied Chemical Corp.** (Fibers Div.); Columbia; broad woven fabric — 1,600. **South Carolina Baptist Hospitals Inc.** (HQ); Columbia; hospital — 1,530.

Eastman Kodak Co. (Carolina Eastman Co.); West Columbia; synthetic fibers — 1,470. **Veterans Administration;** Columbia; veterans' hospital — 1,400. **M. Lowenstein Corp.** (Pacific Columbia Mills Div.); Columbia; cotton textile finishing — 1,300. **First Bankshares Corp. of South Carolina;** Columbia; bank holding company — 1,120. **Southeastern Freight Lines Inc.** (HQ); West Columbia; trucking — 1,050. **Utica Tool Co. Inc.;** Orangeburg; hand tools — 975. **Westinghouse Electric Corp.;** Columbia; nuclear fuel — 960.

Pinkerton's Inc.; Columbia; security services — 800. **Square D Co.;** Columbia; electric motor controls — 800. **Shakespeare Co.** (Fishing Tackle Div.); Columbia; fishing tackle wholesaling — 725. **Blue Cross-Blue Shield of South Carolina** (HQ); Columbia; health insurance — 715. **Colonial Life & Accident Insurance** (HQ); Columbia; accident, life insurance — 700. **Mepco/Electra Inc.;** Columbia; electrical motors, generators — 700. **Southern Security Service Inc.;** Columbia;

security services — 700. **A C Kleening Service & Supply;** West Columbia; janitorial services, supply — 640.

Anchor Continental Inc.; Columbia; paper goods — 625. **Columbia Newspapers Inc.;** Columbia; newspaper publishing — 605. **Ambler Industries Inc.** (Rydal Mfg. Co.); Orangeburg; boys' coats — 550. **Burlington Industries Inc.** (Catlin Farish Co. Div.); Batesburg; broad woven fabrics — 550. **Atlantic Soft Drink Co.** (HQ); Columbia; soft drink bottling — 500. **Canron Corp.** (Tamper Div.); West Columbia; construction machinery — 500. **Citizens & Southern National Bank of South Carolina** (HQ); Columbia; banking — 500. **J. B. Martin Co.;** Leesville; velvet material — 500.

3rd District

West — Anderson, Aiken

Hugging the western border of the state, the 3rd stretches in a band one and two counties wide from the Blue Ridge Mountains in the far north to rural Allendale County, only 60 miles from the Atlantic coast beaches. The district contains two major Republican pockets, created by the same kind of economic development that has occurred across the state. But it remains predominantly rural and is generally Democratic territory.

The Democratic incumbent came through the redistricting process in better shape than was first planned. Instead of giving the district the "mountains-to-the-sea" constituency the state Senate leadership envisioned, the new map added only two small counties, Allendale and Barnwell.

Six rural, securely Democratic counties account for half the district's vote. The two largest, Anderson and Greenwood, are traditional textile counties now making a successful effort to lure other investment. Anderson's new factories have brought housing developments on land once given over to cotton. In Greenwood, where the old families still control mill town patronage and politics, new technology has come in the form of plants making orthopedic devices and synthetic chemicals.

Much of the population remains sunk in poverty, with the sharecroppers of Abbeville and McCormick counties in particular scratching out meager livings from the tobacco, corn and soybeans growing in their poor soil. Racial issues often dominate local politics, and the Ku Klux Klan's strong presence spurs the civil rights organizing carried on throughout the area.

Old-fashioned populism was strong in most of these six counties. Echoes of it remained in 1968 when voters in this portion of the district responded to George C. Wallace's law-and-order call by giving him a vote 15-to-20 percentage points above his statewide average. A more liberal Democratic vote comes from tiny black-majority McCormick County, the only county in the state that is losing population.

The strongest Republican area of the 3rd is Aiken County, Republican Sen. Strom Thurmond's political base and a traditional winter resting place for wealthy Northerners. Its county seat of Aiken boasts a public library built by the du Pont family. The bulk of the county's GOP support comes from the white-collar suburbs clustered north and east of Augusta, Ga., and from the du Pont executives working at or retired from the Savannah River nuclear complex that spans Aiken and Barnwell counties.

Pickens County also has a significant Republican bloc. Local politics remain Democratic there, but growth in the communities nearest to Greenville, in the neighboring 4th District, is increasing the Republican base, and the town of Clemson has a conservative bloc of academics among the mathematics and science faculty at Clemson University.

The two new counties, Barnwell and Allendale, are rural and lean Democratic. But Barnwell, which until the early 1950s had the most acreage in the country planted in watermelons, now houses almost two-thirds of the 300-square-mile Savannah River nuclear plant, which manufactures weapons-grade plutonium and is the largest employer in the district. There are also an unused commercial nuclear fuel reprocessing plant and a commercial burial ground for low-level nuclear waste products. The technicians and employees of these plants who live in Barnwell County provide a steadily conservative and Republican vote in most statewide and national elections.

Election Returns

3rd District		Democrat		Republican	
1976	President	79,979	(59.6%)	53,342	(39.8%)
	House	112,929	(95.6%)	5,098	(4.3%)
1978	Governor	66,279	(65.9%)	33,057	(32.9%)
	Senate	42,833	(42.1%)	58,705	(57.8%)
	House	78,217	(79.1%)	20,695	(20.9%)
1980	President	89,433	(50.9%)	82,493	(46.9%)
	Senate	120,315	(69.6%)	52,632	(30.4%)
	House	86,971	(59.3%)	58,686	(40.0%)
1982	Governor	69,213	(71.4%)	27,747	(28.6%)
	House	77,125	(90.4%)	—	

Demographics

Population: 519,280. **Percent Change from 1970:** 20.2%.

Land Area: 6,163 square miles. **Population per Square Mile:** 84.3.

Counties, 1980 Population: Abbeville — 22,627; Aiken — 105,625; Allendale — 10,700; Anderson — 133,235; Barnwell — 19,868; Edgefield — 17,528; Greenwood — 57,847; McCormick — 7,797; Oconee — 48,611; Pickens — 79,292; Saluda — 16,150.

Cities, 1980 Population: Aiken — 14,978; Anderson — 27,313; Easley — 14,264; Greenwood — 21,613; North Augusta — 13,593.

Race and Ancestry: White — 76.9%; Black — 22.7%; American Indian, Eskimo and Aleut — 0.1%; Asian and Pacific Islander — 0.2%. Spanish Origin — 0.7%. English — 21.8%; French — 0.6%; German — 3.5%; Irish — 6.9%; Scottish — 0.6%.

Universities, Enrollment: Aiken Technical College, Aiken — 1,267; Anderson College, Anderson — 1,160; Central Wesleyan College, Central — 414; Clemson University, Clemson — 11,579; Erskine College, Due West — 730; Lander College, Greenwood — 1,756; Piedmont Technical College, Greenwood — 1,757; Tri-County Technical College, Pendleton — 2,356; University of South Carolina at Aiken, Aiken — 1,793; University of South Carolina at Salkehatchie, Allendale — 479.

Newspapers, Circulation: *Aiken Standard* (e), Aiken — 12,125; *The Independent Mail* (all day, S), Anderson — 45,320; *The Index-Journal* (e), Greenwood — 15,874. *The Greenville News* also circulates in the district.

Commercial Television Stations, Affiliation: WAIM-TV, Anderson (ABC, CBS). District is divided between Greenville-Spartanburg-Asheville (N.C.) ADI and Augusta (Ga.) ADI.

Nuclear Power Plants: Oconee 1, Lake Keowee (Babcock & Wilcox, Duke Power), July 1973; Oconee 2, Lake Keowee (Babcock & Wilcox, Duke Power), September 1974; Oconee 3, Lake Keowee (Babcock & Wilcox, Duke Power), December 1974.

Industries:

E. I. du Pont de Nemours & Co. (Savannah River Plant); Aiken; plutonium — 9,140. **J. P. Stevens & Co. Inc.;** Clemson; broad woven fabrics — 2,200. **Alice Mfg. Co.;** Easley; blended cloth mills — 2,000. **Michelin Tire Corp.;** Anderson; tires, inner tubes — 2,000. **Monsanto Co.;** Greenwood; synthetic organic chemicals — 1,800. **The Singer Co.** (Motor Products Div.); Pickens; power tools — 1,800.

Owens-Corning Fiberglas Corp.; Aiken; fiberglass — 1,700. **Anderson Memorial Hospital;** Anderson; hospital — 1,400. **Owens-Corning Fiberglas Corp.;** Anderson; textile glass fibers — 1,350. **Badische Co.;** Anderson; yarn mills — 1,300. **The Singer Co.;** Anderson; vacuum cleaners — 1,200. **The Kendall Co. Inc.;** Pelzer; cotton goods — 1,100. **Parke Davis & Co. Inc.** (Orthopedic Div.); Greenwood; medical devices — 1,100. **Stone Platt Corp.** (HQ); Easley; textile machinery — 1,100. **United Merchants & Manufacturers Inc.** (Finishing Plant); Clearwater; cotton fabric mills — 1,100. **Platt-Saco-Lowell Corp.** (HQ); Easley; textile machinery — 1,090.

Self Memorial Hospital; Greenwood; hospital — 1,070. **Rheem Mfg. Inc.;** Williston; textile machinery — 1,040. **Akzona Inc.** (American Enka Co.); Central; nylon polyester yarns — 1,000. **Greenwood Mills Inc.** (Matthews Mills - HQ); Greenwood; cotton mills — 1,000. **Sangamo Weston Inc.** (Sangamo Energy Management Div.); West Union; watthour meters — 1,000. **M. Lowenstein Corp.** (Orr-Lyons Mills); Anderson; cotton polyester mills — 925. **Milliken & Co.** (Cushman Mill Div.); Williamston; synthetic fabric, yarn mills — 900. **Riegel Textile Corp.** (La France Industries Div.); La France; broad woven fabric mills — 900. **Sangamo Weston Inc.** (Sangamo Electric Co.); Pickens; electrical industrial appliances — 900. **Therm-O-Disc Inc.;** Aiken; temperature controls — 850.

Andrea Fashions Inc. (HQ); West Union; women's clothing — 800. **NCR Corp.;** Liberty; cash registers — 800. **Kimberly-Clark Corp.;** Beech Island; tissue products — 720. **Clark-Schwebel Fiber Glass;** Anderson; fabric mills — 700. **J. P. Stevens & Co. Inc.;** Seneca; broad woven fabrics — 700. **United Merchants & Manufacturers Inc.;** Bath; cotton fabric mills — 650. **Bigelow-Sanford Inc.** (Rocky River Plant); Calhoun Falls; carpet yarn — 600. **Burlington Industries Inc.** (Calhoun Mills); Calhoun Falls; cotton sheet mills — 600. **The Kendall Co. Inc.;** Seneca; elastic orthopedic products — 600. **Magic Chef Inc.** (Admiral Div.); Williston; freezers, refrigerators — 600. **Milliken & Co.;** McCormick; worsted, woven fabric mills — 600.

Swirl Inc.; Easley; women's loungewear — 575. **Belton Corp.** (HQ); Belton; electrical appliances — 535. **Riegel Textile Corp.** (Consumer Products Div.); Johnston; fabric mills — 535. **Greenwood Mills Inc.;** Ninety Six; cotton fabrics — 521. **M. Lowenstein Corp.** (Chiquola Mfg. Div.); Honea Path; cotton blended fabrics — 500. **Milliken & Co.;** Barnwell; woolen synthetic fabric mills — 500. **Milliken & Co.;** Honea Path; woven fabric mills — 500. **Stauffer Chemical Co. Inc.;** Anderson; fabricated plastics — 500. **J. P. Stevens Co. Inc.** (Appleton Mills); Anderson; broad woven fabric mills — 500. **Textron Inc.** (Shuron Continental Div.); Barnwell; ophthalmic lenses — 500. **West Point-Pepperell Inc.** (Equinox Mill); Anderson; textile mills — 500.

4th District

Northwest — Greenville, Spartanburg

Redistricting did little to change the political complexion of the 4th District. Union County, shifted to the 4th from the 5th District, is heavily Democratic, but accounts for only 6 percent of the district vote.

The nucleus of the 4th is Greenville County, the most populous and most industrialized county in the state and a showplace of the New South. The city of Greenville developed as a center of the textile industry after the Civil War, and it still bustles with mills, clothing manufacturers and textile machinery producers.

Since 1960, however, the city's non-unionized labor force and low wage rate — about $2 per hour less than the national average — have combined with a favorable tax structure and warm climate to draw investment from the Frost Belt and overseas. Union Carbide, General Electric and Michelin have located plants there, and the area's industrial base has expanded dramatically since the early 1960s. With it have grown such towns as Mauldin and Simpsonville, whose new citizens come from out of state and from inner-city Greenville. The city itself lost 5 percent of its population in the 1970s.

Greenville County has a history of conservatism reaching back to its Tory leanings during the Revolution, and it was among the first areas in the state to take to Republicanism following World War II. But its tendency to follow the GOP line in national elections masks a more fragmented political life.

Greenville's Republican Party has been split by maneuvering between its mainstream partisans among the area's corporate management and small-business owners and an intensely conservative wing that takes its cues from fundamentalist Bob Jones University.

Conservative Democrats are in the majority in the outlying parts of Greenville County, in the mountainous north and among the farmers at the southern end. But liberal Democratic strength exists within the city among blacks, organized teachers and textile workers.

Greenville's development has spilled over into Spartanburg County, bringing new industries and political change. But older textile mills and huge peach orchards dominate the area; peaches were painted on the street signs in downtown Spartanburg. Rank-and-file textile employees and farm laborers give Spartanburg much firmer Democratic loyalties than Greenville has, although Spartanburg went Republican for president in 1980 for the first time, handing Ronald Reagan a bare two-point margin over Jimmy Carter.

Union County has not shared in its neighbors' economic fortune. Half of Union County's land area is in the Sumter National Forest area and the lack of any major highway through the county prevented new plants from relocating there. Union relied on the textile industry for more than half its jobs but the hard times affecting the textile business forced several mills to close in 1981. Union remains staunchly Democratic; the only Republican candidate anywhere in the county in 1982 ran for the school board.

Election Returns

4th District		Democrat		Republican	
1976	President	70,211	(52.1%)	63,018	(46.8%)
	House	97,044	(72.1%)	37,511	(27.9%)
1978	Governor	71,682	(67.4%)	33,558	(31.6%)
	Senate	43,367	(40.5%)	63,504	(59.4%)
	House	51,102	(48.8%)	51,377	(49.1%)
1980	President	65,654	(43.8%)	80,298	(53.6%)
	Senate	98,352	(66.9%)	48,582	(33.1%)
	House	8,845	(8.2%)	91,371	(85.0%)
1982	Governor	78,183	(69.3%)	34,615	(30.7%)
	House	40,394	(36.7%)	69,802	(63.3%)

Demographics

Population: 520,525. **Percent Change from 1970:** 17.3%.

Land Area: 2,124 square miles. **Population per Square Mile:** 245.1.

Counties, 1980 Population: Greenville — 287,913; Spartanburg — 201,861; Union — 30,751.

Cities, 1980 Population: Greenville — 58,242; Greer — 10,525; Spartanburg — 43,968; Union — 10,523.

Race and Ancestry: White — 80.1%; Black — 19.4%; American Indian, Eskimo and Aleut — 0.1%; Asian and Pacific Islander — 0.4%. Spanish Origin — 0.8%. English — 22.2%; French — 0.7%; German — 3.2%; Irish — 6.1%; Scottish — 0.7%.

Universities, Enrollment: Converse College, Spartanburg — 1,040; Furman University, Greenville — 3,151; Greenville Technical College, Greenville — 5,918; North Greenville College, Tigerville — 636; Rutledge College, Spartanburg — 678; Spartanburg Methodist College, Spartanburg — 1,038; Spartanburg Technical College, Spartanburg — 1,996; University of South Carolina at Spartanburg, Spartanburg — 2,608; University of South Carolina at Union, Union — 290; Wofford College, Spartanburg — 1,027.

Newspapers, Circulation: *The Greenville News* (mS), Greenville — 85,214; *Greenville Piedmont* (eS), Greenville — 23,926; *Spartanburg Herald* (mS), Spartanburg — 41,156; *Spartanburg Journal* (eS), Spartanburg — 8,022; *Union Daily Times* (e), Union — 6,525.

Commercial Television Stations, Affiliation: WFBC-TV, Greenville (NBC); WGGS-TV, Greenville (None); WLOS-TV, Greenville (ABC); WSPA-TV, Spartanburg (CBS). Entire district is located in Greenville-Spartanburg-Asheville (N.C.) ADI.

Industries:

Greenville Hospital System (HQ); Greenville; hospital — 3,350. **M. Lowenstein Corp.** (Wamdel Div.); Union; knitting mills — 3,000. **American Hoechst Corp.** (Fibers Industries Div.); Spartanburg; polyester fibers — 2,600. **Union Carbide Corp.** (Kemet); Simpsonville; electronic capacitors — 2,500. **M. Lowenstein Corp.** (Printing & Finishing Div.); Lyman; cotton goods — 2,300.

Spartanburg General Hospital; Spartanburg; hospital — 2,000. **Jonathan Logan Inc.** (Butte Knitting Mills Div.); Spartanburg; children's wear — 1,800. **J. P. Stevens & Co. Inc.** (Duncan Plant); Greenville; textile mills — 1,750. **Fiber Industries Inc.;** Greenville; nylon fibers — 1,560. **Stone Mfg. Co. Inc.** (HQ); Greenville; men's, boys' underwear — 1,500. **W. R. Grace & Co.** (Cryovac Div.); Simpsonville; food products machinery — 1,300. **J. E. Sirrine Co. Inc.** (HQ); Greenville; engineering consultants — 1,200. **Steel Heddle Mfg. Co.** (HQ); Greenville; textile machinery — 1,150. **Cone Mills Corp.** (Carlisle Finishing Co.); Carlisle; cotton synthetic finishing — 1,100.

J. P. Stevens & Co. Inc. (Piedmont Plant); Piedmont; broad woven fabrics — 1,100. **Spartan Mills** (HQ); Spartanburg; woven, knit cloth hosiery — 1,100. **Lockwood Greene Engineers Inc.;** Spartanburg; engineering services — 1,050. **Daniel International Corp.** (Daniel Construction Co.); Greenville; general building contracting — 1,010. **J. P. Stevens & Co. Inc.** (Monaghan Plant); Greenville; textile mills — 1,000. **Michelin Tire Corp.;** Greenville; tires, inner tubes — 1,000. **Rockwell International** (Rockwell Draper); Spartanburg; textile machinery — 1,000. **General Electric Co.** (Gas Turbine Div.); Greenville; turbines — 915. **American Hoechst Corp.** (Film Div.); Greer; plastic film — 900.

Milliken & Co. (Judson Mills Div.); Greenville; woven synthetic fabric mills — 900. **S & S Mfg. Co. Inc.;** Spartanburg; women's blouses — 900. **J. P. Stevens & Co.;** Greenville; broad woven fabric mills — 900. **Mayfair Mills Inc.;** Arcadia; cotton prints — 850. **Arrow Automotive Industries;** Spartanburg; electrical engine equipment — 840. **Spartan Mills Inc.;** Startex; cotton fabric mills — 825. **Her Majesty Industries Inc.** (Just Kids - HQ); Mauldin; children's clothing — 800. **Piedmont Industries Inc.** (Kaynee Co. Div. - HQ); Greenville; men's, boys' clothing — 800. **The Torrington Co.** (Tyger River Plant); Union; roller bearings — 800.

Winn-Dixie Greenville Inc. (Economy Wholesale Distributors — HQ); Greenville; grocery chain — 800. **J. P. Stevens & Co. Inc.** (Victor Plant); Greer; cotton fabric — 780. **Kohler Co.;** Spartanburg; plumbing fixtures — 750. **Inman Mills Inc.** (HQ); Inman; broad woven fabric mills — 748. **The Liberty Corp.** (HQ); Greenville; life insurance — 725. **Firestone Tire & Rubber Co.** (Steel Products Div.); Spartanburg; stainless steel fabricating — 700. **Morton Norwich Products Inc.**

(Texize Div.); Mauldin; industrial cleaning chemicals — 700. **J. P. Stevens & Co. Inc.;** Slater; broad woven fabric — 700. **Textron Inc.** (Homelite Div.); Greer; internal combustion engines — 700.

United Merchants & Manufacturers Inc. (Buffalo Mills Div.); Buffalo; broad woven fabric mills — 700. **W. R. Grace & Co.** (Cryovac Div.); Duncan; plastic packaging materials — 700. **United Merchants & Manufacturers Inc.** (Buffalo Mill); Union; synthetic fabrics mill — 670. **J. P. Stevens & Co. Inc.** (Parker Plant); Greenville; cloth fabric — 650. **Emb-Tex Corp.** (Embroidery Emporium - HQ); Travelers Rest; machine embroideries — 600. **Harrison Electrical Constructors;** Greenville; electrical contracting — 600. **Milliken & Co.;** Drayton; synthetic fabric mills — 600. **Milliken & Co.;** Pacolet Mills; cotton fabric mills — 600. **Milliken & Co.;** Spartanburg; women's clothing wholesaling — 600.

Phillips Fibers Corp.; Spartanburg; man-made fibers — 600. **Reeves Bros. Inc.;** Woodruff; cotton, synthetic yarns — 600. **J. P. Stevens & Co. Inc.;** Piedmont; chemicals — 600. **Simpsonville Mills Co.** (HQ); Simpsonville; narrow woven cloth — 595. **Southern Railway Co.;** Spartanburg; railroad operations — 565. **Industrial Housekeeping Inc.;** Greenville; janitorial service — 550. **Raycord Co. Inc.;** Spartanburg; men's sport shirts — 550. **Dan River Inc.** (Woodside Div.); Fountain Inn; synthetic fabrics — 525. **Inman Mills Inc.;** Enoree; broad woven fabric mills — 525. **Cone Mills Corp.** (Union Bleachery Plant); Greenville; corduroy dyeing — 510.

American Fast Print Ltd. (Fryml Fabrics Division); Spartanburg; textile finishing — 500. **Avco Corp.;** Greer; machine tool parts — 500. **Ballenger Corp.;** Greenville; building, highway construction — 500. **Bigelow-Sanford Inc.;** Landrum; carpet mill — 500. **Bi-Lo Inc.** (HQ); Mauldin; grocery chain — 500. **Davis Electrical Constructors** (HQ); Greenville; electrical contracting — 500. **Deering Milliken Service Corp.;** Spartanburg; business consulting — 500. **Harley Corp.** (HQ); Spartanburg; paper bags — 500. **Lucas Industries Inc.;** Greenville; fuel pumps — 500. **Monsanto Co.;** Moore; abrasive products — 500.

5th District

North Central — Rock Hill

Touching on four distinct regions of South Carolina, the 5th sprawls from the hills of Cherokee County to the low country around Sumter, lacking a geographic center or a clear political identity. The area is dependent on yarns and cloth. The largest employer in the 5th is Springs Mills, with plants in Lancaster, Kershaw and Chester; the huge du Pont synthetic fibers plant in Camden runs a close second. Most of the counties in the central section of the district have at least one town whose name ends in "Mills," and millworkers form the base of the area's labor-oriented Democratic vote.

The district is dotted with various other industries, including furniture, hand tools and a soup cannery. Black-majority Fairfield County, the only county in South Carolina to give Hubert H. Humphrey more than 50 percent of the vote in 1968, has a Uniroyal tire-cord plant.

The population of the old 5th increased by only 13 percent in the 1970s, the slowest growth rate in the state. The judicial panel removed Union County from the 5th to enlarge the nearby 4th, but replaced it with two counties, Lee and Newberry, to bring the 5th up to size. Newberry County, in the western half of the district, is the larger of the two. Heavily dependent on the textile and timber industries, its local politics remain traditionally Democratic, although national elections bring out a sizable GOP vote around the county seat of Newberry.

The district's southern and eastern counties remain primarily agricultural. Chesterfield and tiny Lee County grow soybeans, corn, cotton and melons; their politics, centered around the courthouses in Chesterfield and Bishopville, are rigidly Democratic.

The largest city in the district is Rock Hill, a declining textile town in York County, some 25 miles from Charlotte, N.C. The county's last cotton mill, located in Rock Hill, closed in early 1982. Rock Hill remains a blue-collar town, however, with a strong Democratic loyalty. In 1980 it gave Jimmy Carter 67 percent of its vote. The rest of York County has been growing quickly, and several suburban Charlotte communities have sprung up near the North Carolina border. Their residents provide one of the few firm blocs of Republican strength in the district.

The 5th's other GOP pockets are in Sumter and Kershaw counties. Shaw Air Force Base in Sumter has been a major source of federal dollars and conservative votes. Kershaw's county seat of Camden is the home base of some of South Carolina's most prominent Democratic politicians, but its du Pont executives and other wealthy business executives who live outside the city back Republican candidates.

Election Returns

5th District		Democrat		Republican	
1976	President	80,255	(59.4%)	54,153	(40.1%)
	House	74,271	(55.1%)	60,183	(44.7%)
1978	Governor	62,919	(64.5%)	33,816	(34.6%)
	Senate	43,537	(43.9%)	55,529	(56.0%)
	House	68,648	(82.9%)	1,212	(1.5%)
1980	President	74,745	(53.1%)	63,496	(45.1%)
	Senate	105,091	(77.4%)	30,701	(22.6%)
	House	102,044	(83.2%)	6,756	(5.5%)
1982	Governor	75,195	(73.4%)	27,279	(26.6%)
	House	69,345	(67.6%)	33,191	(32.4%)

Demographics

Population: 519,716. **Percent Change from 1970:** 12.9%.

Land Area: 6,845 square miles. **Population per Square Mile:** 75.9.

Counties, 1980 Population: Cherokee — 40,983; Chester — 30,148; Chesterfield — 38,161; Fairfield — 20,700; Kershaw — 39,015; Lancaster — 53,361; Laurens — 52,214; Lee — 18,929; Newberry — 31,242; Sumter — 88,243; York — 106,720.

Cities, 1980 Population: Gaffney — 13,453; Laurens — 10,587; Rock Hill — 35,344; Sumter — 24,890.

Race and Ancestry: White — 66.9%; Black — 32.4%; American Indian, Eskimo and Aleut — 0.3%; Asian and Pacific Islander — 0.2%. Spanish Origin — 0.9%. English — 18.9%; French — 0.5%; German — 3.4%; Irish — 5.2%; Scottish — 0.6%.

Universities, Enrollment: Chesterfield-Marlboro Technical College, Cheraw — 579; Limestone College, Gaffney — 1,418; Morris College, Sumter — 626; Newberry College, Newberry — 819; Presbyterian College, Clinton — 921; Sumter Area Technical College, Sumter — 1,769; University of South Carolina at Lancaster, Lancaster — 742; University of South Carolina at Sumter, Sumter — 1,089; Winthrop College, Rock Hill — 5,040; York Technical College, Rock Hill — 1,655.

Newspapers, Circulation: *The Chronicle-Independent* (e), Camden — 7,000; *Evening Herald* (e), Rock Hill — 24,268; *The Sumter Daily Item* (e), Sumter — 18,856.

Commercial Television Stations, Affiliation: District is divided between

Columbia ADI and Charlotte (N.C.) ADI. Portion is in Greenville-Spartanburg-Asheville (N.C.) ADI.

Military Installations: Shaw Air Force Base, Sumter — 5,701.

Nuclear Power Plants: Catawba 1 and 2, Rock Hill (Westinghouse, Duke Power); Cherokee 1, Spartanburg (Combustion Engineering, Duke Power); Summer 1, Parr (Westinghouse, Daniel International), November 1982.

Industries:

E. I. du Pont de Nemours & Co.; Camden; synthetic yarn — 3,600. **Springs Mills Inc.;** Lancaster; cotton blended fabrics mill — 3,500. **Springs Mills Inc.** (Grace Finishing Plant); Lancaster; fabric finishers — 2,900. **Celanese Corp.;** Rock Hill; man-made fibers — 2,000. **Skyline Mfg. Co. Inc.;** Camden; children's outerwear — 1,750.

M. Lowenstein Corp. (Printing & Finishing Div.); Rock Hill; automotive trimmings — 1,450. **Campbell Soup Co.;** Sumter; canning, packaging — 1,330. **Clinton Mills Inc.** (Bailey Plant - HQ); Clinton; broad woven cloth mill — 1,300. **Springs Mills Inc.** (Grace Finishing Plant); Lancaster; textiles — 1,300. **The Torrington Co.** (Clinton Bearings Div.); Clinton; ball, roller bearings — 1,300. **Georgia-Pacific Corp.** (Williams Furniture Co.); Sumter; furniture — 1,250. **Greenwood Mills Inc.** (Joanna Cotton Mills); Joanna; window shades — 1,100. **Cooper Industries Inc.** (Crescent/Xcelite Div.); Sumter; hand tools — 1,000. **Bowater Carolina Corp.** (HQ); Catawba; sulphate pulp mill — 945. **The Kendall Co. Inc.;** Bethune; textile finishing — 900. **Springs Mills;** Chester; cotton fabrics mill — 900. **J. P. Stevens Co. Inc.;** Whitmire; broad woven cloth — 850. **Santee Print Works Inc.;** Sumter; print cloth processing — 825. **Springs Mills Inc.** (Customer Service Center); Lancaster; administrative offices — 800. **Louis Rich Inc.;** Newberry; poultry processing — 750. **Springs Mills Inc.;** Kershaw; broad woven fabric mills — 750. **Milliken & Co.;** Gaffney; fabric mill — 700. **Uniroyal Inc.** (Fibers & Textile Div.); Winnsboro; tire cord — 651. **Indian Head Inc.** (Glass Div.); Laurens; glass products — 650. **J. P. Stevens & Co. Inc.** (Republic Plant #2); Great Falls; fabric mills — 650.

J. P. Stevens & Co. Inc.; Laurens; broad woven fabric — 650. **Becton Dickinson and Co.** (Vacutainer Systems Div.); Sumter; medical supplies — 600. **Burlington Industries Inc.** (James Fabrics); Cheraw; fiberglass — 600. **Charm Corp. of South Carolina;** Ridgeway; robes, dressing gowns — 600. **M. Lowenstein Corp.** (Limestone Mfg. Div.); Gaffney; sheeting — 600. **Exide Corp.;** Sumter; storage batteries — 564. **J. P. Stevens & Co. Inc.** (Republic Plant #3); Great Falls; cotton fabric mill — 550. **Pioneer Ltd.** (HQ); Sumter; children's wear — 530. **The Kendall Co. Inc.** (Oakland Plant); Newberry; broad woven fabrics mill — 500. **Oxford Industries Inc.** (Carolina Apparel Mfg. Co.); Gaffney; women's blouses — 500.

6th District

East — Florence

Agriculture dominates this district more than any other in South Carolina, and tobacco is the key product. Horry County in the eastern corner of the state has one of the richest tobacco crops in the country. Broadleaf from Horry's fields is stored in warehouses and bid on at auctions throughout the district in such towns as Darlington, Marion and Mullins and in Williamsburg County, farther south. When the federal tobacco quota and price support program was threatened at the end of 1981, a significant part of the 6th's livelihood was threatened as well.

Democratic politics dominate the 6th District, and the addition of the rural, northern section of Berkeley County reinforces that pattern. The poverty that afflicts counties such as Williamsburg and Marion keeps them in the Democratic column in national as well as local elections; in the 1980 election that cost Abscam defendant John W. Jenrette Jr. his seat, these counties gave the three-term Democrat his highest margins in the district.

There is a long history of political corruption in this part of South Carolina; the largest vote fraud investigation in the history of the Southeast took place in Dillon County in 1980. The investigation resulted in the imprisonment of the county Democratic Party chairman.

Blacks make up 41 percent of the population in the new 6th, the largest proportion in any of South Carolina's districts. Williamsburg, Marion and Clarendon counties have black-majority populations, and blacks throughout the area are better organized than in most other parts of the South. It was a solid black vote that allowed Jenrette to come within 5,217 votes of re-election in 1980 even though he had been convicted in the Abscam bribery scandal.

Republican strength has been building in Horry and Florence counties which, despite their ties to tobacco, are also the centers of non-farm income in the district. Coastal Horry County has the fastest-growing tourist industry in South Carolina, drawing visitors year-round from Ohio and down Interstate 95 from New York and New England to the surf and resorts of Myrtle Beach. Military personnel living in the area around Myrtle Beach Air Force Base and the wealthy retirees who have been moving to the area in increasing numbers during the 1970s give the county a more conservative cast.

Although small factories are scattered throughout the 6th — candies are produced in Marion and Tupperware in Hemingway — Florence is the district's industrial center. A railhead since the Civil War, it has drawn new plants and industries, accompanied by an influx of managerial people and Republican votes.

The only other industrial area is Georgetown, where the International Paper Company and Georgetown Steel Corporation dominate the city's port and blue-collar workers provide Democratic margins.

Election Returns

6th District		Democrat		Republican	
1976	President	84,895	(61.4%)	52,984	(38.3%)
	House	78,844	(56.8%)	59,610	(42.9%)
1978	Governor	57,033	(56.8%)	42,639	(42.4%)
	Senate	49,518	(48.1%)	53,388	(51.9%)
	House	70,281	(96.2%)	2,561	(3.5%)
1980	President	79,783	(52.5%)	69,806	(45.9%)
	Senate	111,496	(76.9%)	33,474	(23.1%)
	House	71,292	(47.5%)	78,159	(52.1%)
1982	Governor	88,325	(74.6%)	30,141	(25.4%)
	House	62,582	(52.5%)	56,653	(47.5%)

Demographics

Population: 519,273. **Percent Change from 1970:** 23.6%.

Land Area: 7,247 square miles. **Population per Square Mile:** 71.7.

Counties, 1980 Population: Berkeley (Pt.) — 39,927; Clarendon — 27,464; Darlington — 62,717; Dillon — 31,083; Florence — 110,163; Georgetown — 42,461; Horry — 101,419; Marion — 34,179; Marlboro — 31,634; Williamsburg — 38,226.

Cities, 1980 Population: Conway — 10,240; Florence — 30,062; Georgetown — 10,144; Myrtle Beach — 18,446; North Charleston (Pt.) — 0.

Race and Ancestry: White — 58.6%; Black — 40.9%; American Indian, Eskimo and Aleut — 0.2%; Asian and Pacific Islander — 0.2%. Spanish Origin — 1.1%. English — 19.7%; French — 0.5%; German — 1.9%; Irish — 3.4%; Scottish — 0.5%.

Universities, Enrollment: Coker College, Hartsville — 313; Florence-Darlington Technical College, Florence — 2,344; Francis Marion College, Florence — 2,974; Horry-Georgetown Technical College, Conway — 1,310; University of South Carolina at Coastal Carolina, Conway — 2,243; Williamsburg Technical College, Kingstree — 503.

Newspapers, Circulation: *Florence Morning News* (mS), Florence — 31,232; *Sun News* (mS), Myrtle Beach — 14,677.

Commercial Television Stations, Affiliation: WBTW, Florence (CBS); WPDE-TV, Florence (ABC). Most of district is located in Charleston ADI and Florence ADI. Portions are in Columbia ADI and Wilmington (N.C.) ADI.

Military Installations: Myrtle Beach Air Force Base, Myrtle Beach — 3,614.

Nuclear Power Plants: Robinson 2, Hartsville (Westinghouse, Ebasco Services Inc.), March 1971.

Industries:

Sonoco Products Co. (HQ); Hartsville; paperboard mills — 2,500. **AVX Corp.** (AVX Ceramics); Myrtle Beach; electronic components — 2,050. **Wellman Industries Inc.;** Johnsonville; polyester, nylon, wool fibers, lanolin — 1,600. **General Electric Co.** (Mobile Radio Dept.); Florence; mobile radios — 1,400. **International Paper Co.;** Georgetown; paperboard mills — 1,200.

Fiber Industries Inc.; Florence; polyester fibers — 1,100. **Fiber Industries Inc.;** Darlington; synthetic organic fibers — 1,000. **Georgetown Steel Corp.** (Andrews Wire Div. - HQ); Georgetown; steel bars, wire — 1,000. **E. I. du Pont de Nemours & Co.** (Construction Div.); Florence; polyester products — 900. **Oneita Knitting Mills** (HQ); Andrews; men's, boys' clothing — 900. **Aynor Mfg. Co.;** Aynor; women's outerwear — 850. **Union Carbide Corp.** (Linde Div.); Florence; welding machinery — 850. **Marlene Industries Inc.** (Loris Mfg. Co.); Loris; women's sportswear — 800.

Emerson Electric Co. Inc. (Environmental Products Div.); Bennettsville; heating, ventilation equipment — 750. **Dart Industries Inc.** (Tupperware Div.); Hemingway; plastics products — 727. **James River Corp.** (Dixie Products); Darlington; paper cups, containers — 700. **Travenol Laboratories** (Medical Products Div.); Kingstree; pharmaceutical preparations — 700. **The Hanes Corp.** (L'eggs Products Div.); Hartsville; women's hosiery — 680. **Walter Kidde & Co. Inc.** (Grove Mfg. Co. Div.); Conway; industrial cranes — 670. **McGregory-Doniger Inc.** (Anvil Knitwear Div.); Mullins; men's underwear — 655. **Marlowe Mfg. Co.;** Florence; children's clothes — 650. **Mohasco Corp.** (Cale River Mill); Bennettsville; carpet, yarn mill — 600.

Mohasco Corp. (Dixiana Mills); Dillon; carpet mills — 600. **Russell Stover Candies Inc.;** Marion; candy — 524. **B. E. & K. Inc.;** Florence; industrial construction — 500. **La-Z-Boy Chair Co. Inc.;** Florence; furniture — 500. **The Marmon Group Inc.;** Darlington; motor vehicle parts; 500. **Nucor Corp.** (Steel Div.); Darlington; steel works — 500. **Southern Packaging & Storage Co.;** Mullins; food packaging, storage — 500. **United Merchants & Manufacturers Inc.;** Conway; yarn spinning mills — 500. **Wayne-Gossard Corp.** (Heritage Sportswear Div.); Marion; men's sweaters — 500.

South Dakota

South Dakota lost one of its two congressional districts as a result of the 1980 Census. The loss, due to a modest population increase of 3.7 percent during the 1970s, meant the state would elect one representative at-large for the first time since it entered the union in 1889. South Dakota had three representatives from 1913 to 1933.

South Dakota is a Midwestern state on one side of the Missouri River and a Western state on the other. Crossing the Missouri going west means leaving the Corn Belt and entering ranching country, where in most places there is not enough water for a good crop in an average year.

There are political differences to match the geographical ones. The Corn Belt counties vote much like Iowa and Minnesota across the border — Republican but relatively tolerant of government social services. The western side is more like Wyoming — ornery, individualist and eager for government to leave it alone.

The people are mostly in the east. Throughout the 1970s there were as many people in the 21 eastern counties as there were in the 46 western counties.

The Corn Palace in Mitchell symbolizes the primacy of that crop in the eastern third of the state. An auditorium with mosaics wrought out of various colored corn cobs on the exterior, the Corn Palace has stood as a tourist attraction and a banner of the economic foundation of the area since the last century.

The corn feeds cattle and hogs and provides the largest share of agricultural income in the state. Sioux Falls, the state's main metropolis, is a service center for agricultural interests, with banks, insurance companies and farm implement dealers all tied closely to the agricultural economy. There is also a large meatpacking business.

Unlike other areas in the state, the Sioux Falls metropolitan area maintained a respectable growth rate in the 1970s, with surrounding Minnehaha County gaining 14.9 percent and Lincoln County, with its Sioux Falls suburbs, going up 18.5 percent. Further south, Union County — which gets some spillover from nearby Sioux City, Iowa — gained 13.4 percent. But those were the only gains over 10 percent in any South Dakota county east of the Missouri River.

The wheat-growing counties, between the eastern Corn Belt and the Missouri River, suffered the greatest losses in population, most of them declining by more than 10 percent.

At the polls, eastern South Dakota has been somewhat less staunchly Republican than the area west of the Missouri. It was in this area that George McGovern, who comes from Mitchell, molded a statewide Democratic Party and took a U. S. House seat in 1956, the first Democratic House win in 20 years. In 1976 most of the wheat and corn counties backed Jimmy Carter for president, in response to unpopular Republican farm programs.

On the other side of the river the towns appear less frequently. The land gradually turns from green to brown and is used for grazing. In contrast to the relatively sedate farms of the east, the west is cowboy and rodeo country.

Near the western edge of South Dakota lies the state's second largest metropolitan center, Rapid City. Recovering from a devastating 1972 flood, the city has drawn federal rebuilding money and has become something of a boom town. New industries coming in, a newly constructed convention center and the prospering tourism industry have combined to attract young job-seekers to Rapid City from the farms and ranches. Adding to the population growth are retirees who come to live in the scenic Black Hills. Many Indians have returned to the reservations around Rapid City from jobs that have disappeared in the industrial centers of the Midwest.

Republicans are nearly always dominant on this side of the Missouri. In 1976 Carter carried only six counties west of the river, three of them on Indian reservations.

Age of Population

District	Population Under 18	Voting Age Population	Population 65 & Over (% of VAP)	Median Age
AL	205,606	485,162	91,019 (18.8%)	28.9

Income and Occupation

District	Median Family Income	White Collar Workers	Blue Collar Workers	Service Workers	Farm Workers
AL	$ 15,993	44.9%	24.4%	14.8%	15.9%

SOUTH DAKOTA

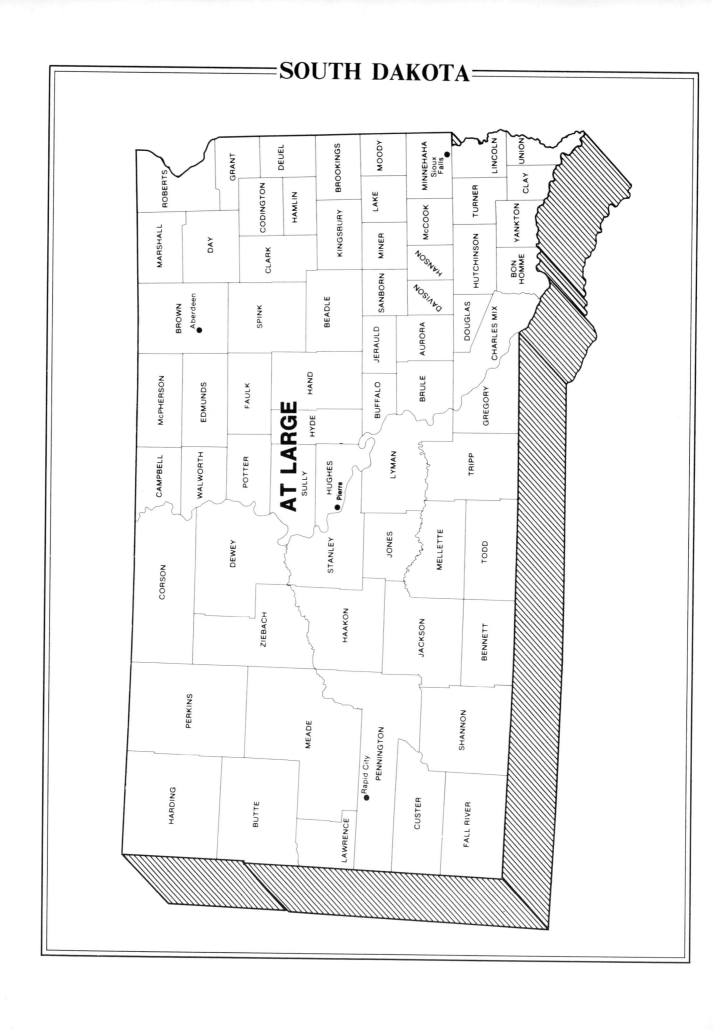

Education: School Years Completed

District	8 Years or Fewer	4 Years of High School	4 Years of College or More	Median School Years
AL	22.0%	36.3%	14.0%	12.5

Housing and Residential Patterns

District	Owner Occupied	Renter Occupied	Urban	Rural
AL	69.3%	30.7%	46.4%	53.6%

Election Returns

At Large		Democrat		Republican	
1976	President	147,068	(48.9%)	151,505	(50.4%)
	House	72,501	(24.6%)	221,188	(75.0%)
1978	Governor	112,679	(43.4%)	147,116	(56.6%)
	Senate	84,767	(33.2%)	170,832	(66.8%)
	House	120,199	(47.0%)	135,324	(53.0%)
1980	President	103,855	(31.7%)	198,343	(60.5%)
	Senate	129,018	(39.4%)	190,594	(58.2%)
	House	173,357	(54.3%)	146,146	(45.7%)
1982	Governor	81,137	(29.1%)	197,425	(70.9%)
	House	142,122	(51.6%)	133,530	(48.4%)

Demographics

Population: 690,768. **Percent Change from 1970:** 3.7%.

Land Area: 75,952 square miles. **Population per Square Mile:** 9.1.

Counties, 1980 Population: Aurora — 3,628; Beadle — 19,195; Bennett — 3,044; Bon Homme — 8,059; Brookings — 24,332; Brown — 36,962; Brule — 5,245; Buffalo — 1,795; Butte — 8,372; Campbell — 2,243; Charles Mix — 9,680; Clark — 4,894; Clay — 13,689; Codington — 20,885; Corson — 5,196; Custer — 6,000; Davison — 17,820; Day — 8,133; Deuel — 5,289; Dewey — 5,366; Douglas — 4,181.

Edmunds — 5,159; Fall River — 8,439; Faulk — 3,327; Grant — 9,013; Gregory — 6,015; Haakon — 2,794; Hamlin — 5,261; Hand — 4,948; Hanson — 3,415; Harding — 1,700; Hughes — 14,220; Hutchinson — 9,350; Hyde — 2,069; Jackson — 3,437; Jerauld — 2,929; Jones — 1,463; Kingsbury — 6,679; Lake — 10,724; Lawrence — 18,339; Lincoln — 13,942; Lyman — 3,864.

Marshall — 5,404; McCook — 6,444; McPherson — 4,027; Meade — 20,717; Mellette — 2,249; Miner — 3,739; Minnehaha — 109,435; Moody — 6,692; Pennington — 70,361; Perkins — 4,700; Potter — 3,674; Roberts — 10,911; Sanborn — 3,213; Shannon —

11,323; Spink — 9,201; Stanley — 2,533; Sully — 1,990; Todd — 7,328; Tripp — 7,268; Turner — 9,255; Union — 10,938; Walworth — 7,011; Yankton — 18,952; Ziebach — 2,308.

Cities, 1980 Population: Aberdeen — 25,956; Brookings — 14,951; Huron — 13,000; Mitchell — 13,916; Pierre — 11,973; Rapid City — 46,492; Sioux Falls — 81,343; Vermillion — 10,136; Watertown — 15,649; Yankton — 12,011.

Race and Ancestry: White — 92.6%; Black — 0.3%; American Indian, Eskimo and Aleut — 6.5%; Asian and Pacific Islander — 0.3%. Spanish Origin — 0.6%. Dutch — 2.0%; English — 4.2%; French — 0.8%; German — 25.9%; Irish — 3.2%; Norwegian — 6.8%; Swedish — 1.7%.

Universities, Enrollment: Augustana College, Sioux Falls — 2,115; Black Hills State College, Spearfish — 2,099; Dakota State College, Madison — 1,000; Dakota Wesleyan University, Mitchell — 543; Huron College, Huron — 321; Mount Marty College, Yankton — 568; National College, Rapid City — 2,285; North American Baptist Seminary, Sioux Falls — 155; Northern State College, Aberdeen — 2,603; Presentation College, Aberdeen — 300; Sioux Falls College, Sioux Falls — 656; South Dakota School of Mines and Technology, Rapid City — 2,393; South Dakota State University, Brookings — 6,848; University of South Dakota (main campus), Vermillion — 5,968; University of South Dakota (Springfield campus), Springfield — 852; Yankton College, Yankton — 272.

Newspapers, Circulation: *Aberdeen American News* (eS), Aberdeen — 21,080; *Argus-Leader* (mS), Sioux Falls — 45,321; *The Brookings Daily Register* (e), Brookings — 5,500; *Call/Pioneer Times* (e), Lead — 2,512; *Daily Capital Journal* (e), Pierre — 4,700; *Huron Daily Plainsman* (eS), Huron — 13,762; *Madison Daily Leader* (e), Madison — 3,808; *Post* (m), Belle Fourche — 3,393; *The Rapid City Journal* (eS), Rapid City — 32,284; *Republic* (e), Mitchell — 13,843; *Watertown Public Opinion* (e), Watertown — 17,350; *Yankton Daily Press & Dakotan* (e), Yankton — 10,814.

Commercial Television Stations, Affiliation: KABY-TV, Aberdeen (NBC); KDLO-TV, Florence (CBS); KELO-TV, Sioux Falls (CBS); KEVN-TV, Rapid City (ABC, CBS); KHSD-TV, Lead (NBC, ABC); KIVV-TV, Lead (ABC, CBS); KOTA-TV, Rapid City (NBC); KPRY-TV, Pierre (NBC); KSFY-TV, Sioux Falls (NBC); KXON-TV, Mitchell (ABC). Most of district is located in Rapid City ADI and Sioux Falls-Mitchell ADI. Portions are in Minot (N.D.)-Bismarck (N.D.)-Dickinson (N.D.) ADI and Sioux City (Iowa) ADI.

Military Installations: Ellsworth Air Force Base, Box Elder — 6,836; Joe Foss Field (Air Force), Sioux Falls — 715.

Industries:

John Morrell & Co.; Sioux Falls; meatpacking — 3,000. **Sioux Valley Hospital Assn.;** Sioux Falls; hospital — 1,830. **Presentation Sisters Inc.;** Sioux Falls; hospital — 1,300. **Magnetic Peripherals Inc.;** Rapid City; computers — 1,100. **Citibank, South Dakota;** Sioux Falls; credit card operations — 1,047. **Midwest Coast Transport Inc.;** Sioux Falls; trucking — 800. **Minnesota Mining & Mfg. Co. Inc.;** Aberdeen; face masks — 600. **Raven Industries Inc.** (HQ); Sioux Falls; insulated ski clothing — 530. **Magnetic Peripherals Inc.;** Aberdeen; computers — 500. **Minnesota Mining & Mfg. Co.;** Brookings; health care products — 500.

Tennessee

The Democratic Party had a classic gerrymander in mind when they drew Tennessee's new congressional districts. Endeavoring to bring two more Democrats into the delegation, which expanded by one seat to nine members, the Democratic state Legislature passed a redistricting bill June 17, 1981, that established two open districts.

One is a sprawling rural catchall of 23 counties in eastern and middle Tennessee. This new 4th District is basically the territory that was left over after five overpopulated districts were trimmed down to the ideal population size. The other open district was the 7th District in west-central Tennessee. The new map threw a Democrat and Republican into the same district, but the Republican already had announced his intention to run for the Senate.

Tennessee Gov. Lamar Alexander, a Republican, took a close look at the map proposed by the Democrats and decided that Republican candidates had a chance in both open districts. Because the map also did nothing to harm East Tennessee's two Republican incumbents, Alexander decided not to veto the Democrats' attempted gerrymander. He allowed the new redistricting proposal to become law without his signature.

In November the Democrats won the 4th convincingly, but Republicans narrowly carried the 7th.

Tennessee earned its new district by taking in nearly 665,000 new residents during the 1970s. But it was merely regaining the seat it had lost after the 1970 Census when it fell just short of the population required for nine seats. None of the districts created in 1981 varied from the ideal population of 510,083 by more than 1.3 percentage points.

Income and Occupation

District	Median Family Income	White Collar Workers	Blue Collar Workers	Service Workers	Farm Workers
1	$ 15,374	42.7%	43.3%	11.0%	3.0%
2	17,196	50.6	35.1	12.6	1.7
3	17,741	49.3	37.3	12.1	1.2
4	13,733	35.6	48.5	10.9	5.1
5	19,528	59.4	26.7	12.8	1.1
6	17,325	44.7	40.8	10.7	3.8
7	18,411	51.0	35.4	10.7	2.9
8	15,200	41.1	42.4	12.2	4.3
9	15,230	52.5	31.2	15.7	0.6
State	$ 16,564	47.8%	37.6%	12.1%	2.6%

Education: School Years Completed

District	8 Years or Fewer	4 Years of High School	4 Years of College or More	Median School Years
1	33.2%	30.4%	10.5%	12.0
2	25.8	31.2	15.0	12.3
3	24.6	31.8	13.9	12.3
4	38.8	29.7	7.5	11.8
5	18.5	32.0	18.6	12.5
6	30.2	32.2	12.0	12.2
7	24.4	33.6	14.6	12.3
8	30.9	32.8	7.8	12.0
9	22.5	31.6	13.3	12.3
State	27.7%	31.7%	12.6%	12.2

Age of Population

District	Population Under 18	Voting Age Population	Population 65 & Over (% of VAP)	Median Age
1	141,525	371,177	57,367 (15.5%)	31.7
2	134,488	375,709	58,457 (15.6%)	30.6
3	146,235	370,457	55,994 (15.1%)	30.6
4	151,572	359,160	61,644 (17.2%)	31.0
5	130,775	384,057	57,539 (15.0%)	30.0
6	149,483	362,322	55,363 (15.3%)	30.2
7	152,410	351,201	46,053 (13.1%)	29.1
8	146,152	358,805	65,163 (18.2%)	29.8
9	145,920	359,672	60,008 (16.7%)	28.4
State	1,298,560	3,292,560	517,588 (15.7%)	30.1

Housing and Residential Patterns

District	Owner Occupied	Renter Occupied	Urban	Rural
1	75.2%	24.8%	48.2%	51.8%
2	68.2	31.8	62.2	37.8
3	68.7	31.3	68.0	32.0
4	75.5	24.5	26.5	73.5
5	58.5	41.5	93.7	6.3
6	74.9	25.1	45.2	54.8
7	73.6	26.4	50.9	49.1
8	69.8	30.2	49.0	51.0
9	54.0	46.0	100.0	0.0
State	68.6%	31.4%	60.4%	39.6%

TENNESSEE

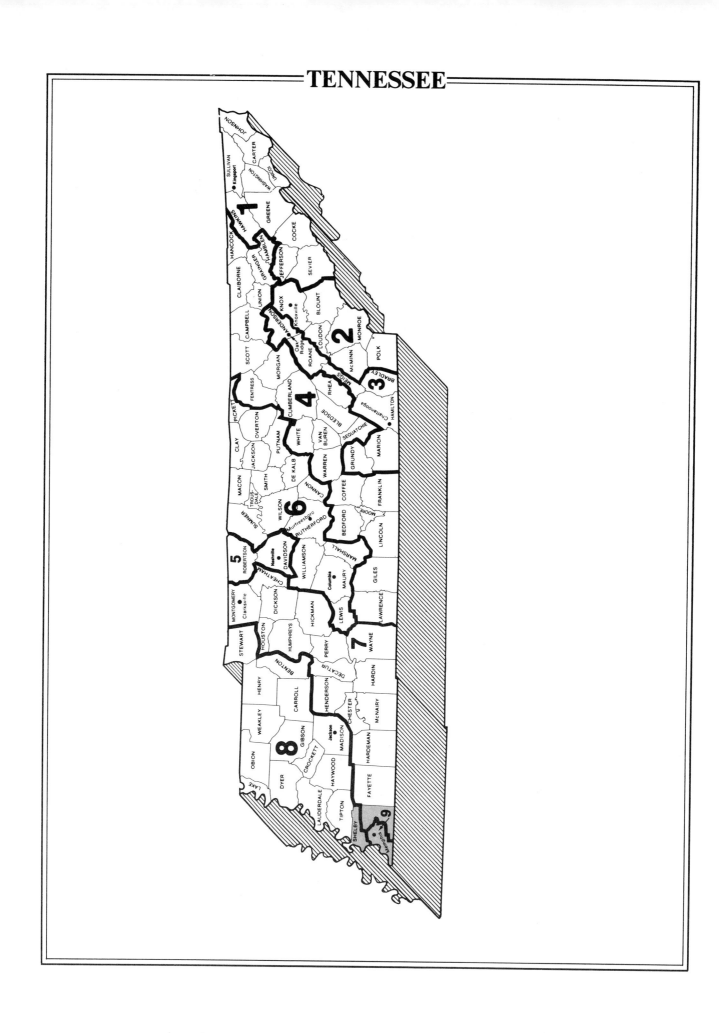

1st District

Northeast — Tri-cities

1st District		Democrat		Republican	
1982	Senate	69,824	(54.9%)	57,306	(45.1%)
	House	27,580	(22.8%)	89,497	(74.1%)

By removing three western counties, the Legislature pushed the 1st District further into the northeastern corner of the state. Hamblen, Grainger and Hancock counties are steadfastly Republican, but their transfer to the new 4th District did not affect GOP control in the 1st. The 10 counties that make up the new 1st gave Ronald Reagan 61 percent of their vote in the 1980 presidential race, his highest percentage in any of Tennessee's congressional districts. The 1st District has not elected a Democrat to the House since 1878.

The Tennessee Valley Authority (TVA) has freed this district and much of East Tennessee from the pervasive rural poverty of an earlier era. Isolated highland towns, tobacco patches and livestock clearings were once the 1st District norm, but in the past generation, small cities have grown up around industries drawn to the area by the availability of TVA power.

Forty-five percent of the people in the 1st District live in Sullivan and Washington counties, which encompass northeast Tennessee's Tri-cities — Johnson City, Kingsport and Bristol. These towns make everything from textiles, paper and chemicals to electronic calculators and communications equipment.

Because of its industrial work force, the Tri-cities area has a respectable Democratic vote. In 1980, Reagan managed only 51 percent in Sullivan County; in 1976, Jimmy Carter narrowly took Sullivan. Reagan was much stronger in Washington County in 1980, but Democrats still held him below 60 percent.

Even when Democrats do well in the Tri-cities, however, they are generally swamped districtwide. More than one-half of the people in the 1st District live in rural and small-town counties where the impact of TVA has not shaken natives from their instinctive suspicion of big government. These counties regularly elect Republican candidates by wide margins.

The rural areas raise tobacco, poultry and livestock. Zinc and limestone are mined, and some people commute to factory jobs in Knoxville or the Tri-cities.

At the southern end of the 1st, Sevier County feeds on tourist dollars. It is the gateway to the Great Smoky Mountains National Park, which draws about 10 million visitors yearly. At the very edge of the park in Sevier County is Gatlinburg, a town of 3,210 people whose motels sleep 40,000.

Election Returns

1st District		Democrat		Republican	
1976	President	72,867	(45.4%)	85,130	(53.1%)
	Senate	68,005	(44.7%)	83,169	(54.6%)
	House	61,789	(41.4%)	86,055	(57.7%)
1978	Governor	42,222	(32.8%)	85,738	(66.6%)
	Senate	38,527	(31.0%)	78,587	(63.3%)
	House	44,916	(36.0%)	79,809	(64.0%)
1980	President	62,841	(36.1%)	105,474	(60.6%)
	House	—		113,840	(85.4%)
1982	Governor	33,387	(26.1%)	94,595	(73.9%)

Demographics

Population: 512,702. **Percent Change from 1970:** 18.9%.

Land Area: 3,958 square miles. **Population per Square Mile:** 129.5.

Counties, 1980 Population: Carter — 50,205; Cocke — 28,792; Greene — 54,422; Hawkins — 43,751; Jefferson — 31,284; Johnson — 13,745; Sevier — 41,418; Sullivan — 143,968; Unicoi — 16,362; Washington — 88,755.

Cities, 1980 Population: Bristol — 23,986; Elizabethton — 12,431; Greeneville — 14,097; Johnson City — 39,753; Kingsport — 32,027.

Race and Ancestry: White — 97.7%; Black — 1.9%; American Indian, Eskimo and Aleut — 0.1%; Asian and Pacific Islander — 0.2%. Spanish Origin — 0.5%. Dutch — 0.7%; English — 31.1%; French — 0.6%; German — 4.9%; Irish — 6.5%; Scottish — 0.5%.

Universities, Enrollment: Bristol College, Bristol — 233; Carson-Newman College, Jefferson City — 1,737; East Tennessee State University, Johnson City — 9,153; Emmanuel School of Religion, Johnson City — 132; King College, Bristol — 277; Milligan College, Milligan College — 754; Steed College, Johnson City — 383; Tri-Cities State Technical School, Blountville — 661; Tusculum College, Greeneville — 375.

Newspapers, Circulation: *Daily News* (mS), Kingsport — 4,100; *Elizabethton Star* (eS), Elizabethton — 8,879; *The Greenville Sun* (e), Greenville — 14,411; *Johnson City Press-Chronicle* (meS), Johnson City — 26,589; *Kingsport Times-News* (all day, S), Kingsport — 43,132.

Commercial Television Stations, Affiliation: WJHL-TV, Johnson City (CBS); WKPT-TV, Kingsport (ABC). District is divided between Knoxville ADI and Bristol (Va.)-Kingsport-Johnson City ADI.

Military Installations: Holston Army Ammunition Plant, Kingsport — 1,082.

Industries:

Eastman Kodak Co. (Tennessee Eastman Co.); Kingsport; chemicals, plastics — 11,400. **N. A. P. Consumer Electronics Corp.;** Greeneville; color televisions — 3,500. **Kingsport Press Inc.** (HQ); Kingsport; book printing — 3,180. **ITT Telecommunications Corp.** (HQ); Johnson City; communications equipment — 3,000. **Sperry Corp.;** Bristol; computerized business machines — 2,000.

Holston Valley Community Hospital; Kingsport; hospital — 1,950. Raytheon Co. (Missile Systems Div.); Bristol; electronic equipment — 1,850. **North American Rayon Corp.;** Elizabethton; rayon — 1,500. **Memorial Hospital Inc.;** Johnson City; hospital — 1,230. **Green Valley Development Center;** Greeneville; state psychiatric hospital — 1,170. **The Mead Corp.;** Kingsport; paper mill — 1,100. **The Mason & Dixon Lines Inc.** (HQ); Kingsport; trucking — 1,060. **Holston Defense Corp.** (Holston Army Ammunition Plant); Kingsport; explosives — 1,030. Bristol Memorial Hospital; Bristol; hospital — 1,020. **Texas Instruments Inc.** (Electronic Controls Div.); Johnson City; electronic components — 1,000. **Burlington Industries Inc.** (Klopman Mills-Volunteer Plant); Bristol; broad woven fabrics — 900. **Cherokee Textile Mills** (HQ); Sevierville; cotton, synthetic fabrics — 900.

N. A. P. Consumer Electronics Corp.; Jefferson City; television cabinets — 837. **Metals Engineering Inc.;** Greeneville; metal stampings — 700. **Mor-Flo Industries Inc.;** Johnson City; household appliances — 700. **J. P. Stevens & Co. Inc.;** Kingsport; broad woven fabric — 700. **Kingsport Press Inc.;** Church Hill; book publishing — 699. **Clinchfield Railroad Co.** (HQ); Erwin; railroad operations — 615. Eastman Chemical Products Inc. (HQ); Kingsport; chemical wholesaling — 610. **AFG Industries Inc.;** Church Hill; glass — 578. **Holliston Mills Inc.;** Church Hill; coated paper, fabric — 526. **Burlington Industries Inc.** (Klopman Div.); Johnson City; broad woven synthetic fabric — 500. **The Holliston Mills Inc.;** Kingsport; fabric finishing — 500. **Nuclear Fuel Services Inc.;** Erwin; nuclear fuel — 500. **Plus Mark Inc.;** Afton; gift wrapping — 500.

2nd District

East — Knoxville

The 2nd has been impeccably Republican for years in nearly every contest for national, congressional and state-wide office. Redistricting altered the appearance of the 2nd, but not its partisan preference.

The remap removed four northern counties and enhanced the already-dominant role of Knoxville and Knox County in the district. Sixty-three percent of the district's residents live in Knox County, compared with 54 percent before redistricting.

With 175,030 residents, Knoxville is the third-largest city in the state. TVA headquarters are there, as is the University of Tennessee's main campus.

The city grew up on textiles, tobacco marketing and meatpacking, but now has a larger role as a regional retail and distribution center. Knoxville was the site of the 1982 World's Fair, staged on a 70-acre site adjoining downtown.

Federal employees who work for TVA are generally Democratic, but the labor vote in private industry is a mixed bag; although union leaders are Democratic, many of the rank-and-file are conservative and vote Republican. The state university also has a conservative orientation, and the outlying rural sections of Knox County are strongly Republican. Democratic candidates consider 45 percent a good showing in Knox County, where the Republican tradition has not abated since the Civil War. Between 1964 and 1982, the Republican House incumbent has been held under 70 percent of the vote just twice — in 1964 when he first won election and 1976.

Blount County, south of Knoxville, has 15 percent of the district's residents. Located there are the sprawling plants of Alcoa Aluminum. In 1980, Blount was Ronald Reagan's best 2nd District county, giving him 64 percent of the vote.

Moving south toward the Georgia line, Democratic strength picks up. McMinn and Monroe counties gave tiny margins to Jimmy Carter in 1976, but reversed field in 1980 and cast more than 55 percent of their vote for Reagan. Polk County, added to the 2nd by redistricting, is the eastern-most county in Tennessee carried by Carter in 1980. But the Democratic votes of Polk's 13,602 residents are barely noticed in the 2nd.

The four northern counties that were moved out of the 2nd into the 4th were Campbell, Claiborne, Scott and Union. All usually vote Republican, but their combined vote seldom was decisive.

Election Returns

2nd District		Democrat		Republican	
1976	President	85,485	(48.7%)	88,130	(50.2%)
	Senate	72,241	(42.6%)	96,219	(56.8%)
	House	64,179	(38.0%)	104,768	(62.0%)
1978	Governor	60,489	(41.1%)	86,162	(58.6%)
	Senate	47,132	(32.7%)	89,058	(61.7%)
	House	26,747	(19.4%)	110,772	(80.5%)
1980	President	71,287	(38.4%)	106,979	(57.6%)
	House	43,339	(24.8%)	131,643	(75.2%)
1982	Governor	34,372	(23.8%)	109,756	(76.2%)

2nd District		Democrat		Republican	
1982	Senate	80,883	(56.1%)	63,281	(43.9%)
	House	—[1]		x[1]	

[1] *No votes tabulated where candidate was unopposed; x indicates winner.*

Demographics

Population: 510,197. **Percent Change from 1970:** 17.3%.

Land Area: 2,814 square miles. **Population per Square Mile:** 181.3.

Counties, 1980 Population: Blount — 77,770; Knox — 319,694; Loudon — 28,553; McMinn — 41,878; Monroe — 28,700; Polk — 13,602.

Cities, 1980 Population: Athens — 12,080; Knoxville — 175,030; Maryville — 17,480.

Race and Ancestry: White — 92.6%; Black — 6.7%; American Indian, Eskimo and Aleut — 0.1%; Asian and Pacific Islander — 0.4%. Spanish Origin — 0.6%. Dutch — 0.8%; English — 24.4%; French — 0.6%; German — 4.7%; Irish — 6.5%; Scottish — 0.5%.

Universities, Enrollment: Cooper Institute, Knoxville — 82; Draughons Junior College of Business, Knoxville — 743; Hiwassee College, Madisonville — 622; Johnson Bible College, Knoxville — 403; Knoxville Business College, Knoxville — 405; Knoxville College, Knoxville — 529; Maryville College, Maryville — 603; State Technical Institute at Knoxville, Knoxville — 2,410; Tennessee Institute of Electronics, Knoxville — 160; Tennessee Wesleyan College, Athens — 467; University of Tennessee at Knoxville, Knoxville — 30,282.

Newspapers, Circulation: *The Daily Times* (e), Maryville — 19,378; *The Knoxville Journal* (m), Knoxville — 56,337; *The Knoxville News-Sentinel* (eS), Knoxville — 102,047; *Post-Athenian* (e), Athens — 8,960.

Commercial Television Stations, Affiliation: WATE-TV, Knoxville (ABC); WBIR-TV, Knoxville (CBS); WTVK, Knoxville (NBC). Most of district is located in Knoxville ADI. Portion is in Chattanooga ADI.

Military Installations: Alcoa Air National Guard Station, Alcoa — 80; McGhee Tyson Airport, Alcoa — 861.

Industries:

Aluminum Co. of America Inc. (Nanthahala Power & Light Div.); Alcoa; aluminum production — 4,000. **Bowater North American Corp.** (Bowater Southern Paper Div.); Calhoun; newsprint — 1,850. **Levi Strauss & Co.**; Knoxville; jeans — 1,800. **St. Mary's Medical Center Inc.**; Knoxville; hospital — 1,750. **Standard Knitting Mills Inc.** (HQ); Knoxville; underwear — 1,721.

Fort Sanders Presbyterian Hospital Inc.; Knoxville; hospital — 1,500. **Cities Service Co.**; Copperhill; copper mining — 1,440. **East Tennessee Baptist Hospital**; Knoxville; hospital — 1,200. **Robertshaw Controls Co.** (Fulton Sylphon Div.); Knoxville; metal bellows — 1,150. **Lakeshore Mental Health Institute**; Knoxville; mental hospital — 1,140. **Maremont Corp.**; Loudon; auto mufflers — 900. **Levi Strauss & Co.**; Maryville; men's, boys' jeans — 900. **Phillips & Jordan Inc.** (HQ); Knoxville; heavy construction contractors — 875. **Rohm & Haas Tennessee Inc.**; Knoxville; plastics — 800. **Scovill Mfg. Co.** (Security Products Div.); Lenoir City; security devices — 800. **Palm Beach Co.** (Mill Outlet); Knoxville; men's suits — 760.

Millers Inc. (HQ); Knoxville; department stores — 750. **Levi Strauss & Co.**; Powell; men's, boys' clothing — 720. **N. A. P. Consumer Electronics Corp.** (HQ); Knoxville; video, audio equipment — 675. **Commercial Maintenance Inc.** (Dixie Janitorial Service - HQ); Knoxville; janitorial services — 600. **Knoxville News-Sentinal Co.**; Knoxville; newspaper publishing — 600. **N. A. P. Consumer Electronics Corp.** (HQ); Knoxville; color televisions, cabinets — 600. **Southeast Services Corp.**; Knoxville; janitorial services — 600. **Asarco Inc.** (Tennessee Mines Div.); Knoxville; zinc mining — 550. **Midland-Ross Corp.** (Electrical Products Div.); Athens; electrical apparatus — 500. **Morgan Mfg. Co. Inc.** (Red Snap Work Clothing); Etowah; men's, boys' overalls — 500. **Schlegel Tennessee Inc.**; Maryville; rubber sealing devices — 500.

3rd District

Southeast — Chattanooga, Oak Ridge

Though the 3rd usually votes Republican in state and national elections, it was expected to remain safe for the incumbent, a conservative Democrat and staunch ally of nuclear power. A pro-nuclear stance is a must in this district: many jobs are tied to the nuclear research and production facilities at Oak Ridge, to the Clinch River breeder reactor and to the Sequoyah nuclear plant in northern Hamilton County.

The population center of the 3rd is Chattanooga, a heavily industrialized city producing iron, steel and textiles. Chattanooga and surrounding Hamilton County contain 56 percent of the 3rd District's residents. There has been some racial tension between Chattanooga's working-class whites, many of whom come from rural backgrounds, and blacks, who make up about one-third of the population — a high percentage by East Tennessee standards.

The district's most loyally Democratic counties are Anderson and Roane, in the northern part of the 3rd. The major city is Oak Ridge. Nearly 18,000 people work at Union Carbide's three Oak Ridge plants, which build weapons components and enrich uranium for use in reactors.

The government workers and scientific intelligentsia at Oak Ridge have traditionally been the most consistent Democratic voting bloc in East Tennessee, but that is changing as the GOP takes the leading role in promoting nuclear energy. In 1976, Jimmy Carter won 56 percent in both Anderson and Roane counties, but in 1980 he averaged only 38 percent there. His attempt to shut down the Clinch River breeder reactor was widely unpopular.

Redistricting removed three counties along the western edge of the 3rd (Rhea, Bledsoe and Sequatchie), plus Morgan County in its northwest corner and Polk County at its eastern edge. Altogether, the counties given up cast only about 10 percent of the total vote in 1980. Grundy County, a small but strongly Democratic area, was added to the 3rd by redistricting.

Election Returns

3rd District		Democrat		Republican	
1976	President	85,514	(51.3%)	79,510	(47.7%)
	Senate	71,324	(43.5%)	92,065	(56.1%)
	House	110,986	(68.0%)	49,767	(30.5%)
1978	Governor	53,951	(43.3%)	70,250	(56.3%)
	Senate	44,649	(36.6%)	69,730	(57.2%)
	House	97,550	(88.8%)	—	
1980	President	74,677	(41.3%)	101,094	(55.9%)
	House	106,012	(61.6%)	66,120	(38.4%)
1982	Governor	48,502	(35.8%)	86,810	(64.2%)
	Senate	77,155	(57.8%)	56,239	(42.2%)
	House	84,967	(61.8%)	49,885	(36.3%)

Demographics

Population: 516,692. **Percent Change from 1970:** 17.1%.

Land Area: 2,625 square miles. **Population per Square Mile:** 196.8.

Counties, 1980 Population: Anderson — 67,346; Bradley — 67,547; Grundy — 13,787; Hamilton — 287,740; Marion — 24,416; Meigs — 7,431; Roane — 48,425.

Cities, 1980 Population: Chattanooga — 169,565; Cleveland — 26,415; East Ridge — 21,236; Oak Ridge — 27,662; Red Bank — 13,297.

Race and Ancestry: White — 87.0%; Black — 12.4%; American Indian, Eskimo and Aleut — 0.1%; Asian and Pacific Islander — 0.4%. Spanish Origin — 0.7%. Dutch — 0.5%; English — 23.4%; French — 0.7%; German — 3.9%; Irish — 5.9%; Scottish — 0.5%.

Universities, Enrollment: Chattanooga State Technical Community College, Chattanooga — 4,933; Cleveland State Community College, Cleveland — 3,595; Edmondson Junior College of Business, Chattanooga — 403; Lee College, Cleveland — 1,335; McKenzie College, Chattanooga — 487; Roane State Community College, Harriman — 3,642; Southern Missionary College, Collegedale — 2,091; University of Tennessee at Chattanooga, Chattanooga — 7,596.

Newspapers, Circulation: *Banner* (eS), Cleveland — 14,933; *The Chattanooga Times* (mS), Chattanooga — 49,031; *News-Free Press* (eS), Chattanooga — 61,735; *The Oak Ridger* (e), Oak Ridge — 11,528.

Commercial Television Stations, Affiliation: WDEF-TV, Chattanooga (CBS); WRCB-TV, Chattanooga (NBC); WRIP-TV, Chattanooga (None); WTVC, Chattanooga (ABC). Most of district is located in Chattanooga ADI. Portion is in Knoxville ADI.

Military Installations: Lovell Field (Air Force), Chattanooga — 189; Volunteer Army Ammunition Plant, Chattanooga — 153.

Nuclear Power Plants: Clinch River, Oak Ridge (Westinghouse, Stone & Webster); Sequoyah 1, Daisy (Westinghouse, Tennessee Valley Authority), July 1981; Sequoyah 2, Daisy (Westinghouse, Tennessee Valley Authority), June 1982.

Industries:

Union Carbide Corp. (Nuclear Div.); Oak Ridge; nuclear materials — 17,654. **Hospital Affiliates International Inc.;** Chattanooga; hospital — 4,000. **Chattanooga-Hamilton County Hospital;** Chattanooga; hospital — 2,700. **E. I. du Pont de Nemours & Co. Inc.;** Chattanooga; textile fibers — 2,300. **Magic Chef Inc.** (HQ); Cleveland; major household appliances — 2,000.

Provident Life & Casualty Co. (HQ); Chattanooga; life, health insurance — 1,960. **McKee Baking Co.;** Collegedale; cakes — 1,500. **Blue Cross & Blue Shield of Tennessee;** Chattanooga; health insurance — 1,440. **Burlington Industries** (Harriman Hosiery Co.); Harriman; women's hosiery — 1,250. **Dixie Yarns Inc.** (HQ); Chattanooga; yarn processing — 1,100. **Duracell International Inc.** (Battery Technology); Cleveland; batteries — 1,100. **American Uniform Co.** (Dust-Tex Co. Div. - HQ); Cleveland; men's, women's work clothing — 1,050. **Standard-Coosa-Thatcher Co.** (HQ); Chattanooga; yarn thread — 1,000. **The Rust Engineering Co.;** Oak Ridge; construction contractors — 977. **Spencer Wright Industries Inc.** (Cobble Div.); Chattanooga; textile machinery — 900. **United States Pipe & Foundry Co.** (Chattanooga Valve Fitting Div.); Chattanooga; foundry — 860. **Olin Corp.;** Charleston; chlorine — 800.

Chattanooga Glass Co. Inc. (HQ); Chattanooga; glass — 700. **AMCA International Corp.** (Lorain Div.); Chattanooga; heavy construction equipment — 686. **Mueller Co.;** Chattanooga; fire hydrants — 685. **Minnesota Mining & Mfg. Co.** (Electronic Products Div.); Chattanooga; ceramics — 680. **Hardwick Stove Co.** (Hardwick Enamel Co. - HQ); Cleveland; kitchen gas ranges —650. **Hardwick Clothes Inc.** (HQ); Cleveland; men's clothing — 556. **The Bendix Corp.** (Friction Materials Div.); Cleveland; brake linings — 500. **Burlington Industries Inc.** (Burlington Socks); Rockwood; hosiery — 500. **Central Soya Co.;** Chattanooga; poultry processors — 500. **Dixie Yarns Inc.;** Lupton City; yarn mills — 500. **Skyland International Corp.** (HQ); Chattanooga; knitwear — 500.

4th District

Northeast and South Central

The all-new 4th slants across the state for approximately 300 miles, from Hancock County in the northeast to Lawrence County on the Alabama border. It crosses one time zone and dips into four major media markets.

After Democrats tightened the boundaries of the three East Tennessee districts to meet population requirements, they were left with 11 counties that had to be attached elsewhere. They joined those 11 to 10 other counties split off from the old mid-state 4th District. Then Democrats threw in two counties from the old 6th District to bring the population of the new district to just under 511,000.

The partisan strains in the 4th District vary from staunch Appalachian Republicanism in the northern counties to plateau Democratic populism at the southern end. In 1980 the 23 counties that make up the new 4th gave Ronald Reagan 49 percent and Jimmy Carter 48 percent of the vote. In 1982 it sent a Democrat to the U.S. House, giving him two-thirds of its vote.

One unifying feature of the district is its rural nature. There is no county with a population greater than 50,000; the district's largest population center is Morristown, in Hamblen County, with 19,683 people.

Morristown is a marketing center for area farms, and a nearby American Enka plant keeps 3,200 people busy making synthetic fibers. Reagan won 61 percent in Hamblen County in 1980, a typical showing for this rugged, traditionally Republican area.

Coal has long been an economic staple here. Underground activity has mostly given way to surface mining, and in some places rapacious strip-mining techniques have defaced the landscape. In recent years exploration for oil and natural gas has helped the economy.

Agriculture focuses on tobacco, poultry and dairying. Those looking for a steady wage commute to factories in Knoxville, Morristown, and a few other towns.

Further south, the terrain levels out and voting habits shift from mountain GOP to populist Democratic. Coffee County, where sour mash whiskey is made, gave Jimmy Carter 57 percent of the vote in 1980. In Bedford County, famous for its Tennessee walking horses, Carter won 63 percent. Democratic strength is less pronounced in Lawrence County, at the extreme southwest end of the district. Reagan won 49 percent there in 1980.

Election Returns

4th District		Democrat		Republican	
1976	President	92,374	(60.3%)	59,365	(38.8%)
	Senate	85,188	(56.7%)	64,474	(42.9%)
	House	79,197	(64.0%)	41,000	(33.1%)
1978	Governor	61,461	(48.5%)	64,888	(51.2%)
	Senate	51,048	(41.9%)	65,300	(53.6%)
	House	63,828	(62.9%)	36,360	(35.8%)
1980	President	80,216	(48.3%)	81,664	(49.2%)
	House	65,463	(49.4%)	65,695	(49.5%)
1982	Governor	62,352	(45.4%)	74,956	(54.6%)
	Senate	90,018	(64.8%)	48,920	(35.2%)
	House	93,453	(66.1%)	47,865	(33.9%)

Demographics

Population: 510,732. **Percent Change from 1970:** 22.2%.

Land Area: 9,445 square miles. **Population per Square Mile:** 54.1.

Counties, 1980 Population: Bedford — 27,916; Bledsoe — 9,478; Campbell — 34,923; Claiborne — 24,595; Coffee — 38,311; Cumberland — 28,676; Fentress — 14,826; Franklin — 31,983; Giles — 24,625; Grainger — 16,751; Hamblen — 49,300; Hancock — 6,887;

Lawrence — 34,110; Lincoln — 26,483; Moore — 4,510; Morgan — 16,604; Rhea — 24,235; Scott — 19,259; Sequatchie — 8,605; Union — 11,707; Van Buren — 4,728; Warren — 32,653; White — 19,567.

Cities, 1980 Population: Lawrenceburg — 10,184; McMinnville — 10,683; Morristown — 19,683; Shelbyville — 13,530; Tullahoma — 15,800.

Race and Ancestry: White — 95.9%; Black — 3.7%; American Indian, Eskimo and Aleut — 0.1%; Asian and Pacific Islander — 0.2%. Spanish Origin — 0.7%. Dutch — 0.5%; English — 28.2%; German — 3.6%; Irish — 7.7%.

Universities, Enrollment: Bryan College, Dayton — 616; Lincoln Memorial University, Harrogate — 1,209; Martin College, Pulaski — 291; Morristown College, Morristown — 114; Motlow State Community College, Tullahoma — 2,207; University of the South, Sewanee — 1,186; Walters State Community College, Morristown — 4,009.

Newspapers, Circulation: *Citizen Tribune* (eS), Morristown — 20,094; *Shelbyville Times-Gazette* (e), Shelbyville — 8,123.

Commercial Television Stations, Affiliation: WCPT-TV, Crossville (None). District is divided between Knoxville ADI and Nashville ADI. Portions are in Chattanooga ADI and Huntsville (Ala.)-Decatur (Ala.)-Florence (Ala.) ADI.

Military Installations: Arnold Air Force Station, Manchester — 1,143.

Nuclear Power Plants: Watts Bar 1 and 2, Spring City (Westinghouse, Tennessee Valley Authority).

Industries:

Murray Ohio Mfg. Co.; Lawrenceburg; bicycles, power motors 3,500. **Akzona Inc.** (American Enka Co.); Lowland; rayon, nylon — 3,000. **Carrier Corp.** (Carrier Air Conditioning Co.); McMinnville; air conditioners — 1,750. **The Berkline Corp.;** Morristown; upholstered furniture — 1,500. **Amana Refrigeration Inc.;** Fayetteville; refrigerators — 1,400. **Maremont Corp.** (Gabriel Div.); Pulaski; motor vehicle parts — 1,400.

Emhart Industries Inc. (Mallory Timers Co.); Sparta; electronic components — 1,350. **Pan American World Service Inc.** (Arnold Air Force Station); Tullahoma; maintenance support — 1,100. **Gould Inc.** (Electric Motor Div.); McMinnville; motors — 1,000. **Magnavox Consumer Electronics Co.** (Jefferson City Cabinet Co.); Morristown; radios, televisions — 1,000. **Shelby Williams Industries Inc.;** Morristown; restaurant chairs — 1,000. **Empire Pencil Corp.;** Shelbyville; pens, pencils — 850. **Batesville Casket Co.;** Manchester; burial caskets — 800. **Serbin Fashion Inc.;** Fayetteville; women's dresses — 800. **Kayser Roth Corp.;** Dayton; women's hosiery — 796. **Ludlow Corp.** (Forest Products Div.); Morristown; bedroom furniture — 700. **Sunbeam Corp.** (Oster Div.); McMinnville; electric blenders — 700. **Eaton Corp.;** Shelbyville; truck transmissions — 670.

Fly Mfg. Co.; Shelbyville; men's work clothes — 600. **Powermatic Houdaille Inc.;** McMinnville; woodworking machinery — 600. **La-Z-Boy Chair Co.;** Dayton; furniture — 575. **Lee Marr Shirt Co. Inc.** (Croton Shirt Co.); Pulaski; men's shirts — 575. **Imperial Reading Corp.** (Britania Sportswear Div.); La Follette; sportswear — 550. **Lannom Mfg.;** Tullahoma; baseballs, bats — 550. **Textron Inc.** (Fafnir Bearing); Pulaski; ball, roller bearings — 550. **Serbin Fashions Inc.** (HQ); Fayetteville; women's dresses — 535. **C. F. W. Construction Co. Inc.** (HQ); Fayetteville; construction — 500. **Cumberland Medical Center Inc.;** Crossville; hospital — 500. **General Electric Co. Inc.** (D & D Div.); Morristown; circuit protectors — 500. **LEA Industries Inc.;** Morristown; furniture — 500. **Suburban Mfg.;** Dayton; heaters, furnaces — 500.

5th District

Nashville

More than 90 percent of the 5th District vote comes from Nashville and surrounding Davidson County, where Democrats are firmly in control. Jimmy Carter carried the

5th with 60 percent in 1980, and it rarely supports a Republican in statewide elections.

Nashville is Tennessee's capital, and state government employees are a large part of the work force. Davidson County is home to more than a dozen colleges and universities, and factories in the area manufacture aircraft parts, glass, clothing, and tires. Nashville is also a banking and insurance center and headquarters for the country music industry and several publishers of religious materials.

The Democratic inclinations of government workers, academic communities and labor unions uphold Nashville's traditional position as the focal point of Middle Tennessee Democratic populism. Populist politics took hold in Nashville early in this century as a reaction to the conservative Democratic machine in Memphis that controlled Tennessee politics until after World War II.

Nashville's population is 23 percent black, a relatively low figure for a large Southern city. Nashville politics has not polarized along racial lines to the degree seen in Memphis and Chattanooga, where blacks make up a higher percentage of the population and whites have drifted away from Democratic loyalties. Most white voters in Nashville are still consistent Democrats.

Robertson County, a rural area north of Nashville, is even more Democratic. Carter won 59 percent in Davidson County in 1980, but took two-thirds of the Robertson vote.

The only change in the 5th District brought about by redistricting was a transfer of 21,616 residents of Cheatham County to the neighboring 7th District. Cheatham, strongly Democratic, cast just 4 percent of the 5th District's total 1980 vote.

Election Returns

5th District		Democrat		Republican	
1976	President	106,554	(62.1%)	63,167	(36.8%)
	Senate	98,913	(58.5%)	68,859	(40.7%)
	House	121,600	(92.3%)	—	
1978	Governor	62,059	(44.0%)	78,521	(55.7%)
	Senate	62,015	(44.6%)	73,033	(52.5%)
	House	65,964	(51.1%)	46,016	(35.7%)
1980	President	111,122	(59.5%)	69,332	(37.1%)
	House	114,100	(65.1%)	61,269	(34.9%)
1982	Governor	59,963	(43.0%)	79,361	(57.0%)
	Senate	95,960	(66.7%)	47,805	(33.3%)
	House	109,282	(80.2%)	27,061	(19.8%)

Demographics

Population: 514,832. **Percent Change from 1970:** 7.9%.

Land Area: 977 square miles. **Population per Square Mile:** 527.0.

Counties, 1980 Population: Davidson — 477,811; Robertson — 37,021.

Cities, 1980 Population: Nashville — 455,651; Springfield — 10,814.

Race and Ancestry: White — 77.4%; Black — 21.6%; American Indian, Eskimo and Aleut — 0.1%; Asian and Pacific Islander — 0.5%. Spanish Origin — 0.8%. English — 17.6%; French — 0.6%; German — 3.5%; Irish — 5.4%; Italian — 0.5%; Scottish — 0.6%.

Universities, Enrollment: American Baptist College, Nashville — 134; Aquinas Junior College, Nashville — 288; Belmont College, Nashville — 1,706; David Lipscomb College, Nashville — 2,316; Draughons Junior College of Business, Nashville — 421; Fisk University, Nashville — 1,009; Free Will Baptist Bible College, Nashville — 513; John A. Gupton College, Nashville — 60; Meharry Medical College, Nashville — 1,066; Nashville State Technical Institute, Nashville — 5,283; Scarritt College for Christian Workers, Nashville — 90; Tennessee State University, Nashville — 8,438; Trevecca Nazarene College, Nashville — 920; Vanderbilt University, Nashville — 8,874.

Newspapers, Circulation: *Nashville Banner* (e), Nashville — 82,743; *The Tennessean* (mS), Nashville — 133,789.

Commercial Television Stations, Affiliation: WSMV-TV, Nashville (NBC); WNGE, Nashville (ABC); WTVF, Nashville (CBS); WZTV, Nashville (None). Entire district is located in Nashville ADI.

Military Installations: Nashville Metropolitan Airport (Air National Guard), Nashville — 1,422.

Industries:

Avco Corp. (Avco Aerostructures Div.); Nashville; aircraft parts — 4,107. **Newspaper Printing Corp.;** Nashville; commercial printing — 2,100. **N. L. T. Corp.** (HQ); Nashville; life, health insurance — 2,000. **St. Thomas Hospital;** Nashville; hospital — 1,930. **Baptist Hospital Inc.;** Nashville; hospital — 1,900.

Louisville & Nashville Railroad Co.; Nashville; railroad — 1,800. **Ford Motor Co. Inc.** (Nashville Glass Plant); Nashville; glass — 1,750. **Aladdin Industries Inc.** (HQ); Nashville; lamps, vacuum bottles, jugs — 1,600. **Genesco Inc.** (HQ); Nashville; footwear — 1,600. **Paccar Inc.** (Peterbilt Motor Co.); Madison; motor vehicle bodies — 1,000. **The Rodgers Companies Inc.;** Nashville; general contracting — 1,000. **Rogers Formfit Inc.;** Nashville; women's underwear — 1,000. **Third National Bank** (HQ); Nashville; banking — 1,000. **United Methodist Publishing House** (HQ); Nashville; book publishing — 1,000. **Aratex Services Inc.** (Cavalier Industries Div.); Nashville; industrial launderers — 925.

Ward Baird Printing Co. Inc.; Nashville; lithography — 900. **Nashville Bridge Co.** (HQ); Nashville; barges, towboats — 830. **Life & Casualty Insurance Co. of Tennessee** (HQ); Nashville; insurance — 825. **American General Life Insurance Co.;** Nashville; life insurance — 800. **Oscar Mayer & Co. Inc.;** Goodlettsville; meatpacking — 800. **Cain-Sloan Co. Inc.** (HQ); Nashville; department stores — 750. **Armstrong Rubber Co.;** Madison; tires — 700. **Clayton Mobile Homes;** Nashville; mobile home dealers — 700. **E. I. du Pont de Nemours & Co. Inc.;** Old Hickory; plastics, explosives — 700.

Northern Telecom Inc.; Nashville; telephone apparatus — 700. **Rent-A-Driver Inc.;** Nashville; freight forwarding — 600. **Tennessee Tufting Corp.** (HQ); Nashville; bath mats, rugs — 600. **Boston Industrial Products Inc.;** Nashville; rubber hoses — 580. **Horace Small Mfg. Co.** (HQ); Nashville; men's uniforms — 550. **Yellow Freight System Inc.;** Nashville; trucking — 534. **John E. Bouchard & Sons Co.;** Nashville; gray iron, brass, aluminum — 500. **Kusan Inc.** (Kusan Mfg. Div.); Nashville; custom plastic products — 500. **McDowell Enterprises Inc.;** Nashville; highway construction — 500. **Nasco Inc.** (Voltex Div. - HQ); Springfield; men's, women's clothing — 500. **Oman Construction Co. Inc.;** Nashville; general construction — 500. **Triangle Pacific Corp.** (E. L. Bruce Hardwood Floors Div.); Nashville; hardwood flooring — 500.

6th District

North Central — Murfreesboro

The Democratic incumbent in the 6th District is so well ensconced that Democrats threw Republican territory into his district in an effort to help Democratic candidates elsewhere in the state.

On its eastern and southern ends, the district gave up 11 counties — nearly all of them strongly Democratic — to the 3rd District and the new 4th. The 6th gained increasingly Republican Williamson County.

Williamson, which contains Nashville's southern suburbs, is the fastest-growing county in the state; it saw a 68.8

percent population increase in the 1970s. Although Jimmy Carter won Williamson narrowly in 1976, GOP gubernatorial candidate Lamar Alexander carried it with 68 percent in 1978, and Ronald Reagan won 55 percent there in 1980.

Though the 6th is mostly rural — Murfreesboro, the largest city, has 32,845 people — there are several other small cities where factories produce furniture, pencils, and textiles.

In Smyrna, a Rutherford County town with 8,839 people, Japan's Nissan Motor Company is building a $300 million truck assembly plant. The factory was the largest single industrial-capital investment in Tennessee history and was expected to employ more than 2,000 people. Industrial expansion is increasing the district's blue-collar work force, and the labor vote seems inclined to hold to the Democratic loyalties that are traditional in middle Tennessee.

In addition to Williamson County, the 6th picked up Maury and Lewis counties. Lewis is small, rural and strongly Democratic. The Democratic grip is not quite as tight in Maury County, but Carter was able to win 53 percent there in 1980. Phosphates are mined in Maury, and the city of Columbia there is a marketing center for surrounding livestock and dairy farms.

Election Returns

6th District		Democrat		Republican	
1976	President	93,751	(64.4%)	49,892	(34.3%)
	Senate	85,561	(60.4%)	55,500	(39.2%)
	House	76,044	(76.4%)	19,416	(19.5%)
1978	Governor	56,597	(44.3%)	70,916	(55.5%)
	Senate	50,721	(40.8%)	69,451	(55.9%)
	House	73,146	(77.3%)	21,456	(22.7%)
1980	President	92,485	(54.6%)	72,526	(42.8%)
	House	86,731	(66.7%)	43,297	(33.3%)
1982	Governor	66,943	(47.3%)	74,642	(52.7%)
	Senate	92,544	(64.9%)	50,158	(35.0%)
	House	x[1]		—[1]	

[1] *No votes tabulated where candidate was unopposed; x indicates winner.*

Demographics

Population: 511,805. **Percent Change from 1970:** 37.0%.

Land Area: 6,381 square miles. **Population per Square Mile:** 80.2.

Counties, 1980 Population: Cannon — 10,234; Clay — 7,676; De Kalb — 13,589; Jackson — 9,398; Lewis — 9,700; Macon — 15,700; Marshall — 19,698; Maury — 51,095; Overton — 17,575; Pickett — 4,358; Putnam — 47,690; Rutherford — 84,058; Smith — 14,935; Sumner — 85,790; Trousdale — 6,137; Williamson — 58,108; Wilson — 56,064.

Cities, 1980 Population: Columbia — 26,372; Cookeville — 20,535; Franklin — 12,407; Gallatin — 17,191; Hendersonville — 26,561; Lebanon — 11,872; Murfreesboro — 32,845.

Race and Ancestry: White — 92.2%; Black — 7.3%; American Indian, Eskimo and Aleut — 0.1%; Asian and Pacific Islander — 0.3%. Spanish Origin — 0.7%. English — 25.3%; French — 0.6%; German — 3.2%; Irish — 6.8%; Scottish — 0.6%.

Universities, Enrollment: Columbia State Community College, Columbia — 2,529; Cumberland College of Tennessee, Lebanon — 501; Cumberland School of Medical Technology, Cookeville — 45; Middle

Tennessee State University, Murfreesboro — 11,275; O'More School of Interior Design, Franklin — 96; Tennessee Technological University, Cookeville — 8,259; Volunteer State Community College, Gallatin — 4,195.

Newspapers, Circulation: *The Daily Herald* (e), Columbia — 12,488; *Daily News Journal* (eS), Murfreesboro — 11,614; *The Dispatch* (mS), Cookeville — 12,039; *Herald-Citizen* (eS), Cookeville — 9,014; *The Lebanon Democrat* (e), Lebanon — 7,477. Nashville *Tennessean* and *Nashville Banner* also circulate in the district.

Commercial Television Stations, Affiliation: Entire district is located in Nashville ADI.

Nuclear Power Plants: Hartsville A-1 and A-2, Hartsville (General Electric, Tennessee Valley Authority).

Industries:

TRW Inc. (Ross Gear Div.); Lebanon; motor vehicle parts — 1,200. **Heil-Quaker Corp.**; Lewisburg; gas heaters — 1,150. **National Savings Life Insurance Co.**; Murfreesboro; insurance — 1,100. **Union Carbide Corp.** (Carbon Products Div.); Columbia; carbon, graphite products — 1,000. **General Electric Co.**; Murfreesboro; motors, generators — 950.

Firestone Tire & Rubber Co.; La Vergne; tires, inner tubes — 890. **Better-Bilt Aluminum Products Co. Inc.**; Smyrna; aluminum doors, windows — 860. **Kayser-Roth Corp.** (Colonial Corp. Div.); Woodbury; shirts, outerwear — 800. **Precision Rubber Products Corp.** (HQ); Lebanon; gaskets, seals — 800. **Samsonite Corp.** (Furniture Div.); Murfreesboro; metal household furniture — 800. **Fleetguard Inc.** (HQ); Cookeville; filters — 750. **Arcata National Corp.** (C. P. S. Industries Div.); Franklin; fabric mills — 700. **United States Shoe Corp.** (Texas Boot Co. Div.); Lebanon; footwear — 700. **Monsanto Co.**; Columbia; industrial inorganic chemicals — 699. **Robertshaw Controls Co.** (Lux Time Div.); Lebanon; industrial controls — 640. **General Electric Co. Inc.**; Hendersonville; electric motors — 630.

Almet-Lawnlite Co.; Portland; aluminum furniture — 600. **Marlene Industries Corp.** (Trousdale Mfg. Co. Inc.); Hartsville; women's outerwear — 600. **R. R. Donnelly & Sons. Co.** (Donnelly Printing Co.); Gallatin; printing — 550. **Faber-Castell Corp.**; Lewisburg; pens, pencils — 550. **Val D'Or Inc.**; Smithville; men's, women's knitwear — 520. **Gary Co. Inc.**; Gallatin; men's shirts — 500. **GF Business Equipment Inc.**; Gallatin; metal office furniture — 500. **Heil-Quaker Corp.**; La Vergne; heating equipment — 500. **Koh-I-Noor Rapidograph Inc.** (Cosmolab); Lewisburg; pencils, crayons, artists' materials — 500. **Lasko Metal Products Inc.**; Franklin; fans, heaters — 500.

7th District

West Central — Clarksville, Part of Shelby County

The 7th was one of the two districts that Democratic legislators wanted to turn into Democratic seats. To that end, they severed Republican Williamson County and placed it in the strongly Democratic 6th where its influence would be diminished.

However, that move did not assure an end to Republican control of this west-central district. The loss of Williamson on the district's eastern end was offset by the loss of four other eastern counties where Democrats have an edge.

And further west, the new 7th gained thousands of staunch Republicans in bedroom communities northeast of Memphis. If these voters had not been added, Democrats would win the district routinely. However, voter turnout in the Shelby County portion of the 7th is high, and Republican margins are phenomenal. The 1982 GOP Senate nominee, who received only 38 percent statewide, took nearly 60 percent in the Shelby portion of the 7th. The Shelby County vote helped put a Republican into the 7th District

House seat in 1982; he won just 50 percent of the vote.

Outside of Shelby County, a couple of counties have sizable black populations, but most of the voters are white, conservative-populist and traditionally Democratic. Six of the 15 counties in this area have not voted for a Republican in a major statewide contest since 1974, and two of these six — Houston and Perry — even went for George McGovern in the 1972 Nixon sweep.

Aside from Shelby, the rural quality of the 7th is broken by only one city, Clarksville (Montgomery County), near the Kentucky border. Once a marketing center for fire-cured tobacco, Clarksville today depends to a greater extent on its factory payroll and the military population at Fort Campbell, west of the city. Republican Gov. Lamar Alexander and Sen. Howard H. Baker Jr. have done well in Montgomery County, but it usually goes Democratic.

There is one pocket of Republican strength outside the Memphis area — a handful of counties along the Highland Rim, in the hilly south-central part of the district. The terrain and voting behavior of this area resemble Republican East Tennessee.

Election Returns

7th District		Democrat		Republican	
1976	President	74,622	(51.3%)	69,443	(47.7%)
	Senate	69,150	(49.4%)	70,410	(50.3%)
	House	45,924	(40.9%)	66,226	(59.0%)
1978	Governor	48,838	(38.8%)	76,506	(60.8%)
	Senate	45,837	(37.3%)	73,496	(59.8%)
	House	43,979	(36.5%)	75,917	(63.0%)
1980	President	73,984	(41.2%)	100,694	(56.0%)
	House	19,739	(17.8%)	90,891	(82.2%)
1982	Governor	55,873	(39.0%)	87,460	(61.0%)
	Senate	78,734	(53.3%)	68,989	(46.7%)
	House	72,359	(49.5%)	73,835	(50.5%)

Demographics

Population: 503,611. **Percent Change from 1970:** 47.4%.

Land Area: 7,723 square miles. **Population per Square Mile:** 65.2.

Counties, 1980 Population: Cheatham — 21,616; Chester — 12,727; Decatur — 10,857; Dickson — 30,037; Fayette — 25,305; Hardeman — 23,873; Hardin — 22,280; Henderson — 21,390; Hickman — 15,151; Houston — 6,871; Humphreys — 15,957; McNairy — 22,525; Montgomery — 83,342; Perry — 6,111; Shelby (Pt.) — 171,623; Wayne — 13,946.

Cities, 1980 Population: Bartlett — 17,170; Clarksville — 54,777; Germantown — 20,459; Memphis (Pt.) — 79,715.

Race and Ancestry: White — 87.1%; Black — 12.0%; American Indian, Eskimo and Aleut — 0.1%; Asian and Pacific Islander — 0.5%. Spanish Origin — 1.0%. English — 21.7%; French — 0.7%; German — 3.7%; Irish — 7.4%; Italian — 0.7%; Scottish — 0.5%.

Universities, Enrollment: Austin Peay State University, Clarksville — 4,968; Freed-Hardeman College, Henderson — 1,544.

Newspapers, Circulation: *The Leaf-Chronicle* (eS), Clarksville — 16,821. Memphis *Commercial Appeal* also circulates in the district.

Commercial Television Stations, Affiliation: District is divided between Memphis ADI and Nashville ADI. Portion is in Jackson ADI.

Military Installations: Fort Campbell, Clarksville — 25,342.

Industries:

St. Francis Hospital Inc.; Memphis; hospital — 1,390. **The Trane Co.;** Clarksville; heating, air conditioning equipment — 1,300. **State Industries Inc.** (HQ); Ashland City; water heaters — 1,200. **Acme Boot Co. Inc.;** Clarksville; men's, children's boots — 1,050. **Carrier Corp;** Collierville; air conditioners — 1,000. **E. I. du Pont de Nemours & Co.;** New Johnsonville; inorganic pigments — 1,000. **Scoville Inc.** (Shrader Automotive Products Div.); Dickson; motor vehicle parts — 1,000.

Decaturville Sportswear Inc.; Decaturville; women's outerwear — 950. **Gould Inc.** (Electric Motor Div.); Lexington; motors — 800. **Harman International Industries** (Harman Automotive Div.); Bolivar; zinc die casting — 800. **Sharp Electronics Corp.** (Sharp Mfg. Co.); Memphis; radios — 800. **Thomson Co.;** Parsons; men's, boys' pants — 600. **Tennessee River Pulp & Paper** (TMA Forest Products Div. - HQ); Counce; container board — 550. **Joseph Schlitz Brewing Co.;** Memphis; brewery — 545. **Burlington Northern Inc.;** Memphis; railroad switching — 500. **Malone & Hyde Inc.** (Super D Drugs); Memphis; warehousing — 500. **Troxel Mfg. Co.** (HQ); Moscow; bicycle seats — 500.

8th District

West — Jackson, Part of Shelby County

Ronald Reagan carried the old mostly rural and suburban 7th District in 1980, but the new district, redrawn and renumbered the 8th, gave Jimmy Carter a majority. The difference is the removal of 75,000 mostly Republican voters in suburban Memphis.

The Legislature kept the Frayser area of Memphis in the new 8th District as well as a significant part of northern Shelby County, where suburbia and GOP dominance give way to farms and Democratic leanings. The Memphis Naval Air Station is in north Shelby, near Millington. Twenty percent of the people in the 8th live in Shelby County.

Madison County (Jackson) is home to another 15 percent of the 8th's residents. Republicans are gaining ground there, thanks in part to an influx of managerial people to Jackson's increasingly diversified industries, among them a Bendix auto parts plant and a Procter & Gamble Co. facility that makes Pringles potato chips. The surrounding farm counties look to Jackson, the district's largest city outside of Memphis, as a source of retail goods and services. Reagan won 50 percent of the Madison County vote in 1980.

Thirteen mostly rural counties account for two-thirds of the 8th District population. This is a region of soybeans, corn, wheat, and cotton. Population grew little during the 1980s. Lake County, the only Tennessee County to lose population during the 1970s, is located at the northwest corner of the 8th. The 13 agricultural counties are nearly always Democratic. Carter took all but one of them in 1980, although Reagan's strong appeal among conservative voters brought him close in a few counties.

Election Returns

8th District		Democrat		Republican	
1976	President	92,833	(60.2%)	59,608	(38.7%)
	Senate	87,221	(57.9%)	62,681	(41.6%)
	House	94,272	(100.0%)	—	
1978	Governor	58,258	(47.2%)	64,822	(52.3%)
	Senate	51,484	(43.6%)	60,857	(51.5%)
	House	86,331	(74.5%)	29,491	(25.5%)

Memphis

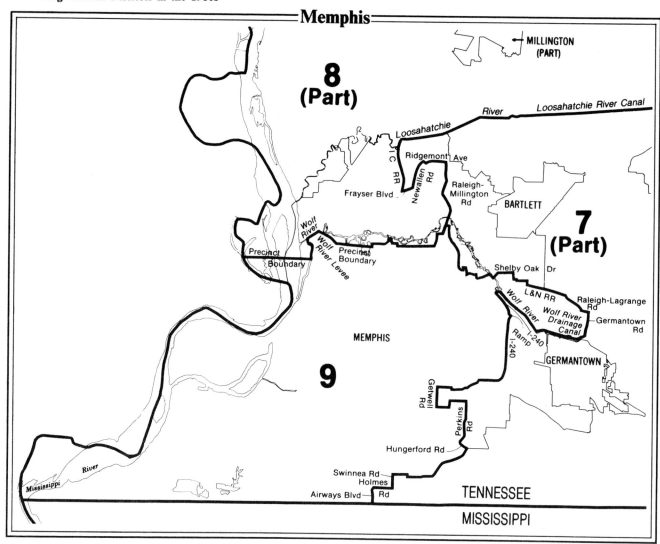

8 (Part)

MILLINGTON (PART)

River   Loosahatchie River Canal

Loosahatchie

Ridgemont Ave

Frayser Blvd

Newallen Rd

Raleigh-Millington Rd

BARTLETT

7 (Part)

Wolf River

Precinct Boundary

Wolf River Levee

Precinct Boundary

Shelby Oak   Dr

L&N RR

Raleigh-Lagrange Rd

Wolf River Drainage Canal

Germantown Rd

I-240 Ramp   I-240

GERMANTOWN

MEMPHIS

9

Getwell Rd

Perkins Rd

Hungerford Rd

Swinnea Rd

Holmes

Airways Blvd   Rd

TENNESSEE

MISSISSIPPI

Mississippi   River

8th District		Democrat		Republican	
1980	President	87,477	(51.2%)	80,238	(46.9%)
	House	117,347	(80.1%)	29,144	(19.9%)
1982	Governor	61,218	(48.9%)	63,891	(51.1%)
	Senate	84,815	(65.9%)	43,954	(34.1%)
	House	93,945	(74.9%)	31,527	(25.1%)

Demographics

Population: 504,957. **Percent Change from 1970:** 12.2%.

Land Area: 7,029 square miles. **Population per Square Mile:** 71.8.

Counties, 1980 Population: Benton — 14,901; Carroll — 28,285; Crockett — 14,941; Dyer — 34,663; Gibson — 49,467; Haywood — 20,318; Henry — 28,656; Lake — 7,455; Lauderdale — 24,555; Madison — 74,546; Obion — 32,781; Shelby (Pt.) — 99,898; Stewart — 8,665; Tipton — 32,930; Weakley — 32,896.

Cities, 1980 Population: Dyersburg — 15,856; Humboldt — 10,209; Jackson — 49,131; Memphis (Pt.) — 61,049; Millington — 20,236; Paris — 10,728; Union City — 10,436.

Race and Ancestry: White — 79.3%; Black — 20.0%; American Indian, Eskimo and Aleut — 0.1%; Asian and Pacific Islander — 0.3%.

Spanish Origin — 0.9%. English — 22.8%; French — 0.6%; German — 2.7%; Irish — 7.2%.

Universities, Enrollment: Bethel College, McKenzie — 446; Dyersburg State Community College, Dyersburg — 1,086; Jackson State Community College, Jackson — 2,651; Lambuth College, Jackson — 754; Lane College, Jackson — 757; Union University, Jackson — 1,345; University of Tennessee at Martin, Martin — 5,375.

Newspapers, Circulation: *The Jackson Sun* (eS), Jackson — 31,821; *The Paris Post Intelligencer* (e), Paris — 8,190; *State Gazette* (e), Dyersburg — 6,178; *Union City Daily Messenger* (e), Union City — 9,346. Memphis *Commercial Appeal* also circulates in the district.

Commercial Television Stations, Affiliation: WBBJ-TV, Jackson (ABC). Most of district is located in Memphis ADI. Portions are in Jackson ADI, Nashville ADI, and Paducah (Ky.)-Cape Girardeau (Mo.)-Harrisburg (Ill.) ADI.

Military Installations: Memphis Naval Air Station, Millington — 14,874; Memphis Naval Regional Medical Center, Millington — 652; Milan Army Ammunition Plant, Milan — 1,346.

Industries:

Goodyear Tire & Rubber Co.; Union City; auto tires — 2,600. **Jackson-Madison County General Hospital;** Jackson; hospital — 1,500. **Martin Marietta Aluminum Inc.** (Army Ammunition Plant); Milan; ammunition — 1,495. **Colt Industries Operating Corp.** (Holley Carburetor Div.); Paris; carburetors — 1,150. **Tennessee Textiles Inc.** (HQ); Bemis; textile, thread mill — 1,150.

Dyersburg Fabrics Inc. (HQ); Dyersburg; knitting mill — 1,000. **E. I. du Pont de Nemours Co.**; Memphis; inorganic chemicals — 900. **Owens-Corning Fiberglas Corp.**; Jackson; fiberglass — 900. **Henry I. Siegel Co. Inc.** (H.I.S. Sportswear); Bruceton; men's sports coats — 900. **Dart Industries Inc.** (Tupperware Co.); Halls; plastic household products — 750. **Colonial Rubber Works Inc.** (HQ); Dyersburg; fabricated rubber products — 700. **Emerson Electric Co.** (Special Products Div.); Paris; power tools — 700. **The Procter & Gamble Co.** (Food Products Div.); Jackson; food products — 700.

W. F. Hall Printing Co.; Dresden; book printing — 600. **International Telephone & Telegraph Corp.** (ITT Telecommunications Apparatus Div.); Milan; communications equipment — 600. **Porter-Cable Corp.**; Jackson; portable power tools — 600. **Consolidated Aluminum Corp.**; Jackson; aluminum sheet, foil — 560. **Bendix Corp.**; Jackson; automobile parts — 550. **Copeland Electric Corp.**; Humboldt; electric motors — 500. **Gaines Mfg. Co. Inc.**; McKenzie; upholstered furniture — 500. **Kellwood Co.**; Rutherford; men's, boys' coats — 500. **Publix Shirt Corp.**; Huntingdon; men's, boys' dress shirts — 500.

9th District

Memphis

While Tennessee's population grew by 16.9 percent during the 1970s, an exodus from center-city Memphis cut population in the old district by a like percentage. As a result, redistricting added about 80,000 people and changed its number from 8 to 9. Nearly all of the district's new residents are suburban Republicans.

Like most heavily-black districts throughout the country, the old 8th District was reliably Democratic in good years and bad. Jimmy Carter won 63 percent of the vote there in 1980, considerably more than in any other Tennessee district and an improvement on his 1976 performance.

Blacks are still a majority in the new 9th, but with the new white communities brought in by redistricting, blacks and whites will be about even among registered voters. Before the remap, blacks enjoyed a 60-40 advantage among registered voters.

In partisan terms the 9th District is still strongly Democratic. But because the black population is lower, the black incumbent must rely on white working-class Democrats more than he has in the past. That was expected to be a challenge in Memphis, where politics often polarizes along racial lines.

The Memphis economy is a mixture of old and new. Cotton marketing, warehousing and processing of cottonseed into oil have been important for more than a century and a half, and still are. But now the emphasis has shifted to manufactured goods such as auto parts, tires and pharmaceuticals. Memphis is also headquarters for the Holiday Inn empire and for the air fleet of Federal Express, the air freight carrier.

Election Returns

9th District		Democrat		Republican	
1976	President	121,879	(59.9%)	79,724	(39.2%)
	Senate	110,697	(57.8%)	79,854	(41.7%)
	House	109,030	(56.0%)	85,727	(44.0%)

9th District		Democrat		Republican	
1978	Governor	79,620	(55.2%)	64,156	(44.5%)
	Senate	74,815	(53.2%)	63,132	(44.9%)
	House	78,156	(60.6%)	49,290	(38.2%)
1980	President	128,962	(63.2%)	69,760	(34.2%)
	House	111,065	(86.7%)	16,977	(13.3%)
1982	Governor	78,327	(54.1%)	66,492	(45.9%)
	Senate	110,180	(71.9%)	42,990	(28.1%)
	House	112,143	(72.4%)	40,812	(26.4%)

Demographics

Population: 505,592. **Percent Change from 1970:** -9.4%.

Land Area: 205 square miles. **Population per Square Mile:** 2,466.3.

Counties, 1980 Population: Shelby (Pt.) — 505,592.

Cities, 1980 Population: Memphis (Pt.) — 505,592.

Race and Ancestry: White — 42.2%; Black — 57.2%; American Indian, Eskimo and Aleut — 0.1%; Asian and Pacific Islander — 0.4%. Spanish Origin — 0.8%. English — 10.7%; German — 2.0%; Irish — 3.5%; Italian — 0.7%.

Universities, Enrollment: Christian Brothers College, Memphis — 1,342; Draughons Junior College, Memphis — 886; Harding Graduate School of Religion, Memphis — 279; LeMoyne-Owen College, Memphis — 1,049; Memphis Academy of Arts, Memphis — 206; Memphis State University, Memphis — 20,784; Memphis Theological Seminary, Memphis — 147.

Mid-South Bible College, Memphis — 147; Shelby State Community College, Memphis — 5,585; Southern College of Optometry, Memphis — 586; Southwestern at Memphis, Memphis — 1,059; State Technical Institute at Memphis, Memphis — 6,277; University of Tennessee Center for the Health Sciences, Memphis — 2,124.

Newspapers, Circulation: *The Commercial Appeal* (mS), Memphis — 203,764.

Commercial Television Stations, Affiliation: WHBQ-TV, Memphis (ABC); WMC-TV, Memphis (NBC); WPTY-TV, Memphis (None); WREG-TV, Memphis (CBS). Entire district is located in Memphis ADI.

Military Installations: Memphis Defense Depot, Memphis — 3,598; Memphis International Airport (Air Force), Oakville — 852.

Industries:

Federal Express Corp. (HQ); Memphis; certified air cargo services — 6,000. **Baptist Memorial Hospital**; Memphis; hospital — 4,500. **Allen & O'Hara Inc.**; Memphis; industrial construction — 3,250. **Methodist Hospital Inc.**; Memphis; hospital — 3,130. **First Tennessee National Corp.** (HQ); Memphis; banking — 2,000. **Veterans Administration**; Memphis; veterans' hospital — 2,000.

Illinois Central Gulf Railroad; Memphis; railroad operations — 1,500. **Plough Inc.** (HQ); Memphis; pharmaceuticals, cosmetics — 1,500. **Hunter Fan & Ventilating Co.** (Pioneer Div.); Memphis; heaters — 1,400. **Kimberly-Clark Corp.** (Consumer Products Div.); Memphis; paper products — 1,400. **Gibson Greeting Cards Inc.** (Cleo Wrap Div.); Memphis; paper conversion — 1,200. **Hunter Fan & Ventilating Co.** (Comfort Conditioning Div. - HQ); Memphis; electric fans — 1,200. **Aeolian Corp.** (HQ); Memphis; pianos, piano parts — 1,000. **Gordon's Transports Inc.** (HQ); Memphis; trucking — 1,000. **Memphis Publishing Co.**; Memphis; newspaper publishing — 1,000.

True Temper Sports Inc.; Memphis; sporting goods — 900. **Holiday Inns Inc.** (HQ); Memphis; hotel operations — 800. **Kellogg Co.**; Memphis; cereals — 750. **Richards Mfg. Co. Inc.** (HQ); Memphis; surgical supplies — 750. **Buckeye Cellulose Corp.** (Cellulose & Specialties Div.); Memphis; pulp mill — 700. **Consolidated Foods Corp.** (Oxford Security Systems Div.); Memphis; security services — 700. **Memphis Furniture Mfg. Co.** (HQ); Memphis; furniture — 660. **ITT Continental Baking Co. Inc.** (Hostess Cake); Memphis; bread, cakes — 650. **Sears, Roebuck & Co.**; Memphis; warehousing — 650. **Republic**

Airlines Inc. (Republic Air Freight); Memphis; commercial airline — 625. **Coca-Cola Bottling Co.;** Memphis; soft drink bottling — 620. **Burlington Northern Inc.;** Memphis; railroad operations — 600. **Fruehauf Corp.** (Fruehauf Trailers); Memphis; trucks, truck trailers — 600.

Holiday Inns Inc. (Product Services Div.); Memphis; motel equipment wholesaling — 590. **McLean Trucking Co. Inc.;** Memphis; trucking — 590. **General Mills Inc.** (Donruss Div.); Memphis; chewing gum — 550. **Kraft Inc.** (Humko Products Div.); Memphis; vegetable oil — 550. **Kimco Auto Products Inc.** (HQ); Memphis; auto parts — 515. **First Tennessee Bank** (HQ); Memphis; banking — 500. **General Electric Co.;** Memphis; miniature lights — 500. **Guardsmark Inc.** (HQ); Memphis; security service — 500. **Louisville & Nashville Railroad;** Memphis; railroad operations — 500. **S. & W. Construction Co. of Tennessee Inc.** (HQ); Memphis; industrial construction — 500. **Union Planters National Bank of Memphis** (HQ); Memphis; banking — 500. **Kroger Co.;** Memphis; bakery, warehousing — more than 500.

Texas

The congressional redistricting process in Texas encountered controversy, Justice Department scrutiny and court review during the first three years of the 1980s. Concern over Hispanic representation caused the Justice Department to overturn Texas' first congressional redistricting map. The second map, drawn by a U.S. federal court, was overturned by the Supreme Court, although House candidates ran under it in the 1982 elections. The third map, drawn by the Legislature in May 1983, was approved by the Justice Department Sept. 27 and was the map expected to remain in place for the rest of the 1980s.

Texas' first congressional redistricting plan was highly touted as a Republican windfall when it passed in August 1981. An alliance between Republican Gov. William Clements and state House Speaker Billy Clayton, a conservative Democrat, produced the plan and a coalition of GOP and conservative Democratic state legislators pushed the map through the solidly Democratic Texas Legislature Aug. 10, 1981.

But soon after Clements signed the bill on Aug. 14, 1981, a group of blacks and Hispanics filed suit in federal court, claiming that voting rights had been curtailed by the Legislature's reshaping of districts in South Texas, the Dallas-Fort Worth area and metropolitan Houston.

Because election law changes in Texas must comply with the provisions of the 1965 Voting Rights Act, the federal judges deferred action on the minorities' suit pending Justice Department review.

The department ruled Jan. 29, 1982, that the map improperly distributed the Hispanic population in two South Texas districts, the 15th and the 27th. The Legislature had made the 15th 80 percent Hispanic and the 27th 52 percent Hispanic; the department said that plan packed the 15th with Hispanics while diluting their strength in the 27th.

The department's rejection of two districts rendered the redistricting bill legally unenforceable because Texas is wholly covered by the Voting Rights Act. Gov. Clements declined to call the Legislature into special session to redraw boundaries, thus setting the stage for court action.

The ruling of the three-judge federal panel, handed down Feb. 27, 1982, rearranged the two South Texas districts to give Hispanics a good chance to win both. In addition, it reshaped four districts in the Dallas-Fort Worth area in a way that dashed GOP hopes of creating a new district for itself in Dallas County.

The Legislature had fashioned a strongly Republican 5th District in Dallas County by transferring most of the minority voters in that district to the Democratic 24th, which would have become 64 percent black and Hispanic. The court felt it was fairer to redistribute minority voters more evenly between the 5th and 24th, giving blacks and Hispanics substantial influence in each district but majority control in neither.

Texas Republicans appealed that decision to the Supreme Court, which ruled April 1, 1982, that the panel had acted improperly in redrawing the four Dallas-Ft. Worth area districts. The justices agreed with GOP arguments that the panel had ignored legislative intent.

But in remanding the case to the federal panel, the Supreme Court left the judges with the option of keeping their plan in place for 1982 because candidates had already filed for the court-drawn districts. The panel chose that option April 5, 1982.

During the 1970s population grew by 27.1 percent in Texas. In the 1980 reapportionment, the state qualified for three additional House seats. Democrats narrowly won in the new 26th, which lies between Dallas and Fort Worth, and won handily in the new South Texas 27th and in Houston's 25th District. The only gain Republicans made occurred in early 1983 when the Democrat in the 6th District resigned his seat, switched parties and regained his seat as a Republican in a special election.

He was one of three incumbents the state Legislature helped when it drew new congressional district lines in May 1983. The 6th District was given some Republican territory from the Tarrant County portion of the 26th. In turn, the 6th relinquished some territory likely to support Democrats to the 24th.

To bolster the freshman Democrat in the 26th, which lies between Dallas and Ft. Worth, the Legislature added Democratic voters by reuniting Arlington in the district. And in the 23rd, the Legislature aided a veteran Democratic incumbent by shifting about 35,000 conservative Republican voters in the San Antonio suburbs to the Republican 21st District. In exchange the 23rd took Val Verde County, a 63 percent Hispanic county on the Mexican border that generally votes Democratic.

The profiles below describe those districts that were in place for the 1982 elections.

TEXAS

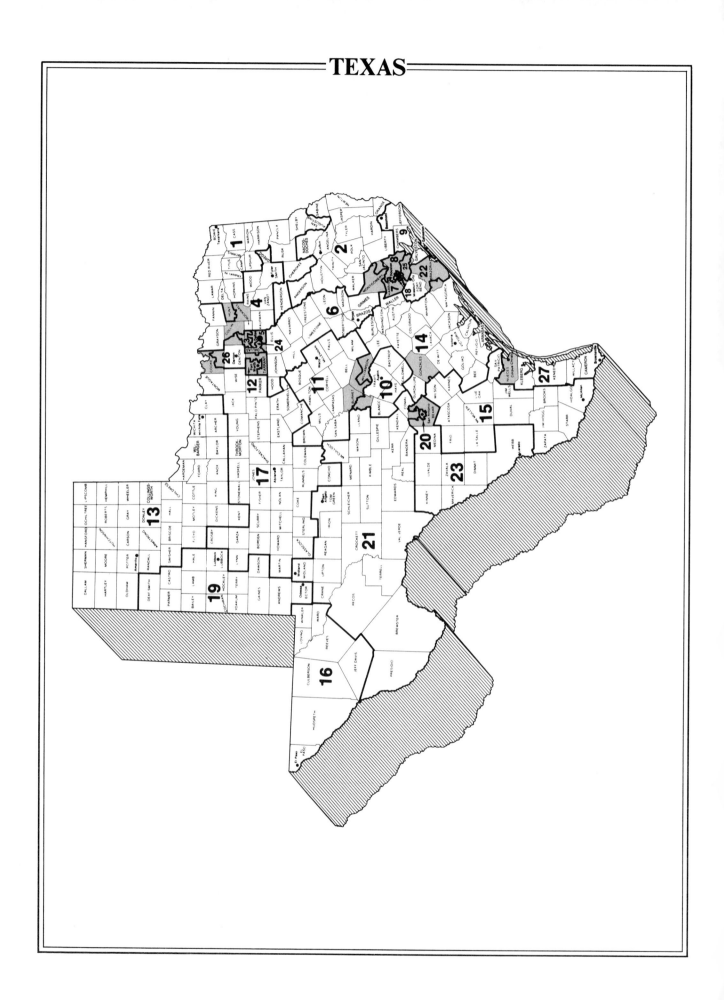

Age of Population

District	Population Under 18	Voting Age Population	Population 65 & Over (% of VAP)	Median Age
1	150,052	376,964	85,485 (22.7%)	32.8
2	153,980	372,792	62,165 (16.7%)	29.5
3	132,315	394,610	39,552 (10.0%)	30.2
4	149,092	377,899	74,813 (19.8%)	31.9
5	151,707	374,926	45,962 (12.3%)	28.1
6	152,154	375,239	63,612 (17.0%)	29.0
7	151,600	375,483	24,749 (6.6%)	29.1
8	179,733	347,798	24,703 (7.1%)	26.2
9	156,081	370,362	48,638 (13.1%)	29.1
10	136,272	390,909	45,569 (11.7%)	26.8
11	146,369	381,013	65,385 (17.2%)	27.8
12	152,495	374,579	53,166 (14.2%)	28.9
13	149,962	376,878	66,383 (17.6%)	30.1
14	158,301	368,619	70,506 (19.1%)	30.0
15	198,180	329,023	52,916 (16.1%)	25.4
16	185,841	341,560	35,953 (10.5%)	25.1
17	146,414	380,499	82,648 (21.7%)	32.2
18	160,969	366,424	50,691 (13.8%)	27.2
19	166,863	360,942	45,903 (12.7%)	26.4
20	167,538	358,812	55,130 (15.4%)	26.3
21	149,432	377,612	64,291 (17.0%)	31.2
22	145,110	381,492	29,577 (7.8%)	27.6
23	190,176	336,355	36,224 (10.8%)	25.8
24	169,490	357,187	37,006 (10.4%)	26.4
25	160,626	366,175	31,561 (8.6%)	27.1
26	159,878	367,421	32,027 (8.7%)	28.3
27	185,476	341,512	46,546 (13.6%)	26.0
State	4,306,106	9,923,085	1,371,161 (13.8%)	28.2

Education: School Years Completed

District	8 Years or Fewer	4 Years of High School	4 Years of College or More	Median School Years
1	23.8%	29.2%	10.1%	12.1
2	22.9	30.8	10.0	12.1
3	4.5	25.4	38.1	13.5
4	19.4	30.1	12.7	12.3
5	18.9	31.5	13.1	12.4
6	19.9	29.3	15.3	12.3
7	5.3	25.9	37.3	13.4
8	15.8	34.0	14.0	12.4
9	16.5	32.3	16.3	12.5
10	15.8	25.4	26.9	12.8
11	20.4	30.9	13.5	12.3
12	17.8	30.9	13.2	12.4
13	18.2	32.0	13.3	12.4
14	30.2	27.1	11.5	12.1
15	45.4	21.4	9.8	11.6
16	29.2	29.2	13.5	12.3
17	23.4	28.4	11.1	12.1
18	31.5	24.0	11.8	11.9
19	23.1	28.4	14.5	12.3
20	33.6	27.7	8.6	12.0
21	18.0	27.7	21.5	12.6
22	11.1	28.0	27.5	13.0
23	28.9	27.6	14.5	12.3
24	17.5	32.9	12.5	12.4
25	12.5	32.1	19.7	12.7
26	7.6	29.6	28.1	13.1
27	34.2	24.1	13.0	12.1
State	20.7%	28.8%	16.9%	12.4

Income and Occupation

District	Median Family Income	White Collar Workers	Blue Collar Workers	Service Workers	Farm Workers
1	$ 16,376	41.7%	40.5%	13.0%	4.8%
2	18,281	41.9	42.3	12.7	3.0
3	29,302	76.7	15.7	7.2	0.5
4	18,592	46.0	38.9	12.5	2.6
5	18,844	50.8	35.0	13.3	0.8
6	20,044	50.8	33.8	11.8	3.7
7	31,395	74.2	19.0	6.2	0.7
8	24,631	51.6	38.1	9.6	0.7
9	22,957	52.3	34.4	12.3	1.1
10	19,457	61.7	22.9	13.7	1.7
11	15,602	48.8	32.6	14.1	4.4
12	19,157	50.0	36.7	12.5	0.8
13	18,620	46.0	33.5	13.2	7.3
14	18,734	42.9	37.2	13.0	6.9
15	13,313	42.8	35.0	12.5	9.7
16	15,476	51.8	33.4	13.2	1.6
17	16,778	42.2	36.5	13.1	8.3
18	15,449	41.8	40.6	16.7	0.9
19	18,294	48.7	32.3	11.5	7.5
20	13,809	47.5	34.5	17.0	0.9
21	20,018	57.7	26.5	11.9	3.9
22	25,922	64.5	25.9	8.4	1.2
23	16,680	55.1	29.5	12.3	3.2
24	18,760	50.1	36.3	12.9	0.7
25	23,778	55.6	33.2	10.8	0.5
26	26,029	66.5	23.8	8.6	1.1
27	16,048	49.6	32.9	13.9	3.6
State	$ 19,618	53.1%	32.1%	11.9%	2.9%

Housing and Residential Patterns

District	Owner Occupied	Renter Occupied	Urban	Rural
1	75.1%	24.9%	41.4%	58.6%
2	74.7	25.3	40.2	59.8
3	57.8	42.2	98.8	1.2
4	72.0	28.0	56.2	43.8
5	53.2	46.8	99.2	0.8
6	71.5	28.5	54.3	45.7
7	62.1	37.9	93.8	6.2
8	69.6	30.4	89.8	10.2
9	68.0	32.0	90.8	9.2
10	54.6	45.4	80.6	19.4
11	63.4	36.6	68.9	31.1
12	64.0	36.0	96.5	3.5
13	70.0	30.0	74.8	25.2
14	72.0	28.0	52.0	48.0
15	72.2	27.8	67.7	32.3
16	60.7	39.3	93.5	6.5
17	72.7	27.3	57.8	42.2
18	42.8	57.2	100.0	0.0
19	65.3	34.7	77.4	22.6
20	57.5	42.5	100.0	0.0
21	69.5	30.5	76.1	23.9
22	53.2	46.8	83.4	16.6
23	69.0	31.0	82.0	18.0
24	55.4	44.6	100.0	0.0
25	58.4	41.6	99.7	0.3
26	72.4	27.6	89.4	10.6
27	62.2	37.8	86.1	13.9
State	64.3%	35.7%	79.6%	20.4%

1st District

Northeast — Texarkana

Republicans have broken the barriers of Democratic domination in many parts of Texas, but the GOP still encounters stiff resistance in the rural 1st in the northeastern corner of the state.

In the early 1980s blacks made up more than 20 percent of the population in half the rural counties of the 1st District. By running well among blacks and appealing to the Southern sympathies of rural whites, Jimmy Carter won the district comfortably in 1976 and edged Ronald Reagan in 1980.

Republicans have made some inroads in Texarkana (Bowie County) and Marshall (Harrison County), both manufacturing centers providing goods and services to the surrounding farms and towns. Texarkana, the twin city of its namesake across the state line in Arkansas, hosts the Red River Army Depot, a largely civilian facility that services Army vehicles. Once the home of an important timber trade, Marshall now harbors light industries related to East Texas' active oil and natural gas wells. The 1st's lumber industry today is centered farther south, in St. Augustine County.

Reagan carried Bowie and Harrison counties in 1980, averaging 53 percent of the vote. But those two urbanized counties cast less than a quarter of the district's 1980 vote; the rural counties still dominate politics in the 1st, and nearly all of them are Democratic.

The 1982 redistricting did not make substantial changes in the character of the district. At its northwest corner, the 1st moved out of Wood, Rains and Fannin counties and added territory in the northern half of Hunt County.

Election Returns

1st District		Democrat		Republican	
1976	President	95,599	(59.1%)	65,538	(40.5%)
	Senate	100,926	(67.0%)	49,278	(32.7%)
	House	125,217	(83.4%)	24,975	(16.6%)
1978	Governor	51,195	(56.7%)	38,897	(43.1%)
	Senate	49,270	(56.1%)	38,375	(43.7%)
	House	66,878	(77.9%)	19,003	(22.1%)
1980	President	90,448	(49.5%)	89,581	(49.0%)
	House	127,635	(98.9%)	1,464	(1.1%)
1982	Governor	77,636	(61.5%)	48,002	(38.0%)
	Senate	83,765	(65.7%)	42,902	(33.6%)
	House	100,685	(97.5%)	—	

Demographics

Population: 527,016. **Percent Change from 1970:** 20.4%.

Land Area: 13,271 square miles. **Population per Square Mile:** 39.7.

Counties, 1980 Population: Bowie — 75,301; Camp — 9,275; Cass — 29,430; Cherokee — 38,127; Delta — 4,839; Franklin — 6,893; Harrison — 52,265; Henderson — 42,606; Hopkins — 25,247; Hunt (Pt.) — 15,775; Lamar — 42,156; Marion — 10,360; Morris — 14,629; Panola — 20,724; Red River — 16,101; Rusk — 41,382; San Augustine — 8,785; Shelby — 23,084; Titus — 21,442; Upshur — 28,595.

Cities, 1980 Population: Athens — 10,197; Henderson — 11,473; Jacksonville — 12,264; Kilgore (Pt.) — 2,543; Longview (Pt.) — 1,677; Marshall — 24,921; Mount Pleasant — 11,003; Paris — 25,498; Sulphur Springs — 12,804; Texarkana — 31,271.

Race and Ancestry: White — 79.2%; Black — 19.6%; American Indian, Eskimo and Aleut — 0.2%; Asian and Pacific Islander — 0.2%. Spanish Origin — 1.6%. English — 16.8%; French — 0.7%; German — 2.7%; Irish — 6.0%.

Universities, Enrollment: East Texas Baptist College, Marshall — 916; East Texas State University, Commerce — 8,322; East Texas State University at Texarkana, Texarkana — 632; Henderson County Junior College, Athens — 2,993; Jacksonville College, Jacksonville — 279; Lon Morris College, Jacksonville — 333; Panola Junior College, Carthage — 963; Paris Junior College, Paris — 2,130; Texarkana Community College, Texarkana — 3,658; Wiley College, Marshall — 665.

Newspapers, Circulation: *Athens Daily Review* (eS), Athens — 5,670; *Henderson Daily News* (eS), Henderson — 5,416; *Jacksonville Daily Progress* (eS), Jacksonville — 6,130; *Marshall News Messenger* (eS), Marshall — 9,615; *Mount Pleasant Daily Tribune* (eS), Mount Pleasant — 4,836; *The Paris News* (eS), Paris — 13,445; *Sulpher Springs News-Telegram* (eS), Sulpher Springs — 6,525; *Texarkana Gazette* (mS), Texarkana — 31,265.

Commercial Television Stations, Affiliation: KTAL, Texarkana (NBC). Most of district is located in Shreveport (La.)-Texarkana ADI. Portions are in Dallas-Fort Worth ADI and Tyler ADI.

Military Installations: Lone Star Army Ammunition Plant, Texarkana — 1,381; Longhorn Army Ammunition Plant, Marshall — 762; Red River Army Depot, Texarkana — 6,719.

Industries:

Lone Star Steel Co.; Lone Star; steel — 5,000. **Campbell Soup Co.;** Paris; canned specialties — 1,650. **Pilgrim Industries Inc.;** Mount Pleasant; poultry processing — 1,500. **Day & Zimmerman Inc.** (Lone Star Div.); Texarkana; small arms ammunition — 1,400. **Texarkana Memorial Hospital;** Texarkana; hospital — 1,050.

The Mathes Co.; Athens; televisions — 1,000. **Thiokol Corp.** (Longhorn Div.); Karnack; ammunition — 1,000. **Fabsteel Co. Inc.;** Waskom; structural metal — 900. **Holly Farms of Texas Inc.** (HQ); Center; poultry processing — 850. **International Paper Co.;** Texarkana; paper mill — 765. **Wales Transportation Inc.;** Lone Star; trucking — 700. **Rockwell International Corp.** (Flow Control Div.); Sulphur Springs; valves, pipe fittings — 668. **Babcock & Wilcox Co. Inc.;** Paris; general construction — 651. **Valmac Industries Inc.;** Tenaha; farm supply wholesaling — 550. **The H. D. Lee Co. Inc.;** Sulphur Springs; men's clothing — 525. **Merico Inc.;** Paris; bakery products — 500. **Nichols-Kusan Inc.** (Old Jacksonville Ceiling Fans); Jacksonville; plastic ceiling fans — 500.

2nd District

East — Lufkin, Orange

Traditionally poor, isolated and dependent on timber, the east Texas piney woods 2nd took on a new prosperity in the 1970s with the growth of the oil industry. Lufkin, the district's largest city, still relies on a large paper mill for many of its jobs. But it also has steel mills and a factory that makes oil and gas drilling equipment.

Heavily industrialized Orange hosts petrochemical facilities and a waning shipbuilding industry. Du Pont, Gulf Oil, and Firestone all maintain plants along Orange's major industrial corridor, known locally as "Chemical Row." Independent oil outfits and cattle ranches are scattered throughout the district.

Like all of East Texas, the 2nd is conservative and has strong ties to Dixie; in 1968, this was the only Texas district carried by George C. Wallace. But it has a residual populist streak in the smaller counties and sometimes has been hospitable to moderate Democrats willing to speak its language. Jimmy Carter carried the territory of the new 2nd easily in 1976, and in 1980, when Carter lost the state by a decisive margin, he won the 2nd with just under 5,000 votes.

Redistricting made the 2nd better territory for the Democrats. The district turned over to the 6th District about 80 percent of the residents of Montgomery County, where politics is dominated by white-collar Houston suburbanites who helped Ronald Reagan win two-thirds of the county's 1980 presidential vote.

Remaining in the 2nd District are 27,000 people in the northeast section of Montgomery County. Although this area is in Houston's sphere of influence, it has much in common with the rest of the district.

In addition to removing most of Montgomery County, redistricting pared away four Democratic-majority counties along the western edge of the 2nd District. Each of the counties voted for Carter in 1980, but they cast less than 5,000 votes apiece, so their loss was not expected to hurt the Democrats.

Election Returns

2nd District		Democrat		Republican	
1976	President	85,850	(58.8%)	59,163	(40.6%)
	Senate	92,833	(67.4%)	44,354	(32.2%)
	House	108,485	(95.0%)	—	
1978	Governor	48,387	(60.0%)	32,147	(39.9%)
	Senate	46,823	(59.7%)	31,444	(40.1%)
	House	56,537	(75.1%)	18,736	(24.9%)
1980	President	86,056	(50.4%)	81,093	(47.5%)
	House	115,378	(71.8%)	43,365	(27.0%)
1982	Governor	82,099	(67.1%)	39,389	(32.2%)
	Senate	81,274	(68.9%)	35,702	(30.3%)
	House	91,762	(94.3%)	—	

Demographics

Population: 526,772. **Percent Change from 1970:** 35.4%.

Land Area: 13,043 square miles. **Population per Square Mile:** 40.4.

Counties, 1980 Population: Anderson — 38,381; Angelina — 64,172; Hardin — 40,721; Houston — 22,299; Jasper — 30,781; Liberty — 47,088; Montgomery (Pt.) — 27,447; Nacogdoches — 46,786; Newton — 13,254; Orange — 83,838; Polk — 24,407; Sabine — 8,702; San Jacinto — 11,434; Trinity — 9,450; Tyler — 16,223; Walker — 41,789.

Cities, 1980 Population: Houston (Pt.) — 19; Huntsville — 23,936; Lufkin — 28,562; Nacogdoches — 27,149; Orange — 23,628; Palestine — 15,948; Vidor — 12,117.

Race and Ancestry: White — 82.3%; Black — 15.5%; American Indian, Eskimo and Aleut — 0.3%; Asian and Pacific Islander — 0.3%. Spanish Origin — 3.2%. English — 16.7%; French — 3.0%; German — 3.6%; Irish — 6.0%.

Universities, Enrollment: Angelina College, Lufkin — 2,074; Sam Houston State University, Huntsville — 10,601; Stephen F. Austin State University, Nacogdoches — 10,768.

Newspapers, Circulation: *The Daily Sentinel* (e), Nacogdoches — 8,761; *The Huntsville Item* (eS), Huntsville — 5,716; *Lufkin News* (eS), Lufkin — 14,312; *The Orange Leader* (eS), Orange — 11,276;

Palestine Herald-Press (eS), Palestine — 8,967. *The Beaumont Enterprise* also circulates in the district.

Commercial Television Stations, Affiliation: KTRE-TV, Lufkin (ABC, NBC). Most of the district is divided between Beaumont-Port Arthur ADI and Houston ADI. Portions are in Shreveport (La.)-Texarkana ADI, Dallas-Fort Worth ADI and Tyler ADI.

Industries:

E. I. du Pont de Nemours & Co.; Orange; plastics — 2,750. **Lufkin Industries Inc.** (HQ); Lufkin; oil field machinery — 2,179. **Levington Industries Inc.** (HQ); Orange; shipbuilding — 1,900. **Kirby Forest Industries Inc.;** Silsbee; sawmill — 1,700. **Temple-Eastex Inc.** (HQ); Diboll; pulp mill, lumber products — 1,200.

Temple-Eastex Inc.; Evadale; pulp mill — 1,100. **Texas Foundries Inc.** (HQ); Lufkin; malleable iron foundries — 1,090. **St. Regis Paper Co.** (Southland Paper Mills Div.); Lufkin; newsprint — 1,070. **United States Steel Corp.** (American Bridge Div.); Orange; structural metal — 1,000. **Georgetown Texas Steel Corp.;** Vidor; steel mill — 900. **Kirby Forest Industries Inc.;** Bon Wier; lumber, plywood — 700. **Missouri-Pacific Railroad Co.;** Palestine; railroad operations — 700.

Owens-Illinois Inc. (Forest Products Div.); Orange; wood fiber boxes — 621. **Firestone Tire & Rubber Co.** (Firestone Synthetic Rubber & Latex Co.); Orange; industrial organic chemicals — 600. **Santa Fe Industries Inc.** (Atchison, Topeka & Santa Fe Railroad); Silsbee; railroad operations — 600. **Western Co. of North America;** Liberty; oil well services — 600. **National Pipe & Tube Co. Inc.** (HQ); Liberty; steel pipes — 550. **Champion International Corp.** (Champion Building Products); Camden; plywood — 500. **Gulf Oil Corp.** (Gulf Oil Chemicals Co.- Plastics Div.); Orange; plastics — 500.

3rd District

North Dallas, Northern Suburbs

The 3rd District is home to many of Dallas' high-status wealthy neighborhoods and northern suburbs. The median housing value here is more than $77,000, by far the highest in the area and second in the state only to the 7th District in Houston. Many of Dallas' top corporate executives maintain their homes here, commuting to work downtown.

Foremost among the affluent communities of North Dallas are Highland Park and University Park, traditional enclaves of the city's economic establishment. Rapid development of high-rise offices and shopping malls is occurring along the Dallas North Tollway leading into the suburbs. Suburban Richardson and Carrollton are filled with young newcomers who work for electronics manufacturers, research firms and corporate branch offices.

More than 250,000 people moved into the 3rd during the 1970s, making it Texas' third fastest-growing district. To bring its population down to ideal district size, the three federal judges who redrew it concentrated it compactly in Dallas and nearby suburbs. The 3rd gave up all of its Denton County territory, all except a segment of Plano in Collin County and most of northwest Dallas County, including Irving. The 3rd added voters in upper-middle-class Republican-voting areas in Garland.

The GOP is firmly in control throughout the redrawn 3rd. Most Republican candidates for statewide and federal office can count on receiving over 65 percent of the districtwide vote. Ronald Reagan did far better than that in 1980 — he outpolled Jimmy Carter within the area of the new 3rd 74 percent to 21 percent. Winning the GOP primary nomination to the U.S. House is tantamount to winning the general election.

Election Returns

3rd District		Democrat		Republican	
1976	President	53,698	(28.5%)	132,653	(70.5%)
	Senate	51,848	(29.3%)	123,900	(70.0%)
	House	51,003	(28.5%)	127,577	(71.3%)
1978	Governor	29,251	(26.2%)	81,444	(73.1%)
	Senate	32,887	(31.3%)	71,588	(68.0%)
	House	3,224	(4.1%)	75,068	(95.8%)
1980	President	45,783	(21.4%)	158,246	(74.0%)
	House	39,704	(19.7%)	155,837	(77.3%)
1982	Governor	48,485	(30.3%)	111,653	(69.7%)
	Senate	49,544	(36.6%)	85,891	(63.4%)
	House	28,223	(21.8%)	99,852	(77.1%)

Demographics

Population: 526,925. **Percent Change from 1970:** 47.8%.

Land Area: 250 square miles. **Population per Square Mile:** 2,107.7.

Counties, 1980 Population: Collin (Pt.) — 24,435; Dallas (Pt.) — 502,490.

Cities, 1980 Population: Carrollton (Pt.) — 26,547; Dallas (Pt.) — 282,408; Farmers Branch (Pt.) — 24,761; Garland (Pt.) — 57,965; Mesquite (Pt.) — 361; Plano (Pt.) — 12,900; Richardson — 72,496; University Park — 22,254.

Race and Ancestry: White — 93.2%; Black — 3.3%; American Indian, Eskimo and Aleut — 0.3%; Asian and Pacific Islander — 1.6%. Spanish Origin — 4.1%. Dutch — 0.5%; English — 16.4%; French — 1.1%; German — 6.7%; Irish — 4.8%; Italian — 1.1%; Polish — 0.8%; Russian — 0.6%; Scottish — 0.8%; Swedish — 0.5%.

Universities, Enrollment: Brookhaven College, Farmers Branch — 4,574; Dallas Christian College, Dallas — 146; Richland College, Dallas — 11,350; Southern Methodist University, Dallas — 9,112; University of Texas at Dallas, Richardson — 6,369.

Newspapers, Circulation: *Arlington Daily News* (eS), Farmers Branch — 5,689; *Garland Daily News* (eS), Garland — 10,360; *Plano Daily Star-Courier* (eS), Plano — 13,891; *Richardson Daily News* (e), Richardson — 6,408. *The Dallas Morning News* and *Dallas Times Herald* also circulate in the district.

Commercial Television Stations, Affiliation: Entire district is located in Dallas-Fort Worth ADI.

Industries:

Texas Instruments Inc. (HQ); Dallas; semiconductors, electronic equipment — 25,000. **Mostek Corp.** (HQ); Carrollton; semiconductors — 5,000. **Rockwell International Corp.** (Collins Transmission Systems Group); Richardson; electronic equipment — 3,900. **Rockwell International Corp.** (Collins Communication Div.); Richardson; electronic equipment — 3,000. **Blue Cross-Blue Shield of Texas** (HQ); Richardson; health insurance — 2,220.

Otis Engineering Corp. (HQ); Carrollton; oil well equipment — 2,000. **Presbyterian Hospital of Dallas;** Dallas; hospital — 1,850. **Electronic Data Systems Corp.;** Dallas; data processing services — 1,400. **Computer Language Research Inc.** (Fast Tax); Carrollton; tax return service — 800. **Humana of Texas Inc.** Dallas; hospital — 800. **Northern Telecom Inc.** (Network Systems Group); Richardson; telecommunications equipment — 800. **Forney Engineering Co.** (General Regulator Div. - HQ); Carrollton; automatic controls — 750. **Sun Oil Co.;** Dallas; oil exploration — 708.

Elfab Corp.; Addison; electronic components — 700. **Occidental Petroleum Corp.** (Zoecon Industries); Dallas; pesticides — 700. **Electrospace Systems Inc.** (HQ); Richardson; communications equipment — 600. **Planned Marketing Associates** (HQ); Dallas; life, fire, casualty insurance — 600. **Sun Gas Co. Inc.** (HQ); Dallas; natural gas production — 600. **Members Insurance Co. Inc.** (HQ); Dallas; insurance — 585. **Southwestern States Bankcard Assn.;** Addison; bank credit card center — 576. **Chilton Corp.** (HQ); Dallas; credit bureau — 550.

Frymire Engineering Co. (HQ); Dallas; plumbing, heating, cooling contracting — 535. **Arrow Industries Inc.** (HQ); Carrollton; dry food packaging — 500. **Travelers Insurance Co.;** Dallas; life, health insurance — 500. **American Petrofina Holding Co.** (HQ); Dallas; oil production, refining — 500. **Fox & Jacobs Inc.** (HQ); Carrollton; construction — 500. **Geophysical Service Inc.** (HQ); Dallas; oil, gas exploration services — 500. **Overhead Door Corp.** (General Aluminum Div.); Carrollton; aluminum doors — 500. **State Farm General Insurance Co.;** Dallas; health insurance — 500.

4th District

Northeast — Tyler, Longview

Three distinct areas constitute the 4th District. At the northern end, slow-growing Grayson and Fannin counties raise livestock, sorghum, peanuts and hay. Sherman, the seat of Grayson County, is an old, cotton-processing town now turning out meat products, electronics and surgical supplies.

The counties in the central part of the district are caught up in the sprawl of metropolitan Dallas; population doubled in both Collin and Rockwall counties during the 1970s. Many people in those counties commute to Dallas jobs.

At the eastern end of the district are two cities that serve as supply and distribution hubs for the East Texas oil fields — Tyler (Smith County) and Longview (Gregg County). Fueled by the expansion of the independent oil industry, those two counties also surpassed the state's 27 percent growth rate during the 1970s.

Democrats have won the 4th by narrow margins in most recent contests for statewide office. But the GOP has continued to make strides — especially in the eastern and central regions.

Ronald Reagan won 68 percent in Gregg County and 65 percent in Smith and took both Rockwall and Collin counties by comfortable margins. All those counties voted for Gerald R. Ford in 1976, but not by such wide margins as Reagan enjoyed.

In the north, Grayson County swung to Reagan in 1980 after voting for Jimmy Carter in 1976. But in 1982 it fell easily to the Democratic candidate for Governor. Despite its proclivity to vote Republican in national elections, the district in 1982 returned its Democratic incumbent to the House with nearly 74 percent of the vote.

In the remap, the 4th lost voters who live directly north of the Dallas-Fort Worth area: Denton County and western Collin County were incorporated into the newly created 26th District. Eastern Collin County remained in the 4th.

The district took in two new counties nearly equal in population, Wood and Fannin. Wood went for Reagan in 1980, but Fannin chose Carter. And in 1982 Fannin gave 75 percent of its vote to the Democratic candidate for governor.

Fannin was the home of U. S. House Speaker Sam Rayburn who represented the 4th for 48 years. The district still covers much of the Rayburn territory.

Election Returns

4th District		Democrat		Republican	
1976	President	79,514	(51.5%)	74,225	(48.0%)
	Senate	80,683	(54.9%)	66,004	(44.9%)
	House	93,1744	(62.4%)	56,046	(37.6%)
1978	Governor	47,216	(50.2%)	46,625	(49.6%)
	Senate	45,746	(50.2%)	45,006	(49.5%)
	House	53,531	(61.7%)	33,261	(38.3%)
1980	President	73,547	(40.8%)	103,771	(57.5%)
	House	94,706	(55.6%)	75,553	(44.4%)
1982	Governor	70,808	(52.8%)	62,399	(46.5%)
	Senate	71,714	(53.7%)	60,297	(45.1%)
	House	94,134	(73.8%)	32,221	(25.3%)

Demographics

Population: 526,991. **Percent Change from 1970:** 25.8%.

Land Area: 6,710 square miles. **Population per Square Mile:** 78.5.

Counties, 1980 Population: Collin (Pt.) — 31,079; Fannin — 24,285; Grayson — 89,796; Gregg — 99,487; Hunt (Pt.) — 39,473; Kaufman — 39,015; Rains — 4,839; Rockwall — 14,528; Smith — 128,366; Van Zandt — 31,426; Wood — 24,697.

Cities, 1980 Population: Dallas (Pt.) — 1; Denison — 23,884; Garland (Pt.) — 0; Greenville — 22,161; Kilgore (Pt.) — 8,425; Longview (Pt.) — 61,085; McKinney (Pt.) — 6,790; Sherman — 30,413; Terrell — 13,225; Tyler — 70,508.

Race and Ancestry: White — 84.0%; Black — 14.0%; American Indian, Eskimo and Aleut — 0.3%; Asian and Pacific Islander — 0.3%. Spanish Origin — 2.7%. English — 16.6%; French — 0.7%; German — 3.5%; Irish — 6.0%.

Universities, Enrollment: Austin College, Sherman — 1,190; Grayson County College, Denison — 3,623; Jarvis Christian College, Hawkins — 619; Kilgore College, Kilgore — 4,095; LeTourneau College, Longview — 1,037; Southwestern Christian College, Terrell — 285; Texas College, Tyler — 476; Tyler Junior College, Tyler — 6,794; University of Texas at Tyler, Tyler — 1,921.

Newspapers, Circulation: *The Denison Herald* (eS), Denison — 13,556; *Favorite* (eS), Bonham — 3,630; *Herald-Banner* (mS), Greenville — 11,803; *Kilgore News Herald* (eS), Kilgore — 5,879; *Longview Morning Journal* (mS), Longview — 14,135; *Longview News* (e), Longview — 16,602; *Sherman Democrat* (eS), Sherman — 19,813; *The Terrell Tribune* (eS), Terrell — 5,733; *Tyler Courier-Times* (eS), Tyler — 9,188; *Tyler Morning Telegraph* (m), Tyler — 35,417; *The Dallas Morning News* and *Dallas Times Herald* also circulate in the district.

Commercial Television Stations, Affiliation: KLTV, Tyler (ABC, NBC, CBS). Most of district is located in Dallas-Fort Worth ADI. Portions are in Tyler ADI and Shreveport (La.)-Texarkana ADI.

Industries:

Texas Instruments Inc.; Sherman; electronics — 3,000. **Tyler Pipe Industries** (HQ); Tyler; cast iron pipes — 2,785. **Eastman Kodak Co. Inc.;** Longview; photographic supplies — 2,700. **E-Systems Inc.;** Greenville; aircraft equipment — 2,700. **Trane CAC;** Tyler; air conditioners — 1,850.

Marathon Le Tourneau Co.; Longview; heavy construction machinery — 1,500. **Kelly-Springfield Tire Co.;** Tyler; auto tires — 1,370. **East Texas Hospital Foundation;** Tyler; hospital — 1,020. **Brown & Root Inc.;** Tyler; heavy construction — 900. **Johnson & Johnson Products Inc.;** Sherman; surgical supplies — 825. **Oscar Mayer & Co. Inc.;** Sherman; meatpacking — 750. **The Southland Corp.** (Distribution Center); Tyler; warehousing — 741.

The L. E. Myers Co. (Southwest Div.); Longview; powerline construction — 700. **Hitchcock Industries Inc.;** Denison; aluminum castings — 600. **U.S. Industries Inc.** (Axelson Inc.); Longview; oil drilling machinery — 600. **Boise Cascade Corp.;** Denison; metal cans — 530.

Carrier Corp.; Tyler; air conditioning equipment — 525. **Burlington Industries Inc.;** Sherman; wool fabric — 500. **Garlock Inc.** (HQ); Longview; plastics products — 500. **Imperial American Co.;** Tyler; exercise equipment — 500.

5th District

Downtown Dallas, Eastern and Southern Suburbs

Few American cities have as controversial a reputation as Dallas. Following the assassination of President Kennedy there in 1963, the city suffered from an image of frontier violence and extremism that was hard to shake. Just as that perception was fading, the television series "Dallas" came along to popularize the image of a metropolis ruled by an oligarchy of oil interests obsessed with money and power.

But Dallas is more than ostentatious wealth and unbridled conservatism. It long has been a cosmopolitan city and a financial center of the Southwest. Northerners looking for a place that fits their definition of a city are much more likely to find it in Dallas than in sloppier, more chaotic Houston.

Sixty percent of the district's residents live in the city of Dallas. The Trinity River is the dividing line in downtown Dallas, with areas immediately east of the river in the 5th and those in the west in the 24th. Minorities make up nearly a third of the 5th District's population; most of them live in a concentrated area adjacent to downtown.

Just northwest of downtown Dallas lies Oaklawn, a fashionable enclave of young professionals. Oaklawn has a sizable gay community. East Dallas is a mix of middle- and upper-middle-class residential neighborhoods and more transient young workers.

Outside of Dallas, the 5th retains white, middle-income suburban communities such as Mesquite, Sunnyvale, Seagoville and Balch Springs. A sizable number of blue-collar workers live in those areas and by the early 1980s many of them had shown waning affection for Democratic policies. However, these areas gave strong support to the Democratic House and gubernatorial candidates in 1982.

In suburbs further south and west, working-class dissatisfaction with Democrats is less evident, though the voters prefer candidates in the moderate-to-conservative mold. Fitting that political profile are Hutchins, Wilmer and Lancaster, three towns that were moved from the 6th into the 5th under the remap.

Election Returns

5th District		Democrat		Republican	
1976	President	57,813	(48.3%)	60,885	(50.8%)
	Senate	47,729	(41.8%)	65,624	(57.5%)
	House	54,798	(47.6%)	58,858	(51.1%)
1978	Governor	39,280	(49.3%)	39,583	(49.7%)
	Senate	41,464	(53.6%)	34,915	(45.2%)
	House	34,590	(47.3%)	38,113	(52.2%)
1980	President	70,128	(44.5%)	80,636	(51.2%)
	House	73,553	(48.2%)	78,460	(51.4%)
1982	Governor	47,668	(56.3%)	36,959	(43.7%)
	Senate	45,554	(60.9%)	29,222	(39.1%)
	House	52,214	(64.8%)	27,121	(33.7%)

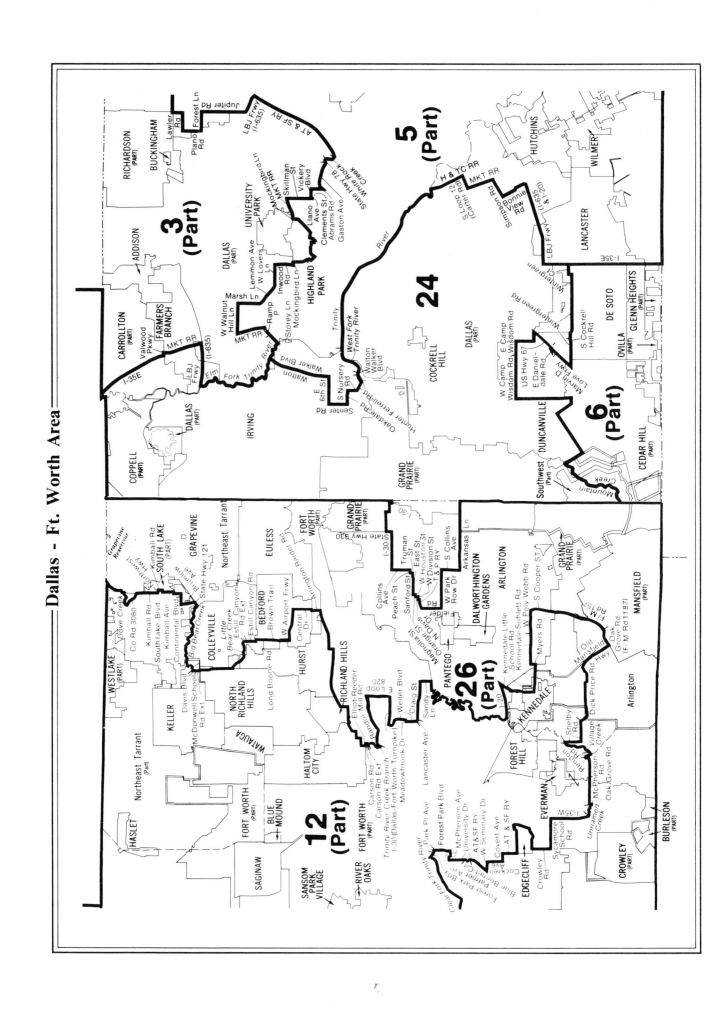

Dallas - Ft. Worth Area

Demographics

Population: 526,633. **Percent Change from 1970:** 0.8%.

Land Area: 362 square miles. **Population per Square Mile:** 1,454.8.

Counties, 1980 Population: Dallas (Pt.) — 526,633.

Cities, 1980 Population: Balch Springs — 13,746; Dallas (Pt.) — 322,568; Garland (Pt.) — 80,892; Irving (Pt.) — 8,079; Lancaster (Pt.) — 14,779; Mesquite (Pt.) — 66,692.

Race and Ancestry: White — 71.6%; Black — 19.6%; American Indian, Eskimo and Aleut — 0.5%; Asian and Pacific Islander — 1.0%. Spanish Origin — 12.2%. English — 13.3%; French — 0.7%; German — 3.7%; Irish — 4.6%; Italian — 0.5%.

Universities, Enrollment: Allstate Business College, Dallas — 1,657; Baylor College of Dentistry, Dallas — 459; Cedar Valley College, Lancaster — 1,874; Criswell Bible College, Dallas — 348; Dallas Bible College, Dallas — 235; Dallas Theological Seminary, Dallas — 1,035; Eastfield College, Mesquite — 8,092; El Centro College, Dallas — 6,479; Miss Wade's Fashion Merchandising College, Dallas — 200; University of Dallas (main campus), Irving — 2,688 *(school straddles line between 5th and 24th districts)*; University of Texas Health Science Center at Dallas, Dallas — 1,355;

Newspapers, Circulation: *The Dallas Morning News* (mS), Dallas — 278,746; *Dallas Times Herald* (all day, S), Dallas — 245,011; *News* (eS), Mesquite — 4,197.

Commercial Television Stations, Affiliation: KDFW-TV, Dallas (CBS); KNBN-TV, Dallas (None, Spanish); KTWS-TV, Dallas (None); KXTX-TV, Dallas (None); WFAA-TV, Dallas (ABC). Entire district is located in Dallas-Fort Worth ADI.

Military Installations: Garland Air National Guard Base, Garland — 175.

Industries:

Atlantic Richfield Co. (Arco Oil & Gas Co.); Dallas; oil, gas exploration — 3,500. **Western Electric Inc.;** Mesquite; telephone apparatus — 3,300. **Dallas County Hospital District;** Dallas; hospital — 3,200. **Republic of Texas Corp.** (HQ); Dallas; bank holding company — 2,740. **First National Bank in Dallas** (HQ); Dallas; banking — 2,000. **Mercantile Texas Corp.** (HQ); Dallas; banking — 2,000. **Sedco International S. A.;** Dallas; oil, gas drilling — 2,000. **Xerox Corp.;** Dallas; copying equipment — 2,000.

St. Paul Hospital; Dallas; hospital — 1,800. **Enserch Corp.** (Lone Star Gas Div. - HQ); Dallas; natural gas distributing — 1,700. **Group Life & Health Insurance Co.;** Dallas; life, health insurance — 1,600. **American Building Maintenance Co.;** Dallas; janitorial services — 1,500. **Cooper Industries Inc.** (Airmotive Div.); Dallas; aircraft — 1,500. **E-Systems Inc.** (Garland Div.); Garland; electronic systems — 1,500. **Taylor Publishing Co.** (HQ); Dallas; yearbook publishing — 1,500. **A. H. Belco Corp.** (The Dallas Morning News); Dallas; newspaper publishing — 1,450. **Times Herald Printing Co.;** Dallas; newspaper publishing — 1,360. **Safeway Stores Inc.;** Garland; warehousing — 1,300. **Central Freight Lines Inc.;** Irving; trucking — 1,240.

Crum & Forster Inc. (Floyd West & Co.); Dallas; life insurance — 1,150. **Blue Ridge Insurance Co.;** Dallas; property, casualty insurance — 1,100. **Dallas Market Center Development Co.;** Dallas; hotel — 1,100. **Pitney-Bowes Inc.** (The Drawing Board); Dallas; greeting cards — 1,100. **Southwestern Life Insurance Co.** (HQ); Dallas; life insurance — 1,030. **Federal Reserve Bank of Dallas** (HQ); Dallas; banking — 1,000. **Frito-Lay Inc.;** Dallas; snack foods — 1,000. **Great Western Coca-Cola Bottling Co.;** Dallas; soft drink bottling — 1,000. **Trailways Inc.** (HQ); Dallas; interstate passenger bus transportation — 961. **The Southland Co.** (HQ); Dallas; groceries — 918.

Affiliated Food Stores Inc. (Thrif-tee Food Stores HQ); Dallas; grocery wholesaling — 900. **Southland Financial Corp.** (HQ); Irving; life, health insurance — 900. **United States Steel Corp.** (Oil Well Div.); Garland; oil wells — 900. **Sammons Enterprises Inc.** (HQ); Dallas; industrial machinery wholesaling, insurance — 830. **Kraft Inc.** (Kraft Foods Div.); Garland; canned, prepared foods — 800. **Republic National Life Insurance Co.** (HQ); Dallas; life, health insurance — 800. **Great American Reserve Insurance Co.** (HQ); Dallas life, health insurance — 737. **ET & WNC Transportation Co.** (HQ); Dallas; trucking — 720. **Union Bankers Insurance Co.;** Dallas; life, health, accident insurance — 715. **Southwest Airlines Co.** (HQ); Dallas; commercial airline — 712. **Atlantic Richfield Co.** (Arco Oil and Gas Co.); Dallas; oil, gas exploration — 700.

Fairmont-Dallas Hotel Corp.; Dallas; hotel — 700. **International Business Machines Corp.;** Irving; management services — 700. **Arthur Andersen & Co.;** Dallas; accounting services — 650. **Dallas Cap & Emblem Mfg. Inc.** (Dal-Cap); Dallas; caps, emblems — 650. **Merchants Fast Motor Lines Inc.;** Dallas; trucking — 650. **American Standard County Mutual Insurance** (HQ); Dallas; auto insurance — 600. **Diversified AP Enterprises** (Byer-Rolnick); Garland; men's hats — 600. **Fidelity Union Life Insurance Co.** (HQ); Dallas; life insurance — 600. **Maryland Cup Corp.** (Sweetheart Cup Corp. Texas Div.); Dallas; paper cups — 600. **Southland Life Insurance Co.** (HQ); Dallas; life, health insurance — 600. **Texas Employers Insurance** (HQ); Dallas; casualty insurance — 600.

University Computing Co. (HQ); Dallas; computer data services — 600. **Varo Inc.** (HQ); Garland; semiconductors — 600. **Wyly Corp.** (HQ); Dallas; computer services — 600. **Core Laboratories Inc.** (HQ); Dallas; oil, field services — 568. **National Bank of Commerce;** Dallas; banking — 563. **Dr. Pepper Metroplex Refreshment** (HQ); Irving; soft drinks — 550. **Haggar Co.;** Dallas; men's, boys' clothing wholesaling — 550. **Associates Financial Services Inc.** (HQ); Irving; consumer finance lending — 525. **Frito-Lay Inc.;** Irving; snack foods — 525. **Republic Financial Services** (HQ); Dallas; life, casualty, fire insurance — 525. **Employers Casualty Co.** (HQ); Dallas; insurance — 512.

First City Bank; Dallas; banking — 509. **Abbott Laboratories** (Abbott Diagnostic Lab); Dallas; pharmaceuticals — 500. **Continental Emsco Co.;** Garland; oil field equipment — 500. **Conwell Corp.** (HQ); Dallas; trucking — 500. **Hilton Hotels Corp.** (Dallas Hilton); Dallas; hotel — 500. **Hyatt Corp.;** Dallas; hotel — 500. **Jerell Inc.** (HQ); Dallas; junior dresses — 500. **Lone Star Life Insurance Co.;** Dallas; life, health, accident insurance — 500. **Procter & Gamble Mfg. Co.;** Dallas; soap — 500. **Tracy-Locke Co. Inc.** (HQ); Dallas; advertising agency — 500. **Work Wear Corp.** (Action Line); Garland; men's, women's clothing — 500.

6th District

Dallas-Fort Worth and Houston Suburbs; Bryan

The 6th District is a long column of counties that begins near Dallas-Fort Worth and runs southeast to the suburbs of Houston, more than 200 miles away. At either end are the two fastest-growing counties in the state. In the northwest corner of the district, spillover from metropolitan Fort Worth nearly tripled the population of Hood County. Far to the south, Montgomery County grew approximately 160 percent, filling up with affluent professionals who commute to their jobs in Houston.

Between those population concentrations lies mostly rural territory. The urban exception in this central part of the district is Bryan (Brazos County), a city with a population of 44,337. Near Bryan is College Station, home of Texas A & M University, which has an enrollment of more than 30,000 students.

The rural counties, most of them more than one-fifth black, have remained loyally Democratic — all eight voted for Jimmy Carter in the 1976 and 1980 presidential elections. But the Democrats' rural strength has to compete with the broadening influence of suburban, white-collar Republicans flooding into the northern and southern ends of the 6th District.

In the Dallas-Fort Worth sphere, Hood, Johnson and Ellis counties each voted for Ronald Reagan in 1980, turning away from their 1976 preference for Carter. Montgomery County supported Gerald R. Ford in 1976 and gave Reagan a 2-to-1 majority. Parts of Montgomery were placed in the redrawn 2nd and 8th districts, but the 6th contains the bulk of the county's voters. Brazos County is also good GOP territory; it gave Reagan 60 percent in 1980.

Redistricting brought in Hood County from the 11th District as well as four rural counties and most of Montgomery from the 2nd. The 6th gave up all its territory in Tarrant County (Fort Worth) and neighboring Parker County and retained only the southwest corner of Dallas County.

Election Returns

6th District		Democrat		Republican	
1976	President	82,688	(54.6%)	68,045	(44.9%)
	Senate	83,947	(57.8%)	59,330	(40.9%)
	House	101,818	(75.0%)	31,799	(23.4%)
1978	Governor	51,283	(55.3%)	41,046	(44.3%)
	Senate	46,229	(52.6%)	41,255	(46.9%)
	House	56,975	(69.2%)	25,289	(30.7%)
1980	President	76,3016	(42.4%)	98,440	(54.7%)
	House	115,211	(72.6%)	42,804	(27.0%)
1982	Governor	67,687	(55.2%)	54,123	(44.2%)
	Senate	71,096	(59.3%)	47,912	(40.0%)
	House	91,546	(94.5%)	—	

Demographics

Population: 527,393. **Percent Change from 1970:** 56.6%.

Land Area: 10,678 square miles. **Population per Square Mile:** 49.4.

Counties, 1980 Population: Brazos — 93,588; Dallas (Pt.) — 46,150; Ellis — 59,743; Freestone — 14,830; Grimes — 13,580; Hill — 25,024; Hood — 17,714; Johnson — 67,649; Leon — 9,594; Limestone — 20,224; Madison — 10,649; Montgomery (Pt.) — 98,672; Navarro — 35,323; Robertson — 14,653.

Cities, 1980 Population: Bryan — 44,337; Burleson (Pt.) — 10,611; Cleburne — 19,218; College Station — 37,272; Conroe — 18,034; Corsicana — 21,712; De Soto (Pt.) — 15,380; Duncanville (Pt.) — 21,684; Ennis — 12,110; Grand Prairie (Pt.) — 7; Houston (Pt.) — 0; Waxahachie — 14,624.

Race and Ancestry: White — 85.6%; Black — 10.8%; American Indian, Eskimo and Aleut — 0.2%; Asian and Pacific Islander — 0.5%. Spanish Origin — 5.9%. English — 15.4%; French — 0.9%; German — 5.4%; Irish — 5.6%; Italian — 0.7%; Polish — 0.7%; Scottish — 0.5%.

Universities, Enrollment: Hill Junior College, Hillsboro — 750; Navarro College, Corsicana — 2,274; Northwood Institute (Cedar Hill campus), Cedar Hill — 1,653; Southwestern Adventist College, Keene — 700; Southwestern Assemblies of God College, Waxahachie — 713; Texas A & M University, College Station — 33,499.

Newspapers, Circulation: *Bryan-College Station Eagle* (eS), Bryan — 18,148; *Cleburne Times-Review* (eS), Cleburne — 8,296; *Corsicana Daily Sun* (eS), Corsicana — 10,300; *The Courier* (eS), Conroe — 11,717; *The Ennis Daily News* (eS), Ennis — 4,500; *Mexia Daily News* (e), Mexia — 3,760; *Waxahachie Daily Light* (eS), Waxahachie — 5,275. *The Dallas Morning News* and *Dallas Times Herald* also circulate in the district.

Commercial Television Stations, Affiliation: KBTX-TV, Bryan (ABC, CBS). Most of district is located in Dallas-Fort Worth ADI. Portions are in Houston ADI and Waco-Temple ADI.

Industries:

Jack Eckerd Corp. (Eckerd Drug Co.) Conroe; drugstore products distributing — 2,500. **Redman Building Products Inc.** (Alenco Div.); Bryan; metal windows, doors — 950. **Austin Power Inc.;** Anderson; general construction — 900. **Owens-Corning Fiberglas Corp.;** Waxahachie; insulation materials — 700. **Chaparral Steel Co.** (HQ); Midlothian; steel — 650. **Ennis Business Forms Inc.** (HQ); Ennis; business forms, office supplies — 500. **International Paper Co.** (Long Bell Div.); Navasota; wood preserving — 500. **Nucor Corp.;** Jewett; steel — 500. **Skytop Rig Co.;** Conroe; oil field machinery — 500.

7th District

Western Houston and Suburbs

As Houston has grown into America's fifth largest city and the commercial center of the Southwest, the 7th has grown dense with the homes of the prosperous corporate community. More than 400,000 people moved into the district during the 1970s, giving the old 7th an 86 percent growth rate, highest of any district in Texas.

To cut the 7th's population down to size, map makers gave more than 340,000 people to neighboring districts. The 22nd and 25th took much of the southwest Houston part of the 7th, and the 8th picked up territory all along the northeastern border of the 7th. As redrawn the 7th runs from the northwest portion of Houston west to the Harris County line. It has the highest housing values in the state.

Although most of Houston's myriad corporate headquarters lie outside the 7th's boundaries, the district has its own mini-downtowns at the numerous freeway interchanges. Office buildings line the east-west Katy Freeway, and small oil-related companies are scattered throughout the district.

Along with the 3rd District in Dallas, the redrawn 7th gives Republicans their highest margins in the state. In 1976 Gerald R. Ford swept the presidential vote in the district by nearly 3-to-1. Ronald Reagan improved on that in 1980, scoring his best Texas showing with 78 percent of the vote.

Election Returns

7th District		Democrat		Republican	
1976	President	51,398	(27.8%)	131,831	(71.2%)
	Senate	63,127	(34.8%)	117,326	(64.7%)
	House	—		124,374	(100.0%)
1978	Governor	28,138	(27.2%)	74,896	(72.3%)
	Senate	25,765	(24.5%)	78,601	(74.7%)
	House	11,662	(11.7%)	88,289	(88.3%)
1980	President	34,478	(18.2%)	147,638	(78.0%)
	House	21,862	(12.2%)	154,351	(86.2%)
1982	Governor	34,013	(27.2%)	90,010	(72.1%)
	Senate	48,464	(38.6%)	76,107	(60.7%)
	House	17,866	(14.0%)	108,718	(85.0%)

Demographics

Population: 527,083. **Percent Change from 1970:** 103.6%.

Land Area: 629 square miles. **Population per Square Mile:** 838.0.

Counties, 1980 Population: Harris (Pt.) — 527,083.

Cities, 1980 Population: Houston (Pt.) — 319,172.

Race and Ancestry: White — 91.6%; Black — 3.2%; American Indian, Eskimo and Aleut — 0.2%; Asian and Pacific Islander — 2.9%. Spanish Origin — 7.1%. English — 12.8%; French — 1.5%; German — 7.4%; Irish — 4.0%; Italian — 1.5%; Polish — 1.1%; Scottish — 0.7%.

Newspapers, Circulation: *Houston Chronicle* and *The Houston Post* circulate in the district.

Commercial Television Stations, Affiliation: KTXH, Houston (None). Entire district is located in Houston ADI. *(For other Houston stations, see 18th and 22nd districts.)*

Industries:

Cameron Iron Works Inc. (HQ); Houston; oil tools — 6,780. **The Dow Chemical Co.** (Dowell Div.); Houston; oil field services — 4,600. **Bechtel Petroleum Inc.**; Houston; engineering, construction — 4,500. **Stewart & Stevenson Services**; Houston; oil field equipment — 3,000. **Occidental of Libya Inc.**; Houston; oil production — 2,300.

Texas Instruments Inc. (Digital Systems Group); Cypress; semiconductors — 2,030. **Dresser Industries Inc.** (Dresser Atlas); Houston; research — 1,600. **Dixilyn-Field Drilling Co. Inc.**; Houston; oil drilling — 1,500. **TRW Inc.** (Mission Mfg. Co.); Houston; castings, valves — 1,380. **Keystone International Inc.** (Valve Div. - HQ); Houston; valves — 1,330. **Western Geophysical Co. of America** (Aero Services - HQ); Houston; oil exploration — 1,200. **Litwin Engineers & Constructors**; Houston; engineering services — 1,100. **Solus Ocean Systems**; Houston; offshore oil field services — 1,100. **Baker International Corp.** (Baker Service Tools); Houston; oil tools wholesaling — 1,000. **Daniel Industries Inc.** (Flow Products Div.); Houston; metering devices — 1,000. **Global Marine Drilling Co.** (HQ); Houston; oil drilling — 1,000.

Houston Northwest Medical Center; Houston; hospital — 1,000. **Igloo Corp.** (HQ); Houston; picnic chests — 1,000. **Oxy Petroleum Inc.**; Houston; oil, gas exploration — 1,000. **Big Three Industries Inc.** (Nitrogen Oil Well Service Co.); Houston; oil well services — 900. **Daniel Industries Inc.** (Flow Products Div.); Houston; valves, measuring devices — 900. **Union Texas Petroleum Corp.** (HQ); Houston; oil exploration — 810. **Armco Inc.** (National Supply); Houston; oil field machinery wholesaling — 800. **FMC Corp.**; Houston; oil well valves — 800. **Industrial Security Service Corp.**; Houston; security services — 750.

NL Industries Inc. (NL Rig Equipment); Houston; oil rigs — 750. **Anderson, Clayton & Co.** (Gulf Atlantic Distribution Services); Houston; general warehousing — 725. **Exxon Corp.**; Houston; credit card center — 715. **Halliburton Co.** (Wellex Div.); Houston; oil field equipment — 700. **Hill Ross Controls Corp.** (HQ); Houston; electrical controls — 665. **J. E. Sirrine Co.**; Houston; consulting engineers — 650. **Commercial Drywall Inc.** (Commercial Paint Co. - HQ); Houston; drywall contracting — 600. **L. B. Foster Co. Inc.**; Houston; metal service center — 600. **Robertson Cartage Co.** (L-M-R Co.); Houston; trucking — 600.

Bechtel Power Corp.; Houston; engineering, construction — 575. **Exxon Corp.** (Marketing & Accounting Center); Houston; administrative offices — 565. **NL Industries Inc.** (Controls System); Houston; oil field equipment — 530. **Armco Steel Corp.** (National Supply Div.); Houston; oil field equipment — 500. **Brown Oil Tools Inc.** (Beta Div. - HQ); Houston; oil field equipment — 500. **National Steel Products Co.** (Stran Steel Building Systems); Houston; prefabricated metal buildings — 500. **PRE Corp.** (Elder International Div.); Houston; mobile housing — 500. **The Randall Corp.**; Houston; gas processing — 500.

8th District

Houston Suburbs, Eastern Harris County

The 1982 redistricting improved the 8th District for its freshman Republican incumbent. The district gave up strong Democratic areas to the underpopulated urban 18th, lost all its blue-collar territory south of the Houston Ship Channel to the 25th and picked up residential and semi-rural areas in northeastern Harris County that had been part of the 7th and 9th districts. It also took in the eastern corner of suburban Montgomery County.

Thousands of middle- and upper-middle-income families moved into the Harris County part of the redrawn 8th during the 1970s, dramatically increasing the Republican voting base. Pollsters found some new subdivisions voting Republican 9-to-1 in the 1980 presidential contest. This influx of GOP-minded voters helped lift Ronald Reagan to victory over Jimmy Carter with 57 percent of the district vote — just two points shy of the 59 percent Carter polled in the areas of the redrawn district four years earlier.

But the 8th is not as monolithically white-collar and Republican as the 7th. Although the 8th lost many of its petrochemical plants in redistricting, a large number of the plants' blue-collar employees maintain their homes in the 8th. In addition, blue-collar Baytown is the site of a huge Exxon refinery and other petroleum-related industries.

The 8th District also kept a significant amount of territory in minority areas on Houston's perimeter. Nearly 30 percent of the people in the 8th are either black or Hispanic. Lakewood, in the southwestern part of the district, has a sizable minority population.

Still, the bulk of the 8th is suburban territory, with many residents commuting to work in downtown Houston. Some of the district's most affluent residents live in Kingwood, a subdivision that sprouted as migrants flocked to the Sun Belt.

Election Returns

8th District		Democrat		Republican	
1976	President	70,107	(59.1%)	47,856	(40.3%)
	Senate	70,334	(63.0%)	40,354	(36.1%)
	House	65,852	(60.5%)	42,836	(39.4%)
1978	Governor	30,517	(53.2%)	26,668	(46.5%)
	Senate	28,943	(50.6%)	27,657	(48.4%)
	House	29,076	(53.1%)	25,660	(46.9%)
1980	President	64,072	(40.6%)	89,301	(56.5%)
	House	51,210	(44.7%)	63,293	(55.2%)
1982	Governor	53,263	(59.8%)	35,215	(39.6%)
	Senate	52,394	(61.5%)	32,097	(37.7%)
	House	38,041	(42.6%)	50,630	(56.8%)

Demographics

Population: 527,531. **Percent Change from 1970:** 65.7%.

Land Area: 639 square miles. **Population per Square Mile:** 825.6.

Counties, 1980 Population: Harris (Pt.) — 525,163; Montgomery (Pt.) — 2,368.

Cities, 1980 Population: Baytown (Pt.) — 56,917; Houston (Pt.) — 168,103.

Race and Ancestry: White — 75.2%; Black — 16.7%; American Indian, Eskimo and Aleut — 0.3%; Asian and Pacific Islander — 1.1%. Spanish Origin — 12.5%. English — 9.5%; French — 1.6%; German — 4.7%; Irish — 3.8%; Italian — 0.7%; Polish — 0.7%.

Universities, Enrollment: Lee College, Baytown — 4,876; North Harris County College, Houston — 6,625; San Jacinto College (North campus), Houston — 2,859; Southern Bible College, Houston — 125.

Newspapers, Circulation: *The Baytown Sun* (eS), Baytown — 19,588. *Houston Chronicle* and *The Houston Post* also circulate in the district.

Commercial Television Stations, Affiliation: Entire district is located in Houston ADI.

Industries:

Armco Steel Corp.; Houston; steel — 4,000. **Exxon Corp.** (Exxon Co. USA Div.); Baytown; petroleum refining — 2,300. **United States Steel Corp.;** Baytown; steel — 2,190. **Mitchell Energy & Development Corp.** (HQ); The Woodlands; oil and gas exploration, production; real estate development — 1,980. **NL Industries Inc.** (NL McCullough); Houston; oil, gas field services — 1,500.

FMC Corp. (Petroleum Equipment Group); Houston; oil field equipment — 1,000. **PRE Corp.** (Pyramid Mfg. Co. Div.); Houston; oil field equipment — 1,000. **Mobay Chemical Corp.;** Baytown; industrial chemicals — 900. **Atlantic Richfield Co. Inc.** (Chemical Div.); Channelview; synthetic rubber — 850. **Central Freight Lines Inc.;** Houston; trucking — 850. **FMC Corp.;** Houston; oil well equipment — 850. **Exxon Chemical Co.;** Baytown; chemical refining — 800. **Gulf Oil Corp.** (Gulf Oil Chemicals Co.); Baytown; olefins — 620. **Hydril Co.** (Technology Center); Houston; oil field equipment — 520. **Anchor Hocking Corp.;** Houston; glass containers — 500. **Challenger Drilling Inc.;** Houston; drilling — 500. **Pan American World Airways Inc.;** Houston; commercial airline — 500.

9th District

Southeast — Beaumont, Galveston

The 9th is dominated by three industrial cities: Beaumont and Port Arthur, near the Louisiana border in Jefferson County, and Galveston, further south along the Gulf of Mexico in Galveston County.

The discovery of oil in the Spindletop Oil Field in January of 1901 triggered Beaumont's modern industrial development. Oil is still pumped at Spindletop within sight of a monument and a museum commemorating the field's contribution to Texas' economy. Port Arthur serves as a shipping center for the district's oil and petrochemical products.

The city of Galveston, located on Pelican Island, is also a major port of entry. Looking out to sea from Galveston Bay, one sees the horizon dotted with off-shore oil rigs. Local merchants have made a business of servicing area off-shore facilities, shipping out food and laundry to the laborers.

This northern coastal area is one of the few strongholds of organized labor in Texas and the unions have helped keep the 9th in the Democratic column. This is also one of the more ethnically diverse parts of Texas. There are Cajuns and blue-collar whites, many of German, Czech or Polish stock. Kemah, a Galveston County town, has a growing population of French-speaking Southeast Asians. Nearly 30 percent of the people are either black or Hispanic.

One of organized labor's few Texas strongholds, the 9th generally votes Democratic in statewide races. Jimmy Carter carried the 9th easily in 1976; he won narrowly in 1980.

Under the remap, the 9th gave all of its northeastern Harris County territory to the 8th; that area was Republican in complexion. In return, the 9th received a smaller section of southeastern Harris County, including part of Clear Lake City, an enclave of Republican engineers who work at the Johnson Space Center.

Election Returns

9th District		**Democrat**		**Republican**	
1976	President	97,831	(58.4%)	68,490	(40.9%)
	Senate	105,826	(65.5%)	54,263	(33.6%)
	House	112,378	(92.9%)	8,564	(7.1%)
1978	Governor	47,230	(56.8%)	35,432	(42.6%)
	Senate	45,695	(55.9%)	35,406	(43.3%)
	House	49,813	(62.6%)	29,706	(37.4%)
1980	President	84,259	(48.9%)	81,669	(47.4%)
	House	102,609	(91.1%)	9,963	(8.8%)
1982	Governor	77,340	(63.6%)	42,896	(35.3%)
	Senate	79,463	(67.4%)	36,961	(31.3%)
	House	78,965	(67.6%)	35,422	(30.3%)

Demographics

Population: 526,443. **Percent Change from 1970:** 17.5%.

Land Area: 1,998 square miles. **Population per Square Mile:** 263.5.

Counties, 1980 Population: Chambers — 18,538; Galveston — 195,940; Harris (Pt.) — 61,027; Jefferson — 250,938.

Cities, 1980 Population: Baytown (Pt.) — 6; Beaumont — 118,102; Friendswood — 10,719; Galveston — 61,902; Groves — 17,090; Houston (Pt.) — 27,296; La Marque — 15,372; League City — 16,578; Nederland — 16,855; Pasadena (Pt.) — 0; Pearland (Pt.) — 787; Port Arthur — 61,251; Port Neches — 13,944; Texas City — 41,403.

Race and Ancestry: White — 74.1%; Black — 21.4%; American Indian, Eskimo and Aleut — 0.2%; Asian and Pacific Islander — 1.6%. Spanish Origin — 7.6%. English — 10.7%; French — 4.8%; German — 4.3%; Irish — 3.8%; Italian — 1.5%.

Universities, Enrollment: College of the Mainland, Texas City — 2,511; Galveston College, Galveston — 1,555; Lamar University, Beaumont — 13,553; Moody College of Texas A & M University, Galveston — 593; San Jacinto College (South campus), Houston — 3,220; University of Houston at Clear Lake City, Houston — 5,592; University of Texas Medical Branch, Galveston — 1,586.

Newspapers, Circulation: *The Beaumont Enterprise* (mS), Beaumont — 65,466; *The Beaumont Journal* (e) — 13,728; *The Daily Citizen* (mS), Clear Lake City — 5,300; *The Galveston Daily News* (mS), Galveston — 27,543; *Port Arthur News* (eS), Port Arthur — 26,213; *Texas City Sun* (eS), Texas City — 12,300. *Houston Chronicle* and *The Houston Post* also circulate in the district.

Commercial Television Stations, Affiliation: KBMT, Beaumont (ABC); KFDM-TV, Beaumont (CBS); KJAC, Beaumont (NBC). District is divided between Beaumont-Port Arthur ADI and Houston ADI.

Military Installations: Nederland Air National Guard Station, Nederland — 14.

Industries:

Gulf Oil Corp.; Port Arthur; oil refining — 3,000. **Union Carbide Corp.;** Texas City; inorganic pigments — 2,350. **Mobil Oil Corp.** (Mobil Chemical Co. Div.); Beaumont; oil refining — 2,200. **Monsanto Co.;** Texas City; chemicals — 2,000. **Amoco Oil Co.** (Amoco Texas Refining); Texas City; oil refining — 1,800.

American National Insurance Co. (HQ); Galveston; life insurance — 1,600. **Bethlehem Steel Corp.** (Beaumont Yard); Beaumont; shipbuilding, repairing — 1,400. **St. Elizabeth Hospital;** Beaumont; hospital — 1,400. **E. I. du Pont de Nemours & Co.;** Beaumont; industrial inorganic chemicals — 1,200. **Lockheed Engineering & Management Service Co.** (HQ); Houston; engineering services — 1,200. **Ford Aerospace & Communications Corp.;** Houston; engineering services — 1,070. **Baptist Hospital of Southeast Texas;** Beaumont; hospital — 1,000. **Union Oil Co.** (Union 76 Div.); Nederland; oil refining — 830. **International Business Machines Corp.;** Houston; computer programming — 800. **George P. Reintjes Co. Inc.;** Groves; industrial process furnaces — 800. **Todd Shipyards Corp.;** Galveston; shipbuilding, repairing — 800.

Texaco Inc.; Port Neches; plastics — 750. **Goodyear Tire & Rubber Co. Inc.** (Beaumont Chemical Plant); Beaumont; auto supplies, synthetic rubber — 680. **Computer Sciences Corp.;** Clear Lake Shores; computer software — 650. **Dresser Industries Inc.** (Ideco Div.); Beaumont; oil field machinery — 625. **B. F. Goodrich Co. Inc.;** Port Neches; synthetic rubber — 600. **The Singer Co.;** Clear Lake Shores; communications equipment — 600. **Texas City Refining Inc.** (HQ); Texas City; oil refining — 543. **Woodfin Shipyard Inc.** (Burton Shipyard); Port Arthur; shipbuilding, repairing — 525. **Neches Butane Products Co. Inc.;** Port Neches; industrial inorganic chemicals — 514. **Helena Laboratories Corp.;** Beaumont; optical instruments — 500. **Grumman Houston Corp.** (HQ); Webster; electronic components — 500.

10th District

Central — Austin

Though the redrawn 10th takes in five counties and most of a sixth, 80 percent of the district's people live either in the state capital of Austin or in surrounding Travis County.

Austin's large state government work force and huge academic community affiliated with the University of Texas make it less conservative than other major cities in the state. Travis County was the only one of the state's large urban counties that did not vote for Ronald Reagan in 1980, and two years later Democrat Mark White won 57 percent of the county's vote in his successful gubernatorial bid. The rest of the 10th has remained loyally Democratic in recent elections for statewide and national office.

The Austin economy has diversified beyond reliance on state government and the university. Electronics and computer companies flocked to the area in the 1970s, luring upwardly mobile, middle-class employees, many of whom are sympathetic to the GOP. The influx of these professionals helped Travis County's population jump by 42 percent in the 1970s, the fastest growth rate among the state's six largest urban counties.

The population boom has also spawned some anti-growth sentiments. In November 1981, Austin residents voted to end the city's financial commitment to a nuclear power generating project plagued by construction delays and cost overruns. Anti-nuclear activists urged energy conservation to trim the city's burgeoning appetite for power.

When a flood swept through the city on Memorial Day 1981, killing 13 and causing millions in property damage, anti-growth forces blamed the destruction on pell-mell development of the area's watershed.

Beyond the Travis County borders, the 10th extends south and west into largely rural Democratic territory. Blanco County has attracted Republican retirees, but the county's small population gives it limited electoral impact. Because of Austin's population growth, the remap moved ten counties either completely or partially within the old 10th into the 14th.

Election Returns

10th District		Democrat		Republican	
1976	President	97,200	(52.9%)	83,817	(45.6%)
	Senate	95,919	(53.8%)	76,611	(43.0%)
	House	134,199	(76.7%)	40,771	(23.3%)

10th District		Democrat		Republican	
1978	Governor	59,104	(55.3%)	46,430	(43.4%)
	Senate	55,274	(52.8%)	47,740	(45.6%)
	House	77,989	(76.4%)	24,042	(23.6%)
1980	President	91,779	(47.1%)	89,926	(46.1%)
	House	111,120	(58.8%)	73,396	(38.8%)
1982	Governor	88,796	(57.3%)	61,279	(39.6%)
	Senate	99,838	(64.9%)	50,547	(32.9%)
	House	121,030	(90.1%)	—	

Demographics

Population: 527,181. **Percent Change from 1970:** 41.0%.

Land Area: 4,206 square miles. **Population per Square Mile:** 125.3.

Counties, 1980 Population: Bastrop — 24,726; Blanco — 4,681; Burnet (Pt.) — 13,970; Caldwell — 23,637; Hays — 40,594; Travis — 419,573.

Cities, 1980 Population: Austin (Pt.) — 345,109; Round Rock (Pt.) — 0; San Marcos — 23,420.

Race and Ancestry: White — 78.7%; Black — 10.4%; American Indian, Eskimo and Aleut — 0.3%; Asian and Pacific Islander — 1.0%. Spanish Origin — 18.5%. English — 11.6%; French — 1.0%; German — 8.4%; Irish — 3.8%; Italian — 0.6%; Polish — 0.5%; Scottish — 0.6%; Swedish — 0.8%.

Universities, Enrollment: Austin Community College, Austin — 12,527; Austin Presbyterian Theological Seminary, Austin — 207; Concordia College, Austin — 360; The Episcopal Theological Seminary of the Southwest, Austin — 76; Houston-Tillotson College, Austin — 692; St. Edward's University, Austin — 2,322; Southwest Texas State University, San Marcos — 15,400; University of Texas at Austin, Austin — 46,148.

Newspapers, Circulation: *Austin American-Statesman* (all day, S) — 124,238; *The Austin Citizen* (e) — 13,614; *San Marcos Daily Record* (eS), San Marcos — 4,744.

Commercial Television Stations, Affiliation: KTBC-TV, Austin (CBS); KTVV, Austin (NBC); KVUE-TV, Austin (ABC). District is divided between Austin ADI and San Antonio ADI.

Military Installations: Bergstrom Air Force Base, Austin — 6,241.

Industries:

International Business Machines Corp. (Entry Systems Div.); Austin; electronic computing equipment, services — 6,500. **Texas Instruments Inc.;** Austin; electronic computing equipment — 3,000. **Tracor Inc.** (HQ); Austin; research and development, navigational equipment, ship repair — 2,000. **Motorola Inc.;** Austin; semiconductors — 1,500. **Seton Hospital Inc.;** Austin; hospital — 1,200.

Capital National Bank; Austin; banking — 944. **Conroy Inc.** (Glastron Boat Div.); Austin; shipbuilding, repairing — 800. **Radian Corp.** (HQ); Austin; scientific research — 675. **Cox Enterprises Inc.** (Austin-American Statesman); Austin; newspaper publishing — 650. **Austin National Bank;** Austin; banking — 609. **Dahlstrom Corp.;** Buda; road construction — 550.

11th District

Central — Waco

Most voters here are Democratic in name but are more loyal to a political philosophy than to a political party. When the Democratic nominee meets local conservative standards, he can carry the 11th. But if the Democrat is tainted with liberalism, the electorate can cross over to the

Republican column.

The areas most prone to flirt with Republicanism are the district's two urbanized counties — McLennan County (Waco) and Bell County (Killeen and Temple). Jimmy Carter carried both counties in 1976, but his margins were unimpressive. Both went for Ronald Reagan in 1980.

Waco, with slightly more than 100,000 people, is sometimes called the "Baptist Rome." It is the home of the largest Baptist-affiliated university in the world, Baylor University. Waco's economy has ridden through recessionary times fairly well because of university-related employment and the city's diversified manufacturing base — products range from plastic bags and tires to candy bars and storage batteries.

Southwest of Waco are rapidly growing Killeen and Temple; during the 1970s the two matured from oversized towns into small cities pushing toward 50,000 in population. The federal government's contribution to the Bell County economy is immense because Fort Hood, the second largest Army base in the country, is located there.

Traditional conservative Democrats hold sway in most of the district's 11 rural counties, where 40 percent of the vote is cast. Though Reagan performed well in the rural areas in 1980, two years later most voters there returned to the fold to support Democratic gubernatorial candidate Mark White.

At the eastern end of the 11th, the fertile Blacklands Prairie soil grows feed grains, cotton, hay and other crops. Livestock raising — beef cattle, sheep and hogs — is a major income producer all across the 11th, especially in the hillier western sections.

The redistricting plan smoothed the 11th District's jagged fringes but made no substantial change in the politics of the area. McLennan County and Bell County account for more than 60 percent of the new district's population.

Election Returns

11th District		Democrat		Republican	
1976	President	83,552	(56.3%)	63,788	(43.0%)
	Senate	83,617	(59.0%)	57,702	(40.7%)
	House	86,254	(56.8%)	65,596	(43.2%)
1978	Governor	48,776	(53.2%)	42,569	(46.4%)
	Senate	48,372	(53.0%)	42,477	(46.6%)
	House	44,218	(50.4%)	43,555	(49.6%)
1980	President	71,042	(44.6%)	84,251	(52.9%)
	House	110,789	(99.2%)	884	(0.8%)
1982	Governor	60,338	(57.1%)	44,825	(42.4%)
	Senate	63,753	(61.3%)	39,611	(38.1%)
	House	83,236	(96.4%)	—	

Demographics

Population: 527,382. **Percent Change from 1970:** 25.3%.

Land Area: 11,474 square miles. **Population per Square Mile:** 46.0.

Counties, 1980 Population: Bell — 157,889; Bosque — 13,401; Brown — 33,057; Burnet (Pt.) — 3,833; Coryell — 56,767; Falls — 17,946; Hamilton — 8,297; Lampasas — 12,005; McLennan — 170,755; Milam — 22,732; Mills — 4,477; San Saba — 6,204; Williamson (Pt.) — 20,019.

Cities, 1980 Population: Austin (Pt.) — 23; Belton — 10,660; Brown-

wood — 19,396; Copperas Cove — 19,469; Fort Hood (CDP) — 31,250; Killeen — 46,296; Temple — 42,483; Waco — 101,261.

Race and Ancestry: White — 79.1%; Black — 14.1%; American Indian, Eskimo and Aleut — 0.3%; Asian and Pacific Islander — 1.1%. Spanish Origin — 9.3%. English — 13.8%; French — 0.8%; German — 8.1%; Irish — 5.2%.

Universities, Enrollment: American Technological University, Killeen — 838; Baylor University, Waco — 10,067; Central Texas College, Killeen — 4,421; Howard Payne University, Brownwood — 1,201; McLennan Community College, Waco — 4,002; Paul Quinn College, Waco — 438; Temple Junior College, Temple — 2,367; Texas State Technical Institute, Waco — 4,236; University of Mary Hardin-Baylor, Belton — 1,034.

Newspapers, Circulation: *Brownwood Bulletin* (eS), Brownwood — 10,702; *Daily Herald* (eS), Killeen — 14,838; *Marlin Daily Democrat* (e), Marlin — 3,286; *Temple Daily Telegram* (mS), Temple — 25,437; *Waco Tribune-Herald* (all day, S), Waco — 49,998.

Commercial Television Stations, Affiliation: KCEN-TV, Temple (NBC, ABC); KWTX-TV, Waco (ABC, CBS). Most of district is located in Waco-Temple ADI. Portions are in Abilene-Sweetwater ADI, Austin ADI and Dallas-Fort Worth ADI.

Military Installations: Fort Hood, Killeen — 49,397.

Industries:

Scott Memorial Hospital; Temple; hospital — 2,600. **General Tire & Rubber Co.;** Waco; tires, inner tubes — 1,460. **Aluminum Co. of America;** Rockdale; aluminum smelting — 1,444. **Veterans Administration;** Waco; veterans' hospital — 1,390. **Hillcrest Baptist Hospital;** Waco; hospital — 1,300.

Veterans Administration; Temple; veterans' hospital — 1,200. **Dart Industries Inc.** (Ralph Wilson Plastics Co.); Temple; plastic products — 1,100. **Owens-Illinois Inc.;** Waco; glass containers — 950. **Mobil Oil Corp.** (Chemical Co. Div.); Temple; plastic bags — 800. **Brown & Root Inc.;** Rockdale; heavy construction — 700. **Texas Plantation Foods Corp.;** Waco; turkey raising, processing — 700.

Atchison, Topeka & Santa Fe Railroad Co.; Temple; railroad operations — 600. **Central Freight Lines Inc.** (HQ); Waco; trucking — 600. **Certain-Teed Products Corp.** (Ideal Millwork Div.); Waco; millwork products — 565. **Marathon Mfg. Co.;** Waco; storage batteries — 560. **Minnesota Mining & Mfg. Co.** (Traffic Control Materials Div.); Brownwood; waterproof paints, varnishes — 530. **Mars Inc.;** Waco; candy — 500.

12th District

Fort Worth; Northwest Tarrant County

Less than half the size of neighboring Dallas and declining in population, Fort Worth projects a blue-collar and Western roughneck image that contrasts with its more sophisticated neighbor.

The city's reputation is not entirely accurate. Cattle marketing and agribusiness are still important in the Fort Worth economy, but since World War II the city has been a major manufacturer of military and aerospace equipment, and electronics is increasingly important. General Dynamics and Bell Helicopter, which lies in the 24th District just beyond the 12th's eastern boundary, are among the area's leading employers. Both firms regularly net huge defense contracts.

Many middle- and upper-income Fort Worth residents have left the city, turning formerly rural territory in surrounding Tarrant County into suburbs. Old residential neighborhoods on the city's Near South Side now are largely black; the Near North Side has a sizable Hispanic community.

The affluent western and southwestern sections of the city and its suburbs give the 12th a Republican vote of some significance. The northeastern Mid-Cities area in the corridor between Fort Worth and Dallas is also a pocket of affluent, GOP-minded voters. The redrawn 12th narrowly favored Ronald Reagan in the 1980 presidential race. But the combined forces of organized labor, liberals, low-income whites and minorities generally lift Democrats to victory here.

Redistricting made the seat even safer for Democrats. The 12th, which needed to add nearly 20,000 residents, picked up blue-collar territory in south Fort Worth that had been part of the 6th District.

Election Returns

12th District		Democrat		Republican	
1976	President	74,856	(53.4%)	63,612	(45.4%)
	Senate	77,806	(58.0%)	54,838	(40.9%)
	House	102,049	(73.0%)	37,138	(26.6%)
1978	Governor	39,096	(53.9%)	33,120	(45.6%)
	Senate	35,293	(52.7%)	31,240	(46.6%)
	House	48,163	(68.0%)	22,702	(32.0%)
1980	President	77,202	(47.9%)	79,254	(49.2%)
	House	104,622	(62.6%)	61,289	(36.7%)
1982	Governor	67,162	(59.0%)	45,977	(40.4%)
	Senate	69,877	(63.4%)	39,429	(35.8%)
	House	78,913	(68.9%)		—

Demographics

Population: 527,074. **Percent Change from 1970:** 5.8%.

Land Area: 463 square miles. **Population per Square Mile:** 1,138.4.

Counties, 1980 Population: Tarrant (Pt.) — 527,074.

Cities, 1980 Population: Arlington (Pt.) — 977; Bedford (Pt.) — 9,933; Benbrook (Pt.) — 0; Euless (Pt.) — 3,518; Forest Hill — 11,684; Fort Worth (Pt.) — 309,249; Haltom City — 29,014; Hurst (Pt.) — 31,355; North Richland Hills — 30,592; Watauga — 10,284; White Settlement — 13,508.

Race and Ancestry: White — 75.9%; Black — 17.3%; American Indian, Eskimo and Aleut — 0.4%; Asian and Pacific Islander — 0.7%. Spanish Origin — 10.4%. English — 12.4%; French — 0.8%; German — 4.2%; Irish — 4.9%; Scottish — 0.5%.

Universities, Enrollment: Southwestern Baptist Theological Seminary, Fort Worth — 3,684; Tarrant County Junior College, Fort Worth — 21,152; Texas Christian University, Forth Worth — 6,283 (school straddles line between 12th and 26th districts); Texas College of Osteopathic Medicine, Fort Worth — 330; Texas Wesleyan College, Fort Worth — 1,667.

Newspapers, Circulation: Fort Worth Star Telegram (all day, S), Fort Worth — 241,246; Mid-Cities Daily News (eS), Hurst — 7,676.

Commercial Television Stations, Affiliation: KTVT, Fort Worth (None); KXAS-TV, Fort Worth (NBC). Entire district is located in Dallas-Forth Worth ADI.

Military Installations: Carswell Air Force Base, Fort Worth — 6,621.

Industries:

General Dynamics Corp. (Fort Worth Div.); Fort Worth; aircraft — 17,000. **Texas American Bankshares Inc.** (HQ); Fort Worth; banking — 2,300. **Harris Methodist Hospital;** Fort Worth; hospital — 2,000. **Gearhart Industries Inc.** (HQ); Fort Worth; oil field equipment — 1,900. **First United Bancorporation;** Fort Worth; bank holding company — 1,540

Miller Brewing Co.; Fort Worth; brewery — 1,500. **Texas Steel Co.;** Fort Worth; steel products — 1,300. **St. Joseph Hospital;** Fort Worth; hospital — 1,170. **Fort Worth & Denver Railway Co.;** Fort Worth; railroad operations — 1,200. **Fruehauf Corp.** (Hobbs Trailer Div.); Fort Worth; truck trailers — 1,200. **All Saints Episcopal Hospital;** Fort Worth; hospital — 1,150. **Tarrant County Hospital District;** Fort Worth; hospital — 1,090. **Arlington Memorial Hospital Foundation;** Arlington; hospital — 1,000.

Lennox Industries Inc.; Fort Worth; gas furnaces, air conditioners — 1,000. **The Fort Worth National Bank;** Fort Worth; banking — 960. **H. J. Justin & Sons Inc.** (Justin Boot Co. - HQ); Fort Worth; boots, shoes — 950. **Harston Gravel Co. Inc.** (HQ); Fort Worth; sand, gravel pit — 930. **First National Bank of Fort Worth;** Fort Worth; banking — 853. **Lone Star Mfg. Co. Inc.** (Frostemp - HQ); Fort Worth; cooling equipment — 805. **A. Brandt Co. Inc.** (Branco Div. - HQ); Fort Worth; upholstered furniture — 800. **Capital Cities Communications;** Fort Worth; newspaper publishing — 800. **Halliburton Co.** (Freight Master Div.); Fort Worth; railroad equipment — 800.

Fort Worth Medical Plaza Inc.; Fort Worth; hospital — 775. **Alcon Laboratories Inc.** (Owen Laboratories - HQ); Fort Worth; pharmaceuticals — 750. **Missouri Pacific Railroad Co.;** Fort Worth; railroad operations — 750. **Volkswagen of America Inc.;** Fort Worth; auto air conditioners — 700. **Stratoflex Inc.** (HQ); Fort Worth; flexible hose — 687. **H. J. Justin & Sons Inc.** (Justin Boot Co.); Fort Worth; boots — 675. **Ben Hogan Co.** (HQ); Fort Worth; golf clubs — 620. **Americana Hotels Corp.;** Fort Worth; hotel — 600. **Champion Parts Rebuilders Inc.;** Fort Worth; auto parts wholesaling — 600. **Coca-Cola Bottling Co. of Fort Worth** (HQ); Fort Worth; soft drink bottling — 600.

Winn-Dixie Texas Inc. (Buddies Super Markets - HQ); Fort Worth; grocery retailing — 600. **Pengo Industries Inc.** (HQ); Fort Worth; oil field equipment — 600. **Mrs. Baird's Bakeries Inc.** (HQ); Fort Worth; bakery products — 550. **Harbison-Fischer Mfg. Co.** (HQ); Fort Worth; oil well pumping equipment — 550. **Western Preferred Corp.** (HQ); Fort Worth; life, accident insurance — 527 **Monning Dry Goods Co.** (HQ); Fort Worth; department store — 518. **Criterion Metals Corp.;** Fort Worth; metal fencing — 500. **James M. Walker Inc.** (Walker Construction Co. - HQ); Fort Worth; construction contracting — 500. **Melody Home Mfg. Co.;** Saginaw; mobile homes — 500. **Williamson-Dickie Mfg. Co.** (HQ); Fort Worth; men's, boy's work clothes — 500.

13th District

The Panhandle — Amarillo, Wichita Falls

The two parties are closely matched in the 13th District; Republicans rule in the Panhandle and Democrats hold sway in the Red River Valley to the south. But the voters are uniformly conservative, and they flocked to Ronald Reagan in 1980. Of the 37 counties in the redrawn 13th District, three-fourths voted for Reagan, many by margins exceeding 2-to-1.

Because of its scant rainfall, most of this region long was used only for cattle grazing. Discovery of underground water supplies in the 1940s sparked cultivation of wheat, cotton and sorghum grains on huge, highly mechanized farms. The agricultural revolution has been so extensive that the underground Ogallala aquifer is being rapidly depleted. Some of the wheat and cattle growers went heavily into debt in the 1970s and have fallen on hard times; the 13th was well represented among the members of the American Agriculture Movement who brought their tractors to Washington in 1979 to protest low farm prices.

Amarillo (Potter and Randall counties) is a city of nearly 150,000 that serves as the focal point of the Panhandle's farm lands. Its factories pack meat, mill flour and handle oil and natural gas drilled locally. Like the rural areas surrounding it, Amarillo is Republican. In 1980, Reagan took 61 percent in Potter County and 74 percent in Randall County.

To the southeast is Wichita Falls (Wichita County), an area with Democratic affections whose votes usually help Democratic candidates compete districtwide. Carter won 53 percent of the Wichita County vote in 1976, but he fell about 2,000 votes short of carrying the old 13th. In 1980, Reagan won 55 percent in Wichita, paving the way for his easy victory in the district.

Wichita Falls' population declined slightly during the 1970s and stood at 94,201 in 1980. The city has a large industrial sector that makes fiberglass products, clothing and mechanical parts. Located north of the city is Sheppard Air Force Base, one of the country's largest Air Force training facilities.

The district's population grew by only 8 percent during the 1970s, so the remap brought the 13th to ideal size by adding just over 21,000 people in four rural counties. The political impact was negligible.

Election Returns

13th District		Democrat		Republican	
1976	President	90,518	(49.8%)	90,173	(49.6%)
	Senate	107,750	(61.6%)	66,358	(38.0%)
	House	106,479	(60.4%)	69,328	(39.3%)
1978	Governor	54,616	(50.0%)	54,268	(49.7%)
	Senate	51,880	(48.7%)	54,244	(51.0%)
	House	79,284	(75.0%)	26,426	(25.0%)
1980	President	68,648	(36.0%)	117,716	(61.7%)
	House	104,703	(56.4%)	80,819	(43.6%)
1982	Governor	77,868	(51.2%)	72,907	(47.9%)
	Senate	82,384	(54.4%)	67,189	(44.4%)
	House	86,376	(63.6%)	47,877	(35.2%)

Demographics

Population: 526,840. **Percent Change from 1970:** 7.7%.

Land Area: 34,619 square miles. **Population per Square Mile:** 15.2.

Counties, 1980 Population: Archer — 7,266; Armstrong — 1,994; Baylor — 4,919; Briscoe — 2,579; Carson — 6,672; Childress — 6,950; Clay — 9,582; Collingsworth — 4,648; Cottle — 2,947; Dallam — 6,531; Dickens — 3,539; Donley — 4,075; Floyd — 9,834; Foard — 2,158; Gray — 26,386; Hall — 5,594; Hansford — 6,209; Hardeman — 6,368; Hartley — 3,987; Hemphill — 5,304; Hutchinson — 26,304.

Kent — 1,145; King — 425; Knox — 5,329; Lipscomb — 3,766; Moore — 16,575; Motley — 1,950; Ochiltree — 9,588; Oldham — 2,283; Potter — 98,637; Randall — 75,062; Roberts — 1,187; Sherman — 3,174; Swisher — 9,723; Wheeler — 7,137; Wichita — 121,082; Wilbarger — 15,931.

Cities, 1980 Population: Amarillo — 149,230; Borger — 15,837; Burkburnett — 10,668; Canyon — 10,724; Dumas — 12,194; Pampa — 21,396; Vernon — 12,695; Wichita Falls — 94,201.

Race and Ancestry: White — 89.3%; Black — 5.1%; American Indian, Eskimo and Aleut — 0.5%; Asian and Pacific Islander — 0.8%. Spanish Origin — 8.9%. Dutch — 0.5%; English — 16.9%; French — 0.8%; German — 6.0%; Irish — 5.8%; Scottish — 0.5%.

Universities, Enrollment: Amarillo College, Amarillo — 5,463; Clarendon College, Clarendon — 646; Frank Phillips College, Borger — 724; Midwestern State University, Wichita Falls — 4,400; Texas State Technical Institute, Amarillo — 1,469; Vernon Regional Junior College, Vernon — 1,368; West Texas State University, Canyon — 6,469.

Newspapers, Circulation: *Amarillo Daily News* (mS), Amarillo — 42,698; *Amarillo Globe-Times* (eS), Amarillo — 29,952; *Borger News-Herald* (eS), Borger — 7,519; *Dalhart Daily Texan* (eS), Dalhart — 2,746; *News* (eS), Pampa — 7,612; *The Vernon Daily Record* (eS), Vernon — 6,010; *Wichita Falls Record-News* (mS), Wichita Falls — 34,216; *Wichita Falls Times* (eS), Wichita Falls — 16,627.

Commercial Television Stations, Affiliation: KAMR-TV, Amarillo (NBC); KAUZ-TV, Wichita Falls (CBS); KFDA-TV, Amarillo (CBS); KFDX-TV, Wichita Falls (NBC); KJTV, Amarillo (None); KVII-TV, Amarillo (ABC). Most of district is located in Amarillo ADI. Portions are in Abilene-Sweetwater ADI, Lubbock ADI and Wichita Falls-Lawton (Okla.) ADI.

Military Installations: Sheppard Air Force Base, Wichita Falls — 6,301.

Industries:

Mason & Hanger-Silas Mason Co.; Amarillo; management services — 2,600. **Iowa Beef Processors Inc.;** Amarillo; meatpacking — 2,000. **Atchison, Topeka & Santa Fe Railway Co.;** Amarillo; railroad operations — 1,500. **Diamond Shamrock Corp.;** Amarillo; oil producing, refining — 1,280. **Phillips Petroleum Co. Inc.;** Borger; oil refining — 1,158.

Swift & Co.; Cactus; meatpacking — 1,100. **PPG Industries Inc.;** Wichita Falls; flat glass — 1,000. **Textron Inc.;** Amarillo; aircraft parts — 1,000. **Wichita Falls State Hospital;** Wichita Falls; mental hospital — 1,000. **Asarco Inc.;** Amarillo; copper refining — 940. **Certain-Teed Corp.;** Wichita Falls; fiberglass — 900. **E. W. Moran Drilling Co. Inc.;** Wichita Falls; oil, gas production — 780. **Ingersoll-Rand Oilfield Products** (HQ); Pampa; oil field machinery — 700.

Fish Engineering & Construction Co.; Borger; oil field services — 600. **Missouri Valley Inc.;** Amarillo; heavy construction — 600. **Levi Strauss & Co.;** Wichita Falls; men's clothing — 550. **Pioneer Corp.** (Energas Co. - HQ); Amarillo; natural gas extraction — 525. **Diamond Shamrock Corp.** (McKee Refinery & Gasoline Plant); Dumas; oil refining — 500. **Kracke-Gober Corp.;** Borger; engineering, surveying services — 500. **The LTV Corp.** (Wilson Mfg. Co.); Wichita Falls; oil drilling rigs — 500. **Phillips Petroleum Co.** (Phillips Chemical Co.); Borger; plastic polymers — 500.

14th District

South Central, Gulf Coast — Victoria

This district is among those significantly altered by the 1982 remap. It lost dependably Democratic Nueces County (Corpus Christi), which cast half the 14th District's vote in the 1980 presidential election.

In return the 14th gained most of Williamson County, an increasingly Republican and fast-growing county north of Austin where Ronald Reagan won 56 percent of the vote in 1980. The 14th also took part or all of several rural conservative counties formerly located in the 10th, 15th, 22nd and 23rd districts.

With Corpus Christi out of the 14th, the district's largest city is Victoria, with a population of just over 50,000 people. Its economy revolves around petrochemicals, oilfield equipment and steel products. Victoria County gave 63 percent of its 1980 presidential vote to Reagan.

North of Victoria, Jackson and Wharton counties are the center of a major southeast Texas rice belt. This part of the district has another, recently publicized claim to fame: LaGrange, the seat of Fayette County, was the site of a brothel made famous in the musical, "The Best Little Whorehouse in Texas."

Minorities make up about one-third of the population in the redrawn 14th. Most of the Hispanics are grouped in the district's southwestern counties and account for 20 percent of the residents. Blacks — 12 percent of the population — are concentrated in the northeastern part of the district. The district also has the highest percentage of persons of German ancestry in the state.

Election Returns

14th District		Democrat		Republican	
1976	President	71,983	(52.5%)	64,145	(46.8%)
	Senate	79,609	(61.2%)	49,767	(38.3%)
	House	78,407	(69.4%)	34,493	(30.5%)
1978	Governor	44,724	(49.9%)	44,499	(49.6%)
	Senate	44,553	(50.2%)	43,642	(49.2%)
	House	65,532	(78.3%)	17,870	(21.3%)
1980	President	67,989	(40.7%)	95,107	(56.9%)
	House	101,262	(65.4%)	53,417	(34.5%)
1982	Governor	63,171	(53.1%)	55,151	(46.4%)
	Senate	69,384	(59.3%)	47,023	(40.2%)
	House	76,851	(60.7%)	48,942	(38.6%)

Demographics

Population: 526,920. **Percent Change from 1970:** 26.0%.

Land Area: 16,679 square miles. **Population per Square Mile:** 31.6.

Counties, 1980 Population: Aransas — 14,260; Austin — 17,726; Bee — 26,030; Brazoria (Pt.) — 15,911; Burleson — 12,313; Calhoun — 19,574; Colorado — 18,823; De Witt — 18,903; Fayette — 18,832; Goliad — 5,193; Gonzales (Pt.) — 14,875; Guadalupe — 46,708; Jackson — 13,352; Lavaca — 19,004; Lee — 10,952; Matagorda — 37,828; Refugio — 9,289; Victoria — 68,807; Waller — 19,798; Washington — 21,998; Wharton — 40,242; Williamson (Pt.) — 56,502.

Cities, 1980 Population: Austin (Pt.) — 364; Bay City — 17,837; Beeville — 14,574; Brenham — 10,966; El Campo — 10,462; New Braunfels (Pt.) — 27; Port Lavaca — 10,911; Round Rock (Pt.) — 11,812; Seguin — 17,854; Taylor — 10,619; Victoria — 50,695.

Race and Ancestry: White — 80.1%; Black — 11.5%; American Indian, Eskimo and Aleut — 0.2%; Asian and Pacific Islander — 0.4%. Spanish Origin — 20.1%. English — 8.2%; French — 0.7%; German — 13.7%; Irish — 3.2%; Polish — 0.8%.

Universities, Enrollment: Bee County College, Beeville — 1,976; Prairie View Agricultural and Mechanical University, Prairie View — 5,528; Southwestern University, Georgetown — 1,029; Texas Lutheran College, Seguin — 1,342; University of Houston at Victoria, Victoria — 803; Victoria College, Victoria — 2,362; Wharton County Junior College, Wharton — 2,056.

Newspapers, Circulation: *Brenham Banner-Press* (e), Brenham — 5,622; *Daily Inquirer* (e), Gonzales — 2,655; *The Daily Tribune* (eS), Bay City — 6,918; *Gazette-Enterprise* (eS), Seguin — 8,125; *The Port Lavaca Wave* (e), Port Lavaca — 3,997; *Taylor Daily Press* (e), Taylor — 4,783; *The Victoria Advocate* (mS), Victoria — 32,138.

Commercial Television Stations, Affiliation: KAVU-TV, Victoria (NBC); KXIX, Victoria (ABC). Most of district is located in Houston ADI. Portions are in Austin ADI, Corpus Christi ADI, San Antonio ADI, Victoria ADI and Waco-Temple ADI.

Military Installations: Chase Field Naval Air Station, Beeville — 2,312.

Nuclear Power Plants: South Texas 1 and 2, Bay City (Westinghouse, Ebasco Services Inc.).

Industries:

Aluminum Co. of America; Point Comfort; aluminum — 1,500. **Motorola Inc.;** Seguin; auto radios — 1,400. **E. I. du Pont de Nemours & Co.;** Victoria; plastic materials — 1,300. **Union Carbide Corp.;** Port Lavaca; industrial organic chemicals — 1,300. **Westinghouse Electric Corp.;** Round Rock; industrial motors — 800.

The Federal Co.; Seguin; poultry dressing — 650. **Skytop Rig Co.;** Victoria; oil field machinery — 650. **Structural Metals Inc.** (Horowitz Salvage - HQ); Seguin; steel — 600. **Holly Farms of Texas Inc.;** Seguin; poultry processing — 500. **Tandy Brands Inc.** (Tex-Tan Welhausen Co. Div.); Yoakum; small leather goods — 500.

15th District

South — McAllen

The remap gave Cameron County (Brownsville) and two other coastal counties to the new 27th District, pushing the 15th District farther north, almost to San Antonio, far from the Rio Grande Valley where the majority of the district's people live. As redrawn, the 15th is still the most heavily Hispanic district in the nation — 71.7 percent.

Although this area is among the poorest in the country — median family income was the 10th lowest in the nation in 1980 — the economic boom that has transformed much of the Southwest is affecting the Rio Grande Valley. Population in the three southernmost counties of the 15th increased by more than 50 percent during the 1970s. McAllen, on the Mexican border, is a major port of entry into Mexico and an important foreign trade center that grew 78 percent during the 1970s to a 1980 population of 66,281. The city and surrounding Hidalgo County together have more than 283,000 residents.

Many of the newcomers to the district have been lured by jobs in small plants that make electronic components, medical equipment and food processing machinery. Tourism is a reliable revenue producer, with visitors drawn by the sun and the chance to sightsee in Mexico.

But the economic underpinning of the valley is agriculture. Freezes are rare, so the almost year-round growing season produces an abundance of citrus fruit, vegetables, cotton and grain. Factories that process, pack and ship the produce are major employers; there is a substantial influx of farm workers during the harvests.

North of the valley, the rolling brush is broken by an occasional stream. There is oil and gas development in this region. Beef cattle and other livestock roam the ranches and feed grains grow well there.

The most populous county outside of Hidalgo is San Patricio County, with 58,013 people. San Patricio, just across the bay from Corpus Christi, is closely linked economically to that city and before the remap was in the same congressional district as Corpus Christi. But to help balance the Hispanic populations in the 15th and 27th districts, the federal judges' map put San Patricio and Corpus Christi into separate districts.

Jimmy Carter's 1980 margin in San Patricio was only 301 votes, and five rural counties in the northern part of the 15th voted for Ronald Reagan. But further south, in such heavily Hispanic rural counties as Duval, Brooks and

Jim Hogg, Carter won huge majorities. This is the area where wealthy Anglo-landlords traditionally have controlled the votes of poor Hispanic farm workers. Hidalgo County is solidly Democratic.

Election Returns

15th District		Democrat		Republican	
1976	President	84,143	(67.0%)	40,776	(32.5%)
	Senate	84,357	(72.4%)	31,366	(26.9%)
	House	89,751	(78.6%)	24,383	(21.4%)
1978	Governor	42,793	(56.9%)	31,028	(41.3%)
	Senate	40,866	(55.8%)	30,983	(42.3%)
	House	51,120	(73.5%)	17,683	(25.4%)
1980	President	79,071	(56.3%)	58,582	(41.7%)
	House	93,049	(70.8%)	38,379	(29.2%)
1982	Governor	71,629	(65.1%)	37,700	(34.3%)
	Senate	77,178	(71.6%)	29,803	(27.7%)
	House	76,544	(95.7%)	—	

Demographics

Population: 527,203. **Percent Change from 1970:** 38.4%.

Land Area: 16,880 square miles. **Population per Square Mile:** 31.2.

Counties, 1980 Population: Atascosa — 25,055; Brooks — 8,428; Duval — 12,517; Frio — 13,785; Gonzales (Pt.) — 2,008; Hidalgo — 283,229; Jim Hogg — 5,168; Jim Wells — 36,498; Karnes — 13,593; La Salle — 5,514; Live Oak — 9,606; McMullen — 789; Nueces (Pt.) — 2,350; San Patricio — 58,013; Starr — 27,266; Wilson — 16,756; Zapata — 6,628.

Cities, 1980 Population: Alice — 20,961; Corpus Christi (Pt.) — 1,967; Edinburg — 24,075; McAllen — 66,281; Mercedes — 11,851; Mission — 22,589; Pharr — 21,381; Portland (Pt.) — 12,023; Weslaco — 19,331.

Race and Ancestry: White — 85.5%; Black — 0.5%; American Indian, Eskimo and Aleut — 0.1%; Asian and Pacific Islander — 0.1%. Spanish Origin — 71.7%. English — 4.1%; German — 3.2%; Irish — 1.6%; Polish — 0.9%.

Universities, Enrollment: Pan American University, Edinburg — 9,715.

Newspapers, Circulation: *Echo-News* (eS), Alice — 7,075; *The Monitor* (eS), McAllen — 21,438; *Review* (eS), Edinburg — 4,100.

Commercial Television Stations, Affiliation: KRGV-TV, Weslaco (ABC). Most of district is divided between Corpus Christi ADI and San Antonio ADI. Portions are in Laredo ADI and McAllen-Brownsville ADI.

Industries:
Waxahachie Garment Co. (Haggar Slacks); Edinburg; men's slacks — 950. **E. I. du Pont de Nemours & Co.;** Ingleside; chlorine, caustic chemicals — 600. **Rome Industries Inc.** (Reynolds Mfg. Co.); McAllen; hydraulic machinery — 600. **Baker Marine Corp.** (HQ); Ingleside; marine oil drilling equipment — 550. **Harkins & Co.** (Cox Cotton Construction Co. Div. - HQ); Alice; oil, gas drilling — 540. **Conoco Inc.** (Conquista Project); Falls City; metal mining — 520.

16th District

West — El Paso

Although the redrawn 16th covers much of far West Texas, 91 percent of its population lives in El Paso and the surrounding county of the same name. El Paso's population increased by nearly one-third during the 1970s, making it the fourth-largest city in Texas. El Paso and Ciudad Juarez — its sister city across the Rio Grande — constitute the largest urban concentration on the Mexican-American border.

The El Paso economy relies heavily on textiles produced with locally grown cotton. Also economically important is the government — the U.S. Army's Fort Bliss is located in El Paso and a number of people work across the New Mexico state line at the White Sands Missile Range.

Hispanics make up 60.2 percent of the population in the redrawn 16th, but they have not generally turned out in large numbers or voted as a bloc for Democrats.

Outside El Paso County, the seven counties that fill out the district are loyally Republican, but consist mostly of desert and prairie grass. Their political impact is minimal. In 1980, for example, Loving County went for Ronald Reagan over Jimmy Carter by more than 2-to-1; the vote was 50-22 and was cast by 79 percent of the county's population. Democrats generally carry the district in statewide races; Democratic gubernatorial candidate Mark White took it with 54 percent of the vote in 1982.

In the only notable boundary change, the remap moved the 16th out of western Odessa (Ector County), a Republican oil-producing center. Ector County voters cast 13 percent of the 16th's 1980 presidential vote, and two-thirds of them chose Reagan.

Hispanics make up 60 percent of the population in the redrawn 16th, making it the fifth largest Hispanic district in the nation. But the Hispanics have not generally turned out in large numbers and voted as a bloc for Democrats.

Election Returns

16th District		Democrat		Republican	
1976	President	52,104	(50.9%)	49,117	(47.9%)
	Senate	64,968	(63.8%)	33,201	(32.6%)
	House	64,087	(60.5%)	41,672	(39.4%)
1978	Governor	36,364	(55.4%)	29,120	(44.4%)
	Senate	33,313	(52.6%)	29,832	(47.1%)
	House	45,630	(70.5%)	19,072	(29.5%)
1980	President	45,471	(40.0%)	61,651	(54.3%)
	House	87,977	(83.8%)	631	(0.6%)
1982	Governor	44,281	(53.9%)	36,903	(44.9%)
	Senate	51,248	(63.2%)	28,698	(35.4%)
	House	44,024	(53.9%)	36,064	(44.2%)

Demographics

Population: 527,401. **Percent Change from 1970:** 29.9%.

Land Area: 16,625 square miles. **Population per Square Mile:** 31.7.

Counties, 1980 Population: Culberson — 3,315; El Paso — 479,899; Hudspeth — 2,728; Jeff Davis — 1,647; Loving — 91; Reeves — 15,801; Ward — 13,976; Winkler — 9,944.

Cities, 1980 Population: El Paso — 425,259; Fort Bliss (CDP) — 12,687; Pecos — 12,855.

Race and Ancestry: White — 60.2%; Black — 3.6%; American Indian, Eskimo and Aleut — 0.3%; Asian and Pacific Islander — 0.9%. Spanish Origin — 60.2%. English — 5.9%; French — 0.5%; German — 3.3%; Irish — 1.9%; Italian — 0.5%.

Universities, Enrollment: El Paso Community College, El Paso — 10,832; University of Texas at El Paso, El Paso — 15,751.

Newspapers, Circulation: *El Paso Herald-Post* (e), El Paso — 34,276; *El Paso Times* (mS), El Paso — 56,414; *Pecos Enterprise* (e), Pecos — 2,324. Foreign language newspaper: *El Continental* (Spanish), El Paso — 3,880.

Commercial Television Stations, Affiliation: KCIK, El Paso (None); KDBC-TV, El Paso (CBS); KEHB-TV, El Paso (None); KTSM-TV, El Paso (NBC); KVIA-TV, El Paso (ABC). District is divided between El Paso ADI and Odessa-Midland ADI.

Military Installations: Fort Bliss, El Paso — 25,298.

Industries:

Farah Mfg. Co. (HQ); El Paso; men's clothing — 4,000. **Providence Memorial Hospital;** El Paso; hospital — 1,260. **Southern Pacific Transport Co.;** El Paso; freight forwarding — 1,200. **Hortex Inc.** (Billy the Kid Div.); El Paso; boys' slacks — 1,100. **Atari Inc.;** El Paso; pre-recorded tape cassettes — 1,000. **El Paso Natural Gas** (HQ); El Paso; natural gas transmission — 1,000. **The Zia Co.** (HQ); El Paso; engineering services — 1,000.

Asarco Inc.; El Paso; copper, lead smelting — 900. **Farah Mfg. Co.;** El Paso; men's clothing — 900. **GTE Lenkurt Inc.;** El Paso; telephone apparatus — 900. **Phelps Dodge Refining Corp.;** El Paso; copper smelting, refining — 850. **Schoenfeld Industries Inc.;** El Paso; men's clothing — 850. **El Paso National Corp.;** El Paso; banking — 750. **Allen-Bradley Co.;** El Paso; general warehousing — 700. **Levi Strauss & Co. Inc.;** El Paso; work clothing — 650. **Continental Air Lines Inc.;** El Paso; commercial airline — 600. **W. R. Weaver Co. Inc.** (Weaver Scopes); El Paso; telescopic instruments — 572. **Mountain Pass Canning Co.** (Old El Paso); Anthony; prepared Mexican-style food — 550. **American Hospital Supply Corp.** (Converter Div.); El Paso; surgical supplies — 500. **Border Steel Rolling Mills Inc.;** El Paso; steel rolling mill — 500. **Maher Mfg. Co.;** El Paso; men's, women's clothing — 500.

17th District

West Central — Abilene

The 17th District stretches across more than 300 miles of rolling West Texas prairie. Its life revolves around cattle, cotton, oil and gas. The 17th was the slowest-growing constituency in Texas during the 1970s — its numbers increased by only 8 percent.

Redistricting added nearly 23,000 people to the 17th to bring it up to ideal size, but the remap did not significantly alter the district's rural, conservative, traditionally Democratic character. While Republicans have made inroads in presidential voting — Ronald Reagan swept more than half the district's counties in 1980 — the GOP has made few dents in Democratic voting habits in state and local races. Between 1966 and 1982, Republicans fielded a congressional candidate in the district just once, in 1978, when the seat was open.

The best Republican territory is the district's largest population center, Taylor County (Abilene), which is home for about one-fifth of the district's residents. Taylor voted for Republican William Clements in both the 1978 and 1982 gubernatorial races and Reagan won 62 percent there in 1980. Abilene's highly successful economy is based on agribusiness, diversified small manufacturing and a major military installation, Dyess Air Force Base.

Other than Taylor County, only six counties in the 17th have more than 20,000 people. Five of them are at the far eastern edge of the district, either in or near the metropolitan sphere of Fort Worth. Population growth there has been brisk. Parker County, for instance, added nearly 11,000 people during the 1970s; Reagan won Parker with 52

percent in 1980. But the bulk of the district's vote is still cast by the normally Democratic voters from small towns, ranches and farms.

In the remap, the 17th gave a tier of its northern counties to the 13th, another slow-growth district that needed to gain population. Along its southern border, the 17th gained territory from the overpopulated 21st and 11th districts.

Election Returns

17th District		Democrat		Republican	
1976	President	99,077	(57.0%)	73,789	(42.5%)
	Senate	104,699	(64.0%)	58,429	(35.7%)
	House	134,298	(97.8%)	2,903	(2.1%)
1978	Governor	55,623	(51.0%)	53,149	(48.7%)
	Senate	55,896	(52.2%)	50,819	(47.5%)
	House	71,038	(66.7%)	35,453	(33.3%)
1980	President	79,143	(46.4%)	87,449	(51.3%)
	House	133,338	(95.0%)	6,939	(4.9%)
1982	Governor	78,253	(56.0%)	61,000	(43.6%)
	Senate	85,605	(61.8%)	52,223	(37.7%)
	House	109,359	(97.1%)	—	

Demographics

Population: 526,913. **Percent Change from 1970:** 9.3%.

Land Area: 31,592 square miles. **Population per Square Mile:** 16.7.

Counties, 1980 Population: Borden — 859; Callahan — 10,992; Coke — 3,196; Coleman — 10,439; Comanche — 12,617; Concho — 2,915; Cooke (Pt.) — 20,791; Crosby — 8,859; Eastland — 19,480; Erath — 22,560; Fisher — 5,891; Garza — 5,336; Glasscock — 1,304; Haskell — 7,725; Howard — 33,142; Jack — 7,408; Jones — 17,268; Lynn — 8,605; Martin — 4,684; Mitchell — 9,088; Montague — 17,410; Nolan — 17,359; Palo Pinto — 24,062; Parker — 44,609; Runnels — 11,872; Scurry — 18,192; Shackelford — 3,915; Somervell — 4,154; Stephens — 9,926; Sterling — 1,206; Stonewall — 2,406; Taylor — 110,932; Throckmorton — 2,053; Wise — 26,575; Young — 19,083.

Cities, 1980 Population: Abilene — 98,315; Big Spring — 24,804; Gainesville — 14,081; Mineral Wells — 14,468; Snyder — 12,705; Stephenville — 11,881; Sweetwater — 12,242; Weatherford — 12,049.

Race and Ancestry: White — 89.4%; Black — 3.2%; American Indian, Eskimo and Aleut — 0.3%; Asian and Pacific Islander — 0.5%. Spanish Origin — 11.2%. Dutch — 0.5%; English — 17.9%; French — 0.7%; German — 5.2%; Irish — 6.3%.

Universities, Enrollment: Abilene Christian University, Abilene — 4,560; Cisco Junior College, Cisco — 1,462; Cooke County College, Gainesville — 1,526; Hardin-Simmons University, Abilene — 1,969; Howard College at Big Spring, Big Spring — 1,091; McMurry College, Abilene — 1,494; Ranger Junior College, Ranger — 717; Tarleton State University, Stephenville — 3,592; Texas State Technical Institute, Sweetwater — 377; Weatherford College, Weatherford — 1,610; Western Texas College, Snyder — 1,164.

Newspapers, Circulation: *Abilene Reporter-News* (all day, S), Abilene — 54,942; *Big Spring Herald* (eS), Big Spring — 10,270; *Gainesville Daily Register* (e), Gainesville — 8,254; *Index* (eS), Mineral Wells — 5,300; *News* (eS), Snyder — 5,251; *Stephenville Empire-Tribune* (eS), Stephenville — 4,784; *Sweetwater Reporter* (eS), Sweetwater — 4,790; *The Weatherford Democrat* (eS), Weatherford — 5,571.

Commercial Television Stations, Affiliation: KRBC-TV, Abilene (NBC); KTAB-TV, Abilene (CBS); KTXS-TV, Sweetwater (ABC); KWAB, Big Spring (ABC). Most of district is divided among Abilene-

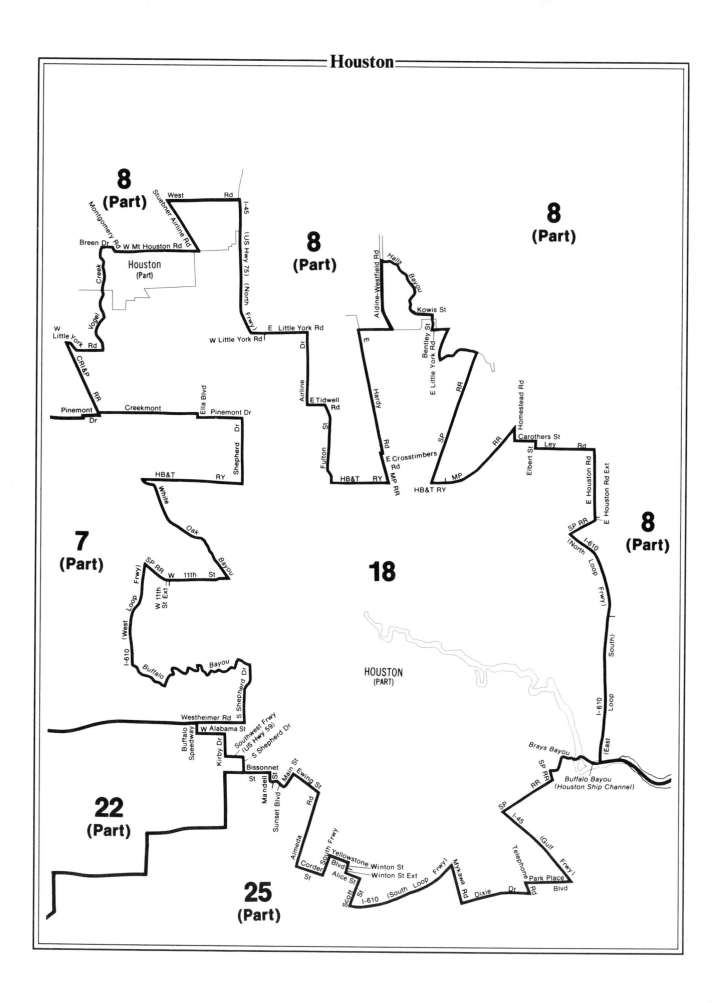

Sweetwater ADI and Dallas-Fort Worth ADI. Portions are in Lubbock ADI, Odessa-Midland ADI, San Angelo ADI and Wichita Falls-Lawton (Okla.) ADI.

Military Installations: Dyess Air Force Base, Abilene — 5,557.

Nuclear Power Plants: Comanche Peak 1 and 2, Glen Rose (Westinghouse, Brown & Root).

Industries:

Brown & Root Inc.; Glen Rose; nuclear power plant construction — 4,013. **Hendrick Medical Center;** Abilene; hospital — 1,300. **Walter Kidde & Co. Inc.** (Weber Aircraft Div.); Gainesville; aircraft parts — 1,200. **Armco Inc.** (National Supply Co. Div.); Gainesville; oil field machinery — 1,000. **Harsco Corp.;** Mineral Wells; structural clay, plastic products — 800. **Mepco/Electra Inc.;** Mineral Wells; electronic equipment — 600.

18th District

Central Houston

The 18th contains the office towers of downtown Houston, a magnet for corporate executives and the focal point of this booming city's infamously long rush hours. The district, 98 percent of which lies within the city's boundaries, also serves as a reminder that Houston has suffered some growing pains in its drive to become a world-class cosmopolitan city.

As Houston's population climbed by nearly one-third between 1970 and 1980, the 18th lost more than 39,000 residents. Many of the whites left for the suburbs of surrounding Harris County, leaving behind a downtown area plagued by tensions arising from the police department's reputation for rough treatment of minorities.

In redistricting, the 18th caught up with some of those who left it in the 1970s, adding nearly 100,000 people, most of whom live in black and Hispanic areas not too far outside the district's former boundaries. The 18th is the only Texas district in which whites do not make up a majority of the total population. It is 41 percent white and, with nearly half of Houston's black community, 41 percent black. Hispanics account for 31 percent of the population.

Residents of the 18th span the economic spectrum. To the northwest, River Oaks, partially contained within the district, is home to some of the 18th's most affluent and most conservative constituents. The Heights area is predominantly middle income and blue collar. There is a large Hispanic community in the Denver Harbor area and a growing Asian population along the fringes of central Houston.

Although blacks, whites and Hispanics have about the same number of people in the 18th, the district has sent a black Democrat to Congress since it was created in 1971. The 18th is the most staunchly Democratic district in the state; George McGovern in 1972 and Jimmy Carter in 1976 won a higher percentage here than in any other Texas district.

Election Returns

18th District		Democrat		Republican	
1976	President	91,624	(70.8%)	36,665	(28.3%)
	Senate	87,106	(73.4%)	29,989	(25.3%)
	House	97,912	(77.8%)	27,468	(21.8%)

18th District		Democrat		Republican	
1978	Governor	44,544	(71.5%)	17,019	(27.3%)
	Senate	41,250	(70.1%)	16,756	(28.5%)
	House	43,766	(87.2%)	5,236	(10.4%)
1980	President	79,143	(68.8%)	31,836	(27.7%)
	House	84,690	(75.3%)	25,790	(22.9%)
1982	Governor	62,508	(79.7%)	15,127	(19.3%)
	Senate	64,560	(82.5%)	12,930	(16.5%)
	House	68,014	(82.6%)	12,104	(14.7%)

Demographics

Population: 527,393. **Percent Change from 1970:** -5.9%.

Land Area: 113 square miles. **Population per Square Mile:** 4,667.2.

Counties, 1980 Population: Harris (Pt.) — 527,393.

Cities, 1980 Population: Houston (Pt.) — 517,010.

Race and Ancestry: White — 41.0%; Black — 40.8%; American Indian, Eskimo and Aleut — 0.2%; Asian and Pacific Islander — 1.4%. Spanish Origin — 31.2%. English — 4.7%; French — 0.8%; German — 2.2%; Irish — 1.8%; Italian — 0.6%; Polish — 0.7%.

Universities, Enrollment: Blinn College, Brenham — 2,502; Gulf-Coast Bible College, Houston — 337; Houston Community College, Houston — 24,431; South Texas College of Law, Houston — 1,248; Texas Southern University, Houston — 8,528; University of Houston (main campus), Houston — 30,692; University of Houston (downtown college), Houston — 4,610; University of St. Thomas, Houston — 1,824.

Newspapers, Circulation: *Houston Chronicle* (all day, S), Houston — 352,475; *The Houston Post* also circulates in the district.

Commercial Television Stations, Affiliation: KHOU-TV, Houston (CBS). Entire district is located in Houston ADI. *(For other Houston stations, see 7th and 22nd districts.)*

Industries:

First City Bank of Texas; Houston; banking — 8,900. **Gulf Oil Corp.** (Operations Headquarters); Houston; administrative offices — 5,500. **Brown & Root Inc.** (Market Operators Div. - HQ); Houston; construction contracting — 5,000. **Exxon Corp.;** Houston; oil, gas production — 4,000. **Southern Pacific Transportation Co.;** Houston; railroad operations — 3,500.

First City Bancorp of Texas Inc.; Houston; banking — 3,000. **Shell Oil Co.** (Shell Chemical Co. Div. - HQ); Houston; oil production, refining — 3,000. **Dresser Industries Inc.;** Houston; oil field equipment — 2,800. **Reed Tool Co.** (HQ); Houston; oil field equipment — 2,500. **St. Joseph's Hospital;** Houston; hospital — 2,500. **Tenneco Inc.** (HQ); Houston; oil production, refining — 2,500. **Mid Valley Inc.;** Houston; general contracting — 2,350. **Hughes Tool Co.** (HQ); Houston; oil field tools — 2,162. **American General Insurance Co.** (HQ); Houston; life, casualty insurance — 2,000.

Combustion Engineering Inc. (Gray Tool Co. Div.); Houston; oil field equipment — 2,000. **Schlumberger Technology Corp.** (HQ); Houston; oil well services — 2,000. **Stewart & Stevenson Service;** Houston; generators — 2,000. **Houston Chronicle Publishing Co. Inc.** (HQ); Houston; newspaper publishing — 1,980. **Allied Maintenance Corp. of Texas;** Houston; janitorial services — 1,800. **American Building Maintenance Co.;** Houston; janitorial services — 1,800. **Gulf Oil Corp.;** Houston; oil refining — 1,800. **Texas Eastern Corp.** (HQ); Houston; natural gas transmission — 1,800. **P A International;** Houston; oil field construction — 1,700. **Texaco Inc.;** Houston; oil, gas production — 1,700.

Texas Commerce Bancshares Inc. (HQ); Houston; banking — 1,700. **Baker International Corp.;** Houston; oil tools — 1,500. **Reed Rock Bit Co.** (HQ); Houston; oil drill rock bits — 1,500. **Aramco Services Co.;** Houston; administrative offices — 1,450. **ARA Services** (Environmental Services); Houston; janitorial services — 1,200. **Digicon Inc.** (HQ); Houston; oil, gas exploring — 1,160. **Coulter Scimed Inc.;** Houston; laboratory, hospital equipment wholesaling — 1,100. **Pritchard Service Inc.;** Houston; janitorial services — 1,100.

Zapata Haynie Corp. Houston; fish oil meal — 1,100. **Lykes Bros. Steamship Co. Inc.** (West Guif Div.); Houston; passenger ships — 1,070.

Arthur Andersen & Co.; Houston; accounting services — 1,050. **Bowen Tools Inc.** (HQ); Houston; oil well tools — 1,000. **Burt Mfg.**; Houston; heating, cooling equipment wholesaling — 1,000. **General Foods Corp.**; Houston; coffee, rice — 1,000. **Grocers Supply Co. Inc.** (HQ); Houston; grocery wholesaling — 1,000. **Joy Mfg. Co.** (Baash-Ross Div.); Houston; oil well equipment — 1,000. **United Energy Resources Inc.** (HQ); Houston; natural gas transmission — 1,000. **Pennzoil Co.** (HQ); Houston; oil refining — 900. **Sakowitz Inc.** (HQ); Houston; department stores — 900. **Hydril Co.** Houston; oil field equipment — 891.

Hyatt Corp. (Hyatt Regency Houston Hotel); Houston; hotel — 850. **Vinson & Elkins** (HQ); Houston; law firm — 850. **Wilson Industries Inc.** (Engineering & Mfg. Div. - HQ); Houston; oil field equipment — 825. **Camco Inc.** (HQ); Houston; oil field equipment — 800. **Houston Oil & Minerals Corp.** (HQ); Houston; oil, gas producing — 800. **Southwest Fab Weld Co.**; Houston; piping — 800. **Zapata Off-Shore Co.**; Houston; oil well drilling — 800. **American General Life Insurance Co.** (HQ); Houston; life insurance — 740. **Nabisco Inc.**; Houston; cookies, crackers — 730. **Port Houston Terminal Inc.**; Houston; marine cargo terminal — 714.

W. S. Bellows Construction Corp.; Houston; general contracting — 700. **Houston National Bank**; Houston; banking — 700. **Fulbright & Jaworski** (HQ); Houston; law firm — 650. **Key International Drilling Co. Ltd.**; Houston; oil, gas drilling — 650. **NL Industries Inc.** (Atlas Bradford Div.); Houston; oil field equipment — 650. **Williams Bros. Construction Co.**; Houston; highway, heavy construction — 650. **Port Terminal Railroad Assn.**; Houston; railroad operations — 620. **Gordon Jewelry Corp.** (Buying and Wholesaling Div. - HQ); Houston; jewelry stores — 600. **Hartney Construction Inc.**; Houston; bricklaying — 600. **Mosher Steel Co.** (HQ); Houston; structural steel — 600.

Cliffs Drilling Co. Inc.; Houston; oil, gas drilling — 580. **Baker & Botts** (HQ); Houston; law firm — 560. **BJ-Hughes Inc.**; Houston; oil field equipment — 550. **Coca-Cola Co. Foods Div.** (Fisher-Spiegel Div.); Houston; coffee wholesaling — 550. **Lomas & Nettleton Co.**; Houston; mortgage banking — 550. **Sunbelt Hotels Inc.** (Ramada North Hotel); Houston; hotel — 520. **Prudential Building Maintenance Corp.**; Houston; janitorial services — 504. **Riviana International Inc.**; Houston; canned foods — 502. **Allied Industries Inc.**; Houston; metal fabrication — 500. **Charter International Oil Co.**; Houston; oil refining — 500.

Daylesteel Co. Inc.; Houston; structural steel — 500. **First International Bank in Houston**; Houston; banking — 500. **Fisk Electric Co.** (HQ); Houston; electrical contracting — 500. **Getty Oil Co.**; Houston; oil exploring — 500. **Manhattan Construction Co.**; Houston; construction — 500. **S & B Industries Inc.** (HQ); Houston; construction — 500. **Standco Industries Inc.** (Bolt and Oilfield Products Div.); Houston; bolts, fasteners — 500. **Tenneco Oil Co.** (United States Producing Div. - HQ); Houston; oil, gas producing — 500. **Texas Electrical Steel Cast Co.**; Houston; steel foundry — 500. **Wyatt Industries Inc.** (HQ); Houston; steel plate — 500.

19th District

Northwest — Lubbock, Odessa

Although it has been in Democratic hands at the congressional level since its creation half a century ago, the 19th has shown pronounced Republican tendencies in state and national politics. The remap deprived it of Midland County, where Ronald Reagan won 77 percent in 1980, but the redrawn 19th takes in all of heavily Republican Ector County (Odessa). Former GOP Gov. William Clements won a majority here in his unsuccessful bid for a second term in 1982.

Odessa, with more than 90,000 residents, refines petroleum and provides equipment and supplies to surround-

ing oil fields. It has a reputation as the blue-collar stronghold of the Midland-Odessa population center, but it is firmly Republican. Clements took 57 percent there in 1982, and Reagan in 1980 won more than 70 percent of the Ector County vote. The county's population is about one-fifth of the district's total.

More than 100 miles north of Odessa is the district's other major urbanized area, Lubbock County. Like Ector, Lubbock nearly always falls in the Republican column. Irrigation has enabled the agricultural region around Lubbock to replace East Texas as the state's predominant cotton-growing area. Lubbock, a city of 174,000 residents, calls itself the world's largest cottonseed processing center. Texas Tech University and Reese Air Force Base are important employers. Lubbock County has 40 percent of the redrawn district's population.

Republicans have also made inroads in the Democratic farming and ranching counties. Jimmy Carter carried most of them in 1976, but four years later Reagan swept them all, taking most by a 2-to-1 margin or better.

Besides giving Midland County to the 21st and incorporating into the 19th territory the part of Ector County formerly in the 16th, the remap placed all of Dawson County in the 19th and gave Martin County to the 17th.

Election Returns

19th District		Democrat		Republican	
1976	President	67,123	(43.7%)	85,190	(55.5%)
	Senate	82,831	(56.7%)	61,975	(42.4%)
	House	81,635	(54.1%)	69,353	(45.9%)
1978	Governor	41,223	(43.4%)	52,553	(55.4%)
	Senate	39,918	(43.9%)	49,888	(54.8%)
	House	57,243	(60.4%)	37,457	(39.6%)
1980	President	46,373	(29.1%)	108,936	(68.3%)
	House	124,608	(92.8%)	—	
1982	Governor	52,408	(46.2%)	60,067	(53.0%)
	Senate	55,933	(50.4%)	54,086	(48.8%)
	House	89,702	(81.6%)	19,062	(17.3%)

Demographics

Population: 527,805. **Percent Change from 1970:** 15.2%.

Land Area: 15,205 square miles. **Population per Square Mile:** 34.7.

Counties, 1980 Population: Andrews — 13,323; Bailey — 8,168; Castro — 10,556; Cochran — 4,825; Dawson — 16,184; Deaf Smith — 21,165; Ector — 115,374; Gaines — 13,150; Hale — 37,592; Hockley — 23,230; Lamb — 18,669; Lubbock — 211,651; Parmer — 11,038; Terry — 14,581; Yoakum — 8,299.

Cities, 1980 Population: Andrews — 11,061; Brownfield — 10,387; Hereford — 15,853; Lamesa — 11,790; Levelland — 13,809; Lubbock — 173,979; Odessa — 90,027; Plainview — 22,187.

Race and Ancestry: White — 82.0%; Black — 5.4%; American Indian, Eskimo and Aleut — 0.3%; Asian and Pacific Islander — 0.5%. Spanish Origin — 25.0%. English — 14.8%; French — 0.6%; German — 4.5%; Irish — 4.5%.

Universities, Enrollment: Lubbock Christian College, Lubbock — 1,238; Odessa College, Odessa — 3,893; South Plains College, Levelland — 2,843; Texas Tech University, Lubbock — 23,043; University of Texas of the Permian Basin, Odessa — 1,580; Wayland Baptist University, Plainview — 1,406.

Newspapers, Circulation: *Hereford Brand* (eS), Hereford — 3,145;

Lubbock Avalanche-Journal (meS), Lubbock — 71,225; *The Odessa American* (eS), Odessa — 36,641; *Plainview Daily Herald* (eS), Plainview — 9,765.

Commercial Television Stations, Affiliation: KAMC, Lubbock (ABC); KCBD-TV, Lubbock (NBC); KJAA, Lubbock (None); KLBK-TV, Lubbock (CBS); KOSA-TV, Odessa (CBS); KTPX, Odessa (ABC). Most of district is located in Lubbock ADI. Portions are in Amarillo ADI and Odessa-Midland ADI.

Military Installations: Reese Air Force Base, Lubbock — 2,954.

Industries:

Texas Instruments Inc.; Lubbock; semiconductors — 1,800. **Methodist Hospital;** Lubbock; hospital — 1,700. **Medical Center Hospital;** Odessa; hospital — 1,030. **MBPXL Corp.;** Plainview; meatpacking — 950. **Phillips Petroleum Co. Inc.;** Odessa; oil exploration brokers — 800. **American Cotton Growers Corp.;** Littlefield; denim textiles — 650. **Amoco Products Co.;** Levelland; oil production — 500. **Meister Industries Inc.** (Longhorn Custom Coating); Odessa; plastic coating — 500.

20th District

Central San Antonio

The new 20th District is firmly anchored in the heart of San Antonio. The city's population exceeds 785,000, making it the third-largest city in Texas and the 10th-largest in the country. It casts 95 percent of the vote in the 20th District.

The 20th is 61.7 percent Hispanic, a percentage exceeded in Texas only by the 15th district south of San Antonio. In 1981 San Antonio became the first major Texas city to elect a Mexican-American mayor, choosing Democrat Henry Cisneros.

Although San Antonio was founded in the early 18th century by the Spanish and has a Hispanic majority, its economy has been controlled by Anglos since its early days as a cattle center. Today federal payrolls are the key economic component. There are seven major military installations in or near San Antonio, including five Air Force bases.

The 20th lost 9 percent of its population during the 1970s, so redistricting extended the perimeter of this circle-shaped district to bring it up to ideal size. Roping in northwestern San Antonio all the way to Loop 410, a major route circling the city, the Legislature added to the 20th a mix of upper middle-class professionals and academics associated with the University of Texas at San Antonio, located in the 21st District.

The district's politics remain solidly Democratic. Residents of the redrawn 20th have given Democratic candidates for statewide and national office over 60 percent of their vote in most recent elections.

Election Returns

20th District		Democrat		Republican	
1976	President	84,087	(67.1%)	39,739	(31.7%)
	Senate	84,808	(71.3%)	31,833	(26.8%)
	House	100,457	(94.4%)	5,508	(5.2%)
1978	Governor	52,848	(64.0%)	27,894	(33.8%)
	Senate	50,347	(64.8%)	25,645	(33.0%)
	House	61,690	(90.4%)	6,358	(9.3%)

20th District		Democrat		Republican	
1980	President	82,513	(63.5%)	43,427	(33.4%)
	House	91,572	(73.2%)	32,409	(25.9%)
1982	Governor	54,516	(69.0%)	23,935	(30.3%)
	Senate	58,233	(75.4%)	18,300	(23.7%)
	House	68,544	(91.5%)	—	

Demographics

Population: 526,350. **Percent Change from 1970:** -5.8%.

Land Area: 119 square miles. **Population per Square Mile:** 4,423.1.

Counties, 1980 Population: Bexar (Pt.) — 526,350.

Cities, 1980 Population: Lackland AFB (CDP) — 14,459; San Antonio (Pt.) — 502,040.

Race and Ancestry: White — 75.5%; Black — 8.8%; American Indian, Eskimo and Aleut — 0.2%; Asian and Pacific Islander — 0.6%. Spanish Origin — 61.7%. English — 3.9%; French — 0.5%; German — 4.0%; Irish — 1.6%; Polish — 0.6%.

Universities, Enrollment: Incarnate Word College, San Antonio — 1,573; Oblate College of the Southwest, San Antonio — 92; Our Lady of the Lake University of San Antonio, San Antonio — 1,768; St. Mary's University, San Antonio — 3,324; St. Philip's College, San Antonio — 7,071; San Antonio College, San Antonio — 21,038; Trinity University, San Antonio — 3,255.

Newspapers, Circulation: *San Antonio Express* (mS), San Antonio — 81,121; *San Antonio Light* (eS), San Antonio — 122,158; *San Antonio News* (e), San Antonio — 75,960.

Commercial Television Stations, Affiliation: KMOL-TV, San Antonio (NBC); KSAT-TV, San Antonio (ABC); KWEX-TV, San Antonio (None, Spanish). Entire district is located in San Antonio ADI.

Military Installations: Fort Sam Houston, San Antonio — 15,624; Kelly Air Force Base, San Antonio — 22,474; Lackland Air Force Base, San Antonio — 9,196.

Industries:

Baptist Memorial Hospital Inc.; San Antonio; hospital — 2,200. **Southwest Research Institute** (HQ); San Antonio; scientific research — 1,990. **Finesilver Mfg. Co.** (HQ); San Antonio; men's, boys' work clothes — 1,500. **Levi Strauss & Co.;** San Antonio; women's clothing — 1,250. **Levi Strauss & Co.;** San Antonio; boys' jeans — 1,200.

Frost National Bank; San Antonio; banking — 1,150. **National Bancshares Corp. of Texas;** San Antonio; bank holding company — 1,020. **Santone Industries Inc.** (HQ); San Antonio; men's suits — 1,000. **Allied Stores of Texas Inc.** (Joskes - HQ); San Antonio; department stores — 975. **The Express-News Corp.;** San Antonio; newspaper publishing — 815. **Coca-Cola Bottling Co. of San Antonio;** San Antonio; soft drink bottling — 745. **Pearl Brewing Co.** (HQ); San Antonio; brewery — 650. **Chromalloy-American Corp.** (Chromalloy Metal Techtronics); San Antonio; industrial coating — 600. **The Hearst Corp.;** San Antonio; newspaper publishing — 600. **The Roegelein Co.** (San Antonio Cold Storage Co. - HQ); San Antonio; meatpacking — 600. **Alamo Iron Works** (HQ); San Antonio; industrial machinery — 550. **Pritchard Services Inc.;** San Antonio; janitorial services — 550. **Valero Energy Corp.** (HQ); San Antonio; natural gas transmission — 550. **Marriott Corp;** San Antonio; hotel — 500.

21st District

San Antonio Suburbs, San Angelo, Midland

Spanning 26 whole counties and part of another, the 21st extends from the suburbs of San Antonio in Bexar County 500 miles west across Texas ranch land to the Mexican border.

=San Antonio=

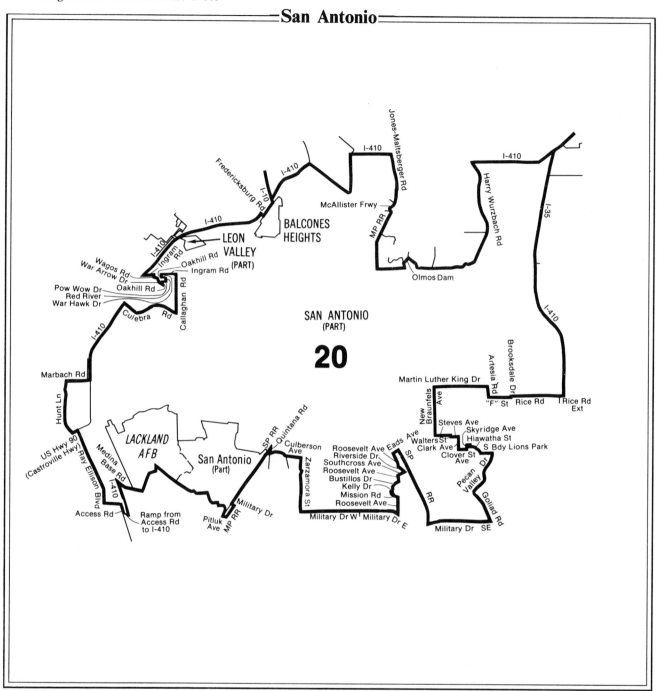

A 72-percent population growth rate in the Bexar County portion of the 21st was the major factor that made the old 21st the fourth fastest-growing district in Texas during the 1970s. In the 1976 and 1980 presidential contests and in the 1978 gubernatorial election, GOP candidates carried all but two of the 26 counties entirely in the redrawn 21st.

More than a quarter of the vote is cast in Bexar County, much of that in a predominantly white-collar portion of northern San Antonio that is the 21st's largest population center. Under the remap, the 21st District traded many faithful Republican voters in the San Antonio suburbs of northern Bexar County for another GOP bas-

tion, Midland County, which gave Ronald Reagan more than three-fourths of its 1980 presidential vote.

Midland votes solidly Republican because it is the white-collar administrative center for the vast oil fields of the Permian Basin in west Texas. Scores of oil companies maintain offices in this city of about 70,000.

Slightly larger and somewhat less Republican than Midland is San Angelo (Tom Green County), also in the northern part of the 21st. That city bills itself "the sheep and wool capital" of the nation and is a center for sheep raising and wool processing and shipping. Reagan took 61 percent of the Tom Green vote in 1980.

There are few other population centers in the sprawling district; the dry range-land of the rural counties is best suited to grazing and oil drilling. Many ranchers receive royalties for oil drilled on their lands.

Besides the boundary changes in Bexar and Midland, the 21st gave five northern rural counties to the underpopulated 17th and took in Presidio County on its western edge and McCulloch County in its northeast corner. Both Presidio and McCulloch have consistently voted Democratic, but together they have fewer than 14,000 people.

The district's Hispanic population — 22.2 percent — is Democratic, but the Hispanic turnout is low and has little impact on the congressional outcome.

Election Returns

21st District		Democrat		Republican	
1976	President	74,912	(39.2%)	114,212	(59.7%)
	Senate	93,270	(50.7%)	88,274	(48.0%)
	House	127,202	(68.5%)	55,225	(29.7%)
1978	Governor	43,444	(34.7%)	81,362	(64.9%)
	Senate	48,226	(38.4%)	76,792	(61.1%)
	House	47,909	(38.1%)	77,785	(61.9%)
1980	President	63,744	(27.4%)	161,863	(69.6%)
	House	60,694	(28.7%)	147,424	(69.8%)
1982	Governor	52,969	(37.2%)	88,302	(62.1%)
	Senate	62,420	(44.6%)	76,679	(54.7%)
	House	35,112	(24.6%)	106,515	(74.5%)

Demographics

Population: 527,044. **Percent Change from 1970:** 31.9%.

Land Area: 44,786 square miles. **Population per Square Mile:** 11.8.

Counties, 1980 Population: Bandera — 7,084; Bexar (Pt.) — 137,492; Brewster — 7,573; Comal — 36,446; Crane — 4,600; Crockett — 4,608; Edwards — 2,033; Gillespie — 13,532; Irion — 1,386; Kendall — 10,635; Kerr — 28,780; Kimble — 4,063; Llano — 10,144; Mason — 3,683; McCulloch — 8,735; Menard — 2,346; Midland — 82,636; Pecos — 14,618; Presidio — 5,188; Reagan — 4,135; Real — 2,469; Schleicher — 2,820; Sutton — 5,130; Terrell — 1,595; Tom Green — 84,784; Upton — 4,619; Val Verde — 35,910.

Cities, 1980 Population: Del Rio — 30,034; Kerrville — 15,276; Midland — 70,525; New Braunfels (Pt.) — 22,375; San Angelo — 73,240; San Antonio (Pt.) — 101,289.

Race and Ancestry: White — 88.5%; Black — 2.9%; American Indian, Eskimo and Aleut — 0.2%; Asian and Pacific Islander — 0.6%. Spanish Origin — 22.2%. English — 12.2%; French — 0.7%; German — 9.9%; Irish — 4.2%; Italian — 0.5%; Scottish — 0.6%.

Universities, Enrollment: Angelo State University, San Angelo — 5,705; Midland College, Midland — 2,759; Schreiner College, Kerrville — 358; Sul Ross State University, Alpine — 2,143; University of Texas at San Antonio, San Antonio — 9,831.

Newspapers, Circulation: *Kerrville Daily Times* (eS), Kerrville — 6,503; *Midland Reporter-Telegram* (eS), Midland — 21,934; *New Braunfels Herald-Zeitung* (eS), New Braunfels — 10,109; *News-Herald* (eS), Del Rio — 6,950; *Standard* (mS), San Angelo — 36,692; *Times* (e), San Angelo — 7,328. *San Antonio Express*, *San Antonio Light* and *San Antonio News* also circulate in the district.

Commercial Television Stations, Affiliation: KCTV, San Angelo (CBS); KMID-TV, Midland (NBC). District is divided among Abilene-Sweetwater ADI, Austin ADI, Odessa-Midland ADI, San Angelo ADI and San Antonio ADI.

Military Installations: Goodfellow Air Force Base, San Angelo — 1,473; Laughlin Air Force, Del Rio — 2,959.

Industries:

Ethicon Inc.; San Angelo; surgical supplies — 1,700. **West Point-Pepperell Inc.** (Mission Valley Mills); New Braunfels; woven fabrics — 1,400. **Fairchild Swearingen Corp.;** San Antonio; aircraft — 1,350. **The Friedrich Co.** (HQ); San Antonio; refrigeration — 1,000. **The First National Bank;** Midland; banking — 700. **C. B. L. & Associates Inc.** (Plaza Del Sol); Del Rio; shopping center operators — 600. **Tesoro Petroleum Corp.** (HQ); San Antonio; oil, gas production — 600. **Salant Corp.** (Texas Apparel Co.); Del Rio; men's clothing — 510. **Mooney Aircraft Corp.;** Kerrville; aircraft — 500.

22nd District

Southwest Houston; Part of Brazoria County

The remap took advantage of rapid growth in the 22nd to give the Republican incumbent a much more reliable district. Population in the territory increased 52 percent during the 1970s, making it the second fastest-growing district in Texas. In redistricting the 22nd shed all its Harris County territory south of the Ship Channel, an area where Republican strength is closely matched by regularly Democratic labor votes and a significant black population.

From the 8th District the 22nd received established residential areas of southwest Houston such as Bellaire, Sharpstown and West University Place, where the people are middle- to high-income Republicans. Also in the redrawn 22nd is Missouri City, which is divided between Harris and Fort Bend counties. It grew phenomenally during the 1970s; population in the Fort Bend part of the city jumped from less than 1,000 in 1970 to nearly 25,000 in 1980.

All of Fort Bend County remains in the 22nd. Although parts of the county are still rural and small-town in character and have little to do with Houston, residential subdivisions with high-priced, single-family homes are becoming the norm. The influx of Houston professionals more than doubled Fort Bend's population in the 1970s; Ronald Reagan won two-thirds of the county's 1980 presidential vote.

Toward the Gulf, the 22nd gave to the 14th the southwestern half of Brazoria County, including the towns of West Columbia and Sweeny. Conservative Democrats are numerous in northeast Brazoria towns such as Alvin, but closer to the coast, Republicans are stronger in Freeport and in Lake Jackson.

Election Returns

22nd District		Democrat		Republican	
1976	President	50,146	(37.3%)	83,150	(61.8%)
	Senate	60,640	(47.0%)	67,205	(52.1%)
	House	31,299	(26.4%)	87,204	(73.6%)
1978	Governor	34,852	(40.6%)	50,608	(59.0%)
	Senate	30,402	(39.2%)	46,606	(60.0%)
	House	25,613	(32.3%)	53,646	(67.7%)
1980	President	48,188	(30.1%)	104,147	(65.1%)
	House	52,190	(33.1%)	103,625	(65.7%)
1982	Governor	47,559	(50.5%)	45,876	(48.7%)
	Senate	51,489	(56.6%)	38,780	(42.6%)
	House	—[1]		x[1]	

[1] *No votes tabulated where candidate was unopposed; x indicates winner.*

Demographics

Population: 526,602. **Percent Change from 1970:** 76.9%.

Land Area: 2,143 square miles. **Population per Square Mile:** 245.7.

Counties, 1980 Population: Brazoria (Pt.) — 153,676; Fort Bend — 130,846; Harris (Pt.) — 242,080.

Cities, 1980 Population: Alvin — 16,515; Angleton — 13,929; Bellaire — 14,950; Freeport — 13,444; Houston (Pt.) — 222,243; Lake Jackson — 19,102; Missouri City (Pt.) — 24,533; Pearland (Pt.) — 12,461; Rosenberg — 17,995; West University Place — 12,010.

Race and Ancestry: White — 81.1%; Black — 9.6%; American Indian, Eskimo and Aleut — 0.2%; Asian and Pacific Islander — 2.9%. Spanish Origin — 13.6%. English — 10.2%; French — 1.5%; German — 6.1%; Irish — 3.5%; Italian — 1.0%; Polish — 0.9%; Scottish — 0.5%.

Universities, Enrollment: Alvin Community College, Alvin — 3,024; Brazosport College, Lake Jackson — 3,660; Houston Baptist University, Houston — 1,996.

Newspapers, Circulation: *The Alvin Sun* (eS), Alvin — 7,102; *The Angleton Times* (mS), Angleton — 4,409; *The Brazosport Facts* (eS), Clute — 18,777; *Herald-Coaster* (eS), Rosenberg — 7,101; *The Houston Post* (mS), Houston — 330,695. *Houston Chronicle* also circulates in the district.

Commercial Television Stations, Affiliation: KHTV, Houston (None); KPRC-TV, Houston (NBC); KRIV-TV, Houston (None); KTRK-TV, Houston (ABC). Entire district is located in Houston ADI. *(For other Houston stations, see 7th and 18th districts.)*

Industries:

The Dow Chemical Co.; Freeport; industrial inorganic chemicals — 7,500. **Lifemark Hospitals Inc.;** Houston; health insurance — 5,300. Texaco Inc. (Texaco International Sales); Bellaire; chemicals wholesaling — 2,500. **Prudential Insurance Co. of America;** Bellaire; life insurance — 2,500. **Mundy Industrial Maintenance Inc.;** Houston; maintenance services — 2,200.

Mobile Producing Texas & New Mexico Inc.; Houston; natural gas drilling — 2,100. **Conoco Inc.** (Chemical Div.); Houston; chemical wholesaling — 2,000. **Gulf Oil Corp.** (Gulf Trading & Transportation); Houston; credit card center — 2,000. **Offshore International;** Houston; oil, gas drilling — 2,000. **ACF Industries Inc.** (W-K-M Valve Div.); Missouri City; oil field valves, pipe fittings — 1,900. **M. W. Kellogg Co.** (HQ); Houston; truck trailers — 1,800. **U.S. Contractors Inc.;** Clute; general construction — 1,800. **Memorial Hospital System** (HQ); Houston; hospital — 1,500. **Raymond Offshore Constructors** (HQ); Houston; fabricated structural metal, barge leasing — 1,500. **The Houston Post Co. Inc.** (HQ); Houston; newspaper publishing — 1,400.

Transco Companies Inc. (HQ); Houston; natural gas transmission — 1,200. **Monsanto Co.;** Alvin; petroleum chemicals — 1,200. **Harvey Construction Co. Inc.** (Westpark Equipment Co. Div.); Houston; general construction — 1,100. **Healthcare International Inc.;** Houston; mental hospital — 1,100. **Reed Tubular Products Co.;** Sugar Land; nonmetallic mineral products — 1,020. **The Coastal Corp.;** Houston; petroleum products wholesaling — 1,000. **Intermedics Inc.** (HQ); Freeport; electronic medical equipment — 1,000. **Memorial Hospital System;** Houston; hospital — 1,000. **Amoco Chemical Corp.** Alvin; plastics products — 900. **Exxon Production Research Co.** (HQ); Houston; research — 875.

The Lummus Co.; Houston; engineering services — 800. **Mark Products Inc.;** Houston; geophysical cable, communications equipment — 800. **Al-Qahtami Pipe Coating;** Houston; pipe coating — 780. **Foster Wheeler Energy Corp.;** Houston; design engineers — 750. **Gulf States Inc.** (HQ); Freeport; electrical, plumbing contracting — 700. **Great West Coca-Cola Bottling Co.** (Houston Coca-Cola Bottling Co. Div. - HQ); Houston; soft drink bottling — 640. **Hudson Engineering Corp.** (HQ); Houston; general construction — 630. **Boehringer Mannheim Diagnostics** (HQ); Houston; blood chemistry equipment — 625. **Anderson Greenwood & Co.** (HQ); Houston; valves — 620. **Imperial Sugar Co.** (HQ); Sugar Land; cane sugar refining — 603. **Bariven;** Houston; crude oil — 600.

CDI Corp.; Houston; engineering services — 600. **Post Oak Western Hotels** (Galleria Plaza Hotel); Houston; hotel — 600. **General Motors Corp.** (Chevrolet Motor Div.); Houston; auto parts wholesaling — 590. **Geosource Inc.** (Technology Div.); Houston; oil exploration — 570. **Allstate Insurance Co. Inc.;** Houston; life insurance — 550. **Digital Equipment Corp.;** Houston; computer services — 550. **D M International Inc.** (Dresser Engineering Div. - HQ); Houston; heavy construction, engineering services — 525. **Schlumberger Technology Corp.** (Vector Cable Div.); Sugar Land; electrical wiring devices — 515. **Armco Inc.** (Baylor Co.); Sugar Land; oil field machinery — 510. **Dravo Utility Contractors Inc.;** Freeport; construction management services — 500. **Dun-Par Engineered Form Co.;** Pearland; road construction — 500.

Ebasco Services Inc.; Thompsons; bridge, tunnel constructing — 500. **Fluor Corp.** (Ocean Services); Houston; engineering, construction services — 500. **Gulf Research & Development Co.** (Houston Technical Service Center); Houston; oil exploration — 500. **Gulf States Toyota Inc.;** Houston; auto wholesaling — 500. **Landmark Management Corp.;** Houston; real estate management — 500. **Mundy Construction Co.;** Houston; heavy construction — 500. **N F Industries Inc.;** Houston; oil, gas exploration services — 500. **Panhandle Eastern Pipeline Co.;** Houston; natural gas extraction, transmission — 500. **Post Oak Hotels Inc.** (Houston Oaks Hotel); Houston; hotel — 500. **Shoreline Geophysical Services** (Southern Operations); Houston; oil, gas exploration services — 500. **Texaco Inc.** (Credit Card Center); Bellaire; credit card operations — 500. **Trunkline Gas Co.** (HQ); Houston; natural gas transmission — 500.

23rd District

Southwest — San Antonio Suburbs, Laredo

The 23rd changed substantially under the remap, adding most of San Antonio's northern Bexar County suburbs and losing all its rural eastern territory to the 14th and 15th districts.

Republican strength in the redrawn 23rd is concentrated in Bexar and three other counties also in the northern part of the district — Medina, Uvalde and Kinney. All of those counties voted for Ronald Reagan in 1980. Uvalde was the home of Democratic U.S. House Speaker and Vice President John Nance "Cactus Jack" Garner.

The San Antonio portion of the 23rd includes communities such as Windcrest, a haven for military retirees who express a conservative bias at the polls. The suburbs of Antonio roll west to the fringes of Medina County; some residents commute nearly 50 miles a day to jobs in the city. Medina generally backed Republicans for statewide office in the late 1970s, but sided with Democrats in the 1982 gubernatorial and senatorial contests.

To the south, the overwhelming Hispanic presence ensures that Democratic voting patterns prevail. The population center in this part of the 23rd is Laredo in Webb County. Nine out of every 10 Webb residents are Hispanic; the county was the largest in Texas to vote for George McGovern in 1972. Jimmy Carter won 67 percent there in 1980 and Democrat Mark White won 70 percent of the gubernatorial ballots there in 1982.

With 91,449 people, Laredo is a gateway for trade and tourism with Mexico and has petroleum operations. It is surrounded by vegetable-growing farmlands irrigated with water from the Rio Grande.

Dry areas to the north and east are best suited to cattle ranches and exploration for oil and gas. Hispanics account for 53 percent of the redrawn district's population, the same as in the old 23rd.

Election Returns

23rd District		Democrat		Republican	
1976	President	64,738	(54.4%)	53,031	(44.6%)
	Senate	69,034	(61.8%)	41,146	(36.8%)
	House	84,738	(89.0%)	9,632	(10.1%)
1978	Governor	35,259	(48.4%)	34,452	(47.3%)
	Senate	35,310	(48.8%)	33,591	(46.5%)
	House	44,686	(71.2%)	12,165	(19.4%)
1980	President	61,509	(45.4%)	69,876	(51.5%)
	House	71,057	(56.0%)	55,563	(43.8%)
1982	Governor	48,692	(54.1%)	40,626	(45.2%)
	Senate	53,717	(61.3%)	33,221	(37.9%)
	House	51,690	(55.3%)	41,363	(44.2%)

Demographics

Population: 526,531. **Percent Change from 1970:** 57.9%.

Land Area: 12,491 square miles. **Population per Square Mile:** 42.2.

Counties, 1980 Population: Bexar (Pt.) — 324,958; Dimmit — 11,367; Kinney — 2,279; Maverick — 31,398; Medina — 23,164; Uvalde — 22,441; Webb — 99,258; Zavala — 11,666.

Cities, 1980 Population: Eagle Pass — 21,407; Laredo — 91,449; San Antonio (Pt.) — 182,551; Universal City — 10,720; Uvalde — 14,178.

Race and Ancestry: White — 84.3%; Black — 4.1%; American Indian, Eskimo and Aleut — 0.3%; Asian and Pacific Islander — 0.7%. Spanish Origin — 53.1%. English — 5.6%; French — 0.6%; German — 5.6%; Irish — 2.2%; Italian — 0.5%; Polish — 0.9%.

Universities, Enrollment: Laredo Junior College, Laredo — 3,107; Laredo State University, Laredo — 788; Southwest Texas Junior College, Uvalde — 2,206; University of Texas Health Science Center at San Antonio, San Antonio — 2,212.

Newspapers, Circulation: *San Antonio Express, San Antonio Light* and *San Antonio News* circulate in the district. Foreign language newspapers: *The Laredo News* (bilingual: English/Spanish), Laredo — 22,544; *Laredo Times* (Spanish), Laredo — 18,383.

Commercial Television Stations, Affiliation: KENS-TV, San Antonio (CBS); KGNS-TV, Laredo (NBC, ABC); KVTV, Laredo (CBS). Most of the district is in San Antonio ADI. Portion is in Laredo ADI.

Military Installations: Brooks Air Force Base, San Antonio — 2,415; Randolph Air Force Base, Universal City — 7,652; San Antonio Air Force Station, San Antonio — 3,154.

Industries:

United Services Auto Assn. (HQ); San Antonio; casualty, life insurance — 4,360. **Datapoint Corp.** (HQ); San Antonio; computing equipment — 3,300. **Bexar County Hospital District;** San Antonio; hospital — 2,530. **Veterans Administration;** San Antonio; veterans' hospital — 1,850. **Southwest Texas Methodist Hospital** (HQ); San Antonio; hospital — 1,260. **Salant Corp.** (Texas Apparel Co.); Eagle Pass; men's coats — 600. **Clarke Printing Packaging Co.;** San Antonio; commercial printing — 590. **Baker International Corp.** (Bakerline Div.); San Antonio; oil field tools — 550. **Del Monte Corp.;** Crystal City; vegetable farming, processing — 500.

24th District

South Dallas and Western Suburbs

The redrawn 24th was one of the districts altered significantly by the federal court. As drawn by the Legislature, the new 24th was more than 60 percent black or Hispanic. The federal court redistributed the minority voters more evenly between the 24th and the neighboring 5th so that neither district had minority control. Still, the 5th has the largest concentration of blacks and Hispanics in the Dallas area.

The black population of the 24th is concentrated at the district's eastern end, south of the Trinity River in Dallas. The Hispanic population is heavier in the central part of the district. The suburbs of Grand Prairie and Irving on the western edge of the 24th are mostly white. The district's white precincts gave Ronald Reagan solid majorities in 1980, but tend to divide about evenly between the parties in statewide contests.

The South Dallas areas with their heavy minority influence are predictably Democratic. The Democratic Party also plays a dominant role in Grand Prairie and Irving, which contain manufacturing and distribution facilities and the homes of many blue-collar factory workers and laborers in construction-related trades. Part of the sprawling Dallas-Fort Worth Airport is located in the northwestern corner of the district and some of the district's residents are employed at the airport or by the airlines that use it.

The 24th also crosses into Tarrant County to pick up a section of Arlington where a General Motors plant is located. Labor delivers a sizable Democratic vote there. The bulk of the Tarrant County territory in the old 24th was incorporated into the newly created 26th District.

Election Returns

24th District		Democrat		Republican	
1976	President	70,306	(54.5%)	57,683	(44.7%)
	Senate	61,202	(49.9%)	60,397	(49.2%)
	House	76,446	(62.8%)	44,657	(36.7%)
1978	Governor	31,747	(48.6%)	32,875	(50.4%)
	Senate	40,939	(57.8%)	29,078	(41.1%)
	House	37,006	(57.2%)	27,718	(42.8%)
1980	President	73,166	(51.3%)	64,612	(45.3%)
	House	83,228	(60.9%)	52,887	(38.7%)
1982	Governor	58,878	(63.2%)	34,230	(36.7%)
	Senate	55,271	(65.0%)	29,725	(34.9%)
	House	63,857	(72.9%)	22,798	(26.0%)

Demographics

Population: 526,677. **Percent Change from 1970:** 7.6%.

Land Area: 275 square miles. **Population per Square Mile:** 1,915.2.

Counties, 1980 Population: Dallas (Pt.) — 481,117; Tarrant (Pt.) — 45,560.

Cities, 1980 Population: Arlington (Pt.) — 42,150; Carrollton (Pt.) — 306; Dallas (Pt.) — 299,000; De Soto (Pt.) — 158; Duncanville (Pt.) — 6,097; Farmers Branch (Pt.) — 102; Grand Prairie (Pt.) — 69,134; Grapevine (Pt.) — 39; Irving (Pt.) — 101,864; Lancaster (Pt.) — 28.

Race and Ancestry: White — 57.7%; Black — 32.2%; American Indian, Eskimo and Aleut — 0.5%; Asian and Pacific Islander — 0.9%. Spanish Origin — 13.4%. English — 10.4%; French — 0.7%; German — 3.2%; Irish — 3.6%.

Universities, Enrollment: Bishop College, Dallas — 945; Dallas Baptist College, Dallas — 1,134; DeVry Institute of Technology, Irving — 1,141; Mountain View College, Dallas — 5,409; North Lake College, Irving — 4,115; University of Dallas (main campus), Irving — 2,688 *(school straddles line between 5th and 24th districts)*; University of Texas at Arlington, Arlington — 20,166.

Newspapers, Circulation: *Grand Prairie Daily News* (eS), Grand Prairie — 6,779; *Irving Daily News* (eS), Irving — 10,909. *The Dallas Morning News, Dallas Times Herald* and *Fort Worth Star-Telegram* also circulate in the district.

Commercial Television Stations, Affiliation: KTXA, Arlington (None). Entire district is located in the Dallas-Fort Worth ADI.

Military Installations: Dallas Naval Air Station, Dallas — 4,680.

Industries:

Vought Corp. (HQ); Grand Prairie; miliary aircraft, missiles — 9,300. **General Motors Corp.**; Arlington; autos — 4,100. **Recognition Equipment Inc.** (HQ); Irving; electronic computing equipment — 2,100. **Methodist Hospitals of Dallas**; Dallas; hospital — 1,780. **Delta Air Lines Inc.**; Dallas; commercial airline — 1,400.

Dresser Industries Inc. (P & M Mfg. Div.); Dallas; oil field equipment — 1,000. **Glitsch Inc.** (HQ); Dallas; chemical processing equipment — 900. **Morse Electro Products Corp.** (Morse Electrophonic); Dallas; stereo units — 725. **Dallas Fort Worth Regional Airport**; Dallas; airport — 711. **NCH Corp.** (Mohawk Laboratories Div. - HQ); Irving; cleaning, sanitation chemicals — 605. **Central Mutual Insurance Co.**; Irving; property, casualty insurance — 600. **Texstar Corp.** (Plastics Div.); Grand Prairie; plastics products — 600.

Sweetheart Cup Corp. of Texas (HQ); Dallas; paper cups — 550. **Bo-Mar Mfg. Co. Inc.** (Dallas Woodcraft Div.); Dallas; wooden products — 500. **Omega Optical Co. Inc.** (HQ); Dallas; ophthalmic goods — 600. **Roadway Express Inc.**; Irving; trucking — 500. **The Southland Corp.** (Oak Farms Div.); Dallas; dairy processing — 500. **Texas Distributors Inc.** (Tempo Mechanical - HQ); Dallas; mechanical contracting — 500. **Texas International Airlines**; Dallas; commercial airline — 500.

25th District

South Houston and Southeast Suburbs

The 25th is one of three new House districts that Texas gained in the 1980 reapportionment. The 25th contains all of Harris County south of the Houston Ship Channel, a waterway lined with heavy industry. The cities of Pasadena and Deer Park are filled with blue-collar workers employed at huge refineries run by Shell, Crown and other petroleum giants.

These working-class people are nearly all nominal Democrats but they are no longer faithful partisan voters. Ronald Reagan's conservative themes played well enough for him to win the blue-collar precincts here in 1980 and that vote, combined with support from GOP regulars in the more affluent parts of Pasadena, Deer Park and neighboring South Houston, enabled him to defeat Jimmy Carter by 4,000 votes in the area within the new 25th.

West of these communities is a concentration of minority voters. Sunnyside, a predominantly black community, is one of Houston's most impoverished areas. The Brentwood neighborhood hosts a large number of middle-class black professionals.

Blacks and Hispanics make up 39 percent of the district's population; among all the Houston-area districts, only central Houston's 18th has a higher minority percentage than the 25th. A small but politically active Jewish community at the district's western end adds to the diversity of its electorate.

Living in the southeastern corner of the 25th are many employees of NASA's Manned Spacecraft Center, which is located across the district boundary in the 9th. Although

Republicans harbored hopes of winning this district, the Democratic House candidate in 1982 amassed more than 60 percent of the vote.

Election Returns

25th District		Democrat		Republican	
1976	President	76,849	(52.3%)	68,959	(46.9%)
	Senate	78,985	(57.7%)	56,681	(41.4%)
	House	89,044	(54.7%)	73,368	(45.1%)
1978	Governor	44,702	(54.8%)	36,368	(44.6%)
	Senate	42,097	(51.1%)	39,452	(47.9%)
	House	41,902	(55.0%)	34,175	(44.9%)
1980	President	68,689	(46.6%)	72,831	(49.4%)
	House	74,092	(51.6%)	68,543	(47.7%)
1982	Governor	60,606	(51.1%)	56,899	(48.0%)
	Senate	71,165	(59.6%)	47,089	(39.4%)
	House	63,974	(60.4%)	40,112	(37.9%)

Demographics

Population: 526,801. **Percent Change from 1970:** 20.4%.

Land Area: 268 square miles. **Population per Square Mile:** 1,965.7.

Counties, 1980 Population: Harris (Pt.) — 526,801.

Cities, 1980 Population: Deer Park — 22,648; Houston (Pt.) — 341,295; La Porte — 14,062; Missouri City (Pt.) — 0; Pasadena (Pt.) — 112,560; South Houston — 13,293.

Race and Ancestry: White — 66.9%; Black — 25.0%; American Indian, Eskimo and Aleut — 0.2%; Asian and Pacific Islander — 1.5%. Spanish Origin — 13.7%. English — 8.8%; French — 1.3%; German — 4.2%; Irish — 3.0%; Italian — 0.7%; Polish — 0.6%.

Universities, Enrollment: Baylor College of Medicine, Houston — 863; Rice University, Houston — 3,476; San Jacinto College (central campus), Pasadena — 9,398; Texas Chiropractic College, Pasadena — 431; University of Texas Health Science Center at Houston, Houston — 2,466.

Newspapers, Circulation: *Pasadena Citizen* (mS), Pasadena — 12,440. *Houston Chronicle* and *The Houston Post* also circulate in the district.

Commercial Television Stations, Affiliation: Entire district is located in Houston ADI.

Military Installations: Ellington Air National Guard Base, Houston — 950; La Porte Air National Guard Station, La Porte — 113.

Industries:

The Methodist Hospital Inc.; Houston; hospital — 4,600. **Hermann Hospital**; Houston; hospital — 2,400. **Diamond Shamrock Corp.**; Deer Park; synthetic rubber — 2,000. **St. Luke's Episcopal Hospital**; Houston; hospital — 2,000. **Texas Children's Hospital**; Houston; children's hospital — 2,000.

Brown & Root Inc.; Pasadena; heavy construction — 1,850. **Fluor Corp.** (Engineers & Constructors); Houston; industrial machinery — 1,800. **Atlantic Richfield Co. Inc.** (Petroleum Products Co.); Houston; petroleum refining — 1,600. **Champion International Inc.** (Paper Div.); Pasadena; paper, paperboard — 1,500. **Shell Oil Co.**; Deer Park; pesticides, chemicals — 1,500. **Amoco Production Co.**; Houston; oil, gas production — 1,350. **E. I. du Pont de Nemours & Co.**; La Porte; inorganic chemicals — 1,300. **Pasadena Bayshore Hospital Inc.**; Pasadena; hospital — 1,060.

Ethyl Corp.; Pasadena; chemicals wholesaling — 1,000. **AMF Tuboscope Inc.** (HQ); Houston; oil field services, plastic coatings — 900. **Rohm & Haas Texas Inc.**; Deer Park; chemicals — 900. **Goodyear Tire & Rubber Co.** (Houston Chemical Plant); Houston; synthetic rubber — 855. **Don Love Inc.** (HQ); Pasadena; general contracting — 850. **The LTV Corp.** (Continental Emsco); Houston; oil field equipment — 800. **Phillips Chemical Co.**; Pasadena; printing ink — 800. **SIP Inc.** (HQ); Houston; general contracting — 700. **The Lubrizol Corp.** Deer Park; chemicals — 600.

F. H. Maloney Co. (HQ); Houston; valves, rubber products — 600. **Marathon Paving & Utility Contractors Inc.**; Houston; sewer, pipeline contracting — 600. **National Distillers & Chemical Corp.** (USI Chemical Div.); Deer Park; plastics materials — 600. **Texas Pipe Bending Co.** (HQ); Houston; fabricated pipe — 600. **Hilton Hotels Corp.** (Shamrock Hilton); Houston; hotel operations — 550. **Fleming Companies Inc.**; Houston; food wholesaling — 525. **Celanese Chemical Co. Inc.**; Houston; industrial inorganic chemicals — 500. **Petromas Inc.**; Houston; engineering, construction services — 500.

26th District

Fort Worth Suburbs; Arlington, Denton

Most of the people in the newly created 26th live in conservative portions of Tarrant County unsuitable for inclusion in the Fort Worth-based 12th District, which was drawn to protect the Democratic House majority leader who represents it.

The suburbs south of Fort Worth are home to doctors, lawyers and other upper-middle-class professionals who are hard-core conservative voters. Much of this area had been part of the 6th District. In the southeastern part of Tarrant County, towns such as Mansfield are growing and becoming more Republican; they appeal to white-collar workers who want to live in a more rural setting that is still within a reasonable commuting distance of their jobs.

The dominant city in the 26th is Arlington, which sits astride the "mid-cities" growth corridor between Dallas and Fort Worth. Arlington grew 78 percent during the 1970s, to a 1980 population of about 160,000. It contains a wide array of industries and tourism and the hotel/motel business are critical to the economy.

A labor-oriented Democratic part of eastern Arlington was placed in the 24th District. The white-collar population that dominates the 26th District portion of Arlington generally prefers Republicans, although a sizable number of people there have voted in House races for Democrats.

Also included in the mid-cities category are the closely linked towns of Hurst, Euless and Bedford, just north of Arlington and demographically similar to it. In northeastern Tarrant County are the small but fast-growing communities of Grapevine and Colleyville, which are near the Dallas-Fort Worth Airport.

North of Tarrant County is Denton County, which is wholly within the 26th. Primarily rural and Democratic not too long ago, Denton County grew 89 percent during the 1970s and is now solidly Republican. There are some liberal votes in older sections of the city of Denton and some traditional Democrats in the areas of the county that are still devoted to farming and ranching. Also in the 26th are portions of Collin and Cooke counties, both politically conservative.

Election Returns

26th District		Democrat		Republican	
1976	President	66,752	(44.2%)	82,893	(54.8%)
	Senate	70,507	(48.6%)	73,376	(50.5%)
	House	81,295	(54.4%)	67,756	(45.3%)
1978	Governor	35,412	(39.6%)	53,827	(60.1%)
	Senate	36,002	(41.1%)	51,319	(58.6%)
	House	31,313	(39.8%)	47,357	(60.2%)
1980	President	56,690	(29.8%)	125,343	(65.8%)
	House	85,290	(43.5%)	110,466	(56.4%)
1982	Governor	56,221	(40.0%)	83,236	(59.2%)
	Senate	60,439	(43.5%)	77,114	(55.5%)
	House	69,782	(50.1%)	69,438	(49.9%)

Demographics

Population: 527,299. **Percent Change from 1970:** 87.3%.

Land Area: 1,921 square miles. **Population per Square Mile:** 274.5.

Counties, 1980 Population: Collin (Pt.) — 89,062; Cooke (Pt.) — 6,865; Denton — 143,126; Tarrant (Pt.) — 288,246.

Cities, 1980 Population: Arlington (Pt.) — 116,986; Bedford (Pt.) — 10,888; Benbrook (Pt.) — 13,579; Burleson (Pt.) — 1,123; Carrollton (Pt.) — 13,742; Dallas (Pt.) — 101; Denton — 48,063; Euless (Pt.) — 20,484; Fort Worth (Pt.) — 75,915; Grand Prairie (Pt.) — 2,321; Grapevine (Pt.) — 11,762; Hurst (Pt.) — 65; Lewisville — 24,273; McKinney (Pt.) — 9,466; Plano (Pt.) — 59,431; The Colony — 11,586.

Race and Ancestry: White — 93.7%; Black — 3.1%; American Indian, Eskimo and Aleut — 0.3%; Asian and Pacific Islander — 1.1%. Spanish Origin — 3.9%. Dutch — 0.5%; English — 16.0%; French — 1.0%; German — 6.4%; Irish — 5.2%; Italian — 0.8%; Polish — 0.5%; Scottish — 0.6%.

Universities, Enrollment: Bauder Fashion College, Arlington — 495; North Texas State University, Denton — 18,201; Texas Christian University, Fort Worth — 6,283 *(school straddles line between 12th and 26th districts)*; Texas Woman's University, Denton — 7,944.

Newspapers, Circulation: *Daily Leader* (eS), Lewisville — 4,736; *Denton Record-Chronicle* (eS), Denton — 14,868; *McKinney Courier-Gazette* (eS), McKinney — 6,475. *The Dallas Morning News, Dallas Times Herald* and *Fort Worth Star-Telegram* also circulate in the district.

Commercial Television Stations, Affiliation: Entire district is located in Dallas-Fort Worth ADI.

Industries:

American Airlines Inc. (HQ); Grapevine; airline operations — 10,061. **Textron Inc.** (Bell Helicopter Co.); Fort Worth; helicopters — 6,100. **Palco Industries Inc.** (Apparatus Div.); Denton; metal working machinery — 1,050. **Skychefs Inc.** (HQ); Grapevine; airline food service — 1,000. **Surgikos Inc.** (HQ); Arlington; surgical gloves — 791.

Atlantic Richfield Co. (Oil & Gas Co.); Plano; petroleum research — 750. **The Texstar Corp.** (Ara Mfg. Co.); Grand Prairie; auto air conditioners — 729. **Maples-Platter Companies** (HQ); Fort Worth; groceries wholesaling — 700. **Reliance Telecommunications Electronics**; Bedford; telephone apparatus — 650. **Menasco Inc.**; Fort Worth; aircraft parts — 520. **Aztec Mfg. Co.** (Drilling Equipment Div. - HQ); Crowley; oil drill pipe — 500.

27th District

Gulf Coast — Corpus Christi, Brownsville

This new district looks tidy and compact: five counties lined up along the Gulf Coast in far southern Texas with the region's two largest cities at either end.

But when the boundaries of the 27th were released by federal judges, there were grumblings in Brownsville, a Mexican border city in the Rio Grande Valley that has never had a great deal of contact with Corpus Christi, its much larger competitor for tourists and seaport trade. Since about 50 percent of the district's population lives in Nueces County (Corpus Christi), some Brownsville residents worry that their interests will take second place to Corpus Christi's in the new 27th.

These people were more comfortable with the old district arrangement, which paired Cameron County (Brownsville) with McAllen, another Mexican-border city just to its west. But the judges disregarded that traditional Brownsville-McAllen affinity to balance the Hispanic populations in the 15th and 27th districts.

Among Texas ports, Corpus Christi is second only to Houston in tonnage handled yearly. The city has large petrochemical and aluminum plants and seafood processing facilities. Tourists are lured to Corpus Christi by its mild climate and direct access to the Padre Island National Seashore.

By comparison, Brownsville offers more of a south-of-the-border flavor than Corpus Christi; Nueces County is not quite half Hispanic, but in Cameron County, 77.1 percent of the residents are Hispanic. Overall the district is nearly two-thirds Hispanic. Export-import trade with Mexico is vital to the economy, and the bounteous harvests of the Rio Grande Valley keep many workers busy with fruit and vegetable processing.

Nueces and Cameron behave similarly at the polls, as reflected in the 1980 presidential results. Jimmy Carter carried both counties, although in each case by less than 3,000 votes over Ronald Reagan. There are three other counties in the 27th, but these sparsely populated ranchlands were expected to have scant electoral impact.

Election Returns

27th District		Democrat		Republican	
1976	President	86,991	(60.9%)	54,623	(38.2%)
	Senate	89,416	(65.8%)	45,225	(33.3%)
	House	90,266	(66.4%)	45,681	(33.6%)
1978	Governor	42,973	(53.9%)	35,412	(44.4%)
	Senate	40,007	(51.3%)	36,417	(46.7%)
	House	49,160	(65.1%)	26,390	(34.9%)
1980	President	72,902	(50.5%)	69,306	(46.7%)
	House	81,821	(57.8%)	59,674	(42.2%)
1982	Governor	62,988	(60.4%)	40,471	(38.8%)
	Senate	68,280	(66.7%)	33,170	(32.4%)
	House	66,604	(64.0%)	35,209	(33.8%)

Demographics

Population: 526,988. **Percent Change from 1970:** 23.7%.

Land Area: 4,580 square miles. **Population per Square Mile:** 115.1.

Counties, 1980 Population: Cameron — 209,727; Kenedy — 543; Kleberg — 33,358; Nueces (Pt.) — 265,865; Willacy — 17,495.

Cities, 1980 Population: Brownsville — 84,997; Corpus Christi (Pt.) — 230,032; Harlingen — 43,543; Kingsville — 28,808; Portland (Pt.) — 0; Robstown — 12,100; San Benito — 17,988.

Race and Ancestry: White — 79.2%; Black — 2.7%; American Indian, Eskimo and Aleut — 0.2%; Asian and Pacific Islander — 0.5%. Spanish Origin — 61.5%. English — 5.5%; French — 0.5%; German — 3.0%; Irish — 1.8%.

Universities, Enrollment: Corpus Christi State University, Corpus Christi — 2,748; Del Mar College, Corpus Christi — 8,273; Texas Southmost College, Brownsville — 4,294; Texas State Technical Institute, Harlingen — 1,642; Texas A & I University, Kingsville — 5,356.

Newspapers, Circulation: *Brownsville Herald* (eS), Brownsville — 13,078; *Corpus Christi Caller* (mS), Corpus Christi — 62,142; *Corpus Christi Times* (e), Corpus Christi — 25,118; *Valley Morning Star* (mS), Harlingen — 22,088.

Commercial Television Stations, Affiliation: KGBT-TV, Harlingen (CBS); KIII, Corpus Christi (ABC); KORO, Corpus Christi (None, Spanish); KRIS-TV, Corpus Christi (NBC); KVEO, Brownsville (NBC); KZTV, Corpus Christi (CBS). District is divided between Corpus Christi ADI and McAllen-Brownsville ADI.

Military Installations: Corpus Christi Naval Air Station, Corpus Christi — 7,159; Corpus Christi Naval Regional Medical Center, Corpus Christi — 347; Kingsville Naval Air Station, Kingsville — 2,384.

Industries:

Memorial Medical Center; Corpus Christi; hospital — 1,590. **Marathon LeTourneau Co.;** Brownsville; offshore oil drilling rigs — 1,200. **Arthur Bros. Inc.;** Kingsville; general contracting — 1,190. **Berry Contracting Inc.** (Fabricators Div.); Corpus Christi; heavy construction — 1,000. **Celanese Corp.** (Plastic Div.); Bishop; inorganic pigments, chemicals — 1,000.

Exxon Corp.; Corpus Christi; oil production — 845. **McKinney Pant Co. Inc.;** Brownsville; men's slacks — 750. **Eagle International Inc.;** Brownsville; buses, vehicle bodies — 690. **Asarco Inc.;** Corpus Christi; electrolytic zinc — 609. **King Ranch Inc.** (Laureles Div. - HQ); Kingsville; livestock ranch, oil production — 600. **Levi Strauss & Co.;** Brownsville; boys' jeans — 600. **The William Carter Co. Inc.;** Harlingen; children's sleepwear — 580. **Sun Oil Co. Inc.;** Corpus Christi; oil, gas exploration — 523. **Champlin Petroleum Co. Inc.;** Corpus Christi; petrochemicals — 500. **Mobil Oil Corp.** (Uranium-Div.); Corpus Christi; oil, gas exploration — 500. **San Antonio Shoe Inc.;** San Antonio; shoes — 500. **Levi Strauss & Co.;** Corpus Christi; women's dresses — 500. **Sunbeam Corp.;** Brownsville; electrical housewares — 500.

Utah

Utah's population grew 37.9 percent during the 1970s, giving the state a third House seat, and the GOP-dominated Legislature drew the map to the Republicans' benefit. All three districts went to the GOP in 1982.

Democratic Gov. Scott M. Matheson decided not to veto the redistricting bill that was sent to him Oct. 30, 1981. He said he thought the measure would stand up to legal challenges, so he allowed it to become law Nov. 11, 1981, without his signature. Republicans had enough votes to override a veto anyway. The vote on passage was 50-21 in the state House and 20-8 in the state Senate.

Gov. Matheson had tried to prevent Republicans from drawing a partisan map by appointing a citizens' panel to devise an "objective" plan. The panel favored creating two solidly Republican districts but keeping a substantial Democratic vote in the Salt Lake City-based 2nd District.

The Legislature accepted the outlines of the commission proposal but helped the 2nd District Republican incumbent by moving Democrats from his district into the new 3rd.

To create the 3rd, the Legislature attached the Democratic southwestern part of Salt Lake County to staunchly Republican Utah County (Provo). The 3rd was fleshed out with lightly populated counties in the eastern part of the state. Its Republican leanings seemed secure. The 1st District was still centered in Davis and Weber counties. But it was given Republican rural territory in the state's western half, which helped nullify Democratic strength in Weber County.

Republican legislators from rural southern Utah were distressed that the metropolitan areas along the Wasatch Range near Salt Lake City would dominate all the districts politically. Several of the rural Republicans joined the minority Democratic legislators in voting against the plan.

Conservative, Mormon Utah is a bastion of Republicanism. The last time it went Democratic for president was in 1948. In 1980, Jimmy Carter scored an embarrassingly low 21 percent of the vote there. That was Carter's poorest showing in the country and worse even than George McGovern's Utah performance eight years earlier. Democrats continued to win House elections into the 1970s, but the last Democratic congressman, Gunn McKay, was ousted in 1980.

Republicans, however, have failed to dislodge the Democratic Party from its last beachhead in the state, the governorship. Democrats have held the governor's chair for 18 years since 1964.

Age of Population

District	Population Under 18	Voting Age Population	Population 65 & Over (% of VAP)	Median Age
1	184,427	303,406	38,009 (12.5%)	24.2
2	161,612	325,863	43,307 (13.3%)	26.4
3	194,066	291,663	27,904 (9.6%)	22.4
State	540,105	920,932	109,220 (11.9%)	24.2

Income and Occupation

District	Median Family Income	White Collar Workers	Blue Collar Workers	Service Workers	Farm Workers
1	$ 19,614	52.9%	30.6%	12.8%	3.6%
2	21,116	60.5	27.5	11.4	0.7
3	19,265	48.1	36.9	12.4	2.6
State	$ 20,024	54.3%	31.4%	12.2%	2.2%

Education: School Years Completed

District	8 Years or Fewer	4 Years of High School	4 Years of College or More	Median School Years
1	6.8%	38.1%	17.9%	12.8
2	7.3	33.7	23.6	12.9
3	7.0	36.4	17.6	12.8
State	7.0%	36.0%	19.9%	12.8

Housing and Residential Patterns

District	Owner Occupied	Renter Occupied	Urban	Rural
1	74.2%	25.8%	77.1%	22.9%
2	64.2	35.8	99.4	0.6
3	74.9	25.1	76.7	23.3
State	70.7%	29.3%	84.4%	15.6%

UTAH

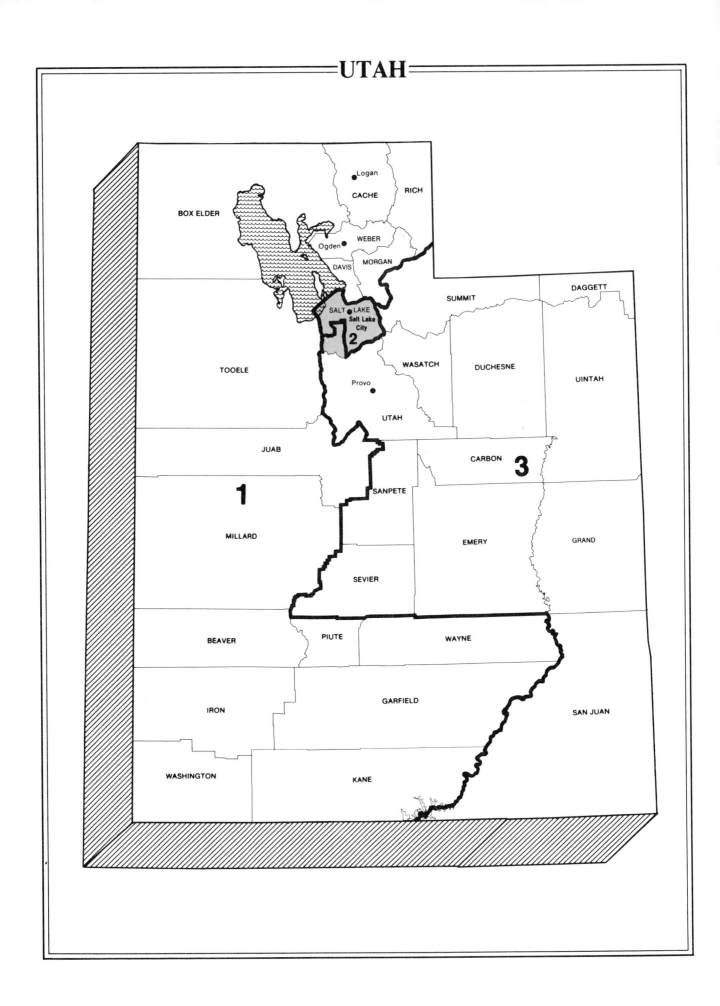

BOX ELDER

Logan
CACHE   RICH

WEBER
Ogden
MORGAN
DAVIS

SALT LAKE   SUMMIT   DAGGETT
Salt Lake
City
2

TOOELE   WASATCH   DUCHESNE   UINTAH

Provo
UTAH

JUAB   CARBON   **3**

SANPETE

1
EMERY   GRAND

MILLARD

SEVIER

BEAVER   PIUTE   WAYNE

IRON   GARFIELD   SAN JUAN

WASHINGTON   KANE

1st District

Ogden and Rural Utah

The railroad center of Ogden and surrounding Weber County comprise what Democratic core Utah has. It was at Promontory, just north of Ogden, that the golden spike was driven in 1869, creating the nation's first transcontinental rail link. The Church of Jesus Christ of Latter-Day Saints (Mormon Church) is an important influence in Weber County, as it is everywhere in Utah, but the railroads brought a higher number of non-Mormons than in other parts of the state.

Weber's Democrats are largely blue-collar workers and union members, a legacy of the railroad era. The county also has a sizable number of federal employees who work at Hill Air Force Base and nearby defense installations. Although he lost statewide, Democrat Sen. Frank Moss in 1976 ran up a good plurality in Weber. But the county is no longer Democratic on the national level. It has not supported a Democratic candidate for president since Lyndon B. Johnson ran in 1964.

Rapidly developing Davis County, also in the 1st District, sits in the corridor between Ogden and Salt Lake City. It is a politically polarized county in which Republicans have the edge. Its northern part, around Clearfield and Sunset, votes Democratic in many contests. In southern Davis, towns such as Bountiful are part of suburban Salt Lake and vote Republican.

The rural remainder of the district has an almost uniformly Republican coloration. An exception is Millard County, which has an influx of blue-collar workers at the Inter-Mountain Power Project. But they are too few to make a difference.

Washington County in the southwest corner of Utah has a devout Republican loyalty. Its population doubled during the 1970s as senior citizens and affluent outsiders looking for winter homes found its semitropical climate attractive. But it is not a major population center; Washington has one-sixth the population of Weber County.

Redistricting removed Utah County (Provo) from the 1st, but the loss of Republican voting strength there was expected to be offset by voters in Davis and the rural counties. The district lost rural counties in the eastern part of the state and gained ones in the west. But both sets were Republican, so the partisan impact of those shifts was minor.

Election Returns

1st District		Democrat		Republican	
1976	President	65,603	(34.5%)	117,288	(61.6%)
	Governor	91,979	(49.9%)	87,746	(47.6%)
	Senate	82,579	(44.8%)	98,971	(53.7%)
	House	100,104	(55.3%)	76,465	(42.2%)
1978	House	59,631	(46.8%)	63,561	(49.9%)
1980	President	39,968	(19.1%)	158,837	(75.8%)
	Governor	108,837	(52.3%)	98,421	(76.9%)
	Senate	46,111	(22.4%)	157,980	(76.9%)
	House	90,079	(43.7%)	115,888	(56.2%)
1982	Senate	68,917	(37.8%)	113,014	(61.9%)
	House	66,006	(37.2%)	111,416	(62.8%)

Demographics

Population: 487,833. **Percent Change from 1970:** 31.0%.

Land Area: 46,994 square miles. **Population per Square Mile:** 10.4.

Counties, 1980 Population: Beaver — 4,378; Box Elder — 33,222; Cache — 57,176; Davis — 146,540; Garfield — 3,673; Iron — 17,349; Juab — 5,530; Kane — 4,024; Millard — 8,970; Morgan — 4,917; Piute — 1,329; Rich — 2,100; Tooele — 26,033; Washington — 26,065; Wayne — 1,911; Weber — 144,616.

Cities, 1980 Population: Bountiful — 32,877; Brigham City — 15,596; Cedar City — 10,972; Clearfield — 17,982; Layton — 22,862; Logan — 26,844; Ogden — 64,407; Roy — 19,694; South Ogden — 11,366; St. George — 11,350; Tooele — 14,335.

Race and Ancestry: White — 94.7%; Black — 1.0%; American Indian, Eskimo and Aleut — 0.9%; Asian and Pacific Islander — 1.1%. Spanish Origin — 4.0%. Dutch — 0.9%; English — 29.6%; French — 0.6%; German — 3.6%; Irish — 1.3%; Italian — 0.6%; Norwegian — 0.5%; Scottish — 0.9%; Swedish — 1.3%.

Universities, Enrollment: Dixie College, St. George — 1,790; Southern Utah State College, Cedar City — 2,058; Utah State University, Logan — 9,939; Weber State College, Ogden — 10,065.

Newspapers, Circulation: *The Herald Journal* (eS), Logan — 12,165; *Ogden Standard-Examiner* (eS), Ogden — 50,532; *Spectrum* (eS), St. George — 5,870.

Commercial Television Stations, Affiliation: Entire district is located in Salt Lake City ADI.

Military Installations: Dugway Proving Ground, Dugway — 1,126; Francis Peak Air National Guard Station, Farmington — 3; Hill Air Force Base, Clearfield — 22,990; Hill Weapons Range, Wendover — 81; Little Mountain Test Annex, Ogden — 1; Ogden Defense Depot, Ogden — 1,654; South Area Tooele Army Depot, Tooele — 548; Tooele Army Depot, Tooele — 3,923.

Industries:

Thiokol Corp.; Corinne; solid chemicals — 4,000. **Intermountain Health Care Inc.;** Ogden; hospital — 1,300. **Max Factor & Co.;** Clearfield; cosmetics — 550. **Western Zirconium Inc.;** Ogden; metal mining — 500. **The Wurlitzer Co.;** Logan; electronic pianos — 500.

2nd District

Salt Lake City

To concentrate the 2nd District entirely within Salt Lake County, which contains more than 42 percent of the state's population, the state Legislature lopped off the 2nd District's rural counties and gave them to the 1st District. Those were dependable Republican votes, but their loss was neutralized by a second change, dropping the Democratic southwestern portion of Salt Lake County and giving it to the new 3rd District.

The 2nd District has had a variety of shapes over the last few decades, but its linchpin always has been Salt Lake City, the governmental, commercial, cultural and spiritual capital of the state. Salt Lake City is the world headquarters of the Church of Jesus Christ of Latter-day Saints, and it exerts great political force there.

The city harbors enough Democratic blue-collar workers and liberal young professionals to lean Democratic in many elections and to give the dominant suburban Republicans an occasional challenge countywide. The portion of Salt Lake County in the new 2nd District, which includes all of the city proper, favored Democratic Gov. Scott Matheson in the 1976 and 1980 gubernatorial elections.

But in both those election years, the same area went heavily against Democratic President Jimmy Carter.

Salt Lake City's working-class West Side, the traditional home for many copper miners, generally votes Democratic, as does the central city section. In the northern hills, called The Avenues, young professionals often vote the Democratic ticket as well. But in the wealthy Wasatch foothills section, called the East Bench, Republicans dominate. More people live in the Salt Lake suburbs than in the city itself. Voters in such suburban communities as Cottonwood and Murray habitually opt for the GOP.

Election Returns

2nd District		Democrat		Republican	
1976	President	72,856	(35.6%)	125,057	(61.1%)
	Governor	113,984	(56.5%)	85,283	(42.3%)
	Senate	97,472	(47.8%)	103,480	(50.8%)
	House	76,630	(38.4%)	106,424	(53.3%)
1978	House	51,214	(36.4%)	86,356	(61.4%)
1980	President	48,612	(23.3%)	137,579	(66.1%)
	Governor	123,965	(60.0%)	81,576	(39.5%)
	Senate	63,061	(30.7%)	139,914	(68.0%)
	House	65,066	(32.0%)	131,867	(64.8%)
1982	Senate	86,457	(47.6%)	94,340	(51.9%)
	House	78,981	(46.2%)	92,109	(53.8%)

Demographics

Population: 487,475. **Percent Change from 1970:** 21.3%.

Land Area: 569 square miles. **Population per Square Mile:** 856.7.

Counties, 1980 Population: Salt Lake (Pt.) — 487,475.

Cities, 1980 Population: Magna — 13,138; Midvale — 10,146; Murray (Pt.) — 25,720; Salt Lake City — 163,033; Sandy City (Pt.) — 50,546; South Salt Lake — 10,561; West Valley (Pt.) — 46,521.

Race and Ancestry: White — 94.0%; Black — 0.7%; American Indian, Eskimo and Aleut — 0.7%; Asian and Pacific Islander — 2.1%. Spanish Origin — 4.9%. Dutch — 1.0%; English — 24.4%; French — 0.5%; German — 4.3%; Greek — 0.6%; Irish — 1.8%; Italian — 1.0%; Norwegian — 0.7%; Scottish — 0.9%; Swedish — 1.5%.

Universities, Enrollment: L.D.S. Business College, Salt Lake City — 983; University of Utah, Salt Lake City — 22,970; Utah Technical College at Salt Lake, Salt Lake City — 5,937; Westminster College, Salt Lake City — 1,049.

Newspapers, Circulation: *The Deseret News* (e), Salt Lake City — 73,372; *The Salt Lake Tribune* (mS), Salt Lake City — 110,747.

Commercial Television Stations, Affiliation: KSL-TV, Salt Lake City (CBS); KSTU, Salt Lake City (None); KTVX, Salt Lake City (ABC); KUTV, Salt Lake City (NBC). Entire district is located in Salt Lake City ADI.

Military Installations: Salt Lake City International Airport (Air Force), Salt Lake City — 1,266.

Industries:

Kennecott Corp. (Utah Copper Div.); Salt Lake City; copper refining — 5,000. **Union Pacific Railroad Co.;** Salt Lake City; railroad operations — 3,000. **Sperry Corp.;** Salt Lake City; guided missiles — 2,600. **Hercules Inc.** (Aerospace Div.); Magna; guided missiles — 2,500. **Deseret Co. Inc.;** Sandy; surgical instruments — 2,000.

First Security Corp. (HQ); Salt Lake City; bank holding company — 1,800. **Denver and Rio Grande Western Railroad Co.;** Salt Lake City; railroad operations — 1,600. **Sisters of the Holy Cross Inc.;** Salt Lake City; hospital — 1,300. **I. M. L. Freight Inc.** (HQ); Salt Lake

City; trucking — 1,000. **O. C. Tanner Mfg. Inc.;** Salt Lake City; jewelry — 1,000. **Pyke Mfg. Co.** (HQ); Salt Lake City; women's clothing — 1,000. **Veterans Administration;** Salt Lake City; veterans' hospital — 1,000. **Envirotech Corp.** (Eimco Process Machinery Div.); Salt Lake City; industrial machinery — 950. **Snowbird Corp.;** Sandy; resort — 850. **Sperry Corp.;** Salt Lake City; computers — 850. **Northwest Energy Co.** (HQ); Salt Lake City; natural gas, coal production, natural gas transmission — 773. **Amax Specialty Metal Corp.** (Magnesium Div.); Salt Lake City; magnesium production — 700. **E-Systems Inc.** (Montek Div.); Salt Lake City; communications equipment — 700. **Mountain Fuel Supply Co.** (HQ); Salt Lake City; natural gas transmission — 660.

Litton Systems Inc.; Salt Lake City; electronic communications equipment — 650. **Varian Associates** (EIMAC); Salt Lake City; TV, radio tubes — 640. **Consolidated Freightways Corp.;** Salt Lake City; trucking — 625. **Zions Cooperative Mercantile Institution** (HQ); Salt Lake City; department store chain — 625. **Arcata Corp.** (Huntsman Container Corp.) Salt Lake City; polystyrene products — 600. **General Telephone & Electronics Corp.;** Salt Lake City; telecommunications equipment — 600. **Newspaper Agency Corp.;** Salt Lake City; newspaper printing — 600. **Associated Food Stores Inc.** (HQ); Salt Lake City; grocery wholesaling — 579. **Gibbons Co.;** Salt Lake City; highway construction — 539. **Evans & Sutherland Computer;** Salt Lake City; video computers — 520. **Holdings Little America;** Salt Lake City; motel — 500. **Shurtleff & Andrews Construction Co.;** Salt Lake City; heavy construction, equipment leasing — 500. **John Wiley & Sons Inc.;** Salt Lake City; warehousing — 500. **Envirotech Corp.;** Salt Lake City; mining machinery — 500.

3rd District

Provo and Rural Utah

Provo and surrounding Utah County are home to the most intense Mormon community in the state. That is in large part because Provo is the location of Brigham Young University, founded in 1875 to prepare Mormon youth for teaching and religious proselytizing.

This influence makes Utah County overwhelmingly Republican. Since 1960 its sole defection to the Democrats on the presidential level came when Barry Goldwater was the GOP nominee in 1964. Goldwater came within about 3,000 votes of taking the county.

The northern section of the county contains Lehi and American Forks — towns whose blue-collar workers are employed at the Geneva Steelworks plant. Even in these communities, however, Mormon values are crucial and Democrats cannot count on a heavy vote.

Democrats do predominate in the southwest part of Salt Lake County, which was moved into this district from the 2nd. Many of the residents, living in towns such as South Jordan and West Valley City, are copper miners. But these voters differ little from those elsewhere in the district when it comes to national elections. The 3rd District part of Salt Lake County voted for Ronald Reagan in 1980 by 2-1.

The rest of the 3rd is rural and sparsely populated. Much of it is mountains or desert. Cattle ranching and mining are leading industries and Republicans dominate.

Democrats, though, are strong in Carbon and Emery counties, where coal mining has taken off. Jimmy Carter carried both counties in 1976, the only counties in the state he won. In 1980, as he was being humiliated statewide, he still came within three votes of carrying Carbon. This is a mostly non-Mormon area, with many residents of Greek, Italian and Mexican descent who came to work in the mines. Uintah County harbors large deposits of oil shale, yet little growth has occurred there so far.

Election Returns

3rd District		Democrat		Republican	
1976	President	43,651	(29.8%)	95,563	(65.3%)
	Governor	74,743	(48.6%)	74,998	(48.8%)
	Senate	61,897	(40.7%)	87,770	(57.8%)
	House	89,828	(55.1%)	68,514	(42.0%)
1978	House	51,946	(46.7%)	56,603	(50.9%)
1980	President	35,686	(19.1%)	143,271	(76.8%)
	Governor	98,172	(53.0%)	86,581	(46.7%)
	Senate	42,282	(23.1%)	139,781	(76.3%)
	House	77,281	(42.3%)	104,241	(57.1%)
1982	Senate	64,108	(38.5%)	101,978	(61.2%)
	House	32,661	(23.1%)	108,478	(76.9%)

Demographics

Population: 485,729. **Percent Change from 1970:** 70.3%.

Land Area: 34,511 square miles. **Population per Square Mile:** 14.1.

Counties, 1980 Population: Carbon — 22,179; Daggett — 769; Duchesne — 12,565; — Emery 11,451; Grand — 8,241; Salt Lake (Pt.) — 131,591; San Juan — 12,253; Sanpete — 14,620; Sevier — 14,727; Summit — 10,198; Uintah — 20,506; Utah — 218,106; Wasatch — 8,523.

Cities, 1980 Population: American Fork — 12,564; Murray (Pt.) — 30; Orem — 52,399; Pleasant Grove — 10,833; Provo — 74,108; Sandy City (Pt.) — 0; Springville — 12,101; West Jordan — 27,192.

Race and Ancestry: White — 95.1%; Black — 0.2%; American Indian, Eskimo and Aleut — 2.3%; Asian and Pacific Islander — 0.9%. Spanish Origin — 3.5%. Dutch — 0.6%; English — 29.1%; French — 0.6%; German — 3.4%; Irish — 1.5%; Italian — 0.8%; Norwegian — 0.5%; Scottish — 0.9%; Swedish — 1.2%.

Universities, Enrollment: Brigham Young University, Provo — 33,266; College of Eastern Utah, Price — 851; Snow College, Ephraim — 1,283; Stevens Henager College, Provo — 348; Utah Technical College at Provo, Provo — 4,481.

Newspapers, Circulation: *The Daily Herald* (eS), Provo — 30,361. *Salt Lake City Deseret News* and *The Salt Lake Tribune* also circulate in the district.

Commercial Television Stations, Affiliation: Entire district is located in Salt Lake City ADI.

Industries:

United States Steel Corp. (Geneva Steelworks); Provo; steel — 2,800. **Sorenson Research Inc.;** Murray; surgical equipment — 1,800. **Intermountain Health Care Inc.;** Provo; hospital — 1,600. **Signetics Corp.;** Orem; electronic components — 1,200. **Emery Mining Corp.;** Huntington; coal mining — 1,000.

California Portland Cement Co. (Soldier Creek Coal Co. Inc.); Price; coal mining — 970. **National Semiconductor Corp.;** West Jordan; electronic computing equipment — 850. **Price River Coal Co.;** Helper; coal mining — 600. **Atlas Corp.** (Big Indian Mine); La Sal; uranium mining — 500. **Kaiser Steel Corp.;** Sunnyside; coal mining — 500.

Vermont

For most of this century, Vermont was the northern counterpart of Dixie — the state where voters marked for the GOP by habit and asked questions later.

That was mostly because it was so thoroughly a rural state. Even after World War II there was little industry in Vermont that did not have to do with the state's forests or stone quarries. There were few immigrant groups and virtually no non-whites. There was little to jar traditional Yankee voting patterns.

The situation has changed in recent years. Vermont now has one of the nation's more independent electorates, although Republicans generally remain the dominant party. Unlike Republicans across the border in New Hampshire who have pursued a policy of partisan controversy, the Vermont GOP has found centrist candidates who have been able to blur party distinctions and appeal to the emerging independent bloc.

Meanwhile, the Democratic Party has been changing, influenced by newcomers from New York and other states. Many of the transplants are committed environmentalists, and this has pulled Democratic candidates to the left in some parts of Vermont, not always helping them in state-wide races.

But Vermont Democrats know they can win with the right sort of candidate in the right year. Their symbol of success is Sen. Patrick Leahy, who got himself elected in the Watergate year of 1974 and then held on for a second term in the much less favorable atmosphere of 1980.

Burlington, population 37,712, is the largest city in Vermont and the only one resembling a metropolitan area. Burlington, situated on Lake Champlain, grew first as a major port and later as a manufacturing center. Recent growth in the electronics industry on the fringes of Burlington has brought some prosperity to the region, but not to the city. Suffering from an acute housing shortage and high unemployment, Burlington in 1981 elected a Socialist mayor.

The home of one in every five Vermonters, Burlington and surrounding Chittenden County are essential to the success of any Democratic statewide campaign. Burlington and the French Canadian mill town of Winooski are solidly Democratic. The other towns in the Burlington orbit — Essex, Colchester, South Burlington — are less predictable, but often back Democrats. In 1980, Leahy's 5,000 vote plurality in Chittenden was nearly twice his overall state-wide margin.

Franklin and Grand Isle counties, located in the northwestern corner of the state, are largely agricultural. With a sizable French Canadian population, the region is almost as Democratic as Chittenden County. Grand Isle, a county consisting of a chain of islands in Lake Champlain, was the smallest but fastest growing county in the state.

Dubbed the "Northeast Kingdom" by former Sen. George Aiken when he was governor in the 1930s, Essex, Orleans and Caledonia counties are the most remote in Vermont. They are more staunchly Republican than any other region. Ronald Reagan's highest percentages came from this area.

For many years the population of this region had been dwindling. But the completion of Interstate 91 in the 1970s made the area more accessible, and the population is now increasing about as fast as the statewide average. Seasonal farming remains the major economic activity, making this the poorest area in the state.

Vermont is remembered for its picturesque villages, dairy farms, ski slopes and maple syrup. All are found throughout the Green Mountains, which stretch nearly the entire length of the state. Politically most of the small towns and villages in the Green Mountains still vote Republican. But in the 1970s there was an influx of younger, city-dwelling professionals. This new immigrant class has brought the area a new lifestyle as well as an increase in the Democratic vote.

Although most of the population is found in the rural areas, a few small industrial centers are scattered around the Green Mountains. Barre, the self-proclaimed "Granite Center of the World," is heavily Democratic, as is Bellows Falls on the Connecticut River. The other small urban centers — Rutland, Brattleboro, Bennington and the state capital, Montpelier — all have some Democratic voters, but exhibit the same streak of political independence found in most of the small villages.

Age of Population

District	Population Under 18	Voting Age Population	Population 65 & Over (% of VAP)	Median Age
AL	145,318	366,138	58,166 (15.9%)	29.4

VERMONT

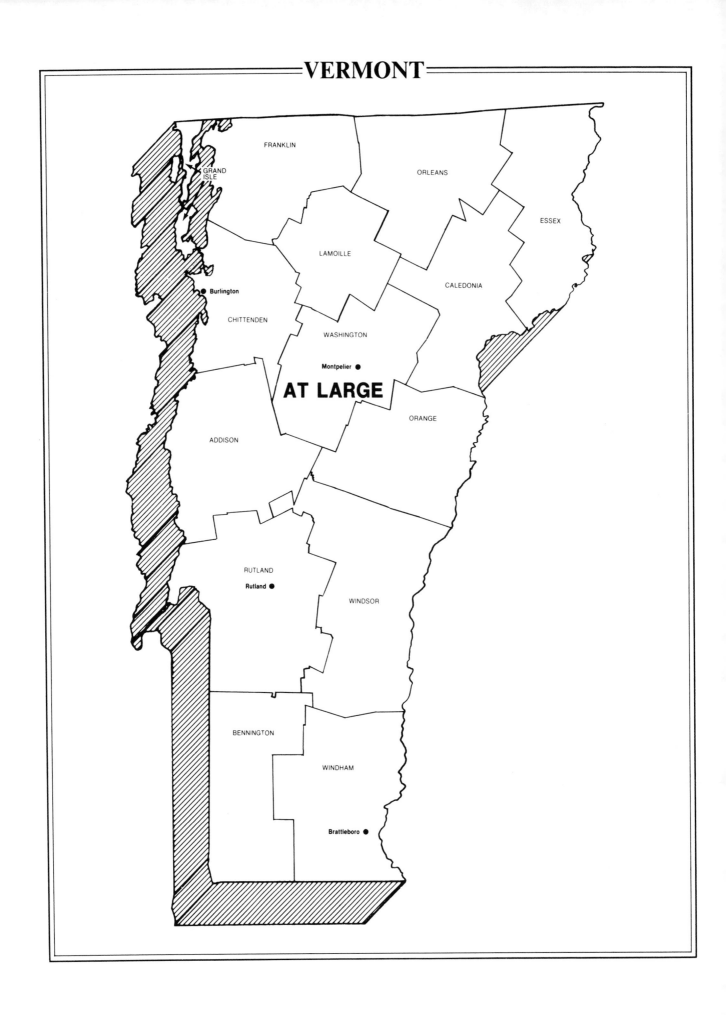

FRANKLIN

GRAND
ISLE

ORLEANS

ESSEX

LAMOILLE

CALEDONIA

● Burlington

CHITTENDEN

WASHINGTON

Montpelier ●

AT LARGE

ORANGE

ADDISON

RUTLAND

Rutland ●

WINDSOR

BENNINGTON

WINDHAM

Brattleboro ●

Income and Occupation

District	Median Family Income	White Collar Workers	Blue Collar Workers	Service Workers	Farm Workers
AL	$ 17,205	50.8%	30.5%	13.4%	5.2%

Education: School Years Completed

District	8 Years or Fewer	4 Years of High School	4 Years of College or More	Median School Years
AL	16.7%	36.4%	19.0%	12.6

Housing and Residential Patterns

District	Owner Occupied	Renter Occupied	Urban	Rural
AL	68.7%	31.3%	33.8%	66.2%

Election Returns

At Large		Democrat		Republican	
1976	President	80,954	(43.1%)	102,085	(54.4%)
	Governor	75,262	(40.5%)	99,268	(53.4%)
	Senate	85,682	(45.3%)	94,481	(50.0%)
	House	60,202	(32.6%)	124,458	(67.4%)
1978	Governor	42,482	(34.1%)	78,181	(62.8%)
	House	23,228	(19.3%)	90,688	(75.3%)
1980	President	81,952	(38.4%)	94,628	(44.4%)
	Governor	77,363	(36.8%)	123,229	(58.6%)
	Senate	104,176	(49.8%)	101,421	(48.5%)
	House	—		154,274	(79.2%)
1982	Governor	74,394	(44.0%)	93,111	(55.0%)
	Senate	79,340	(47.2%)	84,449	(50.3%)
	House	38,296	(23.2%)	114,191	(69.2%)

Demographics

Population: 511,456. **Percent Change from 1970:** 15.0%.

Land Area: 9,273 square miles. **Population per Square Mile:** 55.2.

Counties, 1980 Population: Addison — 29,406; Bennington — 33,345; Caledonia — 25,808; Chittenden — 115,534; Essex — 6,313; Franklin — 34,788; Grand Isle — 4,613; Lamoille — 16,767; Orange — 22,739; Orleans — 23,440; Rutland — 58,347; Washington — 52,393; Windham — 36,933; Windsor — 51,030.

Cities, 1980 Population: Bennington — 15,815; Burlington — 37,712; Colchester — 12,629; Essex — 14,392; Rutland — 18,436; South Burlington — 10,679; Springfield — 10,190.

Race and Ancestry: White — 99.1%; Black — 0.2%; American Indian, Eskimo and Aleut — 0.2%; Asian and Pacific Islander — 0.3%. Spanish Origin — 0.6%. English — 15.4%; French — 11.2%; German — 2.3%; Irish — 4.6%; Italian — 1.7%; Polish — 1.1%; Scottish — 1.2%; Swedish — 0.5%.

Universities, Enrollment: Bennington College, Bennington — 594; Castleton State College, Castleton — 1,842; Champlain College, Burlington — 1,451; College of St. Joseph The Provider, Rutland — 408; Community College of Vermont, Montpelier — 1,816; Goddard College, Plainfield — 1,408; Green Mountain College, Poultney — 472; Johnson State College, Johnson — 1,431; Lyndon State College, Lyndonville — 1,005; Marlboro College, Marlboro — 211; Middlebury College, Middlebury — 1,926.

Norwich University (main campus), Northfield — 1,600; Norwich University (Vermont College campus), Montpelier — 504; St. Michael's College, Winooski — 1,711; School for International Training, Brattleboro — 778; Southern Vermont College, Bennington — 476; Trinity College, Burlington — 770; University of Vermont, Burlington — 10,988; Vermont Law School, South Royalton — 385; Vermont Technical College, Randolph Center — 793.

Newspapers, Circulation: *The Bennington Banner* (e), Bennington — 7,328; *Brattleboro Reformer* (e), Brattleboro — 8,360; *The Burlington Free Press* (mS), Burlington — 48,900; *The Caledonian-Record* (e), St. Johnsburg — 9,348; *The Newport Daily Express* (e), Newport — 4,304; *Rutland Daily Herald* (mS), Rutland — 21,243; *St. Albans Daily Messenger* (e), St. Albans — 3,753; *The Times-Argus* (eS), Barre — 12,345; *Valley News* (e), White River Junction — 13,216.

Commercial Television Stations, Affiliation: WCAX-TV, Burlington (CBS); WEZF-TV, Burlington (ABC); WNNE, Hartford (NBC). Most of district is located in Burlington-Plattsburgh (N.Y.) ADI. Portions are in Albany (N.Y.)-Schenectady (N.Y.)-Troy (N.Y.) ADI, Boston (Mass.) ADI and Portland (Maine)-Poland Spring (Maine) ADI.

Military Installations: Burlington International Airport (Air Force), South Burlington — 626.

Nuclear Power Plants: Vermont Yankee 1, Vernon (General Electric, Ebasco Services), November 1972.

Industries:

International Business Machines Corp.; Essex Junction; computers — 6,000. **General Electric Co.;** Burlington; electrical equipment — 3,300. **General Electric Co.** (Aircraft Equipment Div.); Burlington; weapon systems — 2,200. **Medical Center Hospital of Vermont Inc.;** Burlington; hospital — 2,100. **General Electric Co.;** Rutland; aircraft engine parts — 1,800.

P. & C. Food Markets Inc.; White River Junction; wholesale groceries — 1,400. **Velan Valve Corp.;** Williston; steam valves — 1,170. **Textron Inc.** (Waterbury Farrel Div.); Springfield; machine tools — 1,150. **National Life Insurance Co.** (HQ); Montpelier; life, casualty insurance — 860. **Cone-Blanchard Machine Co.;** Windsor; machine tools — 850. **Simmonds Precision Products** (Instruments Systems Div.); Vergennes; marine engineering devices — 833. **Digital Equipment Corp.;** South Burlington; computer systems — 760. **Book Press Inc.** (HQ); Brattleboro; book printing — 735. **Ethan Allen Inc.;** Orleans; wooden furniture — 717.

Bryant Grinder Corp.; Springfield; grinding machines — 650. **Ethan Allen Inc.;** Beecher Falls; wooden furniture — 600. **Union Carbide Corp.;** Bennington; dry batteries — 600. **Chittenden Corp.;** Burlington; bank holding company — 550. **Colt Industries Operating Corp.** (Fairbank Weighing Div.); St. Johnsbury; weighing equipment — 530.

Virginia

Displaying just a tinge of partisanship, Virginia's Democratic-controlled Legislature adopted a congressional district map designed to undermine the Republican incumbent in the 8th District.

On May 1, 1981, legislators sent this tentative redistricting plan incorporating the 8th District changes to Republican Gov. John Dalton and asked for his comments. Gov. Dalton asked that the 8th District be redrawn to make it more favorable for the incumbent, but the state Legislature rejected that suggestion in a special session held in June 1981. Dalton signed the redistricting bill into law June 12, 1981.

A more ambitiously partisan proposal that might have undermined several other Republican incumbents was rejected by the state Legislature's conservative Democratic Party leadership. Nonetheless, in November 1982 Democrats won three Republican congressional districts, including one that had been under GOP control for 30 years. The sagging economy, rather than redistricting, appeared to be the major factor in these seat shifts; the Democrats made their gains downstate where economic conditions were worst.

The Republicans, however, retained their hold on the 8th District seat. As a result of the 1982 elections, six members of the Virginia delegation were Republicans, four were Democrats. This was an increase of three seats for the Democrats, who had held only one seat in the previous Congress.

Age of Population

District	Population Under 18	Voting Age Population	Population 65 & Over (% of VAP)	Median Age
1	150,764	384,328	53,578 (13.9%)	29.5
2	146,142	383,036	36,388 (9.5%)	26.2
3	138,858	394,810	54,731 (13.9%)	30.2
4	158,632	377,071	53,225 (14.1%)	29.5
5	148,996	382,312	63,859 (16.7%)	31.5
6	137,004	401,356	67,927 (16.9%)	31.8
7	151,269	383,878	53,204 (13.9%)	29.8
8	158,292	376,074	23,284 (6.2%)	29.4
9	150,538	388,333	58,900 (15.2%)	29.4
10	133,839	401,286	40,208 (10.0%)	31.3
State	1,474,334	3,872,484	505,304 (13.0%)	29.8

Income and Occupation

District	Median Family Income	White Collar Workers	Blue Collar Workers	Service Workers	Farm Workers
1	$ 18,348	48.6%	33.6%	14.5%	3.3%
2	18,561	58.8	26.1	14.1	1.1
3	21,598	60.9	26.5	12.1	0.5
4	18,051	44.1	38.6	14.3	3.0
5	16,220	36.7	48.0	10.5	4.8
6	18,309	49.2	33.9	14.1	2.8
7	19,765	50.3	33.3	12.2	4.1
8	29,864	73.5	15.5	10.4	0.6
9	15,526	39.8	45.0	11.9	3.3
10	31,287	76.6	12.7	9.7	1.0
State	$ 20,018	54.8%	30.5%	12.2%	2.4%

Education: School Years Completed

District	8 Years or Fewer	4 Years of High School	4 Years of College or More	Median School Years
1	21.1%	30.5%	14.8%	12.3
2	13.0	35.2	17.5	12.6
3	16.6	27.7	21.2	12.6
4	27.7	28.1	10.3	12.1
5	36.1	25.5	8.6	11.8
6	25.8	29.4	13.6	12.2
7	24.8	29.6	16.0	12.3
8	6.6	29.0	36.6	13.2
9	38.7	24.2	9.4	11.7
10	6.4	25.7	40.9	13.4
State	21.6%	28.4%	19.1%	12.4

Housing and Residential Patterns

District	Owner Occupied	Renter Occupied	Urban	Rural
1	66.2%	33.8%	61.9%	38.1%
2	53.9	46.1	99.1	0.9
3	60.5	39.5	92.2	7.8
4	67.3	32.7	68.1	31.9
5	76.0	24.0	27.5	72.5
6	69.5	30.5	62.2	37.8
7	69.6	30.4	35.7	64.3

VIRGINIA

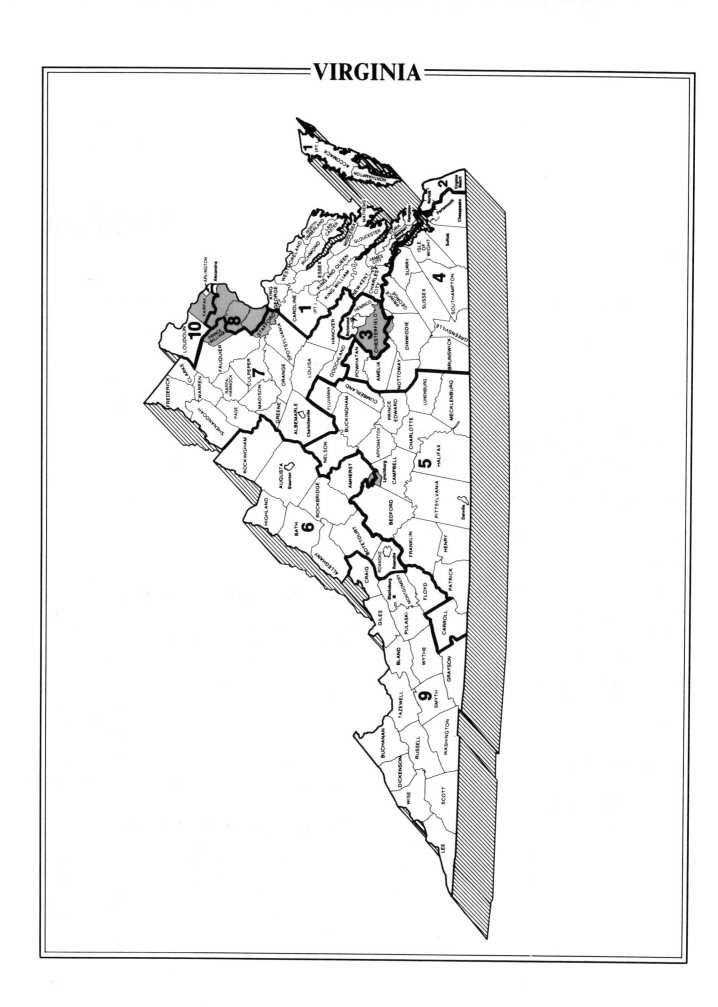

District	Owner Occupied	Renter Occupied	Urban	Rural
8	63.2	36.8	91.2	8.8
9	75.1	24.9	29.5	70.5
10	55.4	44.6	93.3	6.7
State	65.6%	34.4%	66.0%	34.0%

1st District

East — Newport News, Hampton

Traditionally Democratic, the 1st District did not elect its first Republican in this century to Congress until 1976. He held the seat for three terms, and when he retired to run for the Senate in 1982, another Republican captured the office.

But though the district has come loose from its traditional Democratic moorings, it is no Republican stronghold; its significant black and working-class populations make it less than predictable in most contests. In close statewide races, the 1st is a swing district. Jimmy Carter carried it with 50 percent of the vote in 1976. In the 1980 presidential contest, Ronald Reagan finished 5 points ahead of Carter.

Half the people in the 1st live in two cities at the district's southern end — Hampton and Newport News, both ports of the Hampton Roads harbor. These two cities frequently turn in Democratic majorities. In 1980, Carter won Hampton, while Reagan eked out a 357-vote plurality in Newport News.

Both cities are about one-third black, with economies tied to military and shipbuilding facilities; the Newport News Shipbuilding Co. alone employs 26,000 people.

The balance of the district's population is scattered through rural counties along the Chesapeake Bay and inland from it. Colonial Virginia's plantation economy was centered in this area; fishing, oystering, crabbing, corn, soybeans and wheat are important today. Tourism is a major economic factor in the Colonial Williamsburg and Yorktown areas.

This conservative rural territory is where the GOP has made its most significant inroads into the traditional Democratic strength. Of the 18 counties outside Hampton and Newport News, Reagan won all but four in 1980, accumulating an 11,000-vote cushion.

In redistricting, the 1st took Caroline County from the 7th. An agricultural county that is 43 percent black, Caroline gave 56.7 percent of its vote to Carter in 1980. But the county's population is just 3 percent of the district's total, so its impact is minimal.

Election Returns

1st District		Democrat		Republican	
1976	President	83,549	(50.5%)	77,249	(46.7%)
	Senate	55,144	(36.5%)	—[1]	
	House	70,159	(46.4%)	73,914	(48.9%)
1977	Governor	61,484	(47.3%)	67,280	(51.7%)
1978	Senate	66,121	(52.4%)	59,970	(47.6%)
	House	36,364	(28.6%)	90,713	(71.4%)

1st District		Democrat		Republican	
1980	President	80,434	(44.6%)	90,093	(49.9%)
	House	—		132,986	(90.7%)
1981	Governor	77,155	(55.2%)	62,491	(44.7%)
1982	Senate	60,770	(40.5%)	89,145	(59.4%)
	House	62,379	(43.7%)	76,926	(53.9%)

[1] *There was no Republican candidate; Harry F. Byrd Jr. won the election as an Independent, winning 890,778 votes (57.2% of the total statewide vote).*

Demographics

Population: 535,092. **Percent Change from 1970:** 11.3%.

Land Area: 4,257 square miles. **Population per Square Mile:** 125.7.

Counties, 1980 Population: Accomack — 31,268; Caroline — 17,904; Charles City — 6,692; Essex — 8,864; Gloucester — 20,107; Hampton[1] — 122,617; James City — 22,763; King George — 10,543; King William — 9,334; Lancaster — 10,129; Mathews — 7,995; Middlesex — 7,719; New Kent — 8,781; Newport News[1] — 144,903; Northampton — 14,625; Northumberland — 9,828; Poquoson[1] — 8,726; Richmond — 6,952; Westmoreland — 14,041; Williamsburg[1] — 9,870; York — 35,463.

[1] *Independent cities.*

Race and Ancestry: White — 67.0%; Black — 31.3%; American Indian, Eskimo and Aleut — 0.4%; Asian and Pacific Islander — 0.8%. Spanish Origin — 1.3%. English — 19.6%; French — 0.7%; German — 3.8%; Irish — 3.0%; Italian — 0.7%; Polish — 0.5%; Scottish — 0.5%.

Universities, Enrollment: Christopher Newport College, Newport News — 3,897; College of William and Mary in Virginia, Williamsburg — 6,465; Eastern Shore Community College, Melfa — 524; Hampton Institute, Hampton — 3,230; Rappahannock Community College, Glenns — 1,429; Thomas Nelson Community College, Hampton — 6,314.

Newspapers, Circulation: *Daily Press* (mS), Newport News — 57,164; *Times-Herald* (e), Newport News — 41,594.

Commercial Television Stations, Affiliation: WVEC-TV, Hampton (ABC). District is divided between Norfolk-Portsmouth-Newport News-Hampton ADI and Richmond ADI. Portion is in Washington, D.C. ADI.

Military Installations: Cape Charles Air Force Station, Kiptopeke — 6; Fort A. P. Hill, Bowling Green — 3,935; Fort Eustis, Newport News — 14,274; Fort Monroe, Hampton — 2,965; Langley Air Force Base, Hampton — 11,853; Naval Surface Weapons Center, Dahlgren — 2,907; Yorktown Naval Weapons Station, Newport News — 2,770.

Industries:

Newport News Shipbuilding & Drydock Co. (HQ); Newport News; shipbuilding — 26,000. **Colonial Williamsburg Foundation;** Williamsburg; historic village, hotel — 2,800. **Eastern State Hospital;** Williamsburg; state psychiatric hospital — 1,330. **Newport News General Hospital;** Newport News; hospital — 1,250. **Anheuser-Busch Inc.;** Williamsburg; brewery — 1,100. **Perdue Inc.;** Accomac; poultry dressing — 1,100.

Badische Corp. (HQ); Williamsburg; industrial chemicals, synthetic fibers — 1,000. **Holly Farms Poultry Industries;** Temperanceville; poultry processing — 950. **The Chesapeake Corp. of Virginia** (HQ); West Point; paper mills — 900. **Chesapeake & Ohio Railway;** Newport News; railroad operations — 800. **Bendix Corp.;** Newport News; motor vehicle parts — 600. **Daily Press Inc.;** Newport News; newspaper publishing — 600. **Howmet Turbine Components Corp.** (Misco Hampton Div.); Hampton; manufacturing industries — 600. **Williamsburg Pottery Factory** (Williamsburg Glasshouse); Lightfoot; pottery products — 550. **Maida Development Corp.;** Hampton; electronic components — 500. **Standard Products Co. Inc.;** Kilmarnock; animal, marine oils — 500.

2nd District

Norfolk, Virginia Beach

The 2nd is composed of adjacent cities: the fast-growing residential and resort municipality of Virginia Beach and the unionized port city of Norfolk, which lost 13 percent of its population during the 1970s.

The two cities present a stark political contrast. Norfolk, which is 35 percent black, gave Jimmy Carter a 52-41 percent edge in 1980. Virginia Beach, which is 86 percent white, went to Ronald Reagan by nearly 2-1.

Like the southern portion of the 1st District, the 2nd is heavily dependent on the massive concentration of naval installations, shipbuilders and shipping firms in the Hampton Roads harbor area, which ranks first in export tonnage among the nation's Atlantic ports and is the biggest coal shipper in the world.

During the 1970s, many military families, business people and retirees settled in Virginia Beach, adding another dimension to its identity as a summertime tourist center. The city's retail and service trade has boomed in response to this influx of affluence. After growing 52 percent in the previous 10 years, Virginia Beach in 1980 had 263,000 residents and was just 5,000 people short of supplanting Norfolk as Virginia's largest city.

The 2nd was expanded slightly by redistricting. It picked up 35,000 people in the southern part of Virginia Beach who had been in the 4th District. The new territory is a solidly Republican and rural area into which suburbia is encroaching. The Republican incumbent has not had Democratic opposition since 1976.

Election Returns

2nd District		Democrat		Republican	
1976	President	65,119	(48.6%)	62,692	(46.8%)
	Senate	48,255	(39.6%)	—[1]	
	House	43,600	(34.7%)	81,873	(65.3%)
1977	Governor	51,829	(51.5%)	48,330	(48.0%)
1978	Senate	50,047	(50.3%)	49,363	(49.6%)
	House	—		65,850	(100.0%)
1980	President	60,013	(41.0%)	75,443	(51.5%)
	House	2,371	(2.1%)	101,681	(88.4%)
1981	Governor	62,773	(58.9%)	43,586	(40.9%)
1982	Senate	57,886	(51.2%)	54,990	(48.7%)
	House	—		78,108	(99.8%)

[1] *There was no Republican candidate; Harry F. Byrd Jr. won the election as an Independent, winning 890,778 votes (57.2% of the total statewide vote).*

Demographics

Population: 529,178. **Percent Change from 1970:** 10.2%.

Land Area: 309 square miles. **Population per Square Mile:** 1,712.6.

Counties, 1980 Population: Norfolk[1] — 266,979; Virginia Beach[1] — 262,199.

[1] *Independent cities.*

Race and Ancestry: White — 73.5%; Black — 22.7%; American Indian, Eskimo and Aleut — 0.3%; Asian and Pacific Islander — 2.6%. Spanish Origin — 2.1%. English — 14.2%; French — 1.0%; German

— 4.7%; Irish — 3.7%; Italian — 1.6%; Polish — 0.8%; Scottish — 0.8%.

Universities, Enrollment: Eastern Virginia Medical School, Norfolk — 315; Kee's Business College, Norfolk — 524; Norfolk State University, Norfolk — 6,756; Old Dominion University, Norfolk — 16,353; Virginia Wesleyan College, Norfolk — 834.

Newspapers, Circulation: *The Ledger-Star* (eS), Norfolk — 94,130; *The Virginian-Pilot* (mS), Norfolk — 127,791.

Commercial Television Stations, Affiliation: WTKR-TV, Norfolk (CBS); WTVZ, Norfolk (None). Entire district is located in Norfolk-Portsmouth-Newport News-Hampton ADI.

Military Installations: Armed Forces Staff College, Norfolk — 562; Atlantic Fleet Anti-submarine Warfare Training Center, Norfolk — 297; Atlantic Fleet Combat Training Center, Virginia Beach — 4,492; Atlantic Naval Communications Area Master Station, Norfolk — 831; Camp Elmore (Marine Corps), Norfolk — 800; Fort Story, Virginia Beach — 1,696; Little Creek Naval Amphibious Base, Norfolk — 10,014; Norfolk Naval Air Station, Norfolk — 15,281; Norfolk Naval Public Works Center, Norfolk — 1,776; Norfolk Naval Station, Norfolk — 39,244; Norfolk Naval Supply Center, Norfolk — 4,494; Oceana Naval Air Station, Virginia Beach — 9,987.

Industries:

Norfolk Shipbuilding & Drydock Co. (HQ); Norfolk; shipbuilding — 3,200. **Medical Center Hospitals;** Norfolk; hospital — 2,520. **Virginia National Bankshares** (HQ); Norfolk; banking — 2,000. **De Paul Hospital;** Norfolk; hospital — 1,550. **Landmark Communications Inc.** (HQ); Norfolk; newspaper publishing — 1,550.

Norfolk & Western Railway Co.; Norfolk; railroad operations — 1,200. **General Hospital of Virginia Beach Inc.;** Virginia Beach; hospital — 1,010. **Ford Motor Co. Inc.** (Norfolk Assembly Plant); Norfolk; trucks — 1,000. **General Foam Plastics Corp.;** Norfolk; miscellaneous plastics products — 600. **Allied Repair Service Inc.** (HQ); Norfolk; marine repairing services — 520.

3rd District

Richmond and Suburbs

Like the 2nd District, the 3rd has two distinct parts: the black-majority, traditionally Democratic city of Richmond, and the surrounding suburbs in Chesterfield and Henrico counties, which are overwhelmingly white and predominantly Republican.

Because the population grew in the suburbs and shrunk in the city, the 3rd had emerged as a GOP stronghold by the end of the 1970s. Redistricting made the district even more of a Republican bastion. To make up for Richmond's 12 percent population decline in the 1970s, the 3rd picked up 33,000 western Chesterfield voters from the 5th.

The political split between Richmond and its suburbs was obvious in 1980 voting. Jimmy Carter won 55 percent in Richmond, which is home to 41 percent of the people in the redrawn 3rd. But Ronald Reagan took more than two-thirds of the vote in both Henrico and Chesterfield. In one Henrico precinct, Reagan's margin was 8-1.

Richmond, the capital and the third-largest city in the state, has long been the center of Virginia commerce and government. It was also one of the South's early manufacturing centers, originally concentrating on tobacco processing. Over the years, factories have diversified into chemicals, textiles, metals and other products.

Richmond's business elite exercises considerable influence over politics in the district and in the state. The

Republican win in 1980, which marked the first time the district had switched party control since the 19th century, had the backing of the business establishment.

Population trends point toward long-term GOP dominance. With the 1980 census, suburban Henrico and Chesterfield counties together gained enough new residents to exceed Richmond's population for the first time in history.

Election Returns

3rd District		Democrat		Republican	
1976	President	79,505	(41.3%)	109,653	(56.9%)
	Senate	66,116	(36.0%)	—[1]	
	House	134,263	(88.0%)	—	
1977	Governor	55,685	(34.5%)	104,602	(64.8%)
1978	Senate	59,010	(40.7%)	85,747	(59.2%)
	House	111,511	(88.5%)	—	
1980	President	80,943	(37.8%)	121,797	(57.0%)
	House	71,739	(36.6%)	95,481	(48.7%)
1981	Governor	87,998	(50.1%)	87,274	(49.7%)
1982	Senate	70,985	(44.0%)	90,036	(55.9%)
	House	63,946	(40.8%)	92,928	(59.2%)

[1] *There was no Republican candidate; Harry F. Byrd Jr. won the election as an Independent, winning 890,778 votes (57.2% of the total statewide vote).*

Demographics

Population: 533,668. **Percent Change from 1970:** 12.0%.

Land Area: 711 square miles. **Population per Square Mile:** 750.6.

Counties, 1980 Population: Chesterfield (Pt.) — 133,719; Henrico — 180,735; Richmond[1] — 219,214.

[1] *Independent city*

Cities, 1980 Population: Bon Air (CDP) — 16,224; Chester (CDP) — 11,728; East Highland Park (CDP) — 11,797; Highland Springs (CDP) — 12,146; Lakeside (CDP) — 12,289; Laurel (CDP) — 10,569; Richmond — 219,214; Tuckahoe (CDP) — 39,868.

Race and Ancestry: White — 70.6%; Black — 28.3%; American Indian, Eskimo and Aleut — 0.2%; Asian and Pacific Islander — 0.7%. Spanish Origin — 0.9%. English — 20.3%; French — 0.7%; German — 4.3%; Irish — 3.3%; Italian — 0.8%; Polish — 0.5%; Scottish — 0.6%.

Universities, Enrollment: J. Sargeant Reynolds Community College, Richmond — 9,006; John Tyler Community College, Chester — 4,038; Presbyterian School of Christian Education, Richmond — 106; Union Theological Seminary in Virginia, Richmond — 265; University of Richmond, Richmond — 4,189; Virginia Commonwealth University, Richmond — 19,817; Virginia Union University, Richmond — 1,274.

Newspapers, Circulation: *The Richmond News Leader* (e), Richmond — 114,468; *Richmond Times-Dispatch* (mS), Richmond — 134,880.

Commercial Television Stations, Affiliation: WRLH-TV, Richmond (None); WRNX, Richmond (None); WTVR-TV, Richmond (CBS); WWBT, Richmond (NBC). Entire district is located in Richmond ADI.

Military Installations: Byrd Field (Air Force), Sandston — 903; Richmond Defense General Supply Center, Richmond — 2,892.

Industries:

Philip Morris Inc.; Richmond; cigarettes — 14,000. **E. I. du Pont de Nemours & Co.** (Textile Fibers Dept.); Richmond; textile fibers — 3,700. **Reynolds Metals Co.** (HQ); Richmond; primary aluminum production — 3,450. **Thalhimer Brothers Inc.** (HQ); Richmond; department stores — 2,100. **United Bankshares Inc.** (HQ); Richmond; banking — 2,000.

Western Electric Co. Inc.; Richmond; telephone equipment — 1,700. **Media General Inc.** (HQ); Richmond; newspaper publishing — 1,500. **A. H. Robbins Co. Inc.** (HQ); Richmond; pharmaceutical preparations — 1,350. **Richmond Memorial Hospital Inc.;** Richmond; hospital — 1,300. **Holly Farms Poultry Industries;** Glen Allen; poultry processing — 1,220. **Chippenham Hospital Inc.;** Richmond; hospital — 1,100. **Federal Reserve Bank of Richmond** (HQ); Richmond; banking — 1,000. **St. Mary's Hospital;** Richmond; hospital — 1,000. **Blue Cross of Virginia Inc.;** Richmond; health insurance — 950. **Bank of Virginia Co.** (HQ); Richmond; banking — 900. **Nabisco Inc.;** Richmond; cookies — 750. **Interbake Foods Inc.** (HQ); Richmond; cookies — 700. **Basic Construction Co.;** Richmond; hotels, motels — 650.

Life Insurance Co. of Virginia (HQ); Richmond; life insurance — 635. **American Brands Inc.** (Tobacco Div.); Richmond; cigarettes — 600. **Chesapeake & Ohio Railway Co.;** Richmond; railroad operations — 600. **General Electric Co.;** Richmond; refrigerators, freezers — 580. **The William Byrd Press Inc.** (HQ); Richmond; commercial printing — 566. **McLean Trucking Co.;** Richmond; truck terminal — 550. **Overnite Transportation Co.** (HQ); Richmond; trucking — 550. **Philip Morris Inc.;** Richmond; tobacco research — 550. **Richmond, Fredericksburg & Potomac Railroad** (HQ); Richmond; railroad operations — 542. **St. Luke's Hospital;** Richmond; hospital — 524. **E. R. Carpenter Co. Inc.** (HQ); Richmond; urethane foam — 500. **Travelers Insurance Co. Inc.;** Richmond; life insurance — 500. **First & Merchants Corp.** (HQ); Richmond; banking — more than 500.

4th District

Southeast — Chesapeake, Portsmouth

With Portsmouth's large black population and blue-collar work force joining diehard rural Democrats, the 4th is solidly Democratic on paper. It was the only Virginia district to give Jimmy Carter a majority in 1980. Democrat Charles S. Robb won 60 percent here en route to election as governor.

But throughout the 1970s Republicans and conservative Democrats formed a voting majority to send a Republican to the House. Not until 1982 did a Democrat win, picking up nearly 55 percent of the vote.

Portsmouth is 45 percent black and home to nearly a quarter of the people in the redrawn 4th. The city is oriented toward the naval and shipbuilding economy of Norfolk, Hampton and Newport News. In 1980, Carter won 58 percent in Portsmouth, his highest percentage in any of Virginia's major cities.

The neighboring city of Chesapeake, slightly larger than Portsmouth, gave Ronald Reagan a slim victory in 1980. Chesapeake is less black and less industrial than Portsmouth; many who work in Portsmouth's shipyards and factories have homes in Chesapeake.

There is some industry in the smaller cities of the 4th, which together make up another 20 percent of the district's population. Suffolk processes peanuts, Petersburg makes tobacco products, Hopewell calls itself the chemical capital of the South, and Smithfield is home to the meatpackers who cure the hams that bear the town's name. Of these towns, Carter lost only Hopewell in 1980. The most reliably Democratic of the smaller cities is black-majority Petersburg.

Peanuts and tobacco are the important crops in the farm lands of the 4th, where more than one-third of the district's rsidents live. Democratic ties are still strong there. Sussex County, for example, gave Carter 57 percent of the total vote there in 1980. Rural population exodus, a trend that has virtually ended elsewhere in Virginia, still plagues this area; four agricultural counties lost population in the 1970s.

Four counties and part of another joined the 4th District because of redistricting. Along its western border, the district gained Brunswick, Nottoway, Powhatan and Amelia counties and a slice of Chesterfield County. Although much of the new territory is rural, the eastern end of Powhatan is an outlying Richmond suburb, and that county had a growth rate of 70 percent in the 1970s. The district gave up the southern part of Virginia Beach to the 2nd District.

Election Returns

4th District		Democrat		Republican	
1976	President	96,396	(56.4%)	69,501	(40.7%)
	Senate	62,142	(39.9%)	—[1]	
	House	73,863	(50.3%)	72,003	(49.1%)
1977	Governor	71,160	(52.0%)	63,623	(46.5%)
1978	Senate	71,203	(55.7%)	56,576	(44.3%)
	House	9,810	(11.5%)	75,489	(88.3%)
1980	President	91,716	(50.2%)	83,955	(46.0%)
	House	69,083	(43.5%)	89,238	(56.2%)
1981	Governor	187,102	(60.1%)	57,577	(39.7%)
1982	Senate	86,522	(58.4%)	61,619	(41.5%)
	House	80,695	(54.4%)	67,708	(45.6%)

[1] *There was no Republican candidate; Harry F. Byrd Jr. won the election as an Independent, winning 890,778 votes (57.2% of the total statewide vote).*

Demographics

Population: 535,703. **Percent Change from 1970:** 7.1%.

Land Area: 5,114 square miles. **Population per Square Mile:** 104.8.

Counties, 1980 Population: Amelia — 8,405; Brunswick — 15,632; Chesapeake[1] — 114,486; Chesterfield (Pt.) — 7,653; Colonial Heights[1] — 16,509; Dinwiddie — 22,602; Emporia[1] — 4,840; Franklin[1] — 7,308; Greensville — 10,903; Hopewell[1] — 23,397; Isle Of Wight — 21,603; Nottoway — 14,666; Petersburg[1] — 41,055; Portsmouth[1] — 104,577; Powhatan — 13,062; Prince George — 25,733; Southampton — 18,731; Suffolk[1] — 47,621; Surry — 6,046; Sussex — 10,874.

[1] *Independent cities.*

Race and Ancestry: White — 59.2%; Black — 39.7%; American Indian, Eskimo and Aleut — 0.1%; Asian and Pacific Islander — 0.6%. Spanish Origin — 1.1%. English — 19.3%; French — 0.6%; German — 2.6%; Irish — 2.5%; Italian — 0.6%.

Universities, Enrollment: Paul D. Camp Community College, Franklin — 1,096; Richard Bland College, Petersburg — 1,035; St. Paul's College, Lawrenceville — 645; Southside Virginia Community College, Alberta — 1,863; Tidewater Community College, Portsmouth — 14,935; Virginia State University, Petersburg — 4,746.

Newspapers, Circulation: *News* (e), Hopewell — 7,366; *News-Herald* (eS), Suffolk — 7,642; *The Progress-Index* (eS), Petersburg — 23,016.

Commercial Television Stations, Affiliation: WAVY-TV, Portsmouth (NBC); WXEX-TV, Petersburg (ABC); WYAH-TV, Portsmouth (None). District is divided between Norfolk-Portsmouth-Newport News-Hampton ADI and Richmond ADI.

Military Installations: Fort Lee, Petersburg — 8,591; Fort Pickett, Blackstone — 3,414; Norfolk Naval Shipyard, Portsmouth — 14,982; Portsmouth Naval Regional Medical Center, Portsmouth — 2,744.

Nuclear Power Plants: Surry 1, Gravel Neck (Westinghouse, Stone & Webster), December 1972; Surry 2, Gravel Neck (Westinghouse, Stone & Webster), May 1973.

Industries:

Union Camp Corp. (Bleached Div.); Franklin; paper products — 2,380. **Allied Chemical Corp.** (Fibers Div.); Hopewell; nylon fiber — 2,018. **General Electric Co.** (Television Business Div.); Portsmouth; television sets — 1,900. **Brown & Williamson Tobacco Corp.**; Petersburg; cigarettes — 1,720. **Smithfield Packing Co. Inc.** (HQ); Smithfield; meatpacking — 1,600.

ITT Continental Baking Co. Inc. (Gwaltney of Smithfield); Smithfield; meatpacking — 1,500. **Standard Brands Inc.** (Planters Peanut Div.); Suffolk; nuts — 1,500. **Hercules Inc.**; Hopewell; explosives — 1,250. **Allied Chemical Corp.** (Fibers & Plastics Co.); Hopewell; synthetic organic fibers — 1,200. **Firestone Tire & Rubber Co. Inc.** (Synthetic Fibers Div.); Hopewell; synthetic organic fibers — 1,100. **Petersburg General Hospital;** Petersburg; hospital — 1,100. **Central State Hospital;** Petersburg; state psychiatric hospital — 1,000. **Portsmouth General Hospital;** Portsmouth; hospital — 1,000. **Continental Group Inc.** (Forest Industries); Hopewell; paper, paperboard — 540. **Titmus Optical Inc.**; Petersburg; ophthalmic goods — 535. **Allied Chemical Corp.** (Technical Center); Petersburg; cellulosic fibers — 500. **Dayco Corp.** (Seward Luggage Div.); Petersburg; luggage — 500.

5th District

South — Danville

The 5th is in the heart of Virginia's rural "Southside," a largely agricultural region that more closely resembles the Deep South than does any other part of the state. It is relatively poor and has a substantial black population. Tobacco and soybeans are major crops, but this region lacks the rich soil of the Tidewater.

The 5th supports conservative Democrats; its House incumbent is an example of that. But it has long refused to vote for more liberal Democratic candidates at the state and national level. It was one of only two districts in Virginia to back George C. Wallace in 1968 and has not supported a Democrat for president in more than a quarter-century. Even Barry Goldwater in 1964 carried it with 51 percent of the vote.

The district's largest city is Danville, a tobacco market and textile center on the North Carolina border. Ronald Reagan received 61 percent in Danville in 1980. The residents of the city and those of surrounding Pittsylvania County, which Reagan took by 2-1, make up about one-fifth of the district's population.

Most of the people in the 5th are scattered through farming areas and a few factory towns. Most of these areas normally vote Republican at the state level. The best area for Democrats is Henry County. Jimmy Carter won it with 49 percent in 1980 and was beaten by only 96 votes in its county-seat town of Martinsville, a major furniture-producer.

To the north, the district takes in part of Lynchburg. That section of Lynchburg and its southern neighbor, Campbell County, are strongly conservative areas where Reagan won two-thirds of the 1980 vote.

In redistricting, the 5th lost a tier of counties on the eastern end of the district to the 4th — Powhatan, Amelia, Nottoway and Brunswick — and gave to the 3rd the western half of Chesterfield County. On the southwestern edge, the 5th traded Floyd County to the 9th in return for Carroll County. The 5th also picked up Bedford County from the 6th and Fluvanna and Nelson counties from the 7th.

The changes were not expected to have a great impact on the political character of the 5th. Of the counties the district lost, all but one chose Reagan in 1980; of the counties it gained, Carter took only Nelson.

Election Returns

5th District		Democrat		Republican	
1976	President	77,138	(47.9%)	78,306	(48.6%)
	Senate	41,867	(29.5%)	—[1]	
	House	86,667	(84.2%)	14,496	(14.1%)
1977	Governor	45,241	(39.7%)	67,875	(59.6%)
1978	Senate	58,054	(49.0%)	60,391	(51.0%)
	House	69,215	(84.2%)	12,956	(15.8%)
1980	President	73,569	(41.5%)	97,203	(54.8%)
	House	90,000	(81.2%)	20,657	(18.6%)
1981	Governor	70,900	(49.9%)	70,750	(49.8%)
1982	Senate	60,840	(47.0%)	68,375	(52.9%)
	House	88,293	(99.9%)	—	

[1] *There was no Republican candidate; Harry F. Byrd Jr. won the election as an Independent, winning 890,778 votes (57.2% of the total statewide vote).*

Demographics

Population: 531,308. **Percent Change from 1970:** 13.7%.

Land Area: 9,007 square miles. **Population per Square Mile:** 59.0.

Counties, 1980 Population: Appomattox — 11,971; Bedford — 34,927; Bedford[1] — 5,991; Buckingham — 11,751; Campbell — 45,424; Carroll — 27,270; Charlotte — 12,266; Cumberland — 7,881; Danville[1] — 45,642; Fluvanna — 10,244; Franklin — 35,740; Halifax — 30,599; Henry — 57,654; Lunenburg — 12,124; Lynchburg (Pt.)[1] — 14,684; Martinsville[1] — 18,149; Mecklenburg — 29,444; Nelson — 12,204; Patrick — 17,647; Pittsylvania — 66,147; Prince Edward — 16,456; South Boston[1] — 7,093.

[1] *Independent cities.*

Race and Ancestry: White — 74.9%; Black — 24.7%; American Indian, Eskimo and Aleut — 0.1%; Asian and Pacific Islander — 0.2%. Spanish Origin — 0.7%. English — 28.1%; French — 0.5%; German — 3.4%; Irish — 3.8%; Scottish — 0.5%.

Universities, Enrollment: Averett College, Danville — 1,028; Danville Community College, Danville — 2,236; Ferrum College, Ferrum — 1,589; Hampden-Sydney College, Hampden-Sydney — 731; Longwood College, Farmville — 2,470; Patrick Henry Community College, Martinsville — 1,605.

Newspapers, Circulation: *The Bee* (e), Danville — 17,092; *Bulletin* (eS), Martinsville — 17,686; *The Danville Register* (mS), Danville — 9,098.

Commercial Television Stations, Affiliation: Most of district is located in Roanoke-Lynchburg ADI. Portions are in Richmond ADI, Greensboro (N.C.)-Winston Salem (N.C.)-High Point (N.C.) ADI, and Raleigh (N.C.)-Durham (N.C.) ADI.

Industries:

Dan River Inc.; Danville; broad-woven fabric mills — 8,700. **E. I. du Pont de Nemours & Co.;** Martinsville; plastics materials — 3,600. **Bassett Furniture Industries** (HQ); Bassett; wooden household furniture — 3,000. **Stanley Industries Corp.;** (HQ); Stanleytown; wooden household furniture — 2,500. **Goodyear Tire & Rubber Co.;** Danville; tires, inner tubes — 2,150.

The Babcock & Wilcox Co. (Naval Nuclear Fuel Div.); Lynchburg; nuclear fuel — 2,100. **American Furniture Co. Inc.** (HQ); Martinsville; wooden household furniture — 2,000. **Fieldcrest Mills Inc.;** Fieldale; towels — 1,470. **Burlington Industries Inc.** (Klopman Div.); Hurt; men's trousers — 1,400. **Burlington Industries Inc.** (Klopman Div.); Altavista; broad-woven fabric mills — 1,390. **Burlington Industries Inc.** (Menswear Div.); Clarksville; broad-woven fabric mills — 1,300. **The Memorial Hospital Inc.;** Danville; hospital — 1,200. **Rubatex Corp.** (Walltex Corp. - HQ); Bedford; rubber products — 1,200. **Tultex Corp.** (Sale Knitting Co.); South Boston; knit outerwear mills — 1,000.

Bassett-Walker Inc.; Bassett; knit fabric mills — 950. **Thomasville Furniture Industries** (Armstrong Furniture Div.); Appomattox; household furniture — 925. **Bassett-Walker Inc.** (HQ); Martinsville; knit outerwear — 900. **Hampco Apparel Inc.;** Martinsville; men's trousers — 900. **Burlington Industries Inc.;** Halifax; broad-woven fabric mills — 800. **Pannill Knitting Co. Inc.** (HQ); Martinsville; knit outerwear mills — 800.

Health-Tex Inc.; Danville; children's clothing — 735. **J. P. Stevens & Co. Inc.** (United Elastic Div.); Stuart; broad-woven cotton fabric mills — 700. **J. P. Stevens & Co. Inc.;** South Boston; broad-woven fabric mills — 700. **Westinghouse Electric Corp.** (Small Power Transformer Div.); South Boston; power transformers — 650. **Hooker Furniture Corp.** (HQ); Martinsville; wooden household furniture — 600. **The Lane Co. Inc.** (Hickory Chair Co. Div. - HQ); Altavista; wooden household furniture — 600.

Bassett Furniture Industries; Martinsville; wooden household furniture — 550. **The Budd Co.;** Ridgeway; truck trailers — 550. **Martin Processing Inc.;** Rocky Mount; textile finishing — 550. **Russell Stover Candies Inc.;** Clarksville; candy — 550. **U.S. Industries Inc.** (M. W. Manufacturers Div.); Rocky Mount; wood millwork — 525. **Sprague Electric Co.;** Hillsville; electronic components — 500. **Simplimatic Engineering Co.** (Seco Avionics Div. - HQ); Lynchburg; conveyors — 500. **Stackpole Components Co.;** Farmville; refrigerators, freezers — 500.

6th District

West — Roanoke, Lynchburg

The 1982 election ended a 28-year winning streak for Republicans in 6th District House elections. Pockets of Democratic strength show up in state and national elections, and in 1982 they coalesced to elect a Democrat by a narrow margin to the House.

Jimmy Carter won 52 percent of the 1980 vote in the city of Roanoke, which has more than 100,000 people and 19 percent of the district's population. An array of industries in Roanoke make textiles, furniture, and metal and electrical products. Carter also carried towns to the north such as Covington, Buena Vista and Clifton Forge, and the two counties surrounding them, Bath and Allegheny. There are chemical plants and pulpwood and paper mills in that area.

But Democratic support is surpassed by the Republican vote in Roanoke's suburbs, in Lynchburg and in most of the rural areas. Reagan won 56 percent in Roanoke County, took nearly all the rural counties and defeated Carter 59-33 percent in Lynchburg, the home base of evangelist Jerry Falwell and the Moral Majority. Some 52,000 residents of Lynchburg are in the 6th District, the other 15,000 are in the 5th.

Outside of metropolitan Roanoke and Lynchburg, the district is rural and depends primarily on livestock and poultry. Rockingham County, the new addition for 1982, contains the city of Harrisonburg, supplier of turkeys for thousands of Thanksgiving dinners. Rockingham County is more populous and more Republican than Bedford County, which switched from the 6th to the 5th.

Election Returns

6th District		Democrat		Republican	
1976	President	82,111	(46.3%)	90,573	(51.1%)
	Senate	54,366	(32.7%)	—[1]	
	House	520	(0.3%)	100,381	(63.5%)
1977	Governor	52,456	(37.9%)	85,103	(61.5%)
1978	Senate	61,826	(47.0%)	69,458	(52.9%)
	House	4,672	(4.7%)	94,439	(95.1%)
1980	President	82,299	(43.3%)	97,549	(51.3%)
	House	153	(0.1%)	130,098	(99.1%)
1981	Governor	76,490	(50.9%)	73,702	(49.0%)
1982	Senate	62,380	(45.4%)	74,933	(54.5%)
	House	68,192	(49.7%)	66,537	(48.5%)

[1] *There was no Republican candidate; Harry F. Byrd Jr. won the election as an Independent, winning 890,778 votes (57.2% of the statewide total vote).*

Demographics

Population: 538,360. **Percent Change from 1970:** 8.6%.

Land Area: 5,256 square miles. **Population per Square Mile:** 102.4.

Counties, 1980 Population: Alleghany — 14,333; Amherst — 29,122; Augusta — 53,732; Bath — 5,860; Botetourt — 23,270; Buena Vista[1] — 6,717; Clifton Forge[1] — 5,046; Covington[1] — 9,063; Harrisonburg[1] — 19,671; Highland — 2,937; Lexington[1] — 7,292; Lynchburg[1] (Pt.) — 52,059; Roanoke[1] — 72,945; Roanoke — 100,220; Rockbridge — 17,911; Rockingham — 57,038; Salem[1] — 23,958; Staunton[1] — 21,857; Waynesboro[1] — 15,329.

[1] *Independent cities.*

Race and Ancestry: White — 88.6%; Black — 10.8%; American Indian, Eskimo and Aleut — 0.1%; Asian and Pacific Islander — 0.3%. Spanish Origin — 0.6%. Dutch — 0.5%; English — 23.1%; French — 0.7%; German — 9.2%; Irish — 4.6%; Italian — 0.6%; Scottish — 0.7%.

Universities, Enrollment: Blue Ridge Community College, Weyers Cave — 2,322; Bridgewater College, Bridgewater — 950; Central Virginia Community College, Lynchburg — 3,976; Dabney S. Lancaster Community College, Clifton Forge — 1,075; Eastern Mennonite College, Harrisonburg — 1,149; Hollins College, Hollins College — 940; James Madison University, Harrisonburg — 9,468; Liberty Baptist College, Lynchburg — 2,930; Lynchburg College, Lynchburg — 2,486; Mary Baldwin College, Staunton — 839.

National Business College, Roanoke — 728; Phillips Business College, Lynchburg — 107; Randolph-Macon Women's College, Lynchburg — 734; Roanoke College, Salem — 1,374; Southern Seminary Junior College, Buena Vista — 271; Sweet Briar College, Sweet Briar — 650; Virginia Military Institute, Lexington — 1,319; Virginia Western Community College, Roanoke — 5,909; Washington and Lee University, Lexington — 1,622.

Newspapers, Circulation: *Covington Virginian* (e), Covington — 9,219; *The Daily Advance* (e), Lynchburg — 20,640; *Daily News-Record* (m), Harrisonburg — 28,593; *The Lynchburg News* (m), Lynchburg — 20,949; *The News-Virginian* (e), Waynesboro — 13,422; *Review* (e), Clifton Forge — 3,183; *Roanoke Times & World News* (meS), Roanoke — 115,951; *The Staunton Leader* (eS), Staunton — 17,088.

Commercial Television Stations, Affiliation: WDBJ-TV, Roanoke (CBS); WHSV-TV, Harrisonburg (ABC); WSET-TV, Lynchburg (ABC); WSLS-TV, Roanoke (NBC). Most of district is located in Roanoke-Lynchburg ADI. Portions are in Harrisonburg ADI and Richmond ADI.

Industries:

Norfolk & Western Railway Co. (HQ); Roanoke; railroad operations — 4,500. **General Electric Co.** (Drive Systems Dept.); Salem; industrial controls — 3,500. **General Electric Co.** (Mobile Communications Div.); Lynchburg; communications equipment — 3,200. **Lynchburg Training School & Hospital;** Madison Heights; state psychiatric hospital — 2,540. **Roanoke Hospital Assn.;** Roanoke; hospital — 2,200

E. I. du Pont de Nemours & Co.; Waynesboro; yarn texturizing — 2,050. **Westvaco Corp.** (Bleached Board Div.); Covington; paperboard mills — 1,800. **Hercules Inc.;** Covington; plastics materials — 1,400. **Western State Hospital;** Staunton; state psychiatric hospital — 1,350. **General Electric Co.;** Waynesboro; data communications business products — 1,330. **Marvel Poultry Co. Inc.;** Dayton; turkey farm, processing — 1,300. **The Babcock & Wilcox Co.** Lynchburg; nuclear power — 1,150. **Burlington Industries** (Lees Carpet); Glasgow; woven carpets and rugs — 1,100. **Wilson Trucking Corp.** (HQ); Fishersville; trucking — 1,100. **Roanoke Valley Community Hospital;** Roanoke; hospital — 1,060. **Dominion Bankshares Corp.** (HQ); Roanoke; banking — 1,050. **Rockingham Memorial Hospital;** Harrisonburg; hospital — 1,003.

Rowe Furniture Corp. (HQ); Salem; wooden household furniture — 1,000. **Smith's Transfer Corp.** (HQ); Staunton; trucking — 1,000. **Virginia Baptist Hospital;** Lynchburg; hospital — 1,000. **Virginia Hot Springs Inc.;** Hot Springs; hotel — 882. **Merck & Co. Inc.;** Elkton; industrial chemicals — 800. **Meredith/Burda Corp. Inc.;** Lynchburg; rotogravure printing — 800. **Chesapeake & Ohio Railway Co.;** Clifton Forge; railroad operations — 750. **The Singer Co.** (Furniture Div.); Roanoke; wooden household furniture — 717. **Craddock-Terry Shoe Corp.** (HQ); Lynchburg; shoes — 700. **Daniel Construction Co.;** Warm Springs; bridge, elevated highway construction — 700. **H. D. Lee Co. Inc.;** Broadway; leisure wear — 700.

International Telephone & Telegraph Corp. (Electro-Optical Products Div.); Roanoke; radio receiving electron tubes — 700. **Rocco Enterprises, Inc.;** Harrisonburg; poultry production & processing — 700. **Wayn-Tex Inc.** (HQ); Waynesboro; synthetic fibers, carpet backing, industrial fabric — 690. **Holly Farms Inc.;** Harrisonburg; poultry processing — 676. **American Safety Razor Co.** (Personna International Div.); Verona; razor blades, surgical appliances — 650. **Eli Lilly & Co.** (Creative Packaging Co. Div.); Roanoke; plastic products — 650. **Blue Ridge Transfer Co.;** Roanoke; trucking — 629. **AMP Inc.;** Harrisonburg; electrical components — 604. **Amsted Industries Inc.** (Griffin Pipe Products Co.); Lynchburg; foundry — 600. **Burlington Industries Inc.** (Vinton Weaving Co.); Vinton; broad-woven fabric mills — 600. **The Kroger Co.** (Roanoke Meat Plant); Salem; meatpacking — 600. **First National Exchange Bank of Virginia Inc.** (HQ); Roanoke; banking — 594.

Dunham-Bush Inc.; Harrisonburg; air conditioning systems, heating equipment — 550. **Genesco Inc.** (L. Grief & Co. Div.); Verona; men's suits, coats — 550. **Halmode Apparel Inc.** (Althougher Fashions Div. - HQ); Roanoke; women's dresses — 550. **Tenneco Inc.** (Walker Mfg. Co.); Harrisonburg; motor vehicle parts — 540. **Times-World Corp.;** Roanoke; newspaper publishing — 525. **Blue Cross of Southwestern Virginia;** Roanoke; health insurance — 518. **Wampler Foods Inc.;** Harrisonburg; turkey processing — 511. **Maid Bess Corp.** (HQ); Salem; women's apparel — 510. **The Mead Corp.** (Paperboard Products Div.); Lynchburg; paperboard products — 504. **Eaton Corp.;** Salem; industrial trucks — 500. **Rockingham Poultry Marketing Co-op** (HQ); Broadway; poultry processing — 500.

7th District

North — Charlottesville, Winchester

The 7th runs from Richmond's northern suburbs across the Blue Ridge Mountains and up the Shenandoah Valley to Winchester, the center of the state's apple-growing industry and home of Virginia's political dynasty, the Byrd family.

For generations the district was rural, Democratic and conservative. But like Harry F. Byrd Jr., who took over his father's Democratic Senate seat in 1965 and became an independent four years later, the 7th has abandoned its Democratic roots. It has emerged as the state's foremost

Republican stronghold. In the 1981 gubernatorial election, the 7th was the only district carried by unsuccessful Republican candidate J. Marshall Coleman.

With expansion of the Richmond suburbs and steady growth in the upper Shenandoah Valley and most of northern Virginia, population in the 7th increased by 29 percent in the 1970s. This was the fastest growth rate of any district in the state. Because of it, redistricting had to trim the edges of the 7th.

Caroline County moved to the 1st District, Fluvanna and Nelson counties to the 5th and Rockingham County to the 6th. To weaken the Republican incumbent in the neighboring 8th, Democratic cartographers also shifted about 35,000 mostly Republican voters in Prince William County out of the 8th into the 7th.

Two suburban areas contribute heavily to Republican majorities. Hanover County, which is becoming one of Richmond's outlying residential areas, gave Ronald Reagan 70 percent of its 1980 vote. Northwest Prince William County, in the Washington, D. C. suburban sphere, favored Reagan by almost 2-1.

In counties along the Blue Ridge Mountains, a well-developed agricultural economy is keyed to dairying, livestock and fruit. There is also some manufacturing. Reagan won more than 64 percent in both the "apple capital" of Winchester and in surrounding Frederick County, at the northern tip of the 7th.

Reagan's margins were somewhat smaller, though still solid, in Spotsylvania and Stafford counties. Those are longtime farming areas recently adopted by people who depend on long-distance commuter buses to get to jobs in Washington, D. C.

Spotsylvania was Virginia's fastest growing county in the 1970s. Stafford is split between the 7th and 8th districts.

The few Democratic footholds in the 7th are in the southern part of the district. In Charlottesville, the district's largest city and home of the University of Virginia, the academic community boosted Jimmy Carter to 47 percent of the vote; independent candidate John B. Anderson took 10 percent.

Neighboring Louisa and Goochland counties, both about a third black, were almost a dead heat between Carter and Reagan.

Election Returns

7th District		Democrat		Republican	
1976	President	71,046	(44.2%)	86,160	(53.5%)
	Senate	48,281	(31.9%)	—[1]	
	House	6,236	(4.9%)	100,084	(78.1%)
1977	Governor	49,477	(40.9%)	70,826	(58.5%)
1978	Senate	57,437	(48.4%)	61,277	(51.6%)
	House	42,286	(36.6%)	72,911	(63.1%)
1980	President	59,092	(32.3%)	112,099	(51.3%)
	House	5,920	(4.5%)	123,626	(94.9%)
1981	Governor	68,199	(48.5%)	72,148	(51.3%)
1982	Senate	57,237	(44.1%)	72,354	(55.8%)
	House	46,514	(36.3%)	76,752	(59.8%)

[1] *There was no Republican candidate; Harry F. Byrd Jr. won the election as an Independent, winning 890,778 votes (57.2% of the total statewide vote).*

Demographics

Population: 535,147. **Percent Change from 1970:** 31.1%.

Land Area: 6,424 square miles. **Population per Square Mile:** 83.3.

Counties, 1980 Population: Albemarle — 55,783; Charlottesville[1] — 39,916; Clarke — 9,965; Culpeper — 22,620; Fauquier — 35,889; Frederick — 34,150; Fredericksburg[1] — 15,322; Goochland — 11,761; Greene — 7,625; Hanover — 50,398; Louisa — 17,825; Madison — 10,232; Manassas[1] — 15,438; Manassas Park[1] — 6,524; Orange — 18,063; Page — 19,401; Prince William (Pt.) — 34,683; Rappahannock — 6,093; Shenandoah — 27,559; Spotsylvania — 34,435; Stafford (Pt.) — 20,048; Warren — 21,200; Winchester[1] — 20,217.
[1] *Independent cities.*

Race and Ancestry: White — 87.0%; Black — 12.2%; American Indian, Eskimo and Aleut — 0.1%; Asian and Pacific Islander — 0.5%. Spanish Origin — 0.8%. English — 20.7%; French — 0.8%; German — 7.9%; Irish — 4.0%; Italian — 0.8%; Scottish — 0.6%.

Universities, Enrollment: Germanna Community College, Locust Grove — 1,212; Judge Advocate General's School - U.S. Army, Charlottesville — 60; Lord Fairfax Community College, Middletown — 2,027; Mary Washington College, Fredericksburg — 2,628; Piedmont Virginia Community College, Charlottesville — 3,558; Randolph-Macon College, Ashland — 953; Shenandoah College and Conservatory of Music, Winchester — 784; University of Virginia, Charlottesville — 16,441.

Newspapers, Circulation: *The Daily Progress* (eS), Charlottesville — 29,641; *The Free Lance-Star* (e), Fredericksburg — 27,758; *Journal-Messenger* (e), Manassas — 11,023; *Northern Virginia Daily* (m), Strasburg — 14,320; *Star-Exponent* (m), Culpeper — 6,543; *Winchester Evening Star* (e), Winchester — 18,962.

Commercial Television Stations, Affiliation: WTKK, Manassas (None); WVIR-TV, Charlottesville (NBC). District is divided between Richmond ADI and Washington, D.C. ADI. Portion is in Harrisonburg ADI.

Military Installations: Quantico Marine Corps Development and Education Command, Fredericksburg — 6,384; Vint Hill Farms Station (Army), Warrenton — 1,582.

Nuclear Power Plants: North Anna 1, Mineral (Westinghouse, Stone & Webster), June 1978; North Anna 2, Mineral (Westinghouse, Stone & Webster), December 1980.

Industries:

International Business Machines Corp. (Federal Systems Div.); Manassas; electronic computing equipment — 2,500. **Avtex Fibers Inc.;** Front Royal; rayon, polyester fibers — 2,000. **Del Monte Corp.;** Crozet; frozen specialties — 1,350. **Acme Visible Records Inc.** (Data Vue Products); Crozet; metal filing cabinets — 1,210. **Comdial Telephone Systems;** Charlottesville; telephone apparatus — 1,210.

Winchester Memorial Hospital; Winchester; hospital — 1,150. **Abex Corp.** (Friction Products Div.); Winchester; asbestos products — 1,000. **Aileen Inc.;** Edinburg; women's sportswear — 1,000. **Capital Industries Inc.** (Capital Records); Winchester; phonograph records, magnetic tapes — 1,000. **General Electric Co.** (Industrial Control Dept.); Charlottesville; electronic components — 1,000. **Richfood Inc.** (HQ); Mechanicsville; grocery, meat wholesaling — 1,000. **Sperry Corp.** (Marine Systems); Charlottesville; telephone apparatus — 950. **Southland Corp.** (Distribution Center of Virginia); Fredericksburg; general warehousing, storage — 920. **O'Sullivan Corp.** (HQ); Winchester; miscellaneous plastics products — 795. **State Farms Fire & Casualty Co.;** Charlottesville; casualty insurance — 667.

Crouse-Hinds Co. Inc. (Distribution Equipment Div.); Earlysville; switchgear equipment — 650. **Crown Cork & Seal Co. Inc.;** Winchester; metal cans — 650. **Blue Bell Inc.;** Luray; men's work clothes — 600. **American Woodmark Corp.** (HQ); Berryville; wooden kitchen cabinets — 575. **Alfred Teves Inc.;** Culpeper; motor vehicle parts — 550. **Rubbermaid Commercial Products;** Winchester; miscellaneous plastics products — 550. **Atlantic Research Corp.** (Propulsion Div.); Gainesville; research laboratory — 500. **Frank Ix & Son Inc.;** Charlottesville; broad-woven fabric mills — 500. **Rocco Farms Foods Inc.;** Edinburg; poultry processing — 500.

8th District

D. C. Suburbs, Alexandria

The Virginia Legislature's remap was intended to weaken the Republican incumbent in the 8th District. To that end, the cities of Manassas and Manassas Park, outlying suburbs of Washington, D. C., located in Prince William County, were moved to the 7th District.

The redrawn 8th still included most of the southern portion of Virginia's Washington-area suburbs. Growth there has been spurred by the rapid expansion of the federal government and the attraction of a diverse array of white-collar industries to the area.

The district's close-in suburb is Alexandria, with about one-fifth of the population of the 8th. Alexandria is the district's most reliable Democratic territory. The revitalized "Old Town" part of the city is an affluent competitor to the Georgetown section of Washington, and it has thousands of Democratic-voting young professionals. On the fringe of Old Town is a black community that comprises 22 percent of the Alexandria population and adds to Democratic strength.

Beyond Alexandria to the south and southwest, the suburbs are newer, whiter and more Republican. Population in these outlying areas is booming: Fairfax, Prince William and Stafford counties each grew by more than 30 percent during the 1970s.

Once-pastoral Fairfax County is now a suburban colossus of 600,000 people; development is spreading so quickly that the county board enacted tax incentives to encourage preservation of the scarce agricultural land that remains.

More than twice as populous as any other jurisdiction in Virginia, Fairfax is divided nearly evenly between the new 8th and 10th districts. Fairfax residents account for 56 percent of the population in the redrawn 8th.

Party roots in Fairfax County are shallow because rapid growth has blurred community lines and reduced the effectiveness of local party structures. Elections are often close.

The 110,000 residents of southern Prince William County make up one-fifth of the district's population. This area was a ticket-splitter in 1980. Rounding out the district is generally Republican Stafford County; its 40,000 people are split between the 8th and the 7th districts.

Despite the shift out of the district of Manassas and Manassas Park, which had given him his winning margin in 1980, the Republican incumbent overcame his Democratic challenger in 1982, carrying the election with just under 50 percent of the vote. It was the third match between the two candidates.

Election Returns

8th District		Democrat		Republican	
1976	President	75,717	(47.3%)	80,978	(50.6%)
	Senate	71,634	(48.6%)	—¹	
	House	77,009	(51.7%)	63,129	(42.4%)
1977	Governor	43,992	(43.6%)	56,073	(55.5%)
1978	Senate	53,323	(52.2%)	48,779	(47.8%)
	House	52,725	(51.1%)	48,113	(46.6%)

8th District		Democrat		Republican	
1980	President	63,214	(33.4%)	104,891	(55.4%)
	House	88,610	(48.8%)	87,568	(48.3%)
1981	Governor	59,478	(53.6%)	59,875	(46.2%)
1982	Senate	71,439	(51.9%)	66,099	(48.0%)
	House	68,071	(48.6%)	69,620	(49.7%)

¹ *There was no Republican candidate; Harry F. Byrd Jr. won the election as an Independent, winning 890,778 votes (57.2% of the total statewide vote).*

Demographics

Population: 534,366. **Percent Change from 1970:** 25.6%.

Land Area: 580 square miles. **Population per Square Mile:** 921.3.

Counties, 1980 Population: Alexandria¹ — 103,217; Fairfax (Pt.) — 300,707; Prince William (Pt.) — 110,020; Stafford (Pt.) — 20,422.
¹ *Independent cities.*

Cities, 1980 Population: Alexandria — 103,217; Annandale (CDP) (Pt.) — 26,900; Burke (CDP) — 33,835; Chantilly (CDP) (Pt.) — 11,736; Dale City (CDP) — 33,127; Lake Ridge (CDP) — 11,072; Mount Vernon (CDP) — 24,058; Springfield (CDP) (Pt.) — 18,864; West Springfield (CDP) — 25,012; Woodbridge (CDP) — 24,004.

Race and Ancestry: White — 85.6%; Black — 10.1%; American Indian, Eskimo and Aleut — 0.2%; Asian and Pacific Islander — 2.8%. Spanish Origin — 2.9%. English — 12.2%; French — 1.0%; German — 6.5%; Irish — 5.0%; Italian — 2.1%; Polish — 1.1%; Russian — 0.6%; Scottish — 0.7%.

Universities, Enrollment: Northern Virginia Community College, Annandale — 31,447; Protestant Episcopal Theological Seminary in Virginia, Alexandria — 185.

Newspapers, Circulation: *The Alexandria Gazette* (e), Alexandria — 12,523; *The Alexandria Journal* (m), Alexandria — 5,877; *Potomac News* (e), Woodbridge — 19,695. *The Washington Post* and *The Fairfax Journal* also circulate in the district.

Commercial Television Stations, Affiliation: Entire district is located in Washington, D.C., ADI.

Military Installations: Cameron Station (Army), Alexandria — 4,466; Fort Belvoir, Alexandria — 9,917.

Industries:

The Alexandria Hospital; Alexandria; hospital — 1,420. **Atlantic Research Corp.** (HQ); Springfield; guided missile units, signaling equipment — 797. **Fruit Growers Express Co.;** Alexandria; railroad car rental — 721. **V. S. E. Corp.** (HQ); Alexandria; engineering services — 650. **Richmond Fredericksburg & Potomac Railroad;** Alexandria; railroad operations — 540. **Peoples Drug Stores Inc.** (HQ); Alexandria; drug retailing — 500.

9th District

Southwest — Blacksburg, Bristol

This Appalachian district has long been called the "Fighting Ninth" because of its fiercely competitive two-party system and traditional isolation from the Virginia political establishment in Richmond.

Southwestern Virginia was settled by Scots-Irish and German immigrants who had little in common with the English settlers in the Tidewater and Piedmont. In the years when Democrats routinely dominated Virginia politics, the 9th was the only consistently Republican district.

But as the state GOP has moved rightward in recent

years, it has lost part of its historic base in the southwest.

Coal-mining counties along the Kentucky and West Virginia borders now regularly vote Democratic. Nearly half the 9th District's 17 counties went for Jimmy Carter in 1980; Ronald Reagan received only 49 percent overall in the 9th. In 1982, the Democratic challenger beat the Republican incumbent by just over 1,100 votes.

The largest city in the district is Blacksburg, which grew from fewer than 10,000 to more than 30,000 people in the 1970s. Located there is Virginia Tech University, with 20,000 students the largest school in the state. Some residents of northeastern Montgomery County drive to jobs in nearby Roanoke, the commercial center of southwest Virginia. Reagan won Montgomery by less than 800 votes.

The only other city of any size is Bristol, which shares its downtown area with the city of Bristol, Tenn. Redistricting brought Floyd County into the 9th from the 5th and moved Carroll County out of the 9th into the 5th. Carroll has twice as many voters as Floyd and is slightly more Republican.

Election Returns

9th District		Democrat		Republican	
1976	President	87,783	(51.5%)	76,627	(45.0%)
	Senate	57,253	(38.9%)		—[1]
	House	70,076	(43.5%)	90,904	(56.5%)
1977	Governor	55,225	(45.8%)	64,307	(53.3%)
1978	Senate	62,055	(51.9%)	57,562	(48.1%)
	House	46,574	(39.1%)	72,463	(60.9%)
1980	President	84,218	(47.3%)	86,251	(48.4%)
	House	52,325	(31.6%)	113,097	(68.4%)
1981	Governor	76,182	(56.1%)	59,463	(43.8%)
1982	Senate	76,418	(51.9%)	70,600	(48.0%)
	House	76,205	(50.4%)	75,082	(49.6%)

[1] There was no Republican candidate; Harry F. Byrd Jr. won the election as an Independent, winning 890,778 votes (57.2% of the total statewide vote).

Demographics

Population: 538,871. **Percent Change from 1970:** 19.2%.

Land Area: 7,310 square miles. **Population per Square Mile:** 73.7.

Counties, 1980 Population: Bland — 6,349; Bristol[1] — 19,042; Buchanan — 37,989; Craig — 3,948; Dickenson — 19,806; Floyd — 11,563; Galax[1] — 6,524; Giles — 17,810; Grayson — 16,579; Lee — 25,956; Montgomery — 63,516; Norton[1] — 4,757; Pulaski — 35,229; Radford[1] — 13,225; Russell — 31,761; Scott — 25,068; Smyth — 33,366; Tazewell — 50,511; Washington — 46,487; Wise — 43,863; Wythe — 25,522.

[1] Independent cities.

Cities, 1980 Population: Blacksburg — 30,638; Bristol — 19,042; Christiansburg — 10,345; Galax — 6,524; Norton — 4,757; Pulaski — 10,106; Radford — 13,225.

Race and Ancestry: White — 97.1%; Black — 2.4%; American Indian, Eskimo and Aleut — 0.1%; Asian and Pacific Islander — 0.3%. Spanish Origin — 0.6%. Dutch — 0.7%; English — 32.5%; French — 0.5%; German — 5.8%; Irish — 6.2%; Scottish — 0.5%.

Universities, Enrollment: Bluefield College, Bluefield — 428, Emory and Henry College, Emory — 792; Mountain Empire Community College, Big Stone Gap — 2,548; New River Community College, Dublin — 3,185; Radford University, Radford — 5,757; Southwest

Virginia Community College, Richlands — 3,383; University of Virginia, Clinch Valley College, Wise — 1,008; Virginia Highlands Community College, Abingdon — 1,491; Virginia Intermont College, Bristol — 691; Virginia Polytechnic Institute and State University, Blacksburg — 21,069; Wytheville Community College, Wytheville — 1,921.

Newspapers, Circulation: *Herald-Courier* (mS), Bristol — 29,494; *News-Journal* (eS), Radford — 2,355; *The News-Messenger* (e), Christianburg — 6,546; *The Southwest Times* (eS), Pulaski — 6,854; *Virginia-Tennessean* (eS), Bristol — 9,555.

Commercial Television Stations, Affiliation: WCYB-TV, Bristol (NBC). District is divided between Bristol-Kingsport (Tenn.)-Johnson City (Tenn.) ADI and Roanoke-Lynchburg ADI. Portion is in Bluefield (W.Va.)-Beckley (W.Va.)-Oak Hill (W.Va.) ADI.

Military Installations: Radford Army Ammunition Plant, Radford — 3,396.

Industries:

Hercules Inc. (Radford Army Ammunition Plant); Radford; explosives, small arms ammunition — 2,700. **Celanese Corp.** (Fibers Div.); Narrows; cellulosic man-made fibers — 2,200. **Island Creek Coal Co. Inc.;** Oakwood; coal mining — 2,100. **Pittston Co.** (Clinchfield Coal Co. Div.); Dante; coal mining — 2,050. **Westmoreland Coal Co.** (General Coal Co.); Big Stone Gap; coal mining — 1,820.

Jewell Ridge Coal Corp.; Jewell Valley; coal mining — 1,400. **Hanes Corp.** (Knitwear Div.); Galax; men's underwear — 1,100. **Pulaski Furniture Corp.** (HQ); Pulaski; wooden household furniture — 1,000. **Lynchburg Foundry Co. Inc.;** Radford; gray iron foundry — 856. **Consolidation Coal Co. Inc.** (Pocahontas Fuel Div.); Bishop; coal mining — 800. **Virginia House Furniture Corp.;** Atkins; wooden household furniture — 800. **Kahn & Feldman Inc.** (Jefferson Mills); Pulaski; yarn texturizing — 735. **Fries Textile Co.;** Fries; broad-woven fabric mills — 700. **Norris Industries** (Automotive Trim Div.); Duffield; automotive stampings — 700. **Jewell Smokeless Coal Corp.** (Dominion Coal); Vansant; coal mining services — 665. **Litton Systems Inc.** (Poly Scientific Div.); Blacksburg; electronic components — 650.

Valleydale Packers Inc.; Bristol; meatpacking — 650. **Pulaski Furniture Corp.;** Dublin; wooden household furniture — 630. **Coleman Furniture Corp.;** Pulaski; wooden household furniture — 600. **Brunswick Corp.;** Marion; plastics products — 579. **S & S Corp.** (HQ); Cedar Bluff; mining machinery — 575. **Bishop Coal Co.;** Bishop; coal mining — 561. **Federal-Mogul Corp.;** Blacksburg; motor vehicle parts — 555. **Beatrice Pocahontas Co.;** Keen Mountain; coal mining — 550. **Bristol Steel & Iron Works Inc.** (HQ); Bristol; heavy structural metal — 550. **Volvo White Truck Corp.;** Dublin; motor vehicle bodies — 550. **Vaughan Furniture Co. Inc.** (HQ); Galax; wooden household furniture — 540. **Reynolds Metals Co.** (Can Div.); Bristol; aluminum products — 510. **Harvey Hubbell Inc.** (Lighting Div.); Christianburg; outdoor lighting equipment — 500. **Webb Furniture Enterprises Inc.;** Galax; wooden household furniture — 500.

10th District

D. C. Suburbs, Arlington County

The 10th is one of the most affluent districts in the South, but it is hardly fair to identify it as southern. It is mainly a set of bedroom communities for civil servants, Pentagon and nearby military installation employees, and others who work for the federal government. It ranks fifth in the nation in median family income.

Redistricting does not alter the 10th, which had a population gain of 14.9 percent during the 1970s, precisely the statewide average.

Arlington County, just outside Washington, grew rapidly in in the 1950s and 1960s as the federal government expanded. Although suburban sprawl has peaked in Arlington — the county lost 21,685 people in the 1970s — there has been some movement of younger, affluent professionals into the county's condominiums and rental apartments. These people are generally less conservative than the average Virginian, but they are transient and politically unreliable.

There are fewer blacks in Arlington than in neighboring Alexandria, but the county is becoming a melting pot for other minorities. Asians, Hispanics and other minority groups together make up 23 percent of the county's population. Arlington's "Little Saigon" area is a magnet for Vietnamese-owned businesses.

West of Arlington, the 10th takes in nearly 300,000 people living in the northern part of Fairfax County. Like southern Fairfax County, which is part of the 8th District, this part of the county is filling up rapidly with people who commute to work in Washington, D.C., just across the Potomac River. Ronald Reagan took 56 percent in the Fairfax County portion of the new 10th in 1980.

Further northwest is Loudoun County, home base of some long-distance commuters but also a slice of Northern Virginia "hunt" country. Reagan won nearly 60 percent of the Loudoun vote in 1980.

Election Returns

10th District		Democrat		Republican	
1976	President	95,532	(46.8%)	104,815	(51.3%)
	Senate	90,951	(47.5%)	—[1]	
	House	103,689	(54.7%)	73,616	(38.8%)
1977	Governor	54,770	(43.1%)	71,283	(56.1%)
1978	Senate	69,435	(51.9%)	64,109	(47.9%)
	House	70,892	(53.3%)	61,981	(46.6%)
1980	President	76,676	(34.0%)	120,328	(53.4%)
	House	105,883	(48.8%)	110,840	(51.1%)
1981	Governor	84,080	(53.6%)	72,532	(46.2%)
1982	Senate	86,362	(53.0%)	76,420	(46.9%)
	House	75,361	(46.0%)	86,506	(52.7%)

[1] *There was no Republican candidate; Harry F. Byrd Jr. won the election as an Independent, winning 890,778 votes (57.2% of the total statewide vote).*

Demographics

Population: 535,125. **Percent Change from 1970:** 15.1%.

Land Area: 738 square miles. **Population per Square Mile:** 725.1.

Counties, 1980 Population: Arlington — 152,599; Fairfax[1] — 19,390; Fairfax (Pt.) — 296,194; Falls Church[1] — 9,515; Loudoun — 57,427.
[1] *Independent cities.*

Cities, 1980 Population: Annandale (CDP) (Pt.) — 22,624; Arlington — 152,599; Chantilly (CDP) (Pt.) — 523; Fairfax — 19,390; Falls Church — 9,515; Herndon — 11,449; McLean (CDP) — 35,664; Oakton (CDP) — 19,150; Reston (CDP) — 36,407; Springfield (CDP) (Pt.) — 2,571; Sterling Park (CDP) — 16,080; Tysons Corner (CDP) — 10,065; Vienna — 15,469.

Race and Ancestry: White — 87.2%; Black — 6.6%; American Indian, Eskimo and Aleut — 0.2%; Asian and Pacific Islander — 4.3%. Spanish Origin — 4.0%. English — 12.5%; French — 1.0%; German — 6.5%; Greek — 0.5%; Irish — 5.4%; Italian — 2.0%; Polish — 1.1%; Russian — 0.7%; Scottish — 0.7%.

Universities, Enrollment: Marymount College of Virginia, Arlington — 1,174; George Mason University, Fairfax — 13,293.

Newspapers, Circulation: *The Arlington Journal* (m), Arlington — 9,794; *The Fairfax Journal* (m), Fairfax — 44,595; *Northern Virginia Sun* (m), Arlington — 18,405. *The Washington Post* also circulates in the district.

Commercial Television Stations, Affiliation: Entire district is located in Washington, D.C. ADI.

Military Installations: Arlington Hall Station (Army), Arlington — 2,497; Fort Myer, Arlington — 5,700; Henderson Hall Marine Corps Headquarters, Arlington — 2,129.

Industries:

Drug Fair Inc. (HQ); Alexandria; drug stores — 3,800. **First Virginia Banks Inc.;** Falls Church — bank holding company — 2,800. **U.S. Air** (HQ); Arlington; commercial airline — 2,000. **Mobil Oil Corp.** (Marketing & Refining - HQ); Fairfax; administrative offices — 1,400. **Arlington Hospital Assn. Inc.;** Arlington; hospital — 1,300.

HBH Co.; Arlington; engineering services — 1,200. **Mitre Corp.** (Metrek Div.); McLean; research laboratories — 1,150. **E-Systems Inc.** (Melpar Div.); Falls Church; radio and television transmitting equipment — 1,000. **CACI Inc. Federal;** Arlington; management, consulting services — 900. **Honeywell Information Systems;** (Federal Systems Operations Div.); McLean; data systems consulting services — 900. **Western Electric Co. Inc.;** Arlington; electrical apparatus and equipment — 850. **American Automobile Assn.** (HQ); Falls Church; travelers' services — 800. **The BDM Corp.** (HQ); McLean; engineering services — 800. **PRC Data Services Co. Inc.** (HQ); McLean; computer software services — 800. **GTE Telenet Communications;** Vienna; data communication services — 771.

First American Bank of Virginia (HQ); McLean; banking — 750. **National Imperial 400 Inc.** (HQ); Arlington; motels — 750. **American Management Systems** (AMS Computer Center - HQ); Arlington; computer systems services — 746. **Navy Federal Credit Union** (HQ); Vienna; federal credit union — 737. **Satellite Business System** (HQ); McLean; electronic communications equipment — 700. **TRW Inc.** (TRW Defense Space Systems); McLean; research — 625. **The Boeing Co. Inc.** (Computer Services Div.); Vienna; computer consulting services — 600. **General Electric Co.** (Information Services Div. Co.); Fairfax; data processing services — 600. **Hadron Inc.;** McLean; industrial lasers, computer tools — 600. **Advance Security Inc.;** Falls Church; security systems — 500. **Marriott Corp.;** Arlington; hotel — 500.

Washington

Washington's Legislature, faced with the seemingly easy task of dividing up the spoils of the state's brisk population growth during the 1970s, was unable to manage it without months of controversy and an eventual court suit. The first plan approved by the Legislature was vetoed by the governor. A second plan was then approved and put in place for the 1982 elections. But shortly after that the map was thrown out by a federal district court. A third plan, drawn up by a bipartisan commission, was approved by the Legislature and the governor in 1983.

The trouble began when the state was awarded an eighth House seat for the 1980s. With Republicans controlling both legislative chambers and the governorship, prospects for an easy remapping process seemed good. But sparring between the GOP's moderate and conservative factions led to prolonged indecision, which was not resolved until mid-February of 1982. The Legislature's first remap effort — which would have weakened at least one incumbent in each party, drew the unanimous opposition of the state's congressional delegation and was vetoed by Gov. John Spellman, a moderate Republican, in May 1981.

In the legislative wrangling over the second map, the main bone of contention was the city of Everett. The timber and aerospace city, which usually provides Democratic margins, had been the population focus of the old 2nd District. which was represented by a Democrat. But Republican legislators, determined to create a new Republican 8th District in Seattle's southern suburbs, wanted to expand the 1st District northward to pick up Everett's population. Neither incumbent nor the citizens of Everett were enthusiastic about the change.

Their complaints were ignored, however, by a bipartisan majority in the state House. Nine Democrats — at the urging of most of the state's Democratic congressional incumbents — voted with the Republican leadership and gave the new plan a 52-to-44 victory in the Washington House on Jan. 19, 1982. After a final unsuccessful effort by Everett-area state senators to keep Everett within the 2nd, the Senate approved the House plan by a 25-to-21 vote on Feb. 10. Spellman signed the remap bill into law Feb. 17.

Everett residents filed suit in federal court, arguing that the city had little in common with the rest of the 1st District. Ignoring the "community of interests" issue, the three-judge court ruled that the map violated the "one-person, one-vote" rule by allowing too wide a population variation between districts. The judges told the Legislature to come up with a suitable plan within 90 days after convening Jan. 10, 1983, or the court would draw the map itself.

For the first time in Washington's history, the Legislature, which switched to Democratic control after the November 1982 election, gave the redistricting job to a five-member bipartisan citizens' commission. The commission plan solved both the population and the Everett problems. The new population variance is less than one-tenth of 1 percent, while the districts voided by the court varied by 1.4 percent. Everett was restored to the 2nd District.

Washington's new congressional boundaries do little harm to any of the incumbents. The state House unanimously approved the commission map March 18 and the Senate ratified it March 23 by a 44-4 vote. Gov. Spellman signed the plan into law March 29.

In addition to moving Everett, the commission map, which will be in place for the 1984 elections, reunited the contiguous towns of Aberdeen, Hoquiam and Cosmopolis in the 3rd District; the map thrown out by the court had split them between the 2nd and 3rd. Kitsap County, which had been split among the 1st, 2nd and 6th, is divided between just the 1st and the 6th for the 1984 elections. A small portion of Tacoma that had been moved to the 8th was returned to the 6th. And Kent, a blue-collar, industrial suburb of Seattle, was placed in the 7th.

The descriptions below are for the districts that were in place for the 1982 elections.

Age of Population

District	Population Under 18	Voting Age Population	Population 65 & Over (% of VAP)	Median Age
1	138,869	379,960	50,783 (13.4%)	30.9
2	148,530	370,223	59,041 (15.9%)	30.0
3	156,685	359,783	54,034 (15.0%)	29.7
4	155,550	356,411	54,162 (15.2%)	29.2
5	143,779	375,183	59,979 (16.0%)	29.0
6	141,499	374,471	51,951 (13.9%)	28.4
7	98,444	415,596	70,001 (16.8%)	31.4
8	156,004	361,169	31,611 (8.8%)	29.5
State	1,139,360	2,992,796	431,562 (14.4)	29.8

WASHINGTON

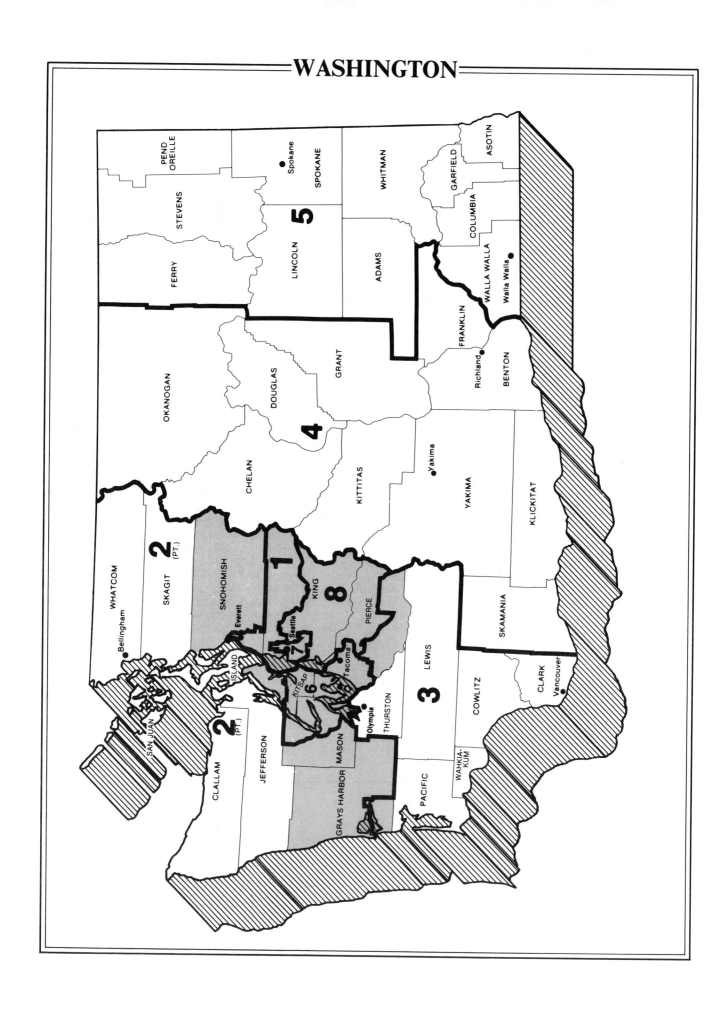

Income and Occupation

District	Median Family Income	White Collar Workers	Blue Collar Workers	Service Workers	Farm Workers
1	$ 25,669	61.9%	25.8%	10.9%	1.3%
2	20,348	46.7	33.5	13.7	6.2
3	20,919	49.6	33.1	12.9	4.4
4	19,713	46.6	29.6	12.5	11.4
5	19,031	53.5	26.3	15.2	4.9
6	19,788	53.0	31.2	14.1	1.7
7	21,728	59.5	25.7	13.9	0.9
8	27,016	61.5	26.9	10.4	1.3
State	$ 21,696	54.6%	28.7%	12.9%	3.8%

Education: School Years Completed

District	8 Years or Fewer	4 Years of High School	4 Years of College or More	Median School Years
1	6.8%	34.7%	25.2%	13.0
2	11.2	40.2	14.9	12.6
3	11.5	40.0	14.3	12.6
4	16.1	36.6	14.6	12.5
5	11.1	37.5	18.0	12.7
6	10.2	41.1	14.8	12.6
7	10.4	32.8	23.7	12.8
8	5.7	36.5	25.1	13.0
State	10.3%	37.4%	19.0%	12.7

Housing and Residential Patterns

District	Owner Occupied	Renter Occupied	Urban	Rural
1	71.1%	28.9%	90.6%	9.4%
2	71.7	28.3	42.5	57.5
3	68.3	31.7	59.4	40.6
4	66.9	33.1	57.7	42.3
5	66.7	33.3	71.5	28.5
6	61.2	38.8	85.1	14.9
7	49.8	50.2	100.0	0.0
8	72.8	27.2	81.3	18.7
State	65.6%	34.4%	73.5%	26.5%

1st District

Northern King County — Everett

In the 1970s the 1st District included a sizable northern portion of Seattle and took its cue from that city. The version in place for the 98th Congress is different, including less of Seattle but all of Everett, the seat of Snohomish County. Those district lines are only temporary, however. A new redistricting plan scheduled to take effect for the 1984 elections removes Everett and restores the focus on the Seattle area. None of the changes altered the political balance, which is toward the Republican Party.

Everett traditionally has depended on timber and shipping. Labor conflict plagued those industries between the two world wars, with unions becoming the foundation of local Democratic strength. Since the 1960s, the city has been closely linked to Boeing's aircraft plants as assembly lines for the jumbo 747 jetliner have provided steady employment. But the 1981-82 economic slump has been felt at Boeing.

In addition to Boeing, electronics and high-technology industries make up Everett's diversified economic base. The heavily timbered coastal areas, dependent on fishing, have a largely Scandinavian population.

For the 98th Congress, the 1st still has portions of northern Seattle, including much of the academic community at the University of Washington, although the campus itself is in the 7th District. The North Seattle vote is moderate-to-liberal, and Republicans here are often distrustful of the more conservative wing of the GOP that vies for control of the state Legislature. The incumbent's moderate Republicanism should be sufficient to hold down defections from the GOP.

The remainder of King County in the 1st includes some northeastern suburbs and, toward the Cascade slopes, some less-developed territory. Republicans run strongly in both areas. In 1980 northeast King County helped offset Seattle's blue-collar vote, tilting the county as a whole to the GOP national and statewide tickets. Across Puget Sound, picturesque Bainbridge Island, which was in the 6th, was moved to the 1st.

Election Returns

1st District		Democrat		Republican	
1976	President	108,345	(44.3%)	126,007	(51.5%)
	Governor	111,659	(45.7%)	126,372	(51.7%)
	Senate	174,015	(73.1%)	52,943	(22.2%)
	House	80,340	(40.1%)	116,181	(57.9%)
1978	House	52,470	(41.3%)	72,874	(57.4%)
1980	President	82,818	(37.5%)	104,923	(47.5%)
	Governor	94,342	(41.9%)	131,030	(58.1%)
	Senate	101,338	(44.9%)	124,159	(55.1%)
	House	69,770	(28.4%)	168,439	(68.6%)
1982	Senate	115,766	(68.0%)	40,855	(24.0%)
	House	59,444	(32.4%)	123,956	(67.6%)

Demographics

Population: 518,829. **Percent Change from 1970:** 21.7%.

Land Area: 986 square miles. **Population per Square Mile:** 526.6.

Counties, 1980 Population: King (Pt.) — 288,546; Kitsap (Pt.) — 12,314; Snohomish (Pt.) — 217,969.

Cities, 1980 Population: Edmonds — 27,679; Everett — 54,413; Kirkland (Pt.) — 15,018; Lynnwood — 22,641; Mountlake Terrace — 16,534; Redmond (Pt.) — 9,922; Seattle (Pt.) — 102,122.

Race and Ancestry: White — 94.7%; Black — 0.8%; American Indian, Eskimo and Aleut — 0.8%; Asian and Pacific Islander — 2.7%. Spanish Origin — 1.6%. Dutch — 0.8%; English — 8.8%; French — 0.9%; German — 6.7%; Irish — 3.2%; Italian — 1.0%; Norwegian — 4.0%; Polish — 0.5%; Scottish — 1.0%; Swedish — 2.0%.

Universities, Enrollment: Edmonds Community College, Lynnwood — 7,322; Everett Community College — 10,170; Northwest College of the Assemblies of God, Kirkland — 825; Puget Sound College of the Bible, Edmonds — 174; Shoreline Community College, Seattle — 7,572.

Newspapers, Circulation: *The Herald* (e), Everett — 60,404. *The Bremerton Sun, Seattle Post-Intelligencer* and *The Seattle Times* also circulate in the district.

Commercial Television Stations, Affiliation: Entire district is located in Seattle-Tacoma ADI.

Military Installations: Paine Field Air National Guard Station, Everett — 115; Seattle Naval Station, Seattle — 2,529.

Industries:

The Boeing Co.; Everett; aircraft — 14,000. **The Boeing Co.** (Seattle Services Div.); Seattle; aircraft — 2,000. **Scott Paper Co.** (Northwest Operation Div.); Everett; pulp, paper products — 2,000. **John Fluke Mfg. Co. Inc.** (HQ); Everett; electricity measuring devices — 1,800. **Children's Orthopedic Hospital;** Seattle; hospital — 1,250.

Blue Cross of Washington & Alaska Inc. (HQ); Seattle; health insurance — 1,070. **Eldec Corp.** (HQ); Lynnwood; aircraft radio equipment — 1,070. **Marine Construction & Design** (HQ); Seattle; ship repairing, hydraulic winches — 745. **Sisters of Providence of Washington;** Everett; hospital — 700. **E. A. Nord Co. Inc.;** Everett; millwork — 650. **Physio-Control Corp.** (HQ); Redmond; medical instruments — 570. **Western Gear Corp.;** Everett; heavy machinery — 500.

2nd District

Northwest — Bellingham; Olympic Peninsula

The 2nd traditionally has been focused on the logging town of Everett, and after 1984 it will be again. The district lines in effect for the 1982 elections, which did not include the city, were overturned by a federal court late in 1982 on grounds of population inequality. When the lines were redrawn a few months later for the 1984 elections, Everett was returned to the district.

For 1983 and 1984, however, the largest city is Bellingham, with a population of about 46,000. Only 23 miles from the Canadian border, Bellingham is a logging center dependent on a large Georgia-Pacific plant. Like most of the northern coast area, Bellingham has a large population of Norwegian descent.

Whatcom County, dominated by Bellingham, gave pluralities to both Gerald R. Ford in 1976 and Ronald Reagan in 1980. Most Democratic statewide candidates have carried the county, but Republican Gov. John Spellman and Sen. Slade Gorton took it as part of the 1980 GOP sweep.

Although Everett is no longer in the district, the 2nd's largest concentration of voters is still in Snohomish County, north of the city along the Interstate 5 corridor. Almost one-third of the district's residents are in Snohomish, where the voting pattern for national and statewide offices changed from a Democratic sweep in 1976 to a GOP triumph in 1980. Reagan in 1980 drew 11,000 votes more in the county than did Ford in 1976.

The 1982 remap restored to the 2nd the northern part of the Olympic Peninsula, which the 1970 redistricting had shifted from the 2nd to the 3rd. Lightly populated, this portion of the peninsula consists of mountains, forests and coastline in Clallam, Jefferson and Mason counties. Most of Grays Harbor County is also in the new 2nd, although a small part of it remains in the 3rd. Grays Harbor, which experienced only modest growth during the 1970s while the other peninsula counties grew swiftly, was one of only two counties in the state that backed Jimmy Carter in 1980. It had taken a similarly lonely stand supporting George McGovern in 1972.

On the eastern edge of the Olympic Peninsula, the 2nd picked up the northern part of Kitsap County, which has stretches of intense development around its logging and shipping centers. Skirting the city limits of Bremerton, the new boundaries make the 2nd home to the Bangor naval installation, where some new Trident submarines are based. The Kitsap territory added to the 2nd shares the usually Democratic leanings of the rest of the county.

San Juan and Island counties, the chains of islands between Juan de Fuca Strait and Puget Sound, are rain-soaked preserves of heavily forested land and vegetable farms. The area includes the Whidbey Island Naval Air Station in Oak Harbor. Although they are sparsely settled, both counties recently have experienced rapid population growth: San Juan County's population has more than doubled, and Island County has grown by two-thirds, since the 1970 census. Voters here tend to be Republican.

Election Returns

2nd District		Democrat		Republican	
1976	President	76,614	(47.8%)	81,677	(51.0%)
	Governor	91,856	(56.2%)	70,420	(42.9%)
	Senate	108,897	(69.9%)	44,745	(28.7%)
	House	85,124	(51.7%)	76,821	(46.7%)
1978	House	61,031	(53.9%)	52,114	(46.0%)
1980	President	79,259	(38.0%)	103,045	(49.4%)
	Governor	92,918	(45.7%)	110,434	(54.3%)
	Senate	87,714	(45.3%)	106,126	(54.7%)
	House	147,618	(74.5%)	45,005	(22.7%)
1982	Senate	118,656	(67.4%)	43,075	(24.5%)
	House	101,383	(59.6%)	68,622	(40.4%)

Demographics

Population: 518,753. **Percent Change from 1970:** 40.2%.

Land Area: 12,231 square miles. **Population per Square Mile:** 42.4.

Counties, 1980 Population: Clallam — 51,648; Grays Harbor (Pt.) — 43,246; Island — 44,048; Jefferson — 15,965; Kitsap (Pt.) — 48,799; Mason (Pt.) — 16,619; San Juan — 7,838; Skagit — 64,138; Snohomish (Pt.) — 119,751; Whatcom — 106,701.

Cities, 1980 Population: Aberdeen (Pt.) — 8; Bellingham — 45,794; Mount Vernon — 13,009; Oak Harbor — 12,271; Port Angeles — 17,311.

Race and Ancestry: White — 94.9%; Black — 0.5%; American Indian, Eskimo and Aleut — 2.4%; Asian and Pacific Islander — 1.1%. Spanish Origin — 1.9%. Dutch — 2.5%; English — 8.9%; French — 1.0%; German — 6.9%; Irish — 3.1%; Italian — 0.6%; Norwegian — 3.3%; Polish — 0.5%; Scottish — 0.9%; Swedish — 2.0%.

Universities, Enrollment: Peninsula College, Port Angeles — 3,577; Skagit Valley College, Mount Vernon — 6,831; Western Washington University, Bellingham — 10,616; Whatcom Community College, Bellingham — 2,335.

Newspapers, Circulation: *The Bellingham Herald* (eS), Bellingham — 22,935; *The Daily News* (eS), Port Angeles — 13,395; *Skagit Valley Herald* (e), Mount Vernon — 16,420. *The Bremerton Sun* and Everett *Herald* also circulate in the district.

Commercial Television Stations, Affiliation: KVOS-TV, Bellingham (CBS). Entire district is located in Seattle-Tacoma ADI.

Military Installations: Bangor Naval Submarine Base, Bremerton — 6,156; Bellingham Municipal Airport (Air Force), Bellingham — 140; Makah Air Force Station, Neah Bay — 115; Naval Underseas Warfare Engineering Station, Keyport — 3,626; Pacific Beach Naval Facility, Pacific Beach — 130; Whidbey Island Naval Air Station, Oak Harbor — 8,446.

Nuclear Power Plants: Washington Nuclear 3, Satsop (Combustion Engineering, Ebasco Services).

Industries:

Intalco Aluminum Corp.; Ferndale; aluminum refining — 1,250. **Georgia-Pacific Corp.;** Bellingham; pulp, paper, alkaline, chlorine — 1,100. **Skagit Corp.;** Sedro-Woolley; construction machinery — 770. **Snelson-Anvil Inc.;** Anacortes; industrial machinery — 750. **Peter Kiewit Sons Co.;** Elma; general contracting — 700. **ITT Rayonier Inc.;** Hoquiam; pulp mill — 550.

3rd District

Southwest — Olympia, Vancouver

The 3rd, stretching from Puget Sound west to the Pacific and south toward the Columbia River border with Oregon, is oriented toward maritime and forestry interests. It contains some of the most Democratic territory in the state. When Richard Nixon's landslide engulfed George McGovern in 1972, Pacific County, then and now in the 3rd District, gave the Democrat his best percentage anywhere in the state. It did the same for Jimmy Carter in 1980.

Lumber dominates the economy of the interior. The 3rd has vast stretches of woodland, including the scenic Coastal Range and much of the Cascade Mountains, with Mount Rainier National Park at the district's eastern border. The area's mills produce paper, timber and cardboard under the state's strict water pollution standards. Along the coast, fishing and dockwork are predominant, and labor unions are well entrenched among longshoremen.

Olympia, the scenic capital city, is dominated by state government. It is the largest city in fast-growing Thurston County. Thurston provided its customary Democratic margins in 1976, but in 1980 the county switched to a straight GOP ticket, although Ronald Reagan won it with just a plurality.

Logging is a central factor in the economy of Cowlitz County, where growth in the cities of Longview and Kelso paced the area's brisk population rise. With a largely blue-collar electorate, Cowlitz County gave majorities to the 1976 Democratic ticket, but Reagan won a plurality in 1980.

The aluminum industry is strong along the Columbia River in Clark County. For 1983 and 1984, the county was reunified in the 3rd after being split between the 3rd and 4th for a decade; for the 1984 elections, the county was again split between the two districts. Under both versions the 3rd regains Vancouver, just upriver from the confluence of the Columbia and the Willamette rivers. It is a major industrial center, with newly arrived electronics firms such as Hewlett-Packard helping the economy diversify. Clark is usually a Democratic county, but Reagan took it in 1980.

With a population that grew by 33 percent during the 1970s, the 3rd had to yield territory for the 1980s. For 1983-84 the 3rd lost all of Clallam, Jefferson and most of Grays Harbor counties to the 2nd; most of Mason County to the 2nd and 6th; and all of its King County areas and much of its Pierce County areas to the new 8th. The new 3rd gained the remainder of Clark County from the 4th.

The subsequent redistricting reunified the towns of Aberdeen, Hoquiam and Cosmopolis in Grays Harbor

County in the 3rd. They were divided between the 2nd and 3rd in 1983-84. For the 1984 elections, 2,200 people in the southeastern corner of Clark County were returned to the 4th.

Election Returns

3rd District		Democrat		Republican	
1976	President	95,027	(51.0%)	84,267	(45.2%)
	Governor	107,441	(57.9%)	72,784	(39.2%)
	Senate	131,416	(73.4%)	40,836	(22.8%)
	House	118,201	(66.0%)	59,063	(33.0%)
1978	House	75,911	(61.3%)	47,972	(38.7%)
1980	President	86,949	(40.0%)	104,332	(48.0%)
	Governor	98,086	(45.1%)	119,388	(54.9%)
	Senate	102,643	(47.3%)	114,195	(52.7%)
	House	127,700	(59.2%)	87,831	(40.8%)
1982	Senate	115,180	(71.7%)	34,921	(21.7%)
	House	97,323	(60.1%)	59,686	(36.8%)

Demographics

Population: 516,468. **Percent Change from 1970:** 39.5%.

Land Area: 6,929 square miles. **Population per Square Mile:** 74.5.

Counties, 1980 Population: Clark — 192,227; Cowlitz — 79,548; Grays Harbor (Pt.) — 23,068; Lewis — 56,025; Pacific — 17,237; Pierce (Pt.) — 20,267; Thurston — 124,264; Wahkiakum — 3,832.

Cities, 1980 Population: Aberdeen (Pt.) — 18,731; Centralia — 11,555; Kelso — 11,129; Lacey — 13,940; Longview — 31,052; Olympia — 27,447; Vancouver — 42,834.

Race and Ancestry: White — 96.0%; Black — 0.6%; American Indian, Eskimo and Aleut — 1.1%; Asian and Pacific Islander — 1.5%. Spanish Origin — 1.6%. Dutch — 0.7%; English — 9.0%; French — 1.0%; German — 8.3%; Irish — 3.4%; Italian — 0.7%; Norwegian — 2.0%; Polish — 0.6%; Scottish — 0.7%; Swedish — 1.5%.

Universities, Enrollment: Centralia College, Centralia — 6,540; Clark College, Vancouver — 9,384; The Evergreen State College, Olympia — 2,805; Grays Harbor College, Aberdeen — 3,445; Lower Columbia College, Longview — 4,914; Olympia Technical Community College, Olympia — 3,642; St. Martin's College, Olympia — 685.

Newspapers, Circulation: *The Columbian* (eS), Vancouver — 45,315; *The Daily Chronicle* (e), Centralia — 16,016; *The Daily News* (e), Longview — 26,799; *The Daily Olympian* (eS), Olympia — 29,952; *The Daily World* (eS), Aberdeen — 19,049.

Commercial Television Stations, Affiliation: District is divided between Seattle-Tacoma ADI and Portland (Ore.) ADI.

Industries:

Weyerhaeuser Co. (Southwest Washington Region); Longview; sawmill, pulp, paper — 3,940. **Crown Zellerbach Corp.** (Mill Div.); Camas; pulp, paper products — 2,200. **Longview Fibre Co.** (HQ); Longview; pulp, paper products — 1,900. **Tektronix Inc.** (Instrument Div.); Vancouver; electronic instruments and accessories — 1,528. **Aluminum Co. of America Inc.;** Vancouver; aluminum smelting — 1,400.

Reynolds Metals Co. (Longview Reduction Plant); Longview; aluminum rolling and drawing — 1,250. **Sisters of Providence of Washington;** Olympia; hospital — 1,100. **Olympia Brewing Co.** (HQ); Olympia; brewery — 750. **Tektronix Inc.;** (Electrical Mechanical Components Mfg. Div.); Vancouver; plastic and wire components — 648. **Washington Irrigation & Development Co.;** Centralia; coal mining — 610. **Jantzen Inc.;** Vancouver; men's, women's clothing — 600. **The Columbian Inc.;** Vancouver; newspaper publishing — 525.

4th District

Central — Yakima, Tri-Cities

Barren brush land filled much of central Washington until federal irrigation and dam-building projects a generation ago made the desert bloom. As a result, the 4th District, cutting a broad swath from the Canadian frontier to the Oregon border, contains some of the richest farm land in the Pacific Northwest. At the same time, its northern tier, home of the Colville Indian Reservation and two national forests, remains heavily wooded and sparsely populated.

The largest concentration of voters is in the "Tri-Cities" area — the new district boundaries encompass largely blue-collar Pasco and white-collar Kennewick and Richland. The population of Kennewick more than doubled in the 1970s, while Richland grew by over one-quarter and Pasco by one-third, pacing Benton and Franklin counties' surge.

The Tri-Cities area is also the center of the district's central political concern: nuclear power and nuclear weapons. Since its development of the Nagasaki atomic warhead during World War II, the Hanford Atomic Works, sprawling over 570 square miles, has produced most of the nation's plutonium for nuclear weapons. Along with a spent-fuel reprocessing facility, the first plutonium-fueled breeder reactor in the United States has been installed at the Hanford site, raising hopes of abundant energy but drawing some concern over proliferation of the weapons-grade fuel.

The entire GOP ticket won Benton and Franklin counties by strong margins in 1980. However, the late Democratic Sen. Henry M. Jackson always ran well there.

Yakima, the largest city in the district, lies in a valley that federal water projects have helped make one of the nation's chief apple-growing areas. The Yakima Valley is also the country's largest producer of cherries and hops. This strongly Republican agricultural region was not particularly proud of its maverick native son, the late Supreme Court Justice William O. Douglas, and Douglas did not look back nostalgically toward his boyhood in Yakima. Yakima County gave Ronald Reagan a 55.2-percent victory in 1980.

On the Columbia River in Grant County, at the border of the 4th and 5th districts, is the Grand Coulee Dam, one of the largest construction projects in human history. Denounced as big-government intrusion when begun under the New Deal, the series of dams along the river has encouraged area industry — particularly electricity-intensive aluminum processing — by providing clean, low-cost energy.

The 4th is also the site of Mount St. Helens, whose eruptions from May 1980 through early 1982 felled thousands of acres of timber. That misfortune came atop the already severe woes of the area's lumber industry, suffering from the national increase in interest rates and consequent decrease in housing starts.

In the 1982 remap, the 4th gained all of Franklin County and the remainder of Grant and Okanogan counties from the 5th and yielded the remainder of Clark County to the 3rd. In the subsequent redistricting, the 4th took back 2,200 people in the southeastern corner of Clark County and gained a small part of Walla Walla from the 5th.

Election Returns

4th District		Democrat		Republican	
1976	President	73,833	(42.1%)	95,427	(54.4%)
	Governor	89,260	(51.7%)	80,402	(46.6%)
	Senate	114,692	(69.5%)	45,356	(27.5%)
	House	98,007	(55.0%)	61,476	(34.5%)
1978	House	69,466	(58.4%)	48,892	(41.1%)
1980	President	64,820	(32.9%)	113,840	(57.8%)
	Governor	75,142	(38.7%)	118,824	(61.3%)
	Senate	82,912	(41.0%)	119,077	(59.0%)
	House	78,070	(41.1%)	112,016	(58.9%)
1982	Senate	114,708	(71.1%)	40,837	(25.3%)
	House	45,990	(28.6%)	112,148	(69.8%)

Demographics

Population: 511,961. **Percent Change from 1970:** 25.7%.

Land Area: 25,778 square miles. **Population per Square Mile:** 19.9.

Counties, 1980 Population: Benton — 109,444; Chelan — 45,061; Douglas — 22,144; Franklin — 35,025; Grant — 48,522; Kittitas — 24,877; Klickitat — 15,822; Okanogan — 30,639; Skamania — 7,919; Yakima — 172,508.

Cities, 1980 Population: Ellensburg — 11,752; Kennewick — 34,397; Moses Lake — 10,629; Pasco — 17,944; Richland — 33,578; Wenatchee — 17,257; Yakima — 49,826.

Race and Ancestry: White — 89.6%; Black — 0.9%; American Indian, Eskimo and Aleut — 2.5%; Asian and Pacific Islander — 1.0%. Spanish Origin — 8.7%. Dutch — 1.0%; English — 9.8%; French — 1.3%; German — 8.9%; Irish — 3.2%; Italian — 0.6%; Norwegian — 1.4%; Scottish — 0.7%; Swedish — 1.0%.

Universities, Enrollment: Big Bend Community College, Moses Lake — 1,326; Central Washington University, Ellensburg — 7,551; Columbia Basin College, Pasco — 9,814; Wenatchee Valley College, Wenatchee — 3,999; Yakima Valley Community College, Yakima — 5,732.

Newspapers, Circulation: *Columbia Basin Herald* (e), Moses Lake — 6,910; *Daily Record* (e), Ellensburg — 5,885; *Tri-City Herald* (eS), Pasco — 39,397; *The Wenatchee World* (eS), Wenatchee — 27,661; *Yakima Herald Republic* (mS), Yakima — 39,763.

Commercial Television Stations, Affiliation: KAPP, Yakima (ABC); KIMA-TV, Yakima (CBS); KNDO, Yakima (NBC); KNDU, Richland (NBC). District is divided between Spokane and Yakima ADIs. Portions are in Seattle-Tacoma ADI and Portland (Ore.) ADI.

Nuclear Power Plants: Skagit 1 and 2, Hanford (General Electric, Bechtel); Washington Nuclear 1, Richland (Babcock & Wilcox, Bechtel); Washington Nuclear 2, Richland (General Electric, Bechtel).

Industries:

Rockwell International Corp.; Richland; nuclear fuel scrap — 4,500. **Battelle Memorial Institute** (Pacific Northwest Laboratories); Richland; scientific research — 2,600. **Westinghouse Hanford Co.** (Hanford Engineering Development Lab); Richland; nuclear research — 2,300. **Aluminum Co. of America Inc.**; Wenatchee; aluminum — 1,000. **Bechtel Power Corp.**; Richland; nuclear power plant construction — 1,000.

Exxon Nuclear Co. Inc.; Richland; nuclear fuels — 930. **Iowa Beef Processors Inc.**; Pasco; meatpacking — 900. **J. A. Jones Construction Co.**; Richland; heavy construction — 900. **Groves-Kiewit-Grant**; North Bonneville; heavy construction — 800. **Boise Cascade Corp.**; Yakima; lumber products — 700. **Martin Marietta Aluminum Inc.**; Goldendale; aluminum — 700. **Twin City Foods Inc.**; Prosser; food processing — 650.

Crown Zellerbach Corp. (Northwest Wood Products Div.); Omak; lumber mill — 600. **Foley-Wismer & Becker**; Richland; electrical contracting — 600. **Wright, Schuchart & Harbor Jr.;** Richland; mechanical contracting — 505. **Amfac Food Inc.** (Lamb-Weston Inc.); Connell; frozen fruits, juices, vegetables — 500. **Burns & Roe Inc.;** Richland; heavy construction — 500. **Fischbach-Lord Electric Co.;** Richland; electrical contracting — 500. **Rogers Walla Walla Inc.** (Country Gardens); Pasco; frozen french fries — 500.

5th District

East — Spokane

Much of eastern Washington likes to call itself the "Inland Empire," taking pride in the agricultural prosperity that sets it apart from Washington-on-the-Pacific. Most of the fertile wheat-growing land of the Inland Empire lies within the broad bend of the Columbia River; potato and vegetable farming is important to the economy of southeastern Washington, where the Snake River branches off toward the Idaho border.

The 5th is largely a rural district despite the presence of metropolitan Spokane, home to more than a quarter-million people. The farm vote is crucial to any congressional election. The area has given its House incumbents prolonged tenure — it has had only two representatives in 40 years — but farm politics are volatile and give any incumbent cause for concern.

Spokane County, which grew in the 1970s by 18.9 percent to nearly 342,000 residents, continues to cast more than half the 5th's vote. The city of Spokane, with a population that remained stable during the same period, is the banking and marketing center of the district, and of the broader Inland Empire counties in Washington, Oregon, Idaho and Montana. Its sizable aluminum industry takes advantage of the low-cost hydroelectric power that comes from New Deal dams along the Columbia.

Comparatively isolated and marked by a stable, non-transient population, Spokane is one of the more conservative of America's large cities. For a time in the early 1960s, its wariness of government intrusion led it to refuse federal assistance for local projects. Spokane County gave 55 percent of its vote to Ronald Reagan in 1980 and 60 percent to GOP Sen. Slade Gorton.

Outside Spokane County, the electorate is even more conservative. The only large county in the southeastern part of the state that differs from this pattern is Whitman, site of the Washington State University campus in Pullman.

The 5th's population within the old district boundaries grew by 19.5 percent in the 1970s, and the 1982 redistricting yielded all of Okanogan and Franklin counties and part of Grant County to the neighboring 4th. The subsequent redistricting required the 5th to give up even more territory, moving a corner of Walla Walla County to the 4th.

Election Returns

5th District		Democrat		Republican	
1976	President	83,059	(42.7%)	104,956	(53.9%)
	Governor	89,780	(46.0%)	100,194	(51.3%)
	Senate	120,414	(62.8%)	63,381	(33.1%)
	House	108,342	(57.0%)	79,050	(41.6%)
1978	House	69,714	(47.6%)	62,942	(43.0%)
1980	President	73,239	(34.1%)	120,364	(56.1%)
	Governor	85,521	(39.8%)	129,218	(60.2%)
	Senate	83,930	(39.0%)	131,261	(61.0%)
	House	109,644	(51.9%)	101,782	(48.1%)
1982	Senate	111,952	(65.3%)	53,475	(31.2%)
	House	109,549	(64.3%)	60,816	(35.7%)

Demographics

Population: 518,962. **Percent Change from 1970:** 18.7%.

Land Area: 17,681 square miles. **Population per Square Mile:** 29.4.

Counties, 1980 Population: Adams — 13,267; Asotin — 16,823; Columbia — 4,057; Ferry — 5,811; Garfield — 2,468; Lincoln — 9,604; Pend Oreille — 8,580; Spokane — 341,835; Stevens — 28,979; Walla Walla — 47,435; Whitman — 40,103.

Cities, 1980 Population: Pullman — 23,579; Spokane — 171,300; Walla Walla — 25,618.

Race and Ancestry: White — 94.8%; Black — 1.1%; American Indian, Eskimo and Aleut — 1.5%; Asian and Pacific Islander — 1.2%. Spanish Origin — 2.3%. Dutch — 0.7%; English — 9.2%; French — 1.2%; German — 11.7%; Irish — 4.2%; Italian — 1.3%; Norwegian — 2.2%; Scottish — 1.0%; Swedish — 1.7%.

Universities, Enrollment: Eastern Washington University, Cheney — 8,333; Fort Wright College, Spokane — 408; Gonzaga University, Spokane — 3,351; Spokane Community College, Spokane — 5,162; Spokane Falls Community College, Spokane — 5,469; Walla Walla College, College Place — 1,911; Walla Walla Community College, Walla Walla — 5,084; Washington State University, Pullman — 17,468; Whitman College, Walla Walla — 1,144; Whitworth College, Spokane — 1,768.

Newspapers, Circulation: *Chronicle* (e), Spokane — 61,235; *Palouse Empire News* (e), Pullman — 1,000; *Spokesman-Review* (mS), Spokane — 75,617; *Walla Walla Union Bulletin* (eS), Walla Walla — 15,911.

Commercial Television Stations, Affiliation: KAYU-TV, Spokane (None); KHQ-TV, Spokane (NBC); KREM-TV, Spokane (CBS); KXLY-TV, Spokane (ABC). Most of district is located in Spokane ADI. Portion is in Yakima ADI.

Military Installations: Fairchild Air Force Base, Airway Heights — 5,393; Spokane International Airport (Air National Guard), Spokane — 264.

Industries:

Kaiser Aluminum & Chemical Corp. (Trentwood Rolling Mill); Spokane; steel rolling mill — 2,600. **Sacred Heart Hospital;** Spokane; hospital — 2,100. **Iowa Beef Processors Inc.;** Wallula; meatpacking — 1,400. **Kaiser Aluminum & Chemical Corp.;** Spokane; aluminum — 1,400. **Deaconess Hospital;** Spokane; hospital — 1,360. **Key Tronic Corp.** (HQ); Spokane; computers — 800. **General Telephone & Electronics Corp.** (Columbia Div.); Spokane; lighting fixtures — 600. **Northwest Alloys Inc.;** Addy; magnesium products — 500. **Rogers Walla Walla Inc.** (HQ); Walla Walla; canned, frozen vegetables — 500.

6th District

Puget Sound — Bremerton, Tacoma

Maritime interests dominate the 6th, which surrounds the sinuous waterways that cut into the shores of Puget Sound and the Hood Canal. Docks, naval installations and shipbuilding facilities maintain the peninsula's historic links with the sea.

The industrial city of Tacoma — overshadowed by its nearby rival, Seattle, and sensitive about it — is the population center of the district with nearly one-quarter of the residents. Tacoma's fortunes follow the cycles of Boeing's aircraft business, but the city is less dependent on the huge aerospace firm than is Seattle. Commerce at the dockyards of Tacoma's deep-water port has enjoyed brisk growth and continues to expand. The wood-products and metal-smelting industries are also vital elements in the city's economy. The Tacoma area is the world headquarters of the Weyerhaeuser Co., although redistricting moved the main offices from the 6th District to the 8th.

Tacoma's blue-collar, heavily unionized electorate generally tilts Pierce County to centrist Democrats. Democrats carried the county by solid margins in 1976 although in 1980 Republicans carried the county in statewide contests.

Across Puget Sound from Tacoma, the largest city in the 6th's part of the Kitsap Peninsula is Bremerton, where shipbuilding and docking remain the backbone of local industry and the U.S. Navy is an important influence. Paper and wood are also central concerns. Although some major naval bases were shifted by redistricting into the 2nd, the 6th retained the Puget Sound Naval Shipyard, including drydocks, supply depots and a refueling and refitting center for nuclear-powered aircraft carriers. Because of the labor vote in Bremerton, surrounding Kitsap County is good territory for most statewide Democrats.

The 26.7 percent population growth within the old district boundaries since the 1970 census required the 6th to shed some territory in the 1982 remap. Although the borders of the 6th changed substantially, the slight Democratic tilt of the district remained. The 6th gained some suburban areas in southwestern Pierce County that often vote Republican, but yielded some equally Republican white-collar towns in Pierce County to the newly created 8th. The 6th lost the northern part of Kitsap County to the 2nd and moved west to include part of Mason County.

The redistricting scheduled to take effect for the 1984 elections moved back into the 6th those portions the earlier redistricting had yielded to the 2nd. It also reunited Tacoma in the 6th.

Election Returns

6th District		Democrat		Republican	
1976	President	91,991	(49.4%)	88,014	(47.3%)
	Governor	117,256	(63.9%)	62,282	(34.0%)
	Senate	135,897	(77.0%)	34,599	(19.6%)
	House	117,828	(73.8%)	39,760	(24.9%)
1978	House	58,356	(60.8%)	35,610	(37.1%)
1980	President	74,592	(36.3%)	103,070	(50.1%)
	Governor	85,587	(42.4%)	116,429	(57.6%)
	Senate	101,301	(50.0%)	101,134	(50.0%)
	House	106,838	(54.3%)	90,079	(45.7%)
1982	Senate	97,291	(71.7%)	31,360	(23.1%)
	House	89,985	(62.5%)	47,720	(33.2%)

Demographics

Population: 515,970. **Percent Change from 1970:** 15.1%.

Land Area: 1,059 square miles. **Population per Square Mile:** 487.2.

Counties, 1980 Population: Kitsap (Pt.) — 86,039; Mason (Pt.) — 14,565; Pierce (Pt.) — 415,366.

Cities, 1980 Population: Bremerton — 36,208; Fort Lewis (CDP) — 23,761; Puyallup — 18,251; Tacoma (Pt.) — 154,254.

Race and Ancestry: White — 87.4%; Black — 6.1%; American Indian, Eskimo and Aleut — 1.3%; Asian and Pacific Islander — 3.6%. Spanish Origin — 2.8%. Dutch — 0.5%; English — 7.7%; French — 1.1%; German — 7.8%; Irish — 3.1%; Italian — 1.2%; Norwegian — 2.8%; Polish — 0.7%; Scottish — 0.7%; Swedish — 1.5%.

Universities, Enrollment: Fort Steilacoom Community Center - Lakewood Center, Tacoma — 8,887; Olympic College, Bremerton — 8,183; Pacific Lutheran University, Tacoma — 3,475; Tacoma Community College, Tacoma — 6,075; University of Puget Sound, Tacoma — 2,877.

Newspapers, Circulation: *The Bremerton Sun* (e), Bremerton — 35,481; *The Tacoma News Tribune* (eS), Tacoma — 106,450.

Commercial Television Stations, Affiliation: KCPQ, Tacoma (None); KQFB, Tacoma (None); KSTW, Tacoma (None). Entire district is located in Seattle-Tacoma ADI.

Military Installations: Bremerton Naval Regional Medical Center, Bremerton — 621; Fort Lewis, Tacoma — 27,199; McChord Air Force Base, Tacoma — 8,864; Puget Sound Naval Shipyard, Bremerton — 11,291; Puget Sound Naval Supply Center, Bremerton — 607.

Industries:

Tacoma Boatbuilding Co. Inc.; Tacoma; shipbuilding — 2,000. **St. Joseph Hospital & Health Care Center Inc.;** Tacoma; hospital — 1,170. **Western State Hospital;** Steilacoom; state mental hospital — 1,000. **Curtice-Burns Inc.** (Nalley's Fine Foods Div.); Tacoma; specialty food items — 820. **Hygrade Food Products Corp.;** Tacoma; meatpacking — 600. **Weyerhaeuser Co.;** Tacoma; administrative offices — 600. **Atlas Foundry & Machine Co.;** Tacoma; steel foundry — 550. **Kaiser Aluminum & Chemical Corp.;** Tacoma; aluminum — 500. **West Coast Grocery Co.;** Takoma; grocery wholesaling — 500.

7th District

Seattle and Suburbs

Scenic Seattle developed a reputation as a "livable city" in the 1970s, although it had some rocky economic times. The aerospace depression that crippled it at the start of the decade gave way to a boom in the late 1970s, but the upturn quickly turned into another recession as both the aircraft and home-building industries stagnated.

The 7th traditionally has been based in Seattle's South Side, one of the few blue-collar and ethnic enclaves in the Northwest. The South Side has a varied working-class population that includes well-defined Scandinavian and Italian communities. The district's geography changed considerably for the 1980s, however. The 1982 remap made up for the district's population deficit by expanding into the city's northern section. This addition made for a substantial cultural change; most of the new North Side voters live in white-collar neighborhoods where middle-class "good government" liberalism is more common than the bread-and-butter politics of the South Side.

During the 1970s the old 7th was the state's most dependable Democratic district, and the 1982 remap made it even more so. Republican cartographers used the 7th as a repository for urban Democrats to help tilt the new, neighboring 8th toward the GOP. Ronald Reagan carried the old 7th by a scant 1,400 votes, while losing the area of the new 7th to Jimmy Carter overwhelmingly.

1 (Part)

DUVALL

COTTAGE LAKE

LAKE FOREST PARK

BOTHELL

KINGSGATE

INGLEWOOD

East Seattle (Part)

JUANITA

ROSE HILL

REDMOND

REDMOND

N 165th St

Aurora Ave N

15th Ave NE

N Z

NE 75th St

20th Ave NE

35th Ave NE

24th Ave NW

N 85th St

15th Ave W

KIRKLAND

NE 80th St

East Seattle (Part)

State Hwy 202

CARNATION

SEATTLE

Seattle (Part)

CLYDE HILL

MEDINA

BELLEVUE

BEAUX ARTS VILLAGE

Puget Sound

7

MERCER ISLAND

Fall City Rd

Raging River

328th Ave SE

BRYN MAWR SKYWAY

ISSAQUAH

BOULEVARD PARK

Issaquah Plateau

I-90

WHITE CENTER SHOREWOOD

RIVERTON

I-405

RENTON (PART)

BURIEN

TUKWILA

NORMANDY PARK

S 1st Ave

SW 43rd St

CASCADE-FAIRWOOD

Vashon Island

NORTH HILL

S 188th St

RENTON (PART)

DES MOINES

KENT

Tahoma-Maple Valley

8 (Part)

BLACK DIAMOND

AUBURN (PART)

Auburn

Muckleshoot Reservation

Enumclaw Plateau

MILTON (PART)

PACIFIC

ENUMCLAW

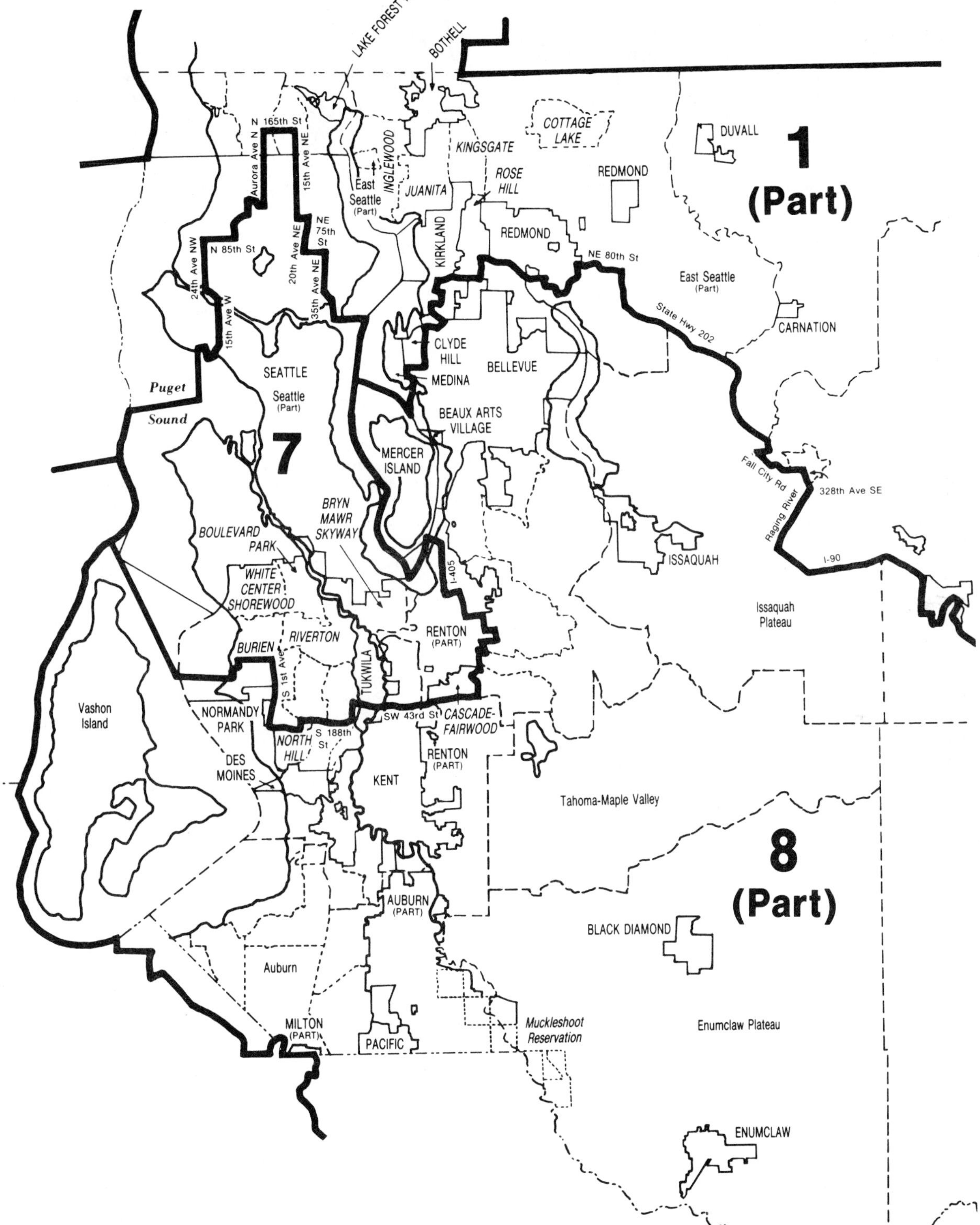

Labor is a crucial element in the district's Democratic politics. The machinists, among the nation's most liberal unions in recent years, are important among the Boeing workers, and there is a tradition of militant unionism along the docks.

Seattle enjoyed boom times through the 1950s and early 1960s as Boeing was awarded contracts for the B-52 bomber and parts of the Minuteman intercontinental ballistic missile and NASA Saturn rockets. During Boeing's slump — between mid-1968 and the end of 1971 — 63,500 blue-collar and 8,000 white-collar workers were laid off, which boosted the area's unemployment rate from 2.5 percent to 13 percent in that four-year period. Unemployment was under control again by 1975, but the 1981-82 recession lifted it above 10 percent in 1982.

The subsequent remap, scheduled to take effect for the 1984 elections, extended the Seattle part of the 7th south about three miles and added the blue-collar industrial suburb of Kent.

Election Returns

7th District		Democrat		Republican	
1976	President	105,246	(48.2%)	104,976	(48.1%)
	Governor	120,725	(55.7%)	91,368	(42.2%)
	Senate	157,067	(75.8%)	42,303	(20.4%)
	House	104,540	(51.7%)	93,767	(46.4%)
1978	House	62,512	(44.4%)	76,759	(54.5%)
1980	President	97,717	(48.2%)	70,762	(34.9%)
	Governor	107,584	(52.2%)	98,437	(47.8%)
	Senate	120,448	(58.7%)	84,748	(41.3%)
	House	103,762	(48.1%)	108,225	(50.1%)
1982	Senate	128,653	(68.7%)	36,775	(19.6%)
	House	126,313	(79.9%)	51,759	(29.1%)

Demographics

Population: 514,040. **Percent Change from 1970:** -7.1%.

Land Area: 110 square miles. **Population per Square Mile:** 4,673.1

Counties, 1980 Population: King (Pt.) — 514,040.

Cities, 1980 Population: Renton (Pt.) — 19,053; Seattle (Pt.) — 391,724.

Race and Ancestry: White — 79.6%; Black — 9.4%; American Indian, Eskimo and Aleut — 1.4%; Asian and Pacific Islander — 7.8%. Spanish Origin — 2.7%. Dutch — 0.5%; English — 7.4%; French — 1.0%; German — 5.9%; Irish — 3.4%; Italian — 1.4%; Norwegian — 2.8%; Polish — 0.6%; Russian — 0.5%; Scottish — 0.9%; Swedish — 1.7%.

Universities, Enrollment: City College, Seattle — 1,663; Cornish Institute, Seattle — 440; Griffin College, Seattle — 181; North Seattle Community College, Seattle — 8,775; Seattle Central Community College, Seattle — 7,360; Seattle Pacific University, Seattle — 2,698; Seattle University, Seattle — 4,343; South Seattle Community College, Seattle — 8,117; University of Washington, Seattle — 36,636.

Newspapers, Circulation: *Seattle Daily Journal of Commerce* (m), Seattle — 5,159; *Seattle Post-Intelligencer* (mS), Seattle — 196,739; *The Seattle Times* (all day, S), Seattle — 257,248.

Commercial Television Stations, Affiliation: KING-TV, Seattle (NBC); KIRO-TV, Seattle (CBS); KOMO-TV, Seattle (ABC). Entire district is located in Seattle-Tacoma ADI.

Military Installations: Seattle Air Guard Base, Seattle — 240.

Industries:

The Boeing Co. (Commercial Airplane Co.); Renton; aircraft — 11,600. **Todd Pacific Shipyards Corp.;** Seattle; shipbuilding, repair — 2,800. **The Swedish Hospital Medical Center;** Seattle; hospital — 2,700. **Lockheed Shipbuilding & Construction Co.;** Seattle; shipbuilding — 2,500. **Burlington Northern Inc.;** Seattle; railroad operations — 2,100.

Group Health Operations of Puget Sound; Seattle; hospital — 2,010. **Paccar Inc.** (Pacific Car & Foundry); Renton; railroad freight cars — 2,000. **SAFECO Corp.** (HQ); Seattle; insurance, real estate — 2,000. **Seafirst Corp.** (HQ); Seattle; banking — 2,000. **United Airlines Inc.;** Seattle; commercial airline — 2,000. **Wright Schuchart Inc.;** Seattle; commercial building contracting — 1,900. **The Boeing Co.;** Seattle; computer services — 1,720. **Northwest Airlines Inc.** (Northwest Orient Airlines); Seattle; commercial airline — 1,500. **Seattle Times Co.;** Seattle; newspaper publishing — 1,500.

Allstate Insurance Co. Inc.; Seattle; insurance — 1,400. **Bethlehem Steel Corp.;** Seattle; steel works, bars, bolts — 1,300. **The Boeing Co.** (Engineering & Construction); Tukwila; engineering, heavy construction —1,300. **Virginia Mason Hospital Assn. Inc.;** Seattle; hospital — 1,300. **Veterans Administration;** Seattle; veterans' hospital — 1,280. **Honeywell Inc.** (Defense Electronics Operations Div.); Seattle; engineering services — 1,250. **Harborview Medical Center;** Seattle; hospital — 1,200. **Valley General Hospital;** Renton; hospital — 1,110. **Port of Seattle** (HQ); Seattle; port authority — 1,010.

C X Corp. (HQ); Seattle; film, film processing — 950. **Fisher Companies Inc.;** Seattle; flour mill; television, radio stations — 860. **Associated Grocers Inc.** (HQ); Seattle; grocery wholesaling — 800. **Markey Machinery Co. Inc.;** Seattle; construction machinery — 800. **Rainier National Bank** (HQ); Seattle; banking — 800. **Schoenfeld Industries Inc.** (Brittania Neckwear - HQ); Seattle; men's, women's sportswear — 800. **The Hearst Corp.** (Seattle Post Intelligencer); Seattle; newspaper publishing — 715. **Foss Launch & Tug Co.** (HQ); Seattle; maritime carrier — 700. **Western Air Lines Inc.;** Seattle; commercial airline — 700.

Paccar Inc. (Kenworth Truck Co. Div.); Seattle; trucks — 675. **The Boeing Co.** (Marine Systems Div.); Seattle; shipbuilding — 650. **Indian Head Inc.** (Northwestern Glass Co.); Seattle; glass containers — 600. **Marine Power & Equipment Inc.;** Seattle; ship repairing, construction — 600. **Republic Airlines West Inc.;** Seattle; commercial airline — 600. **Gais Seattle French Baking;** Seattle; bakery goods — 595. **First Interstate Bank** (HQ); Seattle; banking — 505. **Nordstrom Inc.** (Place Two - HQ); Seattle; family apparel stores — 500. **Northwest Protective Service;** Seattle; security services — 500. **Washington Plaza Hotel Co.;** Seattle; hotel — 500.

8th District

Seattle Suburbs — Bellevue

A new district carved out of the prosperous suburbs and exurbs of Seattle, along with some rural areas toward the slopes of the Cascade Mountains, the 8th is the dividend earned by the state's 21 percent population growth of the 1970s. The Republican legislators who designed it were careful to ensure that it would have a decidedly Republican character. Its medium income is $27,016, the 23rd highest in the nation.

For 1983-84, the 8th District includes the entire southern half of King County. Small communities in the southwestern portion of the county — Auburn, Kent, Algona — send white-collar professionals to jobs in downtown Seattle. In addition the headquarters of Boeing's civilian aviation division in Renton, in the 7th District, supplies numerous managerial and administrative jobs. Blue-collar workers and technicians employed at the Boeing facility in Renton assemble much of the mid-sized 757 jet.

Bellevue, the second-largest city in King County after Seattle, is a bustling white-collar community of nearly 74,000 whose population grew by 20.8 percent in the 1970s. Its residents provide strong Republican majorities. The pressures of unplanned growth have been felt farther south; the highway corridor between the medium-sized cities of Auburn and Kent has been engulfed by strip development.

At the western edge of the district, along Puget Sound, Mercer Island is a wealthy suburb whose population has grown briskly. Once-rural Vashon Island, south of Mercer, is growing quickly as farming gives way to housing tracts. Vashon also has some light manufacturing.

At the eastern edge of the new 8th, residential subdivisions are eclipsing open land, as the district stretches toward the foothills and ski areas of the Cascades. A large chunk of eastern Pierce County is in the new district but this part of Pierce County is sparsely populated and has little political importance.

Under the district lines scheduled to take effect in 1984, the 8th retains its suburban character. The portion of Tacoma it had gained for 1983-84 was returned to the 6th. The 8th yielded Kent, a blue-collar suburb of Seattle to the 7th.

Election Returns

8th District		Democrat		Republican	
1976	President	83,198	(45.5%)	92,377	(50.5%)
	Governor	93,810	(51.7%)	83,195	(45.9%)
	Senate	128,801	(74.2%)	37,372	(21.5%)
	House	105,573	(62.9%)	59,621	(35.5%)
1978	House	57,792	(51.5%)	53,684	(47.8%)
1980	President	65,230	(31.8%)	109,740	(53.5%)
	Governor	81,726	(41.3%)	116,336	(58.7%)
	Senate	77,784	(39.5%)	119,076	(60.5%)
	House	72,731	(47.6%)	79,459	(52.1%)
1982	Senate	91,559	(67.4%)	35,693	(26.3%)
	House	59,824	(43.0%)	79,209	(57.0%)

Demographics

Population: 517,173. **Percent Change from 1970:** 29.1%.

Land Area: 1,739 square miles. **Population per Square Mile:** 297.4.

Counties, 1980 Population: King (Pt.) — 467,163; Pierce (Pt.) — 50,010.

Cities, 1980 Population: Auburn — 26,417; Bellevue — 73,903; Kent — 23,152; Kirkland (Pt.) — 3,761; Mercer Island — 21,522; Redmond (Pt.) — 13,396; Renton (Pt.) — 11,559; Tacoma (Pt.) — 4,247.

Race and Ancestry: White — 94.6%; Black — 1.0%; American Indian, Eskimo and Aleut — 0.8%; Asian and Pacific Islander — 2.7%. Spanish Origin — 1.7%. Dutch — 0.8%; English — 9.0%; French — 1.0%; German — 7.3%; Irish — 3.1%; Italian — 1.2%; Norwegian — 2.5%; Polish — 0.7%; Scottish — 0.8%; Swedish — 1.5%.

Universities, Enrollment: Bellevue Community College, Bellevue — 8,712; Green River Community College, Auburn — 7,130; Highline Community College, Midway — 10,042; Lutheran Bible Institute of Seattle, Issaquah — 280.

Newspapers, Circulation: *Daily Globe News* (mS), Auburn — 7,859; *Daily News Journal* (mS), Kent — 10,244; *Journal-American* (m), Bellevue — 27,612; *Renton Daily Record Chronicle* (mS), Kent — 10,520. *Seattle Post-Intelligencer, The Seattle Times* and *The Tacoma News Tribune* also circulate in the district.

Commercial Television Stations, Affiliation: Entire district is located in Seattle-Tacoma ADI.

Industries:

The Boeing Co.; Kent; aerospace equipment — 16,500. **The Boeing Co. (Fabrication Div.);** Auburn; airplane components — 10,500. **Weyerhaeuser Co. (HQ);** Federal Way; logs, lumber — 3,000. **Sundstrand Corp. (Data Control);** Redmond; aircraft control equipment — 1,900. **Western Electric Co. Inc.;** Kent; electrical equipment wholesaling, repairing — 1,400.

Weyerhaeuser Co.; Snoqualmie; sawmill, hardwood veneer, plywood — 900. **Safeway Stores Inc.;** Bellevue; grocery wholesaling — 850. **K2 Corp.;** Vashon; sports equipment — 700. **Heath Techna Precision Structures Inc.;** Kent; aircraft interiors — 650. **Alaska Airlines Inc. (HQ);** Seattle; commercial airline — 600. **Advanced Technology Labs Inc. (HQ);** Bellevue; medical diagnostic equipment — 575. **Data I/O Corp. (HQ);** Issaquah; electronic computing equipment — 557. **Criton Corp. (Precision Structures Div.);** Kent; aircraft parts — 500. **Farmers New World Life Insurance;** Mercer Island; life, health insurance — 550. **Standard Equipment Inc. (Mullen Construction Co.);** Kent; highway construction — 500.

West Virginia

After considering proposals designed to unseat at least one of the state's two Republican House members, the Democratic-controlled West Virginia Legislature approved a redistricting plan early in 1982 that made only minor alterations in the existing lines.

The plan passed the Legislature Jan. 28 and was signed by Democratic Gov. John D. "Jay" Rockefeller IV on Feb. 8, 1982.

None of the four districts was more than 35,000 out of population balance, so no major surgery was needed. The remap affected only three of West Virginia's 55 counties. All are in the rural north central part of the state and have a combined population of less than 50,000.

The GOP congressional victories in 1980 had tempted legislators to make more drastic changes. The switch of two seats to Republicans ended a 12-year Democratic monopoly of the congressional delegation.

Intent on regaining at least one of the seats, the Democratic House passed a redistricting bill in 1981 aimed at weakening the Republican in the 3rd, who had won the previous year by only 9,603 votes. But state Senate leaders viewed the changes as too drastic. Enthusiasm for the House plan evaporated when the 2nd District Republican announced that he would vacate his House seat to run for the U.S. Senate.

With the 2nd District suddenly open, Democratic leaders shifted targets and endorsed a redistricting plan that left each district basically intact. In 1982 Democrats recaptured both Republican seats, demonstrating that West Virginia's political orientation has not changed very much since the state became federally dependent and viscerally Democratic during the New Deal.

Age of Population

District	Population Under 18	Voting Age Population	Population 65 & Over (% of VAP)	Median Age
1	135,285	353,283	64,928 (18.4%)	31.7
2	137,270	350,168	60,621 (17.3%)	29.7
3	138,965	347,147	57,194 (16.5%)	30.9
4	148,116	339,410	55,125 (16.2%)	29.4
State	559,636	1,390,008	237,868 (17.1%)	30.4

Income and Occupation

District	Median Family Income	White Collar Workers	Blue Collar Workers	Service Workers	Farm Workers
1	$ 18,747	44.3%	41.8%	12.9%	1.0%
2	15,716	42.3	39.9	13.8	3.9
3	18,115	48.7	38.4	11.6	1.3
4	16,746	44.7	42.7	11.8	0.9
State	$ 17,308	45.0%	40.6%	12.6%	1.8%

Education: School Years Completed

District	8 Years or Fewer	4 Years of High School	4 Years of College or More	Median School Years
1	23.0%	40.7%	10.2%	12.3
2	30.7	33.5	11.2	12.1
3	27.7	35.9	11.2	12.2
4	30.8	32.1	9.0	12.0
State	28.0%	35.6%	10.4%	12.2

Housing and Residential Patterns

District	Owner Occupied	Renter Occupied	Urban	Rural
1	73.7%	26.3%	51.9%	48.1%
2	74.2	25.8	20.5	79.5
3	73.2	26.8	39.8	60.2
4	73.2	26.8	32.5	67.5
State	73.6%	26.4%	36.2%	63.8%

1st District

Northern Panhandle — Wheeling

The 1st District's northernmost regions are in the orbit of industrial Pittsburgh. Heavy industry (iron and steel) is concentrated in the Panhandle, a narrow strip of West Virginia crowded between the Pennsylvania border and the

WEST VIRGINIA

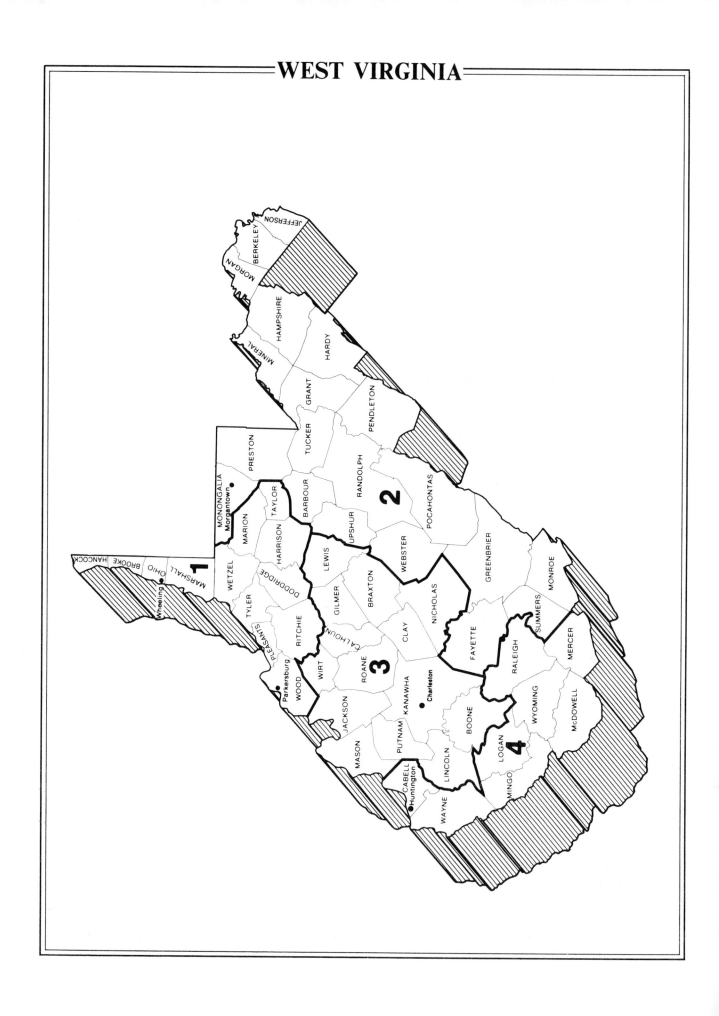

Ohio River. To the southeast, coal is mined in Marion and Harrison counties and shipped up the Monongahela River to the western Pennsylvania metropolis.

Both of these areas are heavily unionized and boast concentrations of Southern and Eastern European ethnics, descendants of immigrants attracted by work in the mines and mills. These areas usually produce Democratic majorities sufficient to carry the district.

Marion and Harrison counties, which also are major glass producers, and Brooke and Hancock counties, at the northern tip of the Panhandle, are the most reliably Democratic counties in the district. All four counties preferred Jimmy Carter by at least 12 percentage points over Ronald Reagan in 1980. Together the four comprise 44 percent of the district population.

Massive layoffs in the steel industry devastated the economy in Brooke and Hancock counties in the early 1980s. Ohio County (Wheeling) has fared better. But like the rest of the West Virginia Panhandle, it has lost population since 1960.

In the 1800s Wheeling was the western terminus of the National Road, a major artery between the Eastern seaboard and the growing frontier. Since then, Wheeling has developed into the Panhandle's commercial center, with a significant white-collar population that often produces GOP majorities. Ohio County voted Republican in the 1972, 1976 and 1980 presidential elections.

To the south is Marshall County, the home base of former Republican Gov. Arch A. Moore. Ohio and Marshall counties, which together make up 21 percent of the district population, gave Moore a strong enough base to win six terms in the U.S. House, from 1957 to 1969.

The only other population center in the 1st is Wood County (Parkersburg), located about midway along the Ohio River between Wheeling and Huntington. The county holds 19 percent of the district voters and anchors the southwestern corner of the 1st. Like the rural counties that separate it from the district's other, more industrialized urban centers, Wood County frequently votes for Republican candidates.

Although the 1st District was long the most prosperous district in West Virginia, its population grew by only about 6 percent during the 1970s — a lower growth rate than in any other district in the state.

Redistricting added Ritchie County from the 3rd District and Taylor County from the 2nd. Both are rural and Republican oriented, but together they make up only 5 percent of the district population.

Election Returns

1st District		Democrat		Republican	
1976	President	111,273	(55.2%)	90,173	(44.7%)
	Governor	137,102	(66.8%)	68,267	(33.2%)
	Senate	155,448	(99.9%)	—	
	House	115,333	(59.1%)	79,791	(40.9%)
1978	Senate	63,091	(46.8%)	71,798	(53.2%)
	House	81,730	(63.2%)	47,676	(36.8%)
1980	President	93,363	(48.0%)	91,307	(47.0%)
	Governor	103,729	(52.7%)	92,131	(46.8%)
	House	111,385	(62.2%)	67,825	(37.8%)
1982	Senate	104,675	(67.6%)	48,757	(31.5%)
	House	79,529	(53.2%)	70,069	(46.8%)

Demographics

Population: 488,568. **Percent Change from 1970:** 6.1%.

Land Area: 3,376 square miles. **Population per Square Mile:** 144.7.

Counties, 1980 Population: Brooke — 31,117; Doddridge — 7,433; Hancock — 40,418; Harrison — 77,710; Marion — 65,789; Marshall — 41,608; Ohio — 61,389; Pleasants — 8,236; Ritchie — 11,442; Taylor — 16,584; Tyler — 11,320; Wetzel — 21,874; Wood — 93,648.

Cities, 1980 Population: Clarksburg — 22,371; Fairmont — 23,863; Moundsville — 12,419; Parkersburg — 39,967; Vienna — 11,618; Weirton — 24,736; Wheeling — 43,070.

Race and Ancestry: White — 98.0%; Black — 1.6%; American Indian, Eskimo and Aleut — 0.1%; Asian and Pacific Islander — 0.2%. Spanish Origin — 0.7%. Dutch — 0.6%; English — 14.9%; French — 0.6%; German — 8.4%; Irish — 5.3%; Italian — 3.5%; Polish — 1.6%.

Universities, Enrollment: Bethany College, Bethany — 886; Fairmont State College, Fairmont — 5,244; Ohio Valley College, Parkersburg — 256; Parkersburg Community College, Parkersburg — 3,206; Salem College, Salem — 870; West Liberty State College, West Liberty — 2,671; West Virginia Business College, Clarksburg — 434; West Virginia Career College, Fairmont — 562; West Virginia Northern Community College, Wheeling — 3,245; Wheeling College, Wheeling — 1,026.

Newspapers, Circulation: *The Clarksburg Exponent* (mS), Clarksburg — 8,576; *Clarksburg Telegram* (eS), Clarksburg — 19,585; *Intelligencer* (m), Wheeling — 24,173; *Moundsville Daily Echo* (e), Moundsville — 5,018; *The Mountain Statesman* (m), Grafton — 3,295; *News-Register* (eS), Wheeling — 27,956; *The Parkersburg News* (mS), 20,869; *The Parkersburg Sentinel* (e), Parkersburg — 17,517; *Times-West Virginian* (mS), Fairmont — 15,659; *Weirton Daily Times* (e), Weirton — 8,224.

Commercial Television Stations, Affiliation: WBOY, Clarksburg (NBC); WLYJ, Clarksburg (None); WTAP, Parkersburg (NBC); WTRF, Wheeling (CBS). Most of district is located in Wheeling-Steubenville (Ohio) ADI. Portions are in Clarksburg-Weston ADI, Parkersburg ADI and Pittsburgh (Pa.) ADI.

Industries:

National Steel Corp. (Weirton Steel Div.); Weirton; tin plates — 7,000. E. I. du Pont de Nemours & Co.; Parkersburg; plastic products — 3,020. Consolidation Coal. Co. (Fairmont Operations); Monongahela; coal mining — 1,615. Ohio Valley Medical Center Inc.; Wheeling; hospital — 1,600. Westinghouse Electric Corp.; Fairmont; light bulbs — 1,600.

Borg-Warner Chemicals Inc.; Parkersburg; plastic resins — 1,500. Borg-Warner Corp.; Washington; engraving — 1,500. Mobay Chemical Corp.; New Martinsville; paints, varnishes — 1,200. St. Joseph Hospital of Parkersburg; Parkersburg; hospital — 1,100. Anchor Hocking Corp.; Clarksburg; glassware — 1,050. United Hospital Center Inc.; Clarksburg; hospital — 1,020. Valley Camp Coal Co. Inc.; Triadelphia; coal mining — 1,000. Homer Laughlin China Co. (HQ); Newell; dinnerware — 897. PPG Industries Inc. (Chemical Div.); New Martinsville; industrial organic chemicals — 850. Wheeling-Pittsburgh Steel Corp. (Wheeling Corrugating Co. Div.); Wheeling; blast furnace, steel products — 750. Southern Ohio Coal Co. (Martinka Mine #1); Fairmont; coal mining — 720.

American Cyanamid Co.; Willow Island; industrial inorganic chemicals — 700. O. Ames Co. (HQ); Parkersburg; lawn, garden tools — 700. Wheeling Machine Products Co. (Wheeling Pacific Div. - HQ); Wheeling; pipe couplings — 700. Wheeling-Pittsburgh Steel Corp.; Benwood; steel pipe, tubes — 700. Wheeling-Pittsburgh Steel Corp. (Wheeling Fabricating Div.); Wheeling; steel sheet, bars — 700. Union Carbide Corp.; Clarksburg; carbon, graphite products — 650. Consolidated Gas Supply Corp. (Hope Natural Gas Co. Div. - HQ); Clarksburg; natural gas production — 632. FMC Corp.; Fairmont; mining machinery — 600. Butler Mfg. Co. (Walker/Parkersburg Div.); Parkersburg; wiring devices — 550. Anchor Hocking Corp. (Ceramic Products Div.); Chester; dinnerware — 500. Corning Glass Works Inc.; Parkersburg; glass tubing — 500.

2nd District

East — Morgantown, Eastern Panhandle

It does not take long for an incumbent to make his position impregnable in the 2nd District because challengers find it difficult to reach the electorate hidden in its hills and hollows.

One of the largest districts east of the Mississippi River, the 2nd has no major media markets. Candidates must buy television time in Pittsburgh, Pa., Harrisonburg, Va., and Washington, D.C., to reach the voters.

Democratic Rep. Harley O. Staggers held the congressional seat for 32 years until his retirement in 1980, and many Democratic leaders virtually had conceded a second term to Staggers' Republican successor before he announced he would seek the Senate seat. In 1982, Staggers' son won the district with 64 percent of the vote.

After several decades of population decline, many counties in the 2nd showed substantial gains in the 1970s. The old district's 20 percent growth rate outstripped other districts in the state and forced the 2nd to shed two counties — Taylor to the 1st and Lewis to the 3rd. Both are small, Republican-leaning counties situated along the district's western border.

Population growth was greatest in the eastern Panhandle, where large numbers of retirees and commuters from the Baltimore, Md. and Washington, D.C., areas have relocated. Jefferson County, located at the tip of the Panhandle, showed a 42 percent population increase during the 1970s, the largest increase of any county in the state.

But most of the district is in the Allegheny Mountains where the standard of living is the lowest in the state. Many mountaineers turn to the large tourist trade to supplement their meager incomes. The luxurious Greenbrier Hotel in White Sulphur Springs is one of the district's major employers.

With mining and industry limited and major agricultural operations restricted to level areas of the Panhandle, neither political party has a large natural constituency in the district. Elections are frequently determined by name recognition.

Democratic strength is greatest in the few mining and industrial areas along the western fringe of the district. Monongalia County, one of the leading coal-producing counties in the state, combines a sizable number of blue-collar voters with the large academic community at West Virginia University in Morgantown. The county holds 15 percent of the district population.

Fayette County, at the southwest corner of the district, is the other major Democratic stronghold. It lies at one end of the industrialized Kanawha Valley and is home for nearly 12 percent of district residents.

Until the New Deal era, Democratic votes in the district were concentrated in the mountain counties along the Virginia border. But these counties often vote Republican now.

Republican Party candidates usually run best in the Panhandle, which includes the fertile farm land of the northern Shenandoah Valley. Pastoral Grant County regularly turns in the highest Republican voting percentages in the state. It gave Ronald Reagan 75 percent of the vote in 1980. But within this area only Berkeley County, with 10 percent of the district residents, constitutes a major population center.

Election Returns

2nd District		Democrat		Republican	
1976	President	105,527	(57.0%)	79,607	(43.0%)
	Governor	116,098	(63.4%)	67,050	(36.6%)
	Senate	143,044	(100.0%)	—	
	House	127,157	(73.3%)	46,297	(26.7%)
1978	Senate	61,258	(51.9%)	56,685	(48.1%)
	House	64,658	(55.9%)	51,067	(44.1%)
1980	President	87,423	(47.5%)	86,471	(47.0%)
	Governor	96,530	(52.3%)	87,138	(47.2%)
	House	75,722	(44.4%)	94,678	(55.6%)
1982	Senate	96,251	(66.9%)	46,578	(32.4%)
	House	87,904	(64.0%)	49,413	(36.0%)

Demographics

Population: 487,438. **Percent Change from 1970:** 20.5%.

Land Area: 10,685 square miles. **Population per Square Mile:** 45.6.

Counties, 1980 Population: Barbour — 16,639; Berkeley — 46,775; Fayette — 57,863; Grant — 10,210; Greenbrier — 37,665; Hampshire — 14,867; Hardy — 10,030; Jefferson — 30,302; Mineral — 27,234; Monongalia — 75,024; Monroe — 12,873; Morgan — 10,711; Pendleton — 7,910; Pocahontas — 9,919; Preston — 30,460; Randolph — 28,734; Summers — 15,875; Tucker — 8,675; Upshur — 23,427; Webster — 12,245.

Cities, 1980 Population: Martinsburg — 13,063; Morgantown — 27,605.

Race and Ancestry: White — 96.3%; Black — 3.1%; American Indian, Eskimo and Aleut — 0.1%; Asian and Pacific Islander — 0.3%. Spanish Origin — 0.7%. Dutch — 0.8%; English — 17.3%; French — 0.7%; German — 10.3%; Irish — 5.3%; Italian — 1.6%; Polish — 0.5%; Scottish — 0.5%.

Universities, Enrollment: Alderson-Broaddus College, Philippi — 811; Davis and Elkins College, Elkins — 980; Potomac State College of West Virginia University, Keyser — 1,104; Shepherd College, Shepherdstown — 3,001; West Virginia Career College, Morgantown — 532; West Virginia Institute of Technology, Montgomery — 3,338; West Virginia School of Osteopathic Medicine, Lewisburg — 231; West Virginia University, Morgantown — 21,220; West Virginia Wesleyan College, Buckhannon — 1,746.

Newspapers, Circulation: *Daily News* (e), Lewisburg — 6,309; *Dominion-Post* (mS), Morgantown — 19,697; *The Evening Journal* (e), Martinsburg — 18,191; *The Inter-Mountain* (e), Elkins — 9,853; *Mineral Daily News Tribune* (e), Keyser — 5,414.

Commercial Television Stations, Affiliation: WOAY, Oak Hill (ABC). District is divided among Bluefield-Beckley-Oak Hill ADI, Clarksburg-Weston ADI, Pittsburgh (Pa.) ADI, Harrisonburg (Va.) ADI and Washington (D.C.) ADI.

Military Installations: Eastern West Virginia Regional Airport (Air Force), Martinsburg — 926.

Industries:

Consolidation Coal Co.; Osage; coal mining — 1,546. **Veterans Administration;** Martinsburg; veterans' hospital — 1,200. **White Sulphur Springs Co.** (Greenbrier Hotel); White Sulphur Springs; resort hotel — 950. **General Motors Corp.;** Martinsburg; automotive parts — 894. **Consolidation Coal Co.** (Blacksville Div.); Wana; coal mining — 797.

Corning Glass Works Inc.; Martinsburg; glassware — 750. **Sterling Faucet Co.;** Morgantown; faucets — 750. **Dixie-Narco Inc.;** Ranson; drink vending machines — 550. **Canaan Valley Resort Inc.;** Davis; resort hotel — 543. **Republic Steel Corp.;** Philippi; coal mining — 525. **Westmoreland Coal Co.** (Imperial Smokeless Div.); Quinwood; coal mining — 521.

3rd District

Central — Charleston

The 3rd District centers on populous Kanawha County (Charleston), which enjoyed an economic comeback in the late 1970s and early 1980s as a center for the temporarily reviving coal industry. Kanawha contains nearly one-half of the district population.

As the seat of state government and commerce, the Charleston area boasts the most diverse economy in the state. The capital city has a large white-collar work force that frequently produces Republican majorities.

But nearly three out of four voters in Kanawha County live outside Charleston. Many are blue-collar workers employed by the numerous chemical companies that line the Kanawha River. These people vote Democratic.

The result is that Kanawha is a crucial swing county, neither reliably Republican nor reliably Democratic. It went Democratic for president and governor in 1980, but put a Republican in the House. In 1982 it replaced the Republican with a Democrat, giving him a scant 52 percent of the vote.

With more than 230,000 residents, Kanawha is the most populous county in West Virginia. Between 1960 and 1980 its population decreased by more than 20,000, due to a decline in the chemical and glass industries and completion of a highway network that encouraged residents to move to bedroom communities outside the county. The coal revival increased population in the surrounding counties, not in Kanawha itself.

Putnam and nearby counties in the Ohio River Valley long have been centers of rural Republican strength. Together they cast about one-quarter of the district vote. Tobacco, corn and livestock provide an agricultural base. Layoffs in 1981 at the large Kaiser Aluminum plant in Ravenswood sent the unemployment rate soaring.

The economy is not much healthier in the rolling countryside to the east. There is some coal and natural gas in these central counties, but little industrialization. An area of poor farms, it has been Democratic for generations. South of Charleston are two counties with coal and natural gas, Lincoln and Boone. These Democratic bastions make up 11 percent of the 3rd's population.

Redistricting made little change in the complexion of the 3rd. The district exchanged one small, normally Republican county (Ritchie) for another (Lewis).

Demographics

Population: 486,112. **Percent Change from 1970:** 10.0%.

Land Area: 6,324 square miles. **Population per Square Mile:** 76.9.

Counties, 1980 Population: Boone — 30,447; Braxton — 13,894; Calhoun — 8,250; Clay — 11,265; Gilmer — 8,334; Jackson — 25,794; Kanawha — 231,414; Lewis — 18,813; Lincoln — 23,675; Mason — 27,045; Nicholas — 28,126; Putnam — 38,181; Roane — 15,952; Wirt — 4,922.

Cities, 1980 Population: Charleston — 63,968; South Charleston — 15,968; St. Albans — 12,402.

Race and Ancestry: White — 96.5%; Black — 3.0%; American Indian, Eskimo and Aleut — 0.1%; Asian and Pacific Islander — 0.4%. Spanish Origin — 0.5%. Dutch — 0.7%; English — 23.0%; French — 0.6%; German — 5.7%; Irish — 5.5%; Italian — 0.7%; Scottish — 0.5%.

Universities, Enrollment: Glenville State College, Glenville — 1,889; University of Charleston, Charleston — 2,039; West Virginia Career College, Charleston — 693; West Virginia College of Graduate Studies, Institute — 3,323; West Virginia College of Technology, Charleston — 310; West Virginia State College, Institute — 4,378.

Newspapers, Circulation: *Charleston Daily Mail* (e), Charleston — 55,825; *The Charleston Gazette* (mS), Charleston — 55,518; *Point Pleasant Register* (e), Point Pleasant — 5,921.

Commercial Television Stations, Affiliation: WCHS, Charleston (CBS); WDTV, Weston (CBS); WVAH, Charleston (None). Most of district is located in Charleston-Huntington ADI. Portion is in Clarksburg-Weston ADI.

Military Installations: Kanawha County Airport (Air Force), Charleston — 927.

Industries:

Union Carbide Corp. (Technical Center); Charleston; research & development — 4,000. **Kaiser Aluminum & Chemical Corp.;** Ravenswood; aluminum production — 2,273. **E. I. du Pont de Nemours & Co.;** Belle; industrial inorganic chemicals — 1,700. **Columbia Gas Transmission Corp.** (HQ); Charleston; natural gas transmission — 1,180. **Union Carbide Corp.** (Agricultural Products Co. Inc.); Institute; pesticide products — 1,300. **Union Carbide Corp.** (Silicones & Urethane Intermediates Div.); South Charleston; chemicals — 1,300.

Carbon Fuel Co.; Winifrede; coal mining — 1,000. **FMC Corp.** (Industrial Chemicals Group); South Charleston; industrial inorganic chemicals — 950. **Libbey-Owens-Ford Co.;** Charleston; plate glass windows — 950. **Cedar Coal Co. Inc.;** Cabin Creek; coal mining — 930. **Valley Camp Coal Co.;** Shrewsbury; coal mining — 725. **Monsanto Co.** (Industrial Chemicals Div.); Nitro; synthetic rubber — 704. **Volkswagen of America;** Charleston; auto assembly — 650. **Smith's Transfer Corp.;** Belle; trucking — 633. **The Carbon Fuel Co. Inc.;** Carbon; coal mining — 597. **S. J. Groves & Sons Co.;** Charleston; mining construction — 500. **Pittston Co.** (Clinchfield Coal Co. Div.); Nettie; coal mining — 500.

Election Returns

3rd District		Democrat		Republican	
1976	President	113,707	(57.9%)	82,475	(42.0%)
	Governor	125,733	(64.4%)	69,468	(35.6%)
	Senate	144,212	(99.0%)	—	
	House	130,448	(98.1%)	2,150	(1.6%)
1978	Senate	67,056	(49.4%)	68,740	(50.6%)
	House	75,914	(58.8%)	53,175	(41.2%)
1980	President	93,700	(48.5%)	89,359	(46.2%)
	Governor	97,027	(49.9%)	96,630	(49.7%)
	House	86,284	(47.3%)	96,323	(52.7%)
1982	Senate	100,722	(67.3%)	47,740	(31.9%)
	House	84,619	(51.9%)	60,844	(41.6%)

4th District

South and West — Huntington, Beckley

The Appalachian 4th is the most staunchly Democratic district in the state. Jimmy Carter carried it in 1980 by more than 25,000 votes, even though he failed to take any of the other districts by more than 4,000. Redistricting made no changes in the district lines.

The 4th is the center of the state's coal-mining industry. The region was loyally Republican early this century when local political bosses were aligned with the mine operators. But the New Deal and the ascendancy of the

United Mine Workers shattered old alliances.

Republican strength is now limited to Mercer (Bluefield) and Cabell (Huntington) counties, which are on the fringes of the coal fields at opposite ends of the district. Mercer County, home for 15 percent of the district population, is located in the mountainous southern end of the district along the Virginia border.

With 22 percent of the district population, Cabell is the largest county in the 4th. Near the junction of the West Virginia, Ohio and Kentucky borders, Huntington grew from a railroad center into the largest city in West Virginia, overtaken in population by Charleston only during the 1970s. Although it has diversified industries, it is not now a boom area. Cabell was one of only three counties in the state to lose population in the 1970s.

Between Huntington and Bluefield is Democratic coal country. The revival of the coal industry has helped to reverse decades of population decline in the region. As the miners returned, all but one of the southern coal counties grew by at least 10 percent in the 1970s.

But even this population surge left some counties below their population levels of a half century earlier. Logan County, for instance, had more registered voters in 1928 than in 1980.

Raleigh County's 24 percent population gain in the 1970s was the highest in the coal region. The county seat of Beckley is a prosperous retail center. About five miles to the southwest is the small town of Sophia, where Senate Democratic Leader Robert C. Byrd grew up.

Further south along the twists and curves of state Route 16 is McDowell County. One of the poorest of the coal counties, it was the only one in the region to lose population in the 1970s. Most of the mines in McDowell's rugged terrain have been played out.

Election Returns

4th District		Democrat		Republican	
1976	President	105,407	(62.4%)	62,505	(37.2%)
	Governor	116,728	(70.5%)	48,635	(29.4%)
	Senate	123,719	(100.0%)	—	
	House	73,626	(45.6%)	28,825	(17.8%)
1978	Senate	57,629	(55.0%)	47,094	(45.0%)
	House	70,035	(100.0%)	—	
1980	President	92,976	(56.0%)	67,069	(40.4%)
	Governor	104,577	(62.8%)	61,341	(36.9%)
	House	117,595	(76.6%)	36,020	(23.4%)

4th District		Democrat		Republican	
1982	Senate	85,522	(73.0%)	30,835	(26.3%)
	House	91,184	(80.5%)	22,054	(19.5%)

Demographics

Population: 487,526. **Percent Change from 1970:** 11.4%.

Land Area: 3,735 square miles. **Population per Square Mile:** 130.5.

Counties, 1980 Population: Cabell — 106,835; Logan — 50,679; McDowell — 49,899; Mercer — 73,942; Mingo — 37,336; Raleigh — 86,821; Wayne — 46,021; Wyoming — 35,993.

Cities, 1980 Population: Beckley — 20,492; Bluefield — 16,060; Huntington — 63,684.

Race and Ancestry: White — 93.9%; Black — 5.6%; American Indian, Eskimo and Aleut — 0.1%; Asian and Pacific Islander — 0.3%. Spanish Origin — 0.7%. Dutch — 0.6%; English — 24.4%; French — 0.6%; German — 4.0%; Irish — 5.8%; Italian — 1.0%.

Universities, Enrollment: Appalachian Bible College, Bradley — 247; Beckley College, Beckley — 1,287; Bluefield State College, Bluefield — 2,340; Concord College, Athens — 2,174; Huntington College of Business, Huntington — 691; Marshall University, Huntington — 11,856; Southern West Virginia Community College, Logan — 2,020; West Virginia Career College, Huntington — 250.

Newspapers, Circulation: *Beckley Post-Herald* (mS), Beckley — 21,343; *Bluefield Daily Telegraph* (mS), Bluefield — 28,560; *Daily News* (e), Williamson — 12,271; *Herald-Dispatch* (mS), Huntington — 48,535; *The Logan Banner* (e), Logan — 11,999; *Raleigh Register* (eS), Beckley — 12,137; *The Welch Daily News* (e), Welch — 10,076.

Commercial Television Stations, Affiliation: WOWK, Huntington (ABC); WSAZ, Huntington (NBC); WVVA, Bluefield (NBC). Most of district is located in Charleston-Huntington ADI. Portion is in Bluefield-Beckley-Oak Hill ADI.

Industries:

Huntington Alloys Inc. (HQ); Huntington; nickel products — 2,500. **Chesapeake & Ohio Railway Co.**; Huntington; railroad operations — 2,200. **Amherst Coal Co.**; Lundale; coal mining — 1,200. **Itmann Coal Co. Inc.**; Itmann; coal mining — 1,200. **Owens-Illinois Glass Co. Inc.**; Huntington; glass containers — 1,130.

Saint Mary's Hospital Inc.; Huntington; hospital — 1,000. **Westmoreland Coal Co.** (Winding Gulf Coals Div.); Tams; coal mining — 984. **Corbin Ltd.** (HQ); Huntington; men's trousers — 802. **Connors Steel Co.** (Hunt Works); Huntington; steel rolling mill — 700. **Ranger Fuel Corp.**; Beckley; coal mining — 700. **Olga Coal Co.**; Coalwood; coal mining — 600. **Pickands Mather & Co.** (Beckley Coal Mining Co.); Glen Daniel; coal mining — 570. **Eastern Associated Coal Corp.**; Herndon; coal mining — 535. **Eagle-Picher Industries Inc.** (Elmac Div.); Huntington; mining machinery — 525. **Consolidation Coal Co.** (Rowland Mine); Beckley; coal mining — 500.

Wisconsin

Wisconsin's new congressional map made two Milwaukee-area districts more competitive, but otherwise brought few immediate changes in the political status quo.

Republican Gov. Lee Sherman Dreyfus vetoed the Democratic Legislature's first remap bill Nov. 27, 1981, partly because it placed the homes of two GOP incumbents in the same constituency and drew an unfavorable district for a freshman Republican.

It appeared for a time that federal judges would intervene to draw the lines, but under the pressure of a court deadline of April 2, 1982, the Legislature agreed to a compromise map that the governor signed into law March 25. Under the compromise, the three Republicans were left in about the same positions they occupied before redistricting. The U. S. House delegation remained 5-4 Democratic after the 1982 elections.

Attention focused on Milwaukee County's two districts because both lost population during the 1970s and had to expand to come up to population equality. Suburban Milwaukee's 9th District and three outstate constituencies — the 3rd, 7th and 8th — enjoyed substantial population gains.

Although most people associate the state's Progressive Party heritage with liberalism, Wisconsin is neither as Democratic nor as liberal as many asume. The Progressive philosophy that lingers can just as easily manifest itself through support for government-baiting Republicans as for socially tolerant Democrats.

Income and Occupation

District	Median Family Income	White Collar Workers	Blue Collar Workers	Service Workers	Farm Workers
1	$ 22,510	44.4%	38.4%	13.9%	3.2%
2	21,188	54.9	23.9	14.3	6.9
3	17,872	42.1	29.8	15.0	13.2
4	23,532	50.6	35.6	13.3	0.5
5	20,645	54.1	30.3	15.2	0.4
6	19,918	40.1	37.8	14.7	7.4
7	17,702	43.0	32.7	14.9	9.4
8	19,456	44.2	35.0	14.3	6.6
9	25,373	51.5	34.0	11.4	3.1
State	$ 20,915	47.5%	33.0%	14.1%	5.5%

Education: School Years Completed

District	8 Years or Fewer	4 Years of High School	4 Years of College or More	Median School Years
1	15.8%	41.8%	12.8%	12.4
2	14.1	37.3	22.9	12.7
3	21.5	40.0	13.7	12.4
4	15.8	42.4	12.4	12.5
5	16.3	34.3	17.5	12.5
6	20.7	43.6	11.2	12.4
7	23.1	40.6	11.4	12.4
8	20.0	43.8	11.9	12.4
9	14.5	40.0	19.5	12.6
State	18.0%	40.4%	14.8%	12.5

Age of Population

District	Population Under 18	Voting Age Population	Population 65 & Over (% of VAP)	Median Age
1	155,914	366,924	56,852 (15.5%)	29.0
2	139,925	383,086	55,870 (14.6%)	28.6
3	148,644	374,265	68,869 (18.4%)	28.5
4	141,058	381,822	57,760 (15.1%)	30.6
5	141,606	381,248	67,138 (17.6%)	28.9
6	151,991	370,486	69,925 (18.9%)	30.2
7	155,940	366,683	70,537 (19.2%)	29.7
8	160,671	362,554	64,184 (17.7%)	29.0
9	162,071	360,879	53,062 (14.7%)	30.4
State	1,357,820	3,347,947	564,197 (16.9%)	29.4

Housing and Residential Patterns

District	Owner Occupied	Renter Occupied	Urban	Rural
1	69.8%	30.2%	68.9%	31.1%
2	62.6	37.4	59.9	40.1
3	72.7	27.3	39.7	60.3
4	61.5	38.5	97.8	2.2
5	47.9	52.1	100.0	0.0
6	74.9	25.1	50.8	49.2
7	76.0	24.0	40.9	59.1
8	75.0	25.0	54.9	45.1
9	76.8	23.2	64.8	35.2
State	68.2%	31.8%	64.2%	35.8%

WISCONSIN

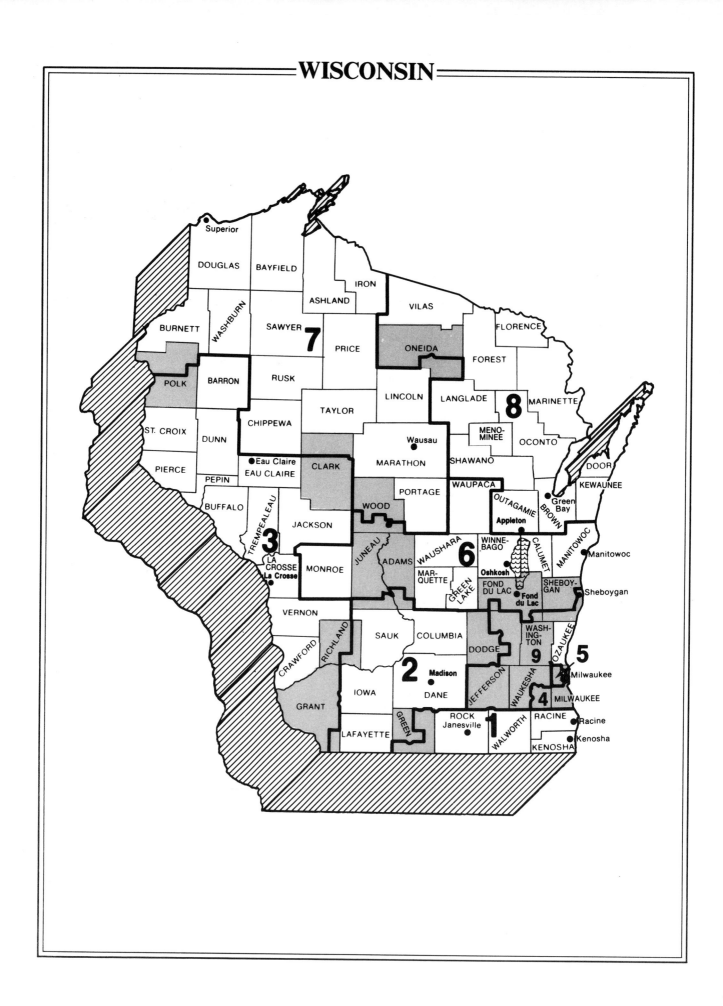

1st District

Southeast — Racine, Kenosha

Although it is dominated by four industrialized cities and has a six-term Democratic incumbent, the 1st is far from a Democratic stronghold. The incumbent's success has more to do with his personal appeal than his party label.

Until his election in 1970, Democrats had won this district only twice in the 20th century — 1958 and 1964. Both were defeated after serving single terms. No Democratic presidential candidate has carried the 1st since Lyndon B. Johnson in 1964.

The district's two largest cities are sandwiched between Milwaukee and Chicago on the Lake Michigan shore. Racine, with a traditional Danish influence, manufactures a wide range of Johnson's Wax products, from Agree shampoo to Pledge furniture polish. Among its hundreds of other manufacturing concerns are the J. I. Case farm machinery plant and the Western Publishing Co., which provides mostly white-collar jobs. Racine County gave the Democratic House incumbent 56 percent of the vote in 1980 but voted Republican for Senate and president.

Kenosha's economic base is not as diversified as Racine's. The city, which boasts a sizable Italian community and a branch of the University of Wisconsin, has suffered because of declining employment at its huge American Motors Corp. (AMC) plant. Although AMC has invested about $60 million to retool its Kenosha facility, increased reliance on labor-saving robots and demand for smaller cars mean that the heyday of automobile-manufacturing employment in this area has passed. Kenosha County voted Democratic in 1980.

In the west-central part of the district are the smaller industrial cities of Janesville and Beloit, both in Rock County. Janesville's General Motors plant has been re-tooled to build smaller cars, but employs nearly 2,000 fewer auto workers in the scaled-down operation.

Perched on the Illinois border just 8 miles south of Janesville, Beloit was settled by a group of immigrants from New Hampshire who founded Beloit College in 1847. The city makes heavy machinery, such as backup engines for nuclear submarines.

The strongest Republican vote in the 1st comes from Walworth County, between Janesville and Racine-Kenosha. Resort complexes around Lake Geneva and Lake Delavan cater to wealthy vacationers from Milwaukee and Chicago. Soybeans grow so well in the farming sections of Walworth County that the Japanese Kikkoman soy sauce company built a plant in Walworth to brew and bottle its product.

Just over 7,500 people came into the 1st through redistricting, all of them from Green County townships that were in the 2nd. Their entry is not likely to have a noticeable impact on elections.

Election Returns

1st District		Democrat		Republican	
1976	President	107,718	(48.4%)	108,964	(49.0%)
	Senate	144,482	(72.6%)	53,158	(26.7%)
	House	137,954	(64.9%)	72,534	(34.1%)

1st District		Democrat		Republican	
1978	Governor	70,309	(48.4%)	74,049	(51.0%)
	House	78,089	(54.4%)	65,384	(45.6%)
1980	President	98,916	(41.7%)	117,710	(49.6%)
	Senate	109,936	(48.4%)	113,267	(49.9%)
	House	127,738	(56.1%)	97,736	(42.9%)
1982	Governor	95,205	(60.0%)	61,687	(38.9%)
	Senate	103,938	(66.7%)	49,611	(31.8%)
	House	95,055	(61.0%)	59,309	(38.1%)

Demographics

Population: 522,838. **Percent Change from 1970:** 5.1%.

Land Area: 2,219 square miles. **Population per Square Mile:** 235.6.

Counties, 1980 Population: Green (Pt.) — 13,220; Jefferson (Pt.) — 2,422; Kenosha — 123,137; Racine — 173,132; Rock — 139,420; Walworth — 71,507.

Cities, 1980 Population: Beloit — 35,207; Janesville — 51,071; Kenosha — 77,685; Racine — 85,725; Whitewater — 11,520.

Race and Ancestry: White — 94.1%; Black — 4.2%; American Indian, Eskimo and Aleut — 0.2%; Asian and Pacific Islander — 0.4%. Spanish Origin — 2.5%. Dutch — 0.7%; English — 4.1%; French — 0.7%; German — 16.7%; Irish — 2.6%; Italian — 2.3%; Norwegian — 2.5%; Polish — 2.4%; Swedish — 0.9%.

Universities, Enrollment: Beloit College, Beloit — 1,058; Blackhawk Technical Institute, Janesville — 2,148; Carthage College, Kenosha — 1,551; Gateway Technical Institute (Kenosha campus), Kenosha — 9,124; Holy Redeemer College, Waterford — 73; Milton College, Milton — 283; North Central Technical Institute, Wausau — 3,390; University of Wisconsin (Parkside campus), Kenosha — 5,368; University of Wisconsin (Whitewater campus), Whitewater — 10,004.

Newspapers, Circulation: *Beloit Daily News* (e), Beloit — 20,105; *The Janesville Gazette* (e), Janesville — 31,459; *The Journal Times* (eS), Racine — 38,796; *Kenosha News* (e), Kenosha — 31,895.

Commercial Television Stations, Affiliation: District is divided among Madison ADI, Milwaukee ADI, Chicago (Ill.) ADI and Rockford (Ill.) ADI.

Industries:

American Motors Corp.; Kenosha; autos — 7,700. **General Motors Corp.** (Assembly Div.); Janesville; autos — 6,550. **J. I. Case Co.** (HQ); Racine; construction, farm equipment — 4,300. **S. C. Johnson & Son Inc.** (HQ); Racine; waxes, polishes — 3,400. **Beloit Corp.** (HQ); Beloit; paper-making machinery — 3,090.

S. C. Johnson & Son Inc. (Johnson Wax); Sturtevant; waxes, polishes — 1,800. **Colt Industries Operating Corp.** (Fairbanks Morse Engine Div.); Beloit; diesel engines — 1,700. **Western Publishing Co. Inc.** (HQ); Racine; children's books, games — 1,500. **The Parker Pen Co. Inc.** (HQ); Janesville; pens, mechanical pencils — 1,430. **Twin Disc Inc.** (HQ); Racine; clutches — 1,390. **Snap-On Tools Corp.** (HQ); Kenosha; wrenches, hand tools — 1,300. **Kenosha Memorial Hospital Inc.;** Kenosha; hospital — 1,100. **St. Catherine's Hospital;** Kenosha; hospital — 1,040. **Evans Products Co.** (Metals Div.); Racine; steel castings — 1,000. **United States Shoe Corp.** (Freeman Shoe Co.); Beloit; men's shoes — 1,000. **Ladish Co. Inc.** (Tri Clover Div.); Kenosha; fabricated pipes — 850. **Eaton Corp.;** Kenosha; speed changers — 800. **Textron Inc.** (Jacobson-Textron); Racine; garden machinery — 800.

Twin Disc Inc.; Racine; clutches — 750. **Dallas & Mavis Forwarding Corp.** (HQ); Kenosha; trucking — 656. **Janesville Auto Transport Co.** (HQ); Janesville; trucking — 600. **Playboy Club of Lake Geneva;** Lake Geneva; resort — 600. **Sta-Rite Industries Inc.** (Water Equipment Div.); Delavan; water pumps, swimming pool equipment — 567. **Massey-Ferguson Inc.** (Central Parts Operations); Racine; farm machinery distributing — 550. **Tenneco Inc.** (Walker Mfg. Co. Div.); Racine; auto equipment — 550. **Modine Mfg. Co.** (HQ); Racine;

vehicle heat transferring equipment — 525. **Rexnord Inc.** (Hydraulic Components Div.); Racine; hydraulic pumps — 525. **Amsted Industries Inc.** (MacWhyte Co. Div.); Kenosha; wire rope — 500. **Jockey International Inc.** (HQ); Kenosha; men's knit underwear — 500. **Wisconsin Associates Inc.**; Kenosha; general contracting — 500. **Young Radiator Co.** (HQ); Racine; vehicle radiators — 500.

2nd District

South — Madison

Redistricting did not alter the most important fact of political life in the 2nd: The Republicans have most of the land and the Democrats have most of the voters. While the 2nd covers a sizable portion of southern Wisconsin's Republican-voting rural areas, its centerpiece is the city of Madison in Dane County. As long as that metropolis continues to vote Democratic, the district is likely to go Democratic.

The 1980 election exhibited the Republican frustration: the Democratic House incumbent lost every county in the district except Dane. But he was re-elected by winning a 3-to-2 margin in Dane, which cast more than 60 percent of the vote.

Madison, the state capital and second largest city in Wisconsin, has its share of industry; meat processor Oscar Mayer, for example, employs more than 2,500 in its Madison plant. But the dominant side of the city's personality is its white-collar sector — the bureaucrats who work in local and state government, the 2,300 educators who teach 40,000 students at the University of Wisconsin, and the large number of insurance company home offices that leads Madison to call itself a midwestern Hartford.

The city has a tradition of political liberalism. Since 1924, when Robert La Follette carried Dane County as the Progressive Party's presidential candidate, Democrats nearly always have won there. In 1972 George McGovern won 58 percent in Dane County, and eight years later, Democratic Sen. Gaylord Nelson took two-thirds of the Dane County vote while losing statewide. Independent John B. Anderson won 12 percent of the county's 1980 presidential vote.

Outside Madison, agriculture and tourism sustain the district's economy. Dairying is important, and there is some beef production, although many livestock farmers have switched to raising corn as a cash crop.

In New Glarus (Green County), which was founded by the Swiss, the downtown has been redone to resemble a village in the mother country. Wisconsin Dells (Columbia County) lures big-city tourists to view the steep ridges and high plateaus along the Wisconsin River.

The majority of farmers and townsfolk in the district are conservative, and they chafe at Madison's dominance of district politics. Many complain that state-paid freeloaders in the capital can afford to be liberal because they are spending other people's hard-earned dollars.

Ronald Reagan's conservatism found many followers in the rural areas of the district. In 1980 Reagan won six of the eight counties partly or wholly within the 2nd, leaving only Dane and its eastern neighbor, Iowa County, in Jimmy Carter's column. But the wide Democratic margin in Dane enabled Carter to carry the district.

The new 2nd District is very similar to the old. Some Democratic votes were lost as seven Green County townships shifted into the 1st, but a comparable number of GOP votes in northeastern Dodge County were transferred to the 9th. Democrats are competitive with Republicans in the few areas new to the 2nd District — southeastern Grant County and eastern Richland County, brought in from the 3rd, and southern portions of Juneau and Adams counties, which moved from the 6th.

Election Returns

2nd District		Democrat		Republican	
1976	President	124,106	(51.1%)	109,405	(45.1%)
	Senate	151,865	(68.2%)	65,708	(29.5%)
	House	151,677	(65.6%)	79,458	(34.4%)
1978	Governor	79,363	(45.3%)	94,333	(53.8%)
	House	98,111	(58.1%)	68,920	(40.8%)
1980	President	124,236	(47.2%)	106,003	(40.3%)
	Senate	147,189	(59.1%)	97,874	(39.3%)
	House	139,798	(54.3%)	115,902	(45.1%)
1982	Governor	118,527	(61.5%)	71,999	(37.3%)
	Senate	115,112	(61.1%)	59,020	(31.3%)
	House	112,677	(60.6%)	71,989	(38.7%)

Demographics

Population: 523,011. **Percent Change from 1970:** 9.8%.

Land Area: 5,477 square miles. **Population per Square Mile:** 95.5.

Counties, 1980 Population: Adams (Pt.) — 1,962; Columbia — 43,222; Dane — 323,545; Dodge (Pt.) — 41,118; Grant (Pt.) — 6,538; Green (Pt.) — 16,792; Iowa — 19,802; Juneau (Pt.) — 4,529; Lafayette — 17,412; Richland (Pt.) — 4,622; Sauk — 43,469.

Cities, 1980 Population: Beaver Dam — 14,149; Madison — 170,616; Middleton — 11,779; Monroe — 10,027; Sun Prairie — 12,931.

Race and Ancestry: White — 97.3%; Black — 1.2%; American Indian, Eskimo and Aleut — 0.3%; Asian and Pacific Islander — 0.8%. Spanish Origin — 0.8%. Dutch — 0.8%; English — 4.9%; French — 0.5%; German — 21.8%; Irish — 2.9%; Italian — 0.7%; Norwegian — 5.0%; Polish — 1.0%; Swedish — 0.5%.

Universities, Enrollment: Edgewood College, Madison — 666; Madison Area Technical College, Madison — 8,335; Madison Business College, Madison — 275; University of Wisconsin (Madison campus), Madison — 41,242; Wisconsin School of Electronics, Madison — 242.

Newspapers, Circulation: *The Capital Times* (e), Madison — 33,938; *Daily Citizen* (e), Beaver Dam — 9,883; *Monroe Evening Times* (e), Monroe — 8,318; *News-Republic* (e), Baraboo — 5,811; *Portage Daily Register* (e), Portage — 7,941; *Wisconsin State Journal* (mS), Madison — 76,479.

Commercial Television Stations, Affiliation: WISC-TV, Madison (CBS); WKOW-TV, Madison (ABC); WMTV, Madison (NBC). Most of district is located in Madison ADI. Portions are in La Crosse-Eau Claire ADI, Milwaukee ADI, Wausau-Rhinelander ADI and Cedar Rapids (Iowa)-Waterloo (Iowa) ADI.

Military Installations: Badger Army Ammunition Plant, Baraboo — 350; Truax Field (Air Force), Madison — 959.

Industries:

Oscar Mayer & Co. Inc. (HQ); Madison; meatpacking — 2,800. **American Family Mutual Insurance Co.** (HQ); Madison; fire, casualty insurance — 1,990. **Madison General Hospital Assn.**; Madison; hospital — 1,900. **St. Mary's Hospital & Medical Center**; Madison; hospital — 1,700. **Wisconsin Physicians' Service Insurance Corp.** (HQ); Madison; health insurance — 1,500.

Deere & Co. Inc.; Horicon; grounds care equipment — 1,400. **CUNA Mutual Insurance Society** (HQ); Madison; life insurance —

1,300. **Airco Inc.** (Ohio Medical Products Div.); Madison; medical instruments — 1,025. **Methodist Hospital;** Madison; hospital — 1,025. **Graber Industries Inc.** (HQ); Middleton; window hardware — 865. **Greyhound Lines Inc.** (Greyhound Lines West); Madison; interstate bus transportation — 720. **Rayovac Corp.** (HQ); Madison; dry cell batteries — 700. **Madison-Kipp Corp.** (HQ); Madison; zinc products — 590. **Beatrice Foods Co.** (Sanna Div.); Madison; dried dairy beverage mixes, puddings — 576. **Nicolet Instrument Corp.** (HQ); Madison; electronic equipment — 560. **Webcrafters Inc.;** Madison; commercial printing — 500. **Marshall Erdmann & Associates;** Madison; architectural services — more than 500.

3rd District

West — Eau Claire, La Crosse

In a state famous for its cows, the 3rd stands at the head of the herd, producing more milk than any congressional district in the nation. The 3rd hugs western Wisconsin's border with Iowa and Minnesota, and most of its people live on farms or in small crossroads towns.

Jimmy Carter learned in 1980 that dairy farmers are a politically volatile group. In 1976 Carter narrowly won the 3rd on his way to a slim victory statewide. Four years later many voters in the district's rural areas turned to the GOP, giving Ronald Reagan a 48-to-43 percent advantage in the 3rd, the same tally with which he carried the state.

This 1980 reversal of Democratic fortunes in the 3rd helped a Republican unseat a three-term Democratic House incumbent. Redistricting made border shifts on the northern and eastern edges of the 3rd, but the territory remains as it was before the remap — a marginal district that either party can win. In 1982 the Republicans held it, winning 56.6 percent of the vote.

There are only two sizable cities, roughly equal in size. Democrats usually hold sway in Eau Claire and the counties near it in the northern part of the district. Republicans are dominant in La Crosse and counties south of it along the Mississippi River.

Eau Claire was once a wild lumber outpost, cutting logs that floated down the Chippewa River from the northern forests. It still has a paper mill producing disposable diapers and napkins, but the largest manufacturer is Uniroyal. There is a branch of the University of Wisconsin in the city.

The Democratic leanings of Eau Claire and the rural northern part of the 3rd are due partly to the influence of the Democratic-Farmer-Labor coalition in Minnesota politics. Eau Claire is only 85 miles east of Minneapolis-St. Paul, and the Twin Cities serve as a source of information and culture for northern 3rd District voters. Eau Claire County went for Carter in both 1976 and 1980.

La Crosse is Wisconsin's only major Mississippi River city, lying roughly halfway between Dubuque, Iowa, and the Twin Cities. Two companies are La Crosse's economic mainstays. The Trane Company, manufacturers of heating and air conditioning equipment, employs about 4,000 and G. Heileman Brewing Inc. provides 1,000 jobs. La Crosse also has a branch of the state university.

La Crosse County voted to keep Gerald R. Ford in the White House in 1976, and it chose to evict Carter in 1980. But Democratic strength in La Crosse should not be overlooked.

In the rural areas Scandinavian lineage is most common, and the farmers tend dairy operations and raise alfalfa, corn and soybeans. Population growth in most of the rural counties helped the 3rd become Wisconsin's second-fastest-growing district during the 1970s. Many of those newly arrived residents are city workers who endure long commutes to live in a pastoral setting.

In redistricting, the 3rd gained from the 7th the southern two-thirds of Clark County. The 3rd moved entirely out of Monroe County, losing Republican votes there to the 6th. Those were offset by a shift of Democratic votes in northern Polk County to the 7th. The 3rd also dropped eastern Richland County and a corner of southern Grant County to the 2nd.

Election Returns

3rd District		Democrat		Republican	
1976	President	114,895	(49.4%)	112,422	(48.3%)
	Senate	148,974	(71.2%)	59,729	(28.5%)
	House	132,271	(58.5%)	93,679	(41.4%)
1978	Governor	68,972	(45.7%)	80,867	(53.5%)
	House	91,431	(62.7%)	54,116	(37.1%)
1980	President	109,434	(42.7%)	123,312	(48.1%)
	Senate	122,107	(50.2%)	118,511	(48.7%)
	House	120,127	(49.3%)	123,708	(50.7%)
1982	Governor	93,648	(53.7%)	78,885	(45.2%)
	Senate	111,019	(65.4%)	56,253	(33.1%)
	House	75,132	(42.8%)	99,304	(56.6%)

Demographics

Population: 522,909. **Percent Change from 1970:** 13.4%.

Land Area: 10,980 square miles. **Population per Square Mile:** 47.6.

Counties, 1980 Population: Barron — 38,730; Buffalo — 14,309; Clark (Pt.) — 18,493; Crawford — 16,556; Dunn — 34,314; Eau Claire — 78,805; Grant (Pt.) — 45,198; Jackson — 16,831; La Crosse — 91,056; Pepin — 7,477; Pierce — 31,149; Polk (Pt.) — 22,075; Richland (Pt.) — 12,854; St. Croix — 43,262; Trempealeau — 26,158; Vernon — 25,642.

Cities, 1980 Population: Eau Claire (Pt.) — 49,852; La Crosse — 48,347; Menomonie — 12,769.

Race and Ancestry: White — 99.1%; Black — 0.2%; American Indian, Eskimo and Aleut — 0.3%; Asian and Pacific Islander — 0.3%. Spanish Origin — 0.3%. Dutch — 0.5%; English — 3.7%; French — 0.8%; German — 20.2%; Irish — 2.4%; Norwegian — 10.3%; Polish — 1.6%; Swedish — 1.5%.

Universities, Enrollment: District One Technical Institute, Eau Claire — 2,751; Southwest Wisconsin Vocational-Technical Institute, Fennimore — 1,058; University of Wisconsin (Eau Claire campus), Eau Claire — 11,054; University of Wisconsin (La Crosse campus), La Crosse — 9,016; University of Wisconsin (Platteville campus), Platteville — 4,955; University of Wisconsin (River Falls campus), River Falls — 5,339; University of Wisconsin (Stout campus), Menomonie — 7,411; Viterbo College, La Crosse — 1,113; Western Wisconsin Technical Institute, La Crosse — 4,936.

Newspapers, Circulation: *La Crosse Tribune* (eS), La Crosse — 34,857; *Leader Telegram* (e), Eau Claire — 33,565.

Commercial Television Stations, Affiliation: WEAU-TV, Eau Claire (NBC); WKBT, La Crosse (CBS); WQOV, Eau Claire (None); WXOW-TV, La Crosse (ABC). Most of district is divided between La Crosse-Eau Claire ADI and Minneapolis (Minn.)-St. Paul (Minn.) ADI. Portions are in Madison ADI, Wausau-Rhinelander ADI and Cedar Rapids (Iowa)-Waterloo (Iowa) ADI.

Nuclear Power Plants: La Crosse, Genoa (Allis Chalmers, Maxon Construction Co.), November 1969.

Industries:

The Trane Co. (HQ); La Crosse; heating, cooling equipment — 3,700. **La Crosse Lutheran Hospital & Community Mental Health Center;** La Crosse; hospital — 1,600. **Uniroyal Inc.** (Uniroyal Tire Co. Div.); Eau Claire; tires — 1,536. **St. Francis Medical Center Inc.;** La Crosse; hospital — 1,400. **G. Heileman Brewing Co. Inc.** (HQ); La Crosse; brewery — 1,000. **Advance Transformer Co.;** Boscobel; transformers — 700. **La Crosse Rubber Mills Co.** (HQ); La Crosse; canvas, rubber footwear — 700. **Pope & Talbut;** Eau Claire; paper mills — 680. **Nordson Corp.** (Doboy Packaging Machinery Div.); New Richmond; food packaging equipment — 650.

4th District

Southern Milwaukee and Suburbs — Waukesha

Redistricting brought nearly 120,000 newcomers to the 4th District. The population of the old 4th declined 7 percent during the 1970s, and redistricting carried the district's border westward from south Milwaukee and the close-in suburbs of West Allis and Franklin into middle-income, residential territory of Waukesha County.

The core of the 4th District's traditional constituency is Milwaukee's South Side, which has been the base of the city's huge Polish community since the turn of the century. Like many of the Eastern Europeans who migrated to industrial cities, the Poles have been loyal, somewhat conservative Democrats.

In the 1960s and 1970s a number of Poles, especially younger ones, left the South Side and relocated in places such as New Berlin and neighboring Muskego. Some of these migrants have drifted from their political moorings, moving into the Republican column in state and national elections. Waukesha County's strong GOP organization helped bring Ronald Reagan 58 percent of the vote there in 1980.

Despite the GOP strength in Waukesha, it was likely to be an uphill struggle for Republicans to win the district. In the areas that comprise the redrawn 4th, Democrats Jimmy Carter and Gaylord Nelson both came out ahead in 1980. The Republicans did not even field a candidate against the longtime Democratic House incumbent in 1982.

The departure of some Poles for the suburbs has made room for a greater ethnic mix on the South Side. Although the area remains predominantly white, there is a sizable Puerto Rican community in the near South Side, close to Lake Michigan and the downtown business district.

Most residents in the city and the suburbs look to Milwaukee's heavy industries for economic sustenance. Many of the district's constituents make machinery for mining, construction and agricultural use. Factories are distributed evenly between the 4th and 5th districts, and people who live in south Milwaukee often commute to jobs in the northern part of the city.

Unemployment is a problem, but the jobless rate is not as high here as in cities dominated by one or two industries, such as Kenosha in the 1st. What worries Milwaukeeans more is the decay of the city's aging industrial plants; many date from the late 19th and early 20th centuries.

Modernization is sorely needed, but some businesses are saying that high labor costs and taxes in Milwaukee discourage investment in new facilities. The city is confronted with the possibility that its tradition of high union wages and expensive city services may deprive local industries of the capital needed to modernize.

Besides the addition of southeast Waukesha County, the other major boundary shift sent the city of Wauwatosa to the 5th District. Wauwatosa is an older residential area with a decided preference for the GOP in most contests.

Election Returns

4th District		Democrat		Republican	
1976	President	129,927	(54.3%)	101,527	(42.4%)
	Senate	183,667	(76.8%)	53,358	(22.3%)
	House	170,149	(87.0%)	25,256	(12.9%)
1978	Governor	88,526	(51.9%)	80,915	(47.4%)
	House	103,806	(64.1%)	58,211	(35.9%)
1980	President	118,444	(47.9%)	108,464	(43.9%)
	Senate	130,969	(52.4%)	115,668	(46.3%)
	House	140,402	(62.7%)	82,119	(36.7%)
1982	Governor	112,082	(65.2%)	57,830	(33.6%)
	Senate	123,059	(72.4%)	44,588	(26.2%)
	House	129,557	(94.5%)		—

Demographics

Population: 522,880. **Percent Change from 1970:** -1.3%.

Land Area: 281 square miles. **Population per Square Mile:** 1,860.8.

Counties, 1980 Population: Milwaukee (Pt.) — 413,303; Waukesha (Pt.) — 109,577.

Cities, 1980 Population: Cudahy — 19,547; Franklin — 16,871; Greendale — 16,928; Greenfield — 31,467; Milwaukee (Pt.) — 205,796; Muskego — 15,277; New Berlin — 30,529; Oak Creek — 16,932; South Milwaukee — 21,069; St. Francis — 10,066; Waukesha (Pt.) — 49,340; West Allis — 63,982.

Race and Ancestry: White — 96.8%; Black — 0.3%; American Indian, Eskimo and Aleut — 0.6%; Asian and Pacific Islander — 0.7%. Spanish Origin — 4.0%. English — 2.0%; French — 0.7%; German — 18.8%; Irish — 2.0%; Italian — 1.6%; Norwegian — 1.1%; Polish — 12.8%; Swedish — 0.5%.

Universities, Enrollment: Alverno College, Milwaukee — 1,363; Carroll College, Waukesha — 1,343; Milwaukee Stratton College, Milwaukee — 318; Sacred Heart School of Theology, Hales Corners — 119; Saint Francis De Sales College, Milwaukee — 83; Saint Francis Seminary, School of Pastoral Ministry, Milwaukee — 85.

Newspapers, Circulation: *The Milwaukee Journal* and *Milwaukee Sentinel* circulate in the district.

Commercial Television Stations, Affiliation: Entire district is located in Milwaukee ADI.

Military Installations: Gen. Billy Mitchell Field (Air Force), Milwaukee — 2,005.

Industries:

General Electric Co. (Medical Systems Div.); Waukesha; x-ray equipment — 5,000. **Allen-Bradley Co.** (HQ); Milwaukee; industrial controls — 4,500. **Ladish Co.** (HQ); Cudahy; valves, pumps — 4,500. **General Electric Co. Inc.** (Medical Systems Operations); Milwaukee; x-ray equipment — 4,460. **Allis-Chalmers Corp.** (HQ); Milwaukee; mining and farm machinery, industrial trucks — 4,000.

St. Luke's Hospital Assn.; Milwaukee; hospital — 3,120. **Harnischfeger Corp.;** Milwaukee; construction machinery — 3,000. **St. Joseph's Hospital;** Milwaukee; hospital — 2,400. **Bucyrus-Erie Co.** (HQ); South Milwaukee; power shovels — 2,300. **General Motors Corp.** (Delco Electronics Div.); Oak Creek; auto safety equipment —

Milwaukee

2,200. **Northwestern Mutual Life Insurance Co.** (HQ); Milwaukee; life insurance — 2,190. **First Wisconsin Corp.** (HQ); Milwaukee; banking — 2,000. **General Motors Corp.** (AC Spark Plug Div.); Oak Creek; motor vehicle parts — 1,980. **Kearney & Trecker Corp.** (HQ); Milwaukee; machine tools — 1,850. **R. T. E. Corp.** (HQ); Waukesha; electrical transformers — 1,700. **Rexnord Inc.** (Nordberg Div.); Milwaukee; conveyors, conveying equipment — 1,650. **Litton Industrial Products Inc.** (Louis Allis Div.); Milwaukee; industrial controls — 1,600. **Dresser Industries Inc.** (Waukesha Engine Div.); Waukesha; internal combustion engines — 1,500. **Waukesha Memorial Hospital Inc.;** Waukesha; hospital — 1,450.**West Allis Memorial Hospital;** Milwaukee; hospital — 1,450.

St. Francis Hospital Inc.; Milwaukee; hospital — 1,100. **Marshall & Ilsley Bank** (HQ); Milwaukee; banking — 1,050. **Babcock & Wilcox Co. Inc.** (Tubular Products Div.); Milwaukee; carbon alloys — 1,000. **Patrick Cudahy of Wisconsin Inc.;** Cudahy; meatpacking — 1,000. **Teledyne Industries Inc.** (Teledyne Wisconsin Motors); Milwaukee; air-cooled engines — 1,000. **Trinity Memorial Hospital of Cudahy;** Cudahy; hospital — 1,000. **Marine Corp.** (HQ); Milwaukee; banking — 906. **Astronautics Corp.** (HQ); Milwaukee; aircraft instruments, electronic communications equipment — 900. **Figgie International Inc.;** Cudahy; food products machinery — 900. **Caterpillar Tractor Co. Inc.;** Milwaukee; construction equipment — 800. **Inryco Inc.;** Milwaukee; wall panels, flooring — 800. **Ampco-Pittsburg Corp.** (Ampco Metal Div.); Milwaukee; bronze castings — 700. **Howmet Turbine Components Corp.** (Crucible Steel Casting Div.); Milwaukee; steel castings — 700. **Armco Insurance Group Inc.** (HQ); Milwaukee; property, casualty insurance — 650. **International Business Machines Corp.;** Milwaukee; office machine wholesaling — 650. **The Heil Co. Inc.** (Truck Equipment Div.); Milwaukee; truck bodies — 637.

American Motors Corp. (Automotive Parts Div.); Milwaukee; parts warehousing — 600. **Peck Meat Packing Corp.** (Emmber Brands Div. - HQ); Milwaukee; beef boning, prepared meats — 600. **E Z Paintr Corp.** (HQ); Milwaukee; paint rollers — 595. **Harnischfeger Corp.** (Material Handling Equipment Systems Div.); Oak Creek; overhead cranes — 593. **McQuay-Perfex Inc.;** Milwaukee; fabricated plate work — 570. **Maynard Steel Casting Co.** (HQ); Milwaukee; steel foundry — 535. **Siemens-Allis Inc.** (Large Rotating Apparatus Div.); Milwaukee; motors, generators — 535. **PPG Industries Inc.;** Oak Creek; paints, varnishes, allied products — 525. **Abex Corp.** (Waukesha Pumps); Waukesha; pumping equipment — 510. **General Casting Corp.;** Waukesha; gray iron foundry — 500. **MGIC Investment Corp.** (HQ); Milwaukee; surety company — 500. **Northwestern National Insurance Co.** (HQ); Milwaukee; fire, accident, health insurance — 500. **Rexnord Inc.;** Milwaukee; mechanical power transmission equipment — 500.

5th District

Northern Milwaukee and Suburbs — Wauwatosa

The 5th lost nearly 11 percent of its population during the 1970s and had to gain 92,954 new people, many of them in Republican suburban areas. But the district is still securely anchored in heavily Democratic north Milwaukee.

The 5th contains 11 of Milwaukee's 16 aldermanic districts; the 4th holds the remainder. The Menomonee River marks part of the boundary between the 4th and the 5th, and most of the German immigrants to Milwaukee settled north of the Menomonee. In recent decades the Germans have fanned out into the suburbs; north Milwaukee is now about one-fourth black.

Virtually all of that black population lives in a concentrated area in the central part of the 5th. In an effort to promote integrated housing patterns, the centrally located Sherman Park neighborhood has tried to draw blacks west and whites east to live as neighbors. That task is not easy in Milwaukee, where racial tension dates back to violent civil rights demonstrations in the 1960s and has been exacerbated more recently by strained relations between minorities and the Milwaukee Police Department.

On the northeast side of the district, between the Milwaukee River and Lake Michigan, is an area marked by large homes, a gathering of academics who work at the Milwaukee branch of the University of Wisconsin, and white-collar professionals who hold middle- and upper-management positions in downtown offices.

In this northeast area, the 5th gained the communities of Shorewood, Glendale and Brown Deer from the 9th District. Although most residents here vote Republican, these areas are not as strong for the GOP as are the nearby lakeside areas of Whitefish Bay, Fox Point, Bayside and River Hills, which are in the 9th District. Brown Deer has a sizable blue-collar bloc that has been leaning Republican but may switch back if influenced by the other Democratic areas in the 5th District.

Moved into the 5th from the 4th was the western Milwaukee suburb of Wauwatosa, a mostly Republican residential area with older housing stock. Wauwatosa voted decisively for Ronald Reagan in 1980.

The 5th is the focal point of Milwaukee's best-known industry, brewing. The giants were Schlitz, Pabst and Miller. Once all three were locally owned, but the structure of the industry has changed. In the early 1970s Miller was bought out by Philip Morris, a New York-based conglomerate. Beset by financial problems, Schlitz in 1981 closed its Milwaukee brewery; no longer is "the beer that made Milwaukee famous" brewed anywhere in the city. Pabst spent millions of dollars to refurbish its Milwaukee headquarters, but in 1983 it too was in some financial trouble.

In 1980 Jimmy Carter won 60 percent of the 5th District vote. Republican additions under the remap reduced his tally to 54 percent in the redrawn 5th. That is a significant drop in Democratic strength, but there is still a margin of safety against GOP takeover.

Election Returns

5th District		Democrat		Republican	
1976	President	135,133	(55.3%)	102,120	(41.8%)
	Senate	170,019	(75.2%)	53,783	(23.6%)
	House	161,384	(75.6%)	50,003	(23.4%)
1978	Governor	90,354	(54.5%)	74,430	(44.9%)
	House	104,098	(66.5%)	51,311	(32.8%)
1980	President	136,084	(54.4%)	91,520	(36.6%)
	Senate	138,975	(57.3%)	100,577	(41.5%)
	House	152,421	(69.6%)	64,863	(29.6%)
1982	Governor	109,882	(68.3%)	49,454	(30.8%)
	Senate	114,778	(73.2%)	38,866	(24.8%)
	House	99,713	(63.6%)	54,826	(34.9%)

Demographics

Population: 522,854. **Percent Change from 1970:** -10.0%.

Land Area: 92 square miles. **Population per Square Mile:** 5,683.2.

Counties, 1980 Population: Milwaukee (Pt.) — 522,852; Washington (Pt.) — 2.

Cities, 1980 Population: Brown Deer — 12,921; Glendale — 13,882; Milwaukee (Pt.) — 430,416; Shorewood — 14,327; Wauwatosa — 51,308.

Race and Ancestry: White — 69.2%; Black — 28.3%; American Indian, Eskimo and Aleut — 0.6%; Asian and Pacific Islander — 0.7%. Spanish Origin — 2.2%. English — 2.3%; French — 0.5%; German — 18.7%; Irish — 2.2%; Italian — 1.7%; Norwegian — 0.8%; Polish — 3.4%; Russian — 0.8%.

Universities, Enrollment: Concordia College, Milwaukee — 505; Marquette University, Milwaukee — 11,205; Medical College of Wisconsin, Milwaukee — 837; Milwaukee Area Technical College, Milwaukee — 21,352; Milwaukee School of Engineering, North Milwaukee — 2,387; Mount Mary College, Milwaukee — 1,170; University of Wisconsin (Milwaukee campus), Milwaukee — 25,933.

Newspapers, Circulation: *The Milwaukee Journal* (eS), Milwaukee — 324,049; *Milwaukee Sentinel* (m), Milwaukee — 163,295. Foreign language newspaper: *Milwaukee Deutsche Zeitung* (German), Milwaukee — 189,000.

Commercial Television Stations, Affiliation: WCGV-TV, Milwaukee (None); WISN-TV, Milwaukee (ABC); WITI-TV, Milwaukee (CBS); WTMJ-TV, Milwaukee (NBC); WVTV, Milwaukee (None). Entire district is located in Milwaukee ADI.

Industries:

A. O. Smith Corp. (HQ); Milwaukee; motor vehicle parts — 5,500. **Briggs & Stratton Corp.**; Wauwatosa; engines — 5,000. **The Falk Corp.** (HQ); Milwaukee; mechanical speed changers — 3,000. **Chicago & North Western Transportation Co.**; Milwaukee; railroad operations — 2,850. **Eaton Corp.** (Cutler-Hammer Group); Milwaukee; industrial controls — 2,500.

Harley-Davidson Motor Co. Inc. (HQ); Milwaukee; motorcycles — 2,200. **Grede Foundries Inc.** (HQ); Milwaukee; gray iron foundry —

2,100. **The Journal Co. Inc.** (HQ); Milwaukee; newspaper publishing — 2,000. **Mount Sinai Medical Center Inc.** (HQ); Milwaukee; hospital — 2,000. **Pabst Brewing Co.** (HQ); Milwaukee; brewery — 2,000. **Miller Brewing Co.** (HQ); Milwaukee; brewery — 1,800. **St. Michael Hospital**; Milwaukee; hospital — 1,790. **Columbia Hospital Inc.**; Milwaukee; hospital — 1,600. **Master Lock Co.**; Milwaukee; padlocks — 1,500. **J. C. Penney Co.**; Milwaukee; catalog distribution center — 1,500. **St. Mary's Hospital of Milwaukee**; Milwaukee; hospital — 1,340.

Milwaukee Children's Hospital Assn.; Milwaukee; children's hospital — 1,150. **Blue Cross/Blue Shield of Wisconsin Inc.** (HQ); Milwaukee; health insurance — 1,100. **Chicago, Milwaukee, St. Paul & Pacific Railroad**; Milwaukee; railroad operations — 1,000. **Continental Can Co. Inc.**; Milwaukee; metal cans — 1,000. **Good Samaritan Medical Center**; Milwaukee; hospital — 1,000. **Outboard Marine Corp.**; Milwaukee; internal combustion engines — 1,000. **Pinkerton's Inc.**; Milwaukee; security services — 1,000. **Sunbeam Corp.** (Oster Div.); Milwaukee; electric housewares — 900. **Eaton Corp.** (Specific Industry Control Div.); Milwaukee; industrial controls — 825.

American Can Co. (Canco Div.); Milwaukee; metal containers — 750. **Outboard Marine Corp.** (Evinrude Motors); Milwaukee; outboard motors — 700. **Square D Co. Inc.**; Milwaukee; industrial controls — 700. **Briggs & Stratton Corp.**; Glendale; engines — 681. **Briggs & Stratton Corp.**; Milwaukee; automotive hardware — 672. **Roundys Inc.** (HQ); Milwaukee; grocery wholesaling — 650. **Johnson Controls Inc.** (Globe Battery Div. - HQ); Milwaukee; measuring instruments, batteries — 600. **The Singer Co.** (Controls Div.); Milwaukee; heating, cooling equipment controls — 560. **The Kane Service** (Merchants Police Div.); Milwaukee; protection services — 550. **Time Insurance Co. Inc.**; Milwaukee; health insurance — 550. **Johnson Controls Inc.** (Globe Battery Div.); Milwaukee; automotive batteries — 520. **Beatrice Foods Co.** (Pfister & Vogel Tanning Co. Div.); Milwaukee; cattle hide tanning — 500.

6th District

Central — Oshkosh, Fond du Lac, Manitowoc

By moving the city of Sheboygan to the 9th District and incorporating into the 6th all of Waupaca and Monroe counties, redistricting made the 6th District constituency considerably more rural and slightly more Republican.

The 6th did not need such substantial alteration — its population grew at nearly the statewide average during the 1970s. But to accommodate population shifts elsewhere in the state, cartographers decided to push the 6th north and west. As redrawn it reaches from Lake Michigan across south-central Wisconsin and stops about 25 miles short of the Mississippi River on the west.

The farms and market towns of the district are generally Republican, while the Democrats' greatest strength is in several small industrialized cities in the eastern part of the 6th — Manitowoc and Two Rivers in Manitowoc County, Oshkosh and Neenah-Menasha in the county of Winnebago and Fond du Lac in Fond du Lac County.

The most Democratic of the bunch is Manitowoc, a prominent Lake Michigan shipbuilding center in the days when wooden vessels plied the seas. More than half the jobs in Manitowoc County are involved with manufacturing and processing, and unions are an important force. Among goods produced are the Mirro Corp.'s aluminum pots and pans as well as construction cranes and motel ice-making machines. Manitowoc went solidly for Jimmy Carter in 1976, but gave Ronald Reagan a slim margin in 1980.

Though nominal Democrats are numerous in Oshkosh and Fond du Lac counties, those who vote Democratic usually find themselves in a minority at election time.

Reagan won both counties in 1980, holding Carter to less than 40 percent of the vote in each.

Oshkosh is on the western shore of Lake Winnebago, the state's largest lake. Tourism and a state university branch boost the economy, and factories turn out auto parts and wood and paper products. Neenah, at the north end of the lake, is headquarters for Kimberly-Clark, the paper-products giant.

At the southern tip of the lake is Fond du Lac, an early French trading post that is now the home of Mercury outboard motors. Fond du Lac has strong historical justification for its GOP leanings: outside the city is Ripon College, the 1854 birthplace of the Republican Party.

After all-important dairying, output from the district's farms is diverse, including corn, peas, beans and cranberries. The peak of Republican strength in the rural part of the 6th is in Green Lake County, a resort area with large summer homes.

In addition to losing the city of Sheboygan, the 6th gave to the 9th the heavily Republican southern tier of townships in Sheboygan County and a corner of Fond du Lac County. On its northern border, the 6th turned over one township in Brown County to the 8th, then gained Republican Waupaca County from the 8th and southern Wood County from the 7th. In the south, portions of Adams and Juneau counties went to the 2nd, and the western border of the 6th was expanded to take in all of Monroe County, which leans Republican.

The 6th has been close in many state and national elections, but it has sent only one Democrat to the U. S. House since 1938. Redistricting should not interrupt that pattern.

Election Returns

6th District		Democrat		Republican	
1976	President	96,131	(45.0%)	112,146	(52.5%)
	Senate	146,319	(69.4%)	63,470	(30.1%)
	House	82,829	(38.2%)	133,722	(61.7%)
1978	Governor	64,137	(41.1%)	90,659	(58.1%)
	House	50,285	(31.2%)	109,559	(68.1%)
1980	President	94,779	(37.9%)	135,709	(54.3%)
	Senate	92,956	(41.3%)	128,456	(57.1%)
	House	95,789	(39.5%)	146,549	(60.5%)
1982	Governor	89,131	(50.0%)	85,814	(48.1%)
	Senate	91,202	(54.0%)	75,071	(44.5%)
	House	59,922	(35.0%)	111,348	(65.0%)

Demographics

Population: 522,477. **Percent Change from 1970:** 7.5%.

Land Area: 6,869 square miles. **Population per Square Mile:** 76.1.

Counties, 1980 Population: Adams (Pt.) — 11,495; Calumet — 30,867; Fond Du Lac (Pt.) — 81,223; Green Lake — 18,370; Juneau (Pt.) — 16,510; Manitowoc — 82,918; Marquette — 11,672; Monroe — 35,074; Sheboygan (Pt.) — 34,811; Waupaca — 42,831; Waushara — 18,526; Winnebago — 131,703; Wood (Pt.) — 6,477.

Cities, 1980 Population: Appleton (Pt.) — 5,501; Fond Du Lac — 35,863; Manitowoc — 32,547; Menasha — 14,728; Neenah — 22,432; Oshkosh — 49,620; Two Rivers — 13,354.

Race and Ancestry: White — 98.9%; Black — 0.2%; American Indian, Eskimo and Aleut — 0.4%; Asian and Pacific Islander — 0.3%. Spanish Origin — 0.6%. Dutch — 1.1%; English — 2.9%; French —

0.7%; German — 34.0%; Irish — 1.7%; Norwegian — 1.8%; Polish — 2.3%.

Universities, Enrollment: Lakeland College, Sheboygan Falls — 721; Lakeshore Technical Institute, Cleveland — 4,878; Marian College of Fond du Lac, Fond du Lac — 516; Moraine Park Vocational, Technical, and Adult Education District, Fond du Lac — 2,461; Ripon College, Ripon — 930; Silver Lake College, Manitowoc — 346; University of Wisconsin (Oshkosh campus), Oshkosh — 10,129.

Newspapers, Circulation: *The Fond Du Lac Reporter* (eS), Fond Du Lac — 22,617; *Herald-Times-Reporter* (eS), Manitowoc — 17,427; *Oshkosh Daily Northwestern* (e), Oshkosh — 28,841. Appleton *Post-Crescent* also circulates in the district.

Commercial Television Stations, Affiliation: WTMB-TV, Tomah (None). Most of district is located in Green Bay ADI. Portions are in La Crosse-Eau Claire ADI, Madison ADI, Milwaukee ADI and Wausau-Rhinelander ADI.

Military Installations: Fort McCoy, Sparta — 5,794; Volk Field Air National Guard Base, Camp Douglas — 123.

Nuclear Power Plants: Point Beach 1, Two Creeks (Westinghouse, Bechtel), December 1970; Point Beach 2, Two Creeks (Westinghouse, Bechtel), October 1972.

Industries:

Kohler Co. (HQ); Kohler; plumbing fixtures — 5,970. **Kimberly-Clark Corp.** (HQ); Neenah; paper products — 4,800. **Brunswick Corp.** (Mercury Marine Div.); Fond du Lac; internal combustion engines — 3,200. **The Manitowoc Co. Inc.** (Manitowoc Engineering Co. - HQ); Manitowoc; cranes, ice making machines, shipbuilding — 2,500. **American Hospital Supply Corp.**; Two Rivers; school, office furniture — 1,830.

Neenah Foundry; Neenah; industrial, construction castings — 1,500. **Mirro Corp.** (HQ); Manitowoc; aluminum housewares — 1,300. **Theda Clark Memorial Hospital**; Neenah; hospital — 1,250. **Tecumseh Products Co. Inc.** (Lauson Engine Div.); New Holstein; gasoline-powered engines — 1,241. **Beatrice Foods Co.** (Brillion Iron Works Div.); Brillion; farm machinery — 1,100. **Giddings & Lewis Inc.** (HQ); Fond du Lac; machine tools — 1,100. **Consolidated Foods Corp.** (Hillshire Farm Co.); New London; meat processing — 1,070. **Mercy Medical Center of Oshkosh**; Oshkosh; hospital — 1,020. **George Banta Co. Inc.** (HQ); Menasha; book printing — 1,000. **Paragon Electric Co. Inc.** (HQ); Two Rivers; electrical controls — 1,000. **Rockwell International Inc.** (Off-Highway Products Div.); Oshkosh; axles — 1,000. **Speed Queen Co.** (Huebsch Originators - HQ); Ripon; laundry equipment — 1,000. **St. Agnes Hospital**; Fond du Lac; hospital — 1,000. **Menasha Corp.**; Neenah; shipping containers — 964. **McQuay-Perfex Inc.** (Berlin Cast Metal Div.); Berlin; foundry, furnaces — 820. **Nekoosa Papers Inc.**; Nekoosa; paper mill — 812. **Oshkosh Truck Corp.** (HQ); Oshkosh; heavy duty trucks — 710.

Wells Mfg. Corp. (HQ); Fond du Lac; ignition parts — 700. **Gilson Brothers Co.** (HQ); Plymouth; power garden equipment — 650. **Borden Inc.** (Borden Food Co. Div.); Plymouth; cheese — 600. **Gould Inc.** (Hose & Coupling Div.); Manitowoc; hydraulic hose — 600. **Waupaca Foundry Inc.** (HQ); Waupaca; gray iron foundry — 600. **P. H. Glatfelter Co.** (Bergstrom Paper Div.); Neenah; paper mill — 557. **Curwood Inc.** (American Packaging Machinery Co. - HQ); New London; packing machinery — 550. **Universal Foundry**; Oshkosh; non-ferrous castings — 550. **American Can Co. Inc.**; Menasha; paper, paperboard mills — 500. **C-E Morgan Inc.**; Oshkosh; millwork — 500. **Northern Engraving Corp.** (HQ); Sparta; engraving services — 500. **Soo Line Railroad Inc.**; Fond du Lac; railroad operations — 500.

7th District

Northwest — Wausau, Superior

The 7th reaches from the center of Wisconsin all the way north to Lake Superior. The southern part of the district is devoted largely to dairy farming; in the north, a booming recreation industry has brought new life to many old mining and lumbering areas that were exploited and abandoned earlier in this century.

In redistricting, parts of three counties moved out of the 7th and part of one county moved in. The shifts did no harm to the Democratic incumbent, who has held the seat since 1969.

A key to the incumbent's success has been his ability to win votes in Marathon and Wood counties, areas in the southern part of the 7th where Republicans generally run well in state and national elections. The major city in Marathon County is Wausau, which has paper mills, prefabricated home builders and white-collar employment in the insurance industry. In Wood County, Wisconsin Rapids has paper mills, and Marshfield has a large medical clinic and research facility. The cities are processing centers for the surrounding dairy lands.

The heaviest Democratic vote in the southern part of the 7th comes out of Portage County. The city of Stevens Point there has a large Polish contingent, a branch of the state university and the headquarters of the Sentry Insurance Co. Moving north, the land becomes hillier and less productive. In 1976 Jimmy Carter carried most of the counties in the central part of the 7th, but four years later he lost them all to Ronald Reagan, who nearly won the district's overall vote.

A generous scattering of streams, rivers, lakes, national forests and state parks covers the northern reaches of the 7th, luring tourists and retirees from the urban centers of the upper Midwest. Population growth and tourism have made the massive Telemark resort in Bayfield County one of Wisconsin's major year-round convention centers.

The northern sections of the 7th share the same solid Democratic traditions found in Minnesota's Iron Range and the nearby western end of Michigan's Upper Peninsula. The major Democratic bastion is the region's only sizable city, Superior, a predominantly working-class town settled by Finns and Swedes.

The port facilities of Superior and its larger neighbor, Duluth, Minn., are a funnel for soybeans, wheat and a wide range of other commodities raised on the farms of the Midwest. Some ore from the Minnesota Iron Range is handled, but not nearly as much as in the past.

In the south, redistricting shifted most of Clark County to the 3rd and much of southern Wood County went to the 6th. The 7th kept the town of Rhinelander, but most of Oneida County joined the 8th. At its western edge, the 7th gained northern Polk County from the 3rd. In the area that makes up the new 7th, Carter won in 1980 by 46 to 45 percent, nearly the same margin he received in the old 7th.

Election Returns

7th District		Democrat		Republican	
1976	President	128,419	(54.9%)	99,145	(42.4%)
	Senate	159,023	(77.6%)	44,405	(21.7%)
	House	162,753	(73.7%)	56,813	(25.7%)
1978	Governor	73,192	(42.1%)	99,050	(57.0%)
	House	104,976	(62.5%)	61,383	(36.6%)
1980	President	118,482	(46.1%)	116,505	(45.3%)
	Senate	122,945	(49.7%)	118,031	(47.8%)
	House	156,270	(65.3%)	83,197	(34.7%)

7th District		Democrat		Republican	
1982	Governor	105,562	(56.4%)	78,314	(41.8%)
	Senate	127,807	(68.1%)	56,886	(30.3%)
	House	122,124	(68.0%)	57,535	(32.0%)

Demographics

Population: 522,623. **Percent Change from 1970:** 11.9%.

Land Area: 16,460 square miles. **Population per Square Mile:** 31.8.

Counties, 1980 Population: Ashland — 16,783; Bayfield — 13,822; Burnett — 12,340; Chippewa — 52,127; Clark (Pt.) — 14,417; Douglas — 44,421; Iron — 6,730; Lincoln — 26,555; Marathon — 111,270; Oneida (Pt.) — 13,929; Polk (Pt.) — 10,276; Portage — 57,420; Price — 15,788; Rusk — 15,589; Sawyer — 12,843; Taylor — 18,817; Washburn — 13,174; Wood (Pt.) — 66,322.

Cities, 1980 Population: Chippewa Falls — 12,270; Eau Claire (Pt.) — 1,657; Marshfield — 18,290; Stevens Point — 22,970; Superior — 29,571; Wausau — 32,426; Wisconsin Rapids — 17,995.

Race and Ancestry: White — 98.4%; Black — 0.1%; American Indian, Eskimo and Aleut — 1.1%; Asian and Pacific Islander — 0.2%. Spanish Origin — 0.3%. Dutch — 0.6%; English — 2.8%; French — 1.1%; German — 24.8%; Irish — 1.9%; Italian — 0.6%; Norwegian — 3.0%; Polish — 6.9%; Swedish — 2.4%.

Universities, Enrollment: Mid-State Vocational, Technical, and Adult Education District, Wisconsin Rapids — 1,332; Mount Senario College, Ladysmith — 448; Nicolet College and Technical Institute, Rhinelander — 1,117; Northland College, Ashland — 691; University of Wisconsin (Stevens Point campus), Stevens Point — 9,183; University of Wisconsin (Superior campus), Superior — 2,322; Wisconsin Indianhead Technical Institute, Shell Lake — 2,752.

Newspapers, Circulation: *Chippewa Herald Telegram* (e), Chippewa Falls — 9,495; *The Daily Herald* (e), Wausau — 29,506; *Daily Tribune* (e), Wisconsin Rapids — 12,925; *The Evening Telegram* (e), Superior — 14,916; *Marshfield News-Herald* (e), Marshfield — 15,332; *Press* (m), Ashland — 8,253; *The Rhinelander Daily News* (eS), Rhinelander — 6,169; *Stevens Point Journal* (e), Stevens Point — 13,704.

Commercial Television Stations, Affiliation: KBJR-TV, Superior (NBC); WAEO-TV, Rhinelander (NBC); WAOW-TV, Wausau (ABC); WSAW-TV, Wausau (CBS). Most of district is divided between Wausau-Rhinelander ADI and Duluth (Minn.)-Superior ADI. Portions are in La Crosse-Eau Claire ADI and Minneapolis (Minn.)-St. Paul (Minn.) ADI.

Industries:

Consolidated Papers Inc. (HQ); Wisconsin Rapids; paper mills — 3,600. **Employers Insurance of Wausau** (Wausau Insurance Companies - HQ); Wausau; casualty insurance — 2,490. **Nekoosa Papers Inc.** (HQ); Port Edwards; fine paper — 2,400. **Sentry Insurance Co.** (HQ); Stevens Point; casualty insurance — 2,120. **St. Joseph's Hospital of Marshfield;** Marshfield; hospital — 1,800.

Marathon Electric Mfg. Corp. (HQ); Wausau; motors, generators — 1,130. **Wausau Hospital Inc.;** Wausau; hospital — 1,100. **J. I. Case Co.** (Drott Div.); Schofield; construction equipment — 900. **Weyerhaeuser Co.** (Marshfield Wood Products); Marshfield; wooden doors — 900. **Rhinelander Paper Co. Inc.** Rhinelander; coated paper — 850. **Weather Shield Mfg. Inc.** (HQ); Medford; wood windows — 850. **Weyerhaeuser Co.;** Rothschild; paper, pulp — 660. **Flambeau Paper Corp.;** Park Falls; paper mill — 610.

Owens-Illinois Inc. (Forest Products Div.); Tomahawk; paperboard mills — 600. **Preway Inc.** (HQ); Wisconsin Rapids; prefabricated fireplaces — 600. **Mosinee Paper Corp.** (Bay West & Calwis Div. - HQ); Mosinee; paper mill, plastic products — 580. **Bata Shoe Co.** (Weinbrenner Shoe Div.); Merrill; men's footwear — 560. **Consolidated Papers Inc.** (Wisconsin River Div.); Whiting; paper mill — 545. **Harris-Crestline Corp.** (HQ); Wausau; windows — 500. **James River Co.** (Paperboard Packaging Div.); Wausau; paper food containers — 500. **Wausau Homes Inc.** (HQ); Wausau; pre-built homes — 500.

8th District

Northeast — Green Bay, Appleton

Despite the transfer of heavily Republican Waupaca County to the 6th District, more than half the ballots in the 8th still are cast in the Fox River Valley counties of Outagamie (Appleton) and Brown (Green Bay).

Germans are the most noticeable ethnic group in the industrialized valley. Most of them are Catholic and conservative, and they have made the 8th a generally Republican district. The areas included in the redrawn district favored Ronald Reagan over Jimmy Carter in 1980 by 55 to 37 percent.

The economy of the valley and the vast wooded area to the north is dependent on trees and paper. Among the economic leaders in Green Bay is the Fort Howard Paper Co. The city also makes wood products, processes dairy products and has a state university campus.

Paper, grain and dairy products go out of the Green Bay port and fertilizer, cement and coal come in. Green Bay, best known for its football Packers, is the smallest city to host a National Football League club.

Thirty miles southwest is Appleton, on the north shore of Lake Winnebago. Again, paper manufacturers and paper-making equipment industries are important employers. Appleton also has white-collar jobs at insurance companies and at Lawrence College, a private liberal arts institution. Appleton is perhaps best known as the home town of the late Republican Senator Joseph R. McCarthy.

Brown County voted for John F. Kennedy, a Catholic, in the 1960 presidential contest, but it traditionally prefers Republican presidential candidates. Ronald Reagan won 57 percent there in 1980. He received 53 percent in Outagamie, where independent John B. Anderson took a respectable 10 percent.

As in the neighboring 7th District, nature has been generous to the 8th. The focal points for tourist resorts and vacation homes are Door County, on a peninsula jutting into Lake Michigan, and Vilas County, in a lakes region on the Michigan border. Both counties vote solidly Republican, influenced by the prosperity that has come from serving nature-seekers from all over the Midwest.

In the rural counties in the north-central part of the district, most of the people are Republican, although there are pockets of Democratic strength. Forest County, where lumbering is important, chose Carter over Reagan in 1980, as did Menominee County, where most of the voters live on the Menominee Indian Reservation.

In addition to the shift of Waupaca County, redistricting brought the 8th most of Oneida County from the 7th. Voters there tend to favor Republicans in national and state elections although they supported the Democratic incumbent in the 7th.

Election Returns

8th District		Democrat		Republican	
1976	President	102,935	(46.0%)	115,804	(51.7%)
	Senate	141,907	(71.6%)	55,150	(27.8%)
	House	114,134	(52.2%)	99,468	(45.6%)
1978	Governor	68,373	(40.2%)	100,310	(59.0%)
	House	73,080	(43.3%)	95,618	(56.7%)

8th District		Democrat		Republican	
1980	President	93,714	(37.1%)	139,698	(55.3%)
	Senate	100,532	(41.5%)	137,984	(57.0%)
	House	81,575	(33.9%)	159,304	(66.1%)
1982	Governor	90,356	(50.1%)	87,566	(48.5%)
	Senate	100,520	(57.2%)	73,070	(41.6%)
	House	74,436	(42.0%)	101,379	(57.2%)

Demographics

Population: 523,225. **Percent Change from 1970:** 12.3%.

Land Area: 9,786 square miles. **Population per Square Mile:** 53.5.

Counties, 1980 Population: Brown — 175,280; Door — 25,029; Florence — 4,172; Forest — 9,044; Kewaunee — 19,539; Langlade — 19,978; Marinette — 39,314; Menominee — 3,373; Oconto — 28,947; Oneida (Pt.) — 17,287; Outagamie — 128,799; Shawano — 35,928; Vilas — 16,535.

Cities, 1980 Population: Appleton (Pt.) — 53,531; Ashwaubenon — 14,486; De Pere — 14,892; Green Bay — 87,899; Kaukauna — 11,310; Marinette — 11,965.

Race and Ancestry: White — 97.3%; Black — 0.1%; American Indian, Eskimo and Aleut — 2.1%; Asian and Pacific Islander — 0.4%. Spanish Origin — 0.4%. Dutch — 2.5%; English — 2.3%; French — 1.9%; German — 23.3%; Irish — 2.0%; Italian — 0.5%; Norwegian — 1.1%; Polish — 3.8%; Swedish — 1.0%.

Universities, Enrollment: Fox Valley Technical Institute, Appleton — 4,627; The Institute of Paper Chemistry, Appleton — 95; Lawrence University, Appleton — 1,137; Northeast Wisconsin Technical Institute, Green Bay — 3,542; St. Norbert College, De Pere — 1,686; University of Wisconsin (Green Bay campus), Green Bay — 4,164.

Newspapers, Circulation: *Antigo Daily Journal* (e), Antigo — 6,554; *Eagle-Star* (e), Marinette — 10,148; *The Green Bay News-Chronicle* (m), Green Bay — 12,744; *Green Bay Press-Gazette* (eS), Green Bay — 58,543; *The Post-Crescent* (eS), Appleton — 52,023; *Shawano Evening Leader* (e), Shawano — 7,709.

Commercial Television Stations, Affiliation: WBAY-TV, Green Bay (CBS); WFRV-TV, Green Bay (NBC); WLRE, Green Bay (None); WLUK, Green Bay (ABC). District is divided between Green Bay ADI and Wausau-Rhinelander ADI.

Nuclear Power Plants: Kewaunee, Green Bay (Westinghouse, Pioneer Services and Engineering), June 1974.

Industries:

Fort Howard Paper Co. (HQ); Green Bay; paper mills — 2,800. **Procter & Gamble Paper Products Co.** (Fox River Mill Div. - HQ); Green Bay; sanitary paper products — 2,100. **Bay Shipbuilding Corp.;** Sturgeon Bay; ship repairing — 1,770. **Hammermill Paper Co.** (Thilmany Pulp & Paper Co. Div.); Kaukauna; paper mill — 1,700. **St. Vincent Hospital;** Green Bay; hospital — 1,650.

Miller Electric Mfg. Co. Inc. (HQ); Appleton; welding equipment — 1,560. **Paper Converting Machine Co.;** Green Bay; paper industries machinery — 1,400. **American Can Co.;** Green Bay; paper products — 1,300. **Midtec Paper Corp.;** Kimberly; coated paper — 1,200. **St. Elizabeth Hospital Inc.;** Appleton; hospital — 1,150. **Appleton Papers Inc.** (HQ); Appleton; coated paper — 1,110. **Bellin Memorial Hospital Inc;** Green Bay; hospital — 1,050. **The Ansul Co.** (HQ); Marinette; fire control products — 1,000. **Schreiber Foods Inc.** (HQ); Green Bay; cheese — 960. **Marinette Marine Corp.;** Marinette; shipbuilding — 950.

Peterson Builders Inc. (HQ); Sturgeon Bay; shipbuilding, repairing — 875. **Zwicker Knitting Mills** (Hansen Knits Div. - HQ); Appleton; knitted gloves — 850. **Scott Paper Co.;** Marinette; paper — 750. **Green Bay Packaging Inc.** (HQ); Green Bay; paperboard mills — 692. **Appleton Papers Inc.;** Combined Locks; paper mill — 650. **Presto Products Inc.** (HQ); Appleton; plastic bags — 600. **Fox Valley Corp.** (Fox River Paper Div. - HQ); Appleton; paper bags — 550. **Safeguard**

Engine Parts Inc. (Manley Valve Div. - HQ); Marinette; valves — 540. Coleman Products Co. (HQ); Coleman; electrical parts for internal combustion engines — 500. Doerr Electric Corp.; Sturgeon Bay; electric motors — 500.

9th District

Milwaukee Suburbs, Sheboygan

The 9th is Wisconsin's only true suburban district; during the 1970s it lured enough people out of Milwaukee's 4th and 5th districts to grow by nearly 18 percent, the fastest of any district in the state. Not surprisingly, the 9th is also Wisconsin's most staunchly Republican district. Jimmy Carter barely managed one-third of the district's vote in 1980.

The strongest GOP support comes from the "Gold Coast" section of the district, a string of exclusive neighborhoods along Lake Michigan north of Milwaukee. In the city's boom days, beer-brewing barons and other industrial kingpins built mansions on the North Shore; today the property values and the GOP turnouts there are stunning. Whitefish Bay, Fox Point and Bayside each voted for Ronald Reagan in 1980 by margins exceeding 2-to-1.

Directly north of those established North Shore communities is Ozaukee County. Mequon and Thiensville, in the southern part of Ozaukee, are becoming extensions of the Gold Coast. Although the middle and northern sections of Ozaukee are somewhat less affluent, they do not reduce Republican margins significantly.

Compared with Milwaukee and Ozaukee counties, the middle-class element is larger in the western sections of the 9th. Washington County is a combination of fast-growing bedroom communities and agricultural lands encroached upon by development, with a smattering of industry.

In earlier generations, the lakes of Waukesha County drew Milwaukee's leading families to buy real estate in the county for summer retreats. But in Pewaukee, Hartland and other parts of the county, suburbanization has taken its toll on those large holdings. In 1980 Reagan won 58 percent of the county's vote. The areas of Waukesha County where Democrats are most numerous — the city of Waukesha and the southeastern part of the county — were transferred to the underpopulated 4th District.

The 9th is filled out with Jefferson and Dodge counties, which are slightly beyond the reach of Milwaukee sprawl and rely on agriculture — primarily dairying, egg production and raising cattle and corn.

The 9th underwent several boundary changes in redistricting, but the transfers had little impact on the partisanship of the electorate. In addition to giving Democratic southeast Waukesha County to the 4th, the remap sent Shorewood, Brown Deer and Glendale in Milwaukee County to the 5th. The 9th received the city of Sheboygan and other parts of Sheboygan County from the 6th and took the northeast quarter of Dodge from the 2nd.

Election Returns

9th District		Democrat		Republican	
1976	President	100,968	(40.2%)	143,454	(57.1%)

9th District		Democrat		Republican	
1976	Senate	149,404	(66.9%)	73,141	(32.7%)
	House	77,136	(34.0%)	149,777	(66.0%)
1978	Governor	70,591	(36.6%)	121,443	(62.9%)
	House	64,660	(36.7%)	111,451	(63.2%)
1980	President	87,405	(33.7%)	149,924	(57.8%)
	Senate	99,878	(35.9%)	175,943	(63.2%)
	House	57,858	(24.1%)	182,094	(75.9%)
1982	Governor	82,419	(46.9%)	91,289	(52.0%)
	Senate	95,876	(55.8%)	73,990	(43.0%)
	House	—[1]		x[1]	

[1] *No votes tabulated where candidate was unopposed; x indicates winner.*

Demographics

Population: 522,950. **Percent Change from 1970:** 15.2%.

Land Area: 2,263 square miles. **Population per Square Mile:** 231.1.

Counties, 1980 Population: Dodge (Pt.) — 33,946; Fond Du Lac (Pt.) — 7,741; Jefferson (Pt.) — 63,730; Milwaukee (Pt.) — 28,833; Ozaukee — 66,981; Sheboygan (Pt.) — 66,124; Washington (Pt.) — 84,846; Waukesha (Pt.) — 170,749.

Cities, 1980 Population: Brookfield — 34,035; Germantown — 10,729; Menomonee Falls — 27,845; Mequon — 16,193; Sheboygan — 48,085; Watertown — 18,113; Waukesha (Pt.) — 979; West Bend — 21,484; Whitefish Bay — 14,930.

Race and Ancestry: White — 98.7%; Black — 0.4%; American Indian, Eskimo and Aleut — 0.2%; Asian and Pacific Islander — 0.4%. Spanish Origin — 0.8%. Dutch — 1.7%; English — 2.8%; French — 0.6%; German — 34.2%; Irish — 1.9%; Italian — 0.8%; Norwegian — 1.0%; Polish — 2.1%; Russian — 0.5%.

Universities, Enrollment: Cardinal Stritch College, Milwaukee — 1,136; Nashotah House, Nashotah — 78; Waukesha County Technical Institute, Pewaukee — 5,100.

Newspapers, Circulation: *Daily Jefferson County Union* (e), Fort Atkinson — 8,745; *The Sheboygan Press* (e), Sheboygan — 32,141; *Watertown Daily Times* (e), Watertown — 10,002; *Waukesha Freeman* (e), Waukesha — 25,461; *West Bend News* (e), West Bend — 10,560. *Fond du Lac Reporter*, *The Milwaukee Journal* and *Milwaukee Sentinel* also circulate in the district.

Commercial Television Stations, Affiliation: Most of district is located in Milwaukee ADI. Portion is in Green Bay ADI.

Industries:

Dart Industries Inc.; West Bend; metal stampings, electrical housewares — 2,000. Tecumseh Products Co. (Power Products Div.); Grafton; gasoline engines — 1,300. Crepaco Inc. (Amerio Refrigeration Equipment); Lake Mills; food products equipment — 1,000. Gehl Co. (HQ); West Bend; agricultural equipment — 950. Briggs and Stratton Corp.; Menominee Falls; engines — 934.

Mayville Metal Products Co. (HQ); Mayville; sheet metal — 875. Amity Leather Products Co. (HQ); West Bend; personal leather goods — 750. Badger Meter Inc. (Electronics Div. - HQ); Milwaukee; flow measurement devices — 725. The Vollrath Co. Inc. (HQ); Sheboygan; stainless steel ware — 700. Sheboygan Paint Co. Inc.; Sheboygan; paint — 680. W. A. Krueger Co.; Brookfield; commercial, book printing — 680. Allis-Chalmers Corp. (Simplicity Mfg. Co. Div.); Port Washington; power garden equipment — 650. Doerr Electric Corp. (HQ); Cedarburg; electric motors, pumps, speed changers — 600. Milwaukee Electric Tool Corp. (HQ); Brookfield; portable power tools — 600. H. C. Prange Co. (HQ); Sheboygan; department stores — 600. Hayssen Mfg. Co. (HQ); Sheboygan; packaging equipment — 550. Broan Mfg. Co. Inc. (Nautilus Industries - HQ); Hartford; kitchen ranges — 525. FMC Corp. (Outdoor Power Equipment Div.); Port Washington; lawn, garden equipment — 525. Hamlin Inc. (HQ); Lake Mills; switches — 510.

Wyoming

Milward Simpson, Wyoming's blunt-spoken ex-governor, once proposed a novel solution to the state's problems: build a fence around the state and keep everyone else out. Instead Wyoming did just the opposite: turned itself into an energy mecca wracked by development, growth and social and political change.

The pace of the change has been staggering. Rural, arid and insular, Wyoming was the slowest-growing state in the nation in the 1960s. In the 1970s it was the third *fastest*-growing state, behind only Nevada and Arizona. Credit it to, or blame it on, the energy crisis. Wyoming has oil, coal, natural gas, uranium and oil shale, all in abundance. And the boom has only just begun. Many of the resources have hardly been tapped. But the signs of change are unmistakable.

Wyoming in 1980 had nearly half a million residents, up from 332,416 in 1970. By 1980 the quiet, pleasant cow towns of a decade earlier were crowded, crime-ridden boom towns, where every motel room was booked up and most of the permanent residents lived in trailers.

Wyoming seems ambivalent about these changes. It is still a pro-growth state where environmental restrictions are viewed skeptically, but its residents also are leery of having their mountains torn up to provide air conditioning for the cities. When governors of other coal states expressed their support for relaxed strip mining restrictions, Wyoming's governor, Ed Herschler, opposed them. In 1978 Democrat Herschler was re-elected in large part by proposing an increased mineral severance tax and calling his Republican opponent "a mouthpiece for the mining industry." In 1982 Herschler was returned to office for an unprecedented third time, taking 63 percent of the vote.

Wyoming always has been fairly easy to explain in terms of partisan politics. Democrats are competitive in the five counties along the state's southern border. North of these five — Albany, Carbon, Laramie, Sweetwater and Uinta counties — Democrats almost never win, and this makes it difficult to succeed statewide.

The Democratic voting tradition in southern Wyoming goes back to the early days of the state when immigrant laborers were imported to build the Union Pacific rail line through those southern counties. The state's first coal miners followed. Many of these people were Italian immigrants; others were Oriental. Like their counterparts in other states most of the workers were drawn into the Democratic Party.

Although the southern counties remain the most Democratic area in the state, its residents are conservative on most issues and on recent issues often have sided with Republicans. Ronald Reagan easily carried all five southern counties in 1980.

The few Democrats who have won statewide in recent years have done so by restraining the growth of the Republican vote in the south. In 1978, when Gov. Ed Herschler was re-elected by less than 2,400 votes statewide, he won the five southern counties by a combined margin of 8,347 votes.

Three of the four largest towns in Wyoming are in this region, including Cheyenne, the state capital, and Laramie. In 1980 slightly more than one third of the state's residents lived here.

Although the northern section as a whole has been gaining population faster than the south, a few areas, particularly Sweetwater County in the southwest, more than doubled in population during the 1970s boom. Rock Springs, an energy boom town that is the county seat, is the state's most important single source of Democratic votes.

The northern part of the state is the Wyoming of rock and ranch. Its dry plateaus and basins accommodate the cattle ranches that make Wyoming the "Cowboy State." The mountains and valleys contain most of the state's mineral wealth.

It is conservative country that Republicans have carried in nearly every election. Ranching interests traditionally have dominated it. The population boom and gradual shift from ranching to mineral development have changed the power structure in some of these counties, but they have done little to shake the region's GOP voting habits. Converse County, the fastest-growing area in the state, gave more than 70 percent of its vote to Reagan in 1980.

Natrona County is the largest in northern Wyoming and a solid Republican area that almost never backs Democrats. Casper, the county seat, is the state's largest city. A boom town with just over 51,000 people, Casper finally passed Cheyenne, the traditional leader, in 1980. Once mainly a trading center, Casper has become the hub of Wyoming's mineral operations.

The population boom is changing the face of northern Wyoming, with new towns and subdivisions sprouting like prairie grass. Nevertheless, the people still are widely scattered. Apart from Casper, Sheridan is still the only town in northern Wyoming with more than 15,000 inhabitants.

WYOMING

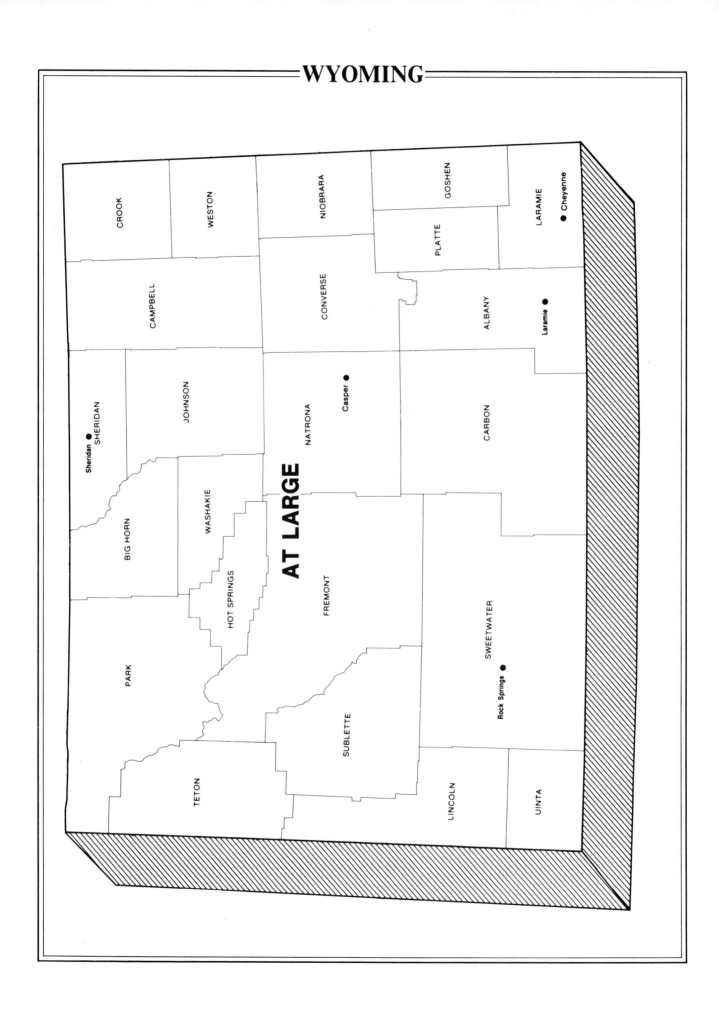

Age of Population

District	Population Under 18	Voting Age Population	Population 65 & Over (% of VAP)	Median Age
AL	145,553	324,004	37,175 (11.5%)	27.1

Income and Occupation

District	Median Family Income	White Collar Workers	Blue Collar Workers	Service Workers	Farm Workers
AL	$ 22,430	46.8%	35.8%	12.5%	5.0%

Education: School Years Completed

District	8 Years or Fewer	4 Years of High School	4 Years of College or More	Median School Years
AL	10.0%	40.0%	17.2%	12.7

Housing and Residential Patterns

District	Owner Occupied	Renter Occupied	Urban	Rural
AL	69.2%	30.8%	62.7%	37.3%

Election Returns

At Large		Democrat		Republican	
1976	President	62,239	(39.8%)	92,717	(59.3%)
	Senate	70,558	(54.6%)	84,810	(45.4%)
	House	85,721	(56.4%)	66,147	(43.6%)
1978	Governor	69,972	(50.9%)	67,595	(49.1%)
	Senate	50,456	(37.8%)	82,908	(62.2%)
	House	53,522	(41.4%)	75,855	(58.6%)
1980	President	49,427	(28.0%)	110,700	(62.6%)
	House	53,338	(31.4%)	116,361	(68.6%)
1982	Governor	106,427	(63.1%)	62,128	(36.9%)
	Senate	72,466	(43.3%)	94,725	(56.7%)
	House	46,041	(28.9%)	113,236	(71.1%)

Demographics

Population: 469,557. Percent Change from 1970: 41.3%.

Land Area: 96,989 square miles. **Population per Square Mile:** 4.8.

Counties, 1980 Population: Albany — 29,062; Big Horn — 11,896; Campbell — 24,367; Carbon — 21,896; Converse — 14,069; Crook — 5,308; Fremont — 38,992; Goshen — 12,040; Hot Springs — 5,710; Johnson — 6,700; Laramie — 68,649; Lincoln — 12,177; Natrona — 71,856; Niobrara — 2,924; Park — 21,639; Platte — 11,975; Sheridan — 25,048; Sublette — 4,548; Sweetwater — 41,723; Teton — 9,355; Uinta — 13,021; Washakie — 9,496; Weston — 7,106.

Cities, 1980 Population: Casper — 51,016; Cheyenne — 47,283; Gillette — 12,134; Green River — 12,807; Laramie — 24,410; Rawlins — 11,547; Rock Springs — 19,458; Sheridan — 15,146.

Race and Ancestry: White — 95.1%; Black — 0.7%; American Indian, Eskimo and Aleut — 1.5%; Asian and Pacific Islander — 0.4%. Spanish Origin — 5.2%. Dutch — 1.0%; English — 11.2%; French — 1.3%; German — 13.4%; Irish — 5.1%; Italian — 1.0%; Norwegian — 1.4%; Polish — 0.8%; Scottish — 1.3%; Swedish — 1.6%.

Universities, Enrollment: Casper College, Casper — 3,311; Central Wyoming College, Riverton — 827; Eastern Wyoming College, Torrington — 861; Laramie County Community College, Cheyenne — 2,487; Northwest Community College, Powell — 1,543; Sheridan College, Sheridan — 1,052; University of Wyoming, Laramie — 9,014; Western Wyoming Community College, Rock Springs — 1,226; Wyoming School of Animal Technology, Thermopolis — 22.

Newspapers, Circulation: *Daily Rocket-Miner* (m), Rock Springs — 7,420; *Laramie Daily Boomerang* (mS), Laramie — 7,487; *News-Record* (e), Gillette — 5,401; *Northern Wyoming Daily News* (m), Worland — 4,422; *Press* (e), Sheridan — 6,842; *Rawlins Times* (m), Rawlins — 4,511; *The Riverton Ranger* (e), Riverton — 7,034; *Star-Tribune* (mS), Casper — 32,957; *Wyoming Eagle* (mS), Cheyenne — 8,561; *Wyoming State Tribune* (eS), Cheyenne — 11,408.

Commercial Television Stations, Affiliation: KCWY-TV, Casper (CBS); KSGW-TV, Sheridan (NBC, ABC, CBS); KTNW, Riverton (NBC); KTUX, Rock Springs (None); KTWO-TV, Casper (ABC, NBC); KYCU-TV, Cheyenne (CBS, ABC, NBC). Most of district is divided between Casper-Riverton ADI and Salt Lake City (Utah) ADI. Portions are in Cheyenne ADI, Rapid City (S.D.) ADI, Billings (Mont.)-Hardin (Mont.) ADI, Denver (Colo.) ADI and Idaho Falls (Idaho)-Pocatello (Idaho) ADI.

Military Installations: Boulder Research Site (Air Force), Boulder — 14; Francis E. Warren Air Force Base, Cheyenne — 4,145.

Industries:

FMC Corp.; Green River; soda ash — 1,350. **Allied Chemical Corp.;** Green River; mineral mining — 1,200. **Brown & Root Inc.;** Green River; industrial building contracting — 640. **Stauffer Chemical Co. of Wyoming (HQ);** Green River; industrial chemicals — 625. **Decker Coal Co.;** Sheridan; coal mine — 623.

Black Butte Coal Co.; Point of Rocks; coal mining — 600. **Getty Oil Co. Inc. (Petrotonics Co.);** Casper; uranium mining — 570. **Bridger Coal Co.;** Rock Springs; coal mine — 525. **Texasgulf Inc.;** Granger; soda ash mining — 510. **Amax Inc.;** Gillette; coal mine — 500. **United States Steel Corp.;** Lander; iron ore mining — 500.

Appendix

Reapportionment and Redistricting

Reapportionment, the redistribution of the 435 seats in the U. S. House of Representatives among the states to reflect shifts in population, and redistricting, the redrawing of congressional district lines within each state, are among the most important processes in the U.S. political system. They help determine whether the House will be dominated by Democrats or Republicans, liberals or conservatives. They help determine whether racial or ethnic minorities receive fair representation.

Reapportionment and redistricting occur every 10 years on the basis of the decennial population census. States whose populations grew quickly over the previous 10 years are given additional congressional seats, while those that lost population or grew much slower than the national average have seats taken away. For the rest, the sizes of their delegations in the House remain unchanged.

The states that gain or lose seats must make extensive changes in their congressional maps. Even those states with stable delegations must make modifications that account for population shifts within their boundaries in accordance with the U. S. Supreme Court "one-person, one-vote" rulings.

Despite their importance to the political process, reapportionment and redistricting draw little interest from the general public. This is ironic, wrote Andrea J. Wollock in the January 1982 issue of *State Legislatures,* because reapportionment is not only a "supremely important" political issue but also "a source of unsurpassed political drama and intrigue." Partisan interests are enhanced, personal political ambitions of powerful politicians are furthered. Incumbents are protected or politically crippled. Tempers flare and fists fly, as they did during a redistricting debate in the Illinois legislature in 1981.

Among the many unique features to emerge in the remarkable nation-creating endeavor of 1787 was a national legislative body whose membership was to be elected by the people and apportioned on the basis of population. But, as with almost everything in the Constitution, only a few basic rules and regulations were laid down. How to interpret and implement the instructions contained in the document was left to future generations. Practical reactions to concrete problems would shape the institutions and create the customs by which the new nation would develop and prosper.

Within this framework, many questions soon arose concerning the House of Representatives. How large was it to be? What mathematical formula was to be used in calculating the distribution of seats among the various states? Were the representatives to be elected at large or by districts? If by districts, what standards should be used in fixing their boundaries? The Congress and the courts have been wrestling with these questions for almost 200 years.

Until the mid-20th century, such questions generally remained in the hands of the legislators. But with growing concentration of the population in urban areas, variations in population among congressional districts became more pronounced — and more noticeable. Efforts to get Congress to redress the grievance of heavily populated but under-represented areas proved unsuccessful. So intent were rural legislators on preventing power from slipping out of their hands that they managed to block reapportionment of the House following the census of 1920.

Not long after that, the focus shifted to the Supreme Court, where litigants tried to persuade the court to order the states to revise congressional district boundaries in line with population shifts. After initial failure, a breakthrough occurred in 1964 in the case of *Wesberry v. Sanders.* The court declared that the Constitution required that "as nearly as practicable, one man's vote in a congressional election is to be worth as much as another's."

In the years that followed, the court repeatedly reaffirmed its "one person, one vote" requirement. In 1983 the court held that no deviation from that principle was permissible unless the state proved that the population variation was necessary to achieve some legitimate goal. This ruling immediately drew fire from those who thought it would allow states to ignore several other traditional factors involved in redistricting — such as compactness of the district or integrity of county and city lines — in their quest for districts of precisely equal populations.

Early History

Modern legislative bodies are descended from the councils of feudal lords and gentry that medieval kings summoned for the purpose of raising revenues and armies. These councils did not represent a king's subjects in any modern sense. They represented certain groups of subjects, such as the nobility, the clergy, the landed gentry and town merchants. Representation was by interest groups and had no relation to equal representation for equal numbers of people. In England, the king's council became Parliament, with the higher nobility and clergy making up the House of Lords and representatives of the gentry and merchants making up the House of Commons.

Beginning as little more than administrative and advisory arms of the throne, royal councils in time developed into lawmaking bodies and acquired powers that eventually eclipsed those of the monarchs they served. The power struggle in England climaxed during the Cromwellian period when the Crown gave way, temporarily, to the Commonwealth. By 1800 Parliament was clearly the superior branch of government.

During the 18th and early 19th centuries, as the power of Parliament grew, the English became increasingly concerned about the "representativeness" of their system of apportionment. Newly developing industrial cities had no more representation in the House of Commons than small, almost deserted country towns. Small constituencies were bought and sold. Men from these empty "rotten boroughs" often were sent to Parliament representing a single "patron" landowner or clique of wealthy men. It was not until the Reform Act of 1832 that Parliament curbed such excesses and turned toward a representative system based on population.

The growth of the powers of Parliament as well as the development of English ideas of representation during the 17th and 18th centuries had a profound effect on the colonists in America. Representative assemblies were unifying forces behind the breakaway of the colonies from England and the establishment of the newly independent country.

Colonists in America, generally modeling their legislatures after England's, used both population and land units as bases for apportionment. Patterns of early representation varied. "Nowhere did representation bear any uniform relation to the number of electors. Here and there the factor of size had been crudely recognized," Robert Luce pointed out in his book *Legislative Principles.*

In New England, the town usually was the basis for representation. In the Middle Atlantic region, the county frequently was used. Virginia used the county with extra representation for specified cities. In many areas, towns and counties were fairly equal in population. Thus territorial representation afforded roughly equal representation for equal numbers of people. Delaware's three counties, for example, were of almost equal population and had the same representation in the legislature. But in Virginia the disparity was enormous (from 951 people in one county to 22,015 in another). Thomas Jefferson criticized the state's constitution on the ground that "among those who share the representation, the shares are unequal."

The Continental Congress, with representation from every colony, proclaimed in the Declaration of Independence in 1776 that governments derive "their just powers from the consent of the governed" and that "the right of representation in the legislature" is an "inestimable right" of the people. The Constitutional Convention of 1787 included representatives from all the states. However, in neither of these bodies were the state delegations or voting powers proportional to population.

Intentions of Founding Fathers

Andrew Hacker, in his book *Congressional Districting,* said that to ascertain what the framers of the Constitution had in mind when they drew up the section concerning the House of Representatives, it was necessary to study closely

several sources: the Constitution itself; the recorded discussions and debates at the Constitutional Convention; *The Federalist Papers* (essays written by Alexander Hamilton, John Jay and James Madison in defense of the Constitution); and the deliberations of the states' ratifying conventions.

The Constitution declares only that each state is to be allotted a certain number of representatives. It does not state specifically that congressional districts must be equal or nearly equal in population. Nor does it even require specifically that a state create districts at all. However, it seems clear that the first clause of Article I, Section 2, providing that House members should be chosen "by the people of the several states," indicated that the House of Representatives, in contrast to the Senate, was to represent people rather than states. "It follows," Hacker wrote, "that if the states are to have equal representation in the upper chamber, then individuals are to be equally represented in the lower body."

The third clause of Article I, Section 2, provided that congressional apportionment among the states must be according to population. But Hacker argued that "there is little point in giving the states congressmen 'according to their respective numbers' if the states do not redistribute the members of their delegations on the same principle. For representatives are not the property of the states, as are the senators, but rather belong to the people who happen to reside within the boundaries of those states. Thus, each citizen has a claim to be regarded as a political unit equal in value to his neighbors." In this and similar ways, constitutional scholars have argued the case for single-member congressional districts deduced from the wording of the Constitution itself.

The issue of unequal representation arose only once during debate in the Constitutional Convention. The occasion was Madison's defense of Article I, Section 4, of the proposed Constitution, giving Congress the power to override state regulations on "the times ... and manner" of holding elections for members of Congress. Madison's argument related to the fact that many state legislatures of the time were badly malapportioned: "The inequality of the representation in the legislatures of particular states would produce a like inequality in their representation in the national legislature, as it was presumable that the counties having the power in the former case would secure it to themselves in the latter."

The implication was that states would create congressional districts and that unequal districting was bad and should be prevented.

Madison made this interpretation even more clear in his contributions to *The Federalist Papers.* Arguing in favor of the relatively small size of the projected House of Representatives, he wrote in No. 56: "Divide the largest state into ten or twelve districts and it will be found that there will be no peculiar local interests ... which will not be within the knowledge of the Representative of the district."

In the same paper, Madison said: "The Representatives of each state will not only bring with them a considerable knowledge of its laws, and a local knowledge of their respective districts, but will probably in all cases have been members, and may even at the very time be members, of the state legislature, where all the local information and interests of the state are assembled, and from whence they may easily be conveyed by a very few hands into the legislature of the United States." And finally, in the next *Federalist* paper (No. 57), Madison made the statement

Constitutional Provisions on Apportionment and Districting

Article I, Section 2: The House of Representatives shall be composed of Members chosen every second Year by the People of the several States, and the Electors in each State shall have the Qualifications requisite for Electors of the most numerous Branch of the State Legislature....

Representatives and direct Taxes shall be apportioned among the several States which may be included within this Union, according to their respective Numbers, which shall be determined by adding to the whole Number of free Persons, including those bound to Service for a Term of Years, and excluding Indians not taxed, three fifths of all other Persons. The actual Enumeration shall be made within three Years after the first Meeting of the Congress of the United States, and within every subsequent Term of ten Years, in such Manner as they shall by Law direct. The Number of Representatives shall not exceed one for every thirty thousand, but each State shall have at least one Representative....

Article I, Section 4: The Times, Places and Manner of holding Elections for Senators and Representatives, shall be prescribed in each State by the Legislature thereof; but the Congress may at any time by Law make or alter such Regulations, except as to the Place of Chusing Senators....

Article (Amendment) XIV, Section 2: Representatives shall be apportioned among the several States according to their respective numbers, counting the whole number of persons in each State, excluding Indians not taxed. But when the right to vote at any election for the choice of electors for President and Vice President of the United States, Representatives in Congress, the Executive and Judicial officers of a State, or the members of the Legislature thereof, is denied to any of the male inhabitants of such State, being twenty-one years of age, and citizens of the United States, or in any way abridged, except for participation in rebellion, or other crime, the basis of representation therein shall be reduced in the proportion which the number of such male citizens shall bear to the whole number of male citizens twenty-one years of age in such state.

that "... each Representative of the United States will be elected by five or six thousand citizens." In making these arguments, Madison seems to have assumed that all or most representatives would be elected by districts rather than at large.

In the states' ratifying conventions, the grant to Congress by Article I, Section 4, of ultimate jurisdiction over the "times, places and manner of holding elections" (except the places of choosing senators) held the attention of many delegates. There were differences over the merits of this section, but no justification of unequal districts was prominently used to attack the grant of power. Further evidence that individual districts were the intention of the Founding Fathers was given in the New York ratifying convention, when Alexander Hamilton said: "The natural and proper mode of holding elections will be to divide the state into districts in proportion to the number to be elected. This state will consequently be divided at first into six."

From his study of the sources relating to the question of congressional districting, Hacker concluded: "There is, then, a good deal of evidence that those who framed and ratified the Constitution intended that the House of Representatives have as its constituency a public in which the votes of all citizens were of equal weight.... The House of Representatives was designed to be a popular chamber, giving the same electoral power to all who had the vote. And the concern of Madison ... that districts be equal in size was an institutional step in the direction of securing this democratic principle."

REAPPORTIONMENT: THE NUMBER OF SEATS

Article I, Section 2, Clause 3, of the Constitution laid down the basic rules for apportionment and reapportionment of seats in the House of Representatives: "Representatives ... shall be apportioned among the several states which may be included within this Union, according to their respective numbers, which shall be determined by adding to the whole number of free persons, including those bound to service for a term of years, and excluding Indians not taxed, three-fifths of all other persons. The actual enumeration shall be made within three years after the first meeting of the Congress of the United States, and within every subsequent term of ten years, in such manner as they shall by law direct. The number of Representatives shall not exceed one for every thirty thousand, but each state shall have at least one Representative...."

The Constitution made the first apportionment, which was to remain in effect until the first census was taken. No reliable figures on the population were available at the time. The 13 states were allocated the following numbers of representatives: New Hampshire, three; Massachusetts, eight; Rhode Island and Providence Plantations, one; Connecticut, five; New York, six; New Jersey, four; Pennsylvania, eight; Delaware, one; Maryland, six; Virginia, ten; North Carolina, five; South Carolina, five; and Georgia, three. The apportionment of seats — 65 in all — thus mandated by the Constitution remained in effect during the First and Second Congresses (1789-93).

Apparently realizing that apportionment of the House was likely to become a major bone of contention, the First Congress submitted to the states a proposed constitutional amendment containing a formula to be used in future reapportionments. The amendment, which was not ratified, provided that following the taking of a decennial census there would be one representative for every 30,000 persons until the House membership reached 100, "after which the proportion shall be so regulated by Congress that there shall be not less than 100 representatives, nor less than one representative for every 40,000 persons, until the number of representatives shall amount to 200, after which the proportion shall be so regulated by Congress, that there shall not be less than 200 representatives, nor more than one representative for every 50,000 persons."

First Apportionment by Congress

The failure to ratify this amendment made it necessary for Congress to enact apportionment legislation after the first census had been taken in 1790. The first apportionment bill was sent to the president on March 23, 1792. Washington sent the bill back to Congress without his signature — the first presidential veto.

The bill had incorporated the constitutional minimum of 30,000 as the size of each district. But the population of each state was not a simple multiple of 30,000. Significant fractions were left over when the number of people in each state was divided by 30,000. Thus, for example, Vermont was found to be entitled to 2.851 representatives, New Jersey to 5.98 and Virginia to 21.018. Therefore, a formula had to be found that would deal in the fairest possible manner with unavoidable variations from exact equality.

Accordingly, Congress proposed in the first apportionment bill to distribute the members on a fixed ratio of one representative per 30,000 inhabitants, and give an additional member to each state with a fraction exceeding one-half. Washington's veto was based on the belief that eight states would receive more than one representative per 30,000 people under this formula.

A motion to override the veto was unsuccessful. A new bill meeting the president's objections was introduced April 9, 1792, and approved April 14. The act provided for a ratio of one member for every 33,000 inhabitants and fixed the exact number of representatives to which each state was entitled. The total membership of the House was to be 105. In dividing the population of the various states by 33,000, all remainders were to be disregarded. This was known as the method of rejected fractions; it was devised by Thomas Jefferson.

Reapportionment by Jefferson's Method

Jefferson's method of reapportionment resulted in great inequalities among states. A Vermont district would contain 42,766 inhabitants, a New Jersey district 35,911 and a Virginia district only 33,187. Emphasis was placed on what was considered the ideal size of a congressional district rather than on what the size of the House ought to be. This method was in use until 1840.

The reapportionment act based on the census of 1800 continued the ratio of 33,000 which provided a House of 141 members. Debate on the third apportionment bill began in the House on Nov. 22, 1811, and the bill was sent to the president on Dec. 21. The ratio was fixed at 35,000, yielding a House of 181 members. Following the census of 1820, Congress approved an apportionment bill providing a ratio of 40,000 inhabitants per district. The sum of the quotas for the various states produced a House of 213 members.

The act of May 22, 1832, fixed the ratio at 47,700, resulting in a House of 240 members. Dissatisfaction with

the method in use continued, and Daniel Webster launched a vigorous attack against it. He urged adoption of a method that would assign an additional representative to each state with a large fraction. His approach to the reapportionment process was made in a report he submitted to Congress in 1832: "The Constitution, therefore, must be understood not as enjoining an absolute relative equality — because that would be demanding an impossibility — but as requiring of Congress to make the apportionment of Representatives among the several states according to their respective numbers, *as near as may be.* That which cannot be done perfectly must be done in a manner as near perfection as can be.... In such a case approximation becomes a rule."

Following the census of 1840, Congress adopted a reapportionment method similar to that advocated by Webster. The method fixed a ratio of one representative for every 70,680 persons. This figure was reached by deciding on a fixed size of the House in advance (223), dividing that figure into the total national "representative population" and using the result (70,680) as the fixed ratio. The population of each state was then divided by this ratio to find the number of its representatives and was assigned an additional representative for each fraction over one-half. Under this method the actual size of the House dropped. *(Congressional apportionment, box, p. 614)*

The modified reapportionment formula adopted by Congress in 1842 was found to be more satisfactory than the previous method, but another change was made following the census of 1850. The new system was proposed by Rep. Samuel F. Vinton of Ohio and became known as the Vinton method.

Vinton Apportionment Formula

Under this formula, Congress first fixed the size of the House and then distributed the seats. The total qualifying population of the country was divided by the desired number of representatives and the resulting number became the ratio of population to each representative. The population of each state was divided by this ratio and each state received the number of representatives equal to the whole number in the quotient for that state. Then, to reach the required size of the House, additional representatives were assigned based on the remaining fractions, beginning with the state having the largest fraction. This procedure differed from the 1842 method only in the last step, which assigned one representative to every state having a fraction larger than one-half.

Proponents of the Vinton method pointed out that it had the distinct advantage of making it possible to fix the size of the House in advance and to take into account at least the largest fractions. The concern of the House turned from the ideal size of a congressional district to the ideal size of the House itself. Under the 1842 reapportionment formula, the exact size of the House could not be fixed in advance. If every state with a fraction over one-half were given an additional representative, the House might wind up with a few more or a few less than the desired number. However, under the Vinton method, only states with the largest fractions were given additional House members and only up to the desired total size of the House.

Reapportionments by Vinton Method

Six reapportionments were carried out under the Vinton method. The 1850 Census Act contained three provisions not included in any previous law. First, it provided not only for reapportionment after the census of 1850 but also for reapportionment after all subsequent censuses; second, it purported to fix the size of the House permanently at 233 members; and third, it provided in advance for an automatic apportionment by the secretary of the interior under the method prescribed in the act.

Following the census of 1860, according to the provisions of the act passed a decade before, an automatic reapportionment was to be carried out by the Interior Department. However, because the size of the House was to remain at the 1850 level, some states faced loss of representation and others would gain less than they expected. To avert that possibility, an act was approved March 4, 1862, increasing the size of the House to 241 and giving an extra representative to eight states — Illinois, Iowa, Kentucky, Minnesota, Ohio, Pennsylvania, Rhode Island and Vermont.

Apportionment legislation following the census of 1870 contained several new provisions. The act of Feb. 2, 1872, fixed the size of the House at 283, with the proviso that the number should be increased if new states were admitted. A supplemental act of May 30, 1872, assigned one additional representative each to Alabama, Florida, Indiana, Louisiana, New Hampshire, New York, Pennsylvania, Tennessee and Vermont.

Another section of the 1872 act provided that no state should thereafter be admitted "without having the necessary population to entitle it to at least one representative fixed by this bill." That provision was found to be unenforceable because no Congress can bind a succeeding Congress. Moreover, no ratio was fixed by the act, although the basis on which the representatives were assigned was 131,425. In 1890 Idaho was admitted with a population of 84,385 and Wyoming with a population of 60,705.

With the Reconstruction era at its height in the South, the reapportionment legislation of 1872 reflected the desire of Congress to enforce Section 2 of the new 14th Amendment. That section attempted to protect the right of blacks to vote by providing for reduction of representation in the House of a state that interfered with the exercise of that right. The number of representatives of such a state was to be reduced in proportion to the number of inhabitants of voting age whose right to go to the polls was denied or abridged. The reapportionment bill repeated the language of the section, but it was never put into effect because of the difficulty of determining the exact number of persons whose right to vote was being abridged.

The reapportionment act of Feb. 25, 1882, provided for a House of 325 members, with additional members for any new states admitted to the Union. No new apportionment provisions were added. The acts of Feb. 7, 1891, and Jan. 16, 1901, were routine as far as apportionment was concerned. The 1891 measure provided for a House of 356 members, and the 1901 statute increased the number to 386.

Despite the apparent advantages of the Vinton method, certain difficulties began to reveal themselves as the formula was applied. Zechariah Chafee Jr. of the Harvard Law School summarized these problems in an article in the *Harvard Law Review* in 1929. The method, he pointed out, suffered from what he called the "Alabama paradox." Under that aberration, an increase in the total size of the House might be accompanied by an actual loss of a seat by some states, even though there had been no corresponding change in population. This phenomenon

first appeared in tables prepared for Congress in 1881, which gave Alabama eight members in a House of 299 but only seven members in a House of 300. It could even happen that the state which lost a seat was the one state that had expanded in population, while all the others had fewer persons.

Chafee concluded from his study of the Vinton method: "Thus, it is unsatisfactory to fix the ratio of population per Representative before seats are distributed. Either the size of the House comes out haphazard, or, if this be determined in advance, the absurdities of the 'Alabama paradox' vitiate the apportionment. Under present conditions, it is essential to determine the size of the House in advance; the problem thereafter is to distribute the required number of seats among the several states as nearly as possible in proportion to their respective populations so that no state is treated unfairly in comparison with any other state."

Maximum Membership of House

On Aug. 8, 1911, the membership of the House was fixed at 433. Provision was made in the reapportionment act of that date for the addition of one representative each from Arizona and New Mexico, which were expected to become states in the near future. Thus, the size of the House reached 435, where it has remained up to the present with the exception of a brief period (1959-63) when the admission of Alaska and Hawaii raised the total temporarily to 437.

Limiting the size of the House amounted to recognition that the body would soon expand to unmanageable proportions if Congress continued the practice of adding new seats every 10 years, to match population gains without depriving any state of its existing representation. Agreement on a fixed number made the task of reapportionment all the more difficult when the population not only increased but became much more mobile. Population shifts brought Congress up hard against the politically painful necessity of taking seats away from slow-growing states to give the fast-growing states adequate representation.

A new mathematical calculation was adopted for the reapportionment following the census of 1910. Devised by Prof. W. F. Willcox of Cornell University, the new system established a priority list which assigned seats progressively beginning with the first seat above the constitutional minimum of at least one seat per state. When there were 48 states, this method was used to assign the 49th member, the 50th member, and so on, until the agreed upon size of the House was reached. The method was called major fractions and was used after the censuses of 1910, 1930 and 1940. There was no reapportionment in 1920.

1920s Struggle

The results of the 14th decennial census were announced Dec. 17, 1920, just after the short session of the 66th Congress convened. The census of 1920 showed that for the first time in history a majority of Americans were urban residents. Disclosure of this fact came as a profound shock to persons used to emphasizing the nation's rural traditions and the virtues of life on farms and in small towns. Rural legislators immediately mounted an attack on the census results and succeeded in postponing reapportionment legislation for almost a decade.

Thomas Jefferson once wrote: "Those who labor in the

Congressional Apportionment, 1789-1980

Year of Census[1]

	Constitution† (1789)	1790	1800	1810	1820	1830	1840	1850	1860	1870	1880	1890	1900	1910	1930#	1940	1950	1960	1970	1980
Ala.				1*	3	5	7	7	6	8	8	9	9	10	9	9	9	8	7	7
Alaska																	1*	1	1	1
Ariz.														1*	1	2	2	3	4	5
Ark.						1*	1	2	3	4	5	6	7	7	7	7	6	4	4	4
Calif.							2*	2	3	4	6	7	8	11	20	23	30	38	43	45
Colo.										1*	1	2	3	4	4	4	4	4	5	6
Conn.	5	7	7	7	6	6	4	4	4	4	4	4	5	5	6	6	6	6	6	6
Del.	1	1	1	2	1	1	1	1	1	1	1	1	1	1	1	1	1	1	1	1
Fla.							1*	1	1	2	2	2	3	4	5	6	8	12	15	19
Ga.	3	2	4	6	7	9	8	8	7	9	10	11	11	12	10	10	10	10	10	10
Hawaii																	1*	2	2	2
Idaho											1*	1	1	2	2	2	2	2	2	2
Ill.				1*	1	3	7	9	14	19	20	22	25	27	27	26	25	24	24	22
Ind.				1*	3	7	10	11	11	13	13	13	13	13	12	11	11	11	11	10
Iowa							2*	2	6	9	11	11	11	11	9	8	8	7	6	6
Kan.									1	3	7	8	8	8	7	6	6	5	5	5
Ky.		2	6	10	12	13	10	10	9	10	11	11	11	11	9	9	8	7	7	7
La.				1*	3	3	4	4	5	6	6	6	7	8	8	8	8	8	8	8
Maine				7*	7	8	7	6	5	5	4	4	4	4	3	3	3	2	2	2
Md.	6	8	9	9	9	8	6	6	5	6	6	6	6	6	6	6	7	8	8	8
Mass.	8	14	17	13‡	13	12	10	11	10	11	12	13	14	16	15	14	14	12	12	11
Mich.						1*	3	4	6	9	11	12	12	13	17	17	18	19	19	18
Minn.								2*	2	3	5	7	9	10	9	9	9	8	8	8
Miss.				1*	1	2	4	5	5	6	7	7	8	8	7	7	6	5	5	5
Mo.					1	2	5	7	9	13	14	15	16	16	13	13	11	10	10	9
Mont.											1*	1	1	2	2	2	2	2	2	2
Neb.									1*	1	3	6	6	6	5	4	4	3	3	3
Nev.									1*	1	1	1	1	1	1	1	1	1	1	2
N.H.	3	4	5	6	6	5	4	3	3	3	2	2	2	2	2	2	2	2	2	2
N.J.	4	5	6	6	6	6	5	5	5	7	7	8	10	12	14	14	14	15	15	14
N.M.														1*	1	2	2	2	2	3
N.Y.	6	10	17	27	34	40	34	33	31	33	34	34	37	43	45	45	43	41	39	34
N.C.	5	10	12	13	13	13	9	8	7	8	9	9	10	10	11	12	12	11	11	11
N.D.											1*	1	2	3	2	2	2	2	1	1
Ohio			1*	6	14	19	21	21	19	20	21	21	21	22	24	23	23	24	23	21
Okla.													5*	8	9	8	6	6	6	6
Ore.								1*	1	1	1	2	2	3	3	4	4	4	4	5
Pa.	8	13	18	23	26	28	24	25	24	27	28	30	32	36	34	33	30	27	25	23
R.I.	1	2	2	2	2	2	2	2	2	2	2	2	2	3	2	2	2	2	2	2
S.C.	5	6	8	9	9	9	7	6	4	5	7	7	7	7	6	6	6	6	6	6
S.D.											2*	2	2	3	2	2	2	2	2	1
Tenn.		1*	3	6	9	13	11	10	8	10	10	10	10	10	9	10	9	9	8	9
Texas							2*	2	4	6	11	13	16	18	21	21	22	23	24	27
Utah												1*	1	2	2	2	2	2	2	3
Vt.		2	4	6	5	5	4	3	3	3	2	2	2	2	1	1	1	1	1	1
Va.	10	19	22	23	22	21	15	13	11	9	10	10	10	10	9	9	10	10	10	10
Wash.											1*	2	3	5	6	6	7	7	7	8
W.Va.										3	4	4	5	6	6	6	6	5	4	4
Wis.							2*	3	6	8	9	10	11	11	10	10	10	10	9	9
Wyo.											1*	1	1	1	1	1	1	1	1	1
Total	65	106	142	186	213	242	232	237	243	293	332	357	391	435	435	435	437**	435	435	435

[1] Apportionment effective with congressional election two years after census.

† Original apportionment made in Constitution, pending first census.

No apportionment was made in 1920.

* These figures are not based on any census, but indicate the provisional representation accorded newly admitted states by the Congress, pending the next census.

‡ Twenty members were assigned to Massachusetts, but seven of these were credited to Maine when that area became a state.

** Normally 435, but temporarily increased two seats by Congress when Alaska and Hawaii became states.

Source: *Biographical Directory of the American Congress* and Bureau of the Census.

earth are the chosen people of God, if ever He had a chosen people, whose breasts He had made His peculiar deposit for substantial and genuine virtue. . . . The mobs of great cities add just as much to the support of pure government as sores do to the strength of the human body. . . . I think our governments will remain virtuous for many centuries as long as they are chiefly agricultural: and this shall be as long as there shall be vacant lands in any part of America. When they get piled up upon one another in large cities as in Europe, they will become corrupt as in Europe."

As their power waned throughout the latter part of the 19th century and the early part of the 20th, farmers and their spokesmen clung to the Jeffersonian belief that they were somehow more pure and virtuous than the growing number of urban residents. When finally faced with the fact that they were in the minority, they put up a strong rear-guard action to prevent the inevitable shift of congressional districts to the cities.

Rural representatives insisted that, since the 1920 census was taken as of Jan. 1, the farm population had been under counted. In support of this contention, they argued that many farm laborers were seasonally employed in the cities at that time of year. Furthermore, mid-winter road conditions probably had prevented enumerators from visiting many farms, they said; and other farmers were said to have been counted incorrectly because they were absent on winter vacation trips. The change of the census date to Jan. 1 in 1920 had been made to conform to recommendations of the Agriculture Department, which had asserted that the census should be taken early in the year if an accurate statistical picture of farming conditions was desired.

Another point raised by rural legislators was that large numbers of unnaturalized aliens were congregated in Northern cities, with the result that these cities gained at the expense of constituencies made up mostly of citizens of the United States. Rep. Homer Hoch, R-Kan., submitted a table showing that, in a House of 435 representatives, exclusion from the census count of persons not naturalized would have altered the allocation of seats of 16 states. Southern and Western farming states would have retained the number of seats allocated to them in 1911 or would have gained, while Northern industrial states and California would have lost or at least would have gained fewer seats.

A constitutional amendment to exclude all aliens from the enumeration for purposes of reapportionment was proposed during the 70th Congress (1927-29) by Rep. Hoch, Sen. Arthur Capper, R-Kan., and others. During the Senate Commerce Committee's bearings on reapportionment, Sen. Frederick M. Sackett, R-Ky., and Sen. Lawrence D. Tyson, D-Tenn., said they too intended to propose amendments to the same effect. But nothing further came of the proposals.

Reapportionment Bills Opposed

The first bill to reapportion the House according to the 1920 census was drafted by the House Census Committee early in 1921. Proceeding on the theory that no state should have its representation reduced, the committee proposed to increase the total number of representatives from 435 to 483. But the House voted 267-76 to keep its membership at 435 and passed the bill so amended on Jan. 19, 1921. Eleven states would have lost seats and eight would have gained. The bill then was blocked by a Senate committee, where it died when the 66th Congress expired March 4, 1921.

Early in the 67th Congress, the House Census Committee again reported a bill, this time fixing the total membership at 460, an increase of 25. Two states — Maine and Massachusetts — would have lost one representative each and 16 states would have gained. On the floor of the House an attempt to fix the number at the existing 435 failed, and the House voted to send the bill back to committee.

During the 68th Congress (1923-25), the House Census Committee failed to report any reapportionment bill, and midway in the 69th Congress (1925-27) it again looked as if no reapportionment measure would come out of the committee. Accordingly, on April 8, 1926, Rep. Henry E. Barbour, R-Calif., moved that the committee be discharged from further consideration of a bill identical with that passed by the House in 1921 keeping the chamber's membership at 435.

Chairman Bertrand H. Snell, R-N.Y., of the House Rules Committee, representing the Republican leadership of the House, raised a point of order against Barbour's motion. The Speaker of the House, Nicholas Longworth, R-Ohio, pointed out that decisions of earlier Speakers tended to indicate that reapportionment had been considered a matter of "constitutional privilege," and that Rep. Barbour's motion must be held in order if these precedents were followed. But the Speaker said he doubted whether the precedents had been interpreted correctly. He therefore submitted to the House the question of whether the pending motion should be considered privileged. The House sustained the Rules Committee by voting 87-265 not to consider the question privileged.

Intervention by President Coolidge

President Coolidge, who previously had made no reference to reapportionment in his communications to Congress, announced in January 1927 that he favored passage of a new apportionment bill during the short session of the 69th Congress, which would end in less than two months. The House Census Committee refused to act. Its chairman, Rep. E. Hart Fenn, R-Conn., therefore moved in the House on March 2, 1927, to suspend the rules and pass a bill he had introduced authorizing the secretary of commerce to reapportion the House immediately after the 1930 census. The motion was voted down 183-197.

The Fenn bill was rewritten early in the 70th Congress (1927-29) to give Congress itself a chance to act before the proposed reapportionment by the secretary of commerce should go into effect. The bill was submitted to the House, which on May 18, 1928, voted 186-165 to recommit it to the Census Committee. After minor changes, the Fenn bill was again reported to the House and was passed on Jan. 11, 1929. No record vote was taken on passage of the bill, but a motion to return it to the committee was rejected 134-227.

Four days later, the reapportionment bill was reported by the Senate Commerce Committee. Repeated efforts to bring it up for floor action ahead of other bills failed. Its supporters gave up the fight on Feb. 27, 1929 — five days before the end of the session, when it became evident that senators from states slated to lose representation were ready to carry on a filibuster that would have blocked not only reapportionment but all other measures.

Intervention by President Hoover

With the time for the next census rapidly approaching, President Hoover listed provision for the 1930 census and reapportionment as "matters of emergency legislation" that should be acted upon in the special session of the 71st Congress that was convened on April 15, 1929. In response to this urgent request, the Senate June 13 passed, 48-37, a combined census-reapportionment bill that had been approved by voice vote of the House two days earlier.

The 1929 law established a permanent system of reapportioning the 435 House seats following each census. It provided that immediately after the convening of the 71st Congress for its short session in December 1930, the president was to transmit to Congress a statement showing the population of each state together with an apportionment of representatives to each state based on the existing size of the House. Failing enactment of new apportionment legislation, that apportionment would go into effect without further action and would remain in effect for ensuing elections to the House of Representatives until another census had been taken and another reapportionment made.

Because two decades had passed between reapportionments, a greater shift than usual took place following the census of 1930. California's House delegation was almost doubled, rising from 11 to 20. Michigan gained four seats, Texas three, and New Jersey, New York and Ohio two each. Twenty-one states lost a total of 27 seats; Missouri lost three and Georgia, Iowa, Kentucky and Pennsylvania each lost two.

The 1929 act required the president to report the distribution of seats by two methods, major fractions and equal proportions. This was in the nature of a test to see which method yielded the fairer result. However, pending legislation to the contrary, the method of major fractions was to be used.

The two methods gave an identical distribution of seats based on 1930 census figures. However, in 1940 the two methods gave different results: under major fractions, Michigan would have gained a seat lost by Arkansas; under equal proportions, there would have been no change in either state. The automatic reapportionment provisions of the 1929 act went into effect in January 1941. But the House Census Committee moved to reverse the result, favoring the certain Democratic seat in Arkansas over a possible Republican gain if the seat were shifted to Michigan. The Democratic-controlled Congress went along, adopting equal proportions as the method to be used in reapportionment calculations after the 1950 and subsequent censuses, and making this action retroactive to January 1941 in order to save Arkansas its seat.

While politics doubtless played a part in timing of the action taken in 1941, the method of equal proportions had come to be accepted as the best available. It had been worked out by Prof. Edward V. Huntington of Harvard in 1921. At the request of the Speaker of the House, all known methods of apportionment were considered in 1929 by the National Academy of Sciences Committee on Apportionment. The committee expressed its preference for equal proportions.

Method of Equal Proportions

This method involves complicated mathematical calculations. In brief, each of the 50 states is initially assigned the one seat to which every state is entitled by the Constitution. Then "priority numbers" for states to receive second seats, third seats and so on are calculated by dividing the state's population by the square root of n(n-1), where "n" is the number of seats for that state. The prior-

ity numbers are then lined up in order and the seats given to the states with priority numbers until 435 are awarded.

The method is designed to make the *proportional* difference between the average district size in any two states as small as possible. For instance, using 1980 census figures, if New Mexico got three seats and Indiana got 10, as occurred under the method of equal proportions, New Mexico would have an average district size of 433,323, and Indiana would have an average district size of 549,018. That makes Indiana's average 27 percent larger than New Mexico's. On the other hand, if New Mexico got two seats and Indiana got 11, as would have happened if the major fractions method had been used in 1980, New Mexico's average district of 649,984 would be 30 percent larger than Indiana's average of 499,107.

Two respected private statisticians, M. L. Balinski and H. P. Young, have argued that the equal proportions method has "cheated the larger states, and given undue representation to the smaller ones," in violation of the Supreme Court's one-man, one-vote rule. They have advocated a return to the Vinton method of apportionment. Such a bill was introduced in Congress in early 1981, but it received little attention and died at the end of the session.

REDISTRICTING: DRAWING THE LINES

Although the Constitution contained provisions for the apportionment of U.S. House seats among the states, it was silent about how these members should be elected. From the beginning most states divided their territory into geographic districts, permitting only one member of Congress to be elected from each district.

But some states allowed would-be House members to run at large, with voters able to cast as many votes as there were seats to be filled. Still other states created what were known as multi-member districts; in these a single geographic unit would elect two or more members of the House. At various times, some states used combinations of these methods. For example, a state might elect 10 representatives from 10 individual districts and two at large.

In the first few elections to the House, New Hampshire, Pennsylvania, New Jersey and Georgia elected their representatives at large, as did Rhode Island and Delaware, the two states with only a single representative. Districts were used in Massachusetts, New York, Maryland, Virginia and South Carolina. In Connecticut, a preliminary election was held to nominate three times as many persons as the number of representatives to be chosen at large in the subsequent election. In 1840, 22 of the 31 states elected their representatives by districts. New Hampshire, New Jersey, Georgia, Alabama, Mississippi and Missouri, with a combined representation of 33 House seats, elected their representatives at large. Three states, Arkansas, Delaware and Florida, had only one representative each.

Those states that used congressional districts quickly developed what came to be known as the gerrymander. This was the practice of drawing district lines so as to maximize the advantage of a political party or interest group. The name originated from a salamander-shaped congressional district created by the Massachusetts Legislature in 1812 when Elbridge Gerry was governor. *(Box, this page)*

Constant efforts had been made during the early 1800s to lay down national rules, by means of a constitutional amendment, for congressional districting. The first resolution proposing a mandatory division of each state into districts was introduced in Congress in 1800. In 1802 the Legislatures of Vermont and North Carolina adopted resolutions in support of such action. From 1816 to 1826, 22 state resolutions were adopted proposing the election of representatives by districts.

In Congress, Sen. Mahlon Dickerson of New Jersey proposed such an amendment regularly almost every year from 1817 to 1826. It was adopted by the Senate three times, in 1819, 1820 and 1822, but each time it failed to reach a vote in the House.

Acceptance by most states of the principle of local representation put an end to congressional efforts in behalf of a constitutional amendment and led to enactment of a law in 1842 requiring contiguous single-member congressional districts. That law required representatives to be "elected by districts composed of contiguous territory equal in number to the representatives to which said state may be entitled, no one district electing more than one Representative."

When President Tyler signed the bill, he appended to it a memorandum voicing doubt as to the constitutionality of the districting provisions. The memorandum precipitated a minor constitutional crisis. The House, urged on by Rep. John Quincy Adams of Massachusetts, appointed a select committee to consider the action of the president. Chaired by the aging former president, the committee drew up a resolution protesting Tyler's action as "unwarranted by the Constitution and laws of the United States, injurious to the public interest, and of evil example for the future; and this House do hereby solemnly protest against the said act of the President and against its ever being repeated or adduced as a precedent hereafter." The House took no action on the resolution; several attempts to call it up under suspension of the rules failed to receive the necessary two-thirds vote.

Districting Legislation, 1850-1910

The districting provisions of the 1842 act were not repeated in the legislation that followed the census of 1850. But in 1862 an act separate from the reapportionment act revived the provisions of the act of 1842 requiring districts to be composed of contiguous territory.

The 1872 reapportionment act again repeated the districting provisions and went even further by adding that districts should contain "as nearly as practicable an equal number of inhabitants." Similar provisions were included in the acts of 1881 and 1891. In the act of Jan. 16, 1901, the words "compact territory" were added, and the clause then read "contiguous and compact territory and containing as nearly as practicable an equal number of inhabitants." This requirement appeared also in the legislation of Aug. 8, 1911. (The "contiguous and compact" provisions of the act subsequently lapsed and, as of 1982, had not been replaced.)

Several attempts, none of them successful, were made to enforce redistricting provisions. Despite the districting requirements of the act of June 25, 1842, New Hampshire, Georgia, Mississippi and Missouri elected their represen-

Origins of the Gerrymander

The practice of "gerrymandering" — the excessive manipulation of the shape of a legislative district to benefit a certain incumbent or party — is probably as old as the republic, but the name originated in 1812.

In that year the Massachusetts Legislature carved out of Essex County a district which historian John Fiske said had a "dragonlike contour." When the painter Gilbert Stuart saw the misshapen district, he penciled in a head, wings and claws and exclaimed: "That will do for a salamander!" — to which editor Benjamin Russell replied: "Better say a Gerrymander" — after Elbridge Gerry, then governor of Massachusetts.

tatives at large that autumn. When the House elected at that time convened for its first session on Dec. 4, 1843, objection was made to seating the representatives of the four states. The matter was referred to the Committee on Elections. The majority report of the committee, submitted by its chairman, Rep. Stephen A. Douglas, D-Ill., asserted that the act of 1842 was not binding upon the states and that the representatives in question were entitled to their seats. An amendment to the majority report deleted all reference to the apportionment law. A minority report by Rep. Garrett David, Whig-Ky., contended that the members had not been elected according to the Constitution and the laws and were not entitled to their seats.

The matter was debated in the House Feb. 6-14, 1844. With the Democratic Party holding a majority of more than 60, and with 18 of the 21 challenged members being Democrats, the House decided to seat the members. However, by 1848 all four states had come around to electing their representatives by districts.

The next challenge to a member of the House based on federal districting laws occurred in 1901. It was charged that the Kentucky redistricting law then in force was contrary to the redistricting provisions of the federal reapportionment law of Jan. 16, 1901. The specific challenge was to Rep. George G. Gilbert, D, of the eighth Kentucky district. The committee assigned to investigate the matter turned aside the challenge, asserting that the federal act was not binding on the states. The reasons given were practical and political:

"Your committee are therefore of opinion that a proper construction of the Constitution does not warrant the conclusion that by that instrument Congress is clothed with power to determine the boundaries of Congressional districts, or to revise the acts of a State Legislature in fixing such boundaries; and your committee is further of opinion that even if such power is to be implied from the language of the Constitution, it would be in the last degree unwise and intolerable that it should exercise it. To do so would be to put into the hands of Congress the ability to disfranchise, in effect, a large body of the electors. It would give Congress the power to apply to all the States, in favor of one party, a general system of gerrymandering. It is true that the same method is to a large degree resorted to by the several states, but the division of political power is so general and diverse that notwithstanding the inherent vice of the system of gerrymandering, some kind of equality of distribution results."

In 1908 the Virginia Legislature transferred Floyd County from the fifth to the sixth congressional district. As a result, the population of the fifth district was reduced from 175,579 to 160,191 and that of the sixth district was increased from 181,571 to 196,959. The average for the state was 185,418.

When the newly elected representative from the fifth district, Edward W. Saunders, D, was challenged by his opponent in the election, the majority of the congressional investigating committee upheld the challenge. They concluded that the Virginia law of 1908 was null and void because it did not conform with the federal law of Jan. 16, 1901, or with the constitution of Virginia, and that the district should be regarded as including the counties that were a part of it before enactment of the 1908 state legislation. In that case Saunders' opponent would have had a majority of the votes, so the committee recommended that he be seated. Thus, for the first time, it looked as though the districting legislation would be enforced, but the House did not take action on the committee's report and Saunders' challenger was not seated.

Court Action on Redistricting

After the long and desultory battle over reapportionment in the 1920s, those who were unhappy over the inaction of Congress and the state legislatures began taking their cases to court. At first, they had no luck. But as the population disparity in both federal and state legislative districts grew and the Supreme Court began to show a tendency to intervene, plaintiffs were more successful.

Finally, in a series of decisions beginning with *Baker v.* *Carr* in 1962 (369 U.S. 186) the court intervened massively in the redistricting process, ordering that congressional districts as well as state and local legislative districts be drawn so that their populations would be as nearly equal as possible.

Supreme Court's 1932 Decision

That ruling essentially reversed the direction the court had taken in 1932. *Wood v. Broom* (287 U.S. 1), was a case challenging the constitutionality of a Mississippi redistricting law. The question was whether the 1911 federal redistricting act, which required that districts be separate, compact, contiguous and equally populated and which had been neither specifically repealed not reaffirmed in the 1929 reapportionment act, was still in effect.

Speaking for the court, Chief Justice Charles Evans Hughes ruled that the 1911 act had, in effect, expired with the approval of the 1929 apportionment act and that the standards of the 1911 act therefore were no longer applicable. The court reversed the decision of a lower federal court, which had permanently enjoined elections under the new Mississippi redistricting act because it violated the standards of the 1911 act.

The fact that the court upheld a state law that failed to provide for districts of equal population was almost less important than the minority opinion that the court should not have heard the case. Four members of the Supreme Court — Justices Louis D. Brandeis, Harlan F. Stone, Owen J. Roberts and Benjamin N. Cardozo — while concurring in the majority opinion, said they would have dismissed the Wood suit for "want of equity." The "want-of-equity" phrase in this context suggested a policy of judicial self-limitation with respect to the entire question of judicial involvement in essentially "political" questions.

'Political Thicket'

Not until 1946, in *Colegrove v. Green* (328 U.S. 549, 1946), did the court again rule in a significant case dealing with congressional redistricting. The case was brought by Kenneth Colegrove, a political science professor at Northwestern University, who alleged that Illinois' congressional districts — varying in size between 112,116 and 914,053 in population — were so unequal that they violated the 14th Amendment's guarantee of equal protection of the laws. A seven-man Supreme Court divided 4-3 in dismissing the suit.

Justice Felix Frankfurter gave the opinion of the court, speaking for himself and Justices Stanley F. Reed and Harold H. Burton. Frankfurter's opinion cited *Wood v. Broom* to indicate that Congress had deliberately removed the standard set by the 1911 act. "We also agree," he said, "with the four Justices (Brandeis, Stone, Roberts and Cardozo) who were of the opinion that the bill in *Wood v. Broom* should be 'dismissed for want of equity.'" The issue, Frankfurter said, was "of a peculiarly political nature and therefore not meant for judicial interpretation.... The short of it is that the Constitution has conferred upon Congress exclusive authority to secure fair representation by the states in the popular House and has left to that House determination whether states have fulfilled their responsibility. If Congress failed in exercising its powers, whereby standards of fairness are offended, the remedy lies ultimately with the people.... To sustain this action would cut very deep into the very being of Congress. Courts ought not to enter this political thicket. The remedy for unfair-

Malapportionment and Gerrymandering

The prevalence of malapportionment and gerrymandering in the creation of U.S. congressional districts was, to many observers, one of the chief evils in the American system before the "one-man, one-vote" ruling by the Supreme Court in 1964. On Feb. 17 of that year, the court, in the case of *Wesberry v. Sanders*, declared that "as nearly as is practicable, one man's vote in a congressional election is to be worth as much as another's."

Malapportionment

Malapportionment occurred when districts of grossly unequal populations were created — either through actions of state legislatures in establishing new districts or, as was the more frequent practice in America, simply by failing to redistrict despite major population shifts.

Within a single state, populations in some congressional districts varied by as much as eight to one. Generally, growing urban areas were under-represented, to the advantage of rural areas.

Examples of great disparity in congressional district sizes in modern U.S. history included: New York (1930), 776,425 residents in the largest district and 90,671 in the smallest district; Ohio (1946), 698,650 and 163,561; Illinois (1946), 914,053 and 112,116; Arkansas (1946), 423,152 and 177,476; Texas (1962), 951,527 and 216,371; Michigan (1962), 802,994 and 177,431; Maryland (1962), 711,045 and 243,570; South Dakota (1962), 497,669 and 182,845.

The decennial census and ensuing reapportionment of House seats eventually forced redistricting in most states, although some resorted to the expedient of electing members at large (this occurred in Texas, Hawaii, Ohio, Michigan and Maryland in 1962) rather than face redrawing district lines.

A 1967 law (PL 90-196) banned at-large elections in states with more than one representative. However, that law has been interpreted variously by the states. And where divided states' legislatures have been unable to agree on a redistricting plan, the courts have had to impose their own plan.

In their 1981 book, *Congress and Its Members*, political scientists Roger H. Davidson and Walter J. Oleszek noted:

"Today, House districts within states start out nearly equal in population. (Sizes vary somewhat because of apportionment, and of course inequalities build during the 10 years.) The goal of population equality, however, has been won at the expense of other goals. Parity in numbers of residents makes it harder to respect political divisions such as county lines. It also makes it hard to follow economic, social, or geographic boundaries. The congressional district, therefore, tends to be an artificial creation with little relationship to real communities of interest — economic or geographic or political. This heightens the congressional district's isolation, forcing candidates to forge their own unique groups and alliances. It also aids incumbents, who have ways of reaching voters without relying on commercial communications media."

Gerrymandering

Gerrymandering was the name given to excessive manipulation of the shape of legislative districts to benefit a particular politician or political party. The gerrymander was named after Democrat Elbridge Gerry, the governor of Massachusetts in 1812 when the Legislature created a peculiar salamander-shaped district to benefit his party.

Unlike malapportionment, gerrymandering has not been prohibited by law. It still is used today by both political parties. In 1961 Republican legislators in New York created one gerrymander-like creature stretching across the greater part of upstate New York, his head hanging over Albany in the east and his tail reaching for Rochester in the west. Such salamander, tadpole and fishlike creatures sprang to life on the maps of New York City's boroughs. In North Carolina after the 1960 Census, Democratic redistricters formed an almost perfect gerrymander shape to throw the state's sole Republican representative in with a strong Democratic opponent.

After the 1980 Census, Democrats in control of California's Legislature drew a district in the San Francisco Bay area in which two segments were linked only by a body of water. New Jersey's map was a gerrymander that boasted some of the most bizarrely shaped districts in the nation. The Supreme Court threw those districts out in 1983 but on the grounds of population inequality, not because they were gerrymandered.

Davidson and Oleszek cite two kinds of gerrymandering: "packing" and "cracking." In the first case, a district line is drawn so as to encompass as many of one party's voters as possible, thus making it "safe." "Cracking" entails diluting one party's strength by dispersing it among two or more districts.

The intent of practically every gerrymander is political — to create a maximum number of districts which would elect the party candidates or types of candidates favored by the controlling group in the state legislature that did the redistricting, thus increasing, or maintaining, the political power of the already politically dominant group.

"The long-range effects of gerrymanders are not easily measured," concluded Davidson and Oleszek. "Marginal or competitive districts (those where the winner gains less than 55 percent of the votes) are tougher for a party to capture and hold, but they have the advantage of yielding legislative seats with a modest number of voters (that is, a minimal winning coalition). Safe districts, while naturally preferred by the incumbents, can waste the majority party's votes by furnishing outsized victories."

ness in districting is to secure state legislatures that will apportion properly, or to invoke the ample powers of Congress." Frankfurter said, in addition, that the court could not affirmatively remap congressional districts and that elections at large would be politically undesirable.

Justice Hugo L. Black, who was joined in a dissenting opinion by Justices William O. Douglas and Frank Murphy, expressed the belief that the district court had jurisdiction under a section of the U.S. Code giving district courts the right to redress deprivations of constitutional rights occurring through action of the states. Black's opinion also rested on a previous case in which the court had indicated that federal constitutional questions, unless "frivolous," fall under the jurisdiction of the federal courts. Black asserted that the appellants had standing to sue, that the population disparities did violate the equal protection clause of the 14th Amendment and that relief should be granted.

With the court split 3-3 on whether the judiciary had or should exercise jurisdiction, the deciding opinion in *Colegrove v. Green* was that of Justice Wiley B. Rutledge. On the question of justiciability, Rutledge agreed with Black, Douglas and Murphy that the issue could be considered by the federal courts. Thus a majority of the court participating in the *Colegrove* case felt that congressional redistricting cases were justiciable.

On the other hand, on the question of granting relief in this specific instance, Rutledge agreed with Frankfurter, Reed and Burton that the case should be dismissed. He pointed out that four of the nine justices in *Wood v. Broom* had felt that dismissal should be for want of equity. Rutledge saw a "want-of-equity" situation in *Colegrove v. Green* as well. "I think the gravity of the constitutional questions raised [are] so great, together with the possibility of collision [with the political departments of the government], that the admonition [against avoidable constitutional decision] is appropriate to be followed here," Rutledge said. Jurisdiction, he thought, should be exercised "only in the most compelling circumstances." He thought that "the shortness of time remaining [before the forthcoming election] makes it doubtful whether action could or would be taken in time to secure for petitioners the effective relief they seek." Rutledge warned that congressional elections at large would deprive citizens of representation by districts, "which the prevailing policy of Congress demands." In the case of at-large elections, he warned, "the cure sought may be worse than the disease." For all these reasons he concluded that the case was "one in which the Court may properly, and should, decline to exercise its jurisdiction."

Changing Views

In the ensuing years, law professors, political scientists and other commentators expressed growing criticism of the *Colegrove* doctrine and growing impatience with the Supreme Court's position. At the same time, the membership of the court was changing, and the new members were more inclined toward judicial action on redistricting.

In the 1950s, the court decided two cases that laid some groundwork for its subsequent reapportionment decisions. The first was *Brown v. Board of Education* (347 U.S. 483, 1954), the historic school desegregation case, in which the court decided that an individual citizen could assert a right to equal protection of the laws under the 14th Amendment, contrary to the "separate but equal" doctrine

of public facilities for white and black citizens. Six years later, in *Gomillion v. Lightfoot* (364 U.S. 339, 1960), the court held that the Alabama Legislature could not draw the city limits of Tuskegee so as to exclude nearly every black vote. In his opinion, Justice Frankfurter drew a clear line between redistricting challenges based on the 14th Amendment, such as *Colgrove*, and 15th Amendment challenges to discriminatory redistricting as in *Gomillion*. But Justice Charles E. Whittaker said that the equal protection clause was the proper constitutional basis for the decision. One commentator later remarked that *Gomillion* amounted to a "dragon" in the "political thicket" of *Colegrove*.

By 1962 only three members of the *Colegrove* court remained: Justices Black and Douglas, dissenters in that case, and Justice Frankfurter, aging spokesman for restraint in the exercise of judicial power.

By then it was clear that malapportionment within the states could no longer be ignored. By 1960 there was not a single legislative body in a single state in which there was not at least a 2-to-1 population disparity between the most and the least heavily populated districts. For example, the disparity was 242-1 in the Connecticut House, 223-1 in the Nevada Senate, 141-1 in the Rhode Island Senate and 9-1 in the Georgia Senate. Studies of the effective vote of large and small counties in state legislatures between 1910 and 1960 showed that the effective vote of the large counties had slipped while their percentage of the national population had more than doubled. The most lightly populated counties, on the other hand, advanced from a position of slight over-representation to one of extreme over-representation, holding almost twice as many seats as they would be entitled to by population size alone. Predictably, the rural-dominated state legislatures resisted every move toward reapportioning districts to reflect new population patterns.

By no means as gross, but still substantial, was population imbalance among congressional districts. In Texas, the census of 1960 showed the most heavily populated district had four times as many inhabitants as the most lightly populated. Arizona, Maryland and Ohio each had at least one district with three times as many inhabitants as the least populated. In a majority of cases, it was rural areas that benefited from the population imbalance in congressional districts. As a result of the postwar population movement out of central cities to the surrounding areas, the suburbs were the most under-represented.

Baker v. Carr

It was against this background that a group of Tennessee city dwellers successfully broke the longstanding precedent against federal court involvement in legislative apportionment problems. For more than half a century, since 1901, the Tennessee Legislature had refused to reapportion itself, even though a decennial reapportionment based on population was specifically required by the state's constitution. In the meantime, Tennessee's population had grown and shifted dramatically to urban areas. By 1960 the House legislative districts ranged from 3,454 to 36,031 in population, while the Senate districts ranged from 39,727 to 108,094. Appeals by urban residents to the rural-controlled Tennessee Legislatures proved fruitless. A suit brought in the state courts to force reapportionment was rejected on the grounds that the courts should stay out of legislative matters.

The urban interests then appealed to the federal courts, stating that they had no redress: the Legislature had refused to act for more than half a century; the state courts had refused to intervene; Tennessee had no referendum or initiative laws. The city dwellers charged that there was "a debasement of their votes by virtue of the incorrect, obsolete and unconstitutional apportionment" to such an extent that they were being deprived of their right to "equal protection of the laws" under the 14th Amendment. (The 14th Amendment reads, in part: "No state shall ... deny to any person within its jurisdiction the equal protection of the laws.")

The Supreme Court on March 26, 1962, handed down its historic decision in *Baker v. Carr,* ruling in favor of the Tennessee city dwellers by a 6-2 margin. In the majority opinion, Justice William J. Brennan Jr. emphasized that the federal judiciary had the power to review the apportionment of state legislatures under the 14th Amendment's equal protection clause. "The mere fact that a suit seeks protection as a political right," Brennan wrote, "does not mean that it presents a political question" that the courts should avoid.

In a vigorous dissent, Justice Frankfurter said the majority decision constituted "a massive repudiation of the experience of our whole past" and was an assertion of "destructively novel judicial power." He contended that the lack of any clear basis for relief "catapults the lower courts" into a "mathematical quagmire." Frankfurter insisted that "there is not under our Constitution a judicial remedy for every political mischief." Appeal for relief, he maintained, should not be made in the courts, but rather "to an informed civically militant electorate."

The court had abandoned the view that malapportionment questions were outside its competence. But it stopped there and in *Baker v. Carr* did not address the merits of the not involve congressional districts.

Gray v. Sanders

The "one person, one vote" rule was first set out by the court almost exactly one year after its decision in *Baker v. Carr.* But the case in which the announcement came did not involve congressional districts.

In the ruling in the case of *Gray v. Sanders,* the court found that Georgia's county-unit primary system for electing state officials — a system which weighted votes to give advantage to rural districts in statewide primary elections — denied voters the equal protection of the laws.

All votes in a statewide election must have equal weight, held the court: "How then can one person be given twice or 10 times the voting power of another person in a statewide election merely because he lives in a rural area or because he lives in the smallest rural county? Once the geographical unit for which a representative is to be chosen is designated, all who participate in the election are to have an equal vote — whatever their race, whatever their sex, whatever their occupation, whatever their income, and wherever their home may be in that geographical unit. This is required by the Equal Protection Clause of the Fourteenth Amendment. The concept of 'we the people' under the Constitution visualizes no preferred class of voters but equality among those who meet the basic qualification. The idea that every voter is equal to every other voter in his State, when he casts his ballot in favor of one of several competing candidates, underlies many of our decisions. ... The conception of political equality from the Declaration of Independence to Lincoln's Gettysburg Address, to the Fifteenth, Seventeenth, and Nineteenth Amendments can mean only one thing — one person, one vote."

The Rule Applied

The court's rulings in *Baker* and *Gray* concerned the equal weighting and counting of votes cast in state elections. In 1964, deciding the case of *Wesberry v. Sanders,* the court applied the "one person, one vote" principle to congressional districts and set equality as the standard for congressional redistricting.

Shortly after the *Baker* decision was handed down, James P. Wesberry Jr., an Atlanta resident and a member of the Georgia Senate, filed suit in federal court in Atlanta claiming that gross disparity in the population of Georgia's congressional districts violated 14th Amendment rights of equal protection of the laws. At the time, Georgia districts ranged in population from 272,154 in the rural 9th District in the northeastern part of the state to 823,860 in the 5th District in Atlanta and its suburbs. District lines had not been changed since 1931. The state's number of House seats remained the same in the interim, but Atlanta's district population — already high in 1931 compared with the others — had more than doubled in 30 years, making a 5th District vote worth about one-third that of a vote in the 9th.

On June 20, 1962, the three-judge federal court divided 2-1 in dismissing Wesberry's suit. The majority reasoned that the precedent of *Colegrove* still controlled in congressional district cases. The judges cautioned against federal judicial interference with Congress and against "depriving others of the right to vote" if the suit should result in at-large elections. They suggested that the Georgia Legislature (under court order to reapportion itself) or the U.S. Congress might better provide relief. Wesberry then appealed to the Supreme Court, which heard arguments in the case in November 1963.

On Feb. 17, 1964, the Supreme Court ruled in the case of *Wesberry v. Sanders* (376 U.S. 1) that congressional districts must be substantially equal in population. The court, which upheld Wesberry's challenge by a 6-3 decision, based its ruling on the history and wording of Article I, Section 2, of the Constitution providing that representatives shall be apportioned among the states according to their respective numbers and be chosen by the people of the several states. This language, the court stated, meant that "as nearly as is practicable, one man's vote in a congressional election is to be worth as much as another's."

The majority opinion, written by Justice Black and supported by Chief Justice Earl Warren and Justices Brennan, Douglas, Arthur J. Goldberg and Byron R. White, said that, "While it may not be possible to draw congressional districts with mathematical precision, that is no excuse for ignoring our Constitution's plain objective of making equal representation for equal numbers of people the fundamental goal for the House of Representatives."

In a strongly worded dissent, Justice John M. Harlan asserted that the Constitution did not establish population as the only criterion of congressional districting and that the subject was left by the Constitution to the discretion of the states, subject only to the supervisory power of Congress. "The constitutional right which the court creates is manufactured out of whole cloth," Harlan concluded.

The *Wesberry* opinion established no precise standards for districting beyond declaring that districts must be as nearly equal in population "as is practicable." In his dissent, Harlan suggested that a disparity of more than 100,000 between a state's largest and smallest districts would "presumably" violate the equality standard enunciated by the majority. On that basis, Harlan estimated, the

The Voting Rights Act

There is one form of gerrymandering that is expressly forbidden by law: redistricting for the purpose of racial discrimination. The Voting Rights Act of 1965, extended in 1970, 1975 and 1982, banned redistricting plans that diluted the voting strength of black communities. Other minorities, including Hispanics, Asian-Americans, American Indians and native Alaskans subsequently were brought under the protection of the law.

The law originally was aimed at those Southern states where blacks had long been targets of discrimination. At the time the original law was passed, racial redistricting was not a great problem since black voting strength was minimal. However, with the enhancement of registration and voting rights for blacks, lawmakers feared that affected states would, through gerrymandering, divide black communities among several congressional districts and lower the chances of electing black representatives. That concern resulted in Section Five, the pre-clearance provisions of the act under which nine states and parts of 13 others must receive Justice Department approval of their congressional redistricting plans.

The Voting Rights Act is widely considered the most effective civil rights measure ever enacted. The voter registration provisions have been the most successful. Black voter registration in Mississippi increased from 6.7 percent in 1964 to 67.4 percent in 1976. Black representation in state legislatures, which also come under the purview of the Voting Rights Act, increased substantially. But black congressional representation has not expanded as greatly. After the 1964 elections the nine states that now must clear entire state plans had 74 seats and no black congressmen. In 1982 they had 79 seats, and just one black representative.

constitutional standards to congressional districting.

In 1967 the court hinted at the strict stance it would adopt two years later. With two unsigned opinions, the court sent back to Indiana and Missouri for revision those two states' congressional redistricting plans because they allowed variations of as much as 20 percent from the average district population.

Two years later, Missouri's revised plan returned to the court for full review. With its decision in the case of *Kirkpatrick v. Preisler* (385 U.S. 450), the court by a 6-3 vote rejected the plan. It was unacceptable, held the majority, because it allowed a variation of as much as 3.1 percent from perfectly equal population districts.

The court thus made clear its strict application of "one person, one vote" to congressional redistricting. Minor deviations from the strict equal-population principle were permissible only when the state provided substantial evidence that the variation was unavoidable.

Writing for the court, Justice Brennan declared that there was no "fixed numerical or percentage population variance small enough to be considered *de minimis* and to satisfy without question the 'as nearly as practicable' standard." "Equal representation for equal numbers of people is a principle designed to prevent debasement of voting power and diminution of access to elected Representatives. Toleration of even small deviations detracts from these purposes," Brennan wrote.

The only permissible variances in population, the court ruled, were those that were unavoidable despite the effort to achieve absolute equality or those that could be legally justified. The variances in Missouri could have been avoided, the court said.

None of Missouri's arguments for the plan qualified as "legally acceptable" justifications. The court rejected the argument that population variance was necessary to allow representation of distinct interest groups. It held acceptance of such variances in order to produce districts with specific interests as "antithetical" to the basic purpose of equal representation.

Justice Byron R. White dissented from the majority opinion, which he characterized as "an unduly rigid and unwarranted application of the Equal Protection Clause which will unnecessarily involve the courts in the abrasive task of drawing district lines." White added that some "acceptably small" population variance could be established. He indicated that considerations of existing political boundaries and geographical compactness could justify to him some variation from "absolute equality" of population.

Justice Harlan, joined by Justice Potter Stewart, objected that "whatever room remained under this Court's prior decisions for the free play of the political process in matters of reapportionment is now all but eliminated by today's Draconian judgments."

districts of 37 states with 398 representatives would be unconstitutional, "leaving a constitutional House of 37 members now sitting."

Neither did the court's decision make any reference to gerrymandering, since it discussed only the population, not the shape of districts. In a separate districting opinion handed down the same day as *Wesberry*, the court dismissed a challenge to congressional districts in New York City, which had been brought by voters who charged that Manhattan's 17th "silk-stocking" District had been gerrymandered to exclude blacks and Puerto Rican citizens.

Strict Equality

Five years elapsed between the court's admonition in *Wesberry v. Sanders* and the court's next application of

Practical Results

As a result of the court decisions of the 1960s, nearly every state was forced to redraw its congressional district lines — sometimes more than once. By the end of the decade, 39 of the 45 states with more than one representative had made the necessary adjustments.

However, the effect of the "one-person, one-vote" standard on congressional districts did not bring about immediate equality in districts in the years 1964-70. Most of the new districts were far from equal in population, because the only official population figures came from the 1960 census. Massive population shifts during the decade rendered most post-*Wesberry* efforts to achieve equality useless.

But following redistricting in 1971-72, based on the 1970 census, the result achieved was that House members elected in November 1972 to the 93rd Congress represented districts that differed only slightly in population from the state average. In 285 of the 435 districts, the district's variance was less than 1 percent from the state average district population.

By contrast, only nine of the districts in the 88th Congress (elected in 1962) deviated less than 1 percent from the state average; 81 were between 1 and 5 percent; 87 from 5 to 10 percent; and in 236 districts, the deviation was 10 percent or greater. Twenty-two House members were elected at large.

The Supreme Court made only one major ruling concerning congressional districts during the 1970s. On June 18, 1973, the court declared the Texas congressional districts, as redrawn in 1971, unconstitutional because of excessive population variance among districts. The variance between the largest and smallest districts was 4.9872 percent. The court returned the case to a three-judge federal panel, which adopted a new congressional district plan, effective Oct. 17, 1973.

Precise Equality

Almost exactly 10 years later, on June 22, 1983, the Supreme Court handed down another redistricting decision with sweeping implications. In a 5-4 decision, the court ruled in *Karcher v. Daggett* that states must adhere as closely as possible to the "one person, one vote" standard and bear the burden of proving that deviations from precise population equality were made in pursuit of a legitimate goal. The decision overturned New Jersey's congressional district map because the variation between the most populated district and the least populated district was 0.69 percent.

Brennan, who wrote the court opinion in *Baker* and *Kirkpatrick*, also wrote the opinion in *Karcher*, contending that population differences between districts "could have been avoided or significantly reduced with a good-faith effort to achieve population equality."

"Adopting any standard other than population equality, using the best census data available, would subtly erode the Constitution's ideal of equal representation," Brennan wrote. "If state legislators knew that a certain *de minimis* level of population differences were acceptable, they would doubtless strive to achieve that level rather than equality. Furthermore, choosing a different standard would import a high degree of arbitrariness into the process of reviewing reapportionment plans. In this case, appellants argue that a maximum deviation of approximately 0.7 percent should be considered *de minimis*. If we accept that argument, how are we to regard deviations of 0.8 percent, 0.95 percent, 1.0 percent or 1.1 percent? ... To accept the legitimacy of unjustified, though small population deviations in this case would mean to reject the basic premise of *Kirkpatrick* and *Wesberry*."

Brennan said that "any number of consistently applied legislative policies might justify" some population variation. These included "making districts compact, respecting municipal boundaries, preserving the cores of prior districts, and avoiding contests between incumbent Represen-

tatives." However, he cautioned, the state must show "with some specificity that a particular objective required the specific deviations in its plan, rather than simply relying on general assertions."

In his dissent Justice White criticized the majority for its "unreasonable insistence on an unattainable perfection in the equalizing of congressional districts." He warned that the decision would invite "further litigation of virtually every congressional redistricting plan in the nation."

The court did not address the underlying political issue in the New Jersey case, which was that its map had been drawn to serve Democratic interests. As a partisan gerrymander, the map had few peers, boasting some of the most oddly-shaped districts in the country. One constituency, known as "the fishhook" by its detractors, twisted through central New Jersey's industrial landscape, picking up Democratic voters along the way. Another stretched from the suburbs of New York to the fringes of Trenton.

In separate dissents Justices Lewis F. Powell Jr. and John Paul Stevens broadly hinted that they were willing to hear constitutional challenges to instances of partisan gerrymandering. "A legislator cannot represent his constitutents properly — nor can voters from a fragmented district exercise the ballot intelligently — when a voting district is nothing more than an artificial unit divorced from, and indeed often in conflict with, the various communities established in the State," wrote Powell.

Congress and Redistricting

Several attempts were made by Congress in the post-war period to enact new legislation on redistricting. Only one of these efforts was successful — enactment of a measure barring at-large elections in states with more than one representative.

On Jan. 9, 1951, President Truman, upon presentation of the official state population figures of the 1950 census, asked for changes in existing law to tighten federal control of state redistricting. Specifically, he asked for a ban on gerrymandering, an end to at-large seats in states having more than one representative and a sharp reduction in the huge differences in size among congressional districts within most states.

On behalf of the administration, House Judiciary Committee Chairman Emanuel Celler, D-N.Y., introduced a bill to require compact and contiguous congressional districts that would not vary by more than 15 percent between districts within a state. The bill also eliminated at-large seats and made redistricting mandatory every 10 years in accordance with population changes. But the House Judiciary Committee took no action on the proposals.

Rep. Celler regularly introduced his bill throughout the 1950s and early 1960s, but it made no headway until the Supreme Court handed down the *Wesberry* decision in 1964. On June 24, 1964, a Celler bill was approved by a House Judiciary subcommittee. But the full committee did not act on the bill before adjournment of Congress.

On March 16, 1965, the House finally passed a redistricting bill. It established 15 percent as the maximum percentage by which a congressional district's population might deviate from the average size of the state's districts; prohibited at-large elections for any state with more than one House seat; required that districts be composed of "contiguous territory in as compact form as practicable," and forbade more than one redistricting of a state between decennial censuses. A major reason for House approval of Celler's bill appeared to be a desire to gain protection from court imposition of even more rigid criteria. But the measure encountered difficulties in the Senate Judiciary Committee. After considerable wrangling over its provisions, the committee voted to report the bill without precise agreement on its wording. No report was ever filed by the committee.

In 1967 a redistricting bill was passed by both the Senate and the House, but not in the same form. And the bill had a different purpose from that of previous bills dealing with the subject. Instead of trying to establish standards of fairness in drawing district lines, the chief purpose in 1967 was to prevent the courts from ordering redistricting of House seats or from ordering any state to hold elections at large — a procedure that many incumbent representatives feared — until after the House had been reapportioned on the basis of the 1970 census.

A combination of liberal Democrats and Republicans in the Senate managed to defeat the conference report Nov. 8, 1967, by a vote of 22-55. Liberals favored court action, which they believed would eliminate many conservative rural districts, while Republicans felt that redistricted areas, especially in the growing suburbs, would elect more Republicans than Democrats.

To avoid at-large elections, the Senate added a rider to a House-passed private bill. Under the rider, at-large elections of U.S. representatives were banned in all states entitled to more than one representative, with the exceptions of New Mexico and Hawaii. Those states had a tradition of electing their two representatives at large. Both of them, however, soon passed districting laws — New Mexico for the 1968 elections and Hawaii for 1970.

In 1971 Celler introduced a new version of his proposed redistricting legislation. Although the House Judiciary Committee reported the measure favorably, no further action was taken on the bill, and it died at the end of the 92nd Congress.

After the 1960 census, an attempt had been made to increase the size of the House to avoid some of the losses of seats that would otherwise be suffered by several states. By a vote of 12-14, the House Judiciary Committee on Sept. 9, 1961, rejected a motion to recommend enlarging the House to 453 seats. And by a vote of 14-15, the same committee rejected a bill reported by a subcommittee that would have increased the permanent size of the House to 438.

House Membership in the 95th Congress

ALABAMA
1. Jack Edwards (R)
2. William L. Dickinson (R)
3. Bill Nichols (D)
4. Tom Bevill (D)
5. Ronnie G. Flippo (D)*
6. John Buchanan (R)
7. Walter Flowers (D)

ALASKA
AL Donald E. Young (R)

ARIZONA
1. John J. Rhodes (R)
2. Morris K. Udall (D)
3. Bob Stump (D)*
4. Eldon D. Rudd (R)*

ARKANSAS
1. Bill Alexander (D)
2. Jim Guy Tucker (D)*
3. John Paul Hammerschmidt (R)
4. Ray Thornton (D)

CALIFORNIA
1. Harold T. Johnson (D)
2. Don H. Clausen (R)
3. John E. Moss (D)
4. Robert L. Leggett (D)
5. John L. Burton (D)
6. Phillip Burton (D)
7. George Miller (D)
8. Ronald V. Dellums (D)
9. Fortney H. (Pete) Stark (D)
10. Don Edwards (D)
11. Leo J. Ryan (D)
12. Paul N. McCloskey Jr. (R)
13. Norman Y. Mineta (D)
14. John J. McFall (D)
15. B. F. Sisk (D)
16. Leon E. Panetta (D)*
17. John Krebs (D)
18. William M. Ketchum (R)
19. Robert J. Lagomarsino (R)
20. Barry M. Goldwater Jr. (R)
21. James C. Corman (D)
22. Carlos J. Moorhead (R)
23. Anthony C. Beilenson (D)*
24. Henry A. Waxman (D)
25. Edward R. Roybal (D)
26. John H. Rousselot (R)
27. Robert K. Dornan (R)*
28. Yvonne Brathwaite Burke (D)
29. Augustus F. Hawkins (D)
30. George E. Danielson (D)
31. Charles H. Wilson (D)
32. Glenn M. Anderson (D)
33. Del Clawson (R)
34. Mark W. Hannaford (D)
35. Jim Lloyd (D)
36. George E. Brown Jr. (D)
37. Shirley N. Pettis (R)
38. Jerry M. Patterson (D)
39. Charles E. Wiggins (R)
40. Robert E. Badham (R)*
41. Bob Wilson (R)
42. Lionel Van Deerlin (D)
43. Clair W. Burgener (R)

House Lineup

Democrats 292   **Republicans 143**

Freshman Democrats - 47   Freshman Republicans - 20
*Freshman Representative   #Former Representative

COLORADO
1. Patricia Schroeder (D)
2. Timothy E. Wirth (D)
3. Frank E. Evans (D)
4. James P. Johnson (R)
5. William L. Armstrong (R)

CONNECTICUT
1. William R. Cotter (D)
2. Christopher J. Dodd (D)
3. Robert N. Giaimo (D)
4. Stewart B. McKinney (R)
5. Ronald A. Sarasin (R)
6. Toby Moffett (D)

DELAWARE
AL Thomas B. Evans Jr. (R)*

FLORIDA
1. Robert L. F. Sikes (D)
2. Don Fuqua (D)
3. Charles E. Bennett (D)
4. Bill Chappell Jr. (D)
5. Richard Kelly (R)
6. C. W. Bill Young (R)
7. Sam Gibbons (D)
8. Andrew P. Ireland (D)*
9. Louis Frey Jr. (R)
10. L. A. (Skip) Bafalis (R)
11. Paul G. Rogers (D)
12. J. Herbert Burke (R)
13. William Lehman (D)
14. Claude Pepper (D)
15. Dante B. Fascell (D)

GEORGIA
1. Ronald B. (Bo) Ginn (D)
2. Dawson Mathis (D)
3. Jack Brinkley (D)
4. Elliott H. Levitas (D)
5. Andrew Young (D)
6. John J. Flynt Jr. (D)
7. Larry P. McDonald (D)
8. Billy Lee Evans (D)*
9. Ed Jenkins (D)*
10. Doug Barnard (D)*

HAWAII
1. Cecil Heftel (D)*
2. Daniel Akaka (D)*

IDAHO
1. Steven D. Symms (R)
2. George Hansen (R)

ILLINOIS
1. Ralph H. Metcalfe (D)
2. Morgan F. Murphy (D)
3. Martin A. Russo (D)
4. Edward J. Derwinski (R)
5. John G. Fary (D)
6. Henry J. Hyde (R)
7. Cardiss Collins (D)
8. Dan Rostenkowski (D)
9. Sidney R. Yates (D)
10. Abner J. Mikva (D)
11. Frank Annunzio (D)
12. Philip M. Crane (R)
13. Robert McClory (R)
14. John N. Erlenborn (R)
15. Tom Corcoran (R)*
16. John B. Anderson (R)
17. George M. O'Brien (R)
18. Robert H. Michel (R)
19. Tom Railsback (R)
20. Paul Findley (R)
21. Edward R. Madigan (R)
22. George E. Shipley (D)
23. Melvin Price (D)
24. Paul Simon (D)

INDIANA
1. Adam Benjamin Jr. (D)*
2. Floyd Fithian (D)
3. John Brademas (D)
4. J. Danforth Quayle (R)*
5. Elwood Hillis (R)
6. David W. Evans (D)
7. John T. Myers (R)
8. David L. Cornwell (D)*
9. Lee H. Hamilton (D)
10. Phil Sharp (D)
11. Andy Jacobs Jr. (D)

IOWA
1. James A. S. Leach (R)*
2. Michael T. Blouin (D)
3. Charles E. Grassley (R)
4. Neal Smith (D)
5. Tom Harkin (D)
6. Berkley Bedell (D)

KANSAS
1. Keith G. Sebelius (R)
2. Martha Keys (D)
3. Larry Winn Jr. (R)
4. Dan Glickman (D)*
5. Joe Skubitz (R)

KENTUCKY
1. Carroll Hubbard Jr. (D)
2. William H. Natcher (D)
3. Romano L. Mazzoli (D)
4. M. G. (Gene) Snyder (R)
5. Tim Lee Carter (R)
6. John B. Breckinridge (D)
7. Carl D. Perkins (D)

LOUISIANA
1. Richard E. Tonry (D)*
2. Corinne C. Boggs (D)
3. David C. Treen (R)
4. Joe D. Waggonner Jr. (D)
5. Jerry Huckaby (D)*
6. W. Henson Moore (R)
7. John B. Breaux (D)
8. Gillis W. Long (D)

MAINE
1. David F. Emery (R)
2. William S. Cohen (R)

MARYLAND
1. Robert E. Bauman (R)
2. Clarence D. Long (D)
3. Barbara A. Mikulski (D)*
4. Marjorie S. Holt (R)
5. Gladys N. Spellman (D)
6. Goodloe E. Byron (D)
7. Parren J. Mitchell (D)
8. Newton I. Steers Jr. (R)*

MASSACHUSETTS
1. Silvio O. Conte (R)
2. Edward P. Boland (D)
3. Joseph D. Early (D)
4. Robert F. Drinan (D)
5. Paul E. Tsongas (D)
6. Michael J. Harrington (D)
7. Edward J. Markey (D)*
8. Thomas P. O'Neill Jr. (D)
9. John Joseph Moakley (D)
10. Margaret M. Heckler (R)
11. James A. Burke (D)
12. Gerry E. Studds (D)

MICHIGAN
1. John Conyers Jr. (D)
2. Carl D. Pursell (R)*
3. Garry Brown (R)
4. David A. Stockman (R)*
5. Harold S. Sawyer (R)*
6. Bob Carr (D)
7. Dale E. Kildee (D)*
8. Bob Traxler (D)
9. Guy Vander Jagt (R)
10. Elford A. Cederberg (R)
11. Philip E. Ruppe (R)
12. David E. Bonior (D)*
13. Charles C. Diggs Jr. (D)
14. Lucien N. Nedzi (D)
15. William D. Ford (D)
16. John D. Dingell (D)
17. William M. Brodhead (D)
18. James J. Blanchard (D)
19. William S. Broomfield (R)

MINNESOTA
1. Albert H. Quie (R)
2. Tom Hagedorn (R)
3. Bill Frenzel (R)
4. Bruce F. Vento (D)*
5. Donald M. Fraser (D)
6. Richard Nolan (D)
7. Bob Bergland (D)
8. James L. Oberstar (D)

House Membership in the 95th Congress

MISSISSIPPI
1. Jamie L. Whitten (D)
2. David R. Bowen (D)
3. G. V. (Sonny) Montgomery (D)
4. Thad Cochran (R)
5. Trent Lott (R)

MISSOURI
1. William (Bill) Clay (D)
2. Robert A. Young (D)*
3. Richard A. Gephardt (D)*
4. Ike Skelton (D)*
5. Richard Bolling (D)
6. E. Thomas Coleman (R)*
7. Gene Taylor (R)
8. Richard H. Ichord (D)
9. Harold L. Volkmer (D)*
10. Bill D. Burlison (D)

MONTANA
1. Max Baucus (D)
2. Ron Marlenee (R)*

NEBRASKA
1. Charles Thone (R)
2. John J. Cavanaugh (D)*
3. Virginia Smith (R)

NEVADA
AL Jim Santini (D)

NEW HAMPSHIRE
1. Norman E. D'Amours (D)
2. James C. Cleveland (R)

NEW JERSEY
1. James J. Florio (D)
2. William J. Hughes (D)
3. James J. Howard (D)
4. Frank Thompson Jr. (D)
5. Millicent Fenwick (R)
6. Edwin B. Forsythe (R)
7. Andrew Maguire (D)
8. Robert A. Roe (D)
9. Harold C. Hollenbeck (R)*
10. Peter W. Rodino Jr. (D)
11. Joseph G. Minish (D)
12. Matthew J. Rinaldo (R)
13. Helen Meyner (D)
14. Joseph A. LeFante (D)*
15. Edward J. Patten (D)

NEW MEXICO
1. Manuel Lujan Jr. (R)
2. Harold Runnels (D)

NEW YORK
1. Otis G. Pike (D)
2. Thomas J. Downey (D)
3. Jerome A. Ambro (D)
4. Norman F. Lent (R)
5. John W. Wydler (R)
6. Lester L. Wolff (D)
7. Joseph P. Addabbo (D)
8. Benjamin S. Rosenthal (D)
9. James J. Delaney (D)
10. Mario Biaggi (D)
11. James H. Scheuer (D)
12. Shirley Chisholm (D)
13. Stephen J. Solarz (D)
14. Frederick W. Richmond (D)
15. Leo C. Zeferetti (D)
16. Elizabeth Holtzman (D)
17. John M. Murphy (D)
18. Edward I. Koch (D)
19. Charles B. Rangel (D)
20. Theodore S. Weiss (D)*
21. Herman Badillo (D)
22. Johathan B. Bingham (D)
23. Bruce F. Caputo (R)*
24. Richard L. Ottinger (D)
25. Hamilton Fish Jr. (R)
26. Benjamin A. Gilman (R)
27. Matthew F. McHugh (D)
28. Samuel S. Stratton (D)
29. Edward W. Pattison (D)
30. Robert C. McEwen (R)
31. Donald J. Mitchell (R)
32. James M. Hanley (D)
33. William F. Walsh (R)
34. Frank J. Horton (R)
35. Barber B. Conable Jr. (R)
36. John J. LaFalce (D)
37. Henry J. Nowak (D)
38. Jack F. Kemp (R)
39. Stanley N. Lundine (D)

NORTH CAROLINA
1. Walter B. Jones (D)
2. L. H. Fountain (D)
3. Charles Whitley (D)*
4. Ike F. Andrews (D)
5. Stephen L. Neal (D)
6. Richardson Preyer (D)
7. Charles G. Rose III (D)
8. W.G. (Bill) Hefner (D)
9. James G. Martin (R)
10. James T. Broyhill (R)
11. Lamar Gudger (D)*

NORTH DAKOTA
AL Mark Andrews (R)

OHIO
1. Bill Gradison (R)
2. Thomas A. Luken (D)#*
3. Charles W. Whalen Jr. (R)
4. Tennyson Guyer (R)
5. Delbert L. Latta (R)
6. William H. Harsha (R)
7. Clarence J. Brown (R)
8. Thomas N. Kindness (R)
9. Thomas L. Ashley (D)
10. Clarence E. Miller (R)
11. J. William Stanton (R)
12. Samuel L. Devine (R)
13. Donald J. Pease (D)*
14. John F. Seiberling (D)
15. Chalmers P. Wylie (R)
16. Ralph S. Regula (R)
17. John M. Ashbrook (R)
18. Douglas Applegate (D)*
19. Charles J. Carney (D)
20. Mary Rose Oakar (D)*
21. Louis Stokes (D)
22. Charles A. Vanik (D)
23. Ronald M. Mottl (D)

OKLAHOMA
1. James R. Jones (D)
2. Ted Risenhoover (D)
3. Wes Watkins (D)*
4. Tom Steed (D)
5. Mickey Edwards (R)*
6. Glenn English (D)

OREGON
1. Les AuCoin (D)
2. Al Ullman (D)
3. Robert Duncan (D)
4. James Weaver (D)

PENNSYLVANIA
1. Michael (Ozzie) Myers (D)*
2. Robert N.C. Nix (D)
3. Raymond F. Lederer (D)*
4. Joshua Eilberg (D)
5. Richard T. Schuize (D)
6. Gus Yatron (D)
7. Robert W. Edgar (D)
8. Peter H. Kostmayer (D)*
9. E.G. Shuster (R)
10. Joseph M. McDade (R)
11. Daniel J. Flood (D)
12. John P. Murtha (D)
13. R. Lawrence Coughlin (R)
14. William S. Moorhead (D)
15. Fred B. Rooney (D)
16. Robert S. Walker (R)*
17. Allen E. Ertel (D)*
18. Doug Walgren (D)*
19. William (Bill) Goodling (R)
20. Joseph M. Gaydos (D)
21. John H. Dent (D)
22. Austin J. Murphy (D)*
23. Joseph S. Ammerman (D)*
24. Marc L. Marks (R)*
25. Gary A. Myers (R)

RHODE ISLAND
1. Fernand J. St Germain (D)
2. Edward P. Beard (D)

SOUTH CAROLINA
1. Mendel J. Davis (D)
2. Floyd Spence (R)
3. Butler Derrick (D)
4. James R. Mann (D)
5. Kenneth L. Holland (D)
6. John W. Jenrette Jr. (D)

SOUTH DAKOTA
1. Larry Pressler (R)
2. James Abdnor (R)

TENNESSEE
1. James H. (Jimmy) Quillen (R)
2. John J. Duncan (R)
3. Marilyn Lloyd (D)
4. Albert Gore Jr. (D)*
5. Clifford Allen (D)
6. Robin L. Beard Jr. (R)
7. Ed Jones (D)
8. Harold E. Ford (D)

TEXAS
1. Sam B. Hall Jr. (D)
2. Charles Wilson (D)
3. James M. Collins (R)
4. Ray Roberts (D)
5. Jim Mattox (D)*
6. Olin E. Teague (D)
7. Bill Archer (R)
8. Bob Eckhardt (D)
9. Jack Brooks (D)
10. J.J. Pickle (D)
11. W.R. Poage (D)
12. Jim Wright (D)
13. Jack Hightower (D)
14. John Young (D)
15. Eligio de la Garza (D)
16. Richard C. White (D)
17. Omar Burleson (D)
18. Barbara C. Jordan (D)
19. George Mahon (D)
20. Henry B. Gonzalez (D)
21. Robert Krueger (D)
22. Bob Gammage (D)*
23. Abraham Kazen Jr. (D)
24. Dale Milford (D)

UTAH
1. Gunn McKay (D)
2. Dan Marriott (R)*

VERMONT
AL James M. Jeffords (R)

VIRGINIA
1. Paul S. Trible Jr. (R)*
2. G. William Whitehurst (R)
3. David E. Satterfield III (D)
4. Robert W. Daniel Jr. (R)
5. W.C. (Dan) Daniel (D)
6. M. Caldwell Butler (R)
7. J. Kenneth Robinson (R)
8. Herbert E. Harris II (D)
9. William C. Wampler (R)
10. Joseph L. Fisher (D)

WASHINGTON
1. Joel Pritchard (R)
2. Lloyd Meeds (D)
3. Don Bonker (D)
4. Mike McCormack (D)
5. Thomas S. Foley (D)
6. Norman D. Dicks (D)*
7. Brock Adams (D)

WEST VIRGINIA
1. Robert H. Mollohan (D)
2. Harley O. Staggers (D)
3. John M. Slack (D)
4. Nick Joe Rahall (D)*

WISCONSIN
1. Les Aspin (D)
2. Robert W. Kastenmeier (D)
3. Alvin Baldus (D)
4. Clement J. Zablocki (D)
5. Henry S. Reuss (D)
6. William A. Steiger (R)
7. David R. Obey (D)
8. Robert J. Cornell (D)
9. Robert W. Kasten Jr. (R)

WYOMING
AL Teno Roncalio (D)

House Membership in the 96th Congress

ALABAMA
1. Jack Edwards (R)
2. William L. Dickinson (R)
3. Bill Nichols (D)
4. Tom Bevill (D)
5. Ronnie G. Flippo (D)
6. John Buchanan (R)
7. Richard C. Shelby (D)*

ALASKA
AL Don Young (R)

ARIZONA
1. John J. Rhodes (R)
2. Morris K. Udall (D)
3. Bob Stump (D)
4. Eldon Rudd (R)

ARKANSAS
1. Bill Alexander (D)
2. Ed Bethune (R)*
3. John Paul Hammerschmidt (R)
4. Beryl Anthony (D)*

CALIFORNIA
1. Harold T. Johnson (D)
2. Don H. Clausen (R)
3. Robert T. Matsui (D)*
4. Vic Fazio (D)*
5. John L. Burton (D)
6. Phillip Burton (D)
7. George Miller (D)
8. Ronald V. Dellums (D)
9. Fortney H. (Pete) Stark (D)
10. Don Edwards (D)
11. Leo J. Ryan (D)
12. Paul N. McCloskey Jr. (R)
13. Norman Y. Mineta (D)
14. Norman D. Shumway (R)*
15. Tom Coelho (D)*
16. Leon E. Panetta (D)
17. Charles (Chip) Pashayan Jr. (R)*
18. William Thomas (R)*
19. Robert J. Lagomarsino (R)
20. Barry M. Goldwater Jr. (R)
21. James C. Corman (D)
22. Carlos J. Moorhead (R)
23. Anthony C. (Tony) Beilenson (D)
24. Henry A. Waxman (D)
25. Edward R. Roybal (D)
26. John H. Rousselot (R)
27. Robert K. Dornan (R)
28. Julian C. Dixon (D)*
29. Augustus F. Hawkins (D)
30. George E. Danielson (D)
31. Charles H. Wilson (D)
32. Glenn M. Anderson (D)
33. Wayne Grisham (R)*
34. Dan Lungren (R)*
35. Jim Lloyd (D)
36. George E. Brown Jr. (D)
37. Jerry Lewis (R)*
38. Jerry M. Patterson (D)
39. William E. Dannemeyer (R)*
40. Robert E. Badham (R)
41. Bob Wilson (R)
42. Lionel Van Deerlin (D)
43. Clair W. Burgener (R)

House Lineup

Democrats 276   Republicans 159

Freshman Democrats - 41
*Freshman Representative

Freshman Republicans - 36
#Former Representative

COLORADO
1. Patricia Schroeder (D)
2. Timothy E. Wirth (D)
3. Ray Kogovsek (D)*
4. James P. Johnson (R)
5. Ken Kramer (R)*

CONNECTICUT
1. William R. Cotter (D)
2. Christopher J. Dodd (D)
3. Robert N. Giaimo (D)
4. Stewart B. McKinney (R)
5. William Ratchford (D)*
6. Toby Moffett (D)

DELAWARE
AL Thomas B. Evans Jr. (R)

FLORIDA
1. Earl Hutto (D)*
2. Don Fuqua (D)
3. Charles E. Bennett (D)
4. Bill Chappell Jr. (D)
5. Richard Kelly (R)
6. C. W. Bill Young (R)
7. Sam Gibbons (D)
8. Andy Ireland (D)
9. Bill Nelson (D)*
10. L. A. (Skip) Bafalis (R)
11. Don Mica (D)*
12. Edward J. Stack (D)*
13. William Lehman (D)
14. Claude Pepper (D)
15. Dante B. Fascell (D)

GEORGIA
1. Bo Ginn (D)
2. Dawson Mathis (D)
3. Jack Brinkley (D)
4. Elliott H. Levitas (D)
5. Wyche Fowler (D)
6. Newt Gingrich (R)*
7. Larry P. McDonald (D)
8. Billy Lee Evans (D)
9. Ed Jenkins (D)
10. Doug Barnard (D)

HAWAII
1. Cecil (Cec) Heftel (D)
2. Daniel K. Akaka (D)

IDAHO
1. Steven D. Symms (R)
2. George Hansen (R)

ILLINOIS
1. Bennett Stewart (D)*
2. Morgan F. Murphy (D)

---

3. Marty Russo (D)
4. Edward J. Derwinski (R)
5. John G. Fary (D)
6. Henry J. Hyde (R)
7. Cardiss Collins (D)
8. Dan Rostenkowski (D)
9. Sidney R. Yates (D)
10. Abner J. Mikva (D)
11. Frank Annunzio (D)
12. Philip M. Crane (R)
13. Robert McClory (R)
14. John N. Erlenborn (R)
15. Tom Corcoran (R)
16. John B. Anderson (R)
17. George M. O'Brien (R)
18. Robert H. Michel (R)
19. Tom Railsback (R)
20. Paul Findley (R)
21. Edward R. Madigan (R)
22. Daniel B. Crane (R)*
23. Melvin Price (D)
24. Paul Simon (D)

INDIANA
1. Adam Benjamin Jr. (D)
2. Floyd Fithian (D)
3. John Brademas (D)
4. Dan Quayle (R)
5. Elwood Hillis (R)
6. David W. Evans (D)
7. John T. Myers (R)
8. H. Joel Deckard (R)*
9. Lee H. Hamilton (D)
10. Phil Sharp (D)
11. Andy Jacobs Jr. (D)

IOWA
1. Jim Leach (R)
2. Tom Tauke (R)*
3. Charles E. Grassley (R)
4. Neal Smith (D)
5. Tom Harkin (D)
6. Berkley Bedell (D)

KANSAS
1. Keith G. Sebelius (R)
2. Jim Jeffries (R)*
3. Larry Winn Jr. (R)
4. Dan Glickman (D)
5. Robert Whittaker (R)*

KENTUCKY
1. Carroll Hubbard Jr. (D)
2. William H. Natcher (D)
3. Romano L. Mazzoli (D)
4. Gene Snyder (R)
5. Tim Lee Carter (R)
6. Larry J. Hopkins (R)*
7. Carl D. Perkins (D)

LOUISIANA
1. Robert L. Livingston (R)
2. Lindy Boggs (D)
3. David C. Treen (R)
4. Claude (Buddy) Leach (D)*
5. Jerry Huckaby (D)
6. W. Henson Moore (R)
7. John B. Breaux (D)
8. Gillis W. Long (D)

MAINE
1. David F. Emery (R)
2. Olympia J. Snowe (R)*

MARYLAND
1. Robert E. Bauman (R)
2. Clarence D. Long (D)
3. Barbara A. Mikulski (D)
4. Marjorie S. Holt (R)
5. Gladys Noon Spellman (D)
6. Beverly Byron (D)*
7. Parren J. Mitchell (D)
8. Michael D. Barnes (D)*

MASSACHUSETTS
1. Silvio O. Conte (R)
2. Edward P. Boland (D)
3. Joseph D. Early (D)
4. Robert F. Drinan (D)
5. James M. Shannon (D)*
6. Nicholas Mavroules (D)*
7. Edward J. Markey (D)
8. Thomas P. O'Neill Jr. (D)
9. Joe Moakley (D)
10. Margaret M. Heckler (R)
11. Brian J. Donnelly (D)*
12. Gerry E. Studds (D)

MICHIGAN
1. John Conyers Jr. (D)
2. Carl D. Pursell (R)
3. Howard Wolpe (D)*
4. Dave Stockman (R)
5. Harold S. Sawyer (R)
6. Bob Carr (D)
7. Dale E. Kildee (D)
8. Bob Traxler (D)
9. Guy Vander Jagt (R)
10. Don Albosta (D)*
11. Robert W. Davis (R)*
12. David E. Bonior (D)
13. Charles C. Diggs Jr. (D)
14. Lucien N. Nedzi (D)
15. William D. Ford (D)
16. John D. Dingell (D)
17. William M. Brodhead (D)
18. James J. Blanchard (D)
19. William S. Broomfield (R)

MINNESOTA
1. Arlen Erdahl (R)*
2. Tom Hagedorn (R)
3. Bill Frenzel (R)
4. Bruce F. Vento (D)
5. Martin Olav Sabo (D)*
6. Richard Nolan (D)
7. Arlan Stangeland (R)
8. James L. Oberstar (D)

House Membership in the 96th Congress

MISSISSIPPI
1. Jamie L. Whitten (D)
2. David R. Bowen (D)
3. G. V. (Sonny) Montgomery (D)
4. Jon C. Hinson (R)*
5. Trent Lott (R)

MISSOURI
1. William (Bill) Clay (D)
2. Robert A. Young (D)
3. Richard A. Gephardt (D)
4. Ike Skelton (D)
5. Richard Bolling (D)
6. E. Thomas Coleman (R)
7. Gene Taylor (R)
8. Richard H. Ichord (D)
9. Harold L. Volkmer (D)
10. Bill D. Burlison (D)

MONTANA
1. Pat Williams (D)*
2. Ron Marlenee (R)

NEBRASKA
1. Douglas K. Bereuter (R)*
2. John J. Cavanaugh (D)
3. Virginia Smith (R)

NEVADA
AL Jim Santini (D)

NEW HAMPSHIRE
1. Norman E. D'Amours (D)
2. James C. Cleveland (R)

NEW JERSEY
1. James J. Florio (D)
2. William J. Hughes (D)
3. James J. Howard (D)
4. Frank Thompson Jr. (D)
5. Millicent Fenwick (R)
6. Edwin B. Forsythe (R)
7. Andrew Maguire (D)
8. Robert A. Roe (D)
9. Harold C. Hollenbeck (R)
10. Peter W. Rodino Jr. (D)
11. Joseph G. Minish (D)
12. Matthew J. Rinaldo (R)
13. Jim Courter (R)*
14. Frank J. Guarini (D)*
15. Edward J. Patten (D)

NEW MEXICO
1. Manuel Lujan Jr. (R)
2. Harold Runnels (D)

NEW YORK
1. William Carney (R)*
2. Thomas J. Downey (D)
3. Jerome A. Ambro (D)
4. Norman F. Lent (R)
5. John W. Wydler (R)
6. Lester L. Wolff (D)
7. Joseph P. Addabbo (D)
8. Benjamin S. Rosenthal (D)
9. Geraldine A. Ferraro (D)*
10. Mario Biaggi (D)
11. James H. Scheuer (D)
12. Shirley Chisholm (D)
13. Stephen J. Solarz (D)
14. Frederick Richmond (D)
15. Leo C. Zeferetti (D)
16. Elizabeth Holtzman (D)
17. John M. Murphy (D)
18. S. William Green (R)
19. Charles B. Rangel (D)
20. Ted Weiss (D)
21. Robert Garcia (D)
22. Jonathan B. Bingham (D)
23. Peter A. Peyser (D)#*
24. Richard L. Ottinger (D)
25. Hamilton Fish Jr. (R)
26. Benjamin A. Gilman (R)
27. Matthew F. McHugh (D)
28. Samuel S. Stratton (D)
29. Gerald B. Solomon (R)*
30. Robert C. McEwen (R)
31. Donald J. Mitchell (R)
32. James M. Hanley (D)
33. Gary A. Lee (R)*
34. Frank Horton (R)
35. Barber B. Conable Jr. (R)
36. John J. LaFalce (D)
37. Henry J. Nowak (D)
38. Jack F. Kemp (R)
39. Stanley N. Lundine (D)

NORTH CAROLINA
1. Walter B. Jones (D)
2. L. H. Fountain (D)
3. Charlie Whitley (D)
4. Ike F. Andrews (D)
5. Stephen L. Neal (D)
6. Richardson Preyer (D)
7. Charlie Rose (D)
8. W. G. (Bill) Hefner (D)
9. James G. Martin (R)
10. James T. Broyhill (R)
11. Lamar Gudger (D)

NORTH DAKOTA
AL Mark Andrews (R)

OHIO
1. Bill Gradison (R)
2. Thomas A. Luken (D)
3. Tony P. Hall (D)*
4. Tennyson Guyer (R)
5. Delbert L. Latta (R)
6. William H. Harsha (R)
7. Clarence J. Brown (R)
8. Thomas N. Kindness (R)
9. Thomas L. Ashley (D)
10. Clarence E. Miller (R)
11. J. William Stanton (R)
12. Samuel L. Devine (R)
13. Don J. Pease (D)
14. John F. Seiberling (D)
15. Chalmers P. Wylie (R)
16. Ralph S. Regula (R)
17. John M. Ashbrook (R)
18. Douglas Applegate (D)
19. Lyle Williams (R)*
20. Mary Rose Oakar (D)
21. Louis Stokes (D)
22. Charles A. Vanik (D)
23. Ronald M. Mottl (D)

OKLAHOMA
1. James R. Jones (D)
2. Mike Synar (D)*
3. Wes Watkins (D)
4. Tom Steed (D)
5. Mickey Edwards (R)
6. Glenn English (D)

OREGON
1. Les AuCoin (D)
2. Al Ullman (D)
3. Robert Duncan (D)
4. James Weaver (D)

PENNSYLVANIA
1. Michael (Ozzie) Myers (D)
2. William H. Gray III (D)*
3. Raymond F. Lederer (D)
4. Charles F. Dougherty (R)*
5. Richard T. Schulze (R)
6. Gus Yatron (D)
7. Robert W. Edgar (D)
8. Peter H. Kostmayer (D)
9. Bud Shuster (R)
10. Joseph M. McDade (R)
11. Daniel J. Flood (D)
12. John P. Murtha (D)
13. Lawrence Coughlin (R)
14. William S. Moorhead (D)
15. Donald L. Ritter (R)*
16. Robert S. Walker (R)
17. Allen E. Ertel (D)
18. Doug Walgren (D)
19. Bill Goodling (R)
20. Joseph M. Gaydos (D)
21. Don Bailey (D)*
22. Austin J. Murphy (D)
23. William F. Clinger Jr. (R)*
24. Marc L. Marks (R)
25. Eugene V. Atkinson (D)*

RHODE ISLAND
1. Fernand J. St Germain (D)
1. Edward P. Beard (D)

SOUTH CAROLINA
1. Mendel J. Davis (D)
2. Floyd Spence (R)
3. Butler Derrick (D)
4. Carroll Campbell (R)*
5. Ken Holland (D)
6. John W. Jenrette Jr. (D)

SOUTH DAKOTA
†1. Leo K. Thorsness (R)*
2. James Abdnor (R)

TENNESSEE
1. James H. (Jimmy) Quillen (R)
2. John J. Duncan (R)
3. Marilyn Lloyd (D)
4. Albert Gore Jr. (D)
5. Bill Boner (D)*
6. Robin L. Beard Jr. (R)
7. Ed Jones (D)
8. Harold E. Ford (D)

TEXAS
1. Sam B. Hall Jr. (D)
2. Charles Wilson (D)
3. James M. Collins (R)
4. Ray Roberts (D)
5. Jim Mattox (D)
6. Phil Gramm (D)*
7. Bill Archer (R)
8. Bob Eckhardt (D)
9. Jack Brooks (D)
10. J. J. Pickle (D)
11. J. Marvin Leath (D)*
12. Jim Wright (D)
13. Jack Hightower (D)
14. Joe Wyatt (D)*
15. E. (Kika) de la Garza (D)
16. Richard C. White (D)
17. Charles Stenholm (D)*
18. Mickey Leland (D)*
19. Kent Hance (D)*
20. Henry B. Gonzalez (D)
21. Tom Loeffler (R)*
22. Ron Paul (R)#*
23. Abraham Kazen Jr. (D)
24. Martin Frost (D)*

UTAH
1. Gunn McKay (D)
2. Dan Marriott (R)

VERMONT
AL James M. Jeffords (R)

VIRGINIA
1. Paul S. Trible Jr. (R)
2. G. William Whitehurst (R)
3. David E. Satterfield III (D)
4. Robert W. Daniel (R)
5. Dan Daniel (D)
6. M. Caldwell Butler (R)
7. J. Kenneth Robinson (R)
8. Herbert E. Harris II (D)
9. William C. Wampler (R)
10. Joseph L. Fisher (D)

WASHINGTON
1. Joel Pritchard (R)
2. Al Swift (D)*
3. Don Bonker (D)
4. Mike McCormack (D)
5. Thomas S. Foley (D)
6. Norman D. Dicks (D)
7. Mike Lowry (D)*

WEST VIRGINIA
1. Robert H. Mollohan (D)
2. Harley O. Staggers (D)
3. John M. Slack (D)
4. Nick J. Rahall (D)

WISCONSIN
1. Les Aspin (D)
2. Robert W. Kastenmeier (D)
3. Alvin Baldus (D)
4. Clement J. Zablocki (D)
5. Henry S. Reuss (D)
6. William A. Steiger (R)
7. David R. Obey (D)
8. Tobias A. Roth (R)*
9. F. James Sensenbrenner Jr. (R)*

WYOMING
AL Richard Cheney (R)*

† Pending recount.

House Membership in the 97th Congress

ALABAMA
1. Jack Edwards (R)
2. William L. Dickinson (R)
3. Bill Nichols (D)
4. Tom Bevill (D)
5. Ronnie G. Flippo (D)
6. Albert Lee Smith Jr. (R)#
7. Richard C. Shelby (D)

ALASKA
AL Don Young (R)

ARIZONA
1. John J. Rhodes (R)
2. Morris K. Udall (D)
3. Bob Stump (D)
4. Eldon Rudd (R)

ARKANSAS
1. Bill Alexander (D)
2. Ed Bethune (R)
3. John Paul Hammerschmidt (R)
4. Beryl Anthony Jr. (D)

CALIFORNIA
1. Eugene A. Chappie (R)#
2. Don H. Clausen (R)
3. Robert T. Matsui (D)
4. Vic Fazio (D)
5. John L. Burton (D)
6. Phillip Burton (D)
7. George Miller (D)
8. Ronald V. Dellums (D)
9. Fortney H. (Pete) Stark (D)
10. Don Edwards (D)
11. Tom Lantos (D)#
12. Paul N. McCloskey Jr. (R)
13. Norman Y. Mineta (D)
14. Norman D. Shumway (R)
15. Tony Coelho (D)
16. Leon E. Panetta (D)
17. Charles (Chip) Pashayan Jr. (R)
18. William M. Thomas (R)
19. Robert J. Lagomarsino (R)
20. Barry M. Goldwater Jr. (R)
21. Bobbi Fiedler (R)#
22. Carlos J. Moorhead (R)
23. Anthony C. Beilenson (D)
24. Henry A. Waxman (D)
25. Edward R. Roybal (D)
26. John H. Rousselot (R)
27. Robert K. Dornan (R)
28. Julian C. Dixon (D)
29. Augustus F. Hawkins (D)
30. George E. Danielson (D)
31. Mervyn M. Dymally (D)#
32. Glenn M. Anderson (D)
33. Wayne Grisham (R)
34. Dan Lungren (R)
35. David Dreier (R)#
36. George E. Brown Jr. (D)
37. Jerry Lewis (R)
38. Jerry M. Patterson (D)
39. William E. Dannemeyer (R)
40. Robert E. Badham (R)
41. Bill Lowery (R)#
42. Duncan L. Hunter (R)#
43. Clair W. Burgener (R)

COLORADO
1. Patricia Schroeder (D)
2. Timothy E. Wirth (D)
3. Ray Kogovsek (D)
4. Hank Brown (R)#
5. Ken Kramer (R)

CONNECTICUT
1. William R. Cotter (D)
2. Samuel Gejdenson (D)#
3. Lawrence J. DeNardis (R)#
4. Stewart B. McKinney (R)
5. William R. Ratchford (D)
6. Toby Moffett (D)

DELAWARE
AL Thomas B. Evans Jr. (R)

FLORIDA
1. Earl Hutto (D)
2. Don Fuqua (D)
3. Charles E. Bennett (D)
4. Bill Chappell Jr. (D)
5. Bill McCollum (R)#
6. C. W. Bill Young (R)
7. Sam Gibbons (D)
8. Andy Ireland (D)
9. Bill Nelson (D)
10. L. A. (Skip) Bafalis (R)
11. Dan Mica (D)
12. Clay Shaw (R)#
13. William Lehman (D)
14. Claude Pepper (D)
15. Dante B. Fascell (D)

GEORGIA
1. Bo Ginn (D)
2. Charles F. Hatcher (D)#
3. Jack Brinkley (D)
4. Elliott H. Levitas (D)
5. Wyche Fowler Jr. (D)
6. Newt Gingrich (R)
7. Larry P. McDonald (D)
8. Billy Lee Evans (D)
9. Ed Jenkins (D)
10. Doug Barnard (D)

HAWAII
1. Cecil Heftel (D)
2. Daniel K. Akaka (D)

IDAHO
1. Larry Craig (R)#
2. George Hansen (R)

ILLINOIS
1. Harold Washington (D)#
2. Gus Savage (D)#
3. Marty Russo (D)
4. Edward J. Derwinski (R)
5. John G. Fary (D)
6. Henry J. Hyde (R)
7. Cardiss Collins (D)
8. Dan Rostenkowski (D)
9. Sidney R. Yates (D)
10. John E. Porter (R)
11. Frank Annunzio (D)
12. Philip M. Crane (R)
13. Robert McClory (R)
14. John N. Erlenborn (R)
15. Tom Corcoran (R)
16. Lynn M. Martin (R)#
17. George M. O'Brien (R)
18. Robert H. Michel (R)
19. Tom Railsback (R)
20. Paul Findley (R)
21. Edward R. Madigan (R)
22. Daniel B. Crane (R)
23. Melvin Price (D)
24. Paul Simon (D)

INDIANA
1. Adam Benjamin Jr. (D)
2. Floyd Fithian (D)
3. John P. Hiler (R)#
4. Daniel R. Coats (R)#
5. Elwood Hillis (R)
6. David W. Evans (D)
7. John T. Myers (R)
8. H. Joel Deckard (R)
9. Lee H. Hamilton (D)
10. Phil Sharp (D)
11. Andy Jacobs Jr. (D)

IOWA
1. Jim Leach (R)
2. Tom Tauke (R)
3. Cooper Evans (R)#
4. Neal Smith (D)
5. Tom Harkin (D)
6. Berkley Bedell (D)

KANSAS
1. Pat Roberts (R)#
2. Jim Jeffries (R)
3. Larry Winn Jr. (R)
4. Dan Glickman (D)
5. Bob Whittaker (R)

KENTUCKY
1. Carroll Hubbard Jr. (D)
2. William H. Natcher (D)
3. Romano L. Mazzoli (D)
4. Gene Snyder (R)
5. Harold Rogers (R)#
6. Larry J. Hopkins (R)
7. Carl D. Perkins (D)

LOUISIANA
1. Robert L. Livingston (R)
2. Lindy Boggs (D)
3. W. J. (Billy) Tauzin (D)
4. Buddy Roemer (D)#
5. Jerry Huckaby (D)
6. W. Henson Moore (R)
7. John B. Breaux (D)
8. Gillis W. Long (D)

MAINE
1. David F. Emery (R)
2. Olympia J. Snowe (R)

MARYLAND
1. Roy Dyson (D)#
2. Clarence D. Long (D)
3. Barbara A. Mikulski (D)
4. Marjorie S. Holt (R)
5. Gladys Noon Spellman (D)
6. Beverly B. Byron (D)
7. Parren J. Mitchell (D)
8. Michael D. Barnes (D)

MASSACHUSETTS
1. Silvio O. Conte (R)
2. Edward P. Boland (D)
3. Joseph D. Early (D)
4. Barney Frank (D)#
5. James M. Shannon (D)
6. Nicholas Mavroules (D)
7. Edward J. Markey (D)
8. Thomas P. O'Neill Jr. (D)
9. Joe Moakley (D)
10. Margaret M. Heckler (R)
11. Brian J. Donnelly (D)
12. Gerry E. Studds (D)

MICHIGAN
1. John Conyers Jr. (D)
2. Carl D. Pursell (R)
3. Howard Wolpe (D)
4. Dave Stockman (R)
5. Harold S. Sawyer (R)
6. Jim Dunn (R)#
7. Dale E. Kildee (D)
8. Bob Traxler (D)
9. Guy Vander Jagt (R)
10. Don Albosta (D)
11. Robert W. Davis (R)
12. David E. Bonior (D)
13. George W. Crockett Jr. (D)#
14. Dennis M. Hertel (D)#
15. William D. Ford (D)
16. John D. Dingell (D)
17. William M. Brodhead (D)
18. James J. Blanchard (D)
19. William S. Broomfield (R)

MINNESOTA
1. Arlen Erdahl (R)
2. Tom Hagedorn (R)
3. Bill Frenzel (R)
4. Bruce F. Vento (D)
5. Martin Olav Sabo (D)
6. Vin Weber (R)#
7. Arlan Stangeland (R)
8. James L. Oberstar (D)

House Lineup

Democrats 243*   **Republicans 192**

Freshman Democrats - 22   Freshman Republicans - 52
#Freshman Representative   †Former Representative

House Membership in the 97th Congress

MISSISSIPPI
1. Jamie L. Whitten (D)
2. David R. Bowen (D)
3. G. V. (Sonny) Montgomery (D)
4. Jon C. Hinson (R)
5. Trent Lott (R)

MISSOURI
1. William Clay (D)
2. Robert A. Young (D)
3. Richard A. Gephardt (D)
4. Ike Skelton (D)
5. Richard Bolling (D)
6. E. Thomas Coleman (R)
7. Gene Taylor (R)
8. Wendell Bailey (R)#
9. Harold L. Volkmer (D)
10. Bill Emerson (R)#

MONTANA
1. Pat Williams (D)
2. Ron Marlenee (R)

NEBRASKA
1. Douglas K. Bereuter (R)
2. Hal Daub (R)#
3. Virginia Smith (R)

NEVADA
AL Jim Santini (D)

NEW HAMPSHIRE
1. Norman E. D'Amours (D)
2. Judd Gregg (R)#

NEW JERSEY
1. James J. Florio (D)
2. William J. Hughes (D)
3. James J. Howard (D)
4. Christopher H. Smith (R)#
5. Millicent Fenwick (R)
6. Edwin B. Forsythe (R)
7. Marge Roukema (R)#
8. Robert A. Roe (D)
9. Harold C. Hollenbeck (R)
10. Peter W. Rodino Jr. (D)
11. Joseph G. Minish (D)
12. Matthew J. Rinaldo (R)
13. Jim Courter (R)
14. Frank J. Guarini (D)
15. Bernard J. Dwyer (D)#

NEW MEXICO
1. Manuel Lujan Jr. (R)
2. Joe Skeen (R)#

NEW YORK
1. William Carney (R)
2. Thomas J. Downey (D)
3. Gregory W. Carman (R)#
4. Norman F. Lent (R)
5. Raymond J. McGrath (R)#
6. John LeBoutillier (R)#
7. Joseph P. Addabbo (D)
8. Benjamin S. Rosenthal (D)
9. Geraldine A. Ferraro (D)
10. Mario Biaggi (D)
11. James H. Scheuer (D)
12. Shirley Chisholm (D)
13. Stephen J. Solarz (D)
14. Fred Richmond (D)
15. Leo C. Zeferetti (D)
16. Charles E. Schumer (D)#
17. Guy V. Molinari (R)#
18. S. William Green (R)
19. Charles B. Rangel (D)
20. Ted Weiss (D)
21. Robert Garcia (D)
22. Jonathan B. Bingham (D)
23. Peter A. Peyser (D)
24. Richard L. Ottinger (D)
25. Hamilton Fish Jr. (R)
26. Benjamin A. Gilman (R)
27. Matthew F. McHugh (D)
28. Samuel S. Stratton (D)
29. Gerald B. Solomon (R)
30. David O'B. Martin (R)#
31. Donald J. Mitchell (R)
32. George Wortley (R)#
33. Gary A. Lee (R)
34. Frank Horton (R)
35. Barber B. Conable Jr. (R)
36. John J. LaFalce (D)
37. Henry J. Nowak (D)
38. Jack F. Kemp (R)
39. Stanley N. Lundine (D)

NORTH CAROLINA
1. Walter B. Jones (D)
2. L. H. Fountain (D)
3. Charles Whitley (D)
4. Ike F. Andrews (D)
5. Stephen L. Neal (D)
6. Eugene Johnston (R)#
7. Charlie Rose (D)
8. W. G. (Bill) Hefner (D)
9. James G. Martin (R)
10. James T. Broyhill (R)
11. William M. Hendon (R)#

NORTH DAKOTA
AL Byron L. Dorgan (D)#

OHIO
1. Bill Gradison (R)
2. Thomas A. Luken (D)
3. Tony P. Hall (D)
4. Tennyson Guyer (R)
5. Delbert L. Latta (R)
6. Bob McEwen (R)#
7. Clarence J. Brown (R)
8. Thomas N. Kindness (R)
9. Ed Weber (R)#
10. Clarence E. Miller (R)
11. J. William Stanton (R)
12. Robert N. Shamansky (D)#
13. Don J. Pease (D)
14. John F. Seiberling (D)
15. Chalmers P. Wylie (R)
16. Ralph S. Regula (R)
17. John M. Ashbrook (R)
18. Douglas Applegate (D)
19. Lyle Williams (R)
20. Mary Rose Oakar (D)
21. Louis Stokes (D)
22. Dennis E. Eckart (D)#
23. Ronald M. Mottl (D)

OKLAHOMA
1. James R. Jones (D)
2. Mike Synar (D)
3. Wes Watkins (D)
4. Dave McCurdy (D)#
5. Mickey Edwards (R)
6. Glenn English (D)

OREGON
1. Les AuCoin (D)
2. Denny Smith (R)#
3. Ron Wyden (D)#
4. James Weaver (D)

PENNSYLVANIA
1. Thomas M. Foglietta (I)#
2. William H. Gray III (D)
3. Raymond F. Lederer (D)
4. Charles F. Dougherty (R)
5. Richard T. Schulze (R)
6. Gus Yatron (D)
7. Robert W. Edgar (D)
8. James K. Coyne (R)#
9. Bud Shuster (R)
10. Joseph M. McDade (R)
11. James L. Nelligan (R)#
12. John P. Murtha (D)
13. Lawrence Coughlin (R)
14. William J. Coyne (D)#
15. Don Ritter (R)
16. Robert S. Walker (R)
17. Allen E. Ertel (D)
18. Doug Walgren (D)
19. Bill Goodling (R)
20. Joseph M. Gaydos (D)
21. Don Bailey (D)
22. Austin J. Murphy (D)
23. William F. Clinger Jr. (R)
24. Marc L. Marks (R)
25. Eugene V. Atkinson (D)

RHODE ISLAND
1. Fernand J. St Germain (D)
2. Claudine Schneider (R)#

SOUTH CAROLINA
1. Thomas F. Hartnett (R)#
2. Floyd Spence (R)
3. Butler Derrick (D)
4. Carroll A. Campbell Jr. (R)
5. Ken Holland (D)
6. John L. Napier (R)#

SOUTH DAKOTA
1. Thomas A. Daschle (D)
2. Clint Roberts (R)#

TENNESSEE
1. James H. Quillen (R)
2. John J. Duncan (R)
3. Marilyn Lloyd Bouquard (D)
4. Albert Gore Jr. (D)
5. Bill Boner (D)
6. Robin L. Beard Jr. (R)
7. Ed Jones (D)
8. Harold E. Ford (D)

TEXAS
1. Sam B. Hall Jr. (D)
2. Charles Wilson (D)
3. James M. Collins (R)
4. Ralph M. Hall (D)#
5. Jim Mattox (D)
6. Phil Gramm (D)
7. Bill Archer (R)
8. Jack Fields (R)#
9. Jack Brooks (D)
10. J. J. Pickle (D)
11. Marvin Leath (D)
12. Jim Wright (D)
13. Jack Hightower (D)
14. William N. Patman (D)#
15. E. (Kika) de la Garza (D)
16. Richard C. White (D)
17. Charles W. Stenholm (D)
18. Mickey Leland (D)
19. Kent Hance (D)
20. Henry B. Gonzalez (D)
21. Tom Loeffler (R)
22. Ron Paul (R)
23. Abraham Kazen Jr. (D)
24. Martin Frost (D)

UTAH
1. James V. Hansen (R)#
2. Dan Marriott (R)

VERMONT
AL James M. Jeffords (R)

VIRGINIA
1. Paul S. Trible Jr. (R)
2. G. William Whitehurst (R)
3. Thomas J. Bliley Jr. (R)#
4. Robert W. Daniel Jr. (R)
5. Dan Daniel (D)
6. M. Caldwell Butler (R)
7. J. Kenneth Robinson (R)
8. Stanford E. Parris (R)# †
9. William C. Wampler (R)
10. Frank R. Wolf (R)#

WASHINGTON
1. Joel Pritchard (R)
2. Al Swift (D)
3. Don Bonker (D)
4. Sid Morrison (R)#
5. Thomas S. Foley (D)
6. Norman D. Dicks (D)
7. Mike Lowry (D)

WEST VIRGINIA
1. Robert H. Mollohan (D)
2. Cleve Benedict (R)#
3. Mick Staton (R)#
4. Nick J. Rahall (D)

WISCONSIN
1. Les Aspin (D)
2. Robert W. Kastenmeier (D)
3. Steven Gunderson (R)#
4. Clement J. Zablocki (D)
5. Henry S. Reuss (D)
6. Thomas E. Petri (R)
7. David R. Obey (D)
8. Toby Roth (R)
9. F. James Sensenbrenner (R)

WYOMING
AL Richard B. Cheney (R)

Includes Foglietta, Pa., elected as an independent.

House Membership in the 98th Congress

ALABAMA
1. Jack Edwards (R)
2. William L. Dickinson (R)
3. Bill Nichols (D)
4. Tom Bevill (D)
5. Ronnie G. Flippo (D)
6. Ben Erdreich (D)#
7. Richard C. Shelby (D)

ALASKA
AL Don Young (R)

ARIZONA
1. John McCain (R)#
2. Morris K. Udall (D)
3. Bob Stump (R)
4. Eldon Rudd (R)
5. Jim McNulty (D)#

ARKANSAS
1. Bill Alexander (D)
2. Ed Bethune (R)
3. John Paul Hammerschmidt (R)
4. Beryl Anthony Jr. (D)

CALIFORNIA
1. Douglas H. Bosco (D)#
2. Gene Chappie (R)
3. Robert T. Matsui (D)
4. Vic Fazio (D)
5. Phillip Burton (D)
6. Barbara Boxer (D)#
7. George Miller (D)
8. Ronald V. Dellums (D)
9. Fortney H. "Pete" Stark (D)
10. Don Edwards (D)
11. Tom Lantos (D)
12. Ed Zschau (R)#
13. Norman Y. Mineta (D)
14. Norman D. Shumway (R)
15. Tony Coelho (D)
16. Leon E. Panetta (D)
17. Charles Pashayan Jr. (R)
18. Richard Lehman (D)#
19. Robert J. Lagomarsino (R)
20. William M. Thomas (R)
21. Bobbi Fiedler (R)
22. Carlos J. Moorhead (R)
23. Anthony C. Beilenson (D)
24. Henry A. Waxman (D)
25. Edward R. Roybal (D)
26. Howard L. Berman (D)#
27. Mel Levine (D)#
28. Julian C. Dixon (D)
29. Augustus F. Hawkins (D)
30. Matthew G. Martinez (D)
31. Mervyn M. Dymally (D)
32. Glenn M. Anderson (D)
33. David Dreier (R)
34. Esteban Torres (D)#
35. Jerry Lewis (R)
36. George E. Brown Jr. (D)
37. Al McCandless (R)#
38. Jerry M. Patterson (D)
39. William E. Dannemeyer (R)
40. Robert E. Badham (R)
41. Bill Lowery (R)
42. Dan Lungren (R)
43. Ron Packard (R)#

44. Jim Bates (D)#
45. Duncan L. Hunter (R)

COLORADO
1. Patricia Schroeder (D)
2. Timothy E. Wirth (D)
3. Ray Kogovsek (D)
4. Hank Brown (R)
5. Ken Kramer (R)
6. Jack Swigert (R)#

CONNECTICUT
1. Barbara B. Kennelly (D)
2. Sam Gejdenson (D)
3. Bruce A. Morrison (D)#
4. Stewart B. McKinney (R)
5. William R. Ratchford (D)
6. Nancy L. Johnson (R)#

DELAWARE
AL Thomas R. Carper (D)#

FLORIDA
1. Earl Hutto (D)
2. Don Fuqua (D)
3. Charles E. Bennett (D)
4. Bill Chappell Jr. (D)
5. Bill McCollum (R)
6. Kenneth H. MacKay (D)#
7. Sam Gibbons (D)
8. C.W. Bill Young (R)
9. Michael Bilirakis (R)#
10. Andy Ireland (D)
11. Bill Nelson (D)
12. Tom Lewis (R)#
13. Connie Mack III (R)#
14. Daniel A. Mica (D)
15. E. Clay Shaw Jr. (R)
16. Larry Smith (D)#
17. William Lehman (D)
18. Claude Pepper (D)
19. Dante B. Fascell (D)

GEORGIA
1. Lindsay Thomas (D)#
2. Charles Hatcher (D)
3. Richard Ray (D)#
4. Elliott H. Levitas (D)
5. Wyche Fowler Jr. (D)
6. Newt Gingrich (R)
7. Larry P. McDonald (D)
8. J. Roy Rowland (D)#
9. Ed Jenkins (D)
10. Doug Barnard Jr. (D)

HAWAII
1. Cecil Heftel (D)
2. Daniel K. Akaka (D)

IDAHO
1. Larry E. Craig (R)
2. George Hansen (R)

ILLINOIS
1. Harold Washington (D)
2. Gus Savage (D)
3. Marty Russo (D)
4. George M. O'Brien (R)
5. William O. Lipinski (D)#
6. Henry J. Hyde (R)
7. Cardiss Collins (D)
8. Dan Rostenkowski (D)
9. Sidney R. Yates (D)
10. John Edward Porter (R)
11. Frank Annunzio (D)
12. Philip M. Crane (R)
13. John N. Erlenborn (R)
14. Tom Corcoran (R)
15. Edward R. Madigan (R)
16. Lynn Martin (R)
17. Lane Evans (D)#
18. Robert H. Michel (R)
19. Daniel B. Crane (R)
20. Richard J. Durbin (D)#
21. Melvin Price (D)
22. Paul Simon (D)

INDIANA
1. Katie Hall (D)#
2. Philip R. Sharp (D)
3. John Hiler (R)
4. Dan Coats (R)
5. Elwood Hillis (R)
6. Dan Burton (R)#
7. John T. Myers (R)
8. Francis X. McCloskey (D)#
9. Lee H. Hamilton (D)
10. Andrew Jacobs Jr. (D)

IOWA
1. Jim Leach (R)
2. Tom Tauke (R)
3. Cooper Evans (R)
4. Neal Smith (D)
5. Tom Harkin (D)
6. Berkley Bedell (D)

KANSAS
1. Pat Roberts (R)
2. Jim Slattery (D)#
3. Larry Winn Jr. (R)
4. Dan Glickman (D)
5. Bob Whittaker (R)

KENTUCKY
1. Carroll Hubbard Jr. (D)
2. William H. Natcher (D)
3. Romano L. Mazzoli (D)

4. Gene Snyder (R)
5. Harold Rogers (R)
6. Larry J. Hopkins (R)
7. Carl D. Perkins (D)

LOUISIANA
1. Bob Livingston (R)
2. Lindy (Mrs. Hale) Boggs (D)
3. W. J. "Billy" Tauzin (D)
4. Buddy Roemer (D)
5. Jerry Huckaby (D)
6. Henson Moore (R)
7. John B. Breaux (D)
8. Gillis W. Long (D)

MAINE
1. John R. McKernan Jr. (R)#
2. Olympia J. Snowe (R)

MARYLAND
1. Roy Dyson (D)
2. Clarence D. Long (D)
3. Barbara A. Mikulski (D)
4. Marjorie S. Holt (R)
5. Steny H. Hoyer (D)
6. Beverly B. Byron (D)
7. Parren J. Mitchell (D)
8. Michael D. Barnes (D)

MASSACHUSETTS
1. Silvio O. Conte (R)
2. Edward P. Boland (D)
3. Joseph D. Early (D)
4. Barney Frank (D)
5. James M. Shannon (D)
6. Nicholas Mavroules (D)
7. Edward J. Markey (D)
8. Thomas P. O'Neill Jr. (D)
9. Joe Moakley (D)
10. Gerry E. Studds (D)
11. Brian J. Donnelly (D)

MICHIGAN
1. John Conyers Jr. (D)
2. Carl D. Pursell (R)
3. Howard Wolpe (D)
4. Mark Siljander (R)
5. Harold S. Sawyer (R)
6. Bob Carr (D)†#
7. Dale E. Kildee (D)
8. Bob Traxler (D)
9. Guy Vander Jagt (R)
10. Don Albosta (D)
11. Robert W. Davis (R)
12. David E. Bonior (D)
13. George W. Crockett Jr. (D)
14. Dennis M. Hertel (D)
15. William D. Ford (D)
16. John D. Dingell (D)
17. Sander Levin (D)#
18. William S. Broomfield (R)

MINNESOTA
1. Timothy J. Penny (D)#
2. Vin Weber (R)
3. Bill Frenzel (R)
4. Bruce F. Vento (D)
5. Martin Olav Sabo (D)
6. Gerry Sikorski (D)#

House Lineup

Democrats 267   **Republicans 166**

Freshman Democrats - 57   Freshman Republicans - 24
#Freshman Representative   †Former Representative

Elections in these districts were held Nov. 30.

House Membership in the 98th Congress

7. Arlan Stangeland (R)
8. James L. Oberstar (D)

MISSISSIPPI
1. Jamie L. Whitten (D)
2. Webb Franklin (R)#
3. G. V. "Sonny" Montgomery (D)
4. Wayne Dowdy (D)
5. Trent Lott (R)

MISSOURI
1. William Clay (D)
2. Robert A. Young (D)
3. Richard A. Gephardt (D)
4. Ike Skelton (D)
5. Alan Wheat (D)#
6. E. Thomas Coleman (R)
7. Gene Taylor (R)
8. Bill Emerson (R)
9. Harold L. Volkmer (D)

MONTANA
1. Pat Williams (D)
2. Ron Marlenee (R)

NEBRASKA
1. Douglas K. Bereuter (R)
2. Hal Daub (R)
3. Virginia Smith (R)

NEVADA
1. Harry Reid (D)#
2. Barbara Vucanovich (R)#

NEW HAMPSHIRE
1. Norman E. D'Amours (D)
2. Judd Gregg (R)

NEW JERSEY
1. James J. Florio (D)
2. William J. Hughes (D)
3. James J. Howard (D)
4. Christopher H. Smith (R)
5. Marge Roukema (R)
6. Bernard J. Dwyer (D)
7. Matthew J. Rinaldo (R)
8. Robert A. Roe (D)
9. Robert G. Torricelli (D)#
10. Peter W. Rodino Jr. (D)
11. Joseph G. Minish (D)
12. Jim Courter (R)
13. Edwin B. Forsythe (R)
14. Frank J. Guarini (D)

NEW MEXICO
1. Manuel Lujan Jr. (R)
2. Joe Skeen (R)
3. Bill Richardson (D)#

NEW YORK
1. William Carney (R)
2. Thomas J. Downey (D)
3. Robert J. Mrazek (D)#
4. Norman F. Lent (R)
5. Raymond J. McGrath (R)
6. Joseph P. Addabbo (D)
7. Benjamin S. Rosenthal (D)
8. James H. Scheuer (D)
9. Geraldine A. Ferraro (D)
10. Charles E. Schumer (D)
11. Edolphus Towns (D)#
12. Major R. Owens (D)#
13. Stephen J. Solarz (D)
14. Guy V. Molinari (R)
15. Bill Green (R)
16. Charles B. Rangel (D)
17. Ted Weiss (D)
18. Robert Garcia (D)
19. Mario Biaggi (D)
20. Richard L. Ottinger (D)
21. Hamilton Fish Jr. (R)
22. Benjamin A. Gilman (R)
23. Samuel S. Stratton (D)
24. Gerald B. H. Solomon (R)
25. Sherwood L. Boehlert (R)#
26. David O'B. Martin (R)
27. George C. Wortley (R)
28. Matthew F. McHugh (D)
29. Frank Horton (R)
30. Barber B. Conable Jr. (R)
31. Jack F. Kemp (R)
32. John J. LaFalce (D)
33. Henry J. Nowak (D)
34. Stanley N. Lundine (D)

NORTH CAROLINA
1. Walter B. Jones (D)
2. I. T. "Tim" Valentine Jr. (D)#
3. Charles Whitley (D)
4. Ike Andrews (D)
5. Stephen L. Neal (D)
6. Charles Robin Britt (D)#
7. Charlie Rose (D)
8. W. G. "Bill" Hefner (D)
9. James G. Martin (R)
10. James T. Broyhill (R)
11. James McClure Clarke (D)#

NORTH DAKOTA
AL Byron L. Dorgan (D)

OHIO
1. Thomas A. Luken (D)
2. Bill Gradison (R)
3. Tony P. Hall (D)
4. Michael G. Oxley (R)
5. Delbert L. Latta (R)
6. Bob McEwen (R)
7. Michael Dewine (R)#
8. Thomas N. Kindness (R)
9. Marcy Kaptur (D)#
10. Clarence E. Miller (R)
11. Dennis E. Eckart (D)
12. John R. Kasich (R)#
13. Don J. Pease (D)
14. John F. Seiberling (D)
15. Chalmers P. Wylie (R)
16. Ralph Regula (R)
17. Lyle Williams (R)
18. Douglas Applegate (D)
19. Edward F. Feighan (D)#
20. Mary Rose Oakar (D)
21. Louis Stokes (D)

OKLAHOMA
1. James R. Jones (D)
2. Mike Synar (D)
3. Wes Watkins (D)
4. Dave McCurdy (D)
5. Mickey Edwards (R)
6. Glenn English (D)

OREGON
1. Les AuCoin (D)
2. Bob Smith (R)#
3. Ron Wyden (D)
4. James Weaver (D)
5. Denny Smith (R)

PENNSYLVANIA
1. Thomas M. Foglietta (D)
2. William H. Gray III (D)
3. Robert A. Borski (D)#
4. Joseph P. Kolter (D)#
5. Richard T. Schulze (R)
6. Gus Yatron (D)
7. Robert W. Edgar (D)
8. Peter H. Kostmayer (D)†#
9. Bud Shuster (R)
10. Joseph M. McDade (R)
11. Frank Harrison (D)#
12. John P. Murtha (D)
13. Lawrence Coughlin (R)
14. William J. Coyne (D)
15. Don Ritter (R)
16. Robert S. Walker (R)
17. George W. Gekas (R)#
18. Doug Walgren (D)
19. Bill Goodling (R)
20. Joseph M. Gaydos (D)
21. Thomas J. Ridge (R)#
22. Austin J. Murphy (D)
23. William F. Clinger Jr. (R)

RHODE ISLAND
1. Fernand J. St Germain (D)
2. Claudine Schneider (R)

SOUTH CAROLINA
1. Thomas F. Hartnett (R)
2. Floyd Spence (R)
3. Butler Derrick (D)
4. Carroll A. Campbell Jr. (R)
5. John Spratt (D)#
6. Robert M. Tallon Jr. (D)#

SOUTH DAKOTA
AL Thomas A. Daschle (D)

TENNESSEE
1. James H. Quillen (R)
2. John J. Duncan (R)
3. Marilyn Lloyd Bouquard (D)
4. Jim Cooper (D)#
5. Bill Boner (D)
6. Albert Gore Jr. (D)
7. Don Sundquist (R)#
8. Ed Jones (D)
9. Harold E. Ford (D)

TEXAS
1. Sam B. Hall Jr. (D)
2. Charles Wilson (D)
3. Steve Bartlett (R)#
4. Ralph M. Hall (D)
5. John Bryant (D)#
6. Phil Gramm (D)
7. Bill Archer (R)
8. Jack Fields (R)
9. Jack Brooks (D)
10. J. J. Pickle (D)
11. Marvin Leath (D)
12. Jim Wright (D)
13. Jack Hightower (D)
14. Bill Patman (D)
15. E. "Kika" de la Garza (D)
16. Ronald Coleman (D)#
17. Charles W. Stenholm (D)
18. Mickey Leland (D)
19. Kent Hance (D)
20. Henry B. Gonzalez (D)
21. Tom Loeffler (R)
22. Ron Paul (R)
23. Abraham Kazen Jr. (D)
24. Martin Frost (D)
25. Mike Andrews (D)#
26. Tom Vandergriff (D)#
27. Solomon P. Ortiz (D)#

UTAH
1. James V. Hansen (R)
2. Dan Marriott (R)
3. Howard C. Nielson (R)#

VERMONT
AL James M. Jeffords (R)

VIRGINIA
1. Herbert H. Bateman (R)#
2. G. William Whitehurst (R)
3. Thomas J. Bliley Jr. (R)
4. Norman Sisisky (D)#
5. Dan Daniel (D)
6. James R. Olin (D)#
7. J. Kenneth Robinson (R)
8. Stan Parris (R)
9. Frederick C. Boucher (D)#
10. Frank R. Wolf (R)

WASHINGTON
1. Joel Pritchard (R)
2. Al Swift (D)
3. Don Bonker (D)
4. Sid Morrison (R)
5. Thomas S. Foley (D)
6. Norman D. Dicks (D)
7. Mike Lowry (D)
8. Rodney Chandler (R)#

WEST VIRGINIA
1. Alan B. Mollohan (D)#
2. Harley O. Staggers Jr. (D)#
3. Bob Wise (D)#
4. Nick J. Rahall II (D)

WISCONSIN
1. Les Aspin (D)
2. Robert W. Kastenmeier (D)
3. Steve Gunderson (R)
4. Clement J. Zablocki (D)
5. Jim Moody (D)#
6. Thomas E. Petri (R)
7. David R. Obey (D)
8. Toby Roth (R)
9. F. James Sensenbrenner Jr. (R)

WYOMING
AL Dick Cheney (R)